Collins

OFFICIAL SCRABBLE™ WORDS

Published by Collins
An imprint of HarperCollins Publishers
Westerhill Road
Bishopbriggs
Glasgow G64 2QT

HarperCollins Publishers
1st Floor, Watermarque Building
Ringsend Road, Dublin 4, Ireland

Sixth Edition 2022

10 9 8 7 6 5 4 3 2 1

ISBN 978-0-00-852388-6

www.collins.co.uk/scrabble

Typeset by Davidson Publishing Solutions, Glasgow

Printed and bound by Replika Press

A catalogue record for this book is available from the British Library.

If you would like to comment on any aspect of this book, please contact us at the given address or online.
E-mail: puzzles@harpercollins.co.uk
facebook.com/collinsdictionary
@collinsdict

MIX
Paper from responsible sources
FSC™ C007454

This book is produced from independently certified FSC™ paper to ensure responsible forest management.

For more information visit: www.harpercollins.co.uk/green

Rules for the Scrabble word list

- Only includes words of between 2 and 15 letters in length
- Does not include proper nouns, place names, and words with an initial capital letter, unless such words can also be spelt with a lower-case initial letter
- Does not include abbreviations, prefixes, suffixes, words requiring apostrophes or hyphens
- Includes foreign words that are considered to have been absorbed into the English language
- Includes inflected forms, such as plurals and verb forms, eg plumb, plumbs, plumbed, plumbing
- Includes words that are old, obsolete, dialectal, historical and/or literary
- Includes World English, including spelling and variants from the US, South Africa, Australia, New Zealand, etc
- Includes words that are denoted contractions, short forms and slang
- Includes words that may be deemed rude or derogatory

Disclaimer

While every effort has been made to exclude words in the category of hate speech, no other word is excluded on the grounds of religion, gender, race, or for any reason other than that it is an invalid word form for the game of Scrabble. The presence or exclusion of any word does not in any way represent the views of the Publisher, HarperCollins.

Other Scrabble resources

Associations

World English-Language Scrabble Players Association (WESPA) –
www.wespa.org

The WESPA website also provides access to resources for national associations, tournament organizers, players and youth players.

Association of British Scrabble Players (ABSP) – www.absp.org.uk

The ABSP website includes details of UK Scrabble clubs and UK tournaments.

North American Scrabble Players Association (NASPA) –
www.scrabbleplayers.org

The NASPA website contains numerous word lists and lists of further Scrabble resources.

Facebook

Several Scrabble groups, including:

World English-Language Scrabble Players Association

Scrabble International

Scrabble Snippetz

Collins Scrabble Players

Contents

Editor
Mary O'Neill

Computing Support
Agnieszka Urbanowicz

For the Publisher
Gerry Breslin
Kerry Ferguson

Collins Scrabble App

Download the Collins Official SCRABBLE™ app from the App Store.

Perfect for adjudication, solving and training.

Collins Scrabble Tools online

www.collinsdictionary.com/scrabble/scrabble-tools

Tools and tips, plus *Collins Scrabble Word Finder*, giving instant access to all official playable Scrabble words and scores.

Alphabetical list of two letter words

AA
AB
AD
AE
AG
AH
AI
AL
AM
AN
AR
AS
AT
AW
AX
AY
BA
BE
BI
BO
BY
CH
DA
DE
DI
DO
EA
ED
EE
EF
EH
EL
EM
EN
ER
ES
ET
EW
EX
FA
FE
FY
GI
GO
GU
HA
HE
HI
HM
HO
ID
IF
IN
IO
IS
IT
JA
JO
KA
KI
KO
KY
LA
LI
LO
MA
ME
MI
MM
MO
MU
MY
NA
NE
NO
NU
NY
OB
OD
OE
OF
OH
OI
OK
OM
ON
OO
OP
OR
OS
OU
OW
OX
OY
PA
PE
PI
PO
QI
RE
SH
SI
SO
ST
TA
TE
TI
TO
UG
UH
UM
UN
UP
UR
US
UT
WE
WO
XI
XU
YA
YE
YO
YU
ZA
ZE
ZO

Alphabetical list of three letter words

AAH
AAL
AAS
ABA
ABB
ABS
ABY
ACE
ACH
ACT
ADD
ADO
ADS
ADZ
AFF
AFT
AGA
AGE
AGO
AGS
AHA
AHI
AHS
AIA
AID
AIL
AIM
AIN
AIR
AIS
AIT
AJI
AKA
AKE
ALA
ALB
ALE
ALF
ALL
ALP
ALS
ALT
ALU
AMA
AME
AMI
AMP
AMU
ANA
AND
ANE
ANI
ANN
ANS
ANT
ANY
APE
APO
APP
APT
ARB
ARC
ARD
ARE
ARF
ARK
ARM
ARS
ART
ARY
ASH
ASK
ASP
ASS
ATE
ATS
ATT
AUA
AUE
AUF
AUK
AVA
AVE
AVO
AWA
AWE
AWK
AWL
AWN
AXE
AYE
AYS
AYU
AZO
BAA
BAC
BAD
BAE
BAG
BAH
BAL
BAM
BAN
BAO
BAP
BAR
BAS
BAT
BAY
BED
BEE
BEG
BEL
BEN
BES
BET
BEY
BEZ
BIB
BID
BIG
BIN
BIO
BIS
BIT
BIZ
BOA
BOB
BOD
BOG
BOH
BOI
BOK
BON
BOO
BOP
BOR
BOS
BOT
BOW
BOX
BOY
BRA
BRO
BRR
BRU
BUB
BUD
BUG
BUM
BUN
BUR
BUS
BUT
BUY
BYE
BYS
CAA
CAB
CAD

CAF
CAG
CAL
CAM
CAN
CAP
CAR
CAT
CAW
CAY
CAZ
CEE
CEL
CEP
CHA
CHE
CHI
CID
CIG
CIS
CIT
CLY
COB
COD
COG
COL
CON
COO
COP
COR
COS
COT
COW
COX
COY
COZ
CRU
CRY
CUB
CUD
CUE
CUM
CUP
CUR
CUT
CUZ
CWM
DAB
DAD
DAE
DAG
DAH
DAK
DAL
DAM
DAN
DAP
DAS
DAW
DAY
DEB
DEE
DEF
DEG
DEI
DEL
DEN
DEP
DEV
DEW
DEX
DEY
DIB
DID
DIE
DIF
DIG
DIM
DIN
DIP
DIS
DIT
DIV
DOB
DOC
DOD
DOE
DOF
DOG
DOH
DOL
DOM
DON
DOO
DOP
DOR
DOS
DOT
DOW
DOX
DOY
DRY
DSO
DUB
DUD
DUE
DUG
DUH
DUI
DUM
DUN
DUO
DUP
DUX
DYE
DZO
EAN
EAR
EAS
EAT
EAU
EBB
ECH
ECO
ECU
EDH
EDS
EEK
EEL
EEN
EEW
EFF
EFS
EFT
EGG
EGO
EHS
EIK
EKE
ELD
ELF
ELK
ELL
ELM
ELS
ELT
EME
EMO
EMS
EMU
END
ENE
ENG
ENS
EON
ERA
ERE
ERF
ERG
ERK
ERM
ERN
ERR
ERS
ESS
EST
ETA
ETH
EUK
EVE

EVO
EWE
EWK
EWT
EXO
EYE
FAA
FAB
FAD
FAE
FAG
FAH
FAN
FAP
FAR
FAS
FAT
FAW
FAX
FAY
FED
FEE
FEG
FEH
FEM
FEN
FER
FES
FET
FEU
FEW
FEY
FEZ
FIB
FID
FIE
FIG
FIL
FIN
FIR
FIT
FIX
FIZ
FLU
FLY
FOB
FOE
FOG
FOH
FON
FOO
FOP
FOR
FOU
FOX
FOY
FRA
FRO
FRY
FUB
FUD
FUG
FUM
FUN
FUR
GAB
GAD
GAE
GAG
GAK
GAL
GAM
GAN
GAP
GAR
GAS
GAT
GAU
GAW
GAY
GED
GEE
GEL
GEM
GEN
GEO
GER
GET
GEY
GHI
GIB
GID
GIE
GIF
GIG
GIN
GIO
GIP
GIS
GIT
GJU
GNU
GOA
GOB
GOD
GOE
GON
GOO
GOR
GOS
GOT
GOV
GOX
GRR
GUB
GUE
GUL
GUM
GUN
GUP
GUR
GUS
GUT
GUV
GUY
GYM
GYP
HAD
HAE
HAG
HAH
HAJ
HAM
HAN
HAO
HAP
HAS
HAT
HAW
HAY
HEH
HEM
HEN
HEP
HER
HES
HET
HEW
HEX
HEY
HIC
HID
HIE
HIM
HIN
HIP
HIS
HIT
HMM
HOA
HOB
HOC
HOD
HOE
HOG
HOH
HOI
HOM
HON
HOO

HOP
HOS
HOT
HOW
HOX
HOY
HUB
HUE
HUG
HUH
HUI
HUM
HUN
HUP
HUT
HYE
HYP
ICE
ICH
ICK
ICY
IDE
IDS
IFF
IFS
IGG
ILK
ILL
IMP
ING
INK
INN
INS
ION
IOS
IRE
IRK
ISH
ISM
ISO
ITA
ITS
IVY
IWI
JAB
JAG
JAI
JAK
JAM
JAP
JAR
JAW
JAY
JEE
JET
JEU
JIB
JIG
JIN
JIZ
JOB
JOE
JOG
JOL
JOR
JOT
JOW
JOY
JUD
JUG
JUN
JUS
JUT
KAB
KAE
KAF
KAI
KAK
KAM
KAS
KAT
KAW
KAY
KEA
KEB
KED
KEF
KEG
KEN
KEP
KET
KEX
KEY
KHI
KID
KIF
KIN
KIP
KIR
KIS
KIT
KOA
KOB
KOI
KON
KOP
KOR
KOS
KOW
KUE
KYE
KYU
LAB
LAC
LAD
LAG
LAH
LAM
LAP
LAR
LAS
LAT
LAV
LAW
LAX
LAY
LEA
LED
LEE
LEG
LEI
LEK
LEP
LET
LEU
LEV
LEW
LEX
LEY
LIB
LID
LIE
LIG
LIN
LIP
LIS
LIT
LOB
LOD
LOG
LOO
LOP
LOR
LOS
LOT
LOU
LOW
LOX
LOY
LUD
LUG
LUM
LUN
LUR
LUV
LUX
LUZ
LYE
LYM
MAA

MAC	MIS	NAG	NOO	OFT
MAD	MIX	NAH	NOR	OHM
MAE	MIZ	NAM	NOS	OHO
MAG	MMM	NAN	NOT	OHS
MAK	MNA	NAP	NOW	OIK
MAL	MOA	NAS	NOX	OIL
MAM	MOB	NAT	NOY	OIS
MAN	MOC	NAV	NTH	OKA
MAP	MOD	NAW	NUB	OKE
MAR	MOE	NAY	NUG	OLD
MAS	MOG	NEB	NUN	OLE
MAT	MOI	NED	NUR	OLM
MAW	MOL	NEE	NUS	OMA
MAX	MOM	NEF	NUT	OMS
MAY	MON	NEG	NYE	ONE
MED	MOO	NEK	NYM	ONO
MEE	MOP	NEP	NYS	ONS
MEG	MOR	NET	OAF	ONY
MEH	MOS	NEW	OAK	OOF
MEL	MOT	NIB	OAR	OOH
MEM	MOU	NID	OAT	OOM
MEN	MOW	NIE	OBA	OON
MES	MOY	NIL	OBE	OOP
MET	MOZ	NIM	OBI	OOR
MEU	MUD	NIP	OBO	OOS
MEW	MUG	NIS	OBS	OOT
MHO	MUM	NIT	OCA	OPA
MIB	MUN	NIX	OCH	OPE
MIC	MUS	NOB	ODA	OPS
MID	MUT	NOD	ODD	OPT
MIG	MUX	NOG	ODE	ORA
MIL	MYC	NOH	ODS	ORB
MIM	NAB	NOM	OES	ORC
MIR	NAE	NON	OFF	ORD

ORE	PAX	POI	RAD	RIA
ORF	PAY	POL	RAG	RIB
ORG	PEA	POM	RAH	RID
ORS	PEC	POO	RAI	RIF
ORT	PED	POP	RAJ	RIG
OSE	PEE	POS	RAM	RIM
OUD	PEG	POT	RAN	RIN
OUK	PEH	POW	RAP	RIP
OUP	PEL	POX	RAS	RIT
OUR	PEN	POZ	RAT	RIZ
OUS	PEP	PRE	RAV	ROB
OUT	PER	PRO	RAW	ROC
OVA	PES	PRY	RAX	ROD
OWE	PET	PSI	RAY	ROE
OWL	PEW	PST	REB	ROK
OWN	PHI	PUB	REC	ROM
OWT	PHO	PUD	RED	ROO
OXO	PHT	PUG	REE	ROT
OXY	PIA	PUH	REF	ROW
OYE	PIC	PUL	REG	RUB
OYS	PIE	PUN	REH	RUC
PAC	PIG	PUP	REI	RUD
PAD	PIN	PUR	REM	RUE
PAH	PIP	PUS	REN	RUG
PAK	PIR	PUT	REO	RUM
PAL	PIS	PUY	REP	RUN
PAM	PIT	PWN	RES	RUT
PAN	PIU	PYA	RET	RYA
PAP	PIX	PYE	REV	RYE
PAR	PLU	PYX	REW	RYU
PAS	PLY	QAT	REX	SAB
PAT	POA	QIN	REZ	SAC
PAV	POD	QIS	RHO	SAD
PAW	POH	QUA	RHY	SAE

SAG
SAI
SAL
SAM
SAN
SAP
SAR
SAT
SAU
SAV
SAW
SAX
SAY
SAZ
SEA
SEC
SED
SEE
SEG
SEI
SEL
SEN
SER
SET
SEV
SEW
SEX
SEY
SEZ
SHA
SHE
SHH
SHO
SHY
SIB
SIC
SIF
SIG
SIK
SIM
SIN
SIP
SIR
SIS
SIT
SIX
SKA
SKI
SKY
SLY
SMA
SNY
SOB
SOC
SOD
SOG
SOH
SOL
SOM
SON
SOP
SOS
SOT
SOU
SOV
SOW
SOX
SOY
SOZ
SPA
SPY
SRI
STY
SUB
SUD
SUE
SUG
SUI
SUK
SUM
SUN
SUP
SUQ
SUR
SUS
SWY
SYE
SYN
TAB
TAD
TAE
TAG
TAI
TAJ
TAK
TAM
TAN
TAO
TAP
TAR
TAS
TAT
TAU
TAV
TAW
TAX
TAY
TEA
TEC
TED
TEE
TEF
TEG
TEL
TEN
TES
TET
TEW
TEX
THE
THO
THY
TIC
TID
TIE
TIG
TIK
TIL
TIN
TIP
TIS
TIT
TIX
TIZ
TOC
TOD
TOE
TOG
TOM
TON
TOO
TOP
TOR
TOT
TOW
TOY
TRY
TSK
TUB
TUG
TUI
TUM
TUN
TUP
TUT
TUX
TWA
TWO
TWP
TYE
TYG
UDO
UDS
UEY
UFO
UGH
UGS
UKE
ULE
ULU

UME
UMM
UMP
UMS
UMU
UNI
UNS
UPO
UPS
URB
URD
URE
URN
URP
USE
UTA
UTE
UTS
UTU
UVA
VAC
VAE
VAG
VAN
VAR
VAS
VAT
VAU
VAV
VAW
VAX
VEE
VEG
VET
VEX
VIA
VID
VIE
VIG
VIM
VIN
VIS
VLY
VOE
VOG
VOL
VOM
VOR
VOW
VOX
VUG
VUM
WAB
WAD
WAE
WAG
WAI
WAN
WAP
WAR
WAS
WAT
WAW
WAX
WAY
WAZ
WEB
WED
WEE
WEM
WEN
WET
WEX
WEY
WHA
WHO
WHY
WIG
WIN
WIS
WIT
WIZ
WOE
WOF
WOK
WON
WOO
WOP
WOS
WOT
WOW
WOX
WRY
WUD
WUS
WUZ
WYE
WYN
XED
XIS
YAD
YAE
YAG
YAH
YAK
YAM
YAP
YAR
YAS
YAW
YAY
YEA
YEH
YEN
YEP
YER
YES
YET
YEW
YEX
YEZ
YGO
YIN
YIP
YOB
YOD
YOK
YOM
YON
YOU
YOW
YUG
YUK
YUM
YUP
YUS
ZAG
ZAP
ZAS
ZAX
ZEA
ZED
ZEE
ZEK
ZEL
ZEN
ZEP
ZEX
ZHO
ZIG
ZIN
ZIP
ZIT
ZIZ
ZOA
ZOL
ZOO
ZOS
ZUZ
ZZZ

Two and three letter words with J, Q, X, and Z

Two letter words with J

JA	JO

Three letter words with J

AJI	JAM	JEU	JOG	JUG
GJU	JAP	JIB	JOL	JUN
HAJ	JAR	JIG	JOR	JUS
JAB	JAW	JIN	JOT	JUT
JAG	JAY	JIZ	JOW	RAJ
JAI	JEE	JOB	JOY	TAJ
JAK	JET	JOE	JUD	

Two letter words with Q

QI

Three letter words with Q

QAT	QIN	QIS	QUA	SUQ

Two letter words with X

AX	EX	OX	XI	XU

Three letter words with X

AXE	GOX	MUX	REX	VEX
BOX	HEX	NIX	SAX	VOX
COX	HOX	NOX	SEX	WAX
DEX	KEX	OXO	SIX	WEX
DOX	LAX	OXY	SOX	WOX
DUX	LEX	PAX	TAX	XED
EXO	LOX	PIX	TEX	XIS
FAX	LUX	POX	TIX	YEX
FIX	MAX	PYX	TUX	ZAX
FOX	MIX	RAX	VAX	ZEX

Two letter words with Z

ZA	ZE	ZO

Three letter words with Z

ADZ	JIZ	TIZ	ZED	ZIP
AZO	LUZ	WAZ	ZEE	ZIT
BEZ	MIZ	WIZ	ZEK	ZIZ
BIZ	MOZ	WUZ	ZEL	ZOA
CAZ	POZ	YEZ	ZEN	ZOL
COZ	REZ	ZAG	ZEP	ZOO
CUZ	RIZ	ZAP	ZEX	ZOS
DZO	SAZ	ZAS	ZHO	ZUZ
FEZ	SEZ	ZAX	ZIG	ZZZ
FIZ	SOZ	ZEA	ZIN	

TWO TO NINE LETTER WORDS

AA
AAH
AAHED
AAHING
AAHS
AAL
AALII
AALIIS
AALS
AARDVARK
AARDVARKS
AARDWOLF
AARGH
AARRGH
AARRGHH
AARTI
AARTIS
AAS
AASVOGEL
AASVOGELS
AB
ABA
ABAC
ABACA
ABACAS
ABACI
ABACK
ABACS
ABACTINAL
ABACTOR
ABACTORS
ABACUS
ABACUSES
ABAFT
ABAKA
ABAKAS
ABALONE
ABALONES
ABAMP
ABAMPERE
ABAMPERES
ABAMPS
ABAND
ABANDED
ABANDING
ABANDON
ABANDONED
ABANDONEE
ABANDONER
ABANDONS
ABANDS
ABAPICAL
ABAS
ABASE
ABASED
ABASEDLY
ABASEMENT
ABASER
ABASERS
ABASES
ABASH
ABASHED
ABASHEDLY
ABASHES
ABASHING
ABASHLESS
ABASHMENT
ABASIA
ABASIAS
ABASING
ABASK
ABATABLE
ABATE
ABATED
ABATEMENT
ABATER
ABATERS
ABATES
ABATING
ABATIS
ABATISES
ABATOR
ABATORS
ABATTIS
ABATTISES
ABATTOIR
ABATTOIRS
ABATTU
ABATURE
ABATURES
ABAXIAL
ABAXILE
ABAYA
ABAYAS
ABB
ABBA
ABBACIES
ABBACY
ABBAS
ABBATIAL
ABBE
ABBED
ABBES
ABBESS
ABBESSES
ABBEY
ABBEYS
ABBOT
ABBOTCIES
ABBOTCY
ABBOTS
ABBOTSHIP
ABBS
ABCEE
ABCEES
ABCOULOMB
ABDABS
ABDICABLE
ABDICANT
ABDICANTS
ABDICATE
ABDICATED
ABDICATES
ABDICATOR
ABDOMEN
ABDOMENS
ABDOMINA
ABDOMINAL
ABDUCE
ABDUCED
ABDUCENS
ABDUCENT
ABDUCES
ABDUCING
ABDUCT
ABDUCTED
ABDUCTEE
ABDUCTEES
ABDUCTING
ABDUCTION
ABDUCTOR
ABDUCTORS
ABDUCTS
ABEAM
ABEAR
ABEARING
ABEARS
ABED
ABEGGING
ABEIGH
ABELE
ABELES
ABELIA
ABELIAN
ABELIAS
ABELMOSK
ABELMOSKS
ABER
ABERNETHY
ABERRANCE
ABERRANCY
ABERRANT
ABERRANTS
ABERRATE
ABERRATED
ABERRATES
ABERS
ABESSIVE
ABESSIVES
ABET
ABETMENT
ABETMENTS
ABETS
ABETTAL
ABETTALS
ABETTED
ABETTER
ABETTERS
ABETTING
ABETTOR
ABETTORS
ABEYANCE
ABEYANCES
ABEYANCY
ABEYANT
ABFARAD
ABFARADS
ABHENRIES
ABHENRY
ABHENRYS
ABHOR
ABHORRED
ABHORRENT
ABHORRER
ABHORRERS
ABHORRING
ABHORS
ABID
ABIDANCE
ABIDANCES
ABIDDEN
ABIDE
ABIDED
ABIDER
ABIDERS
ABIDES
ABIDING
ABIDINGLY
ABIDINGS
ABIES

ABIETES
ABIETIC
ABIGAIL
ABIGAILS
ABILITIES
ABILITY
ABIOGENIC
ABIOSES
ABIOSIS
ABIOTIC
ABITUR
ABITURS
ABJECT
ABJECTED
ABJECTING
ABJECTION
ABJECTLY
ABJECTS
ABJOINT
ABJOINTED
ABJOINTS
ABJURE
ABJURED
ABJURER
ABJURERS
ABJURES
ABJURING
ABLATE
ABLATED
ABLATES
ABLATING
ABLATION
ABLATIONS
ABLATIVAL
ABLATIVE
ABLATIVES
ABLATOR
ABLATORS
ABLAUT
ABLAUTS
ABLAZE
ABLE
ABLED
ABLEGATE
ABLEGATES
ABLEISM
ABLEISMS
ABLEIST
ABLEISTS
ABLER
ABLES
ABLEST
ABLET
ABLETS
ABLING
ABLINGS
ABLINS
ABLOOM
ABLOW
ABLUENT
ABLUENTS
ABLUSH
ABLUTED
ABLUTION
ABLUTIONS
ABLY
ABMHO
ABMHOS
ABNEGATE
ABNEGATED
ABNEGATES
ABNEGATOR
ABNORMAL
ABNORMALS
ABNORMITY
ABNORMOUS
ABOARD
ABODE
ABODED
ABODEMENT
ABODES
ABODING
ABOHM
ABOHMS
ABOIDEAU
ABOIDEAUS
ABOIDEAUX
ABOIL
ABOITEAU
ABOITEAUS
ABOITEAUX
ABOLISH
ABOLISHED
ABOLISHER
ABOLISHES
ABOLITION
ABOLLA
ABOLLAE
ABOLLAS
ABOMA
ABOMAS
ABOMASA
ABOMASAL
ABOMASI
ABOMASUM
ABOMASUS
ABOMINATE
ABONDANCE
ABOON
ABORAL
ABORALLY
ABORD
ABORDED
ABORDING
ABORDS
ABORE
ABORIGEN
ABORIGENS
ABORIGIN
ABORIGINE
ABORIGINS
ABORNE
ABORNING
ABORT
ABORTED
ABORTEE
ABORTEES
ABORTER
ABORTERS
ABORTING
ABORTION
ABORTIONS
ABORTIVE
ABORTS
ABORTUARY
ABORTUS
ABORTUSES
ABOUGHT
ABOULIA
ABOULIAS
ABOULIC
ABOUND
ABOUNDED
ABOUNDING
ABOUNDS
ABOUT
ABOUTS
ABOVE
ABOVES
ABRACHIA
ABRACHIAS
ABRADABLE
ABRADANT
ABRADANTS
ABRADE
ABRADED
ABRADER
ABRADERS
ABRADES
ABRADING
ABRAID
ABRAIDED
ABRAIDING
ABRAIDS
ABRAM
ABRASAX
ABRASAXES
ABRASION
ABRASIONS
ABRASIVE
ABRASIVES
ABRAXAS
ABRAXASES
ABRAY
ABRAYED
ABRAYING
ABRAYS
ABRAZO
ABRAZOS
ABREACT
ABREACTED
ABREACTS
ABREAST
ABREGE
ABREGES
ABRI
ABRICOCK
ABRICOCKS
ABRIDGE
ABRIDGED
ABRIDGER
ABRIDGERS
ABRIDGES
ABRIDGING
ABRIM
ABRIN
ABRINS
ABRIS
ABROACH
ABROAD
ABROADS
ABROGABLE
ABROGATE
ABROGATED
ABROGATES
ABROGATOR
ABROOKE
ABROOKED
ABROOKES
ABROOKING
ABROSIA
ABROSIAS
ABRUPT
ABRUPTER
ABRUPTEST
ABRUPTION
ABRUPTLY
ABRUPTS
ABS
ABSCESS
ABSCESSED
ABSCESSES
ABSCIND
ABSCINDED
ABSCINDS
ABSCISE
ABSCISED
ABSCISES
ABSCISIC
ABSCISIN
ABSCISING
ABSCISINS
ABSCISS
ABSCISSA
ABSCISSAE
ABSCISSAS
ABSCISSE
ABSCISSES
ABSCISSIN
ABSCOND

ABSCONDED
ABSCONDER
ABSCONDS
ABSEIL
ABSEILED
ABSEILER
ABSEILERS
ABSEILING
ABSEILS
ABSENCE
ABSENCES
ABSENT
ABSENTED
ABSENTEE
ABSENTEES
ABSENTER
ABSENTERS
ABSENTING
ABSENTLY
ABSENTS
ABSEY
ABSEYS
ABSINTH
ABSINTHE
ABSINTHES
ABSINTHS
ABSIT
ABSITS
ABSOLUTE
ABSOLUTER
ABSOLUTES
ABSOLVE
ABSOLVED
ABSOLVENT
ABSOLVER
ABSOLVERS
ABSOLVES
ABSOLVING
ABSONANT
ABSORB
ABSORBANT
ABSORBATE
ABSORBED
ABSORBENT
ABSORBER
ABSORBERS
ABSORBING
ABSORBS
ABSTAIN
ABSTAINED
ABSTAINER
ABSTAINS
ABSTERGE
ABSTERGED
ABSTERGES
ABSTINENT
ABSTRACT
ABSTRACTS
ABSTRICT
ABSTRICTS
ABSTRUSE
ABSTRUSER
ABSURD
ABSURDER
ABSURDEST
ABSURDISM
ABSURDIST
ABSURDITY
ABSURDLY
ABSURDS
ABTHANE
ABTHANES
ABUBBLE
ABUILDING
ABULIA
ABULIAS
ABULIC
ABUNA
ABUNAS
ABUNDANCE
ABUNDANCY
ABUNDANT
ABUNE
ABURST
ABUSABLE
ABUSAGE
ABUSAGES
ABUSE
ABUSED
ABUSER
ABUSERS
ABUSES
ABUSING
ABUSION
ABUSIONS
ABUSIVE
ABUSIVELY
ABUT
ABUTILON
ABUTILONS
ABUTMENT
ABUTMENTS
ABUTS
ABUTTAL
ABUTTALS
ABUTTED
ABUTTER
ABUTTERS
ABUTTING
ABUZZ
ABVOLT
ABVOLTS
ABWATT
ABWATTS
ABY
ABYE
ABYEING
ABYES
ABYING
ABYS
ABYSM
ABYSMAL
ABYSMALLY
ABYSMS
ABYSS
ABYSSAL
ABYSSES
ACACIA
ACACIAS
ACADEME
ACADEMES
ACADEMIA
ACADEMIAS
ACADEMIC
ACADEMICS
ACADEMIES
ACADEMISM
ACADEMIST
ACADEMY
ACAI
ACAIS
ACAJOU
ACAJOUS
ACALCULIA
ACALEPH
ACALEPHAE
ACALEPHAN
ACALEPHE
ACALEPHES
ACALEPHS
ACANTH
ACANTHA
ACANTHAE
ACANTHAS
ACANTHI
ACANTHIN
ACANTHINE
ACANTHINS
ACANTHOID
ACANTHOUS
ACANTHS
ACANTHUS
ACAPNIA
ACAPNIAS
ACARBOSE
ACARBOSES
ACARI
ACARIAN
ACARIASES
ACARIASIS
ACARICIDE
ACARID
ACARIDAN
ACARIDANS
ACARIDEAN
ACARIDIAN
ACARIDS
ACARINE
ACARINES
ACAROID
ACAROLOGY
ACARPOUS
ACARUS
ACATER
ACATERS
ACATES
ACATHISIA
ACATOUR
ACATOURS
ACAUDAL
ACAUDATE
ACAULINE
ACAULOSE
ACAULOUS
ACCA
ACCABLE
ACCAS
ACCEDE
ACCEDED
ACCEDENCE
ACCEDER
ACCEDERS
ACCEDES
ACCEDING
ACCEND
ACCENDED
ACCENDING
ACCENDS
ACCENSION
ACCENT
ACCENTED
ACCENTING
ACCENTOR
ACCENTORS
ACCENTS
ACCENTUAL
ACCEPT
ACCEPTANT
ACCEPTED
ACCEPTEE
ACCEPTEES
ACCEPTER
ACCEPTERS
ACCEPTING
ACCEPTIVE
ACCEPTOR
ACCEPTORS
ACCEPTS
ACCESS
ACCESSARY
ACCESSED
ACCESSES
ACCESSING
ACCESSION
ACCESSORY
ACCIDENCE
ACCIDENT
ACCIDENTS
ACCIDIA
ACCIDIAS

ACCIDIE
ACCIDIES
ACCINGE
ACCINGED
ACCINGES
ACCINGING
ACCIPITER
ACCITE
ACCITED
ACCITES
ACCITING
ACCLAIM
ACCLAIMED
ACCLAIMER
ACCLAIMS
ACCLIMATE
ACCLIVITY
ACCLIVOUS
ACCLOY
ACCLOYED
ACCLOYING
ACCLOYS
ACCOAST
ACCOASTED
ACCOASTS
ACCOIED
ACCOIL
ACCOILS
ACCOLADE
ACCOLADED
ACCOLADES
ACCOMPANY
ACCOMPT
ACCOMPTED
ACCOMPTS
ACCORAGE
ACCORAGED
ACCORAGES
ACCORD
ACCORDANT
ACCORDED
ACCORDER
ACCORDERS
ACCORDING
ACCORDION
ACCORDS
ACCOST
ACCOSTED
ACCOSTING
ACCOSTS
ACCOUNT
ACCOUNTED
ACCOUNTS
ACCOURAGE
ACCOURT
ACCOURTED
ACCOURTS
ACCOUTER
ACCOUTERS
ACCOUTRE
ACCOUTRED
ACCOUTRES
ACCOY
ACCOYED
ACCOYING
ACCOYLD
ACCOYS
ACCREDIT
ACCREDITS
ACCRETE
ACCRETED
ACCRETES
ACCRETING
ACCRETION
ACCRETIVE
ACCREW
ACCREWED
ACCREWING
ACCREWS
ACCROIDES
ACCRUABLE
ACCRUAL
ACCRUALS
ACCRUE
ACCRUED
ACCRUES
ACCRUING
ACCUMBENT
ACCURACY
ACCURATE
ACCURSE
ACCURSED
ACCURSES
ACCURSING
ACCURST
ACCUSABLE
ACCUSABLY
ACCUSAL
ACCUSALS
ACCUSANT
ACCUSANTS
ACCUSE
ACCUSED
ACCUSER
ACCUSERS
ACCUSES
ACCUSING
ACCUSTOM
ACCUSTOMS
ACE
ACED
ACEDIA
ACEDIAS
ACELDAMA
ACELDAMAS
ACELLULAR
ACENTRIC
ACENTRICS
ACEPHALIC
ACEQUIA
ACEQUIAS
ACER
ACERATE
ACERATED
ACERB
ACERBATE
ACERBATED
ACERBATES
ACERBER
ACERBEST
ACERBIC
ACERBITY
ACEROLA
ACEROLAS
ACEROSE
ACEROUS
ACERS
ACERVATE
ACERVULI
ACERVULUS
ACES
ACESCENCE
ACESCENCY
ACESCENT
ACESCENTS
ACETA
ACETABULA
ACETAL
ACETALS
ACETAMID
ACETAMIDE
ACETAMIDS
ACETATE
ACETATED
ACETATES
ACETIC
ACETIFIED
ACETIFIER
ACETIFIES
ACETIFY
ACETIN
ACETINS
ACETONE
ACETONES
ACETONIC
ACETOSE
ACETOUS
ACETOXYL
ACETOXYLS
ACETUM
ACETYL
ACETYLATE
ACETYLENE
ACETYLIC
ACETYLIDE
ACETYLS
ACH
ACHAENIA
ACHAENIUM
ACHAGE
ACHAGES
ACHALASIA
ACHAR
ACHARNE
ACHARS
ACHARYA
ACHARYAS
ACHATES
ACHE
ACHED
ACHENE
ACHENES
ACHENIA
ACHENIAL
ACHENIUM
ACHENIUMS
ACHES
ACHIER
ACHIEST
ACHIEVE
ACHIEVED
ACHIEVER
ACHIEVERS
ACHIEVES
ACHIEVING
ACHILLEA
ACHILLEAS
ACHIMENES
ACHINESS
ACHING
ACHINGLY
ACHINGS
ACHIOTE
ACHIOTES
ACHIRAL
ACHKAN
ACHKANS
ACHOLIA
ACHOLIAS
ACHOO
ACHOOS
ACHROMAT
ACHROMATS
ACHROMIC
ACHROMOUS
ACHY
ACICLOVIR
ACICULA
ACICULAE
ACICULAR
ACICULAS
ACICULATE
ACICULUM
ACICULUMS
ACID
ACIDEMIA
ACIDEMIAS
ACIDER
ACIDEST
ACIDHEAD

ACIDHEADS
ACIDIC
ACIDIER
ACIDIEST
ACIDIFIED
ACIDIFIER
ACIDIFIES
ACIDIFY
ACIDITIES
ACIDITY
ACIDLY
ACIDNESS
ACIDOPHIL
ACIDOSES
ACIDOSIS
ACIDOTIC
ACIDS
ACIDULATE
ACIDULENT
ACIDULOUS
ACIDURIA
ACIDURIAS
ACIDY
ACIERAGE
ACIERAGES
ACIERATE
ACIERATED
ACIERATES
ACIFORM
ACINAR
ACING
ACINI
ACINIC
ACINIFORM
ACINOSE
ACINOUS
ACINUS
ACKEE
ACKEES
ACKER
ACKERS
ACKNEW
ACKNOW
ACKNOWING
ACKNOWN
ACKNOWNE
ACKNOWS
ACLINIC
ACMATIC
ACME
ACMES
ACMIC
ACMITE
ACMITES
ACNE
ACNED
ACNES
ACNODAL
ACNODE
ACNODES
ACOCK
ACOELOUS
ACOEMETI
ACOLD
ACOLUTHIC
ACOLYTE
ACOLYTES
ACOLYTH
ACOLYTHS
ACONITE
ACONITES
ACONITIC
ACONITINE
ACONITUM
ACONITUMS
ACORN
ACORNED
ACORNS
ACOSMISM
ACOSMISMS
ACOSMIST
ACOSMISTS
ACOUCHI
ACOUCHIES
ACOUCHIS
ACOUCHY
ACOUSTIC
ACOUSTICS
ACQUAINT
ACQUAINTS
ACQUEST
ACQUESTS
ACQUIESCE
ACQUIGHT
ACQUIGHTS
ACQUIRAL
ACQUIRALS
ACQUIRE
ACQUIRED
ACQUIREE
ACQUIREES
ACQUIRER
ACQUIRERS
ACQUIRES
ACQUIRING
ACQUIS
ACQUIST
ACQUISTS
ACQUIT
ACQUITE
ACQUITES
ACQUITING
ACQUITS
ACQUITTAL
ACQUITTED
ACQUITTER
ACRASIA
ACRASIAS
ACRASIN
ACRASINS
ACRATIC
ACRAWL
ACRE
ACREAGE
ACREAGES
ACRED
ACRES
ACRID
ACRIDER
ACRIDEST
ACRIDIN
ACRIDINE
ACRIDINES
ACRIDINS
ACRIDITY
ACRIDLY
ACRIDNESS
ACRIMONY
ACRITARCH
ACRITICAL
ACRO
ACROBAT
ACROBATIC
ACROBATS
ACRODONT
ACRODONTS
ACRODROME
ACROGEN
ACROGENIC
ACROGENS
ACROLECT
ACROLECTS
ACROLEIN
ACROLEINS
ACROLITH
ACROLITHS
ACROMIA
ACROMIAL
ACROMION
ACRONIC
ACRONICAL
ACRONYCAL
ACRONYM
ACRONYMIC
ACRONYMS
ACROPETAL
ACROPHOBE
ACROPHONY
ACROPOLIS
ACROS
ACROSOMAL
ACROSOME
ACROSOMES
ACROSPIRE
ACROSS
ACROSTIC
ACROSTICS
ACROTER
ACROTERIA
ACROTERS
ACROTIC
ACROTISM
ACROTISMS
ACRYLATE
ACRYLATES
ACRYLIC
ACRYLICS
ACRYLYL
ACRYLYLS
ACT
ACTA
ACTABLE
ACTANT
ACTANTS
ACTED
ACTIN
ACTINAL
ACTINALLY
ACTING
ACTINGS
ACTINIA
ACTINIAE
ACTINIAN
ACTINIANS
ACTINIAS
ACTINIC
ACTINIDE
ACTINIDES
ACTINISM
ACTINISMS
ACTINIUM
ACTINIUMS
ACTINOID
ACTINOIDS
ACTINON
ACTINONS
ACTINOPOD
ACTINS
ACTION
ACTIONED
ACTIONER
ACTIONERS
ACTIONING
ACTIONIST
ACTIONS
ACTIVATE
ACTIVATED
ACTIVATES
ACTIVATOR
ACTIVE
ACTIVELY
ACTIVES
ACTIVISE
ACTIVISED
ACTIVISES
ACTIVISM
ACTIVISMS
ACTIVIST
ACTIVISTS
ACTIVITY

ACTIVIZE
ACTIVIZED
ACTIVIZES
ACTON
ACTONS
ACTOR
ACTORISH
ACTORLIER
ACTORLY
ACTORS
ACTRESS
ACTRESSES
ACTRESSY
ACTS
ACTUAL
ACTUALISE
ACTUALIST
ACTUALITE
ACTUALITY
ACTUALIZE
ACTUALLY
ACTUALS
ACTUARIAL
ACTUARIES
ACTUARY
ACTUATE
ACTUATED
ACTUATES
ACTUATING
ACTUATION
ACTUATOR
ACTUATORS
ACTURE
ACTURES
ACUATE
ACUATED
ACUATES
ACUATING
ACUITIES
ACUITY
ACULEATE
ACULEATED
ACULEATES
ACULEI
ACULEUS
ACUMEN
ACUMENS
ACUMINATE
ACUMINOUS
ACUPOINT
ACUPOINTS
ACUSHLA
ACUSHLAS
ACUTANCE
ACUTANCES
ACUTE
ACUTELY
ACUTENESS
ACUTER
ACUTES
ACUTEST
ACYCLIC
ACYCLOVIR
ACYL
ACYLATE
ACYLATED
ACYLATES
ACYLATING
ACYLATION
ACYLOIN
ACYLOINS
ACYLS
AD
ADAGE
ADAGES
ADAGIAL
ADAGIO
ADAGIOS
ADAMANCE
ADAMANCES
ADAMANCY
ADAMANT
ADAMANTLY
ADAMANTS
ADAMSITE
ADAMSITES
ADAPT
ADAPTABLE
ADAPTED
ADAPTER
ADAPTERS
ADAPTING
ADAPTION
ADAPTIONS
ADAPTIVE
ADAPTOGEN
ADAPTOR
ADAPTORS
ADAPTS
ADAW
ADAWED
ADAWING
ADAWS
ADAXIAL
ADAYS
ADBOT
ADBOTS
ADD
ADDABLE
ADDAX
ADDAXES
ADDEBTED
ADDED
ADDEDLY
ADDEEM
ADDEEMED
ADDEEMING
ADDEEMS
ADDEND
ADDENDA
ADDENDS
ADDENDUM
ADDENDUMS
ADDER
ADDERBEAD
ADDERS
ADDERWORT
ADDIBLE
ADDICT
ADDICTED
ADDICTING
ADDICTION
ADDICTIVE
ADDICTS
ADDIES
ADDING
ADDINGS
ADDIO
ADDIOS
ADDITION
ADDITIONS
ADDITIVE
ADDITIVES
ADDITORY
ADDLE
ADDLED
ADDLEMENT
ADDLES
ADDLING
ADDOOM
ADDOOMED
ADDOOMING
ADDOOMS
ADDORSED
ADDRESS
ADDRESSED
ADDRESSEE
ADDRESSER
ADDRESSES
ADDRESSOR
ADDREST
ADDS
ADDUCE
ADDUCED
ADDUCENT
ADDUCER
ADDUCERS
ADDUCES
ADDUCIBLE
ADDUCING
ADDUCT
ADDUCTED
ADDUCTING
ADDUCTION
ADDUCTIVE
ADDUCTOR
ADDUCTORS
ADDUCTS
ADDY
ADEEM
ADEEMED
ADEEMING
ADEEMS
ADELGID
ADELGIDS
ADEMPTION
ADENINE
ADENINES
ADENITIS
ADENOID
ADENOIDAL
ADENOIDS
ADENOMA
ADENOMAS
ADENOMATA
ADENOSES
ADENOSINE
ADENOSIS
ADENYL
ADENYLATE
ADENYLIC
ADENYLS
ADEPT
ADEPTER
ADEPTEST
ADEPTLY
ADEPTNESS
ADEPTS
ADEQUACY
ADEQUATE
ADERMIN
ADERMINS
ADESPOTA
ADESSIVE
ADESSIVES
ADHAN
ADHANS
ADHARMA
ADHARMAS
ADHERABLE
ADHERE
ADHERED
ADHERENCE
ADHEREND
ADHERENDS
ADHERENT
ADHERENTS
ADHERER
ADHERERS
ADHERES
ADHERING
ADHESION
ADHESIONS
ADHESIVE
ADHESIVES
ADHIBIT
ADHIBITED
ADHIBITS
ADHOCRACY
ADIABATIC

ADIAPHORA
ADIEU
ADIEUS
ADIEUX
ADIOS
ADIOSES
ADIPIC
ADIPOCERE
ADIPOCYTE
ADIPOSE
ADIPOSES
ADIPOSIS
ADIPOSITY
ADIPOUS
ADIPSIA
ADIPSIAS
ADIT
ADITS
ADJACENCE
ADJACENCY
ADJACENT
ADJACENTS
ADJECTIVE
ADJIGO
ADJIGOS
ADJOIN
ADJOINED
ADJOINING
ADJOINS
ADJOINT
ADJOINTS
ADJOURN
ADJOURNED
ADJOURNS
ADJUDGE
ADJUDGED
ADJUDGES
ADJUDGING
ADJUNCT
ADJUNCTLY
ADJUNCTS
ADJURE
ADJURED
ADJURER
ADJURERS
ADJURES
ADJURING
ADJUROR
ADJURORS
ADJUST
ADJUSTED
ADJUSTER
ADJUSTERS
ADJUSTING
ADJUSTIVE
ADJUSTOR
ADJUSTORS
ADJUSTS
ADJUTAGE
ADJUTAGES
ADJUTANCY
ADJUTANT
ADJUTANTS
ADJUVANCY
ADJUVANT
ADJUVANTS
ADLAND
ADLANDS
ADMAN
ADMASS
ADMASSES
ADMEASURE
ADMEN
ADMIN
ADMINICLE
ADMINS
ADMIRABLE
ADMIRABLY
ADMIRAL
ADMIRALS
ADMIRALTY
ADMIRANCE
ADMIRE
ADMIRED
ADMIRER
ADMIRERS
ADMIRES
ADMIRING
ADMISSION
ADMISSIVE
ADMIT
ADMITS
ADMITTED
ADMITTEE
ADMITTEES
ADMITTER
ADMITTERS
ADMITTING
ADMIX
ADMIXED
ADMIXES
ADMIXING
ADMIXT
ADMIXTURE
ADMONISH
ADMONITOR
ADNASCENT
ADNATE
ADNATION
ADNATIONS
ADNEXA
ADNEXAL
ADNOMINAL
ADNOUN
ADNOUNS
ADO
ADOBE
ADOBELIKE
ADOBES
ADOBO
ADOBOS
ADONIS
ADONISE
ADONISED
ADONISES
ADONISING
ADONIZE
ADONIZED
ADONIZES
ADONIZING
ADOORS
ADOPT
ADOPTABLE
ADOPTED
ADOPTEE
ADOPTEES
ADOPTER
ADOPTERS
ADOPTING
ADOPTION
ADOPTIONS
ADOPTIOUS
ADOPTIVE
ADOPTS
ADORABLE
ADORABLY
ADORATION
ADORE
ADORED
ADORER
ADORERS
ADORES
ADORING
ADORINGLY
ADORKABLE
ADORN
ADORNED
ADORNER
ADORNERS
ADORNING
ADORNMENT
ADORNS
ADOS
ADOWN
ADOZE
ADPRESS
ADPRESSED
ADPRESSES
ADRAD
ADRATE
ADRATES
ADREAD
ADREADED
ADREADING
ADREADS
ADRED
ADRENAL
ADRENALIN
ADRENALLY
ADRENALS
ADRIFT
ADROIT
ADROITER
ADROITEST
ADROITLY
ADRY
ADS
ADSCRIPT
ADSCRIPTS
ADSORB
ADSORBATE
ADSORBED
ADSORBENT
ADSORBER
ADSORBERS
ADSORBING
ADSORBS
ADSPEAK
ADSPEAKS
ADSUKI
ADSUKIS
ADSUM
ADUKI
ADUKIS
ADULARIA
ADULARIAS
ADULATE
ADULATED
ADULATES
ADULATING
ADULATION
ADULATOR
ADULATORS
ADULATORY
ADULT
ADULTERER
ADULTERY
ADULTHOOD
ADULTLIKE
ADULTLY
ADULTNESS
ADULTRESS
ADULTS
ADUMBRAL
ADUMBRATE
ADUNC
ADUNCATE
ADUNCATED
ADUNCITY
ADUNCOUS
ADUST
ADUSTED
ADUSTING
ADUSTS
ADVANCE
ADVANCED
ADVANCER
ADVANCERS
ADVANCES
ADVANCING

ADVANTAGE
ADVECT
ADVECTED
ADVECTING
ADVECTION
ADVECTIVE
ADVECTS
ADVENE
ADVENED
ADVENES
ADVENING
ADVENT
ADVENTIVE
ADVENTS
ADVENTURE
ADVERB
ADVERBIAL
ADVERBS
ADVERSARY
ADVERSE
ADVERSELY
ADVERSER
ADVERSEST
ADVERSITY
ADVERT
ADVERTED
ADVERTENT
ADVERTING
ADVERTISE
ADVERTIZE
ADVERTS
ADVEW
ADVEWED
ADVEWING
ADVEWS
ADVICE
ADVICEFUL
ADVICES
ADVISABLE
ADVISABLY
ADVISE
ADVISED
ADVISEDLY
ADVISEE
ADVISEES
ADVISER
ADVISERS
ADVISES
ADVISING
ADVISINGS
ADVISOR
ADVISORS
ADVISORY
ADVOCAAT
ADVOCAATS
ADVOCACY
ADVOCATE
ADVOCATED
ADVOCATES
ADVOCATOR
ADVOUTRER
ADVOUTRY
ADVOWSON
ADVOWSONS
ADWARD
ADWARDED
ADWARDING
ADWARDS
ADWARE
ADWARES
ADWOMAN
ADWOMEN
ADYNAMIA
ADYNAMIAS
ADYNAMIC
ADYTA
ADYTUM
ADZ
ADZE
ADZED
ADZELIKE
ADZES
ADZING
ADZUKI
ADZUKIS
AE
AECIA
AECIAL
AECIDIA
AECIDIAL
AECIDIUM
AECIUM
AEDES
AEDICULE
AEDICULES
AEDILE
AEDILES
AEDINE
AEFALD
AEFAULD
AEGIRINE
AEGIRINES
AEGIRITE
AEGIRITES
AEGIS
AEGISES
AEGLOGUE
AEGLOGUES
AEGROTAT
AEGROTATS
AEMULE
AEMULED
AEMULES
AEMULING
AENEOUS
AENEUS
AENEUSES
AEOLIAN
AEOLIPILE
AEOLIPYLE
AEON
AEONIAN
AEONIC
AEONS
AEPYORNIS
AEQUORIN
AEQUORINS
AERADIO
AERADIOS
AERATE
AERATED
AERATES
AERATING
AERATION
AERATIONS
AERATOR
AERATORS
AERIAL
AERIALIST
AERIALITY
AERIALLY
AERIALS
AERIE
AERIED
AERIER
AERIES
AERIEST
AERIFIED
AERIFIES
AERIFORM
AERIFY
AERIFYING
AERILY
AERO
AEROBAT
AEROBATIC
AEROBATS
AEROBE
AEROBES
AEROBIA
AEROBIC
AEROBICS
AEROBIONT
AEROBIUM
AEROBOMB
AEROBOMBS
AEROBOT
AEROBOTS
AEROBRAKE
AEROBUS
AEROBUSES
AERODART
AERODARTS
AERODROME
AERODUCT
AERODUCTS
AERODYNE
AERODYNES
AEROFOIL
AEROFOILS
AEROGEL
AEROGELS
AEROGRAM
AEROGRAMS
AEROGRAPH
AEROLITE
AEROLITES
AEROLITH
AEROLITHS
AEROLITIC
AEROLOGIC
AEROLOGY
AEROMANCY
AEROMETER
AEROMETRY
AEROMOTOR
AERONAUT
AERONAUTS
AERONOMER
AERONOMIC
AERONOMY
AEROPAUSE
AEROPHAGY
AEROPHOBE
AEROPHONE
AEROPHORE
AEROPHYTE
AEROPLANE
AEROPULSE
AEROS
AEROSAT
AEROSATS
AEROSCOPE
AEROSHELL
AEROSOL
AEROSOLS
AEROSPACE
AEROSPIKE
AEROSTAT
AEROSTATS
AEROTAXES
AEROTAXIS
AEROTONE
AEROTONES
AEROTRAIN
AERUGO
AERUGOS
AERY
AESC
AESCES
AESCULIN
AESCULINS
AESIR
AESTHESES
AESTHESIA
AESTHESIS
AESTHETE
AESTHETES
AESTHETIC
AESTIVAL

AESTIVATE
AETATIS
AETHER
AETHEREAL
AETHERIC
AETHERS
AETIOLOGY
AFALD
AFAR
AFARA
AFARAS
AFARS
AFAWLD
AFEAR
AFEARD
AFEARED
AFEARING
AFEARS
AFEBRILE
AFF
AFFABLE
AFFABLY
AFFAIR
AFFAIRE
AFFAIRES
AFFAIRS
AFFEAR
AFFEARD
AFFEARE
AFFEARED
AFFEARES
AFFEARING
AFFEARS
AFFECT
AFFECTED
AFFECTER
AFFECTERS
AFFECTING
AFFECTION
AFFECTIVE
AFFECTS
AFFEER
AFFEERED
AFFEERING
AFFEERS
AFFERENT
AFFERENTS
AFFIANCE
AFFIANCED
AFFIANCES
AFFIANT
AFFIANTS
AFFICHE
AFFICHES
AFFIDAVIT
AFFIED
AFFIES
AFFILIATE
AFFINAL
AFFINE
AFFINED
AFFINELY
AFFINES
AFFINITY
AFFIRM
AFFIRMANT
AFFIRMED
AFFIRMER
AFFIRMERS
AFFIRMING
AFFIRMS
AFFIX
AFFIXABLE
AFFIXAL
AFFIXED
AFFIXER
AFFIXERS
AFFIXES
AFFIXIAL
AFFIXING
AFFIXMENT
AFFIXTURE
AFFLATED
AFFLATION
AFFLATUS
AFFLICT
AFFLICTED
AFFLICTER
AFFLICTS
AFFLUENCE
AFFLUENCY
AFFLUENT
AFFLUENTS
AFFLUENZA
AFFLUX
AFFLUXES
AFFLUXION
AFFOGATO
AFFOGATOS
AFFOORD
AFFOORDED
AFFOORDS
AFFORCE
AFFORCED
AFFORCES
AFFORCING
AFFORD
AFFORDED
AFFORDING
AFFORDS
AFFOREST
AFFORESTS
AFFRAP
AFFRAPPED
AFFRAPS
AFFRAY
AFFRAYED
AFFRAYER
AFFRAYERS
AFFRAYING
AFFRAYS
AFFRENDED
AFFRET
AFFRETS
AFFRICATE
AFFRIGHT
AFFRIGHTS
AFFRONT
AFFRONTE
AFFRONTED
AFFRONTEE
AFFRONTS
AFFUSION
AFFUSIONS
AFFY
AFFYDE
AFFYING
AFGHAN
AFGHANI
AFGHANIS
AFGHANS
AFIELD
AFIRE
AFLAJ
AFLAME
AFLATOXIN
AFLOAT
AFLUTTER
AFOCAL
AFOOT
AFORE
AFOREHAND
AFORESAID
AFORETIME
AFOUL
AFRAID
AFREET
AFREETS
AFRESH
AFRIT
AFRITS
AFRO
AFRONT
AFROS
AFT
AFTER
AFTERBODY
AFTERBURN
AFTERCARE
AFTERCLAP
AFTERDAMP
AFTERDECK
AFTEREYE
AFTEREYED
AFTEREYES
AFTERGAME
AFTERGLOW
AFTERHEAT
AFTERINGS
AFTERLIFE
AFTERMAST
AFTERMATH
AFTERMOST
AFTERNOON
AFTERPAIN
AFTERPEAK
AFTERS
AFTERSHOW
AFTERSUN
AFTERSUNS
AFTERTAX
AFTERTIME
AFTERWARD
AFTERWORD
AFTMOST
AFTOSA
AFTOSAS
AG
AGA
AGACANT
AGACANTE
AGACERIE
AGACERIES
AGAIN
AGAINST
AGALACTIA
AGALLOCH
AGALLOCHS
AGALWOOD
AGALWOODS
AGAMA
AGAMAS
AGAMETE
AGAMETES
AGAMI
AGAMIC
AGAMID
AGAMIDS
AGAMIS
AGAMOGONY
AGAMOID
AGAMOIDS
AGAMONT
AGAMONTS
AGAMOUS
AGAPAE
AGAPAI
AGAPE
AGAPEIC
AGAPES
AGAR
AGARIC
AGARICS
AGAROSE
AGAROSES
AGARS
AGARWOOD
AGARWOODS
AGAS
AGAST

AGASTED
AGASTING
AGASTS
AGATE
AGATES
AGATEWARE
AGATISE
AGATISED
AGATISES
AGATISING
AGATIZE
AGATIZED
AGATIZES
AGATIZING
AGATOID
AGAVE
AGAVES
AGAZE
AGAZED
AGE
AGED
AGEDLY
AGEDNESS
AGEE
AGEING
AGEINGS
AGEISM
AGEISMS
AGEIST
AGEISTS
AGELAST
AGELASTIC
AGELASTS
AGELESS
AGELESSLY
AGELONG
AGEMATE
AGEMATES
AGEN
AGENCIES
AGENCY
AGENDA
AGENDAS
AGENDER
AGENDUM
AGENDUMS
AGENE
AGENES
AGENESES
AGENESIA
AGENESIAS
AGENESIS
AGENETIC
AGENISE
AGENISED
AGENISES
AGENISING
AGENIZE
AGENIZED
AGENIZES
AGENIZING
AGENT
AGENTED
AGENTIAL
AGENTING
AGENTINGS
AGENTIVAL
AGENTIVE
AGENTIVES
AGENTRIES
AGENTRY
AGENTS
AGER
AGERATUM
AGERATUMS
AGERS
AGES
AGEUSIA
AGEUSIAS
AGFLATION
AGGADA
AGGADAH
AGGADAHS
AGGADAS
AGGADIC
AGGADOT
AGGADOTH
AGGER
AGGERS
AGGIE
AGGIES
AGGRACE
AGGRACED
AGGRACES
AGGRACING
AGGRADE
AGGRADED
AGGRADES
AGGRADING
AGGRATE
AGGRATED
AGGRATES
AGGRATING
AGGRAVATE
AGGREGATE
AGGRESS
AGGRESSED
AGGRESSES
AGGRESSOR
AGGRI
AGGRIEVE
AGGRIEVED
AGGRIEVES
AGGRO
AGGROS
AGGRY
AGHA
AGHAS
AGHAST
AGILA
AGILAS
AGILE
AGILELY
AGILENESS
AGILER
AGILEST
AGILITIES
AGILITY
AGIN
AGING
AGINGS
AGINNER
AGINNERS
AGIO
AGIOS
AGIOTAGE
AGIOTAGES
AGISM
AGISMS
AGIST
AGISTED
AGISTER
AGISTERS
AGISTING
AGISTMENT
AGISTOR
AGISTORS
AGISTS
AGITA
AGITABLE
AGITANS
AGITAS
AGITATE
AGITATED
AGITATES
AGITATING
AGITATION
AGITATIVE
AGITATO
AGITATOR
AGITATORS
AGITPOP
AGITPOPS
AGITPROP
AGITPROPS
AGLARE
AGLEAM
AGLEE
AGLET
AGLETS
AGLEY
AGLIMMER
AGLITTER
AGLOO
AGLOOS
AGLOSSAL
AGLOSSATE
AGLOSSIA
AGLOSSIAS
AGLOW
AGLU
AGLUS
AGLY
AGLYCON
AGLYCONE
AGLYCONES
AGLYCONS
AGMA
AGMAS
AGMINATE
AGNAIL
AGNAILS
AGNAME
AGNAMED
AGNAMES
AGNATE
AGNATES
AGNATHAN
AGNATHANS
AGNATHOUS
AGNATIC
AGNATICAL
AGNATION
AGNATIONS
AGNISE
AGNISED
AGNISES
AGNISING
AGNIZE
AGNIZED
AGNIZES
AGNIZING
AGNOLOTTI
AGNOMEN
AGNOMENS
AGNOMINA
AGNOMINAL
AGNOSIA
AGNOSIAS
AGNOSIC
AGNOSTIC
AGNOSTICS
AGO
AGOG
AGOGE
AGOGES
AGOGIC
AGOGICS
AGOING
AGON
AGONAL
AGONE
AGONES
AGONIC
AGONIES
AGONISE
AGONISED
AGONISES
AGONISING
AGONISM

AGONISMS
AGONIST
AGONISTES
AGONISTIC
AGONISTS
AGONIZE
AGONIZED
AGONIZES
AGONIZING
AGONS
AGONY
AGOOD
AGORA
AGORAE
AGORAS
AGOROT
AGOROTH
AGOUTA
AGOUTAS
AGOUTI
AGOUTIES
AGOUTIS
AGOUTY
AGRAFE
AGRAFES
AGRAFFE
AGRAFFES
AGRAPHA
AGRAPHIA
AGRAPHIAS
AGRAPHIC
AGRAPHON
AGRARIAN
AGRARIANS
AGRASTE
AGRAVIC
AGREE
AGREEABLE
AGREEABLY
AGREED
AGREEING
AGREEMENT
AGREES
AGREGE
AGREGES
AGREMENS
AGREMENT
AGREMENTS
AGRESTAL
AGRESTIAL
AGRESTIC
AGRIA
AGRIAS
AGRIMONY
AGRIN
AGRINS
AGRIOLOGY
AGRISE
AGRISED
AGRISES
AGRISING
AGRIZE
AGRIZED
AGRIZES
AGRIZING
AGRO
AGRODOLCE
AGROLOGIC
AGROLOGY
AGRONOMIC
AGRONOMY
AGROS
AGROUND
AGRYPNIA
AGRYPNIAS
AGRYZE
AGRYZED
AGRYZES
AGRYZING
AGS
AGTERSKOT
AGUACATE
AGUACATES
AGUE
AGUED
AGUELIKE
AGUES
AGUEWEED
AGUEWEEDS
AGUISE
AGUISED
AGUISES
AGUISH
AGUISHLY
AGUISING
AGUIZE
AGUIZED
AGUIZES
AGUIZING
AGUNA
AGUNAH
AGUNOT
AGUNOTH
AGUTI
AGUTIS
AGYRIA
AGYRIAS
AH
AHA
AHCHOO
AHEAD
AHEAP
AHED
AHEIGHT
AHEM
AHEMERAL
AHENT
AHI
AHIGH
AHIMSA
AHIMSAS
AHIND
AHING
AHINT
AHIS
AHISTORIC
AHOLD
AHOLDS
AHORSE
AHOY
AHS
AHULL
AHUNGERED
AHUNGRY
AHURU
AHURUHURU
AHURUS
AI
AIA
AIAS
AIBLINS
AID
AIDA
AIDANCE
AIDANCES
AIDANT
AIDANTS
AIDAS
AIDE
AIDED
AIDER
AIDERS
AIDES
AIDFUL
AIDING
AIDLESS
AIDMAN
AIDMEN
AIDOI
AIDOS
AIDS
AIERIES
AIERY
AIGA
AIGAS
AIGHT
AIGLET
AIGLETS
AIGRET
AIGRETS
AIGRETTE
AIGRETTES
AIGUILLE
AIGUILLES
AIKIDO
AIKIDOS
AIKONA
AIL
AILANTHIC
AILANTHUS
AILANTO
AILANTOS
AILED
AILERON
AILERONS
AILETTE
AILETTES
AILING
AILMENT
AILMENTS
AILS
AIM
AIMED
AIMER
AIMERS
AIMFUL
AIMFULLY
AIMING
AIMLESS
AIMLESSLY
AIMS
AIN
AINE
AINEE
AINGA
AINGAS
AINS
AINSELL
AINSELLS
AIOLI
AIOLIS
AIR
AIRBAG
AIRBAGS
AIRBALL
AIRBALLED
AIRBALLS
AIRBASE
AIRBASES
AIRBOARD
AIRBOARDS
AIRBOAT
AIRBOATS
AIRBORNE
AIRBOUND
AIRBRICK
AIRBRICKS
AIRBRUSH
AIRBURST
AIRBURSTS
AIRBUS
AIRBUSES
AIRBUSSES
AIRCHECK
AIRCHECKS
AIRCOACH
AIRCON
AIRCONS
AIRCRAFT
AIRCREW

A

AIRCREWS
AIRDATE
AIRDATES
AIRDRAWN
AIRDROME
AIRDROMES
AIRDROP
AIRDROPS
AIRED
AIRER
AIRERS
AIREST
AIRFARE
AIRFARES
AIRFIELD
AIRFIELDS
AIRFLOW
AIRFLOWS
AIRFOIL
AIRFOILS
AIRFRAME
AIRFRAMES
AIRGAP
AIRGAPS
AIRGLOW
AIRGLOWS
AIRGRAPH
AIRGRAPHS
AIRGUN
AIRGUNS
AIRHEAD
AIRHEADED
AIRHEADS
AIRHOLE
AIRHOLES
AIRIER
AIRIEST
AIRILY
AIRINESS
AIRING
AIRINGS
AIRLESS
AIRLIFT
AIRLIFTED
AIRLIFTS
AIRLIKE
AIRLINE
AIRLINER
AIRLINERS
AIRLINES
AIRLOCK
AIRLOCKS
AIRMAIL
AIRMAILED
AIRMAILS
AIRMAN
AIRMEN
AIRMOBILE
AIRN
AIRNED
AIRNING
AIRNS
AIRPARK
AIRPARKS
AIRPLANE
AIRPLANES
AIRPLAY
AIRPLAYS
AIRPORT
AIRPORTS
AIRPOST
AIRPOSTS
AIRPOWER
AIRPOWERS
AIRPROOF
AIRPROOFS
AIRPROX
AIRPROXES
AIRS
AIRSCAPE
AIRSCAPES
AIRSCREW
AIRSCREWS
AIRSHAFT
AIRSHAFTS
AIRSHED
AIRSHEDS
AIRSHIP
AIRSHIPS
AIRSHOT
AIRSHOTS
AIRSHOW
AIRSHOWS
AIRSICK
AIRSIDE
AIRSIDES
AIRSOME
AIRSPACE
AIRSPACES
AIRSPEED
AIRSPEEDS
AIRSTOP
AIRSTOPS
AIRSTREAM
AIRSTRIKE
AIRSTRIP
AIRSTRIPS
AIRT
AIRTED
AIRTH
AIRTHED
AIRTHING
AIRTHS
AIRTIGHT
AIRTIME
AIRTIMES
AIRTING
AIRTRAM
AIRTRAMS
AIRTS
AIRVAC
AIRVACS
AIRWARD
AIRWARDS
AIRWAVE
AIRWAVES
AIRWAY
AIRWAYS
AIRWISE
AIRWOMAN
AIRWOMEN
AIRWORTHY
AIRY
AIS
AISLE
AISLED
AISLELESS
AISLES
AISLEWAY
AISLEWAYS
AISLING
AISLINGS
AIT
AITCH
AITCHBONE
AITCHES
AITS
AITU
AITUS
AIVER
AIVERS
AIYEE
AIZLE
AIZLES
AJAR
AJEE
AJI
AJIES
AJIS
AJIVA
AJIVAS
AJOWAN
AJOWANS
AJUGA
AJUGAS
AJUTAGE
AJUTAGES
AJWAN
AJWANS
AKA
AKARYOTE
AKARYOTES
AKARYOTIC
AKAS
AKATEA
AKATEAS
AKATHISIA
AKE
AKEAKE
AKEAKES
AKEBIA
AKEBIAS
AKED
AKEDAH
AKEDAHS
AKEE
AKEES
AKELA
AKELAS
AKENE
AKENES
AKENIAL
AKES
AKHARA
AKHARAS
AKIMBO
AKIN
AKINESES
AKINESIA
AKINESIAS
AKINESIS
AKINETIC
AKING
AKIRAHO
AKIRAHOS
AKITA
AKITAS
AKKAS
AKOLUTHOS
AKRASIA
AKRASIAS
AKRATIC
AKVAVIT
AKVAVITS
AL
ALA
ALAAP
ALAAPS
ALABAMINE
ALABASTER
ALACHLOR
ALACHLORS
ALACK
ALACKADAY
ALACRITY
ALAE
ALAIMENT
ALAIMENTS
ALALAGMOI
ALALAGMOS
ALALIA
ALALIAS
ALAMEDA
ALAMEDAS
ALAMO
ALAMODE
ALAMODES
ALAMORT
ALAMOS
ALAN

ALAND
ALANDS
ALANE
ALANG
ALANGS
ALANIN
ALANINE
ALANINES
ALANINS
ALANNAH
ALANNAHS
ALANS
ALANT
ALANTS
ALANYL
ALANYLS
ALAP
ALAPA
ALAPAS
ALAPS
ALAR
ALARM
ALARMABLE
ALARMED
ALARMEDLY
ALARMING
ALARMISM
ALARMISMS
ALARMIST
ALARMISTS
ALARMS
ALARUM
ALARUMED
ALARUMING
ALARUMS
ALARY
ALAS
ALASKA
ALASKAS
ALASTOR
ALASTORS
ALASTRIM
ALASTRIMS
ALATE
ALATED
ALATES
ALATION
ALATIONS

ALAY
ALAYED
ALAYING
ALAYS
ALB
ALBA
ALBACORE
ALBACORES
ALBARELLI
ALBARELLO
ALBAS
ALBATA
ALBATAS
ALBATROSS
ALBE
ALBEDO
ALBEDOES
ALBEDOS
ALBEE
ALBEIT
ALBERGHI
ALBERGO
ALBERT
ALBERTITE
ALBERTS
ALBESCENT
ALBESPINE
ALBESPYNE
ALBICORE
ALBICORES
ALBINAL
ALBINESS
ALBINIC
ALBINISM
ALBINISMS
ALBINO
ALBINOISM
ALBINOS
ALBINOTIC
ALBITE
ALBITES
ALBITIC
ALBITICAL
ALBITISE
ALBITISED
ALBITISES
ALBITIZE
ALBITIZED

ALBITIZES
ALBIZIA
ALBIZIAS
ALBIZZIA
ALBIZZIAS
ALBRICIAS
ALBS
ALBUGO
ALBUGOS
ALBUM
ALBUMEN
ALBUMENS
ALBUMIN
ALBUMINS
ALBUMOSE
ALBUMOSES
ALBUMS
ALBURNOUS
ALBURNUM
ALBURNUMS
ALBUTEROL
ALCADE
ALCADES
ALCAHEST
ALCAHESTS
ALCAIC
ALCAICS
ALCAIDE
ALCAIDES
ALCALDE
ALCALDES
ALCARRAZA
ALCATRAS
ALCAYDE
ALCAYDES
ALCAZAR
ALCAZARS
ALCHEMIC
ALCHEMIES
ALCHEMISE
ALCHEMIST
ALCHEMIZE
ALCHEMY
ALCHERA
ALCHERAS
ALCHYMIES
ALCHYMY
ALCID

ALCIDINE
ALCIDS
ALCO
ALCOHOL
ALCOHOLIC
ALCOHOLS
ALCOLOCK
ALCOLOCKS
ALCOOL
ALCOOLS
ALCOPOP
ALCOPOPS
ALCORZA
ALCORZAS
ALCOS
ALCOVE
ALCOVED
ALCOVES
ALDEA
ALDEAS
ALDEHYDE
ALDEHYDES
ALDEHYDIC
ALDER
ALDERFLY
ALDERMAN
ALDERMEN
ALDERN
ALDERS
ALDICARB
ALDICARBS
ALDOL
ALDOLASE
ALDOLASES
ALDOLS
ALDOSE
ALDOSES
ALDOXIME
ALDOXIMES
ALDRIN
ALDRINS
ALE
ALEATORIC
ALEATORY
ALEBENCH
ALEC
ALECITHAL
ALECK

ALECKS
ALECOST
ALECOSTS
ALECS
ALECTRYON
ALEE
ALEF
ALEFS
ALEFT
ALEGAR
ALEGARS
ALEGGE
ALEGGED
ALEGGES
ALEGGING
ALEHOUSE
ALEHOUSES
ALEMBIC
ALEMBICS
ALEMBROTH
ALENCON
ALENCONS
ALENGTH
ALEPH
ALEPHS
ALEPINE
ALEPINES
ALERCE
ALERCES
ALERION
ALERIONS
ALERT
ALERTED
ALERTER
ALERTEST
ALERTING
ALERTLY
ALERTNESS
ALERTS
ALES
ALETHIC
ALEURON
ALEURONE
ALEURONES
ALEURONIC
ALEURONS
ALEVIN
ALEVINS

ALEW
ALEWASHED
ALEWIFE
ALEWIVES
ALEWS
ALEXANDER
ALEXIA
ALEXIAS
ALEXIC
ALEXIN
ALEXINE
ALEXINES
ALEXINIC
ALEXINS
ALEYE
ALEYED
ALEYES
ALEYING
ALF
ALFA
ALFAKI
ALFAKIS
ALFALFA
ALFALFAS
ALFAQUI
ALFAQUIN
ALFAQUINS
ALFAQUIS
ALFAS
ALFERECES
ALFEREZ
ALFILARIA
ALFILERIA
ALFORJA
ALFORJAS
ALFREDO
ALFRESCO
ALFS
ALGA
ALGAE
ALGAECIDE
ALGAL
ALGAROBA
ALGAROBAS
ALGARROBA
ALGARROBO
ALGAS
ALGATE
ALGATES
ALGEBRA
ALGEBRAIC
ALGEBRAS
ALGERINE
ALGERINES
ALGESES
ALGESIA
ALGESIAS
ALGESIC
ALGESIS
ALGETIC
ALGICIDAL
ALGICIDE
ALGICIDES
ALGID
ALGIDITY
ALGIDNESS
ALGIN
ALGINATE
ALGINATES
ALGINIC
ALGINS
ALGOID
ALGOLOGY
ALGOMETER
ALGOMETRY
ALGOR
ALGORISM
ALGORISMS
ALGORITHM
ALGORS
ALGUACIL
ALGUACILS
ALGUAZIL
ALGUAZILS
ALGUM
ALGUMS
ALIAS
ALIASED
ALIASES
ALIASING
ALIASINGS
ALIBI
ALIBIED
ALIBIES
ALIBIING
ALIBIS
ALIBLE
ALICANT
ALICANTS
ALICYCLIC
ALIDAD
ALIDADE
ALIDADES
ALIDADS
ALIEN
ALIENABLE
ALIENAGE
ALIENAGES
ALIENATE
ALIENATED
ALIENATES
ALIENATOR
ALIENED
ALIENEE
ALIENEES
ALIENER
ALIENERS
ALIENING
ALIENISM
ALIENISMS
ALIENIST
ALIENISTS
ALIENLY
ALIENNESS
ALIENOR
ALIENORS
ALIENS
ALIF
ALIFORM
ALIFS
ALIGARTA
ALIGARTAS
ALIGHT
ALIGHTED
ALIGHTING
ALIGHTS
ALIGN
ALIGNED
ALIGNER
ALIGNERS
ALIGNING
ALIGNMENT
ALIGNS
ALIKE
ALIKENESS
ALIMENT
ALIMENTAL
ALIMENTED
ALIMENTS
ALIMONIED
ALIMONIES
ALIMONY
ALINE
ALINED
ALINEMENT
ALINER
ALINERS
ALINES
ALINING
ALIPED
ALIPEDS
ALIPHATIC
ALIQUANT
ALIQUOT
ALIQUOTS
ALISMA
ALISMAS
ALISON
ALISONS
ALIST
ALIT
ALITERACY
ALITERATE
ALIUNDE
ALIVE
ALIVENESS
ALIYA
ALIYAH
ALIYAHS
ALIYAS
ALIYOS
ALIYOT
ALIYOTH
ALIZARI
ALIZARIN
ALIZARINE
ALIZARINS
ALIZARIS
ALKAHEST
ALKAHESTS
ALKALI
ALKALIC
ALKALIES
ALKALIFY
ALKALIN
ALKALINE
ALKALIS
ALKALISE
ALKALISED
ALKALISER
ALKALISES
ALKALIZE
ALKALIZED
ALKALIZER
ALKALIZES
ALKALOID
ALKALOIDS
ALKALOSES
ALKALOSIS
ALKALOTIC
ALKANE
ALKANES
ALKANET
ALKANETS
ALKANNIN
ALKANNINS
ALKENE
ALKENES
ALKIE
ALKIES
ALKINE
ALKINES
ALKO
ALKOS
ALKOXIDE
ALKOXIDES
ALKOXY
ALKY
ALKYD
ALKYDS
ALKYL
ALKYLATE
ALKYLATED
ALKYLATES
ALKYLIC
ALKYLS
ALKYNE
ALKYNES
ALL
ALLANITE

ALLANITES
ALLANTOIC
ALLANTOID
ALLANTOIN
ALLANTOIS
ALLATIVE
ALLATIVES
ALLAY
ALLAYED
ALLAYER
ALLAYERS
ALLAYING
ALLAYINGS
ALLAYMENT
ALLAYS
ALLCOMERS
ALLEDGE
ALLEDGED
ALLEDGES
ALLEDGING
ALLEE
ALLEES
ALLEGE
ALLEGED
ALLEGEDLY
ALLEGER
ALLEGERS
ALLEGES
ALLEGGE
ALLEGGED
ALLEGGES
ALLEGGING
ALLEGIANT
ALLEGING
ALLEGORIC
ALLEGORY
ALLEGRO
ALLEGROS
ALLEL
ALLELE
ALLELES
ALLELIC
ALLELISM
ALLELISMS
ALLELS
ALLELUIA
ALLELUIAH
ALLELUIAS
ALLEMANDE
ALLENARLY
ALLERGEN
ALLERGENS
ALLERGIC
ALLERGICS
ALLERGIES
ALLERGIN
ALLERGINS
ALLERGIST
ALLERGY
ALLERION
ALLERIONS
ALLETHRIN
ALLEVIANT
ALLEVIATE
ALLEY
ALLEYCAT
ALLEYCATS
ALLEYED
ALLEYS
ALLEYWAY
ALLEYWAYS
ALLHEAL
ALLHEALS
ALLIABLE
ALLIAK
ALLIAKS
ALLIANCE
ALLIANCES
ALLICE
ALLICES
ALLICHOLY
ALLICIN
ALLICINS
ALLIED
ALLIES
ALLIGARTA
ALLIGATE
ALLIGATED
ALLIGATES
ALLIGATOR
ALLIS
ALLISES
ALLIUM
ALLIUMS
ALLNESS
ALLNESSES
ALLNIGHT
ALLOBAR
ALLOBARS
ALLOCABLE
ALLOCARPY
ALLOCATE
ALLOCATED
ALLOCATES
ALLOCATOR
ALLOD
ALLODIA
ALLODIAL
ALLODIUM
ALLODIUMS
ALLODS
ALLODYNIA
ALLOGAMY
ALLOGENIC
ALLOGRAFT
ALLOGRAPH
ALLOMERIC
ALLOMETRY
ALLOMONE
ALLOMONES
ALLOMORPH
ALLONGE
ALLONGED
ALLONGES
ALLONGING
ALLONS
ALLONYM
ALLONYMS
ALLOPATH
ALLOPATHS
ALLOPATHY
ALLOPATRY
ALLOPHANE
ALLOPHONE
ALLOPLASM
ALLOSAUR
ALLOSAURS
ALLOSTERY
ALLOT
ALLOTMENT
ALLOTROPE
ALLOTROPY
ALLOTS
ALLOTTED
ALLOTTEE
ALLOTTEES
ALLOTTER
ALLOTTERS
ALLOTTERY
ALLOTTING
ALLOTYPE
ALLOTYPES
ALLOTYPIC
ALLOTYPY
ALLOVER
ALLOVERS
ALLOW
ALLOWABLE
ALLOWABLY
ALLOWANCE
ALLOWED
ALLOWEDLY
ALLOWING
ALLOWS
ALLOXAN
ALLOXANS
ALLOY
ALLOYED
ALLOYING
ALLOYS
ALLOZYME
ALLOZYMES
ALLS
ALLSEED
ALLSEEDS
ALLSORTS
ALLSPICE
ALLSPICES
ALLUDE
ALLUDED
ALLUDES
ALLUDING
ALLURE
ALLURED
ALLURER
ALLURERS
ALLURES
ALLURING
ALLUSION
ALLUSIONS
ALLUSIVE
ALLUVIA
ALLUVIAL
ALLUVIALS
ALLUVION
ALLUVIONS
ALLUVIUM
ALLUVIUMS
ALLY
ALLYING
ALLYL
ALLYLIC
ALLYLS
ALLYOU
ALMA
ALMAGEST
ALMAGESTS
ALMAH
ALMAHS
ALMAIN
ALMAINS
ALMANAC
ALMANACK
ALMANACKS
ALMANACS
ALMANDINE
ALMANDITE
ALMAS
ALME
ALMEH
ALMEHS
ALMEMAR
ALMEMARS
ALMERIES
ALMERY
ALMES
ALMIGHTY
ALMIRAH
ALMIRAHS
ALMNER
ALMNERS
ALMOND
ALMONDIER
ALMONDITE
ALMONDS
ALMONDY
ALMONER
ALMONERS
ALMONRIES
ALMONRY

A

ALMOST
ALMOUS
ALMS
ALMSGIVER
ALMSHOUSE
ALMSMAN
ALMSMEN
ALMSWOMAN
ALMSWOMEN
ALMUCE
ALMUCES
ALMUD
ALMUDE
ALMUDES
ALMUDS
ALMUG
ALMUGS
ALNAGE
ALNAGER
ALNAGERS
ALNAGES
ALNICO
ALNICOS
ALOCASIA
ALOCASIAS
ALOD
ALODIA
ALODIAL
ALODIUM
ALODIUMS
ALODS
ALOE
ALOED
ALOES
ALOESWOOD
ALOETIC
ALOETICS
ALOFT
ALOGIA
ALOGIAS
ALOGICAL
ALOHA
ALOHAS
ALOIN
ALOINS
ALONE
ALONELY
ALONENESS
ALONG
ALONGSIDE
ALONGST
ALOO
ALOOF
ALOOFLY
ALOOFNESS
ALOOS
ALOPECIA
ALOPECIAS
ALOPECIC
ALOPECOID
ALOUD
ALOW
ALOWE
ALP
ALPACA
ALPACAS
ALPACCA
ALPACCAS
ALPARGATA
ALPEEN
ALPEENS
ALPENGLOW
ALPENHORN
ALPHA
ALPHABET
ALPHABETS
ALPHAS
ALPHASORT
ALPHATEST
ALPHORN
ALPHORNS
ALPHOSIS
ALPHYL
ALPHYLS
ALPINE
ALPINELY
ALPINES
ALPINISM
ALPINISMS
ALPINIST
ALPINISTS
ALPS
ALREADY
ALRIGHT
ALS
ALSIKE
ALSIKES
ALSO
ALSOON
ALSOONE
ALT
ALTAR
ALTARAGE
ALTARAGES
ALTARS
ALTARWISE
ALTER
ALTERABLE
ALTERABLY
ALTERANT
ALTERANTS
ALTERCATE
ALTERED
ALTERER
ALTERERS
ALTERING
ALTERITY
ALTERN
ALTERNANT
ALTERNAT
ALTERNATE
ALTERNATS
ALTERNE
ALTERNES
ALTERS
ALTESSE
ALTESSES
ALTEZA
ALTEZAS
ALTEZZA
ALTEZZAS
ALTHAEA
ALTHAEAS
ALTHEA
ALTHEAS
ALTHO
ALTHORN
ALTHORNS
ALTHOUGH
ALTIGRAPH
ALTIMETER
ALTIMETRY
ALTIPLANO
ALTISSIMO
ALTITUDE
ALTITUDES
ALTO
ALTOIST
ALTOISTS
ALTOS
ALTRICES
ALTRICIAL
ALTRUISM
ALTRUISMS
ALTRUIST
ALTRUISTS
ALTS
ALU
ALUDEL
ALUDELS
ALULA
ALULAE
ALULAR
ALULAS
ALUM
ALUMIN
ALUMINA
ALUMINAS
ALUMINATE
ALUMINE
ALUMINES
ALUMINIC
ALUMINIDE
ALUMINISE
ALUMINIUM
ALUMINIZE
ALUMINOUS
ALUMINS
ALUMINUM
ALUMINUMS
ALUMISH
ALUMIUM
ALUMIUMS
ALUMNA
ALUMNAE
ALUMNI
ALUMNUS
ALUMROOT
ALUMROOTS
ALUMS
ALUMSTONE
ALUNITE
ALUNITES
ALURE
ALURES
ALUS
ALVAR
ALVARS
ALVEARIES
ALVEARY
ALVEATED
ALVEOLAR
ALVEOLARS
ALVEOLATE
ALVEOLE
ALVEOLES
ALVEOLI
ALVEOLUS
ALVINE
ALWAY
ALWAYS
ALYSSUM
ALYSSUMS
AM
AMA
AMABILE
AMADAVAT
AMADAVATS
AMADODA
AMADOU
AMADOUS
AMAH
AMAHS
AMAIN
AMAKHOSI
AMAKOSI
AMALGAM
AMALGAMS
AMANDINE
AMANDINES
AMANDLA
AMANDLAS
AMANITA
AMANITAS
AMANITIN
AMANITINS
AMARACUS
AMARANT
AMARANTH
AMARANTHS

AMARANTIN
AMARANTS
AMARELLE
AMARELLES
AMARETTI
AMARETTO
AMARETTOS
AMARNA
AMARONE
AMARONES
AMARYLLID
AMARYLLIS
AMAS
AMASS
AMASSABLE
AMASSED
AMASSER
AMASSERS
AMASSES
AMASSING
AMASSMENT
AMATE
AMATED
AMATES
AMATEUR
AMATEURS
AMATING
AMATION
AMATIONS
AMATIVE
AMATIVELY
AMATOL
AMATOLS
AMATORIAL
AMATORIAN
AMATORY
AMAUROSES
AMAUROSIS
AMAUROTIC
AMAUT
AMAUTI
AMAUTIK
AMAUTIKS
AMAUTIS
AMAUTS
AMAZE
AMAZED
AMAZEDLY
AMAZEMENT
AMAZES
AMAZING
AMAZINGLY
AMAZON
AMAZONIAN
AMAZONITE
AMAZONS
AMBACH
AMBACHES
AMBAGE
AMBAGES
AMBAGIOUS
AMBAN
AMBANS
AMBARI
AMBARIES
AMBARIS
AMBARY
AMBASSAGE
AMBASSIES
AMBASSY
AMBATCH
AMBATCHES
AMBEER
AMBEERS
AMBER
AMBERED
AMBERGRIS
AMBERIER
AMBERIES
AMBERIEST
AMBERINA
AMBERINAS
AMBERITE
AMBERITES
AMBERJACK
AMBEROID
AMBEROIDS
AMBEROUS
AMBERS
AMBERY
AMBIANCE
AMBIANCES
AMBIENCE
AMBIENCES
AMBIENT
AMBIENTS
AMBIGUITY
AMBIGUOUS
AMBIPOLAR
AMBIT
AMBITION
AMBITIONS
AMBITIOUS
AMBITS
AMBITTY
AMBIVERT
AMBIVERTS
AMBLE
AMBLED
AMBLER
AMBLERS
AMBLES
AMBLING
AMBLINGS
AMBLYOPIA
AMBLYOPIC
AMBO
AMBOINA
AMBOINAS
AMBONES
AMBOS
AMBOYNA
AMBOYNAS
AMBRIES
AMBROID
AMBROIDS
AMBROSIA
AMBROSIAL
AMBROSIAN
AMBROSIAS
AMBROTYPE
AMBRY
AMBSACE
AMBSACES
AMBULACRA
AMBULANCE
AMBULANT
AMBULANTS
AMBULATE
AMBULATED
AMBULATES
AMBULATOR
AMBULETTE
AMBUSCADE
AMBUSCADO
AMBUSH
AMBUSHED
AMBUSHER
AMBUSHERS
AMBUSHES
AMBUSHING
AME
AMEARST
AMEBA
AMEBAE
AMEBAN
AMEBAS
AMEBEAN
AMEBIASES
AMEBIASIS
AMEBIC
AMEBOCYTE
AMEBOID
AMEER
AMEERATE
AMEERATES
AMEERS
AMEIOSES
AMEIOSIS
AMELCORN
AMELCORNS
AMELIA
AMELIAS
AMEN
AMENABLE
AMENABLY
AMENAGE
AMENAGED
AMENAGES
AMENAGING
AMENAUNCE
AMEND
AMENDABLE
AMENDE
AMENDED
AMENDER
AMENDERS
AMENDES
AMENDING
AMENDMENT
AMENDS
AMENE
AMENED
AMENING
AMENITIES
AMENITY
AMENS
AMENT
AMENTA
AMENTAL
AMENTIA
AMENTIAS
AMENTS
AMENTUM
AMERCE
AMERCED
AMERCER
AMERCERS
AMERCES
AMERCING
AMERICIUM
AMES
AMESACE
AMESACES
AMETHYST
AMETHYSTS
AMETROPIA
AMETROPIC
AMI
AMIA
AMIABLE
AMIABLY
AMIANTHUS
AMIANTUS
AMIAS
AMICABLE
AMICABLY
AMICE
AMICES
AMICI
AMICUS
AMID
AMIDASE
AMIDASES
AMIDE
AMIDES
AMIDIC
AMIDIN
AMIDINE
AMIDINES

AMIDINS
AMIDMOST
AMIDO
AMIDOGEN
AMIDOGENS
AMIDOL
AMIDOLS
AMIDONE
AMIDONES
AMIDS
AMIDSHIP
AMIDSHIPS
AMIDST
AMIE
AMIES
AMIGA
AMIGAS
AMIGO
AMIGOS
AMILDAR
AMILDARS
AMIN
AMINE
AMINES
AMINIC
AMINITIES
AMINITY
AMINO
AMINOS
AMINS
AMIR
AMIRATE
AMIRATES
AMIRS
AMIS
AMISES
AMISS
AMISSES
AMISSIBLE
AMISSING
AMITIES
AMITOSES
AMITOSIS
AMITOTIC
AMITROLE
AMITROLES
AMITY
AMLA
AMLAS
AMMAN
AMMANS
AMMETER
AMMETERS
AMMINE
AMMINES
AMMINO
AMMIRAL
AMMIRALS
AMMO
AMMOCETE
AMMOCETES
AMMOCOETE
AMMOLITE
AMMOLITES
AMMON
AMMONAL
AMMONALS
AMMONATE
AMMONATES
AMMONIA
AMMONIAC
AMMONIACS
AMMONIAS
AMMONIATE
AMMONIC
AMMONICAL
AMMONIFY
AMMONITE
AMMONITES
AMMONITIC
AMMONIUM
AMMONIUMS
AMMONO
AMMONOID
AMMONOIDS
AMMONS
AMMOS
AMNESIA
AMNESIAC
AMNESIACS
AMNESIAS
AMNESIC
AMNESICS
AMNESTIC
AMNESTIED
AMNESTIES
AMNESTY
AMNIA
AMNIC
AMNIO
AMNION
AMNIONIC
AMNIONS
AMNIOS
AMNIOTE
AMNIOTES
AMNIOTIC
AMNIOTOMY
AMOEBA
AMOEBAE
AMOEBAEAN
AMOEBAN
AMOEBAS
AMOEBEAN
AMOEBIC
AMOEBOID
AMOK
AMOKS
AMOKURA
AMOKURAS
AMOLE
AMOLES
AMOMUM
AMOMUMS
AMONG
AMONGST
AMOOVE
AMOOVED
AMOOVES
AMOOVING
AMORAL
AMORALISM
AMORALIST
AMORALITY
AMORALLY
AMORANCE
AMORANCES
AMORANT
AMORCE
AMORCES
AMORET
AMORETS
AMORETTI
AMORETTO
AMORETTOS
AMORINI
AMORINO
AMORISM
AMORISMS
AMORIST
AMORISTIC
AMORISTS
AMORNINGS
AMOROSA
AMOROSAS
AMOROSITY
AMOROSO
AMOROSOS
AMOROUS
AMOROUSLY
AMORPHISM
AMORPHOUS
AMORT
AMORTISE
AMORTISED
AMORTISES
AMORTIZE
AMORTIZED
AMORTIZES
AMOSITE
AMOSITES
AMOTION
AMOTIONS
AMOUNT
AMOUNTED
AMOUNTING
AMOUNTS
AMOUR
AMOURETTE
AMOURS
AMOVE
AMOVED
AMOVES
AMOVING
AMOWT
AMOWTS
AMP
AMPACITY
AMPASSIES
AMPASSY
AMPED
AMPERAGE
AMPERAGES
AMPERE
AMPERES
AMPERSAND
AMPERZAND
AMPHIBIA
AMPHIBIAN
AMPHIBOLE
AMPHIBOLY
AMPHIGORY
AMPHIOXI
AMPHIOXUS
AMPHIPATH
AMPHIPOD
AMPHIPODS
AMPHOLYTE
AMPHORA
AMPHORAE
AMPHORAL
AMPHORAS
AMPHORIC
AMPING
AMPLE
AMPLENESS
AMPLER
AMPLEST
AMPLEXUS
AMPLIDYNE
AMPLIFIED
AMPLIFIER
AMPLIFIES
AMPLIFY
AMPLITUDE
AMPLOSOME
AMPLY
AMPOULE
AMPOULES
AMPS
AMPUL
AMPULE
AMPULES
AMPULLA
AMPULLAE
AMPULLAR
AMPULLARY
AMPULS
AMPUTATE
AMPUTATED

AMPUTATES
AMPUTATOR
AMPUTEE
AMPUTEES
AMREETA
AMREETAS
AMRIT
AMRITA
AMRITAS
AMRITS
AMSINCKIA
AMTMAN
AMTMANS
AMTRAC
AMTRACK
AMTRACKS
AMTRACS
AMTRAK
AMTRAKS
AMU
AMUCK
AMUCKS
AMULET
AMULETIC
AMULETS
AMUS
AMUSABLE
AMUSE
AMUSEABLE
AMUSED
AMUSEDLY
AMUSEMENT
AMUSER
AMUSERS
AMUSES
AMUSETTE
AMUSETTES
AMUSIA
AMUSIAS
AMUSIC
AMUSING
AMUSINGLY
AMUSIVE
AMYGDAL
AMYGDALA
AMYGDALAE
AMYGDALE
AMYGDALES

AMYGDALIN
AMYGDALS
AMYGDULE
AMYGDULES
AMYL
AMYLASE
AMYLASES
AMYLENE
AMYLENES
AMYLIC
AMYLOGEN
AMYLOGENS
AMYLOID
AMYLOIDAL
AMYLOIDS
AMYLOPSIN
AMYLOSE
AMYLOSES
AMYLS
AMYLUM
AMYLUMS
AMYOTONIA
AMYTAL
AMYTALS
AN
ANA
ANABAENA
ANABAENAS
ANABANTID
ANABAS
ANABASES
ANABASIS
ANABATIC
ANABIOSES
ANABIOSIS
ANABIOTIC
ANABLEPS
ANABOLIC
ANABOLISM
ANABOLITE
ANABRANCH
ANACHARIS
ANACLINAL
ANACLISES
ANACLISIS
ANACLITIC
ANACONDA
ANACONDAS

ANACRUSES
ANACRUSIS
ANADEM
ANADEMS
ANAEMIA
ANAEMIAS
ANAEMIC
ANAEROBE
ANAEROBES
ANAEROBIA
ANAEROBIC
ANAGEN
ANAGENS
ANAGLYPH
ANAGLYPHS
ANAGLYPHY
ANAGOGE
ANAGOGES
ANAGOGIC
ANAGOGIES
ANAGOGY
ANAGRAM
ANAGRAMS
ANAL
ANALCIME
ANALCIMES
ANALCIMIC
ANALCITE
ANALCITES
ANALECTA
ANALECTIC
ANALECTS
ANALEMMA
ANALEMMAS
ANALEPTIC
ANALGESIA
ANALGESIC
ANALGETIC
ANALGIA
ANALGIAS
ANALITIES
ANALITY
ANALLY
ANALOG
ANALOGA
ANALOGIC
ANALOGIES
ANALOGISE

ANALOGISM
ANALOGIST
ANALOGIZE
ANALOGON
ANALOGONS
ANALOGOUS
ANALOGS
ANALOGUE
ANALOGUES
ANALOGY
ANALYSAND
ANALYSE
ANALYSED
ANALYSER
ANALYSERS
ANALYSES
ANALYSING
ANALYSIS
ANALYST
ANALYSTS
ANALYTE
ANALYTES
ANALYTIC
ANALYTICS
ANALYZE
ANALYZED
ANALYZER
ANALYZERS
ANALYZES
ANALYZING
ANAMNESES
ANAMNESIS
ANAMNIOTE
ANAN
ANANA
ANANAS
ANANASES
ANANDA
ANANDAS
ANANDROUS
ANANKE
ANANKES
ANANTHOUS
ANAPAEST
ANAPAESTS
ANAPEST
ANAPESTIC
ANAPESTS

ANAPHASE
ANAPHASES
ANAPHASIC
ANAPHOR
ANAPHORA
ANAPHORAL
ANAPHORAS
ANAPHORIC
ANAPHORS
ANAPLASIA
ANAPLASTY
ANAPTYXES
ANAPTYXIS
ANARCH
ANARCHAL
ANARCHIAL
ANARCHIC
ANARCHIES
ANARCHISE
ANARCHISM
ANARCHIST
ANARCHIZE
ANARCHS
ANARCHY
ANARTHRIA
ANARTHRIC
ANAS
ANASARCA
ANASARCAS
ANASTASES
ANASTASIS
ANASTATIC
ANATA
ANATAS
ANATASE
ANATASES
ANATEXES
ANATEXIS
ANATHEMA
ANATHEMAS
ANATMAN
ANATMANS
ANATOMIC
ANATOMIES
ANATOMISE
ANATOMIST
ANATOMIZE
ANATOMY

ANATOXIN
ANATOXINS
ANATROPY
ANATTA
ANATTAS
ANATTO
ANATTOS
ANAXIAL
ANBURIES
ANBURY
ANCE
ANCESTOR
ANCESTORS
ANCESTRAL
ANCESTRY
ANCHO
ANCHOR
ANCHORAGE
ANCHORED
ANCHORESS
ANCHORET
ANCHORETS
ANCHORING
ANCHORITE
ANCHORMAN
ANCHORMEN
ANCHORS
ANCHOS
ANCHOVETA
ANCHOVIES
ANCHOVY
ANCHUSA
ANCHUSAS
ANCHUSIN
ANCHUSINS
ANCHYLOSE
ANCIENT
ANCIENTER
ANCIENTLY
ANCIENTRY
ANCIENTS
ANCILE
ANCILIA
ANCILLA
ANCILLAE
ANCILLARY
ANCILLAS
ANCIPITAL
ANCLE
ANCLES
ANCOME
ANCOMES
ANCON
ANCONAL
ANCONE
ANCONEAL
ANCONES
ANCONOID
ANCORA
ANCRESS
ANCRESSES
AND
ANDANTE
ANDANTES
ANDANTINI
ANDANTINO
ANDESINE
ANDESINES
ANDESITE
ANDESITES
ANDESITIC
ANDESYTE
ANDESYTES
ANDIRON
ANDIRONS
ANDOUILLE
ANDRADITE
ANDRO
ANDROECIA
ANDROGEN
ANDROGENS
ANDROGYNE
ANDROGYNY
ANDROID
ANDROIDS
ANDROLOGY
ANDROMEDA
ANDROS
ANDS
ANDVILE
ANDVILES
ANE
ANEAR
ANEARED
ANEARING
ANEARS
ANEATH
ANECDOTA
ANECDOTAL
ANECDOTE
ANECDOTES
ANECDOTIC
ANECDYSES
ANECDYSIS
ANECHOIC
ANELACE
ANELACES
ANELASTIC
ANELE
ANELED
ANELES
ANELING
ANELLI
ANEMIA
ANEMIAS
ANEMIC
ANEMOGRAM
ANEMOLOGY
ANEMONE
ANEMONES
ANEMOSES
ANEMOSIS
ANENST
ANENT
ANERGIA
ANERGIAS
ANERGIC
ANERGIES
ANERGY
ANERLY
ANEROID
ANEROIDS
ANES
ANESTRA
ANESTRI
ANESTROUS
ANESTRUM
ANESTRUS
ANETHOL
ANETHOLE
ANETHOLES
ANETHOLS
ANETIC
ANEUPLOID
ANEURIN
ANEURINS
ANEURISM
ANEURISMS
ANEURYSM
ANEURYSMS
ANEW
ANGA
ANGAKOK
ANGAKOKS
ANGARIA
ANGARIAS
ANGARIES
ANGARY
ANGAS
ANGASHORE
ANGEKKOK
ANGEKKOKS
ANGEKOK
ANGEKOKS
ANGEL
ANGELED
ANGELFISH
ANGELHOOD
ANGELIC
ANGELICA
ANGELICAL
ANGELICAS
ANGELING
ANGELS
ANGELUS
ANGELUSES
ANGER
ANGERED
ANGERING
ANGERLESS
ANGERLY
ANGERS
ANGICO
ANGICOS
ANGINA
ANGINAL
ANGINAS
ANGINOSE
ANGINOUS
ANGIOGRAM
ANGIOLOGY
ANGIOMA
ANGIOMAS
ANGIOMATA
ANGISHORE
ANGKLUNG
ANGKLUNGS
ANGLE
ANGLED
ANGLEDUG
ANGLEDUGS
ANGLEPOD
ANGLEPODS
ANGLER
ANGLERS
ANGLES
ANGLESITE
ANGLEWISE
ANGLEWORM
ANGLICE
ANGLICISE
ANGLICISM
ANGLICIST
ANGLICIZE
ANGLIFIED
ANGLIFIES
ANGLIFY
ANGLING
ANGLINGS
ANGLIST
ANGLISTS
ANGLO
ANGLOPHIL
ANGLOS
ANGOLA
ANGOPHORA
ANGORA
ANGORAS
ANGOSTURA
ANGRIER
ANGRIES
ANGRIEST
ANGRILY
ANGRINESS
ANGRY
ANGST
ANGSTIER
ANGSTIEST
ANGSTROM
ANGSTROMS

ANGSTS
ANGSTY
ANGUIFORM
ANGUINE
ANGUIPED
ANGUIPEDE
ANGUIPEDS
ANGUISH
ANGUISHED
ANGUISHES
ANGULAR
ANGULARLY
ANGULATE
ANGULATED
ANGULATES
ANGULOSE
ANGULOUS
ANHEDONIA
ANHEDONIC
ANHEDRAL
ANHEDRALS
ANHINGA
ANHINGAS
ANHUNGRED
ANHYDRASE
ANHYDRIDE
ANHYDRITE
ANHYDROUS
ANI
ANICCA
ANICCAS
ANICONIC
ANICONISM
ANICONIST
ANICUT
ANICUTS
ANIDROSES
ANIDROSIS
ANIGH
ANIGHT
ANIL
ANILE
ANILIN
ANILINE
ANILINES
ANILINGUS
ANILINS
ANILITIES
ANILITY
ANILS
ANIMA
ANIMACIES
ANIMACY
ANIMAL
ANIMALIAN
ANIMALIC
ANIMALIER
ANIMALISE
ANIMALISM
ANIMALIST
ANIMALITY
ANIMALIZE
ANIMALLY
ANIMALS
ANIMAS
ANIMATE
ANIMATED
ANIMATELY
ANIMATER
ANIMATERS
ANIMATES
ANIMATEUR
ANIMATI
ANIMATIC
ANIMATICS
ANIMATING
ANIMATION
ANIMATISM
ANIMATIST
ANIMATO
ANIMATOR
ANIMATORS
ANIMATOS
ANIME
ANIMES
ANIMI
ANIMIS
ANIMISM
ANIMISMS
ANIMIST
ANIMISTIC
ANIMISTS
ANIMOSITY
ANIMUS
ANIMUSES
ANION
ANIONIC
ANIONS
ANIRIDIA
ANIRIDIAS
ANIRIDIC
ANIS
ANISE
ANISEED
ANISEEDS
ANISES
ANISETTE
ANISETTES
ANISIC
ANISOGAMY
ANISOLE
ANISOLES
ANKER
ANKERITE
ANKERITES
ANKERS
ANKH
ANKHS
ANKLE
ANKLEBONE
ANKLED
ANKLES
ANKLET
ANKLETS
ANKLING
ANKLONG
ANKLONGS
ANKLUNG
ANKLUNGS
ANKUS
ANKUSES
ANKUSH
ANKUSHES
ANKYLOSE
ANKYLOSED
ANKYLOSES
ANKYLOSIS
ANKYLOTIC
ANLACE
ANLACES
ANLAGE
ANLAGEN
ANLAGES
ANLAS
ANLASES
ANN
ANNA
ANNAL
ANNALISE
ANNALISED
ANNALISES
ANNALIST
ANNALISTS
ANNALIZE
ANNALIZED
ANNALIZES
ANNALS
ANNAS
ANNAT
ANNATES
ANNATS
ANNATTA
ANNATTAS
ANNATTO
ANNATTOS
ANNEAL
ANNEALED
ANNEALER
ANNEALERS
ANNEALING
ANNEALS
ANNECTENT
ANNELID
ANNELIDAN
ANNELIDS
ANNEX
ANNEXABLE
ANNEXE
ANNEXED
ANNEXES
ANNEXING
ANNEXION
ANNEXIONS
ANNEXMENT
ANNEXURE
ANNEXURES
ANNICUT
ANNICUTS
ANNO
ANNONA
ANNONAS
ANNOTATE
ANNOTATED
ANNOTATES
ANNOTATOR
ANNOUNCE
ANNOUNCED
ANNOUNCER
ANNOUNCES
ANNOY
ANNOYANCE
ANNOYED
ANNOYER
ANNOYERS
ANNOYING
ANNOYS
ANNS
ANNUAL
ANNUALISE
ANNUALIZE
ANNUALLY
ANNUALS
ANNUITANT
ANNUITIES
ANNUITISE
ANNUITIZE
ANNUITY
ANNUL
ANNULAR
ANNULARLY
ANNULARS
ANNULATE
ANNULATED
ANNULATES
ANNULET
ANNULETS
ANNULI
ANNULLED
ANNULLING
ANNULMENT
ANNULOSE
ANNULS
ANNULUS
ANNULUSES
ANOA
ANOAS
ANOBIID
ANOBIIDS
ANODAL
ANODALLY

A

ANODE
ANODES
ANODIC
ANODISE
ANODISED
ANODISER
ANODISERS
ANODISES
ANODISING
ANODIZE
ANODIZED
ANODIZER
ANODIZERS
ANODIZES
ANODIZING
ANODONTIA
ANODYNE
ANODYNES
ANODYNIC
ANOESES
ANOESIS
ANOESTRA
ANOESTRI
ANOESTRUM
ANOESTRUS
ANOETIC
ANOINT
ANOINTED
ANOINTER
ANOINTERS
ANOINTING
ANOINTS
ANOLE
ANOLES
ANOLYTE
ANOLYTES
ANOMALIES
ANOMALOUS
ANOMALY
ANOMIC
ANOMIE
ANOMIES
ANOMY
ANON
ANONYM
ANONYMA
ANONYMAS
ANONYMISE
ANONYMITY
ANONYMIZE
ANONYMOUS
ANONYMS
ANOOPSIA
ANOOPSIAS
ANOPHELES
ANOPIA
ANOPIAS
ANOPSIA
ANOPSIAS
ANORAK
ANORAKS
ANORECTAL
ANORECTIC
ANORETIC
ANORETICS
ANOREXIA
ANOREXIAS
ANOREXIC
ANOREXICS
ANOREXIES
ANOREXY
ANORTHIC
ANORTHITE
ANOSMATIC
ANOSMIA
ANOSMIAS
ANOSMIC
ANOTHER
ANOUGH
ANOUROUS
ANOVULANT
ANOVULAR
ANOW
ANOXAEMIA
ANOXAEMIC
ANOXEMIA
ANOXEMIAS
ANOXEMIC
ANOXIA
ANOXIAS
ANOXIC
ANS
ANSA
ANSAE
ANSAPHONE
ANSATE
ANSATED
ANSATZ
ANSATZES
ANSERINE
ANSERINES
ANSEROUS
ANSWER
ANSWERED
ANSWERER
ANSWERERS
ANSWERING
ANSWERS
ANT
ANTA
ANTACID
ANTACIDS
ANTAE
ANTALGIC
ANTALGICS
ANTALKALI
ANTAR
ANTARA
ANTARAS
ANTARCTIC
ANTARS
ANTAS
ANTBEAR
ANTBEARS
ANTBIRD
ANTBIRDS
ANTE
ANTEATER
ANTEATERS
ANTECEDE
ANTECEDED
ANTECEDES
ANTECHOIR
ANTED
ANTEDATE
ANTEDATED
ANTEDATES
ANTEED
ANTEFIX
ANTEFIXA
ANTEFIXAE
ANTEFIXAL
ANTEFIXES
ANTEING
ANTELOPE
ANTELOPES
ANTELUCAN
ANTENATAL
ANTENATI
ANTENNA
ANTENNAE
ANTENNAL
ANTENNARY
ANTENNAS
ANTENNULE
ANTEPAST
ANTEPASTS
ANTERIOR
ANTEROOM
ANTEROOMS
ANTES
ANTETYPE
ANTETYPES
ANTEVERT
ANTEVERTS
ANTHELIA
ANTHELION
ANTHELIX
ANTHEM
ANTHEMED
ANTHEMIA
ANTHEMIC
ANTHEMING
ANTHEMION
ANTHEMIS
ANTHEMS
ANTHER
ANTHERAL
ANTHERID
ANTHERIDS
ANTHERS
ANTHESES
ANTHESIS
ANTHILL
ANTHILLS
ANTHOCARP
ANTHOCYAN
ANTHODIA
ANTHODIUM
ANTHOID
ANTHOLOGY
ANTHOTAXY
ANTHOZOAN
ANTHOZOIC
ANTHRACES
ANTHRACIC
ANTHRAX
ANTHRAXES
ANTHRO
ANTHROPIC
ANTHROS
ANTHURIUM
ANTI
ANTIABUSE
ANTIACNE
ANTIAGING
ANTIAIR
ANTIALIEN
ANTIAR
ANTIARIN
ANTIARINS
ANTIARMOR
ANTIARS
ANTIATOM
ANTIATOMS
ANTIAUXIN
ANTIBIAS
ANTIBLACK
ANTIBODY
ANTIBOSS
ANTIBUG
ANTIBUSER
ANTIC
ANTICAL
ANTICALLY
ANTICAR
ANTICHLOR
ANTICISE
ANTICISED
ANTICISES
ANTICITY
ANTICIVIC
ANTICIZE
ANTICIZED
ANTICIZES
ANTICK
ANTICKE
ANTICKED
ANTICKES
ANTICKING

A

ANTICKS
ANTICLINE
ANTICLING
ANTICLY
ANTICODON
ANTICOLD
ANTICOUS
ANTICRACK
ANTICRIME
ANTICS
ANTICULT
ANTICULTS
ANTIDORA
ANTIDORON
ANTIDOTAL
ANTIDOTE
ANTIDOTED
ANTIDOTES
ANTIDRAFT
ANTIDRUG
ANTIDUNE
ANTIDUNES
ANTIELITE
ANTIENT
ANTIENTS
ANTIFA
ANTIFAS
ANTIFAT
ANTIFLU
ANTIFOAM
ANTIFOG
ANTIFRAUD
ANTIFUR
ANTIGANG
ANTIGAY
ANTIGEN
ANTIGENE
ANTIGENES
ANTIGENIC
ANTIGENS
ANTIGLARE
ANTIGRAFT
ANTIGUN
ANTIHELIX
ANTIHERO
ANTIHUMAN
ANTIJAM
ANTIKING
ANTIKINGS
ANTIKNOCK
ANTILABOR
ANTILEAK
ANTILEFT
ANTILIFE
ANTILIFER
ANTILOCK
ANTILOG
ANTILOGS
ANTILOGY
ANTIMACHO
ANTIMALE
ANTIMAN
ANTIMASK
ANTIMASKS
ANTIMEN
ANTIMERE
ANTIMERES
ANTIMERIC
ANTIMINE
ANTIMONIC
ANTIMONY
ANTIMONYL
ANTIMUON
ANTIMUONS
ANTIMUSIC
ANTIMYCIN
ANTING
ANTINGS
ANTINODAL
ANTINODE
ANTINODES
ANTINOISE
ANTINOME
ANTINOMES
ANTINOMIC
ANTINOMY
ANTINOVEL
ANTINUKE
ANTINUKER
ANTINUKES
ANTIPAPAL
ANTIPARTY
ANTIPASTI
ANTIPASTO
ANTIPATHY
ANTIPHON
ANTIPHONS
ANTIPHONY
ANTIPILL
ANTIPODAL
ANTIPODE
ANTIPODES
ANTIPOLAR
ANTIPOLE
ANTIPOLES
ANTIPOPE
ANTIPOPES
ANTIPORN
ANTIPOT
ANTIPRESS
ANTIPYIC
ANTIPYICS
ANTIQUARK
ANTIQUARY
ANTIQUATE
ANTIQUE
ANTIQUED
ANTIQUELY
ANTIQUER
ANTIQUERS
ANTIQUES
ANTIQUEY
ANTIQUIER
ANTIQUING
ANTIQUITY
ANTIRADAR
ANTIRAPE
ANTIRED
ANTIRIOT
ANTIROCK
ANTIROLL
ANTIROYAL
ANTIRUST
ANTIRUSTS
ANTIS
ANTISAG
ANTISCIAN
ANTISENSE
ANTISERA
ANTISERUM
ANTISEX
ANTISHAKE
ANTISHARK
ANTISHIP
ANTISHOCK
ANTISKID
ANTISLEEP
ANTISLIP
ANTISMOG
ANTISMOKE
ANTISMUT
ANTISNOB
ANTISNOBS
ANTISOLAR
ANTISPAM
ANTISPAST
ANTISTAT
ANTISTATE
ANTISTATS
ANTISTICK
ANTISTORY
ANTISTYLE
ANTITANK
ANTITAX
ANTITHEFT
ANTITHET
ANTITHETS
ANTITOXIC
ANTITOXIN
ANTITRADE
ANTITRAGI
ANTITRUST
ANTITUMOR
ANTITYPAL
ANTITYPE
ANTITYPES
ANTITYPIC
ANTIULCER
ANTIUNION
ANTIURBAN
ANTIVAX
ANTIVAXER
ANTIVENIN
ANTIVENOM
ANTIVIRAL
ANTIVIRUS
ANTIWAR
ANTIWEAR
ANTIWEED
ANTIWHITE
ANTIWOMAN
ANTIWORLD
ANTLER
ANTLERED
ANTLERS
ANTLIA
ANTLIAE
ANTLIATE
ANTLIKE
ANTLION
ANTLIONS
ANTONYM
ANTONYMIC
ANTONYMS
ANTONYMY
ANTPITTA
ANTPITTAS
ANTRA
ANTRAL
ANTRE
ANTRES
ANTRORSE
ANTRUM
ANTRUMS
ANTS
ANTSIER
ANTSIEST
ANTSINESS
ANTSY
ANTWACKIE
ANUCLEATE
ANURA
ANURAL
ANURAN
ANURANS
ANURESES
ANURESIS
ANURETIC
ANURIA
ANURIAS
ANURIC
ANUROUS
ANUS
ANUSES
ANVIL
ANVILED
ANVILING
ANVILLED
ANVILLING
ANVILS

ANVILTOP
ANVILTOPS
ANXIETIES
ANXIETY
ANXIOUS
ANXIOUSLY
ANY
ANYBODIES
ANYBODY
ANYHOW
ANYMORE
ANYON
ANYONE
ANYONES
ANYONS
ANYPLACE
ANYROAD
ANYTHING
ANYTHINGS
ANYTIME
ANYWAY
ANYWAYS
ANYWHEN
ANYWHERE
ANYWHERES
ANYWISE
ANZIANI
AORIST
AORISTIC
AORISTS
AORTA
AORTAE
AORTAL
AORTAS
AORTIC
AORTITIS
AOUDAD
AOUDADS
APACE
APACHE
APACHES
APADANA
APADANAS
APAGE
APAGOGE
APAGOGES
APAGOGIC
APAID
APANAGE
APANAGED
APANAGES
APAREJO
APAREJOS
APART
APARTHEID
APARTMENT
APARTNESS
APATETIC
APATHATON
APATHETIC
APATHIES
APATHY
APATITE
APATITES
APATOSAUR
APAY
APAYD
APAYING
APAYS
APE
APEAK
APED
APEDOM
APEDOMS
APEEK
APEHOOD
APEHOODS
APELIKE
APEMAN
APEMEN
APEPSIA
APEPSIAS
APEPSIES
APEPSY
APER
APERCU
APERCUS
APERIENT
APERIENTS
APERIES
APERIODIC
APERITIF
APERITIFS
APERITIVE
APERS
APERT
APERTNESS
APERTURAL
APERTURE
APERTURED
APERTURES
APERY
APES
APESHIT
APETALIES
APETALOUS
APETALY
APEX
APEXES
APGAR
APHAGIA
APHAGIAS
APHAKIA
APHAKIAS
APHANITE
APHANITES
APHANITIC
APHASIA
APHASIAC
APHASIACS
APHASIAS
APHASIC
APHASICS
APHELIA
APHELIAN
APHELION
APHELIONS
APHERESES
APHERESIS
APHERETIC
APHESES
APHESIS
APHETIC
APHETISE
APHETISED
APHETISES
APHETIZE
APHETIZED
APHETIZES
APHICIDE
APHICIDES
APHID
APHIDES
APHIDIAN
APHIDIANS
APHIDIOUS
APHIDS
APHIS
APHOLATE
APHOLATES
APHONIA
APHONIAS
APHONIC
APHONICS
APHONIES
APHONOUS
APHONY
APHORISE
APHORISED
APHORISER
APHORISES
APHORISM
APHORISMS
APHORIST
APHORISTS
APHORIZE
APHORIZED
APHORIZER
APHORIZES
APHOTIC
APHRODITE
APHTHA
APHTHAE
APHTHOUS
APHYLLIES
APHYLLOUS
APHYLLY
APIACEOUS
APIAN
APIARIAN
APIARIANS
APIARIES
APIARIST
APIARISTS
APIARY
APICAL
APICALLY
APICALS
APICES
APICIAN
APICULATE
APICULI
APICULUS
APIECE
APIEZON
APIMANIA
APIMANIAS
APING
APIOL
APIOLOGY
APIOLS
APISH
APISHLY
APISHNESS
APISM
APISMS
APIVOROUS
APLANAT
APLANATIC
APLANATS
APLANETIC
APLASIA
APLASIAS
APLASTIC
APLENTY
APLITE
APLITES
APLITIC
APLOMB
APLOMBS
APLUSTRE
APLUSTRES
APNEA
APNEAL
APNEAS
APNEIC
APNEUSES
APNEUSIS
APNEUSTIC
APNOEA
APNOEAL
APNOEAS
APNOEIC
APO
APOAPSES
APOAPSIS
APOCARP
APOCARPS
APOCARPY
APOCOPATE

APOCOPE
APOCOPES
APOCOPIC
APOCRINE
APOCRYPHA
APOD
APODAL
APODE
APODES
APODICTIC
APODOSES
APODOSIS
APODOUS
APODS
APOENZYME
APOGAEIC
APOGAMIC
APOGAMIES
APOGAMOUS
APOGAMY
APOGEAL
APOGEAN
APOGEE
APOGEES
APOGEIC
APOGRAPH
APOGRAPHS
APOLLO
APOLLOS
APOLOG
APOLOGAL
APOLOGIA
APOLOGIAE
APOLOGIAS
APOLOGIES
APOLOGISE
APOLOGIST
APOLOGIZE
APOLOGS
APOLOGUE
APOLOGUES
APOLOGY
APOLUNE
APOLUNES
APOMICT
APOMICTIC
APOMICTS
APOMIXES
APOMIXIS
APOOP
APOPHASES
APOPHASIS
APOPHATIC
APOPHENIA
APOPHONY
APOPHYGE
APOPHYGES
APOPHYSES
APOPHYSIS
APOPLAST
APOPLASTS
APOPLEX
APOPLEXED
APOPLEXES
APOPLEXY
APOPTOSES
APOPTOSIS
APOPTOTIC
APORETIC
APORIA
APORIAS
APORT
APOS
APOSITIA
APOSITIAS
APOSITIC
APOSPORIC
APOSPORY
APOSTACY
APOSTASY
APOSTATE
APOSTATES
APOSTATIC
APOSTIL
APOSTILLE
APOSTILS
APOSTLE
APOSTLES
APOSTOLIC
APOTHECE
APOTHECES
APOTHECIA
APOTHEGM
APOTHEGMS
APOTHEM
APOTHEMS
APOZEM
APOZEMS
APP
APPAID
APPAIR
APPAIRED
APPAIRING
APPAIRS
APPAL
APPALL
APPALLED
APPALLING
APPALLS
APPALOOSA
APPALS
APPALTI
APPALTO
APPANAGE
APPANAGED
APPANAGES
APPARAT
APPARATS
APPARATUS
APPAREL
APPARELED
APPARELS
APPARENCY
APPARENT
APPARENTS
APPARITOR
APPAY
APPAYD
APPAYING
APPAYS
APPEACH
APPEACHED
APPEACHES
APPEAL
APPEALED
APPEALER
APPEALERS
APPEALING
APPEALS
APPEAR
APPEARED
APPEARER
APPEARERS
APPEARING
APPEARS
APPEASE
APPEASED
APPEASER
APPEASERS
APPEASES
APPEASING
APPEL
APPELLANT
APPELLATE
APPELLEE
APPELLEES
APPELLOR
APPELLORS
APPELS
APPEND
APPENDAGE
APPENDANT
APPENDED
APPENDENT
APPENDING
APPENDIX
APPENDS
APPERIL
APPERILL
APPERILLS
APPERILS
APPERTAIN
APPESTAT
APPESTATS
APPETENCE
APPETENCY
APPETENT
APPETIBLE
APPETISE
APPETISED
APPETISER
APPETISES
APPETITE
APPETITES
APPETIZE
APPETIZED
APPETIZER
APPETIZES
APPLAUD
APPLAUDED
APPLAUDER
APPLAUDS
APPLAUSE
APPLAUSES
APPLE
APPLECART
APPLEJACK
APPLES
APPLET
APPLETINI
APPLETS
APPLEY
APPLIABLE
APPLIANCE
APPLICANT
APPLICATE
APPLIED
APPLIER
APPLIERS
APPLIES
APPLIEST
APPLIQUE
APPLIQUED
APPLIQUES
APPLY
APPLYING
APPOINT
APPOINTED
APPOINTEE
APPOINTER
APPOINTOR
APPOINTS
APPORT
APPORTION
APPORTS
APPOSABLE
APPOSE
APPOSED
APPOSER
APPOSERS
APPOSES
APPOSING
APPOSITE
APPRAISAL
APPRAISE
APPRAISED
APPRAISEE
APPRAISER
APPRAISES
APPREHEND

APPRESS
APPRESSED
APPRESSES
APPRISE
APPRISED
APPRISER
APPRISERS
APPRISES
APPRISING
APPRIZE
APPRIZED
APPRIZER
APPRIZERS
APPRIZES
APPRIZING
APPRO
APPROACH
APPROBATE
APPROOF
APPROOFS
APPROS
APPROVAL
APPROVALS
APPROVE
APPROVED
APPROVER
APPROVERS
APPROVES
APPROVING
APPS
APPUI
APPUIED
APPUIS
APPULSE
APPULSES
APPULSIVE
APPUY
APPUYED
APPUYING
APPUYS
APRACTIC
APRAXIA
APRAXIAS
APRAXIC
APRES
APRICATE
APRICATED
APRICATES
APRICOCK
APRICOCKS
APRICOT
APRICOTS
APRIORISM
APRIORIST
APRIORITY
APRON
APRONED
APRONFUL
APRONFULS
APRONING
APRONLIKE
APRONS
APROPOS
APROTIC
APSARAS
APSARASES
APSE
APSES
APSIDAL
APSIDES
APSIDIOLE
APSIS
APSO
APSOS
APT
APTAMER
APTAMERS
APTED
APTER
APTERAL
APTERIA
APTERISM
APTERISMS
APTERIUM
APTEROUS
APTERYX
APTERYXES
APTEST
APTING
APTITUDE
APTITUDES
APTLY
APTNESS
APTNESSES
APTOTE
APTOTES
APTOTIC
APTS
APYRASE
APYRASES
APYRETIC
APYREXIA
APYREXIAS
AQUA
AQUABATIC
AQUABOARD
AQUACADE
AQUACADES
AQUADROME
AQUAE
AQUAFABA
AQUAFABAS
AQUAFARM
AQUAFARMS
AQUAFER
AQUAFERS
AQUAFIT
AQUAFITS
AQUALUNG
AQUALUNGS
AQUANAUT
AQUANAUTS
AQUAPHOBE
AQUAPLANE
AQUAPORIN
AQUARELLE
AQUARIA
AQUARIAL
AQUARIAN
AQUARIANS
AQUARIIST
AQUARIST
AQUARISTS
AQUARIUM
AQUARIUMS
AQUAROBIC
AQUAS
AQUASCAPE
AQUASHOW
AQUASHOWS
AQUATIC
AQUATICS
AQUATINT
AQUATINTA
AQUATINTS
AQUATONE
AQUATONES
AQUAVIT
AQUAVITS
AQUEDUCT
AQUEDUCTS
AQUEOUS
AQUEOUSLY
AQUIFER
AQUIFERS
AQUILEGIA
AQUILINE
AQUILON
AQUILONS
AQUIVER
AR
ARAARA
ARAARAS
ARABA
ARABAS
ARABESK
ARABESKS
ARABESQUE
ARABIC
ARABICA
ARABICAS
ARABICISE
ARABICIZE
ARABILITY
ARABIN
ARABINOSE
ARABINS
ARABIS
ARABISE
ARABISED
ARABISES
ARABISING
ARABIZE
ARABIZED
ARABIZES
ARABIZING
ARABLE
ARABLES
ARACEOUS
ARACHIS
ARACHISES
ARACHNID
ARACHNIDS
ARACHNOID
ARAGONITE
ARAHUANA
ARAHUANAS
ARAISE
ARAISED
ARAISES
ARAISING
ARAK
ARAKS
ARALIA
ARALIAS
ARAME
ARAMES
ARAMID
ARAMIDS
ARANCINI
ARANEID
ARANEIDAN
ARANEIDS
ARANEOUS
ARAPAIMA
ARAPAIMAS
ARAPONGA
ARAPONGAS
ARAPUNGA
ARAPUNGAS
ARAR
ARAROBA
ARAROBAS
ARARS
ARAUCARIA
ARAWANA
ARAWANAS
ARAYSE
ARAYSED
ARAYSES
ARAYSING
ARB
ARBA
ARBALEST
ARBALESTS
ARBALIST
ARBALISTS
ARBAS
ARBELEST
ARBELESTS

ARBITER
ARBITERS
ARBITRAGE
ARBITRAL
ARBITRARY
ARBITRATE
ARBITRESS
ARBITRIUM
ARBLAST
ARBLASTER
ARBLASTS
ARBOR
ARBOREAL
ARBORED
ARBOREOUS
ARBORES
ARBORET
ARBORETA
ARBORETS
ARBORETUM
ARBORIO
ARBORIOS
ARBORISE
ARBORISED
ARBORISES
ARBORIST
ARBORISTS
ARBORIZE
ARBORIZED
ARBORIZES
ARBOROUS
ARBORS
ARBOUR
ARBOURED
ARBOURS
ARBOVIRAL
ARBOVIRUS
ARBS
ARBUSCLE
ARBUSCLES
ARBUTE
ARBUTEAN
ARBUTES
ARBUTUS
ARBUTUSES
ARC
ARCADE
ARCADED
ARCADES
ARCADIA
ARCADIAN
ARCADIANS
ARCADIAS
ARCADING
ARCADINGS
ARCANA
ARCANAS
ARCANE
ARCANELY
ARCANIST
ARCANISTS
ARCANUM
ARCANUMS
ARCATURE
ARCATURES
ARCCOSINE
ARCED
ARCH
ARCHAEA
ARCHAEAL
ARCHAEAN
ARCHAEANS
ARCHAEI
ARCHAEON
ARCHAEUS
ARCHAIC
ARCHAICAL
ARCHAISE
ARCHAISED
ARCHAISER
ARCHAISES
ARCHAISM
ARCHAISMS
ARCHAIST
ARCHAISTS
ARCHAIZE
ARCHAIZED
ARCHAIZER
ARCHAIZES
ARCHANGEL
ARCHDRUID
ARCHDUCAL
ARCHDUCHY
ARCHDUKE
ARCHDUKES
ARCHEAN
ARCHED
ARCHEI
ARCHENEMY
ARCHER
ARCHERESS
ARCHERIES
ARCHERS
ARCHERY
ARCHES
ARCHEST
ARCHETYPE
ARCHEUS
ARCHFIEND
ARCHFOE
ARCHFOES
ARCHFOOL
ARCHFOOLS
ARCHI
ARCHICARP
ARCHIL
ARCHILOWE
ARCHILS
ARCHIMAGE
ARCHINE
ARCHINES
ARCHING
ARCHINGS
ARCHITECT
ARCHITYPE
ARCHIVAL
ARCHIVE
ARCHIVED
ARCHIVES
ARCHIVING
ARCHIVIST
ARCHIVOLT
ARCHLET
ARCHLETS
ARCHLIKE
ARCHLUTE
ARCHLUTES
ARCHLY
ARCHNESS
ARCHOLOGY
ARCHON
ARCHONS
ARCHONTIC
ARCHOSAUR
ARCHRIVAL
ARCHSTONE
ARCHWAY
ARCHWAYS
ARCHWISE
ARCIFORM
ARCING
ARCINGS
ARCKED
ARCKING
ARCKINGS
ARCMIN
ARCMINS
ARCMINUTE
ARCO
ARCOGRAPH
ARCOLOGY
ARCOS
ARCS
ARCSEC
ARCSECOND
ARCSECS
ARCSINE
ARCSINES
ARCTIC
ARCTICS
ARCTIID
ARCTIIDS
ARCTOID
ARCTOPHIL
ARCUATE
ARCUATED
ARCUATELY
ARCUATION
ARCUS
ARCUSES
ARD
ARDEB
ARDEBS
ARDENCIES
ARDENCY
ARDENT
ARDENTLY
ARDOR
ARDORS
ARDOUR
ARDOURS
ARDRI
ARDRIGH
ARDRIGHS
ARDRIS
ARDS
ARDUOUS
ARDUOUSLY
ARE
AREA
AREACH
AREACHED
AREACHES
AREACHING
AREAD
AREADING
AREADS
AREAE
AREAL
AREALLY
AREAR
AREARS
AREAS
AREAWAY
AREAWAYS
ARECA
ARECAS
ARECOLINE
ARED
AREDD
AREDE
AREDES
AREDING
AREFIED
AREFIES
AREFY
AREFYING
AREG
AREIC
ARENA
ARENAS
ARENATION
ARENE
ARENES
ARENITE
ARENITES
ARENITIC
ARENOSE
ARENOUS
AREOLA

AREOLAE
AREOLAR
AREOLAS
AREOLATE
AREOLATED
AREOLE
AREOLES
AREOLOGY
AREOMETER
AREOMETRY
AREOSTYLE
AREPA
AREPAS
ARERE
ARES
ARET
ARETE
ARETES
ARETHUSA
ARETHUSAS
ARETS
ARETT
ARETTED
ARETTING
ARETTS
AREW
ARF
ARFS
ARGAL
ARGALA
ARGALAS
ARGALI
ARGALIS
ARGALS
ARGAN
ARGAND
ARGANDS
ARGANS
ARGEMONE
ARGEMONES
ARGENT
ARGENTAL
ARGENTIC
ARGENTINE
ARGENTITE
ARGENTOUS
ARGENTS
ARGENTUM
ARGENTUMS
ARGH
ARGHAN
ARGHANS
ARGIL
ARGILLITE
ARGILS
ARGINASE
ARGINASES
ARGININE
ARGININES
ARGLE
ARGLED
ARGLES
ARGLING
ARGOL
ARGOLS
ARGON
ARGONAUT
ARGONAUTS
ARGONON
ARGONONS
ARGONS
ARGOSIES
ARGOSY
ARGOT
ARGOTIC
ARGOTS
ARGUABLE
ARGUABLY
ARGUE
ARGUED
ARGUER
ARGUERS
ARGUES
ARGUFIED
ARGUFIER
ARGUFIERS
ARGUFIES
ARGUFY
ARGUFYING
ARGUING
ARGULI
ARGULUS
ARGUMENT
ARGUMENTA
ARGUMENTS
ARGUS
ARGUSES
ARGUTE
ARGUTELY
ARGYLE
ARGYLES
ARGYLL
ARGYLLS
ARGYRIA
ARGYRIAS
ARGYRITE
ARGYRITES
ARHAT
ARHATS
ARHATSHIP
ARHYTHMIA
ARHYTHMIC
ARIA
ARIARIES
ARIARY
ARIAS
ARID
ARIDER
ARIDEST
ARIDITIES
ARIDITY
ARIDLY
ARIDNESS
ARIEL
ARIELS
ARIETTA
ARIETTAS
ARIETTE
ARIETTES
ARIGHT
ARIKI
ARIKIS
ARIL
ARILED
ARILLARY
ARILLATE
ARILLATED
ARILLI
ARILLODE
ARILLODES
ARILLOID
ARILLUS
ARILS
ARIOSE
ARIOSI
ARIOSO
ARIOSOS
ARIOT
ARIPPLE
ARIS
ARISE
ARISEN
ARISES
ARISH
ARISHES
ARISING
ARISTA
ARISTAE
ARISTAS
ARISTATE
ARISTO
ARISTOS
ARISTOTLE
ARK
ARKED
ARKING
ARKITE
ARKITES
ARKOSE
ARKOSES
ARKOSIC
ARKS
ARLE
ARLED
ARLES
ARLING
ARM
ARMADA
ARMADAS
ARMADILLO
ARMAGNAC
ARMAGNACS
ARMAMENT
ARMAMENTS
ARMATURE
ARMATURED
ARMATURES
ARMBAND
ARMBANDS
ARMCHAIR
ARMCHAIRS
ARMED
ARMER
ARMERIA
ARMERIAS
ARMERS
ARMET
ARMETS
ARMFUL
ARMFULS
ARMGAUNT
ARMGUARD
ARMGUARDS
ARMHOLE
ARMHOLES
ARMIES
ARMIGER
ARMIGERAL
ARMIGERO
ARMIGEROS
ARMIGERS
ARMIL
ARMILLA
ARMILLAE
ARMILLARY
ARMILLAS
ARMILS
ARMING
ARMINGS
ARMISTICE
ARMLESS
ARMLET
ARMLETS
ARMLIKE
ARMLOAD
ARMLOADS
ARMLOCK
ARMLOCKED
ARMLOCKS
ARMOIRE
ARMOIRES
ARMONICA
ARMONICAS
ARMOR
ARMORED
ARMORER
ARMORERS
ARMORIAL
ARMORIALS
ARMORIES

ARMORING
ARMORIST
ARMORISTS
ARMORLESS
ARMORS
ARMORY
ARMOUR
ARMOURED
ARMOURER
ARMOURERS
ARMOURIES
ARMOURING
ARMOURS
ARMOURY
ARMOZEEN
ARMOZEENS
ARMOZINE
ARMOZINES
ARMPIT
ARMPITS
ARMREST
ARMRESTS
ARMS
ARMSFUL
ARMURE
ARMURES
ARMY
ARMYWORM
ARMYWORMS
ARNA
ARNAS
ARNATTO
ARNATTOS
ARNICA
ARNICAS
ARNOTTO
ARNOTTOS
ARNUT
ARNUTS
AROBA
AROBAS
AROHA
AROHAS
AROID
AROIDS
AROINT
AROINTED
AROINTING
AROINTS
AROLLA
AROLLAS
AROMA
AROMAS
AROMATASE
AROMATIC
AROMATICS
AROMATISE
AROMATIZE
AROSE
AROUND
AROUSABLE
AROUSAL
AROUSALS
AROUSE
AROUSED
AROUSER
AROUSERS
AROUSES
AROUSING
AROW
AROWANA
AROWANAS
AROYNT
AROYNTED
AROYNTING
AROYNTS
ARPA
ARPAS
ARPEGGIO
ARPEGGIOS
ARPEN
ARPENS
ARPENT
ARPENTS
ARPILLERA
ARQUEBUS
ARRACACHA
ARRACK
ARRACKS
ARRAH
ARRAIGN
ARRAIGNED
ARRAIGNER
ARRAIGNS
ARRANGE
ARRANGED
ARRANGER
ARRANGERS
ARRANGES
ARRANGING
ARRANT
ARRANTLY
ARRAS
ARRASED
ARRASENE
ARRASENES
ARRASES
ARRAUGHT
ARRAY
ARRAYAL
ARRAYALS
ARRAYED
ARRAYER
ARRAYERS
ARRAYING
ARRAYMENT
ARRAYS
ARREAR
ARREARAGE
ARREARS
ARRECT
ARREEDE
ARREEDES
ARREEDING
ARREST
ARRESTANT
ARRESTED
ARRESTEE
ARRESTEES
ARRESTER
ARRESTERS
ARRESTING
ARRESTIVE
ARRESTOR
ARRESTORS
ARRESTS
ARRET
ARRETS
ARRHIZAL
ARRIAGE
ARRIAGES
ARRIBA
ARRIDE
ARRIDED
ARRIDES
ARRIDING
ARRIERE
ARRIERO
ARRIEROS
ARRIS
ARRISES
ARRISH
ARRISHES
ARRIVAL
ARRIVALS
ARRIVANCE
ARRIVANCY
ARRIVE
ARRIVED
ARRIVER
ARRIVERS
ARRIVES
ARRIVING
ARRIVISME
ARRIVISTE
ARROBA
ARROBAS
ARROCES
ARROGANCE
ARROGANCY
ARROGANT
ARROGATE
ARROGATED
ARROGATES
ARROGATOR
ARROW
ARROWED
ARROWHEAD
ARROWIER
ARROWIEST
ARROWING
ARROWLESS
ARROWLIKE
ARROWROOT
ARROWS
ARROWWOOD
ARROWWORM
ARROWY
ARROYO
ARROYOS
ARROZ
ARROZES
ARS
ARSE
ARSED
ARSEHOLE
ARSEHOLED
ARSEHOLES
ARSENAL
ARSENALS
ARSENATE
ARSENATES
ARSENIATE
ARSENIC
ARSENICAL
ARSENICS
ARSENIDE
ARSENIDES
ARSENIOUS
ARSENITE
ARSENITES
ARSENO
ARSENOUS
ARSES
ARSEY
ARSHEEN
ARSHEENS
ARSHIN
ARSHINE
ARSHINES
ARSHINS
ARSIER
ARSIEST
ARSINE
ARSINES
ARSING
ARSINO
ARSIS
ARSON
ARSONIST
ARSONISTS
ARSONITE
ARSONITES
ARSONOUS
ARSONS
ARSY
ART
ARTAL
ARTEFACT
ARTEFACTS

A

ARTEL
ARTELS
ARTEMISIA
ARTERIAL
ARTERIALS
ARTERIES
ARTERIOLE
ARTERITIS
ARTERY
ARTESIAN
ARTFUL
ARTFULLY
ARTHOUSE
ARTHOUSES
ARTHRITIC
ARTHRITIS
ARTHRODIA
ARTHROPOD
ARTHROSES
ARTHROSIS
ARTI
ARTIC
ARTICHOKE
ARTICLE
ARTICLED
ARTICLES
ARTICLING
ARTICS
ARTICULAR
ARTIER
ARTIES
ARTIEST
ARTIFACT
ARTIFACTS
ARTIFICE
ARTIFICER
ARTIFICES
ARTIGI
ARTIGIS
ARTILLERY
ARTILY
ARTINESS
ARTIS
ARTISAN
ARTISANAL
ARTISANS
ARTIST
ARTISTE
ARTISTES
ARTISTIC
ARTISTRY
ARTISTS
ARTLESS
ARTLESSLY
ARTMAKER
ARTMAKERS
ARTMAKING
ARTS
ARTSIE
ARTSIER
ARTSIES
ARTSIEST
ARTSINESS
ARTSMAN
ARTSMEN
ARTSY
ARTWORK
ARTWORKS
ARTY
ARUANA
ARUANAS
ARUGOLA
ARUGOLAS
ARUGULA
ARUGULAS
ARUHE
ARUHES
ARUM
ARUMS
ARUSPEX
ARUSPICES
ARVAL
ARVEE
ARVEES
ARVICOLE
ARVICOLES
ARVO
ARVOS
ARY
ARYBALLOS
ARYL
ARYLS
ARYTENOID
ARYTHMIA
ARYTHMIAS
ARYTHMIC
AS
ASAFETIDA
ASANA
ASANAS
ASAR
ASARUM
ASARUMS
ASBESTIC
ASBESTINE
ASBESTOS
ASBESTOUS
ASBESTUS
ASCARED
ASCARID
ASCARIDES
ASCARIDS
ASCARIS
ASCARISES
ASCAUNT
ASCEND
ASCENDANT
ASCENDED
ASCENDENT
ASCENDER
ASCENDERS
ASCENDEUR
ASCENDING
ASCENDS
ASCENSION
ASCENSIVE
ASCENT
ASCENTS
ASCERTAIN
ASCESES
ASCESIS
ASCETIC
ASCETICAL
ASCETICS
ASCI
ASCIAN
ASCIANS
ASCIDIA
ASCIDIAN
ASCIDIANS
ASCIDIATE
ASCIDIUM
ASCITES
ASCITIC
ASCITICAL
ASCLEPIAD
ASCLEPIAS
ASCOCARP
ASCOCARPS
ASCOGONIA
ASCON
ASCONCE
ASCONOID
ASCONS
ASCORBATE
ASCORBIC
ASCOSPORE
ASCOT
ASCOTS
ASCRIBE
ASCRIBED
ASCRIBES
ASCRIBING
ASCUS
ASDIC
ASDICS
ASEA
ASEISMIC
ASEITIES
ASEITY
ASEMANTIC
ASEPALOUS
ASEPSES
ASEPSIS
ASEPTATE
ASEPTIC
ASEPTICS
ASEXUAL
ASEXUALLY
ASH
ASHAKE
ASHAME
ASHAMED
ASHAMEDLY
ASHAMES
ASHAMING
ASHCAKE
ASHCAKES
ASHCAN
ASHCANS
ASHED
ASHEN
ASHERIES
ASHERY
ASHES
ASHET
ASHETS
ASHFALL
ASHFALLS
ASHIER
ASHIEST
ASHINE
ASHINESS
ASHING
ASHIVER
ASHKEY
ASHKEYS
ASHLAR
ASHLARED
ASHLARING
ASHLARS
ASHLER
ASHLERED
ASHLERING
ASHLERS
ASHLESS
ASHMAN
ASHMEN
ASHORE
ASHPAN
ASHPANS
ASHPLANT
ASHPLANTS
ASHRAF
ASHRAM
ASHRAMA
ASHRAMAS
ASHRAMITE
ASHRAMS
ASHTANGA
ASHTANGAS
ASHTRAY
ASHTRAYS
ASHY
ASIAGO
ASIAGOS
ASIDE
ASIDES
ASINICO
ASINICOS

ASININE
ASININELY
ASININITY
ASK
ASKANCE
ASKANCED
ASKANCES
ASKANCING
ASKANT
ASKANTED
ASKANTING
ASKANTS
ASKARI
ASKARIS
ASKED
ASKER
ASKERS
ASKESES
ASKESIS
ASKEW
ASKEWNESS
ASKING
ASKINGS
ASKLENT
ASKOI
ASKOS
ASKS
ASLAKE
ASLAKED
ASLAKES
ASLAKING
ASLANT
ASLEEP
ASLOPE
ASLOSH
ASMEAR
ASMOULDER
ASOCIAL
ASOCIALS
ASP
ASPARAGUS
ASPARKLE
ASPARTAME
ASPARTATE
ASPARTIC
ASPECT
ASPECTED
ASPECTING
ASPECTS
ASPECTUAL
ASPEN
ASPENS
ASPER
ASPERATE
ASPERATED
ASPERATES
ASPERGE
ASPERGED
ASPERGER
ASPERGERS
ASPERGES
ASPERGILL
ASPERGING
ASPERITY
ASPERMIA
ASPERMIAS
ASPEROUS
ASPERS
ASPERSE
ASPERSED
ASPERSER
ASPERSERS
ASPERSES
ASPERSING
ASPERSION
ASPERSIVE
ASPERSOIR
ASPERSOR
ASPERSORS
ASPERSORY
ASPHALT
ASPHALTED
ASPHALTER
ASPHALTIC
ASPHALTS
ASPHALTUM
ASPHERIC
ASPHERICS
ASPHODEL
ASPHODELS
ASPHYXIA
ASPHYXIAL
ASPHYXIAS
ASPHYXIED
ASPHYXIES
ASPHYXY
ASPIC
ASPICK
ASPICKS
ASPICS
ASPIDIA
ASPIDIOID
ASPIDIUM
ASPINE
ASPINES
ASPIRANT
ASPIRANTS
ASPIRATA
ASPIRATAE
ASPIRATE
ASPIRATED
ASPIRATES
ASPIRATOR
ASPIRE
ASPIRED
ASPIRER
ASPIRERS
ASPIRES
ASPIRIN
ASPIRING
ASPIRINS
ASPIS
ASPISES
ASPISH
ASPLENIUM
ASPORT
ASPORTED
ASPORTING
ASPORTS
ASPOUT
ASPRAWL
ASPREAD
ASPRO
ASPROS
ASPROUT
ASPS
ASQUAT
ASQUINT
ASRAMA
ASRAMAS
ASS
ASSAGAI
ASSAGAIED
ASSAGAIS
ASSAI
ASSAIL
ASSAILANT
ASSAILED
ASSAILER
ASSAILERS
ASSAILING
ASSAILS
ASSAIS
ASSAM
ASSAMS
ASSART
ASSARTED
ASSARTING
ASSARTS
ASSASSIN
ASSASSINS
ASSAULT
ASSAULTED
ASSAULTER
ASSAULTS
ASSAY
ASSAYABLE
ASSAYED
ASSAYER
ASSAYERS
ASSAYING
ASSAYINGS
ASSAYS
ASSEGAAI
ASSEGAAIS
ASSEGAI
ASSEGAIED
ASSEGAIS
ASSEMBLE
ASSEMBLED
ASSEMBLER
ASSEMBLES
ASSEMBLY
ASSENT
ASSENTED
ASSENTER
ASSENTERS
ASSENTING
ASSENTIVE
ASSENTOR
ASSENTORS
ASSENTS
ASSERT
ASSERTED
ASSERTER
ASSERTERS
ASSERTING
ASSERTION
ASSERTIVE
ASSERTOR
ASSERTORS
ASSERTORY
ASSERTS
ASSES
ASSESS
ASSESSED
ASSESSES
ASSESSING
ASSESSOR
ASSESSORS
ASSET
ASSETLESS
ASSETS
ASSEVER
ASSEVERED
ASSEVERS
ASSEZ
ASSHOLE
ASSHOLES
ASSIDUITY
ASSIDUOUS
ASSIEGE
ASSIEGED
ASSIEGES
ASSIEGING
ASSIENTO
ASSIENTOS
ASSIGN
ASSIGNAT
ASSIGNATS
ASSIGNED
ASSIGNEE
ASSIGNEES
ASSIGNER
ASSIGNERS
ASSIGNING
ASSIGNOR
ASSIGNORS
ASSIGNS
ASSIST

ASSISTANT
ASSISTED
ASSISTER
ASSISTERS
ASSISTING
ASSISTIVE
ASSISTOR
ASSISTORS
ASSISTS
ASSIZE
ASSIZED
ASSIZER
ASSIZERS
ASSIZES
ASSIZING
ASSLIKE
ASSOCIATE
ASSOIL
ASSOILED
ASSOILING
ASSOILS
ASSOILZIE
ASSONANCE
ASSONANT
ASSONANTS
ASSONATE
ASSONATED
ASSONATES
ASSORT
ASSORTED
ASSORTER
ASSORTERS
ASSORTING
ASSORTIVE
ASSORTS
ASSOT
ASSOTS
ASSOTT
ASSOTTED
ASSOTTING
ASSUAGE
ASSUAGED
ASSUAGER
ASSUAGERS
ASSUAGES
ASSUAGING
ASSUASIVE
ASSUETUDE

ASSUMABLE
ASSUMABLY
ASSUME
ASSUMED
ASSUMEDLY
ASSUMER
ASSUMERS
ASSUMES
ASSUMING
ASSUMINGS
ASSUMPSIT
ASSURABLE
ASSURANCE
ASSURE
ASSURED
ASSUREDLY
ASSUREDS
ASSURER
ASSURERS
ASSURES
ASSURGENT
ASSURING
ASSUROR
ASSURORS
ASSWAGE
ASSWAGED
ASSWAGES
ASSWAGING
ASSWIPE
ASSWIPES
ASTABLE
ASTANGA
ASTANGAS
ASTARE
ASTART
ASTARTED
ASTARTING
ASTARTS
ASTASIA
ASTASIAS
ASTATIC
ASTATIDE
ASTATIDES
ASTATINE
ASTATINES
ASTATKI
ASTATKIS
ASTEISM

ASTEISMS
ASTELIC
ASTELIES
ASTELY
ASTER
ASTERIA
ASTERIAS
ASTERID
ASTERIDS
ASTERISK
ASTERISKS
ASTERISM
ASTERISMS
ASTERN
ASTERNAL
ASTEROID
ASTEROIDS
ASTERS
ASTERT
ASTERTED
ASTERTING
ASTERTS
ASTHANGA
ASTHANGAS
ASTHENIA
ASTHENIAS
ASTHENIC
ASTHENICS
ASTHENIES
ASTHENY
ASTHMA
ASTHMAS
ASTHMATIC
ASTHORE
ASTHORES
ASTICHOUS
ASTIGMIA
ASTIGMIAS
ASTILBE
ASTILBES
ASTIR
ASTOMATAL
ASTOMOUS
ASTONE
ASTONED
ASTONES
ASTONIED
ASTONIES

ASTONING
ASTONISH
ASTONY
ASTONYING
ASTOOP
ASTOUND
ASTOUNDED
ASTOUNDS
ASTRACHAN
ASTRADDLE
ASTRAGAL
ASTRAGALI
ASTRAGALS
ASTRAKHAN
ASTRAL
ASTRALLY
ASTRALS
ASTRAND
ASTRANTIA
ASTRAY
ASTRICT
ASTRICTED
ASTRICTS
ASTRIDE
ASTRINGE
ASTRINGED
ASTRINGER
ASTRINGES
ASTROCYTE
ASTRODOME
ASTROFELL
ASTROID
ASTROIDS
ASTROLABE
ASTROLOGY
ASTRONAUT
ASTRONOMY
ASTROPHEL
ASTRUT
ASTUCIOUS
ASTUCITY
ASTUN
ASTUNNED
ASTUNNING
ASTUNS
ASTUTE
ASTUTELY
ASTUTER

ASTUTEST
ASTYLAR
ASUDDEN
ASUNDER
ASURA
ASURAS
ASWARM
ASWAY
ASWIM
ASWING
ASWIRL
ASWOON
ASYLA
ASYLEE
ASYLEES
ASYLLABIC
ASYLUM
ASYLUMS
ASYMMETRY
ASYMPTOTE
ASYNAPSES
ASYNAPSIS
ASYNDETA
ASYNDETIC
ASYNDETON
ASYNERGIA
ASYNERGY
ASYSTOLE
ASYSTOLES
ASYSTOLIC
AT
ATAATA
ATAATAS
ATABAL
ATABALS
ATABEG
ATABEGS
ATABEK
ATABEKS
ATABRIN
ATABRINE
ATABRINES
ATABRINS
ATACAMITE
ATACTIC
ATAGHAN
ATAGHANS
ATALAYA

ATALAYAS
ATAMAN
ATAMANS
ATAMASCO
ATAMASCOS
ATAP
ATAPS
ATARACTIC
ATARAXIA
ATARAXIAS
ATARAXIC
ATARAXICS
ATARAXIES
ATARAXY
ATAVIC
ATAVISM
ATAVISMS
ATAVIST
ATAVISTIC
ATAVISTS
ATAXIA
ATAXIAS
ATAXIC
ATAXICS
ATAXIES
ATAXY
ATCHIEVE
ATCHIEVED
ATCHIEVES
ATE
ATEBRIN
ATEBRINS
ATECHNIC
ATECHNICS
ATELIC
ATELIER
ATELIERS
ATEMOYA
ATEMOYAS
ATEMPORAL
ATENOLOL
ATENOLOLS
ATES
ATHAME
ATHAMES
ATHANASY
ATHANOR
ATHANORS
ATHEISE
ATHEISED
ATHEISES
ATHEISING
ATHEISM
ATHEISMS
ATHEIST
ATHEISTIC
ATHEISTS
ATHEIZE
ATHEIZED
ATHEIZES
ATHEIZING
ATHELING
ATHELINGS
ATHEMATIC
ATHENAEUM
ATHENEUM
ATHENEUMS
ATHEOLOGY
ATHEOUS
ATHERINE
ATHERINES
ATHEROMA
ATHEROMAS
ATHETESES
ATHETESIS
ATHETISE
ATHETISED
ATHETISES
ATHETIZE
ATHETIZED
ATHETIZES
ATHETOID
ATHETOSES
ATHETOSIC
ATHETOSIS
ATHETOTIC
ATHIRST
ATHLETA
ATHLETAS
ATHLETE
ATHLETES
ATHLETIC
ATHLETICS
ATHODYD
ATHODYDS
ATHRILL
ATHROB
ATHROCYTE
ATHWART
ATIGI
ATIGIS
ATILT
ATIMIES
ATIMY
ATINGLE
ATISHOO
ATISHOOS
ATLANTES
ATLAS
ATLASES
ATLATL
ATLATLS
ATMA
ATMAN
ATMANS
ATMAS
ATMOLOGY
ATMOLYSE
ATMOLYSED
ATMOLYSES
ATMOLYSIS
ATMOLYZE
ATMOLYZED
ATMOLYZES
ATMOMETER
ATMOMETRY
ATMOS
ATMOSES
ATOC
ATOCIA
ATOCIAS
ATOCS
ATOK
ATOKAL
ATOKE
ATOKES
ATOKOUS
ATOKS
ATOLL
ATOLLS
ATOM
ATOMIC
ATOMICAL
ATOMICITY
ATOMICS
ATOMIES
ATOMISE
ATOMISED
ATOMISER
ATOMISERS
ATOMISES
ATOMISING
ATOMISM
ATOMISMS
ATOMIST
ATOMISTIC
ATOMISTS
ATOMIZE
ATOMIZED
ATOMIZER
ATOMIZERS
ATOMIZES
ATOMIZING
ATOMS
ATOMY
ATONABLE
ATONAL
ATONALISM
ATONALIST
ATONALITY
ATONALLY
ATONE
ATONEABLE
ATONED
ATONEMENT
ATONER
ATONERS
ATONES
ATONIA
ATONIAS
ATONIC
ATONICITY
ATONICS
ATONIES
ATONING
ATONINGLY
ATONY
ATOP
ATOPIC
ATOPIES
ATOPY
ATRAMENT
ATRAMENTS
ATRAZINE
ATRAZINES
ATREMBLE
ATRESIA
ATRESIAS
ATRESIC
ATRETIC
ATRIA
ATRIAL
ATRIP
ATRIUM
ATRIUMS
ATROCIOUS
ATROCITY
ATROPHIA
ATROPHIAS
ATROPHIC
ATROPHIED
ATROPHIES
ATROPHY
ATROPIA
ATROPIAS
ATROPIN
ATROPINE
ATROPINES
ATROPINS
ATROPISM
ATROPISMS
ATROPOUS
ATS
ATT
ATTABOY
ATTABOYS
ATTACH
ATTACHE
ATTACHED
ATTACHER
ATTACHERS
ATTACHES
ATTACHING
ATTACK
ATTACKED
ATTACKER
ATTACKERS
ATTACKING
ATTACKMAN
ATTACKMEN

ATTACKS
ATTAGIRL
ATTAIN
ATTAINDER
ATTAINED
ATTAINER
ATTAINERS
ATTAINING
ATTAINS
ATTAINT
ATTAINTED
ATTAINTS
ATTAP
ATTAPS
ATTAR
ATTARS
ATTASK
ATTASKED
ATTASKING
ATTASKS
ATTASKT
ATTEMPER
ATTEMPERS
ATTEMPT
ATTEMPTED
ATTEMPTER
ATTEMPTS
ATTEND
ATTENDANT
ATTENDED
ATTENDEE
ATTENDEES
ATTENDER
ATTENDERS
ATTENDING
ATTENDS
ATTENT
ATTENTAT
ATTENTATS
ATTENTION
ATTENTIVE
ATTENTS
ATTENUANT
ATTENUATE
ATTERCOP
ATTERCOPS
ATTEST
ATTESTANT
ATTESTED
ATTESTER
ATTESTERS
ATTESTING
ATTESTOR
ATTESTORS
ATTESTS
ATTIC
ATTICISE
ATTICISED
ATTICISES
ATTICISM
ATTICISMS
ATTICIST
ATTICISTS
ATTICIZE
ATTICIZED
ATTICIZES
ATTICS
ATTIRE
ATTIRED
ATTIRES
ATTIRING
ATTIRINGS
ATTITUDE
ATTITUDES
ATTOLASER
ATTOLLENS
ATTOLLENT
ATTOMETER
ATTOMETRE
ATTONCE
ATTONE
ATTONED
ATTONES
ATTONING
ATTORN
ATTORNED
ATTORNEY
ATTORNEYS
ATTORNING
ATTORNS
ATTOTESLA
ATTRACT
ATTRACTED
ATTRACTER
ATTRACTOR
ATTRACTS
ATTRAHENS
ATTRAHENT
ATTRAP
ATTRAPPED
ATTRAPS
ATTRIBUTE
ATTRIST
ATTRISTED
ATTRISTS
ATTRIT
ATTRITE
ATTRITED
ATTRITES
ATTRITING
ATTRITION
ATTRITIVE
ATTRITS
ATTRITTED
ATTUENT
ATTUITE
ATTUITED
ATTUITES
ATTUITING
ATTUITION
ATTUITIVE
ATTUNE
ATTUNED
ATTUNES
ATTUNING
ATUA
ATUAS
ATWAIN
ATWEEL
ATWEEN
ATWITTER
ATWIXT
ATYPIC
ATYPICAL
AUA
AUAS
AUBADE
AUBADES
AUBERGE
AUBERGES
AUBERGINE
AUBRETIA
AUBRETIAS
AUBRIETA
AUBRIETAS
AUBRIETIA
AUBURN
AUBURNS
AUCEPS
AUCEPSES
AUCTION
AUCTIONED
AUCTIONS
AUCTORIAL
AUCUBA
AUCUBAS
AUDACIOUS
AUDACITY
AUDAD
AUDADS
AUDIAL
AUDIBLE
AUDIBLED
AUDIBLES
AUDIBLING
AUDIBLY
AUDIENCE
AUDIENCES
AUDIENCIA
AUDIENT
AUDIENTS
AUDILE
AUDILES
AUDING
AUDINGS
AUDIO
AUDIOBOOK
AUDIOGRAM
AUDIOLOGY
AUDIOPHIL
AUDIOS
AUDIOTAPE
AUDIPHONE
AUDISM
AUDISMS
AUDIST
AUDISTS
AUDIT
AUDITABLE
AUDITED
AUDITEE
AUDITEES
AUDITING
AUDITINGS
AUDITION
AUDITIONS
AUDITIVE
AUDITIVES
AUDITOR
AUDITORIA
AUDITORS
AUDITORY
AUDITRESS
AUDITS
AUE
AUF
AUFGABE
AUFGABES
AUFS
AUGEND
AUGENDS
AUGER
AUGERS
AUGH
AUGHT
AUGHTS
AUGITE
AUGITES
AUGITIC
AUGMENT
AUGMENTED
AUGMENTER
AUGMENTOR
AUGMENTS
AUGUR
AUGURAL
AUGURED
AUGURER
AUGURERS
AUGURIES
AUGURING
AUGURS
AUGURSHIP
AUGURY
AUGUST
AUGUSTE
AUGUSTER
AUGUSTES
AUGUSTEST
AUGUSTLY

AUGUSTS
AUK
AUKLET
AUKLETS
AUKS
AULA
AULARIAN
AULARIANS
AULAS
AULD
AULDER
AULDEST
AULIC
AULNAGE
AULNAGER
AULNAGERS
AULNAGES
AULOI
AULOS
AUMAIL
AUMAILED
AUMAILING
AUMAILS
AUMBRIES
AUMBRY
AUMIL
AUMILS
AUNE
AUNES
AUNT
AUNTER
AUNTERS
AUNTHOOD
AUNTHOODS
AUNTIE
AUNTIES
AUNTLIER
AUNTLIEST
AUNTLIKE
AUNTLY
AUNTS
AUNTY
AURA
AURAE
AURAL
AURALITY
AURALLY
AURAR
AURAS
AURATE
AURATED
AURATES
AUREATE
AUREATELY
AUREI
AUREITIES
AUREITY
AURELIA
AURELIAN
AURELIANS
AURELIAS
AUREOLA
AUREOLAE
AUREOLAS
AUREOLE
AUREOLED
AUREOLES
AUREOLING
AURES
AUREUS
AURIC
AURICLE
AURICLED
AURICLES
AURICULA
AURICULAE
AURICULAR
AURICULAS
AURIFIED
AURIFIES
AURIFORM
AURIFY
AURIFYING
AURIS
AURISCOPE
AURIST
AURISTS
AUROCHS
AUROCHSES
AURORA
AURORAE
AURORAL
AURORALLY
AURORAS
AUROREAN
AUROUS
AURUM
AURUMS
AUSFORM
AUSFORMED
AUSFORMS
AUSLANDER
AUSPEX
AUSPICATE
AUSPICE
AUSPICES
AUSTENITE
AUSTERE
AUSTERELY
AUSTERER
AUSTEREST
AUSTERITY
AUSTRAL
AUSTRALES
AUSTRALIS
AUSTRALS
AUSUBO
AUSUBOS
AUTACOID
AUTACOIDS
AUTARCH
AUTARCHIC
AUTARCHS
AUTARCHY
AUTARKIC
AUTARKIES
AUTARKIST
AUTARKY
AUTECIOUS
AUTECISM
AUTECISMS
AUTEUR
AUTEURISM
AUTEURIST
AUTEURS
AUTHENTIC
AUTHOR
AUTHORED
AUTHORESS
AUTHORIAL
AUTHORING
AUTHORISE
AUTHORISH
AUTHORISM
AUTHORITY
AUTHORIZE
AUTHORS
AUTISM
AUTISMS
AUTIST
AUTISTIC
AUTISTICS
AUTISTS
AUTO
AUTOBAHN
AUTOBAHNS
AUTOBANK
AUTOBANKS
AUTOBODY
AUTOBUS
AUTOBUSES
AUTOCADE
AUTOCADES
AUTOCAR
AUTOCARP
AUTOCARPS
AUTOCARS
AUTOCIDAL
AUTOCLAVE
AUTOCOID
AUTOCOIDS
AUTOCRACY
AUTOCRAT
AUTOCRATS
AUTOCRIME
AUTOCRINE
AUTOCROSS
AUTOCUE
AUTOCUES
AUTOCUTIE
AUTOCYCLE
AUTODIAL
AUTODIALS
AUTODROME
AUTODYNE
AUTODYNES
AUTOECISM
AUTOED
AUTOFLARE
AUTOFOCUS
AUTOGAMIC
AUTOGAMY
AUTOGENIC
AUTOGENY
AUTOGIRO
AUTOGIROS
AUTOGRAFT
AUTOGRAPH
AUTOGUIDE
AUTOGYRO
AUTOGYROS
AUTOHARP
AUTOHARPS
AUTOICOUS
AUTOING
AUTOLATRY
AUTOLOAD
AUTOLOADS
AUTOLOGY
AUTOLYSE
AUTOLYSED
AUTOLYSES
AUTOLYSIN
AUTOLYSIS
AUTOLYTIC
AUTOLYZE
AUTOLYZED
AUTOLYZES
AUTOMAGIC
AUTOMAKER
AUTOMAN
AUTOMAT
AUTOMATA
AUTOMATE
AUTOMATED
AUTOMATES
AUTOMATIC
AUTOMATON
AUTOMATS
AUTOMEN
AUTOMETER
AUTONOMIC
AUTONOMY
AUTONYM
AUTONYMS
AUTOPEN
AUTOPENS
AUTOPHAGY
AUTOPHOBY
AUTOPHONY

AUTOPHYTE
AUTOPILOT
AUTOPISTA
AUTOPOINT
AUTOPSIA
AUTOPSIAS
AUTOPSIC
AUTOPSIED
AUTOPSIES
AUTOPSIST
AUTOPSY
AUTOPTIC
AUTOPUT
AUTOPUTS
AUTOREPLY
AUTOROUTE
AUTOS
AUTOSAVE
AUTOSAVED
AUTOSAVES
AUTOSCOPY
AUTOSOMAL
AUTOSOME
AUTOSOMES
AUTOSPORE
AUTOSPORT
AUTOTELIC
AUTOTEST
AUTOTESTS
AUTOTIMER
AUTOTOMIC
AUTOTOMY
AUTOTOXIC
AUTOTOXIN
AUTOTROPH
AUTOTUNE
AUTOTUNES
AUTOTYPE
AUTOTYPED
AUTOTYPES
AUTOTYPIC
AUTOTYPY
AUTOVAC
AUTOVACS
AUTUMN
AUTUMNAL
AUTUMNIER
AUTUMNS
AUTUMNY
AUTUNITE
AUTUNITES
AUXESES
AUXESIS
AUXETIC
AUXETICS
AUXILIAR
AUXILIARS
AUXILIARY
AUXIN
AUXINIC
AUXINS
AUXOCYTE
AUXOCYTES
AUXOMETER
AUXOSPORE
AUXOTONIC
AUXOTROPH
AVA
AVADAVAT
AVADAVATS
AVAIL
AVAILABLE
AVAILABLY
AVAILE
AVAILED
AVAILES
AVAILFUL
AVAILING
AVAILS
AVAL
AVALANCHE
AVALE
AVALED
AVALEMENT
AVALES
AVALING
AVANT
AVANTI
AVANTIST
AVANTISTS
AVARICE
AVARICES
AVAS
AVASCULAR
AVAST
AVATAR
AVATARS
AVAUNT
AVAUNTED
AVAUNTING
AVAUNTS
AVE
AVEL
AVELLAN
AVELLANE
AVELS
AVENGE
AVENGED
AVENGEFUL
AVENGER
AVENGERS
AVENGES
AVENGING
AVENIR
AVENIRS
AVENS
AVENSES
AVENTAIL
AVENTAILE
AVENTAILS
AVENTRE
AVENTRED
AVENTRES
AVENTRING
AVENTURE
AVENTURES
AVENTURIN
AVENUE
AVENUES
AVER
AVERAGE
AVERAGED
AVERAGELY
AVERAGER
AVERAGERS
AVERAGES
AVERAGING
AVERMENT
AVERMENTS
AVERRABLE
AVERRED
AVERRING
AVERS
AVERSE
AVERSELY
AVERSION
AVERSIONS
AVERSIVE
AVERSIVES
AVERT
AVERTABLE
AVERTED
AVERTEDLY
AVERTER
AVERTERS
AVERTIBLE
AVERTING
AVERTS
AVES
AVGAS
AVGASES
AVGASSES
AVIAN
AVIANISE
AVIANISED
AVIANISES
AVIANIZE
AVIANIZED
AVIANIZES
AVIANS
AVIARIES
AVIARIST
AVIARISTS
AVIARY
AVIATE
AVIATED
AVIATES
AVIATIC
AVIATING
AVIATION
AVIATIONS
AVIATOR
AVIATORS
AVIATRESS
AVIATRICE
AVIATRIX
AVICULAR
AVID
AVIDER
AVIDEST
AVIDIN
AVIDINS
AVIDITIES
AVIDITY
AVIDLY
AVIDNESS
AVIETTE
AVIETTES
AVIFAUNA
AVIFAUNAE
AVIFAUNAL
AVIFAUNAS
AVIFORM
AVIGATOR
AVIGATORS
AVINE
AVION
AVIONIC
AVIONICS
AVIONS
AVIRULENT
AVISANDUM
AVISE
AVISED
AVISEMENT
AVISES
AVISING
AVISO
AVISOS
AVITAL
AVIZANDUM
AVIZE
AVIZED
AVIZEFULL
AVIZES
AVIZING
AVO
AVOCADO
AVOCADOES
AVOCADOS
AVOCATION
AVOCET
AVOCETS
AVODIRE
AVODIRES
AVOID
AVOIDABLE
AVOIDABLY
AVOIDANCE
AVOIDANT

AVOIDED
AVOIDER
AVOIDERS
AVOIDING
AVOIDS
AVOISION
AVOISIONS
AVOPARCIN
AVOS
AVOSET
AVOSETS
AVOUCH
AVOUCHED
AVOUCHER
AVOUCHERS
AVOUCHES
AVOUCHING
AVOURE
AVOURES
AVOUTERER
AVOUTRER
AVOUTRERS
AVOUTRIES
AVOUTRY
AVOW
AVOWABLE
AVOWABLY
AVOWAL
AVOWALS
AVOWED
AVOWEDLY
AVOWER
AVOWERS
AVOWING
AVOWRIES
AVOWRY
AVOWS
AVOYER
AVOYERS
AVRUGA
AVRUGAS
AVULSE
AVULSED
AVULSES
AVULSING
AVULSION
AVULSIONS
AVUNCULAR
AVYZE
AVYZED
AVYZES
AVYZING
AW
AWA
AWAIT
AWAITED
AWAITER
AWAITERS
AWAITING
AWAITS
AWAKE
AWAKED
AWAKEN
AWAKENED
AWAKENER
AWAKENERS
AWAKENING
AWAKENS
AWAKES
AWAKING
AWAKINGS
AWANTING
AWARD
AWARDABLE
AWARDED
AWARDEE
AWARDEES
AWARDER
AWARDERS
AWARDING
AWARDS
AWARE
AWARENESS
AWARER
AWAREST
AWARN
AWARNED
AWARNING
AWARNS
AWASH
AWATCH
AWATO
AWATOS
AWAVE
AWAY
AWAYDAY
AWAYDAYS
AWAYES
AWAYNESS
AWAYS
AWDL
AWDLS
AWE
AWEARIED
AWEARY
AWEATHER
AWED
AWEE
AWEEL
AWEIGH
AWEING
AWELESS
AWES
AWESOME
AWESOMELY
AWESTRIKE
AWESTRUCK
AWETO
AWETOS
AWFUL
AWFULLER
AWFULLEST
AWFULLY
AWFULNESS
AWFY
AWHAPE
AWHAPED
AWHAPES
AWHAPING
AWHATO
AWHATOS
AWHEEL
AWHEELS
AWHETO
AWHETOS
AWHILE
AWHIRL
AWING
AWK
AWKS
AWKWARD
AWKWARDER
AWKWARDLY
AWL
AWLBIRD
AWLBIRDS
AWLESS
AWLS
AWLWORT
AWLWORTS
AWMOUS
AWMRIE
AWMRIES
AWMRY
AWN
AWNED
AWNER
AWNERS
AWNIER
AWNIEST
AWNING
AWNINGED
AWNINGS
AWNLESS
AWNS
AWNY
AWOKE
AWOKEN
AWOL
AWOLS
AWORK
AWRACK
AWRONG
AWRY
AWSOME
AX
AXAL
AXE
AXEBIRD
AXEBIRDS
AXED
AXEL
AXELIKE
AXELS
AXEMAN
AXEMEN
AXENIC
AXES
AXIAL
AXIALITY
AXIALLY
AXIL
AXILE
AXILEMMA
AXILEMMAS
AXILLA
AXILLAE
AXILLAR
AXILLARS
AXILLARY
AXILLAS
AXILS
AXING
AXINITE
AXINITES
AXIOLOGY
AXIOM
AXIOMATIC
AXIOMS
AXION
AXIONS
AXIS
AXISED
AXISES
AXITE
AXITES
AXLE
AXLED
AXLES
AXLETREE
AXLETREES
AXLIKE
AXMAN
AXMEN
AXOID
AXOIDS
AXOLEMMA
AXOLEMMAS
AXOLOTL
AXOLOTLS
AXON
AXONAL
AXONE
AXONEMAL
AXONEME
AXONEMES
AXONES
AXONIC
AXONS
AXOPLASM

AXOPLASMS
AXSEED
AXSEEDS
AY
AYAH
AYAHS
AYAHUASCA
AYAHUASCO
AYATOLLAH
AYAYA
AYAYAS
AYE
AYELP
AYENBITE
AYENBITES
AYES
AYGRE
AYIN
AYINS
AYONT
AYRE
AYRES
AYRIE
AYRIES
AYS
AYU
AYURVEDA
AYURVEDAS
AYURVEDIC
AYUS
AYWORD
AYWORDS
AZALEA
AZALEAS
AZAN
AZANS
AZEDARACH
AZEOTROPE
AZEOTROPY
AZERTY
AZIDE
AZIDES
AZIDO
AZIMUTH
AZIMUTHAL
AZIMUTHS
AZINE
AZINES
AZIONE
AZIONES
AZLON
AZLONS
AZO
AZOIC
AZOLE
AZOLES
AZOLLA
AZOLLAS
AZON
AZONAL
AZONIC
AZONS
AZOTAEMIA
AZOTAEMIC
AZOTE
AZOTED
AZOTEMIA
AZOTEMIAS
AZOTEMIC
AZOTES
AZOTH
AZOTHS
AZOTIC
AZOTISE
AZOTISED
AZOTISES
AZOTISING
AZOTIZE
AZOTIZED
AZOTIZES
AZOTIZING
AZOTOUS
AZOTURIA
AZOTURIAS
AZUKI
AZUKIS
AZULEJO
AZULEJOS
AZURE
AZUREAN
AZURES
AZURIES
AZURINE
AZURINES
AZURITE
AZURITES
AZURN
AZURY
AZYGIES
AZYGOS
AZYGOSES
AZYGOUS
AZYGOUSLY
AZYGY
AZYM
AZYME
AZYMES
AZYMITE
AZYMITES
AZYMOUS
AZYMS

B

BA
BAA
BAAED
BAAING
BAAINGS
BAAL
BAALEBOS
BAALIM
BAALISM
BAALISMS
BAALS
BAAS
BAASKAAP
BAASKAAPS
BAASKAP
BAASKAPS
BAASSKAP
BAASSKAPS
BABA
BABACO
BABACOOTE
BABACOS
BABACU
BABACUS
BABALAS
BABAS
BABASSU
BABASSUS
BABBELAS
BABBITRY
BABBITT
BABBITTED
BABBITTRY
BABBITTS
BABBLE
BABBLED
BABBLER
BABBLERS
BABBLES
BABBLIER
BABBLIEST
BABBLING
BABBLINGS
BABBLY
BABE
BABEL
BABELDOM
BABELDOMS
BABELISH
BABELISM
BABELISMS
BABELS
BABES
BABESIA
BABESIAE
BABESIAS
BABICHE
BABICHES
BABIED
BABIER
BABIES
BABIEST
BABIRUSA
BABIRUSAS
BABIRUSSA
BABKA
BABKAS
BABLAH
BABLAHS
BABOO
BABOOL
BABOOLS
BABOON
BABOONERY
BABOONISH
BABOONS
BABOOS
BABOOSH
BABOOSHES
BABOUCHE
BABOUCHES
BABU
BABUCHE
BABUCHES
BABUDOM
BABUDOMS
BABUISM
BABUISMS
BABUL
BABULS
BABUS
BABUSHKA
BABUSHKAS
BABY
BABYCCINO
BABYCINO
BABYCINOS
BABYDADDY
BABYDOLL
BABYDOLLS
BABYFOOD
BABYFOODS
BABYHOOD
BABYHOODS
BABYING
BABYISH
BABYISHLY
BABYLIKE
BABYMOON
BABYMOONS
BABYPROOF
BABYSAT
BABYSIT
BABYSITS
BAC
BACALAO
BACALAOS
BACALHAU
BACALHAUS
BACCA
BACCAE
BACCALA
BACCALAS
BACCARA
BACCARAS
BACCARAT
BACCARATS
BACCARE
BACCAS
BACCATE
BACCATED
BACCHANAL
BACCHANT
BACCHANTE
BACCHANTS
BACCHIAC
BACCHIAN
BACCHIC
BACCHII
BACCHIUS
BACCIES
BACCIFORM
BACCO
BACCOES
BACCOS
BACCY
BACH
BACHA
BACHARACH
BACHAS
BACHATA
BACHATAS
BACHCHA
BACHCHAS
BACHED
BACHELOR
BACHELORS
BACHES
BACHING
BACHS
BACILLAR
BACILLARY
BACILLI
BACILLUS
BACK
BACKACHE
BACKACHES
BACKACTER
BACKARE
BACKBAND
BACKBANDS
BACKBAR
BACKBARS
BACKBEAT
BACKBEATS
BACKBENCH
BACKBEND
BACKBENDS
BACKBIT
BACKBITE
BACKBITER
BACKBITES
BACKBLOCK
BACKBOARD
BACKBOND
BACKBONDS
BACKBONE
BACKBONED
BACKBONES
BACKBURN
BACKBURNS
BACKCAST
BACKCASTS
BACKCHAT
BACKCHATS
BACKCHECK
BACKCLOTH
BACKCOMB
BACKCOMBS
BACKCOURT
BACKCROSS
BACKDATE
BACKDATED
BACKDATES
BACKDOOR
BACKDOWN
BACKDOWNS
BACKDRAFT
BACKDROP
BACKDROPS

B

BACKDROPT
BACKED
BACKER
BACKERS
BACKET
BACKETS
BACKFALL
BACKFALLS
BACKFAT
BACKFATS
BACKFIELD
BACKFILE
BACKFILES
BACKFILL
BACKFILLS
BACKFIRE
BACKFIRED
BACKFIRES
BACKFISCH
BACKFIT
BACKFITS
BACKFLIP
BACKFLIPS
BACKFLOW
BACKFLOWS
BACKHAND
BACKHANDS
BACKHAUL
BACKHAULS
BACKHOE
BACKHOED
BACKHOES
BACKHOUSE
BACKIE
BACKIES
BACKING
BACKINGS
BACKLAND
BACKLANDS
BACKLASH
BACKLESS
BACKLIFT
BACKLIFTS
BACKLIGHT
BACKLINE
BACKLINER
BACKLINES
BACKLIST
BACKLISTS
BACKLIT
BACKLOAD
BACKLOADS
BACKLOG
BACKLOGS
BACKLOT
BACKLOTS
BACKMOST
BACKOUT
BACKOUTS
BACKPACK
BACKPACKS
BACKPEDAL
BACKPIECE
BACKPLANE
BACKPLATE
BACKREST
BACKRESTS
BACKRONYM
BACKROOM
BACKROOMS
BACKRUSH
BACKS
BACKSAW
BACKSAWS
BACKSEAT
BACKSEATS
BACKSET
BACKSETS
BACKSEY
BACKSEYS
BACKSHISH
BACKSHORE
BACKSIDE
BACKSIDES
BACKSIGHT
BACKSLAP
BACKSLAPS
BACKSLASH
BACKSLID
BACKSLIDE
BACKSPACE
BACKSPEER
BACKSPEIR
BACKSPIN
BACKSPINS
BACKSPLIT
BACKSTAB
BACKSTABS
BACKSTAGE
BACKSTAIR
BACKSTALL
BACKSTAMP
BACKSTAY
BACKSTAYS
BACKSTOP
BACKSTOPS
BACKSTORY
BACKSTRAP
BACKSWEPT
BACKSWING
BACKSWORD
BACKTALK
BACKTALKS
BACKTRACK
BACKUP
BACKUPS
BACKVELD
BACKVELDS
BACKWALL
BACKWALLS
BACKWARD
BACKWARDS
BACKWASH
BACKWATER
BACKWIND
BACKWINDS
BACKWOOD
BACKWOODS
BACKWORD
BACKWORDS
BACKWORK
BACKWORKS
BACKWRAP
BACKWRAPS
BACKYARD
BACKYARDS
BACLAVA
BACLAVAS
BACLOFEN
BACLOFENS
BACON
BACONER
BACONERS
BACONS
BACRONYM
BACRONYMS
BACS
BACTERIA
BACTERIAL
BACTERIAN
BACTERIAS
BACTERIC
BACTERIN
BACTERINS
BACTERISE
BACTERIUM
BACTERIZE
BACTEROID
BACULA
BACULINE
BACULITE
BACULITES
BACULUM
BACULUMS
BAD
BADASS
BADASSED
BADASSES
BADDER
BADDEST
BADDIE
BADDIES
BADDISH
BADDY
BADE
BADGE
BADGED
BADGELESS
BADGER
BADGERED
BADGERING
BADGERLY
BADGERS
BADGES
BADGING
BADINAGE
BADINAGED
BADINAGES
BADINERIE
BADIOUS
BADLAND
BADLANDS
BADLY
BADMAN
BADMASH
BADMASHES
BADMEN
BADMINTON
BADMOUTH
BADMOUTHS
BADNESS
BADNESSES
BADS
BADWARE
BADWARES
BAE
BAEL
BAELS
BAES
BAETYL
BAETYLS
BAFF
BAFFED
BAFFIES
BAFFING
BAFFLE
BAFFLED
BAFFLEGAB
BAFFLER
BAFFLERS
BAFFLES
BAFFLING
BAFFS
BAFFY
BAFT
BAFTS
BAG
BAGARRE
BAGARRES
BAGASS
BAGASSE
BAGASSES
BAGATELLE
BAGEL
BAGELED
BAGELING
BAGELLED
BAGELLING
BAGELS
BAGFUL

BAGFULS
BAGGAGE
BAGGAGES
BAGGED
BAGGER
BAGGERS
BAGGIE
BAGGIER
BAGGIES
BAGGIEST
BAGGILY
BAGGINESS
BAGGING
BAGGINGS
BAGGIT
BAGGITS
BAGGY
BAGH
BAGHOUSE
BAGHOUSES
BAGHS
BAGIE
BAGIES
BAGLESS
BAGLIKE
BAGMAN
BAGMEN
BAGNETTE
BAGNETTES
BAGNIO
BAGNIOS
BAGPIPE
BAGPIPED
BAGPIPER
BAGPIPERS
BAGPIPES
BAGPIPING
BAGS
BAGSFUL
BAGUET
BAGUETS
BAGUETTE
BAGUETTES
BAGUIO
BAGUIOS
BAGWASH
BAGWASHES
BAGWIG
BAGWIGS
BAGWORM
BAGWORMS
BAH
BAHADA
BAHADAS
BAHADUR
BAHADURS
BAHOOKIE
BAHOOKIES
BAHT
BAHTS
BAHU
BAHUS
BAHUT
BAHUTS
BAHUVRIHI
BAIDAR
BAIDARKA
BAIDARKAS
BAIDARS
BAIGNOIRE
BAIL
BAILABLE
BAILBOND
BAILBONDS
BAILED
BAILEE
BAILEES
BAILER
BAILERS
BAILEY
BAILEYS
BAILIE
BAILIES
BAILIFF
BAILIFFS
BAILING
BAILIWICK
BAILLI
BAILLIAGE
BAILLIE
BAILLIES
BAILLIS
BAILMENT
BAILMENTS
BAILOR
BAILORS
BAILOUT
BAILOUTS
BAILS
BAILSMAN
BAILSMEN
BAININ
BAININS
BAINITE
BAINITES
BAIRN
BAIRNISH
BAIRNLIER
BAIRNLIKE
BAIRNLY
BAIRNS
BAISA
BAISAS
BAISEMAIN
BAIT
BAITED
BAITER
BAITERS
BAITFISH
BAITH
BAITING
BAITINGS
BAITS
BAIZA
BAIZAS
BAIZE
BAIZED
BAIZES
BAIZING
BAJADA
BAJADAS
BAJAN
BAJANS
BAJILLION
BAJRA
BAJRAS
BAJREE
BAJREES
BAJRI
BAJRIS
BAJU
BAJUS
BAKE
BAKEAPPLE
BAKEBOARD
BAKED
BAKEHOUSE
BAKELITE
BAKELITES
BAKEMEAT
BAKEMEATS
BAKEN
BAKEOFF
BAKEOFFS
BAKER
BAKERIES
BAKERS
BAKERY
BAKES
BAKESHOP
BAKESHOPS
BAKESTONE
BAKEWARE
BAKEWARES
BAKGAT
BAKHSHISH
BAKING
BAKINGS
BAKKIE
BAKKIES
BAKLAVA
BAKLAVAS
BAKLAWA
BAKLAWAS
BAKSHEESH
BAKSHISH
BAL
BALACLAVA
BALADIN
BALADINE
BALADINES
BALADINS
BALAFON
BALAFONS
BALALAIKA
BALANCE
BALANCED
BALANCER
BALANCERS
BALANCES
BALANCING
BALANITIS
BALAS
BALASES
BALATA
BALATAS
BALAYAGE
BALAYAGED
BALAYAGES
BALBOA
BALBOAS
BALCONET
BALCONETS
BALCONIED
BALCONIES
BALCONY
BALD
BALDACHIN
BALDAQUIN
BALDED
BALDER
BALDEST
BALDFACED
BALDHEAD
BALDHEADS
BALDICOOT
BALDIE
BALDIER
BALDIES
BALDIEST
BALDING
BALDISH
BALDLY
BALDMONEY
BALDNESS
BALDPATE
BALDPATED
BALDPATES
BALDRIC
BALDRICK
BALDRICKS
BALDRICS
BALDS
BALDY
BALE
BALECTION
BALED
BALEEN
BALEENS
BALEFIRE

BALEFIRES
BALEFUL
BALEFULLY
BALER
BALERS
BALES
BALING
BALINGS
BALISAUR
BALISAURS
BALISE
BALISES
BALISTA
BALISTAE
BALISTAS
BALK
BALKANISE
BALKANIZE
BALKED
BALKER
BALKERS
BALKIER
BALKIEST
BALKILY
BALKINESS
BALKING
BALKINGLY
BALKINGS
BALKLINE
BALKLINES
BALKS
BALKY
BALL
BALLABILE
BALLABILI
BALLAD
BALLADE
BALLADED
BALLADEER
BALLADES
BALLADIC
BALLADIN
BALLADINE
BALLADING
BALLADINS
BALLADIST
BALLADRY
BALLADS
BALLAN
BALLANS
BALLANT
BALLANTED
BALLANTS
BALLAST
BALLASTED
BALLASTER
BALLASTS
BALLAT
BALLATED
BALLATING
BALLATS
BALLBOY
BALLBOYS
BALLCLAY
BALLCLAYS
BALLCOCK
BALLCOCKS
BALLED
BALLER
BALLERINA
BALLERINE
BALLERS
BALLET
BALLETED
BALLETIC
BALLETING
BALLETS
BALLFIELD
BALLGAME
BALLGAMES
BALLGIRL
BALLGIRLS
BALLGOWN
BALLGOWNS
BALLHAWK
BALLHAWKS
BALLIER
BALLIES
BALLIEST
BALLING
BALLINGS
BALLISTA
BALLISTAE
BALLISTAS
BALLISTIC
BALLIUM
BALLIUMS
BALLOCKS
BALLON
BALLONET
BALLONETS
BALLONNE
BALLONNES
BALLONS
BALLOON
BALLOONED
BALLOONS
BALLOT
BALLOTED
BALLOTEE
BALLOTEES
BALLOTER
BALLOTERS
BALLOTING
BALLOTINI
BALLOTS
BALLOW
BALLOWS
BALLPARK
BALLPARKS
BALLPEEN
BALLPOINT
BALLROOM
BALLROOMS
BALLS
BALLSED
BALLSES
BALLSIER
BALLSIEST
BALLSING
BALLSY
BALLUP
BALLUPS
BALLUTE
BALLUTES
BALLY
BALLYARD
BALLYARDS
BALLYHOO
BALLYHOOS
BALLYRAG
BALLYRAGS
BALM
BALMACAAN
BALMED
BALMIER
BALMIEST
BALMILY
BALMINESS
BALMING
BALMLIKE
BALMORAL
BALMORALS
BALMS
BALMY
BALNEAL
BALNEARY
BALONEY
BALONEYS
BALOO
BALOOS
BALS
BALSA
BALSAM
BALSAMED
BALSAMIC
BALSAMIER
BALSAMING
BALSAMS
BALSAMY
BALSAS
BALSAWOOD
BALTHASAR
BALTHAZAR
BALTI
BALTIC
BALTIS
BALU
BALUN
BALUNS
BALUS
BALUSTER
BALUSTERS
BALZARINE
BAM
BAMBI
BAMBINI
BAMBINO
BAMBINOS
BAMBIS
BAMBOO
BAMBOOS
BAMBOOZLE
BAMMED
BAMMER
BAMMERS
BAMMING
BAMPOT
BAMPOTS
BAMS
BAN
BANAK
BANAKS
BANAL
BANALER
BANALEST
BANALISE
BANALISED
BANALISES
BANALITY
BANALIZE
BANALIZED
BANALIZES
BANALLY
BANANA
BANANAS
BANAUSIAN
BANAUSIC
BANC
BANCO
BANCOS
BANCS
BAND
BANDA
BANDAGE
BANDAGED
BANDAGER
BANDAGERS
BANDAGES
BANDAGING
BANDAID
BANDALORE
BANDANA
BANDANAS
BANDANNA
BANDANNAS
BANDAR
BANDARI
BANDARIS
BANDARS

BANDAS
BANDBOX
BANDBOXES
BANDBRAKE
BANDEAU
BANDEAUS
BANDEAUX
BANDED
BANDEIRA
BANDEIRAS
BANDELET
BANDELETS
BANDELIER
BANDER
BANDEROL
BANDEROLE
BANDEROLS
BANDERS
BANDFISH
BANDH
BANDHS
BANDICOOT
BANDIED
BANDIER
BANDIES
BANDIEST
BANDINESS
BANDING
BANDINGS
BANDIT
BANDITO
BANDITOS
BANDITRY
BANDITS
BANDITTI
BANDITTIS
BANDLIKE
BANDMATE
BANDMATES
BANDOBAST
BANDOBUST
BANDOG
BANDOGS
BANDOLEER
BANDOLEON
BANDOLERO
BANDOLIER
BANDOLINE
BANDONEON
BANDONION
BANDOOK
BANDOOKS
BANDORA
BANDORAS
BANDORE
BANDORES
BANDPASS
BANDROL
BANDROLS
BANDS
BANDSAW
BANDSAWED
BANDSAWS
BANDSHELL
BANDSMAN
BANDSMEN
BANDSTAND
BANDSTER
BANDSTERS
BANDURA
BANDURAS
BANDURIST
BANDWAGON
BANDWIDTH
BANDY
BANDYING
BANDYINGS
BANDYMAN
BANDYMEN
BANE
BANEBERRY
BANED
BANEFUL
BANEFULLY
BANES
BANG
BANGALAY
BANGALAYS
BANGALORE
BANGALOW
BANGALOWS
BANGBELLY
BANGED
BANGER
BANGERS
BANGING
BANGKOK
BANGKOKS
BANGLE
BANGLED
BANGLES
BANGS
BANGSRING
BANGSTER
BANGSTERS
BANGTAIL
BANGTAILS
BANI
BANIA
BANIAN
BANIANS
BANIAS
BANING
BANISH
BANISHED
BANISHER
BANISHERS
BANISHES
BANISHING
BANISTER
BANISTERS
BANJAX
BANJAXED
BANJAXES
BANJAXING
BANJO
BANJOES
BANJOIST
BANJOISTS
BANJOLELE
BANJOS
BANJULELE
BANK
BANKABLE
BANKBOOK
BANKBOOKS
BANKCARD
BANKCARDS
BANKED
BANKER
BANKERLY
BANKERS
BANKET
BANKETS
BANKING
BANKINGS
BANKIT
BANKITS
BANKNOTE
BANKNOTES
BANKROLL
BANKROLLS
BANKRUPT
BANKRUPTS
BANKS
BANKSIA
BANKSIAS
BANKSIDE
BANKSIDES
BANKSMAN
BANKSMEN
BANKSTER
BANKSTERS
BANLIEUE
BANLIEUES
BANNABLE
BANNED
BANNER
BANNERALL
BANNERED
BANNERET
BANNERETS
BANNERING
BANNEROL
BANNEROLS
BANNERS
BANNET
BANNETS
BANNING
BANNINGS
BANNISTER
BANNOCK
BANNOCKS
BANNS
BANOFFEE
BANOFFEES
BANOFFI
BANOFFIS
BANQUET
BANQUETED
BANQUETER
BANQUETS
BANQUETTE
BANS
BANSELA
BANSELAS
BANSHEE
BANSHEES
BANSHIE
BANSHIES
BANT
BANTAM
BANTAMS
BANTED
BANTENG
BANTENGS
BANTER
BANTERED
BANTERER
BANTERERS
BANTERING
BANTERS
BANTIES
BANTING
BANTINGS
BANTLING
BANTLINGS
BANTS
BANTY
BANXRING
BANXRINGS
BANYA
BANYAN
BANYANS
BANYAS
BANZAI
BANZAIS
BAO
BAOBAB
BAOBABS
BAOS
BAP
BAPS
BAPTISE
BAPTISED
BAPTISER
BAPTISERS
BAPTISES
BAPTISIA
BAPTISIAS

B

BAPTISING
BAPTISM
BAPTISMAL
BAPTISMS
BAPTIST
BAPTISTRY
BAPTISTS
BAPTIZE
BAPTIZED
BAPTIZER
BAPTIZERS
BAPTIZES
BAPTIZING
BAPU
BAPUS
BAR
BARACAN
BARACANS
BARACHOIS
BARAGOUIN
BARASINGA
BARATHEA
BARATHEAS
BARATHRUM
BARAZA
BARAZAS
BARB
BARBAL
BARBARIAN
BARBARIC
BARBARISE
BARBARISM
BARBARITY
BARBARIZE
BARBAROUS
BARBASCO
BARBASCOS
BARBASTEL
BARBATE
BARBATED
BARBE
BARBECUE
BARBECUED
BARBECUER
BARBECUES
BARBED
BARBEL
BARBELL
BARBELLS
BARBELS
BARBEQUE
BARBEQUED
BARBEQUES
BARBER
BARBERED
BARBERING
BARBERRY
BARBERS
BARBES
BARBET
BARBETS
BARBETTE
BARBETTES
BARBICAN
BARBICANS
BARBICEL
BARBICELS
BARBIE
BARBIES
BARBING
BARBITAL
BARBITALS
BARBITONE
BARBLESS
BARBOLA
BARBOLAS
BARBOT
BARBOTINE
BARBOTS
BARBOTTE
BARBOTTES
BARBS
BARBULE
BARBULES
BARBUT
BARBUTS
BARBWIRE
BARBWIRES
BARBY
BARCA
BARCAROLE
BARCAS
BARCHAN
BARCHANE
BARCHANES
BARCHANS
BARCODE
BARCODED
BARCODES
BARD
BARDASH
BARDASHES
BARDE
BARDED
BARDES
BARDIC
BARDIE
BARDIER
BARDIES
BARDIEST
BARDING
BARDISM
BARDISMS
BARDLING
BARDLINGS
BARDO
BARDOS
BARDS
BARDSHIP
BARDSHIPS
BARDY
BARE
BAREBACK
BAREBACKS
BAREBOAT
BAREBOATS
BAREBONE
BAREBONED
BAREBONES
BARED
BAREFACED
BAREFIT
BAREFOOT
BAREGE
BAREGES
BAREGINE
BAREGINES
BAREHAND
BAREHANDS
BAREHEAD
BARELAND
BARELY
BARENESS
BARER
BARES
BARESARK
BARESARKS
BAREST
BARF
BARFED
BARFI
BARFING
BARFIS
BARFLIES
BARFLY
BARFS
BARFUL
BARGAIN
BARGAINED
BARGAINER
BARGAINS
BARGANDER
BARGE
BARGED
BARGEE
BARGEES
BARGEESE
BARGELIKE
BARGELLO
BARGELLOS
BARGEMAN
BARGEMEN
BARGEPOLE
BARGES
BARGEST
BARGESTS
BARGHEST
BARGHESTS
BARGING
BARGOON
BARGOONS
BARGOOSE
BARGUEST
BARGUESTS
BARHOP
BARHOPPED
BARHOPS
BARIATRIC
BARIC
BARILLA
BARILLAS
BARING
BARISH
BARISTA
BARISTAS
BARITE
BARITES
BARITONAL
BARITONE
BARITONES
BARIUM
BARIUMS
BARK
BARKAN
BARKANS
BARKED
BARKEEP
BARKEEPER
BARKEEPS
BARKEN
BARKENED
BARKENING
BARKENS
BARKER
BARKERS
BARKHAN
BARKHANS
BARKIER
BARKIEST
BARKING
BARKLESS
BARKLIKE
BARKS
BARKY
BARLEDUC
BARLEDUCS
BARLESS
BARLEY
BARLEYS
BARLOW
BARLOWS
BARM
BARMAID
BARMAIDS
BARMAN
BARMBRACK
BARMEN
BARMIE
BARMIER
BARMIEST

BARMILY
BARMINESS
BARMKIN
BARMKINS
BARMPOT
BARMPOTS
BARMS
BARMY
BARN
BARNACLE
BARNACLED
BARNACLES
BARNBOARD
BARNBRACK
BARNED
BARNET
BARNETS
BARNEY
BARNEYED
BARNEYING
BARNEYS
BARNIER
BARNIEST
BARNING
BARNLIKE
BARNS
BARNSTORM
BARNWOOD
BARNWOODS
BARNY
BARNYARD
BARNYARDS
BAROCCO
BAROCCOS
BAROCK
BAROCKS
BAROGRAM
BAROGRAMS
BAROGRAPH
BAROLO
BAROLOS
BAROMETER
BAROMETRY
BAROMETZ
BARON
BARONAGE
BARONAGES
BARONESS
BARONET
BARONETCY
BARONETS
BARONG
BARONGS
BARONIAL
BARONIES
BARONNE
BARONNES
BARONS
BARONY
BAROPHILE
BAROQUE
BAROQUELY
BAROQUES
BAROSAUR
BAROSAURS
BAROSCOPE
BAROSTAT
BAROSTATS
BAROTITIS
BAROUCHE
BAROUCHES
BARP
BARPERSON
BARPS
BARQUE
BARQUES
BARQUETTE
BARRA
BARRABLE
BARRACAN
BARRACANS
BARRACE
BARRACES
BARRACK
BARRACKED
BARRACKER
BARRACKS
BARRACOON
BARRACUDA
BARRAGE
BARRAGED
BARRAGES
BARRAGING
BARRANCA
BARRANCAS
BARRANCO
BARRANCOS
BARRAS
BARRASWAY
BARRAT
BARRATED
BARRATER
BARRATERS
BARRATING
BARRATOR
BARRATORS
BARRATRY
BARRATS
BARRE
BARRED
BARREED
BARREFULL
BARREING
BARREL
BARRELAGE
BARRELED
BARRELFUL
BARRELING
BARRELLED
BARRELS
BARREN
BARRENER
BARRENEST
BARRENLY
BARRENS
BARRES
BARRET
BARRETOR
BARRETORS
BARRETRY
BARRETS
BARRETTE
BARRETTER
BARRETTES
BARRICADE
BARRICADO
BARRICO
BARRICOES
BARRICOS
BARRIE
BARRIER
BARRIERED
BARRIERS
BARRIES
BARRIEST
BARRING
BARRINGS
BARRIO
BARRIOS
BARRIQUE
BARRIQUES
BARRISTER
BARRO
BARROOM
BARROOMS
BARROW
BARROWFUL
BARROWS
BARRULET
BARRULETS
BARRY
BARS
BARSTOOL
BARSTOOLS
BARTEND
BARTENDED
BARTENDER
BARTENDS
BARTER
BARTERED
BARTERER
BARTERERS
BARTERING
BARTERS
BARTISAN
BARTISANS
BARTIZAN
BARTIZANS
BARTON
BARTONS
BARTSIA
BARTSIAS
BARWARE
BARWARES
BARWOOD
BARWOODS
BARYE
BARYES
BARYON
BARYONIC
BARYONS
BARYTA
BARYTAS
BARYTE
BARYTES
BARYTIC
BARYTON
BARYTONE
BARYTONES
BARYTONS
BAS
BASAL
BASALLY
BASALT
BASALTES
BASALTIC
BASALTINE
BASALTS
BASAN
BASANITE
BASANITES
BASANS
BASANT
BASANTS
BASCINET
BASCINETS
BASCULE
BASCULES
BASE
BASEBALL
BASEBALLS
BASEBAND
BASEBANDS
BASEBOARD
BASEBORN
BASED
BASEEJ
BASEHEAD
BASEHEADS
BASELARD
BASELARDS
BASELESS
BASELINE
BASELINER
BASELINES
BASELOAD
BASELOADS
BASELY
BASEMAN
BASEMEN

B

BASEMENT
BASEMENTS
BASEN
BASENESS
BASENJI
BASENJIS
BASEPATH
BASEPATHS
BASEPLATE
BASER
BASES
BASEST
BASH
BASHAW
BASHAWISM
BASHAWS
BASHED
BASHER
BASHERS
BASHES
BASHFUL
BASHFULLY
BASHING
BASHINGS
BASHLESS
BASHLIK
BASHLIKS
BASHLYK
BASHLYKS
BASHMENT
BASHMENTS
BASHO
BASHTAG
BASHTAGS
BASIC
BASICALLY
BASICITY
BASICS
BASIDIA
BASIDIAL
BASIDIUM
BASIFIED
BASIFIER
BASIFIERS
BASIFIES
BASIFIXED
BASIFUGAL
BASIFY
BASIFYING
BASIJ
BASIL
BASILAR
BASILARY
BASILECT
BASILECTS
BASILIC
BASILICA
BASILICAE
BASILICAL
BASILICAN
BASILICAS
BASILICON
BASILISK
BASILISKS
BASILS
BASIN
BASINAL
BASINED
BASINET
BASINETS
BASINFUL
BASINFULS
BASING
BASINLIKE
BASINS
BASION
BASIONS
BASIPETAL
BASIS
BASK
BASKED
BASKET
BASKETFUL
BASKETRY
BASKETS
BASKING
BASKS
BASMATI
BASMATIS
BASNET
BASNETS
BASOCHE
BASOCHES
BASON
BASONS
BASOPHIL
BASOPHILE
BASOPHILS
BASQUE
BASQUED
BASQUES
BASQUINE
BASQUINES
BASS
BASSE
BASSED
BASSER
BASSERS
BASSES
BASSEST
BASSET
BASSETED
BASSETING
BASSETS
BASSETT
BASSETTED
BASSETTS
BASSI
BASSIER
BASSIEST
BASSINET
BASSINETS
BASSING
BASSIST
BASSISTS
BASSLINE
BASSLINES
BASSLY
BASSNESS
BASSO
BASSOON
BASSOONS
BASSOS
BASSWOOD
BASSWOODS
BASSY
BAST
BASTA
BASTARD
BASTARDLY
BASTARDRY
BASTARDS
BASTARDY
BASTE
BASTED
BASTER
BASTERS
BASTES
BASTI
BASTIDE
BASTIDES
BASTILE
BASTILES
BASTILLE
BASTILLES
BASTINADE
BASTINADO
BASTING
BASTINGS
BASTION
BASTIONED
BASTIONS
BASTIS
BASTLE
BASTLES
BASTO
BASTOS
BASTS
BASUCO
BASUCOS
BAT
BATABLE
BATARD
BATARDS
BATATA
BATATAS
BATAVIA
BATAVIAS
BATBOY
BATBOYS
BATCH
BATCHED
BATCHER
BATCHERS
BATCHES
BATCHING
BATCHINGS
BATE
BATEAU
BATEAUX
BATED
BATELESS
BATELEUR
BATELEURS
BATEMENT
BATEMENTS
BATES
BATFISH
BATFISHES
BATFOWL
BATFOWLED
BATFOWLER
BATFOWLS
BATGIRL
BATGIRLS
BATH
BATHCUBE
BATHCUBES
BATHE
BATHED
BATHER
BATHERS
BATHES
BATHETIC
BATHHOUSE
BATHING
BATHINGS
BATHLESS
BATHMAT
BATHMATS
BATHMIC
BATHMISM
BATHMISMS
BATHOLITE
BATHOLITH
BATHORSE
BATHORSES
BATHOS
BATHOSES
BATHROBE
BATHROBES
BATHROOM
BATHROOMS
BATHS
BATHTUB
BATHTUBS
BATHWATER
BATHYAL
BATHYBIUS
BATHYLITE

BATHYLITH
BATIK
BATIKED
BATIKING
BATIKS
BATING
BATISTE
BATISTES
BATLER
BATLERS
BATLET
BATLETS
BATLIKE
BATMAN
BATMEN
BATOLOGY
BATON
BATONED
BATONING
BATONNIER
BATONS
BATOON
BATOONED
BATOONING
BATOONS
BATRACHIA
BATS
BATSHIT
BATSMAN
BATSMEN
BATSWING
BATSWOMAN
BATSWOMEN
BATT
BATTA
BATTALIA
BATTALIAS
BATTALION
BATTAS
BATTEAU
BATTEAUX
BATTED
BATTEL
BATTELED
BATTELER
BATTELERS
BATTELING
BATTELLED
BATTELS
BATTEMENT
BATTEN
BATTENED
BATTENER
BATTENERS
BATTENING
BATTENS
BATTER
BATTERED
BATTERER
BATTERERS
BATTERIE
BATTERIES
BATTERING
BATTERO
BATTEROS
BATTERS
BATTERY
BATTIER
BATTIES
BATTIEST
BATTIK
BATTIKS
BATTILL
BATTILLED
BATTILLS
BATTILY
BATTINESS
BATTING
BATTINGS
BATTLE
BATTLEAX
BATTLEAXE
BATTLEBUS
BATTLED
BATTLER
BATTLERS
BATTLES
BATTLING
BATTOLOGY
BATTS
BATTU
BATTUE
BATTUES
BATTUTA
BATTUTAS
BATTUTO
BATTUTOS
BATTY
BATWING
BATWOMAN
BATWOMEN
BAUBEE
BAUBEES
BAUBLE
BAUBLES
BAUBLING
BAUCHLE
BAUCHLED
BAUCHLES
BAUCHLING
BAUD
BAUDEKIN
BAUDEKINS
BAUDRIC
BAUDRICK
BAUDRICKE
BAUDRICKS
BAUDRICS
BAUDRONS
BAUDS
BAUERA
BAUERAS
BAUHINIA
BAUHINIAS
BAUK
BAUKED
BAUKING
BAUKS
BAULK
BAULKED
BAULKER
BAULKERS
BAULKIER
BAULKIEST
BAULKILY
BAULKING
BAULKLINE
BAULKS
BAULKY
BAUR
BAURS
BAUSOND
BAUXITE
BAUXITES
BAUXITIC
BAVARDAGE
BAVAROIS
BAVIN
BAVINED
BAVINING
BAVINS
BAWBEE
BAWBEES
BAWBLE
BAWBLES
BAWCOCK
BAWCOCKS
BAWD
BAWDIER
BAWDIES
BAWDIEST
BAWDILY
BAWDINESS
BAWDKIN
BAWDKINS
BAWDRIC
BAWDRICS
BAWDRIES
BAWDRY
BAWDS
BAWDY
BAWK
BAWKS
BAWL
BAWLED
BAWLER
BAWLERS
BAWLEY
BAWLEYS
BAWLING
BAWLINGS
BAWLS
BAWN
BAWNEEN
BAWNEENS
BAWNS
BAWR
BAWRS
BAWSUNT
BAWTIE
BAWTIES
BAWTY
BAXTER
BAXTERS
BAY
BAYADEER
BAYADEERS
BAYADERE
BAYADERES
BAYAMO
BAYAMOS
BAYARD
BAYARDS
BAYBERRY
BAYE
BAYED
BAYER
BAYES
BAYEST
BAYFRONT
BAYFRONTS
BAYING
BAYLE
BAYLES
BAYMAN
BAYMEN
BAYNODDY
BAYONET
BAYONETED
BAYONETS
BAYOU
BAYOUS
BAYS
BAYSIDE
BAYSIDES
BAYT
BAYTED
BAYTING
BAYTS
BAYWOOD
BAYWOODS
BAYWOP
BAYWOPS
BAYYAN
BAYYANS
BAZAAR
BAZAARS
BAZAR
BAZARS
BAZAZZ

B

BAZAZZES
BAZILLION
BAZOO
BAZOOKA
BAZOOKAS
BAZOOM
BAZOOMS
BAZOOS
BAZOUKI
BAZOUKIS
BAZZ
BAZZAZZ
BAZZAZZES
BAZZED
BAZZES
BAZZING
BDELLIUM
BDELLIUMS
BE
BEACH
BEACHBALL
BEACHBOY
BEACHBOYS
BEACHCOMB
BEACHED
BEACHES
BEACHGOER
BEACHHEAD
BEACHIER
BEACHIEST
BEACHING
BEACHSIDE
BEACHWEAR
BEACHY
BEACON
BEACONED
BEACONING
BEACONS
BEAD
BEADBLAST
BEADED
BEADER
BEADERS
BEADHOUSE
BEADIER
BEADIEST
BEADILY
BEADINESS
BEADING
BEADINGS
BEADLE
BEADLEDOM
BEADLES
BEADLIKE
BEADMAN
BEADMEN
BEADROLL
BEADROLLS
BEADS
BEADSMAN
BEADSMEN
BEADWORK
BEADWORKS
BEADY
BEAGLE
BEAGLED
BEAGLER
BEAGLERS
BEAGLES
BEAGLING
BEAGLINGS
BEAK
BEAKED
BEAKER
BEAKERFUL
BEAKERS
BEAKIER
BEAKIEST
BEAKLESS
BEAKLIKE
BEAKS
BEAKY
BEAL
BEALING
BEALINGS
BEALS
BEAM
BEAMED
BEAMER
BEAMERS
BEAMIER
BEAMIEST
BEAMILY
BEAMINESS
BEAMING
BEAMINGLY
BEAMINGS
BEAMISH
BEAMISHLY
BEAMLESS
BEAMLET
BEAMLETS
BEAMLIKE
BEAMS
BEAMY
BEAN
BEANBAG
BEANBAGS
BEANBALL
BEANBALLS
BEANED
BEANERIES
BEANERY
BEANFEAST
BEANIE
BEANIES
BEANING
BEANLIKE
BEANO
BEANOS
BEANPOLE
BEANPOLES
BEANS
BEANSTALK
BEANY
BEAR
BEARABLE
BEARABLY
BEARBERRY
BEARBINE
BEARBINES
BEARCAT
BEARCATS
BEARD
BEARDED
BEARDIE
BEARDIER
BEARDIES
BEARDIEST
BEARDING
BEARDLESS
BEARDLIKE
BEARDS
BEARDY
BEARE
BEARED
BEARER
BEARERS
BEARES
BEARGRASS
BEARHUG
BEARHUGS
BEARING
BEARINGS
BEARISH
BEARISHLY
BEARLIKE
BEARNAISE
BEARPAW
BEARPAWS
BEARS
BEARSKIN
BEARSKINS
BEARWARD
BEARWARDS
BEARWOOD
BEARWOODS
BEAST
BEASTED
BEASTHOOD
BEASTIE
BEASTIES
BEASTILY
BEASTING
BEASTINGS
BEASTLIER
BEASTLIKE
BEASTLY
BEASTS
BEAT
BEATABLE
BEATBOX
BEATBOXED
BEATBOXER
BEATBOXES
BEATDOWN
BEATDOWNS
BEATEN
BEATER
BEATERS
BEATH
BEATHED
BEATHING
BEATHS
BEATIER
BEATIEST
BEATIFIC
BEATIFIED
BEATIFIES
BEATIFY
BEATING
BEATINGS
BEATITUDE
BEATLESS
BEATNIK
BEATNIKS
BEATS
BEATY
BEAU
BEAUCOUP
BEAUCOUPS
BEAUFET
BEAUFETS
BEAUFFET
BEAUFFETS
BEAUFIN
BEAUFINS
BEAUISH
BEAUS
BEAUT
BEAUTEOUS
BEAUTER
BEAUTEST
BEAUTIED
BEAUTIES
BEAUTIFUL
BEAUTIFY
BEAUTS
BEAUTY
BEAUTYING
BEAUX
BEAUXITE
BEAUXITES
BEAVER
BEAVERED
BEAVERIES
BEAVERING
BEAVERS
BEAVERY
BEBEERINE

BEBEERU
BEBEERUS
BEBLOOD
BEBLOODED
BEBLOODS
BEBOP
BEBOPPED
BEBOPPER
BEBOPPERS
BEBOPPING
BEBOPS
BEBUNG
BEBUNGS
BECALL
BECALLED
BECALLING
BECALLS
BECALM
BECALMED
BECALMING
BECALMS
BECAME
BECAP
BECAPPED
BECAPPING
BECAPS
BECARPET
BECARPETS
BECASSE
BECASSES
BECAUSE
BECCACCIA
BECCAFICO
BECHALK
BECHALKED
BECHALKS
BECHAMEL
BECHAMELS
BECHANCE
BECHANCED
BECHANCES
BECHARM
BECHARMED
BECHARMS
BECK
BECKE
BECKED
BECKES
BECKET
BECKETS
BECKING
BECKON
BECKONED
BECKONER
BECKONERS
BECKONING
BECKONS
BECKS
BECLAMOR
BECLAMORS
BECLAMOUR
BECLASP
BECLASPED
BECLASPS
BECLOAK
BECLOAKED
BECLOAKS
BECLOG
BECLOGGED
BECLOGS
BECLOTHE
BECLOTHED
BECLOTHES
BECLOUD
BECLOUDED
BECLOUDS
BECLOWN
BECLOWNED
BECLOWNS
BECOME
BECOMES
BECOMING
BECOMINGS
BECOWARD
BECOWARDS
BECQUEREL
BECRAWL
BECRAWLED
BECRAWLS
BECRIME
BECRIMED
BECRIMES
BECRIMING
BECROWD
BECROWDED
BECROWDS
BECRUST
BECRUSTED
BECRUSTS
BECUDGEL
BECUDGELS
BECURL
BECURLED
BECURLING
BECURLS
BECURSE
BECURSED
BECURSES
BECURSING
BECURST
BED
BEDABBLE
BEDABBLED
BEDABBLES
BEDAD
BEDAGGLE
BEDAGGLED
BEDAGGLES
BEDAMN
BEDAMNED
BEDAMNING
BEDAMNS
BEDARKEN
BEDARKENS
BEDASH
BEDASHED
BEDASHES
BEDASHING
BEDAUB
BEDAUBED
BEDAUBING
BEDAUBS
BEDAWIN
BEDAWINS
BEDAZE
BEDAZED
BEDAZES
BEDAZING
BEDAZZLE
BEDAZZLED
BEDAZZLES
BEDBATH
BEDBATHS
BEDBOARD
BEDBOARDS
BEDBUG
BEDBUGS
BEDCHAIR
BEDCHAIRS
BEDCOVER
BEDCOVERS
BEDDABLE
BEDDED
BEDDER
BEDDERS
BEDDING
BEDDINGS
BEDE
BEDEAFEN
BEDEAFENS
BEDECK
BEDECKED
BEDECKING
BEDECKS
BEDEGUAR
BEDEGUARS
BEDEHOUSE
BEDEL
BEDELL
BEDELLS
BEDELS
BEDELSHIP
BEDEMAN
BEDEMEN
BEDERAL
BEDERALS
BEDES
BEDESMAN
BEDESMEN
BEDEVIL
BEDEVILED
BEDEVILS
BEDEW
BEDEWED
BEDEWING
BEDEWS
BEDFAST
BEDFELLOW
BEDFRAME
BEDFRAMES
BEDGOWN
BEDGOWNS
BEDHEAD
BEDHEADS
BEDIAPER
BEDIAPERS
BEDIDE
BEDIGHT
BEDIGHTED
BEDIGHTS
BEDIM
BEDIMMED
BEDIMMING
BEDIMPLE
BEDIMPLED
BEDIMPLES
BEDIMS
BEDIRTIED
BEDIRTIES
BEDIRTY
BEDIZEN
BEDIZENED
BEDIZENS
BEDLAM
BEDLAMER
BEDLAMERS
BEDLAMISM
BEDLAMITE
BEDLAMP
BEDLAMPS
BEDLAMS
BEDLESS
BEDLIKE
BEDLINER
BEDLINERS
BEDMAKER
BEDMAKERS
BEDMATE
BEDMATES
BEDOTTED
BEDOUIN
BEDOUINS
BEDPAN
BEDPANS
BEDPLATE
BEDPLATES
BEDPOST
BEDPOSTS
BEDQUILT
BEDQUILTS

B

BEDRAGGLE
BEDRAIL
BEDRAILS
BEDRAL
BEDRALS
BEDRAPE
BEDRAPED
BEDRAPES
BEDRAPING
BEDRENCH
BEDREST
BEDRESTS
BEDRID
BEDRIDDEN
BEDRIGHT
BEDRIGHTS
BEDRITE
BEDRITES
BEDRIVEL
BEDRIVELS
BEDROCK
BEDROCKS
BEDROLL
BEDROLLS
BEDROOM
BEDROOMED
BEDROOMS
BEDROP
BEDROPPED
BEDROPS
BEDROPT
BEDRUG
BEDRUGGED
BEDRUGS
BEDS
BEDSHEET
BEDSHEETS
BEDSIDE
BEDSIDES
BEDSIT
BEDSITS
BEDSITTER
BEDSKIRT
BEDSKIRTS
BEDSOCK
BEDSOCKS
BEDSONIA
BEDSONIAS
BEDSORE
BEDSORES
BEDSPREAD
BEDSPRING
BEDSTAND
BEDSTANDS
BEDSTEAD
BEDSTEADS
BEDSTRAW
BEDSTRAWS
BEDTICK
BEDTICKS
BEDTIME
BEDTIMES
BEDU
BEDUCK
BEDUCKED
BEDUCKING
BEDUCKS
BEDUIN
BEDUINS
BEDUMB
BEDUMBED
BEDUMBING
BEDUMBS
BEDUNCE
BEDUNCED
BEDUNCES
BEDUNCING
BEDUNG
BEDUNGED
BEDUNGING
BEDUNGS
BEDUST
BEDUSTED
BEDUSTING
BEDUSTS
BEDWARD
BEDWARDS
BEDWARF
BEDWARFED
BEDWARFS
BEDWARMER
BEDWETTER
BEDYDE
BEDYE
BEDYED
BEDYEING
BEDYES
BEE
BEEBEE
BEEBEES
BEEBREAD
BEEBREADS
BEECH
BEECHEN
BEECHES
BEECHIER
BEECHIEST
BEECHMAST
BEECHNUT
BEECHNUTS
BEECHWOOD
BEECHY
BEEDI
BEEDIE
BEEDIES
BEEF
BEEFALO
BEEFALOES
BEEFALOS
BEEFCAKE
BEEFCAKES
BEEFEATER
BEEFED
BEEFIER
BEEFIEST
BEEFILY
BEEFINESS
BEEFING
BEEFLESS
BEEFS
BEEFSTEAK
BEEFWOOD
BEEFWOODS
BEEFY
BEEGAH
BEEGAHS
BEEHIVE
BEEHIVED
BEEHIVES
BEEKEEPER
BEELIKE
BEELINE
BEELINED
BEELINES
BEELINING
BEEN
BEENAH
BEENAHS
BEENTO
BEENTOS
BEEP
BEEPED
BEEPER
BEEPERS
BEEPING
BEEPS
BEER
BEERAGE
BEERAGES
BEERFEST
BEERFESTS
BEERHALL
BEERHALLS
BEERIER
BEERIEST
BEERILY
BEERINESS
BEERMAT
BEERMATS
BEERNUT
BEERNUTS
BEERS
BEERSIES
BEERY
BEES
BEESOME
BEESTING
BEESTINGS
BEESTUNG
BEESWAX
BEESWAXED
BEESWAXES
BEESWING
BEESWINGS
BEET
BEETED
BEETFLIES
BEETFLY
BEETING
BEETLE
BEETLED
BEETLER
BEETLERS
BEETLES
BEETLING
BEETROOT
BEETROOTS
BEETS
BEEVES
BEEYARD
BEEYARDS
BEEZER
BEEZERS
BEFALL
BEFALLEN
BEFALLING
BEFALLS
BEFANA
BEFANAS
BEFELD
BEFELL
BEFFANA
BEFFANAS
BEFINGER
BEFINGERS
BEFINNED
BEFIT
BEFITS
BEFITTED
BEFITTING
BEFLAG
BEFLAGGED
BEFLAGS
BEFLEA
BEFLEAED
BEFLEAING
BEFLEAS
BEFLECK
BEFLECKED
BEFLECKS
BEFLOWER
BEFLOWERS
BEFLUM
BEFLUMMED
BEFLUMS
BEFOAM
BEFOAMED
BEFOAMING
BEFOAMS
BEFOG

BEFOGGED
BEFOGGING
BEFOGS
BEFOOL
BEFOOLED
BEFOOLING
BEFOOLS
BEFORE
BEFORTUNE
BEFOUL
BEFOULED
BEFOULER
BEFOULERS
BEFOULING
BEFOULS
BEFRET
BEFRETS
BEFRETTED
BEFRIEND
BEFRIENDS
BEFRINGE
BEFRINGED
BEFRINGES
BEFUDDLE
BEFUDDLED
BEFUDDLES
BEG
BEGAD
BEGALL
BEGALLED
BEGALLING
BEGALLS
BEGAN
BEGAR
BEGARS
BEGAT
BEGAZE
BEGAZED
BEGAZES
BEGAZING
BEGEM
BEGEMMED
BEGEMMING
BEGEMS
BEGET
BEGETS
BEGETTER
BEGETTERS
BEGETTING
BEGGAR
BEGGARDOM
BEGGARED
BEGGARIES
BEGGARING
BEGGARLY
BEGGARS
BEGGARY
BEGGED
BEGGING
BEGGINGLY
BEGGINGS
BEGHARD
BEGHARDS
BEGIFT
BEGIFTED
BEGIFTING
BEGIFTS
BEGILD
BEGILDED
BEGILDING
BEGILDS
BEGILT
BEGIN
BEGINNE
BEGINNER
BEGINNERS
BEGINNES
BEGINNING
BEGINS
BEGIRD
BEGIRDED
BEGIRDING
BEGIRDLE
BEGIRDLED
BEGIRDLES
BEGIRDS
BEGIRT
BEGLAD
BEGLADDED
BEGLADS
BEGLAMOR
BEGLAMORS
BEGLAMOUR
BEGLERBEG
BEGLOOM
BEGLOOMED
BEGLOOMS
BEGNAW
BEGNAWED
BEGNAWING
BEGNAWS
BEGO
BEGOES
BEGOGGLED
BEGOING
BEGONE
BEGONIA
BEGONIAS
BEGORAH
BEGORED
BEGORRA
BEGORRAH
BEGOT
BEGOTTEN
BEGRIM
BEGRIME
BEGRIMED
BEGRIMES
BEGRIMING
BEGRIMMED
BEGRIMS
BEGROAN
BEGROANED
BEGROANS
BEGRUDGE
BEGRUDGED
BEGRUDGER
BEGRUDGES
BEGS
BEGUILE
BEGUILED
BEGUILER
BEGUILERS
BEGUILES
BEGUILING
BEGUIN
BEGUINAGE
BEGUINE
BEGUINES
BEGUINS
BEGULF
BEGULFED
BEGULFING
BEGULFS
BEGUM
BEGUMS
BEGUN
BEGUNK
BEGUNKED
BEGUNKING
BEGUNKS
BEHALF
BEHALVES
BEHAPPEN
BEHAPPENS
BEHATTED
BEHAVE
BEHAVED
BEHAVER
BEHAVERS
BEHAVES
BEHAVING
BEHAVIOR
BEHAVIORS
BEHAVIOUR
BEHEAD
BEHEADAL
BEHEADALS
BEHEADED
BEHEADER
BEHEADERS
BEHEADING
BEHEADS
BEHELD
BEHEMOTH
BEHEMOTHS
BEHEST
BEHESTS
BEHIGHT
BEHIGHTED
BEHIGHTS
BEHIND
BEHINDS
BEHOLD
BEHOLDEN
BEHOLDER
BEHOLDERS
BEHOLDING
BEHOLDS
BEHOOF
BEHOOFS
BEHOOVE
BEHOOVED
BEHOOVES
BEHOOVING
BEHOTE
BEHOTES
BEHOTING
BEHOVE
BEHOVED
BEHOVEFUL
BEHOVELY
BEHOVES
BEHOVING
BEHOWL
BEHOWLED
BEHOWLING
BEHOWLS
BEIGE
BEIGEL
BEIGELS
BEIGER
BEIGES
BEIGEST
BEIGIER
BEIGIEST
BEIGNE
BEIGNES
BEIGNET
BEIGNETS
BEIGY
BEIN
BEINED
BEING
BEINGLESS
BEINGNESS
BEINGS
BEINING
BEINKED
BEINNESS
BEINS
BEJABBERS
BEJABERS
BEJADE
BEJADED
BEJADES
BEJADING
BEJANT
BEJANTS
BEJASUS

BEJASUSES
BEJEEBERS
BEJEEZUS
BEJESUIT
BEJESUITS
BEJESUS
BEJESUSES
BEJEWEL
BEJEWELED
BEJEWELS
BEJUMBLE
BEJUMBLED
BEJUMBLES
BEKAH
BEKAHS
BEKISS
BEKISSED
BEKISSES
BEKISSING
BEKNAVE
BEKNAVED
BEKNAVES
BEKNAVING
BEKNIGHT
BEKNIGHTS
BEKNOT
BEKNOTS
BEKNOTTED
BEKNOWN
BEL
BELABOR
BELABORED
BELABORS
BELABOUR
BELABOURS
BELACE
BELACED
BELACES
BELACING
BELADIED
BELADIES
BELADY
BELADYING
BELAH
BELAHS
BELAMIES
BELAMOUR
BELAMOURE
BELAMOURS
BELAMY
BELAR
BELARS
BELATE
BELATED
BELATEDLY
BELATES
BELATING
BELAUD
BELAUDED
BELAUDING
BELAUDS
BELAY
BELAYED
BELAYER
BELAYERS
BELAYING
BELAYS
BELCH
BELCHED
BELCHER
BELCHERS
BELCHES
BELCHING
BELDAM
BELDAME
BELDAMES
BELDAMS
BELEAGUER
BELEAP
BELEAPED
BELEAPING
BELEAPS
BELEAPT
BELEE
BELEED
BELEEING
BELEES
BELEMNITE
BELEMNOID
BELFRIED
BELFRIES
BELFRY
BELGA
BELGARD
BELGARDS
BELGAS
BELGICISM
BELIE
BELIED
BELIEF
BELIEFS
BELIER
BELIERS
BELIES
BELIEVE
BELIEVED
BELIEVER
BELIEVERS
BELIEVES
BELIEVING
BELIKE
BELIQUOR
BELIQUORS
BELITTLE
BELITTLED
BELITTLER
BELITTLES
BELIVE
BELL
BELLBIND
BELLBINDS
BELLBIRD
BELLBIRDS
BELLBOY
BELLBOYS
BELLBUOY
BELLBUOYS
BELLCAST
BELLCOTE
BELLCOTES
BELLE
BELLED
BELLEEK
BELLEEKS
BELLES
BELLETER
BELLETERS
BELLHOP
BELLHOPS
BELLIBONE
BELLICOSE
BELLIED
BELLIES
BELLING
BELLINGS
BELLINI
BELLINIS
BELLMAN
BELLMEN
BELLOCK
BELLOCKED
BELLOCKS
BELLOW
BELLOWED
BELLOWER
BELLOWERS
BELLOWING
BELLOWS
BELLPULL
BELLPULLS
BELLS
BELLWORT
BELLWORTS
BELLY
BELLYACHE
BELLYBAND
BELLYBOAT
BELLYFLOP
BELLYFUL
BELLYFULS
BELLYING
BELLYINGS
BELLYLIKE
BELOMANCY
BELON
BELONG
BELONGED
BELONGER
BELONGERS
BELONGING
BELONGS
BELONS
BELOVE
BELOVED
BELOVEDS
BELOVES
BELOVING
BELOW
BELOWS
BELS
BELT
BELTED
BELTER
BELTERS
BELTING
BELTINGS
BELTLESS
BELTLIKE
BELTLINE
BELTLINES
BELTMAN
BELTMEN
BELTS
BELTWAY
BELTWAYS
BELUGA
BELUGAS
BELVEDERE
BELYING
BEMA
BEMAD
BEMADAM
BEMADAMED
BEMADAMS
BEMADDED
BEMADDEN
BEMADDENS
BEMADDING
BEMADS
BEMAS
BEMATA
BEMAUL
BEMAULED
BEMAULING
BEMAULS
BEMAZED
BEMBEX
BEMBEXES
BEMBIX
BEMBIXES
BEMEAN
BEMEANED
BEMEANING
BEMEANS
BEMEANT
BEMEDAL
BEMEDALED
BEMEDALS
BEMETE
BEMETED

BEMETES
BEMETING
BEMINGLE
BEMINGLED
BEMINGLES
BEMIRE
BEMIRED
BEMIRES
BEMIRING
BEMIST
BEMISTED
BEMISTING
BEMISTS
BEMIX
BEMIXED
BEMIXES
BEMIXING
BEMIXT
BEMOAN
BEMOANED
BEMOANER
BEMOANERS
BEMOANING
BEMOANS
BEMOCK
BEMOCKED
BEMOCKING
BEMOCKS
BEMOIL
BEMOILED
BEMOILING
BEMOILS
BEMONSTER
BEMOUTH
BEMOUTHED
BEMOUTHS
BEMUD
BEMUDDED
BEMUDDING
BEMUDDLE
BEMUDDLED
BEMUDDLES
BEMUDS
BEMUFFLE
BEMUFFLED
BEMUFFLES
BEMURMUR
BEMURMURS
BEMUSE
BEMUSED
BEMUSEDLY
BEMUSES
BEMUSING
BEMUZZLE
BEMUZZLED
BEMUZZLES
BEN
BENADRYL
BENADRYLS
BENAME
BENAMED
BENAMES
BENAMING
BENCH
BENCHED
BENCHER
BENCHERS
BENCHES
BENCHIER
BENCHIEST
BENCHING
BENCHLAND
BENCHLESS
BENCHMARK
BENCHTOP
BENCHTOPS
BENCHY
BEND
BENDABLE
BENDAY
BENDAYED
BENDAYING
BENDAYS
BENDED
BENDEE
BENDEES
BENDER
BENDERS
BENDIER
BENDIEST
BENDINESS
BENDING
BENDINGLY
BENDINGS
BENDLET
BENDLETS
BENDS
BENDWAYS
BENDWISE
BENDY
BENDYS
BENE
BENEATH
BENEDICK
BENEDICKS
BENEDICT
BENEDICTS
BENEDIGHT
BENEFACT
BENEFACTS
BENEFIC
BENEFICE
BENEFICED
BENEFICES
BENEFIT
BENEFITED
BENEFITER
BENEFITS
BENEMPT
BENEMPTED
BENES
BENET
BENETS
BENETTED
BENETTING
BENGA
BENGALINE
BENGAS
BENI
BENIGHT
BENIGHTED
BENIGHTEN
BENIGHTER
BENIGHTS
BENIGN
BENIGNANT
BENIGNER
BENIGNEST
BENIGNITY
BENIGNLY
BENIS
BENISEED
BENISEEDS
BENISON
BENISONS
BENITIER
BENITIERS
BENJ
BENJAMIN
BENJAMINS
BENJES
BENNE
BENNES
BENNET
BENNETS
BENNI
BENNIES
BENNIS
BENNY
BENOMYL
BENOMYLS
BENS
BENT
BENTGRASS
BENTHAL
BENTHIC
BENTHOAL
BENTHON
BENTHONIC
BENTHONS
BENTHOS
BENTHOSES
BENTIER
BENTIEST
BENTO
BENTONITE
BENTOS
BENTS
BENTWOOD
BENTWOODS
BENTY
BENUMB
BENUMBED
BENUMBING
BENUMBS
BENZAL
BENZALS
BENZENE
BENZENES
BENZENOID
BENZIDIN
BENZIDINE
BENZIDINS
BENZIL
BENZILS
BENZIN
BENZINE
BENZINES
BENZINS
BENZOATE
BENZOATES
BENZOIC
BENZOIN
BENZOINS
BENZOL
BENZOLE
BENZOLES
BENZOLINE
BENZOLS
BENZOYL
BENZOYLS
BENZYL
BENZYLIC
BENZYLS
BEPAINT
BEPAINTED
BEPAINTS
BEPAT
BEPATCHED
BEPATS
BEPATTED
BEPATTING
BEPEARL
BEPEARLED
BEPEARLS
BEPELT
BEPELTED
BEPELTING
BEPELTS
BEPEPPER
BEPEPPERS
BEPESTER
BEPESTERS
BEPIMPLE
BEPIMPLED
BEPIMPLES
BEPITIED
BEPITIES
BEPITY
BEPITYING

BEPLASTER
BEPLUMED
BEPOMMEL
BEPOMMELS
BEPOWDER
BEPOWDERS
BEPRAISE
BEPRAISED
BEPRAISES
BEPROSE
BEPROSED
BEPROSES
BEPROSING
BEPUFF
BEPUFFED
BEPUFFING
BEPUFFS
BEQUEATH
BEQUEATHS
BEQUEST
BEQUESTS
BERAKE
BERAKED
BERAKES
BERAKING
BERASCAL
BERASCALS
BERATE
BERATED
BERATES
BERATING
BERAY
BERAYED
BERAYING
BERAYS
BERBER
BERBERE
BERBERES
BERBERIN
BERBERINE
BERBERINS
BERBERIS
BERBERS
BERBICE
BERCEAU
BERCEAUX
BERCEUSE
BERCEUSES
BERDACHE
BERDACHES
BERDASH
BERDASHES
BERE
BEREAVE
BEREAVED
BEREAVEN
BEREAVER
BEREAVERS
BEREAVES
BEREAVING
BEREFT
BERES
BERET
BERETS
BERETTA
BERETTAS
BERG
BERGALL
BERGALLS
BERGAMA
BERGAMAS
BERGAMASK
BERGAMOT
BERGAMOTS
BERGANDER
BERGEN
BERGENIA
BERGENIAS
BERGENS
BERGERE
BERGERES
BERGFALL
BERGFALLS
BERGHAAN
BERGHAANS
BERGMEHL
BERGMEHLS
BERGOMASK
BERGS
BERGYLT
BERGYLTS
BERHYME
BERHYMED
BERHYMES
BERHYMING
BERIBERI
BERIBERIS
BERIMBAU
BERIMBAUS
BERIME
BERIMED
BERIMES
BERIMING
BERINGED
BERK
BERKELIUM
BERKO
BERKS
BERLEY
BERLEYED
BERLEYING
BERLEYS
BERLIN
BERLINE
BERLINES
BERLINS
BERM
BERME
BERMED
BERMES
BERMING
BERMS
BERMUDAS
BERNICLE
BERNICLES
BEROB
BEROBBED
BEROBBING
BEROBED
BEROBS
BEROUGED
BERRET
BERRETS
BERRETTA
BERRETTAS
BERRIED
BERRIES
BERRIGAN
BERRIGANS
BERRY
BERRYING
BERRYINGS
BERRYLESS
BERRYLIKE
BERSEEM
BERSEEMS
BERSERK
BERSERKER
BERSERKLY
BERSERKS
BERTH
BERTHA
BERTHAGE
BERTHAGES
BERTHAS
BERTHE
BERTHED
BERTHES
BERTHING
BERTHINGS
BERTHS
BERYL
BERYLINE
BERYLLIA
BERYLLIAS
BERYLLIUM
BERYLS
BES
BESAINT
BESAINTED
BESAINTS
BESANG
BESAT
BESAW
BESCATTER
BESCORCH
BESCOUR
BESCOURED
BESCOURS
BESCRAWL
BESCRAWLS
BESCREEN
BESCREENS
BESEE
BESEECH
BESEECHED
BESEECHER
BESEECHES
BESEEING
BESEEKE
BESEEKES
BESEEKING
BESEEM
BESEEMED
BESEEMING
BESEEMLY
BESEEMS
BESEEN
BESEES
BESES
BESET
BESETMENT
BESETS
BESETTER
BESETTERS
BESETTING
BESHADOW
BESHADOWS
BESHAME
BESHAMED
BESHAMES
BESHAMING
BESHINE
BESHINES
BESHINING
BESHIVER
BESHIVERS
BESHONE
BESHOUT
BESHOUTED
BESHOUTS
BESHREW
BESHREWED
BESHREWS
BESHROUD
BESHROUDS
BESIDE
BESIDES
BESIEGE
BESIEGED
BESIEGER
BESIEGERS
BESIEGES
BESIEGING
BESIGH
BESIGHED
BESIGHING
BESIGHS
BESING
BESINGING

BESINGS
BESIT
BESITS
BESITTING
BESLAVE
BESLAVED
BESLAVER
BESLAVERS
BESLAVES
BESLAVING
BESLIME
BESLIMED
BESLIMES
BESLIMING
BESLOBBER
BESLUBBER
BESMEAR
BESMEARED
BESMEARER
BESMEARS
BESMILE
BESMILED
BESMILES
BESMILING
BESMIRCH
BESMOKE
BESMOKED
BESMOKES
BESMOKING
BESMOOTH
BESMOOTHS
BESMUDGE
BESMUDGED
BESMUDGES
BESMUT
BESMUTCH
BESMUTS
BESMUTTED
BESNOW
BESNOWED
BESNOWING
BESNOWS
BESOGNIO
BESOGNIOS
BESOIN
BESOINS
BESOM
BESOMED
BESOMING
BESOMS
BESONIAN
BESONIANS
BESOOTHE
BESOOTHED
BESOOTHES
BESORT
BESORTED
BESORTING
BESORTS
BESOT
BESOTS
BESOTTED
BESOTTING
BESOUGHT
BESOULED
BESPAKE
BESPANGLE
BESPAT
BESPATE
BESPATTER
BESPEAK
BESPEAKS
BESPECKLE
BESPED
BESPEED
BESPEEDS
BESPICE
BESPICED
BESPICES
BESPICING
BESPIT
BESPITS
BESPOKE
BESPOKEN
BESPORT
BESPORTED
BESPORTS
BESPOT
BESPOTS
BESPOTTED
BESPOUSE
BESPOUSED
BESPOUSES
BESPOUT
BESPOUTED
BESPOUTS
BESPREAD
BESPREADS
BESPRENT
BEST
BESTAD
BESTADDE
BESTAIN
BESTAINED
BESTAINS
BESTAR
BESTARRED
BESTARS
BESTEAD
BESTEADED
BESTEADS
BESTED
BESTEST
BESTI
BESTIAL
BESTIALLY
BESTIALS
BESTIARY
BESTICK
BESTICKS
BESTIE
BESTIES
BESTILL
BESTILLED
BESTILLS
BESTING
BESTIR
BESTIRRED
BESTIRS
BESTIS
BESTORM
BESTORMED
BESTORMS
BESTOW
BESTOWAL
BESTOWALS
BESTOWED
BESTOWER
BESTOWERS
BESTOWING
BESTOWS
BESTREAK
BESTREAKS
BESTREW
BESTREWED
BESTREWN
BESTREWS
BESTRID
BESTRIDE
BESTRIDES
BESTRODE
BESTROW
BESTROWED
BESTROWN
BESTROWS
BESTS
BESTUCK
BESTUD
BESTUDDED
BESTUDS
BESUITED
BESUNG
BESWARM
BESWARMED
BESWARMS
BET
BETA
BETACISM
BETACISMS
BETAINE
BETAINES
BETAKE
BETAKEN
BETAKES
BETAKING
BETAS
BETATOPIC
BETATRON
BETATRONS
BETATTER
BETATTERS
BETAXED
BETCHA
BETE
BETED
BETEEM
BETEEME
BETEEMED
BETEEMES
BETEEMING
BETEEMS
BETEL
BETELNUT
BETELNUTS
BETELS
BETES
BETH
BETHANK
BETHANKED
BETHANKIT
BETHANKS
BETHEL
BETHELS
BETHESDA
BETHESDAS
BETHINK
BETHINKS
BETHORN
BETHORNED
BETHORNS
BETHOUGHT
BETHRALL
BETHRALLS
BETHS
BETHUMB
BETHUMBED
BETHUMBS
BETHUMP
BETHUMPED
BETHUMPS
BETHWACK
BETHWACKS
BETID
BETIDE
BETIDED
BETIDES
BETIDING
BETIGHT
BETIME
BETIMED
BETIMES
BETIMING
BETING
BETISE
BETISES
BETITLE
BETITLED
BETITLES
BETITLING
BETOIL

B

BETOILED
BETOILING
BETOILS
BETOKEN
BETOKENED
BETOKENS
BETON
BETONIES
BETONS
BETONY
BETOOK
BETOSS
BETOSSED
BETOSSES
BETOSSING
BETRAY
BETRAYAL
BETRAYALS
BETRAYED
BETRAYER
BETRAYERS
BETRAYING
BETRAYS
BETREAD
BETREADS
BETRIM
BETRIMMED
BETRIMS
BETROD
BETRODDEN
BETROTH
BETROTHAL
BETROTHED
BETROTHS
BETS
BETTA
BETTAS
BETTED
BETTER
BETTERED
BETTERING
BETTERS
BETTIES
BETTING
BETTINGS
BETTONG
BETTONGS
BETTOR
BETTORS
BETTY
BETUMBLED
BETWEEN
BETWEENS
BETWIXT
BEUNCLED
BEURRE
BEURRES
BEVATRON
BEVATRONS
BEVEL
BEVELED
BEVELER
BEVELERS
BEVELING
BEVELLED
BEVELLER
BEVELLERS
BEVELLING
BEVELMENT
BEVELS
BEVER
BEVERAGE
BEVERAGES
BEVERED
BEVERING
BEVERS
BEVIES
BEVOMIT
BEVOMITED
BEVOMITS
BEVOR
BEVORS
BEVUE
BEVUES
BEVVIED
BEVVIES
BEVVY
BEVVYING
BEVY
BEWAIL
BEWAILED
BEWAILER
BEWAILERS
BEWAILING
BEWAILS
BEWARE
BEWARED
BEWARES
BEWARING
BEWEARIED
BEWEARIES
BEWEARY
BEWEEP
BEWEEPING
BEWEEPS
BEWENT
BEWEPT
BEWET
BEWETS
BEWETTED
BEWETTING
BEWHORE
BEWHORED
BEWHORES
BEWHORING
BEWIG
BEWIGGED
BEWIGGING
BEWIGS
BEWILDER
BEWILDERS
BEWINGED
BEWITCH
BEWITCHED
BEWITCHER
BEWITCHES
BEWORM
BEWORMED
BEWORMING
BEWORMS
BEWORRIED
BEWORRIES
BEWORRY
BEWRAP
BEWRAPPED
BEWRAPS
BEWRAPT
BEWRAY
BEWRAYED
BEWRAYER
BEWRAYERS
BEWRAYING
BEWRAYS
BEY
BEYLIC
BEYLICS
BEYLIK
BEYLIKS
BEYOND
BEYONDS
BEYS
BEZ
BEZANT
BEZANTS
BEZAZZ
BEZAZZES
BEZEL
BEZELLESS
BEZELS
BEZES
BEZIL
BEZILS
BEZIQUE
BEZIQUES
BEZOAR
BEZOARDIC
BEZOARS
BEZONIAN
BEZONIANS
BEZZANT
BEZZANTS
BEZZAZZ
BEZZAZZES
BEZZIE
BEZZIES
BEZZLE
BEZZLED
BEZZLES
BEZZLING
BEZZY
BHAGEE
BHAGEES
BHAI
BHAIS
BHAJAN
BHAJANS
BHAJEE
BHAJEES
BHAJI
BHAJIA
BHAJIS
BHAKTA
BHAKTAS
BHAKTI
BHAKTIS
BHANG
BHANGRA
BHANGRAS
BHANGS
BHARAL
BHARALS
BHAT
BHATS
BHAVAN
BHAVANS
BHAWAN
BHAWANS
BHEESTIE
BHEESTIES
BHEESTY
BHEL
BHELPURI
BHELPURIS
BHELS
BHIKHU
BHIKHUS
BHIKKHUNI
BHINDI
BHINDIS
BHISHTI
BHISHTIS
BHISTEE
BHISTEES
BHISTI
BHISTIE
BHISTIES
BHISTIS
BHOONA
BHOONAS
BHOOT
BHOOTS
BHUNA
BHUNAS
BHUT
BHUTS
BI
BIACETYL
BIACETYLS
BIACH
BIACHES

BIALI
BIALIES
BIALIS
BIALY
BIALYS
BIANNUAL
BIANNUALS
BIAS
BIASED
BIASEDLY
BIASES
BIASING
BIASINGS
BIASNESS
BIASSED
BIASSEDLY
BIASSES
BIASSING
BIATCH
BIATCHES
BIATHLETE
BIATHLON
BIATHLONS
BIAXAL
BIAXIAL
BIAXIALLY
BIB
BIBACIOUS
BIBASIC
BIBATION
BIBATIONS
BIBB
BIBBED
BIBBER
BIBBERIES
BIBBERS
BIBBERY
BIBBING
BIBBINGS
BIBBLE
BIBBLES
BIBBS
BIBCOCK
BIBCOCKS
BIBE
BIBELOT
BIBELOTS
BIBES
BIBFUL
BIBFULS
BIBIMBAP
BIBIMBAPS
BIBLE
BIBLES
BIBLESS
BIBLICAL
BIBLICISM
BIBLICIST
BIBLIKE
BIBLIOTIC
BIBLIST
BIBLISTS
BIBS
BIBULOUS
BICAMERAL
BICARB
BICARBS
BICAUDAL
BICCIES
BICCY
BICE
BICENTRIC
BICEP
BICEPS
BICEPSES
BICES
BICHIR
BICHIRS
BICHORD
BICHROME
BICIPITAL
BICKER
BICKERED
BICKERER
BICKERERS
BICKERING
BICKERS
BICKIE
BICKIES
BICOASTAL
BICOLOR
BICOLORED
BICOLORS
BICOLOUR
BICOLOURS
BICONCAVE
BICONVEX
BICORN
BICORNATE
BICORNE
BICORNES
BICORNS
BICRON
BICRONS
BICURIOUS
BICUSPID
BICUSPIDS
BICYCLE
BICYCLED
BICYCLER
BICYCLERS
BICYCLES
BICYCLIC
BICYCLING
BICYCLIST
BID
BIDARKA
BIDARKAS
BIDARKEE
BIDARKEES
BIDDABLE
BIDDABLY
BIDDEN
BIDDER
BIDDERS
BIDDIES
BIDDING
BIDDINGS
BIDDY
BIDE
BIDED
BIDENT
BIDENTAL
BIDENTALS
BIDENTATE
BIDENTS
BIDER
BIDERS
BIDES
BIDET
BIDETS
BIDI
BIDING
BIDINGS
BIDIS
BIDON
BIDONS
BIDS
BIELD
BIELDED
BIELDIER
BIELDIEST
BIELDING
BIELDS
BIELDY
BIEN
BIENNALE
BIENNALES
BIENNIA
BIENNIAL
BIENNIALS
BIENNIUM
BIENNIUMS
BIER
BIERS
BIERWURST
BIESTINGS
BIFACE
BIFACES
BIFACIAL
BIFARIOUS
BIFF
BIFFED
BIFFER
BIFFERS
BIFFIES
BIFFIN
BIFFING
BIFFINS
BIFFO
BIFFOS
BIFFS
BIFFY
BIFID
BIFIDA
BIFIDITY
BIFIDLY
BIFIDUM
BIFIDUMS
BIFIDUS
BIFIDUSES
BIFILAR
BIFILARLY
BIFLEX
BIFOCAL
BIFOCALED
BIFOCALS
BIFOLD
BIFOLDS
BIFOLIATE
BIFORATE
BIFORKED
BIFORM
BIFORMED
BIFTAH
BIFTAHS
BIFTER
BIFTERS
BIFURCATE
BIG
BIGA
BIGAE
BIGAMIES
BIGAMIST
BIGAMISTS
BIGAMOUS
BIGAMY
BIGARADE
BIGARADES
BIGAROON
BIGAROONS
BIGARREAU
BIGEMINAL
BIGEMINY
BIGENER
BIGENERIC
BIGENERS
BIGEYE
BIGEYES
BIGFEET
BIGFOOT
BIGFOOTED
BIGFOOTS
BIGG
BIGGED
BIGGER
BIGGEST
BIGGETIER
BIGGETY
BIGGIE

BIGGIES
BIGGIN
BIGGING
BIGGINGS
BIGGINS
BIGGISH
BIGGITIER
BIGGITY
BIGGON
BIGGONS
BIGGS
BIGGY
BIGHA
BIGHAS
BIGHEAD
BIGHEADED
BIGHEADS
BIGHORN
BIGHORNS
BIGHT
BIGHTED
BIGHTING
BIGHTS
BIGLY
BIGMOUTH
BIGMOUTHS
BIGNESS
BIGNESSES
BIGNONIA
BIGNONIAS
BIGOS
BIGOSES
BIGOT
BIGOTED
BIGOTEDLY
BIGOTRIES
BIGOTRY
BIGOTS
BIGS
BIGSTICK
BIGTIME
BIGUANIDE
BIGUINE
BIGUINES
BIGWIG
BIGWIGS
BIHOURLY
BIJECTION
BIJECTIVE
BIJOU
BIJOUS
BIJOUX
BIJUGATE
BIJUGOUS
BIJURAL
BIJWONER
BIJWONERS
BIKE
BIKED
BIKER
BIKERS
BIKES
BIKEWAY
BIKEWAYS
BIKIE
BIKIES
BIKING
BIKINGS
BIKINI
BIKINIED
BIKINIS
BIKKIE
BIKKIES
BILABIAL
BILABIALS
BILABIATE
BILANDER
BILANDERS
BILATERAL
BILAYER
BILAYERS
BILBERRY
BILBIES
BILBO
BILBOA
BILBOAS
BILBOES
BILBOS
BILBY
BILE
BILECTION
BILED
BILES
BILESTONE
BILEVEL
BILEVELS
BILGE
BILGED
BILGES
BILGIER
BILGIEST
BILGING
BILGY
BILHARZIA
BILIAN
BILIANS
BILIARIES
BILIARY
BILIMBI
BILIMBING
BILIMBIS
BILINEAR
BILING
BILINGUAL
BILIOUS
BILIOUSLY
BILIRUBIN
BILITERAL
BILK
BILKED
BILKER
BILKERS
BILKING
BILKS
BILL
BILLABLE
BILLABONG
BILLBOARD
BILLBOOK
BILLBOOKS
BILLBUG
BILLBUGS
BILLED
BILLER
BILLERS
BILLET
BILLETED
BILLETEE
BILLETEES
BILLETER
BILLETERS
BILLETING
BILLETS
BILLFISH
BILLFOLD
BILLFOLDS
BILLHEAD
BILLHEADS
BILLHOOK
BILLHOOKS
BILLIARD
BILLIARDS
BILLIE
BILLIES
BILLING
BILLINGS
BILLION
BILLIONS
BILLIONTH
BILLMAN
BILLMEN
BILLON
BILLONS
BILLOW
BILLOWED
BILLOWIER
BILLOWING
BILLOWS
BILLOWY
BILLS
BILLY
BILLYBOY
BILLYBOYS
BILLYCAN
BILLYCANS
BILLYCOCK
BILLYO
BILLYOH
BILLYOHS
BILLYOS
BILOBAR
BILOBATE
BILOBATED
BILOBED
BILOBULAR
BILOCULAR
BILSTED
BILSTEDS
BILTONG
BILTONGS
BIMA
BIMAH
BIMAHS
BIMANAL
BIMANOUS
BIMANUAL
BIMAS
BIMBASHI
BIMBASHIS
BIMBETTE
BIMBETTES
BIMBLE
BIMBO
BIMBOES
BIMBOS
BIMENSAL
BIMESTER
BIMESTERS
BIMETAL
BIMETALS
BIMETHYL
BIMETHYLS
BIMINI
BIMINIS
BIMODAL
BIMONTHLY
BIMORPH
BIMORPHS
BIN
BINAL
BINARIES
BINARISM
BINARISMS
BINARY
BINATE
BINATELY
BINAURAL
BIND
BINDABLE
BINDER
BINDERIES
BINDERS
BINDERY
BINDHI
BINDHIS
BINDI
BINDING
BINDINGLY
BINDINGS
BINDIS

BINDLE
BINDLES
BINDS
BINDWEED
BINDWEEDS
BINE
BINER
BINERS
BINERVATE
BINES
BING
BINGE
BINGEABLE
BINGED
BINGEING
BINGEINGS
BINGER
BINGERS
BINGES
BINGIES
BINGING
BINGINGS
BINGLE
BINGLED
BINGLES
BINGLING
BINGO
BINGOED
BINGOES
BINGOING
BINGOS
BINGS
BINGY
BINIOU
BINIOUS
BINIT
BINITS
BINK
BINKS
BINMAN
BINMEN
BINNACLE
BINNACLES
BINNED
BINNING
BINOCLE
BINOCLES
BINOCS
BINOCULAR
BINOMIAL
BINOMIALS
BINOMINAL
BINOVULAR
BINS
BINTURONG
BINUCLEAR
BIO
BIOACTIVE
BIOASSAY
BIOASSAYS
BIOBANK
BIOBANKS
BIOBLAST
BIOBLASTS
BIOCENOSE
BIOCHEMIC
BIOCHIP
BIOCHIPS
BIOCIDAL
BIOCIDE
BIOCIDES
BIOCLEAN
BIOCYCLE
BIOCYCLES
BIODATA
BIODIESEL
BIODOT
BIODOTS
BIOENERGY
BIOETHIC
BIOETHICS
BIOFACT
BIOFACTS
BIOFIBERS
BIOFIBRES
BIOFILM
BIOFILMS
BIOFOULER
BIOFUEL
BIOFUELED
BIOFUELS
BIOG
BIOGAS
BIOGASES
BIOGASSES
BIOGEN
BIOGENIC
BIOGENIES
BIOGENOUS
BIOGENS
BIOGENY
BIOGRAPH
BIOGRAPHS
BIOGRAPHY
BIOGS
BIOHACKER
BIOHAZARD
BIOHERM
BIOHERMS
BIOLOGIC
BIOLOGICS
BIOLOGIES
BIOLOGISM
BIOLOGIST
BIOLOGY
BIOLYSES
BIOLYSIS
BIOLYTIC
BIOMARKER
BIOMASS
BIOMASSES
BIOME
BIOMES
BIOMETER
BIOMETERS
BIOMETRIC
BIOMETRY
BIOMINING
BIOMORPH
BIOMORPHS
BIONIC
BIONICS
BIONOMIC
BIONOMICS
BIONOMIES
BIONOMIST
BIONOMY
BIONT
BIONTIC
BIONTS
BIOPARENT
BIOPHILIA
BIOPHOR
BIOPHORE
BIOPHORES
BIOPHORS
BIOPIC
BIOPICS
BIOPIRACY
BIOPIRATE
BIOPLASM
BIOPLASMS
BIOPLAST
BIOPLASTS
BIOPLAY
BIOPLAYS
BIOPSIC
BIOPSIED
BIOPSIES
BIOPSY
BIOPSYING
BIOPTIC
BIOREGION
BIORHYTHM
BIOS
BIOSAFETY
BIOSCOPE
BIOSCOPES
BIOSCOPY
BIOSENSOR
BIOSOCIAL
BIOSOLID
BIOSOLIDS
BIOSPHERE
BIOSTABLE
BIOSTATIC
BIOSTROME
BIOTA
BIOTAS
BIOTECH
BIOTECHS
BIOTERROR
BIOTIC
BIOTICAL
BIOTICS
BIOTIN
BIOTINS
BIOTITE
BIOTITES
BIOTITIC
BIOTOPE
BIOTOPES
BIOTOXIN
BIOTOXINS
BIOTRON
BIOTRONS
BIOTROPH
BIOTROPHS
BIOTURBED
BIOTYPE
BIOTYPES
BIOTYPIC
BIOVULAR
BIOWASTE
BIOWASTES
BIOWEAPON
BIPACK
BIPACKS
BIPAROUS
BIPARTED
BIPARTITE
BIPARTY
BIPED
BIPEDAL
BIPEDALLY
BIPEDS
BIPHASIC
BIPHENYL
BIPHENYLS
BIPINNATE
BIPLANE
BIPLANES
BIPOD
BIPODS
BIPOLAR
BIPRISM
BIPRISMS
BIPYRAMID
BIRACIAL
BIRADIAL
BIRADICAL
BIRAMOSE
BIRAMOUS
BIRCH
BIRCHBARK
BIRCHED
BIRCHEN
BIRCHES
BIRCHING
BIRCHINGS

BIRCHIR
BIRCHIRS
BIRCHWOOD
BIRD
BIRDBATH
BIRDBATHS
BIRDBRAIN
BIRDCAGE
BIRDCAGES
BIRDCALL
BIRDCALLS
BIRDDOG
BIRDDOGS
BIRDED
BIRDER
BIRDERS
BIRDFARM
BIRDFARMS
BIRDFEED
BIRDFEEDS
BIRDHOUSE
BIRDIE
BIRDIED
BIRDIEING
BIRDIES
BIRDING
BIRDINGS
BIRDLIFE
BIRDLIFES
BIRDLIKE
BIRDLIME
BIRDLIMED
BIRDLIMES
BIRDMAN
BIRDMEN
BIRDS
BIRDSEED
BIRDSEEDS
BIRDSEYE
BIRDSEYES
BIRDSFOOT
BIRDSHOT
BIRDSHOTS
BIRDSONG
BIRDSONGS
BIRDWATCH
BIRDWING
BIRDWINGS

BIREME
BIREMES
BIRETTA
BIRETTAS
BIRIANI
BIRIANIS
BIRIYANI
BIRIYANIS
BIRK
BIRKEN
BIRKIE
BIRKIER
BIRKIES
BIRKIEST
BIRKS
BIRL
BIRLE
BIRLED
BIRLER
BIRLERS
BIRLES
BIRLIEMAN
BIRLIEMEN
BIRLING
BIRLINGS
BIRLINN
BIRLINNS
BIRLS
BIRO
BIROS
BIRR
BIRRED
BIRRETTA
BIRRETTAS
BIRRING
BIRROTCH
BIRRS
BIRSE
BIRSED
BIRSES
BIRSIER
BIRSIEST
BIRSING
BIRSLE
BIRSLED
BIRSLES
BIRSLING
BIRSY

BIRTH
BIRTHDATE
BIRTHDAY
BIRTHDAYS
BIRTHDOM
BIRTHDOMS
BIRTHED
BIRTHER
BIRTHERS
BIRTHING
BIRTHINGS
BIRTHMARK
BIRTHNAME
BIRTHRATE
BIRTHROOT
BIRTHS
BIRTHWORT
BIRYANI
BIRYANIS
BIS
BISCACHA
BISCACHAS
BISCOTTI
BISCOTTO
BISCUIT
BISCUITS
BISCUITY
BISE
BISECT
BISECTED
BISECTING
BISECTION
BISECTOR
BISECTORS
BISECTRIX
BISECTS
BISERIAL
BISERIATE
BISERRATE
BISES
BISEXUAL
BISEXUALS
BISH
BISHES
BISHOP
BISHOPDOM
BISHOPED
BISHOPESS

BISHOPING
BISHOPRIC
BISHOPS
BISK
BISKS
BISMAR
BISMARCK
BISMARCKS
BISMARS
BISMILLAH
BISMUTH
BISMUTHAL
BISMUTHIC
BISMUTHS
BISNAGA
BISNAGAS
BISOM
BISOMS
BISON
BISONS
BISONTINE
BISPHENOL
BISQUE
BISQUES
BISSON
BISSONED
BISSONING
BISSONS
BIST
BISTABLE
BISTABLES
BISTATE
BISTER
BISTERED
BISTERS
BISTORT
BISTORTS
BISTOURY
BISTRE
BISTRED
BISTRES
BISTRO
BISTROIC
BISTROS
BISULCATE
BISULFATE
BISULFIDE
BISULFITE

BIT
BITABLE
BITCH
BITCHED
BITCHEN
BITCHERY
BITCHES
BITCHFEST
BITCHIER
BITCHIEST
BITCHILY
BITCHING
BITCHY
BITCOIN
BITCOINS
BITE
BITEABLE
BITEPLATE
BITER
BITERS
BITES
BITESIZE
BITEWING
BITEWINGS
BITING
BITINGLY
BITINGS
BITLESS
BITMAP
BITMAPPED
BITMAPS
BITO
BITONAL
BITOS
BITOU
BITRATE
BITRATES
BITS
BITSER
BITSERS
BITSIER
BITSIEST
BITSTOCK
BITSTOCKS
BITSTREAM
BITSY
BITT
BITTACLE

BITTACLES
BITTE
BITTED
BITTEN
BITTER
BITTERED
BITTERER
BITTEREST
BITTERING
BITTERISH
BITTERLY
BITTERN
BITTERNS
BITTERNUT
BITTERS
BITTIE
BITTIER
BITTIES
BITTIEST
BITTILY
BITTINESS
BITTING
BITTINGS
BITTOCK
BITTOCKS
BITTOR
BITTORS
BITTOUR
BITTOURS
BITTS
BITTUR
BITTURS
BITTY
BITUMED
BITUMEN
BITUMENS
BITURBO
BITURBOS
BITWISE
BIUNIQUE
BIVALENCE
BIVALENCY
BIVALENT
BIVALENTS
BIVALVATE
BIVALVE
BIVALVED
BIVALVES
BIVARIANT
BIVARIATE
BIVIA
BIVINYL
BIVINYLS
BIVIOUS
BIVIUM
BIVOUAC
BIVOUACKS
BIVOUACS
BIVVIED
BIVVIES
BIVVY
BIVVYING
BIWEEKLY
BIYEARLY
BIZ
BIZARRE
BIZARRELY
BIZARRES
BIZARRO
BIZARROS
BIZAZZ
BIZAZZES
BIZCACHA
BIZCACHAS
BIZE
BIZES
BIZJET
BIZJETS
BIZNAGA
BIZNAGAS
BIZONAL
BIZONE
BIZONES
BIZZAZZ
BIZZAZZES
BIZZES
BIZZIES
BIZZO
BIZZOS
BIZZY
BLAB
BLABBED
BLABBER
BLABBERED
BLABBERS
BLABBIER
BLABBIEST
BLABBING
BLABBINGS
BLABBY
BLABS
BLACK
BLACKBALL
BLACKBAND
BLACKBIRD
BLACKBODY
BLACKBOY
BLACKBOYS
BLACKBUCK
BLACKBUTT
BLACKCAP
BLACKCAPS
BLACKCOCK
BLACKDAMP
BLACKED
BLACKEN
BLACKENED
BLACKENER
BLACKENS
BLACKER
BLACKEST
BLACKFACE
BLACKFIN
BLACKFINS
BLACKFISH
BLACKFLY
BLACKGAME
BLACKGUM
BLACKGUMS
BLACKHEAD
BLACKING
BLACKINGS
BLACKISH
BLACKJACK
BLACKLAND
BLACKLEAD
BLACKLEG
BLACKLEGS
BLACKLIST
BLACKLY
BLACKMAIL
BLACKNESS
BLACKOUT
BLACKOUTS
BLACKPOLL
BLACKS
BLACKSPOT
BLACKTAIL
BLACKTIP
BLACKTIPS
BLACKTOP
BLACKTOPS
BLACKWASH
BLACKWOOD
BLAD
BLADDED
BLADDER
BLADDERED
BLADDERS
BLADDERY
BLADDING
BLADE
BLADED
BLADELESS
BLADELIKE
BLADER
BLADERS
BLADES
BLADEWORK
BLADIER
BLADIEST
BLADING
BLADINGS
BLADS
BLADY
BLAE
BLAEBERRY
BLAER
BLAES
BLAEST
BLAFF
BLAFFED
BLAFFING
BLAFFS
BLAG
BLAGGED
BLAGGER
BLAGGERS
BLAGGING
BLAGGINGS
BLAGS
BLAGUE
BLAGUER
BLAGUERS
BLAGUES
BLAGUEUR
BLAGUEURS
BLAH
BLAHED
BLAHER
BLAHEST
BLAHING
BLAHS
BLAIN
BLAINS
BLAISE
BLAIZE
BLAM
BLAMABLE
BLAMABLY
BLAME
BLAMEABLE
BLAMEABLY
BLAMED
BLAMEFUL
BLAMELESS
BLAMER
BLAMERS
BLAMES
BLAMING
BLAMMED
BLAMMING
BLAMS
BLANCH
BLANCHED
BLANCHER
BLANCHERS
BLANCHES
BLANCHING
BLANCO
BLANCOED
BLANCOING
BLANCOS
BLAND
BLANDED
BLANDER
BLANDEST
BLANDING
BLANDISH
BLANDLY

BLANDNESS
BLANDS
BLANK
BLANKED
BLANKER
BLANKEST
BLANKET
BLANKETED
BLANKETS
BLANKETY
BLANKIE
BLANKIES
BLANKING
BLANKINGS
BLANKLY
BLANKNESS
BLANKS
BLANKY
BLANQUET
BLANQUETS
BLARE
BLARED
BLARES
BLARING
BLARNEY
BLARNEYED
BLARNEYS
BLART
BLARTED
BLARTING
BLARTS
BLASE
BLASH
BLASHED
BLASHES
BLASHIER
BLASHIEST
BLASHING
BLASHY
BLASPHEME
BLASPHEMY
BLAST
BLASTED
BLASTEMA
BLASTEMAL
BLASTEMAS
BLASTEMIC
BLASTER
BLASTERS
BLASTHOLE
BLASTIE
BLASTIER
BLASTIES
BLASTIEST
BLASTING
BLASTINGS
BLASTMENT
BLASTOFF
BLASTOFFS
BLASTOID
BLASTOIDS
BLASTOMA
BLASTOMAS
BLASTOPOR
BLASTS
BLASTULA
BLASTULAE
BLASTULAR
BLASTULAS
BLASTY
BLAT
BLATANCY
BLATANT
BLATANTLY
BLATE
BLATED
BLATER
BLATES
BLATEST
BLATHER
BLATHERED
BLATHERER
BLATHERS
BLATING
BLATS
BLATT
BLATTANT
BLATTED
BLATTER
BLATTERED
BLATTERS
BLATTING
BLATTS
BLAUBOK
BLAUBOKS
BLAUD
BLAUDED
BLAUDING
BLAUDS
BLAW
BLAWED
BLAWING
BLAWN
BLAWORT
BLAWORTS
BLAWS
BLAY
BLAYS
BLAZAR
BLAZARS
BLAZE
BLAZED
BLAZER
BLAZERED
BLAZERS
BLAZES
BLAZING
BLAZINGLY
BLAZON
BLAZONED
BLAZONER
BLAZONERS
BLAZONING
BLAZONRY
BLAZONS
BLEACH
BLEACHED
BLEACHER
BLEACHERS
BLEACHERY
BLEACHES
BLEACHING
BLEAK
BLEAKER
BLEAKEST
BLEAKISH
BLEAKLY
BLEAKNESS
BLEAKS
BLEAKY
BLEAR
BLEARED
BLEARER
BLEAREST
BLEAREYED
BLEARIER
BLEARIEST
BLEARILY
BLEARING
BLEARS
BLEARY
BLEAT
BLEATED
BLEATER
BLEATERS
BLEATING
BLEATINGS
BLEATS
BLEB
BLEBBIER
BLEBBIEST
BLEBBING
BLEBBINGS
BLEBBY
BLEBS
BLECH
BLED
BLEE
BLEED
BLEEDER
BLEEDERS
BLEEDING
BLEEDINGS
BLEEDS
BLEEP
BLEEPED
BLEEPER
BLEEPERS
BLEEPING
BLEEPS
BLEES
BLELLUM
BLELLUMS
BLEMISH
BLEMISHED
BLEMISHER
BLEMISHES
BLENCH
BLENCHED
BLENCHER
BLENCHERS
BLENCHES
BLENCHING
BLEND
BLENDABLE
BLENDE
BLENDED
BLENDER
BLENDERS
BLENDES
BLENDING
BLENDINGS
BLENDS
BLENNIES
BLENNIOID
BLENNY
BLENT
BLEOMYCIN
BLERT
BLERTS
BLESBOK
BLESBOKS
BLESBUCK
BLESBUCKS
BLESS
BLESSED
BLESSEDER
BLESSEDLY
BLESSER
BLESSERS
BLESSES
BLESSING
BLESSINGS
BLEST
BLET
BLETHER
BLETHERED
BLETHERER
BLETHERS
BLETS
BLETTED
BLETTING
BLEUATRE
BLEW
BLEWART
BLEWARTS
BLEWIT
BLEWITS
BLEWITSES
BLEY

BLEYS
BLIGHT
BLIGHTED
BLIGHTER
BLIGHTERS
BLIGHTIES
BLIGHTING
BLIGHTS
BLIGHTY
BLIKSEM
BLIMBING
BLIMBINGS
BLIMEY
BLIMP
BLIMPED
BLIMPERY
BLIMPING
BLIMPISH
BLIMPS
BLIMY
BLIN
BLIND
BLINDAGE
BLINDAGES
BLINDED
BLINDER
BLINDERS
BLINDEST
BLINDFISH
BLINDFOLD
BLINDGUT
BLINDGUTS
BLINDING
BLINDINGS
BLINDLESS
BLINDLY
BLINDNESS
BLINDS
BLINDSIDE
BLINDWORM
BLING
BLINGED
BLINGER
BLINGEST
BLINGIER
BLINGIEST
BLINGING
BLINGLISH
BLINGS
BLINGY
BLINI
BLINIS
BLINK
BLINKARD
BLINKARDS
BLINKED
BLINKER
BLINKERED
BLINKERS
BLINKING
BLINKS
BLINNED
BLINNING
BLINS
BLINTZ
BLINTZE
BLINTZES
BLINY
BLIP
BLIPPED
BLIPPING
BLIPS
BLIPVERT
BLIPVERTS
BLISS
BLISSED
BLISSES
BLISSFUL
BLISSING
BLISSLESS
BLIST
BLISTER
BLISTERED
BLISTERS
BLISTERY
BLIT
BLITE
BLITES
BLITHE
BLITHEFUL
BLITHELY
BLITHER
BLITHERED
BLITHERS
BLITHEST
BLITS
BLITTED
BLITTER
BLITTERS
BLITTING
BLITZ
BLITZED
BLITZER
BLITZERS
BLITZES
BLITZING
BLIVE
BLIZZARD
BLIZZARDS
BLIZZARDY
BLOAT
BLOATED
BLOATER
BLOATERS
BLOATING
BLOATINGS
BLOATS
BLOATWARE
BLOB
BLOBBED
BLOBBIER
BLOBBIEST
BLOBBING
BLOBBY
BLOBS
BLOC
BLOCK
BLOCKABLE
BLOCKADE
BLOCKADED
BLOCKADER
BLOCKADES
BLOCKAGE
BLOCKAGES
BLOCKBUST
BLOCKED
BLOCKER
BLOCKERS
BLOCKHEAD
BLOCKHOLE
BLOCKIE
BLOCKIER
BLOCKIES
BLOCKIEST
BLOCKING
BLOCKINGS
BLOCKISH
BLOCKS
BLOCKSHIP
BLOCKWORK
BLOCKY
BLOCS
BLOG
BLOGGABLE
BLOGGED
BLOGGER
BLOGGERS
BLOGGIER
BLOGGIEST
BLOGGING
BLOGGINGS
BLOGGY
BLOGPOST
BLOGPOSTS
BLOGRING
BLOGRINGS
BLOGROLL
BLOGROLLS
BLOGS
BLOKART
BLOKARTS
BLOKE
BLOKEDOM
BLOKEDOMS
BLOKEISH
BLOKES
BLOKEY
BLOKIER
BLOKIEST
BLOKISH
BLONCKET
BLOND
BLONDE
BLONDER
BLONDES
BLONDEST
BLONDINE
BLONDINED
BLONDINES
BLONDING
BLONDINGS
BLONDISH
BLONDNESS
BLONDS
BLOOD
BLOODBATH
BLOODED
BLOODFIN
BLOODFINS
BLOODIED
BLOODIER
BLOODIES
BLOODIEST
BLOODILY
BLOODING
BLOODINGS
BLOODLESS
BLOODLIKE
BLOODLINE
BLOODLUST
BLOODRED
BLOODROOT
BLOODS
BLOODSHED
BLOODSHOT
BLOODWOOD
BLOODWORM
BLOODWORT
BLOODY
BLOODYING
BLOOEY
BLOOIE
BLOOK
BLOOKS
BLOOM
BLOOMED
BLOOMER
BLOOMERS
BLOOMERY
BLOOMIER
BLOOMIEST
BLOOMING
BLOOMINGS
BLOOMLESS
BLOOMS
BLOOMY
BLOOP
BLOOPED
BLOOPER
BLOOPERS

BLOOPIER
BLOOPIEST
BLOOPING
BLOOPS
BLOOPY
BLOOSME
BLOOSMED
BLOOSMES
BLOOSMING
BLOOTERED
BLOQUISTE
BLORE
BLORES
BLOSSOM
BLOSSOMED
BLOSSOMS
BLOSSOMY
BLOT
BLOTCH
BLOTCHED
BLOTCHES
BLOTCHIER
BLOTCHILY
BLOTCHING
BLOTCHY
BLOTLESS
BLOTS
BLOTTED
BLOTTER
BLOTTERS
BLOTTIER
BLOTTIEST
BLOTTING
BLOTTINGS
BLOTTO
BLOTTY
BLOUBOK
BLOUBOKS
BLOUSE
BLOUSED
BLOUSES
BLOUSIER
BLOUSIEST
BLOUSILY
BLOUSING
BLOUSON
BLOUSONS
BLOUSY
BLOVIATE
BLOVIATED
BLOVIATES
BLOW
BLOWBACK
BLOWBACKS
BLOWBALL
BLOWBALLS
BLOWBY
BLOWBYS
BLOWDART
BLOWDARTS
BLOWDOWN
BLOWDOWNS
BLOWED
BLOWER
BLOWERS
BLOWFISH
BLOWFLIES
BLOWFLY
BLOWGUN
BLOWGUNS
BLOWHARD
BLOWHARDS
BLOWHOLE
BLOWHOLES
BLOWIE
BLOWIER
BLOWIES
BLOWIEST
BLOWINESS
BLOWING
BLOWINGS
BLOWJOB
BLOWJOBS
BLOWKART
BLOWKARTS
BLOWLAMP
BLOWLAMPS
BLOWN
BLOWOFF
BLOWOFFS
BLOWOUT
BLOWOUTS
BLOWPIPE
BLOWPIPES
BLOWS
BLOWSE
BLOWSED
BLOWSES
BLOWSIER
BLOWSIEST
BLOWSILY
BLOWSY
BLOWTORCH
BLOWTUBE
BLOWTUBES
BLOWUP
BLOWUPS
BLOWY
BLOWZE
BLOWZED
BLOWZES
BLOWZIER
BLOWZIEST
BLOWZILY
BLOWZY
BLUB
BLUBBED
BLUBBER
BLUBBERED
BLUBBERER
BLUBBERS
BLUBBERY
BLUBBING
BLUBS
BLUCHER
BLUCHERS
BLUD
BLUDE
BLUDES
BLUDGE
BLUDGED
BLUDGEON
BLUDGEONS
BLUDGER
BLUDGERS
BLUDGES
BLUDGING
BLUDIE
BLUDIER
BLUDIEST
BLUDS
BLUDY
BLUE
BLUEBACK
BLUEBACKS
BLUEBALL
BLUEBALLS
BLUEBEARD
BLUEBEAT
BLUEBEATS
BLUEBELL
BLUEBELLS
BLUEBERRY
BLUEBILL
BLUEBILLS
BLUEBIRD
BLUEBIRDS
BLUEBLOOD
BLUEBOOK
BLUEBOOKS
BLUEBUCK
BLUEBUCKS
BLUEBUSH
BLUECAP
BLUECAPS
BLUECOAT
BLUECOATS
BLUECURLS
BLUED
BLUEFIN
BLUEFINS
BLUEFISH
BLUEGILL
BLUEGILLS
BLUEGOWN
BLUEGOWNS
BLUEGRASS
BLUEGUM
BLUEGUMS
BLUEHEAD
BLUEHEADS
BLUEING
BLUEINGS
BLUEISH
BLUEJACK
BLUEJACKS
BLUEJAY
BLUEJAYS
BLUEJEANS
BLUELINE
BLUELINER
BLUELINES
BLUELY
BLUEMOUTH
BLUENESS
BLUENOSE
BLUENOSED
BLUENOSES
BLUEPOINT
BLUEPRINT
BLUER
BLUES
BLUESHIFT
BLUESIER
BLUESIEST
BLUESMAN
BLUESMEN
BLUEST
BLUESTEM
BLUESTEMS
BLUESTONE
BLUESY
BLUET
BLUETICK
BLUETICKS
BLUETIT
BLUETITS
BLUETS
BLUETTE
BLUETTES
BLUEWEED
BLUEWEEDS
BLUEWING
BLUEWINGS
BLUEWOOD
BLUEWOODS
BLUEY
BLUEYS
BLUFF
BLUFFABLE
BLUFFED
BLUFFER
BLUFFERS
BLUFFEST
BLUFFING
BLUFFLY
BLUFFNESS
BLUFFS
BLUGGIER
BLUGGIEST

BLUGGY
BLUID
BLUIDIER
BLUIDIEST
BLUIDS
BLUIDY
BLUIER
BLUIEST
BLUING
BLUINGS
BLUISH
BLUME
BLUMED
BLUMES
BLUMING
BLUNDER
BLUNDERED
BLUNDERER
BLUNDERS
BLUNGE
BLUNGED
BLUNGER
BLUNGERS
BLUNGES
BLUNGING
BLUNK
BLUNKED
BLUNKER
BLUNKERS
BLUNKING
BLUNKS
BLUNT
BLUNTED
BLUNTER
BLUNTEST
BLUNTHEAD
BLUNTING
BLUNTISH
BLUNTLY
BLUNTNESS
BLUNTS
BLUR
BLURB
BLURBED
BLURBING
BLURBIST
BLURBISTS
BLURBS
BLURRED
BLURREDLY
BLURRIER
BLURRIEST
BLURRILY
BLURRING
BLURRY
BLURS
BLURT
BLURTED
BLURTER
BLURTERS
BLURTING
BLURTINGS
BLURTS
BLUSH
BLUSHED
BLUSHER
BLUSHERS
BLUSHES
BLUSHET
BLUSHETS
BLUSHFUL
BLUSHING
BLUSHINGS
BLUSHLESS
BLUSTER
BLUSTERED
BLUSTERER
BLUSTERS
BLUSTERY
BLUSTROUS
BLUTWURST
BLYPE
BLYPES
BO
BOA
BOAB
BOABS
BOAK
BOAKED
BOAKING
BOAKS
BOAR
BOARD
BOARDABLE
BOARDED
BOARDER
BOARDERS
BOARDIES
BOARDING
BOARDINGS
BOARDLIKE
BOARDMAN
BOARDMEN
BOARDROOM
BOARDS
BOARDWALK
BOARFISH
BOARHOUND
BOARISH
BOARISHLY
BOARS
BOART
BOARTS
BOAS
BOAST
BOASTED
BOASTER
BOASTERS
BOASTFUL
BOASTING
BOASTINGS
BOASTLESS
BOASTS
BOAT
BOATABLE
BOATBILL
BOATBILLS
BOATED
BOATEL
BOATELS
BOATER
BOATERS
BOATFUL
BOATFULS
BOATHOOK
BOATHOOKS
BOATHOUSE
BOATIE
BOATIES
BOATING
BOATINGS
BOATLIFT
BOATLIFTS
BOATLIKE
BOATLOAD
BOATLOADS
BOATMAN
BOATMEN
BOATNECK
BOATNECKS
BOATPORT
BOATPORTS
BOATS
BOATSMAN
BOATSMEN
BOATSWAIN
BOATTAIL
BOATTAILS
BOATYARD
BOATYARDS
BOB
BOBA
BOBAC
BOBACS
BOBAK
BOBAKS
BOBAS
BOBBED
BOBBEJAAN
BOBBER
BOBBERIES
BOBBERS
BOBBERY
BOBBIES
BOBBIN
BOBBINET
BOBBINETS
BOBBING
BOBBINS
BOBBISH
BOBBITT
BOBBITTED
BOBBITTS
BOBBLE
BOBBLED
BOBBLES
BOBBLIER
BOBBLIEST
BOBBLING
BOBBLY
BOBBY
BOBBYSOCK
BOBBYSOX
BOBCAT
BOBCATS
BOBECHE
BOBECHES
BOBFLOAT
BOBFLOATS
BOBLET
BOBLETS
BOBO
BOBOL
BOBOLINK
BOBOLINKS
BOBOLLED
BOBOLLING
BOBOLS
BOBOS
BOBOTIE
BOBOTIES
BOBOWLER
BOBOWLERS
BOBS
BOBSKATE
BOBSKATES
BOBSLED
BOBSLEDS
BOBSLEIGH
BOBSTAY
BOBSTAYS
BOBTAIL
BOBTAILED
BOBTAILS
BOBWEIGHT
BOBWHEEL
BOBWHEELS
BOBWHITE
BOBWHITES
BOBWIG
BOBWIGS
BOCACCIO
BOCACCIOS
BOCAGE
BOCAGES
BOCCA
BOCCAS
BOCCE
BOCCES
BOCCI

BOCCIA
BOCCIAS
BOCCIE
BOCCIES
BOCCIS
BOCK
BOCKED
BOCKEDY
BOCKING
BOCKS
BOCONCINI
BOD
BODACH
BODACHS
BODACIOUS
BODDLE
BODDLES
BODE
BODED
BODEFUL
BODEGA
BODEGAS
BODEGUERO
BODEMENT
BODEMENTS
BODES
BODGE
BODGED
BODGER
BODGERS
BODGES
BODGIE
BODGIER
BODGIES
BODGIEST
BODGING
BODHI
BODHIS
BODHRAN
BODHRANS
BODICE
BODICES
BODIED
BODIES
BODIKIN
BODIKINS
BODILESS
BODILY
BODING
BODINGLY
BODINGS
BODKIN
BODKINS
BODLE
BODLES
BODRAG
BODRAGS
BODS
BODY
BODYBOARD
BODYBUILD
BODYBUILT
BODYCHECK
BODYGUARD
BODYING
BODYLINE
BODYLINES
BODYMAN
BODYMEN
BODYSHELL
BODYSIDE
BODYSIDES
BODYSUIT
BODYSUITS
BODYSURF
BODYSURFS
BODYWASH
BODYWORK
BODYWORKS
BOEHMITE
BOEHMITES
BOEP
BOEPS
BOERBUL
BOERBULL
BOERBULLS
BOERBULS
BOEREWORS
BOERTJIE
BOERTJIES
BOET
BOETS
BOEUF
BOEUFS
BOFF
BOFFED
BOFFIN
BOFFING
BOFFINIER
BOFFINS
BOFFINY
BOFFO
BOFFOLA
BOFFOLAS
BOFFOS
BOFFS
BOG
BOGAN
BOGANS
BOGART
BOGARTED
BOGARTING
BOGARTS
BOGBEAN
BOGBEANS
BOGEY
BOGEYED
BOGEYING
BOGEYISM
BOGEYISMS
BOGEYMAN
BOGEYMEN
BOGEYS
BOGGARD
BOGGARDS
BOGGART
BOGGARTS
BOGGED
BOGGER
BOGGERS
BOGGIER
BOGGIEST
BOGGINESS
BOGGING
BOGGISH
BOGGLE
BOGGLED
BOGGLER
BOGGLERS
BOGGLES
BOGGLING
BOGGY
BOGHEAD
BOGHOLE
BOGHOLES
BOGIE
BOGIED
BOGIEING
BOGIES
BOGLAND
BOGLANDS
BOGLE
BOGLED
BOGLES
BOGLING
BOGMAN
BOGMEN
BOGOAK
BOGOAKS
BOGONG
BOGONGS
BOGS
BOGUE
BOGUES
BOGUS
BOGUSLY
BOGUSNESS
BOGWOOD
BOGWOODS
BOGY
BOGYISM
BOGYISMS
BOGYMAN
BOGYMEN
BOH
BOHEA
BOHEAS
BOHEMIA
BOHEMIAN
BOHEMIANS
BOHEMIAS
BOHO
BOHOS
BOHRIUM
BOHRIUMS
BOHS
BOI
BOIL
BOILABLE
BOILED
BOILER
BOILERIES
BOILERMAN
BOILERMEN
BOILERS
BOILERY
BOILING
BOILINGLY
BOILINGS
BOILOFF
BOILOFFS
BOILOVER
BOILOVERS
BOILS
BOING
BOINGED
BOINGING
BOINGS
BOINK
BOINKED
BOINKING
BOINKS
BOIS
BOISERIE
BOISERIES
BOITE
BOITES
BOK
BOKE
BOKED
BOKEH
BOKEHS
BOKES
BOKING
BOKKEN
BOKKENS
BOKO
BOKOS
BOKS
BOLA
BOLAR
BOLAS
BOLASES
BOLD
BOLDED
BOLDEN
BOLDENED
BOLDENING
BOLDENS
BOLDER

BOLDEST
BOLDFACE
BOLDFACED
BOLDFACES
BOLDING
BOLDLY
BOLDNESS
BOLDS
BOLE
BOLECTION
BOLERO
BOLEROS
BOLES
BOLETE
BOLETES
BOLETI
BOLETUS
BOLETUSES
BOLIDE
BOLIDES
BOLINE
BOLINES
BOLIVAR
BOLIVARES
BOLIVARS
BOLIVIA
BOLIVIANO
BOLIVIAS
BOLIX
BOLIXED
BOLIXES
BOLIXING
BOLL
BOLLARD
BOLLARDS
BOLLED
BOLLEN
BOLLETRIE
BOLLING
BOLLIX
BOLLIXED
BOLLIXES
BOLLIXING
BOLLOCK
BOLLOCKED
BOLLOCKS
BOLLOX
BOLLOXED
BOLLOXES
BOLLOXING
BOLLS
BOLLWORM
BOLLWORMS
BOLO
BOLOGNA
BOLOGNAS
BOLOGNESE
BOLOGRAPH
BOLOMETER
BOLOMETRY
BOLONEY
BOLONEYS
BOLOS
BOLSHEVIK
BOLSHIE
BOLSHIER
BOLSHIES
BOLSHIEST
BOLSHY
BOLSON
BOLSONS
BOLSTER
BOLSTERED
BOLSTERER
BOLSTERS
BOLT
BOLTED
BOLTER
BOLTERS
BOLTHEAD
BOLTHEADS
BOLTHOLE
BOLTHOLES
BOLTING
BOLTINGS
BOLTLESS
BOLTLIKE
BOLTONIA
BOLTONIAS
BOLTROPE
BOLTROPES
BOLTS
BOLUS
BOLUSES
BOMA
BOMAS
BOMB
BOMBABLE
BOMBARD
BOMBARDE
BOMBARDED
BOMBARDER
BOMBARDES
BOMBARDON
BOMBARDS
BOMBASINE
BOMBAST
BOMBASTED
BOMBASTER
BOMBASTIC
BOMBASTS
BOMBAX
BOMBAXES
BOMBAZINE
BOMBE
BOMBED
BOMBER
BOMBERS
BOMBES
BOMBESIN
BOMBESINS
BOMBILATE
BOMBINATE
BOMBING
BOMBINGS
BOMBLET
BOMBLETS
BOMBLOAD
BOMBLOADS
BOMBO
BOMBORA
BOMBORAS
BOMBOS
BOMBPROOF
BOMBS
BOMBSHELL
BOMBSIGHT
BOMBSITE
BOMBSITES
BOMBYCID
BOMBYCIDS
BOMBYCOID
BOMBYX
BOMBYXES
BOMMIE
BOMMIES
BON
BONA
BONACI
BONACIS
BONAMANI
BONAMANO
BONAMIA
BONAMIAS
BONANZA
BONANZAS
BONASSUS
BONASUS
BONASUSES
BONBON
BONBONS
BONCE
BONCES
BOND
BONDABLE
BONDAGE
BONDAGER
BONDAGERS
BONDAGES
BONDED
BONDER
BONDERS
BONDING
BONDINGS
BONDLESS
BONDMAID
BONDMAIDS
BONDMAN
BONDMEN
BONDS
BONDSMAN
BONDSMEN
BONDSTONE
BONDUC
BONDUCS
BONDWOMAN
BONDWOMEN
BONE
BONEBED
BONEBEDS
BONEBLACK
BONED
BONEFISH
BONEHEAD
BONEHEADS
BONELESS
BONELIKE
BONEMEAL
BONEMEALS
BONER
BONERS
BONES
BONESET
BONESETS
BONETIRED
BONEY
BONEYARD
BONEYARDS
BONEYER
BONEYEST
BONFIRE
BONFIRES
BONG
BONGED
BONGING
BONGO
BONGOES
BONGOIST
BONGOISTS
BONGOS
BONGRACE
BONGRACES
BONGS
BONHAM
BONHAMS
BONHOMIE
BONHOMIES
BONHOMMIE
BONHOMOUS
BONIATO
BONIATOS
BONIBELL
BONIBELLS
BONIE
BONIER
BONIEST
BONIFACE
BONIFACES
BONILASSE
BONINESS

B

BONING
BONINGS
BONISM
BONISMS
BONIST
BONISTS
BONITA
BONITAS
BONITO
BONITOES
BONITOS
BONJOUR
BONK
BONKED
BONKERS
BONKING
BONKINGS
BONKS
BONNE
BONNES
BONNET
BONNETED
BONNETING
BONNETS
BONNIBELL
BONNIE
BONNIER
BONNIES
BONNIEST
BONNILY
BONNINESS
BONNOCK
BONNOCKS
BONNY
BONOBO
BONOBOS
BONSAI
BONSELA
BONSELAS
BONSELLA
BONSELLAS
BONSOIR
BONSPELL
BONSPELLS
BONSPIEL
BONSPIELS
BONTBOK
BONTBOKS
BONTEBOK
BONTEBOKS
BONUS
BONUSED
BONUSES
BONUSING
BONUSINGS
BONUSSED
BONUSSES
BONUSSING
BONXIE
BONXIES
BONY
BONZA
BONZE
BONZER
BONZES
BOO
BOOAI
BOOAIS
BOOAY
BOOAYS
BOOB
BOOBED
BOOBHEAD
BOOBHEADS
BOOBIALLA
BOOBIE
BOOBIES
BOOBING
BOOBIRD
BOOBIRDS
BOOBISH
BOOBOISIE
BOOBOO
BOOBOOK
BOOBOOKS
BOOBOOS
BOOBS
BOOBY
BOOBYISH
BOOBYISM
BOOBYISMS
BOOCOO
BOOCOOS
BOODIE
BOODIED
BOODIES
BOODLE
BOODLED
BOODLER
BOODLERS
BOODLES
BOODLING
BOODY
BOODYING
BOOED
BOOFHEAD
BOOFHEADS
BOOFIER
BOOFIEST
BOOFY
BOOGALOO
BOOGALOOS
BOOGER
BOOGERMAN
BOOGERMEN
BOOGERS
BOOGEY
BOOGEYED
BOOGEYING
BOOGEYMAN
BOOGEYMEN
BOOGEYS
BOOGIE
BOOGIED
BOOGIEING
BOOGIEMAN
BOOGIEMEN
BOOGIES
BOOGY
BOOGYING
BOOGYMAN
BOOGYMEN
BOOH
BOOHAI
BOOHAIS
BOOHED
BOOHING
BOOHOO
BOOHOOED
BOOHOOING
BOOHOOS
BOOHS
BOOING
BOOINGS
BOOJUM
BOOJUMS
BOOK
BOOKABLE
BOOKBAG
BOOKBAGS
BOOKCASE
BOOKCASES
BOOKED
BOOKEND
BOOKENDED
BOOKENDS
BOOKER
BOOKERS
BOOKFUL
BOOKFULS
BOOKIE
BOOKIER
BOOKIES
BOOKIEST
BOOKING
BOOKINGS
BOOKISH
BOOKISHLY
BOOKLAND
BOOKLANDS
BOOKLESS
BOOKLET
BOOKLETS
BOOKLICE
BOOKLIGHT
BOOKLIKE
BOOKLORE
BOOKLORES
BOOKLOUSE
BOOKMAKER
BOOKMAN
BOOKMARK
BOOKMARKS
BOOKMEN
BOOKOO
BOOKOOS
BOOKPLATE
BOOKRACK
BOOKRACKS
BOOKREST
BOOKRESTS
BOOKS
BOOKSHELF
BOOKSHOP
BOOKSHOPS
BOOKSIE
BOOKSIER
BOOKSIEST
BOOKSTALL
BOOKSTAND
BOOKSTORE
BOOKSY
BOOKWORK
BOOKWORKS
BOOKWORM
BOOKWORMS
BOOKY
BOOL
BOOLED
BOOLING
BOOLS
BOOM
BOOMBOX
BOOMBOXES
BOOMBURB
BOOMBURBS
BOOMED
BOOMER
BOOMERANG
BOOMERS
BOOMIER
BOOMIEST
BOOMING
BOOMINGLY
BOOMINGS
BOOMKIN
BOOMKINS
BOOMLET
BOOMLETS
BOOMS
BOOMSLANG
BOOMSTICK
BOOMTOWN
BOOMTOWNS
BOOMY
BOON
BOONDOCK
BOONDOCKS
BOONER
BOONERS

BOONEST
BOONGARY
BOONIES
BOONLESS
BOONS
BOOR
BOORD
BOORDE
BOORDES
BOORDS
BOORISH
BOORISHLY
BOORKA
BOORKAS
BOORS
BOORTREE
BOORTREES
BOOS
BOOSE
BOOSED
BOOSES
BOOSHIT
BOOSING
BOOST
BOOSTED
BOOSTER
BOOSTERS
BOOSTING
BOOSTS
BOOT
BOOTABLE
BOOTBLACK
BOOTCUT
BOOTED
BOOTEE
BOOTEES
BOOTERIES
BOOTERY
BOOTH
BOOTHOSE
BOOTHS
BOOTIE
BOOTIES
BOOTIKIN
BOOTIKINS
BOOTING
BOOTJACK
BOOTJACKS
BOOTLACE
BOOTLACES
BOOTLAST
BOOTLASTS
BOOTLEG
BOOTLEGS
BOOTLESS
BOOTLICK
BOOTLICKS
BOOTMAKER
BOOTS
BOOTSTRAP
BOOTY
BOOZE
BOOZED
BOOZER
BOOZERS
BOOZES
BOOZEY
BOOZIER
BOOZIEST
BOOZILY
BOOZINESS
BOOZING
BOOZINGS
BOOZY
BOP
BOPEEP
BOPEEPS
BOPPED
BOPPER
BOPPERS
BOPPIER
BOPPIEST
BOPPING
BOPPISH
BOPPY
BOPS
BOR
BORA
BORACES
BORACHIO
BORACHIOS
BORACIC
BORACITE
BORACITES
BORAGE
BORAGES
BORAK
BORAKS
BORAL
BORALS
BORANE
BORANES
BORAS
BORATE
BORATED
BORATES
BORATING
BORAX
BORAXES
BORAZON
BORAZONS
BORD
BORDAR
BORDARS
BORDE
BORDEAUX
BORDEL
BORDELLO
BORDELLOS
BORDELS
BORDER
BORDEREAU
BORDERED
BORDERER
BORDERERS
BORDERING
BORDERS
BORDES
BORDS
BORDURE
BORDURES
BORE
BOREAL
BOREALIS
BOREAS
BOREASES
BORECOLE
BORECOLES
BORED
BOREDOM
BOREDOMS
BOREE
BOREEN
BOREENS
BOREES
BOREHOLE
BOREHOLES
BOREL
BORELS
BORER
BORERS
BORES
BORESCOPE
BORESOME
BORGHETTO
BORGO
BORGOS
BORIC
BORIDE
BORIDES
BORING
BORINGLY
BORINGS
BORK
BORKED
BORKING
BORKINGS
BORKS
BORLOTTI
BORM
BORMED
BORMING
BORMS
BORN
BORNA
BORNE
BORNEOL
BORNEOLS
BORNITE
BORNITES
BORNITIC
BORNYL
BORNYLS
BORON
BORONIA
BORONIAS
BORONIC
BORONS
BOROUGH
BOROUGHS
BORREL
BORRELIA
BORRELIAS
BORRELL
BORROW
BORROWED
BORROWER
BORROWERS
BORROWING
BORROWS
BORS
BORSCH
BORSCHES
BORSCHT
BORSCHTS
BORSHCH
BORSHCHES
BORSHT
BORSHTS
BORSIC
BORSICS
BORSTAL
BORSTALL
BORSTALLS
BORSTALS
BORT
BORTIER
BORTIEST
BORTS
BORTSCH
BORTSCHES
BORTY
BORTZ
BORTZES
BORZOI
BORZOIS
BOS
BOSBERAAD
BOSBOK
BOSBOKS
BOSCAGE
BOSCAGES
BOSCHBOK
BOSCHBOKS
BOSCHVARK
BOSCHVELD
BOSH
BOSHBOK
BOSHBOKS
BOSHES

B

BOSHTA
BOSHTER
BOSHVARK
BOSHVARKS
BOSIE
BOSIES
BOSK
BOSKAGE
BOSKAGES
BOSKER
BOSKET
BOSKETS
BOSKIER
BOSKIEST
BOSKINESS
BOSKS
BOSKY
BOSOM
BOSOMED
BOSOMIER
BOSOMIEST
BOSOMING
BOSOMS
BOSOMY
BOSON
BOSONIC
BOSONS
BOSQUE
BOSQUES
BOSQUET
BOSQUETS
BOSS
BOSSDOM
BOSSDOMS
BOSSED
BOSSER
BOSSES
BOSSEST
BOSSET
BOSSETS
BOSSIER
BOSSIES
BOSSIEST
BOSSILY
BOSSINESS
BOSSING
BOSSINGS
BOSSISM
BOSSISMS
BOSSY
BOSTANGI
BOSTANGIS
BOSTHOON
BOSTHOONS
BOSTON
BOSTONS
BOSTRYX
BOSTRYXES
BOSUN
BOSUNS
BOT
BOTA
BOTANIC
BOTANICA
BOTANICAL
BOTANICAS
BOTANICS
BOTANIES
BOTANISE
BOTANISED
BOTANISER
BOTANISES
BOTANIST
BOTANISTS
BOTANIZE
BOTANIZED
BOTANIZER
BOTANIZES
BOTANY
BOTARGO
BOTARGOES
BOTARGOS
BOTAS
BOTCH
BOTCHED
BOTCHEDLY
BOTCHER
BOTCHERS
BOTCHERY
BOTCHES
BOTCHIER
BOTCHIEST
BOTCHILY
BOTCHING
BOTCHINGS
BOTCHY
BOTE
BOTEL
BOTELS
BOTES
BOTFLIES
BOTFLY
BOTH
BOTHAN
BOTHANS
BOTHER
BOTHERED
BOTHERING
BOTHERS
BOTHIE
BOTHIES
BOTHOLE
BOTHOLES
BOTHRIA
BOTHRIUM
BOTHRIUMS
BOTHY
BOTHYMAN
BOTHYMEN
BOTNET
BOTNETS
BOTONE
BOTONEE
BOTONNEE
BOTOXED
BOTRYOID
BOTRYOSE
BOTRYTIS
BOTS
BOTT
BOTTARGA
BOTTARGAS
BOTTE
BOTTED
BOTTEGA
BOTTEGAS
BOTTES
BOTTIES
BOTTINE
BOTTINES
BOTTING
BOTTLE
BOTTLED
BOTTLEFUL
BOTTLER
BOTTLERS
BOTTLES
BOTTLING
BOTTLINGS
BOTTOM
BOTTOMED
BOTTOMER
BOTTOMERS
BOTTOMING
BOTTOMRY
BOTTOMS
BOTTOMSET
BOTTONY
BOTTS
BOTTY
BOTULIN
BOTULINAL
BOTULINS
BOTULINUM
BOTULINUS
BOTULISM
BOTULISMS
BOUBOU
BOUBOUS
BOUCHE
BOUCHEE
BOUCHEES
BOUCHES
BOUCLE
BOUCLEE
BOUCLEES
BOUCLES
BOUDERIE
BOUDERIES
BOUDIN
BOUDINS
BOUDOIR
BOUDOIRS
BOUFFANT
BOUFFANTS
BOUFFE
BOUFFES
BOUGE
BOUGED
BOUGES
BOUGET
BOUGETS
BOUGH
BOUGHED
BOUGHLESS
BOUGHPOT
BOUGHPOTS
BOUGHS
BOUGHT
BOUGHTEN
BOUGHTS
BOUGIE
BOUGIES
BOUGING
BOUILLI
BOUILLIS
BOUILLON
BOUILLONS
BOUK
BOUKS
BOULDER
BOULDERED
BOULDERER
BOULDERS
BOULDERY
BOULE
BOULES
BOULEVARD
BOULLE
BOULLES
BOULT
BOULTED
BOULTER
BOULTERS
BOULTING
BOULTINGS
BOULTS
BOUN
BOUNCE
BOUNCED
BOUNCER
BOUNCERS
BOUNCES
BOUNCIER
BOUNCIEST
BOUNCILY
BOUNCING
BOUNCY
BOUND
BOUNDABLE

BOUNDARY
BOUNDED
BOUNDEN
BOUNDER
BOUNDERS
BOUNDING
BOUNDLESS
BOUNDNESS
BOUNDS
BOUNED
BOUNING
BOUNS
BOUNTEOUS
BOUNTIED
BOUNTIES
BOUNTIFUL
BOUNTREE
BOUNTREES
BOUNTY
BOUNTYHED
BOUQUET
BOUQUETS
BOURASQUE
BOURBON
BOURBONS
BOURD
BOURDED
BOURDER
BOURDERS
BOURDING
BOURDON
BOURDONS
BOURDS
BOURG
BOURGEOIS
BOURGEON
BOURGEONS
BOURGS
BOURKHA
BOURKHAS
BOURLAW
BOURLAWS
BOURN
BOURNE
BOURNES
BOURNS
BOURREE
BOURREES
BOURRIDE
BOURRIDES
BOURSE
BOURSES
BOURSIER
BOURSIERS
BOURSIN
BOURSINS
BOURTREE
BOURTREES
BOUSE
BOUSED
BOUSES
BOUSIER
BOUSIEST
BOUSING
BOUSOUKI
BOUSOUKIA
BOUSOUKIS
BOUSY
BOUT
BOUTADE
BOUTADES
BOUTIQUE
BOUTIQUES
BOUTIQUEY
BOUTON
BOUTONNE
BOUTONNEE
BOUTONS
BOUTS
BOUVARDIA
BOUVIER
BOUVIERS
BOUZOUKI
BOUZOUKIA
BOUZOUKIS
BOVATE
BOVATES
BOVID
BOVIDS
BOVINE
BOVINELY
BOVINES
BOVINITY
BOVVER
BOVVERS
BOW
BOWAT
BOWATS
BOWBENT
BOWED
BOWEL
BOWELED
BOWELING
BOWELLED
BOWELLESS
BOWELLING
BOWELS
BOWER
BOWERBIRD
BOWERED
BOWERIES
BOWERING
BOWERS
BOWERY
BOWES
BOWET
BOWETS
BOWFIN
BOWFINS
BOWFRONT
BOWGET
BOWGETS
BOWHEAD
BOWHEADS
BOWHUNT
BOWHUNTED
BOWHUNTER
BOWHUNTS
BOWIE
BOWING
BOWINGLY
BOWINGS
BOWKNOT
BOWKNOTS
BOWL
BOWLDER
BOWLDERS
BOWLED
BOWLEG
BOWLEGGED
BOWLEGS
BOWLER
BOWLERS
BOWLESS
BOWLFUL
BOWLFULS
BOWLIKE
BOWLINE
BOWLINES
BOWLING
BOWLINGS
BOWLLIKE
BOWLS
BOWMAN
BOWMEN
BOWNE
BOWNED
BOWNES
BOWNING
BOWPOT
BOWPOTS
BOWR
BOWRS
BOWS
BOWSAW
BOWSAWS
BOWSE
BOWSED
BOWSER
BOWSERS
BOWSES
BOWSEY
BOWSEYS
BOWSHOT
BOWSHOTS
BOWSIE
BOWSIES
BOWSING
BOWSMAN
BOWSMEN
BOWSPRIT
BOWSPRITS
BOWSTRING
BOWSTRUNG
BOWWOOD
BOWWOODS
BOWWOW
BOWWOWED
BOWWOWING
BOWWOWS
BOWYANG
BOWYANGS
BOWYER
BOWYERS
BOX
BOXBALL
BOXBALLS
BOXBERRY
BOXBOARD
BOXBOARDS
BOXCAR
BOXCARS
BOXED
BOXEN
BOXER
BOXERCISE
BOXERS
BOXES
BOXFISH
BOXFISHES
BOXFUL
BOXFULS
BOXHAUL
BOXHAULED
BOXHAULS
BOXIER
BOXIEST
BOXILY
BOXINESS
BOXING
BOXINGS
BOXKEEPER
BOXLA
BOXLAS
BOXLIKE
BOXPLOT
BOXPLOTS
BOXROOM
BOXROOMS
BOXTHORN
BOXTHORNS
BOXTIES
BOXTY
BOXWALLAH
BOXWOOD
BOXWOODS
BOXY
BOY
BOYAR
BOYARD

BOYARDS
BOYARISM
BOYARISMS
BOYARS
BOYAU
BOYAUX
BOYCHICK
BOYCHICKS
BOYCHIK
BOYCHIKS
BOYCOTT
BOYCOTTED
BOYCOTTER
BOYCOTTS
BOYED
BOYF
BOYFRIEND
BOYFS
BOYG
BOYGS
BOYHOOD
BOYHOODS
BOYING
BOYISH
BOYISHLY
BOYKIE
BOYKIES
BOYLA
BOYLAS
BOYO
BOYOS
BOYS
BOYSHORTS
BOYSIER
BOYSIEST
BOYSY
BOZO
BOZOS
BOZZETTI
BOZZETTO
BRA
BRAAI
BRAAIED
BRAAIING
BRAAIS
BRAATA
BRAATAS
BRAATASES
BRABBLE
BRABBLED
BRABBLER
BRABBLERS
BRABBLES
BRABBLING
BRACCATE
BRACCIA
BRACCIO
BRACE
BRACED
BRACELET
BRACELETS
BRACER
BRACERO
BRACEROS
BRACERS
BRACES
BRACH
BRACHAH
BRACHAHS
BRACHES
BRACHET
BRACHETS
BRACHIA
BRACHIAL
BRACHIALS
BRACHIATE
BRACHIUM
BRACHIUMS
BRACHOT
BRACHS
BRACING
BRACINGLY
BRACINGS
BRACIOLA
BRACIOLAS
BRACIOLE
BRACIOLES
BRACK
BRACKEN
BRACKENS
BRACKET
BRACKETED
BRACKETS
BRACKISH
BRACKS
BRACONID
BRACONIDS
BRACT
BRACTEAL
BRACTEATE
BRACTED
BRACTEOLE
BRACTLESS
BRACTLET
BRACTLETS
BRACTS
BRAD
BRADAWL
BRADAWLS
BRADDED
BRADDING
BRADOON
BRADOONS
BRADS
BRAE
BRAEHEID
BRAEHEIDS
BRAES
BRAG
BRAGGART
BRAGGARTS
BRAGGED
BRAGGER
BRAGGERS
BRAGGEST
BRAGGIER
BRAGGIEST
BRAGGING
BRAGGINGS
BRAGGY
BRAGLY
BRAGS
BRAHMA
BRAHMAN
BRAHMANI
BRAHMANIS
BRAHMANS
BRAHMAS
BRAHMIN
BRAHMINS
BRAID
BRAIDE
BRAIDED
BRAIDER
BRAIDERS
BRAIDEST
BRAIDING
BRAIDINGS
BRAIDS
BRAIL
BRAILED
BRAILING
BRAILLE
BRAILLED
BRAILLER
BRAILLERS
BRAILLES
BRAILLING
BRAILLIST
BRAILS
BRAIN
BRAINBOX
BRAINCASE
BRAINDEAD
BRAINED
BRAINFART
BRAINFOOD
BRAINIAC
BRAINIACS
BRAINIER
BRAINIEST
BRAINILY
BRAINING
BRAINISH
BRAINLESS
BRAINPAN
BRAINPANS
BRAINS
BRAINSICK
BRAINSTEM
BRAINWASH
BRAINWAVE
BRAINWORK
BRAINY
BRAIRD
BRAIRDED
BRAIRDING
BRAIRDS
BRAISE
BRAISED
BRAISES
BRAISING
BRAIZE
BRAIZES
BRAK
BRAKE
BRAKEAGE
BRAKEAGES
BRAKED
BRAKELESS
BRAKEMAN
BRAKEMEN
BRAKES
BRAKESMAN
BRAKESMEN
BRAKIER
BRAKIEST
BRAKING
BRAKINGS
BRAKS
BRAKY
BRALESS
BRAMBLE
BRAMBLED
BRAMBLES
BRAMBLIER
BRAMBLING
BRAMBLY
BRAME
BRAMES
BRAN
BRANCARD
BRANCARDS
BRANCH
BRANCHED
BRANCHER
BRANCHERS
BRANCHERY
BRANCHES
BRANCHIA
BRANCHIAE
BRANCHIAL
BRANCHIER
BRANCHING
BRANCHLET
BRANCHY
BRAND
BRANDADE
BRANDADES
BRANDED

BRANDER
BRANDERED
BRANDERS
BRANDIED
BRANDIES
BRANDING
BRANDINGS
BRANDISE
BRANDISES
BRANDISH
BRANDLESS
BRANDLING
BRANDRETH
BRANDS
BRANDY
BRANDYING
BRANE
BRANES
BRANGLE
BRANGLED
BRANGLES
BRANGLING
BRANK
BRANKED
BRANKIER
BRANKIEST
BRANKING
BRANKS
BRANKY
BRANLE
BRANLES
BRANNED
BRANNER
BRANNERS
BRANNIER
BRANNIEST
BRANNIGAN
BRANNING
BRANNY
BRANS
BRANSLE
BRANSLES
BRANT
BRANTAIL
BRANTAILS
BRANTLE
BRANTLES
BRANTS
BRAP
BRAS
BRASCO
BRASCOS
BRASERO
BRASEROS
BRASES
BRASH
BRASHED
BRASHER
BRASHES
BRASHEST
BRASHIER
BRASHIEST
BRASHING
BRASHLY
BRASHNESS
BRASHY
BRASIER
BRASIERS
BRASIL
BRASILEIN
BRASILIN
BRASILINS
BRASILS
BRASS
BRASSAGE
BRASSAGES
BRASSARD
BRASSARDS
BRASSART
BRASSARTS
BRASSED
BRASSERIE
BRASSES
BRASSET
BRASSETS
BRASSICA
BRASSICAS
BRASSIE
BRASSIER
BRASSIERE
BRASSIES
BRASSIEST
BRASSILY
BRASSING
BRASSISH
BRASSWARE
BRASSY
BRAST
BRASTING
BRASTS
BRAT
BRATCHET
BRATCHETS
BRATLING
BRATLINGS
BRATPACK
BRATPACKS
BRATS
BRATTICE
BRATTICED
BRATTICES
BRATTIER
BRATTIEST
BRATTISH
BRATTLE
BRATTLED
BRATTLES
BRATTLING
BRATTY
BRATWURST
BRAUNCH
BRAUNCHED
BRAUNCHES
BRAUNITE
BRAUNITES
BRAVA
BRAVADO
BRAVADOED
BRAVADOES
BRAVADOS
BRAVAS
BRAVE
BRAVED
BRAVELY
BRAVENESS
BRAVER
BRAVERIES
BRAVERS
BRAVERY
BRAVES
BRAVEST
BRAVI
BRAVING
BRAVO
BRAVOED
BRAVOES
BRAVOING
BRAVOS
BRAVURA
BRAVURAS
BRAVURE
BRAW
BRAWER
BRAWEST
BRAWL
BRAWLED
BRAWLER
BRAWLERS
BRAWLIE
BRAWLIER
BRAWLIEST
BRAWLING
BRAWLINGS
BRAWLS
BRAWLY
BRAWN
BRAWNED
BRAWNIER
BRAWNIEST
BRAWNILY
BRAWNS
BRAWNY
BRAWS
BRAXIES
BRAXY
BRAY
BRAYED
BRAYER
BRAYERS
BRAYING
BRAYS
BRAZA
BRAZAS
BRAZE
BRAZED
BRAZELESS
BRAZEN
BRAZENED
BRAZENING
BRAZENLY
BRAZENRY
BRAZENS
BRAZER
BRAZERS
BRAZES
BRAZIER
BRAZIERS
BRAZIERY
BRAZIL
BRAZILEIN
BRAZILIN
BRAZILINS
BRAZILS
BRAZING
BREACH
BREACHED
BREACHER
BREACHERS
BREACHES
BREACHING
BREAD
BREADBIN
BREADBINS
BREADBOX
BREADED
BREADHEAD
BREADIER
BREADIEST
BREADING
BREADLESS
BREADLIKE
BREADLINE
BREADNUT
BREADNUTS
BREADROOM
BREADROOT
BREADS
BREADTH
BREADTHS
BREADY
BREAK
BREAKABLE
BREAKAGE
BREAKAGES
BREAKAWAY
BREAKBACK
BREAKBEAT
BREAKBONE
BREAKDOWN
BREAKER

B

BREAKERS
BREAKEVEN
BREAKFAST
BREAKING
BREAKINGS
BREAKNECK
BREAKOFF
BREAKOFFS
BREAKOUT
BREAKOUTS
BREAKS
BREAKTIME
BREAKUP
BREAKUPS
BREAKWALL
BREAM
BREAMED
BREAMING
BREAMS
BREARE
BREARES
BREASKIT
BREASKITS
BREAST
BREASTED
BREASTFED
BREASTING
BREASTPIN
BREASTS
BREATH
BREATHE
BREATHED
BREATHER
BREATHERS
BREATHES
BREATHFUL
BREATHIER
BREATHILY
BREATHING
BREATHS
BREATHY
BRECCIA
BRECCIAL
BRECCIAS
BRECCIATE
BRECHAM
BRECHAMS
BRECHAN
BRECHANS
BRED
BREDE
BREDED
BREDES
BREDIE
BREDIES
BREDING
BREDREN
BREDRENS
BREDRIN
BREDRINS
BREDS
BREE
BREECH
BREECHED
BREECHES
BREECHING
BREED
BREEDER
BREEDERS
BREEDING
BREEDINGS
BREEDS
BREEKS
BREEM
BREENGE
BREENGED
BREENGES
BREENGING
BREER
BREERED
BREERING
BREERS
BREES
BREESE
BREESES
BREEST
BREESTS
BREEZE
BREEZED
BREEZES
BREEZEWAY
BREEZIER
BREEZIEST
BREEZILY
BREEZING
BREEZY
BREGMA
BREGMAS
BREGMATA
BREGMATE
BREGMATIC
BREHON
BREHONS
BREI
BREID
BREIDS
BREIING
BREINGE
BREINGED
BREINGES
BREINGING
BREIS
BREIST
BREISTS
BREKKIE
BREKKIES
BREKKY
BRELOQUE
BRELOQUES
BREME
BREN
BRENNE
BRENNES
BRENNING
BRENS
BRENT
BRENTER
BRENTEST
BRENTS
BRER
BRERE
BRERES
BRERS
BRESAOLA
BRESAOLAS
BRETASCHE
BRETESSE
BRETESSES
BRETHREN
BRETON
BRETONS
BRETTICE
BRETTICED
BRETTICES
BREVE
BREVES
BREVET
BREVETCY
BREVETE
BREVETED
BREVETING
BREVETS
BREVETTED
BREVIARY
BREVIATE
BREVIATES
BREVIER
BREVIERS
BREVIS
BREVISES
BREVITIES
BREVITY
BREW
BREWAGE
BREWAGES
BREWED
BREWER
BREWERIES
BREWERS
BREWERY
BREWHOUSE
BREWING
BREWINGS
BREWIS
BREWISES
BREWPUB
BREWPUBS
BREWS
BREWSKI
BREWSKIES
BREWSKIS
BREWSTER
BREWSTERS
BREY
BREYED
BREYING
BREYS
BRIAR
BRIARD
BRIARDS
BRIARED
BRIARIER
BRIARIEST
BRIARROOT
BRIARS
BRIARWOOD
BRIARY
BRIBABLE
BRIBE
BRIBEABLE
BRIBED
BRIBEE
BRIBEES
BRIBER
BRIBERIES
BRIBERS
BRIBERY
BRIBES
BRIBING
BRICABRAC
BRICHT
BRICHTER
BRICHTEST
BRICK
BRICKBAT
BRICKBATS
BRICKCLAY
BRICKED
BRICKEN
BRICKIE
BRICKIER
BRICKIES
BRICKIEST
BRICKING
BRICKINGS
BRICKKILN
BRICKLE
BRICKLES
BRICKLIKE
BRICKS
BRICKWALL
BRICKWORK
BRICKY
BRICKYARD
BRICOLAGE
BRICOLE
BRICOLES
BRICOLEUR
BRIDAL
BRIDALLY

B

BRIDALS
BRIDE
BRIDECAKE
BRIDED
BRIDEMAID
BRIDEMAN
BRIDEMEN
BRIDES
BRIDESMAN
BRIDESMEN
BRIDEWELL
BRIDGABLE
BRIDGE
BRIDGED
BRIDGES
BRIDGING
BRIDGINGS
BRIDIE
BRIDIES
BRIDING
BRIDLE
BRIDLED
BRIDLER
BRIDLERS
BRIDLES
BRIDLEWAY
BRIDLING
BRIDOON
BRIDOONS
BRIE
BRIEF
BRIEFCASE
BRIEFED
BRIEFER
BRIEFERS
BRIEFEST
BRIEFING
BRIEFINGS
BRIEFLESS
BRIEFLY
BRIEFNESS
BRIEFS
BRIER
BRIERED
BRIERIER
BRIERIEST
BRIERROOT
BRIERS
BRIERWOOD
BRIERY
BRIES
BRIG
BRIGADE
BRIGADED
BRIGADES
BRIGADIER
BRIGADING
BRIGALOW
BRIGALOWS
BRIGAND
BRIGANDRY
BRIGANDS
BRIGHT
BRIGHTEN
BRIGHTENS
BRIGHTER
BRIGHTEST
BRIGHTISH
BRIGHTLY
BRIGHTS
BRIGS
BRIGUE
BRIGUED
BRIGUES
BRIGUING
BRIGUINGS
BRIK
BRIKI
BRIKIS
BRIKS
BRILL
BRILLER
BRILLEST
BRILLIANT
BRILLO
BRILLOS
BRILLS
BRIM
BRIMFUL
BRIMFULL
BRIMFULLY
BRIMING
BRIMINGS
BRIMLESS
BRIMMED
BRIMMER
BRIMMERS
BRIMMING
BRIMS
BRIMSTONE
BRIMSTONY
BRIN
BRINDED
BRINDISI
BRINDISIS
BRINDLE
BRINDLED
BRINDLES
BRINE
BRINED
BRINELESS
BRINER
BRINERS
BRINES
BRING
BRINGDOWN
BRINGER
BRINGERS
BRINGING
BRINGINGS
BRINGS
BRINIER
BRINIES
BRINIEST
BRININESS
BRINING
BRINISH
BRINJAL
BRINJALS
BRINJARRY
BRINK
BRINKMAN
BRINKMEN
BRINKS
BRINNIES
BRINNY
BRINS
BRINY
BRIO
BRIOCHE
BRIOCHES
BRIOLETTE
BRIONIES
BRIONY
BRIOS
BRIQUET
BRIQUETS
BRIQUETTE
BRIS
BRISANCE
BRISANCES
BRISANT
BRISE
BRISES
BRISK
BRISKED
BRISKEN
BRISKENED
BRISKENS
BRISKER
BRISKEST
BRISKET
BRISKETS
BRISKIER
BRISKIEST
BRISKING
BRISKISH
BRISKLY
BRISKNESS
BRISKS
BRISKY
BRISLING
BRISLINGS
BRISS
BRISSES
BRISTLE
BRISTLED
BRISTLES
BRISTLIER
BRISTLING
BRISTLY
BRISTOL
BRISTOLS
BRISURE
BRISURES
BRIT
BRITANNIA
BRITCHES
BRITH
BRITHS
BRITS
BRITSCHKA
BRITSKA
BRITSKAS
BRITT
BRITTANIA
BRITTLE
BRITTLED
BRITTLELY
BRITTLER
BRITTLES
BRITTLEST
BRITTLING
BRITTLY
BRITTS
BRITZKA
BRITZKAS
BRITZSKA
BRITZSKAS
BRIZE
BRIZES
BRO
BROACH
BROACHED
BROACHER
BROACHERS
BROACHES
BROACHING
BROAD
BROADAX
BROADAXE
BROADAXES
BROADBAND
BROADBEAN
BROADBILL
BROADBRIM
BROADCAST
BROADEN
BROADENED
BROADENER
BROADENS
BROADER
BROADEST
BROADISH
BROADLEAF
BROADLINE
BROADLOOM
BROADLY
BROADNESS
BROADS

BROADSIDE
BROADTAIL
BROADWAY
BROADWAYS
BROADWISE
BROAST
BROASTED
BROASTING
BROASTS
BROCADE
BROCADED
BROCADES
BROCADING
BROCAGE
BROCAGES
BROCARD
BROCARDS
BROCATEL
BROCATELS
BROCCOLI
BROCCOLIS
BROCH
BROCHAN
BROCHANS
BROCHE
BROCHED
BROCHES
BROCHETTE
BROCHING
BROCHO
BROCHOS
BROCHS
BROCHURE
BROCHURES
BROCK
BROCKAGE
BROCKAGES
BROCKED
BROCKET
BROCKETS
BROCKIT
BROCKRAM
BROCKRAMS
BROCKS
BROCOLI
BROCOLIS
BROD
BRODDED
BRODDING
BRODDLE
BRODDLED
BRODDLES
BRODDLING
BRODEKIN
BRODEKINS
BRODKIN
BRODKINS
BRODS
BROEKIES
BROG
BROGAN
BROGANS
BROGGED
BROGGING
BROGH
BROGHS
BROGS
BROGUE
BROGUEISH
BROGUERY
BROGUES
BROGUISH
BROIDER
BROIDERED
BROIDERER
BROIDERS
BROIDERY
BROIL
BROILED
BROILER
BROILERS
BROILING
BROILS
BROKAGE
BROKAGES
BROKE
BROKED
BROKEN
BROKENLY
BROKER
BROKERAGE
BROKERED
BROKERIES
BROKERING
BROKERS
BROKERY
BROKES
BROKING
BROKINGS
BROLGA
BROLGAS
BROLLIES
BROLLY
BROMAL
BROMALS
BROMANCE
BROMANCES
BROMANTIC
BROMATE
BROMATED
BROMATES
BROMATING
BROME
BROMELAIN
BROMELIA
BROMELIAD
BROMELIAS
BROMELIN
BROMELINS
BROMEOSIN
BROMES
BROMIC
BROMID
BROMIDE
BROMIDES
BROMIDIC
BROMIDS
BROMIN
BROMINATE
BROMINE
BROMINES
BROMINISM
BROMINS
BROMISE
BROMISED
BROMISES
BROMISING
BROMISM
BROMISMS
BROMIZE
BROMIZED
BROMIZES
BROMIZING
BROMMER
BROMMERS
BROMO
BROMOFORM
BROMOS
BRONC
BRONCHI
BRONCHIA
BRONCHIAL
BRONCHIUM
BRONCHO
BRONCHOS
BRONCHUS
BRONCO
BRONCOS
BRONCS
BROND
BRONDE
BRONDER
BRONDES
BRONDEST
BRONDS
BRONDYRON
BRONZE
BRONZED
BRONZEN
BRONZER
BRONZERS
BRONZES
BRONZIER
BRONZIEST
BRONZIFY
BRONZING
BRONZINGS
BRONZITE
BRONZITES
BRONZY
BROO
BROOCH
BROOCHED
BROOCHES
BROOCHING
BROOD
BROODED
BROODER
BROODERS
BROODIER
BROODIEST
BROODILY
BROODING
BROODINGS
BROODLESS
BROODMARE
BROODS
BROODY
BROOK
BROOKABLE
BROOKED
BROOKIE
BROOKIES
BROOKING
BROOKITE
BROOKITES
BROOKLET
BROOKLETS
BROOKLIKE
BROOKLIME
BROOKS
BROOKWEED
BROOL
BROOLS
BROOM
BROOMBALL
BROOMCORN
BROOMED
BROOMIER
BROOMIEST
BROOMING
BROOMRAPE
BROOMS
BROOMY
BROOS
BROOSE
BROOSES
BROS
BROSE
BROSES
BROSIER
BROSIEST
BROSY
BROTH
BROTHA
BROTHAS
BROTHEL
BROTHELS
BROTHER
BROTHERED

BROTHERLY
BROTHERS
BROTHIER
BROTHIEST
BROTHS
BROTHY
BROUGH
BROUGHAM
BROUGHAMS
BROUGHS
BROUGHT
BROUGHTA
BROUGHTAS
BROUHAHA
BROUHAHAS
BROUZE
BROUZES
BROW
BROWALLIA
BROWBAND
BROWBANDS
BROWBEAT
BROWBEATS
BROWBONE
BROWBONES
BROWED
BROWLESS
BROWN
BROWNED
BROWNER
BROWNERS
BROWNEST
BROWNIE
BROWNIER
BROWNIES
BROWNIEST
BROWNING
BROWNINGS
BROWNISH
BROWNNESS
BROWNNOSE
BROWNOUT
BROWNOUTS
BROWNS
BROWNTAIL
BROWNY
BROWRIDGE
BROWS
BROWSABLE
BROWSE
BROWSED
BROWSER
BROWSERS
BROWSES
BROWSIER
BROWSIEST
BROWSING
BROWSINGS
BROWST
BROWSTS
BROWSY
BRR
BRRR
BRU
BRUCELLA
BRUCELLAE
BRUCELLAS
BRUCHID
BRUCHIDS
BRUCIN
BRUCINE
BRUCINES
BRUCINS
BRUCITE
BRUCITES
BRUCKLE
BRUGH
BRUGHS
BRUHAHA
BRUHAHAS
BRUILZIE
BRUILZIES
BRUIN
BRUINS
BRUISE
BRUISED
BRUISER
BRUISERS
BRUISES
BRUISING
BRUISINGS
BRUIT
BRUITED
BRUITER
BRUITERS
BRUITING
BRUITS
BRULE
BRULES
BRULOT
BRULOTS
BRULYIE
BRULYIES
BRULZIE
BRULZIES
BRUMAL
BRUMBIES
BRUMBY
BRUME
BRUMES
BRUMMAGEM
BRUMMER
BRUMMERS
BRUMOUS
BRUNCH
BRUNCHED
BRUNCHER
BRUNCHERS
BRUNCHES
BRUNCHING
BRUNET
BRUNETS
BRUNETTE
BRUNETTES
BRUNG
BRUNIZEM
BRUNIZEMS
BRUNT
BRUNTED
BRUNTING
BRUNTS
BRUS
BRUSH
BRUSHABLE
BRUSHBACK
BRUSHED
BRUSHER
BRUSHERS
BRUSHES
BRUSHFIRE
BRUSHIER
BRUSHIEST
BRUSHING
BRUSHINGS
BRUSHLAND
BRUSHLESS
BRUSHLIKE
BRUSHMARK
BRUSHOFF
BRUSHOFFS
BRUSHUP
BRUSHUPS
BRUSHWOOD
BRUSHWORK
BRUSHY
BRUSK
BRUSKER
BRUSKEST
BRUSQUE
BRUSQUELY
BRUSQUER
BRUSQUEST
BRUSSELS
BRUSSEN
BRUST
BRUSTING
BRUSTS
BRUT
BRUTAL
BRUTALISE
BRUTALISM
BRUTALIST
BRUTALITY
BRUTALIZE
BRUTALLY
BRUTE
BRUTED
BRUTELIKE
BRUTELY
BRUTENESS
BRUTER
BRUTERS
BRUTES
BRUTEST
BRUTIFIED
BRUTIFIES
BRUTIFY
BRUTING
BRUTINGS
BRUTISH
BRUTISHLY
BRUTISM
BRUTISMS
BRUTS
BRUX
BRUXED
BRUXES
BRUXING
BRUXISM
BRUXISMS
BRYOLOGY
BRYONIES
BRYONY
BRYOPHYTE
BRYOZOAN
BRYOZOANS
BUAT
BUATS
BUAZE
BUAZES
BUB
BUBA
BUBAL
BUBALE
BUBALES
BUBALINE
BUBALIS
BUBALISES
BUBALS
BUBAS
BUBBE
BUBBES
BUBBIE
BUBBIES
BUBBLE
BUBBLED
BUBBLEGUM
BUBBLER
BUBBLERS
BUBBLES
BUBBLIER
BUBBLIES
BUBBLIEST
BUBBLING
BUBBLY
BUBBY
BUBINGA
BUBINGAS
BUBKES
BUBKIS

B

BUBO
BUBOED
BUBOES
BUBONIC
BUBS
BUBU
BUBUKLE
BUBUKLES
BUBUS
BUCARDO
BUCARDOS
BUCATINI
BUCCAL
BUCCALLY
BUCCANEER
BUCCANIER
BUCCINA
BUCCINAS
BUCELLAS
BUCENTAUR
BUCHU
BUCHUS
BUCK
BUCKAROO
BUCKAROOS
BUCKAYRO
BUCKAYROS
BUCKBEAN
BUCKBEANS
BUCKBOARD
BUCKBRUSH
BUCKED
BUCKEEN
BUCKEENS
BUCKER
BUCKEROO
BUCKEROOS
BUCKERS
BUCKET
BUCKETED
BUCKETFUL
BUCKETING
BUCKETS
BUCKEYE
BUCKEYES
BUCKHORN
BUCKHORNS
BUCKHOUND
BUCKIE
BUCKIES
BUCKING
BUCKINGS
BUCKISH
BUCKISHLY
BUCKLE
BUCKLED
BUCKLER
BUCKLERED
BUCKLERS
BUCKLES
BUCKLING
BUCKLINGS
BUCKO
BUCKOES
BUCKOS
BUCKRAKE
BUCKRAKES
BUCKRAM
BUCKRAMED
BUCKRAMS
BUCKS
BUCKSAW
BUCKSAWS
BUCKSHEE
BUCKSHEES
BUCKSHISH
BUCKSHOT
BUCKSHOTS
BUCKSKIN
BUCKSKINS
BUCKSOM
BUCKTAIL
BUCKTAILS
BUCKTEETH
BUCKTHORN
BUCKTOOTH
BUCKU
BUCKUS
BUCKWHEAT
BUCKYBALL
BUCKYTUBE
BUCOLIC
BUCOLICAL
BUCOLICS
BUD
BUDA
BUDAS
BUDDED
BUDDER
BUDDERS
BUDDHA
BUDDHAS
BUDDIED
BUDDIER
BUDDIES
BUDDIEST
BUDDING
BUDDINGS
BUDDLE
BUDDLED
BUDDLEIA
BUDDLEIAS
BUDDLES
BUDDLING
BUDDY
BUDDYING
BUDGE
BUDGED
BUDGER
BUDGEREE
BUDGERO
BUDGEROS
BUDGEROW
BUDGEROWS
BUDGERS
BUDGES
BUDGET
BUDGETARY
BUDGETED
BUDGETEER
BUDGETER
BUDGETERS
BUDGETING
BUDGETS
BUDGIE
BUDGIES
BUDGING
BUDI
BUDIS
BUDLESS
BUDLIKE
BUDMASH
BUDMASHES
BUDO
BUDOS
BUDS
BUDTENDER
BUDWOOD
BUDWOODS
BUDWORM
BUDWORMS
BUFF
BUFFA
BUFFABLE
BUFFALO
BUFFALOED
BUFFALOES
BUFFALOS
BUFFAS
BUFFE
BUFFED
BUFFEL
BUFFER
BUFFERED
BUFFERING
BUFFERS
BUFFEST
BUFFET
BUFFETED
BUFFETER
BUFFETERS
BUFFETING
BUFFETS
BUFFI
BUFFIER
BUFFIEST
BUFFING
BUFFINGS
BUFFO
BUFFOON
BUFFOONS
BUFFOS
BUFFS
BUFFY
BUFO
BUFOS
BUFOTALIN
BUG
BUGABOO
BUGABOOS
BUGBANE
BUGBANES
BUGBEAR
BUGBEARS
BUGEYE
BUGEYES
BUGGAN
BUGGANE
BUGGANES
BUGGANS
BUGGED
BUGGER
BUGGERED
BUGGERIES
BUGGERING
BUGGERS
BUGGERY
BUGGIER
BUGGIES
BUGGIEST
BUGGIN
BUGGINESS
BUGGING
BUGGINGS
BUGGINS
BUGGY
BUGHOUSE
BUGHOUSES
BUGLE
BUGLED
BUGLER
BUGLERS
BUGLES
BUGLET
BUGLETS
BUGLEWEED
BUGLING
BUGLOSS
BUGLOSSES
BUGONG
BUGONGS
BUGOUT
BUGOUTS
BUGS
BUGSEED
BUGSEEDS
BUGSHA
BUGSHAS
BUGWORT
BUGWORTS

BUHL
BUHLS
BUHLWORK
BUHLWORKS
BUHR
BUHRS
BUHRSTONE
BUHUND
BUHUNDS
BUIBUI
BUIBUIS
BUIK
BUIKS
BUILD
BUILDABLE
BUILDDOWN
BUILDED
BUILDER
BUILDERS
BUILDING
BUILDINGS
BUILDOUT
BUILDOUTS
BUILDS
BUILDUP
BUILDUPS
BUILT
BUIRDLIER
BUIRDLY
BUIST
BUISTED
BUISTING
BUISTS
BUKE
BUKES
BUKKAKE
BUKKAKES
BUKSHEE
BUKSHEES
BUKSHI
BUKSHIS
BULB
BULBAR
BULBED
BULBEL
BULBELS
BULBIL
BULBILS
BULBING
BULBLET
BULBLETS
BULBOSITY
BULBOUS
BULBOUSLY
BULBS
BULBUL
BULBULS
BULGAR
BULGARS
BULGE
BULGED
BULGER
BULGERS
BULGES
BULGHUR
BULGHURS
BULGIER
BULGIEST
BULGINE
BULGINES
BULGINESS
BULGING
BULGINGLY
BULGUR
BULGURS
BULGY
BULIMIA
BULIMIAC
BULIMIACS
BULIMIAS
BULIMIC
BULIMICS
BULIMIES
BULIMUS
BULIMUSES
BULIMY
BULK
BULKAGE
BULKAGES
BULKED
BULKER
BULKERS
BULKHEAD
BULKHEADS
BULKIER
BULKIEST
BULKILY
BULKINESS
BULKING
BULKINGS
BULKS
BULKY
BULL
BULLA
BULLACE
BULLACES
BULLAE
BULLARIES
BULLARY
BULLATE
BULLBARS
BULLBAT
BULLBATS
BULLBRIER
BULLCOOK
BULLCOOKS
BULLDOG
BULLDOGS
BULLDOZE
BULLDOZED
BULLDOZER
BULLDOZES
BULLDUST
BULLDUSTS
BULLED
BULLER
BULLERED
BULLERING
BULLERS
BULLET
BULLETED
BULLETIN
BULLETING
BULLETINS
BULLETRIE
BULLETS
BULLEY
BULLEYS
BULLFIGHT
BULLFINCH
BULLFROG
BULLFROGS
BULLGINE
BULLGINES
BULLHEAD
BULLHEADS
BULLHORN
BULLHORNS
BULLIED
BULLIER
BULLIES
BULLIEST
BULLING
BULLINGS
BULLION
BULLIONS
BULLISH
BULLISHLY
BULLNECK
BULLNECKS
BULLNOSE
BULLNOSED
BULLNOSES
BULLOCK
BULLOCKED
BULLOCKS
BULLOCKY
BULLOSA
BULLOUS
BULLPEN
BULLPENS
BULLPOUT
BULLPOUTS
BULLRING
BULLRINGS
BULLRUSH
BULLS
BULLSEYE
BULLSEYES
BULLSHAT
BULLSHIT
BULLSHITS
BULLSHOT
BULLSHOTS
BULLSNAKE
BULLWADDY
BULLWEED
BULLWEEDS
BULLWHACK
BULLWHIP
BULLWHIPS
BULLY
BULLYBOY
BULLYBOYS
BULLYCIDE
BULLYING
BULLYINGS
BULLYISM
BULLYISMS
BULLYRAG
BULLYRAGS
BULNBULN
BULNBULNS
BULRUSH
BULRUSHES
BULRUSHY
BULSE
BULSES
BULWADDEE
BULWADDY
BULWARK
BULWARKED
BULWARKS
BUM
BUMALO
BUMALOTI
BUMALOTIS
BUMBAG
BUMBAGS
BUMBAZE
BUMBAZED
BUMBAZES
BUMBAZING
BUMBLE
BUMBLEBEE
BUMBLED
BUMBLEDOM
BUMBLER
BUMBLERS
BUMBLES
BUMBLING
BUMBLINGS
BUMBO
BUMBOAT
BUMBOATS
BUMBOS
BUMELIA
BUMELIAS
BUMF
BUMFLUFF

BUMFLUFFS
BUMFS
BUMFUCK
BUMFUCKS
BUMFUZZLE
BUMKIN
BUMKINS
BUMMALO
BUMMALOS
BUMMALOTI
BUMMAREE
BUMMAREES
BUMMED
BUMMEL
BUMMELS
BUMMER
BUMMERS
BUMMEST
BUMMING
BUMMLE
BUMMLED
BUMMLES
BUMMLING
BUMMOCK
BUMMOCKS
BUMP
BUMPED
BUMPER
BUMPERED
BUMPERING
BUMPERS
BUMPH
BUMPHS
BUMPIER
BUMPIEST
BUMPILY
BUMPINESS
BUMPING
BUMPINGS
BUMPKIN
BUMPKINLY
BUMPKINS
BUMPOLOGY
BUMPS
BUMPTIOUS
BUMPY
BUMS
BUMSTER
BUMSTERS
BUMSUCKER
BUMWAD
BUMWADS
BUN
BUNA
BUNAS
BUNBURIED
BUNBURIES
BUNBURY
BUNCE
BUNCED
BUNCES
BUNCH
BUNCHED
BUNCHER
BUNCHERS
BUNCHES
BUNCHIER
BUNCHIEST
BUNCHILY
BUNCHING
BUNCHINGS
BUNCHY
BUNCING
BUNCO
BUNCOED
BUNCOES
BUNCOING
BUNCOMBE
BUNCOMBES
BUNCOS
BUND
BUNDE
BUNDED
BUNDH
BUNDHS
BUNDIED
BUNDIES
BUNDING
BUNDIST
BUNDISTS
BUNDLE
BUNDLED
BUNDLER
BUNDLERS
BUNDLES
BUNDLING
BUNDLINGS
BUNDOBUST
BUNDOOK
BUNDOOKS
BUNDS
BUNDT
BUNDTS
BUNDU
BUNDUS
BUNDWALL
BUNDWALLS
BUNDY
BUNDYING
BUNFIGHT
BUNFIGHTS
BUNG
BUNGALOID
BUNGALOW
BUNGALOWS
BUNGED
BUNGEE
BUNGEES
BUNGER
BUNGERS
BUNGEY
BUNGEYS
BUNGHOLE
BUNGHOLES
BUNGIE
BUNGIES
BUNGING
BUNGLE
BUNGLED
BUNGLER
BUNGLERS
BUNGLES
BUNGLING
BUNGLINGS
BUNGS
BUNGWALL
BUNGWALLS
BUNGY
BUNHEAD
BUNHEADS
BUNIA
BUNIAS
BUNION
BUNIONS
BUNJE
BUNJEE
BUNJEES
BUNJES
BUNJIE
BUNJIES
BUNJY
BUNK
BUNKED
BUNKER
BUNKERED
BUNKERING
BUNKERS
BUNKHOUSE
BUNKIE
BUNKIES
BUNKING
BUNKMATE
BUNKMATES
BUNKO
BUNKOED
BUNKOING
BUNKOS
BUNKS
BUNKUM
BUNKUMS
BUNN
BUNNET
BUNNETS
BUNNIA
BUNNIAS
BUNNIES
BUNNS
BUNNY
BUNODONT
BUNRAKU
BUNRAKUS
BUNS
BUNSEN
BUNSENS
BUNT
BUNTAL
BUNTALS
BUNTED
BUNTER
BUNTERS
BUNTIER
BUNTIEST
BUNTING
BUNTINGS
BUNTLINE
BUNTLINES
BUNTS
BUNTY
BUNYA
BUNYAS
BUNYIP
BUNYIPS
BUOY
BUOYAGE
BUOYAGES
BUOYANCE
BUOYANCES
BUOYANCY
BUOYANT
BUOYANTLY
BUOYED
BUOYING
BUOYS
BUPKES
BUPKIS
BUPKUS
BUPLEVER
BUPLEVERS
BUPPIE
BUPPIES
BUPPY
BUPRESTID
BUPROPION
BUQSHA
BUQSHAS
BUR
BURA
BURAN
BURANS
BURAS
BURB
BURBLE
BURBLED
BURBLER
BURBLERS
BURBLES
BURBLIER
BURBLIEST
BURBLING
BURBLINGS

BURBLY
BURBOT
BURBOTS
BURBS
BURD
BURDASH
BURDASHES
BURDEN
BURDENED
BURDENER
BURDENERS
BURDENING
BURDENOUS
BURDENS
BURDIE
BURDIES
BURDIZZO
BURDIZZOS
BURDOCK
BURDOCKS
BURDS
BUREAU
BUREAUS
BUREAUX
BURET
BURETS
BURETTE
BURETTES
BURFI
BURFIS
BURG
BURGAGE
BURGAGES
BURGANET
BURGANETS
BURGEE
BURGEES
BURGEON
BURGEONED
BURGEONS
BURGER
BURGERS
BURGESS
BURGESSES
BURGH
BURGHAL
BURGHER
BURGHERS
BURGHS
BURGHUL
BURGHULS
BURGLAR
BURGLARED
BURGLARS
BURGLARY
BURGLE
BURGLED
BURGLES
BURGLING
BURGONET
BURGONETS
BURGOO
BURGOOS
BURGOUT
BURGOUTS
BURGRAVE
BURGRAVES
BURGS
BURGUNDY
BURHEL
BURHELS
BURIAL
BURIALS
BURIED
BURIER
BURIERS
BURIES
BURIN
BURINIST
BURINISTS
BURINS
BURITI
BURITIS
BURK
BURKA
BURKAS
BURKE
BURKED
BURKER
BURKERS
BURKES
BURKHA
BURKHAS
BURKING
BURKINI
BURKINIS
BURKITE
BURKITES
BURKS
BURL
BURLADERO
BURLAP
BURLAPS
BURLED
BURLER
BURLERS
BURLESK
BURLESKS
BURLESQUE
BURLETTA
BURLETTAS
BURLEY
BURLEYCUE
BURLEYED
BURLEYING
BURLEYS
BURLIER
BURLIEST
BURLIKE
BURLILY
BURLINESS
BURLING
BURLS
BURLY
BURN
BURNABLE
BURNABLES
BURNED
BURNER
BURNERS
BURNET
BURNETS
BURNIE
BURNIES
BURNING
BURNINGLY
BURNINGS
BURNISH
BURNISHED
BURNISHER
BURNISHES
BURNOOSE
BURNOOSED
BURNOOSES
BURNOUS
BURNOUSE
BURNOUSED
BURNOUSES
BURNOUT
BURNOUTS
BURNS
BURNSIDE
BURNSIDES
BURNT
BUROO
BUROOS
BURP
BURPED
BURPEE
BURPEES
BURPING
BURPS
BURQA
BURQAS
BURQUINI
BURQUINIS
BURR
BURRAMYS
BURRATA
BURRATAS
BURRAWANG
BURRED
BURREL
BURRELL
BURRELLS
BURRELS
BURRER
BURRERS
BURRFISH
BURRHEL
BURRHELS
BURRIER
BURRIEST
BURRING
BURRITO
BURRITOS
BURRO
BURROS
BURROW
BURROWED
BURROWER
BURROWERS
BURROWING
BURROWS
BURRS
BURRSTONE
BURRY
BURS
BURSA
BURSAE
BURSAL
BURSAR
BURSARIAL
BURSARIES
BURSARS
BURSARY
BURSAS
BURSATE
BURSE
BURSEED
BURSEEDS
BURSERA
BURSES
BURSICON
BURSICONS
BURSIFORM
BURSITIS
BURST
BURSTED
BURSTEN
BURSTER
BURSTERS
BURSTIER
BURSTIEST
BURSTING
BURSTONE
BURSTONES
BURSTS
BURSTY
BURTHEN
BURTHENED
BURTHENS
BURTON
BURTONS
BURWEED
BURWEEDS
BURY
BURYING
BUS
BUSBAR

B

BUSBARS
BUSBIES
BUSBOY
BUSBOYS
BUSBY
BUSED
BUSERA
BUSERAS
BUSES
BUSGIRL
BUSGIRLS
BUSH
BUSHBABY
BUSHBUCK
BUSHBUCKS
BUSHCRAFT
BUSHED
BUSHEL
BUSHELED
BUSHELER
BUSHELERS
BUSHELFUL
BUSHELING
BUSHELLED
BUSHELLER
BUSHELMAN
BUSHELMEN
BUSHELS
BUSHER
BUSHERS
BUSHES
BUSHFIRE
BUSHFIRES
BUSHFLIES
BUSHFLY
BUSHGOAT
BUSHGOATS
BUSHIDO
BUSHIDOS
BUSHIE
BUSHIER
BUSHIES
BUSHIEST
BUSHILY
BUSHINESS
BUSHING
BUSHINGS
BUSHLAND
BUSHLANDS
BUSHLESS
BUSHLIKE
BUSHLOT
BUSHLOTS
BUSHMAN
BUSHMEAT
BUSHMEATS
BUSHMEN
BUSHPIG
BUSHPIGS
BUSHTIT
BUSHTITS
BUSHVELD
BUSHVELDS
BUSHWA
BUSHWAH
BUSHWAHS
BUSHWALK
BUSHWALKS
BUSHWAS
BUSHWHACK
BUSHWOMAN
BUSHWOMEN
BUSHY
BUSIED
BUSIER
BUSIES
BUSIEST
BUSILY
BUSINESS
BUSINESSY
BUSING
BUSINGS
BUSK
BUSKED
BUSKER
BUSKERS
BUSKET
BUSKETS
BUSKIN
BUSKINED
BUSKING
BUSKINGS
BUSKINS
BUSKS
BUSKY
BUSLOAD
BUSLOADS
BUSMAN
BUSMEN
BUSS
BUSSED
BUSSES
BUSSING
BUSSINGS
BUSSU
BUSSUS
BUST
BUSTARD
BUSTARDS
BUSTED
BUSTEE
BUSTEES
BUSTER
BUSTERS
BUSTI
BUSTIC
BUSTICATE
BUSTICS
BUSTIER
BUSTIERS
BUSTIEST
BUSTINESS
BUSTING
BUSTINGS
BUSTIS
BUSTLE
BUSTLED
BUSTLER
BUSTLERS
BUSTLES
BUSTLINE
BUSTLINES
BUSTLING
BUSTS
BUSTY
BUSULFAN
BUSULFANS
BUSUUTI
BUSUUTIS
BUSY
BUSYBODY
BUSYING
BUSYNESS
BUSYWORK
BUSYWORKS
BUT
BUTADIENE
BUTANE
BUTANES
BUTANOIC
BUTANOL
BUTANOLS
BUTANONE
BUTANONES
BUTCH
BUTCHER
BUTCHERED
BUTCHERER
BUTCHERLY
BUTCHERS
BUTCHERY
BUTCHES
BUTCHEST
BUTCHING
BUTCHINGS
BUTCHNESS
BUTE
BUTENE
BUTENES
BUTEO
BUTEONINE
BUTEOS
BUTES
BUTLE
BUTLED
BUTLER
BUTLERAGE
BUTLERED
BUTLERIES
BUTLERING
BUTLERS
BUTLERY
BUTLES
BUTLING
BUTMENT
BUTMENTS
BUTOH
BUTOHS
BUTS
BUTSUDAN
BUTSUDANS
BUTT
BUTTALS
BUTTE
BUTTED
BUTTER
BUTTERBUR
BUTTERCUP
BUTTERED
BUTTERFAT
BUTTERFLY
BUTTERIER
BUTTERIES
BUTTERINE
BUTTERING
BUTTERNUT
BUTTERS
BUTTERY
BUTTES
BUTTHEAD
BUTTHEADS
BUTTIES
BUTTING
BUTTINSKI
BUTTINSKY
BUTTLE
BUTTLED
BUTTLES
BUTTLING
BUTTOCK
BUTTOCKED
BUTTOCKS
BUTTON
BUTTONED
BUTTONER
BUTTONERS
BUTTONIER
BUTTONING
BUTTONS
BUTTONY
BUTTRESS
BUTTS
BUTTSTOCK
BUTTY
BUTTYMAN
BUTTYMEN
BUTUT
BUTUTS
BUTYL
BUTYLATE

BUTYLATED
BUTYLATES
BUTYLENE
BUTYLENES
BUTYLS
BUTYRAL
BUTYRALS
BUTYRATE
BUTYRATES
BUTYRIC
BUTYRIN
BUTYRINS
BUTYROUS
BUTYRYL
BUTYRYLS
BUVETTE
BUVETTES
BUXOM
BUXOMER
BUXOMEST
BUXOMLY
BUXOMNESS
BUY
BUYABLE
BUYABLES
BUYBACK
BUYBACKS
BUYER
BUYERS
BUYING
BUYINGS
BUYOFF
BUYOFFS
BUYOUT
BUYOUTS
BUYS
BUZKASHI
BUZKASHIS
BUZUKI
BUZUKIA
BUZUKIS
BUZZ
BUZZARD
BUZZARDS
BUZZBAIT
BUZZBAITS
BUZZCUT
BUZZCUTS
BUZZED
BUZZER
BUZZERS
BUZZES
BUZZIER
BUZZIEST
BUZZING
BUZZINGLY
BUZZINGS
BUZZKILL
BUZZKILLS
BUZZSAW
BUZZSAWS
BUZZWIG
BUZZWIGS
BUZZWORD
BUZZWORDS
BUZZY
BWANA
BWANAS
BWAZI
BWAZIS
BY
BYCATCH
BYCATCHES
BYCOKET
BYCOKETS
BYDE
BYDED
BYDES
BYDING
BYE
BYELAW
BYELAWS
BYES
BYGONE
BYGONES
BYKE
BYKED
BYKES
BYKING
BYLANDER
BYLANDERS
BYLANE
BYLANES
BYLAW
BYLAWS
BYLINE
BYLINED
BYLINER
BYLINERS
BYLINES
BYLINING
BYLIVE
BYNAME
BYNAMES
BYNEMPT
BYPASS
BYPASSED
BYPASSES
BYPASSING
BYPAST
BYPATH
BYPATHS
BYPLACE
BYPLACES
BYPLAY
BYPLAYS
BYPRODUCT
BYRE
BYREMAN
BYREMEN
BYRES
BYREWOMAN
BYREWOMEN
BYRL
BYRLADY
BYRLAKIN
BYRLAW
BYRLAWS
BYRLED
BYRLING
BYRLS
BYRNIE
BYRNIES
BYROAD
BYROADS
BYROOM
BYROOMS
BYS
BYSSAL
BYSSI
BYSSINE
BYSSOID
BYSSUS
BYSSUSES
BYSTANDER
BYSTREET
BYSTREETS
BYTALK
BYTALKS
BYTE
BYTES
BYTOWNITE
BYWAY
BYWAYS
BYWONER
BYWONERS
BYWORD
BYWORDS
BYWORK
BYWORKS
BYZANT
BYZANTINE
BYZANTS

C

CAA
CAAED
CAAING
CAAS
CAATINGA
CAATINGAS
CAB
CABA
CABAL
CABALA
CABALAS
CABALETTA
CABALETTE
CABALISM
CABALISMS
CABALIST
CABALISTS
CABALLED
CABALLER
CABALLERO
CABALLERS
CABALLINE
CABALLING
CABALS
CABANA
CABANAS
CABARET
CABARETS
CABAS
CABBAGE
CABBAGED
CABBAGES
CABBAGEY
CABBAGIER
CABBAGING
CABBAGY
CABBALA
CABBALAH
CABBALAHS
CABBALAS
CABBALISM
CABBALIST
CABBED
CABBIE
CABBIES
CABBING
CABBY
CABDRIVER
CABER
CABERNET
CABERNETS
CABERS
CABESTRO
CABESTROS
CABEZON
CABEZONE
CABEZONES
CABEZONS
CABILDO
CABILDOS
CABIN
CABINED
CABINET
CABINETRY
CABINETS
CABINING
CABINMATE
CABINS
CABLE
CABLECAST
CABLED
CABLEGRAM
CABLER
CABLERS
CABLES
CABLET
CABLETS
CABLEWAY
CABLEWAYS
CABLING
CABLINGS
CABMAN
CABMEN
CABOB
CABOBBED
CABOBBING
CABOBS
CABOC
CABOCEER
CABOCEERS
CABOCHED
CABOCHON
CABOCHONS
CABOCS
CABOMBA
CABOMBAS
CABOODLE
CABOODLES
CABOOSE
CABOOSES
CABOSHED
CABOTAGE
CABOTAGES
CABOVER
CABOVERS
CABRE
CABRESTA
CABRESTAS
CABRESTO
CABRESTOS
CABRETTA
CABRETTAS
CABRIE
CABRIES
CABRILLA
CABRILLAS
CABRIO
CABRIOLE
CABRIOLES
CABRIOLET
CABRIOS
CABRIT
CABRITS
CABS
CABSTAND
CABSTANDS
CACA
CACAFOGO
CACAFOGOS
CACAFUEGO
CACAO
CACAOS
CACAS
CACHACA
CACHACAS
CACHAEMIA
CACHAEMIC
CACHALOT
CACHALOTS
CACHE
CACHECTIC
CACHED
CACHEPOT
CACHEPOTS
CACHES
CACHET
CACHETED
CACHETING
CACHETS
CACHEXIA
CACHEXIAS
CACHEXIC
CACHEXIES
CACHEXY
CACHING
CACHOLONG
CACHOLOT
CACHOLOTS
CACHOU
CACHOUS
CACHUCHA
CACHUCHAS
CACIQUE
CACIQUES
CACIQUISM
CACK
CACKED
CACKIER
CACKIEST
CACKING
CACKLE
CACKLED
CACKLER
CACKLERS
CACKLES
CACKLING
CACKS
CACKY
CACODEMON
CACODOXY
CACODYL
CACODYLIC
CACODYLS
CACOEPIES
CACOEPY
CACOETHES
CACOETHIC
CACOGENIC
CACOLET
CACOLETS
CACOLOGY
CACOMIXL
CACOMIXLE
CACOMIXLS
CACONYM
CACONYMS
CACONYMY
CACOON
CACOONS
CACOPHONY
CACOTOPIA
CACTI
CACTIFORM
CACTOID
CACTUS
CACTUSES
CACUMEN
CACUMENS
CACUMINA
CACUMINAL

CAD
CADAGA
CADAGAS
CADAGI
CADAGIS
CADASTER
CADASTERS
CADASTRAL
CADASTRE
CADASTRES
CADAVER
CADAVERIC
CADAVERS
CADDICE
CADDICES
CADDIE
CADDIED
CADDIES
CADDIS
CADDISED
CADDISES
CADDISFLY
CADDISH
CADDISHLY
CADDY
CADDYING
CADDYSS
CADDYSSES
CADE
CADEAU
CADEAUX
CADEE
CADEES
CADELLE
CADELLES
CADENCE
CADENCED
CADENCES
CADENCIES
CADENCING
CADENCY
CADENT
CADENTIAL
CADENZA
CADENZAS
CADES
CADET
CADETS
CADETSHIP
CADGE
CADGED
CADGER
CADGERS
CADGES
CADGIER
CADGIEST
CADGING
CADGY
CADI
CADIE
CADIES
CADIS
CADMIC
CADMIUM
CADMIUMS
CADRANS
CADRANSES
CADRE
CADRES
CADS
CADUAC
CADUACS
CADUCEAN
CADUCEI
CADUCEUS
CADUCITY
CADUCOUS
CAECA
CAECAL
CAECALLY
CAECILIAN
CAECITIS
CAECUM
CAEOMA
CAEOMAS
CAERULE
CAERULEAN
CAESAR
CAESAREAN
CAESARIAN
CAESARISM
CAESARS
CAESE
CAESIOUS
CAESIUM
CAESIUMS
CAESTUS
CAESTUSES
CAESURA
CAESURAE
CAESURAL
CAESURAS
CAESURIC
CAF
CAFARD
CAFARDS
CAFE
CAFES
CAFETERIA
CAFETIERE
CAFETORIA
CAFF
CAFFEIN
CAFFEINE
CAFFEINES
CAFFEINIC
CAFFEINS
CAFFEISM
CAFFEISMS
CAFFILA
CAFFILAS
CAFFS
CAFILA
CAFILAS
CAFS
CAFTAN
CAFTANED
CAFTANS
CAG
CAGANER
CAGANERS
CAGE
CAGED
CAGEFUL
CAGEFULS
CAGELIKE
CAGELING
CAGELINGS
CAGER
CAGERS
CAGES
CAGEWORK
CAGEWORKS
CAGEY
CAGEYNESS
CAGIER
CAGIEST
CAGILY
CAGINESS
CAGING
CAGMAG
CAGMAGGED
CAGMAGS
CAGOT
CAGOTS
CAGOUL
CAGOULE
CAGOULES
CAGOULS
CAGS
CAGY
CAGYNESS
CAHIER
CAHIERS
CAHOOT
CAHOOTS
CAHOUN
CAHOUNS
CAHOW
CAHOWS
CAID
CAIDS
CAILLACH
CAILLACHS
CAILLE
CAILLEACH
CAILLES
CAILLIACH
CAIMAC
CAIMACAM
CAIMACAMS
CAIMACS
CAIMAN
CAIMANS
CAIN
CAINS
CAIQUE
CAIQUES
CAIRD
CAIRDS
CAIRN
CAIRNED
CAIRNGORM
CAIRNIER
CAIRNIEST
CAIRNS
CAIRNY
CAISSON
CAISSONS
CAITIFF
CAITIFFS
CAITIVE
CAITIVES
CAJAPUT
CAJAPUTS
CAJEPUT
CAJEPUTS
CAJOLE
CAJOLED
CAJOLER
CAJOLERS
CAJOLERY
CAJOLES
CAJOLING
CAJON
CAJONES
CAJUN
CAJUPUT
CAJUPUTS
CAKE
CAKEAGE
CAKEAGES
CAKEBOX
CAKEBOXES
CAKED
CAKEHOLE
CAKEHOLES
CAKES
CAKEWALK
CAKEWALKS
CAKEY
CAKIER
CAKIEST
CAKINESS
CAKING
CAKINGS
CAKY
CAL
CALABASH
CALABAZA

CALABAZAS
CALABOGUS
CALABOOSE
CALABRESE
CALADIUM
CALADIUMS
CALALOO
CALALOOS
CALALU
CALALUS
CALAMANCO
CALAMANSI
CALAMAR
CALAMARI
CALAMARIS
CALAMARS
CALAMARY
CALAMATA
CALAMATAS
CALAMI
CALAMINE
CALAMINED
CALAMINES
CALAMINT
CALAMINTS
CALAMITE
CALAMITES
CALAMITY
CALAMUS
CALAMUSES
CALANDO
CALANDRIA
CALANTHE
CALANTHES
CALASH
CALASHES
CALATHEA
CALATHEAS
CALATHI
CALATHOS
CALATHUS
CALAVANCE
CALCANEA
CALCANEAL
CALCANEAN
CALCANEI
CALCANEUM
CALCANEUS
CALCAR
CALCARATE
CALCARIA
CALCARINE
CALCARS
CALCEATE
CALCEATED
CALCEATES
CALCED
CALCEDONY
CALCES
CALCIC
CALCICOLE
CALCIFIC
CALCIFIED
CALCIFIES
CALCIFUGE
CALCIFY
CALCIMINE
CALCINE
CALCINED
CALCINES
CALCINING
CALCITE
CALCITES
CALCITIC
CALCIUM
CALCIUMS
CALCRETE
CALCRETES
CALCSPAR
CALCSPARS
CALCTUFA
CALCTUFAS
CALCTUFF
CALCTUFFS
CALCULAR
CALCULARY
CALCULATE
CALCULI
CALCULOSE
CALCULOUS
CALCULUS
CALDARIA
CALDARIUM
CALDERA
CALDERAS
CALDRON
CALDRONS
CALECHE
CALECHES
CALEFIED
CALEFIES
CALEFY
CALEFYING
CALEMBOUR
CALENDAL
CALENDAR
CALENDARS
CALENDER
CALENDERS
CALENDRER
CALENDRIC
CALENDRY
CALENDS
CALENDULA
CALENTURE
CALESA
CALESAS
CALESCENT
CALF
CALFDOZER
CALFHOOD
CALFHOODS
CALFLESS
CALFLICK
CALFLICKS
CALFLIKE
CALFS
CALFSKIN
CALFSKINS
CALIATOUR
CALIBER
CALIBERED
CALIBERS
CALIBRATE
CALIBRE
CALIBRED
CALIBRES
CALICES
CALICHE
CALICHES
CALICLE
CALICLES
CALICO
CALICOES
CALICOS
CALICULAR
CALID
CALIDITY
CALIF
CALIFATE
CALIFATES
CALIFONT
CALIFONTS
CALIFS
CALIGO
CALIGOES
CALIGOS
CALIMA
CALIMAS
CALIMOCHO
CALIOLOGY
CALIPASH
CALIPEE
CALIPEES
CALIPER
CALIPERED
CALIPERS
CALIPH
CALIPHAL
CALIPHATE
CALIPHS
CALISAYA
CALISAYAS
CALIVER
CALIVERS
CALIX
CALIXES
CALK
CALKED
CALKER
CALKERS
CALKIN
CALKING
CALKINGS
CALKINS
CALKS
CALL
CALLA
CALLABLE
CALLAIDES
CALLAIS
CALLALOO
CALLALOOS
CALLALOU
CALLALOUS
CALLAN
CALLANS
CALLANT
CALLANTS
CALLAS
CALLBACK
CALLBACKS
CALLBOARD
CALLBOY
CALLBOYS
CALLED
CALLEE
CALLEES
CALLER
CALLERS
CALLET
CALLETS
CALLID
CALLIDITY
CALLIGRAM
CALLING
CALLINGS
CALLIOPE
CALLIOPES
CALLIPASH
CALLIPEE
CALLIPEES
CALLIPER
CALLIPERS
CALLOP
CALLOPS
CALLOSE
CALLOSES
CALLOSITY
CALLOUS
CALLOUSED
CALLOUSES
CALLOUSLY
CALLOUT
CALLOUTS
CALLOW
CALLOWER
CALLOWEST
CALLOWLY
CALLOWS

CALLS
CALLTIME
CALLTIMES
CALLUNA
CALLUNAS
CALLUS
CALLUSED
CALLUSES
CALLUSING
CALM
CALMANT
CALMANTS
CALMATIVE
CALMED
CALMER
CALMEST
CALMIER
CALMIEST
CALMING
CALMINGLY
CALMINGS
CALMLY
CALMNESS
CALMS
CALMSTANE
CALMSTONE
CALMY
CALO
CALOMEL
CALOMELS
CALORIC
CALORICS
CALORIE
CALORIES
CALORIFIC
CALORISE
CALORISED
CALORISES
CALORIST
CALORISTS
CALORIZE
CALORIZED
CALORIZES
CALORY
CALOS
CALOTTE
CALOTTES
CALOTYPE
CALOTYPES
CALOYER
CALOYERS
CALP
CALPA
CALPAC
CALPACK
CALPACKS
CALPACS
CALPAIN
CALPAINS
CALPAS
CALPS
CALQUE
CALQUED
CALQUES
CALQUING
CALS
CALTHA
CALTHAS
CALTHROP
CALTHROPS
CALTRAP
CALTRAPS
CALTROP
CALTROPS
CALUMBA
CALUMBAS
CALUMET
CALUMETS
CALUMNIED
CALUMNIES
CALUMNY
CALUTRON
CALUTRONS
CALVADOS
CALVARIA
CALVARIAE
CALVARIAL
CALVARIAN
CALVARIAS
CALVARIES
CALVARIUM
CALVARY
CALVE
CALVED
CALVER
CALVERED
CALVERING
CALVERS
CALVES
CALVING
CALVITIES
CALX
CALXES
CALYCATE
CALYCEAL
CALYCES
CALYCINAL
CALYCINE
CALYCLE
CALYCLED
CALYCLES
CALYCOID
CALYCULAR
CALYCULE
CALYCULES
CALYCULI
CALYCULUS
CALYPSO
CALYPSOES
CALYPSOS
CALYPTER
CALYPTERA
CALYPTERS
CALYPTRA
CALYPTRAS
CALYX
CALYXES
CALZONE
CALZONES
CALZONI
CAM
CAMA
CAMAIEU
CAMAIEUX
CAMAIL
CAMAILED
CAMAILS
CAMAN
CAMANACHD
CAMANS
CAMARILLA
CAMARON
CAMARONS
CAMAS
CAMASES
CAMASH
CAMASHES
CAMASS
CAMASSES
CAMBER
CAMBERED
CAMBERING
CAMBERS
CAMBIA
CAMBIAL
CAMBIFORM
CAMBISM
CAMBISMS
CAMBIST
CAMBISTRY
CAMBISTS
CAMBIUM
CAMBIUMS
CAMBOGE
CAMBOGES
CAMBOGIA
CAMBOGIAS
CAMBOOSE
CAMBOOSES
CAMBREL
CAMBRELS
CAMBRIC
CAMBRICS
CAMCORD
CAMCORDED
CAMCORDER
CAMCORDS
CAME
CAMEL
CAMELBACK
CAMELEER
CAMELEERS
CAMELEON
CAMELEONS
CAMELHAIR
CAMELIA
CAMELIAS
CAMELID
CAMELIDS
CAMELINE
CAMELINES
CAMELISH
CAMELLIA
CAMELLIAS
CAMELLIKE
CAMELOID
CAMELOIDS
CAMELOT
CAMELOTS
CAMELRIES
CAMELRY
CAMELS
CAMEO
CAMEOED
CAMEOING
CAMEOS
CAMERA
CAMERAE
CAMERAL
CAMERAMAN
CAMERAMEN
CAMERAS
CAMERATED
CAMES
CAMESE
CAMESES
CAMI
CAMION
CAMIONS
CAMIS
CAMISA
CAMISADE
CAMISADES
CAMISADO
CAMISADOS
CAMISAS
CAMISE
CAMISES
CAMISIA
CAMISIAS
CAMISOLE
CAMISOLES
CAMLET
CAMLETS
CAMMED
CAMMIE
CAMMIES
CAMMING
CAMO
CAMOGIE

CAMOGIES
CAMOMILE
CAMOMILES
CAMOODI
CAMOODIS
CAMORRA
CAMORRAS
CAMORRIST
CAMOS
CAMOTE
CAMOTES
CAMOUFLET
CAMP
CAMPAGNA
CAMPAGNAS
CAMPAGNE
CAMPAIGN
CAMPAIGNS
CAMPANA
CAMPANAS
CAMPANERO
CAMPANILE
CAMPANILI
CAMPANIST
CAMPANULA
CAMPCRAFT
CAMPEACHY
CAMPEADOR
CAMPED
CAMPER
CAMPERIES
CAMPERS
CAMPERY
CAMPESINO
CAMPEST
CAMPFIRE
CAMPFIRES
CAMPHANE
CAMPHANES
CAMPHENE
CAMPHENES
CAMPHINE
CAMPHINES
CAMPHIRE
CAMPHIRES
CAMPHOL
CAMPHOLS
CAMPHONE
CAMPHONES
CAMPHOR
CAMPHORIC
CAMPHORS
CAMPI
CAMPIER
CAMPIEST
CAMPILY
CAMPINESS
CAMPING
CAMPINGS
CAMPION
CAMPIONS
CAMPLE
CAMPLED
CAMPLES
CAMPLING
CAMPLY
CAMPNESS
CAMPO
CAMPODEID
CAMPONG
CAMPONGS
CAMPOREE
CAMPOREES
CAMPOS
CAMPOUT
CAMPOUTS
CAMPS
CAMPSHIRT
CAMPSITE
CAMPSITES
CAMPSTOOL
CAMPUS
CAMPUSED
CAMPUSES
CAMPUSING
CAMPY
CAMS
CAMSHAFT
CAMSHAFTS
CAMSHO
CAMSHOCH
CAMSTAIRY
CAMSTANE
CAMSTANES
CAMSTEARY
CAMSTONE
CAMSTONES
CAMUS
CAMUSES
CAMWHORE
CAMWHORED
CAMWHORES
CAMWOOD
CAMWOODS
CAN
CANADA
CANADAS
CANAIGRE
CANAIGRES
CANAILLE
CANAILLES
CANAKIN
CANAKINS
CANAL
CANALBOAT
CANALED
CANALING
CANALISE
CANALISED
CANALISES
CANALIZE
CANALIZED
CANALIZES
CANALLED
CANALLER
CANALLERS
CANALLING
CANALS
CANAPE
CANAPES
CANARD
CANARDS
CANARIED
CANARIES
CANARY
CANARYING
CANASTA
CANASTAS
CANASTER
CANASTERS
CANBANK
CANBANKS
CANCAN
CANCANS
CANCEL
CANCELBOT
CANCELED
CANCELEER
CANCELER
CANCELERS
CANCELIER
CANCELING
CANCELLED
CANCELLER
CANCELLI
CANCELS
CANCER
CANCERATE
CANCERED
CANCEROUS
CANCERS
CANCHA
CANCHAS
CANCRINE
CANCROID
CANCROIDS
CANDELA
CANDELAS
CANDENT
CANDID
CANDIDA
CANDIDACY
CANDIDAL
CANDIDAS
CANDIDATE
CANDIDER
CANDIDEST
CANDIDLY
CANDIDS
CANDIE
CANDIED
CANDIES
CANDIRU
CANDIRUS
CANDLE
CANDLED
CANDLELIT
CANDLENUT
CANDLEPIN
CANDLER
CANDLERS
CANDLES
CANDLING
CANDOCK
CANDOCKS
CANDOR
CANDORS
CANDOUR
CANDOURS
CANDY
CANDYGRAM
CANDYING
CANDYMAN
CANDYMEN
CANDYTUFT
CANE
CANEBRAKE
CANED
CANEFRUIT
CANEGRUB
CANEGRUBS
CANEH
CANEHS
CANELLA
CANELLAS
CANELLINI
CANEPHOR
CANEPHORA
CANEPHORE
CANEPHORS
CANER
CANERS
CANES
CANESCENT
CANEWARE
CANEWARES
CANFIELD
CANFIELDS
CANFUL
CANFULS
CANG
CANGLE
CANGLED
CANGLES
CANGLING
CANGS
CANGUE
CANGUES
CANICULAR
CANID

CANIDS
CANIER
CANIEST
CANIKIN
CANIKINS
CANINE
CANINES
CANING
CANINGS
CANINITY
CANISTEL
CANISTELS
CANISTER
CANISTERS
CANITIES
CANKER
CANKERED
CANKERIER
CANKERING
CANKEROUS
CANKERS
CANKERY
CANKLE
CANKLES
CANN
CANNA
CANNABIC
CANNABIN
CANNABINS
CANNABIS
CANNACH
CANNACHS
CANNAE
CANNAS
CANNED
CANNEL
CANNELON
CANNELONI
CANNELONS
CANNELS
CANNELURE
CANNER
CANNERIES
CANNERS
CANNERY
CANNIBAL
CANNIBALS
CANNIE
CANNIER
CANNIEST
CANNIKIN
CANNIKINS
CANNILY
CANNINESS
CANNING
CANNINGS
CANNISTER
CANNOLI
CANNOLIS
CANNON
CANNONADE
CANNONED
CANNONEER
CANNONIER
CANNONING
CANNONRY
CANNONS
CANNOT
CANNS
CANNULA
CANNULAE
CANNULAR
CANNULAS
CANNULATE
CANNY
CANOE
CANOEABLE
CANOED
CANOEING
CANOEINGS
CANOEIST
CANOEISTS
CANOEMAN
CANOEMEN
CANOER
CANOERS
CANOES
CANOEWOOD
CANOLA
CANOLAS
CANON
CANONESS
CANONIC
CANONICAL
CANONISE
CANONISED
CANONISER
CANONISES
CANONIST
CANONISTS
CANONIZE
CANONIZED
CANONIZER
CANONIZES
CANONRIES
CANONRY
CANONS
CANOODLE
CANOODLED
CANOODLER
CANOODLES
CANOPIC
CANOPIED
CANOPIES
CANOPY
CANOPYING
CANOROUS
CANS
CANSFUL
CANSO
CANSOS
CANST
CANSTICK
CANSTICKS
CANT
CANTABANK
CANTABILE
CANTAL
CANTALA
CANTALAS
CANTALOUP
CANTALS
CANTAR
CANTARS
CANTATA
CANTATAS
CANTATE
CANTATES
CANTDOG
CANTDOGS
CANTED
CANTEEN
CANTEENS
CANTER
CANTERED
CANTERING
CANTERS
CANTEST
CANTHAL
CANTHARI
CANTHARID
CANTHARIS
CANTHARUS
CANTHI
CANTHIC
CANTHITIS
CANTHOOK
CANTHOOKS
CANTHUS
CANTIC
CANTICLE
CANTICLES
CANTICO
CANTICOED
CANTICOS
CANTICOY
CANTICOYS
CANTICUM
CANTICUMS
CANTIER
CANTIEST
CANTILENA
CANTILY
CANTINA
CANTINAS
CANTINESS
CANTING
CANTINGLY
CANTINGS
CANTION
CANTIONS
CANTLE
CANTLED
CANTLES
CANTLET
CANTLETS
CANTLING
CANTO
CANTON
CANTONAL
CANTONED
CANTONING
CANTONISE
CANTONIZE
CANTONS
CANTOR
CANTORIAL
CANTORIS
CANTORS
CANTOS
CANTRAIP
CANTRAIPS
CANTRAP
CANTRAPS
CANTRED
CANTREDS
CANTREF
CANTREFS
CANTRIP
CANTRIPS
CANTS
CANTUS
CANTUSES
CANTY
CANULA
CANULAE
CANULAR
CANULAS
CANULATE
CANULATED
CANULATES
CANVAS
CANVASED
CANVASER
CANVASERS
CANVASES
CANVASING
CANVASS
CANVASSED
CANVASSER
CANVASSES
CANY
CANYON
CANYONEER
CANYONING
CANYONS
CANZONA
CANZONAS
CANZONE
CANZONES

C

CANZONET
CANZONETS
CANZONI
CAP
CAPA
CAPABLE
CAPABLER
CAPABLEST
CAPABLY
CAPACIOUS
CAPACITOR
CAPACITY
CAPARISON
CAPAS
CAPCOM
CAPCOMS
CAPE
CAPED
CAPEESH
CAPELAN
CAPELANS
CAPELET
CAPELETS
CAPELIKE
CAPELIN
CAPELINE
CAPELINES
CAPELINS
CAPELLET
CAPELLETS
CAPELLINE
CAPELLINI
CAPER
CAPERED
CAPERER
CAPERERS
CAPERING
CAPERS
CAPES
CAPESKIN
CAPESKINS
CAPEWORK
CAPEWORKS
CAPEX
CAPEXES
CAPFUL
CAPFULS
CAPH
CAPHS
CAPI
CAPIAS
CAPIASES
CAPICHE
CAPICOLLA
CAPICOLLO
CAPILLARY
CAPING
CAPISCE
CAPISH
CAPITA
CAPITAL
CAPITALLY
CAPITALS
CAPITAN
CAPITANI
CAPITANO
CAPITANOS
CAPITANS
CAPITATE
CAPITATED
CAPITATES
CAPITAYN
CAPITAYNS
CAPITELLA
CAPITOL
CAPITOLS
CAPITULA
CAPITULAR
CAPITULUM
CAPIZ
CAPIZES
CAPLE
CAPLES
CAPLESS
CAPLET
CAPLETS
CAPLIKE
CAPLIN
CAPLINS
CAPMAKER
CAPMAKERS
CAPO
CAPOCCHIA
CAPOEIRA
CAPOEIRAS
CAPON
CAPONATA
CAPONATAS
CAPONIER
CAPONIERE
CAPONIERS
CAPONISE
CAPONISED
CAPONISES
CAPONIZE
CAPONIZED
CAPONIZES
CAPONS
CAPORAL
CAPORALS
CAPOS
CAPOT
CAPOTASTO
CAPOTE
CAPOTES
CAPOTS
CAPOTTED
CAPOTTING
CAPOUCH
CAPOUCHES
CAPPED
CAPPER
CAPPERS
CAPPING
CAPPINGS
CAPRATE
CAPRATES
CAPRESE
CAPRESES
CAPRI
CAPRIC
CAPRICCI
CAPRICCIO
CAPRICE
CAPRICES
CAPRID
CAPRIDS
CAPRIFIED
CAPRIFIES
CAPRIFIG
CAPRIFIGS
CAPRIFOIL
CAPRIFOLE
CAPRIFORM
CAPRIFY
CAPRINE
CAPRIOLE
CAPRIOLED
CAPRIOLES
CAPRIS
CAPROATE
CAPROATES
CAPROCK
CAPROCKS
CAPROIC
CAPRYLATE
CAPRYLIC
CAPS
CAPSAICIN
CAPSICIN
CAPSICINS
CAPSICUM
CAPSICUMS
CAPSID
CAPSIDAL
CAPSIDS
CAPSIZAL
CAPSIZALS
CAPSIZE
CAPSIZED
CAPSIZES
CAPSIZING
CAPSOMER
CAPSOMERE
CAPSOMERS
CAPSTAN
CAPSTANS
CAPSTONE
CAPSTONES
CAPSULAR
CAPSULARY
CAPSULATE
CAPSULE
CAPSULED
CAPSULES
CAPSULING
CAPSULISE
CAPSULIZE
CAPTAIN
CAPTAINCY
CAPTAINED
CAPTAINRY
CAPTAINS
CAPTAN
CAPTANS
CAPTCHA
CAPTCHAS
CAPTION
CAPTIONED
CAPTIONS
CAPTIOUS
CAPTIVATE
CAPTIVE
CAPTIVED
CAPTIVES
CAPTIVING
CAPTIVITY
CAPTOPRIL
CAPTOR
CAPTORS
CAPTURE
CAPTURED
CAPTURER
CAPTURERS
CAPTURES
CAPTURING
CAPUCCIO
CAPUCCIOS
CAPUCHE
CAPUCHED
CAPUCHES
CAPUCHIN
CAPUCHINS
CAPUERA
CAPUERAS
CAPUL
CAPULS
CAPUT
CAPYBARA
CAPYBARAS
CAR
CARABAO
CARABAOS
CARABID
CARABIDS
CARABIN
CARABINE
CARABINER
CARABINES
CARABINS

CARACAL
CARACALS
CARACARA
CARACARAS
CARACK
CARACKS
CARACOL
CARACOLE
CARACOLED
CARACOLER
CARACOLES
CARACOLS
CARACT
CARACTS
CARACUL
CARACULS
CARAFE
CARAFES
CARAGANA
CARAGANAS
CARAGEEN
CARAGEENS
CARAMBA
CARAMBOLA
CARAMBOLE
CARAMEL
CARAMELS
CARANGID
CARANGIDS
CARANGOID
CARANNA
CARANNAS
CARAP
CARAPACE
CARAPACED
CARAPACES
CARAPAX
CARAPAXES
CARAPS
CARASSOW
CARASSOWS
CARAT
CARATE
CARATES
CARATS
CARAUNA
CARAUNAS
CARAVAN
CARAVANCE
CARAVANED
CARAVANER
CARAVANS
CARAVEL
CARAVELLE
CARAVELS
CARAWAY
CARAWAYS
CARB
CARBACHOL
CARBAMATE
CARBAMIC
CARBAMIDE
CARBAMINO
CARBAMOYL
CARBAMYL
CARBAMYLS
CARBANION
CARBARN
CARBARNS
CARBARYL
CARBARYLS
CARBAZOLE
CARBEEN
CARBEENS
CARBENE
CARBENES
CARBIDE
CARBIDES
CARBIDOPA
CARBIES
CARBINE
CARBINEER
CARBINES
CARBINIER
CARBINOL
CARBINOLS
CARBO
CARBOLIC
CARBOLICS
CARBOLISE
CARBOLIZE
CARBON
CARBONADE
CARBONADO
CARBONARA
CARBONATE
CARBONIC
CARBONISE
CARBONIUM
CARBONIZE
CARBONOUS
CARBONS
CARBONYL
CARBONYLS
CARBORA
CARBORAS
CARBORNE
CARBOS
CARBOXYL
CARBOXYLS
CARBOY
CARBOYED
CARBOYS
CARBS
CARBUNCLE
CARBURATE
CARBURET
CARBURETS
CARBURISE
CARBURIZE
CARBY
CARCAJOU
CARCAJOUS
CARCAKE
CARCAKES
CARCANET
CARCANETS
CARCASE
CARCASED
CARCASES
CARCASING
CARCASS
CARCASSED
CARCASSES
CARCEL
CARCELS
CARCERAL
CARCINOID
CARCINOMA
CARD
CARDAMINE
CARDAMOM
CARDAMOMS
CARDAMON
CARDAMONS
CARDAMUM
CARDAMUMS
CARDAN
CARDBOARD
CARDCASE
CARDCASES
CARDECU
CARDECUE
CARDECUES
CARDECUS
CARDED
CARDER
CARDERS
CARDI
CARDIA
CARDIAC
CARDIACAL
CARDIACS
CARDIAE
CARDIALGY
CARDIAS
CARDIE
CARDIES
CARDIGAN
CARDIGANS
CARDINAL
CARDINALS
CARDING
CARDINGS
CARDIO
CARDIOID
CARDIOIDS
CARDIOS
CARDIS
CARDITIC
CARDITIS
CARDON
CARDONS
CARDOON
CARDOONS
CARDPHONE
CARDPUNCH
CARDS
CARDSHARP
CARDUUS
CARDUUSES
CARDY
CARE
CARED
CAREEN
CAREENAGE
CAREENED
CAREENER
CAREENERS
CAREENING
CAREENS
CAREER
CAREERED
CAREERER
CAREERERS
CAREERING
CAREERISM
CAREERIST
CAREERS
CAREFREE
CAREFUL
CAREFULLY
CAREGIVER
CARELESS
CARELINE
CARELINES
CAREME
CAREMES
CARER
CARERS
CARES
CARESS
CARESSED
CARESSER
CARESSERS
CARESSES
CARESSING
CARESSIVE
CARET
CARETAKE
CARETAKEN
CARETAKER
CARETAKES
CARETOOK
CARETS
CAREWARE
CAREWARES
CAREWORN
CAREX
CARFARE

C

CARFARES
CARFAX
CARFAXES
CARFOX
CARFOXES
CARFUFFLE
CARFUL
CARFULS
CARGEESE
CARGO
CARGOED
CARGOES
CARGOING
CARGOOSE
CARGOS
CARHOP
CARHOPPED
CARHOPS
CARIACOU
CARIACOUS
CARIAMA
CARIAMAS
CARIBE
CARIBES
CARIBOO
CARIBOOS
CARIBOU
CARIBOUS
CARICES
CARIED
CARIERE
CARIERES
CARIES
CARILLON
CARILLONS
CARINA
CARINAE
CARINAL
CARINAS
CARINATE
CARINATED
CARING
CARINGLY
CARINGS
CARIOCA
CARIOCAS
CARIOLE
CARIOLES
CARIOSE
CARIOSITY
CARIOUS
CARITAS
CARITASES
CARITATES
CARJACK
CARJACKED
CARJACKER
CARJACKS
CARJACOU
CARJACOUS
CARK
CARKED
CARKING
CARKS
CARL
CARLE
CARLES
CARLESS
CARLIN
CARLINE
CARLINES
CARLING
CARLINGS
CARLINS
CARLISH
CARLOAD
CARLOADS
CARLOCK
CARLOCKS
CARLOT
CARLOTS
CARLS
CARMAKER
CARMAKERS
CARMAN
CARMELITE
CARMEN
CARMINE
CARMINES
CARN
CARNAGE
CARNAGES
CARNAHUBA
CARNAL
CARNALISE
CARNALISM
CARNALIST
CARNALITY
CARNALIZE
CARNALLED
CARNALLY
CARNALS
CARNAROLI
CARNATION
CARNAUBA
CARNAUBAS
CARNELIAN
CARNEOUS
CARNET
CARNETS
CARNEY
CARNEYED
CARNEYING
CARNEYS
CARNIE
CARNIED
CARNIER
CARNIES
CARNIEST
CARNIFEX
CARNIFIED
CARNIFIES
CARNIFY
CARNITINE
CARNIVAL
CARNIVALS
CARNIVORA
CARNIVORE
CARNIVORY
CARNOSAUR
CARNOSE
CARNOSITY
CARNOTITE
CARNS
CARNY
CARNYING
CARNYX
CARNYXES
CAROACH
CAROACHES
CAROB
CAROBS
CAROCH
CAROCHE
CAROCHES
CAROL
CAROLED
CAROLER
CAROLERS
CAROLI
CAROLING
CAROLINGS
CAROLLED
CAROLLER
CAROLLERS
CAROLLING
CAROLS
CAROLUS
CAROLUSES
CAROM
CAROMED
CAROMEL
CAROMELS
CAROMING
CAROMS
CARON
CARONS
CAROTENE
CAROTENES
CAROTID
CAROTIDAL
CAROTIDS
CAROTIN
CAROTINS
CAROUSAL
CAROUSALS
CAROUSE
CAROUSED
CAROUSEL
CAROUSELS
CAROUSER
CAROUSERS
CAROUSES
CAROUSING
CARP
CARPACCIO
CARPAL
CARPALE
CARPALES
CARPALIA
CARPALS
CARPED
CARPEL
CARPELS
CARPENTER
CARPENTRY
CARPER
CARPERS
CARPET
CARPETBAG
CARPETED
CARPETING
CARPETS
CARPHONE
CARPHONES
CARPI
CARPING
CARPINGLY
CARPINGS
CARPLIKE
CARPOLOGY
CARPOOL
CARPOOLED
CARPOOLER
CARPOOLS
CARPORT
CARPORTS
CARPS
CARPUS
CARR
CARRACK
CARRACKS
CARRACT
CARRACTS
CARRAGEEN
CARRAT
CARRATS
CARRAWAY
CARRAWAYS
CARRECT
CARRECTS
CARREFOUR
CARREL
CARRELL
CARRELLS
CARRELS
CARRIAGE
CARRIAGES
CARRICK
CARRIED

CARRIER
CARRIERS
CARRIES
CARRIOLE
CARRIOLES
CARRION
CARRIONS
CARRITCH
CARROCH
CARROCHES
CARROM
CARROMED
CARROMING
CARROMS
CARRON
CARRONADE
CARROT
CARROTIER
CARROTIN
CARROTINS
CARROTS
CARROTTOP
CARROTY
CARROUSEL
CARRS
CARRY
CARRYALL
CARRYALLS
CARRYBACK
CARRYCOT
CARRYCOTS
CARRYING
CARRYON
CARRYONS
CARRYOUT
CARRYOUTS
CARRYOVER
CARRYTALE
CARS
CARSE
CARSES
CARSEY
CARSEYS
CARSHARE
CARSHARED
CARSHARES
CARSICK
CARSPIEL
CARSPIELS
CART
CARTA
CARTABLE
CARTAGE
CARTAGES
CARTAS
CARTE
CARTED
CARTEL
CARTELISE
CARTELISM
CARTELIST
CARTELIZE
CARTELS
CARTER
CARTERS
CARTES
CARTFUL
CARTFULS
CARTHORSE
CARTILAGE
CARTING
CARTLOAD
CARTLOADS
CARTOGRAM
CARTOLOGY
CARTON
CARTONAGE
CARTONED
CARTONING
CARTONS
CARTOON
CARTOONED
CARTOONS
CARTOONY
CARTOP
CARTOPPER
CARTOUCH
CARTOUCHE
CARTRIDGE
CARTROAD
CARTROADS
CARTS
CARTULARY
CARTWAY
CARTWAYS
CARTWHEEL
CARUCAGE
CARUCAGES
CARUCATE
CARUCATES
CARUNCLE
CARUNCLES
CARVACROL
CARVE
CARVED
CARVEL
CARVELS
CARVEN
CARVER
CARVERIES
CARVERS
CARVERY
CARVES
CARVIES
CARVING
CARVINGS
CARVY
CARWASH
CARWASHES
CARYATIC
CARYATID
CARYATIDS
CARYOPSES
CARYOPSIS
CARYOTIN
CARYOTINS
CASA
CASABA
CASABAS
CASAS
CASAVA
CASAVAS
CASBAH
CASBAHS
CASCABEL
CASCABELS
CASCABLE
CASCABLES
CASCADE
CASCADED
CASCADES
CASCADING
CASCADURA
CASCARA
CASCARAS
CASCHROM
CASCHROMS
CASCO
CASCOS
CASE
CASEASE
CASEASES
CASEATE
CASEATED
CASEATES
CASEATING
CASEATION
CASEBOOK
CASEBOOKS
CASEBOUND
CASED
CASEFIED
CASEFIES
CASEFY
CASEFYING
CASEIC
CASEIN
CASEINATE
CASEINS
CASELAW
CASELAWS
CASELOAD
CASELOADS
CASEMAKER
CASEMAN
CASEMATE
CASEMATED
CASEMATES
CASEMEN
CASEMENT
CASEMENTS
CASEMIX
CASEMIXES
CASEOSE
CASEOSES
CASEOUS
CASERN
CASERNE
CASERNES
CASERNS
CASES
CASETTE
CASETTES
CASEVAC
CASEVACED
CASEVACS
CASEWORK
CASEWORKS
CASEWORM
CASEWORMS
CASH
CASHABLE
CASHAW
CASHAWS
CASHBACK
CASHBACKS
CASHBOOK
CASHBOOKS
CASHBOX
CASHBOXES
CASHED
CASHES
CASHEW
CASHEWS
CASHIER
CASHIERED
CASHIERER
CASHIERS
CASHING
CASHLESS
CASHMERE
CASHMERES
CASHOO
CASHOOS
CASHPOINT
CASHSPIEL
CASIMERE
CASIMERES
CASIMIRE
CASIMIRES
CASING
CASINGS
CASINI
CASINO
CASINOS
CASITA
CASITAS
CASK
CASKED
CASKET

CASKETED
CASKETING
CASKETS
CASKIER
CASKIEST
CASKING
CASKS
CASKSTAND
CASKY
CASPASE
CASPASES
CASQUE
CASQUED
CASQUES
CASSABA
CASSABAS
CASSAREEP
CASSATA
CASSATAS
CASSATION
CASSAVA
CASSAVAS
CASSENA
CASSENAS
CASSENE
CASSENES
CASSEROLE
CASSETTE
CASSETTES
CASSIA
CASSIAS
CASSIE
CASSIES
CASSIMERE
CASSINA
CASSINAS
CASSINE
CASSINES
CASSINGLE
CASSINO
CASSINOS
CASSIOPE
CASSIOPES
CASSIS
CASSISES
CASSOCK
CASSOCKED
CASSOCKS
CASSONADE
CASSONE
CASSONES
CASSOULET
CASSOWARY
CASSPIR
CASSPIRS
CAST
CASTABLE
CASTANET
CASTANETS
CASTAWAY
CASTAWAYS
CASTE
CASTED
CASTEISM
CASTEISMS
CASTELESS
CASTELLA
CASTELLAN
CASTELLUM
CASTER
CASTERED
CASTERS
CASTES
CASTIGATE
CASTING
CASTINGS
CASTLE
CASTLED
CASTLES
CASTLING
CASTLINGS
CASTOCK
CASTOCKS
CASTOFF
CASTOFFS
CASTOR
CASTOREUM
CASTORIES
CASTORS
CASTORY
CASTRAL
CASTRATE
CASTRATED
CASTRATER
CASTRATES
CASTRATI
CASTRATO
CASTRATOR
CASTRATOS
CASTS
CASUAL
CASUALISE
CASUALISM
CASUALIZE
CASUALLY
CASUALS
CASUALTY
CASUARINA
CASUIST
CASUISTIC
CASUISTRY
CASUISTS
CASUS
CAT
CATABASES
CATABASIS
CATABATIC
CATABOLIC
CATACLASM
CATACLYSM
CATACOMB
CATACOMBS
CATAFALCO
CATAGEN
CATAGENS
CATALASE
CATALASES
CATALATIC
CATALEPSY
CATALEXES
CATALEXIS
CATALO
CATALOES
CATALOG
CATALOGED
CATALOGER
CATALOGIC
CATALOGNE
CATALOGS
CATALOGUE
CATALOS
CATALPA
CATALPAS
CATALYSE
CATALYSED
CATALYSER
CATALYSES
CATALYSIS
CATALYST
CATALYSTS
CATALYTIC
CATALYZE
CATALYZED
CATALYZER
CATALYZES
CATAMARAN
CATAMENIA
CATAMITE
CATAMITES
CATAMOUNT
CATAPAN
CATAPANS
CATAPHOR
CATAPHORA
CATAPHORS
CATAPHYLL
CATAPLASM
CATAPLEXY
CATAPULT
CATAPULTS
CATARACT
CATARACTS
CATARHINE
CATARRH
CATARRHAL
CATARRHS
CATASTA
CATASTAS
CATATONIA
CATATONIC
CATATONY
CATAWBA
CATAWBAS
CATBIRD
CATBIRDS
CATBOAT
CATBOATS
CATBRIAR
CATBRIARS
CATBRIER
CATBRIERS
CATCALL
CATCALLED
CATCALLER
CATCALLS
CATCH
CATCHABLE
CATCHALL
CATCHALLS
CATCHCRY
CATCHED
CATCHEN
CATCHER
CATCHERS
CATCHES
CATCHFLY
CATCHIER
CATCHIEST
CATCHILY
CATCHING
CATCHINGS
CATCHLINE
CATCHMENT
CATCHPOLE
CATCHPOLL
CATCHT
CATCHUP
CATCHUPS
CATCHWEED
CATCHWORD
CATCHY
CATCLAW
CATCLAWS
CATCON
CATCONS
CATE
CATECHIN
CATECHINS
CATECHISE
CATECHISM
CATECHIST
CATECHIZE
CATECHOL
CATECHOLS
CATECHU
CATECHUS
CATEGORIC
CATEGORY
CATELOG
CATELOGS

CATENA
CATENAE
CATENANE
CATENANES
CATENARY
CATENAS
CATENATE
CATENATED
CATENATES
CATENOID
CATENOIDS
CATER
CATERAN
CATERANS
CATERED
CATERER
CATERERS
CATERESS
CATERING
CATERINGS
CATERS
CATERWAUL
CATES
CATFACE
CATFACES
CATFACING
CATFALL
CATFALLS
CATFIGHT
CATFIGHTS
CATFISH
CATFISHED
CATFISHES
CATFLAP
CATFLAPS
CATFOOD
CATFOODS
CATGUT
CATGUTS
CATHARISE
CATHARIZE
CATHARSES
CATHARSIS
CATHARTIC
CATHEAD
CATHEADS
CATHECT
CATHECTED
CATHECTIC
CATHECTS
CATHEDRA
CATHEDRAE
CATHEDRAL
CATHEDRAS
CATHEPSIN
CATHEPTIC
CATHETER
CATHETERS
CATHETUS
CATHEXES
CATHEXIS
CATHINONE
CATHISMA
CATHISMAS
CATHODAL
CATHODE
CATHODES
CATHODIC
CATHOLE
CATHOLES
CATHOLIC
CATHOLICS
CATHOLYTE
CATHOOD
CATHOODS
CATHOUSE
CATHOUSES
CATION
CATIONIC
CATIONS
CATJANG
CATJANGS
CATKIN
CATKINATE
CATKINS
CATLIKE
CATLIN
CATLING
CATLINGS
CATLINITE
CATLINS
CATMINT
CATMINTS
CATNAP
CATNAPER
CATNAPERS
CATNAPPED
CATNAPPER
CATNAPS
CATNEP
CATNEPS
CATNIP
CATNIPS
CATOLYTE
CATOLYTES
CATOPTRIC
CATRIGGED
CATS
CATSKIN
CATSKINS
CATSPAW
CATSPAWS
CATSUIT
CATSUITS
CATSUP
CATSUPS
CATTABU
CATTABUS
CATTAIL
CATTAILS
CATTALO
CATTALOES
CATTALOS
CATTED
CATTERIES
CATTERY
CATTIE
CATTIER
CATTIES
CATTIEST
CATTILY
CATTINESS
CATTING
CATTISH
CATTISHLY
CATTLE
CATTLEMAN
CATTLEMEN
CATTLEYA
CATTLEYAS
CATTY
CATWALK
CATWALKS
CATWORKS
CATWORM
CATWORMS
CAUCHEMAR
CAUCUS
CAUCUSED
CAUCUSES
CAUCUSING
CAUCUSSED
CAUCUSSES
CAUDA
CAUDAD
CAUDAE
CAUDAL
CAUDALLY
CAUDATE
CAUDATED
CAUDATES
CAUDATION
CAUDEX
CAUDEXES
CAUDICES
CAUDICLE
CAUDICLES
CAUDILLO
CAUDILLOS
CAUDLE
CAUDLED
CAUDLES
CAUDLING
CAUDRON
CAUDRONS
CAUF
CAUGHT
CAUK
CAUKER
CAUKERS
CAUKS
CAUL
CAULD
CAULDER
CAULDEST
CAULDRIFE
CAULDRON
CAULDRONS
CAULDS
CAULES
CAULICLE
CAULICLES
CAULICULI
CAULIFORM
CAULINARY
CAULINE
CAULIS
CAULK
CAULKED
CAULKER
CAULKERS
CAULKING
CAULKINGS
CAULKS
CAULOME
CAULOMES
CAULS
CAUM
CAUMED
CAUMING
CAUMS
CAUMSTANE
CAUMSTONE
CAUP
CAUPS
CAURI
CAURIS
CAUSA
CAUSABLE
CAUSAE
CAUSAL
CAUSALGIA
CAUSALGIC
CAUSALITY
CAUSALLY
CAUSALS
CAUSATION
CAUSATIVE
CAUSE
CAUSED
CAUSELESS
CAUSEN
CAUSER
CAUSERIE
CAUSERIES
CAUSERS
CAUSES
CAUSEWAY
CAUSEWAYS
CAUSEY

CAUSEYED
CAUSEYS
CAUSING
CAUSTIC
CAUSTICAL
CAUSTICS
CAUTEL
CAUTELOUS
CAUTELS
CAUTER
CAUTERANT
CAUTERIES
CAUTERISE
CAUTERISM
CAUTERIZE
CAUTERS
CAUTERY
CAUTION
CAUTIONED
CAUTIONER
CAUTIONRY
CAUTIONS
CAUTIOUS
CAUVES
CAVA
CAVALCADE
CAVALERO
CAVALEROS
CAVALETTI
CAVALIER
CAVALIERS
CAVALLA
CAVALLAS
CAVALLIES
CAVALLY
CAVALRIES
CAVALRY
CAVAS
CAVASS
CAVASSES
CAVATINA
CAVATINAS
CAVATINE
CAVE
CAVEAT
CAVEATED
CAVEATING
CAVEATOR
CAVEATORS
CAVEATS
CAVED
CAVEFISH
CAVEL
CAVELIKE
CAVELS
CAVEMAN
CAVEMEN
CAVENDISH
CAVEOLA
CAVEOLAE
CAVEOLAR
CAVER
CAVERN
CAVERNED
CAVERNING
CAVERNOUS
CAVERNS
CAVERS
CAVES
CAVESSON
CAVESSONS
CAVETTI
CAVETTO
CAVETTOS
CAVIAR
CAVIARE
CAVIARES
CAVIARIE
CAVIARIES
CAVIARS
CAVICORN
CAVICORNS
CAVIE
CAVIER
CAVIERS
CAVIES
CAVIL
CAVILED
CAVILER
CAVILERS
CAVILING
CAVILLED
CAVILLER
CAVILLERS
CAVILLING
CAVILS
CAVING
CAVINGS
CAVITARY
CAVITATE
CAVITATED
CAVITATES
CAVITIED
CAVITIES
CAVITY
CAVORT
CAVORTED
CAVORTER
CAVORTERS
CAVORTING
CAVORTS
CAVY
CAW
CAWED
CAWING
CAWINGS
CAWK
CAWKER
CAWKERS
CAWKS
CAWS
CAXON
CAXONS
CAY
CAYENNE
CAYENNED
CAYENNES
CAYMAN
CAYMANS
CAYS
CAYUSE
CAYUSES
CAZ
CAZH
CAZIQUE
CAZIQUES
CEANOTHUS
CEAS
CEASE
CEASED
CEASEFIRE
CEASELESS
CEASES
CEASING
CEASINGS
CEAZE
CEAZED
CEAZES
CEAZING
CEBADILLA
CEBID
CEBIDS
CEBOID
CEBOIDS
CECA
CECAL
CECALLY
CECILS
CECITIES
CECITIS
CECITISES
CECITY
CECROPIA
CECROPIAS
CECROPIN
CECROPINS
CECUM
CEDAR
CEDARBIRD
CEDARED
CEDARIER
CEDARIEST
CEDARN
CEDARS
CEDARWOOD
CEDARY
CEDE
CEDED
CEDER
CEDERS
CEDES
CEDI
CEDILLA
CEDILLAS
CEDING
CEDIS
CEDRATE
CEDRATES
CEDRINE
CEDULA
CEDULAS
CEE
CEES
CEIBA
CEIBAS
CEIL
CEILED
CEILER
CEILERS
CEILI
CEILIDH
CEILIDHS
CEILING
CEILINGED
CEILINGS
CEILIS
CEILS
CEINTURE
CEINTURES
CEL
CELADON
CELADONS
CELANDINE
CELEB
CELEBRANT
CELEBRATE
CELEBRITY
CELEBS
CELECOXIB
CELERIAC
CELERIACS
CELERIES
CELERITY
CELERY
CELESTA
CELESTAS
CELESTE
CELESTES
CELESTIAL
CELESTINE
CELESTITE
CELIAC
CELIACS
CELIBACY
CELIBATE
CELIBATES
CELIBATIC
CELL
CELLA
CELLAE

CELLAR
CELLARAGE
CELLARED
CELLARER
CELLARERS
CELLARET
CELLARETS
CELLARING
CELLARIST
CELLARMAN
CELLARMEN
CELLAROUS
CELLARS
CELLARWAY
CELLBLOCK
CELLED
CELLI
CELLING
CELLINGS
CELLIST
CELLISTS
CELLMATE
CELLMATES
CELLO
CELLOIDIN
CELLOS
CELLOSE
CELLOSES
CELLPHONE
CELLS
CELLULAR
CELLULARS
CELLULASE
CELLULE
CELLULES
CELLULITE
CELLULOID
CELLULOSE
CELLULOUS
CELOM
CELOMATA
CELOMIC
CELOMS
CELOSIA
CELOSIAS
CELOTEX
CELOTEXES
CELS
CELSITUDE
CELT
CELTS
CEMBALI
CEMBALIST
CEMBALO
CEMBALOS
CEMBRA
CEMBRAS
CEMENT
CEMENTA
CEMENTED
CEMENTER
CEMENTERS
CEMENTING
CEMENTITE
CEMENTS
CEMENTUM
CEMENTUMS
CEMETERY
CEMITARE
CEMITARES
CENACLE
CENACLES
CENDRE
CENOBITE
CENOBITES
CENOBITIC
CENOTAPH
CENOTAPHS
CENOTE
CENOTES
CENOZOIC
CENS
CENSE
CENSED
CENSER
CENSERS
CENSES
CENSING
CENSOR
CENSORED
CENSORIAL
CENSORIAN
CENSORING
CENSORS
CENSUAL
CENSURE
CENSURED
CENSURER
CENSURERS
CENSURES
CENSURING
CENSUS
CENSUSED
CENSUSES
CENSUSING
CENT
CENTAGE
CENTAGES
CENTAI
CENTAL
CENTALS
CENTARE
CENTARES
CENTAS
CENTAUR
CENTAUREA
CENTAURIC
CENTAURS
CENTAURY
CENTAVO
CENTAVOS
CENTENARY
CENTENIER
CENTER
CENTERED
CENTERING
CENTERS
CENTESES
CENTESIMI
CENTESIMO
CENTESIS
CENTIARE
CENTIARES
CENTIGRAM
CENTILE
CENTILES
CENTIME
CENTIMES
CENTIMO
CENTIMOS
CENTINEL
CENTINELL
CENTINELS
CENTIPEDE
CENTNER
CENTNERS
CENTO
CENTOIST
CENTOISTS
CENTONATE
CENTONEL
CENTONELL
CENTONELS
CENTONES
CENTONIST
CENTOS
CENTRA
CENTRAL
CENTRALER
CENTRALLY
CENTRALS
CENTRE
CENTRED
CENTREING
CENTREMAN
CENTREMEN
CENTRES
CENTRIC
CENTRICAL
CENTRIES
CENTRING
CENTRINGS
CENTRIOLE
CENTRISM
CENTRISMS
CENTRIST
CENTRISTS
CENTRODE
CENTRODES
CENTROID
CENTROIDS
CENTRUM
CENTRUMS
CENTRY
CENTS
CENTU
CENTUM
CENTUMS
CENTUMVIR
CENTUPLE
CENTUPLED
CENTUPLES
CENTURIAL
CENTURIES
CENTURION
CENTURY
CEORL
CEORLISH
CEORLS
CEP
CEPACEOUS
CEPAGE
CEPAGES
CEPE
CEPES
CEPHALAD
CEPHALATE
CEPHALIC
CEPHALICS
CEPHALIN
CEPHALINS
CEPHALOUS
CEPHEID
CEPHEIDS
CEPS
CERACEOUS
CERAMAL
CERAMALS
CERAMIC
CERAMICS
CERAMIDE
CERAMIDES
CERAMIST
CERAMISTS
CERASIN
CERASINS
CERASTES
CERASTIUM
CERATE
CERATED
CERATES
CERATIN
CERATINS
CERATITIS
CERATODUS
CERATOID
CERBEREAN
CERBERIAN
CERCAL
CERCARIA

CERCARIAE
CERCARIAL
CERCARIAN
CERCARIAS
CERCI
CERCIS
CERCISES
CERCLAGE
CERCLAGES
CERCOPID
CERCOPIDS
CERCUS
CERE
CEREAL
CEREALIST
CEREALS
CEREBELLA
CEREBRA
CEREBRAL
CEREBRALS
CEREBRATE
CEREBRIC
CEREBROID
CEREBRUM
CEREBRUMS
CERECLOTH
CERED
CEREMENT
CEREMENTS
CEREMONY
CEREOUS
CERES
CERESIN
CERESINE
CERESINES
CERESINS
CEREUS
CEREUSES
CERGE
CERGES
CERIA
CERIAS
CERIC
CERING
CERIPH
CERIPHS
CERISE
CERISES
CERITE
CERITES
CERIUM
CERIUMS
CERMET
CERMETS
CERNE
CERNED
CERNES
CERNING
CERNUOUS
CERO
CEROC
CEROCS
CEROGRAPH
CEROMANCY
CEROON
CEROONS
CEROS
CEROTIC
CEROTYPE
CEROTYPES
CEROUS
CERRADO
CERRADOS
CERRIAL
CERRIS
CERRISES
CERT
CERTAIN
CERTAINER
CERTAINLY
CERTAINTY
CERTES
CERTIE
CERTIFIED
CERTIFIER
CERTIFIES
CERTIFY
CERTITUDE
CERTS
CERTY
CERULE
CERULEAN
CERULEANS
CERULEIN
CERULEINS
CERULEOUS
CERUMEN
CERUMENS
CERUSE
CERUSES
CERUSITE
CERUSITES
CERUSSITE
CERVELAS
CERVELAT
CERVELATS
CERVEZA
CERVEZAS
CERVICAL
CERVICES
CERVICUM
CERVICUMS
CERVID
CERVIDS
CERVINE
CERVIX
CERVIXES
CESAREAN
CESAREANS
CESAREVNA
CESARIAN
CESARIANS
CESIOUS
CESIUM
CESIUMS
CESPITOSE
CESS
CESSATION
CESSE
CESSED
CESSER
CESSERS
CESSES
CESSING
CESSION
CESSIONS
CESSPIT
CESSPITS
CESSPOOL
CESSPOOLS
CESTA
CESTAS
CESTI
CESTODE
CESTODES
CESTOI
CESTOID
CESTOIDS
CESTOS
CESTOSES
CESTUI
CESTUIS
CESTUS
CESTUSES
CESURA
CESURAE
CESURAL
CESURAS
CESURE
CESURES
CETACEAN
CETACEANS
CETACEOUS
CETANE
CETANES
CETE
CETERACH
CETERACHS
CETES
CETOLOGY
CETRIMIDE
CETUXIMAB
CETYL
CETYLS
CETYWALL
CETYWALLS
CEVADILLA
CEVAPCICI
CEVICHE
CEVICHES
CEVITAMIC
CEYLANITE
CEYLONITE
CEZVE
CEZVES
CH
CHA
CHABAZITE
CHABLIS
CHABOUK
CHABOUKS
CHABUK
CHABUKS
CHACE
CHACED
CHACES
CHACHKA
CHACHKAS
CHACING
CHACK
CHACKED
CHACKING
CHACKS
CHACMA
CHACMAS
CHACO
CHACOES
CHACONINE
CHACONNE
CHACONNES
CHACOS
CHAD
CHADAR
CHADARIM
CHADARS
CHADDAR
CHADDARS
CHADDOR
CHADDORS
CHADLESS
CHADO
CHADOR
CHADORS
CHADOS
CHADRI
CHADS
CHAEBOL
CHAEBOLS
CHAETA
CHAETAE
CHAETAL
CHAETODON
CHAETOPOD
CHAFE
CHAFED
CHAFER
CHAFERS
CHAFES
CHAFF
CHAFFED

CHAFFER
CHAFFERED
CHAFFERER
CHAFFERS
CHAFFERY
CHAFFIER
CHAFFIEST
CHAFFINCH
CHAFFING
CHAFFINGS
CHAFFRON
CHAFFRONS
CHAFFS
CHAFFY
CHAFING
CHAFT
CHAFTS
CHAGAN
CHAGANS
CHAGRIN
CHAGRINED
CHAGRINS
CHAI
CHAIN
CHAINE
CHAINED
CHAINER
CHAINERS
CHAINES
CHAINFALL
CHAINING
CHAINLESS
CHAINLET
CHAINLETS
CHAINMAN
CHAINMEN
CHAINS
CHAINSAW
CHAINSAWS
CHAINSHOT
CHAINWORK
CHAIR
CHAIRBACK
CHAIRDAYS
CHAIRED
CHAIRING
CHAIRLIFT
CHAIRMAN
CHAIRMANS
CHAIRMEN
CHAIRS
CHAIS
CHAISE
CHAISES
CHAKALAKA
CHAKRA
CHAKRAS
CHAL
CHALAH
CHALAHS
CHALAN
CHALANED
CHALANING
CHALANNED
CHALANS
CHALAZA
CHALAZAE
CHALAZAL
CHALAZAS
CHALAZIA
CHALAZION
CHALCID
CHALCIDS
CHALCOGEN
CHALDER
CHALDERS
CHALDRON
CHALDRONS
CHALEH
CHALEHS
CHALET
CHALETS
CHALICE
CHALICED
CHALICES
CHALK
CHALKED
CHALKFACE
CHALKIER
CHALKIEST
CHALKING
CHALKLAND
CHALKLIKE
CHALKMARK
CHALKPIT
CHALKPITS
CHALKS
CHALKY
CHALLA
CHALLAH
CHALLAHS
CHALLAN
CHALLANS
CHALLAS
CHALLENGE
CHALLIE
CHALLIES
CHALLIS
CHALLISES
CHALLOT
CHALLOTH
CHALLY
CHALONE
CHALONES
CHALONIC
CHALOT
CHALOTH
CHALS
CHALUMEAU
CHALUPA
CHALUPAS
CHALUTZ
CHALUTZES
CHALUTZIM
CHALYBEAN
CHALYBITE
CHAM
CHAMADE
CHAMADES
CHAMBER
CHAMBERED
CHAMBERER
CHAMBERS
CHAMBRAY
CHAMBRAYS
CHAMBRE
CHAMELEON
CHAMELOT
CHAMELOTS
CHAMETZ
CHAMETZES
CHAMFER
CHAMFERED
CHAMFERER
CHAMFERS
CHAMFRAIN
CHAMFRON
CHAMFRONS
CHAMISA
CHAMISAL
CHAMISALS
CHAMISAS
CHAMISE
CHAMISES
CHAMISO
CHAMISOS
CHAMLET
CHAMLETS
CHAMMIED
CHAMMIES
CHAMMY
CHAMMYING
CHAMOIS
CHAMOISED
CHAMOISES
CHAMOIX
CHAMOMILE
CHAMP
CHAMPAC
CHAMPACA
CHAMPACAS
CHAMPACS
CHAMPAGNE
CHAMPAIGN
CHAMPAK
CHAMPAKS
CHAMPART
CHAMPARTS
CHAMPAS
CHAMPED
CHAMPER
CHAMPERS
CHAMPERTY
CHAMPIER
CHAMPIEST
CHAMPING
CHAMPION
CHAMPIONS
CHAMPLEVE
CHAMPS
CHAMPY
CHAMS
CHANA
CHANAS
CHANCE
CHANCED
CHANCEFUL
CHANCEL
CHANCELS
CHANCER
CHANCERS
CHANCERY
CHANCES
CHANCEY
CHANCIER
CHANCIEST
CHANCILY
CHANCING
CHANCRE
CHANCRES
CHANCROID
CHANCROUS
CHANCY
CHANDELLE
CHANDLER
CHANDLERS
CHANDLERY
CHANFRON
CHANFRONS
CHANG
CHANGA
CHANGE
CHANGED
CHANGEFUL
CHANGER
CHANGERS
CHANGES
CHANGEUP
CHANGEUPS
CHANGING
CHANGS
CHANK
CHANKS
CHANNEL
CHANNELED
CHANNELER
CHANNELS
CHANNER
CHANNERS
CHANOYO

C

CHANOYOS
CHANOYU
CHANOYUS
CHANSON
CHANSONS
CHANT
CHANTABLE
CHANTAGE
CHANTAGES
CHANTED
CHANTER
CHANTERS
CHANTEUSE
CHANTEY
CHANTEYS
CHANTIE
CHANTIES
CHANTILLY
CHANTING
CHANTINGS
CHANTOR
CHANTORS
CHANTRESS
CHANTRIES
CHANTRY
CHANTS
CHANTY
CHANUKIAH
CHAO
CHAOLOGY
CHAORDIC
CHAOS
CHAOSES
CHAOTIC
CHAP
CHAPARRAL
CHAPATI
CHAPATIES
CHAPATIS
CHAPATTI
CHAPATTIS
CHAPBOOK
CHAPBOOKS
CHAPE
CHAPEAU
CHAPEAUS
CHAPEAUX
CHAPEL
CHAPELESS
CHAPELRY
CHAPELS
CHAPERON
CHAPERONE
CHAPERONS
CHAPES
CHAPESS
CHAPESSES
CHAPITER
CHAPITERS
CHAPKA
CHAPKAS
CHAPLAIN
CHAPLAINS
CHAPLESS
CHAPLET
CHAPLETED
CHAPLETS
CHAPMAN
CHAPMEN
CHAPPAL
CHAPPALS
CHAPPATI
CHAPPATIS
CHAPPED
CHAPPESS
CHAPPIE
CHAPPIER
CHAPPIES
CHAPPIEST
CHAPPING
CHAPPY
CHAPRASSI
CHAPS
CHAPSTICK
CHAPT
CHAPTER
CHAPTERAL
CHAPTERED
CHAPTERS
CHAPTREL
CHAPTRELS
CHAQUETA
CHAQUETAS
CHAR
CHARA
CHARABANC
CHARACID
CHARACIDS
CHARACIN
CHARACINS
CHARACT
CHARACTER
CHARACTS
CHARADE
CHARADES
CHARANGA
CHARANGAS
CHARANGO
CHARANGOS
CHARAS
CHARASES
CHARBROIL
CHARCOAL
CHARCOALS
CHARCOALY
CHARD
CHARDS
CHARE
CHARED
CHARES
CHARET
CHARETS
CHARETTE
CHARETTES
CHARGE
CHARGED
CHARGEFUL
CHARGER
CHARGERS
CHARGES
CHARGING
CHARGINGS
CHARGRILL
CHARIDEE
CHARIDEES
CHARIER
CHARIEST
CHARILY
CHARINESS
CHARING
CHARIOT
CHARIOTED
CHARIOTS
CHARISM
CHARISMA
CHARISMAS
CHARISMS
CHARITIES
CHARITY
CHARIVARI
CHARK
CHARKA
CHARKAS
CHARKED
CHARKHA
CHARKHAS
CHARKING
CHARKS
CHARLADY
CHARLATAN
CHARLEY
CHARLEYS
CHARLIE
CHARLIER
CHARLIES
CHARLOCK
CHARLOCKS
CHARLOTTE
CHARM
CHARMED
CHARMER
CHARMERS
CHARMEUSE
CHARMFUL
CHARMING
CHARMLESS
CHARMONIA
CHARMS
CHARNECO
CHARNECOS
CHARNEL
CHARNELS
CHAROSET
CHAROSETH
CHAROSETS
CHARPAI
CHARPAIS
CHARPIE
CHARPIES
CHARPOY
CHARPOYS
CHARQUI
CHARQUID
CHARQUIS
CHARR
CHARREADA
CHARRED
CHARRIER
CHARRIEST
CHARRING
CHARRO
CHARROS
CHARRS
CHARRY
CHARS
CHART
CHARTA
CHARTABLE
CHARTAS
CHARTED
CHARTER
CHARTERED
CHARTERER
CHARTERS
CHARTING
CHARTISM
CHARTISMS
CHARTIST
CHARTISTS
CHARTLESS
CHARTS
CHARVER
CHARVERS
CHARWOMAN
CHARWOMEN
CHARY
CHAS
CHASE
CHASEABLE
CHASED
CHASEPORT
CHASER
CHASERS
CHASES
CHASING
CHASINGS
CHASM
CHASMAL
CHASMED
CHASMIC

CHASMIER
CHASMIEST
CHASMS
CHASMY
CHASSE
CHASSED
CHASSEED
CHASSEING
CHASSEPOT
CHASSES
CHASSEUR
CHASSEURS
CHASSIS
CHASTE
CHASTELY
CHASTEN
CHASTENED
CHASTENER
CHASTENS
CHASTER
CHASTEST
CHASTISE
CHASTISED
CHASTISER
CHASTISES
CHASTITY
CHASUBLE
CHASUBLES
CHAT
CHATBOT
CHATBOTS
CHATCHKA
CHATCHKAS
CHATCHKE
CHATCHKES
CHATEAU
CHATEAUS
CHATEAUX
CHATELAIN
CHATLINE
CHATLINES
CHATON
CHATONS
CHATOYANT
CHATROOM
CHATROOMS
CHATS
CHATTA
CHATTAS
CHATTED
CHATTEL
CHATTELS
CHATTER
CHATTERED
CHATTERER
CHATTERS
CHATTERY
CHATTI
CHATTIER
CHATTIES
CHATTIEST
CHATTILY
CHATTING
CHATTIS
CHATTY
CHAUFE
CHAUFED
CHAUFER
CHAUFERS
CHAUFES
CHAUFF
CHAUFFED
CHAUFFER
CHAUFFERS
CHAUFFEUR
CHAUFFING
CHAUFFS
CHAUFING
CHAUMER
CHAUMERS
CHAUNCE
CHAUNCED
CHAUNCES
CHAUNCING
CHAUNGE
CHAUNGED
CHAUNGES
CHAUNGING
CHAUNT
CHAUNTED
CHAUNTER
CHAUNTERS
CHAUNTING
CHAUNTRY
CHAUNTS
CHAUSSES
CHAUSSURE
CHAUVIN
CHAUVINS
CHAV
CHAVE
CHAVENDER
CHAVETTE
CHAVETTES
CHAVISH
CHAVS
CHAVVIER
CHAVVIEST
CHAVVY
CHAW
CHAWBACON
CHAWDRON
CHAWDRONS
CHAWED
CHAWER
CHAWERS
CHAWING
CHAWK
CHAWKS
CHAWS
CHAY
CHAYA
CHAYAS
CHAYOTE
CHAYOTES
CHAYROOT
CHAYROOTS
CHAYS
CHAZAN
CHAZANIM
CHAZANS
CHAZZAN
CHAZZANIM
CHAZZANS
CHAZZEN
CHAZZENIM
CHAZZENS
CHE
CHEAP
CHEAPED
CHEAPEN
CHEAPENED
CHEAPENER
CHEAPENS
CHEAPER
CHEAPEST
CHEAPIE
CHEAPIES
CHEAPING
CHEAPISH
CHEAPJACK
CHEAPLY
CHEAPNESS
CHEAPO
CHEAPOS
CHEAPS
CHEAPSHOT
CHEAPY
CHEAT
CHEATABLE
CHEATED
CHEATER
CHEATERS
CHEATERY
CHEATING
CHEATINGS
CHEATS
CHEBEC
CHEBECS
CHECHAKO
CHECHAKOS
CHECHAQUO
CHECHIA
CHECHIAS
CHECK
CHECKABLE
CHECKBOOK
CHECKBOX
CHECKED
CHECKER
CHECKERED
CHECKERS
CHECKIER
CHECKIEST
CHECKING
CHECKINGS
CHECKLESS
CHECKLIST
CHECKMARK
CHECKMATE
CHECKOFF
CHECKOFFS
CHECKOUT
CHECKOUTS
CHECKRAIL
CHECKREIN
CHECKROOM
CHECKROW
CHECKROWS
CHECKS
CHECKSTOP
CHECKSUM
CHECKSUMS
CHECKUP
CHECKUPS
CHECKY
CHEDARIM
CHEDDAR
CHEDDARS
CHEDDARY
CHEDDITE
CHEDDITES
CHEDER
CHEDERS
CHEDITE
CHEDITES
CHEECHAKO
CHEEK
CHEEKBONE
CHEEKED
CHEEKFUL
CHEEKFULS
CHEEKIER
CHEEKIEST
CHEEKILY
CHEEKING
CHEEKLESS
CHEEKS
CHEEKY
CHEEP
CHEEPED
CHEEPER
CHEEPERS
CHEEPING
CHEEPS
CHEER
CHEERED
CHEERER
CHEERERS
CHEERFUL

CHEERIER
CHEERIEST
CHEERILY
CHEERING
CHEERINGS
CHEERIO
CHEERIOS
CHEERLEAD
CHEERLED
CHEERLESS
CHEERLY
CHEERO
CHEEROS
CHEERS
CHEERY
CHEESE
CHEESED
CHEESES
CHEESEVAT
CHEESIER
CHEESIEST
CHEESILY
CHEESING
CHEESY
CHEETAH
CHEETAHS
CHEEWINK
CHEEWINKS
CHEF
CHEFDOM
CHEFDOMS
CHEFED
CHEFFED
CHEFFIER
CHEFFIEST
CHEFFING
CHEFFY
CHEFING
CHEFS
CHEGOE
CHEGOES
CHEILITIS
CHEKA
CHEKAS
CHEKIST
CHEKISTS
CHELA
CHELAE
CHELAS
CHELASHIP
CHELATE
CHELATED
CHELATES
CHELATING
CHELATION
CHELATOR
CHELATORS
CHELICERA
CHELIFORM
CHELIPED
CHELIPEDS
CHELLUP
CHELLUPS
CHELOID
CHELOIDAL
CHELOIDS
CHELONE
CHELONES
CHELONIAN
CHELP
CHELPED
CHELPING
CHELPS
CHEM
CHEMIC
CHEMICAL
CHEMICALS
CHEMICKED
CHEMICS
CHEMISE
CHEMISES
CHEMISM
CHEMISMS
CHEMISORB
CHEMIST
CHEMISTRY
CHEMISTS
CHEMITYPE
CHEMITYPY
CHEMMIES
CHEMMY
CHEMO
CHEMOKINE
CHEMOS
CHEMOSORB
CHEMOSTAT
CHEMPADUK
CHEMS
CHEMSEX
CHEMSEXES
CHEMTRAIL
CHEMURGIC
CHEMURGY
CHENAR
CHENARS
CHENET
CHENETS
CHENILLE
CHENILLES
CHENIX
CHENIXES
CHENOPOD
CHENOPODS
CHEONGSAM
CHEQUE
CHEQUER
CHEQUERED
CHEQUERS
CHEQUES
CHEQUIER
CHEQUIEST
CHEQUING
CHEQUY
CHER
CHERALITE
CHERE
CHERIMOYA
CHERISH
CHERISHED
CHERISHER
CHERISHES
CHERMOULA
CHERNOZEM
CHEROOT
CHEROOTS
CHERRIED
CHERRIER
CHERRIES
CHERRIEST
CHERRY
CHERRYING
CHERT
CHERTIER
CHERTIEST
CHERTS
CHERTY
CHERUB
CHERUBIC
CHERUBIM
CHERUBIMS
CHERUBIN
CHERUBINS
CHERUBS
CHERUP
CHERUPED
CHERUPING
CHERUPS
CHERVIL
CHERVILS
CHESHIRE
CHESHIRES
CHESIL
CHESILS
CHESNUT
CHESNUTS
CHESS
CHESSEL
CHESSELS
CHESSES
CHESSMAN
CHESSMEN
CHEST
CHESTED
CHESTFUL
CHESTFULS
CHESTIER
CHESTIEST
CHESTILY
CHESTING
CHESTNUT
CHESTNUTS
CHESTS
CHESTY
CHETAH
CHETAHS
CHETH
CHETHS
CHETNIK
CHETNIKS
CHETRUM
CHETRUMS
CHEVAL
CHEVALET
CHEVALETS
CHEVALIER
CHEVELURE
CHEVEN
CHEVENS
CHEVEREL
CHEVERELS
CHEVERIL
CHEVERILS
CHEVERON
CHEVERONS
CHEVERYE
CHEVERYES
CHEVET
CHEVETS
CHEVIED
CHEVIES
CHEVILLE
CHEVILLES
CHEVIN
CHEVINS
CHEVIOT
CHEVIOTS
CHEVRE
CHEVRES
CHEVRET
CHEVRETS
CHEVRETTE
CHEVRON
CHEVRONED
CHEVRONS
CHEVRONY
CHEVROTIN
CHEVY
CHEVYING
CHEW
CHEWABLE
CHEWED
CHEWER
CHEWERS
CHEWET
CHEWETS
CHEWIE
CHEWIER
CHEWIES
CHEWIEST
CHEWINESS

CHEWING
CHEWINK
CHEWINKS
CHEWS
CHEWY
CHEZ
CHHERTUM
CHI
CHIA
CHIACK
CHIACKED
CHIACKING
CHIACKS
CHIANTI
CHIANTIS
CHIAO
CHIAOS
CHIAREZZA
CHIAREZZE
CHIAS
CHIASM
CHIASMA
CHIASMAL
CHIASMAS
CHIASMATA
CHIASMI
CHIASMIC
CHIASMS
CHIASMUS
CHIASTIC
CHIAUS
CHIAUSED
CHIAUSES
CHIAUSING
CHIB
CHIBBED
CHIBBING
CHIBOL
CHIBOLS
CHIBOUK
CHIBOUKS
CHIBOUQUE
CHIBS
CHIC
CHICA
CHICALOTE
CHICANA
CHICANAS
CHICANE
CHICANED
CHICANER
CHICANERS
CHICANERY
CHICANES
CHICANING
CHICANO
CHICANOS
CHICAS
CHICCORY
CHICER
CHICEST
CHICH
CHICHA
CHICHAS
CHICHES
CHICHI
CHICHIER
CHICHIEST
CHICHIS
CHICK
CHICKADEE
CHICKAREE
CHICKEE
CHICKEES
CHICKEN
CHICKENED
CHICKENS
CHICKLING
CHICKORY
CHICKPEA
CHICKPEAS
CHICKS
CHICKWEED
CHICLE
CHICLES
CHICLY
CHICNESS
CHICO
CHICON
CHICONS
CHICORIES
CHICORY
CHICOS
CHICOT
CHICOTS
CHICS
CHID
CHIDDEN
CHIDE
CHIDED
CHIDER
CHIDERS
CHIDES
CHIDING
CHIDINGLY
CHIDINGS
CHIDLINGS
CHIEF
CHIEFDOM
CHIEFDOMS
CHIEFER
CHIEFERY
CHIEFESS
CHIEFEST
CHIEFLESS
CHIEFLING
CHIEFLY
CHIEFRIES
CHIEFRY
CHIEFS
CHIEFSHIP
CHIEFTAIN
CHIEL
CHIELD
CHIELDS
CHIELS
CHIFFON
CHIFFONS
CHIFFONY
CHIGETAI
CHIGETAIS
CHIGGA
CHIGGAS
CHIGGER
CHIGGERS
CHIGNON
CHIGNONED
CHIGNONS
CHIGOE
CHIGOES
CHIGRE
CHIGRES
CHIHUAHUA
CHIK
CHIKARA
CHIKARAS
CHIKHOR
CHIKHORS
CHIKOR
CHIKORS
CHIKS
CHILBLAIN
CHILD
CHILDBED
CHILDBEDS
CHILDCARE
CHILDE
CHILDED
CHILDER
CHILDES
CHILDHOOD
CHILDING
CHILDISH
CHILDLESS
CHILDLIER
CHILDLIKE
CHILDLY
CHILDNESS
CHILDREN
CHILDS
CHILE
CHILES
CHILI
CHILIAD
CHILIADAL
CHILIADIC
CHILIADS
CHILIAGON
CHILIARCH
CHILIASM
CHILIASMS
CHILIAST
CHILIASTS
CHILIDOG
CHILIDOGS
CHILIES
CHILIS
CHILL
CHILLADA
CHILLADAS
CHILLAX
CHILLAXED
CHILLAXES
CHILLED
CHILLER
CHILLERS
CHILLEST
CHILLI
CHILLIER
CHILLIES
CHILLIEST
CHILLILY
CHILLING
CHILLINGS
CHILLIS
CHILLNESS
CHILLS
CHILLUM
CHILLUMS
CHILLY
CHILOPOD
CHILOPODS
CHILTEPIN
CHIMAERA
CHIMAERAS
CHIMAERIC
CHIMAR
CHIMARS
CHIMB
CHIMBLEY
CHIMBLEYS
CHIMBLIES
CHIMBLY
CHIMBS
CHIME
CHIMED
CHIMENEA
CHIMENEAS
CHIMER
CHIMERA
CHIMERAS
CHIMERE
CHIMERES
CHIMERIC
CHIMERID
CHIMERIDS
CHIMERISM
CHIMERS
CHIMES
CHIMINEA

CHIMINEAS
CHIMING
CHIMLA
CHIMLAS
CHIMLEY
CHIMLEYS
CHIMNEY
CHIMNEYED
CHIMNEYS
CHIMO
CHIMP
CHIMPS
CHIN
CHINA
CHINAMAN
CHINAMEN
CHINAMPA
CHINAMPAS
CHINAR
CHINAROOT
CHINARS
CHINAS
CHINAWARE
CHINBONE
CHINBONES
CHINCAPIN
CHINCH
CHINCHED
CHINCHES
CHINCHIER
CHINCHING
CHINCHY
CHINCOUGH
CHINDIT
CHINDITS
CHINE
CHINED
CHINES
CHINESE
CHING
CHINGS
CHINING
CHINK
CHINKAPIN
CHINKARA
CHINKARAS
CHINKED
CHINKIER
CHINKIEST
CHINKING
CHINKS
CHINKY
CHINLESS
CHINNED
CHINNING
CHINO
CHINOIS
CHINOISES
CHINONE
CHINONES
CHINOOK
CHINOOKS
CHINOS
CHINOVNIK
CHINS
CHINSE
CHINSED
CHINSES
CHINSING
CHINSTRAP
CHINTS
CHINTSES
CHINTZ
CHINTZES
CHINTZIER
CHINTZILY
CHINTZY
CHINWAG
CHINWAGS
CHIP
CHIPBOARD
CHIPMAKER
CHIPMUCK
CHIPMUCKS
CHIPMUNK
CHIPMUNKS
CHIPOCHIA
CHIPOLATA
CHIPOTLE
CHIPOTLES
CHIPPABLE
CHIPPED
CHIPPER
CHIPPERED
CHIPPERER
CHIPPERS
CHIPPIE
CHIPPIER
CHIPPIES
CHIPPIEST
CHIPPING
CHIPPINGS
CHIPPY
CHIPS
CHIPSET
CHIPSETS
CHIRAGRA
CHIRAGRAS
CHIRAGRIC
CHIRAL
CHIRALITY
CHIRIMOYA
CHIRK
CHIRKED
CHIRKER
CHIRKEST
CHIRKING
CHIRKS
CHIRL
CHIRLED
CHIRLING
CHIRLS
CHIRM
CHIRMED
CHIRMING
CHIRMS
CHIRO
CHIROLOGY
CHIRONOMY
CHIROPODY
CHIROPTER
CHIROS
CHIRP
CHIRPED
CHIRPER
CHIRPERS
CHIRPIER
CHIRPIEST
CHIRPILY
CHIRPING
CHIRPINGS
CHIRPS
CHIRPY
CHIRR
CHIRRE
CHIRRED
CHIRREN
CHIRRES
CHIRRING
CHIRRS
CHIRRUP
CHIRRUPED
CHIRRUPER
CHIRRUPS
CHIRRUPY
CHIRT
CHIRTED
CHIRTING
CHIRTS
CHIRU
CHIRUS
CHIS
CHISEL
CHISELED
CHISELER
CHISELERS
CHISELING
CHISELLED
CHISELLER
CHISELS
CHIT
CHITAL
CHITALS
CHITCHAT
CHITCHATS
CHITIN
CHITINOID
CHITINOUS
CHITINS
CHITLIN
CHITLING
CHITLINGS
CHITLINS
CHITON
CHITONS
CHITOSAN
CHITOSANS
CHITS
CHITTED
CHITTER
CHITTERED
CHITTERS
CHITTIER
CHITTIES
CHITTIEST
CHITTING
CHITTY
CHIV
CHIVALRIC
CHIVALRY
CHIVAREE
CHIVAREED
CHIVAREES
CHIVARI
CHIVARIED
CHIVARIES
CHIVE
CHIVED
CHIVES
CHIVIED
CHIVIES
CHIVING
CHIVS
CHIVVED
CHIVVIED
CHIVVIES
CHIVVING
CHIVVY
CHIVVYING
CHIVY
CHIVYING
CHIWEENIE
CHIYOGAMI
CHIZ
CHIZZ
CHIZZED
CHIZZES
CHIZZING
CHLAMYDES
CHLAMYDIA
CHLAMYS
CHLAMYSES
CHLOASMA
CHLOASMAS
CHLORACNE
CHLORAL
CHLORALS
CHLORATE
CHLORATES
CHLORDAN

CHLORDANE
CHLORDANS
CHLORELLA
CHLORIC
CHLORID
CHLORIDE
CHLORIDES
CHLORIDIC
CHLORIDS
CHLORIN
CHLORINE
CHLORINES
CHLORINS
CHLORITE
CHLORITES
CHLORITIC
CHLOROSES
CHLOROSIS
CHLOROTIC
CHLOROUS
CHOANA
CHOANAE
CHOBDAR
CHOBDARS
CHOC
CHOCCIER
CHOCCIES
CHOCCIEST
CHOCCY
CHOCHO
CHOCHOS
CHOCK
CHOCKED
CHOCKER
CHOCKERS
CHOCKFUL
CHOCKFULL
CHOCKIE
CHOCKIER
CHOCKIES
CHOCKIEST
CHOCKING
CHOCKO
CHOCKOS
CHOCKS
CHOCKY
CHOCO
CHOCOLATE
CHOCOLATY
CHOCOS
CHOCS
CHOCTAW
CHOCTAWS
CHODE
CHOENIX
CHOENIXES
CHOG
CHOGS
CHOICE
CHOICEFUL
CHOICELY
CHOICER
CHOICES
CHOICEST
CHOIL
CHOILS
CHOIR
CHOIRBOY
CHOIRBOYS
CHOIRED
CHOIRGIRL
CHOIRING
CHOIRLIKE
CHOIRMAN
CHOIRMEN
CHOIRS
CHOKE
CHOKEABLE
CHOKEBORE
CHOKECOIL
CHOKED
CHOKEDAMP
CHOKEHOLD
CHOKER
CHOKERMAN
CHOKERMEN
CHOKERS
CHOKES
CHOKEY
CHOKEYS
CHOKIDAR
CHOKIDARS
CHOKIER
CHOKIES
CHOKIEST
CHOKING
CHOKINGLY
CHOKO
CHOKOS
CHOKRA
CHOKRAS
CHOKRI
CHOKRIS
CHOKY
CHOLA
CHOLAEMIA
CHOLAEMIC
CHOLAS
CHOLATE
CHOLATES
CHOLECYST
CHOLELITH
CHOLEMIA
CHOLEMIAS
CHOLENT
CHOLENTS
CHOLER
CHOLERA
CHOLERAIC
CHOLERAS
CHOLERIC
CHOLEROID
CHOLERS
CHOLI
CHOLIAMB
CHOLIAMBS
CHOLIC
CHOLINE
CHOLINES
CHOLIS
CHOLLA
CHOLLAS
CHOLLERS
CHOLTRIES
CHOLTRY
CHOMETZ
CHOMETZES
CHOMMIE
CHOMMIES
CHOMP
CHOMPED
CHOMPER
CHOMPERS
CHOMPING
CHOMPS
CHON
CHONDRAL
CHONDRE
CHONDRES
CHONDRI
CHONDRIFY
CHONDRIN
CHONDRINS
CHONDRITE
CHONDROID
CHONDROMA
CHONDRULE
CHONDRUS
CHONS
CHOOF
CHOOFED
CHOOFING
CHOOFS
CHOOK
CHOOKED
CHOOKIE
CHOOKIES
CHOOKING
CHOOKS
CHOOM
CHOOMS
CHOON
CHOONS
CHOOSE
CHOOSER
CHOOSERS
CHOOSES
CHOOSEY
CHOOSIER
CHOOSIEST
CHOOSILY
CHOOSING
CHOOSY
CHOP
CHOPHOUSE
CHOPIN
CHOPINE
CHOPINES
CHOPINS
CHOPLOGIC
CHOPPED
CHOPPER
CHOPPERED
CHOPPERS
CHOPPIER
CHOPPIEST
CHOPPILY
CHOPPING
CHOPPINGS
CHOPPY
CHOPS
CHOPSOCKY
CHOPSTICK
CHORAGI
CHORAGIC
CHORAGUS
CHORAL
CHORALE
CHORALES
CHORALIST
CHORALLY
CHORALS
CHORD
CHORDA
CHORDAE
CHORDAL
CHORDATE
CHORDATES
CHORDED
CHORDEE
CHORDEES
CHORDING
CHORDINGS
CHORDLIKE
CHORDS
CHORDWISE
CHORE
CHOREA
CHOREAL
CHOREAS
CHOREATIC
CHOREBOY
CHOREBOYS
CHORED
CHOREE
CHOREES
CHOREGI
CHOREGIC
CHOREGUS
CHOREIC

C

CHOREMAN
CHOREMEN
CHOREOID
CHORES
CHOREUS
CHOREUSES
CHORIA
CHORIAL
CHORIAMB
CHORIAMBI
CHORIAMBS
CHORIC
CHORINE
CHORINES
CHORING
CHORIOID
CHORIOIDS
CHORION
CHORIONIC
CHORIONS
CHORISES
CHORISIS
CHORISM
CHORISMS
CHORIST
CHORISTER
CHORISTS
CHORIZO
CHORIZONT
CHORIZOS
CHOROID
CHOROIDAL
CHOROIDS
CHOROLOGY
CHORRIE
CHORRIES
CHORTEN
CHORTENS
CHORTLE
CHORTLED
CHORTLER
CHORTLERS
CHORTLES
CHORTLING
CHORUS
CHORUSED
CHORUSES
CHORUSING
CHORUSSED
CHORUSSES
CHOSE
CHOSEN
CHOSES
CHOTA
CHOTT
CHOTTS
CHOU
CHOUGH
CHOUGHS
CHOULTRY
CHOUNTER
CHOUNTERS
CHOUSE
CHOUSED
CHOUSER
CHOUSERS
CHOUSES
CHOUSH
CHOUSHES
CHOUSING
CHOUT
CHOUTS
CHOUX
CHOW
CHOWCHOW
CHOWCHOWS
CHOWDER
CHOWDERED
CHOWDERS
CHOWDOWN
CHOWDOWNS
CHOWED
CHOWHOUND
CHOWING
CHOWK
CHOWKIDAR
CHOWKS
CHOWRI
CHOWRIES
CHOWRIS
CHOWRY
CHOWS
CHOWSE
CHOWSED
CHOWSES
CHOWSING
CHOWTIME
CHOWTIMES
CHRESARD
CHRESARDS
CHRISM
CHRISMA
CHRISMAL
CHRISMALS
CHRISMON
CHRISMONS
CHRISMS
CHRISOM
CHRISOMS
CHRISTEN
CHRISTENS
CHRISTIAN
CHRISTIE
CHRISTIES
CHRISTOM
CHRISTOMS
CHRISTY
CHROMA
CHROMAKEY
CHROMAS
CHROMATE
CHROMATES
CHROMATIC
CHROMATID
CHROMATIN
CHROME
CHROMED
CHROMEL
CHROMELS
CHROMENE
CHROMENES
CHROMES
CHROMIC
CHROMIDE
CHROMIDES
CHROMIDIA
CHROMIER
CHROMIEST
CHROMING
CHROMINGS
CHROMISE
CHROMISED
CHROMISES
CHROMITE
CHROMITES
CHROMIUM
CHROMIUMS
CHROMIZE
CHROMIZED
CHROMIZES
CHROMO
CHROMOGEN
CHROMOLY
CHROMOLYS
CHROMOS
CHROMOUS
CHROMY
CHROMYL
CHROMYLS
CHRONAXIE
CHRONAXY
CHRONIC
CHRONICAL
CHRONICLE
CHRONICS
CHRONON
CHRONONS
CHRYSALID
CHRYSALIS
CHRYSANTH
CHTHONIAN
CHTHONIC
CHUB
CHUBASCO
CHUBASCOS
CHUBBIER
CHUBBIEST
CHUBBILY
CHUBBY
CHUBS
CHUCK
CHUCKED
CHUCKER
CHUCKERS
CHUCKHOLE
CHUCKIE
CHUCKIES
CHUCKING
CHUCKLE
CHUCKLED
CHUCKLER
CHUCKLERS
CHUCKLES
CHUCKLING
CHUCKS
CHUCKY
CHUDDAH
CHUDDAHS
CHUDDAR
CHUDDARS
CHUDDER
CHUDDERS
CHUDDIES
CHUDDY
CHUFA
CHUFAS
CHUFF
CHUFFED
CHUFFER
CHUFFEST
CHUFFIER
CHUFFIEST
CHUFFING
CHUFFS
CHUFFY
CHUG
CHUGALUG
CHUGALUGS
CHUGGED
CHUGGER
CHUGGERS
CHUGGING
CHUGGINGS
CHUGS
CHUKAR
CHUKARS
CHUKKA
CHUKKAR
CHUKKARS
CHUKKAS
CHUKKER
CHUKKERS
CHUKOR
CHUKORS
CHUM
CHUMASH
CHUMASHES
CHUMASHIM
CHUMLEY
CHUMLEYS

CHUMMAGE
CHUMMAGES
CHUMMED
CHUMMIER
CHUMMIES
CHUMMIEST
CHUMMILY
CHUMMING
CHUMMY
CHUMP
CHUMPED
CHUMPING
CHUMPINGS
CHUMPS
CHUMS
CHUMSHIP
CHUMSHIPS
CHUNDER
CHUNDERED
CHUNDERS
CHUNK
CHUNKED
CHUNKIER
CHUNKIEST
CHUNKILY
CHUNKING
CHUNKINGS
CHUNKS
CHUNKY
CHUNNEL
CHUNNELS
CHUNNER
CHUNNERED
CHUNNERS
CHUNTER
CHUNTERED
CHUNTERS
CHUPATI
CHUPATIS
CHUPATTI
CHUPATTIS
CHUPATTY
CHUPPA
CHUPPAH
CHUPPAHS
CHUPPAS
CHUPPOT
CHUPPOTH
CHUPRASSY
CHUR
CHURCH
CHURCHED
CHURCHES
CHURCHIER
CHURCHING
CHURCHISM
CHURCHLY
CHURCHMAN
CHURCHMEN
CHURCHWAY
CHURCHY
CHURIDAR
CHURIDARS
CHURINGA
CHURINGAS
CHURL
CHURLISH
CHURLS
CHURN
CHURNED
CHURNER
CHURNERS
CHURNING
CHURNINGS
CHURNMILK
CHURNS
CHURR
CHURRED
CHURRING
CHURRO
CHURROS
CHURRS
CHURRUS
CHURRUSES
CHUSE
CHUSED
CHUSES
CHUSING
CHUT
CHUTE
CHUTED
CHUTES
CHUTING
CHUTIST
CHUTISTS
CHUTNEE
CHUTNEES
CHUTNEY
CHUTNEYS
CHUTS
CHUTZPA
CHUTZPAH
CHUTZPAHS
CHUTZPAS
CHYACK
CHYACKED
CHYACKING
CHYACKS
CHYLDE
CHYLE
CHYLES
CHYLIFIED
CHYLIFIES
CHYLIFY
CHYLOUS
CHYLURIA
CHYLURIAS
CHYME
CHYMES
CHYMIC
CHYMICS
CHYMIFIED
CHYMIFIES
CHYMIFY
CHYMIST
CHYMISTRY
CHYMISTS
CHYMOSIN
CHYMOSINS
CHYMOUS
CHYND
CHYPRE
CHYPRES
CHYRON
CHYRONS
CHYTRID
CHYTRIDS
CIABATTA
CIABATTAS
CIABATTE
CIAO
CIBATION
CIBATIONS
CIBOL
CIBOLS
CIBORIA
CIBORIUM
CIBORIUMS
CIBOULE
CIBOULES
CICADA
CICADAE
CICADAS
CICALA
CICALAS
CICALE
CICATRICE
CICATRISE
CICATRIX
CICATRIZE
CICELIES
CICELY
CICERO
CICERONE
CICERONED
CICERONES
CICERONI
CICEROS
CICHLID
CICHLIDAE
CICHLIDS
CICHLOID
CICINNUS
CICISBEI
CICISBEO
CICISBEOS
CICLATON
CICLATONS
CICLATOUN
CICOREE
CICOREES
CICUTA
CICUTAS
CICUTINE
CICUTINES
CID
CIDARIS
CIDARISES
CIDE
CIDED
CIDER
CIDERIER
CIDERIEST
CIDERKIN
CIDERKINS
CIDERS
CIDERY
CIDES
CIDING
CIDS
CIEL
CIELED
CIELING
CIELINGS
CIELS
CIERGE
CIERGES
CIG
CIGAR
CIGARET
CIGARETS
CIGARETTE
CIGARILLO
CIGARLIKE
CIGARS
CIGGIE
CIGGIES
CIGGY
CIGS
CIGUATERA
CILANTRO
CILANTROS
CILIA
CILIARY
CILIATE
CILIATED
CILIATELY
CILIATES
CILIATION
CILICE
CILICES
CILICIOUS
CILIOLATE
CILIUM
CILL
CILLS
CIMAR
CIMARS
CIMBALOM
CIMBALOMS

C

CIMELIA	CINEREA	CIRCINATE	CIRSOID	CITATIONS
CIMEX	CINEREAL	CIRCITER	CIS	CITATOR
CIMICES	CINEREAS	CIRCLE	CISALPINE	CITATORS
CIMIER	CINEREOUS	CIRCLED	CISCO	CITATORY
CIMIERS	CINERIN	CIRCLER	CISCOES	CITE
CIMINITE	CINERINS	CIRCLERS	CISCOS	CITEABLE
CIMINITES	CINES	CIRCLES	CISELEUR	CITED
CIMMERIAN	CINGULA	CIRCLET	CISELEURS	CITER
CIMOLITE	CINGULAR	CIRCLETS	CISELURE	CITERS
CIMOLITES	CINGULATE	CIRCLING	CISELURES	CITES
CINCH	CINGULUM	CIRCLINGS	CISGENDER	CITESS
CINCHED	CINNABAR	CIRCLIP	CISLUNAR	CITESSES
CINCHES	CINNABARS	CIRCLIPS	CISPADANE	CITHARA
CINCHING	CINNAMIC	CIRCS	CISPLATIN	CITHARAS
CINCHINGS	CINNAMON	CIRCUIT	CISSIER	CITHARIST
CINCHONA	CINNAMONS	CIRCUITAL	CISSIES	CITHER
CINCHONAS	CINNAMONY	CIRCUITED	CISSIEST	CITHERN
CINCHONIC	CINNAMYL	CIRCUITRY	CISSIFIED	CITHERNS
CINCINNUS	CINNAMYLS	CIRCUITS	CISSING	CITHERS
CINCT	CINQ	CIRCUITY	CISSINGS	CITHREN
CINCTURE	CINQS	CIRCULAR	CISSOID	CITHRENS
CINCTURED	CINQUAIN	CIRCULARS	CISSOIDS	CITIED
CINCTURES	CINQUAINS	CIRCULATE	CISSUS	CITIES
CINDER	CINQUE	CIRCUS	CISSUSES	CITIFIED
CINDERED	CINQUES	CIRCUSES	CISSY	CITIFIES
CINDERIER	CION	CIRCUSIER	CIST	CITIFY
CINDERING	CIONS	CIRCUSSY	CISTED	CITIFYING
CINDEROUS	CIOPPINO	CIRCUSY	CISTERN	CITIGRADE
CINDERS	CIOPPINOS	CIRE	CISTERNA	CITING
CINDERY	CIPAILLE	CIRES	CISTERNAE	CITIZEN
CINE	CIPAILLES	CIRL	CISTERNAL	CITIZENLY
CINEAST	CIPHER	CIRLS	CISTERNS	CITIZENRY
CINEASTE	CIPHERED	CIRQUE	CISTIC	CITIZENS
CINEASTES	CIPHERER	CIRQUES	CISTRON	CITO
CINEASTS	CIPHERERS	CIRRATE	CISTRONIC	CITOLA
CINEMA	CIPHERING	CIRRHOSED	CISTRONS	CITOLAS
CINEMAS	CIPHERS	CIRRHOSES	CISTS	CITOLE
CINEMATIC	CIPHONIES	CIRRHOSIS	CISTUS	CITOLES
CINEOL	CIPHONY	CIRRHOTIC	CISTUSES	CITRAL
CINEOLE	CIPOLIN	CIRRI	CISTVAEN	CITRALS
CINEOLES	CIPOLINS	CIRRIFORM	CISTVAENS	CITRANGE
CINEOLS	CIPOLLINO	CIRRIPED	CIT	CITRANGES
CINEPHILE	CIPPI	CIRRIPEDE	CITABLE	CITRATE
CINEPLEX	CIPPUS	CIRRIPEDS	CITADEL	CITRATED
CINERAMIC	CIRCA	CIRROSE	CITADELS	CITRATES
CINERARIA	CIRCADIAN	CIRROUS	CITAL	CITREOUS
CINERARY	CIRCAR	CIRRUS	CITALS	CITRIC
CINERATOR	CIRCARS	CIRRUSES	CITATION	CITRIN

C

CITRINE
CITRINES
CITRININ
CITRININS
CITRINS
CITRON
CITRONS
CITROUS
CITRUS
CITRUSES
CITRUSIER
CITRUSSY
CITRUSY
CITS
CITTERN
CITTERNS
CITY
CITYFIED
CITYFIES
CITYFY
CITYFYING
CITYSCAPE
CITYWARD
CITYWIDE
CIVE
CIVES
CIVET
CIVETLIKE
CIVETS
CIVIC
CIVICALLY
CIVICISM
CIVICISMS
CIVICS
CIVIE
CIVIES
CIVIL
CIVILIAN
CIVILIANS
CIVILISE
CIVILISED
CIVILISER
CIVILISES
CIVILIST
CIVILISTS
CIVILITY
CIVILIZE
CIVILIZED
CIVILIZER
CIVILIZES
CIVILLY
CIVILNESS
CIVILS
CIVISM
CIVISMS
CIVVIES
CIVVY
CIZERS
CLABBER
CLABBERED
CLABBERS
CLACH
CLACHAN
CLACHANS
CLACHED
CLACHES
CLACHING
CLACHS
CLACK
CLACKBOX
CLACKDISH
CLACKED
CLACKER
CLACKERS
CLACKING
CLACKS
CLAD
CLADDAGH
CLADDAGHS
CLADDED
CLADDER
CLADDERS
CLADDIE
CLADDIES
CLADDING
CLADDINGS
CLADE
CLADES
CLADISM
CLADISMS
CLADIST
CLADISTIC
CLADISTS
CLADODE
CLADODES
CLADODIAL
CLADOGRAM
CLADS
CLAES
CLAFOUTI
CLAFOUTIS
CLAG
CLAGGED
CLAGGIER
CLAGGIEST
CLAGGING
CLAGGY
CLAGS
CLAIM
CLAIMABLE
CLAIMANT
CLAIMANTS
CLAIMED
CLAIMER
CLAIMERS
CLAIMING
CLAIMS
CLAM
CLAMANCY
CLAMANT
CLAMANTLY
CLAMBAKE
CLAMBAKES
CLAMBE
CLAMBER
CLAMBERED
CLAMBERER
CLAMBERS
CLAME
CLAMES
CLAMLIKE
CLAMMED
CLAMMER
CLAMMERS
CLAMMIER
CLAMMIEST
CLAMMILY
CLAMMING
CLAMMY
CLAMOR
CLAMORED
CLAMORER
CLAMORERS
CLAMORING
CLAMOROUS
CLAMORS
CLAMOUR
CLAMOURED
CLAMOURER
CLAMOURS
CLAMP
CLAMPDOWN
CLAMPED
CLAMPER
CLAMPERED
CLAMPERS
CLAMPING
CLAMPINGS
CLAMPS
CLAMS
CLAMSHELL
CLAMWORM
CLAMWORMS
CLAN
CLANG
CLANGBOX
CLANGED
CLANGER
CLANGERS
CLANGING
CLANGINGS
CLANGOR
CLANGORED
CLANGORS
CLANGOUR
CLANGOURS
CLANGS
CLANK
CLANKED
CLANKIER
CLANKIEST
CLANKING
CLANKINGS
CLANKS
CLANKY
CLANNISH
CLANS
CLANSHIP
CLANSHIPS
CLANSMAN
CLANSMEN
CLAP
CLAPBOARD
CLAPBREAD
CLAPDISH
CLAPNET
CLAPNETS
CLAPPED
CLAPPER
CLAPPERED
CLAPPERS
CLAPPING
CLAPPINGS
CLAPS
CLAPT
CLAPTRAP
CLAPTRAPS
CLAQUE
CLAQUER
CLAQUERS
CLAQUES
CLAQUEUR
CLAQUEURS
CLARAIN
CLARAINS
CLARENCE
CLARENCES
CLARENDON
CLARET
CLARETED
CLARETING
CLARETS
CLARIES
CLARIFIED
CLARIFIER
CLARIFIES
CLARIFY
CLARINET
CLARINETS
CLARINI
CLARINO
CLARINOS
CLARION
CLARIONED
CLARIONET
CLARIONS
CLARITIES
CLARITY
CLARKIA
CLARKIAS

CLARO
CLAROES
CLAROS
CLARSACH
CLARSACHS
CLART
CLARTED
CLARTHEAD
CLARTIER
CLARTIEST
CLARTING
CLARTS
CLARTY
CLARY
CLASH
CLASHED
CLASHER
CLASHERS
CLASHES
CLASHING
CLASHINGS
CLASP
CLASPED
CLASPER
CLASPERS
CLASPING
CLASPINGS
CLASPS
CLASPT
CLASS
CLASSABLE
CLASSED
CLASSER
CLASSERS
CLASSES
CLASSIBLE
CLASSIC
CLASSICAL
CLASSICO
CLASSICS
CLASSIER
CLASSIEST
CLASSIFIC
CLASSIFY
CLASSILY
CLASSING
CLASSINGS
CLASSIS
CLASSISM
CLASSISMS
CLASSIST
CLASSISTS
CLASSLESS
CLASSMAN
CLASSMATE
CLASSMEN
CLASSON
CLASSONS
CLASSROOM
CLASSWORK
CLASSY
CLAST
CLASTIC
CLASTICS
CLASTS
CLAT
CLATCH
CLATCHED
CLATCHES
CLATCHING
CLATHRATE
CLATS
CLATTED
CLATTER
CLATTERED
CLATTERER
CLATTERS
CLATTERY
CLATTING
CLAUCHT
CLAUCHTED
CLAUCHTS
CLAUGHT
CLAUGHTED
CLAUGHTS
CLAUSAL
CLAUSE
CLAUSES
CLAUSTRA
CLAUSTRAL
CLAUSTRUM
CLAUSULA
CLAUSULAE
CLAUSULAR
CLAUT
CLAUTED
CLAUTING
CLAUTS
CLAVATE
CLAVATED
CLAVATELY
CLAVATION
CLAVE
CLAVECIN
CLAVECINS
CLAVER
CLAVERED
CLAVERING
CLAVERS
CLAVES
CLAVI
CLAVICLE
CLAVICLES
CLAVICORN
CLAVICULA
CLAVIE
CLAVIER
CLAVIERS
CLAVIES
CLAVIFORM
CLAVIGER
CLAVIGERS
CLAVIS
CLAVULATE
CLAVUS
CLAW
CLAWBACK
CLAWBACKS
CLAWED
CLAWER
CLAWERS
CLAWING
CLAWLESS
CLAWLIKE
CLAWS
CLAXON
CLAXONS
CLAY
CLAYBANK
CLAYBANKS
CLAYED
CLAYEY
CLAYIER
CLAYIEST
CLAYING
CLAYISH
CLAYLIKE
CLAYMORE
CLAYMORES
CLAYPAN
CLAYPANS
CLAYS
CLAYSTONE
CLAYTONIA
CLAYWARE
CLAYWARES
CLEAN
CLEANABLE
CLEANED
CLEANER
CLEANERS
CLEANEST
CLEANING
CLEANINGS
CLEANISH
CLEANLIER
CLEANLILY
CLEANLY
CLEANNESS
CLEANOUT
CLEANOUTS
CLEANS
CLEANSE
CLEANSED
CLEANSER
CLEANSERS
CLEANSES
CLEANSING
CLEANSKIN
CLEANTECH
CLEANUP
CLEANUPS
CLEAR
CLEARABLE
CLEARAGE
CLEARAGES
CLEARANCE
CLEARCOLE
CLEARCUT
CLEARCUTS
CLEARED
CLEARER
CLEARERS
CLEAREST
CLEAREYED
CLEARING
CLEARINGS
CLEARLY
CLEARNESS
CLEAROUT
CLEAROUTS
CLEARS
CLEARSKIN
CLEARWAY
CLEARWAYS
CLEARWEED
CLEARWING
CLEAT
CLEATED
CLEATING
CLEATS
CLEAVABLE
CLEAVAGE
CLEAVAGES
CLEAVE
CLEAVED
CLEAVER
CLEAVERS
CLEAVES
CLEAVING
CLEAVINGS
CLECHE
CLECK
CLECKED
CLECKIER
CLECKIEST
CLECKING
CLECKINGS
CLECKS
CLECKY
CLEEK
CLEEKED
CLEEKING
CLEEKIT
CLEEKS
CLEEP
CLEEPED
CLEEPING
CLEEPS
CLEEVE

CLEEVES
CLEF
CLEFS
CLEFT
CLEFTED
CLEFTING
CLEFTS
CLEG
CLEGS
CLEIDOIC
CLEIK
CLEIKS
CLEITHRAL
CLEM
CLEMATIS
CLEMENCY
CLEMENT
CLEMENTLY
CLEMMED
CLEMMING
CLEMS
CLENCH
CLENCHED
CLENCHER
CLENCHERS
CLENCHES
CLENCHING
CLEOME
CLEOMES
CLEOPATRA
CLEPE
CLEPED
CLEPES
CLEPING
CLEPSYDRA
CLEPT
CLERGIES
CLERGY
CLERGYMAN
CLERGYMEN
CLERIC
CLERICAL
CLERICALS
CLERICATE
CLERICITY
CLERICS
CLERID
CLERIDS
CLERIHEW
CLERIHEWS
CLERISIES
CLERISY
CLERK
CLERKDOM
CLERKDOMS
CLERKED
CLERKESS
CLERKING
CLERKISH
CLERKLIER
CLERKLIKE
CLERKLING
CLERKLY
CLERKS
CLERKSHIP
CLERUCH
CLERUCHIA
CLERUCHS
CLERUCHY
CLEUCH
CLEUCHS
CLEUGH
CLEUGHS
CLEVE
CLEVEITE
CLEVEITES
CLEVER
CLEVERER
CLEVEREST
CLEVERISH
CLEVERLY
CLEVES
CLEVIS
CLEVISES
CLEW
CLEWED
CLEWING
CLEWS
CLIANTHUS
CLICHE
CLICHED
CLICHEED
CLICHES
CLICK
CLICKABLE
CLICKBAIT
CLICKED
CLICKER
CLICKERS
CLICKET
CLICKETED
CLICKETS
CLICKING
CLICKINGS
CLICKLESS
CLICKS
CLICKWRAP
CLIED
CLIENT
CLIENTAGE
CLIENTAL
CLIENTELE
CLIENTS
CLIES
CLIFF
CLIFFED
CLIFFHANG
CLIFFHUNG
CLIFFIER
CLIFFIEST
CLIFFLIKE
CLIFFS
CLIFFSIDE
CLIFFTOP
CLIFFTOPS
CLIFFY
CLIFT
CLIFTED
CLIFTIER
CLIFTIEST
CLIFTS
CLIFTY
CLIMACTIC
CLIMATAL
CLIMATE
CLIMATED
CLIMATES
CLIMATIC
CLIMATING
CLIMATISE
CLIMATIZE
CLIMATURE
CLIMAX
CLIMAXED
CLIMAXES
CLIMAXING
CLIMB
CLIMBABLE
CLIMBDOWN
CLIMBED
CLIMBER
CLIMBERS
CLIMBING
CLIMBINGS
CLIMBS
CLIME
CLIMES
CLINAL
CLINALLY
CLINAMEN
CLINAMENS
CLINCH
CLINCHED
CLINCHER
CLINCHERS
CLINCHES
CLINCHING
CLINE
CLINES
CLING
CLINGED
CLINGER
CLINGERS
CLINGFILM
CLINGFISH
CLINGIER
CLINGIEST
CLINGING
CLINGS
CLINGWRAP
CLINGY
CLINIC
CLINICAL
CLINICIAN
CLINICS
CLINIQUE
CLINIQUES
CLINK
CLINKED
CLINKER
CLINKERED
CLINKERS
CLINKING
CLINKS
CLINOAXES
CLINOAXIS
CLINOSTAT
CLINQUANT
CLINT
CLINTONIA
CLINTS
CLIOMETRY
CLIP
CLIPART
CLIPARTS
CLIPBOARD
CLIPE
CLIPED
CLIPES
CLIPING
CLIPPABLE
CLIPPED
CLIPPER
CLIPPERS
CLIPPIE
CLIPPIES
CLIPPING
CLIPPINGS
CLIPS
CLIPSHEAR
CLIPSHEET
CLIPT
CLIQUE
CLIQUED
CLIQUES
CLIQUEY
CLIQUIER
CLIQUIEST
CLIQUING
CLIQUISH
CLIQUISM
CLIQUISMS
CLIQUY
CLIT
CLITELLA
CLITELLAR
CLITELLUM
CLITHRAL
CLITIC
CLITICISE

CLITICIZE
CLITICS
CLITORAL
CLITORIC
CLITORIS
CLITS
CLITTER
CLITTERED
CLITTERS
CLIVERS
CLIVIA
CLIVIAS
CLOACA
CLOACAE
CLOACAL
CLOACAS
CLOACINAL
CLOACITIS
CLOAK
CLOAKED
CLOAKING
CLOAKROOM
CLOAKS
CLOAM
CLOAMS
CLOBBER
CLOBBERED
CLOBBERS
CLOCHARD
CLOCHARDS
CLOCHE
CLOCHES
CLOCK
CLOCKED
CLOCKER
CLOCKERS
CLOCKFACE
CLOCKING
CLOCKINGS
CLOCKLIKE
CLOCKS
CLOCKWISE
CLOCKWORK
CLOD
CLODDED
CLODDIER
CLODDIEST
CLODDING
CLODDISH
CLODDY
CLODLY
CLODPATE
CLODPATED
CLODPATES
CLODPOLE
CLODPOLES
CLODPOLL
CLODPOLLS
CLODS
CLOFF
CLOFFS
CLOG
CLOGDANCE
CLOGGED
CLOGGER
CLOGGERS
CLOGGIER
CLOGGIEST
CLOGGILY
CLOGGING
CLOGGINGS
CLOGGY
CLOGMAKER
CLOGS
CLOISON
CLOISONNE
CLOISONS
CLOISTER
CLOISTERS
CLOISTRAL
CLOKE
CLOKED
CLOKES
CLOKING
CLOMB
CLOMP
CLOMPED
CLOMPING
CLOMPS
CLON
CLONAL
CLONALLY
CLONE
CLONED
CLONER
CLONERS
CLONES
CLONIC
CLONICITY
CLONIDINE
CLONING
CLONINGS
CLONISM
CLONISMS
CLONK
CLONKED
CLONKIER
CLONKIEST
CLONKING
CLONKS
CLONKY
CLONS
CLONUS
CLONUSES
CLOOP
CLOOPS
CLOOT
CLOOTIE
CLOOTS
CLOP
CLOPPED
CLOPPING
CLOPS
CLOQUE
CLOQUES
CLOSABLE
CLOSE
CLOSEABLE
CLOSED
CLOSEDOWN
CLOSEHEAD
CLOSELY
CLOSENESS
CLOSEOUT
CLOSEOUTS
CLOSER
CLOSERS
CLOSES
CLOSEST
CLOSET
CLOSETED
CLOSETFUL
CLOSETING
CLOSETS
CLOSEUP
CLOSEUPS
CLOSING
CLOSINGS
CLOSURE
CLOSURED
CLOSURES
CLOSURING
CLOT
CLOTBUR
CLOTBURS
CLOTE
CLOTES
CLOTH
CLOTHE
CLOTHED
CLOTHES
CLOTHIER
CLOTHIERS
CLOTHING
CLOTHINGS
CLOTHLIKE
CLOTHS
CLOTPOLL
CLOTPOLLS
CLOTS
CLOTTED
CLOTTER
CLOTTERED
CLOTTERS
CLOTTIER
CLOTTIEST
CLOTTING
CLOTTINGS
CLOTTISH
CLOTTY
CLOTURE
CLOTURED
CLOTURES
CLOTURING
CLOU
CLOUD
CLOUDAGE
CLOUDAGES
CLOUDED
CLOUDIER
CLOUDIEST
CLOUDILY
CLOUDING
CLOUDINGS
CLOUDLAND
CLOUDLESS
CLOUDLET
CLOUDLETS
CLOUDLIKE
CLOUDS
CLOUDTOWN
CLOUDY
CLOUGH
CLOUGHS
CLOUR
CLOURED
CLOURING
CLOURS
CLOUS
CLOUT
CLOUTED
CLOUTER
CLOUTERLY
CLOUTERS
CLOUTING
CLOUTS
CLOVE
CLOVEN
CLOVER
CLOVERED
CLOVERIER
CLOVERS
CLOVERY
CLOVES
CLOVIS
CLOW
CLOWDER
CLOWDERS
CLOWED
CLOWING
CLOWN
CLOWNED
CLOWNERY
CLOWNFISH
CLOWNING
CLOWNINGS
CLOWNISH
CLOWNS
CLOWS
CLOY

CLOYE
CLOYED
CLOYES
CLOYING
CLOYINGLY
CLOYLESS
CLOYMENT
CLOYMENTS
CLOYS
CLOYSOME
CLOZAPINE
CLOZE
CLOZES
CLUB
CLUBABLE
CLUBBABLE
CLUBBED
CLUBBER
CLUBBERS
CLUBBIER
CLUBBIEST
CLUBBILY
CLUBBING
CLUBBINGS
CLUBBISH
CLUBBISM
CLUBBISMS
CLUBBIST
CLUBBISTS
CLUBBY
CLUBFACE
CLUBFACES
CLUBFEET
CLUBFOOT
CLUBHAND
CLUBHANDS
CLUBHAUL
CLUBHAULS
CLUBHEAD
CLUBHEADS
CLUBHOUSE
CLUBLAND
CLUBLANDS
CLUBLIKE
CLUBMAN
CLUBMATE
CLUBMATES
CLUBMEN
CLUBMOSS
CLUBROOM
CLUBROOMS
CLUBROOT
CLUBROOTS
CLUBRUSH
CLUBS
CLUBWOMAN
CLUBWOMEN
CLUCK
CLUCKED
CLUCKER
CLUCKERS
CLUCKIER
CLUCKIEST
CLUCKING
CLUCKS
CLUCKY
CLUDGIE
CLUDGIES
CLUE
CLUED
CLUEING
CLUELESS
CLUES
CLUEY
CLUIER
CLUIEST
CLUING
CLUMBER
CLUMBERS
CLUMP
CLUMPED
CLUMPER
CLUMPERED
CLUMPERS
CLUMPET
CLUMPETS
CLUMPIER
CLUMPIEST
CLUMPING
CLUMPISH
CLUMPLIKE
CLUMPS
CLUMPY
CLUMSIER
CLUMSIEST
CLUMSILY
CLUMSY
CLUNCH
CLUNCHES
CLUNG
CLUNK
CLUNKED
CLUNKER
CLUNKERS
CLUNKIER
CLUNKIEST
CLUNKING
CLUNKS
CLUNKY
CLUPEID
CLUPEIDS
CLUPEOID
CLUPEOIDS
CLUSIA
CLUSIAS
CLUSTER
CLUSTERED
CLUSTERS
CLUSTERY
CLUTCH
CLUTCHED
CLUTCHES
CLUTCHIER
CLUTCHING
CLUTCHY
CLUTTER
CLUTTERED
CLUTTERS
CLUTTERY
CLY
CLYING
CLYPE
CLYPEAL
CLYPEATE
CLYPED
CLYPEI
CLYPES
CLYPEUS
CLYPING
CLYSTER
CLYSTERS
CNEMIAL
CNEMIDES
CNEMIS
CNIDA
CNIDAE
CNIDARIAN
COACH
COACHABLE
COACHDOG
COACHDOGS
COACHED
COACHEE
COACHEES
COACHER
COACHERS
COACHES
COACHIER
COACHIES
COACHIEST
COACHING
COACHINGS
COACHLINE
COACHLOAD
COACHMAN
COACHMEN
COACHROOF
COACHWHIP
COACHWOOD
COACHWORK
COACHY
COACT
COACTED
COACTING
COACTION
COACTIONS
COACTIVE
COACTOR
COACTORS
COACTS
COADAPTED
COADIES
COADJUTOR
COADMIRE
COADMIRED
COADMIRES
COADMIT
COADMITS
COADUNATE
COADY
COAEVAL
COAEVALS
COAGENCY
COAGENT
COAGENTS
COAGULA
COAGULANT
COAGULASE
COAGULATE
COAGULUM
COAGULUMS
COAITA
COAITAS
COAL
COALA
COALAS
COALBALL
COALBALLS
COALBIN
COALBINS
COALBOX
COALBOXES
COALDUST
COALDUSTS
COALED
COALER
COALERS
COALESCE
COALESCED
COALESCES
COALFACE
COALFACES
COALFIELD
COALFISH
COALHOLE
COALHOLES
COALHOUSE
COALIER
COALIEST
COALIFIED
COALIFIES
COALIFY
COALING
COALISE
COALISED
COALISES
COALISING
COALITION
COALIZE
COALIZED

COALIZES
COALIZING
COALLESS
COALMAN
COALMEN
COALMINE
COALMINER
COALMINES
COALPIT
COALPITS
COALS
COALSACK
COALSACKS
COALSHED
COALSHEDS
COALY
COALYARD
COALYARDS
COAMING
COAMINGS
COANCHOR
COANCHORS
COANNEX
COANNEXED
COANNEXES
COAPPEAR
COAPPEARS
COAPT
COAPTED
COAPTING
COAPTS
COARB
COARBS
COARCTATE
COARSE
COARSELY
COARSEN
COARSENED
COARSENS
COARSER
COARSEST
COARSISH
COASSIST
COASSISTS
COASSUME
COASSUMED
COASSUMES
COAST
COASTAL
COASTALLY
COASTED
COASTER
COASTERS
COASTING
COASTINGS
COASTLAND
COASTLINE
COASTS
COASTWARD
COASTWISE
COAT
COATDRESS
COATE
COATED
COATEE
COATEES
COATER
COATERS
COATES
COATI
COATING
COATINGS
COATIS
COATLESS
COATLIKE
COATRACK
COATRACKS
COATROOM
COATROOMS
COATS
COATSTAND
COATTAIL
COATTAILS
COATTEND
COATTENDS
COATTEST
COATTESTS
COAUTHOR
COAUTHORS
COAX
COAXAL
COAXED
COAXER
COAXERS
COAXES
COAXIAL
COAXIALLY
COAXING
COAXINGLY
COAXINGS
COB
COBAEA
COBAEAS
COBALAMIN
COBALT
COBALTIC
COBALTINE
COBALTITE
COBALTOUS
COBALTS
COBB
COBBED
COBBER
COBBERS
COBBIER
COBBIEST
COBBING
COBBLE
COBBLED
COBBLER
COBBLERS
COBBLERY
COBBLES
COBBLING
COBBLINGS
COBBS
COBBY
COBIA
COBIAS
COBLE
COBLES
COBLOAF
COBLOAVES
COBNUT
COBNUTS
COBRA
COBRAS
COBRIC
COBRIFORM
COBS
COBURG
COBURGS
COBWEB
COBWEBBED
COBWEBBY
COBWEBS
COBZA
COBZAS
COCA
COCAIN
COCAINE
COCAINES
COCAINISE
COCAINISM
COCAINIST
COCAINIZE
COCAINS
COCAPTAIN
COCAS
COCCAL
COCCI
COCCIC
COCCID
COCCIDIA
COCCIDIAN
COCCIDIUM
COCCIDS
COCCO
COCCOID
COCCOIDAL
COCCOIDS
COCCOLITE
COCCOLITH
COCCOS
COCCOUS
COCCUS
COCCYGEAL
COCCYGES
COCCYGIAN
COCCYX
COCCYXES
COCH
COCHAIR
COCHAIRED
COCHAIRS
COCHES
COCHIN
COCHINEAL
COCHINS
COCHLEA
COCHLEAE
COCHLEAR
COCHLEARE
COCHLEARS
COCHLEAS
COCHLEATE
COCINERA
COCINERAS
COCK
COCKADE
COCKADED
COCKADES
COCKAMAMY
COCKAPOO
COCKAPOOS
COCKATEEL
COCKATIEL
COCKATOO
COCKATOOS
COCKBILL
COCKBILLS
COCKBIRD
COCKBIRDS
COCKBOAT
COCKBOATS
COCKCROW
COCKCROWS
COCKED
COCKER
COCKERED
COCKEREL
COCKERELS
COCKERING
COCKERS
COCKET
COCKETS
COCKEYE
COCKEYED
COCKEYES
COCKFIGHT
COCKHORSE
COCKIER
COCKIES
COCKIEST
COCKILY
COCKINESS
COCKING
COCKISH
COCKLE
COCKLEBUR

COCKLED
COCKLEERT
COCKLEMAN
COCKLEMEN
COCKLER
COCKLERS
COCKLES
COCKLIKE
COCKLING
COCKLINGS
COCKLOFT
COCKLOFTS
COCKMATCH
COCKNEY
COCKNEYFY
COCKNEYS
COCKNIFY
COCKPIT
COCKPITS
COCKROACH
COCKS
COCKSCOMB
COCKSFOOT
COCKSHIES
COCKSHOT
COCKSHOTS
COCKSHUT
COCKSHUTS
COCKSHY
COCKSIER
COCKSIEST
COCKSMAN
COCKSMEN
COCKSPUR
COCKSPURS
COCKSURE
COCKSWAIN
COCKSY
COCKTAIL
COCKTAILS
COCKUP
COCKUPS
COCKY
COCO
COCOA
COCOANUT
COCOANUTS
COCOAS
COCOBOLA
COCOBOLAS
COCOBOLO
COCOBOLOS
COCOMAT
COCOMATS
COCONUT
COCONUTS
COCONUTTY
COCOON
COCOONED
COCOONER
COCOONERS
COCOONERY
COCOONING
COCOONS
COCOPAN
COCOPANS
COCOPLUM
COCOPLUMS
COCOS
COCOTTE
COCOTTES
COCOUNSEL
COCOYAM
COCOYAMS
COCOZELLE
COCREATE
COCREATED
COCREATES
COCREATOR
COCTILE
COCTION
COCTIONS
COCULTURE
COCURATE
COCURATED
COCURATES
COCURATOR
COCUSWOOD
COD
CODA
CODABLE
CODAS
CODDED
CODDER
CODDERS
CODDING
CODDLE
CODDLED
CODDLER
CODDLERS
CODDLES
CODDLING
CODE
CODEBOOK
CODEBOOKS
CODEBTOR
CODEBTORS
CODEC
CODECS
CODED
CODEIA
CODEIAS
CODEIN
CODEINA
CODEINAS
CODEINE
CODEINES
CODEINS
CODELESS
CODEN
CODENAME
CODENAMES
CODENS
CODER
CODERIVE
CODERIVED
CODERIVES
CODERS
CODES
CODESIGN
CODESIGNS
CODETTA
CODETTAS
CODEVELOP
CODEWORD
CODEWORDS
CODEX
CODEXES
CODFISH
CODFISHES
CODGER
CODGERS
CODICES
CODICIL
CODICILS
CODIFIED
CODIFIER
CODIFIERS
CODIFIES
CODIFY
CODIFYING
CODILLA
CODILLAS
CODILLE
CODILLES
CODING
CODINGS
CODIRECT
CODIRECTS
CODIST
CODISTS
CODLIN
CODLING
CODLINGS
CODLINS
CODOLOGY
CODOMAIN
CODOMAINS
CODON
CODONS
CODPIECE
CODPIECES
CODRIVE
CODRIVEN
CODRIVER
CODRIVERS
CODRIVES
CODRIVING
CODROVE
CODS
COECILIAN
COED
COEDIT
COEDITED
COEDITING
COEDITOR
COEDITORS
COEDITS
COEDS
COEFFECT
COEFFECTS
COEHORN
COEHORNS
COELIAC
COELIACS
COELOM
COELOMATA
COELOMATE
COELOME
COELOMES
COELOMIC
COELOMS
COELOSTAT
COEMBODY
COEMPLOY
COEMPLOYS
COEMPT
COEMPTED
COEMPTING
COEMPTION
COEMPTS
COENACLE
COENACLES
COENACT
COENACTED
COENACTS
COENAMOR
COENAMORS
COENAMOUR
COENDURE
COENDURED
COENDURES
COENOBIA
COENOBITE
COENOBIUM
COENOCYTE
COENOSARC
COENURE
COENURES
COENURI
COENURUS
COENZYME
COENZYMES
COEQUAL
COEQUALLY
COEQUALS
COEQUATE
COEQUATED
COEQUATES
COERCE

C

COERCED
COERCER
COERCERS
COERCES
COERCIBLE
COERCIBLY
COERCING
COERCION
COERCIONS
COERCIVE
COERECT
COERECTED
COERECTS
COESITE
COESITES
COETERNAL
COEVAL
COEVALITY
COEVALLY
COEVALS
COEVOLVE
COEVOLVED
COEVOLVES
COEXERT
COEXERTED
COEXERTS
COEXIST
COEXISTED
COEXISTS
COEXTEND
COEXTENDS
COFACTOR
COFACTORS
COFEATURE
COFF
COFFED
COFFEE
COFFEEPOT
COFFEES
COFFER
COFFERDAM
COFFERED
COFFERING
COFFERS
COFFIN
COFFINED
COFFING
COFFINING
COFFINITE
COFFINS
COFFLE
COFFLED
COFFLES
COFFLING
COFFRET
COFFRETS
COFFS
COFINANCE
COFIRING
COFIRINGS
COFOUND
COFOUNDED
COFOUNDER
COFOUNDS
COFT
COG
COGENCE
COGENCES
COGENCIES
COGENCY
COGENER
COGENERS
COGENT
COGENTLY
COGGED
COGGER
COGGERS
COGGIE
COGGIES
COGGING
COGGINGS
COGGLE
COGGLED
COGGLES
COGGLIER
COGGLIEST
COGGLING
COGGLY
COGIE
COGIES
COGITABLE
COGITATE
COGITATED
COGITATES
COGITATOR
COGITO
COGITOS
COGNAC
COGNACS
COGNATE
COGNATELY
COGNATES
COGNATION
COGNISANT
COGNISE
COGNISED
COGNISER
COGNISERS
COGNISES
COGNISING
COGNITION
COGNITIVE
COGNIZANT
COGNIZE
COGNIZED
COGNIZER
COGNIZERS
COGNIZES
COGNIZING
COGNOMEN
COGNOMENS
COGNOMINA
COGNOSCE
COGNOSCED
COGNOSCES
COGNOVIT
COGNOVITS
COGON
COGONS
COGS
COGUE
COGUES
COGWAY
COGWAYS
COGWHEEL
COGWHEELS
COHAB
COHABIT
COHABITED
COHABITEE
COHABITER
COHABITOR
COHABITS
COHABS
COHEAD
COHEADED
COHEADING
COHEADS
COHEIR
COHEIRESS
COHEIRS
COHEN
COHENS
COHERE
COHERED
COHERENCE
COHERENCY
COHERENT
COHERER
COHERERS
COHERES
COHERING
COHERITOR
COHESIBLE
COHESION
COHESIONS
COHESIVE
COHIBIT
COHIBITED
COHIBITS
COHO
COHOBATE
COHOBATED
COHOBATES
COHOE
COHOES
COHOG
COHOGS
COHOLDER
COHOLDERS
COHORN
COHORNS
COHORT
COHORTS
COHOS
COHOSH
COHOSHES
COHOST
COHOSTED
COHOSTESS
COHOSTING
COHOSTS
COHOUSING
COHUNE
COHUNES
COHYPONYM
COIF
COIFED
COIFFE
COIFFED
COIFFES
COIFFEUR
COIFFEURS
COIFFEUSE
COIFFING
COIFFURE
COIFFURED
COIFFURES
COIFING
COIFS
COIGN
COIGNE
COIGNED
COIGNES
COIGNING
COIGNS
COIL
COILED
COILER
COILERS
COILING
COILS
COIN
COINABLE
COINAGE
COINAGES
COINCIDE
COINCIDED
COINCIDES
COINED
COINER
COINERS
COINFECT
COINFECTS
COINFER
COINFERS
COINHERE
COINHERED
COINHERES
COINING

COININGS
COINMATE
COINMATES
COINOP
COINS
COINSURE
COINSURED
COINSURER
COINSURES
COINTER
COINTERS
COINTREAU
COINVENT
COINVENTS
COINVEST
COINVESTS
COIR
COIRS
COISTREL
COISTRELS
COISTRIL
COISTRILS
COIT
COITAL
COITALLY
COITION
COITIONAL
COITIONS
COITS
COITUS
COITUSES
COJOIN
COJOINED
COJOINING
COJOINS
COJONES
COKE
COKED
COKEHEAD
COKEHEADS
COKELIKE
COKERNUT
COKERNUTS
COKES
COKESES
COKIER
COKIEST
COKING
COKINGS
COKULORIS
COKY
COL
COLA
COLANDER
COLANDERS
COLAS
COLBIES
COLBY
COLBYS
COLCANNON
COLCHICA
COLCHICUM
COLCOTHAR
COLD
COLDBLOOD
COLDCOCK
COLDCOCKS
COLDER
COLDEST
COLDHOUSE
COLDIE
COLDIES
COLDISH
COLDLY
COLDNESS
COLDS
COLE
COLEAD
COLEADER
COLEADERS
COLEADING
COLEADS
COLECTOMY
COLED
COLEOPTER
COLES
COLESEED
COLESEEDS
COLESLAW
COLESLAWS
COLESSEE
COLESSEES
COLESSOR
COLESSORS
COLETIT
COLETITS
COLEUS
COLEUSES
COLEWORT
COLEWORTS
COLEY
COLEYS
COLIBRI
COLIBRIS
COLIC
COLICIN
COLICINE
COLICINES
COLICINS
COLICKIER
COLICKY
COLICROOT
COLICS
COLICWEED
COLIES
COLIFORM
COLIFORMS
COLIN
COLINEAR
COLINS
COLIPHAGE
COLISEUM
COLISEUMS
COLISTIN
COLISTINS
COLITIC
COLITIS
COLITISES
COLL
COLLAB
COLLABS
COLLAGE
COLLAGED
COLLAGEN
COLLAGENS
COLLAGES
COLLAGING
COLLAGIST
COLLAPSAR
COLLAPSE
COLLAPSED
COLLAPSES
COLLAR
COLLARD
COLLARDS
COLLARED
COLLARET
COLLARETS
COLLARING
COLLARS
COLLATE
COLLATED
COLLATES
COLLATING
COLLATION
COLLATIVE
COLLATOR
COLLATORS
COLLEAGUE
COLLECT
COLLECTED
COLLECTOR
COLLECTS
COLLED
COLLEEN
COLLEENS
COLLEGE
COLLEGER
COLLEGERS
COLLEGES
COLLEGIA
COLLEGIAL
COLLEGIAN
COLLEGIUM
COLLET
COLLETED
COLLETING
COLLETS
COLLICULI
COLLIDE
COLLIDED
COLLIDER
COLLIDERS
COLLIDES
COLLIDING
COLLIE
COLLIED
COLLIER
COLLIERS
COLLIERY
COLLIES
COLLIGATE
COLLIMATE
COLLINEAR
COLLING
COLLINGS
COLLINS
COLLINSES
COLLINSIA
COLLISION
COLLOCATE
COLLODION
COLLODIUM
COLLOGUE
COLLOGUED
COLLOGUES
COLLOID
COLLOIDAL
COLLOIDS
COLLOP
COLLOPS
COLLOQUE
COLLOQUED
COLLOQUES
COLLOQUIA
COLLOQUY
COLLOTYPE
COLLOTYPY
COLLS
COLLUDE
COLLUDED
COLLUDER
COLLUDERS
COLLUDES
COLLUDING
COLLUSION
COLLUSIVE
COLLUVIA
COLLUVIAL
COLLUVIES
COLLUVIUM
COLLY
COLLYING
COLLYRIA
COLLYRIUM
COLOBI
COLOBID
COLOBIDS
COLOBOMA
COLOBOMAS

C

COLOBUS
COLOBUSES
COLOCATE
COLOCATED
COLOCATES
COLOCYNTH
COLOG
COLOGNE
COLOGNED
COLOGNES
COLOGS
COLOMBARD
COLON
COLONE
COLONEL
COLONELCY
COLONELS
COLONES
COLONI
COLONIAL
COLONIALS
COLONIC
COLONICS
COLONIES
COLONISE
COLONISED
COLONISER
COLONISES
COLONIST
COLONISTS
COLONITIS
COLONIZE
COLONIZED
COLONIZER
COLONIZES
COLONNADE
COLONS
COLONUS
COLONY
COLOPHON
COLOPHONS
COLOPHONY
COLOR
COLORABLE
COLORABLY
COLORADO
COLORANT
COLORANTS
COLORBRED
COLORCAST
COLORED
COLOREDS
COLORER
COLORERS
COLORFAST
COLORFUL
COLORIER
COLORIEST
COLORIFIC
COLORING
COLORINGS
COLORISE
COLORISED
COLORISER
COLORISES
COLORISM
COLORISMS
COLORIST
COLORISTS
COLORIZE
COLORIZED
COLORIZER
COLORIZES
COLORLESS
COLORMAN
COLORMEN
COLORS
COLORWASH
COLORWAY
COLORWAYS
COLORY
COLOSSAL
COLOSSEUM
COLOSSI
COLOSSUS
COLOSTOMY
COLOSTRAL
COLOSTRIC
COLOSTRUM
COLOTOMY
COLOUR
COLOURANT
COLOURED
COLOUREDS
COLOURER
COLOURERS
COLOURFUL
COLOURIER
COLOURING
COLOURISE
COLOURISM
COLOURIST
COLOURIZE
COLOURMAN
COLOURMEN
COLOURS
COLOURWAY
COLOURY
COLPITIS
COLPOTOMY
COLS
COLT
COLTAN
COLTANS
COLTED
COLTER
COLTERS
COLTHOOD
COLTHOODS
COLTING
COLTISH
COLTISHLY
COLTS
COLTSFOOT
COLTWOOD
COLTWOODS
COLUBRIAD
COLUBRID
COLUBRIDS
COLUBRINE
COLUGO
COLUGOS
COLUMBARY
COLUMBATE
COLUMBIC
COLUMBINE
COLUMBITE
COLUMBIUM
COLUMBOUS
COLUMEL
COLUMELLA
COLUMELS
COLUMN
COLUMNAL
COLUMNALS
COLUMNAR
COLUMNEA
COLUMNEAS
COLUMNED
COLUMNIST
COLUMNS
COLURE
COLURES
COLY
COLZA
COLZAS
COMA
COMADE
COMAE
COMAKE
COMAKER
COMAKERS
COMAKES
COMAKING
COMAL
COMANAGE
COMANAGED
COMANAGER
COMANAGES
COMARB
COMARBS
COMART
COMARTS
COMAS
COMATE
COMATES
COMATIC
COMATIK
COMATIKS
COMATOSE
COMATULA
COMATULAE
COMATULID
COMB
COMBAT
COMBATANT
COMBATED
COMBATER
COMBATERS
COMBATING
COMBATIVE
COMBATS
COMBATTED
COMBE
COMBED
COMBER
COMBERS
COMBES
COMBI
COMBIER
COMBIES
COMBIEST
COMBINATE
COMBINE
COMBINED
COMBINEDS
COMBINER
COMBINERS
COMBINES
COMBING
COMBINGS
COMBINING
COMBIS
COMBLE
COMBLES
COMBLESS
COMBLIKE
COMBO
COMBOS
COMBOVER
COMBOVERS
COMBRETUM
COMBS
COMBUST
COMBUSTED
COMBUSTOR
COMBUSTS
COMBWISE
COMBY
COME
COMEBACK
COMEBACKS
COMEDDLE
COMEDDLED
COMEDDLES
COMEDIAN
COMEDIANS
COMEDIC
COMEDIES
COMEDIST

COMEDISTS
COMEDO
COMEDONES
COMEDOS
COMEDOWN
COMEDOWNS
COMEDY
COMELIER
COMELIEST
COMELILY
COMELY
COMEMBER
COMEMBERS
COMEOVER
COMEOVERS
COMER
COMERS
COMES
COMET
COMETARY
COMETH
COMETHER
COMETHERS
COMETIC
COMETS
COMFIER
COMFIEST
COMFILY
COMFINESS
COMFIT
COMFITS
COMFITURE
COMFORT
COMFORTED
COMFORTER
COMFORTS
COMFREY
COMFREYS
COMFY
COMIC
COMICAL
COMICALLY
COMICE
COMICES
COMICS
COMING
COMINGLE
COMINGLED
COMINGLES
COMINGS
COMIQUE
COMIQUES
COMITADJI
COMITAL
COMITATUS
COMITIA
COMITIAL
COMITIAS
COMITIES
COMITY
COMIX
COMM
COMMA
COMMAND
COMMANDED
COMMANDER
COMMANDO
COMMANDOS
COMMANDS
COMMAS
COMMATA
COMMENCE
COMMENCED
COMMENCER
COMMENCES
COMMEND
COMMENDAM
COMMENDED
COMMENDER
COMMENDS
COMMENSAL
COMMENT
COMMENTED
COMMENTER
COMMENTOR
COMMENTS
COMMER
COMMERCE
COMMERCED
COMMERCES
COMMERE
COMMERES
COMMERGE
COMMERGED
COMMERGES
COMMERS
COMMIE
COMMIES
COMMINATE
COMMINGLE
COMMINUTE
COMMIS
COMMISH
COMMISHES
COMMISSAR
COMMIT
COMMITS
COMMITTAL
COMMITTED
COMMITTEE
COMMITTER
COMMIX
COMMIXED
COMMIXES
COMMIXING
COMMIXT
COMMO
COMMODE
COMMODES
COMMODIFY
COMMODITY
COMMODO
COMMODORE
COMMON
COMMONAGE
COMMONED
COMMONER
COMMONERS
COMMONEST
COMMONEY
COMMONEYS
COMMONING
COMMONLY
COMMONS
COMMORANT
COMMOS
COMMOT
COMMOTE
COMMOTES
COMMOTION
COMMOTS
COMMOVE
COMMOVED
COMMOVES
COMMOVING
COMMS
COMMUNAL
COMMUNARD
COMMUNE
COMMUNED
COMMUNER
COMMUNERS
COMMUNES
COMMUNING
COMMUNION
COMMUNISE
COMMUNISM
COMMUNIST
COMMUNITY
COMMUNIZE
COMMUTATE
COMMUTE
COMMUTED
COMMUTER
COMMUTERS
COMMUTES
COMMUTING
COMMUTUAL
COMMY
COMODO
COMONOMER
COMORBID
COMOSE
COMOUS
COMP
COMPACT
COMPACTED
COMPACTER
COMPACTLY
COMPACTOR
COMPACTS
COMPADRE
COMPADRES
COMPAGE
COMPAGES
COMPAND
COMPANDED
COMPANDER
COMPANDOR
COMPANDS
COMPANIED
COMPANIES
COMPANING
COMPANION
COMPANY
COMPARE
COMPARED
COMPARER
COMPARERS
COMPARES
COMPARING
COMPART
COMPARTED
COMPARTS
COMPAS
COMPASS
COMPASSED
COMPASSES
COMPAST
COMPEAR
COMPEARED
COMPEARS
COMPED
COMPEER
COMPEERED
COMPEERS
COMPEL
COMPELLED
COMPELLER
COMPELS
COMPEND
COMPENDIA
COMPENDS
COMPER
COMPERE
COMPERED
COMPERES
COMPERING
COMPERS
COMPESCE
COMPESCED
COMPESCES
COMPETE
COMPETED
COMPETENT
COMPETES
COMPETING
COMPILE
COMPILED
COMPILER

C

C

COMPILERS
COMPILES
COMPILING
COMPING
COMPINGS
COMPITAL
COMPLAIN
COMPLAINS
COMPLAINT
COMPLEAT
COMPLEATS
COMPLECT
COMPLECTS
COMPLETE
COMPLETED
COMPLETER
COMPLETES
COMPLEX
COMPLEXED
COMPLEXER
COMPLEXES
COMPLEXLY
COMPLEXUS
COMPLIANT
COMPLICE
COMPLICES
COMPLICIT
COMPLIED
COMPLIER
COMPLIERS
COMPLIES
COMPLIN
COMPLINE
COMPLINES
COMPLINS
COMPLISH
COMPLOT
COMPLOTS
COMPLUVIA
COMPLY
COMPLYING
COMPO
COMPONE
COMPONENT
COMPONY
COMPORT
COMPORTED
COMPORTS
COMPOS
COMPOSE
COMPOSED
COMPOSER
COMPOSERS
COMPOSES
COMPOSING
COMPOSITE
COMPOST
COMPOSTED
COMPOSTER
COMPOSTS
COMPOSURE
COMPOT
COMPOTE
COMPOTES
COMPOTIER
COMPOTS
COMPOUND
COMPOUNDS
COMPRADOR
COMPRESS
COMPRINT
COMPRINTS
COMPRISAL
COMPRISE
COMPRISED
COMPRISES
COMPRIZE
COMPRIZED
COMPRIZES
COMPS
COMPT
COMPTABLE
COMPTED
COMPTER
COMPTERS
COMPTIBLE
COMPTING
COMPTROLL
COMPTS
COMPULSE
COMPULSED
COMPULSES
COMPUTANT
COMPUTE
COMPUTED
COMPUTER
COMPUTERS
COMPUTES
COMPUTING
COMPUTIST
COMRADE
COMRADELY
COMRADERY
COMRADES
COMS
COMSAT
COMSATS
COMSYMP
COMSYMPS
COMTE
COMTES
COMUS
COMUSES
CON
CONACRE
CONACRED
CONACRES
CONACRING
CONARIA
CONARIAL
CONARIUM
CONATION
CONATIONS
CONATIVE
CONATUS
CONCAUSE
CONCAUSES
CONCAVE
CONCAVED
CONCAVELY
CONCAVES
CONCAVING
CONCAVITY
CONCEAL
CONCEALED
CONCEALER
CONCEALS
CONCEDE
CONCEDED
CONCEDER
CONCEDERS
CONCEDES
CONCEDING
CONCEDO
CONCEIT
CONCEITED
CONCEITS
CONCEITY
CONCEIVE
CONCEIVED
CONCEIVER
CONCEIVES
CONCENT
CONCENTER
CONCENTRE
CONCENTS
CONCENTUS
CONCEPT
CONCEPTI
CONCEPTS
CONCEPTUS
CONCERN
CONCERNED
CONCERNS
CONCERT
CONCERTED
CONCERTI
CONCERTO
CONCERTOS
CONCERTS
CONCETTI
CONCETTO
CONCH
CONCHA
CONCHAE
CONCHAL
CONCHAS
CONCHATE
CONCHE
CONCHED
CONCHES
CONCHIE
CONCHIES
CONCHING
CONCHITIS
CONCHO
CONCHOID
CONCHOIDS
CONCHOS
CONCHS
CONCHY
CONCIERGE
CONCILIAR
CONCISE
CONCISED
CONCISELY
CONCISER
CONCISES
CONCISEST
CONCISING
CONCISION
CONCLAVE
CONCLAVES
CONCLUDE
CONCLUDED
CONCLUDER
CONCLUDES
CONCOCT
CONCOCTED
CONCOCTER
CONCOCTOR
CONCOCTS
CONCOLOR
CONCORD
CONCORDAL
CONCORDAT
CONCORDED
CONCORDS
CONCOURS
CONCOURSE
CONCREATE
CONCRETE
CONCRETED
CONCRETES
CONCREW
CONCREWED
CONCREWS
CONCUBINE
CONCUPIES
CONCUPY
CONCUR
CONCURRED
CONCURS
CONCUSS
CONCUSSED
CONCUSSES
CONCYCLIC
COND
CONDEMN
CONDEMNED

CONDEMNER
CONDEMNOR
CONDEMNS
CONDENSE
CONDENSED
CONDENSER
CONDENSES
CONDER
CONDERS
CONDIDDLE
CONDIE
CONDIES
CONDIGN
CONDIGNLY
CONDIMENT
CONDITION
CONDO
CONDOES
CONDOLE
CONDOLED
CONDOLENT
CONDOLER
CONDOLERS
CONDOLES
CONDOLING
CONDOM
CONDOMS
CONDONE
CONDONED
CONDONER
CONDONERS
CONDONES
CONDONING
CONDOR
CONDORES
CONDORS
CONDOS
CONDUCE
CONDUCED
CONDUCER
CONDUCERS
CONDUCES
CONDUCING
CONDUCIVE
CONDUCT
CONDUCTED
CONDUCTI
CONDUCTOR
CONDUCTS
CONDUCTUS
CONDUIT
CONDUITS
CONDYLAR
CONDYLE
CONDYLES
CONDYLOID
CONDYLOMA
CONE
CONED
CONELESS
CONELIKE
CONELRAD
CONELRADS
CONENOSE
CONENOSES
CONEPATE
CONEPATES
CONEPATL
CONEPATLS
CONES
CONEY
CONEYS
CONF
CONFAB
CONFABBED
CONFABS
CONFECT
CONFECTED
CONFECTS
CONFER
CONFEREE
CONFEREES
CONFERRAL
CONFERRED
CONFERREE
CONFERRER
CONFERS
CONFERVA
CONFERVAE
CONFERVAL
CONFERVAS
CONFESS
CONFESSED
CONFESSES
CONFESSOR
CONFEST
CONFESTLY
CONFETTI
CONFETTO
CONFIDANT
CONFIDE
CONFIDED
CONFIDENT
CONFIDER
CONFIDERS
CONFIDES
CONFIDING
CONFIGURE
CONFINE
CONFINED
CONFINER
CONFINERS
CONFINES
CONFINING
CONFIRM
CONFIRMED
CONFIRMEE
CONFIRMER
CONFIRMOR
CONFIRMS
CONFISEUR
CONFIT
CONFITEOR
CONFITS
CONFITURE
CONFIX
CONFIXED
CONFIXES
CONFIXING
CONFLATE
CONFLATED
CONFLATES
CONFLICT
CONFLICTS
CONFLUENT
CONFLUX
CONFLUXES
CONFOCAL
CONFORM
CONFORMAL
CONFORMED
CONFORMER
CONFORMS
CONFOUND
CONFOUNDS
CONFRERE
CONFRERES
CONFRERIE
CONFRONT
CONFRONTE
CONFRONTS
CONFS
CONFUSE
CONFUSED
CONFUSES
CONFUSING
CONFUSION
CONFUTE
CONFUTED
CONFUTER
CONFUTERS
CONFUTES
CONFUTING
CONGA
CONGAED
CONGAING
CONGAS
CONGE
CONGEAL
CONGEALED
CONGEALER
CONGEALS
CONGED
CONGEE
CONGEED
CONGEEING
CONGEES
CONGEING
CONGENER
CONGENERS
CONGENIAL
CONGENIC
CONGER
CONGERIES
CONGERS
CONGES
CONGEST
CONGESTED
CONGESTS
CONGIARY
CONGII
CONGIUS
CONGLOBE
CONGLOBED
CONGLOBES
CONGO
CONGOES
CONGOS
CONGOU
CONGOUS
CONGRATS
CONGREE
CONGREED
CONGREES
CONGREET
CONGREETS
CONGRESS
CONGRUE
CONGRUED
CONGRUENT
CONGRUES
CONGRUING
CONGRUITY
CONGRUOUS
CONI
CONIA
CONIAS
CONIC
CONICAL
CONICALLY
CONICINE
CONICINES
CONICITY
CONICS
CONIDIA
CONIDIAL
CONIDIAN
CONIDIUM
CONIES
CONIFER
CONIFERS
CONIFORM
CONIINE
CONIINES
CONIMA
CONIMAS
CONIN
CONINE
CONINES
CONING

CONINS
CONIOLOGY
CONIOSES
CONIOSIS
CONIUM
CONIUMS
CONJECT
CONJECTED
CONJECTS
CONJEE
CONJEED
CONJEEING
CONJEES
CONJOIN
CONJOINED
CONJOINER
CONJOINS
CONJOINT
CONJUGAL
CONJUGANT
CONJUGATE
CONJUNCT
CONJUNCTS
CONJUNTO
CONJUNTOS
CONJURE
CONJURED
CONJURER
CONJURERS
CONJURES
CONJURIES
CONJURING
CONJUROR
CONJURORS
CONJURY
CONK
CONKED
CONKER
CONKERS
CONKIER
CONKIEST
CONKING
CONKOUT
CONKOUTS
CONKS
CONKY
CONLANG
CONLANGER
CONLANGS
CONMAN
CONMEN
CONN
CONNATE
CONNATELY
CONNATION
CONNATURE
CONNE
CONNECT
CONNECTED
CONNECTER
CONNECTOR
CONNECTS
CONNED
CONNER
CONNERS
CONNES
CONNEXION
CONNEXIVE
CONNIE
CONNIES
CONNING
CONNINGS
CONNIVE
CONNIVED
CONNIVENT
CONNIVER
CONNIVERS
CONNIVERY
CONNIVES
CONNIVING
CONNOR
CONNORS
CONNOTATE
CONNOTE
CONNOTED
CONNOTES
CONNOTING
CONNOTIVE
CONNS
CONNUBIAL
CONODONT
CONODONTS
CONOID
CONOIDAL
CONOIDIC
CONOIDS
CONOMINEE
CONQUER
CONQUERED
CONQUERER
CONQUEROR
CONQUERS
CONQUEST
CONQUESTS
CONQUIAN
CONQUIANS
CONS
CONSCIENT
CONSCIOUS
CONSCRIBE
CONSCRIPT
CONSEIL
CONSEILS
CONSENSUS
CONSENT
CONSENTED
CONSENTER
CONSENTS
CONSERVE
CONSERVED
CONSERVER
CONSERVES
CONSIDER
CONSIDERS
CONSIGN
CONSIGNED
CONSIGNEE
CONSIGNER
CONSIGNOR
CONSIGNS
CONSIST
CONSISTED
CONSISTS
CONSOCIES
CONSOL
CONSOLATE
CONSOLE
CONSOLED
CONSOLER
CONSOLERS
CONSOLES
CONSOLING
CONSOLS
CONSOLUTE
CONSOMME
CONSOMMES
CONSONANT
CONSONOUS
CONSORT
CONSORTED
CONSORTER
CONSORTIA
CONSORTS
CONSPIRE
CONSPIRED
CONSPIRER
CONSPIRES
CONSPUE
CONSPUED
CONSPUES
CONSPUING
CONSTABLE
CONSTANCY
CONSTANT
CONSTANTS
CONSTATE
CONSTATED
CONSTATES
CONSTER
CONSTERED
CONSTERS
CONSTRAIN
CONSTRICT
CONSTRUAL
CONSTRUCT
CONSTRUE
CONSTRUED
CONSTRUER
CONSTRUES
CONSUL
CONSULAGE
CONSULAR
CONSULARS
CONSULATE
CONSULS
CONSULT
CONSULTA
CONSULTAS
CONSULTED
CONSULTEE
CONSULTER
CONSULTOR
CONSULTS
CONSUME
CONSUMED
CONSUMER
CONSUMERS
CONSUMES
CONSUMING
CONSUMPT
CONSUMPTS
CONTACT
CONTACTED
CONTACTEE
CONTACTOR
CONTACTS
CONTADINA
CONTADINE
CONTADINI
CONTADINO
CONTAGIA
CONTAGION
CONTAGIUM
CONTAIN
CONTAINED
CONTAINER
CONTAINS
CONTANGO
CONTANGOS
CONTE
CONTECK
CONTECKS
CONTEMN
CONTEMNED
CONTEMNER
CONTEMNOR
CONTEMNS
CONTEMPER
CONTEMPO
CONTEMPT
CONTEMPTS
CONTEND
CONTENDED
CONTENDER
CONTENDS
CONTENT
CONTENTED
CONTENTLY
CONTENTS
CONTES

CONTESSA
CONTESSAS
CONTEST
CONTESTED
CONTESTER
CONTESTS
CONTEXT
CONTEXTS
CONTICENT
CONTINENT
CONTINUA
CONTINUAL
CONTINUE
CONTINUED
CONTINUER
CONTINUES
CONTINUO
CONTINUOS
CONTINUUM
CONTLINE
CONTLINES
CONTO
CONTORNI
CONTORNO
CONTORNOS
CONTORT
CONTORTED
CONTORTS
CONTOS
CONTOUR
CONTOURED
CONTOURS
CONTRA
CONTRACT
CONTRACTS
CONTRAIL
CONTRAILS
CONTRAIR
CONTRALTI
CONTRALTO
CONTRARY
CONTRAS
CONTRAST
CONTRASTS
CONTRASTY
CONTRAT
CONTRATE
CONTRATS
CONTRIST
CONTRISTS
CONTRITE
CONTRIVE
CONTRIVED
CONTRIVER
CONTRIVES
CONTROL
CONTROLE
CONTROLS
CONTROUL
CONTROULS
CONTUMACY
CONTUMELY
CONTUND
CONTUNDED
CONTUNDS
CONTUSE
CONTUSED
CONTUSES
CONTUSING
CONTUSION
CONTUSIVE
CONUNDRUM
CONURBAN
CONURBIA
CONURBIAS
CONURE
CONURES
CONUS
CONVECT
CONVECTED
CONVECTOR
CONVECTS
CONVENE
CONVENED
CONVENER
CONVENERS
CONVENES
CONVENING
CONVENOR
CONVENORS
CONVENT
CONVENTED
CONVENTS
CONVERGE
CONVERGED
CONVERGES
CONVERSE
CONVERSED
CONVERSER
CONVERSES
CONVERSO
CONVERSOS
CONVERT
CONVERTED
CONVERTER
CONVERTOR
CONVERTS
CONVEX
CONVEXED
CONVEXES
CONVEXING
CONVEXITY
CONVEXLY
CONVEY
CONVEYAL
CONVEYALS
CONVEYED
CONVEYER
CONVEYERS
CONVEYING
CONVEYOR
CONVEYORS
CONVEYS
CONVICT
CONVICTED
CONVICTS
CONVINCE
CONVINCED
CONVINCER
CONVINCES
CONVIVE
CONVIVED
CONVIVES
CONVIVIAL
CONVIVING
CONVO
CONVOCATE
CONVOKE
CONVOKED
CONVOKER
CONVOKERS
CONVOKES
CONVOKING
CONVOLUTE
CONVOLVE
CONVOLVED
CONVOLVES
CONVOS
CONVOY
CONVOYED
CONVOYING
CONVOYS
CONVULSE
CONVULSED
CONVULSES
CONWOMAN
CONWOMEN
CONY
COO
COOCH
COOCHES
COOCOO
COOED
COOEE
COOEED
COOEEING
COOEES
COOER
COOERS
COOEY
COOEYED
COOEYING
COOEYS
COOF
COOFS
COOING
COOINGLY
COOINGS
COOK
COOKABLE
COOKABLES
COOKBOOK
COOKBOOKS
COOKED
COOKER
COOKERIES
COOKERS
COOKERY
COOKEY
COOKEYS
COOKHOUSE
COOKIE
COOKIES
COOKING
COOKINGS
COOKLESS
COOKMAID
COOKMAIDS
COOKOFF
COOKOFFS
COOKOUT
COOKOUTS
COOKROOM
COOKROOMS
COOKS
COOKSHACK
COOKSHOP
COOKSHOPS
COOKSTOVE
COOKTOP
COOKTOPS
COOKWARE
COOKWARES
COOKY
COOL
COOLABAH
COOLABAHS
COOLAMON
COOLAMONS
COOLANT
COOLANTS
COOLDOWN
COOLDOWNS
COOLED
COOLER
COOLERS
COOLEST
COOLHOUSE
COOLIBAH
COOLIBAHS
COOLIBAR
COOLIBARS
COOLING
COOLINGLY
COOLINGS
COOLISH
COOLIST
COOLISTS
COOLLY
COOLNESS

COOLS
COOLTH
COOLTHS
COOM
COOMB
COOMBE
COOMBES
COOMBS
COOMED
COOMIER
COOMIEST
COOMING
COOMS
COOMY
COON
COONCAN
COONCANS
COONDOG
COONDOGS
COONHOUND
COONS
COONSHIT
COONSHITS
COONSKIN
COONSKINS
COONTIE
COONTIES
COONTY
COOP
COOPED
COOPER
COOPERAGE
COOPERATE
COOPERED
COOPERIES
COOPERING
COOPERS
COOPERY
COOPING
COOPS
COOPT
COOPTED
COOPTING
COOPTION
COOPTIONS
COOPTS
COORDINAL
COORIE
COORIED
COORIEING
COORIES
COOS
COOSEN
COOSENED
COOSENING
COOSENS
COOSER
COOSERS
COOSIN
COOSINED
COOSINING
COOSINS
COOST
COOT
COOTCH
COOTCHED
COOTCHES
COOTCHING
COOTER
COOTERS
COOTIE
COOTIES
COOTIKIN
COOTIKINS
COOTS
COOZE
COOZES
COP
COPACETIC
COPAIBA
COPAIBAS
COPAIVA
COPAIVAS
COPAL
COPALM
COPALMS
COPALS
COPARCENY
COPARENT
COPARENTS
COPARTNER
COPASETIC
COPASTOR
COPASTORS
COPATAINE
COPATRIOT
COPATRON
COPATRONS
COPAY
COPAYMENT
COPAYS
COPE
COPECK
COPECKS
COPED
COPEMATE
COPEMATES
COPEN
COPENS
COPEPOD
COPEPODS
COPER
COPERED
COPERING
COPERS
COPES
COPESETIC
COPESTONE
COPIABLE
COPIED
COPIER
COPIERS
COPIES
COPIHUE
COPIHUES
COPILOT
COPILOTED
COPILOTS
COPING
COPINGS
COPIOUS
COPIOUSLY
COPITA
COPITAS
COPLANAR
COPLOT
COPLOTS
COPLOTTED
COPOLYMER
COPOUT
COPOUTS
COPPED
COPPER
COPPERAH
COPPERAHS
COPPERAS
COPPERED
COPPERIER
COPPERING
COPPERISH
COPPERS
COPPERY
COPPICE
COPPICED
COPPICES
COPPICING
COPPIES
COPPIN
COPPING
COPPINS
COPPLE
COPPLES
COPPRA
COPPRAS
COPPY
COPRA
COPRAEMIA
COPRAEMIC
COPRAH
COPRAHS
COPRAS
COPREMIA
COPREMIAS
COPREMIC
COPRESENT
COPRINCE
COPRINCES
COPRODUCE
COPRODUCT
COPROLITE
COPROLITH
COPROLOGY
COPROSMA
COPROSMAS
COPROZOIC
COPS
COPSE
COPSED
COPSES
COPSEWOOD
COPSHOP
COPSHOPS
COPSIER
COPSIEST
COPSING
COPSY
COPTER
COPTERS
COPUBLISH
COPULA
COPULAE
COPULAR
COPULAS
COPULATE
COPULATED
COPULATES
COPURIFY
COPY
COPYABLE
COPYBOOK
COPYBOOKS
COPYBOY
COPYBOYS
COPYCAT
COPYCATS
COPYDESK
COPYDESKS
COPYEDIT
COPYEDITS
COPYFIGHT
COPYGIRL
COPYGIRLS
COPYGRAPH
COPYHOLD
COPYHOLDS
COPYING
COPYINGS
COPYISM
COPYISMS
COPYIST
COPYISTS
COPYLEFT
COPYLEFTS
COPYREAD
COPYREADS
COPYRIGHT
COPYTAKER
COQUET
COQUETRY
COQUETS

COQUETTE
COQUETTED
COQUETTES
COQUI
COQUILLA
COQUILLAS
COQUILLE
COQUILLES
COQUINA
COQUINAS
COQUIS
COQUITO
COQUITOS
COR
CORACLE
CORACLES
CORACOID
CORACOIDS
CORAGGIO
CORAL
CORALLA
CORALLINE
CORALLITE
CORALLOID
CORALLUM
CORALROOT
CORALS
CORALWORT
CORAM
CORAMINE
CORAMINES
CORANACH
CORANACHS
CORANTO
CORANTOES
CORANTOS
CORBAN
CORBANS
CORBE
CORBEAU
CORBEAUS
CORBEIL
CORBEILLE
CORBEILS
CORBEL
CORBELED
CORBELING
CORBELLED
CORBELS
CORBES
CORBICULA
CORBIE
CORBIES
CORBINA
CORBINAS
CORBY
CORCASS
CORCASSES
CORD
CORDAGE
CORDAGES
CORDATE
CORDATELY
CORDED
CORDELLE
CORDELLED
CORDELLES
CORDER
CORDERS
CORDGRASS
CORDIAL
CORDIALLY
CORDIALS
CORDIFORM
CORDINER
CORDINERS
CORDING
CORDINGS
CORDITE
CORDITES
CORDLESS
CORDLIKE
CORDOBA
CORDOBAS
CORDON
CORDONED
CORDONING
CORDONNET
CORDONS
CORDOTOMY
CORDOVAN
CORDOVANS
CORDS
CORDUROY
CORDUROYS
CORDWAIN
CORDWAINS
CORDWOOD
CORDWOODS
CORDYLINE
CORE
CORED
COREDEEM
COREDEEMS
COREGENT
COREGENTS
COREIGN
COREIGNS
CORELATE
CORELATED
CORELATES
CORELESS
CORELLA
CORELLAS
COREMIA
COREMIUM
COREOPSIS
CORER
CORERS
CORES
COREY
COREYS
CORF
CORFHOUSE
CORGI
CORGIS
CORIA
CORIANDER
CORIES
CORING
CORIOUS
CORIUM
CORIUMS
CORIVAL
CORIVALRY
CORIVALS
CORIXID
CORIXIDS
CORK
CORKAGE
CORKAGES
CORKBOARD
CORKBORER
CORKED
CORKER
CORKERS
CORKIER
CORKIEST
CORKINESS
CORKING
CORKIR
CORKIRS
CORKLIKE
CORKS
CORKSCREW
CORKTREE
CORKTREES
CORKWING
CORKWINGS
CORKWOOD
CORKWOODS
CORKY
CORM
CORMEL
CORMELS
CORMIDIA
CORMIDIUM
CORMLET
CORMLETS
CORMLIKE
CORMOID
CORMORANT
CORMOUS
CORMS
CORMUS
CORMUSES
CORN
CORNACRE
CORNACRES
CORNAGE
CORNAGES
CORNBALL
CORNBALLS
CORNBORER
CORNBRAID
CORNBRASH
CORNBREAD
CORNCAKE
CORNCAKES
CORNCOB
CORNCOBS
CORNCRAKE
CORNCRIB
CORNCRIBS
CORNEA
CORNEAE
CORNEAL
CORNEAS
CORNED
CORNEITIS
CORNEL
CORNELIAN
CORNELS
CORNEMUSE
CORNEOUS
CORNER
CORNERED
CORNERING
CORNERMAN
CORNERMEN
CORNERS
CORNET
CORNETCY
CORNETIST
CORNETS
CORNETT
CORNETTI
CORNETTO
CORNETTOS
CORNETTS
CORNFED
CORNFIELD
CORNFLAG
CORNFLAGS
CORNFLAKE
CORNFLIES
CORNFLOUR
CORNFLY
CORNHUSK
CORNHUSKS
CORNI
CORNICE
CORNICED
CORNICES
CORNICHE
CORNICHES
CORNICHON
CORNICING
CORNICLE
CORNICLES

C

CORNICULA
CORNIER
CORNIEST
CORNIFIC
CORNIFIED
CORNIFIES
CORNIFORM
CORNIFY
CORNILY
CORNINESS
CORNING
CORNIST
CORNISTS
CORNLAND
CORNLANDS
CORNLOFT
CORNLOFTS
CORNMEAL
CORNMEALS
CORNMILL
CORNMILLS
CORNMOTH
CORNMOTHS
CORNO
CORNOPEAN
CORNPIPE
CORNPIPES
CORNPONE
CORNPONES
CORNRENT
CORNRENTS
CORNROW
CORNROWED
CORNROWS
CORNS
CORNSILK
CORNSILKS
CORNSTALK
CORNSTONE
CORNU
CORNUA
CORNUAL
CORNUS
CORNUSES
CORNUTE
CORNUTED
CORNUTES
CORNUTING
CORNUTO
CORNUTOS
CORNWORM
CORNWORMS
CORNY
COROCORE
COROCORES
COROCORO
COROCOROS
CORODIES
CORODY
COROLLA
COROLLARY
COROLLAS
COROLLATE
COROLLINE
CORONA
CORONACH
CORONACHS
CORONAE
CORONAL
CORONALLY
CORONALS
CORONARY
CORONAS
CORONATE
CORONATED
CORONATES
CORONEL
CORONELS
CORONER
CORONERS
CORONET
CORONETED
CORONETS
CORONIAL
CORONIS
CORONISES
CORONIUM
CORONIUMS
CORONOID
COROTATE
COROTATED
COROTATES
COROZO
COROZOS
CORPORA
CORPORAL
CORPORALE
CORPORALS
CORPORAS
CORPORATE
CORPOREAL
CORPORIFY
CORPOSANT
CORPS
CORPSE
CORPSED
CORPSES
CORPSING
CORPSMAN
CORPSMEN
CORPULENT
CORPUS
CORPUSCLE
CORPUSES
CORRADE
CORRADED
CORRADES
CORRADING
CORRAL
CORRALLED
CORRALS
CORRASION
CORRASIVE
CORREA
CORREAS
CORRECT
CORRECTED
CORRECTER
CORRECTLY
CORRECTOR
CORRECTS
CORRELATE
CORRETTO
CORRETTOS
CORRIDA
CORRIDAS
CORRIDOR
CORRIDORS
CORRIE
CORRIES
CORRIGENT
CORRIVAL
CORRIVALS
CORRODANT
CORRODE
CORRODED
CORRODENT
CORRODER
CORRODERS
CORRODES
CORRODIES
CORRODING
CORRODY
CORROSION
CORROSIVE
CORRUGATE
CORRUPT
CORRUPTED
CORRUPTER
CORRUPTLY
CORRUPTOR
CORRUPTS
CORS
CORSAC
CORSACS
CORSAGE
CORSAGES
CORSAIR
CORSAIRS
CORSE
CORSELET
CORSELETS
CORSES
CORSET
CORSETED
CORSETIER
CORSETING
CORSETRY
CORSETS
CORSEY
CORSEYS
CORSITE
CORSITES
CORSIVE
CORSIVES
CORSLET
CORSLETED
CORSLETS
CORSNED
CORSNEDS
CORSO
CORSOS
CORTEGE
CORTEGES
CORTEX
CORTEXES
CORTICAL
CORTICATE
CORTICES
CORTICOID
CORTICOSE
CORTILE
CORTILI
CORTIN
CORTINA
CORTINAS
CORTINS
CORTISOL
CORTISOLS
CORTISONE
CORULER
CORULERS
CORUNDUM
CORUNDUMS
CORUSCANT
CORUSCATE
CORVEE
CORVEES
CORVES
CORVET
CORVETED
CORVETING
CORVETS
CORVETTE
CORVETTED
CORVETTES
CORVID
CORVIDS
CORVINA
CORVINAS
CORVINE
CORVUS
CORVUSES
CORY
CORYBANT
CORYBANTS
CORYDALIS
CORYLUS
CORYLUSES
CORYMB

CORYMBED
CORYMBOSE
CORYMBOUS
CORYMBS
CORYPHAEI
CORYPHE
CORYPHEE
CORYPHEES
CORYPHENE
CORYPHES
CORYZA
CORYZAL
CORYZAS
COS
COSCRIPT
COSCRIPTS
COSE
COSEC
COSECANT
COSECANTS
COSECH
COSECHS
COSECS
COSED
COSEISMAL
COSEISMIC
COSES
COSET
COSETS
COSEY
COSEYS
COSH
COSHED
COSHER
COSHERED
COSHERER
COSHERERS
COSHERIES
COSHERING
COSHERS
COSHERY
COSHES
COSHING
COSIE
COSIED
COSIER
COSIERS
COSIES
COSIEST
COSIGN
COSIGNED
COSIGNER
COSIGNERS
COSIGNING
COSIGNS
COSILY
COSINE
COSINES
COSINESS
COSING
COSMEA
COSMEAS
COSMESES
COSMESIS
COSMETIC
COSMETICS
COSMIC
COSMICAL
COSMID
COSMIDS
COSMIN
COSMINE
COSMINES
COSMINS
COSMISM
COSMISMS
COSMIST
COSMISTS
COSMOCRAT
COSMOGENY
COSMOGONY
COSMOID
COSMOLINE
COSMOLOGY
COSMONAUT
COSMORAMA
COSMOS
COSMOSES
COSMOTRON
COSPHERED
COSPLAY
COSPLAYS
COSPONSOR
COSS
COSSACK
COSSACKS
COSSES
COSSET
COSSETED
COSSETING
COSSETS
COSSETTED
COSSIE
COSSIES
COST
COSTA
COSTAE
COSTAL
COSTALGIA
COSTALLY
COSTALS
COSTAR
COSTARD
COSTARDS
COSTARRED
COSTARS
COSTATE
COSTATED
COSTE
COSTEAN
COSTEANED
COSTEANS
COSTED
COSTER
COSTERS
COSTES
COSTING
COSTINGS
COSTIVE
COSTIVELY
COSTLESS
COSTLIER
COSTLIEST
COSTLY
COSTMARY
COSTOTOMY
COSTREL
COSTRELS
COSTS
COSTUME
COSTUMED
COSTUMER
COSTUMERS
COSTUMERY
COSTUMES
COSTUMEY
COSTUMIER
COSTUMING
COSTUS
COSTUSES
COSY
COSYING
COT
COTAN
COTANGENT
COTANS
COTE
COTEAU
COTEAUS
COTEAUX
COTED
COTELETTE
COTELINE
COTELINES
COTENANCY
COTENANT
COTENANTS
COTERIE
COTERIES
COTES
COTH
COTHS
COTHURN
COTHURNAL
COTHURNI
COTHURNS
COTHURNUS
COTICULAR
COTIDAL
COTIJA
COTIJAS
COTILLION
COTILLON
COTILLONS
COTING
COTINGA
COTINGAS
COTININE
COTININES
COTISE
COTISED
COTISES
COTISING
COTLAND
COTLANDS
COTQUEAN
COTQUEANS
COTRUSTEE
COTS
COTT
COTTA
COTTABUS
COTTAE
COTTAGE
COTTAGED
COTTAGER
COTTAGERS
COTTAGES
COTTAGEY
COTTAGIER
COTTAGING
COTTAR
COTTARS
COTTAS
COTTED
COTTER
COTTERED
COTTERING
COTTERS
COTTID
COTTIDS
COTTIER
COTTIERS
COTTING
COTTISE
COTTISED
COTTISES
COTTISING
COTTOID
COTTON
COTTONADE
COTTONED
COTTONIER
COTTONING
COTTONS
COTTONY
COTTOWN
COTTOWNS
COTTS
COTTUS

C

COTTUSES
COTURNIX
COTWAL
COTWALS
COTYLAE
COTYLE
COTYLEDON
COTYLES
COTYLOID
COTYLOIDS
COTYPE
COTYPES
COUCAL
COUCALS
COUCH
COUCHANT
COUCHE
COUCHED
COUCHEE
COUCHEES
COUCHER
COUCHERS
COUCHES
COUCHETTE
COUCHING
COUCHINGS
COUDE
COUDES
COUGAN
COUGANS
COUGAR
COUGARS
COUGH
COUGHED
COUGHER
COUGHERS
COUGHING
COUGHINGS
COUGHS
COUGUAR
COUGUARS
COULD
COULDEST
COULDST
COULEE
COULEES
COULIBIAC
COULIS
COULISSE
COULISSES
COULOIR
COULOIRS
COULOMB
COULOMBIC
COULOMBS
COULTER
COULTERS
COUMARIC
COUMARIN
COUMARINS
COUMARONE
COUMAROU
COUMAROUS
COUNCIL
COUNCILOR
COUNCILS
COUNSEL
COUNSELED
COUNSELEE
COUNSELOR
COUNSELS
COUNT
COUNTABLE
COUNTABLY
COUNTBACK
COUNTDOWN
COUNTED
COUNTER
COUNTERED
COUNTERS
COUNTESS
COUNTIAN
COUNTIANS
COUNTIES
COUNTING
COUNTINGS
COUNTLESS
COUNTLINE
COUNTRIES
COUNTROL
COUNTROLS
COUNTRY
COUNTS
COUNTSHIP
COUNTY
COUP
COUPE
COUPED
COUPEE
COUPEES
COUPER
COUPERS
COUPES
COUPING
COUPLE
COUPLED
COUPLEDOM
COUPLER
COUPLERS
COUPLES
COUPLET
COUPLETS
COUPLING
COUPLINGS
COUPON
COUPONING
COUPONS
COUPS
COUPURE
COUPURES
COUR
COURAGE
COURAGES
COURANT
COURANTE
COURANTES
COURANTO
COURANTOS
COURANTS
COURB
COURBARIL
COURBED
COURBETTE
COURBING
COURBS
COURD
COURE
COURED
COURES
COURGETTE
COURIE
COURIED
COURIEING
COURIER
COURIERED
COURIERS
COURIES
COURING
COURLAN
COURLANS
COURS
COURSE
COURSED
COURSER
COURSERS
COURSES
COURSING
COURSINGS
COURT
COURTED
COURTEOUS
COURTER
COURTERS
COURTESAN
COURTESY
COURTEZAN
COURTIER
COURTIERS
COURTING
COURTINGS
COURTLET
COURTLETS
COURTLIER
COURTLIKE
COURTLING
COURTLY
COURTROOM
COURTS
COURTSHIP
COURTSIDE
COURTYARD
COUSCOUS
COUSIN
COUSINAGE
COUSINLY
COUSINRY
COUSINS
COUTA
COUTAS
COUTEAU
COUTEAUX
COUTER
COUTERS
COUTH
COUTHER
COUTHEST
COUTHIE
COUTHIER
COUTHIEST
COUTHS
COUTHY
COUTIL
COUTILLE
COUTILLES
COUTILS
COUTURE
COUTURES
COUTURIER
COUVADE
COUVADES
COUVERT
COUVERTS
COUZIN
COUZINS
COVALENCE
COVALENCY
COVALENT
COVARIANT
COVARIATE
COVARIED
COVARIES
COVARY
COVARYING
COVE
COVED
COVELET
COVELETS
COVELLINE
COVELLITE
COVEN
COVENANT
COVENANTS
COVENS
COVENT
COVENTS
COVER
COVERABLE
COVERAGE
COVERAGES
COVERALL

COVERALLS
COVERED
COVERER
COVERERS
COVERING
COVERINGS
COVERLESS
COVERLET
COVERLETS
COVERLID
COVERLIDS
COVERS
COVERSED
COVERSINE
COVERSLIP
COVERT
COVERTER
COVERTEST
COVERTLY
COVERTS
COVERTURE
COVERUP
COVERUPS
COVES
COVET
COVETABLE
COVETED
COVETER
COVETERS
COVETING
COVETISE
COVETISES
COVETOUS
COVETS
COVEY
COVEYS
COVIN
COVINE
COVINES
COVING
COVINGS
COVINOUS
COVINS
COVYNE
COVYNES
COW
COWABUNGA
COWAGE
COWAGES
COWAL
COWALS
COWAN
COWANS
COWARD
COWARDED
COWARDICE
COWARDING
COWARDLY
COWARDRY
COWARDS
COWBANE
COWBANES
COWBELL
COWBELLS
COWBERRY
COWBIND
COWBINDS
COWBIRD
COWBIRDS
COWBOY
COWBOYED
COWBOYING
COWBOYS
COWED
COWEDLY
COWER
COWERED
COWERING
COWERS
COWFEEDER
COWFISH
COWFISHES
COWFLAP
COWFLAPS
COWFLOP
COWFLOPS
COWGIRL
COWGIRLS
COWGRASS
COWHAGE
COWHAGES
COWHAND
COWHANDS
COWHEARD
COWHEARDS
COWHEEL
COWHEELS
COWHERB
COWHERBS
COWHERD
COWHERDS
COWHIDE
COWHIDED
COWHIDES
COWHIDING
COWHOUSE
COWHOUSES
COWIER
COWIEST
COWING
COWINNER
COWINNERS
COWISH
COWISHES
COWITCH
COWITCHES
COWK
COWKED
COWKING
COWKS
COWL
COWLED
COWLICK
COWLICKS
COWLIKE
COWLING
COWLINGS
COWLS
COWLSTAFF
COWMAN
COWMEN
COWORKER
COWORKERS
COWP
COWPAT
COWPATS
COWPEA
COWPEAS
COWPED
COWPIE
COWPIES
COWPING
COWPLOP
COWPLOPS
COWPOKE
COWPOKES
COWPOX
COWPOXES
COWPS
COWPUNK
COWPUNKS
COWRIE
COWRIES
COWRITE
COWRITER
COWRITERS
COWRITES
COWRITING
COWRITTEN
COWROTE
COWRY
COWS
COWSHED
COWSHEDS
COWSKIN
COWSKINS
COWSLIP
COWSLIPS
COWTOWN
COWTOWNS
COWTREE
COWTREES
COWY
COX
COXA
COXAE
COXAL
COXALGIA
COXALGIAS
COXALGIC
COXALGIES
COXALGY
COXCOMB
COXCOMBIC
COXCOMBRY
COXCOMBS
COXED
COXES
COXIB
COXIBS
COXIER
COXIEST
COXINESS
COXING
COXITIDES
COXITIS
COXLESS
COXSACKIE
COXSWAIN
COXSWAINS
COXY
COY
COYAU
COYAUS
COYDOG
COYDOGS
COYED
COYER
COYEST
COYING
COYISH
COYISHLY
COYLY
COYNESS
COYNESSES
COYOTE
COYOTES
COYOTILLO
COYPOU
COYPOUS
COYPU
COYPUS
COYS
COYSTREL
COYSTRELS
COYSTRIL
COYSTRILS
COZ
COZE
COZED
COZEN
COZENAGE
COZENAGES
COZENED
COZENER
COZENERS
COZENING
COZENS
COZES
COZEY

COZEYS
COZIE
COZIED
COZIER
COZIERS
COZIES
COZIEST
COZILY
COZINESS
COZING
COZY
COZYING
COZZES
COZZIE
COZZIES
CRAAL
CRAALED
CRAALING
CRAALS
CRAB
CRABAPPLE
CRABBED
CRABBEDLY
CRABBER
CRABBERS
CRABBIER
CRABBIEST
CRABBILY
CRABBING
CRABBIT
CRABBY
CRABEATER
CRABGRASS
CRABLIKE
CRABMEAT
CRABMEATS
CRABS
CRABSTICK
CRABWISE
CRABWOOD
CRABWOODS
CRACHACH
CRACK
CRACKBACK
CRACKDOWN
CRACKED
CRACKER
CRACKERS
CRACKET
CRACKETS
CRACKHEAD
CRACKIE
CRACKIER
CRACKIES
CRACKIEST
CRACKING
CRACKINGS
CRACKJAW
CRACKJAWS
CRACKLE
CRACKLED
CRACKLES
CRACKLIER
CRACKLING
CRACKLY
CRACKNEL
CRACKNELS
CRACKPOT
CRACKPOTS
CRACKS
CRACKSMAN
CRACKSMEN
CRACKUP
CRACKUPS
CRACKY
CRACOWE
CRACOWES
CRADLE
CRADLED
CRADLER
CRADLERS
CRADLES
CRADLING
CRADLINGS
CRAFT
CRAFTED
CRAFTER
CRAFTERS
CRAFTIER
CRAFTIEST
CRAFTILY
CRAFTING
CRAFTLESS
CRAFTS
CRAFTSMAN
CRAFTSMEN
CRAFTWORK
CRAFTY
CRAG
CRAGFAST
CRAGGED
CRAGGER
CRAGGERS
CRAGGIER
CRAGGIEST
CRAGGILY
CRAGGY
CRAGS
CRAGSMAN
CRAGSMEN
CRAIC
CRAICS
CRAIG
CRAIGS
CRAKE
CRAKED
CRAKES
CRAKING
CRAM
CRAMBE
CRAMBES
CRAMBO
CRAMBOES
CRAMBOS
CRAME
CRAMES
CRAMESIES
CRAMESY
CRAMFULL
CRAMMABLE
CRAMMED
CRAMMER
CRAMMERS
CRAMMING
CRAMMINGS
CRAMOISIE
CRAMOISY
CRAMP
CRAMPBARK
CRAMPED
CRAMPER
CRAMPERS
CRAMPET
CRAMPETS
CRAMPFISH
CRAMPIER
CRAMPIEST
CRAMPING
CRAMPIT
CRAMPITS
CRAMPON
CRAMPONED
CRAMPONS
CRAMPOON
CRAMPOONS
CRAMPS
CRAMPY
CRAMS
CRAN
CRANACHAN
CRANAGE
CRANAGES
CRANAPPLE
CRANBERRY
CRANCH
CRANCHED
CRANCHES
CRANCHING
CRANE
CRANED
CRANEFLY
CRANELIKE
CRANES
CRANIA
CRANIAL
CRANIALLY
CRANIATE
CRANIATES
CRANING
CRANIUM
CRANIUMS
CRANK
CRANKBAIT
CRANKCASE
CRANKED
CRANKER
CRANKEST
CRANKIER
CRANKIEST
CRANKILY
CRANKING
CRANKISH
CRANKLE
CRANKLED
CRANKLES
CRANKLING
CRANKLY
CRANKNESS
CRANKOUS
CRANKPIN
CRANKPINS
CRANKS
CRANKY
CRANNIED
CRANNIES
CRANNOG
CRANNOGE
CRANNOGES
CRANNOGS
CRANNY
CRANNYING
CRANREUCH
CRANS
CRANTS
CRANTSES
CRAP
CRAPAUD
CRAPAUDS
CRAPE
CRAPED
CRAPELIKE
CRAPES
CRAPIER
CRAPIEST
CRAPING
CRAPLE
CRAPLES
CRAPOLA
CRAPOLAS
CRAPPED
CRAPPER
CRAPPERS
CRAPPIE
CRAPPIER
CRAPPIES
CRAPPIEST
CRAPPING
CRAPPY
CRAPS
CRAPSHOOT

CRAPULENT
CRAPULOUS
CRAPY
CRARE
CRARES
CRASES
CRASH
CRASHED
CRASHER
CRASHERS
CRASHES
CRASHING
CRASHPAD
CRASHPADS
CRASIS
CRASS
CRASSER
CRASSEST
CRASSLY
CRASSNESS
CRATCH
CRATCHES
CRATE
CRATED
CRATEFUL
CRATEFULS
CRATER
CRATERED
CRATERING
CRATERLET
CRATEROUS
CRATERS
CRATES
CRATHUR
CRATHURS
CRATING
CRATON
CRATONIC
CRATONS
CRATUR
CRATURS
CRAUNCH
CRAUNCHED
CRAUNCHES
CRAUNCHY
CRAVAT
CRAVATE
CRAVATES
CRAVATS
CRAVATTED
CRAVE
CRAVED
CRAVEN
CRAVENED
CRAVENER
CRAVENEST
CRAVENING
CRAVENLY
CRAVENS
CRAVER
CRAVERS
CRAVES
CRAVING
CRAVINGS
CRAW
CRAWDAD
CRAWDADDY
CRAWDADS
CRAWFISH
CRAWL
CRAWLED
CRAWLER
CRAWLERS
CRAWLIER
CRAWLIEST
CRAWLING
CRAWLINGS
CRAWLS
CRAWLWAY
CRAWLWAYS
CRAWLY
CRAWS
CRAY
CRAYER
CRAYERS
CRAYEST
CRAYFISH
CRAYON
CRAYONED
CRAYONER
CRAYONERS
CRAYONING
CRAYONIST
CRAYONS
CRAYS
CRAYTHUR
CRAYTHURS
CRAZE
CRAZED
CRAZES
CRAZIER
CRAZIES
CRAZIEST
CRAZILY
CRAZINESS
CRAZING
CRAZINGS
CRAZY
CRAZYWEED
CREACH
CREACHS
CREAGH
CREAGHS
CREAK
CREAKED
CREAKIER
CREAKIEST
CREAKILY
CREAKING
CREAKS
CREAKY
CREAM
CREAMCUPS
CREAMED
CREAMER
CREAMERS
CREAMERY
CREAMIER
CREAMIEST
CREAMILY
CREAMING
CREAMLAID
CREAMLIKE
CREAMPUFF
CREAMS
CREAMWARE
CREAMWOVE
CREAMY
CREANCE
CREANCES
CREANT
CREASE
CREASED
CREASER
CREASERS
CREASES
CREASIER
CREASIEST
CREASING
CREASOTE
CREASOTED
CREASOTES
CREASY
CREATABLE
CREATE
CREATED
CREATES
CREATIC
CREATIN
CREATINE
CREATINES
CREATING
CREATINS
CREATION
CREATIONS
CREATIVE
CREATIVES
CREATOR
CREATORS
CREATRESS
CREATRIX
CREATURAL
CREATURE
CREATURES
CRECHE
CRECHES
CRED
CREDAL
CREDENCE
CREDENCES
CREDENDA
CREDENDUM
CREDENT
CREDENZA
CREDENZAS
CREDIBLE
CREDIBLY
CREDIT
CREDITED
CREDITING
CREDITOR
CREDITORS
CREDITS
CREDO
CREDOS
CREDS
CREDULITY
CREDULOUS
CREE
CREED
CREEDAL
CREEDS
CREEING
CREEK
CREEKIER
CREEKIEST
CREEKS
CREEKSIDE
CREEKY
CREEL
CREELED
CREELING
CREELS
CREEP
CREEPAGE
CREEPAGES
CREEPED
CREEPER
CREEPERED
CREEPERS
CREEPIE
CREEPIER
CREEPIES
CREEPIEST
CREEPILY
CREEPING
CREEPMICE
CREEPS
CREEPY
CREES
CREESE
CREESED
CREESES
CREESH
CREESHED
CREESHES
CREESHIER
CREESHING
CREESHY
CREESING

CREM
CREMAINS
CREMANT
CREMASTER
CREMATE
CREMATED
CREMATES
CREMATING
CREMATION
CREMATOR
CREMATORS
CREMATORY
CREME
CREMES
CREMINI
CREMINIS
CREMOCARP
CREMONA
CREMONAS
CREMOR
CREMORNE
CREMORNES
CREMORS
CREMOSIN
CREMS
CREMSIN
CRENA
CRENAS
CRENATE
CRENATED
CRENATELY
CRENATION
CRENATURE
CRENEL
CRENELATE
CRENELED
CRENELING
CRENELLE
CRENELLED
CRENELLES
CRENELS
CRENSHAW
CRENSHAWS
CRENULATE
CREODONT
CREODONTS
CREOLE
CREOLES
CREOLIAN
CREOLIANS
CREOLISE
CREOLISED
CREOLISES
CREOLIST
CREOLISTS
CREOLIZE
CREOLIZED
CREOLIZES
CREOPHAGY
CREOSOL
CREOSOLS
CREOSOTE
CREOSOTED
CREOSOTES
CREOSOTIC
CREPANCE
CREPANCES
CREPE
CREPED
CREPELIKE
CREPERIE
CREPERIES
CREPES
CREPEY
CREPIER
CREPIEST
CREPINESS
CREPING
CREPITANT
CREPITATE
CREPITUS
CREPOLINE
CREPON
CREPONS
CREPS
CREPT
CREPUSCLE
CREPY
CRESCENDI
CRESCENDO
CRESCENT
CRESCENTS
CRESCIVE
CRESOL
CRESOLS
CRESS
CRESSES
CRESSET
CRESSETS
CRESSIER
CRESSIEST
CRESSY
CREST
CRESTA
CRESTAL
CRESTALS
CRESTED
CRESTING
CRESTINGS
CRESTLESS
CRESTON
CRESTONS
CRESTS
CRESYL
CRESYLIC
CRESYLS
CRETIC
CRETICS
CRETIN
CRETINISE
CRETINISM
CRETINIZE
CRETINOID
CRETINOUS
CRETINS
CRETISM
CRETISMS
CRETONNE
CRETONNES
CRETONS
CREUTZER
CREUTZERS
CREVALLE
CREVALLES
CREVASSE
CREVASSED
CREVASSES
CREVETTE
CREVETTES
CREVICE
CREVICED
CREVICES
CREW
CREWCUT
CREWCUTS
CREWE
CREWED
CREWEL
CREWELIST
CREWELLED
CREWELS
CREWES
CREWING
CREWLESS
CREWMAN
CREWMATE
CREWMATES
CREWMEN
CREWNECK
CREWNECKS
CREWS
CRIA
CRIANT
CRIAS
CRIB
CRIBBAGE
CRIBBAGES
CRIBBED
CRIBBER
CRIBBERS
CRIBBING
CRIBBINGS
CRIBBLE
CRIBBLED
CRIBBLES
CRIBBLING
CRIBELLA
CRIBELLAR
CRIBELLUM
CRIBLE
CRIBLES
CRIBRATE
CRIBROSE
CRIBROUS
CRIBS
CRIBWORK
CRIBWORKS
CRICETID
CRICETIDS
CRICK
CRICKED
CRICKET
CRICKETED
CRICKETER
CRICKETS
CRICKEY
CRICKING
CRICKS
CRICKY
CRICOID
CRICOIDS
CRIED
CRIER
CRIERS
CRIES
CRIKEY
CRIM
CRIME
CRIMED
CRIMEFUL
CRIMELESS
CRIMEN
CRIMES
CRIMEWAVE
CRIMINA
CRIMINAL
CRIMINALS
CRIMINATE
CRIMINE
CRIMING
CRIMINI
CRIMINIS
CRIMINOUS
CRIMINY
CRIMMER
CRIMMERS
CRIMP
CRIMPED
CRIMPER
CRIMPERS
CRIMPIER
CRIMPIEST
CRIMPING
CRIMPLE
CRIMPLED
CRIMPLES
CRIMPLING
CRIMPS
CRIMPY
CRIMS

CRIMSON
CRIMSONED
CRIMSONS
CRINAL
CRINATE
CRINATED
CRINE
CRINED
CRINES
CRINGE
CRINGED
CRINGER
CRINGERS
CRINGES
CRINGEY
CRINGIER
CRINGIEST
CRINGING
CRINGINGS
CRINGLE
CRINGLES
CRINGY
CRINING
CRINITE
CRINITES
CRINKLE
CRINKLED
CRINKLES
CRINKLIER
CRINKLIES
CRINKLING
CRINKLY
CRINOID
CRINOIDAL
CRINOIDS
CRINOLINE
CRINOSE
CRINUM
CRINUMS
CRIOLLO
CRIOLLOS
CRIOS
CRIOSES
CRIPE
CRIPES
CRIPPLE
CRIPPLED
CRIPPLER
CRIPPLERS
CRIPPLES
CRIPPLING
CRIS
CRISE
CRISES
CRISIC
CRISIS
CRISP
CRISPATE
CRISPATED
CRISPED
CRISPEN
CRISPENED
CRISPENS
CRISPER
CRISPERS
CRISPEST
CRISPHEAD
CRISPIER
CRISPIES
CRISPIEST
CRISPILY
CRISPIN
CRISPING
CRISPINS
CRISPLY
CRISPNESS
CRISPS
CRISPY
CRISSA
CRISSAL
CRISSUM
CRISTA
CRISTAE
CRISTATE
CRISTATED
CRIT
CRITERIA
CRITERIAL
CRITERION
CRITERIUM
CRITH
CRITHS
CRITIC
CRITICAL
CRITICISE
CRITICISM
CRITICIZE
CRITICS
CRITIQUE
CRITIQUED
CRITIQUES
CRITS
CRITTER
CRITTERS
CRITTUR
CRITTURS
CRIVENS
CRIVVENS
CROAK
CROAKED
CROAKER
CROAKERS
CROAKIER
CROAKIEST
CROAKILY
CROAKING
CROAKINGS
CROAKS
CROAKY
CROC
CROCEATE
CROCEIN
CROCEINE
CROCEINES
CROCEINS
CROCEOUS
CROCHE
CROCHES
CROCHET
CROCHETED
CROCHETER
CROCHETS
CROCI
CROCINE
CROCK
CROCKED
CROCKERY
CROCKET
CROCKETED
CROCKETS
CROCKING
CROCKPOT
CROCKPOTS
CROCKS
CROCODILE
CROCOITE
CROCOITES
CROCOSMIA
CROCS
CROCUS
CROCUSES
CROFT
CROFTED
CROFTER
CROFTERS
CROFTING
CROFTINGS
CROFTS
CROG
CROGGED
CROGGIES
CROGGING
CROGGY
CROGS
CROISSANT
CROJIK
CROJIKS
CROKINOLE
CROMACK
CROMACKS
CROMB
CROMBEC
CROMBECS
CROMBED
CROMBING
CROMBS
CROME
CROMED
CROMES
CROMING
CROMLECH
CROMLECHS
CROMORNA
CROMORNAS
CROMORNE
CROMORNES
CRON
CRONE
CRONES
CRONET
CRONETS
CRONIES
CRONISH
CRONK
CRONKER
CRONKEST
CRONS
CRONY
CRONYISM
CRONYISMS
CROODLE
CROODLED
CROODLES
CROODLING
CROOK
CROOKBACK
CROOKED
CROOKEDER
CROOKEDLY
CROOKER
CROOKERY
CROOKEST
CROOKING
CROOKNECK
CROOKS
CROOL
CROOLED
CROOLING
CROOLS
CROON
CROONED
CROONER
CROONERS
CROONIER
CROONIEST
CROONING
CROONINGS
CROONS
CROONY
CROOVE
CROOVES
CROP
CROPBOUND
CROPFUL
CROPFULL
CROPFULLS
CROPFULS
CROPLAND
CROPLANDS
CROPLESS

C

CROPPED
CROPPER
CROPPERS
CROPPIE
CROPPIES
CROPPING
CROPPINGS
CROPPY
CROPS
CROPSICK
CROQUANTE
CROQUET
CROQUETED
CROQUETS
CROQUETTE
CROQUIS
CRORE
CROREPATI
CRORES
CROSIER
CROSIERED
CROSIERS
CROSS
CROSSABLE
CROSSARM
CROSSARMS
CROSSBAND
CROSSBAR
CROSSBARS
CROSSBEAM
CROSSBILL
CROSSBIT
CROSSBITE
CROSSBOW
CROSSBOWS
CROSSBRED
CROSSBUCK
CROSSCUT
CROSSCUTS
CROSSE
CROSSED
CROSSER
CROSSERS
CROSSES
CROSSEST
CROSSETTE
CROSSFALL
CROSSFIRE
CROSSFISH
CROSSHAIR
CROSSHEAD
CROSSING
CROSSINGS
CROSSISH
CROSSJACK
CROSSLET
CROSSLETS
CROSSLIKE
CROSSLY
CROSSNESS
CROSSOVER
CROSSPLY
CROSSROAD
CROSSRUFF
CROSSTALK
CROSSTIE
CROSSTIED
CROSSTIES
CROSSTOWN
CROSSTREE
CROSSWALK
CROSSWAY
CROSSWAYS
CROSSWIND
CROSSWIRE
CROSSWISE
CROSSWORD
CROSSWORT
CROST
CROSTATA
CROSTATAS
CROSTINI
CROSTINIS
CROSTINO
CROTAL
CROTALA
CROTALE
CROTALES
CROTALINE
CROTALISM
CROTALS
CROTALUM
CROTCH
CROTCHED
CROTCHES
CROTCHET
CROTCHETS
CROTCHETY
CROTON
CROTONBUG
CROTONIC
CROTONS
CROTTLE
CROTTLES
CROUCH
CROUCHED
CROUCHES
CROUCHING
CROUP
CROUPADE
CROUPADES
CROUPE
CROUPED
CROUPER
CROUPERS
CROUPES
CROUPIER
CROUPIERS
CROUPIEST
CROUPILY
CROUPING
CROUPON
CROUPONS
CROUPOUS
CROUPS
CROUPY
CROUSE
CROUSELY
CROUSTADE
CROUT
CROUTE
CROUTES
CROUTON
CROUTONS
CROUTS
CROW
CROWBAIT
CROWBAITS
CROWBAR
CROWBARS
CROWBERRY
CROWBOOT
CROWBOOTS
CROWD
CROWDED
CROWDEDLY
CROWDER
CROWDERS
CROWDFUND
CROWDIE
CROWDIES
CROWDING
CROWDS
CROWDY
CROWEA
CROWEAS
CROWED
CROWER
CROWERS
CROWFEET
CROWFOOT
CROWFOOTS
CROWING
CROWINGLY
CROWINGS
CROWLIKE
CROWN
CROWNED
CROWNER
CROWNERS
CROWNET
CROWNETS
CROWNING
CROWNINGS
CROWNLAND
CROWNLESS
CROWNLET
CROWNLETS
CROWNLIKE
CROWNS
CROWNWORK
CROWS
CROWSFEET
CROWSFOOT
CROWSTEP
CROWSTEPS
CROZE
CROZER
CROZERS
CROZES
CROZIER
CROZIERS
CROZZLED
CRU
CRUBEEN
CRUBEENS
CRUCES
CRUCIAL
CRUCIALLY
CRUCIAN
CRUCIANS
CRUCIATE
CRUCIATES
CRUCIBLE
CRUCIBLES
CRUCIFER
CRUCIFERS
CRUCIFIED
CRUCIFIER
CRUCIFIES
CRUCIFIX
CRUCIFORM
CRUCIFY
CRUCK
CRUCKS
CRUD
CRUDDED
CRUDDIER
CRUDDIEST
CRUDDING
CRUDDLE
CRUDDLED
CRUDDLES
CRUDDLING
CRUDDY
CRUDE
CRUDELY
CRUDENESS
CRUDER
CRUDES
CRUDEST
CRUDIER
CRUDIEST
CRUDITES
CRUDITIES
CRUDITY
CRUDO
CRUDOS
CRUDS
CRUDY

CRUE
CRUEL
CRUELER
CRUELEST
CRUELLER
CRUELLEST
CRUELLS
CRUELLY
CRUELNESS
CRUELS
CRUELTIES
CRUELTY
CRUES
CRUET
CRUETS
CRUFT
CRUFTS
CRUISE
CRUISED
CRUISER
CRUISERS
CRUISES
CRUISEWAY
CRUISEY
CRUISIE
CRUISIER
CRUISIES
CRUISIEST
CRUISING
CRUISINGS
CRUISY
CRUIVE
CRUIVES
CRUIZIE
CRUIZIES
CRULLER
CRULLERS
CRUMB
CRUMBED
CRUMBER
CRUMBERS
CRUMBIER
CRUMBIEST
CRUMBING
CRUMBLE
CRUMBLED
CRUMBLES
CRUMBLIER
CRUMBLIES
CRUMBLING
CRUMBLY
CRUMBS
CRUMBUM
CRUMBUMS
CRUMBY
CRUMEN
CRUMENAL
CRUMENALS
CRUMENS
CRUMHORN
CRUMHORNS
CRUMMACK
CRUMMACKS
CRUMMIE
CRUMMIER
CRUMMIES
CRUMMIEST
CRUMMILY
CRUMMOCK
CRUMMOCKS
CRUMMY
CRUMP
CRUMPED
CRUMPER
CRUMPEST
CRUMPET
CRUMPETS
CRUMPIER
CRUMPIEST
CRUMPING
CRUMPLE
CRUMPLED
CRUMPLES
CRUMPLIER
CRUMPLING
CRUMPLY
CRUMPS
CRUMPY
CRUNCH
CRUNCHED
CRUNCHER
CRUNCHERS
CRUNCHES
CRUNCHIE
CRUNCHIER
CRUNCHIES
CRUNCHILY
CRUNCHING
CRUNCHY
CRUNK
CRUNKED
CRUNKLE
CRUNKLED
CRUNKLES
CRUNKLING
CRUNKS
CRUNODAL
CRUNODE
CRUNODES
CRUOR
CRUORES
CRUORS
CRUPPER
CRUPPERS
CRURA
CRURAL
CRUS
CRUSADE
CRUSADED
CRUSADER
CRUSADERS
CRUSADES
CRUSADING
CRUSADO
CRUSADOES
CRUSADOS
CRUSE
CRUSES
CRUSET
CRUSETS
CRUSH
CRUSHABLE
CRUSHED
CRUSHER
CRUSHERS
CRUSHES
CRUSHING
CRUSHINGS
CRUSIAN
CRUSIANS
CRUSIE
CRUSIES
CRUSILY
CRUST
CRUSTA
CRUSTACEA
CRUSTAE
CRUSTAL
CRUSTAS
CRUSTATE
CRUSTATED
CRUSTED
CRUSTIER
CRUSTIES
CRUSTIEST
CRUSTILY
CRUSTING
CRUSTLESS
CRUSTLIKE
CRUSTOSE
CRUSTS
CRUSTY
CRUSY
CRUTCH
CRUTCHED
CRUTCHES
CRUTCHING
CRUVE
CRUVES
CRUX
CRUXES
CRUZADO
CRUZADOES
CRUZADOS
CRUZEIRO
CRUZEIROS
CRUZIE
CRUZIES
CRWTH
CRWTHS
CRY
CRYBABIES
CRYBABY
CRYER
CRYERS
CRYING
CRYINGLY
CRYINGS
CRYOBANK
CRYOBANKS
CRYOCABLE
CRYOGEN
CRYOGENIC
CRYOGENS
CRYOGENY
CRYOLITE
CRYOLITES
CRYOMETER
CRYOMETRY
CRYONIC
CRYONICS
CRYOPHYTE
CRYOPROBE
CRYOSCOPE
CRYOSCOPY
CRYOSTAT
CRYOSTATS
CRYOTRON
CRYOTRONS
CRYPT
CRYPTADIA
CRYPTAL
CRYPTIC
CRYPTICAL
CRYPTO
CRYPTOGAM
CRYPTON
CRYPTONS
CRYPTONYM
CRYPTOS
CRYPTS
CRYSTAL
CRYSTALS
CSARDAS
CSARDASES
CTENE
CTENES
CTENIDIA
CTENIDIUM
CTENIFORM
CTENOID
CUADRILLA
CUATRO
CUATROS
CUB
CUBAGE
CUBAGES
CUBANE
CUBANELLE
CUBANES

C

CUBATURE
CUBATURES
CUBBED
CUBBIER
CUBBIES
CUBBIEST
CUBBING
CUBBINGS
CUBBISH
CUBBISHLY
CUBBY
CUBBYHOLE
CUBE
CUBEB
CUBEBS
CUBED
CUBELIKE
CUBER
CUBERS
CUBES
CUBHOOD
CUBHOODS
CUBIC
CUBICA
CUBICAL
CUBICALLY
CUBICAS
CUBICITY
CUBICLE
CUBICLES
CUBICLY
CUBICS
CUBICULA
CUBICULUM
CUBIFORM
CUBING
CUBISM
CUBISMS
CUBIST
CUBISTIC
CUBISTS
CUBIT
CUBITAL
CUBITI
CUBITS
CUBITUS
CUBITUSES
CUBLESS
CUBOID
CUBOIDAL
CUBOIDS
CUBS
CUCKING
CUCKOLD
CUCKOLDED
CUCKOLDLY
CUCKOLDOM
CUCKOLDRY
CUCKOLDS
CUCKOO
CUCKOOED
CUCKOOING
CUCKOOS
CUCULLATE
CUCUMBER
CUCUMBERS
CUCURBIT
CUCURBITS
CUD
CUDBEAR
CUDBEARS
CUDDEN
CUDDENS
CUDDIE
CUDDIES
CUDDIN
CUDDINS
CUDDLE
CUDDLED
CUDDLER
CUDDLERS
CUDDLES
CUDDLIER
CUDDLIEST
CUDDLING
CUDDLY
CUDDY
CUDGEL
CUDGELED
CUDGELER
CUDGELERS
CUDGELING
CUDGELLED
CUDGELLER
CUDGELS
CUDGERIE
CUDGERIES
CUDS
CUDWEED
CUDWEEDS
CUE
CUED
CUEING
CUEINGS
CUEIST
CUEISTS
CUES
CUESTA
CUESTAS
CUFF
CUFFABLE
CUFFED
CUFFIN
CUFFING
CUFFINS
CUFFLE
CUFFLED
CUFFLES
CUFFLESS
CUFFLING
CUFFLINK
CUFFLINKS
CUFFO
CUFFS
CUFFUFFLE
CUIF
CUIFS
CUING
CUIRASS
CUIRASSED
CUIRASSES
CUISH
CUISHES
CUISINART
CUISINE
CUISINES
CUISINIER
CUISSE
CUISSER
CUISSERS
CUISSES
CUIT
CUITER
CUITERED
CUITERING
CUITERS
CUITIKIN
CUITIKINS
CUITS
CUITTLE
CUITTLED
CUITTLES
CUITTLING
CUKE
CUKES
CULCH
CULCHES
CULCHIE
CULCHIER
CULCHIES
CULCHIEST
CULET
CULETS
CULEX
CULEXES
CULICES
CULICID
CULICIDS
CULICINE
CULICINES
CULINARY
CULL
CULLAY
CULLAYS
CULLED
CULLENDER
CULLER
CULLERS
CULLET
CULLETS
CULLIED
CULLIES
CULLING
CULLINGS
CULLION
CULLIONLY
CULLIONS
CULLIS
CULLISES
CULLS
CULLY
CULLYING
CULLYISM
CULLYISMS
CULM
CULMED
CULMEN
CULMINA
CULMINANT
CULMINATE
CULMING
CULMS
CULOTTE
CULOTTES
CULPA
CULPABLE
CULPABLY
CULPAE
CULPATORY
CULPRIT
CULPRITS
CULSHIE
CULSHIER
CULSHIES
CULSHIEST
CULT
CULTCH
CULTCHES
CULTER
CULTERS
CULTI
CULTIC
CULTIER
CULTIEST
CULTIGEN
CULTIGENS
CULTISH
CULTISHLY
CULTISM
CULTISMS
CULTIST
CULTISTS
CULTIVAR
CULTIVARS
CULTIVATE
CULTLIKE
CULTRATE
CULTRATED
CULTS
CULTURAL

CULTURATI
CULTURE
CULTURED
CULTURES
CULTURING
CULTURIST
CULTUS
CULTUSES
CULTY
CULVER
CULVERIN
CULVERINS
CULVERS
CULVERT
CULVERTED
CULVERTS
CUM
CUMACEAN
CUMACEANS
CUMARIC
CUMARIN
CUMARINS
CUMARONE
CUMARONES
CUMBENT
CUMBER
CUMBERED
CUMBERER
CUMBERERS
CUMBERING
CUMBERS
CUMBIA
CUMBIAS
CUMBRANCE
CUMBROUS
CUMBUNGI
CUMBUNGIS
CUMEC
CUMECS
CUMIN
CUMINS
CUMMED
CUMMER
CUMMERS
CUMMIN
CUMMING
CUMMINS
CUMQUAT
CUMQUATS
CUMS
CUMSHAW
CUMSHAWS
CUMULATE
CUMULATED
CUMULATES
CUMULET
CUMULETS
CUMULI
CUMULOSE
CUMULOUS
CUMULUS
CUMULUSES
CUNABULA
CUNCTATOR
CUNDIES
CUNDUM
CUNDUMS
CUNDY
CUNEAL
CUNEATE
CUNEATED
CUNEATELY
CUNEATIC
CUNEI
CUNEIFORM
CUNETTE
CUNETTES
CUNEUS
CUNIFORM
CUNIFORMS
CUNIT
CUNITS
CUNJEVOI
CUNJEVOIS
CUNNER
CUNNERS
CUNNING
CUNNINGER
CUNNINGLY
CUNNINGS
CUNT
CUNTS
CUP
CUPBEARER
CUPBOARD
CUPBOARDS
CUPCAKE
CUPCAKES
CUPEL
CUPELED
CUPELER
CUPELERS
CUPELING
CUPELLED
CUPELLER
CUPELLERS
CUPELLING
CUPELS
CUPFERRON
CUPFUL
CUPFULS
CUPGALL
CUPGALLS
CUPHEAD
CUPHEADS
CUPHOLDER
CUPID
CUPIDITY
CUPIDS
CUPLIKE
CUPMAN
CUPMEN
CUPOLA
CUPOLAED
CUPOLAING
CUPOLAR
CUPOLAS
CUPOLATED
CUPPA
CUPPAS
CUPPED
CUPPER
CUPPERS
CUPPIER
CUPPIEST
CUPPING
CUPPINGS
CUPPY
CUPREOUS
CUPRESSUS
CUPRIC
CUPRITE
CUPRITES
CUPROUS
CUPRUM
CUPRUMS
CUPS
CUPSFUL
CUPULA
CUPULAE
CUPULAR
CUPULATE
CUPULE
CUPULES
CUR
CURABLE
CURABLY
CURACAO
CURACAOS
CURACIES
CURACOA
CURACOAS
CURACY
CURAGH
CURAGHS
CURANDERA
CURANDERO
CURARA
CURARAS
CURARE
CURARES
CURARI
CURARINE
CURARINES
CURARIS
CURARISE
CURARISED
CURARISES
CURARIZE
CURARIZED
CURARIZES
CURASSOW
CURASSOWS
CURAT
CURATE
CURATED
CURATES
CURATING
CURATION
CURATIONS
CURATIVE
CURATIVES
CURATOR
CURATORS
CURATORY
CURATRIX
CURATS
CURB
CURBABLE
CURBED
CURBER
CURBERS
CURBING
CURBINGS
CURBLESS
CURBS
CURBSIDE
CURBSIDES
CURBSTONE
CURCH
CURCHEF
CURCHEFS
CURCHES
CURCULIO
CURCULIOS
CURCUMA
CURCUMAS
CURCUMIN
CURCUMINE
CURCUMINS
CURD
CURDED
CURDIER
CURDIEST
CURDINESS
CURDING
CURDLE
CURDLED
CURDLER
CURDLERS
CURDLES
CURDLING
CURDS
CURDY
CURE
CURED
CURELESS
CURER
CURERS
CURES

C

CURET
CURETS
CURETTAGE
CURETTE
CURETTED
CURETTES
CURETTING
CURF
CURFEW
CURFEWS
CURFS
CURFUFFLE
CURIA
CURIAE
CURIAL
CURIALISM
CURIALIST
CURIAS
CURIE
CURIES
CURIET
CURIETS
CURING
CURINGS
CURIO
CURIOS
CURIOSA
CURIOSITY
CURIOUS
CURIOUSER
CURIOUSLY
CURITE
CURITES
CURIUM
CURIUMS
CURL
CURLED
CURLER
CURLERS
CURLEW
CURLEWS
CURLI
CURLICUE
CURLICUED
CURLICUES
CURLIER
CURLIES
CURLIEST
CURLILY
CURLINESS
CURLING
CURLINGS
CURLPAPER
CURLS
CURLY
CURLYCUE
CURLYCUES
CURN
CURNEY
CURNIER
CURNIEST
CURNS
CURNY
CURPEL
CURPELS
CURR
CURRACH
CURRACHS
CURRAGH
CURRAGHS
CURRAJONG
CURRAN
CURRANS
CURRANT
CURRANTS
CURRANTY
CURRAWONG
CURRED
CURREJONG
CURRENCY
CURRENT
CURRENTLY
CURRENTS
CURRICLE
CURRICLES
CURRICULA
CURRIE
CURRIED
CURRIER
CURRIERS
CURRIERY
CURRIES
CURRIJONG
CURRING
CURRISH
CURRISHLY
CURRS
CURRY
CURRYCOMB
CURRYING
CURRYINGS
CURS
CURSAL
CURSE
CURSED
CURSEDER
CURSEDEST
CURSEDLY
CURSENARY
CURSER
CURSERS
CURSES
CURSI
CURSILLO
CURSILLOS
CURSING
CURSINGS
CURSITOR
CURSITORS
CURSITORY
CURSIVE
CURSIVELY
CURSIVES
CURSOR
CURSORARY
CURSORES
CURSORIAL
CURSORILY
CURSORS
CURSORY
CURST
CURSTNESS
CURSUS
CURT
CURTAIL
CURTAILED
CURTAILER
CURTAILS
CURTAIN
CURTAINED
CURTAINS
CURTAL
CURTALAX
CURTALAXE
CURTALS
CURTANA
CURTANAS
CURTATE
CURTATION
CURTAXE
CURTAXES
CURTER
CURTESIES
CURTEST
CURTESY
CURTILAGE
CURTLY
CURTNESS
CURTSEY
CURTSEYED
CURTSEYS
CURTSIED
CURTSIES
CURTSY
CURTSYING
CURULE
CURVATE
CURVATED
CURVATION
CURVATIVE
CURVATURE
CURVE
CURVEBALL
CURVED
CURVEDLY
CURVES
CURVESOME
CURVET
CURVETED
CURVETING
CURVETS
CURVETTED
CURVEY
CURVIER
CURVIEST
CURVIFORM
CURVINESS
CURVING
CURVITAL
CURVITIES
CURVITY
CURVY
CUSCUS
CUSCUSES
CUSEC
CUSECS
CUSH
CUSHAT
CUSHATS
CUSHAW
CUSHAWS
CUSHES
CUSHIE
CUSHIER
CUSHIES
CUSHIEST
CUSHILY
CUSHINESS
CUSHION
CUSHIONED
CUSHIONET
CUSHIONS
CUSHIONY
CUSHTY
CUSHY
CUSK
CUSKS
CUSP
CUSPAL
CUSPATE
CUSPATED
CUSPED
CUSPID
CUSPIDAL
CUSPIDATE
CUSPIDES
CUSPIDOR
CUSPIDORE
CUSPIDORS
CUSPIDS
CUSPIER
CUSPIEST
CUSPIS
CUSPLIKE
CUSPS
CUSPY
CUSS
CUSSED
CUSSEDLY
CUSSER

CUSSERS
CUSSES
CUSSING
CUSSO
CUSSOS
CUSSWORD
CUSSWORDS
CUSTARD
CUSTARDS
CUSTARDY
CUSTOCK
CUSTOCKS
CUSTODE
CUSTODES
CUSTODIAL
CUSTODIAN
CUSTODIER
CUSTODIES
CUSTODY
CUSTOM
CUSTOMARY
CUSTOMED
CUSTOMER
CUSTOMERS
CUSTOMISE
CUSTOMIZE
CUSTOMS
CUSTOS
CUSTREL
CUSTRELS
CUSTUMAL
CUSTUMALS
CUSTUMARY
CUSUM
CUSUMS
CUT
CUTANEOUS
CUTAWAY
CUTAWAYS
CUTBACK
CUTBACKS
CUTBANK
CUTBANKS
CUTBLOCK
CUTBLOCKS
CUTCH
CUTCHA
CUTCHERRY
CUTCHERY
CUTCHES
CUTDOWN
CUTDOWNS
CUTE
CUTELY
CUTENESS
CUTER
CUTES
CUTESIE
CUTESIER
CUTESIEST
CUTEST
CUTESY
CUTEY
CUTEYS
CUTGLASS
CUTGRASS
CUTICLE
CUTICLES
CUTICULA
CUTICULAE
CUTICULAR
CUTIE
CUTIES
CUTIKIN
CUTIKINS
CUTIN
CUTINISE
CUTINISED
CUTINISES
CUTINIZE
CUTINIZED
CUTINIZES
CUTINS
CUTIS
CUTISES
CUTLAS
CUTLASES
CUTLASS
CUTLASSES
CUTLER
CUTLERIES
CUTLERS
CUTLERY
CUTLET
CUTLETS
CUTLETTE
CUTLETTES
CUTLINE
CUTLINES
CUTOFF
CUTOFFS
CUTOUT
CUTOUTS
CUTOVER
CUTOVERS
CUTPURSE
CUTPURSES
CUTS
CUTSCENE
CUTSCENES
CUTTABLE
CUTTAGE
CUTTAGES
CUTTER
CUTTERS
CUTTHROAT
CUTTIER
CUTTIES
CUTTIEST
CUTTING
CUTTINGLY
CUTTINGS
CUTTLE
CUTTLED
CUTTLES
CUTTLING
CUTTO
CUTTOE
CUTTOES
CUTTY
CUTUP
CUTUPS
CUTWATER
CUTWATERS
CUTWORK
CUTWORKS
CUTWORM
CUTWORMS
CUVEE
CUVEES
CUVETTE
CUVETTES
CUZ
CUZES
CUZZES
CUZZIE
CUZZIES
CWM
CWMS
CWTCH
CWTCHED
CWTCHES
CWTCHING
CYAN
CYANAMID
CYANAMIDE
CYANAMIDS
CYANATE
CYANATES
CYANIC
CYANID
CYANIDE
CYANIDED
CYANIDES
CYANIDING
CYANIDS
CYANIN
CYANINE
CYANINES
CYANINS
CYANISE
CYANISED
CYANISES
CYANISING
CYANITE
CYANITES
CYANITIC
CYANIZE
CYANIZED
CYANIZES
CYANIZING
CYANO
CYANOGEN
CYANOGENS
CYANOSE
CYANOSED
CYANOSES
CYANOSIS
CYANOTIC
CYANOTYPE
CYANS
CYANURATE
CYANURET
CYANURETS
CYANURIC
CYATHI
CYATHIA
CYATHIUM
CYATHUS
CYBER
CYBERCAFE
CYBERCAST
CYBERNATE
CYBERNAUT
CYBERPET
CYBERPETS
CYBERPORN
CYBERPUNK
CYBERSEX
CYBERWAR
CYBERWARS
CYBORG
CYBORGS
CYBRARIAN
CYBRID
CYBRIDS
CYCAD
CYCADEOID
CYCADS
CYCAS
CYCASES
CYCASIN
CYCASINS
CYCLAMATE
CYCLAMEN
CYCLAMENS
CYCLAMIC
CYCLASE
CYCLASES
CYCLE
CYCLECAR
CYCLECARS
CYCLED
CYCLEPATH
CYCLER
CYCLERIES
CYCLERS
CYCLERY
CYCLES
CYCLEWAY

CYCLEWAYS
CYCLIC
CYCLICAL
CYCLICALS
CYCLICISM
CYCLICITY
CYCLICLY
CYCLIN
CYCLING
CYCLINGS
CYCLINS
CYCLISE
CYCLISED
CYCLISES
CYCLISING
CYCLIST
CYCLISTS
CYCLITOL
CYCLITOLS
CYCLIZE
CYCLIZED
CYCLIZES
CYCLIZINE
CYCLIZING
CYCLO
CYCLOGIRO
CYCLOID
CYCLOIDAL
CYCLOIDS
CYCLOLITH
CYCLONAL
CYCLONE
CYCLONES
CYCLONIC
CYCLONITE
CYCLOPEAN
CYCLOPES
CYCLOPIAN
CYCLOPIC
CYCLOPS
CYCLORAMA
CYCLOS
CYCLOSES
CYCLOSIS
CYCLOTRON
CYCLUS
CYCLUSES
CYDER
CYDERS
CYESES
CYESIS
CYGNET
CYGNETS
CYLICES
CYLIKES
CYLINDER
CYLINDERS
CYLINDRIC
CYLIX
CYMA
CYMAE
CYMAGRAPH
CYMAR
CYMARS
CYMAS
CYMATIA
CYMATICS
CYMATIUM
CYMBAL
CYMBALEER
CYMBALER
CYMBALERS
CYMBALIST
CYMBALO
CYMBALOES
CYMBALOM
CYMBALOMS
CYMBALOS
CYMBALS
CYMBIDIA
CYMBIDIUM
CYMBIFORM
CYMBLING
CYMBLINGS
CYME
CYMENE
CYMENES
CYMES
CYMLIN
CYMLING
CYMLINGS
CYMLINS
CYMOGENE
CYMOGENES
CYMOGRAPH
CYMOID
CYMOL
CYMOLS
CYMOPHANE
CYMOSE
CYMOSELY
CYMOUS
CYNANCHE
CYNANCHES
CYNEGETIC
CYNIC
CYNICAL
CYNICALLY
CYNICISM
CYNICISMS
CYNICS
CYNODONT
CYNODONTS
CYNOMOLGI
CYNOSURAL
CYNOSURE
CYNOSURES
CYPHER
CYPHERED
CYPHERING
CYPHERS
CYPRES
CYPRESES
CYPRESS
CYPRESSES
CYPRIAN
CYPRIANS
CYPRID
CYPRIDES
CYPRIDS
CYPRINE
CYPRINES
CYPRINID
CYPRINIDS
CYPRINOID
CYPRIS
CYPRUS
CYPRUSES
CYPSELA
CYPSELAE
CYST
CYSTEIN
CYSTEINE
CYSTEINES
CYSTEINIC
CYSTEINS
CYSTIC
CYSTID
CYSTIDEAN
CYSTIDS
CYSTIFORM
CYSTINE
CYSTINES
CYSTITIS
CYSTOCARP
CYSTOCELE
CYSTOID
CYSTOIDS
CYSTOLITH
CYSTOTOMY
CYSTS
CYTASE
CYTASES
CYTASTER
CYTASTERS
CYTE
CYTES
CYTIDINE
CYTIDINES
CYTIDYLIC
CYTISI
CYTISINE
CYTISINES
CYTISUS
CYTODE
CYTODES
CYTOGENY
CYTOID
CYTOKINE
CYTOKINES
CYTOKININ
CYTOLOGIC
CYTOLOGY
CYTOLYSES
CYTOLYSIN
CYTOLYSIS
CYTOLYTIC
CYTOMETER
CYTOMETRY
CYTON
CYTONS
CYTOPATHY
CYTOPENIA
CYTOPLASM
CYTOPLAST
CYTOSINE
CYTOSINES
CYTOSOL
CYTOSOLIC
CYTOSOLS
CYTOSOME
CYTOSOMES
CYTOTAXES
CYTOTAXIS
CYTOTOXIC
CYTOTOXIN
CZAPKA
CZAPKAS
CZAR
CZARDAS
CZARDASES
CZARDOM
CZARDOMS
CZAREVICH
CZAREVNA
CZAREVNAS
CZARINA
CZARINAS
CZARISM
CZARISMS
CZARIST
CZARISTS
CZARITSA
CZARITSAS
CZARITZA
CZARITZAS
CZARS

D

DA
DAAL
DAALS
DAB
DABBA
DABBAS
DABBED
DABBER
DABBERS
DABBING
DABBITIES
DABBITY
DABBLE
DABBLED
DABBLER
DABBLERS
DABBLES
DABBLING
DABBLINGS
DABCHICK
DABCHICKS
DABS
DABSTER
DABSTERS
DACE
DACES
DACHA
DACHAS
DACHSHUND
DACITE
DACITES
DACK
DACKED
DACKER
DACKERED
DACKERING
DACKERS
DACKING
DACKS
DACOIT
DACOITAGE
DACOITIES
DACOITS
DACOITY
DACQUOISE
DACRON
DACRONS
DACTYL
DACTYLAR
DACTYLI
DACTYLIC
DACTYLICS
DACTYLIST
DACTYLS
DACTYLUS
DAD
DADA
DADAH
DADAHS
DADAISM
DADAISMS
DADAIST
DADAISTIC
DADAISTS
DADAS
DADBOD
DADBODS
DADCHELOR
DADDED
DADDIES
DADDING
DADDLE
DADDLED
DADDLES
DADDLING
DADDOCK
DADDOCKS
DADDY
DADGUM
DADO
DADOED
DADOES
DADOING
DADOS
DADS
DAE
DAEDAL
DAEDALEAN
DAEDALIAN
DAEDALIC
DAEING
DAEMON
DAEMONES
DAEMONIC
DAEMONS
DAES
DAFF
DAFFED
DAFFIER
DAFFIES
DAFFIEST
DAFFILY
DAFFINESS
DAFFING
DAFFINGS
DAFFODIL
DAFFODILS
DAFFS
DAFFY
DAFT
DAFTAR
DAFTARS
DAFTER
DAFTEST
DAFTIE
DAFTIES
DAFTLY
DAFTNESS
DAG
DAGABA
DAGABAS
DAGGA
DAGGAS
DAGGED
DAGGER
DAGGERED
DAGGERING
DAGGERS
DAGGIER
DAGGIEST
DAGGING
DAGGINGS
DAGGLE
DAGGLED
DAGGLES
DAGGLING
DAGGY
DAGLOCK
DAGLOCKS
DAGOBA
DAGOBAS
DAGS
DAGWOOD
DAGWOODS
DAH
DAHABEAH
DAHABEAHS
DAHABEEAH
DAHABIAH
DAHABIAHS
DAHABIEH
DAHABIEHS
DAHABIYA
DAHABIYAH
DAHABIYAS
DAHABIYEH
DAHL
DAHLIA
DAHLIAS
DAHLS
DAHOON
DAHOONS
DAHS
DAIDLE
DAIDLED
DAIDLES
DAIDLING
DAIDZEIN
DAIDZEINS
DAIKER
DAIKERED
DAIKERING
DAIKERS
DAIKO
DAIKON
DAIKONS
DAIKOS
DAILIES
DAILINESS
DAILY
DAILYNESS
DAIMEN
DAIMIO
DAIMIOS
DAIMOKU
DAIMOKUS
DAIMON
DAIMONES
DAIMONIC
DAIMONS
DAIMYO
DAIMYOS
DAINE
DAINED
DAINES
DAINING
DAINT
DAINTIER
DAINTIES
DAINTIEST
DAINTILY
DAINTS
DAINTY
DAIQUIRI
DAIQUIRIS
DAIRIES
DAIRY
DAIRYING
DAIRYINGS
DAIRYMAID

D

DAIRYMAN
DAIRYMEN
DAIS
DAISES
DAISHIKI
DAISHIKIS
DAISIED
DAISIES
DAISY
DAISYLIKE
DAK
DAKER
DAKERED
DAKERHEN
DAKERHENS
DAKERING
DAKERS
DAKOIT
DAKOITI
DAKOITIES
DAKOITIS
DAKOITS
DAKOITY
DAKS
DAL
DALAPON
DALAPONS
DALASI
DALASIS
DALE
DALED
DALEDH
DALEDHS
DALEDS
DALES
DALESMAN
DALESMEN
DALETH
DALETHS
DALGYTE
DALGYTES
DALI
DALIS
DALLE
DALLES
DALLIANCE
DALLIED
DALLIER
DALLIERS
DALLIES
DALLOP
DALLOPS
DALLY
DALLYING
DALMAHOY
DALMAHOYS
DALMATIAN
DALMATIC
DALMATICS
DALS
DALT
DALTON
DALTONIAN
DALTONIC
DALTONISM
DALTONS
DALTS
DAM
DAMAGE
DAMAGED
DAMAGER
DAMAGERS
DAMAGES
DAMAGING
DAMAN
DAMANS
DAMAR
DAMARS
DAMASCENE
DAMASK
DAMASKED
DAMASKEEN
DAMASKIN
DAMASKING
DAMASKINS
DAMASKS
DAMASQUIN
DAMASSIN
DAMASSINS
DAMBOARD
DAMBOARDS
DAMBROD
DAMBRODS
DAME
DAMEHOOD
DAMEHOODS
DAMES
DAMEWORT
DAMEWORTS
DAMFOOL
DAMFOOLS
DAMIANA
DAMIANAS
DAMMAR
DAMMARS
DAMME
DAMMED
DAMMER
DAMMERS
DAMMING
DAMMIT
DAMN
DAMNABLE
DAMNABLY
DAMNATION
DAMNATORY
DAMNDEST
DAMNDESTS
DAMNED
DAMNEDER
DAMNEDEST
DAMNER
DAMNERS
DAMNEST
DAMNESTS
DAMNIFIED
DAMNIFIES
DAMNIFY
DAMNING
DAMNINGLY
DAMNS
DAMOISEL
DAMOISELS
DAMOSEL
DAMOSELS
DAMOZEL
DAMOZELS
DAMP
DAMPED
DAMPEN
DAMPENED
DAMPENER
DAMPENERS
DAMPENING
DAMPENS
DAMPER
DAMPERS
DAMPEST
DAMPIER
DAMPIEST
DAMPING
DAMPINGS
DAMPISH
DAMPLY
DAMPNESS
DAMPS
DAMPY
DAMS
DAMSEL
DAMSELFLY
DAMSELS
DAMSON
DAMSONS
DAN
DANAZOL
DANAZOLS
DANCE
DANCEABLE
DANCECORE
DANCED
DANCEHALL
DANCELIKE
DANCER
DANCERS
DANCES
DANCETTE
DANCETTEE
DANCETTES
DANCETTY
DANCEWEAR
DANCEY
DANCICAL
DANCICALS
DANCIER
DANCIEST
DANCING
DANCINGS
DANCY
DANDELION
DANDER
DANDERED
DANDERING
DANDERS
DANDIACAL
DANDIER
DANDIES
DANDIEST
DANDIFIED
DANDIFIES
DANDIFY
DANDILY
DANDIPRAT
DANDLE
DANDLED
DANDLER
DANDLERS
DANDLES
DANDLING
DANDRIFF
DANDRIFFS
DANDRUFF
DANDRUFFS
DANDRUFFY
DANDY
DANDYFUNK
DANDYISH
DANDYISM
DANDYISMS
DANDYPRAT
DANEGELD
DANEGELDS
DANEGELT
DANEGELTS
DANELAGH
DANELAGHS
DANELAW
DANELAWS
DANEWEED
DANEWEEDS
DANEWORT
DANEWORTS
DANG
DANGED
DANGER
DANGERED
DANGERING
DANGEROUS
DANGERS
DANGEST
DANGING

DANGLE
DANGLED
DANGLER
DANGLERS
DANGLES
DANGLIER
DANGLIEST
DANGLING
DANGLINGS
DANGLY
DANGS
DANIO
DANIOS
DANISH
DANISHES
DANK
DANKER
DANKEST
DANKISH
DANKLY
DANKNESS
DANKS
DANNEBROG
DANNIES
DANNY
DANS
DANSAK
DANSAKS
DANSEUR
DANSEURS
DANSEUSE
DANSEUSES
DANT
DANTED
DANTHONIA
DANTING
DANTON
DANTONED
DANTONING
DANTONS
DANTS
DAP
DAPHNE
DAPHNES
DAPHNIA
DAPHNIAS
DAPHNID
DAPHNIDS
DAPPED
DAPPER
DAPPERER
DAPPEREST
DAPPERLY
DAPPERS
DAPPING
DAPPLE
DAPPLED
DAPPLES
DAPPLING
DAPS
DAPSONE
DAPSONES
DAQUIRI
DAQUIRIS
DARAF
DARAFS
DARB
DARBAR
DARBARS
DARBIES
DARBS
DARCIES
DARCY
DARCYS
DARE
DARED
DAREDEVIL
DAREFUL
DARER
DARERS
DARES
DARESAY
DARG
DARGA
DARGAH
DARGAHS
DARGAS
DARGLE
DARGLES
DARGS
DARI
DARIC
DARICS
DARING
DARINGLY
DARINGS
DARIOLE
DARIOLES
DARIS
DARK
DARKED
DARKEN
DARKENED
DARKENER
DARKENERS
DARKENING
DARKENS
DARKER
DARKEST
DARKFIELD
DARKING
DARKISH
DARKLE
DARKLED
DARKLES
DARKLIER
DARKLIEST
DARKLING
DARKLINGS
DARKLY
DARKMANS
DARKNESS
DARKNET
DARKNETS
DARKROOM
DARKROOMS
DARKS
DARKSOME
DARLING
DARLINGLY
DARLINGS
DARN
DARNATION
DARNDEST
DARNDESTS
DARNED
DARNEDER
DARNEDEST
DARNEL
DARNELS
DARNER
DARNERS
DARNEST
DARNESTS
DARNING
DARNINGS
DARNS
DAROGHA
DAROGHAS
DARRAIGN
DARRAIGNE
DARRAIGNS
DARRAIN
DARRAINE
DARRAINED
DARRAINES
DARRAINS
DARRAYN
DARRAYNED
DARRAYNS
DARRE
DARRED
DARRES
DARRING
DARSHAN
DARSHANS
DART
DARTBOARD
DARTED
DARTER
DARTERS
DARTING
DARTINGLY
DARTITIS
DARTLE
DARTLED
DARTLES
DARTLING
DARTRE
DARTRES
DARTROUS
DARTS
DARZI
DARZIS
DAS
DASH
DASHBOARD
DASHCAM
DASHCAMS
DASHED
DASHEEN
DASHEENS
DASHEKI
DASHEKIS
DASHER
DASHERS
DASHES
DASHI
DASHIER
DASHIEST
DASHIKI
DASHIKIS
DASHING
DASHINGLY
DASHIS
DASHLIGHT
DASHPOT
DASHPOTS
DASHY
DASSIE
DASSIES
DASTARD
DASTARDLY
DASTARDS
DASTARDY
DASYMETER
DASYPOD
DASYPODS
DASYURE
DASYURES
DATA
DATABANK
DATABANKS
DATABASE
DATABASED
DATABASES
DATABLE
DATABUS
DATABUSES
DATACARD
DATACARDS
DATACOMMS
DATAFLOW
DATAGLOVE
DATAGRAM
DATAGRAMS
DATAL
DATALLER
DATALLERS
DATALS

DATARIA
DATARIAS
DATARIES
DATARY
DATCHA
DATCHAS
DATE
DATEABLE
DATEBOOK
DATEBOOKS
DATED
DATEDLY
DATEDNESS
DATELESS
DATELINE
DATELINED
DATELINES
DATER
DATERS
DATES
DATING
DATINGS
DATIVAL
DATIVE
DATIVELY
DATIVES
DATO
DATOLITE
DATOLITES
DATOS
DATTO
DATTOS
DATUM
DATUMS
DATURA
DATURAS
DATURIC
DATURINE
DATURINES
DAUB
DAUBE
DAUBED
DAUBER
DAUBERIES
DAUBERS
DAUBERY
DAUBES
DAUBIER
DAUBIEST
DAUBING
DAUBINGLY
DAUBINGS
DAUBRIES
DAUBRY
DAUBS
DAUBY
DAUD
DAUDED
DAUDING
DAUDS
DAUGHTER
DAUGHTERS
DAULT
DAULTS
DAUNDER
DAUNDERED
DAUNDERS
DAUNER
DAUNERED
DAUNERING
DAUNERS
DAUNT
DAUNTED
DAUNTER
DAUNTERS
DAUNTING
DAUNTLESS
DAUNTON
DAUNTONED
DAUNTONS
DAUNTS
DAUPHIN
DAUPHINE
DAUPHINES
DAUPHINS
DAUR
DAURED
DAURING
DAURS
DAUT
DAUTED
DAUTIE
DAUTIES
DAUTING
DAUTS
DAVEN
DAVENED
DAVENING
DAVENPORT
DAVENS
DAVIDIA
DAVIDIAS
DAVIES
DAVIT
DAVITS
DAVY
DAW
DAWAH
DAWAHS
DAWBAKE
DAWBAKES
DAWBRIES
DAWBRY
DAWCOCK
DAWCOCKS
DAWD
DAWDED
DAWDING
DAWDLE
DAWDLED
DAWDLER
DAWDLERS
DAWDLES
DAWDLING
DAWDLINGS
DAWDS
DAWED
DAWEN
DAWING
DAWISH
DAWK
DAWKS
DAWN
DAWNED
DAWNER
DAWNERED
DAWNERING
DAWNERS
DAWNEY
DAWNING
DAWNINGS
DAWNLIKE
DAWNS
DAWS
DAWSONITE
DAWT
DAWTED
DAWTIE
DAWTIES
DAWTING
DAWTS
DAY
DAYAN
DAYANIM
DAYANS
DAYBED
DAYBEDS
DAYBOAT
DAYBOATS
DAYBOOK
DAYBOOKS
DAYBOY
DAYBOYS
DAYBREAK
DAYBREAKS
DAYCARE
DAYCARES
DAYCATION
DAYCENTRE
DAYCH
DAYCHED
DAYCHES
DAYCHING
DAYDREAM
DAYDREAMS
DAYDREAMT
DAYDREAMY
DAYFLIES
DAYFLOWER
DAYFLY
DAYGIRL
DAYGIRLS
DAYGLO
DAYGLOW
DAYGLOWS
DAYLIGHT
DAYLIGHTS
DAYLILIES
DAYLILY
DAYLIT
DAYLONG
DAYMARE
DAYMARES
DAYMARK
DAYMARKS
DAYNT
DAYNTS
DAYPACK
DAYPACKS
DAYROOM
DAYROOMS
DAYS
DAYSACK
DAYSACKS
DAYSAIL
DAYSAILED
DAYSAILER
DAYSAILOR
DAYSAILS
DAYSHELL
DAYSHELLS
DAYSIDE
DAYSIDES
DAYSMAN
DAYSMEN
DAYSPRING
DAYSTAR
DAYSTARS
DAYTALE
DAYTALER
DAYTALERS
DAYTALES
DAYTIME
DAYTIMES
DAYWEAR
DAYWEARS
DAYWORK
DAYWORKER
DAYWORKS
DAZE
DAZED
DAZEDLY
DAZEDNESS
DAZER
DAZERS
DAZES
DAZING
DAZZLE
DAZZLED
DAZZLER

DAZZLERS
DAZZLES
DAZZLING
DAZZLINGS
DE
DEACIDIFY
DEACON
DEACONED
DEACONESS
DEACONING
DEACONRY
DEACONS
DEAD
DEADBEAT
DEADBEATS
DEADBOLT
DEADBOLTS
DEADBOY
DEADBOYS
DEADED
DEADEN
DEADENED
DEADENER
DEADENERS
DEADENING
DEADENS
DEADER
DEADERS
DEADEST
DEADEYE
DEADEYES
DEADFALL
DEADFALLS
DEADHEAD
DEADHEADS
DEADHOUSE
DEADING
DEADLIER
DEADLIEST
DEADLIFT
DEADLIFTS
DEADLIGHT
DEADLINE
DEADLINED
DEADLINES
DEADLOCK
DEADLOCKS
DEADLY
DEADMAN
DEADMEN
DEADNESS
DEADPAN
DEADPANS
DEADS
DEADSTOCK
DEADWATER
DEADWOOD
DEADWOODS
DEAERATE
DEAERATED
DEAERATES
DEAERATOR
DEAF
DEAFBLIND
DEAFEN
DEAFENED
DEAFENING
DEAFENS
DEAFER
DEAFEST
DEAFISH
DEAFLY
DEAFNESS
DEAIR
DEAIRED
DEAIRING
DEAIRS
DEAL
DEALATE
DEALATED
DEALATES
DEALATION
DEALBATE
DEALER
DEALERS
DEALFISH
DEALIGN
DEALIGNED
DEALIGNS
DEALING
DEALINGS
DEALMAKER
DEALS
DEALT
DEAMINASE
DEAMINATE
DEAMINISE
DEAMINIZE
DEAN
DEANED
DEANER
DEANERIES
DEANERS
DEANERY
DEANING
DEANS
DEANSHIP
DEANSHIPS
DEAR
DEARE
DEARED
DEARER
DEARES
DEAREST
DEARESTS
DEARIE
DEARIES
DEARING
DEARLING
DEARLINGS
DEARLY
DEARN
DEARNED
DEARNESS
DEARNFUL
DEARNING
DEARNLY
DEARNS
DEARS
DEARTH
DEARTHS
DEARY
DEASH
DEASHED
DEASHES
DEASHING
DEASIL
DEASILS
DEASIUL
DEASIULS
DEASOIL
DEASOILS
DEATH
DEATHBED
DEATHBEDS
DEATHBLOW
DEATHCARE
DEATHCUP
DEATHCUPS
DEATHFUL
DEATHIER
DEATHIEST
DEATHLESS
DEATHLIER
DEATHLIKE
DEATHLY
DEATHS
DEATHSMAN
DEATHSMEN
DEATHTRAP
DEATHWARD
DEATHY
DEAVE
DEAVED
DEAVES
DEAVING
DEAW
DEAWED
DEAWIE
DEAWING
DEAWS
DEAWY
DEB
DEBACLE
DEBACLES
DEBAG
DEBAGGED
DEBAGGING
DEBAGS
DEBAR
DEBARK
DEBARKED
DEBARKER
DEBARKERS
DEBARKING
DEBARKS
DEBARMENT
DEBARRASS
DEBARRED
DEBARRING
DEBARS
DEBASE
DEBASED
DEBASER
DEBASERS
DEBASES
DEBASING
DEBATABLE
DEBATABLY
DEBATE
DEBATED
DEBATEFUL
DEBATER
DEBATERS
DEBATES
DEBATING
DEBATINGS
DEBAUCH
DEBAUCHED
DEBAUCHEE
DEBAUCHER
DEBAUCHES
DEBBIER
DEBBIES
DEBBIEST
DEBBY
DEBE
DEBEAK
DEBEAKED
DEBEAKING
DEBEAKS
DEBEARD
DEBEARDED
DEBEARDS
DEBEL
DEBELLED
DEBELLING
DEBELS
DEBENTURE
DEBES
DEBILE
DEBILITY
DEBIT
DEBITED
DEBITING
DEBITOR
DEBITORS
DEBITS
DEBONAIR
DEBONAIRE

DEBONE
DEBONED
DEBONER
DEBONERS
DEBONES
DEBONING
DEBOSH
DEBOSHED
DEBOSHES
DEBOSHING
DEBOSS
DEBOSSED
DEBOSSES
DEBOSSING
DEBOUCH
DEBOUCHE
DEBOUCHED
DEBOUCHES
DEBRIDE
DEBRIDED
DEBRIDES
DEBRIDING
DEBRIEF
DEBRIEFED
DEBRIEFER
DEBRIEFS
DEBRIS
DEBRUISE
DEBRUISED
DEBRUISES
DEBS
DEBT
DEBTED
DEBTEE
DEBTEES
DEBTLESS
DEBTOR
DEBTORS
DEBTS
DEBUD
DEBUDDED
DEBUDDING
DEBUDS
DEBUG
DEBUGGED
DEBUGGER
DEBUGGERS
DEBUGGING
DEBUGS
DEBUNK
DEBUNKED
DEBUNKER
DEBUNKERS
DEBUNKING
DEBUNKS
DEBUR
DEBURR
DEBURRED
DEBURRING
DEBURRS
DEBURS
DEBUS
DEBUSED
DEBUSES
DEBUSING
DEBUSSED
DEBUSSES
DEBUSSING
DEBUT
DEBUTANT
DEBUTANTE
DEBUTANTS
DEBUTED
DEBUTING
DEBUTS
DEBYE
DEBYES
DECACHORD
DECAD
DECADAL
DECADE
DECADENCE
DECADENCY
DECADENT
DECADENTS
DECADES
DECADS
DECAF
DECAFF
DECAFFS
DECAFS
DECAGON
DECAGONAL
DECAGONS
DECAGRAM
DECAGRAMS
DECAHEDRA
DECAL
DECALCIFY
DECALED
DECALING
DECALITER
DECALITRE
DECALLED
DECALLING
DECALOG
DECALOGS
DECALOGUE
DECALS
DECAMETER
DECAMETRE
DECAMP
DECAMPED
DECAMPING
DECAMPS
DECAN
DECANAL
DECANALLY
DECANE
DECANES
DECANI
DECANOIC
DECANS
DECANT
DECANTATE
DECANTED
DECANTER
DECANTERS
DECANTING
DECANTS
DECAPOD
DECAPODAL
DECAPODAN
DECAPODS
DECARB
DECARBED
DECARBING
DECARBS
DECARE
DECARES
DECASTERE
DECASTICH
DECASTYLE
DECATHLON
DECAUDATE
DECAY
DECAYABLE
DECAYED
DECAYER
DECAYERS
DECAYING
DECAYLESS
DECAYS
DECCIE
DECCIES
DECEASE
DECEASED
DECEASEDS
DECEASES
DECEASING
DECEDENT
DECEDENTS
DECEIT
DECEITFUL
DECEITS
DECEIVE
DECEIVED
DECEIVER
DECEIVERS
DECEIVES
DECEIVING
DECELERON
DECEMVIR
DECEMVIRI
DECEMVIRS
DECENARY
DECENCIES
DECENCY
DECENNARY
DECENNIA
DECENNIAL
DECENNIUM
DECENT
DECENTER
DECENTERS
DECENTEST
DECENTLY
DECENTRE
DECENTRED
DECENTRES
DECEPTION
DECEPTIVE
DECEPTORY
DECERN
DECERNED
DECERNING
DECERNS
DECERTIFY
DECESSION
DECHEANCE
DECIARE
DECIARES
DECIBEL
DECIBELS
DECIDABLE
DECIDE
DECIDED
DECIDEDLY
DECIDER
DECIDERS
DECIDES
DECIDING
DECIDUA
DECIDUAE
DECIDUAL
DECIDUAS
DECIDUATE
DECIDUOUS
DECIGRAM
DECIGRAMS
DECILE
DECILES
DECILITER
DECILITRE
DECILLION
DECIMAL
DECIMALLY
DECIMALS
DECIMATE
DECIMATED
DECIMATES
DECIMATOR
DECIME
DECIMES
DECIMETER
DECIMETRE
DECIPHER
DECIPHERS
DECISION
DECISIONS

DECISIVE
DECISORY
DECISTERE
DECK
DECKCHAIR
DECKED
DECKEL
DECKELS
DECKER
DECKERS
DECKHAND
DECKHANDS
DECKHOUSE
DECKING
DECKINGS
DECKLE
DECKLED
DECKLES
DECKLESS
DECKO
DECKOED
DECKOING
DECKOS
DECKS
DECLAIM
DECLAIMED
DECLAIMER
DECLAIMS
DECLARANT
DECLARE
DECLARED
DECLARER
DECLARERS
DECLARES
DECLARING
DECLASS
DECLASSE
DECLASSED
DECLASSEE
DECLASSES
DECLAW
DECLAWED
DECLAWING
DECLAWS
DECLINAL
DECLINALS
DECLINANT
DECLINATE
DECLINE
DECLINED
DECLINER
DECLINERS
DECLINES
DECLINING
DECLINIST
DECLIVITY
DECLIVOUS
DECLUTCH
DECLUTTER
DECO
DECOCT
DECOCTED
DECOCTING
DECOCTION
DECOCTIVE
DECOCTS
DECOCTURE
DECODABLE
DECODE
DECODED
DECODER
DECODERS
DECODES
DECODING
DECODINGS
DECOHERER
DECOKE
DECOKED
DECOKES
DECOKING
DECOLLATE
DECOLLETE
DECOLOR
DECOLORED
DECOLORS
DECOLOUR
DECOLOURS
DECOMMIT
DECOMMITS
DECOMPLEX
DECOMPOSE
DECONGEST
DECONTROL
DECOR
DECORATE
DECORATED
DECORATES
DECORATOR
DECOROUS
DECORS
DECORUM
DECORUMS
DECOS
DECOUPAGE
DECOUPLE
DECOUPLED
DECOUPLER
DECOUPLES
DECOY
DECOYED
DECOYER
DECOYERS
DECOYING
DECOYS
DECREASE
DECREASED
DECREASES
DECREE
DECREED
DECREEING
DECREER
DECREERS
DECREES
DECREET
DECREETS
DECREMENT
DECREPIT
DECRETAL
DECRETALS
DECRETIST
DECRETIVE
DECRETORY
DECREW
DECREWED
DECREWING
DECREWS
DECRIAL
DECRIALS
DECRIED
DECRIER
DECRIERS
DECRIES
DECROWN
DECROWNED
DECROWNS
DECRY
DECRYING
DECRYPT
DECRYPTED
DECRYPTS
DECTET
DECTETS
DECUBITAL
DECUBITI
DECUBITUS
DECUMAN
DECUMANS
DECUMBENT
DECUPLE
DECUPLED
DECUPLES
DECUPLING
DECURIA
DECURIAS
DECURIES
DECURION
DECURIONS
DECURRENT
DECURSION
DECURSIVE
DECURVE
DECURVED
DECURVES
DECURVING
DECURY
DECUSSATE
DEDAL
DEDALIAN
DEDANS
DEDENDA
DEDENDUM
DEDENDUMS
DEDICANT
DEDICANTS
DEDICATE
DEDICATED
DEDICATEE
DEDICATES
DEDICATOR
DEDIMUS
DEDIMUSES
DEDUCE
DEDUCED
DEDUCES
DEDUCIBLE
DEDUCIBLY
DEDUCING
DEDUCT
DEDUCTED
DEDUCTING
DEDUCTION
DEDUCTIVE
DEDUCTS
DEE
DEED
DEEDED
DEEDER
DEEDEST
DEEDFUL
DEEDIER
DEEDIEST
DEEDILY
DEEDING
DEEDLESS
DEEDS
DEEDY
DEEING
DEEJAY
DEEJAYED
DEEJAYING
DEEJAYS
DEEK
DEELY
DEEM
DEEMED
DEEMING
DEEMS
DEEMSTER
DEEMSTERS
DEEN
DEENS
DEEP
DEEPEN
DEEPENED
DEEPENER
DEEPENERS
DEEPENING
DEEPENS
DEEPER
DEEPEST

DEEPFELT
DEEPFROZE
DEEPIE
DEEPIES
DEEPLY
DEEPMOST
DEEPNESS
DEEPS
DEEPWATER
DEER
DEERBERRY
DEERE
DEERES
DEERFLIES
DEERFLY
DEERGRASS
DEERHORN
DEERHORNS
DEERHOUND
DEERLET
DEERLETS
DEERLIKE
DEERS
DEERSKIN
DEERSKINS
DEERWEED
DEERWEEDS
DEERYARD
DEERYARDS
DEES
DEET
DEETS
DEEV
DEEVE
DEEVED
DEEVES
DEEVING
DEEVS
DEEWAN
DEEWANS
DEF
DEFACE
DEFACED
DEFACER
DEFACERS
DEFACES
DEFACING
DEFAECATE
DEFALCATE
DEFAME
DEFAMED
DEFAMER
DEFAMERS
DEFAMES
DEFAMING
DEFAMINGS
DEFANG
DEFANGED
DEFANGING
DEFANGS
DEFAST
DEFASTE
DEFAT
DEFATS
DEFATTED
DEFATTING
DEFAULT
DEFAULTED
DEFAULTER
DEFAULTS
DEFEAT
DEFEATED
DEFEATER
DEFEATERS
DEFEATING
DEFEATISM
DEFEATIST
DEFEATS
DEFEATURE
DEFECATE
DEFECATED
DEFECATES
DEFECATOR
DEFECT
DEFECTED
DEFECTING
DEFECTION
DEFECTIVE
DEFECTOR
DEFECTORS
DEFECTS
DEFENCE
DEFENCED
DEFENCES
DEFENCING
DEFEND
DEFENDANT
DEFENDED
DEFENDER
DEFENDERS
DEFENDING
DEFENDS
DEFENSE
DEFENSED
DEFENSES
DEFENSING
DEFENSIVE
DEFER
DEFERABLE
DEFERENCE
DEFERENT
DEFERENTS
DEFERMENT
DEFERRAL
DEFERRALS
DEFERRED
DEFERRER
DEFERRERS
DEFERRING
DEFERS
DEFFER
DEFFEST
DEFFLY
DEFFO
DEFI
DEFIANCE
DEFIANCES
DEFIANT
DEFIANTLY
DEFICIENT
DEFICIT
DEFICITS
DEFIED
DEFIER
DEFIERS
DEFIES
DEFILADE
DEFILADED
DEFILADES
DEFILE
DEFILED
DEFILER
DEFILERS
DEFILES
DEFILING
DEFINABLE
DEFINABLY
DEFINE
DEFINED
DEFINER
DEFINERS
DEFINES
DEFINIENS
DEFINING
DEFINITE
DEFINITES
DEFIS
DEFLATE
DEFLATED
DEFLATER
DEFLATERS
DEFLATES
DEFLATING
DEFLATION
DEFLATOR
DEFLATORS
DEFLEA
DEFLEAED
DEFLEAING
DEFLEAS
DEFLECT
DEFLECTED
DEFLECTOR
DEFLECTS
DEFLEX
DEFLEXED
DEFLEXES
DEFLEXING
DEFLEXION
DEFLEXURE
DEFLORATE
DEFLOWER
DEFLOWERS
DEFLUENT
DEFLUXION
DEFO
DEFOAM
DEFOAMED
DEFOAMER
DEFOAMERS
DEFOAMING
DEFOAMS
DEFOCUS
DEFOCUSED
DEFOCUSES
DEFOG
DEFOGGED
DEFOGGER
DEFOGGERS
DEFOGGING
DEFOGS
DEFOLIANT
DEFOLIATE
DEFORCE
DEFORCED
DEFORCER
DEFORCERS
DEFORCES
DEFORCING
DEFOREST
DEFORESTS
DEFORM
DEFORMED
DEFORMER
DEFORMERS
DEFORMING
DEFORMITY
DEFORMS
DEFOUL
DEFOULED
DEFOULING
DEFOULS
DEFRAG
DEFRAGGED
DEFRAGGER
DEFRAGS
DEFRAUD
DEFRAUDED
DEFRAUDER
DEFRAUDS
DEFRAY
DEFRAYAL
DEFRAYALS
DEFRAYED
DEFRAYER
DEFRAYERS
DEFRAYING
DEFRAYS
DEFREEZE
DEFREEZES

DEFRIEND
DEFRIENDS
DEFROCK
DEFROCKED
DEFROCKS
DEFROST
DEFROSTED
DEFROSTER
DEFROSTS
DEFROZE
DEFROZEN
DEFT
DEFTER
DEFTEST
DEFTLY
DEFTNESS
DEFUEL
DEFUELED
DEFUELING
DEFUELLED
DEFUELS
DEFUNCT
DEFUNCTS
DEFUND
DEFUNDED
DEFUNDING
DEFUNDS
DEFUSE
DEFUSED
DEFUSER
DEFUSERS
DEFUSES
DEFUSING
DEFUZE
DEFUZED
DEFUZES
DEFUZING
DEFY
DEFYING
DEG
DEGAGE
DEGAME
DEGAMES
DEGAMI
DEGAMIS
DEGARNISH
DEGAS
DEGASES
DEGASSED
DEGASSER
DEGASSERS
DEGASSES
DEGASSING
DEGAUSS
DEGAUSSED
DEGAUSSER
DEGAUSSES
DEGEARING
DEGENDER
DEGENDERS
DEGERM
DEGERMED
DEGERMING
DEGERMS
DEGGED
DEGGING
DEGLAZE
DEGLAZED
DEGLAZES
DEGLAZING
DEGOUT
DEGOUTED
DEGOUTING
DEGOUTS
DEGRADE
DEGRADED
DEGRADER
DEGRADERS
DEGRADES
DEGRADING
DEGRAS
DEGREASE
DEGREASED
DEGREASER
DEGREASES
DEGREE
DEGREED
DEGREES
DEGS
DEGU
DEGUM
DEGUMMED
DEGUMMING
DEGUMS
DEGUS
DEGUST
DEGUSTATE
DEGUSTED
DEGUSTING
DEGUSTS
DEHAIR
DEHAIRED
DEHAIRING
DEHAIRS
DEHISCE
DEHISCED
DEHISCENT
DEHISCES
DEHISCING
DEHORN
DEHORNED
DEHORNER
DEHORNERS
DEHORNING
DEHORNS
DEHORS
DEHORT
DEHORTED
DEHORTER
DEHORTERS
DEHORTING
DEHORTS
DEHYDRATE
DEI
DEICE
DEICED
DEICER
DEICERS
DEICES
DEICIDAL
DEICIDE
DEICIDES
DEICING
DEICTIC
DEICTICS
DEID
DEIDER
DEIDEST
DEIDS
DEIF
DEIFER
DEIFEST
DEIFIC
DEIFICAL
DEIFIED
DEIFIER
DEIFIERS
DEIFIES
DEIFORM
DEIFY
DEIFYING
DEIGN
DEIGNED
DEIGNING
DEIGNS
DEIL
DEILS
DEINDEX
DEINDEXED
DEINDEXES
DEINOSAUR
DEIONISE
DEIONISED
DEIONISER
DEIONISES
DEIONIZE
DEIONIZED
DEIONIZER
DEIONIZES
DEIPAROUS
DEISEAL
DEISEALS
DEISHEAL
DEISHEALS
DEISM
DEISMS
DEIST
DEISTIC
DEISTICAL
DEISTS
DEITIES
DEITY
DEIXES
DEIXIS
DEIXISES
DEJECT
DEJECTA
DEJECTED
DEJECTING
DEJECTION
DEJECTORY
DEJECTS
DEJEUNE
DEJEUNER
DEJEUNERS
DEJEUNES
DEKAGRAM
DEKAGRAMS
DEKALITER
DEKALITRE
DEKALOGY
DEKAMETER
DEKAMETRE
DEKARE
DEKARES
DEKE
DEKED
DEKEING
DEKES
DEKING
DEKKO
DEKKOED
DEKKOING
DEKKOS
DEL
DELAINE
DELAINES
DELAPSE
DELAPSED
DELAPSES
DELAPSING
DELAPSION
DELATE
DELATED
DELATES
DELATING
DELATION
DELATIONS
DELATOR
DELATORS
DELAY
DELAYABLE
DELAYED
DELAYER
DELAYERS
DELAYING
DELAYS
DELE
DELEAD
DELEADED

DELEADING
DELEADS
DELEAVE
DELEAVED
DELEAVES
DELEAVING
DELEBLE
DELECTATE
DELED
DELEGABLE
DELEGACY
DELEGATE
DELEGATED
DELEGATEE
DELEGATES
DELEGATOR
DELEING
DELENDA
DELES
DELETABLE
DELETE
DELETED
DELETES
DELETING
DELETION
DELETIONS
DELETIVE
DELETORY
DELF
DELFS
DELFT
DELFTS
DELFTWARE
DELI
DELIBATE
DELIBATED
DELIBATES
DELIBLE
DELICACY
DELICATE
DELICATES
DELICE
DELICES
DELICIOUS
DELICT
DELICTS
DELIGHT
DELIGHTED
DELIGHTER
DELIGHTS
DELIME
DELIMED
DELIMES
DELIMING
DELIMIT
DELIMITED
DELIMITER
DELIMITS
DELINEATE
DELINK
DELINKED
DELINKING
DELINKS
DELIQUIUM
DELIRIA
DELIRIANT
DELIRIOUS
DELIRIUM
DELIRIUMS
DELIS
DELISH
DELIST
DELISTED
DELISTING
DELISTS
DELIVER
DELIVERED
DELIVERER
DELIVERLY
DELIVERS
DELIVERY
DELL
DELLIER
DELLIES
DELLIEST
DELLS
DELLY
DELO
DELOPE
DELOPED
DELOPES
DELOPING
DELOS
DELOUSE
DELOUSED
DELOUSER
DELOUSERS
DELOUSES
DELOUSING
DELPH
DELPHIC
DELPHIN
DELPHINIA
DELPHINS
DELPHS
DELS
DELT
DELTA
DELTAIC
DELTAS
DELTIC
DELTOID
DELTOIDEI
DELTOIDS
DELTS
DELUBRA
DELUBRUM
DELUBRUMS
DELUDABLE
DELUDE
DELUDED
DELUDER
DELUDERS
DELUDES
DELUDING
DELUGE
DELUGED
DELUGES
DELUGING
DELUNDUNG
DELUSION
DELUSIONS
DELUSIVE
DELUSORY
DELUSTER
DELUSTERS
DELUSTRE
DELUSTRED
DELUSTRES
DELUXE
DELVE
DELVED
DELVER
DELVERS
DELVES
DELVING
DEMAGOG
DEMAGOGED
DEMAGOGIC
DEMAGOGS
DEMAGOGUE
DEMAGOGY
DEMAIN
DEMAINE
DEMAINES
DEMAINS
DEMAN
DEMAND
DEMANDANT
DEMANDED
DEMANDER
DEMANDERS
DEMANDING
DEMANDS
DEMANNED
DEMANNING
DEMANS
DEMANTOID
DEMARCATE
DEMARCHE
DEMARCHES
DEMARK
DEMARKED
DEMARKET
DEMARKETS
DEMARKING
DEMARKS
DEMAST
DEMASTED
DEMASTING
DEMASTS
DEMAYNE
DEMAYNES
DEME
DEMEAN
DEMEANE
DEMEANED
DEMEANES
DEMEANING
DEMEANOR
DEMEANORS
DEMEANOUR
DEMEANS
DEMENT
DEMENTATE
DEMENTED
DEMENTI
DEMENTIA
DEMENTIAL
DEMENTIAS
DEMENTING
DEMENTIS
DEMENTS
DEMERARA
DEMERARAN
DEMERARAS
DEMERGE
DEMERGED
DEMERGER
DEMERGERS
DEMERGES
DEMERGING
DEMERIT
DEMERITED
DEMERITS
DEMERSAL
DEMERSE
DEMERSED
DEMERSES
DEMERSING
DEMERSION
DEMES
DEMESNE
DEMESNES
DEMETON
DEMETONS
DEMIC
DEMIES
DEMIGOD
DEMIGODS
DEMIJOHN
DEMIJOHNS
DEMILUNE
DEMILUNES
DEMIMONDE
DEMINER
DEMINERS
DEMINING
DEMININGS
DEMIPIQUE

DEMIREP
DEMIREPS
DEMISABLE
DEMISE
DEMISED
DEMISES
DEMISING
DEMISS
DEMISSION
DEMISSIVE
DEMISSLY
DEMIST
DEMISTED
DEMISTER
DEMISTERS
DEMISTING
DEMISTS
DEMIT
DEMITASSE
DEMITS
DEMITTED
DEMITTING
DEMIURGE
DEMIURGES
DEMIURGIC
DEMIURGUS
DEMIVEG
DEMIVEGES
DEMIVOLT
DEMIVOLTE
DEMIVOLTS
DEMIWORLD
DEMO
DEMOB
DEMOBBED
DEMOBBING
DEMOBS
DEMOCRACY
DEMOCRAT
DEMOCRATS
DEMOCRATY
DEMODE
DEMODED
DEMOED
DEMOI
DEMOING
DEMOLISH
DEMOLOGY
DEMON
DEMONESS
DEMONIAC
DEMONIACS
DEMONIAN
DEMONIC
DEMONICAL
DEMONISE
DEMONISED
DEMONISES
DEMONISM
DEMONISMS
DEMONIST
DEMONISTS
DEMONIZE
DEMONIZED
DEMONIZES
DEMONRIES
DEMONRY
DEMONS
DEMONYM
DEMONYMS
DEMOS
DEMOSCENE
DEMOSES
DEMOTE
DEMOTED
DEMOTES
DEMOTIC
DEMOTICS
DEMOTING
DEMOTION
DEMOTIONS
DEMOTIST
DEMOTISTS
DEMOUNT
DEMOUNTED
DEMOUNTS
DEMPSTER
DEMPSTERS
DEMPT
DEMULCENT
DEMULSIFY
DEMUR
DEMURE
DEMURED
DEMURELY
DEMURER
DEMURES
DEMUREST
DEMURING
DEMURRAGE
DEMURRAL
DEMURRALS
DEMURRED
DEMURRER
DEMURRERS
DEMURRING
DEMURS
DEMY
DEMYSHIP
DEMYSHIPS
DEMYSTIFY
DEMYTHIFY
DEN
DENAR
DENARI
DENARIES
DENARII
DENARIUS
DENARS
DENARY
DENATURE
DENATURED
DENATURES
DENAY
DENAYED
DENAYING
DENAYS
DENAZIFY
DENCH
DENDRIMER
DENDRITE
DENDRITES
DENDRITIC
DENDROID
DENDROIDS
DENDRON
DENDRONS
DENE
DENERVATE
DENES
DENET
DENETS
DENETTED
DENETTING
DENGUE
DENGUES
DENI
DENIABLE
DENIABLY
DENIAL
DENIALIST
DENIALS
DENIED
DENIER
DENIERS
DENIES
DENIGRATE
DENIM
DENIMED
DENIMS
DENIS
DENITRATE
DENITRIFY
DENIZEN
DENIZENED
DENIZENS
DENNED
DENNET
DENNETS
DENNING
DENOMINAL
DENOTABLE
DENOTATE
DENOTATED
DENOTATES
DENOTE
DENOTED
DENOTES
DENOTING
DENOTIVE
DENOUNCE
DENOUNCED
DENOUNCER
DENOUNCES
DENS
DENSE
DENSELY
DENSENESS
DENSER
DENSEST
DENSIFIED
DENSIFIER
DENSIFIES
DENSIFY
DENSITIES
DENSITY
DENT
DENTAL
DENTALIA
DENTALISE
DENTALITY
DENTALIUM
DENTALIZE
DENTALLY
DENTALS
DENTARIA
DENTARIAS
DENTARIES
DENTARY
DENTATE
DENTATED
DENTATELY
DENTATION
DENTED
DENTEL
DENTELLE
DENTELLES
DENTELS
DENTEX
DENTEXES
DENTICARE
DENTICLE
DENTICLES
DENTIFORM
DENTIL
DENTILED
DENTILS
DENTIN
DENTINAL
DENTINE
DENTINES
DENTING
DENTINS
DENTIST
DENTISTRY
DENTISTS
DENTITION
DENTOID
DENTS
DENTULOUS

DENTURAL
DENTURE
DENTURES
DENTURISM
DENTURIST
DENUDATE
DENUDATED
DENUDATES
DENUDE
DENUDED
DENUDER
DENUDERS
DENUDES
DENUDING
DENY
DENYING
DENYINGLY
DEODAND
DEODANDS
DEODAR
DEODARA
DEODARAS
DEODARS
DEODATE
DEODATES
DEODORANT
DEODORISE
DEODORIZE
DEONTIC
DEONTICS
DEORBIT
DEORBITED
DEORBITS
DEOXIDATE
DEOXIDISE
DEOXIDIZE
DEOXY
DEP
DEPAINT
DEPAINTED
DEPAINTS
DEPANNEUR
DEPART
DEPARTED
DEPARTEDS
DEPARTEE
DEPARTEES
DEPARTER
DEPARTERS
DEPARTING
DEPARTS
DEPARTURE
DEPASTURE
DEPECHE
DEPECHED
DEPECHES
DEPECHING
DEPEINCT
DEPEINCTS
DEPEND
DEPENDANT
DEPENDED
DEPENDENT
DEPENDING
DEPENDS
DEPEOPLE
DEPEOPLED
DEPEOPLES
DEPERM
DEPERMED
DEPERMING
DEPERMS
DEPICT
DEPICTED
DEPICTER
DEPICTERS
DEPICTING
DEPICTION
DEPICTIVE
DEPICTOR
DEPICTORS
DEPICTS
DEPICTURE
DEPIGMENT
DEPILATE
DEPILATED
DEPILATES
DEPILATOR
DEPLANE
DEPLANED
DEPLANES
DEPLANING
DEPLENISH
DEPLETE
DEPLETED
DEPLETER
DEPLETERS
DEPLETES
DEPLETING
DEPLETION
DEPLETIVE
DEPLETORY
DEPLORE
DEPLORED
DEPLORER
DEPLORERS
DEPLORES
DEPLORING
DEPLOY
DEPLOYED
DEPLOYER
DEPLOYERS
DEPLOYING
DEPLOYS
DEPLUME
DEPLUMED
DEPLUMES
DEPLUMING
DEPOLISH
DEPONE
DEPONED
DEPONENT
DEPONENTS
DEPONES
DEPONING
DEPORT
DEPORTED
DEPORTEE
DEPORTEES
DEPORTER
DEPORTERS
DEPORTING
DEPORTS
DEPOSABLE
DEPOSAL
DEPOSALS
DEPOSE
DEPOSED
DEPOSER
DEPOSERS
DEPOSES
DEPOSING
DEPOSIT
DEPOSITED
DEPOSITOR
DEPOSITS
DEPOT
DEPOTS
DEPRAVE
DEPRAVED
DEPRAVER
DEPRAVERS
DEPRAVES
DEPRAVING
DEPRAVITY
DEPRECATE
DEPREDATE
DEPREHEND
DEPRENYL
DEPRENYLS
DEPRESS
DEPRESSED
DEPRESSES
DEPRESSOR
DEPRIME
DEPRIMED
DEPRIMES
DEPRIMING
DEPRIVAL
DEPRIVALS
DEPRIVE
DEPRIVED
DEPRIVER
DEPRIVERS
DEPRIVES
DEPRIVING
DEPROGRAM
DEPS
DEPSIDE
DEPSIDES
DEPTH
DEPTHLESS
DEPTHS
DEPURANT
DEPURANTS
DEPURATE
DEPURATED
DEPURATES
DEPURATOR
DEPUTABLE
DEPUTE
DEPUTED
DEPUTES
DEPUTIES
DEPUTING
DEPUTISE
DEPUTISED
DEPUTISES
DEPUTIZE
DEPUTIZED
DEPUTIZES
DEPUTY
DEQUEUE
DEQUEUED
DEQUEUES
DEQUEUING
DERACINE
DERACINES
DERAIGN
DERAIGNED
DERAIGNS
DERAIL
DERAILED
DERAILER
DERAILERS
DERAILING
DERAILS
DERANGE
DERANGED
DERANGER
DERANGERS
DERANGES
DERANGING
DERAT
DERATE
DERATED
DERATES
DERATING
DERATINGS
DERATION
DERATIONS
DERATS
DERATTED
DERATTING
DERAY
DERAYED
DERAYING
DERAYS
DERBIES
DERBY

DERE
DERECHO
DERECHOS
DERED
DERELICT
DERELICTS
DEREPRESS
DERES
DERHAM
DERHAMS
DERIDE
DERIDED
DERIDER
DERIDERS
DERIDES
DERIDING
DERIG
DERIGGED
DERIGGING
DERIGS
DERING
DERINGER
DERINGERS
DERISIBLE
DERISION
DERISIONS
DERISIVE
DERISORY
DERIVABLE
DERIVABLY
DERIVATE
DERIVATED
DERIVATES
DERIVE
DERIVED
DERIVER
DERIVERS
DERIVES
DERIVING
DERM
DERMA
DERMAL
DERMAS
DERMATIC
DERMATOID
DERMATOME
DERMESTID
DERMIC
DERMIS
DERMISES
DERMOID
DERMOIDS
DERMS
DERN
DERNED
DERNFUL
DERNIER
DERNIES
DERNING
DERNLY
DERNS
DERNY
DERNYS
DERO
DEROGATE
DEROGATED
DEROGATES
DEROS
DERRICK
DERRICKED
DERRICKS
DERRIERE
DERRIERES
DERRIES
DERRINGER
DERRIS
DERRISES
DERRO
DERROS
DERRY
DERTH
DERTHS
DERV
DERVISH
DERVISHES
DERVS
DESALT
DESALTED
DESALTER
DESALTERS
DESALTING
DESALTS
DESAND
DESANDED
DESANDING
DESANDS
DESCALE
DESCALED
DESCALER
DESCALERS
DESCALES
DESCALING
DESCANT
DESCANTED
DESCANTER
DESCANTS
DESCEND
DESCENDED
DESCENDER
DESCENDS
DESCENT
DESCENTS
DESCHOOL
DESCHOOLS
DESCRIBE
DESCRIBED
DESCRIBER
DESCRIBES
DESCRIED
DESCRIER
DESCRIERS
DESCRIES
DESCRIVE
DESCRIVED
DESCRIVES
DESCRY
DESCRYING
DESECRATE
DESEED
DESEEDED
DESEEDER
DESEEDERS
DESEEDING
DESEEDS
DESELECT
DESELECTS
DESERT
DESERTED
DESERTER
DESERTERS
DESERTIC
DESERTIFY
DESERTING
DESERTION
DESERTS
DESERVE
DESERVED
DESERVER
DESERVERS
DESERVES
DESERVING
DESEX
DESEXED
DESEXES
DESEXING
DESHI
DESHIS
DESI
DESICCANT
DESICCATE
DESIGN
DESIGNATE
DESIGNED
DESIGNEE
DESIGNEES
DESIGNER
DESIGNERS
DESIGNFUL
DESIGNING
DESIGNS
DESILVER
DESILVERS
DESINE
DESINED
DESINENCE
DESINENT
DESINES
DESINING
DESIPIENT
DESIRABLE
DESIRABLY
DESIRE
DESIRED
DESIRER
DESIRERS
DESIRES
DESIRING
DESIROUS
DESIS
DESIST
DESISTED
DESISTING
DESISTS
DESK
DESKBOUND
DESKFAST
DESKFASTS
DESKILL
DESKILLED
DESKILLS
DESKING
DESKINGS
DESKMAN
DESKMEN
DESKNOTE
DESKNOTES
DESKS
DESKTOP
DESKTOPS
DESMAN
DESMANS
DESMID
DESMIDIAN
DESMIDS
DESMINE
DESMINES
DESMODIUM
DESMOID
DESMOIDS
DESMOSOME
DESNOOD
DESNOODED
DESNOODS
DESOEUVRE
DESOLATE
DESOLATED
DESOLATER
DESOLATES
DESOLATOR
DESORB
DESORBED
DESORBER
DESORBERS
DESORBING
DESORBS
DESOXY
DESPAIR
DESPAIRED
DESPAIRER
DESPAIRS

D

DESPATCH
DESPERADO
DESPERATE
DESPIGHT
DESPIGHTS
DESPISAL
DESPISALS
DESPISE
DESPISED
DESPISER
DESPISERS
DESPISES
DESPISING
DESPITE
DESPITED
DESPITES
DESPITING
DESPOIL
DESPOILED
DESPOILER
DESPOILS
DESPOND
DESPONDED
DESPONDS
DESPOT
DESPOTAT
DESPOTATE
DESPOTATS
DESPOTIC
DESPOTISM
DESPOTS
DESPUMATE
DESSE
DESSERT
DESSERTS
DESSES
DESSYATIN
DESTAIN
DESTAINED
DESTAINS
DESTEMPER
DESTINATE
DESTINE
DESTINED
DESTINES
DESTINIES
DESTINING
DESTINY
DESTITUTE
DESTOCK
DESTOCKED
DESTOCKS
DESTREAM
DESTREAMS
DESTRESS
DESTRIER
DESTRIERS
DESTROY
DESTROYED
DESTROYER
DESTROYS
DESTRUCT
DESTRUCTO
DESTRUCTS
DESUETUDE
DESUGAR
DESUGARED
DESUGARS
DESULFUR
DESULFURS
DESULPHUR
DESULTORY
DESYATIN
DESYATINS
DESYNE
DESYNED
DESYNES
DESYNING
DETACH
DETACHED
DETACHER
DETACHERS
DETACHES
DETACHING
DETAIL
DETAILED
DETAILER
DETAILERS
DETAILING
DETAILS
DETAIN
DETAINED
DETAINEE
DETAINEES
DETAINER
DETAINERS
DETAINING
DETAINS
DETANGLE
DETANGLED
DETANGLER
DETANGLES
DETASSEL
DETASSELS
DETECT
DETECTED
DETECTER
DETECTERS
DETECTING
DETECTION
DETECTIVE
DETECTOR
DETECTORS
DETECTS
DETENT
DETENTE
DETENTES
DETENTION
DETENTIST
DETENTS
DETENU
DETENUE
DETENUES
DETENUS
DETER
DETERGE
DETERGED
DETERGENT
DETERGER
DETERGERS
DETERGES
DETERGING
DETERMENT
DETERMINE
DETERRED
DETERRENT
DETERRER
DETERRERS
DETERRING
DETERS
DETERSION
DETERSIVE
DETEST
DETESTED
DETESTER
DETESTERS
DETESTING
DETESTS
DETHATCH
DETHRONE
DETHRONED
DETHRONER
DETHRONES
DETICK
DETICKED
DETICKER
DETICKERS
DETICKING
DETICKS
DETINUE
DETINUES
DETONABLE
DETONATE
DETONATED
DETONATES
DETONATOR
DETORSION
DETORT
DETORTED
DETORTING
DETORTION
DETORTS
DETOUR
DETOURED
DETOURING
DETOURS
DETOX
DETOXED
DETOXES
DETOXIFY
DETOXING
DETRACT
DETRACTED
DETRACTOR
DETRACTS
DETRAIN
DETRAINED
DETRAINS
DETRAQUE
DETRAQUEE
DETRAQUES
DETRIMENT
DETRITAL
DETRITION
DETRITUS
DETRUDE
DETRUDED
DETRUDES
DETRUDING
DETRUSION
DETRUSOR
DETRUSORS
DETUNE
DETUNED
DETUNES
DETUNING
DEUCE
DEUCED
DEUCEDLY
DEUCES
DEUCING
DEUDDARN
DEUDDARNS
DEUS
DEUTERATE
DEUTERIC
DEUTERIDE
DEUTERIUM
DEUTERON
DEUTERONS
DEUTON
DEUTONS
DEUTZIA
DEUTZIAS
DEV
DEVA
DEVALL
DEVALLED
DEVALLING
DEVALLS
DEVALUATE
DEVALUE
DEVALUED
DEVALUES
DEVALUING
DEVAS
DEVASTATE
DEVEIN
DEVEINED
DEVEINING

DEVEINS
DEVEL
DEVELED
DEVELING
DEVELLED
DEVELLING
DEVELOP
DEVELOPE
DEVELOPED
DEVELOPER
DEVELOPES
DEVELOPPE
DEVELOPS
DEVELS
DEVERBAL
DEVERBALS
DEVEST
DEVESTED
DEVESTING
DEVESTS
DEVI
DEVIANCE
DEVIANCES
DEVIANCY
DEVIANT
DEVIANTS
DEVIATE
DEVIATED
DEVIATES
DEVIATING
DEVIATION
DEVIATIVE
DEVIATOR
DEVIATORS
DEVIATORY
DEVICE
DEVICEFUL
DEVICES
DEVIL
DEVILDOM
DEVILDOMS
DEVILED
DEVILESS
DEVILET
DEVILETS
DEVILFISH
DEVILING
DEVILINGS
DEVILISH
DEVILISM
DEVILISMS
DEVILKIN
DEVILKINS
DEVILLED
DEVILLING
DEVILMENT
DEVILRIES
DEVILRY
DEVILS
DEVILSHIP
DEVILTRY
DEVILWOOD
DEVIOUS
DEVIOUSLY
DEVIS
DEVISABLE
DEVISAL
DEVISALS
DEVISE
DEVISED
DEVISEE
DEVISEES
DEVISER
DEVISERS
DEVISES
DEVISING
DEVISOR
DEVISORS
DEVITRIFY
DEVLING
DEVLINGS
DEVO
DEVOICE
DEVOICED
DEVOICES
DEVOICING
DEVOID
DEVOIR
DEVOIRS
DEVOLVE
DEVOLVED
DEVOLVES
DEVOLVING
DEVON
DEVONIAN
DEVONPORT
DEVONS
DEVORE
DEVORES
DEVOS
DEVOT
DEVOTE
DEVOTED
DEVOTEDLY
DEVOTEE
DEVOTEES
DEVOTES
DEVOTING
DEVOTION
DEVOTIONS
DEVOTS
DEVOUR
DEVOURED
DEVOURER
DEVOURERS
DEVOURING
DEVOURS
DEVOUT
DEVOUTER
DEVOUTEST
DEVOUTLY
DEVS
DEVVEL
DEVVELLED
DEVVELS
DEW
DEWAN
DEWANI
DEWANIS
DEWANNIES
DEWANNY
DEWANS
DEWAR
DEWARS
DEWATER
DEWATERED
DEWATERER
DEWATERS
DEWAX
DEWAXED
DEWAXES
DEWAXING
DEWBERRY
DEWCLAW
DEWCLAWED
DEWCLAWS
DEWDROP
DEWDROPS
DEWED
DEWFALL
DEWFALLS
DEWFULL
DEWIER
DEWIEST
DEWILY
DEWINESS
DEWING
DEWITT
DEWITTED
DEWITTING
DEWITTS
DEWLAP
DEWLAPPED
DEWLAPS
DEWLAPT
DEWLESS
DEWOOL
DEWOOLED
DEWOOLING
DEWOOLS
DEWORM
DEWORMED
DEWORMER
DEWORMERS
DEWORMING
DEWORMS
DEWPOINT
DEWPOINTS
DEWS
DEWY
DEX
DEXES
DEXIE
DEXIES
DEXTER
DEXTERITY
DEXTEROUS
DEXTERS
DEXTRAL
DEXTRALLY
DEXTRALS
DEXTRAN
DEXTRANS
DEXTRIN
DEXTRINE
DEXTRINES
DEXTRINS
DEXTRO
DEXTRORSE
DEXTROSE
DEXTROSES
DEXTROUS
DEXY
DEY
DEYS
DEZINC
DEZINCED
DEZINCING
DEZINCKED
DEZINCS
DHABA
DHABAS
DHAK
DHAKS
DHAL
DHALS
DHAMMA
DHAMMAS
DHANSAK
DHANSAKS
DHARMA
DHARMAS
DHARMIC
DHARMSALA
DHARNA
DHARNAS
DHIKR
DHIKRS
DHIMMI
DHIMMIS
DHOBI
DHOBIS
DHOL
DHOLAK
DHOLAKS
DHOLE
DHOLES
DHOLL
DHOLLS
DHOLS

D

DHOOLIES
DHOOLY
DHOORA
DHOORAS
DHOOTI
DHOOTIE
DHOOTIES
DHOOTIS
DHOTI
DHOTIS
DHOURRA
DHOURRAS
DHOW
DHOWS
DHURNA
DHURNAS
DHURRA
DHURRAS
DHURRIE
DHURRIES
DHUTI
DHUTIS
DHYANA
DHYANAS
DI
DIABASE
DIABASES
DIABASIC
DIABETES
DIABETIC
DIABETICS
DIABLE
DIABLERIE
DIABLERY
DIABLES
DIABOLIC
DIABOLISE
DIABOLISM
DIABOLIST
DIABOLIZE
DIABOLO
DIABOLOGY
DIABOLOS
DIACETYL
DIACETYLS
DIACHRONY
DIACHYLON
DIACHYLUM
DIACID
DIACIDIC
DIACIDS
DIACODION
DIACODIUM
DIACONAL
DIACONATE
DIACRITIC
DIACT
DIACTINAL
DIACTINE
DIACTINES
DIACTINIC
DIACTS
DIADEM
DIADEMED
DIADEMING
DIADEMS
DIADOCHI
DIADOCHY
DIADROM
DIADROMS
DIAERESES
DIAERESIS
DIAERETIC
DIAGLYPH
DIAGLYPHS
DIAGNOSE
DIAGNOSED
DIAGNOSES
DIAGNOSIS
DIAGONAL
DIAGONALS
DIAGRAM
DIAGRAMED
DIAGRAMS
DIAGRAPH
DIAGRAPHS
DIAGRID
DIAGRIDS
DIAL
DIALECT
DIALECTAL
DIALECTIC
DIALECTS
DIALED
DIALER
DIALERS
DIALING
DIALINGS
DIALIST
DIALISTS
DIALLAGE
DIALLAGES
DIALLAGIC
DIALLED
DIALLEL
DIALLELS
DIALLER
DIALLERS
DIALLING
DIALLINGS
DIALLIST
DIALLISTS
DIALOG
DIALOGED
DIALOGER
DIALOGERS
DIALOGIC
DIALOGING
DIALOGISE
DIALOGISM
DIALOGIST
DIALOGITE
DIALOGIZE
DIALOGS
DIALOGUE
DIALOGUED
DIALOGUER
DIALOGUES
DIALS
DIALYSATE
DIALYSE
DIALYSED
DIALYSER
DIALYSERS
DIALYSES
DIALYSING
DIALYSIS
DIALYTIC
DIALYZATE
DIALYZE
DIALYZED
DIALYZER
DIALYZERS
DIALYZES
DIALYZING
DIAMAGNET
DIAMANTE
DIAMANTES
DIAMETER
DIAMETERS
DIAMETRAL
DIAMETRIC
DIAMIDE
DIAMIDES
DIAMIN
DIAMINE
DIAMINES
DIAMINS
DIAMOND
DIAMONDED
DIAMONDS
DIAMYL
DIANDRIES
DIANDROUS
DIANDRY
DIANE
DIANODAL
DIANOETIC
DIANOIA
DIANOIAS
DIANTHUS
DIAPASE
DIAPASES
DIAPASON
DIAPASONS
DIAPAUSE
DIAPAUSED
DIAPAUSES
DIAPENTE
DIAPENTES
DIAPER
DIAPERED
DIAPERING
DIAPERS
DIAPHONE
DIAPHONES
DIAPHONIC
DIAPHONY
DIAPHRAGM
DIAPHYSES
DIAPHYSIS
DIAPIR
DIAPIRIC
DIAPIRISM
DIAPIRS
DIAPSID
DIAPSIDS
DIAPYESES
DIAPYESIS
DIAPYETIC
DIARCH
DIARCHAL
DIARCHIC
DIARCHIES
DIARCHY
DIARIAL
DIARIAN
DIARIES
DIARISE
DIARISED
DIARISES
DIARISING
DIARIST
DIARISTIC
DIARISTS
DIARIZE
DIARIZED
DIARIZES
DIARIZING
DIARRHEA
DIARRHEAL
DIARRHEAS
DIARRHEIC
DIARRHOEA
DIARY
DIASCIA
DIASCIAS
DIASCOPE
DIASCOPES
DIASPORA
DIASPORAS
DIASPORE
DIASPORES
DIASPORIC
DIASTASE
DIASTASES
DIASTASIC
DIASTASIS
DIASTATIC
DIASTEM

DIASTEMA
DIASTEMAS
DIASTEMS
DIASTER
DIASTERS
DIASTOLE
DIASTOLES
DIASTOLIC
DIASTRAL
DIASTYLE
DIASTYLES
DIATHERMY
DIATHESES
DIATHESIS
DIATHETIC
DIATOM
DIATOMIC
DIATOMIST
DIATOMITE
DIATOMS
DIATONIC
DIATREME
DIATREMES
DIATRETA
DIATRETUM
DIATRIBE
DIATRIBES
DIATRON
DIATRONS
DIATROPIC
DIAXON
DIAXONS
DIAZEPAM
DIAZEPAMS
DIAZEUXES
DIAZEUXIS
DIAZIN
DIAZINE
DIAZINES
DIAZINON
DIAZINONS
DIAZINS
DIAZO
DIAZOES
DIAZOLE
DIAZOLES
DIAZONIUM
DIAZOS
DIAZOTISE
DIAZOTIZE
DIB
DIBASIC
DIBBED
DIBBER
DIBBERS
DIBBING
DIBBLE
DIBBLED
DIBBLER
DIBBLERS
DIBBLES
DIBBLING
DIBBS
DIBBUK
DIBBUKIM
DIBBUKKIM
DIBBUKS
DIBROMIDE
DIBS
DIBUTYL
DICACIOUS
DICACITY
DICACODYL
DICALCIUM
DICAMBA
DICAMBAS
DICAST
DICASTERY
DICASTIC
DICASTS
DICE
DICED
DICELIKE
DICENTRA
DICENTRAS
DICENTRIC
DICER
DICERS
DICES
DICEY
DICH
DICHASIA
DICHASIAL
DICHASIUM
DICHOGAMY
DICHONDRA
DICHOPTIC
DICHORD
DICHORDS
DICHOTIC
DICHOTOMY
DICHROIC
DICHROISM
DICHROITE
DICHROMAT
DICHROMIC
DICHT
DICHTED
DICHTING
DICHTS
DICIER
DICIEST
DICING
DICINGS
DICK
DICKED
DICKENS
DICKENSES
DICKER
DICKERED
DICKERER
DICKERERS
DICKERING
DICKERS
DICKEY
DICKEYS
DICKHEAD
DICKHEADS
DICKIE
DICKIER
DICKIES
DICKIEST
DICKING
DICKINGS
DICKS
DICKTIER
DICKTIEST
DICKTY
DICKY
DICKYBIRD
DICLINIES
DICLINISM
DICLINOUS
DICLINY
DICOT
DICOTS
DICOTYL
DICOTYLS
DICROTAL
DICROTIC
DICROTISM
DICROTOUS
DICT
DICTA
DICTATE
DICTATED
DICTATES
DICTATING
DICTATION
DICTATOR
DICTATORS
DICTATORY
DICTATRIX
DICTATURE
DICTED
DICTIER
DICTIEST
DICTING
DICTION
DICTIONAL
DICTIONS
DICTS
DICTUM
DICTUMS
DICTY
DICTYOGEN
DICUMAROL
DICYCLIC
DICYCLIES
DICYCLY
DID
DIDACT
DIDACTIC
DIDACTICS
DIDACTS
DIDACTYL
DIDACTYLS
DIDAKAI
DIDAKAIS
DIDAKEI
DIDAKEIS
DIDAPPER
DIDAPPERS
DIDDER
DIDDERED
DIDDERING
DIDDERS
DIDDICOY
DIDDICOYS
DIDDIER
DIDDIES
DIDDIEST
DIDDLE
DIDDLED
DIDDLER
DIDDLERS
DIDDLES
DIDDLEY
DIDDLEYS
DIDDLIES
DIDDLING
DIDDLY
DIDDUMS
DIDDY
DIDELPHIC
DIDELPHID
DIDICOI
DIDICOIS
DIDICOY
DIDICOYS
DIDIE
DIDIES
DIDJERIDU
DIDO
DIDOES
DIDOS
DIDRACHM
DIDRACHMA
DIDRACHMS
DIDST
DIDY
DIDYMIUM
DIDYMIUMS
DIDYMO
DIDYMOS
DIDYMOUS
DIDYNAMY
DIE
DIEB
DIEBACK

D

DIEBACKS
DIEBS
DIECIOUS
DIED
DIEDRAL
DIEDRALS
DIEDRE
DIEDRES
DIEGESES
DIEGESIS
DIEGETIC
DIEHARD
DIEHARDS
DIEING
DIEL
DIELDRIN
DIELDRINS
DIELS
DIELYTRA
DIELYTRAS
DIEMAKER
DIEMAKERS
DIENE
DIENES
DIEOFF
DIEOFFS
DIERESES
DIERESIS
DIERETIC
DIES
DIESEL
DIESELED
DIESELING
DIESELISE
DIESELIZE
DIESELS
DIESES
DIESINKER
DIESIS
DIESTER
DIESTERS
DIESTOCK
DIESTOCKS
DIESTROUS
DIESTRUM
DIESTRUMS
DIESTRUS
DIET
DIETARIAN
DIETARIES
DIETARILY
DIETARY
DIETED
DIETER
DIETERS
DIETETIC
DIETETICS
DIETHER
DIETHERS
DIETHYL
DIETHYLS
DIETICIAN
DIETINE
DIETINES
DIETING
DIETINGS
DIETIST
DIETISTS
DIETITIAN
DIETS
DIF
DIFF
DIFFER
DIFFERED
DIFFERENT
DIFFERING
DIFFERS
DIFFICILE
DIFFICULT
DIFFIDENT
DIFFLUENT
DIFFORM
DIFFRACT
DIFFRACTS
DIFFS
DIFFUSE
DIFFUSED
DIFFUSELY
DIFFUSER
DIFFUSERS
DIFFUSES
DIFFUSING
DIFFUSION
DIFFUSIVE
DIFFUSOR
DIFFUSORS
DIFS
DIG
DIGAMIES
DIGAMIST
DIGAMISTS
DIGAMMA
DIGAMMAS
DIGAMOUS
DIGAMY
DIGASTRIC
DIGENESES
DIGENESIS
DIGENETIC
DIGERATI
DIGEST
DIGESTANT
DIGESTED
DIGESTER
DIGESTERS
DIGESTIF
DIGESTIFS
DIGESTING
DIGESTION
DIGESTIVE
DIGESTOR
DIGESTORS
DIGESTS
DIGGABLE
DIGGED
DIGGER
DIGGERS
DIGGING
DIGGINGS
DIGHT
DIGHTED
DIGHTING
DIGHTS
DIGICAM
DIGICAMS
DIGIPACK
DIGIPACKS
DIGIT
DIGITAL
DIGITALIN
DIGITALIS
DIGITALLY
DIGITALS
DIGITATE
DIGITATED
DIGITISE
DIGITISED
DIGITISER
DIGITISES
DIGITIZE
DIGITIZED
DIGITIZER
DIGITIZES
DIGITONIN
DIGITOXIN
DIGITRON
DIGITRONS
DIGITS
DIGITULE
DIGITULES
DIGLOSSIA
DIGLOSSIC
DIGLOT
DIGLOTS
DIGLOTTIC
DIGLYPH
DIGLYPHS
DIGNIFIED
DIGNIFIES
DIGNIFY
DIGNITARY
DIGNITIES
DIGNITY
DIGONAL
DIGOXIN
DIGOXINS
DIGRAPH
DIGRAPHIC
DIGRAPHS
DIGRESS
DIGRESSED
DIGRESSER
DIGRESSES
DIGS
DIGYNIAN
DIGYNOUS
DIHEDRA
DIHEDRAL
DIHEDRALS
DIHEDRON
DIHEDRONS
DIHYBRID
DIHYBRIDS
DIHYDRIC
DIKA
DIKAS
DIKAST
DIKASTS
DIKDIK
DIKDIKS
DIKE
DIKED
DIKER
DIKERS
DIKES
DIKETONE
DIKETONES
DIKING
DIKKOP
DIKKOPS
DIKTAT
DIKTATS
DILATABLE
DILATABLY
DILATANCY
DILATANT
DILATANTS
DILATATE
DILATATOR
DILATE
DILATED
DILATER
DILATERS
DILATES
DILATING
DILATION
DILATIONS
DILATIVE
DILATOR
DILATORS
DILATORY
DILDO
DILDOE
DILDOES
DILDOS
DILEMMA
DILEMMAS
DILEMMIC
DILIGENCE
DILIGENT

DILL
DILLED
DILLI
DILLIER
DILLIES
DILLIEST
DILLING
DILLINGS
DILLIS
DILLS
DILLWEED
DILLWEEDS
DILLY
DILSCOOP
DILSCOOPS
DILTIAZEM
DILUENT
DILUENTS
DILUTABLE
DILUTE
DILUTED
DILUTEE
DILUTEES
DILUTER
DILUTERS
DILUTES
DILUTING
DILUTION
DILUTIONS
DILUTIVE
DILUTOR
DILUTORS
DILUVIA
DILUVIAL
DILUVIAN
DILUVION
DILUVIONS
DILUVIUM
DILUVIUMS
DIM
DIMBLE
DIMBLES
DIMBO
DIMBOES
DIMBOS
DIME
DIMENSION
DIMER
DIMERIC
DIMERISE
DIMERISED
DIMERISES
DIMERISM
DIMERISMS
DIMERIZE
DIMERIZED
DIMERIZES
DIMEROUS
DIMERS
DIMES
DIMETER
DIMETERS
DIMETHYL
DIMETHYLS
DIMETRIC
DIMIDIATE
DIMINISH
DIMISSORY
DIMITIES
DIMITY
DIMLY
DIMMABLE
DIMMED
DIMMER
DIMMERS
DIMMEST
DIMMING
DIMMINGS
DIMMISH
DIMNESS
DIMNESSES
DIMORPH
DIMORPHIC
DIMORPHS
DIMOUT
DIMOUTS
DIMP
DIMPLE
DIMPLED
DIMPLES
DIMPLIER
DIMPLIEST
DIMPLING
DIMPLY
DIMPS
DIMPSIES
DIMPSY
DIMS
DIMWIT
DIMWITS
DIMWITTED
DIMYARIAN
DIMYARY
DIN
DINAR
DINARCHY
DINARS
DINDLE
DINDLED
DINDLES
DINDLING
DINE
DINED
DINER
DINERIC
DINERO
DINEROS
DINERS
DINES
DINETTE
DINETTES
DINFUL
DING
DINGBAT
DINGBATS
DINGDONG
DINGDONGS
DINGE
DINGED
DINGER
DINGERS
DINGES
DINGESES
DINGEY
DINGEYS
DINGHIES
DINGHY
DINGIED
DINGIER
DINGIES
DINGIEST
DINGILY
DINGINESS
DINGING
DINGLE
DINGLES
DINGO
DINGOED
DINGOES
DINGOING
DINGOS
DINGS
DINGUS
DINGUSES
DINGY
DINGYING
DINIC
DINICS
DINING
DININGS
DINITRO
DINK
DINKED
DINKER
DINKEST
DINKEY
DINKEYS
DINKIE
DINKIER
DINKIES
DINKIEST
DINKING
DINKLIER
DINKLIEST
DINKLY
DINKS
DINKUM
DINKUMS
DINKY
DINMONT
DINMONTS
DINNA
DINNAE
DINNED
DINNER
DINNERED
DINNERING
DINNERS
DINNING
DINNLE
DINNLED
DINNLES
DINNLING
DINO
DINOCERAS
DINOMANIA
DINOS
DINOSAUR
DINOSAURS
DINOTHERE
DINS
DINT
DINTED
DINTING
DINTLESS
DINTS
DIOBOL
DIOBOLON
DIOBOLONS
DIOBOLS
DIOCESAN
DIOCESANS
DIOCESE
DIOCESES
DIODE
DIODES
DIOECIES
DIOECIOUS
DIOECISM
DIOECISMS
DIOECY
DIOESTRUS
DIOICOUS
DIOL
DIOLEFIN
DIOLEFINS
DIOLS
DIONYSIAC
DIONYSIAN
DIOPSIDE
DIOPSIDES
DIOPSIDIC
DIOPTASE
DIOPTASES
DIOPTER
DIOPTERS
DIOPTRAL
DIOPTRATE
DIOPTRE
DIOPTRES

D

DIOPTRIC
DIOPTRICS
DIORAMA
DIORAMAS
DIORAMIC
DIORISM
DIORISMS
DIORISTIC
DIORITE
DIORITES
DIORITIC
DIOSGENIN
DIOTA
DIOTAS
DIOXAN
DIOXANE
DIOXANES
DIOXANS
DIOXID
DIOXIDE
DIOXIDES
DIOXIDS
DIOXIN
DIOXINS
DIP
DIPCHICK
DIPCHICKS
DIPEPTIDE
DIPHASE
DIPHASIC
DIPHENYL
DIPHENYLS
DIPHONE
DIPHONES
DIPHTHONG
DIPHYSITE
DIPLEGIA
DIPLEGIAS
DIPLEGIC
DIPLEX
DIPLEXER
DIPLEXERS
DIPLOE
DIPLOES
DIPLOGEN
DIPLOGENS
DIPLOIC
DIPLOID
DIPLOIDIC
DIPLOIDS
DIPLOIDY
DIPLOMA
DIPLOMACY
DIPLOMAED
DIPLOMAS
DIPLOMAT
DIPLOMATA
DIPLOMATE
DIPLOMATS
DIPLON
DIPLONEMA
DIPLONS
DIPLONT
DIPLONTIC
DIPLONTS
DIPLOPIA
DIPLOPIAS
DIPLOPIC
DIPLOPOD
DIPLOPODS
DIPLOSES
DIPLOSIS
DIPLOTENE
DIPLOZOA
DIPLOZOIC
DIPLOZOON
DIPNET
DIPNETS
DIPNETTED
DIPNOAN
DIPNOANS
DIPNOOUS
DIPODIC
DIPODIES
DIPODY
DIPOLAR
DIPOLE
DIPOLES
DIPPABLE
DIPPED
DIPPER
DIPPERFUL
DIPPERS
DIPPIER
DIPPIEST
DIPPINESS
DIPPING
DIPPINGS
DIPPY
DIPROTIC
DIPS
DIPSADES
DIPSAS
DIPSHIT
DIPSHITS
DIPSO
DIPSOS
DIPSTICK
DIPSTICKS
DIPSWITCH
DIPT
DIPTERA
DIPTERAL
DIPTERAN
DIPTERANS
DIPTERAS
DIPTERIST
DIPTEROI
DIPTERON
DIPTERONS
DIPTEROS
DIPTEROUS
DIPTYCA
DIPTYCAS
DIPTYCH
DIPTYCHS
DIQUARK
DIQUARKS
DIQUAT
DIQUATS
DIRAM
DIRAMS
DIRDAM
DIRDAMS
DIRDUM
DIRDUMS
DIRE
DIRECT
DIRECTED
DIRECTER
DIRECTEST
DIRECTING
DIRECTION
DIRECTIVE
DIRECTLY
DIRECTOR
DIRECTORS
DIRECTORY
DIRECTRIX
DIRECTS
DIREFUL
DIREFULLY
DIRELY
DIREMPT
DIREMPTED
DIREMPTS
DIRENESS
DIRER
DIREST
DIRGE
DIRGEFUL
DIRGELIKE
DIRGES
DIRHAM
DIRHAMS
DIRHEM
DIRHEMS
DIRIGE
DIRIGENT
DIRIGES
DIRIGIBLE
DIRIGISM
DIRIGISME
DIRIGISMS
DIRIGISTE
DIRIMENT
DIRK
DIRKE
DIRKED
DIRKES
DIRKING
DIRKS
DIRL
DIRLED
DIRLING
DIRLS
DIRNDL
DIRNDLS
DIRT
DIRTBAG
DIRTBAGS
DIRTBALL
DIRTBALLS
DIRTED
DIRTIED
DIRTIER
DIRTIES
DIRTIEST
DIRTILY
DIRTINESS
DIRTING
DIRTS
DIRTY
DIRTYING
DIS
DISA
DISABLE
DISABLED
DISABLER
DISABLERS
DISABLES
DISABLING
DISABLISM
DISABLIST
DISABUSAL
DISABUSE
DISABUSED
DISABUSES
DISACCORD
DISADORN
DISADORNS
DISAFFECT
DISAFFIRM
DISAGREE
DISAGREED
DISAGREES
DISALLIED
DISALLIES
DISALLOW
DISALLOWS
DISALLY
DISANCHOR
DISANNEX
DISANNUL
DISANNULS
DISANOINT
DISAPPEAR
DISAPPLY
DISARM
DISARMED

DISARMER
DISARMERS
DISARMING
DISARMS
DISARRAY
DISARRAYS
DISAS
DISASTER
DISASTERS
DISATTIRE
DISATTUNE
DISAVOUCH
DISAVOW
DISAVOWAL
DISAVOWED
DISAVOWER
DISAVOWS
DISBAND
DISBANDED
DISBANDS
DISBAR
DISBARK
DISBARKED
DISBARKS
DISBARRED
DISBARS
DISBELIEF
DISBENCH
DISBODIED
DISBOSOM
DISBOSOMS
DISBOUND
DISBOWEL
DISBOWELS
DISBRANCH
DISBUD
DISBUDDED
DISBUDS
DISBURDEN
DISBURSAL
DISBURSE
DISBURSED
DISBURSER
DISBURSES
DISC
DISCAGE
DISCAGED
DISCAGES
DISCAGING
DISCAL
DISCALCED
DISCANDIE
DISCANDY
DISCANT
DISCANTED
DISCANTER
DISCANTS
DISCARD
DISCARDED
DISCARDER
DISCARDS
DISCASE
DISCASED
DISCASES
DISCASING
DISCED
DISCEPT
DISCEPTED
DISCEPTS
DISCERN
DISCERNED
DISCERNER
DISCERNS
DISCERP
DISCERPED
DISCERPS
DISCHARGE
DISCHURCH
DISCI
DISCIDE
DISCIDED
DISCIDES
DISCIDING
DISCIFORM
DISCINCT
DISCING
DISCIPLE
DISCIPLED
DISCIPLES
DISCLAIM
DISCLAIMS
DISCLESS
DISCLIKE
DISCLIMAX
DISCLOSE
DISCLOSED
DISCLOSER
DISCLOSES
DISCLOST
DISCO
DISCOBOLI
DISCOED
DISCOER
DISCOERS
DISCOES
DISCOID
DISCOIDAL
DISCOIDS
DISCOING
DISCOLOGY
DISCOLOR
DISCOLORS
DISCOLOUR
DISCOMFIT
DISCOMMON
DISCORD
DISCORDED
DISCORDS
DISCOS
DISCOUNT
DISCOUNTS
DISCOURE
DISCOURED
DISCOURES
DISCOURSE
DISCOVER
DISCOVERS
DISCOVERT
DISCOVERY
DISCREDIT
DISCREET
DISCRETE
DISCRETER
DISCROWN
DISCROWNS
DISCS
DISCUMBER
DISCURE
DISCURED
DISCURES
DISCURING
DISCURSUS
DISCUS
DISCUSES
DISCUSS
DISCUSSED
DISCUSSER
DISCUSSES
DISDAIN
DISDAINED
DISDAINS
DISEASE
DISEASED
DISEASES
DISEASING
DISEDGE
DISEDGED
DISEDGES
DISEDGING
DISEMBARK
DISEMBODY
DISEMPLOY
DISENABLE
DISENDOW
DISENDOWS
DISENGAGE
DISENROL
DISENROLS
DISENTAIL
DISENTOMB
DISESTEEM
DISEUR
DISEURS
DISEUSE
DISEUSES
DISFAME
DISFAMED
DISFAMES
DISFAMING
DISFAVOR
DISFAVORS
DISFAVOUR
DISFIGURE
DISFLESH
DISFLUENT
DISFOREST
DISFORM
DISFORMED
DISFORMS
DISFROCK
DISFROCKS
DISGAVEL
DISGAVELS
DISGEST
DISGESTED
DISGESTS
DISGODDED
DISGORGE
DISGORGED
DISGORGER
DISGORGES
DISGOWN
DISGOWNED
DISGOWNS
DISGRACE
DISGRACED
DISGRACER
DISGRACES
DISGRADE
DISGRADED
DISGRADES
DISGUISE
DISGUISED
DISGUISER
DISGUISES
DISGUST
DISGUSTED
DISGUSTS
DISH
DISHABIT
DISHABITS
DISHABLE
DISHABLED
DISHABLES
DISHALLOW
DISHCLOTH
DISHCLOUT
DISHDASH
DISHDASHA
DISHED
DISHELM
DISHELMED
DISHELMS
DISHERIT
DISHERITS
DISHES
DISHEVEL
DISHEVELS
DISHFUL
DISHFULS

DISHIER
DISHIEST
DISHING
DISHINGS
DISHLIKE
DISHMOP
DISHMOPS
DISHOARD
DISHOARDS
DISHOME
DISHOMED
DISHOMES
DISHOMING
DISHONEST
DISHONOR
DISHONORS
DISHONOUR
DISHORN
DISHORNED
DISHORNS
DISHORSE
DISHORSED
DISHORSES
DISHOUSE
DISHOUSED
DISHOUSES
DISHPAN
DISHPANS
DISHRAG
DISHRAGS
DISHTOWEL
DISHUMOUR
DISHWARE
DISHWARES
DISHWATER
DISHY
DISILLUDE
DISIMMURE
DISINFECT
DISINFEST
DISINFORM
DISINHUME
DISINTER
DISINTERS
DISINURE
DISINURED
DISINURES
DISINVENT
DISINVEST
DISINVITE
DISJASKIT
DISJECT
DISJECTED
DISJECTS
DISJOIN
DISJOINED
DISJOINS
DISJOINT
DISJOINTS
DISJUNCT
DISJUNCTS
DISJUNE
DISJUNED
DISJUNES
DISJUNING
DISK
DISKED
DISKER
DISKERS
DISKETTE
DISKETTES
DISKING
DISKLESS
DISKLIKE
DISKS
DISLEAF
DISLEAFED
DISLEAFS
DISLEAL
DISLEAVE
DISLEAVED
DISLEAVES
DISLIKE
DISLIKED
DISLIKEN
DISLIKENS
DISLIKER
DISLIKERS
DISLIKES
DISLIKING
DISLIMB
DISLIMBED
DISLIMBS
DISLIMN
DISLIMNED
DISLIMNS
DISLINK
DISLINKED
DISLINKS
DISLOAD
DISLOADED
DISLOADS
DISLOCATE
DISLODGE
DISLODGED
DISLODGES
DISLOIGN
DISLOIGNS
DISLOYAL
DISLUSTRE
DISMAL
DISMALER
DISMALEST
DISMALITY
DISMALLER
DISMALLY
DISMALS
DISMAN
DISMANNED
DISMANS
DISMANTLE
DISMASK
DISMASKED
DISMASKS
DISMAST
DISMASTED
DISMASTS
DISMAY
DISMAYD
DISMAYED
DISMAYFUL
DISMAYING
DISMAYL
DISMAYLED
DISMAYLS
DISMAYS
DISME
DISMEMBER
DISMES
DISMISS
DISMISSAL
DISMISSED
DISMISSES
DISMODED
DISMOUNT
DISMOUNTS
DISNATURE
DISNEST
DISNESTED
DISNESTS
DISOBEY
DISOBEYED
DISOBEYER
DISOBEYS
DISOBLIGE
DISODIUM
DISOMIC
DISOMIES
DISOMY
DISORBED
DISORDER
DISORDERS
DISORIENT
DISOWN
DISOWNED
DISOWNER
DISOWNERS
DISOWNING
DISOWNS
DISPACE
DISPACED
DISPACES
DISPACING
DISPARAGE
DISPARATE
DISPARITY
DISPARK
DISPARKED
DISPARKS
DISPART
DISPARTED
DISPARTS
DISPATCH
DISPATHY
DISPAUPER
DISPEACE
DISPEACES
DISPEL
DISPELLED
DISPELLER
DISPELS
DISPENCE
DISPENCED
DISPENCES
DISPEND
DISPENDED
DISPENDS
DISPENSE
DISPENSED
DISPENSER
DISPENSES
DISPEOPLE
DISPERSAL
DISPERSE
DISPERSED
DISPERSER
DISPERSES
DISPIRIT
DISPIRITS
DISPLACE
DISPLACED
DISPLACER
DISPLACES
DISPLANT
DISPLANTS
DISPLAY
DISPLAYED
DISPLAYER
DISPLAYS
DISPLE
DISPLEASE
DISPLED
DISPLES
DISPLING
DISPLODE
DISPLODED
DISPLODES
DISPLUME
DISPLUMED
DISPLUMES
DISPONDEE
DISPONE
DISPONED
DISPONEE
DISPONEES
DISPONER
DISPONERS
DISPONES
DISPONGE
DISPONGED

DISPONGES
DISPONING
DISPORT
DISPORTED
DISPORTS
DISPOSAL
DISPOSALS
DISPOSE
DISPOSED
DISPOSER
DISPOSERS
DISPOSES
DISPOSING
DISPOST
DISPOSTED
DISPOSTS
DISPOSURE
DISPRAD
DISPRAISE
DISPREAD
DISPREADS
DISPRED
DISPREDS
DISPRISON
DISPRIZE
DISPRIZED
DISPRIZES
DISPROFIT
DISPROOF
DISPROOFS
DISPROOVE
DISPROVAL
DISPROVE
DISPROVED
DISPROVEN
DISPROVER
DISPROVES
DISPUNGE
DISPUNGED
DISPUNGES
DISPURSE
DISPURSED
DISPURSES
DISPURVEY
DISPUTANT
DISPUTE
DISPUTED
DISPUTER
DISPUTERS
DISPUTES
DISPUTING
DISQUIET
DISQUIETS
DISRANK
DISRANKED
DISRANKS
DISRATE
DISRATED
DISRATES
DISRATING
DISREGARD
DISRELISH
DISREPAIR
DISREPUTE
DISROBE
DISROBED
DISROBER
DISROBERS
DISROBES
DISROBING
DISROOT
DISROOTED
DISROOTS
DISRUPT
DISRUPTED
DISRUPTER
DISRUPTOR
DISRUPTS
DISS
DISSAVE
DISSAVED
DISSAVER
DISSAVERS
DISSAVES
DISSAVING
DISSEAT
DISSEATED
DISSEATS
DISSECT
DISSECTED
DISSECTOR
DISSECTS
DISSED
DISSEISE
DISSEISED
DISSEISEE
DISSEISES
DISSEISIN
DISSEISOR
DISSEIZE
DISSEIZED
DISSEIZEE
DISSEIZES
DISSEIZIN
DISSEIZOR
DISSEMBLE
DISSEMBLY
DISSENSUS
DISSENT
DISSENTED
DISSENTER
DISSENTS
DISSERT
DISSERTED
DISSERTS
DISSERVE
DISSERVED
DISSERVES
DISSES
DISSEVER
DISSEVERS
DISSHIVER
DISSIDENT
DISSIGHT
DISSIGHTS
DISSIMILE
DISSING
DISSIPATE
DISSOCIAL
DISSOLUTE
DISSOLVE
DISSOLVED
DISSOLVER
DISSOLVES
DISSONANT
DISSUADE
DISSUADED
DISSUADER
DISSUADES
DISSUNDER
DISTAFF
DISTAFFS
DISTAIN
DISTAINED
DISTAINS
DISTAL
DISTALLY
DISTANCE
DISTANCED
DISTANCES
DISTANT
DISTANTLY
DISTASTE
DISTASTED
DISTASTES
DISTAVES
DISTEMPER
DISTEND
DISTENDED
DISTENDER
DISTENDS
DISTENT
DISTENTS
DISTHENE
DISTHENES
DISTHRONE
DISTICH
DISTICHAL
DISTICHS
DISTIL
DISTILL
DISTILLED
DISTILLER
DISTILLS
DISTILS
DISTINCT
DISTINGUE
DISTOME
DISTOMES
DISTORT
DISTORTED
DISTORTER
DISTORTS
DISTRACT
DISTRACTS
DISTRAIL
DISTRAILS
DISTRAIN
DISTRAINS
DISTRAINT
DISTRAIT
DISTRAITE
DISTRESS
DISTRICT
DISTRICTS
DISTRIX
DISTRIXES
DISTRUST
DISTRUSTS
DISTUNE
DISTUNED
DISTUNES
DISTUNING
DISTURB
DISTURBED
DISTURBER
DISTURBS
DISTYLE
DISTYLES
DISULFATE
DISULFID
DISULFIDE
DISULFIDS
DISUNION
DISUNIONS
DISUNITE
DISUNITED
DISUNITER
DISUNITES
DISUNITY
DISUSAGE
DISUSAGES
DISUSE
DISUSED
DISUSES
DISUSING
DISVALUE
DISVALUED
DISVALUES
DISVOUCH
DISYOKE
DISYOKED
DISYOKES
DISYOKING
DIT
DITA
DITAL
DITALS
DITAS
DITCH

DITCHED
DITCHER
DITCHERS
DITCHES
DITCHING
DITCHLESS
DITE
DITED
DITES
DITHECAL
DITHECOUS
DITHEISM
DITHEISMS
DITHEIST
DITHEISTS
DITHELETE
DITHELISM
DITHER
DITHERED
DITHERER
DITHERERS
DITHERIER
DITHERING
DITHERS
DITHERY
DITHIOL
DITHIOLS
DITHIONIC
DITHYRAMB
DITING
DITOKOUS
DITONE
DITONES
DITROCHEE
DITS
DITSIER
DITSIEST
DITSINESS
DITSY
DITT
DITTANDER
DITTANIES
DITTANY
DITTAY
DITTAYS
DITTED
DITTIED
DITTIES
DITTING
DITTIT
DITTO
DITTOED
DITTOING
DITTOLOGY
DITTOS
DITTS
DITTY
DITTYING
DITZ
DITZES
DITZIER
DITZIEST
DITZINESS
DITZY
DIURESES
DIURESIS
DIURETIC
DIURETICS
DIURNAL
DIURNALLY
DIURNALS
DIURON
DIURONS
DIUTURNAL
DIV
DIVA
DIVAGATE
DIVAGATED
DIVAGATES
DIVALENCE
DIVALENCY
DIVALENT
DIVALENTS
DIVAN
DIVANS
DIVAS
DIVE
DIVEBOMB
DIVEBOMBS
DIVED
DIVELLENT
DIVER
DIVERGE
DIVERGED
DIVERGENT
DIVERGES
DIVERGING
DIVERS
DIVERSE
DIVERSED
DIVERSELY
DIVERSES
DIVERSIFY
DIVERSING
DIVERSION
DIVERSITY
DIVERSLY
DIVERT
DIVERTED
DIVERTER
DIVERTERS
DIVERTING
DIVERTIVE
DIVERTS
DIVES
DIVEST
DIVESTED
DIVESTING
DIVESTS
DIVESTURE
DIVI
DIVIDABLE
DIVIDANT
DIVIDE
DIVIDED
DIVIDEDLY
DIVIDEND
DIVIDENDS
DIVIDER
DIVIDERS
DIVIDES
DIVIDING
DIVIDINGS
DIVIDIVI
DIVIDIVIS
DIVIDUAL
DIVIDUOUS
DIVIED
DIVINABLE
DIVINATOR
DIVINE
DIVINED
DIVINELY
DIVINER
DIVINERS
DIVINES
DIVINEST
DIVING
DIVINGS
DIVINIFY
DIVINING
DIVINISE
DIVINISED
DIVINISES
DIVINITY
DIVINIZE
DIVINIZED
DIVINIZES
DIVIS
DIVISIBLE
DIVISIBLY
DIVISIM
DIVISION
DIVISIONS
DIVISIVE
DIVISOR
DIVISORS
DIVNA
DIVO
DIVORCE
DIVORCED
DIVORCEE
DIVORCEES
DIVORCER
DIVORCERS
DIVORCES
DIVORCING
DIVORCIVE
DIVOS
DIVOT
DIVOTS
DIVS
DIVULGATE
DIVULGE
DIVULGED
DIVULGER
DIVULGERS
DIVULGES
DIVULGING
DIVULSE
DIVULSED
DIVULSES
DIVULSING
DIVULSION
DIVULSIVE
DIVVIED
DIVVIER
DIVVIES
DIVVIEST
DIVVY
DIVVYING
DIVYING
DIWAN
DIWANS
DIXI
DIXIE
DIXIES
DIXIT
DIXITS
DIXY
DIYA
DIYAS
DIZAIN
DIZAINS
DIZEN
DIZENED
DIZENING
DIZENMENT
DIZENS
DIZYGOTIC
DIZYGOUS
DIZZARD
DIZZARDS
DIZZIED
DIZZIER
DIZZIES
DIZZIEST
DIZZILY
DIZZINESS
DIZZY
DIZZYING
DJEBEL
DJEBELS
DJELLABA
DJELLABAH
DJELLABAS
DJEMBE
DJEMBES
DJIBBA
DJIBBAH

DJIBBAHS
DJIBBAS
DJIN
DJINN
DJINNI
DJINNS
DJINNY
DJINS
DO
DOAB
DOABLE
DOABS
DOAT
DOATED
DOATER
DOATERS
DOATING
DOATINGS
DOATS
DOB
DOBBED
DOBBER
DOBBERS
DOBBIE
DOBBIES
DOBBIN
DOBBING
DOBBINS
DOBBY
DOBCHICK
DOBCHICKS
DOBE
DOBES
DOBHASH
DOBHASHES
DOBIE
DOBIES
DOBLA
DOBLAS
DOBLON
DOBLONES
DOBLONS
DOBRA
DOBRAS
DOBRO
DOBROS
DOBS
DOBSON
DOBSONFLY
DOBSONS
DOBY
DOC
DOCENT
DOCENTS
DOCETIC
DOCHMIAC
DOCHMIACS
DOCHMII
DOCHMIUS
DOCHT
DOCIBLE
DOCILE
DOCILELY
DOCILER
DOCILEST
DOCILITY
DOCIMASY
DOCK
DOCKAGE
DOCKAGES
DOCKED
DOCKEN
DOCKENS
DOCKER
DOCKERS
DOCKET
DOCKETED
DOCKETING
DOCKETS
DOCKHAND
DOCKHANDS
DOCKING
DOCKINGS
DOCKISE
DOCKISED
DOCKISES
DOCKISING
DOCKIZE
DOCKIZED
DOCKIZES
DOCKIZING
DOCKLAND
DOCKLANDS
DOCKS
DOCKSIDE
DOCKSIDES
DOCKYARD
DOCKYARDS
DOCO
DOCOS
DOCQUET
DOCQUETED
DOCQUETS
DOCS
DOCTOR
DOCTORAL
DOCTORAND
DOCTORATE
DOCTORED
DOCTORESS
DOCTORIAL
DOCTORING
DOCTORLY
DOCTORS
DOCTRESS
DOCTRINAL
DOCTRINE
DOCTRINES
DOCU
DOCUDRAMA
DOCUMENT
DOCUMENTS
DOCUS
DOCUSOAP
DOCUSOAPS
DOD
DODDARD
DODDARDS
DODDED
DODDER
DODDERED
DODDERER
DODDERERS
DODDERIER
DODDERING
DODDERS
DODDERY
DODDIER
DODDIES
DODDIEST
DODDING
DODDIPOLL
DODDLE
DODDLES
DODDY
DODDYPOLL
DODECAGON
DODGE
DODGEBALL
DODGED
DODGEM
DODGEMS
DODGER
DODGERIES
DODGERS
DODGERY
DODGES
DODGIER
DODGIEST
DODGINESS
DODGING
DODGINGS
DODGY
DODKIN
DODKINS
DODMAN
DODMANS
DODO
DODOES
DODOISM
DODOISMS
DODOS
DODS
DOE
DOEK
DOEKS
DOEN
DOER
DOERS
DOES
DOESKIN
DOESKINS
DOEST
DOETH
DOF
DOFF
DOFFED
DOFFER
DOFFERS
DOFFING
DOFFS
DOG
DOGARESSA
DOGATE
DOGATES
DOGBANE
DOGBANES
DOGBERRY
DOGBOLT
DOGBOLTS
DOGCART
DOGCARTS
DOGDOM
DOGDOMS
DOGE
DOGEAR
DOGEARED
DOGEARING
DOGEARS
DOGEATE
DOGEATES
DOGEDOM
DOGEDOMS
DOGES
DOGESHIP
DOGESHIPS
DOGEY
DOGEYS
DOGFACE
DOGFACES
DOGFIGHT
DOGFIGHTS
DOGFISH
DOGFISHES
DOGFOOD
DOGFOODS
DOGFOUGHT
DOGFOX
DOGFOXES
DOGGED
DOGGEDER
DOGGEDEST
DOGGEDLY
DOGGER
DOGGEREL
DOGGERELS
DOGGERIES
DOGGERMAN
DOGGERMEN
DOGGERS

D

DOGGERY
DOGGESS
DOGGESSES
DOGGIE
DOGGIER
DOGGIES
DOGGIEST
DOGGINESS
DOGGING
DOGGINGS
DOGGISH
DOGGISHLY
DOGGO
DOGGONE
DOGGONED
DOGGONER
DOGGONES
DOGGONEST
DOGGONING
DOGGREL
DOGGRELS
DOGGY
DOGHANGED
DOGHOLE
DOGHOLES
DOGHOUSE
DOGHOUSES
DOGIE
DOGIES
DOGLEG
DOGLEGGED
DOGLEGS
DOGLIKE
DOGMA
DOGMAN
DOGMAS
DOGMATA
DOGMATIC
DOGMATICS
DOGMATISE
DOGMATISM
DOGMATIST
DOGMATIZE
DOGMATORY
DOGMEN
DOGNAP
DOGNAPED
DOGNAPER
DOGNAPERS
DOGNAPING
DOGNAPPED
DOGNAPPER
DOGNAPS
DOGPILE
DOGPILES
DOGREL
DOGRELS
DOGROBBER
DOGS
DOGSBODY
DOGSHIP
DOGSHIPS
DOGSHORES
DOGSHOW
DOGSHOWS
DOGSKIN
DOGSKINS
DOGSLED
DOGSLEDS
DOGSLEEP
DOGSLEEPS
DOGSTAIL
DOGSTAILS
DOGTAIL
DOGTAILS
DOGTEETH
DOGTOOTH
DOGTOWN
DOGTOWNS
DOGTROT
DOGTROTS
DOGVANE
DOGVANES
DOGWATCH
DOGWOOD
DOGWOODS
DOGY
DOH
DOHS
DOHYO
DOHYOS
DOILED
DOILIED
DOILIES
DOILT
DOILTER
DOILTEST
DOILY
DOING
DOINGS
DOIT
DOITED
DOITIT
DOITKIN
DOITKINS
DOITS
DOJO
DOJOS
DOL
DOLABRATE
DOLCE
DOLCES
DOLCETTO
DOLCETTOS
DOLCI
DOLDRUMS
DOLE
DOLED
DOLEFUL
DOLEFULLY
DOLENT
DOLENTE
DOLERITE
DOLERITES
DOLERITIC
DOLES
DOLESOME
DOLIA
DOLICHOS
DOLICHURI
DOLINA
DOLINAS
DOLINE
DOLINES
DOLING
DOLIUM
DOLL
DOLLAR
DOLLARED
DOLLARISE
DOLLARIZE
DOLLARS
DOLLDOM
DOLLDOMS
DOLLED
DOLLHOOD
DOLLHOODS
DOLLHOUSE
DOLLIED
DOLLIER
DOLLIERS
DOLLIES
DOLLINESS
DOLLING
DOLLISH
DOLLISHLY
DOLLOP
DOLLOPED
DOLLOPING
DOLLOPS
DOLLS
DOLLY
DOLLYBIRD
DOLLYING
DOLMA
DOLMADES
DOLMAN
DOLMANS
DOLMAS
DOLMEN
DOLMENIC
DOLMENS
DOLOMITE
DOLOMITES
DOLOMITIC
DOLOR
DOLORIFIC
DOLOROSO
DOLOROUS
DOLORS
DOLOS
DOLOSSE
DOLOSTONE
DOLOUR
DOLOURS
DOLPHIN
DOLPHINET
DOLPHINS
DOLS
DOLT
DOLTISH
DOLTISHLY
DOLTS
DOM
DOMAIN
DOMAINAL
DOMAINE
DOMAINES
DOMAINS
DOMAL
DOMANIAL
DOMATIA
DOMATIUM
DOME
DOMED
DOMELIKE
DOMES
DOMESDAY
DOMESDAYS
DOMESTIC
DOMESTICS
DOMETT
DOMETTS
DOMIC
DOMICAL
DOMICALLY
DOMICIL
DOMICILE
DOMICILED
DOMICILES
DOMICILS
DOMIER
DOMIEST
DOMINANCE
DOMINANCY
DOMINANT
DOMINANTS
DOMINATE
DOMINATED
DOMINATES
DOMINATOR
DOMINE
DOMINEE
DOMINEER
DOMINEERS
DOMINEES
DOMINES
DOMING
DOMINICAL
DOMINICK

DOMINICKS
DOMINIE
DOMINIES
DOMINION
DOMINIONS
DOMINIQUE
DOMINIUM
DOMINIUMS
DOMINO
DOMINOES
DOMINOS
DOMOIC
DOMS
DOMY
DON
DONA
DONAH
DONAHS
DONAIR
DONAIRS
DONARIES
DONARY
DONAS
DONATARY
DONATE
DONATED
DONATES
DONATING
DONATION
DONATIONS
DONATISM
DONATISMS
DONATIVE
DONATIVES
DONATOR
DONATORS
DONATORY
DONDER
DONDERED
DONDERING
DONDERS
DONE
DONEE
DONEES
DONEGAL
DONEGALS
DONENESS
DONEPEZIL
DONER
DONERS
DONG
DONGA
DONGAS
DONGED
DONGING
DONGLE
DONGLES
DONGOLA
DONGOLAS
DONGS
DONING
DONINGS
DONJON
DONJONS
DONKEY
DONKEYMAN
DONKEYMEN
DONKEYS
DONKO
DONKOS
DONNA
DONNARD
DONNART
DONNAS
DONNAT
DONNATS
DONNE
DONNED
DONNEE
DONNEES
DONNERD
DONNERED
DONNERT
DONNES
DONNICKER
DONNIES
DONNIKER
DONNIKERS
DONNING
DONNISH
DONNISHLY
DONNISM
DONNISMS
DONNOT
DONNOTS
DONNY
DONOR
DONORS
DONORSHIP
DONS
DONSHIP
DONSHIPS
DONSIE
DONSIER
DONSIEST
DONSY
DONUT
DONUTS
DONUTTED
DONUTTING
DONZEL
DONZELS
DOO
DOOB
DOOBIE
DOOBIES
DOOBREY
DOOBREYS
DOOBRIE
DOOBRIES
DOOBRY
DOOBS
DOOCE
DOOCED
DOOCES
DOOCING
DOOCOT
DOOCOTS
DOODAD
DOODADS
DOODAH
DOODAHS
DOODIES
DOODLE
DOODLEBUG
DOODLED
DOODLER
DOODLERS
DOODLES
DOODLING
DOODOO
DOODOOS
DOODY
DOOFER
DOOFERS
DOOFUS
DOOFUSES
DOOHICKEY
DOOK
DOOKED
DOOKET
DOOKETS
DOOKING
DOOKS
DOOL
DOOLALLY
DOOLAN
DOOLANS
DOOLE
DOOLEE
DOOLEES
DOOLES
DOOLIE
DOOLIES
DOOLS
DOOLY
DOOM
DOOMED
DOOMFUL
DOOMFULLY
DOOMIER
DOOMIEST
DOOMILY
DOOMING
DOOMS
DOOMSAYER
DOOMSDAY
DOOMSDAYS
DOOMSMAN
DOOMSMEN
DOOMSTER
DOOMSTERS
DOOMWATCH
DOOMY
DOON
DOONA
DOONAS
DOOR
DOORBELL
DOORBELLS
DOORCASE
DOORCASES
DOORED
DOORFRAME
DOORJAMB
DOORJAMBS
DOORKNOB
DOORKNOBS
DOORKNOCK
DOORLESS
DOORLIKE
DOORMAN
DOORMAT
DOORMATS
DOORMEN
DOORN
DOORNAIL
DOORNAILS
DOORNBOOM
DOORNS
DOORPLATE
DOORPOST
DOORPOSTS
DOORS
DOORSILL
DOORSILLS
DOORSMAN
DOORSMEN
DOORSTEP
DOORSTEPS
DOORSTONE
DOORSTOP
DOORSTOPS
DOORWAY
DOORWAYS
DOORWOMAN
DOORWOMEN
DOORYARD
DOORYARDS
DOOS
DOOSES
DOOSRA
DOOSRAS
DOOWOP
DOOWOPS
DOOZER
DOOZERS
DOOZIE
DOOZIES
DOOZY

DOP
DOPA
DOPAMINE
DOPAMINES
DOPANT
DOPANTS
DOPAS
DOPATTA
DOPATTAS
DOPE
DOPED
DOPEHEAD
DOPEHEADS
DOPER
DOPERS
DOPES
DOPESHEET
DOPEST
DOPESTER
DOPESTERS
DOPEY
DOPEYNESS
DOPIAZA
DOPIAZAS
DOPIER
DOPIEST
DOPILY
DOPINESS
DOPING
DOPINGS
DOPPED
DOPPER
DOPPERS
DOPPIE
DOPPIES
DOPPING
DOPPINGS
DOPPIO
DOPPIOS
DOPS
DOPY
DOR
DORAD
DORADO
DORADOS
DORADS
DORB
DORBA
DORBAS
DORBEETLE
DORBS
DORBUG
DORBUGS
DORE
DOREE
DOREES
DORES
DORHAWK
DORHAWKS
DORIC
DORIDOID
DORIDOIDS
DORIES
DORIS
DORISE
DORISED
DORISES
DORISING
DORIZE
DORIZED
DORIZES
DORIZING
DORK
DORKIER
DORKIEST
DORKINESS
DORKISH
DORKS
DORKY
DORLACH
DORLACHS
DORM
DORMANCY
DORMANT
DORMANTS
DORMER
DORMERED
DORMERS
DORMICE
DORMIE
DORMIENT
DORMIN
DORMINS
DORMITION
DORMITIVE
DORMITORY
DORMOUSE
DORMS
DORMY
DORNECK
DORNECKS
DORNICK
DORNICKS
DORNOCK
DORNOCKS
DORONICUM
DORP
DORPER
DORPERS
DORPS
DORR
DORRED
DORRING
DORRS
DORS
DORSA
DORSAD
DORSAL
DORSALLY
DORSALS
DORSE
DORSEL
DORSELS
DORSER
DORSERS
DORSES
DORSIFLEX
DORSUM
DORT
DORTED
DORTER
DORTERS
DORTIER
DORTIEST
DORTINESS
DORTING
DORTOUR
DORTOURS
DORTS
DORTY
DORY
DORYMAN
DORYMEN
DOS
DOSA
DOSAGE
DOSAGES
DOSAI
DOSAS
DOSE
DOSED
DOSEH
DOSEHS
DOSEMETER
DOSER
DOSERS
DOSES
DOSH
DOSHA
DOSHAS
DOSHES
DOSIMETER
DOSIMETRY
DOSING
DOSIOLOGY
DOSOLOGY
DOSS
DOSSAL
DOSSALS
DOSSED
DOSSEL
DOSSELS
DOSSER
DOSSERET
DOSSERETS
DOSSERS
DOSSES
DOSSHOUSE
DOSSIER
DOSSIERS
DOSSIL
DOSSILS
DOSSING
DOST
DOT
DOTAGE
DOTAGES
DOTAL
DOTANT
DOTANTS
DOTARD
DOTARDLY
DOTARDS
DOTATION
DOTATIONS
DOTCOM
DOTCOMMER
DOTCOMS
DOTE
DOTED
DOTER
DOTERS
DOTES
DOTH
DOTIER
DOTIEST
DOTING
DOTINGLY
DOTINGS
DOTISH
DOTS
DOTTED
DOTTEL
DOTTELS
DOTTER
DOTTEREL
DOTTERELS
DOTTERS
DOTTIER
DOTTIEST
DOTTILY
DOTTINESS
DOTTING
DOTTLE
DOTTLED
DOTTLER
DOTTLES
DOTTLEST
DOTTREL
DOTTRELS
DOTTY
DOTY
DOUANE
DOUANES
DOUANIER
DOUANIERS
DOUAR
DOUARS
DOUBLE
DOUBLED

DOUBLER
DOUBLERS
DOUBLES
DOUBLET
DOUBLETON
DOUBLETS
DOUBLING
DOUBLINGS
DOUBLOON
DOUBLOONS
DOUBLURE
DOUBLURES
DOUBLY
DOUBT
DOUBTABLE
DOUBTABLY
DOUBTED
DOUBTER
DOUBTERS
DOUBTFUL
DOUBTFULS
DOUBTING
DOUBTINGS
DOUBTLESS
DOUBTS
DOUC
DOUCE
DOUCELY
DOUCENESS
DOUCEPERE
DOUCER
DOUCEST
DOUCET
DOUCETS
DOUCEUR
DOUCEURS
DOUCHE
DOUCHEBAG
DOUCHED
DOUCHES
DOUCHING
DOUCHINGS
DOUCINE
DOUCINES
DOUCS
DOUGH
DOUGHBALL
DOUGHBOY
DOUGHBOYS
DOUGHFACE
DOUGHIER
DOUGHIEST
DOUGHLIKE
DOUGHNUT
DOUGHNUTS
DOUGHS
DOUGHT
DOUGHTIER
DOUGHTILY
DOUGHTY
DOUGHY
DOUK
DOUKED
DOUKING
DOUKS
DOULA
DOULAS
DOULEIA
DOULEIAS
DOUM
DOUMA
DOUMAS
DOUMS
DOUN
DOUP
DOUPIONI
DOUPIONIS
DOUPPIONI
DOUPS
DOUR
DOURA
DOURAH
DOURAHS
DOURAS
DOURER
DOUREST
DOURINE
DOURINES
DOURLY
DOURNESS
DOUSE
DOUSED
DOUSER
DOUSERS
DOUSES
DOUSING
DOUT
DOUTED
DOUTER
DOUTERS
DOUTING
DOUTS
DOUX
DOUZEPER
DOUZEPERS
DOVE
DOVECOT
DOVECOTE
DOVECOTES
DOVECOTS
DOVED
DOVEISH
DOVEISHLY
DOVEKEY
DOVEKEYS
DOVEKIE
DOVEKIES
DOVELET
DOVELETS
DOVELIKE
DOVEN
DOVENED
DOVENING
DOVENS
DOVER
DOVERED
DOVERING
DOVERS
DOVES
DOVETAIL
DOVETAILS
DOVIE
DOVIER
DOVIEST
DOVING
DOVISH
DOVISHLY
DOW
DOWABLE
DOWAGER
DOWAGERS
DOWAR
DOWARS
DOWD
DOWDIER
DOWDIES
DOWDIEST
DOWDILY
DOWDINESS
DOWDS
DOWDY
DOWDYISH
DOWDYISM
DOWDYISMS
DOWED
DOWEL
DOWELED
DOWELING
DOWELINGS
DOWELLED
DOWELLING
DOWELS
DOWER
DOWERED
DOWERIES
DOWERING
DOWERLESS
DOWERS
DOWERY
DOWF
DOWFNESS
DOWIE
DOWIER
DOWIEST
DOWING
DOWITCHER
DOWL
DOWLAS
DOWLASES
DOWLE
DOWLES
DOWLIER
DOWLIEST
DOWLNE
DOWLNES
DOWLNEY
DOWLS
DOWLY
DOWN
DOWNA
DOWNBEAT
DOWNBEATS
DOWNBOUND
DOWNBOW
DOWNBOWS
DOWNBURST
DOWNCAST
DOWNCASTS
DOWNCOME
DOWNCOMER
DOWNCOMES
DOWNCOURT
DOWNCRIED
DOWNCRIES
DOWNCRY
DOWNDRAFT
DOWNED
DOWNER
DOWNERS
DOWNFALL
DOWNFALLS
DOWNFIELD
DOWNFLOW
DOWNFLOWS
DOWNFORCE
DOWNGRADE
DOWNHAUL
DOWNHAULS
DOWNHILL
DOWNHILLS
DOWNHOLE
DOWNIER
DOWNIES
DOWNIEST
DOWNILY
DOWNINESS
DOWNING
DOWNLAND
DOWNLANDS
DOWNLESS
DOWNLIGHT
DOWNLIKE
DOWNLINK
DOWNLINKS
DOWNLOAD
DOWNLOADS
DOWNLOW
DOWNLOWS
DOWNMOST
DOWNPIPE

D

DOWNPIPES
DOWNPLAY
DOWNPLAYS
DOWNPOUR
DOWNPOURS
DOWNRANGE
DOWNRATE
DOWNRATED
DOWNRATES
DOWNRIGHT
DOWNRIVER
DOWNRUSH
DOWNS
DOWNSCALE
DOWNSHIFT
DOWNSIDE
DOWNSIDES
DOWNSIZE
DOWNSIZED
DOWNSIZER
DOWNSIZES
DOWNSLIDE
DOWNSLOPE
DOWNSPIN
DOWNSPINS
DOWNSPOUT
DOWNSTAGE
DOWNSTAIR
DOWNSTATE
DOWNSWEPT
DOWNSWING
DOWNTHROW
DOWNTICK
DOWNTICKS
DOWNTIME
DOWNTIMES
DOWNTOWN
DOWNTOWNS
DOWNTREND
DOWNTROD
DOWNTURN
DOWNTURNS
DOWNVOTE
DOWNVOTED
DOWNVOTES
DOWNWARD
DOWNWARDS
DOWNWARP
DOWNWARPS
DOWNWASH
DOWNWIND
DOWNY
DOWNZONE
DOWNZONED
DOWNZONES
DOWP
DOWPS
DOWRIES
DOWRY
DOWS
DOWSABEL
DOWSABELS
DOWSE
DOWSED
DOWSER
DOWSERS
DOWSES
DOWSET
DOWSETS
DOWSING
DOWSINGS
DOWT
DOWTS
DOX
DOXAPRAM
DOXAPRAMS
DOXASTIC
DOXASTICS
DOXED
DOXES
DOXIE
DOXIES
DOXING
DOXOLOGY
DOXY
DOY
DOYEN
DOYENNE
DOYENNES
DOYENS
DOYLEY
DOYLEYS
DOYLIES
DOYLY
DOYS
DOZE
DOZED
DOZEN
DOZENED
DOZENING
DOZENS
DOZENTH
DOZENTHS
DOZER
DOZERS
DOZES
DOZIER
DOZIEST
DOZILY
DOZINESS
DOZING
DOZINGS
DOZY
DRAB
DRABBED
DRABBER
DRABBERS
DRABBEST
DRABBET
DRABBETS
DRABBIER
DRABBIEST
DRABBING
DRABBISH
DRABBLE
DRABBLED
DRABBLER
DRABBLERS
DRABBLES
DRABBLING
DRABBY
DRABETTE
DRABETTES
DRABLER
DRABLERS
DRABLY
DRABNESS
DRABS
DRAC
DRACAENA
DRACAENAS
DRACENA
DRACENAS
DRACHM
DRACHMA
DRACHMAE
DRACHMAI
DRACHMAS
DRACHMS
DRACK
DRACO
DRACONE
DRACONES
DRACONIAN
DRACONIC
DRACONISM
DRACONTIC
DRAD
DRAFF
DRAFFIER
DRAFFIEST
DRAFFISH
DRAFFS
DRAFFY
DRAFT
DRAFTABLE
DRAFTED
DRAFTEE
DRAFTEES
DRAFTER
DRAFTERS
DRAFTIER
DRAFTIEST
DRAFTILY
DRAFTING
DRAFTINGS
DRAFTS
DRAFTSMAN
DRAFTSMEN
DRAFTY
DRAG
DRAGEE
DRAGEES
DRAGGED
DRAGGER
DRAGGERS
DRAGGIER
DRAGGIEST
DRAGGING
DRAGGINGS
DRAGGLE
DRAGGLED
DRAGGLES
DRAGGLING
DRAGGY
DRAGHOUND
DRAGLINE
DRAGLINES
DRAGNET
DRAGNETS
DRAGOMAN
DRAGOMANS
DRAGOMEN
DRAGON
DRAGONESS
DRAGONET
DRAGONETS
DRAGONFLY
DRAGONISE
DRAGONISH
DRAGONISM
DRAGONIZE
DRAGONNE
DRAGONS
DRAGOON
DRAGOONED
DRAGOONS
DRAGROPE
DRAGROPES
DRAGS
DRAGSMAN
DRAGSMEN
DRAGSTER
DRAGSTERS
DRAGSTRIP
DRAGWAY
DRAGWAYS
DRAIL
DRAILED
DRAILING
DRAILS
DRAIN
DRAINABLE
DRAINAGE
DRAINAGES
DRAINED
DRAINER
DRAINERS
DRAINING
DRAINPIPE

DRAINS
DRAISENE
DRAISENES
DRAISINE
DRAISINES
DRAKE
DRAKES
DRAM
DRAMA
DRAMADIES
DRAMADY
DRAMAS
DRAMATIC
DRAMATICS
DRAMATISE
DRAMATIST
DRAMATIZE
DRAMATURG
DRAMEDIES
DRAMEDY
DRAMMACH
DRAMMACHS
DRAMMED
DRAMMING
DRAMMOCK
DRAMMOCKS
DRAMS
DRAMSHOP
DRAMSHOPS
DRANGWAY
DRANGWAYS
DRANK
DRANT
DRANTED
DRANTING
DRANTS
DRAP
DRAPABLE
DRAPE
DRAPEABLE
DRAPED
DRAPER
DRAPERIED
DRAPERIES
DRAPERS
DRAPERY
DRAPES
DRAPET
DRAPETS
DRAPEY
DRAPIER
DRAPIERS
DRAPIEST
DRAPING
DRAPPED
DRAPPIE
DRAPPIES
DRAPPING
DRAPPY
DRAPS
DRASTIC
DRASTICS
DRAT
DRATCHELL
DRATS
DRATTED
DRATTING
DRAUGHT
DRAUGHTED
DRAUGHTER
DRAUGHTS
DRAUGHTY
DRAUNT
DRAUNTED
DRAUNTING
DRAUNTS
DRAVE
DRAW
DRAWABLE
DRAWBACK
DRAWBACKS
DRAWBAR
DRAWBARS
DRAWBORE
DRAWBORES
DRAWCARD
DRAWCARDS
DRAWCORD
DRAWCORDS
DRAWDOWN
DRAWDOWNS
DRAWEE
DRAWEES
DRAWER
DRAWERFUL
DRAWERS
DRAWING
DRAWINGS
DRAWKNIFE
DRAWL
DRAWLED
DRAWLER
DRAWLERS
DRAWLIER
DRAWLIEST
DRAWLING
DRAWLS
DRAWLY
DRAWN
DRAWNWORK
DRAWPLATE
DRAWS
DRAWSHAVE
DRAWTUBE
DRAWTUBES
DRAY
DRAYAGE
DRAYAGES
DRAYED
DRAYHORSE
DRAYING
DRAYMAN
DRAYMEN
DRAYS
DRAZEL
DRAZELS
DREAD
DREADED
DREADER
DREADERS
DREADEST
DREADFUL
DREADFULS
DREADING
DREADLESS
DREADLOCK
DREADLY
DREADS
DREAM
DREAMBOAT
DREAMED
DREAMER
DREAMERS
DREAMERY
DREAMFUL
DREAMHOLE
DREAMIER
DREAMIEST
DREAMILY
DREAMING
DREAMINGS
DREAMLAND
DREAMLESS
DREAMLIKE
DREAMS
DREAMT
DREAMTIME
DREAMY
DREAR
DREARE
DREARER
DREARES
DREAREST
DREARIER
DREARIES
DREARIEST
DREARILY
DREARING
DREARINGS
DREARS
DREARY
DRECK
DRECKIER
DRECKIEST
DRECKISH
DRECKS
DRECKSILL
DRECKY
DREDGE
DREDGED
DREDGER
DREDGERS
DREDGES
DREDGING
DREDGINGS
DREE
DREED
DREEING
DREER
DREES
DREEST
DREG
DREGGIER
DREGGIEST
DREGGISH
DREGGY
DREGS
DREICH
DREICHER
DREICHEST
DREIDEL
DREIDELS
DREIDL
DREIDLS
DREIGH
DREIGHER
DREIGHEST
DREK
DREKKIER
DREKKIEST
DREKKY
DREKS
DRENCH
DRENCHED
DRENCHER
DRENCHERS
DRENCHES
DRENCHING
DRENT
DREPANID
DREPANIDS
DREPANIUM
DRERE
DRERES
DRERIHEAD
DRESS
DRESSAGE
DRESSAGES
DRESSED
DRESSER
DRESSERS
DRESSES
DRESSIER
DRESSIEST
DRESSILY
DRESSING
DRESSINGS
DRESSMADE
DRESSMAKE
DRESSY

DREST
DREVILL
DREVILLS
DREW
DREY
DREYS
DRIB
DRIBBED
DRIBBER
DRIBBERS
DRIBBING
DRIBBLE
DRIBBLED
DRIBBLER
DRIBBLERS
DRIBBLES
DRIBBLET
DRIBBLETS
DRIBBLIER
DRIBBLING
DRIBBLY
DRIBLET
DRIBLETS
DRIBS
DRICE
DRICES
DRICKSIE
DRICKSIER
DRIED
DRIEGH
DRIER
DRIERS
DRIES
DRIEST
DRIFT
DRIFTAGE
DRIFTAGES
DRIFTED
DRIFTER
DRIFTERS
DRIFTIER
DRIFTIEST
DRIFTING
DRIFTINGS
DRIFTLESS
DRIFTNET
DRIFTNETS
DRIFTPIN
DRIFTPINS
DRIFTS
DRIFTWOOD
DRIFTY
DRILL
DRILLABLE
DRILLED
DRILLER
DRILLERS
DRILLHOLE
DRILLING
DRILLINGS
DRILLS
DRILLSHIP
DRILY
DRINK
DRINKABLE
DRINKABLY
DRINKER
DRINKERS
DRINKING
DRINKINGS
DRINKS
DRIP
DRIPLESS
DRIPPED
DRIPPER
DRIPPERS
DRIPPIER
DRIPPIEST
DRIPPILY
DRIPPING
DRIPPINGS
DRIPPY
DRIPS
DRIPSTONE
DRIPT
DRISHEEN
DRISHEENS
DRIVABLE
DRIVE
DRIVEABLE
DRIVEL
DRIVELED
DRIVELER
DRIVELERS
DRIVELINE
DRIVELING
DRIVELLED
DRIVELLER
DRIVELS
DRIVEN
DRIVER
DRIVERS
DRIVES
DRIVEWAY
DRIVEWAYS
DRIVING
DRIVINGLY
DRIVINGS
DRIZZLE
DRIZZLED
DRIZZLES
DRIZZLIER
DRIZZLING
DRIZZLY
DROGER
DROGERS
DROGHER
DROGHERS
DROGUE
DROGUES
DROGUET
DROGUETS
DROICH
DROICHIER
DROICHS
DROICHY
DROID
DROIDS
DROIL
DROILED
DROILING
DROILS
DROIT
DROITS
DROKE
DROKES
DROLE
DROLER
DROLES
DROLEST
DROLL
DROLLED
DROLLER
DROLLERY
DROLLEST
DROLLING
DROLLINGS
DROLLISH
DROLLNESS
DROLLS
DROLLY
DROME
DROMEDARE
DROMEDARY
DROMES
DROMIC
DROMICAL
DROMOI
DROMON
DROMOND
DROMONDS
DROMONS
DROMOS
DRONE
DRONED
DRONER
DRONERS
DRONES
DRONGO
DRONGOES
DRONGOS
DRONIER
DRONIEST
DRONING
DRONINGLY
DRONISH
DRONISHLY
DRONKLAP
DRONKLAPS
DRONY
DROOB
DROOBS
DROOG
DROOGISH
DROOGS
DROOK
DROOKED
DROOKING
DROOKINGS
DROOKIT
DROOKS
DROOL
DROOLED
DROOLIER
DROOLIEST
DROOLING
DROOLS
DROOLY
DROOME
DROOMES
DROOP
DROOPED
DROOPIER
DROOPIEST
DROOPILY
DROOPING
DROOPS
DROOPY
DROP
DROPCLOTH
DROPDOWN
DROPDOWNS
DROPFLIES
DROPFLY
DROPFORGE
DROPHEAD
DROPHEADS
DROPKICK
DROPKICKS
DROPLET
DROPLETS
DROPLIGHT
DROPLIKE
DROPLOCK
DROPLOCKS
DROPOUT
DROPOUTS
DROPPABLE
DROPPED
DROPPER
DROPPERS
DROPPING
DROPPINGS
DROPPLE
DROPPLES
DROPS
DROPSEED
DROPSEEDS
DROPSHOT
DROPSHOTS

DROPSICAL
DROPSIED
DROPSIES
DROPSONDE
DROPSTONE
DROPSY
DROPT
DROPTOP
DROPTOPS
DROPWISE
DROPWORT
DROPWORTS
DROSERA
DROSERAS
DROSHKIES
DROSHKY
DROSKIES
DROSKY
DROSS
DROSSES
DROSSIER
DROSSIEST
DROSSY
DROSTDIES
DROSTDY
DROSTDYS
DROUGHT
DROUGHTS
DROUGHTY
DROUK
DROUKED
DROUKING
DROUKINGS
DROUKIT
DROUKS
DROUTH
DROUTHIER
DROUTHS
DROUTHY
DROVE
DROVED
DROVER
DROVERS
DROVES
DROVING
DROVINGS
DROW
DROWN
DROWND
DROWNDED
DROWNDING
DROWNDS
DROWNED
DROWNER
DROWNERS
DROWNING
DROWNINGS
DROWNS
DROWS
DROWSE
DROWSED
DROWSES
DROWSIER
DROWSIEST
DROWSIHED
DROWSILY
DROWSING
DROWSY
DRUB
DRUBBED
DRUBBER
DRUBBERS
DRUBBING
DRUBBINGS
DRUBS
DRUCKEN
DRUDGE
DRUDGED
DRUDGER
DRUDGERS
DRUDGERY
DRUDGES
DRUDGING
DRUDGISM
DRUDGISMS
DRUG
DRUGGED
DRUGGER
DRUGGERS
DRUGGET
DRUGGETS
DRUGGIE
DRUGGIER
DRUGGIES
DRUGGIEST
DRUGGING
DRUGGIST
DRUGGISTS
DRUGGY
DRUGLESS
DRUGLORD
DRUGLORDS
DRUGMAKER
DRUGS
DRUGSTER
DRUGSTERS
DRUGSTORE
DRUID
DRUIDESS
DRUIDIC
DRUIDICAL
DRUIDISM
DRUIDISMS
DRUIDRIES
DRUIDRY
DRUIDS
DRUM
DRUMBEAT
DRUMBEATS
DRUMBLE
DRUMBLED
DRUMBLES
DRUMBLING
DRUMFIRE
DRUMFIRES
DRUMFISH
DRUMHEAD
DRUMHEADS
DRUMLIER
DRUMLIEST
DRUMLIKE
DRUMLIN
DRUMLINS
DRUMLY
DRUMMED
DRUMMER
DRUMMERS
DRUMMIES
DRUMMING
DRUMMINGS
DRUMMOCK
DRUMMOCKS
DRUMMY
DRUMROLL
DRUMROLLS
DRUMS
DRUMSTICK
DRUNK
DRUNKARD
DRUNKARDS
DRUNKEN
DRUNKENLY
DRUNKER
DRUNKEST
DRUNKISH
DRUNKS
DRUPE
DRUPEL
DRUPELET
DRUPELETS
DRUPELS
DRUPES
DRUSE
DRUSEN
DRUSES
DRUSIER
DRUSIEST
DRUSY
DRUTHER
DRUTHERS
DRUXIER
DRUXIEST
DRUXY
DRY
DRYABLE
DRYAD
DRYADES
DRYADIC
DRYADS
DRYAS
DRYASDUST
DRYBEAT
DRYBEATEN
DRYBEATS
DRYER
DRYERS
DRYEST
DRYING
DRYINGS
DRYISH
DRYLAND
DRYLANDS
DRYLOT
DRYLOTS
DRYLY
DRYMOUTH
DRYMOUTHS
DRYNESS
DRYNESSES
DRYPOINT
DRYPOINTS
DRYS
DRYSALTER
DRYSTONE
DRYSUIT
DRYSUITS
DRYWALL
DRYWALLED
DRYWALLER
DRYWALLS
DRYWELL
DRYWELLS
DSO
DSOBO
DSOBOS
DSOMO
DSOMOS
DSOS
DUAD
DUADS
DUAL
DUALIN
DUALINS
DUALISE
DUALISED
DUALISES
DUALISING
DUALISM
DUALISMS
DUALIST
DUALISTIC
DUALISTS
DUALITIES
DUALITY
DUALIZE
DUALIZED
DUALIZES
DUALIZING
DUALLED
DUALLIE

D

DUALLIES DUALLING DUALLY DUALS DUAN DUANS DUAR DUARCHIES DUARCHY DUARS DUATHLETE DUATHLON DUATHLONS DUB DUBBED DUBBER DUBBERS DUBBIN DUBBINED DUBBING DUBBINGS DUBBINING DUBBINS DUBBO DUBBOS DUBIETIES DUBIETY DUBIOSITY DUBIOUS DUBIOUSLY DUBITABLE DUBITABLY DUBITANCY DUBITATE DUBITATED DUBITATES DUBNIUM DUBNIUMS DUBONNET DUBONNETS DUBS DUBSTEP DUBSTEPS DUCAL DUCALLY DUCAT DUCATOON DUCATOONS

DUCATS DUCDAME DUCE DUCES DUCHESS DUCHESSE DUCHESSED DUCHESSES DUCHIES DUCHY DUCI DUCK DUCKBILL DUCKBILLS DUCKBOARD DUCKED DUCKER DUCKERS DUCKFOOT DUCKIE DUCKIER DUCKIES DUCKIEST DUCKING DUCKINGS DUCKISH DUCKISHES DUCKLING DUCKLINGS DUCKMOLE DUCKMOLES DUCKPIN DUCKPINS DUCKS DUCKSHOVE DUCKTAIL DUCKTAILS DUCKWALK DUCKWALKS DUCKWEED DUCKWEEDS DUCKY DUCT DUCTAL DUCTED DUCTILE DUCTILELY DUCTILITY

DUCTING DUCTINGS DUCTLESS DUCTS DUCTULE DUCTULES DUCTWORK DUCTWORKS DUD DUDDER DUDDERED DUDDERIES DUDDERING DUDDERS DUDDERY DUDDIE DUDDIER DUDDIES DUDDIEST DUDDY DUDE DUDED DUDEEN DUDEENS DUDENESS DUDES DUDETTE DUDETTES DUDGEON DUDGEONS DUDHEEN DUDHEENS DUDING DUDISH DUDISHLY DUDISM DUDISMS DUDS DUE DUECENTO DUECENTOS DUED DUEFUL DUEL DUELED DUELER DUELERS DUELING

DUELINGS DUELIST DUELISTS DUELLED DUELLER DUELLERS DUELLI DUELLING DUELLINGS DUELLIST DUELLISTS DUELLO DUELLOS DUELS DUELSOME DUENDE DUENDES DUENESS DUENESSES DUENNA DUENNAS DUES DUET DUETED DUETING DUETS DUETT DUETTED DUETTI DUETTING DUETTINO DUETTINOS DUETTIST DUETTISTS DUETTO DUETTOS DUETTS DUFF DUFFED DUFFEL DUFFELS DUFFER DUFFERDOM DUFFERISM DUFFERS DUFFEST DUFFING DUFFINGS

DUFFLE DUFFLES DUFFS DUFUS DUFUSES DUG DUGITE DUGITES DUGONG DUGONGS DUGOUT DUGOUTS DUGS DUH DUHKHA DUHKHAS DUI DUIKER DUIKERBOK DUIKERS DUING DUIT DUITS DUKA DUKAS DUKE DUKED DUKEDOM DUKEDOMS DUKELING DUKELINGS DUKERIES DUKERY DUKES DUKESHIP DUKESHIPS DUKING DUKKA DUKKAH DUKKAHS DUKKAS DUKKHA DUKKHAS DULCAMARA DULCE DULCES DULCET DULCETLY

DULCETS
DULCIAN
DULCIANA
DULCIANAS
DULCIANS
DULCIFIED
DULCIFIES
DULCIFY
DULCIMER
DULCIMERS
DULCIMORE
DULCINEA
DULCINEAS
DULCITE
DULCITES
DULCITOL
DULCITOLS
DULCITUDE
DULCOSE
DULCOSES
DULE
DULES
DULIA
DULIAS
DULL
DULLARD
DULLARDS
DULLED
DULLER
DULLEST
DULLIER
DULLIEST
DULLING
DULLISH
DULLISHLY
DULLNESS
DULLS
DULLY
DULNESS
DULNESSES
DULOCRACY
DULOSES
DULOSIS
DULOTIC
DULSE
DULSES
DULY
DUM
DUMA
DUMAIST
DUMAISTS
DUMAS
DUMB
DUMBBELL
DUMBBELLS
DUMBCANE
DUMBCANES
DUMBED
DUMBER
DUMBEST
DUMBFOUND
DUMBHEAD
DUMBHEADS
DUMBING
DUMBLY
DUMBNESS
DUMBO
DUMBOS
DUMBS
DUMBSHIT
DUMBSHITS
DUMBSHOW
DUMBSHOWS
DUMBSIZE
DUMBSIZED
DUMBSIZES
DUMDUM
DUMDUMS
DUMELA
DUMFOUND
DUMFOUNDS
DUMKA
DUMKAS
DUMKY
DUMMERER
DUMMERERS
DUMMIED
DUMMIER
DUMMIES
DUMMIEST
DUMMINESS
DUMMKOPF
DUMMKOPFS
DUMMY
DUMMYING
DUMOSE
DUMOSITY
DUMOUS
DUMP
DUMPBIN
DUMPBINS
DUMPCART
DUMPCARTS
DUMPED
DUMPEE
DUMPEES
DUMPER
DUMPERS
DUMPIER
DUMPIES
DUMPIEST
DUMPILY
DUMPINESS
DUMPING
DUMPINGS
DUMPISH
DUMPISHLY
DUMPLE
DUMPLED
DUMPLES
DUMPLING
DUMPLINGS
DUMPS
DUMPSITE
DUMPSITES
DUMPSTER
DUMPSTERS
DUMPTRUCK
DUMPY
DUN
DUNAM
DUNAMS
DUNCE
DUNCEDOM
DUNCEDOMS
DUNCELIKE
DUNCERIES
DUNCERY
DUNCES
DUNCH
DUNCHED
DUNCHES
DUNCHING
DUNCICAL
DUNCISH
DUNCISHLY
DUNDER
DUNDERS
DUNE
DUNELAND
DUNELANDS
DUNELIKE
DUNES
DUNG
DUNGAREE
DUNGAREED
DUNGAREES
DUNGED
DUNGEON
DUNGEONED
DUNGEONER
DUNGEONS
DUNGER
DUNGERS
DUNGHEAP
DUNGHEAPS
DUNGHILL
DUNGHILLS
DUNGIER
DUNGIEST
DUNGING
DUNGMERE
DUNGMERES
DUNGS
DUNGY
DUNITE
DUNITES
DUNITIC
DUNK
DUNKED
DUNKER
DUNKERS
DUNKING
DUNKINGS
DUNKS
DUNLIN
DUNLINS
DUNNAGE
DUNNAGES
DUNNAKIN
DUNNAKINS
DUNNART
DUNNARTS
DUNNED
DUNNER
DUNNESS
DUNNESSES
DUNNEST
DUNNIER
DUNNIES
DUNNIEST
DUNNING
DUNNINGS
DUNNISH
DUNNITE
DUNNITES
DUNNO
DUNNOCK
DUNNOCKS
DUNNY
DUNS
DUNSH
DUNSHED
DUNSHES
DUNSHING
DUNT
DUNTED
DUNTING
DUNTS
DUO
DUOBINARY
DUODECIMO
DUODENA
DUODENAL
DUODENARY
DUODENUM
DUODENUMS
DUOLOG
DUOLOGS
DUOLOGUE
DUOLOGUES
DUOMI
DUOMO
DUOMOS
DUOPOLIES
DUOPOLIST
DUOPOLY
DUOPSONY
DUOS
DUOTONE

D

DUOTONES
DUP
DUPABLE
DUPATTA
DUPATTAS
DUPE
DUPED
DUPER
DUPERIES
DUPERS
DUPERY
DUPES
DUPING
DUPINGS
DUPION
DUPIONS
DUPLE
DUPLET
DUPLETS
DUPLEX
DUPLEXED
DUPLEXER
DUPLEXERS
DUPLEXES
DUPLEXING
DUPLEXITY
DUPLICAND
DUPLICATE
DUPLICITY
DUPLIED
DUPLIES
DUPLY
DUPLYING
DUPONDII
DUPONDIUS
DUPPED
DUPPIES
DUPPING
DUPPY
DUPS
DURA
DURABLE
DURABLES
DURABLY
DURAL
DURALS
DURALUMIN
DURAMEN
DURAMENS
DURANCE
DURANCES
DURANT
DURANTS
DURAS
DURATION
DURATIONS
DURATIVE
DURATIVES
DURBAR
DURBARS
DURDUM
DURDUMS
DURE
DURED
DUREFUL
DURES
DURESS
DURESSE
DURESSES
DURGAH
DURGAHS
DURGAN
DURGANS
DURGIER
DURGIEST
DURGY
DURIAN
DURIANS
DURICRUST
DURING
DURION
DURIONS
DURMAST
DURMASTS
DURN
DURNDEST
DURNED
DURNEDER
DURNEDEST
DURNING
DURNS
DURO
DUROC
DUROCS
DUROMETER
DUROS
DUROY
DUROYS
DURR
DURRA
DURRAS
DURRIE
DURRIES
DURRS
DURRY
DURST
DURUKULI
DURUKULIS
DURUM
DURUMS
DURZI
DURZIS
DUSH
DUSHED
DUSHES
DUSHING
DUSK
DUSKED
DUSKEN
DUSKENED
DUSKENING
DUSKENS
DUSKER
DUSKEST
DUSKIER
DUSKIEST
DUSKILY
DUSKINESS
DUSKING
DUSKISH
DUSKISHLY
DUSKLY
DUSKNESS
DUSKS
DUSKY
DUST
DUSTBALL
DUSTBALLS
DUSTBIN
DUSTBINS
DUSTCART
DUSTCARTS
DUSTCLOTH
DUSTCOAT
DUSTCOATS
DUSTCOVER
DUSTED
DUSTER
DUSTERS
DUSTHEAP
DUSTHEAPS
DUSTIER
DUSTIEST
DUSTILY
DUSTINESS
DUSTING
DUSTINGS
DUSTLESS
DUSTLIKE
DUSTMAN
DUSTMEN
DUSTOFF
DUSTOFFS
DUSTPAN
DUSTPANS
DUSTPROOF
DUSTRAG
DUSTRAGS
DUSTS
DUSTSHEET
DUSTSTORM
DUSTUP
DUSTUPS
DUSTY
DUTCH
DUTCHES
DUTCHMAN
DUTCHMEN
DUTEOUS
DUTEOUSLY
DUTIABLE
DUTIED
DUTIES
DUTIFUL
DUTIFULLY
DUTY
DUUMVIR
DUUMVIRAL
DUUMVIRI
DUUMVIRS
DUVET
DUVETINE
DUVETINES
DUVETS
DUVETYN
DUVETYNE
DUVETYNES
DUVETYNS
DUX
DUXELLES
DUXES
DUYKER
DUYKERS
DVANDVA
DVANDVAS
DVORNIK
DVORNIKS
DWAAL
DWAALS
DWALE
DWALES
DWALM
DWALMED
DWALMING
DWALMS
DWAM
DWAMMED
DWAMMING
DWAMS
DWANG
DWANGS
DWARF
DWARFED
DWARFER
DWARFEST
DWARFING
DWARFISH
DWARFISM
DWARFISMS
DWARFLIKE
DWARFNESS
DWARFS
DWARVES
DWAUM
DWAUMED
DWAUMING
DWAUMS
DWEEB
DWEEBIER
DWEEBIEST

DWEEBISH
DWEEBS
DWEEBY
DWELL
DWELLED
DWELLER
DWELLERS
DWELLING
DWELLINGS
DWELLS
DWELT
DWILE
DWILES
DWINDLE
DWINDLED
DWINDLES
DWINDLING
DWINE
DWINED
DWINES
DWINING
DYABLE
DYAD
DYADIC
DYADICS
DYADS
DYARCHAL
DYARCHIC
DYARCHIES
DYARCHY
DYBBUK
DYBBUKIM
DYBBUKKIM
DYBBUKS
DYE
DYEABLE
DYED
DYEING
DYEINGS
DYELINE
DYELINES
DYER
DYERS
DYES
DYESTER
DYESTERS
DYESTUFF
DYESTUFFS
DYEWEED
DYEWEEDS
DYEWOOD
DYEWOODS
DYEWORKS
DYING
DYINGLY
DYINGNESS
DYINGS
DYKE
DYKED
DYKES
DYKING
DYKON
DYKONS
DYNAMETER
DYNAMIC
DYNAMICAL
DYNAMICS
DYNAMISE
DYNAMISED
DYNAMISES
DYNAMISM
DYNAMISMS
DYNAMIST
DYNAMISTS
DYNAMITE
DYNAMITED
DYNAMITER
DYNAMITES
DYNAMITIC
DYNAMIZE
DYNAMIZED
DYNAMIZES
DYNAMO
DYNAMOS
DYNAMOTOR
DYNAST
DYNASTIC
DYNASTIES
DYNASTS
DYNASTY
DYNATRON
DYNATRONS
DYNE
DYNEIN
DYNEINS
DYNEL
DYNELS
DYNES
DYNODE
DYNODES
DYNORPHIN
DYSBINDIN
DYSCHROA
DYSCHROAS
DYSCHROIA
DYSCRASIA
DYSCRASIC
DYSCRATIC
DYSENTERY
DYSFLUENT
DYSGENIC
DYSGENICS
DYSLALIA
DYSLALIAS
DYSLECTIC
DYSLEXIA
DYSLEXIAS
DYSLEXIC
DYSLEXICS
DYSLOGIES
DYSLOGY
DYSMELIA
DYSMELIAS
DYSMELIC
DYSODIL
DYSODILE
DYSODILES
DYSODILS
DYSODYLE
DYSODYLES
DYSPATHY
DYSPEPSIA
DYSPEPSY
DYSPEPTIC
DYSPHAGIA
DYSPHAGIC
DYSPHAGY
DYSPHASIA
DYSPHASIC
DYSPHONIA
DYSPHONIC
DYSPHORIA
DYSPHORIC
DYSPLASIA
DYSPNEA
DYSPNEAL
DYSPNEAS
DYSPNEIC
DYSPNOEA
DYSPNOEAL
DYSPNOEAS
DYSPNOEIC
DYSPNOIC
DYSPRAXIA
DYSPRAXIC
DYSTAXIA
DYSTAXIAS
DYSTAXIC
DYSTECTIC
DYSTHESIA
DYSTHETIC
DYSTHYMIA
DYSTHYMIC
DYSTOCIA
DYSTOCIAL
DYSTOCIAS
DYSTONIA
DYSTONIAS
DYSTONIC
DYSTOPIA
DYSTOPIAN
DYSTOPIAS
DYSTROPHY
DYSURIA
DYSURIAS
DYSURIC
DYSURIES
DYSURY
DYTISCID
DYTISCIDS
DYVOUR
DYVOURIES
DYVOURS
DYVOURY
DZEREN
DZERENS
DZHO
DZHOS
DZIGGETAI
DZO
DZOS

E

E

EA
EACH
EACHWHERE
EADISH
EADISHES
EAGER
EAGERER
EAGEREST
EAGERLY
EAGERNESS
EAGERS
EAGLE
EAGLED
EAGLEHAWK
EAGLES
EAGLET
EAGLETS
EAGLEWOOD
EAGLING
EAGRE
EAGRES
EALDORMAN
EALDORMEN
EALE
EALED
EALES
EALING
EAN
EANED
EANING
EANLING
EANLINGS
EANS
EAR
EARACHE
EARACHES
EARBALL
EARBALLS
EARBASH
EARBASHED
EARBASHER
EARBASHES
EARBOB
EARBOBS
EARBUD
EARBUDS
EARCON
EARCONS
EARD
EARDED
EARDING
EARDROP
EARDROPS
EARDRUM
EARDRUMS
EARDS
EARED
EARFLAP
EARFLAPS
EARFUL
EARFULS
EARHOLE
EARHOLES
EARING
EARINGS
EARL
EARLAP
EARLAPS
EARLDOM
EARLDOMS
EARLESS
EARLIER
EARLIES
EARLIEST
EARLIKE
EARLINESS
EARLOBE
EARLOBES
EARLOCK
EARLOCKS
EARLS
EARLSHIP
EARLSHIPS
EARLY
EARLYWOOD
EARMARK
EARMARKED
EARMARKS
EARMUFF
EARMUFFS
EARN
EARNED
EARNER
EARNERS
EARNEST
EARNESTLY
EARNESTS
EARNING
EARNINGS
EARNS
EARNT
EARPHONE
EARPHONES
EARPICK
EARPICKS
EARPIECE
EARPIECES
EARPLUG
EARPLUGS
EARRING
EARRINGED
EARRINGS
EARS
EARSHOT
EARSHOTS
EARST
EARSTONE
EARSTONES
EARTH
EARTHBORN
EARTHED
EARTHEN
EARTHFALL
EARTHFAST
EARTHFLAX
EARTHIER
EARTHIEST
EARTHILY
EARTHING
EARTHLIER
EARTHLIES
EARTHLIKE
EARTHLING
EARTHLY
EARTHMAN
EARTHMEN
EARTHNUT
EARTHNUTS
EARTHPEA
EARTHPEAS
EARTHRISE
EARTHS
EARTHSET
EARTHSETS
EARTHSTAR
EARTHWARD
EARTHWAX
EARTHWOLF
EARTHWORK
EARTHWORM
EARTHY
EARWAX
EARWAXES
EARWIG
EARWIGGED
EARWIGGY
EARWIGS
EARWORM
EARWORMS
EAS
EASE
EASED
EASEFUL
EASEFULLY
EASEL
EASELED
EASELESS
EASELS
EASEMENT
EASEMENTS
EASER
EASERS
EASES
EASIED
EASIER
EASIES
EASIEST
EASILY
EASINESS
EASING
EASINGS
EASLE
EASLES
EASSEL
EASSIL
EAST
EASTABOUT
EASTBOUND
EASTED
EASTER
EASTERLY
EASTERN
EASTERNER
EASTERS
EASTING
EASTINGS
EASTLAND
EASTLANDS
EASTLIN
EASTLING
EASTLINGS
EASTLINS
EASTMOST
EASTS
EASTWARD
EASTWARDS
EASY
EASYGOING
EASYING
EAT

EATABLE
EATABLES
EATAGE
EATAGES
EATCHE
EATCHES
EATEN
EATER
EATERIE
EATERIES
EATERS
EATERY
EATH
EATHE
EATHLY
EATING
EATINGS
EATS
EAU
EAUS
EAUX
EAVE
EAVED
EAVES
EAVESDRIP
EAVESDROP
EAVING
EBAUCHE
EBAUCHES
EBAYER
EBAYERS
EBAYING
EBAYINGS
EBB
EBBED
EBBET
EBBETS
EBBING
EBBLESS
EBBS
EBENEZER
EBENEZERS
EBENISTE
EBENISTES
EBIONISE
EBIONISED
EBIONISES
EBIONISM
EBIONISMS
EBIONITIC
EBIONIZE
EBIONIZED
EBIONIZES
EBON
EBONICS
EBONIES
EBONISE
EBONISED
EBONISES
EBONISING
EBONIST
EBONISTS
EBONITE
EBONITES
EBONIZE
EBONIZED
EBONIZES
EBONIZING
EBONS
EBONY
EBOOK
EBOOKS
EBRIATE
EBRIATED
EBRIETIES
EBRIETY
EBRILLADE
EBRIOSE
EBRIOSITY
EBULLIENT
EBURNEAN
EBURNEOUS
ECAD
ECADS
ECARINATE
ECARTE
ECARTES
ECAUDATE
ECBOLE
ECBOLES
ECBOLIC
ECBOLICS
ECCE
ECCENTRIC
ECCLESIA
ECCLESIAE
ECCLESIAL
ECCO
ECCRINE
ECCRISES
ECCRISIS
ECCRITIC
ECCRITICS
ECDEMIC
ECDYSES
ECDYSIAL
ECDYSIAST
ECDYSIS
ECDYSISES
ECDYSON
ECDYSONE
ECDYSONES
ECDYSONS
ECESIC
ECESIS
ECESISES
ECH
ECHAPPE
ECHAPPES
ECHARD
ECHARDS
ECHE
ECHED
ECHELLE
ECHELLES
ECHELON
ECHELONED
ECHELONS
ECHES
ECHEVERIA
ECHIDNA
ECHIDNAE
ECHIDNAS
ECHIDNINE
ECHINACEA
ECHINATE
ECHINATED
ECHING
ECHINI
ECHINOID
ECHINOIDS
ECHINUS
ECHINUSES
ECHIUM
ECHIUMS
ECHIURAN
ECHIURANS
ECHIUROID
ECHO
ECHOED
ECHOER
ECHOERS
ECHOES
ECHOEY
ECHOGRAM
ECHOGRAMS
ECHOGRAPH
ECHOIC
ECHOIER
ECHOIEST
ECHOING
ECHOISE
ECHOISED
ECHOISES
ECHOISING
ECHOISM
ECHOISMS
ECHOIST
ECHOISTS
ECHOIZE
ECHOIZED
ECHOIZES
ECHOIZING
ECHOLALIA
ECHOLALIC
ECHOLESS
ECHOS
ECHOVIRUS
ECHT
ECLAIR
ECLAIRS
ECLAMPSIA
ECLAMPSY
ECLAMPTIC
ECLAT
ECLATS
ECLECTIC
ECLECTICS
ECLIPSE
ECLIPSED
ECLIPSER
ECLIPSERS
ECLIPSES
ECLIPSING
ECLIPSIS
ECLIPTIC
ECLIPTICS
ECLOGITE
ECLOGITES
ECLOGUE
ECLOGUES
ECLOSE
ECLOSED
ECLOSES
ECLOSING
ECLOSION
ECLOSIONS
ECO
ECOCIDAL
ECOCIDE
ECOCIDES
ECOD
ECOFREAK
ECOFREAKS
ECOGIFT
ECOGIFTS
ECOLODGE
ECOLODGES
ECOLOGIC
ECOLOGIES
ECOLOGIST
ECOLOGY
ECOMAP
ECOMAPS
ECOMMERCE
ECOMUSEUM
ECONOBOX
ECONOMIC
ECONOMICS
ECONOMIES
ECONOMISE
ECONOMISM
ECONOMIST
ECONOMIZE
ECONOMY
ECONUT
ECONUTS
ECOPHOBIA
ECORCHE
ECORCHES

ECOREGION
ECOS
ECOSPHERE
ECOSSAISE
ECOSTATE
ECOSYSTEM
ECOTAGE
ECOTAGES
ECOTARIAN
ECOTONAL
ECOTONE
ECOTONES
ECOTOPIA
ECOTOPIAS
ECOTOUR
ECOTOURED
ECOTOURS
ECOTOXIC
ECOTYPE
ECOTYPES
ECOTYPIC
ECOZONE
ECOZONES
ECPHRASES
ECPHRASIS
ECRASEUR
ECRASEURS
ECRITOIRE
ECRU
ECRUS
ECSTASES
ECSTASIED
ECSTASIES
ECSTASIS
ECSTASISE
ECSTASIZE
ECSTASY
ECSTATIC
ECSTATICS
ECTASES
ECTASIA
ECTASIAS
ECTASIS
ECTATIC
ECTHYMA
ECTHYMAS
ECTHYMATA
ECTOBLAST
ECTOCRINE
ECTODERM
ECTODERMS
ECTOGENE
ECTOGENES
ECTOGENIC
ECTOGENY
ECTOMERE
ECTOMERES
ECTOMERIC
ECTOMORPH
ECTOPHYTE
ECTOPIA
ECTOPIAS
ECTOPIC
ECTOPIES
ECTOPLASM
ECTOPROCT
ECTOPY
ECTOSARC
ECTOSARCS
ECTOTHERM
ECTOZOA
ECTOZOAN
ECTOZOANS
ECTOZOIC
ECTOZOON
ECTROPIC
ECTROPION
ECTROPIUM
ECTYPAL
ECTYPE
ECTYPES
ECU
ECUELLE
ECUELLES
ECUMENE
ECUMENES
ECUMENIC
ECUMENICS
ECUMENISM
ECUMENIST
ECURIE
ECURIES
ECUS
ECZEMA
ECZEMAS
ED
EDACIOUS
EDACITIES
EDACITY
EDAMAME
EDAMAMES
EDAPHIC
EDDIED
EDDIES
EDDISH
EDDISHES
EDDO
EDDOES
EDDY
EDDYING
EDELWEISS
EDEMA
EDEMAS
EDEMATA
EDEMATOSE
EDEMATOUS
EDENIC
EDENTAL
EDENTATE
EDENTATES
EDGE
EDGEBONE
EDGEBONES
EDGED
EDGELESS
EDGER
EDGERS
EDGES
EDGEWAYS
EDGEWISE
EDGIER
EDGIEST
EDGILY
EDGINESS
EDGING
EDGINGS
EDGY
EDH
EDHS
EDIBILITY
EDIBLE
EDIBLES
EDICT
EDICTAL
EDICTALLY
EDICTS
EDIFICE
EDIFICES
EDIFICIAL
EDIFIED
EDIFIER
EDIFIERS
EDIFIES
EDIFY
EDIFYING
EDILE
EDILES
EDIT
EDITABLE
EDITED
EDITING
EDITINGS
EDITION
EDITIONED
EDITIONS
EDITOR
EDITORIAL
EDITORS
EDITRESS
EDITRICES
EDITRIX
EDITRIXES
EDITS
EDS
EDUCABLE
EDUCABLES
EDUCATE
EDUCATED
EDUCATES
EDUCATING
EDUCATION
EDUCATIVE
EDUCATOR
EDUCATORS
EDUCATORY
EDUCE
EDUCED
EDUCEMENT
EDUCES
EDUCIBLE
EDUCING
EDUCT
EDUCTION
EDUCTIONS
EDUCTIVE
EDUCTOR
EDUCTORS
EDUCTS
EE
EECH
EECHED
EECHES
EECHING
EEEW
EEJIT
EEJITS
EEK
EEL
EELFARE
EELFARES
EELGRASS
EELIER
EELIEST
EELING
EELINGS
EELLIKE
EELPOUT
EELPOUTS
EELS
EELWORM
EELWORMS
EELWRACK
EELWRACKS
EELY
EEN
EENSIER
EENSIEST
EENSY
EERIE
EERIER
EERIEST
EERILY
EERINESS
EERY
EEVEN
EEVENS
EEVN
EEVNING
EEVNINGS
EEVNS

EEW
EF
EFF
EFFABLE
EFFACE
EFFACED
EFFACER
EFFACERS
EFFACES
EFFACING
EFFECT
EFFECTED
EFFECTER
EFFECTERS
EFFECTING
EFFECTIVE
EFFECTOR
EFFECTORS
EFFECTS
EFFECTUAL
EFFED
EFFEIR
EFFEIRED
EFFEIRING
EFFEIRS
EFFENDI
EFFENDIS
EFFERE
EFFERED
EFFERENCE
EFFERENT
EFFERENTS
EFFERES
EFFERING
EFFETE
EFFETELY
EFFICACY
EFFICIENT
EFFIERCE
EFFIERCED
EFFIERCES
EFFIGIAL
EFFIGIES
EFFIGY
EFFING
EFFINGS
EFFLUENCE
EFFLUENT
EFFLUENTS
EFFLUVIA
EFFLUVIAL
EFFLUVIUM
EFFLUX
EFFLUXES
EFFLUXION
EFFORCE
EFFORCED
EFFORCES
EFFORCING
EFFORT
EFFORTFUL
EFFORTS
EFFRAIDE
EFFRAY
EFFRAYS
EFFS
EFFULGE
EFFULGED
EFFULGENT
EFFULGES
EFFULGING
EFFUSE
EFFUSED
EFFUSES
EFFUSING
EFFUSION
EFFUSIONS
EFFUSIVE
EFS
EFT
EFTEST
EFTS
EFTSOON
EFTSOONS
EGAD
EGADS
EGAL
EGALITE
EGALITES
EGALITIES
EGALITY
EGALLY
EGAREMENT
EGENCE
EGENCES
EGENCIES
EGENCY
EGER
EGERS
EGEST
EGESTA
EGESTED
EGESTING
EGESTION
EGESTIONS
EGESTIVE
EGESTS
EGG
EGGAR
EGGARS
EGGBEATER
EGGCORN
EGGCORNS
EGGCUP
EGGCUPS
EGGED
EGGER
EGGERIES
EGGERS
EGGERY
EGGFRUIT
EGGFRUITS
EGGHEAD
EGGHEADED
EGGHEADS
EGGIER
EGGIEST
EGGING
EGGLER
EGGLERS
EGGLESS
EGGLIKE
EGGMASS
EGGMASSES
EGGNOG
EGGNOGS
EGGPLANT
EGGPLANTS
EGGS
EGGSHELL
EGGSHELLS
EGGWASH
EGGWASHES
EGGWHISK
EGGWHISKS
EGGY
EGIS
EGISES
EGLANTINE
EGLATERE
EGLATERES
EGLOMISE
EGLOMISES
EGMA
EGMAS
EGO
EGOISM
EGOISMS
EGOIST
EGOISTIC
EGOISTS
EGOITIES
EGOITY
EGOLESS
EGOMANIA
EGOMANIAC
EGOMANIAS
EGOS
EGOSURF
EGOSURFED
EGOSURFS
EGOTHEISM
EGOTISE
EGOTISED
EGOTISES
EGOTISING
EGOTISM
EGOTISMS
EGOTIST
EGOTISTIC
EGOTISTS
EGOTIZE
EGOTIZED
EGOTIZES
EGOTIZING
EGREGIOUS
EGRESS
EGRESSED
EGRESSES
EGRESSING
EGRESSION
EGRESSIVE
EGRET
EGRETS
EGYPTIAN
EGYPTIANS
EH
EHED
EHING
EHS
EIDE
EIDENT
EIDER
EIDERDOWN
EIDERS
EIDETIC
EIDETICS
EIDOGRAPH
EIDOLA
EIDOLIC
EIDOLON
EIDOLONS
EIDOS
EIGENMODE
EIGENTONE
EIGHT
EIGHTBALL
EIGHTEEN
EIGHTEENS
EIGHTFOIL
EIGHTFOLD
EIGHTFOOT
EIGHTH
EIGHTHLY
EIGHTHS
EIGHTIES
EIGHTIETH
EIGHTS
EIGHTSMAN
EIGHTSMEN
EIGHTSOME
EIGHTVO
EIGHTVOS
EIGHTY
EIGNE
EIK
EIKED
EIKING
EIKON
EIKONES

EIKONS
EIKS
EILD
EILDING
EILDINGS
EILDS
EINA
EINE
EINKORN
EINKORNS
EINSTEIN
EINSTEINS
EIRACK
EIRACKS
EIRENIC
EIRENICAL
EIRENICON
EIRENICS
EISEGESES
EISEGESIS
EISEL
EISELL
EISELLS
EISELS
EISH
EISWEIN
EISWEINS
EITHER
EJACULATE
EJECT
EJECTA
EJECTABLE
EJECTED
EJECTING
EJECTION
EJECTIONS
EJECTIVE
EJECTIVES
EJECTMENT
EJECTOR
EJECTORS
EJECTS
EJIDO
EJIDOS
EKE
EKED
EKES
EKING
EKISTIC
EKISTICAL
EKISTICS
EKKA
EKKAS
EKLOGITE
EKLOGITES
EKPHRASES
EKPHRASIS
EKPWELE
EKPWELES
EKTEXINE
EKTEXINES
EKUELE
EL
ELABORATE
ELAEAGNUS
ELAEOLITE
ELAIN
ELAINS
ELAIOSOME
ELAN
ELANCE
ELANCED
ELANCES
ELANCING
ELAND
ELANDS
ELANET
ELANETS
ELANS
ELAPHINE
ELAPID
ELAPIDS
ELAPINE
ELAPSE
ELAPSED
ELAPSES
ELAPSING
ELASTANCE
ELASTANE
ELASTANES
ELASTASE
ELASTASES
ELASTIC
ELASTICS
ELASTIN
ELASTINS
ELASTOMER
ELATE
ELATED
ELATEDLY
ELATER
ELATERID
ELATERIDS
ELATERIN
ELATERINS
ELATERITE
ELATERIUM
ELATERS
ELATES
ELATING
ELATION
ELATIONS
ELATIVE
ELATIVES
ELBOW
ELBOWED
ELBOWING
ELBOWINGS
ELBOWROOM
ELBOWS
ELCHEE
ELCHEES
ELCHI
ELCHIS
ELD
ELDER
ELDERCARE
ELDERLIES
ELDERLY
ELDERS
ELDERSHIP
ELDEST
ELDESTS
ELDIN
ELDING
ELDINGS
ELDINS
ELDORADO
ELDORADOS
ELDRESS
ELDRESSES
ELDRICH
ELDRITCH
ELDS
ELECT
ELECTABLE
ELECTED
ELECTEE
ELECTEES
ELECTING
ELECTION
ELECTIONS
ELECTIVE
ELECTIVES
ELECTOR
ELECTORAL
ELECTORS
ELECTRESS
ELECTRET
ELECTRETS
ELECTRIC
ELECTRICS
ELECTRIFY
ELECTRISE
ELECTRIZE
ELECTRO
ELECTRODE
ELECTROED
ELECTRON
ELECTRONS
ELECTROS
ELECTRUM
ELECTRUMS
ELECTS
ELECTUARY
ELEDOISIN
ELEGANCE
ELEGANCES
ELEGANCY
ELEGANT
ELEGANTLY
ELEGIAC
ELEGIACAL
ELEGIACS
ELEGIAST
ELEGIASTS
ELEGIES
ELEGISE
ELEGISED
ELEGISES
ELEGISING
ELEGIST
ELEGISTS
ELEGIT
ELEGITS
ELEGIZE
ELEGIZED
ELEGIZES
ELEGIZING
ELEGY
ELEMENT
ELEMENTAL
ELEMENTS
ELEMI
ELEMIS
ELENCH
ELENCHI
ELENCHIC
ELENCHS
ELENCHTIC
ELENCHUS
ELENCTIC
ELEOPTENE
ELEPHANT
ELEPHANTS
ELEPIDOTE
ELEUTHERI
ELEVATE
ELEVATED
ELEVATEDS
ELEVATES
ELEVATING
ELEVATION
ELEVATOR
ELEVATORS
ELEVATORY
ELEVEN
ELEVENS
ELEVENSES
ELEVENTH
ELEVENTHS
ELEVON
ELEVONS
ELF
ELFED
ELFHOOD
ELFHOODS
ELFIN
ELFING
ELFINS

E

ELFISH
ELFISHES
ELFISHLY
ELFLAND
ELFLANDS
ELFLIKE
ELFLOCK
ELFLOCKS
ELFS
ELHI
ELIAD
ELIADS
ELICHE
ELICHES
ELICIT
ELICITED
ELICITING
ELICITOR
ELICITORS
ELICITS
ELIDE
ELIDED
ELIDES
ELIDIBLE
ELIDING
ELIGIBLE
ELIGIBLES
ELIGIBLY
ELIMINANT
ELIMINATE
ELINT
ELINTS
ELISION
ELISIONS
ELITE
ELITES
ELITISM
ELITISMS
ELITIST
ELITISTS
ELIXIR
ELIXIRS
ELK
ELKHORN
ELKHOUND
ELKHOUNDS
ELKS
ELL
ELLAGIC
ELLIPSE
ELLIPSES
ELLIPSIS
ELLIPSOID
ELLIPTIC
ELLOPS
ELLOPSES
ELLS
ELLWAND
ELLWANDS
ELM
ELMEN
ELMIER
ELMIEST
ELMS
ELMWOOD
ELMWOODS
ELMY
ELOCUTE
ELOCUTED
ELOCUTES
ELOCUTING
ELOCUTION
ELOCUTORY
ELODEA
ELODEAS
ELOGE
ELOGES
ELOGIES
ELOGIST
ELOGISTS
ELOGIUM
ELOGIUMS
ELOGY
ELOIGN
ELOIGNED
ELOIGNER
ELOIGNERS
ELOIGNING
ELOIGNS
ELOIN
ELOINED
ELOINER
ELOINERS
ELOINING
ELOINMENT
ELOINS
ELONGATE
ELONGATED
ELONGATES
ELOPE
ELOPED
ELOPEMENT
ELOPER
ELOPERS
ELOPES
ELOPING
ELOPS
ELOPSES
ELOQUENCE
ELOQUENT
ELPEE
ELPEES
ELS
ELSE
ELSEWHERE
ELSEWISE
ELSHIN
ELSHINS
ELSIN
ELSINS
ELT
ELTCHI
ELTCHIS
ELTS
ELUANT
ELUANTS
ELUATE
ELUATES
ELUCIDATE
ELUDE
ELUDED
ELUDER
ELUDERS
ELUDES
ELUDIBLE
ELUDING
ELUENT
ELUENTS
ELUSION
ELUSIONS
ELUSIVE
ELUSIVELY
ELUSORY
ELUTE
ELUTED
ELUTES
ELUTING
ELUTION
ELUTIONS
ELUTOR
ELUTORS
ELUTRIATE
ELUVIA
ELUVIAL
ELUVIATE
ELUVIATED
ELUVIATES
ELUVIUM
ELUVIUMS
ELVAN
ELVANITE
ELVANITES
ELVANS
ELVEN
ELVER
ELVERS
ELVES
ELVISH
ELVISHES
ELVISHLY
ELYSIAN
ELYTRA
ELYTRAL
ELYTROID
ELYTRON
ELYTROUS
ELYTRUM
EM
EMACIATE
EMACIATED
EMACIATES
EMACS
EMACSEN
EMAIL
EMAILABLE
EMAILED
EMAILER
EMAILERS
EMAILING
EMAILINGS
EMAILS
EMANANT
EMANATE
EMANATED
EMANATES
EMANATING
EMANATION
EMANATIST
EMANATIVE
EMANATOR
EMANATORS
EMANATORY
EMBACE
EMBACES
EMBACING
EMBAIL
EMBAILED
EMBAILING
EMBAILS
EMBALE
EMBALED
EMBALES
EMBALING
EMBALL
EMBALLED
EMBALLING
EMBALLS
EMBALM
EMBALMED
EMBALMER
EMBALMERS
EMBALMING
EMBALMS
EMBANK
EMBANKED
EMBANKER
EMBANKERS
EMBANKING
EMBANKS
EMBAR
EMBARGO
EMBARGOED
EMBARGOES
EMBARK
EMBARKED
EMBARKING
EMBARKS
EMBARRAS
EMBARRASS
EMBARRED

E

EMBARRING
EMBARS
EMBASE
EMBASED
EMBASES
EMBASING
EMBASSADE
EMBASSAGE
EMBASSIES
EMBASSY
EMBASTE
EMBATHE
EMBATHED
EMBATHES
EMBATHING
EMBATTLE
EMBATTLED
EMBATTLES
EMBAY
EMBAYED
EMBAYING
EMBAYLD
EMBAYMENT
EMBAYS
EMBED
EMBEDDED
EMBEDDING
EMBEDMENT
EMBEDS
EMBELLISH
EMBER
EMBERS
EMBEZZLE
EMBEZZLED
EMBEZZLER
EMBEZZLES
EMBIGGEN
EMBIGGENS
EMBITTER
EMBITTERS
EMBLAZE
EMBLAZED
EMBLAZER
EMBLAZERS
EMBLAZES
EMBLAZING
EMBLAZON
EMBLAZONS
EMBLEM
EMBLEMA
EMBLEMATA
EMBLEMED
EMBLEMING
EMBLEMISE
EMBLEMIZE
EMBLEMS
EMBLIC
EMBLICS
EMBLOOM
EMBLOOMED
EMBLOOMS
EMBLOSSOM
EMBODIED
EMBODIER
EMBODIERS
EMBODIES
EMBODY
EMBODYING
EMBOG
EMBOGGED
EMBOGGING
EMBOGS
EMBOGUE
EMBOGUED
EMBOGUES
EMBOGUING
EMBOIL
EMBOILED
EMBOILING
EMBOILS
EMBOLDEN
EMBOLDENS
EMBOLI
EMBOLIC
EMBOLIES
EMBOLISE
EMBOLISED
EMBOLISES
EMBOLISM
EMBOLISMS
EMBOLIZE
EMBOLIZED
EMBOLIZES
EMBOLUS
EMBOLUSES
EMBOLY
EMBORDER
EMBORDERS
EMBOSCATA
EMBOSK
EMBOSKED
EMBOSKING
EMBOSKS
EMBOSOM
EMBOSOMED
EMBOSOMS
EMBOSS
EMBOSSED
EMBOSSER
EMBOSSERS
EMBOSSES
EMBOSSING
EMBOST
EMBOUND
EMBOUNDED
EMBOUNDS
EMBOW
EMBOWED
EMBOWEL
EMBOWELED
EMBOWELS
EMBOWER
EMBOWERED
EMBOWERS
EMBOWING
EMBOWMENT
EMBOWS
EMBOX
EMBOXED
EMBOXES
EMBOXING
EMBRACE
EMBRACED
EMBRACEOR
EMBRACER
EMBRACERS
EMBRACERY
EMBRACES
EMBRACING
EMBRACIVE
EMBRAID
EMBRAIDED
EMBRAIDS
EMBRANGLE
EMBRASOR
EMBRASORS
EMBRASURE
EMBRAVE
EMBRAVED
EMBRAVES
EMBRAVING
EMBRAZURE
EMBREAD
EMBREADED
EMBREADS
EMBREATHE
EMBRITTLE
EMBROCATE
EMBROGLIO
EMBROIDER
EMBROIL
EMBROILED
EMBROILER
EMBROILS
EMBROWN
EMBROWNED
EMBROWNS
EMBRUE
EMBRUED
EMBRUES
EMBRUING
EMBRUTE
EMBRUTED
EMBRUTES
EMBRUTING
EMBRYO
EMBRYOID
EMBRYOIDS
EMBRYON
EMBRYONAL
EMBRYONIC
EMBRYONS
EMBRYOS
EMBRYOTIC
EMBUS
EMBUSED
EMBUSES
EMBUSIED
EMBUSIES
EMBUSING
EMBUSQUE
EMBUSQUES
EMBUSSED
EMBUSSES
EMBUSSING
EMBUSY
EMBUSYING
EMCEE
EMCEED
EMCEEING
EMCEES
EMDASH
EMDASHES
EME
EMEER
EMEERATE
EMEERATES
EMEERS
EMEND
EMENDABLE
EMENDALS
EMENDATE
EMENDATED
EMENDATES
EMENDATOR
EMENDED
EMENDER
EMENDERS
EMENDING
EMENDS
EMERALD
EMERALDS
EMERAUDE
EMERAUDES
EMERG
EMERGE
EMERGED
EMERGENCE
EMERGENCY
EMERGENT
EMERGENTS
EMERGES
EMERGING
EMERGS
EMERIED
EMERIES
EMERITA
EMERITAE
EMERITAS
EMERITI

EMERITUS
EMEROD
EMERODS
EMEROID
EMEROIDS
EMERSE
EMERSED
EMERSION
EMERSIONS
EMERY
EMERYING
EMES
EMESES
EMESIS
EMESISES
EMETIC
EMETICAL
EMETICS
EMETIN
EMETINE
EMETINES
EMETINS
EMEU
EMEUS
EMEUTE
EMEUTES
EMIC
EMICANT
EMICATE
EMICATED
EMICATES
EMICATING
EMICATION
EMICS
EMICTION
EMICTIONS
EMICTORY
EMIGRANT
EMIGRANTS
EMIGRATE
EMIGRATED
EMIGRATES
EMIGRE
EMIGREE
EMIGREES
EMIGRES
EMINENCE
EMINENCES
EMINENCY
EMINENT
EMINENTLY
EMIR
EMIRATE
EMIRATES
EMIRS
EMISSARY
EMISSILE
EMISSION
EMISSIONS
EMISSIVE
EMIT
EMITS
EMITTANCE
EMITTED
EMITTER
EMITTERS
EMITTING
EMLETS
EMMA
EMMARBLE
EMMARBLED
EMMARBLES
EMMAS
EMMER
EMMERS
EMMESH
EMMESHED
EMMESHES
EMMESHING
EMMET
EMMETROPE
EMMETS
EMMEW
EMMEWED
EMMEWING
EMMEWS
EMMOVE
EMMOVED
EMMOVES
EMMOVING
EMMY
EMMYS
EMO
EMOCORE
EMOCORES
EMODIN
EMODINS
EMOJI
EMOJIS
EMOLLIATE
EMOLLIENT
EMOLUMENT
EMONG
EMONGES
EMONGEST
EMONGST
EMOS
EMOTE
EMOTED
EMOTER
EMOTERS
EMOTES
EMOTICON
EMOTICONS
EMOTING
EMOTION
EMOTIONAL
EMOTIONS
EMOTIVE
EMOTIVELY
EMOTIVISM
EMOTIVITY
EMOVE
EMOVED
EMOVES
EMOVING
EMPACKET
EMPACKETS
EMPAESTIC
EMPAIRE
EMPAIRED
EMPAIRES
EMPAIRING
EMPALE
EMPALED
EMPALER
EMPALERS
EMPALES
EMPALING
EMPANADA
EMPANADAS
EMPANEL
EMPANELED
EMPANELS
EMPANOPLY
EMPARE
EMPARED
EMPARES
EMPARING
EMPARL
EMPARLED
EMPARLING
EMPARLS
EMPART
EMPARTED
EMPARTING
EMPARTS
EMPATHIC
EMPATHIES
EMPATHISE
EMPATHIST
EMPATHIZE
EMPATHY
EMPATRON
EMPATRONS
EMPAYRE
EMPAYRED
EMPAYRES
EMPAYRING
EMPEACH
EMPEACHED
EMPEACHES
EMPENNAGE
EMPEOPLE
EMPEOPLED
EMPEOPLES
EMPERCE
EMPERCED
EMPERCES
EMPERCING
EMPERIES
EMPERISE
EMPERISED
EMPERISES
EMPERISH
EMPERIZE
EMPERIZED
EMPERIZES
EMPEROR
EMPERORS
EMPERY
EMPHASES
EMPHASIS
EMPHASISE
EMPHASIZE
EMPHATIC
EMPHATICS
EMPHLYSES
EMPHLYSIS
EMPHYSEMA
EMPIERCE
EMPIERCED
EMPIERCES
EMPIGHT
EMPIGHTED
EMPIGHTS
EMPIRE
EMPIRES
EMPIRIC
EMPIRICAL
EMPIRICS
EMPLACE
EMPLACED
EMPLACES
EMPLACING
EMPLANE
EMPLANED
EMPLANES
EMPLANING
EMPLASTER
EMPLASTIC
EMPLASTRA
EMPLEACH
EMPLECTON
EMPLECTUM
EMPLONGE
EMPLONGED
EMPLONGES
EMPLOY
EMPLOYE
EMPLOYED
EMPLOYEE
EMPLOYEES
EMPLOYER
EMPLOYERS
EMPLOYES
EMPLOYING
EMPLOYS
EMPLUME
EMPLUMED

EMPLUMES
EMPLUMING
EMPOISON
EMPOISONS
EMPOLDER
EMPOLDERS
EMPORIA
EMPORIUM
EMPORIUMS
EMPOWER
EMPOWERED
EMPOWERS
EMPRESS
EMPRESSE
EMPRESSES
EMPRISE
EMPRISES
EMPRIZE
EMPRIZES
EMPT
EMPTED
EMPTIABLE
EMPTIED
EMPTIER
EMPTIERS
EMPTIES
EMPTIEST
EMPTILY
EMPTINESS
EMPTING
EMPTINGS
EMPTINS
EMPTION
EMPTIONAL
EMPTIONS
EMPTS
EMPTY
EMPTYING
EMPTYINGS
EMPTYSES
EMPTYSIS
EMPURPLE
EMPURPLED
EMPURPLES
EMPUSA
EMPUSAS
EMPUSE
EMPUSES
EMPYEMA
EMPYEMAS
EMPYEMATA
EMPYEMIC
EMPYESES
EMPYESIS
EMPYREAL
EMPYREAN
EMPYREANS
EMPYREUMA
EMS
EMU
EMULATE
EMULATED
EMULATES
EMULATING
EMULATION
EMULATIVE
EMULATOR
EMULATORS
EMULE
EMULED
EMULES
EMULGE
EMULGED
EMULGENCE
EMULGENT
EMULGES
EMULGING
EMULING
EMULOUS
EMULOUSLY
EMULSIBLE
EMULSIFY
EMULSIN
EMULSINS
EMULSION
EMULSIONS
EMULSIVE
EMULSOID
EMULSOIDS
EMULSOR
EMULSORS
EMUNCTION
EMUNCTORY
EMUNGE
EMUNGED
EMUNGES
EMUNGING
EMURE
EMURED
EMURES
EMURING
EMUS
EMYD
EMYDE
EMYDES
EMYDS
EMYS
EN
ENABLE
ENABLED
ENABLER
ENABLERS
ENABLES
ENABLING
ENACT
ENACTABLE
ENACTED
ENACTING
ENACTION
ENACTIONS
ENACTIVE
ENACTMENT
ENACTOR
ENACTORS
ENACTORY
ENACTS
ENACTURE
ENACTURES
ENALAPRIL
ENALLAGE
ENALLAGES
ENAMEL
ENAMELED
ENAMELER
ENAMELERS
ENAMELING
ENAMELIST
ENAMELLED
ENAMELLER
ENAMELS
ENAMINE
ENAMINES
ENAMOR
ENAMORADO
ENAMORED
ENAMORING
ENAMORS
ENAMOUR
ENAMOURED
ENAMOURS
ENANTHEMA
ENARCH
ENARCHED
ENARCHES
ENARCHING
ENARGITE
ENARGITES
ENARM
ENARMED
ENARMING
ENARMS
ENATE
ENATES
ENATIC
ENATION
ENATIONS
ENAUNTER
ENCAENIA
ENCAENIAS
ENCAGE
ENCAGED
ENCAGES
ENCAGING
ENCALM
ENCALMED
ENCALMING
ENCALMS
ENCAMP
ENCAMPED
ENCAMPING
ENCAMPS
ENCANTHIS
ENCAPSULE
ENCARPUS
ENCASE
ENCASED
ENCASES
ENCASH
ENCASHED
ENCASHES
ENCASHING
ENCASING
ENCASTRE
ENCAUSTIC
ENCAVE
ENCAVED
ENCAVES
ENCAVING
ENCEINTE
ENCEINTES
ENCEPHALA
ENCHAFE
ENCHAFED
ENCHAFES
ENCHAFING
ENCHAIN
ENCHAINED
ENCHAINS
ENCHANT
ENCHANTED
ENCHANTER
ENCHANTS
ENCHARGE
ENCHARGED
ENCHARGES
ENCHARM
ENCHARMED
ENCHARMS
ENCHASE
ENCHASED
ENCHASER
ENCHASERS
ENCHASES
ENCHASING
ENCHEASON
ENCHEER
ENCHEERED
ENCHEERS
ENCHILADA
ENCHORIAL
ENCHORIC
ENCIERRO
ENCIERROS
ENCINA
ENCINAL
ENCINAS
ENCIPHER
ENCIPHERS
ENCIRCLE
ENCIRCLED

ENCIRCLES
ENCLASP
ENCLASPED
ENCLASPS
ENCLAVE
ENCLAVED
ENCLAVES
ENCLAVING
ENCLISES
ENCLISIS
ENCLITIC
ENCLITICS
ENCLOSE
ENCLOSED
ENCLOSER
ENCLOSERS
ENCLOSES
ENCLOSING
ENCLOSURE
ENCLOTHE
ENCLOTHED
ENCLOTHES
ENCLOUD
ENCLOUDED
ENCLOUDS
ENCODABLE
ENCODE
ENCODED
ENCODER
ENCODERS
ENCODES
ENCODING
ENCODINGS
ENCOLOUR
ENCOLOURS
ENCOLPIA
ENCOLPION
ENCOLPIUM
ENCOLURE
ENCOLURES
ENCOMIA
ENCOMIAST
ENCOMION
ENCOMIUM
ENCOMIUMS
ENCOMPASS
ENCORE
ENCORED
ENCORES
ENCORING
ENCOUNTER
ENCOURAGE
ENCRADLE
ENCRADLED
ENCRADLES
ENCRATIES
ENCRATY
ENCREASE
ENCREASED
ENCREASES
ENCRIMSON
ENCRINAL
ENCRINIC
ENCRINITE
ENCROACH
ENCRUST
ENCRUSTED
ENCRUSTS
ENCRYPT
ENCRYPTED
ENCRYPTS
ENCUMBER
ENCUMBERS
ENCURTAIN
ENCYCLIC
ENCYCLICS
ENCYST
ENCYSTED
ENCYSTING
ENCYSTS
END
ENDAMAGE
ENDAMAGED
ENDAMAGES
ENDAMEBA
ENDAMEBAE
ENDAMEBAS
ENDAMEBIC
ENDAMOEBA
ENDANGER
ENDANGERS
ENDARCH
ENDARCHY
ENDART
ENDARTED
ENDARTING
ENDARTS
ENDASH
ENDASHES
ENDBRAIN
ENDBRAINS
ENDCAP
ENDCAPS
ENDEAR
ENDEARED
ENDEARING
ENDEARS
ENDEAVOR
ENDEAVORS
ENDEAVOUR
ENDECAGON
ENDED
ENDEICTIC
ENDEIXES
ENDEIXIS
ENDEMIAL
ENDEMIC
ENDEMICAL
ENDEMICS
ENDEMISM
ENDEMISMS
ENDENIZEN
ENDER
ENDERMIC
ENDERON
ENDERONS
ENDERS
ENDEW
ENDEWED
ENDEWING
ENDEWS
ENDEXINE
ENDEXINES
ENDGAME
ENDGAMES
ENDGATE
ENDGATES
ENDING
ENDINGS
ENDIRON
ENDIRONS
ENDITE
ENDITED
ENDITES
ENDITING
ENDIVE
ENDIVES
ENDLANG
ENDLEAF
ENDLEAFS
ENDLEAVES
ENDLESS
ENDLESSLY
ENDLONG
ENDMOST
ENDNOTE
ENDNOTES
ENDOBLAST
ENDOCARP
ENDOCARPS
ENDOCAST
ENDOCASTS
ENDOCRINE
ENDOCYTIC
ENDODERM
ENDODERMS
ENDODYNE
ENDOERGIC
ENDOGAMIC
ENDOGAMY
ENDOGEN
ENDOGENIC
ENDOGENS
ENDOGENY
ENDOLYMPH
ENDOMIXES
ENDOMIXIS
ENDOMORPH
ENDOPHAGY
ENDOPHYTE
ENDOPLASM
ENDOPOD
ENDOPODS
ENDOPROCT
ENDORPHIN
ENDORSE
ENDORSED
ENDORSEE
ENDORSEES
ENDORSER
ENDORSERS
ENDORSES
ENDORSING
ENDORSIVE
ENDORSOR
ENDORSORS
ENDOSARC
ENDOSARCS
ENDOSCOPE
ENDOSCOPY
ENDOSMOS
ENDOSMOSE
ENDOSOME
ENDOSOMES
ENDOSPERM
ENDOSPORE
ENDOSS
ENDOSSED
ENDOSSES
ENDOSSING
ENDOSTEA
ENDOSTEAL
ENDOSTEUM
ENDOSTYLE
ENDOTHERM
ENDOTOXIC
ENDOTOXIN
ENDOW
ENDOWED
ENDOWER
ENDOWERS
ENDOWING
ENDOWMENT
ENDOWS
ENDOZOA
ENDOZOIC
ENDOZOON
ENDPAPER
ENDPAPERS
ENDPLATE
ENDPLATES
ENDPLAY
ENDPLAYED
ENDPLAYS
ENDPOINT
ENDPOINTS
ENDRIN
ENDRINS
ENDS
ENDSHIP

ENDSHIPS
ENDUE
ENDUED
ENDUES
ENDUING
ENDUNGEON
ENDURABLE
ENDURABLY
ENDURANCE
ENDURE
ENDURED
ENDURER
ENDURERS
ENDURES
ENDURING
ENDURO
ENDUROS
ENDWAYS
ENDWISE
ENDYSES
ENDYSIS
ENDZONE
ENDZONES
ENE
ENEMA
ENEMAS
ENEMATA
ENEMIES
ENEMY
ENERGETIC
ENERGIC
ENERGID
ENERGIDS
ENERGIES
ENERGISE
ENERGISED
ENERGISER
ENERGISES
ENERGIZE
ENERGIZED
ENERGIZER
ENERGIZES
ENERGUMEN
ENERGY
ENERVATE
ENERVATED
ENERVATES
ENERVATOR
ENERVE
ENERVED
ENERVES
ENERVING
ENES
ENEW
ENEWED
ENEWING
ENEWS
ENFACE
ENFACED
ENFACES
ENFACING
ENFANT
ENFANTS
ENFEEBLE
ENFEEBLED
ENFEEBLER
ENFEEBLES
ENFELON
ENFELONED
ENFELONS
ENFEOFF
ENFEOFFED
ENFEOFFS
ENFESTED
ENFETTER
ENFETTERS
ENFEVER
ENFEVERED
ENFEVERS
ENFIERCE
ENFIERCED
ENFIERCES
ENFILADE
ENFILADED
ENFILADES
ENFILED
ENFIRE
ENFIRED
ENFIRES
ENFIRING
ENFIX
ENFIXED
ENFIXES
ENFIXING
ENFLAME
ENFLAMED
ENFLAMES
ENFLAMING
ENFLESH
ENFLESHED
ENFLESHES
ENFLOWER
ENFLOWERS
ENFOLD
ENFOLDED
ENFOLDER
ENFOLDERS
ENFOLDING
ENFOLDS
ENFORCE
ENFORCED
ENFORCER
ENFORCERS
ENFORCES
ENFORCING
ENFOREST
ENFORESTS
ENFORM
ENFORMED
ENFORMING
ENFORMS
ENFRAME
ENFRAMED
ENFRAMES
ENFRAMING
ENFREE
ENFREED
ENFREEDOM
ENFREEING
ENFREES
ENFREEZE
ENFREEZES
ENFROSEN
ENFROZE
ENFROZEN
ENG
ENGAGE
ENGAGED
ENGAGEDLY
ENGAGEE
ENGAGER
ENGAGERS
ENGAGES
ENGAGING
ENGAOL
ENGAOLED
ENGAOLING
ENGAOLS
ENGARLAND
ENGENDER
ENGENDERS
ENGENDURE
ENGILD
ENGILDED
ENGILDING
ENGILDS
ENGILT
ENGINE
ENGINED
ENGINEER
ENGINEERS
ENGINER
ENGINERS
ENGINERY
ENGINES
ENGINING
ENGINOUS
ENGIRD
ENGIRDED
ENGIRDING
ENGIRDLE
ENGIRDLED
ENGIRDLES
ENGIRDS
ENGIRT
ENGLACIAL
ENGLISH
ENGLISHED
ENGLISHES
ENGLOBE
ENGLOBED
ENGLOBES
ENGLOBING
ENGLOOM
ENGLOOMED
ENGLOOMS
ENGLUT
ENGLUTS
ENGLUTTED
ENGOBE
ENGOBES
ENGORE
ENGORED
ENGORES
ENGORGE
ENGORGED
ENGORGES
ENGORGING
ENGORING
ENGOULED
ENGOUMENT
ENGRACE
ENGRACED
ENGRACES
ENGRACING
ENGRAFF
ENGRAFFED
ENGRAFFS
ENGRAFT
ENGRAFTED
ENGRAFTS
ENGRAIL
ENGRAILED
ENGRAILS
ENGRAIN
ENGRAINED
ENGRAINER
ENGRAINS
ENGRAM
ENGRAMMA
ENGRAMMAS
ENGRAMME
ENGRAMMES
ENGRAMMIC
ENGRAMS
ENGRASP
ENGRASPED
ENGRASPS
ENGRAVE
ENGRAVED
ENGRAVEN
ENGRAVER
ENGRAVERS
ENGRAVERY
ENGRAVES
ENGRAVING
ENGRENAGE
ENGRIEVE
ENGRIEVED
ENGRIEVES

ENGROOVE
ENGROOVED
ENGROOVES
ENGROSS
ENGROSSED
ENGROSSER
ENGROSSES
ENGS
ENGUARD
ENGUARDED
ENGUARDS
ENGULF
ENGULFED
ENGULFING
ENGULFS
ENGULPH
ENGULPHED
ENGULPHS
ENGYSCOPE
ENHALO
ENHALOED
ENHALOES
ENHALOING
ENHALOS
ENHANCE
ENHANCED
ENHANCER
ENHANCERS
ENHANCES
ENHANCING
ENHANCIVE
ENHEARSE
ENHEARSED
ENHEARSES
ENHEARTEN
ENHUNGER
ENHUNGERS
ENHYDRITE
ENHYDROS
ENHYDROUS
ENIAC
ENIACS
ENIGMA
ENIGMAS
ENIGMATA
ENIGMATIC
ENISLE
ENISLED
ENISLES
ENISLING
ENJAMB
ENJAMBED
ENJAMBING
ENJAMBS
ENJOIN
ENJOINDER
ENJOINED
ENJOINER
ENJOINERS
ENJOINING
ENJOINS
ENJOY
ENJOYABLE
ENJOYABLY
ENJOYED
ENJOYER
ENJOYERS
ENJOYING
ENJOYMENT
ENJOYS
ENKERNEL
ENKERNELS
ENKINDLE
ENKINDLED
ENKINDLER
ENKINDLES
ENLACE
ENLACED
ENLACES
ENLACING
ENLARD
ENLARDED
ENLARDING
ENLARDS
ENLARGE
ENLARGED
ENLARGEN
ENLARGENS
ENLARGER
ENLARGERS
ENLARGES
ENLARGING
ENLEVE
ENLIGHT
ENLIGHTED
ENLIGHTEN
ENLIGHTS
ENLINK
ENLINKED
ENLINKING
ENLINKS
ENLIST
ENLISTED
ENLISTEE
ENLISTEES
ENLISTER
ENLISTERS
ENLISTING
ENLISTS
ENLIT
ENLIVEN
ENLIVENED
ENLIVENER
ENLIVENS
ENLOCK
ENLOCKED
ENLOCKING
ENLOCKS
ENLUMINE
ENLUMINED
ENLUMINES
ENMESH
ENMESHED
ENMESHES
ENMESHING
ENMEW
ENMEWED
ENMEWING
ENMEWS
ENMITIES
ENMITY
ENMOSSED
ENMOVE
ENMOVED
ENMOVES
ENMOVING
ENNAGE
ENNAGES
ENNEAD
ENNEADIC
ENNEADS
ENNEAGON
ENNEAGONS
ENNEAGRAM
ENNOBLE
ENNOBLED
ENNOBLER
ENNOBLERS
ENNOBLES
ENNOBLING
ENNOG
ENNOGS
ENNUI
ENNUIED
ENNUIS
ENNUYE
ENNUYED
ENNUYEE
ENNUYING
ENODAL
ENOKI
ENOKIDAKE
ENOKIS
ENOKITAKE
ENOL
ENOLASE
ENOLASES
ENOLIC
ENOLOGIES
ENOLOGIST
ENOLOGY
ENOLS
ENOMOTIES
ENOMOTY
ENOPHILE
ENOPHILES
ENORM
ENORMITY
ENORMOUS
ENOSES
ENOSIS
ENOSISES
ENOUGH
ENOUGHS
ENOUNCE
ENOUNCED
ENOUNCES
ENOUNCING
ENOW
ENOWS
ENPLANE
ENPLANED
ENPLANES
ENPLANING
ENPRINT
ENPRINTS
ENQUEUE
ENQUEUED
ENQUEUES
ENQUEUING
ENQUIRE
ENQUIRED
ENQUIRER
ENQUIRERS
ENQUIRES
ENQUIRIES
ENQUIRING
ENQUIRY
ENRACE
ENRACED
ENRACES
ENRACING
ENRAGE
ENRAGED
ENRAGEDLY
ENRAGES
ENRAGING
ENRANCKLE
ENRANGE
ENRANGED
ENRANGES
ENRANGING
ENRANK
ENRANKED
ENRANKING
ENRANKS
ENRAPT
ENRAPTURE
ENRAUNGE
ENRAUNGED
ENRAUNGES
ENRAVISH
ENRHEUM
ENRHEUMED
ENRHEUMS
ENRICH
ENRICHED
ENRICHER
ENRICHERS
ENRICHES

ENRICHING
ENRIDGED
ENRING
ENRINGED
ENRINGING
ENRINGS
ENRIVEN
ENROBE
ENROBED
ENROBER
ENROBERS
ENROBES
ENROBING
ENROL
ENROLL
ENROLLED
ENROLLEE
ENROLLEES
ENROLLER
ENROLLERS
ENROLLING
ENROLLS
ENROLMENT
ENROLS
ENROOT
ENROOTED
ENROOTING
ENROOTS
ENROUGH
ENROUGHED
ENROUGHS
ENROUND
ENROUNDED
ENROUNDS
ENS
ENSAMPLE
ENSAMPLED
ENSAMPLES
ENSATE
ENSCONCE
ENSCONCED
ENSCONCES
ENSCROLL
ENSCROLLS
ENSEAL
ENSEALED
ENSEALING
ENSEALS
ENSEAM
ENSEAMED
ENSEAMING
ENSEAMS
ENSEAR
ENSEARED
ENSEARING
ENSEARS
ENSEMBLE
ENSEMBLES
ENSERF
ENSERFED
ENSERFING
ENSERFS
ENSEW
ENSEWED
ENSEWING
ENSEWS
ENSHEATH
ENSHEATHE
ENSHEATHS
ENSHELL
ENSHELLED
ENSHELLS
ENSHELTER
ENSHIELD
ENSHIELDS
ENSHRINE
ENSHRINED
ENSHRINEE
ENSHRINES
ENSHROUD
ENSHROUDS
ENSIFORM
ENSIGN
ENSIGNCY
ENSIGNED
ENSIGNING
ENSIGNS
ENSILAGE
ENSILAGED
ENSILAGES
ENSILE
ENSILED
ENSILES
ENSILING
ENSKIED
ENSKIES
ENSKY
ENSKYED
ENSKYING
ENSLAVE
ENSLAVED
ENSLAVER
ENSLAVERS
ENSLAVES
ENSLAVING
ENSNARE
ENSNARED
ENSNARER
ENSNARERS
ENSNARES
ENSNARING
ENSNARL
ENSNARLED
ENSNARLS
ENSORCEL
ENSORCELL
ENSORCELS
ENSOUL
ENSOULED
ENSOULING
ENSOULS
ENSPHERE
ENSPHERED
ENSPHERES
ENSTAMP
ENSTAMPED
ENSTAMPS
ENSTATITE
ENSTEEP
ENSTEEPED
ENSTEEPS
ENSTYLE
ENSTYLED
ENSTYLES
ENSTYLING
ENSUE
ENSUED
ENSUES
ENSUING
ENSUITE
ENSUITES
ENSURE
ENSURED
ENSURER
ENSURERS
ENSURES
ENSURING
ENSWATHE
ENSWATHED
ENSWATHES
ENSWEEP
ENSWEEPS
ENSWEPT
ENTAIL
ENTAILED
ENTAILER
ENTAILERS
ENTAILING
ENTAILS
ENTAME
ENTAMEBA
ENTAMEBAE
ENTAMEBAS
ENTAMED
ENTAMES
ENTAMING
ENTAMOEBA
ENTANGLE
ENTANGLED
ENTANGLER
ENTANGLES
ENTASES
ENTASIA
ENTASIAS
ENTASIS
ENTASTIC
ENTAYLE
ENTAYLED
ENTAYLES
ENTAYLING
ENTELECHY
ENTELLUS
ENTENDER
ENTENDERS
ENTENTE
ENTENTES
ENTER
ENTERA
ENTERABLE
ENTERAL
ENTERALLY
ENTERATE
ENTERED
ENTERER
ENTERERS
ENTERIC
ENTERICS
ENTERING
ENTERINGS
ENTERITIS
ENTERON
ENTERONS
ENTERS
ENTERTAIN
ENTERTAKE
ENTERTOOK
ENTETE
ENTETEE
ENTHALPY
ENTHETIC
ENTHRAL
ENTHRALL
ENTHRALLS
ENTHRALS
ENTHRONE
ENTHRONED
ENTHRONES
ENTHUSE
ENTHUSED
ENTHUSES
ENTHUSING
ENTHYMEME
ENTIA
ENTICE
ENTICED
ENTICER
ENTICERS
ENTICES
ENTICING
ENTICINGS
ENTIRE
ENTIRELY
ENTIRES
ENTIRETY
ENTITIES
ENTITLE
ENTITLED
ENTITLES
ENTITLING
ENTITY

ENTOBLAST
ENTODERM
ENTODERMS
ENTOIL
ENTOILED
ENTOILING
ENTOILS
ENTOMB
ENTOMBED
ENTOMBING
ENTOMBS
ENTOMIC
ENTOPHYTE
ENTOPIC
ENTOPROCT
ENTOPTIC
ENTOPTICS
ENTOTIC
ENTOURAGE
ENTOZOA
ENTOZOAL
ENTOZOAN
ENTOZOANS
ENTOZOIC
ENTOZOON
ENTRAIL
ENTRAILED
ENTRAILS
ENTRAIN
ENTRAINED
ENTRAINER
ENTRAINS
ENTRALL
ENTRALLES
ENTRAMMEL
ENTRANCE
ENTRANCED
ENTRANCES
ENTRANT
ENTRANTS
ENTRAP
ENTRAPPED
ENTRAPPER
ENTRAPS
ENTREAT
ENTREATED
ENTREATS
ENTREATY
ENTRECHAT
ENTRECOTE
ENTREE
ENTREES
ENTREMES
ENTREMETS
ENTRENCH
ENTREPOT
ENTREPOTS
ENTRESOL
ENTRESOLS
ENTREZ
ENTRIES
ENTRISM
ENTRISMS
ENTRIST
ENTRISTS
ENTROLD
ENTROPIC
ENTROPIES
ENTROPION
ENTROPIUM
ENTROPY
ENTRUST
ENTRUSTED
ENTRUSTS
ENTRY
ENTRYISM
ENTRYISMS
ENTRYIST
ENTRYISTS
ENTRYWAY
ENTRYWAYS
ENTS
ENTWINE
ENTWINED
ENTWINES
ENTWINING
ENTWIST
ENTWISTED
ENTWISTS
ENUCLEATE
ENUF
ENUMERATE
ENUNCIATE
ENURE
ENURED
ENUREMENT
ENURES
ENURESES
ENURESIS
ENURETIC
ENURETICS
ENURING
ENURN
ENURNED
ENURNING
ENURNS
ENVASSAL
ENVASSALS
ENVAULT
ENVAULTED
ENVAULTS
ENVEIGLE
ENVEIGLED
ENVEIGLES
ENVELOP
ENVELOPE
ENVELOPED
ENVELOPER
ENVELOPES
ENVELOPS
ENVENOM
ENVENOMED
ENVENOMS
ENVERMEIL
ENVIABLE
ENVIABLY
ENVIED
ENVIER
ENVIERS
ENVIES
ENVIOUS
ENVIOUSLY
ENVIRO
ENVIRON
ENVIRONED
ENVIRONS
ENVIROS
ENVISAGE
ENVISAGED
ENVISAGES
ENVISION
ENVISIONS
ENVOI
ENVOIS
ENVOY
ENVOYS
ENVOYSHIP
ENVY
ENVYING
ENVYINGLY
ENVYINGS
ENWALL
ENWALLED
ENWALLING
ENWALLOW
ENWALLOWS
ENWALLS
ENWHEEL
ENWHEELED
ENWHEELS
ENWIND
ENWINDING
ENWINDS
ENWOMB
ENWOMBED
ENWOMBING
ENWOMBS
ENWOUND
ENWRAP
ENWRAPPED
ENWRAPS
ENWRAPT
ENWREATH
ENWREATHE
ENWREATHS
ENZIAN
ENZIANS
ENZONE
ENZONED
ENZONES
ENZONING
ENZOOTIC
ENZOOTICS
ENZYM
ENZYMATIC
ENZYME
ENZYMES
ENZYMIC
ENZYMS
EOAN
EOBIONT
EOBIONTS
EOCENE
EOHIPPUS
EOLIAN
EOLIENNE
EOLIENNES
EOLIPILE
EOLIPILES
EOLITH
EOLITHIC
EOLITHS
EOLOPILE
EOLOPILES
EON
EONIAN
EONISM
EONISMS
EONS
EORL
EORLS
EOSIN
EOSINE
EOSINES
EOSINIC
EOSINS
EOTHEN
EPACRID
EPACRIDS
EPACRIS
EPACRISES
EPACT
EPACTS
EPAENETIC
EPAGOGE
EPAGOGES
EPAGOGIC
EPANODOS
EPARCH
EPARCHATE
EPARCHIAL
EPARCHIES
EPARCHS
EPARCHY
EPATANT
EPATER
EPATERED
EPATERING
EPATERS
EPAULE

EPAULES
EPAULET
EPAULETED
EPAULETS
EPAULETTE
EPAXIAL
EPAZOTE
EPAZOTES
EPEDAPHIC
EPEE
EPEEIST
EPEEISTS
EPEES
EPEIRA
EPEIRAS
EPEIRIC
EPEIRID
EPEIRIDS
EPENDYMA
EPENDYMAL
EPENDYMAS
EPEOLATRY
EPERDU
EPERDUE
EPERGNE
EPERGNES
EPHA
EPHAH
EPHAHS
EPHAS
EPHEBE
EPHEBES
EPHEBI
EPHEBIC
EPHEBOI
EPHEBOS
EPHEBUS
EPHEDRA
EPHEDRAS
EPHEDRIN
EPHEDRINE
EPHEDRINS
EPHELIDES
EPHELIS
EPHEMERA
EPHEMERAE
EPHEMERAL
EPHEMERAS
EPHEMERID
EPHEMERIS
EPHEMERON
EPHIALTES
EPHOD
EPHODS
EPHOR
EPHORAL
EPHORALTY
EPHORATE
EPHORATES
EPHORI
EPHORS
EPIBIOSES
EPIBIOSIS
EPIBIOTIC
EPIBLAST
EPIBLASTS
EPIBLEM
EPIBLEMS
EPIBOLIC
EPIBOLIES
EPIBOLY
EPIC
EPICAL
EPICALLY
EPICALYX
EPICANTHI
EPICARDIA
EPICARP
EPICARPS
EPICEDE
EPICEDES
EPICEDIA
EPICEDIAL
EPICEDIAN
EPICEDIUM
EPICENE
EPICENES
EPICENISM
EPICENTER
EPICENTRA
EPICENTRE
EPICIER
EPICIERS
EPICISM
EPICISMS
EPICIST
EPICISTS
EPICLESES
EPICLESIS
EPICLIKE
EPICORMIC
EPICOTYL
EPICOTYLS
EPICRANIA
EPICRISES
EPICRISIS
EPICRITIC
EPICS
EPICURE
EPICUREAN
EPICURES
EPICURISE
EPICURISM
EPICURIZE
EPICYCLE
EPICYCLES
EPICYCLIC
EPIDEMIC
EPIDEMICS
EPIDERM
EPIDERMAL
EPIDERMIC
EPIDERMIS
EPIDERMS
EPIDICTIC
EPIDOSITE
EPIDOTE
EPIDOTES
EPIDOTIC
EPIDURAL
EPIDURALS
EPIFAUNA
EPIFAUNAE
EPIFAUNAL
EPIFAUNAS
EPIFOCAL
EPIGAEAL
EPIGAEAN
EPIGAEOUS
EPIGAMIC
EPIGEAL
EPIGEAN
EPIGEIC
EPIGENE
EPIGENIC
EPIGENIST
EPIGENOME
EPIGENOUS
EPIGEOUS
EPIGON
EPIGONE
EPIGONES
EPIGONI
EPIGONIC
EPIGONISM
EPIGONOUS
EPIGONS
EPIGONUS
EPIGRAM
EPIGRAMS
EPIGRAPH
EPIGRAPHS
EPIGRAPHY
EPIGYNIES
EPIGYNOUS
EPIGYNY
EPILATE
EPILATED
EPILATES
EPILATING
EPILATION
EPILATOR
EPILATORS
EPILEPSY
EPILEPTIC
EPILIMNIA
EPILITHIC
EPILOBIUM
EPILOG
EPILOGIC
EPILOGISE
EPILOGIST
EPILOGIZE
EPILOGS
EPILOGUE
EPILOGUED
EPILOGUES
EPIMER
EPIMERASE
EPIMERE
EPIMERES
EPIMERIC
EPIMERISE
EPIMERISM
EPIMERIZE
EPIMERS
EPIMYSIA
EPIMYSIUM
EPINAOI
EPINAOS
EPINASTIC
EPINASTY
EPINEURAL
EPINEURIA
EPINICIAN
EPINICION
EPINIKIAN
EPINIKION
EPINOSIC
EPIPHANIC
EPIPHANY
EPIPHRAGM
EPIPHYSES
EPIPHYSIS
EPIPHYTAL
EPIPHYTE
EPIPHYTES
EPIPHYTIC
EPIPLOA
EPIPLOIC
EPIPLOON
EPIPLOONS
EPIPOLIC
EPIPOLISM
EPIROGENY
EPIRRHEMA
EPISCIA
EPISCIAS
EPISCOPAL
EPISCOPE
EPISCOPES
EPISCOPY
EPISEMON
EPISEMONS
EPISODAL
EPISODE
EPISODES
EPISODIAL
EPISODIC
EPISOMAL

EPISOME
EPISOMES
EPISPERM
EPISPERMS
EPISPORE
EPISPORES
EPISTASES
EPISTASIS
EPISTASY
EPISTATIC
EPISTAXES
EPISTAXIS
EPISTEMIC
EPISTERNA
EPISTLE
EPISTLED
EPISTLER
EPISTLERS
EPISTLES
EPISTLING
EPISTOLER
EPISTOLET
EPISTOLIC
EPISTOME
EPISTOMES
EPISTYLE
EPISTYLES
EPITAPH
EPITAPHED
EPITAPHER
EPITAPHIC
EPITAPHS
EPITASES
EPITASIS
EPITAXES
EPITAXIAL
EPITAXIC
EPITAXIES
EPITAXIS
EPITAXY
EPITHECA
EPITHECAE
EPITHELIA
EPITHEM
EPITHEMA
EPITHEMS
EPITHESES
EPITHESIS
EPITHET
EPITHETED
EPITHETIC
EPITHETON
EPITHETS
EPITOME
EPITOMES
EPITOMIC
EPITOMISE
EPITOMIST
EPITOMIZE
EPITONIC
EPITOPE
EPITOPES
EPITRITE
EPITRITES
EPIZEUXES
EPIZEUXIS
EPIZOA
EPIZOAN
EPIZOANS
EPIZOIC
EPIZOISM
EPIZOISMS
EPIZOITE
EPIZOITES
EPIZOON
EPIZOOTIC
EPIZOOTY
EPOCH
EPOCHA
EPOCHAL
EPOCHALLY
EPOCHAS
EPOCHS
EPODE
EPODES
EPODIC
EPONYM
EPONYMIC
EPONYMIES
EPONYMOUS
EPONYMS
EPONYMY
EPOPEE
EPOPEES
EPOPOEIA
EPOPOEIAS
EPOPT
EPOPTS
EPOS
EPOSES
EPOXIDE
EPOXIDES
EPOXIDISE
EPOXIDIZE
EPOXIED
EPOXIES
EPOXY
EPOXYED
EPOXYING
EPRIS
EPRISE
EPSILON
EPSILONIC
EPSILONS
EPSOMITE
EPSOMITES
EPUISE
EPUISEE
EPULARY
EPULATION
EPULIDES
EPULIS
EPULISES
EPULOTIC
EPULOTICS
EPURATE
EPURATED
EPURATES
EPURATING
EPURATION
EPYLLIA
EPYLLION
EPYLLIONS
EQUABLE
EQUABLY
EQUAL
EQUALED
EQUALI
EQUALING
EQUALISE
EQUALISED
EQUALISER
EQUALISES
EQUALITY
EQUALIZE
EQUALIZED
EQUALIZER
EQUALIZES
EQUALLED
EQUALLING
EQUALLY
EQUALNESS
EQUALS
EQUANT
EQUANTS
EQUATABLE
EQUATE
EQUATED
EQUATES
EQUATING
EQUATION
EQUATIONS
EQUATIVE
EQUATOR
EQUATORS
EQUERRIES
EQUERRY
EQUES
EQUID
EQUIDS
EQUIFINAL
EQUIMOLAL
EQUIMOLAR
EQUINAL
EQUINE
EQUINELY
EQUINES
EQUINIA
EQUINIAS
EQUINITY
EQUINOX
EQUINOXES
EQUIP
EQUIPAGE
EQUIPAGED
EQUIPAGES
EQUIPE
EQUIPES
EQUIPMENT
EQUIPOISE
EQUIPPED
EQUIPPER
EQUIPPERS
EQUIPPING
EQUIPS
EQUISETA
EQUISETIC
EQUISETUM
EQUITABLE
EQUITABLY
EQUITANT
EQUITES
EQUITIES
EQUITY
EQUIVALVE
EQUIVOCAL
EQUIVOKE
EQUIVOKES
EQUIVOQUE
ER
ERA
ERADIATE
ERADIATED
ERADIATES
ERADICANT
ERADICATE
ERAS
ERASABLE
ERASE
ERASED
ERASEMENT
ERASER
ERASERS
ERASES
ERASING
ERASION
ERASIONS
ERASURE
ERASURES
ERATHEM
ERATHEMS
ERBIA
ERBIAS
ERBIUM
ERBIUMS
ERE
ERECT
ERECTABLE
ERECTED
ERECTER

ERECTERS
ERECTILE
ERECTING
ERECTION
ERECTIONS
ERECTIVE
ERECTLY
ERECTNESS
ERECTOR
ERECTORS
ERECTS
ERED
ERELONG
EREMIC
EREMITAL
EREMITE
EREMITES
EREMITIC
EREMITISH
EREMITISM
EREMURI
EREMURUS
ERENOW
EREPSIN
EREPSINS
ERES
ERETHIC
ERETHISM
ERETHISMS
ERETHITIC
EREV
EREVS
EREWHILE
EREWHILES
ERF
ERG
ERGASTIC
ERGATANER
ERGATE
ERGATES
ERGATIVE
ERGATIVES
ERGATOID
ERGATOIDS
ERGO
ERGODIC
ERGOGENIC
ERGOGRAM
ERGOGRAMS
ERGOGRAPH
ERGOMANIA
ERGOMETER
ERGOMETRY
ERGON
ERGONOMIC
ERGONS
ERGOS
ERGOT
ERGOTIC
ERGOTISE
ERGOTISED
ERGOTISES
ERGOTISM
ERGOTISMS
ERGOTIZE
ERGOTIZED
ERGOTIZES
ERGOTS
ERGS
ERHU
ERHUS
ERIACH
ERIACHS
ERIC
ERICA
ERICAS
ERICK
ERICKS
ERICOID
ERICS
ERIGERON
ERIGERONS
ERING
ERINGO
ERINGOES
ERINGOS
ERINITE
ERINITES
ERINUS
ERINUSES
ERIOMETER
ERIONITE
ERIONITES
ERIOPHYID
ERISTIC
ERISTICAL
ERISTICS
ERK
ERKS
ERLANG
ERLANGS
ERLKING
ERLKINGS
ERM
ERMELIN
ERMELINS
ERMINE
ERMINED
ERMINES
ERN
ERNE
ERNED
ERNES
ERNING
ERNS
ERODABLE
ERODE
ERODED
ERODENT
ERODENTS
ERODES
ERODIBLE
ERODING
ERODIUM
ERODIUMS
EROGENIC
EROGENOUS
EROS
EROSE
EROSELY
EROSES
EROSIBLE
EROSION
EROSIONAL
EROSIONS
EROSIVE
EROSIVITY
EROSTRATE
EROTEMA
EROTEMAS
EROTEME
EROTEMES
EROTESES
EROTESIS
EROTETIC
EROTIC
EROTICA
EROTICAL
EROTICAS
EROTICISE
EROTICISM
EROTICIST
EROTICIZE
EROTICS
EROTISE
EROTISED
EROTISES
EROTISING
EROTISM
EROTISMS
EROTIZE
EROTIZED
EROTIZES
EROTIZING
EROTOLOGY
ERR
ERRABLE
ERRANCIES
ERRANCY
ERRAND
ERRANDS
ERRANT
ERRANTLY
ERRANTRY
ERRANTS
ERRATA
ERRATAS
ERRATIC
ERRATICAL
ERRATICS
ERRATUM
ERRED
ERRHINE
ERRHINES
ERRING
ERRINGLY
ERRINGS
ERRONEOUS
ERROR
ERRORIST
ERRORISTS
ERRORLESS
ERRORS
ERRS
ERS
ERSATZ
ERSATZES
ERSES
ERST
ERSTWHILE
ERUCIC
ERUCIFORM
ERUCT
ERUCTATE
ERUCTATED
ERUCTATES
ERUCTED
ERUCTING
ERUCTS
ERUDITE
ERUDITELY
ERUDITES
ERUDITION
ERUGO
ERUGOS
ERUMPENT
ERUPT
ERUPTED
ERUPTIBLE
ERUPTING
ERUPTION
ERUPTIONS
ERUPTIVE
ERUPTIVES
ERUPTS
ERUV
ERUVIM
ERUVIN
ERUVS
ERVALENTA
ERVEN
ERVIL
ERVILS
ERYNGIUM
ERYNGIUMS
ERYNGO
ERYNGOES
ERYNGOS
ERYTHEMA
ERYTHEMAL

ERYTHEMAS
ERYTHEMIC
ERYTHRINA
ERYTHRISM
ERYTHRITE
ERYTHROID
ERYTHRON
ERYTHRONS
ES
ESCABECHE
ESCALADE
ESCALADED
ESCALADER
ESCALADES
ESCALADO
ESCALATE
ESCALATED
ESCALATES
ESCALATOR
ESCALIER
ESCALIERS
ESCALLOP
ESCALLOPS
ESCALOP
ESCALOPE
ESCALOPED
ESCALOPES
ESCALOPS
ESCAPABLE
ESCAPADE
ESCAPADES
ESCAPADO
ESCAPADOS
ESCAPE
ESCAPED
ESCAPEE
ESCAPEES
ESCAPER
ESCAPERS
ESCAPES
ESCAPING
ESCAPISM
ESCAPISMS
ESCAPIST
ESCAPISTS
ESCAR
ESCARGOT
ESCARGOTS
ESCAROLE
ESCAROLES
ESCARP
ESCARPED
ESCARPING
ESCARPS
ESCARS
ESCHALOT
ESCHALOTS
ESCHAR
ESCHARS
ESCHEAT
ESCHEATED
ESCHEATOR
ESCHEATS
ESCHEW
ESCHEWAL
ESCHEWALS
ESCHEWED
ESCHEWER
ESCHEWERS
ESCHEWING
ESCHEWS
ESCLANDRE
ESCOLAR
ESCOLARS
ESCOPETTE
ESCORT
ESCORTAGE
ESCORTED
ESCORTING
ESCORTS
ESCOT
ESCOTED
ESCOTING
ESCOTS
ESCOTTED
ESCOTTING
ESCRIBANO
ESCRIBE
ESCRIBED
ESCRIBES
ESCRIBING
ESCROC
ESCROCS
ESCROL
ESCROLL
ESCROLLS
ESCROLS
ESCROW
ESCROWED
ESCROWING
ESCROWS
ESCUAGE
ESCUAGES
ESCUDO
ESCUDOS
ESCULENT
ESCULENTS
ESEMPLASY
ESERINE
ESERINES
ESES
ESILE
ESILES
ESKAR
ESKARS
ESKER
ESKERS
ESKIES
ESKY
ESLOIN
ESLOINED
ESLOINING
ESLOINS
ESLOYNE
ESLOYNED
ESLOYNES
ESLOYNING
ESNE
ESNECIES
ESNECY
ESNES
ESOPHAGI
ESOPHAGUS
ESOTERIC
ESOTERICA
ESOTERIES
ESOTERISM
ESOTERY
ESOTROPIA
ESOTROPIC
ESPADA
ESPADAS
ESPAGNOLE
ESPALIER
ESPALIERS
ESPANOL
ESPANOLES
ESPARTO
ESPARTOS
ESPECIAL
ESPERANCE
ESPIAL
ESPIALS
ESPIED
ESPIEGLE
ESPIER
ESPIERS
ESPIES
ESPIONAGE
ESPLANADE
ESPOIR
ESPOIRS
ESPOUSAL
ESPOUSALS
ESPOUSE
ESPOUSED
ESPOUSER
ESPOUSERS
ESPOUSES
ESPOUSING
ESPRESSO
ESPRESSOS
ESPRIT
ESPRITS
ESPUMOSO
ESPUMOSOS
ESPY
ESPYING
ESQUIRE
ESQUIRED
ESQUIRES
ESQUIRESS
ESQUIRING
ESQUISSE
ESQUISSES
ESS
ESSAY
ESSAYED
ESSAYER
ESSAYERS
ESSAYETTE
ESSAYING
ESSAYISH
ESSAYIST
ESSAYISTS
ESSAYS
ESSE
ESSENCE
ESSENCES
ESSENTIAL
ESSES
ESSIVE
ESSIVES
ESSOIN
ESSOINED
ESSOINER
ESSOINERS
ESSOINING
ESSOINS
ESSONITE
ESSONITES
ESSOYNE
ESSOYNES
EST
ESTABLISH
ESTACADE
ESTACADES
ESTAFETTE
ESTAMINET
ESTANCIA
ESTANCIAS
ESTATE
ESTATED
ESTATES
ESTATING
ESTEEM
ESTEEMED
ESTEEMING
ESTEEMS
ESTER
ESTERASE
ESTERASES
ESTERIFY
ESTERS
ESTHESES
ESTHESIA
ESTHESIAS
ESTHESIS
ESTHETE
ESTHETES

E

ESTHETIC
ESTHETICS
ESTIMABLE
ESTIMABLY
ESTIMATE
ESTIMATED
ESTIMATES
ESTIMATOR
ESTIVAL
ESTIVATE
ESTIVATED
ESTIVATES
ESTIVATOR
ESTOC
ESTOCS
ESTOILE
ESTOILES
ESTOP
ESTOPPAGE
ESTOPPED
ESTOPPEL
ESTOPPELS
ESTOPPING
ESTOPS
ESTOVER
ESTOVERS
ESTRADE
ESTRADES
ESTRADIOL
ESTRAGON
ESTRAGONS
ESTRAL
ESTRANGE
ESTRANGED
ESTRANGER
ESTRANGES
ESTRAPADE
ESTRAY
ESTRAYED
ESTRAYING
ESTRAYS
ESTREAT
ESTREATED
ESTREATS
ESTREPE
ESTREPED
ESTREPES
ESTREPING
ESTRICH
ESTRICHES
ESTRIDGE
ESTRIDGES
ESTRILDID
ESTRIN
ESTRINS
ESTRIOL
ESTRIOLS
ESTRO
ESTROGEN
ESTROGENS
ESTRONE
ESTRONES
ESTROS
ESTROUS
ESTRUAL
ESTRUM
ESTRUMS
ESTRUS
ESTRUSES
ESTS
ESTUARIAL
ESTUARIAN
ESTUARIES
ESTUARINE
ESTUARY
ESURIENCE
ESURIENCY
ESURIENT
ET
ETA
ETACISM
ETACISMS
ETAERIO
ETAERIOS
ETAGE
ETAGERE
ETAGERES
ETAGES
ETALAGE
ETALAGES
ETALON
ETALONS
ETAMIN
ETAMINE
ETAMINES
ETAMINS
ETAPE
ETAPES
ETAS
ETAT
ETATISM
ETATISME
ETATISMES
ETATISMS
ETATIST
ETATISTE
ETATISTES
ETATS
ETCETERA
ETCETERAS
ETCH
ETCHANT
ETCHANTS
ETCHED
ETCHER
ETCHERS
ETCHES
ETCHING
ETCHINGS
ETEN
ETENS
ETERNAL
ETERNALLY
ETERNALS
ETERNE
ETERNISE
ETERNISED
ETERNISES
ETERNITY
ETERNIZE
ETERNIZED
ETERNIZES
ETESIAN
ETESIANS
ETH
ETHAL
ETHALS
ETHANAL
ETHANALS
ETHANE
ETHANES
ETHANOATE
ETHANOIC
ETHANOL
ETHANOLS
ETHANOYL
ETHANOYLS
ETHE
ETHENE
ETHENES
ETHEPHON
ETHEPHONS
ETHER
ETHERCAP
ETHERCAPS
ETHEREAL
ETHEREOUS
ETHERIAL
ETHERIC
ETHERICAL
ETHERIFY
ETHERION
ETHERIONS
ETHERISE
ETHERISED
ETHERISER
ETHERISES
ETHERISH
ETHERISM
ETHERISMS
ETHERIST
ETHERISTS
ETHERIZE
ETHERIZED
ETHERIZER
ETHERIZES
ETHERS
ETHIC
ETHICAL
ETHICALLY
ETHICALS
ETHICIAN
ETHICIANS
ETHICISE
ETHICISED
ETHICISES
ETHICISM
ETHICISMS
ETHICIST
ETHICISTS
ETHICIZE
ETHICIZED
ETHICIZES
ETHICS
ETHINYL
ETHINYLS
ETHION
ETHIONINE
ETHIONS
ETHIOPS
ETHIOPSES
ETHMOID
ETHMOIDAL
ETHMOIDS
ETHNARCH
ETHNARCHS
ETHNARCHY
ETHNE
ETHNIC
ETHNICAL
ETHNICISM
ETHNICITY
ETHNICS
ETHNOCIDE
ETHNOGENY
ETHNOLOGY
ETHNONYM
ETHNONYMS
ETHNOS
ETHNOSES
ETHOGRAM
ETHOGRAMS
ETHOLOGIC
ETHOLOGY
ETHONONE
ETHONONES
ETHOS
ETHOSES
ETHOXIDE
ETHOXIDES
ETHOXIES
ETHOXY
ETHOXYL
ETHOXYLS
ETHS
ETHYL
ETHYLATE
ETHYLATED
ETHYLATES
ETHYLENE

ETHYLENES
ETHYLENIC
ETHYLIC
ETHYLS
ETHYNE
ETHYNES
ETHYNYL
ETHYNYLS
ETIC
ETICS
ETIOLATE
ETIOLATED
ETIOLATES
ETIOLIN
ETIOLINS
ETIOLOGIC
ETIOLOGY
ETIQUETTE
ETNA
ETNAS
ETOILE
ETOILES
ETOUFFEE
ETOUFFEES
ETOURDI
ETOURDIE
ETRANGER
ETRANGERE
ETRANGERS
ETRENNE
ETRENNES
ETRIER
ETRIERS
ETTERCAP
ETTERCAPS
ETTIN
ETTINS
ETTLE
ETTLED
ETTLES
ETTLING
ETUDE
ETUDES
ETUI
ETUIS
ETWEE
ETWEES
ETYMA
ETYMIC
ETYMOLOGY
ETYMON
ETYMONS
ETYPIC
ETYPICAL
EUCAIN
EUCAINE
EUCAINES
EUCAINS
EUCALYPT
EUCALYPTI
EUCALYPTS
EUCARYON
EUCARYONS
EUCARYOT
EUCARYOTE
EUCARYOTS
EUCHARIS
EUCHLORIC
EUCHLORIN
EUCHOLOGY
EUCHRE
EUCHRED
EUCHRES
EUCHRING
EUCLASE
EUCLASES
EUCLIDEAN
EUCLIDIAN
EUCRITE
EUCRITES
EUCRITIC
EUCRYPHIA
EUCYCLIC
EUDAEMON
EUDAEMONS
EUDAEMONY
EUDAIMON
EUDAIMONS
EUDEMON
EUDEMONIA
EUDEMONIC
EUDEMONS
EUDIALYTE
EUGARIE
EUGARIES
EUGE
EUGENIA
EUGENIAS
EUGENIC
EUGENICAL
EUGENICS
EUGENISM
EUGENISMS
EUGENIST
EUGENISTS
EUGENOL
EUGENOLS
EUGH
EUGHEN
EUGHS
EUGLENA
EUGLENAS
EUGLENID
EUGLENIDS
EUGLENOID
EUK
EUKARYON
EUKARYONS
EUKARYOT
EUKARYOTE
EUKARYOTS
EUKED
EUKING
EUKS
EULACHAN
EULACHANS
EULACHON
EULACHONS
EULOGIA
EULOGIAE
EULOGIAS
EULOGIES
EULOGISE
EULOGISED
EULOGISER
EULOGISES
EULOGIST
EULOGISTS
EULOGIUM
EULOGIUMS
EULOGIZE
EULOGIZED
EULOGIZER
EULOGIZES
EULOGY
EUMELANIN
EUMERISM
EUMERISMS
EUMONG
EUMONGS
EUMUNG
EUMUNGS
EUNUCH
EUNUCHISE
EUNUCHISM
EUNUCHIZE
EUNUCHOID
EUNUCHS
EUOI
EUONYMIN
EUONYMINS
EUONYMUS
EUOUAE
EUOUAES
EUPAD
EUPADS
EUPATRID
EUPATRIDS
EUPEPSIA
EUPEPSIAS
EUPEPSIES
EUPEPSY
EUPEPTIC
EUPHAUSID
EUPHEMISE
EUPHEMISM
EUPHEMIST
EUPHEMIZE
EUPHENIC
EUPHENICS
EUPHOBIA
EUPHOBIAS
EUPHON
EUPHONIA
EUPHONIAS
EUPHONIC
EUPHONIES
EUPHONISE
EUPHONISM
EUPHONIUM
EUPHONIZE
EUPHONS
EUPHONY
EUPHORBIA
EUPHORIA
EUPHORIAS
EUPHORIC
EUPHORIES
EUPHORY
EUPHOTIC
EUPHRASIA
EUPHRASY
EUPHROE
EUPHROES
EUPHUISE
EUPHUISED
EUPHUISES
EUPHUISM
EUPHUISMS
EUPHUIST
EUPHUISTS
EUPHUIZE
EUPHUIZED
EUPHUIZES
EUPLASTIC
EUPLOID
EUPLOIDS
EUPLOIDY
EUPNEA
EUPNEAS
EUPNEIC
EUPNOEA
EUPNOEAS
EUPNOEIC
EUREKA
EUREKAS
EURHYTHMY
EURIPI
EURIPUS
EURIPUSES
EURO
EUROBOND
EUROBONDS
EUROCRAT
EUROCRATS
EUROCREEP
EUROKIES
EUROKOUS
EUROKY
EUROLAND

E

EUROLANDS
EURONOTE
EURONOTES
EUROPHILE
EUROPIUM
EUROPIUMS
EUROPOP
EUROPOPS
EUROS
EUROZONE
EUROZONES
EURYBATH
EURYBATHS
EURYOKIES
EURYOKOUS
EURYOKY
EURYTHERM
EURYTHMIC
EURYTHMY
EURYTOPIC
EUSOCIAL
EUSOL
EUSOLS
EUSTACIES
EUSTACY
EUSTASIES
EUSTASY
EUSTATIC
EUSTELE
EUSTELES
EUSTRESS
EUSTYLE
EUSTYLES
EUTAXIA
EUTAXIAS
EUTAXIES
EUTAXITE
EUTAXITES
EUTAXITIC
EUTAXY
EUTECTIC
EUTECTICS
EUTECTOID
EUTEXIA
EUTEXIAS
EUTHANASE
EUTHANASY
EUTHANAZE
EUTHANISE
EUTHANIZE
EUTHENICS
EUTHENIST
EUTHERIAN
EUTHYMIA
EUTHYMIAS
EUTHYROID
EUTRAPELY
EUTROPHIC
EUTROPHY
EUTROPIC
EUTROPIES
EUTROPOUS
EUTROPY
EUXENITE
EUXENITES
EVACUANT
EVACUANTS
EVACUATE
EVACUATED
EVACUATES
EVACUATOR
EVACUEE
EVACUEES
EVADABLE
EVADE
EVADED
EVADER
EVADERS
EVADES
EVADIBLE
EVADING
EVADINGLY
EVAGATION
EVAGINATE
EVALUABLE
EVALUATE
EVALUATED
EVALUATES
EVALUATOR
EVANESCE
EVANESCED
EVANESCES
EVANGEL
EVANGELIC
EVANGELS
EVANGELY
EVANISH
EVANISHED
EVANISHES
EVANITION
EVAPORATE
EVAPORITE
EVASIBLE
EVASION
EVASIONAL
EVASIONS
EVASIVE
EVASIVELY
EVE
EVECTION
EVECTIONS
EVEJAR
EVEJARS
EVEN
EVENED
EVENEMENT
EVENER
EVENERS
EVENEST
EVENFALL
EVENFALLS
EVENING
EVENINGS
EVENLY
EVENNESS
EVENS
EVENSONG
EVENSONGS
EVENT
EVENTED
EVENTER
EVENTERS
EVENTFUL
EVENTIDE
EVENTIDES
EVENTING
EVENTINGS
EVENTIVE
EVENTLESS
EVENTRATE
EVENTS
EVENTUAL
EVENTUATE
EVER
EVERGLADE
EVERGREEN
EVERMORE
EVERNET
EVERNETS
EVERSIBLE
EVERSION
EVERSIONS
EVERT
EVERTED
EVERTING
EVERTOR
EVERTORS
EVERTS
EVERWHERE
EVERWHICH
EVERY
EVERYBODY
EVERYDAY
EVERYDAYS
EVERYMAN
EVERYMEN
EVERYONE
EVERYWAY
EVERYWHEN
EVES
EVET
EVETS
EVHOE
EVICT
EVICTED
EVICTEE
EVICTEES
EVICTING
EVICTION
EVICTIONS
EVICTOR
EVICTORS
EVICTS
EVIDENCE
EVIDENCED
EVIDENCES
EVIDENT
EVIDENTLY
EVIDENTS
EVIL
EVILDOER
EVILDOERS
EVILDOING
EVILER
EVILEST
EVILLER
EVILLEST
EVILLY
EVILNESS
EVILS
EVINCE
EVINCED
EVINCES
EVINCIBLE
EVINCIBLY
EVINCING
EVINCIVE
EVIRATE
EVIRATED
EVIRATES
EVIRATING
EVITABLE
EVITATE
EVITATED
EVITATES
EVITATING
EVITATION
EVITE
EVITED
EVITERNAL
EVITES
EVITING
EVO
EVOCABLE
EVOCATE
EVOCATED
EVOCATES
EVOCATING
EVOCATION
EVOCATIVE
EVOCATOR
EVOCATORS
EVOCATORY
EVOE
EVOHE
EVOKE
EVOKED
EVOKER
EVOKERS
EVOKES

E

EVOKING
EVOLUE
EVOLUES
EVOLUTE
EVOLUTED
EVOLUTES
EVOLUTING
EVOLUTION
EVOLUTIVE
EVOLVABLE
EVOLVE
EVOLVED
EVOLVENT
EVOLVENTS
EVOLVER
EVOLVERS
EVOLVES
EVOLVING
EVONYMUS
EVOS
EVOVAE
EVOVAES
EVULGATE
EVULGATED
EVULGATES
EVULSE
EVULSED
EVULSES
EVULSING
EVULSION
EVULSIONS
EVZONE
EVZONES
EW
EWE
EWER
EWERS
EWES
EWEST
EWFTES
EWGHEN
EWHOW
EWK
EWKED
EWKING
EWKS
EWT
EWTS
EX
EXABYTE
EXABYTES
EXACT
EXACTA
EXACTABLE
EXACTAS
EXACTED
EXACTER
EXACTERS
EXACTEST
EXACTING
EXACTION
EXACTIONS
EXACTLY
EXACTMENT
EXACTNESS
EXACTOR
EXACTORS
EXACTRESS
EXACTS
EXACUM
EXACUMS
EXAHERTZ
EXALT
EXALTED
EXALTEDLY
EXALTER
EXALTERS
EXALTING
EXALTS
EXAM
EXAMEN
EXAMENS
EXAMETRE
EXAMETRES
EXAMINANT
EXAMINATE
EXAMINE
EXAMINED
EXAMINEE
EXAMINEES
EXAMINER
EXAMINERS
EXAMINES
EXAMINING
EXAMPLAR
EXAMPLARS
EXAMPLE
EXAMPLED
EXAMPLES
EXAMPLING
EXAMS
EXANIMATE
EXANTHEM
EXANTHEMA
EXANTHEMS
EXAPTED
EXAPTIVE
EXARATE
EXARATION
EXARCH
EXARCHAL
EXARCHATE
EXARCHIES
EXARCHIST
EXARCHS
EXARCHY
EXCAMB
EXCAMBED
EXCAMBING
EXCAMBION
EXCAMBIUM
EXCAMBS
EXCARNATE
EXCAUDATE
EXCAVATE
EXCAVATED
EXCAVATES
EXCAVATOR
EXCEED
EXCEEDED
EXCEEDER
EXCEEDERS
EXCEEDING
EXCEEDS
EXCEL
EXCELLED
EXCELLENT
EXCELLING
EXCELS
EXCELSIOR
EXCENTRIC
EXCEPT
EXCEPTANT
EXCEPTED
EXCEPTING
EXCEPTION
EXCEPTIVE
EXCEPTOR
EXCEPTORS
EXCEPTS
EXCERPT
EXCERPTA
EXCERPTED
EXCERPTER
EXCERPTOR
EXCERPTS
EXCERPTUM
EXCESS
EXCESSED
EXCESSES
EXCESSING
EXCESSIVE
EXCHANGE
EXCHANGED
EXCHANGER
EXCHANGES
EXCHEAT
EXCHEATS
EXCHEQUER
EXCIDE
EXCIDED
EXCIDES
EXCIDING
EXCIMER
EXCIMERS
EXCIPIENT
EXCIPLE
EXCIPLES
EXCISABLE
EXCISE
EXCISED
EXCISEMAN
EXCISEMEN
EXCISES
EXCISING
EXCISION
EXCISIONS
EXCITABLE
EXCITABLY
EXCITANCY
EXCITANT
EXCITANTS
EXCITE
EXCITED
EXCITEDLY
EXCITER
EXCITERS
EXCITES
EXCITING
EXCITON
EXCITONIC
EXCITONS
EXCITOR
EXCITORS
EXCLAIM
EXCLAIMED
EXCLAIMER
EXCLAIMS
EXCLAVE
EXCLAVES
EXCLOSURE
EXCLUDE
EXCLUDED
EXCLUDEE
EXCLUDEES
EXCLUDER
EXCLUDERS
EXCLUDES
EXCLUDING
EXCLUSION
EXCLUSIVE
EXCLUSORY
EXCORIATE
EXCREMENT
EXCRETA
EXCRETAL
EXCRETE
EXCRETED
EXCRETER
EXCRETERS
EXCRETES
EXCRETING
EXCRETION
EXCRETIVE
EXCRETORY
EXCUBANT
EXCUDIT
EXCULPATE
EXCURRENT
EXCURSE

EXCURSED
EXCURSES
EXCURSING
EXCURSION
EXCURSIVE
EXCURSUS
EXCUSABLE
EXCUSABLY
EXCUSAL
EXCUSALS
EXCUSE
EXCUSED
EXCUSER
EXCUSERS
EXCUSES
EXCUSING
EXCUSIVE
EXEAT
EXEATS
EXEC
EXECRABLE
EXECRABLY
EXECRATE
EXECRATED
EXECRATES
EXECRATOR
EXECS
EXECUTANT
EXECUTARY
EXECUTE
EXECUTED
EXECUTER
EXECUTERS
EXECUTES
EXECUTING
EXECUTION
EXECUTIVE
EXECUTOR
EXECUTORS
EXECUTORY
EXECUTRIX
EXECUTRY
EXED
EXEDRA
EXEDRAE
EXEDRAS
EXEEM
EXEEMED
EXEEMING
EXEEMS
EXEGESES
EXEGESIS
EXEGETE
EXEGETES
EXEGETIC
EXEGETICS
EXEGETIST
EXEME
EXEMED
EXEMES
EXEMING
EXEMPLA
EXEMPLAR
EXEMPLARS
EXEMPLARY
EXEMPLE
EXEMPLES
EXEMPLIFY
EXEMPLUM
EXEMPT
EXEMPTED
EXEMPTING
EXEMPTION
EXEMPTIVE
EXEMPTS
EXEQUATUR
EXEQUIAL
EXEQUIES
EXEQUY
EXERCISE
EXERCISED
EXERCISER
EXERCISES
EXERCYCLE
EXERGIES
EXERGONIC
EXERGUAL
EXERGUE
EXERGUES
EXERGY
EXERT
EXERTED
EXERTING
EXERTION
EXERTIONS
EXERTIVE
EXERTS
EXES
EXEUNT
EXFIL
EXFILLED
EXFILLING
EXFILS
EXFOLIANT
EXFOLIATE
EXHALABLE
EXHALANT
EXHALANTS
EXHALE
EXHALED
EXHALENT
EXHALENTS
EXHALES
EXHALING
EXHAUST
EXHAUSTED
EXHAUSTER
EXHAUSTS
EXHEDRA
EXHEDRAE
EXHIBIT
EXHIBITED
EXHIBITER
EXHIBITOR
EXHIBITS
EXHORT
EXHORTED
EXHORTER
EXHORTERS
EXHORTING
EXHORTS
EXHUMATE
EXHUMATED
EXHUMATES
EXHUME
EXHUMED
EXHUMER
EXHUMERS
EXHUMES
EXHUMING
EXIES
EXIGEANT
EXIGEANTE
EXIGENCE
EXIGENCES
EXIGENCY
EXIGENT
EXIGENTLY
EXIGENTS
EXIGIBLE
EXIGUITY
EXIGUOUS
EXILABLE
EXILE
EXILED
EXILEMENT
EXILER
EXILERS
EXILES
EXILIAN
EXILIC
EXILING
EXILITIES
EXILITY
EXIMIOUS
EXINE
EXINES
EXING
EXIST
EXISTED
EXISTENCE
EXISTENT
EXISTENTS
EXISTING
EXISTS
EXIT
EXITANCE
EXITANCES
EXITED
EXITING
EXITLESS
EXITS
EXO
EXOCARP
EXOCARPS
EXOCRINE
EXOCRINES
EXOCYCLIC
EXOCYTIC
EXOCYTOSE
EXODE
EXODERM
EXODERMAL
EXODERMIS
EXODERMS
EXODES
EXODIC
EXODIST
EXODISTS
EXODOI
EXODONTIA
EXODOS
EXODUS
EXODUSES
EXOENZYME
EXOERGIC
EXOGAMIC
EXOGAMIES
EXOGAMOUS
EXOGAMY
EXOGEN
EXOGENIC
EXOGENISM
EXOGENOUS
EXOGENS
EXOME
EXOMES
EXOMION
EXOMIONS
EXOMIS
EXOMISES
EXON
EXONERATE
EXONEREE
EXONEREES
EXONIC
EXONS
EXONUMIA
EXONUMIST
EXONYM
EXONYMS
EXOPHAGY
EXOPHORIC
EXOPLANET
EXOPLASM
EXOPLASMS
EXOPOD
EXOPODITE
EXOPODS
EXORABLE

EXORATION
EXORCISE
EXORCISED
EXORCISER
EXORCISES
EXORCISM
EXORCISMS
EXORCIST
EXORCISTS
EXORCIZE
EXORCIZED
EXORCIZER
EXORCIZES
EXORDIA
EXORDIAL
EXORDIUM
EXORDIUMS
EXOSMIC
EXOSMOSE
EXOSMOSES
EXOSMOSIS
EXOSMOTIC
EXOSPHERE
EXOSPORAL
EXOSPORE
EXOSPORES
EXOSPORIA
EXOSTOSES
EXOSTOSIS
EXOTERIC
EXOTIC
EXOTICA
EXOTICISE
EXOTICISM
EXOTICIST
EXOTICIZE
EXOTICS
EXOTISM
EXOTISMS
EXOTOXIC
EXOTOXIN
EXOTOXINS
EXOTROPIA
EXOTROPIC
EXPAND
EXPANDED
EXPANDER
EXPANDERS
EXPANDING
EXPANDOR
EXPANDORS
EXPANDS
EXPANSE
EXPANSES
EXPANSILE
EXPANSION
EXPANSIVE
EXPAT
EXPATIATE
EXPATS
EXPECT
EXPECTANT
EXPECTED
EXPECTER
EXPECTERS
EXPECTING
EXPECTS
EXPEDIENT
EXPEDITE
EXPEDITED
EXPEDITER
EXPEDITES
EXPEDITOR
EXPEL
EXPELLANT
EXPELLED
EXPELLEE
EXPELLEES
EXPELLENT
EXPELLER
EXPELLERS
EXPELLING
EXPELS
EXPEND
EXPENDED
EXPENDER
EXPENDERS
EXPENDING
EXPENDS
EXPENSE
EXPENSED
EXPENSES
EXPENSING
EXPENSIVE
EXPERT
EXPERTED
EXPERTING
EXPERTISE
EXPERTISM
EXPERTIZE
EXPERTLY
EXPERTS
EXPIABLE
EXPIATE
EXPIATED
EXPIATES
EXPIATING
EXPIATION
EXPIATOR
EXPIATORS
EXPIATORY
EXPIRABLE
EXPIRANT
EXPIRANTS
EXPIRE
EXPIRED
EXPIRER
EXPIRERS
EXPIRES
EXPIRIES
EXPIRING
EXPIRY
EXPISCATE
EXPLAIN
EXPLAINED
EXPLAINER
EXPLAINS
EXPLANT
EXPLANTED
EXPLANTS
EXPLETIVE
EXPLETORY
EXPLICATE
EXPLICIT
EXPLICITS
EXPLODE
EXPLODED
EXPLODER
EXPLODERS
EXPLODES
EXPLODING
EXPLOIT
EXPLOITED
EXPLOITER
EXPLOITS
EXPLORE
EXPLORED
EXPLORER
EXPLORERS
EXPLORES
EXPLORING
EXPLOSION
EXPLOSIVE
EXPO
EXPONENT
EXPONENTS
EXPONIBLE
EXPORT
EXPORTED
EXPORTER
EXPORTERS
EXPORTING
EXPORTS
EXPOS
EXPOSABLE
EXPOSAL
EXPOSALS
EXPOSE
EXPOSED
EXPOSER
EXPOSERS
EXPOSES
EXPOSING
EXPOSIT
EXPOSITED
EXPOSITOR
EXPOSITS
EXPOSOME
EXPOSOMES
EXPOSTURE
EXPOSURE
EXPOSURES
EXPOUND
EXPOUNDED
EXPOUNDER
EXPOUNDS
EXPRESS
EXPRESSED
EXPRESSER
EXPRESSES
EXPRESSLY
EXPRESSO
EXPRESSOS
EXPUGN
EXPUGNED
EXPUGNING
EXPUGNS
EXPULSE
EXPULSED
EXPULSES
EXPULSING
EXPULSION
EXPULSIVE
EXPUNCT
EXPUNCTED
EXPUNCTS
EXPUNGE
EXPUNGED
EXPUNGER
EXPUNGERS
EXPUNGES
EXPUNGING
EXPURGATE
EXPURGE
EXPURGED
EXPURGES
EXPURGING
EXQUISITE
EXSCIND
EXSCINDED
EXSCINDS
EXSECANT
EXSECANTS
EXSECT
EXSECTED
EXSECTING
EXSECTION
EXSECTS
EXSERT
EXSERTED
EXSERTILE
EXSERTING
EXSERTION
EXSERTS
EXSICCANT
EXSICCATE
EXSTROPHY
EXSUCCOUS
EXTANT
EXTASIES

EXTASY
EXTATIC
EXTEMPORE
EXTEND
EXTENDANT
EXTENDED
EXTENDER
EXTENDERS
EXTENDING
EXTENDS
EXTENSE
EXTENSES
EXTENSILE
EXTENSION
EXTENSITY
EXTENSIVE
EXTENSOR
EXTENSORS
EXTENT
EXTENTS
EXTENUATE
EXTERIOR
EXTERIORS
EXTERMINE
EXTERN
EXTERNAL
EXTERNALS
EXTERNAT
EXTERNATS
EXTERNE
EXTERNES
EXTERNS
EXTINCT
EXTINCTED
EXTINCTS
EXTINE
EXTINES
EXTIRP
EXTIRPATE
EXTIRPED
EXTIRPING
EXTIRPS
EXTOL
EXTOLD
EXTOLL
EXTOLLED
EXTOLLER
EXTOLLERS
EXTOLLING
EXTOLLS
EXTOLMENT
EXTOLS
EXTORSIVE
EXTORT
EXTORTED
EXTORTER
EXTORTERS
EXTORTING
EXTORTION
EXTORTIVE
EXTORTS
EXTRA
EXTRABOLD
EXTRACT
EXTRACTED
EXTRACTOR
EXTRACTS
EXTRADITE
EXTRADOS
EXTRAIT
EXTRAITS
EXTRALITY
EXTRANET
EXTRANETS
EXTRAPOSE
EXTRAS
EXTRAUGHT
EXTRAVERT
EXTREAT
EXTREATED
EXTREATS
EXTREMA
EXTREMAL
EXTREMALS
EXTREME
EXTREMELY
EXTREMER
EXTREMES
EXTREMEST
EXTREMISM
EXTREMIST
EXTREMITY
EXTREMUM
EXTREMUMS
EXTRICATE
EXTRINSIC
EXTROPIAN
EXTROPIES
EXTROPY
EXTRORSAL
EXTRORSE
EXTROVERT
EXTRUDE
EXTRUDED
EXTRUDER
EXTRUDERS
EXTRUDES
EXTRUDING
EXTRUSILE
EXTRUSION
EXTRUSIVE
EXTRUSORY
EXTUBATE
EXTUBATED
EXTUBATES
EXUBERANT
EXUBERATE
EXUDATE
EXUDATES
EXUDATION
EXUDATIVE
EXUDE
EXUDED
EXUDES
EXUDING
EXUL
EXULLED
EXULLING
EXULS
EXULT
EXULTANCE
EXULTANCY
EXULTANT
EXULTED
EXULTING
EXULTS
EXURB
EXURBAN
EXURBIA
EXURBIAS
EXURBS
EXUVIA
EXUVIAE
EXUVIAL
EXUVIATE
EXUVIATED
EXUVIATES
EXUVIUM
EYALET
EYALETS
EYAS
EYASES
EYASS
EYASSES
EYE
EYEABLE
EYEBALL
EYEBALLED
EYEBALLS
EYEBANK
EYEBANKS
EYEBAR
EYEBARS
EYEBATH
EYEBATHS
EYEBEAM
EYEBEAMS
EYEBLACK
EYEBLACKS
EYEBLINK
EYEBLINKS
EYEBOLT
EYEBOLTS
EYEBRIGHT
EYEBROW
EYEBROWED
EYEBROWS
EYECUP
EYECUPS
EYED
EYEDNESS
EYEDROPS
EYEFOLD
EYEFOLDS
EYEFUL
EYEFULS
EYEGLASS
EYEHOLE
EYEHOLES
EYEHOOK
EYEHOOKS
EYEING
EYELASH
EYELASHES
EYELESS
EYELET
EYELETED
EYELETEER
EYELETING
EYELETS
EYELETTED
EYELEVEL
EYELIAD
EYELIADS
EYELID
EYELIDS
EYELIFT
EYELIFTS
EYELIKE
EYELINE
EYELINER
EYELINERS
EYELINES
EYEN
EYEOPENER
EYEPATCH
EYEPIECE
EYEPIECES
EYEPOINT
EYEPOINTS
EYEPOPPER
EYER
EYERS
EYES
EYESHADE
EYESHADES
EYESHADOW
EYESHINE
EYESHINES
EYESHOT
EYESHOTS
EYESIGHT
EYESIGHTS
EYESOME
EYESORE
EYESORES
EYESPOT
EYESPOTS
EYESTALK
EYESTALKS

EYESTONE
EYESTONES
EYESTRAIN
EYETEETH
EYETOOTH
EYEWASH
EYEWASHES
EYEWATER
EYEWATERS
EYEWEAR
EYEWEARS
EYEWINK
EYEWINKS
EYING
EYLIAD
EYLIADS
EYNE
EYOT
EYOTS
EYRA
EYRAS
EYRE
EYRES
EYRIE
EYRIES
EYRIR
EYRY
EZINE
EZINES

F

FA
FAA
FAAING
FAAN
FAAS
FAB
FABACEOUS
FABBER
FABBEST
FABBIER
FABBIEST
FABBY
FABLE
FABLED
FABLER
FABLERS
FABLES
FABLET
FABLETS
FABLIAU
FABLIAUX
FABLING
FABLINGS
FABRIC
FABRICANT
FABRICATE
FABRICKED
FABRICS
FABRIQUE
FABRIQUES
FABS
FABULAR
FABULATE
FABULATED
FABULATES
FABULATOR
FABULISE
FABULISED
FABULISES
FABULISM
FABULISMS
FABULIST
FABULISTS
FABULIZE
FABULIZED
FABULIZES
FABULOUS
FABURDEN
FABURDENS
FACADE
FACADES
FACE
FACEABLE
FACEBAR
FACEBARS
FACEBOOK
FACEBOOKS
FACECLOTH
FACED
FACEDOWN
FACEDOWNS
FACELESS
FACELIFT
FACELIFTS
FACEMAIL
FACEMAILS
FACEMAN
FACEMASK
FACEMASKS
FACEMEN
FACEOFF
FACEOFFS
FACEPALM
FACEPALMS
FACEPLANT
FACEPLATE
FACEPRINT
FACER
FACERS
FACES
FACET
FACETE
FACETED
FACETELY
FACETIAE
FACETIME
FACETIMED
FACETIMES
FACETING
FACETINGS
FACETIOUS
FACETS
FACETTED
FACETTING
FACEUP
FACIA
FACIAE
FACIAL
FACIALIST
FACIALLY
FACIALS
FACIAS
FACIEND
FACIENDS
FACIES
FACILE
FACILELY
FACILITY
FACING
FACINGS
FACONNE
FACONNES
FACSIMILE
FACT
FACTA
FACTFUL
FACTICE
FACTICES
FACTICITY
FACTION
FACTIONAL
FACTIONS
FACTIOUS
FACTIS
FACTISES
FACTITIVE
FACTIVE
FACTOID
FACTOIDAL
FACTOIDS
FACTOR
FACTORAGE
FACTORED
FACTORIAL
FACTORIES
FACTORING
FACTORISE
FACTORIZE
FACTORS
FACTORY
FACTOTUM
FACTOTUMS
FACTS
FACTSHEET
FACTUAL
FACTUALLY
FACTUM
FACTUMS
FACTURE
FACTURES
FACULA
FACULAE
FACULAR
FACULTIES
FACULTY
FACUNDITY
FAD
FADABLE
FADAISE
FADAISES
FADDIER
FADDIEST
FADDINESS
FADDISH
FADDISHLY
FADDISM
FADDISMS
FADDIST
FADDISTS
FADDLE
FADDLED
FADDLES
FADDLING
FADDY
FADE
FADEAWAY
FADEAWAYS
FADED
FADEDLY
FADEDNESS
FADEIN
FADEINS
FADELESS
FADEOUT
FADEOUTS
FADER
FADERS
FADES
FADEUR
FADEURS
FADGE
FADGED
FADGES
FADGING
FADIER
FADIEST
FADING
FADINGS
FADLIKE
FADO
FADOMETER
FADOS
FADS
FADY
FAE
FAECAL
FAECES
FAENA
FAENAS
FAERIE

FAERIES
FAERY
FAFF
FAFFED
FAFFIER
FAFFIEST
FAFFING
FAFFS
FAFFY
FAG
FAGACEOUS
FAGGED
FAGGING
FAGGINGS
FAGGOT
FAGGOTED
FAGGOTING
FAGGOTS
FAGIN
FAGINS
FAGOT
FAGOTED
FAGOTER
FAGOTERS
FAGOTING
FAGOTINGS
FAGOTS
FAGOTTI
FAGOTTIST
FAGOTTO
FAGOTTOS
FAGS
FAH
FAHLBAND
FAHLBANDS
FAHLERZ
FAHLERZES
FAHLORE
FAHLORES
FAHS
FAIBLE
FAIBLES
FAIENCE
FAIENCES
FAIK
FAIKED
FAIKES
FAIKING
FAIKS
FAIL
FAILED
FAILING
FAILINGLY
FAILINGS
FAILLE
FAILLES
FAILOVER
FAILOVERS
FAILS
FAILURE
FAILURES
FAIN
FAINE
FAINEANCE
FAINEANCY
FAINEANT
FAINEANTS
FAINED
FAINER
FAINES
FAINEST
FAINING
FAINITES
FAINLY
FAINNE
FAINNES
FAINNESS
FAINS
FAINT
FAINTED
FAINTER
FAINTERS
FAINTEST
FAINTIER
FAINTIEST
FAINTING
FAINTINGS
FAINTISH
FAINTLY
FAINTNESS
FAINTS
FAINTY
FAIR
FAIRED
FAIRER
FAIREST
FAIRFACED
FAIRGOER
FAIRGOERS
FAIRIER
FAIRIES
FAIRIEST
FAIRILY
FAIRING
FAIRINGS
FAIRISH
FAIRISHLY
FAIRLEAD
FAIRLEADS
FAIRLY
FAIRNESS
FAIRS
FAIRWAY
FAIRWAYS
FAIRY
FAIRYDOM
FAIRYDOMS
FAIRYHOOD
FAIRYISM
FAIRYISMS
FAIRYLAND
FAIRYLIKE
FAIRYTALE
FAITH
FAITHCURE
FAITHED
FAITHER
FAITHERS
FAITHFUL
FAITHFULS
FAITHING
FAITHINGS
FAITHLESS
FAITHS
FAITOR
FAITORS
FAITOUR
FAITOURS
FAIX
FAJITA
FAJITAS
FAKE
FAKED
FAKEER
FAKEERS
FAKEMENT
FAKEMENTS
FAKER
FAKERIES
FAKERS
FAKERY
FAKES
FAKEST
FAKEY
FAKEYS
FAKIE
FAKIER
FAKIES
FAKIEST
FAKING
FAKIR
FAKIRISM
FAKIRISMS
FAKIRS
FALAFEL
FALAFELS
FALAJ
FALANGISM
FALANGIST
FALBALA
FALBALAS
FALCADE
FALCADES
FALCATE
FALCATED
FALCATION
FALCES
FALCHION
FALCHIONS
FALCIFORM
FALCON
FALCONER
FALCONERS
FALCONET
FALCONETS
FALCONINE
FALCONOID
FALCONRY
FALCONS
FALCULA
FALCULAE
FALCULAS
FALCULATE
FALDAGE
FALDAGES
FALDERAL
FALDERALS
FALDEROL
FALDEROLS
FALDETTA
FALDETTAS
FALDSTOOL
FALL
FALLACIES
FALLACY
FALLAL
FALLALERY
FALLALISH
FALLALS
FALLAWAY
FALLAWAYS
FALLBACK
FALLBACKS
FALLBOARD
FALLEN
FALLER
FALLERS
FALLFISH
FALLIBLE
FALLIBLY
FALLING
FALLINGS
FALLOFF
FALLOFFS
FALLOUT
FALLOUTS
FALLOW
FALLOWED
FALLOWER
FALLOWEST
FALLOWING
FALLOWS
FALLS
FALSE
FALSED
FALSEFACE
FALSEHOOD
FALSELY
FALSENESS
FALSER

FALSERS
FALSES
FALSEST
FALSETTO
FALSETTOS
FALSEWORK
FALSIE
FALSIES
FALSIFIED
FALSIFIER
FALSIFIES
FALSIFY
FALSING
FALSISH
FALSISM
FALSISMS
FALSITIES
FALSITY
FALTBOAT
FALTBOATS
FALTER
FALTERED
FALTERER
FALTERERS
FALTERING
FALTERS
FALX
FAME
FAMED
FAMELESS
FAMES
FAMILIAL
FAMILIAR
FAMILIARS
FAMILIES
FAMILISM
FAMILISMS
FAMILIST
FAMILLE
FAMILLES
FAMILY
FAMINE
FAMINES
FAMING
FAMISH
FAMISHED
FAMISHES
FAMISHING
FAMOUS
FAMOUSED
FAMOUSES
FAMOUSING
FAMOUSLY
FAMULI
FAMULUS
FAN
FANAL
FANALS
FANATIC
FANATICAL
FANATICS
FANBASE
FANBASES
FANBOY
FANBOYS
FANCIABLE
FANCIED
FANCIER
FANCIERS
FANCIES
FANCIEST
FANCIFIED
FANCIFIES
FANCIFUL
FANCIFY
FANCILESS
FANCILY
FANCINESS
FANCY
FANCYING
FANCYWORK
FAND
FANDANGLE
FANDANGO
FANDANGOS
FANDED
FANDING
FANDOM
FANDOMS
FANDS
FANE
FANEGA
FANEGADA
FANEGADAS
FANEGAS
FANES
FANFARADE
FANFARE
FANFARED
FANFARES
FANFARING
FANFARON
FANFARONA
FANFARONS
FANFIC
FANFICS
FANFOLD
FANFOLDED
FANFOLDS
FANG
FANGA
FANGAS
FANGED
FANGING
FANGIRL
FANGIRLS
FANGLE
FANGLED
FANGLES
FANGLESS
FANGLIKE
FANGLING
FANGO
FANGOS
FANGS
FANION
FANIONS
FANJET
FANJETS
FANK
FANKED
FANKING
FANKLE
FANKLED
FANKLES
FANKLING
FANKS
FANLIGHT
FANLIGHTS
FANLIKE
FANNED
FANNEL
FANNELL
FANNELLS
FANNELS
FANNER
FANNERS
FANNIED
FANNIES
FANNING
FANNINGS
FANNY
FANNYING
FANO
FANON
FANONS
FANOS
FANS
FANSITE
FANSITES
FANSUB
FANSUBS
FANTAD
FANTADS
FANTAIL
FANTAILED
FANTAILS
FANTASIA
FANTASIAS
FANTASIE
FANTASIED
FANTASIES
FANTASISE
FANTASIST
FANTASIZE
FANTASM
FANTASMAL
FANTASMIC
FANTASMS
FANTASQUE
FANTAST
FANTASTIC
FANTASTRY
FANTASTS
FANTASY
FANTEEG
FANTEEGS
FANTIGUE
FANTIGUES
FANTOD
FANTODS
FANTOM
FANTOMS
FANTOOSH
FANUM
FANUMS
FANWISE
FANWORT
FANWORTS
FANZINE
FANZINES
FAP
FAQIR
FAQIRS
FAQUIR
FAQUIRS
FAR
FARAD
FARADAIC
FARADAY
FARADAYS
FARADIC
FARADISE
FARADISED
FARADISER
FARADISES
FARADISM
FARADISMS
FARADIZE
FARADIZED
FARADIZER
FARADIZES
FARADS
FARAND
FARANDINE
FARANDOLE
FARANG
FARANGS
FARAWAY
FARAWAYS
FARCE
FARCED
FARCEMEAT
FARCER
FARCERS
FARCES
FARCEUR
FARCEURS
FARCEUSE
FARCEUSES

FARCI
FARCICAL
FARCIE
FARCIED
FARCIES
FARCIFIED
FARCIFIES
FARCIFY
FARCIN
FARCING
FARCINGS
FARCINS
FARCY
FARD
FARDAGE
FARDAGES
FARDED
FARDEL
FARDELS
FARDEN
FARDENS
FARDING
FARDINGS
FARDS
FARE
FAREBOX
FAREBOXES
FARED
FARER
FARERS
FARES
FAREWELL
FAREWELLS
FARFAL
FARFALLE
FARFALLES
FARFALS
FARFEL
FARFELS
FARFET
FARINA
FARINAS
FARING
FARINHA
FARINHAS
FARINOSE
FARL
FARLE
FARLES
FARLS
FARM
FARMABLE
FARMED
FARMER
FARMERESS
FARMERIES
FARMERS
FARMERY
FARMHAND
FARMHANDS
FARMHOUSE
FARMING
FARMINGS
FARMLAND
FARMLANDS
FARMOST
FARMS
FARMSTEAD
FARMWIFE
FARMWIVES
FARMWORK
FARMWORKS
FARMYARD
FARMYARDS
FARNARKEL
FARNESOL
FARNESOLS
FARNESS
FARNESSES
FARO
FAROLITO
FAROLITOS
FAROS
FAROUCHE
FARRAGO
FARRAGOES
FARRAGOS
FARRAND
FARRANT
FARRED
FARREN
FARRENS
FARRIER
FARRIERS
FARRIERY
FARRING
FARRO
FARROS
FARROW
FARROWED
FARROWING
FARROWS
FARRUCA
FARRUCAS
FARS
FARSE
FARSED
FARSEEING
FARSES
FARSIDE
FARSIDES
FARSING
FART
FARTED
FARTHEL
FARTHELS
FARTHER
FARTHEST
FARTHING
FARTHINGS
FARTING
FARTLEK
FARTLEKS
FARTS
FAS
FASCES
FASCI
FASCIA
FASCIAE
FASCIAL
FASCIAS
FASCIATE
FASCIATED
FASCICLE
FASCICLED
FASCICLES
FASCICULE
FASCICULI
FASCIITIS
FASCINATE
FASCINE
FASCINES
FASCIO
FASCIOLA
FASCIOLAS
FASCIOLE
FASCIOLES
FASCIS
FASCISM
FASCISMI
FASCISMO
FASCISMS
FASCIST
FASCISTA
FASCISTI
FASCISTIC
FASCISTS
FASCITIS
FASH
FASHED
FASHERIES
FASHERY
FASHES
FASHING
FASHION
FASHIONED
FASHIONER
FASHIONS
FASHIONY
FASHIOUS
FAST
FASTBACK
FASTBACKS
FASTBALL
FASTBALLS
FASTED
FASTEN
FASTENED
FASTENER
FASTENERS
FASTENING
FASTENS
FASTER
FASTERS
FASTEST
FASTI
FASTIE
FASTIES
FASTIGIUM
FASTING
FASTINGS
FASTISH
FASTLY
FASTNESS
FASTS
FASTUOUS
FAT
FATAL
FATALISM
FATALISMS
FATALIST
FATALISTS
FATALITY
FATALLY
FATALNESS
FATBACK
FATBACKS
FATBERG
FATBERGS
FATBIRD
FATBIRDS
FATE
FATED
FATEFUL
FATEFULLY
FATES
FATHEAD
FATHEADED
FATHEADS
FATHER
FATHERED
FATHERING
FATHERLY
FATHERS
FATHOM
FATHOMED
FATHOMER
FATHOMERS
FATHOMING
FATHOMS
FATIDIC
FATIDICAL
FATIGABLE
FATIGATE
FATIGATED
FATIGATES
FATIGUE
FATIGUED
FATIGUES
FATIGUING

FATING
FATISCENT
FATLESS
FATLIKE
FATLING
FATLINGS
FATLY
FATNESS
FATNESSES
FATS
FATSIA
FATSIAS
FATSO
FATSOES
FATSOS
FATSTOCK
FATSTOCKS
FATTED
FATTEN
FATTENED
FATTENER
FATTENERS
FATTENING
FATTENS
FATTER
FATTEST
FATTIER
FATTIES
FATTIEST
FATTILY
FATTINESS
FATTING
FATTISH
FATTISM
FATTISMS
FATTIST
FATTISTS
FATTRELS
FATTY
FATUITIES
FATUITOUS
FATUITY
FATUOUS
FATUOUSLY
FATWA
FATWAED
FATWAH
FATWAHED
FATWAHING
FATWAHS
FATWAING
FATWAS
FATWOOD
FATWOODS
FAUBOURG
FAUBOURGS
FAUCAL
FAUCALS
FAUCES
FAUCET
FAUCETRY
FAUCETS
FAUCHION
FAUCHIONS
FAUCHON
FAUCHONS
FAUCIAL
FAUGH
FAULCHION
FAULD
FAULDS
FAULT
FAULTED
FAULTFUL
FAULTIER
FAULTIEST
FAULTILY
FAULTING
FAULTLESS
FAULTLINE
FAULTS
FAULTY
FAUN
FAUNA
FAUNAE
FAUNAL
FAUNALLY
FAUNAS
FAUNIST
FAUNISTIC
FAUNISTS
FAUNLIKE
FAUNS
FAUNULA
FAUNULAE
FAUNULE
FAUNULES
FAUR
FAURD
FAURER
FAUREST
FAUSTIAN
FAUT
FAUTED
FAUTEUIL
FAUTEUILS
FAUTING
FAUTOR
FAUTORS
FAUTS
FAUVE
FAUVES
FAUVETTE
FAUVETTES
FAUVISM
FAUVISMS
FAUVIST
FAUVISTS
FAUX
FAUXMANCE
FAVA
FAVAS
FAVE
FAVEL
FAVELA
FAVELAS
FAVELL
FAVELLA
FAVELLAS
FAVELS
FAVEOLATE
FAVER
FAVES
FAVEST
FAVICON
FAVICONS
FAVISM
FAVISMS
FAVONIAN
FAVOR
FAVORABLE
FAVORABLY
FAVORED
FAVORER
FAVORERS
FAVORING
FAVORITE
FAVORITES
FAVORLESS
FAVORS
FAVOSE
FAVOUR
FAVOURED
FAVOURER
FAVOURERS
FAVOURING
FAVOURITE
FAVOURS
FAVOUS
FAVRILE
FAVRILES
FAVUS
FAVUSES
FAW
FAWN
FAWNED
FAWNER
FAWNERS
FAWNIER
FAWNIEST
FAWNING
FAWNINGLY
FAWNINGS
FAWNLIKE
FAWNS
FAWNY
FAWS
FAX
FAXABLE
FAXED
FAXES
FAXING
FAY
FAYALITE
FAYALITES
FAYED
FAYENCE
FAYENCES
FAYER
FAYEST
FAYING
FAYNE
FAYNED
FAYNES
FAYNING
FAYRE
FAYRES
FAYS
FAZE
FAZED
FAZENDA
FAZENDAS
FAZES
FAZING
FE
FEAGUE
FEAGUED
FEAGUES
FEAGUING
FEAL
FEALED
FEALING
FEALS
FEALTIES
FEALTY
FEAR
FEARE
FEARED
FEARER
FEARERS
FEARES
FEARFUL
FEARFULLY
FEARING
FEARLESS
FEARS
FEARSOME
FEART
FEASANCE
FEASANCES
FEASE
FEASED
FEASES
FEASIBLE
FEASIBLY
FEASING
FEAST
FEASTED
FEASTER
FEASTERS

FEASTFUL
FEASTING
FEASTINGS
FEASTLESS
FEASTS
FEAT
FEATED
FEATEOUS
FEATER
FEATEST
FEATHER
FEATHERED
FEATHERS
FEATHERY
FEATING
FEATLIER
FEATLIEST
FEATLY
FEATOUS
FEATS
FEATUOUS
FEATURE
FEATURED
FEATURELY
FEATURES
FEATURING
FEAZE
FEAZED
FEAZES
FEAZING
FEBLESSE
FEBLESSES
FEBRICITY
FEBRICULA
FEBRICULE
FEBRIFIC
FEBRIFUGE
FEBRILE
FEBRILITY
FECAL
FECES
FECHT
FECHTER
FECHTERS
FECHTING
FECHTS
FECIAL
FECIALS
FECIT
FECK
FECKED
FECKIN
FECKING
FECKLESS
FECKLY
FECKS
FECULA
FECULAE
FECULAS
FECULENCE
FECULENCY
FECULENT
FECUND
FECUNDATE
FECUNDITY
FED
FEDARIE
FEDARIES
FEDAYEE
FEDAYEEN
FEDELINI
FEDELINIS
FEDERACY
FEDERAL
FEDERALLY
FEDERALS
FEDERARIE
FEDERARY
FEDERATE
FEDERATED
FEDERATES
FEDERATOR
FEDEX
FEDEXED
FEDEXES
FEDEXING
FEDORA
FEDORAS
FEDS
FEE
FEEB
FEEBLE
FEEBLED
FEEBLER
FEEBLES
FEEBLEST
FEEBLING
FEEBLISH
FEEBLY
FEEBS
FEED
FEEDABLE
FEEDBACK
FEEDBACKS
FEEDBAG
FEEDBAGS
FEEDBOX
FEEDBOXES
FEEDER
FEEDERS
FEEDGRAIN
FEEDHOLE
FEEDHOLES
FEEDING
FEEDINGS
FEEDLOT
FEEDLOTS
FEEDPIPE
FEEDPIPES
FEEDS
FEEDSTOCK
FEEDSTUFF
FEEDWATER
FEEDYARD
FEEDYARDS
FEEING
FEEL
FEELBAD
FEELER
FEELERS
FEELESS
FEELGOOD
FEELING
FEELINGLY
FEELINGS
FEELS
FEEN
FEENS
FEER
FEERED
FEERIE
FEERIES
FEERIN
FEERING
FEERINGS
FEERINS
FEERS
FEES
FEESE
FEESED
FEESES
FEESING
FEET
FEETFIRST
FEETLESS
FEEZE
FEEZED
FEEZES
FEEZING
FEG
FEGARIES
FEGARY
FEGS
FEH
FEHM
FEHME
FEHMIC
FEHS
FEIGN
FEIGNED
FEIGNEDLY
FEIGNER
FEIGNERS
FEIGNING
FEIGNINGS
FEIGNS
FEIJOA
FEIJOADA
FEIJOADAS
FEIJOAS
FEINT
FEINTED
FEINTER
FEINTEST
FEINTING
FEINTS
FEIRIE
FEIRIER
FEIRIEST
FEIS
FEISEANNA
FEIST
FEISTIER
FEISTIEST
FEISTILY
FEISTS
FEISTY
FELAFEL
FELAFELS
FELCH
FELCHED
FELCHES
FELCHING
FELDGRAU
FELDGRAUS
FELDSCHAR
FELDSCHER
FELDSHER
FELDSHERS
FELDSPAR
FELDSPARS
FELDSPATH
FELICIA
FELICIAS
FELICIFIC
FELICITER
FELICITY
FELID
FELIDS
FELINE
FELINELY
FELINES
FELINITY
FELL
FELLA
FELLABLE
FELLAH
FELLAHEEN
FELLAHIN
FELLAHS
FELLAS
FELLATE
FELLATED
FELLATES
FELLATING
FELLATIO
FELLATION
FELLATIOS
FELLATOR
FELLATORS

FELLATRIX
FELLED
FELLER
FELLERS
FELLEST
FELLFIELD
FELLIES
FELLING
FELLINGS
FELLNESS
FELLOE
FELLOES
FELLOW
FELLOWED
FELLOWING
FELLOWLY
FELLOWMAN
FELLOWMEN
FELLOWS
FELLS
FELLY
FELON
FELONIES
FELONIOUS
FELONOUS
FELONRIES
FELONRY
FELONS
FELONY
FELQUISTE
FELSIC
FELSITE
FELSITES
FELSITIC
FELSPAR
FELSPARS
FELSTONE
FELSTONES
FELT
FELTED
FELTER
FELTERED
FELTERING
FELTERS
FELTIER
FELTIEST
FELTING
FELTINGS
FELTLIKE
FELTS
FELTY
FELUCCA
FELUCCAS
FELWORT
FELWORTS
FEM
FEMAL
FEMALE
FEMALES
FEMALITY
FEMALS
FEME
FEMERALL
FEMERALLS
FEMERELL
FEMERELLS
FEMES
FEMETARY
FEMICIDAL
FEMICIDE
FEMICIDES
FEMINACY
FEMINAL
FEMINAZI
FEMINAZIS
FEMINEITY
FEMINIE
FEMINIES
FEMININE
FEMININES
FEMINISE
FEMINISED
FEMINISES
FEMINISM
FEMINISMS
FEMINIST
FEMINISTS
FEMINITY
FEMINIZE
FEMINIZED
FEMINIZES
FEMITER
FEMITERS
FEMME
FEMMES
FEMMIER
FEMMIEST
FEMMY
FEMORA
FEMORAL
FEMS
FEMUR
FEMURS
FEN
FENAGLE
FENAGLED
FENAGLES
FENAGLING
FENCE
FENCED
FENCELESS
FENCELIKE
FENCELINE
FENCER
FENCEROW
FENCEROWS
FENCERS
FENCES
FENCEWIRE
FENCIBLE
FENCIBLES
FENCING
FENCINGS
FEND
FENDED
FENDER
FENDERED
FENDERS
FENDIER
FENDIEST
FENDING
FENDS
FENDY
FENESTRA
FENESTRAE
FENESTRAL
FENESTRAS
FENI
FENING
FENINGA
FENINGS
FENIS
FENITAR
FENITARS
FENKS
FENLAND
FENLANDS
FENMAN
FENMEN
FENNEC
FENNECS
FENNEL
FENNELS
FENNIER
FENNIES
FENNIEST
FENNING
FENNISH
FENNY
FENS
FENT
FENTANYL
FENTANYLS
FENTHION
FENTHIONS
FENTS
FENUGREEK
FENURON
FENURONS
FEOD
FEODAL
FEODARIES
FEODARY
FEODS
FEOFF
FEOFFED
FEOFFEE
FEOFFEES
FEOFFER
FEOFFERS
FEOFFING
FEOFFMENT
FEOFFOR
FEOFFORS
FEOFFS
FER
FERACIOUS
FERACITY
FERAL
FERALISED
FERALIZED
FERALS
FERBAM
FERBAMS
FERE
FERER
FERES
FEREST
FERETORY
FERIA
FERIAE
FERIAL
FERIAS
FERINE
FERITIES
FERITY
FERLIE
FERLIED
FERLIER
FERLIES
FERLIEST
FERLY
FERLYING
FERM
FERMATA
FERMATAS
FERMATE
FERMENT
FERMENTED
FERMENTER
FERMENTOR
FERMENTS
FERMI
FERMION
FERMIONIC
FERMIONS
FERMIS
FERMIUM
FERMIUMS
FERMS
FERN
FERNALLY
FERNBIRD
FERNBIRDS
FERNERIES
FERNERY
FERNIER
FERNIEST
FERNING
FERNINGS

FERNINST
FERNLESS
FERNLIKE
FERNS
FERNSHAW
FERNSHAWS
FERNTICLE
FERNY
FEROCIOUS
FEROCITY
FERRATE
FERRATES
FERREL
FERRELED
FERRELING
FERRELLED
FERRELS
FERREOUS
FERRET
FERRETED
FERRETER
FERRETERS
FERRETIER
FERRETING
FERRETS
FERRETY
FERRIAGE
FERRIAGES
FERRIC
FERRIED
FERRIES
FERRITE
FERRITES
FERRITIC
FERRITIN
FERRITINS
FERROCENE
FERROGRAM
FERROTYPE
FERROUS
FERRUGO
FERRUGOS
FERRULE
FERRULED
FERRULES
FERRULING
FERRUM
FERRUMS
FERRY
FERRYBOAT
FERRYING
FERRYMAN
FERRYMEN
FERTIGATE
FERTILE
FERTILELY
FERTILER
FERTILEST
FERTILISE
FERTILITY
FERTILIZE
FERULA
FERULAE
FERULAS
FERULE
FERULED
FERULES
FERULING
FERVENCY
FERVENT
FERVENTER
FERVENTLY
FERVID
FERVIDER
FERVIDEST
FERVIDITY
FERVIDLY
FERVOR
FERVOROUS
FERVORS
FERVOUR
FERVOURS
FES
FESCUE
FESCUES
FESS
FESSE
FESSED
FESSES
FESSING
FESSWISE
FEST
FESTA
FESTAL
FESTALLY
FESTALS
FESTAS
FESTER
FESTERED
FESTERING
FESTERS
FESTIER
FESTIEST
FESTILOGY
FESTINATE
FESTIVAL
FESTIVALS
FESTIVE
FESTIVELY
FESTIVITY
FESTIVOUS
FESTOLOGY
FESTOON
FESTOONED
FESTOONS
FESTS
FESTY
FET
FETA
FETAL
FETAS
FETATION
FETATIONS
FETCH
FETCHED
FETCHER
FETCHERS
FETCHES
FETCHING
FETE
FETED
FETERITA
FETERITAS
FETES
FETIAL
FETIALES
FETIALIS
FETIALS
FETICH
FETICHE
FETICHES
FETICHISE
FETICHISM
FETICHIST
FETICHIZE
FETICIDAL
FETICIDE
FETICIDES
FETID
FETIDER
FETIDEST
FETIDITY
FETIDLY
FETIDNESS
FETING
FETISH
FETISHES
FETISHISE
FETISHISM
FETISHIST
FETISHIZE
FETLOCK
FETLOCKED
FETLOCKS
FETOLOGY
FETOR
FETORS
FETOSCOPE
FETOSCOPY
FETS
FETT
FETTA
FETTAS
FETTED
FETTER
FETTERED
FETTERER
FETTERERS
FETTERING
FETTERS
FETTING
FETTLE
FETTLED
FETTLER
FETTLERS
FETTLES
FETTLING
FETTLINGS
FETTS
FETTUCINE
FETTUCINI
FETUS
FETUSES
FETWA
FETWAS
FEU
FEUAR
FEUARS
FEUD
FEUDAL
FEUDALISE
FEUDALISM
FEUDALIST
FEUDALITY
FEUDALIZE
FEUDALLY
FEUDARIES
FEUDARY
FEUDATORY
FEUDED
FEUDING
FEUDINGS
FEUDIST
FEUDISTS
FEUDS
FEUED
FEUILLETE
FEUING
FEUS
FEUTRE
FEUTRED
FEUTRES
FEUTRING
FEVER
FEVERED
FEVERFEW
FEVERFEWS
FEVERING
FEVERISH
FEVERLESS
FEVEROUS
FEVERROOT
FEVERS
FEVERWEED
FEVERWORT
FEW
FEWER
FEWEST
FEWMET
FEWMETS

FEWNESS
FEWNESSES
FEWS
FEWTER
FEWTERED
FEWTERING
FEWTERS
FEWTRILS
FEY
FEYED
FEYER
FEYEST
FEYING
FEYLY
FEYNESS
FEYNESSES
FEYS
FEZ
FEZES
FEZZED
FEZZES
FEZZY
FIACRE
FIACRES
FIANCE
FIANCEE
FIANCEES
FIANCES
FIAR
FIARS
FIASCHI
FIASCO
FIASCOES
FIASCOS
FIAT
FIATED
FIATING
FIATS
FIAUNT
FIAUNTS
FIB
FIBBED
FIBBER
FIBBERIES
FIBBERS
FIBBERY
FIBBING
FIBER
FIBERED
FIBERFILL
FIBERISE
FIBERISED
FIBERISES
FIBERIZE
FIBERIZED
FIBERIZES
FIBERLESS
FIBERLIKE
FIBERS
FIBRANNE
FIBRANNES
FIBRATE
FIBRATES
FIBRE
FIBRED
FIBREFILL
FIBRELESS
FIBRELIKE
FIBRES
FIBRIFORM
FIBRIL
FIBRILAR
FIBRILLA
FIBRILLAE
FIBRILLAR
FIBRILLIN
FIBRILS
FIBRIN
FIBRINOID
FIBRINOUS
FIBRINS
FIBRO
FIBROCYTE
FIBROID
FIBROIDS
FIBROIN
FIBROINS
FIBROLINE
FIBROLITE
FIBROMA
FIBROMAS
FIBROMATA
FIBROS
FIBROSE
FIBROSED
FIBROSES
FIBROSING
FIBROSIS
FIBROTIC
FIBROUS
FIBROUSLY
FIBS
FIBSTER
FIBSTERS
FIBULA
FIBULAE
FIBULAR
FIBULAS
FICAIN
FICAINS
FICE
FICES
FICHE
FICHES
FICHU
FICHUS
FICIN
FICINS
FICKLE
FICKLED
FICKLER
FICKLES
FICKLEST
FICKLING
FICKLY
FICO
FICOES
FICOS
FICTILE
FICTION
FICTIONAL
FICTIONS
FICTIVE
FICTIVELY
FICTOR
FICTORS
FICUS
FICUSES
FID
FIDDIOUS
FIDDLE
FIDDLED
FIDDLER
FIDDLERS
FIDDLES
FIDDLEY
FIDDLEYS
FIDDLIER
FIDDLIEST
FIDDLING
FIDDLINGS
FIDDLY
FIDEISM
FIDEISMS
FIDEIST
FIDEISTIC
FIDEISTS
FIDELISMO
FIDELISTA
FIDELITY
FIDES
FIDGE
FIDGED
FIDGES
FIDGET
FIDGETED
FIDGETER
FIDGETERS
FIDGETIER
FIDGETING
FIDGETS
FIDGETY
FIDGING
FIDIBUS
FIDIBUSES
FIDO
FIDOS
FIDS
FIDUCIAL
FIDUCIARY
FIE
FIEF
FIEFDOM
FIEFDOMS
FIEFS
FIELD
FIELDBOOT
FIELDED
FIELDER
FIELDERS
FIELDFARE
FIELDING
FIELDINGS
FIELDMICE
FIELDS
FIELDSMAN
FIELDSMEN
FIELDVOLE
FIELDWARD
FIELDWORK
FIEND
FIENDISH
FIENDLIKE
FIENDS
FIENT
FIENTS
FIER
FIERCE
FIERCELY
FIERCER
FIERCEST
FIERE
FIERES
FIERIER
FIERIEST
FIERILY
FIERINESS
FIERS
FIERY
FIEST
FIESTA
FIESTAS
FIFE
FIFED
FIFER
FIFERS
FIFES
FIFI
FIFING
FIFIS
FIFTEEN
FIFTEENER
FIFTEENS
FIFTEENTH
FIFTH
FIFTHLY
FIFTHS
FIFTIES
FIFTIETH
FIFTIETHS

F

FIFTY
FIFTYFOLD
FIFTYISH
FIG
FIGEATER
FIGEATERS
FIGGED
FIGGERIES
FIGGERY
FIGGIER
FIGGIEST
FIGGING
FIGGY
FIGHT
FIGHTABLE
FIGHTBACK
FIGHTER
FIGHTERS
FIGHTING
FIGHTINGS
FIGHTS
FIGJAM
FIGJAMS
FIGLIKE
FIGMENT
FIGMENTS
FIGO
FIGOS
FIGS
FIGTREE
FIGTREES
FIGULINE
FIGULINES
FIGURABLE
FIGURAL
FIGURALLY
FIGURANT
FIGURANTE
FIGURANTS
FIGURATE
FIGURE
FIGURED
FIGUREDLY
FIGURER
FIGURERS
FIGURES
FIGURINE
FIGURINES
FIGURING
FIGURIST
FIGURISTS
FIGWORT
FIGWORTS
FIKE
FIKED
FIKERIES
FIKERY
FIKES
FIKIER
FIKIEST
FIKING
FIKISH
FIKY
FIL
FILA
FILABEG
FILABEGS
FILACEOUS
FILACER
FILACERS
FILAGGRIN
FILAGREE
FILAGREED
FILAGREES
FILAMENT
FILAMENTS
FILANDER
FILANDERS
FILAR
FILAREE
FILAREES
FILARIA
FILARIAE
FILARIAL
FILARIAN
FILARIID
FILARIIDS
FILASSE
FILASSES
FILATORY
FILATURE
FILATURES
FILAZER
FILAZERS
FILBERD
FILBERDS
FILBERT
FILBERTS
FILCH
FILCHED
FILCHER
FILCHERS
FILCHES
FILCHING
FILCHINGS
FILE
FILEABLE
FILECARD
FILECARDS
FILED
FILEFISH
FILEMOT
FILEMOTS
FILENAME
FILENAMES
FILER
FILERS
FILES
FILET
FILETED
FILETING
FILETS
FILFOT
FILFOTS
FILIAL
FILIALLY
FILIATE
FILIATED
FILIATES
FILIATING
FILIATION
FILIBEG
FILIBEGS
FILICIDAL
FILICIDE
FILICIDES
FILIFORM
FILIGRAIN
FILIGRANE
FILIGREE
FILIGREED
FILIGREES
FILII
FILING
FILINGS
FILIOQUE
FILIOQUES
FILISTER
FILISTERS
FILIUS
FILK
FILKS
FILL
FILLABLE
FILLAGREE
FILLE
FILLED
FILLER
FILLERS
FILLES
FILLESTER
FILLET
FILLETED
FILLETER
FILLETERS
FILLETING
FILLETS
FILLIBEG
FILLIBEGS
FILLIES
FILLING
FILLINGS
FILLIP
FILLIPED
FILLIPEEN
FILLIPING
FILLIPS
FILLISTER
FILLO
FILLOS
FILLS
FILLY
FILM
FILMABLE
FILMCARD
FILMCARDS
FILMDOM
FILMDOMS
FILMED
FILMER
FILMERS
FILMFEST
FILMFESTS
FILMGOER
FILMGOERS
FILMGOING
FILMI
FILMIC
FILMIER
FILMIEST
FILMILY
FILMINESS
FILMING
FILMINGS
FILMIS
FILMISH
FILMLAND
FILMLANDS
FILMLESS
FILMLIKE
FILMMAKER
FILMS
FILMSET
FILMSETS
FILMSTRIP
FILMY
FILO
FILOPLUME
FILOPODIA
FILOS
FILOSE
FILOSELLE
FILOVIRUS
FILS
FILTER
FILTERED
FILTERER
FILTERERS
FILTERING
FILTERS
FILTH
FILTHIER
FILTHIEST
FILTHILY
FILTHS
FILTHY
FILTRABLE
FILTRATE
FILTRATED
FILTRATES

FILTRE
FILUM
FIMBLE
FIMBLES
FIMBRIA
FIMBRIAE
FIMBRIAL
FIMBRIATE
FIN
FINABLE
FINAGLE
FINAGLED
FINAGLER
FINAGLERS
FINAGLES
FINAGLING
FINAL
FINALE
FINALES
FINALIS
FINALISE
FINALISED
FINALISER
FINALISES
FINALISM
FINALISMS
FINALIST
FINALISTS
FINALITY
FINALIZE
FINALIZED
FINALIZER
FINALIZES
FINALLY
FINALS
FINANCE
FINANCED
FINANCES
FINANCIAL
FINANCIER
FINANCING
FINBACK
FINBACKS
FINCA
FINCAS
FINCH
FINCHED
FINCHES
FINCHLIKE
FIND
FINDABLE
FINDER
FINDERS
FINDING
FINDINGS
FINDRAM
FINDRAMS
FINDS
FINE
FINEABLE
FINED
FINEER
FINEERED
FINEERING
FINEERS
FINEISH
FINELESS
FINELY
FINENESS
FINER
FINERIES
FINERS
FINERY
FINES
FINESPUN
FINESSE
FINESSED
FINESSER
FINESSERS
FINESSES
FINESSING
FINEST
FINESTS
FINFISH
FINFISHES
FINFOOT
FINFOOTS
FINGAN
FINGANS
FINGER
FINGERED
FINGERER
FINGERERS
FINGERING
FINGERS
FINGERTIP
FINI
FINIAL
FINIALED
FINIALS
FINICAL
FINICALLY
FINICKETY
FINICKIER
FINICKIN
FINICKING
FINICKY
FINIKIN
FINIKING
FINING
FININGS
FINIS
FINISES
FINISH
FINISHED
FINISHER
FINISHERS
FINISHES
FINISHING
FINITE
FINITELY
FINITES
FINITISM
FINITISMS
FINITIST
FINITISTS
FINITO
FINITUDE
FINITUDES
FINJAN
FINJANS
FINK
FINKED
FINKING
FINKS
FINLESS
FINLIKE
FINLIT
FINLITS
FINMARK
FINMARKS
FINNAC
FINNACK
FINNACKS
FINNACS
FINNAN
FINNANS
FINNED
FINNER
FINNERS
FINNESKO
FINNICKY
FINNIER
FINNIEST
FINNING
FINNMARK
FINNMARKS
FINNOCHIO
FINNOCK
FINNOCKS
FINNSKO
FINNY
FINO
FINOCCHIO
FINOCHIO
FINOCHIOS
FINOS
FINS
FINSKO
FINTECH
FINTECHS
FIORATURA
FIORD
FIORDS
FIORIN
FIORINS
FIORITURA
FIORITURE
FIPPENCE
FIPPENCES
FIPPLE
FIPPLES
FIQH
FIQHS
FIQUE
FIQUES
FIR
FIRE
FIREABLE
FIREARM
FIREARMED
FIREARMS
FIREBACK
FIREBACKS
FIREBALL
FIREBALLS
FIREBASE
FIREBASES
FIREBIRD
FIREBIRDS
FIREBOARD
FIREBOAT
FIREBOATS
FIREBOMB
FIREBOMBS
FIREBOX
FIREBOXES
FIREBRAND
FIREBRAT
FIREBRATS
FIREBREAK
FIREBRICK
FIREBUG
FIREBUGS
FIREBUSH
FIRECLAY
FIRECLAYS
FIRECREST
FIRED
FIREDAMP
FIREDAMPS
FIREDOG
FIREDOGS
FIREDRAKE
FIREFANG
FIREFANGS
FIREFIGHT
FIREFLIES
FIREFLOAT
FIREFLOOD
FIREFLY
FIREGUARD
FIREHALL
FIREHALLS
FIREHOSE
FIREHOSES
FIREHOUSE
FIRELESS
FIRELIGHT
FIRELIT

FIRELOCK
FIRELOCKS
FIREMAN
FIREMANIC
FIREMARK
FIREMARKS
FIREMEN
FIREPAN
FIREPANS
FIREPINK
FIREPINKS
FIREPIT
FIREPITS
FIREPLACE
FIREPLUG
FIREPLUGS
FIREPOT
FIREPOTS
FIREPOWER
FIREPROOF
FIRER
FIREREEL
FIREREELS
FIREROOM
FIREROOMS
FIRERS
FIRES
FIRESCAPE
FIRESHIP
FIRESHIPS
FIRESIDE
FIRESIDES
FIRESTONE
FIRESTORM
FIRETHORN
FIRETRAP
FIRETRAPS
FIRETRUCK
FIREWALL
FIREWALLS
FIREWATER
FIREWEED
FIREWEEDS
FIREWOMAN
FIREWOMEN
FIREWOOD
FIREWOODS
FIREWORK
FIREWORKS
FIREWORM
FIREWORMS
FIRIE
FIRIES
FIRING
FIRINGS
FIRK
FIRKED
FIRKIN
FIRKING
FIRKINS
FIRKS
FIRLOT
FIRLOTS
FIRM
FIRMAMENT
FIRMAN
FIRMANS
FIRMED
FIRMER
FIRMERS
FIRMEST
FIRMING
FIRMLESS
FIRMLY
FIRMNESS
FIRMS
FIRMWARE
FIRMWARES
FIRN
FIRNS
FIRRIER
FIRRIEST
FIRRING
FIRRINGS
FIRRY
FIRS
FIRST
FIRSTBORN
FIRSTHAND
FIRSTLING
FIRSTLY
FIRSTNESS
FIRSTS
FIRTH
FIRTHS
FIRWOOD
FIRWOODS
FISC
FISCAL
FISCALIST
FISCALLY
FISCALS
FISCS
FISGIG
FISGIGS
FISH
FISHABLE
FISHBALL
FISHBALLS
FISHBOAT
FISHBOATS
FISHBOLT
FISHBOLTS
FISHBONE
FISHBONES
FISHBOWL
FISHBOWLS
FISHCAKE
FISHCAKES
FISHED
FISHER
FISHERIES
FISHERMAN
FISHERMEN
FISHERS
FISHERY
FISHES
FISHEYE
FISHEYES
FISHFUL
FISHGIG
FISHGIGS
FISHHOOK
FISHHOOKS
FISHIER
FISHIEST
FISHIFIED
FISHIFIES
FISHIFY
FISHILY
FISHINESS
FISHING
FISHINGS
FISHKILL
FISHKILLS
FISHLESS
FISHLIKE
FISHLINE
FISHLINES
FISHMEAL
FISHMEALS
FISHNET
FISHNETS
FISHPLATE
FISHPOLE
FISHPOLES
FISHPOND
FISHPONDS
FISHSKIN
FISHSKINS
FISHTAIL
FISHTAILS
FISHWAY
FISHWAYS
FISHWIFE
FISHWIVES
FISHWORM
FISHWORMS
FISHY
FISHYBACK
FISK
FISKED
FISKING
FISKS
FISNOMIE
FISNOMIES
FISSATE
FISSILE
FISSILITY
FISSION
FISSIONAL
FISSIONED
FISSIONS
FISSIPED
FISSIPEDE
FISSIPEDS
FISSIVE
FISSLE
FISSLED
FISSLES
FISSLING
FISSURAL
FISSURE
FISSURED
FISSURES
FISSURING
FIST
FISTED
FISTFIGHT
FISTFUL
FISTFULS
FISTIANA
FISTIANAS
FISTIC
FISTICAL
FISTICUFF
FISTIER
FISTIEST
FISTING
FISTINGS
FISTMELE
FISTMELES
FISTNOTE
FISTNOTES
FISTS
FISTULA
FISTULAE
FISTULAR
FISTULAS
FISTULATE
FISTULOSE
FISTULOUS
FISTY
FIT
FITCH
FITCHE
FITCHEE
FITCHES
FITCHET
FITCHETS
FITCHEW
FITCHEWS
FITCHY
FITFUL
FITFULLY
FITLIER
FITLIEST
FITLY
FITMENT
FITMENTS

FITNA
FITNAS
FITNESS
FITNESSES
FITS
FITT
FITTABLE
FITTE
FITTED
FITTER
FITTERS
FITTES
FITTEST
FITTING
FITTINGLY
FITTINGS
FITTS
FIVE
FIVEFOLD
FIVEPENCE
FIVEPENNY
FIVEPIN
FIVEPINS
FIVER
FIVERS
FIVES
FIX
FIXABLE
FIXATE
FIXATED
FIXATES
FIXATIF
FIXATIFS
FIXATING
FIXATION
FIXATIONS
FIXATIVE
FIXATIVES
FIXATURE
FIXATURES
FIXED
FIXEDLY
FIXEDNESS
FIXER
FIXERS
FIXES
FIXING
FIXINGS
FIXIT
FIXITIES
FIXITS
FIXITY
FIXIVE
FIXT
FIXTURE
FIXTURES
FIXURE
FIXURES
FIZ
FIZGIG
FIZGIGGED
FIZGIGS
FIZZ
FIZZED
FIZZEN
FIZZENS
FIZZER
FIZZERS
FIZZES
FIZZGIG
FIZZGIGS
FIZZIER
FIZZIEST
FIZZILY
FIZZINESS
FIZZING
FIZZINGS
FIZZLE
FIZZLED
FIZZLES
FIZZLING
FIZZY
FJELD
FJELDS
FJORD
FJORDIC
FJORDS
FLAB
FLABBIER
FLABBIEST
FLABBILY
FLABBY
FLABELLA
FLABELLUM
FLABS
FLACCID
FLACCIDER
FLACCIDLY
FLACK
FLACKED
FLACKER
FLACKERED
FLACKERS
FLACKERY
FLACKET
FLACKETED
FLACKETS
FLACKING
FLACKS
FLACON
FLACONS
FLAFF
FLAFFED
FLAFFER
FLAFFERED
FLAFFERS
FLAFFING
FLAFFS
FLAG
FLAGELLA
FLAGELLAR
FLAGELLIN
FLAGELLUM
FLAGEOLET
FLAGGED
FLAGGER
FLAGGERS
FLAGGIER
FLAGGIEST
FLAGGING
FLAGGINGS
FLAGGY
FLAGITATE
FLAGLESS
FLAGMAN
FLAGMEN
FLAGON
FLAGONS
FLAGPOLE
FLAGPOLES
FLAGRANCE
FLAGRANCY
FLAGRANT
FLAGS
FLAGSHIP
FLAGSHIPS
FLAGSTAFF
FLAGSTICK
FLAGSTONE
FLAIL
FLAILED
FLAILING
FLAILS
FLAIR
FLAIRS
FLAK
FLAKE
FLAKED
FLAKER
FLAKERS
FLAKES
FLAKEY
FLAKIER
FLAKIES
FLAKIEST
FLAKILY
FLAKINESS
FLAKING
FLAKS
FLAKY
FLAM
FLAMBE
FLAMBEAU
FLAMBEAUS
FLAMBEAUX
FLAMBEE
FLAMBEED
FLAMBEES
FLAMBEING
FLAMBES
FLAME
FLAMED
FLAMELESS
FLAMELET
FLAMELETS
FLAMELIKE
FLAMEN
FLAMENCO
FLAMENCOS
FLAMENS
FLAMEOUT
FLAMEOUTS
FLAMER
FLAMERS
FLAMES
FLAMFEW
FLAMFEWS
FLAMIER
FLAMIEST
FLAMINES
FLAMING
FLAMINGLY
FLAMINGO
FLAMINGOS
FLAMM
FLAMMABLE
FLAMMED
FLAMMING
FLAMMS
FLAMMULE
FLAMMULES
FLAMS
FLAMY
FLAN
FLANCARD
FLANCARDS
FLANCH
FLANCHED
FLANCHES
FLANCHING
FLANE
FLANED
FLANERIE
FLANERIES
FLANES
FLANEUR
FLANEURS
FLANGE
FLANGED
FLANGER
FLANGERS
FLANGES
FLANGING
FLANGINGS
FLANING
FLANK
FLANKED
FLANKEN
FLANKENS
FLANKER

FLANKERED
FLANKERS
FLANKING
FLANKS
FLANNEL
FLANNELED
FLANNELET
FLANNELLY
FLANNELS
FLANNEN
FLANNENS
FLANNIE
FLANNIES
FLANNY
FLANS
FLAP
FLAPERON
FLAPERONS
FLAPJACK
FLAPJACKS
FLAPLESS
FLAPLIKE
FLAPPABLE
FLAPPED
FLAPPER
FLAPPERS
FLAPPIER
FLAPPIEST
FLAPPING
FLAPPINGS
FLAPPY
FLAPS
FLAPTRACK
FLARE
FLAREBACK
FLARED
FLARES
FLAREUP
FLAREUPS
FLARIER
FLARIEST
FLARING
FLARINGLY
FLARY
FLASER
FLASERS
FLASH
FLASHBACK
FLASHBANG
FLASHBULB
FLASHCARD
FLASHCUBE
FLASHED
FLASHER
FLASHERS
FLASHES
FLASHEST
FLASHGUN
FLASHGUNS
FLASHIER
FLASHIEST
FLASHILY
FLASHING
FLASHINGS
FLASHLAMP
FLASHOVER
FLASHTUBE
FLASHY
FLASK
FLASKET
FLASKETS
FLASKS
FLAT
FLATBACK
FLATBACKS
FLATBED
FLATBEDS
FLATBOAT
FLATBOATS
FLATBREAD
FLATBROD
FLATBRODS
FLATCAP
FLATCAPS
FLATCAR
FLATCARS
FLATETTE
FLATETTES
FLATFEET
FLATFISH
FLATFOOT
FLATFOOTS
FLATFORM
FLATFORMS
FLATHEAD
FLATHEADS
FLATIRON
FLATIRONS
FLATLAND
FLATLANDS
FLATLET
FLATLETS
FLATLINE
FLATLINED
FLATLINER
FLATLINES
FLATLING
FLATLINGS
FLATLONG
FLATLY
FLATMATE
FLATMATES
FLATNESS
FLATPACK
FLATPACKS
FLATPICK
FLATPICKS
FLATS
FLATSHARE
FLATSTICK
FLATTED
FLATTEN
FLATTENED
FLATTENER
FLATTENS
FLATTER
FLATTERED
FLATTERER
FLATTERS
FLATTERY
FLATTEST
FLATTIE
FLATTIES
FLATTING
FLATTINGS
FLATTISH
FLATTOP
FLATTOPS
FLATTY
FLATULENT
FLATUOUS
FLATUS
FLATUSES
FLATWARE
FLATWARES
FLATWASH
FLATWATER
FLATWAYS
FLATWISE
FLATWORK
FLATWORKS
FLATWORM
FLATWORMS
FLAUGHT
FLAUGHTED
FLAUGHTER
FLAUGHTS
FLAUNCH
FLAUNCHED
FLAUNCHES
FLAUNE
FLAUNES
FLAUNT
FLAUNTED
FLAUNTER
FLAUNTERS
FLAUNTIER
FLAUNTILY
FLAUNTING
FLAUNTS
FLAUNTY
FLAUTA
FLAUTAS
FLAUTIST
FLAUTISTS
FLAVA
FLAVANOL
FLAVANOLS
FLAVANONE
FLAVAS
FLAVIN
FLAVINE
FLAVINES
FLAVINS
FLAVONE
FLAVONES
FLAVONOID
FLAVONOL
FLAVONOLS
FLAVOR
FLAVORED
FLAVORER
FLAVORERS
FLAVORFUL
FLAVORIER
FLAVORING
FLAVORIST
FLAVOROUS
FLAVORS
FLAVORY
FLAVOUR
FLAVOURED
FLAVOURER
FLAVOURS
FLAVOURY
FLAW
FLAWED
FLAWIER
FLAWIEST
FLAWING
FLAWLESS
FLAWN
FLAWNS
FLAWS
FLAWY
FLAX
FLAXEN
FLAXES
FLAXIER
FLAXIEST
FLAXLIKE
FLAXSEED
FLAXSEEDS
FLAXY
FLAY
FLAYED
FLAYER
FLAYERS
FLAYING
FLAYS
FLAYSOME
FLEA
FLEABAG
FLEABAGS
FLEABANE
FLEABANES
FLEABITE
FLEABITES
FLEADH
FLEADHS

F

FLEAM
FLEAMS
FLEAPIT
FLEAPITS
FLEAS
FLEASOME
FLEAWORT
FLEAWORTS
FLECHE
FLECHES
FLECHETTE
FLECK
FLECKED
FLECKER
FLECKERED
FLECKERS
FLECKIER
FLECKIEST
FLECKING
FLECKLESS
FLECKS
FLECKY
FLECTION
FLECTIONS
FLED
FLEDGE
FLEDGED
FLEDGES
FLEDGIER
FLEDGIEST
FLEDGING
FLEDGLING
FLEDGY
FLEE
FLEECE
FLEECED
FLEECER
FLEECERS
FLEECES
FLEECH
FLEECHED
FLEECHES
FLEECHING
FLEECIE
FLEECIER
FLEECIES
FLEECIEST
FLEECILY
FLEECING
FLEECY
FLEEING
FLEEK
FLEEKS
FLEER
FLEERED
FLEERER
FLEERERS
FLEERING
FLEERINGS
FLEERS
FLEES
FLEET
FLEETED
FLEETER
FLEETERS
FLEETEST
FLEETING
FLEETLY
FLEETNESS
FLEETS
FLEG
FLEGGED
FLEGGING
FLEGS
FLEHMEN
FLEHMENED
FLEHMENS
FLEISHIG
FLEISHIK
FLEME
FLEMED
FLEMES
FLEMING
FLEMISH
FLEMISHED
FLEMISHES
FLEMIT
FLENCH
FLENCHED
FLENCHER
FLENCHERS
FLENCHES
FLENCHING
FLENSE
FLENSED
FLENSER
FLENSERS
FLENSES
FLENSING
FLEROVIUM
FLESH
FLESHED
FLESHER
FLESHERS
FLESHES
FLESHHOOD
FLESHIER
FLESHIEST
FLESHILY
FLESHING
FLESHINGS
FLESHLESS
FLESHLIER
FLESHLING
FLESHLY
FLESHMENT
FLESHPOT
FLESHPOTS
FLESHWORM
FLESHY
FLETCH
FLETCHED
FLETCHER
FLETCHERS
FLETCHES
FLETCHING
FLETTON
FLETTONS
FLEUR
FLEURET
FLEURETS
FLEURETTE
FLEURON
FLEURONS
FLEURS
FLEURY
FLEW
FLEWED
FLEWS
FLEX
FLEXAGON
FLEXAGONS
FLEXED
FLEXES
FLEXI
FLEXIBLE
FLEXIBLY
FLEXILE
FLEXING
FLEXION
FLEXIONAL
FLEXIONS
FLEXIS
FLEXITIME
FLEXO
FLEXOR
FLEXORS
FLEXOS
FLEXTIME
FLEXTIMER
FLEXTIMES
FLEXUOSE
FLEXUOUS
FLEXURAL
FLEXURE
FLEXURES
FLEXWING
FLEXWINGS
FLEY
FLEYED
FLEYING
FLEYS
FLIBBERT
FLIBBERTS
FLIC
FLICHTER
FLICHTERS
FLICK
FLICKABLE
FLICKED
FLICKER
FLICKERED
FLICKERS
FLICKERY
FLICKING
FLICKS
FLICS
FLIED
FLIER
FLIERS
FLIES
FLIEST
FLIGHT
FLIGHTED
FLIGHTIER
FLIGHTILY
FLIGHTING
FLIGHTS
FLIGHTY
FLIM
FLIMFLAM
FLIMFLAMS
FLIMP
FLIMPED
FLIMPING
FLIMPS
FLIMS
FLIMSIER
FLIMSIES
FLIMSIEST
FLIMSILY
FLIMSY
FLINCH
FLINCHED
FLINCHER
FLINCHERS
FLINCHES
FLINCHING
FLINDER
FLINDERED
FLINDERS
FLING
FLINGER
FLINGERS
FLINGING
FLINGS
FLINKITE
FLINKITES
FLINT
FLINTED
FLINTHEAD
FLINTIER
FLINTIEST
FLINTIFY
FLINTILY
FLINTING
FLINTLIKE
FLINTLOCK
FLINTS
FLINTY

FLIP
FLIPBOARD
FLIPBOOK
FLIPBOOKS
FLIPCHART
FLIPFLOP
FLIPFLOPS
FLIPPANCY
FLIPPANT
FLIPPED
FLIPPER
FLIPPERS
FLIPPEST
FLIPPIER
FLIPPIEST
FLIPPING
FLIPPINGS
FLIPPY
FLIPS
FLIPSIDE
FLIPSIDES
FLIR
FLIRS
FLIRT
FLIRTED
FLIRTER
FLIRTERS
FLIRTIER
FLIRTIEST
FLIRTING
FLIRTINGS
FLIRTISH
FLIRTS
FLIRTY
FLISK
FLISKED
FLISKIER
FLISKIEST
FLISKING
FLISKS
FLISKY
FLIT
FLITCH
FLITCHED
FLITCHES
FLITCHING
FLITE
FLITED
FLITES
FLITING
FLITS
FLITT
FLITTED
FLITTER
FLITTERED
FLITTERN
FLITTERNS
FLITTERS
FLITTING
FLITTINGS
FLITTS
FLIVVER
FLIVVERS
FLIX
FLIXED
FLIXES
FLIXING
FLIXWEED
FLIXWEEDS
FLOAT
FLOATABLE
FLOATAGE
FLOATAGES
FLOATANT
FLOATANTS
FLOATBASE
FLOATCUT
FLOATED
FLOATEL
FLOATELS
FLOATER
FLOATERS
FLOATIER
FLOATIEST
FLOATING
FLOATINGS
FLOATS
FLOATY
FLOB
FLOBBED
FLOBBING
FLOBS
FLOC
FLOCCED
FLOCCI
FLOCCING
FLOCCOSE
FLOCCULAR
FLOCCULE
FLOCCULES
FLOCCULI
FLOCCULUS
FLOCCUS
FLOCK
FLOCKED
FLOCKIER
FLOCKIEST
FLOCKING
FLOCKINGS
FLOCKLESS
FLOCKS
FLOCKY
FLOCS
FLOE
FLOES
FLOG
FLOGGABLE
FLOGGED
FLOGGER
FLOGGERS
FLOGGING
FLOGGINGS
FLOGS
FLOKATI
FLOKATIS
FLONG
FLONGS
FLOOD
FLOODABLE
FLOODED
FLOODER
FLOODERS
FLOODGATE
FLOODING
FLOODINGS
FLOODLESS
FLOODLIT
FLOODMARK
FLOODS
FLOODTIDE
FLOODWALL
FLOODWAY
FLOODWAYS
FLOOEY
FLOOIE
FLOOR
FLOORAGE
FLOORAGES
FLOORED
FLOORER
FLOORERS
FLOORHEAD
FLOORING
FLOORINGS
FLOORLESS
FLOORPAN
FLOORPANS
FLOORS
FLOORSHOW
FLOOSIE
FLOOSIES
FLOOSY
FLOOZIE
FLOOZIES
FLOOZY
FLOP
FLOPHOUSE
FLOPOVER
FLOPOVERS
FLOPPED
FLOPPER
FLOPPERS
FLOPPIER
FLOPPIES
FLOPPIEST
FLOPPILY
FLOPPING
FLOPPY
FLOPS
FLOPTICAL
FLOR
FLORA
FLORAE
FLORAL
FLORALLY
FLORALS
FLORAS
FLOREANT
FLOREAT
FLOREATED
FLORENCE
FLORENCES
FLORET
FLORETS
FLORIATED
FLORICANE
FLORID
FLORIDEAN
FLORIDER
FLORIDEST
FLORIDITY
FLORIDLY
FLORIER
FLORIEST
FLORIFORM
FLORIGEN
FLORIGENS
FLORIN
FLORINS
FLORIST
FLORISTIC
FLORISTRY
FLORISTS
FLORS
FLORUIT
FLORUITS
FLORULA
FLORULAE
FLORULE
FLORULES
FLORY
FLOSCULAR
FLOSCULE
FLOSCULES
FLOSH
FLOSHES
FLOSS
FLOSSED
FLOSSER
FLOSSERS
FLOSSES
FLOSSIE
FLOSSIER
FLOSSIES
FLOSSIEST
FLOSSILY
FLOSSING
FLOSSINGS
FLOSSY
FLOTA

FLOTAGE
FLOTAGES
FLOTANT
FLOTAS
FLOTATION
FLOTE
FLOTED
FLOTEL
FLOTELS
FLOTES
FLOTILLA
FLOTILLAS
FLOTING
FLOTSAM
FLOTSAMS
FLOUNCE
FLOUNCED
FLOUNCES
FLOUNCIER
FLOUNCING
FLOUNCY
FLOUNDER
FLOUNDERS
FLOUR
FLOURED
FLOURIER
FLOURIEST
FLOURING
FLOURISH
FLOURISHY
FLOURLESS
FLOURS
FLOURY
FLOUSE
FLOUSED
FLOUSES
FLOUSH
FLOUSHED
FLOUSHES
FLOUSHING
FLOUSING
FLOUT
FLOUTED
FLOUTER
FLOUTERS
FLOUTING
FLOUTS
FLOW
FLOWABLE
FLOWAGE
FLOWAGES
FLOWCHART
FLOWED
FLOWER
FLOWERAGE
FLOWERBED
FLOWERED
FLOWERER
FLOWERERS
FLOWERET
FLOWERETS
FLOWERFUL
FLOWERIER
FLOWERILY
FLOWERING
FLOWERPOT
FLOWERS
FLOWERY
FLOWING
FLOWINGLY
FLOWMETER
FLOWN
FLOWS
FLOWSTONE
FLOX
FLU
FLUATE
FLUATES
FLUB
FLUBBED
FLUBBER
FLUBBERS
FLUBBING
FLUBDUB
FLUBDUBS
FLUBS
FLUCTUANT
FLUCTUATE
FLUE
FLUED
FLUELLEN
FLUELLENS
FLUELLIN
FLUELLINS
FLUENCE
FLUENCES
FLUENCIES
FLUENCY
FLUENT
FLUENTLY
FLUENTS
FLUERIC
FLUERICS
FLUES
FLUEWORK
FLUEWORKS
FLUEY
FLUFF
FLUFFBALL
FLUFFED
FLUFFER
FLUFFERS
FLUFFIER
FLUFFIEST
FLUFFILY
FLUFFING
FLUFFS
FLUFFY
FLUGEL
FLUGELMAN
FLUGELMEN
FLUGELS
FLUID
FLUIDAL
FLUIDALLY
FLUIDIC
FLUIDICS
FLUIDIFY
FLUIDISE
FLUIDISED
FLUIDISER
FLUIDISES
FLUIDITY
FLUIDIZE
FLUIDIZED
FLUIDIZER
FLUIDIZES
FLUIDLIKE
FLUIDLY
FLUIDNESS
FLUIDRAM
FLUIDRAMS
FLUIDS
FLUIER
FLUIEST
FLUISH
FLUKE
FLUKED
FLUKES
FLUKEY
FLUKIER
FLUKIEST
FLUKILY
FLUKINESS
FLUKING
FLUKY
FLUME
FLUMED
FLUMES
FLUMING
FLUMMERY
FLUMMOX
FLUMMOXED
FLUMMOXES
FLUMP
FLUMPED
FLUMPING
FLUMPS
FLUNG
FLUNK
FLUNKED
FLUNKER
FLUNKERS
FLUNKEY
FLUNKEYS
FLUNKIE
FLUNKIES
FLUNKING
FLUNKS
FLUNKY
FLUNKYISM
FLUOR
FLUORENE
FLUORENES
FLUORESCE
FLUORIC
FLUORID
FLUORIDE
FLUORIDES
FLUORIDS
FLUORIN
FLUORINE
FLUORINES
FLUORINS
FLUORITE
FLUORITES
FLUOROSES
FLUOROSIS
FLUOROTIC
FLUORS
FLUORSPAR
FLURR
FLURRED
FLURRIED
FLURRIES
FLURRING
FLURRS
FLURRY
FLURRYING
FLUS
FLUSH
FLUSHABLE
FLUSHED
FLUSHER
FLUSHERS
FLUSHES
FLUSHEST
FLUSHIER
FLUSHIEST
FLUSHING
FLUSHINGS
FLUSHNESS
FLUSHWORK
FLUSHY
FLUSTER
FLUSTERED
FLUSTERS
FLUSTERY
FLUSTRATE
FLUTE
FLUTED
FLUTELIKE
FLUTER
FLUTERS
FLUTES
FLUTEY
FLUTEYER
FLUTEYEST
FLUTIER
FLUTIEST

FLUTINA
FLUTINAS
FLUTING
FLUTINGS
FLUTIST
FLUTISTS
FLUTTER
FLUTTERED
FLUTTERER
FLUTTERS
FLUTTERY
FLUTY
FLUVIAL
FLUVIATIC
FLUX
FLUXED
FLUXES
FLUXGATE
FLUXGATES
FLUXING
FLUXION
FLUXIONAL
FLUXIONS
FLUXIVE
FLUXMETER
FLUYT
FLUYTS
FLY
FLYABLE
FLYAWAY
FLYAWAYS
FLYBACK
FLYBACKS
FLYBANE
FLYBANES
FLYBELT
FLYBELTS
FLYBLEW
FLYBLOW
FLYBLOWN
FLYBLOWS
FLYBOAT
FLYBOATS
FLYBOOK
FLYBOOKS
FLYBOY
FLYBOYS
FLYBRIDGE
FLYBY
FLYBYS
FLYER
FLYERS
FLYEST
FLYFISHER
FLYHAND
FLYHANDS
FLYING
FLYINGS
FLYLEAF
FLYLEAVES
FLYLESS
FLYLINE
FLYLINES
FLYMAKER
FLYMAKERS
FLYMAN
FLYMEN
FLYOFF
FLYOFFS
FLYOVER
FLYOVERS
FLYPAPER
FLYPAPERS
FLYPAST
FLYPASTS
FLYPE
FLYPED
FLYPES
FLYPING
FLYPITCH
FLYPOSTER
FLYRODDER
FLYSCH
FLYSCHES
FLYSCREEN
FLYSHEET
FLYSHEETS
FLYSPECK
FLYSPECKS
FLYSPRAY
FLYSPRAYS
FLYSTRIKE
FLYTE
FLYTED
FLYTES
FLYTIER
FLYTIERS
FLYTING
FLYTINGS
FLYTRAP
FLYTRAPS
FLYWAY
FLYWAYS
FLYWEIGHT
FLYWHEEL
FLYWHEELS
FOAL
FOALED
FOALFOOT
FOALFOOTS
FOALING
FOALINGS
FOALS
FOAM
FOAMABLE
FOAMED
FOAMER
FOAMERS
FOAMIER
FOAMIEST
FOAMILY
FOAMINESS
FOAMING
FOAMINGLY
FOAMINGS
FOAMLESS
FOAMLIKE
FOAMS
FOAMY
FOB
FOBBED
FOBBING
FOBS
FOCACCIA
FOCACCIAS
FOCAL
FOCALISE
FOCALISED
FOCALISES
FOCALIZE
FOCALIZED
FOCALIZES
FOCALLY
FOCI
FOCIMETER
FOCOMETER
FOCUS
FOCUSABLE
FOCUSED
FOCUSER
FOCUSERS
FOCUSES
FOCUSING
FOCUSINGS
FOCUSLESS
FOCUSSED
FOCUSSES
FOCUSSING
FODDER
FODDERED
FODDERER
FODDERERS
FODDERING
FODDERS
FODGEL
FOE
FOEDARIE
FOEDARIES
FOEDERATI
FOEFIE
FOEHN
FOEHNS
FOEMAN
FOEMEN
FOEN
FOES
FOETAL
FOETATION
FOETICIDE
FOETID
FOETIDER
FOETIDEST
FOETIDLY
FOETOR
FOETORS
FOETUS
FOETUSES
FOG
FOGASH
FOGASHES
FOGBOUND
FOGBOW
FOGBOWS
FOGDOG
FOGDOGS
FOGEY
FOGEYDOM
FOGEYDOMS
FOGEYISH
FOGEYISM
FOGEYISMS
FOGEYS
FOGFRUIT
FOGFRUITS
FOGGAGE
FOGGAGES
FOGGED
FOGGER
FOGGERS
FOGGIER
FOGGIEST
FOGGILY
FOGGINESS
FOGGING
FOGGINGS
FOGGY
FOGHORN
FOGHORNS
FOGIE
FOGIES
FOGLE
FOGLES
FOGLESS
FOGLIGHT
FOGLIGHTS
FOGMAN
FOGMEN
FOGOU
FOGOUS
FOGRAM
FOGRAMITE
FOGRAMITY
FOGRAMS
FOGS
FOGY
FOGYDOM
FOGYDOMS
FOGYISH
FOGYISM
FOGYISMS

FOH
FOHN
FOHNS
FOIBLE
FOIBLES
FOID
FOIDS
FOIL
FOILABLE
FOILBORNE
FOILED
FOILING
FOILINGS
FOILIST
FOILISTS
FOILS
FOILSMAN
FOILSMEN
FOIN
FOINED
FOINING
FOININGLY
FOINS
FOISON
FOISONS
FOIST
FOISTED
FOISTER
FOISTERS
FOISTING
FOISTS
FOLACIN
FOLACINS
FOLATE
FOLATES
FOLD
FOLDABLE
FOLDAWAY
FOLDAWAYS
FOLDBACK
FOLDBACKS
FOLDBOAT
FOLDBOATS
FOLDED
FOLDER
FOLDEROL
FOLDEROLS
FOLDERS
FOLDING
FOLDINGS
FOLDOUT
FOLDOUTS
FOLDS
FOLDUP
FOLDUPS
FOLEY
FOLEYS
FOLIA
FOLIAGE
FOLIAGED
FOLIAGES
FOLIAR
FOLIATE
FOLIATED
FOLIATES
FOLIATING
FOLIATION
FOLIATURE
FOLIC
FOLIE
FOLIES
FOLIO
FOLIOED
FOLIOING
FOLIOLATE
FOLIOLE
FOLIOLES
FOLIOLOSE
FOLIOS
FOLIOSE
FOLIOUS
FOLIUM
FOLIUMS
FOLK
FOLKIE
FOLKIER
FOLKIES
FOLKIEST
FOLKINESS
FOLKISH
FOLKLAND
FOLKLANDS
FOLKLIFE
FOLKLIFES
FOLKLIKE
FOLKLIVES
FOLKLORE
FOLKLORES
FOLKLORIC
FOLKMOOT
FOLKMOOTS
FOLKMOT
FOLKMOTE
FOLKMOTES
FOLKMOTS
FOLKS
FOLKSIER
FOLKSIEST
FOLKSILY
FOLKSONG
FOLKSONGS
FOLKSY
FOLKTALE
FOLKTALES
FOLKWAY
FOLKWAYS
FOLKY
FOLLES
FOLLICLE
FOLLICLES
FOLLIED
FOLLIES
FOLLIS
FOLLOW
FOLLOWED
FOLLOWER
FOLLOWERS
FOLLOWING
FOLLOWS
FOLLOWUP
FOLLOWUPS
FOLLY
FOLLYING
FOMENT
FOMENTED
FOMENTER
FOMENTERS
FOMENTING
FOMENTS
FOMES
FOMITE
FOMITES
FON
FOND
FONDA
FONDANT
FONDANTS
FONDAS
FONDED
FONDER
FONDEST
FONDING
FONDLE
FONDLED
FONDLER
FONDLERS
FONDLES
FONDLING
FONDLINGS
FONDLY
FONDNESS
FONDS
FONDU
FONDUE
FONDUED
FONDUEING
FONDUES
FONDUING
FONDUS
FONE
FONES
FONLY
FONNED
FONNING
FONS
FONT
FONTAL
FONTANEL
FONTANELS
FONTANGE
FONTANGES
FONTICULI
FONTINA
FONTINAS
FONTLET
FONTLETS
FONTS
FOO
FOOBAR
FOOD
FOODBANK
FOODBANKS
FOODBORNE
FOODERIES
FOODERY
FOODFUL
FOODIE
FOODIES
FOODISM
FOODISMS
FOODLAND
FOODLANDS
FOODLESS
FOODOIR
FOODOIRS
FOODS
FOODSHED
FOODSHEDS
FOODSTUFF
FOODWAYS
FOODY
FOOFARAW
FOOFARAWS
FOOL
FOOLED
FOOLERIES
FOOLERY
FOOLFISH
FOOLHARDY
FOOLING
FOOLINGS
FOOLISH
FOOLISHER
FOOLISHLY
FOOLPROOF
FOOLS
FOOLSCAP
FOOLSCAPS
FOOS
FOOSBALL
FOOSBALLS
FOOT
FOOTAGE
FOOTAGES
FOOTBAG
FOOTBAGS
FOOTBALL
FOOTBALLS
FOOTBAR
FOOTBARS

FOOTBATH
FOOTBATHS
FOOTBED
FOOTBEDS
FOOTBOARD
FOOTBOY
FOOTBOYS
FOOTBRAKE
FOOTCLOTH
FOOTED
FOOTER
FOOTERED
FOOTERING
FOOTERS
FOOTFALL
FOOTFALLS
FOOTFAULT
FOOTGEAR
FOOTGEARS
FOOTHILL
FOOTHILLS
FOOTHOLD
FOOTHOLDS
FOOTIE
FOOTIER
FOOTIES
FOOTIEST
FOOTING
FOOTINGS
FOOTLE
FOOTLED
FOOTLER
FOOTLERS
FOOTLES
FOOTLESS
FOOTLIGHT
FOOTLIKE
FOOTLING
FOOTLINGS
FOOTLONG
FOOTLONGS
FOOTLOOSE
FOOTMAN
FOOTMARK
FOOTMARKS
FOOTMEN
FOOTMUFF
FOOTMUFFS
FOOTNOTE
FOOTNOTED
FOOTNOTES
FOOTPACE
FOOTPACES
FOOTPAD
FOOTPADS
FOOTPAGE
FOOTPAGES
FOOTPATH
FOOTPATHS
FOOTPLATE
FOOTPOST
FOOTPOSTS
FOOTPRINT
FOOTPUMP
FOOTPUMPS
FOOTRA
FOOTRACE
FOOTRACES
FOOTRAS
FOOTREST
FOOTRESTS
FOOTROPE
FOOTROPES
FOOTRULE
FOOTRULES
FOOTS
FOOTSAL
FOOTSALS
FOOTSIE
FOOTSIES
FOOTSLOG
FOOTSLOGS
FOOTSORE
FOOTSTALK
FOOTSTALL
FOOTSTEP
FOOTSTEPS
FOOTSTOCK
FOOTSTONE
FOOTSTOOL
FOOTSY
FOOTWALL
FOOTWALLS
FOOTWAY
FOOTWAYS
FOOTWEAR
FOOTWEARS
FOOTWEARY
FOOTWELL
FOOTWELLS
FOOTWORK
FOOTWORKS
FOOTWORN
FOOTY
FOOZLE
FOOZLED
FOOZLER
FOOZLERS
FOOZLES
FOOZLING
FOOZLINGS
FOP
FOPLING
FOPLINGS
FOPPED
FOPPERIES
FOPPERY
FOPPING
FOPPISH
FOPPISHLY
FOPS
FOR
FORA
FORAGE
FORAGED
FORAGER
FORAGERS
FORAGES
FORAGING
FORAM
FORAMEN
FORAMENS
FORAMINA
FORAMINAL
FORAMS
FORANE
FORASMUCH
FORAY
FORAYED
FORAYER
FORAYERS
FORAYING
FORAYS
FORB
FORBAD
FORBADE
FORBARE
FORBEAR
FORBEARER
FORBEARS
FORBID
FORBIDAL
FORBIDALS
FORBIDDAL
FORBIDDEN
FORBIDDER
FORBIDS
FORBODE
FORBODED
FORBODES
FORBODING
FORBORE
FORBORNE
FORBS
FORBY
FORBYE
FORCAT
FORCATS
FORCE
FORCEABLE
FORCEABLY
FORCED
FORCEDLY
FORCEFUL
FORCELESS
FORCEMEAT
FORCEOUT
FORCEOUTS
FORCEPS
FORCEPSES
FORCER
FORCERS
FORCES
FORCIBLE
FORCIBLY
FORCING
FORCINGLY
FORCIPATE
FORCIPES
FORD
FORDABLE
FORDED
FORDID
FORDING
FORDLESS
FORDO
FORDOES
FORDOING
FORDONE
FORDONNE
FORDS
FORE
FOREANENT
FOREARM
FOREARMED
FOREARMS
FOREBAY
FOREBAYS
FOREBEAR
FOREBEARS
FOREBITT
FOREBITTS
FOREBODE
FOREBODED
FOREBODER
FOREBODES
FOREBODY
FOREBOOM
FOREBOOMS
FOREBRAIN
FOREBY
FOREBYE
FORECABIN
FORECADDY
FORECAR
FORECARS
FORECAST
FORECASTS
FORECHECK
FORECLOSE
FORECLOTH
FORECOURT
FOREDATE
FOREDATED
FOREDATES
FOREDECK
FOREDECKS
FOREDID
FOREDO
FOREDOES

FOREDOING
FOREDONE
FOREDOOM
FOREDOOMS
FOREFACE
FOREFACES
FOREFEEL
FOREFEELS
FOREFEET
FOREFELT
FOREFEND
FOREFENDS
FOREFOOT
FOREFRONT
FOREGLEAM
FOREGO
FOREGOER
FOREGOERS
FOREGOES
FOREGOING
FOREGONE
FOREGUT
FOREGUTS
FOREHAND
FOREHANDS
FOREHEAD
FOREHEADS
FOREHENT
FOREHENTS
FOREHOCK
FOREHOCKS
FOREHOOF
FOREHOOFS
FOREIGN
FOREIGNER
FOREIGNLY
FOREJUDGE
FOREKING
FOREKINGS
FOREKNEW
FOREKNOW
FOREKNOWN
FOREKNOWS
FOREL
FORELADY
FORELAID
FORELAIN
FORELAND
FORELANDS
FORELAY
FORELAYS
FORELEG
FORELEGS
FORELEND
FORELENDS
FORELENT
FORELIE
FORELIES
FORELIFT
FORELIFTS
FORELIMB
FORELIMBS
FORELLED
FORELLING
FORELOCK
FORELOCKS
FORELS
FORELYING
FOREMAN
FOREMAST
FOREMASTS
FOREMEAN
FOREMEANS
FOREMEANT
FOREMEN
FOREMILK
FOREMILKS
FOREMOST
FORENAME
FORENAMED
FORENAMES
FORENIGHT
FORENOON
FORENOONS
FORENSIC
FORENSICS
FOREPART
FOREPARTS
FOREPAST
FOREPAW
FOREPAWS
FOREPEAK
FOREPEAKS
FOREPLAN
FOREPLANS
FOREPLAY
FOREPLAYS
FOREPOINT
FORERAN
FORERANK
FORERANKS
FOREREACH
FOREREAD
FOREREADS
FORERUN
FORERUNS
FORES
FORESAID
FORESAIL
FORESAILS
FORESAW
FORESAY
FORESAYS
FORESEE
FORESEEN
FORESEER
FORESEERS
FORESEES
FORESHANK
FORESHEET
FORESHEW
FORESHEWN
FORESHEWS
FORESHIP
FORESHIPS
FORESHOCK
FORESHORE
FORESHOW
FORESHOWN
FORESHOWS
FORESIDE
FORESIDES
FORESIGHT
FORESKIN
FORESKINS
FORESKIRT
FORESLACK
FORESLOW
FORESLOWS
FORESPAKE
FORESPEAK
FORESPEND
FORESPENT
FORESPOKE
FOREST
FORESTAGE
FORESTAIR
FORESTAL
FORESTALL
FORESTAY
FORESTAYS
FORESTEAL
FORESTED
FORESTER
FORESTERS
FORESTIAL
FORESTINE
FORESTING
FORESTRY
FORESTS
FORESWEAR
FORESWORE
FORESWORN
FORETASTE
FORETEACH
FORETEETH
FORETELL
FORETELLS
FORETHINK
FORETIME
FORETIMES
FORETOKEN
FORETOLD
FORETOOTH
FORETOP
FORETOPS
FOREVER
FOREVERS
FOREWARD
FOREWARDS
FOREWARN
FOREWARNS
FOREWEIGH
FOREWENT
FOREWIND
FOREWINDS
FOREWING
FOREWINGS
FOREWOMAN
FOREWOMEN
FOREWORD
FOREWORDS
FOREWORN
FOREX
FOREXES
FOREYARD
FOREYARDS
FORFAIR
FORFAIRED
FORFAIRN
FORFAIRS
FORFAITER
FORFAULT
FORFAULTS
FORFEIT
FORFEITED
FORFEITER
FORFEITS
FORFEND
FORFENDED
FORFENDS
FORFEX
FORFEXES
FORFICATE
FORFOCHEN
FORGAT
FORGATHER
FORGAVE
FORGE
FORGEABLE
FORGED
FORGEMAN
FORGEMEN
FORGER
FORGERIES
FORGERS
FORGERY
FORGES
FORGET
FORGETFUL
FORGETIVE
FORGETS
FORGETTER
FORGING
FORGINGS
FORGIVE
FORGIVEN
FORGIVER
FORGIVERS
FORGIVES

FORGIVING
FORGO
FORGOER
FORGOERS
FORGOES
FORGOING
FORGONE
FORGOT
FORGOTTEN
FORHAILE
FORHAILED
FORHAILES
FORHENT
FORHENTS
FORHOO
FORHOOED
FORHOOIE
FORHOOIED
FORHOOIES
FORHOOING
FORHOOS
FORHOW
FORHOWED
FORHOWING
FORHOWS
FORINSEC
FORINT
FORINTS
FORJASKIT
FORJESKIT
FORJUDGE
FORJUDGED
FORJUDGES
FORK
FORKBALL
FORKBALLS
FORKED
FORKEDLY
FORKER
FORKERS
FORKFUL
FORKFULS
FORKHEAD
FORKHEADS
FORKIER
FORKIEST
FORKINESS
FORKING
FORKLESS
FORKLIFT
FORKLIFTS
FORKLIKE
FORKS
FORKSFUL
FORKTAIL
FORKTAILS
FORKY
FORLANA
FORLANAS
FORLEND
FORLENDS
FORLENT
FORLESE
FORLESES
FORLESING
FORLORE
FORLORN
FORLORNER
FORLORNLY
FORLORNS
FORM
FORMABLE
FORMABLY
FORMAL
FORMALIN
FORMALINE
FORMALINS
FORMALISE
FORMALISM
FORMALIST
FORMALITY
FORMALIZE
FORMALLY
FORMALS
FORMAMIDE
FORMANT
FORMANTS
FORMAT
FORMATE
FORMATED
FORMATES
FORMATING
FORMATION
FORMATIVE
FORMATS
FORMATTED
FORMATTER
FORME
FORMED
FORMEE
FORMEES
FORMER
FORMERLY
FORMERS
FORMES
FORMFUL
FORMIATE
FORMIATES
FORMIC
FORMICA
FORMICANT
FORMICARY
FORMICAS
FORMICATE
FORMING
FORMINGS
FORMLESS
FORMOL
FORMOLS
FORMS
FORMULA
FORMULAE
FORMULAIC
FORMULAR
FORMULARS
FORMULARY
FORMULAS
FORMULATE
FORMULISE
FORMULISM
FORMULIST
FORMULIZE
FORMWORK
FORMWORKS
FORMYL
FORMYLS
FORNENST
FORNENT
FORNICAL
FORNICATE
FORNICES
FORNIX
FORPET
FORPETS
FORPINE
FORPINED
FORPINES
FORPINING
FORPIT
FORPITS
FORRAD
FORRADER
FORRADS
FORRARDER
FORRAY
FORRAYED
FORRAYING
FORRAYS
FORREN
FORRIT
FORSAID
FORSAKE
FORSAKEN
FORSAKER
FORSAKERS
FORSAKES
FORSAKING
FORSAY
FORSAYING
FORSAYS
FORSLACK
FORSLACKS
FORSLOE
FORSLOED
FORSLOES
FORSLOW
FORSLOWED
FORSLOWS
FORSOOK
FORSOOTH
FORSPEAK
FORSPEAKS
FORSPEND
FORSPENDS
FORSPENT
FORSPOKE
FORSPOKEN
FORSWATT
FORSWEAR
FORSWEARS
FORSWINK
FORSWINKS
FORSWONCK
FORSWORE
FORSWORN
FORSWUNK
FORSYTHIA
FORT
FORTALICE
FORTE
FORTED
FORTES
FORTH
FORTHCAME
FORTHCOME
FORTHINK
FORTHINKS
FORTHWITH
FORTHY
FORTIES
FORTIETH
FORTIETHS
FORTIFIED
FORTIFIER
FORTIFIES
FORTIFY
FORTILAGE
FORTING
FORTIS
FORTITUDE
FORTLET
FORTLETS
FORTNIGHT
FORTRESS
FORTS
FORTUITY
FORTUNATE
FORTUNE
FORTUNED
FORTUNES
FORTUNING
FORTUNISE
FORTUNIZE
FORTY
FORTYFOLD
FORTYISH
FORUM
FORUMS
FORWANDER
FORWARD

FORWARDED
FORWARDER
FORWARDLY
FORWARDS
FORWARN
FORWARNED
FORWARNS
FORWASTE
FORWASTED
FORWASTES
FORWEARY
FORWENT
FORWHY
FORWORN
FORZA
FORZANDI
FORZANDO
FORZANDOS
FORZATI
FORZATO
FORZATOS
FORZE
FOSCARNET
FOSS
FOSSA
FOSSAE
FOSSAS
FOSSATE
FOSSE
FOSSED
FOSSES
FOSSETTE
FOSSETTES
FOSSICK
FOSSICKED
FOSSICKER
FOSSICKS
FOSSIL
FOSSILISE
FOSSILIZE
FOSSILS
FOSSOR
FOSSORIAL
FOSSORS
FOSSULA
FOSSULAE
FOSSULATE
FOSTER
FOSTERAGE
FOSTERED
FOSTERER
FOSTERERS
FOSTERING
FOSTERS
FOSTRESS
FOTHER
FOTHERED
FOTHERING
FOTHERS
FOU
FOUAT
FOUATS
FOUD
FOUDRIE
FOUDRIES
FOUDS
FOUER
FOUEST
FOUET
FOUETS
FOUETTE
FOUETTES
FOUGADE
FOUGADES
FOUGASSE
FOUGASSES
FOUGHT
FOUGHTEN
FOUGHTIER
FOUGHTY
FOUL
FOULARD
FOULARDS
FOULBROOD
FOULDER
FOULDERED
FOULDERS
FOULE
FOULED
FOULER
FOULES
FOULEST
FOULIE
FOULIES
FOULING
FOULINGS
FOULLY
FOULMART
FOULMARTS
FOULNESS
FOULS
FOUMART
FOUMARTS
FOUND
FOUNDED
FOUNDER
FOUNDERED
FOUNDERS
FOUNDING
FOUNDINGS
FOUNDLING
FOUNDRESS
FOUNDRIES
FOUNDRY
FOUNDS
FOUNT
FOUNTAIN
FOUNTAINS
FOUNTFUL
FOUNTS
FOUR
FOURBALL
FOURBALLS
FOURCHEE
FOURCHEES
FOUREYED
FOURFOLD
FOURGON
FOURGONS
FOURPENCE
FOURPENNY
FOURPLAY
FOURPLAYS
FOURPLEX
FOURS
FOURSCORE
FOURSES
FOURSOME
FOURSOMES
FOURTEEN
FOURTEENS
FOURTH
FOURTHLY
FOURTHS
FOUS
FOUSSA
FOUSSAS
FOUSTIER
FOUSTIEST
FOUSTY
FOUTER
FOUTERED
FOUTERING
FOUTERS
FOUTH
FOUTHS
FOUTRA
FOUTRAS
FOUTRE
FOUTRED
FOUTRES
FOUTRING
FOVEA
FOVEAE
FOVEAL
FOVEAS
FOVEATE
FOVEATED
FOVEIFORM
FOVEOLA
FOVEOLAE
FOVEOLAR
FOVEOLAS
FOVEOLATE
FOVEOLE
FOVEOLES
FOVEOLET
FOVEOLETS
FOWL
FOWLED
FOWLER
FOWLERS
FOWLING
FOWLINGS
FOWLPOX
FOWLPOXES
FOWLS
FOWTH
FOWTHS
FOX
FOXBERRY
FOXED
FOXES
FOXFIRE
FOXFIRES
FOXFISH
FOXFISHES
FOXGLOVE
FOXGLOVES
FOXHOLE
FOXHOLES
FOXHOUND
FOXHOUNDS
FOXHUNT
FOXHUNTED
FOXHUNTER
FOXHUNTS
FOXIE
FOXIER
FOXIES
FOXIEST
FOXILY
FOXINESS
FOXING
FOXINGS
FOXLIKE
FOXSHARK
FOXSHARKS
FOXSHIP
FOXSHIPS
FOXSKIN
FOXSKINS
FOXTAIL
FOXTAILS
FOXTROT
FOXTROTS
FOXY
FOY
FOYBOAT
FOYBOATS
FOYER
FOYERS
FOYLE
FOYLED
FOYLES
FOYLING
FOYNE
FOYNED
FOYNES
FOYNING

F

FOYS
FOZIER
FOZIEST
FOZINESS
FOZY
FRA
FRAB
FRABBED
FRABBING
FRABBIT
FRABJOUS
FRABS
FRACAS
FRACASES
FRACK
FRACKED
FRACKER
FRACKERS
FRACKING
FRACKINGS
FRACKS
FRACT
FRACTAL
FRACTALS
FRACTED
FRACTI
FRACTING
FRACTION
FRACTIONS
FRACTIOUS
FRACTS
FRACTUR
FRACTURAL
FRACTURE
FRACTURED
FRACTURER
FRACTURES
FRACTURS
FRACTUS
FRAE
FRAENA
FRAENUM
FRAENUMS
FRAG
FRAGGED
FRAGGING
FRAGGINGS
FRAGILE
FRAGILELY
FRAGILER
FRAGILEST
FRAGILITY
FRAGMENT
FRAGMENTS
FRAGOR
FRAGORS
FRAGRANCE
FRAGRANCY
FRAGRANT
FRAGS
FRAICHEUR
FRAIL
FRAILER
FRAILEST
FRAILISH
FRAILLY
FRAILNESS
FRAILS
FRAILTEE
FRAILTEES
FRAILTIES
FRAILTY
FRAIM
FRAIMS
FRAISE
FRAISED
FRAISES
FRAISING
FRAKTUR
FRAKTURS
FRAMABLE
FRAMBESIA
FRAMBOISE
FRAME
FRAMEABLE
FRAMED
FRAMELESS
FRAMER
FRAMERS
FRAMES
FRAMEWORK
FRAMING
FRAMINGS
FRAMPAL
FRAMPLER
FRAMPLERS
FRAMPOLD
FRANC
FRANCHISE
FRANCISE
FRANCISED
FRANCISES
FRANCIUM
FRANCIUMS
FRANCIZE
FRANCIZED
FRANCIZES
FRANCO
FRANCOLIN
FRANCS
FRANGER
FRANGERS
FRANGIBLE
FRANGLAIS
FRANION
FRANIONS
FRANK
FRANKABLE
FRANKED
FRANKER
FRANKERS
FRANKEST
FRANKFORT
FRANKFURT
FRANKING
FRANKLIN
FRANKLINS
FRANKLY
FRANKNESS
FRANKS
FRANKUM
FRANKUMS
FRANSERIA
FRANTIC
FRANTICLY
FRANZIER
FRANZIEST
FRANZY
FRAP
FRAPE
FRAPEAGE
FRAPEAGES
FRAPED
FRAPES
FRAPING
FRAPPANT
FRAPPE
FRAPPED
FRAPPEE
FRAPPES
FRAPPING
FRAPS
FRAS
FRASCATI
FRASCATIS
FRASS
FRASSES
FRAT
FRATCH
FRATCHES
FRATCHETY
FRATCHIER
FRATCHING
FRATCHY
FRATE
FRATER
FRATERIES
FRATERNAL
FRATERS
FRATERY
FRATI
FRATRIES
FRATRY
FRATS
FRAU
FRAUD
FRAUDFUL
FRAUDS
FRAUDSMAN
FRAUDSMEN
FRAUDSTER
FRAUGHAN
FRAUGHANS
FRAUGHT
FRAUGHTED
FRAUGHTER
FRAUGHTS
FRAULEIN
FRAULEINS
FRAUS
FRAUTAGE
FRAUTAGES
FRAWZEY
FRAWZEYS
FRAY
FRAYED
FRAYING
FRAYINGS
FRAYS
FRAZIL
FRAZILS
FRAZZLE
FRAZZLED
FRAZZLES
FRAZZLING
FREAK
FREAKED
FREAKERY
FREAKFUL
FREAKIER
FREAKIEST
FREAKILY
FREAKING
FREAKISH
FREAKOUT
FREAKOUTS
FREAKS
FREAKY
FRECKLE
FRECKLED
FRECKLES
FRECKLIER
FRECKLING
FRECKLY
FREDAINE
FREDAINES
FREE
FREEBASE
FREEBASED
FREEBASER
FREEBASES
FREEBEE
FREEBEES
FREEBIE
FREEBIES
FREEBOARD
FREEBOOT
FREEBOOTS
FREEBOOTY
FREEBORN

F

FREECYCLE
FREED
FREEDIVER
FREEDMAN
FREEDMEN
FREEDOM
FREEDOMS
FREEFALL
FREEFORM
FREEGAN
FREEGANS
FREEHAND
FREEHOLD
FREEHOLDS
FREEING
FREEKEH
FREEKEHS
FREELANCE
FREELOAD
FREELOADS
FREELY
FREEMAN
FREEMASON
FREEMEN
FREEMIUM
FREEMIUMS
FREENESS
FREEPHONE
FREEPOST
FREEPOSTS
FREER
FREERIDE
FREERIDES
FREERS
FREES
FREESHEET
FREESIA
FREESIAS
FREEST
FREESTONE
FREESTYLE
FREET
FREETIER
FREETIEST
FREETS
FREETY
FREEWARE
FREEWARES
FREEWAY
FREEWAYS
FREEWHEEL
FREEWILL
FREEWOMAN
FREEWOMEN
FREEWRITE
FREEWROTE
FREEZABLE
FREEZE
FREEZER
FREEZERS
FREEZES
FREEZING
FREEZINGS
FREIGHT
FREIGHTED
FREIGHTER
FREIGHTS
FREIT
FREITIER
FREITIEST
FREITS
FREITY
FREMD
FREMDS
FREMIT
FREMITS
FREMITUS
FRENA
FRENCH
FRENCHED
FRENCHES
FRENCHIFY
FRENCHING
FRENEMIES
FRENEMY
FRENETIC
FRENETICS
FRENNE
FRENNES
FRENULA
FRENULAR
FRENULUM
FRENULUMS
FRENUM
FRENUMS
FRENZICAL
FRENZIED
FRENZIES
FRENZILY
FRENZY
FRENZYING
FREON
FREONS
FREQUENCE
FREQUENCY
FREQUENT
FREQUENTS
FRERE
FRERES
FRESCADE
FRESCADES
FRESCO
FRESCOED
FRESCOER
FRESCOERS
FRESCOES
FRESCOING
FRESCOIST
FRESCOS
FRESH
FRESHED
FRESHEN
FRESHENED
FRESHENER
FRESHENS
FRESHER
FRESHERS
FRESHES
FRESHEST
FRESHET
FRESHETS
FRESHIE
FRESHIES
FRESHING
FRESHISH
FRESHLY
FRESHMAN
FRESHMEN
FRESHNESS
FRESNEL
FRESNELS
FRET
FRETBOARD
FRETFUL
FRETFULLY
FRETLESS
FRETS
FRETSAW
FRETSAWS
FRETSOME
FRETTED
FRETTER
FRETTERS
FRETTIER
FRETTIEST
FRETTING
FRETTINGS
FRETTY
FRETWORK
FRETWORKS
FRIABLE
FRIAND
FRIANDE
FRIANDES
FRIANDS
FRIAR
FRIARBIRD
FRIARIES
FRIARLY
FRIARS
FRIARY
FRIB
FRIBBLE
FRIBBLED
FRIBBLER
FRIBBLERS
FRIBBLES
FRIBBLING
FRIBBLISH
FRIBS
FRICADEL
FRICADELS
FRICANDO
FRICASSEE
FRICATIVE
FRICHT
FRICHTED
FRICHTING
FRICHTS
FRICKING
FRICOT
FRICOTS
FRICTION
FRICTIONS
FRIDGE
FRIDGED
FRIDGES
FRIDGING
FRIED
FRIEDCAKE
FRIEND
FRIENDED
FRIENDING
FRIENDLY
FRIENDS
FRIER
FRIERS
FRIES
FRIEZE
FRIEZED
FRIEZES
FRIEZING
FRIG
FRIGATE
FRIGATES
FRIGATOON
FRIGES
FRIGGED
FRIGGER
FRIGGERS
FRIGGING
FRIGGINGS
FRIGHT
FRIGHTED
FRIGHTEN
FRIGHTENS
FRIGHTFUL
FRIGHTING
FRIGHTS
FRIGID
FRIGIDER
FRIGIDEST
FRIGIDITY
FRIGIDLY
FRIGOT
FRIGOTS
FRIGS
FRIJOL
FRIJOLE
FRIJOLES

FRIKKADEL
FRILL
FRILLED
FRILLER
FRILLERS
FRILLERY
FRILLIER
FRILLIES
FRILLIEST
FRILLING
FRILLINGS
FRILLS
FRILLY
FRINGE
FRINGED
FRINGES
FRINGIER
FRINGIEST
FRINGING
FRINGINGS
FRINGY
FRIPON
FRIPONS
FRIPPER
FRIPPERER
FRIPPERS
FRIPPERY
FRIPPET
FRIPPETS
FRIS
FRISBEE
FRISBEES
FRISE
FRISEE
FRISEES
FRISES
FRISETTE
FRISETTES
FRISEUR
FRISEURS
FRISK
FRISKA
FRISKAS
FRISKED
FRISKER
FRISKERS
FRISKET
FRISKETS
FRISKFUL
FRISKIER
FRISKIEST
FRISKILY
FRISKING
FRISKINGS
FRISKS
FRISKY
FRISSON
FRISSONS
FRIST
FRISTED
FRISTING
FRISTS
FRISURE
FRISURES
FRIT
FRITES
FRITFLIES
FRITFLY
FRITH
FRITHBORH
FRITHS
FRITS
FRITT
FRITTATA
FRITTATAS
FRITTED
FRITTER
FRITTERED
FRITTERER
FRITTERS
FRITTING
FRITTS
FRITURE
FRITURES
FRITZ
FRITZED
FRITZES
FRITZING
FRIULANO
FRIULANOS
FRIVOL
FRIVOLED
FRIVOLER
FRIVOLERS
FRIVOLING
FRIVOLITY
FRIVOLLED
FRIVOLLER
FRIVOLOUS
FRIVOLS
FRIZ
FRIZADO
FRIZADOS
FRIZE
FRIZED
FRIZER
FRIZERS
FRIZES
FRIZETTE
FRIZETTES
FRIZING
FRIZZ
FRIZZANTE
FRIZZED
FRIZZER
FRIZZERS
FRIZZES
FRIZZIER
FRIZZIES
FRIZZIEST
FRIZZILY
FRIZZING
FRIZZLE
FRIZZLED
FRIZZLER
FRIZZLERS
FRIZZLES
FRIZZLIER
FRIZZLING
FRIZZLY
FRIZZY
FRO
FROCK
FROCKED
FROCKING
FROCKINGS
FROCKLESS
FROCKS
FROE
FROES
FROG
FROGBIT
FROGBITS
FROGEYE
FROGEYED
FROGEYES
FROGFISH
FROGGED
FROGGERY
FROGGIER
FROGGIEST
FROGGING
FROGGINGS
FROGGY
FROGLET
FROGLETS
FROGLIKE
FROGLING
FROGLINGS
FROGMAN
FROGMARCH
FROGMEN
FROGMOUTH
FROGS
FROGSPAWN
FROIDEUR
FROIDEURS
FROING
FROINGS
FROISE
FROISES
FROLIC
FROLICKED
FROLICKER
FROLICKY
FROLICS
FROM
FROMAGE
FROMAGES
FROMENTY
FROND
FRONDAGE
FRONDAGES
FRONDED
FRONDENT
FRONDEUR
FRONDEURS
FRONDLESS
FRONDOSE
FRONDOUS
FRONDS
FRONS
FRONT
FRONTAGE
FRONTAGER
FRONTAGES
FRONTAL
FRONTALLY
FRONTALS
FRONTED
FRONTENIS
FRONTER
FRONTERS
FRONTES
FRONTEST
FRONTIER
FRONTIERS
FRONTING
FRONTLESS
FRONTLET
FRONTLETS
FRONTLINE
FRONTLIST
FRONTMAN
FRONTMEN
FRONTON
FRONTONS
FRONTOON
FRONTOONS
FRONTPAGE
FRONTS
FRONTWARD
FRONTWAYS
FRONTWISE
FRORE
FROREN
FRORN
FRORNE
FRORY
FROS
FROSH
FROSHES
FROST
FROSTBIT
FROSTBITE
FROSTED
FROSTEDS
FROSTFISH
FROSTIER
FROSTIEST

FROSTILY
FROSTING
FROSTINGS
FROSTLESS
FROSTLIKE
FROSTLINE
FROSTNIP
FROSTNIPS
FROSTS
FROSTWORK
FROSTY
FROTH
FROTHED
FROTHER
FROTHERS
FROTHERY
FROTHIER
FROTHIEST
FROTHILY
FROTHING
FROTHINGS
FROTHLESS
FROTHS
FROTHY
FROTTAGE
FROTTAGES
FROTTEUR
FROTTEURS
FROUFROU
FROUFROUS
FROUGHIER
FROUGHY
FROUNCE
FROUNCED
FROUNCES
FROUNCING
FROUZIER
FROUZIEST
FROUZILY
FROUZY
FROW
FROWARD
FROWARDLY
FROWARDS
FROWIE
FROWIER
FROWIEST
FROWN
FROWNED
FROWNER
FROWNERS
FROWNIER
FROWNIEST
FROWNING
FROWNS
FROWNY
FROWS
FROWSIER
FROWSIEST
FROWSILY
FROWST
FROWSTED
FROWSTER
FROWSTERS
FROWSTIER
FROWSTING
FROWSTS
FROWSTY
FROWSY
FROWY
FROWZIER
FROWZIEST
FROWZILY
FROWZY
FROZE
FROZEN
FROZENLY
FRUCTAN
FRUCTANS
FRUCTED
FRUCTIFY
FRUCTIVE
FRUCTOSE
FRUCTOSES
FRUCTUARY
FRUCTUATE
FRUCTUOUS
FRUG
FRUGAL
FRUGALIST
FRUGALITY
FRUGALLY
FRUGGED
FRUGGING
FRUGIVORE
FRUGS
FRUICT
FRUICTS
FRUIT
FRUITAGE
FRUITAGES
FRUITCAKE
FRUITED
FRUITER
FRUITERER
FRUITERS
FRUITERY
FRUITFUL
FRUITIER
FRUITIEST
FRUITILY
FRUITING
FRUITINGS
FRUITION
FRUITIONS
FRUITIVE
FRUITLESS
FRUITLET
FRUITLETS
FRUITLIKE
FRUITS
FRUITWOOD
FRUITWORM
FRUITY
FRUMENTY
FRUMP
FRUMPED
FRUMPIER
FRUMPIEST
FRUMPILY
FRUMPING
FRUMPISH
FRUMPLE
FRUMPLED
FRUMPLES
FRUMPLING
FRUMPS
FRUMPY
FRUSEMIDE
FRUSH
FRUSHED
FRUSHES
FRUSHING
FRUST
FRUSTA
FRUSTRATE
FRUSTS
FRUSTULE
FRUSTULES
FRUSTUM
FRUSTUMS
FRUTEX
FRUTICES
FRUTICOSE
FRUTIFIED
FRUTIFIES
FRUTIFY
FRY
FRYABLE
FRYBREAD
FRYBREADS
FRYER
FRYERS
FRYING
FRYINGS
FRYPAN
FRYPANS
FUB
FUBAR
FUBBED
FUBBERIES
FUBBERY
FUBBIER
FUBBIEST
FUBBING
FUBBY
FUBS
FUBSIER
FUBSIEST
FUBSY
FUCHSIA
FUCHSIAS
FUCHSIN
FUCHSINE
FUCHSINES
FUCHSINS
FUCHSITE
FUCHSITES
FUCI
FUCK
FUCKED
FUCKER
FUCKERS
FUCKFACE
FUCKFACES
FUCKHEAD
FUCKHEADS
FUCKING
FUCKINGS
FUCKOFF
FUCKOFFS
FUCKS
FUCKUP
FUCKUPS
FUCKWIT
FUCKWITS
FUCOID
FUCOIDAL
FUCOIDS
FUCOSE
FUCOSES
FUCOUS
FUCUS
FUCUSED
FUCUSES
FUD
FUDDIER
FUDDIES
FUDDIEST
FUDDLE
FUDDLED
FUDDLER
FUDDLERS
FUDDLES
FUDDLING
FUDDLINGS
FUDDY
FUDGE
FUDGED
FUDGES
FUDGIER
FUDGIEST
FUDGING
FUDGY
FUDS
FUEHRER
FUEHRERS
FUEL
FUELED
FUELER

FUELERS
FUELING
FUELLED
FUELLER
FUELLERS
FUELLING
FUELS
FUELWOOD
FUELWOODS
FUERO
FUEROS
FUFF
FUFFED
FUFFIER
FUFFIEST
FUFFING
FUFFS
FUFFY
FUG
FUGACIOUS
FUGACITY
FUGAL
FUGALLY
FUGATO
FUGATOS
FUGGED
FUGGIER
FUGGIEST
FUGGILY
FUGGINESS
FUGGING
FUGGY
FUGHETTA
FUGHETTAS
FUGIE
FUGIES
FUGIO
FUGIOS
FUGITIVE
FUGITIVES
FUGLE
FUGLED
FUGLEMAN
FUGLEMEN
FUGLES
FUGLIER
FUGLIEST
FUGLING
FUGLY
FUGS
FUGU
FUGUE
FUGUED
FUGUELIKE
FUGUES
FUGUING
FUGUIST
FUGUISTS
FUGUS
FUHRER
FUHRERS
FUJI
FUJIS
FULCRA
FULCRATE
FULCRUM
FULCRUMS
FULFIL
FULFILL
FULFILLED
FULFILLER
FULFILLS
FULFILS
FULGENCY
FULGENT
FULGENTLY
FULGID
FULGOR
FULGOROUS
FULGORS
FULGOUR
FULGOURS
FULGURAL
FULGURANT
FULGURATE
FULGURITE
FULGUROUS
FULHAM
FULHAMS
FULL
FULLAGE
FULLAGES
FULLAM
FULLAMS
FULLAN
FULLANS
FULLBACK
FULLBACKS
FULLBLOOD
FULLED
FULLER
FULLERED
FULLERENE
FULLERIDE
FULLERIES
FULLERING
FULLERITE
FULLERS
FULLERY
FULLEST
FULLFACE
FULLFACES
FULLING
FULLISH
FULLNESS
FULLS
FULLY
FULMAR
FULMARS
FULMINANT
FULMINATE
FULMINE
FULMINED
FULMINES
FULMINIC
FULMINING
FULMINOUS
FULNESS
FULNESSES
FULSOME
FULSOMELY
FULSOMER
FULSOMEST
FULVID
FULVOUS
FUM
FUMADO
FUMADOES
FUMADOS
FUMAGE
FUMAGES
FUMARASE
FUMARASES
FUMARATE
FUMARATES
FUMARIC
FUMAROLE
FUMAROLES
FUMAROLIC
FUMATORIA
FUMATORY
FUMBLE
FUMBLED
FUMBLER
FUMBLERS
FUMBLES
FUMBLING
FUME
FUMED
FUMELESS
FUMELIKE
FUMER
FUMEROLE
FUMEROLES
FUMERS
FUMES
FUMET
FUMETS
FUMETTE
FUMETTES
FUMETTI
FUMETTO
FUMETTOS
FUMIER
FUMIEST
FUMIGANT
FUMIGANTS
FUMIGATE
FUMIGATED
FUMIGATES
FUMIGATOR
FUMING
FUMINGLY
FUMITORY
FUMOSITY
FUMOUS
FUMS
FUMULI
FUMULUS
FUMY
FUN
FUNBOARD
FUNBOARDS
FUNCKIA
FUNCKIAS
FUNCTION
FUNCTIONS
FUNCTOR
FUNCTORS
FUND
FUNDABLE
FUNDAMENT
FUNDED
FUNDER
FUNDERS
FUNDI
FUNDIC
FUNDIE
FUNDIES
FUNDING
FUNDINGS
FUNDIS
FUNDLESS
FUNDRAISE
FUNDS
FUNDUS
FUNDY
FUNEBRAL
FUNEBRE
FUNEBRIAL
FUNERAL
FUNERALS
FUNERARY
FUNEREAL
FUNEST
FUNFAIR
FUNFAIRS
FUNFEST
FUNFESTS
FUNG
FUNGAL
FUNGALS
FUNGI
FUNGIBLE
FUNGIBLES
FUNGIC
FUNGICIDE
FUNGIFORM
FUNGISTAT
FUNGO

F

FUNGOED
FUNGOES
FUNGOID
FUNGOIDAL
FUNGOIDS
FUNGOING
FUNGOS
FUNGOSITY
FUNGOUS
FUNGS
FUNGUS
FUNGUSES
FUNHOUSE
FUNHOUSES
FUNICLE
FUNICLES
FUNICULAR
FUNICULI
FUNICULUS
FUNK
FUNKED
FUNKER
FUNKERS
FUNKHOLE
FUNKHOLES
FUNKIA
FUNKIAS
FUNKIER
FUNKIEST
FUNKILY
FUNKINESS
FUNKING
FUNKS
FUNKSTER
FUNKSTERS
FUNKY
FUNNED
FUNNEL
FUNNELED
FUNNELING
FUNNELLED
FUNNELS
FUNNER
FUNNEST
FUNNIER
FUNNIES
FUNNIEST
FUNNILY
FUNNINESS
FUNNING
FUNNY
FUNNYMAN
FUNNYMEN
FUNPLEX
FUNPLEXES
FUNS
FUNSTER
FUNSTERS
FUR
FURACIOUS
FURACITY
FURAL
FURALS
FURAN
FURANE
FURANES
FURANOSE
FURANOSES
FURANS
FURBALL
FURBALLS
FURBEARER
FURBELOW
FURBELOWS
FURBISH
FURBISHED
FURBISHER
FURBISHES
FURCA
FURCAE
FURCAL
FURCATE
FURCATED
FURCATELY
FURCATES
FURCATING
FURCATION
FURCRAEA
FURCRAEAS
FURCULA
FURCULAE
FURCULAR
FURCULUM
FURDER
FUREUR
FUREURS
FURFAIR
FURFAIRS
FURFUR
FURFURAL
FURFURALS
FURFURAN
FURFURANS
FURFURES
FURFUROL
FURFUROLE
FURFUROLS
FURFUROUS
FURFURS
FURIBUND
FURIES
FURIOSITY
FURIOSO
FURIOSOS
FURIOUS
FURIOUSLY
FURKID
FURKIDS
FURL
FURLABLE
FURLANA
FURLANAS
FURLED
FURLER
FURLERS
FURLESS
FURLIKE
FURLING
FURLONG
FURLONGS
FURLOUGH
FURLOUGHS
FURLS
FURMENTY
FURMETIES
FURMETY
FURMITIES
FURMITY
FURNACE
FURNACED
FURNACES
FURNACING
FURNIMENT
FURNISH
FURNISHED
FURNISHER
FURNISHES
FURNITURE
FUROL
FUROLE
FUROLES
FUROLS
FUROR
FURORE
FURORES
FURORS
FURPHIES
FURPHY
FURPIECE
FURPIECES
FURR
FURRED
FURRIER
FURRIERS
FURRIERY
FURRIES
FURRIEST
FURRILY
FURRINER
FURRINERS
FURRINESS
FURRING
FURRINGS
FURROW
FURROWED
FURROWER
FURROWERS
FURROWIER
FURROWING
FURROWS
FURROWY
FURRS
FURRY
FURS
FURTH
FURTHER
FURTHERED
FURTHERER
FURTHERS
FURTHEST
FURTIVE
FURTIVELY
FURUNCLE
FURUNCLES
FURY
FURZE
FURZES
FURZIER
FURZIEST
FURZY
FUSAIN
FUSAINS
FUSARIA
FUSARIUM
FUSARIUMS
FUSAROL
FUSAROLE
FUSAROLES
FUSAROLS
FUSBALL
FUSBALLS
FUSC
FUSCOUS
FUSE
FUSED
FUSEE
FUSEES
FUSEL
FUSELAGE
FUSELAGES
FUSELESS
FUSELIKE
FUSELS
FUSES
FUSHION
FUSHIONS
FUSIBLE
FUSIBLY
FUSIDIC
FUSIFORM
FUSIL
FUSILE
FUSILEER
FUSILEERS
FUSILIER
FUSILIERS
FUSILLADE
FUSILLI
FUSILLIS
FUSILS

FUSING
FUSION
FUSIONAL
FUSIONISM
FUSIONIST
FUSIONS
FUSK
FUSKED
FUSKER
FUSKERED
FUSKERING
FUSKERS
FUSKING
FUSKS
FUSS
FUSSBALL
FUSSBALLS
FUSSED
FUSSER
FUSSERS
FUSSES
FUSSIER
FUSSIEST
FUSSILY
FUSSINESS
FUSSING
FUSSPOT
FUSSPOTS
FUSSY
FUST
FUSTED
FUSTET
FUSTETS
FUSTIAN
FUSTIANS
FUSTIC
FUSTICS
FUSTIER
FUSTIEST
FUSTIGATE
FUSTILUGS
FUSTILY
FUSTINESS
FUSTING
FUSTOC
FUSTOCS
FUSTS
FUSTY
FUSULINID
FUSUMA
FUSUMAS
FUTCHEL
FUTCHELS
FUTHARC
FUTHARCS
FUTHARK
FUTHARKS
FUTHORC
FUTHORCS
FUTHORK
FUTHORKS
FUTILE
FUTILELY
FUTILER
FUTILEST
FUTILITY
FUTON
FUTONS
FUTSAL
FUTSALS
FUTTOCK
FUTTOCKS
FUTURAL
FUTURE
FUTURES
FUTURISM
FUTURISMS
FUTURIST
FUTURISTS
FUTURITY
FUTZ
FUTZED
FUTZES
FUTZING
FUZE
FUZED
FUZEE
FUZEES
FUZELESS
FUZES
FUZIL
FUZILS
FUZING
FUZZ
FUZZBALL
FUZZBALLS
FUZZBOX
FUZZBOXES
FUZZED
FUZZES
FUZZIER
FUZZIEST
FUZZILY
FUZZINESS
FUZZING
FUZZLE
FUZZLED
FUZZLES
FUZZLING
FUZZTONE
FUZZTONES
FUZZY
FY
FYCE
FYCES
FYKE
FYKED
FYKES
FYKING
FYLE
FYLES
FYLFOT
FYLFOTS
FYNBOS
FYNBOSES
FYRD
FYRDS
FYTTE
FYTTES

G

GAB
GABARDINE
GABBA
GABBARD
GABBARDS
GABBART
GABBARTS
GABBAS
GABBED
GABBER
GABBERS
GABBIER
GABBIEST
GABBINESS
GABBING
GABBLE
GABBLED
GABBLER
GABBLERS
GABBLES
GABBLING
GABBLINGS
GABBRO
GABBROIC
GABBROID
GABBROS
GABBY
GABELLE
GABELLED
GABELLER
GABELLERS
GABELLES
GABERDINE
GABFEST
GABFESTS
GABIES
GABION
GABIONADE
GABIONAGE
GABIONED
GABIONS
GABLE
GABLED
GABLELIKE
GABLES
GABLET
GABLETS
GABLING
GABNASH
GABNASHES
GABOON
GABOONS
GABS
GABY
GACH
GACHED
GACHER
GACHERS
GACHES
GACHING
GAD
GADABOUT
GADABOUTS
GADARENE
GADDED
GADDER
GADDERS
GADDI
GADDING
GADDIS
GADE
GADES
GADFLIES
GADFLY
GADGE
GADGES
GADGET
GADGETEER
GADGETIER
GADGETRY
GADGETS
GADGETY
GADGIE
GADGIES
GADI
GADID
GADIDS
GADIS
GADJE
GADJES
GADJO
GADJOS
GADLING
GADLINGS
GADMAN
GADMEN
GADOID
GADOIDS
GADOLINIC
GADROON
GADROONED
GADROONS
GADS
GADSMAN
GADSMEN
GADSO
GADWALL
GADWALLS
GADZOOKS
GAE
GAED
GAEING
GAELICISE
GAELICISM
GAELICIZE
GAEN
GAES
GAFF
GAFFE
GAFFED
GAFFER
GAFFERS
GAFFES
GAFFING
GAFFINGS
GAFFS
GAFFSAIL
GAFFSAILS
GAG
GAGA
GAGAKU
GAGAKUS
GAGE
GAGEABLE
GAGEABLY
GAGED
GAGER
GAGERS
GAGES
GAGGED
GAGGER
GAGGERIES
GAGGERS
GAGGERY
GAGGING
GAGGLE
GAGGLED
GAGGLES
GAGGLING
GAGGLINGS
GAGING
GAGMAN
GAGMEN
GAGS
GAGSTER
GAGSTERS
GAHNITE
GAHNITES
GAID
GAIDS
GAIETIES
GAIETY
GAIJIN
GAILLARD
GAILLARDE
GAILY
GAIN
GAINABLE
GAINED
GAINER
GAINERS
GAINEST
GAINFUL
GAINFULLY
GAINING
GAININGS
GAINLESS
GAINLIER
GAINLIEST
GAINLY
GAINS
GAINSAID
GAINSAY
GAINSAYER
GAINSAYS
GAINST
GAIR
GAIRFOWL
GAIRFOWLS
GAIRS
GAIT
GAITA
GAITAS
GAITED
GAITER
GAITERED
GAITERS
GAITING
GAITS
GAITT
GAITTS
GAJO
GAJOS
GAK
GAKS
GAL
GALA
GALABEA
GALABEAH
GALABEAHS

GALABEAS
GALABIA
GALABIAH
GALABIAHS
GALABIAS
GALABIEH
GALABIEHS
GALABIYA
GALABIYAH
GALABIYAS
GALACTIC
GALACTICO
GALACTOSE
GALAGE
GALAGES
GALAGO
GALAGOS
GALAH
GALAHS
GALANGA
GALANGAL
GALANGALS
GALANGAS
GALANT
GALANTINE
GALANTS
GALANTY
GALAPAGO
GALAPAGOS
GALAS
GALATEA
GALATEAS
GALAVANT
GALAVANTS
GALAX
GALAXES
GALAXIES
GALAXY
GALBANUM
GALBANUMS
GALDRAGON
GALE
GALEA
GALEAE
GALEAS
GALEATE
GALEATED
GALED
GALEIFORM
GALENA
GALENAS
GALENGALE
GALENIC
GALENICAL
GALENITE
GALENITES
GALENOID
GALERE
GALERES
GALES
GALETTE
GALETTES
GALILEE
GALILEES
GALING
GALINGALE
GALIONGEE
GALIOT
GALIOTS
GALIPOT
GALIPOTS
GALIVANT
GALIVANTS
GALL
GALLABEA
GALLABEAH
GALLABEAS
GALLABIA
GALLABIAH
GALLABIAS
GALLABIEH
GALLABIYA
GALLAMINE
GALLANT
GALLANTED
GALLANTER
GALLANTLY
GALLANTRY
GALLANTS
GALLATE
GALLATES
GALLEASS
GALLED
GALLEIN
GALLEINS
GALLEON
GALLEONS
GALLERIA
GALLERIAS
GALLERIED
GALLERIES
GALLERIST
GALLERY
GALLET
GALLETA
GALLETAS
GALLETED
GALLETING
GALLETS
GALLEY
GALLEYS
GALLFLIES
GALLFLY
GALLIARD
GALLIARDS
GALLIASS
GALLIC
GALLICA
GALLICAN
GALLICAS
GALLICISE
GALLICISM
GALLICIZE
GALLIED
GALLIER
GALLIES
GALLIEST
GALLINAZO
GALLING
GALLINGLY
GALLINULE
GALLIOT
GALLIOTS
GALLIPOT
GALLIPOTS
GALLISE
GALLISED
GALLISES
GALLISING
GALLISISE
GALLISIZE
GALLIUM
GALLIUMS
GALLIVANT
GALLIVAT
GALLIVATS
GALLIWASP
GALLIZE
GALLIZED
GALLIZES
GALLIZING
GALLNUT
GALLNUTS
GALLOCK
GALLON
GALLONAGE
GALLONS
GALLOON
GALLOONED
GALLOONS
GALLOOT
GALLOOTS
GALLOP
GALLOPADE
GALLOPED
GALLOPER
GALLOPERS
GALLOPING
GALLOPS
GALLOUS
GALLOW
GALLOWAY
GALLOWAYS
GALLOWED
GALLOWING
GALLOWS
GALLOWSES
GALLS
GALLSTONE
GALLUMPH
GALLUMPHS
GALLUS
GALLUSED
GALLUSES
GALLY
GALLYING
GALOCHE
GALOCHED
GALOCHES
GALOCHING
GALOOT
GALOOTS
GALOP
GALOPADE
GALOPADES
GALOPED
GALOPIN
GALOPING
GALOPINS
GALOPPED
GALOPPING
GALOPS
GALORE
GALORES
GALOSH
GALOSHE
GALOSHED
GALOSHES
GALOSHING
GALOWSES
GALRAVAGE
GALS
GALTONIA
GALTONIAS
GALUMPH
GALUMPHED
GALUMPHER
GALUMPHS
GALUT
GALUTH
GALUTHS
GALUTS
GALVANIC
GALVANISE
GALVANISM
GALVANIST
GALVANIZE
GALVO
GALVOS
GALYAC
GALYACS
GALYAK
GALYAKS
GAM
GAMA
GAMAHUCHE
GAMARUCHE
GAMAS
GAMASH
GAMASHES

GAMAY
GAMAYS
GAMB
GAMBA
GAMBADE
GAMBADES
GAMBADO
GAMBADOED
GAMBADOES
GAMBADOS
GAMBAS
GAMBE
GAMBES
GAMBESON
GAMBESONS
GAMBET
GAMBETS
GAMBETTA
GAMBETTAS
GAMBIA
GAMBIAS
GAMBIER
GAMBIERS
GAMBIR
GAMBIRS
GAMBIST
GAMBISTS
GAMBIT
GAMBITED
GAMBITING
GAMBITS
GAMBLE
GAMBLED
GAMBLER
GAMBLERS
GAMBLES
GAMBLING
GAMBLINGS
GAMBO
GAMBOES
GAMBOGE
GAMBOGES
GAMBOGIAN
GAMBOGIC
GAMBOL
GAMBOLED
GAMBOLING
GAMBOLLED
GAMBOLS
GAMBOS
GAMBREL
GAMBRELS
GAMBROON
GAMBROONS
GAMBS
GAMBUSIA
GAMBUSIAS
GAME
GAMEBAG
GAMEBAGS
GAMEBOOK
GAMEBOOKS
GAMECOCK
GAMECOCKS
GAMED
GAMEFISH
GAMEFOWL
GAMEFOWLS
GAMELAN
GAMELANS
GAMELIKE
GAMELY
GAMENESS
GAMEPLAY
GAMEPLAYS
GAMER
GAMERS
GAMES
GAMESHOW
GAMESHOWS
GAMESIER
GAMESIEST
GAMESMAN
GAMESMEN
GAMESOME
GAMEST
GAMESTER
GAMESTERS
GAMESY
GAMETAL
GAMETE
GAMETES
GAMETIC
GAMEY
GAMEYNESS
GAMGEE
GAMIC
GAMIER
GAMIEST
GAMIFIED
GAMIFIES
GAMIFY
GAMIFYING
GAMILY
GAMIN
GAMINE
GAMINERIE
GAMINES
GAMINESS
GAMING
GAMINGS
GAMINS
GAMMA
GAMMADIA
GAMMADION
GAMMAS
GAMMATIA
GAMMATION
GAMME
GAMMED
GAMMER
GAMMERS
GAMMES
GAMMIER
GAMMIEST
GAMMING
GAMMOCK
GAMMOCKED
GAMMOCKS
GAMMON
GAMMONED
GAMMONER
GAMMONERS
GAMMONING
GAMMONS
GAMMY
GAMODEME
GAMODEMES
GAMONE
GAMONES
GAMP
GAMPISH
GAMPS
GAMS
GAMUT
GAMUTS
GAMY
GAMYNESS
GAN
GANACHE
GANACHES
GANCH
GANCHED
GANCHES
GANCHING
GANDER
GANDERED
GANDERING
GANDERISM
GANDERS
GANDY
GANE
GANEF
GANEFS
GANEV
GANEVS
GANG
GANGBANG
GANGBANGS
GANGBO
GANGBOARD
GANGBOS
GANGED
GANGER
GANGERS
GANGING
GANGINGS
GANGLAND
GANGLANDS
GANGLE
GANGLED
GANGLES
GANGLIA
GANGLIAL
GANGLIAR
GANGLIATE
GANGLIER
GANGLIEST
GANGLING
GANGLION
GANGLIONS
GANGLY
GANGPLANK
GANGPLOW
GANGPLOWS
GANGREL
GANGRELS
GANGRENE
GANGRENED
GANGRENES
GANGS
GANGSHAG
GANGSHAGS
GANGSMAN
GANGSMEN
GANGSTA
GANGSTAS
GANGSTER
GANGSTERS
GANGUE
GANGUES
GANGWAY
GANGWAYS
GANISTER
GANISTERS
GANJA
GANJAH
GANJAHS
GANJAS
GANNED
GANNET
GANNETRY
GANNETS
GANNING
GANNISTER
GANOF
GANOFS
GANOID
GANOIDS
GANOIN
GANOINE
GANOINES
GANOINS
GANS
GANSEY
GANSEYS
GANT
GANTED
GANTELOPE
GANTING

GANTLET
GANTLETED
GANTLETS
GANTLINE
GANTLINES
GANTLOPE
GANTLOPES
GANTRIES
GANTRY
GANTS
GANYMEDE
GANYMEDES
GANZFELD
GANZFELDS
GAOL
GAOLBIRD
GAOLBIRDS
GAOLBREAK
GAOLBROKE
GAOLED
GAOLER
GAOLERESS
GAOLERS
GAOLING
GAOLLESS
GAOLS
GAP
GAPE
GAPED
GAPER
GAPERS
GAPES
GAPESEED
GAPESEEDS
GAPEWORM
GAPEWORMS
GAPIER
GAPIEST
GAPING
GAPINGLY
GAPINGS
GAPLESS
GAPO
GAPOS
GAPOSIS
GAPOSISES
GAPPED
GAPPER
GAPPERS
GAPPIER
GAPPIEST
GAPPING
GAPPINGS
GAPPY
GAPS
GAPY
GAR
GARAGE
GARAGED
GARAGEMAN
GARAGEMEN
GARAGES
GARAGEY
GARAGIER
GARAGIEST
GARAGING
GARAGINGS
GARAGIST
GARAGISTE
GARAGISTS
GARB
GARBAGE
GARBAGES
GARBAGEY
GARBAGIER
GARBAGY
GARBANZO
GARBANZOS
GARBE
GARBED
GARBES
GARBING
GARBLE
GARBLED
GARBLER
GARBLERS
GARBLES
GARBLESS
GARBLING
GARBLINGS
GARBO
GARBOARD
GARBOARDS
GARBOIL
GARBOILS
GARBOLOGY
GARBOS
GARBS
GARBURE
GARBURES
GARCINIA
GARCINIAS
GARCON
GARCONS
GARDA
GARDAI
GARDANT
GARDANTS
GARDEN
GARDENED
GARDENER
GARDENERS
GARDENFUL
GARDENIA
GARDENIAS
GARDENING
GARDENS
GARDEROBE
GARDYLOO
GARDYLOOS
GARE
GAREFOWL
GAREFOWLS
GARES
GARFISH
GARFISHES
GARGANEY
GARGANEYS
GARGANTUA
GARGARISE
GARGARISM
GARGARIZE
GARGET
GARGETS
GARGETY
GARGLE
GARGLED
GARGLER
GARGLERS
GARGLES
GARGLING
GARGOYLE
GARGOYLED
GARGOYLES
GARI
GARIAL
GARIALS
GARIBALDI
GARIGUE
GARIGUES
GARIS
GARISH
GARISHED
GARISHES
GARISHING
GARISHLY
GARJAN
GARJANS
GARLAND
GARLANDED
GARLANDRY
GARLANDS
GARLIC
GARLICKED
GARLICKY
GARLICS
GARMENT
GARMENTED
GARMENTS
GARMS
GARNER
GARNERED
GARNERING
GARNERS
GARNET
GARNETS
GARNI
GARNISH
GARNISHED
GARNISHEE
GARNISHER
GARNISHES
GARNISHOR
GARNISHRY
GARNITURE
GAROTE
GAROTED
GAROTES
GAROTING
GAROTTE
GAROTTED
GAROTTER
GAROTTERS
GAROTTES
GAROTTING
GAROUPA
GAROUPAS
GARPIKE
GARPIKES
GARRAN
GARRANS
GARRE
GARRED
GARRES
GARRET
GARRETED
GARRETEER
GARRETS
GARRIGUE
GARRIGUES
GARRING
GARRISON
GARRISONS
GARRON
GARRONS
GARROT
GARROTE
GARROTED
GARROTER
GARROTERS
GARROTES
GARROTING
GARROTS
GARROTTE
GARROTTED
GARROTTER
GARROTTES
GARRULITY
GARRULOUS
GARRYA
GARRYAS
GARRYOWEN
GARS
GART
GARTER
GARTERED
GARTERING
GARTERS
GARTH
GARTHS

GARUDA
GARUDAS
GARUM
GARUMS
GARVEY
GARVEYS
GARVIE
GARVIES
GARVOCK
GARVOCKS
GAS
GASAHOL
GASAHOLS
GASALIER
GASALIERS
GASBAG
GASBAGGED
GASBAGS
GASCON
GASCONADE
GASCONISM
GASCONS
GASEITIES
GASEITY
GASELIER
GASELIERS
GASEOUS
GASES
GASFIELD
GASFIELDS
GASH
GASHED
GASHER
GASHES
GASHEST
GASHFUL
GASHING
GASHLIER
GASHLIEST
GASHLY
GASHOLDER
GASHOUSE
GASHOUSES
GASIFIED
GASIFIER
GASIFIERS
GASIFIES
GASIFORM
GASIFY
GASIFYING
GASKET
GASKETED
GASKETS
GASKIN
GASKING
GASKINGS
GASKINS
GASLESS
GASLIGHT
GASLIGHTS
GASLIT
GASMAN
GASMEN
GASOGENE
GASOGENES
GASOHOL
GASOHOLS
GASOLENE
GASOLENES
GASOLIER
GASOLIERS
GASOLINE
GASOLINES
GASOLINIC
GASOMETER
GASOMETRY
GASP
GASPED
GASPER
GASPEREAU
GASPERS
GASPIER
GASPIEST
GASPINESS
GASPING
GASPINGLY
GASPINGS
GASPS
GASPY
GASSED
GASSER
GASSERS
GASSES
GASSIER
GASSIEST
GASSILY
GASSINESS
GASSING
GASSINGS
GASSY
GAST
GASTED
GASTER
GASTERED
GASTERING
GASTERS
GASTFULL
GASTHAUS
GASTIGHT
GASTING
GASTNESS
GASTNESSE
GASTRAEA
GASTRAEAS
GASTRAEUM
GASTRAL
GASTREA
GASTREAS
GASTRIC
GASTRIN
GASTRINS
GASTRITIC
GASTRITIS
GASTROPOD
GASTROPUB
GASTRULA
GASTRULAE
GASTRULAR
GASTRULAS
GASTS
GASWORKS
GAT
GATCH
GATCHED
GATCHER
GATCHERS
GATCHES
GATCHING
GATE
GATEAU
GATEAUS
GATEAUX
GATECRASH
GATED
GATEFOLD
GATEFOLDS
GATEHOUSE
GATELEG
GATELEGS
GATELESS
GATELIKE
GATEMAN
GATEMEN
GATEPOST
GATEPOSTS
GATER
GATERS
GATES
GATEWAY
GATEWAYS
GATH
GATHER
GATHERED
GATHERER
GATHERERS
GATHERING
GATHERS
GATHS
GATING
GATINGS
GATLING
GATOR
GATORS
GATS
GATVOL
GAU
GAUCH
GAUCHE
GAUCHED
GAUCHELY
GAUCHER
GAUCHERIE
GAUCHERS
GAUCHES
GAUCHESCO
GAUCHEST
GAUCHING
GAUCHO
GAUCHOS
GAUCIE
GAUCIER
GAUCIEST
GAUCY
GAUD
GAUDEAMUS
GAUDED
GAUDERIES
GAUDERY
GAUDGIE
GAUDGIES
GAUDIER
GAUDIES
GAUDIEST
GAUDILY
GAUDINESS
GAUDING
GAUDS
GAUDY
GAUFER
GAUFERS
GAUFFER
GAUFFERED
GAUFFERS
GAUFRE
GAUFRES
GAUGE
GAUGEABLE
GAUGEABLY
GAUGED
GAUGER
GAUGERS
GAUGES
GAUGING
GAUGINGS
GAUJE
GAUJES
GAULEITER
GAULT
GAULTER
GAULTERS
GAULTS
GAUM
GAUMED
GAUMIER
GAUMIEST
GAUMING
GAUMLESS
GAUMS
GAUMY
GAUN

GAUNCH
GAUNCHED
GAUNCHES
GAUNCHING
GAUNT
GAUNTED
GAUNTER
GAUNTEST
GAUNTING
GAUNTLET
GAUNTLETS
GAUNTLY
GAUNTNESS
GAUNTREE
GAUNTREES
GAUNTRIES
GAUNTRY
GAUNTS
GAUP
GAUPED
GAUPER
GAUPERS
GAUPING
GAUPS
GAUPUS
GAUPUSES
GAUR
GAURS
GAUS
GAUSS
GAUSSES
GAUSSIAN
GAUZE
GAUZELIKE
GAUZES
GAUZIER
GAUZIEST
GAUZILY
GAUZINESS
GAUZY
GAVAGE
GAVAGES
GAVE
GAVEL
GAVELED
GAVELING
GAVELKIND
GAVELLED
GAVELLING
GAVELMAN
GAVELMEN
GAVELOCK
GAVELOCKS
GAVELS
GAVIAL
GAVIALOID
GAVIALS
GAVOT
GAVOTS
GAVOTTE
GAVOTTED
GAVOTTES
GAVOTTING
GAW
GAWCIER
GAWCIEST
GAWCY
GAWD
GAWDS
GAWK
GAWKED
GAWKER
GAWKERS
GAWKIER
GAWKIES
GAWKIEST
GAWKIHOOD
GAWKILY
GAWKINESS
GAWKING
GAWKISH
GAWKISHLY
GAWKS
GAWKY
GAWMOGE
GAWMOGES
GAWP
GAWPED
GAWPER
GAWPERS
GAWPING
GAWPS
GAWPUS
GAWPUSES
GAWS
GAWSIE
GAWSIER
GAWSIEST
GAWSY
GAY
GAYAL
GAYALS
GAYCATION
GAYDAR
GAYDARS
GAYER
GAYEST
GAYETIES
GAYETY
GAYLY
GAYNESS
GAYNESSES
GAYS
GAYSOME
GAYWINGS
GAZABO
GAZABOES
GAZABOS
GAZAL
GAZALS
GAZANG
GAZANGED
GAZANGING
GAZANGS
GAZANIA
GAZANIAS
GAZAR
GAZARS
GAZE
GAZEBO
GAZEBOES
GAZEBOS
GAZED
GAZEFUL
GAZEHOUND
GAZELLE
GAZELLES
GAZEMENT
GAZEMENTS
GAZER
GAZERS
GAZES
GAZETTE
GAZETTED
GAZETTEER
GAZETTES
GAZETTING
GAZIER
GAZIEST
GAZILLION
GAZING
GAZINGS
GAZOGENE
GAZOGENES
GAZON
GAZONS
GAZOO
GAZOOKA
GAZOOKAS
GAZOON
GAZOONS
GAZOOS
GAZPACHO
GAZPACHOS
GAZUMP
GAZUMPED
GAZUMPER
GAZUMPERS
GAZUMPING
GAZUMPS
GAZUNDER
GAZUNDERS
GAZY
GEAL
GEALED
GEALING
GEALOUS
GEALOUSY
GEALS
GEAN
GEANS
GEAR
GEARBOX
GEARBOXES
GEARCASE
GEARCASES
GEARE
GEARED
GEARES
GEARHEAD
GEARHEADS
GEARING
GEARINGS
GEARLESS
GEARS
GEARSHIFT
GEARSTICK
GEARWHEEL
GEASON
GEAT
GEATS
GEBUR
GEBURS
GECK
GECKED
GECKING
GECKO
GECKOES
GECKOS
GECKS
GED
GEDACT
GEDACTS
GEDDIT
GEDECKT
GEDECKTS
GEDS
GEE
GEEBAG
GEEBAGS
GEEBUNG
GEEBUNGS
GEECHEE
GEECHEES
GEED
GEEGAW
GEEGAWS
GEEING
GEEK
GEEKDOM
GEEKDOMS
GEEKED
GEEKERIES
GEEKERY
GEEKIER
GEEKIEST
GEEKINESS
GEEKISH
GEEKISM
GEEKISMS

GEEKS
GEEKSPEAK
GEEKY
GEELBEK
GEELBEKS
GEEP
GEEPOUND
GEEPOUNDS
GEEPS
GEES
GEESE
GEEST
GEESTS
GEEZ
GEEZAH
GEEZAHS
GEEZER
GEEZERS
GEFILTE
GEFUFFLE
GEFUFFLED
GEFUFFLES
GEFULLTE
GEGGIE
GEGGIES
GEHLENITE
GEISHA
GEISHAS
GEIST
GEISTS
GEIT
GEITED
GEITING
GEITS
GEL
GELABLE
GELADA
GELADAS
GELANDE
GELANT
GELANTS
GELASTIC
GELATE
GELATED
GELATES
GELATI
GELATIN
GELATINE
GELATINES
GELATING
GELATINS
GELATION
GELATIONS
GELATIS
GELATO
GELATOS
GELCAP
GELCAPS
GELCOAT
GELCOATS
GELD
GELDED
GELDER
GELDERS
GELDING
GELDINGS
GELDS
GELEE
GELEES
GELID
GELIDER
GELIDEST
GELIDITY
GELIDLY
GELIDNESS
GELIGNITE
GELLANT
GELLANTS
GELLED
GELLIES
GELLING
GELLY
GELOSIES
GELOSY
GELS
GELSEMIA
GELSEMINE
GELSEMIUM
GELT
GELTS
GEM
GEMATRIA
GEMATRIAS
GEMCLIP
GEMCLIPS
GEMEL
GEMELS
GEMFISH
GEMFISHES
GEMINAL
GEMINALLY
GEMINATE
GEMINATED
GEMINATES
GEMINI
GEMINIES
GEMINOUS
GEMINY
GEMLIKE
GEMMA
GEMMAE
GEMMAN
GEMMATE
GEMMATED
GEMMATES
GEMMATING
GEMMATION
GEMMATIVE
GEMMED
GEMMEN
GEMMEOUS
GEMMERIES
GEMMERY
GEMMIER
GEMMIEST
GEMMILY
GEMMINESS
GEMMING
GEMMOLOGY
GEMMULE
GEMMULES
GEMMY
GEMOLOGY
GEMONY
GEMOT
GEMOTE
GEMOTES
GEMOTS
GEMS
GEMSBOK
GEMSBOKS
GEMSBUCK
GEMSBUCKS
GEMSHORN
GEMSHORNS
GEMSTONE
GEMSTONES
GEMUTLICH
GEN
GENA
GENAL
GENAPPE
GENAPPES
GENAS
GENDARME
GENDARMES
GENDER
GENDERED
GENDERING
GENDERISE
GENDERIZE
GENDERS
GENE
GENEALOGY
GENERA
GENERABLE
GENERAL
GENERALCY
GENERALE
GENERALIA
GENERALLY
GENERALS
GENERANT
GENERANTS
GENERATE
GENERATED
GENERATES
GENERATOR
GENERIC
GENERICAL
GENERICS
GENEROUS
GENES
GENESES
GENESIS
GENET
GENETIC
GENETICAL
GENETICS
GENETRIX
GENETS
GENETTE
GENETTES
GENEVA
GENEVAS
GENIAL
GENIALISE
GENIALITY
GENIALIZE
GENIALLY
GENIC
GENICALLY
GENICULAR
GENIE
GENIES
GENII
GENIP
GENIPAP
GENIPAPO
GENIPAPOS
GENIPAPS
GENIPS
GENISTA
GENISTAS
GENISTEIN
GENITAL
GENITALIA
GENITALIC
GENITALLY
GENITALS
GENITIVAL
GENITIVE
GENITIVES
GENITOR
GENITORS
GENITRIX
GENITURE
GENITURES
GENIUS
GENIUSES
GENIZAH
GENIZAHS
GENIZOT
GENIZOTH
GENLOCK
GENLOCKED
GENLOCKS
GENNAKER
GENNAKERS
GENNED

GENNEL
GENNELS
GENNET
GENNETS
GENNIES
GENNING
GENNY
GENOA
GENOAS
GENOCIDAL
GENOCIDE
GENOCIDES
GENOGRAM
GENOGRAMS
GENOISE
GENOISES
GENOM
GENOME
GENOMES
GENOMIC
GENOMICS
GENOMS
GENOTOXIC
GENOTYPE
GENOTYPED
GENOTYPES
GENOTYPIC
GENRE
GENRES
GENRO
GENROS
GENS
GENSENG
GENSENGS
GENT
GENTEEL
GENTEELER
GENTEELLY
GENTES
GENTIAN
GENTIANS
GENTIER
GENTIEST
GENTIL
GENTILE
GENTILES
GENTILIC
GENTILISE
GENTILISH
GENTILISM
GENTILITY
GENTILIZE
GENTLE
GENTLED
GENTLEMAN
GENTLEMEN
GENTLER
GENTLES
GENTLEST
GENTLING
GENTLY
GENTOO
GENTOOS
GENTRICE
GENTRICES
GENTRIES
GENTRIFY
GENTRY
GENTS
GENTY
GENU
GENUA
GENUFLECT
GENUINE
GENUINELY
GENUS
GENUSES
GEO
GEOBOTANY
GEOCACHE
GEOCACHED
GEOCACHER
GEOCACHES
GEOCARPIC
GEOCARPY
GEOCODE
GEOCODED
GEOCODES
GEOCODING
GEOCORONA
GEODATA
GEODE
GEODES
GEODESIC
GEODESICS
GEODESIES
GEODESIST
GEODESY
GEODETIC
GEODETICS
GEODIC
GEODUCK
GEODUCKS
GEOFACT
GEOFACTS
GEOGENIES
GEOGENY
GEOGNOSES
GEOGNOSIS
GEOGNOST
GEOGNOSTS
GEOGNOSY
GEOGONIC
GEOGONIES
GEOGONY
GEOGRAPHY
GEOID
GEOIDAL
GEOIDS
GEOLATRY
GEOLOGER
GEOLOGERS
GEOLOGIAN
GEOLOGIC
GEOLOGIES
GEOLOGISE
GEOLOGIST
GEOLOGIZE
GEOLOGY
GEOMANCER
GEOMANCY
GEOMANT
GEOMANTIC
GEOMANTS
GEOMATICS
GEOMETER
GEOMETERS
GEOMETRIC
GEOMETRID
GEOMETRY
GEOMYOID
GEONOMICS
GEOPHAGIA
GEOPHAGY
GEOPHILIC
GEOPHONE
GEOPHONES
GEOPHYTE
GEOPHYTES
GEOPHYTIC
GEOPONIC
GEOPONICS
GEOPROBE
GEOPROBES
GEORGETTE
GEORGIC
GEORGICAL
GEORGICS
GEOS
GEOSPHERE
GEOSTATIC
GEOTACTIC
GEOTAG
GEOTAGGED
GEOTAGS
GEOTAXES
GEOTAXIS
GEOTHERM
GEOTHERMS
GEOTROPIC
GER
GERAH
GERAHS
GERANIAL
GERANIALS
GERANIOL
GERANIOLS
GERANIUM
GERANIUMS
GERARDIA
GERARDIAS
GERBE
GERBERA
GERBERAS
GERBES
GERBIL
GERBILLE
GERBILLES
GERBILS
GERE
GERENT
GERENTS
GERENUK
GERENUKS
GERES
GERFALCON
GERIATRIC
GERLE
GERLES
GERM
GERMAIN
GERMAINE
GERMAINES
GERMAINS
GERMAN
GERMANDER
GERMANE
GERMANELY
GERMANIC
GERMANISE
GERMANITE
GERMANIUM
GERMANIZE
GERMANOUS
GERMANS
GERMED
GERMEN
GERMENS
GERMFREE
GERMICIDE
GERMIER
GERMIEST
GERMIN
GERMINA
GERMINAL
GERMINANT
GERMINATE
GERMINESS
GERMING
GERMINS
GERMLIKE
GERMPLASM
GERMPROOF
GERMS
GERMY
GERNE
GERNED
GERNES
GERNING
GERONIMO

G

GERONTIC
GEROPIGA
GEROPIGAS
GERS
GERT
GERTCHA
GERUND
GERUNDIAL
GERUNDIVE
GERUNDS
GESNERIA
GESNERIAD
GESNERIAS
GESSAMINE
GESSE
GESSED
GESSES
GESSING
GESSO
GESSOED
GESSOES
GEST
GESTALT
GESTALTEN
GESTALTS
GESTANT
GESTAPO
GESTAPOS
GESTATE
GESTATED
GESTATES
GESTATING
GESTATION
GESTATIVE
GESTATORY
GESTE
GESTES
GESTIC
GESTICAL
GESTS
GESTURAL
GESTURE
GESTURED
GESTURER
GESTURERS
GESTURES
GESTURING
GET
GETA
GETABLE
GETAS
GETATABLE
GETAWAY
GETAWAYS
GETOUT
GETOUTS
GETS
GETTABLE
GETTER
GETTERED
GETTERING
GETTERS
GETTING
GETTINGS
GETUP
GETUPS
GEUM
GEUMS
GEWGAW
GEWGAWED
GEWGAWS
GEY
GEYAN
GEYER
GEYEST
GEYSER
GEYSERED
GEYSERING
GEYSERITE
GEYSERS
GHARIAL
GHARIALS
GHARRI
GHARRIES
GHARRIS
GHARRY
GHAST
GHASTED
GHASTFUL
GHASTING
GHASTLIER
GHASTLY
GHASTNESS
GHASTS
GHAT
GHATS
GHAUT
GHAUTS
GHAZAL
GHAZALS
GHAZEL
GHAZELS
GHAZI
GHAZIES
GHAZIS
GHEE
GHEES
GHERAO
GHERAOED
GHERAOES
GHERAOING
GHERAOS
GHERKIN
GHERKINS
GHESSE
GHESSED
GHESSES
GHESSING
GHEST
GHETTO
GHETTOED
GHETTOES
GHETTOING
GHETTOISE
GHETTOIZE
GHETTOS
GHI
GHIBLI
GHIBLIS
GHILGAI
GHILGAIS
GHILLIE
GHILLIED
GHILLIES
GHILLYING
GHIS
GHOST
GHOSTED
GHOSTIER
GHOSTIEST
GHOSTING
GHOSTINGS
GHOSTLIER
GHOSTLIKE
GHOSTLY
GHOSTS
GHOSTY
GHOUL
GHOULIE
GHOULIES
GHOULISH
GHOULS
GHRELIN
GHRELINS
GHUBAR
GHYLL
GHYLLS
GI
GIAMBEUX
GIANT
GIANTESS
GIANTHOOD
GIANTISM
GIANTISMS
GIANTLIER
GIANTLIKE
GIANTLY
GIANTRIES
GIANTRY
GIANTS
GIANTSHIP
GIAOUR
GIAOURS
GIARDIA
GIARDIAS
GIB
GIBBED
GIBBER
GIBBERED
GIBBERING
GIBBERISH
GIBBERS
GIBBET
GIBBETED
GIBBETING
GIBBETS
GIBBETTED
GIBBING
GIBBON
GIBBONS
GIBBOSE
GIBBOSITY
GIBBOUS
GIBBOUSLY
GIBBSITE
GIBBSITES
GIBE
GIBED
GIBEL
GIBELS
GIBER
GIBERS
GIBES
GIBING
GIBINGLY
GIBLET
GIBLETS
GIBLI
GIBLIS
GIBS
GIBSON
GIBSONS
GIBUS
GIBUSES
GID
GIDDAP
GIDDAY
GIDDIED
GIDDIER
GIDDIES
GIDDIEST
GIDDILY
GIDDINESS
GIDDUP
GIDDY
GIDDYAP
GIDDYING
GIDDYUP
GIDGEE
GIDGEES
GIDJEE
GIDJEES
GIDS
GIE
GIED
GIEING
GIEN
GIES
GIF
GIFS

GIFT
GIFTABLE
GIFTABLES
GIFTED
GIFTEDLY
GIFTEE
GIFTEES
GIFTING
GIFTINGS
GIFTLESS
GIFTS
GIFTSHOP
GIFTSHOPS
GIFTWARE
GIFTWARES
GIFTWRAP
GIFTWRAPS
GIG
GIGA
GIGABIT
GIGABITS
GIGABYTE
GIGABYTES
GIGACYCLE
GIGAFLOP
GIGAFLOPS
GIGAHERTZ
GIGANTEAN
GIGANTIC
GIGANTISM
GIGAS
GIGATON
GIGATONS
GIGAVOLT
GIGAVOLTS
GIGAWATT
GIGAWATTS
GIGGED
GIGGING
GIGGIT
GIGGITED
GIGGITING
GIGGITS
GIGGLE
GIGGLED
GIGGLER
GIGGLERS
GIGGLES
GIGGLIER
GIGGLIEST
GIGGLING
GIGGLINGS
GIGGLY
GIGHE
GIGLET
GIGLETS
GIGLOT
GIGLOTS
GIGMAN
GIGMANITY
GIGMEN
GIGOLO
GIGOLOS
GIGOT
GIGOTS
GIGS
GIGUE
GIGUES
GILA
GILAS
GILBERT
GILBERTS
GILCUP
GILCUPS
GILD
GILDED
GILDEN
GILDER
GILDERS
GILDHALL
GILDHALLS
GILDING
GILDINGS
GILDS
GILDSMAN
GILDSMEN
GILET
GILETS
GILGAI
GILGAIS
GILGIE
GILGIES
GILL
GILLAROO
GILLAROOS
GILLED
GILLER
GILLERS
GILLET
GILLETS
GILLFLIRT
GILLIE
GILLIED
GILLIES
GILLING
GILLION
GILLIONS
GILLNET
GILLNETS
GILLS
GILLY
GILLYING
GILLYVOR
GILLYVORS
GILPEY
GILPEYS
GILPIES
GILPY
GILRAVAGE
GILSONITE
GILT
GILTCUP
GILTCUPS
GILTHEAD
GILTHEADS
GILTS
GILTWOOD
GIMBAL
GIMBALED
GIMBALING
GIMBALLED
GIMBALS
GIMCRACK
GIMCRACKS
GIMEL
GIMELS
GIMLET
GIMLETED
GIMLETING
GIMLETS
GIMMAL
GIMMALLED
GIMMALS
GIMME
GIMMER
GIMMERS
GIMMES
GIMMICK
GIMMICKED
GIMMICKRY
GIMMICKS
GIMMICKY
GIMMIE
GIMMIES
GIMMOR
GIMMORS
GIMP
GIMPED
GIMPIER
GIMPIEST
GIMPING
GIMPS
GIMPY
GIN
GINCH
GINCHES
GING
GINGAL
GINGALL
GINGALLS
GINGALS
GINGE
GINGELEY
GINGELEYS
GINGELI
GINGELIES
GINGELIS
GINGELLI
GINGELLIS
GINGELLY
GINGELY
GINGER
GINGERADE
GINGERED
GINGERIER
GINGERING
GINGERLY
GINGEROUS
GINGERS
GINGERY
GINGES
GINGHAM
GINGHAMS
GINGILI
GINGILIS
GINGILLI
GINGILLIS
GINGIVA
GINGIVAE
GINGIVAL
GINGKO
GINGKOES
GINGKOS
GINGLE
GINGLES
GINGLYMI
GINGLYMUS
GINGS
GINHOUSE
GINHOUSES
GINK
GINKGO
GINKGOES
GINKGOS
GINKS
GINN
GINNED
GINNEL
GINNELS
GINNER
GINNERIES
GINNERS
GINNERY
GINNIER
GINNIEST
GINNING
GINNINGS
GINNY
GINORMOUS
GINS
GINSENG
GINSENGS
GINSHOP
GINSHOPS
GIO
GIOCOSO
GIOS
GIP
GIPON
GIPONS

G

GIPPED
GIPPER
GIPPERS
GIPPIES
GIPPING
GIPPY
GIPS
GIPSEN
GIPSENS
GIPSIED
GIPSIES
GIPSY
GIPSYDOM
GIPSYDOMS
GIPSYHOOD
GIPSYING
GIPSYISH
GIPSYISM
GIPSYISMS
GIPSYWORT
GIRAFFE
GIRAFFES
GIRAFFID
GIRAFFIDS
GIRAFFINE
GIRAFFISH
GIRAFFOID
GIRANDOLA
GIRANDOLE
GIRASOL
GIRASOLE
GIRASOLES
GIRASOLS
GIRD
GIRDED
GIRDER
GIRDERS
GIRDING
GIRDINGLY
GIRDINGS
GIRDLE
GIRDLED
GIRDLER
GIRDLERS
GIRDLES
GIRDLING
GIRDS
GIRKIN
GIRKINS
GIRL
GIRLHOOD
GIRLHOODS
GIRLIE
GIRLIER
GIRLIES
GIRLIEST
GIRLISH
GIRLISHLY
GIRLOND
GIRLONDS
GIRLS
GIRLY
GIRN
GIRNED
GIRNEL
GIRNELS
GIRNER
GIRNERS
GIRNIE
GIRNIER
GIRNIEST
GIRNING
GIRNS
GIRO
GIROLLE
GIROLLES
GIRON
GIRONIC
GIRONNY
GIRONS
GIROS
GIROSOL
GIROSOLS
GIRR
GIRRS
GIRSH
GIRSHES
GIRT
GIRTED
GIRTH
GIRTHED
GIRTHING
GIRTHLINE
GIRTHS
GIRTING
GIRTLINE
GIRTLINES
GIRTS
GIS
GISARME
GISARMES
GISM
GISMO
GISMOLOGY
GISMOS
GISMS
GIST
GISTS
GIT
GITANA
GITANAS
GITANO
GITANOS
GITCH
GITCHES
GITE
GITES
GITS
GITTARONE
GITTED
GITTERN
GITTERNED
GITTERNS
GITTIN
GITTING
GIUST
GIUSTED
GIUSTING
GIUSTO
GIUSTS
GIVABLE
GIVE
GIVEABLE
GIVEAWAY
GIVEAWAYS
GIVEBACK
GIVEBACKS
GIVED
GIVEN
GIVENNESS
GIVENS
GIVER
GIVERS
GIVES
GIVING
GIVINGS
GIZMO
GIZMOLOGY
GIZMOS
GIZZ
GIZZARD
GIZZARDS
GIZZEN
GIZZENED
GIZZENING
GIZZENS
GIZZES
GJETOST
GJETOSTS
GJU
GJUS
GLABELLA
GLABELLAE
GLABELLAR
GLABRATE
GLABROUS
GLACE
GLACED
GLACEED
GLACEING
GLACES
GLACIAL
GLACIALLY
GLACIALS
GLACIATE
GLACIATED
GLACIATES
GLACIER
GLACIERED
GLACIERS
GLACIS
GLACISES
GLAD
GLADDED
GLADDEN
GLADDENED
GLADDENER
GLADDENS
GLADDER
GLADDEST
GLADDIE
GLADDIES
GLADDING
GLADDON
GLADDONS
GLADE
GLADELIKE
GLADES
GLADFUL
GLADIATE
GLADIATOR
GLADIER
GLADIEST
GLADIOLA
GLADIOLAR
GLADIOLAS
GLADIOLE
GLADIOLES
GLADIOLI
GLADIOLUS
GLADIUS
GLADIUSES
GLADLIER
GLADLIEST
GLADLY
GLADNESS
GLADS
GLADSOME
GLADSOMER
GLADSTONE
GLADWRAP
GLADWRAPS
GLADY
GLAIK
GLAIKET
GLAIKIT
GLAIKS
GLAIR
GLAIRE
GLAIRED
GLAIREOUS
GLAIRES
GLAIRIER
GLAIRIEST
GLAIRIN
GLAIRING
GLAIRINS
GLAIRS
GLAIRY
GLAIVE

GLAIVED
GLAIVES
GLAM
GLAMMED
GLAMMER
GLAMMEST
GLAMMIER
GLAMMIEST
GLAMMING
GLAMMY
GLAMOR
GLAMORED
GLAMORING
GLAMORISE
GLAMORIZE
GLAMOROUS
GLAMORS
GLAMOUR
GLAMOURED
GLAMOURS
GLAMPING
GLAMPINGS
GLAMS
GLANCE
GLANCED
GLANCER
GLANCERS
GLANCES
GLANCING
GLANCINGS
GLAND
GLANDERED
GLANDERS
GLANDES
GLANDLESS
GLANDLIKE
GLANDS
GLANDULAR
GLANDULE
GLANDULES
GLANS
GLARE
GLAREAL
GLARED
GLARELESS
GLAREOUS
GLARES
GLARIER
GLARIEST
GLARINESS
GLARING
GLARINGLY
GLARY
GLASNOST
GLASNOSTS
GLASS
GLASSED
GLASSEN
GLASSES
GLASSFUL
GLASSFULS
GLASSIE
GLASSIER
GLASSIES
GLASSIEST
GLASSIFY
GLASSILY
GLASSINE
GLASSINES
GLASSING
GLASSLESS
GLASSLIKE
GLASSMAN
GLASSMEN
GLASSWARE
GLASSWORK
GLASSWORM
GLASSWORT
GLASSY
GLAUCOMA
GLAUCOMAS
GLAUCOUS
GLAUM
GLAUMED
GLAUMING
GLAUMS
GLAUR
GLAURIER
GLAURIEST
GLAURS
GLAURY
GLAZE
GLAZED
GLAZEN
GLAZER
GLAZERS
GLAZES
GLAZIER
GLAZIERS
GLAZIERY
GLAZIEST
GLAZILY
GLAZINESS
GLAZING
GLAZINGS
GLAZY
GLEAM
GLEAMED
GLEAMER
GLEAMERS
GLEAMIER
GLEAMIEST
GLEAMING
GLEAMINGS
GLEAMS
GLEAMY
GLEAN
GLEANABLE
GLEANED
GLEANER
GLEANERS
GLEANING
GLEANINGS
GLEANS
GLEAVE
GLEAVES
GLEBA
GLEBAE
GLEBE
GLEBELESS
GLEBES
GLEBIER
GLEBIEST
GLEBOUS
GLEBY
GLED
GLEDE
GLEDES
GLEDGE
GLEDGED
GLEDGES
GLEDGING
GLEDS
GLEE
GLEED
GLEEDS
GLEEFUL
GLEEFULLY
GLEEING
GLEEK
GLEEKED
GLEEKING
GLEEKS
GLEEMAN
GLEEMEN
GLEENIE
GLEENIES
GLEES
GLEESOME
GLEET
GLEETED
GLEETIER
GLEETIEST
GLEETING
GLEETS
GLEETY
GLEG
GLEGGER
GLEGGEST
GLEGLY
GLEGNESS
GLEI
GLEIS
GLEN
GLENGARRY
GLENLIKE
GLENOID
GLENOIDAL
GLENOIDS
GLENS
GLENT
GLENTED
GLENTING
GLENTS
GLEY
GLEYED
GLEYING
GLEYINGS
GLEYS
GLIA
GLIADIN
GLIADINE
GLIADINES
GLIADINS
GLIAL
GLIAS
GLIB
GLIBBED
GLIBBER
GLIBBERY
GLIBBEST
GLIBBING
GLIBLY
GLIBNESS
GLIBS
GLID
GLIDDER
GLIDDERY
GLIDDEST
GLIDE
GLIDED
GLIDEPATH
GLIDER
GLIDERS
GLIDES
GLIDING
GLIDINGLY
GLIDINGS
GLIFF
GLIFFING
GLIFFINGS
GLIFFS
GLIFT
GLIFTS
GLIKE
GLIKES
GLIM
GLIME
GLIMED
GLIMES
GLIMING
GLIMMER
GLIMMERED
GLIMMERS
GLIMMERY
GLIMPSE
GLIMPSED
GLIMPSER
GLIMPSERS
GLIMPSES

GLIMPSING
GLIMS
GLINT
GLINTED
GLINTIER
GLINTIEST
GLINTING
GLINTS
GLINTY
GLIOMA
GLIOMAS
GLIOMATA
GLIOSES
GLIOSIS
GLISK
GLISKS
GLISSADE
GLISSADED
GLISSADER
GLISSADES
GLISSANDI
GLISSANDO
GLISSE
GLISSES
GLISTEN
GLISTENED
GLISTENS
GLISTER
GLISTERED
GLISTERS
GLIT
GLITCH
GLITCHES
GLITCHIER
GLITCHY
GLITS
GLITTER
GLITTERED
GLITTERS
GLITTERY
GLITZ
GLITZED
GLITZES
GLITZIER
GLITZIEST
GLITZILY
GLITZING
GLITZY
GLOAM
GLOAMING
GLOAMINGS
GLOAMS
GLOAT
GLOATED
GLOATER
GLOATERS
GLOATING
GLOATINGS
GLOATS
GLOB
GLOBAL
GLOBALISE
GLOBALISM
GLOBALIST
GLOBALIZE
GLOBALLY
GLOBATE
GLOBATED
GLOBBIER
GLOBBIEST
GLOBBY
GLOBE
GLOBED
GLOBEFISH
GLOBELIKE
GLOBES
GLOBESITY
GLOBETROT
GLOBI
GLOBIER
GLOBIEST
GLOBIN
GLOBING
GLOBINS
GLOBOID
GLOBOIDS
GLOBOSE
GLOBOSELY
GLOBOSITY
GLOBOUS
GLOBS
GLOBULAR
GLOBULARS
GLOBULE
GLOBULES
GLOBULET
GLOBULETS
GLOBULIN
GLOBULINS
GLOBULITE
GLOBULOUS
GLOBUS
GLOBY
GLOCHID
GLOCHIDIA
GLOCHIDS
GLODE
GLOGG
GLOGGS
GLOIRE
GLOIRES
GLOM
GLOMERA
GLOMERATE
GLOMERULE
GLOMERULI
GLOMMED
GLOMMING
GLOMS
GLOMUS
GLONOIN
GLONOINS
GLOOM
GLOOMED
GLOOMFUL
GLOOMIER
GLOOMIEST
GLOOMILY
GLOOMING
GLOOMINGS
GLOOMLESS
GLOOMS
GLOOMSTER
GLOOMY
GLOOP
GLOOPED
GLOOPIER
GLOOPIEST
GLOOPING
GLOOPS
GLOOPY
GLOP
GLOPPED
GLOPPIER
GLOPPIEST
GLOPPING
GLOPPY
GLOPS
GLORIA
GLORIAS
GLORIED
GLORIES
GLORIFIED
GLORIFIER
GLORIFIES
GLORIFY
GLORIOLE
GLORIOLES
GLORIOSA
GLORIOSAS
GLORIOUS
GLORY
GLORYING
GLOSS
GLOSSA
GLOSSAE
GLOSSAL
GLOSSARY
GLOSSAS
GLOSSATOR
GLOSSED
GLOSSEME
GLOSSEMES
GLOSSER
GLOSSERS
GLOSSES
GLOSSIER
GLOSSIES
GLOSSIEST
GLOSSILY
GLOSSINA
GLOSSINAS
GLOSSING
GLOSSIST
GLOSSISTS
GLOSSITIC
GLOSSITIS
GLOSSLESS
GLOSSY
GLOST
GLOSTS
GLOTTAL
GLOTTIC
GLOTTIDES
GLOTTIS
GLOTTISES
GLOUT
GLOUTED
GLOUTING
GLOUTS
GLOVE
GLOVEBOX
GLOVED
GLOVELESS
GLOVELIKE
GLOVER
GLOVERS
GLOVES
GLOVING
GLOVINGS
GLOW
GLOWED
GLOWER
GLOWERED
GLOWERING
GLOWERS
GLOWFLIES
GLOWFLY
GLOWING
GLOWINGLY
GLOWLAMP
GLOWLAMPS
GLOWS
GLOWSTICK
GLOWWORM
GLOWWORMS
GLOXINIA
GLOXINIAS
GLOZE
GLOZED
GLOZES
GLOZING
GLOZINGS
GLUCAGON
GLUCAGONS
GLUCAN
GLUCANS
GLUCINA
GLUCINAS
GLUCINIC

GLUCINIUM
GLUCINUM
GLUCINUMS
GLUCONATE
GLUCONIC
GLUCOSE
GLUCOSES
GLUCOSIC
GLUCOSIDE
GLUE
GLUEBALL
GLUEBALLS
GLUED
GLUEING
GLUEISH
GLUELIKE
GLUEPOT
GLUEPOTS
GLUER
GLUERS
GLUES
GLUEY
GLUEYNESS
GLUG
GLUGGABLE
GLUGGED
GLUGGING
GLUGS
GLUHWEIN
GLUHWEINS
GLUIER
GLUIEST
GLUILY
GLUINESS
GLUING
GLUISH
GLUM
GLUME
GLUMELIKE
GLUMELLA
GLUMELLAS
GLUMES
GLUMLY
GLUMMER
GLUMMEST
GLUMNESS
GLUMPIER
GLUMPIEST
GLUMPILY
GLUMPISH
GLUMPS
GLUMPY
GLUMS
GLUNCH
GLUNCHED
GLUNCHES
GLUNCHING
GLUON
GLUONS
GLURGE
GLURGES
GLUT
GLUTAEAL
GLUTAEI
GLUTAEUS
GLUTAMATE
GLUTAMIC
GLUTAMINE
GLUTCH
GLUTCHED
GLUTCHES
GLUTCHING
GLUTE
GLUTEAL
GLUTEI
GLUTELIN
GLUTELINS
GLUTEN
GLUTENIN
GLUTENINS
GLUTENOUS
GLUTENS
GLUTES
GLUTEUS
GLUTINOUS
GLUTS
GLUTTED
GLUTTING
GLUTTON
GLUTTONS
GLUTTONY
GLYCAEMIA
GLYCAEMIC
GLYCAN
GLYCANS
GLYCATION
GLYCEMIA
GLYCEMIAS
GLYCEMIC
GLYCERIA
GLYCERIAS
GLYCERIC
GLYCERIDE
GLYCERIN
GLYCERINE
GLYCERINS
GLYCEROL
GLYCEROLS
GLYCERYL
GLYCERYLS
GLYCIN
GLYCINE
GLYCINES
GLYCINS
GLYCOCOLL
GLYCOGEN
GLYCOGENS
GLYCOL
GLYCOLIC
GLYCOLLIC
GLYCOLS
GLYCONIC
GLYCONICS
GLYCOSE
GLYCOSES
GLYCOSIDE
GLYCOSYL
GLYCOSYLS
GLYCYL
GLYCYLS
GLYPH
GLYPHIC
GLYPHS
GLYPTAL
GLYPTALS
GLYPTIC
GLYPTICS
GMELINITE
GNAMMA
GNAR
GNARL
GNARLED
GNARLIER
GNARLIEST
GNARLING
GNARLS
GNARLY
GNARR
GNARRED
GNARRING
GNARRS
GNARS
GNASH
GNASHED
GNASHER
GNASHERS
GNASHES
GNASHING
GNASHINGS
GNAT
GNATHAL
GNATHIC
GNATHION
GNATHIONS
GNATHITE
GNATHITES
GNATHONIC
GNATLIKE
GNATLING
GNATLINGS
GNATS
GNATTIER
GNATTIEST
GNATTY
GNATWREN
GNATWRENS
GNAW
GNAWABLE
GNAWED
GNAWER
GNAWERS
GNAWING
GNAWINGLY
GNAWINGS
GNAWN
GNAWS
GNEISS
GNEISSES
GNEISSIC
GNEISSOID
GNEISSOSE
GNOCCHI
GNOMAE
GNOME
GNOMELIKE
GNOMES
GNOMIC
GNOMICAL
GNOMISH
GNOMIST
GNOMISTS
GNOMON
GNOMONIC
GNOMONICS
GNOMONS
GNOSES
GNOSIS
GNOSTIC
GNOSTICAL
GNOSTICS
GNOW
GNOWS
GNU
GNUS
GO
GOA
GOAD
GOADED
GOADING
GOADLIKE
GOADS
GOADSMAN
GOADSMEN
GOADSTER
GOADSTERS
GOAF
GOAFS
GOAL
GOALBALL
GOALBALLS
GOALED
GOALIE
GOALIES
GOALING
GOALLESS
GOALMOUTH
GOALPOST
GOALPOSTS
GOALS
GOALWARD

G

GOALWARDS
GOANNA
GOANNAS
GOARY
GOAS
GOAT
GOATEE
GOATEED
GOATEES
GOATFISH
GOATHERD
GOATHERDS
GOATIER
GOATIES
GOATIEST
GOATISH
GOATISHLY
GOATLIKE
GOATLING
GOATLINGS
GOATS
GOATSE
GOATSES
GOATSKIN
GOATSKINS
GOATWEED
GOATWEEDS
GOATY
GOB
GOBAN
GOBANG
GOBANGS
GOBANS
GOBAR
GOBBED
GOBBELINE
GOBBET
GOBBETS
GOBBI
GOBBIER
GOBBIEST
GOBBING
GOBBLE
GOBBLED
GOBBLER
GOBBLERS
GOBBLES
GOBBLING
GOBBO
GOBBY
GOBI
GOBIES
GOBIID
GOBIIDS
GOBIOID
GOBIOIDS
GOBIS
GOBLET
GOBLETS
GOBLIN
GOBLINS
GOBO
GOBOES
GOBONEE
GOBONY
GOBOS
GOBS
GOBSHITE
GOBSHITES
GOBURRA
GOBURRAS
GOBY
GOCHUJANG
GOD
GODAWFUL
GODCHILD
GODDAM
GODDAMMED
GODDAMMIT
GODDAMN
GODDAMNED
GODDAMNIT
GODDAMNS
GODDAMS
GODDED
GODDEN
GODDENS
GODDESS
GODDESSES
GODDING
GODET
GODETIA
GODETIAS
GODETS
GODFATHER
GODHEAD
GODHEADS
GODHOOD
GODHOODS
GODLESS
GODLESSLY
GODLIER
GODLIEST
GODLIKE
GODLILY
GODLINESS
GODLING
GODLINGS
GODLY
GODMOTHER
GODOWN
GODOWNS
GODPARENT
GODROON
GODROONED
GODROONS
GODS
GODSEND
GODSENDS
GODSHIP
GODSHIPS
GODSLOT
GODSLOTS
GODSO
GODSON
GODSONS
GODSPEED
GODSPEEDS
GODSQUAD
GODSQUADS
GODWARD
GODWARDS
GODWIT
GODWITS
GOE
GOEL
GOELS
GOER
GOERS
GOES
GOEST
GOETH
GOETHITE
GOETHITES
GOETIC
GOETIES
GOETY
GOEY
GOFER
GOFERS
GOFF
GOFFED
GOFFER
GOFFERED
GOFFERING
GOFFERS
GOFFING
GOFFS
GOGGA
GOGGAS
GOGGLE
GOGGLEBOX
GOGGLED
GOGGLER
GOGGLERS
GOGGLES
GOGGLIER
GOGGLIEST
GOGGLING
GOGGLINGS
GOGGLY
GOGLET
GOGLETS
GOGO
GOGOS
GOHONZON
GOHONZONS
GOIER
GOIEST
GOING
GOINGS
GOITER
GOITERED
GOITERS
GOITRE
GOITRED
GOITRES
GOITROGEN
GOITROUS
GOJI
GOJIS
GOLCONDA
GOLCONDAS
GOLD
GOLDARN
GOLDARNED
GOLDARNS
GOLDBRICK
GOLDBUG
GOLDBUGS
GOLDCREST
GOLDEN
GOLDENED
GOLDENER
GOLDENEST
GOLDENEYE
GOLDENING
GOLDENLY
GOLDENROD
GOLDENS
GOLDER
GOLDEST
GOLDEYE
GOLDEYES
GOLDFIELD
GOLDFINCH
GOLDFINNY
GOLDFISH
GOLDIER
GOLDIES
GOLDIEST
GOLDISH
GOLDLESS
GOLDMINER
GOLDS
GOLDSINNY
GOLDSIZE
GOLDSIZES
GOLDSMITH
GOLDSPINK
GOLDSTICK
GOLDSTONE
GOLDTAIL
GOLDTONE
GOLDTONES
GOLDURN
GOLDURNS
GOLDWORK
GOLDWORKS
GOLDY

GOLE
GOLEM
GOLEMS
GOLES
GOLF
GOLFED
GOLFER
GOLFERS
GOLFIANA
GOLFIANAS
GOLFING
GOLFINGS
GOLFS
GOLGOTHA
GOLGOTHAS
GOLIARD
GOLIARDIC
GOLIARDS
GOLIARDY
GOLIAS
GOLIASED
GOLIASES
GOLIASING
GOLIATH
GOLIATHS
GOLLAN
GOLLAND
GOLLANDS
GOLLANS
GOLLAR
GOLLARED
GOLLARING
GOLLARS
GOLLER
GOLLERED
GOLLERING
GOLLERS
GOLLIED
GOLLIES
GOLLOP
GOLLOPED
GOLLOPER
GOLLOPERS
GOLLOPING
GOLLOPS
GOLLY
GOLLYING
GOLOMYNKA
GOLOSH
GOLOSHE
GOLOSHED
GOLOSHES
GOLOSHING
GOLOSHOES
GOLP
GOLPE
GOLPES
GOLPS
GOMBEEN
GOMBEENS
GOMBO
GOMBOS
GOMBRO
GOMBROON
GOMBROONS
GOMBROS
GOMER
GOMERAL
GOMERALS
GOMEREL
GOMERELS
GOMERIL
GOMERILS
GOMERS
GOMOKU
GOMOKUS
GOMPA
GOMPAS
GOMPHOSES
GOMPHOSIS
GOMUTI
GOMUTIS
GOMUTO
GOMUTOS
GON
GONAD
GONADAL
GONADIAL
GONADIC
GONADS
GONCH
GONCHES
GONDELAY
GONDELAYS
GONDOLA
GONDOLAS
GONDOLIER
GONE
GONEF
GONEFS
GONENESS
GONER
GONERS
GONFALON
GONFALONS
GONFANON
GONFANONS
GONG
GONGED
GONGING
GONGLIKE
GONGS
GONGSTER
GONGSTERS
GONGYO
GONGYOS
GONIA
GONIATITE
GONIDIA
GONIDIAL
GONIDIC
GONIDIUM
GONIF
GONIFF
GONIFFS
GONIFS
GONION
GONIUM
GONK
GONKS
GONNA
GONOCOCCI
GONOCYTE
GONOCYTES
GONODUCT
GONODUCTS
GONOF
GONOFS
GONOPH
GONOPHORE
GONOPHS
GONOPOD
GONOPODS
GONOPORE
GONOPORES
GONORRHEA
GONOSOME
GONOSOMES
GONS
GONYS
GONYSES
GONZO
GONZOS
GOO
GOOBER
GOOBERS
GOOBIES
GOOBY
GOOD
GOODBY
GOODBYE
GOODBYES
GOODBYS
GOODFACED
GOODFELLA
GOODIE
GOODIER
GOODIES
GOODIEST
GOODINESS
GOODISH
GOODLIER
GOODLIEST
GOODLY
GOODMAN
GOODMEN
GOODNESS
GOODNIGHT
GOODS
GOODSIRE
GOODSIRES
GOODTIME
GOODWIFE
GOODWILL
GOODWILLS
GOODWIVES
GOODY
GOODYEAR
GOODYEARS
GOOEY
GOOEYNESS
GOOF
GOOFBALL
GOOFBALLS
GOOFED
GOOFIER
GOOFIEST
GOOFILY
GOOFINESS
GOOFING
GOOFS
GOOFUS
GOOFUSES
GOOFY
GOOG
GOOGLE
GOOGLED
GOOGLES
GOOGLIES
GOOGLING
GOOGLY
GOOGOL
GOOGOLS
GOOGS
GOOIER
GOOIEST
GOOILY
GOOINESS
GOOK
GOOKIER
GOOKIEST
GOOKS
GOOKY
GOOL
GOOLD
GOOLDS
GOOLEY
GOOLEYS
GOOLIE
GOOLIES
GOOLS
GOOLY
GOOMBAH
GOOMBAHS
GOOMBAY
GOOMBAYS
GOON
GOONDA
GOONDAS
GOONERIES

GOONERY
GOONEY
GOONEYS
GOONIE
GOONIER
GOONIES
GOONIEST
GOONS
GOONY
GOOP
GOOPED
GOOPIER
GOOPIEST
GOOPINESS
GOOPS
GOOPY
GOOR
GOORAL
GOORALS
GOORIE
GOORIES
GOOROO
GOOROOS
GOORS
GOORY
GOOS
GOOSANDER
GOOSE
GOOSED
GOOSEFISH
GOOSEFOOT
GOOSEGOB
GOOSEGOBS
GOOSEGOG
GOOSEGOGS
GOOSEHERD
GOOSELIKE
GOOSENECK
GOOSERIES
GOOSERY
GOOSES
GOOSEY
GOOSEYS
GOOSIER
GOOSIES
GOOSIEST
GOOSINESS
GOOSING
GOOSY
GOPAK
GOPAKS
GOPHER
GOPHERED
GOPHERING
GOPHERS
GOPIK
GOPIKS
GOPURA
GOPURAM
GOPURAMS
GOPURAS
GOR
GORA
GORAL
GORALS
GORAMIES
GORAMY
GORAS
GORBELLY
GORBLIMEY
GORBLIMY
GORCOCK
GORCOCKS
GORCROW
GORCROWS
GORDITA
GORDITAS
GORE
GORED
GOREFEST
GOREFESTS
GOREHOUND
GORES
GORGE
GORGEABLE
GORGED
GORGEDLY
GORGEOUS
GORGER
GORGERIN
GORGERINS
GORGERS
GORGES
GORGET
GORGETED
GORGETS
GORGIA
GORGIAS
GORGING
GORGIO
GORGIOS
GORGON
GORGONEIA
GORGONIAN
GORGONISE
GORGONIZE
GORGONS
GORHEN
GORHENS
GORI
GORIER
GORIEST
GORILLA
GORILLAS
GORILLIAN
GORILLINE
GORILLOID
GORILY
GORINESS
GORING
GORINGS
GORIS
GORM
GORMAND
GORMANDS
GORMED
GORMIER
GORMIEST
GORMING
GORMLESS
GORMS
GORMY
GORP
GORPED
GORPING
GORPS
GORS
GORSE
GORSEDD
GORSEDDS
GORSES
GORSIER
GORSIEST
GORSOON
GORSOONS
GORSY
GORY
GOS
GOSH
GOSHAWK
GOSHAWKS
GOSHT
GOSHTS
GOSLARITE
GOSLET
GOSLETS
GOSLING
GOSLINGS
GOSPEL
GOSPELER
GOSPELERS
GOSPELISE
GOSPELIZE
GOSPELLED
GOSPELLER
GOSPELLY
GOSPELS
GOSPODA
GOSPODAR
GOSPODARS
GOSPODIN
GOSPORT
GOSPORTS
GOSS
GOSSAMER
GOSSAMERS
GOSSAMERY
GOSSAN
GOSSANS
GOSSE
GOSSED
GOSSES
GOSSIB
GOSSIBS
GOSSING
GOSSIP
GOSSIPED
GOSSIPER
GOSSIPERS
GOSSIPIER
GOSSIPING
GOSSIPPED
GOSSIPPER
GOSSIPRY
GOSSIPS
GOSSIPY
GOSSOON
GOSSOONS
GOSSYPINE
GOSSYPOL
GOSSYPOLS
GOSTER
GOSTERED
GOSTERING
GOSTERS
GOT
GOTCH
GOTCHA
GOTCHAS
GOTCHES
GOTCHIES
GOTH
GOTHIC
GOTHICISE
GOTHICISM
GOTHICIZE
GOTHICS
GOTHIER
GOTHIEST
GOTHITE
GOTHITES
GOTHS
GOTHY
GOTTA
GOTTEN
GOUACHE
GOUACHES
GOUCH
GOUCHED
GOUCHES
GOUCHING
GOUGE
GOUGED
GOUGER
GOUGERE
GOUGERES
GOUGERS
GOUGES
GOUGING
GOUJEERS

GOUJON
GOUJONS
GOUK
GOUKS
GOULASH
GOULASHES
GOURA
GOURAMI
GOURAMIES
GOURAMIS
GOURAS
GOURD
GOURDE
GOURDES
GOURDFUL
GOURDFULS
GOURDIER
GOURDIEST
GOURDLIKE
GOURDS
GOURDY
GOURMAND
GOURMANDS
GOURMET
GOURMETS
GOUSTIER
GOUSTIEST
GOUSTROUS
GOUSTY
GOUT
GOUTFLIES
GOUTFLY
GOUTIER
GOUTIEST
GOUTILY
GOUTINESS
GOUTS
GOUTTE
GOUTTES
GOUTWEED
GOUTWEEDS
GOUTWORT
GOUTWORTS
GOUTY
GOV
GOVERN
GOVERNALL
GOVERNED
GOVERNESS
GOVERNING
GOVERNOR
GOVERNORS
GOVERNS
GOVS
GOWAN
GOWANED
GOWANS
GOWANY
GOWD
GOWDER
GOWDEST
GOWDS
GOWDSPINK
GOWF
GOWFED
GOWFER
GOWFERS
GOWFING
GOWFS
GOWK
GOWKS
GOWL
GOWLAN
GOWLAND
GOWLANDS
GOWLANS
GOWLED
GOWLING
GOWLS
GOWN
GOWNBOY
GOWNBOYS
GOWNED
GOWNING
GOWNMAN
GOWNMEN
GOWNS
GOWNSMAN
GOWNSMEN
GOWPEN
GOWPENFUL
GOWPENS
GOX
GOXES
GOYLE
GOYLES
GOZZAN
GOZZANS
GRAAL
GRAALS
GRAB
GRABBABLE
GRABBED
GRABBER
GRABBERS
GRABBIER
GRABBIEST
GRABBING
GRABBLE
GRABBLED
GRABBLER
GRABBLERS
GRABBLES
GRABBLING
GRABBY
GRABEN
GRABENS
GRABS
GRACE
GRACED
GRACEFUL
GRACELESS
GRACES
GRACILE
GRACILES
GRACILIS
GRACILITY
GRACING
GRACIOSO
GRACIOSOS
GRACIOUS
GRACKLE
GRACKLES
GRAD
GRADABLE
GRADABLES
GRADATE
GRADATED
GRADATES
GRADATIM
GRADATING
GRADATION
GRADATORY
GRADDAN
GRADDANED
GRADDANS
GRADE
GRADED
GRADELESS
GRADELIER
GRADELY
GRADER
GRADERS
GRADES
GRADIENT
GRADIENTS
GRADIN
GRADINE
GRADINES
GRADING
GRADINGS
GRADINI
GRADINO
GRADINS
GRADS
GRADUAL
GRADUALLY
GRADUALS
GRADUAND
GRADUANDS
GRADUATE
GRADUATED
GRADUATES
GRADUATOR
GRADUS
GRADUSES
GRAECISE
GRAECISED
GRAECISES
GRAECIZE
GRAECIZED
GRAECIZES
GRAFF
GRAFFED
GRAFFING
GRAFFITI
GRAFFITIS
GRAFFITO
GRAFFS
GRAFT
GRAFTAGE
GRAFTAGES
GRAFTED
GRAFTER
GRAFTERS
GRAFTING
GRAFTINGS
GRAFTS
GRAHAM
GRAHAMS
GRAIL
GRAILE
GRAILES
GRAILS
GRAIN
GRAINAGE
GRAINAGES
GRAINE
GRAINED
GRAINER
GRAINERS
GRAINES
GRAINIER
GRAINIEST
GRAINING
GRAININGS
GRAINLESS
GRAINS
GRAINY
GRAIP
GRAIPS
GRAITH
GRAITHED
GRAITHING
GRAITHLY
GRAITHS
GRAKLE
GRAKLES
GRALLOCH
GRALLOCHS
GRAM
GRAMA
GRAMARIES
GRAMARY
GRAMARYE
GRAMARYES
GRAMAS
GRAMASH
GRAMASHES
GRAME

GRAMERCY
GRAMES
GRAMMA
GRAMMAGE
GRAMMAGES
GRAMMAR
GRAMMARS
GRAMMAS
GRAMMATIC
GRAMME
GRAMMES
GRAMOCHE
GRAMOCHES
GRAMP
GRAMPA
GRAMPAS
GRAMPIES
GRAMPS
GRAMPUS
GRAMPUSES
GRAMPY
GRAMS
GRAN
GRANA
GRANARIES
GRANARY
GRAND
GRANDAD
GRANDADDY
GRANDADS
GRANDAM
GRANDAME
GRANDAMES
GRANDAMS
GRANDAUNT
GRANDBABY
GRANDDAD
GRANDDADS
GRANDDAM
GRANDDAMS
GRANDE
GRANDEE
GRANDEES
GRANDER
GRANDEST
GRANDEUR
GRANDEURS
GRANDIOSE
GRANDIOSO
GRANDKID
GRANDKIDS
GRANDLY
GRANDMA
GRANDMAMA
GRANDMAS
GRANDNESS
GRANDPA
GRANDPAPA
GRANDPAS
GRANDS
GRANDSIR
GRANDSIRE
GRANDSIRS
GRANDSON
GRANDSONS
GRANFER
GRANFERS
GRANGE
GRANGER
GRANGERS
GRANGES
GRANITA
GRANITAS
GRANITE
GRANITES
GRANITIC
GRANITISE
GRANITITE
GRANITIZE
GRANITOID
GRANIVORE
GRANNAM
GRANNAMS
GRANNIE
GRANNIED
GRANNIES
GRANNOM
GRANNOMS
GRANNY
GRANNYING
GRANNYISH
GRANOLA
GRANOLAS
GRANOLITH
GRANS
GRANT
GRANTABLE
GRANTED
GRANTEE
GRANTEES
GRANTER
GRANTERS
GRANTING
GRANTOR
GRANTORS
GRANTS
GRANTSMAN
GRANTSMEN
GRANULAR
GRANULARY
GRANULATE
GRANULE
GRANULES
GRANULITE
GRANULOMA
GRANULOSE
GRANULOUS
GRANUM
GRANUMS
GRAPE
GRAPED
GRAPELESS
GRAPELICE
GRAPELIKE
GRAPERIES
GRAPERY
GRAPES
GRAPESEED
GRAPESHOT
GRAPETREE
GRAPEVINE
GRAPEY
GRAPH
GRAPHED
GRAPHEME
GRAPHEMES
GRAPHEMIC
GRAPHENE
GRAPHENES
GRAPHIC
GRAPHICAL
GRAPHICLY
GRAPHICS
GRAPHING
GRAPHITE
GRAPHITES
GRAPHITIC
GRAPHIUM
GRAPHIUMS
GRAPHS
GRAPIER
GRAPIEST
GRAPINESS
GRAPING
GRAPLE
GRAPLES
GRAPLIN
GRAPLINE
GRAPLINES
GRAPLINS
GRAPNEL
GRAPNELS
GRAPPA
GRAPPAS
GRAPPLE
GRAPPLED
GRAPPLER
GRAPPLERS
GRAPPLES
GRAPPLING
GRAPY
GRASP
GRASPABLE
GRASPED
GRASPER
GRASPERS
GRASPING
GRASPLESS
GRASPS
GRASS
GRASSBIRD
GRASSED
GRASSER
GRASSERS
GRASSES
GRASSHOOK
GRASSIER
GRASSIEST
GRASSILY
GRASSING
GRASSINGS
GRASSLAND
GRASSLESS
GRASSLIKE
GRASSPLOT
GRASSQUIT
GRASSROOT
GRASSUM
GRASSUMS
GRASSY
GRASTE
GRAT
GRATE
GRATED
GRATEFUL
GRATELESS
GRATER
GRATERS
GRATES
GRATICULE
GRATIFIED
GRATIFIER
GRATIFIES
GRATIFY
GRATIN
GRATINATE
GRATINE
GRATINEE
GRATINEED
GRATINEES
GRATING
GRATINGLY
GRATINGS
GRATINS
GRATIS
GRATITUDE
GRATTOIR
GRATTOIRS
GRATUITY
GRATULANT
GRATULATE
GRAUNCH
GRAUNCHED
GRAUNCHER
GRAUNCHES
GRAUPEL
GRAUPELS
GRAV
GRAVADLAX
GRAVAMEN

GRAVAMENS
GRAVAMINA
GRAVE
GRAVED
GRAVEL
GRAVELED
GRAVELESS
GRAVELIKE
GRAVELING
GRAVELISH
GRAVELLED
GRAVELLY
GRAVELS
GRAVELY
GRAVEN
GRAVENESS
GRAVER
GRAVERS
GRAVES
GRAVESIDE
GRAVESITE
GRAVEST
GRAVEWARD
GRAVEYARD
GRAVID
GRAVIDA
GRAVIDAE
GRAVIDAS
GRAVIDITY
GRAVIDLY
GRAVIES
GRAVING
GRAVINGS
GRAVIS
GRAVITAS
GRAVITATE
GRAVITIES
GRAVITINO
GRAVITON
GRAVITONS
GRAVITY
GRAVLAKS
GRAVLAX
GRAVLAXES
GRAVS
GRAVURE
GRAVURES
GRAVY
GRAWLIX
GRAWLIXES
GRAY
GRAYBACK
GRAYBACKS
GRAYBEARD
GRAYED
GRAYER
GRAYEST
GRAYFISH
GRAYFLIES
GRAYFLY
GRAYHEAD
GRAYHEADS
GRAYHEN
GRAYHENS
GRAYHOUND
GRAYING
GRAYISH
GRAYLAG
GRAYLAGS
GRAYLE
GRAYLES
GRAYLING
GRAYLINGS
GRAYLIST
GRAYLISTS
GRAYLY
GRAYMAIL
GRAYMAILS
GRAYNESS
GRAYOUT
GRAYOUTS
GRAYS
GRAYSCALE
GRAYSTONE
GRAYWACKE
GRAYWATER
GRAZABLE
GRAZE
GRAZEABLE
GRAZED
GRAZER
GRAZERS
GRAZES
GRAZIER
GRAZIERS
GRAZING
GRAZINGLY
GRAZINGS
GRAZIOSO
GREASE
GREASED
GREASER
GREASERS
GREASES
GREASIER
GREASIES
GREASIEST
GREASILY
GREASING
GREASY
GREAT
GREATCOAT
GREATEN
GREATENED
GREATENS
GREATER
GREATEST
GREATESTS
GREATLY
GREATNESS
GREATS
GREAVE
GREAVED
GREAVES
GREAVING
GREBE
GREBES
GREBO
GREBOES
GREBOS
GRECE
GRECES
GRECIAN
GRECIANS
GRECISE
GRECISED
GRECISES
GRECISING
GRECIZE
GRECIZED
GRECIZES
GRECIZING
GRECQUE
GRECQUES
GREE
GREEBO
GREEBOES
GREEBOS
GREECE
GREECES
GREED
GREEDHEAD
GREEDIER
GREEDIEST
GREEDILY
GREEDLESS
GREEDS
GREEDSOME
GREEDY
GREEGREE
GREEGREES
GREEING
GREEK
GREEKED
GREEKING
GREEKINGS
GREEN
GREENBACK
GREENBELT
GREENBONE
GREENBUG
GREENBUGS
GREENED
GREENER
GREENERS
GREENERY
GREENEST
GREENEYE
GREENEYES
GREENFLY
GREENGAGE
GREENHAND
GREENHEAD
GREENHORN
GREENIE
GREENIER
GREENIES
GREENIEST
GREENING
GREENINGS
GREENISH
GREENLET
GREENLETS
GREENLING
GREENLIT
GREENLY
GREENMAIL
GREENNESS
GREENROOM
GREENS
GREENSAND
GREENSICK
GREENSOME
GREENTH
GREENTHS
GREENWASH
GREENWAY
GREENWAYS
GREENWEED
GREENWING
GREENWOOD
GREENY
GREES
GREESE
GREESES
GREESING
GREESINGS
GREET
GREETE
GREETED
GREETER
GREETERS
GREETES
GREETING
GREETINGS
GREETS
GREFFIER
GREFFIERS
GREGALE
GREGALES
GREGARIAN
GREGARINE
GREGATIM
GREGE
GREGED
GREGES
GREGING
GREGO
GREGOS
GREIGE

G

GREIGES
GREIN
GREINED
GREINING
GREINS
GREISEN
GREISENS
GREISLY
GREMIAL
GREMIALS
GREMLIN
GREMLINS
GREMMIE
GREMMIES
GREMMY
GREMOLATA
GREN
GRENACHE
GRENACHES
GRENADE
GRENADES
GRENADIER
GRENADINE
GRENNED
GRENNING
GRENS
GRESE
GRESES
GRESSING
GRESSINGS
GREVE
GREVES
GREVILLEA
GREW
GREWED
GREWHOUND
GREWING
GREWS
GREWSOME
GREWSOMER
GREX
GREXES
GREY
GREYBACK
GREYBACKS
GREYBEARD
GREYED
GREYER
GREYEST
GREYHEAD
GREYHEADS
GREYHEN
GREYHENS
GREYHOUND
GREYING
GREYINGS
GREYISH
GREYLAG
GREYLAGS
GREYLIST
GREYLISTS
GREYLY
GREYNESS
GREYS
GREYSCALE
GREYSTONE
GREYWACKE
GRIBBLE
GRIBBLES
GRICE
GRICED
GRICER
GRICERS
GRICES
GRICING
GRICINGS
GRID
GRIDDED
GRIDDER
GRIDDERS
GRIDDING
GRIDDLE
GRIDDLED
GRIDDLES
GRIDDLING
GRIDE
GRIDED
GRIDELIN
GRIDELINS
GRIDES
GRIDING
GRIDIRON
GRIDIRONS
GRIDLOCK
GRIDLOCKS
GRIDS
GRIECE
GRIECED
GRIECES
GRIEF
GRIEFER
GRIEFERS
GRIEFFUL
GRIEFLESS
GRIEFS
GRIESIE
GRIESLY
GRIESY
GRIEVANCE
GRIEVANT
GRIEVANTS
GRIEVE
GRIEVED
GRIEVER
GRIEVERS
GRIEVES
GRIEVING
GRIEVINGS
GRIEVOUS
GRIFF
GRIFFE
GRIFFES
GRIFFIN
GRIFFINS
GRIFFON
GRIFFONS
GRIFFS
GRIFT
GRIFTED
GRIFTER
GRIFTERS
GRIFTING
GRIFTS
GRIG
GRIGGED
GRIGGING
GRIGRI
GRIGRIS
GRIGS
GRIKE
GRIKES
GRILL
GRILLADE
GRILLADES
GRILLAGE
GRILLAGES
GRILLE
GRILLED
GRILLER
GRILLERS
GRILLERY
GRILLES
GRILLING
GRILLINGS
GRILLION
GRILLIONS
GRILLROOM
GRILLS
GRILLWORK
GRILSE
GRILSES
GRIM
GRIMACE
GRIMACED
GRIMACER
GRIMACERS
GRIMACES
GRIMACING
GRIMALKIN
GRIME
GRIMED
GRIMES
GRIMIER
GRIMIEST
GRIMILY
GRIMINESS
GRIMING
GRIMLY
GRIMMER
GRIMMEST
GRIMNESS
GRIMOIRE
GRIMOIRES
GRIMY
GRIN
GRINCH
GRINCHES
GRIND
GRINDED
GRINDELIA
GRINDER
GRINDERS
GRINDERY
GRINDING
GRINDINGS
GRINDS
GRINNED
GRINNER
GRINNERS
GRINNING
GRINNINGS
GRINS
GRIOT
GRIOTS
GRIP
GRIPE
GRIPED
GRIPER
GRIPERS
GRIPES
GRIPEY
GRIPIER
GRIPIEST
GRIPING
GRIPINGLY
GRIPINGS
GRIPLE
GRIPMAN
GRIPMEN
GRIPPE
GRIPPED
GRIPPER
GRIPPERS
GRIPPES
GRIPPIER
GRIPPIEST
GRIPPING
GRIPPLE
GRIPPLES
GRIPPY
GRIPS
GRIPSACK
GRIPSACKS
GRIPT
GRIPTAPE
GRIPTAPES
GRIPY
GRIS
GRISAILLE
GRISE

G

GRISED
GRISELY
GRISEOUS
GRISES
GRISETTE
GRISETTES
GRISGRIS
GRISING
GRISKIN
GRISKINS
GRISLED
GRISLIER
GRISLIES
GRISLIEST
GRISLY
GRISON
GRISONS
GRISSINI
GRISSINO
GRIST
GRISTER
GRISTERS
GRISTLE
GRISTLES
GRISTLIER
GRISTLY
GRISTMILL
GRISTS
GRISY
GRIT
GRITH
GRITHS
GRITLESS
GRITS
GRITSTONE
GRITTED
GRITTER
GRITTERS
GRITTEST
GRITTIER
GRITTIEST
GRITTILY
GRITTING
GRITTINGS
GRITTY
GRIVATION
GRIVET
GRIVETS
GRIZ
GRIZE
GRIZES
GRIZZES
GRIZZLE
GRIZZLED
GRIZZLER
GRIZZLERS
GRIZZLES
GRIZZLIER
GRIZZLIES
GRIZZLING
GRIZZLY
GROAN
GROANED
GROANER
GROANERS
GROANFUL
GROANING
GROANINGS
GROANS
GROAT
GROATS
GROCER
GROCERIES
GROCERS
GROCERY
GROCKED
GROCKING
GROCKLE
GROCKLES
GRODIER
GRODIEST
GRODY
GROG
GROGGED
GROGGERY
GROGGIER
GROGGIEST
GROGGILY
GROGGING
GROGGY
GROGRAM
GROGRAMS
GROGS
GROGSHOP
GROGSHOPS
GROIN
GROINED
GROINING
GROININGS
GROINS
GROK
GROKED
GROKING
GROKKED
GROKKING
GROKS
GROMA
GROMAS
GROMET
GROMETS
GROMMET
GROMMETED
GROMMETS
GROMWELL
GROMWELLS
GRONE
GRONED
GRONEFULL
GRONES
GRONING
GROOF
GROOFS
GROOLIER
GROOLIEST
GROOLY
GROOM
GROOMED
GROOMER
GROOMERS
GROOMING
GROOMINGS
GROOMS
GROOMSMAN
GROOMSMEN
GROOVE
GROOVED
GROOVER
GROOVERS
GROOVES
GROOVIER
GROOVIEST
GROOVILY
GROOVING
GROOVY
GROPE
GROPED
GROPER
GROPERS
GROPES
GROPING
GROPINGLY
GROSBEAK
GROSBEAKS
GROSCHEN
GROSCHENS
GROSER
GROSERS
GROSERT
GROSERTS
GROSET
GROSETS
GROSGRAIN
GROSS
GROSSART
GROSSARTS
GROSSED
GROSSER
GROSSERS
GROSSES
GROSSEST
GROSSING
GROSSLY
GROSSNESS
GROSSULAR
GROSZ
GROSZE
GROSZY
GROT
GROTESQUE
GROTS
GROTTIER
GROTTIEST
GROTTO
GROTTOED
GROTTOES
GROTTOS
GROTTY
GROUCH
GROUCHED
GROUCHES
GROUCHIER
GROUCHILY
GROUCHING
GROUCHY
GROUF
GROUFS
GROUGH
GROUGHS
GROUND
GROUNDAGE
GROUNDED
GROUNDEN
GROUNDER
GROUNDERS
GROUNDHOG
GROUNDING
GROUNDMAN
GROUNDMEN
GROUNDNUT
GROUNDOUT
GROUNDS
GROUNDSEL
GROUP
GROUPABLE
GROUPAGE
GROUPAGES
GROUPED
GROUPER
GROUPERS
GROUPIE
GROUPIES
GROUPING
GROUPINGS
GROUPIST
GROUPISTS
GROUPLET
GROUPLETS
GROUPOID
GROUPOIDS
GROUPS
GROUPWARE
GROUPWORK
GROUPY
GROUSE
GROUSED
GROUSER
GROUSERS
GROUSES
GROUSEST
GROUSING

GROUT
GROUTED
GROUTER
GROUTERS
GROUTIER
GROUTIEST
GROUTING
GROUTINGS
GROUTS
GROUTY
GROVE
GROVED
GROVEL
GROVELED
GROVELER
GROVELERS
GROVELESS
GROVELING
GROVELLED
GROVELLER
GROVELS
GROVES
GROVET
GROVETS
GROVIER
GROVIEST
GROVY
GROW
GROWABLE
GROWER
GROWERS
GROWING
GROWINGLY
GROWINGS
GROWL
GROWLED
GROWLER
GROWLERS
GROWLERY
GROWLIER
GROWLIEST
GROWLING
GROWLINGS
GROWLS
GROWLY
GROWN
GROWNUP
GROWNUPS
GROWS
GROWTH
GROWTHIER
GROWTHIST
GROWTHS
GROWTHY
GROYNE
GROYNES
GROZING
GRR
GRRL
GRRLS
GRRRL
GRRRLS
GRUB
GRUBBED
GRUBBER
GRUBBERS
GRUBBIER
GRUBBIEST
GRUBBILY
GRUBBING
GRUBBLE
GRUBBLED
GRUBBLES
GRUBBLING
GRUBBY
GRUBS
GRUBSTAKE
GRUBWORM
GRUBWORMS
GRUDGE
GRUDGED
GRUDGEFUL
GRUDGER
GRUDGERS
GRUDGES
GRUDGING
GRUDGINGS
GRUE
GRUED
GRUEING
GRUEL
GRUELED
GRUELER
GRUELERS
GRUELING
GRUELINGS
GRUELLED
GRUELLER
GRUELLERS
GRUELLING
GRUELS
GRUES
GRUESOME
GRUESOMER
GRUFE
GRUFES
GRUFF
GRUFFED
GRUFFER
GRUFFEST
GRUFFIER
GRUFFIEST
GRUFFILY
GRUFFING
GRUFFISH
GRUFFLY
GRUFFNESS
GRUFFS
GRUFFY
GRUFTED
GRUGRU
GRUGRUS
GRUIFORM
GRUING
GRUM
GRUMBLE
GRUMBLED
GRUMBLER
GRUMBLERS
GRUMBLES
GRUMBLIER
GRUMBLING
GRUMBLY
GRUME
GRUMES
GRUMLY
GRUMMER
GRUMMEST
GRUMMET
GRUMMETED
GRUMMETS
GRUMNESS
GRUMOSE
GRUMOUS
GRUMP
GRUMPED
GRUMPH
GRUMPHED
GRUMPHIE
GRUMPHIES
GRUMPHING
GRUMPHS
GRUMPHY
GRUMPIER
GRUMPIES
GRUMPIEST
GRUMPILY
GRUMPING
GRUMPISH
GRUMPS
GRUMPY
GRUND
GRUNDIES
GRUNDLE
GRUNDLES
GRUNGE
GRUNGER
GRUNGERS
GRUNGES
GRUNGEY
GRUNGIER
GRUNGIEST
GRUNGY
GRUNION
GRUNIONS
GRUNT
GRUNTED
GRUNTER
GRUNTERS
GRUNTING
GRUNTINGS
GRUNTLE
GRUNTLED
GRUNTLES
GRUNTLING
GRUNTS
GRUPPETTI
GRUPPETTO
GRUSHIE
GRUTCH
GRUTCHED
GRUTCHES
GRUTCHING
GRUTTEN
GRUYERE
GRUYERES
GRYCE
GRYCES
GRYDE
GRYDED
GRYDES
GRYDING
GRYESY
GRYFON
GRYFONS
GRYKE
GRYKES
GRYPE
GRYPES
GRYPHON
GRYPHONS
GRYPT
GRYSBOK
GRYSBOKS
GRYSELY
GRYSIE
GU
GUACAMOLE
GUACHARO
GUACHAROS
GUACO
GUACOS
GUAIAC
GUAIACOL
GUAIACOLS
GUAIACS
GUAIACUM
GUAIACUMS
GUAIOCUM
GUAIOCUMS
GUAN
GUANA
GUANABANA
GUANACO
GUANACOS
GUANAS
GUANASE
GUANASES
GUANAY
GUANAYS

GUANAZOLO
GUANGO
GUANGOS
GUANIDIN
GUANIDINE
GUANIDINS
GUANIN
GUANINE
GUANINES
GUANINS
GUANO
GUANOS
GUANOSINE
GUANS
GUANXI
GUANXIS
GUANYLIC
GUAR
GUARACHA
GUARACHAS
GUARACHE
GUARACHES
GUARACHI
GUARACHIS
GUARANA
GUARANAS
GUARANI
GUARANIES
GUARANIS
GUARANTEE
GUARANTOR
GUARANTY
GUARD
GUARDABLE
GUARDAGE
GUARDAGES
GUARDANT
GUARDANTS
GUARDDOG
GUARDDOGS
GUARDED
GUARDEDLY
GUARDEE
GUARDEES
GUARDER
GUARDERS
GUARDIAN
GUARDIANS
GUARDING
GUARDLESS
GUARDLIKE
GUARDRAIL
GUARDROOM
GUARDS
GUARDSHIP
GUARDSMAN
GUARDSMEN
GUARISH
GUARISHED
GUARISHES
GUARS
GUAVA
GUAVAS
GUAYABERA
GUAYULE
GUAYULES
GUB
GUBBAH
GUBBAHS
GUBBED
GUBBING
GUBBINS
GUBBINSES
GUBERNIYA
GUBS
GUCK
GUCKIER
GUCKIEST
GUCKS
GUCKY
GUDDLE
GUDDLED
GUDDLES
GUDDLING
GUDE
GUDEMAN
GUDEMEN
GUDES
GUDESIRE
GUDESIRES
GUDEWIFE
GUDEWIVES
GUDGEON
GUDGEONED
GUDGEONS
GUE
GUELDER
GUENON
GUENONS
GUERDON
GUERDONED
GUERDONER
GUERDONS
GUEREZA
GUEREZAS
GUERIDON
GUERIDONS
GUERILLA
GUERILLAS
GUERITE
GUERITES
GUERNSEY
GUERNSEYS
GUERRILLA
GUES
GUESS
GUESSABLE
GUESSED
GUESSER
GUESSERS
GUESSES
GUESSING
GUESSINGS
GUESSWORK
GUEST
GUESTBOOK
GUESTED
GUESTEN
GUESTENED
GUESTENS
GUESTING
GUESTS
GUESTWISE
GUFF
GUFFAW
GUFFAWED
GUFFAWING
GUFFAWS
GUFFIE
GUFFIES
GUFFS
GUGA
GUGAS
GUGGLE
GUGGLED
GUGGLES
GUGGLING
GUGLET
GUGLETS
GUICHET
GUICHETS
GUID
GUIDABLE
GUIDAGE
GUIDAGES
GUIDANCE
GUIDANCES
GUIDE
GUIDEBOOK
GUIDED
GUIDELESS
GUIDELINE
GUIDEPOST
GUIDER
GUIDERS
GUIDES
GUIDESHIP
GUIDEWAY
GUIDEWAYS
GUIDEWORD
GUIDING
GUIDINGS
GUIDON
GUIDONS
GUIDS
GUILD
GUILDER
GUILDERS
GUILDHALL
GUILDRIES
GUILDRY
GUILDS
GUILDSHIP
GUILDSMAN
GUILDSMEN
GUILE
GUILED
GUILEFUL
GUILELESS
GUILER
GUILERS
GUILES
GUILING
GUILLEMET
GUILLEMOT
GUILLOCHE
GUILT
GUILTED
GUILTIER
GUILTIEST
GUILTILY
GUILTING
GUILTLESS
GUILTS
GUILTY
GUIMBARD
GUIMBARDS
GUIMP
GUIMPE
GUIMPED
GUIMPES
GUIMPING
GUIMPS
GUINEA
GUINEAS
GUINEP
GUINEPS
GUIPURE
GUIPURES
GUIRO
GUIROS
GUISARD
GUISARDS
GUISE
GUISED
GUISER
GUISERS
GUISES
GUISING
GUISINGS
GUITAR
GUITARIST
GUITARS
GUITGUIT
GUITGUITS
GUIZER
GUIZERS
GUL
GULA
GULAG

GULAGS
GULAR
GULARS
GULAS
GULCH
GULCHED
GULCHES
GULCHING
GULDEN
GULDENS
GULE
GULES
GULET
GULETS
GULF
GULFED
GULFIER
GULFIEST
GULFING
GULFLIKE
GULFS
GULFWEED
GULFWEEDS
GULFY
GULL
GULLABLE
GULLABLY
GULLED
GULLER
GULLERIES
GULLERS
GULLERY
GULLET
GULLETS
GULLEY
GULLEYED
GULLEYING
GULLEYS
GULLIBLE
GULLIBLY
GULLIED
GULLIES
GULLING
GULLISH
GULLS
GULLWING
GULLY
GULLYING
GULOSITY
GULP
GULPED
GULPER
GULPERS
GULPH
GULPHS
GULPIER
GULPIEST
GULPING
GULPINGLY
GULPS
GULPY
GULS
GULY
GUM
GUMBALL
GUMBALLS
GUMBO
GUMBOIL
GUMBOILS
GUMBOOT
GUMBOOTS
GUMBOS
GUMBOTIL
GUMBOTILS
GUMDROP
GUMDROPS
GUMLANDS
GUMLESS
GUMLIKE
GUMLINE
GUMLINES
GUMMA
GUMMAS
GUMMATA
GUMMATOUS
GUMMED
GUMMER
GUMMERS
GUMMI
GUMMIER
GUMMIES
GUMMIEST
GUMMILY
GUMMINESS
GUMMING
GUMMINGS
GUMMIS
GUMMITE
GUMMITES
GUMMOSE
GUMMOSES
GUMMOSIS
GUMMOSITY
GUMMOUS
GUMMY
GUMNUT
GUMNUTS
GUMP
GUMPED
GUMPHION
GUMPHIONS
GUMPING
GUMPS
GUMPTION
GUMPTIONS
GUMPTIOUS
GUMS
GUMSHIELD
GUMSHOE
GUMSHOED
GUMSHOES
GUMSUCKER
GUMTREE
GUMTREES
GUMWEED
GUMWEEDS
GUMWOOD
GUMWOODS
GUN
GUNBOAT
GUNBOATS
GUNCOTTON
GUNDIES
GUNDOG
GUNDOGS
GUNDY
GUNFIGHT
GUNFIGHTS
GUNFIRE
GUNFIRES
GUNFLINT
GUNFLINTS
GUNFOUGHT
GUNG
GUNGE
GUNGED
GUNGES
GUNGIER
GUNGIEST
GUNGING
GUNGY
GUNHOUSE
GUNHOUSES
GUNITE
GUNITES
GUNK
GUNKED
GUNKHOLE
GUNKHOLED
GUNKHOLES
GUNKIER
GUNKIEST
GUNKING
GUNKS
GUNKY
GUNLAYER
GUNLAYERS
GUNLESS
GUNLOCK
GUNLOCKS
GUNMAKER
GUNMAKERS
GUNMAN
GUNMEN
GUNMETAL
GUNMETALS
GUNNAGE
GUNNAGES
GUNNED
GUNNEL
GUNNELS
GUNNEN
GUNNER
GUNNERA
GUNNERAS
GUNNERIES
GUNNERS
GUNNERY
GUNNIES
GUNNING
GUNNINGS
GUNNY
GUNNYBAG
GUNNYBAGS
GUNNYSACK
GUNPAPER
GUNPAPERS
GUNPLAY
GUNPLAYS
GUNPOINT
GUNPOINTS
GUNPORT
GUNPORTS
GUNPOWDER
GUNROOM
GUNROOMS
GUNRUNNER
GUNS
GUNSEL
GUNSELS
GUNSHIP
GUNSHIPS
GUNSHOT
GUNSHOTS
GUNSIGHT
GUNSIGHTS
GUNSMITH
GUNSMITHS
GUNSTICK
GUNSTICKS
GUNSTOCK
GUNSTOCKS
GUNSTONE
GUNSTONES
GUNTER
GUNTERS
GUNWALE
GUNWALES
GUNYAH
GUNYAHS
GUP
GUPPIES
GUPPY
GUPS
GUQIN
GUQINS
GUR
GURAMI
GURAMIS
GURDIES

GURDWARA
GURDWARAS
GURDY
GURGE
GURGED
GURGES
GURGING
GURGLE
GURGLED
GURGLES
GURGLET
GURGLETS
GURGLIER
GURGLIEST
GURGLING
GURGLY
GURGOYLE
GURGOYLES
GURJUN
GURJUNS
GURL
GURLED
GURLET
GURLETS
GURLIER
GURLIEST
GURLING
GURLS
GURLY
GURN
GURNARD
GURNARDS
GURNED
GURNET
GURNETS
GURNEY
GURNEYS
GURNING
GURNS
GURRAH
GURRAHS
GURRIER
GURRIERS
GURRIES
GURRY
GURS
GURSH
GURSHES
GURU
GURUDOM
GURUDOMS
GURUISM
GURUISMS
GURUS
GURUSHIP
GURUSHIPS
GUS
GUSH
GUSHED
GUSHER
GUSHERS
GUSHES
GUSHIER
GUSHIEST
GUSHILY
GUSHINESS
GUSHING
GUSHINGLY
GUSHY
GUSLA
GUSLAR
GUSLARS
GUSLAS
GUSLE
GUSLES
GUSLI
GUSLIS
GUSSET
GUSSETED
GUSSETING
GUSSETS
GUSSIE
GUSSIED
GUSSIES
GUSSY
GUSSYING
GUST
GUSTABLE
GUSTABLES
GUSTATION
GUSTATIVE
GUSTATORY
GUSTED
GUSTFUL
GUSTIE
GUSTIER
GUSTIEST
GUSTILY
GUSTINESS
GUSTING
GUSTLESS
GUSTO
GUSTOES
GUSTOS
GUSTS
GUSTY
GUT
GUTBUCKET
GUTCHER
GUTCHERS
GUTFUL
GUTFULS
GUTLESS
GUTLESSLY
GUTLIKE
GUTROT
GUTROTS
GUTS
GUTSED
GUTSER
GUTSERS
GUTSES
GUTSFUL
GUTSFULS
GUTSIER
GUTSIEST
GUTSILY
GUTSINESS
GUTSING
GUTSY
GUTTA
GUTTAE
GUTTAS
GUTTATE
GUTTATED
GUTTATES
GUTTATING
GUTTATION
GUTTED
GUTTER
GUTTERED
GUTTERIER
GUTTERING
GUTTERS
GUTTERY
GUTTIER
GUTTIES
GUTTIEST
GUTTING
GUTTLE
GUTTLED
GUTTLER
GUTTLERS
GUTTLES
GUTTLING
GUTTURAL
GUTTURALS
GUTTY
GUTZER
GUTZERS
GUV
GUVS
GUY
GUYED
GUYING
GUYLE
GUYLED
GUYLER
GUYLERS
GUYLES
GUYLINE
GUYLINER
GUYLINERS
GUYLINES
GUYLING
GUYOT
GUYOTS
GUYS
GUYSE
GUYSES
GUZZLE
GUZZLED
GUZZLER
GUZZLERS
GUZZLES
GUZZLING
GWEDUC
GWEDUCK
GWEDUCKS
GWEDUCS
GWINE
GWINIAD
GWINIADS
GWYNIAD
GWYNIADS
GYAL
GYALS
GYAN
GYANS
GYBE
GYBED
GYBES
GYBING
GYELD
GYELDS
GYLDEN
GYM
GYMBAL
GYMBALS
GYMKHANA
GYMKHANAS
GYMMAL
GYMMALS
GYMNASIA
GYMNASIAL
GYMNASIC
GYMNASIEN
GYMNASIUM
GYMNAST
GYMNASTIC
GYMNASTS
GYMNIC
GYMNOSOPH
GYMP
GYMPED
GYMPIE
GYMPIES
GYMPING
GYMPS
GYMS
GYMSLIP
GYMSLIPS
GYMSUIT
GYMSUITS
GYNAE
GYNAECEA
GYNAECEUM
GYNAECIA
GYNAECIUM
GYNAECOID

G

GYNAES
GYNANDRY
GYNARCHIC
GYNARCHY
GYNECIA
GYNECIC
GYNECIUM
GYNECOID
GYNIATRY
GYNIE
GYNIES
GYNNEY
GYNNEYS
GYNNIES
GYNNY
GYNO
GYNOCRACY
GYNOECIA
GYNOECIUM
GYNOPHOBE
GYNOPHORE
GYNOS
GYNY
GYOZA
GYOZAS
GYP
GYPLURE
GYPLURES
GYPO
GYPOS
GYPPIE
GYPPIES
GYPPY
GYPS
GYPSEIAN
GYPSEOUS
GYPSIED
GYPSIES
GYPSUM
GYPSUMS
GYPSY
GYPSYDOM
GYPSYDOMS
GYPSYHOOD
GYPSYING
GYPSYISH
GYPSYISM
GYPSYISMS
GYPSYWORT
GYRAL
GYRALLY
GYRANT
GYRASE
GYRASES
GYRATE
GYRATED
GYRATES
GYRATING
GYRATION
GYRATIONS
GYRATOR
GYRATORS
GYRATORY
GYRE
GYRED
GYRENE
GYRENES
GYRES
GYRFALCON
GYRI
GYRING
GYRO
GYROCAR
GYROCARS
GYRODYNE
GYRODYNES
GYROIDAL
GYROLITE
GYROLITES
GYROMANCY
GYRON
GYRONIC
GYRONNY
GYRONS
GYROPILOT
GYROPLANE
GYROS
GYROSCOPE
GYROSE
GYROSTAT
GYROSTATS
GYROUS
GYROVAGUE
GYRUS
GYRUSES
GYTE
GYTES
GYTRASH
GYTRASHES
GYTTJA
GYTTJAS
GYVE
GYVED
GYVES
GYVING

HA
HAAF
HAAFS
HAANEPOOT
HAAR
HAARS
HABANERA
HABANERAS
HABANERO
HABANEROS
HABDABS
HABDALAH
HABDALAHS
HABENDUM
HABENDUMS
HABERDINE
HABERGEON
HABILABLE
HABILE
HABIT
HABITABLE
HABITABLY
HABITAN
HABITANS
HABITANT
HABITANTS
HABITAT
HABITATS
HABITED
HABITING
HABITS
HABITUAL
HABITUALS
HABITUATE
HABITUDE
HABITUDES
HABITUE
HABITUES
HABITUS
HABITUSES
HABLE
HABOOB
HABOOBS
HABU
HABUS
HACEK
HACEKS
HACENDADO
HACHIS
HACHURE
HACHURED
HACHURES
HACHURING
HACIENDA
HACIENDAS
HACK
HACKABLE
HACKAMORE
HACKBERRY
HACKBOLT
HACKBOLTS
HACKBUT
HACKBUTS
HACKED
HACKEE
HACKEES
HACKER
HACKERIES
HACKERS
HACKERY
HACKETTE
HACKETTES
HACKIE
HACKIES
HACKING
HACKINGS
HACKLE
HACKLED
HACKLER
HACKLERS
HACKLES
HACKLET
HACKLETS
HACKLIER
HACKLIEST
HACKLING
HACKLY
HACKMAN
HACKMEN
HACKNEY
HACKNEYED
HACKNEYS
HACKS
HACKSAW
HACKSAWED
HACKSAWN
HACKSAWS
HACKWORK
HACKWORKS
HACQUETON
HAD
HADAL
HADARIM
HADAWAY
HADDEN
HADDEST
HADDIE
HADDIES
HADDING
HADDOCK
HADDOCKS
HADE
HADED
HADEDAH
HADEDAHS
HADES
HADING
HADITH
HADITHS
HADJ
HADJEE
HADJEES
HADJES
HADJI
HADJIS
HADROME
HADROMES
HADRON
HADRONIC
HADRONS
HADROSAUR
HADS
HADST
HAE
HAECCEITY
HAED
HAEING
HAEM
HAEMAL
HAEMATAL
HAEMATEIN
HAEMATIC
HAEMATICS
HAEMATIN
HAEMATINS
HAEMATITE
HAEMATOID
HAEMATOMA
HAEMIC
HAEMIN
HAEMINS
HAEMOCOEL
HAEMOCYTE
HAEMOID
HAEMOLYSE
HAEMOLYZE
HAEMONIES
HAEMONY
HAEMOSTAT
HAEMS
HAEN
HAEREDES
HAEREMAI
HAEREMAIS
HAERES
HAES
HAET
HAETS
HAFF
HAFFET
HAFFETS
HAFFIT
HAFFITS
HAFFLIN
HAFFLINS
HAFFS
HAFIZ
HAFIZES
HAFNIUM
HAFNIUMS
HAFT
HAFTARA
HAFTARAH
HAFTARAHS
HAFTARAS
HAFTAROS
HAFTAROT
HAFTAROTH
HAFTED
HAFTER
HAFTERS
HAFTING
HAFTORAH
HAFTORAHS
HAFTOROS
HAFTOROT
HAFTOROTH
HAFTS
HAG
HAGADIC
HAGADIST
HAGADISTS
HAGBERRY
HAGBOLT
HAGBOLTS
HAGBORN
HAGBUSH
HAGBUSHES
HAGBUT
HAGBUTEER

H

HAGBUTS
HAGBUTTER
HAGDEN
HAGDENS
HAGDON
HAGDONS
HAGDOWN
HAGDOWNS
HAGFISH
HAGFISHES
HAGG
HAGGADA
HAGGADAH
HAGGADAHS
HAGGADAS
HAGGADIC
HAGGADIST
HAGGADOT
HAGGADOTH
HAGGARD
HAGGARDLY
HAGGARDS
HAGGED
HAGGING
HAGGIS
HAGGISES
HAGGISH
HAGGISHLY
HAGGLE
HAGGLED
HAGGLER
HAGGLERS
HAGGLES
HAGGLING
HAGGLINGS
HAGGS
HAGIARCHY
HAGIOLOGY
HAGLET
HAGLETS
HAGLIKE
HAGRIDDEN
HAGRIDE
HAGRIDER
HAGRIDERS
HAGRIDES
HAGRIDING
HAGRODE
HAGS
HAH
HAHA
HAHAS
HAHNIUM
HAHNIUMS
HAHS
HAICK
HAICKS
HAIDUK
HAIDUKS
HAIK
HAIKA
HAIKAI
HAIKS
HAIKU
HAIKUS
HAIL
HAILED
HAILER
HAILERS
HAILIER
HAILIEST
HAILING
HAILS
HAILSHOT
HAILSHOTS
HAILSTONE
HAILSTORM
HAILY
HAIMISH
HAIN
HAINCH
HAINCHED
HAINCHES
HAINCHING
HAINED
HAINING
HAININGS
HAINS
HAINT
HAINTS
HAIQUE
HAIQUES
HAIR
HAIRBALL
HAIRBALLS
HAIRBAND
HAIRBANDS
HAIRBELL
HAIRBELLS
HAIRBRUSH
HAIRCAP
HAIRCAPS
HAIRCLOTH
HAIRCUT
HAIRCUTS
HAIRDO
HAIRDOS
HAIRDRIER
HAIRDRYER
HAIRED
HAIRGRIP
HAIRGRIPS
HAIRIER
HAIRIEST
HAIRIF
HAIRIFS
HAIRILY
HAIRINESS
HAIRING
HAIRLESS
HAIRLIKE
HAIRLINE
HAIRLINES
HAIRLOCK
HAIRLOCKS
HAIRNET
HAIRNETS
HAIRPIECE
HAIRPIN
HAIRPINS
HAIRS
HAIRSPRAY
HAIRST
HAIRSTED
HAIRSTING
HAIRSTS
HAIRSTYLE
HAIRTAIL
HAIRTAILS
HAIRWING
HAIRWINGS
HAIRWORK
HAIRWORKS
HAIRWORM
HAIRWORMS
HAIRY
HAIRYBACK
HAITH
HAJ
HAJES
HAJI
HAJIS
HAJJ
HAJJAH
HAJJAHS
HAJJES
HAJJI
HAJJIS
HAKA
HAKAM
HAKAMS
HAKARI
HAKARIS
HAKAS
HAKE
HAKEA
HAKEAS
HAKEEM
HAKEEMS
HAKES
HAKIM
HAKIMS
HAKU
HAKUS
HALACHA
HALACHAS
HALACHIC
HALACHIST
HALACHOT
HALACHOTH
HALAKAH
HALAKAHS
HALAKHA
HALAKHAH
HALAKHAHS
HALAKHAS
HALAKHIC
HALAKHIST
HALAKHOT
HALAKHOTH
HALAKIC
HALAKIST
HALAKISTS
HALAKOTH
HALAL
HALALA
HALALAH
HALALAHS
HALALAS
HALALLED
HALALLING
HALALS
HALATION
HALATIONS
HALAVAH
HALAVAHS
HALAZONE
HALAZONES
HALBERD
HALBERDS
HALBERT
HALBERTS
HALCYON
HALCYONIC
HALCYONS
HALE
HALED
HALENESS
HALER
HALERS
HALERU
HALES
HALEST
HALF
HALFA
HALFAS
HALFBACK
HALFBACKS
HALFBEAK
HALFBEAKS
HALFEN
HALFLIFE
HALFLIN
HALFLING
HALFLINGS
HALFLINS
HALFLIVES
HALFNESS
HALFPACE
HALFPACES

HALFPENCE
HALFPENNY
HALFPIPE
HALFPIPES
HALFS
HALFTIME
HALFTIMES
HALFTONE
HALFTONES
HALFTRACK
HALFWAY
HALFWIT
HALFWITS
HALIBUT
HALIBUTS
HALICORE
HALICORES
HALID
HALIDE
HALIDES
HALIDOM
HALIDOME
HALIDOMES
HALIDOMS
HALIDS
HALIER
HALIEROV
HALIERS
HALIEUTIC
HALIMOT
HALIMOTE
HALIMOTES
HALIMOTS
HALING
HALIOTIS
HALITE
HALITES
HALITOSES
HALITOSIS
HALITOTIC
HALITOUS
HALITUS
HALITUSES
HALL
HALLAH
HALLAHS
HALLAL
HALLALI
HALLALIS
HALLALLED
HALLALOO
HALLALOOS
HALLALS
HALLAN
HALLANS
HALLEL
HALLELS
HALLIAN
HALLIANS
HALLIARD
HALLIARDS
HALLING
HALLINGS
HALLION
HALLIONS
HALLMARK
HALLMARKS
HALLO
HALLOA
HALLOAED
HALLOAING
HALLOAS
HALLOED
HALLOES
HALLOING
HALLOO
HALLOOED
HALLOOING
HALLOOS
HALLOS
HALLOT
HALLOTH
HALLOUMI
HALLOUMIS
HALLOW
HALLOWED
HALLOWER
HALLOWERS
HALLOWING
HALLOWS
HALLS
HALLSTAND
HALLUCAL
HALLUCES
HALLUX
HALLWAY
HALLWAYS
HALLYON
HALLYONS
HALM
HALMA
HALMAS
HALMS
HALO
HALOBIONT
HALOCLINE
HALOED
HALOES
HALOGEN
HALOGENIC
HALOGENS
HALOGETON
HALOID
HALOIDS
HALOING
HALOLIKE
HALON
HALONS
HALOPHILE
HALOPHILY
HALOPHOBE
HALOPHYTE
HALOS
HALOSERE
HALOSERES
HALOTHANE
HALOUMI
HALOUMIS
HALSE
HALSED
HALSER
HALSERS
HALSES
HALSING
HALT
HALTED
HALTER
HALTERE
HALTERED
HALTERES
HALTERING
HALTERS
HALTING
HALTINGLY
HALTINGS
HALTLESS
HALTS
HALUTZ
HALUTZIM
HALVA
HALVAH
HALVAHS
HALVAS
HALVE
HALVED
HALVER
HALVERS
HALVES
HALVING
HALVINGS
HALWA
HALWAS
HALYARD
HALYARDS
HAM
HAMADA
HAMADAS
HAMADRYAD
HAMADRYAS
HAMAL
HAMALS
HAMAMELIS
HAMARTIA
HAMARTIAS
HAMATE
HAMATES
HAMATSA
HAMATSAS
HAMAUL
HAMAULS
HAMBA
HAMBLE
HAMBLED
HAMBLES
HAMBLING
HAMBONE
HAMBONED
HAMBONES
HAMBONING
HAMBURG
HAMBURGER
HAMBURGS
HAME
HAMED
HAMES
HAMEWITH
HAMFAT
HAMFATS
HAMFATTER
HAMING
HAMLET
HAMLETS
HAMMADA
HAMMADAS
HAMMAL
HAMMALS
HAMMAM
HAMMAMS
HAMMED
HAMMER
HAMMERED
HAMMERER
HAMMERERS
HAMMERING
HAMMERKOP
HAMMERMAN
HAMMERMEN
HAMMERS
HAMMERTOE
HAMMIER
HAMMIES
HAMMIEST
HAMMILY
HAMMINESS
HAMMING
HAMMOCK
HAMMOCKS
HAMMY
HAMOSE
HAMOUS
HAMPER
HAMPERED
HAMPERER
HAMPERERS
HAMPERING
HAMPERS
HAMPSTER
HAMPSTERS
HAMS
HAMSTER

H

HAMSTERS
HAMSTRING
HAMSTRUNG
HAMULAR
HAMULATE
HAMULI
HAMULOSE
HAMULOUS
HAMULUS
HAMZA
HAMZAH
HAMZAHS
HAMZAS
HAN
HANAP
HANAPER
HANAPERS
HANAPS
HANCE
HANCES
HANCH
HANCHED
HANCHES
HANCHING
HAND
HANDAX
HANDAXE
HANDAXES
HANDBAG
HANDBAGS
HANDBALL
HANDBALLS
HANDBELL
HANDBELLS
HANDBILL
HANDBILLS
HANDBLOWN
HANDBOOK
HANDBOOKS
HANDBRAKE
HANDCAR
HANDCARS
HANDCART
HANDCARTS
HANDCLAP
HANDCLAPS
HANDCLASP
HANDCRAFT
HANDCUFF
HANDCUFFS
HANDED
HANDER
HANDERS
HANDFAST
HANDFASTS
HANDFED
HANDFEED
HANDFEEDS
HANDFUL
HANDFULS
HANDGLASS
HANDGRIP
HANDGRIPS
HANDGUN
HANDGUNS
HANDHELD
HANDHELDS
HANDHOLD
HANDHOLDS
HANDICAP
HANDICAPS
HANDIER
HANDIEST
HANDILY
HANDINESS
HANDING
HANDISM
HANDISMS
HANDIWORK
HANDJAR
HANDJARS
HANDJOB
HANDJOBS
HANDKNIT
HANDKNITS
HANDLE
HANDLEBAR
HANDLED
HANDLER
HANDLERS
HANDLES
HANDLESS
HANDLIKE
HANDLINE
HANDLINER
HANDLINES
HANDLING
HANDLINGS
HANDLIST
HANDLISTS
HANDLOOM
HANDLOOMS
HANDMADE
HANDMAID
HANDMAIDS
HANDOFF
HANDOFFS
HANDOUT
HANDOUTS
HANDOVER
HANDOVERS
HANDPASS
HANDPHONE
HANDPICK
HANDPICKS
HANDPLAY
HANDPLAYS
HANDPRESS
HANDPRINT
HANDRAIL
HANDRAILS
HANDROLL
HANDROLLS
HANDS
HANDSAW
HANDSAWS
HANDSEL
HANDSELED
HANDSELS
HANDSET
HANDSETS
HANDSEWN
HANDSFUL
HANDSHAKE
HANDSIER
HANDSIEST
HANDSOME
HANDSOMER
HANDSOMES
HANDSPIKE
HANDSTAFF
HANDSTAMP
HANDSTAND
HANDSTURN
HANDSY
HANDTOWEL
HANDWHEEL
HANDWORK
HANDWORKS
HANDWOVEN
HANDWRIT
HANDWRITE
HANDWROTE
HANDY
HANDYMAN
HANDYMEN
HANDYWORK
HANEPOOT
HANEPOOTS
HANG
HANGABLE
HANGAR
HANGARAGE
HANGARED
HANGARING
HANGARS
HANGBIRD
HANGBIRDS
HANGDOG
HANGDOGS
HANGED
HANGER
HANGERS
HANGFIRE
HANGFIRES
HANGI
HANGING
HANGINGS
HANGIS
HANGMAN
HANGMEN
HANGNAIL
HANGNAILS
HANGNEST
HANGNESTS
HANGOUT
HANGOUTS
HANGOVER
HANGOVERS
HANGRIER
HANGRIEST
HANGRY
HANGS
HANGTAG
HANGTAGS
HANGUL
HANGULS
HANGUP
HANGUPS
HANIWA
HANIWAS
HANJAR
HANJARS
HANK
HANKED
HANKER
HANKERED
HANKERER
HANKERERS
HANKERING
HANKERS
HANKIE
HANKIES
HANKING
HANKS
HANKY
HANSA
HANSAS
HANSE
HANSEATIC
HANSEL
HANSELED
HANSELING
HANSELLED
HANSELS
HANSES
HANSOM
HANSOMS
HANT
HANTED
HANTING
HANTLE
HANTLES
HANTS
HANUKIAH
HANUKIAHS
HANUMAN
HANUMANS
HAO
HAOMA

HAOMAS
HAOS
HAP
HAPAX
HAPAXES
HAPHAZARD
HAPHTARA
HAPHTARAH
HAPHTARAS
HAPHTAROT
HAPKIDO
HAPKIDOS
HAPLESS
HAPLESSLY
HAPLITE
HAPLITES
HAPLITIC
HAPLOID
HAPLOIDIC
HAPLOIDS
HAPLOIDY
HAPLOLOGY
HAPLONT
HAPLONTIC
HAPLONTS
HAPLOPIA
HAPLOPIAS
HAPLOSES
HAPLOSIS
HAPLOTYPE
HAPLY
HAPPED
HAPPEN
HAPPENED
HAPPENING
HAPPENS
HAPPI
HAPPIED
HAPPIER
HAPPIES
HAPPIEST
HAPPILY
HAPPINESS
HAPPING
HAPPIS
HAPPOSHU
HAPPOSHUS
HAPPY
HAPPYING
HAPS
HAPTEN
HAPTENE
HAPTENES
HAPTENIC
HAPTENS
HAPTERON
HAPTERONS
HAPTIC
HAPTICAL
HAPTICS
HAPU
HAPUKA
HAPUKAS
HAPUKU
HAPUKUS
HAPUS
HAQUETON
HAQUETONS
HARAAM
HARAKEKE
HARAKEKES
HARAM
HARAMBEE
HARAMBEES
HARAMDA
HARAMDAS
HARAMDI
HARAMDIS
HARAMS
HARAMZADA
HARAMZADI
HARANGUE
HARANGUED
HARANGUER
HARANGUES
HARASS
HARASSED
HARASSER
HARASSERS
HARASSES
HARASSING
HARBINGER
HARBOR
HARBORAGE
HARBORED
HARBORER
HARBORERS
HARBORFUL
HARBORING
HARBOROUS
HARBORS
HARBOUR
HARBOURED
HARBOURER
HARBOURS
HARD
HARDASS
HARDASSES
HARDBACK
HARDBACKS
HARDBAG
HARDBAGS
HARDBAKE
HARDBAKES
HARDBALL
HARDBALLS
HARDBEAM
HARDBEAMS
HARDBOARD
HARDBODY
HARDBOOT
HARDBOOTS
HARDBOUND
HARDCASE
HARDCASES
HARDCORE
HARDCORES
HARDCOURT
HARDCOVER
HARDEDGE
HARDEDGES
HARDEN
HARDENED
HARDENER
HARDENERS
HARDENING
HARDENS
HARDER
HARDEST
HARDFACE
HARDFACES
HARDGOODS
HARDGRASS
HARDHACK
HARDHACKS
HARDHAT
HARDHATS
HARDHEAD
HARDHEADS
HARDIER
HARDIES
HARDIEST
HARDIHEAD
HARDIHOOD
HARDILY
HARDIMENT
HARDINESS
HARDISH
HARDLINE
HARDLINER
HARDLY
HARDMAN
HARDMEN
HARDNESS
HARDNOSE
HARDNOSED
HARDNOSES
HARDOKE
HARDOKES
HARDPACK
HARDPACKS
HARDPAN
HARDPANS
HARDPARTS
HARDROCK
HARDROCKS
HARDS
HARDSCAPE
HARDSET
HARDSHELL
HARDSHIP
HARDSHIPS
HARDSTAND
HARDTACK
HARDTACKS
HARDTAIL
HARDTAILS
HARDTOP
HARDTOPS
HARDWARE
HARDWARES
HARDWIRE
HARDWIRED
HARDWIRES
HARDWOOD
HARDWOODS
HARDY
HARE
HAREBELL
HAREBELLS
HARED
HAREEM
HAREEMS
HARELD
HARELDS
HARELIKE
HAREM
HAREMS
HARES
HARESTAIL
HAREWOOD
HAREWOODS
HARIANA
HARIANAS
HARICOT
HARICOTS
HARIGALDS
HARIGALS
HARIJAN
HARIJANS
HARIM
HARIMS
HARING
HARIOLATE
HARIRA
HARIRAS
HARISH
HARISSA
HARISSAS
HARK
HARKED
HARKEN
HARKENED
HARKENER
HARKENERS
HARKENING
HARKENS
HARKING
HARKS
HARL

HARLED
HARLEQUIN
HARLING
HARLINGS
HARLOT
HARLOTRY
HARLOTS
HARLS
HARM
HARMALA
HARMALAS
HARMALIN
HARMALINE
HARMALINS
HARMAN
HARMANS
HARMATTAN
HARMDOING
HARMED
HARMEL
HARMELS
HARMER
HARMERS
HARMFUL
HARMFULLY
HARMIN
HARMINE
HARMINES
HARMING
HARMINS
HARMLESS
HARMONIC
HARMONICA
HARMONICS
HARMONIES
HARMONISE
HARMONIST
HARMONIUM
HARMONIZE
HARMONY
HARMOST
HARMOSTS
HARMOSTY
HARMOTOME
HARMS
HARN
HARNESS
HARNESSED
HARNESSER
HARNESSES
HARNS
HARO
HAROS
HAROSET
HAROSETH
HAROSETHS
HAROSETS
HARP
HARPED
HARPER
HARPERS
HARPIES
HARPIN
HARPING
HARPINGS
HARPINS
HARPIST
HARPISTS
HARPOON
HARPOONED
HARPOONER
HARPOONS
HARPS
HARPY
HARPYLIKE
HARQUEBUS
HARRIDAN
HARRIDANS
HARRIED
HARRIER
HARRIERS
HARRIES
HARROW
HARROWED
HARROWER
HARROWERS
HARROWING
HARROWS
HARRUMPH
HARRUMPHS
HARRY
HARRYING
HARSH
HARSHED
HARSHEN
HARSHENED
HARSHENS
HARSHER
HARSHES
HARSHEST
HARSHING
HARSHLY
HARSHNESS
HARSLET
HARSLETS
HART
HARTAL
HARTALS
HARTBEES
HARTBEEST
HARTELY
HARTEN
HARTENED
HARTENING
HARTENS
HARTLESSE
HARTS
HARTSHORN
HARUMPH
HARUMPHED
HARUMPHS
HARUSPEX
HARUSPICY
HARVEST
HARVESTED
HARVESTER
HARVESTS
HAS
HASH
HASHED
HASHEESH
HASHES
HASHHEAD
HASHHEADS
HASHIER
HASHIEST
HASHING
HASHINGS
HASHISH
HASHISHES
HASHMARK
HASHMARKS
HASHTAG
HASHTAGS
HASHY
HASK
HASKS
HASLET
HASLETS
HASP
HASPED
HASPING
HASPS
HASS
HASSAR
HASSARS
HASSEL
HASSELS
HASSES
HASSIUM
HASSIUMS
HASSLE
HASSLED
HASSLES
HASSLING
HASSOCK
HASSOCKS
HASSOCKY
HAST
HASTA
HASTATE
HASTATED
HASTATELY
HASTE
HASTED
HASTEFUL
HASTEN
HASTENED
HASTENER
HASTENERS
HASTENING
HASTENS
HASTES
HASTIER
HASTIEST
HASTILY
HASTINESS
HASTING
HASTINGS
HASTY
HAT
HATABLE
HATBAND
HATBANDS
HATBOX
HATBOXES
HATBRUSH
HATCH
HATCHABLE
HATCHBACK
HATCHECK
HATCHECKS
HATCHED
HATCHEL
HATCHELED
HATCHELS
HATCHER
HATCHERS
HATCHERY
HATCHES
HATCHET
HATCHETS
HATCHETY
HATCHING
HATCHINGS
HATCHLING
HATCHMENT
HATCHWAY
HATCHWAYS
HATE
HATEABLE
HATED
HATEFUL
HATEFULLY
HATELESS
HATER
HATERENT
HATERENTS
HATERS
HATES
HATFUL
HATFULS
HATGUARD
HATGUARDS
HATH
HATHA
HATINATOR
HATING
HATLESS
HATLIKE

HATMAKER
HATMAKERS
HATPEG
HATPEGS
HATPIN
HATPINS
HATRACK
HATRACKS
HATRED
HATREDS
HATS
HATSFUL
HATSTAND
HATSTANDS
HATTED
HATTER
HATTERED
HATTERIA
HATTERIAS
HATTERING
HATTERS
HATTING
HATTINGS
HATTOCK
HATTOCKS
HAUBERK
HAUBERKS
HAUBOIS
HAUD
HAUDING
HAUDS
HAUF
HAUFS
HAUGH
HAUGHS
HAUGHT
HAUGHTIER
HAUGHTILY
HAUGHTY
HAUL
HAULAGE
HAULAGES
HAULBACK
HAULBACKS
HAULD
HAULDS
HAULED
HAULER
HAULERS
HAULIER
HAULIERS
HAULING
HAULINGS
HAULM
HAULMIER
HAULMIEST
HAULMS
HAULMY
HAULOUT
HAULOUTS
HAULS
HAULST
HAULT
HAULYARD
HAULYARDS
HAUN
HAUNCH
HAUNCHED
HAUNCHES
HAUNCHING
HAUNS
HAUNT
HAUNTED
HAUNTER
HAUNTERS
HAUNTING
HAUNTINGS
HAUNTS
HAURIANT
HAURIENT
HAUSE
HAUSED
HAUSEN
HAUSENS
HAUSES
HAUSFRAU
HAUSFRAUS
HAUSING
HAUSTELLA
HAUSTORIA
HAUT
HAUTBOIS
HAUTBOY
HAUTBOYS
HAUTE
HAUTER
HAUTEST
HAUTEUR
HAUTEURS
HAUYNE
HAUYNES
HAVARTI
HAVARTIS
HAVDALAH
HAVDALAHS
HAVDOLOH
HAVDOLOHS
HAVE
HAVELOCK
HAVELOCKS
HAVEN
HAVENED
HAVENING
HAVENLESS
HAVENS
HAVEOUR
HAVEOURS
HAVER
HAVERED
HAVEREL
HAVERELS
HAVERING
HAVERINGS
HAVERS
HAVERSACK
HAVERSINE
HAVES
HAVILDAR
HAVILDARS
HAVING
HAVINGS
HAVIOR
HAVIORS
HAVIOUR
HAVIOURS
HAVOC
HAVOCKED
HAVOCKER
HAVOCKERS
HAVOCKING
HAVOCS
HAW
HAWALA
HAWALAS
HAWBUCK
HAWBUCKS
HAWEATER
HAWEATERS
HAWED
HAWFINCH
HAWING
HAWK
HAWKBELL
HAWKBELLS
HAWKBILL
HAWKBILLS
HAWKBIT
HAWKBITS
HAWKED
HAWKER
HAWKERS
HAWKEY
HAWKEYED
HAWKEYS
HAWKIE
HAWKIES
HAWKING
HAWKINGS
HAWKISH
HAWKISHLY
HAWKIT
HAWKLIKE
HAWKMOTH
HAWKMOTHS
HAWKNOSE
HAWKNOSES
HAWKS
HAWKSBILL
HAWKSHAW
HAWKSHAWS
HAWKWEED
HAWKWEEDS
HAWM
HAWMED
HAWMING
HAWMS
HAWS
HAWSE
HAWSED
HAWSEHOLE
HAWSEPIPE
HAWSER
HAWSERS
HAWSES
HAWSING
HAWTHORN
HAWTHORNS
HAWTHORNY
HAY
HAYBAND
HAYBANDS
HAYBOX
HAYBOXES
HAYCATION
HAYCOCK
HAYCOCKS
HAYED
HAYER
HAYERS
HAYEY
HAYFIELD
HAYFIELDS
HAYFORK
HAYFORKS
HAYIER
HAYIEST
HAYING
HAYINGS
HAYLAGE
HAYLAGES
HAYLE
HAYLES
HAYLOFT
HAYLOFTS
HAYMAKER
HAYMAKERS
HAYMAKING
HAYMOW
HAYMOWS
HAYRACK
HAYRACKS
HAYRAKE
HAYRAKES
HAYRICK
HAYRICKS
HAYRIDE
HAYRIDES
HAYS
HAYSEED
HAYSEEDS

HAYSEL
HAYSELS
HAYSTACK
HAYSTACKS
HAYWARD
HAYWARDS
HAYWIRE
HAYWIRES
HAZAN
HAZANIM
HAZANS
HAZARD
HAZARDED
HAZARDER
HAZARDERS
HAZARDING
HAZARDIZE
HAZARDOUS
HAZARDRY
HAZARDS
HAZE
HAZED
HAZEL
HAZELHEN
HAZELHENS
HAZELLY
HAZELNUT
HAZELNUTS
HAZELS
HAZELWOOD
HAZER
HAZERS
HAZES
HAZIER
HAZIEST
HAZILY
HAZINESS
HAZING
HAZINGS
HAZMAT
HAZMATS
HAZY
HAZZAN
HAZZANIM
HAZZANS
HE
HEAD
HEADACHE

HEADACHES
HEADACHEY
HEADACHY
HEADAGE
HEADAGES
HEADBAND
HEADBANDS
HEADBANG
HEADBANGS
HEADBOARD
HEADCASE
HEADCASES
HEADCHAIR
HEADCLOTH
HEADCOUNT
HEADDRESS
HEADED
HEADEND
HEADENDS
HEADER
HEADERS
HEADFAST
HEADFASTS
HEADFIRST
HEADFISH
HEADFRAME
HEADFUCK
HEADFUCKS
HEADFUL
HEADFULS
HEADGATE
HEADGATES
HEADGEAR
HEADGEARS
HEADGUARD
HEADHUNT
HEADHUNTS
HEADIER
HEADIEST
HEADILY
HEADINESS
HEADING
HEADINGS
HEADLAMP
HEADLAMPS
HEADLAND
HEADLANDS
HEADLEASE

HEADLESS
HEADLIGHT
HEADLIKE
HEADLINE
HEADLINED
HEADLINER
HEADLINES
HEADLOCK
HEADLOCKS
HEADLONG
HEADMAN
HEADMARK
HEADMARKS
HEADMEN
HEADMOST
HEADNOTE
HEADNOTES
HEADPEACE
HEADPHONE
HEADPIECE
HEADPIN
HEADPINS
HEADPOND
HEADPONDS
HEADRACE
HEADRACES
HEADRAIL
HEADRAILS
HEADREACH
HEADREST
HEADRESTS
HEADRIG
HEADRIGS
HEADRING
HEADRINGS
HEADROOM
HEADROOMS
HEADROPE
HEADROPES
HEADS
HEADSAIL
HEADSAILS
HEADSCARF
HEADSET
HEADSETS
HEADSHAKE
HEADSHIP
HEADSHIPS

HEADSHOT
HEADSHOTS
HEADSMAN
HEADSMEN
HEADSPACE
HEADSTALL
HEADSTAND
HEADSTAY
HEADSTAYS
HEADSTICK
HEADSTOCK
HEADSTONE
HEADWALL
HEADWALLS
HEADWARD
HEADWARDS
HEADWATER
HEADWAY
HEADWAYS
HEADWIND
HEADWINDS
HEADWORD
HEADWORDS
HEADWORK
HEADWORKS
HEADY
HEAL
HEALABLE
HEALD
HEALDED
HEALDING
HEALDS
HEALED
HEALEE
HEALEES
HEALER
HEALERS
HEALING
HEALINGLY
HEALINGS
HEALS
HEALSOME
HEALTH
HEALTHFUL
HEALTHIER
HEALTHILY
HEALTHISM
HEALTHS

HEALTHY
HEAME
HEAP
HEAPED
HEAPER
HEAPERS
HEAPIER
HEAPIEST
HEAPING
HEAPS
HEAPSTEAD
HEAPY
HEAR
HEARABLE
HEARD
HEARDS
HEARE
HEARER
HEARERS
HEARES
HEARIE
HEARING
HEARINGS
HEARKEN
HEARKENED
HEARKENER
HEARKENS
HEARS
HEARSAY
HEARSAYS
HEARSE
HEARSED
HEARSES
HEARSIER
HEARSIEST
HEARSING
HEARSY
HEART
HEARTACHE
HEARTBEAT
HEARTBURN
HEARTED
HEARTEN
HEARTENED
HEARTENER
HEARTENS
HEARTFELT
HEARTFREE

HEARTH
HEARTHRUG
HEARTHS
HEARTIER
HEARTIES
HEARTIEST
HEARTIKIN
HEARTILY
HEARTING
HEARTLAND
HEARTLESS
HEARTLET
HEARTLETS
HEARTLING
HEARTLY
HEARTPEA
HEARTPEAS
HEARTS
HEARTSEED
HEARTSICK
HEARTSINK
HEARTSOME
HEARTSORE
HEARTWOOD
HEARTWORM
HEARTY
HEAST
HEASTE
HEASTES
HEASTS
HEAT
HEATABLE
HEATED
HEATEDLY
HEATER
HEATERS
HEATH
HEATHBIRD
HEATHCOCK
HEATHEN
HEATHENRY
HEATHENS
HEATHER
HEATHERED
HEATHERS
HEATHERY
HEATHFOWL
HEATHIER
HEATHIEST
HEATHLAND
HEATHLESS
HEATHLIKE
HEATHS
HEATHY
HEATING
HEATINGS
HEATLESS
HEATPROOF
HEATS
HEATSPOT
HEATSPOTS
HEATWAVE
HEATWAVES
HEAUME
HEAUMES
HEAVE
HEAVED
HEAVEN
HEAVENLY
HEAVENS
HEAVER
HEAVERS
HEAVES
HEAVIER
HEAVIES
HEAVIEST
HEAVILY
HEAVINESS
HEAVING
HEAVINGS
HEAVY
HEAVYISH
HEAVYSET
HEBDOMAD
HEBDOMADS
HEBE
HEBEN
HEBENON
HEBENONS
HEBENS
HEBES
HEBETANT
HEBETATE
HEBETATED
HEBETATES
HEBETIC
HEBETUDE
HEBETUDES
HEBONA
HEBONAS
HEBRAISE
HEBRAISED
HEBRAISES
HEBRAIZE
HEBRAIZED
HEBRAIZES
HECATOMB
HECATOMBS
HECH
HECHT
HECHTING
HECHTS
HECK
HECKLE
HECKLED
HECKLER
HECKLERS
HECKLES
HECKLING
HECKLINGS
HECKS
HECKUVA
HECOGENIN
HECTARE
HECTARES
HECTIC
HECTICAL
HECTICLY
HECTICS
HECTOGRAM
HECTOR
HECTORED
HECTORER
HECTORERS
HECTORING
HECTORISM
HECTORLY
HECTORS
HEDARIM
HEDDLE
HEDDLED
HEDDLES
HEDDLING
HEDER
HEDERA
HEDERAL
HEDERAS
HEDERATED
HEDERS
HEDGE
HEDGEBILL
HEDGED
HEDGEHOG
HEDGEHOGS
HEDGEHOP
HEDGEHOPS
HEDGEPIG
HEDGEPIGS
HEDGER
HEDGEROW
HEDGEROWS
HEDGERS
HEDGES
HEDGIER
HEDGIEST
HEDGING
HEDGINGLY
HEDGINGS
HEDGY
HEDONIC
HEDONICS
HEDONISM
HEDONISMS
HEDONIST
HEDONISTS
HEDYPHANE
HEDYSARUM
HEED
HEEDED
HEEDER
HEEDERS
HEEDFUL
HEEDFULLY
HEEDIER
HEEDIEST
HEEDINESS
HEEDING
HEEDLESS
HEEDS
HEEDY
HEEHAW
HEEHAWED
HEEHAWING
HEEHAWS
HEEL
HEELBALL
HEELBALLS
HEELBAR
HEELBARS
HEELED
HEELER
HEELERS
HEELING
HEELINGS
HEELLESS
HEELPIECE
HEELPLATE
HEELPOST
HEELPOSTS
HEELS
HEELTAP
HEELTAPS
HEEZE
HEEZED
HEEZES
HEEZIE
HEEZIES
HEEZING
HEFT
HEFTE
HEFTED
HEFTER
HEFTERS
HEFTIER
HEFTIEST
HEFTILY
HEFTINESS
HEFTING
HEFTS
HEFTY
HEGARI
HEGARIS
HEGEMON
HEGEMONIC
HEGEMONS
HEGEMONY
HEGIRA
HEGIRAS
HEGUMEN
HEGUMENE

H

HEGUMENES
HEGUMENOI
HEGUMENOS
HEGUMENS
HEGUMENY
HEH
HEHS
HEID
HEIDS
HEIDUC
HEIDUCS
HEIFER
HEIFERS
HEIGH
HEIGHT
HEIGHTEN
HEIGHTENS
HEIGHTH
HEIGHTHS
HEIGHTISM
HEIGHTS
HEIL
HEILED
HEILING
HEILS
HEIMISH
HEINIE
HEINIES
HEINOUS
HEINOUSLY
HEIR
HEIRDOM
HEIRDOMS
HEIRED
HEIRESS
HEIRESSES
HEIRING
HEIRLESS
HEIRLOOM
HEIRLOOMS
HEIRS
HEIRSHIP
HEIRSHIPS
HEISHI
HEIST
HEISTED
HEISTER
HEISTERS
HEISTING
HEISTS
HEITIKI
HEITIKIS
HEJAB
HEJABS
HEJIRA
HEJIRAS
HEJRA
HEJRAS
HEKETARA
HEKETARAS
HEKTARE
HEKTARES
HEKTOGRAM
HELCOID
HELD
HELE
HELED
HELENIUM
HELENIUMS
HELES
HELIAC
HELIACAL
HELIAST
HELIASTS
HELIBORNE
HELIBUS
HELIBUSES
HELICAL
HELICALLY
HELICASE
HELICASES
HELICES
HELICITY
HELICLINE
HELICOID
HELICOIDS
HELICON
HELICONIA
HELICONS
HELICOPT
HELICOPTS
HELICTITE
HELIDECK
HELIDECKS
HELIDROME
HELILIFT
HELILIFTS
HELIMAN
HELIMEN
HELING
HELIO
HELIODOR
HELIODORS
HELIOGRAM
HELIOLOGY
HELIOPSES
HELIOPSIS
HELIOS
HELIOSES
HELIOSIS
HELIOSTAT
HELIOTYPE
HELIOTYPY
HELIOZOAN
HELIOZOIC
HELIPAD
HELIPADS
HELIPILOT
HELIPORT
HELIPORTS
HELISKI
HELISKIED
HELISKIS
HELISTOP
HELISTOPS
HELITACK
HELITACKS
HELIUM
HELIUMS
HELIX
HELIXES
HELL
HELLBENT
HELLBOX
HELLBOXES
HELLBROTH
HELLCAT
HELLCATS
HELLDIVER
HELLEBORE
HELLED
HELLENISE
HELLENIZE
HELLER
HELLERI
HELLERIES
HELLERIS
HELLERS
HELLERY
HELLFIRE
HELLFIRES
HELLHOLE
HELLHOLES
HELLHOUND
HELLICAT
HELLICATS
HELLIER
HELLIERS
HELLING
HELLION
HELLIONS
HELLISH
HELLISHLY
HELLKITE
HELLKITES
HELLO
HELLOED
HELLOES
HELLOING
HELLOS
HELLOVA
HELLS
HELLSCAPE
HELLUVA
HELLWARD
HELLWARDS
HELM
HELMED
HELMER
HELMERS
HELMET
HELMETED
HELMETING
HELMETS
HELMING
HELMINTH
HELMINTHS
HELMLESS
HELMS
HELMSMAN
HELMSMEN
HELO
HELOPHYTE
HELOS
HELOT
HELOTAGE
HELOTAGES
HELOTISM
HELOTISMS
HELOTRIES
HELOTRY
HELOTS
HELP
HELPABLE
HELPDESK
HELPDESKS
HELPED
HELPER
HELPERS
HELPFUL
HELPFULLY
HELPING
HELPINGS
HELPLESS
HELPLINE
HELPLINES
HELPMATE
HELPMATES
HELPMEET
HELPMEETS
HELPS
HELVE
HELVED
HELVES
HELVETIUM
HELVING
HEM
HEMAGOG
HEMAGOGS
HEMAGOGUE
HEMAL
HEMATAL
HEMATEIN
HEMATEINS
HEMATIC
HEMATICS
HEMATIN
HEMATINE
HEMATINES
HEMATINIC

HEMATINS
HEMATITE
HEMATITES
HEMATITIC
HEMATOID
HEMATOMA
HEMATOMAS
HEMATOSES
HEMATOSIS
HEMATOZOA
HEMATURIA
HEMATURIC
HEME
HEMELYTRA
HEMES
HEMIALGIA
HEMIC
HEMICYCLE
HEMIHEDRA
HEMIHEDRY
HEMIN
HEMINA
HEMINAS
HEMINS
HEMIOLA
HEMIOLAS
HEMIOLIA
HEMIOLIAS
HEMIOLIC
HEMIONE
HEMIONES
HEMIONUS
HEMIOPIA
HEMIOPIAS
HEMIOPIC
HEMIOPSIA
HEMIPOD
HEMIPODE
HEMIPODES
HEMIPODS
HEMIPTER
HEMIPTERS
HEMISPACE
HEMISTICH
HEMITROPE
HEMITROPY
HEMLINE
HEMLINES

HEMLOCK
HEMLOCKS
HEMMED
HEMMER
HEMMERS
HEMMING
HEMOCOEL
HEMOCOELS
HEMOCONIA
HEMOCYTE
HEMOCYTES
HEMOID
HEMOLYMPH
HEMOLYSE
HEMOLYSED
HEMOLYSES
HEMOLYSIN
HEMOLYSIS
HEMOLYTIC
HEMOLYZE
HEMOLYZED
HEMOLYZES
HEMOPHILE
HEMOSTAT
HEMOSTATS
HEMOTOXIC
HEMOTOXIN
HEMP
HEMPEN
HEMPIE
HEMPIER
HEMPIES
HEMPIEST
HEMPLIKE
HEMPS
HEMPSEED
HEMPSEEDS
HEMPWEED
HEMPWEEDS
HEMPY
HEMS
HEMSTITCH
HEN
HENBANE
HENBANES
HENBIT
HENBITS
HENCE

HENCH
HENCHER
HENCHEST
HENCHMAN
HENCHMEN
HENCOOP
HENCOOPS
HEND
HENDED
HENDIADYS
HENDING
HENDS
HENEQUEN
HENEQUENS
HENEQUIN
HENEQUINS
HENGE
HENGES
HENHOUSE
HENHOUSES
HENIQUEN
HENIQUENS
HENIQUIN
HENIQUINS
HENLEY
HENLEYS
HENLIKE
HENNA
HENNAED
HENNAING
HENNAS
HENNED
HENNER
HENNERIES
HENNERS
HENNERY
HENNIER
HENNIES
HENNIEST
HENNIN
HENNING
HENNINS
HENNISH
HENNISHLY
HENNY
HENOTIC
HENPECK
HENPECKED

HENPECKS
HENRIES
HENRY
HENRYS
HENS
HENT
HENTED
HENTING
HENTS
HEP
HEPAR
HEPARIN
HEPARINS
HEPARS
HEPATIC
HEPATICA
HEPATICAE
HEPATICAL
HEPATICAS
HEPATICS
HEPATISE
HEPATISED
HEPATISES
HEPATITE
HEPATITES
HEPATITIS
HEPATIZE
HEPATIZED
HEPATIZES
HEPATOMA
HEPATOMAS
HEPCAT
HEPCATS
HEPPER
HEPPEST
HEPS
HEPSTER
HEPSTERS
HEPT
HEPTAD
HEPTADS
HEPTAGLOT
HEPTAGON
HEPTAGONS
HEPTANE
HEPTANES
HEPTAPODY
HEPTARCH

HEPTARCHS
HEPTARCHY
HEPTOSE
HEPTOSES
HER
HERALD
HERALDED
HERALDIC
HERALDING
HERALDIST
HERALDRY
HERALDS
HERB
HERBAGE
HERBAGED
HERBAGES
HERBAL
HERBALISM
HERBALIST
HERBALS
HERBAR
HERBARIA
HERBARIAL
HERBARIAN
HERBARIES
HERBARIUM
HERBARS
HERBARY
HERBED
HERBELET
HERBELETS
HERBICIDE
HERBIER
HERBIEST
HERBIST
HERBISTS
HERBIVORA
HERBIVORE
HERBIVORY
HERBLESS
HERBLET
HERBLETS
HERBLIKE
HERBOLOGY
HERBORISE
HERBORIST
HERBORIZE
HERBOSE

H

HERBOUS
HERBS
HERBY
HERCOGAMY
HERCULEAN
HERCULES
HERCYNITE
HERD
HERDBOY
HERDBOYS
HERDED
HERDEN
HERDENS
HERDER
HERDERS
HERDESS
HERDESSES
HERDIC
HERDICS
HERDING
HERDINGS
HERDLIKE
HERDMAN
HERDMEN
HERDS
HERDSMAN
HERDSMEN
HERDWICK
HERDWICKS
HERE
HEREABOUT
HEREAFTER
HEREAT
HEREAWAY
HEREAWAYS
HEREBY
HEREDES
HEREDITY
HEREFROM
HEREIN
HEREINTO
HERENESS
HEREOF
HEREON
HERES
HERESIES
HERESY
HERETIC
HERETICAL
HERETICS
HERETO
HERETRIX
HEREUNDER
HEREUNTO
HEREUPON
HEREWITH
HERIED
HERIES
HERIOT
HERIOTS
HERISSE
HERISSON
HERISSONS
HERITABLE
HERITABLY
HERITAGE
HERITAGES
HERITOR
HERITORS
HERITRESS
HERITRIX
HERKOGAMY
HERL
HERLING
HERLINGS
HERLS
HERM
HERMA
HERMAE
HERMAEAN
HERMAI
HERMANDAD
HERMETIC
HERMETICS
HERMETISM
HERMETIST
HERMIT
HERMITAGE
HERMITESS
HERMITIC
HERMITISM
HERMITRY
HERMITS
HERMS
HERN
HERNIA
HERNIAE
HERNIAL
HERNIAS
HERNIATE
HERNIATED
HERNIATES
HERNS
HERNSHAW
HERNSHAWS
HERO
HEROES
HEROIC
HEROICAL
HEROICISE
HEROICIZE
HEROICLY
HEROICS
HEROIN
HEROINE
HEROINES
HEROINISM
HEROINS
HEROISE
HEROISED
HEROISES
HEROISING
HEROISM
HEROISMS
HEROIZE
HEROIZED
HEROIZES
HEROIZING
HERON
HERONRIES
HERONRY
HERONS
HERONSEW
HERONSEWS
HERONSHAW
HEROON
HEROONS
HEROS
HEROSHIP
HEROSHIPS
HERPES
HERPESES
HERPETIC
HERPETICS
HERPETOID
HERPTILE
HERRIED
HERRIES
HERRIMENT
HERRING
HERRINGER
HERRINGS
HERRY
HERRYING
HERRYMENT
HERS
HERSALL
HERSALLS
HERSE
HERSED
HERSELF
HERSES
HERSHIP
HERSHIPS
HERSTORY
HERTZ
HERTZES
HERY
HERYE
HERYED
HERYES
HERYING
HES
HESITANCE
HESITANCY
HESITANT
HESITATE
HESITATED
HESITATER
HESITATES
HESITATOR
HESP
HESPED
HESPERID
HESPERIDS
HESPING
HESPS
HESSIAN
HESSIANS
HESSITE
HESSITES
HESSONITE
HEST
HESTERNAL
HESTS
HET
HETAERA
HETAERAE
HETAERAS
HETAERIC
HETAERISM
HETAERIST
HETAIRA
HETAIRAI
HETAIRAS
HETAIRIA
HETAIRIAS
HETAIRIC
HETAIRISM
HETAIRIST
HETE
HETERO
HETERODOX
HETERONYM
HETEROPOD
HETEROS
HETEROSES
HETEROSIS
HETEROTIC
HETES
HETH
HETHER
HETHS
HETING
HETMAN
HETMANATE
HETMANS
HETMEN
HETS
HETTIE
HETTIES
HEUCH
HEUCHERA
HEUCHERAS
HEUCHS
HEUGH
HEUGHS
HEUREKA
HEUREKAS
HEURETIC

HEURETICS
HEURISM
HEURISMS
HEURISTIC
HEVEA
HEVEAS
HEW
HEWABLE
HEWED
HEWER
HEWERS
HEWGH
HEWING
HEWINGS
HEWN
HEWS
HEX
HEXACHORD
HEXACT
HEXACTS
HEXAD
HEXADE
HEXADECYL
HEXADES
HEXADIC
HEXADS
HEXAFOIL
HEXAFOILS
HEXAGLOT
HEXAGLOTS
HEXAGON
HEXAGONAL
HEXAGONS
HEXAGRAM
HEXAGRAMS
HEXAHEDRA
HEXAMERAL
HEXAMETER
HEXAMINE
HEXAMINES
HEXANE
HEXANES
HEXANOIC
HEXAPLA
HEXAPLAR
HEXAPLAS
HEXAPLOID
HEXAPOD
HEXAPODAL
HEXAPODIC
HEXAPODS
HEXAPODY
HEXARCH
HEXARCHY
HEXASTICH
HEXASTYLE
HEXATHLON
HEXED
HEXENE
HEXENES
HEXER
HEXEREI
HEXEREIS
HEXERS
HEXES
HEXING
HEXINGS
HEXONE
HEXONES
HEXOSAN
HEXOSANS
HEXOSE
HEXOSES
HEXYL
HEXYLENE
HEXYLENES
HEXYLIC
HEXYLS
HEY
HEYDAY
HEYDAYS
HEYDEY
HEYDEYS
HEYDUCK
HEYDUCKS
HEYED
HEYING
HEYS
HI
HIANT
HIATAL
HIATUS
HIATUSES
HIBACHI
HIBACHIS
HIBAKUSHA
HIBERNAL
HIBERNATE
HIBERNISE
HIBERNIZE
HIBISCUS
HIC
HICATEE
HICATEES
HICCATEE
HICCATEES
HICCOUGH
HICCOUGHS
HICCUP
HICCUPED
HICCUPIER
HICCUPING
HICCUPPED
HICCUPS
HICCUPY
HICK
HICKER
HICKEST
HICKEY
HICKEYS
HICKIE
HICKIES
HICKISH
HICKORIES
HICKORY
HICKS
HICKWALL
HICKWALLS
HICKYMAL
HICKYMALS
HID
HIDABLE
HIDAGE
HIDAGES
HIDALGA
HIDALGAS
HIDALGO
HIDALGOS
HIDDEN
HIDDENITE
HIDDENLY
HIDDER
HIDDERS
HIDE
HIDEAWAY
HIDEAWAYS
HIDEBOUND
HIDED
HIDELESS
HIDEOSITY
HIDEOUS
HIDEOUSLY
HIDEOUT
HIDEOUTS
HIDER
HIDERS
HIDES
HIDING
HIDINGS
HIDLING
HIDLINGS
HIDLINS
HIDROSES
HIDROSIS
HIDROTIC
HIDROTICS
HIE
HIED
HIEING
HIELAMAN
HIELAMANS
HIELAND
HIEMAL
HIEMS
HIERACIUM
HIERARCH
HIERARCHS
HIERARCHY
HIERATIC
HIERATICA
HIERATICS
HIEROCRAT
HIERODULE
HIEROGRAM
HIEROLOGY
HIERURGY
HIES
HIFALUTIN
HIGGLE
HIGGLED
HIGGLER
HIGGLERS
HIGGLES
HIGGLING
HIGGLINGS
HIGH
HIGHBALL
HIGHBALLS
HIGHBORN
HIGHBOY
HIGHBOYS
HIGHBRED
HIGHBROW
HIGHBROWS
HIGHBUSH
HIGHCHAIR
HIGHED
HIGHER
HIGHERED
HIGHERING
HIGHERS
HIGHEST
HIGHFLIER
HIGHFLYER
HIGHING
HIGHISH
HIGHJACK
HIGHJACKS
HIGHJINKS
HIGHLAND
HIGHLANDS
HIGHLIFE
HIGHLIFES
HIGHLIGHT
HIGHLY
HIGHMAN
HIGHMEN
HIGHMOST
HIGHNESS
HIGHRISE
HIGHRISES
HIGHROAD
HIGHROADS
HIGHS
HIGHSPOT
HIGHSPOTS
HIGHT
HIGHTAIL
HIGHTAILS
HIGHTED

HIGHTH
HIGHTHS
HIGHTING
HIGHTINGS
HIGHTOP
HIGHTOPS
HIGHTS
HIGHVELD
HIGHVELDS
HIGHWAY
HIGHWAYS
HIJAB
HIJABS
HIJACK
HIJACKED
HIJACKER
HIJACKERS
HIJACKING
HIJACKS
HIJINKS
HIJRA
HIJRAH
HIJRAHS
HIJRAS
HIKE
HIKED
HIKER
HIKERS
HIKES
HIKING
HIKINGS
HIKOI
HIKOIED
HIKOIING
HIKOIS
HILA
HILAR
HILARIOUS
HILARITY
HILCH
HILCHED
HILCHES
HILCHING
HILD
HILDING
HILDINGS
HILI
HILL
HILLBILLY
HILLCREST
HILLED
HILLER
HILLERS
HILLFOLK
HILLFORT
HILLFORTS
HILLIER
HILLIEST
HILLINESS
HILLING
HILLINGS
HILLMEN
HILLO
HILLOA
HILLOAED
HILLOAING
HILLOAS
HILLOCK
HILLOCKED
HILLOCKS
HILLOCKY
HILLOED
HILLOES
HILLOING
HILLOS
HILLS
HILLSIDE
HILLSIDES
HILLSLOPE
HILLTOP
HILLTOPS
HILLY
HILT
HILTED
HILTING
HILTLESS
HILTS
HILUM
HILUS
HIM
HIMATIA
HIMATION
HIMATIONS
HIMBO
HIMBOS
HIMS
HIMSELF
HIN
HINAHINA
HINAHINAS
HINAU
HINAUS
HIND
HINDBERRY
HINDBRAIN
HINDCAST
HINDCASTS
HINDER
HINDERED
HINDERER
HINDERERS
HINDERING
HINDERS
HINDFEET
HINDFOOT
HINDGUT
HINDGUTS
HINDHEAD
HINDHEADS
HINDLEG
HINDLEGS
HINDMILK
HINDMILKS
HINDMOST
HINDRANCE
HINDS
HINDSHANK
HINDSIGHT
HINDWARD
HINDWING
HINDWINGS
HING
HINGE
HINGED
HINGELESS
HINGELIKE
HINGER
HINGERS
HINGES
HINGING
HINGS
HINKIER
HINKIEST
HINKY
HINNIE
HINNIED
HINNIES
HINNY
HINNYING
HINS
HINT
HINTED
HINTER
HINTERS
HINTING
HINTINGLY
HINTINGS
HINTS
HIOI
HIOIS
HIP
HIPBONE
HIPBONES
HIPHUGGER
HIPLESS
HIPLIKE
HIPLINE
HIPLINES
HIPLY
HIPNESS
HIPNESSES
HIPPARCH
HIPPARCHS
HIPPED
HIPPEN
HIPPENS
HIPPER
HIPPEST
HIPPIATRY
HIPPIC
HIPPIE
HIPPIEDOM
HIPPIEISH
HIPPIER
HIPPIES
HIPPIEST
HIPPIN
HIPPINESS
HIPPING
HIPPINGS
HIPPINS
HIPPISH
HIPPO
HIPPOCRAS
HIPPODAME
HIPPOLOGY
HIPPOS
HIPPURIC
HIPPURITE
HIPPUS
HIPPUSES
HIPPY
HIPPYDOM
HIPPYDOMS
HIPPYISH
HIPS
HIPSHOT
HIPSTER
HIPSTERS
HIPT
HIRABLE
HIRAGANA
HIRAGANAS
HIRAGE
HIRAGES
HIRCINE
HIRCOSITY
HIRE
HIREABLE
HIREAGE
HIREAGES
HIRED
HIREE
HIREES
HIRELING
HIRELINGS
HIRER
HIRERS
HIRES
HIRING
HIRINGS
HIRLING
HIRLINGS
HIRPLE
HIRPLED
HIRPLES
HIRPLING
HIRRIENT
HIRRIENTS
HIRSEL

HIRSELED
HIRSELING
HIRSELLED
HIRSELS
HIRSLE
HIRSLED
HIRSLES
HIRSLING
HIRSTIE
HIRSUTE
HIRSUTISM
HIRUDIN
HIRUDINS
HIRUNDINE
HIS
HISH
HISHED
HISHES
HISHING
HISN
HISPANISM
HISPID
HISPIDITY
HISS
HISSED
HISSELF
HISSER
HISSERS
HISSES
HISSIER
HISSIES
HISSIEST
HISSING
HISSINGLY
HISSINGS
HISSY
HIST
HISTAMIN
HISTAMINE
HISTAMINS
HISTED
HISTIDIN
HISTIDINE
HISTIDINS
HISTIE
HISTING
HISTIOID
HISTOGEN
HISTOGENS
HISTOGENY
HISTOGRAM
HISTOID
HISTOLOGY
HISTONE
HISTONES
HISTORIAN
HISTORIC
HISTORIED
HISTORIES
HISTORIFY
HISTORISM
HISTORY
HISTRIO
HISTRION
HISTRIONS
HISTRIOS
HISTS
HIT
HITCH
HITCHED
HITCHER
HITCHERS
HITCHES
HITCHHIKE
HITCHIER
HITCHIEST
HITCHILY
HITCHING
HITCHY
HITHE
HITHER
HITHERED
HITHERING
HITHERS
HITHERTO
HITHES
HITLESS
HITMAKER
HITMAKERS
HITMAN
HITMEN
HITS
HITTABLE
HITTER
HITTERS
HITTING
HIVE
HIVED
HIVELESS
HIVELIKE
HIVEMIND
HIVEMINDS
HIVER
HIVERS
HIVES
HIVEWARD
HIVEWARDS
HIVING
HIYA
HIZEN
HIZENS
HIZZ
HIZZED
HIZZES
HIZZING
HIZZONER
HIZZONERS
HM
HMM
HMMM
HO
HOA
HOACTZIN
HOACTZINS
HOAED
HOAGIE
HOAGIES
HOAGY
HOAING
HOAR
HOARD
HOARDED
HOARDER
HOARDERS
HOARDING
HOARDINGS
HOARDS
HOARED
HOARFROST
HOARHEAD
HOARHEADS
HOARHOUND
HOARIER
HOARIEST
HOARILY
HOARINESS
HOARING
HOARS
HOARSE
HOARSELY
HOARSEN
HOARSENED
HOARSENS
HOARSER
HOARSEST
HOARY
HOAS
HOAST
HOASTED
HOASTING
HOASTMAN
HOASTMEN
HOASTS
HOATCHING
HOATZIN
HOATZINES
HOATZINS
HOAX
HOAXED
HOAXER
HOAXERS
HOAXES
HOAXING
HOB
HOBBED
HOBBER
HOBBERS
HOBBIES
HOBBING
HOBBISH
HOBBIT
HOBBITRY
HOBBITS
HOBBLE
HOBBLED
HOBBLER
HOBBLERS
HOBBLES
HOBBLING
HOBBLINGS
HOBBY
HOBBYISM
HOBBYISMS
HOBBYIST
HOBBYISTS
HOBBYLESS
HOBDAY
HOBDAYED
HOBDAYING
HOBDAYS
HOBGOBLIN
HOBJOB
HOBJOBBED
HOBJOBBER
HOBJOBS
HOBLIKE
HOBNAIL
HOBNAILED
HOBNAILS
HOBNOB
HOBNOBBED
HOBNOBBER
HOBNOBBY
HOBNOBS
HOBO
HOBODOM
HOBODOMS
HOBOED
HOBOES
HOBOING
HOBOISM
HOBOISMS
HOBOS
HOBS
HOC
HOCK
HOCKED
HOCKER
HOCKERS
HOCKEY
HOCKEYS
HOCKING
HOCKLE
HOCKLED
HOCKLES
HOCKLING
HOCKS
HOCKSHOP
HOCKSHOPS
HOCUS

HOCUSED
HOCUSES
HOCUSING
HOCUSSED
HOCUSSES
HOCUSSING
HOD
HODAD
HODADDIES
HODADDY
HODADS
HODDED
HODDEN
HODDENS
HODDIN
HODDING
HODDINS
HODDLE
HODDLED
HODDLES
HODDLING
HODIERNAL
HODJA
HODJAS
HODMAN
HODMANDOD
HODMEN
HODOGRAPH
HODOMETER
HODOMETRY
HODOSCOPE
HODS
HOE
HOECAKE
HOECAKES
HOED
HOEDOWN
HOEDOWNS
HOEING
HOELIKE
HOER
HOERS
HOES
HOG
HOGAN
HOGANS
HOGBACK
HOGBACKS
HOGEN
HOGENS
HOGFISH
HOGFISHES
HOGG
HOGGED
HOGGER
HOGGEREL
HOGGERELS
HOGGERIES
HOGGERS
HOGGERY
HOGGET
HOGGETS
HOGGIN
HOGGING
HOGGINGS
HOGGINS
HOGGISH
HOGGISHLY
HOGGS
HOGH
HOGHOOD
HOGHOODS
HOGHS
HOGLIKE
HOGMANAY
HOGMANAYS
HOGMANE
HOGMANES
HOGMENAY
HOGMENAYS
HOGNOSE
HOGNOSED
HOGNOSES
HOGNUT
HOGNUTS
HOGS
HOGSHEAD
HOGSHEADS
HOGTIE
HOGTIED
HOGTIEING
HOGTIES
HOGTYING
HOGWARD
HOGWARDS
HOGWASH
HOGWASHES
HOGWEED
HOGWEEDS
HOH
HOHA
HOHED
HOHING
HOHS
HOI
HOICK
HOICKED
HOICKING
HOICKS
HOICKSED
HOICKSES
HOICKSING
HOIDEN
HOIDENED
HOIDENING
HOIDENISH
HOIDENS
HOIED
HOIING
HOIK
HOIKED
HOIKING
HOIKS
HOING
HOIS
HOISE
HOISED
HOISES
HOISIN
HOISING
HOISINS
HOIST
HOISTED
HOISTER
HOISTERS
HOISTING
HOISTINGS
HOISTMAN
HOISTMEN
HOISTS
HOISTWAY
HOISTWAYS
HOKA
HOKAS
HOKE
HOKED
HOKES
HOKEY
HOKEYNESS
HOKI
HOKIER
HOKIEST
HOKILY
HOKINESS
HOKING
HOKIS
HOKKU
HOKONUI
HOKONUIS
HOKUM
HOKUMS
HOKYPOKY
HOLANDRIC
HOLARCHY
HOLARD
HOLARDS
HOLD
HOLDABLE
HOLDALL
HOLDALLS
HOLDBACK
HOLDBACKS
HOLDDOWN
HOLDDOWNS
HOLDEN
HOLDER
HOLDERBAT
HOLDERS
HOLDFAST
HOLDFASTS
HOLDING
HOLDINGS
HOLDOUT
HOLDOUTS
HOLDOVER
HOLDOVERS
HOLDS
HOLDUP
HOLDUPS
HOLE
HOLED
HOLELESS
HOLES
HOLESOM
HOLESOME
HOLEY
HOLEYER
HOLEYEST
HOLIBUT
HOLIBUTS
HOLIDAY
HOLIDAYED
HOLIDAYER
HOLIDAYS
HOLIER
HOLIES
HOLIEST
HOLILY
HOLINESS
HOLING
HOLINGS
HOLISM
HOLISMS
HOLIST
HOLISTIC
HOLISTS
HOLK
HOLKED
HOLKING
HOLKS
HOLLA
HOLLAED
HOLLAING
HOLLAND
HOLLANDS
HOLLAS
HOLLER
HOLLERED
HOLLERING
HOLLERS
HOLLIDAM
HOLLIDAMS
HOLLIES
HOLLO
HOLLOA
HOLLOAED
HOLLOAING
HOLLOAS
HOLLOED
HOLLOES

HOLLOING
HOLLOO
HOLLOOED
HOLLOOING
HOLLOOS
HOLLOS
HOLLOW
HOLLOWARE
HOLLOWED
HOLLOWER
HOLLOWEST
HOLLOWING
HOLLOWLY
HOLLOWS
HOLLY
HOLLYHOCK
HOLM
HOLME
HOLMES
HOLMIA
HOLMIAS
HOLMIC
HOLMIUM
HOLMIUMS
HOLMS
HOLO
HOLOCAINE
HOLOCAUST
HOLOCENE
HOLOCRINE
HOLOGAMY
HOLOGRAM
HOLOGRAMS
HOLOGRAPH
HOLOGYNIC
HOLOGYNY
HOLOHEDRA
HOLON
HOLONIC
HOLONS
HOLOPHOTE
HOLOPHYTE
HOLOPTIC
HOLOS
HOLOTYPE
HOLOTYPES
HOLOTYPIC
HOLOZOIC
HOLP
HOLPEN
HOLS
HOLSTEIN
HOLSTEINS
HOLSTER
HOLSTERED
HOLSTERS
HOLT
HOLTS
HOLUBTSI
HOLY
HOLYDAM
HOLYDAME
HOLYDAMES
HOLYDAMS
HOLYDAY
HOLYDAYS
HOLYSTONE
HOLYTIDE
HOLYTIDES
HOM
HOMA
HOMAGE
HOMAGED
HOMAGER
HOMAGERS
HOMAGES
HOMAGING
HOMALOID
HOMALOIDS
HOMAS
HOMBRE
HOMBRES
HOMBURG
HOMBURGS
HOME
HOMEBIRD
HOMEBIRDS
HOMEBIRTH
HOMEBODY
HOMEBOUND
HOMEBOY
HOMEBOYS
HOMEBRED
HOMEBREDS
HOMEBREW
HOMEBREWS
HOMEBUILT
HOMEBUYER
HOMECOMER
HOMECRAFT
HOMED
HOMEFELT
HOMEGIRL
HOMEGIRLS
HOMEGROWN
HOMELAND
HOMELANDS
HOMELESS
HOMELIER
HOMELIEST
HOMELIKE
HOMELILY
HOMELY
HOMELYN
HOMELYNS
HOMEMADE
HOMEMAKER
HOMEOBOX
HOMEOMERY
HOMEOPATH
HOMEOSES
HOMEOSIS
HOMEOTIC
HOMEOWNER
HOMEPAGE
HOMEPAGES
HOMEPLACE
HOMEPORT
HOMEPORTS
HOMER
HOMERED
HOMERIC
HOMERING
HOMEROOM
HOMEROOMS
HOMERS
HOMES
HOMESICK
HOMESITE
HOMESITES
HOMESPUN
HOMESPUNS
HOMESTALL
HOMESTAND
HOMESTAY
HOMESTAYS
HOMESTEAD
HOMESTYLE
HOMETOWN
HOMETOWNS
HOMEWARD
HOMEWARDS
HOMEWARE
HOMEWARES
HOMEWORK
HOMEWORKS
HOMEY
HOMEYNESS
HOMEYS
HOMICIDAL
HOMICIDE
HOMICIDES
HOMIE
HOMIER
HOMIES
HOMIEST
HOMILETIC
HOMILIES
HOMILIST
HOMILISTS
HOMILY
HOMINES
HOMINESS
HOMING
HOMINGS
HOMINIAN
HOMINIANS
HOMINID
HOMINIDS
HOMINIES
HOMININ
HOMININE
HOMININS
HOMINISE
HOMINISED
HOMINISES
HOMINIZE
HOMINIZED
HOMINIZES
HOMINOID
HOMINOIDS
HOMINY
HOMME
HOMMES
HOMMOCK
HOMMOCKS
HOMMOS
HOMMOSES
HOMO
HOMOCERCY
HOMODONT
HOMODYNE
HOMOEOBOX
HOMOEOSES
HOMOEOSIS
HOMOEOTIC
HOMOGAMIC
HOMOGAMY
HOMOGENY
HOMOGONY
HOMOGRAFT
HOMOGRAPH
HOMOLOG
HOMOLOGIC
HOMOLOGS
HOMOLOGUE
HOMOLOGY
HOMOLYSES
HOMOLYSIS
HOMOLYTIC
HOMOMORPH
HOMONYM
HOMONYMIC
HOMONYMS
HOMONYMY
HOMOPHILE
HOMOPHOBE
HOMOPHONE
HOMOPHONY
HOMOPHYLY
HOMOPLASY
HOMOPOLAR
HOMOS
HOMOSEX
HOMOSEXES
HOMOSPORY
HOMOSTYLY
HOMOTAXES
HOMOTAXIC
HOMOTAXIS

HOMOTONIC
HOMOTONY
HOMOTYPAL
HOMOTYPE
HOMOTYPES
HOMOTYPIC
HOMOTYPY
HOMOUSIAN
HOMS
HOMUNCLE
HOMUNCLES
HOMUNCULE
HOMUNCULI
HOMY
HON
HONAN
HONANS
HONCHO
HONCHOED
HONCHOES
HONCHOING
HONCHOS
HOND
HONDA
HONDAS
HONDLE
HONDLED
HONDLES
HONDLING
HONDS
HONE
HONED
HONER
HONERS
HONES
HONEST
HONESTER
HONESTEST
HONESTIES
HONESTLY
HONESTY
HONEWORT
HONEWORTS
HONEY
HONEYBEE
HONEYBEES
HONEYBELL
HONEYBUN
HONEYBUNS
HONEYCOMB
HONEYDEW
HONEYDEWS
HONEYED
HONEYEDLY
HONEYFUL
HONEYING
HONEYLESS
HONEYMOON
HONEYPOT
HONEYPOTS
HONEYS
HONEYTRAP
HONG
HONGI
HONGIED
HONGIES
HONGIING
HONGING
HONGIS
HONGS
HONIED
HONIEDLY
HONING
HONK
HONKED
HONKER
HONKERS
HONKING
HONKS
HONOR
HONORABLE
HONORABLY
HONORAND
HONORANDS
HONORARIA
HONORARY
HONORED
HONOREE
HONOREES
HONORER
HONORERS
HONORIFIC
HONORING
HONORLESS
HONORS
HONOUR
HONOURARY
HONOURED
HONOUREE
HONOUREES
HONOURER
HONOURERS
HONOURING
HONOURS
HONS
HOO
HOOCH
HOOCHES
HOOCHIE
HOOCHIES
HOOD
HOODED
HOODIA
HOODIAS
HOODIE
HOODIER
HOODIES
HOODIEST
HOODING
HOODLESS
HOODLIKE
HOODLUM
HOODLUMS
HOODMAN
HOODMEN
HOODMOLD
HOODMOLDS
HOODOO
HOODOOED
HOODOOING
HOODOOISM
HOODOOS
HOODS
HOODWINK
HOODWINKS
HOODY
HOOEY
HOOEYS
HOOF
HOOFBEAT
HOOFBEATS
HOOFBOUND
HOOFED
HOOFER
HOOFERS
HOOFING
HOOFLESS
HOOFLIKE
HOOFPRINT
HOOFROT
HOOFROTS
HOOFS
HOOK
HOOKA
HOOKAH
HOOKAHS
HOOKAS
HOOKCHECK
HOOKED
HOOKER
HOOKERS
HOOKEY
HOOKEYS
HOOKIER
HOOKIES
HOOKIEST
HOOKING
HOOKINGS
HOOKLESS
HOOKLET
HOOKLETS
HOOKLIKE
HOOKNOSE
HOOKNOSED
HOOKNOSES
HOOKS
HOOKUP
HOOKUPS
HOOKWORM
HOOKWORMS
HOOKY
HOOLACHAN
HOOLEY
HOOLEYS
HOOLICAN
HOOLICANS
HOOLIE
HOOLIER
HOOLIES
HOOLIEST
HOOLIGAN
HOOLIGANS
HOOLOCK
HOOLOCKS
HOOLY
HOON
HOONED
HOONING
HOONS
HOOP
HOOPED
HOOPER
HOOPERS
HOOPING
HOOPLA
HOOPLAS
HOOPLESS
HOOPLIKE
HOOPOE
HOOPOES
HOOPOO
HOOPOOS
HOOPS
HOOPSKIRT
HOOPSTER
HOOPSTERS
HOOR
HOORAH
HOORAHED
HOORAHING
HOORAHS
HOORAY
HOORAYED
HOORAYING
HOORAYS
HOORD
HOORDS
HOOROO
HOOROOED
HOOROOING
HOOROOS
HOORS
HOOSEGOW
HOOSEGOWS
HOOSGOW
HOOSGOWS
HOOSH
HOOSHED
HOOSHES
HOOSHING

HOOT
HOOTCH
HOOTCHES
HOOTED
HOOTER
HOOTERS
HOOTIER
HOOTIEST
HOOTING
HOOTNANNY
HOOTS
HOOTY
HOOVE
HOOVED
HOOVEN
HOOVER
HOOVERED
HOOVERING
HOOVERS
HOOVES
HOOVING
HOP
HOPAK
HOPAKS
HOPBIND
HOPBINDS
HOPBINE
HOPBINES
HOPDOG
HOPDOGS
HOPE
HOPED
HOPEFUL
HOPEFULLY
HOPEFULS
HOPELESS
HOPER
HOPERS
HOPES
HOPFIELD
HOPFIELDS
HOPHEAD
HOPHEADS
HOPING
HOPINGLY
HOPLITE
HOPLITES
HOPLITIC
HOPLOLOGY
HOPPED
HOPPER
HOPPERCAR
HOPPERS
HOPPIER
HOPPIEST
HOPPINESS
HOPPING
HOPPINGS
HOPPLE
HOPPLED
HOPPLER
HOPPLERS
HOPPLES
HOPPLING
HOPPUS
HOPPY
HOPS
HOPSACK
HOPSACKS
HOPSCOTCH
HOPTOAD
HOPTOADS
HORA
HORAH
HORAHS
HORAL
HORARY
HORAS
HORDE
HORDED
HORDEIN
HORDEINS
HORDEOLA
HORDEOLUM
HORDES
HORDING
HORDOCK
HORDOCKS
HORE
HOREHOUND
HORIATIKI
HORIZON
HORIZONAL
HORIZONS
HORK
HORKED
HORKEY
HORKEYS
HORKING
HORKS
HORLICKS
HORME
HORMES
HORMESES
HORMESIS
HORMETIC
HORMIC
HORMONAL
HORMONE
HORMONES
HORMONIC
HORN
HORNBAG
HORNBAGS
HORNBEAK
HORNBEAKS
HORNBEAM
HORNBEAMS
HORNBILL
HORNBILLS
HORNBOOK
HORNBOOKS
HORNBUG
HORNBUGS
HORNDOG
HORNDOGS
HORNED
HORNER
HORNERS
HORNET
HORNETS
HORNFELS
HORNFISH
HORNFUL
HORNFULS
HORNGELD
HORNGELDS
HORNIER
HORNIEST
HORNILY
HORNINESS
HORNING
HORNINGS
HORNISH
HORNIST
HORNISTS
HORNITO
HORNITOS
HORNLESS
HORNLET
HORNLETS
HORNLIKE
HORNPIPE
HORNPIPES
HORNPOUT
HORNPOUTS
HORNS
HORNSTONE
HORNTAIL
HORNTAILS
HORNWORK
HORNWORKS
HORNWORM
HORNWORMS
HORNWORT
HORNWORTS
HORNWRACK
HORNY
HORNYHEAD
HORNYWINK
HOROEKA
HOROEKAS
HOROKAKA
HOROKAKAS
HOROLOGE
HOROLOGER
HOROLOGES
HOROLOGIA
HOROLOGIC
HOROLOGY
HOROMETRY
HOROPITO
HOROPITOS
HOROPTER
HOROPTERS
HOROSCOPE
HOROSCOPY
HORRENT
HORRIBLE
HORRIBLES
HORRIBLY
HORRID
HORRIDER
HORRIDEST
HORRIDLY
HORRIFIC
HORRIFIED
HORRIFIES
HORRIFY
HORROR
HORRORS
HORS
HORSE
HORSEBACK
HORSEBEAN
HORSEBOX
HORSECAR
HORSECARS
HORSED
HORSEFLY
HORSEHAIR
HORSEHEAD
HORSEHIDE
HORSELESS
HORSELIKE
HORSEMAN
HORSEMEAT
HORSEMEN
HORSEMINT
HORSEPLAY
HORSEPOND
HORSEPOX
HORSERACE
HORSES
HORSESHIT
HORSESHOD
HORSESHOE
HORSETAIL
HORSEWAY
HORSEWAYS
HORSEWEED
HORSEWHIP
HORSEY
HORSIE
HORSIER
HORSIES
HORSIEST
HORSILY
HORSINESS
HORSING

HORSINGS
HORSON
HORSONS
HORST
HORSTE
HORSTES
HORSTS
HORSY
HORTATION
HORTATIVE
HORTATORY
HORTENSIA
HOS
HOSANNA
HOSANNAED
HOSANNAH
HOSANNAHS
HOSANNAS
HOSE
HOSED
HOSEL
HOSELIKE
HOSELS
HOSEMAN
HOSEMEN
HOSEN
HOSEPIPE
HOSEPIPES
HOSER
HOSERS
HOSES
HOSEY
HOSEYED
HOSEYING
HOSEYS
HOSIER
HOSIERIES
HOSIERS
HOSIERY
HOSING
HOSPICE
HOSPICES
HOSPITAGE
HOSPITAL
HOSPITALE
HOSPITALS
HOSPITIA
HOSPITIUM
HOSPODAR
HOSPODARS
HOSS
HOSSES
HOST
HOSTA
HOSTAGE
HOSTAGES
HOSTAS
HOSTED
HOSTEL
HOSTELED
HOSTELER
HOSTELERS
HOSTELING
HOSTELLED
HOSTELLER
HOSTELRY
HOSTELS
HOSTESS
HOSTESSED
HOSTESSES
HOSTIE
HOSTIES
HOSTILE
HOSTILELY
HOSTILES
HOSTILITY
HOSTING
HOSTINGS
HOSTLER
HOSTLERS
HOSTLESS
HOSTLESSE
HOSTLY
HOSTRIES
HOSTRY
HOSTS
HOT
HOTBED
HOTBEDS
HOTBLOOD
HOTBLOODS
HOTBOX
HOTBOXED
HOTBOXES
HOTBOXING
HOTCAKE
HOTCAKES
HOTCH
HOTCHED
HOTCHES
HOTCHING
HOTCHPOT
HOTCHPOTS
HOTDOG
HOTDOGGED
HOTDOGGER
HOTDOGS
HOTE
HOTEL
HOTELDOM
HOTELDOMS
HOTELIER
HOTELIERS
HOTELING
HOTELINGS
HOTELLING
HOTELMAN
HOTELMEN
HOTELS
HOTEN
HOTFOOT
HOTFOOTED
HOTFOOTS
HOTHEAD
HOTHEADED
HOTHEADS
HOTHOUSE
HOTHOUSED
HOTHOUSES
HOTLINE
HOTLINER
HOTLINERS
HOTLINES
HOTLINK
HOTLINKS
HOTLY
HOTNESS
HOTNESSES
HOTPLATE
HOTPLATES
HOTPOT
HOTPOTS
HOTPRESS
HOTROD
HOTRODS
HOTS
HOTSHOT
HOTSHOTS
HOTSPOT
HOTSPOTS
HOTSPUR
HOTSPURS
HOTTED
HOTTENTOT
HOTTER
HOTTERED
HOTTERING
HOTTERS
HOTTEST
HOTTIE
HOTTIES
HOTTING
HOTTINGS
HOTTISH
HOTTY
HOUDAH
HOUDAHS
HOUDAN
HOUDANS
HOUF
HOUFED
HOUFF
HOUFFED
HOUFFING
HOUFFS
HOUFING
HOUFS
HOUGH
HOUGHED
HOUGHING
HOUGHS
HOUHERE
HOUHERES
HOUMMOS
HOUMMOSES
HOUMOUS
HOUMOUSES
HOUMUS
HOUMUSES
HOUND
HOUNDED
HOUNDER
HOUNDERS
HOUNDFISH
HOUNDING
HOUNDS
HOUNGAN
HOUNGANS
HOUR
HOURGLASS
HOURI
HOURIS
HOURLIES
HOURLONG
HOURLY
HOURPLATE
HOURS
HOUSE
HOUSEBOAT
HOUSEBOY
HOUSEBOYS
HOUSECARL
HOUSECOAT
HOUSED
HOUSEFLY
HOUSEFUL
HOUSEFULS
HOUSEHOLD
HOUSEKEEP
HOUSEKEPT
HOUSEL
HOUSELED
HOUSELEEK
HOUSELESS
HOUSELIKE
HOUSELINE
HOUSELING
HOUSELLED
HOUSELS
HOUSEMAID
HOUSEMAN
HOUSEMATE
HOUSEMEN
HOUSER
HOUSEROOM
HOUSERS
HOUSES
HOUSESAT
HOUSESIT
HOUSESITS

HOUSETOP
HOUSETOPS
HOUSEWIFE
HOUSEWORK
HOUSEWRAP
HOUSEY
HOUSIER
HOUSIEST
HOUSING
HOUSINGS
HOUSLING
HOUSLINGS
HOUSTONIA
HOUT
HOUTED
HOUTING
HOUTINGS
HOUTS
HOVE
HOVEA
HOVEAS
HOVED
HOVEL
HOVELED
HOVELING
HOVELLED
HOVELLER
HOVELLERS
HOVELLING
HOVELS
HOVEN
HOVER
HOVERED
HOVERER
HOVERERS
HOVERFLY
HOVERING
HOVERPORT
HOVERS
HOVES
HOVING
HOW
HOWBE
HOWBEIT
HOWDAH
HOWDAHS
HOWDIE
HOWDIED
HOWDIES
HOWDY
HOWDYING
HOWE
HOWES
HOWEVER
HOWF
HOWFED
HOWFF
HOWFFED
HOWFFING
HOWFFS
HOWFING
HOWFS
HOWITZER
HOWITZERS
HOWK
HOWKED
HOWKER
HOWKERS
HOWKING
HOWKS
HOWL
HOWLBACK
HOWLBACKS
HOWLED
HOWLER
HOWLERS
HOWLET
HOWLETS
HOWLING
HOWLINGLY
HOWLINGS
HOWLROUND
HOWLS
HOWRE
HOWRES
HOWS
HOWSO
HOWSOEVER
HOWTOWDIE
HOWZAT
HOWZIT
HOX
HOXED
HOXES
HOXING
HOY
HOYA
HOYAS
HOYDEN
HOYDENED
HOYDENING
HOYDENISH
HOYDENISM
HOYDENS
HOYED
HOYING
HOYLE
HOYLES
HOYS
HRYVNA
HRYVNAS
HRYVNIA
HRYVNIAS
HRYVNYA
HRYVNYAS
HUANACO
HUANACOS
HUAQUERO
HUAQUEROS
HUARACHE
HUARACHES
HUARACHO
HUARACHOS
HUB
HUBBIES
HUBBLIER
HUBBLIEST
HUBBLY
HUBBUB
HUBBUBOO
HUBBUBOOS
HUBBUBS
HUBBY
HUBCAP
HUBCAPS
HUBLESS
HUBRIS
HUBRISES
HUBRISTIC
HUBS
HUCK
HUCKABACK
HUCKED
HUCKERY
HUCKING
HUCKLE
HUCKLED
HUCKLES
HUCKLING
HUCKS
HUCKSTER
HUCKSTERS
HUCKSTERY
HUDDEN
HUDDLE
HUDDLED
HUDDLER
HUDDLERS
HUDDLES
HUDDLING
HUDDUP
HUDNA
HUDNAS
HUDUD
HUDUDS
HUE
HUED
HUELESS
HUER
HUERS
HUES
HUFF
HUFFED
HUFFER
HUFFERS
HUFFIER
HUFFIEST
HUFFILY
HUFFINESS
HUFFING
HUFFINGS
HUFFISH
HUFFISHLY
HUFFKIN
HUFFKINS
HUFFS
HUFFY
HUG
HUGE
HUGELY
HUGENESS
HUGEOUS
HUGEOUSLY
HUGER
HUGEST
HUGGABLE
HUGGED
HUGGER
HUGGERS
HUGGIER
HUGGIEST
HUGGING
HUGGY
HUGS
HUGY
HUH
HUHU
HUHUS
HUI
HUIA
HUIAS
HUIC
HUIPIL
HUIPILES
HUIPILS
HUIS
HUISACHE
HUISACHES
HUISSIER
HUISSIERS
HUITAIN
HUITAINS
HULA
HULAS
HULE
HULES
HULK
HULKED
HULKIER
HULKIEST
HULKING
HULKS
HULKY
HULL
HULLED
HULLER
HULLERS
HULLIER
HULLIEST
HULLING

HULLO
HULLOA
HULLOAED
HULLOAING
HULLOAS
HULLOED
HULLOES
HULLOING
HULLOO
HULLOOED
HULLOOING
HULLOOS
HULLOS
HULLS
HULLY
HUM
HUMA
HUMAN
HUMANE
HUMANELY
HUMANER
HUMANEST
HUMANHOOD
HUMANISE
HUMANISED
HUMANISER
HUMANISES
HUMANISM
HUMANISMS
HUMANIST
HUMANISTS
HUMANITY
HUMANIZE
HUMANIZED
HUMANIZER
HUMANIZES
HUMANKIND
HUMANLIKE
HUMANLY
HUMANNESS
HUMANOID
HUMANOIDS
HUMANS
HUMAS
HUMATE
HUMATES
HUMBLE
HUMBLEBEE
HUMBLED
HUMBLER
HUMBLERS
HUMBLES
HUMBLESSE
HUMBLEST
HUMBLING
HUMBLINGS
HUMBLY
HUMBUCKER
HUMBUG
HUMBUGGED
HUMBUGGER
HUMBUGS
HUMBUZZ
HUMBUZZES
HUMDINGER
HUMDRUM
HUMDRUMS
HUMECT
HUMECTANT
HUMECTATE
HUMECTED
HUMECTING
HUMECTIVE
HUMECTS
HUMEFIED
HUMEFIES
HUMEFY
HUMEFYING
HUMERAL
HUMERALS
HUMERI
HUMERUS
HUMF
HUMFED
HUMFING
HUMFS
HUMHUM
HUMHUMS
HUMIC
HUMICOLE
HUMICOLES
HUMID
HUMIDER
HUMIDEST
HUMIDEX
HUMIDEXES
HUMIDICES
HUMIDIFY
HUMIDITY
HUMIDLY
HUMIDNESS
HUMIDOR
HUMIDORS
HUMIFIED
HUMIFIES
HUMIFY
HUMIFYING
HUMILIANT
HUMILIATE
HUMILITY
HUMINT
HUMINTS
HUMITE
HUMITES
HUMITURE
HUMITURES
HUMLIE
HUMLIES
HUMMABLE
HUMMAUM
HUMMAUMS
HUMMED
HUMMEL
HUMMELLED
HUMMELLER
HUMMELS
HUMMER
HUMMERS
HUMMING
HUMMINGS
HUMMLE
HUMMOCK
HUMMOCKED
HUMMOCKS
HUMMOCKY
HUMMUM
HUMMUMS
HUMMUS
HUMMUSES
HUMOGEN
HUMOGENS
HUMONGOUS
HUMOR
HUMORAL
HUMORALLY
HUMORED
HUMORESK
HUMORESKS
HUMORFUL
HUMORING
HUMORIST
HUMORISTS
HUMORLESS
HUMOROUS
HUMORS
HUMORSOME
HUMOUR
HUMOURED
HUMOURFUL
HUMOURING
HUMOURS
HUMOUS
HUMOUSES
HUMP
HUMPBACK
HUMPBACKS
HUMPED
HUMPEN
HUMPENS
HUMPER
HUMPERS
HUMPH
HUMPHED
HUMPHING
HUMPHS
HUMPIER
HUMPIES
HUMPIEST
HUMPINESS
HUMPING
HUMPLESS
HUMPLIKE
HUMPS
HUMPTIES
HUMPTY
HUMPY
HUMS
HUMSTRUM
HUMSTRUMS
HUMUNGOUS
HUMUS
HUMUSES
HUMUSIER
HUMUSIEST
HUMUSY
HUMVEE
HUMVEES
HUN
HUNCH
HUNCHBACK
HUNCHED
HUNCHES
HUNCHING
HUNDRED
HUNDREDER
HUNDREDOR
HUNDREDS
HUNDREDTH
HUNG
HUNGAN
HUNGANS
HUNGER
HUNGERED
HUNGERFUL
HUNGERING
HUNGERLY
HUNGERS
HUNGOVER
HUNGRIER
HUNGRIEST
HUNGRILY
HUNGRY
HUNH
HUNK
HUNKER
HUNKERED
HUNKERING
HUNKERS
HUNKIER
HUNKIEST
HUNKS
HUNKSES
HUNKY
HUNNISH
HUNS
HUNT
HUNTABLE
HUNTAWAY
HUNTAWAYS
HUNTED

HUNTEDLY
HUNTER
HUNTERS
HUNTING
HUNTINGS
HUNTRESS
HUNTS
HUNTSMAN
HUNTSMEN
HUP
HUPIRO
HUPIROS
HUPPAH
HUPPAHS
HUPPED
HUPPING
HUPPOT
HUPPOTH
HUPS
HURCHEON
HURCHEONS
HURDEN
HURDENS
HURDIES
HURDLE
HURDLED
HURDLER
HURDLERS
HURDLES
HURDLING
HURDLINGS
HURDS
HURL
HURLBAT
HURLBATS
HURLED
HURLER
HURLERS
HURLEY
HURLEYS
HURLIES
HURLING
HURLINGS
HURLS
HURLY
HURRA
HURRAED
HURRAH
HURRAHED
HURRAHING
HURRAHS
HURRAING
HURRAS
HURRAY
HURRAYED
HURRAYING
HURRAYS
HURRICANE
HURRICANO
HURRIED
HURRIEDLY
HURRIER
HURRIERS
HURRIES
HURRY
HURRYING
HURRYINGS
HURST
HURSTS
HURT
HURTER
HURTERS
HURTFUL
HURTFULLY
HURTING
HURTLE
HURTLED
HURTLES
HURTLESS
HURTLING
HURTS
HUSBAND
HUSBANDED
HUSBANDER
HUSBANDLY
HUSBANDRY
HUSBANDS
HUSH
HUSHABIED
HUSHABIES
HUSHABY
HUSHABYE
HUSHED
HUSHEDLY
HUSHER
HUSHERED
HUSHERING
HUSHERS
HUSHES
HUSHFUL
HUSHIER
HUSHIEST
HUSHING
HUSHPUPPY
HUSHY
HUSK
HUSKED
HUSKER
HUSKERS
HUSKIER
HUSKIES
HUSKIEST
HUSKILY
HUSKINESS
HUSKING
HUSKINGS
HUSKLIKE
HUSKS
HUSKY
HUSO
HUSOS
HUSS
HUSSAR
HUSSARS
HUSSES
HUSSIES
HUSSIF
HUSSIFS
HUSSY
HUSTINGS
HUSTLE
HUSTLED
HUSTLER
HUSTLERS
HUSTLES
HUSTLING
HUSTLINGS
HUSWIFE
HUSWIFES
HUSWIVES
HUT
HUTCH
HUTCHED
HUTCHES
HUTCHIE
HUTCHIES
HUTCHING
HUTIA
HUTIAS
HUTLIKE
HUTMENT
HUTMENTS
HUTS
HUTTED
HUTTING
HUTTINGS
HUTZPA
HUTZPAH
HUTZPAHS
HUTZPAS
HUZOOR
HUZOORS
HUZZA
HUZZAED
HUZZAH
HUZZAHED
HUZZAHING
HUZZAHS
HUZZAING
HUZZAS
HUZZIES
HUZZY
HWAN
HWYL
HWYLS
HYACINE
HYACINES
HYACINTH
HYACINTHS
HYAENA
HYAENAS
HYAENIC
HYALIN
HYALINE
HYALINES
HYALINISE
HYALINIZE
HYALINS
HYALITE
HYALITES
HYALOGEN
HYALOGENS
HYALOID
HYALOIDS
HYALONEMA
HYBRID
HYBRIDISE
HYBRIDISM
HYBRIDIST
HYBRIDITY
HYBRIDIZE
HYBRIDOMA
HYBRIDOUS
HYBRIDS
HYBRIS
HYBRISES
HYBRISTIC
HYDANTOIN
HYDATHODE
HYDATID
HYDATIDS
HYDATOID
HYDRA
HYDRACID
HYDRACIDS
HYDRAE
HYDRAEMIA
HYDRAGOG
HYDRAGOGS
HYDRANGEA
HYDRANT
HYDRANTH
HYDRANTHS
HYDRANTS
HYDRAS
HYDRASE
HYDRASES
HYDRASTIS
HYDRATE
HYDRATED
HYDRATES
HYDRATING
HYDRATION
HYDRATOR
HYDRATORS
HYDRAULIC
HYDRAZIDE
HYDRAZINE
HYDRAZOIC
HYDREMIA

HYDREMIAS
HYDRIA
HYDRIAE
HYDRIC
HYDRID
HYDRIDE
HYDRIDES
HYDRIDS
HYDRILLA
HYDRILLAS
HYDRIODIC
HYDRO
HYDROCAST
HYDROCELE
HYDROFOIL
HYDROGEL
HYDROGELS
HYDROGEN
HYDROGENS
HYDROID
HYDROIDS
HYDROLASE
HYDROLOGY
HYDROLYSE
HYDROLYTE
HYDROLYZE
HYDROMA
HYDROMAS
HYDROMATA
HYDROMEL
HYDROMELS
HYDRONAUT
HYDRONIC
HYDRONIUM
HYDROPATH
HYDROPIC
HYDROPS
HYDROPSES
HYDROPSY
HYDROPTIC
HYDROPULT
HYDROS
HYDROSERE
HYDROSKI
HYDROSKIS
HYDROSOL
HYDROSOLS
HYDROSOMA
HYDROSOME
HYDROSTAT
HYDROUS
HYDROVANE
HYDROXIDE
HYDROXIUM
HYDROXY
HYDROXYL
HYDROXYLS
HYDROZOA
HYDROZOAN
HYDROZOON
HYDYNE
HYDYNES
HYE
HYED
HYEING
HYEN
HYENA
HYENAS
HYENIC
HYENINE
HYENOID
HYENS
HYES
HYETAL
HYETOLOGY
HYGEIST
HYGEISTS
HYGGE
HYGGES
HYGIEIST
HYGIEISTS
HYGIENE
HYGIENES
HYGIENIC
HYGIENICS
HYGIENIST
HYGRISTOR
HYGRODEIK
HYGROLOGY
HYGROMA
HYGROMAS
HYGROMATA
HYGROPHIL
HYGROSTAT
HYING
HYKE
HYKES
HYLA
HYLAS
HYLDING
HYLDINGS
HYLE
HYLEG
HYLEGS
HYLES
HYLIC
HYLICISM
HYLICISMS
HYLICIST
HYLICISTS
HYLISM
HYLISMS
HYLIST
HYLISTS
HYLOBATE
HYLOBATES
HYLOIST
HYLOISTS
HYLOPHYTE
HYLOZOIC
HYLOZOISM
HYLOZOIST
HYMEN
HYMENAEAL
HYMENAEAN
HYMENAL
HYMENEAL
HYMENEALS
HYMENEAN
HYMENEANS
HYMENIA
HYMENIAL
HYMENIUM
HYMENIUMS
HYMENS
HYMN
HYMNAL
HYMNALS
HYMNARIES
HYMNARY
HYMNBOOK
HYMNBOOKS
HYMNED
HYMNIC
HYMNING
HYMNIST
HYMNISTS
HYMNLESS
HYMNLIKE
HYMNODIES
HYMNODIST
HYMNODY
HYMNOLOGY
HYMNS
HYNDE
HYNDES
HYOID
HYOIDAL
HYOIDEAN
HYOIDS
HYOSCINE
HYOSCINES
HYP
HYPALGIA
HYPALGIAS
HYPALLAGE
HYPANTHIA
HYPATE
HYPATES
HYPE
HYPED
HYPER
HYPERACID
HYPERARID
HYPERBOLA
HYPERBOLE
HYPERCUBE
HYPEREMIA
HYPEREMIC
HYPERER
HYPEREST
HYPERFINE
HYPERGAMY
HYPERGOL
HYPERGOLS
HYPERICIN
HYPERICUM
HYPERLINK
HYPERMART
HYPERNOVA
HYPERNYM
HYPERNYMS
HYPERNYMY
HYPERON
HYPERONS
HYPEROPE
HYPEROPES
HYPEROPIA
HYPEROPIC
HYPERPNEA
HYPERPURE
HYPERREAL
HYPERS
HYPERTEXT
HYPES
HYPESTER
HYPESTERS
HYPETHRAL
HYPHA
HYPHAE
HYPHAL
HYPHEMIA
HYPHEMIAS
HYPHEN
HYPHENATE
HYPHENED
HYPHENIC
HYPHENING
HYPHENISE
HYPHENISM
HYPHENIZE
HYPHENS
HYPHIES
HYPHY
HYPING
HYPINGS
HYPINOSES
HYPINOSIS
HYPNIC
HYPNICS
HYPNOGENY
HYPNOID
HYPNOIDAL
HYPNOLOGY
HYPNONE
HYPNONES
HYPNOSES
HYPNOSIS
HYPNOTEE
HYPNOTEES

HYPNOTIC
HYPNOTICS
HYPNOTISE
HYPNOTISM
HYPNOTIST
HYPNOTIZE
HYPNOTOID
HYPNUM
HYPNUMS
HYPO
HYPOACID
HYPOBARIC
HYPOBLAST
HYPOBOLE
HYPOBOLES
HYPOCAUST
HYPOCIST
HYPOCISTS
HYPOCOTYL
HYPOCRISY
HYPOCRITE
HYPODERM
HYPODERMA
HYPODERMS
HYPOED
HYPOGAEA
HYPOGAEAL
HYPOGAEAN
HYPOGAEUM
HYPOGEA
HYPOGEAL
HYPOGEAN
HYPOGENE
HYPOGENIC
HYPOGEOUS
HYPOGEUM
HYPOGYNY
HYPOID
HYPOIDS
HYPOING
HYPOMANIA
HYPOMANIC
HYPOMORPH
HYPONASTY
HYPONEA
HYPONEAS
HYPONOIA
HYPONOIAS
HYPONYM
HYPONYMS
HYPONYMY
HYPOPHYGE
HYPOPLOID
HYPOPNEA
HYPOPNEAS
HYPOPNEIC
HYPOPNOEA
HYPOPYON
HYPOPYONS
HYPOS
HYPOSTOME
HYPOSTYLE
HYPOTAXES
HYPOTAXIS
HYPOTHEC
HYPOTHECA
HYPOTHECS
HYPOTONIA
HYPOTONIC
HYPOXEMIA
HYPOXEMIC
HYPOXIA
HYPOXIAS
HYPOXIC
HYPPED
HYPPING
HYPS
HYPURAL
HYRACES
HYRACOID
HYRACOIDS
HYRAX
HYRAXES
HYSON
HYSONS
HYSSOP
HYSSOPS
HYSTERIA
HYSTERIAS
HYSTERIC
HYSTERICS
HYSTEROID
HYTE
HYTHE
HYTHES

I

IAMB
IAMBI
IAMBIC
IAMBICS
IAMBIST
IAMBISTS
IAMBS
IAMBUS
IAMBUSES
IANTHINE
IATRIC
IATRICAL
IATROGENY
IBADAH
IBADAT
IBERIS
IBERISES
IBEX
IBEXES
IBICES
IBIDEM
IBIS
IBISES
IBOGAINE
IBOGAINES
IBRIK
IBRIKS
IBUPROFEN
ICE
ICEBALL
ICEBALLS
ICEBERG
ICEBERGS
ICEBLINK
ICEBLINKS
ICEBOAT
ICEBOATED
ICEBOATER
ICEBOATS
ICEBOUND
ICEBOX
ICEBOXES
ICECAP
ICECAPPED
ICECAPS
ICED
ICEFALL
ICEFALLS
ICEFIELD
ICEFIELDS
ICEFISH
ICEFISHED
ICEFISHES
ICEHOUSE
ICEHOUSES
ICEKHANA
ICEKHANAS
ICELESS
ICELIKE
ICEMAKER
ICEMAKERS
ICEMAN
ICEMEN
ICEPACK
ICEPACKS
ICER
ICERS
ICES
ICESCAPE
ICESCAPES
ICESTONE
ICESTONES
ICEWINE
ICEWINES
ICEWORM
ICEWORMS
ICH
ICHABOD
ICHED
ICHES
ICHING
ICHNEUMON
ICHNITE
ICHNITES
ICHNOLITE
ICHNOLOGY
ICHOR
ICHOROUS
ICHORS
ICHS
ICHTHIC
ICHTHYIC
ICHTHYOID
ICHTHYS
ICHTHYSES
ICICLE
ICICLED
ICICLES
ICIER
ICIEST
ICILY
ICINESS
ICINESSES
ICING
ICINGS
ICK
ICKER
ICKERS
ICKIER
ICKIEST
ICKILY
ICKINESS
ICKLE
ICKLER
ICKLEST
ICKS
ICKY
ICON
ICONES
ICONIC
ICONICAL
ICONICITY
ICONIFIED
ICONIFIES
ICONIFY
ICONISE
ICONISED
ICONISES
ICONISING
ICONIZE
ICONIZED
ICONIZES
ICONIZING
ICONOLOGY
ICONOSTAS
ICONS
ICTAL
ICTERIC
ICTERICAL
ICTERICS
ICTERID
ICTERIDS
ICTERINE
ICTERUS
ICTERUSES
ICTIC
ICTUS
ICTUSES
ICY
ID
IDANT
IDANTS
IDE
IDEA
IDEAED
IDEAL
IDEALESS
IDEALISE
IDEALISED
IDEALISER
IDEALISES
IDEALISM
IDEALISMS
IDEALIST
IDEALISTS
IDEALITY
IDEALIZE
IDEALIZED
IDEALIZER
IDEALIZES
IDEALLESS
IDEALLY
IDEALNESS
IDEALOGUE
IDEALOGY
IDEALS
IDEAS
IDEATA
IDEATE
IDEATED
IDEATES
IDEATING
IDEATION
IDEATIONS
IDEATIVE
IDEATUM
IDEE
IDEES
IDEM
IDENT
IDENTIC
IDENTICAL
IDENTIFY
IDENTIKIT
IDENTITY
IDENTS
IDEOGRAM
IDEOGRAMS
IDEOGRAPH
IDEOLOGIC
IDEOLOGUE
IDEOLOGY
IDEOMOTOR
IDEOPHONE
IDEOPOLIS
IDES
IDIOBLAST
IDIOCIES
IDIOCY
IDIOGRAM

IDIOGRAMS
IDIOGRAPH
IDIOLECT
IDIOLECTS
IDIOM
IDIOMATIC
IDIOMS
IDIOPATHY
IDIOPHONE
IDIOPLASM
IDIOT
IDIOTCIES
IDIOTCY
IDIOTIC
IDIOTICAL
IDIOTICON
IDIOTISH
IDIOTISM
IDIOTISMS
IDIOTS
IDIOTYPE
IDIOTYPES
IDIOTYPIC
IDLE
IDLED
IDLEHOOD
IDLEHOODS
IDLENESS
IDLER
IDLERS
IDLES
IDLESSE
IDLESSES
IDLEST
IDLING
IDLY
IDOCRASE
IDOCRASES
IDOL
IDOLA
IDOLATER
IDOLATERS
IDOLATOR
IDOLATORS
IDOLATRY
IDOLISE
IDOLISED
IDOLISER
IDOLISERS
IDOLISES
IDOLISING
IDOLISM
IDOLISMS
IDOLIST
IDOLISTS
IDOLIZE
IDOLIZED
IDOLIZER
IDOLIZERS
IDOLIZES
IDOLIZING
IDOLON
IDOLS
IDOLUM
IDONEITY
IDONEOUS
IDS
IDYL
IDYLIST
IDYLISTS
IDYLL
IDYLLIAN
IDYLLIC
IDYLLIST
IDYLLISTS
IDYLLS
IDYLS
IF
IFF
IFFIER
IFFIEST
IFFILY
IFFINESS
IFFY
IFS
IFTAR
IFTARS
IGAD
IGAPO
IGAPOS
IGARAPE
IGARAPES
IGG
IGGED
IGGING
IGGS
IGLOO
IGLOOS
IGLU
IGLUS
IGNARO
IGNAROES
IGNAROS
IGNATIA
IGNATIAS
IGNEOUS
IGNESCENT
IGNIFIED
IGNIFIES
IGNIFY
IGNIFYING
IGNITABLE
IGNITE
IGNITED
IGNITER
IGNITERS
IGNITES
IGNITIBLE
IGNITING
IGNITION
IGNITIONS
IGNITOR
IGNITORS
IGNITRON
IGNITRONS
IGNOBLE
IGNOBLER
IGNOBLEST
IGNOBLY
IGNOMIES
IGNOMINY
IGNOMY
IGNORABLE
IGNORAMI
IGNORAMUS
IGNORANCE
IGNORANT
IGNORANTS
IGNORE
IGNORED
IGNORER
IGNORERS
IGNORES
IGNORING
IGUANA
IGUANAS
IGUANIAN
IGUANIANS
IGUANID
IGUANIDS
IGUANODON
IHRAM
IHRAMS
IJTIHAD
IJTIHADS
IKAN
IKANS
IKAT
IKATS
IKEBANA
IKEBANAS
IKON
IKONS
ILEA
ILEAC
ILEAL
ILEITIDES
ILEITIS
ILEITISES
ILEOSTOMY
ILEUM
ILEUS
ILEUSES
ILEX
ILEXES
ILIA
ILIAC
ILIACI
ILIACUS
ILIACUSES
ILIAD
ILIADS
ILIAL
ILICES
ILIUM
ILK
ILKA
ILKADAY
ILKADAYS
ILKS
ILL
ILLAPSE
ILLAPSED
ILLAPSES
ILLAPSING
ILLATION
ILLATIONS
ILLATIVE
ILLATIVES
ILLAWARRA
ILLEGAL
ILLEGALLY
ILLEGALS
ILLEGIBLE
ILLEGIBLY
ILLER
ILLEST
ILLIAD
ILLIADS
ILLIBERAL
ILLICIT
ILLICITLY
ILLIMITED
ILLINIUM
ILLINIUMS
ILLIPE
ILLIPES
ILLIQUID
ILLISION
ILLISIONS
ILLITE
ILLITES
ILLITIC
ILLNESS
ILLNESSES
ILLOGIC
ILLOGICAL
ILLOGICS
ILLS
ILLTH
ILLTHS
ILLUDE
ILLUDED
ILLUDES
ILLUDING
ILLUME
ILLUMED
ILLUMES
ILLUMINE
ILLUMINED

ILLUMINER
ILLUMINES
ILLUMING
ILLUPI
ILLUPIS
ILLUSION
ILLUSIONS
ILLUSIVE
ILLUSORY
ILLUVIA
ILLUVIAL
ILLUVIATE
ILLUVIUM
ILLUVIUMS
ILLY
ILMENITE
ILMENITES
IMAGE
IMAGEABLE
IMAGED
IMAGELESS
IMAGER
IMAGERIES
IMAGERS
IMAGERY
IMAGES
IMAGINAL
IMAGINARY
IMAGINE
IMAGINED
IMAGINEER
IMAGINER
IMAGINERS
IMAGINES
IMAGING
IMAGINGS
IMAGINING
IMAGINIST
IMAGISM
IMAGISMS
IMAGIST
IMAGISTIC
IMAGISTS
IMAGO
IMAGOES
IMAGOS
IMAM
IMAMATE
IMAMATES
IMAMS
IMARET
IMARETS
IMARI
IMARIS
IMAUM
IMAUMS
IMBALANCE
IMBALM
IMBALMED
IMBALMER
IMBALMERS
IMBALMING
IMBALMS
IMBAR
IMBARK
IMBARKED
IMBARKING
IMBARKS
IMBARRED
IMBARRING
IMBARS
IMBASE
IMBASED
IMBASES
IMBASING
IMBATHE
IMBATHED
IMBATHES
IMBATHING
IMBECILE
IMBECILES
IMBECILIC
IMBED
IMBEDDED
IMBEDDING
IMBEDS
IMBIBE
IMBIBED
IMBIBER
IMBIBERS
IMBIBES
IMBIBING
IMBITTER
IMBITTERS
IMBIZO
IMBIZOS
IMBLAZE
IMBLAZED
IMBLAZES
IMBLAZING
IMBODIED
IMBODIES
IMBODY
IMBODYING
IMBOLDEN
IMBOLDENS
IMBORDER
IMBORDERS
IMBOSK
IMBOSKED
IMBOSKING
IMBOSKS
IMBOSOM
IMBOSOMED
IMBOSOMS
IMBOSS
IMBOSSED
IMBOSSES
IMBOSSING
IMBOWER
IMBOWERED
IMBOWERS
IMBRANGLE
IMBRAST
IMBREX
IMBRICATE
IMBRICES
IMBROGLIO
IMBROWN
IMBROWNED
IMBROWNS
IMBRUE
IMBRUED
IMBRUES
IMBRUING
IMBRUTE
IMBRUTED
IMBRUTES
IMBRUTING
IMBUE
IMBUED
IMBUEMENT
IMBUES
IMBUING
IMBURSE
IMBURSED
IMBURSES
IMBURSING
IMID
IMIDAZOLE
IMIDE
IMIDES
IMIDIC
IMIDO
IMIDS
IMINAZOLE
IMINE
IMINES
IMINO
IMINOUREA
IMIPENEM
IMIPENEMS
IMITABLE
IMITANCY
IMITANT
IMITANTS
IMITATE
IMITATED
IMITATES
IMITATING
IMITATION
IMITATIVE
IMITATOR
IMITATORS
IMMANACLE
IMMANE
IMMANELY
IMMANENCE
IMMANENCY
IMMANENT
IMMANITY
IMMANTLE
IMMANTLED
IMMANTLES
IMMASK
IMMASKED
IMMASKING
IMMASKS
IMMATURE
IMMATURER
IMMATURES
IMMEDIACY
IMMEDIATE
IMMENSE
IMMENSELY
IMMENSER
IMMENSEST
IMMENSITY
IMMERGE
IMMERGED
IMMERGES
IMMERGING
IMMERSE
IMMERSED
IMMERSER
IMMERSERS
IMMERSES
IMMERSING
IMMERSION
IMMERSIVE
IMMESH
IMMESHED
IMMESHES
IMMESHING
IMMEW
IMMEWED
IMMEWING
IMMEWS
IMMIES
IMMIGRANT
IMMIGRATE
IMMINENCE
IMMINENCY
IMMINENT
IMMINGLE
IMMINGLED
IMMINGLES
IMMINUTE
IMMISSION
IMMIT
IMMITS
IMMITTED
IMMITTING
IMMIX
IMMIXED
IMMIXES
IMMIXING
IMMIXTURE
IMMOBILE
IMMODEST

IMMODESTY
IMMOLATE
IMMOLATED
IMMOLATES
IMMOLATOR
IMMOMENT
IMMORAL
IMMORALLY
IMMORTAL
IMMORTALS
IMMOTILE
IMMOVABLE
IMMOVABLY
IMMUNE
IMMUNER
IMMUNES
IMMUNEST
IMMUNISE
IMMUNISED
IMMUNISER
IMMUNISES
IMMUNITY
IMMUNIZE
IMMUNIZED
IMMUNIZER
IMMUNIZES
IMMUNOGEN
IMMURE
IMMURED
IMMURES
IMMURING
IMMUTABLE
IMMUTABLY
IMMY
IMP
IMPACABLE
IMPACT
IMPACTED
IMPACTER
IMPACTERS
IMPACTFUL
IMPACTING
IMPACTION
IMPACTITE
IMPACTIVE
IMPACTOR
IMPACTORS
IMPACTS
IMPAINT
IMPAINTED
IMPAINTS
IMPAIR
IMPAIRED
IMPAIRER
IMPAIRERS
IMPAIRING
IMPAIRS
IMPALA
IMPALAS
IMPALE
IMPALED
IMPALER
IMPALERS
IMPALES
IMPALING
IMPANATE
IMPANEL
IMPANELED
IMPANELS
IMPANNEL
IMPANNELS
IMPARITY
IMPARK
IMPARKED
IMPARKING
IMPARKS
IMPARL
IMPARLED
IMPARLING
IMPARLS
IMPART
IMPARTED
IMPARTER
IMPARTERS
IMPARTIAL
IMPARTING
IMPARTS
IMPASSE
IMPASSES
IMPASSION
IMPASSIVE
IMPASTE
IMPASTED
IMPASTES
IMPASTING
IMPASTO
IMPASTOED
IMPASTOS
IMPATIENS
IMPATIENT
IMPAVE
IMPAVED
IMPAVES
IMPAVID
IMPAVIDLY
IMPAVING
IMPAWN
IMPAWNED
IMPAWNING
IMPAWNS
IMPEACH
IMPEACHED
IMPEACHER
IMPEACHES
IMPEARL
IMPEARLED
IMPEARLS
IMPECCANT
IMPED
IMPEDANCE
IMPEDE
IMPEDED
IMPEDER
IMPEDERS
IMPEDES
IMPEDING
IMPEDOR
IMPEDORS
IMPEL
IMPELLED
IMPELLENT
IMPELLER
IMPELLERS
IMPELLING
IMPELLOR
IMPELLORS
IMPELS
IMPEND
IMPENDED
IMPENDENT
IMPENDING
IMPENDS
IMPENNATE
IMPERATOR
IMPERFECT
IMPERIA
IMPERIAL
IMPERIALS
IMPERIL
IMPERILED
IMPERILS
IMPERIOUS
IMPERIUM
IMPERIUMS
IMPETICOS
IMPETIGO
IMPETIGOS
IMPETRATE
IMPETUOUS
IMPETUS
IMPETUSES
IMPHEE
IMPHEES
IMPI
IMPIES
IMPIETIES
IMPIETY
IMPING
IMPINGE
IMPINGED
IMPINGENT
IMPINGER
IMPINGERS
IMPINGES
IMPINGING
IMPINGS
IMPIOUS
IMPIOUSLY
IMPIS
IMPISH
IMPISHLY
IMPLANT
IMPLANTED
IMPLANTER
IMPLANTS
IMPLATE
IMPLATED
IMPLATES
IMPLATING
IMPLEACH
IMPLEAD
IMPLEADED
IMPLEADER
IMPLEADS
IMPLED
IMPLEDGE
IMPLEDGED
IMPLEDGES
IMPLEMENT
IMPLETE
IMPLETED
IMPLETES
IMPLETING
IMPLETION
IMPLEX
IMPLEXES
IMPLEXION
IMPLICATE
IMPLICIT
IMPLICITY
IMPLIED
IMPLIEDLY
IMPLIES
IMPLODE
IMPLODED
IMPLODENT
IMPLODES
IMPLODING
IMPLORE
IMPLORED
IMPLORER
IMPLORERS
IMPLORES
IMPLORING
IMPLOSION
IMPLOSIVE
IMPLUNGE
IMPLUNGED
IMPLUNGES
IMPLUVIA
IMPLUVIUM
IMPLY
IMPLYING
IMPOCKET
IMPOCKETS
IMPOLDER
IMPOLDERS
IMPOLICY
IMPOLITE
IMPOLITER

IMPOLITIC
IMPONE
IMPONED
IMPONENT
IMPONENTS
IMPONES
IMPONING
IMPOROUS
IMPORT
IMPORTANT
IMPORTED
IMPORTER
IMPORTERS
IMPORTING
IMPORTS
IMPORTUNE
IMPOSABLE
IMPOSE
IMPOSED
IMPOSER
IMPOSERS
IMPOSES
IMPOSEX
IMPOSEXES
IMPOSING
IMPOST
IMPOSTED
IMPOSTER
IMPOSTERS
IMPOSTING
IMPOSTOR
IMPOSTORS
IMPOSTS
IMPOSTUME
IMPOSTURE
IMPOT
IMPOTENCE
IMPOTENCY
IMPOTENT
IMPOTENTS
IMPOTS
IMPOUND
IMPOUNDED
IMPOUNDER
IMPOUNDS
IMPOWER
IMPOWERED
IMPOWERS
IMPRECATE
IMPRECISE
IMPREGN
IMPREGNED
IMPREGNS
IMPRESA
IMPRESARI
IMPRESAS
IMPRESE
IMPRESES
IMPRESS
IMPRESSE
IMPRESSED
IMPRESSER
IMPRESSES
IMPREST
IMPRESTS
IMPRIMIS
IMPRINT
IMPRINTED
IMPRINTER
IMPRINTS
IMPRISON
IMPRISONS
IMPRO
IMPROBITY
IMPROMPTU
IMPROPER
IMPROS
IMPROV
IMPROVE
IMPROVED
IMPROVER
IMPROVERS
IMPROVES
IMPROVING
IMPROVISE
IMPROVS
IMPRUDENT
IMPS
IMPSONITE
IMPUDENCE
IMPUDENCY
IMPUDENT
IMPUGN
IMPUGNED
IMPUGNER
IMPUGNERS
IMPUGNING
IMPUGNS
IMPULSE
IMPULSED
IMPULSES
IMPULSING
IMPULSION
IMPULSIVE
IMPUNDULU
IMPUNITY
IMPURE
IMPURELY
IMPURER
IMPUREST
IMPURITY
IMPURPLE
IMPURPLED
IMPURPLES
IMPUTABLE
IMPUTABLY
IMPUTE
IMPUTED
IMPUTER
IMPUTERS
IMPUTES
IMPUTING
IMSHI
IMSHY
IN
INABILITY
INACTION
INACTIONS
INACTIVE
INAIDABLE
INAMORATA
INAMORATI
INAMORATO
INANE
INANELY
INANENESS
INANER
INANES
INANEST
INANGA
INANGAS
INANIMATE
INANITIES
INANITION
INANITY
INAPT
INAPTER
INAPTEST
INAPTLY
INAPTNESS
INARABLE
INARCH
INARCHED
INARCHES
INARCHING
INARM
INARMED
INARMING
INARMS
INASMUCH
INAUDIBLE
INAUDIBLY
INAUGURAL
INAURATE
INAURATED
INAURATES
INBEING
INBEINGS
INBENT
INBOARD
INBOARDS
INBORN
INBOUND
INBOUNDED
INBOUNDS
INBOX
INBOXES
INBREAK
INBREAKS
INBREATHE
INBRED
INBREDS
INBREED
INBREEDER
INBREEDS
INBRING
INBRINGS
INBROUGHT
INBUILT
INBURNING
INBURST
INBURSTS
INBY
INBYE
INCAGE
INCAGED
INCAGES
INCAGING
INCANT
INCANTED
INCANTING
INCANTS
INCAPABLE
INCAPABLY
INCARNATE
INCASE
INCASED
INCASES
INCASING
INCAUTION
INCAVE
INCAVED
INCAVES
INCAVI
INCAVING
INCAVO
INCEDE
INCEDED
INCEDES
INCEDING
INCEL
INCELS
INCENSE
INCENSED
INCENSER
INCENSERS
INCENSES
INCENSING
INCENSOR
INCENSORS
INCENSORY
INCENT
INCENTED
INCENTER
INCENTERS
INCENTING
INCENTIVE
INCENTRE
INCENTRES
INCENTS

INCEPT
INCEPTED
INCEPTING
INCEPTION
INCEPTIVE
INCEPTOR
INCEPTORS
INCEPTS
INCERTAIN
INCESSANT
INCEST
INCESTS
INCH
INCHASE
INCHASED
INCHASES
INCHASING
INCHED
INCHER
INCHERS
INCHES
INCHING
INCHMEAL
INCHOATE
INCHOATED
INCHOATES
INCHPIN
INCHPINS
INCHTAPE
INCHTAPES
INCHWORM
INCHWORMS
INCIDENCE
INCIDENT
INCIDENTS
INCIPIENT
INCIPIT
INCIPITS
INCISAL
INCISE
INCISED
INCISES
INCISING
INCISION
INCISIONS
INCISIVE
INCISOR
INCISORS
INCISORY
INCISURAL
INCISURE
INCISURES
INCITABLE
INCITANT
INCITANTS
INCITE
INCITED
INCITER
INCITERS
INCITES
INCITING
INCIVIL
INCIVISM
INCIVISMS
INCLASP
INCLASPED
INCLASPS
INCLE
INCLEMENT
INCLES
INCLINE
INCLINED
INCLINER
INCLINERS
INCLINES
INCLINING
INCLIP
INCLIPPED
INCLIPS
INCLOSE
INCLOSED
INCLOSER
INCLOSERS
INCLOSES
INCLOSING
INCLOSURE
INCLUDE
INCLUDED
INCLUDES
INCLUDING
INCLUSION
INCLUSIVE
INCOG
INCOGNITA
INCOGNITO
INCOGS
INCOME
INCOMER
INCOMERS
INCOMES
INCOMING
INCOMINGS
INCOMMODE
INCOMPACT
INCONDITE
INCONIE
INCONNU
INCONNUE
INCONNUES
INCONNUS
INCONY
INCORPSE
INCORPSED
INCORPSES
INCORRECT
INCORRUPT
INCREASE
INCREASED
INCREASER
INCREASES
INCREATE
INCREMATE
INCREMENT
INCRETION
INCRETORY
INCROSS
INCROSSED
INCROSSES
INCRUST
INCRUSTED
INCRUSTS
INCUBATE
INCUBATED
INCUBATES
INCUBATOR
INCUBI
INCUBOUS
INCUBUS
INCUBUSES
INCUDAL
INCUDATE
INCUDES
INCULCATE
INCULPATE
INCULT
INCUMBENT
INCUMBER
INCUMBERS
INCUNABLE
INCUR
INCURABLE
INCURABLY
INCURIOUS
INCURRED
INCURRENT
INCURRING
INCURS
INCURSION
INCURSIVE
INCURVATE
INCURVE
INCURVED
INCURVES
INCURVING
INCURVITY
INCUS
INCUSE
INCUSED
INCUSES
INCUSING
INCUT
INCUTS
INDABA
INDABAS
INDAGATE
INDAGATED
INDAGATES
INDAGATOR
INDAMIN
INDAMINE
INDAMINES
INDAMINS
INDART
INDARTED
INDARTING
INDARTS
INDEBTED
INDECENCY
INDECENT
INDECORUM
INDEED
INDEEDY
INDELIBLE
INDELIBLY
INDEMNIFY
INDEMNITY
INDENE
INDENES
INDENT
INDENTED
INDENTER
INDENTERS
INDENTING
INDENTION
INDENTOR
INDENTORS
INDENTS
INDENTURE
INDEVOUT
INDEW
INDEWED
INDEWING
INDEWS
INDEX
INDEXABLE
INDEXAL
INDEXED
INDEXER
INDEXERS
INDEXES
INDEXICAL
INDEXING
INDEXINGS
INDEXLESS
INDIA
INDIAS
INDICAN
INDICANS
INDICANT
INDICANTS
INDICATE
INDICATED
INDICATES
INDICATOR
INDICES
INDICIA
INDICIAL
INDICIAS
INDICIUM
INDICIUMS

INDICT
INDICTED
INDICTEE
INDICTEES
INDICTER
INDICTERS
INDICTING
INDICTION
INDICTOR
INDICTORS
INDICTS
INDIE
INDIES
INDIGEN
INDIGENCE
INDIGENCY
INDIGENE
INDIGENES
INDIGENS
INDIGENT
INDIGENTS
INDIGEST
INDIGESTS
INDIGN
INDIGNANT
INDIGNIFY
INDIGNITY
INDIGNLY
INDIGO
INDIGOES
INDIGOID
INDIGOIDS
INDIGOS
INDIGOTIC
INDIGOTIN
INDINAVIR
INDIRECT
INDIRUBIN
INDISPOSE
INDITE
INDITED
INDITER
INDITERS
INDITES
INDITING
INDIUM
INDIUMS
INDIVIDUA
INDOCIBLE
INDOCILE
INDOL
INDOLE
INDOLENCE
INDOLENCY
INDOLENT
INDOLES
INDOLS
INDOOR
INDOORS
INDORSE
INDORSED
INDORSEE
INDORSEES
INDORSER
INDORSERS
INDORSES
INDORSING
INDORSOR
INDORSORS
INDOW
INDOWED
INDOWING
INDOWS
INDOXYL
INDOXYLS
INDRAFT
INDRAFTS
INDRAUGHT
INDRAWN
INDRENCH
INDRI
INDRIS
INDRISES
INDUBIOUS
INDUCE
INDUCED
INDUCER
INDUCERS
INDUCES
INDUCIAE
INDUCIBLE
INDUCING
INDUCT
INDUCTED
INDUCTEE
INDUCTEES
INDUCTILE
INDUCTING
INDUCTION
INDUCTIVE
INDUCTOR
INDUCTORS
INDUCTS
INDUE
INDUED
INDUES
INDUING
INDULGE
INDULGED
INDULGENT
INDULGER
INDULGERS
INDULGES
INDULGING
INDULIN
INDULINE
INDULINES
INDULINS
INDULT
INDULTS
INDUMENTA
INDUNA
INDUNAS
INDURATE
INDURATED
INDURATES
INDUSIA
INDUSIAL
INDUSIATE
INDUSIUM
INDUSTRY
INDUVIAE
INDUVIAL
INDUVIATE
INDWELL
INDWELLER
INDWELLS
INDWELT
INDYREF
INDYREFS
INEARTH
INEARTHED
INEARTHS
INEBRIANT
INEBRIATE
INEBRIETY
INEBRIOUS
INEDIBLE
INEDIBLY
INEDITA
INEDITED
INEFFABLE
INEFFABLY
INELASTIC
INELEGANT
INEPT
INEPTER
INEPTEST
INEPTLY
INEPTNESS
INEQUABLE
INEQUITY
INERM
INERMOUS
INERRABLE
INERRABLY
INERRANCY
INERRANT
INERT
INERTER
INERTEST
INERTIA
INERTIAE
INERTIAL
INERTIAS
INERTLY
INERTNESS
INERTS
INERUDITE
INESSIVE
INESSIVES
INEXACT
INEXACTLY
INEXPERT
INEXPERTS
INFALL
INFALLING
INFALLS
INFAME
INFAMED
INFAMES
INFAMIES
INFAMING
INFAMISE
INFAMISED
INFAMISES
INFAMIZE
INFAMIZED
INFAMIZES
INFAMOUS
INFAMY
INFANCIES
INFANCY
INFANT
INFANTA
INFANTAS
INFANTE
INFANTEER
INFANTES
INFANTILE
INFANTINE
INFANTRY
INFANTS
INFARCT
INFARCTED
INFARCTS
INFARE
INFARES
INFATUATE
INFAUNA
INFAUNAE
INFAUNAL
INFAUNAS
INFAUST
INFECT
INFECTANT
INFECTED
INFECTER
INFECTERS
INFECTING
INFECTION
INFECTIVE
INFECTOR
INFECTORS
INFECTS
INFECUND
INFEED
INFEEDS
INFEFT
INFEFTED

INFEFTING
INFEFTS
INFELT
INFEOFF
INFEOFFED
INFEOFFS
INFER
INFERABLE
INFERABLY
INFERE
INFERENCE
INFERIAE
INFERIBLE
INFERIOR
INFERIORS
INFERNAL
INFERNO
INFERNOS
INFERRED
INFERRER
INFERRERS
INFERRING
INFERS
INFERTILE
INFEST
INFESTANT
INFESTED
INFESTER
INFESTERS
INFESTING
INFESTS
INFICETE
INFIDEL
INFIDELIC
INFIDELS
INFIELD
INFIELDER
INFIELDS
INFIGHT
INFIGHTER
INFIGHTS
INFILL
INFILLED
INFILLING
INFILLS
INFIMA
INFIMUM
INFIMUMS
INFINITE
INFINITES
INFINITY
INFIRM
INFIRMARY
INFIRMED
INFIRMER
INFIRMEST
INFIRMING
INFIRMITY
INFIRMLY
INFIRMS
INFIX
INFIXED
INFIXES
INFIXING
INFIXION
INFIXIONS
INFLAME
INFLAMED
INFLAMER
INFLAMERS
INFLAMES
INFLAMING
INFLATE
INFLATED
INFLATER
INFLATERS
INFLATES
INFLATING
INFLATION
INFLATIVE
INFLATOR
INFLATORS
INFLATUS
INFLECT
INFLECTED
INFLECTOR
INFLECTS
INFLEXED
INFLEXION
INFLEXURE
INFLICT
INFLICTED
INFLICTER
INFLICTOR
INFLICTS
INFLIGHT
INFLOW
INFLOWING
INFLOWS
INFLUENCE
INFLUENT
INFLUENTS
INFLUENZA
INFLUX
INFLUXES
INFLUXION
INFO
INFOBAHN
INFOBAHNS
INFOLD
INFOLDED
INFOLDER
INFOLDERS
INFOLDING
INFOLDS
INFOMANIA
INFORCE
INFORCED
INFORCES
INFORCING
INFORM
INFORMAL
INFORMANT
INFORMED
INFORMER
INFORMERS
INFORMING
INFORMS
INFORTUNE
INFOS
INFOTECH
INFOTECHS
INFOUGHT
INFRA
INFRACT
INFRACTED
INFRACTOR
INFRACTS
INFRARED
INFRAREDS
INFRINGE
INFRINGED
INFRINGER
INFRINGES
INFRUGAL
INFULA
INFULAE
INFURIATE
INFUSCATE
INFUSE
INFUSED
INFUSER
INFUSERS
INFUSES
INFUSIBLE
INFUSING
INFUSION
INFUSIONS
INFUSIVE
INFUSORIA
INFUSORY
ING
INGAN
INGANS
INGATE
INGATES
INGATHER
INGATHERS
INGENER
INGENERS
INGENIOUS
INGENIUM
INGENIUMS
INGENU
INGENUE
INGENUES
INGENUITY
INGENUOUS
INGENUS
INGEST
INGESTA
INGESTED
INGESTING
INGESTION
INGESTIVE
INGESTS
INGINE
INGINES
INGLE
INGLENEUK
INGLENOOK
INGLES
INGLOBE
INGLOBED
INGLOBES
INGLOBING
INGLUVIAL
INGLUVIES
INGO
INGOES
INGOING
INGOINGS
INGOT
INGOTED
INGOTING
INGOTS
INGRAFT
INGRAFTED
INGRAFTS
INGRAIN
INGRAINED
INGRAINER
INGRAINS
INGRAM
INGRAMS
INGRATE
INGRATELY
INGRATES
INGRESS
INGRESSES
INGROOVE
INGROOVED
INGROOVES
INGROSS
INGROSSED
INGROSSES
INGROUND
INGROUNDS
INGROUP
INGROUPS
INGROWING
INGROWN
INGROWTH
INGROWTHS
INGRUM
INGRUMS
INGS
INGUINAL
INGULF
INGULFED

INGULFING
INGULFS
INGULPH
INGULPHED
INGULPHS
INHABIT
INHABITED
INHABITER
INHABITOR
INHABITS
INHALABLE
INHALANT
INHALANTS
INHALATOR
INHALE
INHALED
INHALER
INHALERS
INHALES
INHALING
INHARMONY
INHAUL
INHAULER
INHAULERS
INHAULS
INHAUST
INHAUSTED
INHAUSTS
INHEARSE
INHEARSED
INHEARSES
INHERCE
INHERCED
INHERCES
INHERCING
INHERE
INHERED
INHERENCE
INHERENCY
INHERENT
INHERES
INHERING
INHERIT
INHERITED
INHERITOR
INHERITS
INHESION
INHESIONS
INHIBIN
INHIBINS
INHIBIT
INHIBITED
INHIBITER
INHIBITOR
INHIBITS
INHOLDER
INHOLDERS
INHOLDING
INHOOP
INHOOPED
INHOOPING
INHOOPS
INHUMAN
INHUMANE
INHUMANER
INHUMANLY
INHUMATE
INHUMATED
INHUMATES
INHUME
INHUMED
INHUMER
INHUMERS
INHUMES
INHUMING
INIA
INIMICAL
INION
INIONS
INIQUITY
INISLE
INISLED
INISLES
INISLING
INITIAL
INITIALED
INITIALER
INITIALLY
INITIALS
INITIATE
INITIATED
INITIATES
INITIATOR
INJECT
INJECTANT
INJECTED
INJECTING
INJECTION
INJECTIVE
INJECTOR
INJECTORS
INJECTS
INJELLIED
INJELLIES
INJELLY
INJERA
INJERAS
INJOINT
INJOINTED
INJOINTS
INJUNCT
INJUNCTED
INJUNCTS
INJURABLE
INJURE
INJURED
INJURER
INJURERS
INJURES
INJURIES
INJURING
INJURIOUS
INJURY
INJUSTICE
INK
INKBERRY
INKBLOT
INKBLOTS
INKED
INKER
INKERS
INKHOLDER
INKHORN
INKHORNS
INKHOSI
INKHOSIS
INKIER
INKIEST
INKINESS
INKING
INKJET
INKJETS
INKLE
INKLED
INKLES
INKLESS
INKLIKE
INKLING
INKLINGS
INKOSI
INKOSIS
INKPAD
INKPADS
INKPOT
INKPOTS
INKS
INKSPOT
INKSPOTS
INKSTAIN
INKSTAINS
INKSTAND
INKSTANDS
INKSTONE
INKSTONES
INKWELL
INKWELLS
INKWOOD
INKWOODS
INKY
INLACE
INLACED
INLACES
INLACING
INLAID
INLAND
INLANDER
INLANDERS
INLANDS
INLAY
INLAYER
INLAYERS
INLAYING
INLAYINGS
INLAYS
INLET
INLETS
INLETTING
INLIER
INLIERS
INLOCK
INLOCKED
INLOCKING
INLOCKS
INLY
INLYING
INMATE
INMATES
INMESH
INMESHED
INMESHES
INMESHING
INMIGRANT
INMOST
INN
INNAGE
INNAGES
INNARDS
INNATE
INNATELY
INNATIVE
INNED
INNER
INNERLY
INNERMOST
INNERNESS
INNERS
INNERSOLE
INNERVATE
INNERVE
INNERVED
INNERVES
INNERVING
INNERWEAR
INNING
INNINGS
INNINGSES
INNIT
INNKEEPER
INNLESS
INNOCENCE
INNOCENCY
INNOCENT
INNOCENTS
INNOCUITY
INNOCUOUS
INNOVATE
INNOVATED
INNOVATES
INNOVATOR
INNOXIOUS

INNS
INNUENDO
INNUENDOS
INNYARD
INNYARDS
INOCULA
INOCULANT
INOCULATE
INOCULUM
INOCULUMS
INODOROUS
INOPINATE
INORB
INORBED
INORBING
INORBS
INORGANIC
INORNATE
INOSINE
INOSINES
INOSITE
INOSITES
INOSITOL
INOSITOLS
INOTROPE
INOTROPES
INOTROPIC
INPATIENT
INPAYMENT
INPHASE
INPOUR
INPOURED
INPOURING
INPOURS
INPUT
INPUTS
INPUTTED
INPUTTER
INPUTTERS
INPUTTING
INQILAB
INQILABS
INQUERE
INQUERED
INQUERES
INQUERING
INQUEST
INQUESTS
INQUIET
INQUIETED
INQUIETLY
INQUIETS
INQUILINE
INQUINATE
INQUIRE
INQUIRED
INQUIRER
INQUIRERS
INQUIRES
INQUIRIES
INQUIRING
INQUIRY
INQUORATE
INRO
INROAD
INROADS
INRUN
INRUNS
INRUSH
INRUSHES
INRUSHING
INS
INSANE
INSANELY
INSANER
INSANEST
INSANIE
INSANIES
INSANITY
INSATIATE
INSATIETY
INSCAPE
INSCAPES
INSCIENCE
INSCIENT
INSCONCE
INSCONCED
INSCONCES
INSCRIBE
INSCRIBED
INSCRIBER
INSCRIBES
INSCROLL
INSCROLLS
INSCULP
INSCULPED
INSCULPS
INSCULPT
INSEAM
INSEAMED
INSEAMING
INSEAMS
INSECT
INSECTAN
INSECTARY
INSECTEAN
INSECTILE
INSECTION
INSECTS
INSECURE
INSECURER
INSEEM
INSEEMED
INSEEMING
INSEEMS
INSELBERG
INSENSATE
INSERT
INSERTED
INSERTER
INSERTERS
INSERTING
INSERTION
INSERTS
INSET
INSETS
INSETTED
INSETTER
INSETTERS
INSETTING
INSHALLAH
INSHEATH
INSHEATHE
INSHEATHS
INSHELL
INSHELLED
INSHELLS
INSHELTER
INSHIP
INSHIPPED
INSHIPS
INSHORE
INSHRINE
INSHRINED
INSHRINES
INSIDE
INSIDER
INSIDERS
INSIDES
INSIDIOUS
INSIGHT
INSIGHTS
INSIGNE
INSIGNIA
INSIGNIAS
INSINCERE
INSINEW
INSINEWED
INSINEWS
INSINUATE
INSIPID
INSIPIDER
INSIPIDLY
INSIPIENT
INSIST
INSISTED
INSISTENT
INSISTER
INSISTERS
INSISTING
INSISTS
INSNARE
INSNARED
INSNARER
INSNARERS
INSNARES
INSNARING
INSOFAR
INSOLATE
INSOLATED
INSOLATES
INSOLE
INSOLENCE
INSOLENT
INSOLENTS
INSOLES
INSOLUBLE
INSOLUBLY
INSOLVENT
INSOMNIA
INSOMNIAC
INSOMNIAS
INSOMUCH
INSOOTH
INSOUL
INSOULED
INSOULING
INSOULS
INSOURCE
INSOURCED
INSOURCES
INSPAN
INSPANNED
INSPANS
INSPECT
INSPECTED
INSPECTOR
INSPECTS
INSPHERE
INSPHERED
INSPHERES
INSPIRE
INSPIRED
INSPIRER
INSPIRERS
INSPIRES
INSPIRING
INSPIRIT
INSPIRITS
INSPO
INSPOS
INSTABLE
INSTAGRAM
INSTAL
INSTALL
INSTALLED
INSTALLER
INSTALLS
INSTALS
INSTANCE
INSTANCED
INSTANCES
INSTANCY
INSTANT
INSTANTER
INSTANTLY
INSTANTS
INSTAR
INSTARRED
INSTARS

INSTATE
INSTATED
INSTATES
INSTATING
INSTEAD
INSTEP
INSTEPS
INSTIGATE
INSTIL
INSTILL
INSTILLED
INSTILLER
INSTILLS
INSTILS
INSTINCT
INSTINCTS
INSTITUTE
INSTRESS
INSTROKE
INSTROKES
INSTRUCT
INSTRUCTS
INSUCKEN
INSULA
INSULAE
INSULANT
INSULANTS
INSULAR
INSULARLY
INSULARS
INSULATE
INSULATED
INSULATES
INSULATOR
INSULIN
INSULINS
INSULSE
INSULSITY
INSULT
INSULTANT
INSULTED
INSULTER
INSULTERS
INSULTING
INSULTS
INSURABLE
INSURANCE
INSURANT
INSURANTS
INSURE
INSURED
INSUREDS
INSURER
INSURERS
INSURES
INSURGENT
INSURING
INSWATHE
INSWATHED
INSWATHES
INSWEPT
INSWING
INSWINGER
INSWINGS
INTACT
INTACTLY
INTAGLI
INTAGLIO
INTAGLIOS
INTAKE
INTAKES
INTARSIA
INTARSIAS
INTEGER
INTEGERS
INTEGRAL
INTEGRALS
INTEGRAND
INTEGRANT
INTEGRATE
INTEGRIN
INTEGRINS
INTEGRITY
INTEL
INTELLECT
INTELS
INTENABLE
INTEND
INTENDANT
INTENDED
INTENDEDS
INTENDER
INTENDERS
INTENDING
INTENDS
INTENIBLE
INTENSATE
INTENSE
INTENSELY
INTENSER
INTENSEST
INTENSIFY
INTENSION
INTENSITY
INTENSIVE
INTENT
INTENTION
INTENTIVE
INTENTLY
INTENTS
INTER
INTERACT
INTERACTS
INTERAGE
INTERARCH
INTERBANK
INTERBED
INTERBEDS
INTERBRED
INTERCEDE
INTERCELL
INTERCEPT
INTERCITY
INTERCLAN
INTERCLUB
INTERCOM
INTERCOMS
INTERCOOL
INTERCROP
INTERCUT
INTERCUTS
INTERDASH
INTERDEAL
INTERDICT
INTERDINE
INTERESS
INTERESSE
INTEREST
INTERESTS
INTERFACE
INTERFERE
INTERFILE
INTERFIRM
INTERFLOW
INTERFOLD
INTERFUSE
INTERGANG
INTERGREW
INTERGROW
INTERIM
INTERIMS
INTERIOR
INTERIORS
INTERJECT
INTERJOIN
INTERKNIT
INTERKNOT
INTERLACE
INTERLAID
INTERLAP
INTERLAPS
INTERLARD
INTERLAY
INTERLAYS
INTERLEAF
INTERLEND
INTERLENT
INTERLINE
INTERLINK
INTERLOAN
INTERLOCK
INTERLOOP
INTERLOPE
INTERLUDE
INTERMALE
INTERMAT
INTERMATS
INTERMENT
INTERMESH
INTERMIT
INTERMITS
INTERMIX
INTERMONT
INTERMURE
INTERN
INTERNAL
INTERNALS
INTERNE
INTERNED
INTERNEE
INTERNEES
INTERNES
INTERNET
INTERNETS
INTERNING
INTERNIST
INTERNODE
INTERNS
INTERPAGE
INTERPLAY
INTERPLED
INTERPONE
INTERPOSE
INTERPRET
INTERRACE
INTERRAIL
INTERRED
INTERREX
INTERRING
INTERROW
INTERRUPT
INTERS
INTERSECT
INTERSERT
INTERSEX
INTERTERM
INTERTEXT
INTERTIE
INTERTIES
INTERTILL
INTERUNIT
INTERVAL
INTERVALE
INTERVALS
INTERVEIN
INTERVENE
INTERVIEW
INTERWAR
INTERWEB
INTERWEBS
INTERWIND
INTERWORD
INTERWORK
INTERWOVE
INTERZONE
INTESTACY
INTESTATE
INTESTINE
INTHRAL
INTHRALL

INTHRALLS
INTHRALS
INTHRONE
INTHRONED
INTHRONES
INTI
INTIFADA
INTIFADAH
INTIFADAS
INTIFADEH
INTIL
INTIMA
INTIMACY
INTIMAE
INTIMAL
INTIMAS
INTIMATE
INTIMATED
INTIMATER
INTIMATES
INTIME
INTIMISM
INTIMISMS
INTIMIST
INTIMISTE
INTIMISTS
INTIMITY
INTINE
INTINES
INTIRE
INTIS
INTITLE
INTITLED
INTITLES
INTITLING
INTITULE
INTITULED
INTITULES
INTO
INTOED
INTOMB
INTOMBED
INTOMBING
INTOMBS
INTONACO
INTONACOS
INTONATE
INTONATED
INTONATES
INTONATOR
INTONE
INTONED
INTONER
INTONERS
INTONES
INTONING
INTONINGS
INTORSION
INTORT
INTORTED
INTORTING
INTORTION
INTORTS
INTOWN
INTRA
INTRACITY
INTRADA
INTRADAS
INTRADAY
INTRADOS
INTRANET
INTRANETS
INTRANT
INTRANTS
INTREAT
INTREATED
INTREATS
INTRENCH
INTREPID
INTRICACY
INTRICATE
INTRIGANT
INTRIGUE
INTRIGUED
INTRIGUER
INTRIGUES
INTRINCE
INTRINSIC
INTRO
INTRODUCE
INTROFIED
INTROFIES
INTROFY
INTROIT
INTROITAL
INTROITS
INTROITUS
INTROJECT
INTROLD
INTROMIT
INTROMITS
INTRON
INTRONIC
INTRONS
INTRORSE
INTROS
INTROVERT
INTRUDE
INTRUDED
INTRUDER
INTRUDERS
INTRUDES
INTRUDING
INTRUSION
INTRUSIVE
INTRUST
INTRUSTED
INTRUSTS
INTUBATE
INTUBATED
INTUBATES
INTUIT
INTUITED
INTUITING
INTUITION
INTUITIVE
INTUITS
INTUMESCE
INTURN
INTURNED
INTURNS
INTUSE
INTUSES
INTWINE
INTWINED
INTWINES
INTWINING
INTWIST
INTWISTED
INTWISTS
INUKSHUIT
INUKSHUK
INUKSHUKS
INUKSUIT
INUKSUK
INUKSUKS
INULA
INULAS
INULASE
INULASES
INULIN
INULINS
INUMBRATE
INUNCTION
INUNDANT
INUNDATE
INUNDATED
INUNDATES
INUNDATOR
INURBANE
INURE
INURED
INUREMENT
INURES
INURING
INURN
INURNED
INURNING
INURNMENT
INURNS
INUSITATE
INUST
INUSTION
INUSTIONS
INUTILE
INUTILELY
INUTILITY
INVADABLE
INVADE
INVADED
INVADER
INVADERS
INVADES
INVADING
INVALID
INVALIDED
INVALIDER
INVALIDLY
INVALIDS
INVAR
INVARIANT
INVARS
INVASION
INVASIONS
INVASIVE
INVEAGLE
INVEAGLED
INVEAGLES
INVECKED
INVECTED
INVECTIVE
INVEIGH
INVEIGHED
INVEIGHER
INVEIGHS
INVEIGLE
INVEIGLED
INVEIGLER
INVEIGLES
INVENIT
INVENT
INVENTED
INVENTER
INVENTERS
INVENTING
INVENTION
INVENTIVE
INVENTOR
INVENTORS
INVENTORY
INVENTS
INVERITY
INVERNESS
INVERSE
INVERSED
INVERSELY
INVERSES
INVERSING
INVERSION
INVERSIVE
INVERT
INVERTASE
INVERTED
INVERTER
INVERTERS
INVERTIN
INVERTING
INVERTINS
INVERTOR
INVERTORS

INVERTS
INVEST
INVESTED
INVESTING
INVESTOR
INVESTORS
INVESTS
INVEXED
INVIABLE
INVIABLY
INVIDIOUS
INVIOLACY
INVIOLATE
INVIOUS
INVIRILE
INVISCID
INVISIBLE
INVISIBLY
INVITAL
INVITE
INVITED
INVITEE
INVITEES
INVITER
INVITERS
INVITES
INVITING
INVITINGS
INVOCABLE
INVOCATE
INVOCATED
INVOCATES
INVOCATOR
INVOICE
INVOICED
INVOICES
INVOICING
INVOKE
INVOKED
INVOKER
INVOKERS
INVOKES
INVOKING
INVOLUCEL
INVOLUCRA
INVOLUCRE
INVOLUTE
INVOLUTED
INVOLUTES
INVOLVE
INVOLVED
INVOLVER
INVOLVERS
INVOLVES
INVOLVING
INWALL
INWALLED
INWALLING
INWALLS
INWARD
INWARDLY
INWARDS
INWEAVE
INWEAVED
INWEAVES
INWEAVING
INWICK
INWICKED
INWICKING
INWICKS
INWIND
INWINDING
INWINDS
INWIT
INWITH
INWITS
INWORK
INWORKED
INWORKING
INWORKS
INWORN
INWOUND
INWOVE
INWOVEN
INWRAP
INWRAPPED
INWRAPS
INWRAPT
INWREATHE
INWROUGHT
INYALA
INYALAS
IO
IODATE
IODATED
IODATES
IODATING
IODATION
IODATIONS
IODIC
IODID
IODIDE
IODIDES
IODIDS
IODIN
IODINATE
IODINATED
IODINATES
IODINE
IODINES
IODINS
IODISE
IODISED
IODISER
IODISERS
IODISES
IODISING
IODISM
IODISMS
IODIZE
IODIZED
IODIZER
IODIZERS
IODIZES
IODIZING
IODOFORM
IODOFORMS
IODOMETRY
IODOPHILE
IODOPHOR
IODOPHORS
IODOPSIN
IODOPSINS
IODOUS
IODURET
IODURETS
IODYRITE
IODYRITES
IOLITE
IOLITES
ION
IONIC
IONICALLY
IONICITY
IONICS
IONISABLE
IONISE
IONISED
IONISER
IONISERS
IONISES
IONISING
IONIUM
IONIUMS
IONIZABLE
IONIZE
IONIZED
IONIZER
IONIZERS
IONIZES
IONIZING
IONOGEN
IONOGENIC
IONOGENS
IONOMER
IONOMERS
IONONE
IONONES
IONOPAUSE
IONOPHORE
IONOSONDE
IONOTROPY
IONS
IOPANOIC
IOS
IOTA
IOTACISM
IOTACISMS
IOTAS
IPECAC
IPECACS
IPOMOEA
IPOMOEAS
IPPON
IPPONS
IPRINDOLE
IRACUND
IRADE
IRADES
IRASCIBLE
IRASCIBLY
IRATE
IRATELY
IRATENESS
IRATER
IRATEST
IRE
IRED
IREFUL
IREFULLY
IRELESS
IRENIC
IRENICAL
IRENICISM
IRENICON
IRENICONS
IRENICS
IRENOLOGY
IRES
IRID
IRIDAL
IRIDEAL
IRIDES
IRIDIAL
IRIDIAN
IRIDIC
IRIDISE
IRIDISED
IRIDISES
IRIDISING
IRIDIUM
IRIDIUMS
IRIDIZE
IRIDIZED
IRIDIZES
IRIDIZING
IRIDOCYTE
IRIDOLOGY
IRIDOTOMY
IRIDS
IRING
IRIS
IRISATE
IRISATED
IRISATES
IRISATING
IRISATION
IRISCOPE
IRISCOPES
IRISED

IRISES
IRISING
IRITIC
IRITIS
IRITISES
IRK
IRKED
IRKING
IRKS
IRKSOME
IRKSOMELY
IROKO
IROKOS
IRON
IRONBARK
IRONBARKS
IRONBOUND
IRONCLAD
IRONCLADS
IRONE
IRONED
IRONER
IRONERS
IRONES
IRONIC
IRONICAL
IRONIER
IRONIES
IRONIEST
IRONING
IRONINGS
IRONISE
IRONISED
IRONISES
IRONISING
IRONIST
IRONISTS
IRONIZE
IRONIZED
IRONIZES
IRONIZING
IRONLESS
IRONLIKE
IRONMAN
IRONMEN
IRONNESS
IRONS
IRONSIDE
IRONSIDES
IRONSMITH
IRONSTONE
IRONWARE
IRONWARES
IRONWEED
IRONWEEDS
IRONWOMAN
IRONWOMEN
IRONWOOD
IRONWOODS
IRONWORK
IRONWORKS
IRONY
IRRADIANT
IRRADIATE
IRREAL
IRREALITY
IRREDENTA
IRREGULAR
IRRELATED
IRRIDENTA
IRRIGABLE
IRRIGABLY
IRRIGATE
IRRIGATED
IRRIGATES
IRRIGATOR
IRRIGUOUS
IRRISION
IRRISIONS
IRRISORY
IRRITABLE
IRRITABLY
IRRITANCY
IRRITANT
IRRITANTS
IRRITATE
IRRITATED
IRRITATES
IRRITATOR
IRRUPT
IRRUPTED
IRRUPTING
IRRUPTION
IRRUPTIVE
IRRUPTS
IRUKANDJI
IS
ISABEL
ISABELLA
ISABELLAS
ISABELS
ISAGOGE
ISAGOGES
ISAGOGIC
ISAGOGICS
ISALLOBAR
ISARITHM
ISARITHMS
ISATIN
ISATINE
ISATINES
ISATINIC
ISATINS
ISBA
ISBAS
ISCHAEMIA
ISCHAEMIC
ISCHEMIA
ISCHEMIAS
ISCHEMIC
ISCHIA
ISCHIADIC
ISCHIAL
ISCHIATIC
ISCHIUM
ISCHURIA
ISCHURIAS
ISEIKONIA
ISEIKONIC
ISENERGIC
ISH
ISHES
ISINGLASS
ISIT
ISLAND
ISLANDED
ISLANDER
ISLANDERS
ISLANDING
ISLANDS
ISLE
ISLED
ISLELESS
ISLEMAN
ISLEMEN
ISLES
ISLESMAN
ISLESMEN
ISLET
ISLETED
ISLETS
ISLING
ISLOMANIA
ISM
ISMATIC
ISMATICAL
ISMS
ISNA
ISNAE
ISO
ISOAMYL
ISOAMYLS
ISOBAR
ISOBARE
ISOBARES
ISOBARIC
ISOBARISM
ISOBARS
ISOBASE
ISOBASES
ISOBATH
ISOBATHIC
ISOBATHS
ISOBRONT
ISOBRONTS
ISOBUTANE
ISOBUTENE
ISOBUTYL
ISOBUTYLS
ISOCHASM
ISOCHASMS
ISOCHEIM
ISOCHEIMS
ISOCHIMAL
ISOCHIME
ISOCHIMES
ISOCHOR
ISOCHORE
ISOCHORES
ISOCHORIC
ISOCHORS
ISOCHRON
ISOCHRONE
ISOCHRONS
ISOCLINAL
ISOCLINE
ISOCLINES
ISOCLINIC
ISOCRACY
ISOCRATIC
ISOCRYMAL
ISOCRYME
ISOCRYMES
ISOCYANIC
ISOCYCLIC
ISODICA
ISODICON
ISODOMA
ISODOMON
ISODOMOUS
ISODOMUM
ISODONT
ISODONTAL
ISODONTS
ISODOSE
ISODOSES
ISOENZYME
ISOETES
ISOFORM
ISOFORMS
ISOGAMETE
ISOGAMIC
ISOGAMIES
ISOGAMOUS
ISOGAMY
ISOGENEIC
ISOGENIC
ISOGENIES
ISOGENOUS
ISOGENY
ISOGLOSS
ISOGON
ISOGONAL
ISOGONALS
ISOGONE
ISOGONES
ISOGONIC
ISOGONICS
ISOGONIES
ISOGONS

ISOGONY
ISOGRAFT
ISOGRAFTS
ISOGRAM
ISOGRAMS
ISOGRAPH
ISOGRAPHS
ISOGRIV
ISOGRIVS
ISOHEL
ISOHELS
ISOHYDRIC
ISOHYET
ISOHYETAL
ISOHYETS
ISOKONT
ISOKONTAN
ISOKONTS
ISOLABLE
ISOLATE
ISOLATED
ISOLATES
ISOLATING
ISOLATION
ISOLATIVE
ISOLATOR
ISOLATORS
ISOLEAD
ISOLEADS
ISOLEX
ISOLEXES
ISOLINE
ISOLINES
ISOLOG
ISOLOGOUS
ISOLOGS
ISOLOGUE
ISOLOGUES
ISOMER
ISOMERASE
ISOMERE
ISOMERES
ISOMERIC
ISOMERISE
ISOMERISM
ISOMERIZE
ISOMEROUS
ISOMERS
ISOMETRIC
ISOMETRY
ISOMORPH
ISOMORPHS
ISONIAZID
ISONOME
ISONOMES
ISONOMIC
ISONOMIES
ISONOMOUS
ISONOMY
ISOOCTANE
ISOPACH
ISOPACHS
ISOPHONE
ISOPHONES
ISOPHOTAL
ISOPHOTE
ISOPHOTES
ISOPLETH
ISOPLETHS
ISOPOD
ISOPODAN
ISOPODANS
ISOPODOUS
ISOPODS
ISOPOLITY
ISOPRENE
ISOPRENES
ISOPROPYL
ISOPTERAN
ISOPYCNAL
ISOPYCNIC
ISOS
ISOSCELES
ISOSMOTIC
ISOSPIN
ISOSPINS
ISOSPORY
ISOSTACY
ISOSTASY
ISOSTATIC
ISOSTERIC
ISOTACH
ISOTACHS
ISOTACTIC
ISOTHERAL
ISOTHERE
ISOTHERES
ISOTHERM
ISOTHERMS
ISOTONE
ISOTONES
ISOTONIC
ISOTOPE
ISOTOPES
ISOTOPIC
ISOTOPIES
ISOTOPY
ISOTRON
ISOTRONS
ISOTROPIC
ISOTROPY
ISOTYPE
ISOTYPES
ISOTYPIC
ISOZYME
ISOZYMES
ISOZYMIC
ISPAGHULA
ISSEI
ISSEIS
ISSUABLE
ISSUABLY
ISSUANCE
ISSUANCES
ISSUANT
ISSUE
ISSUED
ISSUELESS
ISSUER
ISSUERS
ISSUES
ISSUING
ISTANA
ISTANAS
ISTHMI
ISTHMIAN
ISTHMIANS
ISTHMIC
ISTHMOID
ISTHMUS
ISTHMUSES
ISTLE
ISTLES
IT
ITA
ITACISM
ITACISMS
ITACONIC
ITALIC
ITALICISE
ITALICIZE
ITALICS
ITAS
ITCH
ITCHED
ITCHES
ITCHIER
ITCHIEST
ITCHILY
ITCHINESS
ITCHING
ITCHINGS
ITCHWEED
ITCHWEEDS
ITCHY
ITEM
ITEMED
ITEMING
ITEMISE
ITEMISED
ITEMISER
ITEMISERS
ITEMISES
ITEMISING
ITEMIZE
ITEMIZED
ITEMIZER
ITEMIZERS
ITEMIZES
ITEMIZING
ITEMS
ITERANCE
ITERANCES
ITERANT
ITERATE
ITERATED
ITERATES
ITERATING
ITERATION
ITERATIVE
ITERUM
ITHER
ITINERACY
ITINERANT
ITINERARY
ITINERATE
ITS
ITSELF
IURE
IVIED
IVIES
IVORIED
IVORIER
IVORIES
IVORIEST
IVORIST
IVORISTS
IVORY
IVORYBILL
IVORYLIKE
IVORYWOOD
IVRESSE
IVRESSES
IVY
IVYLEAF
IVYLIKE
IWI
IWIS
IXIA
IXIAS
IXNAY
IXODIASES
IXODIASIS
IXODID
IXODIDS
IXORA
IXORAS
IXTLE
IXTLES
IZAR
IZARD
IZARDS
IZARS
IZVESTIA
IZVESTIAS
IZVESTIYA
IZZARD
IZZARDS
IZZAT
IZZATS

J

JA
JAAP
JAAPS
JAB
JABBED
JABBER
JABBERED
JABBERER
JABBERERS
JABBERING
JABBERS
JABBING
JABBINGLY
JABBLE
JABBLED
JABBLES
JABBLING
JABERS
JABIRU
JABIRUS
JABORANDI
JABOT
JABOTS
JABS
JACAL
JACALES
JACALS
JACAMAR
JACAMARS
JACANA
JACANAS
JACARANDA
JACARE
JACARES
JACCHUS
JACCHUSES
JACENT
JACINTH
JACINTHE
JACINTHES
JACINTHS
JACK
JACKAL
JACKALLED
JACKALOPE
JACKALS
JACKAROO
JACKAROOS
JACKASS
JACKASSES
JACKBOOT
JACKBOOTS
JACKDAW
JACKDAWS
JACKED
JACKEEN
JACKEENS
JACKER
JACKEROO
JACKEROOS
JACKERS
JACKET
JACKETED
JACKETING
JACKETS
JACKFISH
JACKFRUIT
JACKIES
JACKING
JACKINGS
JACKKNIFE
JACKLEG
JACKLEGS
JACKLIGHT
JACKLING
JACKLINGS
JACKMAN
JACKMEN
JACKPLANE
JACKPOT
JACKPOTS
JACKROLL
JACKROLLS
JACKS
JACKSCREW
JACKSHAFT
JACKSIE
JACKSIES
JACKSMELT
JACKSMITH
JACKSNIPE
JACKSTAFF
JACKSTAY
JACKSTAYS
JACKSTONE
JACKSTRAW
JACKSY
JACKY
JACOBIN
JACOBINS
JACOBUS
JACOBUSES
JACONET
JACONETS
JACQUARD
JACQUARDS
JACQUERIE
JACTATION
JACULATE
JACULATED
JACULATES
JACULATOR
JACUZZI
JACUZZIS
JADE
JADED
JADEDLY
JADEDNESS
JADEITE
JADEITES
JADELIKE
JADERIES
JADERY
JADES
JADING
JADISH
JADISHLY
JADITIC
JAEGER
JAEGERS
JAFA
JAFAS
JAFFA
JAFFAS
JAG
JAGA
JAGAED
JAGAING
JAGAS
JAGDWURST
JAGER
JAGERS
JAGG
JAGGARIES
JAGGARY
JAGGED
JAGGEDER
JAGGEDEST
JAGGEDLY
JAGGER
JAGGERIES
JAGGERS
JAGGERY
JAGGHERY
JAGGIER
JAGGIES
JAGGIEST
JAGGING
JAGGS
JAGGY
JAGHIR
JAGHIRDAR
JAGHIRE
JAGHIRES
JAGHIRS
JAGIR
JAGIRS
JAGLESS
JAGRA
JAGRAS
JAGS
JAGUAR
JAGUARS
JAI
JAIL
JAILABLE
JAILBAIT
JAILBAITS
JAILBIRD
JAILBIRDS
JAILBREAK
JAILBROKE
JAILED
JAILER
JAILERESS
JAILERS
JAILHOUSE
JAILING
JAILLESS
JAILOR
JAILORESS
JAILORS
JAILS
JAK
JAKE
JAKER
JAKES
JAKESES
JAKEST
JAKEY
JAKEYS
JAKFRUIT
JAKFRUITS
JAKS
JALABIB
JALAP
JALAPENO
JALAPENOS
JALAPIC
JALAPIN

JALAPINS
JALAPS
JALEBI
JALEBIS
JALFREZI
JALFREZIS
JALLEBI
JALLEBIS
JALOP
JALOPIES
JALOPPIES
JALOPPY
JALOPS
JALOPY
JALOUSE
JALOUSED
JALOUSES
JALOUSIE
JALOUSIED
JALOUSIES
JALOUSING
JAM
JAMAAT
JAMAATS
JAMADAR
JAMADARS
JAMB
JAMBALAYA
JAMBART
JAMBARTS
JAMBE
JAMBEAU
JAMBEAUS
JAMBEAUX
JAMBED
JAMBEE
JAMBEES
JAMBER
JAMBERS
JAMBES
JAMBEUX
JAMBIER
JAMBIERS
JAMBING
JAMBIYA
JAMBIYAH
JAMBIYAHS
JAMBIYAS
JAMBO
JAMBOK
JAMBOKKED
JAMBOKS
JAMBOLAN
JAMBOLANA
JAMBOLANS
JAMBONE
JAMBONES
JAMBOOL
JAMBOOLS
JAMBOREE
JAMBOREES
JAMBS
JAMBU
JAMBUL
JAMBULS
JAMBUS
JAMBUSTER
JAMDANI
JAMDANIS
JAMES
JAMESES
JAMJAR
JAMJARS
JAMLIKE
JAMMABLE
JAMMED
JAMMER
JAMMERS
JAMMIER
JAMMIES
JAMMIEST
JAMMING
JAMMINGS
JAMMY
JAMON
JAMPACKED
JAMPAN
JAMPANEE
JAMPANEES
JAMPANI
JAMPANIS
JAMPANS
JAMPOT
JAMPOTS
JAMS
JANE
JANES
JANGLE
JANGLED
JANGLER
JANGLERS
JANGLES
JANGLIER
JANGLIEST
JANGLING
JANGLINGS
JANGLY
JANIFORM
JANISARY
JANISSARY
JANITOR
JANITORS
JANITRESS
JANITRIX
JANIZAR
JANIZARS
JANIZARY
JANKER
JANKERS
JANN
JANNEY
JANNEYED
JANNEYING
JANNEYS
JANNIED
JANNIES
JANNOCK
JANNOCKS
JANNS
JANNY
JANNYING
JANNYINGS
JANSKY
JANSKYS
JANTEE
JANTIER
JANTIES
JANTIEST
JANTY
JAP
JAPAN
JAPANISE
JAPANISED
JAPANISES
JAPANIZE
JAPANIZED
JAPANIZES
JAPANNED
JAPANNER
JAPANNERS
JAPANNING
JAPANS
JAPE
JAPED
JAPER
JAPERIES
JAPERS
JAPERY
JAPES
JAPING
JAPINGLY
JAPINGS
JAPONICA
JAPONICAS
JAPPED
JAPPING
JAPS
JAR
JARARACA
JARARACAS
JARARAKA
JARARAKAS
JARFUL
JARFULS
JARGON
JARGONED
JARGONEER
JARGONEL
JARGONELS
JARGONIER
JARGONING
JARGONISE
JARGONISH
JARGONIST
JARGONIZE
JARGONS
JARGONY
JARGOON
JARGOONS
JARHEAD
JARHEADS
JARINA
JARINAS
JARK
JARKMAN
JARKMEN
JARKS
JARL
JARLDOM
JARLDOMS
JARLS
JARLSBERG
JAROOL
JAROOLS
JAROSITE
JAROSITES
JAROVISE
JAROVISED
JAROVISES
JAROVIZE
JAROVIZED
JAROVIZES
JARP
JARPED
JARPING
JARPS
JARRAH
JARRAHS
JARRED
JARRING
JARRINGLY
JARRINGS
JARS
JARSFUL
JARTA
JARTAS
JARUL
JARULS
JARVEY
JARVEYS
JARVIE
JARVIES
JASEY
JASEYS
JASIES
JASMIN
JASMINE
JASMINES
JASMINS
JASMONATE

JASP
JASPE
JASPER
JASPERIER
JASPERISE
JASPERIZE
JASPEROUS
JASPERS
JASPERY
JASPES
JASPIDEAN
JASPILITE
JASPIS
JASPISES
JASPS
JASS
JASSES
JASSID
JASSIDS
JASY
JATAKA
JATAKAS
JATO
JATOS
JATROPHA
JATROPHAS
JAUK
JAUKED
JAUKING
JAUKS
JAUNCE
JAUNCED
JAUNCES
JAUNCING
JAUNDICE
JAUNDICED
JAUNDICES
JAUNSE
JAUNSED
JAUNSES
JAUNSING
JAUNT
JAUNTED
JAUNTEE
JAUNTIE
JAUNTIER
JAUNTIES
JAUNTIEST
JAUNTILY
JAUNTING
JAUNTS
JAUNTY
JAUP
JAUPED
JAUPING
JAUPS
JAVA
JAVAS
JAVEL
JAVELIN
JAVELINA
JAVELINAS
JAVELINED
JAVELINS
JAVELLE
JAVELS
JAW
JAWAN
JAWANS
JAWARI
JAWARIS
JAWBATION
JAWBONE
JAWBONED
JAWBONER
JAWBONERS
JAWBONES
JAWBONING
JAWBOX
JAWBOXES
JAWED
JAWFALL
JAWFALLS
JAWHOLE
JAWHOLES
JAWING
JAWINGS
JAWLESS
JAWLIKE
JAWLINE
JAWLINES
JAWS
JAXIE
JAXIES
JAXY
JAY
JAYBIRD
JAYBIRDS
JAYCEE
JAYCEES
JAYGEE
JAYGEES
JAYHAWKER
JAYS
JAYVEE
JAYVEES
JAYWALK
JAYWALKED
JAYWALKER
JAYWALKS
JAZERANT
JAZERANTS
JAZIES
JAZY
JAZZ
JAZZBO
JAZZBOS
JAZZED
JAZZER
JAZZERS
JAZZES
JAZZIER
JAZZIEST
JAZZILY
JAZZINESS
JAZZING
JAZZLIKE
JAZZMAN
JAZZMEN
JAZZY
JEALOUS
JEALOUSE
JEALOUSED
JEALOUSER
JEALOUSES
JEALOUSLY
JEALOUSY
JEAN
JEANED
JEANETTE
JEANETTES
JEANS
JEANSWEAR
JEAT
JEATS
JEBEL
JEBELS
JEDI
JEDIS
JEE
JEED
JEEING
JEEL
JEELED
JEELIE
JEELIED
JEELIEING
JEELIES
JEELING
JEELS
JEELY
JEELYING
JEEP
JEEPED
JEEPERS
JEEPING
JEEPNEY
JEEPNEYS
JEEPS
JEER
JEERED
JEERER
JEERERS
JEERING
JEERINGLY
JEERINGS
JEERS
JEES
JEESLY
JEEZ
JEEZE
JEEZELY
JEEZLY
JEFE
JEFES
JEFF
JEFFED
JEFFING
JEFFS
JEGGINGS
JEHAD
JEHADEEN
JEHADI
JEHADIS
JEHADISM
JEHADISMS
JEHADIST
JEHADISTS
JEHADS
JEHU
JEHUS
JEJUNA
JEJUNAL
JEJUNE
JEJUNELY
JEJUNITY
JEJUNUM
JEJUNUMS
JELAB
JELABS
JELL
JELLABA
JELLABAH
JELLABAHS
JELLABAS
JELLED
JELLIED
JELLIES
JELLIFIED
JELLIFIES
JELLIFY
JELLING
JELLO
JELLOS
JELLS
JELLY
JELLYBEAN
JELLYFISH
JELLYING
JELLYLIKE
JELLYROLL
JELUTONG
JELUTONGS
JEMADAR
JEMADARS
JEMBE
JEMBES
JEMIDAR
JEMIDARS
JEMIMA

JEMIMAS
JEMMIED
JEMMIER
JEMMIES
JEMMIEST
JEMMINESS
JEMMY
JEMMYING
JENNET
JENNETING
JENNETS
JENNIES
JENNY
JEOFAIL
JEOFAILS
JEON
JEONS
JEOPARD
JEOPARDED
JEOPARDER
JEOPARDS
JEOPARDY
JEQUERITY
JEQUIRITY
JERBIL
JERBILS
JERBOA
JERBOAS
JEREED
JEREEDS
JEREMIAD
JEREMIADS
JEREPIGO
JEREPIGOS
JERFALCON
JERID
JERIDS
JERK
JERKED
JERKER
JERKERS
JERKIER
JERKIES
JERKIEST
JERKILY
JERKIN
JERKINESS
JERKING
JERKINGLY
JERKINGS
JERKINS
JERKS
JERKWATER
JERKY
JEROBOAM
JEROBOAMS
JERQUE
JERQUED
JERQUER
JERQUERS
JERQUES
JERQUING
JERQUINGS
JERREED
JERREEDS
JERRICAN
JERRICANS
JERRID
JERRIDS
JERRIES
JERRY
JERRYCAN
JERRYCANS
JERSEY
JERSEYED
JERSEYS
JESS
JESSAMIES
JESSAMINE
JESSAMY
JESSANT
JESSE
JESSED
JESSERANT
JESSES
JESSIE
JESSIES
JESSING
JEST
JESTBOOK
JESTBOOKS
JESTED
JESTEE
JESTEES
JESTER
JESTERS
JESTFUL
JESTING
JESTINGLY
JESTINGS
JESTS
JESUS
JET
JETBEAD
JETBEADS
JETE
JETES
JETFOIL
JETFOILS
JETLAG
JETLAGS
JETLIKE
JETLINER
JETLINERS
JETON
JETONS
JETPACK
JETPACKS
JETPORT
JETPORTS
JETS
JETSAM
JETSAMS
JETSOM
JETSOMS
JETSON
JETSONS
JETSTREAM
JETTATURA
JETTED
JETTIED
JETTIER
JETTIES
JETTIEST
JETTINESS
JETTING
JETTISON
JETTISONS
JETTON
JETTONS
JETTY
JETTYING
JETWAY
JETWAYS
JEU
JEUNE
JEUX
JEWEL
JEWELED
JEWELER
JEWELERS
JEWELFISH
JEWELING
JEWELLED
JEWELLER
JEWELLERS
JEWELLERY
JEWELLIKE
JEWELLING
JEWELRIES
JEWELRY
JEWELS
JEWELWEED
JEWFISH
JEWFISHES
JEWIE
JEWIES
JEZAIL
JEZAILS
JEZEBEL
JEZEBELS
JHALA
JHALAS
JHATKA
JHATKAS
JIAO
JIAOS
JIB
JIBB
JIBBA
JIBBAH
JIBBAHS
JIBBAS
JIBBED
JIBBER
JIBBERED
JIBBERING
JIBBERS
JIBBING
JIBBINGS
JIBBONS
JIBBOOM
JIBBOOMS
JIBBS
JIBE
JIBED
JIBER
JIBERS
JIBES
JIBING
JIBINGLY
JIBS
JICAMA
JICAMAS
JICKAJOG
JICKAJOGS
JIFF
JIFFIES
JIFFS
JIFFY
JIG
JIGAJIG
JIGAJIGS
JIGAJOG
JIGAJOGS
JIGAMAREE
JIGGED
JIGGER
JIGGERED
JIGGERING
JIGGERS
JIGGIER
JIGGIEST
JIGGING
JIGGINGS
JIGGISH
JIGGLE
JIGGLED
JIGGLES
JIGGLIER
JIGGLIEST
JIGGLING
JIGGLY
JIGGUMBOB
JIGGY
JIGJIG
JIGJIGS
JIGLIKE
JIGOT
JIGOTS

JIGS
JIGSAW
JIGSAWED
JIGSAWING
JIGSAWN
JIGSAWS
JIHAD
JIHADEEN
JIHADI
JIHADIS
JIHADISM
JIHADISMS
JIHADIST
JIHADISTS
JIHADS
JILBAB
JILBABS
JILGIE
JILGIES
JILL
JILLAROO
JILLAROOS
JILLET
JILLETS
JILLFLIRT
JILLION
JILLIONS
JILLIONTH
JILLS
JILT
JILTED
JILTER
JILTERS
JILTING
JILTS
JIMCRACK
JIMCRACKS
JIMINY
JIMJAM
JIMJAMS
JIMMIE
JIMMIED
JIMMIES
JIMMINY
JIMMY
JIMMYING
JIMP
JIMPER
JIMPEST
JIMPIER
JIMPIEST
JIMPLY
JIMPNESS
JIMPSON
JIMPY
JIMSON
JIMSONS
JIN
JINGAL
JINGALL
JINGALLS
JINGALS
JINGBANG
JINGBANGS
JINGKO
JINGKOES
JINGLE
JINGLED
JINGLER
JINGLERS
JINGLES
JINGLET
JINGLETS
JINGLIER
JINGLIEST
JINGLING
JINGLY
JINGO
JINGOES
JINGOISH
JINGOISM
JINGOISMS
JINGOIST
JINGOISTS
JINJILI
JINJILIS
JINK
JINKED
JINKER
JINKERED
JINKERING
JINKERS
JINKING
JINKS
JINN
JINNE
JINNEE
JINNI
JINNIS
JINNS
JINRIKSHA
JINS
JINX
JINXED
JINXES
JINXING
JIPIJAPA
JIPIJAPAS
JIPYAPA
JIPYAPAS
JIRBLE
JIRBLED
JIRBLES
JIRBLING
JIRD
JIRDS
JIRGA
JIRGAS
JIRKINET
JIRKINETS
JIRRE
JISM
JISMS
JISSOM
JISSOMS
JITNEY
JITNEYS
JITTER
JITTERBUG
JITTERED
JITTERIER
JITTERING
JITTERS
JITTERY
JIUJITSU
JIUJITSUS
JIUJUTSU
JIUJUTSUS
JIVE
JIVEASS
JIVEASSES
JIVED
JIVER
JIVERS
JIVES
JIVEST
JIVEY
JIVIER
JIVIEST
JIVING
JIVY
JIZ
JIZZ
JIZZES
JNANA
JNANAS
JO
JOANNA
JOANNAS
JOANNES
JOANNESES
JOB
JOBATION
JOBATIONS
JOBBED
JOBBER
JOBBERIES
JOBBERS
JOBBERY
JOBBIE
JOBBIES
JOBBING
JOBBINGS
JOBCENTRE
JOBE
JOBED
JOBERNOWL
JOBES
JOBHOLDER
JOBING
JOBLESS
JOBNAME
JOBNAMES
JOBS
JOBSEEKER
JOBSHARE
JOBSHARES
JOBSWORTH
JOCK
JOCKDOM
JOCKDOMS
JOCKETTE
JOCKETTES
JOCKEY
JOCKEYED
JOCKEYING
JOCKEYISH
JOCKEYISM
JOCKEYS
JOCKIER
JOCKIEST
JOCKISH
JOCKNEY
JOCKNEYS
JOCKO
JOCKOS
JOCKS
JOCKSTRAP
JOCKTELEG
JOCKY
JOCO
JOCOS
JOCOSE
JOCOSELY
JOCOSER
JOCOSEST
JOCOSITY
JOCULAR
JOCULARLY
JOCULATOR
JOCUND
JOCUNDER
JOCUNDEST
JOCUNDITY
JOCUNDLY
JODEL
JODELLED
JODELLING
JODELS
JODHPUR
JODHPURS
JOE
JOES
JOEY
JOEYS
JOG
JOGGED
JOGGER
JOGGERS
JOGGING

JOGGINGS
JOGGLE
JOGGLED
JOGGLER
JOGGLERS
JOGGLES
JOGGLING
JOGPANTS
JOGS
JOGTROT
JOGTROTS
JOHANNES
JOHN
JOHNBOAT
JOHNBOATS
JOHNNIE
JOHNNIES
JOHNNY
JOHNS
JOHNSON
JOHNSONS
JOIN
JOINABLE
JOINDER
JOINDERS
JOINED
JOINER
JOINERIES
JOINERS
JOINERY
JOINING
JOININGS
JOINS
JOINT
JOINTED
JOINTEDLY
JOINTER
JOINTERS
JOINTING
JOINTINGS
JOINTLESS
JOINTLY
JOINTNESS
JOINTRESS
JOINTS
JOINTURE
JOINTURED
JOINTURES
JOINTWEED
JOINTWORM
JOIST
JOISTED
JOISTING
JOISTS
JOJOBA
JOJOBAS
JOKE
JOKED
JOKER
JOKERS
JOKES
JOKESMITH
JOKESOME
JOKESTER
JOKESTERS
JOKEY
JOKIER
JOKIEST
JOKILY
JOKINESS
JOKING
JOKINGLY
JOKINGS
JOKOL
JOKY
JOL
JOLE
JOLED
JOLES
JOLING
JOLIOTIUM
JOLL
JOLLED
JOLLER
JOLLERS
JOLLEY
JOLLEYER
JOLLEYERS
JOLLEYING
JOLLEYS
JOLLIED
JOLLIER
JOLLIERS
JOLLIES
JOLLIEST
JOLLIFIED
JOLLIFIES
JOLLIFY
JOLLILY
JOLLIMENT
JOLLINESS
JOLLING
JOLLITIES
JOLLITY
JOLLOF
JOLLOP
JOLLOPS
JOLLS
JOLLY
JOLLYBOAT
JOLLYER
JOLLYERS
JOLLYHEAD
JOLLYING
JOLLYINGS
JOLS
JOLT
JOLTED
JOLTER
JOLTERS
JOLTHEAD
JOLTHEADS
JOLTIER
JOLTIEST
JOLTILY
JOLTING
JOLTINGLY
JOLTINGS
JOLTS
JOLTY
JOMO
JOMON
JOMONS
JOMOS
JONCANOE
JONCANOES
JONES
JONESED
JONESES
JONESING
JONG
JONGLEUR
JONGLEURS
JONGS
JONNOCK
JONNYCAKE
JONQUIL
JONQUILS
JONTIES
JONTY
JOOK
JOOKED
JOOKERIES
JOOKERY
JOOKING
JOOKS
JOR
JORAM
JORAMS
JORDAN
JORDANS
JORDELOO
JORDELOOS
JORS
JORUM
JORUMS
JOSEPH
JOSEPHS
JOSH
JOSHED
JOSHER
JOSHERS
JOSHES
JOSHING
JOSHINGLY
JOSHINGS
JOSKIN
JOSKINS
JOSS
JOSSER
JOSSERS
JOSSES
JOSTLE
JOSTLED
JOSTLER
JOSTLERS
JOSTLES
JOSTLING
JOSTLINGS
JOT
JOTA
JOTAS
JOTS
JOTTED
JOTTER
JOTTERS
JOTTIER
JOTTIEST
JOTTING
JOTTINGS
JOTTY
JOTUN
JOTUNN
JOTUNNS
JOTUNS
JOUAL
JOUALS
JOUGS
JOUISANCE
JOUK
JOUKED
JOUKERIES
JOUKERY
JOUKING
JOUKS
JOULE
JOULED
JOULES
JOULING
JOUNCE
JOUNCED
JOUNCES
JOUNCIER
JOUNCIEST
JOUNCING
JOUNCY
JOUR
JOURNAL
JOURNALED
JOURNALS
JOURNEY
JOURNEYED
JOURNEYER
JOURNEYS
JOURNO
JOURNOS
JOURS
JOUST
JOUSTED
JOUSTER

JOUSTERS
JOUSTING
JOUSTINGS
JOUSTS
JOVIAL
JOVIALITY
JOVIALLY
JOVIALTY
JOW
JOWAR
JOWARI
JOWARIS
JOWARS
JOWED
JOWING
JOWL
JOWLED
JOWLER
JOWLERS
JOWLIER
JOWLIEST
JOWLINESS
JOWLING
JOWLS
JOWLY
JOWS
JOY
JOYANCE
JOYANCES
JOYED
JOYFUL
JOYFULLER
JOYFULLY
JOYING
JOYLESS
JOYLESSLY
JOYOUS
JOYOUSLY
JOYPAD
JOYPADS
JOYPOP
JOYPOPPED
JOYPOPPER
JOYPOPS
JOYRIDDEN
JOYRIDE
JOYRIDER
JOYRIDERS
JOYRIDES
JOYRIDING
JOYRODE
JOYS
JOYSTICK
JOYSTICKS
JUBA
JUBAS
JUBATE
JUBBAH
JUBBAHS
JUBE
JUBES
JUBHAH
JUBHAHS
JUBILANCE
JUBILANCY
JUBILANT
JUBILATE
JUBILATED
JUBILATES
JUBILE
JUBILEE
JUBILEES
JUBILES
JUCO
JUCOS
JUD
JUDAS
JUDASES
JUDDER
JUDDERED
JUDDERIER
JUDDERING
JUDDERS
JUDDERY
JUDGE
JUDGEABLE
JUDGED
JUDGELESS
JUDGELIKE
JUDGEMENT
JUDGER
JUDGERS
JUDGES
JUDGESHIP
JUDGEY
JUDGIER
JUDGIEST
JUDGING
JUDGINGLY
JUDGINGS
JUDGMATIC
JUDGMENT
JUDGMENTS
JUDGY
JUDICABLE
JUDICARE
JUDICARES
JUDICATOR
JUDICIAL
JUDICIARY
JUDICIOUS
JUDIES
JUDO
JUDOGI
JUDOGIS
JUDOIST
JUDOISTS
JUDOKA
JUDOKAS
JUDOS
JUDS
JUDY
JUG
JUGA
JUGAAD
JUGAADS
JUGAL
JUGALS
JUGATE
JUGFUL
JUGFULS
JUGGED
JUGGING
JUGGINGS
JUGGINS
JUGGINSES
JUGGLE
JUGGLED
JUGGLER
JUGGLERS
JUGGLERY
JUGGLES
JUGGLING
JUGGLINGS
JUGHEAD
JUGHEADS
JUGLET
JUGLETS
JUGS
JUGSFUL
JUGULA
JUGULAR
JUGULARS
JUGULATE
JUGULATED
JUGULATES
JUGULUM
JUGUM
JUGUMS
JUICE
JUICED
JUICEHEAD
JUICELESS
JUICER
JUICERS
JUICES
JUICIER
JUICIEST
JUICILY
JUICINESS
JUICING
JUICY
JUJITSU
JUJITSUS
JUJU
JUJUBE
JUJUBES
JUJUISM
JUJUISMS
JUJUIST
JUJUISTS
JUJUS
JUJUTSU
JUJUTSUS
JUKE
JUKEBOX
JUKEBOXES
JUKED
JUKES
JUKING
JUKSKEI
JUKSKEIS
JUKU
JUKUS
JULEP
JULEPS
JULIENNE
JULIENNED
JULIENNES
JULIET
JULIETS
JUMAR
JUMARED
JUMARING
JUMARRED
JUMARRING
JUMARS
JUMART
JUMARTS
JUMBAL
JUMBALS
JUMBIE
JUMBIES
JUMBLE
JUMBLED
JUMBLER
JUMBLERS
JUMBLES
JUMBLIER
JUMBLIEST
JUMBLING
JUMBLY
JUMBO
JUMBOISE
JUMBOISED
JUMBOISES
JUMBOIZE
JUMBOIZED
JUMBOIZES
JUMBOS
JUMBUCK
JUMBUCKS
JUMBY
JUMELLE
JUMELLES
JUMP
JUMPABLE
JUMPED
JUMPER
JUMPERS

JUMPIER
JUMPIEST
JUMPILY
JUMPINESS
JUMPING
JUMPINGLY
JUMPINGS
JUMPOFF
JUMPOFFS
JUMPROPE
JUMPROPES
JUMPS
JUMPSHOT
JUMPSHOTS
JUMPSIES
JUMPSUIT
JUMPSUITS
JUMPY
JUN
JUNCATE
JUNCATES
JUNCO
JUNCOES
JUNCOS
JUNCTION
JUNCTIONS
JUNCTURAL
JUNCTURE
JUNCTURES
JUNCUS
JUNCUSES
JUNEATING
JUNGLE
JUNGLED
JUNGLEGYM
JUNGLES
JUNGLI
JUNGLIER
JUNGLIEST
JUNGLIS
JUNGLIST
JUNGLISTS
JUNGLY
JUNIOR
JUNIORATE
JUNIORED
JUNIORING
JUNIORITY
JUNIORS
JUNIPER
JUNIPERS
JUNK
JUNKANOO
JUNKANOOS
JUNKED
JUNKER
JUNKERDOM
JUNKERS
JUNKET
JUNKETED
JUNKETEER
JUNKETER
JUNKETERS
JUNKETING
JUNKETS
JUNKETTED
JUNKETTER
JUNKIE
JUNKIER
JUNKIES
JUNKIEST
JUNKINESS
JUNKING
JUNKMAN
JUNKMEN
JUNKS
JUNKY
JUNKYARD
JUNKYARDS
JUNTA
JUNTAS
JUNTO
JUNTOS
JUPATI
JUPATIS
JUPE
JUPES
JUPON
JUPONS
JURA
JURAL
JURALLY
JURANT
JURANTS
JURASSIC
JURAT
JURATORY
JURATS
JURE
JUREL
JURELS
JURES
JURIDIC
JURIDICAL
JURIED
JURIES
JURIST
JURISTIC
JURISTS
JUROR
JURORS
JURY
JURYING
JURYLESS
JURYMAN
JURYMAST
JURYMASTS
JURYMEN
JURYWOMAN
JURYWOMEN
JUS
JUSSIVE
JUSSIVES
JUST
JUSTED
JUSTER
JUSTERS
JUSTEST
JUSTICE
JUSTICER
JUSTICERS
JUSTICES
JUSTICIAR
JUSTIFIED
JUSTIFIER
JUSTIFIES
JUSTIFY
JUSTING
JUSTLE
JUSTLED
JUSTLES
JUSTLING
JUSTLY
JUSTNESS
JUSTS
JUT
JUTE
JUTELIKE
JUTES
JUTS
JUTTED
JUTTIED
JUTTIER
JUTTIES
JUTTIEST
JUTTING
JUTTINGLY
JUTTY
JUTTYING
JUVE
JUVENAL
JUVENALS
JUVENILE
JUVENILES
JUVENILIA
JUVES
JUVIE
JUVIES
JUXTAPOSE
JYMOLD
JYNX
JYNXES

K

KA
KAAL
KAAMA
KAAMAS
KAAS
KAB
KABAB
KABABBED
KABABBING
KABABS
KABADDI
KABADDIS
KABAKA
KABAKAS
KABALA
KABALAS
KABALISM
KABALISMS
KABALIST
KABALISTS
KABAR
KABARS
KABAYA
KABAYAS
KABBALA
KABBALAH
KABBALAHS
KABBALAS
KABBALISM
KABBALIST
KABELE
KABELES
KABELJOU
KABELJOUS
KABELJOUW
KABIKI
KABIKIS
KABLOOEY
KABLOOIE
KABLOONA
KABLOONAS
KABLOONAT
KABOB
KABOBBED
KABOBBING
KABOBS
KABOCHA
KABOCHAS
KABOODLE
KABOODLES
KABOOM
KABOOMS
KABS
KABUKI
KABUKIS
KACCHA
KACCHAS
KACHA
KACHAHRI
KACHAHRIS
KACHCHA
KACHERI
KACHERIS
KACHINA
KACHINAS
KACHORI
KACHORIS
KACHUMBER
KACK
KACKS
KADAI
KADAIS
KADAITCHA
KADDISH
KADDISHES
KADDISHIM
KADE
KADES
KADI
KADIS
KAE
KAED
KAEING
KAES
KAF
KAFFIYAH
KAFFIYAHS
KAFFIYEH
KAFFIYEHS
KAFILA
KAFILAS
KAFS
KAFTAN
KAFTANS
KAFUFFLE
KAFUFFLES
KAGO
KAGOOL
KAGOOLS
KAGOS
KAGOUL
KAGOULE
KAGOULES
KAGOULS
KAGU
KAGUS
KAHAL
KAHALS
KAHAWAI
KAHAWAIS
KAHIKATEA
KAHIKATOA
KAHUNA
KAHUNAS
KAI
KAIAK
KAIAKED
KAIAKING
KAIAKS
KAID
KAIDS
KAIE
KAIES
KAIF
KAIFS
KAIK
KAIKA
KAIKAI
KAIKAIS
KAIKAS
KAIKAWAKA
KAIKOMAKO
KAIKS
KAIL
KAILS
KAILYAIRD
KAILYARD
KAILYARDS
KAIM
KAIMAKAM
KAIMAKAMS
KAIMS
KAIN
KAING
KAINGA
KAINGAS
KAINIT
KAINITE
KAINITES
KAINITS
KAINS
KAIROMONE
KAIS
KAISER
KAISERDOM
KAISERIN
KAISERINS
KAISERISM
KAISERS
KAIZEN
KAIZENS
KAJAWAH
KAJAWAHS
KAJEPUT
KAJEPUTS
KAK
KAKA
KAKAPO
KAKAPOS
KAKARIKI
KAKARIKIS
KAKAS
KAKEMONO
KAKEMONOS
KAKI
KAKIEMON
KAKIEMONS
KAKIS
KAKIVAK
KAKIVAKS
KAKODYL
KAKODYLS
KAKS
KAKURO
KAKUROS
KALAM
KALAMANSI
KALAMATA
KALAMATAS
KALAMDAN
KALAMDANS
KALAMKARI
KALAMS
KALANCHOE
KALE
KALENDAR
KALENDARS
KALENDS
KALES
KALEWIFE
KALEWIVES
KALEYARD
KALEYARDS
KALI
KALIAN
KALIANS
KALIF
KALIFATE
KALIFATES
KALIFS

K

KALIMBA
KALIMBAS
KALINITE
KALINITES
KALIPH
KALIPHATE
KALIPHS
KALIS
KALIUM
KALIUMS
KALLIDIN
KALLIDINS
KALLITYPE
KALMIA
KALMIAS
KALONG
KALONGS
KALOOKI
KALOOKIE
KALOOKIES
KALOOKIS
KALOTYPE
KALOTYPES
KALPA
KALPAC
KALPACS
KALPAK
KALPAKS
KALPAS
KALPIS
KALPISES
KALSOMINE
KALUKI
KALUKIS
KALUMPIT
KALUMPITS
KALYPTRA
KALYPTRAS
KAM
KAMA
KAMAAINA
KAMAAINAS
KAMACITE
KAMACITES
KAMAHI
KAMAHIS
KAMALA
KAMALAS
KAMAS
KAME
KAMEES
KAMEESES
KAMEEZ
KAMEEZES
KAMELA
KAMELAS
KAMERAD
KAMERADED
KAMERADS
KAMES
KAMI
KAMICHI
KAMICHIS
KAMIK
KAMIKAZE
KAMIKAZES
KAMIKS
KAMILA
KAMILAS
KAMIS
KAMISES
KAMME
KAMOKAMO
KAMOKAMOS
KAMOTIK
KAMOTIKS
KAMOTIQ
KAMOTIQS
KAMPONG
KAMPONGS
KAMSEEN
KAMSEENS
KAMSIN
KAMSINS
KANA
KANAE
KANAES
KANAMYCIN
KANAS
KANBAN
KANBANS
KANDIES
KANDY
KANE
KANEH
KANEHS
KANES
KANG
KANGA
KANGAROO
KANGAROOS
KANGAS
KANGHA
KANGHAS
KANGS
KANJI
KANJIS
KANS
KANSES
KANT
KANTAR
KANTARS
KANTED
KANTELA
KANTELAS
KANTELE
KANTELES
KANTEN
KANTENS
KANTHA
KANTHAS
KANTIKOY
KANTIKOYS
KANTING
KANTS
KANUKA
KANUKAS
KANZU
KANZUS
KAOLIANG
KAOLIANGS
KAOLIN
KAOLINE
KAOLINES
KAOLINIC
KAOLINISE
KAOLINITE
KAOLINIZE
KAOLINS
KAON
KAONIC
KAONS
KAPA
KAPAS
KAPEEK
KAPEYKA
KAPH
KAPHS
KAPOK
KAPOKS
KAPOW
KAPOWS
KAPPA
KAPPAS
KAPU
KAPUKA
KAPUKAS
KAPUS
KAPUT
KAPUTT
KARA
KARABINER
KARAHI
KARAHIS
KARAISM
KARAISMS
KARAIT
KARAITS
KARAKA
KARAKAS
KARAKIA
KARAKIAS
KARAKUL
KARAKULS
KARAMU
KARAMUS
KARANGA
KARANGAED
KARANGAS
KARAOKE
KARAOKES
KARAS
KARAT
KARATE
KARATEIST
KARATEKA
KARATEKAS
KARATES
KARATS
KAREAREA
KAREAREAS
KARENGO
KARENGOS
KARITE
KARITES
KARK
KARKED
KARKING
KARKS
KARMA
KARMAS
KARMIC
KARN
KARNS
KARO
KAROO
KAROOS
KARORO
KAROROS
KAROS
KAROSHI
KAROSHIS
KAROSS
KAROSSES
KARRI
KARRIS
KARROO
KARROOS
KARSEY
KARSEYS
KARSIES
KARST
KARSTIC
KARSTIFY
KARSTS
KARSY
KART
KARTER
KARTERS
KARTING
KARTINGS
KARTS
KARYOGAMY
KARYOGRAM
KARYOLOGY
KARYON
KARYONS
KARYOSOME
KARYOTIN
KARYOTINS

KARYOTYPE
KARZIES
KARZY
KAS
KASBAH
KASBAHS
KASHA
KASHAS
KASHER
KASHERED
KASHERING
KASHERS
KASHMIR
KASHMIRS
KASHRUS
KASHRUSES
KASHRUT
KASHRUTH
KASHRUTHS
KASHRUTS
KASME
KAT
KATA
KATABASES
KATABASIS
KATABATIC
KATABOLIC
KATAKANA
KATAKANAS
KATAL
KATALS
KATANA
KATANAS
KATAS
KATCHINA
KATCHINAS
KATCINA
KATCINAS
KATHAK
KATHAKALI
KATHAKS
KATHARSES
KATHARSIS
KATHODAL
KATHODE
KATHODES
KATHODIC
KATHUMP
KATHUMPS
KATI
KATION
KATIONS
KATIPO
KATIPOS
KATIS
KATORGA
KATORGAS
KATS
KATSINA
KATSINAM
KATSINAS
KATSURA
KATSURAS
KATTI
KATTIS
KATYDID
KATYDIDS
KAUGH
KAUGHS
KAUMATUA
KAUMATUAS
KAUPAPA
KAUPAPAS
KAURI
KAURIES
KAURIS
KAURU
KAURUS
KAURY
KAVA
KAVAKAVA
KAVAKAVAS
KAVAL
KAVALS
KAVAS
KAVASS
KAVASSES
KAW
KAWA
KAWAII
KAWAIIS
KAWAKAWA
KAWAKAWAS
KAWAS
KAWAU
KAWAUS
KAWED
KAWING
KAWS
KAY
KAYAK
KAYAKED
KAYAKER
KAYAKERS
KAYAKING
KAYAKINGS
KAYAKS
KAYLE
KAYLES
KAYLIED
KAYO
KAYOED
KAYOES
KAYOING
KAYOINGS
KAYOS
KAYS
KAZACHKI
KAZACHOC
KAZACHOCS
KAZACHOK
KAZACHOKS
KAZATSKI
KAZATSKY
KAZATZKA
KAZATZKAS
KAZI
KAZILLION
KAZIS
KAZOO
KAZOOS
KBAR
KBARS
KEA
KEAS
KEASAR
KEASARS
KEAVIE
KEAVIES
KEB
KEBAB
KEBABBED
KEBABBING
KEBABS
KEBAR
KEBARS
KEBBED
KEBBIE
KEBBIES
KEBBING
KEBBOCK
KEBBOCKS
KEBBUCK
KEBBUCKS
KEBELE
KEBELES
KEBLAH
KEBLAHS
KEBOB
KEBOBBED
KEBOBBING
KEBOBS
KEBS
KECK
KECKED
KECKING
KECKLE
KECKLED
KECKLES
KECKLING
KECKLINGS
KECKS
KECKSES
KECKSIES
KECKSY
KED
KEDDAH
KEDDAHS
KEDGE
KEDGED
KEDGER
KEDGEREE
KEDGEREES
KEDGERS
KEDGES
KEDGIER
KEDGIEST
KEDGING
KEDGY
KEDS
KEECH
KEECHES
KEEF
KEEFS
KEEK
KEEKED
KEEKER
KEEKERS
KEEKING
KEEKS
KEEL
KEELAGE
KEELAGES
KEELBOAT
KEELBOATS
KEELED
KEELER
KEELERS
KEELHALE
KEELHALED
KEELHALES
KEELHAUL
KEELHAULS
KEELIE
KEELIES
KEELING
KEELINGS
KEELIVINE
KEELLESS
KEELMAN
KEELMEN
KEELS
KEELSON
KEELSONS
KEELYVINE
KEEMA
KEEMAS
KEEN
KEENED
KEENER
KEENERS
KEENEST
KEENING
KEENINGS
KEENLY
KEENNESS
KEENO
KEENOS
KEENS
KEEP

KEEPABLE
KEEPER
KEEPERS
KEEPING
KEEPINGS
KEEPNET
KEEPNETS
KEEPS
KEEPSAKE
KEEPSAKES
KEEPSAKY
KEESHOND
KEESHONDS
KEESTER
KEESTERS
KEET
KEETS
KEEVE
KEEVES
KEF
KEFFEL
KEFFELS
KEFFIYAH
KEFFIYAHS
KEFFIYEH
KEFFIYEHS
KEFIR
KEFIRS
KEFS
KEFTEDES
KEFUFFLE
KEFUFFLED
KEFUFFLES
KEG
KEGELER
KEGELERS
KEGGED
KEGGER
KEGGERS
KEGGING
KEGLER
KEGLERS
KEGLING
KEGLINGS
KEGS
KEHUA
KEHUAS
KEIGHT
KEIR
KEIREN
KEIRENS
KEIRETSU
KEIRETSUS
KEIRIN
KEIRINS
KEIRS
KEISTER
KEISTERS
KEITLOA
KEITLOAS
KEKENO
KEKENOS
KEKERENGU
KEKS
KEKSYE
KEKSYES
KELEP
KELEPS
KELIM
KELIMS
KELL
KELLAUT
KELLAUTS
KELLIES
KELLS
KELLY
KELOID
KELOIDAL
KELOIDS
KELP
KELPED
KELPER
KELPERS
KELPFISH
KELPIE
KELPIES
KELPING
KELPS
KELPY
KELSON
KELSONS
KELT
KELTER
KELTERS
KELTIE
KELTIES
KELTS
KELTY
KELVIN
KELVINS
KEMB
KEMBED
KEMBING
KEMBLA
KEMBLAS
KEMBO
KEMBOED
KEMBOING
KEMBOS
KEMBS
KEMP
KEMPED
KEMPER
KEMPERS
KEMPIER
KEMPIEST
KEMPING
KEMPINGS
KEMPLE
KEMPLES
KEMPS
KEMPT
KEMPY
KEN
KENAF
KENAFS
KENCH
KENCHES
KENDO
KENDOIST
KENDOISTS
KENDOS
KENNED
KENNEL
KENNELED
KENNELING
KENNELLED
KENNELMAN
KENNELMEN
KENNELS
KENNER
KENNERS
KENNET
KENNETS
KENNETT
KENNETTED
KENNETTS
KENNING
KENNINGS
KENO
KENOS
KENOSES
KENOSIS
KENOSISES
KENOTIC
KENOTICS
KENOTRON
KENOTRONS
KENS
KENSPECK
KENT
KENTE
KENTED
KENTES
KENTIA
KENTIAS
KENTING
KENTLEDGE
KENTS
KEP
KEPHALIC
KEPHALICS
KEPHALIN
KEPHALINS
KEPHIR
KEPHIRS
KEPI
KEPIS
KEPPED
KEPPEN
KEPPING
KEPPIT
KEPS
KEPT
KERAMIC
KERAMICS
KERATIN
KERATINS
KERATITIS
KERATOID
KERATOMA
KERATOMAS
KERATOSE
KERATOSES
KERATOSIC
KERATOSIS
KERATOTIC
KERB
KERBAYA
KERBAYAS
KERBED
KERBING
KERBINGS
KERBLOOEY
KERBS
KERBSIDE
KERBSIDES
KERBSTONE
KERCHIEF
KERCHIEFS
KERCHOO
KEREL
KERELS
KERERU
KERERUS
KERF
KERFED
KERFING
KERFLOOEY
KERFS
KERFUFFLE
KERKIER
KERKIEST
KERKY
KERMA
KERMAS
KERMES
KERMESES
KERMESITE
KERMESS
KERMESSE
KERMESSES
KERMIS
KERMISES
KERMODE
KERMODES
KERN
KERNE
KERNED
KERNEL

KERNELED
KERNELING
KERNELLED
KERNELLY
KERNELS
KERNES
KERNING
KERNINGS
KERNISH
KERNITE
KERNITES
KERNS
KERO
KEROGEN
KEROGENS
KEROS
KEROSENE
KEROSENES
KEROSINE
KEROSINES
KERPLUNK
KERPLUNKS
KERRIA
KERRIAS
KERRIES
KERRY
KERSEY
KERSEYS
KERVE
KERVED
KERVES
KERVING
KERYGMA
KERYGMAS
KERYGMATA
KESAR
KESARS
KESH
KESHES
KEST
KESTING
KESTREL
KESTRELS
KESTS
KET
KETA
KETAINE
KETAMINE
KETAMINES
KETAS
KETCH
KETCHES
KETCHING
KETCHUP
KETCHUPS
KETCHUPY
KETE
KETENE
KETENES
KETES
KETMIA
KETMIAS
KETO
KETOGENIC
KETOL
KETOLS
KETONE
KETONEMIA
KETONES
KETONIC
KETONURIA
KETOSE
KETOSES
KETOSIS
KETOTIC
KETOXIME
KETOXIMES
KETS
KETTLE
KETTLED
KETTLEFUL
KETTLES
KETTLING
KETUBAH
KETUBAHS
KETUBOT
KETUBOTH
KEVEL
KEVELS
KEVIL
KEVILS
KEWL
KEWLER
KEWLEST
KEWPIE
KEWPIES
KEX
KEXES
KEY
KEYBOARD
KEYBOARDS
KEYBUGLE
KEYBUGLES
KEYBUTTON
KEYCARD
KEYCARDS
KEYED
KEYER
KEYERS
KEYEST
KEYFRAME
KEYFRAMES
KEYHOLE
KEYHOLES
KEYING
KEYINGS
KEYLESS
KEYLINE
KEYLINES
KEYLOGGER
KEYNOTE
KEYNOTED
KEYNOTER
KEYNOTERS
KEYNOTES
KEYNOTING
KEYPAD
KEYPADS
KEYPAL
KEYPALS
KEYPRESS
KEYPUNCH
KEYRING
KEYRINGS
KEYS
KEYSET
KEYSETS
KEYSTER
KEYSTERS
KEYSTONE
KEYSTONED
KEYSTONES
KEYSTROKE
KEYWAY
KEYWAYS
KEYWORD
KEYWORDS
KEYWORKER
KGOTLA
KGOTLAS
KHADDAR
KHADDARS
KHADI
KHADIS
KHAF
KHAFS
KHAKI
KHAKILIKE
KHAKIS
KHALAT
KHALATS
KHALIF
KHALIFA
KHALIFAH
KHALIFAHS
KHALIFAS
KHALIFAT
KHALIFATE
KHALIFATS
KHALIFS
KHAMSEEN
KHAMSEENS
KHAMSIN
KHAMSINS
KHAN
KHANATE
KHANATES
KHANDA
KHANDAS
KHANGA
KHANGAS
KHANJAR
KHANJARS
KHANS
KHANSAMA
KHANSAMAH
KHANSAMAS
KHANUM
KHANUMS
KHAPH
KHAPHS
KHARIF
KHARIFS
KHAT
KHATS
KHAYA
KHAYAL
KHAYALS
KHAYAS
KHAZEN
KHAZENIM
KHAZENS
KHAZI
KHAZIS
KHEDA
KHEDAH
KHEDAHS
KHEDAS
KHEDIVA
KHEDIVAL
KHEDIVAS
KHEDIVATE
KHEDIVE
KHEDIVES
KHEDIVIAL
KHET
KHETH
KHETHS
KHETS
KHI
KHILAFAT
KHILAFATS
KHILAT
KHILATS
KHILIM
KHILIMS
KHIMAR
KHIMARS
KHIRKAH
KHIRKAHS
KHIS
KHODJA
KHODJAS
KHOJA
KHOJAS
KHOR
KHORS
KHOTBAH
KHOTBAHS
KHOTBEH

KHOTBEHS
KHOUM
KHOUMS
KHUD
KHUDS
KHURTA
KHURTAS
KHUSKHUS
KHUTBAH
KHUTBAHS
KI
KIAAT
KIAATS
KIACK
KIACKS
KIANG
KIANGS
KIAUGH
KIAUGHS
KIBBE
KIBBEH
KIBBEHS
KIBBES
KIBBI
KIBBIS
KIBBITZ
KIBBITZED
KIBBITZER
KIBBITZES
KIBBLE
KIBBLED
KIBBLES
KIBBLING
KIBBUTZ
KIBBUTZIM
KIBE
KIBEI
KIBEIS
KIBES
KIBIBYTE
KIBIBYTES
KIBITKA
KIBITKAS
KIBITZ
KIBITZED
KIBITZER
KIBITZERS
KIBITZES
KIBITZING
KIBLA
KIBLAH
KIBLAHS
KIBLAS
KIBOSH
KIBOSHED
KIBOSHES
KIBOSHING
KICK
KICKABLE
KICKABOUT
KICKBACK
KICKBACKS
KICKBALL
KICKBALLS
KICKBOARD
KICKBOX
KICKBOXED
KICKBOXER
KICKBOXES
KICKDOWN
KICKDOWNS
KICKED
KICKER
KICKERS
KICKFLIP
KICKFLIPS
KICKIER
KICKIEST
KICKING
KICKINGS
KICKOFF
KICKOFFS
KICKOUT
KICKOUTS
KICKPLATE
KICKS
KICKSHAW
KICKSHAWS
KICKSTAND
KICKSTART
KICKUP
KICKUPS
KICKY
KID
KIDDED
KIDDER
KIDDERS
KIDDIE
KIDDIED
KIDDIER
KIDDIERS
KIDDIES
KIDDING
KIDDINGLY
KIDDINGS
KIDDISH
KIDDLE
KIDDLES
KIDDO
KIDDOES
KIDDOS
KIDDUSH
KIDDUSHES
KIDDY
KIDDYING
KIDDYWINK
KIDEL
KIDELS
KIDGE
KIDGIE
KIDGIER
KIDGIEST
KIDGLOVE
KIDLET
KIDLETS
KIDLIKE
KIDLING
KIDLINGS
KIDLIT
KIDLITS
KIDNAP
KIDNAPED
KIDNAPEE
KIDNAPEES
KIDNAPER
KIDNAPERS
KIDNAPING
KIDNAPPED
KIDNAPPEE
KIDNAPPER
KIDNAPS
KIDNEY
KIDNEYS
KIDOLOGY
KIDS
KIDSKIN
KIDSKINS
KIDSTAKES
KIDULT
KIDULTS
KIDVID
KIDVIDS
KIEF
KIEFS
KIEKIE
KIEKIES
KIELBASA
KIELBASAS
KIELBASI
KIELBASY
KIER
KIERIE
KIERIES
KIERS
KIESELGUR
KIESERITE
KIESTER
KIESTERS
KIEV
KIEVE
KIEVES
KIEVS
KIF
KIFF
KIFS
KIGHT
KIGHTS
KIKOI
KIKOIS
KIKUMON
KIKUMONS
KIKUYU
KIKUYUS
KILD
KILDERKIN
KILERG
KILERGS
KILEY
KILEYS
KILIKITI
KILIKITIS
KILIM
KILIMS
KILL
KILLABLE
KILLADAR
KILLADARS
KILLAS
KILLASES
KILLCOW
KILLCOWS
KILLCROP
KILLCROPS
KILLDEE
KILLDEER
KILLDEERS
KILLDEES
KILLED
KILLER
KILLERS
KILLICK
KILLICKS
KILLIE
KILLIES
KILLIFISH
KILLING
KILLINGLY
KILLINGS
KILLJOY
KILLJOYS
KILLOCK
KILLOCKS
KILLOGIE
KILLOGIES
KILLS
KILLUT
KILLUTS
KILN
KILNED
KILNING
KILNS
KILO
KILOBAR
KILOBARS
KILOBASE
KILOBASES
KILOBAUD
KILOBAUDS
KILOBIT
KILOBITS

KILOBYTE
KILOBYTES
KILOCURIE
KILOCYCLE
KILOGAUSS
KILOGRAM
KILOGRAMS
KILOGRAY
KILOGRAYS
KILOHERTZ
KILOJOULE
KILOLITER
KILOLITRE
KILOMETER
KILOMETRE
KILOMOLE
KILOMOLES
KILOPOND
KILOPONDS
KILORAD
KILORADS
KILOS
KILOTON
KILOTONNE
KILOTONS
KILOVOLT
KILOVOLTS
KILOWATT
KILOWATTS
KILP
KILPS
KILT
KILTED
KILTER
KILTERS
KILTIE
KILTIES
KILTING
KILTINGS
KILTLIKE
KILTS
KILTY
KIMBO
KIMBOED
KIMBOING
KIMBOS
KIMCHEE
KIMCHEES
KIMCHI
KIMCHIS
KIMMER
KIMMERS
KIMONO
KIMONOED
KIMONOS
KIN
KINA
KINAKINA
KINAKINAS
KINARA
KINARAS
KINAS
KINASE
KINASES
KINCHIN
KINCHINS
KINCOB
KINCOBS
KIND
KINDA
KINDED
KINDER
KINDERS
KINDEST
KINDIE
KINDIES
KINDING
KINDLE
KINDLED
KINDLER
KINDLERS
KINDLES
KINDLESS
KINDLIER
KINDLIEST
KINDLILY
KINDLING
KINDLINGS
KINDLY
KINDNESS
KINDRED
KINDREDS
KINDS
KINDY
KINE
KINEMA
KINEMAS
KINEMATIC
KINES
KINESCOPE
KINESES
KINESIC
KINESICS
KINESIS
KINESISES
KINETIC
KINETICAL
KINETICS
KINETIN
KINETINS
KINFOLK
KINFOLKS
KING
KINGBIRD
KINGBIRDS
KINGBOLT
KINGBOLTS
KINGCRAFT
KINGCUP
KINGCUPS
KINGDOM
KINGDOMED
KINGDOMS
KINGED
KINGFISH
KINGHOOD
KINGHOODS
KINGING
KINGKLIP
KINGKLIPS
KINGLE
KINGLES
KINGLESS
KINGLET
KINGLETS
KINGLIER
KINGLIEST
KINGLIKE
KINGLING
KINGLINGS
KINGLY
KINGMAKER
KINGPIN
KINGPINS
KINGPOST
KINGPOSTS
KINGS
KINGSHIP
KINGSHIPS
KINGSIDE
KINGSIDES
KINGSNAKE
KINGWOOD
KINGWOODS
KININ
KININS
KINK
KINKAJOU
KINKAJOUS
KINKED
KINKIER
KINKIEST
KINKILY
KINKINESS
KINKING
KINKLE
KINKLES
KINKS
KINKY
KINLESS
KINO
KINONE
KINONES
KINOS
KINRED
KINREDS
KINS
KINSFOLK
KINSFOLKS
KINSHIP
KINSHIPS
KINSMAN
KINSMEN
KINSWOMAN
KINSWOMEN
KINTLEDGE
KIORE
KIORES
KIOSK
KIOSKS
KIP
KIPE
KIPES
KIPP
KIPPA
KIPPAGE
KIPPAGES
KIPPAH
KIPPAHS
KIPPAS
KIPPED
KIPPEN
KIPPER
KIPPERED
KIPPERER
KIPPERERS
KIPPERING
KIPPERS
KIPPING
KIPPS
KIPS
KIPSKIN
KIPSKINS
KIPUNJI
KIPUNJIS
KIR
KIRANA
KIRANAS
KIRBEH
KIRBEHS
KIRBIGRIP
KIRBY
KIRIGAMI
KIRIGAMIS
KIRIMON
KIRIMONS
KIRK
KIRKED
KIRKING
KIRKINGS
KIRKMAN
KIRKMEN
KIRKS
KIRKTON
KIRKTONS
KIRKWARD
KIRKYAIRD
KIRKYARD
KIRKYARDS
KIRMESS

K

KIRMESSES
KIRN
KIRNED
KIRNING
KIRNS
KIRPAN
KIRPANS
KIRRI
KIRRIS
KIRS
KIRSCH
KIRSCHES
KIRTAN
KIRTANS
KIRTLE
KIRTLED
KIRTLES
KIS
KISAN
KISANS
KISH
KISHES
KISHKA
KISHKAS
KISHKE
KISHKES
KISKADEE
KISKADEES
KISMAT
KISMATS
KISMET
KISMETIC
KISMETS
KISS
KISSABLE
KISSABLY
KISSAGRAM
KISSED
KISSEL
KISSELS
KISSER
KISSERS
KISSES
KISSIER
KISSIEST
KISSING
KISSINGS
KISSOGRAM
KISSY
KIST
KISTED
KISTFUL
KISTFULS
KISTING
KISTS
KISTVAEN
KISTVAENS
KIT
KITBAG
KITBAGS
KITCHEN
KITCHENED
KITCHENER
KITCHENET
KITCHENS
KITE
KITEBOARD
KITED
KITELIKE
KITENGE
KITENGES
KITER
KITERS
KITES
KITH
KITHARA
KITHARAS
KITHE
KITHED
KITHES
KITHING
KITHS
KITING
KITINGS
KITLING
KITLINGS
KITS
KITSCH
KITSCHES
KITSCHIER
KITSCHIFY
KITSCHILY
KITSCHY
KITSET
KITSETS
KITTED
KITTEL
KITTELS
KITTEN
KITTENED
KITTENIER
KITTENING
KITTENISH
KITTENS
KITTENY
KITTIES
KITTING
KITTIWAKE
KITTLE
KITTLED
KITTLER
KITTLES
KITTLEST
KITTLIER
KITTLIEST
KITTLING
KITTLY
KITTUL
KITTULS
KITTY
KITUL
KITULS
KIVA
KIVAS
KIWI
KIWIFRUIT
KIWIS
KLANG
KLANGS
KLAP
KLAPPED
KLAPPING
KLAPS
KLATCH
KLATCHES
KLATSCH
KLATSCHES
KLAVERN
KLAVERNS
KLAVIER
KLAVIERS
KLAXON
KLAXONED
KLAXONING
KLAXONS
KLEAGLE
KLEAGLES
KLEENEX
KLEENEXES
KLEFTIKO
KLEFTIKOS
KLENDUSIC
KLEPHT
KLEPHTIC
KLEPHTISM
KLEPHTS
KLEPTO
KLEPTOS
KLETT
KLETTS
KLEZMER
KLEZMERS
KLEZMORIM
KLICK
KLICKS
KLIEG
KLIEGS
KLIK
KLIKS
KLINKER
KLINKERS
KLINOSTAT
KLIPDAS
KLIPDASES
KLISTER
KLISTERS
KLONDIKE
KLONDIKED
KLONDIKER
KLONDIKES
KLONDYKE
KLONDYKED
KLONDYKER
KLONDYKES
KLONG
KLONGS
KLOOCH
KLOOCHES
KLOOCHMAN
KLOOCHMEN
KLOOF
KLOOFS
KLOOTCH
KLOOTCHES
KLUDGE
KLUDGED
KLUDGES
KLUDGEY
KLUDGIER
KLUDGIEST
KLUDGING
KLUDGY
KLUGE
KLUGED
KLUGES
KLUGING
KLUTZ
KLUTZES
KLUTZIER
KLUTZIEST
KLUTZY
KLYSTRON
KLYSTRONS
KNACK
KNACKED
KNACKER
KNACKERED
KNACKERS
KNACKERY
KNACKIER
KNACKIEST
KNACKING
KNACKISH
KNACKS
KNACKY
KNAG
KNAGGIER
KNAGGIEST
KNAGGY
KNAGS
KNAIDEL
KNAIDELS
KNAIDLACH
KNAP
KNAPPED
KNAPPER
KNAPPERS
KNAPPING
KNAPPLE
KNAPPLED

KNAPPLES
KNAPPLING
KNAPS
KNAPSACK
KNAPSACKS
KNAPWEED
KNAPWEEDS
KNAR
KNARL
KNARLIER
KNARLIEST
KNARLS
KNARLY
KNARRED
KNARRIER
KNARRIEST
KNARRING
KNARRY
KNARS
KNAUR
KNAURS
KNAVE
KNAVERIES
KNAVERY
KNAVES
KNAVESHIP
KNAVISH
KNAVISHLY
KNAWE
KNAWEL
KNAWELS
KNAWES
KNEAD
KNEADABLE
KNEADED
KNEADER
KNEADERS
KNEADING
KNEADS
KNEE
KNEEBOARD
KNEECAP
KNEECAPS
KNEED
KNEEHOLE
KNEEHOLES
KNEEING
KNEEJERK
KNEEL
KNEELED
KNEELER
KNEELERS
KNEELIKE
KNEELING
KNEELS
KNEEPAD
KNEEPADS
KNEEPAN
KNEEPANS
KNEEPIECE
KNEEROOM
KNEEROOMS
KNEES
KNEESIES
KNEESOCK
KNEESOCKS
KNEIDEL
KNEIDELS
KNEIDLACH
KNELL
KNELLED
KNELLING
KNELLS
KNELT
KNESSET
KNESSETS
KNEVELL
KNEVELLED
KNEVELLS
KNEW
KNICKER
KNICKERED
KNICKERS
KNICKS
KNIFE
KNIFED
KNIFELESS
KNIFELIKE
KNIFEMAN
KNIFEMEN
KNIFER
KNIFEREST
KNIFERS
KNIFES
KNIFING
KNIFINGS
KNIGHT
KNIGHTAGE
KNIGHTED
KNIGHTING
KNIGHTLY
KNIGHTS
KNIPHOFIA
KNISH
KNISHES
KNIT
KNITBONE
KNITBONES
KNITCH
KNITCHES
KNITS
KNITTABLE
KNITTED
KNITTER
KNITTERS
KNITTING
KNITTINGS
KNITTLE
KNITTLES
KNITWEAR
KNITWEARS
KNIVE
KNIVED
KNIVES
KNIVING
KNOB
KNOBBED
KNOBBER
KNOBBERS
KNOBBIER
KNOBBIEST
KNOBBING
KNOBBLE
KNOBBLED
KNOBBLES
KNOBBLIER
KNOBBLING
KNOBBLY
KNOBBY
KNOBHEAD
KNOBHEADS
KNOBLIKE
KNOBS
KNOBSTICK
KNOCK
KNOCKBACK
KNOCKDOWN
KNOCKED
KNOCKER
KNOCKERS
KNOCKING
KNOCKINGS
KNOCKLESS
KNOCKOFF
KNOCKOFFS
KNOCKOUT
KNOCKOUTS
KNOCKS
KNOLL
KNOLLED
KNOLLER
KNOLLERS
KNOLLIER
KNOLLIEST
KNOLLING
KNOLLS
KNOLLY
KNOP
KNOPPED
KNOPS
KNOSP
KNOSPS
KNOT
KNOTGRASS
KNOTHEAD
KNOTHEADS
KNOTHOLE
KNOTHOLES
KNOTLESS
KNOTLIKE
KNOTS
KNOTTED
KNOTTER
KNOTTERS
KNOTTIER
KNOTTIEST
KNOTTILY
KNOTTING
KNOTTINGS
KNOTTY
KNOTWEED
KNOTWEEDS
KNOTWORK
KNOTWORKS
KNOUT
KNOUTED
KNOUTING
KNOUTS
KNOW
KNOWABLE
KNOWE
KNOWER
KNOWERS
KNOWES
KNOWHOW
KNOWHOWS
KNOWING
KNOWINGER
KNOWINGLY
KNOWINGS
KNOWLEDGE
KNOWN
KNOWNS
KNOWS
KNUB
KNUBBIER
KNUBBIEST
KNUBBLE
KNUBBLED
KNUBBLES
KNUBBLIER
KNUBBLING
KNUBBLY
KNUBBY
KNUBS
KNUCKLE
KNUCKLED
KNUCKLER
KNUCKLERS
KNUCKLES
KNUCKLIER
KNUCKLING
KNUCKLY
KNUR
KNURL
KNURLED
KNURLIER
KNURLIEST
KNURLING
KNURLINGS

K

KNURLS
KNURLY
KNURR
KNURRS
KNURS
KNUT
KNUTS
KO
KOA
KOALA
KOALAS
KOAN
KOANS
KOAP
KOAPS
KOAS
KOB
KOBAN
KOBANG
KOBANGS
KOBANS
KOBO
KOBOLD
KOBOLDS
KOBOS
KOBS
KOCHIA
KOCHIAS
KOEKOEA
KOEKOEAS
KOEL
KOELS
KOFF
KOFFS
KOFTA
KOFTAS
KOFTGAR
KOFTGARI
KOFTGARIS
KOFTGARS
KOFTWORK
KOFTWORKS
KOGAL
KOGALS
KOHA
KOHANIM
KOHAS
KOHEKOHE
KOHEKOHES
KOHEN
KOHL
KOHLRABI
KOHLRABIS
KOHLS
KOI
KOINE
KOINES
KOIS
KOJI
KOJIS
KOKA
KOKAKO
KOKAKOS
KOKAM
KOKAMS
KOKANEE
KOKANEES
KOKAS
KOKER
KOKERS
KOKIRI
KOKIRIS
KOKOBEH
KOKOPU
KOKOPUS
KOKOWAI
KOKOWAIS
KOKRA
KOKRAS
KOKUM
KOKUMS
KOLA
KOLACKIES
KOLACKY
KOLAS
KOLBASI
KOLBASIS
KOLBASSA
KOLBASSAS
KOLBASSI
KOLBASSIS
KOLHOZ
KOLHOZES
KOLHOZY
KOLINSKI
KOLINSKY
KOLKHOS
KOLKHOSES
KOLKHOSY
KOLKHOZ
KOLKHOZES
KOLKHOZY
KOLKOZ
KOLKOZES
KOLKOZY
KOLO
KOLOS
KOMATIK
KOMATIKS
KOMBU
KOMBUS
KOMISSAR
KOMISSARS
KOMITAJI
KOMITAJIS
KOMONDOR
KOMONDORS
KOMPROMAT
KON
KONAKI
KONAKIS
KONBU
KONBUS
KOND
KONDO
KONDOS
KONEKE
KONEKES
KONFYT
KONFYTS
KONGONI
KONIMETER
KONINI
KONINIS
KONIOLOGY
KONISCOPE
KONK
KONKED
KONKING
KONKS
KONNING
KONS
KOODOO
KOODOOS
KOOK
KOOKED
KOOKIE
KOOKIER
KOOKIEST
KOOKILY
KOOKINESS
KOOKING
KOOKS
KOOKUM
KOOKUMS
KOOKY
KOOLAH
KOOLAHS
KOORI
KOORIES
KOORIS
KOP
KOPASETIC
KOPECK
KOPECKS
KOPEK
KOPEKS
KOPH
KOPHS
KOPIYKA
KOPIYKAS
KOPIYKY
KOPIYOK
KOPJE
KOPJES
KOPPA
KOPPAS
KOPPIE
KOPPIES
KOPS
KOR
KORA
KORAI
KORARI
KORARIS
KORAS
KORAT
KORATS
KORE
KORERO
KOREROED
KOREROING
KOREROS
KORES
KORFBALL
KORFBALLS
KORIMAKO
KORIMAKOS
KORKIR
KORKIRS
KORMA
KORMAS
KORO
KOROMIKO
KOROMIKOS
KORORA
KORORAS
KOROS
KOROWAI
KOROWAIS
KORS
KORU
KORUN
KORUNA
KORUNAS
KORUNY
KORUS
KOS
KOSES
KOSHER
KOSHERED
KOSHERING
KOSHERS
KOSMOS
KOSMOSES
KOSS
KOSSES
KOTARE
KOTARES
KOTCH
KOTCHED
KOTCHES
KOTCHING
KOTO
KOTOS
KOTOW
KOTOWED
KOTOWER
KOTOWERS
KOTOWING

KOTOWS
KOTTABOS
KOTUKU
KOTUKUS
KOTWAL
KOTWALS
KOULAN
KOULANS
KOUMIS
KOUMISES
KOUMISS
KOUMISSES
KOUMYS
KOUMYSES
KOUMYSS
KOUMYSSES
KOUPREY
KOUPREYS
KOURA
KOURAS
KOURBASH
KOUROI
KOUROS
KOUSKOUS
KOUSSO
KOUSSOS
KOW
KOWHAI
KOWHAIS
KOWS
KOWTOW
KOWTOWED
KOWTOWER
KOWTOWERS
KOWTOWING
KOWTOWS
KRAAL
KRAALED
KRAALING
KRAALS
KRAB
KRABS
KRAFT
KRAFTS
KRAI
KRAIS
KRAIT
KRAITS
KRAKEN
KRAKENS
KRAKOWIAK
KRAMERIA
KRAMERIAS
KRANG
KRANGS
KRANS
KRANSES
KRANTZ
KRANTZES
KRANZ
KRANZES
KRATER
KRATERS
KRAUT
KRAUTROCK
KRAUTS
KRAY
KRAYS
KREASOTE
KREASOTED
KREASOTES
KREATINE
KREATINES
KREEP
KREEPS
KREESE
KREESED
KREESES
KREESING
KREMLIN
KREMLINS
KRENG
KRENGS
KREOSOTE
KREOSOTED
KREOSOTES
KREPLACH
KREPLECH
KREUTZER
KREUTZERS
KREUZER
KREUZERS
KREWE
KREWES
KRILL
KRILLS
KRIMMER
KRIMMERS
KRIS
KRISED
KRISES
KRISING
KROMESKY
KRONA
KRONE
KRONEN
KRONER
KRONOR
KRONUR
KROON
KROONI
KROONS
KRUBI
KRUBIS
KRUBUT
KRUBUTS
KRULLER
KRULLERS
KRUMHORN
KRUMHORNS
KRUMKAKE
KRUMKAKES
KRUMMHOLZ
KRUMMHORN
KRUMPER
KRUMPERS
KRUMPING
KRUMPINGS
KRUNK
KRUNKED
KRUNKS
KRYOLITE
KRYOLITES
KRYOLITH
KRYOLITHS
KRYOMETER
KRYPSES
KRYPSIS
KRYPTON
KRYPTONS
KRYTRON
KRYTRONS
KSAR
KSARS
KUBASA
KUBASAS
KUBIE
KUBIES
KUCCHA
KUCCHAS
KUCHCHA
KUCHEN
KUCHENS
KUDLIK
KUDLIKS
KUDO
KUDOS
KUDOSES
KUDU
KUDUS
KUDZU
KUDZUS
KUE
KUEH
KUES
KUFI
KUFIS
KUFIYAH
KUFIYAHS
KUGEL
KUGELS
KUIA
KUIAS
KUKRI
KUKRIS
KUKU
KUKUS
KULA
KULAK
KULAKI
KULAKS
KULAN
KULANS
KULAS
KULBASA
KULBASAS
KULFI
KULFIS
KULTUR
KULTURS
KUMARA
KUMARAHOU
KUMARAS
KUMARI
KUMARIS
KUMBALOI
KUMERA
KUMERAS
KUMIKUMI
KUMIKUMIS
KUMIS
KUMISES
KUMISS
KUMISSES
KUMITE
KUMITES
KUMKUM
KUMKUMS
KUMMEL
KUMMELS
KUMQUAT
KUMQUATS
KUMYS
KUMYSES
KUNA
KUNDALINI
KUNE
KUNEKUNE
KUNEKUNES
KUNJOOS
KUNKAR
KUNKARS
KUNKUR
KUNKURS
KUNZITE
KUNZITES
KURBASH
KURBASHED
KURBASHES
KURFUFFLE
KURGAN
KURGANS
KURI
KURIS
KURRAJONG
KURRE
KURRES
KURSAAL
KURSAALS
KURTA

K

KURTAS
KURTOSES
KURTOSIS
KURU
KURUS
KURUSH
KURUSHES
KURVEY
KURVEYED
KURVEYING
KURVEYOR
KURVEYORS
KURVEYS
KUSSO
KUSSOS
KUTA
KUTAS
KUTCH
KUTCHA
KUTCHES
KUTI
KUTIS
KUTU
KUTUS
KUVASZ
KUVASZOK
KUZU
KUZUS
KVAS
KVASES
KVASS
KVASSES
KVELL
KVELLED
KVELLING
KVELLS
KVETCH
KVETCHED
KVETCHER
KVETCHERS
KVETCHES
KVETCHIER
KVETCHILY
KVETCHING
KVETCHY
KWACHA
KWACHAS
KWAITO
KWAITOS
KWANZA
KWANZAS
KWELA
KWELAS
KY
KYACK
KYACKS
KYAK
KYAKS
KYANG
KYANGS
KYANISE
KYANISED
KYANISES
KYANISING
KYANITE
KYANITES
KYANITIC
KYANIZE
KYANIZED
KYANIZES
KYANIZING
KYAR
KYARS
KYAT
KYATS
KYBO
KYBOS
KYBOSH
KYBOSHED
KYBOSHES
KYBOSHING
KYDST
KYE
KYES
KYLE
KYLES
KYLICES
KYLIE
KYLIES
KYLIKES
KYLIN
KYLINS
KYLIX
KYLIXES
KYLLOSES
KYLLOSIS
KYLOE
KYLOES
KYMOGRAM
KYMOGRAMS
KYMOGRAPH
KYND
KYNDE
KYNDED
KYNDES
KYNDING
KYNDS
KYNE
KYOGEN
KYOGENS
KYPE
KYPES
KYPHOSES
KYPHOSIS
KYPHOTIC
KYRIE
KYRIELLE
KYRIELLES
KYRIES
KYTE
KYTES
KYTHE
KYTHED
KYTHES
KYTHING
KYU
KYUS

K

L

LA
LAAGER
LAAGERED
LAAGERING
LAAGERS
LAARI
LAARIS
LAB
LABARA
LABARUM
LABARUMS
LABDA
LABDACISM
LABDANUM
LABDANUMS
LABDAS
LABEL
LABELABLE
LABELED
LABELER
LABELERS
LABELING
LABELLA
LABELLATE
LABELLED
LABELLER
LABELLERS
LABELLING
LABELLIST
LABELLOID
LABELLUM
LABELMATE
LABELS
LABIA
LABIAL
LABIALISE
LABIALISM
LABIALITY
LABIALIZE
LABIALLY
LABIALS
LABIATE
LABIATED
LABIATES
LABILE
LABILITY
LABIS
LABISES
LABIUM
LABLAB
LABLABS
LABNEH
LABNEHS
LABOR
LABORED
LABOREDLY
LABORER
LABORERS
LABORING
LABORIOUS
LABORISM
LABORISMS
LABORIST
LABORISTS
LABORITE
LABORITES
LABORS
LABORSOME
LABOUR
LABOURED
LABOURER
LABOURERS
LABOURING
LABOURISM
LABOURIST
LABOURITE
LABOURS
LABRA
LABRADOR
LABRADORS
LABRAL
LABRET
LABRETS
LABRID
LABRIDS
LABROID
LABROIDS
LABROSE
LABRUM
LABRUMS
LABRUSCA
LABRUSCAS
LABRYS
LABRYSES
LABS
LABURNUM
LABURNUMS
LABYRINTH
LAC
LACCOLITE
LACCOLITH
LACE
LACEBARK
LACEBARKS
LACED
LACELESS
LACELIKE
LACEMAKER
LACER
LACERABLE
LACERANT
LACERATE
LACERATED
LACERATES
LACERS
LACERTIAN
LACERTID
LACERTIDS
LACERTINE
LACES
LACET
LACETS
LACEWING
LACEWINGS
LACEWOOD
LACEWOODS
LACEWORK
LACEWORKS
LACEY
LACHES
LACHESES
LACHRYMAL
LACIER
LACIEST
LACILY
LACINESS
LACING
LACINGS
LACINIA
LACINIAE
LACINIATE
LACK
LACKADAY
LACKED
LACKER
LACKERED
LACKERING
LACKERS
LACKEY
LACKEYED
LACKEYING
LACKEYS
LACKING
LACKLAND
LACKLANDS
LACKS
LACMUS
LACMUSES
LACONIC
LACONICAL
LACONISM
LACONISMS
LACQUER
LACQUERED
LACQUERER
LACQUERS
LACQUEY
LACQUEYED
LACQUEYS
LACRIMAL
LACRIMALS
LACRIMARY
LACRIMOSO
LACROSSE
LACROSSES
LACRYMAL
LACRYMALS
LACS
LACTAM
LACTAMS
LACTARIAN
LACTARY
LACTASE
LACTASES
LACTATE
LACTATED
LACTATES
LACTATING
LACTATION
LACTEAL
LACTEALLY
LACTEALS
LACTEAN
LACTEOUS
LACTIC
LACTIFIC
LACTITOL
LACTITOLS
LACTIVISM
LACTIVIST
LACTONE
LACTONES
LACTONIC
LACTOSE
LACTOSES
LACTULOSE
LACUNA
LACUNAE
LACUNAL
LACUNAR

L

LACUNARIA
LACUNARS
LACUNARY
LACUNAS
LACUNATE
LACUNE
LACUNES
LACUNOSE
LACY
LAD
LADANUM
LADANUMS
LADDER
LADDERED
LADDERIER
LADDERING
LADDERS
LADDERY
LADDIE
LADDIER
LADDIES
LADDIEST
LADDISH
LADDISHLY
LADDISM
LADDISMS
LADDY
LADE
LADED
LADEN
LADENED
LADENING
LADENS
LADER
LADERS
LADES
LADETTE
LADETTES
LADHOOD
LADHOODS
LADIES
LADIFIED
LADIFIES
LADIFY
LADIFYING
LADING
LADINGS
LADINO
LADINOS
LADLE
LADLED
LADLEFUL
LADLEFULS
LADLER
LADLERS
LADLES
LADLING
LADRON
LADRONE
LADRONES
LADRONS
LADS
LADY
LADYBIRD
LADYBIRDS
LADYBOY
LADYBOYS
LADYBUG
LADYBUGS
LADYCOW
LADYCOWS
LADYFIED
LADYFIES
LADYFISH
LADYFLIES
LADYFLY
LADYFY
LADYFYING
LADYHOOD
LADYHOODS
LADYISH
LADYISM
LADYISMS
LADYKIN
LADYKINS
LADYLIKE
LADYLOVE
LADYLOVES
LADYNESS
LADYPALM
LADYPALMS
LADYSHIP
LADYSHIPS
LAER
LAERED
LAERING
LAERS
LAESIE
LAETARE
LAETARES
LAETRILE
LAETRILES
LAEVIGATE
LAEVO
LAEVULIN
LAEVULINS
LAEVULOSE
LAG
LAGAN
LAGANS
LAGENA
LAGENAS
LAGEND
LAGENDS
LAGER
LAGERED
LAGERING
LAGERS
LAGGARD
LAGGARDLY
LAGGARDS
LAGGED
LAGGEN
LAGGENS
LAGGER
LAGGERS
LAGGIN
LAGGING
LAGGINGLY
LAGGINGS
LAGGINS
LAGNAPPE
LAGNAPPES
LAGNIAPPE
LAGOMORPH
LAGOON
LAGOONAL
LAGOONS
LAGRIMOSO
LAGS
LAGUNA
LAGUNAS
LAGUNE
LAGUNES
LAH
LAHAL
LAHALS
LAHAR
LAHARS
LAHS
LAIC
LAICAL
LAICALLY
LAICH
LAICHS
LAICISE
LAICISED
LAICISES
LAICISING
LAICISM
LAICISMS
LAICITIES
LAICITY
LAICIZE
LAICIZED
LAICIZES
LAICIZING
LAICS
LAID
LAIDED
LAIDING
LAIDLIER
LAIDLIEST
LAIDLY
LAIDS
LAIGH
LAIGHER
LAIGHEST
LAIGHS
LAIK
LAIKA
LAIKAS
LAIKED
LAIKER
LAIKERS
LAIKING
LAIKS
LAIN
LAIPSE
LAIPSED
LAIPSES
LAIPSING
LAIR
LAIRAGE
LAIRAGES
LAIRD
LAIRDLIER
LAIRDLY
LAIRDS
LAIRDSHIP
LAIRED
LAIRIER
LAIRIEST
LAIRING
LAIRISE
LAIRISED
LAIRISES
LAIRISING
LAIRIZE
LAIRIZED
LAIRIZES
LAIRIZING
LAIRS
LAIRY
LAISSE
LAISSES
LAITANCE
LAITANCES
LAITH
LAITHLY
LAITIES
LAITY
LAKE
LAKEBED
LAKEBEDS
LAKED
LAKEFILL
LAKEFILLS
LAKEFRONT
LAKEHEAD
LAKEHEADS
LAKELAND
LAKELANDS
LAKELET
LAKELETS
LAKELIKE
LAKEPORT
LAKEPORTS
LAKER
LAKERS

L

LAKES
LAKESHORE
LAKESIDE
LAKESIDES
LAKEVIEW
LAKEWARD
LAKEWARDS
LAKH
LAKHS
LAKIER
LAKIEST
LAKIN
LAKING
LAKINGS
LAKINS
LAKISH
LAKSA
LAKSAS
LAKY
LALANG
LALANGS
LALDIE
LALDIES
LALDY
LALIQUE
LALIQUES
LALL
LALLAN
LALLAND
LALLANDS
LALLANS
LALLATION
LALLED
LALLING
LALLINGS
LALLS
LALLYGAG
LALLYGAGS
LAM
LAMA
LAMAISTIC
LAMANTIN
LAMANTINS
LAMAS
LAMASERAI
LAMASERY
LAMB
LAMBADA
LAMBADAS
LAMBAST
LAMBASTE
LAMBASTED
LAMBASTES
LAMBASTS
LAMBDA
LAMBDAS
LAMBDOID
LAMBED
LAMBENCY
LAMBENT
LAMBENTLY
LAMBER
LAMBERS
LAMBERT
LAMBERTS
LAMBIE
LAMBIER
LAMBIES
LAMBIEST
LAMBING
LAMBINGS
LAMBITIVE
LAMBKILL
LAMBKILLS
LAMBKIN
LAMBKINS
LAMBLIKE
LAMBLING
LAMBLINGS
LAMBOYS
LAMBRUSCO
LAMBS
LAMBSKIN
LAMBSKINS
LAMBSWOOL
LAMBY
LAME
LAMEBRAIN
LAMED
LAMEDH
LAMEDHS
LAMEDS
LAMELLA
LAMELLAE
LAMELLAR
LAMELLAS
LAMELLATE
LAMELLOID
LAMELLOSE
LAMELY
LAMENESS
LAMENT
LAMENTED
LAMENTER
LAMENTERS
LAMENTING
LAMENTS
LAMER
LAMES
LAMEST
LAMETER
LAMETERS
LAMIA
LAMIAE
LAMIAS
LAMIGER
LAMIGERS
LAMINA
LAMINABLE
LAMINAE
LAMINAL
LAMINALS
LAMINAR
LAMINARIA
LAMINARIN
LAMINARY
LAMINAS
LAMINATE
LAMINATED
LAMINATES
LAMINATOR
LAMING
LAMINGTON
LAMININ
LAMININS
LAMINITIS
LAMINOSE
LAMINOUS
LAMISH
LAMISTER
LAMISTERS
LAMITER
LAMITERS
LAMMED
LAMMER
LAMMERS
LAMMIE
LAMMIES
LAMMIGER
LAMMIGERS
LAMMING
LAMMINGS
LAMMY
LAMP
LAMPAD
LAMPADARY
LAMPADIST
LAMPADS
LAMPAS
LAMPASES
LAMPASSE
LAMPASSES
LAMPBLACK
LAMPBRUSH
LAMPED
LAMPER
LAMPERN
LAMPERNS
LAMPERS
LAMPERSES
LAMPHOLE
LAMPHOLES
LAMPING
LAMPINGS
LAMPION
LAMPIONS
LAMPLESS
LAMPLIGHT
LAMPLIT
LAMPOON
LAMPOONED
LAMPOONER
LAMPOONS
LAMPPOST
LAMPPOSTS
LAMPREY
LAMPREYS
LAMPS
LAMPSHADE
LAMPSHELL
LAMPSTAND
LAMPUKA
LAMPUKAS
LAMPUKI
LAMPUKIS
LAMPYRID
LAMPYRIDS
LAMS
LAMSTER
LAMSTERS
LANA
LANAI
LANAIS
LANAS
LANATE
LANATED
LANCE
LANCED
LANCEGAY
LANCEGAYS
LANCEJACK
LANCELET
LANCELETS
LANCELIKE
LANCEOLAR
LANCER
LANCERS
LANCES
LANCET
LANCETED
LANCETS
LANCEWOOD
LANCH
LANCHED
LANCHES
LANCHING
LANCIERS
LANCIFORM
LANCINATE
LANCING
LAND
LANDAMMAN
LANDAU
LANDAULET
LANDAUS
LANDBOARD
LANDDAMNE
LANDDROS
LANDDROST
LANDE

L

LANDED
LANDER
LANDERS
LANDES
LANDFALL
LANDFALLS
LANDFAST
LANDFILL
LANDFILLS
LANDFORCE
LANDFORM
LANDFORMS
LANDGRAB
LANDGRABS
LANDGRAVE
LANDING
LANDINGS
LANDLADY
LANDLER
LANDLERS
LANDLESS
LANDLINE
LANDLINES
LANDLOPER
LANDLORD
LANDLORDS
LANDMAN
LANDMARK
LANDMARKS
LANDMASS
LANDMEN
LANDMINE
LANDMINED
LANDMINES
LANDOWNER
LANDRACE
LANDRACES
LANDRAIL
LANDRAILS
LANDS
LANDSCAPE
LANDSHARK
LANDSIDE
LANDSIDES
LANDSKIP
LANDSKIPS
LANDSLEIT
LANDSLID
LANDSLIDE
LANDSLIP
LANDSLIPS
LANDSMAN
LANDSMEN
LANDWARD
LANDWARDS
LANDWASH
LANDWIND
LANDWINDS
LANE
LANELY
LANES
LANEWAY
LANEWAYS
LANG
LANGAHA
LANGAHAS
LANGAR
LANGARS
LANGER
LANGERED
LANGERS
LANGEST
LANGLAUF
LANGLAUFS
LANGLEY
LANGLEYS
LANGOUSTE
LANGRAGE
LANGRAGES
LANGREL
LANGRELS
LANGRIDGE
LANGSHAN
LANGSHANS
LANGSPEL
LANGSPELS
LANGSPIEL
LANGSPIL
LANGSPILS
LANGSYNE
LANGSYNES
LANGUAGE
LANGUAGED
LANGUAGES
LANGUE
LANGUED
LANGUES
LANGUET
LANGUETS
LANGUETTE
LANGUID
LANGUIDLY
LANGUISH
LANGUOR
LANGUORS
LANGUR
LANGURS
LANIARD
LANIARDS
LANIARIES
LANIARY
LANITAL
LANITALS
LANK
LANKED
LANKER
LANKEST
LANKIER
LANKIEST
LANKILY
LANKINESS
LANKING
LANKLY
LANKNESS
LANKS
LANKY
LANNER
LANNERET
LANNERETS
LANNERS
LANOLATED
LANOLIN
LANOLINE
LANOLINES
LANOLINS
LANOSE
LANOSITY
LANT
LANTANA
LANTANAS
LANTERLOO
LANTERN
LANTERNED
LANTERNS
LANTHANON
LANTHANUM
LANTHORN
LANTHORNS
LANTS
LANTSKIP
LANTSKIPS
LANUGO
LANUGOS
LANX
LANYARD
LANYARDS
LAODICEAN
LAOGAI
LAOGAIS
LAP
LAPBOARD
LAPBOARDS
LAPDOG
LAPDOGS
LAPEL
LAPELED
LAPELLED
LAPELS
LAPFUL
LAPFULS
LAPHELD
LAPIDARY
LAPIDATE
LAPIDATED
LAPIDATES
LAPIDEOUS
LAPIDES
LAPIDIFIC
LAPIDIFY
LAPIDIST
LAPIDISTS
LAPILLI
LAPILLUS
LAPIN
LAPINS
LAPIS
LAPISES
LAPJE
LAPJES
LAPPED
LAPPEL
LAPPELS
LAPPER
LAPPERED
LAPPERING
LAPPERS
LAPPET
LAPPETED
LAPPETS
LAPPIE
LAPPIES
LAPPING
LAPPINGS
LAPS
LAPSABLE
LAPSANG
LAPSANGS
LAPSE
LAPSED
LAPSER
LAPSERS
LAPSES
LAPSIBLE
LAPSING
LAPSTONE
LAPSTONES
LAPSTRAKE
LAPSTREAK
LAPSUS
LAPTOP
LAPTOPS
LAPTRAY
LAPTRAYS
LAPWING
LAPWINGS
LAPWORK
LAPWORKS
LAQUEARIA
LAR
LARBOARD
LARBOARDS
LARCENER
LARCENERS
LARCENIES
LARCENIST
LARCENOUS
LARCENY
LARCH
LARCHEN
LARCHES

LARCHWOOD
LARD
LARDALITE
LARDED
LARDER
LARDERER
LARDERERS
LARDERS
LARDIER
LARDIEST
LARDING
LARDLIKE
LARDON
LARDONS
LARDOON
LARDOONS
LARDS
LARDY
LARE
LAREE
LAREES
LARES
LARGANDO
LARGE
LARGELY
LARGEN
LARGENED
LARGENESS
LARGENING
LARGENS
LARGER
LARGES
LARGESS
LARGESSE
LARGESSES
LARGEST
LARGHETTO
LARGISH
LARGITION
LARGO
LARGOS
LARI
LARIAT
LARIATED
LARIATING
LARIATS
LARIGAN
LARIGANS
LARINE
LARIS
LARK
LARKED
LARKER
LARKERS
LARKIER
LARKIEST
LARKINESS
LARKING
LARKISH
LARKS
LARKSOME
LARKSPUR
LARKSPURS
LARKY
LARMIER
LARMIERS
LARN
LARNAKES
LARNAX
LARNED
LARNEY
LARNEYS
LARNIER
LARNIEST
LARNING
LARNS
LARNT
LAROID
LARRIGAN
LARRIGANS
LARRIKIN
LARRIKINS
LARRUP
LARRUPED
LARRUPER
LARRUPERS
LARRUPING
LARRUPS
LARS
LARUM
LARUMS
LARVA
LARVAE
LARVAL
LARVAS
LARVATE
LARVATED
LARVICIDE
LARVIFORM
LARVIKITE
LARYNGAL
LARYNGALS
LARYNGEAL
LARYNGES
LARYNX
LARYNXES
LAS
LASAGNA
LASAGNAS
LASAGNE
LASAGNES
LASCAR
LASCARS
LASE
LASED
LASER
LASERDISC
LASERDISK
LASERED
LASERING
LASERS
LASERWORT
LASES
LASH
LASHED
LASHER
LASHERS
LASHES
LASHING
LASHINGLY
LASHINGS
LASHINS
LASHKAR
LASHKARS
LASHLESS
LASING
LASINGS
LASKET
LASKETS
LASQUE
LASQUES
LASS
LASSES
LASSI
LASSIE
LASSIES
LASSIS
LASSITUDE
LASSLORN
LASSO
LASSOCK
LASSOCKS
LASSOED
LASSOER
LASSOERS
LASSOES
LASSOING
LASSOINGS
LASSOS
LASSU
LASSUS
LASSY
LAST
LASTAGE
LASTAGES
LASTBORN
LASTBORNS
LASTED
LASTER
LASTERS
LASTING
LASTINGLY
LASTINGS
LASTLY
LASTS
LAT
LATAH
LATAHS
LATAKIA
LATAKIAS
LATCH
LATCHED
LATCHES
LATCHET
LATCHETS
LATCHING
LATCHKEY
LATCHKEYS
LATE
LATECOMER
LATED
LATEEN
LATEENER
LATEENERS
LATEENS
LATELY
LATEN
LATENCE
LATENCES
LATENCIES
LATENCY
LATENED
LATENESS
LATENING
LATENS
LATENT
LATENTLY
LATENTS
LATER
LATERAD
LATERAL
LATERALED
LATERALLY
LATERALS
LATERBORN
LATERISE
LATERISED
LATERISES
LATERITE
LATERITES
LATERITIC
LATERIZE
LATERIZED
LATERIZES
LATESCENT
LATEST
LATESTS
LATEWAKE
LATEWAKES
LATEWOOD
LATEWOODS
LATEX
LATEXES
LATH
LATHE
LATHED
LATHEE
LATHEES
LATHEN
LATHER

LATHERED
LATHERER
LATHERERS
LATHERIER
LATHERING
LATHERS
LATHERY
LATHES
LATHI
LATHIER
LATHIEST
LATHING
LATHINGS
LATHIS
LATHLIKE
LATHS
LATHWORK
LATHWORKS
LATHY
LATHYRISM
LATHYRUS
LATI
LATICES
LATICIFER
LATICLAVE
LATIFONDI
LATIFONDO
LATIGO
LATIGOES
LATIGOS
LATILLA
LATILLAS
LATIMERIA
LATINA
LATINAS
LATINISE
LATINISED
LATINISES
LATINITY
LATINIZE
LATINIZED
LATINIZES
LATINO
LATINOS
LATISH
LATITANCY
LATITANT
LATITAT
LATITATS
LATITUDE
LATITUDES
LATKE
LATKES
LATOSOL
LATOSOLIC
LATOSOLS
LATRANT
LATRATION
LATRIA
LATRIAS
LATRINE
LATRINES
LATROCINY
LATRON
LATRONS
LATS
LATTE
LATTEN
LATTENS
LATTER
LATTERLY
LATTERS
LATTES
LATTICE
LATTICED
LATTICES
LATTICING
LATTICINI
LATTICINO
LATTIN
LATTINS
LATU
LATUS
LAUAN
LAUANS
LAUCH
LAUCHING
LAUCHS
LAUD
LAUDABLE
LAUDABLY
LAUDANUM
LAUDANUMS
LAUDATION
LAUDATIVE
LAUDATOR
LAUDATORS
LAUDATORY
LAUDED
LAUDER
LAUDERS
LAUDING
LAUDS
LAUF
LAUFS
LAUGH
LAUGHABLE
LAUGHABLY
LAUGHED
LAUGHER
LAUGHERS
LAUGHFUL
LAUGHIER
LAUGHIEST
LAUGHING
LAUGHINGS
LAUGHLINE
LAUGHS
LAUGHSOME
LAUGHTER
LAUGHTERS
LAUGHY
LAUNCE
LAUNCED
LAUNCES
LAUNCH
LAUNCHED
LAUNCHER
LAUNCHERS
LAUNCHES
LAUNCHING
LAUNCHPAD
LAUNCING
LAUND
LAUNDER
LAUNDERED
LAUNDERER
LAUNDERS
LAUNDRESS
LAUNDRIES
LAUNDRY
LAUNDS
LAURA
LAURAE
LAURAS
LAUREATE
LAUREATED
LAUREATES
LAUREL
LAURELED
LAURELING
LAURELLED
LAURELS
LAURIC
LAURYL
LAURYLS
LAUWINE
LAUWINES
LAV
LAVA
LAVABO
LAVABOES
LAVABOS
LAVAFORM
LAVAGE
LAVAGES
LAVAL
LAVALAVA
LAVALAVAS
LAVALIER
LAVALIERE
LAVALIERS
LAVALIKE
LAVANDIN
LAVANDINS
LAVAS
LAVASH
LAVASHES
LAVATERA
LAVATERAS
LAVATION
LAVATIONS
LAVATORY
LAVE
LAVED
LAVEER
LAVEERED
LAVEERING
LAVEERS
LAVEMENT
LAVEMENTS
LAVENDER
LAVENDERS
LAVER
LAVEROCK
LAVEROCKS
LAVERS
LAVES
LAVING
LAVISH
LAVISHED
LAVISHER
LAVISHERS
LAVISHES
LAVISHEST
LAVISHING
LAVISHLY
LAVOLT
LAVOLTA
LAVOLTAED
LAVOLTAS
LAVOLTED
LAVOLTING
LAVOLTS
LAVRA
LAVRAS
LAVROCK
LAVROCKS
LAVS
LAVVIES
LAVVY
LAW
LAWBOOK
LAWBOOKS
LAWCOURT
LAWCOURTS
LAWED
LAWER
LAWEST
LAWFARE
LAWFARES
LAWFUL
LAWFULLY
LAWGIVER
LAWGIVERS
LAWGIVING
LAWIN
LAWINE
LAWINES
LAWING

LAWINGS
LAWINS
LAWK
LAWKS
LAWLAND
LAWLANDS
LAWLESS
LAWLESSLY
LAWLIKE
LAWMAKER
LAWMAKERS
LAWMAKING
LAWMAN
LAWMEN
LAWMONGER
LAWN
LAWNED
LAWNIER
LAWNIEST
LAWNING
LAWNMOWER
LAWNS
LAWNY
LAWS
LAWSUIT
LAWSUITS
LAWYER
LAWYERED
LAWYERING
LAWYERLY
LAWYERS
LAX
LAXATION
LAXATIONS
LAXATIVE
LAXATIVES
LAXATOR
LAXATORS
LAXED
LAXER
LAXES
LAXEST
LAXING
LAXISM
LAXISMS
LAXIST
LAXISTS
LAXITIES
LAXITY
LAXLY
LAXNESS
LAXNESSES
LAY
LAYABOUT
LAYABOUTS
LAYAWAY
LAYAWAYS
LAYBACK
LAYBACKED
LAYBACKS
LAYDEEZ
LAYED
LAYER
LAYERAGE
LAYERAGES
LAYERED
LAYERING
LAYERINGS
LAYERS
LAYETTE
LAYETTES
LAYIN
LAYING
LAYINGS
LAYINS
LAYLOCK
LAYLOCKS
LAYMAN
LAYMANISE
LAYMANIZE
LAYMEN
LAYOFF
LAYOFFS
LAYOUT
LAYOUTS
LAYOVER
LAYOVERS
LAYPEOPLE
LAYPERSON
LAYS
LAYSHAFT
LAYSHAFTS
LAYSTALL
LAYSTALLS
LAYTIME
LAYTIMES
LAYUP
LAYUPS
LAYWOMAN
LAYWOMEN
LAZAR
LAZARET
LAZARETS
LAZARETTE
LAZARETTO
LAZARS
LAZE
LAZED
LAZES
LAZIED
LAZIER
LAZIES
LAZIEST
LAZILY
LAZINESS
LAZING
LAZO
LAZOED
LAZOES
LAZOING
LAZOS
LAZULI
LAZULIS
LAZULITE
LAZULITES
LAZURITE
LAZURITES
LAZY
LAZYBONES
LAZYING
LAZYISH
LAZZARONE
LAZZARONI
LAZZI
LAZZO
LEA
LEACH
LEACHABLE
LEACHATE
LEACHATES
LEACHED
LEACHER
LEACHERS
LEACHES
LEACHIER
LEACHIEST
LEACHING
LEACHINGS
LEACHOUR
LEACHOURS
LEACHY
LEAD
LEADABLE
LEADED
LEADEN
LEADENED
LEADENING
LEADENLY
LEADENS
LEADER
LEADERENE
LEADERS
LEADIER
LEADIEST
LEADING
LEADINGLY
LEADINGS
LEADLESS
LEADMAN
LEADMEN
LEADOFF
LEADOFFS
LEADPLANT
LEADS
LEADSCREW
LEADSMAN
LEADSMEN
LEADWORK
LEADWORKS
LEADWORT
LEADWORTS
LEADY
LEAF
LEAFAGE
LEAFAGES
LEAFBUD
LEAFBUDS
LEAFED
LEAFERIES
LEAFERY
LEAFIER
LEAFIEST
LEAFINESS
LEAFING
LEAFLESS
LEAFLET
LEAFLETED
LEAFLETER
LEAFLETS
LEAFLIKE
LEAFMOLD
LEAFMOLDS
LEAFROLL
LEAFROLLS
LEAFS
LEAFSTALK
LEAFWORM
LEAFWORMS
LEAFY
LEAGUE
LEAGUED
LEAGUER
LEAGUERED
LEAGUERS
LEAGUES
LEAGUING
LEAK
LEAKAGE
LEAKAGES
LEAKED
LEAKER
LEAKERS
LEAKIER
LEAKIEST
LEAKILY
LEAKINESS
LEAKING
LEAKLESS
LEAKPROOF
LEAKS
LEAKY
LEAL
LEALER
LEALEST
LEALLY
LEALTIES
LEALTY
LEAM
LEAMED
LEAMING

LEAMS
LEAN
LEANED
LEANER
LEANERS
LEANEST
LEANING
LEANINGS
LEANLY
LEANNESS
LEANS
LEANT
LEANY
LEAP
LEAPED
LEAPER
LEAPEROUS
LEAPERS
LEAPFROG
LEAPFROGS
LEAPING
LEAPOROUS
LEAPROUS
LEAPS
LEAPT
LEAR
LEARE
LEARED
LEARES
LEARIER
LEARIEST
LEARINESS
LEARING
LEARN
LEARNABLE
LEARNED
LEARNEDLY
LEARNER
LEARNERS
LEARNING
LEARNINGS
LEARNS
LEARNT
LEARS
LEARY
LEAS
LEASABLE
LEASE
LEASEBACK
LEASED
LEASEHOLD
LEASER
LEASERS
LEASES
LEASH
LEASHED
LEASHES
LEASHING
LEASING
LEASINGS
LEASOW
LEASOWE
LEASOWED
LEASOWES
LEASOWING
LEASOWS
LEAST
LEASTS
LEASTWAYS
LEASTWISE
LEASURE
LEASURES
LEAT
LEATHER
LEATHERED
LEATHERN
LEATHERS
LEATHERY
LEATS
LEAVE
LEAVED
LEAVEN
LEAVENED
LEAVENER
LEAVENERS
LEAVENING
LEAVENOUS
LEAVENS
LEAVER
LEAVERS
LEAVES
LEAVIER
LEAVIEST
LEAVING
LEAVINGS
LEAVY
LEAZE
LEAZES
LEBBEK
LEBBEKS
LEBEN
LEBENS
LEBKUCHEN
LECANORA
LECANORAS
LECCIES
LECCY
LECH
LECHAIM
LECHAIMS
LECHAYIM
LECHAYIMS
LECHED
LECHER
LECHERED
LECHERIES
LECHERING
LECHEROUS
LECHERS
LECHERY
LECHES
LECHING
LECHWE
LECHWES
LECITHIN
LECITHINS
LECTERN
LECTERNS
LECTIN
LECTINS
LECTION
LECTIONS
LECTOR
LECTORATE
LECTORS
LECTOTYPE
LECTRESS
LECTURE
LECTURED
LECTURER
LECTURERS
LECTURES
LECTURING
LECTURN
LECTURNS
LECYTHI
LECYTHIS
LECYTHUS
LED
LEDDEN
LEDDENS
LEDE
LEDES
LEDGE
LEDGED
LEDGER
LEDGERED
LEDGERING
LEDGERS
LEDGES
LEDGIER
LEDGIEST
LEDGY
LEDUM
LEDUMS
LEE
LEEAR
LEEARS
LEEBOARD
LEEBOARDS
LEECH
LEECHDOM
LEECHDOMS
LEECHED
LEECHEE
LEECHEES
LEECHES
LEECHING
LEECHLIKE
LEED
LEEING
LEEK
LEEKS
LEEP
LEEPED
LEEPING
LEEPS
LEER
LEERED
LEERIER
LEERIEST
LEERILY
LEERINESS
LEERING
LEERINGLY
LEERINGS
LEERS
LEERY
LEES
LEESE
LEESES
LEESING
LEET
LEETLE
LEETS
LEETSPEAK
LEEWARD
LEEWARDLY
LEEWARDS
LEEWAY
LEEWAYS
LEEZE
LEFT
LEFTE
LEFTER
LEFTEST
LEFTIE
LEFTIES
LEFTISH
LEFTISM
LEFTISMS
LEFTIST
LEFTISTS
LEFTMOST
LEFTMOSTS
LEFTOVER
LEFTOVERS
LEFTS
LEFTWARD
LEFTWARDS
LEFTWING
LEFTY
LEG
LEGACIES
LEGACY
LEGAL
LEGALESE
LEGALESES
LEGALISE
LEGALISED

L

LEGALISER
LEGALISES
LEGALISM
LEGALISMS
LEGALIST
LEGALISTS
LEGALITY
LEGALIZE
LEGALIZED
LEGALIZER
LEGALIZES
LEGALLY
LEGALS
LEGATARY
LEGATE
LEGATED
LEGATEE
LEGATEES
LEGATES
LEGATINE
LEGATING
LEGATION
LEGATIONS
LEGATO
LEGATOR
LEGATORS
LEGATOS
LEGEND
LEGENDARY
LEGENDISE
LEGENDIST
LEGENDIZE
LEGENDRY
LEGENDS
LEGER
LEGERING
LEGERINGS
LEGERITY
LEGERS
LEGES
LEGGE
LEGGED
LEGGER
LEGGERS
LEGGES
LEGGIE
LEGGIER
LEGGIERO
LEGGIES
LEGGIEST
LEGGIN
LEGGINESS
LEGGING
LEGGINGED
LEGGINGS
LEGGINS
LEGGISM
LEGGISMS
LEGGO
LEGGY
LEGHOLD
LEGHOLDS
LEGHORN
LEGHORNS
LEGIBLE
LEGIBLY
LEGION
LEGIONARY
LEGIONED
LEGIONS
LEGISLATE
LEGIST
LEGISTS
LEGIT
LEGITIM
LEGITIMS
LEGITS
LEGLAN
LEGLANS
LEGLEN
LEGLENS
LEGLESS
LEGLET
LEGLETS
LEGLIKE
LEGLIN
LEGLINS
LEGMAN
LEGMEN
LEGONG
LEGONGS
LEGROOM
LEGROOMS
LEGS
LEGSIDE
LEGSIDES
LEGUAAN
LEGUAANS
LEGUAN
LEGUANS
LEGUME
LEGUMES
LEGUMIN
LEGUMINS
LEGWARMER
LEGWEAR
LEGWEARS
LEGWORK
LEGWORKS
LEHAIM
LEHAIMS
LEHAYIM
LEHAYIMS
LEHR
LEHRJAHRE
LEHRS
LEHUA
LEHUAS
LEI
LEIDGER
LEIDGERS
LEIGER
LEIGERS
LEIOMYOMA
LEIPOA
LEIPOAS
LEIR
LEIRED
LEIRING
LEIRS
LEIS
LEISH
LEISHER
LEISHEST
LEISLER
LEISLERS
LEISTER
LEISTERED
LEISTERS
LEISURE
LEISURED
LEISURELY
LEISURES
LEISURING
LEITMOTIF
LEITMOTIV
LEK
LEKE
LEKGOTLA
LEKGOTLAS
LEKKED
LEKKER
LEKKING
LEKKINGS
LEKS
LEKU
LEKVAR
LEKVARS
LEKYTHI
LEKYTHOI
LEKYTHOS
LEKYTHUS
LEMAN
LEMANS
LEME
LEMED
LEMEL
LEMELS
LEMES
LEMING
LEMMA
LEMMAS
LEMMATA
LEMMATISE
LEMMATIZE
LEMME
LEMMING
LEMMINGS
LEMNISCAL
LEMNISCI
LEMNISCUS
LEMON
LEMONADE
LEMONADES
LEMONED
LEMONFISH
LEMONIER
LEMONIEST
LEMONING
LEMONISH
LEMONLIKE
LEMONS
LEMONWOOD
LEMONY
LEMPIRA
LEMPIRAS
LEMUR
LEMURES
LEMURIAN
LEMURIANS
LEMURINE
LEMURINES
LEMURLIKE
LEMUROID
LEMUROIDS
LEMURS
LEND
LENDABLE
LENDER
LENDERS
LENDING
LENDINGS
LENDS
LENES
LENG
LENGED
LENGER
LENGEST
LENGING
LENGS
LENGTH
LENGTHEN
LENGTHENS
LENGTHFUL
LENGTHIER
LENGTHILY
LENGTHMAN
LENGTHMEN
LENGTHS
LENGTHY
LENIENCE
LENIENCES
LENIENCY
LENIENT
LENIENTLY
LENIENTS
LENIFIED
LENIFIES
LENIFY
LENIFYING

LENIS
LENITE
LENITED
LENITES
LENITIES
LENITING
LENITION
LENITIONS
LENITIVE
LENITIVES
LENITY
LENO
LENOS
LENS
LENSE
LENSED
LENSES
LENSING
LENSINGS
LENSLESS
LENSLIKE
LENSMAN
LENSMEN
LENT
LENTANDO
LENTEN
LENTI
LENTIC
LENTICEL
LENTICELS
LENTICLE
LENTICLES
LENTICULE
LENTIFORM
LENTIGO
LENTIL
LENTILS
LENTISC
LENTISCS
LENTISK
LENTISKS
LENTO
LENTOID
LENTOIDS
LENTOR
LENTORS
LENTOS
LENTOUS
LENVOY
LENVOYS
LEONE
LEONES
LEONINE
LEOPARD
LEOPARDS
LEOTARD
LEOTARDED
LEOTARDS
LEP
LEPER
LEPERS
LEPID
LEPIDOTE
LEPIDOTES
LEPORID
LEPORIDAE
LEPORIDS
LEPORINE
LEPPED
LEPPING
LEPRA
LEPRAS
LEPROSE
LEPROSERY
LEPROSIES
LEPROSITY
LEPROSY
LEPROTIC
LEPROUS
LEPROUSLY
LEPS
LEPT
LEPTA
LEPTIN
LEPTINS
LEPTOME
LEPTOMES
LEPTON
LEPTONIC
LEPTONS
LEPTOPHOS
LEPTOSOME
LEPTOTENE
LEQUEAR
LEQUEARS
LERE
LERED
LERES
LERING
LERNAEAN
LERP
LERPS
LESBIAN
LESBIANS
LESBIC
LESBIGAY
LESBIGAYS
LESION
LESIONED
LESIONING
LESIONS
LESPEDEZA
LESS
LESSEE
LESSEES
LESSEN
LESSENED
LESSENING
LESSENS
LESSER
LESSES
LESSON
LESSONED
LESSONING
LESSONS
LESSOR
LESSORS
LEST
LESTED
LESTING
LESTS
LESULA
LESULAS
LET
LETCH
LETCHED
LETCHES
LETCHING
LETCHINGS
LETDOWN
LETDOWNS
LETHAL
LETHALITY
LETHALLY
LETHALS
LETHARGIC
LETHARGY
LETHE
LETHEAN
LETHEE
LETHEES
LETHES
LETHIED
LETOUT
LETOUTS
LETROZOLE
LETS
LETTABLE
LETTED
LETTER
LETTERBOX
LETTERED
LETTERER
LETTERERS
LETTERING
LETTERMAN
LETTERMEN
LETTERN
LETTERNS
LETTERS
LETTERSET
LETTING
LETTINGS
LETTRE
LETTRES
LETTUCE
LETTUCES
LETUP
LETUPS
LEU
LEUCAEMIA
LEUCAEMIC
LEUCEMIA
LEUCEMIAS
LEUCEMIC
LEUCH
LEUCHEN
LEUCIN
LEUCINE
LEUCINES
LEUCINS
LEUCISM
LEUCISMS
LEUCISTIC
LEUCITE
LEUCITES
LEUCITIC
LEUCO
LEUCOCYTE
LEUCOMA
LEUCOMAS
LEUCON
LEUCONS
LEUCOSES
LEUCOSIN
LEUCOSINS
LEUCOSIS
LEUCOTIC
LEUCOTOME
LEUCOTOMY
LEUD
LEUDES
LEUDS
LEUGH
LEUGHEN
LEUKAEMIA
LEUKAEMIC
LEUKEMIA
LEUKEMIAS
LEUKEMIC
LEUKEMICS
LEUKEMOID
LEUKOCYTE
LEUKOMA
LEUKOMAS
LEUKON
LEUKONS
LEUKOSES
LEUKOSIS
LEUKOTIC
LEUKOTOME
LEUKOTOMY
LEV
LEVA
LEVANT
LEVANTED
LEVANTER
LEVANTERS
LEVANTINE
LEVANTING

L

LEVANTS
LEVAS
LEVATOR
LEVATORES
LEVATORS
LEVE
LEVEE
LEVEED
LEVEEING
LEVEES
LEVEL
LEVELED
LEVELER
LEVELERS
LEVELING
LEVELLED
LEVELLER
LEVELLERS
LEVELLEST
LEVELLING
LEVELLY
LEVELNESS
LEVELS
LEVER
LEVERAGE
LEVERAGED
LEVERAGES
LEVERED
LEVERET
LEVERETS
LEVERING
LEVERS
LEVES
LEVIABLE
LEVIATHAN
LEVIED
LEVIER
LEVIERS
LEVIES
LEVIGABLE
LEVIGATE
LEVIGATED
LEVIGATES
LEVIGATOR
LEVIN
LEVINS
LEVIRATE
LEVIRATES
LEVIRATIC
LEVIS
LEVITATE
LEVITATED
LEVITATES
LEVITATOR
LEVITE
LEVITES
LEVITIC
LEVITICAL
LEVITIES
LEVITY
LEVO
LEVODOPA
LEVODOPAS
LEVOGYRE
LEVOGYRES
LEVS
LEVULIN
LEVULINS
LEVULOSE
LEVULOSES
LEVY
LEVYING
LEW
LEWD
LEWDER
LEWDEST
LEWDLY
LEWDNESS
LEWDSBIES
LEWDSBY
LEWDSTER
LEWDSTERS
LEWIS
LEWISES
LEWISIA
LEWISIAS
LEWISITE
LEWISITES
LEWISSON
LEWISSONS
LEX
LEXEME
LEXEMES
LEXEMIC
LEXES
LEXICA
LEXICAL
LEXICALLY
LEXICON
LEXICONS
LEXIGRAM
LEXIGRAMS
LEXIS
LEXISES
LEY
LEYLANDI
LEYLANDII
LEYLANDIS
LEYS
LI
LIABILITY
LIABLE
LIAISE
LIAISED
LIAISES
LIAISING
LIAISON
LIAISONS
LIANA
LIANAS
LIANE
LIANES
LIANG
LIANGS
LIANOID
LIAR
LIARD
LIARDS
LIARS
LIART
LIAS
LIASES
LIASSIC
LIATRIS
LIATRISES
LIB
LIBANT
LIBATE
LIBATED
LIBATES
LIBATING
LIBATION
LIBATIONS
LIBATORY
LIBBARD
LIBBARDS
LIBBED
LIBBER
LIBBERS
LIBBING
LIBECCHIO
LIBECCIO
LIBECCIOS
LIBEL
LIBELANT
LIBELANTS
LIBELED
LIBELEE
LIBELEES
LIBELER
LIBELERS
LIBELING
LIBELINGS
LIBELIST
LIBELISTS
LIBELLANT
LIBELLED
LIBELLEE
LIBELLEES
LIBELLER
LIBELLERS
LIBELLING
LIBELLOUS
LIBELOUS
LIBELS
LIBER
LIBERAL
LIBERALLY
LIBERALS
LIBERATE
LIBERATED
LIBERATES
LIBERATOR
LIBERO
LIBEROS
LIBERS
LIBERTIES
LIBERTINE
LIBERTY
LIBIDINAL
LIBIDO
LIBIDOS
LIBKEN
LIBKENS
LIBLAB
LIBLABS
LIBRA
LIBRAE
LIBRAIRE
LIBRAIRES
LIBRAIRIE
LIBRARIAN
LIBRARIES
LIBRARY
LIBRAS
LIBRATE
LIBRATED
LIBRATES
LIBRATING
LIBRATION
LIBRATORY
LIBRETTI
LIBRETTO
LIBRETTOS
LIBRI
LIBRIFORM
LIBS
LICE
LICENCE
LICENCED
LICENCEE
LICENCEES
LICENCER
LICENCERS
LICENCES
LICENCING
LICENSE
LICENSED
LICENSEE
LICENSEES
LICENSER
LICENSERS
LICENSES
LICENSING
LICENSOR
LICENSORS
LICENSURE
LICENTE
LICH
LICHANOS

LICHEE
LICHEES
LICHEN
LICHENED
LICHENIN
LICHENING
LICHENINS
LICHENISM
LICHENIST
LICHENOID
LICHENOSE
LICHENOUS
LICHENS
LICHES
LICHGATE
LICHGATES
LICHI
LICHIS
LICHT
LICHTED
LICHTER
LICHTEST
LICHTING
LICHTLIED
LICHTLIES
LICHTLY
LICHTS
LICHWAKE
LICHWAKES
LICHWAY
LICHWAYS
LICIT
LICITLY
LICITNESS
LICK
LICKED
LICKER
LICKERISH
LICKERS
LICKING
LICKINGS
LICKPENNY
LICKS
LICKSPIT
LICKSPITS
LICORICE
LICORICES
LICTOR
LICTORIAN
LICTORS
LID
LIDAR
LIDARS
LIDDED
LIDDING
LIDDINGS
LIDGER
LIDGERS
LIDLESS
LIDO
LIDOCAINE
LIDOS
LIDS
LIE
LIED
LIEDER
LIEF
LIEFER
LIEFEST
LIEFLY
LIEFS
LIEGE
LIEGEDOM
LIEGEDOMS
LIEGELESS
LIEGEMAN
LIEGEMEN
LIEGER
LIEGERS
LIEGES
LIEN
LIENABLE
LIENAL
LIENEE
LIENEES
LIENOR
LIENORS
LIENS
LIENTERIC
LIENTERY
LIER
LIERNE
LIERNES
LIERS
LIES
LIEU
LIEUS
LIEVE
LIEVER
LIEVES
LIEVEST
LIFE
LIFEBELT
LIFEBELTS
LIFEBLOOD
LIFEBOAT
LIFEBOATS
LIFEBUOY
LIFEBUOYS
LIFECARE
LIFECARES
LIFEFUL
LIFEGUARD
LIFEHACK
LIFEHACKS
LIFEHOLD
LIFELESS
LIFELIKE
LIFELINE
LIFELINES
LIFELONG
LIFER
LIFERS
LIFES
LIFESAVER
LIFESOME
LIFESPAN
LIFESPANS
LIFESTYLE
LIFETIME
LIFETIMES
LIFEWAY
LIFEWAYS
LIFEWORK
LIFEWORKS
LIFEWORLD
LIFT
LIFTABLE
LIFTBACK
LIFTBACKS
LIFTBOY
LIFTBOYS
LIFTED
LIFTER
LIFTERS
LIFTGATE
LIFTGATES
LIFTING
LIFTMAN
LIFTMEN
LIFTOFF
LIFTOFFS
LIFTS
LIFULL
LIG
LIGAMENT
LIGAMENTS
LIGAN
LIGAND
LIGANDS
LIGANS
LIGASE
LIGASES
LIGATE
LIGATED
LIGATES
LIGATING
LIGATION
LIGATIONS
LIGATIVE
LIGATURE
LIGATURED
LIGATURES
LIGER
LIGERS
LIGGE
LIGGED
LIGGER
LIGGERS
LIGGES
LIGGING
LIGGINGS
LIGHT
LIGHTBULB
LIGHTED
LIGHTEN
LIGHTENED
LIGHTENER
LIGHTENS
LIGHTER
LIGHTERED
LIGHTERS
LIGHTEST
LIGHTFACE
LIGHTFAST
LIGHTFUL
LIGHTING
LIGHTINGS
LIGHTISH
LIGHTLESS
LIGHTLIED
LIGHTLIES
LIGHTLY
LIGHTNESS
LIGHTNING
LIGHTS
LIGHTSHIP
LIGHTSOME
LIGHTWAVE
LIGHTWOOD
LIGNAGE
LIGNAGES
LIGNALOES
LIGNAN
LIGNANS
LIGNE
LIGNEOUS
LIGNES
LIGNICOLE
LIGNIFIED
LIGNIFIES
LIGNIFORM
LIGNIFY
LIGNIN
LIGNINS
LIGNITE
LIGNITES
LIGNITIC
LIGNOSE
LIGNOSES
LIGNUM
LIGNUMS
LIGROIN
LIGROINE
LIGROINES
LIGROINS
LIGS
LIGULA
LIGULAE
LIGULAR

LIGULAS
LIGULATE
LIGULATED
LIGULE
LIGULES
LIGULOID
LIGURE
LIGURES
LIGUSTRUM
LIKABLE
LIKABLY
LIKE
LIKEABLE
LIKEABLY
LIKED
LIKELIER
LIKELIEST
LIKELY
LIKEN
LIKENED
LIKENESS
LIKENING
LIKENS
LIKER
LIKERS
LIKES
LIKEST
LIKEWAKE
LIKEWAKES
LIKEWALK
LIKEWALKS
LIKEWISE
LIKIN
LIKING
LIKINGS
LIKINS
LIKUTA
LILAC
LILACS
LILANGENI
LILIED
LILIES
LILL
LILLED
LILLING
LILLIPUT
LILLIPUTS
LILLS
LILO
LILOS
LILT
LILTED
LILTING
LILTINGLY
LILTS
LILY
LILYLIKE
LIMA
LIMACEL
LIMACELS
LIMACEOUS
LIMACES
LIMACINE
LIMACON
LIMACONS
LIMAIL
LIMAILS
LIMAN
LIMANS
LIMAS
LIMATION
LIMATIONS
LIMAX
LIMB
LIMBA
LIMBAS
LIMBATE
LIMBEC
LIMBECK
LIMBECKS
LIMBECS
LIMBED
LIMBER
LIMBERED
LIMBERER
LIMBEREST
LIMBERING
LIMBERLY
LIMBERS
LIMBI
LIMBIC
LIMBIER
LIMBIEST
LIMBING
LIMBLESS
LIMBMEAL
LIMBO
LIMBOED
LIMBOES
LIMBOING
LIMBOS
LIMBOUS
LIMBS
LIMBUS
LIMBUSES
LIMBY
LIME
LIMEADE
LIMEADES
LIMED
LIMEKILN
LIMEKILNS
LIMELESS
LIMELIGHT
LIMELIT
LIMEN
LIMENS
LIMEPIT
LIMEPITS
LIMERENCE
LIMERICK
LIMERICKS
LIMES
LIMESCALE
LIMESTONE
LIMEWASH
LIMEWATER
LIMEY
LIMEYS
LIMIER
LIMIEST
LIMINA
LIMINAL
LIMINESS
LIMING
LIMINGS
LIMIT
LIMITABLE
LIMITARY
LIMITED
LIMITEDLY
LIMITEDS
LIMITER
LIMITERS
LIMITES
LIMITING
LIMITINGS
LIMITLESS
LIMITS
LIMMA
LIMMAS
LIMMER
LIMMERS
LIMN
LIMNAEID
LIMNAEIDS
LIMNED
LIMNER
LIMNERS
LIMNETIC
LIMNIC
LIMNING
LIMNOLOGY
LIMNS
LIMO
LIMONENE
LIMONENES
LIMONITE
LIMONITES
LIMONITIC
LIMONIUM
LIMONIUMS
LIMOS
LIMOSES
LIMOSIS
LIMOUS
LIMOUSINE
LIMP
LIMPA
LIMPAS
LIMPED
LIMPER
LIMPERS
LIMPEST
LIMPET
LIMPETS
LIMPID
LIMPIDITY
LIMPIDLY
LIMPING
LIMPINGLY
LIMPINGS
LIMPKIN
LIMPKINS
LIMPLY
LIMPNESS
LIMPS
LIMPSEY
LIMPSIER
LIMPSIEST
LIMPSY
LIMULI
LIMULOID
LIMULOIDS
LIMULUS
LIMULUSES
LIMY
LIN
LINABLE
LINAC
LINACS
LINAGE
LINAGES
LINALOL
LINALOLS
LINALOOL
LINALOOLS
LINCH
LINCHES
LINCHET
LINCHETS
LINCHPIN
LINCHPINS
LINCRUSTA
LINCTURE
LINCTURES
LINCTUS
LINCTUSES
LIND
LINDANE
LINDANES
LINDEN
LINDENS
LINDIED
LINDIES
LINDS
LINDWORM
LINDWORMS
LINDY
LINDYING

LINE
LINEABLE
LINEAGE
LINEAGES
LINEAL
LINEALITY
LINEALLY
LINEAMENT
LINEAR
LINEARISE
LINEARITY
LINEARIZE
LINEARLY
LINEATE
LINEATED
LINEATION
LINEBRED
LINECUT
LINECUTS
LINED
LINELESS
LINELIKE
LINEMAN
LINEMATE
LINEMATES
LINEMEN
LINEN
LINENFOLD
LINENIER
LINENIEST
LINENS
LINENY
LINEOLATE
LINER
LINERLESS
LINERS
LINES
LINESCORE
LINESMAN
LINESMEN
LINEUP
LINEUPS
LINEY
LING
LINGA
LINGAM
LINGAMS
LINGAS
LINGBERRY
LINGCOD
LINGCODS
LINGEL
LINGELS
LINGER
LINGERED
LINGERER
LINGERERS
LINGERIE
LINGERIES
LINGERING
LINGERS
LINGIER
LINGIEST
LINGLE
LINGLES
LINGO
LINGOES
LINGOS
LINGOT
LINGOTS
LINGS
LINGSTER
LINGSTERS
LINGUA
LINGUAE
LINGUAL
LINGUALLY
LINGUALS
LINGUAS
LINGUICA
LINGUICAS
LINGUINE
LINGUINES
LINGUINI
LINGUINIS
LINGUISA
LINGUISAS
LINGUIST
LINGUISTS
LINGULA
LINGULAE
LINGULAR
LINGULAS
LINGULATE
LINGY
LINHAY
LINHAYS
LINIER
LINIEST
LINIMENT
LINIMENTS
LININ
LINING
LININGS
LININS
LINISH
LINISHED
LINISHER
LINISHERS
LINISHES
LINISHING
LINK
LINKABLE
LINKAGE
LINKAGES
LINKBOY
LINKBOYS
LINKED
LINKER
LINKERS
LINKIER
LINKIEST
LINKING
LINKMAN
LINKMEN
LINKROT
LINKROTS
LINKS
LINKSLAND
LINKSMAN
LINKSMEN
LINKSPAN
LINKSPANS
LINKSTER
LINKSTERS
LINKUP
LINKUPS
LINKWORK
LINKWORKS
LINKY
LINN
LINNED
LINNET
LINNETS
LINNEY
LINNEYS
LINNIES
LINNING
LINNS
LINNY
LINO
LINOCUT
LINOCUTS
LINOLEATE
LINOLEIC
LINOLENIC
LINOLEUM
LINOLEUMS
LINOS
LINOTYPE
LINOTYPED
LINOTYPER
LINOTYPES
LINS
LINSANG
LINSANGS
LINSEED
LINSEEDS
LINSEY
LINSEYS
LINSTOCK
LINSTOCKS
LINT
LINTED
LINTEL
LINTELED
LINTELLED
LINTELS
LINTER
LINTERS
LINTIE
LINTIER
LINTIES
LINTIEST
LINTING
LINTINGS
LINTLESS
LINTOL
LINTOLS
LINTS
LINTSEED
LINTSEEDS
LINTSTOCK
LINTWHITE
LINTY
LINUM
LINUMS
LINURON
LINURONS
LINUX
LINUXES
LINY
LION
LIONCEL
LIONCELLE
LIONCELS
LIONEL
LIONELS
LIONESS
LIONESSES
LIONET
LIONETS
LIONFISH
LIONHEAD
LIONHEADS
LIONISE
LIONISED
LIONISER
LIONISERS
LIONISES
LIONISING
LIONISM
LIONISMS
LIONIZE
LIONIZED
LIONIZER
LIONIZERS
LIONIZES
LIONIZING
LIONLIER
LIONLIEST
LIONLIKE
LIONLY
LIONS
LIP
LIPA
LIPAEMIA
LIPAEMIAS
LIPARITE
LIPARITES

LIPAS
LIPASE
LIPASES
LIPE
LIPECTOMY
LIPEMIA
LIPEMIAS
LIPES
LIPGLOSS
LIPID
LIPIDE
LIPIDES
LIPIDIC
LIPIDOSES
LIPIDOSIS
LIPIDS
LIPIN
LIPINS
LIPLESS
LIPLIKE
LIPLINER
LIPLINERS
LIPO
LIPOCYTE
LIPOCYTES
LIPOGRAM
LIPOGRAMS
LIPOIC
LIPOID
LIPOIDAL
LIPOIDS
LIPOLITIC
LIPOLYSES
LIPOLYSIS
LIPOLYTIC
LIPOMA
LIPOMAS
LIPOMATA
LIPOPLAST
LIPOS
LIPOSOMAL
LIPOSOME
LIPOSOMES
LIPOSUCK
LIPOSUCKS
LIPOTROPY
LIPPED
LIPPEN
LIPPENED
LIPPENING
LIPPENS
LIPPER
LIPPERED
LIPPERING
LIPPERS
LIPPIE
LIPPIER
LIPPIES
LIPPIEST
LIPPINESS
LIPPING
LIPPINGS
LIPPITUDE
LIPPY
LIPREAD
LIPREADER
LIPREADS
LIPS
LIPSALVE
LIPSALVES
LIPSTICK
LIPSTICKS
LIPURIA
LIPURIAS
LIQUABLE
LIQUATE
LIQUATED
LIQUATES
LIQUATING
LIQUATION
LIQUEFIED
LIQUEFIER
LIQUEFIES
LIQUEFY
LIQUESCE
LIQUESCED
LIQUESCES
LIQUEUR
LIQUEURED
LIQUEURS
LIQUID
LIQUIDATE
LIQUIDIER
LIQUIDISE
LIQUIDITY
LIQUIDIZE
LIQUIDLY
LIQUIDS
LIQUIDUS
LIQUIDY
LIQUIFIED
LIQUIFIER
LIQUIFIES
LIQUIFY
LIQUITAB
LIQUITABS
LIQUOR
LIQUORED
LIQUORICE
LIQUORING
LIQUORISH
LIQUORS
LIRA
LIRAS
LIRE
LIRI
LIRIOPE
LIRIOPES
LIRIPIPE
LIRIPIPES
LIRIPOOP
LIRIPOOPS
LIRK
LIRKED
LIRKING
LIRKS
LIROT
LIROTH
LIS
LISENTE
LISK
LISKS
LISLE
LISLES
LISP
LISPED
LISPER
LISPERS
LISPING
LISPINGLY
LISPINGS
LISPOUND
LISPOUNDS
LISPS
LISPUND
LISPUNDS
LISSES
LISSOM
LISSOME
LISSOMELY
LISSOMLY
LIST
LISTABLE
LISTBOX
LISTBOXES
LISTED
LISTEE
LISTEES
LISTEL
LISTELS
LISTEN
LISTENED
LISTENER
LISTENERS
LISTENING
LISTENS
LISTER
LISTERIA
LISTERIAL
LISTERIAS
LISTERS
LISTETH
LISTFUL
LISTICLE
LISTICLES
LISTING
LISTINGS
LISTLESS
LISTS
LISTSERV
LISTSERVS
LIT
LITAI
LITANIES
LITANY
LITAS
LITCHI
LITCHIS
LITE
LITED
LITENESS
LITER
LITERACY
LITERAL
LITERALLY
LITERALS
LITERARY
LITERATE
LITERATES
LITERATI
LITERATIM
LITERATO
LITERATOR
LITERATUS
LITEROSE
LITERS
LITES
LITEST
LITH
LITHARGE
LITHARGES
LITHATE
LITHATES
LITHE
LITHED
LITHELY
LITHEMIA
LITHEMIAS
LITHEMIC
LITHENESS
LITHER
LITHERLY
LITHES
LITHESOME
LITHEST
LITHIA
LITHIAS
LITHIASES
LITHIASIS
LITHIC
LITHIFIED
LITHIFIES
LITHIFY
LITHING
LITHISTID
LITHITE
LITHITES
LITHIUM
LITHIUMS
LITHO

L

LITHOCYST
LITHOED
LITHOES
LITHOID
LITHOIDAL
LITHOING
LITHOLOGY
LITHOPONE
LITHOPS
LITHOS
LITHOSOL
LITHOSOLS
LITHOTOME
LITHOTOMY
LITHOTYPE
LITHS
LITIGABLE
LITIGANT
LITIGANTS
LITIGATE
LITIGATED
LITIGATES
LITIGATOR
LITIGIOUS
LITING
LITMUS
LITMUSES
LITORAL
LITOTES
LITOTIC
LITRE
LITREAGE
LITREAGES
LITRES
LITS
LITTEN
LITTER
LITTERBAG
LITTERBUG
LITTERED
LITTERER
LITTERERS
LITTERIER
LITTERING
LITTERS
LITTERY
LITTLE
LITTLER
LITTLES
LITTLEST
LITTLIE
LITTLIES
LITTLIN
LITTLING
LITTLINGS
LITTLINS
LITTLISH
LITTORAL
LITTORALS
LITU
LITURGIC
LITURGICS
LITURGIES
LITURGISM
LITURGIST
LITURGY
LITUUS
LITUUSES
LIVABLE
LIVE
LIVEABLE
LIVEBLOG
LIVEBLOGS
LIVED
LIVEDO
LIVEDOS
LIVELIER
LIVELIEST
LIVELILY
LIVELOD
LIVELODS
LIVELONG
LIVELONGS
LIVELOOD
LIVELOODS
LIVELY
LIVEN
LIVENED
LIVENER
LIVENERS
LIVENESS
LIVENING
LIVENS
LIVER
LIVERED
LIVERIED
LIVERIES
LIVERING
LIVERINGS
LIVERISH
LIVERLEAF
LIVERLESS
LIVERS
LIVERWORT
LIVERY
LIVERYMAN
LIVERYMEN
LIVES
LIVEST
LIVESTOCK
LIVETRAP
LIVETRAPS
LIVEWARE
LIVEWARES
LIVEWELL
LIVEWELLS
LIVEYER
LIVEYERE
LIVEYERES
LIVEYERS
LIVID
LIVIDER
LIVIDEST
LIVIDITY
LIVIDLY
LIVIDNESS
LIVIER
LIVIERS
LIVING
LIVINGLY
LIVINGS
LIVOR
LIVORS
LIVRAISON
LIVRE
LIVRES
LIVYER
LIVYERS
LIXIVIA
LIXIVIAL
LIXIVIATE
LIXIVIOUS
LIXIVIUM
LIXIVIUMS
LIZARD
LIZARDS
LIZZIE
LIZZIES
LLAMA
LLAMAS
LLANERO
LLANEROS
LLANO
LLANOS
LO
LOACH
LOACHES
LOAD
LOADABLE
LOADED
LOADEN
LOADENED
LOADENING
LOADENS
LOADER
LOADERS
LOADING
LOADINGS
LOADS
LOADSPACE
LOADSTAR
LOADSTARS
LOADSTONE
LOAF
LOAFED
LOAFER
LOAFERISH
LOAFERS
LOAFING
LOAFINGS
LOAFS
LOAM
LOAMED
LOAMIER
LOAMIEST
LOAMINESS
LOAMING
LOAMLESS
LOAMS
LOAMY
LOAN
LOANABLE
LOANBACK
LOANBACKS
LOANED
LOANEE
LOANEES
LOANER
LOANERS
LOANING
LOANINGS
LOANS
LOANSHIFT
LOANWORD
LOANWORDS
LOAST
LOATH
LOATHE
LOATHED
LOATHER
LOATHERS
LOATHES
LOATHEST
LOATHFUL
LOATHING
LOATHINGS
LOATHLIER
LOATHLY
LOATHNESS
LOATHSOME
LOATHY
LOAVE
LOAVED
LOAVES
LOAVING
LOB
LOBAR
LOBATE
LOBATED
LOBATELY
LOBATION
LOBATIONS
LOBBED
LOBBER
LOBBERS
LOBBIED
LOBBIES
LOBBING
LOBBY
LOBBYER

LOBBYERS
LOBBYGOW
LOBBYGOWS
LOBBYING
LOBBYINGS
LOBBYISM
LOBBYISMS
LOBBYIST
LOBBYISTS
LOBE
LOBECTOMY
LOBED
LOBEFIN
LOBEFINS
LOBELESS
LOBELET
LOBELETS
LOBELIA
LOBELIAS
LOBELIKE
LOBELINE
LOBELINES
LOBES
LOBI
LOBING
LOBINGS
LOBIPED
LOBLOLLY
LOBO
LOBOLA
LOBOLAS
LOBOLO
LOBOLOS
LOBOS
LOBOSE
LOBOTOMY
LOBS
LOBSCOUSE
LOBSTER
LOBSTERED
LOBSTERER
LOBSTERS
LOBSTICK
LOBSTICKS
LOBTAIL
LOBTAILED
LOBTAILS
LOBULAR
LOBULARLY
LOBULATE
LOBULATED
LOBULE
LOBULES
LOBULI
LOBULOSE
LOBULUS
LOBUS
LOBWORM
LOBWORMS
LOCA
LOCAL
LOCALE
LOCALES
LOCALISE
LOCALISED
LOCALISER
LOCALISES
LOCALISM
LOCALISMS
LOCALIST
LOCALISTS
LOCALITE
LOCALITES
LOCALITY
LOCALIZE
LOCALIZED
LOCALIZER
LOCALIZES
LOCALLY
LOCALNESS
LOCALS
LOCATABLE
LOCATE
LOCATED
LOCATER
LOCATERS
LOCATES
LOCATING
LOCATION
LOCATIONS
LOCATIVE
LOCATIVES
LOCATOR
LOCATORS
LOCAVORE
LOCAVORES
LOCELLATE
LOCH
LOCHAN
LOCHANS
LOCHE
LOCHES
LOCHIA
LOCHIAL
LOCHIAS
LOCHS
LOCI
LOCIE
LOCIES
LOCIS
LOCK
LOCKABLE
LOCKAGE
LOCKAGES
LOCKAWAY
LOCKAWAYS
LOCKBOX
LOCKBOXES
LOCKDOWN
LOCKDOWNS
LOCKED
LOCKER
LOCKERS
LOCKET
LOCKETS
LOCKFAST
LOCKFUL
LOCKFULS
LOCKHOUSE
LOCKING
LOCKINGS
LOCKJAW
LOCKJAWS
LOCKLESS
LOCKMAKER
LOCKMAN
LOCKMEN
LOCKNUT
LOCKNUTS
LOCKOUT
LOCKOUTS
LOCKPICK
LOCKPICKS
LOCKRAM
LOCKRAMS
LOCKS
LOCKSET
LOCKSETS
LOCKSMAN
LOCKSMEN
LOCKSMITH
LOCKSTEP
LOCKSTEPS
LOCKUP
LOCKUPS
LOCO
LOCOED
LOCOES
LOCOFOCO
LOCOFOCOS
LOCOING
LOCOISM
LOCOISMS
LOCOMAN
LOCOMEN
LOCOMOTE
LOCOMOTED
LOCOMOTES
LOCOMOTOR
LOCOPLANT
LOCOS
LOCOWEED
LOCOWEEDS
LOCULAR
LOCULATE
LOCULATED
LOCULE
LOCULED
LOCULES
LOCULI
LOCULUS
LOCUM
LOCUMS
LOCUPLETE
LOCUS
LOCUST
LOCUSTA
LOCUSTAE
LOCUSTAL
LOCUSTED
LOCUSTING
LOCUSTS
LOCUTION
LOCUTIONS
LOCUTORY
LOD
LODE
LODEN
LODENS
LODES
LODESMAN
LODESMEN
LODESTAR
LODESTARS
LODESTONE
LODGE
LODGEABLE
LODGED
LODGEMENT
LODGEPOLE
LODGER
LODGERS
LODGES
LODGING
LODGINGS
LODGMENT
LODGMENTS
LODICULA
LODICULAE
LODICULE
LODICULES
LODS
LOERIE
LOERIES
LOESS
LOESSAL
LOESSES
LOESSIAL
LOESSIC
LOFT
LOFTED
LOFTER
LOFTERS
LOFTIER
LOFTIEST
LOFTILY
LOFTINESS
LOFTING
LOFTLESS
LOFTLIKE

LOFTS
LOFTSMAN
LOFTSMEN
LOFTY
LOG
LOGAN
LOGANIA
LOGANIAS
LOGANS
LOGAOEDIC
LOGARITHM
LOGBOARD
LOGBOARDS
LOGBOOK
LOGBOOKS
LOGE
LOGES
LOGGAT
LOGGATS
LOGGED
LOGGER
LOGGERS
LOGGETS
LOGGIA
LOGGIAS
LOGGIE
LOGGIER
LOGGIEST
LOGGING
LOGGINGS
LOGGISH
LOGGY
LOGIA
LOGIC
LOGICAL
LOGICALLY
LOGICIAN
LOGICIANS
LOGICISE
LOGICISED
LOGICISES
LOGICISM
LOGICISMS
LOGICIST
LOGICISTS
LOGICIZE
LOGICIZED
LOGICIZES
LOGICLESS
LOGICS
LOGIE
LOGIER
LOGIES
LOGIEST
LOGILY
LOGIN
LOGINESS
LOGINS
LOGION
LOGIONS
LOGISTIC
LOGISTICS
LOGJAM
LOGJAMMED
LOGJAMS
LOGJUICE
LOGJUICES
LOGLINE
LOGLINES
LOGLOG
LOGLOGS
LOGNORMAL
LOGO
LOGOED
LOGOFF
LOGOFFS
LOGOGRAM
LOGOGRAMS
LOGOGRAPH
LOGOGRIPH
LOGOI
LOGOMACH
LOGOMACHS
LOGOMACHY
LOGON
LOGONS
LOGOPEDIC
LOGOPHILE
LOGORRHEA
LOGOS
LOGOTHETE
LOGOTYPE
LOGOTYPES
LOGOTYPY
LOGOUT
LOGOUTS
LOGROLL
LOGROLLED
LOGROLLER
LOGROLLS
LOGS
LOGWAY
LOGWAYS
LOGWOOD
LOGWOODS
LOGY
LOHAN
LOHANS
LOIASES
LOIASIS
LOIASISES
LOID
LOIDED
LOIDING
LOIDS
LOIN
LOINCLOTH
LOINS
LOIPE
LOIPEN
LOIR
LOIRS
LOITER
LOITERED
LOITERER
LOITERERS
LOITERING
LOITERS
LOKE
LOKES
LOKSHEN
LOLIGO
LOLIGOS
LOLIUM
LOLIUMS
LOLL
LOLLED
LOLLER
LOLLERS
LOLLIES
LOLLING
LOLLINGLY
LOLLIPOP
LOLLIPOPS
LOLLOP
LOLLOPED
LOLLOPIER
LOLLOPING
LOLLOPS
LOLLOPY
LOLLS
LOLLY
LOLLYGAG
LOLLYGAGS
LOLLYPOP
LOLLYPOPS
LOLOG
LOLOGS
LOLZ
LOMA
LOMAS
LOMATA
LOME
LOMED
LOMEIN
LOMEINS
LOMENT
LOMENTA
LOMENTS
LOMENTUM
LOMENTUMS
LOMES
LOMING
LOMPISH
LONE
LONELIER
LONELIEST
LONELILY
LONELY
LONENESS
LONER
LONERS
LONESOME
LONESOMES
LONG
LONGA
LONGAEVAL
LONGAN
LONGANS
LONGAS
LONGBOARD
LONGBOAT
LONGBOATS
LONGBOW
LONGBOWS
LONGCASE
LONGCLOTH
LONGE
LONGED
LONGEING
LONGER
LONGERON
LONGERONS
LONGERS
LONGES
LONGEST
LONGEVAL
LONGEVITY
LONGEVOUS
LONGFORM
LONGHAIR
LONGHAIRS
LONGHAND
LONGHANDS
LONGHEAD
LONGHEADS
LONGHORN
LONGHORNS
LONGHOUSE
LONGICORN
LONGIES
LONGING
LONGINGLY
LONGINGS
LONGISH
LONGITUDE
LONGJUMP
LONGJUMPS
LONGLEAF
LONGLINE
LONGLINER
LONGLINES
LONGLIST
LONGLISTS
LONGLY
LONGNECK
LONGNECKS
LONGNESS
LONGS
LONGSHIP

LONGSHIPS
LONGSHORE
LONGSOME
LONGSPUR
LONGSPURS
LONGTIME
LONGUEUR
LONGUEURS
LONGWALL
LONGWALLS
LONGWAYS
LONGWISE
LONGWORM
LONGWORMS
LONICERA
LONICERAS
LOO
LOOBIER
LOOBIES
LOOBIEST
LOOBILY
LOOBY
LOOED
LOOEY
LOOEYS
LOOF
LOOFA
LOOFAH
LOOFAHS
LOOFAS
LOOFFUL
LOOFFULS
LOOFS
LOOGIE
LOOGIES
LOOIE
LOOIES
LOOING
LOOK
LOOKALIKE
LOOKDOWN
LOOKDOWNS
LOOKED
LOOKER
LOOKERS
LOOKIE
LOOKING
LOOKISM
LOOKISMS
LOOKIST
LOOKISTS
LOOKIT
LOOKOUT
LOOKOUTS
LOOKOVER
LOOKOVERS
LOOKS
LOOKSISM
LOOKSISMS
LOOKUP
LOOKUPS
LOOKY
LOOM
LOOMED
LOOMING
LOOMS
LOON
LOONEY
LOONEYS
LOONIE
LOONIER
LOONIES
LOONIEST
LOONILY
LOONINESS
LOONING
LOONINGS
LOONS
LOONY
LOOP
LOOPED
LOOPER
LOOPERS
LOOPHOLE
LOOPHOLED
LOOPHOLES
LOOPIER
LOOPIEST
LOOPILY
LOOPINESS
LOOPING
LOOPINGS
LOOPLIKE
LOOPS
LOOPY
LOOR
LOORD
LOORDS
LOOS
LOOSE
LOOSEBOX
LOOSED
LOOSELY
LOOSEN
LOOSENED
LOOSENER
LOOSENERS
LOOSENESS
LOOSENING
LOOSENS
LOOSER
LOOSES
LOOSEST
LOOSIE
LOOSIES
LOOSING
LOOSINGS
LOOT
LOOTED
LOOTEN
LOOTER
LOOTERS
LOOTING
LOOTINGS
LOOTS
LOOVES
LOP
LOPE
LOPED
LOPER
LOPERS
LOPES
LOPGRASS
LOPHODONT
LOPING
LOPINGLY
LOPOLITH
LOPOLITHS
LOPPED
LOPPER
LOPPERED
LOPPERING
LOPPERS
LOPPET
LOPPETS
LOPPIER
LOPPIES
LOPPIEST
LOPPING
LOPPINGS
LOPPY
LOPS
LOPSIDED
LOPSTICK
LOPSTICKS
LOQUACITY
LOQUAT
LOQUATS
LOQUITUR
LOR
LORAL
LORAN
LORANS
LORATE
LORAZEPAM
LORCHA
LORCHAS
LORD
LORDED
LORDING
LORDINGS
LORDKIN
LORDKINS
LORDLESS
LORDLIER
LORDLIEST
LORDLIKE
LORDLING
LORDLINGS
LORDLY
LORDOMA
LORDOMAS
LORDOSES
LORDOSIS
LORDOTIC
LORDS
LORDSHIP
LORDSHIPS
LORDY
LORE
LOREAL
LOREL
LORELS
LORES
LORETTE
LORETTES
LORGNETTE
LORGNON
LORGNONS
LORIC
LORICA
LORICAE
LORICAS
LORICATE
LORICATED
LORICATES
LORICS
LORIES
LORIKEET
LORIKEETS
LORIMER
LORIMERS
LORINER
LORINERS
LORING
LORINGS
LORIOT
LORIOTS
LORIS
LORISES
LORN
LORNER
LORNEST
LORNNESS
LORRELL
LORRELLS
LORRIES
LORRY
LORY
LOS
LOSABLE
LOSE
LOSED
LOSEL
LOSELS
LOSEN
LOSER
LOSERS
LOSES
LOSH

LOSING
LOSINGEST
LOSINGLY
LOSINGS
LOSLYF
LOSLYFS
LOSS
LOSSES
LOSSIER
LOSSIEST
LOSSLESS
LOSSMAKER
LOSSY
LOST
LOSTNESS
LOT
LOTA
LOTAH
LOTAHS
LOTAS
LOTE
LOTES
LOTH
LOTHARIO
LOTHARIOS
LOTHEFULL
LOTHER
LOTHEST
LOTHFULL
LOTHNESS
LOTHSOME
LOTI
LOTIC
LOTION
LOTIONS
LOTO
LOTOS
LOTOSES
LOTS
LOTSA
LOTTA
LOTTE
LOTTED
LOTTER
LOTTERIES
LOTTERS
LOTTERY
LOTTES
LOTTING
LOTTO
LOTTOS
LOTUS
LOTUSES
LOTUSLAND
LOU
LOUCHE
LOUCHELY
LOUCHER
LOUCHEST
LOUD
LOUDEN
LOUDENED
LOUDENING
LOUDENS
LOUDER
LOUDEST
LOUDISH
LOUDLIER
LOUDLIEST
LOUDLY
LOUDMOUTH
LOUDNESS
LOUED
LOUGH
LOUGHS
LOUIE
LOUIES
LOUING
LOUIS
LOUMA
LOUMAS
LOUN
LOUND
LOUNDED
LOUNDER
LOUNDERED
LOUNDERS
LOUNDING
LOUNDS
LOUNED
LOUNGE
LOUNGED
LOUNGER
LOUNGERS
LOUNGES
LOUNGEY
LOUNGIER
LOUNGIEST
LOUNGING
LOUNGINGS
LOUNGY
LOUNING
LOUNS
LOUP
LOUPE
LOUPED
LOUPEN
LOUPES
LOUPING
LOUPIT
LOUPS
LOUR
LOURE
LOURED
LOURES
LOURIE
LOURIER
LOURIES
LOURIEST
LOURING
LOURINGLY
LOURINGS
LOURS
LOURY
LOUS
LOUSE
LOUSED
LOUSER
LOUSERS
LOUSES
LOUSEWORT
LOUSIER
LOUSIEST
LOUSILY
LOUSINESS
LOUSING
LOUSINGS
LOUSY
LOUT
LOUTED
LOUTERIES
LOUTERY
LOUTING
LOUTISH
LOUTISHLY
LOUTS
LOUVAR
LOUVARS
LOUVER
LOUVERED
LOUVERS
LOUVRE
LOUVRED
LOUVRES
LOVABLE
LOVABLY
LOVAGE
LOVAGES
LOVAT
LOVATS
LOVE
LOVEABLE
LOVEABLY
LOVEBIRD
LOVEBIRDS
LOVEBITE
LOVEBITES
LOVEBUG
LOVEBUGS
LOVED
LOVEFEST
LOVEFESTS
LOVELESS
LOVELIER
LOVELIES
LOVELIEST
LOVELIGHT
LOVELILY
LOVELOCK
LOVELOCKS
LOVELORN
LOVELY
LOVEMAKER
LOVER
LOVERED
LOVERLESS
LOVERLY
LOVERS
LOVES
LOVESEAT
LOVESEATS
LOVESICK
LOVESOME
LOVEVINE
LOVEVINES
LOVEY
LOVEYS
LOVIE
LOVIER
LOVIES
LOVIEST
LOVING
LOVINGLY
LOVINGS
LOW
LOWAN
LOWANS
LOWBALL
LOWBALLED
LOWBALLS
LOWBORN
LOWBOY
LOWBOYS
LOWBRED
LOWBROW
LOWBROWED
LOWBROWS
LOWBUSH
LOWBUSHES
LOWDOWN
LOWDOWNS
LOWE
LOWED
LOWER
LOWERABLE
LOWERCASE
LOWERED
LOWERIER
LOWERIEST
LOWERING
LOWERINGS
LOWERMOST
LOWERS
LOWERY
LOWES
LOWEST
LOWING
LOWINGS
LOWISH
LOWLAND

LOWLANDER
LOWLANDS
LOWLIER
LOWLIEST
LOWLIFE
LOWLIFER
LOWLIFERS
LOWLIFES
LOWLIGHT
LOWLIGHTS
LOWLIHEAD
LOWLILY
LOWLINESS
LOWLIVES
LOWLY
LOWN
LOWND
LOWNDED
LOWNDING
LOWNDS
LOWNE
LOWNED
LOWNES
LOWNESS
LOWNESSES
LOWNING
LOWNS
LOWP
LOWPASS
LOWPED
LOWPING
LOWPS
LOWRIDER
LOWRIDERS
LOWRIE
LOWRIES
LOWRY
LOWS
LOWSE
LOWSED
LOWSENING
LOWSER
LOWSES
LOWSEST
LOWSING
LOWSIT
LOWT
LOWTED
LOWTING
LOWTS
LOWVELD
LOWVELDS
LOX
LOXED
LOXES
LOXING
LOXODROME
LOXODROMY
LOXYGEN
LOXYGENS
LOY
LOYAL
LOYALER
LOYALEST
LOYALISM
LOYALISMS
LOYALIST
LOYALISTS
LOYALLER
LOYALLEST
LOYALLY
LOYALNESS
LOYALTIES
LOYALTY
LOYS
LOZELL
LOZELLS
LOZEN
LOZENGE
LOZENGED
LOZENGES
LOZENGIER
LOZENGY
LOZENS
LUACH
LUAU
LUAUS
LUBBARD
LUBBARDS
LUBBER
LUBBERLY
LUBBERS
LUBE
LUBED
LUBES
LUBFISH
LUBFISHES
LUBING
LUBRIC
LUBRICAL
LUBRICANT
LUBRICATE
LUBRICITY
LUBRICOUS
LUCARNE
LUCARNES
LUCE
LUCENCE
LUCENCES
LUCENCIES
LUCENCY
LUCENT
LUCENTLY
LUCERN
LUCERNE
LUCERNES
LUCERNS
LUCES
LUCHOT
LUCHOTH
LUCID
LUCIDER
LUCIDEST
LUCIDITY
LUCIDLY
LUCIDNESS
LUCIFER
LUCIFERIN
LUCIFERS
LUCIGEN
LUCIGENS
LUCITE
LUCITES
LUCK
LUCKED
LUCKEN
LUCKIE
LUCKIER
LUCKIES
LUCKIEST
LUCKILY
LUCKINESS
LUCKING
LUCKLESS
LUCKPENNY
LUCKS
LUCKY
LUCRATIVE
LUCRE
LUCRES
LUCTATION
LUCUBRATE
LUCULENT
LUCUMA
LUCUMAS
LUCUMO
LUCUMONES
LUCUMOS
LUD
LUDE
LUDERICK
LUDERICKS
LUDES
LUDIC
LUDICALLY
LUDICROUS
LUDO
LUDOS
LUDS
LUDSHIP
LUDSHIPS
LUES
LUETIC
LUETICS
LUFF
LUFFA
LUFFAS
LUFFED
LUFFING
LUFFS
LUG
LUGE
LUGED
LUGEING
LUGEINGS
LUGER
LUGERS
LUGES
LUGGABLE
LUGGABLES
LUGGAGE
LUGGAGES
LUGGED
LUGGER
LUGGERS
LUGGIE
LUGGIES
LUGGING
LUGHOLE
LUGHOLES
LUGING
LUGINGS
LUGS
LUGSAIL
LUGSAILS
LUGWORM
LUGWORMS
LUIT
LUITEN
LUKE
LUKEWARM
LULIBUB
LULIBUBS
LULL
LULLABIED
LULLABIES
LULLABY
LULLED
LULLER
LULLERS
LULLING
LULLINGLY
LULLS
LULU
LULUS
LULZ
LUM
LUMA
LUMAS
LUMBAGO
LUMBAGOS
LUMBANG
LUMBANGS
LUMBAR
LUMBARS
LUMBER
LUMBERED
LUMBERER
LUMBERERS
LUMBERING

LUMBERLY
LUMBERMAN
LUMBERMEN
LUMBERS
LUMBI
LUMBRICAL
LUMBRICI
LUMBRICUS
LUMBUS
LUMEN
LUMENAL
LUMENS
LUMINA
LUMINAIRE
LUMINAL
LUMINANCE
LUMINANT
LUMINANTS
LUMINARIA
LUMINARY
LUMINE
LUMINED
LUMINES
LUMINESCE
LUMINING
LUMINISM
LUMINISMS
LUMINIST
LUMINISTS
LUMINOUS
LUMME
LUMMIER
LUMMIEST
LUMMOX
LUMMOXES
LUMMY
LUMP
LUMPED
LUMPEN
LUMPENLY
LUMPENS
LUMPER
LUMPERS
LUMPFISH
LUMPIA
LUMPIAS
LUMPIER
LUMPIEST
LUMPILY
LUMPINESS
LUMPING
LUMPINGLY
LUMPISH
LUMPISHLY
LUMPKIN
LUMPKINS
LUMPS
LUMPY
LUMS
LUN
LUNA
LUNACIES
LUNACY
LUNANAUT
LUNANAUTS
LUNAR
LUNARIAN
LUNARIANS
LUNARIES
LUNARIST
LUNARISTS
LUNARNAUT
LUNARS
LUNARY
LUNAS
LUNATE
LUNATED
LUNATELY
LUNATES
LUNATIC
LUNATICAL
LUNATICS
LUNATION
LUNATIONS
LUNCH
LUNCHBOX
LUNCHED
LUNCHEON
LUNCHEONS
LUNCHER
LUNCHERS
LUNCHES
LUNCHING
LUNCHMEAT
LUNCHPAIL
LUNCHROOM
LUNCHTIME
LUNE
LUNES
LUNET
LUNETS
LUNETTE
LUNETTES
LUNG
LUNGAN
LUNGANS
LUNGE
LUNGED
LUNGEE
LUNGEES
LUNGEING
LUNGER
LUNGERS
LUNGES
LUNGFISH
LUNGFUL
LUNGFULS
LUNGI
LUNGIE
LUNGIES
LUNGING
LUNGIS
LUNGLESS
LUNGLIKE
LUNGS
LUNGWORM
LUNGWORMS
LUNGWORT
LUNGWORTS
LUNGYI
LUNGYIS
LUNIER
LUNIES
LUNIEST
LUNINESS
LUNISOLAR
LUNITIDAL
LUNK
LUNKER
LUNKERS
LUNKHEAD
LUNKHEADS
LUNKS
LUNS
LUNT
LUNTED
LUNTING
LUNTS
LUNULA
LUNULAE
LUNULAR
LUNULATE
LUNULATED
LUNULE
LUNULES
LUNY
LUNYIE
LUNYIES
LUPANAR
LUPANARS
LUPIN
LUPINE
LUPINES
LUPINS
LUPOID
LUPOUS
LUPPEN
LUPULIN
LUPULINE
LUPULINIC
LUPULINS
LUPUS
LUPUSES
LUR
LURCH
LURCHED
LURCHER
LURCHERS
LURCHES
LURCHING
LURDAN
LURDANE
LURDANES
LURDANS
LURDEN
LURDENS
LURE
LURED
LURER
LURERS
LURES
LUREX
LUREXES
LURGI
LURGIES
LURGIS
LURGY
LURID
LURIDER
LURIDEST
LURIDLY
LURIDNESS
LURING
LURINGLY
LURINGS
LURK
LURKED
LURKER
LURKERS
LURKING
LURKINGLY
LURKINGS
LURKS
LURRIES
LURRY
LURS
LURVE
LURVES
LUSCIOUS
LUSER
LUSERS
LUSH
LUSHED
LUSHER
LUSHERS
LUSHES
LUSHEST
LUSHIER
LUSHIES
LUSHIEST
LUSHING
LUSHLY
LUSHNESS
LUSHY
LUSK
LUSKED
LUSKING
LUSKISH
LUSKS
LUST

LUSTED
LUSTER
LUSTERED
LUSTERING
LUSTERS
LUSTFUL
LUSTFULLY
LUSTICK
LUSTIER
LUSTIEST
LUSTIHEAD
LUSTIHOOD
LUSTILY
LUSTINESS
LUSTING
LUSTIQUE
LUSTLESS
LUSTRA
LUSTRAL
LUSTRATE
LUSTRATED
LUSTRATES
LUSTRE
LUSTRED
LUSTRES
LUSTRINE
LUSTRINES
LUSTRING
LUSTRINGS
LUSTROUS
LUSTRUM
LUSTRUMS
LUSTS
LUSTY
LUSUS
LUSUSES
LUTANIST
LUTANISTS
LUTE
LUTEA
LUTEAL
LUTECIUM
LUTECIUMS
LUTED
LUTEFISK
LUTEFISKS
LUTEIN
LUTEINISE
LUTEINIZE
LUTEINS
LUTELIKE
LUTENIST
LUTENISTS
LUTEOLIN
LUTEOLINS
LUTEOLOUS
LUTEOUS
LUTER
LUTERS
LUTES
LUTESCENT
LUTETIUM
LUTETIUMS
LUTEUM
LUTFISK
LUTFISKS
LUTHERN
LUTHERNS
LUTHIER
LUTHIERS
LUTING
LUTINGS
LUTIST
LUTISTS
LUTITE
LUTITES
LUTTEN
LUTZ
LUTZES
LUV
LUVS
LUVVED
LUVVIE
LUVVIEDOM
LUVVIES
LUVVING
LUVVY
LUX
LUXATE
LUXATED
LUXATES
LUXATING
LUXATION
LUXATIONS
LUXE
LUXED
LUXER
LUXES
LUXEST
LUXING
LUXMETER
LUXMETERS
LUXURIANT
LUXURIATE
LUXURIES
LUXURIOUS
LUXURIST
LUXURISTS
LUXURY
LUZ
LUZERN
LUZERNS
LUZZES
LWEI
LWEIS
LYAM
LYAMS
LYARD
LYART
LYASE
LYASES
LYCAENID
LYCAENIDS
LYCEA
LYCEE
LYCEES
LYCEUM
LYCEUMS
LYCH
LYCHEE
LYCHEES
LYCHES
LYCHGATE
LYCHGATES
LYCHNIS
LYCHNISES
LYCOPENE
LYCOPENES
LYCOPOD
LYCOPODS
LYCOPSID
LYCOPSIDS
LYCRA
LYCRAS
LYDDITE
LYDDITES
LYE
LYES
LYFULL
LYING
LYINGLY
LYINGS
LYKEWAKE
LYKEWAKES
LYKEWALK
LYKEWALKS
LYM
LYME
LYMES
LYMITER
LYMITERS
LYMPH
LYMPHAD
LYMPHADS
LYMPHATIC
LYMPHOID
LYMPHOMA
LYMPHOMAS
LYMPHOUS
LYMPHS
LYMS
LYNAGE
LYNAGES
LYNCEAN
LYNCH
LYNCHED
LYNCHER
LYNCHERS
LYNCHES
LYNCHET
LYNCHETS
LYNCHING
LYNCHINGS
LYNCHPIN
LYNCHPINS
LYNE
LYNES
LYNX
LYNXES
LYNXLIKE
LYOLYSES
LYOLYSIS
LYOMEROUS
LYONNAISE
LYOPHIL
LYOPHILE
LYOPHILED
LYOPHILIC
LYOPHOBE
LYOPHOBIC
LYRA
LYRATE
LYRATED
LYRATELY
LYRE
LYREBIRD
LYREBIRDS
LYRES
LYRIC
LYRICAL
LYRICALLY
LYRICISE
LYRICISED
LYRICISES
LYRICISM
LYRICISMS
LYRICIST
LYRICISTS
LYRICIZE
LYRICIZED
LYRICIZES
LYRICON
LYRICONS
LYRICS
LYRIFORM
LYRISM
LYRISMS
LYRIST
LYRISTS
LYSATE
LYSATES
LYSE
LYSED
LYSERGIC
LYSERGIDE
LYSES
LYSIGENIC
LYSIMETER
LYSIN
LYSINE

L

LYSINES
LYSING
LYSINS
LYSIS
LYSOGEN
LYSOGENIC
LYSOGENS
LYSOGENY
LYSOL
LYSOLS
LYSOSOMAL
LYSOSOME
LYSOSOMES
LYSOZYME
LYSOZYMES
LYSSA
LYSSAS
LYTE
LYTED
LYTES
LYTHE
LYTHES
LYTHRUM
LYTHRUMS
LYTIC
LYTICALLY
LYTING
LYTTA
LYTTAE
LYTTAS

L

M

MA
MAA
MAAED
MAAING
MAAR
MAARE
MAARS
MAAS
MAASES
MAATJES
MABE
MABELA
MABELAS
MABES
MAC
MACA
MACABER
MACABRE
MACABRELY
MACABRER
MACABREST
MACACO
MACACOS
MACADAM
MACADAMED
MACADAMIA
MACADAMS
MACAHUBA
MACAHUBAS
MACALLUM
MACALLUMS
MACAQUE
MACAQUES
MACARISE
MACARISED
MACARISES
MACARISM
MACARISMS
MACARIZE
MACARIZED
MACARIZES
MACARON
MACARONI
MACARONIC
MACARONIS
MACARONS
MACAROON
MACAROONS
MACAS
MACASSAR
MACASSARS
MACAW
MACAWS
MACCABAW
MACCABAWS
MACCABOY
MACCABOYS
MACCARONI
MACCHIA
MACCHIATO
MACCHIE
MACCOBOY
MACCOBOYS
MACE
MACED
MACEDOINE
MACER
MACERAL
MACERALS
MACERATE
MACERATED
MACERATER
MACERATES
MACERATOR
MACERS
MACES
MACH
MACHACA
MACHACAS
MACHAIR
MACHAIRS
MACHAN
MACHANS
MACHE
MACHER
MACHERS
MACHES
MACHETE
MACHETES
MACHI
MACHINATE
MACHINE
MACHINED
MACHINERY
MACHINES
MACHINIMA
MACHINING
MACHINIST
MACHISMO
MACHISMOS
MACHMETER
MACHO
MACHOISM
MACHOISMS
MACHOS
MACHREE
MACHREES
MACHS
MACHZOR
MACHZORIM
MACHZORS
MACING
MACINTOSH
MACK
MACKEREL
MACKERELS
MACKINAW
MACKINAWS
MACKLE
MACKLED
MACKLES
MACKLING
MACKS
MACLE
MACLED
MACLES
MACON
MACONS
MACOYA
MACOYAS
MACRAME
MACRAMES
MACRAMI
MACRAMIS
MACRO
MACROBIAN
MACROCODE
MACROCOPY
MACROCOSM
MACROCYST
MACROCYTE
MACRODOME
MACRODONT
MACROGLIA
MACROLIDE
MACROLOGY
MACROMERE
MACROMOLE
MACRON
MACRONS
MACROPOD
MACROPODS
MACROPSIA
MACROS
MACROTOUS
MACRURAL
MACRURAN
MACRURANS
MACRUROID
MACRUROUS
MACS
MACTATION
MACULA
MACULAE
MACULAR
MACULAS
MACULATE
MACULATED
MACULATES
MACULE
MACULED
MACULES
MACULING
MACULOSE
MACUMBA
MACUMBAS
MAD
MADAFU
MADAFUS
MADAM
MADAME
MADAMED
MADAMES
MADAMING
MADAMS
MADAROSES
MADAROSIS
MADBRAIN
MADBRAINS
MADCAP
MADCAPS
MADDED
MADDEN
MADDENED
MADDENING
MADDENS
MADDER
MADDERS
MADDEST
MADDING
MADDINGLY
MADDISH
MADDOCK
MADDOCKS
MADE
MADEFIED
MADEFIES
MADEFY
MADEFYING
MADEIRA

MADEIRAS
MADELEINE
MADERISE
MADERISED
MADERISES
MADERIZE
MADERIZED
MADERIZES
MADEUPPY
MADGE
MADGES
MADHOUSE
MADHOUSES
MADID
MADISON
MADISONS
MADLING
MADLINGS
MADLY
MADMAN
MADMEN
MADNESS
MADNESSES
MADONNA
MADONNAS
MADOQUA
MADOQUAS
MADRAS
MADRASA
MADRASAH
MADRASAHS
MADRASAS
MADRASES
MADRASSA
MADRASSAH
MADRASSAS
MADRE
MADREPORE
MADRES
MADRIGAL
MADRIGALS
MADRILENE
MADRONA
MADRONAS
MADRONE
MADRONES
MADRONO
MADRONOS
MADS
MADTOM
MADTOMS
MADURO
MADUROS
MADWOMAN
MADWOMEN
MADWORT
MADWORTS
MADZOON
MADZOONS
MAE
MAELID
MAELIDS
MAELSTROM
MAENAD
MAENADES
MAENADIC
MAENADISM
MAENADS
MAERL
MAERLS
MAES
MAESTOSO
MAESTOSOS
MAESTRI
MAESTRO
MAESTROS
MAFFIA
MAFFIAS
MAFFICK
MAFFICKED
MAFFICKER
MAFFICKS
MAFFLED
MAFFLIN
MAFFLING
MAFFLINGS
MAFFLINS
MAFIA
MAFIAS
MAFIC
MAFICS
MAFIOSI
MAFIOSO
MAFIOSOS
MAFTED
MAFTIR
MAFTIRS
MAG
MAGAININ
MAGAININS
MAGALOG
MAGALOGS
MAGALOGUE
MAGAZINE
MAGAZINES
MAGDALEN
MAGDALENE
MAGDALENS
MAGE
MAGENTA
MAGENTAS
MAGES
MAGESHIP
MAGESHIPS
MAGG
MAGGED
MAGGIE
MAGGIES
MAGGING
MAGGOT
MAGGOTIER
MAGGOTS
MAGGOTY
MAGGS
MAGI
MAGIAN
MAGIANISM
MAGIANS
MAGIC
MAGICAL
MAGICALLY
MAGICIAN
MAGICIANS
MAGICKED
MAGICKING
MAGICS
MAGILP
MAGILPS
MAGISM
MAGISMS
MAGISTER
MAGISTERS
MAGISTERY
MAGISTRAL
MAGLEV
MAGLEVS
MAGMA
MAGMAS
MAGMATA
MAGMATIC
MAGMATISM
MAGNALIUM
MAGNATE
MAGNATES
MAGNES
MAGNESES
MAGNESIA
MAGNESIAL
MAGNESIAN
MAGNESIAS
MAGNESIC
MAGNESITE
MAGNESIUM
MAGNET
MAGNETAR
MAGNETARS
MAGNETIC
MAGNETICS
MAGNETISE
MAGNETISM
MAGNETIST
MAGNETITE
MAGNETIZE
MAGNETO
MAGNETON
MAGNETONS
MAGNETOS
MAGNETRON
MAGNETS
MAGNIFIC
MAGNIFICO
MAGNIFIED
MAGNIFIER
MAGNIFIES
MAGNIFY
MAGNITUDE
MAGNOLIA
MAGNOLIAS
MAGNON
MAGNONS
MAGNOX
MAGNOXES
MAGNUM
MAGNUMS
MAGNUS
MAGOT
MAGOTS
MAGPIE
MAGPIES
MAGS
MAGSMAN
MAGSMEN
MAGUEY
MAGUEYS
MAGUS
MAGYAR
MAHA
MAHANT
MAHANTS
MAHARAJA
MAHARAJAH
MAHARAJAS
MAHARANEE
MAHARANI
MAHARANIS
MAHARISHI
MAHATMA
MAHATMAS
MAHEWU
MAHEWUS
MAHIMAHI
MAHIMAHIS
MAHJONG
MAHJONGG
MAHJONGGS
MAHJONGS
MAHLSTICK
MAHMAL
MAHMALS
MAHOE
MAHOES
MAHOGANY
MAHONIA
MAHONIAS
MAHOUT
MAHOUTS
MAHSEER
MAHSEERS
MAHSIR
MAHSIRS

M

MAHUA
MAHUANG
MAHUANGS
MAHUAS
MAHWA
MAHWAS
MAHZOR
MAHZORIM
MAHZORS
MAIASAUR
MAIASAURA
MAIASAURS
MAID
MAIDAN
MAIDANS
MAIDED
MAIDEN
MAIDENISH
MAIDENLY
MAIDENS
MAIDHOOD
MAIDHOODS
MAIDING
MAIDISH
MAIDISM
MAIDISMS
MAIDLESS
MAIDS
MAIEUTIC
MAIEUTICS
MAIGRE
MAIGRES
MAIHEM
MAIHEMS
MAIK
MAIKO
MAIKOS
MAIKS
MAIL
MAILABLE
MAILBAG
MAILBAGS
MAILBOAT
MAILBOATS
MAILBOX
MAILBOXES
MAILCAR
MAILCARS
MAILCOACH
MAILE
MAILED
MAILER
MAILERS
MAILES
MAILGRAM
MAILGRAMS
MAILING
MAILINGS
MAILL
MAILLESS
MAILLOT
MAILLOTS
MAILLS
MAILMAN
MAILMEN
MAILMERGE
MAILPOUCH
MAILROOM
MAILROOMS
MAILS
MAILSACK
MAILSACKS
MAILSHOT
MAILSHOTS
MAILVAN
MAILVANS
MAIM
MAIMED
MAIMER
MAIMERS
MAIMING
MAIMINGS
MAIMS
MAIN
MAINBOOM
MAINBOOMS
MAINBRACE
MAINDOOR
MAINDOORS
MAINED
MAINER
MAINEST
MAINFRAME
MAINING
MAINLAND
MAINLANDS
MAINLINE
MAINLINED
MAINLINER
MAINLINES
MAINLY
MAINMAST
MAINMASTS
MAINOR
MAINORS
MAINOUR
MAINOURS
MAINPRISE
MAINS
MAINSAIL
MAINSAILS
MAINSHEET
MAINSTAGE
MAINSTAY
MAINSTAYS
MAINTAIN
MAINTAINS
MAINTOP
MAINTOPS
MAINYARD
MAINYARDS
MAIOLICA
MAIOLICAS
MAIR
MAIRE
MAIREHAU
MAIREHAUS
MAIRES
MAIRS
MAISE
MAISES
MAIST
MAISTER
MAISTERED
MAISTERS
MAISTRIES
MAISTRING
MAISTRY
MAISTS
MAIZE
MAIZES
MAJAGUA
MAJAGUAS
MAJESTIC
MAJESTIES
MAJESTY
MAJLIS
MAJLISES
MAJOLICA
MAJOLICAS
MAJOR
MAJORAT
MAJORATS
MAJORDOMO
MAJORED
MAJORETTE
MAJORING
MAJORITY
MAJORLY
MAJORS
MAJORSHIP
MAJUSCULE
MAK
MAKABLE
MAKAR
MAKARS
MAKE
MAKEABLE
MAKEABLES
MAKEBATE
MAKEBATES
MAKEFAST
MAKEFASTS
MAKELESS
MAKEOVER
MAKEOVERS
MAKER
MAKEREADY
MAKERS
MAKES
MAKESHIFT
MAKEUP
MAKEUPS
MAKHANI
MAKHANIS
MAKI
MAKIMONO
MAKIMONOS
MAKING
MAKINGS
MAKIS
MAKO
MAKOS
MAKS
MAKUTA
MAKUTU
MAKUTUED
MAKUTUING
MAKUTUS
MAL
MALA
MALACCA
MALACCAS
MALACHITE
MALACIA
MALACIAS
MALADIES
MALADROIT
MALADY
MALAGUENA
MALAISE
MALAISES
MALAM
MALAMS
MALAMUTE
MALAMUTES
MALANDER
MALANDERS
MALANGA
MALANGAS
MALAPERT
MALAPERTS
MALAPROP
MALAPROPS
MALAR
MALARIA
MALARIAL
MALARIAN
MALARIAS
MALARIOUS
MALARKEY
MALARKEYS
MALARKIES
MALARKY
MALAROMA
MALAROMAS
MALARS
MALAS
MALATE
MALATES

M

MALATHION
MALAX
MALAXAGE
MALAXAGES
MALAXATE
MALAXATED
MALAXATES
MALAXATOR
MALAXED
MALAXES
MALAXING
MALE
MALEATE
MALEATES
MALEDICT
MALEDICTS
MALEFFECT
MALEFIC
MALEFICE
MALEFICES
MALEIC
MALEMIUT
MALEMIUTS
MALEMUTE
MALEMUTES
MALENESS
MALENGINE
MALES
MALFED
MALFORMED
MALGRADO
MALGRE
MALGRED
MALGRES
MALGRING
MALI
MALIBU
MALIC
MALICE
MALICED
MALICES
MALICHO
MALICHOS
MALICING
MALICIOUS
MALIGN
MALIGNANT
MALIGNED
MALIGNER
MALIGNERS
MALIGNING
MALIGNITY
MALIGNLY
MALIGNS
MALIHINI
MALIHINIS
MALIK
MALIKS
MALINE
MALINES
MALINGER
MALINGERS
MALINGERY
MALIS
MALISM
MALISMS
MALISON
MALISONS
MALIST
MALKIN
MALKINS
MALL
MALLAM
MALLAMS
MALLANDER
MALLARD
MALLARDS
MALLCORE
MALLCORES
MALLEABLE
MALLEABLY
MALLEATE
MALLEATED
MALLEATES
MALLECHO
MALLECHOS
MALLED
MALLEE
MALLEES
MALLEI
MALLEMUCK
MALLENDER
MALLEOLAR
MALLEOLI
MALLEOLUS
MALLET
MALLETS
MALLEUS
MALLEUSES
MALLING
MALLINGS
MALLOW
MALLOWS
MALLS
MALM
MALMAG
MALMAGS
MALMIER
MALMIEST
MALMS
MALMSEY
MALMSEYS
MALMSTONE
MALMY
MALODOR
MALODORS
MALODOUR
MALODOURS
MALONATE
MALONATES
MALONIC
MALOTI
MALPIGHIA
MALPOSED
MALS
MALSTICK
MALSTICKS
MALT
MALTALENT
MALTASE
MALTASES
MALTED
MALTEDS
MALTESE
MALTHA
MALTHAS
MALTIER
MALTIEST
MALTINESS
MALTING
MALTINGS
MALTIPOO
MALTIPOOS
MALTMAN
MALTMEN
MALTOL
MALTOLS
MALTOSE
MALTOSES
MALTREAT
MALTREATS
MALTS
MALTSTER
MALTSTERS
MALTWORM
MALTWORMS
MALTY
MALUS
MALUSES
MALVA
MALVAS
MALVASIA
MALVASIAN
MALVASIAS
MALVESIE
MALVESIES
MALVOISIE
MALWA
MALWARE
MALWARES
MALWAS
MAM
MAMA
MAMAGUY
MAMAGUYED
MAMAGUYS
MAMAKAU
MAMAKAUS
MAMAKO
MAMAKOS
MAMAKU
MAMAKUS
MAMALIGA
MAMALIGAS
MAMAS
MAMASAN
MAMASANS
MAMATEEK
MAMATEEKS
MAMBA
MAMBAS
MAMBO
MAMBOED
MAMBOES
MAMBOING
MAMBOS
MAMEE
MAMEES
MAMELON
MAMELONS
MAMELUCO
MAMELUCOS
MAMELUKE
MAMELUKES
MAMEY
MAMEYES
MAMEYS
MAMIE
MAMIES
MAMILLA
MAMILLAE
MAMILLAR
MAMILLARY
MAMILLATE
MAMLUK
MAMLUKS
MAMMA
MAMMAE
MAMMAL
MAMMALIAN
MAMMALITY
MAMMALOGY
MAMMALS
MAMMARIES
MAMMARY
MAMMAS
MAMMATE
MAMMATI
MAMMATUS
MAMMEE
MAMMEES
MAMMER
MAMMERED
MAMMERING
MAMMERS
MAMMET
MAMMETRY
MAMMETS
MAMMEY
MAMMEYS

M

MAMMIE
MAMMIES
MAMMIFER
MAMMIFERS
MAMMIFORM
MAMMILLA
MAMMILLAE
MAMMILLAR
MAMMITIS
MAMMOCK
MAMMOCKED
MAMMOCKS
MAMMOGRAM
MAMMON
MAMMONISH
MAMMONISM
MAMMONIST
MAMMONITE
MAMMONS
MAMMOTH
MAMMOTHS
MAMMY
MAMPARA
MAMPARAS
MAMPOER
MAMPOERS
MAMS
MAMSELLE
MAMSELLES
MAMZER
MAMZERIM
MAMZERS
MAN
MANA
MANACLE
MANACLED
MANACLES
MANACLING
MANAGE
MANAGED
MANAGER
MANAGERS
MANAGES
MANAGING
MANAIA
MANAIAS
MANAKIN
MANAKINS
MANANA
MANANAS
MANAS
MANAT
MANATEE
MANATEES
MANATI
MANATIS
MANATOID
MANATS
MANATU
MANATUS
MANAWA
MANAWAS
MANBAG
MANBAGS
MANBAND
MANBANDS
MANCALA
MANCALAS
MANCANDO
MANCHE
MANCHEGO
MANCHEGOS
MANCHES
MANCHET
MANCHETS
MANCIPATE
MANCIPLE
MANCIPLES
MANCUS
MANCUSES
MAND
MANDALA
MANDALAS
MANDALIC
MANDAMUS
MANDARIN
MANDARINE
MANDARINS
MANDATARY
MANDATE
MANDATED
MANDATES
MANDATING
MANDATOR
MANDATORS
MANDATORY
MANDI
MANDIBLE
MANDIBLES
MANDILION
MANDIOC
MANDIOCA
MANDIOCAS
MANDIOCCA
MANDIOCS
MANDIR
MANDIRA
MANDIRAS
MANDIRS
MANDIS
MANDOLA
MANDOLAS
MANDOLIN
MANDOLINE
MANDOLINS
MANDOM
MANDOMS
MANDORA
MANDORAS
MANDORLA
MANDORLAS
MANDRAKE
MANDRAKES
MANDREL
MANDRELS
MANDRIL
MANDRILL
MANDRILLS
MANDRILS
MANDUCATE
MANDYLION
MANE
MANEB
MANEBS
MANED
MANEGE
MANEGED
MANEGES
MANEGING
MANEH
MANEHS
MANELESS
MANENT
MANES
MANET
MANEUVER
MANEUVERS
MANFUL
MANFULLER
MANFULLY
MANG
MANGA
MANGABEY
MANGABEYS
MANGABIES
MANGABY
MANGAL
MANGALS
MANGANATE
MANGANESE
MANGANIC
MANGANIN
MANGANINS
MANGANITE
MANGANOUS
MANGAS
MANGE
MANGEAO
MANGEAOS
MANGED
MANGEL
MANGELS
MANGER
MANGERS
MANGES
MANGETOUT
MANGEY
MANGIER
MANGIEST
MANGILY
MANGINESS
MANGING
MANGLE
MANGLED
MANGLER
MANGLERS
MANGLES
MANGLING
MANGO
MANGOES
MANGOLD
MANGOLDS
MANGONEL
MANGONELS
MANGOS
MANGOSTAN
MANGOUSTE
MANGROVE
MANGROVES
MANGS
MANGULATE
MANGY
MANHANDLE
MANHATTAN
MANHOLE
MANHOLES
MANHOOD
MANHOODS
MANHUNT
MANHUNTER
MANHUNTS
MANI
MANIA
MANIAC
MANIACAL
MANIACS
MANIAS
MANIC
MANICALLY
MANICOTTI
MANICS
MANICURE
MANICURED
MANICURES
MANIES
MANIFEST
MANIFESTO
MANIFESTS
MANIFOLD
MANIFOLDS
MANIFORM
MANIHOC
MANIHOCS
MANIHOT
MANIHOTS
MANIKIN
MANIKINS
MANILA
MANILAS
MANILLA

M

MANILLAS
MANILLE
MANILLES
MANIOC
MANIOCA
MANIOCAS
MANIOCS
MANIPLE
MANIPLES
MANIPLIES
MANIPULAR
MANIS
MANISES
MANITO
MANITOS
MANITOU
MANITOUS
MANITU
MANITUS
MANJACK
MANJACKS
MANKIER
MANKIEST
MANKIND
MANKINDS
MANKINI
MANKINIS
MANKY
MANLESS
MANLIER
MANLIEST
MANLIKE
MANLIKELY
MANLILY
MANLINESS
MANLY
MANMADE
MANNA
MANNAN
MANNANS
MANNAS
MANNED
MANNEQUIN
MANNER
MANNERED
MANNERISM
MANNERIST
MANNERLY
MANNERS
MANNIKIN
MANNIKINS
MANNING
MANNISH
MANNISHLY
MANNITE
MANNITES
MANNITIC
MANNITOL
MANNITOLS
MANNOSE
MANNOSES
MANO
MANOAO
MANOAOS
MANOES
MANOEUVER
MANOEUVRE
MANOMETER
MANOMETRY
MANOR
MANORIAL
MANORS
MANOS
MANOSCOPY
MANPACK
MANPACKS
MANPOWER
MANPOWERS
MANQUE
MANQUES
MANRED
MANREDS
MANRENT
MANRENTS
MANRIDER
MANRIDERS
MANRIDING
MANROPE
MANROPES
MANS
MANSARD
MANSARDED
MANSARDS
MANSCAPE
MANSCAPED
MANSCAPES
MANSE
MANSES
MANSHIFT
MANSHIFTS
MANSION
MANSIONS
MANSLAYER
MANSONRY
MANSPLAIN
MANSPREAD
MANSUETE
MANSWORN
MANSWORNS
MANTA
MANTAS
MANTEAU
MANTEAUS
MANTEAUX
MANTEEL
MANTEELS
MANTEL
MANTELET
MANTELETS
MANTELS
MANTES
MANTIC
MANTICORA
MANTICORE
MANTID
MANTIDS
MANTIES
MANTILLA
MANTILLAS
MANTIS
MANTISES
MANTISSA
MANTISSAS
MANTLE
MANTLED
MANTLES
MANTLET
MANTLETS
MANTLING
MANTLINGS
MANTO
MANTOES
MANTOS
MANTRA
MANTRAM
MANTRAMS
MANTRAP
MANTRAPS
MANTRAS
MANTRIC
MANTUA
MANTUAS
MANTY
MANTYHOSE
MANUAL
MANUALLY
MANUALS
MANUARY
MANUBRIA
MANUBRIAL
MANUBRIUM
MANUCODE
MANUCODES
MANUHIRI
MANUHIRIS
MANUKA
MANUKAS
MANUL
MANULS
MANUMATIC
MANUMEA
MANUMEAS
MANUMIT
MANUMITS
MANURANCE
MANURE
MANURED
MANURER
MANURERS
MANURES
MANURIAL
MANURING
MANURINGS
MANUS
MANWARD
MANWARDS
MANWISE
MANY
MANYATA
MANYATAS
MANYATTA
MANYATTAS
MANYFOLD
MANYPLIES
MANZANITA
MANZELLO
MANZELLOS
MAOMAO
MAOMAOS
MAORMOR
MAORMORS
MAP
MAPAU
MAPAUS
MAPLE
MAPLELIKE
MAPLES
MAPLESS
MAPLIKE
MAPMAKER
MAPMAKERS
MAPMAKING
MAPPABLE
MAPPED
MAPPEMOND
MAPPER
MAPPERIES
MAPPERS
MAPPERY
MAPPING
MAPPINGS
MAPPIST
MAPPISTS
MAPS
MAPSTICK
MAPSTICKS
MAPWISE
MAQUETTE
MAQUETTES
MAQUI
MAQUILA
MAQUILAS
MAQUIS
MAQUISARD
MAR
MARA
MARABI
MARABIS
MARABOU
MARABOUS

MARABOUT
MARABOUTS
MARABUNTA
MARACA
MARACAS
MARAE
MARAES
MARAGING
MARAGINGS
MARAH
MARAHS
MARAKA
MARANATHA
MARANTA
MARANTAS
MARARI
MARARIS
MARAS
MARASCA
MARASCAS
MARASMIC
MARASMOID
MARASMUS
MARATHON
MARATHONS
MARAUD
MARAUDED
MARAUDER
MARAUDERS
MARAUDING
MARAUDS
MARAVEDI
MARAVEDIS
MARBELISE
MARBELIZE
MARBLE
MARBLED
MARBLEISE
MARBLEIZE
MARBLER
MARBLERS
MARBLES
MARBLIER
MARBLIEST
MARBLING
MARBLINGS
MARBLY
MARC
MARCASITE
MARCATO
MARCATOS
MARCEL
MARCELLA
MARCELLAS
MARCELLED
MARCELLER
MARCELS
MARCH
MARCHED
MARCHEN
MARCHER
MARCHERS
MARCHES
MARCHESA
MARCHESAS
MARCHESE
MARCHESI
MARCHING
MARCHLAND
MARCHLIKE
MARCHMAN
MARCHMEN
MARCHPANE
MARCONI
MARCONIED
MARCONIS
MARCS
MARD
MARDIED
MARDIER
MARDIES
MARDIEST
MARDY
MARDYING
MARE
MAREMMA
MAREMMAS
MAREMME
MARENGO
MARERO
MAREROS
MARES
MARESCHAL
MARG
MARGARIC
MARGARIN
MARGARINE
MARGARINS
MARGARITA
MARGARITE
MARGATE
MARGATES
MARGAY
MARGAYS
MARGE
MARGENT
MARGENTED
MARGENTS
MARGES
MARGIN
MARGINAL
MARGINALS
MARGINATE
MARGINED
MARGINING
MARGINS
MARGOSA
MARGOSAS
MARGRAVE
MARGRAVES
MARGS
MARIA
MARIACHI
MARIACHIS
MARIALITE
MARID
MARIDS
MARIES
MARIGOLD
MARIGOLDS
MARIGRAM
MARIGRAMS
MARIGRAPH
MARIHUANA
MARIJUANA
MARIMBA
MARIMBAS
MARIMBIST
MARINA
MARINADE
MARINADED
MARINADES
MARINARA
MARINARAS
MARINAS
MARINATE
MARINATED
MARINATES
MARINE
MARINER
MARINERA
MARINERAS
MARINERS
MARINES
MARINIERE
MARIPOSA
MARIPOSAS
MARISCHAL
MARISH
MARISHES
MARITAGE
MARITAGES
MARITAL
MARITALLY
MARITIME
MARJORAM
MARJORAMS
MARK
MARKA
MARKAS
MARKDOWN
MARKDOWNS
MARKED
MARKEDLY
MARKER
MARKERS
MARKET
MARKETED
MARKETEER
MARKETER
MARKETERS
MARKETING
MARKETISE
MARKETIZE
MARKETS
MARKHOOR
MARKHOORS
MARKHOR
MARKHORS
MARKING
MARKINGS
MARKKA
MARKKAA
MARKKAS
MARKMAN
MARKMEN
MARKS
MARKSMAN
MARKSMEN
MARKUP
MARKUPS
MARL
MARLE
MARLED
MARLES
MARLIER
MARLIEST
MARLIN
MARLINE
MARLINES
MARLING
MARLINGS
MARLINS
MARLITE
MARLITES
MARLITIC
MARLS
MARLSTONE
MARLY
MARM
MARMALADE
MARMALISE
MARMALIZE
MARMARISE
MARMARIZE
MARMELISE
MARMELIZE
MARMEM
MARMITE
MARMITES
MARMOREAL
MARMOREAN
MARMOSE
MARMOSES
MARMOSET
MARMOSETS
MARMOT
MARMOTS
MARMS
MAROCAIN

M

MAROCAINS
MARON
MARONS
MAROON
MAROONED
MAROONER
MAROONERS
MAROONING
MAROONS
MAROQUIN
MAROQUINS
MAROR
MARORS
MARPLOT
MARPLOTS
MARQUE
MARQUEE
MARQUEES
MARQUES
MARQUESS
MARQUETRY
MARQUIS
MARQUISE
MARQUISES
MARRA
MARRAM
MARRAMS
MARRANO
MARRANOS
MARRAS
MARRED
MARRELS
MARRER
MARRERS
MARRI
MARRIAGE
MARRIAGES
MARRIED
MARRIEDS
MARRIER
MARRIERS
MARRIES
MARRING
MARRIS
MARRON
MARRONS
MARROW
MARROWED
MARROWFAT
MARROWIER
MARROWING
MARROWISH
MARROWS
MARROWSKY
MARROWY
MARRUM
MARRUMS
MARRY
MARRYING
MARRYINGS
MARS
MARSALA
MARSALAS
MARSE
MARSEILLE
MARSES
MARSH
MARSHAL
MARSHALCY
MARSHALED
MARSHALER
MARSHALL
MARSHALLS
MARSHALS
MARSHBUCK
MARSHED
MARSHES
MARSHIER
MARSHIEST
MARSHLAND
MARSHLIKE
MARSHWORT
MARSHY
MARSPORT
MARSPORTS
MARSQUAKE
MARSUPIA
MARSUPIAL
MARSUPIAN
MARSUPIUM
MART
MARTAGON
MARTAGONS
MARTED
MARTEL
MARTELLED
MARTELLO
MARTELLOS
MARTELS
MARTEN
MARTENS
MARTEXT
MARTEXTS
MARTIAL
MARTIALLY
MARTIALS
MARTIAN
MARTIANS
MARTIN
MARTINET
MARTINETS
MARTING
MARTINGAL
MARTINI
MARTINIS
MARTINS
MARTLET
MARTLETS
MARTS
MARTYR
MARTYRDOM
MARTYRED
MARTYRIA
MARTYRIES
MARTYRING
MARTYRISE
MARTYRISH
MARTYRIUM
MARTYRIZE
MARTYRLY
MARTYRS
MARTYRY
MARVEL
MARVELED
MARVELER
MARVELERS
MARVELING
MARVELLED
MARVELLER
MARVELOUS
MARVELS
MARVER
MARVERED
MARVERING
MARVERS
MARVIER
MARVIEST
MARVY
MARXISANT
MARY
MARYBUD
MARYBUDS
MARYJANE
MARYJANES
MARZIPAN
MARZIPANS
MAS
MASA
MASALA
MASALAS
MASAS
MASCARA
MASCARAED
MASCARAS
MASCARON
MASCARONS
MASCLE
MASCLED
MASCLES
MASCON
MASCONS
MASCOT
MASCOTS
MASCULINE
MASCULIST
MASCULY
MASE
MASED
MASER
MASERS
MASES
MASH
MASHALLAH
MASHED
MASHER
MASHERS
MASHES
MASHGIACH
MASHGIAH
MASHGIHIM
MASHIACH
MASHIACHS
MASHIE
MASHIER
MASHIES
MASHIEST
MASHING
MASHINGS
MASHLAM
MASHLAMS
MASHLIM
MASHLIMS
MASHLIN
MASHLINS
MASHLOCH
MASHLOCHS
MASHLUM
MASHLUMS
MASHMAN
MASHMEN
MASHUA
MASHUAS
MASHUP
MASHUPS
MASHY
MASING
MASJID
MASJIDS
MASK
MASKABLE
MASKED
MASKEG
MASKEGS
MASKER
MASKERS
MASKING
MASKINGS
MASKLIKE
MASKS
MASLIN
MASLINS
MASOCHISM
MASOCHIST
MASON
MASONED
MASONIC
MASONING
MASONITE
MASONITES
MASONRIED

MASONRIES
MASONRY
MASONS
MASOOLAH
MASOOLAHS
MASQUE
MASQUER
MASQUERS
MASQUES
MASS
MASSA
MASSACRE
MASSACRED
MASSACRER
MASSACRES
MASSAGE
MASSAGED
MASSAGER
MASSAGERS
MASSAGES
MASSAGING
MASSAGIST
MASSAS
MASSCULT
MASSCULTS
MASSE
MASSED
MASSEDLY
MASSES
MASSETER
MASSETERS
MASSEUR
MASSEURS
MASSEUSE
MASSEUSES
MASSICOT
MASSICOTS
MASSIER
MASSIEST
MASSIF
MASSIFS
MASSINESS
MASSING
MASSIVE
MASSIVELY
MASSIVES
MASSLESS
MASSOOLA
MASSOOLAS
MASSTIGE
MASSTIGES
MASSY
MASSYMORE
MAST
MASTABA
MASTABAH
MASTABAHS
MASTABAS
MASTED
MASTER
MASTERATE
MASTERDOM
MASTERED
MASTERFUL
MASTERIES
MASTERING
MASTERLY
MASTERS
MASTERY
MASTFUL
MASTHEAD
MASTHEADS
MASTHOUSE
MASTIC
MASTICATE
MASTICH
MASTICHE
MASTICHES
MASTICHS
MASTICOT
MASTICOTS
MASTICS
MASTIER
MASTIEST
MASTIFF
MASTIFFS
MASTING
MASTITIC
MASTITIS
MASTIX
MASTIXES
MASTLESS
MASTLIKE
MASTODON
MASTODONS
MASTODONT
MASTOID
MASTOIDAL
MASTOIDS
MASTOPEXY
MASTS
MASTY
MASU
MASULA
MASULAS
MASURIUM
MASURIUMS
MASUS
MAT
MATACHIN
MATACHINA
MATACHINI
MATACHINS
MATADOR
MATADORA
MATADORAS
MATADORE
MATADORES
MATADORS
MATAGOURI
MATAI
MATAIS
MATAMATA
MATAMATAS
MATAMBALA
MATATA
MATATAS
MATATU
MATATUS
MATCH
MATCHA
MATCHABLE
MATCHAS
MATCHBOOK
MATCHBOX
MATCHED
MATCHER
MATCHERS
MATCHES
MATCHET
MATCHETS
MATCHING
MATCHLESS
MATCHLOCK
MATCHMADE
MATCHMAKE
MATCHMARK
MATCHPLAY
MATCHUP
MATCHUPS
MATCHWOOD
MATE
MATED
MATELASSE
MATELESS
MATELOT
MATELOTE
MATELOTES
MATELOTS
MATELOTTE
MATER
MATERIAL
MATERIALS
MATERIEL
MATERIELS
MATERNAL
MATERNITY
MATERS
MATES
MATESHIP
MATESHIPS
MATEY
MATEYNESS
MATEYS
MATFELLON
MATFELON
MATFELONS
MATGRASS
MATH
MATHESES
MATHESIS
MATHS
MATICO
MATICOS
MATIER
MATIES
MATIEST
MATILDA
MATILDAS
MATILY
MATIN
MATINAL
MATINEE
MATINEES
MATINESS
MATING
MATINGS
MATINS
MATIPO
MATIPOS
MATJES
MATLESS
MATLO
MATLOS
MATLOW
MATLOWS
MATOKE
MATOKES
MATOOKE
MATOOKES
MATRASS
MATRASSES
MATRES
MATRIARCH
MATRIC
MATRICE
MATRICES
MATRICIDE
MATRICS
MATRICULA
MATRILINY
MATRIMONY
MATRIX
MATRIXES
MATRON
MATRONAGE
MATRONAL
MATRONISE
MATRONIZE
MATRONLY
MATRONS
MATROSS
MATROSSES
MATS
MATSAH
MATSAHS
MATSURI
MATSURIS
MATSUTAKE
MATT

M

MATTAMORE
MATTE
MATTED
MATTEDLY
MATTER
MATTERED
MATTERFUL
MATTERIER
MATTERING
MATTERS
MATTERY
MATTES
MATTIE
MATTIES
MATTIFIED
MATTIFIES
MATTIFY
MATTIN
MATTING
MATTINGS
MATTINS
MATTOCK
MATTOCKS
MATTOID
MATTOIDS
MATTRASS
MATTRESS
MATTS
MATURABLE
MATURATE
MATURATED
MATURATES
MATURE
MATURED
MATURELY
MATURER
MATURERS
MATURES
MATUREST
MATURING
MATURITY
MATUTINAL
MATUTINE
MATWEED
MATWEEDS
MATY
MATZA
MATZAH
MATZAHS
MATZAS
MATZO
MATZOH
MATZOHS
MATZOON
MATZOONS
MATZOS
MATZOT
MATZOTH
MAUBIES
MAUBY
MAUD
MAUDLIN
MAUDLINLY
MAUDS
MAUGER
MAUGRE
MAUGRED
MAUGRES
MAUGRING
MAUL
MAULED
MAULER
MAULERS
MAULGRE
MAULGRED
MAULGRES
MAULGRING
MAULING
MAULINGS
MAULS
MAULSTICK
MAULVI
MAULVIS
MAUMET
MAUMETRY
MAUMETS
MAUN
MAUND
MAUNDED
MAUNDER
MAUNDERED
MAUNDERER
MAUNDERS
MAUNDIES
MAUNDING
MAUNDS
MAUNDY
MAUNGIER
MAUNGIEST
MAUNGY
MAUNNA
MAURI
MAURIS
MAUSIER
MAUSIEST
MAUSOLEA
MAUSOLEAN
MAUSOLEUM
MAUSY
MAUT
MAUTHER
MAUTHERS
MAUTS
MAUVAIS
MAUVAISE
MAUVE
MAUVEIN
MAUVEINE
MAUVEINES
MAUVEINS
MAUVER
MAUVES
MAUVEST
MAUVIN
MAUVINE
MAUVINES
MAUVINS
MAUZIER
MAUZIEST
MAUZY
MAVEN
MAVENS
MAVERICK
MAVERICKS
MAVIE
MAVIES
MAVIN
MAVINS
MAVIS
MAVISES
MAVOURNIN
MAW
MAWBOUND
MAWED
MAWGER
MAWING
MAWK
MAWKIER
MAWKIEST
MAWKIN
MAWKINS
MAWKISH
MAWKISHLY
MAWKS
MAWKY
MAWMET
MAWMETRY
MAWMETS
MAWN
MAWNS
MAWPUS
MAWPUSES
MAWR
MAWRS
MAWS
MAWSEED
MAWSEEDS
MAWTHER
MAWTHERS
MAX
MAXED
MAXES
MAXI
MAXIBOAT
MAXIBOATS
MAXICOAT
MAXICOATS
MAXIDRESS
MAXILLA
MAXILLAE
MAXILLAR
MAXILLARY
MAXILLAS
MAXILLULA
MAXIM
MAXIMA
MAXIMAL
MAXIMALLY
MAXIMALS
MAXIMAND
MAXIMANDS
MAXIMIN
MAXIMINS
MAXIMISE
MAXIMISED
MAXIMISER
MAXIMISES
MAXIMIST
MAXIMISTS
MAXIMITE
MAXIMITES
MAXIMIZE
MAXIMIZED
MAXIMIZER
MAXIMIZES
MAXIMS
MAXIMUM
MAXIMUMLY
MAXIMUMS
MAXIMUS
MAXIMUSES
MAXING
MAXIS
MAXIXE
MAXIXES
MAXWELL
MAXWELLS
MAY
MAYA
MAYAN
MAYAPPLE
MAYAPPLES
MAYAS
MAYBE
MAYBES
MAYBIRD
MAYBIRDS
MAYBUSH
MAYBUSHES
MAYDAY
MAYDAYS
MAYED
MAYEST
MAYFISH
MAYFISHES
MAYFLIES
MAYFLOWER
MAYFLY
MAYHAP
MAYHAPPEN

M

MAYHEM
MAYHEMS
MAYING
MAYINGS
MAYO
MAYOR
MAYORAL
MAYORALTY
MAYORESS
MAYORS
MAYORSHIP
MAYOS
MAYPOLE
MAYPOLES
MAYPOP
MAYPOPS
MAYS
MAYST
MAYSTER
MAYSTERS
MAYVIN
MAYVINS
MAYWEED
MAYWEEDS
MAZAEDIA
MAZAEDIUM
MAZARD
MAZARDS
MAZARINE
MAZARINES
MAZE
MAZED
MAZEDLY
MAZEDNESS
MAZEFUL
MAZELIKE
MAZELTOV
MAZEMENT
MAZEMENTS
MAZER
MAZERS
MAZES
MAZEY
MAZHBI
MAZHBIS
MAZIER
MAZIEST
MAZILY
MAZINESS
MAZING
MAZOURKA
MAZOURKAS
MAZOUT
MAZOUTS
MAZUMA
MAZUMAS
MAZURKA
MAZURKAS
MAZUT
MAZUTS
MAZY
MAZZARD
MAZZARDS
MBAQANGA
MBAQANGAS
MBIRA
MBIRAS
ME
MEACOCK
MEACOCKS
MEAD
MEADOW
MEADOWIER
MEADOWS
MEADOWY
MEADS
MEAGER
MEAGERER
MEAGEREST
MEAGERLY
MEAGRE
MEAGRELY
MEAGRER
MEAGRES
MEAGREST
MEAL
MEALED
MEALER
MEALERS
MEALIE
MEALIER
MEALIES
MEALIEST
MEALINESS
MEALING
MEALLESS
MEALS
MEALTIME
MEALTIMES
MEALWORM
MEALWORMS
MEALY
MEALYBUG
MEALYBUGS
MEAN
MEANDER
MEANDERED
MEANDERER
MEANDERS
MEANDRIAN
MEANDROUS
MEANE
MEANED
MEANER
MEANERS
MEANES
MEANEST
MEANIE
MEANIES
MEANING
MEANINGLY
MEANINGS
MEANLY
MEANNESS
MEANS
MEANT
MEANTIME
MEANTIMES
MEANWHILE
MEANY
MEARE
MEARES
MEARING
MEASE
MEASED
MEASES
MEASING
MEASLE
MEASLED
MEASLES
MEASLIER
MEASLIEST
MEASLING
MEASLY
MEASURE
MEASURED
MEASURER
MEASURERS
MEASURES
MEASURING
MEAT
MEATAL
MEATAXE
MEATAXES
MEATBALL
MEATBALLS
MEATED
MEATH
MEATHE
MEATHEAD
MEATHEADS
MEATHES
MEATHOOK
MEATHOOKS
MEATHS
MEATIER
MEATIEST
MEATILY
MEATINESS
MEATLESS
MEATLOAF
MEATMAN
MEATMEN
MEATS
MEATSPACE
MEATUS
MEATUSES
MEATY
MEAWES
MEAZEL
MEAZELS
MEBIBYTE
MEBIBYTES
MEBOS
MEBOSES
MECCA
MECCAS
MECH
MECHANIC
MECHANICS
MECHANISE
MECHANISM
MECHANIST
MECHANIZE
MECHITZA
MECHITZAS
MECHITZOT
MECHOUI
MECHOUIS
MECHS
MECK
MECKS
MECLIZINE
MECONATE
MECONATES
MECONIC
MECONIN
MECONINS
MECONIUM
MECONIUMS
MED
MEDACCA
MEDACCAS
MEDAILLON
MEDAKA
MEDAKAS
MEDAL
MEDALED
MEDALET
MEDALETS
MEDALING
MEDALIST
MEDALISTS
MEDALLED
MEDALLIC
MEDALLING
MEDALLION
MEDALLIST
MEDALPLAY
MEDALS
MEDCINAL
MEDDLE
MEDDLED
MEDDLER
MEDDLERS
MEDDLES
MEDDLING
MEDDLINGS
MEDEVAC
MEDEVACED

M

MEDEVACS
MEDFLIES
MEDFLY
MEDIA
MEDIACIES
MEDIACY
MEDIAD
MEDIAE
MEDIAEVAL
MEDIAL
MEDIALLY
MEDIALS
MEDIAN
MEDIANLY
MEDIANS
MEDIANT
MEDIANTS
MEDIAS
MEDIATE
MEDIATED
MEDIATELY
MEDIATES
MEDIATING
MEDIATION
MEDIATISE
MEDIATIVE
MEDIATIZE
MEDIATOR
MEDIATORS
MEDIATORY
MEDIATRIX
MEDIC
MEDICABLE
MEDICABLY
MEDICAID
MEDICAIDS
MEDICAL
MEDICALLY
MEDICALS
MEDICANT
MEDICANTS
MEDICARE
MEDICARES
MEDICATE
MEDICATED
MEDICATES
MEDICIDE
MEDICIDES
MEDICINAL
MEDICINE
MEDICINED
MEDICINER
MEDICINES
MEDICK
MEDICKS
MEDICO
MEDICOS
MEDICS
MEDIEVAL
MEDIEVALS
MEDIGAP
MEDIGAPS
MEDII
MEDINA
MEDINAS
MEDIOCRE
MEDITATE
MEDITATED
MEDITATES
MEDITATOR
MEDIUM
MEDIUMS
MEDIUS
MEDIUSES
MEDIVAC
MEDIVACED
MEDIVACS
MEDLAR
MEDLARS
MEDLE
MEDLED
MEDLES
MEDLEY
MEDLEYS
MEDLING
MEDRESA
MEDRESAS
MEDRESE
MEDRESES
MEDRESSEH
MEDS
MEDULLA
MEDULLAE
MEDULLAR
MEDULLARY
MEDULLAS
MEDULLATE
MEDUSA
MEDUSAE
MEDUSAL
MEDUSAN
MEDUSANS
MEDUSAS
MEDUSOID
MEDUSOIDS
MEE
MEED
MEEDS
MEEK
MEEKEN
MEEKENED
MEEKENING
MEEKENS
MEEKER
MEEKEST
MEEKLY
MEEKNESS
MEEMIE
MEEMIES
MEER
MEERCAT
MEERCATS
MEERED
MEERING
MEERKAT
MEERKATS
MEERS
MEES
MEET
MEETER
MEETERS
MEETEST
MEETING
MEETINGS
MEETLY
MEETNESS
MEETS
MEFF
MEFFS
MEG
MEGA
MEGABAR
MEGABARS
MEGABIT
MEGABITS
MEGABUCK
MEGABUCKS
MEGABYTE
MEGABYTES
MEGACITY
MEGACURIE
MEGACYCLE
MEGADEAL
MEGADEALS
MEGADEATH
MEGADOSE
MEGADOSES
MEGADYNE
MEGADYNES
MEGAFARAD
MEGAFAUNA
MEGAFLOP
MEGAFLOPS
MEGAFLORA
MEGAFOG
MEGAFOGS
MEGAGAUSS
MEGAHERTZ
MEGAHIT
MEGAHITS
MEGAJOULE
MEGALITH
MEGALITHS
MEGALITRE
MEGALODON
MEGALOPIC
MEGALOPS
MEGAMALL
MEGAMALLS
MEGAPHONE
MEGAPHYLL
MEGAPIXEL
MEGAPLEX
MEGAPOD
MEGAPODE
MEGAPODES
MEGAPODS
MEGAQUAKE
MEGARA
MEGARAD
MEGARADS
MEGARON
MEGARONS
MEGASCOPE
MEGASPORE
MEGASS
MEGASSE
MEGASSES
MEGASTAR
MEGASTARS
MEGASTORE
MEGASTORM
MEGATHERE
MEGATON
MEGATONIC
MEGATONS
MEGAVOLT
MEGAVOLTS
MEGAWATT
MEGAWATTS
MEGILLA
MEGILLAH
MEGILLAHS
MEGILLAS
MEGILLOTH
MEGILP
MEGILPH
MEGILPHS
MEGILPS
MEGOHM
MEGOHMS
MEGRIM
MEGRIMS
MEGS
MEH
MEHNDI
MEHNDIS
MEIBOMIAN
MEIKLE
MEIN
MEINED
MEINEY
MEINEYS
MEINIE
MEINIES
MEINING
MEINS
MEINT
MEINY
MEIOCYTE

M

MEIOCYTES
MEIOFAUNA
MEIONITE
MEIONITES
MEIOSES
MEIOSIS
MEIOSPORE
MEIOTIC
MEISHI
MEISHIS
MEISTER
MEISTERS
MEITH
MEITHS
MEJLIS
MEJLISES
MEKKA
MEKKAS
MEKOMETER
MEL
MELA
MELAENA
MELAENAS
MELALEUCA
MELAMDIM
MELAMED
MELAMINE
MELAMINES
MELAMPODE
MELANGE
MELANGES
MELANIAN
MELANIANS
MELANIC
MELANICS
MELANIN
MELANINS
MELANISE
MELANISED
MELANISES
MELANISM
MELANISMS
MELANIST
MELANISTS
MELANITE
MELANITES
MELANITIC
MELANIZE
MELANIZED
MELANIZES
MELANO
MELANOID
MELANOIDS
MELANOMA
MELANOMAS
MELANOS
MELANOSES
MELANOSIS
MELANOTIC
MELANOUS
MELANURIA
MELANURIC
MELAPHYRE
MELAS
MELASTOME
MELATONIN
MELBA
MELD
MELDED
MELDER
MELDERS
MELDING
MELDS
MELEE
MELEES
MELENA
MELENAS
MELIC
MELICK
MELICKS
MELICS
MELIK
MELIKS
MELILITE
MELILITES
MELILOT
MELILOTS
MELINITE
MELINITES
MELIORATE
MELIORISM
MELIORIST
MELIORITY
MELISMA
MELISMAS
MELISMATA
MELITTIN
MELITTINS
MELL
MELLAY
MELLAYS
MELLED
MELLIFIC
MELLING
MELLITE
MELLITES
MELLITIC
MELLOTRON
MELLOW
MELLOWED
MELLOWER
MELLOWEST
MELLOWIER
MELLOWING
MELLOWLY
MELLOWS
MELLOWY
MELLS
MELOCOTON
MELODEON
MELODEONS
MELODIA
MELODIAS
MELODIC
MELODICA
MELODICAS
MELODICS
MELODIES
MELODION
MELODIONS
MELODIOUS
MELODISE
MELODISED
MELODISER
MELODISES
MELODIST
MELODISTS
MELODIZE
MELODIZED
MELODIZER
MELODIZES
MELODRAMA
MELODRAME
MELODY
MELOID
MELOIDS
MELOMANIA
MELOMANIC
MELON
MELONGENE
MELONIER
MELONIEST
MELONS
MELONY
MELOXICAM
MELPHALAN
MELS
MELT
MELTABLE
MELTAGE
MELTAGES
MELTDOWN
MELTDOWNS
MELTED
MELTEMI
MELTEMIS
MELTER
MELTERS
MELTIER
MELTIEST
MELTING
MELTINGLY
MELTINGS
MELTITH
MELTITHS
MELTON
MELTONS
MELTS
MELTWATER
MELTY
MELUNGEON
MEM
MEMBER
MEMBERED
MEMBERS
MEMBRAL
MEMBRANAL
MEMBRANE
MEMBRANED
MEMBRANES
MEME
MEMENTO
MEMENTOES
MEMENTOS
MEMES
MEMETIC
MEMETICS
MEMO
MEMOIR
MEMOIRISM
MEMOIRIST
MEMOIRS
MEMORABLE
MEMORABLY
MEMORANDA
MEMORIAL
MEMORIALS
MEMORIES
MEMORISE
MEMORISED
MEMORISER
MEMORISES
MEMORITER
MEMORIZE
MEMORIZED
MEMORIZER
MEMORIZES
MEMORY
MEMOS
MEMS
MEMSAHIB
MEMSAHIBS
MEN
MENACE
MENACED
MENACER
MENACERS
MENACES
MENACING
MENAD
MENADIONE
MENADS
MENAGE
MENAGED
MENAGERIE
MENAGES
MENAGING
MENARCHE
MENARCHES
MENAZON

MENAZONS
MEND
MENDABLE
MENDACITY
MENDED
MENDER
MENDERS
MENDICANT
MENDICITY
MENDIGO
MENDIGOS
MENDING
MENDINGS
MENDS
MENE
MENED
MENEER
MENEERS
MENES
MENFOLK
MENFOLKS
MENG
MENGE
MENGED
MENGES
MENGING
MENGS
MENHADEN
MENHADENS
MENHIR
MENHIRS
MENIAL
MENIALLY
MENIALS
MENILITE
MENILITES
MENING
MENINGEAL
MENINGES
MENINX
MENISCAL
MENISCATE
MENISCI
MENISCOID
MENISCUS
MENO
MENOLOGY
MENOMINEE
MENOMINI
MENOMINIS
MENOPAUSE
MENOPOLIS
MENOPOME
MENOPOMES
MENORAH
MENORAHS
MENORRHEA
MENSA
MENSAE
MENSAL
MENSAS
MENSCH
MENSCHEN
MENSCHES
MENSCHIER
MENSCHY
MENSE
MENSED
MENSEFUL
MENSELESS
MENSES
MENSH
MENSHED
MENSHEN
MENSHES
MENSHING
MENSING
MENSTRUA
MENSTRUAL
MENSTRUUM
MENSUAL
MENSURAL
MENSWEAR
MENSWEARS
MENT
MENTA
MENTAL
MENTALESE
MENTALISM
MENTALIST
MENTALITY
MENTALLY
MENTATION
MENTEE
MENTEES
MENTHENE
MENTHENES
MENTHOL
MENTHOLS
MENTICIDE
MENTION
MENTIONED
MENTIONER
MENTIONS
MENTO
MENTOR
MENTORED
MENTORIAL
MENTORING
MENTORS
MENTOS
MENTUM
MENU
MENUDO
MENUDOS
MENUISIER
MENUS
MENYIE
MENYIES
MEOU
MEOUED
MEOUING
MEOUS
MEOW
MEOWED
MEOWING
MEOWS
MEPACRINE
MEPHITIC
MEPHITIS
MEPHITISM
MERANTI
MERANTIS
MERBROMIN
MERC
MERCADO
MERCADOS
MERCAPTAN
MERCAPTO
MERCAT
MERCATS
MERCENARY
MERCER
MERCERIES
MERCERISE
MERCERIZE
MERCERS
MERCERY
MERCES
MERCH
MERCHANT
MERCHANTS
MERCHES
MERCHET
MERCHETS
MERCHILD
MERCIABLE
MERCIES
MERCIFIDE
MERCIFIED
MERCIFIES
MERCIFUL
MERCIFY
MERCILESS
MERCS
MERCURATE
MERCURIAL
MERCURIC
MERCURIES
MERCURISE
MERCURIZE
MERCUROUS
MERCURY
MERCY
MERDE
MERDES
MERE
MERED
MEREL
MERELL
MERELLS
MERELS
MERELY
MERENGUE
MERENGUES
MEREOLOGY
MERER
MERES
MERESMAN
MERESMEN
MEREST
MERESTONE
MERFOLK
MERFOLKS
MERGANSER
MERGE
MERGED
MERGEE
MERGEES
MERGENCE
MERGENCES
MERGER
MERGERS
MERGES
MERGING
MERGINGS
MERGUEZ
MERI
MERICARP
MERICARPS
MERIDIAN
MERIDIANS
MERIL
MERILS
MERIMAKE
MERIMAKES
MERING
MERINGS
MERINGUE
MERINGUES
MERINO
MERINOS
MERIS
MERISES
MERISIS
MERISM
MERISMS
MERISTEM
MERISTEMS
MERISTIC
MERIT
MERITED
MERITING
MERITLESS
MERITS
MERK
MERKIN
MERKINS
MERKS
MERL

MERLE
MERLES
MERLIN
MERLING
MERLINGS
MERLINS
MERLON
MERLONS
MERLOT
MERLOTS
MERLS
MERMAID
MERMAIDEN
MERMAIDS
MERMAN
MERMEN
MEROCRINE
MEROGONY
MEROISTIC
MEROME
MEROMES
MERONYM
MERONYMS
MERONYMY
MEROPIA
MEROPIAS
MEROPIC
MEROPIDAN
MEROSOME
MEROSOMES
MEROZOITE
MERPEOPLE
MERRIE
MERRIER
MERRIES
MERRIEST
MERRILY
MERRIMENT
MERRINESS
MERRY
MERRYMAN
MERRYMEN
MERSALYL
MERSALYLS
MERSE
MERSES
MERSION
MERSIONS
MERYCISM
MERYCISMS
MES
MESA
MESAIL
MESAILS
MESAL
MESALLY
MESARAIC
MESARCH
MESAS
MESCAL
MESCALIN
MESCALINE
MESCALINS
MESCALISM
MESCALS
MESCLUM
MESCLUMS
MESCLUN
MESCLUNS
MESDAMES
MESE
MESEEMED
MESEEMETH
MESEEMS
MESEL
MESELED
MESELS
MESENTERA
MESENTERY
MESES
MESETA
MESETAS
MESH
MESHED
MESHES
MESHIER
MESHIEST
MESHING
MESHINGS
MESHUGA
MESHUGAAS
MESHUGAH
MESHUGAS
MESHUGGA
MESHUGGAH
MESHUGGE
MESHWORK
MESHWORKS
MESHY
MESIAD
MESIAL
MESIALLY
MESIAN
MESIC
MESICALLY
MESMERIC
MESMERISE
MESMERISM
MESMERIST
MESMERIZE
MESNALTY
MESNE
MESNES
MESOBLAST
MESOCARP
MESOCARPS
MESOCRANY
MESODERM
MESODERMS
MESOGLEA
MESOGLEAL
MESOGLEAS
MESOGLOEA
MESOLITE
MESOLITES
MESOMERE
MESOMERES
MESOMORPH
MESON
MESONIC
MESONS
MESOPAUSE
MESOPHILE
MESOPHYL
MESOPHYLL
MESOPHYLS
MESOPHYTE
MESOSAUR
MESOSAURS
MESOSCALE
MESOSOME
MESOSOMES
MESOTRON
MESOTRONS
MESOZOAN
MESOZOANS
MESOZOIC
MESPIL
MESPILS
MESPRISE
MESPRISES
MESPRIZE
MESPRIZES
MESQUIN
MESQUINE
MESQUIT
MESQUITE
MESQUITES
MESQUITS
MESS
MESSAGE
MESSAGED
MESSAGES
MESSAGING
MESSALINE
MESSAN
MESSANS
MESSED
MESSENGER
MESSES
MESSIAH
MESSIAHS
MESSIANIC
MESSIAS
MESSIASES
MESSIER
MESSIEST
MESSIEURS
MESSILY
MESSINESS
MESSING
MESSMAN
MESSMATE
MESSMATES
MESSMEN
MESSUAGE
MESSUAGES
MESSY
MESTEE
MESTEES
MESTER
MESTERS
MESTESO
MESTESOES
MESTESOS
MESTINO
MESTINOES
MESTINOS
MESTIZA
MESTIZAS
MESTIZO
MESTIZOES
MESTIZOS
MESTO
MESTOM
MESTOME
MESTOMES
MESTOMS
MESTRANOL
MET
META
METABASES
METABASIS
METABATIC
METABOLIC
METABOLY
METACARPI
METADATA
METADATAS
METAFILE
METAFILES
METAGE
METAGENIC
METAGES
METAIRIE
METAIRIES
METAL
METALED
METALHEAD
METALING
METALISE
METALISED
METALISES
METALIST
METALISTS
METALIZE
METALIZED
METALIZES
METALLED
METALLIC

M

METALLICS
METALLIKE
METALLINE
METALLING
METALLISE
METALLIST
METALLIZE
METALLOID
METALLY
METALMARK
METALS
METALWARE
METALWORK
METAMALE
METAMALES
METAMER
METAMERAL
METAMERE
METAMERES
METAMERIC
METAMERS
METAMICT
METANOIA
METANOIAS
METAPELET
METAPHASE
METAPHOR
METAPHORS
METAPLASM
METAPLOT
METARCHON
METASOMA
METASOMAS
METATAG
METATAGS
METATARSI
METATE
METATES
METAVERSE
METAXYLEM
METAYAGE
METAYAGES
METAYER
METAYERS
METAZOA
METAZOAL
METAZOAN
METAZOANS
METAZOIC
METAZOON
METCAST
METCASTS
METE
METED
METEOR
METEORIC
METEORISM
METEORIST
METEORITE
METEOROID
METEOROUS
METEORS
METEPA
METEPAS
METER
METERAGE
METERAGES
METERED
METERING
METERS
METES
METESTICK
METESTRUS
METEWAND
METEWANDS
METEYARD
METEYARDS
METFORMIN
METH
METHADON
METHADONE
METHADONS
METHANAL
METHANALS
METHANE
METHANES
METHANOIC
METHANOL
METHANOLS
METHANOYL
METHEGLIN
METHINK
METHINKS
METHO
METHOD
METHODIC
METHODISE
METHODISM
METHODIST
METHODIZE
METHODS
METHOS
METHOUGHT
METHOXIDE
METHOXIES
METHOXY
METHOXYL
METHOXYLS
METHS
METHYL
METHYLAL
METHYLALS
METHYLASE
METHYLATE
METHYLENE
METHYLIC
METHYLS
METHYSES
METHYSIS
METHYSTIC
METIC
METICA
METICAIS
METICAL
METICALS
METICAS
METICS
METIER
METIERS
METIF
METIFS
METING
METIS
METISSE
METISSES
METOL
METOLS
METONYM
METONYMIC
METONYMS
METONYMY
METOPAE
METOPE
METOPES
METOPIC
METOPISM
METOPISMS
METOPON
METOPONS
METOPRYL
METOPRYLS
METRALGIA
METRAZOL
METRAZOLS
METRE
METRED
METRES
METRIC
METRICAL
METRICATE
METRICIAN
METRICISE
METRICISM
METRICIST
METRICIZE
METRICS
METRIFIED
METRIFIER
METRIFIES
METRIFY
METRING
METRIST
METRISTS
METRITIS
METRO
METROLOGY
METRONOME
METROPLEX
METROS
METS
METTLE
METTLED
METTLES
METUMP
METUMPS
MEU
MEUNIERE
MEUS
MEUSE
MEUSED
MEUSES
MEUSING
MEVE
MEVED
MEVES
MEVING
MEVROU
MEVROUS
MEW
MEWED
MEWING
MEWL
MEWLED
MEWLER
MEWLERS
MEWLING
MEWLS
MEWS
MEWSED
MEWSES
MEWSING
MEYNT
MEZAIL
MEZAILS
MEZCAL
MEZCALINE
MEZCALS
MEZE
MEZEREON
MEZEREONS
MEZEREUM
MEZEREUMS
MEZES
MEZQUIT
MEZQUITE
MEZQUITES
MEZQUITS
MEZUZA
MEZUZAH
MEZUZAHS
MEZUZAS
MEZUZOT
MEZUZOTH
MEZZ
MEZZALUNA
MEZZANINE
MEZZE
MEZZES
MEZZO
MEZZOS

MEZZOTINT
MGANGA
MGANGAS
MHO
MHORR
MHORRS
MHOS
MI
MIAOU
MIAOUED
MIAOUING
MIAOUS
MIAOW
MIAOWED
MIAOWING
MIAOWS
MIASM
MIASMA
MIASMAL
MIASMAS
MIASMATA
MIASMATIC
MIASMIC
MIASMOUS
MIASMS
MIAUL
MIAULED
MIAULING
MIAULS
MIB
MIBS
MIBUNA
MIBUNAS
MIC
MICA
MICACEOUS
MICAS
MICATE
MICATED
MICATES
MICATING
MICAWBER
MICAWBERS
MICE
MICELL
MICELLA
MICELLAE
MICELLAR
MICELLAS
MICELLE
MICELLES
MICELLS
MICH
MICHAEL
MICHAELS
MICHE
MICHED
MICHER
MICHERS
MICHES
MICHIGAN
MICHIGANS
MICHING
MICHINGS
MICHT
MICHTS
MICKERIES
MICKERY
MICKEY
MICKEYED
MICKEYING
MICKEYS
MICKIES
MICKLE
MICKLER
MICKLES
MICKLEST
MICKY
MICO
MICOS
MICRA
MICRIFIED
MICRIFIES
MICRIFY
MICRO
MICROBAR
MICROBARS
MICROBE
MICROBEAD
MICROBEAM
MICROBES
MICROBIAL
MICROBIAN
MICROBIC
MICROBLOG
MICROBREW
MICROBUS
MICROCAP
MICROCAR
MICROCARD
MICROCARS
MICROCHIP
MICROCODE
MICROCOPY
MICROCOSM
MICROCYTE
MICRODONT
MICRODOT
MICRODOTS
MICROFILM
MICROFINE
MICROFORM
MICROGLIA
MICROGRAM
MICROHM
MICROHMS
MICROINCH
MICROJET
MICROJETS
MICROLITE
MICROLITH
MICROLOAN
MICROLOGY
MICROLUX
MICROMERE
MICROMESH
MICROMHO
MICROMHOS
MICROMINI
MICROMOLE
MICROMORT
MICRON
MICRONISE
MICRONIZE
MICRONS
MICROPORE
MICROPSIA
MICROPUMP
MICROPYLE
MICROS
MICROSITE
MICROSOME
MICROTOME
MICROTOMY
MICROTONE
MICROTUBE
MICROVOLT
MICROWATT
MICROWAVE
MICROWIRE
MICRURGY
MICS
MICTION
MICTIONS
MICTURATE
MID
MIDAIR
MIDAIRS
MIDBAND
MIDBRAIN
MIDBRAINS
MIDCALF
MIDCALVES
MIDCAP
MIDCOURSE
MIDCULT
MIDCULTS
MIDDAY
MIDDAYS
MIDDEN
MIDDENS
MIDDEST
MIDDIE
MIDDIES
MIDDLE
MIDDLED
MIDDLEMAN
MIDDLEMEN
MIDDLER
MIDDLERS
MIDDLES
MIDDLING
MIDDLINGS
MIDDORSAL
MIDDY
MIDFIELD
MIDFIELDS
MIDGE
MIDGES
MIDGET
MIDGETS
MIDGIE
MIDGIER
MIDGIES
MIDGIEST
MIDGUT
MIDGUTS
MIDGY
MIDI
MIDIBUS
MIDIBUSES
MIDINETTE
MIDIRON
MIDIRONS
MIDIS
MIDISKIRT
MIDLAND
MIDLANDER
MIDLANDS
MIDLEG
MIDLEGS
MIDLIFE
MIDLIFER
MIDLIFERS
MIDLINE
MIDLINES
MIDLIST
MIDLISTS
MIDLIVES
MIDMONTH
MIDMONTHS
MIDMOST
MIDMOSTS
MIDNIGHT
MIDNIGHTS
MIDNOON
MIDNOONS
MIDPAY
MIDPOINT
MIDPOINTS
MIDRANGE
MIDRANGES
MIDRASH
MIDRASHIC
MIDRASHIM
MIDRASHOT
MIDRIB
MIDRIBS
MIDRIFF
MIDRIFFS

M

MIDS
MIDSEASON
MIDSHIP
MIDSHIPS
MIDSHORE
MIDSIZE
MIDSIZED
MIDSOLE
MIDSOLES
MIDSPACE
MIDSPACES
MIDST
MIDSTORY
MIDSTREAM
MIDSTS
MIDSUMMER
MIDTERM
MIDTERMS
MIDTHIGH
MIDTHIGHS
MIDTOWN
MIDTOWNS
MIDWATCH
MIDWATER
MIDWATERS
MIDWAY
MIDWAYS
MIDWEEK
MIDWEEKLY
MIDWEEKS
MIDWIFE
MIDWIFED
MIDWIFERY
MIDWIFES
MIDWIFING
MIDWINTER
MIDWIVE
MIDWIVED
MIDWIVES
MIDWIVING
MIDYEAR
MIDYEARS
MIELIE
MIELIES
MIEN
MIENS
MIEVE
MIEVED
MIEVES
MIEVING
MIFF
MIFFED
MIFFIER
MIFFIEST
MIFFILY
MIFFINESS
MIFFING
MIFFS
MIFFY
MIFTY
MIG
MIGAWD
MIGG
MIGGLE
MIGGLES
MIGGS
MIGHT
MIGHTEST
MIGHTFUL
MIGHTIER
MIGHTIEST
MIGHTILY
MIGHTS
MIGHTST
MIGHTY
MIGMATITE
MIGNON
MIGNONNE
MIGNONNES
MIGNONS
MIGRAINE
MIGRAINES
MIGRANT
MIGRANTS
MIGRATE
MIGRATED
MIGRATES
MIGRATING
MIGRATION
MIGRATOR
MIGRATORS
MIGRATORY
MIGS
MIHA
MIHAS
MIHI
MIHIED
MIHIING
MIHIS
MIHRAB
MIHRABS
MIJNHEER
MIJNHEERS
MIKADO
MIKADOS
MIKE
MIKED
MIKES
MIKING
MIKRA
MIKRON
MIKRONS
MIKVA
MIKVAH
MIKVAHS
MIKVAS
MIKVEH
MIKVEHS
MIKVOS
MIKVOT
MIKVOTH
MIL
MILADI
MILADIES
MILADIS
MILADY
MILAGE
MILAGES
MILCH
MILCHIG
MILCHIK
MILD
MILDED
MILDEN
MILDENED
MILDENING
MILDENS
MILDER
MILDEST
MILDEW
MILDEWED
MILDEWIER
MILDEWING
MILDEWS
MILDEWY
MILDING
MILDISH
MILDLY
MILDNESS
MILDS
MILE
MILEAGE
MILEAGES
MILEPOST
MILEPOSTS
MILER
MILERS
MILES
MILESIAN
MILESIMO
MILESIMOS
MILESTONE
MILF
MILFOIL
MILFOILS
MILFS
MILIA
MILIARIA
MILIARIAL
MILIARIAS
MILIARY
MILIEU
MILIEUS
MILIEUX
MILING
MILINGS
MILITANCE
MILITANCY
MILITANT
MILITANTS
MILITAR
MILITARIA
MILITARY
MILITATE
MILITATED
MILITATES
MILITIA
MILITIAS
MILIUM
MILK
MILKED
MILKEN
MILKER
MILKERS
MILKFISH
MILKIER
MILKIEST
MILKILY
MILKINESS
MILKING
MILKINGS
MILKLESS
MILKLIKE
MILKMAID
MILKMAIDS
MILKMAN
MILKMEN
MILKO
MILKOS
MILKS
MILKSHAKE
MILKSHED
MILKSHEDS
MILKSOP
MILKSOPPY
MILKSOPS
MILKTOAST
MILKWEED
MILKWEEDS
MILKWOOD
MILKWOODS
MILKWORT
MILKWORTS
MILKY
MILL
MILLABLE
MILLAGE
MILLAGES
MILLBOARD
MILLCAKE
MILLCAKES
MILLDAM
MILLDAMS
MILLE
MILLED
MILLENARY
MILLENNIA
MILLEPED
MILLEPEDE
MILLEPEDS

M

MILLEPORE
MILLER
MILLERITE
MILLERS
MILLES
MILLET
MILLETS
MILLHAND
MILLHANDS
MILLHOUSE
MILLIAMP
MILLIAMPS
MILLIARD
MILLIARDS
MILLIARE
MILLIARES
MILLIARY
MILLIBAR
MILLIBARS
MILLIE
MILLIEME
MILLIEMES
MILLIER
MILLIERS
MILLIES
MILLIGAL
MILLIGALS
MILLIGRAM
MILLILUX
MILLIME
MILLIMES
MILLIMHO
MILLIMHOS
MILLIMOLE
MILLINE
MILLINER
MILLINERS
MILLINERY
MILLINES
MILLING
MILLINGS
MILLIOHM
MILLIOHMS
MILLION
MILLIONS
MILLIONTH
MILLIPED
MILLIPEDE
MILLIPEDS
MILLIREM
MILLIREMS
MILLIVOLT
MILLIWATT
MILLOCRAT
MILLPOND
MILLPONDS
MILLRACE
MILLRACES
MILLRIND
MILLRINDS
MILLRUN
MILLRUNS
MILLS
MILLSCALE
MILLSTONE
MILLTAIL
MILLTAILS
MILLWHEEL
MILLWORK
MILLWORKS
MILNEB
MILNEBS
MILO
MILOMETER
MILOR
MILORD
MILORDS
MILORS
MILOS
MILPA
MILPAS
MILREIS
MILS
MILSEY
MILSEYS
MILT
MILTED
MILTER
MILTERS
MILTIER
MILTIEST
MILTING
MILTONIA
MILTONIAS
MILTS
MILTY
MILTZ
MILTZES
MILVINE
MIM
MIMBAR
MIMBARS
MIME
MIMED
MIMEO
MIMEOED
MIMEOING
MIMEOS
MIMER
MIMERS
MIMES
MIMESES
MIMESIS
MIMESISES
MIMESTER
MIMESTERS
MIMETIC
MIMETICAL
MIMETITE
MIMETITES
MIMIC
MIMICAL
MIMICKED
MIMICKER
MIMICKERS
MIMICKING
MIMICRIES
MIMICRY
MIMICS
MIMING
MIMIVIRUS
MIMMER
MIMMEST
MIMMICK
MIMMICKED
MIMMICKS
MIMOSA
MIMOSAE
MIMOSAS
MIMSEY
MIMSIER
MIMSIEST
MIMSY
MIMULUS
MIMULUSES
MINA
MINABLE
MINACIOUS
MINACITY
MINAE
MINAR
MINARET
MINARETED
MINARETS
MINARS
MINAS
MINATORY
MINBAR
MINBARS
MINCE
MINCED
MINCEMEAT
MINCER
MINCERS
MINCES
MINCEUR
MINCIER
MINCIEST
MINCING
MINCINGLY
MINCY
MIND
MINDED
MINDEDLY
MINDER
MINDERS
MINDFUCK
MINDFUCKS
MINDFUL
MINDFULLY
MINDING
MINDINGS
MINDLESS
MINDS
MINDSCAPE
MINDSET
MINDSETS
MINDSHARE
MINE
MINEABLE
MINED
MINEFIELD
MINELAYER
MINEOLA
MINEOLAS
MINER
MINERAL
MINERALS
MINERS
MINES
MINESHAFT
MINESTONE
MINETTE
MINETTES
MINEVER
MINEVERS
MING
MINGE
MINGED
MINGER
MINGERS
MINGES
MINGIER
MINGIEST
MINGILY
MINGINESS
MINGING
MINGLE
MINGLED
MINGLER
MINGLERS
MINGLES
MINGLING
MINGLINGS
MINGS
MINGY
MINI
MINIATE
MINIATED
MINIATES
MINIATING
MINIATION
MINIATURE
MINIBAR
MINIBARS
MINIBIKE
MINIBIKER
MINIBIKES
MINIBREAK
MINIBUS

MINIBUSES
MINICAB
MINICABS
MINICAM
MINICAMP
MINICAMPS
MINICAMS
MINICAR
MINICARS
MINICOM
MINICOMS
MINIDISC
MINIDISCS
MINIDISH
MINIDISK
MINIDISKS
MINIDRESS
MINIER
MINIEST
MINIFIED
MINIFIES
MINIFY
MINIFYING
MINIGOLF
MINIGOLFS
MINIKIN
MINIKINS
MINILAB
MINILABS
MINIM
MINIMA
MINIMAL
MINIMALLY
MINIMALS
MINIMART
MINIMARTS
MINIMAX
MINIMAXED
MINIMAXES
MINIMENT
MINIMENTS
MINIMILL
MINIMILLS
MINIMISE
MINIMISED
MINIMISER
MINIMISES
MINIMISM
MINIMISMS
MINIMIST
MINIMISTS
MINIMIZE
MINIMIZED
MINIMIZER
MINIMIZES
MINIMOTO
MINIMOTOS
MINIMS
MINIMUM
MINIMUMS
MINIMUS
MINIMUSES
MINING
MININGS
MINION
MINIONS
MINIPARK
MINIPARKS
MINIPILL
MINIPILLS
MINIRUGBY
MINIS
MINISCULE
MINISH
MINISHED
MINISHES
MINISHING
MINISKI
MINISKIRT
MINISKIS
MINISODE
MINISODES
MINISTATE
MINISTER
MINISTERS
MINISTRY
MINITOWER
MINITRACK
MINIUM
MINIUMS
MINIVAN
MINIVANS
MINIVER
MINIVERS
MINIVET
MINIVETS
MINK
MINKE
MINKES
MINKS
MINNEOLA
MINNEOLAS
MINNICK
MINNICKED
MINNICKS
MINNIE
MINNIES
MINNOCK
MINNOCKED
MINNOCKS
MINNOW
MINNOWS
MINNY
MINO
MINOR
MINORCA
MINORCAS
MINORED
MINORING
MINORITY
MINORS
MINORSHIP
MINOS
MINOTAUR
MINOXIDIL
MINSHUKU
MINSHUKUS
MINSTER
MINSTERS
MINSTREL
MINSTRELS
MINT
MINTAGE
MINTAGES
MINTED
MINTER
MINTERS
MINTIER
MINTIEST
MINTING
MINTLIKE
MINTS
MINTY
MINUEND
MINUENDS
MINUET
MINUETED
MINUETING
MINUETS
MINUS
MINUSCULE
MINUSES
MINUTE
MINUTED
MINUTELY
MINUTEMAN
MINUTEMEN
MINUTER
MINUTES
MINUTEST
MINUTIA
MINUTIAE
MINUTIAL
MINUTING
MINUTIOSE
MINX
MINXES
MINXISH
MINY
MINYAN
MINYANIM
MINYANS
MIOCENE
MIOMBO
MIOMBOS
MIOSES
MIOSIS
MIOSISES
MIOTIC
MIOTICS
MIPS
MIQUELET
MIQUELETS
MIR
MIRABELLE
MIRABILIA
MIRABILIS
MIRABLE
MIRACIDIA
MIRACLE
MIRACLES
MIRADOR
MIRADORS
MIRAGE
MIRAGES
MIRANDISE
MIRANDIZE
MIRBANE
MIRBANES
MIRCHI
MIRE
MIRED
MIREPOIX
MIRES
MIREX
MIREXES
MIRI
MIRID
MIRIDS
MIRIER
MIRIEST
MIRIFIC
MIRIFICAL
MIRIN
MIRINESS
MIRING
MIRINS
MIRITI
MIRITIS
MIRK
MIRKER
MIRKEST
MIRKIER
MIRKIEST
MIRKILY
MIRKINESS
MIRKS
MIRKY
MIRLIER
MIRLIEST
MIRLIGOES
MIRLITON
MIRLITONS
MIRLY
MIRO
MIROMIRO
MIROMIROS
MIROS
MIRROR
MIRRORED

MIRRORING
MIRRORS
MIRS
MIRTH
MIRTHFUL
MIRTHLESS
MIRTHS
MIRV
MIRVED
MIRVING
MIRVS
MIRY
MIRZA
MIRZAS
MIS
MISACT
MISACTED
MISACTING
MISACTS
MISADAPT
MISADAPTS
MISADD
MISADDED
MISADDING
MISADDS
MISADJUST
MISADVICE
MISADVISE
MISAGENT
MISAGENTS
MISAIM
MISAIMED
MISAIMING
MISAIMS
MISALIGN
MISALIGNS
MISALLEGE
MISALLIED
MISALLIES
MISALLOT
MISALLOTS
MISALLY
MISALTER
MISALTERS
MISANDRY
MISAPPLY
MISARRAY
MISARRAYS
MISASSAY
MISASSAYS
MISASSIGN
MISASSUME
MISATE
MISATONE
MISATONED
MISATONES
MISAUNTER
MISAVER
MISAVERS
MISAVISED
MISAWARD
MISAWARDS
MISBECAME
MISBECOME
MISBEGAN
MISBEGIN
MISBEGINS
MISBEGOT
MISBEGUN
MISBEHAVE
MISBELIEF
MISBESEEM
MISBESTOW
MISBIAS
MISBIASED
MISBIASES
MISBILL
MISBILLED
MISBILLS
MISBIND
MISBINDS
MISBIRTH
MISBIRTHS
MISBORN
MISBOUND
MISBRAND
MISBRANDS
MISBUILD
MISBUILDS
MISBUILT
MISBUTTON
MISCALL
MISCALLED
MISCALLER
MISCALLS
MISCARRY
MISCAST
MISCASTS
MISCEGEN
MISCEGENE
MISCEGENS
MISCEGINE
MISCH
MISCHANCE
MISCHANCY
MISCHARGE
MISCHIEF
MISCHIEFS
MISCHOICE
MISCHOOSE
MISCHOSE
MISCHOSEN
MISCIBLE
MISCITE
MISCITED
MISCITES
MISCITING
MISCLAIM
MISCLAIMS
MISCLASS
MISCODE
MISCODED
MISCODES
MISCODING
MISCOIN
MISCOINED
MISCOINS
MISCOLOR
MISCOLORS
MISCOLOUR
MISCOOK
MISCOOKED
MISCOOKS
MISCOPIED
MISCOPIES
MISCOPY
MISCOUNT
MISCOUNTS
MISCREANT
MISCREATE
MISCREDIT
MISCREED
MISCREEDS
MISCUE
MISCUED
MISCUEING
MISCUES
MISCUING
MISCUT
MISCUTS
MISDATE
MISDATED
MISDATES
MISDATING
MISDEAL
MISDEALER
MISDEALS
MISDEALT
MISDEED
MISDEEDS
MISDEEM
MISDEEMED
MISDEEMS
MISDEFINE
MISDEMEAN
MISDEMPT
MISDESERT
MISDIAL
MISDIALED
MISDIALS
MISDID
MISDIET
MISDIETED
MISDIETS
MISDIGHT
MISDIGHTS
MISDIRECT
MISDIVIDE
MISDO
MISDOER
MISDOERS
MISDOES
MISDOING
MISDOINGS
MISDONE
MISDONNE
MISDOUBT
MISDOUBTS
MISDRAW
MISDRAWN
MISDRAWS
MISDREAD
MISDREADS
MISDREW
MISDRIVE
MISDRIVEN
MISDRIVES
MISDROVE
MISE
MISEASE
MISEASES
MISEAT
MISEATEN
MISEATING
MISEATS
MISEDIT
MISEDITED
MISEDITS
MISEMPLOY
MISENROL
MISENROLL
MISENROLS
MISENTER
MISENTERS
MISENTRY
MISER
MISERABLE
MISERABLY
MISERE
MISERERE
MISERERES
MISERES
MISERIES
MISERLIER
MISERLY
MISERS
MISERY
MISES
MISESTEEM
MISEVENT
MISEVENTS
MISFAITH
MISFAITHS
MISFALL
MISFALLEN
MISFALLS
MISFALNE
MISFARE
MISFARED
MISFARES

MISFARING
MISFEASOR
MISFED
MISFEED
MISFEEDS
MISFEIGN
MISFEIGNS
MISFELL
MISFIELD
MISFIELDS
MISFILE
MISFILED
MISFILES
MISFILING
MISFIRE
MISFIRED
MISFIRES
MISFIRING
MISFIT
MISFITS
MISFITTED
MISFOCUS
MISFOLD
MISFOLDED
MISFOLDS
MISFORM
MISFORMED
MISFORMS
MISFRAME
MISFRAMED
MISFRAMES
MISGAGE
MISGAGED
MISGAGES
MISGAGING
MISGAUGE
MISGAUGED
MISGAUGES
MISGAVE
MISGENDER
MISGIVE
MISGIVEN
MISGIVES
MISGIVING
MISGO
MISGOES
MISGOING
MISGONE
MISGOTTEN
MISGOVERN
MISGRADE
MISGRADED
MISGRADES
MISGRAFF
MISGRAFT
MISGRAFTS
MISGREW
MISGROW
MISGROWN
MISGROWS
MISGROWTH
MISGUESS
MISGUGGLE
MISGUIDE
MISGUIDED
MISGUIDER
MISGUIDES
MISHANDLE
MISHANTER
MISHAP
MISHAPPED
MISHAPPEN
MISHAPS
MISHAPT
MISHEAR
MISHEARD
MISHEARS
MISHEGAAS
MISHEGOSS
MISHIT
MISHITS
MISHMASH
MISHMEE
MISHMEES
MISHMI
MISHMIS
MISHMOSH
MISHUGAS
MISINFER
MISINFERS
MISINFORM
MISINTEND
MISINTER
MISINTERS
MISJOIN
MISJOINED
MISJOINS
MISJUDGE
MISJUDGED
MISJUDGER
MISJUDGES
MISKAL
MISKALS
MISKEEP
MISKEEPS
MISKEN
MISKENNED
MISKENS
MISKENT
MISKEPT
MISKEY
MISKEYED
MISKEYING
MISKEYS
MISKICK
MISKICKED
MISKICKS
MISKNEW
MISKNOW
MISKNOWN
MISKNOWS
MISLABEL
MISLABELS
MISLABOR
MISLABORS
MISLABOUR
MISLAID
MISLAIN
MISLAY
MISLAYER
MISLAYERS
MISLAYING
MISLAYS
MISLEAD
MISLEADER
MISLEADS
MISLEARED
MISLEARN
MISLEARNS
MISLEARNT
MISLED
MISLEEKE
MISLEEKED
MISLEEKES
MISLETOE
MISLETOES
MISLIE
MISLIES
MISLIGHT
MISLIGHTS
MISLIKE
MISLIKED
MISLIKER
MISLIKERS
MISLIKES
MISLIKING
MISLIPPEN
MISLIT
MISLIVE
MISLIVED
MISLIVES
MISLIVING
MISLOCATE
MISLODGE
MISLODGED
MISLODGES
MISLUCK
MISLUCKED
MISLUCKS
MISLYING
MISMADE
MISMAKE
MISMAKES
MISMAKING
MISMANAGE
MISMARK
MISMARKED
MISMARKS
MISMARRY
MISMATCH
MISMATE
MISMATED
MISMATES
MISMATING
MISMEET
MISMEETS
MISMET
MISMETRE
MISMETRED
MISMETRES
MISMOVE
MISMOVED
MISMOVES
MISMOVING
MISNAME
MISNAMED
MISNAMES
MISNAMING
MISNOMER
MISNOMERS
MISNUMBER
MISO
MISOCLERE
MISOGAMIC
MISOGAMY
MISOGYNIC
MISOGYNY
MISOLOGY
MISONEISM
MISONEIST
MISORDER
MISORDERS
MISORIENT
MISOS
MISPAGE
MISPAGED
MISPAGES
MISPAGING
MISPAINT
MISPAINTS
MISPARSE
MISPARSED
MISPARSES
MISPART
MISPARTED
MISPARTS
MISPATCH
MISPEN
MISPENNED
MISPENS
MISPHRASE
MISPICKEL
MISPLACE
MISPLACED
MISPLACES
MISPLAN
MISPLANS
MISPLANT
MISPLANTS
MISPLAY

MISPLAYED
MISPLAYS
MISPLEAD
MISPLEADS
MISPLEASE
MISPLED
MISPOINT
MISPOINTS
MISPOISE
MISPOISED
MISPOISES
MISPRAISE
MISPRICE
MISPRICED
MISPRICES
MISPRINT
MISPRINTS
MISPRISE
MISPRISED
MISPRISES
MISPRIZE
MISPRIZED
MISPRIZER
MISPRIZES
MISPROUD
MISQUOTE
MISQUOTED
MISQUOTER
MISQUOTES
MISRAISE
MISRAISED
MISRAISES
MISRATE
MISRATED
MISRATES
MISRATING
MISREAD
MISREADS
MISRECKON
MISRECORD
MISREFER
MISREFERS
MISREGARD
MISRELATE
MISRELIED
MISRELIES
MISRELY
MISRENDER
MISREPORT
MISRHYMED
MISROUTE
MISROUTED
MISROUTES
MISRULE
MISRULED
MISRULES
MISRULING
MISS
MISSA
MISSABLE
MISSAE
MISSAID
MISSAL
MISSALS
MISSAW
MISSAY
MISSAYING
MISSAYS
MISSEAT
MISSEATED
MISSEATS
MISSED
MISSEE
MISSEEING
MISSEEM
MISSEEMED
MISSEEMS
MISSEEN
MISSEES
MISSEL
MISSELL
MISSELLS
MISSELS
MISSEND
MISSENDS
MISSENSE
MISSENSED
MISSENSES
MISSENT
MISSES
MISSET
MISSETS
MISSHAPE
MISSHAPED
MISSHAPEN
MISSHAPER
MISSHAPES
MISSHOD
MISSHOOD
MISSHOODS
MISSIER
MISSIES
MISSIEST
MISSILE
MISSILEER
MISSILERY
MISSILES
MISSILRY
MISSING
MISSINGLY
MISSION
MISSIONAL
MISSIONED
MISSIONER
MISSIONS
MISSIS
MISSISES
MISSISH
MISSIVE
MISSIVES
MISSOLD
MISSORT
MISSORTED
MISSORTS
MISSOUND
MISSOUNDS
MISSOUT
MISSOUTS
MISSPACE
MISSPACED
MISSPACES
MISSPEAK
MISSPEAKS
MISSPELL
MISSPELLS
MISSPELT
MISSPEND
MISSPENDS
MISSPENT
MISSPOKE
MISSPOKEN
MISSTAMP
MISSTAMPS
MISSTART
MISSTARTS
MISSTATE
MISSTATED
MISSTATES
MISSTEER
MISSTEERS
MISSTEP
MISSTEPS
MISSTOP
MISSTOPS
MISSTRIKE
MISSTRUCK
MISSTYLE
MISSTYLED
MISSTYLES
MISSUIT
MISSUITED
MISSUITS
MISSUS
MISSUSES
MISSY
MIST
MISTAKE
MISTAKEN
MISTAKER
MISTAKERS
MISTAKES
MISTAKING
MISTAL
MISTALS
MISTAUGHT
MISTBOW
MISTBOWS
MISTEACH
MISTED
MISTELL
MISTELLS
MISTEMPER
MISTEND
MISTENDED
MISTENDS
MISTER
MISTERED
MISTERIES
MISTERING
MISTERM
MISTERMED
MISTERMS
MISTERS
MISTERY
MISTEUK
MISTFUL
MISTHINK
MISTHINKS
MISTHREW
MISTHROW
MISTHROWN
MISTHROWS
MISTICO
MISTICOS
MISTIER
MISTIEST
MISTIGRIS
MISTILY
MISTIME
MISTIMED
MISTIMES
MISTIMING
MISTINESS
MISTING
MISTINGS
MISTITLE
MISTITLED
MISTITLES
MISTLE
MISTLED
MISTLES
MISTLETOE
MISTLING
MISTOLD
MISTOOK
MISTOUCH
MISTRACE
MISTRACED
MISTRACES
MISTRAIN
MISTRAINS
MISTRAL
MISTRALS
MISTREAT
MISTREATS
MISTRESS
MISTRIAL
MISTRIALS
MISTRUST
MISTRUSTS

M

MISTRUTH
MISTRUTHS
MISTRYST
MISTRYSTS
MISTS
MISTUNE
MISTUNED
MISTUNES
MISTUNING
MISTUTOR
MISTUTORS
MISTY
MISTYPE
MISTYPED
MISTYPES
MISTYPING
MISUNION
MISUNIONS
MISUSAGE
MISUSAGES
MISUSE
MISUSED
MISUSER
MISUSERS
MISUSES
MISUSING
MISUST
MISVALUE
MISVALUED
MISVALUES
MISWEEN
MISWEENED
MISWEENS
MISWEND
MISWENDS
MISWENT
MISWORD
MISWORDED
MISWORDS
MISWRIT
MISWRITE
MISWRITES
MISWROTE
MISYOKE
MISYOKED
MISYOKES
MISYOKING
MITCH
MITCHED
MITCHES
MITCHING
MITE
MITER
MITERED
MITERER
MITERERS
MITERING
MITERS
MITERWORT
MITES
MITHER
MITHERED
MITHERING
MITHERS
MITICIDAL
MITICIDE
MITICIDES
MITIER
MITIEST
MITIGABLE
MITIGANT
MITIGANTS
MITIGATE
MITIGATED
MITIGATES
MITIGATOR
MITIS
MITISES
MITOGEN
MITOGENIC
MITOGENS
MITOMYCIN
MITOSES
MITOSIS
MITOTIC
MITRAILLE
MITRAL
MITRE
MITRED
MITRES
MITREWORT
MITRIFORM
MITRING
MITSVAH
MITSVAHS
MITSVOTH
MITT
MITTEN
MITTENED
MITTENS
MITTIMUS
MITTS
MITUMBA
MITUMBAS
MITY
MITZVAH
MITZVAHS
MITZVOTH
MIURUS
MIURUSES
MIX
MIXABLE
MIXDOWN
MIXDOWNS
MIXED
MIXEDLY
MIXEDNESS
MIXEN
MIXENS
MIXER
MIXERS
MIXES
MIXIBLE
MIXIER
MIXIEST
MIXING
MIXINGS
MIXMASTER
MIXOLOGY
MIXT
MIXTAPE
MIXTAPES
MIXTE
MIXTION
MIXTIONS
MIXTURE
MIXTURES
MIXUP
MIXUPS
MIXY
MIZ
MIZEN
MIZENMAST
MIZENS
MIZMAZE
MIZMAZES
MIZUNA
MIZUNAS
MIZZ
MIZZEN
MIZZENS
MIZZES
MIZZLE
MIZZLED
MIZZLES
MIZZLIER
MIZZLIEST
MIZZLING
MIZZLINGS
MIZZLY
MIZZONITE
MIZZY
MM
MMM
MNA
MNAS
MNEME
MNEMES
MNEMIC
MNEMON
MNEMONIC
MNEMONICS
MNEMONIST
MNEMONS
MO
MOA
MOAI
MOAN
MOANED
MOANER
MOANERS
MOANFUL
MOANFULLY
MOANING
MOANINGLY
MOANINGS
MOANS
MOAS
MOAT
MOATED
MOATING
MOATLIKE
MOATS
MOB
MOBBED
MOBBER
MOBBERS
MOBBIE
MOBBIES
MOBBING
MOBBINGS
MOBBISH
MOBBISHLY
MOBBISM
MOBBISMS
MOBBLE
MOBBLED
MOBBLES
MOBBLING
MOBBY
MOBCAP
MOBCAPS
MOBCAST
MOBCASTED
MOBCASTS
MOBE
MOBES
MOBEY
MOBEYS
MOBIE
MOBIES
MOBILE
MOBILES
MOBILISE
MOBILISED
MOBILISER
MOBILISES
MOBILITY
MOBILIZE
MOBILIZED
MOBILIZER
MOBILIZES
MOBISODE
MOBISODES
MOBLE
MOBLED
MOBLES
MOBLING
MOBLOG
MOBLOGGER

MOBLOGS
MOBOCRACY
MOBOCRAT
MOBOCRATS
MOBS
MOBSMAN
MOBSMEN
MOBSTER
MOBSTERS
MOBY
MOC
MOCASSIN
MOCASSINS
MOCCASIN
MOCCASINS
MOCCIES
MOCH
MOCHA
MOCHAS
MOCHED
MOCHELL
MOCHELLS
MOCHI
MOCHIE
MOCHIER
MOCHIEST
MOCHILA
MOCHILAS
MOCHINESS
MOCHING
MOCHIS
MOCHS
MOCHY
MOCK
MOCKABLE
MOCKADO
MOCKADOES
MOCKAGE
MOCKAGES
MOCKED
MOCKER
MOCKERED
MOCKERIES
MOCKERING
MOCKERNUT
MOCKERS
MOCKERY
MOCKING
MOCKINGLY
MOCKINGS
MOCKNEY
MOCKNEYS
MOCKS
MOCKTAIL
MOCKTAILS
MOCKUP
MOCKUPS
MOCOCK
MOCOCKS
MOCS
MOCUCK
MOCUCKS
MOCUDDUM
MOCUDDUMS
MOD
MODAFINIL
MODAL
MODALISM
MODALISMS
MODALIST
MODALISTS
MODALITY
MODALLY
MODALS
MODDED
MODDER
MODDERS
MODDING
MODDINGS
MODE
MODEL
MODELED
MODELER
MODELERS
MODELING
MODELINGS
MODELIST
MODELISTS
MODELLED
MODELLER
MODELLERS
MODELLI
MODELLING
MODELLIST
MODELLO
MODELLOS
MODELS
MODEM
MODEMED
MODEMING
MODEMS
MODENA
MODENAS
MODER
MODERATE
MODERATED
MODERATES
MODERATO
MODERATOR
MODERATOS
MODERN
MODERNE
MODERNER
MODERNES
MODERNEST
MODERNISE
MODERNISM
MODERNIST
MODERNITY
MODERNIZE
MODERNLY
MODERNS
MODERS
MODES
MODEST
MODESTER
MODESTEST
MODESTIES
MODESTLY
MODESTY
MODGE
MODGED
MODGES
MODGING
MODI
MODICA
MODICUM
MODICUMS
MODIFIED
MODIFIER
MODIFIERS
MODIFIES
MODIFY
MODIFYING
MODII
MODILLION
MODIOLAR
MODIOLI
MODIOLUS
MODISH
MODISHLY
MODIST
MODISTE
MODISTES
MODISTS
MODIUS
MODIWORT
MODIWORTS
MODS
MODULAR
MODULARLY
MODULARS
MODULATE
MODULATED
MODULATES
MODULATOR
MODULE
MODULES
MODULI
MODULO
MODULUS
MODUS
MOE
MOELLON
MOELLONS
MOER
MOERED
MOERING
MOERS
MOES
MOFETTE
MOFETTES
MOFFETTE
MOFFETTES
MOFO
MOFOS
MOFUSSIL
MOFUSSILS
MOG
MOGGAN
MOGGANS
MOGGED
MOGGIE
MOGGIES
MOGGING
MOGGY
MOGHUL
MOGHULS
MOGS
MOGUL
MOGULED
MOGULS
MOHAIR
MOHAIRS
MOHALIM
MOHAWK
MOHAWKS
MOHEL
MOHELIM
MOHELS
MOHICAN
MOHICANS
MOHO
MOHOS
MOHR
MOHRS
MOHUA
MOHUAS
MOHUR
MOHURS
MOI
MOIDER
MOIDERED
MOIDERING
MOIDERS
MOIDORE
MOIDORES
MOIETIES
MOIETY
MOIL
MOILE
MOILED
MOILER
MOILERS
MOILES
MOILING
MOILINGLY
MOILS
MOINEAU
MOINEAUS

M

MOIRA
MOIRAI
MOIRE
MOIRES
MOISER
MOISERS
MOIST
MOISTED
MOISTEN
MOISTENED
MOISTENER
MOISTENS
MOISTER
MOISTEST
MOISTFUL
MOISTIFY
MOISTING
MOISTLY
MOISTNESS
MOISTS
MOISTURE
MOISTURES
MOIT
MOITHER
MOITHERED
MOITHERS
MOITS
MOJAHEDIN
MOJARRA
MOJARRAS
MOJITO
MOJITOS
MOJO
MOJOES
MOJOS
MOKADDAM
MOKADDAMS
MOKE
MOKES
MOKI
MOKIHI
MOKIHIS
MOKIS
MOKO
MOKOMOKO
MOKOMOKOS
MOKOPUNA
MOKOPUNAS
MOKORO
MOKOROS
MOKOS
MOKSHA
MOKSHAS
MOL
MOLA
MOLAL
MOLALITY
MOLAR
MOLARITY
MOLARS
MOLAS
MOLASSE
MOLASSES
MOLD
MOLDABLE
MOLDAVITE
MOLDBOARD
MOLDED
MOLDER
MOLDERED
MOLDERING
MOLDERS
MOLDIER
MOLDIEST
MOLDINESS
MOLDING
MOLDINGS
MOLDS
MOLDWARP
MOLDWARPS
MOLDY
MOLE
MOLECAST
MOLECASTS
MOLECULAR
MOLECULE
MOLECULES
MOLED
MOLEHILL
MOLEHILLS
MOLEHUNT
MOLEHUNTS
MOLELIKE
MOLES
MOLESKIN
MOLESKINS
MOLEST
MOLESTED
MOLESTER
MOLESTERS
MOLESTFUL
MOLESTING
MOLESTS
MOLIES
MOLIMEN
MOLIMENS
MOLINE
MOLINES
MOLINET
MOLINETS
MOLING
MOLL
MOLLA
MOLLAH
MOLLAHS
MOLLAS
MOLLIE
MOLLIES
MOLLIFIED
MOLLIFIER
MOLLIFIES
MOLLIFY
MOLLITIES
MOLLS
MOLLUSC
MOLLUSCA
MOLLUSCAN
MOLLUSCS
MOLLUSCUM
MOLLUSK
MOLLUSKAN
MOLLUSKS
MOLLY
MOLLYHAWK
MOLLYMAWK
MOLOCH
MOLOCHISE
MOLOCHIZE
MOLOCHS
MOLOSSI
MOLOSSUS
MOLS
MOLT
MOLTED
MOLTEN
MOLTENLY
MOLTER
MOLTERS
MOLTING
MOLTO
MOLTS
MOLY
MOLYBDATE
MOLYBDIC
MOLYBDOUS
MOLYS
MOM
MOME
MOMENT
MOMENTA
MOMENTANY
MOMENTARY
MOMENTLY
MOMENTO
MOMENTOES
MOMENTOS
MOMENTOUS
MOMENTS
MOMENTUM
MOMENTUMS
MOMES
MOMI
MOMISM
MOMISMS
MOMMA
MOMMAS
MOMMET
MOMMETS
MOMMIES
MOMMY
MOMOIR
MOMOIRS
MOMS
MOMSER
MOMSERS
MOMUS
MOMUSES
MOMZER
MOMZERIM
MOMZERS
MON
MONA
MONACHAL
MONACHISM
MONACHIST
MONACID
MONACIDIC
MONACIDS
MONACT
MONACTINE
MONACTS
MONAD
MONADAL
MONADES
MONADIC
MONADICAL
MONADISM
MONADISMS
MONADNOCK
MONADS
MONAL
MONALS
MONAMINE
MONAMINES
MONANDRY
MONARCH
MONARCHAL
MONARCHIC
MONARCHS
MONARCHY
MONARDA
MONARDAS
MONAS
MONASES
MONASTERY
MONASTIC
MONASTICS
MONATOMIC
MONAUL
MONAULS
MONAURAL
MONAXIAL
MONAXON
MONAXONIC
MONAXONS
MONAZITE
MONAZITES
MONDAIN
MONDAINE
MONDAINES

MONDAINS
MONDE
MONDES
MONDIAL
MONDO
MONDOS
MONECIAN
MONECIOUS
MONELLIN
MONELLINS
MONEME
MONEMES
MONER
MONERA
MONERAN
MONERANS
MONERGISM
MONERON
MONETARY
MONETH
MONETHS
MONETISE
MONETISED
MONETISES
MONETIZE
MONETIZED
MONETIZES
MONEY
MONEYBAG
MONEYBAGS
MONEYBELT
MONEYBOX
MONEYED
MONEYER
MONEYERS
MONEYLESS
MONEYMAN
MONEYMEN
MONEYS
MONEYWORT
MONG
MONGCORN
MONGCORNS
MONGEESE
MONGER
MONGERED
MONGERIES
MONGERING
MONGERS
MONGERY
MONGO
MONGOE
MONGOES
MONGOOSE
MONGOOSES
MONGOS
MONGREL
MONGRELLY
MONGRELS
MONGS
MONGST
MONIAL
MONIALS
MONIC
MONICKER
MONICKERS
MONIE
MONIED
MONIES
MONIKER
MONIKERED
MONIKERS
MONILIA
MONILIAE
MONILIAL
MONILIAS
MONIMENT
MONIMENTS
MONIPLIES
MONISH
MONISHED
MONISHES
MONISHING
MONISM
MONISMS
MONIST
MONISTIC
MONISTS
MONITION
MONITIONS
MONITIVE
MONITOR
MONITORED
MONITORS
MONITORY
MONITRESS
MONK
MONKERIES
MONKERY
MONKEY
MONKEYED
MONKEYING
MONKEYISH
MONKEYISM
MONKEYPOD
MONKEYPOT
MONKEYPOX
MONKEYS
MONKFISH
MONKHOOD
MONKHOODS
MONKISH
MONKISHLY
MONKS
MONKSHOOD
MONO
MONOACID
MONOACIDS
MONOAMINE
MONOAO
MONOAOS
MONOBASIC
MONOBLOC
MONOBROW
MONOBROWS
MONOCARP
MONOCARPS
MONOCEROS
MONOCHORD
MONOCLE
MONOCLED
MONOCLES
MONOCLINE
MONOCOQUE
MONOCOT
MONOCOTS
MONOCOTYL
MONOCRACY
MONOCRAT
MONOCRATS
MONOCROP
MONOCROPS
MONOCULAR
MONOCYCLE
MONOCYTE
MONOCYTES
MONOCYTIC
MONODIC
MONODICAL
MONODIES
MONODIST
MONODISTS
MONODONT
MONODRAMA
MONODY
MONOECIES
MONOECISM
MONOECY
MONOESTER
MONOFIL
MONOFILS
MONOFUEL
MONOFUELS
MONOGAMIC
MONOGAMY
MONOGENIC
MONOGENY
MONOGERM
MONOGLOT
MONOGLOTS
MONOGONY
MONOGRAM
MONOGRAMS
MONOGRAPH
MONOGYNY
MONOHULL
MONOHULLS
MONOICOUS
MONOKINE
MONOKINES
MONOKINI
MONOKINIS
MONOLATER
MONOLATRY
MONOLAYER
MONOLINE
MONOLITH
MONOLITHS
MONOLOG
MONOLOGIC
MONOLOGS
MONOLOGUE
MONOLOGY
MONOMACHY
MONOMANIA
MONOMARK
MONOMARKS
MONOMER
MONOMERIC
MONOMERS
MONOMETER
MONOMIAL
MONOMIALS
MONOMODE
MONONYM
MONONYMS
MONOPHAGY
MONOPHASE
MONOPHONY
MONOPHYLY
MONOPITCH
MONOPLANE
MONOPLOID
MONOPOD
MONOPODE
MONOPODES
MONOPODIA
MONOPODS
MONOPODY
MONOPOLE
MONOPOLES
MONOPOLY
MONOPRINT
MONOPSONY
MONOPTERA
MONOPTOTE
MONOPULSE
MONORAIL
MONORAILS
MONORCHID
MONORHINE
MONORHYME
MONOS
MONOSEMIC
MONOSEMY
MONOSES
MONOSIES
MONOSIS
MONOSKI
MONOSKIED

M

MONOSKIER
MONOSKIS
MONOSOME
MONOSOMES
MONOSOMIC
MONOSOMY
MONOSTELE
MONOSTELY
MONOSTICH
MONOSTOME
MONOSTYLE
MONOSY
MONOTASK
MONOTASKS
MONOTINT
MONOTINTS
MONOTONE
MONOTONED
MONOTONES
MONOTONIC
MONOTONY
MONOTREME
MONOTROCH
MONOTYPE
MONOTYPES
MONOTYPIC
MONOVULAR
MONOXIDE
MONOXIDES
MONOXYLON
MONS
MONSIEUR
MONSIGNOR
MONSOON
MONSOONAL
MONSOONS
MONSTER
MONSTERA
MONSTERAS
MONSTERED
MONSTERS
MONSTROUS
MONTADALE
MONTAGE
MONTAGED
MONTAGES
MONTAGING
MONTAN
MONTANE
MONTANES
MONTANT
MONTANTO
MONTANTOS
MONTANTS
MONTARIA
MONTARIAS
MONTE
MONTEITH
MONTEITHS
MONTEM
MONTEMS
MONTERO
MONTEROS
MONTES
MONTH
MONTHLIES
MONTHLING
MONTHLONG
MONTHLY
MONTHS
MONTICLE
MONTICLES
MONTICULE
MONTIES
MONTRE
MONTRES
MONTURE
MONTURES
MONTY
MONUMENT
MONUMENTS
MONURON
MONURONS
MONY
MONYPLIES
MONZONITE
MOO
MOOBIES
MOOBS
MOOCH
MOOCHED
MOOCHER
MOOCHERS
MOOCHES
MOOCHING
MOOD
MOODIED
MOODIER
MOODIES
MOODIEST
MOODILY
MOODINESS
MOODS
MOODY
MOODYING
MOOED
MOOI
MOOING
MOOK
MOOKS
MOOKTAR
MOOKTARS
MOOL
MOOLA
MOOLAH
MOOLAHS
MOOLAS
MOOLED
MOOLEY
MOOLEYS
MOOLI
MOOLIES
MOOLING
MOOLIS
MOOLOO
MOOLOOS
MOOLS
MOOLVI
MOOLVIE
MOOLVIES
MOOLVIS
MOOLY
MOON
MOONBEAM
MOONBEAMS
MOONBLIND
MOONBOOTS
MOONBOW
MOONBOWS
MOONCAKE
MOONCAKES
MOONCALF
MOONCHILD
MOONCRAFT
MOONDOG
MOONDOGS
MOONDUST
MOONDUSTS
MOONED
MOONER
MOONERS
MOONEYE
MOONEYES
MOONFACE
MOONFACED
MOONFACES
MOONFISH
MOONG
MOONGATE
MOONGATES
MOONIER
MOONIES
MOONIEST
MOONILY
MOONINESS
MOONING
MOONISH
MOONISHLY
MOONLESS
MOONLET
MOONLETS
MOONLIGHT
MOONLIKE
MOONLIT
MOONPHASE
MOONPORT
MOONPORTS
MOONQUAKE
MOONRAKER
MOONRISE
MOONRISES
MOONROCK
MOONROCKS
MOONROOF
MOONROOFS
MOONS
MOONSAIL
MOONSAILS
MOONSCAPE
MOONSEED
MOONSEEDS
MOONSET
MOONSETS
MOONSHEE
MOONSHEES
MOONSHINE
MOONSHINY
MOONSHIP
MOONSHIPS
MOONSHOT
MOONSHOTS
MOONSTONE
MOONWALK
MOONWALKS
MOONWARD
MOONWARDS
MOONWORT
MOONWORTS
MOONY
MOOP
MOOPED
MOOPING
MOOPS
MOOR
MOORAGE
MOORAGES
MOORBURN
MOORBURNS
MOORCOCK
MOORCOCKS
MOORED
MOORFOWL
MOORFOWLS
MOORHEN
MOORHENS
MOORIER
MOORIEST
MOORILL
MOORILLS
MOORING
MOORINGS
MOORISH
MOORLAND
MOORLANDS
MOORLOG
MOORLOGS
MOORMAN
MOORMEN
MOORS
MOORVA

MOORVAS
MOORWORT
MOORWORTS
MOORY
MOOS
MOOSE
MOOSEBIRD
MOOSEHAIR
MOOSEHIDE
MOOSEWOOD
MOOSEYARD
MOOT
MOOTABLE
MOOTED
MOOTER
MOOTERS
MOOTEST
MOOTING
MOOTINGS
MOOTMAN
MOOTMEN
MOOTNESS
MOOTS
MOOVE
MOOVED
MOOVES
MOOVING
MOP
MOPANE
MOPANES
MOPANI
MOPANIS
MOPBOARD
MOPBOARDS
MOPE
MOPED
MOPEDS
MOPEHAWK
MOPEHAWKS
MOPER
MOPERIES
MOPERS
MOPERY
MOPES
MOPEY
MOPHEAD
MOPHEADS
MOPIER
MOPIEST
MOPILY
MOPINESS
MOPING
MOPINGLY
MOPISH
MOPISHLY
MOPOKE
MOPOKES
MOPPED
MOPPER
MOPPERS
MOPPET
MOPPETS
MOPPIER
MOPPIEST
MOPPING
MOPPY
MOPS
MOPSIES
MOPSTICK
MOPSTICKS
MOPSY
MOPUS
MOPUSES
MOPY
MOQUETTE
MOQUETTES
MOR
MORA
MORACEOUS
MORAE
MORAINAL
MORAINE
MORAINES
MORAINIC
MORAL
MORALE
MORALES
MORALISE
MORALISED
MORALISER
MORALISES
MORALISM
MORALISMS
MORALIST
MORALISTS
MORALITY
MORALIZE
MORALIZED
MORALIZER
MORALIZES
MORALL
MORALLED
MORALLER
MORALLERS
MORALLING
MORALLS
MORALLY
MORALS
MORAS
MORASS
MORASSES
MORASSIER
MORASSY
MORAT
MORATORIA
MORATORY
MORATS
MORAY
MORAYS
MORBID
MORBIDER
MORBIDEST
MORBIDITY
MORBIDLY
MORBIFIC
MORBILLI
MORBUS
MORBUSES
MORCEAU
MORCEAUX
MORCHA
MORCHAS
MORDACITY
MORDANCY
MORDANT
MORDANTED
MORDANTLY
MORDANTS
MORDENT
MORDENTS
MORE
MOREEN
MOREENS
MOREISH
MOREL
MORELLE
MORELLES
MORELLO
MORELLOS
MORELS
MORENDO
MORENDOS
MORENESS
MOREOVER
MOREPORK
MOREPORKS
MORES
MORESQUE
MORESQUES
MORGAN
MORGANITE
MORGANS
MORGAY
MORGAYS
MORGEN
MORGENS
MORGUE
MORGUES
MORIA
MORIAS
MORIBUND
MORICHE
MORICHES
MORION
MORIONS
MORISCO
MORISCOES
MORISCOS
MORISH
MORKIN
MORKINS
MORLING
MORLINGS
MORMAOR
MORMAORS
MORN
MORNAY
MORNAYS
MORNE
MORNED
MORNES
MORNING
MORNINGS
MORNS
MOROCCO
MOROCCOS
MORON
MORONIC
MORONISM
MORONISMS
MORONITY
MORONS
MOROSE
MOROSELY
MOROSER
MOROSEST
MOROSITY
MORPH
MORPHEAN
MORPHED
MORPHEME
MORPHEMES
MORPHEMIC
MORPHETIC
MORPHEW
MORPHEWS
MORPHIA
MORPHIAS
MORPHIC
MORPHIN
MORPHINE
MORPHINES
MORPHING
MORPHINGS
MORPHINIC
MORPHINS
MORPHO
MORPHOGEN
MORPHOS
MORPHOSES
MORPHOSIS
MORPHOTIC
MORPHS
MORRA
MORRAS
MORRELL
MORRELLS
MORRHUA
MORRHUAS
MORRICE

M

MORRICES
MORRION
MORRIONS
MORRIS
MORRISED
MORRISES
MORRISING
MORRO
MORROS
MORROW
MORROWS
MORS
MORSAL
MORSALS
MORSE
MORSEL
MORSELED
MORSELING
MORSELLED
MORSELS
MORSES
MORSURE
MORSURES
MORT
MORTAL
MORTALISE
MORTALITY
MORTALIZE
MORTALLY
MORTALS
MORTAR
MORTARED
MORTARIER
MORTARING
MORTARMAN
MORTARMEN
MORTARS
MORTARY
MORTBELL
MORTBELLS
MORTCLOTH
MORTGAGE
MORTGAGED
MORTGAGEE
MORTGAGER
MORTGAGES
MORTGAGOR
MORTICE
MORTICED
MORTICER
MORTICERS
MORTICES
MORTICIAN
MORTICING
MORTIFIC
MORTIFIED
MORTIFIER
MORTIFIES
MORTIFY
MORTISE
MORTISED
MORTISER
MORTISERS
MORTISES
MORTISING
MORTLING
MORTLINGS
MORTMAIN
MORTMAINS
MORTS
MORTSAFE
MORTSAFES
MORTUARY
MORULA
MORULAE
MORULAR
MORULAS
MORWONG
MORWONGS
MORYAH
MOS
MOSAIC
MOSAICISM
MOSAICIST
MOSAICKED
MOSAICS
MOSASAUR
MOSASAURI
MOSASAURS
MOSCATO
MOSCATOS
MOSCHATE
MOSCHATEL
MOSCOVIUM
MOSE
MOSED
MOSELLE
MOSELLES
MOSES
MOSEY
MOSEYED
MOSEYING
MOSEYS
MOSH
MOSHAV
MOSHAVIM
MOSHED
MOSHER
MOSHERS
MOSHES
MOSHING
MOSHINGS
MOSING
MOSK
MOSKONFYT
MOSKS
MOSLINGS
MOSQUE
MOSQUES
MOSQUITO
MOSQUITOS
MOSS
MOSSBACK
MOSSBACKS
MOSSED
MOSSER
MOSSERS
MOSSES
MOSSGROWN
MOSSIE
MOSSIER
MOSSIES
MOSSIEST
MOSSINESS
MOSSING
MOSSLAND
MOSSLANDS
MOSSLIKE
MOSSO
MOSSPLANT
MOSSY
MOST
MOSTE
MOSTEST
MOSTESTS
MOSTLY
MOSTS
MOSTWHAT
MOT
MOTE
MOTED
MOTEL
MOTELIER
MOTELIERS
MOTELS
MOTEN
MOTES
MOTET
MOTETS
MOTETT
MOTETTIST
MOTETTS
MOTEY
MOTEYS
MOTH
MOTHBALL
MOTHBALLS
MOTHED
MOTHER
MOTHERED
MOTHERESE
MOTHERIER
MOTHERING
MOTHERLY
MOTHERS
MOTHERY
MOTHIER
MOTHIEST
MOTHLIKE
MOTHPROOF
MOTHS
MOTHY
MOTI
MOTIER
MOTIEST
MOTIF
MOTIFIC
MOTIFS
MOTILE
MOTILES
MOTILITY
MOTION
MOTIONAL
MOTIONED
MOTIONER
MOTIONERS
MOTIONING
MOTIONIST
MOTIONS
MOTIS
MOTIVATE
MOTIVATED
MOTIVATES
MOTIVATOR
MOTIVE
MOTIVED
MOTIVES
MOTIVIC
MOTIVING
MOTIVITY
MOTLEY
MOTLEYER
MOTLEYEST
MOTLEYS
MOTLIER
MOTLIEST
MOTMOT
MOTMOTS
MOTOCROSS
MOTOR
MOTORABLE
MOTORAIL
MOTORAILS
MOTORBIKE
MOTORBOAT
MOTORBUS
MOTORCADE
MOTORCAR
MOTORCARS
MOTORDOM
MOTORDOMS
MOTORED
MOTORHOME
MOTORIAL
MOTORIC
MOTORICS
MOTORING
MOTORINGS
MOTORISE
MOTORISED

M

MOTORISES
MOTORIST
MOTORISTS
MOTORIUM
MOTORIUMS
MOTORIZE
MOTORIZED
MOTORIZES
MOTORLESS
MOTORMAN
MOTORMEN
MOTORS
MOTORSHIP
MOTORWAY
MOTORWAYS
MOTORY
MOTOSCAFI
MOTOSCAFO
MOTS
MOTSER
MOTSERS
MOTT
MOTTE
MOTTES
MOTTIER
MOTTIES
MOTTIEST
MOTTLE
MOTTLED
MOTTLER
MOTTLERS
MOTTLES
MOTTLING
MOTTLINGS
MOTTO
MOTTOED
MOTTOES
MOTTOS
MOTTS
MOTTY
MOTU
MOTUCA
MOTUCAS
MOTUS
MOTZA
MOTZAS
MOU
MOUCH
MOUCHARD
MOUCHARDS
MOUCHED
MOUCHER
MOUCHERS
MOUCHES
MOUCHING
MOUCHOIR
MOUCHOIRS
MOUDIWART
MOUDIWORT
MOUE
MOUES
MOUFFLON
MOUFFLONS
MOUFLON
MOUFLONS
MOUGHT
MOUILLE
MOUJIK
MOUJIKS
MOULAGE
MOULAGES
MOULD
MOULDABLE
MOULDED
MOULDER
MOULDERED
MOULDERS
MOULDIER
MOULDIEST
MOULDING
MOULDINGS
MOULDS
MOULDWARP
MOULDY
MOULIN
MOULINET
MOULINETS
MOULINS
MOULS
MOULT
MOULTED
MOULTEN
MOULTER
MOULTERS
MOULTING
MOULTINGS
MOULTS
MOUND
MOUNDBIRD
MOUNDED
MOUNDING
MOUNDS
MOUNSEER
MOUNSEERS
MOUNT
MOUNTABLE
MOUNTAIN
MOUNTAINS
MOUNTAINY
MOUNTANT
MOUNTANTS
MOUNTED
MOUNTER
MOUNTERS
MOUNTING
MOUNTINGS
MOUNTS
MOUP
MOUPED
MOUPING
MOUPS
MOURN
MOURNED
MOURNER
MOURNERS
MOURNFUL
MOURNING
MOURNINGS
MOURNIVAL
MOURNS
MOURVEDRE
MOUS
MOUSAKA
MOUSAKAS
MOUSE
MOUSEBIRD
MOUSED
MOUSEKIN
MOUSEKINS
MOUSELIKE
MOUSEMAT
MOUSEMATS
MOUSEOVER
MOUSEPAD
MOUSEPADS
MOUSER
MOUSERIES
MOUSERS
MOUSERY
MOUSES
MOUSETAIL
MOUSETRAP
MOUSEY
MOUSIE
MOUSIER
MOUSIES
MOUSIEST
MOUSILY
MOUSINESS
MOUSING
MOUSINGS
MOUSLE
MOUSLED
MOUSLES
MOUSLING
MOUSME
MOUSMEE
MOUSMEES
MOUSMES
MOUSSAKA
MOUSSAKAS
MOUSSE
MOUSSED
MOUSSES
MOUSSEUX
MOUSSING
MOUST
MOUSTACHE
MOUSTED
MOUSTING
MOUSTS
MOUSY
MOUTAN
MOUTANS
MOUTER
MOUTERED
MOUTERER
MOUTERERS
MOUTERING
MOUTERS
MOUTH
MOUTHABLE
MOUTHED
MOUTHER
MOUTHERS
MOUTHFEEL
MOUTHFUL
MOUTHFULS
MOUTHIER
MOUTHIEST
MOUTHILY
MOUTHING
MOUTHLESS
MOUTHLIKE
MOUTHPART
MOUTHS
MOUTHWASH
MOUTHY
MOUTON
MOUTONNEE
MOUTONS
MOVABLE
MOVABLES
MOVABLY
MOVANT
MOVANTS
MOVE
MOVEABLE
MOVEABLES
MOVEABLY
MOVED
MOVELESS
MOVEMENT
MOVEMENTS
MOVER
MOVERS
MOVES
MOVIE
MOVIEDOM
MOVIEDOMS
MOVIEGOER
MOVIELAND
MOVIEOKE
MOVIEOKES
MOVIEOLA
MOVIEOLAS
MOVIES
MOVING
MOVINGLY
MOVIOLA

MOVIOLAS
MOW
MOWA
MOWAS
MOWBURN
MOWBURNED
MOWBURNS
MOWBURNT
MOWDIE
MOWDIES
MOWED
MOWER
MOWERS
MOWING
MOWINGS
MOWN
MOWRA
MOWRAS
MOWS
MOXA
MOXAS
MOXIE
MOXIES
MOY
MOYA
MOYAS
MOYGASHEL
MOYITIES
MOYITY
MOYL
MOYLE
MOYLED
MOYLES
MOYLING
MOYLS
MOYS
MOZ
MOZE
MOZED
MOZES
MOZETTA
MOZETTAS
MOZETTE
MOZING
MOZO
MOZOS
MOZZ
MOZZES
MOZZETTA
MOZZETTAS
MOZZETTE
MOZZIE
MOZZIES
MOZZLE
MOZZLED
MOZZLES
MOZZLING
MPRET
MPRETS
MRIDAMGAM
MRIDANG
MRIDANGA
MRIDANGAM
MRIDANGAS
MRIDANGS
MU
MUCATE
MUCATES
MUCH
MUCHACHA
MUCHACHAS
MUCHACHO
MUCHACHOS
MUCHEL
MUCHELL
MUCHELLS
MUCHELS
MUCHES
MUCHLY
MUCHNESS
MUCHO
MUCIC
MUCID
MUCIDITY
MUCIDNESS
MUCIGEN
MUCIGENS
MUCILAGE
MUCILAGES
MUCIN
MUCINOGEN
MUCINOID
MUCINOUS
MUCINS
MUCK
MUCKAMUCK
MUCKED
MUCKENDER
MUCKER
MUCKERED
MUCKERING
MUCKERISH
MUCKERS
MUCKHEAP
MUCKHEAPS
MUCKIER
MUCKIEST
MUCKILY
MUCKINESS
MUCKING
MUCKLE
MUCKLER
MUCKLES
MUCKLEST
MUCKLUCK
MUCKLUCKS
MUCKRAKE
MUCKRAKED
MUCKRAKER
MUCKRAKES
MUCKS
MUCKSWEAT
MUCKWORM
MUCKWORMS
MUCKY
MUCKYMUCK
MUCLUC
MUCLUCS
MUCOID
MUCOIDAL
MUCOIDS
MUCOLYTIC
MUCOR
MUCORS
MUCOSA
MUCOSAE
MUCOSAL
MUCOSAS
MUCOSE
MUCOSITY
MUCOUS
MUCRO
MUCRONATE
MUCRONES
MUCROS
MUCULENT
MUCUS
MUCUSES
MUD
MUDBANK
MUDBANKS
MUDBATH
MUDBATHS
MUDBUG
MUDBUGS
MUDCAP
MUDCAPPED
MUDCAPS
MUDCAT
MUDCATS
MUDDED
MUDDER
MUDDERS
MUDDIED
MUDDIER
MUDDIES
MUDDIEST
MUDDILY
MUDDINESS
MUDDING
MUDDLE
MUDDLED
MUDDLER
MUDDLERS
MUDDLES
MUDDLIER
MUDDLIEST
MUDDLING
MUDDLINGS
MUDDLY
MUDDY
MUDDYING
MUDEJAR
MUDEJARES
MUDEYE
MUDEYES
MUDFISH
MUDFISHES
MUDFLAP
MUDFLAPS
MUDFLAT
MUDFLATS
MUDFLOW
MUDFLOWS
MUDGE
MUDGED
MUDGER
MUDGERS
MUDGES
MUDGING
MUDGUARD
MUDGUARDS
MUDHEN
MUDHENS
MUDHOLE
MUDHOLES
MUDHOOK
MUDHOOKS
MUDHOPPER
MUDIR
MUDIRIA
MUDIRIAS
MUDIRIEH
MUDIRIEHS
MUDIRS
MUDLARK
MUDLARKED
MUDLARKS
MUDLOGGER
MUDPACK
MUDPACKS
MUDPIE
MUDPIES
MUDPUPPY
MUDRA
MUDRAS
MUDROCK
MUDROCKS
MUDROOM
MUDROOMS
MUDS
MUDSCOW
MUDSCOWS
MUDSILL
MUDSILLS
MUDSLIDE
MUDSLIDES
MUDSLING
MUDSLINGS
MUDSLUNG

MUDSTONE
MUDSTONES
MUDWORT
MUDWORTS
MUEDDIN
MUEDDINS
MUENSTER
MUENSTERS
MUESLI
MUESLIS
MUEZZIN
MUEZZINS
MUFF
MUFFED
MUFFETTEE
MUFFIN
MUFFINEER
MUFFING
MUFFINS
MUFFISH
MUFFLE
MUFFLED
MUFFLER
MUFFLERED
MUFFLERS
MUFFLES
MUFFLING
MUFFS
MUFLON
MUFLONS
MUFTI
MUFTIS
MUG
MUGEARITE
MUGFUL
MUGFULS
MUGG
MUGGA
MUGGAR
MUGGARS
MUGGAS
MUGGED
MUGGEE
MUGGEES
MUGGER
MUGGERS
MUGGIER
MUGGIEST
MUGGILY
MUGGINESS
MUGGING
MUGGINGS
MUGGINS
MUGGINSES
MUGGISH
MUGGLE
MUGGLES
MUGGS
MUGGUR
MUGGURS
MUGGY
MUGHAL
MUGHALS
MUGS
MUGSHOT
MUGSHOTS
MUGWORT
MUGWORTS
MUGWUMP
MUGWUMPS
MUHLIES
MUHLY
MUID
MUIDS
MUIL
MUILS
MUIR
MUIRBURN
MUIRBURNS
MUIRS
MUIST
MUISTED
MUISTING
MUISTS
MUJAHEDIN
MUJAHIDIN
MUJIK
MUJIKS
MUKHTAR
MUKHTARS
MUKLUK
MUKLUKS
MUKTUK
MUKTUKS
MULBERRY
MULCH
MULCHED
MULCHES
MULCHING
MULCT
MULCTED
MULCTING
MULCTS
MULE
MULED
MULES
MULESED
MULESES
MULESING
MULESINGS
MULETA
MULETAS
MULETEER
MULETEERS
MULEY
MULEYS
MULGA
MULGAS
MULIE
MULIES
MULING
MULISH
MULISHLY
MULL
MULLA
MULLAH
MULLAHED
MULLAHING
MULLAHISM
MULLAHS
MULLARKY
MULLAS
MULLED
MULLEIN
MULLEINS
MULLEN
MULLENS
MULLER
MULLERED
MULLERIAN
MULLERING
MULLERS
MULLET
MULLETS
MULLEY
MULLEYS
MULLIGAN
MULLIGANS
MULLING
MULLION
MULLIONED
MULLIONS
MULLITE
MULLITES
MULLOCK
MULLOCKS
MULLOCKY
MULLOWAY
MULLOWAYS
MULLS
MULMUL
MULMULL
MULMULLS
MULMULS
MULSE
MULSES
MULSH
MULSHED
MULSHES
MULSHING
MULTEITY
MULTIAGE
MULTIATOM
MULTIBAND
MULTIBANK
MULTICAR
MULTICAST
MULTICELL
MULTICIDE
MULTICITY
MULTICOPY
MULTICORE
MULTICULT
MULTIDAY
MULTIDISC
MULTIDISK
MULTIDRUG
MULTIFID
MULTIFIL
MULTIFILS
MULTIFOIL
MULTIFOLD
MULTIFORM
MULTIGENE
MULTIGERM
MULTIGRID
MULTIGYM
MULTIGYMS
MULTIHUED
MULTIHULL
MULTIJET
MULTILANE
MULTILINE
MULTILOBE
MULTIMODE
MULTIPACK
MULTIPAGE
MULTIPARA
MULTIPART
MULTIPATH
MULTIPED
MULTIPEDE
MULTIPEDS
MULTIPION
MULTIPLE
MULTIPLES
MULTIPLET
MULTIPLEX
MULTIPLY
MULTIPOLE
MULTIPORT
MULTIRISK
MULTIROLE
MULTIROOM
MULTISITE
MULTISIZE
MULTISTEP
MULTITASK
MULTITIER
MULTITON
MULTITONE
MULTITOOL
MULTITUDE
MULTIUNIT
MULTIUSE
MULTIUSER
MULTIWALL
MULTIWAY
MULTIYEAR
MULTUM

MULTUMS
MULTURE
MULTURED
MULTURER
MULTURERS
MULTURES
MULTURING
MUM
MUMBLE
MUMBLED
MUMBLER
MUMBLERS
MUMBLES
MUMBLIER
MUMBLIEST
MUMBLING
MUMBLINGS
MUMBLY
MUMCHANCE
MUMM
MUMMED
MUMMER
MUMMERED
MUMMERIES
MUMMERING
MUMMERS
MUMMERY
MUMMIA
MUMMIAS
MUMMICHOG
MUMMIED
MUMMIES
MUMMIFIED
MUMMIFIES
MUMMIFORM
MUMMIFY
MUMMING
MUMMINGS
MUMMOCK
MUMMOCKS
MUMMS
MUMMY
MUMMYING
MUMP
MUMPED
MUMPER
MUMPERS
MUMPING
MUMPISH
MUMPISHLY
MUMPS
MUMPSIMUS
MUMS
MUMSIER
MUMSIES
MUMSIEST
MUMSINESS
MUMSY
MUMU
MUMUS
MUN
MUNCH
MUNCHABLE
MUNCHED
MUNCHER
MUNCHERS
MUNCHES
MUNCHIE
MUNCHIER
MUNCHIES
MUNCHIEST
MUNCHING
MUNCHKIN
MUNCHKINS
MUNCHY
MUNDANE
MUNDANELY
MUNDANER
MUNDANEST
MUNDANITY
MUNDIC
MUNDICS
MUNDIFIED
MUNDIFIES
MUNDIFY
MUNDUNGO
MUNDUNGOS
MUNDUNGUS
MUNG
MUNGA
MUNGAS
MUNGCORN
MUNGCORNS
MUNGE
MUNGED
MUNGES
MUNGING
MUNGO
MUNGOES
MUNGOOSE
MUNGOOSES
MUNGOS
MUNGS
MUNI
MUNICIPAL
MUNIFIED
MUNIFIES
MUNIFY
MUNIFYING
MUNIMENT
MUNIMENTS
MUNIS
MUNITE
MUNITED
MUNITES
MUNITING
MUNITION
MUNITIONS
MUNNION
MUNNIONS
MUNS
MUNSHI
MUNSHIS
MUNSTER
MUNSTERS
MUNTED
MUNTER
MUNTERS
MUNTIN
MUNTINED
MUNTING
MUNTINGS
MUNTINS
MUNTJAC
MUNTJACS
MUNTJAK
MUNTJAKS
MUNTRIE
MUNTRIES
MUON
MUONIC
MUONIUM
MUONIUMS
MUONS
MUPPET
MUPPETS
MUQADDAM
MUQADDAMS
MURA
MURAENA
MURAENAS
MURAENID
MURAENIDS
MURAGE
MURAGES
MURAL
MURALED
MURALIST
MURALISTS
MURALLED
MURALS
MURAS
MURDABAD
MURDER
MURDERED
MURDEREE
MURDEREES
MURDERER
MURDERERS
MURDERESS
MURDERING
MURDEROUS
MURDERS
MURE
MURED
MUREIN
MUREINS
MURENA
MURENAS
MURES
MUREX
MUREXES
MURGEON
MURGEONED
MURGEONS
MURIATE
MURIATED
MURIATES
MURIATIC
MURICATE
MURICATED
MURICES
MURID
MURIDS
MURIFORM
MURINE
MURINES
MURING
MURK
MURKED
MURKER
MURKEST
MURKIER
MURKIEST
MURKILY
MURKINESS
MURKING
MURKISH
MURKLY
MURKS
MURKSOME
MURKY
MURL
MURLAIN
MURLAINS
MURLAN
MURLANS
MURLED
MURLIER
MURLIEST
MURLIN
MURLING
MURLINS
MURLS
MURLY
MURMUR
MURMURED
MURMURER
MURMURERS
MURMURING
MURMUROUS
MURMURS
MURPHIES
MURPHY
MURR
MURRA
MURRAGH
MURRAGHS
MURRAIN
MURRAINED

MURRAINS
MURRAM
MURRAMS
MURRAS
MURRAY
MURRAYS
MURRE
MURREE
MURREES
MURRELET
MURRELETS
MURREN
MURRENS
MURRES
MURREY
MURREYS
MURRHA
MURRHAS
MURRHINE
MURRHINES
MURRI
MURRIES
MURRIN
MURRINE
MURRINES
MURRINS
MURRION
MURRIONS
MURRIS
MURRS
MURRY
MURSHID
MURSHIDS
MURTHER
MURTHERED
MURTHERER
MURTHERS
MURTI
MURTIS
MURVA
MURVAS
MUS
MUSACEOUS
MUSANG
MUSANGS
MUSAR
MUSARS
MUSCA
MUSCADEL
MUSCADELS
MUSCADET
MUSCADETS
MUSCADIN
MUSCADINE
MUSCADINS
MUSCAE
MUSCARINE
MUSCAT
MUSCATEL
MUSCATELS
MUSCATS
MUSCAVADO
MUSCID
MUSCIDS
MUSCLE
MUSCLED
MUSCLEMAN
MUSCLEMEN
MUSCLES
MUSCLEY
MUSCLIER
MUSCLIEST
MUSCLING
MUSCLINGS
MUSCLY
MUSCOID
MUSCOIDS
MUSCOLOGY
MUSCONE
MUSCONES
MUSCOSE
MUSCOVADO
MUSCOVITE
MUSCOVY
MUSCULAR
MUSCULOUS
MUSE
MUSED
MUSEFUL
MUSEFULLY
MUSEOLOGY
MUSER
MUSERS
MUSES
MUSET
MUSETS
MUSETTE
MUSETTES
MUSEUM
MUSEUMS
MUSH
MUSHA
MUSHED
MUSHER
MUSHERS
MUSHES
MUSHIE
MUSHIER
MUSHIES
MUSHIEST
MUSHILY
MUSHINESS
MUSHING
MUSHINGS
MUSHMOUTH
MUSHRAT
MUSHRATS
MUSHROOM
MUSHROOMS
MUSHROOMY
MUSHY
MUSIC
MUSICAL
MUSICALE
MUSICALES
MUSICALLY
MUSICALS
MUSICIAN
MUSICIANS
MUSICK
MUSICKED
MUSICKER
MUSICKERS
MUSICKING
MUSICKS
MUSICLESS
MUSICS
MUSIMON
MUSIMONS
MUSING
MUSINGLY
MUSINGS
MUSIT
MUSITS
MUSIVE
MUSJID
MUSJIDS
MUSK
MUSKED
MUSKEG
MUSKEGS
MUSKET
MUSKETEER
MUSKETOON
MUSKETRY
MUSKETS
MUSKIE
MUSKIER
MUSKIES
MUSKIEST
MUSKILY
MUSKINESS
MUSKING
MUSKIT
MUSKITS
MUSKLE
MUSKLES
MUSKMELON
MUSKONE
MUSKONES
MUSKOX
MUSKOXEN
MUSKRAT
MUSKRATS
MUSKROOT
MUSKROOTS
MUSKS
MUSKY
MUSLIN
MUSLINED
MUSLINET
MUSLINETS
MUSLINS
MUSMON
MUSMONS
MUSO
MUSOS
MUSPIKE
MUSPIKES
MUSQUASH
MUSROL
MUSROLS
MUSS
MUSSE
MUSSED
MUSSEL
MUSSELLED
MUSSELS
MUSSES
MUSSIER
MUSSIEST
MUSSILY
MUSSINESS
MUSSING
MUSSITATE
MUSSY
MUST
MUSTACHE
MUSTACHED
MUSTACHES
MUSTACHIO
MUSTANG
MUSTANGS
MUSTARD
MUSTARDS
MUSTARDY
MUSTED
MUSTEE
MUSTEES
MUSTELID
MUSTELIDS
MUSTELINE
MUSTER
MUSTERED
MUSTERER
MUSTERERS
MUSTERING
MUSTERS
MUSTH
MUSTHS
MUSTIER
MUSTIEST
MUSTILY
MUSTINESS
MUSTING
MUSTS
MUSTY
MUT
MUTABLE
MUTABLY

M

MUTAGEN
MUTAGENIC
MUTAGENS
MUTANDA
MUTANDUM
MUTANT
MUTANTS
MUTASE
MUTASES
MUTATE
MUTATED
MUTATES
MUTATING
MUTATION
MUTATIONS
MUTATIVE
MUTATOR
MUTATORS
MUTATORY
MUTCH
MUTCHED
MUTCHES
MUTCHING
MUTCHKIN
MUTCHKINS
MUTE
MUTED
MUTEDLY
MUTELY
MUTENESS
MUTER
MUTES
MUTEST
MUTHA
MUTHAS
MUTI
MUTICATE
MUTICOUS
MUTILATE
MUTILATED
MUTILATES
MUTILATOR
MUTINE
MUTINED
MUTINEER
MUTINEERS
MUTINES
MUTING
MUTINIED
MUTINIES
MUTINING
MUTINOUS
MUTINY
MUTINYING
MUTIS
MUTISM
MUTISMS
MUTON
MUTONS
MUTOSCOPE
MUTS
MUTT
MUTTER
MUTTERED
MUTTERER
MUTTERERS
MUTTERING
MUTTERS
MUTTON
MUTTONIER
MUTTONS
MUTTONY
MUTTS
MUTUAL
MUTUALISE
MUTUALISM
MUTUALIST
MUTUALITY
MUTUALIZE
MUTUALLY
MUTUALS
MUTUCA
MUTUCAS
MUTUEL
MUTUELS
MUTULAR
MUTULE
MUTULES
MUTUUM
MUTUUMS
MUUMUU
MUUMUUS
MUX
MUXED
MUXES
MUXING
MUZAK
MUZAKIER
MUZAKIEST
MUZAKS
MUZAKY
MUZHIK
MUZHIKS
MUZJIK
MUZJIKS
MUZZ
MUZZED
MUZZES
MUZZIER
MUZZIEST
MUZZILY
MUZZINESS
MUZZING
MUZZLE
MUZZLED
MUZZLER
MUZZLERS
MUZZLES
MUZZLING
MUZZY
MVULE
MVULES
MWAH
MWALIMU
MWALIMUS
MY
MYAL
MYALGIA
MYALGIAS
MYALGIC
MYALISM
MYALISMS
MYALIST
MYALISTS
MYALL
MYALLS
MYASES
MYASIS
MYC
MYCELE
MYCELES
MYCELIA
MYCELIAL
MYCELIAN
MYCELIUM
MYCELLA
MYCELLAS
MYCELOID
MYCETES
MYCETOMA
MYCETOMAS
MYCOBIONT
MYCOFLORA
MYCOLOGIC
MYCOLOGY
MYCOPHAGY
MYCOPHILE
MYCORHIZA
MYCOSES
MYCOSIS
MYCOTIC
MYCOTOXIN
MYCOVIRUS
MYCS
MYDRIASES
MYDRIASIS
MYDRIATIC
MYELIN
MYELINE
MYELINES
MYELINIC
MYELINS
MYELITES
MYELITIS
MYELOCYTE
MYELOGRAM
MYELOID
MYELOMA
MYELOMAS
MYELOMATA
MYELON
MYELONS
MYGALE
MYGALES
MYIASES
MYIASIS
MYIOPHILY
MYLAR
MYLARS
MYLODON
MYLODONS
MYLODONT
MYLODONTS
MYLOHYOID
MYLONITE
MYLONITES
MYLONITIC
MYNA
MYNAH
MYNAHS
MYNAS
MYNHEER
MYNHEERS
MYOBLAST
MYOBLASTS
MYOCARDIA
MYOCLONIC
MYOCLONUS
MYOFIBRIL
MYOGEN
MYOGENIC
MYOGENS
MYOGLOBIN
MYOGRAM
MYOGRAMS
MYOGRAPH
MYOGRAPHS
MYOGRAPHY
MYOID
MYOIDS
MYOLOGIC
MYOLOGIES
MYOLOGIST
MYOLOGY
MYOMA
MYOMANCY
MYOMANTIC
MYOMAS
MYOMATA
MYOMATOUS
MYOMERE
MYOMERES
MYONEURAL
MYOPATHIC
MYOPATHY
MYOPE
MYOPES
MYOPHILY
MYOPIA
MYOPIAS

MYOPIC
MYOPICS
MYOPIES
MYOPS
MYOPSES
MYOPY
MYOSCOPE
MYOSCOPES
MYOSES
MYOSIN
MYOSINS
MYOSIS
MYOSISES
MYOSITIS
MYOSOTE
MYOSOTES
MYOSOTIS
MYOSTATIN
MYOTIC
MYOTICS
MYOTOME
MYOTOMES
MYOTONIA
MYOTONIAS
MYOTONIC
MYOTUBE
MYOTUBES
MYRBANE
MYRBANES
MYRIAD
MYRIADS
MYRIADTH
MYRIADTHS
MYRIAPOD
MYRIAPODS
MYRICA
MYRICAS
MYRINGA
MYRINGAS
MYRIOPOD
MYRIOPODS
MYRIORAMA
MYRISTIC
MYRMECOID
MYRMIDON
MYRMIDONS
MYROBALAN
MYRRH
MYRRHIC
MYRRHIER
MYRRHIEST
MYRRHINE
MYRRHOL
MYRRHOLS
MYRRHS
MYRRHY
MYRTLE
MYRTLES
MYSELF
MYSID
MYSIDS
MYSOST
MYSOSTS
MYSPACE
MYSPACED
MYSPACES
MYSPACING
MYSTAGOG
MYSTAGOGS
MYSTAGOGY
MYSTERIES
MYSTERY
MYSTIC
MYSTICAL
MYSTICETE
MYSTICISM
MYSTICLY
MYSTICS
MYSTIFIED
MYSTIFIER
MYSTIFIES
MYSTIFY
MYSTIQUE
MYSTIQUES
MYTH
MYTHI
MYTHIC
MYTHICAL
MYTHICISE
MYTHICISM
MYTHICIST
MYTHICIZE
MYTHIER
MYTHIEST
MYTHISE
MYTHISED
MYTHISES
MYTHISING
MYTHISM
MYTHISMS
MYTHIST
MYTHISTS
MYTHIZE
MYTHIZED
MYTHIZES
MYTHIZING
MYTHMAKER
MYTHOI
MYTHOLOGY
MYTHOMANE
MYTHOPEIC
MYTHOPOET
MYTHOS
MYTHS
MYTHUS
MYTHY
MYTILOID
MYXAMEBA
MYXAMEBAE
MYXAMEBAS
MYXAMOEBA
MYXEDEMA
MYXEDEMAS
MYXEDEMIC
MYXO
MYXOCYTE
MYXOCYTES
MYXOEDEMA
MYXOID
MYXOMA
MYXOMAS
MYXOMATA
MYXOS
MYXOVIRAL
MYXOVIRUS
MZEE
MZEES
MZUNGU
MZUNGUS

N

NA
NAAM
NAAMS
NAAN
NAANS
NAARTJE
NAARTJES
NAARTJIE
NAARTJIES
NAB
NABBED
NABBER
NABBERS
NABBING
NABE
NABES
NABIS
NABK
NABKS
NABLA
NABLAS
NABOB
NABOBERY
NABOBESS
NABOBISH
NABOBISM
NABOBISMS
NABOBS
NABS
NACARAT
NACARATS
NACELLE
NACELLES
NACH
NACHAS
NACHE
NACHES
NACHO
NACHOS
NACHTMAAL
NACKET
NACKETS
NACRE
NACRED
NACREOUS
NACRES
NACRITE
NACRITES
NACROUS
NADA
NADAS
NADIR
NADIRAL
NADIRS
NADORS
NADS
NAE
NAEBODIES
NAEBODY
NAES
NAETHING
NAETHINGS
NAEVE
NAEVES
NAEVI
NAEVOID
NAEVUS
NAFF
NAFFED
NAFFER
NAFFEST
NAFFING
NAFFLY
NAFFNESS
NAFFS
NAG
NAGA
NAGANA
NAGANAS
NAGAPIE
NAGAPIES
NAGARI
NAGARIS
NAGAS
NAGGED
NAGGER
NAGGERS
NAGGIER
NAGGIEST
NAGGING
NAGGINGLY
NAGGINGS
NAGGY
NAGMAAL
NAGMAALS
NAGOR
NAGORS
NAGS
NAGWARE
NAGWARES
NAH
NAHAL
NAHALS
NAIAD
NAIADES
NAIADS
NAIANT
NAIF
NAIFER
NAIFEST
NAIFLY
NAIFNESS
NAIFS
NAIK
NAIKS
NAIL
NAILBITER
NAILBRUSH
NAILED
NAILER
NAILERIES
NAILERS
NAILERY
NAILFILE
NAILFILES
NAILFOLD
NAILFOLDS
NAILHEAD
NAILHEADS
NAILING
NAILINGS
NAILLESS
NAILS
NAILSET
NAILSETS
NAIN
NAINSELL
NAINSELLS
NAINSOOK
NAINSOOKS
NAIRA
NAIRAS
NAIRU
NAIRUS
NAISSANCE
NAISSANT
NAIVE
NAIVELY
NAIVENESS
NAIVER
NAIVES
NAIVEST
NAIVETE
NAIVETES
NAIVETIES
NAIVETY
NAIVIST
NAKED
NAKEDER
NAKEDEST
NAKEDLY
NAKEDNESS
NAKER
NAKERS
NAKFA
NAKFAS
NALA
NALAS
NALED
NALEDS
NALIDIXIC
NALLA
NALLAH
NALLAHS
NALLAS
NALOXONE
NALOXONES
NAM
NAMABLE
NAMASKAR
NAMASKARS
NAMASTE
NAMASTES
NAMAYCUSH
NAME
NAMEABLE
NAMECHECK
NAMED
NAMELESS
NAMELY
NAMEPLATE
NAMER
NAMERS
NAMES
NAMESAKE
NAMESAKES
NAMETAG
NAMETAGS
NAMETAPE
NAMETAPES
NAMING
NAMINGS
NAMMA
NAMS
NAMU
NAMUS
NAN
NANA
NANAS
NANDIN

NANDINA
NANDINAS
NANDINE
NANDINES
NANDINS
NANDOO
NANDOOS
NANDU
NANDUS
NANE
NANG
NANISM
NANISMS
NANITE
NANITES
NANKEEN
NANKEENS
NANKIN
NANKINS
NANNA
NANNAS
NANNIE
NANNIED
NANNIES
NANNY
NANNYGAI
NANNYGAIS
NANNYING
NANNYINGS
NANNYISH
NANO
NANOBE
NANOBEE
NANOBEES
NANOBES
NANOBOT
NANOBOTS
NANODOT
NANODOTS
NANOGRAM
NANOGRAMS
NANOGRASS
NANOMETER
NANOMETRE
NANOOK
NANOOKS
NANOPORE
NANOPORES
NANOS
NANOSCALE
NANOTECH
NANOTECHS
NANOTESLA
NANOTUBE
NANOTUBES
NANOWATT
NANOWATTS
NANOWIRE
NANOWIRES
NANOWORLD
NANS
NANUA
NANUAS
NAOI
NAOS
NAOSES
NAP
NAPA
NAPALM
NAPALMED
NAPALMING
NAPALMS
NAPAS
NAPE
NAPED
NAPERIES
NAPERY
NAPES
NAPHTHA
NAPHTHAS
NAPHTHENE
NAPHTHOL
NAPHTHOLS
NAPHTHOUS
NAPHTHYL
NAPHTHYLS
NAPHTOL
NAPHTOLS
NAPIFORM
NAPING
NAPKIN
NAPKINS
NAPLESS
NAPOLEON
NAPOLEONS
NAPOO
NAPOOED
NAPOOING
NAPOOS
NAPPA
NAPPAS
NAPPE
NAPPED
NAPPER
NAPPERS
NAPPES
NAPPIE
NAPPIER
NAPPIES
NAPPIEST
NAPPINESS
NAPPING
NAPPY
NAPRON
NAPRONS
NAPROXEN
NAPROXENS
NAPS
NARAS
NARASES
NARC
NARCEEN
NARCEENS
NARCEIN
NARCEINE
NARCEINES
NARCEINS
NARCISM
NARCISMS
NARCISSI
NARCISSUS
NARCIST
NARCISTIC
NARCISTS
NARCO
NARCOMA
NARCOMAS
NARCOMATA
NARCOS
NARCOSE
NARCOSES
NARCOSIS
NARCOTIC
NARCOTICS
NARCOTINE
NARCOTISE
NARCOTISM
NARCOTIST
NARCOTIZE
NARCS
NARD
NARDED
NARDINE
NARDING
NARDOO
NARDOOS
NARDS
NARE
NARES
NARGHILE
NARGHILES
NARGHILLY
NARGHILY
NARGILE
NARGILEH
NARGILEHS
NARGILES
NARGILIES
NARGILY
NARGUILEH
NARIAL
NARIC
NARICORN
NARICORNS
NARINE
NARIS
NARK
NARKED
NARKIER
NARKIEST
NARKING
NARKS
NARKY
NARQUOIS
NARRAS
NARRASES
NARRATE
NARRATED
NARRATER
NARRATERS
NARRATES
NARRATING
NARRATION
NARRATIVE
NARRATOR
NARRATORS
NARRATORY
NARRE
NARROW
NARROWED
NARROWER
NARROWEST
NARROWING
NARROWISH
NARROWLY
NARROWS
NARTHEX
NARTHEXES
NARTJIE
NARTJIES
NARWAL
NARWALS
NARWHAL
NARWHALE
NARWHALES
NARWHALS
NARY
NAS
NASAL
NASALISE
NASALISED
NASALISES
NASALISM
NASALISMS
NASALITY
NASALIZE
NASALIZED
NASALIZES
NASALLY
NASALS
NASARD
NASARDS
NASCENCE
NASCENCES
NASCENCY
NASCENT
NASEBERRY
NASHGAB
NASHGABS
NASHI

N

NASHIS
NASIAL
NASION
NASIONS
NASSELLA
NASTALIK
NASTALIKS
NASTIC
NASTIER
NASTIES
NASTIEST
NASTILY
NASTINESS
NASTY
NASUTE
NASUTES
NAT
NATAL
NATALITY
NATANT
NATANTLY
NATATION
NATATIONS
NATATORIA
NATATORY
NATCH
NATCHES
NATES
NATHELESS
NATHEMO
NATHEMORE
NATHLESS
NATIFORM
NATION
NATIONAL
NATIONALS
NATIONS
NATIS
NATIVE
NATIVELY
NATIVES
NATIVISM
NATIVISMS
NATIVIST
NATIVISTS
NATIVITY
NATRIUM
NATRIUMS
NATROLITE
NATRON
NATRONS
NATS
NATTER
NATTERED
NATTERER
NATTERERS
NATTERIER
NATTERING
NATTERS
NATTERY
NATTIER
NATTIEST
NATTILY
NATTINESS
NATTY
NATURA
NATURAE
NATURAL
NATURALLY
NATURALS
NATURE
NATURED
NATURES
NATURING
NATURISM
NATURISMS
NATURIST
NATURISTS
NAUCH
NAUCHES
NAUGAHYDE
NAUGHT
NAUGHTIER
NAUGHTIES
NAUGHTILY
NAUGHTS
NAUGHTY
NAUMACHIA
NAUMACHY
NAUNT
NAUNTS
NAUPLIAL
NAUPLII
NAUPLIOID
NAUPLIUS
NAUSEA
NAUSEANT
NAUSEANTS
NAUSEAS
NAUSEATE
NAUSEATED
NAUSEATES
NAUSEOUS
NAUTCH
NAUTCHES
NAUTIC
NAUTICAL
NAUTICS
NAUTILI
NAUTILOID
NAUTILUS
NAV
NAVAID
NAVAIDS
NAVAL
NAVALISM
NAVALISMS
NAVALLY
NAVAR
NAVARCH
NAVARCHS
NAVARCHY
NAVARHO
NAVARHOS
NAVARIN
NAVARINS
NAVARS
NAVE
NAVEL
NAVELS
NAVELWORT
NAVES
NAVETTE
NAVETTES
NAVEW
NAVEWS
NAVICERT
NAVICERTS
NAVICULA
NAVICULAR
NAVICULAS
NAVIES
NAVIGABLE
NAVIGABLY
NAVIGATE
NAVIGATED
NAVIGATES
NAVIGATOR
NAVS
NAVVIED
NAVVIES
NAVVY
NAVVYING
NAVY
NAW
NAWAB
NAWABS
NAY
NAYS
NAYSAID
NAYSAY
NAYSAYER
NAYSAYERS
NAYSAYING
NAYSAYS
NAYTHLES
NAYWARD
NAYWARDS
NAYWORD
NAYWORDS
NAZE
NAZES
NAZI
NAZIFIED
NAZIFIES
NAZIFY
NAZIFYING
NAZIR
NAZIRS
NAZIS
NDUJA
NDUJAS
NE
NEAFE
NEAFES
NEAFFE
NEAFFES
NEAL
NEALED
NEALING
NEALS
NEANIC
NEAP
NEAPED
NEAPING
NEAPS
NEAR
NEARBY
NEARED
NEARER
NEAREST
NEARING
NEARISH
NEARLIER
NEARLIEST
NEARLY
NEARNESS
NEARS
NEARSHORE
NEARSIDE
NEARSIDES
NEAT
NEATEN
NEATENED
NEATENING
NEATENS
NEATER
NEATEST
NEATH
NEATHERD
NEATHERDS
NEATLY
NEATNESS
NEATNIK
NEATNIKS
NEATS
NEB
NEBBED
NEBBICH
NEBBICHS
NEBBING
NEBBISH
NEBBISHE
NEBBISHER
NEBBISHES
NEBBISHY
NEBBUK
NEBBUKS
NEBECK
NEBECKS

N

NEBEK
NEBEKS
NEBEL
NEBELS
NEBENKERN
NEBISH
NEBISHES
NEBRIS
NEBRISES
NEBS
NEBULA
NEBULAE
NEBULAR
NEBULAS
NEBULE
NEBULES
NEBULISE
NEBULISED
NEBULISER
NEBULISES
NEBULIUM
NEBULIUMS
NEBULIZE
NEBULIZED
NEBULIZER
NEBULIZES
NEBULOSE
NEBULOUS
NEBULY
NECESSARY
NECESSITY
NECK
NECKATEE
NECKATEES
NECKBAND
NECKBANDS
NECKBEEF
NECKBEEFS
NECKCLOTH
NECKED
NECKER
NECKERS
NECKGEAR
NECKGEARS
NECKING
NECKINGS
NECKLACE
NECKLACED
NECKLACES
NECKLESS
NECKLET
NECKLETS
NECKLIKE
NECKLINE
NECKLINES
NECKPIECE
NECKS
NECKSHOT
NECKSHOTS
NECKTIE
NECKTIES
NECKVERSE
NECKWEAR
NECKWEARS
NECKWEED
NECKWEEDS
NECROLOGY
NECROPHIL
NECROPOLI
NECROPSY
NECROSE
NECROSED
NECROSES
NECROSING
NECROSIS
NECROTIC
NECROTISE
NECROTIZE
NECROTOMY
NECTAR
NECTAREAL
NECTAREAN
NECTARED
NECTARIAL
NECTARIED
NECTARIES
NECTARINE
NECTAROUS
NECTARS
NECTARY
NED
NEDDIER
NEDDIES
NEDDIEST
NEDDISH
NEDDY
NEDETTE
NEDETTES
NEDS
NEE
NEED
NEEDED
NEEDER
NEEDERS
NEEDFIRE
NEEDFIRES
NEEDFUL
NEEDFULLY
NEEDFULS
NEEDIER
NEEDIEST
NEEDILY
NEEDINESS
NEEDING
NEEDLE
NEEDLED
NEEDLEFUL
NEEDLER
NEEDLERS
NEEDLES
NEEDLESS
NEEDLIER
NEEDLIEST
NEEDLING
NEEDLINGS
NEEDLY
NEEDMENT
NEEDMENTS
NEEDS
NEEDY
NEELD
NEELDS
NEELE
NEELES
NEEM
NEEMB
NEEMBS
NEEMS
NEEP
NEEPS
NEESBERRY
NEESE
NEESED
NEESES
NEESING
NEEZE
NEEZED
NEEZES
NEEZING
NEF
NEFANDOUS
NEFARIOUS
NEFAST
NEFS
NEG
NEGATE
NEGATED
NEGATER
NEGATERS
NEGATES
NEGATING
NEGATION
NEGATIONS
NEGATIVE
NEGATIVED
NEGATIVES
NEGATON
NEGATONS
NEGATOR
NEGATORS
NEGATORY
NEGATRON
NEGATRONS
NEGLECT
NEGLECTED
NEGLECTER
NEGLECTOR
NEGLECTS
NEGLIGE
NEGLIGEE
NEGLIGEES
NEGLIGENT
NEGLIGES
NEGOCIANT
NEGOTIANT
NEGOTIATE
NEGRITUDE
NEGRONI
NEGRONIS
NEGS
NEGUS
NEGUSES
NEIF
NEIFS
NEIGH
NEIGHBOR
NEIGHBORS
NEIGHBOUR
NEIGHED
NEIGHING
NEIGHINGS
NEIGHS
NEINEI
NEINEIS
NEIST
NEITHER
NEIVE
NEIVES
NEK
NEKS
NEKTON
NEKTONIC
NEKTONS
NELIES
NELIS
NELLIE
NELLIES
NELLY
NELSON
NELSONS
NELUMBIUM
NELUMBO
NELUMBOS
NEMA
NEMAS
NEMATIC
NEMATICS
NEMATODE
NEMATODES
NEMATOID
NEMERTEAN
NEMERTIAN
NEMERTINE
NEMESES
NEMESIA
NEMESIAS
NEMESIS
NEMN
NEMNED
NEMNING

NEMNS
NEMOPHILA
NEMORAL
NEMOROUS
NEMPT
NENE
NENES
NENNIGAI
NENNIGAIS
NENUPHAR
NENUPHARS
NEOBLAST
NEOBLASTS
NEOCON
NEOCONS
NEOCORTEX
NEODYMIUM
NEOGENE
NEOGOTHIC
NEOLITH
NEOLITHIC
NEOLITHS
NEOLOGIAN
NEOLOGIC
NEOLOGIES
NEOLOGISE
NEOLOGISM
NEOLOGIST
NEOLOGIZE
NEOLOGY
NEOMORPH
NEOMORPHS
NEOMYCIN
NEOMYCINS
NEON
NEONATAL
NEONATE
NEONATES
NEONED
NEONOMIAN
NEONS
NEOPAGAN
NEOPAGANS
NEOPHILE
NEOPHILES
NEOPHILIA
NEOPHOBE
NEOPHOBES
NEOPHOBIA
NEOPHOBIC
NEOPHYTE
NEOPHYTES
NEOPHYTIC
NEOPILINA
NEOPLASIA
NEOPLASM
NEOPLASMS
NEOPLASTY
NEOPRENE
NEOPRENES
NEOSOUL
NEOSOULS
NEOTEINIA
NEOTENIC
NEOTENIES
NEOTENOUS
NEOTENY
NEOTERIC
NEOTERICS
NEOTERISE
NEOTERISM
NEOTERIST
NEOTERIZE
NEOTOXIN
NEOTOXINS
NEOTROPIC
NEOTYPE
NEOTYPES
NEP
NEPENTHE
NEPENTHES
NEPER
NEPERS
NEPETA
NEPETAS
NEPHALISM
NEPHALIST
NEPHELINE
NEPHELITE
NEPHEW
NEPHEWS
NEPHOGRAM
NEPHOLOGY
NEPHRALGY
NEPHRIC
NEPHRIDIA
NEPHRISM
NEPHRISMS
NEPHRITE
NEPHRITES
NEPHRITIC
NEPHRITIS
NEPHROID
NEPHRON
NEPHRONS
NEPHROSES
NEPHROSIS
NEPHROTIC
NEPIONIC
NEPIT
NEPITS
NEPOTIC
NEPOTISM
NEPOTISMS
NEPOTIST
NEPOTISTS
NEPS
NEPTUNIUM
NERAL
NERALS
NERD
NERDIC
NERDICS
NERDIER
NERDIEST
NERDINESS
NERDISH
NERDS
NERDY
NEREID
NEREIDES
NEREIDS
NEREIS
NERINE
NERINES
NERITE
NERITES
NERITIC
NERK
NERKA
NERKAS
NERKS
NEROL
NEROLI
NEROLIS
NEROLS
NERTS
NERTZ
NERVAL
NERVATE
NERVATION
NERVATURE
NERVE
NERVED
NERVELESS
NERVELET
NERVELETS
NERVER
NERVERS
NERVES
NERVIER
NERVIEST
NERVILY
NERVINE
NERVINES
NERVINESS
NERVING
NERVINGS
NERVOSITY
NERVOUS
NERVOUSLY
NERVULAR
NERVULE
NERVULES
NERVURE
NERVURES
NERVY
NESCIENCE
NESCIENT
NESCIENTS
NESH
NESHER
NESHEST
NESHNESS
NESS
NESSES
NEST
NESTABLE
NESTED
NESTER
NESTERS
NESTFUL
NESTFULS
NESTING
NESTINGS
NESTLE
NESTLED
NESTLER
NESTLERS
NESTLES
NESTLIKE
NESTLING
NESTLINGS
NESTMATE
NESTMATES
NESTOR
NESTORS
NESTS
NET
NETBALL
NETBALLER
NETBALLS
NETBOOK
NETBOOKS
NETE
NETES
NETFUL
NETFULS
NETHEAD
NETHEADS
NETHELESS
NETHER
NETIZEN
NETIZENS
NETLESS
NETLIKE
NETMINDER
NETOP
NETOPS
NETROOT
NETROOTS
NETS
NETSPEAK
NETSPEAKS
NETSUKE
NETSUKES
NETSURF
NETSURFED
NETSURFER
NETSURFS

NETT
NETTABLE
NETTED
NETTER
NETTERS
NETTIE
NETTIER
NETTIES
NETTIEST
NETTING
NETTINGS
NETTLE
NETTLED
NETTLER
NETTLERS
NETTLES
NETTLIER
NETTLIEST
NETTLING
NETTLY
NETTS
NETTY
NETWORK
NETWORKED
NETWORKER
NETWORKS
NEUK
NEUKS
NEUM
NEUMATIC
NEUME
NEUMES
NEUMIC
NEUMS
NEURAL
NEURALGIA
NEURALGIC
NEURALLY
NEURATION
NEURAXON
NEURAXONS
NEURILITY
NEURINE
NEURINES
NEURISM
NEURISMS
NEURITE
NEURITES
NEURITIC
NEURITICS
NEURITIS
NEUROCHIP
NEUROCOEL
NEUROGLIA
NEUROGRAM
NEUROID
NEUROIDS
NEUROLOGY
NEUROMA
NEUROMAS
NEUROMAST
NEUROMATA
NEURON
NEURONAL
NEURONE
NEURONES
NEURONIC
NEURONS
NEUROPATH
NEUROPIL
NEUROPILS
NEUROSAL
NEUROSES
NEUROSIS
NEUROTIC
NEUROTICS
NEUROTOMY
NEURULA
NEURULAE
NEURULAR
NEURULAS
NEUSTIC
NEUSTICS
NEUSTON
NEUSTONIC
NEUSTONS
NEUTER
NEUTERED
NEUTERING
NEUTERS
NEUTRAL
NEUTRALLY
NEUTRALS
NEUTRETTO
NEUTRINO
NEUTRINOS
NEUTRON
NEUTRONIC
NEUTRONS
NEVE
NEVEL
NEVELLED
NEVELLING
NEVELS
NEVER
NEVERMIND
NEVERMORE
NEVES
NEVI
NEVOID
NEVUS
NEW
NEWB
NEWBIE
NEWBIES
NEWBORN
NEWBORNS
NEWBS
NEWCOME
NEWCOMER
NEWCOMERS
NEWED
NEWEL
NEWELL
NEWELLED
NEWELLS
NEWELS
NEWER
NEWEST
NEWFANGLE
NEWFOUND
NEWIE
NEWIES
NEWING
NEWISH
NEWISHLY
NEWLY
NEWLYWED
NEWLYWEDS
NEWMARKET
NEWMOWN
NEWNESS
NEWNESSES
NEWS
NEWSAGENT
NEWSBEAT
NEWSBEATS
NEWSBOY
NEWSBOYS
NEWSBREAK
NEWSCAST
NEWSCASTS
NEWSCLIP
NEWSCLIPS
NEWSDESK
NEWSDESKS
NEWSED
NEWSES
NEWSFEED
NEWSFEEDS
NEWSFLASH
NEWSGIRL
NEWSGIRLS
NEWSGROUP
NEWSHAWK
NEWSHAWKS
NEWSHOUND
NEWSIE
NEWSIER
NEWSIES
NEWSIEST
NEWSINESS
NEWSING
NEWSLESS
NEWSMAKER
NEWSMAN
NEWSMEN
NEWSPAPER
NEWSPEAK
NEWSPEAKS
NEWSPRINT
NEWSREEL
NEWSREELS
NEWSROOM
NEWSROOMS
NEWSSHEET
NEWSSTAND
NEWSTRADE
NEWSWIRE
NEWSWIRES
NEWSWOMAN
NEWSWOMEN
NEWSY
NEWT
NEWTON
NEWTONS
NEWTS
NEWWAVER
NEWWAVERS
NEXT
NEXTDOOR
NEXTLY
NEXTNESS
NEXTS
NEXUS
NEXUSES
NGAI
NGAIO
NGAIOS
NGANA
NGANAS
NGARARA
NGARARAS
NGATI
NGATIS
NGOMA
NGOMAS
NGULTRUM
NGULTRUMS
NGWEE
NGWEES
NHANDU
NHANDUS
NIACIN
NIACINS
NIAGARA
NIAGARAS
NIAISERIE
NIALAMIDE
NIB
NIBBED
NIBBING
NIBBLE
NIBBLED
NIBBLER
NIBBLERS
NIBBLES
NIBBLIES
NIBBLING
NIBBLINGS

NIBBLY
NIBLET
NIBLETS
NIBLICK
NIBLICKS
NIBLIKE
NIBS
NICAD
NICADS
NICCOLITE
NICE
NICEISH
NICELY
NICENESS
NICER
NICEST
NICETIES
NICETY
NICHE
NICHED
NICHER
NICHERED
NICHERING
NICHERS
NICHES
NICHING
NICHROME
NICHROMES
NICHT
NICHTS
NICISH
NICK
NICKAR
NICKARS
NICKED
NICKEL
NICKELED
NICKELIC
NICKELINE
NICKELING
NICKELISE
NICKELIZE
NICKELLED
NICKELOUS
NICKELS
NICKER
NICKERED
NICKERING
NICKERNUT
NICKERS
NICKING
NICKLE
NICKLED
NICKLES
NICKLING
NICKNACK
NICKNACKS
NICKNAME
NICKNAMED
NICKNAMER
NICKNAMES
NICKPOINT
NICKS
NICKSTICK
NICKUM
NICKUMS
NICOISE
NICOL
NICOLS
NICOMPOOP
NICOTIAN
NICOTIANA
NICOTIANS
NICOTIN
NICOTINE
NICOTINED
NICOTINES
NICOTINIC
NICOTINS
NICTATE
NICTATED
NICTATES
NICTATING
NICTATION
NICTITANT
NICTITATE
NID
NIDAL
NIDAMENTA
NIDATE
NIDATED
NIDATES
NIDATING
NIDATION
NIDATIONS
NIDDERING
NIDDICK
NIDDICKS
NIDE
NIDED
NIDERING
NIDERINGS
NIDERLING
NIDES
NIDGET
NIDGETED
NIDGETING
NIDGETS
NIDI
NIDIFIED
NIDIFIES
NIDIFY
NIDIFYING
NIDING
NIDINGS
NIDOR
NIDOROUS
NIDORS
NIDS
NIDUS
NIDUSES
NIE
NIECE
NIECES
NIED
NIEF
NIEFS
NIELLATED
NIELLI
NIELLIST
NIELLISTS
NIELLO
NIELLOED
NIELLOING
NIELLOS
NIENTE
NIES
NIEVE
NIEVEFUL
NIEVEFULS
NIEVES
NIFE
NIFES
NIFF
NIFFED
NIFFER
NIFFERED
NIFFERING
NIFFERS
NIFFIER
NIFFIEST
NIFFING
NIFFNAFF
NIFFNAFFS
NIFFS
NIFFY
NIFTIER
NIFTIES
NIFTIEST
NIFTILY
NIFTINESS
NIFTY
NIGELLA
NIGELLAS
NIGGARD
NIGGARDED
NIGGARDLY
NIGGARDS
NIGGLE
NIGGLED
NIGGLER
NIGGLERS
NIGGLES
NIGGLIER
NIGGLIEST
NIGGLING
NIGGLINGS
NIGGLY
NIGH
NIGHED
NIGHER
NIGHEST
NIGHING
NIGHLY
NIGHNESS
NIGHS
NIGHT
NIGHTBIRD
NIGHTCAP
NIGHTCAPS
NIGHTCLUB
NIGHTED
NIGHTFALL
NIGHTFIRE
NIGHTGEAR
NIGHTGLOW
NIGHTGOWN
NIGHTHAWK
NIGHTIE
NIGHTIES
NIGHTJAR
NIGHTJARS
NIGHTLESS
NIGHTLIFE
NIGHTLIKE
NIGHTLONG
NIGHTLY
NIGHTMARE
NIGHTMARY
NIGHTS
NIGHTSIDE
NIGHTSPOT
NIGHTTIDE
NIGHTTIME
NIGHTWARD
NIGHTWEAR
NIGHTY
NIGIRI
NIGIRIS
NIGRICANT
NIGRIFIED
NIGRIFIES
NIGRIFY
NIGRITUDE
NIGROSIN
NIGROSINE
NIGROSINS
NIHIL
NIHILISM
NIHILISMS
NIHILIST
NIHILISTS
NIHILITY
NIHILS
NIHONGA
NIHONGAS
NIHONIUM
NIHONIUMS
NIKAB
NIKABS

NIKAH
NIKAHS
NIKAU
NIKAUS
NIL
NILGAI
NILGAIS
NILGAU
NILGAUS
NILGHAI
NILGHAIS
NILGHAU
NILGHAUS
NILL
NILLED
NILLING
NILLS
NILPOTENT
NILS
NIM
NIMB
NIMBED
NIMBI
NIMBLE
NIMBLER
NIMBLESSE
NIMBLEST
NIMBLEWIT
NIMBLY
NIMBS
NIMBUS
NIMBUSED
NIMBUSES
NIMBYISM
NIMBYISMS
NIMBYNESS
NIMIETIES
NIMIETY
NIMIOUS
NIMMED
NIMMER
NIMMERS
NIMMING
NIMONIC
NIMPS
NIMROD
NIMRODS
NIMS
NINCOM
NINCOMS
NINCUM
NINCUMS
NINE
NINEBARK
NINEBARKS
NINEFOLD
NINEHOLES
NINEPENCE
NINEPENNY
NINEPIN
NINEPINS
NINER
NINERS
NINES
NINESCORE
NINETEEN
NINETEENS
NINETIES
NINETIETH
NINETY
NINHYDRIN
NINJA
NINJAS
NINJITSU
NINJITSUS
NINJUTSU
NINJUTSUS
NINNIES
NINNY
NINNYISH
NINON
NINONS
NINTH
NINTHLY
NINTHS
NIOBATE
NIOBATES
NIOBIC
NIOBITE
NIOBITES
NIOBIUM
NIOBIUMS
NIOBOUS
NIP
NIPA
NIPAS
NIPCHEESE
NIPPED
NIPPER
NIPPERED
NIPPERING
NIPPERKIN
NIPPERS
NIPPIER
NIPPIEST
NIPPILY
NIPPINESS
NIPPING
NIPPINGLY
NIPPLE
NIPPLED
NIPPLES
NIPPLING
NIPPY
NIPS
NIPTER
NIPTERS
NIQAAB
NIQAABS
NIQAB
NIQABS
NIRAMIAI
NIRAMIAIS
NIRL
NIRLED
NIRLIE
NIRLIER
NIRLIEST
NIRLING
NIRLIT
NIRLS
NIRLY
NIRVANA
NIRVANAS
NIRVANIC
NIS
NISBERRY
NISEI
NISEIS
NISGUL
NISGULS
NISH
NISHES
NISI
NISSE
NISSES
NISUS
NIT
NITE
NITER
NITERIE
NITERIES
NITERS
NITERY
NITES
NITHER
NITHERED
NITHERING
NITHERS
NITHING
NITHINGS
NITID
NITINOL
NITINOLS
NITON
NITONS
NITPICK
NITPICKED
NITPICKER
NITPICKS
NITPICKY
NITRAMINE
NITRATE
NITRATED
NITRATES
NITRATINE
NITRATING
NITRATION
NITRATOR
NITRATORS
NITRE
NITREOUS
NITRES
NITRIC
NITRID
NITRIDE
NITRIDED
NITRIDES
NITRIDING
NITRIDS
NITRIFIED
NITRIFIER
NITRIFIES
NITRIFY
NITRIL
NITRILE
NITRILES
NITRILS
NITRITE
NITRITES
NITRO
NITROGEN
NITROGENS
NITROLIC
NITROS
NITROSO
NITROSYL
NITROSYLS
NITROUS
NITROX
NITROXES
NITROXYL
NITROXYLS
NITRY
NITRYL
NITRYLS
NITS
NITTIER
NITTIEST
NITTY
NITWIT
NITWITS
NITWITTED
NIVAL
NIVATION
NIVATIONS
NIVEOUS
NIX
NIXE
NIXED
NIXER
NIXERS
NIXES
NIXIE
NIXIES
NIXING
NIXY
NIZAM
NIZAMATE
NIZAMATES

N

NIZAMS
NKOSI
NKOSIS
NO
NOAH
NOAHS
NOB
NOBBIER
NOBBIEST
NOBBILY
NOBBINESS
NOBBLE
NOBBLED
NOBBLER
NOBBLERS
NOBBLES
NOBBLING
NOBBUT
NOBBY
NOBELIUM
NOBELIUMS
NOBILESSE
NOBILIARY
NOBILITY
NOBLE
NOBLEMAN
NOBLEMEN
NOBLENESS
NOBLER
NOBLES
NOBLESSE
NOBLESSES
NOBLEST
NOBLY
NOBODIES
NOBODY
NOBS
NOCAKE
NOCAKES
NOCEBO
NOCEBOS
NOCENT
NOCENTLY
NOCENTS
NOCHEL
NOCHELED
NOCHELING
NOCHELLED
NOCHELS
NOCK
NOCKED
NOCKET
NOCKETS
NOCKING
NOCKS
NOCTILIO
NOCTILIOS
NOCTILUCA
NOCTUA
NOCTUARY
NOCTUAS
NOCTUID
NOCTUIDS
NOCTULE
NOCTULES
NOCTUOID
NOCTUOIDS
NOCTURIA
NOCTURIAS
NOCTURN
NOCTURNAL
NOCTURNE
NOCTURNES
NOCTURNS
NOCUOUS
NOCUOUSLY
NOD
NODAL
NODALISE
NODALISED
NODALISES
NODALITY
NODALIZE
NODALIZED
NODALIZES
NODALLY
NODATED
NODATION
NODATIONS
NODDED
NODDER
NODDERS
NODDIER
NODDIES
NODDIEST
NODDING
NODDINGLY
NODDINGS
NODDLE
NODDLED
NODDLES
NODDLING
NODDY
NODE
NODES
NODI
NODICAL
NODOSE
NODOSITY
NODOUS
NODS
NODULAR
NODULATED
NODULE
NODULED
NODULES
NODULOSE
NODULOUS
NODUS
NOEL
NOELS
NOES
NOESES
NOESIS
NOESISES
NOETIC
NOG
NOGAKU
NOGG
NOGGED
NOGGIN
NOGGING
NOGGINGS
NOGGINS
NOGGS
NOGOODNIK
NOGS
NOH
NOHOW
NOHOWISH
NOIL
NOILIER
NOILIES
NOILIEST
NOILS
NOILY
NOINT
NOINTED
NOINTER
NOINTERS
NOINTING
NOINTS
NOIR
NOIRISH
NOIRS
NOISE
NOISED
NOISEFUL
NOISELESS
NOISENIK
NOISENIKS
NOISES
NOISETTE
NOISETTES
NOISIER
NOISIEST
NOISILY
NOISINESS
NOISING
NOISOME
NOISOMELY
NOISY
NOLE
NOLES
NOLITION
NOLITIONS
NOLL
NOLLS
NOLO
NOLOS
NOM
NOMA
NOMAD
NOMADE
NOMADES
NOMADIC
NOMADIES
NOMADISE
NOMADISED
NOMADISES
NOMADISM
NOMADISMS
NOMADIZE
NOMADIZED
NOMADIZES
NOMADS
NOMADY
NOMARCH
NOMARCHS
NOMARCHY
NOMAS
NOMBLES
NOMBRIL
NOMBRILS
NOME
NOMEN
NOMENS
NOMES
NOMIC
NOMINA
NOMINABLE
NOMINAL
NOMINALLY
NOMINALS
NOMINATE
NOMINATED
NOMINATES
NOMINATOR
NOMINEE
NOMINEES
NOMISM
NOMISMS
NOMISTIC
NOMOCRACY
NOMOGENY
NOMOGRAM
NOMOGRAMS
NOMOGRAPH
NOMOI
NOMOLOGIC
NOMOLOGY
NOMOS
NOMOTHETE
NOMS
NON
NONA
NONACID
NONACIDIC
NONACIDS
NONACTING

NONACTION
NONACTIVE
NONACTOR
NONACTORS
NONADDICT
NONADULT
NONADULTS
NONAGE
NONAGED
NONAGES
NONAGON
NONAGONAL
NONAGONS
NONANE
NONANES
NONANIMAL
NONANOIC
NONANSWER
NONARABLE
NONARIES
NONART
NONARTIST
NONARTS
NONARY
NONAS
NONATOMIC
NONAUTHOR
NONAVIAN
NONBANK
NONBANKS
NONBASIC
NONBEING
NONBEINGS
NONBELIEF
NONBINARY
NONBITING
NONBLACK
NONBLACKS
NONBODIES
NONBODY
NONBONDED
NONBOOK
NONBOOKS
NONBRAND
NONBUYING
NONCAKING
NONCAMPUS
NONCAREER
NONCASH
NONCASUAL
NONCAUSAL
NONCE
NONCEREAL
NONCES
NONCHURCH
NONCLASS
NONCLING
NONCODING
NONCOITAL
NONCOKING
NONCOLA
NONCOLAS
NONCOLOR
NONCOLORS
NONCOLOUR
NONCOM
NONCOMBAT
NONCOMS
NONCONCUR
NONCORE
NONCOUNT
NONCOUNTY
NONCREDIT
NONCRIME
NONCRIMES
NONCRISES
NONCRISIS
NONCYCLIC
NONDAIRY
NONDANCE
NONDANCER
NONDANCES
NONDEALER
NONDEGREE
NONDEMAND
NONDESERT
NONDOCTOR
NONDOLLAR
NONDRIP
NONDRIVER
NONDRUG
NONDRYING
NONE
NONEDIBLE
NONEGO
NONEGOS
NONELECT
NONELECTS
NONELITE
NONEMPTY
NONENDING
NONENERGY
NONENTITY
NONENTRY
NONEQUAL
NONEQUALS
NONEROTIC
NONES
NONESUCH
NONET
NONETHNIC
NONETS
NONETTE
NONETTES
NONETTI
NONETTO
NONETTOS
NONEVENT
NONEVENTS
NONEXEMPT
NONEXOTIC
NONEXPERT
NONEXTANT
NONFACT
NONFACTOR
NONFACTS
NONFADING
NONFAMILY
NONFAN
NONFANS
NONFARM
NONFARMER
NONFAT
NONFATAL
NONFATTY
NONFEUDAL
NONFILIAL
NONFINAL
NONFINITE
NONFISCAL
NONFLUID
NONFLUIDS
NONFLYING
NONFOCAL
NONFOOD
NONFOODS
NONFORMAL
NONFOSSIL
NONFROZEN
NONFUEL
NONFUELS
NONFUNDED
NONG
NONGAME
NONGAY
NONGAYS
NONGHETTO
NONGLARE
NONGLARES
NONGLAZED
NONGLOSSY
NONGOLFER
NONGRADED
NONGREASY
NONGREEN
NONGROWTH
NONGS
NONGUEST
NONGUESTS
NONGUILT
NONGUILTS
NONHARDY
NONHEME
NONHERO
NONHEROES
NONHEROIC
NONHOME
NONHUMAN
NONHUMANS
NONHUNTER
NONI
NONIDEAL
NONILLION
NONIMAGE
NONIMAGES
NONIMMUNE
NONIMPACT
NONINERT
NONINJURY
NONINSECT
NONIONIC
NONIRON
NONIS
NONISSUE
NONISSUES
NONJOINER
NONJURIES
NONJURING
NONJUROR
NONJURORS
NONJURY
NONKIN
NONKINS
NONKOSHER
NONLABOR
NONLABOUR
NONLAWYER
NONLEADED
NONLEAFY
NONLEAGUE
NONLEGAL
NONLEGUME
NONLETHAL
NONLEVEL
NONLIABLE
NONLIFE
NONLINEAL
NONLINEAR
NONLIQUID
NONLIVES
NONLIVING
NONLOCAL
NONLOCALS
NONLOVING
NONLOYAL
NONLYRIC
NONMAJOR
NONMAJORS
NONMAN
NONMANUAL
NONMARKET
NONMATURE
NONMEAT
NONMEATS
NONMEMBER
NONMEN
NONMENTAL
NONMETAL
NONMETALS
NONMETRIC

N

NONMETRO
NONMOBILE
NONMODAL
NONMODERN
NONMONEY
NONMORAL
NONMORTAL
NONMOTILE
NONMOVING
NONMUSIC
NONMUSICS
NONMUTANT
NONMUTUAL
NONNASAL
NONNATIVE
NONNAVAL
NONNEURAL
NONNEWS
NONNIES
NONNOBLE
NONNORMAL
NONNOVEL
NONNOVELS
NONNY
NONOBESE
NONOHMIC
NONOILY
NONORAL
NONORALLY
NONOWNER
NONOWNERS
NONPAGAN
NONPAGANS
NONPAID
NONPAPAL
NONPAR
NONPAREIL
NONPARENT
NONPARITY
NONPAROUS
NONPARTY
NONPAST
NONPASTS
NONPAYING
NONPEAK
NONPEAKS
NONPERSON
NONPLANAR
NONPLAY
NONPLAYER
NONPLAYS
NONPLIANT
NONPLUS
NONPLUSED
NONPLUSES
NONPOETIC
NONPOINT
NONPOLAR
NONPOLICE
NONPOOR
NONPOORS
NONPOROUS
NONPOSTAL
NONPRINT
NONPROFIT
NONPROS
NONPROVEN
NONPUBLIC
NONQUOTA
NONRACIAL
NONRACISM
NONRANDOM
NONRATED
NONREADER
NONRETURN
NONRHOTIC
NONRIGID
NONRIOTER
NONRIVAL
NONRIVALS
NONROYAL
NONROYALS
NONRUBBER
NONRULING
NONRUN
NONRUNNER
NONRURAL
NONSACRED
NONSALINE
NONSCHOOL
NONSECRET
NONSECURE
NONSELF
NONSELVES
NONSENSE
NONSENSES
NONSERIAL
NONSEXIST
NONSEXUAL
NONSHRINK
NONSIGNER
NONSKATER
NONSKED
NONSKEDS
NONSKID
NONSKIER
NONSKIERS
NONSLIP
NONSMOKER
NONSOCIAL
NONSOLAR
NONSOLID
NONSOLIDS
NONSPEECH
NONSTAPLE
NONSTATE
NONSTATIC
NONSTEADY
NONSTICK
NONSTICKY
NONSTOP
NONSTOPS
NONSTORY
NONSTYLE
NONSTYLES
NONSUCH
NONSUCHES
NONSUGAR
NONSUGARS
NONSUIT
NONSUITED
NONSUITS
NONSYSTEM
NONTALKER
NONTARGET
NONTARIFF
NONTAX
NONTAXES
NONTHEISM
NONTHEIST
NONTIDAL
NONTITLE
NONTONAL
NONTONIC
NONTOXIC
NONTOXICS
NONTRAGIC
NONTRIBAL
NONTRUMP
NONTRUTH
NONTRUTHS
NONUNION
NONUNIONS
NONUNIQUE
NONUPLE
NONUPLES
NONUPLET
NONUPLETS
NONURBAN
NONURGENT
NONUSABLE
NONUSE
NONUSER
NONUSERS
NONUSES
NONUSING
NONVACANT
NONVALID
NONVECTOR
NONVENOUS
NONVERBAL
NONVESTED
NONVIABLE
NONVIEWER
NONVIRAL
NONVIRGIN
NONVIRILE
NONVISUAL
NONVITAL
NONVOCAL
NONVOCALS
NONVOTER
NONVOTERS
NONVOTING
NONWAGE
NONWAR
NONWARS
NONWHITE
NONWHITES
NONWINGED
NONWOODY
NONWOOL
NONWORD
NONWORDS
NONWORK
NONWORKER
NONWORKS
NONWOVEN
NONWOVENS
NONWRITER
NONYL
NONYLS
NONZERO
NOO
NOOB
NOOBS
NOODGE
NOODGED
NOODGES
NOODGING
NOODLE
NOODLED
NOODLEDOM
NOODLES
NOODLING
NOODLINGS
NOOGIE
NOOGIES
NOOIT
NOOK
NOOKIE
NOOKIER
NOOKIES
NOOKIEST
NOOKLIKE
NOOKS
NOOKY
NOOLOGIES
NOOLOGY
NOOMETRY
NOON
NOONDAY
NOONDAYS
NOONED
NOONER
NOONERS
NOONING
NOONINGS
NOONS
NOONTIDE

N

NOONTIDES
NOONTIME
NOONTIMES
NOOP
NOOPS
NOOSE
NOOSED
NOOSELIKE
NOOSER
NOOSERS
NOOSES
NOOSING
NOOSPHERE
NOOTROPIC
NOPAL
NOPALES
NOPALITO
NOPALITOS
NOPALS
NOPE
NOPLACE
NOR
NORDIC
NORDICITY
NORI
NORIA
NORIAS
NORIMON
NORIMONS
NORIS
NORITE
NORITES
NORITIC
NORK
NORKS
NORLAND
NORLANDS
NORM
NORMA
NORMAL
NORMALCY
NORMALISE
NORMALITY
NORMALIZE
NORMALLY
NORMALS
NORMAN
NORMANDE
NORMANDES
NORMANS
NORMAS
NORMATIVE
NORMCORE
NORMCORES
NORMED
NORMLESS
NORMS
NOROVIRUS
NORSEL
NORSELLED
NORSELLER
NORSELS
NORTENA
NORTENAS
NORTENO
NORTENOS
NORTH
NORTHEAST
NORTHED
NORTHER
NORTHERED
NORTHERLY
NORTHERN
NORTHERNS
NORTHERS
NORTHING
NORTHINGS
NORTHLAND
NORTHMOST
NORTHS
NORTHWARD
NORTHWEST
NORWARD
NORWARDS
NOS
NOSE
NOSEAN
NOSEANS
NOSEBAG
NOSEBAGS
NOSEBAND
NOSEBANDS
NOSEBLEED
NOSED
NOSEDIVE
NOSEDIVED
NOSEDIVES
NOSEDOVE
NOSEGAY
NOSEGAYS
NOSEGUARD
NOSELESS
NOSELIKE
NOSELITE
NOSELITES
NOSEPIECE
NOSER
NOSERS
NOSES
NOSEWHEEL
NOSEY
NOSEYS
NOSH
NOSHED
NOSHER
NOSHERIE
NOSHERIES
NOSHERS
NOSHERY
NOSHES
NOSHING
NOSIER
NOSIES
NOSIEST
NOSILY
NOSINESS
NOSING
NOSINGS
NOSODE
NOSODES
NOSOLOGIC
NOSOLOGY
NOSTALGIA
NOSTALGIC
NOSTOC
NOSTOCS
NOSTOI
NOSTOLOGY
NOSTOS
NOSTRIL
NOSTRILS
NOSTRO
NOSTRUM
NOSTRUMS
NOSY
NOT
NOTA
NOTABILIA
NOTABLE
NOTABLES
NOTABLY
NOTAEUM
NOTAEUMS
NOTAIRE
NOTAIRES
NOTAL
NOTANDA
NOTANDUM
NOTAPHILY
NOTARIAL
NOTARIES
NOTARISE
NOTARISED
NOTARISES
NOTARIZE
NOTARIZED
NOTARIZES
NOTARY
NOTATE
NOTATED
NOTATES
NOTATING
NOTATION
NOTATIONS
NOTATOR
NOTATORS
NOTCH
NOTCHBACK
NOTCHED
NOTCHEL
NOTCHELED
NOTCHELS
NOTCHER
NOTCHERS
NOTCHES
NOTCHIER
NOTCHIEST
NOTCHING
NOTCHINGS
NOTCHY
NOTE
NOTEBANDI
NOTEBOOK
NOTEBOOKS
NOTECARD
NOTECARDS
NOTECASE
NOTECASES
NOTED
NOTEDLY
NOTEDNESS
NOTELESS
NOTELET
NOTELETS
NOTEPAD
NOTEPADS
NOTEPAPER
NOTER
NOTERS
NOTES
NOTHER
NOTHING
NOTHINGS
NOTICE
NOTICED
NOTICER
NOTICERS
NOTICES
NOTICING
NOTIFIED
NOTIFIER
NOTIFIERS
NOTIFIES
NOTIFY
NOTIFYING
NOTING
NOTION
NOTIONAL
NOTIONIST
NOTIONS
NOTITIA
NOTITIAE
NOTITIAS
NOTOCHORD
NOTORIETY
NOTORIOUS
NOTORNIS
NOTOUR
NOTT
NOTTURNI

NOTTURNO
NOTUM
NOUGAT
NOUGATINE
NOUGATS
NOUGHT
NOUGHTIES
NOUGHTS
NOUL
NOULD
NOULDE
NOULE
NOULES
NOULS
NOUMENA
NOUMENAL
NOUMENON
NOUN
NOUNAL
NOUNALLY
NOUNIER
NOUNIEST
NOUNLESS
NOUNS
NOUNY
NOUP
NOUPS
NOURICE
NOURICES
NOURISH
NOURISHED
NOURISHER
NOURISHES
NOURITURE
NOURSLE
NOURSLED
NOURSLES
NOURSLING
NOUS
NOUSELL
NOUSELLED
NOUSELLS
NOUSES
NOUSLE
NOUSLED
NOUSLES
NOUSLING
NOUT
NOUVEAU
NOUVEAUX
NOUVELLE
NOUVELLES
NOVA
NOVAE
NOVALIA
NOVALIKE
NOVAS
NOVATE
NOVATED
NOVATES
NOVATING
NOVATION
NOVATIONS
NOVEL
NOVELDOM
NOVELDOMS
NOVELESE
NOVELESES
NOVELETTE
NOVELISE
NOVELISED
NOVELISER
NOVELISES
NOVELISH
NOVELISM
NOVELISMS
NOVELIST
NOVELISTS
NOVELIZE
NOVELIZED
NOVELIZER
NOVELIZES
NOVELLA
NOVELLAE
NOVELLAS
NOVELLE
NOVELLY
NOVELS
NOVELTIES
NOVELTY
NOVEMBER
NOVEMBERS
NOVENA
NOVENAE
NOVENARY
NOVENAS
NOVENNIAL
NOVERCAL
NOVERINT
NOVERINTS
NOVICE
NOVICES
NOVICHOK
NOVICHOKS
NOVICIATE
NOVITIATE
NOVITIES
NOVITY
NOVOCAINE
NOVODAMUS
NOVUM
NOVUMS
NOW
NOWADAYS
NOWAY
NOWAYS
NOWCAST
NOWCASTS
NOWED
NOWHENCE
NOWHERE
NOWHERES
NOWHITHER
NOWISE
NOWL
NOWLS
NOWN
NOWNESS
NOWNESSES
NOWS
NOWT
NOWTIER
NOWTIEST
NOWTS
NOWTY
NOWY
NOX
NOXAL
NOXES
NOXIOUS
NOXIOUSLY
NOY
NOYADE
NOYADES
NOYANCE
NOYANCES
NOYAU
NOYAUS
NOYAUX
NOYED
NOYES
NOYESES
NOYING
NOYOUS
NOYS
NOYSOME
NOZZER
NOZZERS
NOZZLE
NOZZLES
NTH
NU
NUANCE
NUANCED
NUANCES
NUANCING
NUB
NUBBED
NUBBER
NUBBERS
NUBBIER
NUBBIEST
NUBBIN
NUBBINESS
NUBBING
NUBBINGS
NUBBINS
NUBBLE
NUBBLED
NUBBLES
NUBBLIER
NUBBLIEST
NUBBLING
NUBBLY
NUBBY
NUBECULA
NUBECULAE
NUBIA
NUBIAS
NUBIFORM
NUBILE
NUBILITY
NUBILOSE
NUBILOUS
NUBS
NUBUCK
NUBUCKS
NUCELLAR
NUCELLI
NUCELLUS
NUCHA
NUCHAE
NUCHAL
NUCHALS
NUCLEAL
NUCLEAR
NUCLEASE
NUCLEASES
NUCLEATE
NUCLEATED
NUCLEATES
NUCLEATOR
NUCLEI
NUCLEIC
NUCLEIDE
NUCLEIDES
NUCLEIN
NUCLEINIC
NUCLEINS
NUCLEOID
NUCLEOIDS
NUCLEOLAR
NUCLEOLE
NUCLEOLES
NUCLEOLI
NUCLEOLUS
NUCLEON
NUCLEONIC
NUCLEONS
NUCLEUS
NUCLEUSES
NUCLIDE
NUCLIDES
NUCLIDIC
NUCULE
NUCULES
NUDATION
NUDATIONS
NUDDIES
NUDDY

NUDE
NUDELY
NUDENESS
NUDER
NUDES
NUDEST
NUDGE
NUDGED
NUDGER
NUDGERS
NUDGES
NUDGING
NUDICAUL
NUDIE
NUDIES
NUDISM
NUDISMS
NUDIST
NUDISTS
NUDITIES
NUDITY
NUDNICK
NUDNICKS
NUDNIK
NUDNIKS
NUDZH
NUDZHED
NUDZHES
NUDZHING
NUFF
NUFFIN
NUFFINS
NUFFS
NUG
NUGAE
NUGATORY
NUGGAR
NUGGARS
NUGGET
NUGGETED
NUGGETIER
NUGGETING
NUGGETS
NUGGETTED
NUGGETY
NUGS
NUISANCE
NUISANCER
NUISANCES
NUKE
NUKED
NUKES
NUKING
NULL
NULLA
NULLAH
NULLAHS
NULLAS
NULLED
NULLIFIED
NULLIFIER
NULLIFIES
NULLIFY
NULLING
NULLINGS
NULLIPARA
NULLIPORE
NULLITIES
NULLITY
NULLNESS
NULLS
NUMB
NUMBAT
NUMBATS
NUMBED
NUMBER
NUMBERED
NUMBERER
NUMBERERS
NUMBERING
NUMBERS
NUMBEST
NUMBFISH
NUMBHEAD
NUMBHEADS
NUMBING
NUMBINGLY
NUMBLES
NUMBLY
NUMBNESS
NUMBNUT
NUMBNUTS
NUMBS
NUMBSKULL
NUMCHUCK
NUMCHUCKS
NUMDAH
NUMDAHS
NUMEN
NUMERABLE
NUMERABLY
NUMERACY
NUMERAIRE
NUMERAL
NUMERALLY
NUMERALS
NUMERARY
NUMERATE
NUMERATED
NUMERATES
NUMERATOR
NUMERIC
NUMERICAL
NUMERICS
NUMEROUS
NUMINA
NUMINOUS
NUMMARY
NUMMIER
NUMMIEST
NUMMULAR
NUMMULARY
NUMMULINE
NUMMULITE
NUMMY
NUMNAH
NUMNAHS
NUMPKIN
NUMPKINS
NUMPTIES
NUMPTY
NUMSKULL
NUMSKULLS
NUN
NUNATAK
NUNATAKER
NUNATAKS
NUNCHAKU
NUNCHAKUS
NUNCHEON
NUNCHEONS
NUNCHUCK
NUNCHUCKS
NUNCHUK
NUNCHUKS
NUNCIO
NUNCIOS
NUNCLE
NUNCLES
NUNCUPATE
NUNDINAL
NUNDINALS
NUNDINE
NUNDINES
NUNHOOD
NUNHOODS
NUNLIKE
NUNNATION
NUNNERIES
NUNNERY
NUNNISH
NUNNY
NUNS
NUNSHIP
NUNSHIPS
NUPTIAL
NUPTIALLY
NUPTIALS
NUR
NURAGHE
NURAGHI
NURAGHIC
NURD
NURDIER
NURDIEST
NURDISH
NURDLE
NURDLED
NURDLES
NURDLING
NURDS
NURDY
NURHAG
NURHAGS
NURL
NURLED
NURLING
NURLS
NURR
NURRS
NURS
NURSE
NURSED
NURSELIKE
NURSELING
NURSEMAID
NURSER
NURSERIES
NURSERS
NURSERY
NURSES
NURSING
NURSINGS
NURSLE
NURSLED
NURSLES
NURSLING
NURSLINGS
NURTURAL
NURTURANT
NURTURE
NURTURED
NURTURER
NURTURERS
NURTURES
NURTURING
NUS
NUT
NUTANT
NUTARIAN
NUTARIANS
NUTATE
NUTATED
NUTATES
NUTATING
NUTATION
NUTATIONS
NUTBAR
NUTBARS
NUTBROWN
NUTBUTTER
NUTCASE
NUTCASES
NUTGALL
NUTGALLS
NUTGRASS
NUTHATCH
NUTHIN
NUTHOUSE
NUTHOUSES

NUTJOB
NUTJOBBER
NUTJOBS
NUTLET
NUTLETS
NUTLIKE
NUTLOAF
NUTLOAVES
NUTMEAL
NUTMEALS
NUTMEAT
NUTMEATS
NUTMEG
NUTMEGGED
NUTMEGGY
NUTMEGS
NUTPECKER
NUTPICK
NUTPICKS
NUTRIA
NUTRIAS
NUTRIENT
NUTRIENTS
NUTRIMENT
NUTRITION
NUTRITIVE
NUTS
NUTSEDGE
NUTSEDGES
NUTSHELL
NUTSHELLS
NUTSIER
NUTSIEST
NUTSO
NUTSOS
NUTSY
NUTTED
NUTTER
NUTTERIES
NUTTERS
NUTTERY
NUTTIER
NUTTIEST
NUTTILY
NUTTINESS
NUTTING
NUTTINGS
NUTTY
NUTWOOD
NUTWOODS
NUZZER
NUZZERS
NUZZLE
NUZZLED
NUZZLER
NUZZLERS
NUZZLES
NUZZLING
NY
NYAFF
NYAFFED
NYAFFING
NYAFFS
NYAH
NYALA
NYALAS
NYANZA
NYANZAS
NYAOPE
NYAOPES
NYAS
NYASES
NYBBLE
NYBBLES
NYCTALOPE
NYCTALOPS
NYE
NYED
NYES
NYING
NYLGHAI
NYLGHAIS
NYLGHAU
NYLGHAUS
NYLON
NYLONED
NYLONS
NYM
NYMPH
NYMPHA
NYMPHAE
NYMPHAEA
NYMPHAEAS
NYMPHAEUM
NYMPHAL
NYMPHALID
NYMPHEAN
NYMPHED
NYMPHET
NYMPHETIC
NYMPHETS
NYMPHETTE
NYMPHIC
NYMPHICAL
NYMPHING
NYMPHISH
NYMPHLIER
NYMPHLIKE
NYMPHLY
NYMPHO
NYMPHOS
NYMPHS
NYS
NYSSA
NYSSAS
NYSTAGMIC
NYSTAGMUS
NYSTATIN
NYSTATINS

N

O

OAF
OAFISH
OAFISHLY
OAFS
OAK
OAKED
OAKEN
OAKENSHAW
OAKER
OAKERS
OAKIER
OAKIES
OAKIEST
OAKINESS
OAKLEAF
OAKLEAVES
OAKLIKE
OAKLING
OAKLINGS
OAKMOSS
OAKMOSSES
OAKS
OAKUM
OAKUMS
OAKWOOD
OAKWOODS
OAKY
OANSHAGH
OANSHAGHS
OAR
OARAGE
OARAGES
OARED
OARFISH
OARFISHES
OARIER
OARIEST
OARING
OARLESS
OARLIKE
OARLOCK
OARLOCKS
OARS
OARSMAN
OARSMEN
OARSWOMAN
OARSWOMEN
OARWEED
OARWEEDS
OARY
OASES
OASIS
OAST
OASTHOUSE
OASTS
OAT
OATCAKE
OATCAKES
OATEN
OATER
OATERS
OATH
OATHABLE
OATHS
OATIER
OATIEST
OATLIKE
OATMEAL
OATMEALS
OATS
OATY
OAVES
OB
OBA
OBANG
OBANGS
OBAS
OBBLIGATI
OBBLIGATO
OBCONIC
OBCONICAL
OBCORDATE
OBDURACY
OBDURATE
OBDURATED
OBDURATES
OBDURE
OBDURED
OBDURES
OBDURING
OBE
OBEAH
OBEAHED
OBEAHING
OBEAHISM
OBEAHISMS
OBEAHS
OBECHE
OBECHES
OBEDIENCE
OBEDIENT
OBEISANCE
OBEISANT
OBEISM
OBEISMS
OBELI
OBELIA
OBELIAS
OBELION
OBELISCAL
OBELISE
OBELISED
OBELISES
OBELISING
OBELISK
OBELISKS
OBELISM
OBELISMS
OBELIZE
OBELIZED
OBELIZES
OBELIZING
OBELUS
OBENTO
OBENTOS
OBES
OBESE
OBESELY
OBESENESS
OBESER
OBESEST
OBESITIES
OBESITY
OBESOGEN
OBESOGENS
OBEY
OBEYABLE
OBEYED
OBEYER
OBEYERS
OBEYING
OBEYS
OBFUSCATE
OBI
OBIA
OBIAS
OBIED
OBIING
OBIISM
OBIISMS
OBIIT
OBIS
OBIT
OBITAL
OBITER
OBITS
OBITUAL
OBITUARY
OBJECT
OBJECTED
OBJECTIFY
OBJECTING
OBJECTION
OBJECTIVE
OBJECTOR
OBJECTORS
OBJECTS
OBJET
OBJETS
OBJURE
OBJURED
OBJURES
OBJURGATE
OBJURING
OBLAST
OBLASTI
OBLASTS
OBLATE
OBLATELY
OBLATES
OBLATION
OBLATIONS
OBLATORY
OBLIGABLE
OBLIGANT
OBLIGANTS
OBLIGATE
OBLIGATED
OBLIGATES
OBLIGATI
OBLIGATO
OBLIGATOR
OBLIGATOS
OBLIGE
OBLIGED
OBLIGEE
OBLIGEES
OBLIGER
OBLIGERS
OBLIGES
OBLIGING
OBLIGOR
OBLIGORS
OBLIQUE
OBLIQUED
OBLIQUELY
OBLIQUER
OBLIQUES
OBLIQUEST
OBLIQUID

OBLIQUING
OBLIQUITY
OBLIVION
OBLIVIONS
OBLIVIOUS
OBLONG
OBLONGLY
OBLONGS
OBLOQUIAL
OBLOQUIES
OBLOQUY
OBNOXIOUS
OBO
OBOE
OBOES
OBOIST
OBOISTS
OBOL
OBOLARY
OBOLE
OBOLES
OBOLI
OBOLS
OBOLUS
OBOS
OBOVATE
OBOVATELY
OBOVOID
OBREPTION
OBS
OBSCENE
OBSCENELY
OBSCENER
OBSCENEST
OBSCENITY
OBSCURANT
OBSCURE
OBSCURED
OBSCURELY
OBSCURER
OBSCURERS
OBSCURES
OBSCUREST
OBSCURING
OBSCURITY
OBSECRATE
OBSEQUENT
OBSEQUIAL
OBSEQUIE
OBSEQUIES
OBSEQUY
OBSERVANT
OBSERVE
OBSERVED
OBSERVER
OBSERVERS
OBSERVES
OBSERVING
OBSESS
OBSESSED
OBSESSES
OBSESSING
OBSESSION
OBSESSIVE
OBSESSOR
OBSESSORS
OBSIDIAN
OBSIDIANS
OBSIGN
OBSIGNATE
OBSIGNED
OBSIGNING
OBSIGNS
OBSOLESCE
OBSOLETE
OBSOLETED
OBSOLETES
OBSTACLE
OBSTACLES
OBSTETRIC
OBSTINACY
OBSTINATE
OBSTRUCT
OBSTRUCTS
OBSTRUENT
OBTAIN
OBTAINED
OBTAINER
OBTAINERS
OBTAINING
OBTAINS
OBTECT
OBTECTED
OBTEMPER
OBTEMPERS
OBTEND
OBTENDED
OBTENDING
OBTENDS
OBTENTION
OBTEST
OBTESTED
OBTESTING
OBTESTS
OBTRUDE
OBTRUDED
OBTRUDER
OBTRUDERS
OBTRUDES
OBTRUDING
OBTRUSION
OBTRUSIVE
OBTUND
OBTUNDED
OBTUNDENT
OBTUNDING
OBTUNDITY
OBTUNDS
OBTURATE
OBTURATED
OBTURATES
OBTURATOR
OBTUSE
OBTUSELY
OBTUSER
OBTUSEST
OBTUSITY
OBUMBRATE
OBVENTION
OBVERSE
OBVERSELY
OBVERSES
OBVERSION
OBVERT
OBVERTED
OBVERTING
OBVERTS
OBVIABLE
OBVIATE
OBVIATED
OBVIATES
OBVIATING
OBVIATION
OBVIATOR
OBVIATORS
OBVIOUS
OBVIOUSLY
OBVOLUTE
OBVOLUTED
OBVOLVENT
OBVS
OCA
OCARINA
OCARINAS
OCAS
OCCAM
OCCAMIES
OCCAMS
OCCAMY
OCCASION
OCCASIONS
OCCIDENT
OCCIDENTS
OCCIES
OCCIPITA
OCCIPITAL
OCCIPUT
OCCIPUTS
OCCLUDE
OCCLUDED
OCCLUDENT
OCCLUDER
OCCLUDERS
OCCLUDES
OCCLUDING
OCCLUSAL
OCCLUSION
OCCLUSIVE
OCCLUSOR
OCCLUSORS
OCCULT
OCCULTED
OCCULTER
OCCULTERS
OCCULTING
OCCULTISM
OCCULTIST
OCCULTLY
OCCULTS
OCCUPANCE
OCCUPANCY
OCCUPANT
OCCUPANTS
OCCUPATE
OCCUPATED
OCCUPATES
OCCUPIED
OCCUPIER
OCCUPIERS
OCCUPIES
OCCUPY
OCCUPYING
OCCUR
OCCURRED
OCCURRENT
OCCURRING
OCCURS
OCCY
OCEAN
OCEANARIA
OCEANAUT
OCEANAUTS
OCEANIC
OCEANID
OCEANIDES
OCEANIDS
OCEANS
OCEANSIDE
OCEANVIEW
OCEANWARD
OCELLAR
OCELLATE
OCELLATED
OCELLI
OCELLUS
OCELOID
OCELOT
OCELOTS
OCH
OCHE
OCHER
OCHERED
OCHERIER
OCHERIEST
OCHERING
OCHERISH
OCHEROID
OCHEROUS
OCHERS
OCHERY

O

OCHES
OCHIDORE
OCHIDORES
OCHLOCRAT
OCHONE
OCHRE
OCHREA
OCHREAE
OCHREAS
OCHREATE
OCHRED
OCHREOUS
OCHRES
OCHREY
OCHRIER
OCHRIEST
OCHRING
OCHROID
OCHROUS
OCHRY
OCICAT
OCICATS
OCKER
OCKERISM
OCKERISMS
OCKERS
OCKODOLS
OCOTILLO
OCOTILLOS
OCREA
OCREAE
OCREAS
OCREATE
OCTA
OCTACHORD
OCTAD
OCTADIC
OCTADS
OCTAGON
OCTAGONAL
OCTAGONS
OCTAHEDRA
OCTAL
OCTALS
OCTAMETER
OCTAN
OCTANE
OCTANES
OCTANGLE
OCTANGLES
OCTANOL
OCTANOLS
OCTANS
OCTANT
OCTANTAL
OCTANTS
OCTAPLA
OCTAPLAS
OCTAPLOID
OCTAPODIC
OCTAPODY
OCTARCHY
OCTAS
OCTASTICH
OCTASTYLE
OCTAVAL
OCTAVE
OCTAVES
OCTAVO
OCTAVOS
OCTENNIAL
OCTET
OCTETS
OCTETT
OCTETTE
OCTETTES
OCTETTS
OCTILLION
OCTOFID
OCTOHEDRA
OCTONARII
OCTONARY
OCTOPI
OCTOPLOID
OCTOPOD
OCTOPODAN
OCTOPODES
OCTOPODS
OCTOPOID
OCTOPUS
OCTOPUSES
OCTOPUSH
OCTOSTYLE
OCTOTHORP
OCTROI
OCTROIS
OCTUOR
OCTUORS
OCTUPLE
OCTUPLED
OCTUPLES
OCTUPLET
OCTUPLETS
OCTUPLEX
OCTUPLING
OCTUPLY
OCTYL
OCTYLS
OCULAR
OCULARIST
OCULARLY
OCULARS
OCULATE
OCULATED
OCULI
OCULIST
OCULISTS
OCULUS
OD
ODA
ODAH
ODAHS
ODAL
ODALIQUE
ODALIQUES
ODALISK
ODALISKS
ODALISQUE
ODALLER
ODALLERS
ODALS
ODAS
ODD
ODDBALL
ODDBALLS
ODDER
ODDEST
ODDISH
ODDITIES
ODDITY
ODDLY
ODDMENT
ODDMENTS
ODDNESS
ODDNESSES
ODDS
ODDSMAKER
ODDSMAN
ODDSMEN
ODE
ODEA
ODEON
ODEONS
ODES
ODEUM
ODEUMS
ODIC
ODIFEROUS
ODIOUS
ODIOUSLY
ODISM
ODISMS
ODIST
ODISTS
ODIUM
ODIUMS
ODOGRAPH
ODOGRAPHS
ODOMETER
ODOMETERS
ODOMETRY
ODONATA
ODONATE
ODONATES
ODONATIST
ODONTALGY
ODONTIC
ODONTIST
ODONTISTS
ODONTOID
ODONTOIDS
ODONTOMA
ODONTOMAS
ODOR
ODORANT
ODORANTS
ODORATE
ODORED
ODORFUL
ODORISE
ODORISED
ODORISER
ODORISERS
ODORISES
ODORISING
ODORIZE
ODORIZED
ODORIZER
ODORIZERS
ODORIZES
ODORIZING
ODORLESS
ODOROUS
ODOROUSLY
ODORS
ODOUR
ODOURED
ODOURFUL
ODOURLESS
ODOURS
ODS
ODSO
ODYL
ODYLE
ODYLES
ODYLISM
ODYLISMS
ODYLS
ODYSSEAN
ODYSSEY
ODYSSEYS
ODZOOKS
OE
OECIST
OECISTS
OECOLOGIC
OECOLOGY
OECUMENIC
OEDEMA
OEDEMAS
OEDEMATA
OEDIPAL
OEDIPALLY
OEDIPEAN
OEDOMETER
OEILLADE
OEILLADES
OENANTHIC
OENOLOGY
OENOMANCY

O

OENOMANIA
OENOMEL
OENOMELS
OENOMETER
OENOPHIL
OENOPHILE
OENOPHILS
OENOPHILY
OENOTHERA
OERLIKON
OERLIKONS
OERSTED
OERSTEDS
OES
OESOPHAGI
OESTRAL
OESTRIN
OESTRINS
OESTRIOL
OESTRIOLS
OESTROGEN
OESTRONE
OESTRONES
OESTROUS
OESTRUAL
OESTRUM
OESTRUMS
OESTRUS
OESTRUSES
OEUVRE
OEUVRES
OF
OFF
OFFA
OFFAL
OFFALS
OFFBEAT
OFFBEATS
OFFCAST
OFFCASTS
OFFCUT
OFFCUTS
OFFED
OFFENCE
OFFENCES
OFFEND
OFFENDED
OFFENDER
OFFENDERS
OFFENDING
OFFENDS
OFFENSE
OFFENSES
OFFENSIVE
OFFER
OFFERABLE
OFFERED
OFFEREE
OFFEREES
OFFERER
OFFERERS
OFFERING
OFFERINGS
OFFEROR
OFFERORS
OFFERS
OFFERTORY
OFFHAND
OFFHANDED
OFFICE
OFFICER
OFFICERED
OFFICERS
OFFICES
OFFICIAL
OFFICIALS
OFFICIANT
OFFICIARY
OFFICIATE
OFFICINAL
OFFICIOUS
OFFIE
OFFIES
OFFING
OFFINGS
OFFISH
OFFISHLY
OFFKEY
OFFLINE
OFFLOAD
OFFLOADED
OFFLOADS
OFFPEAK
OFFPRINT
OFFPRINTS
OFFPUT
OFFPUTS
OFFRAMP
OFFRAMPS
OFFS
OFFSADDLE
OFFSCREEN
OFFSCUM
OFFSCUMS
OFFSEASON
OFFSET
OFFSETS
OFFSHOOT
OFFSHOOTS
OFFSHORE
OFFSHORED
OFFSHORES
OFFSIDE
OFFSIDER
OFFSIDERS
OFFSIDES
OFFSPRING
OFFSTAGE
OFFSTAGES
OFFTAKE
OFFTAKES
OFFTRACK
OFFY
OFLAG
OFLAGS
OFT
OFTEN
OFTENER
OFTENEST
OFTENNESS
OFTER
OFTEST
OFTTIMES
OGAM
OGAMIC
OGAMS
OGANESSON
OGDOAD
OGDOADS
OGEE
OGEED
OGEES
OGGIN
OGGINS
OGHAM
OGHAMIC
OGHAMIST
OGHAMISTS
OGHAMS
OGIVAL
OGIVE
OGIVES
OGLE
OGLED
OGLER
OGLERS
OGLES
OGLING
OGLINGS
OGMIC
OGRE
OGREISH
OGREISHLY
OGREISM
OGREISMS
OGRES
OGRESS
OGRESSES
OGRISH
OGRISHLY
OGRISM
OGRISMS
OH
OHED
OHIA
OHIAS
OHING
OHM
OHMAGE
OHMAGES
OHMIC
OHMICALLY
OHMMETER
OHMMETERS
OHMS
OHO
OHONE
OHS
OI
OIDIA
OIDIOID
OIDIUM
OIK
OIKIST
OIKISTS
OIKS
OIL
OILBIRD
OILBIRDS
OILCAMP
OILCAMPS
OILCAN
OILCANS
OILCLOTH
OILCLOTHS
OILCUP
OILCUPS
OILED
OILER
OILERIES
OILERS
OILERY
OILFIELD
OILFIELDS
OILFIRED
OILGAS
OILGASES
OILHOLE
OILHOLES
OILIER
OILIEST
OILILY
OILINESS
OILING
OILLET
OILLETS
OILMAN
OILMEN
OILNUT
OILNUTS
OILPAN
OILPANS
OILPAPER
OILPAPERS
OILPROOF
OILS
OILSEED
OILSEEDS
OILSKIN
OILSKINS

O

OILSTONE
OILSTONES
OILTIGHT
OILWAY
OILWAYS
OILY
OINK
OINKED
OINKING
OINKS
OINOLOGY
OINOMEL
OINOMELS
OINT
OINTED
OINTING
OINTMENT
OINTMENTS
OINTS
OIS
OITICICA
OITICICAS
OJIME
OJIMES
OK
OKA
OKAPI
OKAPIS
OKAS
OKAY
OKAYED
OKAYING
OKAYS
OKE
OKEH
OKEHS
OKES
OKEYDOKE
OKEYDOKEY
OKIMONO
OKIMONOS
OKRA
OKRAS
OKTA
OKTAS
OLD
OLDE
OLDEN
OLDENED
OLDENING
OLDENS
OLDER
OLDEST
OLDIE
OLDIES
OLDISH
OLDNESS
OLDNESSES
OLDS
OLDSQUAW
OLDSQUAWS
OLDSTER
OLDSTERS
OLDSTYLE
OLDSTYLES
OLDWIFE
OLDWIVES
OLDY
OLE
OLEA
OLEACEOUS
OLEANDER
OLEANDERS
OLEARIA
OLEARIAS
OLEASTER
OLEASTERS
OLEATE
OLEATES
OLECRANAL
OLECRANON
OLEFIANT
OLEFIN
OLEFINE
OLEFINES
OLEFINIC
OLEFINS
OLEIC
OLEIN
OLEINE
OLEINES
OLEINS
OLENT
OLEO
OLEOGRAPH
OLEORESIN
OLEOS
OLES
OLESTRA
OLESTRAS
OLEUM
OLEUMS
OLFACT
OLFACTED
OLFACTING
OLFACTION
OLFACTIVE
OLFACTORY
OLFACTS
OLIBANUM
OLIBANUMS
OLICOOK
OLICOOKS
OLID
OLIGAEMIA
OLIGAEMIC
OLIGARCH
OLIGARCHS
OLIGARCHY
OLIGEMIA
OLIGEMIAS
OLIGEMIC
OLIGIST
OLIGISTS
OLIGOCENE
OLIGOGENE
OLIGOMER
OLIGOMERS
OLIGOPOLY
OLIGURIA
OLIGURIAS
OLIGURIC
OLINGO
OLINGOS
OLINGUITO
OLIO
OLIOS
OLIPHANT
OLIPHANTS
OLITORIES
OLITORY
OLIVARY
OLIVE
OLIVENITE
OLIVER
OLIVERS
OLIVES
OLIVET
OLIVETS
OLIVEWOOD
OLIVINE
OLIVINES
OLIVINIC
OLLA
OLLAMH
OLLAMHS
OLLAS
OLLAV
OLLAVS
OLLER
OLLERS
OLLIE
OLLIED
OLLIEING
OLLIES
OLM
OLMS
OLOGIES
OLOGIST
OLOGISTS
OLOGOAN
OLOGOANED
OLOGOANS
OLOGY
OLOLIUQUI
OLOROSO
OLOROSOS
OLPAE
OLPE
OLPES
OLYCOOK
OLYCOOKS
OLYKOEK
OLYKOEKS
OLYMPIAD
OLYMPIADS
OLYMPICS
OM
OMA
OMADHAUN
OMADHAUNS
OMAS
OMASA
OMASAL
OMASUM
OMBER
OMBERS
OMBRE
OMBRELLA
OMBRELLAS
OMBRES
OMBROPHIL
OMBU
OMBUDSMAN
OMBUDSMEN
OMBUS
OMEGA
OMEGAS
OMELET
OMELETS
OMELETTE
OMELETTES
OMEN
OMENED
OMENING
OMENS
OMENTA
OMENTAL
OMENTUM
OMENTUMS
OMER
OMERS
OMERTA
OMERTAS
OMICRON
OMICRONS
OMIGOD
OMIKRON
OMIKRONS
OMINOUS
OMINOUSLY
OMISSIBLE
OMISSION
OMISSIONS
OMISSIVE
OMIT
OMITS
OMITTANCE
OMITTED
OMITTER

O

OMITTERS
OMITTING
OMLAH
OMLAHS
OMMATEA
OMMATEUM
OMMATIDIA
OMNEITIES
OMNEITY
OMNIANA
OMNIANAS
OMNIARCH
OMNIARCHS
OMNIBUS
OMNIBUSES
OMNIETIES
OMNIETY
OMNIFIC
OMNIFIED
OMNIFIES
OMNIFORM
OMNIFY
OMNIFYING
OMNIMODE
OMNIRANGE
OMNIUM
OMNIUMS
OMNIVORA
OMNIVORE
OMNIVORES
OMNIVORY
OMOHYOID
OMOHYOIDS
OMOPHAGIA
OMOPHAGIC
OMOPHAGY
OMOPHORIA
OMOPLATE
OMOPLATES
OMOV
OMOVS
OMPHACITE
OMPHALI
OMPHALIC
OMPHALOI
OMPHALOID
OMPHALOS
OMRAH
OMRAHS
OMS
ON
ONAGER
ONAGERS
ONAGRI
ONANISM
ONANISMS
ONANIST
ONANISTIC
ONANISTS
ONBEAT
ONBEATS
ONBOARD
ONBOARDED
ONBOARDS
ONCE
ONCER
ONCERS
ONCES
ONCET
ONCIDIUM
ONCIDIUMS
ONCOGEN
ONCOGENE
ONCOGENES
ONCOGENIC
ONCOGENS
ONCOLOGIC
ONCOLOGY
ONCOLYSES
ONCOLYSIS
ONCOLYTIC
ONCOME
ONCOMES
ONCOMETER
ONCOMICE
ONCOMING
ONCOMINGS
ONCOMOUSE
ONCOST
ONCOSTMAN
ONCOSTMEN
ONCOSTS
ONCOTOMY
ONCOVIRUS
ONCUS
ONDATRA
ONDATRAS
ONDINE
ONDINES
ONDING
ONDINGS
ONDOGRAM
ONDOGRAMS
ONDOGRAPH
ONE
ONEFOLD
ONEIRIC
ONELY
ONENESS
ONENESSES
ONER
ONERIER
ONERIEST
ONEROUS
ONEROUSLY
ONERS
ONERY
ONES
ONESELF
ONESIE
ONESIES
ONETIME
ONEYER
ONEYERS
ONEYRE
ONEYRES
ONFALL
ONFALLS
ONFLOW
ONFLOWS
ONGAONGA
ONGAONGAS
ONGOING
ONGOINGS
ONIE
ONION
ONIONED
ONIONIER
ONIONIEST
ONIONING
ONIONS
ONIONSKIN
ONIONY
ONIRIC
ONISCOID
ONIUM
ONIUMS
ONKUS
ONLAY
ONLAYS
ONLIEST
ONLINE
ONLINER
ONLINERS
ONLOAD
ONLOADED
ONLOADING
ONLOADS
ONLOOKER
ONLOOKERS
ONLOOKING
ONLY
ONNED
ONNING
ONO
ONOMAST
ONOMASTIC
ONOMASTS
ONOS
ONRUSH
ONRUSHES
ONRUSHING
ONS
ONSCREEN
ONSET
ONSETS
ONSETTER
ONSETTERS
ONSETTING
ONSHORE
ONSHORING
ONSIDE
ONSIDES
ONSLAUGHT
ONST
ONSTAGE
ONSTEAD
ONSTEADS
ONSTREAM
ONTIC
ONTICALLY
ONTO
ONTOGENIC
ONTOGENY
ONTOLOGIC
ONTOLOGY
ONUS
ONUSES
ONWARD
ONWARDLY
ONWARDS
ONY
ONYCHA
ONYCHAS
ONYCHIA
ONYCHIAS
ONYCHITE
ONYCHITES
ONYCHITIS
ONYCHIUM
ONYCHIUMS
ONYMOUS
ONYX
ONYXES
OO
OOBIT
OOBITS
OOCYST
OOCYSTS
OOCYTE
OOCYTES
OODLES
OODLINS
OOF
OOFIER
OOFIEST
OOFS
OOFTISH
OOFTISHES
OOFY
OOGAMETE
OOGAMETES
OOGAMIES
OOGAMOUS
OOGAMY
OOGENESES
OOGENESIS
OOGENETIC
OOGENIES
OOGENY

OOGONIA
OOGONIAL
OOGONIUM
OOGONIUMS
OOH
OOHED
OOHING
OOHINGS
OOHS
OOIDAL
OOLACHAN
OOLACHANS
OOLAKAN
OOLAKANS
OOLICHAN
OOLICHANS
OOLITE
OOLITES
OOLITH
OOLITHS
OOLITIC
OOLOGIC
OOLOGICAL
OOLOGIES
OOLOGIST
OOLOGISTS
OOLOGY
OOLONG
OOLONGS
OOM
OOMIAC
OOMIACK
OOMIACKS
OOMIACS
OOMIAK
OOMIAKS
OOMPAH
OOMPAHED
OOMPAHING
OOMPAHPAH
OOMPAHS
OOMPH
OOMPHS
OOMS
OOMYCETE
OOMYCETES
OON
OONS
OONT
OONTS
OOP
OOPED
OOPHORON
OOPHORONS
OOPHYTE
OOPHYTES
OOPHYTIC
OOPING
OOPS
OOR
OORALI
OORALIS
OORIAL
OORIALS
OORIE
OORIER
OORIEST
OOS
OOSE
OOSES
OOSIER
OOSIEST
OOSPERM
OOSPERMS
OOSPHERE
OOSPHERES
OOSPORE
OOSPORES
OOSPORIC
OOSPOROUS
OOSY
OOT
OOTHECA
OOTHECAE
OOTHECAL
OOTID
OOTIDS
OOTS
OOZE
OOZED
OOZES
OOZIER
OOZIEST
OOZILY
OOZINESS
OOZING
OOZY
OP
OPA
OPACIFIED
OPACIFIER
OPACIFIES
OPACIFY
OPACITIES
OPACITY
OPACOUS
OPAH
OPAHS
OPAL
OPALED
OPALESCE
OPALESCED
OPALESCES
OPALINE
OPALINES
OPALISED
OPALIZED
OPALS
OPAQUE
OPAQUED
OPAQUELY
OPAQUER
OPAQUES
OPAQUEST
OPAQUING
OPAS
OPCODE
OPCODES
OPE
OPED
OPEN
OPENABLE
OPENCAST
OPENED
OPENER
OPENERS
OPENEST
OPENING
OPENINGS
OPENLY
OPENNESS
OPENS
OPENSIDE
OPENSIDES
OPENWORK
OPENWORKS
OPEPE
OPEPES
OPERA
OPERABLE
OPERABLY
OPERAGOER
OPERAND
OPERANDS
OPERANT
OPERANTLY
OPERANTS
OPERAS
OPERATE
OPERATED
OPERATES
OPERATIC
OPERATICS
OPERATING
OPERATION
OPERATISE
OPERATIVE
OPERATIZE
OPERATOR
OPERATORS
OPERCELE
OPERCELES
OPERCULA
OPERCULAR
OPERCULE
OPERCULES
OPERCULUM
OPERETTA
OPERETTAS
OPERON
OPERONS
OPEROSE
OPEROSELY
OPEROSITY
OPES
OPGEFOK
OPHIDIAN
OPHIDIANS
OPHIOLITE
OPHIOLOGY
OPHITE
OPHITES
OPHITIC
OPHIURA
OPHIURAN
OPHIURANS
OPHIURAS
OPHIURID
OPHIURIDS
OPHIUROID
OPIATE
OPIATED
OPIATES
OPIATING
OPIFICER
OPIFICERS
OPINABLE
OPINE
OPINED
OPINES
OPING
OPINICUS
OPINING
OPINION
OPINIONED
OPINIONS
OPIOID
OPIOIDS
OPIUM
OPIUMISM
OPIUMISMS
OPIUMS
OPOBALSAM
OPODELDOC
OPOPANAX
OPORICE
OPORICES
OPOSSUM
OPOSSUMS
OPPIDAN
OPPIDANS
OPPILANT
OPPILATE
OPPILATED
OPPILATES
OPPO
OPPONENCY
OPPONENS
OPPONENT
OPPONENTS

OPPORTUNE
OPPOS
OPPOSABLE
OPPOSABLY
OPPOSE
OPPOSED
OPPOSER
OPPOSERS
OPPOSES
OPPOSING
OPPOSITE
OPPOSITES
OPPRESS
OPPRESSED
OPPRESSES
OPPRESSOR
OPPUGN
OPPUGNANT
OPPUGNED
OPPUGNER
OPPUGNERS
OPPUGNING
OPPUGNS
OPS
OPSIMATH
OPSIMATHS
OPSIMATHY
OPSIN
OPSINS
OPSOMANIA
OPSONIC
OPSONIFY
OPSONIN
OPSONINS
OPSONISE
OPSONISED
OPSONISES
OPSONIUM
OPSONIUMS
OPSONIZE
OPSONIZED
OPSONIZES
OPT
OPTANT
OPTANTS
OPTATIVE
OPTATIVES
OPTED
OPTER
OPTERS
OPTIC
OPTICAL
OPTICALLY
OPTICIAN
OPTICIANS
OPTICIST
OPTICISTS
OPTICS
OPTIMA
OPTIMAL
OPTIMALLY
OPTIMATE
OPTIMATES
OPTIME
OPTIMES
OPTIMISE
OPTIMISED
OPTIMISER
OPTIMISES
OPTIMISM
OPTIMISMS
OPTIMIST
OPTIMISTS
OPTIMIZE
OPTIMIZED
OPTIMIZER
OPTIMIZES
OPTIMUM
OPTIMUMS
OPTING
OPTION
OPTIONAL
OPTIONALS
OPTIONED
OPTIONEE
OPTIONEES
OPTIONING
OPTIONS
OPTOLOGY
OPTOMETER
OPTOMETRY
OPTOPHONE
OPTRONIC
OPTRONICS
OPTS
OPULENCE
OPULENCES
OPULENCY
OPULENT
OPULENTLY
OPULUS
OPULUSES
OPUNTIA
OPUNTIAS
OPUS
OPUSCLE
OPUSCLES
OPUSCULA
OPUSCULAR
OPUSCULE
OPUSCULES
OPUSCULUM
OPUSES
OQUASSA
OQUASSAS
OR
ORA
ORACH
ORACHE
ORACHES
ORACIES
ORACLE
ORACLED
ORACLES
ORACLING
ORACULAR
ORACULOUS
ORACY
ORAD
ORAGIOUS
ORAL
ORALISM
ORALISMS
ORALIST
ORALISTS
ORALITIES
ORALITY
ORALLY
ORALS
ORANG
ORANGE
ORANGEADE
ORANGER
ORANGERIE
ORANGERY
ORANGES
ORANGEST
ORANGEY
ORANGIER
ORANGIEST
ORANGISH
ORANGS
ORANGUTAN
ORANGY
ORANT
ORANTS
ORARIA
ORARIAN
ORARIANS
ORARION
ORARIONS
ORARIUM
ORATE
ORATED
ORATES
ORATING
ORATION
ORATIONS
ORATOR
ORATORIAL
ORATORIAN
ORATORIES
ORATORIO
ORATORIOS
ORATORS
ORATORY
ORATRESS
ORATRICES
ORATRIX
ORATRIXES
ORATURE
ORATURES
ORB
ORBED
ORBICULAR
ORBIER
ORBIEST
ORBING
ORBIT
ORBITA
ORBITAL
ORBITALLY
ORBITALS
ORBITAS
ORBITED
ORBITER
ORBITERS
ORBITIES
ORBITING
ORBITS
ORBITY
ORBLESS
ORBLIKE
ORBS
ORBY
ORC
ORCA
ORCAS
ORCEIN
ORCEINS
ORCHARD
ORCHARDS
ORCHAT
ORCHATS
ORCHEL
ORCHELLA
ORCHELLAS
ORCHELS
ORCHESES
ORCHESIS
ORCHESTIC
ORCHESTRA
ORCHID
ORCHIDIST
ORCHIDS
ORCHIL
ORCHILLA
ORCHILLAS
ORCHILS
ORCHIS
ORCHISES
ORCHITIC
ORCHITIS
ORCIN
ORCINE
ORCINES
ORCINOL
ORCINOLS
ORCINS
ORCS

ORD
ORDAIN
ORDAINED
ORDAINER
ORDAINERS
ORDAINING
ORDAINS
ORDALIAN
ORDALIUM
ORDALIUMS
ORDEAL
ORDEALS
ORDER
ORDERABLE
ORDERED
ORDERER
ORDERERS
ORDERING
ORDERINGS
ORDERLESS
ORDERLIES
ORDERLY
ORDERS
ORDINAIRE
ORDINAL
ORDINALLY
ORDINALS
ORDINANCE
ORDINAND
ORDINANDS
ORDINANT
ORDINANTS
ORDINAR
ORDINARS
ORDINARY
ORDINATE
ORDINATED
ORDINATES
ORDINEE
ORDINEES
ORDINES
ORDNANCE
ORDNANCES
ORDO
ORDOS
ORDS
ORDURE
ORDURES
ORDUROUS
ORE
OREAD
OREADES
OREADS
OREBODIES
OREBODY
ORECTIC
ORECTIVE
OREGANO
OREGANOS
OREIDE
OREIDES
OREODONT
OREODONTS
OREOLOGY
OREPEARCH
ORES
ORESTUNCK
OREWEED
OREWEEDS
OREXIN
OREXINS
OREXIS
OREXISES
ORF
ORFE
ORFES
ORFRAY
ORFRAYS
ORFS
ORG
ORGAN
ORGANA
ORGANDIE
ORGANDIES
ORGANDY
ORGANELLE
ORGANIC
ORGANICAL
ORGANICS
ORGANISE
ORGANISED
ORGANISER
ORGANISES
ORGANISM
ORGANISMS
ORGANIST
ORGANISTS
ORGANITY
ORGANIZE
ORGANIZED
ORGANIZER
ORGANIZES
ORGANON
ORGANONS
ORGANOSOL
ORGANOTIN
ORGANS
ORGANUM
ORGANUMS
ORGANZA
ORGANZAS
ORGANZINE
ORGASM
ORGASMED
ORGASMIC
ORGASMING
ORGASMS
ORGASTIC
ORGEAT
ORGEATS
ORGIA
ORGIAC
ORGIAS
ORGIAST
ORGIASTIC
ORGIASTS
ORGIC
ORGIES
ORGILLOUS
ORGONE
ORGONES
ORGS
ORGUE
ORGUES
ORGULOUS
ORGY
ORIBATID
ORIBATIDS
ORIBI
ORIBIS
ORICALCHE
ORICHALC
ORICHALCS
ORIEL
ORIELLED
ORIELS
ORIENCIES
ORIENCY
ORIENT
ORIENTAL
ORIENTALS
ORIENTATE
ORIENTED
ORIENTEER
ORIENTER
ORIENTERS
ORIENTING
ORIENTS
ORIFEX
ORIFEXES
ORIFICE
ORIFICES
ORIFICIAL
ORIFLAMME
ORIGAMI
ORIGAMIS
ORIGAN
ORIGANE
ORIGANES
ORIGANS
ORIGANUM
ORIGANUMS
ORIGIN
ORIGINAL
ORIGINALS
ORIGINARY
ORIGINATE
ORIGINS
ORIHOU
ORIHOUS
ORILLION
ORILLIONS
ORINASAL
ORINASALS
ORIOLE
ORIOLES
ORISHA
ORISHAS
ORISON
ORISONS
ORIXA
ORIXAS
ORLE
ORLEANS
ORLEANSES
ORLES
ORLISTAT
ORLISTATS
ORLON
ORLONS
ORLOP
ORLOPS
ORMER
ORMERS
ORMOLU
ORMOLUS
ORNAMENT
ORNAMENTS
ORNATE
ORNATELY
ORNATER
ORNATEST
ORNERIER
ORNERIEST
ORNERY
ORNIS
ORNISES
ORNITHES
ORNITHIC
ORNITHINE
ORNITHOID
OROGEN
OROGENIC
OROGENIES
OROGENS
OROGENY
OROGRAPHY
OROIDE
OROIDES
OROLOGIES
OROLOGIST
OROLOGY
OROMETER
OROMETERS
ORONASAL
OROPESA
OROPESAS
OROTUND
OROTUNDLY
ORPHAN

O

ORPHANAGE
ORPHANED
ORPHANING
ORPHANISM
ORPHANS
ORPHARION
ORPHIC
ORPHICAL
ORPHISM
ORPHISMS
ORPHREY
ORPHREYED
ORPHREYS
ORPIMENT
ORPIMENTS
ORPIN
ORPINE
ORPINES
ORPINS
ORRA
ORRAMAN
ORRAMEN
ORRERIES
ORRERY
ORRICE
ORRICES
ORRIS
ORRISES
ORRISROOT
ORS
ORSEILLE
ORSEILLES
ORSELLIC
ORT
ORTANIQUE
ORTHIAN
ORTHICON
ORTHICONS
ORTHO
ORTHOAXES
ORTHOAXIS
ORTHODOX
ORTHODOXY
ORTHOEPIC
ORTHOEPY
ORTHOPEDY
ORTHOPOD
ORTHOPODS
ORTHOPTER
ORTHOPTIC
ORTHOS
ORTHOSES
ORTHOSIS
ORTHOTIC
ORTHOTICS
ORTHOTIST
ORTHOTONE
ORTHROS
ORTHROSES
ORTOLAN
ORTOLANS
ORTS
ORVAL
ORVALS
ORYX
ORYXES
ORZO
ORZOS
OS
OSAR
OSCAR
OSCARS
OSCHEAL
OSCILLATE
OSCINE
OSCINES
OSCININE
OSCITANCE
OSCITANCY
OSCITANT
OSCITATE
OSCITATED
OSCITATES
OSCULA
OSCULANT
OSCULAR
OSCULATE
OSCULATED
OSCULATES
OSCULE
OSCULES
OSCULUM
OSE
OSES
OSETRA
OSETRAS
OSHAC
OSHACS
OSIER
OSIERED
OSIERIES
OSIERS
OSIERY
OSMATE
OSMATES
OSMATIC
OSMETERIA
OSMIATE
OSMIATES
OSMIC
OSMICALLY
OSMICS
OSMIOUS
OSMIUM
OSMIUMS
OSMOL
OSMOLAL
OSMOLAR
OSMOLE
OSMOLES
OSMOLS
OSMOMETER
OSMOMETRY
OSMOSE
OSMOSED
OSMOSES
OSMOSING
OSMOSIS
OSMOTIC
OSMOUS
OSMUND
OSMUNDA
OSMUNDAS
OSMUNDINE
OSMUNDS
OSNABURG
OSNABURGS
OSPREY
OSPREYS
OSSA
OSSARIUM
OSSARIUMS
OSSATURE
OSSATURES
OSSEIN
OSSEINS
OSSELET
OSSELETS
OSSEOUS
OSSEOUSLY
OSSETER
OSSETERS
OSSETRA
OSSETRAS
OSSIA
OSSIAS
OSSICLE
OSSICLES
OSSICULAR
OSSIFIC
OSSIFIED
OSSIFIER
OSSIFIERS
OSSIFIES
OSSIFRAGA
OSSIFRAGE
OSSIFY
OSSIFYING
OSSOBUCO
OSSOBUCOS
OSSUARIES
OSSUARY
OSTEAL
OSTEITIC
OSTEITIS
OSTENSIVE
OSTENSORY
OSTENT
OSTENTED
OSTENTING
OSTENTS
OSTEOCYTE
OSTEODERM
OSTEOGEN
OSTEOGENS
OSTEOGENY
OSTEOID
OSTEOIDS
OSTEOLOGY
OSTEOMA
OSTEOMAS
OSTEOMATA
OSTEOPATH
OSTEOSES
OSTEOSIS
OSTEOTOME
OSTEOTOMY
OSTIA
OSTIAL
OSTIARIES
OSTIARY
OSTIATE
OSTINATI
OSTINATO
OSTINATOS
OSTIOLAR
OSTIOLATE
OSTIOLE
OSTIOLES
OSTIUM
OSTLER
OSTLERESS
OSTLERS
OSTMARK
OSTMARKS
OSTOMATE
OSTOMATES
OSTOMIES
OSTOMY
OSTOSES
OSTOSIS
OSTOSISES
OSTRACA
OSTRACEAN
OSTRACISE
OSTRACISM
OSTRACIZE
OSTRACOD
OSTRACODE
OSTRACODS
OSTRACON
OSTRAKA
OSTRAKON
OSTREGER
OSTREGERS
OSTRICH
OSTRICHES
OTAKU
OTAKUS
OTALGIA

OTALGIAS
OTALGIC
OTALGIES
OTALGY
OTARID
OTARIES
OTARINE
OTARY
OTHER
OTHERED
OTHERING
OTHERNESS
OTHERS
OTHERWISE
OTIC
OTIOSE
OTIOSELY
OTIOSITY
OTITIC
OTITIDES
OTITIS
OTITISES
OTOCYST
OTOCYSTIC
OTOCYSTS
OTOLITH
OTOLITHIC
OTOLITHS
OTOLOGIC
OTOLOGIES
OTOLOGIST
OTOLOGY
OTOPLASTY
OTORRHOEA
OTOSCOPE
OTOSCOPES
OTOSCOPIC
OTOSCOPY
OTOTOXIC
OTTAR
OTTARS
OTTAVA
OTTAVAS
OTTAVINO
OTTAVINOS
OTTER
OTTERED
OTTERING
OTTERS
OTTO
OTTOMAN
OTTOMANS
OTTOS
OTTRELITE
OU
OUABAIN
OUABAINS
OUAKARI
OUAKARIS
OUBAAS
OUBAASES
OUBIT
OUBITS
OUBLIETTE
OUCH
OUCHED
OUCHES
OUCHING
OUCHT
OUCHTS
OUD
OUDS
OUENS
OUGHLIED
OUGHLIES
OUGHLY
OUGHLYING
OUGHT
OUGHTED
OUGHTING
OUGHTNESS
OUGHTS
OUGIYA
OUGIYAS
OUGLIE
OUGLIED
OUGLIEING
OUGLIES
OUGUIYA
OUGUIYAS
OUIJA
OUIJAS
OUISTITI
OUISTITIS
OUK
OUKS
OULACHON
OULACHONS
OULAKAN
OULAKANS
OULD
OULDER
OULDEST
OULK
OULKS
OULONG
OULONGS
OUMA
OUMAS
OUNCE
OUNCES
OUNDIER
OUNDIEST
OUNDY
OUP
OUPA
OUPAS
OUPED
OUPH
OUPHE
OUPHES
OUPHS
OUPING
OUPS
OUR
OURALI
OURALIS
OURANG
OURANGS
OURARI
OURARIS
OUREBI
OUREBIS
OURIE
OURIER
OURIEST
OURN
OUROBOROS
OUROLOGY
OUROSCOPY
OURS
OURSELF
OURSELVES
OUS
OUSEL
OUSELS
OUST
OUSTED
OUSTER
OUSTERS
OUSTING
OUSTITI
OUSTITIS
OUSTS
OUT
OUTA
OUTACT
OUTACTED
OUTACTING
OUTACTS
OUTADD
OUTADDED
OUTADDING
OUTADDS
OUTAGE
OUTAGES
OUTARGUE
OUTARGUED
OUTARGUES
OUTASIGHT
OUTASITE
OUTASK
OUTASKED
OUTASKING
OUTASKS
OUTATE
OUTBACK
OUTBACKER
OUTBACKS
OUTBAKE
OUTBAKED
OUTBAKES
OUTBAKING
OUTBAR
OUTBARK
OUTBARKED
OUTBARKS
OUTBARRED
OUTBARS
OUTBAWL
OUTBAWLED
OUTBAWLS
OUTBEAM
OUTBEAMED
OUTBEAMS
OUTBEG
OUTBEGGED
OUTBEGS
OUTBID
OUTBIDDEN
OUTBIDDER
OUTBIDS
OUTBITCH
OUTBLAZE
OUTBLAZED
OUTBLAZES
OUTBLEAT
OUTBLEATS
OUTBLESS
OUTBLOOM
OUTBLOOMS
OUTBLUFF
OUTBLUFFS
OUTBLUSH
OUTBOARD
OUTBOARDS
OUTBOAST
OUTBOASTS
OUTBOUGHT
OUTBOUND
OUTBOUNDS
OUTBOX
OUTBOXED
OUTBOXES
OUTBOXING
OUTBRAG
OUTBRAGS
OUTBRAVE
OUTBRAVED
OUTBRAVES
OUTBRAWL
OUTBRAWLS
OUTBRAZEN
OUTBREAK
OUTBREAKS
OUTBRED
OUTBREED
OUTBREEDS
OUTBRIBE
OUTBRIBED

OUTBRIBES
OUTBROKE
OUTBROKEN
OUTBUILD
OUTBUILDS
OUTBUILT
OUTBULGE
OUTBULGED
OUTBULGES
OUTBULK
OUTBULKED
OUTBULKS
OUTBULLY
OUTBURN
OUTBURNED
OUTBURNS
OUTBURNT
OUTBURST
OUTBURSTS
OUTBUY
OUTBUYING
OUTBUYS
OUTBY
OUTBYE
OUTCALL
OUTCALLED
OUTCALLS
OUTCAPER
OUTCAPERS
OUTCAST
OUTCASTE
OUTCASTED
OUTCASTES
OUTCASTS
OUTCATCH
OUTCAUGHT
OUTCAVIL
OUTCAVILS
OUTCHARGE
OUTCHARM
OUTCHARMS
OUTCHEAT
OUTCHEATS
OUTCHID
OUTCHIDE
OUTCHIDED
OUTCHIDES
OUTCITIES
OUTCITY
OUTCLASS
OUTCLIMB
OUTCLIMBS
OUTCLOMB
OUTCOACH
OUTCOME
OUTCOMES
OUTCOOK
OUTCOOKED
OUTCOOKS
OUTCOUNT
OUTCOUNTS
OUTCRAFTY
OUTCRAWL
OUTCRAWLS
OUTCRIED
OUTCRIES
OUTCROP
OUTCROPS
OUTCROSS
OUTCROW
OUTCROWD
OUTCROWDS
OUTCROWED
OUTCROWS
OUTCRY
OUTCRYING
OUTCURSE
OUTCURSED
OUTCURSES
OUTCURVE
OUTCURVES
OUTDANCE
OUTDANCED
OUTDANCES
OUTDARE
OUTDARED
OUTDARES
OUTDARING
OUTDATE
OUTDATED
OUTDATES
OUTDATING
OUTDAZZLE
OUTDEBATE
OUTDESIGN
OUTDID
OUTDO
OUTDODGE
OUTDODGED
OUTDODGES
OUTDOER
OUTDOERS
OUTDOES
OUTDOING
OUTDONE
OUTDOOR
OUTDOORS
OUTDOORSY
OUTDRAG
OUTDRAGS
OUTDRANK
OUTDRAW
OUTDRAWN
OUTDRAWS
OUTDREAM
OUTDREAMS
OUTDREAMT
OUTDRESS
OUTDREW
OUTDRINK
OUTDRINKS
OUTDRIVE
OUTDRIVEN
OUTDRIVES
OUTDROP
OUTDROPS
OUTDROVE
OUTDRUNK
OUTDUEL
OUTDUELED
OUTDUELS
OUTDURE
OUTDURED
OUTDURES
OUTDURING
OUTDWELL
OUTDWELLS
OUTDWELT
OUTEARN
OUTEARNED
OUTEARNS
OUTEAT
OUTEATEN
OUTEATING
OUTEATS
OUTECHO
OUTECHOED
OUTECHOES
OUTED
OUTEDGE
OUTEDGES
OUTER
OUTERCOAT
OUTERMOST
OUTERS
OUTERWEAR
OUTFABLE
OUTFABLED
OUTFABLES
OUTFACE
OUTFACED
OUTFACES
OUTFACING
OUTFALL
OUTFALLS
OUTFAST
OUTFASTED
OUTFASTS
OUTFAWN
OUTFAWNED
OUTFAWNS
OUTFEAST
OUTFEASTS
OUTFEEL
OUTFEELS
OUTFELT
OUTFENCE
OUTFENCED
OUTFENCES
OUTFIELD
OUTFIELDS
OUTFIGHT
OUTFIGHTS
OUTFIGURE
OUTFIND
OUTFINDS
OUTFIRE
OUTFIRED
OUTFIRES
OUTFIRING
OUTFISH
OUTFISHED
OUTFISHES
OUTFIT
OUTFITS
OUTFITTED
OUTFITTER
OUTFLANK
OUTFLANKS
OUTFLASH
OUTFLEW
OUTFLIES
OUTFLING
OUTFLINGS
OUTFLOAT
OUTFLOATS
OUTFLOW
OUTFLOWED
OUTFLOWN
OUTFLOWS
OUTFLUNG
OUTFLUSH
OUTFLY
OUTFLYING
OUTFOOL
OUTFOOLED
OUTFOOLS
OUTFOOT
OUTFOOTED
OUTFOOTS
OUTFOUGHT
OUTFOUND
OUTFOX
OUTFOXED
OUTFOXES
OUTFOXING
OUTFROWN
OUTFROWNS
OUTFUMBLE
OUTGAIN
OUTGAINED
OUTGAINS
OUTGALLOP
OUTGAMBLE
OUTGAS
OUTGASES
OUTGASSED
OUTGASSES
OUTGATE
OUTGATES

O

OUTGAVE
OUTGAZE
OUTGAZED
OUTGAZES
OUTGAZING
OUTGIVE
OUTGIVEN
OUTGIVES
OUTGIVING
OUTGLARE
OUTGLARED
OUTGLARES
OUTGLEAM
OUTGLEAMS
OUTGLOW
OUTGLOWED
OUTGLOWS
OUTGNAW
OUTGNAWED
OUTGNAWN
OUTGNAWS
OUTGO
OUTGOER
OUTGOERS
OUTGOES
OUTGOING
OUTGOINGS
OUTGONE
OUTGREW
OUTGRIN
OUTGRINS
OUTGROSS
OUTGROUP
OUTGROUPS
OUTGROW
OUTGROWN
OUTGROWS
OUTGROWTH
OUTGUARD
OUTGUARDS
OUTGUESS
OUTGUIDE
OUTGUIDED
OUTGUIDES
OUTGUN
OUTGUNNED
OUTGUNS
OUTGUSH
OUTGUSHED
OUTGUSHES
OUTHANDLE
OUTHARBOR
OUTHAUL
OUTHAULER
OUTHAULS
OUTHEAR
OUTHEARD
OUTHEARS
OUTHER
OUTHIRE
OUTHIRED
OUTHIRES
OUTHIRING
OUTHIT
OUTHITS
OUTHOMER
OUTHOMERS
OUTHOUSE
OUTHOUSES
OUTHOWL
OUTHOWLED
OUTHOWLS
OUTHUMOR
OUTHUMORS
OUTHUMOUR
OUTHUNT
OUTHUNTED
OUTHUNTS
OUTHUSTLE
OUTHYRE
OUTHYRED
OUTHYRES
OUTHYRING
OUTING
OUTINGS
OUTJEST
OUTJESTED
OUTJESTS
OUTJET
OUTJETS
OUTJINX
OUTJINXED
OUTJINXES
OUTJOCKEY
OUTJUGGLE
OUTJUMP
OUTJUMPED
OUTJUMPS
OUTJUT
OUTJUTS
OUTJUTTED
OUTKEEP
OUTKEEPS
OUTKEPT
OUTKICK
OUTKICKED
OUTKICKS
OUTKILL
OUTKILLED
OUTKILLS
OUTKISS
OUTKISSED
OUTKISSES
OUTLAID
OUTLAIN
OUTLAND
OUTLANDER
OUTLANDS
OUTLASH
OUTLASHED
OUTLASHES
OUTLAST
OUTLASTED
OUTLASTS
OUTLAUGH
OUTLAUGHS
OUTLAUNCE
OUTLAUNCH
OUTLAW
OUTLAWED
OUTLAWING
OUTLAWRY
OUTLAWS
OUTLAY
OUTLAYING
OUTLAYS
OUTLEAD
OUTLEADS
OUTLEAP
OUTLEAPED
OUTLEAPS
OUTLEAPT
OUTLEARN
OUTLEARNS
OUTLEARNT
OUTLED
OUTLER
OUTLERS
OUTLET
OUTLETS
OUTLIE
OUTLIED
OUTLIER
OUTLIERS
OUTLIES
OUTLINE
OUTLINEAR
OUTLINED
OUTLINER
OUTLINERS
OUTLINES
OUTLINING
OUTLIVE
OUTLIVED
OUTLIVER
OUTLIVERS
OUTLIVES
OUTLIVING
OUTLOOK
OUTLOOKED
OUTLOOKS
OUTLOVE
OUTLOVED
OUTLOVES
OUTLOVING
OUTLUSTER
OUTLUSTRE
OUTLYING
OUTMAN
OUTMANNED
OUTMANS
OUTMANTLE
OUTMARCH
OUTMASTER
OUTMATCH
OUTMODE
OUTMODED
OUTMODES
OUTMODING
OUTMOST
OUTMOVE
OUTMOVED
OUTMOVES
OUTMOVING
OUTMUSCLE
OUTNAME
OUTNAMED
OUTNAMES
OUTNAMING
OUTNESS
OUTNESSES
OUTNIGHT
OUTNIGHTS
OUTNUMBER
OUTOFFICE
OUTPACE
OUTPACED
OUTPACES
OUTPACING
OUTPAINT
OUTPAINTS
OUTPART
OUTPARTS
OUTPASS
OUTPASSED
OUTPASSES
OUTPEEP
OUTPEEPED
OUTPEEPS
OUTPEER
OUTPEERED
OUTPEERS
OUTPEOPLE
OUTPITCH
OUTPITIED
OUTPITIES
OUTPITY
OUTPLACE
OUTPLACED
OUTPLACER
OUTPLACES
OUTPLAN
OUTPLANS
OUTPLAY
OUTPLAYED
OUTPLAYS
OUTPLOD
OUTPLODS
OUTPLOT
OUTPLOTS

OUTPOINT
OUTPOINTS
OUTPOLL
OUTPOLLED
OUTPOLLS
OUTPORT
OUTPORTER
OUTPORTS
OUTPOST
OUTPOSTS
OUTPOUR
OUTPOURED
OUTPOURER
OUTPOURS
OUTPOWER
OUTPOWERS
OUTPRAY
OUTPRAYED
OUTPRAYS
OUTPREACH
OUTPREEN
OUTPREENS
OUTPRESS
OUTPRICE
OUTPRICED
OUTPRICES
OUTPRIZE
OUTPRIZED
OUTPRIZES
OUTPSYCH
OUTPSYCHS
OUTPULL
OUTPULLED
OUTPULLS
OUTPUNCH
OUTPUPIL
OUTPUPILS
OUTPURSUE
OUTPUSH
OUTPUSHED
OUTPUSHES
OUTPUT
OUTPUTS
OUTPUTTED
OUTQUOTE
OUTQUOTED
OUTQUOTES
OUTRACE
OUTRACED
OUTRACES
OUTRACING
OUTRAGE
OUTRAGED
OUTRAGES
OUTRAGING
OUTRAISE
OUTRAISED
OUTRAISES
OUTRAN
OUTRANCE
OUTRANCES
OUTRANG
OUTRANGE
OUTRANGED
OUTRANGES
OUTRANK
OUTRANKED
OUTRANKS
OUTRATE
OUTRATED
OUTRATES
OUTRATING
OUTRAVE
OUTRAVED
OUTRAVES
OUTRAVING
OUTRE
OUTREACH
OUTREAD
OUTREADS
OUTREASON
OUTRECKON
OUTRED
OUTREDDED
OUTREDDEN
OUTREDS
OUTREIGN
OUTREIGNS
OUTRELIEF
OUTREMER
OUTREMERS
OUTRIDDEN
OUTRIDE
OUTRIDER
OUTRIDERS
OUTRIDES
OUTRIDING
OUTRIG
OUTRIGGED
OUTRIGGER
OUTRIGHT
OUTRIGS
OUTRING
OUTRINGS
OUTRIVAL
OUTRIVALS
OUTRO
OUTROAR
OUTROARED
OUTROARS
OUTROCK
OUTROCKED
OUTROCKS
OUTRODE
OUTROLL
OUTROLLED
OUTROLLS
OUTROOP
OUTROOPER
OUTROOPS
OUTROOT
OUTROOTED
OUTROOTS
OUTROPE
OUTROPER
OUTROPERS
OUTROPES
OUTROS
OUTROW
OUTROWED
OUTROWING
OUTROWS
OUTRUN
OUTRUNG
OUTRUNNER
OUTRUNS
OUTRUSH
OUTRUSHED
OUTRUSHES
OUTS
OUTSAID
OUTSAIL
OUTSAILED
OUTSAILS
OUTSANG
OUTSAT
OUTSAVOR
OUTSAVORS
OUTSAVOUR
OUTSAW
OUTSAY
OUTSAYING
OUTSAYS
OUTSCHEME
OUTSCOLD
OUTSCOLDS
OUTSCOOP
OUTSCOOPS
OUTSCORE
OUTSCORED
OUTSCORES
OUTSCORN
OUTSCORNS
OUTSCREAM
OUTSEE
OUTSEEING
OUTSEEN
OUTSEES
OUTSELL
OUTSELLS
OUTSERT
OUTSERTS
OUTSERVE
OUTSERVED
OUTSERVES
OUTSET
OUTSETS
OUTSHAME
OUTSHAMED
OUTSHAMES
OUTSHINE
OUTSHINED
OUTSHINES
OUTSHONE
OUTSHOOT
OUTSHOOTS
OUTSHOT
OUTSHOTS
OUTSHOUT
OUTSHOUTS
OUTSIDE
OUTSIDER
OUTSIDERS
OUTSIDES
OUTSIGHT
OUTSIGHTS
OUTSIN
OUTSING
OUTSINGS
OUTSINNED
OUTSINS
OUTSIT
OUTSITS
OUTSIZE
OUTSIZED
OUTSIZES
OUTSKATE
OUTSKATED
OUTSKATES
OUTSKIRT
OUTSKIRTS
OUTSLEEP
OUTSLEEPS
OUTSLEPT
OUTSLICK
OUTSLICKS
OUTSMART
OUTSMARTS
OUTSMELL
OUTSMELLS
OUTSMELT
OUTSMILE
OUTSMILED
OUTSMILES
OUTSMOKE
OUTSMOKED
OUTSMOKES
OUTSNORE
OUTSNORED
OUTSNORES
OUTSOAR
OUTSOARED
OUTSOARS
OUTSOLD
OUTSOLE
OUTSOLES
OUTSOURCE
OUTSPAN
OUTSPANS
OUTSPEAK

OUTSPEAKS
OUTSPED
OUTSPEED
OUTSPEEDS
OUTSPELL
OUTSPELLS
OUTSPELT
OUTSPEND
OUTSPENDS
OUTSPENT
OUTSPOKE
OUTSPOKEN
OUTSPORT
OUTSPORTS
OUTSPRANG
OUTSPREAD
OUTSPRING
OUTSPRINT
OUTSPRUNG
OUTSTAND
OUTSTANDS
OUTSTARE
OUTSTARED
OUTSTARES
OUTSTART
OUTSTARTS
OUTSTATE
OUTSTATED
OUTSTATES
OUTSTAY
OUTSTAYED
OUTSTAYS
OUTSTEER
OUTSTEERS
OUTSTEP
OUTSTEPS
OUTSTOOD
OUTSTRAIN
OUTSTRIDE
OUTSTRIKE
OUTSTRIP
OUTSTRIPS
OUTSTRIVE
OUTSTRODE
OUTSTROKE
OUTSTROVE
OUTSTRUCK
OUTSTUDY
OUTSTUNT
OUTSTUNTS
OUTSULK
OUTSULKED
OUTSULKS
OUTSUM
OUTSUMMED
OUTSUMS
OUTSUNG
OUTSWAM
OUTSWARE
OUTSWEAR
OUTSWEARS
OUTSWEEP
OUTSWEEPS
OUTSWELL
OUTSWELLS
OUTSWEPT
OUTSWIM
OUTSWIMS
OUTSWING
OUTSWINGS
OUTSWORE
OUTSWORN
OUTSWUM
OUTSWUNG
OUTTA
OUTTAKE
OUTTAKEN
OUTTAKES
OUTTAKING
OUTTALK
OUTTALKED
OUTTALKS
OUTTASK
OUTTASKED
OUTTASKS
OUTTELL
OUTTELLS
OUTTHANK
OUTTHANKS
OUTTHIEVE
OUTTHINK
OUTTHINKS
OUTTHREW
OUTTHROB
OUTTHROBS
OUTTHROW
OUTTHROWN
OUTTHROWS
OUTTHRUST
OUTTOLD
OUTTONGUE
OUTTOOK
OUTTOP
OUTTOPPED
OUTTOPS
OUTTOWER
OUTTOWERS
OUTTRADE
OUTTRADED
OUTTRADES
OUTTRAVEL
OUTTRICK
OUTTRICKS
OUTTROT
OUTTROTS
OUTTRUMP
OUTTRUMPS
OUTTURN
OUTTURNS
OUTVALUE
OUTVALUED
OUTVALUES
OUTVAUNT
OUTVAUNTS
OUTVENOM
OUTVENOMS
OUTVIE
OUTVIED
OUTVIES
OUTVOICE
OUTVOICED
OUTVOICES
OUTVOTE
OUTVOTED
OUTVOTER
OUTVOTERS
OUTVOTES
OUTVOTING
OUTVYING
OUTWAIT
OUTWAITED
OUTWAITS
OUTWALK
OUTWALKED
OUTWALKS
OUTWAR
OUTWARD
OUTWARDLY
OUTWARDS
OUTWARRED
OUTWARS
OUTWASH
OUTWASHES
OUTWASTE
OUTWASTED
OUTWASTES
OUTWATCH
OUTWEAR
OUTWEARS
OUTWEARY
OUTWEED
OUTWEEDED
OUTWEEDS
OUTWEEP
OUTWEEPS
OUTWEIGH
OUTWEIGHS
OUTWELL
OUTWELLED
OUTWELLS
OUTWENT
OUTWEPT
OUTWHIRL
OUTWHIRLS
OUTWICK
OUTWICKED
OUTWICKS
OUTWILE
OUTWILED
OUTWILES
OUTWILING
OUTWILL
OUTWILLED
OUTWILLS
OUTWIN
OUTWIND
OUTWINDED
OUTWINDS
OUTWING
OUTWINGED
OUTWINGS
OUTWINS
OUTWISH
OUTWISHED
OUTWISHES
OUTWIT
OUTWITH
OUTWITS
OUTWITTED
OUTWON
OUTWORE
OUTWORK
OUTWORKED
OUTWORKER
OUTWORKS
OUTWORN
OUTWORTH
OUTWORTHS
OUTWOUND
OUTWREST
OUTWRESTS
OUTWRIT
OUTWRITE
OUTWRITES
OUTWROTE
OUTYELL
OUTYELLED
OUTYELLS
OUTYELP
OUTYELPED
OUTYELPS
OUTYIELD
OUTYIELDS
OUVERT
OUVERTE
OUVRAGE
OUVRAGES
OUVRIER
OUVRIERE
OUVRIERES
OUVRIERS
OUZEL
OUZELS
OUZO
OUZOS
OVA
OVAL
OVALBUMIN
OVALITIES
OVALITY

OVALLY
OVALNESS
OVALS
OVARIAL
OVARIAN
OVARIES
OVARIOLE
OVARIOLES
OVARIOUS
OVARITIS
OVARY
OVATE
OVATED
OVATELY
OVATES
OVATING
OVATION
OVATIONAL
OVATIONS
OVATOR
OVATORS
OVEL
OVELS
OVEN
OVENABLE
OVENBIRD
OVENBIRDS
OVENED
OVENING
OVENLIKE
OVENPROOF
OVENS
OVENWARE
OVENWARES
OVENWOOD
OVENWOODS
OVER
OVERABLE
OVERACT
OVERACTED
OVERACTS
OVERACUTE
OVERAGE
OVERAGED
OVERAGES
OVERALERT
OVERALL
OVERALLED
OVERALLS
OVERAPT
OVERARCH
OVERARM
OVERARMED
OVERARMS
OVERATE
OVERAWE
OVERAWED
OVERAWES
OVERAWING
OVERBAKE
OVERBAKED
OVERBAKES
OVERBANK
OVERBANKS
OVERBEAR
OVERBEARS
OVERBEAT
OVERBEATS
OVERBED
OVERBET
OVERBETS
OVERBID
OVERBIDS
OVERBIG
OVERBILL
OVERBILLS
OVERBITE
OVERBITES
OVERBLEW
OVERBLOW
OVERBLOWN
OVERBLOWS
OVERBOARD
OVERBOIL
OVERBOILS
OVERBOLD
OVERBOOK
OVERBOOKS
OVERBOOT
OVERBOOTS
OVERBORE
OVERBORN
OVERBORNE
OVERBOUND
OVERBRAKE
OVERBRED
OVERBREED
OVERBRIEF
OVERBRIM
OVERBRIMS
OVERBROAD
OVERBROW
OVERBROWS
OVERBUILD
OVERBUILT
OVERBULK
OVERBULKS
OVERBURN
OVERBURNS
OVERBURNT
OVERBUSY
OVERBUY
OVERBUYS
OVERBY
OVERCALL
OVERCALLS
OVERCAME
OVERCARRY
OVERCAST
OVERCASTS
OVERCATCH
OVERCHEAP
OVERCHECK
OVERCHILL
OVERCIVIL
OVERCLAD
OVERCLAIM
OVERCLASS
OVERCLEAN
OVERCLEAR
OVERCLOCK
OVERCLOSE
OVERCLOUD
OVERCLOY
OVERCLOYS
OVERCLUB
OVERCLUBS
OVERCOACH
OVERCOAT
OVERCOATS
OVERCOLD
OVERCOLOR
OVERCOME
OVERCOMER
OVERCOMES
OVERCOOK
OVERCOOKS
OVERCOOL
OVERCOOLS
OVERCOUNT
OVERCOVER
OVERCOY
OVERCRAM
OVERCRAMS
OVERCRAW
OVERCRAWS
OVERCROP
OVERCROPS
OVERCROW
OVERCROWD
OVERCROWS
OVERCURE
OVERCURED
OVERCURES
OVERCUT
OVERCUTS
OVERDARE
OVERDARED
OVERDARES
OVERDATED
OVERDEAR
OVERDECK
OVERDECKS
OVERDID
OVERDIGHT
OVERDO
OVERDOER
OVERDOERS
OVERDOES
OVERDOG
OVERDOGS
OVERDOING
OVERDONE
OVERDOSE
OVERDOSED
OVERDOSES
OVERDRAFT
OVERDRANK
OVERDRAW
OVERDRAWN
OVERDRAWS
OVERDRESS
OVERDREW
OVERDRIED
OVERDRIES
OVERDRINK
OVERDRIVE
OVERDROVE
OVERDRUNK
OVERDRY
OVERDUB
OVERDUBS
OVERDUE
OVERDUST
OVERDUSTS
OVERDYE
OVERDYED
OVERDYER
OVERDYERS
OVERDYES
OVEREAGER
OVEREASY
OVEREAT
OVEREATEN
OVEREATER
OVEREATS
OVERED
OVEREDIT
OVEREDITS
OVEREGG
OVEREGGED
OVEREGGS
OVEREMOTE
OVEREQUIP
OVEREXERT
OVEREYE
OVEREYED
OVEREYES
OVEREYING
OVERFALL
OVERFALLS
OVERFAR
OVERFAST
OVERFAT
OVERFAVOR
OVERFEAR
OVERFEARS
OVERFED
OVERFEED
OVERFEEDS

OVERFELL
OVERFILL
OVERFILLS
OVERFINE
OVERFISH
OVERFIT
OVERFLEW
OVERFLIES
OVERFLOOD
OVERFLOW
OVERFLOWN
OVERFLOWS
OVERFLUSH
OVERFLY
OVERFOCUS
OVERFOLD
OVERFOLDS
OVERFOND
OVERFOUL
OVERFRANK
OVERFREE
OVERFULL
OVERFUND
OVERFUNDS
OVERFUSSY
OVERGALL
OVERGALLS
OVERGANG
OVERGANGS
OVERGAVE
OVERGEAR
OVERGEARS
OVERGET
OVERGETS
OVERGILD
OVERGILDS
OVERGILT
OVERGIRD
OVERGIRDS
OVERGIRT
OVERGIVE
OVERGIVEN
OVERGIVES
OVERGLAD
OVERGLAZE
OVERGLOOM
OVERGO
OVERGOAD
OVERGOADS
OVERGOES
OVERGOING
OVERGONE
OVERGORGE
OVERGOT
OVERGRADE
OVERGRAIN
OVERGRASS
OVERGRAZE
OVERGREAT
OVERGREEN
OVERGREW
OVERGROW
OVERGROWN
OVERGROWS
OVERHAILE
OVERHAIR
OVERHAIRS
OVERHALE
OVERHALED
OVERHALES
OVERHAND
OVERHANDS
OVERHANG
OVERHANGS
OVERHAPPY
OVERHARD
OVERHASTE
OVERHASTY
OVERHATE
OVERHATED
OVERHATES
OVERHAUL
OVERHAULS
OVERHEAD
OVERHEADS
OVERHEAP
OVERHEAPS
OVERHEAR
OVERHEARD
OVERHEARS
OVERHEAT
OVERHEATS
OVERHELD
OVERHENT
OVERHENTS
OVERHIGH
OVERHIT
OVERHITS
OVERHOLD
OVERHOLDS
OVERHOLY
OVERHONOR
OVERHOPE
OVERHOPED
OVERHOPES
OVERHOT
OVERHUNG
OVERHUNT
OVERHUNTS
OVERHYPE
OVERHYPED
OVERHYPES
OVERIDLE
OVERING
OVERINKED
OVERISSUE
OVERJOY
OVERJOYED
OVERJOYS
OVERJUMP
OVERJUMPS
OVERJUST
OVERKEEN
OVERKEEP
OVERKEEPS
OVERKEPT
OVERKEST
OVERKILL
OVERKILLS
OVERKIND
OVERKING
OVERKINGS
OVERKNEE
OVERLABOR
OVERLADE
OVERLADED
OVERLADEN
OVERLADES
OVERLAID
OVERLAIN
OVERLAND
OVERLANDS
OVERLAP
OVERLAPS
OVERLARD
OVERLARDS
OVERLARGE
OVERLATE
OVERLAX
OVERLAY
OVERLAYS
OVERLEAF
OVERLEAP
OVERLEAPS
OVERLEAPT
OVERLEARN
OVERLEND
OVERLENDS
OVERLENT
OVERLET
OVERLETS
OVERLEWD
OVERLIE
OVERLIER
OVERLIERS
OVERLIES
OVERLIGHT
OVERLIT
OVERLIVE
OVERLIVED
OVERLIVES
OVERLOAD
OVERLOADS
OVERLOCK
OVERLOCKS
OVERLONG
OVERLOOK
OVERLOOKS
OVERLORD
OVERLORDS
OVERLOUD
OVERLOVE
OVERLOVED
OVERLOVES
OVERLUSH
OVERLUSTY
OVERLY
OVERLYING
OVERMAN
OVERMANS
OVERMANY
OVERMAST
OVERMASTS
OVERMATCH
OVERMEEK
OVERMELT
OVERMELTS
OVERMEN
OVERMERRY
OVERMILD
OVERMILK
OVERMILKS
OVERMINE
OVERMINED
OVERMINES
OVERMIX
OVERMIXED
OVERMIXES
OVERMOUNT
OVERMUCH
OVERNAME
OVERNAMED
OVERNAMES
OVERNEAR
OVERNEAT
OVERNET
OVERNETS
OVERNEW
OVERNICE
OVERNIGHT
OVERPACK
OVERPACKS
OVERPAGE
OVERPAID
OVERPAINT
OVERPART
OVERPARTS
OVERPASS
OVERPAST
OVERPAY
OVERPAYS
OVERPEDAL
OVERPEER
OVERPEERS
OVERPERCH
OVERPERT
OVERPITCH
OVERPLAID
OVERPLAN
OVERPLANS

O

OVERPLANT
OVERPLAST
OVERPLAY
OVERPLAYS
OVERPLIED
OVERPLIES
OVERPLOT
OVERPLOTS
OVERPLUS
OVERPLY
OVERPOISE
OVERPOST
OVERPOSTS
OVERPOWER
OVERPRESS
OVERPRICE
OVERPRINT
OVERPRIZE
OVERPROOF
OVERPROUD
OVERPUMP
OVERPUMPS
OVERQUICK
OVERRACK
OVERRACKS
OVERRAKE
OVERRAKED
OVERRAKES
OVERRAN
OVERRANK
OVERRANKS
OVERRASH
OVERRATE
OVERRATED
OVERRATES
OVERREACH
OVERREACT
OVERREAD
OVERREADS
OVERRED
OVERREDS
OVERREN
OVERRENS
OVERRICH
OVERRIDE
OVERRIDER
OVERRIDES
OVERRIFE
OVERRIGID
OVERRIPE
OVERRIPEN
OVERROAST
OVERRODE
OVERRUDE
OVERRUFF
OVERRUFFS
OVERRULE
OVERRULED
OVERRULER
OVERRULES
OVERRUN
OVERRUNS
OVERS
OVERSAD
OVERSAIL
OVERSAILS
OVERSALE
OVERSALES
OVERSALT
OVERSALTS
OVERSAUCE
OVERSAVE
OVERSAVED
OVERSAVES
OVERSAW
OVERSCALE
OVERSCORE
OVERSEA
OVERSEAS
OVERSEE
OVERSEED
OVERSEEDS
OVERSEEN
OVERSEER
OVERSEERS
OVERSEES
OVERSELL
OVERSELLS
OVERSET
OVERSETS
OVERSEW
OVERSEWED
OVERSEWN
OVERSEWS
OVERSEXED
OVERSHADE
OVERSHARE
OVERSHARP
OVERSHINE
OVERSHIRT
OVERSHOE
OVERSHOES
OVERSHONE
OVERSHOOT
OVERSHOT
OVERSHOTS
OVERSICK
OVERSIDE
OVERSIDES
OVERSIGHT
OVERSIZE
OVERSIZED
OVERSIZES
OVERSKATE
OVERSKIP
OVERSKIPS
OVERSKIRT
OVERSLEEP
OVERSLEPT
OVERSLIP
OVERSLIPS
OVERSLIPT
OVERSLOW
OVERSMAN
OVERSMEN
OVERSMOKE
OVERSOAK
OVERSOAKS
OVERSOFT
OVERSOLD
OVERSOON
OVERSOUL
OVERSOULS
OVERSOW
OVERSOWED
OVERSOWN
OVERSOWS
OVERSPEND
OVERSPENT
OVERSPICE
OVERSPILL
OVERSPILT
OVERSPIN
OVERSPINS
OVERSTAFF
OVERSTAIN
OVERSTAND
OVERSTANK
OVERSTARE
OVERSTATE
OVERSTAY
OVERSTAYS
OVERSTEER
OVERSTEP
OVERSTEPS
OVERSTINK
OVERSTIR
OVERSTIRS
OVERSTOCK
OVERSTOOD
OVERSTORY
OVERSTREW
OVERSTUDY
OVERSTUFF
OVERSTUNK
OVERSUDS
OVERSUP
OVERSUPS
OVERSURE
OVERSWAM
OVERSWAY
OVERSWAYS
OVERSWEAR
OVERSWEET
OVERSWELL
OVERSWIM
OVERSWIMS
OVERSWING
OVERSWORE
OVERSWORN
OVERSWUM
OVERSWUNG
OVERT
OVERTAKE
OVERTAKEN
OVERTAKES
OVERTALK
OVERTALKS
OVERTAME
OVERTART
OVERTASK
OVERTASKS
OVERTAX
OVERTAXED
OVERTAXES
OVERTEACH
OVERTEEM
OVERTEEMS
OVERTHICK
OVERTHIN
OVERTHINK
OVERTHINS
OVERTHREW
OVERTHROW
OVERTIGHT
OVERTIME
OVERTIMED
OVERTIMER
OVERTIMES
OVERTIMID
OVERTIP
OVERTIPS
OVERTIRE
OVERTIRED
OVERTIRES
OVERTLY
OVERTNESS
OVERTOIL
OVERTOILS
OVERTONE
OVERTONES
OVERTOOK
OVERTOP
OVERTOPS
OVERTOWER
OVERTRADE
OVERTRAIN
OVERTREAT
OVERTRICK
OVERTRIM
OVERTRIMS
OVERTRIP
OVERTRIPS
OVERTRUMP
OVERTRUST
OVERTURE
OVERTURED
OVERTURES
OVERTURN
OVERTURNS

OVERTYPE
OVERTYPED
OVERTYPES
OVERURGE
OVERURGED
OVERURGES
OVERUSE
OVERUSED
OVERUSES
OVERUSING
OVERVALUE
OVERVEIL
OVERVEILS
OVERVIEW
OVERVIEWS
OVERVIVID
OVERVOTE
OVERVOTED
OVERVOTES
OVERWARM
OVERWARMS
OVERWARY
OVERWASH
OVERWATCH
OVERWATER
OVERWEAK
OVERWEAR
OVERWEARS
OVERWEARY
OVERWEEN
OVERWEENS
OVERWEIGH
OVERWENT
OVERWET
OVERWETS
OVERWHELM
OVERWIDE
OVERWILY
OVERWIND
OVERWINDS
OVERWING
OVERWINGS
OVERWISE
OVERWORD
OVERWORDS
OVERWORE
OVERWORK
OVERWORKS
OVERWORN
OVERWOUND
OVERWRAP
OVERWRAPS
OVERWRAPT
OVERWREST
OVERWRITE
OVERWROTE
OVERYEAR
OVERYEARS
OVERZEAL
OVERZEALS
OVIBOS
OVIBOSES
OVIBOVINE
OVICIDAL
OVICIDE
OVICIDES
OVIDUCAL
OVIDUCT
OVIDUCTAL
OVIDUCTS
OVIFEROUS
OVIFORM
OVIGEROUS
OVINE
OVINES
OVIPARA
OVIPARITY
OVIPAROUS
OVIPOSIT
OVIPOSITS
OVIRAPTOR
OVISAC
OVISACS
OVIST
OVISTS
OVOID
OVOIDAL
OVOIDALS
OVOIDS
OVOLI
OVOLO
OVOLOS
OVONIC
OVONICS
OVOTESTES
OVOTESTIS
OVULAR
OVULARY
OVULATE
OVULATED
OVULATES
OVULATING
OVULATION
OVULATORY
OVULE
OVULES
OVUM
OW
OWCHE
OWCHES
OWE
OWED
OWELTIES
OWELTY
OWER
OWERBY
OWERLOUP
OWERLOUPS
OWES
OWIE
OWIES
OWING
OWL
OWLED
OWLER
OWLERIES
OWLERS
OWLERY
OWLET
OWLETS
OWLIER
OWLIEST
OWLING
OWLISH
OWLISHLY
OWLLIKE
OWLS
OWLY
OWN
OWNABLE
OWNED
OWNER
OWNERLESS
OWNERS
OWNERSHIP
OWNING
OWNS
OWNSOME
OWNSOMES
OWRE
OWRECAME
OWRECOME
OWRECOMES
OWRELAY
OWRELAYS
OWRES
OWREWORD
OWREWORDS
OWRIE
OWRIER
OWRIEST
OWSE
OWSEN
OWT
OWTS
OX
OXACILLIN
OXALATE
OXALATED
OXALATES
OXALATING
OXALIC
OXALIS
OXALISES
OXAZEPAM
OXAZEPAMS
OXAZINE
OXAZINES
OXAZOLE
OXAZOLES
OXBLOOD
OXBLOODS
OXBOW
OXBOWS
OXCART
OXCARTS
OXEN
OXER
OXERS
OXES
OXEYE
OXEYES
OXFORD
OXFORDS
OXGANG
OXGANGS
OXGATE
OXGATES
OXHEAD
OXHEADS
OXHEART
OXHEARTS
OXHERD
OXHERDS
OXHIDE
OXHIDES
OXIC
OXID
OXIDABLE
OXIDANT
OXIDANTS
OXIDASE
OXIDASES
OXIDASIC
OXIDATE
OXIDATED
OXIDATES
OXIDATING
OXIDATION
OXIDATIVE
OXIDE
OXIDES
OXIDIC
OXIDISE
OXIDISED
OXIDISER
OXIDISERS
OXIDISES
OXIDISING
OXIDIZE
OXIDIZED
OXIDIZER
OXIDIZERS
OXIDIZES
OXIDIZING
OXIDS
OXIES
OXIM
OXIME
OXIMES

OXIMETER
OXIMETERS
OXIMETRY
OXIMS
OXLAND
OXLANDS
OXLIKE
OXLIP
OXLIPS
OXO
OXONIUM
OXONIUMS
OXPECKER
OXPECKERS
OXSLIP
OXSLIPS
OXTAIL
OXTAILS
OXTER
OXTERED
OXTERING
OXTERS
OXTONGUE
OXTONGUES
OXY
OXYACID
OXYACIDS
OXYANION
OXYANIONS
OXYCODONE
OXYGEN
OXYGENASE
OXYGENATE
OXYGENIC
OXYGENISE
OXYGENIZE
OXYGENOUS
OXYGENS
OXYMEL
OXYMELS
OXYMORA
OXYMORON
OXYMORONS
OXYNTIC
OXYPHIL
OXYPHILE
OXYPHILES
OXYPHILIC
OXYPHILS
OXYSALT
OXYSALTS
OXYSOME
OXYSOMES
OXYTOCIC
OXYTOCICS
OXYTOCIN
OXYTOCINS
OXYTONE
OXYTONES
OXYTONIC
OXYTROPE
OXYTROPES
OY
OYE
OYER
OYERS
OYES
OYESES
OYESSES
OYEZ
OYEZES
OYS
OYSTER
OYSTERED
OYSTERER
OYSTERERS
OYSTERING
OYSTERMAN
OYSTERMEN
OYSTERS
OYSTRIGE
OYSTRIGES
OZAENA
OZAENAS
OZALID
OZALIDS
OZEKI
OZEKIS
OZOCERITE
OZOKERITE
OZONATE
OZONATED
OZONATES
OZONATING
OZONATION
OZONE
OZONES
OZONIC
OZONIDE
OZONIDES
OZONISE
OZONISED
OZONISER
OZONISERS
OZONISES
OZONISING
OZONIZE
OZONIZED
OZONIZER
OZONIZERS
OZONIZES
OZONIZING
OZONOUS
OZZIE
OZZIES

O

P

PA
PAAL
PAALS
PAAN
PAANS
PABLUM
PABLUMS
PABOUCHE
PABOUCHES
PABULAR
PABULOUS
PABULUM
PABULUMS
PAC
PACA
PACABLE
PACAS
PACATION
PACATIONS
PACE
PACED
PACEMAKER
PACEMAN
PACEMEN
PACER
PACERS
PACES
PACEWAY
PACEWAYS
PACEY
PACHA
PACHADOM
PACHADOMS
PACHAK
PACHAKS
PACHALIC
PACHALICS
PACHAS
PACHINKO
PACHINKOS
PACHISI
PACHISIS
PACHOULI
PACHOULIS
PACHUCO
PACHUCOS
PACHYDERM
PACHYTENE
PACIER
PACIEST
PACIFIC
PACIFICAE
PACIFICAL
PACIFIED
PACIFIER
PACIFIERS
PACIFIES
PACIFISM
PACIFISMS
PACIFIST
PACIFISTS
PACIFY
PACIFYING
PACING
PACINGS
PACK
PACKABLE
PACKAGE
PACKAGED
PACKAGER
PACKAGERS
PACKAGES
PACKAGING
PACKBOARD
PACKCLOTH
PACKED
PACKER
PACKERS
PACKET
PACKETED
PACKETING
PACKETISE
PACKETIZE
PACKETS
PACKFONG
PACKFONGS
PACKFRAME
PACKHORSE
PACKING
PACKINGS
PACKLY
PACKMAN
PACKMEN
PACKMULE
PACKMULES
PACKNESS
PACKS
PACKSACK
PACKSACKS
PACKSHEET
PACKSTAFF
PACKWAX
PACKWAXES
PACKWAY
PACKWAYS
PACO
PACOS
PACS
PACT
PACTA
PACTION
PACTIONAL
PACTIONED
PACTIONS
PACTS
PACTUM
PACY
PACZKI
PACZKIS
PAD
PADANG
PADANGS
PADAUK
PADAUKS
PADDED
PADDER
PADDERS
PADDIES
PADDING
PADDINGS
PADDLE
PADDLED
PADDLER
PADDLERS
PADDLES
PADDLING
PADDLINGS
PADDOCK
PADDOCKED
PADDOCKS
PADDY
PADDYWACK
PADELLA
PADELLAS
PADEMELON
PADERERO
PADEREROS
PADI
PADIS
PADISHAH
PADISHAHS
PADKOS
PADLE
PADLES
PADLOCK
PADLOCKED
PADLOCKS
PADMA
PADMAS
PADNAG
PADNAGS
PADOUK
PADOUKS
PADRE
PADRES
PADRI
PADRONA
PADRONAS
PADRONE
PADRONES
PADRONI
PADRONISM
PADS
PADSAW
PADSAWS
PADSHAH
PADSHAHS
PADUASOY
PADUASOYS
PADYMELON
PAEAN
PAEANISM
PAEANISMS
PAEANS
PAEDERAST
PAEDEUTIC
PAEDIATRY
PAEDO
PAEDOLOGY
PAEDOS
PAELLA
PAELLAS
PAENULA
PAENULAE
PAENULAS
PAEON
PAEONIC
PAEONICS
PAEONIES
PAEONS
PAEONY
PAESAN
PAESANI
PAESANO
PAESANOS
PAESANS
PAGAN
PAGANDOM
PAGANDOMS
PAGANISE

P

PAGANISED
PAGANISER
PAGANISES
PAGANISH
PAGANISM
PAGANISMS
PAGANIST
PAGANISTS
PAGANIZE
PAGANIZED
PAGANIZER
PAGANIZES
PAGANS
PAGE
PAGEANT
PAGEANTRY
PAGEANTS
PAGEBOY
PAGEBOYS
PAGED
PAGEFUL
PAGEFULS
PAGEHOOD
PAGEHOODS
PAGER
PAGERS
PAGES
PAGEVIEW
PAGEVIEWS
PAGINAL
PAGINATE
PAGINATED
PAGINATES
PAGING
PAGINGS
PAGLE
PAGLES
PAGOD
PAGODA
PAGODAS
PAGODITE
PAGODITES
PAGODS
PAGRI
PAGRIS
PAGURIAN
PAGURIANS
PAGURID
PAGURIDS
PAH
PAHAUTEA
PAHAUTEAS
PAHLAVI
PAHLAVIS
PAHOEHOE
PAHOEHOES
PAHS
PAID
PAIDEUTIC
PAIDLE
PAIDLES
PAIGLE
PAIGLES
PAIK
PAIKED
PAIKING
PAIKS
PAIL
PAILFUL
PAILFULS
PAILLARD
PAILLARDS
PAILLASSE
PAILLETTE
PAILLON
PAILLONS
PAILS
PAILSFUL
PAIN
PAINCH
PAINCHES
PAINED
PAINFUL
PAINFULLY
PAINIM
PAINIMS
PAINING
PAINLESS
PAINS
PAINT
PAINTABLE
PAINTBALL
PAINTBOX
PAINTED
PAINTER
PAINTERLY
PAINTERS
PAINTIER
PAINTIEST
PAINTING
PAINTINGS
PAINTPOT
PAINTPOTS
PAINTRESS
PAINTS
PAINTURE
PAINTURES
PAINTWORK
PAINTY
PAIOCK
PAIOCKE
PAIOCKES
PAIOCKS
PAIR
PAIRE
PAIRED
PAIRER
PAIRES
PAIREST
PAIRIAL
PAIRIALS
PAIRING
PAIRINGS
PAIRS
PAIRWISE
PAIS
PAISA
PAISAN
PAISANA
PAISANAS
PAISANO
PAISANOS
PAISANS
PAISAS
PAISE
PAISLEY
PAISLEYS
PAITRICK
PAITRICKS
PAJAMA
PAJAMAED
PAJAMAS
PAJOCK
PAJOCKE
PAJOCKES
PAJOCKS
PAK
PAKAHI
PAKAHIS
PAKAPOO
PAKAPOOS
PAKEHA
PAKEHAS
PAKFONG
PAKFONGS
PAKIHI
PAKIHIS
PAKKA
PAKOKO
PAKOKOS
PAKORA
PAKORAS
PAKS
PAKTHONG
PAKTHONGS
PAKTONG
PAKTONGS
PAL
PALABRA
PALABRAS
PALACE
PALACED
PALACES
PALACINKE
PALADIN
PALADINS
PALAEOSOL
PALAESTRA
PALAFITTE
PALAGI
PALAGIS
PALAIS
PALAMA
PALAMAE
PALAMATE
PALAMINO
PALAMINOS
PALAMPORE
PALANKEEN
PALANQUIN
PALAPA
PALAPAS
PALAS
PALASES
PALATABLE
PALATABLY
PALATAL
PALATALLY
PALATALS
PALATE
PALATED
PALATES
PALATIAL
PALATINE
PALATINES
PALATING
PALAVER
PALAVERED
PALAVERER
PALAVERS
PALAY
PALAYS
PALAZZI
PALAZZO
PALAZZOS
PALE
PALEA
PALEAE
PALEAL
PALEATE
PALEBUCK
PALEBUCKS
PALED
PALEFACE
PALEFACES
PALELY
PALEMPORE
PALENESS
PALEOCENE
PALEOCON
PALEOCONS
PALEOGENE
PALEOLITH
PALEOLOGY
PALEOSOL
PALEOSOLS
PALEOZOIC
PALER
PALES
PALEST

PALESTRA
PALESTRAE
PALESTRAL
PALESTRAS
PALET
PALETOT
PALETOTS
PALETS
PALETTE
PALETTES
PALEWAYS
PALEWISE
PALFREY
PALFREYED
PALFREYS
PALI
PALIER
PALIEST
PALIFORM
PALIKAR
PALIKARS
PALILALIA
PALILLOGY
PALIMONY
PALING
PALINGS
PALINKA
PALINKAS
PALINODE
PALINODES
PALINODY
PALINOPIA
PALIS
PALISADE
PALISADED
PALISADES
PALISADO
PALISH
PALKEE
PALKEES
PALKI
PALKIS
PALL
PALLA
PALLADIA
PALLADIC
PALLADIUM
PALLADOUS
PALLAE
PALLAH
PALLAHS
PALLASITE
PALLED
PALLET
PALLETED
PALLETING
PALLETISE
PALLETIZE
PALLETS
PALLETTE
PALLETTES
PALLIA
PALLIAL
PALLIARD
PALLIARDS
PALLIASSE
PALLIATE
PALLIATED
PALLIATES
PALLIATOR
PALLID
PALLIDER
PALLIDEST
PALLIDITY
PALLIDLY
PALLIED
PALLIER
PALLIES
PALLIEST
PALLING
PALLIUM
PALLIUMS
PALLONE
PALLONES
PALLOR
PALLORS
PALLS
PALLY
PALLYING
PALM
PALMAR
PALMARIAN
PALMARY
PALMATE
PALMATED
PALMATELY
PALMATION
PALMBALL
PALMBALLS
PALMED
PALMER
PALMERS
PALMETTE
PALMETTES
PALMETTO
PALMETTOS
PALMFUL
PALMFULS
PALMHOUSE
PALMIE
PALMIER
PALMIERS
PALMIES
PALMIEST
PALMIET
PALMIETS
PALMING
PALMIPED
PALMIPEDE
PALMIPEDS
PALMIST
PALMISTER
PALMISTRY
PALMISTS
PALMITATE
PALMITIC
PALMITIN
PALMITINS
PALMLIKE
PALMPRINT
PALMS
PALMTOP
PALMTOPS
PALMY
PALMYRA
PALMYRAS
PALOLO
PALOLOS
PALOMINO
PALOMINOS
PALOOKA
PALOOKAS
PALOVERDE
PALP
PALPABLE
PALPABLY
PALPAL
PALPATE
PALPATED
PALPATES
PALPATING
PALPATION
PALPATOR
PALPATORS
PALPATORY
PALPEBRA
PALPEBRAE
PALPEBRAL
PALPEBRAS
PALPED
PALPI
PALPING
PALPITANT
PALPITATE
PALPS
PALPUS
PALPUSES
PALS
PALSA
PALSAS
PALSGRAVE
PALSHIP
PALSHIPS
PALSIED
PALSIER
PALSIES
PALSIEST
PALSTAFF
PALSTAFFS
PALSTAVE
PALSTAVES
PALSY
PALSYING
PALSYLIKE
PALTER
PALTERED
PALTERER
PALTERERS
PALTERING
PALTERS
PALTRIER
PALTRIEST
PALTRILY
PALTRY
PALUDAL
PALUDIC
PALUDINAL
PALUDINE
PALUDISM
PALUDISMS
PALUDOSE
PALUDOUS
PALUSTRAL
PALY
PAM
PAMPA
PAMPAS
PAMPASES
PAMPEAN
PAMPEANS
PAMPER
PAMPERED
PAMPERER
PAMPERERS
PAMPERING
PAMPERO
PAMPEROS
PAMPERS
PAMPHLET
PAMPHLETS
PAMPHREY
PAMPHREYS
PAMPOEN
PAMPOENS
PAMPOOTIE
PAMS
PAN
PANACEA
PANACEAN
PANACEAS
PANACHAEA
PANACHE
PANACHES
PANADA
PANADAS
PANAMA
PANAMAS
PANARIES
PANARY
PANATELA

PANATELAS
PANATELLA
PANAX
PANAXES
PANBROIL
PANBROILS
PANCAKE
PANCAKED
PANCAKES
PANCAKING
PANCE
PANCES
PANCETTA
PANCETTAS
PANCHAX
PANCHAXES
PANCHAYAT
PANCHEON
PANCHEONS
PANCHION
PANCHIONS
PANCOSMIC
PANCRATIA
PANCRATIC
PANCREAS
PAND
PANDA
PANDAN
PANDANI
PANDANIS
PANDANS
PANDANUS
PANDAR
PANDARED
PANDARING
PANDARS
PANDAS
PANDATION
PANDECT
PANDECTS
PANDEMIA
PANDEMIAN
PANDEMIAS
PANDEMIC
PANDEMICS
PANDER
PANDERED
PANDERER
PANDERERS
PANDERESS
PANDERING
PANDERISM
PANDERLY
PANDEROUS
PANDERS
PANDIED
PANDIES
PANDIT
PANDITS
PANDOOR
PANDOORS
PANDORA
PANDORAS
PANDORE
PANDORES
PANDOUR
PANDOURS
PANDOWDY
PANDROP
PANDROPS
PANDS
PANDURA
PANDURAS
PANDURATE
PANDY
PANDYING
PANE
PANED
PANEER
PANEERS
PANEGOISM
PANEGYRIC
PANEGYRY
PANEITIES
PANEITY
PANEL
PANELED
PANELESS
PANELING
PANELINGS
PANELISED
PANELIST
PANELISTS
PANELIZED
PANELLED
PANELLING
PANELLIST
PANELS
PANES
PANETELA
PANETELAS
PANETELLA
PANETTONE
PANETTONI
PANFISH
PANFISHED
PANFISHES
PANFORTE
PANFORTES
PANFRIED
PANFRIES
PANFRY
PANFRYING
PANFUL
PANFULS
PANG
PANGA
PANGAMIC
PANGAMIES
PANGAMY
PANGAS
PANGED
PANGEN
PANGENE
PANGENES
PANGENS
PANGING
PANGLESS
PANGOLIN
PANGOLINS
PANGRAM
PANGRAMS
PANGS
PANHANDLE
PANHUMAN
PANIC
PANICALLY
PANICK
PANICKED
PANICKIER
PANICKING
PANICKS
PANICKY
PANICLE
PANICLED
PANICLES
PANICS
PANICUM
PANICUMS
PANIER
PANIERS
PANIM
PANIMS
PANING
PANINI
PANINIS
PANINO
PANISC
PANISCS
PANISK
PANISKS
PANISLAM
PANISLAMS
PANJANDRA
PANKO
PANKOS
PANLIKE
PANLOGISM
PANMICTIC
PANMIXES
PANMIXIA
PANMIXIAS
PANMIXIS
PANNAGE
PANNAGES
PANNE
PANNED
PANNELLED
PANNER
PANNERS
PANNES
PANNI
PANNICK
PANNICKS
PANNICLE
PANNICLES
PANNIER
PANNIERED
PANNIERS
PANNIKEL
PANNIKELL
PANNIKELS
PANNIKIN
PANNIKINS
PANNING
PANNINGS
PANNIST
PANNISTS
PANNOSE
PANNUS
PANNUSES
PANOCHA
PANOCHAS
PANOCHE
PANOCHES
PANOISTIC
PANOPLIED
PANOPLIES
PANOPLY
PANOPTIC
PANORAMA
PANORAMAS
PANORAMIC
PANPIPE
PANPIPES
PANS
PANSEXUAL
PANSIED
PANSIES
PANSOPHIC
PANSOPHY
PANSPERMY
PANSTICK
PANSTICKS
PANSY
PANT
PANTABLE
PANTABLES
PANTAGAMY
PANTALEON
PANTALET
PANTALETS
PANTALON
PANTALONE
PANTALONS
PANTALOON
PANTDRESS
PANTED
PANTER
PANTERS

PANTHEISM
PANTHEIST
PANTHENOL
PANTHEON
PANTHEONS
PANTHER
PANTHERS
PANTIE
PANTIES
PANTIHOSE
PANTILE
PANTILED
PANTILES
PANTILING
PANTINE
PANTINES
PANTING
PANTINGLY
PANTINGS
PANTLEG
PANTLEGS
PANTLER
PANTLERS
PANTO
PANTOFFLE
PANTOFLE
PANTOFLES
PANTOMIME
PANTON
PANTONS
PANTOS
PANTOUFLE
PANTOUM
PANTOUMS
PANTRIES
PANTROPIC
PANTRY
PANTRYMAN
PANTRYMEN
PANTS
PANTSUIT
PANTSUITS
PANTUN
PANTUNS
PANTY
PANTYHOSE
PANZER
PANZERS
PANZOOTIC
PAOLI
PAOLO
PAP
PAPA
PAPABLE
PAPACIES
PAPACY
PAPADAM
PAPADAMS
PAPADOM
PAPADOMS
PAPADUM
PAPADUMS
PAPAIN
PAPAINS
PAPAL
PAPALISE
PAPALISED
PAPALISES
PAPALISM
PAPALISMS
PAPALIST
PAPALISTS
PAPALIZE
PAPALIZED
PAPALIZES
PAPALLY
PAPARAZZI
PAPARAZZO
PAPAS
PAPASAN
PAPASANS
PAPAUMA
PAPAUMAS
PAPAVER
PAPAVERS
PAPAW
PAPAWS
PAPAYA
PAPAYAN
PAPAYAS
PAPE
PAPER
PAPERBACK
PAPERBARK
PAPERBOY
PAPERBOYS
PAPERCLIP
PAPERED
PAPERER
PAPERERS
PAPERGIRL
PAPERIER
PAPERIEST
PAPERING
PAPERINGS
PAPERLESS
PAPERS
PAPERWARE
PAPERWORK
PAPERY
PAPES
PAPETERIE
PAPHIAN
PAPHIANS
PAPILIO
PAPILIOS
PAPILLA
PAPILLAE
PAPILLAR
PAPILLARY
PAPILLATE
PAPILLOMA
PAPILLON
PAPILLONS
PAPILLOSE
PAPILLOTE
PAPILLOUS
PAPILLULE
PAPOOSE
PAPOOSES
PAPPADAM
PAPPADAMS
PAPPADOM
PAPPADOMS
PAPPADUM
PAPPADUMS
PAPPED
PAPPI
PAPPIER
PAPPIES
PAPPIEST
PAPPING
PAPPOOSE
PAPPOOSES
PAPPOSE
PAPPOUS
PAPPUS
PAPPUSES
PAPPY
PAPRICA
PAPRICAS
PAPRIKA
PAPRIKAS
PAPRIKASH
PAPS
PAPULA
PAPULAE
PAPULAR
PAPULAS
PAPULE
PAPULES
PAPULOSE
PAPULOUS
PAPYRAL
PAPYRI
PAPYRIAN
PAPYRINE
PAPYRUS
PAPYRUSES
PAR
PARA
PARABASES
PARABASIS
PARABEMA
PARABEN
PARABENS
PARABLAST
PARABLE
PARABLED
PARABLES
PARABLING
PARABOLA
PARABOLAE
PARABOLAS
PARABOLE
PARABOLES
PARABOLIC
PARABRAKE
PARACHOR
PARACHORS
PARACHUTE
PARACLETE
PARACME
PARACMES
PARACRINE
PARACUSES
PARACUSIS
PARADE
PARADED
PARADER
PARADERS
PARADES
PARADIGM
PARADIGMS
PARADING
PARADISAL
PARADISE
PARADISES
PARADISIC
PARADOR
PARADORES
PARADORS
PARADOS
PARADOSES
PARADOX
PARADOXAL
PARADOXER
PARADOXES
PARADOXY
PARADROP
PARADROPS
PARAE
PARAFFIN
PARAFFINE
PARAFFINS
PARAFFINY
PARAFFLE
PARAFFLES
PARAFLE
PARAFLES
PARAFOIL
PARAFOILS
PARAFORM
PARAFORMS
PARAGE
PARAGES
PARAGLIDE
PARAGOGE
PARAGOGES
PARAGOGIC

PARAGOGUE
PARAGON
PARAGONED
PARAGONS
PARAGRAM
PARAGRAMS
PARAGRAPH
PARAKEET
PARAKEETS
PARAKELIA
PARAKITE
PARAKITES
PARALALIA
PARALEGAL
PARALEXIA
PARALEXIC
PARALLAX
PARALLEL
PARALLELS
PARALOGIA
PARALOGUE
PARALOGY
PARALYSE
PARALYSED
PARALYSER
PARALYSES
PARALYSIS
PARALYTIC
PARALYZE
PARALYZED
PARALYZER
PARALYZES
PARAMATTA
PARAMECIA
PARAMEDIC
PARAMENT
PARAMENTA
PARAMENTS
PARAMESE
PARAMESES
PARAMETER
PARAMO
PARAMORPH
PARAMOS
PARAMOUNT
PARAMOUR
PARAMOURS
PARAMYLUM
PARANETE
PARANETES
PARANG
PARANGS
PARANOEA
PARANOEAS
PARANOEIC
PARANOIA
PARANOIAC
PARANOIAS
PARANOIC
PARANOICS
PARANOID
PARANOIDS
PARANYM
PARANYMPH
PARANYMS
PARAPARA
PARAPARAS
PARAPENTE
PARAPET
PARAPETED
PARAPETS
PARAPH
PARAPHED
PARAPHING
PARAPHS
PARAPODIA
PARAQUAT
PARAQUATS
PARAQUET
PARAQUETS
PARAQUITO
PARARHYME
PARAS
PARASAIL
PARASAILS
PARASANG
PARASANGS
PARASCEVE
PARASHAH
PARASHAHS
PARASHOT
PARASHOTH
PARASITE
PARASITES
PARASITIC
PARASOL
PARASOLED
PARASOLS
PARATAXES
PARATAXIS
PARATHA
PARATHAS
PARATHION
PARATONIC
PARATROOP
PARAVAIL
PARAVANE
PARAVANES
PARAVANT
PARAVANTS
PARAVAUNT
PARAWING
PARAWINGS
PARAXIAL
PARAZOA
PARAZOAN
PARAZOANS
PARAZOON
PARBAKE
PARBAKED
PARBAKES
PARBAKING
PARBOIL
PARBOILED
PARBOILS
PARBREAK
PARBREAKS
PARBUCKLE
PARCEL
PARCELED
PARCELING
PARCELLED
PARCELS
PARCENARY
PARCENER
PARCENERS
PARCH
PARCHED
PARCHEDLY
PARCHEESI
PARCHES
PARCHESI
PARCHESIS
PARCHING
PARCHISI
PARCHISIS
PARCHMENT
PARCIMONY
PARCLOSE
PARCLOSES
PARD
PARDAH
PARDAHS
PARDAL
PARDALE
PARDALES
PARDALIS
PARDALOTE
PARDALS
PARDED
PARDEE
PARDI
PARDIE
PARDINE
PARDNER
PARDNERS
PARDON
PARDONED
PARDONER
PARDONERS
PARDONING
PARDONS
PARDS
PARDY
PARE
PARECIOUS
PARECISM
PARECISMS
PARED
PAREGORIC
PAREIRA
PAREIRAS
PARELLA
PARELLAS
PARELLE
PARELLES
PAREN
PARENESES
PARENESIS
PARENS
PARENT
PARENTAGE
PARENTAL
PARENTED
PARENTING
PARENTS
PAREO
PAREOS
PARER
PARERA
PARERAS
PARERGA
PARERGON
PARERS
PARES
PARESES
PARESIS
PARETIC
PARETICS
PAREU
PAREUS
PAREV
PAREVE
PARFAIT
PARFAITS
PARFLECHE
PARFLESH
PARFOCAL
PARGANA
PARGANAS
PARGASITE
PARGE
PARGED
PARGES
PARGET
PARGETED
PARGETER
PARGETERS
PARGETING
PARGETS
PARGETTED
PARGETTER
PARGING
PARGINGS
PARGO
PARGOES
PARGOS
PARGYLINE
PARHELIA
PARHELIC

PARHELION
PARHYPATE
PARIAH
PARIAHS
PARIAL
PARIALS
PARIAN
PARIANS
PARIES
PARIETAL
PARIETALS
PARIETES
PARING
PARINGS
PARIS
PARISCHAN
PARISES
PARISH
PARISHAD
PARISHADS
PARISHEN
PARISHENS
PARISHES
PARISON
PARISONS
PARITIES
PARITOR
PARITORS
PARITY
PARK
PARKA
PARKADE
PARKADES
PARKAS
PARKED
PARKEE
PARKEES
PARKER
PARKERS
PARKETTE
PARKETTES
PARKI
PARKIE
PARKIER
PARKIES
PARKIEST
PARKIN
PARKING
PARKINGS
PARKINS
PARKIS
PARKISH
PARKLAND
PARKLANDS
PARKLIKE
PARKLY
PARKOUR
PARKOURS
PARKS
PARKWARD
PARKWARDS
PARKWAY
PARKWAYS
PARKY
PARLANCE
PARLANCES
PARLANDO
PARLANTE
PARLAY
PARLAYED
PARLAYING
PARLAYS
PARLE
PARLED
PARLEMENT
PARLES
PARLEY
PARLEYED
PARLEYER
PARLEYERS
PARLEYING
PARLEYS
PARLEYVOO
PARLIES
PARLING
PARLOR
PARLORS
PARLOUR
PARLOURS
PARLOUS
PARLOUSLY
PARLY
PARMA
PARMAS
PARMESAN
PARMESANS
PAROCHIAL
PAROCHIN
PAROCHINE
PAROCHINS
PARODIC
PARODICAL
PARODIED
PARODIES
PARODIST
PARODISTS
PARODOI
PARODOS
PARODY
PARODYING
PAROECISM
PAROEMIA
PAROEMIAC
PAROEMIAL
PAROEMIAS
PAROICOUS
PAROL
PAROLABLE
PAROLE
PAROLED
PAROLEE
PAROLEES
PAROLES
PAROLING
PAROLS
PARONYM
PARONYMIC
PARONYMS
PARONYMY
PAROQUET
PAROQUETS
PARORE
PARORES
PAROSMIA
PAROSMIAS
PAROTIC
PAROTID
PAROTIDES
PAROTIDS
PAROTIS
PAROTISES
PAROTITIC
PAROTITIS
PAROTOID
PAROTOIDS
PAROUS
PAROUSIA
PAROUSIAS
PAROXYSM
PAROXYSMS
PARP
PARPANE
PARPANES
PARPED
PARPEN
PARPEND
PARPENDS
PARPENS
PARPENT
PARPENTS
PARPING
PARPOINT
PARPOINTS
PARPS
PARQUET
PARQUETED
PARQUETRY
PARQUETS
PARR
PARRA
PARRAKEET
PARRAL
PARRALS
PARRAS
PARRED
PARREL
PARRELS
PARRHESIA
PARRICIDE
PARRIDGE
PARRIDGES
PARRIED
PARRIER
PARRIERS
PARRIES
PARRING
PARRITCH
PARROCK
PARROCKED
PARROCKS
PARROKET
PARROKETS
PARROQUET
PARROT
PARROTED
PARROTER
PARROTERS
PARROTIER
PARROTING
PARROTRY
PARROTS
PARROTY
PARRS
PARRY
PARRYING
PARS
PARSABLE
PARSE
PARSEC
PARSECS
PARSED
PARSER
PARSERS
PARSES
PARSIMONY
PARSING
PARSINGS
PARSLEY
PARSLEYED
PARSLEYS
PARSLIED
PARSNEP
PARSNEPS
PARSNIP
PARSNIPS
PARSON
PARSONAGE
PARSONIC
PARSONISH
PARSONS
PART
PARTAKE
PARTAKEN
PARTAKER
PARTAKERS
PARTAKES
PARTAKING
PARTAN
PARTANS
PARTED

PARTER
PARTERRE
PARTERRES
PARTERS
PARTI
PARTIAL
PARTIALLY
PARTIALS
PARTIBLE
PARTICLE
PARTICLES
PARTIED
PARTIER
PARTIERS
PARTIES
PARTIEST
PARTIM
PARTING
PARTINGS
PARTIS
PARTISAN
PARTISANS
PARTITA
PARTITAS
PARTITE
PARTITION
PARTITIVE
PARTITURA
PARTIZAN
PARTIZANS
PARTLET
PARTLETS
PARTLY
PARTNER
PARTNERED
PARTNERS
PARTON
PARTONS
PARTOOK
PARTRIDGE
PARTS
PARTURE
PARTURES
PARTWAY
PARTWORK
PARTWORKS
PARTY
PARTYER

PARTYERS
PARTYGOER
PARTYING
PARTYINGS
PARTYISM
PARTYISMS
PARULIDES
PARULIS
PARULISES
PARURA
PARURAS
PARURE
PARURES
PARURESES
PARURESIS
PARURETIC
PARVE
PARVENU
PARVENUE
PARVENUES
PARVENUS
PARVIS
PARVISE
PARVISES
PARVO
PARVOLIN
PARVOLINE
PARVOLINS
PARVOS
PAS
PASCAL
PASCALS
PASCHAL
PASCHALS
PASCUAL
PASCUALS
PASE
PASEAR
PASEARED
PASEARING
PASEARS
PASELA
PASELAS
PASEO
PASEOS
PASES
PASH
PASHA

PASHADOM
PASHADOMS
PASHALIC
PASHALICS
PASHALIK
PASHALIKS
PASHAS
PASHED
PASHES
PASHIM
PASHIMS
PASHING
PASHKA
PASHKAS
PASHM
PASHMINA
PASHMINAS
PASHMS
PASKA
PASKAS
PASKHA
PASKHAS
PASODOBLE
PASPALUM
PASPALUMS
PASPIES
PASPY
PASQUIL
PASQUILER
PASQUILS
PASS
PASSABLE
PASSABLY
PASSADE
PASSADES
PASSADO
PASSADOES
PASSADOS
PASSAGE
PASSAGED
PASSAGER
PASSAGES
PASSAGING
PASSALONG
PASSAMENT
PASSANT
PASSATA
PASSATAS

PASSBAND
PASSBANDS
PASSBOOK
PASSBOOKS
PASSCODE
PASSCODES
PASSE
PASSED
PASSEE
PASSEL
PASSELS
PASSEMENT
PASSENGER
PASSEPIED
PASSER
PASSERBY
PASSERINE
PASSERS
PASSERSBY
PASSES
PASSIBLE
PASSIBLY
PASSIM
PASSING
PASSINGLY
PASSINGS
PASSION
PASSIONAL
PASSIONED
PASSIONS
PASSIVATE
PASSIVE
PASSIVELY
PASSIVES
PASSIVISM
PASSIVIST
PASSIVITY
PASSKEY
PASSKEYS
PASSLESS
PASSMAN
PASSMEN
PASSMENT
PASSMENTS
PASSOUT
PASSOUTS
PASSOVER
PASSOVERS

PASSPORT
PASSPORTS
PASSUS
PASSUSES
PASSWORD
PASSWORDS
PAST
PASTA
PASTALIKE
PASTANCE
PASTANCES
PASTAS
PASTE
PASTED
PASTEDOWN
PASTEL
PASTELIKE
PASTELIST
PASTELS
PASTER
PASTERN
PASTERNS
PASTERS
PASTES
PASTEUP
PASTEUPS
PASTICCI
PASTICCIO
PASTICHE
PASTICHES
PASTIE
PASTIER
PASTIES
PASTIEST
PASTIL
PASTILLE
PASTILLES
PASTILS
PASTILY
PASTIME
PASTIMES
PASTINA
PASTINAS
PASTINESS
PASTING
PASTINGS
PASTIS
PASTISES

PASTITSIO
PASTITSO
PASTITSOS
PASTLESS
PASTNESS
PASTOR
PASTORAL
PASTORALE
PASTORALI
PASTORALS
PASTORATE
PASTORED
PASTORING
PASTORIUM
PASTORLY
PASTORS
PASTRAMI
PASTRAMIS
PASTRIES
PASTROMI
PASTROMIS
PASTRY
PASTS
PASTURAGE
PASTURAL
PASTURE
PASTURED
PASTURER
PASTURERS
PASTURES
PASTURING
PASTY
PAT
PATACA
PATACAS
PATAGIA
PATAGIAL
PATAGIUM
PATAKA
PATAKAS
PATAMAR
PATAMARS
PATBALL
PATBALLS
PATCH
PATCHABLE
PATCHED
PATCHER
PATCHERS
PATCHERY
PATCHES
PATCHIER
PATCHIEST
PATCHILY
PATCHING
PATCHINGS
PATCHOCKE
PATCHOULI
PATCHOULY
PATCHWORK
PATCHY
PATE
PATED
PATELLA
PATELLAE
PATELLAR
PATELLAS
PATELLATE
PATEN
PATENCIES
PATENCY
PATENS
PATENT
PATENTED
PATENTEE
PATENTEES
PATENTING
PATENTLY
PATENTOR
PATENTORS
PATENTS
PATER
PATERA
PATERAE
PATERCOVE
PATERERO
PATEREROS
PATERNAL
PATERNITY
PATERS
PATES
PATH
PATHED
PATHETIC
PATHETICS
PATHIC
PATHICS
PATHING
PATHLESS
PATHNAME
PATHNAMES
PATHOGEN
PATHOGENE
PATHOGENS
PATHOGENY
PATHOLOGY
PATHOS
PATHOSES
PATHS
PATHWAY
PATHWAYS
PATIBLE
PATIENCE
PATIENCES
PATIENT
PATIENTED
PATIENTER
PATIENTLY
PATIENTS
PATIKI
PATIKIS
PATIN
PATINA
PATINAE
PATINAED
PATINAS
PATINATE
PATINATED
PATINATES
PATINE
PATINED
PATINES
PATINING
PATINISE
PATINISED
PATINISES
PATINIZE
PATINIZED
PATINIZES
PATINS
PATIO
PATIOS
PATISSIER
PATKA
PATKAS
PATLY
PATNESS
PATNESSES
PATOIS
PATONCE
PATOOT
PATOOTIE
PATOOTIES
PATOOTS
PATRIAL
PATRIALS
PATRIARCH
PATRIATE
PATRIATED
PATRIATES
PATRICIAN
PATRICIDE
PATRICK
PATRICKS
PATRICO
PATRICOES
PATRICOS
PATRILINY
PATRIMONY
PATRIOT
PATRIOTIC
PATRIOTS
PATRISTIC
PATROL
PATROLLED
PATROLLER
PATROLMAN
PATROLMEN
PATROLOGY
PATROLS
PATRON
PATRONAGE
PATRONAL
PATRONESS
PATRONISE
PATRONIZE
PATRONLY
PATRONNE
PATRONNES
PATRONS
PATROON
PATROONS
PATS
PATSIES
PATSY
PATTAMAR
PATTAMARS
PATTE
PATTED
PATTEE
PATTEN
PATTENED
PATTENING
PATTENS
PATTER
PATTERED
PATTERER
PATTERERS
PATTERING
PATTERN
PATTERNED
PATTERNS
PATTERS
PATTES
PATTEST
PATTIE
PATTIES
PATTING
PATTLE
PATTLES
PATTRESS
PATTY
PATTYPAN
PATTYPANS
PATU
PATULENT
PATULIN
PATULINS
PATULOUS
PATUS
PATUTUKI
PATUTUKIS
PATY
PATZER
PATZERS
PAUA
PAUAS
PAUCAL
PAUCALS
PAUCITIES

P

PAUCITY
PAUGHTIER
PAUGHTY
PAUL
PAULDRON
PAULDRONS
PAULIN
PAULINS
PAULOWNIA
PAULS
PAUNCE
PAUNCES
PAUNCH
PAUNCHED
PAUNCHES
PAUNCHIER
PAUNCHING
PAUNCHY
PAUPER
PAUPERDOM
PAUPERED
PAUPERESS
PAUPERING
PAUPERISE
PAUPERISM
PAUPERIZE
PAUPERS
PAUPIETTE
PAURAQUE
PAURAQUES
PAUROPOD
PAUROPODS
PAUSAL
PAUSE
PAUSED
PAUSEFUL
PAUSELESS
PAUSER
PAUSERS
PAUSES
PAUSING
PAUSINGLY
PAUSINGS
PAV
PAVAGE
PAVAGES
PAVAN
PAVANE
PAVANES
PAVANS
PAVE
PAVED
PAVEED
PAVEMENT
PAVEMENTS
PAVEN
PAVENS
PAVER
PAVERS
PAVES
PAVID
PAVILION
PAVILIONS
PAVILLON
PAVILLONS
PAVIN
PAVING
PAVINGS
PAVINS
PAVIOR
PAVIORS
PAVIOUR
PAVIOURS
PAVIS
PAVISE
PAVISER
PAVISERS
PAVISES
PAVISSE
PAVISSES
PAVLOVA
PAVLOVAS
PAVONAZZO
PAVONE
PAVONES
PAVONIAN
PAVONINE
PAVS
PAW
PAWA
PAWAS
PAWAW
PAWAWED
PAWAWING
PAWAWS
PAWED
PAWER
PAWERS
PAWING
PAWK
PAWKIER
PAWKIEST
PAWKILY
PAWKINESS
PAWKS
PAWKY
PAWL
PAWLS
PAWN
PAWNABLE
PAWNAGE
PAWNAGES
PAWNCE
PAWNCES
PAWNED
PAWNEE
PAWNEES
PAWNER
PAWNERS
PAWNING
PAWNOR
PAWNORS
PAWNS
PAWNSHOP
PAWNSHOPS
PAWPAW
PAWPAWS
PAWS
PAX
PAXES
PAXIUBA
PAXIUBAS
PAXWAX
PAXWAXES
PAY
PAYABLE
PAYABLES
PAYABLY
PAYBACK
PAYBACKS
PAYCHECK
PAYCHECKS
PAYCHEQUE
PAYDAY
PAYDAYS
PAYDOWN
PAYDOWNS
PAYED
PAYEE
PAYEES
PAYER
PAYERS
PAYESS
PAYFONE
PAYFONES
PAYGRADE
PAYGRADES
PAYING
PAYINGS
PAYLIST
PAYLISTS
PAYLOAD
PAYLOADS
PAYMASTER
PAYMENT
PAYMENTS
PAYNIM
PAYNIMRY
PAYNIMS
PAYOFF
PAYOFFS
PAYOLA
PAYOLAS
PAYOR
PAYORS
PAYOUT
PAYOUTS
PAYPHONE
PAYPHONES
PAYROLL
PAYROLLS
PAYS
PAYSAGE
PAYSAGES
PAYSAGIST
PAYSD
PAYSLIP
PAYSLIPS
PAYWALL
PAYWALLS
PAZAZZ
PAZAZZES
PAZZAZZ
PAZZAZZES
PE
PEA
PEABERRY
PEABRAIN
PEABRAINS
PEACE
PEACEABLE
PEACEABLY
PEACED
PEACEFUL
PEACELESS
PEACENIK
PEACENIKS
PEACES
PEACETIME
PEACH
PEACHBLOW
PEACHED
PEACHER
PEACHERS
PEACHES
PEACHICK
PEACHICKS
PEACHIER
PEACHIEST
PEACHILY
PEACHING
PEACHY
PEACING
PEACOAT
PEACOATS
PEACOCK
PEACOCKED
PEACOCKS
PEACOCKY
PEACOD
PEACODS
PEAFOWL
PEAFOWLS
PEAG
PEAGE
PEAGES
PEAGS
PEAHEN
PEAHENS
PEAK

PEAKED
PEAKIER
PEAKIEST
PEAKINESS
PEAKING
PEAKINGS
PEAKISH
PEAKLESS
PEAKLIKE
PEAKS
PEAKY
PEAL
PEALED
PEALIKE
PEALING
PEALS
PEAN
PEANED
PEANING
PEANS
PEANUT
PEANUTS
PEANUTTY
PEAPOD
PEAPODS
PEAR
PEARCE
PEARCED
PEARCES
PEARCING
PEARE
PEARES
PEARL
PEARLASH
PEARLED
PEARLER
PEARLERS
PEARLIER
PEARLIES
PEARLIEST
PEARLIN
PEARLING
PEARLINGS
PEARLINS
PEARLISED
PEARLITE
PEARLITES
PEARLITIC
PEARLIZED
PEARLS
PEARLWARE
PEARLWORT
PEARLY
PEARMAIN
PEARMAINS
PEARS
PEARST
PEART
PEARTER
PEARTEST
PEARTLY
PEARTNESS
PEARWOOD
PEARWOODS
PEAS
PEASANT
PEASANTRY
PEASANTS
PEASANTY
PEASCOD
PEASCODS
PEASE
PEASECOD
PEASECODS
PEASED
PEASEN
PEASES
PEASING
PEASON
PEASOUPER
PEAT
PEATARIES
PEATARY
PEATERIES
PEATERY
PEATIER
PEATIEST
PEATLAND
PEATLANDS
PEATMAN
PEATMEN
PEATS
PEATSHIP
PEATSHIPS
PEATY
PEAVEY
PEAVEYS
PEAVIES
PEAVY
PEAZE
PEAZED
PEAZES
PEAZING
PEBA
PEBAS
PEBBLE
PEBBLED
PEBBLES
PEBBLIER
PEBBLIEST
PEBBLING
PEBBLINGS
PEBBLY
PEBIBYTE
PEBIBYTES
PEBRINE
PEBRINES
PEC
PECAN
PECANS
PECCABLE
PECCANCY
PECCANT
PECCANTLY
PECCARIES
PECCARY
PECCAVI
PECCAVIS
PECH
PECHAN
PECHANS
PECHED
PECHING
PECHS
PECK
PECKE
PECKED
PECKER
PECKERS
PECKES
PECKIER
PECKIEST
PECKING
PECKINGS
PECKISH
PECKISHLY
PECKS
PECKY
PECORINI
PECORINO
PECORINOS
PECS
PECTASE
PECTASES
PECTATE
PECTATES
PECTEN
PECTENS
PECTIC
PECTIN
PECTINAL
PECTINALS
PECTINATE
PECTINEAL
PECTINEI
PECTINES
PECTINEUS
PECTINOUS
PECTINS
PECTISE
PECTISED
PECTISES
PECTISING
PECTIZE
PECTIZED
PECTIZES
PECTIZING
PECTOLITE
PECTORAL
PECTORALS
PECTOSE
PECTOSES
PECULATE
PECULATED
PECULATES
PECULATOR
PECULIA
PECULIAR
PECULIARS
PECULIUM
PECUNIARY
PECUNIOUS
PED
PEDAGOG
PEDAGOGIC
PEDAGOGS
PEDAGOGUE
PEDAGOGY
PEDAL
PEDALBOAT
PEDALCAR
PEDALCARS
PEDALED
PEDALER
PEDALERS
PEDALFER
PEDALFERS
PEDALIER
PEDALIERS
PEDALING
PEDALLED
PEDALLER
PEDALLERS
PEDALLING
PEDALO
PEDALOES
PEDALOS
PEDALS
PEDANT
PEDANTIC
PEDANTISE
PEDANTISM
PEDANTIZE
PEDANTRY
PEDANTS
PEDATE
PEDATELY
PEDATIFID
PEDDER
PEDDERS
PEDDLE
PEDDLED
PEDDLER
PEDDLERS
PEDDLERY
PEDDLES
PEDDLING
PEDDLINGS
PEDERAST
PEDERASTS

PEDERASTY
PEDERERO
PEDEREROS
PEDES
PEDESES
PEDESIS
PEDESTAL
PEDESTALS
PEDETIC
PEDI
PEDIATRIC
PEDICAB
PEDICABS
PEDICEL
PEDICELS
PEDICLE
PEDICLED
PEDICLES
PEDICULAR
PEDICULI
PEDICULUS
PEDICURE
PEDICURED
PEDICURES
PEDIFORM
PEDIGREE
PEDIGREED
PEDIGREES
PEDIMENT
PEDIMENTS
PEDIPALP
PEDIPALPI
PEDIPALPS
PEDIS
PEDLAR
PEDLARIES
PEDLARS
PEDLARY
PEDLER
PEDLERIES
PEDLERS
PEDLERY
PEDOCAL
PEDOCALIC
PEDOCALS
PEDOGENIC
PEDOLOGIC
PEDOLOGY
PEDOMETER
PEDOPHILE
PEDORTHIC
PEDRAIL
PEDRAILS
PEDRERO
PEDREROES
PEDREROS
PEDRO
PEDROS
PEDS
PEDUNCLE
PEDUNCLED
PEDUNCLES
PEDWAY
PEDWAYS
PEE
PEEBEEN
PEEBEENS
PEECE
PEECES
PEED
PEEING
PEEK
PEEKABO
PEEKABOO
PEEKABOOS
PEEKABOS
PEEKAPOO
PEEKAPOOS
PEEKED
PEEKING
PEEKS
PEEL
PEELABLE
PEELED
PEELER
PEELERS
PEELING
PEELINGS
PEELS
PEEN
PEENED
PEENGE
PEENGED
PEENGEING
PEENGES
PEENGING
PEENING
PEENINGS
PEENS
PEEOY
PEEOYS
PEEP
PEEPBO
PEEPBOS
PEEPE
PEEPED
PEEPER
PEEPERS
PEEPES
PEEPHOLE
PEEPHOLES
PEEPING
PEEPS
PEEPSHOW
PEEPSHOWS
PEEPTOE
PEEPUL
PEEPULS
PEER
PEERAGE
PEERAGES
PEERED
PEERESS
PEERESSES
PEERIE
PEERIER
PEERIES
PEERIEST
PEERING
PEERLESS
PEERS
PEERY
PEES
PEESWEEP
PEESWEEPS
PEETWEET
PEETWEETS
PEEVE
PEEVED
PEEVER
PEEVERS
PEEVES
PEEVING
PEEVISH
PEEVISHLY
PEEWEE
PEEWEES
PEEWIT
PEEWITS
PEG
PEGASUS
PEGASUSES
PEGBOARD
PEGBOARDS
PEGBOX
PEGBOXES
PEGGED
PEGGIER
PEGGIES
PEGGIEST
PEGGING
PEGGINGS
PEGGY
PEGH
PEGHED
PEGHING
PEGHS
PEGLEGGED
PEGLESS
PEGLIKE
PEGMATITE
PEGS
PEGTOP
PEGTOPS
PEH
PEHS
PEIGNOIR
PEIGNOIRS
PEIN
PEINCT
PEINCTED
PEINCTING
PEINCTS
PEINED
PEINING
PEINS
PEIRASTIC
PEISE
PEISED
PEISES
PEISHWA
PEISHWAH
PEISHWAHS
PEISHWAS
PEISING
PEIZE
PEIZED
PEIZES
PEIZING
PEJORATE
PEJORATED
PEJORATES
PEKAN
PEKANS
PEKE
PEKEPOO
PEKEPOOS
PEKES
PEKIN
PEKINS
PEKOE
PEKOES
PEL
PELA
PELAGE
PELAGES
PELAGIAL
PELAGIALS
PELAGIAN
PELAGIANS
PELAGIC
PELAGICS
PELAS
PELAU
PELAUS
PELE
PELECYPOD
PELERINE
PELERINES
PELES
PELF
PELFS
PELHAM
PELHAMS
PELICAN
PELICANS
PELISSE
PELISSES
PELITE
PELITES

PELITIC
PELL
PELLACH
PELLACHS
PELLACK
PELLACKS
PELLAGRA
PELLAGRAS
PELLAGRIN
PELLED
PELLET
PELLETAL
PELLETED
PELLETIFY
PELLETING
PELLETISE
PELLETIZE
PELLETS
PELLICLE
PELLICLES
PELLING
PELLITORY
PELLMELL
PELLMELLS
PELLOCK
PELLOCKS
PELLS
PELLUCID
PELLUM
PELLUMS
PELMA
PELMANISM
PELMAS
PELMATIC
PELMET
PELMETS
PELOID
PELOIDS
PELOLOGY
PELON
PELONS
PELORIA
PELORIAN
PELORIAS
PELORIC
PELORIES
PELORISED
PELORISM
PELORISMS
PELORIZED
PELORUS
PELORUSES
PELORY
PELOTA
PELOTAS
PELOTON
PELOTONS
PELS
PELT
PELTA
PELTAE
PELTAS
PELTAST
PELTASTS
PELTATE
PELTATELY
PELTATION
PELTED
PELTER
PELTERED
PELTERING
PELTERS
PELTING
PELTINGLY
PELTINGS
PELTLESS
PELTRIES
PELTRY
PELTS
PELVES
PELVIC
PELVICS
PELVIFORM
PELVIS
PELVISES
PEMBINA
PEMBINAS
PEMBROKE
PEMBROKES
PEMICAN
PEMICANS
PEMMICAN
PEMMICANS
PEMOLINE
PEMOLINES
PEMPHIGI
PEMPHIGUS
PEMPHIX
PEMPHIXES
PEN
PENAL
PENALISE
PENALISED
PENALISES
PENALITY
PENALIZE
PENALIZED
PENALIZES
PENALLY
PENALTIES
PENALTY
PENANCE
PENANCED
PENANCES
PENANCING
PENANG
PENANGS
PENATES
PENCE
PENCEL
PENCELS
PENCES
PENCHANT
PENCHANTS
PENCIL
PENCILED
PENCILER
PENCILERS
PENCILING
PENCILLED
PENCILLER
PENCILS
PENCRAFT
PENCRAFTS
PEND
PENDANT
PENDANTLY
PENDANTS
PENDED
PENDENCY
PENDENT
PENDENTLY
PENDENTS
PENDICLE
PENDICLER
PENDICLES
PENDING
PENDRAGON
PENDS
PENDU
PENDULAR
PENDULATE
PENDULE
PENDULES
PENDULINE
PENDULOUS
PENDULUM
PENDULUMS
PENE
PENED
PENEPLAIN
PENEPLANE
PENES
PENETRANT
PENETRATE
PENFOLD
PENFOLDS
PENFRIEND
PENFUL
PENFULS
PENGO
PENGOS
PENGUIN
PENGUINRY
PENGUINS
PENHOLDER
PENI
PENIAL
PENICIL
PENICILLI
PENICILS
PENIE
PENIES
PENILE
PENILL
PENILLION
PENING
PENINSULA
PENIS
PENISES
PENISTONE
PENITENCE
PENITENCY
PENITENT
PENITENTS
PENK
PENKNIFE
PENKNIVES
PENKS
PENLIGHT
PENLIGHTS
PENLIKE
PENLITE
PENLITES
PENMAN
PENMEN
PENNA
PENNAE
PENNAL
PENNALISM
PENNALS
PENNAME
PENNAMES
PENNANT
PENNANTS
PENNATE
PENNATED
PENNATULA
PENNE
PENNED
PENNEECH
PENNEECHS
PENNEECK
PENNEECKS
PENNER
PENNERS
PENNES
PENNI
PENNIA
PENNIED
PENNIES
PENNIFORM
PENNILESS
PENNILL
PENNINE
PENNINES
PENNING
PENNINITE
PENNIS
PENNON

P

PENNONCEL
PENNONED
PENNONS
PENNY
PENNYBOY
PENNYBOYS
PENNYFEE
PENNYFEES
PENNYLAND
PENNYWISE
PENNYWORT
PENOCHE
PENOCHES
PENOLOGY
PENONCEL
PENONCELS
PENPOINT
PENPOINTS
PENPUSHER
PENS
PENSEE
PENSEES
PENSEL
PENSELS
PENSEROSO
PENSIL
PENSILE
PENSILITY
PENSILS
PENSION
PENSIONE
PENSIONED
PENSIONER
PENSIONES
PENSIONI
PENSIONS
PENSIVE
PENSIVELY
PENSTEMON
PENSTER
PENSTERS
PENSTOCK
PENSTOCKS
PENSUM
PENSUMS
PENT
PENTACLE
PENTACLES
PENTACT
PENTACTS
PENTAD
PENTADIC
PENTADS
PENTAGON
PENTAGONS
PENTAGRAM
PENTALOGY
PENTALPHA
PENTAMERY
PENTANE
PENTANES
PENTANGLE
PENTANOIC
PENTANOL
PENTANOLS
PENTAPODY
PENTARCH
PENTARCHS
PENTARCHY
PENTATHLA
PENTEL
PENTELS
PENTENE
PENTENES
PENTHIA
PENTHIAS
PENTHOUSE
PENTICE
PENTICED
PENTICES
PENTICING
PENTISE
PENTISED
PENTISES
PENTISING
PENTITI
PENTITO
PENTODE
PENTODES
PENTOMIC
PENTOSAN
PENTOSANE
PENTOSANS
PENTOSE
PENTOSES
PENTOSIDE
PENTOXIDE
PENTROOF
PENTROOFS
PENTS
PENTYL
PENTYLENE
PENTYLS
PENUCHE
PENUCHES
PENUCHI
PENUCHIS
PENUCHLE
PENUCHLES
PENUCKLE
PENUCKLES
PENULT
PENULTIMA
PENULTS
PENUMBRA
PENUMBRAE
PENUMBRAL
PENUMBRAS
PENURIES
PENURIOUS
PENURY
PENWIPER
PENWIPERS
PENWOMAN
PENWOMEN
PEON
PEONAGE
PEONAGES
PEONES
PEONIES
PEONISM
PEONISMS
PEONS
PEONY
PEOPLE
PEOPLED
PEOPLER
PEOPLERS
PEOPLES
PEOPLING
PEP
PEPERINO
PEPERINOS
PEPEROMIA
PEPERONI
PEPERONIS
PEPFUL
PEPINO
PEPINOS
PEPITA
PEPITAS
PEPLA
PEPLOS
PEPLOSES
PEPLUM
PEPLUMED
PEPLUMS
PEPLUS
PEPLUSES
PEPO
PEPONIDA
PEPONIDAS
PEPONIUM
PEPONIUMS
PEPOS
PEPPED
PEPPER
PEPPERBOX
PEPPERED
PEPPERER
PEPPERERS
PEPPERIER
PEPPERING
PEPPERONI
PEPPERS
PEPPERY
PEPPIER
PEPPIEST
PEPPILY
PEPPINESS
PEPPING
PEPPY
PEPS
PEPSI
PEPSIN
PEPSINATE
PEPSINE
PEPSINES
PEPSINS
PEPSIS
PEPTALK
PEPTALKED
PEPTALKS
PEPTIC
PEPTICITY
PEPTICS
PEPTID
PEPTIDASE
PEPTIDE
PEPTIDES
PEPTIDIC
PEPTIDS
PEPTISE
PEPTISED
PEPTISER
PEPTISERS
PEPTISES
PEPTISING
PEPTIZE
PEPTIZED
PEPTIZER
PEPTIZERS
PEPTIZES
PEPTIZING
PEPTONE
PEPTONES
PEPTONIC
PEPTONISE
PEPTONIZE
PEQUISTE
PEQUISTES
PER
PERACID
PERACIDS
PERACUTE
PERAEA
PERAEON
PERAEONS
PERAEOPOD
PERAI
PERAIS
PERBORATE
PERBORIC
PERC
PERCALE
PERCALES
PERCALINE
PERCASE
PERCE
PERCEABLE

P

PERCEANT
PERCED
PERCEIVE
PERCEIVED
PERCEIVER
PERCEIVES
PERCEN
PERCENT
PERCENTAL
PERCENTS
PERCEPT
PERCEPTS
PERCES
PERCH
PERCHANCE
PERCHED
PERCHER
PERCHERON
PERCHERS
PERCHERY
PERCHES
PERCHING
PERCHINGS
PERCID
PERCIDS
PERCIFORM
PERCINE
PERCINES
PERCING
PERCOCT
PERCOCTED
PERCOCTS
PERCOID
PERCOIDS
PERCOLATE
PERCOLIN
PERCOLINS
PERCS
PERCUSS
PERCUSSED
PERCUSSES
PERCUSSOR
PERDENDO
PERDIE
PERDITION
PERDU
PERDUE
PERDUES
PERDURE
PERDURED
PERDURES
PERDURING
PERDUS
PERDY
PERE
PEREA
PEREGAL
PEREGALS
PEREGRIN
PEREGRINE
PEREGRINS
PEREIA
PEREION
PEREIONS
PEREIOPOD
PEREIRA
PEREIRAS
PERENNATE
PERENNIAL
PERENNITY
PERENTIE
PERENTIES
PERENTY
PEREON
PEREONS
PEREOPOD
PEREOPODS
PERES
PERFAY
PERFECT
PERFECTA
PERFECTAS
PERFECTED
PERFECTER
PERFECTI
PERFECTLY
PERFECTO
PERFECTOR
PERFECTOS
PERFECTS
PERFERVID
PERFERVOR
PERFET
PERFIDIES
PERFIDY
PERFIN
PERFING
PERFINGS
PERFINS
PERFORANS
PERFORANT
PERFORATE
PERFORCE
PERFORM
PERFORMED
PERFORMER
PERFORMS
PERFUME
PERFUMED
PERFUMER
PERFUMERS
PERFUMERY
PERFUMES
PERFUMIER
PERFUMING
PERFUMY
PERFUSATE
PERFUSE
PERFUSED
PERFUSES
PERFUSING
PERFUSION
PERFUSIVE
PERGOLA
PERGOLAS
PERGUNNAH
PERHAPS
PERHAPSES
PERI
PERIAGUA
PERIAGUAS
PERIAKTOI
PERIAKTOS
PERIANTH
PERIANTHS
PERIAPSES
PERIAPSIS
PERIAPT
PERIAPTS
PERIBLAST
PERIBLEM
PERIBLEMS
PERIBOLI
PERIBOLOI
PERIBOLOS
PERIBOLUS
PERICARP
PERICARPS
PERICLASE
PERICLINE
PERICON
PERICONES
PERICOPAE
PERICOPAL
PERICOPE
PERICOPES
PERICOPIC
PERICYCLE
PERIDERM
PERIDERMS
PERIDIA
PERIDIAL
PERIDINIA
PERIDIUM
PERIDIUMS
PERIDOT
PERIDOTE
PERIDOTES
PERIDOTIC
PERIDOTS
PERIDROME
PERIGEAL
PERIGEAN
PERIGEE
PERIGEES
PERIGON
PERIGONE
PERIGONES
PERIGONIA
PERIGONS
PERIGYNY
PERIHELIA
PERIKARYA
PERIL
PERILED
PERILING
PERILLA
PERILLAS
PERILLED
PERILLING
PERILOUS
PERILS
PERILUNE
PERILUNES
PERILYMPH
PERIMETER
PERIMETRY
PERIMORPH
PERIMYSIA
PERINAEUM
PERINATAL
PERINEA
PERINEAL
PERINEUM
PERINEUMS
PERIOD
PERIODATE
PERIODED
PERIODIC
PERIODID
PERIODIDE
PERIODIDS
PERIODING
PERIODISE
PERIODIZE
PERIODS
PERIOST
PERIOSTEA
PERIOSTS
PERIOTIC
PERIOTICS
PERIPATUS
PERIPETIA
PERIPETY
PERIPHERY
PERIPLASM
PERIPLAST
PERIPLUS
PERIPROCT
PERIPTER
PERIPTERS
PERIPTERY
PERIQUE
PERIQUES
PERIS
PERISARC
PERISARCS
PERISCIAN
PERISCOPE
PERISH

P

PERISHED
PERISHER
PERISHERS
PERISHES
PERISHING
PERISPERM
PERISTOME
PERISTYLE
PERITI
PERITONEA
PERITRACK
PERITRICH
PERITUS
PERIWIG
PERIWIGS
PERJINK
PERJURE
PERJURED
PERJURER
PERJURERS
PERJURES
PERJURIES
PERJURING
PERJUROUS
PERJURY
PERK
PERKED
PERKIER
PERKIEST
PERKILY
PERKIN
PERKINESS
PERKING
PERKINS
PERKISH
PERKS
PERKY
PERLEMOEN
PERLITE
PERLITES
PERLITIC
PERLOUS
PERM
PERMABEAR
PERMABULL
PERMALINK
PERMALLOY
PERMANENT
PERMATAN
PERMATANS
PERMEABLE
PERMEABLY
PERMEANCE
PERMEANT
PERMEANTS
PERMEASE
PERMEASES
PERMEATE
PERMEATED
PERMEATES
PERMEATOR
PERMED
PERMIAN
PERMIE
PERMIES
PERMING
PERMIT
PERMITS
PERMITTED
PERMITTEE
PERMITTER
PERMS
PERMUTATE
PERMUTE
PERMUTED
PERMUTES
PERMUTING
PERN
PERNANCY
PERNED
PERNING
PERNIO
PERNIONES
PERNOD
PERNODS
PERNS
PEROG
PEROGEN
PEROGI
PEROGIE
PEROGIES
PEROGIS
PEROGS
PEROGY
PERONE
PERONEAL
PERONEI
PERONES
PERONEUS
PERORAL
PERORALLY
PERORATE
PERORATED
PERORATES
PERORATOR
PEROVSKIA
PEROXID
PEROXIDE
PEROXIDED
PEROXIDES
PEROXIDIC
PEROXIDS
PEROXO
PEROXY
PERP
PERPEND
PERPENDED
PERPENDS
PERPENT
PERPENTS
PERPETUAL
PERPLEX
PERPLEXED
PERPLEXER
PERPLEXES
PERPS
PERRADIAL
PERRADII
PERRADIUS
PERRIER
PERRIERS
PERRIES
PERRON
PERRONS
PERRUQUE
PERRUQUES
PERRY
PERSALT
PERSALTS
PERSANT
PERSAUNT
PERSE
PERSECUTE
PERSEITY
PERSELINE
PERSES
PERSEVERE
PERSICO
PERSICOS
PERSICOT
PERSICOTS
PERSIENNE
PERSIMMON
PERSING
PERSIST
PERSISTED
PERSISTER
PERSISTS
PERSON
PERSONA
PERSONAE
PERSONAGE
PERSONAL
PERSONALS
PERSONAS
PERSONATE
PERSONIFY
PERSONISE
PERSONIZE
PERSONNED
PERSONNEL
PERSONS
PERSPEX
PERSPEXES
PERSPIRE
PERSPIRED
PERSPIRES
PERSPIRY
PERST
PERSUADE
PERSUADED
PERSUADER
PERSUADES
PERSUE
PERSUED
PERSUES
PERSUING
PERSWADE
PERSWADED
PERSWADES
PERT
PERTAIN
PERTAINED
PERTAINS
PERTAKE
PERTAKEN
PERTAKES
PERTAKING
PERTER
PERTEST
PERTHITE
PERTHITES
PERTHITIC
PERTINENT
PERTLY
PERTNESS
PERTOOK
PERTS
PERTURB
PERTURBED
PERTURBER
PERTURBS
PERTUSATE
PERTUSE
PERTUSED
PERTUSION
PERTUSSAL
PERTUSSES
PERTUSSIS
PERUKE
PERUKED
PERUKES
PERUSABLE
PERUSAL
PERUSALS
PERUSE
PERUSED
PERUSER
PERUSERS
PERUSES
PERUSING
PERV
PERVADE
PERVADED
PERVADER
PERVADERS
PERVADES
PERVADING
PERVASION
PERVASIVE

P

PERVE
PERVED
PERVERSE
PERVERSER
PERVERT
PERVERTED
PERVERTER
PERVERTS
PERVES
PERVIATE
PERVIATED
PERVIATES
PERVICACY
PERVIER
PERVIEST
PERVING
PERVIOUS
PERVO
PERVOS
PERVS
PERVY
PES
PESADE
PESADES
PESANT
PESANTE
PESANTS
PESAUNT
PESAUNTS
PESETA
PESETAS
PESEWA
PESEWAS
PESHMERGA
PESHWA
PESHWAS
PESKIER
PESKIEST
PESKILY
PESKINESS
PESKY
PESO
PESOS
PESSARIES
PESSARY
PESSIMA
PESSIMAL
PESSIMISM
PESSIMIST
PESSIMUM
PEST
PESTER
PESTERED
PESTERER
PESTERERS
PESTERING
PESTEROUS
PESTERS
PESTFUL
PESTHOLE
PESTHOLES
PESTHOUSE
PESTICIDE
PESTIER
PESTIEST
PESTILENT
PESTLE
PESTLED
PESTLES
PESTLING
PESTO
PESTOLOGY
PESTOS
PESTS
PESTY
PET
PETABYTE
PETABYTES
PETAFLOP
PETAFLOPS
PETAHERTZ
PETAL
PETALED
PETALINE
PETALISM
PETALISMS
PETALLED
PETALLIKE
PETALODIC
PETALODY
PETALOID
PETALOUS
PETALS
PETAMETER
PETAMETRE
PETANQUE
PETANQUES
PETAR
PETARA
PETARAS
PETARD
PETARDS
PETARIES
PETARS
PETARY
PETASOS
PETASOSES
PETASUS
PETASUSES
PETAURINE
PETAURIST
PETCHARY
PETCOCK
PETCOCKS
PETECHIA
PETECHIAE
PETECHIAL
PETER
PETERED
PETERING
PETERMAN
PETERMEN
PETERS
PETERSHAM
PETHER
PETHERS
PETHIDINE
PETILLANT
PETIOLAR
PETIOLATE
PETIOLE
PETIOLED
PETIOLES
PETIOLULE
PETIT
PETITE
PETITES
PETITIO
PETITION
PETITIONS
PETITIOS
PETITORY
PETNAP
PETNAPER
PETNAPERS
PETNAPING
PETNAPPED
PETNAPPER
PETNAPS
PETRALE
PETRALES
PETRARIES
PETRARY
PETRE
PETREL
PETRELS
PETRES
PETRI
PETRICHOR
PETRIFIC
PETRIFIED
PETRIFIER
PETRIFIES
PETRIFY
PETROGENY
PETROGRAM
PETROL
PETROLAGE
PETROLEUM
PETROLEUR
PETROLIC
PETROLLED
PETROLOGY
PETROLS
PETRONEL
PETRONELS
PETROSAL
PETROSALS
PETROUS
PETS
PETSAI
PETSAIS
PETTABLE
PETTED
PETTEDLY
PETTER
PETTERS
PETTI
PETTICOAT
PETTIER
PETTIES
PETTIEST
PETTIFOG
PETTIFOGS
PETTILY
PETTINESS
PETTING
PETTINGS
PETTIS
PETTISH
PETTISHLY
PETTITOES
PETTLE
PETTLED
PETTLES
PETTLING
PETTO
PETTY
PETULANCE
PETULANCY
PETULANT
PETUNIA
PETUNIAS
PETUNTSE
PETUNTSES
PETUNTZE
PETUNTZES
PEW
PEWEE
PEWEES
PEWHOLDER
PEWIT
PEWITS
PEWS
PEWTER
PEWTERER
PEWTERERS
PEWTERIER
PEWTERS
PEWTERY
PEYOTE
PEYOTES
PEYOTISM
PEYOTISMS
PEYOTIST
PEYOTISTS
PEYOTL
PEYOTLS
PEYSE
PEYSED

P

PEYSES
PEYSING
PEYTRAL
PEYTRALS
PEYTREL
PEYTRELS
PEZANT
PEZANTS
PEZIZOID
PFENNIG
PFENNIGE
PFENNIGS
PFENNING
PFENNINGS
PFFT
PFUI
PHABLET
PHABLETS
PHACELIA
PHACELIAS
PHACOID
PHACOIDAL
PHACOLITE
PHACOLITH
PHAEIC
PHAEISM
PHAEISMS
PHAENOGAM
PHAETON
PHAETONS
PHAGE
PHAGEDENA
PHAGES
PHAGOCYTE
PHAGOSOME
PHALANGAL
PHALANGE
PHALANGER
PHALANGES
PHALANGID
PHALANX
PHALANXES
PHALAROPE
PHALLI
PHALLIC
PHALLIN
PHALLINS
PHALLISM
PHALLISMS
PHALLIST
PHALLISTS
PHALLOID
PHALLUS
PHALLUSES
PHANG
PHANGED
PHANGING
PHANGS
PHANSIGAR
PHANTASIM
PHANTASM
PHANTASMA
PHANTASMS
PHANTAST
PHANTASTS
PHANTASY
PHANTOM
PHANTOMS
PHANTOMY
PHANTOSME
PHARAOH
PHARAOHS
PHARAONIC
PHARE
PHARES
PHARISAIC
PHARISEE
PHARISEES
PHARM
PHARMA
PHARMACY
PHARMAS
PHARMED
PHARMER
PHARMERS
PHARMING
PHARMINGS
PHARMS
PHAROS
PHAROSES
PHARYNGAL
PHARYNGES
PHARYNX
PHARYNXES
PHASE
PHASEAL
PHASED
PHASEDOWN
PHASELESS
PHASEOLIN
PHASEOUT
PHASEOUTS
PHASER
PHASERS
PHASES
PHASIC
PHASING
PHASINGS
PHASIS
PHASMID
PHASMIDS
PHASOR
PHASORS
PHAT
PHATIC
PHATTER
PHATTEST
PHEASANT
PHEASANTS
PHEAZAR
PHEAZARS
PHEER
PHEERE
PHEERES
PHEERS
PHEESE
PHEESED
PHEESES
PHEESING
PHEEZE
PHEEZED
PHEEZES
PHEEZING
PHELLEM
PHELLEMS
PHELLOGEN
PHELLOID
PHELONIA
PHELONION
PHENACITE
PHENAKISM
PHENAKITE
PHENATE
PHENATES
PHENAZIN
PHENAZINE
PHENAZINS
PHENE
PHENES
PHENETIC
PHENETICS
PHENETOL
PHENETOLE
PHENETOLS
PHENGITE
PHENGITES
PHENIC
PHENIX
PHENIXES
PHENOBARB
PHENOCOPY
PHENOGAM
PHENOGAMS
PHENOL
PHENOLATE
PHENOLIC
PHENOLICS
PHENOLOGY
PHENOLS
PHENOM
PHENOME
PHENOMENA
PHENOMES
PHENOMS
PHENOTYPE
PHENOXIDE
PHENOXY
PHENYL
PHENYLENE
PHENYLIC
PHENYLS
PHENYTOIN
PHEON
PHEONS
PHERESES
PHERESIS
PHEROMONE
PHESE
PHESED
PHESES
PHESING
PHEW
PHI
PHIAL
PHIALLED
PHIALLING
PHIALS
PHILABEG
PHILABEGS
PHILAMOT
PHILAMOTS
PHILANDER
PHILATELY
PHILAVERY
PHILHORSE
PHILIBEG
PHILIBEGS
PHILIPPIC
PHILISTIA
PHILLABEG
PHILLIBEG
PHILOGYNY
PHILOLOGY
PHILOMATH
PHILOMEL
PHILOMELA
PHILOMELS
PHILOMOT
PHILOMOTS
PHILOPENA
PHILTER
PHILTERED
PHILTERS
PHILTRA
PHILTRE
PHILTRED
PHILTRES
PHILTRING
PHILTRUM
PHIMOSES
PHIMOSIS
PHIMOTIC
PHINNOCK
PHINNOCKS
PHIS
PHISH
PHISHED
PHISHER
PHISHERS
PHISHES

PHISHING
PHISHINGS
PHISNOMY
PHIZ
PHIZES
PHIZOG
PHIZOGS
PHIZZ
PHIZZES
PHLEBITIC
PHLEBITIS
PHLEGM
PHLEGMIER
PHLEGMON
PHLEGMONS
PHLEGMS
PHLEGMY
PHLOEM
PHLOEMS
PHLOMIS
PHLOMISES
PHLORIZIN
PHLOX
PHLOXES
PHLYCTENA
PHO
PHOBIA
PHOBIAS
PHOBIC
PHOBICS
PHOBISM
PHOBISMS
PHOBIST
PHOBISTS
PHOCA
PHOCAE
PHOCAS
PHOCINE
PHOCOMELY
PHOEBE
PHOEBES
PHOEBUS
PHOEBUSES
PHOENIX
PHOENIXES
PHOH
PHOLADES
PHOLAS
PHON
PHONAL
PHONATE
PHONATED
PHONATES
PHONATHON
PHONATING
PHONATION
PHONATORY
PHONE
PHONECAM
PHONECAMS
PHONECARD
PHONED
PHONEME
PHONEMES
PHONEMIC
PHONEMICS
PHONER
PHONERS
PHONES
PHONETIC
PHONETICS
PHONETISE
PHONETISM
PHONETIST
PHONETIZE
PHONEY
PHONEYED
PHONEYING
PHONEYS
PHONIC
PHONICS
PHONIED
PHONIER
PHONIES
PHONIEST
PHONILY
PHONINESS
PHONING
PHONMETER
PHONO
PHONOGRAM
PHONOLITE
PHONOLOGY
PHONON
PHONONS
PHONOPORE
PHONOS
PHONOTYPE
PHONOTYPY
PHONS
PHONY
PHONYING
PHOOEY
PHORATE
PHORATES
PHORESIES
PHORESY
PHORETIC
PHORMINX
PHORMIUM
PHORMIUMS
PHORONID
PHORONIDS
PHOS
PHOSGENE
PHOSGENES
PHOSPHATE
PHOSPHENE
PHOSPHID
PHOSPHIDE
PHOSPHIDS
PHOSPHIN
PHOSPHINE
PHOSPHINS
PHOSPHITE
PHOSPHOR
PHOSPHORE
PHOSPHORI
PHOSPHORS
PHOSSY
PHOT
PHOTIC
PHOTICS
PHOTINIA
PHOTINIAS
PHOTINO
PHOTINOS
PHOTISM
PHOTISMS
PHOTO
PHOTOBLOG
PHOTOBOMB
PHOTOCALL
PHOTOCARD
PHOTOCELL
PHOTOCOPY
PHOTODISK
PHOTOED
PHOTOFIT
PHOTOFITS
PHOTOG
PHOTOGEN
PHOTOGENE
PHOTOGENS
PHOTOGENY
PHOTOGRAM
PHOTOGS
PHOTOING
PHOTOLYSE
PHOTOLYZE
PHOTOMAP
PHOTOMAPS
PHOTOMASK
PHOTON
PHOTONIC
PHOTONICS
PHOTONS
PHOTOPHIL
PHOTOPIA
PHOTOPIAS
PHOTOPIC
PHOTOPLAY
PHOTOPSIA
PHOTOPSY
PHOTOS
PHOTOSCAN
PHOTOSET
PHOTOSETS
PHOTOSHOP
PHOTOSTAT
PHOTOTAXY
PHOTOTUBE
PHOTOTYPE
PHOTOTYPY
PHOTS
PHPHT
PHRASAL
PHRASALLY
PHRASE
PHRASED
PHRASEMAN
PHRASEMEN
PHRASER
PHRASERS
PHRASES
PHRASIER
PHRASIEST
PHRASING
PHRASINGS
PHRASY
PHRATRAL
PHRATRIC
PHRATRIES
PHRATRY
PHREAK
PHREAKED
PHREAKER
PHREAKERS
PHREAKING
PHREAKS
PHREATIC
PHRENESES
PHRENESIS
PHRENETIC
PHRENIC
PHRENICS
PHRENISM
PHRENISMS
PHRENITIC
PHRENITIS
PHRENSIED
PHRENSIES
PHRENSY
PHRENTICK
PHRYGANA
PHRYGANAS
PHT
PHTHALATE
PHTHALEIN
PHTHALIC
PHTHALIN
PHTHALINS
PHTHISES
PHTHISIC
PHTHISICS
PHTHISIS
PHUT
PHUTS
PHUTTED
PHUTTING

P

PHWOAH
PHWOAR
PHYCOCYAN
PHYCOLOGY
PHYLA
PHYLACTIC
PHYLAE
PHYLAR
PHYLARCH
PHYLARCHS
PHYLARCHY
PHYLAXIS
PHYLE
PHYLESES
PHYLESIS
PHYLETIC
PHYLETICS
PHYLIC
PHYLLARY
PHYLLID
PHYLLIDS
PHYLLITE
PHYLLITES
PHYLLITIC
PHYLLO
PHYLLODE
PHYLLODES
PHYLLODIA
PHYLLODY
PHYLLOID
PHYLLOIDS
PHYLLOME
PHYLLOMES
PHYLLOMIC
PHYLLOPOD
PHYLLOS
PHYLOGENY
PHYLON
PHYLUM
PHYSALIA
PHYSALIAS
PHYSALIS
PHYSED
PHYSEDS
PHYSES
PHYSETER
PHYSETERS
PHYSIATRY
PHYSIC
PHYSICAL
PHYSICALS
PHYSICIAN
PHYSICISM
PHYSICIST
PHYSICKED
PHYSICKY
PHYSICS
PHYSIO
PHYSIOS
PHYSIQUE
PHYSIQUED
PHYSIQUES
PHYSIS
PHYTANE
PHYTANES
PHYTIN
PHYTINS
PHYTOGENY
PHYTOID
PHYTOL
PHYTOLITH
PHYTOLOGY
PHYTOLS
PHYTON
PHYTONIC
PHYTONS
PHYTOSES
PHYTOSIS
PHYTOTOMY
PHYTOTRON
PI
PIA
PIACEVOLE
PIACULAR
PIAFFE
PIAFFED
PIAFFER
PIAFFERS
PIAFFES
PIAFFING
PIAL
PIAN
PIANETTE
PIANETTES
PIANI
PIANIC
PIANINO
PIANINOS
PIANISM
PIANISMS
PIANIST
PIANISTE
PIANISTES
PIANISTIC
PIANISTS
PIANO
PIANOLA
PIANOLAS
PIANOLESS
PIANOLIST
PIANOS
PIANS
PIARIST
PIARISTS
PIAS
PIASABA
PIASABAS
PIASAVA
PIASAVAS
PIASSABA
PIASSABAS
PIASSAVA
PIASSAVAS
PIASTER
PIASTERS
PIASTRE
PIASTRES
PIAZZA
PIAZZAS
PIAZZE
PIAZZIAN
PIBAL
PIBALS
PIBROCH
PIBROCHS
PIC
PICA
PICACHO
PICACHOS
PICADILLO
PICADOR
PICADORES
PICADORS
PICAL
PICAMAR
PICAMARS
PICANTE
PICARA
PICARAS
PICARIAN
PICARIANS
PICARO
PICAROON
PICAROONS
PICAROS
PICAS
PICAYUNE
PICAYUNES
PICCADILL
PICCATA
PICCATAS
PICCIES
PICCOLO
PICCOLOS
PICCY
PICE
PICENE
PICENES
PICEOUS
PICHOLINE
PICHURIM
PICHURIMS
PICIFORM
PICINE
PICK
PICKABACK
PICKABLE
PICKADIL
PICKADILL
PICKADILS
PICKAPACK
PICKAROON
PICKAX
PICKAXE
PICKAXED
PICKAXES
PICKAXING
PICKBACK
PICKBACKS
PICKED
PICKEER
PICKEERED
PICKEERER
PICKEERS
PICKER
PICKEREL
PICKERELS
PICKERIES
PICKERS
PICKERY
PICKET
PICKETED
PICKETER
PICKETERS
PICKETING
PICKETS
PICKIER
PICKIEST
PICKILY
PICKIN
PICKINESS
PICKING
PICKINGS
PICKINS
PICKLE
PICKLED
PICKLER
PICKLERS
PICKLES
PICKLING
PICKLOCK
PICKLOCKS
PICKMAW
PICKMAWS
PICKOFF
PICKOFFS
PICKPROOF
PICKS
PICKTHANK
PICKUP
PICKUPS
PICKWICK
PICKWICKS
PICKY
PICLORAM
PICLORAMS
PICNIC
PICNICKED
PICNICKER
PICNICKY

P

PICNICS
PICOCURIE
PICOFARAD
PICOGRAM
PICOGRAMS
PICOLIN
PICOLINE
PICOLINES
PICOLINIC
PICOLINS
PICOMETER
PICOMETRE
PICOMOLE
PICOMOLES
PICONG
PICONGS
PICOT
PICOTE
PICOTED
PICOTEE
PICOTEES
PICOTING
PICOTITE
PICOTITES
PICOTS
PICOWAVE
PICOWAVED
PICOWAVES
PICQUET
PICQUETED
PICQUETS
PICRA
PICRAS
PICRATE
PICRATED
PICRATES
PICRIC
PICRITE
PICRITES
PICRITIC
PICS
PICTARNIE
PICTOGRAM
PICTORIAL
PICTURAL
PICTURALS
PICTURE
PICTURED
PICTURES
PICTURING
PICTURISE
PICTURIZE
PICUL
PICULET
PICULETS
PICULS
PIDDLE
PIDDLED
PIDDLER
PIDDLERS
PIDDLES
PIDDLIER
PIDDLIEST
PIDDLING
PIDDLY
PIDDOCK
PIDDOCKS
PIDGEON
PIDGEONS
PIDGIN
PIDGINISE
PIDGINIZE
PIDGINS
PIE
PIEBALD
PIEBALDS
PIECE
PIECED
PIECELESS
PIECEMEAL
PIECEN
PIECENED
PIECENER
PIECENERS
PIECENING
PIECENS
PIECER
PIECERS
PIECES
PIECEWISE
PIECEWORK
PIECING
PIECINGS
PIECRUST
PIECRUSTS
PIED
PIEDFORT
PIEDFORTS
PIEDISH
PIEDISHES
PIEDMONT
PIEDMONTS
PIEDNESS
PIEFORT
PIEFORTS
PIEHOLE
PIEHOLES
PIEING
PIEINGS
PIEMAN
PIEMEN
PIEND
PIENDS
PIEPLANT
PIEPLANTS
PIEPOWDER
PIER
PIERAGE
PIERAGES
PIERCE
PIERCED
PIERCER
PIERCERS
PIERCES
PIERCING
PIERCINGS
PIERHEAD
PIERHEADS
PIERID
PIERIDINE
PIERIDS
PIERIS
PIERISES
PIEROG
PIEROGEN
PIEROGI
PIEROGIES
PIEROGS
PIERRETTE
PIERROT
PIERROTS
PIERS
PIERST
PIERT
PIERTS
PIES
PIET
PIETA
PIETAS
PIETIES
PIETISM
PIETISMS
PIETIST
PIETISTIC
PIETISTS
PIETS
PIETY
PIEZO
PIFFERARI
PIFFERARO
PIFFERO
PIFFEROS
PIFFLE
PIFFLED
PIFFLER
PIFFLERS
PIFFLES
PIFFLING
PIG
PIGBOAT
PIGBOATS
PIGEON
PIGEONED
PIGEONING
PIGEONITE
PIGEONRY
PIGEONS
PIGFACE
PIGFACES
PIGFEED
PIGFEEDS
PIGFISH
PIGFISHES
PIGGED
PIGGERIES
PIGGERY
PIGGIE
PIGGIER
PIGGIES
PIGGIEST
PIGGIN
PIGGINESS
PIGGING
PIGGINGS
PIGGINS
PIGGISH
PIGGISHLY
PIGGY
PIGGYBACK
PIGHEADED
PIGHT
PIGHTED
PIGHTING
PIGHTLE
PIGHTLES
PIGHTS
PIGLET
PIGLETS
PIGLIKE
PIGLING
PIGLINGS
PIGMAEAN
PIGMAN
PIGMEAN
PIGMEAT
PIGMEATS
PIGMEN
PIGMENT
PIGMENTAL
PIGMENTED
PIGMENTS
PIGMIES
PIGMOID
PIGMOIDS
PIGMY
PIGNERATE
PIGNOLI
PIGNOLIA
PIGNOLIAS
PIGNOLIS
PIGNORA
PIGNORATE
PIGNUS
PIGNUT
PIGNUTS
PIGOUT
PIGOUTS
PIGPEN
PIGPENS
PIGS

P

PIGSCONCE
PIGSKIN
PIGSKINS
PIGSNEY
PIGSNEYS
PIGSNIE
PIGSNIES
PIGSNY
PIGSTICK
PIGSTICKS
PIGSTIES
PIGSTUCK
PIGSTY
PIGSWILL
PIGSWILLS
PIGTAIL
PIGTAILED
PIGTAILS
PIGWASH
PIGWASHES
PIGWEED
PIGWEEDS
PIHOIHOI
PIHOIHOIS
PIING
PIKA
PIKAKE
PIKAKES
PIKAS
PIKAU
PIKAUS
PIKE
PIKED
PIKELET
PIKELETS
PIKELIKE
PIKEMAN
PIKEMEN
PIKEPERCH
PIKER
PIKERS
PIKES
PIKESTAFF
PIKI
PIKING
PIKINGS
PIKIS
PIKUL
PIKULS
PILA
PILAE
PILAF
PILAFF
PILAFFS
PILAFS
PILAO
PILAOS
PILAR
PILASTER
PILASTERS
PILAU
PILAUS
PILAW
PILAWS
PILCH
PILCHARD
PILCHARDS
PILCHER
PILCHERS
PILCHES
PILCORN
PILCORNS
PILCROW
PILCROWS
PILE
PILEA
PILEAS
PILEATE
PILEATED
PILED
PILEI
PILELESS
PILEOUS
PILER
PILERS
PILES
PILEUM
PILEUP
PILEUPS
PILEUS
PILEWORK
PILEWORKS
PILEWORT
PILEWORTS
PILFER
PILFERAGE
PILFERED
PILFERER
PILFERERS
PILFERIES
PILFERING
PILFERS
PILFERY
PILGARLIC
PILGRIM
PILGRIMED
PILGRIMER
PILGRIMS
PILI
PILIER
PILIEST
PILIFORM
PILING
PILINGS
PILINUT
PILINUTS
PILIS
PILL
PILLAGE
PILLAGED
PILLAGER
PILLAGERS
PILLAGES
PILLAGING
PILLAR
PILLARED
PILLARING
PILLARIST
PILLARS
PILLAU
PILLAUS
PILLBOX
PILLBOXES
PILLBUG
PILLBUGS
PILLED
PILLHEAD
PILLHEADS
PILLICOCK
PILLIE
PILLIES
PILLING
PILLINGS
PILLION
PILLIONED
PILLIONS
PILLOCK
PILLOCKS
PILLORIED
PILLORIES
PILLORISE
PILLORIZE
PILLORY
PILLOW
PILLOWED
PILLOWIER
PILLOWING
PILLOWS
PILLOWY
PILLS
PILLWORM
PILLWORMS
PILLWORT
PILLWORTS
PILOMOTOR
PILONIDAL
PILOSE
PILOSITY
PILOT
PILOTAGE
PILOTAGES
PILOTED
PILOTFISH
PILOTING
PILOTINGS
PILOTIS
PILOTLESS
PILOTMAN
PILOTMEN
PILOTS
PILOUS
PILOW
PILOWS
PILSENER
PILSENERS
PILSNER
PILSNERS
PILULA
PILULAE
PILULAR
PILULAS
PILULE
PILULES
PILUM
PILUS
PILY
PIMA
PIMAS
PIMENT
PIMENTO
PIMENTON
PIMENTONS
PIMENTOS
PIMENTS
PIMIENTO
PIMIENTOS
PIMP
PIMPED
PIMPERNEL
PIMPING
PIMPINGS
PIMPLE
PIMPLED
PIMPLES
PIMPLIER
PIMPLIEST
PIMPLY
PIMPS
PIN
PINA
PINACEOUS
PINACOID
PINACOIDS
PINAFORE
PINAFORED
PINAFORES
PINAKOID
PINAKOIDS
PINANG
PINANGS
PINAS
PINASTER
PINASTERS
PINATA
PINATAS
PINBALL
PINBALLED
PINBALLS
PINBOARD
PINBOARDS

P

PINBONE
PINBONES
PINCASE
PINCASES
PINCER
PINCERED
PINCERING
PINCERS
PINCH
PINCHBECK
PINCHBUG
PINCHBUGS
PINCHCOCK
PINCHECK
PINCHECKS
PINCHED
PINCHER
PINCHERS
PINCHES
PINCHFIST
PINCHGUT
PINCHGUTS
PINCHING
PINCHINGS
PINCURL
PINCURLS
PINDAN
PINDANS
PINDAREE
PINDAREES
PINDARI
PINDARIS
PINDER
PINDERS
PINDLING
PINDOWN
PINDOWNS
PINE
PINEAL
PINEALS
PINEAPPLE
PINECONE
PINECONES
PINED
PINEDROPS
PINELAND
PINELANDS
PINELIKE
PINENE
PINENES
PINERIES
PINERY
PINES
PINESAP
PINESAPS
PINETA
PINETUM
PINEWOOD
PINEWOODS
PINEY
PINFALL
PINFALLS
PINFISH
PINFISHES
PINFOLD
PINFOLDED
PINFOLDS
PING
PINGED
PINGER
PINGERS
PINGING
PINGLE
PINGLED
PINGLER
PINGLERS
PINGLES
PINGLING
PINGO
PINGOES
PINGOS
PINGPONG
PINGPONGS
PINGRASS
PINGS
PINGUEFY
PINGUID
PINGUIN
PINGUINS
PINHEAD
PINHEADED
PINHEADS
PINHOLE
PINHOLES
PINHOOKER
PINIER
PINIES
PINIEST
PINING
PINION
PINIONED
PINIONING
PINIONS
PINITE
PINITES
PINITOL
PINITOLS
PINK
PINKED
PINKEN
PINKENED
PINKENING
PINKENS
PINKER
PINKERS
PINKERTON
PINKEST
PINKEY
PINKEYE
PINKEYES
PINKEYS
PINKIE
PINKIER
PINKIES
PINKIEST
PINKINESS
PINKING
PINKINGS
PINKISH
PINKLY
PINKNESS
PINKO
PINKOES
PINKOS
PINKROOT
PINKROOTS
PINKS
PINKY
PINLESS
PINNA
PINNACE
PINNACES
PINNACLE
PINNACLED
PINNACLES
PINNAE
PINNAL
PINNAS
PINNATE
PINNATED
PINNATELY
PINNATION
PINNED
PINNER
PINNERS
PINNET
PINNETS
PINNIE
PINNIES
PINNING
PINNINGS
PINNIPED
PINNIPEDE
PINNIPEDS
PINNOCK
PINNOCKS
PINNOED
PINNULA
PINNULAE
PINNULAR
PINNULAS
PINNULATE
PINNULE
PINNULES
PINNY
PINOCHLE
PINOCHLES
PINOCLE
PINOCLES
PINOCYTIC
PINOLE
PINOLES
PINON
PINONES
PINONS
PINOT
PINOTAGE
PINOTAGES
PINOTS
PINPOINT
PINPOINTS
PINPRICK
PINPRICKS
PINS
PINSCHER
PINSCHERS
PINSETTER
PINSPOT
PINSPOTS
PINSTRIPE
PINSWELL
PINSWELLS
PINT
PINTA
PINTABLE
PINTABLES
PINTADA
PINTADAS
PINTADERA
PINTADO
PINTADOES
PINTADOS
PINTAIL
PINTAILED
PINTAILS
PINTANO
PINTANOS
PINTAS
PINTLE
PINTLES
PINTO
PINTOES
PINTOS
PINTS
PINTSIZE
PINTSIZED
PINTUCK
PINTUCKED
PINTUCKS
PINUP
PINUPS
PINWALE
PINWALES
PINWEED
PINWEEDS
PINWHEEL
PINWHEELS
PINWORK
PINWORKS
PINWORM

P

PINWORMS
PINWRENCH
PINXIT
PINY
PINYIN
PINYINS
PINYON
PINYONS
PIOLET
PIOLETS
PION
PIONED
PIONEER
PIONEERED
PIONEERS
PIONER
PIONERS
PIONEY
PIONEYS
PIONIC
PIONIES
PIONING
PIONINGS
PIONS
PIONY
PIOPIO
PIOPIOS
PIOSITIES
PIOSITY
PIOTED
PIOUS
PIOUSLY
PIOUSNESS
PIOY
PIOYE
PIOYES
PIOYS
PIP
PIPA
PIPAGE
PIPAGES
PIPAL
PIPALS
PIPAS
PIPE
PIPEAGE
PIPEAGES
PIPECLAY
PIPECLAYS
PIPED
PIPEFISH
PIPEFUL
PIPEFULS
PIPELESS
PIPELIKE
PIPELINE
PIPELINED
PIPELINES
PIPER
PIPERIC
PIPERINE
PIPERINES
PIPERONAL
PIPERS
PIPES
PIPESTEM
PIPESTEMS
PIPESTONE
PIPET
PIPETS
PIPETTE
PIPETTED
PIPETTES
PIPETTING
PIPEWORK
PIPEWORKS
PIPEWORT
PIPEWORTS
PIPI
PIPIER
PIPIEST
PIPINESS
PIPING
PIPINGLY
PIPINGS
PIPIS
PIPISTREL
PIPIT
PIPITS
PIPKIN
PIPKINS
PIPLESS
PIPPED
PIPPIER
PIPPIEST
PIPPIN
PIPPING
PIPPINS
PIPPY
PIPS
PIPSQUEAK
PIPUL
PIPULS
PIPY
PIQUANCE
PIQUANCES
PIQUANCY
PIQUANT
PIQUANTLY
PIQUE
PIQUED
PIQUES
PIQUET
PIQUETED
PIQUETING
PIQUETS
PIQUILLO
PIQUILLOS
PIQUING
PIR
PIRACETAM
PIRACIES
PIRACY
PIRAGUA
PIRAGUAS
PIRAI
PIRAIS
PIRANA
PIRANAS
PIRANHA
PIRANHAS
PIRARUCU
PIRARUCUS
PIRATE
PIRATED
PIRATES
PIRATIC
PIRATICAL
PIRATING
PIRATINGS
PIRAYA
PIRAYAS
PIRIFORM
PIRL
PIRLICUE
PIRLICUED
PIRLICUES
PIRLS
PIRN
PIRNIE
PIRNIES
PIRNIT
PIRNS
PIROG
PIROGEN
PIROGHI
PIROGI
PIROGIES
PIROGUE
PIROGUES
PIROJKI
PIROPLASM
PIROQUE
PIROQUES
PIROSHKI
PIROUETTE
PIROZHKI
PIROZHOK
PIRS
PIS
PISCARIES
PISCARY
PISCATOR
PISCATORS
PISCATORY
PISCATRIX
PISCIFORM
PISCINA
PISCINAE
PISCINAL
PISCINAS
PISCINE
PISCINES
PISCIVORE
PISCO
PISCOS
PISE
PISES
PISH
PISHED
PISHEOG
PISHEOGS
PISHER
PISHERS
PISHES
PISHING
PISHOGE
PISHOGES
PISHOGUE
PISHOGUES
PISIFORM
PISIFORMS
PISKIES
PISKY
PISMIRE
PISMIRES
PISO
PISOLITE
PISOLITES
PISOLITH
PISOLITHS
PISOLITIC
PISOS
PISS
PISSANT
PISSANTS
PISSED
PISSER
PISSERS
PISSES
PISSHEAD
PISSHEADS
PISSHOLE
PISSHOLES
PISSIER
PISSIEST
PISSING
PISSOIR
PISSOIRS
PISSY
PISTACHE
PISTACHES
PISTACHIO
PISTAREEN
PISTE
PISTED
PISTES
PISTIL
PISTILLAR
PISTILS

PISTOL
PISTOLE
PISTOLED
PISTOLEER
PISTOLERO
PISTOLES
PISTOLET
PISTOLETS
PISTOLIER
PISTOLING
PISTOLLED
PISTOLS
PISTON
PISTONS
PISTOU
PISTOUS
PIT
PITA
PITAHAYA
PITAHAYAS
PITAPAT
PITAPATS
PITARA
PITARAH
PITARAHS
PITARAS
PITAS
PITAYA
PITAYAS
PITCH
PITCHBEND
PITCHED
PITCHER
PITCHERS
PITCHES
PITCHFORK
PITCHIER
PITCHIEST
PITCHILY
PITCHING
PITCHINGS
PITCHMAN
PITCHMEN
PITCHOUT
PITCHOUTS
PITCHPINE
PITCHPIPE
PITCHPOLE
PITCHY
PITEOUS
PITEOUSLY
PITFALL
PITFALLS
PITH
PITHBALL
PITHBALLS
PITHEAD
PITHEADS
PITHECOID
PITHED
PITHFUL
PITHIER
PITHIEST
PITHILY
PITHINESS
PITHING
PITHLESS
PITHLIKE
PITHOI
PITHOS
PITHS
PITHY
PITIABLE
PITIABLY
PITIED
PITIER
PITIERS
PITIES
PITIETH
PITIFUL
PITIFULLY
PITIKINS
PITILESS
PITLIKE
PITMAN
PITMANS
PITMEN
PITON
PITONS
PITOT
PITOTS
PITPROP
PITPROPS
PITS
PITSAW
PITSAWS
PITTA
PITTANCE
PITTANCES
PITTAS
PITTED
PITTEN
PITTER
PITTERED
PITTERING
PITTERS
PITTING
PITTINGS
PITTITE
PITTITES
PITUITA
PITUITARY
PITUITAS
PITUITE
PITUITES
PITUITRIN
PITURI
PITURIS
PITY
PITYING
PITYINGLY
PITYROID
PIU
PIUM
PIUMS
PIUPIU
PIUPIUS
PIVOT
PIVOTABLE
PIVOTAL
PIVOTALLY
PIVOTED
PIVOTER
PIVOTERS
PIVOTING
PIVOTINGS
PIVOTMAN
PIVOTMEN
PIVOTS
PIX
PIXEL
PIXELATE
PIXELATED
PIXELATES
PIXELLATE
PIXELS
PIXES
PIXIE
PIXIEISH
PIXIES
PIXILATE
PIXILATED
PIXILATES
PIXILLATE
PIXINESS
PIXY
PIXYISH
PIZAZZ
PIZAZZES
PIZAZZIER
PIZAZZY
PIZE
PIZED
PIZES
PIZING
PIZZA
PIZZAIOLA
PIZZALIKE
PIZZAS
PIZZAZ
PIZZAZES
PIZZAZZ
PIZZAZZES
PIZZAZZY
PIZZELLE
PIZZELLES
PIZZERIA
PIZZERIAS
PIZZICATI
PIZZICATO
PIZZLE
PIZZLES
PLAAS
PLAASES
PLACABLE
PLACABLY
PLACARD
PLACARDED
PLACARDS
PLACATE
PLACATED
PLACATER
PLACATERS
PLACATES
PLACATING
PLACATION
PLACATIVE
PLACATORY
PLACCAT
PLACCATE
PLACCATES
PLACCATS
PLACE
PLACEABLE
PLACEBO
PLACEBOES
PLACEBOS
PLACED
PLACEKICK
PLACELESS
PLACEMAN
PLACEMAT
PLACEMATS
PLACEMEN
PLACEMENT
PLACENTA
PLACENTAE
PLACENTAL
PLACENTAS
PLACER
PLACERS
PLACES
PLACET
PLACETS
PLACID
PLACIDER
PLACIDEST
PLACIDITY
PLACIDLY
PLACING
PLACINGS
PLACIT
PLACITA
PLACITORY
PLACITS
PLACITUM
PLACK
PLACKET
PLACKETS
PLACKLESS

P

PLACKS
PLACODERM
PLACOID
PLACOIDS
PLAFOND
PLAFONDS
PLAGAL
PLAGE
PLAGES
PLAGIARY
PLAGIUM
PLAGIUMS
PLAGUE
PLAGUED
PLAGUER
PLAGUERS
PLAGUES
PLAGUEY
PLAGUIER
PLAGUIEST
PLAGUILY
PLAGUING
PLAGUY
PLAICE
PLAICES
PLAID
PLAIDED
PLAIDING
PLAIDINGS
PLAIDMAN
PLAIDMEN
PLAIDS
PLAIN
PLAINANT
PLAINANTS
PLAINED
PLAINER
PLAINEST
PLAINFUL
PLAINING
PLAININGS
PLAINISH
PLAINLY
PLAINNESS
PLAINS
PLAINSMAN
PLAINSMEN
PLAINSONG
PLAINT
PLAINTEXT
PLAINTFUL
PLAINTIFF
PLAINTIVE
PLAINTS
PLAINWORK
PLAISTER
PLAISTERS
PLAIT
PLAITED
PLAITER
PLAITERS
PLAITING
PLAITINGS
PLAITS
PLAN
PLANAR
PLANARIA
PLANARIAN
PLANARIAS
PLANARITY
PLANATE
PLANATION
PLANCH
PLANCHE
PLANCHED
PLANCHES
PLANCHET
PLANCHETS
PLANCHING
PLANE
PLANED
PLANELOAD
PLANENESS
PLANER
PLANERS
PLANES
PLANESIDE
PLANET
PLANETARY
PLANETIC
PLANETOID
PLANETS
PLANFORM
PLANFORMS
PLANGENCY
PLANGENT
PLANIGRAM
PLANING
PLANISH
PLANISHED
PLANISHER
PLANISHES
PLANK
PLANKED
PLANKING
PLANKINGS
PLANKLIKE
PLANKS
PLANKTER
PLANKTERS
PLANKTIC
PLANKTON
PLANKTONS
PLANLESS
PLANNED
PLANNER
PLANNERS
PLANNING
PLANNINGS
PLANOGRAM
PLANOSOL
PLANOSOLS
PLANS
PLANT
PLANTA
PLANTABLE
PLANTAE
PLANTAGE
PLANTAGES
PLANTAIN
PLANTAINS
PLANTAR
PLANTAS
PLANTED
PLANTER
PLANTERS
PLANTING
PLANTINGS
PLANTLESS
PLANTLET
PLANTLETS
PLANTLIKE
PLANTLING
PLANTS
PLANTSMAN
PLANTSMEN
PLANTULE
PLANTULES
PLANULA
PLANULAE
PLANULAR
PLANULATE
PLANULOID
PLANURIA
PLANURIAS
PLANURIES
PLANURY
PLANXTIES
PLANXTY
PLAP
PLAPPED
PLAPPING
PLAPS
PLAQUE
PLAQUES
PLAQUETTE
PLASH
PLASHED
PLASHER
PLASHERS
PLASHES
PLASHET
PLASHETS
PLASHIER
PLASHIEST
PLASHING
PLASHINGS
PLASHY
PLASM
PLASMA
PLASMAGEL
PLASMAS
PLASMASOL
PLASMATIC
PLASMIC
PLASMID
PLASMIDS
PLASMIN
PLASMINS
PLASMODIA
PLASMOID
PLASMOIDS
PLASMON
PLASMONS
PLASMS
PLAST
PLASTE
PLASTER
PLASTERED
PLASTERER
PLASTERS
PLASTERY
PLASTIC
PLASTICKY
PLASTICLY
PLASTICS
PLASTID
PLASTIDS
PLASTIQUE
PLASTISOL
PLASTRAL
PLASTRON
PLASTRONS
PLASTRUM
PLASTRUMS
PLAT
PLATAN
PLATANE
PLATANES
PLATANNA
PLATANNAS
PLATANS
PLATBAND
PLATBANDS
PLATE
PLATEASM
PLATEASMS
PLATEAU
PLATEAUED
PLATEAUS
PLATEAUX
PLATED
PLATEFUL
PLATEFULS
PLATELESS
PLATELET
PLATELETS
PLATELIKE
PLATEMAN
PLATEMARK

PLATEMEN
PLATEN
PLATENS
PLATER
PLATERS
PLATES
PLATESFUL
PLATFORM
PLATFORMS
PLATIER
PLATIES
PLATIEST
PLATINA
PLATINAS
PLATING
PLATINGS
PLATINIC
PLATINISE
PLATINIZE
PLATINOID
PLATINOUS
PLATINUM
PLATINUMS
PLATITUDE
PLATONIC
PLATONICS
PLATONISM
PLATOON
PLATOONED
PLATOONS
PLATS
PLATT
PLATTED
PLATTER
PLATTERS
PLATTING
PLATTINGS
PLATY
PLATYFISH
PLATYPI
PLATYPUS
PLATYS
PLATYSMA
PLATYSMAS
PLAUDIT
PLAUDITE
PLAUDITS
PLAUSIBLE
PLAUSIBLY
PLAUSIVE
PLAUSTRAL
PLAY
PLAYA
PLAYABLE
PLAYACT
PLAYACTED
PLAYACTOR
PLAYACTS
PLAYAS
PLAYBACK
PLAYBACKS
PLAYBILL
PLAYBILLS
PLAYBOOK
PLAYBOOKS
PLAYBOY
PLAYBOYS
PLAYBUS
PLAYBUSES
PLAYDATE
PLAYDATES
PLAYDAY
PLAYDAYS
PLAYDOUGH
PLAYDOWN
PLAYDOWNS
PLAYED
PLAYER
PLAYERS
PLAYFIELD
PLAYFUL
PLAYFULLY
PLAYGIRL
PLAYGIRLS
PLAYGOER
PLAYGOERS
PLAYGOING
PLAYGROUP
PLAYHOUSE
PLAYING
PLAYINGS
PLAYLAND
PLAYLANDS
PLAYLESS
PLAYLET
PLAYLETS
PLAYLIKE
PLAYLIST
PLAYLISTS
PLAYMAKER
PLAYMATE
PLAYMATES
PLAYOFF
PLAYOFFS
PLAYPEN
PLAYPENS
PLAYROOM
PLAYROOMS
PLAYS
PLAYSET
PLAYSETS
PLAYSLIP
PLAYSLIPS
PLAYSOME
PLAYSUIT
PLAYSUITS
PLAYTHING
PLAYTIME
PLAYTIMES
PLAYWEAR
PLAYWEARS
PLAZA
PLAZAS
PLEA
PLEACH
PLEACHED
PLEACHES
PLEACHING
PLEAD
PLEADABLE
PLEADED
PLEADER
PLEADERS
PLEADING
PLEADINGS
PLEADS
PLEAED
PLEAING
PLEAS
PLEASABLE
PLEASANCE
PLEASANT
PLEASE
PLEASED
PLEASEDLY
PLEASEMAN
PLEASEMEN
PLEASER
PLEASERS
PLEASES
PLEASETH
PLEASING
PLEASINGS
PLEASURE
PLEASURED
PLEASURER
PLEASURES
PLEAT
PLEATED
PLEATER
PLEATERS
PLEATHER
PLEATHERS
PLEATING
PLEATINGS
PLEATLESS
PLEATS
PLEB
PLEBBIER
PLEBBIEST
PLEBBY
PLEBE
PLEBEAN
PLEBEIAN
PLEBEIANS
PLEBES
PLEBIFIED
PLEBIFIES
PLEBIFY
PLEBS
PLECTRA
PLECTRE
PLECTRES
PLECTRON
PLECTRONS
PLECTRUM
PLECTRUMS
PLED
PLEDGABLE
PLEDGE
PLEDGED
PLEDGEE
PLEDGEES
PLEDGEOR
PLEDGEORS
PLEDGER
PLEDGERS
PLEDGES
PLEDGET
PLEDGETS
PLEDGING
PLEDGOR
PLEDGORS
PLEIAD
PLEIADES
PLEIADS
PLEIOCENE
PLEIOMERY
PLEIOTAXY
PLENA
PLENARIES
PLENARILY
PLENARTY
PLENARY
PLENCH
PLENCHES
PLENILUNE
PLENIPO
PLENIPOES
PLENIPOS
PLENISH
PLENISHED
PLENISHER
PLENISHES
PLENISM
PLENISMS
PLENIST
PLENISTS
PLENITUDE
PLENTEOUS
PLENTIES
PLENTIFUL
PLENTY
PLENUM
PLENUMS
PLEON
PLEONAL
PLEONASM
PLEONASMS
PLEONAST

P

PLEONASTE
PLEONASTS
PLEONEXIA
PLEONIC
PLEONS
PLEOPOD
PLEOPODS
PLERION
PLERIONS
PLEROMA
PLEROMAS
PLEROME
PLEROMES
PLESH
PLESHES
PLESSOR
PLESSORS
PLETHORA
PLETHORAS
PLETHORIC
PLEUCH
PLEUCHED
PLEUCHING
PLEUCHS
PLEUGH
PLEUGHED
PLEUGHING
PLEUGHS
PLEURA
PLEURAE
PLEURAL
PLEURAS
PLEURISY
PLEURITIC
PLEURITIS
PLEURON
PLEURONIA
PLEUSTON
PLEUSTONS
PLEW
PLEWS
PLEX
PLEXAL
PLEXED
PLEXES
PLEXIFORM
PLEXING
PLEXOR
PLEXORS
PLEXURE
PLEXURES
PLEXUS
PLEXUSES
PLIABLE
PLIABLY
PLIANCIES
PLIANCY
PLIANT
PLIANTLY
PLICA
PLICAE
PLICAL
PLICAS
PLICATE
PLICATED
PLICATELY
PLICATES
PLICATING
PLICATION
PLICATURE
PLIE
PLIED
PLIER
PLIERS
PLIES
PLIGHT
PLIGHTED
PLIGHTER
PLIGHTERS
PLIGHTFUL
PLIGHTING
PLIGHTS
PLIM
PLIMMED
PLIMMING
PLIMS
PLIMSOL
PLIMSOLE
PLIMSOLES
PLIMSOLL
PLIMSOLLS
PLIMSOLS
PLING
PLINGED
PLINGING
PLINGS
PLINK
PLINKED
PLINKER
PLINKERS
PLINKIER
PLINKIEST
PLINKING
PLINKINGS
PLINKS
PLINKY
PLINTH
PLINTHS
PLIOCENE
PLIOFILM
PLIOFILMS
PLIOSAUR
PLIOSAURS
PLIOTRON
PLIOTRONS
PLISKIE
PLISKIER
PLISKIES
PLISKIEST
PLISKY
PLISSE
PLISSES
PLOAT
PLOATED
PLOATING
PLOATS
PLOD
PLODDED
PLODDER
PLODDERS
PLODDING
PLODDINGS
PLODGE
PLODGED
PLODGES
PLODGING
PLODS
PLOGGING
PLOGGINGS
PLOIDIES
PLOIDY
PLONG
PLONGD
PLONGE
PLONGED
PLONGES
PLONGING
PLONGS
PLONK
PLONKED
PLONKER
PLONKERS
PLONKIER
PLONKIEST
PLONKING
PLONKINGS
PLONKO
PLONKOS
PLONKS
PLONKY
PLOOK
PLOOKIE
PLOOKIER
PLOOKIEST
PLOOKS
PLOOKY
PLOP
PLOPPED
PLOPPING
PLOPS
PLOSION
PLOSIONS
PLOSIVE
PLOSIVES
PLOT
PLOTFUL
PLOTLESS
PLOTLINE
PLOTLINES
PLOTS
PLOTTAGE
PLOTTAGES
PLOTTED
PLOTTER
PLOTTERED
PLOTTERS
PLOTTIE
PLOTTIER
PLOTTIES
PLOTTIEST
PLOTTING
PLOTTINGS
PLOTTY
PLOTZ
PLOTZED
PLOTZES
PLOTZING
PLOUGH
PLOUGHBOY
PLOUGHED
PLOUGHER
PLOUGHERS
PLOUGHING
PLOUGHMAN
PLOUGHMEN
PLOUGHS
PLOUK
PLOUKIE
PLOUKIER
PLOUKIEST
PLOUKS
PLOUKY
PLOUTER
PLOUTERED
PLOUTERS
PLOVER
PLOVERIER
PLOVERS
PLOVERY
PLOW
PLOWABLE
PLOWBACK
PLOWBACKS
PLOWBOY
PLOWBOYS
PLOWED
PLOWER
PLOWERS
PLOWHEAD
PLOWHEADS
PLOWING
PLOWINGS
PLOWLAND
PLOWLANDS
PLOWMAN
PLOWMEN
PLOWS
PLOWSHARE
PLOWSTAFF
PLOWTAIL

PLOWTAILS
PLOWTER
PLOWTERED
PLOWTERS
PLOWWISE
PLOY
PLOYE
PLOYED
PLOYES
PLOYING
PLOYS
PLU
PLUCK
PLUCKED
PLUCKER
PLUCKERS
PLUCKIER
PLUCKIEST
PLUCKILY
PLUCKING
PLUCKS
PLUCKY
PLUE
PLUES
PLUFF
PLUFFED
PLUFFIER
PLUFFIEST
PLUFFING
PLUFFS
PLUFFY
PLUG
PLUGBOARD
PLUGGED
PLUGGER
PLUGGERS
PLUGGING
PLUGGINGS
PLUGHOLE
PLUGHOLES
PLUGLESS
PLUGOLA
PLUGOLAS
PLUGS
PLUGUGLY
PLUM
PLUMAGE
PLUMAGED
PLUMAGES
PLUMATE
PLUMB
PLUMBABLE
PLUMBAGO
PLUMBAGOS
PLUMBATE
PLUMBATES
PLUMBED
PLUMBEOUS
PLUMBER
PLUMBERS
PLUMBERY
PLUMBIC
PLUMBING
PLUMBINGS
PLUMBISM
PLUMBISMS
PLUMBITE
PLUMBITES
PLUMBLESS
PLUMBNESS
PLUMBOUS
PLUMBS
PLUMBUM
PLUMBUMS
PLUMCAKE
PLUMCAKES
PLUMCOT
PLUMCOTS
PLUMDAMAS
PLUME
PLUMED
PLUMELESS
PLUMELET
PLUMELETS
PLUMELIKE
PLUMERIA
PLUMERIAS
PLUMERIES
PLUMERY
PLUMES
PLUMIER
PLUMIEST
PLUMING
PLUMIPED
PLUMIPEDS
PLUMIST
PLUMISTS
PLUMLIKE
PLUMMER
PLUMMEST
PLUMMET
PLUMMETED
PLUMMETS
PLUMMIER
PLUMMIEST
PLUMMY
PLUMOSE
PLUMOSELY
PLUMOSITY
PLUMOUS
PLUMP
PLUMPED
PLUMPEN
PLUMPENED
PLUMPENS
PLUMPER
PLUMPERS
PLUMPEST
PLUMPIE
PLUMPIER
PLUMPIEST
PLUMPING
PLUMPISH
PLUMPLY
PLUMPNESS
PLUMPS
PLUMPY
PLUMS
PLUMULA
PLUMULAE
PLUMULAR
PLUMULATE
PLUMULE
PLUMULES
PLUMULOSE
PLUMY
PLUNDER
PLUNDERED
PLUNDERER
PLUNDERS
PLUNGE
PLUNGED
PLUNGER
PLUNGERS
PLUNGES
PLUNGING
PLUNGINGS
PLUNK
PLUNKED
PLUNKER
PLUNKERS
PLUNKIER
PLUNKIEST
PLUNKING
PLUNKS
PLUNKY
PLUOT
PLUOTS
PLURAL
PLURALISE
PLURALISM
PLURALIST
PLURALITY
PLURALIZE
PLURALLY
PLURALS
PLURIPARA
PLURISIE
PLURISIES
PLURRY
PLUS
PLUSAGE
PLUSAGES
PLUSED
PLUSES
PLUSH
PLUSHED
PLUSHER
PLUSHES
PLUSHEST
PLUSHIER
PLUSHIEST
PLUSHILY
PLUSHLY
PLUSHNESS
PLUSHY
PLUSING
PLUSSAGE
PLUSSAGES
PLUSSED
PLUSSES
PLUSSING
PLUTEAL
PLUTEI
PLUTEUS
PLUTEUSES
PLUTO
PLUTOCRAT
PLUTOED
PLUTOES
PLUTOID
PLUTOIDS
PLUTOING
PLUTOLOGY
PLUTON
PLUTONIAN
PLUTONIC
PLUTONISM
PLUTONIUM
PLUTONOMY
PLUTONS
PLUTOS
PLUVIAL
PLUVIALS
PLUVIAN
PLUVIANS
PLUVIOSE
PLUVIOUS
PLUVIUS
PLY
PLYER
PLYERS
PLYING
PLYINGLY
PLYWOOD
PLYWOODS
PNEUMA
PNEUMAS
PNEUMATIC
PNEUMONIA
PNEUMONIC
PO
POA
POACEOUS
POACH
POACHABLE
POACHED
POACHER
POACHERS
POACHES

POACHIER
POACHIEST
POACHING
POACHINGS
POACHY
POAKA
POAKAS
POAKE
POAKES
POAS
POBLANO
POBLANOS
POBOY
POBOYS
POCHARD
POCHARDS
POCHAY
POCHAYED
POCHAYING
POCHAYS
POCHETTE
POCHETTES
POCHOIR
POCHOIRS
POCK
POCKARD
POCKARDS
POCKED
POCKET
POCKETED
POCKETER
POCKETERS
POCKETFUL
POCKETING
POCKETS
POCKIER
POCKIES
POCKIEST
POCKILY
POCKING
POCKMANKY
POCKMARK
POCKMARKS
POCKPIT
POCKPITS
POCKS
POCKY
POCO
POCOSEN
POCOSENS
POCOSIN
POCOSINS
POCOSON
POCOSONS
POD
PODAGRA
PODAGRAL
PODAGRAS
PODAGRIC
PODAGROUS
PODAL
PODALIC
PODARGUS
PODCAST
PODCASTED
PODCASTER
PODCASTS
PODDED
PODDIE
PODDIER
PODDIES
PODDIEST
PODDING
PODDLE
PODDLED
PODDLES
PODDLING
PODDY
PODESTA
PODESTAS
PODEX
PODEXES
PODGE
PODGES
PODGIER
PODGIEST
PODGILY
PODGINESS
PODGY
PODIA
PODIAL
PODIATRIC
PODIATRY
PODITE
PODITES
PODITIC
PODIUM
PODIUMED
PODIUMING
PODIUMS
PODLEY
PODLEYS
PODLIKE
PODOCARP
PODOCARPS
PODOLOGY
PODOMERE
PODOMERES
PODS
PODSOL
PODSOLIC
PODSOLISE
PODSOLIZE
PODSOLS
PODUNK
PODUNKS
PODZOL
PODZOLIC
PODZOLISE
PODZOLIZE
PODZOLS
POECHORE
POECHORES
POEM
POEMATIC
POEMS
POENOLOGY
POEP
POEPED
POEPING
POEPOL
POEPOLS
POEPS
POESIED
POESIES
POESY
POESYING
POET
POETASTER
POETASTRY
POETESS
POETESSES
POETIC
POETICAL
POETICALS
POETICISE
POETICISM
POETICIZE
POETICS
POETICULE
POETISE
POETISED
POETISER
POETISERS
POETISES
POETISING
POETIZE
POETIZED
POETIZER
POETIZERS
POETIZES
POETIZING
POETLESS
POETLIKE
POETRESSE
POETRIES
POETRY
POETS
POETSHIP
POETSHIPS
POFFLE
POFFLES
POGEY
POGEYS
POGGE
POGGES
POGIES
POGO
POGOED
POGOER
POGOERS
POGOES
POGOING
POGONIA
POGONIAS
POGONIP
POGONIPS
POGOS
POGROM
POGROMED
POGROMING
POGROMIST
POGROMS
POGY
POH
POHED
POHING
POHIRI
POHIRIS
POHS
POI
POIGNADO
POIGNANCE
POIGNANCY
POIGNANT
POILU
POILUS
POINADO
POINADOES
POINCIANA
POIND
POINDED
POINDER
POINDERS
POINDING
POINDINGS
POINDS
POINT
POINTABLE
POINTE
POINTED
POINTEDLY
POINTEL
POINTELLE
POINTELS
POINTER
POINTERS
POINTES
POINTIER
POINTIEST
POINTILLE
POINTING
POINTINGS
POINTLESS
POINTLIKE
POINTMAN
POINTMEN
POINTS
POINTSMAN
POINTSMEN

POINTY
POIS
POISE
POISED
POISER
POISERS
POISES
POISHA
POISHAS
POISING
POISON
POISONED
POISONER
POISONERS
POISONING
POISONOUS
POISONS
POISSON
POISSONS
POITIN
POITINS
POITREL
POITRELS
POITRINE
POITRINES
POKABLE
POKAL
POKALS
POKE
POKEBERRY
POKED
POKEFUL
POKEFULS
POKELOGAN
POKER
POKERISH
POKEROOT
POKEROOTS
POKERS
POKERWORK
POKES
POKEWEED
POKEWEEDS
POKEY
POKEYS
POKIE
POKIER
POKIES
POKIEST
POKILY
POKINESS
POKING
POKY
POL
POLACCA
POLACCAS
POLACRE
POLACRES
POLAR
POLARISE
POLARISED
POLARISER
POLARISES
POLARITY
POLARIZE
POLARIZED
POLARIZER
POLARIZES
POLARON
POLARONS
POLARS
POLDER
POLDERED
POLDERING
POLDERS
POLE
POLEAX
POLEAXE
POLEAXED
POLEAXES
POLEAXING
POLECAT
POLECATS
POLED
POLEIS
POLELESS
POLEMARCH
POLEMIC
POLEMICAL
POLEMICS
POLEMISE
POLEMISED
POLEMISES
POLEMIST
POLEMISTS
POLEMIZE
POLEMIZED
POLEMIZES
POLENTA
POLENTAS
POLER
POLERS
POLES
POLESTAR
POLESTARS
POLEWARD
POLEY
POLEYN
POLEYNS
POLEYS
POLIANITE
POLICE
POLICED
POLICEMAN
POLICEMEN
POLICER
POLICERS
POLICES
POLICIER
POLICIERS
POLICIES
POLICING
POLICINGS
POLICY
POLIES
POLING
POLINGS
POLIO
POLIOS
POLIS
POLISES
POLISH
POLISHED
POLISHER
POLISHERS
POLISHES
POLISHING
POLITBURO
POLITE
POLITELY
POLITER
POLITESSE
POLITEST
POLITIC
POLITICAL
POLITICK
POLITICKS
POLITICLY
POLITICO
POLITICOS
POLITICS
POLITIES
POLITIQUE
POLITY
POLJE
POLJES
POLK
POLKA
POLKAED
POLKAING
POLKAS
POLKED
POLKING
POLKS
POLL
POLLACK
POLLACKS
POLLAN
POLLANS
POLLARD
POLLARDED
POLLARDS
POLLAXE
POLLAXED
POLLAXES
POLLAXING
POLLED
POLLEE
POLLEES
POLLEN
POLLENATE
POLLENED
POLLENING
POLLENS
POLLENT
POLLER
POLLERS
POLLEX
POLLICAL
POLLICES
POLLICIE
POLLICIES
POLLICY
POLLIES
POLLINATE
POLLING
POLLINGS
POLLINIA
POLLINIC
POLLINISE
POLLINIUM
POLLINIZE
POLLIST
POLLISTS
POLLIWIG
POLLIWIGS
POLLIWOG
POLLIWOGS
POLLMAN
POLLMEN
POLLOCK
POLLOCKS
POLLS
POLLSTER
POLLSTERS
POLLTAKER
POLLUCITE
POLLUSION
POLLUTANT
POLLUTE
POLLUTED
POLLUTER
POLLUTERS
POLLUTES
POLLUTING
POLLUTION
POLLUTIVE
POLLY
POLLYANNA
POLLYWIG
POLLYWIGS
POLLYWOG
POLLYWOGS
POLO
POLOIDAL
POLOIST
POLOISTS
POLONAISE
POLONIE
POLONIES

POLONISE
POLONISED
POLONISES
POLONISM
POLONISMS
POLONIUM
POLONIUMS
POLONIZE
POLONIZED
POLONIZES
POLONY
POLOS
POLS
POLT
POLTED
POLTFEET
POLTFOOT
POLTING
POLTROON
POLTROONS
POLTS
POLVERINE
POLY
POLYACID
POLYACIDS
POLYACT
POLYADIC
POLYAMIDE
POLYAMINE
POLYAMORY
POLYANDRY
POLYANTHA
POLYANTHI
POLYARCH
POLYARCHY
POLYAXIAL
POLYAXON
POLYAXONS
POLYBAG
POLYBAGS
POLYBASIC
POLYBRID
POLYBRIDS
POLYCARPY
POLYCHETE
POLYCONIC
POLYCOT
POLYCOTS
POLYDEMIC
POLYDRUG
POLYENE
POLYENES
POLYENIC
POLYESTER
POLYGALA
POLYGALAS
POLYGAM
POLYGAMIC
POLYGAMS
POLYGAMY
POLYGENE
POLYGENES
POLYGENIC
POLYGENY
POLYGLOT
POLYGLOTS
POLYGLOTT
POLYGON
POLYGONAL
POLYGONS
POLYGONUM
POLYGONY
POLYGRAPH
POLYGYNE
POLYGYNY
POLYHEDRA
POLYIMIDE
POLYLEMMA
POLYMASTY
POLYMATH
POLYMATHS
POLYMATHY
POLYMER
POLYMERIC
POLYMERS
POLYMERY
POLYMORPH
POLYMYXIN
POLYNIA
POLYNIAS
POLYNYA
POLYNYAS
POLYNYI
POLYOL
POLYOLS
POLYOMA
POLYOMAS
POLYOMINO
POLYONYM
POLYONYMS
POLYONYMY
POLYP
POLYPARIA
POLYPARY
POLYPE
POLYPED
POLYPEDS
POLYPES
POLYPHAGY
POLYPHASE
POLYPHON
POLYPHONE
POLYPHONS
POLYPHONY
POLYPI
POLYPIDE
POLYPIDES
POLYPIDOM
POLYPILL
POLYPILLS
POLYPINE
POLYPITE
POLYPITES
POLYPLOID
POLYPNEA
POLYPNEAS
POLYPNEIC
POLYPOD
POLYPODS
POLYPODY
POLYPOID
POLYPORE
POLYPORES
POLYPOSES
POLYPOSIS
POLYPOUS
POLYPS
POLYPTYCH
POLYPUS
POLYPUSES
POLYS
POLYSEME
POLYSEMES
POLYSEMIC
POLYSEMY
POLYSOME
POLYSOMES
POLYSOMIC
POLYSOMY
POLYSTYLE
POLYTENE
POLYTENY
POLYTHENE
POLYTONAL
POLYTYPE
POLYTYPED
POLYTYPES
POLYTYPIC
POLYURIA
POLYURIAS
POLYURIC
POLYVINYL
POLYWATER
POLYZOA
POLYZOAN
POLYZOANS
POLYZOARY
POLYZOIC
POLYZONAL
POLYZOOID
POLYZOON
POM
POMACE
POMACEOUS
POMACES
POMADE
POMADED
POMADES
POMADING
POMANDER
POMANDERS
POMATO
POMATOES
POMATUM
POMATUMED
POMATUMS
POMBE
POMBES
POME
POMELIKE
POMELO
POMELOS
POMEROY
POMEROYS
POMES
POMFRET
POMFRETS
POMMEE
POMMEL
POMMELE
POMMELED
POMMELING
POMMELLED
POMMELS
POMMETTY
POMMIE
POMMIES
POMMY
POMO
POMOERIUM
POMOLOGY
POMOS
POMP
POMPADOUR
POMPANO
POMPANOS
POMPELO
POMPELOS
POMPEY
POMPEYED
POMPEYING
POMPEYS
POMPHOLYX
POMPIER
POMPIERS
POMPILID
POMPILIDS
POMPION
POMPIONS
POMPOM
POMPOMS
POMPON
POMPONS
POMPOON
POMPOONS
POMPOSITY
POMPOSO
POMPOUS
POMPOUSLY
POMPS

POMROY
POMROYS
POMS
POMWATER
POMWATERS
PONCE
PONCEAU
PONCEAUS
PONCEAUX
PONCED
PONCES
PONCEY
PONCHO
PONCHOED
PONCHOS
PONCIER
PONCIEST
PONCING
PONCY
POND
PONDAGE
PONDAGES
PONDED
PONDER
PONDERAL
PONDERATE
PONDERED
PONDERER
PONDERERS
PONDERING
PONDEROSA
PONDEROUS
PONDERS
PONDING
PONDOK
PONDOKKIE
PONDOKS
PONDS
PONDWEED
PONDWEEDS
PONE
PONENT
PONENTS
PONES
PONEY
PONEYS
PONG
PONGA
PONGAL
PONGALS
PONGAS
PONGED
PONGEE
PONGEES
PONGID
PONGIDS
PONGIER
PONGIEST
PONGING
PONGO
PONGOES
PONGOS
PONGS
PONGY
PONIARD
PONIARDED
PONIARDS
PONIED
PONIES
PONK
PONKED
PONKING
PONKS
PONS
PONT
PONTAGE
PONTAGES
PONTAL
PONTES
PONTIANAC
PONTIANAK
PONTIC
PONTIE
PONTIES
PONTIFEX
PONTIFF
PONTIFFS
PONTIFIC
PONTIFICE
PONTIFIED
PONTIFIES
PONTIFY
PONTIL
PONTILE
PONTILES
PONTILS
PONTINE
PONTLEVIS
PONTON
PONTONEER
PONTONIER
PONTONS
PONTOON
PONTOONED
PONTOONER
PONTOONS
PONTS
PONTY
PONY
PONYING
PONYSKIN
PONYSKINS
PONYTAIL
PONYTAILS
PONZU
PONZUS
POO
POOBAH
POOBAHS
POOCH
POOCHED
POOCHES
POOCHING
POOD
POODLE
POODLES
POODS
POOED
POOF
POOGYE
POOGYES
POOH
POOHED
POOHING
POOHS
POOING
POOJA
POOJAH
POOJAHS
POOJAS
POOK
POOKA
POOKAS
POOKING
POOKIT
POOKS
POOL
POOLED
POOLER
POOLERS
POOLHALL
POOLHALLS
POOLING
POOLROOM
POOLROOMS
POOLS
POOLSIDE
POOLSIDES
POON
POONAC
POONACS
POONCE
POONCED
POONCES
POONCING
POONS
POONTANG
POONTANGS
POOP
POOPED
POOPER
POOPERS
POOPIER
POOPIEST
POOPING
POOPS
POOPY
POOR
POORBOX
POORBOXES
POORER
POOREST
POORHOUSE
POORI
POORIS
POORISH
POORLIER
POORLIEST
POORLY
POORMOUTH
POORNESS
POORT
POORTITH
POORTITHS
POORTS
POORWILL
POORWILLS
POOS
POOT
POOTED
POOTER
POOTERED
POOTERING
POOTERS
POOTING
POOTLE
POOTLED
POOTLES
POOTLING
POOTS
POP
POPADUM
POPADUMS
POPCORN
POPCORNS
POPE
POPEDOM
POPEDOMS
POPEHOOD
POPEHOODS
POPELESS
POPELIKE
POPELING
POPELINGS
POPERA
POPERAS
POPERIN
POPERINS
POPES
POPESEYE
POPESHIP
POPESHIPS
POPETTE
POPETTES
POPEYED
POPGUN
POPGUNS
POPINAC
POPINACK
POPINACKS

P

POPINACS
POPINJAY
POPINJAYS
POPJOY
POPJOYED
POPJOYING
POPJOYS
POPLAR
POPLARS
POPLIN
POPLINS
POPLITEAL
POPLITEI
POPLITEUS
POPLITIC
POPOUT
POPOUTS
POPOVER
POPOVERS
POPPA
POPPADOM
POPPADOMS
POPPADUM
POPPADUMS
POPPAS
POPPED
POPPER
POPPERING
POPPERS
POPPET
POPPETS
POPPIED
POPPIER
POPPIES
POPPIEST
POPPING
POPPISH
POPPIT
POPPITS
POPPLE
POPPLED
POPPLES
POPPLIER
POPPLIEST
POPPLING
POPPLY
POPPY
POPPYCOCK
POPPYHEAD
POPPYSEED
POPRIN
POPS
POPSICLE
POPSICLES
POPSIE
POPSIES
POPSOCK
POPSOCKS
POPSTER
POPSTERS
POPSTREL
POPSTRELS
POPSY
POPTASTIC
POPULACE
POPULACES
POPULAR
POPULARLY
POPULARS
POPULATE
POPULATED
POPULATES
POPULISM
POPULISMS
POPULIST
POPULISTS
POPULOUS
PORAE
PORAES
PORAL
PORANGI
PORBEAGLE
PORCELAIN
PORCH
PORCHED
PORCHES
PORCHETTA
PORCHLESS
PORCINE
PORCINI
PORCINIS
PORCINO
PORCUPINE
PORCUPINY
PORE
PORED
PORER
PORERS
PORES
PORGE
PORGED
PORGES
PORGIE
PORGIES
PORGING
PORGY
PORIER
PORIEST
PORIFER
PORIFERAL
PORIFERAN
PORIFERS
PORIN
PORINA
PORINAS
PORINESS
PORING
PORINS
PORISM
PORISMS
PORISTIC
PORK
PORKED
PORKER
PORKERS
PORKIER
PORKIES
PORKIEST
PORKINESS
PORKING
PORKLING
PORKLINGS
PORKPIE
PORKPIES
PORKS
PORKWOOD
PORKWOODS
PORKY
PORLOCK
PORLOCKED
PORLOCKS
PORN
PORNIER
PORNIEST
PORNO
PORNOMAG
PORNOMAGS
PORNOS
PORNS
PORNY
POROGAMIC
POROGAMY
POROMERIC
POROSCOPE
POROSCOPY
POROSE
POROSES
POROSIS
POROSITY
POROUS
POROUSLY
PORPESS
PORPESSE
PORPESSES
PORPHYRIA
PORPHYRIC
PORPHYRIN
PORPHYRIO
PORPHYRY
PORPOISE
PORPOISED
PORPOISES
PORPORATE
PORRECT
PORRECTED
PORRECTS
PORRENGER
PORRIDGE
PORRIDGES
PORRIDGY
PORRIGO
PORRIGOS
PORRINGER
PORT
PORTA
PORTABLE
PORTABLES
PORTABLY
PORTAGE
PORTAGED
PORTAGES
PORTAGING
PORTAGUE
PORTAGUES
PORTAL
PORTALED
PORTALS
PORTANCE
PORTANCES
PORTAPACK
PORTAPAK
PORTAPAKS
PORTAS
PORTASES
PORTATE
PORTATILE
PORTATIVE
PORTED
PORTEND
PORTENDED
PORTENDS
PORTENT
PORTENTS
PORTEOUS
PORTER
PORTERAGE
PORTERED
PORTERESS
PORTERING
PORTERLY
PORTERS
PORTESS
PORTESSE
PORTESSES
PORTFIRE
PORTFIRES
PORTFOLIO
PORTHOLE
PORTHOLES
PORTHORS
PORTHOS
PORTHOSES
PORTHOUSE
PORTICO
PORTICOED
PORTICOES
PORTICOS
PORTIER
PORTIERE
PORTIERED

PORTIERES
PORTIEST
PORTIGUE
PORTIGUES
PORTING
PORTION
PORTIONED
PORTIONER
PORTIONS
PORTLAND
PORTLANDS
PORTLAST
PORTLASTS
PORTLESS
PORTLIER
PORTLIEST
PORTLY
PORTMAN
PORTMEN
PORTOISE
PORTOISES
PORTOLAN
PORTOLANI
PORTOLANO
PORTOLANS
PORTOUS
PORTOUSES
PORTRAIT
PORTRAITS
PORTRAY
PORTRAYAL
PORTRAYED
PORTRAYER
PORTRAYS
PORTREEVE
PORTRESS
PORTS
PORTSIDE
PORTULACA
PORTULAN
PORTULANS
PORTY
PORWIGGLE
PORY
POS
POSABLE
POSADA
POSADAS
POSAUNE
POSAUNES
POSE
POSEABLE
POSED
POSER
POSERISH
POSERS
POSES
POSEUR
POSEURS
POSEUSE
POSEUSES
POSEY
POSH
POSHED
POSHER
POSHES
POSHEST
POSHING
POSHLY
POSHNESS
POSHO
POSHOS
POSHTEEN
POSHTEENS
POSIDRIVE
POSIER
POSIES
POSIEST
POSIGRADE
POSING
POSINGLY
POSINGS
POSIT
POSITED
POSITIF
POSITIFS
POSITING
POSITION
POSITIONS
POSITIVE
POSITIVER
POSITIVES
POSITON
POSITONS
POSITRON
POSITRONS
POSITS
POSNET
POSNETS
POSOLE
POSOLES
POSOLOGIC
POSOLOGY
POSS
POSSE
POSSED
POSSER
POSSERS
POSSES
POSSESS
POSSESSED
POSSESSES
POSSESSOR
POSSET
POSSETED
POSSETING
POSSETS
POSSIBLE
POSSIBLER
POSSIBLES
POSSIBLY
POSSIE
POSSIES
POSSING
POSSUM
POSSUMED
POSSUMING
POSSUMS
POST
POSTAGE
POSTAGES
POSTAL
POSTALLY
POSTALS
POSTANAL
POSTAXIAL
POSTBAG
POSTBAGS
POSTBASE
POSTBASES
POSTBOX
POSTBOXES
POSTBOY
POSTBOYS
POSTBURN
POSTBUS
POSTBUSES
POSTCARD
POSTCARDS
POSTCAVA
POSTCAVAE
POSTCAVAL
POSTCAVAS
POSTCODE
POSTCODED
POSTCODES
POSTCOUP
POSTCRASH
POSTDATE
POSTDATED
POSTDATES
POSTDIVE
POSTDOC
POSTDOCS
POSTDRUG
POSTED
POSTEEN
POSTEENS
POSTER
POSTERED
POSTERING
POSTERIOR
POSTERISE
POSTERITY
POSTERIZE
POSTERN
POSTERNS
POSTERS
POSTFACE
POSTFACES
POSTFACT
POSTFAULT
POSTFIRE
POSTFIX
POSTFIXAL
POSTFIXED
POSTFIXES
POSTFORM
POSTFORMS
POSTGAME
POSTGRAD
POSTGRADS
POSTHASTE
POSTHEAT
POSTHEATS
POSTHOLE
POSTHOLES
POSTHORSE
POSTHOUSE
POSTICAL
POSTICHE
POSTICHES
POSTICOUS
POSTIE
POSTIES
POSTIL
POSTILED
POSTILING
POSTILION
POSTILLED
POSTILLER
POSTILS
POSTIN
POSTING
POSTINGS
POSTINS
POSTIQUE
POSTIQUES
POSTLIKE
POSTLUDE
POSTLUDES
POSTMAN
POSTMARK
POSTMARKS
POSTMEN
POSTNASAL
POSTNATAL
POSTNATI
POSTOP
POSTOPS
POSTORAL
POSTPAID
POSTPONE
POSTPONED
POSTPONER
POSTPONES
POSTPOSE
POSTPOSED
POSTPOSES
POSTPUNK

P

POSTPUNKS
POSTRACE
POSTRIDER
POSTRIOT
POSTS
POSTSHOW
POSTSYNC
POSTSYNCS
POSTTAX
POSTTEEN
POSTTEENS
POSTTEST
POSTTESTS
POSTTRIAL
POSTTRUTH
POSTULANT
POSTULATA
POSTULATE
POSTURAL
POSTURE
POSTURED
POSTURER
POSTURERS
POSTURES
POSTURING
POSTURISE
POSTURIST
POSTURIZE
POSTVIRAL
POSTWAR
POSTWOMAN
POSTWOMEN
POSY
POT
POTABLE
POTABLES
POTAE
POTAES
POTAGE
POTAGER
POTAGERS
POTAGES
POTALE
POTALES
POTAMIC
POTASH
POTASHED
POTASHES
POTASHING
POTASS
POTASSA
POTASSAS
POTASSES
POTASSIC
POTASSIUM
POTATION
POTATIONS
POTATO
POTATOBUG
POTATOES
POTATORY
POTBELLY
POTBOIL
POTBOILED
POTBOILER
POTBOILS
POTBOUND
POTBOY
POTBOYS
POTCH
POTCHE
POTCHED
POTCHER
POTCHERS
POTCHES
POTCHING
POTE
POTED
POTEEN
POTEENS
POTENCE
POTENCES
POTENCIES
POTENCY
POTENT
POTENTATE
POTENTIAL
POTENTISE
POTENTIZE
POTENTLY
POTENTS
POTES
POTFUL
POTFULS
POTGUN
POTGUNS
POTHEAD
POTHEADS
POTHECARY
POTHEEN
POTHEENS
POTHER
POTHERB
POTHERBS
POTHERED
POTHERIER
POTHERING
POTHERS
POTHERY
POTHOLDER
POTHOLE
POTHOLED
POTHOLER
POTHOLERS
POTHOLES
POTHOLING
POTHOOK
POTHOOKS
POTHOS
POTHOSES
POTHOUSE
POTHOUSES
POTHUNTER
POTICARY
POTICHE
POTICHES
POTIN
POTING
POTINS
POTION
POTIONS
POTJIE
POTJIES
POTLACH
POTLACHE
POTLACHES
POTLATCH
POTLIKE
POTLINE
POTLINES
POTLUCK
POTLUCKS
POTMAN
POTMEN
POTOMETER
POTOO
POTOOS
POTOROO
POTOROOS
POTPIE
POTPIES
POTPOURRI
POTS
POTSHARD
POTSHARDS
POTSHARE
POTSHARES
POTSHERD
POTSHERDS
POTSHOP
POTSHOPS
POTSHOT
POTSHOTS
POTSIE
POTSIES
POTSTONE
POTSTONES
POTSY
POTT
POTTABLE
POTTAGE
POTTAGES
POTTED
POTTEEN
POTTEENS
POTTER
POTTERED
POTTERER
POTTERERS
POTTERIES
POTTERING
POTTERS
POTTERY
POTTIER
POTTIES
POTTIEST
POTTINESS
POTTING
POTTINGAR
POTTINGER
POTTLE
POTTLES
POTTO
POTTOS
POTTS
POTTY
POTWALLER
POTZER
POTZERS
POUCH
POUCHED
POUCHES
POUCHFUL
POUCHFULS
POUCHIER
POUCHIEST
POUCHING
POUCHLIKE
POUCHY
POUDER
POUDERS
POUDRE
POUDRES
POUF
POUFED
POUFF
POUFFE
POUFFED
POUFFES
POUFFIER
POUFFIEST
POUFFING
POUFFS
POUFFY
POUFING
POUFS
POUK
POUKE
POUKES
POUKING
POUKIT
POUKS
POULAINE
POULAINES
POULARD
POULARDE
POULARDES
POULARDS
POULDER
POULDERS

P

POULDRE
POULDRES
POULDRON
POULDRONS
POULE
POULES
POULP
POULPE
POULPES
POULPS
POULT
POULTER
POULTERER
POULTERS
POULTICE
POULTICED
POULTICES
POULTRIES
POULTRY
POULTS
POUNCE
POUNCED
POUNCER
POUNCERS
POUNCES
POUNCET
POUNCETS
POUNCHING
POUNCING
POUND
POUNDAGE
POUNDAGES
POUNDAL
POUNDALS
POUNDCAKE
POUNDED
POUNDER
POUNDERS
POUNDING
POUNDINGS
POUNDS
POUPE
POUPED
POUPES
POUPING
POUPT
POUR
POURABLE
POURBOIRE
POURED
POURER
POURERS
POURIE
POURIES
POURING
POURINGLY
POURINGS
POURPOINT
POURS
POURSEW
POURSEWED
POURSEWS
POURSUE
POURSUED
POURSUES
POURSUING
POURSUIT
POURSUITS
POURTRAY
POURTRAYD
POURTRAYS
POUSADA
POUSADAS
POUSOWDIE
POUSSE
POUSSES
POUSSETTE
POUSSIE
POUSSIES
POUSSIN
POUSSINS
POUT
POUTASSOU
POUTED
POUTER
POUTERS
POUTFUL
POUTHER
POUTHERED
POUTHERS
POUTIER
POUTIEST
POUTINE
POUTINES
POUTING
POUTINGLY
POUTINGS
POUTS
POUTY
POVERTIES
POVERTY
POW
POWAN
POWANS
POWDER
POWDERED
POWDERER
POWDERERS
POWDERIER
POWDERING
POWDERMAN
POWDERMEN
POWDERS
POWDERY
POWELLISE
POWELLITE
POWELLIZE
POWER
POWERBAND
POWERBOAT
POWERED
POWERFUL
POWERING
POWERLESS
POWERPLAY
POWERS
POWFAGGED
POWHIRI
POWHIRIS
POWIN
POWINS
POWN
POWND
POWNDED
POWNDING
POWNDS
POWNEY
POWNEYS
POWNIE
POWNIES
POWNS
POWNY
POWRE
POWRED
POWRES
POWRING
POWS
POWSOWDY
POWTER
POWTERED
POWTERING
POWTERS
POWWAW
POWWOW
POWWOWED
POWWOWING
POWWOWS
POX
POXED
POXES
POXIER
POXIEST
POXING
POXVIRUS
POXY
POYNANT
POYNT
POYNTED
POYNTING
POYNTS
POYOU
POYOUS
POYSE
POYSED
POYSES
POYSING
POYSON
POYSONED
POYSONING
POYSONS
POZ
POZIDRIVE
POZOLE
POZOLES
POZZ
POZZIES
POZZOLAN
POZZOLANA
POZZOLANS
POZZY
PRAAM
PRAAMS
PRABBLE
PRABBLES
PRACHARAK
PRACTIC
PRACTICAL
PRACTICE
PRACTICED
PRACTICER
PRACTICES
PRACTICK
PRACTICKS
PRACTICS
PRACTICUM
PRACTIQUE
PRACTISE
PRACTISED
PRACTISER
PRACTISES
PRACTIVE
PRACTOLOL
PRAD
PRADHAN
PRADHANS
PRADS
PRAEAMBLE
PRAECIPE
PRAECIPES
PRAECOCES
PRAEDIAL
PRAEDIALS
PRAEFECT
PRAEFECTS
PRAELECT
PRAELECTS
PRAELUDIA
PRAENOMEN
PRAESES
PRAESIDIA
PRAETOR
PRAETORS
PRAGMATIC
PRAHU
PRAHUS
PRAIRIE
PRAIRIED
PRAIRIES
PRAISE
PRAISEACH

P

PRAISED
PRAISEFUL
PRAISER
PRAISERS
PRAISES
PRAISING
PRAISINGS
PRAJNA
PRAJNAS
PRALINE
PRALINES
PRAM
PRAMS
PRANA
PRANAS
PRANAYAMA
PRANCE
PRANCED
PRANCER
PRANCERS
PRANCES
PRANCING
PRANCINGS
PRANCK
PRANCKE
PRANCKED
PRANCKES
PRANCKING
PRANCKS
PRANDIAL
PRANG
PRANGED
PRANGING
PRANGS
PRANK
PRANKED
PRANKFUL
PRANKIER
PRANKIEST
PRANKING
PRANKINGS
PRANKISH
PRANKLE
PRANKLED
PRANKLES
PRANKLING
PRANKS
PRANKSOME
PRANKSTER
PRANKY
PRAO
PRAOS
PRASE
PRASES
PRAT
PRATE
PRATED
PRATER
PRATERS
PRATES
PRATFALL
PRATFALLS
PRATFELL
PRATIE
PRATIES
PRATING
PRATINGLY
PRATINGS
PRATIQUE
PRATIQUES
PRATS
PRATT
PRATTED
PRATTING
PRATTLE
PRATTLED
PRATTLER
PRATTLERS
PRATTLES
PRATTLING
PRATTS
PRATY
PRAU
PRAUNCE
PRAUNCED
PRAUNCES
PRAUNCING
PRAUS
PRAVITIES
PRAVITY
PRAWLE
PRAWLES
PRAWLIN
PRAWLINS
PRAWN
PRAWNED
PRAWNER
PRAWNERS
PRAWNING
PRAWNS
PRAXES
PRAXIS
PRAXISES
PRAY
PRAYED
PRAYER
PRAYERFUL
PRAYERS
PRAYING
PRAYINGLY
PRAYINGS
PRAYS
PRE
PREABSORB
PREACCUSE
PREACE
PREACED
PREACES
PREACH
PREACHED
PREACHER
PREACHERS
PREACHES
PREACHIER
PREACHIFY
PREACHILY
PREACHING
PREACHY
PREACING
PREACT
PREACTED
PREACTING
PREACTS
PREADAMIC
PREADAPT
PREADAPTS
PREADJUST
PREADMIT
PREADMITS
PREADOPT
PREADOPTS
PREADULT
PREADULTS
PREAGED
PREALLOT
PREALLOTS
PREALTER
PREALTERS
PREAMBLE
PREAMBLED
PREAMBLES
PREAMP
PREAMPS
PREANAL
PREAPPLY
PREARM
PREARMED
PREARMING
PREARMS
PREASE
PREASED
PREASES
PREASING
PREASSE
PREASSED
PREASSES
PREASSIGN
PREASSING
PREASSURE
PREATOMIC
PREATTUNE
PREAUDIT
PREAUDITS
PREAVER
PREAVERS
PREAXIAL
PREBADE
PREBAKE
PREBAKED
PREBAKES
PREBAKING
PREBASAL
PREBATTLE
PREBEND
PREBENDAL
PREBENDS
PREBID
PREBIDDEN
PREBIDS
PREBILL
PREBILLED
PREBILLS
PREBIND
PREBINDS
PREBIOTIC
PREBIRTH
PREBIRTHS
PREBLESS
PREBOARD
PREBOARDS
PREBOIL
PREBOILED
PREBOILS
PREBOOK
PREBOOKED
PREBOOKS
PREBOOM
PREBORN
PREBOUGHT
PREBOUND
PREBUDGET
PREBUILD
PREBUILDS
PREBUILT
PREBUTTAL
PREBUY
PREBUYING
PREBUYS
PRECANCEL
PRECANCER
PRECARIAT
PRECAST
PRECASTS
PRECATIVE
PRECATORY
PRECAUDAL
PRECAVA
PRECAVAE
PRECAVAL
PRECAVALS
PRECEDE
PRECEDED
PRECEDENT
PRECEDES
PRECEDING
PRECEESE
PRECENSOR
PRECENT
PRECENTED
PRECENTOR

PRECENTS
PRECEPIT
PRECEPITS
PRECEPT
PRECEPTOR
PRECEPTS
PRECES
PRECESS
PRECESSED
PRECESSES
PRECHARGE
PRECHECK
PRECHECKS
PRECHILL
PRECHILLS
PRECHOOSE
PRECHOSE
PRECHOSEN
PRECIEUSE
PRECIEUX
PRECINCT
PRECINCTS
PRECIOUS
PRECIP
PRECIPE
PRECIPES
PRECIPICE
PRECIPS
PRECIS
PRECISE
PRECISED
PRECISELY
PRECISER
PRECISES
PRECISEST
PRECISIAN
PRECISING
PRECISION
PRECISIVE
PRECITED
PRECLEAN
PRECLEANS
PRECLEAR
PRECLEARS
PRECLUDE
PRECLUDED
PRECLUDES
PRECOCIAL
PRECOCITY
PRECODE
PRECODED
PRECODES
PRECODING
PRECOITAL
PRECONISE
PRECONIZE
PRECOOK
PRECOOKED
PRECOOKER
PRECOOKS
PRECOOL
PRECOOLED
PRECOOLS
PRECOUP
PRECRASH
PRECREASE
PRECRISIS
PRECURE
PRECURED
PRECURES
PRECURING
PRECURRER
PRECURSE
PRECURSED
PRECURSES
PRECURSOR
PRECUT
PRECUTS
PRECYCLE
PRECYCLED
PRECYCLES
PREDACITY
PREDATE
PREDATED
PREDATES
PREDATING
PREDATION
PREDATISM
PREDATIVE
PREDATOR
PREDATORS
PREDATORY
PREDAWN
PREDAWNS
PREDEATH
PREDEATHS
PREDEBATE
PREDEDUCT
PREDEFINE
PREDELLA
PREDELLAS
PREDELLE
PREDESIGN
PREDEVOTE
PREDIAL
PREDIALS
PREDICANT
PREDICATE
PREDICT
PREDICTED
PREDICTER
PREDICTOR
PREDICTS
PREDIED
PREDIES
PREDIGEST
PREDIKANT
PREDILECT
PREDINNER
PREDIVE
PREDOOM
PREDOOMED
PREDOOMS
PREDRAFT
PREDRAFTS
PREDRIED
PREDRIES
PREDRILL
PREDRILLS
PREDRY
PREDRYING
PREDUSK
PREDUSKS
PREDY
PREDYING
PREE
PREED
PREEDIT
PREEDITED
PREEDITS
PREEING
PREELECT
PREELECTS
PREEMIE
PREEMIES
PREEMPT
PREEMPTED
PREEMPTOR
PREEMPTS
PREEN
PREENACT
PREENACTS
PREENED
PREENER
PREENERS
PREENING
PREENS
PREERECT
PREERECTS
PREES
PREEVE
PREEVED
PREEVES
PREEVING
PREEXCITE
PREEXEMPT
PREEXILIC
PREEXIST
PREEXISTS
PREEXPOSE
PREFAB
PREFABBED
PREFABS
PREFACE
PREFACED
PREFACER
PREFACERS
PREFACES
PREFACIAL
PREFACING
PREFADE
PREFADED
PREFADES
PREFADING
PREFARD
PREFATORY
PREFECT
PREFECTS
PREFER
PREFERRED
PREFERRER
PREFERS
PREFEUDAL
PREFIGHT
PREFIGURE
PREFILE
PREFILED
PREFILES
PREFILING
PREFILLED
PREFIRE
PREFIRED
PREFIRES
PREFIRING
PREFIX
PREFIXAL
PREFIXED
PREFIXES
PREFIXING
PREFIXION
PREFLAME
PREFLIGHT
PREFOCUS
PREFORM
PREFORMAT
PREFORMED
PREFORMS
PREFRANK
PREFRANKS
PREFREEZE
PREFROZE
PREFROZEN
PREFUND
PREFUNDED
PREFUNDS
PREGAME
PREGAMED
PREGAMES
PREGAMING
PREGGERS
PREGGIER
PREGGIEST
PREGGO
PREGGY
PREGNABLE
PREGNANCE
PREGNANCY
PREGNANT
PREGROWTH
PREGUIDE

P

PREGUIDED
PREGUIDES
PREHAB
PREHABS
PREHALLUX
PREHANDLE
PREHARDEN
PREHEAT
PREHEATED
PREHEATER
PREHEATS
PREHEND
PREHENDED
PREHENDS
PREHENSOR
PREHIRING
PREHNITE
PREHNITES
PREHUMAN
PREHUMANS
PREIF
PREIFE
PREIFES
PREIFS
PREIMPOSE
PREINFORM
PREINSERT
PREINVITE
PREJINK
PREJUDGE
PREJUDGED
PREJUDGER
PREJUDGES
PREJUDICE
PREJUDIZE
PRELACIES
PRELACY
PRELATE
PRELATES
PRELATESS
PRELATIAL
PRELATIC
PRELATIES
PRELATION
PRELATISE
PRELATISH
PRELATISM
PRELATIST
PRELATIZE
PRELATURE
PRELATY
PRELAUNCH
PRELAW
PRELECT
PRELECTED
PRELECTOR
PRELECTS
PRELEGAL
PRELIFE
PRELIM
PRELIMIT
PRELIMITS
PRELIMS
PRELIVES
PRELOAD
PRELOADED
PRELOADS
PRELOCATE
PRELOVED
PRELUDE
PRELUDED
PRELUDER
PRELUDERS
PRELUDES
PRELUDI
PRELUDIAL
PRELUDING
PRELUDIO
PRELUDIOS
PRELUNCH
PRELUSION
PRELUSIVE
PRELUSORY
PREM
PREMADE
PREMAKE
PREMAKES
PREMAKING
PREMAN
PREMARKET
PREMATURE
PREMEAL
PREMED
PREMEDIC
PREMEDICS
PREMEDS
PREMEET
PREMEN
PREMERGER
PREMIA
PREMIE
PREMIER
PREMIERE
PREMIERED
PREMIERES
PREMIERS
PREMIES
PREMISE
PREMISED
PREMISES
PREMISING
PREMISS
PREMISSED
PREMISSES
PREMIUM
PREMIUMS
PREMIX
PREMIXED
PREMIXES
PREMIXING
PREMIXT
PREMODERN
PREMODIFY
PREMOLAR
PREMOLARS
PREMOLD
PREMOLDED
PREMOLDS
PREMOLT
PREMONISH
PREMORAL
PREMORSE
PREMOSAIC
PREMOTION
PREMOTOR
PREMOULD
PREMOULDS
PREMOULT
PREMOVE
PREMOVED
PREMOVES
PREMOVING
PREMS
PREMUNE
PREMY
PRENAME
PRENAMES
PRENASAL
PRENASALS
PRENATAL
PRENATALS
PRENEED
PRENOMEN
PRENOMENS
PRENOMINA
PRENOON
PRENOTIFY
PRENOTION
PRENT
PRENTED
PRENTICE
PRENTICED
PRENTICES
PRENTING
PRENTS
PRENUBILE
PRENUMBER
PRENUP
PRENUPS
PRENZIE
PREOBTAIN
PREOCCUPY
PREOCULAR
PREON
PREONS
PREOP
PREOPS
PREOPTION
PREORAL
PREORDAIN
PREORDER
PREORDERS
PREOWNED
PREP
PREPACK
PREPACKED
PREPACKS
PREPAID
PREPARE
PREPARED
PREPARER
PREPARERS
PREPARES
PREPARING
PREPASTE
PREPASTED
PREPASTES
PREPAVE
PREPAVED
PREPAVES
PREPAVING
PREPAY
PREPAYING
PREPAYS
PREPENSE
PREPENSED
PREPENSES
PREPILL
PREPLACE
PREPLACED
PREPLACES
PREPLAN
PREPLANS
PREPLANT
PREPOLLEX
PREPONE
PREPONED
PREPONES
PREPONING
PREPOSE
PREPOSED
PREPOSES
PREPOSING
PREPOSTOR
PREPOTENT
PREPPED
PREPPIE
PREPPIER
PREPPIES
PREPPIEST
PREPPILY
PREPPING
PREPPY
PREPREG
PREPREGS
PREPRESS
PREPRICE
PREPRICED
PREPRICES
PREPRINT

PREPRINTS
PREPS
PREPUBES
PREPUBIS
PREPUCE
PREPUCES
PREPUEBLO
PREPUNCH
PREPUPA
PREPUPAE
PREPUPAL
PREPUPAS
PREPUTIAL
PREQUEL
PREQUELS
PRERACE
PRERADIO
PRERECORD
PRERECTAL
PREREFORM
PRERENAL
PRERETURN
PREREVIEW
PRERINSE
PRERINSED
PRERINSES
PRERIOT
PREROCK
PRERUPT
PRESA
PRESAGE
PRESAGED
PRESAGER
PRESAGERS
PRESAGES
PRESAGING
PRESALE
PRESALES
PRESBYOPE
PRESBYOPY
PRESBYTE
PRESBYTER
PRESBYTES
PRESBYTIC
PRESCHOOL
PRESCIENT
PRESCIND
PRESCINDS
PRESCIOUS
PRESCORE
PRESCORED
PRESCORES
PRESCREEN
PRESCRIBE
PRESCRIPT
PRESCUTA
PRESCUTUM
PRESE
PRESEASON
PRESELECT
PRESELL
PRESELLS
PRESENCE
PRESENCES
PRESENILE
PRESENT
PRESENTED
PRESENTEE
PRESENTER
PRESENTLY
PRESENTS
PRESERVE
PRESERVED
PRESERVER
PRESERVES
PRESES
PRESET
PRESETS
PRESETTLE
PRESHAPE
PRESHAPED
PRESHAPES
PRESHIP
PRESHIPS
PRESHOW
PRESHOWED
PRESHOWN
PRESHOWS
PRESHRANK
PRESHRINK
PRESHRUNK
PRESIDE
PRESIDED
PRESIDENT
PRESIDER
PRESIDERS
PRESIDES
PRESIDIA
PRESIDIAL
PRESIDING
PRESIDIO
PRESIDIOS
PRESIDIUM
PRESIFT
PRESIFTED
PRESIFTS
PRESIGNAL
PRESLEEP
PRESLICE
PRESLICED
PRESLICES
PRESOAK
PRESOAKED
PRESOAKS
PRESOLD
PRESOLVE
PRESOLVED
PRESOLVES
PRESONG
PRESORT
PRESORTED
PRESORTS
PRESPLIT
PRESS
PRESSBACK
PRESSED
PRESSER
PRESSERS
PRESSES
PRESSFAT
PRESSFATS
PRESSFUL
PRESSFULS
PRESSGANG
PRESSIE
PRESSIES
PRESSING
PRESSINGS
PRESSION
PRESSIONS
PRESSMAN
PRESSMARK
PRESSMEN
PRESSOR
PRESSORS
PRESSROOM
PRESSRUN
PRESSRUNS
PRESSURE
PRESSURED
PRESSURES
PRESSWORK
PRESSY
PREST
PRESTAMP
PRESTAMPS
PRESTED
PRESTER
PRESTERNA
PRESTERS
PRESTIGE
PRESTIGES
PRESTING
PRESTO
PRESTORE
PRESTORED
PRESTORES
PRESTOS
PRESTRESS
PRESTRIKE
PRESTS
PRESUME
PRESUMED
PRESUMER
PRESUMERS
PRESUMES
PRESUMING
PRESUMMIT
PRESURVEY
PRETAPE
PRETAPED
PRETAPES
PRETAPING
PRETASTE
PRETASTED
PRETASTES
PRETAX
PRETEEN
PRETEENS
PRETELL
PRETELLS
PRETENCE
PRETENCES
PRETEND
PRETENDED
PRETENDER
PRETENDS
PRETENSE
PRETENSES
PRETERIST
PRETERIT
PRETERITE
PRETERITS
PRETERM
PRETERMIT
PRETERMS
PRETEST
PRETESTED
PRETESTS
PRETEXT
PRETEXTED
PRETEXTS
PRETOLD
PRETONIC
PRETOR
PRETORIAL
PRETORIAN
PRETORS
PRETRAIN
PRETRAINS
PRETRAVEL
PRETREAT
PRETREATS
PRETRIAL
PRETRIALS
PRETRIM
PRETRIMS
PRETTIED
PRETTIER
PRETTIES
PRETTIEST
PRETTIFY
PRETTILY
PRETTY
PRETTYING
PRETTYISH
PRETTYISM
PRETYPE
PRETYPED
PRETYPES

P

PRETYPING
PRETZEL
PRETZELS
PREUNION
PREUNIONS
PREUNITE
PREUNITED
PREUNITES
PREVAIL
PREVAILED
PREVAILER
PREVAILS
PREVALENT
PREVALUE
PREVALUED
PREVALUES
PREVE
PREVED
PREVENE
PREVENED
PREVENES
PREVENING
PREVENT
PREVENTED
PREVENTER
PREVENTS
PREVERB
PREVERBAL
PREVERBS
PREVES
PREVIABLE
PREVIEW
PREVIEWED
PREVIEWER
PREVIEWS
PREVING
PREVIOUS
PREVISE
PREVISED
PREVISES
PREVISING
PREVISION
PREVISIT
PREVISITS
PREVISOR
PREVISORS
PREVUE
PREVUED
PREVUES
PREVUING
PREWAR
PREWARM
PREWARMED
PREWARMS
PREWARN
PREWARNED
PREWARNS
PREWASH
PREWASHED
PREWASHES
PREWEANED
PREWEIGH
PREWEIGHS
PREWIRE
PREWIRED
PREWIRES
PREWIRING
PREWORK
PREWORKED
PREWORKS
PREWORN
PREWRAP
PREWRAPS
PREWRITE
PREWRITES
PREWROTE
PREWYN
PREWYNS
PREX
PREXES
PREXIE
PREXIES
PREXY
PREY
PREYED
PREYER
PREYERS
PREYFUL
PREYING
PREYS
PREZ
PREZES
PREZZIE
PREZZIES
PRIAL
PRIALS
PRIAPEAN
PRIAPI
PRIAPIC
PRIAPISM
PRIAPISMS
PRIAPUS
PRIAPUSES
PRIBBLE
PRIBBLES
PRICE
PRICEABLE
PRICED
PRICELESS
PRICER
PRICERS
PRICES
PRICEY
PRICIER
PRICIEST
PRICILY
PRICINESS
PRICING
PRICINGS
PRICK
PRICKED
PRICKER
PRICKERS
PRICKET
PRICKETS
PRICKIER
PRICKIEST
PRICKING
PRICKINGS
PRICKLE
PRICKLED
PRICKLES
PRICKLIER
PRICKLING
PRICKLY
PRICKS
PRICKWOOD
PRICKY
PRICY
PRIDE
PRIDED
PRIDEFUL
PRIDELESS
PRIDES
PRIDIAN
PRIDING
PRIED
PRIEDIEU
PRIEDIEUS
PRIEDIEUX
PRIEF
PRIEFE
PRIEFES
PRIEFS
PRIER
PRIERS
PRIES
PRIEST
PRIESTED
PRIESTESS
PRIESTING
PRIESTLY
PRIESTS
PRIEVE
PRIEVED
PRIEVES
PRIEVING
PRIG
PRIGGED
PRIGGER
PRIGGERS
PRIGGERY
PRIGGING
PRIGGINGS
PRIGGISH
PRIGGISM
PRIGGISMS
PRIGS
PRILL
PRILLED
PRILLING
PRILLS
PRIM
PRIMA
PRIMACIES
PRIMACY
PRIMAEVAL
PRIMAGE
PRIMAGES
PRIMAL
PRIMALITY
PRIMALLY
PRIMARIES
PRIMARILY
PRIMARY
PRIMAS
PRIMATAL
PRIMATALS
PRIMATE
PRIMATES
PRIMATIAL
PRIMATIC
PRIMAVERA
PRIME
PRIMED
PRIMELY
PRIMENESS
PRIMER
PRIMERO
PRIMEROS
PRIMERS
PRIMES
PRIMETIME
PRIMEUR
PRIMEURS
PRIMEVAL
PRIMI
PRIMINE
PRIMINES
PRIMING
PRIMINGS
PRIMIPARA
PRIMITIAE
PRIMITIAL
PRIMITIAS
PRIMITIVE
PRIMLY
PRIMMED
PRIMMER
PRIMMERS
PRIMMEST
PRIMMING
PRIMNESS
PRIMO
PRIMORDIA
PRIMOS
PRIMP
PRIMPED
PRIMPING
PRIMPS

PRIMROSE
PRIMROSED
PRIMROSES
PRIMROSY
PRIMS
PRIMSIE
PRIMSIER
PRIMSIEST
PRIMULA
PRIMULAS
PRIMULINE
PRIMUS
PRIMUSES
PRIMY
PRINCE
PRINCED
PRINCEDOM
PRINCEKIN
PRINCELET
PRINCELY
PRINCES
PRINCESS
PRINCESSE
PRINCING
PRINCIPAL
PRINCIPE
PRINCIPI
PRINCIPIA
PRINCIPLE
PRINCOCK
PRINCOCKS
PRINCOX
PRINCOXES
PRINK
PRINKED
PRINKER
PRINKERS
PRINKING
PRINKS
PRINT
PRINTABLE
PRINTED
PRINTER
PRINTERS
PRINTERY
PRINTHEAD
PRINTING
PRINTINGS
PRINTLESS
PRINTOUT
PRINTOUTS
PRINTS
PRION
PRIONS
PRIOR
PRIORATE
PRIORATES
PRIORESS
PRIORIES
PRIORITY
PRIORLY
PRIORS
PRIORSHIP
PRIORY
PRISAGE
PRISAGES
PRISE
PRISED
PRISER
PRISERE
PRISERES
PRISERS
PRISES
PRISING
PRISM
PRISMATIC
PRISMOID
PRISMOIDS
PRISMS
PRISMY
PRISON
PRISONED
PRISONER
PRISONERS
PRISONING
PRISONOUS
PRISONS
PRISS
PRISSED
PRISSES
PRISSIER
PRISSIES
PRISSIEST
PRISSILY
PRISSING
PRISSY
PRISTANE
PRISTANES
PRISTINE
PRITHEE
PRIVACIES
PRIVACY
PRIVADO
PRIVADOES
PRIVADOS
PRIVATE
PRIVATEER
PRIVATELY
PRIVATER
PRIVATES
PRIVATEST
PRIVATION
PRIVATISE
PRIVATISM
PRIVATIST
PRIVATIVE
PRIVATIZE
PRIVET
PRIVETS
PRIVIER
PRIVIES
PRIVIEST
PRIVILEGE
PRIVILY
PRIVITIES
PRIVITY
PRIVY
PRIZABLE
PRIZE
PRIZED
PRIZEMAN
PRIZEMEN
PRIZER
PRIZERS
PRIZES
PRIZING
PRO
PROA
PROACTION
PROACTIVE
PROAS
PROB
PROBABLE
PROBABLES
PROBABLY
PROBALL
PROBAND
PROBANDS
PROBANG
PROBANGS
PROBATE
PROBATED
PROBATES
PROBATING
PROBATION
PROBATIVE
PROBATORY
PROBE
PROBEABLE
PROBED
PROBER
PROBERS
PROBES
PROBING
PROBINGLY
PROBINGS
PROBIOTIC
PROBIT
PROBITIES
PROBITS
PROBITY
PROBLEM
PROBLEMS
PROBOSCIS
PROBS
PROCACITY
PROCAINE
PROCAINES
PROCAMBIA
PROCARP
PROCARPS
PROCARYON
PROCEDURE
PROCEED
PROCEEDED
PROCEEDER
PROCEEDS
PROCERITY
PROCESS
PROCESSED
PROCESSER
PROCESSES
PROCESSOR
PROCHAIN
PROCHEIN
PROCHOICE
PROCHURCH
PROCIDENT
PROCINCT
PROCINCTS
PROCLAIM
PROCLAIMS
PROCLISES
PROCLISIS
PROCLITIC
PROCLIVE
PROCONSUL
PROCREANT
PROCREATE
PROCTAL
PROCTITIS
PROCTODEA
PROCTOR
PROCTORED
PROCTORS
PROCURACY
PROCURAL
PROCURALS
PROCURE
PROCURED
PROCURER
PROCURERS
PROCURES
PROCURESS
PROCUREUR
PROCURING
PROCYONID
PROD
PRODDED
PRODDER
PRODDERS
PRODDING
PRODDINGS
PRODIGAL
PRODIGALS
PRODIGIES
PRODIGY
PRODITOR
PRODITORS
PRODITORY

PRODNOSE
PRODNOSED
PRODNOSES
PRODROMA
PRODROMAL
PRODROME
PRODROMES
PRODROMI
PRODROMIC
PRODROMUS
PRODRUG
PRODRUGS
PRODS
PRODUCE
PRODUCED
PRODUCER
PRODUCERS
PRODUCES
PRODUCING
PRODUCT
PRODUCTS
PROEM
PROEMBRYO
PROEMIAL
PROEMS
PROENZYME
PROESTRUS
PROETTE
PROETTES
PROF
PROFACE
PROFAMILY
PROFANE
PROFANED
PROFANELY
PROFANER
PROFANERS
PROFANES
PROFANING
PROFANITY
PROFESS
PROFESSED
PROFESSES
PROFESSOR
PROFFER
PROFFERED
PROFFERER
PROFFERS
PROFILE
PROFILED
PROFILER
PROFILERS
PROFILES
PROFILING
PROFILIST
PROFIT
PROFITED
PROFITEER
PROFITER
PROFITERS
PROFITING
PROFITS
PROFLUENT
PROFORMA
PROFORMAS
PROFOUND
PROFOUNDS
PROFS
PROFUSE
PROFUSELY
PROFUSER
PROFUSERS
PROFUSION
PROFUSIVE
PROG
PROGENIES
PROGENY
PROGERIA
PROGERIAS
PROGESTIN
PROGGED
PROGGER
PROGGERS
PROGGING
PROGGINS
PROGNOSE
PROGNOSED
PROGNOSES
PROGNOSIS
PROGRADE
PROGRADED
PROGRADES
PROGRAM
PROGRAMED
PROGRAMER
PROGRAMME
PROGRAMS
PROGRESS
PROGS
PROGUN
PROHIBIT
PROHIBITS
PROIGN
PROIGNED
PROIGNING
PROIGNS
PROIN
PROINE
PROINED
PROINES
PROINING
PROINS
PROJECT
PROJECTED
PROJECTOR
PROJECTS
PROJET
PROJETS
PROKARYON
PROKARYOT
PROKE
PROKED
PROKER
PROKERS
PROKES
PROKING
PROLABOR
PROLABOUR
PROLACTIN
PROLAMIN
PROLAMINE
PROLAMINS
PROLAN
PROLANS
PROLAPSE
PROLAPSED
PROLAPSES
PROLAPSUS
PROLATE
PROLATED
PROLATELY
PROLATES
PROLATING
PROLATION
PROLATIVE
PROLE
PROLED
PROLEG
PROLEGS
PROLEPSES
PROLEPSIS
PROLEPTIC
PROLER
PROLERS
PROLES
PROLETARY
PROLICIDE
PROLIFIC
PROLINE
PROLINES
PROLING
PROLIX
PROLIXITY
PROLIXLY
PROLL
PROLLED
PROLLER
PROLLERS
PROLLING
PROLLS
PROLLY
PROLOG
PROLOGED
PROLOGING
PROLOGISE
PROLOGIST
PROLOGIZE
PROLOGS
PROLOGUE
PROLOGUED
PROLOGUES
PROLONG
PROLONGE
PROLONGED
PROLONGER
PROLONGES
PROLONGS
PROLUSION
PROLUSORY
PROM
PROMACHOS
PROMENADE
PROMETAL
PROMETALS
PROMETRIC
PROMINE
PROMINENT
PROMINES
PROMISE
PROMISED
PROMISEE
PROMISEES
PROMISER
PROMISERS
PROMISES
PROMISING
PROMISOR
PROMISORS
PROMISSOR
PROMMER
PROMMERS
PROMO
PROMODERN
PROMOED
PROMOING
PROMOS
PROMOTE
PROMOTED
PROMOTER
PROMOTERS
PROMOTES
PROMOTING
PROMOTION
PROMOTIVE
PROMOTOR
PROMOTORS
PROMPT
PROMPTED
PROMPTER
PROMPTERS
PROMPTEST
PROMPTING
PROMPTLY
PROMPTS
PROMPTURE
PROMS
PROMULGE
PROMULGED
PROMULGES
PROMUSCES

P

PROMUSCIS
PRONAOI
PRONAOS
PRONATE
PRONATED
PRONATES
PRONATING
PRONATION
PRONATOR
PRONATORS
PRONE
PRONELY
PRONENESS
PRONEPHRA
PRONER
PRONES
PRONEST
PRONEUR
PRONEURS
PRONG
PRONGBUCK
PRONGED
PRONGHORN
PRONGING
PRONGS
PRONK
PRONKED
PRONKING
PRONKINGS
PRONKS
PRONOTA
PRONOTAL
PRONOTUM
PRONOUN
PRONOUNCE
PRONOUNS
PRONTO
PRONUCLEI
PRONUNCIO
PROO
PROOEMION
PROOEMIUM
PROOF
PROOFED
PROOFER
PROOFERS
PROOFING
PROOFINGS
PROOFLESS
PROOFREAD
PROOFROOM
PROOFS
PROOTIC
PROOTICS
PROP
PROPAGATE
PROPAGE
PROPAGED
PROPAGES
PROPAGING
PROPAGULA
PROPAGULE
PROPALE
PROPALED
PROPALES
PROPALING
PROPANE
PROPANES
PROPANOIC
PROPANOL
PROPANOLS
PROPANONE
PROPEL
PROPELLED
PROPELLER
PROPELLOR
PROPELS
PROPENAL
PROPENALS
PROPEND
PROPENDED
PROPENDS
PROPENE
PROPENES
PROPENOIC
PROPENOL
PROPENOLS
PROPENSE
PROPENYL
PROPENYLS
PROPER
PROPERDIN
PROPERER
PROPEREST
PROPERLY
PROPERS
PROPERTY
PROPHAGE
PROPHAGES
PROPHASE
PROPHASES
PROPHASIC
PROPHECY
PROPHESY
PROPHET
PROPHETIC
PROPHETS
PROPHYLL
PROPHYLLS
PROPINE
PROPINED
PROPINES
PROPINING
PROPIONIC
PROPJET
PROPJETS
PROPMAN
PROPMEN
PROPODEON
PROPODEUM
PROPOLIS
PROPONE
PROPONED
PROPONENT
PROPONES
PROPONING
PROPOSAL
PROPOSALS
PROPOSE
PROPOSED
PROPOSER
PROPOSERS
PROPOSES
PROPOSING
PROPOSITA
PROPOSITI
PROPOUND
PROPOUNDS
PROPPANT
PROPPANTS
PROPPED
PROPPING
PROPRETOR
PROPRIA
PROPRIETY
PROPRIUM
PROPS
PROPTOSES
PROPTOSIS
PROPULSOR
PROPYL
PROPYLA
PROPYLAEA
PROPYLENE
PROPYLIC
PROPYLITE
PROPYLON
PROPYLONS
PROPYLS
PROPYNE
PROPYNES
PRORATE
PRORATED
PRORATES
PRORATING
PRORATION
PRORE
PRORECTOR
PROREFORM
PRORES
PROROGATE
PROROGUE
PROROGUED
PROROGUES
PROS
PROSAIC
PROSAICAL
PROSAISM
PROSAISMS
PROSAIST
PROSAISTS
PROSATEUR
PROSCENIA
PROSCRIBE
PROSCRIPT
PROSE
PROSECCO
PROSECCOS
PROSECT
PROSECTED
PROSECTOR
PROSECTS
PROSECUTE
PROSED
PROSELIKE
PROSELYTE
PROSEMAN
PROSEMEN
PROSER
PROSERS
PROSES
PROSEUCHA
PROSEUCHE
PROSIER
PROSIEST
PROSIFIED
PROSIFIES
PROSIFY
PROSILY
PROSIMIAN
PROSINESS
PROSING
PROSINGS
PROSIT
PROSO
PROSOCIAL
PROSODIAL
PROSODIAN
PROSODIC
PROSODIES
PROSODIST
PROSODY
PROSOMA
PROSOMAL
PROSOMAS
PROSOMATA
PROSOPON
PROSOPONS
PROSOS
PROSPECT
PROSPECTS
PROSPER
PROSPERED
PROSPERS
PROSS
PROSSES
PROSSIE
PROSSIES
PROST
PROSTATE

P

PROSTATES
PROSTATIC
PROSTERNA
PROSTIE
PROSTIES
PROSTOMIA
PROSTRATE
PROSTYLE
PROSTYLES
PROSUMER
PROSUMERS
PROSY
PROTAMIN
PROTAMINE
PROTAMINS
PROTANDRY
PROTANOPE
PROTASES
PROTASIS
PROTATIC
PROTEA
PROTEAN
PROTEANS
PROTEAS
PROTEASE
PROTEASES
PROTECT
PROTECTED
PROTECTER
PROTECTOR
PROTECTS
PROTEGE
PROTEGEE
PROTEGEES
PROTEGES
PROTEI
PROTEID
PROTEIDE
PROTEIDES
PROTEIDS
PROTEIN
PROTEINIC
PROTEINS
PROTEND
PROTENDED
PROTENDS
PROTENSE
PROTENSES
PROTEOME
PROTEOMES
PROTEOMIC
PROTEOSE
PROTEOSES
PROTEST
PROTESTED
PROTESTER
PROTESTOR
PROTESTS
PROTEUS
PROTEUSES
PROTHALLI
PROTHESES
PROTHESIS
PROTHETIC
PROTHORAX
PROTHYL
PROTHYLS
PROTIST
PROTISTAN
PROTISTIC
PROTISTS
PROTIUM
PROTIUMS
PROTO
PROTOAVIS
PROTOCOL
PROTOCOLS
PROTODERM
PROTOGINE
PROTOGYNY
PROTON
PROTONATE
PROTONEMA
PROTONIC
PROTONS
PROTOPOD
PROTOPODS
PROTORE
PROTORES
PROTOSTAR
PROTOTYPE
PROTOXID
PROTOXIDE
PROTOXIDS
PROTOZOA
PROTOZOAL
PROTOZOAN
PROTOZOIC
PROTOZOON
PROTRACT
PROTRACTS
PROTRADE
PROTRUDE
PROTRUDED
PROTRUDES
PROTURAN
PROTURANS
PROTYL
PROTYLE
PROTYLES
PROTYLS
PROUD
PROUDER
PROUDEST
PROUDFUL
PROUDISH
PROUDLY
PROUDNESS
PROUL
PROULED
PROULER
PROULERS
PROULING
PROULS
PROUNION
PROUSTITE
PROVABLE
PROVABLY
PROVAND
PROVANDS
PROVANT
PROVANTED
PROVANTS
PROVE
PROVEABLE
PROVEABLY
PROVED
PROVEDOR
PROVEDORE
PROVEDORS
PROVEN
PROVEND
PROVENDER
PROVENDS
PROVENLY
PROVER
PROVERB
PROVERBED
PROVERBS
PROVERS
PROVES
PROVIANT
PROVIANTS
PROVIDE
PROVIDED
PROVIDENT
PROVIDER
PROVIDERS
PROVIDES
PROVIDING
PROVIDOR
PROVIDORS
PROVINCE
PROVINCES
PROVINE
PROVINED
PROVINES
PROVING
PROVINGS
PROVINING
PROVIRAL
PROVIRUS
PROVISION
PROVISO
PROVISOES
PROVISOR
PROVISORS
PROVISORY
PROVISOS
PROVOCANT
PROVOKE
PROVOKED
PROVOKER
PROVOKERS
PROVOKES
PROVOKING
PROVOLONE
PROVOST
PROVOSTRY
PROVOSTS
PROW
PROWAR
PROWER
PROWESS
PROWESSED
PROWESSES
PROWEST
PROWL
PROWLED
PROWLER
PROWLERS
PROWLING
PROWLINGS
PROWLS
PROWS
PROXEMIC
PROXEMICS
PROXIES
PROXIMAL
PROXIMATE
PROXIMITY
PROXIMO
PROXY
PROYN
PROYNE
PROYNED
PROYNES
PROYNING
PROYNS
PROZYMITE
PROZZIE
PROZZIES
PRUDE
PRUDENCE
PRUDENCES
PRUDENT
PRUDENTLY
PRUDERIES
PRUDERY
PRUDES
PRUDISH
PRUDISHLY
PRUH
PRUINA
PRUINAS
PRUINE
PRUINES
PRUINOSE
PRUNABLE
PRUNE

PRUNED
PRUNELLA
PRUNELLAS
PRUNELLE
PRUNELLES
PRUNELLO
PRUNELLOS
PRUNER
PRUNERS
PRUNES
PRUNEY
PRUNIER
PRUNIEST
PRUNING
PRUNINGS
PRUNT
PRUNTED
PRUNTS
PRUNUS
PRUNUSES
PRURIENCE
PRURIENCY
PRURIENT
PRURIGO
PRURIGOS
PRURITIC
PRURITUS
PRUSIK
PRUSIKED
PRUSIKING
PRUSIKS
PRUSSIAN
PRUSSIATE
PRUSSIC
PRUTA
PRUTAH
PRUTOT
PRUTOTH
PRY
PRYER
PRYERS
PRYING
PRYINGLY
PRYINGS
PRYS
PRYSE
PRYSED
PRYSES
PRYSING
PRYTANEA
PRYTANEUM
PRYTHEE
PSALM
PSALMBOOK
PSALMED
PSALMIC
PSALMING
PSALMIST
PSALMISTS
PSALMODIC
PSALMODY
PSALMS
PSALTER
PSALTERIA
PSALTERS
PSALTERY
PSALTRESS
PSALTRIES
PSALTRY
PSAMMITE
PSAMMITES
PSAMMITIC
PSAMMON
PSAMMONS
PSCHENT
PSCHENTS
PSELLISM
PSELLISMS
PSEPHISM
PSEPHISMS
PSEPHITE
PSEPHITES
PSEPHITIC
PSEUD
PSEUDAXES
PSEUDAXIS
PSEUDERY
PSEUDISH
PSEUDO
PSEUDONYM
PSEUDOPOD
PSEUDOS
PSEUDS
PSHAW
PSHAWED
PSHAWING
PSHAWS
PSI
PSILOCIN
PSILOCINS
PSILOSES
PSILOSIS
PSILOTIC
PSION
PSIONIC
PSIONICS
PSIONS
PSIS
PSOAE
PSOAI
PSOAS
PSOASES
PSOATIC
PSOCID
PSOCIDS
PSORA
PSORALEA
PSORALEAS
PSORALEN
PSORALENS
PSORAS
PSORIASES
PSORIASIS
PSORIATIC
PSORIC
PSST
PST
PSYCH
PSYCHE
PSYCHED
PSYCHES
PSYCHIC
PSYCHICAL
PSYCHICS
PSYCHING
PSYCHISM
PSYCHISMS
PSYCHIST
PSYCHISTS
PSYCHO
PSYCHOGAS
PSYCHOID
PSYCHOIDS
PSYCHOS
PSYCHOSES
PSYCHOSIS
PSYCHOTIC
PSYCHS
PSYLLA
PSYLLAS
PSYLLID
PSYLLIDS
PSYLLIUM
PSYLLIUMS
PSYOP
PSYOPS
PSYWAR
PSYWARS
PTARMIC
PTARMICS
PTARMIGAN
PTERIA
PTERIDINE
PTERIN
PTERINS
PTERION
PTEROIC
PTEROPOD
PTEROPODS
PTEROSAUR
PTERYGIA
PTERYGIAL
PTERYGIUM
PTERYGOID
PTERYLA
PTERYLAE
PTILOSES
PTILOSIS
PTISAN
PTISANS
PTOMAIN
PTOMAINE
PTOMAINES
PTOMAINIC
PTOMAINS
PTOOEY
PTOSES
PTOSIS
PTOTIC
PTUI
PTYALIN
PTYALINS
PTYALISE
PTYALISED
PTYALISES
PTYALISM
PTYALISMS
PTYALIZE
PTYALIZED
PTYALIZES
PTYXES
PTYXIS
PTYXISES
PUB
PUBBED
PUBBING
PUBBINGS
PUBCO
PUBCOS
PUBE
PUBERAL
PUBERTAL
PUBERTIES
PUBERTY
PUBES
PUBESCENT
PUBIC
PUBIS
PUBISES
PUBLIC
PUBLICAN
PUBLICANS
PUBLICISE
PUBLICIST
PUBLICITY
PUBLICIZE
PUBLICLY
PUBLICS
PUBLISH
PUBLISHED
PUBLISHER
PUBLISHES
PUBS
PUCAN
PUCANS
PUCCOON
PUCCOONS
PUCE
PUCELAGE
PUCELAGES

P

PUCELLE
PUCELLES
PUCER
PUCES
PUCEST
PUCK
PUCKA
PUCKED
PUCKER
PUCKERED
PUCKERER
PUCKERERS
PUCKERIER
PUCKERIES
PUCKERING
PUCKEROOD
PUCKERS
PUCKERY
PUCKFIST
PUCKFISTS
PUCKING
PUCKISH
PUCKISHLY
PUCKLE
PUCKLES
PUCKOUT
PUCKOUTS
PUCKS
PUCKSTER
PUCKSTERS
PUD
PUDDEN
PUDDENING
PUDDENS
PUDDER
PUDDERED
PUDDERING
PUDDERS
PUDDIER
PUDDIES
PUDDIEST
PUDDING
PUDDINGS
PUDDINGY
PUDDLE
PUDDLED
PUDDLER
PUDDLERS
PUDDLES
PUDDLIER
PUDDLIEST
PUDDLING
PUDDLINGS
PUDDLY
PUDDOCK
PUDDOCKS
PUDDY
PUDENCIES
PUDENCY
PUDENDA
PUDENDAL
PUDENDOUS
PUDENDUM
PUDENT
PUDEUR
PUDEURS
PUDGE
PUDGES
PUDGIER
PUDGIEST
PUDGILY
PUDGINESS
PUDGY
PUDIBUND
PUDIC
PUDICITY
PUDOR
PUDORS
PUDS
PUDSEY
PUDSIER
PUDSIES
PUDSIEST
PUDSY
PUDU
PUDUS
PUEBLO
PUEBLOS
PUER
PUERED
PUERILE
PUERILELY
PUERILISM
PUERILITY
PUERING
PUERPERA
PUERPERAE
PUERPERAL
PUERPERIA
PUERS
PUFF
PUFFA
PUFFBACK
PUFFBACKS
PUFFBALL
PUFFBALLS
PUFFBIRD
PUFFBIRDS
PUFFED
PUFFER
PUFFERIES
PUFFERS
PUFFERY
PUFFIER
PUFFIEST
PUFFILY
PUFFIN
PUFFINESS
PUFFING
PUFFINGLY
PUFFINGS
PUFFINS
PUFFS
PUFFY
PUFTALOON
PUG
PUGAREE
PUGAREES
PUGGAREE
PUGGAREES
PUGGED
PUGGERIES
PUGGERY
PUGGIE
PUGGIER
PUGGIES
PUGGIEST
PUGGINESS
PUGGING
PUGGINGS
PUGGISH
PUGGLE
PUGGLED
PUGGLES
PUGGLING
PUGGREE
PUGGREES
PUGGRIES
PUGGRY
PUGGY
PUGH
PUGIL
PUGILISM
PUGILISMS
PUGILIST
PUGILISTS
PUGILS
PUGMARK
PUGMARKS
PUGNACITY
PUGREE
PUGREES
PUGS
PUH
PUHA
PUHAS
PUIR
PUIRER
PUIREST
PUIRTITH
PUIRTITHS
PUISNE
PUISNES
PUISNY
PUISSANCE
PUISSANT
PUISSAUNT
PUJA
PUJAH
PUJAHS
PUJARI
PUJARIS
PUJAS
PUKA
PUKAS
PUKATEA
PUKATEAS
PUKE
PUKED
PUKEKO
PUKEKOS
PUKER
PUKERS
PUKES
PUKEY
PUKIER
PUKIEST
PUKING
PUKKA
PUKKAH
PUKU
PUKUS
PUKY
PUL
PULA
PULAO
PULAOS
PULAS
PULDRON
PULDRONS
PULE
PULED
PULER
PULERS
PULES
PULI
PULICENE
PULICIDE
PULICIDES
PULIER
PULIEST
PULIK
PULING
PULINGLY
PULINGS
PULIS
PULK
PULKA
PULKAS
PULKHA
PULKHAS
PULKS
PULL
PULLBACK
PULLBACKS
PULLED
PULLER
PULLERS
PULLET
PULLETS

PULLEY
PULLEYED
PULLEYING
PULLEYS
PULLI
PULLIES
PULLING
PULLMAN
PULLMANS
PULLORUM
PULLOUT
PULLOUTS
PULLOVER
PULLOVERS
PULLS
PULLULATE
PULLUP
PULLUPS
PULLUS
PULLY
PULMO
PULMONARY
PULMONATE
PULMONES
PULMONIC
PULMONICS
PULMOTOR
PULMOTORS
PULP
PULPAL
PULPALLY
PULPBOARD
PULPED
PULPER
PULPERS
PULPIER
PULPIEST
PULPIFIED
PULPIFIES
PULPIFY
PULPILY
PULPINESS
PULPING
PULPINGS
PULPIT
PULPITAL
PULPITED
PULPITEER
PULPITER
PULPITERS
PULPITRY
PULPITS
PULPITUM
PULPITUMS
PULPLESS
PULPMILL
PULPMILLS
PULPOUS
PULPS
PULPSTONE
PULPWOOD
PULPWOODS
PULPY
PULQUE
PULQUES
PULS
PULSANT
PULSAR
PULSARS
PULSATE
PULSATED
PULSATES
PULSATILE
PULSATING
PULSATION
PULSATIVE
PULSATOR
PULSATORS
PULSATORY
PULSE
PULSEBEAT
PULSED
PULSEJET
PULSEJETS
PULSELESS
PULSER
PULSERS
PULSES
PULSIDGE
PULSIDGES
PULSIFIC
PULSING
PULSION
PULSIONS
PULSOJET
PULSOJETS
PULTAN
PULTANS
PULTON
PULTONS
PULTOON
PULTOONS
PULTRUDE
PULTRUDED
PULTRUDES
PULTUN
PULTUNS
PULTURE
PULTURES
PULU
PULUS
PULVER
PULVERED
PULVERINE
PULVERING
PULVERISE
PULVERIZE
PULVEROUS
PULVERS
PULVIL
PULVILIO
PULVILIOS
PULVILLAR
PULVILLE
PULVILLED
PULVILLES
PULVILLI
PULVILLIO
PULVILLUS
PULVILS
PULVINAR
PULVINARS
PULVINATE
PULVINI
PULVINULE
PULVINUS
PULWAR
PULWARS
PULY
PUMA
PUMAS
PUMELO
PUMELOS
PUMICATE
PUMICATED
PUMICATES
PUMICE
PUMICED
PUMICEOUS
PUMICER
PUMICERS
PUMICES
PUMICING
PUMICITE
PUMICITES
PUMIE
PUMIES
PUMMEL
PUMMELED
PUMMELING
PUMMELLED
PUMMELO
PUMMELOS
PUMMELS
PUMP
PUMPABLE
PUMPED
PUMPER
PUMPERS
PUMPHOOD
PUMPHOODS
PUMPHOUSE
PUMPING
PUMPINGS
PUMPION
PUMPIONS
PUMPJACK
PUMPJACKS
PUMPKIN
PUMPKING
PUMPKINGS
PUMPKINS
PUMPLESS
PUMPLIKE
PUMPS
PUMY
PUN
PUNA
PUNAANI
PUNAANY
PUNALUA
PUNALUAN
PUNALUAS
PUNANI
PUNANY
PUNAS
PUNCE
PUNCED
PUNCES
PUNCH
PUNCHBAG
PUNCHBAGS
PUNCHBALL
PUNCHBOWL
PUNCHED
PUNCHEON
PUNCHEONS
PUNCHER
PUNCHERS
PUNCHES
PUNCHIER
PUNCHIEST
PUNCHILY
PUNCHING
PUNCHLESS
PUNCHLINE
PUNCHOUT
PUNCHOUTS
PUNCHY
PUNCING
PUNCTA
PUNCTATE
PUNCTATED
PUNCTATOR
PUNCTILIO
PUNCTO
PUNCTOS
PUNCTUAL
PUNCTUATE
PUNCTULE
PUNCTULES
PUNCTUM
PUNCTUMS
PUNCTURE
PUNCTURED
PUNCTURER
PUNCTURES
PUNDIT
PUNDITIC
PUNDITRY

P

PUNDITS
PUNDONOR
PUNG
PUNGA
PUNGAS
PUNGENCE
PUNGENCES
PUNGENCY
PUNGENT
PUNGENTLY
PUNGLE
PUNGLED
PUNGLES
PUNGLING
PUNGS
PUNIER
PUNIEST
PUNILY
PUNINESS
PUNISH
PUNISHED
PUNISHER
PUNISHERS
PUNISHES
PUNISHING
PUNITION
PUNITIONS
PUNITIVE
PUNITORY
PUNJI
PUNJIED
PUNJIES
PUNJIING
PUNJIS
PUNK
PUNKA
PUNKAH
PUNKAHS
PUNKAS
PUNKER
PUNKERS
PUNKEST
PUNKETTE
PUNKETTES
PUNKEY
PUNKEYS
PUNKIE
PUNKIER
PUNKIES
PUNKIEST
PUNKIN
PUNKINESS
PUNKINS
PUNKISH
PUNKS
PUNKY
PUNNED
PUNNER
PUNNERS
PUNNET
PUNNETS
PUNNIER
PUNNIEST
PUNNING
PUNNINGLY
PUNNINGS
PUNNY
PUNS
PUNSTER
PUNSTERS
PUNT
PUNTED
PUNTEE
PUNTEES
PUNTER
PUNTERS
PUNTIES
PUNTING
PUNTO
PUNTOS
PUNTS
PUNTSMAN
PUNTSMEN
PUNTY
PUNY
PUP
PUPA
PUPAE
PUPAL
PUPARIA
PUPARIAL
PUPARIUM
PUPAS
PUPATE
PUPATED
PUPATES
PUPATING
PUPATION
PUPATIONS
PUPFISH
PUPFISHES
PUPIL
PUPILAGE
PUPILAGES
PUPILAR
PUPILARY
PUPILLAGE
PUPILLAR
PUPILLARY
PUPILLATE
PUPILS
PUPILSHIP
PUPPED
PUPPET
PUPPETEER
PUPPETRY
PUPPETS
PUPPIED
PUPPIES
PUPPING
PUPPODUM
PUPPODUMS
PUPPY
PUPPYDOM
PUPPYDOMS
PUPPYHOOD
PUPPYING
PUPPYISH
PUPPYISM
PUPPYISMS
PUPPYLIKE
PUPS
PUPU
PUPUNHA
PUPUNHAS
PUPUS
PUR
PURANA
PURANAS
PURANIC
PURBLIND
PURCHASE
PURCHASED
PURCHASER
PURCHASES
PURDA
PURDAH
PURDAHED
PURDAHS
PURDAS
PURDONIUM
PURE
PUREBLOOD
PUREBRED
PUREBREDS
PURED
PUREE
PUREED
PUREEING
PUREES
PURELY
PURENESS
PURER
PURES
PUREST
PURFLE
PURFLED
PURFLER
PURFLERS
PURFLES
PURFLING
PURFLINGS
PURFLY
PURGATION
PURGATIVE
PURGATORY
PURGE
PURGEABLE
PURGED
PURGER
PURGERS
PURGES
PURGING
PURGINGS
PURI
PURIFIED
PURIFIER
PURIFIERS
PURIFIES
PURIFY
PURIFYING
PURIN
PURINE
PURINES
PURING
PURINS
PURIRI
PURIRIS
PURIS
PURISM
PURISMS
PURIST
PURISTIC
PURISTS
PURITAN
PURITANIC
PURITANS
PURITIES
PURITY
PURL
PURLED
PURLER
PURLERS
PURLICUE
PURLICUED
PURLICUES
PURLIEU
PURLIEUS
PURLIEUX
PURLIN
PURLINE
PURLINES
PURLING
PURLINGS
PURLINS
PURLOIN
PURLOINED
PURLOINER
PURLOINS
PURLS
PUROMYCIN
PURPIE
PURPIES
PURPLE
PURPLED
PURPLER
PURPLES
PURPLEST
PURPLIER
PURPLIEST

P

PURPLING
PURPLISH
PURPLY
PURPORT
PURPORTED
PURPORTS
PURPOSE
PURPOSED
PURPOSELY
PURPOSES
PURPOSING
PURPOSIVE
PURPURA
PURPURAS
PURPURE
PURPUREAL
PURPURES
PURPURIC
PURPURIN
PURPURINS
PURPY
PURR
PURRED
PURRING
PURRINGLY
PURRINGS
PURRS
PURS
PURSE
PURSED
PURSEFUL
PURSEFULS
PURSELIKE
PURSER
PURSERS
PURSES
PURSEW
PURSEWED
PURSEWING
PURSEWS
PURSIER
PURSIEST
PURSILY
PURSINESS
PURSING
PURSLAIN
PURSLAINS
PURSLANE
PURSLANES
PURSUABLE
PURSUAL
PURSUALS
PURSUANCE
PURSUANT
PURSUE
PURSUED
PURSUER
PURSUERS
PURSUES
PURSUING
PURSUINGS
PURSUIT
PURSUITS
PURSY
PURTIER
PURTIEST
PURTRAID
PURTRAYD
PURTY
PURULENCE
PURULENCY
PURULENT
PURVEY
PURVEYED
PURVEYING
PURVEYOR
PURVEYORS
PURVEYS
PURVIEW
PURVIEWS
PUS
PUSES
PUSH
PUSHBACK
PUSHBACKS
PUSHBALL
PUSHBALLS
PUSHBIKE
PUSHBIKES
PUSHCART
PUSHCARTS
PUSHCHAIR
PUSHDOWN
PUSHDOWNS
PUSHED
PUSHER
PUSHERS
PUSHES
PUSHFUL
PUSHFULLY
PUSHIER
PUSHIEST
PUSHILY
PUSHINESS
PUSHING
PUSHINGLY
PUSHOVER
PUSHOVERS
PUSHPIN
PUSHPINS
PUSHPIT
PUSHPITS
PUSHROD
PUSHRODS
PUSHUP
PUSHUPS
PUSHY
PUSLE
PUSLED
PUSLES
PUSLEY
PUSLEYS
PUSLIKE
PUSLING
PUSS
PUSSEL
PUSSELS
PUSSER
PUSSERS
PUSSES
PUSSIER
PUSSIES
PUSSIEST
PUSSLEY
PUSSLEYS
PUSSLIES
PUSSLIKE
PUSSLY
PUSSY
PUSSYCAT
PUSSYCATS
PUSSYFOOT
PUSSYTOES
PUSTULANT
PUSTULAR
PUSTULATE
PUSTULE
PUSTULED
PUSTULES
PUSTULOUS
PUT
PUTAMEN
PUTAMENS
PUTAMINA
PUTATIVE
PUTCHEON
PUTCHEONS
PUTCHER
PUTCHERS
PUTCHOCK
PUTCHOCKS
PUTCHUK
PUTCHUKS
PUTDOWN
PUTDOWNS
PUTEAL
PUTEALS
PUTELI
PUTELIS
PUTID
PUTLOCK
PUTLOCKS
PUTLOG
PUTLOGS
PUTOFF
PUTOFFS
PUTOIS
PUTON
PUTONGHUA
PUTONS
PUTOUT
PUTOUTS
PUTREFIED
PUTREFIER
PUTREFIES
PUTREFY
PUTRID
PUTRIDER
PUTRIDEST
PUTRIDITY
PUTRIDLY
PUTS
PUTSCH
PUTSCHES
PUTSCHIST
PUTT
PUTTED
PUTTEE
PUTTEES
PUTTEN
PUTTER
PUTTERED
PUTTERER
PUTTERERS
PUTTERING
PUTTERS
PUTTI
PUTTIE
PUTTIED
PUTTIER
PUTTIERS
PUTTIES
PUTTING
PUTTINGS
PUTTO
PUTTOCK
PUTTOCKS
PUTTS
PUTTY
PUTTYING
PUTTYLESS
PUTTYLIKE
PUTTYROOT
PUTURE
PUTURES
PUTZ
PUTZED
PUTZES
PUTZING
PUY
PUYS
PUZEL
PUZELS
PUZZEL
PUZZELS
PUZZLE
PUZZLED
PUZZLEDLY
PUZZLEDOM
PUZZLER

PUZZLERS
PUZZLES
PUZZLING
PUZZOLANA
PWN
PWNED
PWNING
PWNS
PYA
PYAEMIA
PYAEMIAS
PYAEMIC
PYAS
PYAT
PYATS
PYCNIC
PYCNIDIA
PYCNIDIAL
PYCNIDIUM
PYCNITE
PYCNITES
PYCNON
PYCNONS
PYCNOSES
PYCNOSIS
PYCNOSOME
PYCNOTIC
PYE
PYEBALD
PYEBALDS
PYEING
PYELITIC
PYELITIS
PYELOGRAM
PYEMIA
PYEMIAS
PYEMIC
PYENGADU
PYENGADUS
PYES
PYET
PYETS
PYGAL
PYGALS
PYGARG
PYGARGS
PYGARGUS
PYGIDIA
PYGIDIAL
PYGIDIUM
PYGMAEAN
PYGMEAN
PYGMIES
PYGMOID
PYGMOIDS
PYGMY
PYGMYISH
PYGMYISM
PYGMYISMS
PYGOSTYLE
PYIC
PYIN
PYINKADO
PYINKADOS
PYINS
PYJAMA
PYJAMAED
PYJAMAS
PYKNIC
PYKNICS
PYKNOSES
PYKNOSIS
PYKNOSOME
PYKNOTIC
PYLON
PYLONS
PYLORI
PYLORIC
PYLORUS
PYLORUSES
PYNE
PYNED
PYNES
PYNING
PYODERMA
PYODERMAS
PYODERMIC
PYOGENIC
PYOID
PYONER
PYONERS
PYONINGS
PYORRHEA
PYORRHEAL
PYORRHEAS
PYORRHEIC
PYORRHOEA
PYOSES
PYOSIS
PYOT
PYOTS
PYRACANTH
PYRAL
PYRALID
PYRALIDID
PYRALIDS
PYRALIS
PYRALISES
PYRAMID
PYRAMIDAL
PYRAMIDED
PYRAMIDES
PYRAMIDIA
PYRAMIDIC
PYRAMIDON
PYRAMIDS
PYRAMIS
PYRAMISES
PYRAN
PYRANOID
PYRANOSE
PYRANOSES
PYRANS
PYRAZOLE
PYRAZOLES
PYRE
PYRENE
PYRENEITE
PYRENES
PYRENOID
PYRENOIDS
PYRES
PYRETHRIN
PYRETHRUM
PYRETIC
PYREX
PYREXES
PYREXIA
PYREXIAL
PYREXIAS
PYREXIC
PYRIC
PYRIDIC
PYRIDINE
PYRIDINES
PYRIDOXAL
PYRIDOXIN
PYRIFORM
PYRITE
PYRITES
PYRITIC
PYRITICAL
PYRITISE
PYRITISED
PYRITISES
PYRITIZE
PYRITIZED
PYRITIZES
PYRITOUS
PYRO
PYROBORIC
PYROCERAM
PYROCLAST
PYROGEN
PYROGENIC
PYROGENS
PYROGIES
PYROGY
PYROHIES
PYROHY
PYROLA
PYROLAS
PYROLATER
PYROLATRY
PYROLISE
PYROLISED
PYROLISES
PYROLIZE
PYROLIZED
PYROLIZES
PYROLOGY
PYROLYSE
PYROLYSED
PYROLYSER
PYROLYSES
PYROLYSIS
PYROLYTIC
PYROLYZE
PYROLYZED
PYROLYZER
PYROLYZES
PYROMANCY
PYROMANIA
PYROMETER
PYROMETRY
PYRONE
PYRONES
PYRONIN
PYRONINE
PYRONINES
PYRONINS
PYROPE
PYROPES
PYROPHONE
PYROPUS
PYROPUSES
PYROS
PYROSCOPE
PYROSES
PYROSIS
PYROSISES
PYROSOME
PYROSOMES
PYROSTAT
PYROSTATS
PYROXENE
PYROXENES
PYROXENIC
PYROXYLE
PYROXYLES
PYROXYLIC
PYROXYLIN
PYRRHIC
PYRRHICS
PYRRHOUS
PYRROL
PYRROLE
PYRROLES
PYRROLIC
PYRROLS
PYRUVATE
PYRUVATES
PYRUVIC
PYSANKA
PYSANKY
PYTHIUM
PYTHIUMS
PYTHON
PYTHONESS
PYTHONIC

PYTHONS
PYURIA
PYURIAS
PYX
PYXED
PYXES
PYXIDES
PYXIDIA
PYXIDIUM
PYXIE
PYXIES
PYXING
PYXIS
PZAZZ
PZAZZES

P

Q

QABALA
QABALAH
QABALAHS
QABALAS
QABALISM
QABALISMS
QABALIST
QABALISTS
QADI
QADIS
QAID
QAIDS
QAIMAQAM
QAIMAQAMS
QAJAQ
QAJAQS
QALAMDAN
QALAMDANS
QAMUTIK
QAMUTIKS
QANAT
QANATS
QAPIK
QAPIKS
QASIDA
QASIDAS
QAT
QATS
QAWWAL
QAWWALI
QAWWALIS
QAWWALS
QI
QIBLA
QIBLAS
QIGONG
QIGONGS
QIN
QINDAR
QINDARKA
QINDARS
QINGHAOSU
QINS
QINTAR
QINTARKA
QINTARS
QIS
QIVIUT
QIVIUTS
QOPH
QOPHS
QORMA
QORMAS
QUA
QUAALUDE
QUAALUDES
QUACK
QUACKED
QUACKER
QUACKERS
QUACKERY
QUACKIER
QUACKIEST
QUACKING
QUACKISH
QUACKISM
QUACKISMS
QUACKLE
QUACKLED
QUACKLES
QUACKLING
QUACKS
QUACKY
QUAD
QUADDED
QUADDING
QUADDINGS
QUADPLAY
QUADPLAYS
QUADPLEX
QUADRANS
QUADRANT
QUADRANTS
QUADRAT
QUADRATE
QUADRATED
QUADRATES
QUADRATI
QUADRATIC
QUADRATS
QUADRATUS
QUADRELLA
QUADRIC
QUADRICEP
QUADRICS
QUADRIFID
QUADRIGA
QUADRIGAE
QUADRIGAS
QUADRILLE
QUADRIVIA
QUADRUMAN
QUADRUPED
QUADRUPLE
QUADRUPLY
QUADS
QUAERE
QUAERED
QUAEREING
QUAERES
QUAERITUR
QUAESITUM
QUAESTOR
QUAESTORS
QUAFF
QUAFFABLE
QUAFFED
QUAFFER
QUAFFERS
QUAFFING
QUAFFS
QUAG
QUAGGA
QUAGGAS
QUAGGIER
QUAGGIEST
QUAGGY
QUAGMIRE
QUAGMIRED
QUAGMIRES
QUAGMIRY
QUAGS
QUAHAUG
QUAHAUGS
QUAHOG
QUAHOGS
QUAI
QUAICH
QUAICHES
QUAICHS
QUAIGH
QUAIGHS
QUAIL
QUAILED
QUAILING
QUAILINGS
QUAILS
QUAINT
QUAINTER
QUAINTEST
QUAINTLY
QUAIR
QUAIRS
QUAIS
QUAKE
QUAKED
QUAKER
QUAKERS
QUAKES
QUAKIER
QUAKIEST
QUAKILY
QUAKINESS
QUAKING
QUAKINGLY
QUAKINGS
QUAKY
QUALE
QUALIA
QUALIFIED
QUALIFIER
QUALIFIES
QUALIFY
QUALITIED
QUALITIES
QUALITY
QUALM
QUALMIER
QUALMIEST
QUALMING
QUALMINGS
QUALMISH
QUALMLESS
QUALMS
QUALMY
QUAMASH
QUAMASHES
QUANDANG
QUANDANGS
QUANDARY
QUANDONG
QUANDONGS
QUANGO
QUANGOS
QUANNET
QUANNETS
QUANT
QUANTA
QUANTAL
QUANTALLY
QUANTED
QUANTIC
QUANTICAL
QUANTICS
QUANTIFY
QUANTILE
QUANTILES
QUANTING
QUANTISE
QUANTISED

QUANTISER
QUANTISES
QUANTITY
QUANTIZE
QUANTIZED
QUANTIZER
QUANTIZES
QUANTONG
QUANTONGS
QUANTS
QUANTUM
QUANTUMS
QUARE
QUARENDEN
QUARENDER
QUARER
QUAREST
QUARK
QUARKS
QUARREL
QUARRELED
QUARRELER
QUARRELS
QUARRIAN
QUARRIANS
QUARRIED
QUARRIER
QUARRIERS
QUARRIES
QUARRION
QUARRIONS
QUARRY
QUARRYING
QUARRYMAN
QUARRYMEN
QUART
QUARTAN
QUARTANS
QUARTE
QUARTER
QUARTERED
QUARTERER
QUARTERLY
QUARTERN
QUARTERNS
QUARTERS
QUARTES
QUARTET
QUARTETS
QUARTETT
QUARTETTE
QUARTETTI
QUARTETTO
QUARTETTS
QUARTIC
QUARTICS
QUARTIER
QUARTIERS
QUARTILE
QUARTILES
QUARTO
QUARTOS
QUARTS
QUARTZ
QUARTZES
QUARTZIER
QUARTZITE
QUARTZOSE
QUARTZOUS
QUARTZY
QUASAR
QUASARS
QUASH
QUASHED
QUASHER
QUASHERS
QUASHES
QUASHING
QUASI
QUASS
QUASSES
QUASSIA
QUASSIAS
QUASSIN
QUASSINS
QUAT
QUATCH
QUATCHED
QUATCHES
QUATCHING
QUATE
QUATES
QUATORZE
QUATORZES
QUATRAIN
QUATRAINS
QUATRE
QUATRES
QUATS
QUATTED
QUATTING
QUAVER
QUAVERED
QUAVERER
QUAVERERS
QUAVERIER
QUAVERING
QUAVERS
QUAVERY
QUAY
QUAYAGE
QUAYAGES
QUAYD
QUAYLIKE
QUAYS
QUAYSIDE
QUAYSIDES
QUAZZIER
QUAZZIEST
QUAZZY
QUBIT
QUBITS
QUBYTE
QUBYTES
QUEACH
QUEACHES
QUEACHIER
QUEACHY
QUEAN
QUEANS
QUEASIER
QUEASIEST
QUEASILY
QUEASY
QUEAZIER
QUEAZIEST
QUEAZY
QUEBEC
QUEBECS
QUEBRACHO
QUEECHIER
QUEECHY
QUEEN
QUEENCAKE
QUEENCUP
QUEENCUPS
QUEENDOM
QUEENDOMS
QUEENED
QUEENFISH
QUEENHOOD
QUEENIE
QUEENIER
QUEENIES
QUEENIEST
QUEENING
QUEENINGS
QUEENITE
QUEENITES
QUEENLESS
QUEENLET
QUEENLETS
QUEENLIER
QUEENLIKE
QUEENLY
QUEENS
QUEENSHIP
QUEENSIDE
QUEENY
QUEER
QUEERCORE
QUEERED
QUEERER
QUEEREST
QUEERING
QUEERISH
QUEERITY
QUEERLY
QUEERNESS
QUEERS
QUEEST
QUEESTS
QUEINT
QUELCH
QUELCHED
QUELCHES
QUELCHING
QUELEA
QUELEAS
QUELL
QUELLABLE
QUELLED
QUELLER
QUELLERS
QUELLING
QUELLS
QUEME
QUEMED
QUEMES
QUEMING
QUENA
QUENAS
QUENCH
QUENCHED
QUENCHER
QUENCHERS
QUENCHES
QUENCHING
QUENELLE
QUENELLES
QUEP
QUERCETIC
QUERCETIN
QUERCETUM
QUERCINE
QUERCITIN
QUERIDA
QUERIDAS
QUERIED
QUERIER
QUERIERS
QUERIES
QUERIMONY
QUERIST
QUERISTS
QUERN
QUERNS
QUERULOUS
QUERY
QUERYING
QUERYINGS
QUEST
QUESTANT
QUESTANTS
QUESTED
QUESTER
QUESTERS
QUESTING
QUESTINGS
QUESTION

QUESTIONS
QUESTOR
QUESTORS
QUESTRIST
QUESTS
QUETCH
QUETCHED
QUETCHES
QUETCHING
QUETHE
QUETHES
QUETHING
QUETSCH
QUETSCHES
QUETZAL
QUETZALES
QUETZALS
QUEUE
QUEUED
QUEUEING
QUEUEINGS
QUEUER
QUEUERS
QUEUES
QUEUING
QUEUINGS
QUEY
QUEYN
QUEYNIE
QUEYNIES
QUEYNS
QUEYS
QUEZAL
QUEZALES
QUEZALS
QUIBBLE
QUIBBLED
QUIBBLER
QUIBBLERS
QUIBBLES
QUIBBLING
QUIBLIN
QUIBLINS
QUICH
QUICHE
QUICHED
QUICHES
QUICHING
QUICK
QUICKBEAM
QUICKEN
QUICKENED
QUICKENER
QUICKENS
QUICKER
QUICKEST
QUICKFIRE
QUICKIE
QUICKIES
QUICKLIME
QUICKLY
QUICKNESS
QUICKS
QUICKSAND
QUICKSET
QUICKSETS
QUICKSTEP
QUICKY
QUID
QUIDAM
QUIDAMS
QUIDDANY
QUIDDIT
QUIDDITCH
QUIDDITS
QUIDDITY
QUIDDLE
QUIDDLED
QUIDDLER
QUIDDLERS
QUIDDLES
QUIDDLING
QUIDNUNC
QUIDNUNCS
QUIDS
QUIESCE
QUIESCED
QUIESCENT
QUIESCES
QUIESCING
QUIET
QUIETED
QUIETEN
QUIETENED
QUIETENER
QUIETENS
QUIETER
QUIETERS
QUIETEST
QUIETING
QUIETINGS
QUIETISM
QUIETISMS
QUIETIST
QUIETISTS
QUIETIVE
QUIETIVES
QUIETLY
QUIETNESS
QUIETS
QUIETSOME
QUIETUDE
QUIETUDES
QUIETUS
QUIETUSES
QUIFF
QUIFFED
QUIFFS
QUIGHT
QUIGHTED
QUIGHTING
QUIGHTS
QUILL
QUILLAI
QUILLAIA
QUILLAIAS
QUILLAIS
QUILLAJA
QUILLAJAS
QUILLBACK
QUILLED
QUILLET
QUILLETS
QUILLING
QUILLINGS
QUILLMAN
QUILLMEN
QUILLON
QUILLONS
QUILLOW
QUILLOWS
QUILLS
QUILLWORK
QUILLWORT
QUILT
QUILTED
QUILTER
QUILTERS
QUILTING
QUILTINGS
QUILTS
QUIM
QUIMS
QUIN
QUINA
QUINARIES
QUINARY
QUINAS
QUINATE
QUINCE
QUINCES
QUINCHE
QUINCHED
QUINCHES
QUINCHING
QUINCUNX
QUINE
QUINELA
QUINELAS
QUINELLA
QUINELLAS
QUINES
QUINIC
QUINIDINE
QUINIE
QUINIELA
QUINIELAS
QUINIES
QUININ
QUININA
QUININAS
QUININE
QUININES
QUININS
QUINNAT
QUINNATS
QUINO
QUINOA
QUINOAS
QUINOID
QUINOIDAL
QUINOIDS
QUINOL
QUINOLIN
QUINOLINE
QUINOLINS
QUINOLONE
QUINOLS
QUINONE
QUINONES
QUINONOID
QUINOS
QUINQUINA
QUINS
QUINSIED
QUINSIES
QUINSY
QUINT
QUINTA
QUINTAIN
QUINTAINS
QUINTAL
QUINTALS
QUINTAN
QUINTANS
QUINTAR
QUINTARS
QUINTAS
QUINTE
QUINTES
QUINTET
QUINTETS
QUINTETT
QUINTETTE
QUINTETTI
QUINTETTO
QUINTETTS
QUINTIC
QUINTICS
QUINTILE
QUINTILES
QUINTIN
QUINTINS
QUINTS
QUINTUPLE
QUINTUPLY
QUINZE
QUINZES
QUINZHEE
QUINZHEES

QUINZIE
QUINZIES
QUIP
QUIPO
QUIPOS
QUIPPED
QUIPPER
QUIPPERS
QUIPPIER
QUIPPIEST
QUIPPING
QUIPPISH
QUIPPU
QUIPPUS
QUIPPY
QUIPS
QUIPSTER
QUIPSTERS
QUIPU
QUIPUS
QUIRE
QUIRED
QUIRES
QUIRING
QUIRISTER
QUIRK
QUIRKED
QUIRKIER
QUIRKIEST
QUIRKILY
QUIRKING
QUIRKISH
QUIRKS
QUIRKY
QUIRT
QUIRTED
QUIRTING
QUIRTS
QUISLING
QUISLINGS
QUIST
QUISTS
QUIT
QUITCH
QUITCHED
QUITCHES
QUITCHING
QUITCLAIM
QUITE
QUITED
QUITES
QUITING
QUITRENT
QUITRENTS
QUITS
QUITTAL
QUITTALS
QUITTANCE
QUITTED
QUITTER
QUITTERS
QUITTING
QUITTOR
QUITTORS
QUIVER
QUIVERED
QUIVERER
QUIVERERS
QUIVERFUL
QUIVERIER
QUIVERING
QUIVERISH
QUIVERS
QUIVERY
QUIXOTE
QUIXOTES
QUIXOTIC
QUIXOTISM
QUIXOTRY
QUIZ
QUIZZED
QUIZZER
QUIZZERS
QUIZZERY
QUIZZES
QUIZZICAL
QUIZZIFY
QUIZZING
QUIZZINGS
QULLIQ
QULLIQS
QUOAD
QUOD
QUODDED
QUODDING
QUODLIBET
QUODLIN
QUODLINS
QUODS
QUOHOG
QUOHOGS
QUOIF
QUOIFED
QUOIFING
QUOIFS
QUOIN
QUOINED
QUOINING
QUOININGS
QUOINS
QUOIST
QUOISTS
QUOIT
QUOITED
QUOITER
QUOITERS
QUOITING
QUOITS
QUOKKA
QUOKKAS
QUOLL
QUOLLS
QUOMODO
QUOMODOS
QUONDAM
QUONK
QUONKED
QUONKING
QUONKS
QUOOKE
QUOP
QUOPPED
QUOPPING
QUOPS
QUORATE
QUORUM
QUORUMS
QUOTA
QUOTABLE
QUOTABLY
QUOTAS
QUOTATION
QUOTATIVE
QUOTE
QUOTED
QUOTER
QUOTERS
QUOTES
QUOTH
QUOTHA
QUOTIDIAN
QUOTIENT
QUOTIENTS
QUOTING
QUOTITION
QUOTUM
QUOTUMS
QURSH
QURSHES
QURUSH
QURUSHES
QUYTE
QUYTED
QUYTES
QUYTING
QWERTIES
QWERTY
QWERTYS

R

RABANNA
RABANNAS
RABASKA
RABASKAS
RABAT
RABATINE
RABATINES
RABATMENT
RABATO
RABATOES
RABATOS
RABATS
RABATTE
RABATTED
RABATTES
RABATTING
RABBET
RABBETED
RABBETING
RABBETS
RABBI
RABBIES
RABBIN
RABBINATE
RABBINIC
RABBINICS
RABBINISM
RABBINIST
RABBINITE
RABBINS
RABBIS
RABBIT
RABBITED
RABBITER
RABBITERS
RABBITIER
RABBITING
RABBITO
RABBITOH
RABBITOHS
RABBITOS
RABBITRY
RABBITS
RABBITY
RABBLE
RABBLED
RABBLER
RABBLERS
RABBLES
RABBLING
RABBLINGS
RABBONI
RABBONIS
RABI
RABIC
RABID
RABIDER
RABIDEST
RABIDITY
RABIDLY
RABIDNESS
RABIES
RABIETIC
RABIS
RABONA
RABONAS
RACA
RACAHOUT
RACAHOUTS
RACCAHOUT
RACCOON
RACCOONS
RACE
RACEABLE
RACECARD
RACECARDS
RACED
RACEGOER
RACEGOERS
RACEGOING
RACEHORSE
RACEMATE
RACEMATES
RACEME
RACEMED
RACEMES
RACEMIC
RACEMISE
RACEMISED
RACEMISES
RACEMISM
RACEMISMS
RACEMIZE
RACEMIZED
RACEMIZES
RACEMOID
RACEMOSE
RACEMOUS
RACEPATH
RACEPATHS
RACER
RACERS
RACES
RACETRACK
RACEWALK
RACEWALKS
RACEWAY
RACEWAYS
RACH
RACHE
RACHES
RACHET
RACHETED
RACHETING
RACHETS
RACHIAL
RACHIDES
RACHIDIAL
RACHIDIAN
RACHILLA
RACHILLAE
RACHILLAS
RACHIS
RACHISES
RACHITIC
RACHITIS
RACIAL
RACIALISE
RACIALISM
RACIALIST
RACIALIZE
RACIALLY
RACIATION
RACIER
RACIEST
RACILY
RACINESS
RACING
RACINGS
RACINO
RACINOS
RACISM
RACISMS
RACIST
RACISTS
RACK
RACKED
RACKER
RACKERS
RACKET
RACKETED
RACKETEER
RACKETER
RACKETERS
RACKETIER
RACKETING
RACKETRY
RACKETS
RACKETT
RACKETTS
RACKETY
RACKFUL
RACKFULS
RACKING
RACKINGLY
RACKINGS
RACKLE
RACKLES
RACKS
RACKWORK
RACKWORKS
RACLETTE
RACLETTES
RACLOIR
RACLOIRS
RACON
RACONS
RACONTEUR
RACOON
RACOONS
RACQUET
RACQUETED
RACQUETS
RACY
RAD
RADAR
RADARS
RADDED
RADDER
RADDEST
RADDING
RADDLE
RADDLED
RADDLEMAN
RADDLEMEN
RADDLES
RADDLING
RADDOCKE
RADDOCKES
RADE
RADGE
RADGER
RADGES
RADGEST
RADIABLE
RADIAL
RADIALE
RADIALIA
RADIALISE
RADIALITY

R

RADIALIZE
RADIALLY
RADIALS
RADIAN
RADIANCE
RADIANCES
RADIANCY
RADIANS
RADIANT
RADIANTLY
RADIANTS
RADIATA
RADIATAS
RADIATE
RADIATED
RADIATELY
RADIATES
RADIATING
RADIATION
RADIATIVE
RADIATOR
RADIATORS
RADIATORY
RADICAL
RADICALLY
RADICALS
RADICAND
RADICANDS
RADICANT
RADICATE
RADICATED
RADICATES
RADICCHIO
RADICEL
RADICELS
RADICES
RADICLE
RADICLES
RADICULAR
RADICULE
RADICULES
RADII
RADIO
RADIOED
RADIOES
RADIOGOLD
RADIOGRAM
RADIOING
RADIOLOGY
RADIOMAN
RADIOMEN
RADIONICS
RADIOS
RADIOTHON
RADISH
RADISHES
RADIUM
RADIUMS
RADIUS
RADIUSED
RADIUSES
RADIUSING
RADIX
RADIXES
RADOME
RADOMES
RADON
RADONS
RADS
RADULA
RADULAE
RADULAR
RADULAS
RADULATE
RADWASTE
RADWASTES
RAFALE
RAFALES
RAFF
RAFFIA
RAFFIAS
RAFFINATE
RAFFINOSE
RAFFISH
RAFFISHLY
RAFFLE
RAFFLED
RAFFLER
RAFFLERS
RAFFLES
RAFFLESIA
RAFFLING
RAFFS
RAFT
RAFTED
RAFTER
RAFTERED
RAFTERING
RAFTERS
RAFTING
RAFTINGS
RAFTMAN
RAFTMEN
RAFTS
RAFTSMAN
RAFTSMEN
RAG
RAGA
RAGAS
RAGBAG
RAGBAGS
RAGBOLT
RAGBOLTS
RAGDE
RAGDOLL
RAGDOLLS
RAGE
RAGED
RAGEE
RAGEES
RAGEFUL
RAGER
RAGERS
RAGES
RAGG
RAGGA
RAGGAS
RAGGED
RAGGEDER
RAGGEDEST
RAGGEDIER
RAGGEDLY
RAGGEDY
RAGGEE
RAGGEES
RAGGERIES
RAGGERY
RAGGIER
RAGGIES
RAGGIEST
RAGGING
RAGGINGS
RAGGLE
RAGGLED
RAGGLES
RAGGLING
RAGGS
RAGGY
RAGI
RAGING
RAGINGLY
RAGINGS
RAGINI
RAGINIS
RAGIS
RAGLAN
RAGLANS
RAGMAN
RAGMANS
RAGMEN
RAGMENT
RAGMENTS
RAGOUT
RAGOUTED
RAGOUTING
RAGOUTS
RAGPICKER
RAGS
RAGSTONE
RAGSTONES
RAGTAG
RAGTAGS
RAGTAIL
RAGTIME
RAGTIMER
RAGTIMERS
RAGTIMES
RAGTOP
RAGTOPS
RAGU
RAGULED
RAGULY
RAGUS
RAGWEED
RAGWEEDS
RAGWHEEL
RAGWHEELS
RAGWORK
RAGWORKS
RAGWORM
RAGWORMS
RAGWORT
RAGWORTS
RAH
RAHED
RAHING
RAHS
RAHUI
RAHUIS
RAI
RAIA
RAIAS
RAID
RAIDED
RAIDER
RAIDERS
RAIDING
RAIDINGS
RAIDS
RAIK
RAIKED
RAIKING
RAIKS
RAIL
RAILAGE
RAILAGES
RAILBED
RAILBEDS
RAILBIRD
RAILBIRDS
RAILBUS
RAILBUSES
RAILCAR
RAILCARD
RAILCARDS
RAILCARS
RAILE
RAILED
RAILER
RAILERS
RAILES
RAILHEAD
RAILHEADS
RAILING
RAILINGLY
RAILINGS
RAILLERY
RAILLESS
RAILLIES
RAILLY

R

RAILMAN
RAILMEN
RAILROAD
RAILROADS
RAILS
RAILWAY
RAILWAYS
RAILWOMAN
RAILWOMEN
RAIMENT
RAIMENTS
RAIN
RAINBAND
RAINBANDS
RAINBIRD
RAINBIRDS
RAINBOW
RAINBOWED
RAINBOWS
RAINBOWY
RAINCHECK
RAINCOAT
RAINCOATS
RAINDATE
RAINDATES
RAINDROP
RAINDROPS
RAINE
RAINED
RAINES
RAINFALL
RAINFALLS
RAINIER
RAINIEST
RAINILY
RAININESS
RAINING
RAINLESS
RAINMAKER
RAINOUT
RAINOUTS
RAINPROOF
RAINS
RAINSPOUT
RAINSTICK
RAINSTORM
RAINSUIT
RAINSUITS
RAINSWEPT
RAINTIGHT
RAINWASH
RAINWATER
RAINWEAR
RAINWEARS
RAINY
RAIRD
RAIRDS
RAIS
RAISABLE
RAISE
RAISEABLE
RAISED
RAISER
RAISERS
RAISES
RAISIN
RAISING
RAISINGS
RAISINIER
RAISINS
RAISINY
RAISONNE
RAIT
RAITA
RAITAS
RAITED
RAITING
RAITS
RAIYAT
RAIYATS
RAJ
RAJA
RAJAH
RAJAHS
RAJAHSHIP
RAJAS
RAJASHIP
RAJASHIPS
RAJES
RAKE
RAKED
RAKEE
RAKEES
RAKEHELL
RAKEHELLS
RAKEHELLY
RAKELIKE
RAKEOFF
RAKEOFFS
RAKER
RAKERIES
RAKERS
RAKERY
RAKES
RAKESHAME
RAKI
RAKIA
RAKIAS
RAKIJA
RAKIJAS
RAKING
RAKINGS
RAKIS
RAKISH
RAKISHLY
RAKSHAS
RAKSHASA
RAKSHASAS
RAKSHASES
RAKU
RAKUS
RALE
RALES
RALLIED
RALLIER
RALLIERS
RALLIES
RALLIFORM
RALLINE
RALLY
RALLYE
RALLYES
RALLYING
RALLYINGS
RALLYIST
RALLYISTS
RALPH
RALPHED
RALPHING
RALPHS
RAM
RAMADA
RAMADAS
RAMAKIN
RAMAKINS
RAMAL
RAMATE
RAMBLA
RAMBLAS
RAMBLE
RAMBLED
RAMBLER
RAMBLERS
RAMBLES
RAMBLING
RAMBLINGS
RAMBUTAN
RAMBUTANS
RAMCAT
RAMCATS
RAMEAL
RAMEE
RAMEES
RAMEKIN
RAMEKINS
RAMEN
RAMENS
RAMENTA
RAMENTUM
RAMEOUS
RAMEQUIN
RAMEQUINS
RAMET
RAMETS
RAMI
RAMIE
RAMIES
RAMIFIED
RAMIFIES
RAMIFORM
RAMIFY
RAMIFYING
RAMILIE
RAMILIES
RAMILLIE
RAMILLIES
RAMIN
RAMINS
RAMIS
RAMJET
RAMJETS
RAMMED
RAMMEL
RAMMELS
RAMMER
RAMMERS
RAMMIER
RAMMIES
RAMMIEST
RAMMING
RAMMISH
RAMMISHLY
RAMMLE
RAMMLES
RAMMY
RAMONA
RAMONAS
RAMOSE
RAMOSELY
RAMOSITY
RAMOUS
RAMOUSLY
RAMP
RAMPAGE
RAMPAGED
RAMPAGER
RAMPAGERS
RAMPAGES
RAMPAGING
RAMPANCY
RAMPANT
RAMPANTLY
RAMPART
RAMPARTED
RAMPARTS
RAMPAUGE
RAMPAUGED
RAMPAUGES
RAMPED
RAMPER
RAMPERS
RAMPICK
RAMPICKED
RAMPICKS
RAMPIKE
RAMPIKES
RAMPING
RAMPINGS
RAMPION
RAMPIONS

R

RAMPIRE
RAMPIRED
RAMPIRES
RAMPOLE
RAMPOLES
RAMPS
RAMPSMAN
RAMPSMEN
RAMROD
RAMRODDED
RAMRODS
RAMS
RAMSHORN
RAMSHORNS
RAMSON
RAMSONS
RAMSTAM
RAMTIL
RAMTILLA
RAMTILLAS
RAMTILS
RAMULAR
RAMULI
RAMULOSE
RAMULOUS
RAMULUS
RAMUS
RAN
RANA
RANARIAN
RANARIUM
RANARIUMS
RANAS
RANCE
RANCED
RANCEL
RANCELLED
RANCELS
RANCES
RANCH
RANCHED
RANCHER
RANCHERA
RANCHERAS
RANCHERIA
RANCHERIE
RANCHERO
RANCHEROS
RANCHERS
RANCHES
RANCHETTE
RANCHING
RANCHINGS
RANCHLAND
RANCHLESS
RANCHLIKE
RANCHMAN
RANCHMEN
RANCHO
RANCHOS
RANCID
RANCIDER
RANCIDEST
RANCIDITY
RANCIDLY
RANCING
RANCOR
RANCORED
RANCOROUS
RANCORS
RANCOUR
RANCOURED
RANCOURS
RAND
RANDAN
RANDANS
RANDED
RANDEM
RANDEMS
RANDIE
RANDIER
RANDIES
RANDIEST
RANDILY
RANDINESS
RANDING
RANDLORD
RANDLORDS
RANDOM
RANDOMISE
RANDOMIZE
RANDOMLY
RANDOMS
RANDON
RANDONS
RANDS
RANDY
RANEE
RANEES
RANG
RANGA
RANGAS
RANGATIRA
RANGE
RANGED
RANGELAND
RANGER
RANGERS
RANGES
RANGI
RANGIER
RANGIEST
RANGILY
RANGINESS
RANGING
RANGINGS
RANGIORA
RANGIORAS
RANGIS
RANGOLI
RANGOLIS
RANGS
RANGY
RANI
RANID
RANIDS
RANIFORM
RANINE
RANIS
RANK
RANKE
RANKED
RANKER
RANKERS
RANKES
RANKEST
RANKING
RANKINGS
RANKISH
RANKISM
RANKISMS
RANKIST
RANKISTS
RANKLE
RANKLED
RANKLES
RANKLESS
RANKLING
RANKLY
RANKNESS
RANKS
RANKSHIFT
RANPIKE
RANPIKES
RANSACK
RANSACKED
RANSACKER
RANSACKS
RANSEL
RANSELS
RANSHAKLE
RANSOM
RANSOMED
RANSOMER
RANSOMERS
RANSOMING
RANSOMS
RANT
RANTED
RANTER
RANTERISM
RANTERS
RANTING
RANTINGLY
RANTINGS
RANTIPOLE
RANTS
RANULA
RANULAR
RANULAS
RANUNCULI
RANZEL
RANZELMAN
RANZELMEN
RANZELS
RAOULIA
RAOULIAS
RAP
RAPACIOUS
RAPACITY
RAPE
RAPED
RAPER
RAPERS
RAPES
RAPESEED
RAPESEEDS
RAPHAE
RAPHANIA
RAPHANIAS
RAPHE
RAPHES
RAPHIA
RAPHIAS
RAPHIDE
RAPHIDES
RAPHIS
RAPID
RAPIDER
RAPIDEST
RAPIDITY
RAPIDLY
RAPIDNESS
RAPIDS
RAPIER
RAPIERED
RAPIERS
RAPINE
RAPINES
RAPING
RAPINI
RAPINIS
RAPIST
RAPISTS
RAPLOCH
RAPLOCHS
RAPPAREE
RAPPAREES
RAPPE
RAPPED
RAPPEE
RAPPEES
RAPPEL
RAPPELED
RAPPELING
RAPPELLED
RAPPELS
RAPPEN
RAPPER
RAPPERS

R

RAPPES
RAPPING
RAPPINGS
RAPPINI
RAPPORT
RAPPORTS
RAPS
RAPT
RAPTLY
RAPTNESS
RAPTOR
RAPTORIAL
RAPTORS
RAPTURE
RAPTURED
RAPTURES
RAPTURING
RAPTURISE
RAPTURIST
RAPTURIZE
RAPTUROUS
RARE
RAREBIT
RAREBITS
RARED
RAREE
RAREFIED
RAREFIER
RAREFIERS
RAREFIES
RAREFY
RAREFYING
RARELY
RARENESS
RARER
RARERIPE
RARERIPES
RARES
RAREST
RARIFIED
RARIFIES
RARIFY
RARIFYING
RARING
RARITIES
RARITY
RARK
RARKED
RARKING
RARKS
RAS
RASBORA
RASBORAS
RASCAILLE
RASCAL
RASCALDOM
RASCALISM
RASCALITY
RASCALLY
RASCALS
RASCASSE
RASCASSES
RASCHEL
RASCHELS
RASE
RASED
RASER
RASERS
RASES
RASH
RASHED
RASHER
RASHERS
RASHES
RASHEST
RASHIE
RASHIES
RASHING
RASHLIKE
RASHLY
RASHNESS
RASING
RASMALAI
RASMALAIS
RASORIAL
RASP
RASPATORY
RASPBERRY
RASPED
RASPER
RASPERS
RASPIER
RASPIEST
RASPINESS
RASPING
RASPINGLY
RASPINGS
RASPISH
RASPS
RASPY
RASSE
RASSES
RASSLE
RASSLED
RASSLER
RASSLERS
RASSLES
RASSLING
RAST
RASTA
RASTAFARI
RASTER
RASTERED
RASTERING
RASTERISE
RASTERIZE
RASTERS
RASTRUM
RASTRUMS
RASURE
RASURES
RAT
RATA
RATABLE
RATABLES
RATABLY
RATAFEE
RATAFEES
RATAFIA
RATAFIAS
RATAL
RATALS
RATAN
RATANIES
RATANS
RATANY
RATAPLAN
RATAPLANS
RATAS
RATATAT
RATATATS
RATBAG
RATBAGS
RATBITE
RATCH
RATCHED
RATCHES
RATCHET
RATCHETED
RATCHETS
RATCHING
RATE
RATEABLE
RATEABLES
RATEABLY
RATED
RATEEN
RATEENS
RATEL
RATELS
RATEMETER
RATEPAYER
RATER
RATERS
RATES
RATFINK
RATFINKS
RATFISH
RATFISHES
RATH
RATHA
RATHAS
RATHE
RATHER
RATHEREST
RATHERIPE
RATHERISH
RATHEST
RATHOLE
RATHOLES
RATHOUSE
RATHOUSES
RATHRIPE
RATHRIPES
RATHS
RATICIDE
RATICIDES
RATIFIED
RATIFIER
RATIFIERS
RATIFIES
RATIFY
RATIFYING
RATINE
RATINES
RATING
RATINGS
RATIO
RATION
RATIONAL
RATIONALE
RATIONALS
RATIONED
RATIONING
RATIONS
RATIOS
RATITE
RATITES
RATLIKE
RATLIN
RATLINE
RATLINES
RATLING
RATLINGS
RATLINS
RATO
RATOO
RATOON
RATOONED
RATOONER
RATOONERS
RATOONING
RATOONS
RATOOS
RATOS
RATPACK
RATPACKS
RATPROOF
RATS
RATSBANE
RATSBANES
RATTAIL
RATTAILED
RATTAILS
RATTAN
RATTANS
RATTED
RATTEEN
RATTEENS
RATTEN

RATTENED
RATTENER
RATTENERS
RATTENING
RATTENS
RATTER
RATTERIES
RATTERS
RATTERY
RATTIER
RATTIEST
RATTILY
RATTINESS
RATTING
RATTINGS
RATTISH
RATTLE
RATTLEBAG
RATTLEBOX
RATTLED
RATTLER
RATTLERS
RATTLES
RATTLIER
RATTLIEST
RATTLIN
RATTLINE
RATTLINES
RATTLING
RATTLINGS
RATTLINS
RATTLY
RATTON
RATTONS
RATTOON
RATTOONED
RATTOONS
RATTRAP
RATTRAPS
RATTY
RATU
RATUS
RAUCID
RAUCITIES
RAUCITY
RAUCLE
RAUCLER
RAUCLEST
RAUCOUS
RAUCOUSLY
RAUGHT
RAUN
RAUNCH
RAUNCHED
RAUNCHES
RAUNCHIER
RAUNCHILY
RAUNCHING
RAUNCHY
RAUNGE
RAUNGED
RAUNGES
RAUNGING
RAUNS
RAUPATU
RAUPATUS
RAUPO
RAUPOS
RAURIKI
RAURIKIS
RAUWOLFIA
RAV
RAVAGE
RAVAGED
RAVAGER
RAVAGERS
RAVAGES
RAVAGING
RAVE
RAVED
RAVEL
RAVELED
RAVELER
RAVELERS
RAVELIN
RAVELING
RAVELINGS
RAVELINS
RAVELLED
RAVELLER
RAVELLERS
RAVELLIER
RAVELLING
RAVELLY
RAVELMENT
RAVELS
RAVEN
RAVENED
RAVENER
RAVENERS
RAVENEST
RAVENING
RAVENINGS
RAVENLIKE
RAVENOUS
RAVENS
RAVER
RAVERS
RAVES
RAVEY
RAVIER
RAVIEST
RAVIGOTE
RAVIGOTES
RAVIGOTTE
RAVIN
RAVINE
RAVINED
RAVINES
RAVING
RAVINGLY
RAVINGS
RAVINING
RAVINS
RAVIOLI
RAVIOLIS
RAVISH
RAVISHED
RAVISHER
RAVISHERS
RAVISHES
RAVISHING
RAVS
RAW
RAWARU
RAWARUS
RAWBONE
RAWBONED
RAWER
RAWEST
RAWHEAD
RAWHEADS
RAWHIDE
RAWHIDED
RAWHIDES
RAWHIDING
RAWIN
RAWING
RAWINGS
RAWINS
RAWISH
RAWLY
RAWMAISH
RAWN
RAWNESS
RAWNESSES
RAWNS
RAWS
RAX
RAXED
RAXES
RAXING
RAY
RAYA
RAYAH
RAYAHS
RAYAS
RAYED
RAYGRASS
RAYING
RAYLE
RAYLED
RAYLES
RAYLESS
RAYLESSLY
RAYLET
RAYLETS
RAYLIKE
RAYLING
RAYNE
RAYNES
RAYON
RAYONS
RAYS
RAZE
RAZED
RAZEE
RAZEED
RAZEEING
RAZEES
RAZER
RAZERS
RAZES
RAZING
RAZMATAZ
RAZOO
RAZOOS
RAZOR
RAZORABLE
RAZORBACK
RAZORBILL
RAZORCLAM
RAZORED
RAZORFISH
RAZORING
RAZORS
RAZURE
RAZURES
RAZZ
RAZZBERRY
RAZZED
RAZZES
RAZZIA
RAZZIAS
RAZZING
RAZZINGS
RAZZLE
RAZZLES
RE
REABSORB
REABSORBS
REACCEDE
REACCEDED
REACCEDES
REACCENT
REACCENTS
REACCEPT
REACCEPTS
REACCLAIM
REACCUSE
REACCUSED
REACCUSES
REACH
REACHABLE
REACHED
REACHER
REACHERS
REACHES
REACHING
REACHLESS

R

REACQUIRE
REACT
REACTANCE
REACTANT
REACTANTS
REACTED
REACTING
REACTION
REACTIONS
REACTIVE
REACTOR
REACTORS
REACTS
REACTUATE
READ
READABLE
READABLY
READAPT
READAPTED
READAPTS
READD
READDED
READDICT
READDICTS
READDING
READDRESS
READDS
READER
READERLY
READERS
READIED
READIER
READIES
READIEST
READILY
READINESS
READING
READINGS
READJUST
READJUSTS
README
READMES
READMIT
READMITS
READOPT
READOPTED
READOPTS
READORN
READORNED
READORNS
READOUT
READOUTS
READS
READVANCE
READVISE
READVISED
READVISES
READY
READYING
READYMADE
REAEDIFY
REAEDIFYE
REAFFIRM
REAFFIRMS
REAFFIX
REAFFIXED
REAFFIXES
REAGENCY
REAGENT
REAGENTS
REAGIN
REAGINIC
REAGINS
REAIS
REAK
REAKED
REAKING
REAKS
REAL
REALER
REALES
REALEST
REALGAR
REALGARS
REALIA
REALIGN
REALIGNED
REALIGNS
REALISE
REALISED
REALISER
REALISERS
REALISES
REALISING
REALISM
REALISMS
REALIST
REALISTIC
REALISTS
REALITIES
REALITY
REALIZE
REALIZED
REALIZER
REALIZERS
REALIZES
REALIZING
REALLIE
REALLIED
REALLIES
REALLOT
REALLOTS
REALLY
REALLYING
REALM
REALMLESS
REALMS
REALNESS
REALO
REALOS
REALS
REALTER
REALTERED
REALTERS
REALTIE
REALTIES
REALTIME
REALTONE
REALTONES
REALTOR
REALTORS
REALTY
REAM
REAME
REAMED
REAMEND
REAMENDED
REAMENDS
REAMER
REAMERS
REAMES
REAMIER
REAMIEST
REAMING
REAMS
REAMY
REAN
REANALYSE
REANALYZE
REANIMATE
REANNEX
REANNEXED
REANNEXES
REANOINT
REANOINTS
REANS
REANSWER
REANSWERS
REAP
REAPABLE
REAPED
REAPER
REAPERS
REAPHOOK
REAPHOOKS
REAPING
REAPINGS
REAPPAREL
REAPPEAR
REAPPEARS
REAPPLIED
REAPPLIES
REAPPLY
REAPPOINT
REAPPROVE
REAPS
REAR
REARED
REARER
REARERS
REARGUARD
REARGUE
REARGUED
REARGUES
REARGUING
REARHORSE
REARING
REARINGS
REARISE
REARISEN
REARISES
REARISING
REARLY
REARM
REARMED
REARMICE
REARMING
REARMOST
REARMOUSE
REARMS
REAROSE
REAROUSAL
REAROUSE
REAROUSED
REAROUSES
REARRANGE
REARREST
REARRESTS
REARS
REARWARD
REARWARDS
REASCEND
REASCENDS
REASCENT
REASCENTS
REASON
REASONED
REASONER
REASONERS
REASONING
REASONS
REASSAIL
REASSAILS
REASSERT
REASSERTS
REASSESS
REASSIGN
REASSIGNS
REASSORT
REASSORTS
REASSUME
REASSUMED
REASSUMES
REASSURE
REASSURED
REASSURER
REASSURES
REAST
REASTED
REASTIER

REASTIEST
REASTING
REASTS
REASTY
REATA
REATAS
REATE
REATES
REATTACH
REATTACK
REATTACKS
REATTAIN
REATTAINS
REATTEMPT
REAVAIL
REAVAILED
REAVAILS
REAVE
REAVED
REAVER
REAVERS
REAVES
REAVING
REAVOW
REAVOWED
REAVOWING
REAVOWS
REAWAKE
REAWAKED
REAWAKEN
REAWAKENS
REAWAKES
REAWAKING
REAWOKE
REAWOKEN
REB
REBACK
REBACKED
REBACKING
REBACKS
REBADGE
REBADGED
REBADGES
REBADGING
REBAIT
REBAITED
REBAITING
REBAITS
REBALANCE
REBAPTISE
REBAPTISM
REBAPTIZE
REBAR
REBARS
REBASE
REBASED
REBASES
REBASING
REBATABLE
REBATE
REBATED
REBATER
REBATERS
REBATES
REBATING
REBATO
REBATOES
REBATOS
REBBE
REBBES
REBBETZIN
REBEC
REBECK
REBECKS
REBECS
REBEGAN
REBEGIN
REBEGINS
REBEGUN
REBEL
REBELDOM
REBELDOMS
REBELLED
REBELLER
REBELLERS
REBELLING
REBELLION
REBELLOW
REBELLOWS
REBELS
REBID
REBIDDEN
REBIDDING
REBIDS
REBILL
REBILLED
REBILLING
REBILLS
REBIND
REBINDING
REBINDS
REBIRTH
REBIRTHER
REBIRTHS
REBIT
REBITE
REBITES
REBITING
REBITTEN
REBLEND
REBLENDED
REBLENDS
REBLENT
REBLOCHON
REBLOOM
REBLOOMED
REBLOOMER
REBLOOMS
REBLOSSOM
REBOANT
REBOARD
REBOARDED
REBOARDS
REBOATION
REBODIED
REBODIES
REBODY
REBODYING
REBOIL
REBOILED
REBOILING
REBOILS
REBOOK
REBOOKED
REBOOKING
REBOOKS
REBOOT
REBOOTED
REBOOTING
REBOOTS
REBOP
REBOPS
REBORE
REBORED
REBORES
REBORING
REBORN
REBORROW
REBORROWS
REBOTTLE
REBOTTLED
REBOTTLES
REBOUGHT
REBOUND
REBOUNDED
REBOUNDER
REBOUNDS
REBOZO
REBOZOS
REBRACE
REBRACED
REBRACES
REBRACING
REBRANCH
REBRAND
REBRANDED
REBRANDS
REBRED
REBREED
REBREEDS
REBS
REBUFF
REBUFFED
REBUFFING
REBUFFS
REBUILD
REBUILDED
REBUILDS
REBUILT
REBUKABLE
REBUKE
REBUKED
REBUKEFUL
REBUKER
REBUKERS
REBUKES
REBUKING
REBURIAL
REBURIALS
REBURIED
REBURIES
REBURY
REBURYING
REBUS
REBUSES
REBUT
REBUTMENT
REBUTS
REBUTTAL
REBUTTALS
REBUTTED
REBUTTER
REBUTTERS
REBUTTING
REBUTTON
REBUTTONS
REBUY
REBUYING
REBUYS
REC
RECAL
RECALESCE
RECALL
RECALLED
RECALLER
RECALLERS
RECALLING
RECALLS
RECALMENT
RECALS
RECAMIER
RECAMIERS
RECANE
RECANED
RECANES
RECANING
RECANT
RECANTED
RECANTER
RECANTERS
RECANTING
RECANTS
RECAP
RECAPPED
RECAPPING
RECAPS
RECAPTION
RECAPTOR
RECAPTORS
RECAPTURE

RECARPET
RECARPETS
RECARRIED
RECARRIES
RECARRY
RECAST
RECASTING
RECASTS
RECATALOG
RECATCH
RECATCHES
RECAUGHT
RECAUTION
RECCE
RECCED
RECCEED
RECCEING
RECCES
RECCIED
RECCIES
RECCO
RECCOS
RECCY
RECCYING
RECEDE
RECEDED
RECEDES
RECEDING
RECEIPT
RECEIPTED
RECEIPTOR
RECEIPTS
RECEIVAL
RECEIVALS
RECEIVE
RECEIVED
RECEIVER
RECEIVERS
RECEIVES
RECEIVING
RECEMENT
RECEMENTS
RECENCIES
RECENCY
RECENSE
RECENSED
RECENSES
RECENSING
RECENSION
RECENSOR
RECENSORS
RECENT
RECENTER
RECENTEST
RECENTLY
RECENTRE
RECENTRED
RECENTRES
RECEPT
RECEPTION
RECEPTIVE
RECEPTOR
RECEPTORS
RECEPTS
RECERTIFY
RECESS
RECESSED
RECESSES
RECESSING
RECESSION
RECESSIVE
RECHANGE
RECHANGED
RECHANGES
RECHANNEL
RECHARGE
RECHARGED
RECHARGER
RECHARGES
RECHART
RECHARTED
RECHARTER
RECHARTS
RECHATE
RECHATES
RECHAUFFE
RECHEAT
RECHEATED
RECHEATS
RECHECK
RECHECKED
RECHECKS
RECHERCHE
RECHEW
RECHEWED
RECHEWING
RECHEWS
RECHIE
RECHIP
RECHIPPED
RECHIPS
RECHLESSE
RECHOOSE
RECHOOSES
RECHOSE
RECHOSEN
RECIPE
RECIPES
RECIPIENT
RECIRCLE
RECIRCLED
RECIRCLES
RECISION
RECISIONS
RECIT
RECITABLE
RECITAL
RECITALS
RECITE
RECITED
RECITER
RECITERS
RECITES
RECITING
RECITS
RECK
RECKAN
RECKANS
RECKED
RECKING
RECKLESS
RECKLING
RECKLINGS
RECKON
RECKONED
RECKONER
RECKONERS
RECKONING
RECKONS
RECKS
RECLAD
RECLADDED
RECLADS
RECLAIM
RECLAIMED
RECLAIMER
RECLAIMS
RECLAME
RECLAMES
RECLASP
RECLASPED
RECLASPS
RECLEAN
RECLEANED
RECLEANS
RECLIMB
RECLIMBED
RECLIMBS
RECLINATE
RECLINE
RECLINED
RECLINER
RECLINERS
RECLINES
RECLINING
RECLOSE
RECLOSED
RECLOSES
RECLOSING
RECLOTHE
RECLOTHED
RECLOTHES
RECLUSE
RECLUSELY
RECLUSES
RECLUSION
RECLUSIVE
RECLUSORY
RECOAL
RECOALED
RECOALING
RECOALS
RECOAT
RECOATED
RECOATING
RECOATS
RECOCK
RECOCKED
RECOCKING
RECOCKS
RECODE
RECODED
RECODES
RECODIFY
RECODING
RECOGNISE
RECOGNIZE
RECOIL
RECOILED
RECOILER
RECOILERS
RECOILING
RECOILS
RECOIN
RECOINAGE
RECOINED
RECOINING
RECOINS
RECOLLECT
RECOLLET
RECOLLETS
RECOLOR
RECOLORED
RECOLORS
RECOLOUR
RECOLOURS
RECOMB
RECOMBED
RECOMBINE
RECOMBING
RECOMBS
RECOMFORT
RECOMMEND
RECOMMIT
RECOMMITS
RECOMPACT
RECOMPILE
RECOMPOSE
RECOMPUTE
RECON
RECONCILE
RECONDITE
RECONDUCT
RECONFER
RECONFERS
RECONFINE
RECONFIRM
RECONNECT
RECONNED
RECONNING

R

RECONQUER
RECONS
RECONSIGN
RECONSOLE
RECONSULT
RECONTACT
RECONTOUR
RECONVENE
RECONVERT
RECONVEY
RECONVEYS
RECONVICT
RECOOK
RECOOKED
RECOOKING
RECOOKS
RECOPIED
RECOPIES
RECOPY
RECOPYING
RECORD
RECORDED
RECORDER
RECORDERS
RECORDING
RECORDIST
RECORDS
RECORK
RECORKED
RECORKING
RECORKS
RECOUNT
RECOUNTAL
RECOUNTED
RECOUNTER
RECOUNTS
RECOUP
RECOUPE
RECOUPED
RECOUPES
RECOUPING
RECOUPLE
RECOUPLED
RECOUPLES
RECOUPS
RECOURE
RECOURED
RECOURES
RECOURING
RECOURSE
RECOURSED
RECOURSES
RECOVER
RECOVERED
RECOVEREE
RECOVERER
RECOVEROR
RECOVERS
RECOVERY
RECOWER
RECOWERED
RECOWERS
RECOYLE
RECOYLED
RECOYLES
RECOYLING
RECRATE
RECRATED
RECRATES
RECRATING
RECREANCE
RECREANCY
RECREANT
RECREANTS
RECREATE
RECREATED
RECREATES
RECREATOR
RECREMENT
RECROSS
RECROSSED
RECROSSES
RECROWN
RECROWNED
RECROWNS
RECRUIT
RECRUITAL
RECRUITED
RECRUITER
RECRUITS
RECS
RECTA
RECTAL
RECTALLY
RECTANGLE
RECTI
RECTIFIED
RECTIFIER
RECTIFIES
RECTIFY
RECTION
RECTIONS
RECTITIC
RECTITIS
RECTITUDE
RECTO
RECTOCELE
RECTOR
RECTORAL
RECTORATE
RECTORESS
RECTORIAL
RECTORIES
RECTORS
RECTORY
RECTOS
RECTRESS
RECTRICES
RECTRIX
RECTUM
RECTUMS
RECTUS
RECUILE
RECUILED
RECUILES
RECUILING
RECULE
RECULED
RECULES
RECULING
RECUMBENT
RECUR
RECURE
RECURED
RECURES
RECURING
RECURRED
RECURRENT
RECURRING
RECURS
RECURSION
RECURSIVE
RECURVATE
RECURVE
RECURVED
RECURVES
RECURVING
RECUSAL
RECUSALS
RECUSANCE
RECUSANCY
RECUSANT
RECUSANTS
RECUSE
RECUSED
RECUSES
RECUSING
RECUT
RECUTS
RECUTTING
RECYCLATE
RECYCLE
RECYCLED
RECYCLER
RECYCLERS
RECYCLES
RECYCLING
RECYCLIST
RED
REDACT
REDACTED
REDACTING
REDACTION
REDACTOR
REDACTORS
REDACTS
REDAMAGE
REDAMAGED
REDAMAGES
REDAN
REDANS
REDARGUE
REDARGUED
REDARGUES
REDATE
REDATED
REDATES
REDATING
REDBACK
REDBACKS
REDBAIT
REDBAITED
REDBAITER
REDBAITS
REDBAY
REDBAYS
REDBELLY
REDBIRD
REDBIRDS
REDBONE
REDBONES
REDBREAST
REDBRICK
REDBRICKS
REDBUD
REDBUDS
REDBUG
REDBUGS
REDCAP
REDCAPS
REDCOAT
REDCOATS
REDD
REDDED
REDDEN
REDDENDA
REDDENDO
REDDENDOS
REDDENDUM
REDDENED
REDDENING
REDDENS
REDDER
REDDERS
REDDEST
REDDIER
REDDIEST
REDDING
REDDINGS
REDDISH
REDDISHLY
REDDLE
REDDLED
REDDLEMAN
REDDLEMEN
REDDLES
REDDLING
REDDS
REDDY
REDE

R

REDEAL
REDEALING
REDEALS
REDEALT
REDEAR
REDEARS
REDECIDE
REDECIDED
REDECIDES
REDECRAFT
REDED
REDEEM
REDEEMED
REDEEMER
REDEEMERS
REDEEMING
REDEEMS
REDEFEAT
REDEFEATS
REDEFECT
REDEFECTS
REDEFIED
REDEFIES
REDEFINE
REDEFINED
REDEFINES
REDEFY
REDEFYING
REDELESS
REDELIVER
REDEMAND
REDEMANDS
REDENIED
REDENIES
REDENY
REDENYING
REDEPLOY
REDEPLOYS
REDEPOSIT
REDES
REDESCEND
REDESIGN
REDESIGNS
REDEVELOP
REDEYE
REDEYES
REDFIN
REDFINS
REDFISH
REDFISHES
REDFOOT
REDFOOTS
REDHANDED
REDHEAD
REDHEADED
REDHEADS
REDHORSE
REDHORSES
REDIA
REDIAE
REDIAL
REDIALED
REDIALING
REDIALLED
REDIALS
REDIAS
REDICTATE
REDID
REDIGEST
REDIGESTS
REDIGRESS
REDING
REDINGOTE
REDIP
REDIPPED
REDIPPING
REDIPS
REDIPT
REDIRECT
REDIRECTS
REDISCUSS
REDISPLAY
REDISPOSE
REDISTIL
REDISTILL
REDISTILS
REDIVIDE
REDIVIDED
REDIVIDES
REDIVIVUS
REDIVORCE
REDLEG
REDLEGS
REDLINE
REDLINED
REDLINER
REDLINERS
REDLINES
REDLINING
REDLY
REDNESS
REDNESSES
REDO
REDOCK
REDOCKED
REDOCKING
REDOCKS
REDOES
REDOING
REDOLENCE
REDOLENCY
REDOLENT
REDON
REDONE
REDONNED
REDONNING
REDONS
REDOS
REDOUBLE
REDOUBLED
REDOUBLER
REDOUBLES
REDOUBT
REDOUBTED
REDOUBTS
REDOUND
REDOUNDED
REDOUNDS
REDOUT
REDOUTS
REDOWA
REDOWAS
REDOX
REDOXES
REDPOLL
REDPOLLS
REDRAFT
REDRAFTED
REDRAFTS
REDRAW
REDRAWER
REDRAWERS
REDRAWING
REDRAWN
REDRAWS
REDREAM
REDREAMED
REDREAMS
REDREAMT
REDRESS
REDRESSAL
REDRESSED
REDRESSER
REDRESSES
REDRESSOR
REDREW
REDRIED
REDRIES
REDRILL
REDRILLED
REDRILLS
REDRIVE
REDRIVEN
REDRIVES
REDRIVING
REDROOT
REDROOTS
REDROVE
REDRY
REDRYING
REDS
REDSEAR
REDSHANK
REDSHANKS
REDSHARE
REDSHIFT
REDSHIFTS
REDSHIRE
REDSHIRT
REDSHIRTS
REDSHORT
REDSTART
REDSTARTS
REDSTREAK
REDTAIL
REDTAILS
REDTOP
REDTOPS
REDUB
REDUBBED
REDUBBING
REDUBS
REDUCE
REDUCED
REDUCER
REDUCERS
REDUCES
REDUCIBLE
REDUCIBLY
REDUCING
REDUCTANT
REDUCTASE
REDUCTION
REDUCTIVE
REDUCTOR
REDUCTORS
REDUIT
REDUITS
REDUNDANT
REDUVIID
REDUVIIDS
REDUX
REDWARE
REDWARES
REDWATER
REDWATERS
REDWING
REDWINGS
REDWOOD
REDWOODS
REDYE
REDYED
REDYEING
REDYES
REE
REEARN
REEARNED
REEARNING
REEARNS
REEBOK
REEBOKS
REECH
REECHED
REECHES
REECHIE
REECHIER
REECHIEST
REECHING
REECHO
REECHOED

REECHOES
REECHOING
REECHY
REED
REEDBED
REEDBEDS
REEDBIRD
REEDBIRDS
REEDBUCK
REEDBUCKS
REEDE
REEDED
REEDEN
REEDER
REEDERS
REEDES
REEDIER
REEDIEST
REEDIFIED
REEDIFIES
REEDIFY
REEDILY
REEDINESS
REEDING
REEDINGS
REEDIT
REEDITED
REEDITING
REEDITION
REEDITS
REEDLIKE
REEDLING
REEDLINGS
REEDMAN
REEDMEN
REEDS
REEDSTOP
REEDSTOPS
REEDUCATE
REEDY
REEF
REEFABLE
REEFED
REEFER
REEFERS
REEFIER
REEFIEST
REEFING
REEFINGS
REEFPOINT
REEFS
REEFY
REEJECT
REEJECTED
REEJECTS
REEK
REEKED
REEKER
REEKERS
REEKIE
REEKIER
REEKIEST
REEKING
REEKINGLY
REEKS
REEKY
REEL
REELABLE
REELECT
REELECTED
REELECTS
REELED
REELER
REELERS
REELEVATE
REELING
REELINGLY
REELINGS
REELMAN
REELMEN
REELS
REEMBARK
REEMBARKS
REEMBODY
REEMBRACE
REEMERGE
REEMERGED
REEMERGES
REEMIT
REEMITS
REEMITTED
REEMPLOY
REEMPLOYS
REEN
REENACT
REENACTED
REENACTOR
REENACTS
REENDOW
REENDOWED
REENDOWS
REENFORCE
REENGAGE
REENGAGED
REENGAGES
REENGRAVE
REENJOY
REENJOYED
REENJOYS
REENLARGE
REENLIST
REENLISTS
REENROLL
REENROLLS
REENS
REENSLAVE
REENTER
REENTERED
REENTERS
REENTRANT
REENTRIES
REENTRY
REEQUIP
REEQUIPS
REERECT
REERECTED
REERECTS
REES
REEST
REESTED
REESTIER
REESTIEST
REESTING
REESTS
REESTY
REEVE
REEVED
REEVES
REEVESHIP
REEVING
REEVOKE
REEVOKED
REEVOKES
REEVOKING
REEXAMINE
REEXECUTE
REEXHIBIT
REEXPEL
REEXPELS
REEXPLAIN
REEXPLORE
REEXPORT
REEXPORTS
REEXPOSE
REEXPOSED
REEXPOSES
REEXPRESS
REF
REFACE
REFACED
REFACES
REFACING
REFALL
REFALLEN
REFALLING
REFALLS
REFASHION
REFASTEN
REFASTENS
REFECT
REFECTED
REFECTING
REFECTION
REFECTIVE
REFECTORY
REFECTS
REFED
REFEED
REFEEDING
REFEEDS
REFEEL
REFEELING
REFEELS
REFEL
REFELL
REFELLED
REFELLING
REFELS
REFELT
REFENCE
REFENCED
REFENCES
REFENCING
REFER
REFERABLE
REFEREE
REFEREED
REFEREES
REFERENCE
REFERENDA
REFERENT
REFERENTS
REFERRAL
REFERRALS
REFERRED
REFERRER
REFERRERS
REFERRING
REFERS
REFFED
REFFING
REFFINGS
REFI
REFIGHT
REFIGHTS
REFIGURE
REFIGURED
REFIGURES
REFILE
REFILED
REFILES
REFILING
REFILL
REFILLED
REFILLING
REFILLS
REFILM
REFILMED
REFILMING
REFILMS
REFILTER
REFILTERS
REFINABLE
REFINANCE
REFIND
REFINDING
REFINDS
REFINE
REFINED
REFINEDLY

R

REFINER
REFINERS
REFINERY
REFINES
REFINING
REFININGS
REFINISH
REFIRE
REFIRED
REFIRES
REFIRING
REFIS
REFIT
REFITMENT
REFITS
REFITTED
REFITTING
REFIX
REFIXED
REFIXES
REFIXING
REFLAG
REFLAGGED
REFLAGS
REFLATE
REFLATED
REFLATES
REFLATING
REFLATION
REFLECT
REFLECTED
REFLECTER
REFLECTOR
REFLECTS
REFLET
REFLETS
REFLEW
REFLEX
REFLEXED
REFLEXES
REFLEXING
REFLEXION
REFLEXIVE
REFLEXLY
REFLIES
REFLOAT
REFLOATED
REFLOATS
REFLOOD
REFLOODED
REFLOODS
REFLOW
REFLOWED
REFLOWER
REFLOWERS
REFLOWING
REFLOWN
REFLOWS
REFLUENCE
REFLUENT
REFLUX
REFLUXED
REFLUXES
REFLUXING
REFLY
REFLYING
REFOCUS
REFOCUSED
REFOCUSES
REFOLD
REFOLDED
REFOLDING
REFOLDS
REFOOT
REFOOTED
REFOOTING
REFOOTS
REFOREST
REFORESTS
REFORGE
REFORGED
REFORGES
REFORGING
REFORM
REFORMADE
REFORMADO
REFORMAT
REFORMATE
REFORMATS
REFORMED
REFORMER
REFORMERS
REFORMING
REFORMISM
REFORMIST
REFORMS
REFORTIFY
REFOUGHT
REFOUND
REFOUNDED
REFOUNDER
REFOUNDS
REFRACT
REFRACTED
REFRACTOR
REFRACTS
REFRAIN
REFRAINED
REFRAINER
REFRAINS
REFRAME
REFRAMED
REFRAMES
REFRAMING
REFREEZE
REFREEZES
REFRESH
REFRESHED
REFRESHEN
REFRESHER
REFRESHES
REFRIED
REFRIES
REFRINGE
REFRINGED
REFRINGES
REFRONT
REFRONTED
REFRONTS
REFROZE
REFROZEN
REFRY
REFRYING
REFS
REFT
REFUEL
REFUELED
REFUELING
REFUELLED
REFUELS
REFUGE
REFUGED
REFUGEE
REFUGEES
REFUGES
REFUGIA
REFUGING
REFUGIUM
REFULGENT
REFUND
REFUNDED
REFUNDER
REFUNDERS
REFUNDING
REFUNDS
REFURB
REFURBED
REFURBING
REFURBISH
REFURBS
REFURNISH
REFUSABLE
REFUSAL
REFUSALS
REFUSE
REFUSED
REFUSENIK
REFUSER
REFUSERS
REFUSES
REFUSING
REFUSION
REFUSIONS
REFUSNIK
REFUSNIKS
REFUTABLE
REFUTABLY
REFUTAL
REFUTALS
REFUTE
REFUTED
REFUTER
REFUTERS
REFUTES
REFUTING
REG
REGAIN
REGAINED
REGAINER
REGAINERS
REGAINING
REGAINS
REGAL
REGALE
REGALED
REGALER
REGALERS
REGALES
REGALIA
REGALIAN
REGALIAS
REGALING
REGALISM
REGALISMS
REGALIST
REGALISTS
REGALITY
REGALLY
REGALNESS
REGALS
REGAR
REGARD
REGARDANT
REGARDED
REGARDER
REGARDERS
REGARDFUL
REGARDING
REGARDS
REGARS
REGATHER
REGATHERS
REGATTA
REGATTAS
REGAUGE
REGAUGED
REGAUGES
REGAUGING
REGAVE
REGEAR
REGEARED
REGEARING
REGEARS
REGELATE
REGELATED
REGELATES
REGENCE
REGENCES
REGENCIES
REGENCY

R

REGENT
REGENTAL
REGENTS
REGES
REGEST
REGESTED
REGESTING
REGESTS
REGGAE
REGGAES
REGGAETON
REGGO
REGGOS
REGICIDAL
REGICIDE
REGICIDES
REGIE
REGIES
REGIFT
REGIFTED
REGIFTER
REGIFTERS
REGIFTING
REGIFTS
REGILD
REGILDED
REGILDING
REGILDS
REGILT
REGIME
REGIMEN
REGIMENS
REGIMENT
REGIMENTS
REGIMES
REGIMINAL
REGINA
REGINAE
REGINAL
REGINAS
REGION
REGIONAL
REGIONALS
REGIONARY
REGIONS
REGISSEUR
REGISTER
REGISTERS
REGISTRAR
REGISTRY
REGIUS
REGIVE
REGIVEN
REGIVES
REGIVING
REGLAZE
REGLAZED
REGLAZES
REGLAZING
REGLET
REGLETS
REGLORIFY
REGLOSS
REGLOSSED
REGLOSSES
REGLOW
REGLOWED
REGLOWING
REGLOWS
REGLUE
REGLUED
REGLUES
REGLUING
REGMA
REGMAKER
REGMAKERS
REGMATA
REGNA
REGNAL
REGNANCY
REGNANT
REGNUM
REGO
REGOLITH
REGOLITHS
REGORGE
REGORGED
REGORGES
REGORGING
REGOS
REGOSOL
REGOSOLS
REGRADE
REGRADED
REGRADES
REGRADING
REGRAFT
REGRAFTED
REGRAFTS
REGRANT
REGRANTED
REGRANTS
REGRATE
REGRATED
REGRATER
REGRATERS
REGRATES
REGRATING
REGRATOR
REGRATORS
REGREDE
REGREDED
REGREDES
REGREDING
REGREEN
REGREENED
REGREENS
REGREET
REGREETED
REGREETS
REGRESS
REGRESSED
REGRESSES
REGRESSOR
REGRET
REGRETFUL
REGRETS
REGRETTED
REGRETTER
REGREW
REGRIND
REGRINDS
REGROOM
REGROOMED
REGROOMS
REGROOVE
REGROOVED
REGROOVES
REGROUND
REGROUP
REGROUPED
REGROUPS
REGROW
REGROWING
REGROWN
REGROWS
REGROWTH
REGROWTHS
REGS
REGUERDON
REGULA
REGULABLE
REGULAE
REGULAR
REGULARLY
REGULARS
REGULATE
REGULATED
REGULATES
REGULATOR
REGULI
REGULINE
REGULISE
REGULISED
REGULISES
REGULIZE
REGULIZED
REGULIZES
REGULO
REGULOS
REGULUS
REGULUSES
REGUR
REGURS
REH
REHAB
REHABBED
REHABBER
REHABBERS
REHABBING
REHABS
REHAMMER
REHAMMERS
REHANDLE
REHANDLED
REHANDLES
REHANG
REHANGED
REHANGING
REHANGS
REHARDEN
REHARDENS
REHASH
REHASHED
REHASHES
REHASHING
REHEAR
REHEARD
REHEARING
REHEARS
REHEARSAL
REHEARSE
REHEARSED
REHEARSER
REHEARSES
REHEAT
REHEATED
REHEATER
REHEATERS
REHEATING
REHEATS
REHEEL
REHEELED
REHEELING
REHEELS
REHEM
REHEMMED
REHEMMING
REHEMS
REHINGE
REHINGED
REHINGES
REHINGING
REHIRE
REHIRED
REHIRES
REHIRING
REHOBOAM
REHOBOAMS
REHOME
REHOMED
REHOMES
REHOMING
REHOMINGS
REHOUSE
REHOUSED
REHOUSES
REHOUSING
REHS
REHUNG

R

REHYDRATE
REI
REIF
REIFIED
REIFIER
REIFIERS
REIFIES
REIFS
REIFY
REIFYING
REIGN
REIGNED
REIGNING
REIGNITE
REIGNITED
REIGNITES
REIGNS
REIK
REIKI
REIKIS
REIKS
REILLUME
REILLUMED
REILLUMES
REIMAGE
REIMAGED
REIMAGES
REIMAGINE
REIMAGING
REIMBURSE
REIMMERSE
REIMPLANT
REIMPORT
REIMPORTS
REIMPOSE
REIMPOSED
REIMPOSES
REIN
REINCITE
REINCITED
REINCITES
REINCUR
REINCURS
REINDEER
REINDEERS
REINDEX
REINDEXED
REINDEXES
REINDICT
REINDICTS
REINDUCE
REINDUCED
REINDUCES
REINDUCT
REINDUCTS
REINED
REINETTE
REINETTES
REINFECT
REINFECTS
REINFLAME
REINFLATE
REINFORCE
REINFORM
REINFORMS
REINFUND
REINFUNDS
REINFUSE
REINFUSED
REINFUSES
REINHABIT
REINING
REINJECT
REINJECTS
REINJURE
REINJURED
REINJURES
REINJURY
REINK
REINKED
REINKING
REINKS
REINLESS
REINS
REINSERT
REINSERTS
REINSMAN
REINSMEN
REINSPECT
REINSPIRE
REINSTAL
REINSTALL
REINSTALS
REINSTATE
REINSURE
REINSURED
REINSURER
REINSURES
REINTER
REINTERS
REINVADE
REINVADED
REINVADES
REINVENT
REINVENTS
REINVEST
REINVESTS
REINVITE
REINVITED
REINVITES
REINVOKE
REINVOKED
REINVOKES
REINVOLVE
REIRD
REIRDS
REIS
REISES
REISHI
REISHIS
REISSUE
REISSUED
REISSUER
REISSUERS
REISSUES
REISSUING
REIST
REISTAFEL
REISTED
REISTING
REISTS
REITBOK
REITBOKS
REITER
REITERANT
REITERATE
REITERED
REITERING
REITERS
REIVE
REIVED
REIVER
REIVERS
REIVES
REIVING
REIVINGS
REJACKET
REJACKETS
REJECT
REJECTED
REJECTEE
REJECTEES
REJECTER
REJECTERS
REJECTING
REJECTION
REJECTIVE
REJECTOR
REJECTORS
REJECTS
REJIG
REJIGGED
REJIGGER
REJIGGERS
REJIGGING
REJIGS
REJOICE
REJOICED
REJOICER
REJOICERS
REJOICES
REJOICING
REJOIN
REJOINDER
REJOINED
REJOINING
REJOINS
REJON
REJONEO
REJONEOS
REJONES
REJOURN
REJOURNED
REJOURNS
REJUDGE
REJUDGED
REJUDGES
REJUDGING
REJUGGLE
REJUGGLED
REJUGGLES
REJUSTIFY
REKE
REKED
REKES
REKEY
REKEYED
REKEYING
REKEYS
REKINDLE
REKINDLED
REKINDLES
REKING
REKNIT
REKNITS
REKNITTED
REKNOT
REKNOTS
REKNOTTED
RELABEL
RELABELED
RELABELS
RELACE
RELACED
RELACES
RELACHE
RELACHES
RELACING
RELACQUER
RELAID
RELAND
RELANDED
RELANDING
RELANDS
RELAPSE
RELAPSED
RELAPSER
RELAPSERS
RELAPSES
RELAPSING
RELATA
RELATABLE
RELATE
RELATED
RELATEDLY
RELATER
RELATERS
RELATES
RELATING
RELATION

R

RELATIONS
RELATIVAL
RELATIVE
RELATIVES
RELATOR
RELATORS
RELATUM
RELAUNCH
RELAUNDER
RELAX
RELAXABLE
RELAXANT
RELAXANTS
RELAXED
RELAXEDLY
RELAXER
RELAXERS
RELAXES
RELAXIN
RELAXING
RELAXINS
RELAY
RELAYED
RELAYING
RELAYS
RELEARN
RELEARNED
RELEARNS
RELEARNT
RELEASE
RELEASED
RELEASEE
RELEASEES
RELEASER
RELEASERS
RELEASES
RELEASING
RELEASOR
RELEASORS
RELEGABLE
RELEGATE
RELEGATED
RELEGATES
RELEND
RELENDING
RELENDS
RELENT
RELENTED
RELENTING
RELENTS
RELET
RELETS
RELETTER
RELETTERS
RELETTING
RELEVANCE
RELEVANCY
RELEVANT
RELEVE
RELEVES
RELIABLE
RELIABLES
RELIABLY
RELIANCE
RELIANCES
RELIANT
RELIANTLY
RELIC
RELICENSE
RELICS
RELICT
RELICTION
RELICTS
RELIDE
RELIE
RELIED
RELIEF
RELIEFS
RELIER
RELIERS
RELIES
RELIEVE
RELIEVED
RELIEVER
RELIEVERS
RELIEVES
RELIEVING
RELIEVO
RELIEVOS
RELIGHT
RELIGHTED
RELIGHTS
RELIGIEUX
RELIGION
RELIGIONS
RELIGIOSE
RELIGIOSO
RELIGIOUS
RELINE
RELINED
RELINES
RELINING
RELINK
RELINKED
RELINKING
RELINKS
RELIQUARY
RELIQUE
RELIQUEFY
RELIQUES
RELIQUIAE
RELIQUIFY
RELISH
RELISHED
RELISHES
RELISHING
RELIST
RELISTED
RELISTEN
RELISTENS
RELISTING
RELISTS
RELIT
RELIVABLE
RELIVE
RELIVED
RELIVER
RELIVERED
RELIVERS
RELIVES
RELIVING
RELLENO
RELLENOS
RELLIE
RELLIES
RELLISH
RELLISHED
RELLISHES
RELLO
RELLOS
RELOAD
RELOADED
RELOADER
RELOADERS
RELOADING
RELOADS
RELOAN
RELOANED
RELOANING
RELOANS
RELOCATE
RELOCATED
RELOCATEE
RELOCATES
RELOCATOR
RELOCK
RELOCKED
RELOCKING
RELOCKS
RELOOK
RELOOKED
RELOOKING
RELOOKS
RELUCENT
RELUCT
RELUCTANT
RELUCTATE
RELUCTED
RELUCTING
RELUCTS
RELUME
RELUMED
RELUMES
RELUMINE
RELUMINED
RELUMINES
RELUMING
RELY
RELYING
REM
REMADE
REMADES
REMAIL
REMAILED
REMAILER
REMAILERS
REMAILING
REMAILS
REMAIN
REMAINDER
REMAINED
REMAINER
REMAINERS
REMAINING
REMAINS
REMAKE
REMAKER
REMAKERS
REMAKES
REMAKING
REMAN
REMAND
REMANDED
REMANDING
REMANDS
REMANENCE
REMANENCY
REMANENT
REMANENTS
REMANET
REMANETS
REMANIE
REMANIES
REMANNED
REMANNING
REMANS
REMAP
REMAPPED
REMAPPING
REMAPS
REMARK
REMARKED
REMARKER
REMARKERS
REMARKET
REMARKETS
REMARKING
REMARKS
REMARQUE
REMARQUED
REMARQUES
REMARRIED
REMARRIES
REMARRY
REMASTER
REMASTERS
REMATCH
REMATCHED
REMATCHES
REMATE

REMATED
REMATES
REMATING
REMBLAI
REMBLAIS
REMBLE
REMBLED
REMBLES
REMBLING
REMEAD
REMEADED
REMEADING
REMEADS
REMEASURE
REMEDE
REMEDED
REMEDES
REMEDIAL
REMEDIAT
REMEDIATE
REMEDIED
REMEDIES
REMEDING
REMEDY
REMEDYING
REMEET
REMEETING
REMEETS
REMEID
REMEIDED
REMEIDING
REMEIDS
REMELT
REMELTED
REMELTING
REMELTS
REMEMBER
REMEMBERS
REMEN
REMEND
REMENDED
REMENDING
REMENDS
REMENS
REMERCIED
REMERCIES
REMERCY
REMERGE
REMERGED
REMERGES
REMERGING
REMET
REMEX
REMIGATE
REMIGATED
REMIGATES
REMIGES
REMIGIAL
REMIGRATE
REMIND
REMINDED
REMINDER
REMINDERS
REMINDFUL
REMINDING
REMINDS
REMINISCE
REMINT
REMINTED
REMINTING
REMINTS
REMISE
REMISED
REMISES
REMISING
REMISS
REMISSION
REMISSIVE
REMISSLY
REMISSORY
REMIT
REMITMENT
REMITS
REMITTAL
REMITTALS
REMITTED
REMITTEE
REMITTEES
REMITTENT
REMITTER
REMITTERS
REMITTING
REMITTOR
REMITTORS
REMIX
REMIXED
REMIXER
REMIXERS
REMIXES
REMIXING
REMIXT
REMIXTURE
REMNANT
REMNANTAL
REMNANTS
REMODEL
REMODELED
REMODELER
REMODELS
REMODIFY
REMOISTEN
REMOLADE
REMOLADES
REMOLD
REMOLDED
REMOLDING
REMOLDS
REMONTANT
REMONTOIR
REMORA
REMORAS
REMORID
REMORSE
REMORSES
REMOTE
REMOTELY
REMOTER
REMOTES
REMOTEST
REMOTION
REMOTIONS
REMOUD
REMOULADE
REMOULD
REMOULDED
REMOULDS
REMOUNT
REMOUNTED
REMOUNTS
REMOVABLE
REMOVABLY
REMOVAL
REMOVALS
REMOVE
REMOVED
REMOVEDLY
REMOVER
REMOVERS
REMOVES
REMOVING
REMS
REMUAGE
REMUAGES
REMUDA
REMUDAS
REMUEUR
REMUEURS
REMURMUR
REMURMURS
REN
RENAGUE
RENAGUED
RENAGUES
RENAGUING
RENAIL
RENAILED
RENAILING
RENAILS
RENAL
RENAME
RENAMED
RENAMES
RENAMING
RENASCENT
RENATURE
RENATURED
RENATURES
RENAY
RENAYED
RENAYING
RENAYS
RENCONTRE
REND
RENDANG
RENDANGS
RENDED
RENDER
RENDERED
RENDERER
RENDERERS
RENDERING
RENDERS
RENDIBLE
RENDING
RENDITION
RENDS
RENDZINA
RENDZINAS
RENEAGUE
RENEAGUED
RENEAGUES
RENEGADE
RENEGADED
RENEGADES
RENEGADO
RENEGADOS
RENEGATE
RENEGATES
RENEGE
RENEGED
RENEGER
RENEGERS
RENEGES
RENEGING
RENEGUE
RENEGUED
RENEGUER
RENEGUERS
RENEGUES
RENEGUING
RENEST
RENESTED
RENESTING
RENESTS
RENEW
RENEWABLE
RENEWABLY
RENEWAL
RENEWALS
RENEWED
RENEWEDLY
RENEWER
RENEWERS
RENEWING
RENEWINGS
RENEWS
RENEY
RENEYED
RENEYING
RENEYS

R

RENFIERST
RENFORCE
RENFORCED
RENFORCES
RENFORST
RENGA
RENGAS
RENIED
RENIES
RENIFORM
RENIG
RENIGGED
RENIGGING
RENIGS
RENIN
RENINS
RENITENCE
RENITENCY
RENITENT
RENK
RENKER
RENKEST
RENMINBI
RENMINBIS
RENNASE
RENNASES
RENNE
RENNED
RENNES
RENNET
RENNETS
RENNIN
RENNING
RENNINGS
RENNINS
RENO
RENOGRAM
RENOGRAMS
RENOS
RENOTIFY
RENOUNCE
RENOUNCED
RENOUNCER
RENOUNCES
RENOVATE
RENOVATED
RENOVATES
RENOVATOR
RENOWN
RENOWNED
RENOWNER
RENOWNERS
RENOWNING
RENOWNS
RENS
RENT
RENTABLE
RENTAL
RENTALLER
RENTALS
RENTE
RENTED
RENTER
RENTERS
RENTES
RENTIER
RENTIERS
RENTING
RENTINGS
RENTS
RENUMBER
RENUMBERS
RENVERSE
RENVERSED
RENVERSES
RENVERST
RENVOI
RENVOIS
RENVOY
RENVOYS
RENY
RENYING
REO
REOBJECT
REOBJECTS
REOBSERVE
REOBTAIN
REOBTAINS
REOCCUPY
REOCCUR
REOCCURS
REOFFEND
REOFFENDS
REOFFER
REOFFERED
REOFFERS
REOIL
REOILED
REOILING
REOILS
REOPEN
REOPENED
REOPENER
REOPENERS
REOPENING
REOPENS
REOPERATE
REOPPOSE
REOPPOSED
REOPPOSES
REORDAIN
REORDAINS
REORDER
REORDERED
REORDERS
REORG
REORGED
REORGING
REORGS
REORIENT
REORIENTS
REOS
REOUTFIT
REOUTFITS
REOVIRUS
REOXIDISE
REOXIDIZE
REP
REPACIFY
REPACK
REPACKAGE
REPACKED
REPACKING
REPACKS
REPAID
REPAINT
REPAINTED
REPAINTS
REPAIR
REPAIRED
REPAIRER
REPAIRERS
REPAIRING
REPAIRMAN
REPAIRMEN
REPAIRS
REPAND
REPANDLY
REPANEL
REPANELED
REPANELS
REPAPER
REPAPERED
REPAPERS
REPARABLE
REPARABLY
REPARK
REPARKED
REPARKING
REPARKS
REPARTEE
REPARTEED
REPARTEES
REPASS
REPASSAGE
REPASSED
REPASSES
REPASSING
REPAST
REPASTED
REPASTING
REPASTS
REPASTURE
REPATCH
REPATCHED
REPATCHES
REPATTERN
REPAVE
REPAVED
REPAVES
REPAVING
REPAY
REPAYABLE
REPAYING
REPAYMENT
REPAYS
REPEAL
REPEALED
REPEALER
REPEALERS
REPEALING
REPEALS
REPEAT
REPEATED
REPEATER
REPEATERS
REPEATING
REPEATS
REPECHAGE
REPEG
REPEGGED
REPEGGING
REPEGS
REPEL
REPELLANT
REPELLED
REPELLENT
REPELLER
REPELLERS
REPELLING
REPELS
REPENT
REPENTANT
REPENTED
REPENTER
REPENTERS
REPENTING
REPENTS
REPEOPLE
REPEOPLED
REPEOPLES
REPERCUSS
REPEREPE
REPEREPES
REPERK
REPERKED
REPERKING
REPERKS
REPERTORY
REPERUSAL
REPERUSE
REPERUSED
REPERUSES
REPETEND
REPETENDS
REPHRASE
REPHRASED
REPHRASES
REPIGMENT
REPIN

R

REPINE
REPINED
REPINER
REPINERS
REPINES
REPINING
REPININGS
REPINNED
REPINNING
REPINS
REPIQUE
REPIQUED
REPIQUES
REPIQUING
REPLA
REPLACE
REPLACED
REPLACER
REPLACERS
REPLACES
REPLACING
REPLAN
REPLANNED
REPLANS
REPLANT
REPLANTED
REPLANTS
REPLASTER
REPLATE
REPLATED
REPLATES
REPLATING
REPLAY
REPLAYED
REPLAYING
REPLAYS
REPLEAD
REPLEADED
REPLEADER
REPLEADS
REPLED
REPLEDGE
REPLEDGED
REPLEDGES
REPLENISH
REPLETE
REPLETED
REPLETELY
REPLETES
REPLETING
REPLETION
REPLEVIED
REPLEVIES
REPLEVIN
REPLEVINS
REPLEVY
REPLICA
REPLICANT
REPLICAS
REPLICASE
REPLICATE
REPLICON
REPLICONS
REPLIED
REPLIER
REPLIERS
REPLIES
REPLOT
REPLOTS
REPLOTTED
REPLOUGH
REPLOUGHS
REPLOW
REPLOWED
REPLOWING
REPLOWS
REPLUM
REPLUMB
REPLUMBED
REPLUMBS
REPLUNGE
REPLUNGED
REPLUNGES
REPLY
REPLYING
REPO
REPOINT
REPOINTED
REPOINTS
REPOLISH
REPOLL
REPOLLED
REPOLLING
REPOLLS
REPOMAN
REPOMEN
REPONE
REPONED
REPONES
REPONING
REPORT
REPORTAGE
REPORTED
REPORTER
REPORTERS
REPORTING
REPORTS
REPOS
REPOSAL
REPOSALL
REPOSALLS
REPOSALS
REPOSE
REPOSED
REPOSEDLY
REPOSEFUL
REPOSER
REPOSERS
REPOSES
REPOSING
REPOSIT
REPOSITED
REPOSITOR
REPOSITS
REPOSSESS
REPOST
REPOSTED
REPOSTING
REPOSTS
REPOSURE
REPOSURES
REPOT
REPOTS
REPOTTED
REPOTTING
REPOUR
REPOURED
REPOURING
REPOURS
REPOUSSE
REPOUSSES
REPOWER
REPOWERED
REPOWERS
REPP
REPPED
REPPING
REPPINGS
REPPS
REPREEVE
REPREEVED
REPREEVES
REPREHEND
REPRESENT
REPRESS
REPRESSED
REPRESSER
REPRESSES
REPRESSOR
REPRICE
REPRICED
REPRICES
REPRICING
REPRIEFE
REPRIEFES
REPRIEVAL
REPRIEVE
REPRIEVED
REPRIEVER
REPRIEVES
REPRIMAND
REPRIME
REPRIMED
REPRIMES
REPRIMING
REPRINT
REPRINTED
REPRINTER
REPRINTS
REPRISAL
REPRISALS
REPRISE
REPRISED
REPRISES
REPRISING
REPRIVE
REPRIVED
REPRIVES
REPRIVING
REPRIZE
REPRIZED
REPRIZES
REPRIZING
REPRO
REPROACH
REPROBACY
REPROBATE
REPROBE
REPROBED
REPROBES
REPROBING
REPROCESS
REPRODUCE
REPROGRAM
REPROOF
REPROOFED
REPROOFS
REPROS
REPROVAL
REPROVALS
REPROVE
REPROVED
REPROVER
REPROVERS
REPROVES
REPROVING
REPRYVE
REPRYVED
REPRYVES
REPRYVING
REPS
REPTANT
REPTATION
REPTILE
REPTILES
REPTILIA
REPTILIAN
REPTILIUM
REPTILOID
REPUBLIC
REPUBLICS
REPUBLISH
REPUDIATE
REPUGN
REPUGNANT
REPUGNED
REPUGNING
REPUGNS
REPULP
REPULPED

REPULPING
REPULPS
REPULSE
REPULSED
REPULSER
REPULSERS
REPULSES
REPULSING
REPULSION
REPULSIVE
REPUMP
REPUMPED
REPUMPING
REPUMPS
REPUNIT
REPUNITS
REPURE
REPURED
REPURES
REPURIFY
REPURING
REPURPOSE
REPURSUE
REPURSUED
REPURSUES
REPUTABLE
REPUTABLY
REPUTE
REPUTED
REPUTEDLY
REPUTES
REPUTING
REPUTINGS
REQUALIFY
REQUERE
REQUERED
REQUERES
REQUERING
REQUEST
REQUESTED
REQUESTER
REQUESTOR
REQUESTS
REQUICKEN
REQUIEM
REQUIEMS
REQUIGHT
REQUIGHTS
REQUIN
REQUINS
REQUINTO
REQUINTOS
REQUIRE
REQUIRED
REQUIRER
REQUIRERS
REQUIRES
REQUIRING
REQUISITE
REQUIT
REQUITAL
REQUITALS
REQUITE
REQUITED
REQUITER
REQUITERS
REQUITES
REQUITING
REQUITS
REQUITTED
REQUOTE
REQUOTED
REQUOTES
REQUOTING
REQUOYLE
REQUOYLED
REQUOYLES
RERACK
RERACKED
RERACKING
RERACKS
RERADIATE
RERAIL
RERAILED
RERAILING
RERAILS
RERAISE
RERAISED
RERAISES
RERAISING
RERAN
REREAD
REREADING
REREADS
REREBRACE
RERECORD
RERECORDS
REREDOS
REREDOSES
REREDOSSE
RERELEASE
REREMAI
REREMAIS
REREMICE
REREMIND
REREMINDS
REREMOUSE
RERENT
RERENTED
RERENTING
RERENTS
REREPEAT
REREPEATS
REREVIEW
REREVIEWS
REREVISE
REREVISED
REREVISES
REREWARD
REREWARDS
RERIG
RERIGGED
RERIGGING
RERIGS
RERISE
RERISEN
RERISES
RERISING
REROLL
REROLLED
REROLLER
REROLLERS
REROLLING
REROLLS
REROOF
REROOFED
REROOFING
REROOFS
REROSE
REROUTE
REROUTED
REROUTES
REROUTING
RERUN
RERUNNING
RERUNS
RES
RESADDLE
RESADDLED
RESADDLES
RESAID
RESAIL
RESAILED
RESAILING
RESAILS
RESALABLE
RESALE
RESALES
RESALGAR
RESALGARS
RESALUTE
RESALUTED
RESALUTES
RESAMPLE
RESAMPLED
RESAMPLES
RESAT
RESAW
RESAWED
RESAWING
RESAWN
RESAWS
RESAY
RESAYING
RESAYS
RESCALE
RESCALED
RESCALES
RESCALING
RESCHOOL
RESCHOOLS
RESCIND
RESCINDED
RESCINDER
RESCINDS
RESCORE
RESCORED
RESCORES
RESCORING
RESCREEN
RESCREENS
RESCRIPT
RESCRIPTS
RESCUABLE
RESCUE
RESCUED
RESCUEE
RESCUEES
RESCUER
RESCUERS
RESCUES
RESCUING
RESCULPT
RESCULPTS
RESEAL
RESEALED
RESEALING
RESEALS
RESEARCH
RESEASON
RESEASONS
RESEAT
RESEATED
RESEATING
RESEATS
RESEAU
RESEAUS
RESEAUX
RESECT
RESECTED
RESECTING
RESECTION
RESECTS
RESECURE
RESECURED
RESECURES
RESEDA
RESEDAS
RESEE
RESEED
RESEEDED
RESEEDING
RESEEDS
RESEEING
RESEEK
RESEEKING
RESEEKS
RESEEN
RESEES
RESEIZE

RESEIZED
RESEIZES
RESEIZING
RESEIZURE
RESELECT
RESELECTS
RESELL
RESELLER
RESELLERS
RESELLING
RESELLS
RESEMBLE
RESEMBLED
RESEMBLER
RESEMBLES
RESEND
RESENDING
RESENDS
RESENT
RESENTED
RESENTER
RESENTERS
RESENTFUL
RESENTING
RESENTIVE
RESENTS
RESERPINE
RESERVE
RESERVED
RESERVER
RESERVERS
RESERVES
RESERVICE
RESERVING
RESERVIST
RESERVOIR
RESES
RESET
RESETS
RESETTED
RESETTER
RESETTERS
RESETTING
RESETTLE
RESETTLED
RESETTLES
RESEW
RESEWED
RESEWING
RESEWN
RESEWS
RESH
RESHAPE
RESHAPED
RESHAPER
RESHAPERS
RESHAPES
RESHAPING
RESHARPEN
RESHAVE
RESHAVED
RESHAVEN
RESHAVES
RESHAVING
RESHES
RESHINE
RESHINED
RESHINES
RESHINGLE
RESHINING
RESHIP
RESHIPPED
RESHIPPER
RESHIPS
RESHOD
RESHOE
RESHOED
RESHOEING
RESHOES
RESHONE
RESHOOT
RESHOOTS
RESHOT
RESHOW
RESHOWED
RESHOWER
RESHOWERS
RESHOWING
RESHOWN
RESHOWS
RESHUFFLE
RESIANCE
RESIANCES
RESIANT
RESIANTS
RESID
RESIDE
RESIDED
RESIDENCE
RESIDENCY
RESIDENT
RESIDENTS
RESIDER
RESIDERS
RESIDES
RESIDING
RESIDS
RESIDUA
RESIDUAL
RESIDUALS
RESIDUARY
RESIDUE
RESIDUES
RESIDUOUS
RESIDUUM
RESIDUUMS
RESIFT
RESIFTED
RESIFTING
RESIFTS
RESIGHT
RESIGHTED
RESIGHTS
RESIGN
RESIGNED
RESIGNER
RESIGNERS
RESIGNING
RESIGNS
RESILE
RESILED
RESILES
RESILIENT
RESILIN
RESILING
RESILINS
RESILVER
RESILVERS
RESIN
RESINATA
RESINATAS
RESINATE
RESINATED
RESINATES
RESINED
RESINER
RESINERS
RESINIER
RESINIEST
RESINIFY
RESINING
RESINISE
RESINISED
RESINISES
RESINIZE
RESINIZED
RESINIZES
RESINLIKE
RESINOID
RESINOIDS
RESINOSES
RESINOSIS
RESINOUS
RESINS
RESINY
RESIST
RESISTANT
RESISTED
RESISTENT
RESISTER
RESISTERS
RESISTING
RESISTIVE
RESISTOR
RESISTORS
RESISTS
RESIT
RESITE
RESITED
RESITES
RESITING
RESITS
RESITTING
RESITUATE
RESIZABLE
RESIZE
RESIZED
RESIZES
RESIZING
RESKETCH
RESKEW
RESKEWED
RESKEWING
RESKEWS
RESKILL
RESKILLED
RESKILLS
RESKIN
RESKINNED
RESKINS
RESKUE
RESKUED
RESKUES
RESKUING
RESLATE
RESLATED
RESLATES
RESLATING
RESMELT
RESMELTED
RESMELTS
RESMOOTH
RESMOOTHS
RESNATRON
RESOAK
RESOAKED
RESOAKING
RESOAKS
RESOD
RESODDED
RESODDING
RESODS
RESOFTEN
RESOFTENS
RESOJET
RESOJETS
RESOLD
RESOLDER
RESOLDERS
RESOLE
RESOLED
RESOLES
RESOLING
RESOLUBLE
RESOLUTE
RESOLUTER
RESOLUTES
RESOLVE
RESOLVED
RESOLVENT

RESOLVER
RESOLVERS
RESOLVES
RESOLVING
RESONANCE
RESONANT
RESONANTS
RESONATE
RESONATED
RESONATES
RESONATOR
RESORB
RESORBED
RESORBENT
RESORBING
RESORBS
RESORCIN
RESORCINS
RESORT
RESORTED
RESORTER
RESORTERS
RESORTING
RESORTS
RESOUGHT
RESOUND
RESOUNDED
RESOUNDS
RESOURCE
RESOURCED
RESOURCES
RESOW
RESOWED
RESOWING
RESOWN
RESOWS
RESPACE
RESPACED
RESPACES
RESPACING
RESPADE
RESPADED
RESPADES
RESPADING
RESPEAK
RESPEAKS
RESPECIFY
RESPECT
RESPECTED
RESPECTER
RESPECTS
RESPELL
RESPELLED
RESPELLS
RESPELT
RESPIRE
RESPIRED
RESPIRES
RESPIRING
RESPITE
RESPITED
RESPITES
RESPITING
RESPLEND
RESPLENDS
RESPLICE
RESPLICED
RESPLICES
RESPLIT
RESPLITS
RESPOKE
RESPOKEN
RESPOND
RESPONDED
RESPONDER
RESPONDS
RESPONSA
RESPONSE
RESPONSER
RESPONSES
RESPONSOR
RESPONSUM
RESPOOL
RESPOOLED
RESPOOLS
RESPOT
RESPOTS
RESPOTTED
RESPRANG
RESPRAY
RESPRAYED
RESPRAYS
RESPREAD
RESPREADS
RESPRING
RESPRINGS
RESPROUT
RESPROUTS
RESPRUNG
RESSALDAR
REST
RESTABLE
RESTABLED
RESTABLES
RESTACK
RESTACKED
RESTACKS
RESTAFF
RESTAFFED
RESTAFFS
RESTAGE
RESTAGED
RESTAGES
RESTAGING
RESTAMP
RESTAMPED
RESTAMPS
RESTART
RESTARTED
RESTARTER
RESTARTS
RESTATE
RESTATED
RESTATES
RESTATING
RESTATION
RESTED
RESTEM
RESTEMMED
RESTEMS
RESTER
RESTERS
RESTFUL
RESTFULLY
RESTIER
RESTIEST
RESTIFF
RESTIFORM
RESTING
RESTINGS
RESTITCH
RESTITUTE
RESTIVE
RESTIVELY
RESTLESS
RESTO
RESTOCK
RESTOCKED
RESTOCKS
RESTOKE
RESTOKED
RESTOKES
RESTOKING
RESTORAL
RESTORALS
RESTORE
RESTORED
RESTORER
RESTORERS
RESTORES
RESTORING
RESTOS
RESTRAIN
RESTRAINS
RESTRAINT
RESTRESS
RESTRETCH
RESTRICT
RESTRICTS
RESTRIKE
RESTRIKES
RESTRING
RESTRINGE
RESTRINGS
RESTRIVE
RESTRIVEN
RESTRIVES
RESTROOM
RESTROOMS
RESTROVE
RESTRUCK
RESTRUNG
RESTS
RESTUDIED
RESTUDIES
RESTUDY
RESTUFF
RESTUFFED
RESTUFFS
RESTUMP
RESTUMPED
RESTUMPS
RESTY
RESTYLE
RESTYLED
RESTYLES
RESTYLING
RESUBJECT
RESUBMIT
RESUBMITS
RESULT
RESULTANT
RESULTED
RESULTFUL
RESULTING
RESULTS
RESUMABLE
RESUME
RESUMED
RESUMER
RESUMERS
RESUMES
RESUMING
RESUMMON
RESUMMONS
RESUPINE
RESUPPLY
RESURFACE
RESURGE
RESURGED
RESURGENT
RESURGES
RESURGING
RESURRECT
RESURVEY
RESURVEYS
RESUS
RESUSES
RESUSPEND
RESUSSES
RESWALLOW
RET
RETABLE
RETABLES
RETABLO
RETABLOS
RETACK
RETACKED
RETACKING
RETACKLE

R

RETACKLED
RETACKLES
RETACKS
RETAG
RETAGGED
RETAGGING
RETAGS
RETAIL
RETAILED
RETAILER
RETAILERS
RETAILING
RETAILOR
RETAILORS
RETAILS
RETAIN
RETAINED
RETAINER
RETAINERS
RETAINING
RETAINS
RETAKE
RETAKEN
RETAKER
RETAKERS
RETAKES
RETAKING
RETAKINGS
RETALIATE
RETALLIED
RETALLIES
RETALLY
RETAMA
RETAMAS
RETAPE
RETAPED
RETAPES
RETAPING
RETARD
RETARDANT
RETARDED
RETARDER
RETARDERS
RETARDING
RETARDS
RETARGET
RETARGETS
RETASTE
RETASTED
RETASTES
RETASTING
RETAUGHT
RETAX
RETAXED
RETAXES
RETAXING
RETCH
RETCHED
RETCHES
RETCHING
RETCHINGS
RETCHLESS
RETE
RETEACH
RETEACHES
RETEAM
RETEAMED
RETEAMING
RETEAMS
RETEAR
RETEARING
RETEARS
RETELL
RETELLER
RETELLERS
RETELLING
RETELLS
RETEM
RETEMPER
RETEMPERS
RETEMS
RETENE
RETENES
RETENTION
RETENTIVE
RETEST
RETESTED
RETESTIFY
RETESTING
RETESTS
RETEXTURE
RETHINK
RETHINKER
RETHINKS
RETHOUGHT
RETHREAD
RETHREADS
RETIA
RETIAL
RETIARII
RETIARIUS
RETIARY
RETICELLA
RETICENCE
RETICENCY
RETICENT
RETICLE
RETICLES
RETICULA
RETICULAR
RETICULE
RETICULES
RETICULUM
RETIE
RETIED
RETIEING
RETIES
RETIFORM
RETIGHTEN
RETILE
RETILED
RETILES
RETILING
RETIME
RETIMED
RETIMES
RETIMING
RETINA
RETINAE
RETINAL
RETINALS
RETINAS
RETINE
RETINENE
RETINENES
RETINES
RETINITE
RETINITES
RETINITIS
RETINOIC
RETINOID
RETINOIDS
RETINOL
RETINOLS
RETINT
RETINTED
RETINTING
RETINTS
RETINUE
RETINUED
RETINUES
RETINULA
RETINULAE
RETINULAR
RETINULAS
RETIRACY
RETIRAL
RETIRALS
RETIRANT
RETIRANTS
RETIRE
RETIRED
RETIREDLY
RETIREE
RETIREES
RETIRER
RETIRERS
RETIRES
RETIRING
RETITLE
RETITLED
RETITLES
RETITLING
RETOLD
RETOOK
RETOOL
RETOOLED
RETOOLING
RETOOLS
RETORE
RETORN
RETORSION
RETORT
RETORTED
RETORTER
RETORTERS
RETORTING
RETORTION
RETORTIVE
RETORTS
RETOTAL
RETOTALED
RETOTALS
RETOUCH
RETOUCHED
RETOUCHER
RETOUCHES
RETOUR
RETOURED
RETOURING
RETOURS
RETOX
RETOXED
RETOXES
RETOXING
RETRACE
RETRACED
RETRACER
RETRACERS
RETRACES
RETRACING
RETRACK
RETRACKED
RETRACKS
RETRACT
RETRACTED
RETRACTOR
RETRACTS
RETRAICT
RETRAICTS
RETRAIN
RETRAINED
RETRAINEE
RETRAINS
RETRAIT
RETRAITE
RETRAITES
RETRAITS
RETRAITT
RETRAITTS
RETRAL
RETRALLY
RETRATE
RETRATED
RETRATES
RETRATING
RETREAD
RETREADED
RETREADS
RETREAT

R

RETREATED
RETREATER
RETREATS
RETREE
RETREES
RETRENCH
RETRIAL
RETRIALS
RETRIBUTE
RETRIED
RETRIES
RETRIEVAL
RETRIEVE
RETRIEVED
RETRIEVER
RETRIEVES
RETRIM
RETRIMMED
RETRIMS
RETRO
RETROACT
RETROACTS
RETROCEDE
RETROD
RETRODDEN
RETRODICT
RETROFIRE
RETROFIT
RETROFITS
RETROFLEX
RETROJECT
RETRONYM
RETRONYMS
RETROPACK
RETRORSE
RETROS
RETROUSSE
RETROVERT
RETRY
RETRYING
RETS
RETSINA
RETSINAS
RETTED
RETTERIES
RETTERY
RETTING
RETUND
RETUNDED
RETUNDING
RETUNDS
RETUNE
RETUNED
RETUNES
RETUNING
RETURF
RETURFED
RETURFING
RETURFS
RETURN
RETURNED
RETURNEE
RETURNEES
RETURNER
RETURNERS
RETURNIK
RETURNIKS
RETURNING
RETURNS
RETUSE
RETWEET
RETWEETED
RETWEETS
RETWIST
RETWISTED
RETWISTS
RETYING
RETYPE
RETYPED
RETYPES
RETYPING
REUNIFIED
REUNIFIES
REUNIFY
REUNION
REUNIONS
REUNITE
REUNITED
REUNITER
REUNITERS
REUNITES
REUNITING
REUPTAKE
REUPTAKEN
REUPTAKES
REUPTOOK
REURGE
REURGED
REURGES
REURGING
REUSABLE
REUSABLES
REUSE
REUSED
REUSES
REUSING
REUTILISE
REUTILIZE
REUTTER
REUTTERED
REUTTERS
REV
REVALENTA
REVALUATE
REVALUE
REVALUED
REVALUES
REVALUING
REVAMP
REVAMPED
REVAMPER
REVAMPERS
REVAMPING
REVAMPS
REVANCHE
REVANCHES
REVARNISH
REVEAL
REVEALED
REVEALER
REVEALERS
REVEALING
REVEALS
REVEHENT
REVEILLE
REVEILLES
REVEL
REVELATOR
REVELED
REVELER
REVELERS
REVELING
REVELLED
REVELLER
REVELLERS
REVELLING
REVELMENT
REVELRIES
REVELROUS
REVELRY
REVELS
REVENANT
REVENANTS
REVENGE
REVENGED
REVENGER
REVENGERS
REVENGES
REVENGING
REVENGIVE
REVENUAL
REVENUE
REVENUED
REVENUER
REVENUERS
REVENUES
REVERABLE
REVERB
REVERBED
REVERBING
REVERBS
REVERE
REVERED
REVERENCE
REVEREND
REVERENDS
REVERENT
REVERER
REVERERS
REVERES
REVERIE
REVERIES
REVERIFY
REVERING
REVERIST
REVERISTS
REVERS
REVERSAL
REVERSALS
REVERSE
REVERSED
REVERSELY
REVERSER
REVERSERS
REVERSES
REVERSI
REVERSING
REVERSION
REVERSIS
REVERSO
REVERSOS
REVERT
REVERTANT
REVERTED
REVERTER
REVERTERS
REVERTING
REVERTIVE
REVERTS
REVERY
REVEST
REVESTED
REVESTING
REVESTRY
REVESTS
REVET
REVETMENT
REVETS
REVETTED
REVETTING
REVEUR
REVEURS
REVEUSE
REVEUSES
REVIBRATE
REVICTUAL
REVIE
REVIED
REVIES
REVIEW
REVIEWAL
REVIEWALS
REVIEWED
REVIEWER
REVIEWERS
REVIEWING
REVIEWS
REVILE
REVILED
REVILER

R

REVILERS
REVILES
REVILING
REVILINGS
REVIOLATE
REVISABLE
REVISAL
REVISALS
REVISE
REVISED
REVISER
REVISERS
REVISES
REVISING
REVISION
REVISIONS
REVISIT
REVISITED
REVISITS
REVISOR
REVISORS
REVISORY
REVIVABLE
REVIVABLY
REVIVAL
REVIVALS
REVIVE
REVIVED
REVIVER
REVIVERS
REVIVES
REVIVIFY
REVIVING
REVIVINGS
REVIVOR
REVIVORS
REVOCABLE
REVOCABLY
REVOICE
REVOICED
REVOICES
REVOICING
REVOKABLE
REVOKABLY
REVOKE
REVOKED
REVOKER
REVOKERS
REVOKES
REVOKING
REVOLT
REVOLTED
REVOLTER
REVOLTERS
REVOLTING
REVOLTS
REVOLUTE
REVOLVE
REVOLVED
REVOLVER
REVOLVERS
REVOLVES
REVOLVING
REVOTE
REVOTED
REVOTES
REVOTING
REVS
REVUE
REVUES
REVUIST
REVUISTS
REVULSED
REVULSION
REVULSIVE
REVVED
REVVING
REVYING
REW
REWAKE
REWAKED
REWAKEN
REWAKENED
REWAKENS
REWAKES
REWAKING
REWAN
REWARD
REWARDED
REWARDER
REWARDERS
REWARDFUL
REWARDING
REWARDS
REWAREWA
REWAREWAS
REWARM
REWARMED
REWARMING
REWARMS
REWASH
REWASHED
REWASHES
REWASHING
REWATER
REWATERED
REWATERS
REWAX
REWAXED
REWAXES
REWAXING
REWEAR
REWEARING
REWEARS
REWEAVE
REWEAVED
REWEAVES
REWEAVING
REWED
REWEDDED
REWEDDING
REWEDS
REWEIGH
REWEIGHED
REWEIGHS
REWELD
REWELDED
REWELDING
REWELDS
REWET
REWETS
REWETTED
REWETTING
REWIDEN
REWIDENED
REWIDENS
REWILD
REWILDED
REWILDING
REWILDS
REWIN
REWIND
REWINDED
REWINDER
REWINDERS
REWINDING
REWINDS
REWINNING
REWINS
REWIRABLE
REWIRE
REWIRED
REWIRES
REWIRING
REWIRINGS
REWOKE
REWOKEN
REWON
REWORD
REWORDED
REWORDING
REWORDS
REWORE
REWORK
REWORKED
REWORKING
REWORKS
REWORN
REWOUND
REWOVE
REWOVEN
REWRAP
REWRAPPED
REWRAPS
REWRAPT
REWRITE
REWRITER
REWRITERS
REWRITES
REWRITING
REWRITTEN
REWROTE
REWROUGHT
REWS
REWTH
REWTHS
REX
REXES
REXINE
REXINES
REYNARD
REYNARDS
REZ
REZERO
REZEROED
REZEROES
REZEROING
REZEROS
REZES
REZONE
REZONED
REZONES
REZONING
REZONINGS
REZZES
RHABDOID
RHABDOIDS
RHABDOM
RHABDOMAL
RHABDOME
RHABDOMES
RHABDOMS
RHABDUS
RHABDUSES
RHACHIAL
RHACHIDES
RHACHILLA
RHACHIS
RHACHISES
RHACHITIS
RHAGADES
RHAMNOSE
RHAMNOSES
RHAMNUS
RHAMNUSES
RHAMPHOID
RHANJA
RHANJAS
RHAPHAE
RHAPHE
RHAPHES
RHAPHIDE
RHAPHIDES
RHAPHIS
RHAPONTIC
RHAPSODE
RHAPSODES
RHAPSODIC
RHAPSODY
RHATANIES

RHATANY
RHEA
RHEAS
RHEBOK
RHEBOKS
RHEMATIC
RHEME
RHEMES
RHENIUM
RHENIUMS
RHEOBASE
RHEOBASES
RHEOBASIC
RHEOCHORD
RHEOCORD
RHEOCORDS
RHEOLOGIC
RHEOLOGY
RHEOMETER
RHEOMETRY
RHEOPHIL
RHEOPHILE
RHEOSCOPE
RHEOSTAT
RHEOSTATS
RHEOTAXES
RHEOTAXIS
RHEOTOME
RHEOTOMES
RHEOTROPE
RHESUS
RHESUSES
RHETOR
RHETORIC
RHETORICS
RHETORISE
RHETORIZE
RHETORS
RHEUM
RHEUMATIC
RHEUMATIZ
RHEUMED
RHEUMIC
RHEUMIER
RHEUMIEST
RHEUMS
RHEUMY
RHEXES
RHEXIS
RHEXISES
RHIES
RHIGOLENE
RHIME
RHIMES
RHINAL
RHINE
RHINES
RHINITIC
RHINITIS
RHINO
RHINOCERI
RHINOLITH
RHINOLOGY
RHINOS
RHIPIDATE
RHIPIDION
RHIPIDIUM
RHIZIC
RHIZINE
RHIZINES
RHIZOBIA
RHIZOBIAL
RHIZOBIUM
RHIZOCARP
RHIZOCAUL
RHIZOID
RHIZOIDAL
RHIZOIDS
RHIZOMA
RHIZOMATA
RHIZOME
RHIZOMES
RHIZOMIC
RHIZOPI
RHIZOPOD
RHIZOPODS
RHIZOPUS
RHIZOTOMY
RHO
RHODAMIN
RHODAMINE
RHODAMINS
RHODANATE
RHODANIC
RHODANISE
RHODANIZE
RHODIC
RHODIE
RHODIES
RHODINAL
RHODINALS
RHODIUM
RHODIUMS
RHODOLITE
RHODONITE
RHODOPSIN
RHODORA
RHODORAS
RHODOUS
RHODY
RHOEADINE
RHOMB
RHOMBI
RHOMBIC
RHOMBICAL
RHOMBOI
RHOMBOID
RHOMBOIDS
RHOMBOS
RHOMBS
RHOMBUS
RHOMBUSES
RHONCHAL
RHONCHI
RHONCHIAL
RHONCHUS
RHONCUS
RHONCUSES
RHONE
RHONES
RHOPALIC
RHOPALISM
RHOS
RHOTACISE
RHOTACISM
RHOTACIST
RHOTACIZE
RHOTIC
RHOTICITY
RHUBARB
RHUBARBED
RHUBARBS
RHUBARBY
RHUMB
RHUMBA
RHUMBAED
RHUMBAING
RHUMBAS
RHUMBS
RHUS
RHUSES
RHY
RHYME
RHYMED
RHYMELESS
RHYMER
RHYMERS
RHYMES
RHYMESTER
RHYMING
RHYMIST
RHYMISTS
RHYNE
RHYNES
RHYOLITE
RHYOLITES
RHYOLITIC
RHYTA
RHYTHM
RHYTHMAL
RHYTHMED
RHYTHMI
RHYTHMIC
RHYTHMICS
RHYTHMISE
RHYTHMIST
RHYTHMIZE
RHYTHMS
RHYTHMUS
RHYTIDOME
RHYTINA
RHYTINAS
RHYTON
RHYTONS
RIA
RIAD
RIADS
RIAL
RIALS
RIALTO
RIALTOS
RIANCIES
RIANCY
RIANT
RIANTLY
RIAS
RIATA
RIATAS
RIB
RIBA
RIBALD
RIBALDER
RIBALDEST
RIBALDLY
RIBALDRY
RIBALDS
RIBAND
RIBANDS
RIBAS
RIBATTUTA
RIBAUD
RIBAUDRED
RIBAUDRY
RIBAUDS
RIBAVIRIN
RIBBAND
RIBBANDS
RIBBED
RIBBER
RIBBERS
RIBBIE
RIBBIER
RIBBIES
RIBBIEST
RIBBING
RIBBINGS
RIBBIT
RIBBITS
RIBBON
RIBBONED
RIBBONIER
RIBBONING
RIBBONRY
RIBBONS
RIBBONY
RIBBY
RIBCAGE
RIBCAGES
RIBES
RIBEYE

R

RIBEYES
RIBGRASS
RIBIBE
RIBIBES
RIBIBLE
RIBIBLES
RIBIER
RIBIERS
RIBLESS
RIBLET
RIBLETS
RIBLIKE
RIBOSE
RIBOSES
RIBOSOMAL
RIBOSOME
RIBOSOMES
RIBOZYMAL
RIBOZYME
RIBOZYMES
RIBS
RIBSTON
RIBSTONE
RIBSTONES
RIBSTONS
RIBULOSE
RIBULOSES
RIBWORK
RIBWORKS
RIBWORT
RIBWORTS
RICE
RICEBIRD
RICEBIRDS
RICED
RICEFIELD
RICEGRASS
RICER
RICERCAR
RICERCARE
RICERCARI
RICERCARS
RICERCATA
RICERS
RICES
RICEY
RICH
RICHED
RICHEN
RICHENED
RICHENING
RICHENS
RICHER
RICHES
RICHESSE
RICHESSES
RICHEST
RICHING
RICHLY
RICHNESS
RICHT
RICHTED
RICHTER
RICHTEST
RICHTING
RICHTS
RICHWEED
RICHWEEDS
RICIER
RICIEST
RICIN
RICING
RICINS
RICINUS
RICINUSES
RICK
RICKED
RICKER
RICKERS
RICKET
RICKETIER
RICKETILY
RICKETS
RICKETTY
RICKETY
RICKEY
RICKEYS
RICKING
RICKLE
RICKLES
RICKLIER
RICKLIEST
RICKLY
RICKRACK
RICKRACKS
RICKS
RICKSHA
RICKSHAS
RICKSHAW
RICKSHAWS
RICKSTAND
RICKSTICK
RICKYARD
RICKYARDS
RICOCHET
RICOCHETS
RICOTTA
RICOTTAS
RICRAC
RICRACS
RICTAL
RICTUS
RICTUSES
RICY
RID
RIDABLE
RIDDANCE
RIDDANCES
RIDDED
RIDDEN
RIDDER
RIDDERS
RIDDING
RIDDLE
RIDDLED
RIDDLER
RIDDLERS
RIDDLES
RIDDLING
RIDDLINGS
RIDE
RIDEABLE
RIDENT
RIDER
RIDERED
RIDERLESS
RIDERS
RIDERSHIP
RIDES
RIDGE
RIDGEBACK
RIDGED
RIDGEL
RIDGELIKE
RIDGELINE
RIDGELING
RIDGELS
RIDGEPOLE
RIDGER
RIDGERS
RIDGES
RIDGETOP
RIDGETOPS
RIDGETREE
RIDGEWAY
RIDGEWAYS
RIDGIER
RIDGIEST
RIDGIL
RIDGILS
RIDGING
RIDGINGS
RIDGLING
RIDGLINGS
RIDGY
RIDIC
RIDICULE
RIDICULED
RIDICULER
RIDICULES
RIDING
RIDINGS
RIDLEY
RIDLEYS
RIDOTTO
RIDOTTOS
RIDS
RIEL
RIELS
RIEM
RIEMPIE
RIEMPIES
RIEMS
RIESLING
RIESLINGS
RIEVE
RIEVED
RIEVER
RIEVERS
RIEVES
RIEVING
RIF
RIFAMPIN
RIFAMPINS
RIFAMYCIN
RIFE
RIFELY
RIFENESS
RIFER
RIFEST
RIFF
RIFFAGE
RIFFAGES
RIFFED
RIFFING
RIFFLE
RIFFLED
RIFFLER
RIFFLERS
RIFFLES
RIFFLING
RIFFOLA
RIFFOLAS
RIFFRAFF
RIFFRAFFS
RIFFS
RIFLE
RIFLEBIRD
RIFLED
RIFLEMAN
RIFLEMEN
RIFLER
RIFLERIES
RIFLERS
RIFLERY
RIFLES
RIFLING
RIFLINGS
RIFLIP
RIFLIPS
RIFS
RIFT
RIFTE
RIFTED
RIFTIER
RIFTIEST
RIFTING
RIFTLESS
RIFTS
RIFTY

R

RIG
RIGADOON
RIGADOONS
RIGATONI
RIGATONIS
RIGAUDON
RIGAUDONS
RIGG
RIGGALD
RIGGALDS
RIGGED
RIGGER
RIGGERS
RIGGING
RIGGINGS
RIGGISH
RIGGS
RIGHT
RIGHTABLE
RIGHTABLY
RIGHTED
RIGHTEN
RIGHTENED
RIGHTENS
RIGHTEOUS
RIGHTER
RIGHTERS
RIGHTEST
RIGHTFUL
RIGHTIER
RIGHTIES
RIGHTIEST
RIGHTING
RIGHTINGS
RIGHTISH
RIGHTISM
RIGHTISMS
RIGHTIST
RIGHTISTS
RIGHTLESS
RIGHTLY
RIGHTMOST
RIGHTNESS
RIGHTO
RIGHTS
RIGHTSIZE
RIGHTWARD
RIGHTY
RIGID
RIGIDER
RIGIDEST
RIGIDIFY
RIGIDISE
RIGIDISED
RIGIDISES
RIGIDITY
RIGIDIZE
RIGIDIZED
RIGIDIZES
RIGIDLY
RIGIDNESS
RIGIDS
RIGLIN
RIGLING
RIGLINGS
RIGLINS
RIGMAROLE
RIGOL
RIGOLL
RIGOLLS
RIGOLS
RIGOR
RIGORISM
RIGORISMS
RIGORIST
RIGORISTS
RIGOROUS
RIGORS
RIGOUR
RIGOURS
RIGOUT
RIGOUTS
RIGS
RIGSDALER
RIGWIDDIE
RIGWOODIE
RIJSTAFEL
RIKISHA
RIKISHAS
RIKISHI
RIKSHAW
RIKSHAWS
RILE
RILED
RILES
RILEY
RILIER
RILIEST
RILIEVI
RILIEVO
RILING
RILL
RILLE
RILLED
RILLES
RILLET
RILLETS
RILLETTES
RILLING
RILLMARK
RILLMARKS
RILLS
RIM
RIMA
RIMAE
RIMAYE
RIMAYES
RIME
RIMED
RIMELESS
RIMER
RIMERS
RIMES
RIMESTER
RIMESTERS
RIMFIRE
RIMFIRES
RIMIER
RIMIEST
RIMINESS
RIMING
RIMLAND
RIMLANDS
RIMLESS
RIMMED
RIMMER
RIMMERS
RIMMING
RIMMINGS
RIMOSE
RIMOSELY
RIMOSITY
RIMOUS
RIMPLE
RIMPLED
RIMPLES
RIMPLING
RIMROCK
RIMROCKS
RIMS
RIMSHOT
RIMSHOTS
RIMU
RIMUS
RIMY
RIN
RIND
RINDED
RINDIER
RINDIEST
RINDING
RINDLESS
RINDS
RINDY
RINE
RINES
RING
RINGBARK
RINGBARKS
RINGBIT
RINGBITS
RINGBOLT
RINGBOLTS
RINGBONE
RINGBONES
RINGDOVE
RINGDOVES
RINGED
RINGENT
RINGER
RINGERS
RINGETTE
RINGETTES
RINGGIT
RINGGITS
RINGHALS
RINGING
RINGINGLY
RINGINGS
RINGLESS
RINGLET
RINGLETED
RINGLETS
RINGLETY
RINGLIKE
RINGMAN
RINGMEN
RINGNECK
RINGNECKS
RINGS
RINGSIDE
RINGSIDER
RINGSIDES
RINGSTAND
RINGSTER
RINGSTERS
RINGTAIL
RINGTAILS
RINGTAW
RINGTAWS
RINGTONE
RINGTONES
RINGTOSS
RINGWAY
RINGWAYS
RINGWISE
RINGWOMB
RINGWOMBS
RINGWORK
RINGWORKS
RINGWORM
RINGWORMS
RINK
RINKED
RINKHALS
RINKING
RINKS
RINKSIDE
RINKSIDES
RINNING
RINS
RINSABLE
RINSE
RINSEABLE
RINSED
RINSER
RINSERS
RINSES
RINSIBLE
RINSING

RINSINGS
RIOJA
RIOJAS
RIOT
RIOTED
RIOTER
RIOTERS
RIOTING
RIOTINGS
RIOTISE
RIOTISES
RIOTIZE
RIOTIZES
RIOTOUS
RIOTOUSLY
RIOTRIES
RIOTRY
RIOTS
RIP
RIPARIAL
RIPARIALS
RIPARIAN
RIPARIANS
RIPCORD
RIPCORDS
RIPE
RIPECK
RIPECKS
RIPED
RIPELY
RIPEN
RIPENED
RIPENER
RIPENERS
RIPENESS
RIPENING
RIPENS
RIPER
RIPERS
RIPES
RIPEST
RIPIENI
RIPIENIST
RIPIENO
RIPIENOS
RIPING
RIPOFF
RIPOFFS
RIPOST
RIPOSTE
RIPOSTED
RIPOSTES
RIPOSTING
RIPOSTS
RIPP
RIPPABLE
RIPPED
RIPPER
RIPPERS
RIPPIER
RIPPIERS
RIPPING
RIPPINGLY
RIPPINGS
RIPPLE
RIPPLED
RIPPLER
RIPPLERS
RIPPLES
RIPPLET
RIPPLETS
RIPPLIER
RIPPLIEST
RIPPLING
RIPPLINGS
RIPPLY
RIPPS
RIPRAP
RIPRAPPED
RIPRAPS
RIPS
RIPSAW
RIPSAWED
RIPSAWING
RIPSAWN
RIPSAWS
RIPSTOP
RIPSTOPS
RIPT
RIPTIDE
RIPTIDES
RIRORIRO
RIRORIROS
RISALDAR
RISALDARS
RISE
RISEN
RISER
RISERS
RISES
RISHI
RISHIS
RISIBLE
RISIBLES
RISIBLY
RISING
RISINGS
RISK
RISKED
RISKER
RISKERS
RISKFUL
RISKIER
RISKIEST
RISKILY
RISKINESS
RISKING
RISKLESS
RISKS
RISKY
RISOLUTO
RISORII
RISORIUS
RISOTTO
RISOTTOS
RISP
RISPED
RISPETTI
RISPETTO
RISPING
RISPINGS
RISPS
RISQUE
RISQUES
RISSOLE
RISSOLES
RISTRA
RISTRAS
RISTRETTO
RISUS
RISUSES
RIT
RITARD
RITARDS
RITE
RITELESS
RITENUTO
RITENUTOS
RITES
RITONAVIR
RITORNEL
RITORNELL
RITORNELS
RITS
RITT
RITTED
RITTER
RITTERS
RITTING
RITTS
RITUAL
RITUALISE
RITUALISM
RITUALIST
RITUALIZE
RITUALLY
RITUALS
RITUXIMAB
RITZ
RITZES
RITZIER
RITZIEST
RITZILY
RITZINESS
RITZY
RIVA
RIVAGE
RIVAGES
RIVAL
RIVALED
RIVALESS
RIVALING
RIVALISE
RIVALISED
RIVALISES
RIVALITY
RIVALIZE
RIVALIZED
RIVALIZES
RIVALLED
RIVALLESS
RIVALLING
RIVALRIES
RIVALROUS
RIVALRY
RIVALS
RIVALSHIP
RIVAS
RIVE
RIVED
RIVEL
RIVELLED
RIVELLING
RIVELS
RIVEN
RIVER
RIVERAIN
RIVERAINS
RIVERBANK
RIVERBED
RIVERBEDS
RIVERBOAT
RIVERED
RIVERET
RIVERETS
RIVERHEAD
RIVERIER
RIVERIEST
RIVERINE
RIVERLESS
RIVERLIKE
RIVERMAN
RIVERMEN
RIVERS
RIVERSIDE
RIVERWALK
RIVERWARD
RIVERWAY
RIVERWAYS
RIVERWEED
RIVERY
RIVES
RIVET
RIVETED
RIVETER
RIVETERS
RIVETING
RIVETINGS
RIVETS
RIVETTED

RIVETTING
RIVIERA
RIVIERAS
RIVIERE
RIVIERES
RIVING
RIVLIN
RIVLINS
RIVO
RIVULET
RIVULETS
RIVULOSE
RIVULUS
RIVULUSES
RIYAL
RIYALS
RIZ
RIZA
RIZARD
RIZARDS
RIZAS
RIZZAR
RIZZARED
RIZZARING
RIZZARS
RIZZART
RIZZARTS
RIZZER
RIZZERED
RIZZERING
RIZZERS
RIZZOR
RIZZORED
RIZZORING
RIZZORS
ROACH
ROACHED
ROACHES
ROACHING
ROAD
ROADBED
ROADBEDS
ROADBLOCK
ROADCRAFT
ROADEO
ROADEOS
ROADHOG
ROADHOGS
ROADHOUSE
ROADIE
ROADIES
ROADING
ROADINGS
ROADKILL
ROADKILLS
ROADLESS
ROADMAN
ROADMEN
ROADS
ROADSHOW
ROADSHOWS
ROADSIDE
ROADSIDES
ROADSMAN
ROADSMEN
ROADSTEAD
ROADSTER
ROADSTERS
ROADWAY
ROADWAYS
ROADWORK
ROADWORKS
ROAM
ROAMED
ROAMER
ROAMERS
ROAMING
ROAMINGS
ROAMS
ROAN
ROANPIPE
ROANPIPES
ROANS
ROAR
ROARED
ROARER
ROARERS
ROARIE
ROARIER
ROARIEST
ROARING
ROARINGLY
ROARINGS
ROARMING
ROARS
ROARY
ROAST
ROASTED
ROASTER
ROASTERS
ROASTIE
ROASTIES
ROASTING
ROASTINGS
ROASTS
ROATE
ROATED
ROATES
ROATING
ROB
ROBALO
ROBALOS
ROBAND
ROBANDS
ROBATA
ROBATAS
ROBBED
ROBBER
ROBBERIES
ROBBERS
ROBBERY
ROBBIN
ROBBING
ROBBINS
ROBE
ROBED
ROBELIKE
ROBES
ROBIN
ROBING
ROBINGS
ROBINIA
ROBINIAS
ROBINS
ROBLE
ROBLES
ROBOCALL
ROBOCALLS
ROBORANT
ROBORANTS
ROBOT
ROBOTIC
ROBOTICS
ROBOTISE
ROBOTISED
ROBOTISES
ROBOTISM
ROBOTISMS
ROBOTIZE
ROBOTIZED
ROBOTIZES
ROBOTRIES
ROBOTRY
ROBOTS
ROBS
ROBURITE
ROBURITES
ROBUST
ROBUSTA
ROBUSTAS
ROBUSTER
ROBUSTEST
ROBUSTLY
ROC
ROCAILLE
ROCAILLES
ROCAMBOLE
ROCH
ROCHES
ROCHET
ROCHETS
ROCK
ROCKABIES
ROCKABLE
ROCKABY
ROCKABYE
ROCKABYES
ROCKAWAY
ROCKAWAYS
ROCKBOUND
ROCKBURST
ROCKCRESS
ROCKED
ROCKER
ROCKERIES
ROCKERS
ROCKERY
ROCKET
ROCKETED
ROCKETEER
ROCKETER
ROCKETERS
ROCKETING
ROCKETRY
ROCKETS
ROCKFALL
ROCKFALLS
ROCKFISH
ROCKHOUND
ROCKIER
ROCKIERS
ROCKIEST
ROCKILY
ROCKINESS
ROCKING
ROCKINGLY
ROCKINGS
ROCKLAY
ROCKLAYS
ROCKLESS
ROCKLIKE
ROCKLING
ROCKLINGS
ROCKOON
ROCKOONS
ROCKROSE
ROCKROSES
ROCKS
ROCKSHAFT
ROCKSLIDE
ROCKWATER
ROCKWEED
ROCKWEEDS
ROCKWOOL
ROCKWOOLS
ROCKWORK
ROCKWORKS
ROCKY
ROCOCO
ROCOCOS
ROCQUET
ROCQUETS
ROCS
ROD
RODDED
RODDING
RODDINGS
RODE
RODED
RODENT

R

RODENTIAL
RODENTS
RODEO
RODEOED
RODEOING
RODEOS
RODES
RODEWAY
RODEWAYS
RODFISHER
RODGERSIA
RODING
RODINGS
RODLESS
RODLIKE
RODMAN
RODMEN
RODNEY
RODNEYS
RODS
RODSMAN
RODSMEN
RODSTER
RODSTERS
ROE
ROEBUCK
ROEBUCKS
ROED
ROEMER
ROEMERS
ROENTGEN
ROENTGENS
ROES
ROESTI
ROESTIS
ROESTONE
ROESTONES
ROGALLO
ROGALLOS
ROGATION
ROGATIONS
ROGATORY
ROGER
ROGERED
ROGERING
ROGERINGS
ROGERS
ROGNON
ROGNONS
ROGUE
ROGUED
ROGUEING
ROGUER
ROGUERIES
ROGUERS
ROGUERY
ROGUES
ROGUESHIP
ROGUIER
ROGUIEST
ROGUING
ROGUISH
ROGUISHLY
ROGUY
ROHE
ROHES
ROID
ROIDS
ROIL
ROILED
ROILIER
ROILIEST
ROILING
ROILS
ROILY
ROIN
ROINED
ROINING
ROINISH
ROINS
ROIST
ROISTED
ROISTER
ROISTERED
ROISTERER
ROISTERS
ROISTING
ROISTS
ROJAK
ROJAKS
ROJI
ROJIS
ROK
ROKE
ROKED
ROKELAY
ROKELAYS
ROKER
ROKERS
ROKES
ROKIER
ROKIEST
ROKING
ROKKAKU
ROKS
ROKY
ROLAG
ROLAGS
ROLAMITE
ROLAMITES
ROLE
ROLES
ROLF
ROLFED
ROLFER
ROLFERS
ROLFING
ROLFINGS
ROLFS
ROLL
ROLLABLE
ROLLAWAY
ROLLAWAYS
ROLLBACK
ROLLBACKS
ROLLBAR
ROLLBARS
ROLLED
ROLLER
ROLLERS
ROLLICK
ROLLICKED
ROLLICKS
ROLLICKY
ROLLIE
ROLLIES
ROLLING
ROLLINGS
ROLLMOP
ROLLMOPS
ROLLNECK
ROLLNECKS
ROLLOCK
ROLLOCKS
ROLLOUT
ROLLOUTS
ROLLOVER
ROLLOVERS
ROLLS
ROLLTOP
ROLLUP
ROLLUPS
ROLLWAY
ROLLWAYS
ROM
ROMA
ROMAGE
ROMAGES
ROMAIKA
ROMAIKAS
ROMAINE
ROMAINES
ROMAJI
ROMAJIS
ROMAL
ROMALS
ROMAN
ROMANCE
ROMANCED
ROMANCER
ROMANCERS
ROMANCES
ROMANCING
ROMANESCO
ROMANISE
ROMANISED
ROMANISES
ROMANIZE
ROMANIZED
ROMANIZES
ROMANO
ROMANOS
ROMANS
ROMANTIC
ROMANTICS
ROMANZA
ROMANZAS
ROMAUNT
ROMAUNTS
ROMCOM
ROMCOMS
ROMELDALE
ROMEO
ROMEOS
ROMNEYA
ROMNEYAS
ROMP
ROMPED
ROMPER
ROMPERS
ROMPING
ROMPINGLY
ROMPISH
ROMPISHLY
ROMPS
ROMS
RONCADOR
RONCADORS
RONDACHE
RONDACHES
RONDAVEL
RONDAVELS
RONDE
RONDEAU
RONDEAUX
RONDEL
RONDELET
RONDELETS
RONDELLE
RONDELLES
RONDELS
RONDES
RONDINO
RONDINOS
RONDO
RONDOS
RONDURE
RONDURES
RONE
RONEO
RONEOED
RONEOING
RONEOS
RONEPIPE
RONEPIPES
RONES
RONG
RONGGENG
RONGGENGS
RONIN

R

RONINS
RONION
RONIONS
RONNE
RONNEL
RONNELS
RONNIE
RONNIES
RONNING
RONT
RONTE
RONTES
RONTGEN
RONTGENS
RONTS
RONYON
RONYONS
RONZ
RONZER
RONZERS
ROO
ROOD
ROODS
ROOF
ROOFED
ROOFER
ROOFERS
ROOFIE
ROOFIER
ROOFIES
ROOFIEST
ROOFING
ROOFINGS
ROOFLESS
ROOFLIKE
ROOFLINE
ROOFLINES
ROOFS
ROOFSCAPE
ROOFTOP
ROOFTOPS
ROOFTREE
ROOFTREES
ROOFY
ROOIBOS
ROOIBOSES
ROOIKAT
ROOIKATS
ROOINEK
ROOINEKS
ROOK
ROOKED
ROOKERIES
ROOKERY
ROOKIE
ROOKIER
ROOKIES
ROOKIEST
ROOKING
ROOKISH
ROOKS
ROOKY
ROOM
ROOMED
ROOMER
ROOMERS
ROOMETTE
ROOMETTES
ROOMFUL
ROOMFULS
ROOMIE
ROOMIER
ROOMIES
ROOMIEST
ROOMILY
ROOMINESS
ROOMING
ROOMMATE
ROOMMATES
ROOMS
ROOMSFUL
ROOMSOME
ROOMY
ROON
ROONS
ROOP
ROOPED
ROOPIER
ROOPIEST
ROOPING
ROOPIT
ROOPS
ROOPY
ROORBACH
ROORBACHS
ROORBACK
ROORBACKS
ROOS
ROOSA
ROOSAS
ROOSE
ROOSED
ROOSER
ROOSERS
ROOSES
ROOSING
ROOST
ROOSTED
ROOSTER
ROOSTERS
ROOSTING
ROOSTS
ROOT
ROOTAGE
ROOTAGES
ROOTBALL
ROOTBALLS
ROOTBOUND
ROOTCAP
ROOTCAPS
ROOTED
ROOTEDLY
ROOTER
ROOTERS
ROOTHOLD
ROOTHOLDS
ROOTIER
ROOTIES
ROOTIEST
ROOTINESS
ROOTING
ROOTINGS
ROOTKIT
ROOTKITS
ROOTLE
ROOTLED
ROOTLES
ROOTLESS
ROOTLET
ROOTLETS
ROOTLIKE
ROOTLING
ROOTS
ROOTSIER
ROOTSIEST
ROOTSTALK
ROOTSTOCK
ROOTSY
ROOTWORM
ROOTWORMS
ROOTY
ROPABLE
ROPE
ROPEABLE
ROPED
ROPELIKE
ROPER
ROPERIES
ROPERS
ROPERY
ROPES
ROPEWALK
ROPEWALKS
ROPEWAY
ROPEWAYS
ROPEWORK
ROPEWORKS
ROPEY
ROPIER
ROPIEST
ROPILY
ROPINESS
ROPING
ROPINGS
ROPY
ROQUE
ROQUEFORT
ROQUES
ROQUET
ROQUETED
ROQUETING
ROQUETS
ROQUETTE
ROQUETTES
RORAL
RORE
RORES
RORIC
RORID
RORIE
RORIER
RORIEST
RORQUAL
RORQUALS
RORT
RORTED
RORTER
RORTERS
RORTIER
RORTIEST
RORTING
RORTINGS
RORTS
RORTY
RORY
ROSACE
ROSACEA
ROSACEAS
ROSACEOUS
ROSACES
ROSAKER
ROSAKERS
ROSALIA
ROSALIAS
ROSANILIN
ROSARIA
ROSARIAN
ROSARIANS
ROSARIES
ROSARIUM
ROSARIUMS
ROSARY
ROSBIF
ROSBIFS
ROSCID
ROSCOE
ROSCOES
ROSE
ROSEAL
ROSEATE
ROSEATELY
ROSEBAY
ROSEBAYS
ROSEBED
ROSEBEDS
ROSEBOWL
ROSEBOWLS
ROSEBUD
ROSEBUDS
ROSEBUSH

R

ROSED
ROSEFINCH
ROSEFISH
ROSEHIP
ROSEHIPS
ROSELESS
ROSELIKE
ROSELLA
ROSELLAS
ROSELLE
ROSELLES
ROSEMARY
ROSEOLA
ROSEOLAR
ROSEOLAS
ROSERIES
ROSEROOT
ROSEROOTS
ROSERY
ROSES
ROSESLUG
ROSESLUGS
ROSET
ROSETED
ROSETING
ROSETS
ROSETTE
ROSETTED
ROSETTES
ROSETTING
ROSETTY
ROSETY
ROSEWATER
ROSEWOOD
ROSEWOODS
ROSHAMBO
ROSHAMBOS
ROSHI
ROSHIS
ROSIED
ROSIER
ROSIERE
ROSIERES
ROSIERS
ROSIES
ROSIEST
ROSILY
ROSIN
ROSINATE
ROSINATES
ROSINED
ROSINER
ROSINERS
ROSINESS
ROSING
ROSINIER
ROSINIEST
ROSINING
ROSINOL
ROSINOLS
ROSINOUS
ROSINS
ROSINWEED
ROSINY
ROSIT
ROSITED
ROSITING
ROSITS
ROSMARINE
ROSOGLIO
ROSOGLIOS
ROSOLIO
ROSOLIOS
ROSSER
ROSSERS
ROST
ROSTED
ROSTELLA
ROSTELLAR
ROSTELLUM
ROSTER
ROSTERED
ROSTERING
ROSTERS
ROSTI
ROSTING
ROSTIS
ROSTRA
ROSTRAL
ROSTRALLY
ROSTRATE
ROSTRATED
ROSTRUM
ROSTRUMS
ROSTS
ROSULA
ROSULAS
ROSULATE
ROSY
ROSYING
ROT
ROTA
ROTACHUTE
ROTAL
ROTAMETER
ROTAN
ROTANS
ROTAPLANE
ROTARIES
ROTARY
ROTAS
ROTATABLE
ROTATE
ROTATED
ROTATES
ROTATING
ROTATION
ROTATIONS
ROTATIVE
ROTATOR
ROTATORES
ROTATORS
ROTATORY
ROTAVATE
ROTAVATED
ROTAVATES
ROTAVATOR
ROTAVIRAL
ROTAVIRUS
ROTCH
ROTCHE
ROTCHES
ROTCHIE
ROTCHIES
ROTE
ROTED
ROTELY
ROTENONE
ROTENONES
ROTES
ROTGRASS
ROTGUT
ROTGUTS
ROTHER
ROTHERS
ROTI
ROTIFER
ROTIFERAL
ROTIFERAN
ROTIFERS
ROTIFORM
ROTING
ROTINI
ROTINIS
ROTIS
ROTL
ROTLS
ROTO
ROTOGRAPH
ROTOLI
ROTOLO
ROTOLOS
ROTON
ROTONS
ROTOR
ROTORS
ROTOS
ROTOSCOPE
ROTOTILL
ROTOTILLS
ROTOVATE
ROTOVATED
ROTOVATES
ROTOVATOR
ROTPROOF
ROTS
ROTTAN
ROTTANS
ROTTE
ROTTED
ROTTEN
ROTTENER
ROTTENEST
ROTTENLY
ROTTENS
ROTTER
ROTTERS
ROTTES
ROTTING
ROTULA
ROTULAE
ROTULAS
ROTUND
ROTUNDA
ROTUNDAS
ROTUNDATE
ROTUNDED
ROTUNDER
ROTUNDEST
ROTUNDING
ROTUNDITY
ROTUNDLY
ROTUNDS
ROTURIER
ROTURIERS
ROUBLE
ROUBLES
ROUCHE
ROUCHED
ROUCHES
ROUCHING
ROUCHINGS
ROUCOU
ROUCOUS
ROUE
ROUEN
ROUENS
ROUES
ROUGE
ROUGED
ROUGES
ROUGH
ROUGHAGE
ROUGHAGES
ROUGHBACK
ROUGHCAST
ROUGHDRY
ROUGHED
ROUGHEN
ROUGHENED
ROUGHENS
ROUGHER
ROUGHERS
ROUGHEST
ROUGHHEW
ROUGHHEWN
ROUGHHEWS
ROUGHIE
ROUGHIES
ROUGHING

ROUGHINGS
ROUGHISH
ROUGHLEG
ROUGHLEGS
ROUGHLY
ROUGHNECK
ROUGHNESS
ROUGHOUT
ROUGHOUTS
ROUGHS
ROUGHSHOD
ROUGHT
ROUGHY
ROUGING
ROUILLE
ROUILLES
ROUL
ROULADE
ROULADES
ROULE
ROULEAU
ROULEAUS
ROULEAUX
ROULES
ROULETTE
ROULETTED
ROULETTES
ROULS
ROUM
ROUMING
ROUMINGS
ROUMS
ROUNCE
ROUNCES
ROUNCEVAL
ROUNCIES
ROUNCY
ROUND
ROUNDARCH
ROUNDBALL
ROUNDED
ROUNDEDLY
ROUNDEL
ROUNDELAY
ROUNDELS
ROUNDER
ROUNDERS
ROUNDEST
ROUNDHAND
ROUNDHEEL
ROUNDING
ROUNDINGS
ROUNDISH
ROUNDLE
ROUNDLES
ROUNDLET
ROUNDLETS
ROUNDLY
ROUNDNESS
ROUNDS
ROUNDSMAN
ROUNDSMEN
ROUNDTRIP
ROUNDUP
ROUNDUPS
ROUNDURE
ROUNDURES
ROUNDWOOD
ROUNDWORM
ROUP
ROUPED
ROUPET
ROUPIER
ROUPIEST
ROUPILY
ROUPING
ROUPIT
ROUPS
ROUPY
ROUSABLE
ROUSANT
ROUSE
ROUSED
ROUSEMENT
ROUSER
ROUSERS
ROUSES
ROUSING
ROUSINGLY
ROUSSEAU
ROUSSEAUS
ROUSSETTE
ROUST
ROUSTED
ROUSTER
ROUSTERS
ROUSTING
ROUSTS
ROUT
ROUTE
ROUTED
ROUTEING
ROUTEMAN
ROUTEMEN
ROUTER
ROUTERS
ROUTES
ROUTEWAY
ROUTEWAYS
ROUTH
ROUTHIE
ROUTHIER
ROUTHIEST
ROUTHS
ROUTINE
ROUTINEER
ROUTINELY
ROUTINES
ROUTING
ROUTINGS
ROUTINISE
ROUTINISM
ROUTINIST
ROUTINIZE
ROUTOUS
ROUTOUSLY
ROUTS
ROUX
ROVE
ROVED
ROVEN
ROVER
ROVERS
ROVES
ROVING
ROVINGLY
ROVINGS
ROW
ROWABLE
ROWAN
ROWANS
ROWBOAT
ROWBOATS
ROWDEDOW
ROWDEDOWS
ROWDIER
ROWDIES
ROWDIEST
ROWDILY
ROWDINESS
ROWDY
ROWDYDOW
ROWDYDOWS
ROWDYISH
ROWDYISM
ROWDYISMS
ROWED
ROWEL
ROWELED
ROWELING
ROWELLED
ROWELLING
ROWELS
ROWEN
ROWENS
ROWER
ROWERS
ROWIE
ROWIES
ROWING
ROWINGS
ROWLOCK
ROWLOCKS
ROWME
ROWMES
ROWND
ROWNDED
ROWNDELL
ROWNDELLS
ROWNDING
ROWNDS
ROWOVER
ROWOVERS
ROWS
ROWT
ROWTED
ROWTH
ROWTHS
ROWTING
ROWTS
ROYAL
ROYALET
ROYALETS
ROYALISE
ROYALISED
ROYALISES
ROYALISM
ROYALISMS
ROYALIST
ROYALISTS
ROYALIZE
ROYALIZED
ROYALIZES
ROYALLER
ROYALLEST
ROYALLY
ROYALMAST
ROYALS
ROYALTIES
ROYALTY
ROYNE
ROYNED
ROYNES
ROYNING
ROYNISH
ROYST
ROYSTED
ROYSTER
ROYSTERED
ROYSTERER
ROYSTERS
ROYSTING
ROYSTS
ROZELLE
ROZELLES
ROZET
ROZETED
ROZETING
ROZETS
ROZIT
ROZITED
ROZITING
ROZITS
ROZZER
ROZZERS
RUANA
RUANAS
RUB
RUBABOO
RUBABOOS

R

RUBACE
RUBACES
RUBAI
RUBAIS
RUBAIYAT
RUBASSE
RUBASSES
RUBATI
RUBATO
RUBATOS
RUBBABOO
RUBBABOOS
RUBBED
RUBBER
RUBBERED
RUBBERIER
RUBBERING
RUBBERISE
RUBBERIZE
RUBBERS
RUBBERY
RUBBET
RUBBIDIES
RUBBIDY
RUBBIES
RUBBING
RUBBINGS
RUBBISH
RUBBISHED
RUBBISHES
RUBBISHLY
RUBBISHY
RUBBIT
RUBBITIES
RUBBITY
RUBBLE
RUBBLED
RUBBLES
RUBBLIER
RUBBLIEST
RUBBLING
RUBBLY
RUBBOARD
RUBBOARDS
RUBBY
RUBBYDUB
RUBBYDUBS
RUBDOWN
RUBDOWNS
RUBE
RUBEFIED
RUBEFIES
RUBEFY
RUBEFYING
RUBEL
RUBELLA
RUBELLAN
RUBELLANS
RUBELLAS
RUBELLITE
RUBELS
RUBEOLA
RUBEOLAR
RUBEOLAS
RUBES
RUBESCENT
RUBICELLE
RUBICON
RUBICONED
RUBICONS
RUBICUND
RUBIDIC
RUBIDIUM
RUBIDIUMS
RUBIED
RUBIER
RUBIES
RUBIEST
RUBIFIED
RUBIFIES
RUBIFY
RUBIFYING
RUBIGO
RUBIGOS
RUBIN
RUBINE
RUBINEOUS
RUBINES
RUBINS
RUBIOUS
RUBLE
RUBLES
RUBLI
RUBOFF
RUBOFFS
RUBOUT
RUBOUTS
RUBRIC
RUBRICAL
RUBRICATE
RUBRICIAN
RUBRICS
RUBS
RUBSTONE
RUBSTONES
RUBUS
RUBUSES
RUBY
RUBYING
RUBYLIKE
RUC
RUCHE
RUCHED
RUCHES
RUCHING
RUCHINGS
RUCK
RUCKED
RUCKING
RUCKLE
RUCKLED
RUCKLES
RUCKLING
RUCKMAN
RUCKMEN
RUCKS
RUCKSACK
RUCKSACKS
RUCKSEAT
RUCKSEATS
RUCKUS
RUCKUSES
RUCOLA
RUCOLAS
RUCS
RUCTATION
RUCTION
RUCTIONS
RUCTIOUS
RUD
RUDACEOUS
RUDAS
RUDASES
RUDBECKIA
RUDD
RUDDED
RUDDER
RUDDERS
RUDDIED
RUDDIER
RUDDIES
RUDDIEST
RUDDILY
RUDDINESS
RUDDING
RUDDLE
RUDDLED
RUDDLEMAN
RUDDLEMEN
RUDDLES
RUDDLING
RUDDOCK
RUDDOCKS
RUDDS
RUDDY
RUDDYING
RUDE
RUDELY
RUDENESS
RUDER
RUDERAL
RUDERALS
RUDERIES
RUDERY
RUDES
RUDESBIES
RUDESBY
RUDEST
RUDI
RUDIE
RUDIES
RUDIMENT
RUDIMENTS
RUDIS
RUDISH
RUDIST
RUDISTID
RUDISTIDS
RUDISTS
RUDS
RUDY
RUE
RUED
RUEDA
RUEDAS
RUEFUL
RUEFULLY
RUEING
RUEINGS
RUELLE
RUELLES
RUELLIA
RUELLIAS
RUER
RUERS
RUES
RUFESCENT
RUFF
RUFFE
RUFFED
RUFFES
RUFFIAN
RUFFIANED
RUFFIANLY
RUFFIANS
RUFFIN
RUFFING
RUFFINS
RUFFLE
RUFFLED
RUFFLER
RUFFLERS
RUFFLES
RUFFLIER
RUFFLIEST
RUFFLIKE
RUFFLING
RUFFLINGS
RUFFLY
RUFFS
RUFIYAA
RUFIYAAS
RUFOUS
RUFOUSES
RUG
RUGA
RUGAE
RUGAL
RUGALACH
RUGATE

RUGBIES
RUGBY
RUGELACH
RUGELACHS
RUGGED
RUGGEDER
RUGGEDEST
RUGGEDISE
RUGGEDIZE
RUGGEDLY
RUGGELACH
RUGGER
RUGGERS
RUGGIER
RUGGIEST
RUGGING
RUGGINGS
RUGGY
RUGLIKE
RUGOLA
RUGOLAS
RUGOSA
RUGOSAS
RUGOSE
RUGOSELY
RUGOSITY
RUGOUS
RUGRAT
RUGRATS
RUGS
RUGULOSE
RUIN
RUINABLE
RUINATE
RUINATED
RUINATES
RUINATING
RUINATION
RUINED
RUINER
RUINERS
RUING
RUINGS
RUINING
RUININGS
RUINOUS
RUINOUSLY
RUINS
RUKH
RUKHS
RULABLE
RULE
RULED
RULELESS
RULER
RULERED
RULERING
RULERS
RULERSHIP
RULES
RULESSE
RULIER
RULIEST
RULING
RULINGS
RULLION
RULLIONS
RULLOCK
RULLOCKS
RULY
RUM
RUMAKI
RUMAKIS
RUMAL
RUMALS
RUMBA
RUMBAED
RUMBAING
RUMBAS
RUMBELOW
RUMBELOWS
RUMBLE
RUMBLED
RUMBLER
RUMBLERS
RUMBLES
RUMBLIER
RUMBLIEST
RUMBLING
RUMBLINGS
RUMBLY
RUMBO
RUMBOS
RUMDUM
RUMDUMS
RUME
RUMEN
RUMENS
RUMES
RUMINA
RUMINAL
RUMINANT
RUMINANTS
RUMINATE
RUMINATED
RUMINATES
RUMINATOR
RUMKIN
RUMKINS
RUMLY
RUMMAGE
RUMMAGED
RUMMAGER
RUMMAGERS
RUMMAGES
RUMMAGING
RUMMER
RUMMERS
RUMMEST
RUMMIER
RUMMIES
RUMMIEST
RUMMILY
RUMMINESS
RUMMISH
RUMMISHED
RUMMISHES
RUMMY
RUMNESS
RUMNESSES
RUMOR
RUMORED
RUMORER
RUMORERS
RUMORING
RUMOROUS
RUMORS
RUMOUR
RUMOURED
RUMOURER
RUMOURERS
RUMOURING
RUMOURS
RUMP
RUMPED
RUMPIER
RUMPIES
RUMPIEST
RUMPING
RUMPLE
RUMPLED
RUMPLES
RUMPLESS
RUMPLIER
RUMPLIEST
RUMPLING
RUMPLY
RUMPO
RUMPOS
RUMPOT
RUMPOTS
RUMPS
RUMPUS
RUMPUSES
RUMPY
RUMRUNNER
RUMS
RUN
RUNABOUT
RUNABOUTS
RUNAGATE
RUNAGATES
RUNANGA
RUNANGAS
RUNAROUND
RUNAWAY
RUNAWAYS
RUNBACK
RUNBACKS
RUNCH
RUNCHES
RUNCIBLE
RUNCINATE
RUND
RUNDALE
RUNDALES
RUNDLE
RUNDLED
RUNDLES
RUNDLET
RUNDLETS
RUNDOWN
RUNDOWNS
RUNDS
RUNE
RUNECRAFT
RUNED
RUNELIKE
RUNES
RUNFLAT
RUNFLATS
RUNG
RUNGED
RUNGLESS
RUNGS
RUNIC
RUNKLE
RUNKLED
RUNKLES
RUNKLING
RUNLESS
RUNLET
RUNLETS
RUNNABLE
RUNNEL
RUNNELS
RUNNER
RUNNERS
RUNNET
RUNNETS
RUNNIER
RUNNIEST
RUNNINESS
RUNNING
RUNNINGLY
RUNNINGS
RUNNION
RUNNIONS
RUNNY
RUNOFF
RUNOFFS
RUNOUT
RUNOUTS
RUNOVER
RUNOVERS
RUNPROOF
RUNRIG
RUNRIGS
RUNROUND
RUNROUNDS

R

RUNS
RUNT
RUNTED
RUNTIER
RUNTIEST
RUNTINESS
RUNTISH
RUNTISHLY
RUNTS
RUNTY
RUNWAY
RUNWAYS
RUPEE
RUPEES
RUPIA
RUPIAH
RUPIAHS
RUPIAS
RUPTURE
RUPTURED
RUPTURES
RUPTURING
RURAL
RURALISE
RURALISED
RURALISES
RURALISM
RURALISMS
RURALIST
RURALISTS
RURALITE
RURALITES
RURALITY
RURALIZE
RURALIZED
RURALIZES
RURALLY
RURALNESS
RURALS
RURBAN
RURP
RURPS
RURU
RURUS
RUSA
RUSALKA
RUSALKAS
RUSAS
RUSCUS
RUSCUSES
RUSE
RUSES
RUSH
RUSHED
RUSHEE
RUSHEES
RUSHEN
RUSHER
RUSHERS
RUSHES
RUSHIER
RUSHIEST
RUSHINESS
RUSHING
RUSHINGS
RUSHLIGHT
RUSHLIKE
RUSHY
RUSINE
RUSK
RUSKS
RUSMA
RUSMAS
RUSSE
RUSSEL
RUSSELS
RUSSET
RUSSETED
RUSSETIER
RUSSETING
RUSSETS
RUSSETY
RUSSIA
RUSSIAS
RUSSIFIED
RUSSIFIES
RUSSIFY
RUSSULA
RUSSULAE
RUSSULAS
RUST
RUSTABLE
RUSTED
RUSTIC
RUSTICAL
RUSTICALS
RUSTICANA
RUSTICATE
RUSTICIAL
RUSTICISE
RUSTICISM
RUSTICITY
RUSTICIZE
RUSTICLY
RUSTICS
RUSTIER
RUSTIEST
RUSTILY
RUSTINESS
RUSTING
RUSTINGS
RUSTLE
RUSTLED
RUSTLER
RUSTLERS
RUSTLES
RUSTLESS
RUSTLING
RUSTLINGS
RUSTPROOF
RUSTRE
RUSTRED
RUSTRES
RUSTS
RUSTY
RUT
RUTABAGA
RUTABAGAS
RUTACEOUS
RUTH
RUTHENIC
RUTHENIUM
RUTHER
RUTHFUL
RUTHFULLY
RUTHLESS
RUTHS
RUTILANT
RUTILATED
RUTILE
RUTILES
RUTIN
RUTINS
RUTS
RUTTED
RUTTER
RUTTERS
RUTTIER
RUTTIEST
RUTTILY
RUTTINESS
RUTTING
RUTTINGS
RUTTISH
RUTTISHLY
RUTTY
RYA
RYAL
RYALS
RYAS
RYBAT
RYBATS
RYBAUDRYE
RYE
RYEBREAD
RYEBREADS
RYEFLOUR
RYEFLOURS
RYEGRASS
RYEPECK
RYEPECKS
RYES
RYFE
RYKE
RYKED
RYKES
RYKING
RYMME
RYMMED
RYMMES
RYMMING
RYND
RYNDS
RYOKAN
RYOKANS
RYOT
RYOTS
RYOTWARI
RYOTWARIS
RYPE
RYPECK
RYPECKS
RYPER
RYU
RYUS

S

SAAG
SAAGS
SAB
SABADILLA
SABAL
SABALS
SABATON
SABATONS
SABAYON
SABAYONS
SABBAT
SABBATH
SABBATHS
SABBATIC
SABBATICS
SABBATINE
SABBATISE
SABBATISM
SABBATIZE
SABBATS
SABBED
SABBING
SABBINGS
SABE
SABED
SABEING
SABELLA
SABELLAS
SABER
SABERED
SABERING
SABERLIKE
SABERS
SABES
SABHA
SABHAS
SABICU
SABICUS
SABIN
SABINE
SABINES
SABINS
SABIR
SABIRS
SABKHA
SABKHAH
SABKHAHS
SABKHAS
SABKHAT
SABKHATS
SABLE
SABLED
SABLEFISH
SABLER
SABLES
SABLEST
SABLING
SABOT
SABOTAGE
SABOTAGED
SABOTAGES
SABOTED
SABOTEUR
SABOTEURS
SABOTIER
SABOTIERS
SABOTS
SABRA
SABRAS
SABRE
SABRED
SABRELIKE
SABRES
SABREUR
SABREURS
SABREWING
SABRING
SABS
SABULINE
SABULOSE
SABULOUS
SABURRA
SABURRAL
SABURRAS
SAC
SACATON
SACATONS
SACBUT
SACBUTS
SACCADE
SACCADES
SACCADIC
SACCATE
SACCHARIC
SACCHARIN
SACCHARUM
SACCIFORM
SACCOI
SACCOS
SACCOSES
SACCULAR
SACCULATE
SACCULE
SACCULES
SACCULI
SACCULUS
SACELLA
SACELLUM
SACHEM
SACHEMDOM
SACHEMIC
SACHEMS
SACHET
SACHETED
SACHETS
SACK
SACKABLE
SACKAGE
SACKAGED
SACKAGES
SACKAGING
SACKBUT
SACKBUTS
SACKCLOTH
SACKED
SACKER
SACKERS
SACKFUL
SACKFULS
SACKING
SACKINGS
SACKLESS
SACKLIKE
SACKLOAD
SACKLOADS
SACKS
SACKSFUL
SACLESS
SACLIKE
SACQUE
SACQUES
SACRA
SACRAL
SACRALGIA
SACRALISE
SACRALITY
SACRALIZE
SACRALS
SACRAMENT
SACRARIA
SACRARIAL
SACRARIUM
SACRED
SACREDER
SACREDEST
SACREDLY
SACRIFICE
SACRIFIDE
SACRIFIED
SACRIFIES
SACRIFY
SACRILEGE
SACRING
SACRINGS
SACRIST
SACRISTAN
SACRISTS
SACRISTY
SACRUM
SACRUMS
SACS
SAD
SADDED
SADDEN
SADDENED
SADDENING
SADDENS
SADDER
SADDEST
SADDHU
SADDHUS
SADDIE
SADDIES
SADDING
SADDISH
SADDLE
SADDLEBAG
SADDLEBOW
SADDLED
SADDLER
SADDLERS
SADDLERY
SADDLES
SADDLING
SADDO
SADDOES
SADDOS
SADE
SADES
SADHANA
SADHANAS
SADHE
SADHES
SADHU
SADHUS
SADI
SADIRON
SADIRONS
SADIS
SADISM

S

SADISMS
SADIST
SADISTIC
SADISTS
SADLY
SADNESS
SADNESSES
SADO
SADOS
SADS
SADZA
SADZAS
SAE
SAECULA
SAECULUM
SAECULUMS
SAETER
SAETERS
SAFARI
SAFARIED
SAFARIING
SAFARIS
SAFARIST
SAFARISTS
SAFE
SAFED
SAFEGUARD
SAFELIGHT
SAFELY
SAFENESS
SAFER
SAFES
SAFEST
SAFETIED
SAFETIES
SAFETY
SAFETYING
SAFETYMAN
SAFETYMEN
SAFFIAN
SAFFIANS
SAFFLOWER
SAFFRON
SAFFRONED
SAFFRONS
SAFFRONY
SAFING
SAFRANIN
SAFRANINE
SAFRANINS
SAFROL
SAFROLE
SAFROLES
SAFROLS
SAFRONAL
SAFRONALS
SAFT
SAFTER
SAFTEST
SAG
SAGA
SAGACIOUS
SAGACITY
SAGAMAN
SAGAMEN
SAGAMORE
SAGAMORES
SAGANASH
SAGAPENUM
SAGAS
SAGATHIES
SAGATHY
SAGBUT
SAGBUTS
SAGE
SAGEBRUSH
SAGEHOOD
SAGEHOODS
SAGELY
SAGENE
SAGENES
SAGENESS
SAGENITE
SAGENITES
SAGENITIC
SAGER
SAGES
SAGEST
SAGGAR
SAGGARD
SAGGARDS
SAGGARED
SAGGARING
SAGGARS
SAGGED
SAGGER
SAGGERED
SAGGERING
SAGGERS
SAGGIER
SAGGIEST
SAGGING
SAGGINGS
SAGGY
SAGIER
SAGIEST
SAGINATE
SAGINATED
SAGINATES
SAGITTA
SAGITTAL
SAGITTARY
SAGITTAS
SAGITTATE
SAGO
SAGOIN
SAGOINS
SAGOS
SAGOUIN
SAGOUINS
SAGRADA
SAGS
SAGUARO
SAGUAROS
SAGUIN
SAGUINS
SAGUM
SAGY
SAHEB
SAHEBS
SAHIB
SAHIBA
SAHIBAH
SAHIBAHS
SAHIBAS
SAHIBS
SAHIWAL
SAHIWALS
SAHUARO
SAHUAROS
SAI
SAIBLING
SAIBLINGS
SAIC
SAICE
SAICES
SAICK
SAICKS
SAICS
SAID
SAIDEST
SAIDS
SAIDST
SAIGA
SAIGAS
SAIKEI
SAIKEIS
SAIKLESS
SAIL
SAILABLE
SAILBOARD
SAILBOAT
SAILBOATS
SAILCLOTH
SAILED
SAILER
SAILERS
SAILFISH
SAILING
SAILINGS
SAILLESS
SAILMAKER
SAILOR
SAILORING
SAILORLY
SAILORS
SAILPAST
SAILPASTS
SAILPLANE
SAILROOM
SAILROOMS
SAILS
SAIM
SAIMIN
SAIMINS
SAIMIRI
SAIMIRIS
SAIMS
SAIN
SAINE
SAINED
SAINFOIN
SAINFOINS
SAINING
SAINS
SAINT
SAINTDOM
SAINTDOMS
SAINTED
SAINTESS
SAINTFOIN
SAINTHOOD
SAINTING
SAINTISH
SAINTISM
SAINTISMS
SAINTLESS
SAINTLIER
SAINTLIKE
SAINTLILY
SAINTLING
SAINTLY
SAINTS
SAINTSHIP
SAIQUE
SAIQUES
SAIR
SAIRED
SAIRER
SAIREST
SAIRING
SAIRS
SAIS
SAIST
SAITH
SAITHE
SAITHES
SAITHS
SAIYID
SAIYIDS
SAJOU
SAJOUS
SAKE
SAKER
SAKERET
SAKERETS
SAKERS
SAKES
SAKI
SAKIA

SAKIAS
SAKIEH
SAKIEHS
SAKIS
SAKIYEH
SAKIYEHS
SAKKOI
SAKKOS
SAKKOSES
SAKSAUL
SAKSAULS
SAKTI
SAKTIS
SAL
SALAAM
SALAAMED
SALAAMING
SALAAMS
SALABLE
SALABLY
SALACIOUS
SALACITY
SALAD
SALADANG
SALADANGS
SALADE
SALADES
SALADING
SALADINGS
SALADS
SALAL
SALALS
SALAMI
SALAMIS
SALAMON
SALAMONS
SALANGANE
SALARIAT
SALARIATS
SALARIED
SALARIES
SALARY
SALARYING
SALARYMAN
SALARYMEN
SALAT
SALATS
SALBAND
SALBANDS
SALCHOW
SALCHOWS
SALE
SALEABLE
SALEABLY
SALEP
SALEPS
SALERATUS
SALERING
SALERINGS
SALEROOM
SALEROOMS
SALES
SALESGIRL
SALESLADY
SALESMAN
SALESMEN
SALESROOM
SALET
SALETS
SALEWD
SALEYARD
SALEYARDS
SALFERN
SALFERNS
SALIAUNCE
SALIC
SALICES
SALICET
SALICETA
SALICETS
SALICETUM
SALICIN
SALICINE
SALICINES
SALICINS
SALICYLIC
SALIENCE
SALIENCES
SALIENCY
SALIENT
SALIENTLY
SALIENTS
SALIFIED
SALIFIES
SALIFY
SALIFYING
SALIGOT
SALIGOTS
SALIMETER
SALIMETRY
SALINA
SALINAS
SALINE
SALINES
SALINISE
SALINISED
SALINISES
SALINITY
SALINIZE
SALINIZED
SALINIZES
SALIVA
SALIVAL
SALIVARY
SALIVAS
SALIVATE
SALIVATED
SALIVATES
SALIVATOR
SALIX
SALL
SALLAD
SALLADS
SALLAL
SALLALS
SALLE
SALLEE
SALLEES
SALLES
SALLET
SALLETS
SALLIED
SALLIER
SALLIERS
SALLIES
SALLOW
SALLOWED
SALLOWER
SALLOWEST
SALLOWIER
SALLOWING
SALLOWISH
SALLOWLY
SALLOWS
SALLOWY
SALLY
SALLYING
SALLYPORT
SALMI
SALMIS
SALMON
SALMONET
SALMONETS
SALMONID
SALMONIDS
SALMONIER
SALMONOID
SALMONS
SALMONY
SALOL
SALOLS
SALOMETER
SALON
SALONS
SALOON
SALOONS
SALOOP
SALOOPS
SALOP
SALOPIAN
SALOPS
SALP
SALPA
SALPAE
SALPAS
SALPIAN
SALPIANS
SALPICON
SALPICONS
SALPID
SALPIDS
SALPIFORM
SALPINGES
SALPINX
SALPINXES
SALPS
SALS
SALSA
SALSAED
SALSAING
SALSAS
SALSE
SALSES
SALSIFIES
SALSIFY
SALSILLA
SALSILLAS
SALT
SALTANDO
SALTANDOS
SALTANT
SALTANTS
SALTATE
SALTATED
SALTATES
SALTATING
SALTATION
SALTATO
SALTATORY
SALTATOS
SALTBOX
SALTBOXES
SALTBUSH
SALTCAT
SALTCATS
SALTCHUCK
SALTED
SALTER
SALTERIES
SALTERN
SALTERNS
SALTERS
SALTERY
SALTEST
SALTFISH
SALTIE
SALTIER
SALTIERS
SALTIES
SALTIEST
SALTILY
SALTINE
SALTINES
SALTINESS
SALTING
SALTINGS
SALTIRE
SALTIRES
SALTISH
SALTISHLY

SALTLESS
SALTLIKE
SALTLY
SALTNESS
SALTO
SALTOED
SALTOING
SALTOS
SALTPAN
SALTPANS
SALTPETER
SALTPETRE
SALTS
SALTUS
SALTUSES
SALTWATER
SALTWORK
SALTWORKS
SALTWORT
SALTWORTS
SALTY
SALUBRITY
SALUE
SALUED
SALUES
SALUING
SALUKI
SALUKIS
SALURETIC
SALUT
SALUTARY
SALUTE
SALUTED
SALUTER
SALUTERS
SALUTES
SALUTING
SALVABLE
SALVABLY
SALVAGE
SALVAGED
SALVAGEE
SALVAGEES
SALVAGER
SALVAGERS
SALVAGES
SALVAGING
SALVARSAN
SALVATION
SALVATORY
SALVE
SALVED
SALVER
SALVERS
SALVES
SALVETE
SALVETES
SALVIA
SALVIAS
SALVIFIC
SALVING
SALVINGS
SALVO
SALVOED
SALVOES
SALVOING
SALVOR
SALVORS
SALVOS
SALWAR
SALWARS
SAM
SAMA
SAMAAN
SAMAANS
SAMADHI
SAMADHIS
SAMAN
SAMANS
SAMARA
SAMARAS
SAMARITAN
SAMARIUM
SAMARIUMS
SAMAS
SAMBA
SAMBAED
SAMBAING
SAMBAL
SAMBALS
SAMBAR
SAMBARS
SAMBAS
SAMBHAR
SAMBHARS
SAMBHUR
SAMBHURS
SAMBO
SAMBOES
SAMBOS
SAMBUCA
SAMBUCAS
SAMBUKE
SAMBUKES
SAMBUR
SAMBURS
SAME
SAMECH
SAMECHS
SAMEK
SAMEKH
SAMEKHS
SAMEKS
SAMEL
SAMELY
SAMEN
SAMENESS
SAMES
SAMEY
SAMEYNESS
SAMFOO
SAMFOOS
SAMFU
SAMFUS
SAMIEL
SAMIELS
SAMIER
SAMIEST
SAMISEN
SAMISENS
SAMITE
SAMITES
SAMITHI
SAMITHIS
SAMITI
SAMITIS
SAMIZDAT
SAMIZDATS
SAMLET
SAMLETS
SAMLOR
SAMLORS
SAMMED
SAMMIE
SAMMIES
SAMMING
SAMMY
SAMNITIS
SAMOSA
SAMOSAS
SAMOVAR
SAMOVARS
SAMOYED
SAMOYEDS
SAMP
SAMPAN
SAMPANS
SAMPHIRE
SAMPHIRES
SAMPI
SAMPIRE
SAMPIRES
SAMPIS
SAMPLE
SAMPLED
SAMPLER
SAMPLERS
SAMPLERY
SAMPLES
SAMPLING
SAMPLINGS
SAMPS
SAMS
SAMSARA
SAMSARAS
SAMSARIC
SAMSHOO
SAMSHOOS
SAMSHU
SAMSHUS
SAMSKARA
SAMSKARAS
SAMURAI
SAMURAIS
SAN
SANATIVE
SANATORIA
SANATORY
SANBENITO
SANCAI
SANCAIS
SANCHO
SANCHOS
SANCTA
SANCTIFY
SANCTION
SANCTIONS
SANCTITY
SANCTUARY
SANCTUM
SANCTUMS
SAND
SANDABLE
SANDAL
SANDALED
SANDALING
SANDALLED
SANDALS
SANDARAC
SANDARACH
SANDARACS
SANDBAG
SANDBAGS
SANDBANK
SANDBANKS
SANDBAR
SANDBARS
SANDBLAST
SANDBOX
SANDBOXES
SANDBOY
SANDBOYS
SANDBUR
SANDBURR
SANDBURRS
SANDBURS
SANDCRACK
SANDDAB
SANDDABS
SANDED
SANDEK
SANDEKS
SANDER
SANDERS
SANDERSES
SANDFISH
SANDFLIES
SANDFLY
SANDGLASS
SANDHEAP

SANDHEAPS
SANDHI
SANDHILL
SANDHILLS
SANDHIS
SANDHOG
SANDHOGS
SANDIER
SANDIEST
SANDINESS
SANDING
SANDINGS
SANDIVER
SANDIVERS
SANDLESS
SANDLIKE
SANDLING
SANDLINGS
SANDLOT
SANDLOTS
SANDMAN
SANDMEN
SANDPAPER
SANDPEEP
SANDPEEPS
SANDPILE
SANDPILES
SANDPIPER
SANDPIT
SANDPITS
SANDPUMP
SANDPUMPS
SANDS
SANDSHOE
SANDSHOES
SANDSOAP
SANDSOAPS
SANDSPIT
SANDSPITS
SANDSPOUT
SANDSPUR
SANDSPURS
SANDSTONE
SANDSTORM
SANDWICH
SANDWORM
SANDWORMS
SANDWORT
SANDWORTS
SANDY
SANDYISH
SANE
SANED
SANELY
SANENESS
SANER
SANES
SANEST
SANG
SANGA
SANGAR
SANGAREE
SANGAREES
SANGARS
SANGAS
SANGEET
SANGEETS
SANGER
SANGERS
SANGFROID
SANGH
SANGHA
SANGHAS
SANGHAT
SANGHATS
SANGHS
SANGLIER
SANGLIERS
SANGO
SANGOMA
SANGOMAS
SANGOS
SANGRAIL
SANGRAILS
SANGREAL
SANGREALS
SANGRIA
SANGRIAS
SANGS
SANGUIFY
SANGUINE
SANGUINED
SANGUINES
SANICLE
SANICLES
SANIDINE
SANIDINES
SANIES
SANIFIED
SANIFIES
SANIFY
SANIFYING
SANING
SANIOUS
SANITARIA
SANITARY
SANITATE
SANITATED
SANITATES
SANITIES
SANITISE
SANITISED
SANITISER
SANITISES
SANITIZE
SANITIZED
SANITIZER
SANITIZES
SANITORIA
SANITY
SANJAK
SANJAKS
SANK
SANKO
SANKOS
SANNIE
SANNIES
SANNOP
SANNOPS
SANNUP
SANNUPS
SANNYASI
SANNYASIN
SANNYASIS
SANPAN
SANPANS
SANPRO
SANPROS
SANS
SANSA
SANSAR
SANSARS
SANSAS
SANSEI
SANSEIS
SANSERIF
SANSERIFS
SANT
SANTAL
SANTALIC
SANTALIN
SANTALINS
SANTALOL
SANTALOLS
SANTALS
SANTERA
SANTERAS
SANTERIA
SANTERIAS
SANTERO
SANTEROS
SANTIM
SANTIMI
SANTIMS
SANTIMU
SANTIR
SANTIRS
SANTO
SANTOKU
SANTOKUS
SANTOL
SANTOLINA
SANTOLS
SANTON
SANTONICA
SANTONIN
SANTONINS
SANTONS
SANTOOR
SANTOORS
SANTOS
SANTOUR
SANTOURS
SANTS
SANTUR
SANTURS
SANYASI
SANYASIS
SAOLA
SAOLAS
SAOUARI
SAOUARIS
SAP
SAPAJOU
SAPAJOUS
SAPAN
SAPANS
SAPANWOOD
SAPEGO
SAPEGOES
SAPELE
SAPELES
SAPFUL
SAPHEAD
SAPHEADED
SAPHEADS
SAPHENA
SAPHENAE
SAPHENAS
SAPHENOUS
SAPID
SAPIDER
SAPIDEST
SAPIDITY
SAPIDLESS
SAPIDNESS
SAPIENCE
SAPIENCES
SAPIENCY
SAPIENS
SAPIENT
SAPIENTLY
SAPIENTS
SAPLESS
SAPLING
SAPLINGS
SAPODILLA
SAPOGENIN
SAPONARIA
SAPONATED
SAPONIFY
SAPONIN
SAPONINE
SAPONINES
SAPONINS
SAPONITE
SAPONITES
SAPOR
SAPORIFIC
SAPOROUS

S

SAPORS
SAPOTA
SAPOTAS
SAPOTE
SAPOTES
SAPOUR
SAPOURS
SAPPAN
SAPPANS
SAPPED
SAPPER
SAPPERS
SAPPHIC
SAPPHICS
SAPPHIRE
SAPPHIRED
SAPPHIRES
SAPPHISM
SAPPHISMS
SAPPHIST
SAPPHISTS
SAPPIER
SAPPIEST
SAPPILY
SAPPINESS
SAPPING
SAPPINGS
SAPPLE
SAPPLED
SAPPLES
SAPPLING
SAPPY
SAPRAEMIA
SAPRAEMIC
SAPREMIA
SAPREMIAS
SAPREMIC
SAPROBE
SAPROBES
SAPROBIAL
SAPROBIC
SAPROBITY
SAPROLITE
SAPROPEL
SAPROPELS
SAPROZOIC
SAPS
SAPSAGO
SAPSAGOS
SAPSUCKER
SAPUCAIA
SAPUCAIAS
SAPWOOD
SAPWOODS
SAR
SARABAND
SARABANDE
SARABANDS
SARAFAN
SARAFANS
SARAN
SARANGI
SARANGIS
SARANS
SARAPE
SARAPES
SARBACANE
SARCASM
SARCASMS
SARCASTIC
SARCENET
SARCENETS
SARCINA
SARCINAE
SARCINAS
SARCOCARP
SARCODE
SARCODES
SARCODIC
SARCOID
SARCOIDS
SARCOLOGY
SARCOMA
SARCOMAS
SARCOMATA
SARCOMERE
SARCONET
SARCONETS
SARCOPTIC
SARCOSOME
SARCOUS
SARD
SARDANA
SARDANAS
SARDAR
SARDARS
SARDEL
SARDELLE
SARDELLES
SARDELS
SARDINE
SARDINED
SARDINES
SARDINING
SARDIUS
SARDIUSES
SARDONIAN
SARDONIC
SARDONYX
SARDS
SARED
SAREE
SAREES
SARGASSA
SARGASSO
SARGASSOS
SARGASSUM
SARGE
SARGES
SARGO
SARGOS
SARGOSES
SARGUS
SARGUSES
SARI
SARIN
SARING
SARINS
SARIS
SARK
SARKIER
SARKIEST
SARKILY
SARKINESS
SARKING
SARKINGS
SARKS
SARKY
SARMENT
SARMENTA
SARMENTS
SARMENTUM
SARMIE
SARMIES
SARNEY
SARNEYS
SARNIE
SARNIES
SAROD
SARODE
SARODES
SARODIST
SARODISTS
SARODS
SARONG
SARONGS
SARONIC
SAROS
SAROSES
SARPANCH
SARRASIN
SARRASINS
SARRAZIN
SARRAZINS
SARS
SARSAR
SARSARS
SARSDEN
SARSDENS
SARSEN
SARSENET
SARSENETS
SARSENS
SARSNET
SARSNETS
SARTOR
SARTORIAL
SARTORIAN
SARTORII
SARTORIUS
SARTORS
SARUS
SARUSES
SASANQUA
SASANQUAS
SASARARA
SASARARAS
SASER
SASERS
SASH
SASHAY
SASHAYED
SASHAYING
SASHAYS
SASHED
SASHES
SASHIMI
SASHIMIS
SASHING
SASHLESS
SASIN
SASINE
SASINES
SASINS
SASKATOON
SASQUATCH
SASS
SASSABIES
SASSABY
SASSAFRAS
SASSARARA
SASSE
SASSED
SASSES
SASSIER
SASSIES
SASSIEST
SASSILY
SASSINESS
SASSING
SASSOLIN
SASSOLINS
SASSOLITE
SASSWOOD
SASSWOODS
SASSY
SASSYWOOD
SASTRA
SASTRAS
SASTRUGA
SASTRUGI
SAT
SATAI
SATAIS
SATANG
SATANGS
SATANIC
SATANICAL
SATANISM
SATANISMS

SATANIST
SATANISTS
SATANITY
SATARA
SATARAS
SATAY
SATAYS
SATCHEL
SATCHELED
SATCHELS
SATCOM
SATCOMS
SATE
SATED
SATEDNESS
SATEEN
SATEENS
SATELESS
SATELLES
SATELLITE
SATEM
SATES
SATI
SATIABLE
SATIABLY
SATIATE
SATIATED
SATIATES
SATIATING
SATIATION
SATIETIES
SATIETY
SATIN
SATINED
SATINET
SATINETS
SATINETTA
SATINETTE
SATING
SATINIER
SATINIEST
SATINING
SATINPOD
SATINPODS
SATINS
SATINWOOD
SATINY
SATIRE
SATIRES
SATIRIC
SATIRICAL
SATIRISE
SATIRISED
SATIRISER
SATIRISES
SATIRIST
SATIRISTS
SATIRIZE
SATIRIZED
SATIRIZER
SATIRIZES
SATIS
SATISFICE
SATISFIED
SATISFIER
SATISFIES
SATISFY
SATIVE
SATNAV
SATNAVS
SATORI
SATORIS
SATRAP
SATRAPAL
SATRAPIES
SATRAPS
SATRAPY
SATSANG
SATSANGS
SATSUMA
SATSUMAS
SATURABLE
SATURANT
SATURANTS
SATURATE
SATURATED
SATURATER
SATURATES
SATURATOR
SATURNIC
SATURNIID
SATURNINE
SATURNISM
SATURNIST
SATYR
SATYRA
SATYRAL
SATYRALS
SATYRAS
SATYRE
SATYRES
SATYRESS
SATYRIC
SATYRICAL
SATYRID
SATYRIDS
SATYRISK
SATYRISKS
SATYRLIKE
SATYRS
SAU
SAUBA
SAUBAS
SAUCE
SAUCEBOAT
SAUCEBOX
SAUCED
SAUCELESS
SAUCEPAN
SAUCEPANS
SAUCEPOT
SAUCEPOTS
SAUCER
SAUCERFUL
SAUCERS
SAUCES
SAUCH
SAUCHS
SAUCIER
SAUCIERS
SAUCIEST
SAUCILY
SAUCINESS
SAUCING
SAUCISSE
SAUCISSES
SAUCISSON
SAUCY
SAUFGARD
SAUFGARDS
SAUGER
SAUGERS
SAUGH
SAUGHS
SAUGHY
SAUL
SAULGE
SAULGES
SAULIE
SAULIES
SAULS
SAULT
SAULTS
SAUNA
SAUNAED
SAUNAING
SAUNAS
SAUNT
SAUNTED
SAUNTER
SAUNTERED
SAUNTERER
SAUNTERS
SAUNTING
SAUNTS
SAUREL
SAURELS
SAURIAN
SAURIANS
SAURIES
SAUROID
SAUROIDS
SAUROPOD
SAUROPODS
SAURY
SAUSAGE
SAUSAGES
SAUT
SAUTE
SAUTED
SAUTEED
SAUTEEING
SAUTEING
SAUTERNE
SAUTERNES
SAUTES
SAUTING
SAUTOIR
SAUTOIRE
SAUTOIRES
SAUTOIRS
SAUTS
SAV
SAVABLE
SAVAGE
SAVAGED
SAVAGEDOM
SAVAGELY
SAVAGER
SAVAGERY
SAVAGES
SAVAGEST
SAVAGING
SAVAGISM
SAVAGISMS
SAVANNA
SAVANNAH
SAVANNAHS
SAVANNAS
SAVANT
SAVANTE
SAVANTES
SAVANTS
SAVARIN
SAVARINS
SAVASANA
SAVASANAS
SAVATE
SAVATES
SAVE
SAVEABLE
SAVED
SAVEGARD
SAVEGARDS
SAVELOY
SAVELOYS
SAVER
SAVERS
SAVES
SAVEY
SAVEYED
SAVEYING
SAVEYS
SAVIN
SAVINE
SAVINES
SAVING
SAVINGLY
SAVINGS
SAVINS

SAVIOR
SAVIORS
SAVIOUR
SAVIOURS
SAVOR
SAVORED
SAVORER
SAVORERS
SAVORIER
SAVORIES
SAVORIEST
SAVORILY
SAVORING
SAVORLESS
SAVOROUS
SAVORS
SAVORY
SAVOUR
SAVOURED
SAVOURER
SAVOURERS
SAVOURIER
SAVOURIES
SAVOURILY
SAVOURING
SAVOURLY
SAVOURS
SAVOURY
SAVOY
SAVOYARD
SAVOYARDS
SAVOYS
SAVS
SAVVEY
SAVVEYED
SAVVEYING
SAVVEYS
SAVVIED
SAVVIER
SAVVIES
SAVVIEST
SAVVILY
SAVVINESS
SAVVY
SAVVYING
SAW
SAWAH
SAWAHS
SAWBILL
SAWBILLS
SAWBLADE
SAWBLADES
SAWBONES
SAWBUCK
SAWBUCKS
SAWDER
SAWDERED
SAWDERING
SAWDERS
SAWDUST
SAWDUSTED
SAWDUSTS
SAWDUSTY
SAWED
SAWER
SAWERS
SAWFISH
SAWFISHES
SAWFLIES
SAWFLY
SAWGRASS
SAWHORSE
SAWHORSES
SAWING
SAWINGS
SAWLIKE
SAWLOG
SAWLOGS
SAWMILL
SAWMILLER
SAWMILLS
SAWN
SAWNEY
SAWNEYS
SAWPIT
SAWPITS
SAWS
SAWSHARK
SAWSHARKS
SAWTEETH
SAWTIMBER
SAWTOOTH
SAWYER
SAWYERS
SAX
SAXATILE
SAXAUL
SAXAULS
SAXE
SAXES
SAXHORN
SAXHORNS
SAXICOLE
SAXIFRAGE
SAXIST
SAXISTS
SAXITOXIN
SAXMAN
SAXMEN
SAXONIES
SAXONITE
SAXONITES
SAXONY
SAXOPHONE
SAXTUBA
SAXTUBAS
SAY
SAYABLE
SAYABLES
SAYED
SAYEDS
SAYER
SAYERS
SAYEST
SAYID
SAYIDS
SAYING
SAYINGS
SAYNE
SAYON
SAYONARA
SAYONARAS
SAYONS
SAYS
SAYST
SAYYID
SAYYIDS
SAZ
SAZERAC
SAZERACS
SAZES
SAZHEN
SAZHENS
SAZZES
SBIRRI
SBIRRO
SCAB
SCABBARD
SCABBARDS
SCABBED
SCABBIER
SCABBIEST
SCABBILY
SCABBING
SCABBLE
SCABBLED
SCABBLES
SCABBLING
SCABBY
SCABIES
SCABIETIC
SCABIOSA
SCABIOSAS
SCABIOUS
SCABLAND
SCABLANDS
SCABLIKE
SCABRID
SCABROUS
SCABS
SCAD
SCADS
SCAFF
SCAFFED
SCAFFIE
SCAFFIER
SCAFFIES
SCAFFIEST
SCAFFING
SCAFFOLD
SCAFFOLDS
SCAFFS
SCAFFY
SCAG
SCAGGED
SCAGGING
SCAGLIA
SCAGLIAS
SCAGLIOLA
SCAGS
SCAIL
SCAILED
SCAILING
SCAILS
SCAITH
SCAITHED
SCAITHING
SCAITHS
SCALA
SCALABLE
SCALABLY
SCALADE
SCALADES
SCALADO
SCALADOS
SCALAE
SCALAGE
SCALAGES
SCALAR
SCALARE
SCALARES
SCALARS
SCALATION
SCALAWAG
SCALAWAGS
SCALD
SCALDED
SCALDER
SCALDERS
SCALDFISH
SCALDHEAD
SCALDIC
SCALDING
SCALDINGS
SCALDINI
SCALDINO
SCALDS
SCALDSHIP
SCALE
SCALEABLE
SCALEABLY
SCALED
SCALELESS
SCALELIKE
SCALENE
SCALENES
SCALENI
SCALENUS
SCALEPAN
SCALEPANS

S

SCALER
SCALERS
SCALES
SCALETAIL
SCALEUP
SCALEUPS
SCALEWORK
SCALIER
SCALIEST
SCALINESS
SCALING
SCALINGS
SCALL
SCALLAWAG
SCALLED
SCALLIES
SCALLION
SCALLIONS
SCALLOP
SCALLOPED
SCALLOPER
SCALLOPS
SCALLS
SCALLY
SCALLYWAG
SCALOGRAM
SCALP
SCALPED
SCALPEL
SCALPELS
SCALPER
SCALPERS
SCALPING
SCALPINGS
SCALPINS
SCALPLESS
SCALPRUM
SCALPRUMS
SCALPS
SCALY
SCAM
SCAMBLE
SCAMBLED
SCAMBLER
SCAMBLERS
SCAMBLES
SCAMBLING
SCAMEL
SCAMELS
SCAMMED
SCAMMER
SCAMMERS
SCAMMING
SCAMMONY
SCAMP
SCAMPED
SCAMPER
SCAMPERED
SCAMPERER
SCAMPERS
SCAMPI
SCAMPIES
SCAMPING
SCAMPINGS
SCAMPIS
SCAMPISH
SCAMPS
SCAMS
SCAMSTER
SCAMSTERS
SCAMTO
SCAMTOS
SCAN
SCAND
SCANDAL
SCANDALED
SCANDALS
SCANDENT
SCANDIA
SCANDIAS
SCANDIC
SCANDIUM
SCANDIUMS
SCANNABLE
SCANNED
SCANNER
SCANNERS
SCANNING
SCANNINGS
SCANS
SCANSION
SCANSIONS
SCANT
SCANTED
SCANTER
SCANTEST
SCANTIER
SCANTIES
SCANTIEST
SCANTILY
SCANTING
SCANTITY
SCANTLE
SCANTLED
SCANTLES
SCANTLING
SCANTLY
SCANTNESS
SCANTS
SCANTY
SCAPA
SCAPAED
SCAPAING
SCAPAS
SCAPE
SCAPED
SCAPEGOAT
SCAPELESS
SCAPEMENT
SCAPES
SCAPHOID
SCAPHOIDS
SCAPHOPOD
SCAPI
SCAPING
SCAPOLITE
SCAPOSE
SCAPPLE
SCAPPLED
SCAPPLES
SCAPPLING
SCAPULA
SCAPULAE
SCAPULAR
SCAPULARS
SCAPULARY
SCAPULAS
SCAPUS
SCAR
SCARAB
SCARABAEI
SCARABEE
SCARABEES
SCARABOID
SCARABS
SCARCE
SCARCELY
SCARCER
SCARCEST
SCARCITY
SCARE
SCARECROW
SCARED
SCAREDER
SCAREDEST
SCAREDIES
SCAREDY
SCAREHEAD
SCARER
SCARERS
SCARES
SCAREWARE
SCAREY
SCARF
SCARFED
SCARFER
SCARFERS
SCARFING
SCARFINGS
SCARFISH
SCARFPIN
SCARFPINS
SCARFS
SCARFSKIN
SCARFWISE
SCARIER
SCARIEST
SCARIFIED
SCARIFIER
SCARIFIES
SCARIFY
SCARILY
SCARINESS
SCARING
SCARIOSE
SCARIOUS
SCARLESS
SCARLET
SCARLETED
SCARLETS
SCARMOGE
SCARMOGES
SCARP
SCARPA
SCARPAED
SCARPAING
SCARPAS
SCARPED
SCARPER
SCARPERED
SCARPERS
SCARPETTI
SCARPETTO
SCARPH
SCARPHED
SCARPHING
SCARPHS
SCARPINES
SCARPING
SCARPINGS
SCARPS
SCARRE
SCARRED
SCARRES
SCARRIER
SCARRIEST
SCARRING
SCARRINGS
SCARRY
SCARS
SCART
SCARTED
SCARTH
SCARTHS
SCARTING
SCARTS
SCARVED
SCARVES
SCARY
SCAT
SCATBACK
SCATBACKS
SCATCH
SCATCHES
SCATH
SCATHE
SCATHED
SCATHEFUL
SCATHES
SCATHING

S

SCATHS
SCATOLE
SCATOLES
SCATOLOGY
SCATS
SCATT
SCATTED
SCATTER
SCATTERED
SCATTERER
SCATTERS
SCATTERY
SCATTIER
SCATTIEST
SCATTILY
SCATTING
SCATTINGS
SCATTS
SCATTY
SCAUD
SCAUDED
SCAUDING
SCAUDS
SCAUP
SCAUPED
SCAUPER
SCAUPERS
SCAUPING
SCAUPS
SCAUR
SCAURED
SCAURIES
SCAURING
SCAURS
SCAURY
SCAVAGE
SCAVAGED
SCAVAGER
SCAVAGERS
SCAVAGES
SCAVAGING
SCAVENGE
SCAVENGED
SCAVENGER
SCAVENGES
SCAW
SCAWS
SCAWTITE
SCAWTITES
SCAZON
SCAZONS
SCAZONTES
SCAZONTIC
SCEAT
SCEATS
SCEATT
SCEATTAS
SCEATTS
SCEDULE
SCEDULED
SCEDULES
SCEDULING
SCELERAT
SCELERATE
SCELERATS
SCENA
SCENARIES
SCENARIO
SCENARIOS
SCENARISE
SCENARIST
SCENARIZE
SCENARY
SCENAS
SCEND
SCENDED
SCENDING
SCENDS
SCENE
SCENED
SCENEMAN
SCENEMEN
SCENERIES
SCENERY
SCENES
SCENESTER
SCENIC
SCENICAL
SCENICS
SCENING
SCENT
SCENTED
SCENTFUL
SCENTING
SCENTINGS
SCENTLESS
SCENTS
SCEPSIS
SCEPSISES
SCEPTER
SCEPTERED
SCEPTERS
SCEPTIC
SCEPTICAL
SCEPTICS
SCEPTRAL
SCEPTRE
SCEPTRED
SCEPTRES
SCEPTRING
SCEPTRY
SCERNE
SCERNED
SCERNES
SCERNING
SCHANSE
SCHANSES
SCHANTZE
SCHANTZES
SCHANZE
SCHANZES
SCHAPPE
SCHAPPED
SCHAPPES
SCHAPSKA
SCHAPSKAS
SCHATCHEN
SCHAV
SCHAVS
SCHECHITA
SCHEDULAR
SCHEDULE
SCHEDULED
SCHEDULER
SCHEDULES
SCHEELITE
SCHELLIES
SCHELLUM
SCHELLUMS
SCHELLY
SCHELM
SCHELMS
SCHEMA
SCHEMAS
SCHEMATA
SCHEMATIC
SCHEME
SCHEMED
SCHEMER
SCHEMERS
SCHEMES
SCHEMIE
SCHEMIES
SCHEMING
SCHEMINGS
SCHERZI
SCHERZO
SCHERZOS
SCHIAVONE
SCHIEDAM
SCHIEDAMS
SCHILLER
SCHILLERS
SCHILLING
SCHIMMEL
SCHIMMELS
SCHISM
SCHISMA
SCHISMAS
SCHISMS
SCHIST
SCHISTOSE
SCHISTOUS
SCHISTS
SCHIZOID
SCHIZOIDS
SCHIZONT
SCHIZONTS
SCHIZOPOD
SCHLAGER
SCHLAGERS
SCHLEMIEL
SCHLEMIHL
SCHLEP
SCHLEPP
SCHLEPPED
SCHLEPPER
SCHLEPPS
SCHLEPPY
SCHLEPS
SCHLICH
SCHLICHS
SCHLIERE
SCHLIEREN
SCHLIERIC
SCHLOCK
SCHLOCKER
SCHLOCKEY
SCHLOCKS
SCHLOCKY
SCHLONG
SCHLONGS
SCHLOSS
SCHLOSSES
SCHLUB
SCHLUBS
SCHLUMP
SCHLUMPED
SCHLUMPS
SCHLUMPY
SCHMALTZ
SCHMALTZY
SCHMALZ
SCHMALZES
SCHMALZY
SCHMATTE
SCHMATTES
SCHMEAR
SCHMEARED
SCHMEARS
SCHMECK
SCHMECKED
SCHMECKER
SCHMECKS
SCHMEER
SCHMEERED
SCHMEERS
SCHMELZ
SCHMELZE
SCHMELZES
SCHMICK
SCHMICKER
SCHMO
SCHMOCK
SCHMOCKS
SCHMOE
SCHMOES
SCHMOOS
SCHMOOSE
SCHMOOSED

S

SCHMOOSES
SCHMOOZ
SCHMOOZE
SCHMOOZED
SCHMOOZER
SCHMOOZES
SCHMOOZY
SCHMOS
SCHMUCK
SCHMUCKED
SCHMUCKS
SCHMUCKY
SCHMUTTER
SCHMUTZ
SCHMUTZES
SCHNAPPER
SCHNAPPS
SCHNAPS
SCHNAPSES
SCHNAUZER
SCHNECKE
SCHNECKEN
SCHNEID
SCHNEIDS
SCHNELL
SCHNITZEL
SCHNOODLE
SCHNOOK
SCHNOOKS
SCHNORKEL
SCHNORR
SCHNORRED
SCHNORRER
SCHNORRS
SCHNOZ
SCHNOZES
SCHNOZZ
SCHNOZZES
SCHNOZZLE
SCHOLAR
SCHOLARCH
SCHOLARLY
SCHOLARS
SCHOLIA
SCHOLIAST
SCHOLION
SCHOLIUM
SCHOLIUMS
SCHOOL
SCHOOLBAG
SCHOOLBOY
SCHOOLDAY
SCHOOLE
SCHOOLED
SCHOOLER
SCHOOLERS
SCHOOLERY
SCHOOLES
SCHOOLIE
SCHOOLIES
SCHOOLING
SCHOOLKID
SCHOOLMAN
SCHOOLMEN
SCHOOLS
SCHOONER
SCHOONERS
SCHORL
SCHORLS
SCHOUT
SCHOUTS
SCHRIK
SCHRIKS
SCHROD
SCHRODS
SCHTICK
SCHTICKS
SCHTIK
SCHTIKS
SCHTOOK
SCHTOOKS
SCHTOOM
SCHTUCK
SCHTUCKS
SCHTUM
SCHTUP
SCHTUPPED
SCHTUPS
SCHUIT
SCHUITS
SCHUL
SCHULN
SCHULS
SCHUSS
SCHUSSED
SCHUSSER
SCHUSSERS
SCHUSSES
SCHUSSING
SCHUYT
SCHUYTS
SCHVITZ
SCHVITZED
SCHVITZES
SCHWA
SCHWAG
SCHWAGS
SCHWAS
SCIAENID
SCIAENIDS
SCIAENOID
SCIAMACHY
SCIARID
SCIARIDS
SCIATIC
SCIATICA
SCIATICAL
SCIATICAS
SCIATICS
SCIENCE
SCIENCED
SCIENCES
SCIENT
SCIENTER
SCIENTIAL
SCIENTISE
SCIENTISM
SCIENTIST
SCIENTIZE
SCILICET
SCILLA
SCILLAS
SCIMETAR
SCIMETARS
SCIMITAR
SCIMITARS
SCIMITER
SCIMITERS
SCINCOID
SCINCOIDS
SCINTILLA
SCIOLISM
SCIOLISMS
SCIOLIST
SCIOLISTS
SCIOLOUS
SCIOLTO
SCIOMACHY
SCIOMANCY
SCION
SCIONS
SCIOPHYTE
SCIOSOPHY
SCIROC
SCIROCCO
SCIROCCOS
SCIROCS
SCIRRHI
SCIRRHOID
SCIRRHOUS
SCIRRHUS
SCISSEL
SCISSELS
SCISSIL
SCISSILE
SCISSILS
SCISSION
SCISSIONS
SCISSOR
SCISSORED
SCISSORER
SCISSORS
SCISSURE
SCISSURES
SCIURID
SCIURIDS
SCIURINE
SCIURINES
SCIUROID
SCLAFF
SCLAFFED
SCLAFFER
SCLAFFERS
SCLAFFING
SCLAFFS
SCLATE
SCLATED
SCLATES
SCLATING
SCLAUNDER
SCLAVE
SCLAVES
SCLERA
SCLERAE
SCLERAL
SCLERAS
SCLERE
SCLEREID
SCLEREIDE
SCLEREIDS
SCLEREMA
SCLEREMAS
SCLERES
SCLERITE
SCLERITES
SCLERITIC
SCLERITIS
SCLEROID
SCLEROMA
SCLEROMAS
SCLEROSAL
SCLEROSE
SCLEROSED
SCLEROSES
SCLEROSIS
SCLEROTAL
SCLEROTIA
SCLEROTIC
SCLEROTIN
SCLEROUS
SCLIFF
SCLIFFS
SCLIM
SCLIMMED
SCLIMMING
SCLIMS
SCODIER
SCODIEST
SCODY
SCOFF
SCOFFED
SCOFFER
SCOFFERS
SCOFFING
SCOFFINGS
SCOFFLAW
SCOFFLAWS
SCOFFS
SCOG
SCOGGED

SCOGGING
SCOGS
SCOINSON
SCOINSONS
SCOLD
SCOLDABLE
SCOLDED
SCOLDER
SCOLDERS
SCOLDING
SCOLDINGS
SCOLDS
SCOLECES
SCOLECID
SCOLECIDS
SCOLECITE
SCOLECOID
SCOLEX
SCOLIA
SCOLICES
SCOLIOMA
SCOLIOMAS
SCOLION
SCOLIOSES
SCOLIOSIS
SCOLIOTIC
SCOLLOP
SCOLLOPED
SCOLLOPS
SCOLYTID
SCOLYTIDS
SCOLYTOID
SCOMBRID
SCOMBRIDS
SCOMBROID
SCOMFISH
SCONCE
SCONCED
SCONCES
SCONCHEON
SCONCING
SCONE
SCONES
SCONTION
SCONTIONS
SCOOBIES
SCOOBY
SCOOCH
SCOOCHED
SCOOCHES
SCOOCHING
SCOOG
SCOOGED
SCOOGING
SCOOGS
SCOOP
SCOOPABLE
SCOOPED
SCOOPER
SCOOPERS
SCOOPFUL
SCOOPFULS
SCOOPING
SCOOPINGS
SCOOPS
SCOOPSFUL
SCOOSH
SCOOSHED
SCOOSHES
SCOOSHING
SCOOT
SCOOTCH
SCOOTCHED
SCOOTCHES
SCOOTED
SCOOTER
SCOOTERED
SCOOTERS
SCOOTING
SCOOTS
SCOP
SCOPA
SCOPAE
SCOPAS
SCOPATE
SCOPE
SCOPED
SCOPELID
SCOPELIDS
SCOPELOID
SCOPES
SCOPING
SCOPOLINE
SCOPS
SCOPULA
SCOPULAE
SCOPULAS
SCOPULATE
SCORBUTIC
SCORCH
SCORCHED
SCORCHER
SCORCHERS
SCORCHES
SCORCHING
SCORDATO
SCORE
SCORECARD
SCORED
SCORELESS
SCORELINE
SCOREPAD
SCOREPADS
SCORER
SCORERS
SCORES
SCORIA
SCORIAC
SCORIAE
SCORIFIED
SCORIFIER
SCORIFIES
SCORIFY
SCORING
SCORINGS
SCORIOUS
SCORN
SCORNED
SCORNER
SCORNERS
SCORNFUL
SCORNING
SCORNINGS
SCORNS
SCORODITE
SCORPER
SCORPERS
SCORPIOID
SCORPION
SCORPIONS
SCORRENDO
SCORSE
SCORSED
SCORSER
SCORSERS
SCORSES
SCORSING
SCOT
SCOTCH
SCOTCHED
SCOTCHES
SCOTCHING
SCOTER
SCOTERS
SCOTIA
SCOTIAS
SCOTOMA
SCOTOMAS
SCOTOMATA
SCOTOMIA
SCOTOMIAS
SCOTOMIES
SCOTOMY
SCOTOPHIL
SCOTOPIA
SCOTOPIAS
SCOTOPIC
SCOTS
SCOTTIE
SCOTTIES
SCOUG
SCOUGED
SCOUGING
SCOUGS
SCOUNDREL
SCOUP
SCOUPED
SCOUPING
SCOUPS
SCOUR
SCOURED
SCOURER
SCOURERS
SCOURGE
SCOURGED
SCOURGER
SCOURGERS
SCOURGES
SCOURGING
SCOURIE
SCOURIES
SCOURING
SCOURINGS
SCOURS
SCOURSE
SCOURSED
SCOURSES
SCOURSING
SCOUSE
SCOUSER
SCOUSERS
SCOUSES
SCOUT
SCOUTED
SCOUTER
SCOUTERS
SCOUTH
SCOUTHER
SCOUTHERS
SCOUTHERY
SCOUTHS
SCOUTING
SCOUTINGS
SCOUTS
SCOW
SCOWDER
SCOWDERED
SCOWDERS
SCOWED
SCOWING
SCOWL
SCOWLED
SCOWLER
SCOWLERS
SCOWLING
SCOWLS
SCOWP
SCOWPED
SCOWPING
SCOWPS
SCOWRER
SCOWRERS
SCOWRIE
SCOWRIES
SCOWS
SCOWTH
SCOWTHER
SCOWTHERS
SCOWTHS
SCOZZA

SCOZZAS
SCRAB
SCRABBED
SCRABBING
SCRABBLE
SCRABBLED
SCRABBLER
SCRABBLES
SCRABBLY
SCRABS
SCRAE
SCRAES
SCRAG
SCRAGGED
SCRAGGIER
SCRAGGILY
SCRAGGING
SCRAGGLY
SCRAGGY
SCRAGS
SCRAICH
SCRAICHED
SCRAICHS
SCRAIGH
SCRAIGHED
SCRAIGHS
SCRAM
SCRAMB
SCRAMBED
SCRAMBING
SCRAMBLE
SCRAMBLED
SCRAMBLER
SCRAMBLES
SCRAMBS
SCRAMJET
SCRAMJETS
SCRAMMED
SCRAMMING
SCRAMS
SCRAN
SCRANCH
SCRANCHED
SCRANCHES
SCRANNEL
SCRANNELS
SCRANNIER
SCRANNY
SCRANS
SCRAP
SCRAPABLE
SCRAPBOOK
SCRAPE
SCRAPED
SCRAPEGUT
SCRAPER
SCRAPERS
SCRAPES
SCRAPHEAP
SCRAPIE
SCRAPIES
SCRAPING
SCRAPINGS
SCRAPPAGE
SCRAPPED
SCRAPPER
SCRAPPERS
SCRAPPIER
SCRAPPILY
SCRAPPING
SCRAPPLE
SCRAPPLES
SCRAPPY
SCRAPS
SCRAPYARD
SCRAT
SCRATCH
SCRATCHED
SCRATCHER
SCRATCHES
SCRATCHIE
SCRATCHY
SCRATS
SCRATTED
SCRATTING
SCRATTLE
SCRATTLED
SCRATTLES
SCRAUCH
SCRAUCHED
SCRAUCHS
SCRAUGH
SCRAUGHED
SCRAUGHS
SCRAVEL
SCRAVELED
SCRAVELS
SCRAW
SCRAWB
SCRAWBED
SCRAWBING
SCRAWBS
SCRAWL
SCRAWLED
SCRAWLER
SCRAWLERS
SCRAWLIER
SCRAWLING
SCRAWLS
SCRAWLY
SCRAWM
SCRAWMED
SCRAWMING
SCRAWMS
SCRAWNIER
SCRAWNILY
SCRAWNY
SCRAWP
SCRAWPED
SCRAWPING
SCRAWPS
SCRAWS
SCRAY
SCRAYE
SCRAYES
SCRAYS
SCREAK
SCREAKED
SCREAKIER
SCREAKING
SCREAKS
SCREAKY
SCREAM
SCREAMED
SCREAMER
SCREAMERS
SCREAMING
SCREAMO
SCREAMOS
SCREAMS
SCREE
SCREECH
SCREECHED
SCREECHER
SCREECHES
SCREECHY
SCREED
SCREEDED
SCREEDER
SCREEDERS
SCREEDING
SCREEDS
SCREEN
SCREENED
SCREENER
SCREENERS
SCREENFUL
SCREENIE
SCREENIES
SCREENING
SCREENS
SCREES
SCREET
SCREETED
SCREETING
SCREETS
SCREEVE
SCREEVED
SCREEVER
SCREEVERS
SCREEVES
SCREEVING
SCREICH
SCREICHED
SCREICHS
SCREIGH
SCREIGHED
SCREIGHS
SCREW
SCREWABLE
SCREWBALL
SCREWBEAN
SCREWED
SCREWER
SCREWERS
SCREWHEAD
SCREWIER
SCREWIEST
SCREWING
SCREWINGS
SCREWLIKE
SCREWS
SCREWTOP
SCREWTOPS
SCREWUP
SCREWUPS
SCREWWORM
SCREWY
SCRIBABLE
SCRIBAL
SCRIBBLE
SCRIBBLED
SCRIBBLER
SCRIBBLES
SCRIBBLY
SCRIBE
SCRIBED
SCRIBER
SCRIBERS
SCRIBES
SCRIBING
SCRIBINGS
SCRIBISM
SCRIBISMS
SCRIECH
SCRIECHED
SCRIECHS
SCRIED
SCRIENE
SCRIENES
SCRIES
SCRIEVE
SCRIEVED
SCRIEVES
SCRIEVING
SCRIGGLE
SCRIGGLED
SCRIGGLES
SCRIGGLY
SCRIKE
SCRIKED
SCRIKES
SCRIKING
SCRIM
SCRIMMAGE
SCRIMP
SCRIMPED
SCRIMPER
SCRIMPERS
SCRIMPIER

S

SCRIMPILY
SCRIMPING
SCRIMPIT
SCRIMPLY
SCRIMPS
SCRIMPY
SCRIMS
SCRIMSHAW
SCRIMURE
SCRIMURES
SCRINE
SCRINES
SCRIP
SCRIPPAGE
SCRIPS
SCRIPT
SCRIPTED
SCRIPTER
SCRIPTERS
SCRIPTING
SCRIPTORY
SCRIPTS
SCRIPTURE
SCRITCH
SCRITCHED
SCRITCHES
SCRIVE
SCRIVED
SCRIVENER
SCRIVES
SCRIVING
SCROB
SCROBBED
SCROBBING
SCROBBLE
SCROBBLED
SCROBBLES
SCROBE
SCROBES
SCROBS
SCROD
SCRODDLED
SCRODS
SCROFULA
SCROFULAS
SCROG
SCROGGIE
SCROGGIER
SCROGGIN
SCROGGINS
SCROGGY
SCROGS
SCROLL
SCROLLED
SCROLLER
SCROLLERS
SCROLLING
SCROLLS
SCROME
SCROMED
SCROMES
SCROMING
SCROOCH
SCROOCHED
SCROOCHES
SCROOGE
SCROOGED
SCROOGES
SCROOGING
SCROOP
SCROOPED
SCROOPING
SCROOPS
SCROOTCH
SCRORP
SCRORPS
SCROTA
SCROTAL
SCROTE
SCROTES
SCROTUM
SCROTUMS
SCROUGE
SCROUGED
SCROUGER
SCROUGERS
SCROUGES
SCROUGING
SCROUNGE
SCROUNGED
SCROUNGER
SCROUNGES
SCROUNGY
SCROW
SCROWDGE
SCROWDGED
SCROWDGES
SCROWL
SCROWLE
SCROWLED
SCROWLES
SCROWLING
SCROWLS
SCROWS
SCROYLE
SCROYLES
SCRUB
SCRUBBED
SCRUBBER
SCRUBBERS
SCRUBBIER
SCRUBBILY
SCRUBBING
SCRUBBY
SCRUBLAND
SCRUBS
SCRUFF
SCRUFFED
SCRUFFIER
SCRUFFILY
SCRUFFING
SCRUFFS
SCRUFFY
SCRUM
SCRUMDOWN
SCRUMMAGE
SCRUMMED
SCRUMMIE
SCRUMMIER
SCRUMMIES
SCRUMMING
SCRUMMY
SCRUMP
SCRUMPED
SCRUMPIES
SCRUMPING
SCRUMPLE
SCRUMPLED
SCRUMPLES
SCRUMPOX
SCRUMPS
SCRUMPY
SCRUMS
SCRUNCH
SCRUNCHED
SCRUNCHES
SCRUNCHIE
SCRUNCHIN
SCRUNCHY
SCRUNT
SCRUNTIER
SCRUNTS
SCRUNTY
SCRUPLE
SCRUPLED
SCRUPLER
SCRUPLERS
SCRUPLES
SCRUPLING
SCRUTABLE
SCRUTATOR
SCRUTINY
SCRUTO
SCRUTOIRE
SCRUTOS
SCRUZE
SCRUZED
SCRUZES
SCRUZING
SCRY
SCRYDE
SCRYER
SCRYERS
SCRYING
SCRYINGS
SCRYNE
SCRYNES
SCUBA
SCUBAED
SCUBAING
SCUBAS
SCUCHIN
SCUCHINS
SCUD
SCUDDALER
SCUDDED
SCUDDER
SCUDDERS
SCUDDING
SCUDDLE
SCUDDLED
SCUDDLES
SCUDDLING
SCUDI
SCUDLER
SCUDLERS
SCUDO
SCUDS
SCUFF
SCUFFED
SCUFFER
SCUFFERS
SCUFFING
SCUFFLE
SCUFFLED
SCUFFLER
SCUFFLERS
SCUFFLES
SCUFFLING
SCUFFS
SCUFT
SCUFTS
SCUG
SCUGGED
SCUGGING
SCUGS
SCUL
SCULCH
SCULCHES
SCULK
SCULKED
SCULKER
SCULKERS
SCULKING
SCULKS
SCULL
SCULLE
SCULLED
SCULLER
SCULLERS
SCULLERY
SCULLES
SCULLING
SCULLINGS
SCULLION
SCULLIONS
SCULLS
SCULP
SCULPED
SCULPIN

S

SCULPING
SCULPINS
SCULPS
SCULPSIT
SCULPT
SCULPTED
SCULPTING
SCULPTOR
SCULPTORS
SCULPTS
SCULPTURE
SCULS
SCULTCH
SCULTCHES
SCUM
SCUMBAG
SCUMBAGS
SCUMBALL
SCUMBALLS
SCUMBER
SCUMBERED
SCUMBERS
SCUMBLE
SCUMBLED
SCUMBLES
SCUMBLING
SCUMFISH
SCUMLESS
SCUMLIKE
SCUMMED
SCUMMER
SCUMMERS
SCUMMIER
SCUMMIEST
SCUMMILY
SCUMMING
SCUMMINGS
SCUMMY
SCUMS
SCUNCHEON
SCUNDERED
SCUNGE
SCUNGED
SCUNGES
SCUNGIER
SCUNGIEST
SCUNGILE
SCUNGILI
SCUNGILLE
SCUNGILLI
SCUNGING
SCUNGY
SCUNNER
SCUNNERED
SCUNNERS
SCUP
SCUPPAUG
SCUPPAUGS
SCUPPER
SCUPPERED
SCUPPERS
SCUPS
SCUR
SCURF
SCURFIER
SCURFIEST
SCURFS
SCURFY
SCURRED
SCURRIED
SCURRIER
SCURRIERS
SCURRIES
SCURRIL
SCURRILE
SCURRING
SCURRIOUR
SCURRY
SCURRYING
SCURS
SCURVIER
SCURVIES
SCURVIEST
SCURVILY
SCURVY
SCUSE
SCUSED
SCUSES
SCUSING
SCUT
SCUTA
SCUTAGE
SCUTAGES
SCUTAL
SCUTATE
SCUTATION
SCUTCH
SCUTCHED
SCUTCHEON
SCUTCHER
SCUTCHERS
SCUTCHES
SCUTCHING
SCUTE
SCUTELLA
SCUTELLAR
SCUTELLUM
SCUTES
SCUTIFORM
SCUTIGER
SCUTIGERS
SCUTS
SCUTTER
SCUTTERED
SCUTTERS
SCUTTLE
SCUTTLED
SCUTTLER
SCUTTLERS
SCUTTLES
SCUTTLING
SCUTUM
SCUTWORK
SCUTWORKS
SCUZZ
SCUZZBAG
SCUZZBAGS
SCUZZBALL
SCUZZES
SCUZZIER
SCUZZIEST
SCUZZY
SCYBALA
SCYBALOUS
SCYBALUM
SCYE
SCYES
SCYPHATE
SCYPHI
SCYPHUS
SCYTALE
SCYTALES
SCYTHE
SCYTHED
SCYTHEMAN
SCYTHEMEN
SCYTHER
SCYTHERS
SCYTHES
SCYTHING
SDAINE
SDAINED
SDAINES
SDAINING
SDAYN
SDAYNED
SDAYNING
SDAYNS
SDEIGN
SDEIGNE
SDEIGNED
SDEIGNES
SDEIGNING
SDEIGNS
SDEIN
SDEINED
SDEINING
SDEINS
SEA
SEABAG
SEABAGS
SEABANK
SEABANKS
SEABEACH
SEABED
SEABEDS
SEABIRD
SEABIRDS
SEABLITE
SEABLITES
SEABOARD
SEABOARDS
SEABOOT
SEABOOTS
SEABORNE
SEABOTTLE
SEABREAM
SEABREAMS
SEACOAST
SEACOASTS
SEACOCK
SEACOCKS
SEACRAFT
SEACRAFTS
SEACUNNY
SEADOG
SEADOGS
SEADROME
SEADROMES
SEAFARER
SEAFARERS
SEAFARING
SEAFLOOR
SEAFLOORS
SEAFOAM
SEAFOAMS
SEAFOLK
SEAFOLKS
SEAFOOD
SEAFOODS
SEAFOWL
SEAFOWLS
SEAFRONT
SEAFRONTS
SEAGIRT
SEAGOING
SEAGRASS
SEAGULL
SEAGULLS
SEAHAWK
SEAHAWKS
SEAHOG
SEAHOGS
SEAHORSE
SEAHORSES
SEAHOUND
SEAHOUNDS
SEAKALE
SEAKALES
SEAKINDLY
SEAL
SEALABLE
SEALANT
SEALANTS
SEALCH
SEALCHS
SEALED
SEALER
SEALERIES
SEALERS

S

SEALERY
SEALGH
SEALGHS
SEALIFT
SEALIFTED
SEALIFTS
SEALINE
SEALINES
SEALING
SEALINGS
SEALLIKE
SEALPOINT
SEALS
SEALSKIN
SEALSKINS
SEALWAX
SEALWAXES
SEALYHAM
SEALYHAMS
SEAM
SEAMAID
SEAMAIDS
SEAMAN
SEAMANLY
SEAMARK
SEAMARKS
SEAME
SEAMED
SEAMEN
SEAMER
SEAMERS
SEAMES
SEAMFREE
SEAMIER
SEAMIEST
SEAMINESS
SEAMING
SEAMINGS
SEAMLESS
SEAMLIKE
SEAMOUNT
SEAMOUNTS
SEAMS
SEAMSET
SEAMSETS
SEAMSTER
SEAMSTERS
SEAMY
SEAN
SEANCE
SEANCES
SEANED
SEANING
SEANNACHY
SEANS
SEAPIECE
SEAPIECES
SEAPLANE
SEAPLANES
SEAPORT
SEAPORTS
SEAQUAKE
SEAQUAKES
SEAQUARIA
SEAR
SEARAT
SEARATS
SEARCE
SEARCED
SEARCES
SEARCH
SEARCHED
SEARCHER
SEARCHERS
SEARCHES
SEARCHING
SEARCING
SEARE
SEARED
SEARER
SEAREST
SEARING
SEARINGLY
SEARINGS
SEARNESS
SEAROBIN
SEAROBINS
SEARS
SEAS
SEASCAPE
SEASCAPES
SEASCOUT
SEASCOUTS
SEASE
SEASED
SEASES
SEASHELL
SEASHELLS
SEASHORE
SEASHORES
SEASICK
SEASICKER
SEASIDE
SEASIDES
SEASING
SEASON
SEASONAL
SEASONALS
SEASONED
SEASONER
SEASONERS
SEASONING
SEASONS
SEASPEAK
SEASPEAKS
SEASTRAND
SEASURE
SEASURES
SEAT
SEATBACK
SEATBACKS
SEATBELT
SEATBELTS
SEATED
SEATER
SEATERS
SEATING
SEATINGS
SEATLESS
SEATMATE
SEATMATES
SEATRAIN
SEATRAINS
SEATROUT
SEATROUTS
SEATS
SEATWORK
SEATWORKS
SEAWALL
SEAWALLED
SEAWALLS
SEAWAN
SEAWANS
SEAWANT
SEAWANTS
SEAWARD
SEAWARDLY
SEAWARDS
SEAWARE
SEAWARES
SEAWATER
SEAWATERS
SEAWAY
SEAWAYS
SEAWEED
SEAWEEDS
SEAWEEDY
SEAWIFE
SEAWIVES
SEAWOMAN
SEAWOMEN
SEAWORM
SEAWORMS
SEAWORTHY
SEAZE
SEAZED
SEAZES
SEAZING
SEBACEOUS
SEBACIC
SEBASIC
SEBATE
SEBATES
SEBESTEN
SEBESTENS
SEBIFIC
SEBORRHEA
SEBUM
SEBUMS
SEBUNDIES
SEBUNDY
SEC
SECALOSE
SECALOSES
SECANT
SECANTLY
SECANTS
SECATEUR
SECATEURS
SECCO
SECCOS
SECEDE
SECEDED
SECEDER
SECEDERS
SECEDES
SECEDING
SECERN
SECERNED
SECERNENT
SECERNING
SECERNS
SECESH
SECESHER
SECESHERS
SECESHES
SECESSION
SECH
SECHS
SECKEL
SECKELS
SECKLE
SECKLES
SECLUDE
SECLUDED
SECLUDES
SECLUDING
SECLUSION
SECLUSIVE
SECO
SECODONT
SECODONTS
SECONAL
SECONALS
SECOND
SECONDARY
SECONDE
SECONDED
SECONDEE
SECONDEES
SECONDER
SECONDERS
SECONDES
SECONDI
SECONDING
SECONDLY
SECONDO
SECONDS
SECPAR
SECPARS

SECRECIES
SECRECY
SECRET
SECRETA
SECRETAGE
SECRETARY
SECRETE
SECRETED
SECRETER
SECRETES
SECRETEST
SECRETIN
SECRETING
SECRETINS
SECRETION
SECRETIVE
SECRETLY
SECRETOR
SECRETORS
SECRETORY
SECRETS
SECS
SECT
SECTARIAL
SECTARIAN
SECTARIES
SECTARY
SECTATOR
SECTATORS
SECTILE
SECTILITY
SECTION
SECTIONAL
SECTIONED
SECTIONS
SECTOR
SECTORAL
SECTORED
SECTORIAL
SECTORING
SECTORISE
SECTORIZE
SECTORS
SECTS
SECULA
SECULAR
SECULARLY
SECULARS
SECULUM
SECULUMS
SECUND
SECUNDINE
SECUNDLY
SECUNDUM
SECURABLE
SECURANCE
SECURE
SECURED
SECURELY
SECURER
SECURERS
SECURES
SECUREST
SECURING
SECURITAN
SECURITY
SED
SEDAN
SEDANS
SEDARIM
SEDATE
SEDATED
SEDATELY
SEDATER
SEDATES
SEDATEST
SEDATING
SEDATION
SEDATIONS
SEDATIVE
SEDATIVES
SEDENT
SEDENTARY
SEDER
SEDERS
SEDERUNT
SEDERUNTS
SEDES
SEDGE
SEDGED
SEDGELAND
SEDGES
SEDGIER
SEDGIEST
SEDGY
SEDILE
SEDILIA
SEDILIUM
SEDIMENT
SEDIMENTS
SEDITION
SEDITIONS
SEDITIOUS
SEDUCE
SEDUCED
SEDUCER
SEDUCERS
SEDUCES
SEDUCIBLE
SEDUCING
SEDUCINGS
SEDUCIVE
SEDUCTION
SEDUCTIVE
SEDUCTOR
SEDUCTORS
SEDULITY
SEDULOUS
SEDUM
SEDUMS
SEE
SEEABLE
SEECATCH
SEED
SEEDBED
SEEDBEDS
SEEDBOX
SEEDBOXES
SEEDCAKE
SEEDCAKES
SEEDCASE
SEEDCASES
SEEDEATER
SEEDED
SEEDER
SEEDERS
SEEDHEAD
SEEDHEADS
SEEDIER
SEEDIEST
SEEDILY
SEEDINESS
SEEDING
SEEDINGS
SEEDLESS
SEEDLIKE
SEEDLING
SEEDLINGS
SEEDLIP
SEEDLIPS
SEEDMAN
SEEDMEN
SEEDNESS
SEEDPOD
SEEDPODS
SEEDS
SEEDSMAN
SEEDSMEN
SEEDSTOCK
SEEDTIME
SEEDTIMES
SEEDY
SEEING
SEEINGS
SEEK
SEEKER
SEEKERS
SEEKING
SEEKS
SEEL
SEELD
SEELED
SEELIE
SEELIER
SEELIEST
SEELING
SEELINGS
SEELS
SEELY
SEEM
SEEMED
SEEMER
SEEMERS
SEEMING
SEEMINGLY
SEEMINGS
SEEMLESS
SEEMLIER
SEEMLIEST
SEEMLIHED
SEEMLY
SEEMLYHED
SEEMS
SEEN
SEEP
SEEPAGE
SEEPAGES
SEEPED
SEEPIER
SEEPIEST
SEEPING
SEEPS
SEEPY
SEER
SEERESS
SEERESSES
SEERS
SEES
SEESAW
SEESAWED
SEESAWING
SEESAWS
SEETHE
SEETHED
SEETHER
SEETHERS
SEETHES
SEETHING
SEETHINGS
SEEWING
SEEWINGS
SEFER
SEG
SEGAR
SEGARS
SEGETAL
SEGGAR
SEGGARS
SEGHOL
SEGHOLATE
SEGHOLS
SEGMENT
SEGMENTAL
SEGMENTED
SEGMENTS
SEGNI
SEGNO
SEGNOS
SEGO
SEGOL

S

SEGOLATE
SEGOLATES
SEGOLS
SEGOS
SEGREANT
SEGREGANT
SEGREGATE
SEGS
SEGUE
SEGUED
SEGUEING
SEGUES
SEGUGIO
SEGUGIOS
SEHRI
SEHRIS
SEI
SEICENTO
SEICENTOS
SEICHE
SEICHES
SEIDEL
SEIDELS
SEIF
SEIFS
SEIGNEUR
SEIGNEURS
SEIGNEURY
SEIGNIOR
SEIGNIORS
SEIGNIORY
SEIGNORAL
SEIGNORY
SEIK
SEIKER
SEIKEST
SEIL
SEILED
SEILING
SEILS
SEINE
SEINED
SEINER
SEINERS
SEINES
SEINING
SEININGS
SEIR
SEIRS
SEIS
SEISABLE
SEISE
SEISED
SEISER
SEISERS
SEISES
SEISIN
SEISING
SEISINGS
SEISINS
SEISM
SEISMAL
SEISMIC
SEISMICAL
SEISMISM
SEISMISMS
SEISMS
SEISOR
SEISORS
SEISURE
SEISURES
SEITAN
SEITANS
SEITEN
SEITENS
SEITIES
SEITY
SEIZA
SEIZABLE
SEIZAS
SEIZE
SEIZED
SEIZER
SEIZERS
SEIZES
SEIZIN
SEIZING
SEIZINGS
SEIZINS
SEIZOR
SEIZORS
SEIZURE
SEIZURES
SEJANT
SEJEANT
SEKOS
SEKOSES
SEKT
SEKTS
SEL
SELACHIAN
SELADANG
SELADANGS
SELAH
SELAHS
SELAMLIK
SELAMLIKS
SELCOUTH
SELD
SELDOM
SELDOMLY
SELDSEEN
SELDSHOWN
SELE
SELECT
SELECTA
SELECTAS
SELECTED
SELECTEE
SELECTEES
SELECTING
SELECTION
SELECTIVE
SELECTLY
SELECTMAN
SELECTMEN
SELECTOR
SELECTORS
SELECTS
SELENATE
SELENATES
SELENIAN
SELENIC
SELENIDE
SELENIDES
SELENIOUS
SELENITE
SELENITES
SELENITIC
SELENIUM
SELENIUMS
SELENOSES
SELENOSIS
SELENOUS
SELES
SELF
SELFDOM
SELFDOMS
SELFED
SELFHEAL
SELFHEALS
SELFHOOD
SELFHOODS
SELFIE
SELFIES
SELFING
SELFINGS
SELFISH
SELFISHLY
SELFISM
SELFISMS
SELFIST
SELFISTS
SELFLESS
SELFNESS
SELFS
SELFSAME
SELFWARD
SELFWARDS
SELICTAR
SELICTARS
SELKIE
SELKIES
SELL
SELLA
SELLABLE
SELLAE
SELLAS
SELLE
SELLER
SELLERS
SELLES
SELLING
SELLINGS
SELLOFF
SELLOFFS
SELLOTAPE
SELLOUT
SELLOUTS
SELLS
SELS
SELSYN
SELSYNS
SELTZER
SELTZERS
SELVA
SELVAGE
SELVAGED
SELVAGEE
SELVAGEES
SELVAGES
SELVAGING
SELVAS
SELVEDGE
SELVEDGED
SELVEDGES
SELVES
SEMAINIER
SEMANTEME
SEMANTIC
SEMANTICS
SEMANTIDE
SEMANTRA
SEMANTRON
SEMAPHORE
SEMATIC
SEMBLABLE
SEMBLABLY
SEMBLANCE
SEMBLANT
SEMBLANTS
SEMBLE
SEMBLED
SEMBLES
SEMBLING
SEME
SEMEE
SEMEED
SEMEIA
SEMEION
SEMEIOTIC
SEMEME
SEMEMES
SEMEMIC
SEMEN
SEMENS
SEMES
SEMESTER
SEMESTERS
SEMESTRAL

SEMI
SEMIANGLE
SEMIARID
SEMIBALD
SEMIBOLD
SEMIBOLDS
SEMIBREVE
SEMIBULL
SEMIBULLS
SEMICOLON
SEMICOMA
SEMICOMAS
SEMICURED
SEMIDEAF
SEMIDEIFY
SEMIDOME
SEMIDOMED
SEMIDOMES
SEMIDRIER
SEMIDRY
SEMIDWARF
SEMIE
SEMIERECT
SEMIES
SEMIFINAL
SEMIFIT
SEMIFLUID
SEMIGALA
SEMIGALAS
SEMIGLOBE
SEMIGLOSS
SEMIGROUP
SEMIHARD
SEMIHIGH
SEMIHOBO
SEMIHOBOS
SEMILLON
SEMILLONS
SEMILOG
SEMILUNAR
SEMILUNE
SEMILUNES
SEMIMAT
SEMIMATT
SEMIMATTE
SEMIMETAL
SEMIMICRO
SEMIMILD
SEMIMOIST
SEMINA
SEMINAL
SEMINALLY
SEMINAR
SEMINARS
SEMINARY
SEMINATE
SEMINATED
SEMINATES
SEMINOMA
SEMINOMAD
SEMINOMAS
SEMINUDE
SEMIOLOGY
SEMIOPEN
SEMIOSES
SEMIOSIS
SEMIOTIC
SEMIOTICS
SEMIOVAL
SEMIPED
SEMIPEDS
SEMIPIOUS
SEMIPLUME
SEMIPOLAR
SEMIPRO
SEMIPROS
SEMIRAW
SEMIRIGID
SEMIROUND
SEMIRURAL
SEMIS
SEMISES
SEMISOFT
SEMISOLID
SEMISOLUS
SEMISTIFF
SEMISWEET
SEMITAR
SEMITARS
SEMITAUR
SEMITAURS
SEMITIST
SEMITISTS
SEMITONAL
SEMITONE
SEMITONES
SEMITONIC
SEMITRUCK
SEMIURBAN
SEMIVOCAL
SEMIVOWEL
SEMIWATER
SEMIWILD
SEMIWORKS
SEMMIT
SEMMITS
SEMOLINA
SEMOLINAS
SEMPER
SEMPLE
SEMPLER
SEMPLEST
SEMPLICE
SEMPRE
SEMPSTER
SEMPSTERS
SEMSEM
SEMSEMS
SEMUNCIA
SEMUNCIAE
SEMUNCIAL
SEMUNCIAS
SEN
SENA
SENARIES
SENARII
SENARIUS
SENARY
SENAS
SENATE
SENATES
SENATOR
SENATORS
SEND
SENDABLE
SENDAL
SENDALS
SENDED
SENDER
SENDERS
SENDING
SENDINGS
SENDOFF
SENDOFFS
SENDS
SENDUP
SENDUPS
SENE
SENECA
SENECAS
SENECIO
SENECIOS
SENEGA
SENEGAS
SENES
SENESCE
SENESCED
SENESCENT
SENESCES
SENESCHAL
SENESCING
SENGI
SENGIS
SENGREEN
SENGREENS
SENHOR
SENHORA
SENHORAS
SENHORES
SENHORITA
SENHORS
SENILE
SENILELY
SENILES
SENILITY
SENIOR
SENIORITY
SENIORS
SENITI
SENITIS
SENNA
SENNACHIE
SENNAS
SENNET
SENNETS
SENNIGHT
SENNIGHTS
SENNIT
SENNITS
SENOPIA
SENOPIAS
SENOR
SENORA
SENORAS
SENORES
SENORITA
SENORITAS
SENORS
SENRYU
SENS
SENSA
SENSATE
SENSATED
SENSATELY
SENSATES
SENSATING
SENSATION
SENSE
SENSED
SENSEFUL
SENSEI
SENSEIS
SENSELESS
SENSES
SENSI
SENSIBLE
SENSIBLER
SENSIBLES
SENSIBLY
SENSILE
SENSILLA
SENSILLAE
SENSILLUM
SENSING
SENSINGS
SENSIS
SENSISM
SENSISMS
SENSIST
SENSISTS
SENSITISE
SENSITIVE
SENSITIZE
SENSOR
SENSORIA
SENSORIAL
SENSORILY
SENSORIUM
SENSORS
SENSORY

S

SENSUAL
SENSUALLY
SENSUM
SENSUOUS
SENT
SENTE
SENTED
SENTENCE
SENTENCED
SENTENCER
SENTENCES
SENTENTIA
SENTI
SENTIENCE
SENTIENCY
SENTIENT
SENTIENTS
SENTIMENT
SENTIMO
SENTIMOS
SENTINEL
SENTINELS
SENTING
SENTRIES
SENTRY
SENTS
SENVIES
SENVY
SENZA
SEPAD
SEPADDED
SEPADDING
SEPADS
SEPAL
SEPALED
SEPALINE
SEPALLED
SEPALODY
SEPALOID
SEPALOUS
SEPALS
SEPARABLE
SEPARABLY
SEPARATA
SEPARATE
SEPARATED
SEPARATES
SEPARATOR
SEPARATUM
SEPHEN
SEPHENS
SEPIA
SEPIAS
SEPIC
SEPIMENT
SEPIMENTS
SEPIOLITE
SEPIOST
SEPIOSTS
SEPIUM
SEPIUMS
SEPMAG
SEPOY
SEPOYS
SEPPUKU
SEPPUKUS
SEPS
SEPSES
SEPSIS
SEPT
SEPTA
SEPTAGE
SEPTAGES
SEPTAL
SEPTARIA
SEPTARIAN
SEPTARIUM
SEPTATE
SEPTATION
SEPTEMFID
SEPTEMVIR
SEPTENARY
SEPTENNIA
SEPTET
SEPTETS
SEPTETTE
SEPTETTES
SEPTIC
SEPTICAL
SEPTICITY
SEPTICS
SEPTIFORM
SEPTIMAL
SEPTIME
SEPTIMES
SEPTIMOLE
SEPTLEVA
SEPTLEVAS
SEPTORIA
SEPTORIAS
SEPTS
SEPTUM
SEPTUMS
SEPTUOR
SEPTUORS
SEPTUPLE
SEPTUPLED
SEPTUPLES
SEPTUPLET
SEPULCHER
SEPULCHRE
SEPULTURE
SEQUACITY
SEQUEL
SEQUELA
SEQUELAE
SEQUELISE
SEQUELIZE
SEQUELS
SEQUENCE
SEQUENCED
SEQUENCER
SEQUENCES
SEQUENCY
SEQUENT
SEQUENTLY
SEQUENTS
SEQUESTER
SEQUESTRA
SEQUIN
SEQUINED
SEQUINING
SEQUINNED
SEQUINS
SEQUITUR
SEQUITURS
SEQUOIA
SEQUOIAS
SER
SERA
SERAC
SERACS
SERAFILE
SERAFILES
SERAFIN
SERAFINS
SERAGLIO
SERAGLIOS
SERAI
SERAIL
SERAILS
SERAIS
SERAL
SERANG
SERANGS
SERAPE
SERAPES
SERAPH
SERAPHIC
SERAPHIM
SERAPHIMS
SERAPHIN
SERAPHINE
SERAPHINS
SERAPHS
SERASKIER
SERDAB
SERDABS
SERE
SERED
SEREIN
SEREINS
SERENADE
SERENADED
SERENADER
SERENADES
SERENATA
SERENATAS
SERENATE
SERENATED
SERENATES
SERENE
SERENED
SERENELY
SERENER
SERENES
SERENEST
SERENING
SERENITY
SERER
SERES
SEREST
SERF
SERFAGE
SERFAGES
SERFDOM
SERFDOMS
SERFHOOD
SERFHOODS
SERFISH
SERFLIKE
SERFS
SERFSHIP
SERFSHIPS
SERGE
SERGEANCY
SERGEANT
SERGEANTS
SERGEANTY
SERGED
SERGER
SERGERS
SERGES
SERGING
SERGINGS
SERIAL
SERIALISE
SERIALISM
SERIALIST
SERIALITY
SERIALIZE
SERIALLY
SERIALS
SERIATE
SERIATED
SERIATELY
SERIATES
SERIATIM
SERIATING
SERIATION
SERIC
SERICEOUS
SERICIN
SERICINS
SERICITE
SERICITES
SERICITIC
SERICON
SERICONS
SERIEMA

SERIEMAS
SERIES
SERIF
SERIFED
SERIFFED
SERIFS
SERIGRAPH
SERIN
SERINE
SERINES
SERINETTE
SERING
SERINGA
SERINGAS
SERINS
SERIOUS
SERIOUSLY
SERIPH
SERIPHS
SERJEANCY
SERJEANT
SERJEANTS
SERJEANTY
SERK
SERKALI
SERKALIS
SERKS
SERMON
SERMONED
SERMONEER
SERMONER
SERMONERS
SERMONET
SERMONETS
SERMONIC
SERMONING
SERMONISE
SERMONIZE
SERMONS
SEROGROUP
SEROLOGIC
SEROLOGY
SEROMA
SEROMAS
SERON
SERONS
SEROON
SEROONS
SEROPUS
SEROPUSES
SEROSA
SEROSAE
SEROSAL
SEROSAS
SEROSITY
SEROTINAL
SEROTINE
SEROTINES
SEROTINY
SEROTONIN
SEROTYPE
SEROTYPED
SEROTYPES
SEROTYPIC
SEROUS
SEROVAR
SEROVARS
SEROW
SEROWS
SERPENT
SERPENTRY
SERPENTS
SERPIGO
SERPIGOES
SERPIGOS
SERPULA
SERPULAE
SERPULAS
SERPULID
SERPULIDS
SERPULITE
SERR
SERRA
SERRAE
SERRAN
SERRANID
SERRANIDS
SERRANO
SERRANOID
SERRANOS
SERRANS
SERRAS
SERRATE
SERRATED
SERRATES
SERRATI
SERRATING
SERRATION
SERRATURE
SERRATUS
SERRE
SERRED
SERREFILE
SERRES
SERRICORN
SERRIED
SERRIEDLY
SERRIES
SERRIFORM
SERRING
SERRS
SERRULATE
SERRY
SERRYING
SERS
SERUEWE
SERUEWED
SERUEWES
SERUEWING
SERUM
SERUMAL
SERUMS
SERVABLE
SERVAL
SERVALS
SERVANT
SERVANTED
SERVANTRY
SERVANTS
SERVE
SERVEABLE
SERVED
SERVER
SERVERIES
SERVERS
SERVERY
SERVES
SERVEWARE
SERVEWE
SERVEWED
SERVEWES
SERVEWING
SERVICE
SERVICED
SERVICER
SERVICERS
SERVICES
SERVICING
SERVIENT
SERVIETTE
SERVILE
SERVILELY
SERVILES
SERVILISM
SERVILITY
SERVING
SERVINGS
SERVITOR
SERVITORS
SERVITUDE
SERVLET
SERVLETS
SERVO
SERVOS
SERVQUAL
SERVQUALS
SESAME
SESAMES
SESAMOID
SESAMOIDS
SESE
SESELI
SESELIS
SESEY
SESH
SESHES
SESS
SESSA
SESSED
SESSES
SESSILE
SESSILITY
SESSING
SESSION
SESSIONAL
SESSIONS
SESSPOOL
SESSPOOLS
SESTERCE
SESTERCES
SESTERTIA
SESTERTII
SESTET
SESTETS
SESTETT
SESTETTE
SESTETTES
SESTETTO
SESTETTOS
SESTETTS
SESTINA
SESTINAS
SESTINE
SESTINES
SESTON
SESTONS
SET
SETA
SETACEOUS
SETAE
SETAL
SETBACK
SETBACKS
SETENANT
SETENANTS
SETIFORM
SETLINE
SETLINES
SETNESS
SETNESSES
SETOFF
SETOFFS
SETON
SETONS
SETOSE
SETOUS
SETOUT
SETOUTS
SETS
SETSCREW
SETSCREWS
SETT
SETTEE
SETTEES
SETTER
SETTERED
SETTERING
SETTERS
SETTING
SETTINGS

SETTLE
SETTLED
SETTLER
SETTLERS
SETTLES
SETTLING
SETTLINGS
SETTLOR
SETTLORS
SETTS
SETUALE
SETUALES
SETULE
SETULES
SETULOSE
SETULOUS
SETUP
SETUPS
SETWALL
SETWALLS
SEV
SEVEN
SEVENFOLD
SEVENISH
SEVENS
SEVENTEEN
SEVENTH
SEVENTHLY
SEVENTHS
SEVENTIES
SEVENTY
SEVER
SEVERABLE
SEVERAL
SEVERALLY
SEVERALS
SEVERALTY
SEVERANCE
SEVERE
SEVERED
SEVERELY
SEVERER
SEVEREST
SEVERIES
SEVERING
SEVERITY
SEVERS
SEVERY
SEVICHE
SEVICHES
SEVRUGA
SEVRUGAS
SEVS
SEW
SEWABLE
SEWAGE
SEWAGES
SEWAN
SEWANS
SEWAR
SEWARS
SEWED
SEWEL
SEWELLEL
SEWELLELS
SEWELS
SEWEN
SEWENS
SEWER
SEWERAGE
SEWERAGES
SEWERED
SEWERING
SEWERINGS
SEWERLESS
SEWERLIKE
SEWERS
SEWIN
SEWING
SEWINGS
SEWINS
SEWN
SEWS
SEX
SEXAHOLIC
SEXCAPADE
SEXED
SEXENNIAL
SEXER
SEXERCISE
SEXERS
SEXES
SEXFID
SEXFOIL
SEXFOILS
SEXIER
SEXIEST
SEXILY
SEXINESS
SEXING
SEXINGS
SEXISM
SEXISMS
SEXIST
SEXISTS
SEXLESS
SEXLESSLY
SEXLINKED
SEXOLOGIC
SEXOLOGY
SEXPERT
SEXPERTS
SEXPOT
SEXPOTS
SEXT
SEXTAIN
SEXTAINS
SEXTAN
SEXTANS
SEXTANSES
SEXTANT
SEXTANTAL
SEXTANTS
SEXTARII
SEXTARIUS
SEXTED
SEXTET
SEXTETS
SEXTETT
SEXTETTE
SEXTETTES
SEXTETTS
SEXTILE
SEXTILES
SEXTING
SEXTINGS
SEXTO
SEXTOLET
SEXTOLETS
SEXTON
SEXTONESS
SEXTONS
SEXTOS
SEXTS
SEXTUOR
SEXTUORS
SEXTUPLE
SEXTUPLED
SEXTUPLES
SEXTUPLET
SEXTUPLY
SEXUAL
SEXUALISE
SEXUALISM
SEXUALIST
SEXUALITY
SEXUALIZE
SEXUALLY
SEXVALENT
SEXY
SEY
SEYEN
SEYENS
SEYS
SEYSURE
SEYSURES
SEZ
SFERICS
SFORZANDI
SFORZANDO
SFORZATI
SFORZATO
SFORZATOS
SFUMATO
SFUMATOS
SGRAFFITI
SGRAFFITO
SH
SHA
SHABASH
SHABBATOT
SHABBIER
SHABBIEST
SHABBILY
SHABBLE
SHABBLES
SHABBY
SHABRACK
SHABRACKS
SHACK
SHACKED
SHACKIER
SHACKIEST
SHACKING
SHACKLE
SHACKLED
SHACKLER
SHACKLERS
SHACKLES
SHACKLING
SHACKO
SHACKOES
SHACKOS
SHACKS
SHACKTOWN
SHACKY
SHAD
SHADBERRY
SHADBLOW
SHADBLOWS
SHADBUSH
SHADCHAN
SHADCHANS
SHADDOCK
SHADDOCKS
SHADDUP
SHADE
SHADED
SHADELESS
SHADER
SHADERS
SHADES
SHADFLIES
SHADFLY
SHADIER
SHADIEST
SHADILY
SHADINESS
SHADING
SHADINGS
SHADKHAN
SHADKHANS
SHADOOF
SHADOOFS
SHADOW
SHADOWBOX
SHADOWED
SHADOWER
SHADOWERS
SHADOWIER

S

SHADOWILY
SHADOWING
SHADOWS
SHADOWY
SHADRACH
SHADRACHS
SHADS
SHADUF
SHADUFS
SHADY
SHAFT
SHAFTED
SHAFTER
SHAFTERS
SHAFTING
SHAFTINGS
SHAFTLESS
SHAFTS
SHAG
SHAGBARK
SHAGBARKS
SHAGGABLE
SHAGGED
SHAGGER
SHAGGERS
SHAGGIER
SHAGGIEST
SHAGGILY
SHAGGING
SHAGGY
SHAGPILE
SHAGREEN
SHAGREENS
SHAGROON
SHAGROONS
SHAGS
SHAH
SHAHADA
SHAHADAH
SHAHADAHS
SHAHADAS
SHAHDOM
SHAHDOMS
SHAHEED
SHAHEEDS
SHAHID
SHAHIDS
SHAHS
SHAHTOOSH
SHAIKH
SHAIKHS
SHAIRD
SHAIRDS
SHAIRN
SHAIRNS
SHAITAN
SHAITANS
SHAKABLE
SHAKE
SHAKEABLE
SHAKED
SHAKEDOWN
SHAKEN
SHAKEOUT
SHAKEOUTS
SHAKER
SHAKERS
SHAKES
SHAKEUP
SHAKEUPS
SHAKIER
SHAKIEST
SHAKILY
SHAKINESS
SHAKING
SHAKINGS
SHAKO
SHAKOES
SHAKOS
SHAKT
SHAKUDO
SHAKUDOS
SHAKY
SHALE
SHALED
SHALELIKE
SHALES
SHALEY
SHALIER
SHALIEST
SHALING
SHALL
SHALLI
SHALLIS
SHALLON
SHALLONS
SHALLOON
SHALLOONS
SHALLOP
SHALLOPS
SHALLOT
SHALLOTS
SHALLOW
SHALLOWED
SHALLOWER
SHALLOWLY
SHALLOWS
SHALM
SHALMS
SHALOM
SHALOMS
SHALOT
SHALOTS
SHALT
SHALWAR
SHALWARS
SHALY
SHAM
SHAMA
SHAMABLE
SHAMABLY
SHAMAL
SHAMALS
SHAMAN
SHAMANIC
SHAMANISM
SHAMANIST
SHAMANS
SHAMAS
SHAMATEUR
SHAMBA
SHAMBAS
SHAMBLE
SHAMBLED
SHAMBLES
SHAMBLIER
SHAMBLING
SHAMBLY
SHAMBOLIC
SHAME
SHAMEABLE
SHAMEABLY
SHAMED
SHAMEFAST
SHAMEFUL
SHAMELESS
SHAMER
SHAMERS
SHAMES
SHAMIANA
SHAMIANAH
SHAMIANAS
SHAMINA
SHAMINAS
SHAMING
SHAMINGS
SHAMISEN
SHAMISENS
SHAMMAS
SHAMMASH
SHAMMASIM
SHAMMED
SHAMMER
SHAMMERS
SHAMMES
SHAMMIED
SHAMMIES
SHAMMING
SHAMMOS
SHAMMOSIM
SHAMMY
SHAMMYING
SHAMOIS
SHAMOISED
SHAMOISES
SHAMOS
SHAMOSIM
SHAMOY
SHAMOYED
SHAMOYING
SHAMOYS
SHAMPOO
SHAMPOOED
SHAMPOOER
SHAMPOOS
SHAMROCK
SHAMROCKS
SHAMS
SHAMUS
SHAMUSES
SHAN
SHANACHIE
SHAND
SHANDIES
SHANDRIES
SHANDRY
SHANDS
SHANDY
SHANGHAI
SHANGHAIS
SHANK
SHANKBONE
SHANKED
SHANKING
SHANKS
SHANNIES
SHANNY
SHANS
SHANTEY
SHANTEYS
SHANTI
SHANTIES
SHANTIH
SHANTIHS
SHANTIS
SHANTUNG
SHANTUNGS
SHANTY
SHANTYMAN
SHANTYMEN
SHAPABLE
SHAPE
SHAPEABLE
SHAPED
SHAPELESS
SHAPELIER
SHAPELY
SHAPEN
SHAPENED
SHAPENING
SHAPENS
SHAPER
SHAPERS
SHAPES
SHAPEUP
SHAPEUPS
SHAPEWEAR
SHAPING
SHAPINGS
SHAPS

SHARABLE
SHARD
SHARDED
SHARDS
SHARE
SHAREABLE
SHARECROP
SHARED
SHAREMAN
SHAREMEN
SHARER
SHARERS
SHARES
SHARESMAN
SHARESMEN
SHAREWARE
SHARIA
SHARIAH
SHARIAHS
SHARIAS
SHARIAT
SHARIATS
SHARIF
SHARIFIAN
SHARIFS
SHARING
SHARINGS
SHARK
SHARKED
SHARKER
SHARKERS
SHARKING
SHARKINGS
SHARKISH
SHARKLIKE
SHARKS
SHARKSKIN
SHARN
SHARNIER
SHARNIES
SHARNIEST
SHARNS
SHARNY
SHARON
SHARP
SHARPED
SHARPEN
SHARPENED
SHARPENER
SHARPENS
SHARPER
SHARPERS
SHARPEST
SHARPIE
SHARPIES
SHARPING
SHARPINGS
SHARPISH
SHARPLY
SHARPNESS
SHARPS
SHARPTAIL
SHARPY
SHASH
SHASHED
SHASHES
SHASHING
SHASHLICK
SHASHLIK
SHASHLIKS
SHASLIK
SHASLIKS
SHASTA
SHASTAS
SHASTER
SHASTERS
SHASTRA
SHASTRAS
SHAT
SHATOOSH
SHATTER
SHATTERED
SHATTERER
SHATTERS
SHATTERY
SHAUCHLE
SHAUCHLED
SHAUCHLES
SHAUCHLY
SHAUGH
SHAUGHS
SHAUL
SHAULED
SHAULING
SHAULS
SHAVABLE
SHAVASANA
SHAVE
SHAVEABLE
SHAVED
SHAVELING
SHAVEN
SHAVER
SHAVERS
SHAVES
SHAVETAIL
SHAVIE
SHAVIES
SHAVING
SHAVINGS
SHAW
SHAWARMA
SHAWARMAS
SHAWED
SHAWING
SHAWL
SHAWLED
SHAWLEY
SHAWLEYS
SHAWLIE
SHAWLIES
SHAWLING
SHAWLINGS
SHAWLLESS
SHAWLS
SHAWM
SHAWMS
SHAWN
SHAWS
SHAY
SHAYA
SHAYAS
SHAYKH
SHAYKHS
SHAYS
SHAZAM
SHCHI
SHCHIS
SHE
SHEA
SHEADING
SHEADINGS
SHEAF
SHEAFED
SHEAFIER
SHEAFIEST
SHEAFING
SHEAFLIKE
SHEAFS
SHEAFY
SHEAL
SHEALED
SHEALING
SHEALINGS
SHEALS
SHEAR
SHEARED
SHEARER
SHEARERS
SHEARING
SHEARINGS
SHEARLEG
SHEARLEGS
SHEARLING
SHEARMAN
SHEARMEN
SHEARS
SHEAS
SHEATFISH
SHEATH
SHEATHE
SHEATHED
SHEATHER
SHEATHERS
SHEATHES
SHEATHIER
SHEATHING
SHEATHS
SHEATHY
SHEAVE
SHEAVED
SHEAVES
SHEAVING
SHEBANG
SHEBANGS
SHEBEAN
SHEBEANS
SHEBEEN
SHEBEENED
SHEBEENER
SHEBEENS
SHECHITA
SHECHITAH
SHECHITAS
SHED
SHEDABLE
SHEDDABLE
SHEDDED
SHEDDER
SHEDDERS
SHEDDING
SHEDDINGS
SHEDFUL
SHEDFULS
SHEDHAND
SHEDHANDS
SHEDLIKE
SHEDLOAD
SHEDLOADS
SHEDS
SHEEL
SHEELED
SHEELING
SHEELS
SHEEN
SHEENED
SHEENFUL
SHEENIER
SHEENIEST
SHEENING
SHEENS
SHEENY
SHEEP
SHEEPCOT
SHEEPCOTE
SHEEPCOTS
SHEEPDOG
SHEEPDOGS
SHEEPFOLD
SHEEPHEAD
SHEEPIER
SHEEPIEST
SHEEPISH
SHEEPLE
SHEEPLES
SHEEPLIKE
SHEEPMAN
SHEEPMEN
SHEEPO
SHEEPOS

S

SHEEPSKIN
SHEEPWALK
SHEEPY
SHEER
SHEERED
SHEERER
SHEEREST
SHEERING
SHEERLEG
SHEERLEGS
SHEERLY
SHEERNESS
SHEERS
SHEESH
SHEESHA
SHEESHAS
SHEET
SHEETED
SHEETER
SHEETERS
SHEETFED
SHEETIER
SHEETIEST
SHEETING
SHEETINGS
SHEETLESS
SHEETLIKE
SHEETROCK
SHEETS
SHEETY
SHEEVE
SHEEVES
SHEHITA
SHEHITAH
SHEHITAHS
SHEHITAS
SHEHNAI
SHEHNAIS
SHEIK
SHEIKDOM
SHEIKDOMS
SHEIKH
SHEIKHA
SHEIKHAS
SHEIKHDOM
SHEIKHS
SHEIKS
SHEILA

SHEILAS
SHEILING
SHEILINGS
SHEITAN
SHEITANS
SHEITEL
SHEITELS
SHEKALIM
SHEKEL
SHEKELIM
SHEKELS
SHELDDUCK
SHELDRAKE
SHELDUCK
SHELDUCKS
SHELF
SHELFED
SHELFFUL
SHELFFULS
SHELFIER
SHELFIEST
SHELFING
SHELFLIKE
SHELFROOM
SHELFS
SHELFY
SHELL
SHELLAC
SHELLACK
SHELLACKS
SHELLACS
SHELLBACK
SHELLBARK
SHELLDUCK
SHELLED
SHELLER
SHELLERS
SHELLFIRE
SHELLFISH
SHELLFUL
SHELLFULS
SHELLIER
SHELLIEST
SHELLING
SHELLINGS
SHELLS
SHELLWORK
SHELLY

SHELTA
SHELTAS
SHELTER
SHELTERED
SHELTERER
SHELTERS
SHELTERY
SHELTIE
SHELTIES
SHELTY
SHELVE
SHELVED
SHELVER
SHELVERS
SHELVES
SHELVIER
SHELVIEST
SHELVING
SHELVINGS
SHELVY
SHEMOZZLE
SHEN
SHENAI
SHENAIS
SHEND
SHENDING
SHENDS
SHENT
SHEOL
SHEOLS
SHEPHERD
SHEPHERDS
SHEQALIM
SHEQEL
SHEQELS
SHERANG
SHERANGS
SHERBERT
SHERBERTS
SHERBET
SHERBETS
SHERD
SHERDS
SHERE
SHEREEF
SHEREEFS
SHERIA
SHERIAS

SHERIAT
SHERIATS
SHERIF
SHERIFF
SHERIFFS
SHERIFIAN
SHERIFS
SHERLOCK
SHERLOCKS
SHERO
SHEROES
SHEROOT
SHEROOTS
SHERPA
SHERPAS
SHERRIED
SHERRIES
SHERRIS
SHERRISES
SHERRY
SHERWANI
SHERWANIS
SHES
SHET
SHETLAND
SHETLANDS
SHETS
SHETTING
SHEUCH
SHEUCHED
SHEUCHING
SHEUCHS
SHEUGH
SHEUGHED
SHEUGHING
SHEUGHS
SHEVA
SHEVAS
SHEW
SHEWBREAD
SHEWED
SHEWEL
SHEWELS
SHEWER
SHEWERS
SHEWING
SHEWN
SHEWS

SHH
SHHH
SHIAI
SHIAIS
SHIATSU
SHIATSUS
SHIATZU
SHIATZUS
SHIBAH
SHIBAHS
SHIBUICHI
SHICKER
SHICKERED
SHICKERS
SHIDDER
SHIDDERS
SHIDDUCH
SHIED
SHIEL
SHIELD
SHIELDED
SHIELDER
SHIELDERS
SHIELDING
SHIELDS
SHIELED
SHIELING
SHIELINGS
SHIELS
SHIER
SHIERS
SHIES
SHIEST
SHIFT
SHIFTABLE
SHIFTED
SHIFTER
SHIFTERS
SHIFTIER
SHIFTIEST
SHIFTILY
SHIFTING
SHIFTINGS
SHIFTLESS
SHIFTS
SHIFTWORK
SHIFTY
SHIGELLA

SHIGELLAE
SHIGELLAS
SHIITAKE
SHIITAKES
SHIKAR
SHIKARA
SHIKARAS
SHIKAREE
SHIKAREES
SHIKARI
SHIKARIS
SHIKARRED
SHIKARS
SHIKKER
SHIKKERED
SHIKKERS
SHIKRA
SHIKRAS
SHILINGI
SHILINGIS
SHILL
SHILLABER
SHILLALA
SHILLALAH
SHILLALAS
SHILLED
SHILLELAH
SHILLING
SHILLINGS
SHILLS
SHILPIT
SHILY
SHIM
SHIMAAL
SHIMAALS
SHIMMED
SHIMMER
SHIMMERED
SHIMMERS
SHIMMERY
SHIMMEY
SHIMMEYS
SHIMMIED
SHIMMIES
SHIMMING
SHIMMY
SHIMMYING
SHIMOZZLE
SHIMS
SHIN
SHINBONE
SHINBONES
SHINDIES
SHINDIG
SHINDIGS
SHINDY
SHINDYS
SHINE
SHINED
SHINELESS
SHINER
SHINERS
SHINES
SHINESS
SHINESSES
SHINGLE
SHINGLED
SHINGLER
SHINGLERS
SHINGLES
SHINGLIER
SHINGLING
SHINGLY
SHINGUARD
SHINIER
SHINIES
SHINIEST
SHINILY
SHININESS
SHINING
SHININGLY
SHINJU
SHINJUS
SHINKIN
SHINKINS
SHINLEAF
SHINLEAFS
SHINNE
SHINNED
SHINNERY
SHINNES
SHINNEY
SHINNEYED
SHINNEYS
SHINNIED
SHINNIES
SHINNING
SHINNY
SHINNYING
SHINOLA
SHINOLAS
SHINS
SHINTIED
SHINTIES
SHINTY
SHINTYING
SHINY
SHIP
SHIPBOARD
SHIPBORNE
SHIPFUL
SHIPFULS
SHIPLAP
SHIPLAPS
SHIPLESS
SHIPLOAD
SHIPLOADS
SHIPMAN
SHIPMATE
SHIPMATES
SHIPMEN
SHIPMENT
SHIPMENTS
SHIPOWNER
SHIPPABLE
SHIPPED
SHIPPEN
SHIPPENS
SHIPPER
SHIPPERS
SHIPPIE
SHIPPIES
SHIPPING
SHIPPINGS
SHIPPO
SHIPPON
SHIPPONS
SHIPPOS
SHIPPOUND
SHIPS
SHIPSHAPE
SHIPSIDE
SHIPSIDES
SHIPTIME
SHIPTIMES
SHIPWAY
SHIPWAYS
SHIPWORM
SHIPWORMS
SHIPWRECK
SHIPYARD
SHIPYARDS
SHIR
SHIRALEE
SHIRALEES
SHIRAZ
SHIRAZES
SHIRE
SHIRED
SHIREMAN
SHIREMEN
SHIRES
SHIRETOWN
SHIRING
SHIRK
SHIRKED
SHIRKER
SHIRKERS
SHIRKING
SHIRKS
SHIRR
SHIRRA
SHIRRALEE
SHIRRAS
SHIRRED
SHIRRING
SHIRRINGS
SHIRRS
SHIRS
SHIRT
SHIRTBAND
SHIRTED
SHIRTIER
SHIRTIEST
SHIRTILY
SHIRTING
SHIRTINGS
SHIRTLESS
SHIRTLIKE
SHIRTS
SHIRTTAIL
SHIRTY
SHISH
SHISHA
SHISHAS
SHISO
SHISOS
SHIST
SHISTS
SHIT
SHITAKE
SHITAKES
SHITBAG
SHITBAGS
SHITCAN
SHITCANS
SHITE
SHITED
SHITES
SHITFACE
SHITFACED
SHITFACES
SHITHEAD
SHITHEADS
SHITHEEL
SHITHEELS
SHITHOLE
SHITHOLES
SHITHOUSE
SHITING
SHITLESS
SHITLIST
SHITLISTS
SHITLOAD
SHITLOADS
SHITS
SHITSTORM
SHITTAH
SHITTAHS
SHITTED
SHITTER
SHITTERS
SHITTIER
SHITTIEST
SHITTILY
SHITTIM
SHITTIMS
SHITTING
SHITTY
SHITWORK

SHITWORKS
SHITZU
SHITZUS
SHIUR
SHIURIM
SHIV
SHIVA
SHIVAH
SHIVAHS
SHIVAREE
SHIVAREED
SHIVAREES
SHIVAS
SHIVE
SHIVER
SHIVERED
SHIVERER
SHIVERERS
SHIVERIER
SHIVERING
SHIVERS
SHIVERY
SHIVES
SHIVITI
SHIVITIS
SHIVOO
SHIVOOS
SHIVS
SHIVVED
SHIVVING
SHIZZLE
SHIZZLES
SHLEMIEHL
SHLEMIEL
SHLEMIELS
SHLEP
SHLEPP
SHLEPPED
SHLEPPER
SHLEPPERS
SHLEPPIER
SHLEPPING
SHLEPPS
SHLEPPY
SHLEPS
SHLIMAZEL
SHLOCK
SHLOCKIER
SHLOCKS
SHLOCKY
SHLONG
SHLONGS
SHLOSHIM
SHLOSHIMS
SHLUB
SHLUBS
SHLUMP
SHLUMPED
SHLUMPIER
SHLUMPING
SHLUMPS
SHLUMPY
SHMALTZ
SHMALTZES
SHMALTZY
SHMATTE
SHMATTES
SHMEAR
SHMEARED
SHMEARING
SHMEARS
SHMEER
SHMEERED
SHMEERING
SHMEERS
SHMEK
SHMEKS
SHMO
SHMOCK
SHMOCKS
SHMOE
SHMOES
SHMOOSE
SHMOOSED
SHMOOSES
SHMOOSING
SHMOOZE
SHMOOZED
SHMOOZER
SHMOOZERS
SHMOOZES
SHMOOZIER
SHMOOZING
SHMOOZY
SHMUCK
SHMUCKIER
SHMUCKS
SHMUCKY
SHNAPPS
SHNAPS
SHNOOK
SHNOOKS
SHNORRER
SHNORRERS
SHO
SHOAL
SHOALED
SHOALER
SHOALEST
SHOALIER
SHOALIEST
SHOALING
SHOALINGS
SHOALNESS
SHOALS
SHOALWISE
SHOALY
SHOAT
SHOATS
SHOCHET
SHOCHETIM
SHOCHETS
SHOCHU
SHOCHUS
SHOCK
SHOCKABLE
SHOCKED
SHOCKER
SHOCKERS
SHOCKING
SHOCKS
SHOD
SHODDEN
SHODDIER
SHODDIES
SHODDIEST
SHODDILY
SHODDY
SHODER
SHODERS
SHOE
SHOEBILL
SHOEBILLS
SHOEBLACK
SHOEBOX
SHOEBOXES
SHOEBRUSH
SHOED
SHOEHORN
SHOEHORNS
SHOEING
SHOEINGS
SHOELACE
SHOELACES
SHOELESS
SHOEMAKER
SHOEPAC
SHOEPACK
SHOEPACKS
SHOEPACS
SHOER
SHOERS
SHOES
SHOESHINE
SHOETREE
SHOETREES
SHOFAR
SHOFARS
SHOFROTH
SHOG
SHOGGED
SHOGGING
SHOGGLE
SHOGGLED
SHOGGLES
SHOGGLIER
SHOGGLING
SHOGGLY
SHOGI
SHOGIS
SHOGS
SHOGUN
SHOGUNAL
SHOGUNATE
SHOGUNS
SHOJI
SHOJIS
SHOJO
SHOLA
SHOLAS
SHOLOM
SHOLOMS
SHONE
SHONEEN
SHONEENS
SHONKIER
SHONKIEST
SHONKY
SHOO
SHOOED
SHOOFLIES
SHOOFLY
SHOOGIE
SHOOGIED
SHOOGIES
SHOOGLE
SHOOGLED
SHOOGLES
SHOOGLIER
SHOOGLING
SHOOGLY
SHOOING
SHOOK
SHOOKS
SHOOL
SHOOLE
SHOOLED
SHOOLES
SHOOLING
SHOOLS
SHOON
SHOORA
SHOORAS
SHOOS
SHOOSH
SHOOSHED
SHOOSHES
SHOOSHING
SHOOT
SHOOTABLE
SHOOTDOWN
SHOOTER
SHOOTERS
SHOOTIE
SHOOTIES
SHOOTING
SHOOTINGS
SHOOTIST
SHOOTISTS
SHOOTOUT

SHOOTOUTS
SHOOTS
SHOP
SHOPBOARD
SHOPBOT
SHOPBOTS
SHOPBOY
SHOPBOYS
SHOPE
SHOPFRONT
SHOPFUL
SHOPFULS
SHOPGIRL
SHOPGIRLS
SHOPHAR
SHOPHARS
SHOPHOUSE
SHOPHROTH
SHOPLESS
SHOPLIFT
SHOPLIFTS
SHOPMAN
SHOPMEN
SHOPPE
SHOPPED
SHOPPER
SHOPPERS
SHOPPES
SHOPPIER
SHOPPIES
SHOPPIEST
SHOPPING
SHOPPINGS
SHOPPY
SHOPS
SHOPTALK
SHOPTALKS
SHOPWOMAN
SHOPWOMEN
SHOPWORN
SHORAN
SHORANS
SHORE
SHOREBIRD
SHORED
SHOREFAST
SHORELESS
SHORELINE
SHOREMAN
SHOREMEN
SHORER
SHORERS
SHORES
SHORESIDE
SHORESMAN
SHORESMEN
SHOREWARD
SHOREWEED
SHORING
SHORINGS
SHORL
SHORLS
SHORN
SHORT
SHORTAGE
SHORTAGES
SHORTARM
SHORTARSE
SHORTCAKE
SHORTCUT
SHORTCUTS
SHORTED
SHORTEN
SHORTENED
SHORTENER
SHORTENS
SHORTER
SHORTEST
SHORTFALL
SHORTGOWN
SHORTHAIR
SHORTHAND
SHORTHEAD
SHORTHOLD
SHORTHORN
SHORTIA
SHORTIAS
SHORTIE
SHORTIES
SHORTING
SHORTISH
SHORTLIST
SHORTLY
SHORTNESS
SHORTS
SHORTSTOP
SHORTWAVE
SHORTY
SHOT
SHOTCRETE
SHOTE
SHOTES
SHOTFIRER
SHOTGUN
SHOTGUNS
SHOTHOLE
SHOTHOLES
SHOTMAKER
SHOTPROOF
SHOTS
SHOTT
SHOTTE
SHOTTED
SHOTTEN
SHOTTES
SHOTTING
SHOTTLE
SHOTTLES
SHOTTS
SHOUGH
SHOUGHS
SHOULD
SHOULDER
SHOULDERS
SHOULDEST
SHOULDST
SHOUSE
SHOUSES
SHOUT
SHOUTED
SHOUTER
SHOUTERS
SHOUTHER
SHOUTHERS
SHOUTIER
SHOUTIEST
SHOUTING
SHOUTINGS
SHOUTLINE
SHOUTOUT
SHOUTOUTS
SHOUTS
SHOUTY
SHOVE
SHOVED
SHOVEL
SHOVELED
SHOVELER
SHOVELERS
SHOVELFUL
SHOVELING
SHOVELLED
SHOVELLER
SHOVELS
SHOVER
SHOVERS
SHOVES
SHOVING
SHOVINGS
SHOW
SHOWABLE
SHOWBIZ
SHOWBIZZY
SHOWBOAT
SHOWBOATS
SHOWBOX
SHOWBOXES
SHOWBREAD
SHOWCASE
SHOWCASED
SHOWCASES
SHOWD
SHOWDED
SHOWDING
SHOWDOWN
SHOWDOWNS
SHOWDS
SHOWED
SHOWER
SHOWERED
SHOWERER
SHOWERERS
SHOWERFUL
SHOWERIER
SHOWERING
SHOWERS
SHOWERY
SHOWGHE
SHOWGHES
SHOWGIRL
SHOWGIRLS
SHOWGOER
SHOWGOERS
SHOWIER
SHOWIEST
SHOWILY
SHOWINESS
SHOWING
SHOWINGS
SHOWJUMP
SHOWJUMPS
SHOWMAN
SHOWMANCE
SHOWMANLY
SHOWMEN
SHOWN
SHOWOFF
SHOWOFFS
SHOWPIECE
SHOWPLACE
SHOWRING
SHOWRINGS
SHOWROOM
SHOWROOMS
SHOWS
SHOWTIME
SHOWTIMES
SHOWY
SHOWYARD
SHOWYARDS
SHOYU
SHOYUS
SHRADDHA
SHRADDHAS
SHRANK
SHRAPNEL
SHRAPNELS
SHRED
SHREDDED
SHREDDER
SHREDDERS
SHREDDIER
SHREDDING
SHREDDY
SHREDLESS
SHREDS
SHREEK
SHREEKED
SHREEKING
SHREEKS

S

SHREIK
SHREIKED
SHREIKING
SHREIKS
SHREW
SHREWD
SHREWDER
SHREWDEST
SHREWDIE
SHREWDIES
SHREWDLY
SHREWED
SHREWING
SHREWISH
SHREWLIKE
SHREWMICE
SHREWS
SHRI
SHRIECH
SHRIECHED
SHRIECHES
SHRIEK
SHRIEKED
SHRIEKER
SHRIEKERS
SHRIEKIER
SHRIEKING
SHRIEKS
SHRIEKY
SHRIEVAL
SHRIEVE
SHRIEVED
SHRIEVES
SHRIEVING
SHRIFT
SHRIFTS
SHRIGHT
SHRIGHTS
SHRIKE
SHRIKED
SHRIKES
SHRIKING
SHRILL
SHRILLED
SHRILLER
SHRILLEST
SHRILLIER
SHRILLING
SHRILLS
SHRILLY
SHRIMP
SHRIMPED
SHRIMPER
SHRIMPERS
SHRIMPIER
SHRIMPING
SHRIMPS
SHRIMPY
SHRINAL
SHRINE
SHRINED
SHRINES
SHRINING
SHRINK
SHRINKAGE
SHRINKER
SHRINKERS
SHRINKING
SHRINKS
SHRIS
SHRITCH
SHRITCHED
SHRITCHES
SHRIVE
SHRIVED
SHRIVEL
SHRIVELED
SHRIVELS
SHRIVEN
SHRIVER
SHRIVERS
SHRIVES
SHRIVING
SHRIVINGS
SHROFF
SHROFFAGE
SHROFFED
SHROFFING
SHROFFS
SHROOM
SHROOMED
SHROOMER
SHROOMERS
SHROOMING
SHROOMS
SHROUD
SHROUDED
SHROUDIER
SHROUDING
SHROUDS
SHROUDY
SHROVE
SHROVED
SHROVES
SHROVING
SHROW
SHROWD
SHROWED
SHROWING
SHROWS
SHRUB
SHRUBBED
SHRUBBERY
SHRUBBIER
SHRUBBING
SHRUBBY
SHRUBLAND
SHRUBLESS
SHRUBLIKE
SHRUBS
SHRUG
SHRUGGED
SHRUGGING
SHRUGS
SHRUNK
SHRUNKEN
SHTCHI
SHTCHIS
SHTETEL
SHTETELS
SHTETL
SHTETLACH
SHTETLS
SHTICK
SHTICKIER
SHTICKS
SHTICKY
SHTIK
SHTIKS
SHTOOK
SHTOOKS
SHTOOM
SHTOOMER
SHTOOMEST
SHTREIMEL
SHTUCK
SHTUCKS
SHTUM
SHTUMM
SHTUMMER
SHTUMMEST
SHTUP
SHTUPPED
SHTUPPING
SHTUPS
SHUBUNKIN
SHUCK
SHUCKED
SHUCKER
SHUCKERS
SHUCKING
SHUCKINGS
SHUCKS
SHUDDER
SHUDDERED
SHUDDERS
SHUDDERY
SHUFFLE
SHUFFLED
SHUFFLER
SHUFFLERS
SHUFFLES
SHUFFLING
SHUFTI
SHUFTIES
SHUFTIS
SHUFTY
SHUGGIES
SHUGGY
SHUL
SHULE
SHULED
SHULES
SHULING
SHULN
SHULS
SHUMAI
SHUN
SHUNLESS
SHUNNABLE
SHUNNED
SHUNNER
SHUNNERS
SHUNNING
SHUNPIKE
SHUNPIKED
SHUNPIKER
SHUNPIKES
SHUNS
SHUNT
SHUNTED
SHUNTER
SHUNTERS
SHUNTING
SHUNTINGS
SHUNTS
SHURA
SHURAS
SHURIKEN
SHURIKENS
SHUSH
SHUSHED
SHUSHER
SHUSHERS
SHUSHES
SHUSHING
SHUT
SHUTDOWN
SHUTDOWNS
SHUTE
SHUTED
SHUTES
SHUTEYE
SHUTEYES
SHUTING
SHUTOFF
SHUTOFFS
SHUTOUT
SHUTOUTS
SHUTS
SHUTTER
SHUTTERED
SHUTTERS
SHUTTING
SHUTTLE
SHUTTLED
SHUTTLER
SHUTTLERS
SHUTTLES
SHUTTLING

S

SHVITZ
SHVITZED
SHVITZES
SHVITZING
SHWA
SHWANPAN
SHWANPANS
SHWAS
SHWESHWE
SHWESHWES
SHY
SHYER
SHYERS
SHYEST
SHYING
SHYISH
SHYLOCK
SHYLOCKED
SHYLOCKS
SHYLY
SHYNESS
SHYNESSES
SHYPOO
SHYPOOS
SHYSTER
SHYSTERS
SI
SIAL
SIALIC
SIALID
SIALIDAN
SIALIDANS
SIALIDS
SIALOGRAM
SIALOID
SIALOLITH
SIALON
SIALONS
SIALS
SIAMANG
SIAMANGS
SIAMESE
SIAMESED
SIAMESES
SIAMESING
SIAMEZE
SIAMEZED
SIAMEZES
SIAMEZING
SIB
SIBB
SIBBS
SIBILANCE
SIBILANCY
SIBILANT
SIBILANTS
SIBILATE
SIBILATED
SIBILATES
SIBILATOR
SIBILOUS
SIBLING
SIBLINGS
SIBS
SIBSHIP
SIBSHIPS
SIBYL
SIBYLIC
SIBYLLIC
SIBYLLINE
SIBYLS
SIC
SICARIO
SICARIOS
SICCAN
SICCAR
SICCATIVE
SICCED
SICCING
SICCITIES
SICCITY
SICE
SICES
SICH
SICHT
SICHTED
SICHTING
SICHTS
SICILIANA
SICILIANE
SICILIANO
SICK
SICKBAY
SICKBAYS
SICKBED
SICKBEDS
SICKED
SICKEE
SICKEES
SICKEN
SICKENED
SICKENER
SICKENERS
SICKENING
SICKENS
SICKER
SICKERLY
SICKEST
SICKIE
SICKIES
SICKING
SICKISH
SICKISHLY
SICKLE
SICKLED
SICKLEMAN
SICKLEMEN
SICKLEMIA
SICKLEMIC
SICKLES
SICKLIED
SICKLIER
SICKLIES
SICKLIEST
SICKLILY
SICKLING
SICKLY
SICKLYING
SICKNESS
SICKNURSE
SICKO
SICKOS
SICKOUT
SICKOUTS
SICKROOM
SICKROOMS
SICKS
SICKY
SICLIKE
SICS
SIDA
SIDALCEA
SIDALCEAS
SIDAS
SIDDHA
SIDDHAS
SIDDHI
SIDDHIS
SIDDHUISM
SIDDUR
SIDDURIM
SIDDURS
SIDE
SIDEARM
SIDEARMED
SIDEARMER
SIDEARMS
SIDEBAND
SIDEBANDS
SIDEBAR
SIDEBARS
SIDEBOARD
SIDEBONE
SIDEBONES
SIDEBURN
SIDEBURNS
SIDECAR
SIDECARS
SIDECHAIR
SIDECHECK
SIDED
SIDEDLY
SIDEDNESS
SIDEDRESS
SIDEHILL
SIDEHILLS
SIDEKICK
SIDEKICKS
SIDELESS
SIDELIGHT
SIDELINE
SIDELINED
SIDELINER
SIDELINES
SIDELING
SIDELINGS
SIDELOCK
SIDELOCKS
SIDELONG
SIDEMAN
SIDEMEAT
SIDEMEATS
SIDEMEN
SIDENOTE
SIDENOTES
SIDEPATH
SIDEPATHS
SIDEPIECE
SIDER
SIDERAL
SIDERATE
SIDERATED
SIDERATES
SIDEREAL
SIDERITE
SIDERITES
SIDERITIC
SIDEROAD
SIDEROADS
SIDEROSES
SIDEROSIS
SIDEROTIC
SIDERS
SIDES
SIDESHOOT
SIDESHOW
SIDESHOWS
SIDESLIP
SIDESLIPS
SIDESMAN
SIDESMEN
SIDESPIN
SIDESPINS
SIDESPLIT
SIDESTEP
SIDESTEPS
SIDESWIPE
SIDETABLE
SIDETRACK
SIDEWALK
SIDEWALKS
SIDEWALL
SIDEWALLS
SIDEWARD
SIDEWARDS
SIDEWAY
SIDEWAYS
SIDEWHEEL
SIDEWISE
SIDH

SIDHA
SIDHAS
SIDHE
SIDHUISM
SIDHUISMS
SIDING
SIDINGS
SIDLE
SIDLED
SIDLER
SIDLERS
SIDLES
SIDLING
SIDLINGLY
SIECLE
SIECLES
SIEGE
SIEGED
SIEGER
SIEGERS
SIEGES
SIEGING
SIELD
SIEMENS
SIEMENSES
SIEN
SIENITE
SIENITES
SIENNA
SIENNAS
SIENS
SIENT
SIENTS
SIEROZEM
SIEROZEMS
SIERRA
SIERRAN
SIERRAS
SIES
SIESTA
SIESTAS
SIETH
SIETHS
SIEUR
SIEURS
SIEVE
SIEVED
SIEVELIKE
SIEVERT
SIEVERTS
SIEVES
SIEVING
SIF
SIFAKA
SIFAKAS
SIFFLE
SIFFLED
SIFFLES
SIFFLEUR
SIFFLEURS
SIFFLEUSE
SIFFLING
SIFREI
SIFT
SIFTED
SIFTER
SIFTERS
SIFTING
SIFTINGLY
SIFTINGS
SIFTS
SIG
SIGANID
SIGANIDS
SIGH
SIGHED
SIGHER
SIGHERS
SIGHFUL
SIGHING
SIGHINGLY
SIGHINGS
SIGHLESS
SIGHLIKE
SIGHS
SIGHT
SIGHTABLE
SIGHTED
SIGHTER
SIGHTERS
SIGHTING
SIGHTINGS
SIGHTLESS
SIGHTLIER
SIGHTLINE
SIGHTLY
SIGHTS
SIGHTSAW
SIGHTSEE
SIGHTSEEN
SIGHTSEER
SIGHTSEES
SIGHTSMAN
SIGHTSMEN
SIGIL
SIGILLARY
SIGILLATE
SIGILS
SIGISBEI
SIGISBEO
SIGLA
SIGLAS
SIGLOI
SIGLOS
SIGLUM
SIGMA
SIGMAS
SIGMATE
SIGMATED
SIGMATES
SIGMATIC
SIGMATING
SIGMATION
SIGMATISM
SIGMATRON
SIGMOID
SIGMOIDAL
SIGMOIDS
SIGN
SIGNA
SIGNABLE
SIGNAGE
SIGNAGES
SIGNAL
SIGNALED
SIGNALER
SIGNALERS
SIGNALING
SIGNALISE
SIGNALIZE
SIGNALLED
SIGNALLER
SIGNALLY
SIGNALMAN
SIGNALMEN
SIGNALS
SIGNARIES
SIGNARY
SIGNATORY
SIGNATURE
SIGNBOARD
SIGNED
SIGNEE
SIGNEES
SIGNER
SIGNERS
SIGNET
SIGNETED
SIGNETING
SIGNETS
SIGNEUR
SIGNEURIE
SIGNIEUR
SIGNIEURS
SIGNIFICS
SIGNIFIED
SIGNIFIER
SIGNIFIES
SIGNIFY
SIGNING
SIGNINGS
SIGNIOR
SIGNIORI
SIGNIORS
SIGNIORY
SIGNLESS
SIGNOR
SIGNORA
SIGNORAS
SIGNORE
SIGNORES
SIGNORI
SIGNORIA
SIGNORIAL
SIGNORIAS
SIGNORIES
SIGNORINA
SIGNORINE
SIGNORINI
SIGNORINO
SIGNORS
SIGNORY
SIGNPOST
SIGNPOSTS
SIGNS
SIGS
SIJO
SIJOS
SIK
SIKA
SIKAS
SIKE
SIKER
SIKES
SIKORSKY
SIKSIK
SIKSIKS
SILAGE
SILAGED
SILAGEING
SILAGES
SILAGING
SILANE
SILANES
SILASTIC
SILASTICS
SILD
SILDS
SILE
SILED
SILEN
SILENCE
SILENCED
SILENCER
SILENCERS
SILENCES
SILENCING
SILENE
SILENES
SILENI
SILENS
SILENT
SILENTER
SILENTEST
SILENTLY
SILENTS
SILENUS
SILER
SILERS
SILES

S

SILESIA
SILESIAS
SILEX
SILEXES
SILICA
SILICAS
SILICATE
SILICATED
SILICATES
SILICEOUS
SILICIC
SILICIDE
SILICIDES
SILICIFY
SILICIOUS
SILICIUM
SILICIUMS
SILICLE
SILICLES
SILICON
SILICONE
SILICONES
SILICONS
SILICOSES
SILICOSIS
SILICOTIC
SILICULA
SILICULAE
SILICULAS
SILICULE
SILICULES
SILING
SILIQUA
SILIQUAE
SILIQUAS
SILIQUE
SILIQUES
SILIQUOSE
SILIQUOUS
SILK
SILKALENE
SILKALINE
SILKED
SILKEN
SILKENED
SILKENING
SILKENS
SILKIE
SILKIER
SILKIES
SILKIEST
SILKILY
SILKINESS
SILKING
SILKLIKE
SILKOLINE
SILKS
SILKTAIL
SILKTAILS
SILKWEED
SILKWEEDS
SILKWORM
SILKWORMS
SILKY
SILL
SILLABUB
SILLABUBS
SILLADAR
SILLADARS
SILLER
SILLERS
SILLIBUB
SILLIBUBS
SILLIER
SILLIES
SILLIEST
SILLILY
SILLINESS
SILLOCK
SILLOCKS
SILLS
SILLY
SILO
SILOED
SILOING
SILOS
SILOXANE
SILOXANES
SILPHIA
SILPHIUM
SILPHIUMS
SILT
SILTATION
SILTED
SILTIER
SILTIEST
SILTING
SILTS
SILTSTONE
SILTY
SILURIAN
SILURID
SILURIDS
SILURIST
SILURISTS
SILUROID
SILUROIDS
SILVA
SILVAE
SILVAN
SILVANS
SILVAS
SILVATIC
SILVER
SILVERED
SILVERER
SILVERERS
SILVEREYE
SILVERIER
SILVERING
SILVERISE
SILVERIZE
SILVERLY
SILVERN
SILVERS
SILVERTIP
SILVERY
SILVEX
SILVEXES
SILVICAL
SILVICS
SILYMARIN
SIM
SIMA
SIMAR
SIMAROUBA
SIMARRE
SIMARRES
SIMARS
SIMARUBA
SIMARUBAS
SIMAS
SIMATIC
SIMAZINE
SIMAZINES
SIMBA
SIMBAS
SIMCHA
SIMCHAS
SIMI
SIMIAL
SIMIAN
SIMIANS
SIMILAR
SIMILARLY
SIMILE
SIMILES
SIMILISE
SIMILISED
SIMILISES
SIMILIZE
SIMILIZED
SIMILIZES
SIMILOR
SIMILORS
SIMIOID
SIMIOUS
SIMIS
SIMITAR
SIMITARS
SIMKIN
SIMKINS
SIMLIN
SIMLINS
SIMMER
SIMMERED
SIMMERING
SIMMERS
SIMNEL
SIMNELS
SIMOLEON
SIMOLEONS
SIMONIAC
SIMONIACS
SIMONIES
SIMONIOUS
SIMONISE
SIMONISED
SIMONISES
SIMONIST
SIMONISTS
SIMONIZE
SIMONIZED
SIMONIZES
SIMONY
SIMOOM
SIMOOMS
SIMOON
SIMOONS
SIMORG
SIMORGS
SIMP
SIMPAI
SIMPAIS
SIMPATICO
SIMPER
SIMPERED
SIMPERER
SIMPERERS
SIMPERING
SIMPERS
SIMPKIN
SIMPKINS
SIMPLE
SIMPLED
SIMPLER
SIMPLERS
SIMPLES
SIMPLESSE
SIMPLEST
SIMPLETON
SIMPLEX
SIMPLEXES
SIMPLICES
SIMPLICIA
SIMPLIFY
SIMPLING
SIMPLINGS
SIMPLISM
SIMPLISMS
SIMPLIST
SIMPLISTE
SIMPLISTS
SIMPLY
SIMPS
SIMS
SIMUL
SIMULACRA
SIMULACRE
SIMULANT

SIMULANTS
SIMULAR
SIMULARS
SIMULATE
SIMULATED
SIMULATES
SIMULATOR
SIMULCAST
SIMULIUM
SIMULIUMS
SIMULS
SIMURG
SIMURGH
SIMURGHS
SIMURGS
SIN
SINAPISM
SINAPISMS
SINCE
SINCERE
SINCERELY
SINCERER
SINCEREST
SINCERITY
SINCIPITA
SINCIPUT
SINCIPUTS
SIND
SINDED
SINDING
SINDINGS
SINDON
SINDONS
SINDS
SINE
SINECURE
SINECURES
SINED
SINES
SINEW
SINEWED
SINEWIER
SINEWIEST
SINEWING
SINEWLESS
SINEWS
SINEWY
SINFONIA
SINFONIAS
SINFONIE
SINFUL
SINFULLY
SING
SINGABLE
SINGALONG
SINGE
SINGED
SINGEING
SINGER
SINGERS
SINGES
SINGING
SINGINGLY
SINGINGS
SINGLE
SINGLED
SINGLEDOM
SINGLES
SINGLET
SINGLETON
SINGLETS
SINGLING
SINGLINGS
SINGLY
SINGS
SINGSONG
SINGSONGS
SINGSONGY
SINGSPIEL
SINGULAR
SINGULARS
SINGULARY
SINGULT
SINGULTS
SINGULTUS
SINH
SINHS
SINICAL
SINICISE
SINICISED
SINICISES
SINICIZE
SINICIZED
SINICIZES
SINING
SINISTER
SINISTRAL
SINK
SINKABLE
SINKAGE
SINKAGES
SINKER
SINKERS
SINKFUL
SINKFULS
SINKHOLE
SINKHOLES
SINKIER
SINKIEST
SINKING
SINKINGS
SINKS
SINKY
SINLESS
SINLESSLY
SINNED
SINNER
SINNERED
SINNERING
SINNERS
SINNET
SINNETS
SINNING
SINNINGIA
SINOLOGUE
SINOLOGY
SINOPIA
SINOPIAS
SINOPIE
SINOPIS
SINOPISES
SINOPITE
SINOPITES
SINS
SINSYNE
SINTER
SINTERED
SINTERIER
SINTERING
SINTERS
SINTERY
SINUATE
SINUATED
SINUATELY
SINUATES
SINUATING
SINUATION
SINUITIS
SINUOSE
SINUOSITY
SINUOUS
SINUOUSLY
SINUS
SINUSES
SINUSITIS
SINUSLIKE
SINUSOID
SINUSOIDS
SIP
SIPE
SIPED
SIPES
SIPHON
SIPHONAGE
SIPHONAL
SIPHONATE
SIPHONED
SIPHONET
SIPHONETS
SIPHONIC
SIPHONING
SIPHONS
SIPHUNCLE
SIPING
SIPPABLE
SIPPED
SIPPER
SIPPERS
SIPPET
SIPPETS
SIPPING
SIPPLE
SIPPLED
SIPPLES
SIPPLING
SIPPY
SIPS
SIR
SIRCAR
SIRCARS
SIRDAR
SIRDARS
SIRE
SIRED
SIREE
SIREES
SIREN
SIRENIAN
SIRENIANS
SIRENIC
SIRENISE
SIRENISED
SIRENISES
SIRENIZE
SIRENIZED
SIRENIZES
SIRENS
SIRES
SIRGANG
SIRGANGS
SIRI
SIRIASES
SIRIASIS
SIRIH
SIRIHS
SIRING
SIRINGS
SIRIS
SIRKAR
SIRKARS
SIRLOIN
SIRLOINS
SIRNAME
SIRNAMED
SIRNAMES
SIRNAMING
SIROC
SIROCCO
SIROCCOS
SIROCS
SIRONISE
SIRONISED
SIRONISES
SIRONIZE
SIRONIZED
SIRONIZES
SIROSET
SIRRA
SIRRAH
SIRRAHS

S

SIRRAS
SIRRED
SIRREE
SIRREES
SIRRING
SIRS
SIRTUIN
SIRTUINS
SIRUP
SIRUPED
SIRUPIER
SIRUPIEST
SIRUPING
SIRUPS
SIRUPY
SIRVENTE
SIRVENTES
SIS
SISAL
SISALS
SISERARY
SISES
SISKIN
SISKINS
SISS
SISSES
SISSIER
SISSIES
SISSIEST
SISSIFIED
SISSINESS
SISSOO
SISSOOS
SISSY
SISSYISH
SISSYNESS
SIST
SISTA
SISTAS
SISTED
SISTER
SISTERED
SISTERING
SISTERLY
SISTERS
SISTING
SISTRA
SISTROID
SISTRUM
SISTRUMS
SISTS
SIT
SITAR
SITARIST
SITARISTS
SITARS
SITATUNGA
SITCOM
SITCOMS
SITE
SITED
SITELLA
SITELLAS
SITES
SITFAST
SITFASTS
SITH
SITHE
SITHED
SITHEE
SITHEN
SITHENCE
SITHENS
SITHES
SITHING
SITING
SITINGS
SITIOLOGY
SITKA
SITKAMER
SITKAMERS
SITOLOGY
SITREP
SITREPS
SITS
SITTAR
SITTARS
SITTELLA
SITTELLAS
SITTEN
SITTER
SITTERS
SITTINE
SITTINES
SITTING
SITTINGS
SITUATE
SITUATED
SITUATES
SITUATING
SITUATION
SITULA
SITULAE
SITUP
SITUPS
SITUS
SITUSES
SITUTUNGA
SITZ
SITZKRIEG
SITZMARK
SITZMARKS
SIVER
SIVERS
SIWASH
SIWASHED
SIWASHES
SIWASHING
SIX
SIXAIN
SIXAINE
SIXAINES
SIXAINS
SIXER
SIXERS
SIXES
SIXFOLD
SIXISH
SIXMO
SIXMOS
SIXPENCE
SIXPENCES
SIXPENNY
SIXSCORE
SIXSCORES
SIXTE
SIXTEEN
SIXTEENER
SIXTEENMO
SIXTEENS
SIXTEENTH
SIXTES
SIXTH
SIXTHLY
SIXTHS
SIXTIES
SIXTIETH
SIXTIETHS
SIXTY
SIXTYFOLD
SIXTYISH
SIZABLE
SIZABLY
SIZAR
SIZARS
SIZARSHIP
SIZE
SIZEABLE
SIZEABLY
SIZED
SIZEISM
SIZEISMS
SIZEIST
SIZEISTS
SIZEL
SIZELS
SIZER
SIZERS
SIZES
SIZIER
SIZIEST
SIZINESS
SIZING
SIZINGS
SIZISM
SIZISMS
SIZIST
SIZISTS
SIZY
SIZZLE
SIZZLED
SIZZLER
SIZZLERS
SIZZLES
SIZZLING
SIZZLINGS
SJAMBOK
SJAMBOKED
SJAMBOKS
SJOE
SKA
SKAG
SKAGS
SKAIL
SKAILED
SKAILING
SKAILS
SKAITH
SKAITHED
SKAITHING
SKAITHS
SKALD
SKALDIC
SKALDS
SKALDSHIP
SKANGER
SKANGERS
SKANK
SKANKED
SKANKER
SKANKERS
SKANKIER
SKANKIEST
SKANKING
SKANKINGS
SKANKS
SKANKY
SKART
SKARTH
SKARTHS
SKARTS
SKAS
SKAT
SKATE
SKATED
SKATEPARK
SKATEPUNK
SKATER
SKATERS
SKATES
SKATING
SKATINGS
SKATOL
SKATOLE
SKATOLES
SKATOLS
SKATS
SKATT
SKATTS
SKAW

S

SKAWS
SKEAN
SKEANE
SKEANES
SKEANS
SKEAR
SKEARED
SKEARIER
SKEARIEST
SKEARING
SKEARS
SKEARY
SKED
SKEDADDLE
SKEDDED
SKEDDING
SKEDS
SKEE
SKEECHAN
SKEECHANS
SKEED
SKEEF
SKEEING
SKEELIER
SKEELIEST
SKEELY
SKEEN
SKEENS
SKEER
SKEERED
SKEERIER
SKEERIEST
SKEERING
SKEERS
SKEERY
SKEES
SKEESICKS
SKEET
SKEETER
SKEETERS
SKEETS
SKEEVIER
SKEEVIEST
SKEEVY
SKEG
SKEGG
SKEGGER
SKEGGERS
SKEGGS
SKEGS
SKEIGH
SKEIGHER
SKEIGHEST
SKEIN
SKEINED
SKEINING
SKEINS
SKELDER
SKELDERED
SKELDERS
SKELETAL
SKELETON
SKELETONS
SKELF
SKELFS
SKELL
SKELLIE
SKELLIED
SKELLIER
SKELLIES
SKELLIEST
SKELLOCH
SKELLOCHS
SKELLS
SKELLUM
SKELLUMS
SKELLY
SKELLYING
SKELM
SKELMS
SKELP
SKELPED
SKELPING
SKELPINGS
SKELPIT
SKELPS
SKELTER
SKELTERED
SKELTERS
SKELUM
SKELUMS
SKEN
SKENE
SKENES
SKENNED
SKENNING
SKENS
SKEO
SKEOES
SKEOS
SKEP
SKEPFUL
SKEPFULS
SKEPPED
SKEPPING
SKEPS
SKEPSIS
SKEPSISES
SKEPTIC
SKEPTICAL
SKEPTICS
SKER
SKERRED
SKERRICK
SKERRICKS
SKERRIES
SKERRING
SKERRY
SKERS
SKET
SKETCH
SKETCHED
SKETCHER
SKETCHERS
SKETCHES
SKETCHIER
SKETCHILY
SKETCHING
SKETCHPAD
SKETCHY
SKETS
SKETTED
SKETTING
SKEW
SKEWBACK
SKEWBACKS
SKEWBALD
SKEWBALDS
SKEWED
SKEWER
SKEWERED
SKEWERING
SKEWERS
SKEWEST
SKEWING
SKEWNESS
SKEWS
SKEWWHIFF
SKI
SKIABLE
SKIAGRAM
SKIAGRAMS
SKIAGRAPH
SKIAMACHY
SKIASCOPE
SKIASCOPY
SKIATRON
SKIATRONS
SKIBOB
SKIBOBBED
SKIBOBBER
SKIBOBS
SKID
SKIDDED
SKIDDER
SKIDDERS
SKIDDIER
SKIDDIEST
SKIDDING
SKIDDINGS
SKIDDOO
SKIDDOOED
SKIDDOOS
SKIDDY
SKIDLID
SKIDLIDS
SKIDMARK
SKIDMARKS
SKIDOO
SKIDOOED
SKIDOOER
SKIDOOERS
SKIDOOING
SKIDOOS
SKIDPAD
SKIDPADS
SKIDPAN
SKIDPANS
SKIDPROOF
SKIDS
SKIDWAY
SKIDWAYS
SKIED
SKIER
SKIERS
SKIES
SKIEY
SKIEYER
SKIEYEST
SKIFF
SKIFFED
SKIFFING
SKIFFLE
SKIFFLED
SKIFFLES
SKIFFLESS
SKIFFLING
SKIFFS
SKIING
SKIINGS
SKIJORER
SKIJORERS
SKIJORING
SKIJUMPER
SKIKJORER
SKILFUL
SKILFULL
SKILFULLY
SKILL
SKILLED
SKILLESS
SKILLET
SKILLETS
SKILLFUL
SKILLIER
SKILLIES
SKILLIEST
SKILLING
SKILLINGS
SKILLION
SKILLIONS
SKILLS
SKILLY
SKIM
SKIMBOARD
SKIMMED
SKIMMER
SKIMMERS
SKIMMIA
SKIMMIAS

S

SKIMMING
SKIMMINGS
SKIMOBILE
SKIMP
SKIMPED
SKIMPIER
SKIMPIEST
SKIMPILY
SKIMPING
SKIMPS
SKIMPY
SKIMS
SKIN
SKINCARE
SKINCARES
SKINFLICK
SKINFLINT
SKINFOOD
SKINFOODS
SKINFUL
SKINFULS
SKINHEAD
SKINHEADS
SKINK
SKINKED
SKINKER
SKINKERS
SKINKING
SKINKS
SKINLESS
SKINLIKE
SKINNED
SKINNER
SKINNERS
SKINNIER
SKINNIES
SKINNIEST
SKINNING
SKINNY
SKINS
SKINSUIT
SKINSUITS
SKINT
SKINTER
SKINTEST
SKINTIGHT
SKIO
SKIOES
SKIORER
SKIORERS
SKIORING
SKIORINGS
SKIOS
SKIP
SKIPJACK
SKIPJACKS
SKIPLANE
SKIPLANES
SKIPPABLE
SKIPPED
SKIPPER
SKIPPERED
SKIPPERS
SKIPPET
SKIPPETS
SKIPPIER
SKIPPIEST
SKIPPING
SKIPPINGS
SKIPPY
SKIPS
SKIRL
SKIRLED
SKIRLING
SKIRLINGS
SKIRLS
SKIRMISH
SKIRR
SKIRRED
SKIRRET
SKIRRETS
SKIRRING
SKIRRS
SKIRT
SKIRTED
SKIRTER
SKIRTERS
SKIRTING
SKIRTINGS
SKIRTLESS
SKIRTLIKE
SKIRTS
SKIS
SKIT
SKITCH
SKITCHED
SKITCHES
SKITCHING
SKITE
SKITED
SKITES
SKITING
SKITS
SKITTER
SKITTERED
SKITTERS
SKITTERY
SKITTISH
SKITTLE
SKITTLED
SKITTLES
SKITTLING
SKIVE
SKIVED
SKIVER
SKIVERED
SKIVERING
SKIVERS
SKIVES
SKIVIE
SKIVIER
SKIVIEST
SKIVING
SKIVINGS
SKIVVIED
SKIVVIES
SKIVVY
SKIVVYING
SKIVY
SKIWEAR
SKIWEARS
SKLATE
SKLATED
SKLATES
SKLATING
SKLENT
SKLENTED
SKLENTING
SKLENTS
SKLIFF
SKLIFFED
SKLIFFING
SKLIFFS
SKLIM
SKLIMMED
SKLIMMING
SKLIMS
SKOAL
SKOALED
SKOALING
SKOALS
SKODIER
SKODIEST
SKODY
SKOFF
SKOFFED
SKOFFING
SKOFFS
SKOG
SKOGGED
SKOGGING
SKOGS
SKOKIAAN
SKOKIAANS
SKOL
SKOLED
SKOLIA
SKOLING
SKOLION
SKOLLED
SKOLLIE
SKOLLIES
SKOLLING
SKOLLY
SKOLS
SKOOKUM
SKOOKUMS
SKOOL
SKOOLS
SKOOSH
SKOOSHED
SKOOSHES
SKOOSHING
SKORDALIA
SKORT
SKORTS
SKOSH
SKOSHES
SKRAN
SKRANS
SKREEGH
SKREEGHED
SKREEGHS
SKREEN
SKREENS
SKREIGH
SKREIGHED
SKREIGHS
SKRIECH
SKRIECHED
SKRIECHS
SKRIED
SKRIEGH
SKRIEGHED
SKRIEGHS
SKRIES
SKRIK
SKRIKE
SKRIKED
SKRIKES
SKRIKING
SKRIKS
SKRIMMAGE
SKRIMP
SKRIMPED
SKRIMPING
SKRIMPS
SKRONK
SKRONKS
SKRUMP
SKRUMPED
SKRUMPING
SKRUMPS
SKRY
SKRYER
SKRYERS
SKRYING
SKUA
SKUAS
SKUDLER
SKUDLERS
SKUG
SKUGGED
SKUGGING
SKUGS
SKULK
SKULKED
SKULKER
SKULKERS
SKULKING

SKULKINGS
SKULKS
SKULL
SKULLCAP
SKULLCAPS
SKULLED
SKULLING
SKULLS
SKULPIN
SKULPINS
SKUMMER
SKUMMERED
SKUMMERS
SKUNK
SKUNKBIRD
SKUNKED
SKUNKIER
SKUNKIEST
SKUNKING
SKUNKS
SKUNKWEED
SKUNKY
SKURRIED
SKURRIES
SKURRY
SKURRYING
SKUTTLE
SKUTTLED
SKUTTLES
SKUTTLING
SKY
SKYBOARD
SKYBOARDS
SKYBORN
SKYBORNE
SKYBOX
SKYBOXES
SKYBRIDGE
SKYCAP
SKYCAPS
SKYCLAD
SKYDIVE
SKYDIVED
SKYDIVER
SKYDIVERS
SKYDIVES
SKYDIVING
SKYDOVE
SKYED
SKYER
SKYERS
SKYEY
SKYEYER
SKYEYEST
SKYF
SKYFED
SKYFING
SKYFS
SKYGLOW
SKYGLOWS
SKYHOME
SKYHOMES
SKYHOOK
SKYHOOKS
SKYIER
SKYIEST
SKYING
SKYISH
SKYJACK
SKYJACKED
SKYJACKER
SKYJACKS
SKYLAB
SKYLABS
SKYLARK
SKYLARKED
SKYLARKER
SKYLARKS
SKYLESS
SKYLIGHT
SKYLIGHTS
SKYLIKE
SKYLINE
SKYLINES
SKYLIT
SKYMAN
SKYMEN
SKYPHOI
SKYPHOS
SKYR
SKYRE
SKYRED
SKYRES
SKYRING
SKYRMION
SKYRMIONS
SKYROCKET
SKYRS
SKYSAIL
SKYSAILS
SKYSCAPE
SKYSCAPES
SKYSURF
SKYSURFED
SKYSURFER
SKYSURFS
SKYTE
SKYTED
SKYTES
SKYTING
SKYWALK
SKYWALKS
SKYWARD
SKYWARDS
SKYWATCH
SKYWAY
SKYWAYS
SKYWRITE
SKYWRITER
SKYWRITES
SKYWROTE
SLAB
SLABBED
SLABBER
SLABBERED
SLABBERER
SLABBERS
SLABBERY
SLABBIER
SLABBIES
SLABBIEST
SLABBING
SLABBINGS
SLABBY
SLABLIKE
SLABS
SLABSTONE
SLACK
SLACKED
SLACKEN
SLACKENED
SLACKENER
SLACKENS
SLACKER
SLACKERS
SLACKEST
SLACKING
SLACKLY
SLACKNESS
SLACKS
SLADANG
SLADANGS
SLADE
SLADES
SLAE
SLAES
SLAG
SLAGGED
SLAGGIER
SLAGGIEST
SLAGGING
SLAGGINGS
SLAGGY
SLAGHEAP
SLAGHEAPS
SLAGS
SLAHAL
SLAHALS
SLAID
SLAIDS
SLAIN
SLAINTE
SLAIRG
SLAIRGED
SLAIRGING
SLAIRGS
SLAISTER
SLAISTERS
SLAISTERY
SLAKABLE
SLAKE
SLAKEABLE
SLAKED
SLAKELESS
SLAKER
SLAKERS
SLAKES
SLAKING
SLALOM
SLALOMED
SLALOMER
SLALOMERS
SLALOMING
SLALOMIST
SLALOMS
SLAM
SLAMDANCE
SLAMMAKIN
SLAMMED
SLAMMER
SLAMMERS
SLAMMING
SLAMMINGS
SLAMS
SLANDER
SLANDERED
SLANDERER
SLANDERS
SLANE
SLANES
SLANG
SLANGED
SLANGER
SLANGERS
SLANGIER
SLANGIEST
SLANGILY
SLANGING
SLANGINGS
SLANGISH
SLANGS
SLANGUAGE
SLANGULAR
SLANGY
SLANK
SLANT
SLANTED
SLANTER
SLANTERS
SLANTIER
SLANTIEST
SLANTING
SLANTLY
SLANTS
SLANTWAYS
SLANTWISE
SLANTY
SLAP
SLAPDASH
SLAPHAPPY

S

SLAPHEAD
SLAPHEADS
SLAPJACK
SLAPJACKS
SLAPPED
SLAPPER
SLAPPERS
SLAPPING
SLAPPINGS
SLAPS
SLAPSHOT
SLAPSHOTS
SLAPSTICK
SLART
SLARTED
SLARTING
SLARTS
SLASH
SLASHED
SLASHER
SLASHERS
SLASHES
SLASHFEST
SLASHING
SLASHINGS
SLAT
SLATCH
SLATCHES
SLATE
SLATED
SLATELIKE
SLATER
SLATERS
SLATES
SLATEY
SLATHER
SLATHERED
SLATHERS
SLATIER
SLATIEST
SLATINESS
SLATING
SLATINGS
SLATS
SLATTED
SLATTER
SLATTERED
SLATTERN
SLATTERNS
SLATTERS
SLATTERY
SLATTING
SLATTINGS
SLATY
SLAUGHTER
SLAVE
SLAVED
SLAVER
SLAVERED
SLAVERER
SLAVERERS
SLAVERIES
SLAVERING
SLAVERS
SLAVERY
SLAVES
SLAVEY
SLAVEYS
SLAVING
SLAVISH
SLAVISHLY
SLAVOCRAT
SLAVOPHIL
SLAW
SLAWS
SLAY
SLAYABLE
SLAYED
SLAYER
SLAYERS
SLAYING
SLAYINGS
SLAYS
SLEAVE
SLEAVED
SLEAVES
SLEAVING
SLEAZE
SLEAZEBAG
SLEAZED
SLEAZES
SLEAZIER
SLEAZIEST
SLEAZILY
SLEAZING
SLEAZO
SLEAZOID
SLEAZOIDS
SLEAZOS
SLEAZY
SLEB
SLEBS
SLED
SLEDDED
SLEDDER
SLEDDERS
SLEDDING
SLEDDINGS
SLEDED
SLEDGE
SLEDGED
SLEDGER
SLEDGERS
SLEDGES
SLEDGING
SLEDGINGS
SLEDS
SLEE
SLEECH
SLEECHES
SLEECHIER
SLEECHY
SLEEK
SLEEKED
SLEEKEN
SLEEKENED
SLEEKENS
SLEEKER
SLEEKERS
SLEEKEST
SLEEKIER
SLEEKIEST
SLEEKING
SLEEKINGS
SLEEKIT
SLEEKLY
SLEEKNESS
SLEEKS
SLEEKY
SLEEP
SLEEPAWAY
SLEEPER
SLEEPERS
SLEEPERY
SLEEPIER
SLEEPIEST
SLEEPILY
SLEEPING
SLEEPINGS
SLEEPLESS
SLEEPLIKE
SLEEPOUT
SLEEPOUTS
SLEEPOVER
SLEEPRY
SLEEPS
SLEEPSUIT
SLEEPWALK
SLEEPWEAR
SLEEPY
SLEER
SLEEST
SLEET
SLEETED
SLEETIER
SLEETIEST
SLEETING
SLEETS
SLEETY
SLEEVE
SLEEVED
SLEEVEEN
SLEEVEENS
SLEEVELET
SLEEVER
SLEEVERS
SLEEVES
SLEEVING
SLEEVINGS
SLEEZIER
SLEEZIEST
SLEEZY
SLEIDED
SLEIGH
SLEIGHED
SLEIGHER
SLEIGHERS
SLEIGHING
SLEIGHS
SLEIGHT
SLEIGHTS
SLENDER
SLENDERER
SLENDERLY
SLENTER
SLENTERS
SLEPT
SLEUTH
SLEUTHED
SLEUTHING
SLEUTHS
SLEW
SLEWED
SLEWING
SLEWS
SLEY
SLEYS
SLICE
SLICEABLE
SLICED
SLICER
SLICERS
SLICES
SLICING
SLICINGS
SLICK
SLICKED
SLICKEN
SLICKENED
SLICKENER
SLICKENS
SLICKER
SLICKERED
SLICKERS
SLICKEST
SLICKING
SLICKINGS
SLICKLY
SLICKNESS
SLICKROCK
SLICKS
SLICKSTER
SLID
SLIDABLE
SLIDDEN
SLIDDER
SLIDDERED
SLIDDERS
SLIDDERY
SLIDE

SLIDED
SLIDER
SLIDERS
SLIDES
SLIDESHOW
SLIDEWAY
SLIDEWAYS
SLIDING
SLIDINGLY
SLIDINGS
SLIER
SLIEST
SLIEVE
SLIEVES
SLIGHT
SLIGHTED
SLIGHTER
SLIGHTERS
SLIGHTEST
SLIGHTING
SLIGHTISH
SLIGHTLY
SLIGHTS
SLILY
SLIM
SLIMDOWN
SLIMDOWNS
SLIME
SLIMEBAG
SLIMEBAGS
SLIMEBALL
SLIMED
SLIMES
SLIMIER
SLIMIEST
SLIMILY
SLIMINESS
SLIMING
SLIMLINE
SLIMLY
SLIMMED
SLIMMER
SLIMMERS
SLIMMEST
SLIMMING
SLIMMINGS
SLIMMISH
SLIMNESS
SLIMPSIER
SLIMPSY
SLIMS
SLIMSIER
SLIMSIEST
SLIMSY
SLIMY
SLING
SLINGBACK
SLINGER
SLINGERS
SLINGIER
SLINGIEST
SLINGING
SLINGS
SLINGSHOT
SLINGY
SLINK
SLINKED
SLINKER
SLINKERS
SLINKIER
SLINKIEST
SLINKILY
SLINKING
SLINKS
SLINKSKIN
SLINKWEED
SLINKY
SLINTER
SLINTERS
SLIOTAR
SLIOTARS
SLIP
SLIPCASE
SLIPCASED
SLIPCASES
SLIPCOVER
SLIPDRESS
SLIPE
SLIPED
SLIPES
SLIPFORM
SLIPFORMS
SLIPING
SLIPKNOT
SLIPKNOTS
SLIPLESS
SLIPNOOSE
SLIPOUT
SLIPOUTS
SLIPOVER
SLIPOVERS
SLIPPAGE
SLIPPAGES
SLIPPED
SLIPPER
SLIPPERED
SLIPPERS
SLIPPERY
SLIPPIER
SLIPPIEST
SLIPPILY
SLIPPING
SLIPPY
SLIPRAIL
SLIPRAILS
SLIPS
SLIPSHEET
SLIPSHOD
SLIPSLOP
SLIPSLOPS
SLIPSOLE
SLIPSOLES
SLIPT
SLIPUP
SLIPUPS
SLIPWARE
SLIPWARES
SLIPWAY
SLIPWAYS
SLISH
SLISHES
SLIT
SLITHER
SLITHERED
SLITHERS
SLITHERY
SLITLESS
SLITLIKE
SLITS
SLITTED
SLITTER
SLITTERS
SLITTIER
SLITTIEST
SLITTING
SLITTY
SLIVE
SLIVED
SLIVEN
SLIVER
SLIVERED
SLIVERER
SLIVERERS
SLIVERING
SLIVERS
SLIVES
SLIVING
SLIVOVIC
SLIVOVICA
SLIVOVITZ
SLIVOWITZ
SLOAN
SLOANS
SLOB
SLOBBED
SLOBBER
SLOBBERED
SLOBBERER
SLOBBERS
SLOBBERY
SLOBBIER
SLOBBIEST
SLOBBING
SLOBBISH
SLOBBY
SLOBLAND
SLOBLANDS
SLOBS
SLOCKEN
SLOCKENED
SLOCKENS
SLOE
SLOEBUSH
SLOES
SLOETHORN
SLOETREE
SLOETREES
SLOG
SLOGAN
SLOGANED
SLOGANEER
SLOGANISE
SLOGANIZE
SLOGANS
SLOGGED
SLOGGER
SLOGGERS
SLOGGING
SLOGS
SLOID
SLOIDS
SLOJD
SLOJDS
SLOKEN
SLOKENED
SLOKENING
SLOKENS
SLOMMOCK
SLOMMOCKS
SLOMO
SLOMOS
SLOOM
SLOOMED
SLOOMIER
SLOOMIEST
SLOOMING
SLOOMS
SLOOMY
SLOOP
SLOOPS
SLOOSH
SLOOSHED
SLOOSHES
SLOOSHING
SLOOT
SLOOTS
SLOP
SLOPE
SLOPED
SLOPER
SLOPERS
SLOPES
SLOPESIDE
SLOPEWISE
SLOPIER
SLOPIEST
SLOPING
SLOPINGLY
SLOPPED
SLOPPIER

SLOPPIEST
SLOPPILY
SLOPPING
SLOPPY
SLOPS
SLOPWORK
SLOPWORKS
SLOPY
SLORM
SLORMED
SLORMING
SLORMS
SLOSH
SLOSHED
SLOSHES
SLOSHIER
SLOSHIEST
SLOSHING
SLOSHINGS
SLOSHY
SLOT
SLOTBACK
SLOTBACKS
SLOTH
SLOTHED
SLOTHFUL
SLOTHING
SLOTHS
SLOTS
SLOTTED
SLOTTER
SLOTTERS
SLOTTING
SLOUCH
SLOUCHED
SLOUCHER
SLOUCHERS
SLOUCHES
SLOUCHIER
SLOUCHILY
SLOUCHING
SLOUCHY
SLOUGH
SLOUGHED
SLOUGHI
SLOUGHIER
SLOUGHING
SLOUGHIS
SLOUGHS
SLOUGHY
SLOVE
SLOVEN
SLOVENLY
SLOVENRY
SLOVENS
SLOW
SLOWBACK
SLOWBACKS
SLOWCOACH
SLOWDOWN
SLOWDOWNS
SLOWED
SLOWER
SLOWEST
SLOWING
SLOWINGS
SLOWISH
SLOWLY
SLOWNESS
SLOWPOKE
SLOWPOKES
SLOWS
SLOWWORM
SLOWWORMS
SLOYD
SLOYDS
SLUB
SLUBB
SLUBBED
SLUBBER
SLUBBERED
SLUBBERS
SLUBBEST
SLUBBIER
SLUBBIEST
SLUBBING
SLUBBINGS
SLUBBS
SLUBBY
SLUBS
SLUDGE
SLUDGED
SLUDGES
SLUDGIER
SLUDGIEST
SLUDGING
SLUDGY
SLUE
SLUED
SLUEING
SLUES
SLUFF
SLUFFED
SLUFFING
SLUFFS
SLUG
SLUGABED
SLUGABEDS
SLUGFEST
SLUGFESTS
SLUGGABED
SLUGGARD
SLUGGARDS
SLUGGED
SLUGGER
SLUGGERS
SLUGGING
SLUGGISH
SLUGHORN
SLUGHORNE
SLUGHORNS
SLUGLIKE
SLUGS
SLUICE
SLUICED
SLUICES
SLUICEWAY
SLUICIER
SLUICIEST
SLUICING
SLUICY
SLUING
SLUIT
SLUITS
SLUM
SLUMBER
SLUMBERED
SLUMBERER
SLUMBERS
SLUMBERY
SLUMBROUS
SLUMBRY
SLUMGUM
SLUMGUMS
SLUMISM
SLUMISMS
SLUMLORD
SLUMLORDS
SLUMMED
SLUMMER
SLUMMERS
SLUMMIER
SLUMMIEST
SLUMMING
SLUMMINGS
SLUMMOCK
SLUMMOCKS
SLUMMY
SLUMP
SLUMPED
SLUMPIER
SLUMPIEST
SLUMPING
SLUMPS
SLUMPY
SLUMS
SLUNG
SLUNGSHOT
SLUNK
SLUR
SLURB
SLURBAN
SLURBS
SLURP
SLURPED
SLURPER
SLURPERS
SLURPIER
SLURPIEST
SLURPING
SLURPS
SLURPY
SLURRED
SLURRIED
SLURRIES
SLURRING
SLURRY
SLURRYING
SLURS
SLURVE
SLURVES
SLUSE
SLUSES
SLUSH
SLUSHED
SLUSHES
SLUSHIER
SLUSHIES
SLUSHIEST
SLUSHILY
SLUSHING
SLUSHY
SLUT
SLUTCH
SLUTCHES
SLUTCHIER
SLUTCHY
SLUTS
SLUTTERY
SLUTTIER
SLUTTIEST
SLUTTILY
SLUTTISH
SLUTTY
SLY
SLYBOOTS
SLYER
SLYEST
SLYISH
SLYLY
SLYNESS
SLYNESSES
SLYPE
SLYPES
SMA
SMAAK
SMAAKED
SMAAKING
SMAAKS
SMACK
SMACKDOWN
SMACKED
SMACKER
SMACKEROO
SMACKERS
SMACKHEAD
SMACKING
SMACKINGS
SMACKS
SMAIK

S

SMAIKS
SMALL
SMALLAGE
SMALLAGES
SMALLBOY
SMALLBOYS
SMALLED
SMALLER
SMALLEST
SMALLING
SMALLISH
SMALLNESS
SMALLPOX
SMALLS
SMALLSAT
SMALLSATS
SMALLTIME
SMALM
SMALMED
SMALMIER
SMALMIEST
SMALMILY
SMALMING
SMALMS
SMALMY
SMALT
SMALTI
SMALTINE
SMALTINES
SMALTITE
SMALTITES
SMALTO
SMALTOS
SMALTS
SMARAGD
SMARAGDE
SMARAGDES
SMARAGDS
SMARM
SMARMED
SMARMIER
SMARMIEST
SMARMILY
SMARMING
SMARMS
SMARMY
SMART
SMARTARSE
SMARTASS
SMARTED
SMARTEN
SMARTENED
SMARTENS
SMARTER
SMARTEST
SMARTIE
SMARTIES
SMARTING
SMARTISH
SMARTLY
SMARTNESS
SMARTS
SMARTWEED
SMARTY
SMASH
SMASHABLE
SMASHED
SMASHER
SMASHEROO
SMASHERS
SMASHES
SMASHING
SMASHINGS
SMASHUP
SMASHUPS
SMATCH
SMATCHED
SMATCHES
SMATCHING
SMATTER
SMATTERED
SMATTERER
SMATTERS
SMAZE
SMAZES
SMEAR
SMEARCASE
SMEARED
SMEARER
SMEARERS
SMEARIER
SMEARIEST
SMEARILY
SMEARING
SMEARS
SMEARY
SMEATH
SMEATHS
SMECTIC
SMECTITE
SMECTITES
SMECTITIC
SMEDDUM
SMEDDUMS
SMEE
SMEECH
SMEECHED
SMEECHES
SMEECHING
SMEEK
SMEEKED
SMEEKING
SMEEKS
SMEES
SMEETH
SMEETHED
SMEETHING
SMEETHS
SMEGMA
SMEGMAS
SMEIK
SMEIKED
SMEIKING
SMEIKS
SMEKE
SMEKED
SMEKES
SMEKING
SMELL
SMELLABLE
SMELLED
SMELLER
SMELLERS
SMELLIER
SMELLIES
SMELLIEST
SMELLING
SMELLINGS
SMELLS
SMELLY
SMELT
SMELTED
SMELTER
SMELTERS
SMELTERY
SMELTING
SMELTINGS
SMELTS
SMERK
SMERKED
SMERKING
SMERKS
SMEUSE
SMEUSES
SMEW
SMEWS
SMICKER
SMICKERED
SMICKERS
SMICKET
SMICKETS
SMICKLY
SMIDDIED
SMIDDIES
SMIDDY
SMIDDYING
SMIDGE
SMIDGEN
SMIDGENS
SMIDGEON
SMIDGEONS
SMIDGES
SMIDGIN
SMIDGINS
SMIERCASE
SMIGHT
SMIGHTING
SMIGHTS
SMILAX
SMILAXES
SMILE
SMILED
SMILEFUL
SMILELESS
SMILER
SMILERS
SMILES
SMILET
SMILETS
SMILEY
SMILEYS
SMILIER
SMILIES
SMILIEST
SMILING
SMILINGLY
SMILINGS
SMILODON
SMILODONS
SMIR
SMIRCH
SMIRCHED
SMIRCHER
SMIRCHERS
SMIRCHES
SMIRCHING
SMIRK
SMIRKED
SMIRKER
SMIRKERS
SMIRKIER
SMIRKIEST
SMIRKILY
SMIRKING
SMIRKS
SMIRKY
SMIRR
SMIRRED
SMIRRIER
SMIRRIEST
SMIRRING
SMIRRS
SMIRRY
SMIRS
SMIRTING
SMIRTINGS
SMISHING
SMISHINGS
SMIT
SMITE
SMITER
SMITERS
SMITES
SMITH
SMITHED
SMITHERS
SMITHERY
SMITHIED
SMITHIES
SMITHING

S

SMITHINGS
SMITHS
SMITHY
SMITHYING
SMITING
SMITS
SMITTED
SMITTEN
SMITTING
SMITTLE
SMOCK
SMOCKED
SMOCKING
SMOCKINGS
SMOCKLIKE
SMOCKS
SMOG
SMOGGIER
SMOGGIEST
SMOGGY
SMOGLESS
SMOGS
SMOILE
SMOILED
SMOILES
SMOILING
SMOKABLE
SMOKE
SMOKEABLE
SMOKEBOX
SMOKEBUSH
SMOKED
SMOKEHO
SMOKEHOOD
SMOKEHOS
SMOKEJACK
SMOKELESS
SMOKELIKE
SMOKEPOT
SMOKEPOTS
SMOKER
SMOKERS
SMOKES
SMOKEY
SMOKEYS
SMOKIE
SMOKIER
SMOKIES
SMOKIEST
SMOKILY
SMOKINESS
SMOKING
SMOKINGS
SMOKO
SMOKOS
SMOKY
SMOLDER
SMOLDERED
SMOLDERS
SMOLT
SMOLTS
SMOOCH
SMOOCHED
SMOOCHER
SMOOCHERS
SMOOCHES
SMOOCHIER
SMOOCHING
SMOOCHY
SMOODGE
SMOODGED
SMOODGES
SMOODGING
SMOOGE
SMOOGED
SMOOGES
SMOOGING
SMOOR
SMOORED
SMOORING
SMOORS
SMOOSH
SMOOSHED
SMOOSHES
SMOOSHING
SMOOT
SMOOTED
SMOOTH
SMOOTHE
SMOOTHED
SMOOTHEN
SMOOTHENS
SMOOTHER
SMOOTHERS
SMOOTHES
SMOOTHEST
SMOOTHIE
SMOOTHIES
SMOOTHING
SMOOTHISH
SMOOTHLY
SMOOTHS
SMOOTHY
SMOOTING
SMOOTS
SMORBROD
SMORBRODS
SMORE
SMORED
SMORES
SMORG
SMORGS
SMORING
SMORZANDO
SMORZATO
SMOTE
SMOTHER
SMOTHERED
SMOTHERER
SMOTHERS
SMOTHERY
SMOUCH
SMOUCHED
SMOUCHES
SMOUCHING
SMOULDER
SMOULDERS
SMOULDRY
SMOUSE
SMOUSED
SMOUSER
SMOUSERS
SMOUSES
SMOUSING
SMOUT
SMOUTED
SMOUTING
SMOUTS
SMOWT
SMOWTS
SMOYLE
SMOYLED
SMOYLES
SMOYLING
SMRITI
SMRITIS
SMUDGE
SMUDGED
SMUDGEDLY
SMUDGER
SMUDGERS
SMUDGES
SMUDGIER
SMUDGIEST
SMUDGILY
SMUDGING
SMUDGINGS
SMUDGY
SMUG
SMUGGED
SMUGGER
SMUGGERY
SMUGGEST
SMUGGING
SMUGGLE
SMUGGLED
SMUGGLER
SMUGGLERS
SMUGGLES
SMUGGLING
SMUGLY
SMUGNESS
SMUGS
SMUR
SMURFING
SMURFINGS
SMURRED
SMURRIER
SMURRIEST
SMURRING
SMURRY
SMURS
SMUSH
SMUSHED
SMUSHES
SMUSHING
SMUT
SMUTCH
SMUTCHED
SMUTCHES
SMUTCHIER
SMUTCHING
SMUTCHY
SMUTS
SMUTTED
SMUTTIER
SMUTTIEST
SMUTTILY
SMUTTING
SMUTTY
SMYTRIE
SMYTRIES
SNAB
SNABBLE
SNABBLED
SNABBLES
SNABBLING
SNABS
SNACK
SNACKED
SNACKER
SNACKERS
SNACKETTE
SNACKIER
SNACKIEST
SNACKING
SNACKS
SNACKY
SNAFFLE
SNAFFLED
SNAFFLES
SNAFFLING
SNAFU
SNAFUED
SNAFUING
SNAFUS
SNAG
SNAGGED
SNAGGER
SNAGGERS
SNAGGIER
SNAGGIEST
SNAGGING
SNAGGLE
SNAGGLES
SNAGGY
SNAGLIKE
SNAGS
SNAIL
SNAILED

S

SNAILERY
SNAILFISH
SNAILIER
SNAILIEST
SNAILING
SNAILLIKE
SNAILS
SNAILY
SNAKE
SNAKEBIRD
SNAKEBIT
SNAKEBITE
SNAKED
SNAKEFISH
SNAKEHEAD
SNAKELIKE
SNAKEPIT
SNAKEPITS
SNAKEROOT
SNAKES
SNAKESKIN
SNAKEWEED
SNAKEWISE
SNAKEWOOD
SNAKEY
SNAKIER
SNAKIEST
SNAKILY
SNAKINESS
SNAKING
SNAKISH
SNAKY
SNAP
SNAPBACK
SNAPBACKS
SNAPHANCE
SNAPLESS
SNAPLINK
SNAPLINKS
SNAPPABLE
SNAPPED
SNAPPER
SNAPPERED
SNAPPERS
SNAPPIER
SNAPPIEST
SNAPPILY
SNAPPING
SNAPPINGS
SNAPPISH
SNAPPY
SNAPS
SNAPSHOT
SNAPSHOTS
SNAPTIN
SNAPTINS
SNAPWEED
SNAPWEEDS
SNAR
SNARE
SNARED
SNARELESS
SNARER
SNARERS
SNARES
SNARF
SNARFED
SNARFING
SNARFLE
SNARFLED
SNARFLES
SNARFLING
SNARFS
SNARIER
SNARIEST
SNARING
SNARINGS
SNARK
SNARKIER
SNARKIEST
SNARKILY
SNARKS
SNARKY
SNARL
SNARLED
SNARLER
SNARLERS
SNARLIER
SNARLIEST
SNARLING
SNARLINGS
SNARLS
SNARLY
SNARRED
SNARRING
SNARS
SNARY
SNASH
SNASHED
SNASHES
SNASHING
SNASTE
SNASTES
SNATCH
SNATCHED
SNATCHER
SNATCHERS
SNATCHES
SNATCHIER
SNATCHILY
SNATCHING
SNATCHY
SNATH
SNATHE
SNATHES
SNATHS
SNAW
SNAWED
SNAWING
SNAWS
SNAZZIER
SNAZZIEST
SNAZZILY
SNAZZY
SNEAD
SNEADS
SNEAK
SNEAKBOX
SNEAKED
SNEAKER
SNEAKERED
SNEAKERS
SNEAKEUP
SNEAKEUPS
SNEAKIER
SNEAKIEST
SNEAKILY
SNEAKING
SNEAKISH
SNEAKS
SNEAKSBY
SNEAKY
SNEAP
SNEAPED
SNEAPING
SNEAPS
SNEATH
SNEATHS
SNEB
SNEBBE
SNEBBED
SNEBBES
SNEBBING
SNEBS
SNECK
SNECKED
SNECKING
SNECKS
SNED
SNEDDED
SNEDDING
SNEDS
SNEE
SNEED
SNEEING
SNEER
SNEERED
SNEERER
SNEERERS
SNEERFUL
SNEERIER
SNEERIEST
SNEERING
SNEERINGS
SNEERS
SNEERY
SNEES
SNEESH
SNEESHAN
SNEESHANS
SNEESHED
SNEESHES
SNEESHIN
SNEESHING
SNEESHINS
SNEEZE
SNEEZED
SNEEZER
SNEEZERS
SNEEZES
SNEEZIER
SNEEZIEST
SNEEZING
SNEEZINGS
SNEEZY
SNELL
SNELLED
SNELLER
SNELLEST
SNELLING
SNELLS
SNELLY
SNIB
SNIBBED
SNIBBING
SNIBS
SNICK
SNICKED
SNICKER
SNICKERED
SNICKERER
SNICKERS
SNICKERY
SNICKET
SNICKETS
SNICKING
SNICKS
SNIDE
SNIDED
SNIDELY
SNIDENESS
SNIDER
SNIDES
SNIDEST
SNIDEY
SNIDIER
SNIDIEST
SNIDING
SNIES
SNIFF
SNIFFABLE
SNIFFED
SNIFFER
SNIFFERS
SNIFFIER
SNIFFIEST
SNIFFILY
SNIFFING
SNIFFINGS
SNIFFISH

SNIFFLE
SNIFFLED
SNIFFLER
SNIFFLERS
SNIFFLES
SNIFFLIER
SNIFFLING
SNIFFLY
SNIFFS
SNIFFY
SNIFT
SNIFTED
SNIFTER
SNIFTERED
SNIFTERS
SNIFTIER
SNIFTIEST
SNIFTING
SNIFTS
SNIFTY
SNIG
SNIGGED
SNIGGER
SNIGGERED
SNIGGERER
SNIGGERS
SNIGGING
SNIGGLE
SNIGGLED
SNIGGLER
SNIGGLERS
SNIGGLES
SNIGGLING
SNIGLET
SNIGLETS
SNIGS
SNIP
SNIPE
SNIPED
SNIPEFISH
SNIPELIKE
SNIPER
SNIPERS
SNIPES
SNIPIER
SNIPIEST
SNIPING
SNIPINGS
SNIPPED
SNIPPER
SNIPPERS
SNIPPET
SNIPPETS
SNIPPETY
SNIPPIER
SNIPPIEST
SNIPPILY
SNIPPING
SNIPPINGS
SNIPPY
SNIPS
SNIPY
SNIRT
SNIRTED
SNIRTING
SNIRTLE
SNIRTLED
SNIRTLES
SNIRTLING
SNIRTS
SNIT
SNITCH
SNITCHED
SNITCHER
SNITCHERS
SNITCHES
SNITCHIER
SNITCHING
SNITCHY
SNITS
SNITTIER
SNITTIEST
SNITTY
SNIVEL
SNIVELED
SNIVELER
SNIVELERS
SNIVELIER
SNIVELING
SNIVELLED
SNIVELLER
SNIVELLY
SNIVELS
SNIVELY
SNOB
SNOBBERY
SNOBBIER
SNOBBIEST
SNOBBILY
SNOBBISH
SNOBBISM
SNOBBISMS
SNOBBY
SNOBLING
SNOBLINGS
SNOBS
SNOCOACH
SNOD
SNODDED
SNODDER
SNODDEST
SNODDING
SNODDIT
SNODS
SNOEK
SNOEKS
SNOEP
SNOG
SNOGGED
SNOGGER
SNOGGERS
SNOGGING
SNOGS
SNOKE
SNOKED
SNOKES
SNOKING
SNOOD
SNOODED
SNOODING
SNOODS
SNOOK
SNOOKED
SNOOKER
SNOOKERED
SNOOKERS
SNOOKING
SNOOKS
SNOOL
SNOOLED
SNOOLING
SNOOLS
SNOOP
SNOOPED
SNOOPER
SNOOPERS
SNOOPIER
SNOOPIEST
SNOOPILY
SNOOPING
SNOOPS
SNOOPY
SNOOSE
SNOOSES
SNOOT
SNOOTED
SNOOTFUL
SNOOTFULS
SNOOTIER
SNOOTIEST
SNOOTILY
SNOOTING
SNOOTS
SNOOTY
SNOOZE
SNOOZED
SNOOZER
SNOOZERS
SNOOZES
SNOOZIER
SNOOZIEST
SNOOZING
SNOOZLE
SNOOZLED
SNOOZLES
SNOOZLING
SNOOZY
SNORE
SNORED
SNORER
SNORERS
SNORES
SNORING
SNORINGS
SNORKEL
SNORKELED
SNORKELER
SNORKELS
SNORT
SNORTED
SNORTER
SNORTERS
SNORTIER
SNORTIEST
SNORTING
SNORTINGS
SNORTS
SNORTY
SNOT
SNOTRAG
SNOTRAGS
SNOTS
SNOTTED
SNOTTER
SNOTTERED
SNOTTERS
SNOTTERY
SNOTTIE
SNOTTIER
SNOTTIES
SNOTTIEST
SNOTTILY
SNOTTING
SNOTTY
SNOUT
SNOUTED
SNOUTIER
SNOUTIEST
SNOUTING
SNOUTISH
SNOUTLESS
SNOUTLIKE
SNOUTS
SNOUTY
SNOW
SNOWBALL
SNOWBALLS
SNOWBANK
SNOWBANKS
SNOWBELL
SNOWBELLS
SNOWBELT
SNOWBELTS
SNOWBERRY
SNOWBIRD
SNOWBIRDS
SNOWBLINK
SNOWBOARD
SNOWBOOT
SNOWBOOTS

SNOWBOUND
SNOWBRUSH
SNOWBUSH
SNOWCAP
SNOWCAPS
SNOWCAT
SNOWCATS
SNOWCLONE
SNOWCOACH
SNOWDOME
SNOWDOMES
SNOWDRIFT
SNOWDROP
SNOWDROPS
SNOWED
SNOWFALL
SNOWFALLS
SNOWFIELD
SNOWFLAKE
SNOWFLEA
SNOWFLEAS
SNOWFLECK
SNOWFLICK
SNOWGLOBE
SNOWIER
SNOWIEST
SNOWILY
SNOWINESS
SNOWING
SNOWISH
SNOWK
SNOWKED
SNOWKING
SNOWKS
SNOWLAND
SNOWLANDS
SNOWLESS
SNOWLIKE
SNOWLINE
SNOWLINES
SNOWMAKER
SNOWMAN
SNOWMELT
SNOWMELTS
SNOWMEN
SNOWMOLD
SNOWMOLDS
SNOWMOULD
SNOWPACK
SNOWPACKS
SNOWPLOW
SNOWPLOWS
SNOWS
SNOWSCAPE
SNOWSHED
SNOWSHEDS
SNOWSHOE
SNOWSHOED
SNOWSHOER
SNOWSHOES
SNOWSLIDE
SNOWSLIP
SNOWSLIPS
SNOWSNAKE
SNOWSTORM
SNOWSUIT
SNOWSUITS
SNOWY
SNUB
SNUBBE
SNUBBED
SNUBBER
SNUBBERS
SNUBBES
SNUBBEST
SNUBBIER
SNUBBIEST
SNUBBING
SNUBBINGS
SNUBBISH
SNUBBY
SNUBFIN
SNUBNESS
SNUBS
SNUCK
SNUDGE
SNUDGED
SNUDGES
SNUDGING
SNUFF
SNUFFBOX
SNUFFED
SNUFFER
SNUFFERS
SNUFFIER
SNUFFIEST
SNUFFILY
SNUFFING
SNUFFINGS
SNUFFLE
SNUFFLED
SNUFFLER
SNUFFLERS
SNUFFLES
SNUFFLIER
SNUFFLING
SNUFFLY
SNUFFS
SNUFFY
SNUG
SNUGGED
SNUGGER
SNUGGERIE
SNUGGERY
SNUGGEST
SNUGGIES
SNUGGING
SNUGGLE
SNUGGLED
SNUGGLES
SNUGGLIER
SNUGGLING
SNUGGLY
SNUGLY
SNUGNESS
SNUGS
SNUSH
SNUSHED
SNUSHES
SNUSHING
SNUZZLE
SNUZZLED
SNUZZLES
SNUZZLING
SNY
SNYE
SNYES
SO
SOAK
SOAKAGE
SOAKAGES
SOAKAWAY
SOAKAWAYS
SOAKED
SOAKEN
SOAKER
SOAKERS
SOAKING
SOAKINGLY
SOAKINGS
SOAKS
SOAP
SOAPBARK
SOAPBARKS
SOAPBERRY
SOAPBOX
SOAPBOXED
SOAPBOXES
SOAPDISH
SOAPED
SOAPER
SOAPERS
SOAPFISH
SOAPIE
SOAPIER
SOAPIES
SOAPIEST
SOAPILY
SOAPINESS
SOAPING
SOAPLAND
SOAPLANDS
SOAPLESS
SOAPLIKE
SOAPROOT
SOAPROOTS
SOAPS
SOAPSTONE
SOAPSUDS
SOAPSUDSY
SOAPWORT
SOAPWORTS
SOAPY
SOAR
SOARAWAY
SOARE
SOARED
SOARER
SOARERS
SOARES
SOARING
SOARINGLY
SOARINGS
SOARS
SOAVE
SOAVES
SOB
SOBA
SOBAS
SOBBED
SOBBER
SOBBERS
SOBBING
SOBBINGLY
SOBBINGS
SOBEIT
SOBER
SOBERED
SOBERER
SOBEREST
SOBERING
SOBERISE
SOBERISED
SOBERISES
SOBERIZE
SOBERIZED
SOBERIZES
SOBERLY
SOBERNESS
SOBERS
SOBFUL
SOBOLE
SOBOLES
SOBRIETY
SOBRIQUET
SOBS
SOC
SOCA
SOCAGE
SOCAGER
SOCAGERS
SOCAGES
SOCAS
SOCCAGE
SOCCAGES
SOCCER
SOCCERS
SOCES
SOCIABLE
SOCIABLES

SOCIABLY
SOCIAL
SOCIALISE
SOCIALISM
SOCIALIST
SOCIALITE
SOCIALITY
SOCIALIZE
SOCIALLY
SOCIALS
SOCIATE
SOCIATES
SOCIATION
SOCIATIVE
SOCIETAL
SOCIETIES
SOCIETY
SOCIOGRAM
SOCIOLECT
SOCIOLOGY
SOCIOPATH
SOCK
SOCKED
SOCKET
SOCKETED
SOCKETING
SOCKETS
SOCKETTE
SOCKETTES
SOCKEYE
SOCKEYES
SOCKING
SOCKLESS
SOCKMAN
SOCKMEN
SOCKO
SOCKS
SOCLE
SOCLES
SOCMAN
SOCMEN
SOCS
SOD
SODA
SODAIC
SODAIN
SODAINE
SODALESS
SODALIST
SODALISTS
SODALITE
SODALITES
SODALITY
SODAMIDE
SODAMIDES
SODAS
SODBUSTER
SODDED
SODDEN
SODDENED
SODDENING
SODDENLY
SODDENS
SODDIE
SODDIER
SODDIES
SODDIEST
SODDING
SODDY
SODGER
SODGERED
SODGERING
SODGERS
SODIC
SODICITY
SODIUM
SODIUMS
SODOM
SODOMIES
SODOMISE
SODOMISED
SODOMISES
SODOMIST
SODOMISTS
SODOMITE
SODOMITES
SODOMITIC
SODOMIZE
SODOMIZED
SODOMIZES
SODOMS
SODOMY
SODS
SOEVER
SOFA
SOFABED
SOFABEDS
SOFAR
SOFARS
SOFAS
SOFFIONI
SOFFIT
SOFFITS
SOFT
SOFTA
SOFTAS
SOFTBACK
SOFTBACKS
SOFTBALL
SOFTBALLS
SOFTBOUND
SOFTCORE
SOFTCOVER
SOFTED
SOFTEN
SOFTENED
SOFTENER
SOFTENERS
SOFTENING
SOFTENS
SOFTER
SOFTEST
SOFTGOODS
SOFTHEAD
SOFTHEADS
SOFTIE
SOFTIES
SOFTING
SOFTISH
SOFTLING
SOFTLINGS
SOFTLY
SOFTNESS
SOFTPASTE
SOFTS
SOFTSCAPE
SOFTSHELL
SOFTWARE
SOFTWARES
SOFTWOOD
SOFTWOODS
SOFTY
SOG
SOGER
SOGERS
SOGGED
SOGGIER
SOGGIEST
SOGGILY
SOGGINESS
SOGGING
SOGGINGS
SOGGY
SOGS
SOH
SOHO
SOHS
SOHUR
SOHURS
SOIGNE
SOIGNEE
SOIL
SOILAGE
SOILAGES
SOILBORNE
SOILED
SOILIER
SOILIEST
SOILINESS
SOILING
SOILINGS
SOILLESS
SOILS
SOILURE
SOILURES
SOILY
SOIREE
SOIREES
SOJA
SOJAS
SOJOURN
SOJOURNED
SOJOURNER
SOJOURNS
SOJU
SOJUS
SOKAH
SOKAHS
SOKAIYA
SOKE
SOKEMAN
SOKEMANRY
SOKEMEN
SOKEN
SOKENS
SOKES
SOKOL
SOKOLS
SOL
SOLA
SOLACE
SOLACED
SOLACER
SOLACERS
SOLACES
SOLACING
SOLACIOUS
SOLAH
SOLAHS
SOLAN
SOLAND
SOLANDER
SOLANDERS
SOLANDS
SOLANIN
SOLANINE
SOLANINES
SOLANINS
SOLANO
SOLANOS
SOLANS
SOLANUM
SOLANUMS
SOLAR
SOLARIA
SOLARISE
SOLARISED
SOLARISES
SOLARISM
SOLARISMS
SOLARIST
SOLARISTS
SOLARIUM
SOLARIUMS
SOLARIZE
SOLARIZED
SOLARIZES
SOLARS
SOLAS
SOLATE

SOLATED
SOLATES
SOLATIA
SOLATING
SOLATION
SOLATIONS
SOLATIUM
SOLD
SOLDADO
SOLDADOES
SOLDADOS
SOLDAN
SOLDANS
SOLDE
SOLDER
SOLDERED
SOLDERER
SOLDERERS
SOLDERING
SOLDERS
SOLDES
SOLDI
SOLDIER
SOLDIERED
SOLDIERLY
SOLDIERS
SOLDIERY
SOLDO
SOLDS
SOLE
SOLECISE
SOLECISED
SOLECISES
SOLECISM
SOLECISMS
SOLECIST
SOLECISTS
SOLECIZE
SOLECIZED
SOLECIZES
SOLED
SOLEI
SOLEIN
SOLELESS
SOLELY
SOLEMN
SOLEMNER
SOLEMNESS
SOLEMNEST
SOLEMNIFY
SOLEMNISE
SOLEMNITY
SOLEMNIZE
SOLEMNLY
SOLENESS
SOLENETTE
SOLENODON
SOLENOID
SOLENOIDS
SOLEPLATE
SOLEPRINT
SOLER
SOLERA
SOLERAS
SOLERET
SOLERETS
SOLERS
SOLES
SOLEUS
SOLEUSES
SOLFATARA
SOLFEGE
SOLFEGES
SOLFEGGI
SOLFEGGIO
SOLFERINO
SOLGEL
SOLI
SOLICIT
SOLICITED
SOLICITOR
SOLICITS
SOLICITY
SOLID
SOLIDAGO
SOLIDAGOS
SOLIDARE
SOLIDARES
SOLIDARY
SOLIDATE
SOLIDATED
SOLIDATES
SOLIDER
SOLIDEST
SOLIDI
SOLIDIFY
SOLIDISH
SOLIDISM
SOLIDISMS
SOLIDIST
SOLIDISTS
SOLIDITY
SOLIDLY
SOLIDNESS
SOLIDS
SOLIDUM
SOLIDUMS
SOLIDUS
SOLILOQUY
SOLING
SOLION
SOLIONS
SOLIPED
SOLIPEDS
SOLIPSISM
SOLIPSIST
SOLIQUID
SOLIQUIDS
SOLITAIRE
SOLITARY
SOLITO
SOLITON
SOLITONS
SOLITUDE
SOLITUDES
SOLIVE
SOLIVES
SOLLAR
SOLLARED
SOLLARING
SOLLARS
SOLLER
SOLLERET
SOLLERETS
SOLLERS
SOLLICKER
SOLO
SOLOED
SOLOES
SOLOING
SOLOIST
SOLOISTIC
SOLOISTS
SOLON
SOLONCHAK
SOLONETS
SOLONETZ
SOLONS
SOLOS
SOLPUGID
SOLPUGIDS
SOLS
SOLSTICE
SOLSTICES
SOLUBLE
SOLUBLES
SOLUBLY
SOLUM
SOLUMS
SOLUNAR
SOLUS
SOLUSES
SOLUTAL
SOLUTE
SOLUTES
SOLUTION
SOLUTIONS
SOLUTIVE
SOLUTIVES
SOLVABLE
SOLVATE
SOLVATED
SOLVATES
SOLVATING
SOLVATION
SOLVE
SOLVED
SOLVENCY
SOLVENT
SOLVENTLY
SOLVENTS
SOLVER
SOLVERS
SOLVES
SOLVING
SOM
SOMA
SOMAN
SOMANS
SOMAS
SOMASCOPE
SOMATA
SOMATIC
SOMATISM
SOMATISMS
SOMATIST
SOMATISTS
SOMBER
SOMBERED
SOMBERER
SOMBEREST
SOMBERING
SOMBERLY
SOMBERS
SOMBRE
SOMBRED
SOMBRELY
SOMBRER
SOMBRERO
SOMBREROS
SOMBRES
SOMBREST
SOMBRING
SOMBROUS
SOME
SOMEBODY
SOMEDAY
SOMEDEAL
SOMEDEALS
SOMEDELE
SOMEGATE
SOMEHOW
SOMEONE
SOMEONES
SOMEPLACE
SOMERSET
SOMERSETS
SOMETHING
SOMETIME
SOMETIMES
SOMEWAY
SOMEWAYS
SOMEWHAT
SOMEWHATS
SOMEWHEN
SOMEWHERE
SOMEWHILE
SOMEWHY
SOMEWISE
SOMITAL

SOMITE
SOMITES
SOMITIC
SOMMELIER
SOMNIAL
SOMNIATE
SOMNIATED
SOMNIATES
SOMNIFIC
SOMNOLENT
SOMONI
SOMONIS
SOMS
SOMY
SON
SONANCE
SONANCES
SONANCIES
SONANCY
SONANT
SONANTAL
SONANTIC
SONANTS
SONAR
SONARMAN
SONARMEN
SONARS
SONATA
SONATAS
SONATINA
SONATINAS
SONATINE
SONCE
SONCES
SONDAGE
SONDAGES
SONDE
SONDELI
SONDELIS
SONDER
SONDERS
SONDES
SONE
SONERI
SONERIS
SONES
SONG
SONGBIRD
SONGBIRDS
SONGBOOK
SONGBOOKS
SONGCRAFT
SONGFEST
SONGFESTS
SONGFUL
SONGFULLY
SONGKOK
SONGKOKS
SONGLESS
SONGLIKE
SONGMAN
SONGMEN
SONGOLOLO
SONGS
SONGSHEET
SONGSMITH
SONGSTER
SONGSTERS
SONHOOD
SONHOODS
SONIC
SONICALLY
SONICATE
SONICATED
SONICATES
SONICATOR
SONICS
SONLESS
SONLIER
SONLIEST
SONLIKE
SONLY
SONNE
SONNES
SONNET
SONNETARY
SONNETED
SONNETEER
SONNETING
SONNETISE
SONNETIZE
SONNETS
SONNETTED
SONNIES
SONNY
SONOBUOY
SONOBUOYS
SONOGRAM
SONOGRAMS
SONOGRAPH
SONOMETER
SONORANT
SONORANTS
SONORITY
SONOROUS
SONOVOX
SONOVOXES
SONS
SONSE
SONSES
SONSHIP
SONSHIPS
SONSIE
SONSIER
SONSIEST
SONSY
SONTAG
SONTAGS
SONTIES
SOOCHONG
SOOCHONGS
SOOEY
SOOGEE
SOOGEED
SOOGEEING
SOOGEES
SOOGIE
SOOGIED
SOOGIEING
SOOGIES
SOOJEY
SOOJEYS
SOOK
SOOKED
SOOKIER
SOOKIEST
SOOKING
SOOKS
SOOKY
SOOL
SOOLE
SOOLED
SOOLER
SOOLERS
SOOLES
SOOLING
SOOLS
SOOM
SOOMED
SOOMING
SOOMS
SOON
SOONER
SOONERS
SOONEST
SOONISH
SOOP
SOOPED
SOOPING
SOOPINGS
SOOPS
SOOPSTAKE
SOOT
SOOTE
SOOTED
SOOTERKIN
SOOTES
SOOTFLAKE
SOOTH
SOOTHE
SOOTHED
SOOTHER
SOOTHERED
SOOTHERS
SOOTHES
SOOTHEST
SOOTHFAST
SOOTHFUL
SOOTHING
SOOTHINGS
SOOTHLICH
SOOTHLY
SOOTHS
SOOTHSAID
SOOTHSAY
SOOTHSAYS
SOOTIER
SOOTIEST
SOOTILY
SOOTINESS
SOOTING
SOOTINGS
SOOTLESS
SOOTS
SOOTY
SOP
SOPAPILLA
SOPH
SOPHERIC
SOPHERIM
SOPHIES
SOPHISM
SOPHISMS
SOPHIST
SOPHISTER
SOPHISTIC
SOPHISTRY
SOPHISTS
SOPHOMORE
SOPHS
SOPHY
SOPITE
SOPITED
SOPITES
SOPITING
SOPOR
SOPORIFIC
SOPOROSE
SOPOROUS
SOPORS
SOPPED
SOPPIER
SOPPIEST
SOPPILY
SOPPINESS
SOPPING
SOPPINGS
SOPPY
SOPRA
SOPRANI
SOPRANINI
SOPRANINO
SOPRANIST
SOPRANO
SOPRANOS
SOPS
SORA
SORAGE
SORAGES
SORAL

S

SORAS
SORB
SORBABLE
SORBARIA
SORBARIAS
SORBATE
SORBATES
SORBED
SORBENT
SORBENTS
SORBET
SORBETS
SORBIC
SORBING
SORBITAN
SORBITANS
SORBITE
SORBITES
SORBITIC
SORBITISE
SORBITIZE
SORBITOL
SORBITOLS
SORBO
SORBOSE
SORBOSES
SORBS
SORBUS
SORBUSES
SORCERER
SORCERERS
SORCERESS
SORCERIES
SORCEROUS
SORCERY
SORD
SORDA
SORDED
SORDES
SORDID
SORDIDER
SORDIDEST
SORDIDLY
SORDINE
SORDINES
SORDING
SORDINI
SORDINO
SORDO
SORDOR
SORDORS
SORDS
SORE
SORED
SOREDIA
SOREDIAL
SOREDIATE
SOREDIUM
SOREE
SOREES
SOREHEAD
SOREHEADS
SOREHON
SOREHONS
SOREL
SORELL
SORELLS
SORELS
SORELY
SORENESS
SORER
SORES
SOREST
SOREX
SOREXES
SORGHO
SORGHOS
SORGHUM
SORGHUMS
SORGO
SORGOS
SORI
SORICINE
SORICOID
SORING
SORINGS
SORITES
SORITIC
SORITICAL
SORN
SORNED
SORNER
SORNERS
SORNING
SORNINGS
SORNS
SOROBAN
SOROBANS
SOROCHE
SOROCHES
SORORAL
SORORALLY
SORORATE
SORORATES
SORORIAL
SORORISE
SORORISED
SORORISES
SORORITY
SORORIZE
SORORIZED
SORORIZES
SOROSES
SOROSIS
SOROSISES
SORPTION
SORPTIONS
SORPTIVE
SORRA
SORRAS
SORREL
SORRELS
SORRIER
SORRIEST
SORRILY
SORRINESS
SORROW
SORROWED
SORROWER
SORROWERS
SORROWFUL
SORROWING
SORROWS
SORRY
SORRYISH
SORT
SORTA
SORTABLE
SORTABLY
SORTAL
SORTALS
SORTANCE
SORTANCES
SORTATION
SORTED
SORTER
SORTERS
SORTES
SORTIE
SORTIED
SORTIEING
SORTIES
SORTILEGE
SORTILEGY
SORTING
SORTINGS
SORTITION
SORTMENT
SORTMENTS
SORTS
SORUS
SOS
SOSATIE
SOSATIES
SOSS
SOSSED
SOSSES
SOSSING
SOSSINGS
SOSTENUTI
SOSTENUTO
SOT
SOTERIAL
SOTH
SOTHS
SOTOL
SOTOLS
SOTS
SOTTED
SOTTEDLY
SOTTING
SOTTINGS
SOTTISH
SOTTISHLY
SOTTISIER
SOU
SOUARI
SOUARIS
SOUBISE
SOUBISES
SOUBRETTE
SOUCAR
SOUCARS
SOUCE
SOUCED
SOUCES
SOUCHONG
SOUCHONGS
SOUCING
SOUCT
SOUDAN
SOUDANS
SOUFFLE
SOUFFLED
SOUFFLEED
SOUFFLES
SOUGH
SOUGHED
SOUGHING
SOUGHS
SOUGHT
SOUK
SOUKED
SOUKING
SOUKOUS
SOUKOUSES
SOUKS
SOUL
SOULDAN
SOULDANS
SOULDIER
SOULDIERS
SOULED
SOULFUL
SOULFULLY
SOULLESS
SOULLIKE
SOULMATE
SOULMATES
SOULS
SOULSTER
SOULSTERS
SOUM
SOUMED
SOUMING
SOUMINGS
SOUMS
SOUND
SOUNDABLE
SOUNDBAR

SOUNDBARS
SOUNDBITE
SOUNDBOX
SOUNDCARD
SOUNDED
SOUNDER
SOUNDERS
SOUNDEST
SOUNDING
SOUNDINGS
SOUNDLESS
SOUNDLY
SOUNDMAN
SOUNDMEN
SOUNDNESS
SOUNDPOST
SOUNDS
SOUP
SOUPCON
SOUPCONS
SOUPED
SOUPER
SOUPERS
SOUPFIN
SOUPFINS
SOUPIER
SOUPIEST
SOUPILY
SOUPINESS
SOUPING
SOUPLE
SOUPLED
SOUPLES
SOUPLESS
SOUPLIKE
SOUPLING
SOUPS
SOUPSPOON
SOUPY
SOUR
SOURBALL
SOURBALLS
SOURCE
SOURCED
SOURCEFUL
SOURCES
SOURCING
SOURCINGS
SOURDINE
SOURDINES
SOURDOUGH
SOURED
SOURER
SOUREST
SOURGUM
SOURGUMS
SOURING
SOURINGS
SOURISH
SOURISHLY
SOURLY
SOURNESS
SOUROCK
SOUROCKS
SOURPUSS
SOURS
SOURSE
SOURSES
SOURSOP
SOURSOPS
SOURVELD
SOURVELDS
SOURWOOD
SOURWOODS
SOUS
SOUSE
SOUSED
SOUSER
SOUSERS
SOUSES
SOUSING
SOUSINGS
SOUSLIK
SOUSLIKS
SOUT
SOUTACHE
SOUTACHES
SOUTANE
SOUTANES
SOUTAR
SOUTARS
SOUTENEUR
SOUTER
SOUTERLY
SOUTERS
SOUTH
SOUTHEAST
SOUTHED
SOUTHER
SOUTHERED
SOUTHERLY
SOUTHERN
SOUTHERNS
SOUTHERS
SOUTHING
SOUTHINGS
SOUTHLAND
SOUTHMOST
SOUTHPAW
SOUTHPAWS
SOUTHRON
SOUTHRONS
SOUTHS
SOUTHSAID
SOUTHSAY
SOUTHSAYS
SOUTHWARD
SOUTHWEST
SOUTIE
SOUTIES
SOUTPIEL
SOUTPIELS
SOUTS
SOUVENIR
SOUVENIRS
SOUVLAKI
SOUVLAKIA
SOUVLAKIS
SOV
SOVENANCE
SOVEREIGN
SOVIET
SOVIETIC
SOVIETISE
SOVIETISM
SOVIETIST
SOVIETIZE
SOVIETS
SOVKHOZ
SOVKHOZES
SOVKHOZY
SOVRAN
SOVRANLY
SOVRANS
SOVRANTY
SOVS
SOW
SOWABLE
SOWANS
SOWAR
SOWARREE
SOWARREES
SOWARRIES
SOWARRY
SOWARS
SOWBACK
SOWBACKS
SOWBELLY
SOWBREAD
SOWBREADS
SOWBUG
SOWBUGS
SOWCAR
SOWCARS
SOWCE
SOWCED
SOWCES
SOWCING
SOWDER
SOWDERS
SOWED
SOWENS
SOWER
SOWERS
SOWF
SOWFED
SOWFF
SOWFFED
SOWFFING
SOWFFS
SOWFING
SOWFS
SOWING
SOWINGS
SOWL
SOWLE
SOWLED
SOWLES
SOWLING
SOWLS
SOWM
SOWMED
SOWMING
SOWMS
SOWN
SOWND
SOWNDED
SOWNDING
SOWNDS
SOWNE
SOWNES
SOWP
SOWPED
SOWPING
SOWPS
SOWS
SOWSE
SOWSED
SOWSES
SOWSING
SOWSSE
SOWSSED
SOWSSES
SOWSSING
SOWTER
SOWTERS
SOWTH
SOWTHED
SOWTHING
SOWTHS
SOX
SOY
SOYA
SOYAS
SOYBEAN
SOYBEANS
SOYBURGER
SOYLE
SOYLED
SOYLES
SOYLING
SOYMEAL
SOYMEALS
SOYMILK
SOYMILKS
SOYS
SOYUZ
SOYUZES
SOZ
SOZIN

S

SOZINE
SOZINES
SOZINS
SOZZLE
SOZZLED
SOZZLES
SOZZLIER
SOZZLIEST
SOZZLING
SOZZLY
SPA
SPACE
SPACEBAND
SPACED
SPACELAB
SPACELABS
SPACELESS
SPACEMAN
SPACEMEN
SPACEPORT
SPACER
SPACERS
SPACES
SPACESHIP
SPACESUIT
SPACETIME
SPACEWALK
SPACEWARD
SPACEY
SPACIAL
SPACIALLY
SPACIER
SPACIEST
SPACINESS
SPACING
SPACINGS
SPACIOUS
SPACKLE
SPACKLED
SPACKLES
SPACKLING
SPACY
SPADASSIN
SPADE
SPADED
SPADEFEET
SPADEFISH
SPADEFOOT
SPADEFUL
SPADEFULS
SPADELIKE
SPADEMAN
SPADEMEN
SPADER
SPADERS
SPADES
SPADESMAN
SPADESMEN
SPADEWORK
SPADGER
SPADGERS
SPADICES
SPADILLE
SPADILLES
SPADILLIO
SPADILLO
SPADILLOS
SPADING
SPADIX
SPADIXES
SPADO
SPADOES
SPADONES
SPADOS
SPADROON
SPADROONS
SPAE
SPAED
SPAEING
SPAEINGS
SPAEMAN
SPAEMEN
SPAER
SPAERS
SPAES
SPAETZLE
SPAETZLES
SPAEWIFE
SPAEWIVES
SPAG
SPAGERIC
SPAGGED
SPAGGING
SPAGHETTI
SPAGIRIC
SPAGIRIST
SPAGS
SPAGYRIC
SPAGYRICS
SPAGYRIST
SPAHEE
SPAHEES
SPAHI
SPAHIS
SPAIL
SPAILS
SPAIN
SPAINED
SPAING
SPAINGS
SPAINING
SPAINS
SPAIRGE
SPAIRGED
SPAIRGES
SPAIRGING
SPAIT
SPAITS
SPAKE
SPALD
SPALDEEN
SPALDEENS
SPALDS
SPALE
SPALES
SPALL
SPALLABLE
SPALLE
SPALLED
SPALLER
SPALLERS
SPALLES
SPALLING
SPALLINGS
SPALLS
SPALPEEN
SPALPEENS
SPALT
SPALTED
SPALTING
SPALTS
SPAM
SPAMBOT
SPAMBOTS
SPAMMED
SPAMMER
SPAMMERS
SPAMMIE
SPAMMIER
SPAMMIES
SPAMMIEST
SPAMMING
SPAMMINGS
SPAMMY
SPAMS
SPAN
SPANAEMIA
SPANAEMIC
SPANCEL
SPANCELED
SPANCELS
SPANDEX
SPANDEXED
SPANDEXES
SPANDREL
SPANDRELS
SPANDRIL
SPANDRILS
SPANE
SPANED
SPANES
SPANG
SPANGED
SPANGHEW
SPANGHEWS
SPANGING
SPANGLE
SPANGLED
SPANGLER
SPANGLERS
SPANGLES
SPANGLET
SPANGLETS
SPANGLIER
SPANGLING
SPANGLY
SPANGS
SPANIEL
SPANIELS
SPANING
SPANK
SPANKED
SPANKER
SPANKERS
SPANKING
SPANKINGS
SPANKS
SPANLESS
SPANNED
SPANNER
SPANNERS
SPANNING
SPANS
SPANSPEK
SPANSPEKS
SPANSULE
SPANSULES
SPANWORM
SPANWORMS
SPAR
SPARABLE
SPARABLES
SPARAXIS
SPARD
SPARE
SPAREABLE
SPARED
SPARELESS
SPARELY
SPARENESS
SPARER
SPARERIB
SPARERIBS
SPARERS
SPARES
SPAREST
SPARGE
SPARGED
SPARGER
SPARGERS
SPARGES
SPARGING
SPARID
SPARIDS
SPARING
SPARINGLY
SPARK
SPARKE
SPARKED
SPARKER

S

SPARKERS
SPARKES
SPARKIE
SPARKIER
SPARKIES
SPARKIEST
SPARKILY
SPARKING
SPARKISH
SPARKLE
SPARKLED
SPARKLER
SPARKLERS
SPARKLES
SPARKLESS
SPARKLET
SPARKLETS
SPARKLIER
SPARKLIES
SPARKLING
SPARKLY
SPARKPLUG
SPARKS
SPARKY
SPARLIKE
SPARLING
SPARLINGS
SPAROID
SPAROIDS
SPARRE
SPARRED
SPARRER
SPARRERS
SPARRES
SPARRIER
SPARRIEST
SPARRING
SPARRINGS
SPARROW
SPARROWS
SPARRY
SPARS
SPARSE
SPARSEDLY
SPARSELY
SPARSER
SPARSEST
SPARSITY
SPART
SPARTAN
SPARTANS
SPARTEINE
SPARTERIE
SPARTH
SPARTHE
SPARTHES
SPARTHS
SPARTICLE
SPARTINA
SPARTINAS
SPARTS
SPAS
SPASM
SPASMATIC
SPASMED
SPASMIC
SPASMING
SPASMODIC
SPASMS
SPASTIC
SPAT
SPATE
SPATES
SPATFALL
SPATFALLS
SPATHAL
SPATHE
SPATHED
SPATHES
SPATHIC
SPATHOSE
SPATIAL
SPATIALLY
SPATLESE
SPATLESEN
SPATLESES
SPATS
SPATTED
SPATTEE
SPATTEES
SPATTER
SPATTERED
SPATTERS
SPATTING
SPATULA
SPATULAR
SPATULAS
SPATULATE
SPATULE
SPATULES
SPATZLE
SPATZLES
SPAUL
SPAULD
SPAULDS
SPAULS
SPAVIE
SPAVIES
SPAVIET
SPAVIN
SPAVINED
SPAVINS
SPAW
SPAWL
SPAWLED
SPAWLING
SPAWLS
SPAWN
SPAWNED
SPAWNER
SPAWNERS
SPAWNIER
SPAWNIEST
SPAWNING
SPAWNINGS
SPAWNS
SPAWNY
SPAWS
SPAY
SPAYAD
SPAYADS
SPAYD
SPAYDS
SPAYED
SPAYING
SPAYS
SPAZA
SPEAK
SPEAKABLE
SPEAKEASY
SPEAKER
SPEAKERS
SPEAKING
SPEAKINGS
SPEAKOUT
SPEAKOUTS
SPEAKS
SPEAL
SPEALS
SPEAN
SPEANED
SPEANING
SPEANS
SPEAR
SPEARED
SPEARER
SPEARERS
SPEARFISH
SPEARGUN
SPEARGUNS
SPEARHEAD
SPEARIER
SPEARIEST
SPEARING
SPEARINGS
SPEARLIKE
SPEARMAN
SPEARMEN
SPEARMINT
SPEARS
SPEARWORT
SPEARY
SPEAT
SPEATS
SPEC
SPECCED
SPECCIER
SPECCIES
SPECCIEST
SPECCING
SPECCY
SPECIAL
SPECIALER
SPECIALLY
SPECIALS
SPECIALTY
SPECIATE
SPECIATED
SPECIATES
SPECIE
SPECIES
SPECIFIC
SPECIFICS
SPECIFIED
SPECIFIER
SPECIFIES
SPECIFY
SPECIMEN
SPECIMENS
SPECIOUS
SPECK
SPECKED
SPECKIER
SPECKIES
SPECKIEST
SPECKING
SPECKLE
SPECKLED
SPECKLES
SPECKLESS
SPECKLING
SPECKS
SPECKY
SPECS
SPECT
SPECTACLE
SPECTATE
SPECTATED
SPECTATES
SPECTATOR
SPECTED
SPECTER
SPECTERS
SPECTING
SPECTRA
SPECTRAL
SPECTRE
SPECTRES
SPECTRIN
SPECTRINS
SPECTRUM
SPECTRUMS
SPECTS
SPECULA
SPECULAR
SPECULATE
SPECULUM
SPECULUMS
SPED
SPEECH

SPEECHED
SPEECHES
SPEECHFUL
SPEECHIFY
SPEECHING
SPEED
SPEEDBALL
SPEEDBOAT
SPEEDED
SPEEDER
SPEEDERS
SPEEDFUL
SPEEDIER
SPEEDIEST
SPEEDILY
SPEEDING
SPEEDINGS
SPEEDLESS
SPEEDO
SPEEDOS
SPEEDREAD
SPEEDS
SPEEDSTER
SPEEDUP
SPEEDUPS
SPEEDWALK
SPEEDWAY
SPEEDWAYS
SPEEDWELL
SPEEDY
SPEEL
SPEELED
SPEELER
SPEELERS
SPEELING
SPEELS
SPEER
SPEERED
SPEERING
SPEERINGS
SPEERS
SPEIL
SPEILED
SPEILING
SPEILS
SPEIR
SPEIRED
SPEIRING
SPEIRINGS
SPEIRS
SPEISE
SPEISES
SPEISS
SPEISSES
SPEK
SPEKBOOM
SPEKBOOMS
SPEKS
SPELAEAN
SPELD
SPELDED
SPELDER
SPELDERED
SPELDERS
SPELDIN
SPELDING
SPELDINGS
SPELDINS
SPELDRIN
SPELDRING
SPELDRINS
SPELDS
SPELEAN
SPELK
SPELKS
SPELL
SPELLABLE
SPELLBIND
SPELLDOWN
SPELLED
SPELLER
SPELLERS
SPELLFUL
SPELLICAN
SPELLING
SPELLINGS
SPELLS
SPELT
SPELTER
SPELTERS
SPELTS
SPELTZ
SPELTZES
SPELUNK
SPELUNKED
SPELUNKER
SPELUNKS
SPENCE
SPENCER
SPENCERS
SPENCES
SPEND
SPENDABLE
SPENDALL
SPENDALLS
SPENDER
SPENDERS
SPENDIER
SPENDIEST
SPENDING
SPENDINGS
SPENDS
SPENDY
SPENSE
SPENSES
SPENT
SPEOS
SPEOSES
SPERLING
SPERLINGS
SPERM
SPERMARIA
SPERMARY
SPERMATIA
SPERMATIC
SPERMATID
SPERMIC
SPERMINE
SPERMINES
SPERMOUS
SPERMS
SPERRE
SPERRED
SPERRES
SPERRING
SPERSE
SPERSED
SPERSES
SPERSING
SPERST
SPERTHE
SPERTHES
SPET
SPETCH
SPETCHED
SPETCHES
SPETCHING
SPETS
SPETSNAZ
SPETTING
SPETZNAZ
SPEUG
SPEUGS
SPEW
SPEWED
SPEWER
SPEWERS
SPEWIER
SPEWIEST
SPEWINESS
SPEWING
SPEWS
SPEWY
SPHACELUS
SPHAER
SPHAERE
SPHAERES
SPHAERITE
SPHAERS
SPHAGNOUS
SPHAGNUM
SPHAGNUMS
SPHAIREE
SPHAIREES
SPHEAR
SPHEARE
SPHEARES
SPHEARS
SPHENDONE
SPHENE
SPHENES
SPHENIC
SPHENODON
SPHENOID
SPHENOIDS
SPHERAL
SPHERE
SPHERED
SPHERES
SPHERIC
SPHERICAL
SPHERICS
SPHERIER
SPHERIEST
SPHERING
SPHEROID
SPHEROIDS
SPHERULAR
SPHERULE
SPHERULES
SPHERY
SPHINCTER
SPHINGES
SPHINGID
SPHINGIDS
SPHINX
SPHINXES
SPHYGMIC
SPHYGMOID
SPHYGMUS
SPHYNX
SPHYNXES
SPIAL
SPIALS
SPICA
SPICAE
SPICAS
SPICATE
SPICATED
SPICCATO
SPICCATOS
SPICE
SPICEBUSH
SPICED
SPICELESS
SPICER
SPICERIES
SPICERS
SPICERY
SPICES
SPICEY
SPICIER
SPICIEST
SPICILEGE
SPICILY
SPICINESS
SPICING
SPICK
SPICKER
SPICKEST

S

SPICKNEL
SPICKNELS
SPICULA
SPICULAE
SPICULAR
SPICULATE
SPICULE
SPICULES
SPICULUM
SPICY
SPIDE
SPIDER
SPIDERED
SPIDERIER
SPIDERING
SPIDERISH
SPIDERMAN
SPIDERMEN
SPIDERS
SPIDERWEB
SPIDERY
SPIDES
SPIE
SPIED
SPIEGEL
SPIEGELS
SPIEL
SPIELED
SPIELER
SPIELERS
SPIELING
SPIELS
SPIER
SPIERED
SPIERING
SPIERS
SPIES
SPIF
SPIFF
SPIFFED
SPIFFIED
SPIFFIER
SPIFFIES
SPIFFIEST
SPIFFILY
SPIFFING
SPIFFS
SPIFFY
SPIFFYING
SPIFS
SPIGHT
SPIGHTED
SPIGHTING
SPIGHTS
SPIGNEL
SPIGNELS
SPIGOT
SPIGOTS
SPIKE
SPIKED
SPIKEFISH
SPIKELET
SPIKELETS
SPIKELIKE
SPIKENARD
SPIKER
SPIKERIES
SPIKERS
SPIKERY
SPIKES
SPIKEY
SPIKIER
SPIKIEST
SPIKILY
SPIKINESS
SPIKING
SPIKY
SPILE
SPILED
SPILES
SPILIKIN
SPILIKINS
SPILING
SPILINGS
SPILITE
SPILITES
SPILITIC
SPILL
SPILLABLE
SPILLAGE
SPILLAGES
SPILLED
SPILLER
SPILLERS
SPILLIKIN
SPILLING
SPILLINGS
SPILLOVER
SPILLS
SPILLWAY
SPILLWAYS
SPILOSITE
SPILT
SPILTH
SPILTHS
SPIM
SPIMMER
SPIMMERS
SPIMMING
SPIMMINGS
SPIMS
SPIN
SPINA
SPINACENE
SPINACH
SPINACHES
SPINACHY
SPINAE
SPINAGE
SPINAGES
SPINAL
SPINALLY
SPINALS
SPINAR
SPINARAMA
SPINARS
SPINAS
SPINATE
SPINDLE
SPINDLED
SPINDLER
SPINDLERS
SPINDLES
SPINDLIER
SPINDLING
SPINDLY
SPINDRIFT
SPINE
SPINED
SPINEL
SPINELESS
SPINELIKE
SPINELLE
SPINELLES
SPINELS
SPINES
SPINET
SPINETS
SPINETTE
SPINETTES
SPINIER
SPINIEST
SPINIFEX
SPINIFORM
SPININESS
SPINK
SPINKED
SPINKING
SPINKS
SPINLESS
SPINNAKER
SPINNER
SPINNERET
SPINNERS
SPINNERY
SPINNET
SPINNETS
SPINNEY
SPINNEYS
SPINNIER
SPINNIES
SPINNIEST
SPINNING
SPINNINGS
SPINNY
SPINODE
SPINODES
SPINOFF
SPINOFFS
SPINONE
SPINONI
SPINOR
SPINORS
SPINOSE
SPINOSELY
SPINOSITY
SPINOUS
SPINOUT
SPINOUTS
SPINS
SPINSTER
SPINSTERS
SPINTEXT
SPINTEXTS
SPINTO
SPINTOS
SPINULA
SPINULAE
SPINULATE
SPINULE
SPINULES
SPINULOSE
SPINULOUS
SPINY
SPIRACLE
SPIRACLES
SPIRACULA
SPIRAEA
SPIRAEAS
SPIRAL
SPIRALED
SPIRALING
SPIRALISM
SPIRALIST
SPIRALITY
SPIRALLED
SPIRALLY
SPIRALS
SPIRANT
SPIRANTS
SPIRASTER
SPIRATED
SPIRATION
SPIRE
SPIREA
SPIREAS
SPIRED
SPIRELESS
SPIRELET
SPIRELETS
SPIREM
SPIREME
SPIREMES
SPIREMS
SPIRES
SPIREWISE
SPIRIC
SPIRICS
SPIRIER
SPIRIEST

SPIRILLA
SPIRILLAR
SPIRILLUM
SPIRING
SPIRIT
SPIRITED
SPIRITFUL
SPIRITING
SPIRITISM
SPIRITIST
SPIRITOSO
SPIRITOUS
SPIRITS
SPIRITUAL
SPIRITUEL
SPIRITUS
SPIRITY
SPIRLING
SPIRLINGS
SPIROGRAM
SPIROGYRA
SPIROID
SPIRT
SPIRTED
SPIRTING
SPIRTLE
SPIRTLES
SPIRTS
SPIRULA
SPIRULAE
SPIRULAS
SPIRULINA
SPIRY
SPIT
SPITAL
SPITALS
SPITBALL
SPITBALLS
SPITCHER
SPITCHERS
SPITE
SPITED
SPITEFUL
SPITES
SPITFIRE
SPITFIRES
SPITING
SPITS
SPITTED
SPITTEN
SPITTER
SPITTERS
SPITTIER
SPITTIEST
SPITTING
SPITTINGS
SPITTLE
SPITTLES
SPITTLIER
SPITTLY
SPITTOON
SPITTOONS
SPITTY
SPITZ
SPITZES
SPIV
SPIVS
SPIVVERY
SPIVVIER
SPIVVIEST
SPIVVISH
SPIVVY
SPLAKE
SPLAKES
SPLASH
SPLASHED
SPLASHER
SPLASHERS
SPLASHES
SPLASHIER
SPLASHILY
SPLASHING
SPLASHY
SPLAT
SPLATCH
SPLATCHED
SPLATCHES
SPLATS
SPLATTED
SPLATTER
SPLATTERS
SPLATTING
SPLAY
SPLAYED
SPLAYFEET
SPLAYFOOT
SPLAYING
SPLAYS
SPLEEN
SPLEENFUL
SPLEENIER
SPLEENISH
SPLEENS
SPLEENY
SPLENDENT
SPLENDID
SPLENDOR
SPLENDORS
SPLENDOUR
SPLENETIC
SPLENIA
SPLENIAL
SPLENIC
SPLENII
SPLENITIS
SPLENIUM
SPLENIUMS
SPLENIUS
SPLENT
SPLENTS
SPLEUCHAN
SPLICE
SPLICED
SPLICER
SPLICERS
SPLICES
SPLICING
SPLICINGS
SPLIFF
SPLIFFS
SPLINE
SPLINED
SPLINES
SPLINING
SPLINT
SPLINTED
SPLINTER
SPLINTERS
SPLINTERY
SPLINTING
SPLINTS
SPLISH
SPLISHED
SPLISHES
SPLISHING
SPLIT
SPLITS
SPLITTED
SPLITTER
SPLITTERS
SPLITTING
SPLITTISM
SPLITTIST
SPLODGE
SPLODGED
SPLODGES
SPLODGIER
SPLODGILY
SPLODGING
SPLODGY
SPLOG
SPLOGS
SPLOOSH
SPLOOSHED
SPLOOSHES
SPLORE
SPLORES
SPLOSH
SPLOSHED
SPLOSHES
SPLOSHING
SPLOTCH
SPLOTCHED
SPLOTCHES
SPLOTCHY
SPLURGE
SPLURGED
SPLURGER
SPLURGERS
SPLURGES
SPLURGIER
SPLURGING
SPLURGY
SPLURT
SPLURTED
SPLURTING
SPLURTS
SPLUTTER
SPLUTTERS
SPLUTTERY
SPOD
SPODDIER
SPODDIEST
SPODDY
SPODE
SPODES
SPODIUM
SPODIUMS
SPODOGRAM
SPODOSOL
SPODOSOLS
SPODS
SPODUMENE
SPOFFISH
SPOFFY
SPOIL
SPOILABLE
SPOILAGE
SPOILAGES
SPOILED
SPOILER
SPOILERS
SPOILFIVE
SPOILFUL
SPOILING
SPOILS
SPOILSMAN
SPOILSMEN
SPOILT
SPOKE
SPOKED
SPOKEN
SPOKES
SPOKESMAN
SPOKESMEN
SPOKEWISE
SPOKING
SPOLIATE
SPOLIATED
SPOLIATES
SPOLIATOR
SPONDAIC
SPONDAICS
SPONDEE
SPONDEES
SPONDULIX
SPONDYL
SPONDYLS
SPONGE
SPONGEBAG

SPONGED
SPONGEING
SPONGEOUS
SPONGER
SPONGERS
SPONGES
SPONGIER
SPONGIEST
SPONGILY
SPONGIN
SPONGING
SPONGINS
SPONGIOSE
SPONGIOUS
SPONGOID
SPONGY
SPONSAL
SPONSALIA
SPONSIBLE
SPONSING
SPONSINGS
SPONSION
SPONSIONS
SPONSON
SPONSONS
SPONSOR
SPONSORED
SPONSORS
SPONTOON
SPONTOONS
SPOOF
SPOOFED
SPOOFER
SPOOFERS
SPOOFERY
SPOOFIER
SPOOFIEST
SPOOFING
SPOOFINGS
SPOOFS
SPOOFY
SPOOK
SPOOKED
SPOOKERY
SPOOKIER
SPOOKIEST
SPOOKILY
SPOOKING
SPOOKISH
SPOOKS
SPOOKY
SPOOL
SPOOLED
SPOOLER
SPOOLERS
SPOOLING
SPOOLINGS
SPOOLS
SPOOM
SPOOMED
SPOOMING
SPOOMS
SPOON
SPOONBAIT
SPOONBILL
SPOONED
SPOONER
SPOONERS
SPOONEY
SPOONEYS
SPOONFED
SPOONFUL
SPOONFULS
SPOONHOOK
SPOONIER
SPOONIES
SPOONIEST
SPOONILY
SPOONING
SPOONLIKE
SPOONS
SPOONSFUL
SPOONWAYS
SPOONWISE
SPOONWORM
SPOONY
SPOOR
SPOORED
SPOORER
SPOORERS
SPOORING
SPOORS
SPOOT
SPOOTS
SPORADIC
SPORAL
SPORANGIA
SPORE
SPORED
SPORELIKE
SPORES
SPORICIDE
SPORIDESM
SPORIDIA
SPORIDIAL
SPORIDIUM
SPORING
SPORK
SPORKS
SPOROCARP
SPOROCYST
SPOROCYTE
SPOROGENY
SPOROGONY
SPOROID
SPOROPHYL
SPOROZOA
SPOROZOAL
SPOROZOAN
SPOROZOIC
SPOROZOON
SPORRAN
SPORRANS
SPORT
SPORTABLE
SPORTANCE
SPORTBIKE
SPORTCOAT
SPORTED
SPORTER
SPORTERS
SPORTFUL
SPORTIER
SPORTIES
SPORTIEST
SPORTIF
SPORTIFS
SPORTILY
SPORTING
SPORTIVE
SPORTLESS
SPORTS
SPORTSMAN
SPORTSMEN
SPORTY
SPORULAR
SPORULATE
SPORULE
SPORULES
SPOSH
SPOSHES
SPOSHIER
SPOSHIEST
SPOSHY
SPOT
SPOTLESS
SPOTLIGHT
SPOTLIT
SPOTS
SPOTTABLE
SPOTTED
SPOTTER
SPOTTERS
SPOTTIE
SPOTTIER
SPOTTIES
SPOTTIEST
SPOTTILY
SPOTTING
SPOTTINGS
SPOTTY
SPOUSAGE
SPOUSAGES
SPOUSAL
SPOUSALLY
SPOUSALS
SPOUSE
SPOUSED
SPOUSES
SPOUSING
SPOUT
SPOUTED
SPOUTER
SPOUTERS
SPOUTIER
SPOUTIEST
SPOUTING
SPOUTINGS
SPOUTLESS
SPOUTS
SPOUTY
SPRACK
SPRACKLE
SPRACKLED
SPRACKLES
SPRAD
SPRADDLE
SPRADDLED
SPRADDLES
SPRAG
SPRAGGED
SPRAGGING
SPRAGS
SPRAID
SPRAIN
SPRAINED
SPRAINING
SPRAINS
SPRAINT
SPRAINTS
SPRANG
SPRANGLE
SPRANGLED
SPRANGLES
SPRANGS
SPRAT
SPRATS
SPRATTLE
SPRATTLED
SPRATTLES
SPRAUCHLE
SPRAUNCY
SPRAWL
SPRAWLED
SPRAWLER
SPRAWLERS
SPRAWLIER
SPRAWLING
SPRAWLS
SPRAWLY
SPRAY
SPRAYED
SPRAYER
SPRAYERS
SPRAYEY
SPRAYIER
SPRAYIEST
SPRAYING
SPRAYINGS
SPRAYS

SPREAD
SPREADER
SPREADERS
SPREADING
SPREADS
SPREAGH
SPREAGHS
SPREATHE
SPREATHED
SPREATHES
SPREAZE
SPREAZED
SPREAZES
SPREAZING
SPRECHERY
SPRECKLED
SPRED
SPREDD
SPREDDE
SPREDDEN
SPREDDES
SPREDDING
SPREDDS
SPREDS
SPREE
SPREED
SPREEING
SPREES
SPREETHE
SPREETHED
SPREETHES
SPREEZE
SPREEZED
SPREEZES
SPREEZING
SPREKELIA
SPRENT
SPRENTED
SPRENTING
SPRENTS
SPREW
SPREWS
SPRIER
SPRIEST
SPRIG
SPRIGGED
SPRIGGER
SPRIGGERS
SPRIGGIER
SPRIGGING
SPRIGGY
SPRIGHT
SPRIGHTED
SPRIGHTLY
SPRIGHTS
SPRIGS
SPRIGTAIL
SPRING
SPRINGAL
SPRINGALD
SPRINGALS
SPRINGBOK
SPRINGE
SPRINGED
SPRINGER
SPRINGERS
SPRINGES
SPRINGIER
SPRINGILY
SPRINGING
SPRINGLE
SPRINGLES
SPRINGLET
SPRINGS
SPRINGY
SPRINKLE
SPRINKLED
SPRINKLER
SPRINKLES
SPRINT
SPRINTED
SPRINTER
SPRINTERS
SPRINTING
SPRINTS
SPRIT
SPRITE
SPRITEFUL
SPRITELY
SPRITES
SPRITS
SPRITSAIL
SPRITZ
SPRITZED
SPRITZER
SPRITZERS
SPRITZES
SPRITZIER
SPRITZIG
SPRITZIGS
SPRITZING
SPRITZY
SPROCKET
SPROCKETS
SPROD
SPRODS
SPROG
SPROGLET
SPROGLETS
SPROGS
SPRONG
SPROUT
SPROUTED
SPROUTING
SPROUTS
SPRUCE
SPRUCED
SPRUCELY
SPRUCER
SPRUCES
SPRUCEST
SPRUCIER
SPRUCIEST
SPRUCING
SPRUCY
SPRUE
SPRUES
SPRUG
SPRUGS
SPRUIK
SPRUIKED
SPRUIKER
SPRUIKERS
SPRUIKING
SPRUIKS
SPRUIT
SPRUITS
SPRUNG
SPRUSH
SPRUSHED
SPRUSHES
SPRUSHING
SPRY
SPRYER
SPRYEST
SPRYLY
SPRYNESS
SPUD
SPUDDED
SPUDDER
SPUDDERS
SPUDDIER
SPUDDIEST
SPUDDING
SPUDDINGS
SPUDDLE
SPUDDLES
SPUDDY
SPUDGEL
SPUDGELS
SPUDS
SPUE
SPUED
SPUEING
SPUER
SPUERS
SPUES
SPUG
SPUGGIES
SPUGGY
SPUGS
SPUILZIE
SPUILZIED
SPUILZIES
SPUING
SPULE
SPULES
SPULYE
SPULYED
SPULYEING
SPULYES
SPULYIE
SPULYIED
SPULYIES
SPULZIE
SPULZIED
SPULZIES
SPUMANTE
SPUMANTES
SPUME
SPUMED
SPUMES
SPUMIER
SPUMIEST
SPUMING
SPUMONE
SPUMONES
SPUMONI
SPUMONIS
SPUMOUS
SPUMY
SPUN
SPUNGE
SPUNGES
SPUNK
SPUNKED
SPUNKIE
SPUNKIER
SPUNKIES
SPUNKIEST
SPUNKILY
SPUNKING
SPUNKS
SPUNKY
SPUNYARN
SPUNYARNS
SPUR
SPURDOG
SPURDOGS
SPURGALL
SPURGALLS
SPURGE
SPURGES
SPURIAE
SPURIOUS
SPURLESS
SPURLIKE
SPURLING
SPURLINGS
SPURN
SPURNE
SPURNED
SPURNER
SPURNERS
SPURNES
SPURNING
SPURNINGS
SPURNS
SPURRED
SPURRER

SPURRERS
SPURREY
SPURREYS
SPURRIER
SPURRIERS
SPURRIES
SPURRIEST
SPURRING
SPURRINGS
SPURRY
SPURS
SPURT
SPURTED
SPURTER
SPURTERS
SPURTING
SPURTLE
SPURTLES
SPURTS
SPURWAY
SPURWAYS
SPUTA
SPUTNIK
SPUTNIKS
SPUTTER
SPUTTERED
SPUTTERER
SPUTTERS
SPUTTERY
SPUTUM
SPUTUMS
SPY
SPYAL
SPYALS
SPYCAM
SPYCAMS
SPYGLASS
SPYHOLE
SPYHOLES
SPYING
SPYINGS
SPYMASTER
SPYPLANE
SPYPLANES
SPYRE
SPYRES
SPYWARE
SPYWARES
SQUAB
SQUABASH
SQUABBED
SQUABBER
SQUABBEST
SQUABBIER
SQUABBING
SQUABBISH
SQUABBLE
SQUABBLED
SQUABBLER
SQUABBLES
SQUABBY
SQUABS
SQUACCO
SQUACCOS
SQUAD
SQUADDED
SQUADDIE
SQUADDIES
SQUADDING
SQUADDY
SQUADOOSH
SQUADRON
SQUADRONE
SQUADRONS
SQUADS
SQUAIL
SQUAILED
SQUAILER
SQUAILERS
SQUAILING
SQUAILS
SQUALENE
SQUALENES
SQUALID
SQUALIDER
SQUALIDLY
SQUALL
SQUALLED
SQUALLER
SQUALLERS
SQUALLIER
SQUALLING
SQUALLISH
SQUALLS
SQUALLY
SQUALOID
SQUALOR
SQUALORS
SQUAMA
SQUAMAE
SQUAMATE
SQUAMATES
SQUAME
SQUAMELLA
SQUAMES
SQUAMOSAL
SQUAMOSE
SQUAMOUS
SQUAMULA
SQUAMULAS
SQUAMULE
SQUAMULES
SQUANDER
SQUANDERS
SQUARE
SQUARED
SQUARELY
SQUARER
SQUARERS
SQUARES
SQUAREST
SQUARIAL
SQUARIALS
SQUARING
SQUARINGS
SQUARISH
SQUARK
SQUARKS
SQUARROSE
SQUARSON
SQUARSONS
SQUASH
SQUASHED
SQUASHER
SQUASHERS
SQUASHES
SQUASHIER
SQUASHILY
SQUASHING
SQUASHY
SQUAT
SQUATLY
SQUATNESS
SQUATS
SQUATTED
SQUATTER
SQUATTERS
SQUATTEST
SQUATTIER
SQUATTILY
SQUATTING
SQUATTLE
SQUATTLED
SQUATTLES
SQUATTY
SQUAWBUSH
SQUAWFISH
SQUAWK
SQUAWKED
SQUAWKER
SQUAWKERS
SQUAWKIER
SQUAWKING
SQUAWKS
SQUAWKY
SQUAWROOT
SQUEAK
SQUEAKED
SQUEAKER
SQUEAKERS
SQUEAKERY
SQUEAKIER
SQUEAKILY
SQUEAKING
SQUEAKS
SQUEAKY
SQUEAL
SQUEALED
SQUEALER
SQUEALERS
SQUEALING
SQUEALS
SQUEAMISH
SQUEEGEE
SQUEEGEED
SQUEEGEES
SQUEEZE
SQUEEZED
SQUEEZER
SQUEEZERS
SQUEEZES
SQUEEZIER
SQUEEZING
SQUEEZY
SQUEG
SQUEGGED
SQUEGGER
SQUEGGERS
SQUEGGING
SQUEGS
SQUELCH
SQUELCHED
SQUELCHER
SQUELCHES
SQUELCHY
SQUIB
SQUIBBED
SQUIBBER
SQUIBBERS
SQUIBBING
SQUIBS
SQUID
SQUIDDED
SQUIDDING
SQUIDGE
SQUIDGED
SQUIDGES
SQUIDGIER
SQUIDGING
SQUIDGY
SQUIDLIKE
SQUIDS
SQUIER
SQUIERS
SQUIFF
SQUIFFED
SQUIFFER
SQUIFFERS
SQUIFFIER
SQUIFFY
SQUIGGLE
SQUIGGLED
SQUIGGLER
SQUIGGLES
SQUIGGLY
SQUILGEE
SQUILGEED
SQUILGEES
SQUILL
SQUILLA

SQUILLAE
SQUILLAS
SQUILLION
SQUILLS
SQUINANCY
SQUINCH
SQUINCHED
SQUINCHES
SQUINIED
SQUINIES
SQUINNIED
SQUINNIER
SQUINNIES
SQUINNY
SQUINT
SQUINTED
SQUINTER
SQUINTERS
SQUINTEST
SQUINTIER
SQUINTING
SQUINTS
SQUINTY
SQUINY
SQUINYING
SQUIRAGE
SQUIRAGES
SQUIRALTY
SQUIRARCH
SQUIRE
SQUIREAGE
SQUIRED
SQUIREDOM
SQUIREEN
SQUIREENS
SQUIRELY
SQUIRES
SQUIRESS
SQUIRING
SQUIRISH
SQUIRL
SQUIRLS
SQUIRM
SQUIRMED
SQUIRMER
SQUIRMERS
SQUIRMIER
SQUIRMING
SQUIRMS
SQUIRMY
SQUIRR
SQUIRRED
SQUIRREL
SQUIRRELS
SQUIRRELY
SQUIRRING
SQUIRRS
SQUIRT
SQUIRTED
SQUIRTER
SQUIRTERS
SQUIRTING
SQUIRTS
SQUISH
SQUISHED
SQUISHES
SQUISHIER
SQUISHING
SQUISHY
SQUIT
SQUITCH
SQUITCHES
SQUITS
SQUITTERS
SQUIZ
SQUIZZES
SQUOOSH
SQUOOSHED
SQUOOSHES
SQUOOSHY
SQUUSH
SQUUSHED
SQUUSHES
SQUUSHING
SRADDHA
SRADDHAS
SRADHA
SRADHAS
SRI
SRIRACHA
SRIRACHAS
SRIS
ST
STAB
STABBED
STABBER
STABBERS
STABBING
STABBINGS
STABILATE
STABILE
STABILES
STABILISE
STABILITY
STABILIZE
STABLE
STABLEBOY
STABLED
STABLEMAN
STABLEMEN
STABLER
STABLERS
STABLES
STABLEST
STABLING
STABLINGS
STABLISH
STABLY
STABS
STACATION
STACCATI
STACCATO
STACCATOS
STACHYS
STACHYSES
STACK
STACKABLE
STACKED
STACKER
STACKERS
STACKET
STACKETS
STACKING
STACKINGS
STACKLESS
STACKROOM
STACKS
STACKUP
STACKUPS
STACKYARD
STACTE
STACTES
STADDA
STADDAS
STADDLE
STADDLES
STADE
STADES
STADIA
STADIAL
STADIALS
STADIAS
STADIUM
STADIUMS
STAFF
STAFFAGE
STAFFAGES
STAFFED
STAFFER
STAFFERS
STAFFING
STAFFINGS
STAFFMAN
STAFFMEN
STAFFROOM
STAFFS
STAG
STAGE
STAGEABLE
STAGED
STAGEFUL
STAGEFULS
STAGEHAND
STAGEHEAD
STAGELIKE
STAGER
STAGERIES
STAGERS
STAGERY
STAGES
STAGETTE
STAGETTES
STAGEY
STAGGARD
STAGGARDS
STAGGART
STAGGARTS
STAGGED
STAGGER
STAGGERED
STAGGERER
STAGGERS
STAGGERY
STAGGIE
STAGGIER
STAGGIES
STAGGIEST
STAGGING
STAGGY
STAGHORN
STAGHORNS
STAGHOUND
STAGIER
STAGIEST
STAGILY
STAGINESS
STAGING
STAGINGS
STAGNANCE
STAGNANCY
STAGNANT
STAGNATE
STAGNATED
STAGNATES
STAGS
STAGY
STAID
STAIDER
STAIDEST
STAIDLY
STAIDNESS
STAIG
STAIGS
STAIN
STAINABLE
STAINED
STAINER
STAINERS
STAINING
STAININGS
STAINLESS
STAINS
STAIR
STAIRCASE
STAIRED
STAIRFOOT
STAIRHEAD
STAIRLESS
STAIRLIFT
STAIRLIKE

S

STAIRS
STAIRSTEP
STAIRWAY
STAIRWAYS
STAIRWELL
STAIRWISE
STAIRWORK
STAITH
STAITHE
STAITHES
STAITHS
STAKE
STAKED
STAKEOUT
STAKEOUTS
STAKER
STAKERS
STAKES
STAKING
STALACTIC
STALAG
STALAGMA
STALAGMAS
STALAGS
STALE
STALED
STALELY
STALEMATE
STALENESS
STALER
STALES
STALEST
STALING
STALK
STALKED
STALKER
STALKERS
STALKIER
STALKIEST
STALKILY
STALKING
STALKINGS
STALKLESS
STALKLIKE
STALKO
STALKOES
STALKOS
STALKS
STALKY
STALL
STALLAGE
STALLAGES
STALLED
STALLING
STALLINGS
STALLION
STALLIONS
STALLMAN
STALLMEN
STALLS
STALWART
STALWARTS
STALWORTH
STAMEN
STAMENED
STAMENS
STAMINA
STAMINAL
STAMINAS
STAMINATE
STAMINEAL
STAMINODE
STAMINODY
STAMINOID
STAMMEL
STAMMELS
STAMMER
STAMMERED
STAMMERER
STAMMERS
STAMNOI
STAMNOS
STAMP
STAMPED
STAMPEDE
STAMPEDED
STAMPEDER
STAMPEDES
STAMPEDO
STAMPEDOS
STAMPER
STAMPERS
STAMPING
STAMPINGS
STAMPLESS
STAMPS
STANCE
STANCES
STANCH
STANCHED
STANCHEL
STANCHELS
STANCHER
STANCHERS
STANCHES
STANCHEST
STANCHING
STANCHION
STANCHLY
STANCK
STAND
STANDARD
STANDARDS
STANDAWAY
STANDBY
STANDBYS
STANDDOWN
STANDEE
STANDEES
STANDEN
STANDER
STANDERS
STANDFAST
STANDGALE
STANDING
STANDINGS
STANDISH
STANDOFF
STANDOFFS
STANDOUT
STANDOUTS
STANDOVER
STANDPAT
STANDPIPE
STANDS
STANDUP
STANDUPS
STANE
STANED
STANES
STANG
STANGED
STANGING
STANGS
STANHOPE
STANHOPES
STANIEL
STANIELS
STANINE
STANINES
STANING
STANK
STANKED
STANKING
STANKS
STANNARY
STANNATE
STANNATES
STANNATOR
STANNEL
STANNELS
STANNIC
STANNITE
STANNITES
STANNOUS
STANNUM
STANNUMS
STANOL
STANOLS
STANYEL
STANYELS
STANZA
STANZAED
STANZAIC
STANZAS
STANZE
STANZES
STANZO
STANZOES
STANZOS
STAP
STAPEDES
STAPEDIAL
STAPEDII
STAPEDIUS
STAPELIA
STAPELIAS
STAPES
STAPH
STAPHS
STAPLE
STAPLED
STAPLER
STAPLERS
STAPLES
STAPLING
STAPLINGS
STAPPED
STAPPING
STAPPLE
STAPPLES
STAPS
STAR
STARAGEN
STARAGENS
STARBOARD
STARBURST
STARCH
STARCHED
STARCHER
STARCHERS
STARCHES
STARCHIER
STARCHILY
STARCHING
STARCHY
STARDOM
STARDOMS
STARDRIFT
STARDUST
STARDUSTS
STARE
STARED
STARER
STARERS
STARES
STARETS
STARETSES
STARETZ
STARETZES
STARFISH
STARFRUIT
STARGAZE
STARGAZED
STARGAZER
STARGAZES
STARGAZEY
STARING
STARINGLY
STARINGS

STARK
STARKED
STARKEN
STARKENED
STARKENS
STARKER
STARKERS
STARKEST
STARKING
STARKLY
STARKNESS
STARKS
STARLESS
STARLET
STARLETS
STARLIGHT
STARLIKE
STARLING
STARLINGS
STARLIT
STARN
STARNED
STARNIE
STARNIES
STARNING
STARNOSE
STARNOSES
STARNS
STAROSTA
STAROSTAS
STAROSTY
STARR
STARRED
STARRIER
STARRIEST
STARRILY
STARRING
STARRINGS
STARRS
STARRY
STARS
STARSHINE
STARSHIP
STARSHIPS
STARSPOT
STARSPOTS
STARSTONE
START
STARTED
STARTER
STARTERS
STARTFUL
STARTING
STARTINGS
STARTISH
STARTLE
STARTLED
STARTLER
STARTLERS
STARTLES
STARTLIER
STARTLING
STARTLISH
STARTLY
STARTS
STARTSY
STARTUP
STARTUPS
STARVE
STARVED
STARVER
STARVERS
STARVES
STARVING
STARVINGS
STARWORT
STARWORTS
STASES
STASH
STASHED
STASHES
STASHIE
STASHIES
STASHING
STASIDION
STASIMA
STASIMON
STASIS
STAT
STATABLE
STATAL
STATANT
STATE
STATEABLE
STATED
STATEDLY
STATEHOOD
STATELESS
STATELET
STATELETS
STATELIER
STATELILY
STATELY
STATEMENT
STATER
STATEROOM
STATERS
STATES
STATESIDE
STATESMAN
STATESMEN
STATEWIDE
STATIC
STATICAL
STATICE
STATICES
STATICKY
STATICS
STATIM
STATIN
STATING
STATINS
STATION
STATIONAL
STATIONED
STATIONER
STATIONS
STATISM
STATISMS
STATIST
STATISTIC
STATISTS
STATIVE
STATIVES
STATOCYST
STATOLITH
STATOR
STATORS
STATS
STATTO
STATTOS
STATUA
STATUARY
STATUAS
STATUE
STATUED
STATUES
STATUETTE
STATURE
STATURED
STATURES
STATUS
STATUSES
STATUSIER
STATUSY
STATUTE
STATUTES
STATUTORY
STAUMREL
STAUMRELS
STAUN
STAUNCH
STAUNCHED
STAUNCHER
STAUNCHES
STAUNCHLY
STAUNING
STAUNS
STAVE
STAVED
STAVES
STAVING
STAVUDINE
STAW
STAWED
STAWING
STAWS
STAY
STAYAWAY
STAYAWAYS
STAYED
STAYER
STAYERS
STAYING
STAYLESS
STAYMAKER
STAYNE
STAYNED
STAYNES
STAYNING
STAYRE
STAYRES
STAYS
STAYSAIL
STAYSAILS
STEAD
STEADED
STEADFAST
STEADIED
STEADIER
STEADIERS
STEADIES
STEADIEST
STEADILY
STEADING
STEADINGS
STEADS
STEADY
STEADYING
STEAK
STEAKETTE
STEAKS
STEAL
STEALABLE
STEALAGE
STEALAGES
STEALE
STEALED
STEALER
STEALERS
STEALES
STEALING
STEALINGS
STEALS
STEALT
STEALTH
STEALTHED
STEALTHS
STEALTHY
STEAM
STEAMBOAT
STEAMED
STEAMER
STEAMERED
STEAMERS
STEAMIE
STEAMIER
STEAMIES
STEAMIEST
STEAMILY

STEAMING
STEAMINGS
STEAMPUNK
STEAMROLL
STEAMS
STEAMSHIP
STEAMY
STEAN
STEANE
STEANED
STEANES
STEANING
STEANINGS
STEANS
STEAPSIN
STEAPSINS
STEAR
STEARAGE
STEARAGES
STEARATE
STEARATES
STEARD
STEARE
STEARED
STEARES
STEARIC
STEARIN
STEARINE
STEARINES
STEARING
STEARINS
STEARS
STEARSMAN
STEARSMEN
STEATITE
STEATITES
STEATITIC
STEATOMA
STEATOMAS
STEATOSES
STEATOSIS
STED
STEDD
STEDDE
STEDDED
STEDDES
STEDDIED
STEDDIES
STEDDING
STEDDS
STEDDY
STEDDYING
STEDE
STEDED
STEDES
STEDFAST
STEDING
STEDS
STEED
STEEDED
STEEDIED
STEEDIES
STEEDING
STEEDLIKE
STEEDS
STEEDY
STEEDYING
STEEK
STEEKED
STEEKING
STEEKIT
STEEKS
STEEL
STEELBOW
STEELBOWS
STEELD
STEELED
STEELHEAD
STEELIE
STEELIER
STEELIES
STEELIEST
STEELING
STEELINGS
STEELMAN
STEELMEN
STEELS
STEELWARE
STEELWORK
STEELY
STEELYARD
STEEM
STEEMED
STEEMING
STEEMS
STEEN
STEENBOK
STEENBOKS
STEENBRAS
STEENBUCK
STEENED
STEENING
STEENINGS
STEENKIRK
STEENS
STEEP
STEEPED
STEEPEN
STEEPENED
STEEPENS
STEEPER
STEEPERS
STEEPEST
STEEPEUP
STEEPIER
STEEPIEST
STEEPING
STEEPISH
STEEPLE
STEEPLED
STEEPLES
STEEPLING
STEEPLY
STEEPNESS
STEEPS
STEEPUP
STEEPY
STEER
STEERABLE
STEERAGE
STEERAGES
STEERED
STEERER
STEERERS
STEERIER
STEERIES
STEERIEST
STEERING
STEERINGS
STEERLING
STEERS
STEERSMAN
STEERSMEN
STEERY
STEEVE
STEEVED
STEEVELY
STEEVER
STEEVES
STEEVEST
STEEVING
STEEVINGS
STEGNOSES
STEGNOSIS
STEGNOTIC
STEGODON
STEGODONS
STEGODONT
STEGOMYIA
STEGOSAUR
STEIL
STEILS
STEIN
STEINBOCK
STEINBOK
STEINBOKS
STEINED
STEINING
STEININGS
STEINKIRK
STEINS
STELA
STELAE
STELAI
STELAR
STELE
STELENE
STELES
STELIC
STELL
STELLA
STELLAR
STELLAS
STELLATE
STELLATED
STELLED
STELLERID
STELLIFY
STELLING
STELLIO
STELLION
STELLIONS
STELLITE
STELLITES
STELLS
STELLULAR
STEM
STEMBOK
STEMBOKS
STEMBUCK
STEMBUCKS
STEME
STEMED
STEMES
STEMHEAD
STEMHEADS
STEMING
STEMLESS
STEMLET
STEMLETS
STEMLIKE
STEMMA
STEMMAS
STEMMATA
STEMMATIC
STEMME
STEMMED
STEMMER
STEMMERS
STEMMERY
STEMMES
STEMMIER
STEMMIEST
STEMMING
STEMMINGS
STEMMY
STEMPEL
STEMPELS
STEMPLE
STEMPLES
STEMS
STEMSON
STEMSONS
STEMWARE
STEMWARES
STEN
STENCH
STENCHED
STENCHES
STENCHFUL

STENCHIER
STENCHING
STENCHY
STENCIL
STENCILED
STENCILER
STENCILS
STEND
STENDED
STENDING
STENDS
STENGAH
STENGAHS
STENLOCK
STENLOCKS
STENNED
STENNING
STENO
STENOBATH
STENOKIES
STENOKOUS
STENOKY
STENOPAIC
STENOS
STENOSED
STENOSES
STENOSING
STENOSIS
STENOTIC
STENOTYPE
STENOTYPY
STENS
STENT
STENTED
STENTING
STENTOR
STENTORS
STENTOUR
STENTOURS
STENTS
STEP
STEPBAIRN
STEPCHILD
STEPDAD
STEPDADS
STEPDAME
STEPDAMES
STEPHANE
STEPHANES
STEPLESS
STEPLIKE
STEPMOM
STEPMOMS
STEPNEY
STEPNEYS
STEPOVER
STEPOVERS
STEPPE
STEPPED
STEPPER
STEPPERS
STEPPES
STEPPING
STEPS
STEPSON
STEPSONS
STEPSTOOL
STEPT
STEPWISE
STERADIAN
STERANE
STERANES
STERCORAL
STERCULIA
STERE
STEREO
STEREOED
STEREOING
STEREOME
STEREOMES
STEREOS
STERES
STERIC
STERICAL
STERIGMA
STERIGMAS
STERILANT
STERILE
STERILELY
STERILISE
STERILITY
STERILIZE
STERLET
STERLETS
STERLING
STERLINGS
STERN
STERNA
STERNAGE
STERNAGES
STERNAL
STERNEBRA
STERNED
STERNER
STERNEST
STERNFAST
STERNING
STERNITE
STERNITES
STERNITIC
STERNLY
STERNMOST
STERNNESS
STERNPORT
STERNPOST
STERNS
STERNSON
STERNSONS
STERNUM
STERNUMS
STERNWARD
STERNWAY
STERNWAYS
STEROID
STEROIDAL
STEROIDS
STEROL
STEROLS
STERTOR
STERTORS
STERVE
STERVED
STERVES
STERVING
STET
STETS
STETSON
STETSONS
STETTED
STETTING
STEVEDORE
STEVEN
STEVENS
STEVIA
STEVIAS
STEW
STEWABLE
STEWARD
STEWARDED
STEWARDRY
STEWARDS
STEWARTRY
STEWBUM
STEWBUMS
STEWED
STEWER
STEWERS
STEWIER
STEWIEST
STEWING
STEWINGS
STEWPAN
STEWPANS
STEWPOND
STEWPONDS
STEWPOT
STEWPOTS
STEWS
STEWY
STEY
STEYER
STEYEST
STEYS
STHENIA
STHENIAS
STHENIC
STIBBLE
STIBBLER
STIBBLERS
STIBBLES
STIBIAL
STIBINE
STIBINES
STIBIUM
STIBIUMS
STIBNITE
STIBNITES
STICCADO
STICCADOS
STICCATO
STICCATOS
STICH
STICHARIA
STICHERA
STICHERON
STICHIC
STICHIDIA
STICHOI
STICHOS
STICHS
STICK
STICKABLE
STICKBALL
STICKED
STICKER
STICKERED
STICKERS
STICKFUL
STICKFULS
STICKIE
STICKIED
STICKIER
STICKIES
STICKIEST
STICKILY
STICKING
STICKINGS
STICKIT
STICKJAW
STICKJAWS
STICKLE
STICKLED
STICKLER
STICKLERS
STICKLES
STICKLIKE
STICKLING
STICKMAN
STICKMEN
STICKOUT
STICKOUTS
STICKPIN
STICKPINS
STICKS
STICKSEED
STICKUM
STICKUMS
STICKUP
STICKUPS
STICKWEED

S

STICKWORK
STICKY
STICKYING
STICTION
STICTIONS
STIDDIE
STIDDIED
STIDDIES
STIE
STIED
STIES
STIEVE
STIEVELY
STIEVER
STIEVEST
STIFF
STIFFED
STIFFEN
STIFFENED
STIFFENER
STIFFENS
STIFFER
STIFFEST
STIFFIE
STIFFIES
STIFFING
STIFFISH
STIFFLY
STIFFNESS
STIFFS
STIFFWARE
STIFFY
STIFLE
STIFLED
STIFLER
STIFLERS
STIFLES
STIFLING
STIFLINGS
STIGMA
STIGMAL
STIGMAS
STIGMATA
STIGMATIC
STIGME
STIGMES
STILB
STILBENE
STILBENES
STILBITE
STILBITES
STILBS
STILE
STILED
STILES
STILET
STILETS
STILETTO
STILETTOS
STILING
STILL
STILLAGE
STILLAGES
STILLBORN
STILLED
STILLER
STILLERS
STILLEST
STILLIER
STILLIEST
STILLING
STILLINGS
STILLION
STILLIONS
STILLMAN
STILLMEN
STILLNESS
STILLROOM
STILLS
STILLSON
STILLSONS
STILLY
STILT
STILTBIRD
STILTED
STILTEDLY
STILTER
STILTERS
STILTIER
STILTIEST
STILTING
STILTINGS
STILTISH
STILTLIKE
STILTS
STILTY
STIM
STIME
STIMED
STIMES
STIMIE
STIMIED
STIMIES
STIMING
STIMS
STIMULANT
STIMULATE
STIMULI
STIMULUS
STIMY
STIMYING
STING
STINGAREE
STINGBULL
STINGE
STINGED
STINGER
STINGERS
STINGES
STINGFISH
STINGIER
STINGIES
STINGIEST
STINGILY
STINGING
STINGINGS
STINGLESS
STINGO
STINGOS
STINGRAY
STINGRAYS
STINGS
STINGY
STINK
STINKARD
STINKARDS
STINKBIRD
STINKBUG
STINKBUGS
STINKER
STINKEROO
STINKERS
STINKHORN
STINKIER
STINKIEST
STINKING
STINKO
STINKPOT
STINKPOTS
STINKS
STINKWEED
STINKWOOD
STINKY
STINT
STINTED
STINTEDLY
STINTER
STINTERS
STINTIER
STINTIEST
STINTING
STINTINGS
STINTLESS
STINTS
STINTY
STIPA
STIPAS
STIPE
STIPED
STIPEL
STIPELS
STIPEND
STIPENDS
STIPES
STIPIFORM
STIPITATE
STIPITES
STIPPLE
STIPPLED
STIPPLER
STIPPLERS
STIPPLES
STIPPLING
STIPULAR
STIPULARY
STIPULATE
STIPULE
STIPULED
STIPULES
STIR
STIRABOUT
STIRE
STIRED
STIRES
STIRING
STIRK
STIRKS
STIRLESS
STIRP
STIRPES
STIRPS
STIRRA
STIRRABLE
STIRRAH
STIRRAHS
STIRRAS
STIRRE
STIRRED
STIRRER
STIRRERS
STIRRES
STIRRING
STIRRINGS
STIRRUP
STIRRUPS
STIRS
STISHIE
STISHIES
STITCH
STITCHED
STITCHER
STITCHERS
STITCHERY
STITCHES
STITCHING
STITHIED
STITHIES
STITHY
STITHYING
STIVE
STIVED
STIVER
STIVERS
STIVES
STIVIER
STIVIEST
STIVING
STIVY
STOA
STOAE

STOAI
STOAS
STOAT
STOATS
STOB
STOBBED
STOBBING
STOBIE
STOBS
STOCCADO
STOCCADOS
STOCCATA
STOCCATAS
STOCIOUS
STOCK
STOCKADE
STOCKADED
STOCKADES
STOCKAGE
STOCKAGES
STOCKCAR
STOCKCARS
STOCKED
STOCKER
STOCKERS
STOCKFISH
STOCKHORN
STOCKIER
STOCKIEST
STOCKILY
STOCKINET
STOCKING
STOCKINGS
STOCKISH
STOCKIST
STOCKISTS
STOCKLESS
STOCKLIST
STOCKLOCK
STOCKMAN
STOCKMEN
STOCKPILE
STOCKPOT
STOCKPOTS
STOCKROOM
STOCKS
STOCKTAKE
STOCKTOOK
STOCKWORK
STOCKY
STOCKYARD
STODGE
STODGED
STODGER
STODGERS
STODGES
STODGIER
STODGIEST
STODGILY
STODGING
STODGY
STOEP
STOEPS
STOGEY
STOGEYS
STOGIE
STOGIES
STOGY
STOIC
STOICAL
STOICALLY
STOICISM
STOICISMS
STOICS
STOIT
STOITED
STOITER
STOITERED
STOITERS
STOITING
STOITS
STOKE
STOKED
STOKEHOLD
STOKEHOLE
STOKER
STOKERS
STOKES
STOKESIA
STOKESIAS
STOKING
STOKVEL
STOKVELS
STOLE
STOLED
STOLEN
STOLES
STOLID
STOLIDER
STOLIDEST
STOLIDITY
STOLIDLY
STOLLEN
STOLLENS
STOLN
STOLON
STOLONATE
STOLONIC
STOLONS
STOLPORT
STOLPORTS
STOMA
STOMACH
STOMACHAL
STOMACHED
STOMACHER
STOMACHIC
STOMACHS
STOMACHY
STOMACK
STOMACKS
STOMAL
STOMAS
STOMATA
STOMATAL
STOMATE
STOMATES
STOMATIC
STOMATOUS
STOMIA
STOMIUM
STOMIUMS
STOMODAEA
STOMODEA
STOMODEAL
STOMODEUM
STOMP
STOMPED
STOMPER
STOMPERS
STOMPIE
STOMPIER
STOMPIES
STOMPIEST
STOMPING
STOMPS
STOMPY
STONABLE
STOND
STONDS
STONE
STONEABLE
STONEBOAT
STONECAST
STONECHAT
STONECROP
STONECUT
STONECUTS
STONED
STONEFISH
STONEFLY
STONEHAND
STONELESS
STONELIKE
STONEN
STONER
STONERAG
STONERAGS
STONERAW
STONERAWS
STONERN
STONERS
STONES
STONESHOT
STONEWALL
STONEWARE
STONEWASH
STONEWORK
STONEWORT
STONEY
STONG
STONIED
STONIER
STONIES
STONIEST
STONILY
STONINESS
STONING
STONINGS
STONISH
STONISHED
STONISHES
STONK
STONKED
STONKER
STONKERED
STONKERS
STONKING
STONKS
STONN
STONNE
STONNED
STONNES
STONNING
STONNS
STONY
STONYING
STOOD
STOODEN
STOOGE
STOOGED
STOOGES
STOOGING
STOOK
STOOKED
STOOKER
STOOKERS
STOOKIE
STOOKIES
STOOKING
STOOKINGS
STOOKS
STOOL
STOOLBALL
STOOLED
STOOLIE
STOOLIES
STOOLING
STOOLS
STOOLY
STOOP
STOOPBALL
STOOPE
STOOPED
STOOPER
STOOPERS
STOOPES
STOOPING
STOOPS
STOOR

S

STOORS
STOOSHIE
STOOSHIES
STOOZE
STOOZED
STOOZER
STOOZERS
STOOZES
STOOZING
STOOZINGS
STOP
STOPBAND
STOPBANDS
STOPBANK
STOPBANKS
STOPCOCK
STOPCOCKS
STOPE
STOPED
STOPER
STOPERS
STOPES
STOPGAP
STOPGAPS
STOPING
STOPINGS
STOPLESS
STOPLIGHT
STOPOFF
STOPOFFS
STOPOVER
STOPOVERS
STOPPABLE
STOPPAGE
STOPPAGES
STOPPED
STOPPER
STOPPERED
STOPPERS
STOPPING
STOPPINGS
STOPPLE
STOPPLED
STOPPLES
STOPPLING
STOPS
STOPT
STOPWATCH
STOPWORD
STOPWORDS
STORABLE
STORABLES
STORAGE
STORAGES
STORAX
STORAXES
STORE
STORECARD
STORED
STOREMAN
STOREMEN
STORER
STOREROOM
STORERS
STORES
STORESHIP
STOREWIDE
STOREY
STOREYED
STOREYS
STORGE
STORGES
STORIATED
STORIED
STORIES
STORIETTE
STORING
STORK
STORKS
STORM
STORMBIRD
STORMCOCK
STORMED
STORMER
STORMERS
STORMFUL
STORMIER
STORMIEST
STORMILY
STORMING
STORMINGS
STORMLESS
STORMLIKE
STORMS
STORMY
STORNELLI
STORNELLO
STORY
STORYBOOK
STORYETTE
STORYING
STORYINGS
STORYLESS
STORYLINE
STORYTIME
STOSS
STOSSES
STOT
STOTIN
STOTINKA
STOTINKAS
STOTINKI
STOTINOV
STOTINS
STOTIOUS
STOTS
STOTT
STOTTED
STOTTER
STOTTERED
STOTTERS
STOTTIE
STOTTIES
STOTTING
STOTTS
STOTTY
STOUN
STOUND
STOUNDED
STOUNDING
STOUNDS
STOUNING
STOUNS
STOUP
STOUPS
STOUR
STOURE
STOURES
STOURIE
STOURIER
STOURIEST
STOURS
STOURY
STOUSH
STOUSHED
STOUSHES
STOUSHIE
STOUSHIES
STOUSHING
STOUT
STOUTEN
STOUTENED
STOUTENS
STOUTER
STOUTEST
STOUTH
STOUTHS
STOUTISH
STOUTLY
STOUTNESS
STOUTS
STOVAINE
STOVAINES
STOVE
STOVED
STOVEPIPE
STOVER
STOVERS
STOVES
STOVETOP
STOVETOPS
STOVEWOOD
STOVIES
STOVING
STOVINGS
STOW
STOWABLE
STOWAGE
STOWAGES
STOWAWAY
STOWAWAYS
STOWDOWN
STOWDOWNS
STOWED
STOWER
STOWERS
STOWING
STOWINGS
STOWLINS
STOWN
STOWND
STOWNDED
STOWNDING
STOWNDS
STOWNLINS
STOWP
STOWPS
STOWRE
STOWRES
STOWS
STRABISM
STRABISMS
STRACK
STRAD
STRADDLE
STRADDLED
STRADDLER
STRADDLES
STRADIOT
STRADIOTS
STRADS
STRAE
STRAES
STRAFE
STRAFED
STRAFER
STRAFERS
STRAFES
STRAFF
STRAFFED
STRAFFING
STRAFFS
STRAFING
STRAFINGS
STRAG
STRAGGLE
STRAGGLED
STRAGGLER
STRAGGLES
STRAGGLY
STRAGS
STRAICHT
STRAIGHT
STRAIGHTS
STRAIK
STRAIKED
STRAIKING
STRAIKS
STRAIN
STRAINED

STRAINER
STRAINERS
STRAINING
STRAINS
STRAINT
STRAINTS
STRAIT
STRAITED
STRAITEN
STRAITENS
STRAITER
STRAITEST
STRAITING
STRAITLY
STRAITS
STRAK
STRAKE
STRAKED
STRAKES
STRAMACON
STRAMASH
STRAMAZON
STRAMMEL
STRAMMELS
STRAMONY
STRAMP
STRAMPED
STRAMPING
STRAMPS
STRAND
STRANDED
STRANDER
STRANDERS
STRANDING
STRANDS
STRANG
STRANGE
STRANGELY
STRANGER
STRANGERS
STRANGES
STRANGEST
STRANGLE
STRANGLED
STRANGLER
STRANGLES
STRANGURY
STRAP
STRAPHANG
STRAPHUNG
STRAPLESS
STRAPLIKE
STRAPLINE
STRAPPADO
STRAPPED
STRAPPER
STRAPPERS
STRAPPIER
STRAPPING
STRAPPY
STRAPS
STRAPWORT
STRASS
STRASSES
STRATA
STRATAGEM
STRATAL
STRATAS
STRATEGIC
STRATEGY
STRATH
STRATHS
STRATI
STRATIFY
STRATONIC
STRATOSE
STRATOUS
STRATUM
STRATUMS
STRATUS
STRATUSES
STRAUCHT
STRAUCHTS
STRAUGHT
STRAUGHTS
STRAUNGE
STRAVAGE
STRAVAGED
STRAVAGES
STRAVAIG
STRAVAIGS
STRAW
STRAWED
STRAWEN
STRAWHAT
STRAWIER
STRAWIEST
STRAWING
STRAWLESS
STRAWLIKE
STRAWN
STRAWS
STRAWWORM
STRAWY
STRAY
STRAYED
STRAYER
STRAYERS
STRAYING
STRAYINGS
STRAYLING
STRAYS
STRAYVE
STRAYVED
STRAYVES
STRAYVING
STREAK
STREAKED
STREAKER
STREAKERS
STREAKIER
STREAKILY
STREAKING
STREAKS
STREAKY
STREAM
STREAMBED
STREAMED
STREAMER
STREAMERS
STREAMIER
STREAMING
STREAMLET
STREAMS
STREAMY
STREEK
STREEKED
STREEKER
STREEKERS
STREEKING
STREEKS
STREEL
STREELED
STREELING
STREELS
STREET
STREETAGE
STREETBOY
STREETCAR
STREETED
STREETFUL
STREETIER
STREETING
STREETS
STREETY
STREIGHT
STREIGHTS
STREIGNE
STREIGNED
STREIGNES
STRELITZ
STRELITZI
STRENE
STRENES
STRENGTH
STRENGTHS
STRENUITY
STRENUOUS
STREP
STREPENT
STREPS
STRESS
STRESSED
STRESSES
STRESSFUL
STRESSIER
STRESSING
STRESSOR
STRESSORS
STRESSY
STRETCH
STRETCHED
STRETCHER
STRETCHES
STRETCHY
STRETTA
STRETTAS
STRETTE
STRETTI
STRETTO
STRETTOS
STREUSEL
STREUSELS
STREW
STREWAGE
STREWAGES
STREWED
STREWER
STREWERS
STREWING
STREWINGS
STREWMENT
STREWN
STREWS
STREWTH
STRIA
STRIAE
STRIATA
STRIATAL
STRIATE
STRIATED
STRIATES
STRIATING
STRIATION
STRIATUM
STRIATUMS
STRIATURE
STRICH
STRICHES
STRICK
STRICKEN
STRICKLE
STRICKLED
STRICKLES
STRICKS
STRICT
STRICTER
STRICTEST
STRICTION
STRICTISH
STRICTLY
STRICTURE
STRIDDEN
STRIDDLE
STRIDDLED
STRIDDLES
STRIDE
STRIDENCE
STRIDENCY
STRIDENT

STRIDER
STRIDERS
STRIDES
STRIDING
STRIDLING
STRIDOR
STRIDORS
STRIFE
STRIFEFUL
STRIFES
STRIFT
STRIFTS
STRIG
STRIGA
STRIGAE
STRIGATE
STRIGGED
STRIGGING
STRIGIL
STRIGILS
STRIGINE
STRIGOSE
STRIGS
STRIKABLE
STRIKE
STRIKEOUT
STRIKER
STRIKERS
STRIKES
STRIKING
STRIKINGS
STRIM
STRIMMED
STRIMMING
STRIMS
STRINE
STRINES
STRING
STRINGED
STRINGENT
STRINGER
STRINGERS
STRINGIER
STRINGILY
STRINGING
STRINGS
STRINGY
STRINKLE
STRINKLED
STRINKLES
STRIP
STRIPE
STRIPED
STRIPER
STRIPERS
STRIPES
STRIPEY
STRIPIER
STRIPIEST
STRIPING
STRIPINGS
STRIPLING
STRIPPED
STRIPPER
STRIPPERS
STRIPPING
STRIPS
STRIPT
STRIPY
STRIVE
STRIVED
STRIVEN
STRIVER
STRIVERS
STRIVES
STRIVING
STRIVINGS
STROAM
STROAMED
STROAMING
STROAMS
STROBE
STROBED
STROBES
STROBIC
STROBIL
STROBILA
STROBILAE
STROBILAR
STROBILE
STROBILES
STROBILI
STROBILS
STROBILUS
STROBING
STROBINGS
STRODDLE
STRODDLED
STRODDLES
STRODE
STRODLE
STRODLED
STRODLES
STRODLING
STROKABLE
STROKE
STROKED
STROKEN
STROKER
STROKERS
STROKES
STROKING
STROKINGS
STROLL
STROLLED
STROLLER
STROLLERS
STROLLING
STROLLS
STROMA
STROMAL
STROMATA
STROMATIC
STROMB
STROMBS
STROMBUS
STROND
STRONDS
STRONG
STRONGARM
STRONGBOX
STRONGER
STRONGEST
STRONGISH
STRONGLY
STRONGMAN
STRONGMEN
STRONGYL
STRONGYLE
STRONGYLS
STRONTIA
STRONTIAN
STRONTIAS
STRONTIC
STRONTIUM
STROOK
STROOKE
STROOKEN
STROOKES
STROP
STROPHE
STROPHES
STROPHIC
STROPHOID
STROPHULI
STROPPED
STROPPER
STROPPERS
STROPPIER
STROPPILY
STROPPING
STROPPY
STROPS
STROSSERS
STROUD
STROUDING
STROUDS
STROUP
STROUPACH
STROUPAN
STROUPANS
STROUPS
STROUT
STROUTED
STROUTING
STROUTS
STROVE
STROW
STROWED
STROWER
STROWERS
STROWING
STROWINGS
STROWN
STROWS
STROY
STROYED
STROYER
STROYERS
STROYING
STROYS
STRUCK
STRUCKEN
STRUCTURE
STRUDEL
STRUDELS
STRUGGLE
STRUGGLED
STRUGGLER
STRUGGLES
STRUM
STRUMA
STRUMAE
STRUMAS
STRUMATIC
STRUMITIS
STRUMMED
STRUMMEL
STRUMMELS
STRUMMER
STRUMMERS
STRUMMING
STRUMOSE
STRUMOUS
STRUMPET
STRUMPETS
STRUMS
STRUNG
STRUNT
STRUNTED
STRUNTING
STRUNTS
STRUT
STRUTS
STRUTTED
STRUTTER
STRUTTERS
STRUTTING
STRYCHNIA
STRYCHNIC
STUB
STUBBED
STUBBIE
STUBBIER
STUBBIES
STUBBIEST
STUBBILY
STUBBING
STUBBLE
STUBBLED

STUBBLES
STUBBLIER
STUBBLY
STUBBORN
STUBBORNS
STUBBY
STUBS
STUCCO
STUCCOED
STUCCOER
STUCCOERS
STUCCOES
STUCCOING
STUCCOS
STUCK
STUCKS
STUD
STUDBOOK
STUDBOOKS
STUDDED
STUDDEN
STUDDIE
STUDDIES
STUDDING
STUDDINGS
STUDDLE
STUDDLES
STUDE
STUDENT
STUDENTRY
STUDENTS
STUDENTY
STUDFARM
STUDFARMS
STUDFISH
STUDHORSE
STUDIED
STUDIEDLY
STUDIER
STUDIERS
STUDIES
STUDIO
STUDIOS
STUDIOUS
STUDLIER
STUDLIEST
STUDLIKE
STUDLY
STUDS
STUDWORK
STUDWORKS
STUDY
STUDYING
STUFF
STUFFED
STUFFER
STUFFERS
STUFFIER
STUFFIEST
STUFFILY
STUFFING
STUFFINGS
STUFFLESS
STUFFS
STUFFY
STUGGIER
STUGGIEST
STUGGY
STUIVER
STUIVERS
STUKKEND
STULL
STULLS
STULM
STULMS
STULTIFY
STUM
STUMBLE
STUMBLED
STUMBLER
STUMBLERS
STUMBLES
STUMBLIER
STUMBLING
STUMBLY
STUMER
STUMERS
STUMM
STUMMED
STUMMEL
STUMMELS
STUMMING
STUMP
STUMPAGE
STUMPAGES
STUMPED
STUMPER
STUMPERS
STUMPIER
STUMPIES
STUMPIEST
STUMPILY
STUMPING
STUMPINGS
STUMPS
STUMPWORK
STUMPY
STUMS
STUN
STUNG
STUNK
STUNKARD
STUNNED
STUNNER
STUNNERS
STUNNING
STUNNINGS
STUNS
STUNSAIL
STUNSAILS
STUNT
STUNTED
STUNTING
STUNTMAN
STUNTMEN
STUNTS
STUPA
STUPAS
STUPE
STUPED
STUPEFIED
STUPEFIER
STUPEFIES
STUPEFY
STUPENT
STUPES
STUPID
STUPIDER
STUPIDEST
STUPIDITY
STUPIDLY
STUPIDS
STUPING
STUPOR
STUPOROUS
STUPORS
STUPRATE
STUPRATED
STUPRATES
STURDIED
STURDIER
STURDIES
STURDIEST
STURDILY
STURDY
STURE
STURGEON
STURGEONS
STURMER
STURMERS
STURNINE
STURNOID
STURNUS
STURNUSES
STURT
STURTED
STURTING
STURTS
STUSHIE
STUSHIES
STUTTER
STUTTERED
STUTTERER
STUTTERS
STY
STYE
STYED
STYES
STYGIAN
STYING
STYLAR
STYLATE
STYLE
STYLEBOOK
STYLED
STYLEE
STYLEES
STYLELESS
STYLER
STYLERS
STYLES
STYLET
STYLETS
STYLI
STYLIE
STYLIER
STYLIEST
STYLIFORM
STYLING
STYLINGS
STYLISE
STYLISED
STYLISER
STYLISERS
STYLISES
STYLISH
STYLISHLY
STYLISING
STYLIST
STYLISTIC
STYLISTS
STYLITE
STYLITES
STYLITIC
STYLITISM
STYLIZE
STYLIZED
STYLIZER
STYLIZERS
STYLIZES
STYLIZING
STYLO
STYLOBATE
STYLOID
STYLOIDS
STYLOLITE
STYLOPES
STYLOPID
STYLOPIDS
STYLOPISE
STYLOPIZE
STYLOPS
STYLOS
STYLUS
STYLUSES
STYME
STYMED
STYMES
STYMIE
STYMIED

S

STYMIEING
STYMIES
STYMING
STYMY
STYMYING
STYPSIS
STYPSISES
STYPTIC
STYPTICAL
STYPTICS
STYRAX
STYRAXES
STYRE
STYRED
STYRENE
STYRENES
STYRES
STYRING
STYROFOAM
STYTE
STYTED
STYTES
STYTING
SUABILITY
SUABLE
SUABLY
SUASIBLE
SUASION
SUASIONS
SUASIVE
SUASIVELY
SUASORY
SUAVE
SUAVELY
SUAVENESS
SUAVER
SUAVEST
SUAVITIES
SUAVITY
SUB
SUBA
SUBABBOT
SUBABBOTS
SUBACID
SUBACIDLY
SUBACRID
SUBACT
SUBACTED
SUBACTING
SUBACTION
SUBACTS
SUBACUTE
SUBADAR
SUBADARS
SUBADULT
SUBADULTS
SUBAERIAL
SUBAGENCY
SUBAGENT
SUBAGENTS
SUBAH
SUBAHDAR
SUBAHDARS
SUBAHDARY
SUBAHS
SUBAHSHIP
SUBALAR
SUBALPINE
SUBALTERN
SUBAPICAL
SUBAQUA
SUBARCTIC
SUBAREA
SUBAREAS
SUBARID
SUBAS
SUBASTRAL
SUBATOM
SUBATOMIC
SUBATOMS
SUBAUDIO
SUBAURAL
SUBAXIAL
SUBBASAL
SUBBASE
SUBBASES
SUBBASIN
SUBBASINS
SUBBASS
SUBBASSES
SUBBED
SUBBIE
SUBBIES
SUBBING
SUBBINGS
SUBBLOCK
SUBBLOCKS
SUBBRANCH
SUBBREED
SUBBREEDS
SUBBUREAU
SUBBY
SUBCANTOR
SUBCASTE
SUBCASTES
SUBCAUDAL
SUBCAUSE
SUBCAUSES
SUBCAVITY
SUBCELL
SUBCELLAR
SUBCELLS
SUBCENTER
SUBCENTRE
SUBCHASER
SUBCHIEF
SUBCHIEFS
SUBCHORD
SUBCHORDS
SUBCLAIM
SUBCLAIMS
SUBCLAN
SUBCLANS
SUBCLASS
SUBCLAUSE
SUBCLERK
SUBCLERKS
SUBCLIMAX
SUBCODE
SUBCODES
SUBCOLONY
SUBCONSUL
SUBCOOL
SUBCOOLED
SUBCOOLS
SUBCORTEX
SUBCOSTA
SUBCOSTAE
SUBCOSTAL
SUBCOUNTY
SUBCRUST
SUBCRUSTS
SUBCULT
SUBCULTS
SUBCUTES
SUBCUTIS
SUBDEACON
SUBDEALER
SUBDEAN
SUBDEANS
SUBDEB
SUBDEBS
SUBDEPOT
SUBDEPOTS
SUBDEPUTY
SUBDERMAL
SUBDEW
SUBDEWED
SUBDEWING
SUBDEWS
SUBDIVIDE
SUBDOLOUS
SUBDORSAL
SUBDUABLE
SUBDUABLY
SUBDUAL
SUBDUALS
SUBDUCE
SUBDUCED
SUBDUCES
SUBDUCING
SUBDUCT
SUBDUCTED
SUBDUCTS
SUBDUE
SUBDUED
SUBDUEDLY
SUBDUER
SUBDUERS
SUBDUES
SUBDUING
SUBDUPLE
SUBDURAL
SUBDWARF
SUBDWARFS
SUBECHO
SUBECHOES
SUBEDAR
SUBEDARS
SUBEDIT
SUBEDITED
SUBEDITOR
SUBEDITS
SUBENTIRE
SUBENTRY
SUBEPOCH
SUBEPOCHS
SUBEQUAL
SUBER
SUBERATE
SUBERATES
SUBERECT
SUBEREOUS
SUBERIC
SUBERIN
SUBERINS
SUBERISE
SUBERISED
SUBERISES
SUBERIZE
SUBERIZED
SUBERIZES
SUBEROSE
SUBEROUS
SUBERS
SUBFAMILY
SUBFEU
SUBFEUED
SUBFEUING
SUBFEUS
SUBFIELD
SUBFIELDS
SUBFILE
SUBFILES
SUBFIX
SUBFIXES
SUBFLOOR
SUBFLOORS
SUBFLUID
SUBFOLDER
SUBFOSSIL
SUBFRAME
SUBFRAMES
SUBFUSC
SUBFUSCS
SUBFUSK
SUBFUSKS
SUBGENERA
SUBGENRE
SUBGENRES

SUBGENUS
SUBGOAL
SUBGOALS
SUBGRADE
SUBGRADES
SUBGRAPH
SUBGRAPHS
SUBGROUP
SUBGROUPS
SUBGUM
SUBGUMS
SUBHA
SUBHAS
SUBHEAD
SUBHEADS
SUBHEDRAL
SUBHUMAN
SUBHUMANS
SUBHUMID
SUBIDEA
SUBIDEAS
SUBIMAGO
SUBIMAGOS
SUBINCISE
SUBINDEX
SUBINFEUD
SUBITEM
SUBITEMS
SUBITISE
SUBITISED
SUBITISES
SUBITIZE
SUBITIZED
SUBITIZES
SUBITO
SUBJACENT
SUBJECT
SUBJECTED
SUBJECTS
SUBJOIN
SUBJOINED
SUBJOINS
SUBJUGATE
SUBLATE
SUBLATED
SUBLATES
SUBLATING
SUBLATION
SUBLEASE
SUBLEASED
SUBLEASES
SUBLESSEE
SUBLESSOR
SUBLET
SUBLETHAL
SUBLETS
SUBLETTER
SUBLEVEL
SUBLEVELS
SUBLIMATE
SUBLIME
SUBLIMED
SUBLIMELY
SUBLIMER
SUBLIMERS
SUBLIMES
SUBLIMEST
SUBLIMING
SUBLIMISE
SUBLIMIT
SUBLIMITS
SUBLIMITY
SUBLIMIZE
SUBLINE
SUBLINEAR
SUBLINES
SUBLOT
SUBLOTS
SUBLUNAR
SUBLUNARY
SUBLUNATE
SUBLUXATE
SUBMAN
SUBMARINE
SUBMARKET
SUBMATRIX
SUBMEN
SUBMENTA
SUBMENTAL
SUBMENTUM
SUBMENU
SUBMENUS
SUBMERGE
SUBMERGED
SUBMERGES
SUBMERSE
SUBMERSED
SUBMERSES
SUBMICRON
SUBMISS
SUBMISSLY
SUBMIT
SUBMITS
SUBMITTAL
SUBMITTED
SUBMITTER
SUBMUCOSA
SUBMUCOUS
SUBNASAL
SUBNET
SUBNETS
SUBNEURAL
SUBNICHE
SUBNICHES
SUBNIVEAL
SUBNIVEAN
SUBNODAL
SUBNORMAL
SUBNUCLEI
SUBOCEAN
SUBOCTAVE
SUBOCULAR
SUBOFFICE
SUBOPTIC
SUBORAL
SUBORDER
SUBORDERS
SUBORN
SUBORNED
SUBORNER
SUBORNERS
SUBORNING
SUBORNS
SUBOSCINE
SUBOVAL
SUBOVATE
SUBOXIDE
SUBOXIDES
SUBPANEL
SUBPANELS
SUBPAR
SUBPART
SUBPARTS
SUBPENA
SUBPENAED
SUBPENAS
SUBPERIOD
SUBPHASE
SUBPHASES
SUBPHYLA
SUBPHYLAR
SUBPHYLUM
SUBPLOT
SUBPLOTS
SUBPOENA
SUBPOENAS
SUBPOLAR
SUBPOTENT
SUBPRIME
SUBPRIMES
SUBPRIOR
SUBPRIORS
SUBPUBIC
SUBRACE
SUBRACES
SUBREGION
SUBRENT
SUBRENTED
SUBRENTS
SUBRING
SUBRINGS
SUBROGATE
SUBRULE
SUBRULES
SUBS
SUBSACRAL
SUBSALE
SUBSALES
SUBSAMPLE
SUBSCALE
SUBSCALES
SUBSCHEMA
SUBSCRIBE
SUBSCRIPT
SUBSEA
SUBSECIVE
SUBSECT
SUBSECTOR
SUBSECTS
SUBSELLIA
SUBSENSE
SUBSENSES
SUBSERE
SUBSERES
SUBSERIES
SUBSERVE
SUBSERVED
SUBSERVES
SUBSET
SUBSETS
SUBSHAFT
SUBSHAFTS
SUBSHELL
SUBSHELLS
SUBSHRUB
SUBSHRUBS
SUBSIDE
SUBSIDED
SUBSIDER
SUBSIDERS
SUBSIDES
SUBSIDIES
SUBSIDING
SUBSIDISE
SUBSIDIZE
SUBSIDY
SUBSIST
SUBSISTED
SUBSISTER
SUBSISTS
SUBSITE
SUBSITES
SUBSIZAR
SUBSIZARS
SUBSKILL
SUBSKILLS
SUBSOCIAL
SUBSOIL
SUBSOILED
SUBSOILER
SUBSOILS
SUBSOLAR
SUBSONG
SUBSONGS
SUBSONIC
SUBSPACE
SUBSPACES
SUBSTAGE
SUBSTAGES
SUBSTANCE

SUBSTATE
SUBSTATES
SUBSTORM
SUBSTORMS
SUBSTRACT
SUBSTRATA
SUBSTRATE
SUBSTRUCT
SUBSTYLAR
SUBSTYLE
SUBSTYLES
SUBSULTUS
SUBSUME
SUBSUMED
SUBSUMES
SUBSUMING
SUBSYSTEM
SUBTACK
SUBTACKS
SUBTALAR
SUBTASK
SUBTASKS
SUBTAXA
SUBTAXON
SUBTAXONS
SUBTEEN
SUBTEENS
SUBTENANT
SUBTEND
SUBTENDED
SUBTENDS
SUBTENSE
SUBTENSES
SUBTENURE
SUBTEST
SUBTESTS
SUBTEXT
SUBTEXTS
SUBTHEME
SUBTHEMES
SUBTIDAL
SUBTIL
SUBTILE
SUBTILELY
SUBTILER
SUBTILEST
SUBTILIN
SUBTILINS
SUBTILISE
SUBTILITY
SUBTILIZE
SUBTILTY
SUBTITLE
SUBTITLED
SUBTITLES
SUBTLE
SUBTLER
SUBTLEST
SUBTLETY
SUBTLY
SUBTONE
SUBTONES
SUBTONIC
SUBTONICS
SUBTOPIA
SUBTOPIAN
SUBTOPIAS
SUBTOPIC
SUBTOPICS
SUBTORRID
SUBTOTAL
SUBTOTALS
SUBTRACT
SUBTRACTS
SUBTRADE
SUBTRADES
SUBTREND
SUBTRENDS
SUBTRIBE
SUBTRIBES
SUBTRIST
SUBTROPIC
SUBTRUDE
SUBTRUDED
SUBTRUDES
SUBTUNIC
SUBTUNICS
SUBTWEET
SUBTWEETS
SUBTYPE
SUBTYPES
SUBUCULA
SUBUCULAS
SUBULATE
SUBUNIT
SUBUNITS
SUBURB
SUBURBAN
SUBURBANS
SUBURBED
SUBURBIA
SUBURBIAS
SUBURBS
SUBURSINE
SUBVASSAL
SUBVENE
SUBVENED
SUBVENES
SUBVENING
SUBVERSAL
SUBVERSE
SUBVERSED
SUBVERSES
SUBVERST
SUBVERT
SUBVERTED
SUBVERTER
SUBVERTS
SUBVICAR
SUBVICARS
SUBVIRAL
SUBVIRUS
SUBVISUAL
SUBVOCAL
SUBWARDEN
SUBWAY
SUBWAYED
SUBWAYING
SUBWAYS
SUBWOOFER
SUBWORLD
SUBWORLDS
SUBWRITER
SUBZERO
SUBZONAL
SUBZONE
SUBZONES
SUCCADE
SUCCADES
SUCCAH
SUCCAHS
SUCCEDENT
SUCCEED
SUCCEEDED
SUCCEEDER
SUCCEEDS
SUCCENTOR
SUCCES
SUCCESS
SUCCESSES
SUCCESSOR
SUCCI
SUCCINATE
SUCCINCT
SUCCINIC
SUCCINITE
SUCCINYL
SUCCINYLS
SUCCISE
SUCCOR
SUCCORED
SUCCORER
SUCCORERS
SUCCORIES
SUCCORING
SUCCORS
SUCCORY
SUCCOS
SUCCOSE
SUCCOT
SUCCOTASH
SUCCOTH
SUCCOUR
SUCCOURED
SUCCOURER
SUCCOURS
SUCCOUS
SUCCUBA
SUCCUBAE
SUCCUBAS
SUCCUBI
SUCCUBINE
SUCCUBOUS
SUCCUBUS
SUCCULENT
SUCCUMB
SUCCUMBED
SUCCUMBER
SUCCUMBS
SUCCURSAL
SUCCUS
SUCCUSS
SUCCUSSED
SUCCUSSES
SUCH
SUCHLIKE
SUCHLIKES
SUCHNESS
SUCHWISE
SUCK
SUCKED
SUCKEN
SUCKENER
SUCKENERS
SUCKENS
SUCKER
SUCKERED
SUCKERING
SUCKERS
SUCKET
SUCKETS
SUCKFISH
SUCKHOLE
SUCKHOLED
SUCKHOLES
SUCKIER
SUCKIEST
SUCKINESS
SUCKING
SUCKINGS
SUCKLE
SUCKLED
SUCKLER
SUCKLERS
SUCKLES
SUCKLESS
SUCKLING
SUCKLINGS
SUCKS
SUCKY
SUCRALOSE
SUCRASE
SUCRASES
SUCRE
SUCRES
SUCRIER
SUCRIERS
SUCROSE
SUCROSES
SUCTION

S

SUCTIONAL
SUCTIONED
SUCTIONS
SUCTORIAL
SUCTORIAN
SUCURUJU
SUCURUJUS
SUD
SUDAMEN
SUDAMENS
SUDAMINA
SUDAMINAL
SUDARIA
SUDARIES
SUDARIUM
SUDARY
SUDATE
SUDATED
SUDATES
SUDATING
SUDATION
SUDATIONS
SUDATORIA
SUDATORY
SUDD
SUDDEN
SUDDENLY
SUDDENS
SUDDENTY
SUDDER
SUDDERS
SUDDS
SUDOKU
SUDOKUS
SUDOR
SUDORAL
SUDORIFIC
SUDOROUS
SUDORS
SUDS
SUDSED
SUDSER
SUDSERS
SUDSES
SUDSIER
SUDSIEST
SUDSING
SUDSLESS
SUDSY
SUE
SUEABLE
SUED
SUEDE
SUEDED
SUEDELIKE
SUEDES
SUEDETTE
SUEDETTES
SUEDING
SUENT
SUER
SUERS
SUES
SUET
SUETE
SUETES
SUETIER
SUETIEST
SUETS
SUETTIER
SUETTIEST
SUETTY
SUETY
SUFFARI
SUFFARIS
SUFFECT
SUFFECTS
SUFFER
SUFFERED
SUFFERER
SUFFERERS
SUFFERING
SUFFERS
SUFFETE
SUFFETES
SUFFICE
SUFFICED
SUFFICER
SUFFICERS
SUFFICES
SUFFICING
SUFFIX
SUFFIXAL
SUFFIXED
SUFFIXES
SUFFIXING
SUFFIXION
SUFFLATE
SUFFLATED
SUFFLATES
SUFFOCATE
SUFFRAGAN
SUFFRAGE
SUFFRAGES
SUFFUSE
SUFFUSED
SUFFUSES
SUFFUSING
SUFFUSION
SUFFUSIVE
SUG
SUGAN
SUGANS
SUGAR
SUGARALLY
SUGARBUSH
SUGARCANE
SUGARCOAT
SUGARED
SUGARER
SUGARERS
SUGARIER
SUGARIEST
SUGARING
SUGARINGS
SUGARLESS
SUGARLIKE
SUGARLOAF
SUGARPLUM
SUGARS
SUGARY
SUGGED
SUGGEST
SUGGESTED
SUGGESTER
SUGGESTS
SUGGING
SUGGINGS
SUGH
SUGHED
SUGHING
SUGHS
SUGO
SUGOS
SUGS
SUHUR
SUHURS
SUI
SUICIDAL
SUICIDE
SUICIDED
SUICIDES
SUICIDING
SUID
SUIDIAN
SUIDIANS
SUIDS
SUILLINE
SUING
SUINGS
SUINT
SUINTS
SUIPLAP
SUIPLAPS
SUIT
SUITABLE
SUITABLY
SUITCASE
SUITCASES
SUITE
SUITED
SUITER
SUITERS
SUITES
SUITING
SUITINGS
SUITLIKE
SUITOR
SUITORED
SUITORING
SUITORS
SUITRESS
SUITS
SUIVANTE
SUIVANTES
SUIVEZ
SUJEE
SUJEES
SUK
SUKH
SUKHS
SUKIYAKI
SUKIYAKIS
SUKKAH
SUKKAHS
SUKKOS
SUKKOT
SUKKOTH
SUKS
SUKUK
SUKUKS
SULCAL
SULCALISE
SULCALIZE
SULCATE
SULCATED
SULCATION
SULCI
SULCUS
SULDAN
SULDANS
SULFA
SULFAS
SULFATASE
SULFATE
SULFATED
SULFATES
SULFATIC
SULFATING
SULFATION
SULFID
SULFIDE
SULFIDES
SULFIDS
SULFINYL
SULFINYLS
SULFITE
SULFITES
SULFITIC
SULFO
SULFONATE
SULFONE
SULFONES
SULFONIC
SULFONIUM
SULFONYL
SULFONYLS
SULFOXIDE
SULFUR
SULFURATE

S

SULFURED
SULFURET
SULFURETS
SULFURIC
SULFURIER
SULFURING
SULFURISE
SULFURIZE
SULFUROUS
SULFURS
SULFURY
SULFURYL
SULFURYLS
SULK
SULKED
SULKER
SULKERS
SULKIER
SULKIES
SULKIEST
SULKILY
SULKINESS
SULKING
SULKS
SULKY
SULLAGE
SULLAGES
SULLEN
SULLENER
SULLENEST
SULLENLY
SULLENS
SULLIABLE
SULLIED
SULLIES
SULLY
SULLYING
SULPH
SULPHA
SULPHAS
SULPHATE
SULPHATED
SULPHATES
SULPHATIC
SULPHID
SULPHIDE
SULPHIDES
SULPHIDS
SULPHINYL
SULPHITE
SULPHITES
SULPHITIC
SULPHONE
SULPHONES
SULPHONIC
SULPHONYL
SULPHS
SULPHUR
SULPHURED
SULPHURET
SULPHURIC
SULPHURS
SULPHURY
SULPHURYL
SULTAN
SULTANA
SULTANAS
SULTANATE
SULTANESS
SULTANIC
SULTANS
SULTRIER
SULTRIEST
SULTRILY
SULTRY
SULU
SULUS
SUM
SUMAC
SUMACH
SUMACHS
SUMACS
SUMATRA
SUMATRAS
SUMBITCH
SUMI
SUMIS
SUMLESS
SUMMA
SUMMABLE
SUMMAE
SUMMAND
SUMMANDS
SUMMAR
SUMMARIES
SUMMARILY
SUMMARISE
SUMMARIST
SUMMARIZE
SUMMARY
SUMMAS
SUMMAT
SUMMATE
SUMMATED
SUMMATES
SUMMATING
SUMMATION
SUMMATIVE
SUMMATS
SUMMED
SUMMER
SUMMERED
SUMMERIER
SUMMERING
SUMMERLY
SUMMERS
SUMMERSET
SUMMERY
SUMMING
SUMMINGS
SUMMIST
SUMMISTS
SUMMIT
SUMMITAL
SUMMITED
SUMMITEER
SUMMITING
SUMMITRY
SUMMITS
SUMMON
SUMMONED
SUMMONER
SUMMONERS
SUMMONING
SUMMONS
SUMMONSED
SUMMONSES
SUMO
SUMOIST
SUMOISTS
SUMOS
SUMOTORI
SUMOTORIS
SUMP
SUMPH
SUMPHISH
SUMPHS
SUMPIT
SUMPITAN
SUMPITANS
SUMPITS
SUMPS
SUMPSIMUS
SUMPTER
SUMPTERS
SUMPTUARY
SUMPTUOUS
SUMPWEED
SUMPWEEDS
SUMS
SUMY
SUN
SUNBACK
SUNBAKE
SUNBAKED
SUNBAKES
SUNBAKING
SUNBATH
SUNBATHE
SUNBATHED
SUNBATHER
SUNBATHES
SUNBATHS
SUNBEAM
SUNBEAMED
SUNBEAMS
SUNBEAMY
SUNBEAT
SUNBEATEN
SUNBED
SUNBEDS
SUNBELT
SUNBELTS
SUNBERRY
SUNBIRD
SUNBIRDS
SUNBLIND
SUNBLINDS
SUNBLOCK
SUNBLOCKS
SUNBONNET
SUNBOW
SUNBOWS
SUNBRIGHT
SUNBURN
SUNBURNED
SUNBURNS
SUNBURNT
SUNBURST
SUNBURSTS
SUNCARE
SUNCARES
SUNCHOKE
SUNCHOKES
SUNDAE
SUNDAES
SUNDARI
SUNDARIS
SUNDECK
SUNDECKS
SUNDER
SUNDERED
SUNDERER
SUNDERERS
SUNDERING
SUNDERS
SUNDEW
SUNDEWS
SUNDIAL
SUNDIALS
SUNDOG
SUNDOGS
SUNDOWN
SUNDOWNED
SUNDOWNER
SUNDOWNS
SUNDRA
SUNDRAS
SUNDRESS
SUNDRI
SUNDRIES
SUNDRILY
SUNDRIS
SUNDROPS
SUNDRY
SUNFAST
SUNFISH
SUNFISHES
SUNFLOWER
SUNG

SUNGAR
SUNGARS
SUNGAZER
SUNGAZERS
SUNGAZING
SUNGLASS
SUNGLOW
SUNGLOWS
SUNGREBE
SUNGREBES
SUNHAT
SUNHATS
SUNI
SUNIS
SUNK
SUNKEN
SUNKER
SUNKERS
SUNKET
SUNKETS
SUNKIE
SUNKIES
SUNKS
SUNLAMP
SUNLAMPS
SUNLAND
SUNLANDS
SUNLESS
SUNLESSLY
SUNLIGHT
SUNLIGHTS
SUNLIKE
SUNLIT
SUNN
SUNNA
SUNNAH
SUNNAHS
SUNNAS
SUNNED
SUNNIER
SUNNIES
SUNNIEST
SUNNILY
SUNNINESS
SUNNING
SUNNS
SUNNY
SUNPORCH
SUNPROOF
SUNRAY
SUNRAYS
SUNRISE
SUNRISES
SUNRISING
SUNROOF
SUNROOFS
SUNROOM
SUNROOMS
SUNS
SUNSCALD
SUNSCALDS
SUNSCREEN
SUNSEEKER
SUNSET
SUNSETS
SUNSETTED
SUNSHADE
SUNSHADES
SUNSHINE
SUNSHINES
SUNSHINY
SUNSPECS
SUNSPOT
SUNSPOTS
SUNSTAR
SUNSTARS
SUNSTONE
SUNSTONES
SUNSTROKE
SUNSTRUCK
SUNSUIT
SUNSUITS
SUNTAN
SUNTANNED
SUNTANS
SUNTRAP
SUNTRAPS
SUNUP
SUNUPS
SUNWARD
SUNWARDS
SUNWISE
SUP
SUPAWN
SUPAWNS
SUPE
SUPER
SUPERABLE
SUPERABLY
SUPERADD
SUPERADDS
SUPERATE
SUPERATED
SUPERATES
SUPERATOM
SUPERB
SUPERBAD
SUPERBANK
SUPERBER
SUPERBEST
SUPERBIKE
SUPERBITY
SUPERBLY
SUPERBOLD
SUPERBOMB
SUPERBRAT
SUPERBUG
SUPERBUGS
SUPERCAR
SUPERCARS
SUPERCEDE
SUPERCELL
SUPERCHIC
SUPERCITY
SUPERCLUB
SUPERCOIL
SUPERCOLD
SUPERCOOL
SUPERCOP
SUPERCOPS
SUPERCOW
SUPERCOWS
SUPERCUTE
SUPERED
SUPEREGO
SUPEREGOS
SUPERETTE
SUPERFAN
SUPERFANS
SUPERFARM
SUPERFAST
SUPERFINE
SUPERFIRM
SUPERFIT
SUPERFIX
SUPERFLUX
SUPERFLY
SUPERFOOD
SUPERFUND
SUPERFUSE
SUPERGENE
SUPERGLUE
SUPERGOOD
SUPERGUN
SUPERGUNS
SUPERHARD
SUPERHEAT
SUPERHERO
SUPERHET
SUPERHETS
SUPERHIGH
SUPERHIT
SUPERHITS
SUPERHIVE
SUPERHOT
SUPERHYPE
SUPERING
SUPERIOR
SUPERIORS
SUPERJET
SUPERJETS
SUPERJOCK
SUPERLAIN
SUPERLAY
SUPERLIE
SUPERLIES
SUPERLOAD
SUPERLONG
SUPERLOO
SUPERLOOS
SUPERMALE
SUPERMAN
SUPERMART
SUPERMAX
SUPERMEN
SUPERMIND
SUPERMINI
SUPERMOM
SUPERMOMS
SUPERMOON
SUPERMOTO
SUPERNAL
SUPERNATE
SUPERNOVA
SUPERPIMP
SUPERPLUS
SUPERPORT
SUPERPOSE
SUPERPRO
SUPERPROS
SUPERRACE
SUPERREAL
SUPERRICH
SUPERROAD
SUPERS
SUPERSAFE
SUPERSALE
SUPERSALT
SUPERSAUR
SUPERSEDE
SUPERSELL
SUPERSET
SUPERSETS
SUPERSEX
SUPERSHOW
SUPERSIZE
SUPERSOFT
SUPERSOLD
SUPERSPY
SUPERSTAR
SUPERSTUD
SUPERTAX
SUPERTHIN
SUPERTRAM
SUPERUSER
SUPERVENE
SUPERVISE
SUPERWAIF
SUPERWAVE
SUPERWEED
SUPERWIDE
SUPERWIFE
SUPES
SUPINATE
SUPINATED
SUPINATES
SUPINATOR
SUPINE
SUPINELY
SUPINES

S

SUPLEX
SUPLEXES
SUPPAWN
SUPPAWNS
SUPPEAGO
SUPPED
SUPPER
SUPPERED
SUPPERING
SUPPERS
SUPPING
SUPPLANT
SUPPLANTS
SUPPLE
SUPPLED
SUPPLELY
SUPPLER
SUPPLES
SUPPLEST
SUPPLIAL
SUPPLIALS
SUPPLIANT
SUPPLICAT
SUPPLIED
SUPPLIER
SUPPLIERS
SUPPLIES
SUPPLING
SUPPLY
SUPPLYING
SUPPORT
SUPPORTED
SUPPORTER
SUPPORTS
SUPPOSAL
SUPPOSALS
SUPPOSE
SUPPOSED
SUPPOSER
SUPPOSERS
SUPPOSES
SUPPOSING
SUPPRESS
SUPPURATE
SUPRA
SUPREMA
SUPREMACY
SUPREME
SUPREMELY
SUPREMER
SUPREMES
SUPREMEST
SUPREMITY
SUPREMO
SUPREMOS
SUPREMUM
SUPREMUMS
SUPS
SUQ
SUQS
SUR
SURA
SURAH
SURAHS
SURAL
SURAMIN
SURAMINS
SURANCE
SURANCES
SURAS
SURAT
SURATS
SURBAHAR
SURBAHARS
SURBASE
SURBASED
SURBASES
SURBATE
SURBATED
SURBATES
SURBATING
SURBED
SURBEDDED
SURBEDS
SURBET
SURCEASE
SURCEASED
SURCEASES
SURCHARGE
SURCINGLE
SURCOAT
SURCOATS
SURCULI
SURCULOSE
SURCULUS
SURD
SURDITIES
SURDITY
SURDS
SURE
SURED
SUREFIRE
SURELY
SURENESS
SURER
SURES
SUREST
SURETIED
SURETIES
SURETY
SURETYING
SURF
SURFABLE
SURFACE
SURFACED
SURFACER
SURFACERS
SURFACES
SURFACING
SURFBIRD
SURFBIRDS
SURFBOARD
SURFBOAT
SURFBOATS
SURFED
SURFEIT
SURFEITED
SURFEITER
SURFEITS
SURFER
SURFERS
SURFFISH
SURFICIAL
SURFIE
SURFIER
SURFIES
SURFIEST
SURFING
SURFINGS
SURFLIKE
SURFMAN
SURFMEN
SURFPERCH
SURFRIDE
SURFRIDER
SURFRIDES
SURFRODE
SURFS
SURFSIDE
SURFY
SURGE
SURGED
SURGEFUL
SURGELESS
SURGENT
SURGEON
SURGEONCY
SURGEONS
SURGER
SURGERIES
SURGERS
SURGERY
SURGES
SURGICAL
SURGIER
SURGIEST
SURGING
SURGINGS
SURGY
SURICATE
SURICATES
SURIMI
SURIMIS
SURING
SURLIER
SURLIEST
SURLILY
SURLINESS
SURLOIN
SURLOINS
SURLY
SURMASTER
SURMISAL
SURMISALS
SURMISE
SURMISED
SURMISER
SURMISERS
SURMISES
SURMISING
SURMOUNT
SURMOUNTS
SURMULLET
SURNAME
SURNAMED
SURNAMER
SURNAMERS
SURNAMES
SURNAMING
SURPASS
SURPASSED
SURPASSER
SURPASSES
SURPLICE
SURPLICED
SURPLICES
SURPLUS
SURPLUSED
SURPLUSES
SURPRINT
SURPRINTS
SURPRISAL
SURPRISE
SURPRISED
SURPRISER
SURPRISES
SURPRIZE
SURPRIZED
SURPRIZES
SURQUEDRY
SURQUEDY
SURRA
SURRAS
SURREAL
SURREALLY
SURREALS
SURREBUT
SURREBUTS
SURREINED
SURREJOIN
SURRENDER
SURRENDRY
SURREY
SURREYS
SURROGACY
SURROGATE
SURROUND
SURROUNDS
SURROYAL
SURROYALS

SURTAX
SURTAXED
SURTAXES
SURTAXING
SURTITLE
SURTITLES
SURTOUT
SURTOUTS
SURUCUCU
SURUCUCUS
SURVEIL
SURVEILED
SURVEILLE
SURVEILS
SURVEY
SURVEYAL
SURVEYALS
SURVEYED
SURVEYING
SURVEYOR
SURVEYORS
SURVEYS
SURVIEW
SURVIEWED
SURVIEWS
SURVIVAL
SURVIVALS
SURVIVE
SURVIVED
SURVIVER
SURVIVERS
SURVIVES
SURVIVING
SURVIVOR
SURVIVORS
SUS
SUSCEPTOR
SUSCITATE
SUSED
SUSES
SUSHI
SUSHIS
SUSING
SUSLIK
SUSLIKS
SUSPECT
SUSPECTED
SUSPECTER
SUSPECTS
SUSPENCE
SUSPEND
SUSPENDED
SUSPENDER
SUSPENDS
SUSPENS
SUSPENSE
SUSPENSER
SUSPENSES
SUSPENSOR
SUSPICION
SUSPIRE
SUSPIRED
SUSPIRES
SUSPIRING
SUSS
SUSSED
SUSSES
SUSSING
SUSTAIN
SUSTAINED
SUSTAINER
SUSTAINS
SUSTINENT
SUSU
SUSURRANT
SUSURRATE
SUSURROUS
SUSURRUS
SUSUS
SUTILE
SUTLER
SUTLERIES
SUTLERS
SUTLERY
SUTOR
SUTORIAL
SUTORIAN
SUTORS
SUTRA
SUTRAS
SUTTA
SUTTAS
SUTTEE
SUTTEEISM
SUTTEES
SUTTLE
SUTTLED
SUTTLES
SUTTLETIE
SUTTLING
SUTTLY
SUTURAL
SUTURALLY
SUTURE
SUTURED
SUTURES
SUTURING
SUZERAIN
SUZERAINS
SVARAJ
SVARAJES
SVASTIKA
SVASTIKAS
SVEDBERG
SVEDBERGS
SVELTE
SVELTELY
SVELTER
SVELTEST
SWAB
SWABBED
SWABBER
SWABBERS
SWABBIE
SWABBIES
SWABBING
SWABBY
SWABS
SWACHH
SWACK
SWACKED
SWACKING
SWACKS
SWAD
SWADDIE
SWADDIES
SWADDLE
SWADDLED
SWADDLER
SWADDLERS
SWADDLES
SWADDLING
SWADDY
SWADS
SWAG
SWAGE
SWAGED
SWAGER
SWAGERS
SWAGES
SWAGGED
SWAGGER
SWAGGERED
SWAGGERER
SWAGGERS
SWAGGIE
SWAGGIES
SWAGGING
SWAGING
SWAGMAN
SWAGMEN
SWAGS
SWAGSHOP
SWAGSHOPS
SWAGSMAN
SWAGSMEN
SWAIL
SWAILS
SWAIN
SWAINING
SWAININGS
SWAINISH
SWAINS
SWALE
SWALED
SWALES
SWALIER
SWALIEST
SWALING
SWALINGS
SWALLET
SWALLETS
SWALLIES
SWALLOW
SWALLOWED
SWALLOWER
SWALLOWS
SWALLY
SWALY
SWAM
SWAMI
SWAMIES
SWAMIS
SWAMP
SWAMPED
SWAMPER
SWAMPERS
SWAMPIER
SWAMPIEST
SWAMPING
SWAMPISH
SWAMPLAND
SWAMPLESS
SWAMPS
SWAMPY
SWAMY
SWAN
SWANG
SWANHERD
SWANHERDS
SWANK
SWANKED
SWANKER
SWANKERS
SWANKEST
SWANKEY
SWANKEYS
SWANKIE
SWANKIER
SWANKIES
SWANKIEST
SWANKILY
SWANKING
SWANKPOT
SWANKPOTS
SWANKS
SWANKY
SWANLIKE
SWANNED
SWANNERY
SWANNIE
SWANNIER
SWANNIES
SWANNIEST
SWANNING
SWANNINGS
SWANNY
SWANPAN
SWANPANS
SWANS

S

SWANSDOWN
SWANSKIN
SWANSKINS
SWANSONG
SWANSONGS
SWAP
SWAPFILE
SWAPFILES
SWAPPABLE
SWAPPED
SWAPPER
SWAPPERS
SWAPPING
SWAPPINGS
SWAPS
SWAPT
SWAPTION
SWAPTIONS
SWARAJ
SWARAJES
SWARAJISM
SWARAJIST
SWARD
SWARDED
SWARDIER
SWARDIEST
SWARDING
SWARDS
SWARDY
SWARE
SWARF
SWARFED
SWARFING
SWARFS
SWARM
SWARMED
SWARMER
SWARMERS
SWARMING
SWARMINGS
SWARMS
SWART
SWARTH
SWARTHIER
SWARTHILY
SWARTHS
SWARTHY
SWARTIER
SWARTIEST
SWARTNESS
SWARTY
SWARVE
SWARVED
SWARVES
SWARVING
SWASH
SWASHED
SWASHER
SWASHERS
SWASHES
SWASHIER
SWASHIEST
SWASHING
SWASHINGS
SWASHWORK
SWASHY
SWASTICA
SWASTICAS
SWASTIKA
SWASTIKAS
SWAT
SWATCH
SWATCHES
SWATH
SWATHABLE
SWATHE
SWATHED
SWATHER
SWATHERS
SWATHES
SWATHIER
SWATHIEST
SWATHING
SWATHINGS
SWATHS
SWATHY
SWATS
SWATTED
SWATTER
SWATTERED
SWATTERS
SWATTIER
SWATTIEST
SWATTING
SWATTINGS
SWATTY
SWAY
SWAYABLE
SWAYBACK
SWAYBACKS
SWAYED
SWAYER
SWAYERS
SWAYFUL
SWAYING
SWAYINGS
SWAYL
SWAYLED
SWAYLING
SWAYLINGS
SWAYLS
SWAYS
SWAZZLE
SWAZZLES
SWEAL
SWEALED
SWEALING
SWEALINGS
SWEALS
SWEAR
SWEARD
SWEARDS
SWEARER
SWEARERS
SWEARIER
SWEARIEST
SWEARING
SWEARINGS
SWEARS
SWEARWORD
SWEARY
SWEAT
SWEATBAND
SWEATBOX
SWEATED
SWEATER
SWEATERED
SWEATERS
SWEATIER
SWEATIEST
SWEATILY
SWEATING
SWEATINGS
SWEATLESS
SWEATS
SWEATSHOP
SWEATSUIT
SWEATY
SWEDE
SWEDES
SWEDGER
SWEDGERS
SWEE
SWEED
SWEEING
SWEEL
SWEELED
SWEELING
SWEELS
SWEENEY
SWEENEYS
SWEENIES
SWEENY
SWEEP
SWEEPBACK
SWEEPER
SWEEPERS
SWEEPIER
SWEEPIEST
SWEEPING
SWEEPINGS
SWEEPS
SWEEPY
SWEER
SWEERED
SWEERING
SWEERS
SWEERT
SWEES
SWEET
SWEETCORN
SWEETED
SWEETEN
SWEETENED
SWEETENER
SWEETENS
SWEETER
SWEETEST
SWEETFISH
SWEETIE
SWEETIES
SWEETING
SWEETINGS
SWEETISH
SWEETLIP
SWEETLIPS
SWEETLY
SWEETMAN
SWEETMEAL
SWEETMEAT
SWEETMEN
SWEETNESS
SWEETS
SWEETSHOP
SWEETSOP
SWEETSOPS
SWEETVELD
SWEETWOOD
SWEETY
SWEIR
SWEIRED
SWEIRER
SWEIREST
SWEIRING
SWEIRNESS
SWEIRS
SWEIRT
SWELCHIE
SWELCHIES
SWELL
SWELLDOM
SWELLDOMS
SWELLED
SWELLER
SWELLERS
SWELLEST
SWELLFISH
SWELLHEAD
SWELLING
SWELLINGS
SWELLISH
SWELLS
SWELT
SWELTED
SWELTER
SWELTERED
SWELTERS
SWELTING
SWELTRIER
SWELTRY

SWELTS
SWEPT
SWEPTBACK
SWEPTWING
SWERF
SWERFED
SWERFING
SWERFS
SWERVABLE
SWERVE
SWERVED
SWERVER
SWERVERS
SWERVES
SWERVING
SWERVINGS
SWEVEN
SWEVENS
SWEY
SWEYED
SWEYING
SWEYS
SWIDDEN
SWIDDENS
SWIES
SWIFT
SWIFTED
SWIFTER
SWIFTERS
SWIFTEST
SWIFTIE
SWIFTIES
SWIFTING
SWIFTLET
SWIFTLETS
SWIFTLY
SWIFTNESS
SWIFTS
SWIFTY
SWIG
SWIGGED
SWIGGER
SWIGGERS
SWIGGING
SWIGS
SWILE
SWILER
SWILERS
SWILES
SWILING
SWILINGS
SWILL
SWILLED
SWILLER
SWILLERS
SWILLING
SWILLINGS
SWILLS
SWIM
SWIMMABLE
SWIMMER
SWIMMERET
SWIMMERS
SWIMMIER
SWIMMIEST
SWIMMILY
SWIMMING
SWIMMINGS
SWIMMY
SWIMS
SWIMSUIT
SWIMSUITS
SWIMWEAR
SWIMWEARS
SWINDGE
SWINDGED
SWINDGES
SWINDGING
SWINDLE
SWINDLED
SWINDLER
SWINDLERS
SWINDLES
SWINDLING
SWINE
SWINEHERD
SWINEHOOD
SWINELIKE
SWINEPOX
SWINERIES
SWINERY
SWINES
SWING
SWINGARM
SWINGARMS
SWINGBEAT
SWINGBIN
SWINGBINS
SWINGBOAT
SWINGBY
SWINGBYS
SWINGE
SWINGED
SWINGEING
SWINGER
SWINGERS
SWINGES
SWINGIER
SWINGIEST
SWINGING
SWINGINGS
SWINGISM
SWINGISMS
SWINGLE
SWINGLED
SWINGLES
SWINGLING
SWINGMAN
SWINGMEN
SWINGS
SWINGTAIL
SWINGTREE
SWINGY
SWINISH
SWINISHLY
SWINK
SWINKED
SWINKER
SWINKERS
SWINKING
SWINKS
SWINNEY
SWINNEYS
SWIPE
SWIPED
SWIPER
SWIPERS
SWIPES
SWIPEY
SWIPIER
SWIPIEST
SWIPING
SWIPLE
SWIPLES
SWIPPLE
SWIPPLES
SWIRE
SWIRES
SWIRL
SWIRLED
SWIRLIER
SWIRLIEST
SWIRLING
SWIRLS
SWIRLY
SWISH
SWISHED
SWISHER
SWISHERS
SWISHES
SWISHEST
SWISHIER
SWISHIEST
SWISHING
SWISHINGS
SWISHY
SWISS
SWISSES
SWISSING
SWISSINGS
SWITCH
SWITCHED
SWITCHEL
SWITCHELS
SWITCHER
SWITCHERS
SWITCHES
SWITCHIER
SWITCHING
SWITCHMAN
SWITCHMEN
SWITCHY
SWITH
SWITHE
SWITHER
SWITHERED
SWITHERS
SWITHLY
SWITS
SWITSES
SWIVE
SWIVED
SWIVEL
SWIVELED
SWIVELING
SWIVELLED
SWIVELS
SWIVES
SWIVET
SWIVETS
SWIVING
SWIZ
SWIZZ
SWIZZED
SWIZZES
SWIZZING
SWIZZLE
SWIZZLED
SWIZZLER
SWIZZLERS
SWIZZLES
SWIZZLING
SWOB
SWOBBED
SWOBBER
SWOBBERS
SWOBBING
SWOBS
SWOFFER
SWOFFERS
SWOFFING
SWOFFINGS
SWOLE
SWOLER
SWOLEST
SWOLLEN
SWOLLENLY
SWOLN
SWOON
SWOONED
SWOONER
SWOONERS
SWOONIER
SWOONIEST
SWOONING
SWOONINGS
SWOONS
SWOONY
SWOOP
SWOOPED

SWOOPER
SWOOPERS
SWOOPIER
SWOOPIEST
SWOOPING
SWOOPS
SWOOPY
SWOOSH
SWOOSHED
SWOOSHES
SWOOSHING
SWOP
SWOPPABLE
SWOPPED
SWOPPER
SWOPPERS
SWOPPING
SWOPPINGS
SWOPS
SWOPT
SWORD
SWORDBILL
SWORDED
SWORDER
SWORDERS
SWORDFERN
SWORDFISH
SWORDING
SWORDLESS
SWORDLIKE
SWORDMAN
SWORDMEN
SWORDPLAY
SWORDS
SWORDSMAN
SWORDSMEN
SWORDTAIL
SWORE
SWORN
SWOT
SWOTS
SWOTTED
SWOTTER
SWOTTERS
SWOTTIER
SWOTTIEST
SWOTTING
SWOTTINGS
SWOTTY
SWOUN
SWOUND
SWOUNDED
SWOUNDING
SWOUNDS
SWOUNE
SWOUNED
SWOUNES
SWOUNING
SWOUNS
SWOWND
SWOWNDS
SWOWNE
SWOWNES
SWOZZLE
SWOZZLES
SWUM
SWUNG
SWY
SYBARITE
SYBARITES
SYBARITIC
SYBBE
SYBBES
SYBIL
SYBILS
SYBO
SYBOE
SYBOES
SYBOTIC
SYBOTISM
SYBOTISMS
SYBOW
SYBOWS
SYCAMINE
SYCAMINES
SYCAMORE
SYCAMORES
SYCE
SYCEE
SYCEES
SYCES
SYCOMORE
SYCOMORES
SYCON
SYCONIA
SYCONIUM
SYCONOID
SYCONS
SYCOPHANT
SYCOSES
SYCOSIS
SYE
SYED
SYEING
SYEN
SYENITE
SYENITES
SYENITIC
SYENS
SYES
SYKE
SYKER
SYKES
SYLI
SYLIS
SYLLABARY
SYLLABI
SYLLABIC
SYLLABICS
SYLLABIFY
SYLLABISE
SYLLABISM
SYLLABIZE
SYLLABLE
SYLLABLED
SYLLABLES
SYLLABUB
SYLLABUBS
SYLLABUS
SYLLEPSES
SYLLEPSIS
SYLLEPTIC
SYLLOGE
SYLLOGES
SYLLOGISE
SYLLOGISM
SYLLOGIST
SYLLOGIZE
SYLPH
SYLPHIC
SYLPHID
SYLPHIDE
SYLPHIDES
SYLPHIDS
SYLPHIER
SYLPHIEST
SYLPHINE
SYLPHISH
SYLPHLIKE
SYLPHS
SYLPHY
SYLVA
SYLVAE
SYLVAN
SYLVANER
SYLVANERS
SYLVANITE
SYLVANS
SYLVAS
SYLVATIC
SYLVIA
SYLVIAS
SYLVIINE
SYLVIN
SYLVINE
SYLVINES
SYLVINITE
SYLVINS
SYLVITE
SYLVITES
SYMAR
SYMARS
SYMBION
SYMBIONS
SYMBIONT
SYMBIONTS
SYMBIOSES
SYMBIOSIS
SYMBIOT
SYMBIOTE
SYMBIOTES
SYMBIOTIC
SYMBIOTS
SYMBOL
SYMBOLE
SYMBOLED
SYMBOLES
SYMBOLIC
SYMBOLICS
SYMBOLING
SYMBOLISE
SYMBOLISM
SYMBOLIST
SYMBOLIZE
SYMBOLLED
SYMBOLOGY
SYMBOLS
SYMITAR
SYMITARE
SYMITARES
SYMITARS
SYMMETRAL
SYMMETRIC
SYMMETRY
SYMPATHIN
SYMPATHY
SYMPATICO
SYMPATRIC
SYMPATRY
SYMPETALY
SYMPHILE
SYMPHILES
SYMPHILY
SYMPHONIC
SYMPHONY
SYMPHYSES
SYMPHYSIS
SYMPHYTIC
SYMPLAST
SYMPLASTS
SYMPLOCE
SYMPLOCES
SYMPODIA
SYMPODIAL
SYMPODIUM
SYMPOSIA
SYMPOSIAC
SYMPOSIAL
SYMPOSIUM
SYMPTOM
SYMPTOMS
SYMPTOSES
SYMPTOSIS
SYMPTOTIC
SYN
SYNAGOG
SYNAGOGAL
SYNAGOGS
SYNAGOGUE
SYNALEPHA

S

SYNANDRIA
SYNANGIA
SYNANGIUM
SYNANON
SYNANONS
SYNANTHIC
SYNANTHY
SYNAPHEA
SYNAPHEAS
SYNAPHEIA
SYNAPSE
SYNAPSED
SYNAPSES
SYNAPSID
SYNAPSIDS
SYNAPSING
SYNAPSIS
SYNAPTASE
SYNAPTE
SYNAPTES
SYNAPTIC
SYNARCHY
SYNASTRY
SYNAXARIA
SYNAXES
SYNAXIS
SYNBIOTIC
SYNC
SYNCARP
SYNCARPS
SYNCARPY
SYNCED
SYNCH
SYNCHED
SYNCHING
SYNCHRO
SYNCHRONY
SYNCHROS
SYNCHS
SYNCHYSES
SYNCHYSIS
SYNCING
SYNCLINAL
SYNCLINE
SYNCLINES
SYNCOM
SYNCOMS
SYNCOPAL
SYNCOPATE
SYNCOPE
SYNCOPES
SYNCOPIC
SYNCOPTIC
SYNCRETIC
SYNCS
SYNCYTIA
SYNCYTIAL
SYNCYTIUM
SYND
SYNDACTYL
SYNDED
SYNDESES
SYNDESIS
SYNDET
SYNDETIC
SYNDETON
SYNDETONS
SYNDETS
SYNDIC
SYNDICAL
SYNDICATE
SYNDICS
SYNDING
SYNDINGS
SYNDROME
SYNDROMES
SYNDROMIC
SYNDS
SYNE
SYNECHIA
SYNECHIAS
SYNECIOUS
SYNECTIC
SYNECTICS
SYNED
SYNEDRIA
SYNEDRIAL
SYNEDRION
SYNEDRIUM
SYNERESES
SYNERESIS
SYNERGIA
SYNERGIAS
SYNERGIC
SYNERGID
SYNERGIDS
SYNERGIES
SYNERGISE
SYNERGISM
SYNERGIST
SYNERGIZE
SYNERGY
SYNES
SYNESES
SYNESIS
SYNESISES
SYNFUEL
SYNFUELS
SYNGAMIC
SYNGAMIES
SYNGAMOUS
SYNGAMY
SYNGAS
SYNGASES
SYNGASSES
SYNGENEIC
SYNGENIC
SYNGRAPH
SYNGRAPHS
SYNING
SYNIZESES
SYNIZESIS
SYNKARYA
SYNKARYON
SYNOD
SYNODAL
SYNODALS
SYNODIC
SYNODICAL
SYNODS
SYNODSMAN
SYNODSMEN
SYNOECETE
SYNOECISE
SYNOECISM
SYNOECIZE
SYNOEKETE
SYNOICOUS
SYNONYM
SYNONYME
SYNONYMES
SYNONYMIC
SYNONYMS
SYNONYMY
SYNOPSES
SYNOPSIS
SYNOPSISE
SYNOPSIZE
SYNOPTIC
SYNOPTICS
SYNOPTIST
SYNOVIA
SYNOVIAL
SYNOVIAS
SYNOVITIC
SYNOVITIS
SYNROC
SYNROCS
SYNTACTIC
SYNTAGM
SYNTAGMA
SYNTAGMAS
SYNTAGMIC
SYNTAGMS
SYNTAN
SYNTANS
SYNTAX
SYNTAXES
SYNTECTIC
SYNTENIC
SYNTENIES
SYNTENY
SYNTEXIS
SYNTH
SYNTHASE
SYNTHASES
SYNTHESES
SYNTHESIS
SYNTHETIC
SYNTHON
SYNTHONS
SYNTHPOP
SYNTHPOPS
SYNTHRONI
SYNTHS
SYNTONE
SYNTONES
SYNTONIC
SYNTONIES
SYNTONIN
SYNTONINS
SYNTONISE
SYNTONIZE
SYNTONOUS
SYNTONY
SYNTYPE
SYNTYPES
SYNURA
SYNURAE
SYPE
SYPED
SYPES
SYPH
SYPHER
SYPHERED
SYPHERING
SYPHERS
SYPHILIS
SYPHILISE
SYPHILIZE
SYPHILOID
SYPHILOMA
SYPHON
SYPHONAGE
SYPHONAL
SYPHONED
SYPHONIC
SYPHONING
SYPHONS
SYPHS
SYPING
SYRAH
SYRAHS
SYREN
SYRENS
SYRETTE
SYRETTES
SYRINGA
SYRINGAS
SYRINGE
SYRINGEAL
SYRINGED
SYRINGES
SYRINGING
SYRINX
SYRINXES
SYRPHIAN
SYRPHIANS
SYRPHID
SYRPHIDS

SYRTES
SYRTIS
SYRUP
SYRUPED
SYRUPIER
SYRUPIEST
SYRUPING
SYRUPLIKE
SYRUPS
SYRUPY
SYSADMIN
SYSADMINS
SYSOP
SYSOPS
SYSSITIA
SYSSITIAS
SYSTALTIC
SYSTEM
SYSTEMED
SYSTEMIC
SYSTEMICS
SYSTEMISE
SYSTEMIZE
SYSTEMS
SYSTOLE
SYSTOLES
SYSTOLIC
SYSTYLE
SYSTYLES
SYTHE
SYTHES
SYVER
SYVERS
SYZYGAL
SYZYGETIC
SYZYGIAL
SYZYGIES
SYZYGY

T

TA
TAAL
TAALS
TAATA
TAATAS
TAB
TABANID
TABANIDS
TABARD
TABARDED
TABARDS
TABARET
TABARETS
TABASHEER
TABASHIR
TABASHIRS
TABBED
TABBIED
TABBIER
TABBIES
TABBIEST
TABBINET
TABBINETS
TABBING
TABBINGS
TABBIS
TABBISES
TABBOULEH
TABBOULI
TABBOULIS
TABBY
TABBYHOOD
TABBYING
TABEFIED
TABEFIES
TABEFY
TABEFYING
TABELLION
TABER
TABERD
TABERDAR
TABERDARS
TABERDS
TABERED
TABERING
TABERS
TABES
TABESCENT
TABETIC
TABETICS
TABI
TABID
TABINET
TABINETS
TABIS
TABLA
TABLAS
TABLATURE
TABLE
TABLEAU
TABLEAUS
TABLEAUX
TABLED
TABLEFUL
TABLEFULS
TABLELAND
TABLELESS
TABLEMAT
TABLEMATE
TABLEMATS
TABLES
TABLESFUL
TABLESIDE
TABLET
TABLETED
TABLETING
TABLETOP
TABLETOPS
TABLETS
TABLETTED
TABLEWARE
TABLEWISE
TABLIER
TABLIERS
TABLING
TABLINGS
TABLOID
TABLOIDS
TABLOIDY
TABOGGAN
TABOGGANS
TABOO
TABOOED
TABOOING
TABOOLEY
TABOOLEYS
TABOOS
TABOR
TABORED
TABORER
TABORERS
TABORET
TABORETS
TABORIN
TABORINE
TABORINES
TABORING
TABORINS
TABORS
TABOULEH
TABOULEHS
TABOULI
TABOULIS
TABOUR
TABOURED
TABOURER
TABOURERS
TABOURET
TABOURETS
TABOURIN
TABOURING
TABOURINS
TABOURS
TABRERE
TABRERES
TABRET
TABRETS
TABS
TABU
TABUED
TABUING
TABULA
TABULABLE
TABULAE
TABULAR
TABULARLY
TABULATE
TABULATED
TABULATES
TABULATOR
TABULI
TABULIS
TABUN
TABUNS
TABUS
TACAHOUT
TACAHOUTS
TACAMAHAC
TACAN
TACANS
TACE
TACES
TACET
TACH
TACHE
TACHES
TACHINA
TACHINID
TACHINIDS
TACHISM
TACHISME
TACHISMES
TACHISMS
TACHIST
TACHISTE
TACHISTES
TACHISTS
TACHO
TACHOGRAM
TACHOS
TACHS
TACHYLITE
TACHYLYTE
TACHYON
TACHYONIC
TACHYONS
TACHYPNEA
TACIT
TACITLY
TACITNESS
TACITURN
TACK
TACKBOARD
TACKED
TACKER
TACKERS
TACKET
TACKETIER
TACKETS
TACKETY
TACKEY
TACKIER
TACKIES
TACKIEST
TACKIFIED
TACKIFIER
TACKIFIES
TACKIFY
TACKILY
TACKINESS
TACKING
TACKINGS
TACKLE
TACKLED
TACKLER
TACKLERS
TACKLES
TACKLESS
TACKLING
TACKLINGS

TACKS
TACKSMAN
TACKSMEN
TACKY
TACMAHACK
TACNODE
TACNODES
TACO
TACONITE
TACONITES
TACOS
TACRINE
TACRINES
TACT
TACTFUL
TACTFULLY
TACTIC
TACTICAL
TACTICIAN
TACTICITY
TACTICS
TACTILE
TACTILELY
TACTILIST
TACTILITY
TACTION
TACTIONS
TACTISM
TACTISMS
TACTLESS
TACTS
TACTUAL
TACTUALLY
TAD
TADALAFIL
TADDIE
TADDIES
TADPOLE
TADPOLES
TADS
TAE
TAED
TAEDIUM
TAEDIUMS
TAEING
TAEKWONDO
TAEL
TAELS
TAENIA
TAENIAE
TAENIAS
TAENIASES
TAENIASIS
TAENIATE
TAENIOID
TAENITE
TAENITES
TAES
TAFFAREL
TAFFARELS
TAFFEREL
TAFFERELS
TAFFETA
TAFFETAS
TAFFETIER
TAFFETY
TAFFIA
TAFFIAS
TAFFIES
TAFFRAIL
TAFFRAILS
TAFFY
TAFIA
TAFIAS
TAG
TAGALONG
TAGALONGS
TAGAREEN
TAGAREENS
TAGBOARD
TAGBOARDS
TAGETES
TAGGANT
TAGGANTS
TAGGED
TAGGEE
TAGGEES
TAGGER
TAGGERS
TAGGIER
TAGGIEST
TAGGING
TAGGINGS
TAGGY
TAGHAIRM
TAGHAIRMS
TAGINE
TAGINES
TAGLESS
TAGLIKE
TAGLINE
TAGLINES
TAGLIONI
TAGLIONIS
TAGMA
TAGMATA
TAGMEME
TAGMEMES
TAGMEMIC
TAGMEMICS
TAGRAG
TAGRAGS
TAGS
TAGUAN
TAGUANS
TAHA
TAHAS
TAHINA
TAHINAS
TAHINI
TAHINIS
TAHR
TAHRS
TAHSIL
TAHSILDAR
TAHSILS
TAI
TAIAHA
TAIAHAS
TAIGA
TAIGAS
TAIGLACH
TAIGLE
TAIGLED
TAIGLES
TAIGLING
TAIHOA
TAIHOAED
TAIHOAING
TAIHOAS
TAIKO
TAIKONAUT
TAIKOS
TAIL
TAILARD
TAILARDS
TAILBACK
TAILBACKS
TAILBOARD
TAILBONE
TAILBONES
TAILCOAT
TAILCOATS
TAILED
TAILENDER
TAILER
TAILERON
TAILERONS
TAILERS
TAILFAN
TAILFANS
TAILFIN
TAILFINS
TAILFLIES
TAILFLY
TAILGATE
TAILGATED
TAILGATER
TAILGATES
TAILHOOK
TAILHOOKS
TAILING
TAILINGS
TAILLAMP
TAILLAMPS
TAILLE
TAILLES
TAILLESS
TAILLEUR
TAILLEURS
TAILLIE
TAILLIES
TAILLIGHT
TAILLIKE
TAILOR
TAILORED
TAILORESS
TAILORING
TAILORS
TAILPIECE
TAILPIPE
TAILPIPED
TAILPIPES
TAILPLANE
TAILRACE
TAILRACES
TAILS
TAILSKID
TAILSKIDS
TAILSLIDE
TAILSPIN
TAILSPINS
TAILSPUN
TAILSTOCK
TAILWATER
TAILWHEEL
TAILWIND
TAILWINDS
TAILYE
TAILYES
TAILZIE
TAILZIES
TAIN
TAINS
TAINT
TAINTED
TAINTING
TAINTLESS
TAINTS
TAINTURE
TAINTURES
TAIPAN
TAIPANS
TAIRA
TAIRAS
TAIS
TAISCH
TAISCHES
TAISH
TAISHES
TAIT
TAITS
TAIVER
TAIVERED
TAIVERING
TAIVERS
TAIVERT
TAJ
TAJES
TAJINE

TAJINES
TAK
TAKA
TAKABLE
TAKAHE
TAKAHES
TAKAMAKA
TAKAMAKAS
TAKAS
TAKE
TAKEABLE
TAKEAWAY
TAKEAWAYS
TAKEDOWN
TAKEDOWNS
TAKEN
TAKEOFF
TAKEOFFS
TAKEOUT
TAKEOUTS
TAKEOVER
TAKEOVERS
TAKER
TAKERS
TAKES
TAKEUP
TAKEUPS
TAKHI
TAKHIS
TAKI
TAKIER
TAKIEST
TAKIN
TAKING
TAKINGLY
TAKINGS
TAKINS
TAKIS
TAKKIES
TAKKY
TAKS
TAKY
TALA
TALAK
TALAKS
TALANT
TALANTS
TALAPOIN
TALAPOINS
TALAQ
TALAQS
TALAR
TALARIA
TALARS
TALAS
TALAUNT
TALAUNTS
TALAYOT
TALAYOTS
TALBOT
TALBOTS
TALBOTYPE
TALC
TALCED
TALCIER
TALCIEST
TALCING
TALCKED
TALCKIER
TALCKIEST
TALCKING
TALCKY
TALCOSE
TALCOUS
TALCS
TALCUM
TALCUMED
TALCUMING
TALCUMS
TALCY
TALE
TALEA
TALEAE
TALEFUL
TALEGALLA
TALEGGIO
TALEGGIOS
TALENT
TALENTED
TALENTS
TALER
TALERS
TALES
TALESMAN
TALESMEN
TALEYSIM
TALI
TALIGRADE
TALION
TALIONIC
TALIONS
TALIPAT
TALIPATS
TALIPED
TALIPEDS
TALIPES
TALIPOT
TALIPOTS
TALISMAN
TALISMANS
TALK
TALKABLE
TALKATHON
TALKATIVE
TALKBACK
TALKBACKS
TALKBOX
TALKBOXES
TALKED
TALKER
TALKERS
TALKFEST
TALKFESTS
TALKIE
TALKIER
TALKIES
TALKIEST
TALKINESS
TALKING
TALKINGS
TALKS
TALKTIME
TALKTIMES
TALKY
TALL
TALLAGE
TALLAGED
TALLAGES
TALLAGING
TALLAISIM
TALLAT
TALLATS
TALLBOY
TALLBOYS
TALLENT
TALLENTS
TALLER
TALLEST
TALLET
TALLETS
TALLGRASS
TALLIABLE
TALLIATE
TALLIATED
TALLIATES
TALLIED
TALLIER
TALLIERS
TALLIES
TALLIS
TALLISES
TALLISH
TALLISIM
TALLIT
TALLITES
TALLITH
TALLITHES
TALLITHIM
TALLITHS
TALLITIM
TALLITOT
TALLITOTH
TALLITS
TALLNESS
TALLOL
TALLOLS
TALLOT
TALLOTS
TALLOW
TALLOWED
TALLOWIER
TALLOWING
TALLOWISH
TALLOWS
TALLOWY
TALLS
TALLY
TALLYHO
TALLYHOED
TALLYHOES
TALLYHOS
TALLYING
TALLYMAN
TALLYMEN
TALLYSHOP
TALMA
TALMAS
TALMUD
TALMUDIC
TALMUDISM
TALMUDS
TALON
TALONED
TALONS
TALOOKA
TALOOKAS
TALPA
TALPAE
TALPAS
TALUK
TALUKA
TALUKAS
TALUKDAR
TALUKDARS
TALUKS
TALUS
TALUSES
TALWEG
TALWEGS
TAM
TAMABLE
TAMAL
TAMALE
TAMALES
TAMALS
TAMANDU
TAMANDUA
TAMANDUAS
TAMANDUS
TAMANOIR
TAMANOIRS
TAMANU
TAMANUS
TAMARA
TAMARACK
TAMARACKS
TAMARAO
TAMARAOS
TAMARAS
TAMARAU

TAMARAUS
TAMARI
TAMARILLO
TAMARIN
TAMARIND
TAMARINDS
TAMARINS
TAMARIS
TAMARISK
TAMARISKS
TAMASHA
TAMASHAS
TAMBAC
TAMBACS
TAMBAK
TAMBAKS
TAMBALA
TAMBALAS
TAMBER
TAMBERS
TAMBOUR
TAMBOURA
TAMBOURAS
TAMBOURED
TAMBOURER
TAMBOURIN
TAMBOURS
TAMBUR
TAMBURA
TAMBURAS
TAMBURIN
TAMBURINS
TAMBURS
TAME
TAMEABLE
TAMED
TAMEIN
TAMEINS
TAMELESS
TAMELY
TAMENESS
TAMER
TAMERS
TAMES
TAMEST
TAMIN
TAMINE
TAMINES
TAMING
TAMINGS
TAMINS
TAMIS
TAMISE
TAMISES
TAMMAR
TAMMARS
TAMMIE
TAMMIED
TAMMIES
TAMMY
TAMMYING
TAMOXIFEN
TAMP
TAMPALA
TAMPALAS
TAMPAN
TAMPANS
TAMPED
TAMPER
TAMPERED
TAMPERER
TAMPERERS
TAMPERING
TAMPERS
TAMPING
TAMPINGS
TAMPION
TAMPIONS
TAMPON
TAMPONADE
TAMPONAGE
TAMPONED
TAMPONING
TAMPONS
TAMPS
TAMS
TAMWORTH
TAMWORTHS
TAN
TANA
TANADAR
TANADARS
TANAGER
TANAGERS
TANAGRA
TANAGRAS
TANAGRINE
TANAISTE
TANAISTES
TANALISED
TANALIZED
TANAS
TANBARK
TANBARKS
TANDEM
TANDEMS
TANDOOR
TANDOORI
TANDOORIS
TANDOORS
TANE
TANG
TANGA
TANGAS
TANGED
TANGELO
TANGELOS
TANGENCE
TANGENCES
TANGENCY
TANGENT
TANGENTAL
TANGENTS
TANGERINE
TANGHIN
TANGHININ
TANGHINS
TANGI
TANGIBLE
TANGIBLES
TANGIBLY
TANGIE
TANGIER
TANGIES
TANGIEST
TANGINESS
TANGING
TANGIS
TANGLE
TANGLED
TANGLER
TANGLERS
TANGLES
TANGLIER
TANGLIEST
TANGLING
TANGLINGS
TANGLY
TANGO
TANGOED
TANGOES
TANGOING
TANGOIST
TANGOISTS
TANGOLIKE
TANGOS
TANGRAM
TANGRAMS
TANGS
TANGUN
TANGUNS
TANGY
TANH
TANHS
TANIST
TANISTRY
TANISTS
TANIWHA
TANIWHAS
TANK
TANKA
TANKAGE
TANKAGES
TANKARD
TANKARDS
TANKAS
TANKED
TANKER
TANKERED
TANKERING
TANKERS
TANKFUL
TANKFULS
TANKIA
TANKIAS
TANKIES
TANKING
TANKINGS
TANKINI
TANKINIS
TANKLESS
TANKLIKE
TANKS
TANKSHIP
TANKSHIPS
TANKY
TANLING
TANLINGS
TANNA
TANNABLE
TANNAGE
TANNAGES
TANNAH
TANNAHS
TANNAS
TANNATE
TANNATES
TANNED
TANNER
TANNERIES
TANNERS
TANNERY
TANNEST
TANNIC
TANNIE
TANNIES
TANNIN
TANNING
TANNINGS
TANNINS
TANNISH
TANNOY
TANNOYED
TANNOYING
TANNOYS
TANOREXIC
TANREC
TANRECS
TANS
TANSIES
TANSY
TANTALATE
TANTALIC
TANTALISE
TANTALISM
TANTALITE
TANTALIZE
TANTALOUS
TANTALUM
TANTALUMS

TANTALUS
TANTARA
TANTARARA
TANTARAS
TANTI
TANTIES
TANTIVIES
TANTIVY
TANTO
TANTONIES
TANTONY
TANTOS
TANTRA
TANTRAS
TANTRIC
TANTRISM
TANTRISMS
TANTRIST
TANTRISTS
TANTRUM
TANTRUMS
TANTY
TANUKI
TANUKIS
TANYARD
TANYARDS
TANZANITE
TAO
TAONGA
TAONGAS
TAOS
TAP
TAPA
TAPACOLO
TAPACOLOS
TAPACULO
TAPACULOS
TAPADERA
TAPADERAS
TAPADERO
TAPADEROS
TAPALO
TAPALOS
TAPAS
TAPE
TAPEABLE
TAPED
TAPELESS
TAPELIKE
TAPELINE
TAPELINES
TAPEN
TAPENADE
TAPENADES
TAPER
TAPERED
TAPERER
TAPERERS
TAPERING
TAPERINGS
TAPERNESS
TAPERS
TAPERWISE
TAPES
TAPESTRY
TAPET
TAPETA
TAPETAL
TAPETED
TAPETI
TAPETING
TAPETIS
TAPETS
TAPETUM
TAPETUMS
TAPEWORM
TAPEWORMS
TAPHOLE
TAPHOLES
TAPHONOMY
TAPHOUSE
TAPHOUSES
TAPING
TAPINGS
TAPIOCA
TAPIOCAS
TAPIR
TAPIROID
TAPIROIDS
TAPIRS
TAPIS
TAPISES
TAPIST
TAPISTS
TAPLASH
TAPLASHES
TAPLESS
TAPPA
TAPPABLE
TAPPAS
TAPPED
TAPPER
TAPPERS
TAPPET
TAPPETS
TAPPICE
TAPPICED
TAPPICES
TAPPICING
TAPPING
TAPPINGS
TAPPIT
TAPROOM
TAPROOMS
TAPROOT
TAPROOTED
TAPROOTS
TAPS
TAPSMAN
TAPSMEN
TAPSTER
TAPSTERS
TAPSTRESS
TAPSTRIES
TAPSTRY
TAPU
TAPUED
TAPUING
TAPUS
TAQUERIA
TAQUERIAS
TAR
TARA
TARABISH
TARAIRE
TARAIRES
TARAKIHI
TARAKIHIS
TARAMA
TARAMAS
TARAMEA
TARAMEAS
TARAND
TARANDS
TARANTARA
TARANTAS
TARANTASS
TARANTISM
TARANTIST
TARANTULA
TARAS
TARAXACUM
TARBOGGIN
TARBOOSH
TARBOUCHE
TARBOUSH
TARBOY
TARBOYS
TARBUSH
TARBUSHES
TARCEL
TARCELS
TARDIED
TARDIER
TARDIES
TARDIEST
TARDILY
TARDINESS
TARDIVE
TARDO
TARDY
TARDYING
TARDYON
TARDYONS
TARE
TARED
TARES
TARGA
TARGAS
TARGE
TARGED
TARGES
TARGET
TARGETED
TARGETEER
TARGETING
TARGETS
TARGING
TARIFF
TARIFFED
TARIFFING
TARIFFS
TARING
TARINGS
TARLATAN
TARLATANS
TARLETAN
TARLETANS
TARMAC
TARMACKED
TARMACS
TARN
TARNAL
TARNALLY
TARNATION
TARNISH
TARNISHED
TARNISHER
TARNISHES
TARNS
TARO
TAROC
TAROCS
TAROK
TAROKS
TAROS
TAROT
TAROTS
TARP
TARPAN
TARPANS
TARPAPER
TARPAPERS
TARPAULIN
TARPON
TARPONS
TARPS
TARRAGON
TARRAGONS
TARRAS
TARRASES
TARRE
TARRED
TARRES
TARRIANCE
TARRIED
TARRIER
TARRIERS
TARRIES
TARRIEST

T

TARRINESS
TARRING
TARRINGS
TARROCK
TARROCKS
TARROW
TARROWED
TARROWING
TARROWS
TARRY
TARRYING
TARS
TARSAL
TARSALGIA
TARSALS
TARSEAL
TARSEALS
TARSEL
TARSELS
TARSI
TARSIA
TARSIAS
TARSIER
TARSIERS
TARSIOID
TARSIOIDS
TARSIPED
TARSIPEDS
TARSUS
TART
TARTAN
TARTANA
TARTANAS
TARTANE
TARTANED
TARTANES
TARTANRY
TARTANS
TARTAR
TARTARE
TARTARES
TARTARIC
TARTARISE
TARTARIZE
TARTARLY
TARTAROUS
TARTARS
TARTED
TARTER
TARTEST
TARTIER
TARTIEST
TARTILY
TARTINE
TARTINES
TARTINESS
TARTING
TARTISH
TARTISHLY
TARTLET
TARTLETS
TARTLY
TARTNESS
TARTRATE
TARTRATED
TARTRATES
TARTS
TARTUFE
TARTUFES
TARTUFFE
TARTUFFES
TARTUFI
TARTUFO
TARTUFOS
TARTY
TARWEED
TARWEEDS
TARWHINE
TARWHINES
TARZAN
TARZANS
TAS
TASAR
TASARS
TASBIH
TASBIHS
TASE
TASED
TASER
TASERED
TASERING
TASERS
TASES
TASH
TASHED
TASHES
TASHING
TASIMETER
TASIMETRY
TASING
TASK
TASKBAR
TASKBARS
TASKED
TASKER
TASKERS
TASKING
TASKINGS
TASKLESS
TASKS
TASKWORK
TASKWORKS
TASLET
TASLETS
TASS
TASSA
TASSAS
TASSE
TASSEL
TASSELED
TASSELIER
TASSELING
TASSELL
TASSELLED
TASSELLS
TASSELLY
TASSELS
TASSELY
TASSES
TASSET
TASSETS
TASSIE
TASSIES
TASSO
TASSOS
TASSWAGE
TASTABLE
TASTE
TASTEABLE
TASTED
TASTEFUL
TASTELESS
TASTER
TASTERS
TASTES
TASTEVIN
TASTEVINS
TASTIER
TASTIEST
TASTILY
TASTINESS
TASTING
TASTINGS
TASTY
TAT
TATAHASH
TATAMI
TATAMIS
TATAR
TATARS
TATE
TATER
TATERS
TATES
TATH
TATHATA
TATHATAS
TATHED
TATHING
TATHS
TATIE
TATIES
TATLER
TATLERS
TATOU
TATOUAY
TATOUAYS
TATOUS
TATS
TATSOI
TATSOIS
TATT
TATTED
TATTER
TATTERED
TATTERIER
TATTERING
TATTERS
TATTERY
TATTIE
TATTIER
TATTIES
TATTIEST
TATTILY
TATTINESS
TATTING
TATTINGS
TATTLE
TATTLED
TATTLER
TATTLERS
TATTLES
TATTLING
TATTLINGS
TATTOO
TATTOOED
TATTOOER
TATTOOERS
TATTOOING
TATTOOIST
TATTOOS
TATTOW
TATTOWED
TATTOWING
TATTOWS
TATTS
TATTY
TATU
TATUED
TATUING
TATUS
TAU
TAUBE
TAUBES
TAUGHT
TAUHINU
TAUHINUS
TAUHOU
TAUHOUS
TAUIWI
TAUIWIS
TAULD
TAUNT
TAUNTED
TAUNTER
TAUNTERS
TAUNTING
TAUNTINGS
TAUNTS
TAUON

TAUONS
TAUPATA
TAUPATAS
TAUPE
TAUPES
TAUPIE
TAUPIES
TAUREAN
TAURIC
TAURIFORM
TAURINE
TAURINES
TAUS
TAUT
TAUTAUG
TAUTAUGS
TAUTED
TAUTEN
TAUTENED
TAUTENING
TAUTENS
TAUTER
TAUTEST
TAUTING
TAUTIT
TAUTLY
TAUTNESS
TAUTOG
TAUTOGS
TAUTOLOGY
TAUTOMER
TAUTOMERS
TAUTONYM
TAUTONYMS
TAUTONYMY
TAUTS
TAV
TAVA
TAVAH
TAVAHS
TAVAS
TAVER
TAVERED
TAVERING
TAVERN
TAVERNA
TAVERNAS
TAVERNER
TAVERNERS
TAVERNS
TAVERS
TAVERT
TAVS
TAW
TAWA
TAWAI
TAWAIS
TAWAS
TAWDRIER
TAWDRIES
TAWDRIEST
TAWDRILY
TAWDRY
TAWED
TAWER
TAWERIES
TAWERS
TAWERY
TAWHAI
TAWHAIS
TAWHIRI
TAWHIRIS
TAWIE
TAWIER
TAWIEST
TAWING
TAWINGS
TAWNEY
TAWNEYS
TAWNIER
TAWNIES
TAWNIEST
TAWNILY
TAWNINESS
TAWNY
TAWPIE
TAWPIES
TAWS
TAWSE
TAWSED
TAWSES
TAWSING
TAWT
TAWTED
TAWTIE
TAWTIER
TAWTIEST
TAWTING
TAWTS
TAX
TAXA
TAXABLE
TAXABLES
TAXABLY
TAXACEOUS
TAXAMETER
TAXATION
TAXATIONS
TAXATIVE
TAXED
TAXEME
TAXEMES
TAXEMIC
TAXER
TAXERS
TAXES
TAXI
TAXIARCH
TAXIARCHS
TAXICAB
TAXICABS
TAXIDERMY
TAXIED
TAXIES
TAXIING
TAXIMAN
TAXIMEN
TAXIMETER
TAXING
TAXINGLY
TAXINGS
TAXIPLANE
TAXIS
TAXISES
TAXITE
TAXITES
TAXITIC
TAXIWAY
TAXIWAYS
TAXLESS
TAXMAN
TAXMEN
TAXOL
TAXOLS
TAXON
TAXONOMER
TAXONOMIC
TAXONOMY
TAXONS
TAXOR
TAXORS
TAXPAID
TAXPAYER
TAXPAYERS
TAXPAYING
TAXUS
TAXWISE
TAXYING
TAY
TAYASSUID
TAYBERRY
TAYRA
TAYRAS
TAYS
TAZZA
TAZZAS
TAZZE
TCHICK
TCHICKED
TCHICKING
TCHICKS
TCHOTCHKE
TE
TEA
TEABAG
TEABAGS
TEABERRY
TEABOARD
TEABOARDS
TEABOWL
TEABOWLS
TEABOX
TEABOXES
TEABREAD
TEABREADS
TEACAKE
TEACAKES
TEACART
TEACARTS
TEACH
TEACHABLE
TEACHABLY
TEACHER
TEACHERLY
TEACHERS
TEACHES
TEACHIE
TEACHING
TEACHINGS
TEACHLESS
TEACUP
TEACUPFUL
TEACUPS
TEAD
TEADE
TEADES
TEADS
TEAED
TEAGLE
TEAGLED
TEAGLES
TEAGLING
TEAHOUSE
TEAHOUSES
TEAING
TEAK
TEAKETTLE
TEAKS
TEAKWOOD
TEAKWOODS
TEAL
TEALIGHT
TEALIGHTS
TEALIKE
TEALS
TEAM
TEAMAKER
TEAMAKERS
TEAMED
TEAMER
TEAMERS
TEAMING
TEAMINGS
TEAMMATE
TEAMMATES
TEAMS
TEAMSTER
TEAMSTERS
TEAMWISE
TEAMWORK

TEAMWORKS
TEAPOT
TEAPOTS
TEAPOY
TEAPOYS
TEAR
TEARABLE
TEARAWAY
TEARAWAYS
TEARDOWN
TEARDOWNS
TEARDROP
TEARDROPS
TEARED
TEARER
TEARERS
TEARFUL
TEARFULLY
TEARGAS
TEARGASES
TEARIER
TEARIEST
TEARILY
TEARINESS
TEARING
TEARLESS
TEARLIKE
TEAROOM
TEAROOMS
TEARS
TEARSHEET
TEARSTAIN
TEARSTRIP
TEARY
TEAS
TEASABLE
TEASE
TEASED
TEASEL
TEASELED
TEASELER
TEASELERS
TEASELING
TEASELLED
TEASELLER
TEASELS
TEASER
TEASERS
TEASES
TEASHOP
TEASHOPS
TEASING
TEASINGLY
TEASINGS
TEASPOON
TEASPOONS
TEAT
TEATASTER
TEATED
TEATIME
TEATIMES
TEATS
TEAWARE
TEAWARES
TEAZE
TEAZED
TEAZEL
TEAZELED
TEAZELING
TEAZELLED
TEAZELS
TEAZES
TEAZING
TEAZLE
TEAZLED
TEAZLES
TEAZLING
TEBBAD
TEBBADS
TEBIBYTE
TEBIBYTES
TEC
TECH
TECHED
TECHIE
TECHIER
TECHIES
TECHIEST
TECHILY
TECHINESS
TECHNIC
TECHNICAL
TECHNICS
TECHNIKON
TECHNIQUE
TECHNO
TECHNOID
TECHNOIDS
TECHNOPOP
TECHNOS
TECHS
TECHY
TECKEL
TECKELS
TECS
TECTA
TECTAL
TECTIFORM
TECTITE
TECTITES
TECTONIC
TECTONICS
TECTONISM
TECTORIAL
TECTRICES
TECTRIX
TECTUM
TECTUMS
TED
TEDDED
TEDDER
TEDDERED
TEDDERING
TEDDERS
TEDDIE
TEDDIES
TEDDING
TEDDY
TEDIER
TEDIEST
TEDIOSITY
TEDIOUS
TEDIOUSLY
TEDISOME
TEDIUM
TEDIUMS
TEDS
TEDY
TEE
TEED
TEEING
TEEK
TEEL
TEELS
TEEM
TEEMED
TEEMER
TEEMERS
TEEMFUL
TEEMING
TEEMINGLY
TEEMLESS
TEEMS
TEEN
TEENAGE
TEENAGED
TEENAGER
TEENAGERS
TEENAGES
TEEND
TEENDED
TEENDING
TEENDOM
TEENDOMS
TEENDS
TEENE
TEENED
TEENER
TEENERS
TEENES
TEENFUL
TEENIER
TEENIEST
TEENING
TEENS
TEENSIER
TEENSIEST
TEENSY
TEENTIER
TEENTIEST
TEENTSIER
TEENTSY
TEENTY
TEENY
TEENYBOP
TEEPEE
TEEPEES
TEER
TEERED
TEERING
TEERS
TEES
TEETER
TEETERED
TEETERING
TEETERS
TEETH
TEETHE
TEETHED
TEETHER
TEETHERS
TEETHES
TEETHING
TEETHINGS
TEETHLESS
TEETOTAL
TEETOTALS
TEETOTUM
TEETOTUMS
TEEVEE
TEEVEES
TEF
TEFF
TEFFS
TEFILLAH
TEFILLIN
TEFLON
TEFLONS
TEFS
TEG
TEGG
TEGGS
TEGMEN
TEGMENTA
TEGMENTAL
TEGMENTUM
TEGMINA
TEGMINAL
TEGS
TEGU
TEGUA
TEGUAS
TEGUEXIN
TEGUEXINS
TEGULA
TEGULAE
TEGULAR
TEGULARLY
TEGULATED
TEGUMEN

TEGUMENT
TEGUMENTS
TEGUMINA
TEGUS
TEHR
TEHRS
TEHSIL
TEHSILDAR
TEHSILS
TEIGLACH
TEIID
TEIIDS
TEIL
TEILS
TEIN
TEIND
TEINDED
TEINDING
TEINDS
TEINS
TEKKIE
TEKKIES
TEKNONYMY
TEKTITE
TEKTITES
TEKTITIC
TEL
TELA
TELAE
TELAMON
TELAMONES
TELAMONS
TELARY
TELCO
TELCOS
TELD
TELE
TELECAST
TELECASTS
TELECHIR
TELECHIRS
TELECINE
TELECINES
TELECOM
TELECOMM
TELECOMMS
TELECOMS
TELECON
TELECONS
TELECOPY
TELEDU
TELEDUS
TELEFAX
TELEFAXED
TELEFAXES
TELEFILM
TELEFILMS
TELEGA
TELEGAS
TELEGENIC
TELEGONIC
TELEGONY
TELEGRAM
TELEGRAMS
TELEGRAPH
TELEMAN
TELEMARK
TELEMARKS
TELEMATIC
TELEMEN
TELEMETER
TELEMETRY
TELEOLOGY
TELEONOMY
TELEOSAUR
TELEOST
TELEOSTS
TELEPATH
TELEPATHS
TELEPATHY
TELEPHEME
TELEPHONE
TELEPHONY
TELEPHOTO
TELEPIC
TELEPICS
TELEPLAY
TELEPLAYS
TELEPOINT
TELEPORT
TELEPORTS
TELEPRINT
TELERAN
TELERANS
TELERGIC
TELERGIES
TELERGY
TELEROBOT
TELES
TELESALE
TELESALES
TELESCOPE
TELESCOPY
TELESEME
TELESEMES
TELESES
TELESHOP
TELESHOPS
TELESIS
TELESM
TELESMS
TELESTIC
TELESTICH
TELESTICS
TELETEX
TELETEXES
TELETEXT
TELETEXTS
TELETHON
TELETHONS
TELETRON
TELETRONS
TELETYPE
TELETYPED
TELETYPES
TELEVIEW
TELEVIEWS
TELEVISE
TELEVISED
TELEVISER
TELEVISES
TELEVISOR
TELEWORK
TELEWORKS
TELEX
TELEXED
TELEXES
TELEXING
TELFER
TELFERAGE
TELFERED
TELFERIC
TELFERING
TELFERS
TELFORD
TELFORDS
TELIA
TELIAL
TELIC
TELICALLY
TELICITY
TELIUM
TELL
TELLABLE
TELLAR
TELLARED
TELLARING
TELLARS
TELLEN
TELLENS
TELLER
TELLERED
TELLERING
TELLERS
TELLIES
TELLIN
TELLING
TELLINGLY
TELLINGS
TELLINOID
TELLINS
TELLS
TELLTALE
TELLTALES
TELLURAL
TELLURATE
TELLURIAN
TELLURIC
TELLURIDE
TELLURION
TELLURISE
TELLURITE
TELLURIUM
TELLURIZE
TELLUROUS
TELLUS
TELLUSES
TELLY
TELLYS
TELNET
TELNETED
TELNETING
TELNETS
TELNETTED
TELOGEN
TELOGENS
TELOI
TELOME
TELOMERE
TELOMERES
TELOMES
TELOMIC
TELOPHASE
TELOS
TELOTAXES
TELOTAXIS
TELPHER
TELPHERED
TELPHERIC
TELPHERS
TELS
TELSON
TELSONIC
TELSONS
TELT
TEMAZEPAM
TEMBLOR
TEMBLORES
TEMBLORS
TEME
TEMED
TEMENE
TEMENOS
TEMERITY
TEMEROUS
TEMES
TEMP
TEMPED
TEMPEH
TEMPEHS
TEMPER
TEMPERA
TEMPERAS
TEMPERATE
TEMPERED
TEMPERER
TEMPERERS
TEMPERING
TEMPERS
TEMPEST

TEMPESTED
TEMPESTS
TEMPI
TEMPING
TEMPINGS
TEMPLAR
TEMPLARS
TEMPLATE
TEMPLATES
TEMPLE
TEMPLED
TEMPLES
TEMPLET
TEMPLETS
TEMPO
TEMPORAL
TEMPORALS
TEMPORARY
TEMPORE
TEMPORISE
TEMPORIZE
TEMPOS
TEMPS
TEMPT
TEMPTABLE
TEMPTED
TEMPTER
TEMPTERS
TEMPTING
TEMPTINGS
TEMPTRESS
TEMPTS
TEMPURA
TEMPURAS
TEMS
TEMSE
TEMSED
TEMSES
TEMSING
TEMULENCE
TEMULENCY
TEMULENT
TEN
TENABLE
TENABLY
TENACE
TENACES
TENACIOUS
TENACITY
TENACULA
TENACULUM
TENAIL
TENAILLE
TENAILLES
TENAILLON
TENAILS
TENANCIES
TENANCY
TENANT
TENANTED
TENANTING
TENANTRY
TENANTS
TENCH
TENCHES
TEND
TENDANCE
TENDANCES
TENDED
TENDENCE
TENDENCES
TENDENCY
TENDENZ
TENDENZEN
TENDER
TENDERED
TENDERER
TENDERERS
TENDEREST
TENDERING
TENDERISE
TENDERIZE
TENDERLY
TENDERS
TENDING
TENDINOUS
TENDON
TENDONS
TENDRE
TENDRES
TENDRESSE
TENDRIL
TENDRILED
TENDRILLY
TENDRILS
TENDRON
TENDRONS
TENDS
TENDU
TENDUS
TENE
TENEBRAE
TENEBRIO
TENEBRIOS
TENEBRISM
TENEBRIST
TENEBRITY
TENEBROSE
TENEBROUS
TENEMENT
TENEMENTS
TENENDA
TENENDUM
TENENDUMS
TENES
TENESI
TENESMIC
TENESMUS
TENET
TENETS
TENFOLD
TENFOLDS
TENGE
TENGES
TENIA
TENIACIDE
TENIAE
TENIAFUGE
TENIAS
TENIASES
TENIASIS
TENIOID
TENNE
TENNER
TENNERS
TENNES
TENNESI
TENNIES
TENNIS
TENNISES
TENNIST
TENNISTS
TENNO
TENNOS
TENNY
TENON
TENONED
TENONER
TENONERS
TENONING
TENONS
TENOR
TENORINI
TENORINO
TENORIST
TENORISTS
TENORITE
TENORITES
TENORLESS
TENORMAN
TENORMEN
TENOROON
TENOROONS
TENORS
TENOTOMY
TENOUR
TENOURS
TENPENCE
TENPENCES
TENPENNY
TENPIN
TENPINNER
TENPINS
TENREC
TENRECS
TENS
TENSE
TENSED
TENSELESS
TENSELY
TENSENESS
TENSER
TENSES
TENSEST
TENSIBLE
TENSIBLY
TENSILE
TENSILELY
TENSILITY
TENSING
TENSION
TENSIONAL
TENSIONED
TENSIONER
TENSIONS
TENSITIES
TENSITY
TENSIVE
TENSON
TENSONS
TENSOR
TENSORIAL
TENSORS
TENT
TENTACLE
TENTACLED
TENTACLES
TENTACULA
TENTAGE
TENTAGES
TENTATION
TENTATIVE
TENTED
TENTER
TENTERED
TENTERING
TENTERS
TENTFUL
TENTFULS
TENTH
TENTHLY
TENTHS
TENTIE
TENTIER
TENTIEST
TENTIGO
TENTIGOS
TENTING
TENTINGS
TENTLESS
TENTLIKE
TENTMAKER
TENTORIA
TENTORIAL
TENTORIUM
TENTPOLE
TENTPOLES
TENTS
TENTWISE
TENTY

TENUE
TENUES
TENUIOUS
TENUIS
TENUITIES
TENUITY
TENUOUS
TENUOUSLY
TENURABLE
TENURE
TENURED
TENURES
TENURIAL
TENURING
TENUTI
TENUTO
TENUTOS
TENZON
TENZONS
TEOCALLI
TEOCALLIS
TEOPAN
TEOPANS
TEOSINTE
TEOSINTES
TEPA
TEPACHE
TEPACHES
TEPAL
TEPALS
TEPAS
TEPEE
TEPEES
TEPEFIED
TEPEFIES
TEPEFY
TEPEFYING
TEPHIGRAM
TEPHILLAH
TEPHILLIN
TEPHRA
TEPHRAS
TEPHRITE
TEPHRITES
TEPHRITIC
TEPHROITE
TEPID
TEPIDARIA
TEPIDER
TEPIDEST
TEPIDITY
TEPIDLY
TEPIDNESS
TEPOY
TEPOYS
TEQUILA
TEQUILAS
TEQUILLA
TEQUILLAS
TERABYTE
TERABYTES
TERAFLOP
TERAFLOPS
TERAGLIN
TERAGLINS
TERAHERTZ
TERAI
TERAIS
TERAKIHI
TERAKIHIS
TERAMETER
TERAOHM
TERAOHMS
TERAPH
TERAPHIM
TERAPHIMS
TERAS
TERATA
TERATISM
TERATISMS
TERATOGEN
TERATOID
TERATOMA
TERATOMAS
TERAWATT
TERAWATTS
TERBIA
TERBIAS
TERBIC
TERBIUM
TERBIUMS
TERCE
TERCEL
TERCELET
TERCELETS
TERCELS
TERCES
TERCET
TERCETS
TERCIO
TERCIOS
TEREBENE
TEREBENES
TEREBIC
TEREBINTH
TEREBRA
TEREBRAE
TEREBRANT
TEREBRAS
TEREBRATE
TEREDINES
TEREDO
TEREDOS
TEREFA
TEREFAH
TEREK
TEREKS
TERES
TERESES
TERETE
TERETES
TERF
TERFE
TERFES
TERFS
TERGA
TERGAL
TERGITE
TERGITES
TERGUM
TERIYAKI
TERIYAKIS
TERM
TERMAGANT
TERMED
TERMER
TERMERS
TERMINAL
TERMINALS
TERMINATE
TERMINER
TERMINERS
TERMING
TERMINI
TERMINISM
TERMINIST
TERMINUS
TERMITARY
TERMITE
TERMITES
TERMITIC
TERMLESS
TERMLIES
TERMLY
TERMOR
TERMORS
TERMS
TERMTIME
TERMTIMES
TERN
TERNAL
TERNARIES
TERNARY
TERNATE
TERNATELY
TERNE
TERNED
TERNES
TERNING
TERNION
TERNIONS
TERNS
TERPENE
TERPENES
TERPENIC
TERPENOID
TERPINE
TERPINEOL
TERPINES
TERPINOL
TERPINOLS
TERRA
TERRACE
TERRACED
TERRACES
TERRACING
TERRAE
TERRAFORM
TERRAIN
TERRAINS
TERRAMARA
TERRAMARE
TERRANE
TERRANES
TERRAPIN
TERRAPINS
TERRARIA
TERRARIUM
TERRAS
TERRASES
TERRASSE
TERRASSES
TERRAZZO
TERRAZZOS
TERREEN
TERREENS
TERRELLA
TERRELLAS
TERRENE
TERRENELY
TERRENES
TERRET
TERRETS
TERRIBLE
TERRIBLES
TERRIBLY
TERRICOLE
TERRIER
TERRIERS
TERRIES
TERRIFIC
TERRIFIED
TERRIFIER
TERRIFIES
TERRIFY
TERRINE
TERRINES
TERRIT
TERRITORY
TERRITS
TERROIR
TERROIRS
TERROR
TERRORFUL
TERRORISE
TERRORISM
TERRORIST
TERRORIZE
TERRORS
TERRY

T

TERSE
TERSELY
TERSENESS
TERSER
TERSEST
TERSION
TERSIONS
TERTIA
TERTIAL
TERTIALS
TERTIAN
TERTIANS
TERTIARY
TERTIAS
TERTIUM
TERTIUS
TERTIUSES
TERTS
TERVALENT
TERYLENE
TERYLENES
TERZETTA
TERZETTAS
TERZETTI
TERZETTO
TERZETTOS
TES
TESLA
TESLAS
TESSELATE
TESSELLA
TESSELLAE
TESSELLAR
TESSERA
TESSERACT
TESSERAE
TESSERAL
TESSITURA
TESSITURE
TEST
TESTA
TESTABLE
TESTACEAN
TESTACIES
TESTACY
TESTAE
TESTAMENT
TESTAMUR
TESTAMURS
TESTATA
TESTATE
TESTATES
TESTATION
TESTATOR
TESTATORS
TESTATRIX
TESTATUM
TESTATUMS
TESTCROSS
TESTE
TESTED
TESTEE
TESTEES
TESTER
TESTERN
TESTERNED
TESTERNS
TESTERS
TESTES
TESTICLE
TESTICLES
TESTIER
TESTIEST
TESTIFIED
TESTIFIER
TESTIFIES
TESTIFY
TESTILY
TESTIMONY
TESTINESS
TESTING
TESTINGS
TESTIS
TESTON
TESTONS
TESTOON
TESTOONS
TESTRIL
TESTRILL
TESTRILLS
TESTRILS
TESTS
TESTUDO
TESTUDOS
TESTY
TET
TETANAL
TETANIC
TETANICAL
TETANICS
TETANIES
TETANISE
TETANISED
TETANISES
TETANIZE
TETANIZED
TETANIZES
TETANOID
TETANUS
TETANUSES
TETANY
TETCHED
TETCHIER
TETCHIEST
TETCHILY
TETCHY
TETE
TETES
TETH
TETHER
TETHERED
TETHERING
TETHERS
TETHS
TETOTUM
TETOTUMS
TETRA
TETRACID
TETRACIDS
TETRACT
TETRACTS
TETRAD
TETRADIC
TETRADITE
TETRADS
TETRAGON
TETRAGONS
TETRAGRAM
TETRALOGY
TETRAMER
TETRAMERS
TETRAPLA
TETRAPLAS
TETRAPOD
TETRAPODS
TETRAPODY
TETRARCH
TETRARCHS
TETRARCHY
TETRAS
TETRAXON
TETRAXONS
TETRI
TETRIS
TETRODE
TETRODES
TETRONAL
TETRONALS
TETROSE
TETROSES
TETROXID
TETROXIDE
TETROXIDS
TETRYL
TETRYLS
TETS
TETTER
TETTERED
TETTERING
TETTEROUS
TETTERS
TETTIX
TETTIXES
TEUCH
TEUCHAT
TEUCHATS
TEUCHER
TEUCHEST
TEUCHTER
TEUCHTERS
TEUGH
TEUGHER
TEUGHEST
TEUGHLY
TEUTONISE
TEUTONIZE
TEVATRON
TEVATRONS
TEW
TEWART
TEWARTS
TEWED
TEWEL
TEWELS
TEWHIT
TEWHITS
TEWING
TEWIT
TEWITS
TEWS
TEX
TEXAS
TEXASES
TEXES
TEXT
TEXTBOOK
TEXTBOOKS
TEXTED
TEXTER
TEXTERS
TEXTILE
TEXTILES
TEXTING
TEXTINGS
TEXTISM
TEXTISMS
TEXTLESS
TEXTONYM
TEXTONYMS
TEXTORIAL
TEXTPHONE
TEXTS
TEXTSPEAK
TEXTUAL
TEXTUALLY
TEXTUARY
TEXTURAL
TEXTURE
TEXTURED
TEXTURES
TEXTURING
TEXTURISE
TEXTURIZE
TEXTUROUS
THACK
THACKED
THACKING
THACKS
THAE
THAGI

THAGIS
THAIM
THAIRM
THAIRMS
THALAMI
THALAMIC
THALAMUS
THALASSIC
THALE
THALER
THALERS
THALI
THALIAN
THALIS
THALLI
THALLIC
THALLINE
THALLINES
THALLIOUS
THALLIUM
THALLIUMS
THALLOID
THALLOUS
THALLUS
THALLUSES
THALWEG
THALWEGS
THAN
THANA
THANADAR
THANADARS
THANAGE
THANAGES
THANAH
THANAHS
THANAS
THANATISM
THANATIST
THANATOID
THANATOS
THANE
THANEDOM
THANEDOMS
THANEHOOD
THANES
THANESHIP
THANG
THANGKA
THANGKAS
THANGS
THANK
THANKED
THANKEE
THANKER
THANKERS
THANKFUL
THANKING
THANKINGS
THANKIT
THANKLESS
THANKS
THANKYOU
THANKYOUS
THANNA
THANNAH
THANNAHS
THANNAS
THANS
THANX
THAR
THARM
THARMS
THARS
THAT
THATAWAY
THATCH
THATCHED
THATCHER
THATCHERS
THATCHES
THATCHIER
THATCHING
THATCHT
THATCHY
THATNESS
THAUMATIN
THAW
THAWED
THAWER
THAWERS
THAWIER
THAWIEST
THAWING
THAWINGS
THAWLESS
THAWS
THAWY
THE
THEACEOUS
THEANDRIC
THEANINE
THEANINES
THEARCHIC
THEARCHY
THEATER
THEATERS
THEATRAL
THEATRE
THEATRES
THEATRIC
THEATRICS
THEAVE
THEAVES
THEBAINE
THEBAINES
THEBE
THEBES
THECA
THECAE
THECAL
THECATE
THECODONT
THEE
THEED
THEEING
THEEK
THEEKED
THEEKING
THEEKS
THEELIN
THEELINS
THEELOL
THEELOLS
THEES
THEFT
THEFTLESS
THEFTS
THEFTUOUS
THEGITHER
THEGN
THEGNLIER
THEGNLY
THEGNS
THEIC
THEICS
THEIN
THEINE
THEINES
THEINS
THEIR
THEIRS
THEIRSELF
THEISM
THEISMS
THEIST
THEISTIC
THEISTS
THELEMENT
THELF
THELITIS
THELVES
THELYTOKY
THEM
THEMA
THEMATA
THEMATIC
THEMATICS
THEMATISE
THEMATIZE
THEME
THEMED
THEMELESS
THEMES
THEMING
THEMSELF
THEN
THENABOUT
THENAGE
THENAGES
THENAL
THENAR
THENARS
THENCE
THENS
THEOCON
THEOCONS
THEOCRACY
THEOCRASY
THEOCRAT
THEOCRATS
THEODICY
THEOGONIC
THEOGONY
THEOLOG
THEOLOGER
THEOLOGIC
THEOLOGS
THEOLOGUE
THEOLOGY
THEOMACHY
THEOMANCY
THEOMANIA
THEONOMY
THEOPATHY
THEOPHAGY
THEOPHANY
THEORBIST
THEORBO
THEORBOS
THEOREM
THEOREMIC
THEOREMS
THEORETIC
THEORIC
THEORICS
THEORIES
THEORIQUE
THEORISE
THEORISED
THEORISER
THEORISES
THEORIST
THEORISTS
THEORIZE
THEORIZED
THEORIZER
THEORIZES
THEORY
THEOSOPH
THEOSOPHS
THEOSOPHY
THEOTOKOI
THEOTOKOS
THEOW
THEOWS
THERALITE
THERAPIES
THERAPISE
THERAPIST
THERAPIZE

T

THERAPSID
THERAPY
THERBLIG
THERBLIGS
THERE
THEREAT
THEREAWAY
THEREBY
THEREFOR
THEREFORE
THEREFROM
THEREIN
THEREINTO
THEREMIN
THEREMINS
THERENESS
THEREOF
THEREON
THEREOUT
THERES
THERETO
THEREUNTO
THEREUPON
THEREWITH
THERIAC
THERIACA
THERIACAL
THERIACAS
THERIACS
THERIAN
THERIANS
THERM
THERMAE
THERMAL
THERMALLY
THERMALS
THERME
THERMEL
THERMELS
THERMES
THERMETTE
THERMIC
THERMICAL
THERMIDOR
THERMION
THERMIONS
THERMIT
THERMITE
THERMITES
THERMITS
THERMOS
THERMOSES
THERMOSET
THERMOTIC
THERMS
THEROID
THEROLOGY
THEROPOD
THEROPODS
THESAURAL
THESAURI
THESAURUS
THESE
THESES
THESIS
THESP
THESPIAN
THESPIANS
THESPS
THETA
THETAS
THETCH
THETCHED
THETCHES
THETCHING
THETE
THETES
THETHER
THETIC
THETICAL
THETRI
THETRIS
THEURGIC
THEURGIES
THEURGIST
THEURGY
THEW
THEWED
THEWES
THEWIER
THEWIEST
THEWLESS
THEWS
THEWY
THEY
THIAMIN
THIAMINE
THIAMINES
THIAMINS
THIASUS
THIASUSES
THIAZIDE
THIAZIDES
THIAZIN
THIAZINE
THIAZINES
THIAZINS
THIAZOL
THIAZOLE
THIAZOLES
THIAZOLS
THIBET
THIBETS
THIBLE
THIBLES
THICK
THICKED
THICKEN
THICKENED
THICKENER
THICKENS
THICKER
THICKEST
THICKET
THICKETED
THICKETS
THICKETY
THICKHEAD
THICKIE
THICKIES
THICKING
THICKISH
THICKLEAF
THICKLY
THICKNESS
THICKO
THICKOES
THICKOS
THICKS
THICKSET
THICKSETS
THICKSKIN
THICKY
THIEF
THIEFLIKE
THIEVE
THIEVED
THIEVERY
THIEVES
THIEVING
THIEVINGS
THIEVISH
THIG
THIGGED
THIGGER
THIGGERS
THIGGING
THIGGINGS
THIGGIT
THIGH
THIGHBONE
THIGHED
THIGHS
THIGS
THILK
THILL
THILLER
THILLERS
THILLS
THIMBLE
THIMBLED
THIMBLES
THIMBLING
THIN
THINCLAD
THINCLADS
THINDOWN
THINDOWNS
THINE
THING
THINGAMY
THINGHOOD
THINGIER
THINGIES
THINGIEST
THINGNESS
THINGO
THINGOS
THINGS
THINGUMMY
THINGY
THINK
THINKABLE
THINKABLY
THINKER
THINKERS
THINKING
THINKINGS
THINKS
THINLY
THINNED
THINNER
THINNERS
THINNESS
THINNEST
THINNING
THINNINGS
THINNISH
THINS
THIO
THIOFURAN
THIOL
THIOLIC
THIOLS
THIONATE
THIONATES
THIONIC
THIONIN
THIONINE
THIONINES
THIONINS
THIONYL
THIONYLS
THIOPHEN
THIOPHENE
THIOPHENS
THIOPHIL
THIOTEPA
THIOTEPAS
THIOUREA
THIOUREAS
THIR
THIRAM
THIRAMS
THIRD
THIRDED
THIRDHAND
THIRDING
THIRDINGS
THIRDLY

THIRDS
THIRDSMAN
THIRDSMEN
THIRL
THIRLAGE
THIRLAGES
THIRLED
THIRLING
THIRLS
THIRST
THIRSTED
THIRSTER
THIRSTERS
THIRSTFUL
THIRSTIER
THIRSTILY
THIRSTING
THIRSTS
THIRSTY
THIRTEEN
THIRTEENS
THIRTIES
THIRTIETH
THIRTY
THIRTYISH
THIS
THISAWAY
THISNESS
THISTLE
THISTLES
THISTLIER
THISTLY
THITHER
THITHERTO
THIVEL
THIVELS
THLIPSES
THLIPSIS
THO
THOFT
THOFTS
THOLE
THOLED
THOLEIITE
THOLEPIN
THOLEPINS
THOLES
THOLI
THOLING
THOLOBATE
THOLOI
THOLOS
THOLUS
THON
THONDER
THONG
THONGED
THONGIER
THONGIEST
THONGING
THONGS
THONGY
THORACAL
THORACES
THORACIC
THORAX
THORAXES
THORIA
THORIAS
THORIC
THORITE
THORITES
THORIUM
THORIUMS
THORN
THORNBACK
THORNBILL
THORNBIRD
THORNBUSH
THORNED
THORNIER
THORNIEST
THORNILY
THORNING
THORNLESS
THORNLIKE
THORNS
THORNSET
THORNTAIL
THORNTREE
THORNY
THORO
THORON
THORONS
THOROUGH
THOROUGHS
THORP
THORPE
THORPES
THORPS
THOSE
THOTHER
THOU
THOUED
THOUGH
THOUGHT
THOUGHTED
THOUGHTEN
THOUGHTS
THOUING
THOUS
THOUSAND
THOUSANDS
THOWEL
THOWELS
THOWL
THOWLESS
THOWLS
THRAE
THRAIPING
THRALDOM
THRALDOMS
THRALL
THRALLDOM
THRALLED
THRALLING
THRALLS
THRANG
THRANGED
THRANGING
THRANGS
THRAPPLE
THRAPPLED
THRAPPLES
THRASH
THRASHED
THRASHER
THRASHERS
THRASHES
THRASHIER
THRASHING
THRASHY
THRASONIC
THRAVE
THRAVES
THRAW
THRAWARD
THRAWART
THRAWED
THRAWING
THRAWN
THRAWNLY
THRAWS
THREAD
THREADED
THREADEN
THREADER
THREADERS
THREADFIN
THREADIER
THREADING
THREADS
THREADY
THREAP
THREAPED
THREAPER
THREAPERS
THREAPING
THREAPIT
THREAPS
THREAT
THREATED
THREATEN
THREATENS
THREATFUL
THREATING
THREATS
THREAVE
THREAVES
THREE
THREEFOLD
THREENESS
THREEP
THREEPEAT
THREEPED
THREEPER
THREEPERS
THREEPING
THREEPIT
THREEPS
THREEQUEL
THREES
THREESOME
THRENE
THRENES
THRENETIC
THRENODE
THRENODES
THRENODIC
THRENODY
THRENOS
THRENOSES
THREONINE
THRESH
THRESHED
THRESHEL
THRESHELS
THRESHER
THRESHERS
THRESHES
THRESHING
THRESHOLD
THRETTIES
THRETTY
THREW
THRICE
THRID
THRIDACE
THRIDACES
THRIDDED
THRIDDING
THRIDS
THRIFT
THRIFTIER
THRIFTILY
THRIFTS
THRIFTY
THRILL
THRILLANT
THRILLED
THRILLER
THRILLERS
THRILLIER
THRILLING
THRILLS
THRILLY
THRIMSA
THRIMSAS
THRIP
THRIPS

THRIPSES
THRISSEL
THRISSELS
THRIST
THRISTED
THRISTING
THRISTLE
THRISTLES
THRISTS
THRISTY
THRIVE
THRIVED
THRIVEN
THRIVER
THRIVERS
THRIVES
THRIVING
THRIVINGS
THRO
THROAT
THROATED
THROATIER
THROATILY
THROATING
THROATS
THROATY
THROB
THROBBED
THROBBER
THROBBERS
THROBBING
THROBLESS
THROBS
THROE
THROED
THROEING
THROES
THROMBI
THROMBIN
THROMBINS
THROMBOSE
THROMBUS
THRONE
THRONED
THRONES
THRONG
THRONGED
THRONGFUL
THRONGING
THRONGS
THRONING
THRONNER
THRONNERS
THROPPLE
THROPPLED
THROPPLES
THROSTLE
THROSTLES
THROTTLE
THROTTLED
THROTTLER
THROTTLES
THROUGH
THROUGHLY
THROVE
THROW
THROWABLE
THROWAWAY
THROWBACK
THROWDOWN
THROWE
THROWER
THROWERS
THROWES
THROWING
THROWINGS
THROWN
THROWOVER
THROWS
THROWSTER
THRU
THRUM
THRUMMED
THRUMMER
THRUMMERS
THRUMMIER
THRUMMING
THRUMMY
THRUMS
THRUPENNY
THRUPUT
THRUPUTS
THRUSH
THRUSHES
THRUST
THRUSTED
THRUSTER
THRUSTERS
THRUSTFUL
THRUSTING
THRUSTOR
THRUSTORS
THRUSTS
THRUTCH
THRUTCHED
THRUTCHES
THRUWAY
THRUWAYS
THRYMSA
THRYMSAS
THUD
THUDDED
THUDDING
THUDDINGS
THUDS
THUG
THUGGEE
THUGGEES
THUGGERY
THUGGISH
THUGGISM
THUGGISMS
THUGGO
THUGGOS
THUGS
THUJA
THUJAS
THULIA
THULIAS
THULITE
THULITES
THULIUM
THULIUMS
THUMB
THUMBED
THUMBHOLE
THUMBIER
THUMBIEST
THUMBING
THUMBKIN
THUMBKINS
THUMBLESS
THUMBLIKE
THUMBLING
THUMBNAIL
THUMBNUT
THUMBNUTS
THUMBPOT
THUMBPOTS
THUMBS
THUMBTACK
THUMBY
THUMP
THUMPED
THUMPER
THUMPERS
THUMPING
THUMPS
THUNDER
THUNDERED
THUNDERER
THUNDERS
THUNDERY
THUNDROUS
THUNK
THUNKED
THUNKING
THUNKS
THURIBLE
THURIBLES
THURIFER
THURIFERS
THURIFIED
THURIFIES
THURIFY
THURL
THURLS
THUS
THUSES
THUSLY
THUSNESS
THUSWISE
THUYA
THUYAS
THWACK
THWACKED
THWACKER
THWACKERS
THWACKING
THWACKS
THWAITE
THWAITES
THWART
THWARTED
THWARTER
THWARTERS
THWARTING
THWARTLY
THWARTS
THY
THYINE
THYLACINE
THYLAKOID
THYLOSE
THYLOSES
THYLOSIS
THYME
THYMES
THYMEY
THYMI
THYMIC
THYMIDINE
THYMIER
THYMIEST
THYMINE
THYMINES
THYMOCYTE
THYMOL
THYMOLS
THYMOMA
THYMOMAS
THYMOMATA
THYMOSIN
THYMOSINS
THYMUS
THYMUSES
THYMY
THYRATRON
THYREOID
THYREOIDS
THYRISTOR
THYROID
THYROIDAL
THYROIDS
THYROXIN
THYROXINE
THYROXINS
THYRSE
THYRSES
THYRSI

THYRSOID
THYRSUS
THYSELF
TI
TIAN
TIANS
TIAR
TIARA
TIARAED
TIARAS
TIARS
TIBIA
TIBIAE
TIBIAL
TIBIALES
TIBIALIS
TIBIAS
TIC
TICAL
TICALS
TICCA
TICCED
TICCING
TICE
TICED
TICES
TICH
TICHES
TICHIER
TICHIEST
TICHY
TICING
TICK
TICKED
TICKEN
TICKENS
TICKER
TICKERS
TICKET
TICKETED
TICKETING
TICKETS
TICKEY
TICKEYS
TICKIES
TICKING
TICKINGS
TICKLACE
TICKLACES
TICKLE
TICKLEASS
TICKLED
TICKLER
TICKLERS
TICKLES
TICKLIER
TICKLIEST
TICKLING
TICKLINGS
TICKLISH
TICKLY
TICKS
TICKSEED
TICKSEEDS
TICKTACK
TICKTACKS
TICKTOCK
TICKTOCKS
TICKY
TICS
TICTAC
TICTACKED
TICTACS
TICTOC
TICTOCKED
TICTOCS
TID
TIDAL
TIDALLY
TIDBIT
TIDBITS
TIDDIER
TIDDIES
TIDDIEST
TIDDLE
TIDDLED
TIDDLER
TIDDLERS
TIDDLES
TIDDLEY
TIDDLEYS
TIDDLIER
TIDDLIES
TIDDLIEST
TIDDLING
TIDDLY
TIDDY
TIDE
TIDED
TIDELAND
TIDELANDS
TIDELESS
TIDELIKE
TIDELINE
TIDELINES
TIDEMARK
TIDEMARKS
TIDEMILL
TIDEMILLS
TIDERIP
TIDERIPS
TIDES
TIDESMAN
TIDESMEN
TIDEWATER
TIDEWAVE
TIDEWAVES
TIDEWAY
TIDEWAYS
TIDIED
TIDIER
TIDIERS
TIDIES
TIDIEST
TIDILY
TIDINESS
TIDING
TIDINGS
TIDIVATE
TIDIVATED
TIDIVATES
TIDS
TIDY
TIDYING
TIDYTIPS
TIE
TIEBACK
TIEBACKS
TIEBREAK
TIEBREAKS
TIECLASP
TIECLASPS
TIED
TIEING
TIELESS
TIEPIN
TIEPINS
TIER
TIERCE
TIERCED
TIERCEL
TIERCELET
TIERCELS
TIERCERON
TIERCES
TIERCET
TIERCETS
TIERED
TIERING
TIERS
TIES
TIETAC
TIETACK
TIETACKS
TIETACS
TIFF
TIFFANIES
TIFFANY
TIFFED
TIFFIN
TIFFINED
TIFFING
TIFFINGS
TIFFINING
TIFFINS
TIFFS
TIFO
TIFOS
TIFOSI
TIFOSO
TIFOSOS
TIFT
TIFTED
TIFTING
TIFTS
TIG
TIGE
TIGER
TIGEREYE
TIGEREYES
TIGERIER
TIGERIEST
TIGERISH
TIGERISM
TIGERISMS
TIGERLIER
TIGERLIKE
TIGERLY
TIGERS
TIGERWOOD
TIGERY
TIGES
TIGGED
TIGGER
TIGGERED
TIGGERING
TIGGERS
TIGGING
TIGHT
TIGHTASS
TIGHTEN
TIGHTENED
TIGHTENER
TIGHTENS
TIGHTER
TIGHTEST
TIGHTISH
TIGHTKNIT
TIGHTLY
TIGHTNESS
TIGHTROPE
TIGHTS
TIGHTWAD
TIGHTWADS
TIGHTWIRE
TIGLIC
TIGLON
TIGLONS
TIGNON
TIGNONS
TIGON
TIGONS
TIGRESS
TIGRESSES
TIGRIDIA
TIGRIDIAS
TIGRINE
TIGRISH
TIGRISHLY
TIGROID

TIGS
TIK
TIKA
TIKANGA
TIKANGAS
TIKAS
TIKE
TIKES
TIKI
TIKIED
TIKIING
TIKINAGAN
TIKIS
TIKKA
TIKKAS
TIKOLOSHE
TIKS
TIKTAALIK
TIL
TILAK
TILAKS
TILAPIA
TILAPIAS
TILBURIES
TILBURY
TILDE
TILDES
TILE
TILED
TILEFISH
TILELIKE
TILER
TILERIES
TILERS
TILERY
TILES
TILING
TILINGS
TILL
TILLABLE
TILLAGE
TILLAGES
TILLED
TILLER
TILLERED
TILLERING
TILLERMAN
TILLERMEN
TILLERS
TILLICUM
TILLICUMS
TILLIER
TILLIEST
TILLING
TILLINGS
TILLITE
TILLITES
TILLS
TILLY
TILS
TILT
TILTABLE
TILTED
TILTER
TILTERS
TILTH
TILTHS
TILTING
TILTINGS
TILTMETER
TILTROTOR
TILTS
TILTYARD
TILTYARDS
TIMARAU
TIMARAUS
TIMARIOT
TIMARIOTS
TIMBAL
TIMBALE
TIMBALES
TIMBALS
TIMBER
TIMBERED
TIMBERIER
TIMBERING
TIMBERMAN
TIMBERMEN
TIMBERS
TIMBERY
TIMBO
TIMBOS
TIMBRAL
TIMBRE
TIMBREL
TIMBRELS
TIMBRES
TIME
TIMEBOMB
TIMEBOMBS
TIMECARD
TIMECARDS
TIMED
TIMEFRAME
TIMELESS
TIMELIER
TIMELIEST
TIMELINE
TIMELINES
TIMELY
TIMENOGUY
TIMEOUS
TIMEOUSLY
TIMEOUT
TIMEOUTS
TIMEPASS
TIMEPIECE
TIMER
TIMERS
TIMES
TIMESAVER
TIMESCALE
TIMESHARE
TIMESHIFT
TIMESTAMP
TIMETABLE
TIMEWORK
TIMEWORKS
TIMEWORN
TIMID
TIMIDER
TIMIDEST
TIMIDITY
TIMIDLY
TIMIDNESS
TIMING
TIMINGS
TIMIST
TIMISTS
TIMOCRACY
TIMOLOL
TIMOLOLS
TIMON
TIMONEER
TIMONEERS
TIMONS
TIMOROUS
TIMORSOME
TIMOTHIES
TIMOTHY
TIMOUS
TIMOUSLY
TIMPANA
TIMPANAS
TIMPANI
TIMPANIST
TIMPANO
TIMPANUM
TIMPANUMS
TIMPS
TIN
TINA
TINAJA
TINAJAS
TINAMOU
TINAMOUS
TINAS
TINCAL
TINCALS
TINCHEL
TINCHELS
TINCT
TINCTED
TINCTING
TINCTS
TINCTURE
TINCTURED
TINCTURES
TIND
TINDAL
TINDALS
TINDED
TINDER
TINDERBOX
TINDERIER
TINDERS
TINDERY
TINDING
TINDS
TINE
TINEA
TINEAL
TINEAS
TINED
TINEID
TINEIDS
TINES
TINFOIL
TINFOILS
TINFUL
TINFULS
TING
TINGE
TINGED
TINGEING
TINGES
TINGING
TINGLE
TINGLED
TINGLER
TINGLERS
TINGLES
TINGLIER
TINGLIEST
TINGLING
TINGLINGS
TINGLISH
TINGLY
TINGS
TINGUAITE
TINHORN
TINHORNS
TINIER
TINIES
TINIEST
TINILY
TININESS
TINING
TINK
TINKED
TINKER
TINKERED
TINKERER
TINKERERS
TINKERING
TINKERMAN
TINKERMEN
TINKERS
TINKERTOY
TINKING

TINKLE
TINKLED
TINKLER
TINKLERS
TINKLES
TINKLIER
TINKLIEST
TINKLING
TINKLINGS
TINKLY
TINKS
TINLIKE
TINMAN
TINMEN
TINNED
TINNER
TINNERS
TINNIE
TINNIER
TINNIES
TINNIEST
TINNILY
TINNINESS
TINNING
TINNINGS
TINNITUS
TINNY
TINPLATE
TINPLATED
TINPLATES
TINPOT
TINPOTS
TINS
TINSEL
TINSELED
TINSELIER
TINSELING
TINSELLED
TINSELLY
TINSELRY
TINSELS
TINSELY
TINSEY
TINSEYS
TINSMITH
TINSMITHS
TINSNIPS
TINSTONE
TINSTONES
TINT
TINTACK
TINTACKS
TINTED
TINTER
TINTERS
TINTIER
TINTIEST
TINTINESS
TINTING
TINTINGS
TINTLESS
TINTOOKIE
TINTS
TINTY
TINTYPE
TINTYPES
TINWARE
TINWARES
TINWORK
TINWORKS
TINY
TIP
TIPCART
TIPCARTS
TIPCAT
TIPCATS
TIPI
TIPIS
TIPLESS
TIPOFF
TIPOFFS
TIPPABLE
TIPPED
TIPPEE
TIPPEES
TIPPER
TIPPERS
TIPPET
TIPPETS
TIPPIER
TIPPIEST
TIPPING
TIPPINGS
TIPPLE
TIPPLED
TIPPLER
TIPPLERS
TIPPLES
TIPPLING
TIPPY
TIPPYTOE
TIPPYTOED
TIPPYTOES
TIPS
TIPSHEET
TIPSHEETS
TIPSIER
TIPSIEST
TIPSIFIED
TIPSIFIES
TIPSIFY
TIPSILY
TIPSINESS
TIPSTAFF
TIPSTAFFS
TIPSTAVES
TIPSTER
TIPSTERS
TIPSTOCK
TIPSTOCKS
TIPSY
TIPT
TIPTOE
TIPTOED
TIPTOEING
TIPTOES
TIPTOP
TIPTOPS
TIPTRONIC
TIPULA
TIPULAS
TIPUNA
TIPUNAS
TIRADE
TIRADES
TIRAGE
TIRAGES
TIRAMISU
TIRAMISUS
TIRASSE
TIRASSES
TIRE
TIRED
TIREDER
TIREDEST
TIREDLY
TIREDNESS
TIRELESS
TIRELING
TIRELINGS
TIREMAKER
TIRES
TIRESOME
TIREWOMAN
TIREWOMEN
TIRING
TIRINGS
TIRITI
TIRITIS
TIRL
TIRLED
TIRLING
TIRLS
TIRO
TIROES
TIRONIC
TIROS
TIRR
TIRRED
TIRRING
TIRRIT
TIRRITS
TIRRIVEE
TIRRIVEES
TIRRIVIE
TIRRIVIES
TIRRS
TIS
TISANE
TISANES
TISICK
TISICKS
TISSUAL
TISSUE
TISSUED
TISSUES
TISSUEY
TISSUIER
TISSUIEST
TISSUING
TISSULAR
TISWAS
TISWASES
TIT
TITAN
TITANATE
TITANATES
TITANESS
TITANIA
TITANIAS
TITANIC
TITANIS
TITANISES
TITANISM
TITANISMS
TITANITE
TITANITES
TITANIUM
TITANIUMS
TITANOUS
TITANS
TITBIT
TITBITS
TITCH
TITCHES
TITCHIE
TITCHIER
TITCHIEST
TITCHY
TITE
TITELY
TITER
TITERS
TITFER
TITFERS
TITHABLE
TITHE
TITHED
TITHER
TITHERS
TITHES
TITHING
TITHINGS
TITHONIA
TITHONIAS
TITI
TITIAN
TITIANS
TITILLATE
TITIS

TITIVATE
TITIVATED
TITIVATES
TITIVATOR
TITLARK
TITLARKS
TITLE
TITLED
TITLELESS
TITLER
TITLERS
TITLES
TITLIKE
TITLING
TITLINGS
TITLIST
TITLISTS
TITMAN
TITMEN
TITMICE
TITMOSE
TITMOUSE
TITOKI
TITOKIS
TITRABLE
TITRANT
TITRANTS
TITRATE
TITRATED
TITRATES
TITRATING
TITRATION
TITRATOR
TITRATORS
TITRE
TITRES
TITS
TITTED
TITTER
TITTERED
TITTERER
TITTERERS
TITTERING
TITTERS
TITTIE
TITTIES
TITTING
TITTISH
TITTIVATE
TITTLE
TITTLEBAT
TITTLED
TITTLES
TITTLING
TITTUP
TITTUPED
TITTUPIER
TITTUPING
TITTUPPED
TITTUPPY
TITTUPS
TITTUPY
TITTY
TITUBANCY
TITUBANT
TITUBATE
TITUBATED
TITUBATES
TITULAR
TITULARLY
TITULARS
TITULARY
TITULE
TITULED
TITULES
TITULI
TITULING
TITULUS
TITUP
TITUPED
TITUPIER
TITUPIEST
TITUPING
TITUPPED
TITUPPING
TITUPS
TITUPY
TIVY
TIX
TIYIN
TIYINS
TIYN
TIYNS
TIZ
TIZES
TIZWAS
TIZWASES
TIZZ
TIZZES
TIZZIES
TIZZY
TJANTING
TJANTINGS
TMESES
TMESIS
TO
TOAD
TOADEATER
TOADFISH
TOADFLAX
TOADGRASS
TOADIED
TOADIES
TOADISH
TOADLESS
TOADLET
TOADLETS
TOADLIKE
TOADRUSH
TOADS
TOADSTONE
TOADSTOOL
TOADY
TOADYING
TOADYINGS
TOADYISH
TOADYISM
TOADYISMS
TOAST
TOASTED
TOASTER
TOASTERS
TOASTIE
TOASTIER
TOASTIES
TOASTIEST
TOASTING
TOASTINGS
TOASTS
TOASTY
TOAZE
TOAZED
TOAZES
TOAZING
TOBACCO
TOBACCOES
TOBACCOS
TOBIES
TOBOGGAN
TOBOGGANS
TOBOGGIN
TOBOGGINS
TOBY
TOC
TOCCATA
TOCCATAS
TOCCATE
TOCCATINA
TOCHER
TOCHERED
TOCHERING
TOCHERS
TOCK
TOCKED
TOCKIER
TOCKIEST
TOCKING
TOCKLEY
TOCKLEYS
TOCKS
TOCKY
TOCO
TOCOLOGY
TOCOS
TOCS
TOCSIN
TOCSINS
TOD
TODAY
TODAYS
TODDE
TODDED
TODDES
TODDIES
TODDING
TODDLE
TODDLED
TODDLER
TODDLERS
TODDLES
TODDLING
TODDY
TODGER
TODGERS
TODIES
TODS
TODY
TOE
TOEA
TOEAS
TOEBIE
TOEBIES
TOECAP
TOECAPS
TOECLIP
TOECLIPS
TOED
TOEHOLD
TOEHOLDS
TOEIER
TOEIEST
TOEING
TOELESS
TOELIKE
TOENAIL
TOENAILED
TOENAILS
TOEPIECE
TOEPIECES
TOEPLATE
TOEPLATES
TOERAG
TOERAGGER
TOERAGS
TOES
TOESHOE
TOESHOES
TOETOE
TOETOES
TOEY
TOFF
TOFFEE
TOFFEES
TOFFIER
TOFFIES
TOFFIEST
TOFFISH
TOFFS
TOFFY
TOFORE

TOFT
TOFTS
TOFU
TOFUS
TOFUTTI
TOFUTTIS
TOG
TOGA
TOGAE
TOGAED
TOGAS
TOGATE
TOGATED
TOGAVIRUS
TOGE
TOGED
TOGES
TOGETHER
TOGGED
TOGGER
TOGGERED
TOGGERIES
TOGGERING
TOGGERS
TOGGERY
TOGGING
TOGGLE
TOGGLED
TOGGLER
TOGGLERS
TOGGLES
TOGGLING
TOGROG
TOGROGS
TOGS
TOGUE
TOGUES
TOHEROA
TOHEROAS
TOHO
TOHOS
TOHUNGA
TOHUNGAS
TOIL
TOILE
TOILED
TOILER
TOILERS
TOILES
TOILET
TOILETED
TOILETING
TOILETRY
TOILETS
TOILETTE
TOILETTES
TOILFUL
TOILFULLY
TOILINET
TOILINETS
TOILING
TOILINGS
TOILLESS
TOILS
TOILSOME
TOILWORN
TOING
TOINGS
TOISE
TOISEACH
TOISEACHS
TOISECH
TOISECHS
TOISES
TOISON
TOISONS
TOIT
TOITED
TOITING
TOITOI
TOITOIS
TOITS
TOKAMAK
TOKAMAKS
TOKAY
TOKAYS
TOKE
TOKED
TOKEN
TOKENED
TOKENING
TOKENISM
TOKENISMS
TOKENS
TOKER
TOKERS
TOKES
TOKING
TOKO
TOKOLOGY
TOKOLOSHE
TOKOLOSHI
TOKOMAK
TOKOMAKS
TOKONOMA
TOKONOMAS
TOKOS
TOKOTOKO
TOKOTOKOS
TOKTOKKIE
TOLA
TOLAN
TOLANE
TOLANES
TOLANS
TOLAR
TOLARJEV
TOLARJI
TOLARS
TOLAS
TOLBOOTH
TOLBOOTHS
TOLD
TOLE
TOLED
TOLEDO
TOLEDOS
TOLERABLE
TOLERABLY
TOLERANCE
TOLERANT
TOLERATE
TOLERATED
TOLERATES
TOLERATOR
TOLES
TOLEWARE
TOLEWARES
TOLIDIN
TOLIDINE
TOLIDINES
TOLIDINS
TOLING
TOLINGS
TOLL
TOLLABLE
TOLLAGE
TOLLAGES
TOLLBAR
TOLLBARS
TOLLBOOTH
TOLLDISH
TOLLED
TOLLER
TOLLERS
TOLLEY
TOLLEYS
TOLLGATE
TOLLGATED
TOLLGATES
TOLLHOUSE
TOLLIE
TOLLIES
TOLLING
TOLLINGS
TOLLMAN
TOLLMEN
TOLLS
TOLLWAY
TOLLWAYS
TOLLY
TOLSEL
TOLSELS
TOLSEY
TOLSEYS
TOLT
TOLTER
TOLTERED
TOLTERING
TOLTERS
TOLTS
TOLU
TOLUATE
TOLUATES
TOLUENE
TOLUENES
TOLUIC
TOLUID
TOLUIDE
TOLUIDES
TOLUIDIDE
TOLUIDIN
TOLUIDINE
TOLUIDINS
TOLUIDS
TOLUOL
TOLUOLE
TOLUOLES
TOLUOLS
TOLUS
TOLUYL
TOLUYLS
TOLYL
TOLYLS
TOLZEY
TOLZEYS
TOM
TOMAHAWK
TOMAHAWKS
TOMALLEY
TOMALLEYS
TOMAN
TOMANS
TOMATILLO
TOMATO
TOMATOES
TOMATOEY
TOMATOIER
TOMB
TOMBAC
TOMBACK
TOMBACKS
TOMBACS
TOMBAK
TOMBAKS
TOMBAL
TOMBED
TOMBIC
TOMBING
TOMBLESS
TOMBLIKE
TOMBOC
TOMBOCS
TOMBOLA
TOMBOLAS
TOMBOLO
TOMBOLOS
TOMBOY
TOMBOYISH
TOMBOYS

TOMBS
TOMBSTONE
TOMCAT
TOMCATS
TOMCATTED
TOMCOD
TOMCODS
TOME
TOMENTA
TOMENTOSE
TOMENTOUS
TOMENTUM
TOMES
TOMFOOL
TOMFOOLED
TOMFOOLS
TOMIA
TOMIAL
TOMIUM
TOMMED
TOMMIED
TOMMIES
TOMMING
TOMMY
TOMMYCOD
TOMMYCODS
TOMMYING
TOMMYROT
TOMMYROTS
TOMO
TOMOGRAM
TOMOGRAMS
TOMOGRAPH
TOMORROW
TOMORROWS
TOMOS
TOMPION
TOMPIONS
TOMPON
TOMPONED
TOMPONING
TOMPONS
TOMPOT
TOMS
TOMTIT
TOMTITS
TON
TONAL
TONALITE
TONALITES
TONALITIC
TONALITY
TONALLY
TONANT
TONDI
TONDINI
TONDINO
TONDINOS
TONDO
TONDOS
TONE
TONEARM
TONEARMS
TONED
TONELESS
TONEME
TONEMES
TONEMIC
TONEPAD
TONEPADS
TONER
TONERS
TONES
TONETIC
TONETICS
TONETTE
TONETTES
TONEY
TONG
TONGA
TONGAS
TONGED
TONGER
TONGERS
TONGING
TONGMAN
TONGMEN
TONGS
TONGSTER
TONGSTERS
TONGUE
TONGUED
TONGUELET
TONGUES
TONGUING
TONGUINGS
TONIC
TONICALLY
TONICITY
TONICS
TONIER
TONIES
TONIEST
TONIFIED
TONIFIES
TONIFY
TONIFYING
TONIGHT
TONIGHTS
TONING
TONINGS
TONISH
TONISHLY
TONITE
TONITES
TONK
TONKA
TONKED
TONKER
TONKERS
TONKING
TONKS
TONLET
TONLETS
TONNAG
TONNAGE
TONNAGES
TONNAGS
TONNE
TONNEAU
TONNEAUS
TONNEAUX
TONNELL
TONNELLS
TONNER
TONNERS
TONNES
TONNISH
TONNISHLY
TONOMETER
TONOMETRY
TONOPLAST
TONS
TONSIL
TONSILAR
TONSILLAR
TONSILS
TONSOR
TONSORIAL
TONSORS
TONSURE
TONSURED
TONSURES
TONSURING
TONTINE
TONTINER
TONTINERS
TONTINES
TONUS
TONUSES
TONY
TOO
TOOART
TOOARTS
TOODLE
TOODLED
TOODLES
TOODLING
TOOK
TOOL
TOOLBAG
TOOLBAGS
TOOLBAR
TOOLBARS
TOOLBOX
TOOLBOXES
TOOLCASE
TOOLCASES
TOOLCHEST
TOOLED
TOOLER
TOOLERS
TOOLHEAD
TOOLHEADS
TOOLHOUSE
TOOLIE
TOOLIES
TOOLING
TOOLINGS
TOOLKIT
TOOLKITS
TOOLLESS
TOOLMAKER
TOOLMAN
TOOLMEN
TOOLPUSH
TOOLROOM
TOOLROOMS
TOOLS
TOOLSET
TOOLSETS
TOOLSHED
TOOLSHEDS
TOOLTIP
TOOLTIPS
TOOM
TOOMED
TOOMER
TOOMEST
TOOMING
TOOMS
TOON
TOONIE
TOONIES
TOONS
TOORIE
TOORIES
TOOSHIE
TOOSHIER
TOOSHIEST
TOOT
TOOTED
TOOTER
TOOTERS
TOOTH
TOOTHACHE
TOOTHCOMB
TOOTHED
TOOTHFISH
TOOTHFUL
TOOTHFULS
TOOTHIER
TOOTHIEST
TOOTHILY
TOOTHING
TOOTHINGS
TOOTHLESS
TOOTHLIKE
TOOTHPICK
TOOTHS

TOOTHSOME
TOOTHWASH
TOOTHWORT
TOOTHY
TOOTING
TOOTLE
TOOTLED
TOOTLER
TOOTLERS
TOOTLES
TOOTLING
TOOTS
TOOTSED
TOOTSES
TOOTSIE
TOOTSIES
TOOTSING
TOOTSY
TOP
TOPALGIA
TOPALGIAS
TOPARCH
TOPARCHS
TOPARCHY
TOPAZ
TOPAZES
TOPAZINE
TOPCOAT
TOPCOATS
TOPCROSS
TOPE
TOPECTOMY
TOPED
TOPEE
TOPEES
TOPEK
TOPEKS
TOPER
TOPERS
TOPES
TOPFLIGHT
TOPFUL
TOPFULL
TOPH
TOPHE
TOPHES
TOPHI
TOPHS
TOPHUS
TOPI
TOPIARIAN
TOPIARIES
TOPIARIST
TOPIARY
TOPIC
TOPICAL
TOPICALLY
TOPICALS
TOPICS
TOPING
TOPIS
TOPKICK
TOPKICKS
TOPKNOT
TOPKNOTS
TOPLESS
TOPLINE
TOPLINED
TOPLINER
TOPLINERS
TOPLINES
TOPLINING
TOPLOFTY
TOPMAKER
TOPMAKERS
TOPMAKING
TOPMAN
TOPMAST
TOPMASTS
TOPMEN
TOPMINNOW
TOPMOST
TOPNOTCH
TOPO
TOPOGRAPH
TOPOI
TOPOLOGIC
TOPOLOGY
TOPOMETRY
TOPONYM
TOPONYMAL
TOPONYMIC
TOPONYMS
TOPONYMY
TOPOS
TOPOTYPE
TOPOTYPES
TOPPED
TOPPER
TOPPERS
TOPPIER
TOPPIEST
TOPPING
TOPPINGLY
TOPPINGS
TOPPLE
TOPPLED
TOPPLES
TOPPLING
TOPPY
TOPRAIL
TOPRAILS
TOPS
TOPSAIL
TOPSAILS
TOPSCORE
TOPSCORED
TOPSCORES
TOPSIDE
TOPSIDER
TOPSIDERS
TOPSIDES
TOPSMAN
TOPSMEN
TOPSOIL
TOPSOILED
TOPSOILS
TOPSPIN
TOPSPINS
TOPSTITCH
TOPSTONE
TOPSTONES
TOPWATER
TOPWORK
TOPWORKED
TOPWORKS
TOQUE
TOQUES
TOQUET
TOQUETS
TOQUILLA
TOQUILLAS
TOR
TORA
TORAH
TORAHS
TORAN
TORANA
TORANAS
TORANS
TORAS
TORBANITE
TORC
TORCH
TORCHABLE
TORCHED
TORCHER
TORCHERE
TORCHERES
TORCHERS
TORCHES
TORCHIER
TORCHIERE
TORCHIERS
TORCHIEST
TORCHING
TORCHINGS
TORCHLIKE
TORCHLIT
TORCHON
TORCHONS
TORCHWOOD
TORCHY
TORCS
TORCULAR
TORCULARS
TORDION
TORDIONS
TORE
TOREADOR
TOREADORS
TORERO
TOREROS
TORES
TOREUTIC
TOREUTICS
TORGOCH
TORGOCHS
TORI
TORIC
TORICS
TORIES
TORII
TORMENT
TORMENTA
TORMENTED
TORMENTER
TORMENTIL
TORMENTOR
TORMENTS
TORMENTUM
TORMINA
TORMINAL
TORMINOUS
TORN
TORNADE
TORNADES
TORNADIC
TORNADO
TORNADOES
TORNADOS
TORNILLO
TORNILLOS
TORO
TOROID
TOROIDAL
TOROIDS
TOROS
TOROSE
TOROSITY
TOROT
TOROTH
TOROUS
TORPEDO
TORPEDOED
TORPEDOER
TORPEDOES
TORPEDOS
TORPEFIED
TORPEFIES
TORPEFY
TORPID
TORPIDITY
TORPIDLY
TORPIDS
TORPITUDE
TORPOR
TORPORS
TORQUATE
TORQUATED

TORQUE
TORQUED
TORQUER
TORQUERS
TORQUES
TORQUESES
TORQUEY
TORQUIER
TORQUIEST
TORQUING
TORR
TORREFIED
TORREFIES
TORREFY
TORRENT
TORRENTS
TORRET
TORRETS
TORRID
TORRIDER
TORRIDEST
TORRIDITY
TORRIDLY
TORRIFIED
TORRIFIES
TORRIFY
TORRS
TORS
TORSADE
TORSADES
TORSE
TORSEL
TORSELS
TORSES
TORSI
TORSION
TORSIONAL
TORSIONS
TORSIVE
TORSK
TORSKS
TORSO
TORSOS
TORT
TORTA
TORTAS
TORTE
TORTELLI
TORTELLIS
TORTEN
TORTES
TORTIE
TORTIES
TORTILE
TORTILITY
TORTILLA
TORTILLAS
TORTILLON
TORTIOUS
TORTIVE
TORTOISE
TORTOISES
TORTONI
TORTONIS
TORTRICES
TORTRICID
TORTRIX
TORTRIXES
TORTS
TORTUOUS
TORTURE
TORTURED
TORTURER
TORTURERS
TORTURES
TORTURING
TORTUROUS
TORULA
TORULAE
TORULAS
TORULI
TORULIN
TORULINS
TORULOSE
TORULOSES
TORULOSIS
TORULUS
TORUS
TORUSES
TORY
TOSA
TOSAS
TOSE
TOSED
TOSES
TOSH
TOSHACH
TOSHACHS
TOSHED
TOSHER
TOSHERS
TOSHES
TOSHIER
TOSHIEST
TOSHING
TOSHY
TOSING
TOSS
TOSSED
TOSSEN
TOSSER
TOSSERS
TOSSES
TOSSIER
TOSSIEST
TOSSILY
TOSSING
TOSSINGS
TOSSPOT
TOSSPOTS
TOSSUP
TOSSUPS
TOSSY
TOST
TOSTADA
TOSTADAS
TOSTADO
TOSTADOS
TOSTONE
TOSTONES
TOT
TOTABLE
TOTAL
TOTALED
TOTALING
TOTALISE
TOTALISED
TOTALISER
TOTALISES
TOTALISM
TOTALISMS
TOTALIST
TOTALISTS
TOTALITY
TOTALIZE
TOTALIZED
TOTALIZER
TOTALIZES
TOTALLED
TOTALLING
TOTALLY
TOTALS
TOTANUS
TOTANUSES
TOTAQUINE
TOTARA
TOTARAS
TOTE
TOTEABLE
TOTED
TOTEM
TOTEMIC
TOTEMISM
TOTEMISMS
TOTEMIST
TOTEMISTS
TOTEMITE
TOTEMITES
TOTEMS
TOTER
TOTERS
TOTES
TOTHER
TOTHERS
TOTIENT
TOTIENTS
TOTING
TOTITIVE
TOTITIVES
TOTS
TOTTED
TOTTER
TOTTERED
TOTTERER
TOTTERERS
TOTTERIER
TOTTERING
TOTTERS
TOTTERY
TOTTIE
TOTTIER
TOTTIES
TOTTIEST
TOTTING
TOTTINGS
TOTTRING
TOTTY
TOUCAN
TOUCANET
TOUCANETS
TOUCANS
TOUCH
TOUCHABLE
TOUCHABLY
TOUCHBACK
TOUCHDOWN
TOUCHE
TOUCHED
TOUCHER
TOUCHERS
TOUCHES
TOUCHHOLE
TOUCHIER
TOUCHIEST
TOUCHILY
TOUCHING
TOUCHINGS
TOUCHLESS
TOUCHLINE
TOUCHMARK
TOUCHPAD
TOUCHPADS
TOUCHTONE
TOUCHUP
TOUCHUPS
TOUCHWOOD
TOUCHY
TOUGH
TOUGHED
TOUGHEN
TOUGHENED
TOUGHENER
TOUGHENS
TOUGHER
TOUGHEST
TOUGHIE
TOUGHIES
TOUGHING
TOUGHISH
TOUGHLY

TOUGHNESS
TOUGHS
TOUGHY
TOUK
TOUKED
TOUKING
TOUKS
TOULADI
TOULADIS
TOUN
TOUNS
TOUPEE
TOUPEED
TOUPEES
TOUPET
TOUPETS
TOUPIE
TOUPIES
TOUR
TOURACO
TOURACOS
TOURED
TOURER
TOURERS
TOURIE
TOURIES
TOURING
TOURINGS
TOURISM
TOURISMS
TOURIST
TOURISTA
TOURISTAS
TOURISTED
TOURISTIC
TOURISTS
TOURISTY
TOURNEDOS
TOURNEY
TOURNEYED
TOURNEYER
TOURNEYS
TOURNURE
TOURNURES
TOURS
TOURTIERE
TOUSE
TOUSED
TOUSER
TOUSERS
TOUSES
TOUSIER
TOUSIEST
TOUSING
TOUSINGS
TOUSLE
TOUSLED
TOUSLES
TOUSLING
TOUSTIE
TOUSTIER
TOUSTIEST
TOUSY
TOUT
TOUTED
TOUTER
TOUTERS
TOUTIE
TOUTIER
TOUTIEST
TOUTING
TOUTON
TOUTONS
TOUTS
TOUZE
TOUZED
TOUZES
TOUZIER
TOUZIEST
TOUZING
TOUZLE
TOUZLED
TOUZLES
TOUZLING
TOUZY
TOVARICH
TOVARISCH
TOVARISH
TOW
TOWABLE
TOWAGE
TOWAGES
TOWARD
TOWARDLY
TOWARDS
TOWAWAY
TOWAWAYS
TOWBAR
TOWBARS
TOWBOAT
TOWBOATS
TOWED
TOWEL
TOWELED
TOWELETTE
TOWELING
TOWELINGS
TOWELLED
TOWELLING
TOWELS
TOWER
TOWERED
TOWERIER
TOWERIEST
TOWERING
TOWERLESS
TOWERLIKE
TOWERS
TOWERY
TOWHEAD
TOWHEADED
TOWHEADS
TOWHEE
TOWHEES
TOWIE
TOWIER
TOWIES
TOWIEST
TOWING
TOWINGS
TOWKAY
TOWKAYS
TOWLINE
TOWLINES
TOWMON
TOWMOND
TOWMONDS
TOWMONS
TOWMONT
TOWMONTS
TOWN
TOWNEE
TOWNEES
TOWNFOLK
TOWNHALL
TOWNHOME
TOWNHOMES
TOWNHOUSE
TOWNIE
TOWNIER
TOWNIES
TOWNIEST
TOWNISH
TOWNLAND
TOWNLANDS
TOWNLESS
TOWNLET
TOWNLETS
TOWNLIER
TOWNLIEST
TOWNLING
TOWNLINGS
TOWNLY
TOWNS
TOWNSCAPE
TOWNSFOLK
TOWNSHIP
TOWNSHIPS
TOWNSITE
TOWNSITES
TOWNSKIP
TOWNSKIPS
TOWNSMAN
TOWNSMEN
TOWNWARD
TOWNWEAR
TOWNWEARS
TOWNY
TOWPATH
TOWPATHS
TOWPLANE
TOWPLANES
TOWROPE
TOWROPES
TOWS
TOWSACK
TOWSACKS
TOWSE
TOWSED
TOWSER
TOWSERS
TOWSES
TOWSIER
TOWSIEST
TOWSING
TOWSY
TOWT
TOWTED
TOWTING
TOWTS
TOWY
TOWZE
TOWZED
TOWZES
TOWZIER
TOWZIEST
TOWZING
TOWZY
TOXAEMIA
TOXAEMIAS
TOXAEMIC
TOXAPHENE
TOXEMIA
TOXEMIAS
TOXEMIC
TOXIC
TOXICAL
TOXICALLY
TOXICANT
TOXICANTS
TOXICITY
TOXICOSES
TOXICOSIS
TOXICS
TOXIGENIC
TOXIN
TOXINE
TOXINES
TOXINS
TOXOCARA
TOXOCARAL
TOXOCARAS
TOXOID
TOXOIDS
TOXOPHILY
TOY
TOYBOX
TOYBOXES
TOYCHEST
TOYCHESTS

TOYED
TOYER
TOYERS
TOYETIC
TOYING
TOYINGS
TOYISH
TOYISHLY
TOYLAND
TOYLANDS
TOYLESOME
TOYLESS
TOYLIKE
TOYLSOM
TOYMAN
TOYMEN
TOYO
TOYON
TOYONS
TOYOS
TOYS
TOYSHOP
TOYSHOPS
TOYSOME
TOYTOWN
TOYTOWNS
TOYWOMAN
TOYWOMEN
TOZE
TOZED
TOZES
TOZIE
TOZIES
TOZING
TRABEATE
TRABEATED
TRABECULA
TRABS
TRACE
TRACEABLE
TRACEABLY
TRACED
TRACELESS
TRACER
TRACERIED
TRACERIES
TRACERS
TRACERY
TRACES
TRACEUR
TRACEURS
TRACHEA
TRACHEAE
TRACHEAL
TRACHEARY
TRACHEAS
TRACHEATE
TRACHEID
TRACHEIDE
TRACHEIDS
TRACHEOLE
TRACHINUS
TRACHITIS
TRACHLE
TRACHLED
TRACHLES
TRACHLING
TRACHOMA
TRACHOMAS
TRACHYTE
TRACHYTES
TRACHYTIC
TRACING
TRACINGS
TRACK
TRACKABLE
TRACKAGE
TRACKAGES
TRACKBALL
TRACKBED
TRACKBEDS
TRACKED
TRACKER
TRACKERS
TRACKIE
TRACKIES
TRACKING
TRACKINGS
TRACKLESS
TRACKMAN
TRACKMEN
TRACKPAD
TRACKPADS
TRACKROAD
TRACKS
TRACKSIDE
TRACKSUIT
TRACKWAY
TRACKWAYS
TRACT
TRACTABLE
TRACTABLY
TRACTATE
TRACTATES
TRACTATOR
TRACTED
TRACTILE
TRACTING
TRACTION
TRACTIONS
TRACTIVE
TRACTOR
TRACTORS
TRACTRIX
TRACTS
TRACTUS
TRACTUSES
TRAD
TRADABLE
TRADE
TRADEABLE
TRADED
TRADEFUL
TRADELESS
TRADEMARK
TRADENAME
TRADEOFF
TRADEOFFS
TRADER
TRADERS
TRADES
TRADESMAN
TRADESMEN
TRADIE
TRADIES
TRADING
TRADINGS
TRADITION
TRADITIVE
TRADITOR
TRADITORS
TRADS
TRADUCE
TRADUCED
TRADUCER
TRADUCERS
TRADUCES
TRADUCIAN
TRADUCING
TRAFFIC
TRAFFICKY
TRAFFICS
TRAGAL
TRAGEDIAN
TRAGEDIES
TRAGEDY
TRAGELAPH
TRAGI
TRAGIC
TRAGICAL
TRAGICS
TRAGOPAN
TRAGOPANS
TRAGULE
TRAGULES
TRAGULINE
TRAGUS
TRAHISON
TRAHISONS
TRAIK
TRAIKED
TRAIKING
TRAIKIT
TRAIKS
TRAIL
TRAILABLE
TRAILED
TRAILER
TRAILERED
TRAILERS
TRAILHEAD
TRAILING
TRAILLESS
TRAILS
TRAILSIDE
TRAIN
TRAINABLE
TRAINBAND
TRAINED
TRAINEE
TRAINEES
TRAINER
TRAINERS
TRAINFUL
TRAINFULS
TRAINING
TRAININGS
TRAINLESS
TRAINLOAD
TRAINMAN
TRAINMEN
TRAINS
TRAINWAY
TRAINWAYS
TRAIPSE
TRAIPSED
TRAIPSES
TRAIPSING
TRAIT
TRAITOR
TRAITORLY
TRAITORS
TRAITRESS
TRAITS
TRAJECT
TRAJECTED
TRAJECTS
TRAM
TRAMCAR
TRAMCARS
TRAMEL
TRAMELED
TRAMELING
TRAMELL
TRAMELLED
TRAMELLS
TRAMELS
TRAMLESS
TRAMLINE
TRAMLINED
TRAMLINES
TRAMMED
TRAMMEL
TRAMMELED
TRAMMELER
TRAMMELS
TRAMMIE
TRAMMIES
TRAMMING
TRAMP

TRAMPED
TRAMPER
TRAMPERS
TRAMPET
TRAMPETS
TRAMPETTE
TRAMPIER
TRAMPIEST
TRAMPING
TRAMPINGS
TRAMPISH
TRAMPLE
TRAMPLED
TRAMPLER
TRAMPLERS
TRAMPLES
TRAMPLING
TRAMPOLIN
TRAMPS
TRAMPY
TRAMROAD
TRAMROADS
TRAMS
TRAMWAY
TRAMWAYS
TRANCE
TRANCED
TRANCEDLY
TRANCES
TRANCEY
TRANCHE
TRANCHES
TRANCHET
TRANCHETS
TRANCIER
TRANCIEST
TRANCING
TRANECT
TRANECTS
TRANGAM
TRANGAMS
TRANGLE
TRANGLES
TRANK
TRANKED
TRANKING
TRANKS
TRANKUM
TRANKUMS
TRANNIE
TRANNIES
TRANNY
TRANQ
TRANQS
TRANQUIL
TRANS
TRANSACT
TRANSACTS
TRANSAXLE
TRANSCEND
TRANSCODE
TRANSDUCE
TRANSE
TRANSECT
TRANSECTS
TRANSENNA
TRANSEPT
TRANSEPTS
TRANSES
TRANSEUNT
TRANSFARD
TRANSFECT
TRANSFER
TRANSFERS
TRANSFIX
TRANSFIXT
TRANSFORM
TRANSFUSE
TRANSGENE
TRANSHIP
TRANSHIPS
TRANSHUME
TRANSIENT
TRANSIRE
TRANSIRES
TRANSIT
TRANSITED
TRANSITS
TRANSLATE
TRANSMAN
TRANSMEN
TRANSMEW
TRANSMEWS
TRANSMIT
TRANSMITS
TRANSMOVE
TRANSMUTE
TRANSOM
TRANSOMED
TRANSOMS
TRANSONIC
TRANSPIRE
TRANSPORT
TRANSPOSE
TRANSSHIP
TRANSUDE
TRANSUDED
TRANSUDES
TRANSUME
TRANSUMED
TRANSUMES
TRANSUMPT
TRANSVEST
TRANT
TRANTED
TRANTER
TRANTERS
TRANTING
TRANTS
TRAP
TRAPAN
TRAPANNED
TRAPANNER
TRAPANS
TRAPBALL
TRAPBALLS
TRAPDOOR
TRAPDOORS
TRAPE
TRAPED
TRAPES
TRAPESED
TRAPESES
TRAPESING
TRAPEZE
TRAPEZED
TRAPEZES
TRAPEZIA
TRAPEZIAL
TRAPEZII
TRAPEZING
TRAPEZIST
TRAPEZIUM
TRAPEZIUS
TRAPEZOID
TRAPFALL
TRAPFALLS
TRAPING
TRAPLIKE
TRAPLINE
TRAPLINES
TRAPNEST
TRAPNESTS
TRAPPEAN
TRAPPED
TRAPPER
TRAPPERS
TRAPPIER
TRAPPIEST
TRAPPING
TRAPPINGS
TRAPPOSE
TRAPPOUS
TRAPPY
TRAPROCK
TRAPROCKS
TRAPS
TRAPSE
TRAPSED
TRAPSES
TRAPSING
TRAPT
TRAPUNTO
TRAPUNTOS
TRASH
TRASHCAN
TRASHCANS
TRASHED
TRASHER
TRASHERS
TRASHERY
TRASHES
TRASHIER
TRASHIEST
TRASHILY
TRASHING
TRASHMAN
TRASHMEN
TRASHTRIE
TRASHY
TRASS
TRASSES
TRAT
TRATS
TRATT
TRATTORIA
TRATTORIE
TRATTS
TRAUCHLE
TRAUCHLED
TRAUCHLES
TRAUMA
TRAUMAS
TRAUMATA
TRAUMATIC
TRAVAIL
TRAVAILED
TRAVAILS
TRAVE
TRAVEL
TRAVELED
TRAVELER
TRAVELERS
TRAVELING
TRAVELLED
TRAVELLER
TRAVELOG
TRAVELOGS
TRAVELS
TRAVERSAL
TRAVERSE
TRAVERSED
TRAVERSER
TRAVERSES
TRAVERTIN
TRAVES
TRAVESTY
TRAVIS
TRAVISES
TRAVOIS
TRAVOISE
TRAVOISES
TRAWL
TRAWLED
TRAWLER
TRAWLERS
TRAWLEY
TRAWLEYS
TRAWLING
TRAWLINGS

T

TRAWLNET
TRAWLNETS
TRAWLS
TRAY
TRAYBAKE
TRAYBAKES
TRAYBIT
TRAYBITS
TRAYCLOTH
TRAYF
TRAYFUL
TRAYFULS
TRAYNE
TRAYNED
TRAYNES
TRAYNING
TRAYS
TRAZODONE
TREACHER
TREACHERS
TREACHERY
TREACHOUR
TREACLE
TREACLED
TREACLES
TREACLIER
TREACLING
TREACLY
TREAD
TREADED
TREADER
TREADERS
TREADING
TREADINGS
TREADLE
TREADLED
TREADLER
TREADLERS
TREADLES
TREADLESS
TREADLING
TREADMILL
TREADS
TREAGUE
TREAGUES
TREASON
TREASONS
TREASURE
TREASURED
TREASURER
TREASURES
TREASURY
TREAT
TREATABLE
TREATED
TREATER
TREATERS
TREATIES
TREATING
TREATINGS
TREATISE
TREATISES
TREATMENT
TREATS
TREATY
TREBBIANO
TREBLE
TREBLED
TREBLES
TREBLIER
TREBLIEST
TREBLING
TREBLINGS
TREBLY
TREBUCHET
TREBUCKET
TRECENTO
TRECENTOS
TRECK
TRECKED
TRECKING
TRECKS
TREDDLE
TREDDLED
TREDDLES
TREDDLING
TREDILLE
TREDILLES
TREDRILLE
TREE
TREED
TREEHOUSE
TREEING
TREELAWN
TREELAWNS
TREELESS
TREELIKE
TREELINE
TREELINES
TREEN
TREENAIL
TREENAILS
TREENS
TREENWARE
TREES
TREESHIP
TREESHIPS
TREETOP
TREETOPS
TREEWARE
TREEWARES
TREEWAX
TREEWAXES
TREF
TREFA
TREFAH
TREFOIL
TREFOILED
TREFOILS
TREGETOUR
TREGGINGS
TREHALA
TREHALAS
TREHALOSE
TREIF
TREIFA
TREILLAGE
TREILLE
TREILLES
TREK
TREKKED
TREKKER
TREKKERS
TREKKING
TREKKINGS
TREKS
TRELLIS
TRELLISED
TRELLISES
TREM
TREMA
TREMAS
TREMATIC
TREMATODE
TREMATOID
TREMBLANT
TREMBLE
TREMBLED
TREMBLER
TREMBLERS
TREMBLES
TREMBLIER
TREMBLING
TREMBLOR
TREMBLORS
TREMBLY
TREMIE
TREMIES
TREMOLANT
TREMOLITE
TREMOLO
TREMOLOS
TREMOR
TREMORED
TREMORING
TREMOROUS
TREMORS
TREMS
TREMULANT
TREMULATE
TREMULOUS
TRENAIL
TRENAILS
TRENCH
TRENCHAND
TRENCHANT
TRENCHARD
TRENCHED
TRENCHER
TRENCHERS
TRENCHES
TRENCHING
TREND
TRENDED
TRENDIER
TRENDIES
TRENDIEST
TRENDIFY
TRENDILY
TRENDING
TRENDOID
TRENDOIDS
TRENDS
TRENDY
TRENDYISM
TRENISE
TRENISES
TRENTAL
TRENTALS
TREPAN
TREPANG
TREPANGS
TREPANNED
TREPANNER
TREPANS
TREPHINE
TREPHINED
TREPHINER
TREPHINES
TREPID
TREPIDANT
TREPONEMA
TREPONEME
TRES
TRESPASS
TRESS
TRESSED
TRESSEL
TRESSELS
TRESSES
TRESSIER
TRESSIEST
TRESSING
TRESSOUR
TRESSOURS
TRESSURE
TRESSURED
TRESSURES
TRESSY
TREST
TRESTLE
TRESTLES
TRESTS
TRET
TRETINOIN
TRETS
TREVALLY
TREVALLYS
TREVET
TREVETS

T

TREVIS
TREVISES
TREVISS
TREVISSES
TREW
TREWS
TREWSMAN
TREWSMEN
TREY
TREYBIT
TREYBITS
TREYF
TREYFA
TREYS
TREZ
TREZES
TRIABLE
TRIAC
TRIACID
TRIACIDS
TRIACS
TRIACT
TRIACTINE
TRIACTOR
TRIACTORS
TRIACTS
TRIAD
TRIADIC
TRIADICS
TRIADISM
TRIADISMS
TRIADIST
TRIADISTS
TRIADS
TRIAGE
TRIAGED
TRIAGES
TRIAGING
TRIAL
TRIALED
TRIALING
TRIALISM
TRIALISMS
TRIALIST
TRIALISTS
TRIALITY
TRIALLED
TRIALLING
TRIALLIST
TRIALOGUE
TRIALS
TRIALWARE
TRIANGLE
TRIANGLED
TRIANGLES
TRIAPSAL
TRIARCH
TRIARCHS
TRIARCHY
TRIASSIC
TRIATHLON
TRIATIC
TRIATICS
TRIATOMIC
TRIAXIAL
TRIAXIALS
TRIAXON
TRIAXONS
TRIAZIN
TRIAZINE
TRIAZINES
TRIAZINS
TRIAZOLE
TRIAZOLES
TRIAZOLIC
TRIBADE
TRIBADES
TRIBADIC
TRIBADIES
TRIBADISM
TRIBADY
TRIBAL
TRIBALISM
TRIBALIST
TRIBALLY
TRIBALS
TRIBASIC
TRIBBLE
TRIBBLES
TRIBE
TRIBELESS
TRIBES
TRIBESMAN
TRIBESMEN
TRIBLET
TRIBLETS
TRIBOLOGY
TRIBRACH
TRIBRACHS
TRIBULATE
TRIBUNAL
TRIBUNALS
TRIBUNARY
TRIBUNATE
TRIBUNE
TRIBUNES
TRIBUTARY
TRIBUTE
TRIBUTER
TRIBUTERS
TRIBUTES
TRICAR
TRICARS
TRICE
TRICED
TRICEP
TRICEPS
TRICEPSES
TRICERION
TRICES
TRICHINA
TRICHINAE
TRICHINAL
TRICHINAS
TRICHITE
TRICHITES
TRICHITIC
TRICHOID
TRICHOME
TRICHOMES
TRICHOMIC
TRICHORD
TRICHORDS
TRICHOSES
TRICHOSIS
TRICHROIC
TRICHROME
TRICING
TRICITIES
TRICITY
TRICK
TRICKED
TRICKER
TRICKERS
TRICKERY
TRICKIE
TRICKIER
TRICKIEST
TRICKILY
TRICKING
TRICKINGS
TRICKISH
TRICKLE
TRICKLED
TRICKLES
TRICKLESS
TRICKLET
TRICKLETS
TRICKLIER
TRICKLING
TRICKLY
TRICKS
TRICKSIER
TRICKSILY
TRICKSOME
TRICKSTER
TRICKSY
TRICKY
TRICLAD
TRICLADS
TRICLINIA
TRICLINIC
TRICLOSAN
TRICOLOR
TRICOLORS
TRICOLOUR
TRICORN
TRICORNE
TRICORNES
TRICORNS
TRICOT
TRICOTINE
TRICOTS
TRICROTIC
TRICTRAC
TRICTRACS
TRICUSPID
TRICYCLE
TRICYCLED
TRICYCLER
TRICYCLES
TRICYCLIC
TRIDACNA
TRIDACNAS
TRIDACTYL
TRIDARN
TRIDARNS
TRIDE
TRIDENT
TRIDENTAL
TRIDENTED
TRIDENTS
TRIDUAN
TRIDUUM
TRIDUUMS
TRIDYMITE
TRIE
TRIECIOUS
TRIED
TRIELLA
TRIELLAS
TRIENE
TRIENES
TRIENNIA
TRIENNIAL
TRIENNIUM
TRIENS
TRIENTES
TRIER
TRIERARCH
TRIERS
TRIES
TRIETERIC
TRIETHYL
TRIFACIAL
TRIFECTA
TRIFECTAS
TRIFF
TRIFFER
TRIFFEST
TRIFFIC
TRIFFID
TRIFFIDS
TRIFFIDY
TRIFID
TRIFLE
TRIFLED
TRIFLER
TRIFLERS
TRIFLES

T

TRIFLING
TRIFLINGS
TRIFOCAL
TRIFOCALS
TRIFOLD
TRIFOLIA
TRIFOLIES
TRIFOLIUM
TRIFOLY
TRIFORIA
TRIFORIAL
TRIFORIUM
TRIFORM
TRIFORMED
TRIG
TRIGAMIES
TRIGAMIST
TRIGAMOUS
TRIGAMY
TRIGEMINI
TRIGGED
TRIGGER
TRIGGERED
TRIGGERS
TRIGGEST
TRIGGING
TRIGLOT
TRIGLOTS
TRIGLY
TRIGLYPH
TRIGLYPHS
TRIGNESS
TRIGO
TRIGON
TRIGONAL
TRIGONIC
TRIGONOUS
TRIGONS
TRIGOS
TRIGRAM
TRIGRAMS
TRIGRAPH
TRIGRAPHS
TRIGS
TRIGYNIAN
TRIGYNOUS
TRIHEDRA
TRIHEDRAL
TRIHEDRON
TRIHYBRID
TRIHYDRIC
TRIJET
TRIJETS
TRIJUGATE
TRIJUGOUS
TRIKE
TRIKES
TRILBIED
TRILBIES
TRILBY
TRILBYS
TRILD
TRILEMMA
TRILEMMAS
TRILINEAR
TRILITH
TRILITHIC
TRILITHON
TRILITHS
TRILL
TRILLED
TRILLER
TRILLERS
TRILLING
TRILLINGS
TRILLION
TRILLIONS
TRILLIUM
TRILLIUMS
TRILLO
TRILLOES
TRILLS
TRILOBAL
TRILOBATE
TRILOBE
TRILOBED
TRILOBES
TRILOBITE
TRILOGIES
TRILOGY
TRIM
TRIMARAN
TRIMARANS
TRIMER
TRIMERIC
TRIMERISM
TRIMEROUS
TRIMERS
TRIMESTER
TRIMETER
TRIMETERS
TRIMETHYL
TRIMETRIC
TRIMIX
TRIMIXES
TRIMLY
TRIMMED
TRIMMER
TRIMMERS
TRIMMEST
TRIMMING
TRIMMINGS
TRIMNESS
TRIMORPH
TRIMORPHS
TRIMOTOR
TRIMOTORS
TRIMPHONE
TRIMPOT
TRIMPOTS
TRIMS
TRIMTAB
TRIMTABS
TRIN
TRINAL
TRINARY
TRINDLE
TRINDLED
TRINDLES
TRINDLING
TRINE
TRINED
TRINES
TRINGLE
TRINGLES
TRINING
TRINITIES
TRINITRIN
TRINITY
TRINKET
TRINKETED
TRINKETER
TRINKETRY
TRINKETS
TRINKUM
TRINKUMS
TRINODAL
TRINOMIAL
TRINS
TRIO
TRIODE
TRIODES
TRIOL
TRIOLEIN
TRIOLEINS
TRIOLET
TRIOLETS
TRIOLS
TRIONES
TRIONYM
TRIONYMAL
TRIONYMS
TRIOR
TRIORS
TRIOS
TRIOSE
TRIOSES
TRIOXID
TRIOXIDE
TRIOXIDES
TRIOXIDS
TRIOXYGEN
TRIP
TRIPACK
TRIPACKS
TRIPART
TRIPE
TRIPEDAL
TRIPERIES
TRIPERY
TRIPES
TRIPEY
TRIPHASE
TRIPHONE
TRIPHONES
TRIPIER
TRIPIEST
TRIPITAKA
TRIPLANE
TRIPLANES
TRIPLE
TRIPLED
TRIPLES
TRIPLET
TRIPLETS
TRIPLEX
TRIPLEXED
TRIPLEXES
TRIPLIED
TRIPLIES
TRIPLING
TRIPLINGS
TRIPLITE
TRIPLITES
TRIPLOID
TRIPLOIDS
TRIPLOIDY
TRIPLY
TRIPLYING
TRIPMAN
TRIPMEN
TRIPMETER
TRIPOD
TRIPODAL
TRIPODIC
TRIPODIES
TRIPODS
TRIPODY
TRIPOLI
TRIPOLIS
TRIPOS
TRIPOSES
TRIPPANT
TRIPPED
TRIPPER
TRIPPERS
TRIPPERY
TRIPPET
TRIPPETS
TRIPPIER
TRIPPIEST
TRIPPING
TRIPPINGS
TRIPPLE
TRIPPLED
TRIPPLER
TRIPPLERS
TRIPPLES
TRIPPLING
TRIPPY

T

TRIPS
TRIPSES
TRIPSIS
TRIPTAN
TRIPTANE
TRIPTANES
TRIPTANS
TRIPTOTE
TRIPTOTES
TRIPTYCA
TRIPTYCAS
TRIPTYCH
TRIPTYCHS
TRIPTYQUE
TRIPUDIA
TRIPUDIUM
TRIPWIRE
TRIPWIRES
TRIPY
TRIQUETRA
TRIRADIAL
TRIREME
TRIREMES
TRISAGION
TRISCELE
TRISCELES
TRISECT
TRISECTED
TRISECTOR
TRISECTS
TRISEME
TRISEMES
TRISEMIC
TRISERIAL
TRISHAW
TRISHAWS
TRISKELE
TRISKELES
TRISKELIA
TRISMIC
TRISMUS
TRISMUSES
TRISODIUM
TRISOME
TRISOMES
TRISOMIC
TRISOMICS
TRISOMIES
TRISOMY
TRIST
TRISTATE
TRISTE
TRISTESSE
TRISTEZA
TRISTEZAS
TRISTFUL
TRISTICH
TRISTICHS
TRISUL
TRISULA
TRISULAS
TRISULS
TRITANOPE
TRITE
TRITELY
TRITENESS
TRITER
TRITES
TRITEST
TRITHEISM
TRITHEIST
TRITHING
TRITHINGS
TRITIATE
TRITIATED
TRITIATES
TRITICAL
TRITICALE
TRITICISM
TRITICUM
TRITICUMS
TRITIDE
TRITIDES
TRITIUM
TRITIUMS
TRITOMA
TRITOMAS
TRITON
TRITONE
TRITONES
TRITONIA
TRITONIAS
TRITONS
TRITURATE
TRIUMPH
TRIUMPHAL
TRIUMPHED
TRIUMPHER
TRIUMPHS
TRIUMVIR
TRIUMVIRI
TRIUMVIRS
TRIUMVIRY
TRIUNE
TRIUNES
TRIUNITY
TRIVALENT
TRIVALVE
TRIVALVED
TRIVALVES
TRIVET
TRIVETS
TRIVIA
TRIVIAL
TRIVIALLY
TRIVIUM
TRIVIUMS
TRIWEEKLY
TRIZONAL
TRIZONE
TRIZONES
TROAD
TROADE
TROADES
TROADS
TROAK
TROAKED
TROAKING
TROAKS
TROAT
TROATED
TROATING
TROATS
TROCAR
TROCARS
TROCHAIC
TROCHAICS
TROCHAL
TROCHAR
TROCHARS
TROCHE
TROCHEE
TROCHEES
TROCHES
TROCHI
TROCHIL
TROCHILI
TROCHILIC
TROCHILS
TROCHILUS
TROCHISCI
TROCHISK
TROCHISKS
TROCHITE
TROCHITES
TROCHLEA
TROCHLEAE
TROCHLEAR
TROCHLEAS
TROCHOID
TROCHOIDS
TROCHUS
TROCHUSES
TROCK
TROCKED
TROCKEN
TROCKING
TROCKS
TROD
TRODDEN
TRODE
TRODES
TRODS
TROELIE
TROELIES
TROELY
TROFFER
TROFFERS
TROG
TROGGED
TROGGING
TROGGS
TROGON
TROGONS
TROGS
TROIKA
TROIKAS
TROILISM
TROILISMS
TROILIST
TROILISTS
TROILITE
TROILITES
TROILUS
TROILUSES
TROIS
TROJAN
TROJANS
TROKE
TROKED
TROKES
TROKING
TROLAND
TROLANDS
TROLL
TROLLED
TROLLER
TROLLERS
TROLLEY
TROLLEYED
TROLLEYS
TROLLIED
TROLLIES
TROLLING
TROLLINGS
TROLLISH
TROLLIUS
TROLLOP
TROLLOPED
TROLLOPEE
TROLLOPS
TROLLOPY
TROLLS
TROLLY
TROLLYING
TROMBONE
TROMBONES
TROMINO
TROMINOES
TROMINOS
TROMMEL
TROMMELS
TROMP
TROMPE
TROMPED
TROMPES
TROMPING
TROMPS
TRON
TRONA

TRONAS
TRONC
TRONCS
TRONE
TRONES
TRONK
TRONKS
TRONS
TROOLIE
TROOLIES
TROOP
TROOPED
TROOPER
TROOPERS
TROOPIAL
TROOPIALS
TROOPING
TROOPS
TROOPSHIP
TROOSTITE
TROOZ
TROP
TROPAEOLA
TROPARIA
TROPARION
TROPE
TROPED
TROPEOLIN
TROPES
TROPHESY
TROPHI
TROPHIC
TROPHIED
TROPHIES
TROPHY
TROPHYING
TROPIC
TROPICAL
TROPICALS
TROPICS
TROPIN
TROPINE
TROPINES
TROPING
TROPINS
TROPISM
TROPISMS
TROPIST
TROPISTIC
TROPISTS
TROPOLOGY
TROPONIN
TROPONINS
TROPPO
TROSSERS
TROT
TROTH
TROTHED
TROTHFUL
TROTHING
TROTHLESS
TROTHS
TROTLINE
TROTLINES
TROTS
TROTTED
TROTTER
TROTTERS
TROTTING
TROTTINGS
TROTTOIR
TROTTOIRS
TROTYL
TROTYLS
TROU
TROUBLE
TROUBLED
TROUBLER
TROUBLERS
TROUBLES
TROUBLING
TROUBLOUS
TROUCH
TROUCHES
TROUGH
TROUGHED
TROUGHING
TROUGHS
TROULE
TROULED
TROULES
TROULING
TROUNCE
TROUNCED
TROUNCER
TROUNCERS
TROUNCES
TROUNCING
TROUPE
TROUPED
TROUPER
TROUPERS
TROUPES
TROUPIAL
TROUPIALS
TROUPING
TROUSE
TROUSER
TROUSERED
TROUSERS
TROUSES
TROUSSEAU
TROUT
TROUTER
TROUTERS
TROUTFUL
TROUTIER
TROUTIEST
TROUTING
TROUTINGS
TROUTLESS
TROUTLET
TROUTLETS
TROUTLIKE
TROUTLING
TROUTS
TROUTY
TROUVERE
TROUVERES
TROUVEUR
TROUVEURS
TROVE
TROVER
TROVERS
TROVES
TROW
TROWED
TROWEL
TROWELED
TROWELER
TROWELERS
TROWELING
TROWELLED
TROWELLER
TROWELS
TROWING
TROWS
TROWSERS
TROWTH
TROWTHS
TROY
TROYS
TRUANCIES
TRUANCY
TRUANT
TRUANTED
TRUANTING
TRUANTLY
TRUANTRY
TRUANTS
TRUCAGE
TRUCAGES
TRUCE
TRUCED
TRUCELESS
TRUCES
TRUCHMAN
TRUCHMANS
TRUCHMEN
TRUCIAL
TRUCING
TRUCK
TRUCKABLE
TRUCKAGE
TRUCKAGES
TRUCKED
TRUCKER
TRUCKERS
TRUCKFUL
TRUCKFULS
TRUCKIE
TRUCKIES
TRUCKING
TRUCKINGS
TRUCKLE
TRUCKLED
TRUCKLER
TRUCKLERS
TRUCKLES
TRUCKLINE
TRUCKLING
TRUCKLOAD
TRUCKMAN
TRUCKMEN
TRUCKS
TRUCKSTOP
TRUCULENT
TRUDGE
TRUDGED
TRUDGEN
TRUDGENS
TRUDGEON
TRUDGEONS
TRUDGER
TRUDGERS
TRUDGES
TRUDGING
TRUDGINGS
TRUE
TRUEBLUE
TRUEBLUES
TRUEBORN
TRUEBRED
TRUED
TRUEING
TRUELOVE
TRUELOVES
TRUEMAN
TRUEMEN
TRUENESS
TRUEPENNY
TRUER
TRUES
TRUEST
TRUFFE
TRUFFES
TRUFFLE
TRUFFLED
TRUFFLES
TRUFFLING
TRUG
TRUGO
TRUGOS
TRUGS
TRUING
TRUISM
TRUISMS
TRUISTIC
TRULL
TRULLS

TRULY
TRUMEAU
TRUMEAUX
TRUMP
TRUMPED
TRUMPERY
TRUMPET
TRUMPETED
TRUMPETER
TRUMPETS
TRUMPING
TRUMPINGS
TRUMPLESS
TRUMPS
TRUNCAL
TRUNCATE
TRUNCATED
TRUNCATES
TRUNCHEON
TRUNDLE
TRUNDLED
TRUNDLER
TRUNDLERS
TRUNDLES
TRUNDLING
TRUNK
TRUNKED
TRUNKFISH
TRUNKFUL
TRUNKFULS
TRUNKING
TRUNKINGS
TRUNKLESS
TRUNKLIKE
TRUNKS
TRUNKWORK
TRUNNEL
TRUNNELS
TRUNNION
TRUNNIONS
TRUQUAGE
TRUQUAGES
TRUQUEUR
TRUQUEURS
TRUSS
TRUSSED
TRUSSER
TRUSSERS
TRUSSES
TRUSSING
TRUSSINGS
TRUST
TRUSTABLE
TRUSTED
TRUSTEE
TRUSTEED
TRUSTEES
TRUSTER
TRUSTERS
TRUSTFUL
TRUSTIER
TRUSTIES
TRUSTIEST
TRUSTILY
TRUSTING
TRUSTLESS
TRUSTOR
TRUSTORS
TRUSTS
TRUSTY
TRUTH
TRUTHER
TRUTHERS
TRUTHFUL
TRUTHIER
TRUTHIEST
TRUTHLESS
TRUTHLIKE
TRUTHS
TRUTHY
TRY
TRYE
TRYER
TRYERS
TRYING
TRYINGLY
TRYINGS
TRYKE
TRYKES
TRYMA
TRYMATA
TRYOUT
TRYOUTS
TRYP
TRYPAN
TRYPS
TRYPSIN
TRYPSINS
TRYPTIC
TRYSAIL
TRYSAILS
TRYST
TRYSTE
TRYSTED
TRYSTER
TRYSTERS
TRYSTES
TRYSTING
TRYSTS
TRYWORKS
TSADDIK
TSADDIKIM
TSADDIKS
TSADDIQ
TSADDIQIM
TSADDIQS
TSADE
TSADES
TSADI
TSADIK
TSADIKS
TSADIS
TSAMBA
TSAMBAS
TSANTSA
TSANTSAS
TSAR
TSARDOM
TSARDOMS
TSAREVICH
TSAREVNA
TSAREVNAS
TSARINA
TSARINAS
TSARISM
TSARISMS
TSARIST
TSARISTS
TSARITSA
TSARITSAS
TSARITZA
TSARITZAS
TSARS
TSATSKE
TSATSKES
TSESSEBE
TSESSEBES
TSETSE
TSETSES
TSIGANE
TSIGANES
TSIMMES
TSITSITH
TSK
TSKED
TSKING
TSKS
TSKTSK
TSKTSKED
TSKTSKING
TSKTSKS
TSOORIS
TSORES
TSORIS
TSORRISS
TSOTSI
TSOTSIS
TSOURIS
TSOURISES
TSUBA
TSUBAS
TSUBO
TSUBOS
TSUNAMI
TSUNAMIC
TSUNAMIS
TSURIS
TSURISES
TSUTSUMU
TSUTSUMUS
TUAN
TUANS
TUART
TUARTS
TUATARA
TUATARAS
TUATERA
TUATERAS
TUATH
TUATHS
TUATUA
TUATUAS
TUB
TUBA
TUBAE
TUBAGE
TUBAGES
TUBAIST
TUBAISTS
TUBAL
TUBAR
TUBAS
TUBATE
TUBBABLE
TUBBED
TUBBER
TUBBERS
TUBBIER
TUBBIEST
TUBBINESS
TUBBING
TUBBINGS
TUBBISH
TUBBY
TUBE
TUBECTOMY
TUBED
TUBEFUL
TUBEFULS
TUBELESS
TUBELIKE
TUBENOSE
TUBENOSES
TUBER
TUBERCLE
TUBERCLED
TUBERCLES
TUBERCULA
TUBERCULE
TUBEROID
TUBEROIDS
TUBEROSE
TUBEROSES
TUBEROUS
TUBERS
TUBES
TUBEWELL
TUBEWELLS
TUBEWORK
TUBEWORKS

T

TUBEWORM
TUBEWORMS
TUBFAST
TUBFASTS
TUBFISH
TUBFISHES
TUBFUL
TUBFULS
TUBICOLAR
TUBICOLE
TUBICOLES
TUBIFEX
TUBIFEXES
TUBIFICID
TUBIFORM
TUBING
TUBINGS
TUBIST
TUBISTS
TUBLIKE
TUBS
TUBULAR
TUBULARLY
TUBULARS
TUBULATE
TUBULATED
TUBULATES
TUBULATOR
TUBULE
TUBULES
TUBULIN
TUBULINS
TUBULOSE
TUBULOUS
TUBULURE
TUBULURES
TUCHIS
TUCHISES
TUCHUN
TUCHUNS
TUCHUS
TUCHUSES
TUCK
TUCKAHOE
TUCKAHOES
TUCKAMORE
TUCKBOX
TUCKBOXES
TUCKED
TUCKER
TUCKERBAG
TUCKERBOX
TUCKERED
TUCKERING
TUCKERS
TUCKET
TUCKETS
TUCKING
TUCKINGS
TUCKS
TUCKSHOP
TUCKSHOPS
TUCOTUCO
TUCOTUCOS
TUCUTUCO
TUCUTUCOS
TUCUTUCU
TUCUTUCUS
TUFA
TUFACEOUS
TUFAS
TUFF
TUFFE
TUFFES
TUFFET
TUFFETS
TUFFS
TUFOLI
TUFOLIS
TUFT
TUFTED
TUFTER
TUFTERS
TUFTIER
TUFTIEST
TUFTILY
TUFTING
TUFTINGS
TUFTS
TUFTY
TUG
TUGBOAT
TUGBOATS
TUGGED
TUGGER
TUGGERS
TUGGING
TUGGINGLY
TUGGINGS
TUGHRA
TUGHRAS
TUGHRIK
TUGHRIKS
TUGLESS
TUGRA
TUGRAS
TUGRIK
TUGRIKS
TUGS
TUI
TUILE
TUILES
TUILLE
TUILLES
TUILLETTE
TUILYIE
TUILYIED
TUILYIES
TUILZIE
TUILZIED
TUILZIES
TUINA
TUINAS
TUIS
TUISM
TUISMS
TUITION
TUITIONAL
TUITIONS
TUKTOO
TUKTOOS
TUKTU
TUKTUS
TULADI
TULADIS
TULAREMIA
TULAREMIC
TULBAN
TULBANS
TULCHAN
TULCHANS
TULE
TULES
TULIP
TULIPANT
TULIPANTS
TULIPLIKE
TULIPS
TULIPWOOD
TULLE
TULLES
TULLIBEE
TULLIBEES
TULPA
TULPAS
TULSI
TULSIS
TULWAR
TULWARS
TUM
TUMBLE
TUMBLEBUG
TUMBLED
TUMBLER
TUMBLERS
TUMBLES
TUMBLESET
TUMBLING
TUMBLINGS
TUMBREL
TUMBRELS
TUMBRIL
TUMBRILS
TUMEFIED
TUMEFIES
TUMEFY
TUMEFYING
TUMESCE
TUMESCED
TUMESCENT
TUMESCES
TUMESCING
TUMID
TUMIDITY
TUMIDLY
TUMIDNESS
TUMMIES
TUMMLER
TUMMLERS
TUMMY
TUMOR
TUMORAL
TUMORLIKE
TUMOROUS
TUMORS
TUMOUR
TUMOURS
TUMP
TUMPED
TUMPHIES
TUMPHY
TUMPIER
TUMPIEST
TUMPING
TUMPLINE
TUMPLINES
TUMPS
TUMPY
TUMS
TUMSHIE
TUMSHIES
TUMULAR
TUMULARY
TUMULI
TUMULOSE
TUMULOUS
TUMULT
TUMULTED
TUMULTING
TUMULTS
TUMULUS
TUMULUSES
TUN
TUNA
TUNABLE
TUNABLY
TUNAS
TUNBELLY
TUND
TUNDED
TUNDING
TUNDISH
TUNDISHES
TUNDRA
TUNDRAS
TUNDS
TUNDUN
TUNDUNS
TUNE
TUNEABLE

TUNEABLY
TUNEAGE
TUNEAGES
TUNED
TUNEFUL
TUNEFULLY
TUNELESS
TUNER
TUNERS
TUNES
TUNESMITH
TUNEUP
TUNEUPS
TUNG
TUNGS
TUNGSTATE
TUNGSTEN
TUNGSTENS
TUNGSTIC
TUNGSTITE
TUNGSTOUS
TUNIC
TUNICA
TUNICAE
TUNICATE
TUNICATED
TUNICATES
TUNICIN
TUNICINS
TUNICKED
TUNICLE
TUNICLES
TUNICS
TUNIER
TUNIEST
TUNING
TUNINGS
TUNKET
TUNKETS
TUNNAGE
TUNNAGES
TUNNED
TUNNEL
TUNNELED
TUNNELER
TUNNELERS
TUNNELING
TUNNELLED
TUNNELLER
TUNNELS
TUNNIES
TUNNING
TUNNINGS
TUNNY
TUNS
TUNY
TUP
TUPEK
TUPEKS
TUPELO
TUPELOS
TUPIK
TUPIKS
TUPLE
TUPLES
TUPPED
TUPPENCE
TUPPENCES
TUPPENNY
TUPPING
TUPPINGS
TUPS
TUPTOWING
TUPUNA
TUPUNAS
TUQUE
TUQUES
TURACIN
TURACINS
TURACO
TURACOS
TURACOU
TURACOUS
TURBAN
TURBAND
TURBANDS
TURBANED
TURBANNED
TURBANS
TURBANT
TURBANTS
TURBARIES
TURBARY
TURBETH
TURBETHS
TURBID
TURBIDITE
TURBIDITY
TURBIDLY
TURBINAL
TURBINALS
TURBINATE
TURBINE
TURBINED
TURBINES
TURBIT
TURBITH
TURBITHS
TURBITS
TURBO
TURBOCAR
TURBOCARS
TURBOFAN
TURBOFANS
TURBOJET
TURBOJETS
TURBOND
TURBONDS
TURBOPROP
TURBOS
TURBOT
TURBOTS
TURBULENT
TURCOPOLE
TURD
TURDINE
TURDION
TURDIONS
TURDOID
TURDS
TURDUCKEN
TUREEN
TUREENS
TURF
TURFED
TURFEN
TURFGRASS
TURFIER
TURFIEST
TURFINESS
TURFING
TURFINGS
TURFITE
TURFITES
TURFLESS
TURFLIKE
TURFMAN
TURFMEN
TURFS
TURFSKI
TURFSKIS
TURFY
TURGENCY
TURGENT
TURGENTLY
TURGID
TURGIDER
TURGIDEST
TURGIDITY
TURGIDLY
TURGITE
TURGITES
TURGOR
TURGORS
TURION
TURIONS
TURISTA
TURISTAS
TURK
TURKEY
TURKEYS
TURKIES
TURKIESES
TURKIS
TURKISES
TURKOIS
TURKOISES
TURKS
TURLOUGH
TURLOUGHS
TURM
TURME
TURMERIC
TURMERICS
TURMES
TURMOIL
TURMOILED
TURMOILS
TURMS
TURN
TURNABLE
TURNABOUT
TURNAGAIN
TURNBACK
TURNBACKS
TURNCOAT
TURNCOATS
TURNCOCK
TURNCOCKS
TURNDOWN
TURNDOWNS
TURNDUN
TURNDUNS
TURNED
TURNER
TURNERIES
TURNERS
TURNERY
TURNHALL
TURNHALLS
TURNING
TURNINGS
TURNIP
TURNIPED
TURNIPIER
TURNIPING
TURNIPS
TURNIPY
TURNKEY
TURNKEYS
TURNOFF
TURNOFFS
TURNON
TURNONS
TURNOUT
TURNOUTS
TURNOVER
TURNOVERS
TURNPIKE
TURNPIKES
TURNROUND
TURNS
TURNSKIN
TURNSKINS
TURNSOLE
TURNSOLES
TURNSPIT
TURNSPITS
TURNSTILE
TURNSTONE

TURNT
TURNTABLE
TURNUP
TURNUPS
TUROPHILE
TURPETH
TURPETHS
TURPITUDE
TURPS
TURQUOIS
TURQUOISE
TURR
TURRET
TURRETED
TURRETS
TURRIBANT
TURRICAL
TURRS
TURTLE
TURTLED
TURTLER
TURTLERS
TURTLES
TURTLING
TURTLINGS
TURVES
TUSCHE
TUSCHES
TUSH
TUSHED
TUSHERIES
TUSHERY
TUSHES
TUSHIE
TUSHIES
TUSHING
TUSHKAR
TUSHKARS
TUSHKER
TUSHKERS
TUSHY
TUSK
TUSKAR
TUSKARS
TUSKED
TUSKER
TUSKERS
TUSKIER
TUSKIEST
TUSKING
TUSKINGS
TUSKLESS
TUSKLIKE
TUSKS
TUSKY
TUSSAC
TUSSAH
TUSSAHS
TUSSAL
TUSSAR
TUSSARS
TUSSEH
TUSSEHS
TUSSER
TUSSERS
TUSSES
TUSSIS
TUSSISES
TUSSIVE
TUSSLE
TUSSLED
TUSSLES
TUSSLING
TUSSOCK
TUSSOCKED
TUSSOCKS
TUSSOCKY
TUSSOR
TUSSORE
TUSSORES
TUSSORS
TUSSUCK
TUSSUCKS
TUSSUR
TUSSURS
TUT
TUTANIA
TUTANIAS
TUTEE
TUTEES
TUTELAGE
TUTELAGES
TUTELAR
TUTELARS
TUTELARY
TUTENAG
TUTENAGS
TUTIORISM
TUTIORIST
TUTMAN
TUTMEN
TUTOR
TUTORAGE
TUTORAGES
TUTORED
TUTORESS
TUTORIAL
TUTORIALS
TUTORING
TUTORINGS
TUTORISE
TUTORISED
TUTORISES
TUTORISM
TUTORISMS
TUTORIZE
TUTORIZED
TUTORIZES
TUTORS
TUTORSHIP
TUTOYED
TUTOYER
TUTOYERED
TUTOYERS
TUTRESS
TUTRESSES
TUTRICES
TUTRIX
TUTRIXES
TUTS
TUTSAN
TUTSANS
TUTSED
TUTSES
TUTSING
TUTTED
TUTTI
TUTTIES
TUTTING
TUTTINGS
TUTTIS
TUTTY
TUTU
TUTUED
TUTUS
TUTWORK
TUTWORKER
TUTWORKS
TUX
TUXEDO
TUXEDOED
TUXEDOES
TUXEDOS
TUXES
TUYER
TUYERE
TUYERES
TUYERS
TUZZ
TUZZES
TWA
TWADDLE
TWADDLED
TWADDLER
TWADDLERS
TWADDLES
TWADDLIER
TWADDLING
TWADDLY
TWAE
TWAES
TWAFALD
TWAIN
TWAINS
TWAITE
TWAITES
TWAL
TWALPENNY
TWALS
TWANG
TWANGED
TWANGER
TWANGERS
TWANGIER
TWANGIEST
TWANGING
TWANGINGS
TWANGLE
TWANGLED
TWANGLER
TWANGLERS
TWANGLES
TWANGLING
TWANGS
TWANGY
TWANK
TWANKAY
TWANKAYS
TWANKED
TWANKIES
TWANKING
TWANKS
TWANKY
TWAS
TWASOME
TWASOMES
TWAT
TWATS
TWATTED
TWATTING
TWATTLE
TWATTLED
TWATTLER
TWATTLERS
TWATTLES
TWATTLING
TWAY
TWAYBLADE
TWAYS
TWEAK
TWEAKED
TWEAKER
TWEAKERS
TWEAKIER
TWEAKIEST
TWEAKING
TWEAKINGS
TWEAKS
TWEAKY
TWEE
TWEED
TWEEDIER
TWEEDIEST
TWEEDILY
TWEEDLE
TWEEDLED
TWEEDLER
TWEEDLERS
TWEEDLES
TWEEDLING

TWEEDS
TWEEDY
TWEEL
TWEELED
TWEELING
TWEELS
TWEELY
TWEEN
TWEENAGE
TWEENAGER
TWEENER
TWEENERS
TWEENESS
TWEENIE
TWEENIES
TWEENS
TWEENY
TWEEP
TWEEPLE
TWEEPS
TWEER
TWEERED
TWEERING
TWEERS
TWEEST
TWEET
TWEETABLE
TWEETED
TWEETER
TWEETERS
TWEETING
TWEETS
TWEETUP
TWEETUPS
TWEEZE
TWEEZED
TWEEZER
TWEEZERS
TWEEZES
TWEEZING
TWELFTH
TWELFTHLY
TWELFTHS
TWELVE
TWELVEMO
TWELVEMOS
TWELVES
TWENTIES
TWENTIETH
TWENTY
TWENTYISH
TWERK
TWERKED
TWERKING
TWERKINGS
TWERKS
TWERP
TWERPIER
TWERPIEST
TWERPS
TWERPY
TWIBIL
TWIBILL
TWIBILLS
TWIBILS
TWICE
TWICER
TWICERS
TWICHILD
TWIDDLE
TWIDDLED
TWIDDLER
TWIDDLERS
TWIDDLES
TWIDDLIER
TWIDDLING
TWIDDLY
TWIER
TWIERS
TWIFOLD
TWIFORKED
TWIFORMED
TWIG
TWIGGED
TWIGGEN
TWIGGER
TWIGGERS
TWIGGIER
TWIGGIEST
TWIGGING
TWIGGY
TWIGHT
TWIGHTED
TWIGHTING
TWIGHTS
TWIGLESS
TWIGLET
TWIGLETS
TWIGLIKE
TWIGLOO
TWIGLOOS
TWIGS
TWIGSOME
TWILIGHT
TWILIGHTS
TWILIT
TWILL
TWILLED
TWILLIES
TWILLING
TWILLINGS
TWILLS
TWILLY
TWILT
TWILTED
TWILTING
TWILTS
TWIN
TWINBERRY
TWINBORN
TWINE
TWINED
TWINER
TWINERS
TWINES
TWINGE
TWINGED
TWINGEING
TWINGES
TWINGING
TWINIER
TWINIEST
TWINIGHT
TWINING
TWININGLY
TWININGS
TWINJET
TWINJETS
TWINK
TWINKED
TWINKIE
TWINKIES
TWINKING
TWINKLE
TWINKLED
TWINKLER
TWINKLERS
TWINKLES
TWINKLIER
TWINKLING
TWINKLY
TWINKS
TWINKY
TWINLING
TWINLINGS
TWINNED
TWINNING
TWINNINGS
TWINS
TWINSET
TWINSETS
TWINSHIP
TWINSHIPS
TWINTER
TWINTERS
TWINY
TWIRE
TWIRED
TWIRES
TWIRING
TWIRL
TWIRLED
TWIRLER
TWIRLERS
TWIRLIER
TWIRLIEST
TWIRLING
TWIRLS
TWIRLY
TWIRP
TWIRPIER
TWIRPIEST
TWIRPS
TWIRPY
TWISCAR
TWISCARS
TWIST
TWISTABLE
TWISTED
TWISTER
TWISTERS
TWISTIER
TWISTIEST
TWISTING
TWISTINGS
TWISTOR
TWISTORS
TWISTS
TWISTY
TWIT
TWITCH
TWITCHED
TWITCHER
TWITCHERS
TWITCHES
TWITCHIER
TWITCHILY
TWITCHING
TWITCHY
TWITE
TWITES
TWITS
TWITTED
TWITTEN
TWITTENS
TWITTER
TWITTERED
TWITTERER
TWITTERS
TWITTERY
TWITTING
TWITTINGS
TWITTISH
TWIXT
TWIZZLE
TWIZZLED
TWIZZLES
TWIZZLING
TWO
TWOCCER
TWOCCERS
TWOCCING
TWOCCINGS
TWOCKER
TWOCKERS
TWOCKING
TWOCKINGS
TWOER
TWOERS
TWOFER

T

TWOFERS
TWOFOLD
TWOFOLDS
TWONESS
TWONESSES
TWONIE
TWONIES
TWOONIE
TWOONIES
TWOPENCE
TWOPENCES
TWOPENNY
TWOS
TWOSEATER
TWOSOME
TWOSOMES
TWOSTROKE
TWP
TWYER
TWYERE
TWYERES
TWYERS
TWYFOLD
TYCHISM
TYCHISMS
TYCOON
TYCOONATE
TYCOONERY
TYCOONS
TYDE
TYE
TYED
TYEE
TYEES
TYEING
TYER
TYERS
TYES
TYG
TYGS
TYIN
TYING
TYIYN
TYIYNS
TYKE
TYKES
TYKISH
TYLECTOMY
TYLER
TYLERS
TYLOPOD
TYLOPODS
TYLOSES
TYLOSIN
TYLOSINS
TYLOSIS
TYLOTE
TYLOTES
TYMBAL
TYMBALS
TYMP
TYMPAN
TYMPANA
TYMPANAL
TYMPANI
TYMPANIC
TYMPANICS
TYMPANIES
TYMPANIST
TYMPANO
TYMPANS
TYMPANUM
TYMPANUMS
TYMPANY
TYMPS
TYND
TYNDE
TYNE
TYNED
TYNES
TYNING
TYPABLE
TYPAL
TYPE
TYPEABLE
TYPEBAR
TYPEBARS
TYPECASE
TYPECASES
TYPECAST
TYPECASTS
TYPED
TYPEFACE
TYPEFACES
TYPES
TYPESET
TYPESETS
TYPESTYLE
TYPEWRITE
TYPEWROTE
TYPEY
TYPHLITIC
TYPHLITIS
TYPHOID
TYPHOIDAL
TYPHOIDIN
TYPHOIDS
TYPHON
TYPHONIAN
TYPHONIC
TYPHONS
TYPHOON
TYPHOONS
TYPHOSE
TYPHOUS
TYPHUS
TYPHUSES
TYPIC
TYPICAL
TYPICALLY
TYPIER
TYPIEST
TYPIFIED
TYPIFIER
TYPIFIERS
TYPIFIES
TYPIFY
TYPIFYING
TYPING
TYPINGS
TYPIST
TYPISTS
TYPO
TYPOGRAPH
TYPOLOGIC
TYPOLOGY
TYPOMANIA
TYPOS
TYPP
TYPPS
TYPTO
TYPTOED
TYPTOING
TYPTOS
TYPY
TYRAMINE
TYRAMINES
TYRAN
TYRANED
TYRANING
TYRANNE
TYRANNED
TYRANNES
TYRANNESS
TYRANNIC
TYRANNIES
TYRANNING
TYRANNIS
TYRANNISE
TYRANNIZE
TYRANNOUS
TYRANNY
TYRANS
TYRANT
TYRANTED
TYRANTING
TYRANTS
TYRE
TYRED
TYRELESS
TYREMAKER
TYRES
TYRING
TYRO
TYROCIDIN
TYROES
TYRONES
TYRONIC
TYROPITA
TYROPITAS
TYROPITTA
TYROS
TYROSINE
TYROSINES
TYSTIE
TYSTIES
TYTE
TYTHE
TYTHED
TYTHES
TYTHING
TZADDI
TZADDIK
TZADDIKIM
TZADDIKS
TZADDIQ
TZADDIQIM
TZADDIQS
TZADDIS
TZADIK
TZADIKS
TZAR
TZARDOM
TZARDOMS
TZAREVNA
TZAREVNAS
TZARINA
TZARINAS
TZARISM
TZARISMS
TZARIST
TZARISTS
TZARITZA
TZARITZAS
TZARS
TZATZIKI
TZATZIKIS
TZEDAKAH
TZEDAKAHS
TZETSE
TZETSES
TZETZE
TZETZES
TZIGANE
TZIGANES
TZIGANIES
TZIGANY
TZIMMES
TZITZIS
TZITZIT
TZITZITH
TZURIS
TZURISES

U

UAKARI
UAKARIS
UBEROUS
UBERTIES
UBERTY
UBIETIES
UBIETY
UBIQUE
UBIQUITIN
UBIQUITY
UBUNTU
UBUNTUS
UCKERS
UDAL
UDALLER
UDALLERS
UDALS
UDDER
UDDERED
UDDERFUL
UDDERFULS
UDDERLESS
UDDERS
UDO
UDOMETER
UDOMETERS
UDOMETRIC
UDOMETRY
UDON
UDONS
UDOS
UDS
UEY
UEYS
UFO
UFOLOGIES
UFOLOGIST
UFOLOGY
UFOS
UG
UGALI
UGALIS
UGGED
UGGING
UGH
UGHS
UGLIED
UGLIER
UGLIES
UGLIEST
UGLIFIED
UGLIFIER
UGLIFIERS
UGLIFIES
UGLIFY
UGLIFYING
UGLILY
UGLINESS
UGLY
UGLYING
UGS
UGSOME
UH
UHLAN
UHLANS
UHURU
UHURUS
UILLEAN
UILLEANN
UINTAHITE
UINTAITE
UINTAITES
UITLANDER
UJAMAA
UJAMAAS
UKASE
UKASES
UKE
UKELELE
UKELELES
UKES
UKULELE
UKULELES
ULAMA
ULAMAS
ULAN
ULANS
ULCER
ULCERATE
ULCERATED
ULCERATES
ULCERED
ULCERING
ULCEROUS
ULCERS
ULE
ULEMA
ULEMAS
ULES
ULEX
ULEXES
ULEXITE
ULEXITES
ULICES
ULICON
ULICONS
ULIGINOSE
ULIGINOUS
ULIKON
ULIKONS
ULITIS
ULITISES
ULLAGE
ULLAGED
ULLAGES
ULLAGING
ULLING
ULLINGS
ULMACEOUS
ULMIN
ULMINS
ULNA
ULNAD
ULNAE
ULNAR
ULNARE
ULNARIA
ULNAS
ULOSES
ULOSIS
ULOTRICHY
ULPAN
ULPANIM
ULSTER
ULSTERED
ULSTERS
ULTERIOR
ULTIMA
ULTIMACY
ULTIMAS
ULTIMATA
ULTIMATE
ULTIMATED
ULTIMATES
ULTIMATUM
ULTIMO
ULTION
ULTIONS
ULTISOL
ULTISOLS
ULTRA
ULTRACHIC
ULTRACOLD
ULTRACOOL
ULTRADRY
ULTRAFAST
ULTRAFINE
ULTRAHEAT
ULTRAHIGH
ULTRAHIP
ULTRAHOT
ULTRAISM
ULTRAISMS
ULTRAIST
ULTRAISTS
ULTRALEFT
ULTRALOW
ULTRAPOSH
ULTRAPURE
ULTRARARE
ULTRARED
ULTRAREDS
ULTRARICH
ULTRAS
ULTRASAFE
ULTRASLOW
ULTRASOFT
ULTRATHIN
ULTRATINY
ULTRAWIDE
ULU
ULULANT
ULULATE
ULULATED
ULULATES
ULULATING
ULULATION
ULUS
ULVA
ULVAS
ULYIE
ULYIES
ULZIE
ULZIES
UM
UMAMI
UMAMIS
UMANGITE
UMANGITES
UMBEL
UMBELED
UMBELLAR
UMBELLATE
UMBELLED
UMBELLET
UMBELLETS
UMBELLULE
UMBELS
UMBELULE
UMBELULES

UMBER
UMBERED
UMBERIER
UMBERIEST
UMBERING
UMBERS
UMBERY
UMBILICAL
UMBILICI
UMBILICUS
UMBLE
UMBLES
UMBO
UMBONAL
UMBONATE
UMBONES
UMBONIC
UMBOS
UMBRA
UMBRACULA
UMBRAE
UMBRAGE
UMBRAGED
UMBRAGES
UMBRAGING
UMBRAL
UMBRAS
UMBRATED
UMBRATIC
UMBRATILE
UMBRE
UMBREL
UMBRELLA
UMBRELLAS
UMBRELLO
UMBRELLOS
UMBRELS
UMBRERE
UMBRERES
UMBRES
UMBRETTE
UMBRETTES
UMBRIERE
UMBRIERES
UMBRIL
UMBRILS
UMBROSE
UMBROUS
UME
UMEBOSHI
UMEBOSHIS
UMES
UMFAZI
UMFAZIS
UMIAC
UMIACK
UMIACKS
UMIACS
UMIAK
UMIAKS
UMIAQ
UMIAQS
UMLAUT
UMLAUTED
UMLAUTING
UMLAUTS
UMM
UMMA
UMMAH
UMMAHS
UMMAS
UMMED
UMMING
UMP
UMPED
UMPH
UMPHS
UMPIE
UMPIES
UMPING
UMPIRAGE
UMPIRAGES
UMPIRE
UMPIRED
UMPIRES
UMPIRING
UMPS
UMPTEEN
UMPTEENTH
UMPTIER
UMPTIEST
UMPTIETH
UMPTY
UMPY
UMQUHILE
UMRA
UMRAH
UMRAHS
UMRAS
UMS
UMTEENTH
UMU
UMUS
UMWELT
UMWELTS
UMWHILE
UN
UNABASHED
UNABATED
UNABATING
UNABETTED
UNABIDING
UNABJURED
UNABLE
UNABORTED
UNABRADED
UNABUSED
UNABUSIVE
UNACCRUED
UNACCUSED
UNACERBIC
UNACHING
UNACIDIC
UNACTABLE
UNACTED
UNACTIVE
UNACTIVED
UNACTIVES
UNADAPTED
UNADDED
UNADEPT
UNADEPTLY
UNADEPTS
UNADMIRED
UNADOPTED
UNADORED
UNADORNED
UNADULT
UNADVISED
UNAFRAID
UNAGED
UNAGEING
UNAGILE
UNAGING
UNAGREED
UNAI
UNAIDABLE
UNAIDED
UNAIDEDLY
UNAIMED
UNAIRED
UNAIS
UNAKIN
UNAKING
UNAKITE
UNAKITES
UNALARMED
UNALERTED
UNALIGNED
UNALIKE
UNALIST
UNALISTS
UNALIVE
UNALLAYED
UNALLEGED
UNALLIED
UNALLOWED
UNALLOYED
UNALTERED
UNAMASSED
UNAMAZED
UNAMENDED
UNAMERCED
UNAMIABLE
UNAMUSED
UNAMUSING
UNANCHOR
UNANCHORS
UNANELED
UNANIMITY
UNANIMOUS
UNANNEXED
UNANNOYED
UNANXIOUS
UNAPPAREL
UNAPPLIED
UNAPT
UNAPTLY
UNAPTNESS
UNARCHED
UNARGUED
UNARISEN
UNARM
UNARMED
UNARMING
UNARMORED
UNARMS
UNAROUSED
UNARRAYED
UNARTFUL
UNARY
UNASHAMED
UNASKED
UNASSAYED
UNASSUMED
UNASSURED
UNATONED
UNATTIRED
UNATTUNED
UNAU
UNAUDITED
UNAUS
UNAVENGED
UNAVERAGE
UNAVERTED
UNAVOIDED
UNAVOWED
UNAWAKE
UNAWAKED
UNAWARDED
UNAWARE
UNAWARELY
UNAWARES
UNAWED
UNAWESOME
UNAXED
UNBACKED
UNBAFFLED
UNBAG
UNBAGGED
UNBAGGING
UNBAGS
UNBAITED
UNBAKED
UNBALANCE
UNBALE
UNBALED
UNBALES
UNBALING
UNBAN

UNBANDAGE
UNBANDED
UNBANKED
UNBANNED
UNBANNING
UNBANS
UNBAPTISE
UNBAPTIZE
UNBAR
UNBARBED
UNBARE
UNBARED
UNBARES
UNBARING
UNBARK
UNBARKED
UNBARKING
UNBARKS
UNBARRED
UNBARRING
UNBARS
UNBASED
UNBASHFUL
UNBASTED
UNBATED
UNBATHED
UNBE
UNBEAR
UNBEARDED
UNBEARED
UNBEARING
UNBEARS
UNBEATEN
UNBED
UNBEDDED
UNBEDDING
UNBEDS
UNBEEN
UNBEGET
UNBEGETS
UNBEGGED
UNBEGOT
UNBEGUILE
UNBEGUN
UNBEING
UNBEINGS
UNBEKNOWN
UNBELIEF
UNBELIEFS
UNBELIEVE
UNBELOVED
UNBELT
UNBELTED
UNBELTING
UNBELTS
UNBEMUSED
UNBEND
UNBENDED
UNBENDING
UNBENDS
UNBENIGN
UNBENT
UNBEREFT
UNBERUFEN
UNBESEEM
UNBESEEMS
UNBESPEAK
UNBESPOKE
UNBIAS
UNBIASED
UNBIASES
UNBIASING
UNBIASSED
UNBIASSES
UNBID
UNBIDDEN
UNBIGOTED
UNBILLED
UNBIND
UNBINDING
UNBINDS
UNBISHOP
UNBISHOPS
UNBITT
UNBITTED
UNBITTEN
UNBITTER
UNBITTING
UNBITTS
UNBLAMED
UNBLENDED
UNBLENT
UNBLESS
UNBLESSED
UNBLESSES
UNBLEST
UNBLIND
UNBLINDED
UNBLINDS
UNBLOCK
UNBLOCKED
UNBLOCKS
UNBLOODED
UNBLOODY
UNBLOTTED
UNBLOWED
UNBLOWN
UNBLUNTED
UNBLURRED
UNBOARDED
UNBOBBED
UNBODIED
UNBODING
UNBOILED
UNBOLT
UNBOLTED
UNBOLTING
UNBOLTS
UNBONDED
UNBONE
UNBONED
UNBONES
UNBONING
UNBONNET
UNBONNETS
UNBOOKED
UNBOOKISH
UNBOOT
UNBOOTED
UNBOOTING
UNBOOTS
UNBORE
UNBORN
UNBORNE
UNBOSOM
UNBOSOMED
UNBOSOMER
UNBOSOMS
UNBOTTLE
UNBOTTLED
UNBOTTLES
UNBOUGHT
UNBOUNCY
UNBOUND
UNBOUNDED
UNBOWED
UNBOWING
UNBOX
UNBOXED
UNBOXES
UNBOXING
UNBRACE
UNBRACED
UNBRACES
UNBRACING
UNBRAID
UNBRAIDED
UNBRAIDS
UNBRAKE
UNBRAKED
UNBRAKES
UNBRAKING
UNBRANDED
UNBRASTE
UNBRED
UNBREECH
UNBRIDGED
UNBRIDLE
UNBRIDLED
UNBRIDLES
UNBRIEFED
UNBRIGHT
UNBRIZZED
UNBROILED
UNBROKE
UNBROKEN
UNBROWNED
UNBRUISED
UNBRUSED
UNBRUSHED
UNBUCKLE
UNBUCKLED
UNBUCKLES
UNBUDDED
UNBUDGING
UNBUILD
UNBUILDS
UNBUILT
UNBULKIER
UNBULKY
UNBUNDLE
UNBUNDLED
UNBUNDLER
UNBUNDLES
UNBURDEN
UNBURDENS
UNBURIED
UNBURIES
UNBURNED
UNBURNT
UNBURROW
UNBURROWS
UNBURTHEN
UNBURY
UNBURYING
UNBUSIED
UNBUSIER
UNBUSIES
UNBUSIEST
UNBUSTED
UNBUSY
UNBUSYING
UNBUTTON
UNBUTTONS
UNCAGE
UNCAGED
UNCAGES
UNCAGING
UNCAKE
UNCAKED
UNCAKES
UNCAKING
UNCALLED
UNCANDID
UNCANDLED
UNCANDOR
UNCANDORS
UNCANDOUR
UNCANNED
UNCANNIER
UNCANNILY
UNCANNY
UNCANONIC
UNCAP
UNCAPABLE
UNCAPE
UNCAPED
UNCAPES
UNCAPING
UNCAPPED

U

UNCAPPING
UNCAPS
UNCARDED
UNCARED
UNCAREFUL
UNCARING
UNCART
UNCARTED
UNCARTING
UNCARTS
UNCARVED
UNCASE
UNCASED
UNCASES
UNCASHED
UNCASING
UNCASKED
UNCAST
UNCASTED
UNCASTING
UNCASTS
UNCATCHY
UNCATE
UNCATERED
UNCAUGHT
UNCAUSED
UNCE
UNCEASING
UNCEDED
UNCERTAIN
UNCES
UNCESSANT
UNCHAIN
UNCHAINED
UNCHAINS
UNCHAIR
UNCHAIRED
UNCHAIRS
UNCHANCY
UNCHANGED
UNCHARGE
UNCHARGED
UNCHARGES
UNCHARIER
UNCHARITY
UNCHARM
UNCHARMED
UNCHARMS
UNCHARNEL
UNCHARRED
UNCHARTED
UNCHARY
UNCHASTE
UNCHASTER
UNCHECK
UNCHECKED
UNCHECKS
UNCHEERED
UNCHEWED
UNCHIC
UNCHICLY
UNCHILD
UNCHILDED
UNCHILDS
UNCHILLED
UNCHOKE
UNCHOKED
UNCHOKES
UNCHOKING
UNCHOSEN
UNCHRISOM
UNCHURCH
UNCI
UNCIA
UNCIAE
UNCIAL
UNCIALLY
UNCIALS
UNCIFORM
UNCIFORMS
UNCINAL
UNCINARIA
UNCINATE
UNCINATED
UNCINI
UNCINUS
UNCIPHER
UNCIPHERS
UNCITED
UNCIVIL
UNCIVILLY
UNCLAD
UNCLAIMED
UNCLAMP
UNCLAMPED
UNCLAMPS
UNCLARITY
UNCLASP
UNCLASPED
UNCLASPS
UNCLASSED
UNCLASSY
UNCLAWED
UNCLE
UNCLEAN
UNCLEANED
UNCLEANER
UNCLEANLY
UNCLEAR
UNCLEARED
UNCLEARER
UNCLEARLY
UNCLED
UNCLEFT
UNCLENCH
UNCLES
UNCLESHIP
UNCLEW
UNCLEWED
UNCLEWING
UNCLEWS
UNCLICHED
UNCLIMBED
UNCLINCH
UNCLING
UNCLIP
UNCLIPPED
UNCLIPS
UNCLIPT
UNCLOAK
UNCLOAKED
UNCLOAKS
UNCLOG
UNCLOGGED
UNCLOGS
UNCLONED
UNCLOSE
UNCLOSED
UNCLOSES
UNCLOSING
UNCLOTHE
UNCLOTHED
UNCLOTHES
UNCLOUD
UNCLOUDED
UNCLOUDS
UNCLOUDY
UNCLOVEN
UNCLOYED
UNCLOYING
UNCLUTCH
UNCLUTTER
UNCO
UNCOATED
UNCOATING
UNCOBBLED
UNCOCK
UNCOCKED
UNCOCKING
UNCOCKS
UNCODED
UNCOER
UNCOERCED
UNCOES
UNCOEST
UNCOFFIN
UNCOFFINS
UNCOIL
UNCOILED
UNCOILING
UNCOILS
UNCOINED
UNCOLORED
UNCOLT
UNCOLTED
UNCOLTING
UNCOLTS
UNCOMBED
UNCOMBINE
UNCOMELY
UNCOMFIER
UNCOMFY
UNCOMIC
UNCOMMON
UNCONCERN
UNCONFINE
UNCONFORM
UNCONFUSE
UNCONGEAL
UNCOOKED
UNCOOL
UNCOOLED
UNCOPE
UNCOPED
UNCOPES
UNCOPING
UNCORD
UNCORDED
UNCORDIAL
UNCORDING
UNCORDS
UNCORK
UNCORKED
UNCORKING
UNCORKS
UNCORRUPT
UNCOS
UNCOSTLY
UNCOUNTED
UNCOUPLE
UNCOUPLED
UNCOUPLER
UNCOUPLES
UNCOURTLY
UNCOUTH
UNCOUTHER
UNCOUTHLY
UNCOVER
UNCOVERED
UNCOVERS
UNCOWL
UNCOWLED
UNCOWLING
UNCOWLS
UNCOY
UNCOYNED
UNCRACKED
UNCRATE
UNCRATED
UNCRATES
UNCRATING
UNCRAZIER
UNCRAZY
UNCREASED
UNCREATE
UNCREATED
UNCREATES
UNCREWED
UNCROPPED
UNCROSS

UNCROSSED
UNCROSSES
UNCROWDED
UNCROWN
UNCROWNED
UNCROWNS
UNCRUDDED
UNCRUMPLE
UNCRUSHED
UNCTION
UNCTIONS
UNCTUOUS
UNCUFF
UNCUFFED
UNCUFFING
UNCUFFS
UNCULLED
UNCURABLE
UNCURABLY
UNCURB
UNCURBED
UNCURBING
UNCURBS
UNCURDLED
UNCURED
UNCURIOUS
UNCURL
UNCURLED
UNCURLING
UNCURLS
UNCURRENT
UNCURSE
UNCURSED
UNCURSES
UNCURSING
UNCURTAIN
UNCURVED
UNCUS
UNCUT
UNCUTE
UNCYNICAL
UNDAM
UNDAMAGED
UNDAMMED
UNDAMMING
UNDAMNED
UNDAMPED
UNDAMS
UNDARING
UNDASHED
UNDATABLE
UNDATE
UNDATED
UNDATES
UNDATING
UNDAUNTED
UNDAWNING
UNDAZZLE
UNDAZZLED
UNDAZZLES
UNDE
UNDEAD
UNDEAF
UNDEAFED
UNDEAFING
UNDEAFS
UNDEALT
UNDEAR
UNDEBASED
UNDEBATED
UNDECAGON
UNDECAYED
UNDECEIVE
UNDECENT
UNDECIDED
UNDECIMAL
UNDECK
UNDECKED
UNDECKING
UNDECKS
UNDEE
UNDEEDED
UNDEFACED
UNDEFIDE
UNDEFIED
UNDEFILED
UNDEFINED
UNDEIFIED
UNDEIFIES
UNDEIFY
UNDELAYED
UNDELETE
UNDELETED
UNDELETES
UNDELIGHT
UNDELUDED
UNDENIED
UNDENTED
UNDER
UNDERACT
UNDERACTS
UNDERAGE
UNDERAGED
UNDERAGES
UNDERARM
UNDERARMS
UNDERATE
UNDERBAKE
UNDERBEAR
UNDERBID
UNDERBIDS
UNDERBIT
UNDERBITE
UNDERBODY
UNDERBORE
UNDERBOSS
UNDERBRED
UNDERBRIM
UNDERBUD
UNDERBUDS
UNDERBUSH
UNDERBUY
UNDERBUYS
UNDERCARD
UNDERCART
UNDERCAST
UNDERCLAD
UNDERCLAY
UNDERCLUB
UNDERCOAT
UNDERCOOK
UNDERCOOL
UNDERCUT
UNDERCUTS
UNDERDAKS
UNDERDECK
UNDERDID
UNDERDO
UNDERDOER
UNDERDOES
UNDERDOG
UNDERDOGS
UNDERDONE
UNDERDOSE
UNDERDRAW
UNDERDREW
UNDEREAT
UNDEREATS
UNDERFED
UNDERFEED
UNDERFELT
UNDERFIRE
UNDERFISH
UNDERFLOW
UNDERFONG
UNDERFOOT
UNDERFUND
UNDERFUR
UNDERFURS
UNDERGIRD
UNDERGIRT
UNDERGO
UNDERGOD
UNDERGODS
UNDERGOER
UNDERGOES
UNDERGONE
UNDERGOWN
UNDERGRAD
UNDERHAIR
UNDERHAND
UNDERHEAT
UNDERHUNG
UNDERIVED
UNDERJAW
UNDERJAWS
UNDERKEEP
UNDERKEPT
UNDERKILL
UNDERKING
UNDERLAID
UNDERLAIN
UNDERLAP
UNDERLAPS
UNDERLAY
UNDERLAYS
UNDERLEAF
UNDERLET
UNDERLETS
UNDERLIE
UNDERLIER
UNDERLIES
UNDERLINE
UNDERLING
UNDERLIP
UNDERLIPS
UNDERLIT
UNDERLOAD
UNDERMAN
UNDERMANS
UNDERMEN
UNDERMINE
UNDERMOST
UNDERN
UNDERNOTE
UNDERNS
UNDERPAD
UNDERPADS
UNDERPAID
UNDERPART
UNDERPASS
UNDERPAY
UNDERPAYS
UNDERPEEP
UNDERPIN
UNDERPINS
UNDERPLAY
UNDERPLOT
UNDERPROP
UNDERRAN
UNDERRATE
UNDERRIPE
UNDERRUN
UNDERRUNS
UNDERSAID
UNDERSAY
UNDERSAYS
UNDERSEA
UNDERSEAL
UNDERSEAS
UNDERSELF
UNDERSELL
UNDERSET
UNDERSETS
UNDERSHOT
UNDERSIDE
UNDERSIGN
UNDERSIZE
UNDERSKY
UNDERSOIL

UNDERSOLD
UNDERSONG
UNDERSOW
UNDERSOWN
UNDERSOWS
UNDERSPIN
UNDERTAKE
UNDERTANE
UNDERTAX
UNDERTIME
UNDERTINT
UNDERTONE
UNDERTOOK
UNDERTOW
UNDERTOWS
UNDERUSE
UNDERUSED
UNDERUSES
UNDERVEST
UNDERVOTE
UNDERWAY
UNDERWEAR
UNDERWENT
UNDERWING
UNDERWIRE
UNDERWIT
UNDERWITS
UNDERWOOD
UNDERWOOL
UNDERWORK
UNDESERT
UNDESERTS
UNDESERVE
UNDESIRED
UNDEVOUT
UNDID
UNDIES
UNDIGHT
UNDIGHTS
UNDIGNIFY
UNDILUTED
UNDIMMED
UNDINE
UNDINES
UNDINISM
UNDINISMS
UNDINTED
UNDIPPED
UNDIVIDED
UNDIVINE
UNDO
UNDOABLE
UNDOCILE
UNDOCK
UNDOCKED
UNDOCKING
UNDOCKS
UNDOER
UNDOERS
UNDOES
UNDOING
UNDOINGS
UNDONE
UNDOOMED
UNDOS
UNDOTTED
UNDOUBLE
UNDOUBLED
UNDOUBLES
UNDOUBTED
UNDOWERED
UNDRAINED
UNDRAPE
UNDRAPED
UNDRAPES
UNDRAPING
UNDRAW
UNDRAWING
UNDRAWN
UNDRAWS
UNDREADED
UNDREAMED
UNDREAMT
UNDRESS
UNDRESSED
UNDRESSES
UNDREST
UNDREW
UNDRIED
UNDRILLED
UNDRIVEN
UNDROSSY
UNDROWNED
UNDRUNK
UNDUBBED
UNDUE
UNDUG
UNDULANCE
UNDULANCY
UNDULANT
UNDULAR
UNDULATE
UNDULATED
UNDULATES
UNDULATOR
UNDULLED
UNDULOSE
UNDULOUS
UNDULY
UNDUTEOUS
UNDUTIFUL
UNDY
UNDYED
UNDYING
UNDYINGLY
UNDYNAMIC
UNEAGER
UNEAGERLY
UNEARED
UNEARNED
UNEARTH
UNEARTHED
UNEARTHLY
UNEARTHS
UNEASE
UNEASES
UNEASIER
UNEASIEST
UNEASILY
UNEASY
UNEATABLE
UNEATEN
UNEATH
UNEATHES
UNEDGE
UNEDGED
UNEDGES
UNEDGING
UNEDIBLE
UNEDITED
UNEFFACED
UNELATED
UNELECTED
UNEMPTIED
UNENDED
UNENDING
UNENDOWED
UNENGAGED
UNENJOYED
UNENSURED
UNENTERED
UNENVIED
UNENVIOUS
UNENVYING
UNEQUABLE
UNEQUAL
UNEQUALED
UNEQUALLY
UNEQUALS
UNERASED
UNEROTIC
UNERRING
UNERUPTED
UNESPIED
UNESSAYED
UNESSENCE
UNETH
UNETHICAL
UNEVADED
UNEVEN
UNEVENER
UNEVENEST
UNEVENLY
UNEVOLVED
UNEXALTED
UNEXCITED
UNEXCUSED
UNEXOTIC
UNEXPERT
UNEXPIRED
UNEXPOSED
UNEXTINCT
UNEXTREME
UNEYED
UNFABLED
UNFACETED
UNFACT
UNFACTS
UNFADABLE
UNFADED
UNFADING
UNFAILING
UNFAIR
UNFAIRED
UNFAIRER
UNFAIREST
UNFAIRING
UNFAIRLY
UNFAIRS
UNFAITH
UNFAITHS
UNFAKED
UNFALLEN
UNFAMED
UNFAMOUS
UNFANCIED
UNFANCIER
UNFANCY
UNFANNED
UNFASTEN
UNFASTENS
UNFAULTY
UNFAVORED
UNFAZABLE
UNFAZED
UNFEARED
UNFEARFUL
UNFEARING
UNFED
UNFEED
UNFEELING
UNFEIGNED
UNFELLED
UNFELT
UNFELTED
UNFENCE
UNFENCED
UNFENCES
UNFENCING
UNFERTILE
UNFETTER
UNFETTERS
UNFEUDAL
UNFEUED
UNFIGURED
UNFILDE
UNFILED
UNFILIAL
UNFILLED
UNFILMED

U

UNFINE
UNFIRED
UNFIRM
UNFISHED
UNFIT
UNFITLY
UNFITNESS
UNFITS
UNFITTED
UNFITTER
UNFITTEST
UNFITTING
UNFIX
UNFIXED
UNFIXES
UNFIXING
UNFIXITY
UNFIXT
UNFLAPPED
UNFLASHY
UNFLAWED
UNFLEDGED
UNFLESH
UNFLESHED
UNFLESHES
UNFLESHLY
UNFLEXED
UNFLOORED
UNFLUSH
UNFLUSHED
UNFLUSHES
UNFLUTED
UNFLYABLE
UNFOCUSED
UNFOILED
UNFOLD
UNFOLDED
UNFOLDER
UNFOLDERS
UNFOLDING
UNFOLDS
UNFOLLOW
UNFOLLOWS
UNFOND
UNFONDLY
UNFOOL
UNFOOLED
UNFOOLING
UNFOOLS
UNFOOTED
UNFORBID
UNFORCED
UNFORGED
UNFORGOT
UNFORKED
UNFORM
UNFORMAL
UNFORMED
UNFORMING
UNFORMS
UNFORTUNE
UNFOUGHT
UNFOUND
UNFOUNDED
UNFRAMED
UNFRANKED
UNFRAUGHT
UNFREE
UNFREED
UNFREEDOM
UNFREEING
UNFREEMAN
UNFREEMEN
UNFREES
UNFREEZE
UNFREEZES
UNFRETTED
UNFRIEND
UNFRIENDS
UNFROCK
UNFROCKED
UNFROCKS
UNFROZE
UNFROZEN
UNFUELLED
UNFUMED
UNFUNDED
UNFUNNIER
UNFUNNILY
UNFUNNY
UNFURL
UNFURLED
UNFURLING
UNFURLS
UNFURNISH
UNFURRED
UNFUSED
UNFUSSED
UNFUSSIER
UNFUSSILY
UNFUSSY
UNGAG
UNGAGGED
UNGAGGING
UNGAGS
UNGAIN
UNGAINFUL
UNGAINLY
UNGALLANT
UNGALLED
UNGARBED
UNGARBLED
UNGATED
UNGAUGED
UNGAZED
UNGAZING
UNGEAR
UNGEARED
UNGEARING
UNGEARS
UNGELDED
UNGENIAL
UNGENTEEL
UNGENTLE
UNGENTLER
UNGENTLY
UNGENUINE
UNGERMANE
UNGET
UNGETS
UNGETTING
UNGHOSTED
UNGHOSTLY
UNGIFTED
UNGILD
UNGILDED
UNGILDING
UNGILDS
UNGILT
UNGIRD
UNGIRDED
UNGIRDING
UNGIRDS
UNGIRT
UNGIRTH
UNGIRTHED
UNGIRTHS
UNGIVING
UNGLAD
UNGLAZED
UNGLITZY
UNGLOSSED
UNGLOVE
UNGLOVED
UNGLOVES
UNGLOVING
UNGLUE
UNGLUED
UNGLUES
UNGLUING
UNGOD
UNGODDED
UNGODDING
UNGODLIER
UNGODLIKE
UNGODLILY
UNGODLY
UNGODS
UNGORD
UNGORED
UNGORGED
UNGOT
UNGOTTEN
UNGOWN
UNGOWNED
UNGOWNING
UNGOWNS
UNGRACED
UNGRADED
UNGRASSED
UNGRAVELY
UNGRAZED
UNGREASED
UNGREEDY
UNGREEN
UNGREENER
UNGROOMED
UNGROUND
UNGROUP
UNGROUPED
UNGROUPS
UNGROWN
UNGRUDGED
UNGUAL
UNGUARD
UNGUARDED
UNGUARDS
UNGUENT
UNGUENTA
UNGUENTS
UNGUENTUM
UNGUES
UNGUESSED
UNGUIDED
UNGUIFORM
UNGUILTY
UNGUINOUS
UNGUIS
UNGULA
UNGULAE
UNGULAR
UNGULATE
UNGULATES
UNGULED
UNGUM
UNGUMMED
UNGUMMING
UNGUMS
UNGYVE
UNGYVED
UNGYVES
UNGYVING
UNHABLE
UNHACKED
UNHAILED
UNHAIR
UNHAIRED
UNHAIRER
UNHAIRERS
UNHAIRING
UNHAIRS
UNHALLOW
UNHALLOWS
UNHALSED
UNHALVED
UNHAND
UNHANDED
UNHANDIER
UNHANDILY
UNHANDING

U

UNHANDLED
UNHANDS
UNHANDY
UNHANG
UNHANGED
UNHANGING
UNHANGS
UNHAPPEN
UNHAPPENS
UNHAPPIED
UNHAPPIER
UNHAPPIES
UNHAPPILY
UNHAPPY
UNHARBOUR
UNHARDIER
UNHARDY
UNHARMED
UNHARMFUL
UNHARMING
UNHARNESS
UNHARRIED
UNHASP
UNHASPED
UNHASPING
UNHASPS
UNHASTIER
UNHASTING
UNHASTY
UNHAT
UNHATCHED
UNHATS
UNHATTED
UNHATTING
UNHAUNTED
UNHEAD
UNHEADED
UNHEADING
UNHEADS
UNHEAL
UNHEALED
UNHEALING
UNHEALS
UNHEALTH
UNHEALTHS
UNHEALTHY
UNHEARD
UNHEARSE
UNHEARSED
UNHEARSES
UNHEART
UNHEARTED
UNHEARTS
UNHEATED
UNHEDGED
UNHEEDED
UNHEEDFUL
UNHEEDIER
UNHEEDILY
UNHEEDING
UNHEEDY
UNHELE
UNHELED
UNHELES
UNHELING
UNHELM
UNHELMED
UNHELMING
UNHELMS
UNHELPED
UNHELPFUL
UNHEMMED
UNHEPPEN
UNHEROIC
UNHERST
UNHEWN
UNHIDDEN
UNHINGE
UNHINGED
UNHINGES
UNHINGING
UNHIP
UNHIPPER
UNHIPPEST
UNHIRABLE
UNHIRED
UNHITCH
UNHITCHED
UNHITCHES
UNHIVE
UNHIVED
UNHIVES
UNHIVING
UNHOARD
UNHOARDED
UNHOARDS
UNHOLIER
UNHOLIEST
UNHOLILY
UNHOLPEN
UNHOLSTER
UNHOLY
UNHOMELY
UNHONEST
UNHONORED
UNHOOD
UNHOODED
UNHOODING
UNHOODS
UNHOOK
UNHOOKED
UNHOOKING
UNHOOKS
UNHOOP
UNHOOPED
UNHOOPING
UNHOOPS
UNHOPED
UNHOPEFUL
UNHORSE
UNHORSED
UNHORSES
UNHORSING
UNHOSTILE
UNHOUSE
UNHOUSED
UNHOUSES
UNHOUSING
UNHUMAN
UNHUMANLY
UNHUMBLED
UNHUNG
UNHUNTED
UNHURRIED
UNHURT
UNHURTFUL
UNHUSK
UNHUSKED
UNHUSKING
UNHUSKS
UNI
UNIALGAL
UNIAXIAL
UNIBODIES
UNIBODY
UNIBROW
UNIBROWS
UNICA
UNICED
UNICITIES
UNICITY
UNICOLOR
UNICOLOUR
UNICOM
UNICOMS
UNICORN
UNICORNS
UNICUM
UNICYCLE
UNICYCLED
UNICYCLES
UNIDEAED
UNIDEAL
UNIFACE
UNIFACES
UNIFIABLE
UNIFIC
UNIFIED
UNIFIER
UNIFIERS
UNIFIES
UNIFILAR
UNIFORM
UNIFORMED
UNIFORMER
UNIFORMLY
UNIFORMS
UNIFY
UNIFYING
UNIFYINGS
UNIGNITED
UNIJUGATE
UNILINEAL
UNILINEAR
UNILLUMED
UNILOBAR
UNILOBED
UNIMBUED
UNIMODAL
UNIMPEDED
UNIMPOSED
UNINCITED
UNINDEXED
UNINJURED
UNINSTAL
UNINSTALL
UNINSTALS
UNINSURED
UNINURED
UNINVITED
UNINVOKED
UNION
UNIONISE
UNIONISED
UNIONISER
UNIONISES
UNIONISM
UNIONISMS
UNIONIST
UNIONISTS
UNIONIZE
UNIONIZED
UNIONIZER
UNIONIZES
UNIONS
UNIPAROUS
UNIPED
UNIPEDS
UNIPLANAR
UNIPOD
UNIPODS
UNIPOLAR
UNIPOTENT
UNIQUE
UNIQUELY
UNIQUER
UNIQUES
UNIQUEST
UNIRAMOSE
UNIRAMOUS
UNIRONED
UNIRONIC
UNIS
UNISERIAL
UNISEX
UNISEXES
UNISEXUAL
UNISIZE
UNISON
UNISONAL

UNISONANT
UNISONOUS
UNISONS
UNISSUED
UNIT
UNITAGE
UNITAGES
UNITAL
UNITARD
UNITARDS
UNITARIAN
UNITARILY
UNITARITY
UNITARY
UNITE
UNITED
UNITEDLY
UNITER
UNITERS
UNITES
UNITIES
UNITING
UNITINGS
UNITION
UNITIONS
UNITISE
UNITISED
UNITISER
UNITISERS
UNITISES
UNITISING
UNITIVE
UNITIVELY
UNITIZE
UNITIZED
UNITIZER
UNITIZERS
UNITIZES
UNITIZING
UNITRUST
UNITRUSTS
UNITS
UNITY
UNIVALENT
UNIVALVE
UNIVALVED
UNIVALVES
UNIVERSAL
UNIVERSE
UNIVERSES
UNIVOCAL
UNIVOCALS
UNJADED
UNJAM
UNJAMMED
UNJAMMING
UNJAMS
UNJEALOUS
UNJOINED
UNJOINT
UNJOINTED
UNJOINTS
UNJOYFUL
UNJOYOUS
UNJUDGED
UNJUST
UNJUSTER
UNJUSTEST
UNJUSTLY
UNKED
UNKEELED
UNKEMPT
UNKEMPTLY
UNKEND
UNKENNED
UNKENNEL
UNKENNELS
UNKENT
UNKEPT
UNKET
UNKID
UNKIND
UNKINDER
UNKINDEST
UNKINDLED
UNKINDLY
UNKING
UNKINGED
UNKINGING
UNKINGLY
UNKINGS
UNKINK
UNKINKED
UNKINKING
UNKINKS
UNKISS
UNKISSED
UNKISSES
UNKISSING
UNKNELLED
UNKNIGHT
UNKNIGHTS
UNKNIT
UNKNITS
UNKNITTED
UNKNOT
UNKNOTS
UNKNOTTED
UNKNOWING
UNKNOWN
UNKNOWNS
UNKOSHER
UNLABELED
UNLABORED
UNLACE
UNLACED
UNLACES
UNLACING
UNLADE
UNLADED
UNLADEN
UNLADES
UNLADING
UNLADINGS
UNLAID
UNLASH
UNLASHED
UNLASHES
UNLASHING
UNLAST
UNLASTE
UNLATCH
UNLATCHED
UNLATCHES
UNLAW
UNLAWED
UNLAWFUL
UNLAWING
UNLAWS
UNLAY
UNLAYING
UNLAYS
UNLEAD
UNLEADED
UNLEADEDS
UNLEADING
UNLEADS
UNLEAL
UNLEARN
UNLEARNED
UNLEARNS
UNLEARNT
UNLEASED
UNLEASH
UNLEASHED
UNLEASHES
UNLED
UNLESS
UNLET
UNLETHAL
UNLETTED
UNLEVEL
UNLEVELED
UNLEVELS
UNLEVIED
UNLICH
UNLICKED
UNLID
UNLIDDED
UNLIDDING
UNLIDS
UNLIGHTED
UNLIKABLE
UNLIKE
UNLIKED
UNLIKELY
UNLIKES
UNLIMBER
UNLIMBERS
UNLIME
UNLIMED
UNLIMES
UNLIMING
UNLIMITED
UNLINE
UNLINEAL
UNLINED
UNLINES
UNLINING
UNLINK
UNLINKED
UNLINKING
UNLINKS
UNLISTED
UNLIT
UNLIVABLE
UNLIVE
UNLIVED
UNLIVELY
UNLIVES
UNLIVING
UNLOAD
UNLOADED
UNLOADER
UNLOADERS
UNLOADING
UNLOADS
UNLOBED
UNLOCATED
UNLOCK
UNLOCKED
UNLOCKING
UNLOCKS
UNLOGICAL
UNLOOKED
UNLOOSE
UNLOOSED
UNLOOSEN
UNLOOSENS
UNLOOSES
UNLOOSING
UNLOPPED
UNLORD
UNLORDED
UNLORDING
UNLORDLY
UNLORDS
UNLOSABLE
UNLOST
UNLOVABLE
UNLOVE
UNLOVED
UNLOVELY
UNLOVES
UNLOVING
UNLUCKIER
UNLUCKILY
UNLUCKY
UNLYRICAL
UNMACHO

U

UNMADE
UNMAILED
UNMAIMED
UNMAKABLE
UNMAKE
UNMAKER
UNMAKERS
UNMAKES
UNMAKING
UNMAKINGS
UNMAN
UNMANACLE
UNMANAGED
UNMANFUL
UNMANLIER
UNMANLIKE
UNMANLY
UNMANNED
UNMANNING
UNMANNISH
UNMANS
UNMANTLE
UNMANTLED
UNMANTLES
UNMANURED
UNMAPPED
UNMARD
UNMARKED
UNMARRED
UNMARRIED
UNMARRIES
UNMARRY
UNMASK
UNMASKED
UNMASKER
UNMASKERS
UNMASKING
UNMASKS
UNMATCHED
UNMATED
UNMATTED
UNMATURED
UNMEANING
UNMEANT
UNMEEK
UNMEET
UNMEETLY
UNMELLOW
UNMELTED
UNMENDED
UNMERITED
UNMERRIER
UNMERRY
UNMESH
UNMESHED
UNMESHES
UNMESHING
UNMET
UNMETED
UNMETERED
UNMEW
UNMEWED
UNMEWING
UNMEWS
UNMILKED
UNMILLED
UNMINDED
UNMINDFUL
UNMINED
UNMINGLE
UNMINGLED
UNMINGLES
UNMIRIER
UNMIRIEST
UNMIRY
UNMISSED
UNMITER
UNMITERED
UNMITERS
UNMITRE
UNMITRED
UNMITRES
UNMITRING
UNMIX
UNMIXABLE
UNMIXED
UNMIXEDLY
UNMIXES
UNMIXING
UNMIXT
UNMOANED
UNMODISH
UNMOLD
UNMOLDED
UNMOLDING
UNMOLDS
UNMOLTEN
UNMONEYED
UNMONIED
UNMOOR
UNMOORED
UNMOORING
UNMOORS
UNMORAL
UNMORALLY
UNMORTISE
UNMOTIVED
UNMOULD
UNMOULDED
UNMOULDS
UNMOUNT
UNMOUNTED
UNMOUNTS
UNMOURNED
UNMOVABLE
UNMOVABLY
UNMOVED
UNMOVEDLY
UNMOVING
UNMOWN
UNMUFFLE
UNMUFFLED
UNMUFFLES
UNMUSICAL
UNMUZZLE
UNMUZZLED
UNMUZZLES
UNNAIL
UNNAILED
UNNAILING
UNNAILS
UNNAMABLE
UNNAMED
UNNANELD
UNNATIVE
UNNATIVED
UNNATIVES
UNNATURAL
UNNEATH
UNNEEDED
UNNEEDFUL
UNNERVE
UNNERVED
UNNERVES
UNNERVING
UNNEST
UNNESTED
UNNESTING
UNNESTS
UNNETHES
UNNETTED
UNNOBLE
UNNOBLED
UNNOBLES
UNNOBLING
UNNOISIER
UNNOISY
UNNOTED
UNNOTICED
UNNUANCED
UNOAKED
UNOBEYED
UNOBVIOUS
UNOFFERED
UNOFTEN
UNOILED
UNOPEN
UNOPENED
UNOPPOSED
UNORDER
UNORDERED
UNORDERLY
UNORDERS
UNORNATE
UNOWED
UNOWNED
UNPACED
UNPACK
UNPACKED
UNPACKER
UNPACKERS
UNPACKING
UNPACKS
UNPADDED
UNPAGED
UNPAID
UNPAINED
UNPAINFUL
UNPAINT
UNPAINTED
UNPAINTS
UNPAIRED
UNPALSIED
UNPANEL
UNPANELS
UNPANGED
UNPANNEL
UNPANNELS
UNPAPER
UNPAPERED
UNPAPERS
UNPARED
UNPARTED
UNPARTIAL
UNPATCHED
UNPATHED
UNPAVED
UNPAY
UNPAYABLE
UNPAYING
UNPAYS
UNPEELED
UNPEERED
UNPEG
UNPEGGED
UNPEGGING
UNPEGS
UNPEN
UNPENNED
UNPENNIED
UNPENNING
UNPENS
UNPENT
UNPEOPLE
UNPEOPLED
UNPEOPLES
UNPERCH
UNPERCHED
UNPERCHES
UNPERFECT
UNPERPLEX
UNPERSON
UNPERSONS
UNPERVERT
UNPICK
UNPICKED
UNPICKING
UNPICKS
UNPIERCED
UNPILE

UNPILED
UNPILES
UNPILING
UNPILOTED
UNPIN
UNPINKED
UNPINKT
UNPINNED
UNPINNING
UNPINS
UNPITIED
UNPITIFUL
UNPITTED
UNPITYING
UNPLACE
UNPLACED
UNPLACES
UNPLACING
UNPLAGUED
UNPLAINED
UNPLAIT
UNPLAITED
UNPLAITS
UNPLANKED
UNPLANNED
UNPLANTED
UNPLAYED
UNPLEASED
UNPLEATED
UNPLEDGED
UNPLIABLE
UNPLIABLY
UNPLIANT
UNPLOWED
UNPLUCKED
UNPLUG
UNPLUGGED
UNPLUGS
UNPLUMB
UNPLUMBED
UNPLUMBS
UNPLUME
UNPLUMED
UNPLUMES
UNPLUMING
UNPOETIC
UNPOINTED
UNPOISED
UNPOISON
UNPOISONS
UNPOLICED
UNPOLISH
UNPOLITE
UNPOLITIC
UNPOLLED
UNPOPE
UNPOPED
UNPOPES
UNPOPING
UNPOPULAR
UNPOSED
UNPOSTED
UNPOTABLE
UNPOTTED
UNPOURED
UNPOWERED
UNPRAISE
UNPRAISED
UNPRAISES
UNPRAY
UNPRAYED
UNPRAYING
UNPRAYS
UNPREACH
UNPRECISE
UNPREDICT
UNPREPARE
UNPRESSED
UNPRETTY
UNPRICED
UNPRIEST
UNPRIESTS
UNPRIMED
UNPRINTED
UNPRISON
UNPRISONS
UNPRIZED
UNPROBED
UNPROP
UNPROPER
UNPROPPED
UNPROPS
UNPROVED
UNPROVEN
UNPROVIDE
UNPROVOKE
UNPRUNED
UNPUCKER
UNPUCKERS
UNPULLED
UNPURE
UNPURELY
UNPURGED
UNPURSE
UNPURSED
UNPURSES
UNPURSING
UNPURSUED
UNPUZZLE
UNPUZZLED
UNPUZZLES
UNQUAKING
UNQUALIFY
UNQUEEN
UNQUEENED
UNQUEENLY
UNQUEENS
UNQUELLED
UNQUIET
UNQUIETED
UNQUIETER
UNQUIETLY
UNQUIETS
UNQUOTE
UNQUOTED
UNQUOTES
UNQUOTING
UNRACED
UNRACKED
UNRAISED
UNRAKE
UNRAKED
UNRAKES
UNRAKING
UNRANKED
UNRATED
UNRAVAGED
UNRAVEL
UNRAVELED
UNRAVELS
UNRAZED
UNRAZORED
UNREACHED
UNREAD
UNREADIER
UNREADILY
UNREADY
UNREAL
UNREALISE
UNREALISM
UNREALITY
UNREALIZE
UNREALLY
UNREAPED
UNREASON
UNREASONS
UNREAVE
UNREAVED
UNREAVES
UNREAVING
UNREBATED
UNREBUKED
UNRECKED
UNRED
UNREDREST
UNREDUCED
UNREDY
UNREEL
UNREELED
UNREELER
UNREELERS
UNREELING
UNREELS
UNREEVE
UNREEVED
UNREEVES
UNREEVING
UNREFINED
UNREFUTED
UNREIN
UNREINED
UNREINING
UNREINS
UNRELATED
UNRELAXED
UNREMOVED
UNRENEWED
UNRENT
UNRENTED
UNREPAID
UNREPAIR
UNREPAIRS
UNRESERVE
UNREST
UNRESTED
UNRESTFUL
UNRESTING
UNRESTS
UNRETIRE
UNRETIRED
UNRETIRES
UNREVISED
UNREVOKED
UNRHYMED
UNRIBBED
UNRID
UNRIDABLE
UNRIDDEN
UNRIDDLE
UNRIDDLED
UNRIDDLER
UNRIDDLES
UNRIDGED
UNRIFLED
UNRIG
UNRIGGED
UNRIGGING
UNRIGHT
UNRIGHTED
UNRIGHTS
UNRIGS
UNRIMED
UNRINGED
UNRINSED
UNRIP
UNRIPE
UNRIPELY
UNRIPENED
UNRIPER
UNRIPEST
UNRIPPED
UNRIPPING
UNRIPS
UNRISEN
UNRIVALED
UNRIVEN
UNRIVET
UNRIVETED
UNRIVETS
UNROASTED

UNROBE
UNROBED
UNROBES
UNROBING
UNROLL
UNROLLED
UNROLLING
UNROLLS
UNROOF
UNROOFED
UNROOFING
UNROOFS
UNROOST
UNROOSTED
UNROOSTS
UNROOT
UNROOTED
UNROOTING
UNROOTS
UNROPE
UNROPED
UNROPES
UNROPING
UNROSINED
UNROTTED
UNROTTEN
UNROUGED
UNROUGH
UNROUND
UNROUNDED
UNROUNDS
UNROUSED
UNROVE
UNROVEN
UNROYAL
UNROYALLY
UNRUBBED
UNRUDE
UNRUFFE
UNRUFFLE
UNRUFFLED
UNRUFFLES
UNRULE
UNRULED
UNRULES
UNRULIER
UNRULIEST
UNRULY
UNRUMPLED
UNRUSHED
UNRUSTED
UNS
UNSADDLE
UNSADDLED
UNSADDLES
UNSAFE
UNSAFELY
UNSAFER
UNSAFEST
UNSAFETY
UNSAID
UNSAILED
UNSAINED
UNSAINT
UNSAINTED
UNSAINTLY
UNSAINTS
UNSALABLE
UNSALABLY
UNSALTED
UNSALUTED
UNSAMPLED
UNSAPPED
UNSASHED
UNSATABLE
UNSATED
UNSATIATE
UNSATING
UNSAVED
UNSAVORY
UNSAVOURY
UNSAW
UNSAWED
UNSAWN
UNSAY
UNSAYABLE
UNSAYING
UNSAYS
UNSCALE
UNSCALED
UNSCALES
UNSCALING
UNSCANNED
UNSCARIER
UNSCARRED
UNSCARY
UNSCATHED
UNSCENTED
UNSCOURED
UNSCREW
UNSCREWED
UNSCREWS
UNSCYTHED
UNSEAL
UNSEALED
UNSEALING
UNSEALS
UNSEAM
UNSEAMED
UNSEAMING
UNSEAMS
UNSEARED
UNSEASON
UNSEASONS
UNSEAT
UNSEATED
UNSEATING
UNSEATS
UNSECRET
UNSECRETS
UNSECULAR
UNSECURED
UNSEDUCED
UNSEE
UNSEEABLE
UNSEEDED
UNSEEING
UNSEEL
UNSEELED
UNSEELIE
UNSEELING
UNSEELS
UNSEEMING
UNSEEMLY
UNSEEN
UNSEENS
UNSEES
UNSEIZED
UNSELDOM
UNSELF
UNSELFED
UNSELFING
UNSELFISH
UNSELFS
UNSELL
UNSELLING
UNSELLS
UNSELVES
UNSENSE
UNSENSED
UNSENSES
UNSENSING
UNSENT
UNSERIOUS
UNSERVED
UNSET
UNSETS
UNSETTING
UNSETTLE
UNSETTLED
UNSETTLES
UNSEVERED
UNSEW
UNSEWED
UNSEWING
UNSEWN
UNSEWS
UNSEX
UNSEXED
UNSEXES
UNSEXIER
UNSEXIEST
UNSEXILY
UNSEXING
UNSEXIST
UNSEXUAL
UNSEXY
UNSHACKLE
UNSHADED
UNSHADOW
UNSHADOWS
UNSHAKED
UNSHAKEN
UNSHALE
UNSHALED
UNSHALES
UNSHALING
UNSHAMED
UNSHAPE
UNSHAPED
UNSHAPELY
UNSHAPEN
UNSHAPES
UNSHAPING
UNSHARED
UNSHARP
UNSHAVED
UNSHAVEN
UNSHEATHE
UNSHED
UNSHELL
UNSHELLED
UNSHELLS
UNSHENT
UNSHEWN
UNSHIFT
UNSHIFTED
UNSHIFTS
UNSHIP
UNSHIPPED
UNSHIPS
UNSHIRTED
UNSHOCKED
UNSHOD
UNSHOE
UNSHOED
UNSHOEING
UNSHOES
UNSHOOT
UNSHOOTED
UNSHOOTS
UNSHORN
UNSHOT
UNSHOTS
UNSHOTTED
UNSHOUT
UNSHOUTED
UNSHOUTS
UNSHOWIER
UNSHOWN
UNSHOWY
UNSHRIVED
UNSHRIVEN
UNSHROUD
UNSHROUDS
UNSHRUBD
UNSHRUNK
UNSHUNNED
UNSHUT
UNSHUTS

U

UNSHUTTER
UNSICKER
UNSICKLED
UNSIFTED
UNSIGHING
UNSIGHT
UNSIGHTED
UNSIGHTLY
UNSIGHTS
UNSIGNED
UNSILENT
UNSIMILAR
UNSINEW
UNSINEWED
UNSINEWS
UNSINFUL
UNSISTING
UNSIZABLE
UNSIZED
UNSKILFUL
UNSKILLED
UNSKIMMED
UNSKINNED
UNSLAIN
UNSLAKED
UNSLICED
UNSLICK
UNSLING
UNSLINGS
UNSLUICE
UNSLUICED
UNSLUICES
UNSLUNG
UNSMART
UNSMILING
UNSMITTEN
UNSMOKED
UNSMOOTH
UNSMOOTHS
UNSMOTE
UNSNAG
UNSNAGGED
UNSNAGS
UNSNAP
UNSNAPPED
UNSNAPS
UNSNARL
UNSNARLED
UNSNARLS
UNSNECK
UNSNECKED
UNSNECKS
UNSNUFFED
UNSOAKED
UNSOAPED
UNSOBER
UNSOBERED
UNSOBERLY
UNSOBERS
UNSOCIAL
UNSOCKET
UNSOCKETS
UNSOD
UNSODDEN
UNSOFT
UNSOILED
UNSOLACED
UNSOLD
UNSOLDER
UNSOLDERS
UNSOLEMN
UNSOLID
UNSOLIDLY
UNSOLVED
UNSONCY
UNSONSIE
UNSONSIER
UNSONSY
UNSOOTE
UNSOOTHED
UNSORTED
UNSOUGHT
UNSOUL
UNSOULED
UNSOULING
UNSOULS
UNSOUND
UNSOUNDED
UNSOUNDER
UNSOUNDLY
UNSOURCED
UNSOURED
UNSOWED
UNSOWN
UNSPAR
UNSPARED
UNSPARING
UNSPARRED
UNSPARS
UNSPEAK
UNSPEAKS
UNSPED
UNSPELL
UNSPELLED
UNSPELLS
UNSPENT
UNSPHERE
UNSPHERED
UNSPHERES
UNSPIDE
UNSPIED
UNSPILLED
UNSPILT
UNSPLIT
UNSPOILED
UNSPOILT
UNSPOKE
UNSPOKEN
UNSPOOL
UNSPOOLED
UNSPOOLS
UNSPOTTED
UNSPRAYED
UNSPRUNG
UNSPUN
UNSQUARED
UNSTABLE
UNSTABLER
UNSTABLY
UNSTACK
UNSTACKED
UNSTACKS
UNSTAGED
UNSTAID
UNSTAINED
UNSTALKED
UNSTAMPED
UNSTARCH
UNSTARRED
UNSTARRY
UNSTATE
UNSTATED
UNSTATES
UNSTATING
UNSTAYED
UNSTAYING
UNSTEADY
UNSTEEL
UNSTEELED
UNSTEELS
UNSTEMMED
UNSTEP
UNSTEPPED
UNSTEPS
UNSTERILE
UNSTICK
UNSTICKS
UNSTIFFEN
UNSTIFLED
UNSTILLED
UNSTINTED
UNSTIRRED
UNSTITCH
UNSTOCK
UNSTOCKED
UNSTOCKS
UNSTONED
UNSTOP
UNSTOPPED
UNSTOPPER
UNSTOPS
UNSTOW
UNSTOWED
UNSTOWING
UNSTOWS
UNSTRAP
UNSTRAPS
UNSTRESS
UNSTRING
UNSTRINGS
UNSTRIP
UNSTRIPED
UNSTRIPS
UNSTRUCK
UNSTRUNG
UNSTUCK
UNSTUDIED
UNSTUFFED
UNSTUFFY
UNSTUFT
UNSTUNG
UNSTYLISH
UNSUBDUED
UNSUBJECT
UNSUBTLE
UNSUBTLER
UNSUBTLY
UNSUCCESS
UNSUCKED
UNSUIT
UNSUITED
UNSUITING
UNSUITS
UNSULLIED
UNSUMMED
UNSUNG
UNSUNK
UNSUNNED
UNSUNNIER
UNSUNNY
UNSUPPLE
UNSURE
UNSURED
UNSURELY
UNSURER
UNSUREST
UNSUSPECT
UNSWADDLE
UNSWATHE
UNSWATHED
UNSWATHES
UNSWAYED
UNSWEAR
UNSWEARS
UNSWEET
UNSWEPT
UNSWOLLEN
UNSWORE
UNSWORN
UNTACK
UNTACKED
UNTACKING
UNTACKLE
UNTACKLED
UNTACKLES
UNTACKS
UNTACTFUL
UNTAGGED
UNTAILED
UNTAINTED

U

UNTAKEN
UNTAMABLE
UNTAMABLY
UNTAME
UNTAMED
UNTAMES
UNTAMING
UNTANGLE
UNTANGLED
UNTANGLES
UNTANNED
UNTAPPED
UNTARRED
UNTASTED
UNTAUGHT
UNTAX
UNTAXABLE
UNTAXED
UNTAXES
UNTAXING
UNTEACH
UNTEACHES
UNTEAM
UNTEAMED
UNTEAMING
UNTEAMS
UNTEMPER
UNTEMPERS
UNTEMPTED
UNTENABLE
UNTENABLY
UNTENANT
UNTENANTS
UNTENDED
UNTENDER
UNTENT
UNTENTED
UNTENTIER
UNTENTING
UNTENTS
UNTENTY
UNTENURED
UNTESTED
UNTETHER
UNTETHERS
UNTHANKED
UNTHATCH
UNTHAW
UNTHAWED
UNTHAWING
UNTHAWS
UNTHINK
UNTHINKS
UNTHOUGHT
UNTHREAD
UNTHREADS
UNTHRIFT
UNTHRIFTS
UNTHRIFTY
UNTHRONE
UNTHRONED
UNTHRONES
UNTIDIED
UNTIDIER
UNTIDIES
UNTIDIEST
UNTIDILY
UNTIDY
UNTIDYING
UNTIE
UNTIED
UNTIEING
UNTIES
UNTIL
UNTILE
UNTILED
UNTILES
UNTILING
UNTILLED
UNTILTED
UNTIMED
UNTIMELY
UNTIMEOUS
UNTIN
UNTINGED
UNTINNED
UNTINNING
UNTINS
UNTIPPED
UNTIRABLE
UNTIRED
UNTIRING
UNTITLED
UNTO
UNTOILING
UNTOLD
UNTOMB
UNTOMBED
UNTOMBING
UNTOMBS
UNTONED
UNTOOLED
UNTOOTHED
UNTORN
UNTOUCHED
UNTOWARD
UNTRACE
UNTRACED
UNTRACES
UNTRACING
UNTRACK
UNTRACKED
UNTRACKS
UNTRADED
UNTRAINED
UNTRAPPED
UNTREAD
UNTREADED
UNTREADS
UNTREATED
UNTRENDY
UNTRESSED
UNTRIDE
UNTRIED
UNTRIM
UNTRIMMED
UNTRIMS
UNTROD
UNTRODDEN
UNTRUE
UNTRUER
UNTRUEST
UNTRUISM
UNTRUISMS
UNTRULY
UNTRUSS
UNTRUSSED
UNTRUSSER
UNTRUSSES
UNTRUST
UNTRUSTED
UNTRUSTS
UNTRUSTY
UNTRUTH
UNTRUTHS
UNTUCK
UNTUCKED
UNTUCKING
UNTUCKS
UNTUFTED
UNTUMBLED
UNTUNABLE
UNTUNABLY
UNTUNE
UNTUNED
UNTUNEFUL
UNTUNES
UNTUNING
UNTURBID
UNTURF
UNTURFED
UNTURFING
UNTURFS
UNTURN
UNTURNED
UNTURNING
UNTURNS
UNTUTORED
UNTWILLED
UNTWINE
UNTWINED
UNTWINES
UNTWINING
UNTWIST
UNTWISTED
UNTWISTS
UNTYING
UNTYINGS
UNTYPABLE
UNTYPICAL
UNUNBIUM
UNUNBIUMS
UNUNITED
UNUNUNIUM
UNURGED
UNUSABLE
UNUSABLY
UNUSED
UNUSEFUL
UNUSHERED
UNUSUAL
UNUSUALLY
UNUTTERED
UNVAIL
UNVAILE
UNVAILED
UNVAILES
UNVAILING
UNVAILS
UNVALUED
UNVARIED
UNVARYING
UNVEIL
UNVEILED
UNVEILER
UNVEILERS
UNVEILING
UNVEILS
UNVEINED
UNVENTED
UNVERSED
UNVESTED
UNVETTED
UNVEXED
UNVEXT
UNVIABLE
UNVIEWED
UNVIRTUE
UNVIRTUES
UNVISITED
UNVISOR
UNVISORED
UNVISORS
UNVITAL
UNVIZARD
UNVIZARDS
UNVOCAL
UNVOICE
UNVOICED
UNVOICES
UNVOICING
UNVULGAR
UNWAGED
UNWAISTED
UNWAKED
UNWAKENED
UNWALLED
UNWANING
UNWANTED
UNWARDED

UNWARE
UNWARELY
UNWARES
UNWARIE
UNWARIER
UNWARIEST
UNWARILY
UNWARLIKE
UNWARMED
UNWARNED
UNWARPED
UNWARY
UNWASHED
UNWASHEDS
UNWASHEN
UNWASTED
UNWASTING
UNWATCHED
UNWATER
UNWATERED
UNWATERS
UNWATERY
UNWAXED
UNWAYED
UNWEAL
UNWEALS
UNWEANED
UNWEAPON
UNWEAPONS
UNWEARIED
UNWEARIER
UNWEARIES
UNWEARY
UNWEAVE
UNWEAVES
UNWEAVING
UNWEBBED
UNWED
UNWEDDED
UNWEEDED
UNWEENED
UNWEETING
UNWEIGHED
UNWEIGHT
UNWEIGHTS
UNWELCOME
UNWELDED
UNWELDY
UNWELL
UNWEPT
UNWET
UNWETTED
UNWHIPPED
UNWHIPT
UNWHITE
UNWIELDLY
UNWIELDY
UNWIFELY
UNWIGGED
UNWILFUL
UNWILL
UNWILLED
UNWILLING
UNWILLS
UNWIND
UNWINDER
UNWINDERS
UNWINDING
UNWINDS
UNWINGED
UNWINKING
UNWIPED
UNWIRE
UNWIRED
UNWIRES
UNWIRING
UNWISDOM
UNWISDOMS
UNWISE
UNWISELY
UNWISER
UNWISEST
UNWISH
UNWISHED
UNWISHES
UNWISHFUL
UNWISHING
UNWIST
UNWIT
UNWITCH
UNWITCHED
UNWITCHES
UNWITS
UNWITTED
UNWITTIER
UNWITTILY
UNWITTING
UNWITTY
UNWIVE
UNWIVED
UNWIVES
UNWIVING
UNWOMAN
UNWOMANED
UNWOMANLY
UNWOMANS
UNWON
UNWONT
UNWONTED
UNWOODED
UNWOOED
UNWORDED
UNWORK
UNWORKED
UNWORKING
UNWORKS
UNWORLDLY
UNWORMED
UNWORN
UNWORRIED
UNWORTH
UNWORTHS
UNWORTHY
UNWOUND
UNWOUNDED
UNWOVE
UNWOVEN
UNWRAP
UNWRAPPED
UNWRAPS
UNWREAKED
UNWREATHE
UNWRINKLE
UNWRITE
UNWRITES
UNWRITING
UNWRITTEN
UNWROTE
UNWROUGHT
UNWRUNG
UNYEANED
UNYIELDED
UNYOKE
UNYOKED
UNYOKES
UNYOKING
UNYOUNG
UNZEALOUS
UNZIP
UNZIPPED
UNZIPPING
UNZIPS
UNZONED
UP
UPADAISY
UPAITHRIC
UPALONG
UPALONGS
UPAS
UPASES
UPBEAR
UPBEARER
UPBEARERS
UPBEARING
UPBEARS
UPBEAT
UPBEATS
UPBIND
UPBINDING
UPBINDS
UPBLEW
UPBLOW
UPBLOWING
UPBLOWN
UPBLOWS
UPBOIL
UPBOILED
UPBOILING
UPBOILS
UPBORE
UPBORNE
UPBOUND
UPBOUNDEN
UPBOW
UPBOWS
UPBRAID
UPBRAIDED
UPBRAIDER
UPBRAIDS
UPBRAST
UPBRAY
UPBRAYED
UPBRAYING
UPBRAYS
UPBREAK
UPBREAKS
UPBRING
UPBRINGS
UPBROKE
UPBROKEN
UPBROUGHT
UPBUILD
UPBUILDER
UPBUILDS
UPBUILT
UPBURNING
UPBURST
UPBURSTS
UPBY
UPBYE
UPCAST
UPCASTING
UPCASTS
UPCATCH
UPCATCHES
UPCAUGHT
UPCHEER
UPCHEERED
UPCHEERS
UPCHUCK
UPCHUCKED
UPCHUCKS
UPCLIMB
UPCLIMBED
UPCLIMBS
UPCLOSE
UPCLOSED
UPCLOSES
UPCLOSING
UPCOAST
UPCOIL
UPCOILED
UPCOILING
UPCOILS
UPCOME
UPCOMES
UPCOMING
UPCOUNTRY
UPCOURT
UPCURL

U

UPCURLED
UPCURLING
UPCURLS
UPCURVE
UPCURVED
UPCURVES
UPCURVING
UPCYCLE
UPCYCLED
UPCYCLES
UPCYCLING
UPDART
UPDARTED
UPDARTING
UPDARTS
UPDATABLE
UPDATE
UPDATED
UPDATER
UPDATERS
UPDATES
UPDATING
UPDIVE
UPDIVED
UPDIVES
UPDIVING
UPDO
UPDOMING
UPDOMINGS
UPDOS
UPDOVE
UPDRAFT
UPDRAFTS
UPDRAG
UPDRAGGED
UPDRAGS
UPDRAUGHT
UPDRAW
UPDRAWING
UPDRAWN
UPDRAWS
UPDREW
UPDRIED
UPDRIES
UPDRY
UPDRYING
UPEND
UPENDED
UPENDING
UPENDS
UPFIELD
UPFILL
UPFILLED
UPFILLING
UPFILLS
UPFLING
UPFLINGS
UPFLOW
UPFLOWED
UPFLOWING
UPFLOWS
UPFLUNG
UPFOLD
UPFOLDED
UPFOLDING
UPFOLDS
UPFOLLOW
UPFOLLOWS
UPFRONT
UPFURL
UPFURLED
UPFURLING
UPFURLS
UPGANG
UPGANGS
UPGATHER
UPGATHERS
UPGAZE
UPGAZED
UPGAZES
UPGAZING
UPGIRD
UPGIRDED
UPGIRDING
UPGIRDS
UPGIRT
UPGIRTED
UPGIRTING
UPGIRTS
UPGO
UPGOES
UPGOING
UPGOINGS
UPGONE
UPGRADE
UPGRADED
UPGRADER
UPGRADERS
UPGRADES
UPGRADING
UPGREW
UPGROW
UPGROWING
UPGROWN
UPGROWS
UPGROWTH
UPGROWTHS
UPGUSH
UPGUSHED
UPGUSHES
UPGUSHING
UPHAND
UPHANG
UPHANGING
UPHANGS
UPHAUD
UPHAUDING
UPHAUDS
UPHEAP
UPHEAPED
UPHEAPING
UPHEAPS
UPHEAVAL
UPHEAVALS
UPHEAVE
UPHEAVED
UPHEAVER
UPHEAVERS
UPHEAVES
UPHEAVING
UPHELD
UPHILD
UPHILL
UPHILLS
UPHOARD
UPHOARDED
UPHOARDS
UPHOIST
UPHOISTED
UPHOISTS
UPHOLD
UPHOLDER
UPHOLDERS
UPHOLDING
UPHOLDS
UPHOLSTER
UPHOORD
UPHOORDED
UPHOORDS
UPHOVE
UPHROE
UPHROES
UPHUDDEN
UPHUNG
UPHURL
UPHURLED
UPHURLING
UPHURLS
UPJET
UPJETS
UPJETTED
UPJETTING
UPKEEP
UPKEEPS
UPKNIT
UPKNITS
UPKNITTED
UPLAID
UPLAND
UPLANDER
UPLANDERS
UPLANDISH
UPLANDS
UPLAY
UPLAYING
UPLAYS
UPLEAD
UPLEADING
UPLEADS
UPLEAN
UPLEANED
UPLEANING
UPLEANS
UPLEANT
UPLEAP
UPLEAPED
UPLEAPING
UPLEAPS
UPLEAPT
UPLED
UPLIFT
UPLIFTED
UPLIFTER
UPLIFTERS
UPLIFTING
UPLIFTS
UPLIGHT
UPLIGHTED
UPLIGHTER
UPLIGHTS
UPLINK
UPLINKED
UPLINKING
UPLINKS
UPLIT
UPLOAD
UPLOADED
UPLOADING
UPLOADS
UPLOCK
UPLOCKED
UPLOCKING
UPLOCKS
UPLOOK
UPLOOKED
UPLOOKING
UPLOOKS
UPLYING
UPMADE
UPMAKE
UPMAKER
UPMAKERS
UPMAKES
UPMAKING
UPMAKINGS
UPMANSHIP
UPMARKET
UPMARKETS
UPMOST
UPO
UPON
UPPED
UPPER
UPPERCASE
UPPERCUT
UPPERCUTS
UPPERMOST
UPPERPART
UPPERS
UPPILE

UPPILED
UPPILES
UPPILING
UPPING
UPPINGS
UPPISH
UPPISHLY
UPPITIER
UPPITIEST
UPPITY
UPPROP
UPPROPPED
UPPROPS
UPRAISE
UPRAISED
UPRAISER
UPRAISERS
UPRAISES
UPRAISING
UPRAN
UPRATE
UPRATED
UPRATES
UPRATING
UPREACH
UPREACHED
UPREACHES
UPREAR
UPREARED
UPREARING
UPREARS
UPREST
UPRESTS
UPRIGHT
UPRIGHTED
UPRIGHTLY
UPRIGHTS
UPRISAL
UPRISALS
UPRISE
UPRISEN
UPRISER
UPRISERS
UPRISES
UPRISING
UPRISINGS
UPRIST
UPRISTS
UPRIVER
UPRIVERS
UPROAR
UPROARED
UPROARING
UPROARS
UPROLL
UPROLLED
UPROLLING
UPROLLS
UPROOT
UPROOTAL
UPROOTALS
UPROOTED
UPROOTER
UPROOTERS
UPROOTING
UPROOTS
UPROSE
UPROUSE
UPROUSED
UPROUSES
UPROUSING
UPRUN
UPRUNNING
UPRUNS
UPRUSH
UPRUSHED
UPRUSHES
UPRUSHING
UPRYST
UPS
UPSADAISY
UPSCALE
UPSCALED
UPSCALES
UPSCALING
UPSEE
UPSEES
UPSELL
UPSELLING
UPSELLS
UPSEND
UPSENDING
UPSENDS
UPSENT
UPSET
UPSETS
UPSETTER
UPSETTERS
UPSETTING
UPSEY
UPSEYS
UPSHIFT
UPSHIFTED
UPSHIFTS
UPSHOOT
UPSHOOTS
UPSHOT
UPSHOTS
UPSIDE
UPSIDES
UPSIES
UPSILON
UPSILONS
UPSITTING
UPSIZE
UPSIZED
UPSIZES
UPSIZING
UPSKILL
UPSKILLED
UPSKILLS
UPSKIRT
UPSKIRTS
UPSLOPE
UPSLOPES
UPSOAR
UPSOARED
UPSOARING
UPSOARS
UPSOLD
UPSPAKE
UPSPEAK
UPSPEAKS
UPSPEAR
UPSPEARED
UPSPEARS
UPSPOKE
UPSPOKEN
UPSPRANG
UPSPRING
UPSPRINGS
UPSPRUNG
UPSTAGE
UPSTAGED
UPSTAGER
UPSTAGERS
UPSTAGES
UPSTAGING
UPSTAIR
UPSTAIRS
UPSTAND
UPSTANDS
UPSTARE
UPSTARED
UPSTARES
UPSTARING
UPSTART
UPSTARTED
UPSTARTS
UPSTATE
UPSTATER
UPSTATERS
UPSTATES
UPSTAY
UPSTAYED
UPSTAYING
UPSTAYS
UPSTEP
UPSTEPPED
UPSTEPS
UPSTIR
UPSTIRRED
UPSTIRS
UPSTOOD
UPSTREAM
UPSTREAMS
UPSTROKE
UPSTROKES
UPSURGE
UPSURGED
UPSURGES
UPSURGING
UPSWARM
UPSWARMED
UPSWARMS
UPSWAY
UPSWAYED
UPSWAYING
UPSWAYS
UPSWEEP
UPSWEEPS
UPSWELL
UPSWELLED
UPSWELLS
UPSWEPT
UPSWING
UPSWINGS
UPSWOLLEN
UPSWUNG
UPSY
UPTA
UPTAK
UPTAKE
UPTAKEN
UPTAKES
UPTAKING
UPTAKS
UPTALK
UPTALKED
UPTALKING
UPTALKS
UPTEAR
UPTEARING
UPTEARS
UPTEMPO
UPTEMPOS
UPTER
UPTHREW
UPTHROW
UPTHROWN
UPTHROWS
UPTHRUST
UPTHRUSTS
UPTHUNDER
UPTICK
UPTICKS
UPTIE
UPTIED
UPTIES
UPTIGHT
UPTIGHTER
UPTILT
UPTILTED
UPTILTING
UPTILTS
UPTIME
UPTIMES
UPTITLING
UPTOOK
UPTORE

U

UPTORN
UPTOSS
UPTOSSED
UPTOSSES
UPTOSSING
UPTOWN
UPTOWNER
UPTOWNERS
UPTOWNS
UPTRAIN
UPTRAINED
UPTRAINS
UPTREND
UPTRENDS
UPTRILLED
UPTURN
UPTURNED
UPTURNING
UPTURNS
UPTYING
UPVALUE
UPVALUED
UPVALUES
UPVALUING
UPVOTE
UPVOTED
UPVOTES
UPVOTING
UPWAFT
UPWAFTED
UPWAFTING
UPWAFTS
UPWARD
UPWARDLY
UPWARDS
UPWELL
UPWELLED
UPWELLING
UPWELLS
UPWENT
UPWHIRL
UPWHIRLED
UPWHIRLS
UPWIND
UPWINDING
UPWINDS
UPWOUND
UPWRAP
UPWRAPS
UPWROUGHT
UR
URACHI
URACHUS
URACHUSES
URACIL
URACILS
URAEI
URAEMIA
URAEMIAS
URAEMIC
URAEUS
URAEUSES
URALI
URALIS
URALITE
URALITES
URALITIC
URALITISE
URALITIZE
URANIA
URANIAN
URANIAS
URANIC
URANIDE
URANIDES
URANIN
URANINITE
URANINS
URANISCI
URANISCUS
URANISM
URANISMS
URANITE
URANITES
URANITIC
URANIUM
URANIUMS
URANOLOGY
URANOUS
URANYL
URANYLIC
URANYLS
URAO
URAOS
URARE
URARES
URARI
URARIS
URASE
URASES
URATE
URATES
URATIC
URB
URBAN
URBANE
URBANELY
URBANER
URBANEST
URBANISE
URBANISED
URBANISES
URBANISM
URBANISMS
URBANIST
URBANISTS
URBANITE
URBANITES
URBANITY
URBANIZE
URBANIZED
URBANIZES
URBEX
URBEXES
URBIA
URBIAS
URBS
URCEOLATE
URCEOLI
URCEOLUS
URCHIN
URCHINS
URD
URDE
URDEE
URDS
URDY
URE
UREA
UREAL
UREAS
UREASE
UREASES
UREDIA
UREDIAL
UREDINE
UREDINES
UREDINIA
UREDINIAL
UREDINIUM
UREDINOUS
UREDIUM
UREDO
UREDOS
UREDOSORI
UREIC
UREIDE
UREIDES
UREMIA
UREMIAS
UREMIC
URENA
URENAS
URENT
UREOTELIC
URES
URESES
URESIS
URETER
URETERAL
URETERIC
URETERS
URETHAN
URETHANE
URETHANED
URETHANES
URETHANS
URETHRA
URETHRAE
URETHRAL
URETHRAS
URETIC
URGE
URGED
URGENCE
URGENCES
URGENCIES
URGENCY
URGENT
URGENTLY
URGER
URGERS
URGES
URGING
URGINGLY
URGINGS
URIAL
URIALS
URIC
URICASE
URICASES
URIDINE
URIDINES
URIDYLIC
URINAL
URINALS
URINANT
URINARIES
URINARY
URINATE
URINATED
URINATES
URINATING
URINATION
URINATIVE
URINATOR
URINATORS
URINE
URINED
URINEMIA
URINEMIAS
URINEMIC
URINES
URINING
URINOLOGY
URINOSE
URINOUS
URITE
URITES
URMAN
URMANS
URN
URNAL
URNED
URNFIELD
URNFIELDS
URNFUL
URNFULS
URNING
URNINGS

URNLIKE
URNS
UROBILIN
UROBILINS
UROBORIC
UROBOROS
UROCHORD
UROCHORDS
UROCHROME
URODELAN
URODELANS
URODELE
URODELES
URODELOUS
UROGENOUS
UROGRAM
UROGRAMS
UROGRAPHY
UROKINASE
UROLAGNIA
UROLITH
UROLITHIC
UROLITHS
UROLOGIC
UROLOGIES
UROLOGIST
UROLOGY
UROMERE
UROMERES
UROPOD
UROPODAL
UROPODOUS
UROPODS
UROPYGIA
UROPYGIAL
UROPYGIUM
UROSCOPIC
UROSCOPY
UROSES
UROSIS
UROSOME
UROSOMES
UROSTEGE
UROSTEGES
UROSTOMY
UROSTYLE
UROSTYLES
URP
URPED
URPING
URPS
URSA
URSAE
URSID
URSIDS
URSIFORM
URSINE
URSON
URSONS
URTEXT
URTEXTE
URTEXTS
URTICA
URTICANT
URTICANTS
URTICARIA
URTICAS
URTICATE
URTICATED
URTICATES
URUBU
URUBUS
URUS
URUSES
URUSHIOL
URUSHIOLS
URVA
URVAS
US
USABILITY
USABLE
USABLY
USAGE
USAGER
USAGERS
USAGES
USANCE
USANCES
USAUNCE
USAUNCES
USE
USEABLE
USEABLY
USED
USEFUL
USEFULLY
USEFULS
USELESS
USELESSLY
USER
USERNAME
USERNAMES
USERS
USES
USHER
USHERED
USHERESS
USHERETTE
USHERING
USHERINGS
USHERS
USHERSHIP
USING
USNEA
USNEAS
USQUABAE
USQUABAES
USQUE
USQUEBAE
USQUEBAES
USQUES
USTION
USTIONS
USTULATE
USTULATED
USTULATES
USUAL
USUALLY
USUALNESS
USUALS
USUCAPION
USUCAPT
USUCAPTED
USUCAPTS
USUFRUCT
USUFRUCTS
USURE
USURED
USURER
USURERS
USURES
USURESS
USURESSES
USURIES
USURING
USURIOUS
USUROUS
USURP
USURPED
USURPEDLY
USURPER
USURPERS
USURPING
USURPINGS
USURPS
USURY
USWARD
USWARDS
UT
UTA
UTAS
UTASES
UTE
UTENSIL
UTENSILS
UTERI
UTERINE
UTERITIS
UTEROTOMY
UTERUS
UTERUSES
UTES
UTILE
UTILES
UTILIDOR
UTILIDORS
UTILISE
UTILISED
UTILISER
UTILISERS
UTILISES
UTILISING
UTILITIES
UTILITY
UTILIZE
UTILIZED
UTILIZER
UTILIZERS
UTILIZES
UTILIZING
UTIS
UTISES
UTMOST
UTMOSTS
UTOPIA
UTOPIAN
UTOPIANS
UTOPIAS
UTOPIAST
UTOPIASTS
UTOPISM
UTOPISMS
UTOPIST
UTOPISTIC
UTOPISTS
UTRICLE
UTRICLES
UTRICULAR
UTRICULI
UTRICULUS
UTS
UTTER
UTTERABLE
UTTERANCE
UTTERED
UTTERER
UTTERERS
UTTEREST
UTTERING
UTTERINGS
UTTERLESS
UTTERLY
UTTERMOST
UTTERNESS
UTTERS
UTU
UTUS
UVA
UVAE
UVAROVITE
UVAS
UVEA
UVEAL
UVEAS
UVEITIC
UVEITIS
UVEITISES
UVEOUS
UVULA
UVULAE

UVULAR	UVULARS	UVULITIS	UXORIALLY	UXORIOUS
UVULARLY	UVULAS	UXORIAL	UXORICIDE	

U

V

VAC
VACANCE
VACANCES
VACANCIES
VACANCY
VACANT
VACANTLY
VACATABLE
VACATE
VACATED
VACATES
VACATING
VACATION
VACATIONS
VACATUR
VACATURS
VACCINA
VACCINAL
VACCINAS
VACCINATE
VACCINE
VACCINEE
VACCINEES
VACCINES
VACCINIA
VACCINIAL
VACCINIAS
VACCINIUM
VACHERIN
VACHERINS
VACILLANT
VACILLATE
VACKED
VACKING
VACS
VACUA
VACUATE
VACUATED
VACUATES
VACUATING
VACUATION
VACUIST
VACUISTS
VACUITIES
VACUITY
VACUOLAR
VACUOLATE
VACUOLE
VACUOLES
VACUOUS
VACUOUSLY
VACUUM
VACUUMED
VACUUMING
VACUUMS
VADE
VADED
VADES
VADING
VADOSE
VAE
VAES
VAG
VAGABOND
VAGABONDS
VAGAL
VAGALLY
VAGARIES
VAGARIOUS
VAGARISH
VAGARY
VAGGED
VAGGING
VAGI
VAGILE
VAGILITY
VAGINA
VAGINAE
VAGINAL
VAGINALLY
VAGINANT
VAGINAS
VAGINATE
VAGINATED
VAGINITIS
VAGINOSES
VAGINOSIS
VAGINULA
VAGINULAE
VAGINULE
VAGINULES
VAGITUS
VAGITUSES
VAGOTOMY
VAGOTONIA
VAGOTONIC
VAGRANCY
VAGRANT
VAGRANTLY
VAGRANTS
VAGROM
VAGS
VAGUE
VAGUED
VAGUELY
VAGUENESS
VAGUER
VAGUES
VAGUEST
VAGUING
VAGUISH
VAGUS
VAHANA
VAHANAS
VAHINE
VAHINES
VAIL
VAILED
VAILING
VAILS
VAIN
VAINER
VAINESSE
VAINESSES
VAINEST
VAINGLORY
VAINLY
VAINNESS
VAIR
VAIRE
VAIRIER
VAIRIEST
VAIRS
VAIRY
VAIVODE
VAIVODES
VAJAZZLE
VAJAZZLED
VAJAZZLES
VAKAS
VAKASES
VAKASS
VAKASSES
VAKEEL
VAKEELS
VAKIL
VAKILS
VALANCE
VALANCED
VALANCES
VALANCING
VALE
VALENCE
VALENCES
VALENCIA
VALENCIAS
VALENCIES
VALENCY
VALENTINE
VALERATE
VALERATES
VALERIAN
VALERIANS
VALERIC
VALES
VALET
VALETA
VALETAS
VALETE
VALETED
VALETES
VALETING
VALETINGS
VALETS
VALGOID
VALGOUS
VALGUS
VALGUSES
VALI
VALIANCE
VALIANCES
VALIANCY
VALIANT
VALIANTLY
VALIANTS
VALID
VALIDATE
VALIDATED
VALIDATES
VALIDATOR
VALIDER
VALIDEST
VALIDITY
VALIDLY
VALIDNESS
VALINE
VALINES
VALIS
VALISE
VALISES
VALIUM
VALIUMS
VALKYR
VALKYRIE
VALKYRIES
VALKYRS
VALLAR
VALLARIES
VALLARS
VALLARY

VALLATE
VALLATION
VALLECULA
VALLEY
VALLEYED
VALLEYS
VALLHUND
VALLHUNDS
VALLONIA
VALLONIAS
VALLUM
VALLUMS
VALONEA
VALONEAS
VALONIA
VALONIAS
VALOR
VALORISE
VALORISED
VALORISES
VALORIZE
VALORIZED
VALORIZES
VALOROUS
VALORS
VALOUR
VALOURS
VALPROATE
VALPROIC
VALSE
VALSED
VALSES
VALSING
VALUABLE
VALUABLES
VALUABLY
VALUATE
VALUATED
VALUATES
VALUATING
VALUATION
VALUATOR
VALUATORS
VALUE
VALUED
VALUELESS
VALUER
VALUERS
VALUES
VALUING
VALUTA
VALUTAS
VALVAL
VALVAR
VALVASSOR
VALVATE
VALVE
VALVED
VALVELESS
VALVELET
VALVELETS
VALVELIKE
VALVES
VALVING
VALVULA
VALVULAE
VALVULAR
VALVULE
VALVULES
VAMBRACE
VAMBRACED
VAMBRACES
VAMOOSE
VAMOOSED
VAMOOSES
VAMOOSING
VAMOSE
VAMOSED
VAMOSES
VAMOSING
VAMP
VAMPED
VAMPER
VAMPERS
VAMPIER
VAMPIEST
VAMPING
VAMPINGS
VAMPIRE
VAMPIRED
VAMPIRES
VAMPIRIC
VAMPIRING
VAMPIRISE
VAMPIRISH
VAMPIRISM
VAMPIRIZE
VAMPISH
VAMPISHLY
VAMPLATE
VAMPLATES
VAMPS
VAMPY
VAN
VANADATE
VANADATES
VANADIATE
VANADIC
VANADIUM
VANADIUMS
VANADOUS
VANASPATI
VANDA
VANDAL
VANDALIC
VANDALISE
VANDALISH
VANDALISM
VANDALIZE
VANDALS
VANDAS
VANDYKE
VANDYKED
VANDYKES
VANDYKING
VANE
VANED
VANELESS
VANES
VANESSA
VANESSAS
VANESSID
VANESSIDS
VANG
VANGS
VANGUARD
VANGUARDS
VANILLA
VANILLAS
VANILLIC
VANILLIN
VANILLINS
VANISH
VANISHED
VANISHER
VANISHERS
VANISHES
VANISHING
VANITAS
VANITASES
VANITIED
VANITIES
VANITORY
VANITY
VANLIKE
VANLOAD
VANLOADS
VANMAN
VANMEN
VANNED
VANNER
VANNERS
VANNING
VANNINGS
VANPOOL
VANPOOLS
VANQUISH
VANS
VANT
VANTAGE
VANTAGED
VANTAGES
VANTAGING
VANTBRACE
VANTBRASS
VANTS
VANWARD
VAPE
VAPED
VAPER
VAPERS
VAPES
VAPID
VAPIDER
VAPIDEST
VAPIDITY
VAPIDLY
VAPIDNESS
VAPING
VAPINGS
VAPOR
VAPORABLE
VAPORED
VAPORER
VAPORERS
VAPORETTI
VAPORETTO
VAPORIER
VAPORIEST
VAPORIFIC
VAPORING
VAPORINGS
VAPORISE
VAPORISED
VAPORISER
VAPORISES
VAPORISH
VAPORIZE
VAPORIZED
VAPORIZER
VAPORIZES
VAPORLESS
VAPORLIKE
VAPOROUS
VAPORS
VAPORWARE
VAPORY
VAPOUR
VAPOURED
VAPOURER
VAPOURERS
VAPOURIER
VAPOURING
VAPOURISH
VAPOUROUS
VAPOURS
VAPOURY
VAPULATE
VAPULATED
VAPULATES
VAQUERO
VAQUEROS
VAR
VARA
VARACTOR
VARACTORS
VARAN
VARANS
VARAS
VARDIES

VARDY
VARE
VAREC
VARECH
VARECHS
VARECS
VARENYKY
VARES
VAREUSE
VAREUSES
VARGUENO
VARGUENOS
VARIA
VARIABLE
VARIABLES
VARIABLY
VARIANCE
VARIANCES
VARIANT
VARIANTS
VARIAS
VARIATE
VARIATED
VARIATES
VARIATING
VARIATION
VARIATIVE
VARICEAL
VARICELLA
VARICES
VARICOID
VARICOSE
VARICOSED
VARICOSES
VARICOSIS
VARIED
VARIEDLY
VARIEGATE
VARIER
VARIERS
VARIES
VARIETAL
VARIETALS
VARIETIES
VARIETY
VARIFOCAL
VARIFORM
VARIOLA
VARIOLAR
VARIOLAS
VARIOLATE
VARIOLE
VARIOLES
VARIOLITE
VARIOLOID
VARIOLOUS
VARIORUM
VARIORUMS
VARIOUS
VARIOUSLY
VARISCITE
VARISIZED
VARISTOR
VARISTORS
VARITYPE
VARITYPED
VARITYPES
VARIX
VARLET
VARLETESS
VARLETRY
VARLETS
VARLETTO
VARLETTOS
VARMENT
VARMENTS
VARMINT
VARMINTS
VARNA
VARNAS
VARNISH
VARNISHED
VARNISHER
VARNISHES
VARNISHY
VAROOM
VAROOMED
VAROOMING
VAROOMS
VARROA
VARROAS
VARS
VARSAL
VARSITIES
VARSITY
VARTABED
VARTABEDS
VARUS
VARUSES
VARVE
VARVED
VARVEL
VARVELLED
VARVELS
VARVES
VARY
VARYING
VARYINGLY
VARYINGS
VAS
VASA
VASAL
VASCULA
VASCULAR
VASCULUM
VASCULUMS
VASE
VASECTOMY
VASEFUL
VASEFULS
VASELIKE
VASELINE
VASELINED
VASELINES
VASES
VASIFORM
VASOMOTOR
VASOSPASM
VASOTOCIN
VASOTOMY
VASOVAGAL
VASSAIL
VASSAILS
VASSAL
VASSALAGE
VASSALESS
VASSALISE
VASSALIZE
VASSALLED
VASSALRY
VASSALS
VAST
VASTER
VASTEST
VASTIDITY
VASTIER
VASTIEST
VASTITIES
VASTITUDE
VASTITY
VASTLY
VASTNESS
VASTS
VASTY
VAT
VATABLE
VATFUL
VATFULS
VATIC
VATICAL
VATICIDE
VATICIDES
VATICINAL
VATMAN
VATMEN
VATS
VATTED
VATTER
VATTERS
VATTING
VATU
VATUS
VAU
VAUCH
VAUCHED
VAUCHES
VAUCHING
VAUDOO
VAUDOOS
VAUDOUX
VAULT
VAULTAGE
VAULTAGES
VAULTED
VAULTER
VAULTERS
VAULTIER
VAULTIEST
VAULTING
VAULTINGS
VAULTLIKE
VAULTS
VAULTY
VAUNCE
VAUNCED
VAUNCES
VAUNCING
VAUNT
VAUNTAGE
VAUNTAGES
VAUNTED
VAUNTER
VAUNTERS
VAUNTERY
VAUNTFUL
VAUNTIE
VAUNTIER
VAUNTIEST
VAUNTING
VAUNTINGS
VAUNTS
VAUNTY
VAURIEN
VAURIENS
VAUS
VAUT
VAUTE
VAUTED
VAUTES
VAUTING
VAUTS
VAV
VAVASOR
VAVASORS
VAVASORY
VAVASOUR
VAVASOURS
VAVASSOR
VAVASSORS
VAVS
VAW
VAWARD
VAWARDS
VAWNTIE
VAWNTIER
VAWNTIEST
VAWS
VAWTE
VAWTED
VAWTES

VAWTING
VAX
VAXES
VEAL
VEALE
VEALED
VEALER
VEALERS
VEALES
VEALIER
VEALIEST
VEALING
VEALS
VEALY
VECTOR
VECTORED
VECTORIAL
VECTORING
VECTORISE
VECTORIZE
VECTORS
VEDALIA
VEDALIAS
VEDETTE
VEDETTES
VEDUTA
VEDUTAS
VEDUTE
VEDUTISTA
VEDUTISTE
VEDUTISTI
VEE
VEEJAY
VEEJAYS
VEENA
VEENAS
VEEP
VEEPEE
VEEPEES
VEEPS
VEER
VEERED
VEERIES
VEERING
VEERINGLY
VEERINGS
VEERS
VEERY
VEES
VEG
VEGA
VEGAN
VEGANIC
VEGANISM
VEGANISMS
VEGANS
VEGAS
VEGELATE
VEGELATES
VEGEMITE
VEGEMITES
VEGES
VEGETABLE
VEGETABLY
VEGETAL
VEGETALLY
VEGETALS
VEGETANT
VEGETATE
VEGETATED
VEGETATES
VEGETE
VEGETIST
VEGETISTS
VEGETIVE
VEGETIVES
VEGGED
VEGGES
VEGGIE
VEGGIER
VEGGIES
VEGGIEST
VEGGING
VEGIE
VEGIER
VEGIES
VEGIEST
VEGO
VEGOS
VEHEMENCE
VEHEMENCY
VEHEMENT
VEHICLE
VEHICLES
VEHICULAR
VEHM
VEHME
VEHMIC
VEHMIQUE
VEIL
VEILED
VEILEDLY
VEILER
VEILERS
VEILIER
VEILIEST
VEILING
VEILINGS
VEILLESS
VEILLEUSE
VEILLIKE
VEILS
VEILY
VEIN
VEINAL
VEINED
VEINER
VEINERS
VEINIER
VEINIEST
VEINING
VEININGS
VEINLESS
VEINLET
VEINLETS
VEINLIKE
VEINOUS
VEINS
VEINSTONE
VEINSTUFF
VEINULE
VEINULES
VEINULET
VEINULETS
VEINY
VELA
VELAMEN
VELAMINA
VELAR
VELARIA
VELARIC
VELARISE
VELARISED
VELARISES
VELARIUM
VELARIZE
VELARIZED
VELARIZES
VELARS
VELATE
VELATED
VELATURA
VELATURAS
VELCRO
VELCROS
VELD
VELDS
VELDSKOEN
VELDT
VELDTS
VELE
VELES
VELETA
VELETAS
VELIGER
VELIGERS
VELITES
VELL
VELLEITY
VELLENAGE
VELLET
VELLETS
VELLICATE
VELLON
VELLONS
VELLS
VELLUM
VELLUMS
VELLUS
VELOCE
VELOCITY
VELODROME
VELOUR
VELOURS
VELOUTE
VELOUTES
VELOUTINE
VELSKOEN
VELSKOENS
VELUM
VELURE
VELURED
VELURES
VELURING
VELVERET
VELVERETS
VELVET
VELVETED
VELVETEEN
VELVETIER
VELVETING
VELVETS
VELVETY
VENA
VENAE
VENAL
VENALITY
VENALLY
VENATIC
VENATICAL
VENATION
VENATIONS
VENATOR
VENATORS
VEND
VENDABLE
VENDABLES
VENDACE
VENDACES
VENDAGE
VENDAGES
VENDANGE
VENDANGES
VENDED
VENDEE
VENDEES
VENDER
VENDERS
VENDETTA
VENDETTAS
VENDEUSE
VENDEUSES
VENDIBLE
VENDIBLES
VENDIBLY
VENDING
VENDINGS
VENDIS
VENDISES
VENDISS

VENDISSES
VENDITION
VENDOR
VENDORS
VENDS
VENDUE
VENDUES
VENEER
VENEERED
VENEERER
VENEERERS
VENEERING
VENEERS
VENEFIC
VENEFICAL
VENENATE
VENENATED
VENENATES
VENENE
VENENES
VENENOSE
VENERABLE
VENERABLY
VENERATE
VENERATED
VENERATES
VENERATOR
VENEREAL
VENEREAN
VENEREANS
VENEREOUS
VENERER
VENERERS
VENERIES
VENERY
VENETIAN
VENETIANS
VENEWE
VENEWES
VENEY
VENEYS
VENGE
VENGEABLE
VENGEABLY
VENGEANCE
VENGED
VENGEFUL
VENGEMENT
VENGER
VENGERS
VENGES
VENGING
VENIAL
VENIALITY
VENIALLY
VENIDIUM
VENIDIUMS
VENIN
VENINE
VENINES
VENINS
VENIRE
VENIREMAN
VENIREMEN
VENIRES
VENISON
VENISONS
VENITE
VENITES
VENNEL
VENNELS
VENOGRAM
VENOGRAMS
VENOLOGY
VENOM
VENOMED
VENOMER
VENOMERS
VENOMING
VENOMLESS
VENOMOUS
VENOMS
VENOSE
VENOSITY
VENOUS
VENOUSLY
VENT
VENTAGE
VENTAGES
VENTAIL
VENTAILE
VENTAILES
VENTAILS
VENTANA
VENTANAS
VENTAYLE
VENTAYLES
VENTED
VENTER
VENTERS
VENTIDUCT
VENTIFACT
VENTIGE
VENTIGES
VENTIL
VENTILATE
VENTILS
VENTING
VENTINGS
VENTLESS
VENTOSE
VENTOSES
VENTOSITY
VENTOUSE
VENTOUSES
VENTRAL
VENTRALLY
VENTRALS
VENTRE
VENTRED
VENTRES
VENTRICLE
VENTRING
VENTRINGS
VENTROUS
VENTS
VENTURE
VENTURED
VENTURER
VENTURERS
VENTURES
VENTURI
VENTURING
VENTURIS
VENTUROUS
VENUE
VENUES
VENULAR
VENULE
VENULES
VENULOSE
VENULOUS
VENUS
VENUSES
VENVILLE
VENVILLES
VERA
VERACIOUS
VERACITY
VERANDA
VERANDAED
VERANDAH
VERANDAHS
VERANDAS
VERAPAMIL
VERATRIA
VERATRIAS
VERATRIN
VERATRINE
VERATRINS
VERATRUM
VERATRUMS
VERB
VERBAL
VERBALISE
VERBALISM
VERBALIST
VERBALITY
VERBALIZE
VERBALLED
VERBALLY
VERBALS
VERBARIAN
VERBASCUM
VERBATIM
VERBENA
VERBENAS
VERBERATE
VERBIAGE
VERBIAGES
VERBICIDE
VERBID
VERBIDS
VERBIFIED
VERBIFIES
VERBIFY
VERBILE
VERBILES
VERBING
VERBINGS
VERBLESS
VERBOSE
VERBOSELY
VERBOSER
VERBOSEST
VERBOSITY
VERBOTEN
VERBS
VERD
VERDANCY
VERDANT
VERDANTLY
VERDELHO
VERDELHOS
VERDERER
VERDERERS
VERDEROR
VERDERORS
VERDET
VERDETS
VERDICT
VERDICTS
VERDIGRIS
VERDIN
VERDINS
VERDIT
VERDITE
VERDITER
VERDITERS
VERDITES
VERDITS
VERDOY
VERDOYS
VERDURE
VERDURED
VERDURES
VERDUROUS
VERECUND
VERGE
VERGED
VERGENCE
VERGENCES
VERGENCY
VERGER
VERGERS
VERGES
VERGING
VERGLAS
VERGLASES
VERIDIC

V

VERIDICAL
VERIER
VERIEST
VERIFIED
VERIFIER
VERIFIERS
VERIFIES
VERIFY
VERIFYING
VERILY
VERISM
VERISMO
VERISMOS
VERISMS
VERIST
VERISTIC
VERISTS
VERITABLE
VERITABLY
VERITAS
VERITATES
VERITE
VERITES
VERITIES
VERITY
VERJUICE
VERJUICED
VERJUICES
VERJUS
VERJUSES
VERKLEMPT
VERKRAMP
VERLAN
VERLANS
VERLIG
VERLIGTE
VERLIGTES
VERMAL
VERMEIL
VERMEILED
VERMEILLE
VERMEILS
VERMELL
VERMELLS
VERMES
VERMIAN
VERMICIDE
VERMICULE
VERMIFORM
VERMIFUGE
VERMIL
VERMILIES
VERMILION
VERMILLED
VERMILS
VERMILY
VERMIN
VERMINATE
VERMINED
VERMINIER
VERMINOUS
VERMINS
VERMINY
VERMIS
VERMOULU
VERMOUTH
VERMOUTHS
VERMUTH
VERMUTHS
VERNACLE
VERNACLES
VERNAL
VERNALISE
VERNALITY
VERNALIZE
VERNALLY
VERNANT
VERNATION
VERNICLE
VERNICLES
VERNIER
VERNIERS
VERNIX
VERNIXES
VERONAL
VERONALS
VERONICA
VERONICAS
VERONIQUE
VERQUERE
VERQUERES
VERQUIRE
VERQUIRES
VERRA
VERREL
VERRELS
VERREY
VERRINE
VERRINES
VERRUCA
VERRUCAE
VERRUCAS
VERRUCOSE
VERRUCOUS
VERRUGA
VERRUGAS
VERRY
VERS
VERSAL
VERSALS
VERSANT
VERSANTS
VERSATILE
VERSE
VERSED
VERSELET
VERSELETS
VERSEMAN
VERSEMEN
VERSER
VERSERS
VERSES
VERSET
VERSETS
VERSICLE
VERSICLES
VERSIFIED
VERSIFIER
VERSIFIES
VERSIFORM
VERSIFY
VERSIN
VERSINE
VERSINES
VERSING
VERSINGS
VERSINS
VERSION
VERSIONAL
VERSIONED
VERSIONER
VERSIONS
VERSO
VERSOS
VERST
VERSTE
VERSTES
VERSTS
VERSUS
VERSUTE
VERT
VERTEBRA
VERTEBRAE
VERTEBRAL
VERTEBRAS
VERTED
VERTEX
VERTEXES
VERTICAL
VERTICALS
VERTICES
VERTICIL
VERTICILS
VERTICITY
VERTIGO
VERTIGOES
VERTIGOS
VERTING
VERTIPORT
VERTISOL
VERTISOLS
VERTS
VERTU
VERTUE
VERTUES
VERTUOUS
VERTUS
VERVAIN
VERVAINS
VERVE
VERVEL
VERVELLED
VERVELS
VERVEN
VERVENS
VERVES
VERVET
VERVETS
VERY
VESICA
VESICAE
VESICAL
VESICANT
VESICANTS
VESICAS
VESICATE
VESICATED
VESICATES
VESICLE
VESICLES
VESICULA
VESICULAE
VESICULAR
VESPA
VESPAS
VESPER
VESPERAL
VESPERALS
VESPERS
VESPIARY
VESPID
VESPIDS
VESPINE
VESPOID
VESSAIL
VESSAILS
VESSEL
VESSELED
VESSELS
VEST
VESTA
VESTAL
VESTALLY
VESTALS
VESTAS
VESTED
VESTEE
VESTEES
VESTIARY
VESTIBULA
VESTIBULE
VESTIGE
VESTIGES
VESTIGIA
VESTIGIAL
VESTIGIUM
VESTIMENT
VESTING
VESTINGS
VESTITURE

VESTLESS
VESTLIKE
VESTMENT
VESTMENTS
VESTRAL
VESTRIES
VESTRY
VESTRYMAN
VESTRYMEN
VESTS
VESTURAL
VESTURE
VESTURED
VESTURER
VESTURERS
VESTURES
VESTURING
VESUVIAN
VESUVIANS
VET
VETCH
VETCHES
VETCHIER
VETCHIEST
VETCHLING
VETCHY
VETERAN
VETERANS
VETIVER
VETIVERS
VETIVERT
VETIVERTS
VETKOEK
VETKOEKS
VETO
VETOED
VETOER
VETOERS
VETOES
VETOING
VETOLESS
VETS
VETTED
VETTER
VETTERS
VETTING
VETTINGS
VETTURA
VETTURAS
VETTURINI
VETTURINO
VEX
VEXATION
VEXATIONS
VEXATIOUS
VEXATORY
VEXED
VEXEDLY
VEXEDNESS
VEXER
VEXERS
VEXES
VEXIL
VEXILLA
VEXILLAR
VEXILLARY
VEXILLATE
VEXILLUM
VEXILS
VEXING
VEXINGLY
VEXINGS
VEXT
VEZIR
VEZIRS
VIA
VIABILITY
VIABLE
VIABLY
VIADUCT
VIADUCTS
VIAE
VIAL
VIALED
VIALFUL
VIALFULS
VIALING
VIALLED
VIALLING
VIALS
VIAMETER
VIAMETERS
VIAND
VIANDS
VIAS
VIATIC
VIATICA
VIATICAL
VIATICALS
VIATICUM
VIATICUMS
VIATOR
VIATORES
VIATORIAL
VIATORS
VIBE
VIBES
VIBEX
VIBEY
VIBICES
VIBIER
VIBIEST
VIBIST
VIBISTS
VIBRACULA
VIBRAHARP
VIBRANCE
VIBRANCES
VIBRANCY
VIBRANT
VIBRANTLY
VIBRANTS
VIBRATE
VIBRATED
VIBRATES
VIBRATILE
VIBRATING
VIBRATION
VIBRATIVE
VIBRATO
VIBRATOR
VIBRATORS
VIBRATORY
VIBRATOS
VIBRIO
VIBRIOID
VIBRION
VIBRIONIC
VIBRIONS
VIBRIOS
VIBRIOSES
VIBRIOSIS
VIBRISSA
VIBRISSAE
VIBRISSAL
VIBRONIC
VIBS
VIBURNUM
VIBURNUMS
VICAR
VICARAGE
VICARAGES
VICARATE
VICARATES
VICARESS
VICARIAL
VICARIANT
VICARIATE
VICARIES
VICARIOUS
VICARLIER
VICARLY
VICARS
VICARSHIP
VICARY
VICE
VICED
VICEGERAL
VICELESS
VICELIKE
VICENARY
VICENNIAL
VICEREGAL
VICEREINE
VICEROY
VICEROYS
VICES
VICESIMAL
VICHIES
VICHY
VICIATE
VICIATED
VICIATES
VICIATING
VICINAGE
VICINAGES
VICINAL
VICING
VICINITY
VICIOSITY
VICIOUS
VICIOUSLY
VICOMTE
VICOMTES
VICTIM
VICTIMISE
VICTIMIZE
VICTIMS
VICTOR
VICTORESS
VICTORIA
VICTORIAS
VICTORIES
VICTORINE
VICTORS
VICTORY
VICTRESS
VICTRIX
VICTRIXES
VICTROLA
VICTROLAS
VICTUAL
VICTUALED
VICTUALER
VICTUALS
VICUGNA
VICUGNAS
VICUNA
VICUNAS
VID
VIDALIA
VIDALIAS
VIDAME
VIDAMES
VIDE
VIDELICET
VIDENDA
VIDENDUM
VIDEO
VIDEOCAM
VIDEOCAMS
VIDEODISC
VIDEODISK
VIDEOED
VIDEOFIT
VIDEOFITS
VIDEOGRAM
VIDEOING
VIDEOLAND
VIDEOS

V

VIDEOTAPE
VIDEOTEX
VIDEOTEXT
VIDETTE
VIDETTES
VIDICON
VIDICONS
VIDIMUS
VIDIMUSES
VIDIOT
VIDIOTS
VIDS
VIDSCREEN
VIDUAGE
VIDUAGES
VIDUAL
VIDUITIES
VIDUITY
VIDUOUS
VIE
VIED
VIELLE
VIELLES
VIENNA
VIER
VIERS
VIES
VIEW
VIEWABLE
VIEWBOOK
VIEWBOOKS
VIEWDATA
VIEWDATAS
VIEWED
VIEWER
VIEWERS
VIEWIER
VIEWIEST
VIEWINESS
VIEWING
VIEWINGS
VIEWLESS
VIEWLY
VIEWPHONE
VIEWPOINT
VIEWPORT
VIEWPORTS
VIEWS
VIEWSHED
VIEWSHEDS
VIEWY
VIFDA
VIFDAS
VIFF
VIFFED
VIFFING
VIFFS
VIG
VIGA
VIGAS
VIGESIMAL
VIGIA
VIGIAS
VIGIL
VIGILANCE
VIGILANT
VIGILANTE
VIGILS
VIGNERON
VIGNERONS
VIGNETTE
VIGNETTED
VIGNETTER
VIGNETTES
VIGOR
VIGORISH
VIGORO
VIGOROS
VIGOROSO
VIGOROUS
VIGORS
VIGOUR
VIGOURS
VIGS
VIHARA
VIHARAS
VIHUELA
VIHUELAS
VIKING
VIKINGISM
VIKINGS
VILAYET
VILAYETS
VILD
VILDE
VILDLY
VILDNESS
VILE
VILELY
VILENESS
VILER
VILEST
VILIACO
VILIACOES
VILIACOS
VILIAGO
VILIAGOES
VILIAGOS
VILIFIED
VILIFIER
VILIFIERS
VILIFIES
VILIFY
VILIFYING
VILIPEND
VILIPENDS
VILL
VILLA
VILLADOM
VILLADOMS
VILLAE
VILLAGE
VILLAGER
VILLAGERS
VILLAGERY
VILLAGES
VILLAGEY
VILLAGIER
VILLAGIO
VILLAGIOS
VILLAGREE
VILLAIN
VILLAINS
VILLAINY
VILLAN
VILLANAGE
VILLANIES
VILLANOUS
VILLANS
VILLANY
VILLAR
VILLAS
VILLATIC
VILLEIN
VILLEINS
VILLENAGE
VILLI
VILLIACO
VILLIACOS
VILLIAGO
VILLIAGOS
VILLIFORM
VILLOSE
VILLOSITY
VILLOUS
VILLOUSLY
VILLS
VILLUS
VIM
VIMANA
VIMANAS
VIMEN
VIMINA
VIMINAL
VIMINEOUS
VIMS
VIN
VINA
VINACEOUS
VINAL
VINALS
VINAS
VINASSE
VINASSES
VINCA
VINCAS
VINCIBLE
VINCIBLY
VINCULA
VINCULAR
VINCULUM
VINCULUMS
VINDALOO
VINDALOOS
VINDEMIAL
VINDICATE
VINE
VINEAL
VINED
VINEGAR
VINEGARED
VINEGARS
VINEGARY
VINELESS
VINELIKE
VINER
VINERIES
VINERS
VINERY
VINES
VINEW
VINEWED
VINEWING
VINEWS
VINEYARD
VINEYARDS
VINIC
VINIER
VINIEST
VINIFERA
VINIFERAS
VINIFIED
VINIFIES
VINIFY
VINIFYING
VINING
VINO
VINOLENT
VINOLOGY
VINOS
VINOSITY
VINOUS
VINOUSLY
VINS
VINT
VINTAGE
VINTAGED
VINTAGER
VINTAGERS
VINTAGES
VINTAGING
VINTED
VINTING
VINTNER
VINTNERS
VINTRIES
VINTRY
VINTS
VINY
VINYL

VINYLIC
VINYLS
VIOL
VIOLA
VIOLABLE
VIOLABLY
VIOLAS
VIOLATE
VIOLATED
VIOLATER
VIOLATERS
VIOLATES
VIOLATING
VIOLATION
VIOLATIVE
VIOLATOR
VIOLATORS
VIOLD
VIOLENCE
VIOLENCES
VIOLENT
VIOLENTED
VIOLENTLY
VIOLENTS
VIOLER
VIOLERS
VIOLET
VIOLETS
VIOLIN
VIOLINIST
VIOLINS
VIOLIST
VIOLISTS
VIOLONE
VIOLONES
VIOLS
VIOMYCIN
VIOMYCINS
VIOSTEROL
VIPASSANA
VIPER
VIPERFISH
VIPERINE
VIPERISH
VIPERLIKE
VIPEROUS
VIPERS
VIRAEMIA
VIRAEMIAS
VIRAEMIC
VIRAGO
VIRAGOES
VIRAGOISH
VIRAGOS
VIRAL
VIRALITY
VIRALLY
VIRALS
VIRANDA
VIRANDAS
VIRANDO
VIRANDOS
VIRE
VIRED
VIRELAI
VIRELAIS
VIRELAY
VIRELAYS
VIREMENT
VIREMENTS
VIREMIA
VIREMIAS
VIREMIC
VIRENT
VIREO
VIREONINE
VIREOS
VIRES
VIRESCENT
VIRETOT
VIRETOTS
VIRGA
VIRGAE
VIRGAS
VIRGATE
VIRGATES
VIRGE
VIRGER
VIRGERS
VIRGES
VIRGIN
VIRGINAL
VIRGINALS
VIRGINED
VIRGINIA
VIRGINIAS
VIRGINING
VIRGINITY
VIRGINIUM
VIRGINLY
VIRGINS
VIRGULATE
VIRGULE
VIRGULES
VIRICIDAL
VIRICIDE
VIRICIDES
VIRID
VIRIDIAN
VIRIDIANS
VIRIDITE
VIRIDITES
VIRIDITY
VIRILE
VIRILELY
VIRILISE
VIRILISED
VIRILISES
VIRILISM
VIRILISMS
VIRILITY
VIRILIZE
VIRILIZED
VIRILIZES
VIRILOCAL
VIRING
VIRINO
VIRINOS
VIRION
VIRIONS
VIRL
VIRLS
VIROGENE
VIROGENES
VIROID
VIROIDS
VIROLOGIC
VIROLOGY
VIROSE
VIROSES
VIROSIS
VIROUS
VIRTU
VIRTUAL
VIRTUALLY
VIRTUE
VIRTUES
VIRTUOSA
VIRTUOSAS
VIRTUOSE
VIRTUOSI
VIRTUOSIC
VIRTUOSO
VIRTUOSOS
VIRTUOUS
VIRTUS
VIRUCIDAL
VIRUCIDE
VIRUCIDES
VIRULENCE
VIRULENCY
VIRULENT
VIRUS
VIRUSES
VIRUSLIKE
VIRUSOID
VIRUSOIDS
VIS
VISA
VISAED
VISAGE
VISAGED
VISAGES
VISAGIST
VISAGISTE
VISAGISTS
VISAING
VISARD
VISARDS
VISAS
VISCACHA
VISCACHAS
VISCARIA
VISCARIAS
VISCERA
VISCERAL
VISCERATE
VISCID
VISCIDITY
VISCIDLY
VISCIN
VISCINS
VISCOID
VISCOIDAL
VISCOSE
VISCOSES
VISCOSITY
VISCOUNT
VISCOUNTS
VISCOUNTY
VISCOUS
VISCOUSLY
VISCUM
VISCUMS
VISCUS
VISE
VISED
VISEED
VISEING
VISELIKE
VISES
VISHING
VISHINGS
VISIBLE
VISIBLES
VISIBLY
VISIE
VISIED
VISIEING
VISIER
VISIERS
VISIES
VISILE
VISILES
VISING
VISION
VISIONAL
VISIONARY
VISIONED
VISIONER
VISIONERS
VISIONING
VISIONIST
VISIONS
VISIT
VISITABLE
VISITANT
VISITANTS
VISITATOR
VISITE

V

VISITED
VISITEE
VISITEES
VISITER
VISITERS
VISITES
VISITING
VISITINGS
VISITOR
VISITORS
VISITRESS
VISITS
VISIVE
VISNE
VISNES
VISNOMIE
VISNOMIES
VISNOMY
VISON
VISONS
VISOR
VISORED
VISORING
VISORLESS
VISORS
VISTA
VISTAED
VISTAING
VISTAL
VISTALESS
VISTAS
VISTO
VISTOS
VISUAL
VISUALISE
VISUALIST
VISUALITY
VISUALIZE
VISUALLY
VISUALS
VITA
VITACEOUS
VITAE
VITAL
VITALISE
VITALISED
VITALISER
VITALISES
VITALISM
VITALISMS
VITALIST
VITALISTS
VITALITY
VITALIZE
VITALIZED
VITALIZER
VITALIZES
VITALLY
VITALNESS
VITALS
VITAMER
VITAMERS
VITAMIN
VITAMINE
VITAMINES
VITAMINIC
VITAMINS
VITAS
VITASCOPE
VITATIVE
VITE
VITELLARY
VITELLI
VITELLIN
VITELLINE
VITELLINS
VITELLUS
VITESSE
VITESSES
VITEX
VITEXES
VITIABLE
VITIATE
VITIATED
VITIATES
VITIATING
VITIATION
VITIATOR
VITIATORS
VITICETA
VITICETUM
VITICIDE
VITICIDES
VITILIGO
VITILIGOS
VITIOSITY
VITIOUS
VITRAGE
VITRAGES
VITRAIL
VITRAIN
VITRAINS
VITRAUX
VITREOUS
VITREUM
VITREUMS
VITRIC
VITRICS
VITRIFIED
VITRIFIES
VITRIFORM
VITRIFY
VITRINE
VITRINES
VITRIOL
VITRIOLED
VITRIOLIC
VITRIOLS
VITRO
VITTA
VITTAE
VITTATE
VITTLE
VITTLED
VITTLES
VITTLING
VITULAR
VITULINE
VIVA
VIVACE
VIVACES
VIVACIOUS
VIVACITY
VIVAED
VIVAING
VIVAMENTE
VIVANDIER
VIVARIA
VIVARIES
VIVARIUM
VIVARIUMS
VIVARY
VIVAS
VIVAT
VIVATS
VIVDA
VIVDAS
VIVE
VIVELY
VIVENCIES
VIVENCY
VIVER
VIVERRA
VIVERRAS
VIVERRID
VIVERRIDS
VIVERRINE
VIVERS
VIVES
VIVIANITE
VIVID
VIVIDER
VIVIDEST
VIVIDITY
VIVIDLY
VIVIDNESS
VIVIFIC
VIVIFIED
VIVIFIER
VIVIFIERS
VIVIFIES
VIVIFY
VIVIFYING
VIVIPARA
VIVIPARY
VIVISECT
VIVISECTS
VIVO
VIVRES
VIXEN
VIXENISH
VIXENLY
VIXENS
VIZAMENT
VIZAMENTS
VIZARD
VIZARDED
VIZARDING
VIZARDS
VIZCACHA
VIZCACHAS
VIZIED
VIZIER
VIZIERATE
VIZIERIAL
VIZIERS
VIZIES
VIZIR
VIZIRATE
VIZIRATES
VIZIRIAL
VIZIRS
VIZIRSHIP
VIZOR
VIZORED
VIZORING
VIZORLESS
VIZORS
VIZSLA
VIZSLAS
VIZY
VIZYING
VIZZIE
VIZZIED
VIZZIEING
VIZZIES
VLEI
VLEIS
VLIES
VLOG
VLOGGED
VLOGGER
VLOGGERS
VLOGGING
VLOGGINGS
VLOGS
VLY
VOAR
VOARS
VOCAB
VOCABLE
VOCABLES
VOCABLY
VOCABS
VOCABULAR
VOCAL
VOCALESE
VOCALESES
VOCALIC
VOCALICS

VOCALION
VOCALIONS
VOCALISE
VOCALISED
VOCALISER
VOCALISES
VOCALISM
VOCALISMS
VOCALIST
VOCALISTS
VOCALITY
VOCALIZE
VOCALIZED
VOCALIZER
VOCALIZES
VOCALLY
VOCALNESS
VOCALS
VOCATION
VOCATIONS
VOCATIVE
VOCATIVES
VOCES
VOCODER
VOCODERED
VOCODERS
VOCULAR
VOCULE
VOCULES
VODCAST
VODCASTED
VODCASTER
VODCASTS
VODDIES
VODDY
VODKA
VODKAS
VODOU
VODOUN
VODOUNS
VODOUS
VODUN
VODUNS
VOE
VOEMA
VOEMAS
VOERTSAK
VOERTSEK
VOES
VOETSAK
VOETSEK
VOG
VOGIE
VOGIER
VOGIEST
VOGS
VOGUE
VOGUED
VOGUEING
VOGUEINGS
VOGUER
VOGUERS
VOGUES
VOGUEY
VOGUIER
VOGUIEST
VOGUING
VOGUINGS
VOGUISH
VOGUISHLY
VOICE
VOICED
VOICEFUL
VOICELESS
VOICEMAIL
VOICEOVER
VOICER
VOICERS
VOICES
VOICING
VOICINGS
VOID
VOIDABLE
VOIDANCE
VOIDANCES
VOIDED
VOIDEE
VOIDEES
VOIDER
VOIDERS
VOIDING
VOIDINGS
VOIDNESS
VOIDS
VOILA
VOILE
VOILES
VOIP
VOIPS
VOISINAGE
VOITURE
VOITURES
VOITURIER
VOIVODE
VOIVODES
VOL
VOLA
VOLABLE
VOLAE
VOLAGE
VOLANT
VOLANTE
VOLANTES
VOLAR
VOLARIES
VOLARY
VOLATIC
VOLATICS
VOLATILE
VOLATILES
VOLCANIAN
VOLCANIC
VOLCANICS
VOLCANISE
VOLCANISM
VOLCANIST
VOLCANIZE
VOLCANO
VOLCANOES
VOLCANOS
VOLE
VOLED
VOLELIKE
VOLENS
VOLERIES
VOLERY
VOLES
VOLET
VOLETS
VOLING
VOLITANT
VOLITATE
VOLITATED
VOLITATES
VOLITIENT
VOLITION
VOLITIONS
VOLITIVE
VOLITIVES
VOLK
VOLKS
VOLKSLIED
VOLKSRAAD
VOLLEY
VOLLEYED
VOLLEYER
VOLLEYERS
VOLLEYING
VOLLEYS
VOLOST
VOLOSTS
VOLPINO
VOLPINOS
VOLPLANE
VOLPLANED
VOLPLANES
VOLS
VOLT
VOLTA
VOLTAGE
VOLTAGES
VOLTAIC
VOLTAISM
VOLTAISMS
VOLTE
VOLTED
VOLTES
VOLTI
VOLTIGEUR
VOLTING
VOLTINISM
VOLTIS
VOLTMETER
VOLTS
VOLUBIL
VOLUBLE
VOLUBLY
VOLUCRINE
VOLUME
VOLUMED
VOLUMES
VOLUMETER
VOLUMETRY
VOLUMINAL
VOLUMING
VOLUMISE
VOLUMISED
VOLUMISER
VOLUMISES
VOLUMIST
VOLUMISTS
VOLUMIZE
VOLUMIZED
VOLUMIZER
VOLUMIZES
VOLUNTARY
VOLUNTEER
VOLUSPA
VOLUSPAS
VOLUTE
VOLUTED
VOLUTES
VOLUTIN
VOLUTINS
VOLUTION
VOLUTIONS
VOLUTOID
VOLVA
VOLVAE
VOLVAS
VOLVATE
VOLVE
VOLVED
VOLVES
VOLVING
VOLVOX
VOLVOXES
VOLVULI
VOLVULUS
VOM
VOMER
VOMERINE
VOMERS
VOMICA
VOMICAE
VOMICAS
VOMIT
VOMITED
VOMITER
VOMITERS

VOMITIER
VOMITIEST
VOMITING
VOMITINGS
VOMITIVE
VOMITIVES
VOMITO
VOMITORIA
VOMITORY
VOMITOS
VOMITOUS
VOMITS
VOMITUS
VOMITUSES
VOMITY
VOMMED
VOMMING
VOMS
VONGOLE
VOODOO
VOODOOED
VOODOOING
VOODOOISM
VOODOOIST
VOODOOS
VOORKAMER
VOORSKOT
VOORSKOTS
VOR
VORACIOUS
VORACITY
VORAGO
VORAGOES
VORAGOS
VORANT
VORLAGE
VORLAGES
VORPAL
VORRED
VORRING
VORS
VORTEX
VORTEXES
VORTICAL
VORTICES
VORTICISM
VORTICIST
VORTICITY
VORTICOSE
VOSTRO
VOTABLE
VOTARESS
VOTARIES
VOTARIST
VOTARISTS
VOTARY
VOTE
VOTEABLE
VOTED
VOTEEN
VOTEENS
VOTELESS
VOTER
VOTERS
VOTES
VOTING
VOTINGS
VOTIVE
VOTIVELY
VOTIVES
VOTRESS
VOTRESSES
VOUCH
VOUCHED
VOUCHEE
VOUCHEES
VOUCHER
VOUCHERED
VOUCHERS
VOUCHES
VOUCHING
VOUCHSAFE
VOUDON
VOUDONS
VOUDOU
VOUDOUED
VOUDOUING
VOUDOUN
VOUDOUNS
VOUDOUS
VOUGE
VOUGES
VOULGE
VOULGES
VOULU
VOUSSOIR
VOUSSOIRS
VOUTSAFE
VOUTSAFED
VOUTSAFES
VOUVRAY
VOUVRAYS
VOW
VOWED
VOWEL
VOWELED
VOWELISE
VOWELISED
VOWELISES
VOWELIZE
VOWELIZED
VOWELIZES
VOWELLED
VOWELLESS
VOWELLIER
VOWELLING
VOWELLY
VOWELS
VOWER
VOWERS
VOWESS
VOWESSES
VOWING
VOWLESS
VOWS
VOX
VOXEL
VOXELS
VOYAGE
VOYAGED
VOYAGER
VOYAGERS
VOYAGES
VOYAGEUR
VOYAGEURS
VOYAGING
VOYAGINGS
VOYEUR
VOYEURISM
VOYEURS
VOZHD
VOZHDS
VRAIC
VRAICKER
VRAICKERS
VRAICKING
VRAICS
VRIL
VRILS
VROOM
VROOMED
VROOMING
VROOMS
VROT
VROU
VROUS
VROUW
VROUWS
VROW
VROWS
VRYSTATER
VUG
VUGG
VUGGIER
VUGGIEST
VUGGS
VUGGY
VUGH
VUGHIER
VUGHIEST
VUGHS
VUGHY
VUGS
VUGULAR
VULCAN
VULCANIAN
VULCANIC
VULCANISE
VULCANISM
VULCANIST
VULCANITE
VULCANIZE
VULCANS
VULGAR
VULGARER
VULGAREST
VULGARIAN
VULGARISE
VULGARISM
VULGARITY
VULGARIZE
VULGARLY
VULGARS
VULGATE
VULGATES
VULGO
VULGUS
VULGUSES
VULN
VULNED
VULNERARY
VULNERATE
VULNING
VULNS
VULPICIDE
VULPINE
VULPINISM
VULPINITE
VULSELLA
VULSELLAE
VULSELLUM
VULTURE
VULTURES
VULTURINE
VULTURISH
VULTURISM
VULTURN
VULTURNS
VULTUROUS
VULVA
VULVAE
VULVAL
VULVAR
VULVAS
VULVATE
VULVIFORM
VULVITIS
VUM
VUMMED
VUMMING
VUMS
VUTTIER
VUTTIEST
VUTTY
VUVUZELA
VUVUZELAS
VYING
VYINGLY
VYINGS

V

W

WAAC
WAACS
WAAH
WAB
WABAIN
WABAINS
WABBIT
WABBLE
WABBLED
WABBLER
WABBLERS
WABBLES
WABBLIER
WABBLIEST
WABBLING
WABBLY
WABOOM
WABOOMS
WABS
WABSTER
WABSTERS
WACK
WACKE
WACKED
WACKER
WACKERS
WACKES
WACKEST
WACKIER
WACKIEST
WACKILY
WACKINESS
WACKO
WACKOES
WACKOS
WACKS
WACKY
WACONDA
WACONDAS
WAD
WADABLE
WADD
WADDED
WADDER
WADDERS
WADDIE
WADDIED
WADDIES
WADDING
WADDINGS
WADDLE
WADDLED
WADDLER
WADDLERS
WADDLES
WADDLIER
WADDLIEST
WADDLING
WADDLY
WADDS
WADDY
WADDYING
WADE
WADEABLE
WADED
WADER
WADERS
WADES
WADGE
WADGES
WADI
WADIES
WADING
WADINGS
WADIS
WADMAAL
WADMAALS
WADMAL
WADMALS
WADMEL
WADMELS
WADMOL
WADMOLL
WADMOLLS
WADMOLS
WADS
WADSET
WADSETS
WADSETT
WADSETTED
WADSETTER
WADSETTS
WADT
WADTS
WADY
WAE
WAEFUL
WAENESS
WAENESSES
WAES
WAESOME
WAESUCK
WAESUCKS
WAFER
WAFERED
WAFERIER
WAFERIEST
WAFERING
WAFERS
WAFERY
WAFF
WAFFED
WAFFIE
WAFFIES
WAFFING
WAFFLE
WAFFLED
WAFFLER
WAFFLERS
WAFFLES
WAFFLIER
WAFFLIEST
WAFFLING
WAFFLINGS
WAFFLY
WAFFS
WAFT
WAFTAGE
WAFTAGES
WAFTED
WAFTER
WAFTERS
WAFTING
WAFTINGS
WAFTS
WAFTURE
WAFTURES
WAG
WAGE
WAGED
WAGELESS
WAGENBOOM
WAGER
WAGERED
WAGERER
WAGERERS
WAGERING
WAGERINGS
WAGERS
WAGES
WAGGA
WAGGAS
WAGGED
WAGGER
WAGGERIES
WAGGERS
WAGGERY
WAGGING
WAGGISH
WAGGISHLY
WAGGLE
WAGGLED
WAGGLER
WAGGLERS
WAGGLES
WAGGLIER
WAGGLIEST
WAGGLING
WAGGLY
WAGGON
WAGGONED
WAGGONER
WAGGONERS
WAGGONING
WAGGONS
WAGHALTER
WAGING
WAGMOIRE
WAGMOIRES
WAGON
WAGONAGE
WAGONAGES
WAGONED
WAGONER
WAGONERS
WAGONETTE
WAGONFUL
WAGONFULS
WAGONING
WAGONLESS
WAGONLOAD
WAGONS
WAGS
WAGSOME
WAGTAIL
WAGTAILS
WAGYU
WAGYUS
WAHCONDA
WAHCONDAS
WAHINE
WAHINES
WAHOO
WAHOOS
WAI
WAIATA
WAIATAS
WAID
WAIDE
WAIF

WAIFED
WAIFING
WAIFISH
WAIFLIKE
WAIFS
WAIFT
WAIFTS
WAIL
WAILED
WAILER
WAILERS
WAILFUL
WAILFULLY
WAILING
WAILINGLY
WAILINGS
WAILS
WAILSOME
WAIN
WAINAGE
WAINAGES
WAINED
WAINING
WAINS
WAINSCOT
WAINSCOTS
WAIR
WAIRED
WAIRING
WAIRS
WAIRSH
WAIRSHER
WAIRSHEST
WAIRUA
WAIRUAS
WAIS
WAIST
WAISTBAND
WAISTBELT
WAISTCOAT
WAISTED
WAISTER
WAISTERS
WAISTING
WAISTINGS
WAISTLESS
WAISTLINE
WAISTS
WAIT
WAITE
WAITED
WAITER
WAITERAGE
WAITERED
WAITERING
WAITERS
WAITES
WAITING
WAITINGLY
WAITINGS
WAITLIST
WAITLISTS
WAITRESS
WAITRON
WAITRONS
WAITS
WAITSTAFF
WAIVE
WAIVED
WAIVER
WAIVERS
WAIVES
WAIVING
WAIVODE
WAIVODES
WAIWODE
WAIWODES
WAKA
WAKAME
WAKAMES
WAKANDA
WAKANDAS
WAKANE
WAKANES
WAKAS
WAKE
WAKEBOARD
WAKED
WAKEFUL
WAKEFULLY
WAKELESS
WAKEMAN
WAKEMEN
WAKEN
WAKENED
WAKENER
WAKENERS
WAKENING
WAKENINGS
WAKENS
WAKER
WAKERIFE
WAKERS
WAKES
WAKF
WAKFS
WAKIKI
WAKIKIS
WAKING
WAKINGS
WALD
WALDFLUTE
WALDGRAVE
WALDHORN
WALDHORNS
WALDO
WALDOES
WALDOS
WALDRAPP
WALDRAPPS
WALDS
WALE
WALED
WALER
WALERS
WALES
WALI
WALIE
WALIER
WALIES
WALIEST
WALING
WALIS
WALISE
WALISES
WALK
WALKABLE
WALKABOUT
WALKATHON
WALKAWAY
WALKAWAYS
WALKED
WALKER
WALKERS
WALKIES
WALKING
WALKINGS
WALKMILL
WALKMILLS
WALKOUT
WALKOUTS
WALKOVER
WALKOVERS
WALKS
WALKUP
WALKUPS
WALKWAY
WALKWAYS
WALKYRIE
WALKYRIES
WALL
WALLA
WALLABA
WALLABAS
WALLABIES
WALLABY
WALLAH
WALLAHS
WALLAROO
WALLAROOS
WALLAS
WALLBOARD
WALLCHART
WALLED
WALLER
WALLERS
WALLET
WALLETS
WALLEY
WALLEYE
WALLEYED
WALLEYES
WALLEYS
WALLFISH
WALLIE
WALLIER
WALLIES
WALLIEST
WALLING
WALLINGS
WALLOP
WALLOPED
WALLOPER
WALLOPERS
WALLOPING
WALLOPS
WALLOW
WALLOWED
WALLOWER
WALLOWERS
WALLOWING
WALLOWS
WALLPAPER
WALLS
WALLSEND
WALLSENDS
WALLWORT
WALLWORTS
WALLY
WALLYBALL
WALLYDRAG
WALNUT
WALNUTS
WALRUS
WALRUSES
WALTIER
WALTIEST
WALTY
WALTZ
WALTZED
WALTZER
WALTZERS
WALTZES
WALTZING
WALTZINGS
WALTZLIKE
WALY
WAMBENGER
WAMBLE
WAMBLED
WAMBLES
WAMBLIER
WAMBLIEST
WAMBLING
WAMBLINGS
WAMBLY
WAME
WAMED
WAMEFOU
WAMEFOUS

WAMEFUL
WAMEFULS
WAMES
WAMMUL
WAMMULS
WAMMUS
WAMMUSES
WAMPEE
WAMPEES
WAMPISH
WAMPISHED
WAMPISHES
WAMPUM
WAMPUMS
WAMPUS
WAMPUSES
WAMUS
WAMUSES
WAN
WANCHANCY
WAND
WANDER
WANDERED
WANDERER
WANDERERS
WANDERING
WANDEROO
WANDEROOS
WANDERS
WANDLE
WANDLED
WANDLES
WANDLIKE
WANDLING
WANDOO
WANDOOS
WANDS
WANE
WANED
WANES
WANEY
WANG
WANGAN
WANGANS
WANGLE
WANGLED
WANGLER
WANGLERS
WANGLES
WANGLING
WANGLINGS
WANGS
WANGUN
WANGUNS
WANHOPE
WANHOPES
WANIER
WANIEST
WANIGAN
WANIGANS
WANING
WANINGS
WANION
WANIONS
WANK
WANKED
WANKER
WANKERS
WANKIER
WANKIEST
WANKING
WANKLE
WANKS
WANKSTA
WANKSTAS
WANKY
WANLE
WANLY
WANNA
WANNABE
WANNABEE
WANNABEES
WANNABES
WANNED
WANNEL
WANNER
WANNESS
WANNESSES
WANNEST
WANNIGAN
WANNIGANS
WANNING
WANNION
WANNIONS
WANNISH
WANS
WANT
WANTAGE
WANTAGES
WANTAWAY
WANTAWAYS
WANTED
WANTER
WANTERS
WANTHILL
WANTHILLS
WANTIES
WANTING
WANTON
WANTONED
WANTONER
WANTONERS
WANTONEST
WANTONING
WANTONISE
WANTONIZE
WANTONLY
WANTONS
WANTS
WANTY
WANWORDY
WANWORTH
WANWORTHS
WANY
WANZE
WANZED
WANZES
WANZING
WAP
WAPENSHAW
WAPENTAKE
WAPINSHAW
WAPITI
WAPITIS
WAPPED
WAPPEND
WAPPER
WAPPERED
WAPPERING
WAPPERS
WAPPING
WAPS
WAQF
WAQFS
WAR
WARAGI
WARAGIS
WARATAH
WARATAHS
WARB
WARBIER
WARBIEST
WARBIRD
WARBIRDS
WARBLE
WARBLED
WARBLER
WARBLERS
WARBLES
WARBLIER
WARBLIEST
WARBLING
WARBLINGS
WARBLY
WARBONNET
WARBOT
WARBOTS
WARBS
WARBY
WARCRAFT
WARCRAFTS
WARD
WARDCORN
WARDCORNS
WARDED
WARDEN
WARDENED
WARDENING
WARDENRY
WARDENS
WARDER
WARDERED
WARDERING
WARDERS
WARDIAN
WARDING
WARDINGS
WARDLESS
WARDMOTE
WARDMOTES
WARDOG
WARDOGS
WARDRESS
WARDROBE
WARDROBED
WARDROBER
WARDROBES
WARDROOM
WARDROOMS
WARDROP
WARDROPS
WARDS
WARDSHIP
WARDSHIPS
WARE
WARED
WAREHOU
WAREHOUS
WAREHOUSE
WARELESS
WAREROOM
WAREROOMS
WARES
WAREZ
WARFARE
WARFARED
WARFARER
WARFARERS
WARFARES
WARFARIN
WARFARING
WARFARINS
WARGAME
WARGAMED
WARGAMER
WARGAMERS
WARGAMES
WARGAMING
WARHABLE
WARHEAD
WARHEADS
WARHORSE
WARHORSES
WARIBASHI
WARIER
WARIEST
WARILY
WARIMENT
WARIMENTS
WARINESS

W

WARING
WARISON
WARISONS
WARK
WARKED
WARKING
WARKS
WARLESS
WARLIKE
WARLING
WARLINGS
WARLOCK
WARLOCKRY
WARLOCKS
WARLORD
WARLORDS
WARM
WARMAKER
WARMAKERS
WARMAN
WARMBLOOD
WARMED
WARMEN
WARMER
WARMERS
WARMEST
WARMING
WARMINGS
WARMISH
WARMIST
WARMISTS
WARMLY
WARMNESS
WARMONGER
WARMOUTH
WARMOUTHS
WARMS
WARMTH
WARMTHS
WARMUP
WARMUPS
WARN
WARNED
WARNER
WARNERS
WARNING
WARNINGLY
WARNINGS
WARNS
WARP
WARPAGE
WARPAGES
WARPAINT
WARPAINTS
WARPATH
WARPATHS
WARPED
WARPER
WARPERS
WARPING
WARPINGS
WARPLANE
WARPLANES
WARPOWER
WARPOWERS
WARPS
WARPWISE
WARRAGAL
WARRAGALS
WARRAGLE
WARRAGLES
WARRAGUL
WARRAGULS
WARRAN
WARRAND
WARRANDED
WARRANDS
WARRANED
WARRANING
WARRANS
WARRANT
WARRANTED
WARRANTEE
WARRANTER
WARRANTOR
WARRANTS
WARRANTY
WARRAY
WARRAYED
WARRAYING
WARRAYS
WARRE
WARRED
WARREN
WARRENER
WARRENERS
WARRENS
WARREY
WARREYED
WARREYING
WARREYS
WARRIGAL
WARRIGALS
WARRING
WARRIOR
WARRIORS
WARRISON
WARRISONS
WARS
WARSAW
WARSAWS
WARSHIP
WARSHIPS
WARSLE
WARSLED
WARSLER
WARSLERS
WARSLES
WARSLING
WARST
WARSTLE
WARSTLED
WARSTLER
WARSTLERS
WARSTLES
WARSTLING
WART
WARTED
WARTHOG
WARTHOGS
WARTIER
WARTIEST
WARTIME
WARTIMES
WARTLESS
WARTLIKE
WARTS
WARTWEED
WARTWEEDS
WARTWORT
WARTWORTS
WARTY
WARWOLF
WARWOLVES
WARWORK
WARWORKS
WARWORN
WARY
WARZONE
WARZONES
WAS
WASABI
WASABIS
WASE
WASES
WASH
WASHABLE
WASHABLES
WASHAWAY
WASHAWAYS
WASHBAG
WASHBAGS
WASHBALL
WASHBALLS
WASHBASIN
WASHBOARD
WASHBOWL
WASHBOWLS
WASHCLOTH
WASHDAY
WASHDAYS
WASHDOWN
WASHDOWNS
WASHED
WASHEN
WASHER
WASHERED
WASHERIES
WASHERING
WASHERMAN
WASHERMEN
WASHERS
WASHERY
WASHES
WASHFAST
WASHHAND
WASHHOUSE
WASHIER
WASHIEST
WASHILY
WASHIN
WASHINESS
WASHING
WASHINGS
WASHINS
WASHLAND
WASHLANDS
WASHOUT
WASHOUTS
WASHPOT
WASHPOTS
WASHRAG
WASHRAGS
WASHROOM
WASHROOMS
WASHSTAND
WASHTUB
WASHTUBS
WASHUP
WASHUPS
WASHWIPE
WASHWIPES
WASHWOMAN
WASHWOMEN
WASHY
WASM
WASMS
WASP
WASPIE
WASPIER
WASPIES
WASPIEST
WASPILY
WASPINESS
WASPISH
WASPISHLY
WASPLIKE
WASPNEST
WASPNESTS
WASPS
WASPY
WASSAIL
WASSAILED
WASSAILER
WASSAILRY
WASSAILS
WASSERMAN
WASSERMEN
WASSUP
WAST

W

WASTABLE
WASTAGE
WASTAGES
WASTE
WASTEBIN
WASTEBINS
WASTED
WASTEFUL
WASTEL
WASTELAND
WASTELOT
WASTELOTS
WASTELS
WASTENESS
WASTER
WASTERED
WASTERFUL
WASTERIE
WASTERIES
WASTERING
WASTERS
WASTERY
WASTES
WASTEWAY
WASTEWAYS
WASTEWEIR
WASTFULL
WASTING
WASTINGLY
WASTINGS
WASTNESS
WASTREL
WASTRELS
WASTRIE
WASTRIES
WASTRIFE
WASTRIFES
WASTRY
WASTS
WAT
WATAP
WATAPE
WATAPES
WATAPS
WATCH
WATCHA
WATCHABLE
WATCHBAND
WATCHBOX
WATCHCASE
WATCHCRY
WATCHDOG
WATCHDOGS
WATCHED
WATCHER
WATCHERS
WATCHES
WATCHET
WATCHETS
WATCHEYE
WATCHEYES
WATCHFUL
WATCHING
WATCHLIST
WATCHMAN
WATCHMEN
WATCHOUT
WATCHOUTS
WATCHWORD
WATE
WATER
WATERAGE
WATERAGES
WATERBED
WATERBEDS
WATERBIRD
WATERBUCK
WATERBUS
WATERDOG
WATERDOGS
WATERED
WATERER
WATERERS
WATERFALL
WATERFOWL
WATERGATE
WATERHEAD
WATERHEN
WATERHENS
WATERHOLE
WATERIER
WATERIEST
WATERILY
WATERING
WATERINGS
WATERISH
WATERJET
WATERJETS
WATERLEAF
WATERLESS
WATERLILY
WATERLINE
WATERLOG
WATERLOGS
WATERLOO
WATERLOOS
WATERMAN
WATERMARK
WATERMEN
WATERMILL
WATERPOX
WATERS
WATERSHED
WATERSIDE
WATERSKI
WATERSKIS
WATERWAY
WATERWAYS
WATERWEED
WATERWORK
WATERWORN
WATERY
WATERZOOI
WATS
WATT
WATTAGE
WATTAGES
WATTAPE
WATTAPES
WATTER
WATTEST
WATTHOUR
WATTHOURS
WATTLE
WATTLED
WATTLES
WATTLESS
WATTLING
WATTLINGS
WATTMETER
WATTS
WAUCHT
WAUCHTED
WAUCHTING
WAUCHTS
WAUFF
WAUFFED
WAUFFING
WAUFFS
WAUGH
WAUGHED
WAUGHING
WAUGHS
WAUGHT
WAUGHTED
WAUGHTING
WAUGHTS
WAUK
WAUKED
WAUKER
WAUKERS
WAUKING
WAUKMILL
WAUKMILLS
WAUKRIFE
WAUKS
WAUL
WAULED
WAULING
WAULINGS
WAULK
WAULKED
WAULKER
WAULKERS
WAULKING
WAULKMILL
WAULKS
WAULS
WAUR
WAURED
WAURING
WAURS
WAURST
WAVE
WAVEBAND
WAVEBANDS
WAVED
WAVEFORM
WAVEFORMS
WAVEFRONT
WAVEGUIDE
WAVELESS
WAVELET
WAVELETS
WAVELIKE
WAVELLITE
WAVEMETER
WAVEOFF
WAVEOFFS
WAVER
WAVERED
WAVERER
WAVERERS
WAVERIER
WAVERIEST
WAVERING
WAVERINGS
WAVEROUS
WAVERS
WAVERY
WAVES
WAVESHAPE
WAVESON
WAVESONS
WAVETABLE
WAVEY
WAVEYS
WAVICLE
WAVICLES
WAVIER
WAVIES
WAVIEST
WAVILY
WAVINESS
WAVING
WAVINGS
WAVY
WAW
WAWA
WAWAED
WAWAING
WAWAS
WAWE
WAWES
WAWL
WAWLED
WAWLING
WAWLINGS
WAWLS
WAWS

W

WAX
WAXABLE
WAXBERRY
WAXBILL
WAXBILLS
WAXCLOTH
WAXCLOTHS
WAXED
WAXEN
WAXER
WAXERS
WAXES
WAXEYE
WAXEYES
WAXFLOWER
WAXIER
WAXIEST
WAXILY
WAXINESS
WAXING
WAXINGS
WAXLIKE
WAXPLANT
WAXPLANTS
WAXWEED
WAXWEEDS
WAXWING
WAXWINGS
WAXWORK
WAXWORKER
WAXWORKS
WAXWORM
WAXWORMS
WAXY
WAY
WAYANG
WAYANGS
WAYBACK
WAYBACKS
WAYBILL
WAYBILLS
WAYBOARD
WAYBOARDS
WAYBREAD
WAYBREADS
WAYED
WAYFARE
WAYFARED
WAYFARER
WAYFARERS
WAYFARES
WAYFARING
WAYGOING
WAYGOINGS
WAYGONE
WAYGOOSE
WAYGOOSES
WAYING
WAYLAID
WAYLAY
WAYLAYER
WAYLAYERS
WAYLAYING
WAYLAYS
WAYLEAVE
WAYLEAVES
WAYLEGGO
WAYLESS
WAYMARK
WAYMARKED
WAYMARKS
WAYMENT
WAYMENTED
WAYMENTS
WAYPOINT
WAYPOINTS
WAYPOST
WAYPOSTS
WAYS
WAYSIDE
WAYSIDES
WAYWARD
WAYWARDLY
WAYWISER
WAYWISERS
WAYWODE
WAYWODES
WAYWORN
WAYZGOOSE
WAZ
WAZIR
WAZIRS
WAZOO
WAZOOS
WAZZ
WAZZED
WAZZES
WAZZING
WAZZOCK
WAZZOCKS
WE
WEAK
WEAKEN
WEAKENED
WEAKENER
WEAKENERS
WEAKENING
WEAKENS
WEAKER
WEAKEST
WEAKFISH
WEAKISH
WEAKISHLY
WEAKLIER
WEAKLIEST
WEAKLING
WEAKLINGS
WEAKLY
WEAKNESS
WEAKON
WEAKONS
WEAKSIDE
WEAKSIDES
WEAL
WEALD
WEALDS
WEALS
WEALSMAN
WEALSMEN
WEALTH
WEALTHIER
WEALTHILY
WEALTHS
WEALTHY
WEAMB
WEAMBS
WEAN
WEANED
WEANEL
WEANELS
WEANER
WEANERS
WEANING
WEANINGS
WEANLING
WEANLINGS
WEANS
WEAPON
WEAPONED
WEAPONEER
WEAPONING
WEAPONISE
WEAPONIZE
WEAPONRY
WEAPONS
WEAR
WEARABLE
WEARABLES
WEARED
WEARER
WEARERS
WEARIED
WEARIER
WEARIES
WEARIEST
WEARIFUL
WEARILESS
WEARILY
WEARINESS
WEARING
WEARINGLY
WEARINGS
WEARISH
WEARISOME
WEARPROOF
WEARS
WEARY
WEARYING
WEASAND
WEASANDS
WEASEL
WEASELED
WEASELER
WEASELERS
WEASELIER
WEASELING
WEASELLED
WEASELLER
WEASELLY
WEASELS
WEASELY
WEASON
WEASONS
WEATHER
WEATHERED
WEATHERER
WEATHERLY
WEATHERS
WEAVE
WEAVED
WEAVER
WEAVERS
WEAVES
WEAVING
WEAVINGS
WEAZAND
WEAZANDS
WEAZEN
WEAZENED
WEAZENING
WEAZENS
WEB
WEBAPP
WEBAPPS
WEBBED
WEBBIE
WEBBIER
WEBBIES
WEBBIEST
WEBBING
WEBBINGS
WEBBY
WEBCAM
WEBCAMS
WEBCAST
WEBCASTED
WEBCASTER
WEBCASTS
WEBCHAT
WEBCHATS
WEBER
WEBERS
WEBFED
WEBFEET
WEBFOOT
WEBFOOTED
WEBHEAD
WEBHEADS
WEBIFIED
WEBIFIES

W

WEBIFY
WEBIFYING
WEBINAR
WEBINARS
WEBISODE
WEBISODES
WEBLESS
WEBLIKE
WEBLISH
WEBLISHES
WEBLOG
WEBLOGGER
WEBLOGS
WEBMAIL
WEBMAILS
WEBMASTER
WEBPAGE
WEBPAGES
WEBRING
WEBRINGS
WEBS
WEBSITE
WEBSITES
WEBSPACE
WEBSPACES
WEBSTER
WEBSTERS
WEBWHEEL
WEBWHEELS
WEBWORK
WEBWORKS
WEBWORM
WEBWORMS
WEBZINE
WEBZINES
WECHT
WECHTED
WECHTING
WECHTS
WED
WEDDED
WEDDER
WEDDERED
WEDDERING
WEDDERS
WEDDING
WEDDINGS
WEDEL
WEDELED
WEDELING
WEDELN
WEDELNED
WEDELNING
WEDELNS
WEDELS
WEDGE
WEDGED
WEDGELIKE
WEDGES
WEDGEWISE
WEDGIE
WEDGIER
WEDGIES
WEDGIEST
WEDGING
WEDGINGS
WEDGY
WEDLOCK
WEDLOCKS
WEDS
WEE
WEED
WEEDBED
WEEDBEDS
WEEDED
WEEDER
WEEDERIES
WEEDERS
WEEDERY
WEEDHEAD
WEEDHEADS
WEEDICIDE
WEEDIER
WEEDIEST
WEEDILY
WEEDINESS
WEEDING
WEEDINGS
WEEDLESS
WEEDLIKE
WEEDLINE
WEEDLINES
WEEDS
WEEDY
WEEING
WEEJUNS
WEEK
WEEKDAY
WEEKDAYS
WEEKE
WEEKEND
WEEKENDED
WEEKENDER
WEEKENDS
WEEKES
WEEKLIES
WEEKLONG
WEEKLY
WEEKNIGHT
WEEKS
WEEL
WEELS
WEEM
WEEMS
WEEN
WEENED
WEENIE
WEENIER
WEENIES
WEENIEST
WEENING
WEENS
WEENSIER
WEENSIEST
WEENSY
WEENY
WEEP
WEEPER
WEEPERS
WEEPHOLE
WEEPHOLES
WEEPIE
WEEPIER
WEEPIES
WEEPIEST
WEEPILY
WEEPINESS
WEEPING
WEEPINGLY
WEEPINGS
WEEPS
WEEPY
WEER
WEES
WEEST
WEET
WEETE
WEETED
WEETEN
WEETER
WEETEST
WEETING
WEETINGLY
WEETLESS
WEETS
WEEVER
WEEVERS
WEEVIL
WEEVILED
WEEVILIER
WEEVILLED
WEEVILLY
WEEVILS
WEEVILY
WEEWEE
WEEWEED
WEEWEEING
WEEWEES
WEFT
WEFTAGE
WEFTAGES
WEFTE
WEFTED
WEFTES
WEFTING
WEFTS
WEFTWISE
WEID
WEIDS
WEIGELA
WEIGELAS
WEIGELIA
WEIGELIAS
WEIGH
WEIGHABLE
WEIGHAGE
WEIGHAGES
WEIGHED
WEIGHER
WEIGHERS
WEIGHING
WEIGHINGS
WEIGHMAN
WEIGHMEN
WEIGHS
WEIGHT
WEIGHTAGE
WEIGHTED
WEIGHTER
WEIGHTERS
WEIGHTIER
WEIGHTILY
WEIGHTING
WEIGHTS
WEIGHTY
WEIL
WEILS
WEINER
WEINERS
WEIR
WEIRD
WEIRDED
WEIRDER
WEIRDEST
WEIRDIE
WEIRDIES
WEIRDING
WEIRDLY
WEIRDNESS
WEIRDO
WEIRDOES
WEIRDOS
WEIRDS
WEIRDY
WEIRED
WEIRING
WEIRS
WEISE
WEISED
WEISES
WEISING
WEIZE
WEIZED
WEIZES
WEIZING
WEKA
WEKAS
WELAWAY
WELCH
WELCHED

WELCHER
WELCHERS
WELCHES
WELCHING
WELCOME
WELCOMED
WELCOMELY
WELCOMER
WELCOMERS
WELCOMES
WELCOMING
WELD
WELDABLE
WELDED
WELDER
WELDERS
WELDING
WELDINGS
WELDLESS
WELDMENT
WELDMENTS
WELDMESH
WELDOR
WELDORS
WELDS
WELFARE
WELFARES
WELFARISM
WELFARIST
WELFARITE
WELK
WELKE
WELKED
WELKES
WELKIN
WELKING
WELKINS
WELKS
WELKT
WELL
WELLADAY
WELLADAYS
WELLANEAR
WELLAWAY
WELLAWAYS
WELLBEING
WELLBORN
WELLCURB
WELLCURBS
WELLDOER
WELLDOERS
WELLED
WELLHEAD
WELLHEADS
WELLHOLE
WELLHOLES
WELLHOUSE
WELLIE
WELLIES
WELLING
WELLINGS
WELLNESS
WELLS
WELLSITE
WELLSITES
WELLY
WELS
WELSH
WELSHED
WELSHER
WELSHERS
WELSHES
WELSHING
WELT
WELTED
WELTER
WELTERED
WELTERING
WELTERS
WELTING
WELTINGS
WELTS
WEM
WEMB
WEMBS
WEMS
WEN
WENA
WENCH
WENCHED
WENCHER
WENCHERS
WENCHES
WENCHING
WEND
WENDED
WENDIGO
WENDIGOES
WENDIGOS
WENDING
WENDS
WENGE
WENGES
WENNIER
WENNIEST
WENNISH
WENNY
WENS
WENT
WENTS
WEPT
WERE
WEREGILD
WEREGILDS
WEREWOLF
WERGELD
WERGELDS
WERGELT
WERGELTS
WERGILD
WERGILDS
WERNERITE
WERO
WEROS
WERRIS
WERRISES
WERSH
WERSHER
WERSHEST
WERT
WERWOLF
WERWOLVES
WESAND
WESANDS
WESKIT
WESKITS
WESSAND
WESSANDS
WEST
WESTABOUT
WESTBOUND
WESTED
WESTER
WESTERED
WESTERING
WESTERLY
WESTERN
WESTERNER
WESTERNS
WESTERS
WESTIE
WESTIES
WESTING
WESTINGS
WESTLIN
WESTLINS
WESTMOST
WESTS
WESTWARD
WESTWARDS
WET
WETA
WETAS
WETHER
WETHERS
WETLAND
WETLANDS
WETLY
WETNESS
WETNESSES
WETPROOF
WETS
WETSUIT
WETSUITS
WETTABLE
WETTED
WETTER
WETTERS
WETTEST
WETTIE
WETTIES
WETTING
WETTINGS
WETTISH
WETWARE
WETWARES
WEX
WEXE
WEXED
WEXES
WEXING
WEY
WEYARD
WEYS
WEYWARD
WEZAND
WEZANDS
WHA
WHACK
WHACKED
WHACKER
WHACKERS
WHACKIER
WHACKIEST
WHACKING
WHACKINGS
WHACKO
WHACKOES
WHACKOS
WHACKS
WHACKY
WHAE
WHAISLE
WHAISLED
WHAISLES
WHAISLING
WHAIZLE
WHAIZLED
WHAIZLES
WHAIZLING
WHAKAIRO
WHAKAIROS
WHAKAPAPA
WHALE
WHALEBACK
WHALEBOAT
WHALEBONE
WHALED
WHALELIKE
WHALEMAN
WHALEMEN
WHALER
WHALERIES
WHALERS
WHALERY
WHALES
WHALING
WHALINGS
WHALLY
WHAM

W

WHAMMED
WHAMMIES
WHAMMING
WHAMMO
WHAMMOS
WHAMMY
WHAMO
WHAMPLE
WHAMPLES
WHAMS
WHANAU
WHANAUS
WHANG
WHANGAM
WHANGAMS
WHANGED
WHANGEE
WHANGEES
WHANGING
WHANGS
WHAP
WHAPPED
WHAPPER
WHAPPERS
WHAPPING
WHAPS
WHARE
WHARENUI
WHARENUIS
WHAREPUNI
WHARES
WHARF
WHARFAGE
WHARFAGES
WHARFED
WHARFIE
WHARFIES
WHARFING
WHARFINGS
WHARFS
WHARVE
WHARVES
WHAT
WHATA
WHATAS
WHATCHA
WHATEN
WHATEVER

WHATEVS
WHATNA
WHATNESS
WHATNOT
WHATNOTS
WHATS
WHATSIS
WHATSISES
WHATSIT
WHATSITS
WHATSO
WHATTEN
WHAUP
WHAUPS
WHAUR
WHAURS
WHEAL
WHEALS
WHEAR
WHEARE
WHEAT
WHEATEAR
WHEATEARS
WHEATEN
WHEATENS
WHEATGERM
WHEATIER
WHEATIEST
WHEATLAND
WHEATLESS
WHEATLIKE
WHEATMEAL
WHEATS
WHEATWORM
WHEATY
WHEE
WHEECH
WHEECHED
WHEECHING
WHEECHS
WHEEDLE
WHEEDLED
WHEEDLER
WHEEDLERS
WHEEDLES
WHEEDLING
WHEEL
WHEELBASE

WHEELED
WHEELER
WHEELERS
WHEELIE
WHEELIER
WHEELIES
WHEELIEST
WHEELING
WHEELINGS
WHEELLESS
WHEELMAN
WHEELMEN
WHEELS
WHEELSMAN
WHEELSMEN
WHEELSPIN
WHEELWORK
WHEELY
WHEEN
WHEENGE
WHEENGED
WHEENGES
WHEENGING
WHEENS
WHEEP
WHEEPED
WHEEPING
WHEEPLE
WHEEPLED
WHEEPLES
WHEEPLING
WHEEPS
WHEESH
WHEESHED
WHEESHES
WHEESHING
WHEESHT
WHEESHTED
WHEESHTS
WHEEZE
WHEEZED
WHEEZER
WHEEZERS
WHEEZES
WHEEZIER
WHEEZIEST
WHEEZILY
WHEEZING

WHEEZINGS
WHEEZLE
WHEEZLED
WHEEZLES
WHEEZLING
WHEEZY
WHEFT
WHEFTS
WHELK
WHELKED
WHELKIER
WHELKIEST
WHELKS
WHELKY
WHELM
WHELMED
WHELMING
WHELMS
WHELP
WHELPED
WHELPING
WHELPLESS
WHELPS
WHEMMLE
WHEMMLED
WHEMMLES
WHEMMLING
WHEN
WHENAS
WHENCE
WHENCES
WHENCEVER
WHENEVER
WHENS
WHENUA
WHENUAS
WHENWE
WHENWES
WHERE
WHEREAS
WHEREASES
WHEREAT
WHEREBY
WHEREFOR
WHEREFORE
WHEREFORS
WHEREFROM
WHEREIN

WHEREINTO
WHERENESS
WHEREOF
WHEREON
WHEREOUT
WHERES
WHERESO
WHERETO
WHEREUNTO
WHEREUPON
WHEREVER
WHEREWITH
WHERRET
WHERRETED
WHERRETS
WHERRIED
WHERRIES
WHERRIT
WHERRITED
WHERRITS
WHERRY
WHERRYING
WHERRYMAN
WHERRYMEN
WHERVE
WHERVES
WHET
WHETHER
WHETS
WHETSTONE
WHETTED
WHETTER
WHETTERS
WHETTING
WHEUGH
WHEUGHED
WHEUGHING
WHEUGHS
WHEW
WHEWED
WHEWING
WHEWS
WHEY
WHEYEY
WHEYFACE
WHEYFACED
WHEYFACES
WHEYIER

W

WHEYIEST
WHEYISH
WHEYLIKE
WHEYS
WHICH
WHICHEVER
WHICKER
WHICKERED
WHICKERS
WHID
WHIDAH
WHIDAHS
WHIDDED
WHIDDER
WHIDDERED
WHIDDERS
WHIDDING
WHIDS
WHIFF
WHIFFED
WHIFFER
WHIFFERS
WHIFFET
WHIFFETS
WHIFFIER
WHIFFIEST
WHIFFING
WHIFFINGS
WHIFFLE
WHIFFLED
WHIFFLER
WHIFFLERS
WHIFFLERY
WHIFFLES
WHIFFLING
WHIFFS
WHIFFY
WHIFT
WHIFTS
WHIG
WHIGGED
WHIGGING
WHIGS
WHILE
WHILED
WHILERE
WHILES
WHILEVER
WHILING
WHILK
WHILLIED
WHILLIES
WHILLY
WHILLYING
WHILLYWHA
WHILOM
WHILST
WHIM
WHIMBERRY
WHIMBREL
WHIMBRELS
WHIMMED
WHIMMIER
WHIMMIEST
WHIMMING
WHIMMY
WHIMPER
WHIMPERED
WHIMPERER
WHIMPERS
WHIMPLE
WHIMPLED
WHIMPLES
WHIMPLING
WHIMS
WHIMSEY
WHIMSEYS
WHIMSICAL
WHIMSIED
WHIMSIER
WHIMSIES
WHIMSIEST
WHIMSILY
WHIMSY
WHIN
WHINBERRY
WHINCHAT
WHINCHATS
WHINE
WHINED
WHINER
WHINERS
WHINES
WHINEY
WHINGDING
WHINGE
WHINGED
WHINGEING
WHINGER
WHINGERS
WHINGES
WHINGIER
WHINGIEST
WHINGING
WHINGY
WHINIARD
WHINIARDS
WHINIER
WHINIEST
WHININESS
WHINING
WHININGLY
WHININGS
WHINNIED
WHINNIER
WHINNIES
WHINNIEST
WHINNY
WHINNYING
WHINS
WHINSTONE
WHINY
WHINYARD
WHINYARDS
WHIO
WHIOS
WHIP
WHIPBIRD
WHIPBIRDS
WHIPCAT
WHIPCATS
WHIPCORD
WHIPCORDS
WHIPCORDY
WHIPCRACK
WHIPJACK
WHIPJACKS
WHIPLASH
WHIPLESS
WHIPLIKE
WHIPPED
WHIPPER
WHIPPERS
WHIPPET
WHIPPETS
WHIPPIER
WHIPPIEST
WHIPPING
WHIPPINGS
WHIPPIT
WHIPPITS
WHIPPY
WHIPRAY
WHIPRAYS
WHIPS
WHIPSAW
WHIPSAWED
WHIPSAWN
WHIPSAWS
WHIPSNAKE
WHIPSTAFF
WHIPSTALL
WHIPSTER
WHIPSTERS
WHIPSTOCK
WHIPT
WHIPTAIL
WHIPTAILS
WHIPWORM
WHIPWORMS
WHIR
WHIRL
WHIRLBAT
WHIRLBATS
WHIRLED
WHIRLER
WHIRLERS
WHIRLIER
WHIRLIES
WHIRLIEST
WHIRLIGIG
WHIRLING
WHIRLINGS
WHIRLPOOL
WHIRLS
WHIRLWIND
WHIRLY
WHIRR
WHIRRA
WHIRRED
WHIRRET
WHIRRETED
WHIRRETS
WHIRRIED
WHIRRIER
WHIRRIES
WHIRRIEST
WHIRRING
WHIRRINGS
WHIRRS
WHIRRY
WHIRRYING
WHIRS
WHIRTLE
WHIRTLES
WHISH
WHISHED
WHISHES
WHISHING
WHISHT
WHISHTED
WHISHTING
WHISHTS
WHISK
WHISKED
WHISKER
WHISKERED
WHISKERS
WHISKERY
WHISKET
WHISKETS
WHISKEY
WHISKEYS
WHISKIES
WHISKING
WHISKS
WHISKY
WHISPER
WHISPERED
WHISPERER
WHISPERS
WHISPERY
WHISS
WHISSED
WHISSES
WHISSING
WHIST
WHISTED
WHISTING
WHISTLE

WHISTLED
WHISTLER
WHISTLERS
WHISTLES
WHISTLING
WHISTS
WHIT
WHITE
WHITEBAIT
WHITEBASS
WHITEBEAM
WHITECAP
WHITECAPS
WHITECOAT
WHITECOMB
WHITED
WHITEDAMP
WHITEFACE
WHITEFISH
WHITEFLY
WHITEHEAD
WHITELIST
WHITELY
WHITEN
WHITENED
WHITENER
WHITENERS
WHITENESS
WHITENING
WHITENS
WHITEOUT
WHITEOUTS
WHITEPOT
WHITEPOTS
WHITER
WHITES
WHITEST
WHITETAIL
WHITEWALL
WHITEWARE
WHITEWASH
WHITEWING
WHITEWOOD
WHITEY
WHITHER
WHITHERED
WHITHERS
WHITIER
WHITIEST
WHITING
WHITINGS
WHITISH
WHITLING
WHITLINGS
WHITLOW
WHITLOWS
WHITRACK
WHITRACKS
WHITRET
WHITRETS
WHITRICK
WHITRICKS
WHITS
WHITSTER
WHITSTERS
WHITTAW
WHITTAWER
WHITTAWS
WHITTER
WHITTERED
WHITTERS
WHITTLE
WHITTLED
WHITTLER
WHITTLERS
WHITTLES
WHITTLING
WHITTRET
WHITTRETS
WHITY
WHIZ
WHIZBANG
WHIZBANGS
WHIZZ
WHIZZBANG
WHIZZED
WHIZZER
WHIZZERS
WHIZZES
WHIZZIER
WHIZZIEST
WHIZZING
WHIZZINGS
WHIZZO
WHIZZY
WHO
WHOA
WHODUNIT
WHODUNITS
WHODUNNIT
WHOEVER
WHOLE
WHOLEFOOD
WHOLEMEAL
WHOLENESS
WHOLES
WHOLESALE
WHOLESOME
WHOLISM
WHOLISMS
WHOLIST
WHOLISTIC
WHOLISTS
WHOLLY
WHOLPHIN
WHOLPHINS
WHOM
WHOMBLE
WHOMBLED
WHOMBLES
WHOMBLING
WHOMEVER
WHOMMLE
WHOMMLED
WHOMMLES
WHOMMLING
WHOMP
WHOMPED
WHOMPING
WHOMPS
WHOMSO
WHOOBUB
WHOOBUBS
WHOOF
WHOOFED
WHOOFING
WHOOFS
WHOOMP
WHOOMPH
WHOOMPHS
WHOOMPS
WHOONGA
WHOONGAS
WHOOP
WHOOPED
WHOOPEE
WHOOPEES
WHOOPER
WHOOPERS
WHOOPIE
WHOOPIES
WHOOPING
WHOOPINGS
WHOOPLA
WHOOPLAS
WHOOPS
WHOOPSIE
WHOOPSIES
WHOOSH
WHOOSHED
WHOOSHES
WHOOSHING
WHOOSIS
WHOOSISES
WHOOT
WHOOTED
WHOOTING
WHOOTS
WHOP
WHOPPED
WHOPPER
WHOPPERS
WHOPPING
WHOPPINGS
WHOPS
WHORE
WHORED
WHOREDOM
WHOREDOMS
WHORES
WHORESON
WHORESONS
WHORING
WHORINGS
WHORISH
WHORISHLY
WHORL
WHORLBAT
WHORLBATS
WHORLED
WHORLING
WHORLS
WHORT
WHORTLE
WHORTLES
WHORTS
WHOSE
WHOSESO
WHOSEVER
WHOSIS
WHOSISES
WHOSIT
WHOSITS
WHOSO
WHOSOEVER
WHOT
WHOW
WHOWED
WHOWING
WHOWS
WHUMMLE
WHUMMLED
WHUMMLES
WHUMMLING
WHUMP
WHUMPED
WHUMPING
WHUMPS
WHUNSTANE
WHUP
WHUPPED
WHUPPING
WHUPPINGS
WHUPS
WHY
WHYDA
WHYDAH
WHYDAHS
WHYDAS
WHYDUNIT
WHYDUNITS
WHYDUNNIT
WHYEVER
WHYS
WIBBLE
WIBBLED
WIBBLES
WIBBLING
WICCA
WICCAN

W

WICCANS
WICCAS
WICE
WICH
WICHES
WICK
WICKAPE
WICKAPES
WICKED
WICKEDER
WICKEDEST
WICKEDLY
WICKEDS
WICKEN
WICKENS
WICKER
WICKERED
WICKERS
WICKET
WICKETS
WICKIES
WICKING
WICKINGS
WICKIUP
WICKIUPS
WICKLESS
WICKS
WICKTHING
WICKY
WICKYUP
WICKYUPS
WICOPIES
WICOPY
WIDDER
WIDDERS
WIDDIE
WIDDIES
WIDDLE
WIDDLED
WIDDLES
WIDDLING
WIDDY
WIDE
WIDEAWAKE
WIDEBAND
WIDEBANDS
WIDEBODY
WIDELY
WIDEN
WIDENED
WIDENER
WIDENERS
WIDENESS
WIDENING
WIDENINGS
WIDENS
WIDEOUT
WIDEOUTS
WIDER
WIDES
WIDEST
WIDGEON
WIDGEONS
WIDGET
WIDGETS
WIDGIE
WIDGIES
WIDISH
WIDOW
WIDOWBIRD
WIDOWED
WIDOWER
WIDOWERED
WIDOWERS
WIDOWHOOD
WIDOWING
WIDOWMAN
WIDOWMEN
WIDOWS
WIDTH
WIDTHS
WIDTHWAY
WIDTHWAYS
WIDTHWISE
WIEL
WIELD
WIELDABLE
WIELDED
WIELDER
WIELDERS
WIELDIER
WIELDIEST
WIELDING
WIELDLESS
WIELDS
WIELDY
WIELS
WIENER
WIENERS
WIENIE
WIENIES
WIFE
WIFED
WIFEDOM
WIFEDOMS
WIFEHOOD
WIFEHOODS
WIFELESS
WIFELIER
WIFELIEST
WIFELIKE
WIFELY
WIFES
WIFEY
WIFEYS
WIFIE
WIFIES
WIFING
WIFTIER
WIFTIEST
WIFTY
WIG
WIGAN
WIGANS
WIGEON
WIGEONS
WIGGED
WIGGERIES
WIGGERY
WIGGIER
WIGGIEST
WIGGING
WIGGINGS
WIGGLE
WIGGLED
WIGGLER
WIGGLERS
WIGGLES
WIGGLIER
WIGGLIEST
WIGGLING
WIGGLY
WIGGY
WIGHT
WIGHTED
WIGHTING
WIGHTLY
WIGHTS
WIGLESS
WIGLET
WIGLETS
WIGLIKE
WIGMAKER
WIGMAKERS
WIGS
WIGWAG
WIGWAGGED
WIGWAGGER
WIGWAGS
WIGWAM
WIGWAMS
WIKI
WIKIALITY
WIKIS
WIKIUP
WIKIUPS
WILCO
WILD
WILDCARD
WILDCARDS
WILDCAT
WILDCATS
WILDED
WILDER
WILDERED
WILDERING
WILDERS
WILDEST
WILDFIRE
WILDFIRES
WILDFOWL
WILDFOWLS
WILDGRAVE
WILDING
WILDINGS
WILDISH
WILDLAND
WILDLANDS
WILDLIFE
WILDLIFES
WILDLING
WILDLINGS
WILDLY
WILDMAN
WILDMEN
WILDNESS
WILDS
WILDWOOD
WILDWOODS
WILE
WILED
WILEFUL
WILES
WILFUL
WILFULLY
WILGA
WILGAS
WILI
WILIER
WILIEST
WILILY
WILINESS
WILING
WILIS
WILJA
WILJAS
WILL
WILLABLE
WILLED
WILLEMITE
WILLER
WILLERS
WILLEST
WILLET
WILLETS
WILLEY
WILLEYED
WILLEYING
WILLEYS
WILLFUL
WILLFULLY
WILLIAM
WILLIAMS
WILLIE
WILLIED
WILLIES
WILLING
WILLINGER
WILLINGLY
WILLIWAU

WILLIWAUS
WILLIWAW
WILLIWAWS
WILLOW
WILLOWED
WILLOWER
WILLOWERS
WILLOWIER
WILLOWING
WILLOWISH
WILLOWS
WILLOWY
WILLPOWER
WILLS
WILLY
WILLYARD
WILLYART
WILLYING
WILLYWAW
WILLYWAWS
WILT
WILTED
WILTING
WILTJA
WILTJAS
WILTS
WILY
WIMBLE
WIMBLED
WIMBLES
WIMBLING
WIMBREL
WIMBRELS
WIMMIN
WIMP
WIMPED
WIMPIER
WIMPIEST
WIMPINESS
WIMPING
WIMPISH
WIMPISHLY
WIMPLE
WIMPLED
WIMPLES
WIMPLING
WIMPS
WIMPY
WIN
WINCE
WINCED
WINCER
WINCERS
WINCES
WINCEY
WINCEYS
WINCH
WINCHED
WINCHER
WINCHERS
WINCHES
WINCHING
WINCHMAN
WINCHMEN
WINCING
WINCINGLY
WINCINGS
WINCOPIPE
WIND
WINDABLE
WINDAC
WINDACS
WINDAGE
WINDAGES
WINDAS
WINDASES
WINDBAG
WINDBAGS
WINDBELL
WINDBELLS
WINDBILL
WINDBILLS
WINDBLAST
WINDBLOW
WINDBLOWN
WINDBLOWS
WINDBORNE
WINDBOUND
WINDBREAK
WINDBURN
WINDBURNS
WINDBURNT
WINDCHILL
WINDED
WINDER
WINDERS
WINDFALL
WINDFALLS
WINDFLAW
WINDFLAWS
WINDGALL
WINDGALLS
WINDGUN
WINDGUNS
WINDHOVER
WINDIER
WINDIEST
WINDIGO
WINDIGOES
WINDIGOS
WINDILY
WINDINESS
WINDING
WINDINGLY
WINDINGS
WINDLASS
WINDLE
WINDLED
WINDLES
WINDLESS
WINDLING
WINDLINGS
WINDLOAD
WINDLOADS
WINDMILL
WINDMILLS
WINDOCK
WINDOCKS
WINDORE
WINDORES
WINDOW
WINDOWED
WINDOWIER
WINDOWING
WINDOWS
WINDOWY
WINDPACK
WINDPACKS
WINDPIPE
WINDPIPES
WINDPROOF
WINDRING
WINDROW
WINDROWED
WINDROWER
WINDROWS
WINDS
WINDSAIL
WINDSAILS
WINDSES
WINDSHAKE
WINDSHIP
WINDSHIPS
WINDSLAB
WINDSLABS
WINDSOCK
WINDSOCKS
WINDSTORM
WINDSURF
WINDSURFS
WINDSWEPT
WINDTHROW
WINDTIGHT
WINDUP
WINDUPS
WINDWARD
WINDWARDS
WINDWAY
WINDWAYS
WINDY
WINE
WINEBERRY
WINED
WINEGLASS
WINELESS
WINEMAKER
WINEPRESS
WINERIES
WINERY
WINES
WINESAP
WINESAPS
WINESHOP
WINESHOPS
WINESKIN
WINESKINS
WINESOP
WINESOPS
WINEY
WING
WINGBACK
WINGBACKS
WINGBEAT
WINGBEATS
WINGBOW
WINGBOWS
WINGCHAIR
WINGDING
WINGDINGS
WINGE
WINGED
WINGEDLY
WINGEING
WINGER
WINGERS
WINGES
WINGIER
WINGIEST
WINGING
WINGLESS
WINGLET
WINGLETS
WINGLIKE
WINGMAN
WINGMEN
WINGNUT
WINGNUTS
WINGOVER
WINGOVERS
WINGS
WINGSPAN
WINGSPANS
WINGSUIT
WINGSUITS
WINGTIP
WINGTIPS
WINGY
WINIER
WINIEST
WINING
WINISH
WINK
WINKED
WINKER
WINKERS
WINKING
WINKINGLY
WINKINGS
WINKLE
WINKLED

WINKLER
WINKLERS
WINKLES
WINKLING
WINKS
WINLESS
WINN
WINNA
WINNABLE
WINNARD
WINNARDS
WINNED
WINNER
WINNERS
WINNING
WINNINGLY
WINNINGS
WINNLE
WINNLES
WINNOCK
WINNOCKS
WINNOW
WINNOWED
WINNOWER
WINNOWERS
WINNOWING
WINNOWS
WINNS
WINO
WINOES
WINOS
WINS
WINSEY
WINSEYS
WINSOME
WINSOMELY
WINSOMER
WINSOMEST
WINTER
WINTERED
WINTERER
WINTERERS
WINTERFED
WINTERIER
WINTERING
WINTERISE
WINTERISH
WINTERIZE
WINTERLY
WINTERS
WINTERY
WINTLE
WINTLED
WINTLES
WINTLING
WINTRIER
WINTRIEST
WINTRILY
WINTRY
WINY
WINZE
WINZES
WIPE
WIPEABLE
WIPED
WIPEOUT
WIPEOUTS
WIPER
WIPERS
WIPES
WIPING
WIPINGS
WIPPEN
WIPPENS
WIRABLE
WIRE
WIRED
WIREDRAW
WIREDRAWN
WIREDRAWS
WIREDREW
WIREFRAME
WIREGRASS
WIREHAIR
WIREHAIRS
WIRELESS
WIRELIKE
WIRELINE
WIRELINES
WIREMAN
WIREMEN
WIREPHOTO
WIRER
WIRERS
WIRES
WIRETAP
WIRETAPS
WIREWAY
WIREWAYS
WIREWORK
WIREWORKS
WIREWORM
WIREWORMS
WIREWOVE
WIRIER
WIRIEST
WIRILDA
WIRILDAS
WIRILY
WIRINESS
WIRING
WIRINGS
WIRRA
WIRRAH
WIRRAHS
WIRRICOW
WIRRICOWS
WIRY
WIS
WISARD
WISARDS
WISDOM
WISDOMS
WISE
WISEACRE
WISEACRES
WISEASS
WISEASSES
WISECRACK
WISED
WISEGUY
WISEGUYS
WISELIER
WISELIEST
WISELING
WISELINGS
WISELY
WISENESS
WISENT
WISENTS
WISER
WISES
WISEST
WISEWOMAN
WISEWOMEN
WISH
WISHA
WISHBONE
WISHBONES
WISHED
WISHER
WISHERS
WISHES
WISHFUL
WISHFULLY
WISHING
WISHINGS
WISHLESS
WISHT
WISING
WISKET
WISKETS
WISP
WISPED
WISPIER
WISPIEST
WISPILY
WISPINESS
WISPING
WISPISH
WISPLIKE
WISPS
WISPY
WISS
WISSED
WISSES
WISSING
WIST
WISTARIA
WISTARIAS
WISTED
WISTERIA
WISTERIAS
WISTFUL
WISTFULLY
WISTING
WISTITI
WISTITIS
WISTLY
WISTS
WIT
WITAN
WITANS
WITBLITS
WITCH
WITCHED
WITCHEN
WITCHENS
WITCHERY
WITCHES
WITCHETTY
WITCHHOOD
WITCHIER
WITCHIEST
WITCHING
WITCHINGS
WITCHKNOT
WITCHLIKE
WITCHWEED
WITCHY
WITE
WITED
WITELESS
WITES
WITGAT
WITGATS
WITH
WITHAL
WITHDRAW
WITHDRAWN
WITHDRAWS
WITHDREW
WITHE
WITHED
WITHER
WITHERED
WITHERER
WITHERERS
WITHERING
WITHERITE
WITHEROD
WITHERODS
WITHERS
WITHES
WITHHAULT
WITHHELD
WITHHOLD
WITHHOLDS
WITHIER
WITHIES

WITHIEST
WITHIN
WITHING
WITHINS
WITHOUT
WITHOUTEN
WITHOUTS
WITHS
WITHSTAND
WITHSTOOD
WITHWIND
WITHWINDS
WITHY
WITHYWIND
WITING
WITLESS
WITLESSLY
WITLING
WITLINGS
WITLOOF
WITLOOFS
WITNESS
WITNESSED
WITNESSER
WITNESSES
WITNEY
WITNEYS
WITS
WITTED
WITTER
WITTERED
WITTERING
WITTERS
WITTICISM
WITTIER
WITTIEST
WITTILY
WITTINESS
WITTING
WITTINGLY
WITTINGS
WITTOL
WITTOLLY
WITTOLS
WITTY
WITWALL
WITWALLS
WITWANTON
WIVE
WIVED
WIVEHOOD
WIVEHOODS
WIVER
WIVERN
WIVERNS
WIVERS
WIVES
WIVING
WIZ
WIZARD
WIZARDER
WIZARDEST
WIZARDLY
WIZARDRY
WIZARDS
WIZEN
WIZENED
WIZENER
WIZENEST
WIZENING
WIZENS
WIZES
WIZIER
WIZIERS
WIZZEN
WIZZENS
WIZZES
WO
WOAD
WOADED
WOADS
WOADWAX
WOADWAXEN
WOADWAXES
WOAH
WOALD
WOALDS
WOBBEGONG
WOBBLE
WOBBLED
WOBBLER
WOBBLERS
WOBBLES
WOBBLIER
WOBBLIES
WOBBLIEST
WOBBLING
WOBBLINGS
WOBBLY
WOBEGONE
WOCK
WOCKS
WODGE
WODGES
WOE
WOEBEGONE
WOEFUL
WOEFULLER
WOEFULLY
WOENESS
WOENESSES
WOES
WOESOME
WOF
WOFS
WOFUL
WOFULLER
WOFULLEST
WOFULLY
WOFULNESS
WOGGLE
WOGGLES
WOIWODE
WOIWODES
WOJUS
WOK
WOKE
WOKEN
WOKER
WOKEST
WOKKA
WOKS
WOLD
WOLDS
WOLF
WOLFBERRY
WOLFED
WOLFER
WOLFERS
WOLFFISH
WOLFHOUND
WOLFING
WOLFINGS
WOLFISH
WOLFISHLY
WOLFKIN
WOLFKINS
WOLFLIKE
WOLFLING
WOLFLINGS
WOLFRAM
WOLFRAMS
WOLFS
WOLFSBANE
WOLFSKIN
WOLFSKINS
WOLLIES
WOLLY
WOLVE
WOLVED
WOLVER
WOLVERENE
WOLVERINE
WOLVERS
WOLVES
WOLVING
WOLVINGS
WOLVISH
WOLVISHLY
WOMAN
WOMANED
WOMANHOOD
WOMANING
WOMANISE
WOMANISED
WOMANISER
WOMANISES
WOMANISH
WOMANISM
WOMANISMS
WOMANIST
WOMANISTS
WOMANIZE
WOMANIZED
WOMANIZER
WOMANIZES
WOMANKIND
WOMANLESS
WOMANLIER
WOMANLIKE
WOMANLY
WOMANNED
WOMANNESS
WOMANNING
WOMANS
WOMB
WOMBAT
WOMBATS
WOMBED
WOMBIER
WOMBIEST
WOMBING
WOMBLIKE
WOMBS
WOMBY
WOMEN
WOMENFOLK
WOMENKIND
WOMERA
WOMERAS
WOMMERA
WOMMERAS
WOMMIT
WOMMITS
WOMYN
WON
WONDER
WONDERED
WONDERER
WONDERERS
WONDERFUL
WONDERING
WONDERKID
WONDEROUS
WONDERS
WONDRED
WONDROUS
WONGA
WONGAS
WONGI
WONGIED
WONGIING
WONGIS
WONING
WONINGS
WONK
WONKERIES
WONKERY
WONKIER
WONKIEST

W

WONKILY
WONKINESS
WONKISH
WONKS
WONKY
WONNED
WONNER
WONNERS
WONNING
WONNINGS
WONS
WONT
WONTED
WONTEDLY
WONTING
WONTLESS
WONTON
WONTONS
WONTS
WOO
WOOABLE
WOOBUT
WOOBUTS
WOOD
WOODBIN
WOODBIND
WOODBINDS
WOODBINE
WOODBINES
WOODBINS
WOODBLOCK
WOODBORER
WOODBOX
WOODBOXES
WOODCHAT
WOODCHATS
WOODCHIP
WOODCHIPS
WOODCHOP
WOODCHOPS
WOODCHUCK
WOODCOCK
WOODCOCKS
WOODCRAFT
WOODCUT
WOODCUTS
WOODED
WOODEN
WOODENED
WOODENER
WOODENEST
WOODENING
WOODENLY
WOODENS
WOODENTOP
WOODFERN
WOODFERNS
WOODFREE
WOODGRAIN
WOODHEN
WOODHENS
WOODHOLE
WOODHOLES
WOODHORSE
WOODHOUSE
WOODIE
WOODIER
WOODIES
WOODIEST
WOODINESS
WOODING
WOODLAND
WOODLANDS
WOODLARK
WOODLARKS
WOODLESS
WOODLICE
WOODLORE
WOODLORES
WOODLOT
WOODLOTS
WOODLOUSE
WOODMAN
WOODMEAL
WOODMEALS
WOODMEN
WOODMICE
WOODMOUSE
WOODNESS
WOODNOTE
WOODNOTES
WOODPILE
WOODPILES
WOODPRINT
WOODRAT
WOODRATS
WOODREEVE
WOODROOF
WOODROOFS
WOODRUFF
WOODRUFFS
WOODRUSH
WOODS
WOODSCREW
WOODSHED
WOODSHEDS
WOODSHOCK
WOODSIA
WOODSIAS
WOODSIER
WOODSIEST
WOODSKIN
WOODSKINS
WOODSMAN
WOODSMEN
WOODSMOKE
WOODSPITE
WOODSTONE
WOODSTOVE
WOODSY
WOODTONE
WOODTONES
WOODWALE
WOODWALES
WOODWARD
WOODWARDS
WOODWASP
WOODWASPS
WOODWAX
WOODWAXEN
WOODWAXES
WOODWIND
WOODWINDS
WOODWORK
WOODWORKS
WOODWORM
WOODWORMS
WOODWOSE
WOODWOSES
WOODY
WOODYARD
WOODYARDS
WOOED
WOOER
WOOERS
WOOF
WOOFED
WOOFER
WOOFERS
WOOFIER
WOOFIEST
WOOFING
WOOFS
WOOFY
WOOHOO
WOOING
WOOINGLY
WOOINGS
WOOL
WOOLD
WOOLDED
WOOLDER
WOOLDERS
WOOLDING
WOOLDINGS
WOOLDS
WOOLED
WOOLEN
WOOLENS
WOOLER
WOOLERS
WOOLFAT
WOOLFATS
WOOLFELL
WOOLFELLS
WOOLHAT
WOOLHATS
WOOLIE
WOOLIER
WOOLIES
WOOLIEST
WOOLILY
WOOLINESS
WOOLLED
WOOLLEN
WOOLLENS
WOOLLIER
WOOLLIES
WOOLLIEST
WOOLLIKE
WOOLLILY
WOOLLY
WOOLMAN
WOOLMEN
WOOLPACK
WOOLPACKS
WOOLS
WOOLSACK
WOOLSACKS
WOOLSEY
WOOLSEYS
WOOLSHED
WOOLSHEDS
WOOLSKIN
WOOLSKINS
WOOLWARD
WOOLWORK
WOOLWORKS
WOOLY
WOOMERA
WOOMERANG
WOOMERAS
WOON
WOONED
WOONERF
WOONERFS
WOONING
WOONS
WOOPIE
WOOPIES
WOOPS
WOOPSED
WOOPSES
WOOPSING
WOOPY
WOORALI
WOORALIS
WOORARA
WOORARAS
WOORARI
WOORARIS
WOOS
WOOSE
WOOSEL
WOOSELL
WOOSELLS
WOOSELS
WOOSES
WOOSH
WOOSHED

W

WOOSHES
WOOSHING
WOOT
WOOTZ
WOOTZES
WOOZIER
WOOZIEST
WOOZILY
WOOZINESS
WOOZY
WOP
WOPPED
WOPPING
WOPS
WORCESTER
WORD
WORDAGE
WORDAGES
WORDBOOK
WORDBOOKS
WORDBOUND
WORDBREAK
WORDCOUNT
WORDED
WORDGAME
WORDGAMES
WORDIE
WORDIER
WORDIES
WORDIEST
WORDILY
WORDINESS
WORDING
WORDINGS
WORDISH
WORDLESS
WORDLORE
WORDLORES
WORDPLAY
WORDPLAYS
WORDS
WORDSMITH
WORDWRAP
WORDWRAPS
WORDY
WORE
WORK
WORKABLE
WORKABLY
WORKADAY
WORKADAYS
WORKBAG
WORKBAGS
WORKBENCH
WORKBOAT
WORKBOATS
WORKBOOK
WORKBOOKS
WORKBOOT
WORKBOOTS
WORKBOX
WORKBOXES
WORKDAY
WORKDAYS
WORKED
WORKER
WORKERIST
WORKERS
WORKFARE
WORKFARES
WORKFLOW
WORKFLOWS
WORKFOLK
WORKFOLKS
WORKFORCE
WORKFUL
WORKGIRL
WORKGIRLS
WORKGROUP
WORKHORSE
WORKHOUR
WORKHOURS
WORKHOUSE
WORKING
WORKINGS
WORKLESS
WORKLOAD
WORKLOADS
WORKMAN
WORKMANLY
WORKMATE
WORKMATES
WORKMEN
WORKOUT
WORKOUTS
WORKPIECE
WORKPLACE
WORKPRINT
WORKROOM
WORKROOMS
WORKS
WORKSAFE
WORKSHEET
WORKSHOP
WORKSHOPS
WORKSHY
WORKSITE
WORKSITES
WORKSOME
WORKSONG
WORKSONGS
WORKSPACE
WORKTABLE
WORKTOP
WORKTOPS
WORKUP
WORKUPS
WORKWEAR
WORKWEARS
WORKWEEK
WORKWEEKS
WORKWOMAN
WORKWOMEN
WORLD
WORLDBEAT
WORLDED
WORLDER
WORLDERS
WORLDIE
WORLDIES
WORLDLIER
WORLDLING
WORLDLY
WORLDS
WORLDVIEW
WORLDWIDE
WORM
WORMCAST
WORMCASTS
WORMED
WORMER
WORMERIES
WORMERS
WORMERY
WORMFLIES
WORMFLY
WORMGEAR
WORMGEARS
WORMHOLE
WORMHOLED
WORMHOLES
WORMIER
WORMIEST
WORMIL
WORMILS
WORMINESS
WORMING
WORMISH
WORMLIKE
WORMROOT
WORMROOTS
WORMS
WORMSEED
WORMSEEDS
WORMWHEEL
WORMWOOD
WORMWOODS
WORMY
WORN
WORNNESS
WORRAL
WORRALS
WORREL
WORRELS
WORRICOW
WORRICOWS
WORRIED
WORRIEDLY
WORRIER
WORRIERS
WORRIES
WORRIMENT
WORRISOME
WORRIT
WORRITED
WORRITING
WORRITS
WORRY
WORRYCOW
WORRYCOWS
WORRYGUTS
WORRYING
WORRYINGS
WORRYWART
WORSE
WORSED
WORSEN
WORSENED
WORSENESS
WORSENING
WORSENS
WORSER
WORSES
WORSET
WORSETS
WORSHIP
WORSHIPED
WORSHIPER
WORSHIPS
WORSING
WORST
WORSTED
WORSTEDS
WORSTING
WORSTS
WORT
WORTH
WORTHED
WORTHFUL
WORTHIED
WORTHIER
WORTHIES
WORTHIEST
WORTHILY
WORTHING
WORTHLESS
WORTHS
WORTHY
WORTHYING
WORTLE
WORTLES
WORTS
WOS
WOSBIRD
WOSBIRDS
WOST
WOT
WOTCHA
WOTCHER
WOTS

WOTTED
WOTTEST
WOTTETH
WOTTING
WOUBIT
WOUBITS
WOULD
WOULDEST
WOULDS
WOULDST
WOUND
WOUNDABLE
WOUNDED
WOUNDEDLY
WOUNDER
WOUNDERS
WOUNDIER
WOUNDIEST
WOUNDILY
WOUNDING
WOUNDINGS
WOUNDLESS
WOUNDS
WOUNDWORT
WOUNDY
WOURALI
WOURALIS
WOVE
WOVEN
WOVENS
WOW
WOWED
WOWEE
WOWF
WOWFER
WOWFEST
WOWING
WOWS
WOWSER
WOWSERS
WOX
WOXEN
WRACK
WRACKED
WRACKFUL
WRACKING
WRACKS
WRAITH
WRAITHS
WRANG
WRANGED
WRANGING
WRANGLE
WRANGLED
WRANGLER
WRANGLERS
WRANGLES
WRANGLING
WRANGS
WRAP
WRAPOVER
WRAPOVERS
WRAPPAGE
WRAPPAGES
WRAPPED
WRAPPER
WRAPPERED
WRAPPERS
WRAPPING
WRAPPINGS
WRAPROUND
WRAPS
WRAPT
WRASSE
WRASSES
WRASSLE
WRASSLED
WRASSLES
WRASSLING
WRAST
WRASTED
WRASTING
WRASTLE
WRASTLED
WRASTLES
WRASTLING
WRASTS
WRATE
WRATH
WRATHED
WRATHFUL
WRATHIER
WRATHIEST
WRATHILY
WRATHING
WRATHLESS
WRATHS
WRATHY
WRAWL
WRAWLED
WRAWLING
WRAWLS
WRAXLE
WRAXLED
WRAXLES
WRAXLING
WRAXLINGS
WREAK
WREAKED
WREAKER
WREAKERS
WREAKFUL
WREAKING
WREAKLESS
WREAKS
WREATH
WREATHE
WREATHED
WREATHEN
WREATHER
WREATHERS
WREATHES
WREATHIER
WREATHING
WREATHS
WREATHY
WRECK
WRECKAGE
WRECKAGES
WRECKED
WRECKER
WRECKERS
WRECKFISH
WRECKFUL
WRECKING
WRECKINGS
WRECKS
WREN
WRENCH
WRENCHED
WRENCHER
WRENCHERS
WRENCHES
WRENCHING
WRENS
WRENTIT
WRENTITS
WREST
WRESTED
WRESTER
WRESTERS
WRESTING
WRESTLE
WRESTLED
WRESTLER
WRESTLERS
WRESTLES
WRESTLING
WRESTS
WRETCH
WRETCHED
WRETCHES
WRETHE
WRETHED
WRETHES
WRETHING
WRICK
WRICKED
WRICKING
WRICKS
WRIED
WRIER
WRIES
WRIEST
WRIGGLE
WRIGGLED
WRIGGLER
WRIGGLERS
WRIGGLES
WRIGGLIER
WRIGGLING
WRIGGLY
WRIGHT
WRIGHTS
WRING
WRINGED
WRINGER
WRINGERS
WRINGING
WRINGS
WRINKLE
WRINKLED
WRINKLES
WRINKLIE
WRINKLIER
WRINKLIES
WRINKLING
WRINKLY
WRIST
WRISTBAND
WRISTED
WRISTER
WRISTERS
WRISTIER
WRISTIEST
WRISTING
WRISTLET
WRISTLETS
WRISTLOCK
WRISTS
WRISTY
WRIT
WRITABLE
WRITATIVE
WRITE
WRITEABLE
WRITEDOWN
WRITEOFF
WRITEOFFS
WRITER
WRITERESS
WRITERLY
WRITERS
WRITES
WRITHE
WRITHED
WRITHEN
WRITHER
WRITHERS
WRITHES
WRITHING
WRITHINGS
WRITHLED
WRITING
WRITINGS
WRITS
WRITTEN
WRIZLED
WROATH
WROATHS

WROKE
WROKEN
WRONG
WRONGDOER
WRONGED
WRONGER
WRONGERS
WRONGEST
WRONGFUL
WRONGING
WRONGLY
WRONGNESS
WRONGOUS
WRONGS
WROOT
WROOTED
WROOTING
WROOTS
WROTE
WROTH
WROTHFUL
WROUGHT
WRUNG
WRY
WRYBILL
WRYBILLS
WRYER
WRYEST
WRYING
WRYLY
WRYNECK
WRYNECKS
WRYNESS
WRYNESSES
WRYTHEN
WUD
WUDDED
WUDDIES
WUDDING
WUDDY
WUDJULA
WUDJULAS
WUDS
WUDU
WUDUS
WUKKAS
WULFENITE
WULL
WULLED
WULLING
WULLS
WUNNER
WUNNERS
WURLEY
WURLEYS
WURLIE
WURLIES
WURST
WURSTS
WURTZITE
WURTZITES
WURZEL
WURZELS
WUS
WUSES
WUSHU
WUSHUS
WUSS
WUSSES
WUSSIER
WUSSIES
WUSSIEST
WUSSY
WUTHER
WUTHERED
WUTHERING
WUTHERS
WUXIA
WUXIAS
WUZ
WUZZLE
WUZZLED
WUZZLES
WUZZLING
WYANDOTTE
WYCH
WYCHES
WYE
WYES
WYLE
WYLED
WYLES
WYLIECOAT
WYLING
WYN
WYND
WYNDS
WYNN
WYNNS
WYNS
WYSIWYG
WYTE
WYTED
WYTES
WYTING
WYVERN
WYVERNS

X

XANTHAM
XANTHAMS
XANTHAN
XANTHANS
XANTHATE
XANTHATES
XANTHEIN
XANTHEINS
XANTHENE
XANTHENES
XANTHIC
XANTHIN
XANTHINE
XANTHINES
XANTHINS
XANTHISM
XANTHISMS
XANTHOMA
XANTHOMAS
XANTHONE
XANTHONES
XANTHOUS
XANTHOXYL
XEBEC
XEBECS
XED
XENIA
XENIAL
XENIAS
XENIC
XENIUM
XENOBLAST
XENOCRYST
XENOGAMY
XENOGENIC
XENOGENY
XENOGRAFT
XENOLITH
XENOLITHS
XENOMANIA
XENOMENIA
XENON
XENONS
XENOPHILE
XENOPHOBE
XENOPHOBY
XENOPHYA
XENOPUS
XENOPUSES
XENOTIME
XENOTIMES
XENURINE
XENURINES
XERAFIN
XERAFINS
XERANSES
XERANSIS
XERANTIC
XERAPHIN
XERAPHINS
XERARCH
XERASIA
XERASIAS
XERIC
XERICALLY
XERISCAPE
XEROCHASY
XERODERMA
XEROMA
XEROMAS
XEROMATA
XEROMORPH
XEROPHAGY
XEROPHILE
XEROPHILY
XEROPHYTE
XEROSERE
XEROSERES
XEROSES
XEROSIS
XEROSTOMA
XEROTES
XEROTIC
XEROX
XEROXED
XEROXES
XEROXING
XERUS
XERUSES
XI
XIPHOID
XIPHOIDAL
XIPHOIDS
XIPHOPAGI
XIS
XOANA
XOANON
XRAY
XRAYS
XU
XYLAN
XYLANS
XYLEM
XYLEMS
XYLENE
XYLENES
XYLENOL
XYLENOLS
XYLIC
XYLIDIN
XYLIDINE
XYLIDINES
XYLIDINS
XYLITOL
XYLITOLS
XYLOCARP
XYLOCARPS
XYLOGEN
XYLOGENS
XYLOGRAPH
XYLOID
XYLOIDIN
XYLOIDINE
XYLOIDINS
XYLOL
XYLOLOGY
XYLOLS
XYLOMA
XYLOMAS
XYLOMATA
XYLOMETER
XYLONIC
XYLONITE
XYLONITES
XYLOPHAGE
XYLOPHONE
XYLORIMBA
XYLOSE
XYLOSES
XYLOTOMY
XYLYL
XYLYLS
XYST
XYSTER
XYSTERS
XYSTI
XYSTOI
XYSTOS
XYSTS
XYSTUS

Y

YA
YAAR
YAARS
YABA
YABAS
YABBA
YABBAS
YABBER
YABBERED
YABBERING
YABBERS
YABBIE
YABBIED
YABBIES
YABBY
YABBYING
YACCA
YACCAS
YACHT
YACHTED
YACHTER
YACHTERS
YACHTIE
YACHTIES
YACHTING
YACHTINGS
YACHTMAN
YACHTMEN
YACHTS
YACHTSMAN
YACHTSMEN
YACK
YACKA
YACKAS
YACKED
YACKER
YACKERS
YACKING
YACKS
YAD
YADS
YAE
YAFF
YAFFED
YAFFING
YAFFLE
YAFFLES
YAFFS
YAG
YAGE
YAGER
YAGERS
YAGES
YAGGER
YAGGERS
YAGI
YAGIS
YAGS
YAH
YAHOO
YAHOOISM
YAHOOISMS
YAHOOS
YAHRZEIT
YAHRZEITS
YAHS
YAIRD
YAIRDS
YAK
YAKHDAN
YAKHDANS
YAKIMONO
YAKIMONOS
YAKITORI
YAKITORIS
YAKKA
YAKKAS
YAKKED
YAKKER
YAKKERS
YAKKING
YAKOW
YAKOWS
YAKS
YAKUZA
YALD
YALE
YALES
YAM
YAMALKA
YAMALKAS
YAMEN
YAMENS
YAMMER
YAMMERED
YAMMERER
YAMMERERS
YAMMERING
YAMMERS
YAMPIES
YAMPY
YAMS
YAMULKA
YAMULKAS
YAMUN
YAMUNS
YANG
YANGS
YANK
YANKED
YANKEE
YANKEES
YANKER
YANKERS
YANKIE
YANKIES
YANKING
YANKS
YANQUI
YANQUIS
YANTRA
YANTRAS
YAOURT
YAOURTS
YAP
YAPOCK
YAPOCKS
YAPOK
YAPOKS
YAPON
YAPONS
YAPP
YAPPED
YAPPER
YAPPERS
YAPPIE
YAPPIER
YAPPIES
YAPPIEST
YAPPING
YAPPINGLY
YAPPINGS
YAPPS
YAPPY
YAPS
YAPSTER
YAPSTERS
YAQONA
YAQONAS
YAR
YARAK
YARAKS
YARCO
YARCOS
YARD
YARDAGE
YARDAGES
YARDANG
YARDANGS
YARDARM
YARDARMS
YARDBIRD
YARDBIRDS
YARDED
YARDER
YARDERS
YARDING
YARDINGS
YARDLAND
YARDLANDS
YARDLIGHT
YARDMAN
YARDMEN
YARDS
YARDSTICK
YARDWAND
YARDWANDS
YARDWORK
YARDWORKS
YARE
YARELY
YARER
YAREST
YARFA
YARFAS
YARK
YARKED
YARKING
YARKS
YARMELKE
YARMELKES
YARMULKA
YARMULKAS
YARMULKE
YARMULKES
YARN
YARNED
YARNER
YARNERS
YARNING
YARNS
YARPHA
YARPHAS
YARR
YARRAMAN
YARRAMANS
YARRAMEN
YARRAN
YARRANS
YARRED

YARRING
YARROW
YARROWS
YARRS
YARTA
YARTAS
YARTO
YARTOS
YAS
YASHMAC
YASHMACS
YASHMAK
YASHMAKS
YASMAK
YASMAKS
YATAGAN
YATAGANS
YATAGHAN
YATAGHANS
YATE
YATES
YATTER
YATTERED
YATTERING
YATTERS
YAUD
YAUDS
YAULD
YAUP
YAUPED
YAUPER
YAUPERS
YAUPING
YAUPON
YAUPONS
YAUPS
YAUTIA
YAUTIAS
YAW
YAWED
YAWEY
YAWIER
YAWIEST
YAWING
YAWL
YAWLED
YAWLING
YAWLS
YAWMETER
YAWMETERS
YAWN
YAWNED
YAWNER
YAWNERS
YAWNIER
YAWNIEST
YAWNING
YAWNINGLY
YAWNINGS
YAWNS
YAWNSOME
YAWNY
YAWP
YAWPED
YAWPER
YAWPERS
YAWPING
YAWPINGS
YAWPS
YAWS
YAWY
YAY
YAYS
YBET
YBLENT
YBORE
YBOUND
YBOUNDEN
YBRENT
YCLAD
YCLED
YCLEEPE
YCLEEPED
YCLEEPES
YCLEEPING
YCLEPED
YCLEPT
YCOND
YDRAD
YDRED
YE
YEA
YEAD
YEADING
YEADS
YEAH
YEAHS
YEALDON
YEALDONS
YEALING
YEALINGS
YEALM
YEALMED
YEALMING
YEALMS
YEAN
YEANED
YEANING
YEANLING
YEANLINGS
YEANS
YEAR
YEARBOOK
YEARBOOKS
YEARD
YEARDED
YEARDING
YEARDS
YEAREND
YEARENDS
YEARLIES
YEARLING
YEARLINGS
YEARLONG
YEARLY
YEARN
YEARNED
YEARNER
YEARNERS
YEARNING
YEARNINGS
YEARNS
YEARS
YEAS
YEASAYER
YEASAYERS
YEAST
YEASTED
YEASTIER
YEASTIEST
YEASTILY
YEASTING
YEASTLESS
YEASTLIKE
YEASTS
YEASTY
YEBO
YECCH
YECCHS
YECH
YECHIER
YECHIEST
YECHS
YECHY
YEDE
YEDES
YEDING
YEED
YEEDING
YEEDS
YEELIN
YEELINS
YEESH
YEGG
YEGGMAN
YEGGMEN
YEGGS
YEH
YELD
YELDRING
YELDRINGS
YELDROCK
YELDROCKS
YELK
YELKS
YELL
YELLED
YELLER
YELLERS
YELLING
YELLINGS
YELLOCH
YELLOCHED
YELLOCHS
YELLOW
YELLOWED
YELLOWER
YELLOWEST
YELLOWFIN
YELLOWIER
YELLOWING
YELLOWISH
YELLOWLY
YELLOWS
YELLOWY
YELLS
YELM
YELMED
YELMING
YELMS
YELP
YELPED
YELPER
YELPERS
YELPING
YELPINGS
YELPS
YELT
YELTS
YEMMER
YEMMERS
YEN
YENNED
YENNING
YENS
YENTA
YENTAS
YENTE
YENTES
YEOMAN
YEOMANLY
YEOMANRY
YEOMEN
YEOW
YEP
YEPS
YER
YERBA
YERBAS
YERD
YERDED
YERDING
YERDS
YERK
YERKED
YERKING
YERKS
YERSINIA
YERSINIAE
YERSINIAS

YES
YESES
YESHIVA
YESHIVAH
YESHIVAHS
YESHIVAS
YESHIVOT
YESHIVOTH
YESK
YESKED
YESKING
YESKS
YESSED
YESSES
YESSING
YESSIR
YESSIREE
YESSUM
YEST
YESTER
YESTERDAY
YESTEREVE
YESTERN
YESTREEN
YESTREENS
YESTS
YESTY
YET
YETI
YETIS
YETT
YETTIE
YETTIES
YETTS
YEUK
YEUKED
YEUKIER
YEUKIEST
YEUKING
YEUKS
YEUKY
YEVE
YEVEN
YEVES
YEVING
YEW
YEWEN
YEWS
YEX
YEXED
YEXES
YEXING
YEZ
YFERE
YFERES
YGLAUNST
YGO
YGOE
YIBBLES
YICKER
YICKERED
YICKERING
YICKERS
YIDAKI
YIDAKIS
YIELD
YIELDABLE
YIELDED
YIELDER
YIELDERS
YIELDING
YIELDINGS
YIELDS
YIKE
YIKED
YIKES
YIKING
YIKKER
YIKKERED
YIKKERING
YIKKERS
YILL
YILLED
YILLING
YILLS
YIN
YINCE
YINDIE
YINDIES
YINGYANG
YINGYANGS
YINS
YIP
YIPE
YIPES
YIPPED
YIPPEE
YIPPER
YIPPERS
YIPPIE
YIPPIES
YIPPING
YIPPY
YIPS
YIRD
YIRDED
YIRDING
YIRDS
YIRK
YIRKED
YIRKING
YIRKS
YIRR
YIRRED
YIRRING
YIRRS
YIRTH
YIRTHS
YITE
YITES
YITIE
YITIES
YITTEN
YLEM
YLEMS
YLIKE
YLKE
YLKES
YMOLT
YMOLTEN
YMPE
YMPES
YMPING
YMPT
YNAMBU
YNAMBUS
YO
YOB
YOBBERIES
YOBBERY
YOBBIER
YOBBIEST
YOBBISH
YOBBISHLY
YOBBISM
YOBBISMS
YOBBO
YOBBOES
YOBBOS
YOBBY
YOBS
YOCK
YOCKED
YOCKING
YOCKS
YOD
YODE
YODEL
YODELED
YODELER
YODELERS
YODELING
YODELINGS
YODELLED
YODELLER
YODELLERS
YODELLING
YODELS
YODH
YODHS
YODLE
YODLED
YODLER
YODLERS
YODLES
YODLING
YODS
YOGA
YOGAS
YOGEE
YOGEES
YOGH
YOGHOURT
YOGHOURTS
YOGHS
YOGHURT
YOGHURTS
YOGI
YOGIC
YOGIN
YOGINI
YOGINIS
YOGINS
YOGIS
YOGISM
YOGISMS
YOGOURT
YOGOURTS
YOGURT
YOGURTS
YOHIMBE
YOHIMBES
YOHIMBINE
YOICK
YOICKED
YOICKING
YOICKS
YOICKSED
YOICKSES
YOICKSING
YOJAN
YOJANA
YOJANAS
YOJANS
YOK
YOKE
YOKED
YOKEL
YOKELESS
YOKELISH
YOKELS
YOKEMATE
YOKEMATES
YOKER
YOKERED
YOKERING
YOKERS
YOKES
YOKING
YOKINGS
YOKKED
YOKKING
YOKOZUNA
YOKOZUNAS
YOKS
YOKUL
YOLD
YOLDRING
YOLDRINGS
YOLK

Y

YOLKED
YOLKIER
YOLKIEST
YOLKLESS
YOLKS
YOLKY
YOM
YOMIM
YOMP
YOMPED
YOMPING
YOMPS
YON
YOND
YONDER
YONDERLY
YONDERS
YONI
YONIC
YONIS
YONKER
YONKERS
YONKS
YONNIE
YONNIES
YONT
YOOF
YOOFS
YOOP
YOOPS
YOPPER
YOPPERS
YORE
YORES
YORK
YORKED
YORKER
YORKERS
YORKIE
YORKIES
YORKING
YORKS
YORLING
YORLINGS
YORP
YORPED
YORPING
YORPS
YOTTABYTE
YOU
YOUK
YOUKED
YOUKING
YOUKS
YOUNG
YOUNGER
YOUNGERS
YOUNGEST
YOUNGISH
YOUNGLING
YOUNGLY
YOUNGNESS
YOUNGS
YOUNGSTER
YOUNGTH
YOUNGTHLY
YOUNGTHS
YOUNKER
YOUNKERS
YOUPON
YOUPONS
YOUR
YOURN
YOURS
YOURSELF
YOURT
YOURTS
YOUS
YOUSE
YOUTH
YOUTHEN
YOUTHENED
YOUTHENS
YOUTHFUL
YOUTHHEAD
YOUTHHOOD
YOUTHIER
YOUTHIEST
YOUTHLESS
YOUTHLY
YOUTHS
YOUTHSOME
YOUTHY
YOW
YOWE
YOWED
YOWES
YOWIE
YOWIES
YOWING
YOWL
YOWLED
YOWLER
YOWLERS
YOWLEY
YOWLEYS
YOWLING
YOWLINGS
YOWLS
YOWS
YOWZA
YPERITE
YPERITES
YPIGHT
YPLAST
YPLIGHT
YPSILOID
YPSILON
YPSILONS
YRAPT
YRAVISHED
YRENT
YRIVD
YRNEH
YRNEHS
YSAME
YSHEND
YSHENDING
YSHENDS
YSHENT
YSLAKED
YTOST
YTTERBIA
YTTERBIAS
YTTERBIC
YTTERBITE
YTTERBIUM
YTTERBOUS
YTTRIA
YTTRIAS
YTTRIC
YTTRIOUS
YTTRIUM
YTTRIUMS
YU
YUAN
YUANS
YUCA
YUCAS
YUCCA
YUCCAS
YUCCH
YUCH
YUCK
YUCKED
YUCKER
YUCKERS
YUCKIER
YUCKIEST
YUCKINESS
YUCKING
YUCKO
YUCKS
YUCKY
YUFT
YUFTS
YUG
YUGA
YUGARIE
YUGARIES
YUGAS
YUGS
YUK
YUKATA
YUKATAS
YUKE
YUKED
YUKES
YUKIER
YUKIEST
YUKING
YUKKED
YUKKIER
YUKKIEST
YUKKING
YUKKY
YUKO
YUKOS
YUKS
YUKY
YULAN
YULANS
YULE
YULES
YULETIDE
YULETIDES
YUM
YUMBERRY
YUMMIER
YUMMIES
YUMMIEST
YUMMINESS
YUMMO
YUMMY
YUMP
YUMPED
YUMPIE
YUMPIES
YUMPING
YUMPS
YUNX
YUNXES
YUP
YUPON
YUPONS
YUPPIE
YUPPIEDOM
YUPPIEISH
YUPPIES
YUPPIFIED
YUPPIFIES
YUPPIFY
YUPPY
YUPPYDOM
YUPPYDOMS
YUPS
YUPSTER
YUPSTERS
YURT
YURTA
YURTAS
YURTS
YUS
YUTZ
YUTZES
YUZU
YUZUS
YWIS
YWROKE

Y

Z

ZA
ZABAIONE
ZABAIONES
ZABAJONE
ZABAJONES
ZABETA
ZABETAS
ZABRA
ZABRAS
ZABTIEH
ZABTIEHS
ZACATON
ZACATONS
ZACK
ZACKS
ZADDICK
ZADDICKS
ZADDIK
ZADDIKIM
ZADDIKS
ZAFFAR
ZAFFARS
ZAFFER
ZAFFERS
ZAFFIR
ZAFFIRS
ZAFFRE
ZAFFRES
ZAFTIG
ZAG
ZAGGED
ZAGGING
ZAGS
ZAIBATSU
ZAIBATSUS
ZAIDA
ZAIDAS
ZAIDEH
ZAIDEHS
ZAIDIES
ZAIDY
ZAIKAI
ZAIKAIS
ZAIRE
ZAIRES
ZAITECH
ZAITECHS
ZAKAT
ZAKATS
ZAKOUSKA
ZAKOUSKI
ZAKUSKA
ZAKUSKI
ZAMAN
ZAMANG
ZAMANGS
ZAMANS
ZAMARRA
ZAMARRAS
ZAMARRO
ZAMARROS
ZAMBOMBA
ZAMBOMBAS
ZAMBOORAK
ZAMBUCK
ZAMBUCKS
ZAMBUK
ZAMBUKS
ZAMIA
ZAMIAS
ZAMINDAR
ZAMINDARI
ZAMINDARS
ZAMINDARY
ZAMOUSE
ZAMOUSES
ZAMPOGNA
ZAMPOGNAS
ZAMPONE
ZAMPONI
ZAMZAWED
ZANAMIVIR
ZANANA
ZANANAS
ZANDER
ZANDERS
ZANELLA
ZANELLAS
ZANIED
ZANIER
ZANIES
ZANIEST
ZANILY
ZANINESS
ZANJA
ZANJAS
ZANJERO
ZANJEROS
ZANTE
ZANTES
ZANTEWOOD
ZANTHOXYL
ZANY
ZANYING
ZANYISH
ZANYISM
ZANYISMS
ZANZA
ZANZAS
ZANZE
ZANZES
ZAP
ZAPATA
ZAPATEADO
ZAPATEO
ZAPATEOS
ZAPOTILLA
ZAPPED
ZAPPER
ZAPPERS
ZAPPIER
ZAPPIEST
ZAPPING
ZAPPY
ZAPS
ZAPTIAH
ZAPTIAHS
ZAPTIEH
ZAPTIEHS
ZARAPE
ZARAPES
ZARATITE
ZARATITES
ZAREBA
ZAREBAS
ZAREEBA
ZAREEBAS
ZARF
ZARFS
ZARI
ZARIBA
ZARIBAS
ZARIS
ZARNEC
ZARNECS
ZARNICH
ZARNICHS
ZARZUELA
ZARZUELAS
ZAS
ZASTRUGA
ZASTRUGI
ZATI
ZATIS
ZAX
ZAXES
ZAYIN
ZAYINS
ZAZEN
ZAZENS
ZE
ZEA
ZEAL
ZEALANT
ZEALANTS
ZEALFUL
ZEALLESS
ZEALOT
ZEALOTISM
ZEALOTRY
ZEALOTS
ZEALOUS
ZEALOUSLY
ZEALS
ZEAS
ZEATIN
ZEATINS
ZEBEC
ZEBECK
ZEBECKS
ZEBECS
ZEBRA
ZEBRAFISH
ZEBRAIC
ZEBRANO
ZEBRANOS
ZEBRAS
ZEBRASS
ZEBRASSES
ZEBRAWOOD
ZEBRINA
ZEBRINAS
ZEBRINE
ZEBRINES
ZEBRINNY
ZEBROID
ZEBRULA
ZEBRULAS
ZEBRULE
ZEBRULES
ZEBU
ZEBUB
ZEBUBS
ZEBUS
ZECCHIN
ZECCHINE
ZECCHINES
ZECCHINI
ZECCHINO
ZECCHINOS

ZECCHINS
ZECHIN
ZECHINS
ZED
ZEDA
ZEDAS
ZEDOARIES
ZEDOARY
ZEDS
ZEE
ZEES
ZEIN
ZEINS
ZEITGEBER
ZEITGEIST
ZEK
ZEKS
ZEL
ZELANT
ZELANTS
ZELATOR
ZELATORS
ZELATRICE
ZELATRIX
ZELKOVA
ZELKOVAS
ZELOSO
ZELOTYPIA
ZELS
ZEMINDAR
ZEMINDARI
ZEMINDARS
ZEMINDARY
ZEMSTVA
ZEMSTVO
ZEMSTVOS
ZEN
ZENAIDA
ZENAIDAS
ZENANA
ZENANAS
ZENDIK
ZENDIKS
ZENDO
ZENDOS
ZENITH
ZENITHAL
ZENITHS
ZENS
ZEOLITE
ZEOLITES
ZEOLITIC
ZEP
ZEPHYR
ZEPHYRS
ZEPPELIN
ZEPPELINS
ZEPPOLE
ZEPPOLES
ZEPPOLI
ZEPS
ZERDA
ZERDAS
ZEREBA
ZEREBAS
ZERIBA
ZERIBAS
ZERK
ZERKS
ZERO
ZEROED
ZEROES
ZEROING
ZEROS
ZEROTH
ZERUMBET
ZERUMBETS
ZEST
ZESTED
ZESTER
ZESTERS
ZESTFUL
ZESTFULLY
ZESTIER
ZESTIEST
ZESTILY
ZESTINESS
ZESTING
ZESTLESS
ZESTS
ZESTY
ZETA
ZETAS
ZETETIC
ZETETICS
ZETTABYTE
ZEUGMA
ZEUGMAS
ZEUGMATIC
ZEUXITE
ZEUXITES
ZEX
ZEXES
ZEZE
ZEZES
ZHO
ZHOMO
ZHOMOS
ZHOOSH
ZHOOSHED
ZHOOSHES
ZHOOSHING
ZHOS
ZIBELINE
ZIBELINES
ZIBELLINE
ZIBET
ZIBETH
ZIBETHS
ZIBETS
ZIFF
ZIFFIUS
ZIFFIUSES
ZIFFS
ZIG
ZIGAN
ZIGANKA
ZIGANKAS
ZIGANS
ZIGGED
ZIGGING
ZIGGURAT
ZIGGURATS
ZIGS
ZIGZAG
ZIGZAGGED
ZIGZAGGER
ZIGZAGGY
ZIGZAGS
ZIKKURAT
ZIKKURATS
ZIKURAT
ZIKURATS
ZILA
ZILAS
ZILCH
ZILCHES
ZILL
ZILLA
ZILLAH
ZILLAHS
ZILLAS
ZILLION
ZILLIONS
ZILLIONTH
ZILLS
ZIMB
ZIMBI
ZIMBIS
ZIMBS
ZIMOCCA
ZIMOCCAS
ZIN
ZINC
ZINCATE
ZINCATES
ZINCED
ZINCIC
ZINCIER
ZINCIEST
ZINCIFIED
ZINCIFIES
ZINCIFY
ZINCING
ZINCITE
ZINCITES
ZINCKED
ZINCKIER
ZINCKIEST
ZINCKIFY
ZINCKING
ZINCKY
ZINCO
ZINCODE
ZINCODES
ZINCOID
ZINCOS
ZINCOUS
ZINCS
ZINCY
ZINDABAD
ZINE
ZINEB
ZINEBS
ZINES
ZINFANDEL
ZING
ZINGANI
ZINGANO
ZINGARA
ZINGARE
ZINGARI
ZINGARO
ZINGED
ZINGEL
ZINGELS
ZINGER
ZINGERS
ZINGIBER
ZINGIBERS
ZINGIER
ZINGIEST
ZINGING
ZINGS
ZINGY
ZINKE
ZINKED
ZINKENITE
ZINKES
ZINKIER
ZINKIEST
ZINKIFIED
ZINKIFIES
ZINKIFY
ZINKING
ZINKY
ZINNIA
ZINNIAS
ZINS
ZIP
ZIPLESS
ZIPLINE
ZIPLINES
ZIPLOCK
ZIPLOCKED
ZIPLOCKS
ZIPOLA
ZIPOLAS
ZIPPED
ZIPPER

Z

ZIPPERED
ZIPPERING
ZIPPERS
ZIPPIER
ZIPPIEST
ZIPPILY
ZIPPINESS
ZIPPING
ZIPPO
ZIPPOS
ZIPPY
ZIPS
ZIPTOP
ZIPWIRE
ZIPWIRES
ZIRAM
ZIRAMS
ZIRCALLOY
ZIRCALOY
ZIRCALOYS
ZIRCON
ZIRCONIA
ZIRCONIAS
ZIRCONIC
ZIRCONIUM
ZIRCONS
ZIT
ZITE
ZITHER
ZITHERIST
ZITHERN
ZITHERNS
ZITHERS
ZITI
ZITIS
ZITS
ZIZ
ZIZANIA
ZIZANIAS
ZIZEL
ZIZELS
ZIZIT
ZIZITH
ZIZYPHUS
ZIZZ
ZIZZED
ZIZZES
ZIZZING
ZIZZLE
ZIZZLED
ZIZZLES
ZIZZLING
ZLOTE
ZLOTIES
ZLOTY
ZLOTYCH
ZLOTYS
ZO
ZOA
ZOAEA
ZOAEAE
ZOAEAS
ZOARIA
ZOARIAL
ZOARIUM
ZOBO
ZOBOS
ZOBU
ZOBUS
ZOCALO
ZOCALOS
ZOCCO
ZOCCOLO
ZOCCOLOS
ZOCCOS
ZODIAC
ZODIACAL
ZODIACS
ZOEA
ZOEAE
ZOEAL
ZOEAS
ZOECHROME
ZOECIA
ZOECIUM
ZOEFORM
ZOETIC
ZOETROPE
ZOETROPES
ZOETROPIC
ZOFTIG
ZOIATRIA
ZOIATRIAS
ZOIATRICS
ZOIC
ZOISITE
ZOISITES
ZOISM
ZOISMS
ZOIST
ZOISTS
ZOL
ZOLPIDEM
ZOLPIDEMS
ZOLS
ZOMBI
ZOMBIE
ZOMBIES
ZOMBIFIED
ZOMBIFIES
ZOMBIFY
ZOMBIISM
ZOMBIISMS
ZOMBIS
ZOMBOID
ZOMBORUK
ZOMBORUKS
ZONA
ZONAE
ZONAL
ZONALLY
ZONARY
ZONATE
ZONATED
ZONATION
ZONATIONS
ZONDA
ZONDAS
ZONE
ZONED
ZONELESS
ZONER
ZONERS
ZONES
ZONETIME
ZONETIMES
ZONING
ZONINGS
ZONK
ZONKED
ZONKING
ZONKS
ZONOID
ZONOIDS
ZONULA
ZONULAE
ZONULAR
ZONULAS
ZONULE
ZONULES
ZONULET
ZONULETS
ZONURE
ZONURES
ZOO
ZOOBIOTIC
ZOOBLAST
ZOOBLASTS
ZOOCHORE
ZOOCHORES
ZOOCHORY
ZOOCYTIA
ZOOCYTIUM
ZOOEA
ZOOEAE
ZOOEAL
ZOOEAS
ZOOECIA
ZOOECIUM
ZOOEY
ZOOGAMETE
ZOOGAMIES
ZOOGAMOUS
ZOOGAMY
ZOOGENIC
ZOOGENIES
ZOOGENOUS
ZOOGENY
ZOOGLEA
ZOOGLEAE
ZOOGLEAL
ZOOGLEAS
ZOOGLOEA
ZOOGLOEAE
ZOOGLOEAL
ZOOGLOEAS
ZOOGLOEIC
ZOOGONIES
ZOOGONOUS
ZOOGONY
ZOOGRAFT
ZOOGRAFTS
ZOOGRAPHY
ZOOID
ZOOIDAL
ZOOIDS
ZOOIER
ZOOIEST
ZOOKEEPER
ZOOKS
ZOOLATER
ZOOLATERS
ZOOLATRIA
ZOOLATRY
ZOOLITE
ZOOLITES
ZOOLITH
ZOOLITHIC
ZOOLITHS
ZOOLITIC
ZOOLOGIC
ZOOLOGIES
ZOOLOGIST
ZOOLOGY
ZOOM
ZOOMABLE
ZOOMANCY
ZOOMANIA
ZOOMANIAS
ZOOMANTIC
ZOOMED
ZOOMETRIC
ZOOMETRY
ZOOMING
ZOOMORPH
ZOOMORPHS
ZOOMORPHY
ZOOMS
ZOON
ZOONAL
ZOONED
ZOONIC
ZOONING
ZOONITE
ZOONITES
ZOONITIC
ZOONOMIA
ZOONOMIAS
ZOONOMIC
ZOONOMIES

Z

ZOONOMIST
ZOONOMY
ZOONOSES
ZOONOSIS
ZOONOTIC
ZOONS
ZOOPATHY
ZOOPERAL
ZOOPERIES
ZOOPERIST
ZOOPERY
ZOOPHAGAN
ZOOPHAGY
ZOOPHILE
ZOOPHILES
ZOOPHILIA
ZOOPHILIC
ZOOPHILY
ZOOPHOBE
ZOOPHOBES
ZOOPHOBIA
ZOOPHORI
ZOOPHORIC
ZOOPHORUS
ZOOPHYTE
ZOOPHYTES
ZOOPHYTIC
ZOOPLASTY
ZOOS
ZOOSCOPIC
ZOOSCOPY
ZOOSPERM
ZOOSPERMS
ZOOSPORE
ZOOSPORES
ZOOSPORIC
ZOOSTEROL
ZOOT
ZOOTAXIES
ZOOTAXY
ZOOTECHNY
ZOOTHECIA
ZOOTHEISM
ZOOTHOME
ZOOTHOMES
ZOOTIER
ZOOTIEST
ZOOTOMIC
ZOOTOMIES
ZOOTOMIST
ZOOTOMY
ZOOTOXIC
ZOOTOXIN
ZOOTOXINS
ZOOTROPE
ZOOTROPES
ZOOTROPHY
ZOOTY
ZOOTYPE
ZOOTYPES
ZOOTYPIC
ZOOZOO
ZOOZOOS
ZOPILOTE
ZOPILOTES
ZOPPA
ZOPPO
ZORBING
ZORBINGS
ZORBONAUT
ZORGITE
ZORGITES
ZORI
ZORIL
ZORILLA
ZORILLAS
ZORILLE
ZORILLES
ZORILLO
ZORILLOS
ZORILS
ZORINO
ZORINOS
ZORIS
ZORRO
ZORROS
ZOS
ZOSTER
ZOSTERS
ZOUAVE
ZOUAVES
ZOUK
ZOUKS
ZOUNDS
ZOWEE
ZOWIE
ZOYSIA
ZOYSIAS
ZUCCHETTI
ZUCCHETTO
ZUCCHINI
ZUCCHINIS
ZUCHETTA
ZUCHETTAS
ZUCHETTO
ZUCHETTOS
ZUFFOLI
ZUFFOLO
ZUFOLI
ZUFOLO
ZUFOLOS
ZUGZWANG
ZUGZWANGS
ZULU
ZULUS
ZUMBOORUK
ZUPA
ZUPAN
ZUPANS
ZUPAS
ZUPPA
ZUPPAS
ZURF
ZURFS
ZUZ
ZUZIM
ZUZZIM
ZWANZIGER
ZWIEBACK
ZWIEBACKS
ZYDECO
ZYDECOS
ZYGA
ZYGAENID
ZYGAENOID
ZYGAL
ZYGANTRA
ZYGANTRUM
ZYGOCACTI
ZYGODONT
ZYGOID
ZYGOMA
ZYGOMAS
ZYGOMATA
ZYGOMATIC
ZYGON
ZYGOPHYTE
ZYGOSE
ZYGOSES
ZYGOSIS
ZYGOSITY
ZYGOSPERM
ZYGOSPORE
ZYGOTE
ZYGOTENE
ZYGOTENES
ZYGOTES
ZYGOTIC
ZYLONITE
ZYLONITES
ZYMASE
ZYMASES
ZYME
ZYMES
ZYMIC
ZYMITE
ZYMITES
ZYMOGEN
ZYMOGENE
ZYMOGENES
ZYMOGENIC
ZYMOGENS
ZYMOGRAM
ZYMOGRAMS
ZYMOID
ZYMOLOGIC
ZYMOLOGY
ZYMOLYSES
ZYMOLYSIS
ZYMOLYTIC
ZYMOME
ZYMOMES
ZYMOMETER
ZYMOSAN
ZYMOSANS
ZYMOSES
ZYMOSIS
ZYMOTIC
ZYMOTICS
ZYMURGIES
ZYMURGY
ZYTHUM
ZYTHUMS
ZYZZYVA
ZYZZYVAS
ZZZ
ZZZS

TEN TO FIFTEEN LETTER WORDS

AARDWOLVES
ABACTERIAL
ABACTINALLY
ABANDONEDLY
ABANDONEES
ABANDONERS
ABANDONING
ABANDONMENT
ABANDONMENTS
ABANDONWARE
ABANDONWARES
ABASEMENTS
ABASHMENTS
ABATEMENTS
ABBOTSHIPS
ABBREVIATE
ABBREVIATED
ABBREVIATES
ABBREVIATING
ABBREVIATION
ABBREVIATIONS
ABBREVIATOR
ABBREVIATORS
ABBREVIATORY
ABBREVIATURE
ABBREVIATURES
ABCOULOMBS
ABDICATING
ABDICATION
ABDICATIONS
ABDICATIVE
ABDICATORS
ABDOMINALLY
ABDOMINALS
ABDOMINOPLASTY
ABDOMINOUS
ABDUCENTES
ABDUCTIONS
ABDUCTORES
ABECEDARIAN
ABECEDARIANS
ABERDEVINE
ABERDEVINES
ABERNETHIES
ABERRANCES
ABERRANCIES
ABERRANTLY
ABERRATING
ABERRATION
ABERRATIONAL
ABERRATIONS
ABEYANCIES
ABHOMINABLE
ABHORRENCE
ABHORRENCES
ABHORRENCIES
ABHORRENCY
ABHORRENTLY
ABHORRINGS
ABIOGENESES
ABIOGENESIS
ABIOGENETIC
ABIOGENETICALLY
ABIOGENICALLY
ABIOGENIST
ABIOGENISTS
ABIOLOGICAL
ABIOTICALLY
ABIOTROPHIC
ABIOTROPHIES
ABIOTROPHY
ABIRRITANT
ABIRRITANTS
ABIRRITATE
ABIRRITATED
ABIRRITATES
ABIRRITATING
ABITURIENT
ABITURIENTS
ABJECTIONS
ABJECTNESS
ABJECTNESSES
ABJOINTING
ABJUNCTION
ABJUNCTIONS
ABJURATION
ABJURATIONS
ABLACTATION
ABLACTATIONS
ABLATITIOUS
ABLATIVELY
ABLUTIONARY
ABLUTOMANE
ABLUTOMANES
ABNEGATING
ABNEGATION
ABNEGATIONS
ABNEGATORS
ABNORMALISM
ABNORMALISMS
ABNORMALITIES
ABNORMALITY
ABNORMALLY
ABNORMITIES
ABODEMENTS
ABOLISHABLE
ABOLISHERS
ABOLISHING
ABOLISHMENT
ABOLISHMENTS
ABOLITIONAL
ABOLITIONARY
ABOLITIONISM
ABOLITIONISMS
ABOLITIONIST
ABOLITIONISTS
ABOLITIONS
ABOMINABLE
ABOMINABLENESS
ABOMINABLY
ABOMINATED
ABOMINATES
ABOMINATING
ABOMINATION
ABOMINATIONS
ABOMINATOR
ABOMINATORS
ABONDANCES
ABONNEMENT
ABONNEMENTS
ABORIGINAL
ABORIGINALISM
ABORIGINALISMS
ABORIGINALITIES
ABORIGINALITY
ABORIGINALLY
ABORIGINALS
ABORIGINES
ABORTICIDE
ABORTICIDES
ABORTIFACIENT
ABORTIFACIENTS
ABORTIONAL
ABORTIONIST
ABORTIONISTS
ABORTIVELY
ABORTIVENESS
ABORTIVENESSES
ABORTUARIES
ABOVEBOARD
ABOVEGROUND
ABRACADABRA
ABRACADABRAS
ABRANCHIAL
ABRANCHIATE
ABRASIVELY
ABRASIVENESS
ABRASIVENESSES
ABREACTING
ABREACTION
ABREACTIONS
ABREACTIVE
ABRIDGABLE
ABRIDGEABLE
ABRIDGEMENT
ABRIDGEMENTS
ABRIDGMENT
ABRIDGMENTS
ABROGATING
ABROGATION
ABROGATIONS
ABROGATIVE
ABROGATORS
ABRUPTIONS
ABRUPTNESS
ABRUPTNESSES
ABSCESSING
ABSCINDING
ABSCISSINS
ABSCISSION
ABSCISSIONS
ABSCONDENCE
ABSCONDENCES
ABSCONDERS
ABSCONDING
ABSCONDINGS
ABSEILINGS
ABSENTEEISM
ABSENTEEISMS
ABSENTMINDED
ABSENTMINDEDLY
ABSINTHIATED
ABSINTHISM
ABSINTHISMS
ABSOLUTELY
ABSOLUTENESS
ABSOLUTENESSES
ABSOLUTEST
ABSOLUTION
ABSOLUTIONS
ABSOLUTISE
ABSOLUTISED
ABSOLUTISES
ABSOLUTISING
ABSOLUTISM
ABSOLUTISMS
ABSOLUTIST
ABSOLUTISTIC
ABSOLUTISTS
ABSOLUTIVE

ABSOLUTIVES
ABSOLUTIZE
ABSOLUTIZED
ABSOLUTIZES
ABSOLUTIZING
ABSOLUTORY
ABSOLVABLE
ABSOLVENTS
ABSOLVITOR
ABSOLVITORS
ABSORBABILITIES
ABSORBABILITY
ABSORBABLE
ABSORBANCE
ABSORBANCES
ABSORBANCIES
ABSORBANCY
ABSORBANTS
ABSORBATES
ABSORBEDLY
ABSORBEFACIENT
ABSORBEFACIENTS
ABSORBENCIES
ABSORBENCY
ABSORBENTS
ABSORBINGLY
ABSORPTANCE
ABSORPTANCES
ABSORPTIOMETER
ABSORPTIOMETERS
ABSORPTION
ABSORPTIONS
ABSORPTIVE
ABSORPTIVENESS
ABSORPTIVITIES
ABSORPTIVITY
ABSQUATULATE
ABSQUATULATED
ABSQUATULATES
ABSQUATULATING
ABSTAINERS
ABSTAINING
ABSTEMIOUS
ABSTEMIOUSLY
ABSTEMIOUSNESS
ABSTENTION
ABSTENTIONISM
ABSTENTIONISMS
ABSTENTIONIST
ABSTENTIONISTS
ABSTENTIONS
ABSTENTIOUS
ABSTERGENT
ABSTERGENTS
ABSTERGING
ABSTERSION
ABSTERSIONS
ABSTERSIVE
ABSTERSIVES
ABSTINENCE
ABSTINENCES
ABSTINENCIES
ABSTINENCY
ABSTINENTLY
ABSTRACTABLE
ABSTRACTED
ABSTRACTEDLY
ABSTRACTEDNESS
ABSTRACTER
ABSTRACTERS
ABSTRACTEST
ABSTRACTING
ABSTRACTION
ABSTRACTIONAL
ABSTRACTIONISM
ABSTRACTIONISMS
ABSTRACTIONIST
ABSTRACTIONISTS
ABSTRACTIONS
ABSTRACTIVE
ABSTRACTIVELY
ABSTRACTIVES
ABSTRACTLY
ABSTRACTNESS
ABSTRACTNESSES
ABSTRACTOR
ABSTRACTORS
ABSTRICTED
ABSTRICTING
ABSTRICTION
ABSTRICTIONS
ABSTRUSELY
ABSTRUSENESS
ABSTRUSENESSES
ABSTRUSEST
ABSTRUSITIES
ABSTRUSITY
ABSURDISMS
ABSURDISTS
ABSURDITIES
ABSURDNESS
ABSURDNESSES
ABUNDANCES
ABUNDANCIES
ABUNDANTLY
ABUSIVENESS
ABUSIVENESSES
ABYSSOPELAGIC
ACADEMICAL
ACADEMICALISM
ACADEMICALISMS
ACADEMICALLY
ACADEMICALS
ACADEMICIAN
ACADEMICIANS
ACADEMICISM
ACADEMICISMS
ACADEMISMS
ACADEMISTS
ACALCULIAS
ACALEPHANS
ACANACEOUS
ACANTHACEOUS
ACANTHOCEPHALAN
ACANTHUSES
ACARICIDAL
ACARICIDES
ACARIDEANS
ACARIDIANS
ACARIDOMATIA
ACARIDOMATIUM
ACARODOMATIA
ACARODOMATIUM
ACAROLOGIES
ACAROLOGIST
ACAROLOGISTS
ACAROPHILIES
ACAROPHILY
ACARPELLOUS
ACARPELOUS
ACATALECTIC
ACATALECTICS
ACATALEPSIES
ACATALEPSY
ACATALEPTIC
ACATALEPTICS
ACATAMATHESIA
ACATAMATHESIAS
ACATHISIAS
ACAULESCENT
ACCEDENCES
ACCELERABLE
ACCELERANDO
ACCELERANDOS
ACCELERANT
ACCELERANTS
ACCELERATE
ACCELERATED
ACCELERATES
ACCELERATING
ACCELERATINGLY
ACCELERATION
ACCELERATIONS
ACCELERATIVE
ACCELERATOR
ACCELERATORS
ACCELERATORY
ACCELEROMETER
ACCELEROMETERS
ACCENSIONS
ACCENTLESS
ACCENTUALITIES
ACCENTUALITY
ACCENTUALLY
ACCENTUATE
ACCENTUATED
ACCENTUATES
ACCENTUATING
ACCENTUATION
ACCENTUATIONS
ACCEPTABILITIES
ACCEPTABILITY
ACCEPTABLE
ACCEPTABLENESS
ACCEPTABLY
ACCEPTANCE
ACCEPTANCES
ACCEPTANCIES
ACCEPTANCY
ACCEPTANTS
ACCEPTATION
ACCEPTATIONS
ACCEPTEDLY
ACCEPTILATION
ACCEPTILATIONS
ACCEPTINGLY
ACCEPTINGNESS
ACCEPTINGNESSES
ACCEPTIVITIES
ACCEPTIVITY
ACCESSARIES
ACCESSARILY
ACCESSARINESS
ACCESSARINESSES
ACCESSIBILITIES
ACCESSIBILITY
ACCESSIBLE
ACCESSIBLENESS
ACCESSIBLY
ACCESSIONAL
ACCESSIONED
ACCESSIONING
ACCESSIONS
ACCESSORIAL
ACCESSORIES
ACCESSORII
ACCESSORILY
ACCESSORINESS
ACCESSORINESSES
ACCESSORISE
ACCESSORISED
ACCESSORISES
ACCESSORISING
ACCESSORIUS
ACCESSORIZE
ACCESSORIZED
ACCESSORIZES
ACCESSORIZING
ACCIACCATURA
ACCIACCATURAS
ACCIACCATURE
ACCIDENCES
ACCIDENTAL
ACCIDENTALISM
ACCIDENTALISMS
ACCIDENTALITIES
ACCIDENTALITY
ACCIDENTALLY
ACCIDENTALNESS
ACCIDENTALS

ACCIDENTED
ACCIDENTLY
ACCIDENTOLOGIES
ACCIDENTOLOGY
ACCIPITERS
ACCIPITRAL
ACCIPITRINE
ACCIPITRINES
ACCLAIMERS
ACCLAIMING
ACCLAMATION
ACCLAMATIONS
ACCLAMATORY
ACCLIMATABLE
ACCLIMATATION
ACCLIMATATIONS
ACCLIMATED
ACCLIMATES
ACCLIMATING
ACCLIMATION
ACCLIMATIONS
ACCLIMATISABLE
ACCLIMATISATION
ACCLIMATISE
ACCLIMATISED
ACCLIMATISER
ACCLIMATISERS
ACCLIMATISES
ACCLIMATISING
ACCLIMATIZABLE
ACCLIMATIZATION
ACCLIMATIZE
ACCLIMATIZED
ACCLIMATIZER
ACCLIMATIZERS
ACCLIMATIZES
ACCLIMATIZING
ACCLIVITIES
ACCLIVITOUS
ACCOASTING
ACCOLADING
ACCOMMODABLE
ACCOMMODATE
ACCOMMODATED
ACCOMMODATES
ACCOMMODATING
ACCOMMODATINGLY
ACCOMMODATION
ACCOMMODATIONAL
ACCOMMODATIONS
ACCOMMODATIVE
ACCOMMODATOR
ACCOMMODATORS
ACCOMPANIED
ACCOMPANIER
ACCOMPANIERS
ACCOMPANIES
ACCOMPANIMENT
ACCOMPANIMENTS
ACCOMPANIST
ACCOMPANISTS
ACCOMPANYING
ACCOMPANYIST
ACCOMPANYISTS
ACCOMPLICE
ACCOMPLICES
ACCOMPLISH
ACCOMPLISHABLE
ACCOMPLISHED
ACCOMPLISHER
ACCOMPLISHERS
ACCOMPLISHES
ACCOMPLISHING
ACCOMPLISHMENT
ACCOMPLISHMENTS
ACCOMPTABLE
ACCOMPTANT
ACCOMPTANTS
ACCOMPTING
ACCORAGING
ACCORDABLE
ACCORDANCE
ACCORDANCES
ACCORDANCIES
ACCORDANCY
ACCORDANTLY
ACCORDINGLY
ACCORDIONIST
ACCORDIONISTS
ACCORDIONS
ACCOSTABLE
ACCOUCHEMENT
ACCOUCHEMENTS
ACCOUCHEUR
ACCOUCHEURS
ACCOUCHEUSE
ACCOUCHEUSES
ACCOUNTABILITY
ACCOUNTABLE
ACCOUNTABLENESS
ACCOUNTABLY
ACCOUNTANCIES
ACCOUNTANCY
ACCOUNTANT
ACCOUNTANTS
ACCOUNTANTSHIP
ACCOUNTANTSHIPS
ACCOUNTING
ACCOUNTINGS
ACCOUPLEMENT
ACCOUPLEMENTS
ACCOURAGED
ACCOURAGES
ACCOURAGING
ACCOURTING
ACCOUSTREMENT
ACCOUSTREMENTS
ACCOUTERED
ACCOUTERING
ACCOUTERMENT
ACCOUTERMENTS
ACCOUTREMENT
ACCOUTREMENTS
ACCOUTRING
ACCREDITABLE
ACCREDITATION
ACCREDITATIONS
ACCREDITED
ACCREDITING
ACCRESCENCE
ACCRESCENCES
ACCRESCENT
ACCRETIONARY
ACCRETIONS
ACCRUEMENT
ACCRUEMENTS
ACCUBATION
ACCUBATIONS
ACCULTURAL
ACCULTURATE
ACCULTURATED
ACCULTURATES
ACCULTURATING
ACCULTURATION
ACCULTURATIONAL
ACCULTURATIONS
ACCULTURATIVE
ACCUMBENCIES
ACCUMBENCY
ACCUMULABLE
ACCUMULATE
ACCUMULATED
ACCUMULATES
ACCUMULATING
ACCUMULATION
ACCUMULATIONS
ACCUMULATIVE
ACCUMULATIVELY
ACCUMULATOR
ACCUMULATORS
ACCURACIES
ACCURATELY
ACCURATENESS
ACCURATENESSES
ACCURSEDLY
ACCURSEDNESS
ACCURSEDNESSES
ACCUSATION
ACCUSATIONS
ACCUSATIVAL
ACCUSATIVE
ACCUSATIVELY
ACCUSATIVES
ACCUSATORIAL
ACCUSATORY
ACCUSEMENT
ACCUSEMENTS
ACCUSINGLY
ACCUSTOMARY
ACCUSTOMATION
ACCUSTOMATIONS
ACCUSTOMED
ACCUSTOMEDNESS
ACCUSTOMING
ACCUSTREMENT
ACCUSTREMENTS
ACEPHALOUS
ACERACEOUS
ACERBATING
ACERBICALLY
ACERBITIES
ACERVATELY
ACERVATION
ACERVATIONS
ACESCENCES
ACESCENCIES
ACETABULAR
ACETABULUM
ACETABULUMS
ACETALDEHYDE
ACETALDEHYDES
ACETAMIDES
ACETAMINOPHEN
ACETAMINOPHENS
ACETANILID
ACETANILIDE
ACETANILIDES
ACETANILIDS
ACETAZOLAMIDE
ACETAZOLAMIDES
ACETIFICATION
ACETIFICATIONS
ACETIFIERS
ACETIFYING
ACETOACETIC
ACETOMETER
ACETOMETERS
ACETONAEMIA
ACETONAEMIAS
ACETONEMIA
ACETONEMIAS
ACETONITRILE
ACETONITRILES
ACETONURIA
ACETONURIAS
ACETOPHENETIDIN
ACETYLATED
ACETYLATES
ACETYLATING
ACETYLATION
ACETYLATIONS
ACETYLATIVE
ACETYLCHOLINE
ACETYLCHOLINES
ACETYLENES
ACETYLENIC
ACETYLIDES
ACETYLSALICYLIC
ACHAENIUMS
ACHAENOCARP

A

ACHAENOCARPS
ACHALASIAS
ACHIEVABLE
ACHIEVEMENT
ACHIEVEMENTS
ACHINESSES
ACHLAMYDEOUS
ACHLORHYDRIA
ACHLORHYDRIAS
ACHLORHYDRIC
ACHONDRITE
ACHONDRITES
ACHONDRITIC
ACHONDROPLASIA
ACHONDROPLASIAS
ACHONDROPLASTIC
ACHROMATIC
ACHROMATICALLY
ACHROMATICITIES
ACHROMATICITY
ACHROMATIN
ACHROMATINS
ACHROMATISATION
ACHROMATISE
ACHROMATISED
ACHROMATISES
ACHROMATISING
ACHROMATISM
ACHROMATISMS
ACHROMATIZATION
ACHROMATIZE
ACHROMATIZED
ACHROMATIZES
ACHROMATIZING
ACHROMATOPSIA
ACHROMATOPSIAS
ACHROMATOUS
ACICLOVIRS
ACICULATED
ACIDANTHERA
ACIDANTHERAS
ACIDICALLY
ACIDIFIABLE
ACIDIFICATION
ACIDIFICATIONS
ACIDIFIERS
ACIDIFYING
ACIDIMETER
ACIDIMETERS
ACIDIMETRIC
ACIDIMETRICAL
ACIDIMETRICALLY
ACIDIMETRIES
ACIDIMETRY
ACIDNESSES
ACIDOMETER
ACIDOMETERS
ACIDOPHILE
ACIDOPHILES
ACIDOPHILIC
ACIDOPHILOUS
ACIDOPHILS
ACIDOPHILUS
ACIDOPHILUSES
ACIDULATED
ACIDULATES
ACIDULATING
ACIDULATION
ACIDULATIONS
ACIERATING
ACIERATION
ACIERATIONS
ACINACEOUS
ACINACIFORM
ACINETOBACTER
ACINETOBACTERS
ACKNOWLEDGE
ACKNOWLEDGEABLE
ACKNOWLEDGEABLY
ACKNOWLEDGED
ACKNOWLEDGEDLY
ACKNOWLEDGEMENT
ACKNOWLEDGER
ACKNOWLEDGERS
ACKNOWLEDGES
ACKNOWLEDGING
ACKNOWLEDGMENT
ACKNOWLEDGMENTS
ACOELOMATE
ACOELOMATES
ACOLOUTHIC
ACOLOUTHITE
ACOLOUTHITES
ACOLOUTHOS
ACOLOUTHOSES
ACONITINES
ACOTYLEDON
ACOTYLEDONOUS
ACOTYLEDONS
ACOUSTICAL
ACOUSTICALLY
ACOUSTICIAN
ACOUSTICIANS
ACQUAINTANCE
ACQUAINTANCES
ACQUAINTED
ACQUAINTING
ACQUIESCED
ACQUIESCENCE
ACQUIESCENCES
ACQUIESCENT
ACQUIESCENTLY
ACQUIESCENTS
ACQUIESCES
ACQUIESCING
ACQUIESCINGLY
ACQUIGHTING
ACQUIRABILITIES
ACQUIRABILITY
ACQUIRABLE
ACQUIREMENT
ACQUIREMENTS
ACQUISITION
ACQUISITIONAL
ACQUISITIONS
ACQUISITIVE
ACQUISITIVELY
ACQUISITIVENESS
ACQUISITOR
ACQUISITORS
ACQUITMENT
ACQUITMENTS
ACQUITTALS
ACQUITTANCE
ACQUITTANCED
ACQUITTANCES
ACQUITTANCING
ACQUITTERS
ACQUITTING
ACRIDITIES
ACRIDNESSES
ACRIFLAVIN
ACRIFLAVINE
ACRIFLAVINES
ACRIFLAVINS
ACRIMONIES
ACRIMONIOUS
ACRIMONIOUSLY
ACRIMONIOUSNESS
ACRITARCHS
ACROAMATIC
ACROAMATICAL
ACROBATICALLY
ACROBATICS
ACROBATISM
ACROBATISMS
ACROCARPOUS
ACROCENTRIC
ACROCENTRICS
ACROCYANOSES
ACROCYANOSIS
ACRODROMOUS
ACROGENOUS
ACROGENOUSLY
ACROLITHIC
ACROMEGALIC
ACROMEGALICS
ACROMEGALIES
ACROMEGALY
ACRONICALLY
ACRONYCALLY
ACRONYCHAL
ACRONYCHALLY
ACRONYMANIA
ACRONYMANIAS
ACRONYMICALLY
ACRONYMOUS
ACROPARESTHESIA
ACROPETALLY
ACROPHOBES
ACROPHOBIA
ACROPHOBIAS
ACROPHOBIC
ACROPHOBICS
ACROPHONETIC
ACROPHONIC
ACROPHONIES
ACROPOLISES
ACROSPIRES
ACROSTICAL
ACROSTICALLY
ACROTERIAL
ACROTERION
ACROTERIUM
ACRYLAMIDE
ACRYLAMIDES
ACRYLONITRILE
ACRYLONITRILES
ACTABILITIES
ACTABILITY
ACTINICALLY
ACTINIFORM
ACTINOBACILLI
ACTINOBACILLUS
ACTINOBIOLOGIES
ACTINOBIOLOGY
ACTINOCHEMISTRY
ACTINOLITE
ACTINOLITES
ACTINOMERE
ACTINOMERES
ACTINOMETER
ACTINOMETERS
ACTINOMETRIC
ACTINOMETRICAL
ACTINOMETRIES
ACTINOMETRY
ACTINOMORPHIC
ACTINOMORPHIES
ACTINOMORPHOUS
ACTINOMORPHY
ACTINOMYCES
ACTINOMYCETE
ACTINOMYCETES
ACTINOMYCETOUS
ACTINOMYCIN
ACTINOMYCINS
ACTINOMYCOSES
ACTINOMYCOSIS
ACTINOMYCOTIC
ACTINOPODS
ACTINOTHERAPIES
ACTINOTHERAPY
ACTINOURANIUM
ACTINOURANIUMS
ACTINOZOAN
ACTINOZOANS
ACTIONABLE
ACTIONABLY
ACTIONISTS

A

ACTIONLESS
ACTIVATING
ACTIVATION
ACTIVATIONS
ACTIVATORS
ACTIVENESS
ACTIVENESSES
ACTIVISING
ACTIVISTIC
ACTIVITIES
ACTIVIZING
ACTOMYOSIN
ACTOMYOSINS
ACTORLIEST
ACTRESSIER
ACTRESSIEST
ACTUALISATION
ACTUALISATIONS
ACTUALISED
ACTUALISES
ACTUALISING
ACTUALISTS
ACTUALITES
ACTUALITIES
ACTUALIZATION
ACTUALIZATIONS
ACTUALIZED
ACTUALIZES
ACTUALIZING
ACTUARIALLY
ACTUATIONS
ACUMINATED
ACUMINATES
ACUMINATING
ACUMINATION
ACUMINATIONS
ACUPRESSURE
ACUPRESSURES
ACUPUNCTURAL
ACUPUNCTURE
ACUPUNCTURES
ACUPUNCTURIST
ACUPUNCTURISTS
ACUTENESSES
ACYCLOVIRS
ACYLATIONS
ADACTYLOUS
ADAMANCIES
ADAMANTEAN
ADAMANTINE
ADAPTABILITIES
ADAPTABILITY
ADAPTABLENESS
ADAPTABLENESSES
ADAPTATION
ADAPTATIONAL
ADAPTATIONALLY
ADAPTATIONS
ADAPTATIVE
ADAPTEDNESS
ADAPTEDNESSES
ADAPTIVELY
ADAPTIVENESS
ADAPTIVENESSES
ADAPTIVITIES
ADAPTIVITY
ADAPTOGENIC
ADAPTOGENS
ADDERBEADS
ADDERSTONE
ADDERSTONES
ADDERWORTS
ADDICTEDNESS
ADDICTEDNESSES
ADDICTIONS
ADDICTIVENESS
ADDICTIVENESSES
ADDITAMENT
ADDITAMENTS
ADDITIONAL
ADDITIONALITIES
ADDITIONALITY
ADDITIONALLY
ADDITITIOUS
ADDITIVELY
ADDITIVITIES
ADDITIVITY
ADDLEMENTS
ADDLEPATED
ADDRESSABILITY
ADDRESSABLE
ADDRESSEES
ADDRESSERS
ADDRESSING
ADDRESSINGS
ADDRESSORS
ADDUCEABLE
ADDUCTIONS
ADELANTADO
ADELANTADOS
ADEMPTIONS
ADENECTOMIES
ADENECTOMY
ADENITISES
ADENOCARCINOMA
ADENOCARCINOMAS
ADENOHYPOPHYSES
ADENOHYPOPHYSIS
ADENOIDECTOMIES
ADENOIDECTOMY
ADENOMATOUS
ADENOPATHIES
ADENOPATHY
ADENOSINES
ADENOVIRAL
ADENOVIRUS
ADENOVIRUSES
ADENYLATES
ADEPTNESSES
ADEQUACIES
ADEQUATELY
ADEQUATENESS
ADEQUATENESSES
ADEQUATIVE
ADHERENCES
ADHERENTLY
ADHESIONAL
ADHESIVELY
ADHESIVENESS
ADHESIVENESSES
ADHIBITING
ADHIBITION
ADHIBITIONS
ADHOCRACIES
ADIABATICALLY
ADIABATICS
ADIACTINIC
ADIAPHORISM
ADIAPHORISMS
ADIAPHORIST
ADIAPHORISTIC
ADIAPHORISTS
ADIAPHORON
ADIAPHOROUS
ADIATHERMANCIES
ADIATHERMANCY
ADIATHERMANOUS
ADIATHERMIC
ADIPOCERES
ADIPOCEROUS
ADIPOCYTES
ADIPOSITIES
ADJACENCES
ADJACENCIES
ADJACENTLY
ADJECTIVAL
ADJECTIVALLY
ADJECTIVELY
ADJECTIVES
ADJOURNING
ADJOURNMENT
ADJOURNMENTS
ADJUDGEMENT
ADJUDGEMENTS
ADJUDGMENT
ADJUDGMENTS
ADJUDICATE
ADJUDICATED
ADJUDICATES
ADJUDICATING
ADJUDICATION
ADJUDICATIONS
ADJUDICATIVE
ADJUDICATOR
ADJUDICATORS
ADJUDICATORY
ADJUNCTION
ADJUNCTIONS
ADJUNCTIVE
ADJUNCTIVELY
ADJURATION
ADJURATIONS
ADJURATORY
ADJUSTABILITIES
ADJUSTABILITY
ADJUSTABLE
ADJUSTABLY
ADJUSTMENT
ADJUSTMENTAL
ADJUSTMENTS
ADJUTANCIES
ADJUVANCIES
ADMEASURED
ADMEASUREMENT
ADMEASUREMENTS
ADMEASURES
ADMEASURING
ADMINICLES
ADMINICULAR
ADMINICULATE
ADMINICULATED
ADMINICULATES
ADMINICULATING
ADMINISTER
ADMINISTERED
ADMINISTERING
ADMINISTERS
ADMINISTRABLE
ADMINISTRANT
ADMINISTRANTS
ADMINISTRATE
ADMINISTRATED
ADMINISTRATES
ADMINISTRATING
ADMINISTRATION
ADMINISTRATIONS
ADMINISTRATIVE
ADMINISTRATOR
ADMINISTRATORS
ADMINISTRATRIX
ADMIRABILITIES
ADMIRABILITY
ADMIRABLENESS
ADMIRABLENESSES
ADMIRALSHIP
ADMIRALSHIPS
ADMIRALTIES
ADMIRANCES
ADMIRATION
ADMIRATIONS
ADMIRATIVE
ADMIRAUNCE
ADMIRAUNCES
ADMIRINGLY
ADMISSIBILITIES
ADMISSIBILITY
ADMISSIBLE
ADMISSIBLENESS
ADMISSIONS
ADMITTABLE

A

ADMITTANCE
ADMITTANCES
ADMITTEDLY
ADMIXTURES
ADMONISHED
ADMONISHER
ADMONISHERS
ADMONISHES
ADMONISHING
ADMONISHINGLY
ADMONISHMENT
ADMONISHMENTS
ADMONITION
ADMONITIONS
ADMONITIVE
ADMONITORILY
ADMONITORS
ADMONITORY
ADNOMINALS
ADOLESCENCE
ADOLESCENCES
ADOLESCENT
ADOLESCENTLY
ADOLESCENTS
ADOPTABILITIES
ADOPTABILITY
ADOPTIANISM
ADOPTIANISMS
ADOPTIANIST
ADOPTIANISTS
ADOPTIONISM
ADOPTIONISMS
ADOPTIONIST
ADOPTIONISTS
ADOPTIVELY
ADORABILITIES
ADORABILITY
ADORABLENESS
ADORABLENESSES
ADORATIONS
ADORNMENTS
ADPRESSING
ADRENALECTOMIES
ADRENALECTOMY
ADRENALINE
ADRENALINES
ADRENALINS
ADRENALISED
ADRENALIZED
ADRENERGIC
ADRENERGICALLY
ADRENOCEPTOR
ADRENOCEPTORS
ADRENOCHROME
ADRENOCHROMES
ADRENOCORTICAL
ADRIAMYCIN
ADRIAMYCINS
ADROITNESS
ADROITNESSES
ADSCITITIOUS
ADSCITITIOUSLY
ADSCRIPTION
ADSCRIPTIONS
ADSORBABILITIES
ADSORBABILITY
ADSORBABLE
ADSORBATES
ADSORBENTS
ADSORPTION
ADSORPTIONS
ADSORPTIVE
ADULARESCENCE
ADULARESCENCES
ADULARESCENT
ADULATIONS
ADULTERANT
ADULTERANTS
ADULTERATE
ADULTERATED
ADULTERATES
ADULTERATING
ADULTERATION
ADULTERATIONS
ADULTERATOR
ADULTERATORS
ADULTERERS
ADULTERESS
ADULTERESSES
ADULTERIES
ADULTERINE
ADULTERINES
ADULTERISE
ADULTERISED
ADULTERISES
ADULTERISING
ADULTERIZE
ADULTERIZED
ADULTERIZES
ADULTERIZING
ADULTEROUS
ADULTEROUSLY
ADULTESCENT
ADULTESCENTS
ADULTHOODS
ADULTNESSES
ADULTRESSES
ADUMBRATED
ADUMBRATES
ADUMBRATING
ADUMBRATION
ADUMBRATIONS
ADUMBRATIVE
ADUMBRATIVELY
ADUNCITIES
ADVANCEMENT
ADVANCEMENTS
ADVANCINGLY
ADVANTAGEABLE
ADVANTAGED
ADVANTAGEOUS
ADVANTAGEOUSLY
ADVANTAGES
ADVANTAGING
ADVECTIONS
ADVENTITIA
ADVENTITIAL
ADVENTITIAS
ADVENTITIOUS
ADVENTITIOUSLY
ADVENTIVES
ADVENTURED
ADVENTUREFUL
ADVENTURER
ADVENTURERS
ADVENTURES
ADVENTURESOME
ADVENTURESS
ADVENTURESSES
ADVENTURING
ADVENTURINGS
ADVENTURISM
ADVENTURISMS
ADVENTURIST
ADVENTURISTIC
ADVENTURISTS
ADVENTUROUS
ADVENTUROUSLY
ADVENTUROUSNESS
ADVERBIALISE
ADVERBIALISED
ADVERBIALISES
ADVERBIALISING
ADVERBIALIZE
ADVERBIALIZED
ADVERBIALIZES
ADVERBIALIZING
ADVERBIALLY
ADVERBIALS
ADVERGAMING
ADVERGAMINGS
ADVERSARIA
ADVERSARIAL
ADVERSARIES
ADVERSARINESS
ADVERSARINESSES
ADVERSATIVE
ADVERSATIVELY
ADVERSATIVES
ADVERSENESS
ADVERSENESSES
ADVERSITIES
ADVERTENCE
ADVERTENCES
ADVERTENCIES
ADVERTENCY
ADVERTENTLY
ADVERTISED
ADVERTISEMENT
ADVERTISEMENTS
ADVERTISER
ADVERTISERS
ADVERTISES
ADVERTISING
ADVERTISINGS
ADVERTIZED
ADVERTIZEMENT
ADVERTIZEMENTS
ADVERTIZER
ADVERTIZERS
ADVERTIZES
ADVERTIZING
ADVERTIZINGS
ADVERTORIAL
ADVERTORIALS
ADVISABILITIES
ADVISABILITY
ADVISABLENESS
ADVISABLENESSES
ADVISATORY
ADVISEDNESS
ADVISEDNESSES
ADVISEMENT
ADVISEMENTS
ADVISERSHIP
ADVISERSHIPS
ADVISORATE
ADVISORATES
ADVISORIES
ADVOCACIES
ADVOCATING
ADVOCATION
ADVOCATIONS
ADVOCATIVE
ADVOCATORS
ADVOCATORY
ADVOUTRERS
ADVOUTRIES
AECIDIOSPORE
AECIDIOSPORES
AECIDOSPORE
AECIDOSPORES
AECIOSPORE
AECIOSPORES
AEDILESHIP
AEDILESHIPS
AEOLIPILES
AEOLIPYLES
AEOLOTROPIC
AEOLOTROPIES
AEOLOTROPY
AEPYORNISES
AERENCHYMA
AERENCHYMAS
AERENCHYMATOUS
AERIALISTS
AERIALITIES
AERIFICATION
AERIFICATIONS
AEROACOUSTICS

AEROBALLISTICS
AEROBATICS
AEROBICALLY
AEROBICISE
AEROBICISED
AEROBICISES
AEROBICISING
AEROBICIST
AEROBICISTS
AEROBICIZE
AEROBICIZED
AEROBICIZES
AEROBICIZING
AEROBIOLOGICAL
AEROBIOLOGIES
AEROBIOLOGIST
AEROBIOLOGISTS
AEROBIOLOGY
AEROBIONTS
AEROBIOSES
AEROBIOSIS
AEROBIOTIC
AEROBIOTICALLY
AEROBRAKED
AEROBRAKES
AEROBRAKING
AEROBRAKINGS
AEROBUSSES
AERODIGESTIVE
AERODONETICS
AERODROMES
AERODYNAMIC
AERODYNAMICAL
AERODYNAMICALLY
AERODYNAMICIST
AERODYNAMICISTS
AERODYNAMICS
AEROELASTIC
AEROELASTICIAN
AEROELASTICIANS
AEROELASTICITY
AEROEMBOLISM
AEROEMBOLISMS
AEROGENERATOR
AEROGENERATORS
AEROGRAMME
AEROGRAMMES
AEROGRAPHIES
AEROGRAPHS
AEROGRAPHY
AEROHYDROPLANE
AEROHYDROPLANES
AEROLITHOLOGIES
AEROLITHOLOGY
AEROLOGICAL
AEROLOGIES
AEROLOGIST
AEROLOGISTS
AEROMAGNETIC
AEROMANCIES
AEROMECHANIC
AEROMECHANICAL
AEROMECHANICS
AEROMEDICAL
AEROMEDICINE
AEROMEDICINES
AEROMETERS
AEROMETRIC
AEROMETRIES
AEROMODELLING
AEROMODELLINGS
AEROMOTORS
AERONAUTIC
AERONAUTICAL
AERONAUTICALLY
AERONAUTICS
AERONEUROSES
AERONEUROSIS
AERONOMERS
AERONOMICAL
AERONOMIES
AERONOMIST
AERONOMISTS
AEROPAUSES
AEROPHAGIA
AEROPHAGIAS
AEROPHAGIES
AEROPHOBES
AEROPHOBIA
AEROPHOBIAS
AEROPHOBIC
AEROPHONES
AEROPHORES
AEROPHYTES
AEROPLANES
AEROPLANKTON
AEROPLANKTONS
AEROPULSES
AEROSCOPES
AEROSHELLS
AEROSIDERITE
AEROSIDERITES
AEROSOLISATION
AEROSOLISATIONS
AEROSOLISE
AEROSOLISED
AEROSOLISES
AEROSOLISING
AEROSOLIZATION
AEROSOLIZATIONS
AEROSOLIZE
AEROSOLIZED
AEROSOLIZES
AEROSOLIZING
AEROSPACES
AEROSPHERE
AEROSPHERES
AEROSPIKES
AEROSTATIC
AEROSTATICAL
AEROSTATICS
AEROSTATION
AEROSTATIONS
AEROSTRUCTURE
AEROSTRUCTURES
AEROTACTIC
AEROTRAINS
AEROTROPIC
AEROTROPISM
AEROTROPISMS
AERUGINOUS
AESTHESIAS
AESTHESIOGEN
AESTHESIOGENIC
AESTHESIOGENS
AESTHETICAL
AESTHETICALLY
AESTHETICIAN
AESTHETICIANS
AESTHETICISE
AESTHETICISED
AESTHETICISES
AESTHETICISING
AESTHETICISM
AESTHETICISMS
AESTHETICIST
AESTHETICISTS
AESTHETICIZE
AESTHETICIZED
AESTHETICIZES
AESTHETICIZING
AESTHETICS
AESTIVATED
AESTIVATES
AESTIVATING
AESTIVATION
AESTIVATIONS
AESTIVATOR
AESTIVATORS
AETHEREALITIES
AETHEREALITY
AETHEREALLY
AETHRIOSCOPE
AETHRIOSCOPES
AETIOLOGICAL
AETIOLOGICALLY
AETIOLOGIES
AETIOLOGIST
AETIOLOGISTS
AFFABILITIES
AFFABILITY
AFFECTABILITIES
AFFECTABILITY
AFFECTABLE
AFFECTATION
AFFECTATIONS
AFFECTEDLY
AFFECTEDNESS
AFFECTEDNESSES
AFFECTINGLY
AFFECTIONAL
AFFECTIONALLY
AFFECTIONATE
AFFECTIONATELY
AFFECTIONED
AFFECTIONING
AFFECTIONLESS
AFFECTIONS
AFFECTIVELY
AFFECTIVENESS
AFFECTIVENESSES
AFFECTIVITIES
AFFECTIVITY
AFFECTLESS
AFFECTLESSNESS
AFFEERMENT
AFFEERMENTS
AFFENPINSCHER
AFFENPINSCHERS
AFFERENTLY
AFFETTUOSO
AFFIANCING
AFFICIONADO
AFFICIONADOS
AFFIDAVITS
AFFILIABLE
AFFILIATED
AFFILIATES
AFFILIATING
AFFILIATION
AFFILIATIONS
AFFINITIES
AFFINITIVE
AFFIRMABLE
AFFIRMANCE
AFFIRMANCES
AFFIRMANTS
AFFIRMATION
AFFIRMATIONS
AFFIRMATIVE
AFFIRMATIVELY
AFFIRMATIVES
AFFIRMATORY
AFFIRMINGLY
AFFIXATION
AFFIXATIONS
AFFIXMENTS
AFFIXTURES
AFFLATIONS
AFFLATUSES
AFFLICTERS
AFFLICTING
AFFLICTINGS
AFFLICTION
AFFLICTIONS
AFFLICTIVE
AFFLICTIVELY
AFFLUENCES
AFFLUENCIES
AFFLUENTIAL

AFFLUENTIALS
AFFLUENTLY
AFFLUENTNESS
AFFLUENTNESSES
AFFLUENZAS
AFFLUXIONS
AFFOORDING
AFFORCEMENT
AFFORCEMENTS
AFFORDABILITIES
AFFORDABILITY
AFFORDABLE
AFFORDABLY
AFFORESTABLE
AFFORESTATION
AFFORESTATIONS
AFFORESTED
AFFORESTING
AFFRANCHISE
AFFRANCHISED
AFFRANCHISEMENT
AFFRANCHISES
AFFRANCHISING
AFFRAPPING
AFFREIGHTMENT
AFFREIGHTMENTS
AFFRICATED
AFFRICATES
AFFRICATING
AFFRICATION
AFFRICATIONS
AFFRICATIVE
AFFRICATIVES
AFFRIGHTED
AFFRIGHTEDLY
AFFRIGHTEN
AFFRIGHTENED
AFFRIGHTENING
AFFRIGHTENS
AFFRIGHTFUL
AFFRIGHTING
AFFRIGHTMENT
AFFRIGHTMENTS
AFFRONTING
AFFRONTINGLY
AFFRONTINGS
AFFRONTIVE
AFICIONADA
AFICIONADAS
AFICIONADO
AFICIONADOS
AFLATOXINS
AFOREMENTIONED
AFORETHOUGHT
AFORETHOUGHTS
AFRORMOSIA
AFRORMOSIAS
AFTERBIRTH
AFTERBIRTHS
AFTERBODIES
AFTERBRAIN
AFTERBRAINS
AFTERBURNER
AFTERBURNERS
AFTERBURNING
AFTERBURNINGS
AFTERBURNS
AFTERCARES
AFTERCLAPS
AFTERDAMPS
AFTERDECKS
AFTEREFFECT
AFTEREFFECTS
AFTEREYEING
AFTEREYING
AFTERGAMES
AFTERGLOWS
AFTERGRASS
AFTERGRASSES
AFTERGROWTH
AFTERGROWTHS
AFTERGUARD
AFTERGUARDS
AFTERHEATS
AFTERIMAGE
AFTERIMAGES
AFTERLIFES
AFTERLIVES
AFTERMARKET
AFTERMARKETS
AFTERMASTS
AFTERMATHS
AFTERNOONS
AFTERPAINS
AFTERPARTIES
AFTERPARTY
AFTERPEAKS
AFTERPIECE
AFTERPIECES
AFTERSALES
AFTERSENSATION
AFTERSENSATIONS
AFTERSHAFT
AFTERSHAFTS
AFTERSHAVE
AFTERSHAVES
AFTERSHOCK
AFTERSHOCKS
AFTERSHOWS
AFTERSUPPER
AFTERSUPPERS
AFTERSWARM
AFTERSWARMS
AFTERTASTE
AFTERTASTES
AFTERTHOUGHT
AFTERTHOUGHTS
AFTERTIMES
AFTERTREATMENT
AFTERTREATMENTS
AFTERWARDS
AFTERWORDS
AFTERWORLD
AFTERWORLDS
AGALACTIAS
AGALMATOLITE
AGALMATOLITES
AGAMICALLY
AGAMOGENESES
AGAMOGENESIS
AGAMOGENETIC
AGAMOGONIES
AGAMOSPERMIES
AGAMOSPERMY
AGAPANTHUS
AGAPANTHUSES
AGARICACEOUS
AGATEWARES
AGATHODAIMON
AGATHODAIMONS
AGEDNESSES
AGELESSNESS
AGELESSNESSES
AGENDALESS
AGENTIVITIES
AGENTIVITY
AGFLATIONS
AGGIORNAMENTI
AGGIORNAMENTO
AGGIORNAMENTOS
AGGLOMERATE
AGGLOMERATED
AGGLOMERATES
AGGLOMERATING
AGGLOMERATION
AGGLOMERATIONS
AGGLOMERATIVE
AGGLUTINABILITY
AGGLUTINABLE
AGGLUTINANT
AGGLUTINANTS
AGGLUTINATE
AGGLUTINATED
AGGLUTINATES
AGGLUTINATING
AGGLUTINATION
AGGLUTINATIONS
AGGLUTINATIVE
AGGLUTININ
AGGLUTININS
AGGLUTINOGEN
AGGLUTINOGENIC
AGGLUTINOGENS
AGGRADATION
AGGRADATIONS
AGGRANDISE
AGGRANDISED
AGGRANDISEMENT
AGGRANDISEMENTS
AGGRANDISER
AGGRANDISERS
AGGRANDISES
AGGRANDISING
AGGRANDIZE
AGGRANDIZED
AGGRANDIZEMENT
AGGRANDIZEMENTS
AGGRANDIZER
AGGRANDIZERS
AGGRANDIZES
AGGRANDIZING
AGGRAVATED
AGGRAVATES
AGGRAVATING
AGGRAVATINGLY
AGGRAVATION
AGGRAVATIONS
AGGREGATED
AGGREGATELY
AGGREGATENESS
AGGREGATENESSES
AGGREGATES
AGGREGATING
AGGREGATION
AGGREGATIONAL
AGGREGATIONS
AGGREGATIVE
AGGREGATIVELY
AGGREGATOR
AGGREGATORS
AGGRESSING
AGGRESSION
AGGRESSIONS
AGGRESSIVE
AGGRESSIVELY
AGGRESSIVENESS
AGGRESSIVITIES
AGGRESSIVITY
AGGRESSORS
AGGRIEVEDLY
AGGRIEVEMENT
AGGRIEVEMENTS
AGGRIEVING
AGILENESSES
AGISTMENTS
AGITATEDLY
AGITATIONAL
AGITATIONS
AGNATICALLY
AGNOIOLOGIES
AGNOIOLOGY
AGNOLOTTIS
AGNOSTICISM
AGNOSTICISMS
AGONISEDLY
AGONISINGLY
AGONISTICAL
AGONISTICALLY
AGONISTICS
AGONIZEDLY

AGONIZINGLY
AGONOTHETES
AGORAPHOBE
AGORAPHOBES
AGORAPHOBIA
AGORAPHOBIAS
AGORAPHOBIC
AGORAPHOBICS
AGRAMMATICAL
AGRANULOCYTE
AGRANULOCYTES
AGRANULOCYTOSES
AGRANULOCYTOSIS
AGRANULOSES
AGRANULOSIS
AGRARIANISM
AGRARIANISMS
AGREEABILITIES
AGREEABILITY
AGREEABLENESS
AGREEABLENESSES
AGREEMENTS
AGREGATION
AGREGATIONS
AGRIBUSINESS
AGRIBUSINESSES
AGRIBUSINESSMAN
AGRIBUSINESSMEN
AGRICHEMICAL
AGRICHEMICALS
AGRICULTURAL
AGRICULTURALIST
AGRICULTURALLY
AGRICULTURE
AGRICULTURES
AGRICULTURIST
AGRICULTURISTS
AGRIFOODSTUFFS
AGRIMONIES
AGRIOLOGIES
AGRIPRODUCT
AGRIPRODUCTS
AGRITOURISM
AGRITOURISMS
AGRITOURIST
AGRITOURISTS
AGROBIOLOGICAL
AGROBIOLOGIES
AGROBIOLOGIST
AGROBIOLOGISTS
AGROBIOLOGY
AGROBUSINESS
AGROBUSINESSES
AGROCHEMICAL
AGROCHEMICALS
AGRODOLCES
AGROFORESTER
AGROFORESTERS
AGROFORESTRIES
AGROFORESTRY
AGROINDUSTRIAL
AGROINDUSTRIES
AGROINDUSTRY
AGROLOGICAL
AGROLOGIES
AGROLOGIST
AGROLOGISTS
AGRONOMIAL
AGRONOMICAL
AGRONOMICALLY
AGRONOMICS
AGRONOMIES
AGRONOMIST
AGRONOMISTS
AGROSTEMMA
AGROSTEMMAS
AGROSTEMMATA
AGROSTOLOGIC
AGROSTOLOGICAL
AGROSTOLOGIES
AGROSTOLOGIST
AGROSTOLOGISTS
AGROSTOLOGY
AGROTERRORISM
AGROTERRORISMS
AGROTOURISM
AGROTOURISMS
AGROTOURIST
AGROTOURISTS
AGRYPNOTIC
AGRYPNOTICS
AGTERSKOTS
AGUARDIENTE
AGUARDIENTES
AHISTORICAL
AHORSEBACK
AHURUHURUS
AICHMOPHOBIA
AICHMOPHOBIAS
AIGUILLETTE
AIGUILLETTES
AILANTHUSES
AILOUROPHILE
AILOUROPHILES
AILOUROPHILIA
AILOUROPHILIAS
AILOUROPHILIC
AILOUROPHOBE
AILOUROPHOBES
AILOUROPHOBIA
AILOUROPHOBIAS
AILOUROPHOBIC
AILUROPHILE
AILUROPHILES
AILUROPHILIA
AILUROPHILIAS
AILUROPHILIC
AILUROPHOBE
AILUROPHOBES
AILUROPHOBIA
AILUROPHOBIAS
AILUROPHOBIC
AIMLESSNESS
AIMLESSNESSES
AIRBALLING
AIRBOARDING
AIRBOARDINGS
AIRBRUSHED
AIRBRUSHES
AIRBRUSHING
AIRBURSTED
AIRBURSTING
AIRCOACHES
AIRCRAFTMAN
AIRCRAFTMEN
AIRCRAFTSMAN
AIRCRAFTSMEN
AIRCRAFTSWOMAN
AIRCRAFTSWOMEN
AIRCRAFTWOMAN
AIRCRAFTWOMEN
AIRDROPPED
AIRDROPPING
AIRFREIGHT
AIRFREIGHTED
AIRFREIGHTING
AIRFREIGHTS
AIRINESSES
AIRLESSNESS
AIRLESSNESSES
AIRLIFTING
AIRMAILING
AIRMANSHIP
AIRMANSHIPS
AIRPROOFED
AIRPROOFING
AIRSICKNESS
AIRSICKNESSES
AIRSTREAMS
AIRSTRIKES
AIRTIGHTNESS
AIRTIGHTNESSES
AIRWORTHIER
AIRWORTHIEST
AIRWORTHINESS
AIRWORTHINESSES
AITCHBONES
AKATHISIAS
AKOLOUTHOS
AKOLOUTHOSES
AKOLUTHOSES
ALABAMINES
ALABANDINE
ALABANDINES
ALABANDITE
ALABANDITES
ALABASTERS
ALABASTRINE
ALABLASTER
ALABLASTERS
ALACRITIES
ALACRITOUS
ALARMINGLY
ALBARELLOS
ALBATROSSES
ALBERTITES
ALBESCENCE
ALBESCENCES
ALBESPINES
ALBESPYNES
ALBINESSES
ALBINISTIC
ALBINOISMS
ALBITISING
ALBITIZING
ALBUGINEOUS
ALBUMBLATT
ALBUMBLATTER
ALBUMBLATTS
ALBUMENISE
ALBUMENISED
ALBUMENISES
ALBUMENISING
ALBUMENIZE
ALBUMENIZED
ALBUMENIZES
ALBUMENIZING
ALBUMINATE
ALBUMINATES
ALBUMINISE
ALBUMINISED
ALBUMINISES
ALBUMINISING
ALBUMINIZE
ALBUMINIZED
ALBUMINIZES
ALBUMINIZING
ALBUMINOID
ALBUMINOIDS
ALBUMINOUS
ALBUMINURIA
ALBUMINURIAS
ALBUMINURIC
ALBUTEROLS
ALCAICERIA
ALCAICERIAS
ALCARRAZAS
ALCATRASES
ALCHEMICAL
ALCHEMICALLY
ALCHEMISED
ALCHEMISES
ALCHEMISING
ALCHEMISTIC
ALCHEMISTICAL
ALCHEMISTS
ALCHEMIZED
ALCHEMIZES
ALCHEMIZING
ALCHERINGA

A

ALCHERINGAS
ALCOHOLICALLY
ALCOHOLICITIES
ALCOHOLICITY
ALCOHOLICS
ALCOHOLISATION
ALCOHOLISATIONS
ALCOHOLISE
ALCOHOLISED
ALCOHOLISES
ALCOHOLISING
ALCOHOLISM
ALCOHOLISMS
ALCOHOLIZATION
ALCOHOLIZATIONS
ALCOHOLIZE
ALCOHOLIZED
ALCOHOLIZES
ALCOHOLIZING
ALCOHOLOMETER
ALCOHOLOMETERS
ALCOHOLOMETRIES
ALCOHOLOMETRY
ALCYONARIAN
ALCYONARIANS
ALDERFLIES
ALDERMANIC
ALDERMANITIES
ALDERMANITY
ALDERMANLIER
ALDERMANLIEST
ALDERMANLIKE
ALDERMANLY
ALDERMANRIES
ALDERMANRY
ALDERMANSHIP
ALDERMANSHIPS
ALDERWOMAN
ALDERWOMEN
ALDOHEXOSE
ALDOHEXOSES
ALDOLISATION
ALDOLISATIONS
ALDOLIZATION
ALDOLIZATIONS
ALDOPENTOSE
ALDOPENTOSES
ALDOSTERONE
ALDOSTERONES
ALDOSTERONISM
ALDOSTERONISMS
ALEATORIES
ALEBENCHES
ALECTRYONS
ALEGGEAUNCE
ALEGGEAUNCES
ALEMBICATED
ALEMBICATION
ALEMBICATIONS
ALEMBROTHS
ALERTNESSES
ALEXANDERS
ALEXANDERSES
ALEXANDRINE
ALEXANDRINES
ALEXANDRITE
ALEXANDRITES
ALEXIPHARMAKON
ALEXIPHARMAKONS
ALEXIPHARMIC
ALEXIPHARMICS
ALEXITHYMIA
ALEXITHYMIAS
ALFILARIAS
ALFILERIAS
ALGAECIDES
ALGARROBAS
ALGARROBOS
ALGEBRAICAL
ALGEBRAICALLY
ALGEBRAIST
ALGEBRAISTS
ALGIDITIES
ALGIDNESSES
ALGOLAGNIA
ALGOLAGNIAC
ALGOLAGNIACS
ALGOLAGNIAS
ALGOLAGNIC
ALGOLAGNIST
ALGOLAGNISTS
ALGOLOGICAL
ALGOLOGICALLY
ALGOLOGIES
ALGOLOGIST
ALGOLOGISTS
ALGOMETERS
ALGOMETRIES
ALGOPHOBIA
ALGOPHOBIAS
ALGORISMIC
ALGORITHMIC
ALGORITHMICALLY
ALGORITHMS
ALIENABILITIES
ALIENABILITY
ALIENATING
ALIENATION
ALIENATIONS
ALIENATORS
ALIENNESSES
ALIGHTMENT
ALIGHTMENTS
ALIGNMENTS
ALIKENESSES
ALIMENTARY
ALIMENTATION
ALIMENTATIONS
ALIMENTATIVE
ALIMENTING
ALIMENTIVENESS
ALINEATION
ALINEATIONS
ALINEMENTS
ALISMACEOUS
ALITERACIES
ALITERATES
ALIVENESSES
ALIZARINES
ALKAHESTIC
ALKALESCENCE
ALKALESCENCES
ALKALESCENCIES
ALKALESCENCY
ALKALESCENT
ALKALIFIED
ALKALIFIES
ALKALIFYING
ALKALIMETER
ALKALIMETERS
ALKALIMETRIC
ALKALIMETRIES
ALKALIMETRY
ALKALINISATION
ALKALINISATIONS
ALKALINISE
ALKALINISED
ALKALINISES
ALKALINISING
ALKALINITIES
ALKALINITY
ALKALINIZATION
ALKALINIZATIONS
ALKALINIZE
ALKALINIZED
ALKALINIZES
ALKALINIZING
ALKALISABLE
ALKALISERS
ALKALISING
ALKALIZABLE
ALKALIZERS
ALKALIZING
ALKALOIDAL
ALKYLATING
ALKYLATION
ALKYLATIONS
ALLANTOIDAL
ALLANTOIDES
ALLANTOIDS
ALLANTOINS
ALLANTOISES
ALLARGANDO
ALLAYMENTS
ALLEGATION
ALLEGATIONS
ALLEGEANCE
ALLEGEANCES
ALLEGIANCE
ALLEGIANCES
ALLEGIANTS
ALLEGORICAL
ALLEGORICALLY
ALLEGORICALNESS
ALLEGORIES
ALLEGORISATION
ALLEGORISATIONS
ALLEGORISE
ALLEGORISED
ALLEGORISER
ALLEGORISERS
ALLEGORISES
ALLEGORISING
ALLEGORIST
ALLEGORISTS
ALLEGORIZATION
ALLEGORIZATIONS
ALLEGORIZE
ALLEGORIZED
ALLEGORIZER
ALLEGORIZERS
ALLEGORIZES
ALLEGORIZING
ALLEGRETTO
ALLEGRETTOS
ALLELOMORPH
ALLELOMORPHIC
ALLELOMORPHISM
ALLELOMORPHISMS
ALLELOMORPHS
ALLELOPATHIC
ALLELOPATHIES
ALLELOPATHY
ALLELUIAHS
ALLEMANDES
ALLERGENIC
ALLERGENICITIES
ALLERGENICITY
ALLERGISTS
ALLETHRINS
ALLEVIANTS
ALLEVIATED
ALLEVIATES
ALLEVIATING
ALLEVIATION
ALLEVIATIONS
ALLEVIATIVE
ALLEVIATOR
ALLEVIATORS
ALLEVIATORY
ALLHALLOND
ALLHALLOWEN
ALLHALLOWN
ALLHOLLOWN
ALLIACEOUS
ALLICHOLIES
ALLIGARTAS
ALLIGATING
ALLIGATION
ALLIGATIONS

ALLIGATORS
ALLINEATION
ALLINEATIONS
ALLITERATE
ALLITERATED
ALLITERATES
ALLITERATING
ALLITERATION
ALLITERATIONS
ALLITERATIVE
ALLITERATIVELY
ALLNIGHTER
ALLNIGHTERS
ALLOANTIBODIES
ALLOANTIBODY
ALLOANTIGEN
ALLOANTIGENS
ALLOCARPIES
ALLOCATABLE
ALLOCATING
ALLOCATION
ALLOCATIONS
ALLOCATORS
ALLOCHEIRIA
ALLOCHEIRIAS
ALLOCHIRIA
ALLOCHIRIAS
ALLOCHTHONOUS
ALLOCUTION
ALLOCUTIONS
ALLODYNIAS
ALLOGAMIES
ALLOGAMOUS
ALLOGENEIC
ALLOGRAFTED
ALLOGRAFTING
ALLOGRAFTS
ALLOGRAPHIC
ALLOGRAPHS
ALLOIOSTROPHOS
ALLOMERISM
ALLOMERISMS
ALLOMEROUS
ALLOMETRIC
ALLOMETRIES
ALLOMORPHIC
ALLOMORPHISM
ALLOMORPHISMS
ALLOMORPHS
ALLONYMOUS
ALLOPATHIC
ALLOPATHICALLY
ALLOPATHIES
ALLOPATHIST
ALLOPATHISTS
ALLOPATRIC
ALLOPATRICALLY
ALLOPATRIES
ALLOPHANES
ALLOPHONES
ALLOPHONIC
ALLOPLASMIC
ALLOPLASMS
ALLOPLASTIC
ALLOPOLYPLOID
ALLOPOLYPLOIDS
ALLOPOLYPLOIDY
ALLOPURINOL
ALLOPURINOLS
ALLOSAURUS
ALLOSAURUSES
ALLOSTERIC
ALLOSTERICALLY
ALLOSTERIES
ALLOTETRAPLOID
ALLOTETRAPLOIDS
ALLOTETRAPLOIDY
ALLOTHEISM
ALLOTHEISMS
ALLOTMENTS
ALLOTRIOMORPHIC
ALLOTROPES
ALLOTROPIC
ALLOTROPICALLY
ALLOTROPIES
ALLOTROPISM
ALLOTROPISMS
ALLOTROPOUS
ALLOTTERIES
ALLOTYPICALLY
ALLOTYPIES
ALLOWABILITIES
ALLOWABILITY
ALLOWABLENESS
ALLOWABLENESSES
ALLOWABLES
ALLOWANCED
ALLOWANCES
ALLOWANCING
ALLUREMENT
ALLUREMENTS
ALLURINGLY
ALLUSIVELY
ALLUSIVENESS
ALLUSIVENESSES
ALLWEATHER
ALLWEATHERS
ALLYCHOLLIES
ALLYCHOLLY
ALMACANTAR
ALMACANTARS
ALMANDINES
ALMANDITES
ALMIGHTIER
ALMIGHTIEST
ALMIGHTILY
ALMIGHTINESS
ALMIGHTINESSES
ALMONDIEST
ALMONDITES
ALMSGIVERS
ALMSGIVING
ALMSGIVINGS
ALMSHOUSES
ALMUCANTAR
ALMUCANTARS
ALOESWOODS
ALOGICALLY
ALONENESSES
ALONGSHORE
ALONGSHOREMAN
ALONGSHOREMEN
ALOOFNESSES
ALOPECOIDS
ALPARGATAS
ALPENGLOWS
ALPENHORNS
ALPENSTOCK
ALPENSTOCKS
ALPESTRINE
ALPHABETARIAN
ALPHABETARIANS
ALPHABETED
ALPHABETIC
ALPHABETICAL
ALPHABETICALLY
ALPHABETIFORM
ALPHABETING
ALPHABETISATION
ALPHABETISE
ALPHABETISED
ALPHABETISER
ALPHABETISERS
ALPHABETISES
ALPHABETISING
ALPHABETIZATION
ALPHABETIZE
ALPHABETIZED
ALPHABETIZER
ALPHABETIZERS
ALPHABETIZES
ALPHABETIZING
ALPHAMERIC
ALPHAMERICAL
ALPHAMERICALLY
ALPHAMETIC
ALPHAMETICS
ALPHANUMERIC
ALPHANUMERICAL
ALPHANUMERICS
ALPHASORTED
ALPHASORTING
ALPHASORTS
ALPHATESTED
ALPHATESTING
ALPHATESTS
ALPHOSISES
ALSTROEMERIA
ALSTROEMERIAS
ALTALTISSIMO
ALTALTISSIMOS
ALTARPIECE
ALTARPIECES
ALTAZIMUTH
ALTAZIMUTHS
ALTERABILITIES
ALTERABILITY
ALTERATION
ALTERATIONS
ALTERATIVE
ALTERATIVES
ALTERCATED
ALTERCATES
ALTERCATING
ALTERCATION
ALTERCATIONS
ALTERCATIVE
ALTERITIES
ALTERNANCE
ALTERNANCES
ALTERNANTS
ALTERNATED
ALTERNATELY
ALTERNATES
ALTERNATIM
ALTERNATING
ALTERNATION
ALTERNATIONS
ALTERNATIVE
ALTERNATIVELY
ALTERNATIVENESS
ALTERNATIVES
ALTERNATOR
ALTERNATORS
ALTIGRAPHS
ALTIMETERS
ALTIMETRICAL
ALTIMETRICALLY
ALTIMETRIES
ALTIPLANOS
ALTISONANT
ALTISSIMOS
ALTITONANT
ALTITUDINAL
ALTITUDINARIAN
ALTITUDINARIANS
ALTITUDINOUS
ALTOCUMULI
ALTOCUMULUS
ALTOGETHER
ALTOGETHERS
ALTORUFFLED
ALTOSTRATI
ALTOSTRATUS
ALTRICIALS
ALTRUISTIC
ALTRUISTICALLY
ALUMINATES
ALUMINIDES
ALUMINIFEROUS

A

ALUMINISED
ALUMINISES
ALUMINISING
ALUMINIUMS
ALUMINIZED
ALUMINIZES
ALUMINIZING
ALUMINOSILICATE
ALUMINOSITIES
ALUMINOSITY
ALUMINOTHERMIES
ALUMINOTHERMY
ALUMSTONES
ALVEOLARLY
ALVEOLATION
ALVEOLATIONS
ALVEOLITIS
ALVEOLITISES
ALYCOMPAINE
ALYCOMPAINES
AMALGAMATE
AMALGAMATED
AMALGAMATES
AMALGAMATING
AMALGAMATION
AMALGAMATIONS
AMALGAMATIVE
AMALGAMATOR
AMALGAMATORS
AMANTADINE
AMANTADINES
AMANUENSES
AMANUENSIS
AMARACUSES
AMARANTACEOUS
AMARANTHACEOUS
AMARANTHINE
AMARANTINE
AMARANTINS
AMARYLLIDACEOUS
AMARYLLIDS
AMARYLLISES
AMASSMENTS
AMATEURISH
AMATEURISHLY
AMATEURISHNESS
AMATEURISM
AMATEURISMS
AMATEURSHIP
AMATEURSHIPS
AMATIVENESS
AMATIVENESSES
AMATORIALLY
AMATORIOUS
AMAZEBALLS
AMAZEDNESS
AMAZEDNESSES
AMAZEMENTS
AMAZONIANS
AMAZONITES
AMAZONSTONE
AMAZONSTONES
AMBAGITORY
AMBASSADOR
AMBASSADORIAL
AMBASSADORS
AMBASSADORSHIP
AMBASSADORSHIPS
AMBASSADRESS
AMBASSADRESSES
AMBASSAGES
AMBERGRISES
AMBERJACKS
AMBIDENTATE
AMBIDEXTER
AMBIDEXTERITIES
AMBIDEXTERITY
AMBIDEXTEROUS
AMBIDEXTERS
AMBIDEXTROUS
AMBIDEXTROUSLY
AMBIGUITIES
AMBIGUOUSLY
AMBIGUOUSNESS
AMBIGUOUSNESSES
AMBILATERAL
AMBIOPHONIES
AMBIOPHONY
AMBISEXUAL
AMBISEXUALITIES
AMBISEXUALITY
AMBISEXUALS
AMBISONICS
AMBITIONED
AMBITIONING
AMBITIONLESS
AMBITIOUSLY
AMBITIOUSNESS
AMBITIOUSNESSES
AMBIVALENCE
AMBIVALENCES
AMBIVALENCIES
AMBIVALENCY
AMBIVALENT
AMBIVALENTLY
AMBIVERSION
AMBIVERSIONS
AMBLYGONITE
AMBLYGONITES
AMBLYOPIAS
AMBOCEPTOR
AMBOCEPTORS
AMBOSEXUAL
AMBROSIALLY
AMBROTYPES
AMBULACRAL
AMBULACRUM
AMBULANCEMAN
AMBULANCEMEN
AMBULANCES
AMBULANCEWOMAN
AMBULANCEWOMEN
AMBULATING
AMBULATION
AMBULATIONS
AMBULATORIES
AMBULATORILY
AMBULATORS
AMBULATORY
AMBULETTES
AMBUSCADED
AMBUSCADER
AMBUSCADERS
AMBUSCADES
AMBUSCADING
AMBUSCADOES
AMBUSCADOS
AMBUSHMENT
AMBUSHMENTS
AMEBOCYTES
AMELIORABLE
AMELIORANT
AMELIORANTS
AMELIORATE
AMELIORATED
AMELIORATES
AMELIORATING
AMELIORATION
AMELIORATIONS
AMELIORATIVE
AMELIORATOR
AMELIORATORS
AMELIORATORY
AMELOBLAST
AMELOBLASTS
AMELOGENESES
AMELOGENESIS
AMENABILITIES
AMENABILITY
AMENABLENESS
AMENABLENESSES
AMENAUNCES
AMENDATORY
AMENDMENTS
AMENORRHEA
AMENORRHEAS
AMENORRHEIC
AMENORRHOEA
AMENORRHOEAS
AMENTACEOUS
AMENTIFEROUS
AMERCEABLE
AMERCEMENT
AMERCEMENTS
AMERCIABLE
AMERCIAMENT
AMERCIAMENTS
AMERICIUMS
AMETABOLIC
AMETABOLISM
AMETABOLISMS
AMETABOLOUS
AMETHYSTINE
AMETROPIAS
AMIABILITIES
AMIABILITY
AMIABLENESS
AMIABLENESSES
AMIANTHINE
AMIANTHOID
AMIANTHOIDAL
AMIANTHUSES
AMIANTUSES
AMICABILITIES
AMICABILITY
AMICABLENESS
AMICABLENESSES
AMINOACETIC
AMINOACIDURIA
AMINOACIDURIAS
AMINOBENZOIC
AMINOBUTENE
AMINOBUTENES
AMINOPEPTIDASE
AMINOPEPTIDASES
AMINOPHENAZONE
AMINOPHENAZONES
AMINOPHENOL
AMINOPHENOLS
AMINOPHYLLINE
AMINOPHYLLINES
AMINOPTERIN
AMINOPTERINS
AMINOPYRINE
AMINOPYRINES
AMINOTOLUENE
AMINOTOLUENES
AMISSIBILITIES
AMISSIBILITY
AMITOTICALLY
AMITRIPTYLINE
AMITRIPTYLINES
AMITRYPTYLINE
AMITRYPTYLINES
AMMOCOETES
AMMONIACAL
AMMONIACUM
AMMONIACUMS
AMMONIATED
AMMONIATES
AMMONIATING
AMMONIATION
AMMONIATIONS
AMMONIFICATION
AMMONIFICATIONS
AMMONIFIED
AMMONIFIES
AMMONIFYING
AMMONOLYSES
AMMONOLYSIS

AMMOPHILOUS
AMMUNITION
AMMUNITIONED
AMMUNITIONING
AMMUNITIONS
AMNESTYING
AMNIOCENTESES
AMNIOCENTESIS
AMNIOTOMIES
AMOBARBITAL
AMOBARBITALS
AMOEBIASES
AMOEBIASIS
AMOEBIFORM
AMOEBOCYTE
AMOEBOCYTES
AMONTILLADO
AMONTILLADOS
AMORALISMS
AMORALISTS
AMORALITIES
AMOROSITIES
AMOROUSNESS
AMOROUSNESSES
AMORPHISMS
AMORPHOUSLY
AMORPHOUSNESS
AMORPHOUSNESSES
AMORTISABLE
AMORTISATION
AMORTISATIONS
AMORTISEMENT
AMORTISEMENTS
AMORTISING
AMORTIZABLE
AMORTIZATION
AMORTIZATIONS
AMORTIZEMENT
AMORTIZEMENTS
AMORTIZING
AMOURETTES
AMOXICILLIN
AMOXICILLINS
AMOXYCILLIN
AMOXYCILLINS
AMPACITIES
AMPELOGRAPHIES
AMPELOGRAPHY
AMPELOPSES
AMPELOPSIS
AMPELOPSISES
AMPEROMETRIC
AMPERSANDS
AMPERZANDS
AMPHETAMINE
AMPHETAMINES
AMPHIARTHROSES
AMPHIARTHROSIS
AMPHIASTER
AMPHIASTERS
AMPHIBIANS
AMPHIBIOTIC
AMPHIBIOUS
AMPHIBIOUSLY
AMPHIBIOUSNESS
AMPHIBLASTIC
AMPHIBLASTULA
AMPHIBLASTULAE
AMPHIBOLES
AMPHIBOLIC
AMPHIBOLIES
AMPHIBOLITE
AMPHIBOLITES
AMPHIBOLOGICAL
AMPHIBOLOGIES
AMPHIBOLOGY
AMPHIBOLOUS
AMPHIBRACH
AMPHIBRACHIC
AMPHIBRACHS
AMPHICHROIC
AMPHICHROMATIC
AMPHICOELOUS
AMPHICTYON
AMPHICTYONIC
AMPHICTYONIES
AMPHICTYONS
AMPHICTYONY
AMPHIDENTATE
AMPHIDIPLOID
AMPHIDIPLOIDIES
AMPHIDIPLOIDS
AMPHIDIPLOIDY
AMPHIGASTRIA
AMPHIGASTRIUM
AMPHIGORIC
AMPHIGORIES
AMPHIGOURI
AMPHIGOURIS
AMPHIMACER
AMPHIMACERS
AMPHIMICTIC
AMPHIMIXES
AMPHIMIXIS
AMPHIOXUSES
AMPHIPATHIC
AMPHIPHILE
AMPHIPHILES
AMPHIPHILIC
AMPHIPLOID
AMPHIPLOIDIES
AMPHIPLOIDS
AMPHIPLOIDY
AMPHIPODOUS
AMPHIPROSTYLAR
AMPHIPROSTYLE
AMPHIPROSTYLES
AMPHIPROTIC
AMPHISBAENA
AMPHISBAENAE
AMPHISBAENAS
AMPHISBAENIC
AMPHISCIAN
AMPHISCIANS
AMPHISTOMATAL
AMPHISTOMATIC
AMPHISTOMOUS
AMPHISTYLAR
AMPHISTYLARS
AMPHITHEATER
AMPHITHEATERS
AMPHITHEATRAL
AMPHITHEATRE
AMPHITHEATRES
AMPHITHEATRIC
AMPHITHEATRICAL
AMPHITHECIA
AMPHITHECIUM
AMPHITRICHA
AMPHITRICHOUS
AMPHITROPOUS
AMPHOLYTES
AMPHOTERIC
AMPICILLIN
AMPICILLINS
AMPLENESSES
AMPLEXICAUL
AMPLEXUSES
AMPLIATION
AMPLIATIONS
AMPLIATIVE
AMPLIDYNES
AMPLIFIABLE
AMPLIFICATION
AMPLIFICATIONS
AMPLIFIERS
AMPLIFYING
AMPLITUDES
AMPLOSOMES
AMPULLACEAL
AMPULLACEOUS
AMPULLOSITIES
AMPULLOSITY
AMPUTATING
AMPUTATION
AMPUTATIONS
AMPUTATORS
AMRITATTVA
AMRITATTVAS
AMSINCKIAS
AMUSEMENTS
AMUSINGNESS
AMUSINGNESSES
AMUSIVENESS
AMUSIVENESSES
AMYGDALACEOUS
AMYGDALATE
AMYGDALINE
AMYGDALINS
AMYGDALOID
AMYGDALOIDAL
AMYGDALOIDS
AMYLACEOUS
AMYLOBARBITONE
AMYLOBARBITONES
AMYLOIDOSES
AMYLOIDOSIS
AMYLOLYSES
AMYLOLYSIS
AMYLOLYTIC
AMYLOPECTIN
AMYLOPECTINS
AMYLOPLAST
AMYLOPLASTS
AMYLOPSINS
AMYOTONIAS
AMYOTROPHIC
AMYOTROPHIES
AMYOTROPHY
ANABANTIDS
ANABAPTISE
ANABAPTISED
ANABAPTISES
ANABAPTISING
ANABAPTISM
ANABAPTISMS
ANABAPTIST
ANABAPTISTIC
ANABAPTISTS
ANABAPTIZE
ANABAPTIZED
ANABAPTIZES
ANABAPTIZING
ANABLEPSES
ANABOLISMS
ANABOLITES
ANABOLITIC
ANABRANCHES
ANACARDIACEOUS
ANACARDIUM
ANACARDIUMS
ANACATHARSES
ANACATHARSIS
ANACATHARTIC
ANACATHARTICS
ANACHARISES
ANACHORISM
ANACHORISMS
ANACHRONIC
ANACHRONICAL
ANACHRONICALLY
ANACHRONISM
ANACHRONISMS
ANACHRONISTIC
ANACHRONOUS
ANACHRONOUSLY
ANACLASTIC
ANACOLUTHA
ANACOLUTHIA
ANACOLUTHIAS

A

ANACOLUTHIC
ANACOLUTHICALLY
ANACOLUTHON
ANACOLUTHONS
ANACOUSTIC
ANACREONTIC
ANACREONTICALLY
ANACREONTICS
ANACRUSTIC
ANADIPLOSES
ANADIPLOSIS
ANADROMOUS
ANADYOMENE
ANAEMICALLY
ANAEROBICALLY
ANAEROBIONT
ANAEROBIONTS
ANAEROBIOSES
ANAEROBIOSIS
ANAEROBIOTIC
ANAEROBIUM
ANAESTHESES
ANAESTHESIA
ANAESTHESIAS
ANAESTHESIOLOGY
ANAESTHESIS
ANAESTHETIC
ANAESTHETICALLY
ANAESTHETICS
ANAESTHETISE
ANAESTHETISED
ANAESTHETISES
ANAESTHETISING
ANAESTHETIST
ANAESTHETISTS
ANAESTHETIZE
ANAESTHETIZED
ANAESTHETIZES
ANAESTHETIZING
ANAGENESES
ANAGENESIS
ANAGLYPHIC
ANAGLYPHICAL
ANAGLYPHIES
ANAGLYPTIC
ANAGLYPTICAL
ANAGNORISES
ANAGNORISIS
ANAGOGICAL
ANAGOGICALLY
ANAGRAMMATIC
ANAGRAMMATICAL
ANAGRAMMATISE
ANAGRAMMATISED
ANAGRAMMATISES
ANAGRAMMATISING
ANAGRAMMATISM
ANAGRAMMATISMS
ANAGRAMMATIST
ANAGRAMMATISTS
ANAGRAMMATIZE
ANAGRAMMATIZED
ANAGRAMMATIZES
ANAGRAMMATIZING
ANAGRAMMED
ANAGRAMMER
ANAGRAMMERS
ANAGRAMMING
ANALEMMATA
ANALEMMATIC
ANALEPTICS
ANALGESIAS
ANALGESICS
ANALGETICS
ANALOGICAL
ANALOGICALLY
ANALOGISED
ANALOGISES
ANALOGISING
ANALOGISMS
ANALOGISTS
ANALOGIZED
ANALOGIZES
ANALOGIZING
ANALOGOUSLY
ANALOGOUSNESS
ANALOGOUSNESSES
ANALPHABET
ANALPHABETE
ANALPHABETES
ANALPHABETIC
ANALPHABETICS
ANALPHABETISM
ANALPHABETISMS
ANALPHABETS
ANALYSABILITIES
ANALYSABILITY
ANALYSABLE
ANALYSANDS
ANALYSATION
ANALYSATIONS
ANALYTICAL
ANALYTICALLY
ANALYTICITIES
ANALYTICITY
ANALYZABILITIES
ANALYZABILITY
ANALYZABLE
ANALYZATION
ANALYZATIONS
ANAMNESTIC
ANAMNESTICALLY
ANAMNIOTES
ANAMNIOTIC
ANAMORPHIC
ANAMORPHISM
ANAMORPHISMS
ANAMORPHOSCOPE
ANAMORPHOSCOPES
ANAMORPHOSES
ANAMORPHOSIS
ANAMORPHOUS
ANANDAMIDE
ANANDAMIDES
ANAPAESTIC
ANAPAESTICAL
ANAPESTICS
ANAPHORESES
ANAPHORESIS
ANAPHORICAL
ANAPHORICALLY
ANAPHRODISIA
ANAPHRODISIAC
ANAPHRODISIACS
ANAPHRODISIAS
ANAPHYLACTIC
ANAPHYLACTOID
ANAPHYLAXES
ANAPHYLAXIES
ANAPHYLAXIS
ANAPHYLAXY
ANAPLASIAS
ANAPLASMOSES
ANAPLASMOSIS
ANAPLASTIC
ANAPLASTIES
ANAPLEROSES
ANAPLEROSIS
ANAPLEROTIC
ANAPTYCTIC
ANAPTYCTICAL
ANARCHICAL
ANARCHICALLY
ANARCHISED
ANARCHISES
ANARCHISING
ANARCHISMS
ANARCHISTIC
ANARCHISTICALLY
ANARCHISTS
ANARCHIZED
ANARCHIZES
ANARCHIZING
ANARTHRIAS
ANARTHROUS
ANARTHROUSLY
ANARTHROUSNESS
ANASARCOUS
ANASTIGMAT
ANASTIGMATIC
ANASTIGMATISM
ANASTIGMATISMS
ANASTIGMATS
ANASTOMOSE
ANASTOMOSED
ANASTOMOSES
ANASTOMOSING
ANASTOMOSIS
ANASTOMOTIC
ANASTROPHE
ANASTROPHES
ANASTROZOLE
ANASTROZOLES
ANATHEMATA
ANATHEMATICAL
ANATHEMATICALS
ANATHEMATISE
ANATHEMATISED
ANATHEMATISES
ANATHEMATISING
ANATHEMATIZE
ANATHEMATIZED
ANATHEMATIZES
ANATHEMATIZING
ANATOMICAL
ANATOMICALLY
ANATOMISATION
ANATOMISATIONS
ANATOMISED
ANATOMISER
ANATOMISERS
ANATOMISES
ANATOMISING
ANATOMISTS
ANATOMIZATION
ANATOMIZATIONS
ANATOMIZED
ANATOMIZER
ANATOMIZERS
ANATOMIZES
ANATOMIZING
ANATROPIES
ANATROPOUS
ANCESTORED
ANCESTORIAL
ANCESTORING
ANCESTRALLY
ANCESTRALS
ANCESTRESS
ANCESTRESSES
ANCESTRIES
ANCHORAGES
ANCHORESSES
ANCHORETIC
ANCHORETICAL
ANCHORETTE
ANCHORETTES
ANCHORITES
ANCHORITIC
ANCHORITICAL
ANCHORITICALLY
ANCHORLESS
ANCHORPEOPLE
ANCHORPERSON
ANCHORPERSONS
ANCHORWOMAN
ANCHORWOMEN
ANCHOVETAS
ANCHOVETTA
ANCHOVETTAS

ANCHYLOSED
ANCHYLOSES
ANCHYLOSING
ANCHYLOSIS
ANCHYLOTIC
ANCIENTEST
ANCIENTNESS
ANCIENTNESSES
ANCIENTRIES
ANCILLARIES
ANCIPITOUS
ANCYLOSTOMIASES
ANCYLOSTOMIASIS
ANDALUSITE
ANDALUSITES
ANDANTINOS
ANDOUILLES
ANDOUILLETTE
ANDOUILLETTES
ANDRADITES
ANDROCENTRIC
ANDROCENTRISM
ANDROCENTRISMS
ANDROCEPHALOUS
ANDROCLINIA
ANDROCLINIUM
ANDRODIOECIOUS
ANDRODIOECISM
ANDRODIOECISMS
ANDROECIAL
ANDROECIUM
ANDROGENESES
ANDROGENESIS
ANDROGENETIC
ANDROGENIC
ANDROGENOUS
ANDROGYNES
ANDROGYNIES
ANDROGYNOPHORE
ANDROGYNOPHORES
ANDROGYNOUS
ANDROLOGIES
ANDROLOGIST
ANDROLOGISTS
ANDROMEDAS
ANDROMEDOTOXIN
ANDROMEDOTOXINS
ANDROMONOECIOUS
ANDROMONOECISM
ANDROMONOECISMS
ANDROPAUSE
ANDROPAUSES
ANDROPHORE
ANDROPHORES
ANDROSPHINGES
ANDROSPHINX
ANDROSPHINXES
ANDROSTERONE
ANDROSTERONES
ANECDOTAGE
ANECDOTAGES
ANECDOTALISM
ANECDOTALISMS
ANECDOTALIST
ANECDOTALISTS
ANECDOTALLY
ANECDOTICAL
ANECDOTICALLY
ANECDOTIST
ANECDOTISTS
ANELASTICITIES
ANELASTICITY
ANEMICALLY
ANEMOCHORE
ANEMOCHORES
ANEMOCHOROUS
ANEMOGRAMS
ANEMOGRAPH
ANEMOGRAPHIC
ANEMOGRAPHIES
ANEMOGRAPHS
ANEMOGRAPHY
ANEMOLOGIES
ANEMOMETER
ANEMOMETERS
ANEMOMETRIC
ANEMOMETRICAL
ANEMOMETRIES
ANEMOMETRY
ANEMOPHILIES
ANEMOPHILOUS
ANEMOPHILY
ANEMOPHOBIA
ANEMOPHOBIAS
ANEMOSCOPE
ANEMOSCOPES
ANENCEPHALIA
ANENCEPHALIAS
ANENCEPHALIC
ANENCEPHALIES
ANENCEPHALY
ANESTHESIA
ANESTHESIAS
ANESTHESIOLOGY
ANESTHETIC
ANESTHETICALLY
ANESTHETICS
ANESTHETISATION
ANESTHETISE
ANESTHETISED
ANESTHETISES
ANESTHETISING
ANESTHETIST
ANESTHETISTS
ANESTHETIZATION
ANESTHETIZE
ANESTHETIZED
ANESTHETIZES
ANESTHETIZING
ANEUPLOIDIES
ANEUPLOIDS
ANEUPLOIDY
ANEURISMAL
ANEURISMALLY
ANEURISMATIC
ANEURYSMAL
ANEURYSMALLY
ANEURYSMATIC
ANFRACTUOSITIES
ANFRACTUOSITY
ANFRACTUOUS
ANGASHORES
ANGELFISHES
ANGELHOODS
ANGELICALLY
ANGELOLATRIES
ANGELOLATRY
ANGELOLOGIES
ANGELOLOGIST
ANGELOLOGISTS
ANGELOLOGY
ANGELOPHANIES
ANGELOPHANY
ANGIOCARPOUS
ANGIOGENESES
ANGIOGENESIS
ANGIOGENIC
ANGIOGRAMS
ANGIOGRAPHIC
ANGIOGRAPHIES
ANGIOGRAPHY
ANGIOLOGIES
ANGIOMATOUS
ANGIOPLASTIES
ANGIOPLASTY
ANGIOSARCOMA
ANGIOSARCOMAS
ANGIOSARCOMATA
ANGIOSPERM
ANGIOSPERMAL
ANGIOSPERMOUS
ANGIOSPERMS
ANGIOSTOMATOUS
ANGIOSTOMOUS
ANGIOTENSIN
ANGIOTENSINS
ANGISHORES
ANGLEBERRIES
ANGLEBERRY
ANGLEDOZER
ANGLEDOZERS
ANGLERFISH
ANGLERFISHES
ANGLESITES
ANGLETWITCH
ANGLETWITCHES
ANGLEWORMS
ANGLICISATION
ANGLICISATIONS
ANGLICISED
ANGLICISES
ANGLICISING
ANGLICISMS
ANGLICISTS
ANGLICIZATION
ANGLICIZATIONS
ANGLICIZED
ANGLICIZES
ANGLICIZING
ANGLIFYING
ANGLISTICS
ANGLOMANIA
ANGLOMANIAC
ANGLOMANIACS
ANGLOMANIAS
ANGLOPHILE
ANGLOPHILES
ANGLOPHILIA
ANGLOPHILIAS
ANGLOPHILIC
ANGLOPHILS
ANGLOPHOBE
ANGLOPHOBES
ANGLOPHOBIA
ANGLOPHOBIAC
ANGLOPHOBIACS
ANGLOPHOBIAS
ANGLOPHOBIC
ANGLOPHONE
ANGLOPHONES
ANGLOPHONIC
ANGOPHORAS
ANGOSTURAS
ANGRINESSES
ANGUIFAUNA
ANGUIFAUNAE
ANGUIFAUNAS
ANGUILLIFORM
ANGUIPEDES
ANGUISHING
ANGULARITIES
ANGULARITY
ANGULARNESS
ANGULARNESSES
ANGULATING
ANGULATION
ANGULATIONS
ANGUSTIFOLIATE
ANGUSTIROSTRATE
ANGWANTIBO
ANGWANTIBOS
ANHARMONIC
ANHEDONIAS
ANHELATION
ANHELATIONS
ANHIDROSES
ANHIDROSIS
ANHIDROTIC
ANHIDROTICS
ANHUNGERED

ANHYDRASES
ANHYDRIDES
ANHYDRITES
ANICONISMS
ANICONISTS
ANILINCTUS
ANILINCTUSES
ANILINGUSES
ANIMADVERSION
ANIMADVERSIONS
ANIMADVERT
ANIMADVERTED
ANIMADVERTER
ANIMADVERTERS
ANIMADVERTING
ANIMADVERTS
ANIMALCULA
ANIMALCULAR
ANIMALCULE
ANIMALCULES
ANIMALCULISM
ANIMALCULISMS
ANIMALCULIST
ANIMALCULISTS
ANIMALCULUM
ANIMALIERS
ANIMALISATION
ANIMALISATIONS
ANIMALISED
ANIMALISES
ANIMALISING
ANIMALISMS
ANIMALISTIC
ANIMALISTS
ANIMALITIES
ANIMALIZATION
ANIMALIZATIONS
ANIMALIZED
ANIMALIZES
ANIMALIZING
ANIMALLIKE
ANIMATEDLY
ANIMATENESS
ANIMATENESSES
ANIMATEURS
ANIMATINGLY
ANIMATIONS
ANIMATISMS
ANIMATISTS
ANIMATRONIC
ANIMATRONICALLY
ANIMATRONICS
ANIMOSITIES
ANISEIKONIA
ANISEIKONIAS
ANISEIKONIC
ANISOCERCAL
ANISODACTYL
ANISODACTYLOUS
ANISODACTYLS
ANISOGAMIES
ANISOGAMOUS
ANISOMERIC
ANISOMEROUS
ANISOMETRIC
ANISOMETROPIA
ANISOMETROPIAS
ANISOMETROPIC
ANISOMORPHIC
ANISOPHYLLIES
ANISOPHYLLOUS
ANISOPHYLLY
ANISOTROPIC
ANISOTROPICALLY
ANISOTROPIES
ANISOTROPISM
ANISOTROPISMS
ANISOTROPY
ANKLEBONES
ANKYLOSAUR
ANKYLOSAURS
ANKYLOSAURUS
ANKYLOSAURUSES
ANKYLOSING
ANKYLOSTOMIASES
ANKYLOSTOMIASIS
ANNABERGITE
ANNABERGITES
ANNALISING
ANNALISTIC
ANNALIZING
ANNEALINGS
ANNELIDANS
ANNEXATION
ANNEXATIONAL
ANNEXATIONISM
ANNEXATIONISMS
ANNEXATIONIST
ANNEXATIONISTS
ANNEXATIONS
ANNEXMENTS
ANNIHILABLE
ANNIHILATE
ANNIHILATED
ANNIHILATES
ANNIHILATING
ANNIHILATION
ANNIHILATIONISM
ANNIHILATIONS
ANNIHILATIVE
ANNIHILATOR
ANNIHILATORS
ANNIHILATORY
ANNIVERSARIES
ANNIVERSARY
ANNOTATABLE
ANNOTATING
ANNOTATION
ANNOTATIONS
ANNOTATIVE
ANNOTATORS
ANNOUNCEMENT
ANNOUNCEMENTS
ANNOUNCERS
ANNOUNCING
ANNOYANCES
ANNOYINGLY
ANNUALISED
ANNUALISES
ANNUALISING
ANNUALIZED
ANNUALIZES
ANNUALIZING
ANNUITANTS
ANNUITISED
ANNUITISES
ANNUITISING
ANNUITIZED
ANNUITIZES
ANNUITIZING
ANNULARITIES
ANNULARITY
ANNULATION
ANNULATIONS
ANNULLABLE
ANNULMENTS
ANNUNCIATE
ANNUNCIATED
ANNUNCIATES
ANNUNCIATING
ANNUNCIATION
ANNUNCIATIONS
ANNUNCIATIVE
ANNUNCIATOR
ANNUNCIATORS
ANNUNCIATORY
ANNUNTIATE
ANNUNTIATED
ANNUNTIATES
ANNUNTIATING
ANODICALLY
ANODISATION
ANODISATIONS
ANODIZATION
ANODIZATIONS
ANODONTIAS
ANOESTROUS
ANOINTINGS
ANOINTMENT
ANOINTMENTS
ANOMALISTIC
ANOMALISTICAL
ANOMALISTICALLY
ANOMALOUSLY
ANOMALOUSNESS
ANOMALOUSNESSES
ANONACEOUS
ANONYMISED
ANONYMISES
ANONYMISING
ANONYMITIES
ANONYMIZED
ANONYMIZES
ANONYMIZING
ANONYMOUSLY
ANONYMOUSNESS
ANONYMOUSNESSES
ANOPHELINE
ANOPHELINES
ANORECTICS
ANOREXIGENIC
ANORTHITES
ANORTHITIC
ANORTHOSITE
ANORTHOSITES
ANORTHOSITIC
ANOTHERGUESS
ANOVULANTS
ANOVULATION
ANOVULATIONS
ANOVULATORY
ANOXAEMIAS
ANSAPHONES
ANSWERABILITIES
ANSWERABILITY
ANSWERABLE
ANSWERABLENESS
ANSWERABLY
ANSWERLESS
ANSWERPHONE
ANSWERPHONES
ANTAGONISABLE
ANTAGONISATION
ANTAGONISATIONS
ANTAGONISE
ANTAGONISED
ANTAGONISES
ANTAGONISING
ANTAGONISM
ANTAGONISMS
ANTAGONIST
ANTAGONISTIC
ANTAGONISTS
ANTAGONIZABLE
ANTAGONIZATION
ANTAGONIZATIONS
ANTAGONIZE
ANTAGONIZED
ANTAGONIZES
ANTAGONIZING
ANTALKALIES
ANTALKALINE
ANTALKALINES
ANTALKALIS
ANTAPHRODISIAC
ANTAPHRODISIACS
ANTARTHRITIC
ANTARTHRITICS
ANTASTHMATIC
ANTASTHMATICS

ANTEBELLUM
ANTECEDENCE
ANTECEDENCES
ANTECEDENT
ANTECEDENTLY
ANTECEDENTS
ANTECEDING
ANTECESSOR
ANTECESSORS
ANTECHAMBER
ANTECHAMBERS
ANTECHAPEL
ANTECHAPELS
ANTECHOIRS
ANTEDATING
ANTEDATINGS
ANTEDILUVIAL
ANTEDILUVIALLY
ANTEDILUVIAN
ANTEDILUVIANS
ANTEMERIDIAN
ANTEMORTEM
ANTEMUNDANE
ANTENATALLY
ANTENATALS
ANTENNIFEROUS
ANTENNIFORM
ANTENNULAR
ANTENNULES
ANTENUPTIAL
ANTENUPTIALS
ANTEORBITAL
ANTEPENDIA
ANTEPENDIUM
ANTEPENDIUMS
ANTEPENULT
ANTEPENULTIMA
ANTEPENULTIMAS
ANTEPENULTIMATE
ANTEPENULTS
ANTEPOSITION
ANTEPOSITIONS
ANTEPRANDIAL
ANTERIORITIES
ANTERIORITY
ANTERIORLY
ANTEROGRADE
ANTEVERSION
ANTEVERSIONS
ANTEVERTED
ANTEVERTING
ANTHELICES
ANTHELIONS
ANTHELIXES
ANTHELMINTHIC
ANTHELMINTHICS
ANTHELMINTIC
ANTHELMINTICS
ANTHEMISES
ANTHEMWISE
ANTHERIDIA
ANTHERIDIAL
ANTHERIDIUM
ANTHEROZOID
ANTHEROZOIDS
ANTHEROZOOID
ANTHEROZOOIDS
ANTHERSMUT
ANTHERSMUTS
ANTHOCARPOUS
ANTHOCARPS
ANTHOCHLORE
ANTHOCHLORES
ANTHOCYANIN
ANTHOCYANINS
ANTHOCYANS
ANTHOLOGICAL
ANTHOLOGIES
ANTHOLOGISE
ANTHOLOGISED
ANTHOLOGISER
ANTHOLOGISERS
ANTHOLOGISES
ANTHOLOGISING
ANTHOLOGIST
ANTHOLOGISTS
ANTHOLOGIZE
ANTHOLOGIZED
ANTHOLOGIZER
ANTHOLOGIZERS
ANTHOLOGIZES
ANTHOLOGIZING
ANTHOMANIA
ANTHOMANIAC
ANTHOMANIACS
ANTHOMANIAS
ANTHOPHILOUS
ANTHOPHORE
ANTHOPHORES
ANTHOPHYLLITE
ANTHOPHYLLITES
ANTHOTAXIES
ANTHOXANTHIN
ANTHOXANTHINS
ANTHOZOANS
ANTHRACENE
ANTHRACENES
ANTHRACITE
ANTHRACITES
ANTHRACITIC
ANTHRACNOSE
ANTHRACNOSES
ANTHRACOID
ANTHRACOSES
ANTHRACOSIS
ANTHRACYCLINE
ANTHRACYCLINES
ANTHRANILATE
ANTHRANILATES
ANTHRANILIC
ANTHRAQUINONE
ANTHRAQUINONES
ANTHROPICAL
ANTHROPOBIOLOGY
ANTHROPOCENTRIC
ANTHROPOGENESES
ANTHROPOGENESIS
ANTHROPOGENETIC
ANTHROPOGENIC
ANTHROPOGENIES
ANTHROPOGENY
ANTHROPOGONIES
ANTHROPOGONY
ANTHROPOGRAPHY
ANTHROPOID
ANTHROPOIDAL
ANTHROPOIDS
ANTHROPOLATRIES
ANTHROPOLATRY
ANTHROPOLOGICAL
ANTHROPOLOGIES
ANTHROPOLOGIST
ANTHROPOLOGISTS
ANTHROPOLOGY
ANTHROPOMETRIC
ANTHROPOMETRIES
ANTHROPOMETRIST
ANTHROPOMETRY
ANTHROPOMORPH
ANTHROPOMORPHIC
ANTHROPOMORPHS
ANTHROPOPATHIC
ANTHROPOPATHIES
ANTHROPOPATHISM
ANTHROPOPATHY
ANTHROPOPHAGI
ANTHROPOPHAGIC
ANTHROPOPHAGIES
ANTHROPOPHAGITE
ANTHROPOPHAGOUS
ANTHROPOPHAGUS
ANTHROPOPHAGY
ANTHROPOPHOBIA
ANTHROPOPHOBIAS
ANTHROPOPHOBIC
ANTHROPOPHOBICS
ANTHROPOPHUISM
ANTHROPOPHUISMS
ANTHROPOPHYTE
ANTHROPOPHYTES
ANTHROPOPSYCHIC
ANTHROPOSOPHIC
ANTHROPOSOPHIES
ANTHROPOSOPHIST
ANTHROPOSOPHY
ANTHROPOTOMIES
ANTHROPOTOMY
ANTHURIUMS
ANTIABORTION
ANTIABORTIONIST
ANTIACADEMIC
ANTIADITIS
ANTIADITISES
ANTIAGGRESSION
ANTIAIRCRAFT
ANTIAIRCRAFTS
ANTIALCOHOL
ANTIALCOHOLISM
ANTIALCOHOLISMS
ANTIALLERGENIC
ANTIANDROGEN
ANTIANDROGENS
ANTIANEMIA
ANTIANXIETY
ANTIAPARTHEID
ANTIAPHRODISIAC
ANTIARMOUR
ANTIARRHYTHMIC
ANTIARRHYTHMICS
ANTIARTHRITIC
ANTIARTHRITICS
ANTIARTHRITIS
ANTIASTHMA
ANTIASTHMATIC
ANTIASTHMATICS
ANTIAUTHORITY
ANTIAUXINS
ANTIBACCHII
ANTIBACCHIUS
ANTIBACKLASH
ANTIBACTERIAL
ANTIBACTERIALS
ANTIBALLISTIC
ANTIBARBARUS
ANTIBARBARUSES
ANTIBARYON
ANTIBARYONS
ANTIBILIOUS
ANTIBILLBOARD
ANTIBIOSES
ANTIBIOSIS
ANTIBIOTIC
ANTIBIOTICALLY
ANTIBIOTICS
ANTIBLACKISM
ANTIBLACKISMS
ANTIBODIES
ANTIBOURGEOIS
ANTIBOYCOTT
ANTIBURGLAR
ANTIBURGLARY
ANTIBUSERS
ANTIBUSINESS
ANTIBUSING
ANTICAKING
ANTICANCER
ANTICAPITALISM
ANTICAPITALISMS
ANTICAPITALIST
ANTICAPITALISTS

ANTICARCINOGEN
ANTICARCINOGENS
ANTICARIES
ANTICATALYST
ANTICATALYSTS
ANTICATHODE
ANTICATHODES
ANTICATHOLIC
ANTICELLULITE
ANTICENSORSHIP
ANTICHLORISTIC
ANTICHLORS
ANTICHOICE
ANTICHOICER
ANTICHOICERS
ANTICHOLESTEROL
ANTICHOLINERGIC
ANTICHRIST
ANTICHRISTIAN
ANTICHRISTIANLY
ANTICHRISTS
ANTICHTHONES
ANTICHURCH
ANTICIGARETTE
ANTICIPANT
ANTICIPANTS
ANTICIPATABLE
ANTICIPATE
ANTICIPATED
ANTICIPATES
ANTICIPATING
ANTICIPATION
ANTICIPATIONS
ANTICIPATIVE
ANTICIPATIVELY
ANTICIPATOR
ANTICIPATORILY
ANTICIPATORS
ANTICIPATORY
ANTICISING
ANTICIVISM
ANTICIVISMS
ANTICIZING
ANTICLASSICAL
ANTICLASTIC
ANTICLERICAL
ANTICLERICALISM
ANTICLERICALS
ANTICLIMACTIC
ANTICLIMACTICAL
ANTICLIMAX
ANTICLIMAXES
ANTICLINAL
ANTICLINALS
ANTICLINES
ANTICLINORIA
ANTICLINORIUM
ANTICLOCKWISE
ANTICLOTTING
ANTICOAGULANT
ANTICOAGULANTS
ANTICODONS
ANTICOINCIDENCE
ANTICOLLISION
ANTICOLONIAL
ANTICOLONIALISM
ANTICOLONIALIST
ANTICOLONIALS
ANTICOMMERCIAL
ANTICOMMUNISM
ANTICOMMUNISMS
ANTICOMMUNIST
ANTICOMMUNISTS
ANTICOMPETITIVE
ANTICONSUMER
ANTICONVULSANT
ANTICONVULSANTS
ANTICONVULSIVE
ANTICONVULSIVES
ANTICORPORATE
ANTICORROSION
ANTICORROSIONS
ANTICORROSIVE
ANTICORROSIVES
ANTICORRUPTION
ANTICREATIVE
ANTICRUELTY
ANTICULTURAL
ANTICYCLONE
ANTICYCLONES
ANTICYCLONIC
ANTIDANDRUFF
ANTIDAZZLE
ANTIDEFAMATION
ANTIDEMOCRATIC
ANTIDEPRESSANT
ANTIDEPRESSANTS
ANTIDEPRESSION
ANTIDERIVATIVE
ANTIDERIVATIVES
ANTIDESICCANT
ANTIDESICCANTS
ANTIDEVELOPMENT
ANTIDIABETIC
ANTIDIABETICS
ANTIDIARRHEAL
ANTIDIARRHEALS
ANTIDIARRHOEAL
ANTIDIARRHOEALS
ANTIDILUTION
ANTIDIURETIC
ANTIDIURETICS
ANTIDOGMATIC
ANTIDOTALLY
ANTIDOTING
ANTIDROMIC
ANTIDROMICALLY
ANTIDUMPING
ANTIDUMPINGS
ANTIECONOMIC
ANTIEDUCATIONAL
ANTIEGALITARIAN
ANTIELECTRON
ANTIELECTRONS
ANTIELITES
ANTIELITISM
ANTIELITISMS
ANTIELITIST
ANTIELITISTS
ANTIEMETIC
ANTIEMETICS
ANTIENTROPIC
ANTIEPILEPSY
ANTIEPILEPTIC
ANTIEPILEPTICS
ANTIEROTIC
ANTIESTROGEN
ANTIESTROGENS
ANTIEVOLUTION
ANTIEVOLUTIONS
ANTIFAMILY
ANTIFASCISM
ANTIFASCISMS
ANTIFASCIST
ANTIFASCISTS
ANTIFASHION
ANTIFASHIONABLE
ANTIFASHIONS
ANTIFATIGUE
ANTIFEBRILE
ANTIFEBRILES
ANTIFEDERALIST
ANTIFEDERALISTS
ANTIFEMALE
ANTIFEMININE
ANTIFEMINISM
ANTIFEMINISMS
ANTIFEMINIST
ANTIFEMINISTS
ANTIFERROMAGNET
ANTIFERTILITY
ANTIFILIBUSTER
ANTIFILIBUSTERS
ANTIFOAMING
ANTIFOGGING
ANTIFORECLOSURE
ANTIFOREIGN
ANTIFOREIGNER
ANTIFORMALIST
ANTIFOULING
ANTIFOULINGS
ANTIFREEZE
ANTIFREEZES
ANTIFRICTION
ANTIFUNGAL
ANTIFUNGALS
ANTIGAMBLING
ANTIGENICALLY
ANTIGENICITIES
ANTIGENICITY
ANTIGLOBULIN
ANTIGLOBULINS
ANTIGOVERNMENT
ANTIGRAVITIES
ANTIGRAVITY
ANTIGROPELOES
ANTIGROPELOS
ANTIGROWTH
ANTIGUERRILLA
ANTIHALATION
ANTIHALATIONS
ANTIHELICES
ANTIHELIXES
ANTIHELMINTHIC
ANTIHELMINTHICS
ANTIHEROES
ANTIHEROIC
ANTIHEROINE
ANTIHEROINES
ANTIHERPES
ANTIHIJACK
ANTIHISTAMINE
ANTIHISTAMINES
ANTIHISTAMINIC
ANTIHISTAMINICS
ANTIHISTORICAL
ANTIHOMOSEXUAL
ANTIHUMANISM
ANTIHUMANISMS
ANTIHUMANISTIC
ANTIHUNTER
ANTIHUNTERS
ANTIHUNTING
ANTIHYDROGEN
ANTIHYDROGENS
ANTIHYSTERIC
ANTIHYSTERICS
ANTIJACOBIN
ANTIJACOBINS
ANTIJAMMING
ANTIJAMMINGS
ANTIKICKBACK
ANTIKNOCKS
ANTILEGOMENA
ANTILEPROSY
ANTILEPTON
ANTILEPTONS
ANTILEUKEMIC
ANTILIBERAL
ANTILIBERALISM
ANTILIBERALISMS
ANTILIBERALS
ANTILIBERTARIAN
ANTILIFERS
ANTILITERATE
ANTILITTER
ANTILITTERING
ANTILOGARITHM
ANTILOGARITHMIC
ANTILOGARITHMS

ANTILOGICAL
ANTILOGIES
ANTILOGOUS
ANTILOPINE
ANTILYNCHING
ANTIMACASSAR
ANTIMACASSARS
ANTIMAGNETIC
ANTIMALARIA
ANTIMALARIAL
ANTIMALARIALS
ANTIMANAGEMENT
ANTIMARIJUANA
ANTIMARKET
ANTIMARKETEER
ANTIMARKETEERS
ANTIMASQUE
ANTIMASQUES
ANTIMATERIALISM
ANTIMATERIALIST
ANTIMATTER
ANTIMATTERS
ANTIMECHANIST
ANTIMECHANISTS
ANTIMERGER
ANTIMERISM
ANTIMERISMS
ANTIMETABOLE
ANTIMETABOLES
ANTIMETABOLIC
ANTIMETABOLITE
ANTIMETABOLITES
ANTIMETATHESES
ANTIMETATHESIS
ANTIMICROBIAL
ANTIMICROBIALS
ANTIMILITARISM
ANTIMILITARISMS
ANTIMILITARIST
ANTIMILITARISTS
ANTIMILITARY
ANTIMISSILE
ANTIMISSILES
ANTIMITOTIC
ANTIMITOTICS
ANTIMNEMONIC
ANTIMNEMONICS
ANTIMODERN
ANTIMODERNIST
ANTIMODERNISTS
ANTIMONARCHICAL
ANTIMONARCHIST
ANTIMONARCHISTS
ANTIMONATE
ANTIMONATES
ANTIMONIAL
ANTIMONIALS
ANTIMONIATE
ANTIMONIATES
ANTIMONIDE
ANTIMONIDES
ANTIMONIES
ANTIMONIOUS
ANTIMONITE
ANTIMONITES
ANTIMONOPOLIST
ANTIMONOPOLISTS
ANTIMONOPOLY
ANTIMONOUS
ANTIMONYLS
ANTIMOSQUITO
ANTIMUSICAL
ANTIMUSICS
ANTIMUTAGEN
ANTIMUTAGENS
ANTIMYCINS
ANTIMYCOTIC
ANTINARRATIVE
ANTINARRATIVES
ANTINATIONAL
ANTINATIONALIST
ANTINATURAL
ANTINATURE
ANTINAUSEA
ANTINEOPLASTIC
ANTINEOPLASTICS
ANTINEPHRITIC
ANTINEPHRITICS
ANTINEPOTISM
ANTINEUTRINO
ANTINEUTRINOS
ANTINEUTRON
ANTINEUTRONS
ANTINOISES
ANTINOMIAN
ANTINOMIANISM
ANTINOMIANISMS
ANTINOMIANS
ANTINOMICAL
ANTINOMICALLY
ANTINOMIES
ANTINOVELIST
ANTINOVELISTS
ANTINOVELS
ANTINUCLEAR
ANTINUCLEARIST
ANTINUCLEARISTS
ANTINUCLEON
ANTINUCLEONS
ANTINUKERS
ANTIOBESITY
ANTIOBSCENITY
ANTIODONTALGIC
ANTIODONTALGICS
ANTIOESTROGEN
ANTIOESTROGENS
ANTIOXIDANT
ANTIOXIDANTS
ANTIOZONANT
ANTIOZONANTS
ANTIPARALLEL
ANTIPARALLELS
ANTIPARASITIC
ANTIPARASITICS
ANTIPARTICLE
ANTIPARTICLES
ANTIPARTIES
ANTIPASTOS
ANTIPATHETIC
ANTIPATHETICAL
ANTIPATHIC
ANTIPATHIES
ANTIPATHIST
ANTIPATHISTS
ANTIPERIODIC
ANTIPERIODICS
ANTIPERISTALSES
ANTIPERISTALSIS
ANTIPERISTALTIC
ANTIPERISTASES
ANTIPERISTASIS
ANTIPERSONNEL
ANTIPERSPIRANT
ANTIPERSPIRANTS
ANTIPESTICIDE
ANTIPETALOUS
ANTIPHLOGISTIC
ANTIPHLOGISTICS
ANTIPHONAL
ANTIPHONALLY
ANTIPHONALS
ANTIPHONARIES
ANTIPHONARY
ANTIPHONER
ANTIPHONERS
ANTIPHONIC
ANTIPHONICAL
ANTIPHONICALLY
ANTIPHONIES
ANTIPHRASES
ANTIPHRASIS
ANTIPHRASTIC
ANTIPHRASTICAL
ANTIPIRACY
ANTIPLAGUE
ANTIPLAQUE
ANTIPLEASURE
ANTIPOACHING
ANTIPODALS
ANTIPODEAN
ANTIPODEANS
ANTIPOETIC
ANTIPOLICE
ANTIPOLITICAL
ANTIPOLITICS
ANTIPOLLUTION
ANTIPOLLUTIONS
ANTIPOPULAR
ANTIPORNOGRAPHY
ANTIPORTER
ANTIPORTERS
ANTIPOVERTY
ANTIPREDATOR
ANTIPRIESTLY
ANTIPROGRESSIVE
ANTIPROTON
ANTIPROTONS
ANTIPRURITIC
ANTIPRURITICS
ANTIPSYCHIATRY
ANTIPSYCHOTIC
ANTIPSYCHOTICS
ANTIPYRESES
ANTIPYRESIS
ANTIPYRETIC
ANTIPYRETICS
ANTIPYRINE
ANTIPYRINES
ANTIQUARIAN
ANTIQUARIANISM
ANTIQUARIANISMS
ANTIQUARIANS
ANTIQUARIES
ANTIQUARKS
ANTIQUATED
ANTIQUATEDNESS
ANTIQUATES
ANTIQUATING
ANTIQUATION
ANTIQUATIONS
ANTIQUENESS
ANTIQUENESSES
ANTIQUIEST
ANTIQUITARIAN
ANTIQUITARIANS
ANTIQUITIES
ANTIRABIES
ANTIRACHITIC
ANTIRACHITICS
ANTIRACISM
ANTIRACISMS
ANTIRACIST
ANTIRACISTS
ANTIRADARS
ANTIRADICAL
ANTIRADICALISM
ANTIRADICALISMS
ANTIRATIONAL
ANTIRATIONALISM
ANTIRATIONALIST
ANTIRATIONALITY
ANTIREALISM
ANTIREALISMS
ANTIREALIST
ANTIREALISTS
ANTIRECESSION
ANTIREFLECTION
ANTIREFLECTIVE
ANTIREFORM
ANTIREGULATORY

A

ANTIREJECTION
ANTIRELIGION
ANTIRELIGIONS
ANTIRELIGIOUS
ANTIREPUBLICAN
ANTIREPUBLICANS
ANTIRETROVIRAL
ANTIRETROVIRALS
ANTIRHEUMATIC
ANTIRHEUMATICS
ANTIRITUALISM
ANTIRITUALISMS
ANTIROMANTIC
ANTIROMANTICISM
ANTIROMANTICS
ANTIROYALIST
ANTIROYALISTS
ANTIRRHINUM
ANTIRRHINUMS
ANTISATELLITE
ANTISCIANS
ANTISCIENCE
ANTISCIENCES
ANTISCIENTIFIC
ANTISCORBUTIC
ANTISCORBUTICS
ANTISCRIPTURAL
ANTISECRECY
ANTISEGREGATION
ANTISEIZURE
ANTISENTIMENTAL
ANTISEPALOUS
ANTISEPARATIST
ANTISEPARATISTS
ANTISEPSES
ANTISEPSIS
ANTISEPTIC
ANTISEPTICALLY
ANTISEPTICISE
ANTISEPTICISED
ANTISEPTICISES
ANTISEPTICISING
ANTISEPTICISM
ANTISEPTICISMS
ANTISEPTICIZE
ANTISEPTICIZED
ANTISEPTICIZES
ANTISEPTICIZING
ANTISEPTICS
ANTISERUMS
ANTISEXIST
ANTISEXISTS
ANTISEXUAL
ANTISEXUALITIES
ANTISEXUALITY
ANTISEXUALS
ANTISHAKES
ANTISHOCKS
ANTISHOPLIFTING
ANTISLAVERY
ANTISMOKER
ANTISMOKERS
ANTISMOKING
ANTISMUGGLING
ANTISOCIAL
ANTISOCIALISM
ANTISOCIALISMS
ANTISOCIALIST
ANTISOCIALISTS
ANTISOCIALITIES
ANTISOCIALITY
ANTISOCIALLY
ANTISOCIALS
ANTISPASMODIC
ANTISPASMODICS
ANTISPASTIC
ANTISPASTICS
ANTISPASTS
ANTISPECULATION
ANTISPECULATIVE
ANTISPENDING
ANTISTATIC
ANTISTATICS
ANTISTORIES
ANTISTRESS
ANTISTRIKE
ANTISTROPHE
ANTISTROPHES
ANTISTROPHIC
ANTISTROPHON
ANTISTROPHONS
ANTISTUDENT
ANTISTYLES
ANTISUBMARINE
ANTISUBSIDY
ANTISUBVERSION
ANTISUBVERSIVE
ANTISUICIDE
ANTISYMMETRIC
ANTISYPHILITIC
ANTISYPHILITICS
ANTISYZYGIES
ANTISYZYGY
ANTITAKEOVER
ANTITARNISH
ANTITECHNOLOGY
ANTITERRORISM
ANTITERRORISMS
ANTITERRORIST
ANTITERRORISTS
ANTITHALIAN
ANTITHEISM
ANTITHEISMS
ANTITHEIST
ANTITHEISTIC
ANTITHEISTS
ANTITHEORETICAL
ANTITHESES
ANTITHESIS
ANTITHETIC
ANTITHETICAL
ANTITHETICALLY
ANTITHROMBIN
ANTITHROMBINS
ANTITHROMBOTIC
ANTITHROMBOTICS
ANTITHYROID
ANTITOBACCO
ANTITOXINS
ANTITRADES
ANTITRADITIONAL
ANTITRAGUS
ANTITRANSPIRANT
ANTITRINITARIAN
ANTITRUSTER
ANTITRUSTERS
ANTITUBERCULAR
ANTITUBERCULOUS
ANTITUMORAL
ANTITUMORS
ANTITUMOUR
ANTITUMOURAL
ANTITUSSIVE
ANTITUSSIVES
ANTITYPHOID
ANTITYPICAL
ANTITYPICALLY
ANTIUNIVERSITY
ANTIVAXERS
ANTIVAXXER
ANTIVAXXERS
ANTIVENENE
ANTIVENENES
ANTIVENINS
ANTIVENOMS
ANTIVIOLENCE
ANTIVIRALS
ANTIVIRUSES
ANTIVITAMIN
ANTIVITAMINS
ANTIVIVISECTION
ANTIWELFARE
ANTIWHALING
ANTIWORLDS
ANTIWRINKLE
ANTONINIANUS
ANTONINIANUSES
ANTONOMASIA
ANTONOMASIAS
ANTONOMASTIC
ANTONYMIES
ANTONYMOUS
ANTRORSELY
ANTSINESSES
ANUCLEATED
ANXIOLYTIC
ANXIOLYTICS
ANXIOUSNESS
ANXIOUSNESSES
ANYTHINGARIAN
ANYTHINGARIANS
ANYWHITHER
AORISTICALLY
AORTITISES
AORTOGRAPHIC
AORTOGRAPHIES
AORTOGRAPHY
APAGOGICAL
APAGOGICALLY
APARTHEIDS
APARTHOTEL
APARTHOTELS
APARTMENTAL
APARTMENTS
APARTNESSES
APATHATONS
APATHETICAL
APATHETICALLY
APATOSAURS
APATOSAURUS
APATOSAURUSES
APERIODICALLY
APERIODICITIES
APERIODICITY
APERITIVES
APERTNESSES
APFELSTRUDEL
APFELSTRUDELS
APHAERESES
APHAERESIS
APHAERETIC
APHANIPTEROUS
APHELANDRA
APHELANDRAS
APHELIOTROPIC
APHELIOTROPISM
APHELIOTROPISMS
APHETICALLY
APHETISING
APHETIZING
APHIDICIDE
APHIDICIDES
APHORISERS
APHORISING
APHORISTIC
APHORISTICALLY
APHORIZERS
APHORIZING
APHRODISIA
APHRODISIAC
APHRODISIACAL
APHRODISIACS
APHRODISIAS
APHRODITES
APICULTURAL
APICULTURE
APICULTURES
APICULTURIST
APICULTURISTS
APIOLOGIES

APISHNESSES
APITHERAPIES
APITHERAPY
APLACENTAL
APLANATICALLY
APLANATISM
APLANATISMS
APLANOGAMETE
APLANOGAMETES
APLANOSPORE
APLANOSPORES
APOAPSIDES
APOCALYPSE
APOCALYPSES
APOCALYPTIC
APOCALYPTICAL
APOCALYPTICALLY
APOCALYPTICISM
APOCALYPTICISMS
APOCALYPTISM
APOCALYPTISMS
APOCALYPTIST
APOCALYPTISTS
APOCARPIES
APOCARPOUS
APOCATASTASES
APOCATASTASIS
APOCHROMAT
APOCHROMATIC
APOCHROMATISM
APOCHROMATISMS
APOCHROMATS
APOCOPATED
APOCOPATES
APOCOPATING
APOCOPATION
APOCOPATIONS
APOCRYPHAL
APOCRYPHALLY
APOCRYPHALNESS
APOCRYPHON
APOCYNACEOUS
APOCYNTHION
APOCYNTHIONS
APODEICTIC
APODEICTICAL
APODEICTICALLY
APODICTICAL
APODICTICALLY
APODYTERIUM
APODYTERIUMS
APOENZYMES
APOGAMOUSLY
APOGEOTROPIC
APOGEOTROPISM
APOGEOTROPISMS
APOLAUSTIC
APOLAUSTICS
APOLIPOPROTEIN
APOLIPOPROTEINS
APOLITICAL
APOLITICALITIES
APOLITICALITY
APOLITICALLY
APOLITICISM
APOLITICISMS
APOLLONIAN
APOLLONICON
APOLLONICONS
APOLOGETIC
APOLOGETICAL
APOLOGETICALLY
APOLOGETICS
APOLOGISED
APOLOGISER
APOLOGISERS
APOLOGISES
APOLOGISING
APOLOGISTS
APOLOGIZED
APOLOGIZER
APOLOGIZERS
APOLOGIZES
APOLOGIZING
APOMICTICAL
APOMICTICALLY
APOMORPHIA
APOMORPHIAS
APOMORPHINE
APOMORPHINES
APONEUROSES
APONEUROSIS
APONEUROTIC
APOPEMPTIC
APOPEMPTICS
APOPHENIAS
APOPHLEGMATIC
APOPHLEGMATICS
APOPHONIES
APOPHTHEGM
APOPHTHEGMATIC
APOPHTHEGMATISE
APOPHTHEGMATIST
APOPHTHEGMATIZE
APOPHTHEGMS
APOPHYLLITE
APOPHYLLITES
APOPHYSATE
APOPHYSEAL
APOPHYSIAL
APOPLECTIC
APOPLECTICAL
APOPLECTICALLY
APOPLECTICS
APOPLEXIES
APOPLEXING
APOPROTEIN
APOPROTEINS
APOSEMATIC
APOSEMATICALLY
APOSIOPESES
APOSIOPESIS
APOSIOPETIC
APOSPORIES
APOSPOROUS
APOSTACIES
APOSTASIES
APOSTATICAL
APOSTATISE
APOSTATISED
APOSTATISES
APOSTATISING
APOSTATIZE
APOSTATIZED
APOSTATIZES
APOSTATIZING
APOSTILLES
APOSTLESHIP
APOSTLESHIPS
APOSTOLATE
APOSTOLATES
APOSTOLICAL
APOSTOLICALLY
APOSTOLICISM
APOSTOLICISMS
APOSTOLICITIES
APOSTOLICITY
APOSTOLISE
APOSTOLISED
APOSTOLISES
APOSTOLISING
APOSTOLIZE
APOSTOLIZED
APOSTOLIZES
APOSTOLIZING
APOSTROPHE
APOSTROPHES
APOSTROPHIC
APOSTROPHISE
APOSTROPHISED
APOSTROPHISES
APOSTROPHISING
APOSTROPHIZE
APOSTROPHIZED
APOSTROPHIZES
APOSTROPHIZING
APOSTROPHUS
APOSTROPHUSES
APOTHECARIES
APOTHECARY
APOTHECIAL
APOTHECIUM
APOTHEGMATIC
APOTHEGMATICAL
APOTHEGMATISE
APOTHEGMATISED
APOTHEGMATISES
APOTHEGMATISING
APOTHEGMATIST
APOTHEGMATISTS
APOTHEGMATIZE
APOTHEGMATIZED
APOTHEGMATIZES
APOTHEGMATIZING
APOTHEOSES
APOTHEOSIS
APOTHEOSISE
APOTHEOSISED
APOTHEOSISES
APOTHEOSISING
APOTHEOSIZE
APOTHEOSIZED
APOTHEOSIZES
APOTHEOSIZING
APOTROPAIC
APOTROPAICALLY
APOTROPAISM
APOTROPAISMS
APOTROPOUS
APPALLINGLY
APPALOOSAS
APPARATCHIK
APPARATCHIKI
APPARATCHIKS
APPARATUSES
APPARELING
APPARELLED
APPARELLING
APPARELMENT
APPARELMENTS
APPARENCIES
APPARENTLY
APPARENTNESS
APPARENTNESSES
APPARITION
APPARITIONAL
APPARITIONS
APPARITORS
APPARTEMENT
APPARTEMENTS
APPASSIONATO
APPEACHING
APPEACHMENT
APPEACHMENTS
APPEALABILITIES
APPEALABILITY
APPEALABLE
APPEALINGLY
APPEALINGNESS
APPEALINGNESSES
APPEARANCE
APPEARANCES
APPEASABLE
APPEASEMENT
APPEASEMENTS
APPEASINGLY
APPELLANTS
APPELLATION
APPELLATIONAL
APPELLATIONS

A

APPELLATIVE
APPELLATIVELY
APPELLATIVES
APPENDAGES
APPENDANTS
APPENDECTOMIES
APPENDECTOMY
APPENDENTS
APPENDICECTOMY
APPENDICES
APPENDICITIS
APPENDICITISES
APPENDICLE
APPENDICLES
APPENDICULAR
APPENDICULARIAN
APPENDICULATE
APPENDIXES
APPERCEIVE
APPERCEIVED
APPERCEIVES
APPERCEIVING
APPERCEPTION
APPERCEPTIONS
APPERCEPTIVE
APPERCIPIENT
APPERTAINANCE
APPERTAINANCES
APPERTAINED
APPERTAINING
APPERTAINMENT
APPERTAINMENTS
APPERTAINS
APPERTINENT
APPERTINENTS
APPETEEZEMENT
APPETEEZEMENTS
APPETENCES
APPETENCIES
APPETISEMENT
APPETISEMENTS
APPETISERS
APPETISING
APPETISINGLY
APPETITION
APPETITIONS
APPETITIVE
APPETIZERS
APPETIZING
APPETIZINGLY
APPLAUDABLE
APPLAUDABLY
APPLAUDERS
APPLAUDING
APPLAUDINGLY
APPLAUSIVE
APPLAUSIVELY
APPLECARTS
APPLEDRAIN
APPLEDRAINS
APPLEJACKS
APPLERINGIE
APPLERINGIES
APPLESAUCE
APPLESAUCES
APPLETINIS
APPLIANCES
APPLICABILITIES
APPLICABILITY
APPLICABLE
APPLICABLENESS
APPLICABLY
APPLICANTS
APPLICATION
APPLICATIONS
APPLICATIVE
APPLICATIVELY
APPLICATOR
APPLICATORS
APPLICATORY
APPLIQUEING
APPOGGIATURA
APPOGGIATURAS
APPOGGIATURE
APPOINTEES
APPOINTERS
APPOINTING
APPOINTIVE
APPOINTMENT
APPOINTMENTS
APPOINTORS
APPORTIONABLE
APPORTIONED
APPORTIONER
APPORTIONERS
APPORTIONING
APPORTIONMENT
APPORTIONMENTS
APPORTIONS
APPOSITELY
APPOSITENESS
APPOSITENESSES
APPOSITION
APPOSITIONAL
APPOSITIONS
APPOSITIVE
APPOSITIVELY
APPOSITIVES
APPRAISABLE
APPRAISALS
APPRAISEES
APPRAISEMENT
APPRAISEMENTS
APPRAISERS
APPRAISING
APPRAISINGLY
APPRAISIVE
APPRAISIVELY
APPRECIABLE
APPRECIABLY
APPRECIATE
APPRECIATED
APPRECIATES
APPRECIATING
APPRECIATION
APPRECIATIONS
APPRECIATIVE
APPRECIATIVELY
APPRECIATOR
APPRECIATORILY
APPRECIATORS
APPRECIATORY
APPREHENDED
APPREHENDING
APPREHENDS
APPREHENSIBLE
APPREHENSIBLY
APPREHENSION
APPREHENSIONS
APPREHENSIVE
APPREHENSIVELY
APPRENTICE
APPRENTICED
APPRENTICEHOOD
APPRENTICEHOODS
APPRENTICEMENT
APPRENTICEMENTS
APPRENTICES
APPRENTICESHIP
APPRENTICESHIPS
APPRENTICING
APPRESSING
APPRESSORIA
APPRESSORIUM
APPRISINGS
APPRIZINGS
APPROACHABILITY
APPROACHABLE
APPROACHED
APPROACHES
APPROACHING
APPROBATED
APPROBATES
APPROBATING
APPROBATION
APPROBATIONS
APPROBATIVE
APPROBATORY
APPROPINQUATE
APPROPINQUATED
APPROPINQUATES
APPROPINQUATING
APPROPINQUATION
APPROPINQUE
APPROPINQUED
APPROPINQUES
APPROPINQUING
APPROPINQUITIES
APPROPINQUITY
APPROPRIABLE
APPROPRIACIES
APPROPRIACY
APPROPRIATE
APPROPRIATED
APPROPRIATELY
APPROPRIATENESS
APPROPRIATES
APPROPRIATING
APPROPRIATION
APPROPRIATIONS
APPROPRIATIVE
APPROPRIATOR
APPROPRIATORS
APPROVABLE
APPROVABLY
APPROVANCE
APPROVANCES
APPROVINGLY
APPROXIMAL
APPROXIMATE
APPROXIMATED
APPROXIMATELY
APPROXIMATES
APPROXIMATING
APPROXIMATION
APPROXIMATIONS
APPROXIMATIVE
APPROXIMEETING
APPROXIMEETINGS
APPULSIVELY
APPURTENANCE
APPURTENANCES
APPURTENANT
APPURTENANTS
APRICATING
APRICATION
APRICATIONS
APRIORISMS
APRIORISTS
APRIORITIES
APSIDIOLES
APTERYGIAL
APTITUDINAL
APTITUDINALLY
AQUABATICS
AQUABOARDS
AQUACEUTICAL
AQUACEUTICALS
AQUACULTURAL
AQUACULTURE
AQUACULTURES
AQUACULTURIST
AQUACULTURISTS
AQUADROMES
AQUAEROBICS
AQUAFARMED
AQUAFARMING
AQUAFARMINGS
AQUAFITNESS
AQUAFITNESSES

AQUAFORTIS
AQUAFORTISES
AQUAFORTIST
AQUAFORTISTS
AQUALEATHER
AQUALEATHERS
AQUAMANALE
AQUAMANALES
AQUAMANILE
AQUAMANILES
AQUAMARINE
AQUAMARINES
AQUANAUTICS
AQUAPHOBES
AQUAPHOBIA
AQUAPHOBIAS
AQUAPHOBIC
AQUAPHOBICS
AQUAPLANED
AQUAPLANER
AQUAPLANERS
AQUAPLANES
AQUAPLANING
AQUAPLANINGS
AQUAPORINS
AQUARELLES
AQUARELLIST
AQUARELLISTS
AQUARIISTS
AQUAROBICS
AQUASCAPES
AQUATICALLY
AQUATINTAS
AQUATINTED
AQUATINTER
AQUATINTERS
AQUATINTING
AQUATINTIST
AQUATINTISTS
AQUICULTURAL
AQUICULTURE
AQUICULTURES
AQUICULTURIST
AQUICULTURISTS
AQUIFEROUS
AQUIFOLIACEOUS
AQUILEGIAS
AQUILINITIES
AQUILINITY
ARABESQUED
ARABESQUES
ARABICISATION
ARABICISATIONS
ARABICISED
ARABICISES
ARABICISING
ARABICIZATION
ARABICIZATIONS
ARABICIZED
ARABICIZES
ARABICIZING
ARABILITIES
ARABINOSES
ARABINOSIDE
ARABINOSIDES
ARABISATION
ARABISATIONS
ARABIZATION
ARABIZATIONS
ARACHIDONIC
ARACHNIDAN
ARACHNIDANS
ARACHNOIDAL
ARACHNOIDITIS
ARACHNOIDITISES
ARACHNOIDS
ARACHNOLOGICAL
ARACHNOLOGIES
ARACHNOLOGIST
ARACHNOLOGISTS
ARACHNOLOGY
ARACHNOPHOBE
ARACHNOPHOBES
ARACHNOPHOBIA
ARACHNOPHOBIAS
ARACHNOPHOBIC
ARACHNOPHOBICS
ARAEOMETER
ARAEOMETERS
ARAEOMETRIC
ARAEOMETRICAL
ARAEOMETRIES
ARAEOMETRY
ARAEOSTYLE
ARAEOSTYLES
ARAEOSYSTYLE
ARAEOSYSTYLES
ARAGONITES
ARAGONITIC
ARALIACEOUS
ARAUCARIAN
ARAUCARIAS
ARBALESTER
ARBALESTERS
ARBALISTER
ARBALISTERS
ARBITRABLE
ARBITRAGED
ARBITRAGER
ARBITRAGERS
ARBITRAGES
ARBITRAGEUR
ARBITRAGEURS
ARBITRAGING
ARBITRAMENT
ARBITRAMENTS
ARBITRARILY
ARBITRARINESS
ARBITRARINESSES
ARBITRATED
ARBITRATES
ARBITRATING
ARBITRATION
ARBITRATIONAL
ARBITRATIONS
ARBITRATIVE
ARBITRATOR
ARBITRATORS
ARBITRATRICES
ARBITRATRIX
ARBITRATRIXES
ARBITREMENT
ARBITREMENTS
ARBITRESSES
ARBITRIUMS
ARBLASTERS
ARBORACEOUS
ARBOREALLY
ARBORESCENCE
ARBORESCENCES
ARBORESCENT
ARBORETUMS
ARBORICULTURAL
ARBORICULTURE
ARBORICULTURES
ARBORICULTURIST
ARBORISATION
ARBORISATIONS
ARBORISING
ARBORIZATION
ARBORIZATIONS
ARBORIZING
ARBORVITAE
ARBORVITAES
ARBOVIRUSES
ARBUSCULAR
ARCANENESS
ARCANENESSES
ARCCOSINES
ARCHAEBACTERIA
ARCHAEBACTERIUM
ARCHAEOBOTANIES
ARCHAEOBOTANIST
ARCHAEOBOTANY
ARCHAEOLOGICAL
ARCHAEOLOGIES
ARCHAEOLOGIST
ARCHAEOLOGISTS
ARCHAEOLOGY
ARCHAEOMETRIC
ARCHAEOMETRIES
ARCHAEOMETRIST
ARCHAEOMETRISTS
ARCHAEOMETRY
ARCHAEOPTERYX
ARCHAEOPTERYXES
ARCHAEORNIS
ARCHAEORNISES
ARCHAEOZOOLOGY
ARCHAEZOOLOGIES
ARCHAEZOOLOGY
ARCHAICALLY
ARCHAICISM
ARCHAICISMS
ARCHAISERS
ARCHAISING
ARCHAISTIC
ARCHAIZERS
ARCHAIZING
ARCHANGELIC
ARCHANGELS
ARCHBISHOP
ARCHBISHOPRIC
ARCHBISHOPRICS
ARCHBISHOPS
ARCHDEACON
ARCHDEACONRIES
ARCHDEACONRY
ARCHDEACONS
ARCHDIOCESAN
ARCHDIOCESE
ARCHDIOCESES
ARCHDRUIDS
ARCHDUCHESS
ARCHDUCHESSES
ARCHDUCHIES
ARCHDUKEDOM
ARCHDUKEDOMS
ARCHEGONIA
ARCHEGONIAL
ARCHEGONIATE
ARCHEGONIATES
ARCHEGONIUM
ARCHENEMIES
ARCHENTERA
ARCHENTERIC
ARCHENTERON
ARCHENTERONS
ARCHEOASTRONOMY
ARCHEOBOTANIES
ARCHEOBOTANIST
ARCHEOBOTANISTS
ARCHEOBOTANY
ARCHEOLOGICAL
ARCHEOLOGICALLY
ARCHEOLOGIES
ARCHEOLOGIST
ARCHEOLOGISTS
ARCHEOLOGY
ARCHEOMAGNETISM
ARCHEOMETRIES
ARCHEOMETRY
ARCHEOZOOLOGIES
ARCHEOZOOLOGIST
ARCHEOZOOLOGY
ARCHERESSES
ARCHERFISH
ARCHERFISHES
ARCHESPORE
ARCHESPORES

A

ARCHESPORIA
ARCHESPORIAL
ARCHESPORIUM
ARCHETYPAL
ARCHETYPALLY
ARCHETYPES
ARCHETYPICAL
ARCHETYPICALLY
ARCHFIENDS
ARCHGENETHLIAC
ARCHGENETHLIACS
ARCHICARPS
ARCHIDIACONAL
ARCHIDIACONATE
ARCHIDIACONATES
ARCHIEPISCOPACY
ARCHIEPISCOPAL
ARCHIEPISCOPATE
ARCHILOWES
ARCHIMAGES
ARCHIMANDRITE
ARCHIMANDRITES
ARCHIPELAGIAN
ARCHIPELAGIC
ARCHIPELAGO
ARCHIPELAGOES
ARCHIPELAGOS
ARCHIPHONEME
ARCHIPHONEMES
ARCHIPLASM
ARCHIPLASMIC
ARCHIPLASMS
ARCHITECTED
ARCHITECTING
ARCHITECTONIC
ARCHITECTONICS
ARCHITECTS
ARCHITECTURAL
ARCHITECTURALLY
ARCHITECTURE
ARCHITECTURES
ARCHITRAVE
ARCHITRAVED
ARCHITRAVES
ARCHITYPES
ARCHIVISTS
ARCHIVOLTS
ARCHNESSES
ARCHOLOGIES
ARCHONSHIP
ARCHONSHIPS
ARCHONTATE
ARCHONTATES
ARCHOPLASM
ARCHOPLASMIC
ARCHOPLASMS
ARCHOSAURIAN
ARCHOSAURIANS
ARCHOSAURS
ARCHPRIEST
ARCHPRIESTHOOD
ARCHPRIESTHOODS
ARCHPRIESTS
ARCHPRIESTSHIP
ARCHPRIESTSHIPS
ARCHRIVALS
ARCHSTONES
ARCMINUTES
ARCOGRAPHS
ARCOLOGIES
ARCSECONDS
ARCTANGENT
ARCTANGENTS
ARCTICALLY
ARCTOPHILE
ARCTOPHILES
ARCTOPHILIA
ARCTOPHILIAS
ARCTOPHILIES
ARCTOPHILIST
ARCTOPHILISTS
ARCTOPHILS
ARCTOPHILY
ARCUATIONS
ARCUBALIST
ARCUBALISTS
ARDUOUSNESS
ARDUOUSNESSES
ARECOLINES
AREFACTION
AREFACTIONS
ARENACEOUS
ARENATIONS
ARENICOLOUS
AREOCENTRIC
AREOGRAPHIC
AREOGRAPHIES
AREOGRAPHY
AREOLATION
AREOLATIONS
AREOLOGIES
AREOMETERS
AREOMETRIES
AREOSTYLES
AREOSYSTILE
AREOSYSTILES
ARFVEDSONITE
ARFVEDSONITES
ARGENTIFEROUS
ARGENTINES
ARGENTITES
ARGILLACEOUS
ARGILLIFEROUS
ARGILLITES
ARGILLITIC
ARGONAUTIC
ARGUMENTATION
ARGUMENTATIONS
ARGUMENTATIVE
ARGUMENTATIVELY
ARGUMENTIVE
ARGUMENTUM
ARGUMENTUMS
ARGUTENESS
ARGUTENESSES
ARGYRODITE
ARGYRODITES
ARHATSHIPS
ARHYTHMIAS
ARIBOFLAVINOSES
ARIBOFLAVINOSIS
ARIDNESSES
ARISTOCRACIES
ARISTOCRACY
ARISTOCRAT
ARISTOCRATIC
ARISTOCRATICAL
ARISTOCRATISM
ARISTOCRATISMS
ARISTOCRATS
ARISTOLOCHIA
ARISTOLOCHIAS
ARISTOLOGIES
ARISTOLOGY
ARISTOTLES
ARITHMETIC
ARITHMETICAL
ARITHMETICALLY
ARITHMETICIAN
ARITHMETICIANS
ARITHMETICS
ARITHMOMANIA
ARITHMOMANIAS
ARITHMOMETER
ARITHMOMETERS
ARITHMOPHOBIA
ARITHMOPHOBIAS
ARMADILLOS
ARMAMENTARIA
ARMAMENTARIUM
ARMAMENTARIUMS
ARMATURING
ARMIGEROUS
ARMILLARIA
ARMILLARIAS
ARMIPOTENCE
ARMIPOTENCES
ARMIPOTENT
ARMISTICES
ARMLOCKING
ARMORIALLY
ARMOURLESS
AROMATASES
AROMATHERAPIES
AROMATHERAPIST
AROMATHERAPISTS
AROMATHERAPY
AROMATICALLY
AROMATICITIES
AROMATICITY
AROMATISATION
AROMATISATIONS
AROMATISED
AROMATISES
AROMATISING
AROMATIZATION
AROMATIZATIONS
AROMATIZED
AROMATIZES
AROMATIZING
ARPEGGIATE
ARPEGGIATED
ARPEGGIATES
ARPEGGIATING
ARPEGGIATION
ARPEGGIATIONS
ARPEGGIONE
ARPEGGIONES
ARPILLERAS
ARQUEBUSADE
ARQUEBUSADES
ARQUEBUSES
ARQUEBUSIER
ARQUEBUSIERS
ARRACACHAS
ARRAGONITE
ARRAGONITES
ARRAGONITIC
ARRAIGNERS
ARRAIGNING
ARRAIGNINGS
ARRAIGNMENT
ARRAIGNMENTS
ARRANGEABLE
ARRANGEMENT
ARRANGEMENTS
ARRAYMENTS
ARREARAGES
ARRESTABLE
ARRESTANTS
ARRESTATION
ARRESTATIONS
ARRESTINGLY
ARRESTMENT
ARRESTMENTS
ARRHENOTOKIES
ARRHENOTOKY
ARRHYTHMIA
ARRHYTHMIAS
ARRHYTHMIC
ARRIVANCES
ARRIVANCIES
ARRIVEDERCI
ARRIVISMES
ARRIVISTES
ARROGANCES
ARROGANCIES
ARROGANTLY
ARROGATING
ARROGATION

ARROGATIONS
ARROGATIVE
ARROGATORS
ARRONDISSEMENT
ARRONDISSEMENTS
ARROWGRASS
ARROWGRASSES
ARROWHEADS
ARROWROOTS
ARROWWOODS
ARROWWORMS
ARSENIATES
ARSENICALS
ARSENOPYRITE
ARSENOPYRITES
ARSMETRICK
ARSMETRICKS
ARSPHENAMINE
ARSPHENAMINES
ARTEFACTUAL
ARTEMISIAS
ARTEMISININ
ARTEMISININS
ARTERIALISATION
ARTERIALISE
ARTERIALISED
ARTERIALISES
ARTERIALISING
ARTERIALIZATION
ARTERIALIZE
ARTERIALIZED
ARTERIALIZES
ARTERIALIZING
ARTERIALLY
ARTERIOGRAM
ARTERIOGRAMS
ARTERIOGRAPHIC
ARTERIOGRAPHIES
ARTERIOGRAPHY
ARTERIOLAR
ARTERIOLES
ARTERIOTOMIES
ARTERIOTOMY
ARTERIOVENOUS
ARTERITIDES
ARTERITISES
ARTFULNESS
ARTFULNESSES
ARTHRALGIA
ARTHRALGIAS
ARTHRALGIC
ARTHRECTOMIES
ARTHRECTOMY
ARTHRITICALLY
ARTHRITICS
ARTHRITIDES
ARTHRITISES
ARTHRODESES
ARTHRODESIS
ARTHRODIAE
ARTHRODIAL
ARTHROGRAPHIES
ARTHROGRAPHY
ARTHROMERE
ARTHROMERES
ARTHROMERIC
ARTHROPATHIES
ARTHROPATHY
ARTHROPLASTIES
ARTHROPLASTY
ARTHROPODAL
ARTHROPODAN
ARTHROPODOUS
ARTHROPODS
ARTHROSCOPE
ARTHROSCOPES
ARTHROSCOPIC
ARTHROSCOPIES
ARTHROSCOPY
ARTHROSPORE
ARTHROSPORES
ARTHROSPORIC
ARTHROSPOROUS
ARTICHOKES
ARTICULABLE
ARTICULACIES
ARTICULACY
ARTICULATE
ARTICULATED
ARTICULATELY
ARTICULATENESS
ARTICULATES
ARTICULATING
ARTICULATION
ARTICULATIONS
ARTICULATIVE
ARTICULATOR
ARTICULATORS
ARTICULATORY
ARTIFACTUAL
ARTIFICERS
ARTIFICIAL
ARTIFICIALISE
ARTIFICIALISED
ARTIFICIALISES
ARTIFICIALISING
ARTIFICIALITIES
ARTIFICIALITY
ARTIFICIALIZE
ARTIFICIALIZED
ARTIFICIALIZES
ARTIFICIALIZING
ARTIFICIALLY
ARTIFICIALNESS
ARTILLERIES
ARTILLERIST
ARTILLERISTS
ARTILLERYMAN
ARTILLERYMEN
ARTINESSES
ARTIODACTYL
ARTIODACTYLOUS
ARTIODACTYLS
ARTISANSHIP
ARTISANSHIPS
ARTISTICAL
ARTISTICALLY
ARTISTRIES
ARTLESSNESS
ARTLESSNESSES
ARTMAKINGS
ARTOCARPUS
ARTOCARPUSES
ARTSINESSES
ARUNDINACEOUS
ARVICOLINE
ARYBALLOID
ARYBALLOSES
ARYTAENOID
ARYTAENOIDS
ARYTENOIDAL
ARYTENOIDS
ASAFETIDAS
ASAFOETIDA
ASAFOETIDAS
ASARABACCA
ASARABACCAS
ASBESTIFORM
ASBESTOSES
ASBESTOSIS
ASBESTUSES
ASCARIASES
ASCARIASIS
ASCENDABLE
ASCENDANCE
ASCENDANCES
ASCENDANCIES
ASCENDANCY
ASCENDANTLY
ASCENDANTS
ASCENDENCE
ASCENDENCES
ASCENDENCIES
ASCENDENCY
ASCENDENTS
ASCENDEURS
ASCENDIBLE
ASCENSIONAL
ASCENSIONIST
ASCENSIONISTS
ASCENSIONS
ASCERTAINABLE
ASCERTAINABLY
ASCERTAINED
ASCERTAINING
ASCERTAINMENT
ASCERTAINMENTS
ASCERTAINS
ASCETICALLY
ASCETICISM
ASCETICISMS
ASCITITIOUS
ASCLEPIADACEOUS
ASCLEPIADS
ASCLEPIASES
ASCOCARPIC
ASCOGONIUM
ASCOMYCETE
ASCOMYCETES
ASCOMYCETOUS
ASCORBATES
ASCOSPORES
ASCOSPORIC
ASCRIBABLE
ASCRIPTION
ASCRIPTIONS
ASCRIPTIVE
ASEPTICALLY
ASEPTICISE
ASEPTICISED
ASEPTICISES
ASEPTICISING
ASEPTICISM
ASEPTICISMS
ASEPTICIZE
ASEPTICIZED
ASEPTICIZES
ASEPTICIZING
ASEXUALITIES
ASEXUALITY
ASHAMEDNESS
ASHAMEDNESSES
ASHINESSES
ASHLARINGS
ASHLERINGS
ASHRAMITES
ASININITIES
ASKEWNESSES
ASPARAGINASE
ASPARAGINASES
ASPARAGINE
ASPARAGINES
ASPARAGUSES
ASPARTAMES
ASPARTATES
ASPECTABLE
ASPERATING
ASPERGATION
ASPERGATIONS
ASPERGILLA
ASPERGILLI
ASPERGILLOSES
ASPERGILLOSIS
ASPERGILLS
ASPERGILLUM
ASPERGILLUMS
ASPERGILLUS
ASPERITIES
ASPERSIONS
ASPERSIVELY

ASPERSOIRS
ASPERSORIA
ASPERSORIES
ASPERSORIUM
ASPERSORIUMS
ASPHALTERS
ASPHALTING
ASPHALTITE
ASPHALTITES
ASPHALTUMS
ASPHERICAL
ASPHETERISE
ASPHETERISED
ASPHETERISES
ASPHETERISING
ASPHETERISM
ASPHETERISMS
ASPHETERIZE
ASPHETERIZED
ASPHETERIZES
ASPHETERIZING
ASPHYXIANT
ASPHYXIANTS
ASPHYXIATE
ASPHYXIATED
ASPHYXIATES
ASPHYXIATING
ASPHYXIATION
ASPHYXIATIONS
ASPHYXIATOR
ASPHYXIATORS
ASPHYXYING
ASPIDISTRA
ASPIDISTRAS
ASPIRATING
ASPIRATION
ASPIRATIONAL
ASPIRATIONS
ASPIRATORS
ASPIRATORY
ASPIRINGLY
ASPIRINGNESS
ASPIRINGNESSES
ASPLANCHNIC
ASPLENIUMS
ASPORTATION
ASPORTATIONS
ASSAFETIDA
ASSAFETIDAS
ASSAFOETIDA
ASSAFOETIDAS
ASSAGAIING
ASSAILABLE
ASSAILANTS
ASSAILMENT
ASSAILMENTS
ASSASSINATE
ASSASSINATED
ASSASSINATES
ASSASSINATING
ASSASSINATION
ASSASSINATIONS
ASSASSINATOR
ASSASSINATORS
ASSAULTERS
ASSAULTING
ASSAULTIVE
ASSAULTIVELY
ASSAULTIVENESS
ASSEGAAIED
ASSEGAAIING
ASSEGAIING
ASSEMBLAGE
ASSEMBLAGES
ASSEMBLAGIST
ASSEMBLAGISTS
ASSEMBLANCE
ASSEMBLANCES
ASSEMBLAUNCE
ASSEMBLAUNCES
ASSEMBLERS
ASSEMBLIES
ASSEMBLING
ASSEMBLYMAN
ASSEMBLYMEN
ASSEMBLYWOMAN
ASSEMBLYWOMEN
ASSENTANEOUS
ASSENTATION
ASSENTATIONS
ASSENTATOR
ASSENTATORS
ASSENTIENT
ASSENTIENTS
ASSENTINGLY
ASSENTIVENESS
ASSENTIVENESSES
ASSERTABLE
ASSERTEDLY
ASSERTIBLE
ASSERTIONS
ASSERTIVELY
ASSERTIVENESS
ASSERTIVENESSES
ASSERTORIC
ASSESSABLE
ASSESSMENT
ASSESSMENTS
ASSESSORIAL
ASSESSORSHIP
ASSESSORSHIPS
ASSEVERATE
ASSEVERATED
ASSEVERATES
ASSEVERATING
ASSEVERATINGLY
ASSEVERATION
ASSEVERATIONS
ASSEVERATIVE
ASSEVERING
ASSIBILATE
ASSIBILATED
ASSIBILATES
ASSIBILATING
ASSIBILATION
ASSIBILATIONS
ASSIDUITIES
ASSIDUOUSLY
ASSIDUOUSNESS
ASSIDUOUSNESSES
ASSIGNABILITIES
ASSIGNABILITY
ASSIGNABLE
ASSIGNABLY
ASSIGNATION
ASSIGNATIONS
ASSIGNMENT
ASSIGNMENTS
ASSIMILABILITY
ASSIMILABLE
ASSIMILABLY
ASSIMILATE
ASSIMILATED
ASSIMILATES
ASSIMILATING
ASSIMILATION
ASSIMILATIONISM
ASSIMILATIONIST
ASSIMILATIONS
ASSIMILATIVE
ASSIMILATIVELY
ASSIMILATOR
ASSIMILATORS
ASSIMILATORY
ASSISTANCE
ASSISTANCES
ASSISTANTS
ASSISTANTSHIP
ASSISTANTSHIPS
ASSOCIABILITIES
ASSOCIABILITY
ASSOCIABLE
ASSOCIATED
ASSOCIATES
ASSOCIATESHIP
ASSOCIATESHIPS
ASSOCIATING
ASSOCIATION
ASSOCIATIONAL
ASSOCIATIONISM
ASSOCIATIONISMS
ASSOCIATIONIST
ASSOCIATIONISTS
ASSOCIATIONS
ASSOCIATIVE
ASSOCIATIVELY
ASSOCIATIVITIES
ASSOCIATIVITY
ASSOCIATOR
ASSOCIATORS
ASSOCIATORY
ASSOILMENT
ASSOILMENTS
ASSOILZIED
ASSOILZIEING
ASSOILZIES
ASSONANCES
ASSONANTAL
ASSONATING
ASSORTATIVE
ASSORTATIVELY
ASSORTEDNESS
ASSORTEDNESSES
ASSORTMENT
ASSORTMENTS
ASSUAGEMENT
ASSUAGEMENTS
ASSUAGINGS
ASSUBJUGATE
ASSUBJUGATED
ASSUBJUGATES
ASSUBJUGATING
ASSUEFACTION
ASSUEFACTIONS
ASSUETUDES
ASSUMABILITIES
ASSUMABILITY
ASSUMINGLY
ASSUMPSITS
ASSUMPTION
ASSUMPTIONS
ASSUMPTIVE
ASSUMPTIVELY
ASSURANCES
ASSUREDNESS
ASSUREDNESSES
ASSURGENCIES
ASSURGENCY
ASSYTHMENT
ASSYTHMENTS
ASTACOLOGICAL
ASTACOLOGIES
ASTACOLOGIST
ASTACOLOGISTS
ASTACOLOGY
ASTARBOARD
ASTATICALLY
ASTATICISM
ASTATICISMS
ASTEREOGNOSES
ASTEREOGNOSIS
ASTERIATED
ASTERIDIAN
ASTERIDIANS
ASTERISKED
ASTERISKING
ASTERISKLESS
ASTEROIDAL
ASTEROIDEAN
ASTEROIDEANS

ASTHENOPIA
ASTHENOPIAS
ASTHENOPIC
ASTHENOSPHERE
ASTHENOSPHERES
ASTHENOSPHERIC
ASTHMATICAL
ASTHMATICALLY
ASTHMATICS
ASTIGMATIC
ASTIGMATICALLY
ASTIGMATICS
ASTIGMATISM
ASTIGMATISMS
ASTOMATOUS
ASTONISHED
ASTONISHES
ASTONISHING
ASTONISHINGLY
ASTONISHMENT
ASTONISHMENTS
ASTOUNDING
ASTOUNDINGLY
ASTOUNDMENT
ASTOUNDMENTS
ASTRACHANS
ASTRAGALUS
ASTRAKHANS
ASTRANTIAS
ASTRAPHOBIA
ASTRAPHOBIAS
ASTRAPHOBIC
ASTRAPOPHOBIA
ASTRAPOPHOBIAS
ASTRICTING
ASTRICTION
ASTRICTIONS
ASTRICTIVE
ASTRICTIVELY
ASTRINGENCE
ASTRINGENCES
ASTRINGENCIES
ASTRINGENCY
ASTRINGENT
ASTRINGENTLY
ASTRINGENTS
ASTRINGERS
ASTRINGING
ASTROBIOLOGIES
ASTROBIOLOGIST
ASTROBIOLOGISTS
ASTROBIOLOGY
ASTROBLEME
ASTROBLEMES
ASTROBOTANIES
ASTROBOTANY
ASTROCHEMISTRY
ASTROCOMPASS
ASTROCOMPASSES
ASTROCYTES
ASTROCYTIC
ASTROCYTOMA
ASTROCYTOMAS
ASTROCYTOMATA
ASTRODOMES
ASTRODYNAMICIST
ASTRODYNAMICS
ASTROFELLS
ASTROGEOLOGIES
ASTROGEOLOGIST
ASTROGEOLOGISTS
ASTROGEOLOGY
ASTROHATCH
ASTROHATCHES
ASTROLABES
ASTROLATRIES
ASTROLATRY
ASTROLOGER
ASTROLOGERS
ASTROLOGIC
ASTROLOGICAL
ASTROLOGICALLY
ASTROLOGIES
ASTROLOGIST
ASTROLOGISTS
ASTROMETRIC
ASTROMETRICAL
ASTROMETRIES
ASTROMETRY
ASTRONAUTIC
ASTRONAUTICAL
ASTRONAUTICALLY
ASTRONAUTICS
ASTRONAUTS
ASTRONAVIGATION
ASTRONAVIGATOR
ASTRONAVIGATORS
ASTRONOMER
ASTRONOMERS
ASTRONOMIC
ASTRONOMICAL
ASTRONOMICALLY
ASTRONOMIES
ASTRONOMISE
ASTRONOMISED
ASTRONOMISES
ASTRONOMISING
ASTRONOMIZE
ASTRONOMIZED
ASTRONOMIZES
ASTRONOMIZING
ASTROPHELS
ASTROPHOBIA
ASTROPHOBIAS
ASTROPHOBIC
ASTROPHOTOGRAPH
ASTROPHYSICAL
ASTROPHYSICALLY
ASTROPHYSICIST
ASTROPHYSICISTS
ASTROPHYSICS
ASTROSPHERE
ASTROSPHERES
ASTROTOURISM
ASTROTOURISMS
ASTROTOURIST
ASTROTOURISTS
ASTROTURFER
ASTROTURFERS
ASTROTURFING
ASTROTURFINGS
ASTUCIOUSLY
ASTUCITIES
ASTUTENESS
ASTUTENESSES
ASYMMETRIC
ASYMMETRICAL
ASYMMETRICALLY
ASYMMETRIES
ASYMPTOMATIC
ASYMPTOTES
ASYMPTOTIC
ASYMPTOTICAL
ASYMPTOTICALLY
ASYNARTETE
ASYNARTETES
ASYNARTETIC
ASYNCHRONIES
ASYNCHRONISM
ASYNCHRONISMS
ASYNCHRONOUS
ASYNCHRONOUSLY
ASYNCHRONY
ASYNDETICALLY
ASYNDETONS
ASYNERGIAS
ASYNERGIES
ASYNTACTIC
ASYSTOLISM
ASYSTOLISMS
ATACAMITES
ATARACTICS
ATAVISTICALLY
ATCHIEVING
ATELECTASES
ATELECTASIS
ATELECTATIC
ATELEIOSES
ATELEIOSIS
ATHANASIES
ATHEISTICAL
ATHEISTICALLY
ATHEMATICALLY
ATHENAEUMS
ATHEOLOGICAL
ATHEOLOGIES
ATHEORETICAL
ATHERMANCIES
ATHERMANCY
ATHERMANOUS
ATHEROGENESES
ATHEROGENESIS
ATHEROGENIC
ATHEROMATA
ATHEROMATOUS
ATHEROSCLEROSES
ATHEROSCLEROSIS
ATHEROSCLEROTIC
ATHETISING
ATHETIZING
ATHLEISURE
ATHLEISURES
ATHLETICALLY
ATHLETICISM
ATHLETICISMS
ATHROCYTES
ATHROCYTOSES
ATHROCYTOSIS
ATHWARTSHIP
ATHWARTSHIPS
ATMOLOGIES
ATMOLOGIST
ATMOLOGISTS
ATMOLYSING
ATMOLYZING
ATMOMETERS
ATMOMETRIES
ATMOSPHERE
ATMOSPHERED
ATMOSPHERES
ATMOSPHERIC
ATMOSPHERICAL
ATMOSPHERICALLY
ATMOSPHERICS
ATOMICALLY
ATOMICITIES
ATOMISATION
ATOMISATIONS
ATOMISTICAL
ATOMISTICALLY
ATOMIZATION
ATOMIZATIONS
ATONALISMS
ATONALISTS
ATONALITIES
ATONEMENTS
ATONICITIES
ATORVASTATIN
ATORVASTATINS
ATRABILIAR
ATRABILIOUS
ATRABILIOUSNESS
ATRACURIUM
ATRACURIUMS
ATRAMENTAL
ATRAMENTOUS
ATROCIOUSLY
ATROCIOUSNESS
ATROCIOUSNESSES
ATROCITIES

A

ATROPHYING
ATTACHABLE
ATTACHMENT
ATTACHMENTS
ATTACKABLE
ATTAINABILITIES
ATTAINABILITY
ATTAINABLE
ATTAINABLENESS
ATTAINDERS
ATTAINMENT
ATTAINMENTS
ATTAINTING
ATTAINTMENT
ATTAINTMENTS
ATTAINTURE
ATTAINTURES
ATTEMPERED
ATTEMPERING
ATTEMPERMENT
ATTEMPERMENTS
ATTEMPTABILITY
ATTEMPTABLE
ATTEMPTERS
ATTEMPTING
ATTENDANCE
ATTENDANCES
ATTENDANCIES
ATTENDANCY
ATTENDANTS
ATTENDEMENT
ATTENDEMENTS
ATTENDINGS
ATTENDMENT
ATTENDMENTS
ATTENTIONAL
ATTENTIONS
ATTENTIVELY
ATTENTIVENESS
ATTENTIVENESSES
ATTENUANTS
ATTENUATED
ATTENUATES
ATTENUATING
ATTENUATION
ATTENUATIONS
ATTENUATOR
ATTENUATORS
ATTESTABLE
ATTESTANTS
ATTESTATION
ATTESTATIONS
ATTESTATIVE
ATTESTATOR
ATTESTATORS
ATTICISING
ATTICIZING
ATTIREMENT
ATTIREMENTS
ATTITUDINAL
ATTITUDINALLY
ATTITUDINARIAN
ATTITUDINARIANS
ATTITUDINISE
ATTITUDINISED
ATTITUDINISER
ATTITUDINISERS
ATTITUDINISES
ATTITUDINISING
ATTITUDINISINGS
ATTITUDINIZE
ATTITUDINIZED
ATTITUDINIZER
ATTITUDINIZERS
ATTITUDINIZES
ATTITUDINIZING
ATTITUDINIZINGS
ATTOLASERS
ATTOLLENTS
ATTOMETERS
ATTOMETRES
ATTOPHYSICS
ATTORNEYDOM
ATTORNEYDOMS
ATTORNEYED
ATTORNEYING
ATTORNEYISM
ATTORNEYISMS
ATTORNEYSHIP
ATTORNEYSHIPS
ATTORNMENT
ATTORNMENTS
ATTOSECOND
ATTOSECONDS
ATTOTESLAS
ATTRACTABLE
ATTRACTANCE
ATTRACTANCES
ATTRACTANCIES
ATTRACTANCY
ATTRACTANT
ATTRACTANTS
ATTRACTERS
ATTRACTING
ATTRACTINGLY
ATTRACTION
ATTRACTIONS
ATTRACTIVE
ATTRACTIVELY
ATTRACTIVENESS
ATTRACTORS
ATTRAHENTS
ATTRAPPING
ATTRIBUTABLE
ATTRIBUTED
ATTRIBUTER
ATTRIBUTERS
ATTRIBUTES
ATTRIBUTING
ATTRIBUTION
ATTRIBUTIONAL
ATTRIBUTIONS
ATTRIBUTIVE
ATTRIBUTIVELY
ATTRIBUTIVENESS
ATTRIBUTIVES
ATTRIBUTOR
ATTRIBUTORS
ATTRISTING
ATTRITIONAL
ATTRITIONS
ATTRITTING
ATTUITIONAL
ATTUITIONS
ATTUITIVELY
ATTUNEMENT
ATTUNEMENTS
ATYPICALITIES
ATYPICALITY
ATYPICALLY
AUBERGINES
AUBERGISTE
AUBERGISTES
AUBRIETIAS
AUCTIONARY
AUCTIONEER
AUCTIONEERED
AUCTIONEERING
AUCTIONEERS
AUCTIONING
AUDACIOUSLY
AUDACIOUSNESS
AUDACIOUSNESSES
AUDACITIES
AUDIBILITIES
AUDIBILITY
AUDIBLENESS
AUDIBLENESSES
AUDIENCIAS
AUDIOBOOKS
AUDIOCASSETTE
AUDIOCASSETTES
AUDIOGENIC
AUDIOGRAMS
AUDIOGRAPH
AUDIOGRAPHS
AUDIOLOGIC
AUDIOLOGICAL
AUDIOLOGICALLY
AUDIOLOGIES
AUDIOLOGIST
AUDIOLOGISTS
AUDIOMETER
AUDIOMETERS
AUDIOMETRIC
AUDIOMETRICALLY
AUDIOMETRICIAN
AUDIOMETRICIANS
AUDIOMETRIES
AUDIOMETRIST
AUDIOMETRISTS
AUDIOMETRY
AUDIOPHILE
AUDIOPHILES
AUDIOPHILS
AUDIOTAPED
AUDIOTAPES
AUDIOTAPING
AUDIOTYPING
AUDIOTYPINGS
AUDIOTYPIST
AUDIOTYPISTS
AUDIOVISUAL
AUDIOVISUALLY
AUDIOVISUALS
AUDIPHONES
AUDITIONED
AUDITIONER
AUDITIONERS
AUDITIONING
AUDITORIAL
AUDITORIES
AUDITORILY
AUDITORIUM
AUDITORIUMS
AUDITORSHIP
AUDITORSHIPS
AUDITRESSES
AUGMENTABLE
AUGMENTATION
AUGMENTATIONS
AUGMENTATIVE
AUGMENTATIVELY
AUGMENTATIVES
AUGMENTERS
AUGMENTING
AUGMENTORS
AUGURSHIPS
AUGUSTNESS
AUGUSTNESSES
AURALITIES
AUREATENESS
AUREATENESSES
AURICULARLY
AURICULARS
AURICULATE
AURICULATED
AURICULATELY
AURIFEROUS
AURISCOPES
AURISCOPIC
AUSCULTATE
AUSCULTATED
AUSCULTATES
AUSCULTATING
AUSCULTATION
AUSCULTATIONS
AUSCULTATIVE
AUSCULTATOR
AUSCULTATORS

AUSCULTATORY
AUSFORMING
AUSFORMINGS
AUSLANDERS
AUSPICATED
AUSPICATES
AUSPICATING
AUSPICIOUS
AUSPICIOUSLY
AUSPICIOUSNESS
AUSTENITES
AUSTENITIC
AUSTERENESS
AUSTERENESSES
AUSTERITIES
AUSTRALITE
AUSTRALITES
AUSTRINGER
AUSTRINGERS
AUTARCHICAL
AUTARCHIES
AUTARCHIST
AUTARCHISTS
AUTARKICAL
AUTARKISTS
AUTECOLOGIC
AUTECOLOGICAL
AUTECOLOGIES
AUTECOLOGY
AUTEURISMS
AUTEURISTS
AUTHENTICAL
AUTHENTICALLY
AUTHENTICATE
AUTHENTICATED
AUTHENTICATES
AUTHENTICATING
AUTHENTICATION
AUTHENTICATIONS
AUTHENTICATOR
AUTHENTICATORS
AUTHENTICITIES
AUTHENTICITY
AUTHIGENIC
AUTHORCRAFT
AUTHORCRAFTS
AUTHORESSES
AUTHORINGS
AUTHORISABLE
AUTHORISATION
AUTHORISATIONS
AUTHORISED
AUTHORISER
AUTHORISERS
AUTHORISES
AUTHORISING
AUTHORISMS
AUTHORITARIAN
AUTHORITARIANS
AUTHORITATIVE
AUTHORITATIVELY
AUTHORITIES
AUTHORIZABLE
AUTHORIZATION
AUTHORIZATIONS
AUTHORIZED
AUTHORIZER
AUTHORIZERS
AUTHORIZES
AUTHORIZING
AUTHORLESS
AUTHORSHIP
AUTHORSHIPS
AUTISTICALLY
AUTOALLOGAMIES
AUTOALLOGAMY
AUTOANTIBODIES
AUTOANTIBODY
AUTOBAHNEN
AUTOBIOGRAPHER
AUTOBIOGRAPHERS
AUTOBIOGRAPHIC
AUTOBIOGRAPHIES
AUTOBIOGRAPHY
AUTOBODIES
AUTOBUSSES
AUTOCATALYSE
AUTOCATALYSED
AUTOCATALYSES
AUTOCATALYSING
AUTOCATALYSIS
AUTOCATALYTIC
AUTOCATALYZE
AUTOCATALYZED
AUTOCATALYZES
AUTOCATALYZING
AUTOCEPHALIC
AUTOCEPHALIES
AUTOCEPHALOUS
AUTOCEPHALY
AUTOCHANGER
AUTOCHANGERS
AUTOCHTHON
AUTOCHTHONAL
AUTOCHTHONES
AUTOCHTHONIC
AUTOCHTHONIES
AUTOCHTHONISM
AUTOCHTHONISMS
AUTOCHTHONOUS
AUTOCHTHONOUSLY
AUTOCHTHONS
AUTOCHTHONY
AUTOCLAVED
AUTOCLAVES
AUTOCLAVING
AUTOCOMPLETE
AUTOCOMPLETES
AUTOCOPROPHAGY
AUTOCORRECT
AUTOCORRECTS
AUTOCORRELATION
AUTOCRACIES
AUTOCRATIC
AUTOCRATICAL
AUTOCRATICALLY
AUTOCRIMES
AUTOCRITIQUE
AUTOCRITIQUES
AUTOCROSSES
AUTOCUTIES
AUTOCYCLES
AUTODESTRUCT
AUTODESTRUCTED
AUTODESTRUCTING
AUTODESTRUCTIVE
AUTODESTRUCTS
AUTODIALED
AUTODIALING
AUTODIALLED
AUTODIALLING
AUTODIDACT
AUTODIDACTIC
AUTODIDACTICISM
AUTODIDACTS
AUTODROMES
AUTOECIOUS
AUTOECIOUSLY
AUTOECISMS
AUTOEROTIC
AUTOEROTICISM
AUTOEROTICISMS
AUTOEROTISM
AUTOEROTISMS
AUTOEXPOSURE
AUTOEXPOSURES
AUTOFLARES
AUTOFOCUSES
AUTOGAMIES
AUTOGAMOUS
AUTOGENESES
AUTOGENESIS
AUTOGENETIC
AUTOGENICS
AUTOGENIES
AUTOGENOUS
AUTOGENOUSLY
AUTOGRAFTED
AUTOGRAFTING
AUTOGRAFTS
AUTOGRAPHED
AUTOGRAPHIC
AUTOGRAPHICAL
AUTOGRAPHICALLY
AUTOGRAPHIES
AUTOGRAPHING
AUTOGRAPHS
AUTOGRAPHY
AUTOGRAVURE
AUTOGRAVURES
AUTOGUIDES
AUTOHYPNOSES
AUTOHYPNOSIS
AUTOHYPNOTIC
AUTOIMMUNE
AUTOIMMUNITIES
AUTOIMMUNITY
AUTOINFECTION
AUTOINFECTIONS
AUTOINOCULATION
AUTOIONISATION
AUTOIONISATIONS
AUTOIONIZATION
AUTOIONIZATIONS
AUTOJUMBLE
AUTOJUMBLES
AUTOKINESES
AUTOKINESIS
AUTOKINETIC
AUTOLATRIES
AUTOLOADED
AUTOLOADING
AUTOLOGIES
AUTOLOGOUS
AUTOLYSATE
AUTOLYSATES
AUTOLYSING
AUTOLYSINS
AUTOLYZATE
AUTOLYZATES
AUTOLYZING
AUTOMAGICALLY
AUTOMAKERS
AUTOMATABLE
AUTOMATICAL
AUTOMATICALLY
AUTOMATICITIES
AUTOMATICITY
AUTOMATICS
AUTOMATING
AUTOMATION
AUTOMATIONS
AUTOMATISATION
AUTOMATISATIONS
AUTOMATISE
AUTOMATISED
AUTOMATISES
AUTOMATISING
AUTOMATISM
AUTOMATISMS
AUTOMATIST
AUTOMATISTS
AUTOMATIZATION
AUTOMATIZATIONS
AUTOMATIZE
AUTOMATIZED
AUTOMATIZES
AUTOMATIZING
AUTOMATONS
AUTOMATOUS

A

AUTOMETERS
AUTOMOBILE
AUTOMOBILED
AUTOMOBILES
AUTOMOBILIA
AUTOMOBILING
AUTOMOBILISM
AUTOMOBILISMS
AUTOMOBILIST
AUTOMOBILISTS
AUTOMOBILITIES
AUTOMOBILITY
AUTOMORPHIC
AUTOMORPHICALLY
AUTOMORPHISM
AUTOMORPHISMS
AUTOMOTIVE
AUTONOMICAL
AUTONOMICALLY
AUTONOMICS
AUTONOMIES
AUTONOMIST
AUTONOMISTS
AUTONOMOUS
AUTONOMOUSLY
AUTONYMOUS
AUTOPHAGIA
AUTOPHAGIAS
AUTOPHAGIES
AUTOPHAGOUS
AUTOPHANOUS
AUTOPHOBIA
AUTOPHOBIAS
AUTOPHOBIES
AUTOPHONIES
AUTOPHYTES
AUTOPHYTIC
AUTOPHYTICALLY
AUTOPILOTS
AUTOPISTAS
AUTOPLASTIC
AUTOPLASTIES
AUTOPLASTY
AUTOPOINTS
AUTOPOLYPLOID
AUTOPOLYPLOIDS
AUTOPOLYPLOIDY
AUTOPSISTS
AUTOPSYING
AUTOPTICAL
AUTOPTICALLY
AUTORADIOGRAM
AUTORADIOGRAMS
AUTORADIOGRAPH
AUTORADIOGRAPHS
AUTORADIOGRAPHY
AUTOREPLIES
AUTOREVERSE
AUTOREVERSES
AUTORICKSHAW
AUTORICKSHAWS
AUTOROTATE
AUTOROTATED
AUTOROTATES
AUTOROTATING
AUTOROTATION
AUTOROTATIONS
AUTOROUTES
AUTOSAVING
AUTOSCHEDIASM
AUTOSCHEDIASMS
AUTOSCHEDIASTIC
AUTOSCHEDIAZE
AUTOSCHEDIAZED
AUTOSCHEDIAZES
AUTOSCHEDIAZING
AUTOSCOPIC
AUTOSCOPIES
AUTOSEXING
AUTOSEXINGS
AUTOSOMALLY
AUTOSPORES
AUTOSPORTS
AUTOSTABILITIES
AUTOSTABILITY
AUTOSTRADA
AUTOSTRADAS
AUTOSTRADE
AUTOSUGGEST
AUTOSUGGESTED
AUTOSUGGESTING
AUTOSUGGESTION
AUTOSUGGESTIONS
AUTOSUGGESTIVE
AUTOSUGGESTS
AUTOTELLER
AUTOTELLERS
AUTOTETRAPLOID
AUTOTETRAPLOIDS
AUTOTETRAPLOIDY
AUTOTHEISM
AUTOTHEISMS
AUTOTHEIST
AUTOTHEISTS
AUTOTIMERS
AUTOTOMIES
AUTOTOMISE
AUTOTOMISED
AUTOTOMISES
AUTOTOMISING
AUTOTOMIZE
AUTOTOMIZED
AUTOTOMIZES
AUTOTOMIZING
AUTOTOMOUS
AUTOTOXAEMIA
AUTOTOXAEMIAS
AUTOTOXEMIA
AUTOTOXEMIAS
AUTOTOXINS
AUTOTRANSFORMER
AUTOTRANSFUSION
AUTOTROPHIC
AUTOTROPHICALLY
AUTOTROPHIES
AUTOTROPHS
AUTOTROPHY
AUTOTYPIES
AUTOTYPING
AUTOTYPOGRAPHY
AUTOWINDER
AUTOWINDERS
AUTOWORKER
AUTOWORKERS
AUTOXIDATION
AUTOXIDATIONS
AUTUMNALLY
AUTUMNIEST
AUXANOMETER
AUXANOMETERS
AUXILIARIES
AUXOCHROME
AUXOCHROMES
AUXOMETERS
AUXOSPORES
AUXOTROPHIC
AUXOTROPHIES
AUXOTROPHS
AUXOTROPHY
AVAILABILITIES
AVAILABILITY
AVAILABLENESS
AVAILABLENESSES
AVAILINGLY
AVALANCHED
AVALANCHES
AVALANCHING
AVALEMENTS
AVANTURINE
AVANTURINES
AVARICIOUS
AVARICIOUSLY
AVARICIOUSNESS
AVASCULARITIES
AVASCULARITY
AVENACEOUS
AVENGEMENT
AVENGEMENTS
AVENGERESS
AVENGERESSES
AVENTAILES
AVENTURINE
AVENTURINES
AVENTURINS
AVERAGENESS
AVERAGENESSES
AVERAGINGS
AVERRUNCATE
AVERRUNCATED
AVERRUNCATES
AVERRUNCATING
AVERRUNCATION
AVERRUNCATIONS
AVERRUNCATOR
AVERRUNCATORS
AVERSENESS
AVERSENESSES
AVERSIVELY
AVERSIVENESS
AVERSIVENESSES
AVERTIMENT
AVERTIMENTS
AVGOLEMONO
AVGOLEMONOS
AVIANISING
AVIANIZING
AVIATRESSES
AVIATRICES
AVIATRIXES
AVICULTURE
AVICULTURES
AVICULTURIST
AVICULTURISTS
AVIDNESSES
AVISANDUMS
AVISEMENTS
AVITAMINOSES
AVITAMINOSIS
AVITAMINOTIC
AVIZANDUMS
AVOCATIONAL
AVOCATIONALLY
AVOCATIONS
AVOIDANCES
AVOIRDUPOIS
AVOIRDUPOISES
AVOPARCINS
AVOUCHABLE
AVOUCHMENT
AVOUCHMENTS
AVOUTERERS
AVOWABLENESS
AVOWABLENESSES
AVUNCULARITIES
AVUNCULARITY
AVUNCULARLY
AVUNCULATE
AVUNCULATES
AVVOGADORE
AVVOGADORES
AWAKENINGS
AWARENESSES
AWAYNESSES
AWELESSNESS
AWELESSNESSES
AWESOMENESS
AWESOMENESSES
AWESTRICKEN
AWESTRIKES
AWESTRIKING

AWFULNESSES
AWKWARDEST
AWKWARDISH
AWKWARDNESS
AWKWARDNESSES
AXENICALLY
AXEROPHTHOL
AXEROPHTHOLS
AXIALITIES
AXILLARIES
AXINOMANCIES
AXINOMANCY
AXIOLOGICAL
AXIOLOGICALLY
AXIOLOGIES
AXIOLOGIST
AXIOLOGISTS
AXIOMATICAL
AXIOMATICALLY
AXIOMATICS
AXIOMATISATION
AXIOMATISATIONS
AXIOMATISE
AXIOMATISED
AXIOMATISES
AXIOMATISING
AXIOMATIZATION
AXIOMATIZATIONS
AXIOMATIZE
AXIOMATIZED
AXIOMATIZES
AXIOMATIZING
AXISYMMETRIC
AXISYMMETRICAL
AXISYMMETRIES
AXISYMMETRY
AXOLEMMATA
AXONOMETRIC
AXONOMETRIES
AXONOMETRY
AXOPLASMIC
AYAHUASCAS
AYAHUASCOS
AYATOLLAHS
AYUNTAMIENTO
AYUNTAMIENTOS
AYURVEDICS
AZATHIOPRINE
AZATHIOPRINES
AZEDARACHS
AZEOTROPES
AZEOTROPIC
AZEOTROPIES
AZIDOTHYMIDINE
AZIDOTHYMIDINES
AZIMUTHALLY
AZOBENZENE
AZOBENZENES
AZOOSPERMIA
AZOOSPERMIAS
AZOOSPERMIC
AZOTAEMIAS
AZOTOBACTER
AZOTOBACTERS
AZYGOSPORE
AZYGOSPORES

B

BAALEBATIM
BABACOOTES
BABBITRIES
BABBITTING
BABBITTRIES
BABBLATIVE
BABBLEMENT
BABBLEMENTS
BABELESQUE
BABESIASES
BABESIASIS
BABESIOSES
BABESIOSIS
BABINGTONITE
BABINGTONITES
BABIROUSSA
BABIROUSSAS
BABIRUSSAS
BABOONERIES
BABYCCINOS
BABYDADDIES
BABYPROOFED
BABYPROOFING
BABYPROOFS
BABYSITTING
BACCALAUREAN
BACCALAUREATE
BACCALAUREATES
BACCHANALIA
BACCHANALIAN
BACCHANALIANISM
BACCHANALIANS
BACCHANALS
BACCHANTES
BACCIFEROUS
BACCIVOROUS
BACHARACHS
BACHELORDOM
BACHELORDOMS
BACHELORETTE
BACHELORETTES
BACHELORHOOD
BACHELORHOODS
BACHELORISM
BACHELORISMS
BACHELORSHIP
BACHELORSHIPS
BACILLAEMIA
BACILLAEMIAS
BACILLEMIA
BACILLEMIAS
BACILLICIDE
BACILLICIDES
BACILLIFORM
BACILLURIA
BACILLURIAS
BACITRACIN
BACITRACINS
BACKACTERS
BACKBENCHER
BACKBENCHERS
BACKBENCHES
BACKBITERS
BACKBITING
BACKBITINGS
BACKBITTEN
BACKBLOCKER
BACKBLOCKERS
BACKBLOCKS
BACKBOARDS
BACKBONELESS
BACKBREAKER
BACKBREAKERS
BACKBREAKING
BACKBURNED
BACKBURNING
BACKCASTING
BACKCHANNEL
BACKCHANNELS
BACKCHATTED
BACKCHATTING
BACKCHECKED
BACKCHECKING
BACKCHECKS
BACKCLOTHS
BACKCOMBED
BACKCOMBING
BACKCOUNTRIES
BACKCOUNTRY
BACKCOURTMAN
BACKCOURTMEN
BACKCOURTS
BACKCROSSED
BACKCROSSES
BACKCROSSING
BACKDATING
BACKDRAFTS
BACKDRAUGHT
BACKDRAUGHTS
BACKDROPPED
BACKDROPPING
BACKFIELDS
BACKFILLED
BACKFILLING
BACKFILLINGS
BACKFIRING
BACKFISCHES
BACKFITTED
BACKFITTING
BACKFITTINGS
BACKFLIPPED
BACKFLIPPING
BACKFLIPPINGS
BACKGAMMON
BACKGAMMONED
BACKGAMMONING
BACKGAMMONS
BACKGROUND
BACKGROUNDED
BACKGROUNDER
BACKGROUNDERS
BACKGROUNDING
BACKGROUNDS
BACKHANDED
BACKHANDEDLY
BACKHANDEDNESS
BACKHANDER
BACKHANDERS
BACKHANDING
BACKHAULED
BACKHAULING
BACKHOEING
BACKHOUSES
BACKLASHED
BACKLASHER
BACKLASHERS
BACKLASHES
BACKLASHING
BACKLIGHTED
BACKLIGHTING
BACKLIGHTS
BACKLINERS
BACKLISTED
BACKLISTING
BACKLOADED
BACKLOADING
BACKLOGGED
BACKLOGGING
BACKMARKER
BACKMARKERS
BACKPACKED
BACKPACKER
BACKPACKERS
BACKPACKING
BACKPACKINGS
BACKPEDALED
BACKPEDALING
BACKPEDALLED
BACKPEDALLING
BACKPEDALS
BACKPIECES
BACKPLANES
BACKPLATES
BACKRONYMS
BACKRUSHES
BACKSCATTER
BACKSCATTERED
BACKSCATTERING
BACKSCATTERINGS
BACKSCATTERS
BACKSCRATCH
BACKSCRATCHED
BACKSCRATCHER
BACKSCRATCHERS
BACKSCRATCHES
BACKSCRATCHING
BACKSCRATCHINGS
BACKSETTING
BACKSHEESH
BACKSHEESHED
BACKSHEESHES
BACKSHEESHING
BACKSHISHED
BACKSHISHES
BACKSHISHING
BACKSHORES
BACKSIGHTS
BACKSLAPPED
BACKSLAPPER
BACKSLAPPERS
BACKSLAPPING
BACKSLASHES
BACKSLIDDEN
BACKSLIDER
BACKSLIDERS
BACKSLIDES
BACKSLIDING
BACKSLIDINGS
BACKSPACED
BACKSPACER
BACKSPACERS
BACKSPACES
BACKSPACING
BACKSPEERED
BACKSPEERING
BACKSPEERS
BACKSPEIRED
BACKSPEIRING
BACKSPEIRS
BACKSPLASH

BACKSPLASHES
BACKSPLITS
BACKSTABBED
BACKSTABBER
BACKSTABBERS
BACKSTABBING
BACKSTABBINGS
BACKSTAGES
BACKSTAIRS
BACKSTALLED
BACKSTALLING
BACKSTALLS
BACKSTAMPED
BACKSTAMPING
BACKSTAMPS
BACKSTARTING
BACKSTARTINGS
BACKSTITCH
BACKSTITCHED
BACKSTITCHES
BACKSTITCHING
BACKSTOPPED
BACKSTOPPING
BACKSTORIES
BACKSTRAPS
BACKSTREET
BACKSTREETS
BACKSTRETCH
BACKSTRETCHES
BACKSTROKE
BACKSTROKED
BACKSTROKES
BACKSTROKING
BACKSWIMMER
BACKSWIMMERS
BACKSWINGS
BACKSWORDMAN
BACKSWORDMEN
BACKSWORDS
BACKSWORDSMAN
BACKSWORDSMEN
BACKTRACKED
BACKTRACKING
BACKTRACKINGS
BACKTRACKS
BACKVELDER
BACKVELDERS
BACKWARDATION
BACKWARDATIONS
BACKWARDLY
BACKWARDNESS
BACKWARDNESSES
BACKWASHED
BACKWASHES
BACKWASHING
BACKWATERS
BACKWINDED
BACKWINDING
BACKWOODSIER
BACKWOODSIEST
BACKWOODSMAN
BACKWOODSMEN
BACKWOODSY
BACKWORKER
BACKWORKERS
BACTERAEMIA
BACTERAEMIAS
BACTERAEMIC
BACTEREMIA
BACTEREMIAS
BACTEREMIC
BACTERIALLY
BACTERIALS
BACTERICIDAL
BACTERICIDALLY
BACTERICIDE
BACTERICIDES
BACTERIOCIN
BACTERIOCINS
BACTERIOID
BACTERIOIDS
BACTERIOLOGIC
BACTERIOLOGICAL
BACTERIOLOGIES
BACTERIOLOGIST
BACTERIOLOGISTS
BACTERIOLOGY
BACTERIOLYSES
BACTERIOLYSIN
BACTERIOLYSINS
BACTERIOLYSIS
BACTERIOLYTIC
BACTERIOPHAGE
BACTERIOPHAGES
BACTERIOPHAGIC
BACTERIOPHAGIES
BACTERIOPHAGOUS
BACTERIOPHAGY
BACTERIOSES
BACTERIOSIS
BACTERIOSTASES
BACTERIOSTASIS
BACTERIOSTAT
BACTERIOSTATIC
BACTERIOSTATS
BACTERIOTOXIN
BACTERIOTOXINS
BACTERISATION
BACTERISATIONS
BACTERISED
BACTERISES
BACTERISING
BACTERIURIA
BACTERIURIAS
BACTERIZATION
BACTERIZATIONS
BACTERIZED
BACTERIZES
BACTERIZING
BACTEROIDS
BACTERURIA
BACTERURIAS
BACULIFORM
BACULOVIRUS
BACULOVIRUSES
BADDELEYITE
BADDELEYITES
BADDERLOCK
BADDERLOCKS
BADGERLIER
BADGERLIEST
BADINAGING
BADINERIES
BADMINTONS
BADMOUTHED
BADMOUTHING
BAFFLEGABS
BAFFLEMENT
BAFFLEMENTS
BAFFLINGLY
BAGASSOSES
BAGASSOSIS
BAGATELLES
BAGGINESSES
BAGPIPINGS
BAGSWINGER
BAGSWINGERS
BAHUVRIHIS
BAIGNOIRES
BAILIESHIP
BAILIESHIPS
BAILIFFSHIP
BAILIFFSHIPS
BAILIWICKS
BAILLIAGES
BAILLIESHIP
BAILLIESHIPS
BAIRNLIEST
BAISEMAINS
BAITFISHES
BAJILLIONS
BAKEAPPLES
BAKEBOARDS
BAKEHOUSES
BAKESTONES
BAKHSHISHED
BAKHSHISHES
BAKHSHISHING
BAKSHEESHED
BAKSHEESHES
BAKSHEESHING
BAKSHISHED
BAKSHISHES
BAKSHISHING
BALACLAVAS
BALALAIKAS
BALANCEABLE
BALANCINGS
BALANITISES
BALAYAGING
BALBRIGGAN
BALBRIGGANS
BALBUTIENT
BALCONETTE
BALCONETTES
BALDACHINO
BALDACHINOS
BALDACHINS
BALDAQUINS
BALDERDASH
BALDERDASHES
BALDERLOCKS
BALDERLOCKSES
BALDHEADED
BALDICOOTS
BALDMONEYS
BALDNESSES
BALECTIONS
BALEFULNESS
BALEFULNESSES
BALIBUNTAL
BALIBUNTALS
BALKANISATION
BALKANISATIONS
BALKANISED
BALKANISES
BALKANISING
BALKANIZATION
BALKANIZATIONS
BALKANIZED
BALKANIZES
BALKANIZING
BALKINESSES
BALLABILES
BALLADEERED
BALLADEERING
BALLADEERS
BALLADINES
BALLADISTS
BALLADMONGER
BALLADMONGERS
BALLADRIES
BALLANTING
BALLANWRASSE
BALLANWRASSES
BALLASTERS
BALLASTING
BALLBREAKER
BALLBREAKERS
BALLCARRIER
BALLCARRIERS
BALLERINAS
BALLETICALLY
BALLETOMANE
BALLETOMANES
BALLETOMANIA
BALLETOMANIAS
BALLFIELDS
BALLFLOWER
BALLFLOWERS

BALLHANDLING
BALLHANDLINGS
BALLHAWKED
BALLHAWKING
BALLICATTER
BALLICATTERS
BALLISTICALLY
BALLISTICS
BALLISTITE
BALLISTITES
BALLISTOSPORE
BALLISTOSPORES
BALLOCKSED
BALLOCKSES
BALLOCKSING
BALLOONING
BALLOONINGS
BALLOONIST
BALLOONISTS
BALLOTINGS
BALLOTTEMENT
BALLOTTEMENTS
BALLPLAYER
BALLPLAYERS
BALLPOINTS
BALLSINESS
BALLSINESSES
BALLYHOOED
BALLYHOOING
BALLYRAGGED
BALLYRAGGING
BALMACAANS
BALMINESSES
BALMORALITIES
BALMORALITY
BALNEARIES
BALNEATION
BALNEATIONS
BALNEOLOGICAL
BALNEOLOGIES
BALNEOLOGIST
BALNEOLOGISTS
BALNEOLOGY
BALNEOTHERAPIES
BALNEOTHERAPY
BALSAMIEST
BALSAMIFEROUS
BALSAMINACEOUS
BALSAWOODS
BALTHASARS
BALTHAZARS
BALUSTERED
BALUSTRADE
BALUSTRADED
BALUSTRADES
BALZARINES
BAMBOOZLED
BAMBOOZLEMENT
BAMBOOZLEMENTS
BAMBOOZLER
BAMBOOZLERS
BAMBOOZLES
BAMBOOZLING
BANALISATION
BANALISATIONS
BANALISING
BANALITIES
BANALIZATION
BANALIZATIONS
BANALIZING
BANCASSURANCE
BANCASSURANCES
BANCASSURER
BANCASSURERS
BANDAGINGS
BANDALORES
BANDBRAKES
BANDEIRANTE
BANDEIRANTES
BANDELIERS
BANDERILLA
BANDERILLAS
BANDERILLERO
BANDERILLEROS
BANDEROLES
BANDERSNATCH
BANDERSNATCHES
BANDFISHES
BANDICOOTED
BANDICOOTING
BANDICOOTS
BANDINESSES
BANDITRIES
BANDLEADER
BANDLEADERS
BANDMASTER
BANDMASTERS
BANDOBASTS
BANDOBUSTS
BANDOLEERED
BANDOLEERS
BANDOLEONS
BANDOLEROS
BANDOLIERED
BANDOLIERS
BANDOLINED
BANDOLINES
BANDOLINING
BANDONEONS
BANDONIONS
BANDPASSES
BANDSAWING
BANDSHELLS
BANDSPREADING
BANDSPREADINGS
BANDSTANDS
BANDURISTS
BANDWAGONS
BANDWIDTHS
BANEBERRIES
BANEFULNESS
BANEFULNESSES
BANGBELLIES
BANGSRINGS
BANISHMENT
BANISHMENTS
BANISTERED
BANJOLELES
BANJULELES
BANKABILITIES
BANKABILITY
BANKERLIER
BANKERLIEST
BANKROLLED
BANKROLLER
BANKROLLERS
BANKROLLING
BANKRUPTCIES
BANKRUPTCY
BANKRUPTED
BANKRUPTING
BANNERALLS
BANNERETTE
BANNERETTES
BANNISTERS
BANQUETEER
BANQUETEERS
BANQUETERS
BANQUETING
BANQUETINGS
BANQUETTES
BANTAMWEIGHT
BANTAMWEIGHTS
BANTERINGLY
BANTERINGS
BANTINGISM
BANTINGISMS
BAPHOMETIC
BAPTISMALLY
BAPTISTERIES
BAPTISTERY
BAPTISTRIES
BARACHOISES
BARAESTHESIA
BARAESTHESIAS
BARAGOUINS
BARASINGAS
BARASINGHA
BARASINGHAS
BARATHRUMS
BARBARESQUE
BARBARIANISM
BARBARIANISMS
BARBARIANS
BARBARICALLY
BARBARISATION
BARBARISATIONS
BARBARISED
BARBARISES
BARBARISING
BARBARISMS
BARBARITIES
BARBARIZATION
BARBARIZATIONS
BARBARIZED
BARBARIZES
BARBARIZING
BARBAROUSLY
BARBAROUSNESS
BARBAROUSNESSES
BARBASCOES
BARBASTELLE
BARBASTELLES
BARBASTELS
BARBECUERS
BARBECUING
BARBELLATE
BARBEQUING
BARBERRIES
BARBERSHOP
BARBERSHOPS
BARBITONES
BARBITURATE
BARBITURATES
BARBITURIC
BARBOTINES
BARCAROLES
BARCAROLLE
BARCAROLLES
BARDOLATER
BARDOLATERS
BARDOLATRIES
BARDOLATROUS
BARDOLATRY
BAREBACKED
BAREBACKING
BAREBACKINGS
BAREFACEDLY
BAREFACEDNESS
BAREFACEDNESSES
BAREFOOTED
BAREHANDED
BAREHANDING
BAREHEADED
BARELEGGED
BARENESSES
BARESTHESIA
BARESTHESIAS
BARGAINERS
BARGAINING
BARGAININGS
BARGANDERS
BARGEBOARD
BARGEBOARDS
BARGEMASTER
BARGEMASTERS
BARGEPOLES
BARHOPPING
BARIATRICS
BARKANTINE

BARKANTINES
BARKEEPERS
BARKENTINE
BARKENTINES
BARLEYCORN
BARLEYCORNS
BARMBRACKS
BARMINESSES
BARMITSVAH
BARMITSVAHS
BARMITZVAH
BARMITZVAHS
BARNBOARDS
BARNBRACKS
BARNSBREAKING
BARNSBREAKINGS
BARNSTORMED
BARNSTORMER
BARNSTORMERS
BARNSTORMING
BARNSTORMINGS
BARNSTORMS
BAROCEPTOR
BAROCEPTORS
BARODYNAMICS
BAROGNOSES
BAROGNOSIS
BAROGRAPHIC
BAROGRAPHS
BAROMETERS
BAROMETRIC
BAROMETRICAL
BAROMETRICALLY
BAROMETRIES
BAROMETZES
BARONESSES
BARONETAGE
BARONETAGES
BARONETCIES
BARONETESS
BARONETESSES
BARONETICAL
BAROPHILES
BAROPHILIC
BAROPHORESES
BAROPHORESIS
BARORECEPTOR
BARORECEPTORS
BAROSCOPES
BAROSCOPIC
BAROTITISES
BAROTRAUMA
BAROTRAUMAS
BAROTRAUMATA
BARPERSONS
BARQUANTINE
BARQUANTINES
BARQUENTINE
BARQUENTINES
BARQUETTES
BARRACKERS
BARRACKING
BARRACKINGS
BARRACOONS
BARRACOUTA
BARRACOUTAS
BARRACUDAS
BARRAMUNDA
BARRAMUNDAS
BARRAMUNDI
BARRAMUNDIES
BARRAMUNDIS
BARRASWAYS
BARRATRIES
BARRATROUS
BARRATROUSLY
BARRELAGES
BARRELFULS
BARRELHEAD
BARRELHEADS
BARRELHOUSE
BARRELHOUSES
BARRELLING
BARRELSFUL
BARRENNESS
BARRENNESSES
BARRENWORT
BARRENWORTS
BARRETRIES
BARRETROUS
BARRETROUSLY
BARRETTERS
BARRICADED
BARRICADER
BARRICADERS
BARRICADES
BARRICADING
BARRICADOED
BARRICADOES
BARRICADOING
BARRICADOS
BARRIERING
BARRISTERIAL
BARRISTERS
BARRISTERSHIP
BARRISTERSHIPS
BARROWFULS
BARTENDERS
BARTENDING
BARTENDINGS
BARTIZANED
BARYCENTRE
BARYCENTRES
BARYCENTRIC
BARYSPHERE
BARYSPHERES
BASALTINES
BASALTWARE
BASALTWARES
BASEBALLER
BASEBALLERS
BASEBOARDS
BASEBURNER
BASEBURNERS
BASELESSLY
BASELESSNESS
BASELESSNESSES
BASELINERS
BASEMENTLESS
BASENESSES
BASEPLATES
BASERUNNER
BASERUNNERS
BASERUNNING
BASERUNNINGS
BASHAWISMS
BASHAWSHIP
BASHAWSHIPS
BASHFULLER
BASHFULLEST
BASHFULNESS
BASHFULNESSES
BASHIBAZOUK
BASHIBAZOUKS
BASICITIES
BASICRANIAL
BASIDIOCARP
BASIDIOCARPS
BASIDIOMYCETE
BASIDIOMYCETES
BASIDIOMYCETOUS
BASIDIOSPORE
BASIDIOSPORES
BASIDIOSPOROUS
BASIFICATION
BASIFICATIONS
BASILICONS
BASIPETALLY
BASKETBALL
BASKETBALLS
BASKETFULS
BASKETLIKE
BASKETRIES
BASKETSFUL
BASKETWEAVE
BASKETWEAVER
BASKETWEAVERS
BASKETWEAVES
BASKETWORK
BASKETWORKS
BASMITZVAH
BASMITZVAHS
BASOPHILES
BASOPHILIA
BASOPHILIAS
BASOPHILIC
BASSETTING
BASSNESSES
BASSOONIST
BASSOONISTS
BASTARDIES
BASTARDISATION
BASTARDISATIONS
BASTARDISE
BASTARDISED
BASTARDISES
BASTARDISING
BASTARDISM
BASTARDISMS
BASTARDIZATION
BASTARDIZATIONS
BASTARDIZE
BASTARDIZED
BASTARDIZES
BASTARDIZING
BASTARDLIER
BASTARDLIEST
BASTARDRIES
BASTINADED
BASTINADES
BASTINADING
BASTINADOED
BASTINADOES
BASTINADOING
BASTNAESITE
BASTNAESITES
BASTNASITE
BASTNASITES
BATFOWLERS
BATFOWLING
BATFOWLINGS
BATHETICALLY
BATHHOUSES
BATHMITSVAH
BATHMITSVAHS
BATHMITZVAH
BATHMITZVAHS
BATHMIZVAH
BATHMIZVAHS
BATHOCHROME
BATHOCHROMES
BATHOCHROMIC
BATHOLITES
BATHOLITHIC
BATHOLITHS
BATHOLITIC
BATHOMETER
BATHOMETERS
BATHOMETRIC
BATHOMETRICALLY
BATHOMETRIES
BATHOMETRY
BATHOPHILOUS
BATHOPHOBIA
BATHOPHOBIAS
BATHWATERS
BATHYBIUSES
BATHYGRAPHIC
BATHYGRAPHICAL
BATHYLIMNETIC

BATHYLITES
BATHYLITHIC
BATHYLITHS
BATHYLITIC
BATHYMETER
BATHYMETERS
BATHYMETRIC
BATHYMETRICAL
BATHYMETRICALLY
BATHYMETRIES
BATHYMETRY
BATHYPELAGIC
BATHYSCAPE
BATHYSCAPES
BATHYSCAPH
BATHYSCAPHE
BATHYSCAPHES
BATHYSCAPHS
BATHYSPHERE
BATHYSPHERES
BATMITZVAH
BATMITZVAHS
BATOLOGICAL
BATOLOGIES
BATOLOGIST
BATOLOGISTS
BATONNIERS
BATRACHIAN
BATRACHIANS
BATRACHOPHOBIA
BATRACHOPHOBIAS
BATRACHOPHOBIC
BATSMANSHIP
BATSMANSHIPS
BATTAILOUS
BATTALIONS
BATTEILANT
BATTELLING
BATTEMENTS
BATTENINGS
BATTERINGS
BATTILLING
BATTINESSES
BATTLEAXES
BATTLEBUSES
BATTLEBUSSES
BATTLEDOOR
BATTLEDOORS
BATTLEDORE
BATTLEDORES
BATTLEDRESS
BATTLEDRESSES
BATTLEFIELD
BATTLEFIELDS
BATTLEFRONT
BATTLEFRONTS
BATTLEGROUND
BATTLEGROUNDS
BATTLEMENT
BATTLEMENTED
BATTLEMENTS
BATTLEPIECE
BATTLEPIECES
BATTLEPLANE
BATTLEPLANES
BATTLESHIP
BATTLESHIPS
BATTLESPACE
BATTLESPACES
BATTLEWAGON
BATTLEWAGONS
BATTOLOGICAL
BATTOLOGIES
BAUDRICKES
BAUDRONSES
BAULKINESS
BAULKINESSES
BAULKINGLY
BAULKLINES
BAVARDAGES
BAVAROISES
BAWDINESSES
BAWDYHOUSE
BAWDYHOUSES
BAYBERRIES
BAYNODDIES
BAYONETING
BAYONETTED
BAYONETTING
BAZILLIONS
BEACHBALLS
BEACHCOMBED
BEACHCOMBER
BEACHCOMBERS
BEACHCOMBING
BEACHCOMBINGS
BEACHCOMBS
BEACHFRONT
BEACHFRONTS
BEACHGOERS
BEACHHEADS
BEACHWEARS
BEADBLASTED
BEADBLASTER
BEADBLASTERS
BEADBLASTING
BEADBLASTS
BEADHOUSES
BEADINESSES
BEADLEDOMS
BEADLEHOOD
BEADLEHOODS
BEADLESHIP
BEADLESHIPS
BEADSWOMAN
BEADSWOMEN
BEAKERFULS
BEAMINESSES
BEANFEASTS
BEANSPROUT
BEANSPROUTS
BEANSTALKS
BEARABILITIES
BEARABILITY
BEARABLENESS
BEARABLENESSES
BEARBAITING
BEARBAITINGS
BEARBERRIES
BEARDEDNESS
BEARDEDNESSES
BEARDLESSNESS
BEARDLESSNESSES
BEARDTONGUE
BEARDTONGUES
BEARGRASSES
BEARHUGGED
BEARHUGGING
BEARISHNESS
BEARISHNESSES
BEARNAISES
BEASTHOODS
BEASTLIEST
BEASTLINESS
BEASTLINESSES
BEATBOXERS
BEATBOXING
BEATBOXINGS
BEATIFICAL
BEATIFICALLY
BEATIFICATION
BEATIFICATIONS
BEATIFYING
BEATITUDES
BEAUJOLAIS
BEAUJOLAISES
BEAUMONTAGE
BEAUMONTAGES
BEAUMONTAGUE
BEAUMONTAGUES
BEAUTEOUSLY
BEAUTEOUSNESS
BEAUTEOUSNESSES
BEAUTICIAN
BEAUTICIANS
BEAUTIFICATION
BEAUTIFICATIONS
BEAUTIFIED
BEAUTIFIER
BEAUTIFIERS
BEAUTIFIES
BEAUTIFULLER
BEAUTIFULLEST
BEAUTIFULLY
BEAUTIFULNESS
BEAUTIFULNESSES
BEAUTIFYING
BEAVERBOARD
BEAVERBOARDS
BEBEERINES
BEBLOODING
BEBLUBBERED
BECARPETED
BECARPETING
BECCACCIAS
BECCAFICOS
BECHALKING
BECHANCING
BECHARMING
BECKONINGLY
BECKONINGS
BECLAMORED
BECLAMORING
BECLAMOURED
BECLAMOURING
BECLAMOURS
BECLASPING
BECLOAKING
BECLOGGING
BECLOTHING
BECLOUDING
BECLOWNING
BECOMINGLY
BECOMINGNESS
BECOMINGNESSES
BECOWARDED
BECOWARDING
BECQUERELS
BECRAWLING
BECROWDING
BECRUSTING
BECUDGELED
BECUDGELING
BECUDGELLED
BECUDGELLING
BEDABBLING
BEDAGGLING
BEDARKENED
BEDARKENING
BEDAZZLEMENT
BEDAZZLEMENTS
BEDAZZLING
BEDCHAMBER
BEDCHAMBERS
BEDCLOTHES
BEDCOVERING
BEDCOVERINGS
BEDEAFENED
BEDEAFENING
BEDEHOUSES
BEDELLSHIP
BEDELLSHIPS
BEDELSHIPS
BEDEVILING
BEDEVILLED
BEDEVILLING
BEDEVILMENT
BEDEVILMENTS
BEDFELLOWS
BEDIAPERED

BEDIAPERING
BEDIGHTING
BEDIMMINGS
BEDIMPLING
BEDIRTYING
BEDIZENING
BEDIZENMENT
BEDIZENMENTS
BEDLAMISMS
BEDLAMITES
BEDPRESSER
BEDPRESSERS
BEDRAGGLED
BEDRAGGLES
BEDRAGGLING
BEDRENCHED
BEDRENCHES
BEDRENCHING
BEDRIVELED
BEDRIVELING
BEDRIVELLED
BEDRIVELLING
BEDROPPING
BEDRUGGING
BEDSITTERS
BEDSITTING
BEDSPREADS
BEDSPRINGS
BEDWARFING
BEDWARMERS
BEDWETTERS
BEECHDROPS
BEECHMASTS
BEECHWOODS
BEEFBURGER
BEEFBURGERS
BEEFEATERS
BEEFINESSES
BEEFSTEAKS
BEEKEEPERS
BEEKEEPING
BEEKEEPINGS
BEERINESSES
BEESWAXING
BEESWINGED
BEETLEBRAIN
BEETLEBRAINED
BEETLEBRAINS
BEETLEHEAD
BEETLEHEADED
BEETLEHEADS
BEETMASTER
BEETMASTERS
BEETMISTER
BEETMISTERS
BEFINGERED
BEFINGERING
BEFITTINGLY
BEFLAGGING
BEFLECKING
BEFLOWERED
BEFLOWERING
BEFLUMMING
BEFOREHAND
BEFORETIME
BEFORTUNED
BEFORTUNES
BEFORTUNING
BEFOULMENT
BEFOULMENTS
BEFRETTING
BEFRIENDED
BEFRIENDER
BEFRIENDERS
BEFRIENDING
BEFRINGING
BEFUDDLEMENT
BEFUDDLEMENTS
BEFUDDLING
BEGGARDOMS
BEGGARHOOD
BEGGARHOODS
BEGGARLIER
BEGGARLIEST
BEGGARLINESS
BEGGARLINESSES
BEGGARWEED
BEGGARWEEDS
BEGINNINGLESS
BEGINNINGS
BEGIRDLING
BEGLADDING
BEGLAMORED
BEGLAMORING
BEGLAMOURED
BEGLAMOURING
BEGLAMOURS
BEGLERBEGS
BEGLOOMING
BEGRIMMING
BEGROANING
BEGRUDGERIES
BEGRUDGERS
BEGRUDGERY
BEGRUDGING
BEGRUDGINGLY
BEGUILEMENT
BEGUILEMENTS
BEGUILINGLY
BEGUINAGES
BEHAPPENED
BEHAPPENING
BEHAVIORAL
BEHAVIORALLY
BEHAVIORISM
BEHAVIORISMS
BEHAVIORIST
BEHAVIORISTIC
BEHAVIORISTS
BEHAVIOURAL
BEHAVIOURALLY
BEHAVIOURISM
BEHAVIOURISMS
BEHAVIOURIST
BEHAVIOURISTIC
BEHAVIOURISTS
BEHAVIOURS
BEHEADINGS
BEHIGHTING
BEHINDHAND
BEHOLDINGS
BEINGNESSES
BEINNESSES
BEJABERSES
BEJEEZUSES
BEJESUITED
BEJESUITING
BEJEWELING
BEJEWELLED
BEJEWELLING
BEJUMBLING
BEKNIGHTED
BEKNIGHTING
BEKNOTTING
BELABORING
BELABOURED
BELABOURING
BELAMOURES
BELATEDNESS
BELATEDNESSES
BELEAGUERED
BELEAGUERING
BELEAGUERMENT
BELEAGUERMENTS
BELEAGUERS
BELEMNITES
BELGICISMS
BELIEFLESS
BELIEVABILITIES
BELIEVABILITY
BELIEVABLE
BELIEVABLY
BELIEVINGLY
BELIEVINGS
BELIQUORED
BELIQUORING
BELITTLEMENT
BELITTLEMENTS
BELITTLERS
BELITTLING
BELITTLINGLY
BELLADONNA
BELLADONNAS
BELLAMOURE
BELLAMOURES
BELLARMINE
BELLARMINES
BELLETRISM
BELLETRISMS
BELLETRIST
BELLETRISTIC
BELLETRISTICAL
BELLETRISTS
BELLETTRIST
BELLETTRISTS
BELLFLOWER
BELLFLOWERS
BELLFOUNDER
BELLFOUNDERS
BELLFOUNDRIES
BELLFOUNDRY
BELLHANGER
BELLHANGERS
BELLIBONES
BELLICOSELY
BELLICOSITIES
BELLICOSITY
BELLIGERATI
BELLIGERENCE
BELLIGERENCES
BELLIGERENCIES
BELLIGERENCY
BELLIGERENT
BELLIGERENTLY
BELLIGERENTS
BELLOCKING
BELLOWINGS
BELLWETHER
BELLWETHERS
BELLYACHED
BELLYACHER
BELLYACHERS
BELLYACHES
BELLYACHING
BELLYACHINGS
BELLYBANDS
BELLYBOATS
BELLYBUTTON
BELLYBUTTONS
BELLYFLOPPED
BELLYFLOPPING
BELLYFLOPS
BELOMANCIES
BELONGINGNESS
BELONGINGNESSES
BELONGINGS
BELOWDECKS
BELOWGROUND
BELOWSTAIRS
BELSHAZZAR
BELSHAZZARS
BELTCOURSE
BELTCOURSES
BELVEDERES
BEMADAMING
BEMADDENED
BEMADDENING
BEMEDALING
BEMEDALLED
BEMEDALLING

BEMINGLING
BEMOANINGS
BEMONSTERED
BEMONSTERING
BEMONSTERS
BEMOUTHING
BEMUDDLING
BEMUFFLING
BEMURMURED
BEMURMURING
BEMUSEMENT
BEMUSEMENTS
BEMUZZLING
BENCHERSHIP
BENCHERSHIPS
BENCHLANDS
BENCHMARKED
BENCHMARKING
BENCHMARKINGS
BENCHMARKS
BENCHWARMER
BENCHWARMERS
BENDINESSES
BENEDICITE
BENEDICITES
BENEDICTION
BENEDICTIONAL
BENEDICTIONALS
BENEDICTIONS
BENEDICTIVE
BENEDICTORY
BENEDICTUS
BENEDICTUSES
BENEFACTED
BENEFACTING
BENEFACTION
BENEFACTIONS
BENEFACTOR
BENEFACTORS
BENEFACTORY
BENEFACTRESS
BENEFACTRESSES
BENEFICENCE
BENEFICENCES
BENEFICENT
BENEFICENTIAL
BENEFICENTLY
BENEFICIAL
BENEFICIALLY
BENEFICIALNESS
BENEFICIALS
BENEFICIARIES
BENEFICIARY
BENEFICIATE
BENEFICIATED
BENEFICIATES
BENEFICIATING
BENEFICIATION
BENEFICIATIONS
BENEFICING
BENEFITERS
BENEFITING
BENEFITTED
BENEFITTING
BENEPLACITO
BENEVOLENCE
BENEVOLENCES
BENEVOLENT
BENEVOLENTLY
BENEVOLENTNESS
BENGALINES
BENIGHTEDLY
BENIGHTEDNESS
BENIGHTEDNESSES
BENIGHTENED
BENIGHTENING
BENIGHTENINGS
BENIGHTENS
BENIGHTERS
BENIGHTING
BENIGHTINGS
BENIGHTMENT
BENIGHTMENTS
BENIGNANCIES
BENIGNANCY
BENIGNANTLY
BENIGNITIES
BENTGRASSES
BENTHOPELAGIC
BENTHOSCOPE
BENTHOSCOPES
BENTONITES
BENTONITIC
BENUMBEDNESS
BENUMBEDNESSES
BENUMBINGLY
BENUMBMENT
BENUMBMENTS
BENZALDEHYDE
BENZALDEHYDES
BENZANTHRACENE
BENZANTHRACENES
BENZENECARBONYL
BENZENOIDS
BENZIDINES
BENZIMIDAZOLE
BENZIMIDAZOLES
BENZOAPYRENE
BENZOAPYRENES
BENZOCAINE
BENZOCAINES
BENZODIAZEPINE
BENZODIAZEPINES
BENZOFURAN
BENZOFURANS
BENZOLINES
BENZOPHENONE
BENZOPHENONES
BENZOQUINONE
BENZOQUINONES
BENZPYRENE
BENZPYRENES
BENZYLIDINE
BENZYLIDINES
BEPAINTING
BEPEARLING
BEPEPPERED
BEPEPPERING
BEPESTERED
BEPESTERING
BEPIMPLING
BEPLASTERED
BEPLASTERING
BEPLASTERS
BEPOMMELLED
BEPOMMELLING
BEPOWDERED
BEPOWDERING
BEPRAISING
BEQUEATHABLE
BEQUEATHAL
BEQUEATHALS
BEQUEATHED
BEQUEATHER
BEQUEATHERS
BEQUEATHING
BEQUEATHMENT
BEQUEATHMENTS
BERASCALED
BERASCALING
BERBERIDACEOUS
BERBERINES
BERBERISES
BEREAVEMENT
BEREAVEMENTS
BERGAMASKO
BERGAMASKOS
BERGAMASKS
BERGANDERS
BERGOMASKS
BERGSCHRUND
BERGSCHRUNDS
BERIBBONED
BERKELIUMS
BERRYFRUIT
BERRYFRUITS
BERSAGLIERE
BERSAGLIERI
BERSERKERS
BERTILLONAGE
BERTILLONAGES
BERYLLIOSES
BERYLLIOSIS
BERYLLIUMS
BESAINTING
BESCATTERED
BESCATTERING
BESCATTERS
BESCORCHED
BESCORCHES
BESCORCHING
BESCOURING
BESCRAWLED
BESCRAWLING
BESCREENED
BESCREENING
BESCRIBBLE
BESCRIBBLED
BESCRIBBLES
BESCRIBBLING
BESEECHERS
BESEECHING
BESEECHINGLY
BESEECHINGNESS
BESEECHINGS
BESEEMINGLY
BESEEMINGNESS
BESEEMINGNESSES
BESEEMINGS
BESEEMLIER
BESEEMLIEST
BESETMENTS
BESHADOWED
BESHADOWING
BESHIVERED
BESHIVERING
BESHOUTING
BESHREWING
BESHROUDED
BESHROUDING
BESIEGEMENT
BESIEGEMENTS
BESIEGINGLY
BESIEGINGS
BESLAVERED
BESLAVERING
BESLOBBERED
BESLOBBERING
BESLOBBERS
BESLUBBERED
BESLUBBERING
BESLUBBERS
BESMEARERS
BESMEARING
BESMIRCHED
BESMIRCHES
BESMIRCHING
BESMOOTHED
BESMOOTHING
BESMUDGING
BESMUTCHED
BESMUTCHES
BESMUTCHING
BESMUTTING
BESOOTHING
BESOTTEDLY
BESOTTEDNESS
BESOTTEDNESSES
BESPANGLED
BESPANGLES

BESPANGLING
BESPATTERED
BESPATTERING
BESPATTERS
BESPEAKING
BESPECKLED
BESPECKLES
BESPECKLING
BESPECTACLED
BESPEEDING
BESPITTING
BESPORTING
BESPOTTEDNESS
BESPOTTEDNESSES
BESPOTTING
BESPOUSING
BESPOUTING
BESPREADING
BESPRINKLE
BESPRINKLED
BESPRINKLES
BESPRINKLING
BESTAINING
BESTARRING
BESTEADING
BESTIALISE
BESTIALISED
BESTIALISES
BESTIALISING
BESTIALISM
BESTIALISMS
BESTIALITIES
BESTIALITY
BESTIALIZE
BESTIALIZED
BESTIALIZES
BESTIALIZING
BESTIARIES
BESTICKING
BESTILLING
BESTIRRING
BESTORMING
BESTOWMENT
BESTOWMENTS
BESTRADDLE
BESTRADDLED
BESTRADDLES
BESTRADDLING
BESTRAUGHT
BESTREAKED
BESTREAKING
BESTREWING
BESTRIDABLE
BESTRIDDEN
BESTRIDING
BESTROWING
BESTSELLER
BESTSELLERDOM
BESTSELLERDOMS
BESTSELLERS
BESTSELLING
BESTUDDING
BESWARMING
BETACAROTENE
BETACAROTENES
BETACYANIN
BETACYANINS
BETATTERED
BETATTERING
BETHANKING
BETHANKITS
BETHINKING
BETHORNING
BETHRALLED
BETHRALLING
BETHUMBING
BETHUMPING
BETHWACKED
BETHWACKING
BETOKENING
BETREADING
BETRIMMING
BETROTHALS
BETROTHEDS
BETROTHING
BETROTHMENT
BETROTHMENTS
BETTERINGS
BETTERMENT
BETTERMENTS
BETTERMOST
BETTERNESS
BETTERNESSES
BETULACEOUS
BETWEENBRAIN
BETWEENBRAINS
BETWEENITIES
BETWEENITY
BETWEENNESS
BETWEENNESSES
BETWEENTIME
BETWEENTIMES
BETWEENWHILES
BEVELLINGS
BEVELMENTS
BEVOMITING
BEWAILINGLY
BEWAILINGS
BEWEARYING
BEWELTERED
BEWHISKERED
BEWILDERED
BEWILDEREDLY
BEWILDEREDNESS
BEWILDERING
BEWILDERINGLY
BEWILDERMENT
BEWILDERMENTS
BEWITCHERIES
BEWITCHERS
BEWITCHERY
BEWITCHING
BEWITCHINGLY
BEWITCHMENT
BEWITCHMENTS
BEWORRYING
BEWRAPPING
BHIKKHUNIS
BIANNUALLY
BIANNULATE
BIASNESSES
BIATHLETES
BIAURICULAR
BIAURICULATE
BIBLICALLY
BIBLICISMS
BIBLICISTS
BIBLIOGRAPHER
BIBLIOGRAPHERS
BIBLIOGRAPHIC
BIBLIOGRAPHICAL
BIBLIOGRAPHIES
BIBLIOGRAPHY
BIBLIOLATER
BIBLIOLATERS
BIBLIOLATRIES
BIBLIOLATRIST
BIBLIOLATRISTS
BIBLIOLATROUS
BIBLIOLATRY
BIBLIOLOGICAL
BIBLIOLOGIES
BIBLIOLOGIST
BIBLIOLOGISTS
BIBLIOLOGY
BIBLIOMANCIES
BIBLIOMANCY
BIBLIOMANE
BIBLIOMANES
BIBLIOMANIA
BIBLIOMANIAC
BIBLIOMANIACAL
BIBLIOMANIACS
BIBLIOMANIAS
BIBLIOPEGIC
BIBLIOPEGIES
BIBLIOPEGIST
BIBLIOPEGISTS
BIBLIOPEGY
BIBLIOPHAGIST
BIBLIOPHAGISTS
BIBLIOPHIL
BIBLIOPHILE
BIBLIOPHILES
BIBLIOPHILIC
BIBLIOPHILIES
BIBLIOPHILISM
BIBLIOPHILISMS
BIBLIOPHILIST
BIBLIOPHILISTIC
BIBLIOPHILISTS
BIBLIOPHILS
BIBLIOPHILY
BIBLIOPHOBIA
BIBLIOPHOBIAS
BIBLIOPOLE
BIBLIOPOLES
BIBLIOPOLIC
BIBLIOPOLICAL
BIBLIOPOLIES
BIBLIOPOLIST
BIBLIOPOLISTS
BIBLIOPOLY
BIBLIOTHECA
BIBLIOTHECAE
BIBLIOTHECAL
BIBLIOTHECARIES
BIBLIOTHECARY
BIBLIOTHECAS
BIBLIOTHERAPIES
BIBLIOTHERAPY
BIBLIOTICS
BIBLIOTIST
BIBLIOTISTS
BIBULOUSLY
BIBULOUSNESS
BIBULOUSNESSES
BICAMERALISM
BICAMERALISMS
BICAMERALIST
BICAMERALISTS
BICAPSULAR
BICARBONATE
BICARBONATES
BICARPELLARY
BICENTENARIES
BICENTENARY
BICENTENNIAL
BICENTENNIALS
BICEPHALOUS
BICHLORIDE
BICHLORIDES
BICHROMATE
BICHROMATED
BICHROMATES
BICKERINGS
BICOLLATERAL
BICOLOURED
BICOMPONENT
BICOMPONENTS
BICONCAVITIES
BICONCAVITY
BICONDITIONAL
BICONDITIONALS
BICONVEXITIES
BICONVEXITY
BICORNUATE
BICORPORATE
BICULTURAL
BICULTURALISM

BICULTURALISMS
BICUSPIDATE
BICUSPIDATES
BICYCLICAL
BICYCLISTS
BIDDABILITIES
BIDDABILITY
BIDDABLENESS
BIDDABLENESSES
BIDENTATED
BIDIALECTAL
BIDIALECTALISM
BIDIALECTALISMS
BIDIRECTIONAL
BIDIRECTIONALLY
BIDONVILLE
BIDONVILLES
BIENNIALLY
BIENSEANCE
BIENSEANCES
BIERKELLER
BIERKELLERS
BIERWURSTS
BIFACIALLY
BIFARIOUSLY
BIFIDITIES
BIFLAGELLATE
BIFOLIOLATE
BIFUNCTIONAL
BIFURCATED
BIFURCATES
BIFURCATING
BIFURCATION
BIFURCATIONS
BIGAMOUSLY
BIGARREAUS
BIGEMINIES
BIGFOOTING
BIGGETIEST
BIGGITIEST
BIGHEADEDLY
BIGHEADEDNESS
BIGHEADEDNESSES
BIGHEARTED
BIGHEARTEDLY
BIGHEARTEDNESS
BIGMOUTHED
BIGNONIACEOUS
BIGUANIDES
BIJECTIONS
BIJOUTERIE
BIJOUTERIES
BILATERALISM
BILATERALISMS
BILATERALLY
BILBERRIES
BILDUNGSROMAN
BILDUNGSROMANS
BILECTIONS
BILESTONES
BILGEWATER
BILGEWATERS
BILHARZIAL
BILHARZIAS
BILHARZIASES
BILHARZIASIS
BILHARZIOSES
BILHARZIOSIS
BILIMBINGS
BILINGUALISM
BILINGUALISMS
BILINGUALLY
BILINGUALS
BILINGUIST
BILINGUISTS
BILIOUSNESS
BILIOUSNESSES
BILIRUBINS
BILIVERDIN
BILIVERDINS
BILLABONGS
BILLBOARDED
BILLBOARDING
BILLBOARDS
BILLETINGS
BILLFISHES
BILLINGSGATE
BILLINGSGATES
BILLIONAIRE
BILLIONAIRES
BILLIONTHS
BILLOWIEST
BILLOWINESS
BILLOWINESSES
BILLOWINGS
BILLPOSTER
BILLPOSTERS
BILLPOSTING
BILLPOSTINGS
BILLSTICKER
BILLSTICKERS
BILLSTICKING
BILLSTICKINGS
BILLYCOCKS
BILOCATION
BILOCATIONS
BILOCULATE
BIMANUALLY
BIMATERNAL
BIMESTRIAL
BIMESTRIALLY
BIMETALLIC
BIMETALLICS
BIMETALLISM
BIMETALLISMS
BIMETALLIST
BIMETALLISTIC
BIMETALLISTS
BIMILLENARIES
BIMILLENARY
BIMILLENNIA
BIMILLENNIAL
BIMILLENNIALS
BIMILLENNIUM
BIMILLENNIUMS
BIMODALITIES
BIMODALITY
BIMOLECULAR
BIMOLECULARLY
BIMONTHLIES
BIMORPHEMIC
BINATIONAL
BINAURALLY
BINDINGNESS
BINDINGNESSES
BINOCULARITIES
BINOCULARITY
BINOCULARLY
BINOCULARS
BINOMIALLY
BINOMINALS
BINTURONGS
BINUCLEATE
BINUCLEATED
BIOACCUMULATE
BIOACCUMULATED
BIOACCUMULATES
BIOACCUMULATING
BIOACCUMULATION
BIOACOUSTICS
BIOACTIVITIES
BIOACTIVITY
BIOAERATION
BIOAERATIONS
BIOAERONAUTICS
BIOARCHAEOLOGY
BIOASSAYED
BIOASSAYING
BIOASTRONAUTICS
BIOASTRONOMIES
BIOASTRONOMY
BIOAVAILABILITY
BIOAVAILABLE
BIOBANKING
BIOBANKINGS
BIOCATALYST
BIOCATALYSTS
BIOCATALYTIC
BIOCELLATE
BIOCENOLOGIES
BIOCENOLOGY
BIOCENOSES
BIOCENOSIS
BIOCENOTIC
BIOCHEMICAL
BIOCHEMICALLY
BIOCHEMICALS
BIOCHEMIST
BIOCHEMISTRIES
BIOCHEMISTRY
BIOCHEMISTS
BIOCLASTIC
BIOCLIMATIC
BIOCLIMATOLOGY
BIOCOENOLOGIES
BIOCOENOLOGY
BIOCOENOSES
BIOCOENOSIS
BIOCOENOTIC
BIOCOMPATIBLE
BIOCOMPUTING
BIOCOMPUTINGS
BIOCONTROL
BIOCONTROLS
BIOCONVERSION
BIOCONVERSIONS
BIODEGRADABLE
BIODEGRADABLES
BIODEGRADATION
BIODEGRADATIONS
BIODEGRADE
BIODEGRADED
BIODEGRADES
BIODEGRADING
BIODESTRUCTIBLE
BIODIESELS
BIODIVERSE
BIODIVERSITIES
BIODIVERSITY
BIODYNAMIC
BIODYNAMICAL
BIODYNAMICS
BIOECOLOGICAL
BIOECOLOGICALLY
BIOECOLOGIES
BIOECOLOGIST
BIOECOLOGISTS
BIOECOLOGY
BIOELECTRIC
BIOELECTRICAL
BIOELECTRICITY
BIOENERGETIC
BIOENERGETICS
BIOENERGIES
BIOENGINEER
BIOENGINEERED
BIOENGINEERING
BIOENGINEERINGS
BIOENGINEERS
BIOETHANOL
BIOETHANOLS
BIOETHICAL
BIOETHICIST
BIOETHICISTS
BIOFEEDBACK
BIOFEEDBACKS
BIOFLAVONOID
BIOFLAVONOIDS
BIOFOULERS
BIOFOULING

B

BIOFOULINGS
BIOFUELLED
BIOGENESES
BIOGENESIS
BIOGENETIC
BIOGENETICAL
BIOGENETICALLY
BIOGENETICS
BIOGEOCHEMICAL
BIOGEOCHEMICALS
BIOGEOCHEMISTRY
BIOGEOGRAPHER
BIOGEOGRAPHERS
BIOGEOGRAPHIC
BIOGEOGRAPHICAL
BIOGEOGRAPHIES
BIOGEOGRAPHY
BIOGRAPHED
BIOGRAPHEE
BIOGRAPHEES
BIOGRAPHER
BIOGRAPHERS
BIOGRAPHIC
BIOGRAPHICAL
BIOGRAPHICALLY
BIOGRAPHIES
BIOGRAPHING
BIOGRAPHISE
BIOGRAPHISED
BIOGRAPHISES
BIOGRAPHISING
BIOGRAPHIZE
BIOGRAPHIZED
BIOGRAPHIZES
BIOGRAPHIZING
BIOHACKERS
BIOHAZARDOUS
BIOHAZARDS
BIOINDUSTRIES
BIOINDUSTRY
BIOINFORMATICS
BIOLOGICAL
BIOLOGICALLY
BIOLOGICALS
BIOLOGISMS
BIOLOGISTIC
BIOLOGISTS
BIOLUMINESCENCE
BIOLUMINESCENT
BIOMAGNETICS
BIOMARKERS
BIOMATERIAL
BIOMATERIALS
BIOMATHEMATICAL
BIOMATHEMATICS
BIOMECHANICAL
BIOMECHANICALLY
BIOMECHANICS
BIOMEDICAL
BIOMEDICINE
BIOMEDICINES
BIOMETEOROLOGY
BIOMETRICAL
BIOMETRICALLY
BIOMETRICIAN
BIOMETRICIANS
BIOMETRICS
BIOMETRIES
BIOMIMETIC
BIOMIMETICS
BIOMIMICRIES
BIOMIMICRY
BIOMININGS
BIOMOLECULAR
BIOMOLECULE
BIOMOLECULES
BIOMORPHIC
BIONOMICALLY
BIONOMISTS
BIOPARENTS
BIOPESTICIDAL
BIOPESTICIDE
BIOPESTICIDES
BIOPHILIAS
BIOPHYSICAL
BIOPHYSICALLY
BIOPHYSICIST
BIOPHYSICISTS
BIOPHYSICS
BIOPIRACIES
BIOPIRATES
BIOPLASMIC
BIOPLASTIC
BIOPLASTICS
BIOPOIESES
BIOPOIESIS
BIOPOLYMER
BIOPOLYMERS
BIOPRINTING
BIOPRINTINGS
BIOPRIVACIES
BIOPRIVACY
BIOPROSPECTING
BIOPROSPECTINGS
BIOPSYCHOLOGIES
BIOPSYCHOLOGY
BIOREACTOR
BIOREACTORS
BIOREAGENT
BIOREAGENTS
BIOREGIONAL
BIOREGIONALISM
BIOREGIONALISMS
BIOREGIONALIST
BIOREGIONALISTS
BIOREGIONS
BIOREMEDIATION
BIOREMEDIATIONS
BIORHYTHMIC
BIORHYTHMICALLY
BIORHYTHMICS
BIORHYTHMS
BIOSAFETIES
BIOSATELLITE
BIOSATELLITES
BIOSCIENCE
BIOSCIENCES
BIOSCIENTIFIC
BIOSCIENTIST
BIOSCIENTISTS
BIOSCOPIES
BIOSENSORS
BIOSOCIALLY
BIOSPHERES
BIOSPHERIC
BIOSTATICALLY
BIOSTATICS
BIOSTATISTICAL
BIOSTATISTICIAN
BIOSTATISTICS
BIOSTRATIGRAPHY
BIOSTROMES
BIOSURGERIES
BIOSURGERY
BIOSYNTHESES
BIOSYNTHESIS
BIOSYNTHETIC
BIOSYSTEMATIC
BIOSYSTEMATICS
BIOSYSTEMATIST
BIOSYSTEMATISTS
BIOTECHNICAL
BIOTECHNOLOGIES
BIOTECHNOLOGIST
BIOTECHNOLOGY
BIOTELEMETRIC
BIOTELEMETRIES
BIOTELEMETRY
BIOTERRORS
BIOTICALLY
BIOTURBATION
BIOTURBATIONS
BIOWEAPONS
BIPARENTAL
BIPARENTALLY
BIPARIETAL
BIPARTISAN
BIPARTISANISM
BIPARTISANISMS
BIPARTISANSHIP
BIPARTISANSHIPS
BIPARTITELY
BIPARTITION
BIPARTITIONS
BIPEDALISM
BIPEDALISMS
BIPEDALITIES
BIPEDALITY
BIPETALOUS
BIPINNARIA
BIPINNARIAS
BIPINNATELY
BIPOLARISATION
BIPOLARISATIONS
BIPOLARISE
BIPOLARISED
BIPOLARISES
BIPOLARISING
BIPOLARITIES
BIPOLARITY
BIPOLARIZATION
BIPOLARIZATIONS
BIPOLARIZE
BIPOLARIZED
BIPOLARIZES
BIPOLARIZING
BIPROPELLANT
BIPROPELLANTS
BIPYRAMIDAL
BIPYRAMIDS
BIQUADRATE
BIQUADRATES
BIQUADRATIC
BIQUADRATICS
BIQUARTERLY
BIQUINTILE
BIQUINTILES
BIRACIALISM
BIRACIALISMS
BIRACIALLY
BIRADICALS
BIRCHBARKS
BIRCHWOODS
BIRDBRAINED
BIRDBRAINS
BIRDDOGGED
BIRDDOGGING
BIRDDOGGINGS
BIRDHOUSES
BIRDLIMING
BIRDSFOOTS
BIRDWATCHED
BIRDWATCHER
BIRDWATCHERS
BIRDWATCHES
BIRDWATCHING
BIRDWATCHINGS
BIREFRINGENCE
BIREFRINGENCES
BIREFRINGENT
BIROSTRATE
BIRTHDATES
BIRTHMARKS
BIRTHNAMES
BIRTHNIGHT
BIRTHNIGHTS
BIRTHPLACE
BIRTHPLACES
BIRTHRATES
BIRTHRIGHT

BIRTHRIGHTS
BIRTHROOTS
BIRTHSTONE
BIRTHSTONES
BIRTHWORTS
BISCUITIER
BISCUITIEST
BISECTIONAL
BISECTIONALLY
BISECTIONS
BISECTRICES
BISEXUALISM
BISEXUALISMS
BISEXUALITIES
BISEXUALITY
BISEXUALLY
BISHOPBIRD
BISHOPBIRDS
BISHOPDOMS
BISHOPESSES
BISHOPRICS
BISHOPWEED
BISHOPWEEDS
BISMUTHINITE
BISMUTHINITES
BISMUTHOUS
BISOCIATION
BISOCIATIONS
BISOCIATIVE
BISPHENOLS
BISPHOSPHONATE
BISPHOSPHONATES
BISSEXTILE
BISSEXTILES
BISTOURIES
BISULFATES
BISULFIDES
BISULFITES
BISULPHATE
BISULPHATES
BISULPHIDE
BISULPHIDES
BISULPHITE
BISULPHITES
BISYMMETRIC
BISYMMETRICAL
BISYMMETRICALLY
BISYMMETRIES
BISYMMETRY
BITARTRATE
BITARTRATES
BITCHERIES
BITCHFESTS
BITCHINESS
BITCHINESSES
BITEPLATES
BITMAPPING
BITONALITIES
BITONALITY
BITSTREAMS
BITTERBARK
BITTERBARKS
BITTERBRUSH
BITTERBRUSHES
BITTERCRESS
BITTERCRESSES
BITTERLING
BITTERLINGS
BITTERNESS
BITTERNESSES
BITTERNUTS
BITTERROOT
BITTERROOTS
BITTERSWEET
BITTERSWEETLY
BITTERSWEETNESS
BITTERSWEETS
BITTERWEED
BITTERWEEDS
BITTERWOOD
BITTERWOODS
BITTINESSES
BITUMINATE
BITUMINATED
BITUMINATES
BITUMINATING
BITUMINISATION
BITUMINISATIONS
BITUMINISE
BITUMINISED
BITUMINISES
BITUMINISING
BITUMINIZATION
BITUMINIZATIONS
BITUMINIZE
BITUMINIZED
BITUMINIZES
BITUMINIZING
BITUMINOUS
BIUNIQUENESS
BIUNIQUENESSES
BIVALENCES
BIVALENCIES
BIVALVULAR
BIVARIANTS
BIVARIATES
BIVOUACKED
BIVOUACKING
BIWEEKLIES
BIZARRENESS
BIZARRENESSES
BIZARRERIE
BIZARRERIES
BLABBERING
BLABBERMOUTH
BLABBERMOUTHS
BLACKBALLED
BLACKBALLING
BLACKBALLINGS
BLACKBALLS
BLACKBANDS
BLACKBERRIED
BLACKBERRIES
BLACKBERRY
BLACKBERRYING
BLACKBERRYINGS
BLACKBIRDED
BLACKBIRDER
BLACKBIRDERS
BLACKBIRDING
BLACKBIRDINGS
BLACKBIRDS
BLACKBOARD
BLACKBOARDS
BLACKBODIES
BLACKBUCKS
BLACKBUTTS
BLACKCOCKS
BLACKCURRANT
BLACKCURRANTS
BLACKDAMPS
BLACKENERS
BLACKENING
BLACKENINGS
BLACKFACED
BLACKFACES
BLACKFISHES
BLACKFLIES
BLACKGAMES
BLACKGUARD
BLACKGUARDED
BLACKGUARDING
BLACKGUARDISM
BLACKGUARDISMS
BLACKGUARDLIER
BLACKGUARDLIEST
BLACKGUARDLY
BLACKGUARDS
BLACKHANDER
BLACKHANDERS
BLACKHEADED
BLACKHEADS
BLACKHEART
BLACKHEARTS
BLACKISHLY
BLACKJACKED
BLACKJACKING
BLACKJACKS
BLACKLANDS
BLACKLEADED
BLACKLEADING
BLACKLEADS
BLACKLEGGED
BLACKLEGGING
BLACKLISTED
BLACKLISTER
BLACKLISTERS
BLACKLISTING
BLACKLISTINGS
BLACKLISTS
BLACKMAILED
BLACKMAILER
BLACKMAILERS
BLACKMAILING
BLACKMAILS
BLACKNESSES
BLACKPOLLS
BLACKSMITH
BLACKSMITHING
BLACKSMITHINGS
BLACKSMITHS
BLACKSNAKE
BLACKSNAKES
BLACKSPOTS
BLACKSTRAP
BLACKSTRAPS
BLACKTAILS
BLACKTHORN
BLACKTHORNS
BLACKTOPPED
BLACKTOPPING
BLACKWASHED
BLACKWASHES
BLACKWASHING
BLACKWATER
BLACKWATERS
BLACKWOODS
BLADDERIER
BLADDERIEST
BLADDERLIKE
BLADDERNOSE
BLADDERNOSES
BLADDERNUT
BLADDERNUTS
BLADDERWORT
BLADDERWORTS
BLADDERWRACK
BLADDERWRACKS
BLADEWORKS
BLAEBERRIES
BLAMABLENESS
BLAMABLENESSES
BLAMEABLENESS
BLAMEABLENESSES
BLAMEFULLY
BLAMEFULNESS
BLAMEFULNESSES
BLAMELESSLY
BLAMELESSNESS
BLAMELESSNESSES
BLAMESTORM
BLAMESTORMED
BLAMESTORMING
BLAMESTORMINGS
BLAMESTORMS
BLAMEWORTHIER
BLAMEWORTHIEST
BLAMEWORTHINESS
BLAMEWORTHY
BLANCHISSEUSE

BLANCHISSEUSES
BLANCMANGE
BLANCMANGES
BLANDISHED
BLANDISHER
BLANDISHERS
BLANDISHES
BLANDISHING
BLANDISHMENT
BLANDISHMENTS
BLANDNESSES
BLANKETFLOWER
BLANKETFLOWERS
BLANKETIES
BLANKETING
BLANKETINGS
BLANKETLIKE
BLANKETWEED
BLANKETWEEDS
BLANKNESSES
BLANQUETTE
BLANQUETTES
BLARNEYING
BLASPHEMED
BLASPHEMER
BLASPHEMERS
BLASPHEMES
BLASPHEMIES
BLASPHEMING
BLASPHEMOUS
BLASPHEMOUSLY
BLASPHEMOUSNESS
BLASTEMATA
BLASTEMATIC
BLASTHOLES
BLASTMENTS
BLASTOCHYLE
BLASTOCHYLES
BLASTOCOEL
BLASTOCOELE
BLASTOCOELES
BLASTOCOELIC
BLASTOCOELS
BLASTOCYST
BLASTOCYSTS
BLASTODERM
BLASTODERMIC
BLASTODERMS
BLASTODISC
BLASTODISCS
BLASTOGENESES
BLASTOGENESIS
BLASTOGENETIC
BLASTOGENIC
BLASTOMATA
BLASTOMERE
BLASTOMERES
BLASTOMERIC
BLASTOMYCOSES
BLASTOMYCOSIS
BLASTOPORAL
BLASTOPORE
BLASTOPORES
BLASTOPORIC
BLASTOPORS
BLASTOSPHERE
BLASTOSPHERES
BLASTOSPORE
BLASTOSPORES
BLASTULATION
BLASTULATIONS
BLATANCIES
BLATHERERS
BLATHERING
BLATHERINGS
BLATHERSKITE
BLATHERSKITES
BLATTERING
BLAXPLOITATION
BLAXPLOITATIONS
BLAZONINGS
BLAZONRIES
BLEACHABLE
BLEACHERIES
BLEACHERITE
BLEACHERITES
BLEACHINGS
BLEAKNESSES
BLEARINESS
BLEARINESSES
BLEMISHERS
BLEMISHING
BLEMISHMENT
BLEMISHMENTS
BLENNIOIDS
BLENNORRHEA
BLENNORRHEAS
BLENNORRHOEA
BLENNORRHOEAS
BLEOMYCINS
BLEPHARISM
BLEPHARISMS
BLEPHARITIC
BLEPHARITIS
BLEPHARITISES
BLEPHAROPLAST
BLEPHAROPLASTS
BLEPHAROPLASTY
BLEPHAROSPASM
BLEPHAROSPASMS
BLESSEDEST
BLESSEDNESS
BLESSEDNESSES
BLETHERANSKATE
BLETHERANSKATES
BLETHERATION
BLETHERATIONS
BLETHERERS
BLETHERING
BLETHERINGS
BLETHERSKATE
BLETHERSKATES
BLIGHTINGLY
BLIGHTINGS
BLIMPERIES
BLIMPISHLY
BLIMPISHNESS
BLIMPISHNESSES
BLINDFISHES
BLINDFOLDED
BLINDFOLDING
BLINDFOLDS
BLINDINGLY
BLINDNESSES
BLINDSIDED
BLINDSIDES
BLINDSIDING
BLINDSIGHT
BLINDSIGHTS
BLINDSTOREY
BLINDSTOREYS
BLINDSTORIES
BLINDSTORY
BLINDWORMS
BLINGLISHES
BLINKERING
BLISSFULLY
BLISSFULNESS
BLISSFULNESSES
BLISTERIER
BLISTERIEST
BLISTERING
BLISTERINGLY
BLITHENESS
BLITHENESSES
BLITHERING
BLITHESOME
BLITHESOMELY
BLITHESOMENESS
BLITZKRIEG
BLITZKRIEGS
BLIZZARDED
BLIZZARDIER
BLIZZARDIEST
BLIZZARDING
BLIZZARDLY
BLOATEDNESS
BLOATEDNESSES
BLOATWARES
BLOCKADERS
BLOCKADING
BLOCKBOARD
BLOCKBOARDS
BLOCKBUSTED
BLOCKBUSTER
BLOCKBUSTERS
BLOCKBUSTING
BLOCKBUSTINGS
BLOCKBUSTS
BLOCKCHAIN
BLOCKCHAINS
BLOCKHEADED
BLOCKHEADEDLY
BLOCKHEADEDNESS
BLOCKHEADS
BLOCKHOLES
BLOCKHOUSE
BLOCKHOUSES
BLOCKINESS
BLOCKINESSES
BLOCKISHLY
BLOCKISHNESS
BLOCKISHNESSES
BLOCKSHIPS
BLOCKWORKS
BLOGGERATI
BLOGJACKING
BLOGJACKINGS
BLOGOSPHERE
BLOGOSPHERES
BLOGSTREAM
BLOGSTREAMS
BLOKARTING
BLOKARTINGS
BLOKEISHNESS
BLOKEISHNESSES
BLOKISHNESS
BLOKISHNESSES
BLONDENESS
BLONDENESSES
BLONDINING
BLONDNESSES
BLOODBATHS
BLOODCURDLING
BLOODCURDLINGLY
BLOODGUILT
BLOODGUILTIER
BLOODGUILTIEST
BLOODGUILTINESS
BLOODGUILTS
BLOODGUILTY
BLOODHOUND
BLOODHOUNDS
BLOODINESS
BLOODINESSES
BLOODLESSLY
BLOODLESSNESS
BLOODLESSNESSES
BLOODLETTER
BLOODLETTERS
BLOODLETTING
BLOODLETTINGS
BLOODLINES
BLOODLUSTS
BLOODMOBILE
BLOODMOBILES
BLOODROOTS
BLOODSHEDS
BLOODSPRENT
BLOODSTAIN

B

BLOODSTAINED
BLOODSTAINS
BLOODSTOCK
BLOODSTOCKS
BLOODSTONE
BLOODSTONES
BLOODSTREAM
BLOODSTREAMS
BLOODSUCKER
BLOODSUCKERS
BLOODSUCKING
BLOODTHIRSTIER
BLOODTHIRSTIEST
BLOODTHIRSTILY
BLOODTHIRSTY
BLOODWOODS
BLOODWORMS
BLOODWORTS
BLOOMERIES
BLOQUISTES
BLOSSOMIER
BLOSSOMIEST
BLOSSOMING
BLOSSOMINGS
BLOSSOMLESS
BLOTCHIEST
BLOTCHINESS
BLOTCHINESSES
BLOTCHINGS
BLOTTESQUE
BLOTTESQUES
BLOVIATING
BLOVIATION
BLOVIATIONS
BLOWFISHES
BLOWINESSES
BLOWSINESS
BLOWSINESSES
BLOWTORCHED
BLOWTORCHES
BLOWTORCHING
BLOWZINESS
BLOWZINESSES
BLUBBERERS
BLUBBERIER
BLUBBERIEST
BLUBBERING
BLUDGEONED
BLUDGEONER
BLUDGEONERS
BLUDGEONING
BLUEBEARDS
BLUEBERRIES
BLUEBLOODS
BLUEBONNET
BLUEBONNETS
BLUEBOTTLE
BLUEBOTTLES
BLUEBREAST
BLUEBREASTS
BLUEBUSHES
BLUEFISHES
BLUEGRASSES
BLUEISHNESS
BLUEISHNESSES
BLUEJACKET
BLUEJACKETS
BLUEJACKING
BLUEJACKINGS
BLUELINERS
BLUEMOUTHS
BLUENESSES
BLUEPOINTS
BLUEPRINTED
BLUEPRINTING
BLUEPRINTS
BLUESHIFTED
BLUESHIFTS
BLUESNARFING
BLUESNARFINGS
BLUESTOCKING
BLUESTOCKINGS
BLUESTONES
BLUETHROAT
BLUETHROATS
BLUETONGUE
BLUETONGUES
BLUFFNESSES
BLUISHNESS
BLUISHNESSES
BLUNDERBUSS
BLUNDERBUSSES
BLUNDERERS
BLUNDERING
BLUNDERINGLY
BLUNDERINGS
BLUNTHEADS
BLUNTNESSES
BLURREDNESS
BLURREDNESSES
BLURRINESS
BLURRINESSES
BLURRINGLY
BLUSHINGLY
BLUSHLESSLY
BLUSTERERS
BLUSTERIER
BLUSTERIEST
BLUSTERING
BLUSTERINGLY
BLUSTERINGS
BLUSTEROUS
BLUSTEROUSLY
BLUTWURSTS
BOARDINGHOUSE
BOARDINGHOUSES
BOARDROOMS
BOARDSAILING
BOARDSAILINGS
BOARDSAILOR
BOARDSAILORS
BOARDWALKS
BOARFISHES
BOARHOUNDS
BOARISHNESS
BOARISHNESSES
BOASTFULLY
BOASTFULNESS
BOASTFULNESSES
BOASTINGLY
BOATBUILDER
BOATBUILDERS
BOATBUILDING
BOATBUILDINGS
BOATHOUSES
BOATLIFTED
BOATLIFTING
BOATSWAINS
BOBBEJAANS
BOBBITTING
BOBBLEHEAD
BOBBLEHEADS
BOBBYSOCKS
BOBBYSOXER
BOBBYSOXERS
BOBSLEDDED
BOBSLEDDER
BOBSLEDDERS
BOBSLEDDING
BOBSLEDDINGS
BOBSLEIGHED
BOBSLEIGHING
BOBSLEIGHINGS
BOBSLEIGHS
BOBTAILING
BOBWEIGHTS
BOCCONCINI
BODACIOUSLY
BODDHISATTVA
BODDHISATTVAS
BODEGUEROS
BODHISATTVA
BODHISATTVAS
BODYBOARDED
BODYBOARDING
BODYBOARDINGS
BODYBOARDS
BODYBUILDER
BODYBUILDERS
BODYBUILDING
BODYBUILDINGS
BODYBUILDS
BODYCHECKED
BODYCHECKING
BODYCHECKS
BODYGUARDED
BODYGUARDING
BODYGUARDS
BODYSHAPER
BODYSHAPERS
BODYSHELLS
BODYSNATCHER
BODYSNATCHERS
BODYSURFED
BODYSURFER
BODYSURFERS
BODYSURFING
BODYSURFINGS
BODYWASHES
BODYWORKER
BODYWORKERS
BOEREMUSIEK
BOEREMUSIEKS
BOEREWORSES
BOFFINIEST
BOGGINESSES
BOGTROTTING
BOGTROTTINGS
BOGUSNESSES
BOHEMIANISM
BOHEMIANISMS
BOILERMAKER
BOILERMAKERS
BOILERMAKING
BOILERMAKINGS
BOILERPLATE
BOILERPLATED
BOILERPLATES
BOILERPLATING
BOILERSUIT
BOILERSUITS
BOISTEROUS
BOISTEROUSLY
BOISTEROUSNESS
BOKMAKIERIE
BOKMAKIERIES
BOLDFACING
BOLDNESSES
BOLECTIONS
BOLIVIANOS
BOLLETRIES
BOLLOCKING
BOLLOCKINGS
BOLLOCKSED
BOLLOCKSES
BOLLOCKSING
BOLOGNESES
BOLOGRAPHS
BOLOMETERS
BOLOMETRIC
BOLOMETRICALLY
BOLOMETRIES
BOLSHEVIKI
BOLSHEVIKS
BOLSHEVISE
BOLSHEVISED
BOLSHEVISES
BOLSHEVISING
BOLSHEVISM
BOLSHEVISMS

BOLSHEVIZE
BOLSHEVIZED
BOLSHEVIZES
BOLSHEVIZING
BOLSTERERS
BOLSTERING
BOLSTERINGS
BOMBACACEOUS
BOMBARDERS
BOMBARDIER
BOMBARDIERS
BOMBARDING
BOMBARDMENT
BOMBARDMENTS
BOMBARDONS
BOMBASINES
BOMBASTERS
BOMBASTICALLY
BOMBASTING
BOMBAZINES
BOMBILATED
BOMBILATES
BOMBILATING
BOMBILATION
BOMBILATIONS
BOMBINATED
BOMBINATES
BOMBINATING
BOMBINATION
BOMBINATIONS
BOMBPROOFED
BOMBPROOFING
BOMBPROOFS
BOMBSHELLS
BOMBSIGHTS
BONAMIASES
BONAMIASIS
BONASSUSES
BONBONNIERE
BONBONNIERES
BONDHOLDER
BONDHOLDERS
BONDMANSHIP
BONDMANSHIPS
BONDSERVANT
BONDSERVANTS
BONDSTONES
BONDSWOMAN
BONDSWOMEN
BONEBLACKS
BONEFISHES
BONEFISHING
BONEFISHINGS
BONEHEADED
BONEHEADEDNESS
BONESETTER
BONESETTERS
BONESHAKER
BONESHAKERS
BONHOMMIES
BONILASSES
BONINESSES
BONKBUSTER
BONKBUSTERS
BONNIBELLS
BONNILASSE
BONNILASSES
BONNINESSES
BONNYCLABBER
BONNYCLABBERS
BOOBIALLAS
BOOBOISIES
BOOGALOOED
BOOGALOOING
BOOKBINDER
BOOKBINDERIES
BOOKBINDERS
BOOKBINDERY
BOOKBINDING
BOOKBINDINGS
BOOKCROSSING
BOOKCROSSINGS
BOOKENDING
BOOKISHNESS
BOOKISHNESSES
BOOKKEEPER
BOOKKEEPERS
BOOKKEEPING
BOOKKEEPINGS
BOOKLIGHTS
BOOKMAKERS
BOOKMAKING
BOOKMAKINGS
BOOKMARKED
BOOKMARKER
BOOKMARKERS
BOOKMARKING
BOOKMOBILE
BOOKMOBILES
BOOKPLATES
BOOKSELLER
BOOKSELLERS
BOOKSELLING
BOOKSELLINGS
BOOKSHELVES
BOOKSTALLS
BOOKSTANDS
BOOKSTORES
BOOMERANGED
BOOMERANGING
BOOMERANGS
BOOMSLANGS
BOOMSTICKS
BOONDOGGLE
BOONDOGGLED
BOONDOGGLER
BOONDOGGLERS
BOONDOGGLES
BOONDOGGLING
BOONGARIES
BOORISHNESS
BOORISHNESSES
BOOSTERISH
BOOSTERISM
BOOSTERISMS
BOOTBLACKS
BOOTLEGGED
BOOTLEGGER
BOOTLEGGERS
BOOTLEGGING
BOOTLEGGINGS
BOOTLESSLY
BOOTLESSNESS
BOOTLESSNESSES
BOOTLICKED
BOOTLICKER
BOOTLICKERS
BOOTLICKING
BOOTLICKINGS
BOOTLOADER
BOOTLOADERS
BOOTMAKERS
BOOTMAKING
BOOTMAKINGS
BOOTSTRAPPED
BOOTSTRAPPING
BOOTSTRAPS
BOOTYLICIOUS
BOOZEHOUND
BOOZEHOUNDS
BOOZINESSES
BORAGINACEOUS
BORBORYGMAL
BORBORYGMI
BORBORYGMIC
BORBORYGMUS
BORDEREAUX
BORDERLAND
BORDERLANDS
BORDERLESS
BORDERLINE
BORDERLINES
BORDRAGING
BORDRAGINGS
BORESCOPES
BORGHETTOS
BORINGNESS
BORINGNESSES
BOROHYDRIDE
BOROHYDRIDES
BOROSILICATE
BOROSILICATES
BORROWINGS
BOSBERAADS
BOSCHVARKS
BOSCHVELDS
BOSKINESSES
BOSSINESSES
BOSSNAPPING
BOSSNAPPINGS
BOSSYBOOTS
BOTANICALLY
BOTANICALS
BOTANISERS
BOTANISING
BOTANIZERS
BOTANIZING
BOTANOMANCIES
BOTANOMANCY
BOTCHERIES
BOTCHINESS
BOTCHINESSES
BOTHERATION
BOTHERATIONS
BOTHERSOME
BOTRYOIDAL
BOTRYTISES
BOTTLEBRUSH
BOTTLEBRUSHES
BOTTLEFULS
BOTTLENECK
BOTTLENECKED
BOTTLENECKING
BOTTLENECKS
BOTTLENOSE
BOTTLENOSES
BOTTOMINGS
BOTTOMLAND
BOTTOMLANDS
BOTTOMLESS
BOTTOMLESSLY
BOTTOMLESSNESS
BOTTOMMOST
BOTTOMNESS
BOTTOMNESSES
BOTTOMRIES
BOTULINUMS
BOTULINUSES
BOUGAINVILIA
BOUGAINVILIAS
BOUGAINVILLAEA
BOUGAINVILLAEAS
BOUGAINVILLEA
BOUGAINVILLEAS
BOUILLABAISSE
BOUILLABAISSES
BOUILLOTTE
BOUILLOTTES
BOULDERERS
BOULDERIER
BOULDERIEST
BOULDERING
BOULDERINGS
BOULEVARDIER
BOULEVARDIERS
BOULEVARDS
BOULEVERSEMENT
BOULEVERSEMENTS
BOULLEWORK
BOULLEWORKS

B

BOUNCEDOWN
BOUNCEDOWNS
BOUNCINESS
BOUNCINESSES
BOUNCINGLY
BOUNDARIES
BOUNDEDNESS
BOUNDEDNESSES
BOUNDERISH
BOUNDLESSLY
BOUNDLESSNESS
BOUNDLESSNESSES
BOUNDNESSES
BOUNTEOUSLY
BOUNTEOUSNESS
BOUNTEOUSNESSES
BOUNTIFULLY
BOUNTIFULNESS
BOUNTIFULNESSES
BOUNTYHEDS
BOUQUETIERE
BOUQUETIERES
BOURASQUES
BOURBONISM
BOURBONISMS
BOURGEOISE
BOURGEOISES
BOURGEOISIE
BOURGEOISIES
BOURGEOISIFIED
BOURGEOISIFIES
BOURGEOISIFY
BOURGEOISIFYING
BOURGEONED
BOURGEONING
BOURGUIGNON
BOURGUIGNONNE
BOURGUIGNONNES
BOURGUIGNONS
BOUSINGKEN
BOUSINGKENS
BOUSTROPHEDON
BOUSTROPHEDONIC
BOUSTROPHEDONS
BOUTIQUIER
BOUTIQUIEST
BOUTONNIERE
BOUTONNIERES
BOUVARDIAS
BOVINITIES
BOWDLERISATION
BOWDLERISATIONS
BOWDLERISE
BOWDLERISED
BOWDLERISER
BOWDLERISERS
BOWDLERISES
BOWDLERISING
BOWDLERISM
BOWDLERISMS
BOWDLERIZATION
BOWDLERIZATIONS
BOWDLERIZE
BOWDLERIZED
BOWDLERIZER
BOWDLERIZERS
BOWDLERIZES
BOWDLERIZING
BOWERBIRDS
BOWERWOMAN
BOWERWOMEN
BOWHUNTERS
BOWHUNTING
BOWHUNTINGS
BOWLINGUAL
BOWLINGUALS
BOWSTRINGED
BOWSTRINGING
BOWSTRINGS
BOXBERRIES
BOXERCISES
BOXHAULING
BOXINESSES
BOXKEEPERS
BOXWALLAHS
BOYCOTTERS
BOYCOTTING
BOYFRIENDS
BOYISHNESS
BOYISHNESSES
BOYSENBERRIES
BOYSENBERRY
BRAAIVLEIS
BRAAIVLEISES
BRABBLEMENT
BRABBLEMENTS
BRACHIATED
BRACHIATES
BRACHIATING
BRACHIATION
BRACHIATIONS
BRACHIATOR
BRACHIATORS
BRACHIOCEPHALIC
BRACHIOPOD
BRACHIOPODS
BRACHIOSAURUS
BRACHIOSAURUSES
BRACHISTOCHRONE
BRACHYAXES
BRACHYAXIS
BRACHYCEPHAL
BRACHYCEPHALIC
BRACHYCEPHALICS
BRACHYCEPHALIES
BRACHYCEPHALISM
BRACHYCEPHALOUS
BRACHYCEPHALS
BRACHYCEPHALY
BRACHYCEROUS
BRACHYDACTYL
BRACHYDACTYLIC
BRACHYDACTYLIES
BRACHYDACTYLISM
BRACHYDACTYLOUS
BRACHYDACTYLY
BRACHYDIAGONAL
BRACHYDIAGONALS
BRACHYDOME
BRACHYDOMES
BRACHYGRAPHIES
BRACHYGRAPHY
BRACHYLOGIES
BRACHYLOGOUS
BRACHYLOGY
BRACHYODONT
BRACHYPINAKOID
BRACHYPINAKOIDS
BRACHYPRISM
BRACHYPRISMS
BRACHYPTERISM
BRACHYPTERISMS
BRACHYPTEROUS
BRACHYTHERAPIES
BRACHYTHERAPY
BRACHYURAL
BRACHYURAN
BRACHYURANS
BRACHYUROUS
BRACKETING
BRACKETINGS
BRACKISHNESS
BRACKISHNESSES
BRACTEATES
BRACTEOLATE
BRACTEOLES
BRADYCARDIA
BRADYCARDIAC
BRADYCARDIAS
BRADYKINESIA
BRADYKINESIAS
BRADYKININ
BRADYKININS
BRADYPEPTIC
BRADYPEPTICS
BRADYSEISM
BRADYSEISMS
BRAGADISME
BRAGADISMES
BRAGGADOCIO
BRAGGADOCIOS
BRAGGADOCIOUS
BRAGGARTISM
BRAGGARTISMS
BRAGGARTLIER
BRAGGARTLIEST
BRAGGARTLY
BRAGGINGLY
BRAHMANISM
BRAHMANISMS
BRAHMANIST
BRAHMANISTS
BRAHMINISM
BRAHMINISMS
BRAHMINIST
BRAHMINISTS
BRAILLEWRITER
BRAILLEWRITERS
BRAILLISTS
BRAINBOXES
BRAINCASES
BRAINCHILD
BRAINCHILDREN
BRAINFARTS
BRAINFOODS
BRAININESS
BRAININESSES
BRAINLESSLY
BRAINLESSNESS
BRAINLESSNESSES
BRAINPOWER
BRAINPOWERS
BRAINSICKLY
BRAINSICKNESS
BRAINSICKNESSES
BRAINSTEMS
BRAINSTORM
BRAINSTORMED
BRAINSTORMER
BRAINSTORMERS
BRAINSTORMING
BRAINSTORMINGS
BRAINSTORMS
BRAINTEASER
BRAINTEASERS
BRAINWASHED
BRAINWASHER
BRAINWASHERS
BRAINWASHES
BRAINWASHING
BRAINWASHINGS
BRAINWAVES
BRAINWORKS
BRAMBLIEST
BRAMBLINGS
BRANCHERIES
BRANCHIATE
BRANCHIEST
BRANCHINGS
BRANCHIOPOD
BRANCHIOPODS
BRANCHIOSTEGAL
BRANCHLESS
BRANCHLETS
BRANCHLIKE
BRANCHLINE
BRANCHLINES
BRANDERING
BRANDISHED
BRANDISHER

BRANDISHERS
BRANDISHES
BRANDISHING
BRANDLINGS
BRANDRETHS
BRANFULNESS
BRANFULNESSES
BRANGLINGS
BRANKURSINE
BRANKURSINES
BRANNIGANS
BRASHINESS
BRASHINESSES
BRASHNESSES
BRASILEINS
BRASSBOUND
BRASSERIES
BRASSFOUNDER
BRASSFOUNDERS
BRASSFOUNDING
BRASSFOUNDINGS
BRASSICACEOUS
BRASSIERES
BRASSINESS
BRASSINESSES
BRASSWARES
BRATPACKER
BRATPACKERS
BRATTICING
BRATTICINGS
BRATTINESS
BRATTINESSES
BRATTISHED
BRATTISHES
BRATTISHING
BRATTISHINGS
BRATTLINGS
BRATWURSTS
BRAUNCHING
BRAUNSCHWEIGER
BRAUNSCHWEIGERS
BRAVADOING
BRAVENESSES
BRAVISSIMO
BRAWNINESS
BRAWNINESSES
BRAZENNESS
BRAZENNESSES
BRAZENRIES
BRAZIERIES
BRAZILEINS
BRAZILWOOD
BRAZILWOODS
BREADBASKET
BREADBASKETS
BREADBERRIES
BREADBERRY
BREADBOARD
BREADBOARDED
BREADBOARDING
BREADBOARDS
BREADBOXES
BREADCRUMB
BREADCRUMBED
BREADCRUMBING
BREADCRUMBS
BREADFRUIT
BREADFRUITS
BREADHEADS
BREADKNIFE
BREADKNIVES
BREADLINES
BREADROOMS
BREADROOTS
BREADSTICK
BREADSTICKS
BREADSTUFF
BREADSTUFFS
BREADTHWAYS
BREADTHWISE
BREADWINNER
BREADWINNERS
BREADWINNING
BREADWINNINGS
BREAKABLENESS
BREAKABLENESSES
BREAKABLES
BREAKAWAYS
BREAKBEATS
BREAKDANCE
BREAKDANCED
BREAKDANCER
BREAKDANCERS
BREAKDANCES
BREAKDANCING
BREAKDANCINGS
BREAKDOWNS
BREAKEVENS
BREAKFASTED
BREAKFASTER
BREAKFASTERS
BREAKFASTING
BREAKFASTS
BREAKFRONT
BREAKFRONTS
BREAKPOINT
BREAKPOINTS
BREAKTHROUGH
BREAKTHROUGHS
BREAKTIMES
BREAKWALLS
BREAKWATER
BREAKWATERS
BREASTBONE
BREASTBONES
BREASTFEED
BREASTFEEDING
BREASTFEEDINGS
BREASTFEEDS
BREASTPINS
BREASTPLATE
BREASTPLATES
BREASTPLOUGH
BREASTPLOUGHS
BREASTRAIL
BREASTRAILS
BREASTSTROKE
BREASTSTROKER
BREASTSTROKERS
BREASTSTROKES
BREASTSUMMER
BREASTSUMMERS
BREASTWORK
BREASTWORKS
BREATHABILITIES
BREATHABILITY
BREATHABLE
BREATHALYSE
BREATHALYSED
BREATHALYSER
BREATHALYSERS
BREATHALYSES
BREATHALYSING
BREATHALYZE
BREATHALYZED
BREATHALYZER
BREATHALYZERS
BREATHALYZES
BREATHALYZING
BREATHARIAN
BREATHARIANISM
BREATHARIANISMS
BREATHARIANS
BREATHIEST
BREATHINESS
BREATHINESSES
BREATHINGS
BREATHLESS
BREATHLESSLY
BREATHLESSNESS
BREATHTAKING
BREATHTAKINGLY
BRECCIATED
BRECCIATES
BRECCIATING
BRECCIATION
BRECCIATIONS
BREECHBLOCK
BREECHBLOCKS
BREECHCLOTH
BREECHCLOTHS
BREECHCLOUT
BREECHCLOUTS
BREECHINGS
BREECHLESS
BREECHLOADER
BREECHLOADERS
BREEZELESS
BREEZEWAYS
BREEZINESS
BREEZINESSES
BREMSSTRAHLUNG
BREMSSTRAHLUNGS
BRESSUMMER
BRESSUMMERS
BRETASCHES
BRETTICING
BREUNNERITE
BREUNNERITES
BREVETCIES
BREVETTING
BREVIARIES
BREVIPENNATE
BREWHOUSES
BREWMASTER
BREWMASTERS
BRIARROOTS
BRIARWOODS
BRICABRACS
BRICKCLAYS
BRICKEARTH
BRICKEARTHS
BRICKFIELD
BRICKFIELDER
BRICKFIELDERS
BRICKFIELDS
BRICKKILNS
BRICKLAYER
BRICKLAYERS
BRICKLAYING
BRICKLAYINGS
BRICKMAKER
BRICKMAKERS
BRICKMAKING
BRICKMAKINGS
BRICKSHAPED
BRICKWALLS
BRICKWORKS
BRICKYARDS
BRICOLAGES
BRICOLEURS
BRIDECAKES
BRIDEGROOM
BRIDEGROOMS
BRIDEMAIDEN
BRIDEMAIDENS
BRIDEMAIDS
BRIDESMAID
BRIDESMAIDS
BRIDEWEALTH
BRIDEWEALTHS
BRIDEWELLS
BRIDEZILLA
BRIDEZILLAS
BRIDGEABLE
BRIDGEBOARD
BRIDGEBOARDS
BRIDGEHEAD
BRIDGEHEADS
BRIDGELESS

BRIDGELIKE
BRIDGEWORK
BRIDGEWORKS
BRIDLEWAYS
BRIDLEWISE
BRIEFCASES
BRIEFNESSES
BRIERROOTS
BRIERWOODS
BRIGADIERS
BRIGANDAGE
BRIGANDAGES
BRIGANDINE
BRIGANDINES
BRIGANDRIES
BRIGANTINE
BRIGANTINES
BRIGHTENED
BRIGHTENER
BRIGHTENERS
BRIGHTENING
BRIGHTNESS
BRIGHTNESSES
BRIGHTSOME
BRIGHTWORK
BRIGHTWORKS
BRILLIANCE
BRILLIANCES
BRILLIANCIES
BRILLIANCY
BRILLIANTE
BRILLIANTED
BRILLIANTINE
BRILLIANTINED
BRILLIANTINES
BRILLIANTING
BRILLIANTLY
BRILLIANTNESS
BRILLIANTNESSES
BRILLIANTS
BRIMFULLNESS
BRIMFULLNESSES
BRIMFULNESS
BRIMFULNESSES
BRIMSTONES
BRIMSTONIER
BRIMSTONIEST
BRINELLING
BRINELLINGS
BRINGDOWNS
BRININESSES
BRINJARRIES
BRINKMANSHIP
BRINKMANSHIPS
BRINKSMANSHIP
BRINKSMANSHIPS
BRIOLETTES
BRIQUETTED
BRIQUETTES
BRIQUETTING
BRISKENING
BRISKNESSES
BRISTLECONE
BRISTLECONES
BRISTLELIKE
BRISTLETAIL
BRISTLETAILS
BRISTLIEST
BRISTLINESS
BRISTLINESSES
BRITANNIAS
BRITSCHKAS
BRITTANIAS
BRITTLENESS
BRITTLENESSES
BROADBANDS
BROADBEANS
BROADBILLS
BROADBRIMS
BROADBRUSH
BROADCASTED
BROADCASTER
BROADCASTERS
BROADCASTING
BROADCASTINGS
BROADCASTS
BROADCLOTH
BROADCLOTHS
BROADENERS
BROADENING
BROADLEAVED
BROADLEAVES
BROADLINES
BROADLOOMS
BROADNESSES
BROADPIECE
BROADPIECES
BROADSCALE
BROADSHEET
BROADSHEETS
BROADSIDED
BROADSIDES
BROADSIDING
BROADSWORD
BROADSWORDS
BROADTAILS
BROBDINGNAGIAN
BROCATELLE
BROCATELLES
BROCCOLINI
BROCCOLINIS
BROCHETTES
BROGUERIES
BROIDERERS
BROIDERIES
BROIDERING
BROIDERINGS
BROKENHEARTED
BROKENHEARTEDLY
BROKENNESS
BROKENNESSES
BROKERAGES
BROKERINGS
BROMEGRASS
BROMEGRASSES
BROMELAINS
BROMELIACEOUS
BROMELIADS
BROMEOSINS
BROMHIDROSES
BROMHIDROSIS
BROMIDROSES
BROMIDROSIS
BROMINATED
BROMINATES
BROMINATING
BROMINATION
BROMINATIONS
BROMINISMS
BROMOCRIPTINE
BROMOCRIPTINES
BROMOFORMS
BROMOURACIL
BROMOURACILS
BRONCHIALLY
BRONCHIECTASES
BRONCHIECTASIS
BRONCHIOLAR
BRONCHIOLE
BRONCHIOLES
BRONCHIOLITIS
BRONCHIOLITISES
BRONCHITIC
BRONCHITICS
BRONCHITIS
BRONCHITISES
BRONCHODILATOR
BRONCHODILATORS
BRONCHOGENIC
BRONCHOGRAPHIES
BRONCHOGRAPHY
BRONCHOSCOPE
BRONCHOSCOPES
BRONCHOSCOPIC
BRONCHOSCOPICAL
BRONCHOSCOPIES
BRONCHOSCOPIST
BRONCHOSCOPISTS
BRONCHOSCOPY
BRONCHOSPASM
BRONCHOSPASMS
BRONCHOSPASTIC
BRONCOBUSTER
BRONCOBUSTERS
BRONDYRONS
BRONTOBYTE
BRONTOBYTES
BRONTOSAUR
BRONTOSAURS
BRONTOSAURUS
BRONTOSAURUSES
BRONZIFIED
BRONZIFIES
BRONZIFYING
BROODINESS
BROODINESSES
BROODINGLY
BROODMARES
BROOKLIMES
BROOKWEEDS
BROOMBALLER
BROOMBALLERS
BROOMBALLS
BROOMCORNS
BROOMRAPES
BROOMSTAFF
BROOMSTAFFS
BROOMSTICK
BROOMSTICKS
BROTHERHOOD
BROTHERHOODS
BROTHERING
BROTHERLIER
BROTHERLIEST
BROTHERLIKE
BROTHERLINESS
BROTHERLINESSES
BROUGHTASES
BROWALLIAS
BROWBEATEN
BROWBEATER
BROWBEATERS
BROWBEATING
BROWBEATINGS
BROWNFIELD
BROWNFIELDS
BROWNNESSES
BROWNNOSED
BROWNNOSER
BROWNNOSERS
BROWNNOSES
BROWNNOSING
BROWNSHIRT
BROWNSHIRTS
BROWNSTONE
BROWNSTONES
BROWRIDGES
BROWSABLES
BRUCELLOSES
BRUCELLOSIS
BRUGMANSIA
BRUGMANSIAS
BRUMMAGEMS
BRUSCHETTA
BRUSCHETTAS
BRUSCHETTE
BRUSHABILITIES
BRUSHABILITY
BRUSHBACKS
BRUSHFIRES

BRUSHLANDS
BRUSHMARKS
BRUSHSTROKE
BRUSHSTROKES
BRUSHWHEEL
BRUSHWHEELS
BRUSHWOODS
BRUSHWORKS
BRUSQUENESS
BRUSQUENESSES
BRUSQUERIE
BRUSQUERIES
BRUTALISATION
BRUTALISATIONS
BRUTALISED
BRUTALISES
BRUTALISING
BRUTALISMS
BRUTALISTS
BRUTALITIES
BRUTALIZATION
BRUTALIZATIONS
BRUTALIZED
BRUTALIZES
BRUTALIZING
BRUTENESSES
BRUTIFYING
BRUTISHNESS
BRUTISHNESSES
BRYOLOGICAL
BRYOLOGIES
BRYOLOGIST
BRYOLOGISTS
BRYOPHYLLUM
BRYOPHYLLUMS
BRYOPHYTES
BRYOPHYTIC
BUBBLEGUMS
BUBBLEHEAD
BUBBLEHEADED
BUBBLEHEADS
BUBONOCELE
BUBONOCELES
BUCCANEERED
BUCCANEERING
BUCCANEERINGS
BUCCANEERISH
BUCCANEERS
BUCCANIERED
BUCCANIERING
BUCCANIERS
BUCCINATOR
BUCCINATORS
BUCCINATORY
BUCELLASES
BUCENTAURS
BUCKBOARDS
BUCKBRUSHES
BUCKETFULS
BUCKETINGS
BUCKETSFUL
BUCKHOUNDS
BUCKJUMPER
BUCKJUMPERS
BUCKJUMPING
BUCKJUMPINGS
BUCKLERING
BUCKRAMING
BUCKSHISHED
BUCKSHISHES
BUCKSHISHING
BUCKSKINNED
BUCKTHORNS
BUCKTOOTHED
BUCKWHEATS
BUCKYBALLS
BUCKYTUBES
BUCOLICALLY
BUDGERIGAR
BUDGERIGARS
BUDGETEERS
BUDGETINGS
BUDTENDERS
BUFFALOBERRIES
BUFFALOBERRY
BUFFALOFISH
BUFFALOFISHES
BUFFALOING
BUFFERINGS
BUFFETINGS
BUFFLEHEAD
BUFFLEHEADS
BUFFOONERIES
BUFFOONERY
BUFFOONISH
BUFOTALINS
BUFOTENINE
BUFOTENINES
BUGGINESSES
BUGLEWEEDS
BUHRSTONES
BUILDDOWNS
BUIRDLIEST
BULBIFEROUS
BULBOSITIES
BULBOUSNESS
BULBOUSNESSES
BULGINESSES
BULKHEADED
BULKINESSES
BULLBAITING
BULLBAITINGS
BULLBRIERS
BULLDOGGED
BULLDOGGER
BULLDOGGERS
BULLDOGGING
BULLDOGGINGS
BULLDOZERS
BULLDOZING
BULLETINED
BULLETINING
BULLETPROOF
BULLETPROOFED
BULLETPROOFING
BULLETPROOFS
BULLETRIES
BULLETWOOD
BULLETWOODS
BULLFIGHTER
BULLFIGHTERS
BULLFIGHTING
BULLFIGHTINGS
BULLFIGHTS
BULLFINCHES
BULLHEADED
BULLHEADEDLY
BULLHEADEDNESS
BULLIONIST
BULLIONISTS
BULLISHNESS
BULLISHNESSES
BULLMASTIFF
BULLMASTIFFS
BULLNECKED
BULLOCKIER
BULLOCKIES
BULLOCKIEST
BULLOCKING
BULLROARER
BULLROARERS
BULLRUSHES
BULLSHITTED
BULLSHITTER
BULLSHITTERS
BULLSHITTING
BULLSHITTINGS
BULLSNAKES
BULLTERRIER
BULLTERRIERS
BULLWADDIE
BULLWADDIES
BULLWHACKED
BULLWHACKING
BULLWHACKS
BULLWHIPPED
BULLWHIPPING
BULLYCIDES
BULLYRAGGED
BULLYRAGGING
BULRUSHIER
BULRUSHIEST
BULWADDEES
BULWADDIES
BULWARKING
BUMBAILIFF
BUMBAILIFFS
BUMBERSHOOT
BUMBERSHOOTS
BUMBLEBEES
BUMBLEBERRIES
BUMBLEBERRY
BUMBLEDOMS
BUMBLINGLY
BUMFREEZER
BUMFREEZERS
BUMFUZZLED
BUMFUZZLES
BUMFUZZLING
BUMMALOTIS
BUMPINESSES
BUMPKINISH
BUMPKINLIER
BUMPKINLIEST
BUMPOLOGIES
BUMPSADAISY
BUMPTIOUSLY
BUMPTIOUSNESS
BUMPTIOUSNESSES
BUMSUCKERS
BUMSUCKING
BUMSUCKINGS
BUNBURYING
BUNCHBERRIES
BUNCHBERRY
BUNCHGRASS
BUNCHGRASSES
BUNCHINESS
BUNCHINESSES
BUNDOBUSTS
BUNGALOIDS
BUNGLESOME
BUNGLINGLY
BUNKHOUSES
BUOYANCIES
BUOYANTNESS
BUOYANTNESSES
BUPIVACAINE
BUPIVACAINES
BUPRENORPHINE
BUPRENORPHINES
BUPRESTIDS
BUPROPIONS
BURDENSOME
BUREAUCRACIES
BUREAUCRACY
BUREAUCRAT
BUREAUCRATESE
BUREAUCRATESES
BUREAUCRATIC
BUREAUCRATISE
BUREAUCRATISED
BUREAUCRATISES
BUREAUCRATISING
BUREAUCRATISM
BUREAUCRATISMS
BUREAUCRATIST
BUREAUCRATISTS
BUREAUCRATIZE
BUREAUCRATIZED

BUREAUCRATIZES
BUREAUCRATIZING
BUREAUCRATS
BURGEONING
BURGLARIES
BURGLARING
BURGLARIOUS
BURGLARIOUSLY
BURGLARISE
BURGLARISED
BURGLARISES
BURGLARISING
BURGLARIZE
BURGLARIZED
BURGLARIZES
BURGLARIZING
BURGLARPROOF
BURGOMASTER
BURGOMASTERS
BURGUNDIES
BURLADEROS
BURLESQUED
BURLESQUELY
BURLESQUER
BURLESQUERS
BURLESQUES
BURLESQUING
BURLEYCUES
BURLINESSES
BURNETTISE
BURNETTISED
BURNETTISES
BURNETTISING
BURNETTIZE
BURNETTIZED
BURNETTIZES
BURNETTIZING
BURNISHABLE
BURNISHERS
BURNISHING
BURNISHINGS
BURNISHMENT
BURNISHMENTS
BURRAMUNDI
BURRAMUNDIS
BURRAMYSES
BURRAWANGS
BURRFISHES
BURROWSTOWN
BURROWSTOWNS
BURRSTONES
BURSARSHIP
BURSARSHIPS
BURSERACEOUS
BURSICULATE
BURSITISES
BURTHENING
BURTHENSOME
BUSHBABIES
BUSHBASHING
BUSHBASHINGS
BUSHCRAFTS
BUSHELFULS
BUSHELLERS
BUSHELLING
BUSHELLINGS
BUSHELWOMAN
BUSHELWOMEN
BUSHFIGHTING
BUSHFIGHTINGS
BUSHHAMMER
BUSHHAMMERS
BUSHINESSES
BUSHMANSHIP
BUSHMANSHIPS
BUSHMASTER
BUSHMASTERS
BUSHRANGER
BUSHRANGERS
BUSHRANGING
BUSHRANGINGS
BUSHWALKED
BUSHWALKER
BUSHWALKERS
BUSHWALKING
BUSHWALKINGS
BUSHWHACKED
BUSHWHACKER
BUSHWHACKERS
BUSHWHACKING
BUSHWHACKINGS
BUSHWHACKS
BUSINESSES
BUSINESSIER
BUSINESSIEST
BUSINESSLIKE
BUSINESSMAN
BUSINESSMEN
BUSINESSPEOPLE
BUSINESSPERSON
BUSINESSPERSONS
BUSINESSWOMAN
BUSINESSWOMEN
BUSTICATED
BUSTICATES
BUSTICATING
BUSTINESSES
BUSTLINGLY
BUSYBODIED
BUSYBODIES
BUSYBODYING
BUSYBODYINGS
BUSYNESSES
BUTADIENES
BUTCHERBIRD
BUTCHERBIRDS
BUTCHERERS
BUTCHERIES
BUTCHERING
BUTCHERINGS
BUTCHERLIER
BUTCHERLIEST
BUTCHNESSES
BUTENEDIOIC
BUTEONINES
BUTLERAGES
BUTLERSHIP
BUTLERSHIPS
BUTTERBALL
BUTTERBALLS
BUTTERBURS
BUTTERCREAM
BUTTERCREAMS
BUTTERCUPS
BUTTERDOCK
BUTTERDOCKS
BUTTERFATS
BUTTERFINGERED
BUTTERFINGERS
BUTTERFISH
BUTTERFISHES
BUTTERFLIED
BUTTERFLIES
BUTTERFLYER
BUTTERFLYERS
BUTTERFLYFISH
BUTTERFLYFISHES
BUTTERFLYING
BUTTERIEST
BUTTERINES
BUTTERINESS
BUTTERINESSES
BUTTERLESS
BUTTERMILK
BUTTERMILKS
BUTTERNUTS
BUTTERSCOTCH
BUTTERSCOTCHES
BUTTERWEED
BUTTERWEEDS
BUTTERWORT
BUTTERWORTS
BUTTINSKIES
BUTTINSKIS
BUTTOCKING
BUTTONBALL
BUTTONBALLS
BUTTONBUSH
BUTTONBUSHES
BUTTONHELD
BUTTONHOLD
BUTTONHOLDING
BUTTONHOLDS
BUTTONHOLE
BUTTONHOLED
BUTTONHOLER
BUTTONHOLERS
BUTTONHOLES
BUTTONHOLING
BUTTONHOOK
BUTTONHOOKED
BUTTONHOOKING
BUTTONHOOKS
BUTTONIEST
BUTTONLESS
BUTTONMOULD
BUTTONMOULDS
BUTTONWOOD
BUTTONWOODS
BUTTRESSED
BUTTRESSES
BUTTRESSING
BUTTSTOCKS
BUTYLATING
BUTYLATION
BUTYLATIONS
BUTYRACEOUS
BUTYRALDEHYDE
BUTYRALDEHYDES
BUTYROPHENONE
BUTYROPHENONES
BUXOMNESSES
BUZZKILLER
BUZZKILLERS
BYPRODUCTS
BYSSACEOUS
BYSSINOSES
BYSSINOSIS
BYSTANDERS
BYTOWNITES

C

CABALETTAS
CABALISTIC
CABALISTICAL
CABALLEROS
CABBAGETOWN
CABBAGETOWNS
CABBAGEWORM
CABBAGEWORMS
CABBAGIEST
CABBALISMS
CABBALISTIC
CABBALISTICAL
CABBALISTS
CABDRIVERS
CABINETMAKER
CABINETMAKERS
CABINETMAKING
CABINETMAKINGS
CABINETRIES
CABINETWORK
CABINETWORKS
CABINMATES
CABLECASTED
CABLECASTING
CABLECASTS
CABLEGRAMS
CABLEVISION
CABLEVISIONS
CABRIOLETS
CACAFUEGOS
CACCIATORA
CACCIATORE
CACHAEMIAS
CACHECTICAL
CACHINNATE
CACHINNATED
CACHINNATES
CACHINNATING
CACHINNATION
CACHINNATIONS
CACHINNATORY
CACHOLONGS
CACIQUISMS
CACKERMANDER
CACKERMANDERS
CACKLEBERRIES
CACKLEBERRY
CACODAEMON
CACODAEMONS
CACODEMONIC
CACODEMONS
CACODOXIES
CACOEPISTIC
CACOGASTRIC
CACOGENICS
CACOGRAPHER
CACOGRAPHERS
CACOGRAPHIC
CACOGRAPHICAL
CACOGRAPHIES
CACOGRAPHY
CACOLOGIES
CACOMISTLE
CACOMISTLES
CACOMIXLES
CACONYMIES
CACOPHONIC
CACOPHONICAL
CACOPHONICALLY
CACOPHONIES
CACOPHONIOUS
CACOPHONOUS
CACOPHONOUSLY
CACOTOPIAN
CACOTOPIAS
CACOTROPHIES
CACOTROPHY
CACTACEOUS
CACTOBLASTES
CACTOBLASTIS
CACUMINALS
CACUMINOUS
CADASTRALLY
CADAVERINE
CADAVERINES
CADAVEROUS
CADAVEROUSLY
CADAVEROUSNESS
CADDISFLIES
CADDISHNESS
CADDISHNESSES
CADDISWORM
CADDISWORMS
CADETSHIPS
CADUCITIES
CAECILIANS
CAECITISES
CAENOGENESES
CAENOGENESIS
CAENOGENETIC
CAESALPINOID
CAESAREANS
CAESARIANS
CAESARISMS
CAESAROPAPISM
CAESAROPAPISMS
CAESPITOSE
CAESPITOSELY
CAFETERIAS
CAFETIERES
CAFETORIUM
CAFETORIUMS
CAFFEINATED
CAFFEINISM
CAFFEINISMS
CAGEYNESSES
CAGINESSES
CAGMAGGING
CAGYNESSES
CAILLEACHS
CAILLIACHS
CAINOGENESES
CAINOGENESIS
CAINOGENETIC
CAIRNGORMS
CAJOLEMENT
CAJOLEMENTS
CAJOLERIES
CAJOLINGLY
CAKEWALKED
CAKEWALKER
CAKEWALKERS
CAKEWALKING
CAKINESSES
CALABASHES
CALABOGUSES
CALABOOSES
CALABRESES
CALAMANCOES
CALAMANCOS
CALAMANDER
CALAMANDERS
CALAMARIES
CALAMINING
CALAMITIES
CALAMITOUS
CALAMITOUSLY
CALAMITOUSNESS
CALAMONDIN
CALAMONDINS
CALANDRIAS
CALAVANCES
CALAVERITE
CALAVERITES
CALCAREOUS
CALCAREOUSLY
CALCARIFEROUS
CALCARIFORM
CALCEAMENTA
CALCEAMENTUM
CALCEATING
CALCEDONIES
CALCEDONIO
CALCEDONIOS
CALCEIFORM
CALCEOLARIA
CALCEOLARIAS
CALCEOLATE
CALCICOLES
CALCICOLOUS
CALCIFEROL
CALCIFEROLS
CALCIFEROUS
CALCIFICATION
CALCIFICATIONS
CALCIFUGAL
CALCIFUGES
CALCIFUGOUS
CALCIFYING
CALCIGEROUS
CALCIMINED
CALCIMINES
CALCIMINING
CALCINABLE
CALCINATION
CALCINATIONS
CALCINOSES
CALCINOSIS
CALCITONIN
CALCITONINS
CALCSINTER
CALCSINTERS
CALCULABILITIES
CALCULABILITY
CALCULABLE
CALCULABLY
CALCULATED
CALCULATEDLY
CALCULATEDNESS
CALCULATES
CALCULATING
CALCULATINGLY
CALCULATION
CALCULATIONAL
CALCULATIONS
CALCULATIVE
CALCULATOR
CALCULATORS
CALCULUSES
CALEFACIENT

CALEFACIENTS
CALEFACTION
CALEFACTIONS
CALEFACTIVE
CALEFACTOR
CALEFACTORIES
CALEFACTORS
CALEFACTORY
CALEMBOURS
CALENDARED
CALENDARER
CALENDARERS
CALENDARING
CALENDARISATION
CALENDARISE
CALENDARISED
CALENDARISES
CALENDARISING
CALENDARIST
CALENDARISTS
CALENDARIZATION
CALENDARIZE
CALENDARIZED
CALENDARIZES
CALENDARIZING
CALENDERED
CALENDERER
CALENDERERS
CALENDERING
CALENDERINGS
CALENDRERS
CALENDRICAL
CALENDRIES
CALENDULAS
CALENTURES
CALESCENCE
CALESCENCES
CALFDOZERS
CALIATOURS
CALIBRATED
CALIBRATER
CALIBRATERS
CALIBRATES
CALIBRATING
CALIBRATION
CALIBRATIONS
CALIBRATOR
CALIBRATORS
CALIDITIES
CALIFORNIUM
CALIFORNIUMS
CALIGINOSITIES
CALIGINOSITY
CALIGINOUS
CALIMOCHOS
CALIOLOGIES
CALIPASHES
CALIPERING
CALIPHATES
CALISTHENIC
CALISTHENICS
CALLBOARDS
CALLIATURE
CALLIATURES
CALLIDITIES
CALLIGRAMME
CALLIGRAMMES
CALLIGRAMS
CALLIGRAPHER
CALLIGRAPHERS
CALLIGRAPHIC
CALLIGRAPHICAL
CALLIGRAPHIES
CALLIGRAPHIST
CALLIGRAPHISTS
CALLIGRAPHY
CALLIOPSIS
CALLIPASHES
CALLIPERED
CALLIPERING
CALLIPYGEAN
CALLIPYGIAN
CALLIPYGOUS
CALLISTEMON
CALLISTEMONS
CALLISTHENIC
CALLISTHENICS
CALLITHUMP
CALLITHUMPIAN
CALLITHUMPS
CALLOSITIES
CALLOUSING
CALLOUSNESS
CALLOUSNESSES
CALLOWNESS
CALLOWNESSES
CALMATIVES
CALMNESSES
CALMODULIN
CALMODULINS
CALMSTANES
CALMSTONES
CALORESCENCE
CALORESCENCES
CALORESCENT
CALORICALLY
CALORICITIES
CALORICITY
CALORIFICALLY
CALORIFICATION
CALORIFICATIONS
CALORIFIER
CALORIFIERS
CALORIMETER
CALORIMETERS
CALORIMETRIC
CALORIMETRICAL
CALORIMETRIES
CALORIMETRY
CALORISING
CALORIZING
CALOTYPIST
CALOTYPISTS
CALUMNIABLE
CALUMNIATE
CALUMNIATED
CALUMNIATES
CALUMNIATING
CALUMNIATION
CALUMNIATIONS
CALUMNIATOR
CALUMNIATORS
CALUMNIATORY
CALUMNIOUS
CALUMNIOUSLY
CALUMNYING
CALVADOSES
CALVARIUMS
CALYCANTHEMIES
CALYCANTHEMY
CALYCANTHUS
CALYCANTHUSES
CALYCIFORM
CALYCOIDEOUS
CALYCULATE
CALYPSONIAN
CALYPSONIANS
CALYPTERAS
CALYPTRATE
CALYPTROGEN
CALYPTROGENS
CAMANACHDS
CAMARADERIE
CAMARADERIES
CAMARILLAS
CAMBERINGS
CAMBISTRIES
CAMCORDERS
CAMCORDING
CAMELBACKS
CAMELEOPARD
CAMELEOPARDS
CAMELHAIRS
CAMELOPARD
CAMELOPARDS
CAMERAPERSON
CAMERAPERSONS
CAMERAPHONE
CAMERAPHONES
CAMERATION
CAMERATIONS
CAMERAWOMAN
CAMERAWOMEN
CAMERAWORK
CAMERAWORKS
CAMERLENGO
CAMERLENGOS
CAMERLINGO
CAMERLINGOS
CAMIKNICKERS
CAMIKNICKS
CAMISADOES
CAMORRISTA
CAMORRISTI
CAMORRISTS
CAMOUFLAGE
CAMOUFLAGEABLE
CAMOUFLAGED
CAMOUFLAGES
CAMOUFLAGIC
CAMOUFLAGING
CAMOUFLETS
CAMOUFLEUR
CAMOUFLEURS
CAMPAIGNED
CAMPAIGNER
CAMPAIGNERS
CAMPAIGNING
CAMPANEROS
CAMPANIFORM
CAMPANILES
CAMPANISTS
CAMPANOLOGER
CAMPANOLOGERS
CAMPANOLOGICAL
CAMPANOLOGIES
CAMPANOLOGIST
CAMPANOLOGISTS
CAMPANOLOGY
CAMPANULACEOUS
CAMPANULAR
CAMPANULAS
CAMPANULATE
CAMPCRAFTS
CAMPEADORS
CAMPESINOS
CAMPESTRAL
CAMPESTRIAN
CAMPGROUND
CAMPGROUNDS
CAMPHORACEOUS
CAMPHORATE
CAMPHORATED
CAMPHORATES
CAMPHORATING
CAMPIMETRIES
CAMPIMETRY
CAMPINESSES
CAMPNESSES
CAMPODEIDS
CAMPODEIFORM
CAMPSHIRTS
CAMPSTOOLS
CAMPYLOBACTER
CAMPYLOBACTERS
CAMPYLOTROPOUS
CAMSTEERIE
CAMWHORING
CANALBOATS
CANALICULAR

CANALICULATE
CANALICULATED
CANALICULI
CANALICULUS
CANALISATION
CANALISATIONS
CANALISING
CANALIZATION
CANALIZATIONS
CANALIZING
CANCELABLE
CANCELATION
CANCELATIONS
CANCELBOTS
CANCELEERED
CANCELEERING
CANCELEERS
CANCELIERED
CANCELIERING
CANCELIERS
CANCELLABLE
CANCELLARIAL
CANCELLARIAN
CANCELLARIATE
CANCELLARIATES
CANCELLATE
CANCELLATED
CANCELLATION
CANCELLATIONS
CANCELLERS
CANCELLING
CANCELLOUS
CANCERATED
CANCERATES
CANCERATING
CANCERATION
CANCERATIONS
CANCEROPHOBIA
CANCEROPHOBIAS
CANCEROUSLY
CANCERPHOBIA
CANCERPHOBIAS
CANCIONERO
CANCIONEROS
CANCRIFORM
CANCRIZANS
CANDELABRA
CANDELABRAS
CANDELABRUM
CANDELABRUMS
CANDELILLA
CANDELILLAS
CANDESCENCE
CANDESCENCES
CANDESCENT
CANDESCENTLY
CANDIDACIES
CANDIDATES
CANDIDATESHIP
CANDIDATESHIPS
CANDIDATURE
CANDIDATURES
CANDIDIASES
CANDIDIASIS
CANDIDNESS
CANDIDNESSES
CANDLEBERRIES
CANDLEBERRY
CANDLEFISH
CANDLEFISHES
CANDLEHOLDER
CANDLEHOLDERS
CANDLELIGHT
CANDLELIGHTED
CANDLELIGHTER
CANDLELIGHTERS
CANDLELIGHTS
CANDLENUTS
CANDLEPINS
CANDLEPOWER
CANDLEPOWERS
CANDLESNUFFER
CANDLESNUFFERS
CANDLESTICK
CANDLESTICKS
CANDLEWICK
CANDLEWICKS
CANDLEWOOD
CANDLEWOODS
CANDYFLOSS
CANDYFLOSSES
CANDYGRAMS
CANDYTUFTS
CANEBRAKES
CANEFRUITS
CANEPHORAS
CANEPHORES
CANEPHORUS
CANEPHORUSES
CANESCENCE
CANESCENCES
CANINITIES
CANISTERED
CANISTERING
CANISTERISATION
CANISTERISE
CANISTERISED
CANISTERISES
CANISTERISING
CANISTERIZATION
CANISTERIZE
CANISTERIZED
CANISTERIZES
CANISTERIZING
CANKEREDLY
CANKEREDNESS
CANKEREDNESSES
CANKERIEST
CANKERWORM
CANKERWORMS
CANNABINOID
CANNABINOIDS
CANNABINOL
CANNABINOLS
CANNABISES
CANNELLINI
CANNELLINIS
CANNELLONI
CANNELURES
CANNIBALISATION
CANNIBALISE
CANNIBALISED
CANNIBALISES
CANNIBALISING
CANNIBALISM
CANNIBALISMS
CANNIBALISTIC
CANNIBALIZATION
CANNIBALIZE
CANNIBALIZED
CANNIBALIZES
CANNIBALIZING
CANNIBALLY
CANNINESSES
CANNISTERS
CANNONADED
CANNONADES
CANNONADING
CANNONBALL
CANNONBALLED
CANNONBALLING
CANNONBALLS
CANNONEERS
CANNONIERS
CANNONRIES
CANNULATED
CANNULATES
CANNULATING
CANNULATION
CANNULATIONS
CANOEWOODS
CANONESSES
CANONICALLY
CANONICALS
CANONICATE
CANONICATES
CANONICITIES
CANONICITY
CANONISATION
CANONISATIONS
CANONISERS
CANONISING
CANONISTIC
CANONIZATION
CANONIZATIONS
CANONIZERS
CANONIZING
CANOODLERS
CANOODLING
CANOPHILIA
CANOPHILIAS
CANOPHILIST
CANOPHILISTS
CANOPHOBIA
CANOPHOBIAS
CANOROUSLY
CANOROUSNESS
CANOROUSNESSES
CANTABANKS
CANTABILES
CANTALOUPE
CANTALOUPES
CANTALOUPS
CANTANKEROUS
CANTANKEROUSLY
CANTATRICE
CANTATRICES
CANTATRICI
CANTERBURIES
CANTERBURY
CANTERBURYS
CANTHARIDAL
CANTHARIDES
CANTHARIDIAN
CANTHARIDIC
CANTHARIDIN
CANTHARIDINS
CANTHARIDS
CANTHAXANTHIN
CANTHAXANTHINE
CANTHAXANTHINES
CANTHAXANTHINS
CANTHITISES
CANTICOING
CANTICOYED
CANTICOYING
CANTILENAS
CANTILEVER
CANTILEVERED
CANTILEVERING
CANTILEVERS
CANTILLATE
CANTILLATED
CANTILLATES
CANTILLATING
CANTILLATION
CANTILLATIONS
CANTILLATORY
CANTINESSES
CANTONISATION
CANTONISATIONS
CANTONISED
CANTONISES
CANTONISING
CANTONIZATION
CANTONIZATIONS
CANTONIZED
CANTONIZES
CANTONIZING
CANTONMENT

CANTONMENTS
CANULATING
CANULATION
CANULATIONS
CANVASBACK
CANVASBACKS
CANVASLIKE
CANVASSERS
CANVASSING
CANVASSINGS
CANYONEERS
CANYONINGS
CANZONETTA
CANZONETTAS
CANZONETTE
CAOUTCHOUC
CAOUTCHOUCS
CAPABILITIES
CAPABILITY
CAPABLENESS
CAPABLENESSES
CAPACIOUSLY
CAPACIOUSNESS
CAPACIOUSNESSES
CAPACITANCE
CAPACITANCES
CAPACITATE
CAPACITATED
CAPACITATES
CAPACITATING
CAPACITATION
CAPACITATIONS
CAPACITIES
CAPACITIVE
CAPACITIVELY
CAPACITORS
CAPARISONED
CAPARISONING
CAPARISONS
CAPELLINES
CAPELLINIS
CAPELLMEISTER
CAPELLMEISTERS
CAPERCAILLIE
CAPERCAILLIES
CAPERCAILZIE
CAPERCAILZIES
CAPERINGLY
CAPERNOITED
CAPERNOITIE
CAPERNOITIES
CAPERNOITY
CAPICOLLAS
CAPICOLLOS
CAPILLACEOUS
CAPILLAIRE
CAPILLAIRES
CAPILLARIES
CAPILLARITIES
CAPILLARITY
CAPILLITIA
CAPILLITIUM
CAPITALISATION
CAPITALISATIONS
CAPITALISE
CAPITALISED
CAPITALISES
CAPITALISING
CAPITALISM
CAPITALISMS
CAPITALIST
CAPITALISTIC
CAPITALISTS
CAPITALIZATION
CAPITALIZATIONS
CAPITALIZE
CAPITALIZED
CAPITALIZES
CAPITALIZING
CAPITATION
CAPITATIONS
CAPITATIVE
CAPITELLUM
CAPITOLIAN
CAPITOLINE
CAPITULANT
CAPITULANTS
CAPITULARIES
CAPITULARLY
CAPITULARS
CAPITULARY
CAPITULATE
CAPITULATED
CAPITULATES
CAPITULATING
CAPITULATION
CAPITULATIONS
CAPITULATOR
CAPITULATORS
CAPITULATORY
CAPNOMANCIES
CAPNOMANCY
CAPOCCHIAS
CAPODASTRO
CAPODASTROS
CAPONIERES
CAPONISING
CAPONIZING
CAPOTASTOS
CAPPARIDACEOUS
CAPPELLETTI
CAPPERNOITIES
CAPPERNOITY
CAPPUCCINI
CAPPUCCINO
CAPPUCCINOS
CAPREOLATE
CAPRICCIOS
CAPRICCIOSO
CAPRICIOUS
CAPRICIOUSLY
CAPRICIOUSNESS
CAPRIFICATION
CAPRIFICATIONS
CAPRIFOILS
CAPRIFOLES
CAPRIFOLIACEOUS
CAPRIFYING
CAPRIOLING
CAPROLACTAM
CAPROLACTAMS
CAPRYLATES
CAPSAICINS
CAPSIZABLE
CAPSOMERES
CAPSULATED
CAPSULATION
CAPSULATIONS
CAPSULISED
CAPSULISES
CAPSULISING
CAPSULIZED
CAPSULIZES
CAPSULIZING
CAPTAINCIES
CAPTAINING
CAPTAINRIES
CAPTAINSHIP
CAPTAINSHIPS
CAPTIONING
CAPTIONLESS
CAPTIOUSLY
CAPTIOUSNESS
CAPTIOUSNESSES
CAPTIVANCE
CAPTIVANCES
CAPTIVATED
CAPTIVATES
CAPTIVATING
CAPTIVATINGLY
CAPTIVATION
CAPTIVATIONS
CAPTIVATOR
CAPTIVATORS
CAPTIVAUNCE
CAPTIVAUNCES
CAPTIVITIES
CAPTOPRILS
CARABINEER
CARABINEERS
CARABINERO
CARABINEROS
CARABINERS
CARABINIER
CARABINIERE
CARABINIERI
CARABINIERS
CARACOLERS
CARACOLING
CARACOLLED
CARACOLLING
CARAGEENAN
CARAGEENANS
CARAMBOLAS
CARAMBOLED
CARAMBOLES
CARAMBOLING
CARAMELISATION
CARAMELISATIONS
CARAMELISE
CARAMELISED
CARAMELISES
CARAMELISING
CARAMELIZATION
CARAMELIZATIONS
CARAMELIZE
CARAMELIZED
CARAMELIZES
CARAMELIZING
CARAMELLED
CARAMELLING
CARANGOIDS
CARAPACIAL
CARAVANCES
CARAVANEER
CARAVANEERS
CARAVANERS
CARAVANETTE
CARAVANETTES
CARAVANING
CARAVANINGS
CARAVANNED
CARAVANNER
CARAVANNERS
CARAVANNING
CARAVANNINGS
CARAVANSARAI
CARAVANSARAIS
CARAVANSARIES
CARAVANSARY
CARAVANSERAI
CARAVANSERAIS
CARAVELLES
CARBACHOLS
CARBAMATES
CARBAMAZEPINE
CARBAMAZEPINES
CARBAMIDES
CARBAMIDINE
CARBAMIDINES
CARBAMOYLS
CARBANIONS
CARBAZOLES
CARBIDOPAS
CARBIMAZOLE
CARBIMAZOLES
CARBINEERS
CARBINIERS
CARBOCYCLIC
CARBOHYDRASE

CARBOHYDRASES
CARBOHYDRATE
CARBOHYDRATES
CARBOLATED
CARBOLISED
CARBOLISES
CARBOLISING
CARBOLIZED
CARBOLIZES
CARBOLIZING
CARBONACEOUS
CARBONADES
CARBONADOED
CARBONADOES
CARBONADOING
CARBONADOS
CARBONARAS
CARBONATED
CARBONATES
CARBONATING
CARBONATION
CARBONATIONS
CARBONATITE
CARBONATITES
CARBONETTE
CARBONETTES
CARBONIFEROUS
CARBONISATION
CARBONISATIONS
CARBONISED
CARBONISER
CARBONISERS
CARBONISES
CARBONISING
CARBONIUMS
CARBONIZATION
CARBONIZATIONS
CARBONIZED
CARBONIZER
CARBONIZERS
CARBONIZES
CARBONIZING
CARBONLESS
CARBONNADE
CARBONNADES
CARBONYLATE
CARBONYLATED
CARBONYLATES
CARBONYLATING
CARBONYLATION
CARBONYLATIONS
CARBONYLIC
CARBOREXIC
CARBOREXICS
CARBOXYLASE
CARBOXYLASES
CARBOXYLATE
CARBOXYLATED
CARBOXYLATES
CARBOXYLATING
CARBOXYLATION
CARBOXYLATIONS
CARBOXYLIC
CARBUNCLED
CARBUNCLES
CARBUNCULAR
CARBURATED
CARBURATES
CARBURATING
CARBURATION
CARBURATIONS
CARBURETED
CARBURETER
CARBURETERS
CARBURETING
CARBURETION
CARBURETIONS
CARBURETOR
CARBURETORS
CARBURETTED
CARBURETTER
CARBURETTERS
CARBURETTING
CARBURETTOR
CARBURETTORS
CARBURISATION
CARBURISATIONS
CARBURISED
CARBURISES
CARBURISING
CARBURIZATION
CARBURIZATIONS
CARBURIZED
CARBURIZES
CARBURIZING
CARBYLAMINE
CARBYLAMINES
CARCASSING
CARCINOGEN
CARCINOGENESES
CARCINOGENESIS
CARCINOGENIC
CARCINOGENICITY
CARCINOGENS
CARCINOIDS
CARCINOLOGICAL
CARCINOLOGIES
CARCINOLOGIST
CARCINOLOGISTS
CARCINOLOGY
CARCINOMAS
CARCINOMATA
CARCINOMATOID
CARCINOMATOSES
CARCINOMATOSIS
CARCINOMATOUS
CARCINOSARCOMA
CARCINOSARCOMAS
CARCINOSES
CARCINOSIS
CARDAMINES
CARDBOARDIER
CARDBOARDIEST
CARDBOARDS
CARDBOARDY
CARDCASTLE
CARDCASTLES
CARDHOLDER
CARDHOLDERS
CARDIALGIA
CARDIALGIAS
CARDIALGIC
CARDIALGIES
CARDIGANED
CARDINALATE
CARDINALATES
CARDINALATIAL
CARDINALITIAL
CARDINALITIES
CARDINALITY
CARDINALLY
CARDINALSHIP
CARDINALSHIPS
CARDIOCENTESES
CARDIOCENTESIS
CARDIOGENIC
CARDIOGRAM
CARDIOGRAMS
CARDIOGRAPH
CARDIOGRAPHER
CARDIOGRAPHERS
CARDIOGRAPHIC
CARDIOGRAPHICAL
CARDIOGRAPHIES
CARDIOGRAPHS
CARDIOGRAPHY
CARDIOLOGICAL
CARDIOLOGIES
CARDIOLOGIST
CARDIOLOGISTS
CARDIOLOGY
CARDIOMEGALIES
CARDIOMEGALY
CARDIOMOTOR
CARDIOMYOPATHY
CARDIOPATHIES
CARDIOPATHY
CARDIOPLEGIA
CARDIOPLEGIAS
CARDIOPULMONARY
CARDIOTHORACIC
CARDIOTONIC
CARDIOTONICS
CARDIOVASCULAR
CARDITISES
CARDOPHAGI
CARDOPHAGUS
CARDPHONES
CARDPLAYER
CARDPLAYERS
CARDPUNCHES
CARDSHARPER
CARDSHARPERS
CARDSHARPING
CARDSHARPINGS
CARDSHARPS
CARDUACEOUS
CAREENAGES
CAREERISMS
CAREERISTS
CAREFREENESS
CAREFREENESSES
CAREFULLER
CAREFULLEST
CAREFULNESS
CAREFULNESSES
CAREGIVERS
CAREGIVING
CAREGIVINGS
CARELESSLY
CARELESSNESS
CARELESSNESSES
CARESSINGLY
CARESSINGS
CARESSIVELY
CARETAKERS
CARETAKING
CARETAKINGS
CAREWORKER
CAREWORKERS
CARFUFFLED
CARFUFFLES
CARFUFFLING
CARHOPPING
CARHOPPINGS
CARICATURA
CARICATURAL
CARICATURAS
CARICATURE
CARICATURED
CARICATURES
CARICATURING
CARICATURIST
CARICATURISTS
CARILLONED
CARILLONING
CARILLONIST
CARILLONISTS
CARILLONNED
CARILLONNEUR
CARILLONNEURS
CARILLONNING
CARIOGENIC
CARIOSITIES
CARIOUSNESS
CARIOUSNESSES
CARJACKERS
CARJACKING
CARJACKINGS
CARMAGNOLE

CARMAGNOLES
CARMELITES
CARMINATIVE
CARMINATIVES
CARNAHUBAS
CARNALISED
CARNALISES
CARNALISING
CARNALISMS
CARNALISTS
CARNALITIES
CARNALIZED
CARNALIZES
CARNALIZING
CARNALLING
CARNALLITE
CARNALLITES
CARNAPTIOUS
CARNAROLIS
CARNASSIAL
CARNASSIALS
CARNATIONED
CARNATIONS
CARNELIANS
CARNIFEXES
CARNIFICATION
CARNIFICATIONS
CARNIFICIAL
CARNIFYING
CARNITINES
CARNIVALESQUE
CARNIVORES
CARNIVORIES
CARNIVOROUS
CARNIVOROUSLY
CARNIVOROUSNESS
CARNOSAURS
CARNOSITIES
CARNOTITES
CAROLLINGS
CAROMELLED
CAROMELLING
CAROTENOID
CAROTENOIDS
CAROTINOID
CAROTINOIDS
CAROUSINGLY
CAROUSINGS
CARPACCIOS
CARPELLARY
CARPELLATE
CARPELLATES
CARPENTARIA
CARPENTARIAS
CARPENTERED
CARPENTERING
CARPENTERS
CARPENTRIES
CARPETBAGGED
CARPETBAGGER
CARPETBAGGERIES
CARPETBAGGERS
CARPETBAGGERY
CARPETBAGGING
CARPETBAGGINGS
CARPETBAGS
CARPETINGS
CARPETLIKE
CARPETMONGER
CARPETMONGERS
CARPETWEED
CARPETWEEDS
CARPHOLOGIES
CARPHOLOGY
CARPOGONIA
CARPOGONIAL
CARPOGONIUM
CARPOLOGICAL
CARPOLOGIES
CARPOLOGIST
CARPOLOGISTS
CARPOMETACARPI
CARPOMETACARPUS
CARPOOLERS
CARPOOLING
CARPOOLINGS
CARPOPHAGOUS
CARPOPHORE
CARPOPHORES
CARPOSPORE
CARPOSPORES
CARRAGEENAN
CARRAGEENANS
CARRAGEENIN
CARRAGEENINS
CARRAGEENS
CARRAGHEEN
CARRAGHEENAN
CARRAGHEENANS
CARRAGHEENIN
CARRAGHEENINS
CARRAGHEENS
CARREFOURS
CARRIAGEABLE
CARRIAGEWAY
CARRIAGEWAYS
CARRITCHES
CARRIWITCHET
CARRIWITCHETS
CARRONADES
CARROTIEST
CARROTTOPPED
CARROTTOPS
CARROUSELS
CARRYBACKS
CARRYFORWARD
CARRYFORWARDS
CARRYOVERS
CARRYTALES
CARSHARING
CARSHARINGS
CARSICKNESS
CARSICKNESSES
CARTELISATION
CARTELISATIONS
CARTELISED
CARTELISES
CARTELISING
CARTELISMS
CARTELISTS
CARTELIZATION
CARTELIZATIONS
CARTELIZED
CARTELIZES
CARTELIZING
CARTHAMINE
CARTHAMINES
CARTHORSES
CARTILAGES
CARTILAGINOUS
CARTOGRAMS
CARTOGRAPHER
CARTOGRAPHERS
CARTOGRAPHIC
CARTOGRAPHICAL
CARTOGRAPHIES
CARTOGRAPHY
CARTOLOGICAL
CARTOLOGIES
CARTOMANCIES
CARTOMANCY
CARTONAGES
CARTONNAGE
CARTONNAGES
CARTOONIER
CARTOONIEST
CARTOONING
CARTOONINGS
CARTOONISH
CARTOONISHLY
CARTOONIST
CARTOONISTS
CARTOONLIKE
CARTOPHILE
CARTOPHILES
CARTOPHILIC
CARTOPHILIES
CARTOPHILIST
CARTOPHILISTS
CARTOPHILY
CARTOPPERS
CARTOUCHES
CARTRIDGES
CARTULARIES
CARTWHEELED
CARTWHEELER
CARTWHEELERS
CARTWHEELING
CARTWHEELS
CARTWRIGHT
CARTWRIGHTS
CARUNCULAR
CARUNCULATE
CARUNCULATED
CARUNCULOUS
CARVACROLS
CARYATIDAL
CARYATIDEAN
CARYATIDES
CARYATIDIC
CARYOPSIDES
CARYOPTERIS
CARYOPTERISES
CASCADURAS
CASCARILLA
CASCARILLAS
CASEATIONS
CASEBEARER
CASEBEARERS
CASEINATES
CASEINOGEN
CASEINOGENS
CASEMAKERS
CASEMENTED
CASEVACING
CASEWORKER
CASEWORKERS
CASHIERERS
CASHIERING
CASHIERINGS
CASHIERMENT
CASHIERMENTS
CASHMOBBING
CASHMOBBINGS
CASHPOINTS
CASHSPIELS
CASINGHEAD
CASINGHEADS
CASKSTANDS
CASSAREEPS
CASSATIONS
CASSEROLED
CASSEROLES
CASSEROLING
CASSIMERES
CASSINGLES
CASSIOPEIUM
CASSIOPEIUMS
CASSITERITE
CASSITERITES
CASSOLETTE
CASSOLETTES
CASSONADES
CASSOULETS
CASSOWARIES
CASSUMUNAR
CASSUMUNARS
CASTABILITIES
CASTABILITY
CASTANOSPERMINE

CASTELLANS
CASTELLATED
CASTELLATION
CASTELLATIONS
CASTELLUMS
CASTIGATED
CASTIGATES
CASTIGATING
CASTIGATION
CASTIGATIONS
CASTIGATOR
CASTIGATORS
CASTIGATORY
CASTOREUMS
CASTRAMETATION
CASTRAMETATIONS
CASTRATERS
CASTRATING
CASTRATION
CASTRATIONS
CASTRATORS
CASTRATORY
CASUALISATION
CASUALISATIONS
CASUALISED
CASUALISES
CASUALISING
CASUALISMS
CASUALIZATION
CASUALIZATIONS
CASUALIZED
CASUALIZES
CASUALIZING
CASUALNESS
CASUALNESSES
CASUALTIES
CASUARINAS
CASUISTICAL
CASUISTICALLY
CASUISTRIES
CATABOLICALLY
CATABOLISE
CATABOLISED
CATABOLISES
CATABOLISING
CATABOLISM
CATABOLISMS
CATABOLITE
CATABOLITES
CATABOLIZE
CATABOLIZED
CATABOLIZES
CATABOLIZING
CATACAUSTIC
CATACAUSTICS
CATACHRESES
CATACHRESIS
CATACHRESTIC
CATACHRESTICAL
CATACLASES
CATACLASIS
CATACLASMIC
CATACLASMS
CATACLASTIC
CATACLINAL
CATACLYSMAL
CATACLYSMIC
CATACLYSMICALLY
CATACLYSMS
CATACOUSTICS
CATACUMBAL
CATADIOPTRIC
CATADIOPTRICAL
CATADROMOUS
CATAFALCOES
CATAFALQUE
CATAFALQUES
CATALECTIC
CATALECTICS
CATALEPSIES
CATALEPTIC
CATALEPTICALLY
CATALEPTICS
CATALLACTIC
CATALLACTICALLY
CATALLACTICS
CATALOGERS
CATALOGING
CATALOGISE
CATALOGISED
CATALOGISES
CATALOGISING
CATALOGIZE
CATALOGIZED
CATALOGIZES
CATALOGIZING
CATALOGNES
CATALOGUED
CATALOGUER
CATALOGUERS
CATALOGUES
CATALOGUING
CATALOGUISE
CATALOGUISED
CATALOGUISES
CATALOGUISING
CATALOGUIST
CATALOGUISTS
CATALOGUIZE
CATALOGUIZED
CATALOGUIZES
CATALOGUIZING
CATALYSERS
CATALYSING
CATALYTICAL
CATALYTICALLY
CATALYZERS
CATALYZING
CATAMARANS
CATAMENIAL
CATAMOUNTAIN
CATAMOUNTAINS
CATAMOUNTS
CATANANCHE
CATANANCHES
CATAPHONIC
CATAPHONICS
CATAPHORAS
CATAPHORESES
CATAPHORESIS
CATAPHORETIC
CATAPHORIC
CATAPHORICALLY
CATAPHRACT
CATAPHRACTIC
CATAPHRACTS
CATAPHYLLARY
CATAPHYLLS
CATAPHYSICAL
CATAPLASIA
CATAPLASIAS
CATAPLASMS
CATAPLASTIC
CATAPLECTIC
CATAPLEXIES
CATAPULTED
CATAPULTIC
CATAPULTIER
CATAPULTIERS
CATAPULTING
CATARACTOUS
CATARHINES
CATARRHALLY
CATARRHINE
CATARRHINES
CATARRHOUS
CATASTASES
CATASTASIS
CATASTROPHE
CATASTROPHES
CATASTROPHIC
CATASTROPHISM
CATASTROPHISMS
CATASTROPHIST
CATASTROPHISTS
CATATONIAS
CATATONICALLY
CATATONICS
CATATONIES
CATCALLERS
CATCALLING
CATCHCRIES
CATCHFLIES
CATCHINESS
CATCHINESSES
CATCHLINES
CATCHMENTS
CATCHPENNIES
CATCHPENNY
CATCHPHRASE
CATCHPHRASES
CATCHPOLES
CATCHPOLLS
CATCHWATER
CATCHWATERS
CATCHWEEDS
CATCHWEIGHT
CATCHWORDS
CATECHESES
CATECHESIS
CATECHESISES
CATECHETIC
CATECHETICAL
CATECHETICALLY
CATECHETICS
CATECHISATION
CATECHISATIONS
CATECHISED
CATECHISER
CATECHISERS
CATECHISES
CATECHISING
CATECHISINGS
CATECHISMAL
CATECHISMS
CATECHISTIC
CATECHISTICAL
CATECHISTICALLY
CATECHISTS
CATECHIZATION
CATECHIZATIONS
CATECHIZED
CATECHIZER
CATECHIZERS
CATECHIZES
CATECHIZING
CATECHIZINGS
CATECHOLAMINE
CATECHOLAMINES
CATECHUMEN
CATECHUMENAL
CATECHUMENATE
CATECHUMENATES
CATECHUMENICAL
CATECHUMENISM
CATECHUMENISMS
CATECHUMENS
CATECHUMENSHIP
CATECHUMENSHIPS
CATEGOREMATIC
CATEGORIAL
CATEGORIALLY
CATEGORICAL
CATEGORICALLY
CATEGORICALNESS
CATEGORIES
CATEGORISATION
CATEGORISATIONS
CATEGORISE
CATEGORISED

C

CATEGORISES
CATEGORISING
CATEGORIST
CATEGORISTS
CATEGORIZATION
CATEGORIZATIONS
CATEGORIZE
CATEGORIZED
CATEGORIZES
CATEGORIZING
CATENACCIO
CATENACCIOS
CATENARIAN
CATENARIES
CATENATING
CATENATION
CATENATIONS
CATENULATE
CATERCORNER
CATERCORNERED
CATERESSES
CATERPILLAR
CATERPILLARS
CATERWAULED
CATERWAULER
CATERWAULERS
CATERWAULING
CATERWAULINGS
CATERWAULS
CATFACINGS
CATFISHING
CATHARISED
CATHARISES
CATHARISING
CATHARIZED
CATHARIZES
CATHARIZING
CATHARTICAL
CATHARTICALLY
CATHARTICS
CATHECTING
CATHEDRALS
CATHEDRATIC
CATHEPSINS
CATHETERISATION
CATHETERISE
CATHETERISED
CATHETERISES
CATHETERISING
CATHETERISM
CATHETERISMS
CATHETERIZATION
CATHETERIZE
CATHETERIZED
CATHETERIZES
CATHETERIZING
CATHETOMETER
CATHETOMETERS
CATHETUSES
CATHINONES
CATHIODERMIE
CATHIODERMIES
CATHODALLY
CATHODICAL
CATHODICALLY
CATHODOGRAPH
CATHODOGRAPHER
CATHODOGRAPHERS
CATHODOGRAPHIES
CATHODOGRAPHS
CATHODOGRAPHY
CATHOLICALLY
CATHOLICATE
CATHOLICATES
CATHOLICISATION
CATHOLICISE
CATHOLICISED
CATHOLICISES
CATHOLICISING
CATHOLICISM
CATHOLICISMS
CATHOLICITIES
CATHOLICITY
CATHOLICIZATION
CATHOLICIZE
CATHOLICIZED
CATHOLICIZES
CATHOLICIZING
CATHOLICLY
CATHOLICOI
CATHOLICON
CATHOLICONS
CATHOLICOS
CATHOLICOSES
CATHOLYTES
CATIONICALLY
CATLINITES
CATNAPPERS
CATNAPPING
CATOPTRICAL
CATOPTRICS
CATTINESSES
CATTISHNESS
CATTISHNESSES
CAUCHEMARS
CAUCUSSING
CAUCUSSINGS
CAUDATIONS
CAUDILLISMO
CAUDILLISMOS
CAULESCENT
CAULICOLOUS
CAULICULATE
CAULICULUS
CAULICULUSES
CAULIFLORIES
CAULIFLOROUS
CAULIFLORY
CAULIFLOWER
CAULIFLOWERET
CAULIFLOWERETS
CAULIFLOWERS
CAULIGENOUS
CAUMSTANES
CAUMSTONES
CAUSABILITIES
CAUSABILITY
CAUSALGIAS
CAUSALITIES
CAUSATIONAL
CAUSATIONISM
CAUSATIONISMS
CAUSATIONIST
CAUSATIONISTS
CAUSATIONS
CAUSATIVELY
CAUSATIVENESS
CAUSATIVENESSES
CAUSATIVES
CAUSELESSLY
CAUSELESSNESS
CAUSELESSNESSES
CAUSEWAYED
CAUSEWAYING
CAUSTICALLY
CAUSTICITIES
CAUSTICITY
CAUSTICNESS
CAUSTICNESSES
CAUTERANTS
CAUTERISATION
CAUTERISATIONS
CAUTERISED
CAUTERISES
CAUTERISING
CAUTERISMS
CAUTERIZATION
CAUTERIZATIONS
CAUTERIZED
CAUTERIZES
CAUTERIZING
CAUTIONARY
CAUTIONERS
CAUTIONING
CAUTIONRIES
CAUTIOUSLY
CAUTIOUSNESS
CAUTIOUSNESSES
CAVALCADED
CAVALCADES
CAVALCADING
CAVALIERED
CAVALIERING
CAVALIERISH
CAVALIERISM
CAVALIERISMS
CAVALIERLY
CAVALLETTI
CAVALRYMAN
CAVALRYMEN
CAVEFISHES
CAVENDISHES
CAVERNICOLOUS
CAVERNOUSLY
CAVERNULOUS
CAVILLATION
CAVILLATIONS
CAVILLINGS
CAVITATING
CAVITATION
CAVITATIONS
CAVORTINGS
CEANOTHUSES
CEASEFIRES
CEASELESSLY
CEASELESSNESS
CEASELESSNESSES
CEBADILLAS
CECUTIENCIES
CECUTIENCY
CEDARBIRDS
CEDARWOODS
CEDRELACEOUS
CEILOMETER
CEILOMETERS
CELANDINES
CELEBRANTS
CELEBRATED
CELEBRATEDNESS
CELEBRATES
CELEBRATING
CELEBRATION
CELEBRATIONS
CELEBRATIVE
CELEBRATOR
CELEBRATORS
CELEBRATORY
CELEBREALITIES
CELEBREALITY
CELEBRITIES
CELEBUTANTE
CELEBUTANTES
CELECOXIBS
CELERITIES
CELERYLIKE
CELESTIALLY
CELESTIALS
CELESTINES
CELESTITES
CELIBACIES
CELIBATARIAN
CELIBATARIANS
CELLARAGES
CELLARETTE
CELLARETTES
CELLARISTS
CELLARWAYS
CELLBLOCKS
CELLENTANI
CELLENTANIS

CELLIFEROUS
CELLOBIOSE
CELLOBIOSES
CELLOIDINS
CELLOPHANE
CELLOPHANES
CELLPHONES
CELLULARITIES
CELLULARITY
CELLULASES
CELLULATED
CELLULIFEROUS
CELLULITES
CELLULITIS
CELLULITISES
CELLULOIDS
CELLULOLYTIC
CELLULOSES
CELLULOSIC
CELLULOSICS
CELSITUDES
CEMBALISTS
CEMENTATION
CEMENTATIONS
CEMENTATORY
CEMENTITES
CEMENTITIOUS
CEMETERIES
CENESTHESES
CENESTHESIA
CENESTHESIAS
CENESTHESIS
CENESTHETIC
CENOBITICAL
CENOGENESES
CENOGENESIS
CENOGENETIC
CENOGENETICALLY
CENOSPECIES
CENOTAPHIC
CENSORABLE
CENSORIOUS
CENSORIOUSLY
CENSORIOUSNESS
CENSORSHIP
CENSORSHIPS
CENSURABILITIES
CENSURABILITY
CENSURABLE
CENSURABLENESS
CENSURABLY
CENTAUREAS
CENTAURIAN
CENTAURIES
CENTENARIAN
CENTENARIANISM
CENTENARIANISMS
CENTENARIANS
CENTENARIES
CENTENIERS
CENTENNIAL
CENTENNIALLY
CENTENNIALS
CENTERBOARD
CENTERBOARDS
CENTEREDNESS
CENTEREDNESSES
CENTERFOLD
CENTERFOLDS
CENTERINGS
CENTERLESS
CENTERLINE
CENTERLINES
CENTERPIECE
CENTERPIECES
CENTESIMAL
CENTESIMALLY
CENTESIMALS
CENTESIMOS
CENTIGRADE
CENTIGRADES
CENTIGRAMME
CENTIGRAMMES
CENTIGRAMS
CENTILITER
CENTILITERS
CENTILITRE
CENTILITRES
CENTILLION
CENTILLIONS
CENTILLIONTH
CENTILLIONTHS
CENTIMETER
CENTIMETERS
CENTIMETRE
CENTIMETRES
CENTIMETRIC
CENTIMORGAN
CENTIMORGANS
CENTINELLS
CENTIPEDES
CENTIPOISE
CENTIPOISES
CENTONATES
CENTONELLS
CENTONISTS
CENTRALEST
CENTRALISATION
CENTRALISATIONS
CENTRALISE
CENTRALISED
CENTRALISER
CENTRALISERS
CENTRALISES
CENTRALISING
CENTRALISM
CENTRALISMS
CENTRALIST
CENTRALISTIC
CENTRALISTS
CENTRALITIES
CENTRALITY
CENTRALIZATION
CENTRALIZATIONS
CENTRALIZE
CENTRALIZED
CENTRALIZER
CENTRALIZERS
CENTRALIZES
CENTRALIZING
CENTREBOARD
CENTREBOARDS
CENTREDNESS
CENTREDNESSES
CENTREFOLD
CENTREFOLDS
CENTREINGS
CENTRELESS
CENTRELINE
CENTRELINES
CENTREPIECE
CENTREPIECES
CENTRICALLY
CENTRICALNESS
CENTRICALNESSES
CENTRICITIES
CENTRICITY
CENTRIFUGAL
CENTRIFUGALISE
CENTRIFUGALISED
CENTRIFUGALISES
CENTRIFUGALIZE
CENTRIFUGALIZED
CENTRIFUGALIZES
CENTRIFUGALLY
CENTRIFUGALS
CENTRIFUGATION
CENTRIFUGATIONS
CENTRIFUGE
CENTRIFUGED
CENTRIFUGENCE
CENTRIFUGENCES
CENTRIFUGES
CENTRIFUGING
CENTRIOLES
CENTRIPETAL
CENTRIPETALISM
CENTRIPETALISMS
CENTRIPETALLY
CENTROBARIC
CENTROCLINAL
CENTROIDAL
CENTROLECITHAL
CENTROMERE
CENTROMERES
CENTROMERIC
CENTROSOME
CENTROSOMES
CENTROSOMIC
CENTROSPHERE
CENTROSPHERES
CENTROSYMMETRIC
CENTUMVIRATE
CENTUMVIRATES
CENTUMVIRI
CENTUMVIRS
CENTUPLICATE
CENTUPLICATED
CENTUPLICATES
CENTUPLICATING
CENTUPLICATION
CENTUPLICATIONS
CENTUPLING
CENTURIATION
CENTURIATIONS
CENTURIATOR
CENTURIATORS
CENTURIONS
CEPHALAGRA
CEPHALAGRAS
CEPHALALGIA
CEPHALALGIAS
CEPHALALGIC
CEPHALALGICS
CEPHALEXIN
CEPHALEXINS
CEPHALICALLY
CEPHALISATION
CEPHALISATIONS
CEPHALITIS
CEPHALITISES
CEPHALIZATION
CEPHALIZATIONS
CEPHALOCELE
CEPHALOCELES
CEPHALOCHORDATE
CEPHALOMETER
CEPHALOMETERS
CEPHALOMETRIC
CEPHALOMETRIES
CEPHALOMETRY
CEPHALOPOD
CEPHALOPODAN
CEPHALOPODANS
CEPHALOPODIC
CEPHALOPODOUS
CEPHALOPODS
CEPHALORIDINE
CEPHALORIDINES
CEPHALOSPORIN
CEPHALOSPORINS
CEPHALOTHIN
CEPHALOTHINS
CEPHALOTHORACES
CEPHALOTHORACIC
CEPHALOTHORAX
CEPHALOTHORAXES
CEPHALOTOMIES
CEPHALOTOMY
CERAMICIST

CERAMICISTS
CERAMOGRAPHIES
CERAMOGRAPHY
CERARGYRITE
CERARGYRITES
CERASTIUMS
CERATITISES
CERATODUSES
CERATOPSIAN
CERATOPSIANS
CERATOPSID
CERATOPSIDS
CERAUNOGRAPH
CERAUNOGRAPHS
CERCARIANS
CERCOPITHECID
CERCOPITHECIDS
CERCOPITHECOID
CERCOPITHECOIDS
CEREALISTS
CEREBELLAR
CEREBELLIC
CEREBELLOUS
CEREBELLUM
CEREBELLUMS
CEREBRALISM
CEREBRALISMS
CEREBRALIST
CEREBRALISTS
CEREBRALLY
CEREBRATED
CEREBRATES
CEREBRATING
CEREBRATION
CEREBRATIONS
CEREBRIFORM
CEREBRITIS
CEREBRITISES
CEREBROSIDE
CEREBROSIDES
CEREBROSPINAL
CEREBROTONIA
CEREBROTONIAS
CEREBROTONIC
CEREBROTONICS
CEREBROVASCULAR
CERECLOTHS
CEREMONIAL
CEREMONIALISM
CEREMONIALISMS
CEREMONIALIST
CEREMONIALISTS
CEREMONIALLY
CEREMONIALS
CEREMONIES
CEREMONIOUS
CEREMONIOUSLY
CEREMONIOUSNESS
CERIFEROUS
CEROGRAPHIC
CEROGRAPHICAL
CEROGRAPHIES
CEROGRAPHIST
CEROGRAPHISTS
CEROGRAPHS
CEROGRAPHY
CEROMANCIES
CEROPLASTIC
CEROPLASTICS
CERTAINEST
CERTAINTIES
CERTIFIABLE
CERTIFIABLY
CERTIFICATE
CERTIFICATED
CERTIFICATES
CERTIFICATING
CERTIFICATION
CERTIFICATIONS
CERTIFICATORIES
CERTIFICATORY
CERTIFIERS
CERTIFYING
CERTIORARI
CERTIORARIS
CERTITUDES
CERULOPLASMIN
CERULOPLASMINS
CERUMINOUS
CERUSSITES
CERVELASES
CERVICITIS
CERVICITISES
CERVICOGRAPHIES
CERVICOGRAPHY
CESAREVICH
CESAREVICHES
CESAREVITCH
CESAREVITCHES
CESAREVNAS
CESAREWICH
CESAREWICHES
CESAREWITCH
CESAREWITCHES
CESPITOSELY
CESSATIONS
CESSIONARIES
CESSIONARY
CESTOIDEAN
CESTOIDEANS
CETEOSAURUS
CETEOSAURUSES
CETOLOGICAL
CETOLOGIES
CETOLOGIST
CETOLOGISTS
CETRIMIDES
CETUXIMABS
CEVADILLAS
CEYLANITES
CEYLONITES
CHABAZITES
CHACONINES
CHAENOMELES
CHAENOMELESES
CHAETIFEROUS
CHAETODONS
CHAETOGNATH
CHAETOGNATHS
CHAETOPODS
CHAFFERERS
CHAFFERIES
CHAFFERING
CHAFFINCHES
CHAFFINGLY
CHAGRINING
CHAGRINNED
CHAGRINNING
CHAINBRAKE
CHAINBRAKES
CHAINFALLS
CHAINPLATE
CHAINPLATES
CHAINSAWED
CHAINSAWING
CHAINSHOTS
CHAINSTITCH
CHAINSTITCHES
CHAINWHEEL
CHAINWHEELS
CHAINWORKS
CHAIRBACKS
CHAIRBORNE
CHAIRBOUND
CHAIRLIFTS
CHAIRMANED
CHAIRMANING
CHAIRMANNED
CHAIRMANNING
CHAIRMANSHIP
CHAIRMANSHIPS
CHAIRPERSON
CHAIRPERSONS
CHAIRWARMER
CHAIRWARMERS
CHAIRWOMAN
CHAIRWOMEN
CHAISELESS
CHAKALAKAS
CHALANNING
CHALAZIONS
CHALAZOGAMIC
CHALAZOGAMIES
CHALAZOGAMY
CHALCANTHITE
CHALCANTHITES
CHALCEDONIC
CHALCEDONIES
CHALCEDONY
CHALCEDONYX
CHALCEDONYXES
CHALCOCITE
CHALCOCITES
CHALCOGENIDE
CHALCOGENIDES
CHALCOGENS
CHALCOGRAPHER
CHALCOGRAPHERS
CHALCOGRAPHIC
CHALCOGRAPHICAL
CHALCOGRAPHIES
CHALCOGRAPHIST
CHALCOGRAPHISTS
CHALCOGRAPHY
CHALCOLITHIC
CHALCOPYRITE
CHALCOPYRITES
CHALICOTHERE
CHALICOTHERES
CHALKBOARD
CHALKBOARDS
CHALKFACES
CHALKINESS
CHALKINESSES
CHALKLANDS
CHALKMARKS
CHALKSTONE
CHALKSTONES
CHALKSTRIPE
CHALKSTRIPES
CHALLENGEABLE
CHALLENGED
CHALLENGER
CHALLENGERS
CHALLENGES
CHALLENGING
CHALLENGINGLY
CHALUMEAUS
CHALUMEAUX
CHALYBEATE
CHALYBEATES
CHALYBITES
CHAMAELEON
CHAMAELEONS
CHAMAEPHYTE
CHAMAEPHYTES
CHAMBERERS
CHAMBERHAND
CHAMBERHANDS
CHAMBERING
CHAMBERINGS
CHAMBERLAIN
CHAMBERLAINS
CHAMBERLAINSHIP
CHAMBERMAID
CHAMBERMAIDS
CHAMBERPOT
CHAMBERPOTS
CHAMBRANLE
CHAMBRANLES

CHAMELEONIC
CHAMELEONLIKE
CHAMELEONS
CHAMFERERS
CHAMFERING
CHAMFRAINS
CHAMOISING
CHAMOMILES
CHAMPAGNES
CHAMPAIGNS
CHAMPERTIES
CHAMPERTOUS
CHAMPIGNON
CHAMPIGNONS
CHAMPIONED
CHAMPIONESS
CHAMPIONESSES
CHAMPIONING
CHAMPIONSHIP
CHAMPIONSHIPS
CHAMPLEVES
CHANCELESS
CHANCELLERIES
CHANCELLERY
CHANCELLOR
CHANCELLORIES
CHANCELLORS
CHANCELLORSHIP
CHANCELLORSHIPS
CHANCELLORY
CHANCERIES
CHANCINESS
CHANCINESSES
CHANCROIDAL
CHANCROIDS
CHANDELIER
CHANDELIERED
CHANDELIERS
CHANDELLED
CHANDELLES
CHANDELLING
CHANDLERIES
CHANDLERING
CHANDLERINGS
CHANDLERLY
CHANGEABILITIES
CHANGEABILITY
CHANGEABLE
CHANGEABLENESS
CHANGEABLY
CHANGEAROUND
CHANGEAROUNDS
CHANGEFULLY
CHANGEFULNESS
CHANGEFULNESSES
CHANGELESS
CHANGELESSLY
CHANGELESSNESS
CHANGELING
CHANGELINGS
CHANGEOVER
CHANGEOVERS
CHANGEROUND
CHANGEROUNDS
CHANNELERS
CHANNELING
CHANNELISATION
CHANNELISATIONS
CHANNELISE
CHANNELISED
CHANNELISES
CHANNELISING
CHANNELIZATION
CHANNELIZATIONS
CHANNELIZE
CHANNELIZED
CHANNELIZES
CHANNELIZING
CHANNELLED
CHANNELLER
CHANNELLERS
CHANNELLING
CHANSONETTE
CHANSONETTES
CHANSONNIER
CHANSONNIERS
CHANTARELLE
CHANTARELLES
CHANTECLER
CHANTECLERS
CHANTERELLE
CHANTERELLES
CHANTEUSES
CHANTICLEER
CHANTICLEERS
CHANTINGLY
CHANTRESSES
CHANUKIAHS
CHAOLOGIES
CHAOLOGIST
CHAOLOGISTS
CHAOTICALLY
CHAPARAJOS
CHAPAREJOS
CHAPARRALS
CHAPATTIES
CHAPELRIES
CHAPERONAGE
CHAPERONAGES
CHAPERONED
CHAPERONES
CHAPERONING
CHAPFALLEN
CHAPLAINCIES
CHAPLAINCY
CHAPLAINRIES
CHAPLAINRY
CHAPLAINSHIP
CHAPLAINSHIPS
CHAPMANSHIP
CHAPMANSHIPS
CHAPPESSES
CHAPRASSIES
CHAPRASSIS
CHAPSTICKS
CHAPTALISATION
CHAPTALISATIONS
CHAPTALISE
CHAPTALISED
CHAPTALISES
CHAPTALISING
CHAPTALIZATION
CHAPTALIZATIONS
CHAPTALIZE
CHAPTALIZED
CHAPTALIZES
CHAPTALIZING
CHAPTERHOUSE
CHAPTERHOUSES
CHAPTERING
CHARABANCS
CHARACINOID
CHARACTERED
CHARACTERFUL
CHARACTERIES
CHARACTERING
CHARACTERISABLE
CHARACTERISE
CHARACTERISED
CHARACTERISER
CHARACTERISERS
CHARACTERISES
CHARACTERISING
CHARACTERISM
CHARACTERISMS
CHARACTERISTIC
CHARACTERISTICS
CHARACTERIZABLE
CHARACTERIZE
CHARACTERIZED
CHARACTERIZER
CHARACTERIZERS
CHARACTERIZES
CHARACTERIZING
CHARACTERLESS
CHARACTEROLOGY
CHARACTERS
CHARACTERY
CHARBROILED
CHARBROILER
CHARBROILERS
CHARBROILING
CHARBROILS
CHARCOALED
CHARCOALIER
CHARCOALIEST
CHARCOALING
CHARCUTERIE
CHARCUTERIES
CHARDONNAY
CHARDONNAYS
CHARGEABILITIES
CHARGEABILITY
CHARGEABLE
CHARGEABLENESS
CHARGEABLY
CHARGEBACK
CHARGEBACKS
CHARGEHAND
CHARGEHANDS
CHARGELESS
CHARGESHEET
CHARGESHEETS
CHARGRILLED
CHARGRILLING
CHARGRILLS
CHARINESSES
CHARIOTEER
CHARIOTEERED
CHARIOTEERING
CHARIOTEERS
CHARIOTING
CHARISMATA
CHARISMATIC
CHARISMATICS
CHARITABLE
CHARITABLENESS
CHARITABLY
CHARIVARIED
CHARIVARIING
CHARIVARIS
CHARLADIES
CHARLATANIC
CHARLATANICAL
CHARLATANISM
CHARLATANISMS
CHARLATANISTIC
CHARLATANRIES
CHARLATANRY
CHARLATANS
CHARLESTON
CHARLESTONED
CHARLESTONING
CHARLESTONS
CHARLOTTES
CHARMEUSES
CHARMINGER
CHARMINGEST
CHARMINGLY
CHARMLESSLY
CHARMONIUM
CHAROSETHS
CHARREADAS
CHARTACEOUS
CHARTERERS
CHARTERING
CHARTERPARTIES
CHARTERPARTY
CHARTHOUSE
CHARTHOUSES

CHARTOGRAPHER
CHARTOGRAPHERS
CHARTOGRAPHIC
CHARTOGRAPHICAL
CHARTOGRAPHIES
CHARTOGRAPHY
CHARTREUSE
CHARTREUSES
CHARTULARIES
CHARTULARY
CHASEPORTS
CHASMOGAMIC
CHASMOGAMIES
CHASMOGAMOUS
CHASMOGAMY
CHASSEPOTS
CHASTENERS
CHASTENESS
CHASTENESSES
CHASTENING
CHASTENINGLY
CHASTENMENT
CHASTENMENTS
CHASTISABLE
CHASTISEMENT
CHASTISEMENTS
CHASTISERS
CHASTISING
CHASTITIES
CHATEAUBRIAND
CHATEAUBRIANDS
CHATELAINE
CHATELAINES
CHATELAINS
CHATOYANCE
CHATOYANCES
CHATOYANCIES
CHATOYANCY
CHATOYANTS
CHATTERATI
CHATTERBOX
CHATTERBOXES
CHATTERERS
CHATTERIER
CHATTERIEST
CHATTERING
CHATTERINGS
CHATTINESS
CHATTINESSES
CHAUDFROID
CHAUDFROIDS
CHAUFFEURED
CHAUFFEURING
CHAUFFEURS
CHAUFFEUSE
CHAUFFEUSED
CHAUFFEUSES
CHAUFFEUSING
CHAULMOOGRA
CHAULMOOGRAS
CHAULMUGRA
CHAULMUGRAS
CHAUNTRESS
CHAUNTRESSES
CHAUNTRIES
CHAUSSURES
CHAUTAUQUA
CHAUTAUQUAS
CHAUVINISM
CHAUVINISMS
CHAUVINIST
CHAUVINISTIC
CHAUVINISTS
CHAVENDERS
CHAVTASTIC
CHAWBACONS
CHEAPENERS
CHEAPENING
CHEAPISHLY
CHEAPJACKS
CHEAPNESSES
CHEAPSHOTS
CHEAPSKATE
CHEAPSKATES
CHEATERIES
CHEATINGLY
CHECHAKOES
CHECHAQUOS
CHECKBOOKS
CHECKBOXES
CHECKCLERK
CHECKCLERKS
CHECKERBERRIES
CHECKERBERRY
CHECKERBLOOM
CHECKERBLOOMS
CHECKERBOARD
CHECKERBOARDS
CHECKERING
CHECKLATON
CHECKLATONS
CHECKLISTED
CHECKLISTING
CHECKLISTS
CHECKMARKED
CHECKMARKING
CHECKMARKS
CHECKMATED
CHECKMATES
CHECKMATING
CHECKPOINT
CHECKPOINTS
CHECKRAILS
CHECKREINS
CHECKROOMS
CHECKROWED
CHECKROWING
CHECKSTOPS
CHECKWEIGHER
CHECKWEIGHERS
CHEDDARIER
CHEDDARIEST
CHEECHAKOES
CHEECHAKOS
CHEECHALKO
CHEECHALKOES
CHEECHALKOS
CHEEKBONES
CHEEKINESS
CHEEKINESSES
CHEEKPIECE
CHEEKPIECES
CHEEKPOUCH
CHEEKPOUCHES
CHEEKTEETH
CHEEKTOOTH
CHEERFULLER
CHEERFULLEST
CHEERFULLY
CHEERFULNESS
CHEERFULNESSES
CHEERINESS
CHEERINESSES
CHEERINGLY
CHEERISHNESS
CHEERISHNESSES
CHEERLEADER
CHEERLEADERS
CHEERLEADING
CHEERLEADS
CHEERLESSLY
CHEERLESSNESS
CHEERLESSNESSES
CHEESEBOARD
CHEESEBOARDS
CHEESEBURGER
CHEESEBURGERS
CHEESECAKE
CHEESECAKES
CHEESECLOTH
CHEESECLOTHS
CHEESECUTTER
CHEESECUTTERS
CHEESEHOPPER
CHEESEHOPPERS
CHEESELIKE
CHEESEMITE
CHEESEMITES
CHEESEMONGER
CHEESEMONGERS
CHEESEPARER
CHEESEPARERS
CHEESEPARING
CHEESEPARINGS
CHEESEPRESS
CHEESEPRESSES
CHEESESTEAK
CHEESESTEAKS
CHEESETASTER
CHEESETASTERS
CHEESEVATS
CHEESEWIRE
CHEESEWIRES
CHEESEWOOD
CHEESEWOODS
CHEESEWRING
CHEESEWRINGS
CHEESINESS
CHEESINESSES
CHEILITISES
CHEIROMANCER
CHEIROMANCERS
CHEIROMANCIES
CHEIROMANCY
CHELASHIPS
CHELATABLE
CHELATIONS
CHELICERAE
CHELICERAL
CHELICERATE
CHELICERATES
CHELIFEROUS
CHELONIANS
CHELUVIATION
CHELUVIATIONS
CHEMAUTOTROPH
CHEMAUTOTROPHIC
CHEMAUTOTROPHS
CHEMIATRIC
CHEMICALLY
CHEMICKING
CHEMICKINGS
CHEMICOPHYSICAL
CHEMIOSMOSES
CHEMIOSMOSIS
CHEMIOSMOTIC
CHEMISETTE
CHEMISETTES
CHEMISORBED
CHEMISORBING
CHEMISORBS
CHEMISORPTION
CHEMISORPTIONS
CHEMISTRIES
CHEMITYPES
CHEMITYPIES
CHEMOATTRACTANT
CHEMOAUTOTROPH
CHEMOAUTOTROPHS
CHEMOAUTOTROPHY
CHEMOAUTROPH
CHEMOAUTROPHS
CHEMOCEPTOR
CHEMOCEPTORS
CHEMOKINES
CHEMOKINESES
CHEMOKINESIS
CHEMOLITHOTROPH
CHEMONASTIES
CHEMONASTY

CHEMOPREVENTION
CHEMOPSYCHIATRY
CHEMORECEPTION
CHEMORECEPTIONS
CHEMORECEPTIVE
CHEMORECEPTOR
CHEMORECEPTORS
CHEMOSMOSES
CHEMOSMOSIS
CHEMOSMOTIC
CHEMOSORBED
CHEMOSORBING
CHEMOSORBS
CHEMOSPHERE
CHEMOSPHERES
CHEMOSPHERIC
CHEMOSTATS
CHEMOSURGERIES
CHEMOSURGERY
CHEMOSURGICAL
CHEMOSYNTHESES
CHEMOSYNTHESIS
CHEMOSYNTHETIC
CHEMOTACTIC
CHEMOTACTICALLY
CHEMOTAXES
CHEMOTAXIS
CHEMOTAXISES
CHEMOTAXONOMIC
CHEMOTAXONOMIES
CHEMOTAXONOMIST
CHEMOTAXONOMY
CHEMOTHERAPIES
CHEMOTHERAPIST
CHEMOTHERAPISTS
CHEMOTHERAPY
CHEMOTROPIC
CHEMOTROPICALLY
CHEMOTROPISM
CHEMOTROPISMS
CHEMPADUKS
CHEMTRAILS
CHEMURGICAL
CHEMURGIES
CHENOPODIACEOUS
CHEONGSAMS
CHEQUEBOOK
CHEQUEBOOKS
CHEQUERBOARD
CHEQUERBOARDS
CHEQUERING
CHEQUERWISE
CHEQUERWORK
CHEQUERWORKS
CHERALITES
CHERIMOYAS
CHERIMOYER
CHERIMOYERS
CHERISHABLE
CHERISHERS
CHERISHING
CHERISHINGLY
CHERISHMENT
CHERISHMENTS
CHERMOULAS
CHERNOZEMIC
CHERNOZEMS
CHERRYLIKE
CHERRYSTONE
CHERRYSTONES
CHERSONESE
CHERSONESES
CHERUBICAL
CHERUBICALLY
CHERUBIMIC
CHERUBLIKE
CHERVONETS
CHESSBOARD
CHESSBOARDS
CHESSBOXING
CHESSBOXINGS
CHESSPIECE
CHESSPIECES
CHESSPLAYER
CHESSPLAYERS
CHESSYLITE
CHESSYLITES
CHESTERFIELD
CHESTERFIELDS
CHESTINESS
CHESTINESSES
CHEVALIERS
CHEVELURES
CHEVESAILE
CHEVESAILES
CHEVISANCE
CHEVISANCES
CHEVRETTES
CHEVROTAIN
CHEVROTAINS
CHEVROTINS
CHEWINESSES
CHIACKINGS
CHIAREZZAS
CHIAROSCURISM
CHIAROSCURISMS
CHIAROSCURIST
CHIAROSCURISTS
CHIAROSCURO
CHIAROSCUROS
CHIASMATIC
CHIASTOLITE
CHIASTOLITES
CHIBOUQUES
CHICALOTES
CHICANERIES
CHICANINGS
CHICCORIES
CHICKABIDDIES
CHICKABIDDY
CHICKADEES
CHICKAREES
CHICKENHEARTED
CHICKENING
CHICKENPOX
CHICKENPOXES
CHICKENSHIT
CHICKENSHITS
CHICKLINGS
CHICKORIES
CHICKWEEDS
CHICNESSES
CHIEFERIES
CHIEFESSES
CHIEFLINGS
CHIEFSHIPS
CHIEFTAINCIES
CHIEFTAINCY
CHIEFTAINESS
CHIEFTAINESSES
CHIEFTAINRIES
CHIEFTAINRY
CHIEFTAINS
CHIEFTAINSHIP
CHIEFTAINSHIPS
CHIFFCHAFF
CHIFFCHAFFS
CHIFFONADE
CHIFFONADES
CHIFFONIER
CHIFFONIERS
CHIFFONNIER
CHIFFONNIERS
CHIFFONNIEST
CHIFFOROBE
CHIFFOROBES
CHIHUAHUAS
CHILBLAINED
CHILBLAINS
CHILDBEARING
CHILDBEARINGS
CHILDBIRTH
CHILDBIRTHS
CHILDCARES
CHILDCROWING
CHILDCROWINGS
CHILDERMAS
CHILDERMASES
CHILDHOODS
CHILDISHLY
CHILDISHNESS
CHILDISHNESSES
CHILDLESSNESS
CHILDLESSNESSES
CHILDLIEST
CHILDLIKENESS
CHILDLIKENESSES
CHILDMINDER
CHILDMINDERS
CHILDMINDING
CHILDMINDINGS
CHILDNESSES
CHILDPROOF
CHILDPROOFED
CHILDPROOFING
CHILDPROOFS
CHILDRENSWEAR
CHILDRENSWEARS
CHILIAGONS
CHILIAHEDRA
CHILIAHEDRON
CHILIAHEDRONS
CHILIARCHIES
CHILIARCHS
CHILIARCHY
CHILIASTIC
CHILLAXING
CHILLINESS
CHILLINESSES
CHILLINGLY
CHILLNESSES
CHILOPODAN
CHILOPODANS
CHILOPODOUS
CHILTEPINS
CHIMAERISM
CHIMAERISMS
CHIMERICAL
CHIMERICALLY
CHIMERICALNESS
CHIMERISMS
CHIMICHANGA
CHIMICHANGAS
CHIMNEYBOARD
CHIMNEYBOARDS
CHIMNEYBREAST
CHIMNEYBREASTS
CHIMNEYING
CHIMNEYLIKE
CHIMNEYPIECE
CHIMNEYPIECES
CHIMNEYPOT
CHIMNEYPOTS
CHIMPANZEE
CHIMPANZEES
CHINABERRIES
CHINABERRY
CHINACHINA
CHINACHINAS
CHINAROOTS
CHINAWARES
CHINCAPINS
CHINCHERINCHEE
CHINCHERINCHEES
CHINCHIEST
CHINCHILLA
CHINCHILLAS
CHINCOUGHS
CHINKAPINS
CHINKERINCHEE

CHINKERINCHEES
CHINOISERIE
CHINOISERIES
CHINOVNIKS
CHINQUAPIN
CHINQUAPINS
CHINSTRAPS
CHINTZIEST
CHINWAGGED
CHINWAGGING
CHIONODOXA
CHIONODOXAS
CHIPBOARDS
CHIPMAKERS
CHIPOCHIAS
CHIPOLATAS
CHIPPEREST
CHIPPERING
CHIPPINESS
CHIPPINESSES
CHIQUICHIQUI
CHIQUICHIQUIS
CHIRAGRICAL
CHIRALITIES
CHIRIMOYAS
CHIROGNOMIES
CHIROGNOMIST
CHIROGNOMISTS
CHIROGNOMY
CHIROGRAPH
CHIROGRAPHER
CHIROGRAPHERS
CHIROGRAPHIC
CHIROGRAPHICAL
CHIROGRAPHIES
CHIROGRAPHIST
CHIROGRAPHISTS
CHIROGRAPHS
CHIROGRAPHY
CHIROLOGIES
CHIROLOGIST
CHIROLOGISTS
CHIROMANCER
CHIROMANCERS
CHIROMANCIES
CHIROMANCY
CHIROMANTIC
CHIROMANTICAL
CHIRONOMER
CHIRONOMERS
CHIRONOMIC
CHIRONOMID
CHIRONOMIDS
CHIRONOMIES
CHIROPODIAL
CHIROPODIES
CHIROPODIST
CHIROPODISTS
CHIROPRACTIC
CHIROPRACTICS
CHIROPRACTOR
CHIROPRACTORS
CHIROPTERAN
CHIROPTERANS
CHIROPTEROUS
CHIROPTERS
CHIRPINESS
CHIRPINESSES
CHIRRUPERS
CHIRRUPIER
CHIRRUPIEST
CHIRRUPING
CHIRURGEON
CHIRURGEONLY
CHIRURGEONS
CHIRURGERIES
CHIRURGERY
CHIRURGICAL
CHISELLERS
CHISELLING
CHISELLINGS
CHITARRONE
CHITARRONI
CHITCHATTED
CHITCHATTING
CHITTAGONG
CHITTAGONGS
CHITTERING
CHITTERINGS
CHITTERLING
CHITTERLINGS
CHIVALRESQUE
CHIVALRIES
CHIVALROUS
CHIVALROUSLY
CHIVALROUSNESS
CHIVAREEING
CHIVARIING
CHIWEENIES
CHIYOGAMIS
CHLAMYDATE
CHLAMYDEOUS
CHLAMYDIAE
CHLAMYDIAL
CHLAMYDIAS
CHLAMYDOMONADES
CHLAMYDOMONAS
CHLAMYDOSPORE
CHLAMYDOSPORES
CHLOANTHITE
CHLOANTHITES
CHLOASMATA
CHLORACETIC
CHLORACNES
CHLORALISM
CHLORALISMS
CHLORALOSE
CHLORALOSED
CHLORALOSES
CHLORAMBUCIL
CHLORAMBUCILS
CHLORAMINE
CHLORAMINES
CHLORAMPHENICOL
CHLORARGYRITE
CHLORARGYRITES
CHLORDANES
CHLORELLAS
CHLORENCHYMA
CHLORENCHYMAS
CHLORHEXIDINE
CHLORHEXIDINES
CHLORIDATE
CHLORIDATED
CHLORIDATES
CHLORIDATING
CHLORIDISE
CHLORIDISED
CHLORIDISES
CHLORIDISING
CHLORIDIZE
CHLORIDIZED
CHLORIDIZES
CHLORIDIZING
CHLORIMETER
CHLORIMETERS
CHLORIMETRIC
CHLORIMETRIES
CHLORIMETRY
CHLORINATE
CHLORINATED
CHLORINATES
CHLORINATING
CHLORINATION
CHLORINATIONS
CHLORINATOR
CHLORINATORS
CHLORINISE
CHLORINISED
CHLORINISES
CHLORINISING
CHLORINITIES
CHLORINITY
CHLORINIZE
CHLORINIZED
CHLORINIZES
CHLORINIZING
CHLORITISATION
CHLORITISATIONS
CHLORITIZATION
CHLORITIZATIONS
CHLOROACETIC
CHLOROARGYRITE
CHLOROBENZENE
CHLOROBENZENES
CHLOROBROMIDE
CHLOROBROMIDES
CHLOROCALCITE
CHLOROCALCITES
CHLOROCRUORIN
CHLOROCRUORINS
CHLORODYNE
CHLORODYNES
CHLOROETHENE
CHLOROETHENES
CHLOROETHYLENE
CHLOROETHYLENES
CHLOROFORM
CHLOROFORMED
CHLOROFORMER
CHLOROFORMERS
CHLOROFORMING
CHLOROFORMIST
CHLOROFORMISTS
CHLOROFORMS
CHLOROHYDRIN
CHLOROHYDRINS
CHLOROMETER
CHLOROMETERS
CHLOROMETHANE
CHLOROMETHANES
CHLOROMETRIC
CHLOROMETRIES
CHLOROMETRY
CHLOROPHYL
CHLOROPHYLL
CHLOROPHYLLOID
CHLOROPHYLLOUS
CHLOROPHYLLS
CHLOROPHYLS
CHLOROPHYTUM
CHLOROPHYTUMS
CHLOROPICRIN
CHLOROPICRINS
CHLOROPLAST
CHLOROPLASTAL
CHLOROPLASTIC
CHLOROPLASTS
CHLOROPRENE
CHLOROPRENES
CHLOROQUIN
CHLOROQUINE
CHLOROQUINES
CHLOROQUINS
CHLOROSISES
CHLOROTHIAZIDE
CHLOROTHIAZIDES
CHLORPICRIN
CHLORPICRINS
CHLORPROMAZINE
CHLORPROMAZINES
CHLORPROPAMIDE
CHLORPROPAMIDES
CHLORTHALIDONE
CHLORTHALIDONES
CHOANOCYTE
CHOANOCYTES
CHOCAHOLIC
CHOCAHOLICS
CHOCKABLOCK

CHOCKSTONE
CHOCKSTONES
CHOCOHOLIC
CHOCOHOLICS
CHOCOLATES
CHOCOLATEY
CHOCOLATIER
CHOCOLATIERS
CHOCOLATIEST
CHOICENESS
CHOICENESSES
CHOIRGIRLS
CHOIRMASTER
CHOIRMASTERS
CHOIRSCREEN
CHOIRSCREENS
CHOIRSTALL
CHOIRSTALLS
CHOKEBERRIES
CHOKEBERRY
CHOKEBORES
CHOKECHERRIES
CHOKECHERRY
CHOKECOILS
CHOKEDAMPS
CHOKEHOLDS
CHOLAEMIAS
CHOLAGOGIC
CHOLAGOGUE
CHOLAGOGUES
CHOLANGIOGRAM
CHOLANGIOGRAMS
CHOLANGIOGRAPHY
CHOLECALCIFEROL
CHOLECYSTECTOMY
CHOLECYSTITIDES
CHOLECYSTITIS
CHOLECYSTITISES
CHOLECYSTOKININ
CHOLECYSTOSTOMY
CHOLECYSTOTOMY
CHOLECYSTS
CHOLELITHIASES
CHOLELITHIASIS
CHOLELITHS
CHOLERICALLY
CHOLERICLY
CHOLESTASES
CHOLESTASIS
CHOLESTATIC
CHOLESTERATE
CHOLESTERATES
CHOLESTERIC
CHOLESTERIN
CHOLESTERINS
CHOLESTEROL
CHOLESTEROLEMIA
CHOLESTEROLS
CHOLESTYRAMINE
CHOLESTYRAMINES
CHOLIAMBIC
CHOLIAMBICS
CHOLINERGIC
CHOLINERGICALLY
CHOLINESTERASE
CHOLINESTERASES
CHOMOPHYTE
CHOMOPHYTES
CHONDRICHTHYAN
CHONDRICHTHYANS
CHONDRIFICATION
CHONDRIFIED
CHONDRIFIES
CHONDRIFYING
CHONDRIOSOMAL
CHONDRIOSOME
CHONDRIOSOMES
CHONDRITES
CHONDRITIC
CHONDRITIS
CHONDRITISES
CHONDROBLAST
CHONDROBLASTS
CHONDROCRANIA
CHONDROCRANIUM
CHONDROCRANIUMS
CHONDROCYTE
CHONDROCYTES
CHONDROGENESES
CHONDROGENESIS
CHONDROITIN
CHONDROITINS
CHONDROMAS
CHONDROMATA
CHONDROMATOSES
CHONDROMATOSIS
CHONDROMATOUS
CHONDROPHORE
CHONDROPHORES
CHONDROPHORINE
CHONDROPHORINES
CHONDROSAMINE
CHONDROSAMINES
CHONDROSKELETON
CHONDROSTIAN
CHONDROSTIANS
CHONDRULES
CHOPFALLEN
CHOPHOUSES
CHOPLOGICS
CHOPPERING
CHOPPINESS
CHOPPINESSES
CHOPSOCKIES
CHOPSTICKS
CHORAGUSES
CHORALISTS
CHORDAMESODERM
CHORDAMESODERMS
CHORDOPHONE
CHORDOPHONES
CHORDOPHONIC
CHORDOTOMIES
CHORDOTOMY
CHOREGRAPH
CHOREGRAPHED
CHOREGRAPHER
CHOREGRAPHERS
CHOREGRAPHIC
CHOREGRAPHIES
CHOREGRAPHING
CHOREGRAPHS
CHOREGRAPHY
CHOREGUSES
CHOREIFORM
CHOREODRAMA
CHOREODRAMAS
CHOREOGRAPH
CHOREOGRAPHED
CHOREOGRAPHER
CHOREOGRAPHERS
CHOREOGRAPHIC
CHOREOGRAPHIES
CHOREOGRAPHING
CHOREOGRAPHS
CHOREOGRAPHY
CHOREOLOGIES
CHOREOLOGIST
CHOREOLOGISTS
CHOREOLOGY
CHOREPISCOPAL
CHORIAMBIC
CHORIAMBICS
CHORIAMBUS
CHORIAMBUSES
CHORIOALLANTOIC
CHORIOALLANTOIS
CHORIOCARCINOMA
CHORISATION
CHORISATIONS
CHORISTERS
CHORIZATION
CHORIZATIONS
CHORIZONTIST
CHORIZONTISTS
CHORIZONTS
CHOROGRAPHER
CHOROGRAPHERS
CHOROGRAPHIC
CHOROGRAPHICAL
CHOROGRAPHIES
CHOROGRAPHY
CHOROIDITIS
CHOROIDITISES
CHOROLOGICAL
CHOROLOGIES
CHOROLOGIST
CHOROLOGISTS
CHOROPLETH
CHOROPLETHS
CHORUSMASTER
CHORUSMASTERS
CHORUSSING
CHOUCROUTE
CHOUCROUTES
CHOULTRIES
CHOUNTERED
CHOUNTERING
CHOWDERHEAD
CHOWDERHEADED
CHOWDERHEADS
CHOWDERING
CHOWHOUNDS
CHOWKIDARS
CHREMATIST
CHREMATISTIC
CHREMATISTICS
CHREMATISTS
CHRESTOMATHIC
CHRESTOMATHICAL
CHRESTOMATHIES
CHRESTOMATHY
CHRISMATION
CHRISMATIONS
CHRISMATORIES
CHRISMATORY
CHRISTCROSS
CHRISTCROSSES
CHRISTENED
CHRISTENER
CHRISTENERS
CHRISTENING
CHRISTENINGS
CHRISTIANIA
CHRISTIANIAS
CHRISTOPHANIES
CHRISTOPHANY
CHROMAFFIN
CHROMAKEYS
CHROMATICALLY
CHROMATICISM
CHROMATICISMS
CHROMATICITIES
CHROMATICITY
CHROMATICNESS
CHROMATICNESSES
CHROMATICS
CHROMATIDS
CHROMATINIC
CHROMATINS
CHROMATIST
CHROMATISTS
CHROMATOGRAM
CHROMATOGRAMS
CHROMATOGRAPH
CHROMATOGRAPHED
CHROMATOGRAPHER
CHROMATOGRAPHIC
CHROMATOGRAPHS
CHROMATOGRAPHY

CHROMATOID
CHROMATOLOGIES
CHROMATOLOGIST
CHROMATOLOGISTS
CHROMATOLOGY
CHROMATOLYSES
CHROMATOLYSIS
CHROMATOLYTIC
CHROMATOPHORE
CHROMATOPHORES
CHROMATOPHORIC
CHROMATOPHOROUS
CHROMATOPSIA
CHROMATOPSIAS
CHROMATOSPHERE
CHROMATOSPHERES
CHROMATYPE
CHROMATYPES
CHROMIDIUM
CHROMINANCE
CHROMINANCES
CHROMISING
CHROMIZING
CHROMOCENTER
CHROMOCENTERS
CHROMOCENTRE
CHROMOCENTRES
CHROMODYNAMICS
CHROMOGENIC
CHROMOGENS
CHROMOGRAM
CHROMOGRAMS
CHROMOLIES
CHROMOMERE
CHROMOMERES
CHROMOMERIC
CHROMONEMA
CHROMONEMAL
CHROMONEMATA
CHROMONEMATIC
CHROMONEMIC
CHROMOPHIL
CHROMOPHILIC
CHROMOPHILS
CHROMOPHOBE
CHROMOPHOBES
CHROMOPHORE
CHROMOPHORES
CHROMOPHORIC
CHROMOPHOROUS
CHROMOPLAST
CHROMOPLASTS
CHROMOPROTEIN
CHROMOPROTEINS
CHROMOSCOPE
CHROMOSCOPES
CHROMOSOMAL
CHROMOSOMALLY
CHROMOSOME
CHROMOSOMES
CHROMOSPHERE
CHROMOSPHERES
CHROMOSPHERIC
CHROMOTHERAPIES
CHROMOTHERAPY
CHROMOTYPE
CHROMOTYPES
CHROMOXYLOGRAPH
CHRONAXIES
CHRONICALLY
CHRONICITIES
CHRONICITY
CHRONICLED
CHRONICLER
CHRONICLERS
CHRONICLES
CHRONICLING
CHRONOBIOLOGIC
CHRONOBIOLOGIES
CHRONOBIOLOGIST
CHRONOBIOLOGY
CHRONOGRAM
CHRONOGRAMMATIC
CHRONOGRAMS
CHRONOGRAPH
CHRONOGRAPHER
CHRONOGRAPHERS
CHRONOGRAPHIC
CHRONOGRAPHIES
CHRONOGRAPHS
CHRONOGRAPHY
CHRONOLOGER
CHRONOLOGERS
CHRONOLOGIC
CHRONOLOGICAL
CHRONOLOGICALLY
CHRONOLOGIES
CHRONOLOGISE
CHRONOLOGISED
CHRONOLOGISES
CHRONOLOGISING
CHRONOLOGIST
CHRONOLOGISTS
CHRONOLOGIZE
CHRONOLOGIZED
CHRONOLOGIZES
CHRONOLOGIZING
CHRONOLOGY
CHRONOMETER
CHRONOMETERS
CHRONOMETRIC
CHRONOMETRICAL
CHRONOMETRIES
CHRONOMETRY
CHRONOSCOPE
CHRONOSCOPES
CHRONOSCOPIC
CHRONOTHERAPIES
CHRONOTHERAPY
CHRONOTRON
CHRONOTRONS
CHRYSALIDAL
CHRYSALIDES
CHRYSALIDS
CHRYSALISES
CHRYSANTHEMUM
CHRYSANTHEMUMS
CHRYSANTHS
CHRYSAROBIN
CHRYSAROBINS
CHRYSOBERYL
CHRYSOBERYLS
CHRYSOCOLLA
CHRYSOCOLLAS
CHRYSOCRACIES
CHRYSOCRACY
CHRYSOLITE
CHRYSOLITES
CHRYSOLITIC
CHRYSOMELID
CHRYSOMELIDS
CHRYSOPHAN
CHRYSOPHANS
CHRYSOPHILITE
CHRYSOPHILITES
CHRYSOPHYTE
CHRYSOPHYTES
CHRYSOPRASE
CHRYSOPRASES
CHRYSOTILE
CHRYSOTILES
CHUBBINESS
CHUBBINESSES
CHUCKAWALLA
CHUCKAWALLAS
CHUCKHOLES
CHUCKLEHEAD
CHUCKLEHEADED
CHUCKLEHEADS
CHUCKLESOME
CHUCKLINGLY
CHUCKLINGS
CHUCKWALLA
CHUCKWALLAS
CHUFFINESS
CHUFFINESSES
CHUGALUGGED
CHUGALUGGING
CHUMMINESS
CHUMMINESSES
CHUNDERING
CHUNDEROUS
CHUNKINESS
CHUNKINESSES
CHUNNERING
CHUNTERING
CHUPATTIES
CHUPRASSIES
CHURCHGOER
CHURCHGOERS
CHURCHGOING
CHURCHGOINGS
CHURCHIANITIES
CHURCHIANITY
CHURCHIEST
CHURCHINGS
CHURCHISMS
CHURCHLESS
CHURCHLIER
CHURCHLIEST
CHURCHLINESS
CHURCHLINESSES
CHURCHMANLIER
CHURCHMANLIEST
CHURCHMANLY
CHURCHMANSHIP
CHURCHMANSHIPS
CHURCHPEOPLE
CHURCHWARD
CHURCHWARDEN
CHURCHWARDENS
CHURCHWARDS
CHURCHWAYS
CHURCHWOMAN
CHURCHWOMEN
CHURCHYARD
CHURCHYARDS
CHURLISHLY
CHURLISHNESS
CHURLISHNESSES
CHURNALISM
CHURNALISMS
CHURNMILKS
CHURRIGUERESCO
CHURRIGUERESQUE
CHYLACEOUS
CHYLIFEROUS
CHYLIFICATION
CHYLIFICATIONS
CHYLIFYING
CHYLOMICRON
CHYLOMICRONS
CHYMIFEROUS
CHYMIFICATION
CHYMIFICATIONS
CHYMIFYING
CHYMISTRIES
CHYMOTRYPSIN
CHYMOTRYPSINS
CHYMOTRYPTIC
CIBACHROME
CIBACHROMES
CICADELLID
CICADELLIDS
CICATRICES
CICATRICHULE
CICATRICHULES
CICATRICIAL
CICATRICLE
CICATRICLES

CICATRICOSE
CICATRICULA
CICATRICULAS
CICATRISANT
CICATRISATION
CICATRISATIONS
CICATRISED
CICATRISER
CICATRISERS
CICATRISES
CICATRISING
CICATRIXES
CICATRIZANT
CICATRIZATION
CICATRIZATIONS
CICATRIZED
CICATRIZER
CICATRIZERS
CICATRIZES
CICATRIZING
CICERONEING
CICHORACEOUS
CICINNUSES
CICISBEISM
CICISBEISMS
CICLATOUNS
CICLOSPORIN
CICLOSPORINS
CIGARETTES
CIGARILLOS
CIGUATERAS
CIGUATOXIN
CIGUATOXINS
CILIATIONS
CIMETIDINE
CIMETIDINES
CINCHONACEOUS
CINCHONIDINE
CINCHONIDINES
CINCHONINE
CINCHONINES
CINCHONINIC
CINCHONISATION
CINCHONISATIONS
CINCHONISE
CINCHONISED
CINCHONISES
CINCHONISING
CINCHONISM
CINCHONISMS
CINCHONIZATION
CINCHONIZATIONS
CINCHONIZE
CINCHONIZED
CINCHONIZES
CINCHONIZING
CINCINNATE
CINCINNUSES
CINCTURING
CINDERIEST
CINEANGIOGRAPHY
CINEMAGOER
CINEMAGOERS
CINEMATHEQUE
CINEMATHEQUES
CINEMATICALLY
CINEMATISE
CINEMATISED
CINEMATISES
CINEMATISING
CINEMATIZE
CINEMATIZED
CINEMATIZES
CINEMATIZING
CINEMATOGRAPH
CINEMATOGRAPHED
CINEMATOGRAPHER
CINEMATOGRAPHIC
CINEMATOGRAPHS
CINEMATOGRAPHY
CINEMICROGRAPHY
CINEPHILES
CINEPLEXES
CINERARIAS
CINERARIUM
CINERARIUMS
CINERATION
CINERATIONS
CINERATORS
CINERITIOUS
CINGULATED
CINNABARIC
CINNABARINE
CINNAMONIC
CINNAMONIER
CINNAMONIEST
CINNARIZINE
CINNARIZINES
CINQUECENTIST
CINQUECENTISTS
CINQUECENTO
CINQUECENTOS
CINQUEFOIL
CINQUEFOILS
CIPHERINGS
CIPHERTEXT
CIPHERTEXTS
CIPOLLINOS
CIPROFLOXACIN
CIPROFLOXACINS
CIRCASSIAN
CIRCASSIANS
CIRCASSIENNE
CIRCASSIENNES
CIRCENSIAL
CIRCENSIAN
CIRCINATELY
CIRCUITEER
CIRCUITEERED
CIRCUITEERING
CIRCUITEERS
CIRCUITIES
CIRCUITING
CIRCUITOUS
CIRCUITOUSLY
CIRCUITOUSNESS
CIRCUITRIES
CIRCULABLE
CIRCULARISATION
CIRCULARISE
CIRCULARISED
CIRCULARISER
CIRCULARISERS
CIRCULARISES
CIRCULARISING
CIRCULARITIES
CIRCULARITY
CIRCULARIZATION
CIRCULARIZE
CIRCULARIZED
CIRCULARIZER
CIRCULARIZERS
CIRCULARIZES
CIRCULARIZING
CIRCULARLY
CIRCULARNESS
CIRCULARNESSES
CIRCULATABLE
CIRCULATED
CIRCULATES
CIRCULATING
CIRCULATINGS
CIRCULATION
CIRCULATIONS
CIRCULATIVE
CIRCULATOR
CIRCULATORS
CIRCULATORY
CIRCUMAMBAGES
CIRCUMAMBAGIOUS
CIRCUMAMBIENCE
CIRCUMAMBIENCES
CIRCUMAMBIENCY
CIRCUMAMBIENT
CIRCUMAMBIENTLY
CIRCUMAMBULATE
CIRCUMAMBULATED
CIRCUMAMBULATES
CIRCUMAMBULATOR
CIRCUMBENDIBUS
CIRCUMCENTER
CIRCUMCENTERS
CIRCUMCENTRE
CIRCUMCENTRES
CIRCUMCIRCLE
CIRCUMCIRCLES
CIRCUMCISE
CIRCUMCISED
CIRCUMCISER
CIRCUMCISERS
CIRCUMCISES
CIRCUMCISING
CIRCUMCISION
CIRCUMCISIONS
CIRCUMDUCE
CIRCUMDUCED
CIRCUMDUCES
CIRCUMDUCING
CIRCUMDUCT
CIRCUMDUCTED
CIRCUMDUCTING
CIRCUMDUCTION
CIRCUMDUCTIONS
CIRCUMDUCTORY
CIRCUMDUCTS
CIRCUMFERENCE
CIRCUMFERENCES
CIRCUMFERENTIAL
CIRCUMFERENTOR
CIRCUMFERENTORS
CIRCUMFLECT
CIRCUMFLECTED
CIRCUMFLECTING
CIRCUMFLECTS
CIRCUMFLEX
CIRCUMFLEXES
CIRCUMFLEXION
CIRCUMFLEXIONS
CIRCUMFLUENCE
CIRCUMFLUENCES
CIRCUMFLUENT
CIRCUMFLUOUS
CIRCUMFORANEAN
CIRCUMFORANEOUS
CIRCUMFUSE
CIRCUMFUSED
CIRCUMFUSES
CIRCUMFUSILE
CIRCUMFUSING
CIRCUMFUSION
CIRCUMFUSIONS
CIRCUMGYRATE
CIRCUMGYRATED
CIRCUMGYRATES
CIRCUMGYRATING
CIRCUMGYRATION
CIRCUMGYRATIONS
CIRCUMGYRATORY
CIRCUMINCESSION
CIRCUMINSESSION
CIRCUMJACENCIES
CIRCUMJACENCY
CIRCUMJACENT
CIRCUMLITTORAL
CIRCUMLOCUTE
CIRCUMLOCUTED
CIRCUMLOCUTES
CIRCUMLOCUTING
CIRCUMLOCUTION
CIRCUMLOCUTIONS

CIRCUMLOCUTORY
CIRCUMLUNAR
CIRCUMMURE
CIRCUMMURED
CIRCUMMURES
CIRCUMMURING
CIRCUMNAVIGABLE
CIRCUMNAVIGATE
CIRCUMNAVIGATED
CIRCUMNAVIGATES
CIRCUMNAVIGATOR
CIRCUMNUTATE
CIRCUMNUTATED
CIRCUMNUTATES
CIRCUMNUTATING
CIRCUMNUTATION
CIRCUMNUTATIONS
CIRCUMNUTATORY
CIRCUMPOLAR
CIRCUMPOSE
CIRCUMPOSED
CIRCUMPOSES
CIRCUMPOSING
CIRCUMPOSITION
CIRCUMPOSITIONS
CIRCUMROTATE
CIRCUMROTATED
CIRCUMROTATES
CIRCUMROTATING
CIRCUMSCISSILE
CIRCUMSCRIBABLE
CIRCUMSCRIBE
CIRCUMSCRIBED
CIRCUMSCRIBER
CIRCUMSCRIBERS
CIRCUMSCRIBES
CIRCUMSCRIBING
CIRCUMSCRIPTION
CIRCUMSCRIPTIVE
CIRCUMSOLAR
CIRCUMSPECT
CIRCUMSPECTION
CIRCUMSPECTIONS
CIRCUMSPECTIVE
CIRCUMSPECTLY
CIRCUMSPECTNESS
CIRCUMSTANCE
CIRCUMSTANCED
CIRCUMSTANCES
CIRCUMSTANCING
CIRCUMSTANTIAL
CIRCUMSTANTIALS
CIRCUMSTANTIATE
CIRCUMSTELLAR
CIRCUMVALLATE
CIRCUMVALLATED
CIRCUMVALLATES
CIRCUMVALLATING
CIRCUMVALLATION
CIRCUMVENT
CIRCUMVENTED
CIRCUMVENTER
CIRCUMVENTERS
CIRCUMVENTING
CIRCUMVENTION
CIRCUMVENTIONS
CIRCUMVENTIVE
CIRCUMVENTOR
CIRCUMVENTORS
CIRCUMVENTS
CIRCUMVOLUTION
CIRCUMVOLUTIONS
CIRCUMVOLUTORY
CIRCUMVOLVE
CIRCUMVOLVED
CIRCUMVOLVES
CIRCUMVOLVING
CIRCUSIEST
CIRCUSSIER
CIRCUSSIEST
CIRRHIPEDE
CIRRHIPEDES
CIRRHOTICS
CIRRIGRADE
CIRRIPEDES
CIRROCUMULI
CIRROCUMULUS
CIRROSTRATI
CIRROSTRATIVE
CIRROSTRATUS
CISGENDERED
CISMONTANE
CISPLATINS
CISPONTINE
CISTACEOUS
CITATIONAL
CITHARISTIC
CITHARISTS
CITIFICATION
CITIFICATIONS
CITIZENESS
CITIZENESSES
CITIZENISE
CITIZENISED
CITIZENISES
CITIZENISING
CITIZENIZE
CITIZENIZED
CITIZENIZES
CITIZENIZING
CITIZENLIER
CITIZENLIEST
CITIZENRIES
CITIZENSHIP
CITIZENSHIPS
CITRICULTURE
CITRICULTURES
CITRICULTURIST
CITRICULTURISTS
CITRONELLA
CITRONELLAL
CITRONELLALS
CITRONELLAS
CITRONELLOL
CITRONELLOLS
CITRULLINE
CITRULLINES
CITRUSIEST
CITRUSSIER
CITRUSSIEST
CITYFICATION
CITYFICATIONS
CITYSCAPES
CIVILIANISATION
CIVILIANISE
CIVILIANISED
CIVILIANISES
CIVILIANISING
CIVILIANIZATION
CIVILIANIZE
CIVILIANIZED
CIVILIANIZES
CIVILIANIZING
CIVILISABLE
CIVILISATION
CIVILISATIONAL
CIVILISATIONS
CIVILISERS
CIVILISING
CIVILITIES
CIVILIZABLE
CIVILIZATION
CIVILIZATIONAL
CIVILIZATIONS
CIVILIZERS
CIVILIZING
CIVILNESSES
CLABBERING
CLACKBOXES
CLACKDISHES
CLADISTICALLY
CLADISTICS
CLADOCERAN
CLADOCERANS
CLADOGENESES
CLADOGENESIS
CLADOGENETIC
CLADOGRAMS
CLADOPHYLL
CLADOPHYLLS
CLADOSPORIA
CLADOSPORIUM
CLAIRAUDIENCE
CLAIRAUDIENCES
CLAIRAUDIENT
CLAIRAUDIENTLY
CLAIRAUDIENTS
CLAIRCOLLE
CLAIRCOLLES
CLAIRSCHACH
CLAIRSCHACHS
CLAIRVOYANCE
CLAIRVOYANCES
CLAIRVOYANCIES
CLAIRVOYANCY
CLAIRVOYANT
CLAIRVOYANTLY
CLAIRVOYANTS
CLAMANCIES
CLAMATORIAL
CLAMBERERS
CLAMBERING
CLAMJAMFRIES
CLAMJAMFRY
CLAMJAMPHRIE
CLAMJAMPHRIES
CLAMMINESS
CLAMMINESSES
CLAMOROUSLY
CLAMOROUSNESS
CLAMOROUSNESSES
CLAMOURERS
CLAMOURING
CLAMPDOWNS
CLAMPERING
CLAMSHELLS
CLANDESTINE
CLANDESTINELY
CLANDESTINENESS
CLANDESTINITIES
CLANDESTINITY
CLANGBOXES
CLANGORING
CLANGOROUS
CLANGOROUSLY
CLANGOURED
CLANGOURING
CLANJAMFRAY
CLANJAMFRAYS
CLANKINGLY
CLANNISHLY
CLANNISHNESS
CLANNISHNESSES
CLANSWOMAN
CLANSWOMEN
CLAPBOARDED
CLAPBOARDING
CLAPBOARDS
CLAPBREADS
CLAPDISHES
CLAPOMETER
CLAPOMETERS
CLAPPERBOARD
CLAPPERBOARDS
CLAPPERBOY
CLAPPERBOYS
CLAPPERCLAW
CLAPPERCLAWED
CLAPPERCLAWER
CLAPPERCLAWERS

CLAPPERCLAWING
CLAPPERCLAWS
CLAPPERING
CLAPPERINGS
CLAPTRAPPERIES
CLAPTRAPPERY
CLARABELLA
CLARABELLAS
CLARENDONS
CLARIBELLA
CLARIBELLAS
CLARICHORD
CLARICHORDS
CLARIFICATION
CLARIFICATIONS
CLARIFIERS
CLARIFYING
CLARINETIST
CLARINETISTS
CLARINETTIST
CLARINETTISTS
CLARIONETS
CLARIONING
CLARTHEADS
CLASHINGLY
CLASSICALISM
CLASSICALISMS
CLASSICALIST
CLASSICALISTS
CLASSICALITIES
CLASSICALITY
CLASSICALLY
CLASSICALNESS
CLASSICALNESSES
CLASSICALS
CLASSICISE
CLASSICISED
CLASSICISES
CLASSICISING
CLASSICISM
CLASSICISMS
CLASSICIST
CLASSICISTIC
CLASSICISTS
CLASSICIZE
CLASSICIZED
CLASSICIZES
CLASSICIZING
CLASSIFIABLE
CLASSIFICATION
CLASSIFICATIONS
CLASSIFICATORY
CLASSIFIED
CLASSIFIEDS
CLASSIFIER
CLASSIFIERS
CLASSIFIES
CLASSIFYING
CLASSINESS
CLASSINESSES
CLASSLESSNESS
CLASSLESSNESSES
CLASSMATES
CLASSROOMS
CLASSWORKS
CLATHRATES
CLATTERERS
CLATTERIER
CLATTERIEST
CLATTERING
CLATTERINGLY
CLAUCHTING
CLAUDICATION
CLAUDICATIONS
CLAUGHTING
CLAUSTRATION
CLAUSTRATIONS
CLAUSTROPHILIA
CLAUSTROPHILIAS
CLAUSTROPHOBE
CLAUSTROPHOBES
CLAUSTROPHOBIA
CLAUSTROPHOBIAS
CLAUSTROPHOBIC
CLAVATIONS
CLAVECINIST
CLAVECINISTS
CLAVICEMBALO
CLAVICEMBALOS
CLAVICHORD
CLAVICHORDIST
CLAVICHORDISTS
CLAVICHORDS
CLAVICORNS
CLAVICULAE
CLAVICULAR
CLAVICULATE
CLAVICYTHERIA
CLAVICYTHERIUM
CLAVIERIST
CLAVIERISTIC
CLAVIERISTS
CLAVIGEROUS
CLAWHAMMER
CLAWHAMMERS
CLAYMATION
CLAYMATIONS
CLAYSTONES
CLAYTONIAS
CLEANABILITIES
CLEANABILITY
CLEANHANDED
CLEANLIEST
CLEANLINESS
CLEANLINESSES
CLEANNESSES
CLEANSABLE
CLEANSINGS
CLEANSKINS
CLEANTECHS
CLEARANCES
CLEARCOLED
CLEARCOLES
CLEARCOLING
CLEARCUTTING
CLEARCUTTINGS
CLEARHEADED
CLEARHEADEDLY
CLEARHEADEDNESS
CLEARINGHOUSE
CLEARINGHOUSES
CLEARNESSES
CLEARSKINS
CLEARSTORIED
CLEARSTORIES
CLEARSTORY
CLEARWEEDS
CLEARWINGS
CLEAVABILITIES
CLEAVABILITY
CLEAVABLENESS
CLEAVABLENESSES
CLEISTOGAMIC
CLEISTOGAMIES
CLEISTOGAMOUS
CLEISTOGAMOUSLY
CLEISTOGAMY
CLEMATISES
CLEMENCIES
CLEMENTINE
CLEMENTINES
CLENBUTEROL
CLENBUTEROLS
CLEOPATRAS
CLEPSYDRAE
CLEPSYDRAS
CLEPTOCRACIES
CLEPTOCRACY
CLEPTOMANIA
CLEPTOMANIAC
CLEPTOMANIACS
CLEPTOMANIAS
CLERESTORIED
CLERESTORIES
CLERESTORY
CLERGIABLE
CLERGYABLE
CLERGYWOMAN
CLERGYWOMEN
CLERICALISM
CLERICALISMS
CLERICALIST
CLERICALISTS
CLERICALLY
CLERICATES
CLERICITIES
CLERKESSES
CLERKLIEST
CLERKLINESS
CLERKLINESSES
CLERKLINGS
CLERKSHIPS
CLEROMANCIES
CLEROMANCY
CLERUCHIAL
CLERUCHIAS
CLERUCHIES
CLEVERALITIES
CLEVERALITY
CLEVERDICK
CLEVERDICKS
CLEVERNESS
CLEVERNESSES
CLIANTHUSES
CLICKBAITS
CLICKETING
CLICKJACKING
CLICKJACKINGS
CLICKSTREAM
CLICKSTREAMS
CLICKTIVISM
CLICKTIVISMS
CLICKWRAPS
CLIENTAGES
CLIENTELES
CLIENTLESS
CLIENTSHIP
CLIENTSHIPS
CLIFFHANGER
CLIFFHANGERS
CLIFFHANGING
CLIFFHANGINGS
CLIFFHANGS
CLIFFSIDES
CLIMACTERIC
CLIMACTERICAL
CLIMACTERICALLY
CLIMACTERICS
CLIMACTICAL
CLIMACTICALLY
CLIMATICAL
CLIMATICALLY
CLIMATISED
CLIMATISES
CLIMATISING
CLIMATIZED
CLIMATIZES
CLIMATIZING
CLIMATOGRAPHIES
CLIMATOGRAPHY
CLIMATOLOGIC
CLIMATOLOGICAL
CLIMATOLOGIES
CLIMATOLOGIST
CLIMATOLOGISTS
CLIMATOLOGY
CLIMATURES
CLIMAXLESS
CLIMBDOWNS
CLINANDRIA

C

CLINANDRIUM
CLINCHINGLY
CLINDAMYCIN
CLINDAMYCINS
CLINGFILMS
CLINGFISHES
CLINGINESS
CLINGINESSES
CLINGINGLY
CLINGINGNESS
CLINGINGNESSES
CLINGSTONE
CLINGSTONES
CLINGWRAPS
CLINICALLY
CLINICALNESS
CLINICALNESSES
CLINICIANS
CLINKERING
CLINKSTONE
CLINKSTONES
CLINOCHLORE
CLINOCHLORES
CLINODIAGONAL
CLINODIAGONALS
CLINOMETER
CLINOMETERS
CLINOMETRIC
CLINOMETRICAL
CLINOMETRIES
CLINOMETRY
CLINOPINACOID
CLINOPINACOIDS
CLINOPINAKOID
CLINOPINAKOIDS
CLINOPYROXENE
CLINOPYROXENES
CLINOSTATS
CLINQUANTS
CLINTONIAS
CLIOMETRIC
CLIOMETRICAL
CLIOMETRICIAN
CLIOMETRICIANS
CLIOMETRICS
CLIOMETRIES
CLIPBOARDS
CLIPSHEARS
CLIPSHEETS
CLIQUINESS
CLIQUINESSES
CLIQUISHLY
CLIQUISHNESS
CLIQUISHNESSES
CLISHMACLAVER
CLISHMACLAVERS
CLISTOGAMIES
CLISTOGAMY
CLITICISED
CLITICISES
CLITICISING
CLITICIZED
CLITICIZES
CLITICIZING
CLITORECTOMIES
CLITORECTOMY
CLITORIDECTOMY
CLITORIDES
CLITORISES
CLITTERING
CLOACALINE
CLOACITISES
CLOAKROOMS
CLOBBERING
CLOCKFACES
CLOCKMAKER
CLOCKMAKERS
CLOCKWORKS
CLODDISHLY
CLODDISHNESS
CLODDISHNESSES
CLODHOPPER
CLODHOPPERS
CLODHOPPING
CLOFIBRATE
CLOFIBRATES
CLOGDANCES
CLOGGINESS
CLOGGINESSES
CLOGMAKERS
CLOISONNAGE
CLOISONNAGES
CLOISONNES
CLOISTERED
CLOISTERER
CLOISTERERS
CLOISTERING
CLOISTRESS
CLOISTRESSES
CLOMIPHENE
CLOMIPHENES
CLONAZEPAM
CLONAZEPAMS
CLONICITIES
CLONIDINES
CLOSEDOWNS
CLOSEFISTED
CLOSEHEADS
CLOSEMOUTHED
CLOSENESSES
CLOSESTOOL
CLOSESTOOLS
CLOSETFULS
CLOSTRIDIA
CLOSTRIDIAL
CLOSTRIDIAN
CLOSTRIDIUM
CLOSTRIDIUMS
CLOTHBOUND
CLOTHESHORSE
CLOTHESHORSES
CLOTHESLINE
CLOTHESLINED
CLOTHESLINES
CLOTHESLINING
CLOTHESPIN
CLOTHESPINS
CLOTHESPRESS
CLOTHESPRESSES
CLOTTERING
CLOTTINESS
CLOTTINESSES
CLOUDBERRIES
CLOUDBERRY
CLOUDBURST
CLOUDBURSTS
CLOUDINESS
CLOUDINESSES
CLOUDLANDS
CLOUDLESSLY
CLOUDLESSNESS
CLOUDLESSNESSES
CLOUDSCAPE
CLOUDSCAPES
CLOUDTOWNS
CLOVERGRASS
CLOVERGRASSES
CLOVERIEST
CLOVERLEAF
CLOVERLEAFS
CLOVERLEAVES
CLOVERLIKE
CLOWNERIES
CLOWNFISHES
CLOWNISHLY
CLOWNISHNESS
CLOWNISHNESSES
CLOXACILLIN
CLOXACILLINS
CLOZAPINES
CLUBABILITIES
CLUBABILITY
CLUBBABILITIES
CLUBBABILITY
CLUBBINESS
CLUBBINESSES
CLUBFOOTED
CLUBHAULED
CLUBHAULING
CLUBHOUSES
CLUBMANSHIP
CLUBMANSHIPS
CLUBMASTER
CLUBMASTERS
CLUBMOSSES
CLUBRUSHES
CLUMPERING
CLUMPINESS
CLUMPINESSES
CLUMSINESS
CLUMSINESSES
CLUSTERIER
CLUSTERIEST
CLUSTERING
CLUSTERINGLY
CLUTCHIEST
CLUTTERIER
CLUTTERIEST
CLUTTERING
CLYPEIFORM
CNIDARIANS
CNIDOBLAST
CNIDOBLASTS
COACERVATE
COACERVATED
COACERVATES
COACERVATING
COACERVATION
COACERVATIONS
COACHBUILDER
COACHBUILDERS
COACHBUILDING
COACHBUILDINGS
COACHBUILT
COACHLINES
COACHLOADS
COACHROOFS
COACHWHIPS
COACHWOODS
COACHWORKS
COACTIVELY
COACTIVITIES
COACTIVITY
COADAPTATION
COADAPTATIONS
COADJACENCIES
COADJACENCY
COADJACENT
COADJACENTS
COADJUTANT
COADJUTANTS
COADJUTORS
COADJUTORSHIP
COADJUTORSHIPS
COADJUTRESS
COADJUTRESSES
COADJUTRICES
COADJUTRIX
COADJUTRIXES
COADMIRING
COADMITTED
COADMITTING
COADUNATED
COADUNATES
COADUNATING
COADUNATION
COADUNATIONS
COADUNATIVE
COAGENCIES
COAGULABILITIES

COAGULABILITY
COAGULABLE
COAGULANTS
COAGULASES
COAGULATED
COAGULATES
COAGULATING
COAGULATION
COAGULATIONS
COAGULATIVE
COAGULATOR
COAGULATORS
COAGULATORY
COALESCENCE
COALESCENCES
COALESCENT
COALESCING
COALFIELDS
COALFISHES
COALHOUSES
COALIFICATION
COALIFICATIONS
COALIFYING
COALITIONAL
COALITIONER
COALITIONERS
COALITIONISM
COALITIONISMS
COALITIONIST
COALITIONISTS
COALITIONS
COALMASTER
COALMASTERS
COALMINERS
COANCHORED
COANCHORING
COANNEXING
COAPPEARED
COAPPEARING
COAPTATION
COAPTATIONS
COARCTATED
COARCTATES
COARCTATING
COARCTATION
COARCTATIONS
COARSENESS
COARSENESSES
COARSENING
COASSISTED
COASSISTING
COASSUMING
COASTEERING
COASTEERINGS
COASTGUARD
COASTGUARDMAN
COASTGUARDMEN
COASTGUARDS
COASTGUARDSMAN
COASTGUARDSMEN
COASTLANDS
COASTLINES
COASTWARDS
COATDRESSES
COATIMUNDI
COATIMUNDIS
COATSTANDS
COATTENDED
COATTENDING
COATTESTED
COATTESTING
COAUTHORED
COAUTHORING
COAUTHORSHIP
COAUTHORSHIPS
COBALAMINS
COBALTIFEROUS
COBALTINES
COBALTITES
COBBLERIES
COBBLESTONE
COBBLESTONED
COBBLESTONES
COBBLESTONING
COBELLIGERENT
COBELLIGERENTS
COBWEBBERIES
COBWEBBERY
COBWEBBIER
COBWEBBIEST
COBWEBBING
COCAINISATION
COCAINISATIONS
COCAINISED
COCAINISES
COCAINISING
COCAINISMS
COCAINISTS
COCAINIZATION
COCAINIZATIONS
COCAINIZED
COCAINIZES
COCAINIZING
COCAPTAINED
COCAPTAINING
COCAPTAINS
COCARBOXYLASE
COCARBOXYLASES
COCARCINOGEN
COCARCINOGENIC
COCARCINOGENS
COCATALYST
COCATALYSTS
COCCIDIANS
COCCIDIOSES
COCCIDIOSIS
COCCIDIOSTAT
COCCIDIOSTATS
COCCIFEROUS
COCCINEOUS
COCCOLITES
COCCOLITHS
COCHAIRING
COCHAIRMAN
COCHAIRMANSHIP
COCHAIRMANSHIPS
COCHAIRMEN
COCHAIRPERSON
COCHAIRPERSONS
COCHAIRWOMAN
COCHAIRWOMEN
COCHAMPION
COCHAMPIONS
COCHINEALS
COCHLEARES
COCHLEARIFORM
COCHLEATED
COCKABULLIES
COCKABULLY
COCKALEEKIE
COCKALEEKIES
COCKALORUM
COCKALORUMS
COCKAMAMIE
COCKAMAMIER
COCKAMAMIEST
COCKATEELS
COCKATIELS
COCKATRICE
COCKATRICES
COCKBILLED
COCKBILLING
COCKCHAFER
COCKCHAFERS
COCKCROWING
COCKCROWINGS
COCKERNONIES
COCKERNONY
COCKEYEDLY
COCKEYEDNESS
COCKEYEDNESSES
COCKFIGHTING
COCKFIGHTINGS
COCKFIGHTS
COCKHORSES
COCKIELEEKIE
COCKIELEEKIES
COCKINESSES
COCKLEBOAT
COCKLEBOATS
COCKLEBURS
COCKLEERTS
COCKLESHELL
COCKLESHELLS
COCKMATCHES
COCKNEYDOM
COCKNEYDOMS
COCKNEYFICATION
COCKNEYFIED
COCKNEYFIES
COCKNEYFYING
COCKNEYISH
COCKNEYISM
COCKNEYISMS
COCKNIFICATION
COCKNIFICATIONS
COCKNIFIED
COCKNIFIES
COCKNIFYING
COCKROACHES
COCKSCOMBS
COCKSFOOTS
COCKSINESS
COCKSINESSES
COCKSURELY
COCKSURENESS
COCKSURENESSES
COCKSWAINED
COCKSWAINING
COCKSWAINS
COCKTAILED
COCKTAILING
COCKTEASER
COCKTEASERS
COCKTHROWING
COCKTHROWINGS
COCKYLEEKIES
COCKYLEEKY
COCOMPOSER
COCOMPOSERS
COCONSCIOUS
COCONSCIOUSES
COCONSCIOUSNESS
COCONSPIRATOR
COCONSPIRATORS
COCONUTTIER
COCONUTTIEST
COCOONERIES
COCOONINGS
COCOUNSELED
COCOUNSELING
COCOUNSELLED
COCOUNSELLING
COCOUNSELS
COCOZELLES
COCREATING
COCREATORS
COCULTIVATE
COCULTIVATED
COCULTIVATES
COCULTIVATING
COCULTIVATION
COCULTIVATIONS
COCULTURED
COCULTURES
COCULTURING
COCURATING
COCURATORS
COCURRICULAR
COCUSWOODS

C

CODEBREAKER
CODEBREAKERS
CODECLINATION
CODECLINATIONS
CODEFENDANT
CODEFENDANTS
CODEPENDENCE
CODEPENDENCES
CODEPENDENCIES
CODEPENDENCY
CODEPENDENT
CODEPENDENTS
CODERIVING
CODESIGNED
CODESIGNING
CODETERMINATION
CODEVELOPED
CODEVELOPER
CODEVELOPERS
CODEVELOPING
CODEVELOPS
CODICILLARY
CODICOLOGICAL
CODICOLOGIES
CODICOLOGY
CODIFIABILITIES
CODIFIABILITY
CODIFIABLE
CODIFICATION
CODIFICATIONS
CODIRECTED
CODIRECTING
CODIRECTION
CODIRECTIONS
CODIRECTOR
CODIRECTORS
CODISCOVER
CODISCOVERED
CODISCOVERER
CODISCOVERERS
CODISCOVERING
CODISCOVERS
CODOLOGIES
CODOMINANCE
CODOMINANCES
CODOMINANT
CODOMINANTS
CODSWALLOP
CODSWALLOPS
COECILIANS
COEDUCATION
COEDUCATIONAL
COEDUCATIONALLY
COEDUCATIONS
COEFFICIENT
COEFFICIENTS
COELACANTH
COELACANTHIC
COELACANTHS
COELANAGLYPHIC
COELENTERA
COELENTERATE
COELENTERATES
COELENTERIC
COELENTERON
COELENTERONS
COELIOSCOPIES
COELIOSCOPY
COELOMATES
COELOMATIC
COELOSTATS
COELUROSAUR
COELUROSAURS
COEMBODIED
COEMBODIES
COEMBODYING
COEMPLOYED
COEMPLOYING
COEMPTIONS
COENACTING
COENAESTHESES
COENAESTHESIA
COENAESTHESIAS
COENAESTHESIS
COENAMORED
COENAMORING
COENAMOURED
COENAMOURING
COENAMOURS
COENDURING
COENENCHYMA
COENENCHYMAS
COENENCHYMATA
COENENCHYME
COENENCHYMES
COENESTHESES
COENESTHESIA
COENESTHESIAS
COENESTHESIS
COENESTHETIC
COENOBITES
COENOBITIC
COENOBITICAL
COENOBITISM
COENOBITISMS
COENOCYTES
COENOCYTIC
COENOSARCS
COENOSPECIES
COENOSTEUM
COENOSTEUMS
COENZYMATIC
COENZYMATICALLY
COEQUALITIES
COEQUALITY
COEQUALNESS
COEQUALNESSES
COEQUATING
COERCIMETER
COERCIMETERS
COERCIONIST
COERCIONISTS
COERCIVELY
COERCIVENESS
COERCIVENESSES
COERCIVITIES
COERCIVITY
COERECTING
COESSENTIAL
COESSENTIALITY
COESSENTIALLY
COESSENTIALNESS
COETANEOUS
COETANEOUSLY
COETANEOUSNESS
COETERNALLY
COETERNITIES
COETERNITY
COEVALITIES
COEVOLUTION
COEVOLUTIONARY
COEVOLUTIONS
COEVOLVING
COEXECUTOR
COEXECUTORS
COEXECUTRICES
COEXECUTRIX
COEXECUTRIXES
COEXERTING
COEXISTENCE
COEXISTENCES
COEXISTENT
COEXISTING
COEXTENDED
COEXTENDING
COEXTENSION
COEXTENSIONS
COEXTENSIVE
COEXTENSIVELY
COFAVORITE
COFAVORITES
COFEATURED
COFEATURES
COFEATURING
COFFEEHOUSE
COFFEEHOUSES
COFFEEMAKER
COFFEEMAKERS
COFFEEPOTS
COFFERDAMS
COFFINITES
COFINANCED
COFINANCES
COFINANCING
COFOUNDERS
COFOUNDING
COFUNCTION
COFUNCTIONS
COGENERATION
COGENERATIONS
COGENERATOR
COGENERATORS
COGITATING
COGITATINGLY
COGITATION
COGITATIONS
COGITATIVE
COGITATIVELY
COGITATIVENESS
COGITATORS
COGNATENESS
COGNATENESSES
COGNATIONS
COGNISABLE
COGNISABLY
COGNISANCE
COGNISANCES
COGNITIONAL
COGNITIONS
COGNITIVELY
COGNITIVISM
COGNITIVISMS
COGNITIVITIES
COGNITIVITY
COGNIZABLE
COGNIZABLY
COGNIZANCE
COGNIZANCES
COGNOMINAL
COGNOMINALLY
COGNOMINATE
COGNOMINATED
COGNOMINATES
COGNOMINATING
COGNOMINATION
COGNOMINATIONS
COGNOSCENTE
COGNOSCENTI
COGNOSCIBLE
COGNOSCING
COHABITANT
COHABITANTS
COHABITATION
COHABITATIONS
COHABITEES
COHABITERS
COHABITING
COHABITORS
COHEIRESSES
COHERENCES
COHERENCIES
COHERENTLY
COHERITORS
COHESIBILITIES
COHESIBILITY
COHESIONLESS
COHESIVELY
COHESIVENESS
COHESIVENESSES
COHIBITING

COHIBITION
COHIBITIONS
COHIBITIVE
COHOBATING
COHOMOLOGICAL
COHOMOLOGIES
COHOMOLOGY
COHORTATIVE
COHORTATIVES
COHOSTESSED
COHOSTESSES
COHOSTESSING
COHOUSINGS
COHYPONYMS
COIFFEUSES
COIFFURING
COILABILITIES
COILABILITY
COINCIDENCE
COINCIDENCES
COINCIDENCIES
COINCIDENCY
COINCIDENT
COINCIDENTAL
COINCIDENTALLY
COINCIDENTLY
COINCIDING
COINFECTED
COINFECTING
COINFERRED
COINFERRING
COINHERENCE
COINHERENCES
COINHERING
COINHERITANCE
COINHERITANCES
COINHERITOR
COINHERITORS
COINSTANTANEITY
COINSTANTANEOUS
COINSURANCE
COINSURANCES
COINSURERS
COINSURING
COINTERRED
COINTERRING
COINTREAUS
COINVENTED
COINVENTING
COINVENTOR
COINVENTORS
COINVESTED
COINVESTIGATOR
COINVESTIGATORS
COINVESTING
COINVESTOR
COINVESTORS
COKULORISES
COLATITUDE
COLATITUDES
COLCANNONS
COLCHICINE
COLCHICINES
COLCHICUMS
COLCOTHARS
COLDBLOODS
COLDCOCKED
COLDCOCKING
COLDHEARTED
COLDHEARTEDLY
COLDHEARTEDNESS
COLDHOUSES
COLDNESSES
COLECTOMIES
COLEMANITE
COLEMANITES
COLEOPTERA
COLEOPTERAL
COLEOPTERAN
COLEOPTERANS
COLEOPTERIST
COLEOPTERISTS
COLEOPTERON
COLEOPTERONS
COLEOPTEROUS
COLEOPTERS
COLEOPTILE
COLEOPTILES
COLEORHIZA
COLEORHIZAE
COLEORRHIZA
COLEORRHIZAE
COLESTIPOL
COLESTIPOLS
COLICKIEST
COLICROOTS
COLICWEEDS
COLINEARITIES
COLINEARITY
COLIPHAGES
COLLABORATE
COLLABORATED
COLLABORATES
COLLABORATING
COLLABORATION
COLLABORATIONS
COLLABORATIVE
COLLABORATIVELY
COLLABORATIVES
COLLABORATOR
COLLABORATORS
COLLAGENASE
COLLAGENASES
COLLAGENIC
COLLAGENOUS
COLLAGISTS
COLLAPSABILITY
COLLAPSABLE
COLLAPSARS
COLLAPSIBILITY
COLLAPSIBLE
COLLAPSING
COLLARBONE
COLLARBONES
COLLARETTE
COLLARETTES
COLLARLESS
COLLARSTUD
COLLARSTUDS
COLLATABLE
COLLATERAL
COLLATERALISE
COLLATERALISED
COLLATERALISES
COLLATERALISING
COLLATERALITIES
COLLATERALITY
COLLATERALIZE
COLLATERALIZED
COLLATERALIZES
COLLATERALIZING
COLLATERALLY
COLLATERALS
COLLATIONS
COLLEAGUED
COLLEAGUES
COLLEAGUESHIP
COLLEAGUESHIPS
COLLEAGUING
COLLECTABLE
COLLECTABLES
COLLECTANEA
COLLECTEDLY
COLLECTEDNESS
COLLECTEDNESSES
COLLECTIBLE
COLLECTIBLES
COLLECTING
COLLECTINGS
COLLECTION
COLLECTIONS
COLLECTIVE
COLLECTIVELY
COLLECTIVENESS
COLLECTIVES
COLLECTIVISE
COLLECTIVISED
COLLECTIVISES
COLLECTIVISING
COLLECTIVISM
COLLECTIVISMS
COLLECTIVIST
COLLECTIVISTIC
COLLECTIVISTS
COLLECTIVITIES
COLLECTIVITY
COLLECTIVIZE
COLLECTIVIZED
COLLECTIVIZES
COLLECTIVIZING
COLLECTORATE
COLLECTORATES
COLLECTORS
COLLECTORSHIP
COLLECTORSHIPS
COLLEGIALISM
COLLEGIALISMS
COLLEGIALITIES
COLLEGIALITY
COLLEGIALLY
COLLEGIANER
COLLEGIANERS
COLLEGIANS
COLLEGIATE
COLLEGIATELY
COLLEGIATES
COLLEGIUMS
COLLEMBOLAN
COLLEMBOLANS
COLLEMBOLOUS
COLLENCHYMA
COLLENCHYMAS
COLLENCHYMATA
COLLENCHYMATOUS
COLLETERIAL
COLLICULUS
COLLIERIES
COLLIESHANGIE
COLLIESHANGIES
COLLIGATED
COLLIGATES
COLLIGATING
COLLIGATION
COLLIGATIONS
COLLIGATIVE
COLLIMATED
COLLIMATES
COLLIMATING
COLLIMATION
COLLIMATIONS
COLLIMATOR
COLLIMATORS
COLLINEARITIES
COLLINEARITY
COLLINEARLY
COLLINSIAS
COLLIQUABLE
COLLIQUANT
COLLIQUATE
COLLIQUATED
COLLIQUATES
COLLIQUATING
COLLIQUATION
COLLIQUATIONS
COLLIQUATIVE
COLLIQUESCENCE
COLLIQUESCENCES
COLLISIONAL
COLLISIONALLY
COLLISIONS

C

COLLOCATED
COLLOCATES
COLLOCATING
COLLOCATION
COLLOCATIONAL
COLLOCATIONS
COLLOCUTOR
COLLOCUTORS
COLLOCUTORY
COLLODIONS
COLLODIUMS
COLLOGUING
COLLOIDALITIES
COLLOIDALITY
COLLOIDALLY
COLLOQUIAL
COLLOQUIALISM
COLLOQUIALISMS
COLLOQUIALIST
COLLOQUIALISTS
COLLOQUIALITIES
COLLOQUIALITY
COLLOQUIALLY
COLLOQUIALNESS
COLLOQUIALS
COLLOQUIED
COLLOQUIES
COLLOQUING
COLLOQUISE
COLLOQUISED
COLLOQUISES
COLLOQUISING
COLLOQUIST
COLLOQUISTS
COLLOQUIUM
COLLOQUIUMS
COLLOQUIZE
COLLOQUIZED
COLLOQUIZES
COLLOQUIZING
COLLOQUYING
COLLOTYPES
COLLOTYPIC
COLLOTYPIES
COLLUCTATION
COLLUCTATIONS
COLLUSIONS
COLLUSIVELY
COLLUVIUMS
COLLYRIUMS
COLLYWOBBLES
COLOBOMATA
COLOCATING
COLOCYNTHS
COLOGARITHM
COLOGARITHMS
COLOMBARDS
COLONELCIES
COLONELLING
COLONELLINGS
COLONELSHIP
COLONELSHIPS
COLONIALISE
COLONIALISED
COLONIALISES
COLONIALISING
COLONIALISM
COLONIALISMS
COLONIALIST
COLONIALISTIC
COLONIALISTS
COLONIALIZE
COLONIALIZED
COLONIALIZES
COLONIALIZING
COLONIALLY
COLONIALNESS
COLONIALNESSES
COLONISABLE
COLONISATION
COLONISATIONIST
COLONISATIONS
COLONISERS
COLONISING
COLONITISES
COLONIZABLE
COLONIZATION
COLONIZATIONIST
COLONIZATIONS
COLONIZERS
COLONIZING
COLONNADED
COLONNADES
COLONOSCOPE
COLONOSCOPES
COLONOSCOPIES
COLONOSCOPY
COLOPHONIES
COLOQUINTIDA
COLOQUINTIDAS
COLORABILITIES
COLORABILITY
COLORABLENESS
COLORABLENESSES
COLORATION
COLORATIONS
COLORATURA
COLORATURAS
COLORATURE
COLORATURES
COLORBREED
COLORBREEDING
COLORBREEDS
COLORCASTED
COLORCASTING
COLORCASTS
COLORECTAL
COLORFASTNESS
COLORFASTNESSES
COLORFULLY
COLORFULNESS
COLORFULNESSES
COLORIMETER
COLORIMETERS
COLORIMETRIC
COLORIMETRICAL
COLORIMETRIES
COLORIMETRY
COLORISATION
COLORISATIONS
COLORISERS
COLORISING
COLORISTIC
COLORISTICALLY
COLORIZATION
COLORIZATIONS
COLORIZERS
COLORIZING
COLORLESSLY
COLORLESSNESS
COLORLESSNESSES
COLORPOINT
COLORPOINTS
COLORWASHED
COLORWASHES
COLORWASHING
COLOSSALLY
COLOSSEUMS
COLOSSUSES
COLOSTOMIES
COLOSTROUS
COLOSTRUMS
COLOTOMIES
COLOURABILITIES
COLOURABILITY
COLOURABLE
COLOURABLENESS
COLOURABLY
COLOURANTS
COLOURATION
COLOURATIONS
COLOURBRED
COLOURBREED
COLOURBREEDING
COLOURBREEDS
COLOURCAST
COLOURCASTED
COLOURCASTING
COLOURCASTS
COLOURFAST
COLOURFASTNESS
COLOURFULLY
COLOURFULNESS
COLOURFULNESSES
COLOURIEST
COLOURINGS
COLOURISATION
COLOURISATIONS
COLOURISED
COLOURISER
COLOURISERS
COLOURISES
COLOURISING
COLOURISMS
COLOURISTIC
COLOURISTICALLY
COLOURISTS
COLOURIZATION
COLOURIZATIONS
COLOURIZED
COLOURIZER
COLOURIZERS
COLOURIZES
COLOURIZING
COLOURLESS
COLOURLESSLY
COLOURLESSNESS
COLOURPOINT
COLOURPOINTS
COLOURWASH
COLOURWASHED
COLOURWASHES
COLOURWASHING
COLOURWAYS
COLPITISES
COLPORTAGE
COLPORTAGES
COLPORTEUR
COLPORTEURS
COLPOSCOPE
COLPOSCOPES
COLPOSCOPICAL
COLPOSCOPICALLY
COLPOSCOPIES
COLPOSCOPY
COLPOTOMIES
COLTISHNESS
COLTISHNESSES
COLTSFOOTS
COLUBRIADS
COLUBRIFORM
COLUMBARIA
COLUMBARIES
COLUMBARIUM
COLUMBATES
COLUMBINES
COLUMBITES
COLUMBIUMS
COLUMELLAE
COLUMELLAR
COLUMNARITIES
COLUMNARITY
COLUMNATED
COLUMNIATED
COLUMNIATION
COLUMNIATIONS
COLUMNISTIC
COLUMNISTS
COMANAGEMENT
COMANAGEMENTS

COMANAGERS
COMANAGING
COMANCHERO
COMANCHEROS
COMATOSELY
COMATULIDS
COMBATABLE
COMBATANTS
COMBATIVELY
COMBATIVENESS
COMBATIVENESSES
COMBATTING
COMBINABILITIES
COMBINABILITY
COMBINABLE
COMBINATION
COMBINATIONAL
COMBINATIONS
COMBINATIVE
COMBINATORIAL
COMBINATORIALLY
COMBINATORICS
COMBINATORY
COMBININGS
COMBRETUMS
COMBURGESS
COMBURGESSES
COMBUSTIBILITY
COMBUSTIBLE
COMBUSTIBLENESS
COMBUSTIBLES
COMBUSTIBLY
COMBUSTING
COMBUSTION
COMBUSTIONS
COMBUSTIOUS
COMBUSTIVE
COMBUSTIVES
COMBUSTORS
COMEDDLING
COMEDICALLY
COMEDIENNE
COMEDIENNES
COMEDIETTA
COMEDIETTAS
COMEDOGENIC
COMELINESS
COMELINESSES
COMESTIBLE
COMESTIBLES
COMETOGRAPHIES
COMETOGRAPHY
COMETOLOGIES
COMETOLOGY
COMEUPPANCE
COMEUPPANCES
COMFINESSES
COMFITURES
COMFORTABLE
COMFORTABLENESS
COMFORTABLY
COMFORTERS
COMFORTING
COMFORTINGLY
COMFORTLESS
COMFORTLESSLY
COMFORTLESSNESS
COMICALITIES
COMICALITY
COMICALNESS
COMICALNESSES
COMINGLING
COMITADJIS
COMITATIVE
COMITATIVES
COMITATUSES
COMMANDABLE
COMMANDANT
COMMANDANTS
COMMANDANTSHIP
COMMANDANTSHIPS
COMMANDEER
COMMANDEERED
COMMANDEERING
COMMANDEERS
COMMANDERIES
COMMANDERS
COMMANDERSHIP
COMMANDERSHIPS
COMMANDERY
COMMANDING
COMMANDINGLY
COMMANDMENT
COMMANDMENTS
COMMANDOES
COMMEASURABLE
COMMEASURE
COMMEASURED
COMMEASURES
COMMEASURING
COMMEMORABLE
COMMEMORATE
COMMEMORATED
COMMEMORATES
COMMEMORATING
COMMEMORATION
COMMEMORATIONAL
COMMEMORATIONS
COMMEMORATIVE
COMMEMORATIVELY
COMMEMORATIVES
COMMEMORATOR
COMMEMORATORS
COMMEMORATORY
COMMENCEMENT
COMMENCEMENTS
COMMENCERS
COMMENCING
COMMENDABLE
COMMENDABLENESS
COMMENDABLY
COMMENDAMS
COMMENDATION
COMMENDATIONS
COMMENDATOR
COMMENDATORS
COMMENDATORY
COMMENDERS
COMMENDING
COMMENSALISM
COMMENSALISMS
COMMENSALITIES
COMMENSALITY
COMMENSALLY
COMMENSALS
COMMENSURABLE
COMMENSURABLY
COMMENSURATE
COMMENSURATELY
COMMENSURATION
COMMENSURATIONS
COMMENTARIAL
COMMENTARIAT
COMMENTARIATS
COMMENTARIES
COMMENTARY
COMMENTATE
COMMENTATED
COMMENTATES
COMMENTATING
COMMENTATION
COMMENTATIONS
COMMENTATOR
COMMENTATORIAL
COMMENTATORS
COMMENTERS
COMMENTING
COMMENTORS
COMMERCIAL
COMMERCIALESE
COMMERCIALESES
COMMERCIALISE
COMMERCIALISED
COMMERCIALISES
COMMERCIALISING
COMMERCIALISM
COMMERCIALISMS
COMMERCIALIST
COMMERCIALISTIC
COMMERCIALISTS
COMMERCIALITIES
COMMERCIALITY
COMMERCIALIZE
COMMERCIALIZED
COMMERCIALIZES
COMMERCIALIZING
COMMERCIALLY
COMMERCIALS
COMMERCING
COMMERGING
COMMINATED
COMMINATES
COMMINATING
COMMINATION
COMMINATIONS
COMMINATIVE
COMMINATORY
COMMINGLED
COMMINGLES
COMMINGLING
COMMINUTED
COMMINUTES
COMMINUTING
COMMINUTION
COMMINUTIONS
COMMISERABLE
COMMISERATE
COMMISERATED
COMMISERATES
COMMISERATING
COMMISERATINGLY
COMMISERATION
COMMISERATIONS
COMMISERATIVE
COMMISERATIVELY
COMMISERATOR
COMMISERATORS
COMMISSAIRE
COMMISSAIRES
COMMISSARIAL
COMMISSARIAT
COMMISSARIATS
COMMISSARIES
COMMISSARS
COMMISSARY
COMMISSARYSHIP
COMMISSARYSHIPS
COMMISSION
COMMISSIONAIRE
COMMISSIONAIRES
COMMISSIONAL
COMMISSIONARY
COMMISSIONED
COMMISSIONER
COMMISSIONERS
COMMISSIONING
COMMISSIONS
COMMISSURAL
COMMISSURE
COMMISSURES
COMMITMENT
COMMITMENTS
COMMITTABLE
COMMITTALS
COMMITTEEMAN
COMMITTEEMEN
COMMITTEES
COMMITTEESHIP
COMMITTEESHIPS
COMMITTEEWOMAN

COMMITTEEWOMEN
COMMITTERS
COMMITTING
COMMIXTION
COMMIXTIONS
COMMIXTURE
COMMIXTURES
COMMODIFICATION
COMMODIFIED
COMMODIFIES
COMMODIFYING
COMMODIOUS
COMMODIOUSLY
COMMODIOUSNESS
COMMODITIES
COMMODITISE
COMMODITISED
COMMODITISES
COMMODITISING
COMMODITIZE
COMMODITIZED
COMMODITIZES
COMMODITIZING
COMMODORES
COMMONABLE
COMMONAGES
COMMONALITIES
COMMONALITY
COMMONALTIES
COMMONALTY
COMMONHOLD
COMMONHOLDS
COMMONINGS
COMMONNESS
COMMONNESSES
COMMONPLACE
COMMONPLACED
COMMONPLACENESS
COMMONPLACES
COMMONPLACING
COMMONSENSE
COMMONSENSIBLE
COMMONSENSICAL
COMMONWEAL
COMMONWEALS
COMMONWEALTH
COMMONWEALTHS
COMMORANTS
COMMORIENTES
COMMOTIONAL
COMMOTIONS
COMMUNALISATION
COMMUNALISE
COMMUNALISED
COMMUNALISER
COMMUNALISERS
COMMUNALISES
COMMUNALISING
COMMUNALISM
COMMUNALISMS
COMMUNALIST
COMMUNALISTIC
COMMUNALISTS
COMMUNALITIES
COMMUNALITY
COMMUNALIZATION
COMMUNALIZE
COMMUNALIZED
COMMUNALIZER
COMMUNALIZERS
COMMUNALIZES
COMMUNALIZING
COMMUNALLY
COMMUNARDS
COMMUNAUTAIRE
COMMUNAUTAIRES
COMMUNICABILITY
COMMUNICABLE
COMMUNICABLY
COMMUNICANT
COMMUNICANTS
COMMUNICATE
COMMUNICATED
COMMUNICATEE
COMMUNICATEES
COMMUNICATES
COMMUNICATING
COMMUNICATION
COMMUNICATIONAL
COMMUNICATIONS
COMMUNICATIVE
COMMUNICATIVELY
COMMUNICATOR
COMMUNICATORS
COMMUNICATORY
COMMUNINGS
COMMUNIONAL
COMMUNIONALLY
COMMUNIONS
COMMUNIQUE
COMMUNIQUES
COMMUNISATION
COMMUNISATIONS
COMMUNISED
COMMUNISES
COMMUNISING
COMMUNISMS
COMMUNISTIC
COMMUNISTICALLY
COMMUNISTS
COMMUNITAIRE
COMMUNITAIRES
COMMUNITARIAN
COMMUNITARIANS
COMMUNITIES
COMMUNIZATION
COMMUNIZATIONS
COMMUNIZED
COMMUNIZES
COMMUNIZING
COMMUTABILITIES
COMMUTABILITY
COMMUTABLE
COMMUTABLENESS
COMMUTATED
COMMUTATES
COMMUTATING
COMMUTATION
COMMUTATIONS
COMMUTATIVE
COMMUTATIVELY
COMMUTATIVITIES
COMMUTATIVITY
COMMUTATOR
COMMUTATORS
COMMUTINGS
COMONOMERS
COMORBIDITIES
COMORBIDITY
COMPACTEDLY
COMPACTEDNESS
COMPACTEDNESSES
COMPACTERS
COMPACTEST
COMPACTIBLE
COMPACTIFIED
COMPACTIFIES
COMPACTIFY
COMPACTIFYING
COMPACTING
COMPACTION
COMPACTIONS
COMPACTNESS
COMPACTNESSES
COMPACTORS
COMPACTURE
COMPACTURES
COMPAGINATE
COMPAGINATED
COMPAGINATES
COMPAGINATING
COMPAGINATION
COMPAGINATIONS
COMPANDERS
COMPANDING
COMPANDORS
COMPANIABLE
COMPANIONABLE
COMPANIONABLY
COMPANIONATE
COMPANIONED
COMPANIONHOOD
COMPANIONHOODS
COMPANIONING
COMPANIONLESS
COMPANIONS
COMPANIONSHIP
COMPANIONSHIPS
COMPANIONWAY
COMPANIONWAYS
COMPANYING
COMPARABILITIES
COMPARABILITY
COMPARABLE
COMPARABLENESS
COMPARABLY
COMPARATIST
COMPARATISTS
COMPARATIVE
COMPARATIVELY
COMPARATIVENESS
COMPARATIVES
COMPARATIVIST
COMPARATIVISTS
COMPARATOR
COMPARATORS
COMPARISON
COMPARISONS
COMPARTING
COMPARTMENT
COMPARTMENTAL
COMPARTMENTALLY
COMPARTMENTED
COMPARTMENTING
COMPARTMENTS
COMPASSABLE
COMPASSING
COMPASSINGS
COMPASSION
COMPASSIONABLE
COMPASSIONATE
COMPASSIONATED
COMPASSIONATELY
COMPASSIONATES
COMPASSIONATING
COMPASSIONED
COMPASSIONING
COMPASSIONLESS
COMPASSIONS
COMPATIBILITIES
COMPATIBILITY
COMPATIBLE
COMPATIBLENESS
COMPATIBLES
COMPATIBLY
COMPATRIOT
COMPATRIOTIC
COMPATRIOTISM
COMPATRIOTISMS
COMPATRIOTS
COMPEARANCE
COMPEARANCES
COMPEARANT
COMPEARANTS
COMPEARING
COMPEERING
COMPELLABLE
COMPELLABLY
COMPELLATION
COMPELLATIONS

COMPELLATIVE
COMPELLATIVES
COMPELLERS
COMPELLING
COMPELLINGLY
COMPENDIOUS
COMPENDIOUSLY
COMPENDIOUSNESS
COMPENDIUM
COMPENDIUMS
COMPENSABILITY
COMPENSABLE
COMPENSATE
COMPENSATED
COMPENSATES
COMPENSATING
COMPENSATION
COMPENSATIONAL
COMPENSATIONS
COMPENSATIVE
COMPENSATOR
COMPENSATORS
COMPENSATORY
COMPESCING
COMPETENCE
COMPETENCES
COMPETENCIES
COMPETENCY
COMPETENTLY
COMPETENTNESS
COMPETENTNESSES
COMPETITION
COMPETITIONS
COMPETITIVE
COMPETITIVELY
COMPETITIVENESS
COMPETITOR
COMPETITORS
COMPILATION
COMPILATIONS
COMPILATOR
COMPILATORS
COMPILATORY
COMPILEMENT
COMPILEMENTS
COMPLACENCE
COMPLACENCES
COMPLACENCIES
COMPLACENCY
COMPLACENT
COMPLACENTLY
COMPLAINANT
COMPLAINANTS
COMPLAINED
COMPLAINER
COMPLAINERS
COMPLAINING
COMPLAININGLY
COMPLAININGS
COMPLAINTS
COMPLAISANCE
COMPLAISANCES
COMPLAISANT
COMPLAISANTLY
COMPLANATE
COMPLANATION
COMPLANATIONS
COMPLEATED
COMPLEATING
COMPLECTED
COMPLECTING
COMPLEMENT
COMPLEMENTAL
COMPLEMENTALLY
COMPLEMENTARIES
COMPLEMENTARILY
COMPLEMENTARITY
COMPLEMENTARY
COMPLEMENTATION
COMPLEMENTED
COMPLEMENTING
COMPLEMENTISER
COMPLEMENTISERS
COMPLEMENTIZER
COMPLEMENTIZERS
COMPLEMENTS
COMPLETABLE
COMPLETEDNESS
COMPLETEDNESSES
COMPLETELY
COMPLETENESS
COMPLETENESSES
COMPLETERS
COMPLETEST
COMPLETING
COMPLETION
COMPLETIONS
COMPLETIST
COMPLETISTS
COMPLETIVE
COMPLETORIES
COMPLETORY
COMPLEXATION
COMPLEXATIONS
COMPLEXEDNESS
COMPLEXEDNESSES
COMPLEXEST
COMPLEXIFIED
COMPLEXIFIES
COMPLEXIFY
COMPLEXIFYING
COMPLEXING
COMPLEXION
COMPLEXIONAL
COMPLEXIONED
COMPLEXIONLESS
COMPLEXIONS
COMPLEXITIES
COMPLEXITY
COMPLEXNESS
COMPLEXNESSES
COMPLEXOMETRIC
COMPLEXONE
COMPLEXONES
COMPLEXUSES
COMPLIABLE
COMPLIABLENESS
COMPLIABLY
COMPLIANCE
COMPLIANCES
COMPLIANCIES
COMPLIANCY
COMPLIANTLY
COMPLIANTNESS
COMPLIANTNESSES
COMPLICACIES
COMPLICACY
COMPLICANT
COMPLICATE
COMPLICATED
COMPLICATEDLY
COMPLICATEDNESS
COMPLICATES
COMPLICATING
COMPLICATION
COMPLICATIONS
COMPLICATIVE
COMPLICITIES
COMPLICITLY
COMPLICITOUS
COMPLICITY
COMPLIMENT
COMPLIMENTAL
COMPLIMENTARILY
COMPLIMENTARY
COMPLIMENTED
COMPLIMENTER
COMPLIMENTERS
COMPLIMENTING
COMPLIMENTS
COMPLISHED
COMPLISHES
COMPLISHING
COMPLOTTED
COMPLOTTER
COMPLOTTERS
COMPLOTTING
COMPLUVIUM
COMPLUVIUMS
COMPONENCIES
COMPONENCY
COMPONENTAL
COMPONENTIAL
COMPONENTS
COMPORTANCE
COMPORTANCES
COMPORTING
COMPORTMENT
COMPORTMENTS
COMPOSEDLY
COMPOSEDNESS
COMPOSEDNESSES
COMPOSITED
COMPOSITELY
COMPOSITENESS
COMPOSITENESSES
COMPOSITES
COMPOSITING
COMPOSITION
COMPOSITIONAL
COMPOSITIONALLY
COMPOSITIONS
COMPOSITIVE
COMPOSITOR
COMPOSITORIAL
COMPOSITORS
COMPOSITOUS
COMPOSSIBILITY
COMPOSSIBLE
COMPOSTABLE
COMPOSTERS
COMPOSTING
COMPOSTINGS
COMPOSTURE
COMPOSTURED
COMPOSTURES
COMPOSTURING
COMPOSURES
COMPOTATION
COMPOTATIONS
COMPOTATIONSHIP
COMPOTATOR
COMPOTATORS
COMPOTATORY
COMPOTIERS
COMPOUNDABLE
COMPOUNDED
COMPOUNDER
COMPOUNDERS
COMPOUNDING
COMPOUNDINGS
COMPRADORE
COMPRADORES
COMPRADORS
COMPREHEND
COMPREHENDED
COMPREHENDIBLE
COMPREHENDING
COMPREHENDS
COMPREHENSIBLE
COMPREHENSIBLY
COMPREHENSION
COMPREHENSIONS
COMPREHENSIVE
COMPREHENSIVELY
COMPREHENSIVES
COMPREHENSIVISE
COMPREHENSIVIZE
COMPRESSED
COMPRESSEDLY

COMPRESSES
COMPRESSIBILITY
COMPRESSIBLE
COMPRESSIBLY
COMPRESSING
COMPRESSION
COMPRESSIONAL
COMPRESSIONS
COMPRESSIVE
COMPRESSIVELY
COMPRESSOR
COMPRESSORS
COMPRESSURE
COMPRESSURES
COMPRIMARIO
COMPRIMARIOS
COMPRINTED
COMPRINTING
COMPRISABLE
COMPRISALS
COMPRISING
COMPRIZING
COMPROMISE
COMPROMISED
COMPROMISER
COMPROMISERS
COMPROMISES
COMPROMISING
COMPROMISINGLY
COMPROVINCIAL
COMPTROLLED
COMPTROLLER
COMPTROLLERS
COMPTROLLERSHIP
COMPTROLLING
COMPTROLLS
COMPULSATIVE
COMPULSATORY
COMPULSING
COMPULSION
COMPULSIONIST
COMPULSIONISTS
COMPULSIONS
COMPULSITOR
COMPULSITORS
COMPULSIVE
COMPULSIVELY
COMPULSIVENESS
COMPULSIVES
COMPULSIVITIES
COMPULSIVITY
COMPULSORIES
COMPULSORILY
COMPULSORINESS
COMPULSORY
COMPUNCTION
COMPUNCTIONS
COMPUNCTIOUS
COMPUNCTIOUSLY
COMPURGATION
COMPURGATIONS
COMPURGATOR
COMPURGATORIAL
COMPURGATORS
COMPURGATORY
COMPURSION
COMPURSIONS
COMPUTABILITIES
COMPUTABILITY
COMPUTABLE
COMPUTANTS
COMPUTATION
COMPUTATIONAL
COMPUTATIONALLY
COMPUTATIONS
COMPUTATIVE
COMPUTATOR
COMPUTATORS
COMPUTERATE
COMPUTERDOM
COMPUTERDOMS
COMPUTERESE
COMPUTERESES
COMPUTERISABLE
COMPUTERISATION
COMPUTERISE
COMPUTERISED
COMPUTERISES
COMPUTERISING
COMPUTERIST
COMPUTERISTS
COMPUTERITIS
COMPUTERITISES
COMPUTERIZABLE
COMPUTERIZATION
COMPUTERIZE
COMPUTERIZED
COMPUTERIZES
COMPUTERIZING
COMPUTERLESS
COMPUTERLIKE
COMPUTERNIK
COMPUTERNIKS
COMPUTERPHOBE
COMPUTERPHOBES
COMPUTERPHOBIA
COMPUTERPHOBIAS
COMPUTERPHOBIC
COMPUTERPHOBICS
COMPUTINGS
COMPUTISTS
COMRADELIER
COMRADELIEST
COMRADELINESS
COMRADELINESSES
COMRADERIES
COMRADESHIP
COMRADESHIPS
COMSTOCKER
COMSTOCKERIES
COMSTOCKERS
COMSTOCKERY
COMSTOCKISM
COMSTOCKISMS
CONACREISM
CONACREISMS
CONATIONAL
CONCANAVALIN
CONCANAVALINS
CONCATENATE
CONCATENATED
CONCATENATES
CONCATENATING
CONCATENATION
CONCATENATIONS
CONCAVENESS
CONCAVENESSES
CONCAVITIES
CONCEALABLE
CONCEALERS
CONCEALING
CONCEALINGLY
CONCEALMENT
CONCEALMENTS
CONCEDEDLY
CONCEITEDLY
CONCEITEDNESS
CONCEITEDNESSES
CONCEITFUL
CONCEITING
CONCEITLESS
CONCEIVABILITY
CONCEIVABLE
CONCEIVABLENESS
CONCEIVABLY
CONCEIVERS
CONCEIVING
CONCELEBRANT
CONCELEBRANTS
CONCELEBRATE
CONCELEBRATED
CONCELEBRATES
CONCELEBRATING
CONCELEBRATION
CONCELEBRATIONS
CONCENTERED
CONCENTERING
CONCENTERS
CONCENTRATE
CONCENTRATED
CONCENTRATEDLY
CONCENTRATES
CONCENTRATING
CONCENTRATION
CONCENTRATIONS
CONCENTRATIVE
CONCENTRATIVELY
CONCENTRATOR
CONCENTRATORS
CONCENTRED
CONCENTRES
CONCENTRIC
CONCENTRICAL
CONCENTRICALLY
CONCENTRICITIES
CONCENTRICITY
CONCENTRING
CONCEPTACLE
CONCEPTACLES
CONCEPTION
CONCEPTIONAL
CONCEPTIONS
CONCEPTIOUS
CONCEPTIVE
CONCEPTUAL
CONCEPTUALISE
CONCEPTUALISED
CONCEPTUALISER
CONCEPTUALISERS
CONCEPTUALISES
CONCEPTUALISING
CONCEPTUALISM
CONCEPTUALISMS
CONCEPTUALIST
CONCEPTUALISTIC
CONCEPTUALISTS
CONCEPTUALITIES
CONCEPTUALITY
CONCEPTUALIZE
CONCEPTUALIZED
CONCEPTUALIZER
CONCEPTUALIZERS
CONCEPTUALIZES
CONCEPTUALIZING
CONCEPTUALLY
CONCEPTUSES
CONCERNANCIES
CONCERNANCY
CONCERNEDLY
CONCERNEDNESS
CONCERNEDNESSES
CONCERNING
CONCERNMENT
CONCERNMENTS
CONCERTANTE
CONCERTANTES
CONCERTANTI
CONCERTEDLY
CONCERTEDNESS
CONCERTEDNESSES
CONCERTGOER
CONCERTGOERS
CONCERTGOING
CONCERTGOINGS
CONCERTINA
CONCERTINAED
CONCERTINAING
CONCERTINAS
CONCERTING
CONCERTINI

CONCERTINIST
CONCERTINISTS
CONCERTINO
CONCERTINOS
CONCERTISE
CONCERTISED
CONCERTISES
CONCERTISING
CONCERTIZE
CONCERTIZED
CONCERTIZES
CONCERTIZING
CONCERTMASTER
CONCERTMASTERS
CONCERTMEISTER
CONCERTMEISTERS
CONCERTMISTRESS
CONCERTSTUCK
CONCERTSTUCKS
CONCESSIBLE
CONCESSION
CONCESSIONAIRE
CONCESSIONAIRES
CONCESSIONAL
CONCESSIONARIES
CONCESSIONARY
CONCESSIONER
CONCESSIONERS
CONCESSIONIST
CONCESSIONISTS
CONCESSIONNAIRE
CONCESSIONS
CONCESSIVE
CONCESSIVELY
CONCETTISM
CONCETTISMS
CONCETTIST
CONCETTISTS
CONCHIFEROUS
CONCHIFORM
CONCHIGLIE
CONCHIOLIN
CONCHIOLINS
CONCHITISES
CONCHOIDAL
CONCHOIDALLY
CONCHOLOGICAL
CONCHOLOGIES
CONCHOLOGIST
CONCHOLOGISTS
CONCHOLOGY
CONCIERGES
CONCILIABLE
CONCILIARLY
CONCILIARY
CONCILIATE
CONCILIATED
CONCILIATES
CONCILIATING
CONCILIATION
CONCILIATIONS
CONCILIATIVE
CONCILIATOR
CONCILIATORILY
CONCILIATORS
CONCILIATORY
CONCINNITIES
CONCINNITY
CONCINNOUS
CONCIPIENCIES
CONCIPIENCY
CONCIPIENT
CONCISENESS
CONCISENESSES
CONCISIONS
CONCLAMATION
CONCLAMATIONS
CONCLAVISM
CONCLAVISMS
CONCLAVIST
CONCLAVISTS
CONCLUDERS
CONCLUDING
CONCLUSION
CONCLUSIONARY
CONCLUSIONS
CONCLUSIVE
CONCLUSIVELY
CONCLUSIVENESS
CONCLUSORY
CONCOCTERS
CONCOCTING
CONCOCTION
CONCOCTIONS
CONCOCTIVE
CONCOCTORS
CONCOLORATE
CONCOLOROUS
CONCOMITANCE
CONCOMITANCES
CONCOMITANCIES
CONCOMITANCY
CONCOMITANT
CONCOMITANTLY
CONCOMITANTS
CONCORDANCE
CONCORDANCES
CONCORDANT
CONCORDANTLY
CONCORDATS
CONCORDIAL
CONCORDING
CONCORPORATE
CONCORPORATED
CONCORPORATES
CONCORPORATING
CONCOURSES
CONCREATED
CONCREATES
CONCREATING
CONCREMATION
CONCREMATIONS
CONCRESCENCE
CONCRESCENCES
CONCRESCENT
CONCRETELY
CONCRETENESS
CONCRETENESSES
CONCRETING
CONCRETION
CONCRETIONARY
CONCRETIONS
CONCRETISATION
CONCRETISATIONS
CONCRETISE
CONCRETISED
CONCRETISES
CONCRETISING
CONCRETISM
CONCRETISMS
CONCRETIST
CONCRETISTS
CONCRETIVE
CONCRETIVELY
CONCRETIZATION
CONCRETIZATIONS
CONCRETIZE
CONCRETIZED
CONCRETIZES
CONCRETIZING
CONCREWING
CONCUBINAGE
CONCUBINAGES
CONCUBINARIES
CONCUBINARY
CONCUBINES
CONCUBITANCIES
CONCUBITANCY
CONCUBITANT
CONCUBITANTS
CONCUPISCENCE
CONCUPISCENCES
CONCUPISCENT
CONCUPISCIBLE
CONCURRENCE
CONCURRENCES
CONCURRENCIES
CONCURRENCY
CONCURRENT
CONCURRENTLY
CONCURRENTS
CONCURRING
CONCURRINGLY
CONCUSSING
CONCUSSION
CONCUSSIONS
CONCUSSIVE
CONCYCLICALLY
CONDEMNABLE
CONDEMNABLY
CONDEMNATION
CONDEMNATIONS
CONDEMNATORY
CONDEMNERS
CONDEMNING
CONDEMNINGLY
CONDEMNORS
CONDENSABILITY
CONDENSABLE
CONDENSATE
CONDENSATED
CONDENSATES
CONDENSATING
CONDENSATION
CONDENSATIONAL
CONDENSATIONS
CONDENSERIES
CONDENSERS
CONDENSERY
CONDENSIBILITY
CONDENSIBLE
CONDENSING
CONDESCEND
CONDESCENDED
CONDESCENDENCE
CONDESCENDENCES
CONDESCENDING
CONDESCENDINGLY
CONDESCENDS
CONDESCENSION
CONDESCENSIONS
CONDIDDLED
CONDIDDLES
CONDIDDLING
CONDIGNNESS
CONDIGNNESSES
CONDIMENTAL
CONDIMENTED
CONDIMENTING
CONDIMENTS
CONDISCIPLE
CONDISCIPLES
CONDITIONABLE
CONDITIONAL
CONDITIONALITY
CONDITIONALLY
CONDITIONALS
CONDITIONATE
CONDITIONATED
CONDITIONATES
CONDITIONATING
CONDITIONED
CONDITIONER
CONDITIONERS
CONDITIONING
CONDITIONINGS
CONDITIONS
CONDOLATORY
CONDOLEMENT
CONDOLEMENTS

C

CONDOLENCE
CONDOLENCES
CONDOLINGLY
CONDOMINIA
CONDOMINIUM
CONDOMINIUMS
CONDONABLE
CONDONATION
CONDONATIONS
CONDOTTIERE
CONDOTTIERI
CONDUCEMENT
CONDUCEMENTS
CONDUCIBLE
CONDUCINGLY
CONDUCIVENESS
CONDUCIVENESSES
CONDUCTANCE
CONDUCTANCES
CONDUCTIBILITY
CONDUCTIBLE
CONDUCTIMETRIC
CONDUCTING
CONDUCTIOMETRIC
CONDUCTION
CONDUCTIONAL
CONDUCTIONS
CONDUCTIVE
CONDUCTIVELY
CONDUCTIVITIES
CONDUCTIVITY
CONDUCTOMETRIC
CONDUCTORIAL
CONDUCTORS
CONDUCTORSHIP
CONDUCTORSHIPS
CONDUCTRESS
CONDUCTRESSES
CONDUPLICATE
CONDUPLICATION
CONDUPLICATIONS
CONDYLOMAS
CONDYLOMATA
CONDYLOMATOUS
CONEFLOWER
CONEFLOWERS
CONFABBING
CONFABULAR
CONFABULATE
CONFABULATED
CONFABULATES
CONFABULATING
CONFABULATION
CONFABULATIONS
CONFABULATOR
CONFABULATORS
CONFABULATORY
CONFARREATE
CONFARREATION
CONFARREATIONS
CONFECTING
CONFECTION
CONFECTIONARIES
CONFECTIONARY
CONFECTIONER
CONFECTIONERIES
CONFECTIONERS
CONFECTIONERY
CONFECTIONS
CONFEDERACIES
CONFEDERACY
CONFEDERAL
CONFEDERATE
CONFEDERATED
CONFEDERATES
CONFEDERATING
CONFEDERATION
CONFEDERATIONS
CONFEDERATIVE
CONFERENCE
CONFERENCES
CONFERENCIER
CONFERENCIERS
CONFERENCING
CONFERENCINGS
CONFERENTIAL
CONFERMENT
CONFERMENTS
CONFERRABLE
CONFERRALS
CONFERREES
CONFERRENCE
CONFERRENCES
CONFERRERS
CONFERRING
CONFERVOID
CONFERVOIDS
CONFESSABLE
CONFESSANT
CONFESSANTS
CONFESSEDLY
CONFESSING
CONFESSION
CONFESSIONAL
CONFESSIONALISM
CONFESSIONALIST
CONFESSIONALLY
CONFESSIONALS
CONFESSIONARIES
CONFESSIONARY
CONFESSIONS
CONFESSORESS
CONFESSORESSES
CONFESSORS
CONFESSORSHIP
CONFESSORSHIPS
CONFIDANTE
CONFIDANTES
CONFIDANTS
CONFIDENCE
CONFIDENCES
CONFIDENCIES
CONFIDENCY
CONFIDENTIAL
CONFIDENTIALITY
CONFIDENTIALLY
CONFIDENTLY
CONFIDENTS
CONFIDINGLY
CONFIDINGNESS
CONFIDINGNESSES
CONFIGURATE
CONFIGURATED
CONFIGURATES
CONFIGURATING
CONFIGURATION
CONFIGURATIONAL
CONFIGURATIONS
CONFIGURATIVE
CONFIGURATOR
CONFIGURATORS
CONFIGURED
CONFIGURES
CONFIGURING
CONFINABLE
CONFINEABLE
CONFINEDLY
CONFINEDNESS
CONFINEDNESSES
CONFINELESS
CONFINEMENT
CONFINEMENTS
CONFIRMABILITY
CONFIRMABLE
CONFIRMAND
CONFIRMANDS
CONFIRMATION
CONFIRMATIONAL
CONFIRMATIONS
CONFIRMATIVE
CONFIRMATOR
CONFIRMATORS
CONFIRMATORY
CONFIRMEDLY
CONFIRMEDNESS
CONFIRMEDNESSES
CONFIRMEES
CONFIRMERS
CONFIRMING
CONFIRMINGS
CONFIRMORS
CONFISCABLE
CONFISCATABLE
CONFISCATE
CONFISCATED
CONFISCATES
CONFISCATING
CONFISCATION
CONFISCATIONS
CONFISCATOR
CONFISCATORS
CONFISCATORY
CONFISERIE
CONFISERIES
CONFISEURS
CONFITEORS
CONFITURES
CONFLAGRANT
CONFLAGRATE
CONFLAGRATED
CONFLAGRATES
CONFLAGRATING
CONFLAGRATION
CONFLAGRATIONS
CONFLAGRATIVE
CONFLATING
CONFLATION
CONFLATIONS
CONFLICTED
CONFLICTFUL
CONFLICTING
CONFLICTINGLY
CONFLICTION
CONFLICTIONS
CONFLICTIVE
CONFLICTORY
CONFLICTUAL
CONFLUENCE
CONFLUENCES
CONFLUENTLY
CONFLUENTS
CONFOCALLY
CONFORMABILITY
CONFORMABLE
CONFORMABLENESS
CONFORMABLY
CONFORMANCE
CONFORMANCES
CONFORMATION
CONFORMATIONAL
CONFORMATIONS
CONFORMERS
CONFORMING
CONFORMINGLY
CONFORMISM
CONFORMISMS
CONFORMIST
CONFORMISTS
CONFORMITIES
CONFORMITY
CONFOUNDABLE
CONFOUNDED
CONFOUNDEDLY
CONFOUNDEDNESS
CONFOUNDER
CONFOUNDERS
CONFOUNDING
CONFOUNDINGLY
CONFRATERNAL
CONFRATERNITIES

CONFRATERNITY
CONFRERIES
CONFRONTAL
CONFRONTALS
CONFRONTATION
CONFRONTATIONAL
CONFRONTATIONS
CONFRONTED
CONFRONTER
CONFRONTERS
CONFRONTING
CONFRONTMENT
CONFRONTMENTS
CONFUSABILITIES
CONFUSABILITY
CONFUSABLE
CONFUSABLES
CONFUSEDLY
CONFUSEDNESS
CONFUSEDNESSES
CONFUSIBLE
CONFUSIBLES
CONFUSINGLY
CONFUSIONAL
CONFUSIONS
CONFUTABLE
CONFUTATION
CONFUTATIONS
CONFUTATIVE
CONFUTEMENT
CONFUTEMENTS
CONGEALABLE
CONGEALABLENESS
CONGEALERS
CONGEALING
CONGEALMENT
CONGEALMENTS
CONGELATION
CONGELATIONS
CONGENERIC
CONGENERICAL
CONGENERICS
CONGENEROUS
CONGENETIC
CONGENIALITIES
CONGENIALITY
CONGENIALLY
CONGENIALNESS
CONGENIALNESSES
CONGENITAL
CONGENITALLY
CONGENITALNESS
CONGESTIBLE
CONGESTING
CONGESTION
CONGESTIONS
CONGESTIVE
CONGIARIES
CONGLOBATE
CONGLOBATED
CONGLOBATES
CONGLOBATING
CONGLOBATION
CONGLOBATIONS
CONGLOBING
CONGLOBULATE
CONGLOBULATED
CONGLOBULATES
CONGLOBULATING
CONGLOBULATION
CONGLOBULATIONS
CONGLOMERATE
CONGLOMERATED
CONGLOMERATES
CONGLOMERATEUR
CONGLOMERATEURS
CONGLOMERATIC
CONGLOMERATING
CONGLOMERATION
CONGLOMERATIONS
CONGLOMERATIVE
CONGLOMERATOR
CONGLOMERATORS
CONGLUTINANT
CONGLUTINATE
CONGLUTINATED
CONGLUTINATES
CONGLUTINATING
CONGLUTINATION
CONGLUTINATIONS
CONGLUTINATIVE
CONGLUTINATOR
CONGLUTINATORS
CONGRATTERS
CONGRATULABLE
CONGRATULANT
CONGRATULANTS
CONGRATULATE
CONGRATULATED
CONGRATULATES
CONGRATULATING
CONGRATULATION
CONGRATULATIONS
CONGRATULATIVE
CONGRATULATOR
CONGRATULATORS
CONGRATULATORY
CONGREEING
CONGREETED
CONGREETING
CONGREGANT
CONGREGANTS
CONGREGATE
CONGREGATED
CONGREGATES
CONGREGATING
CONGREGATION
CONGREGATIONAL
CONGREGATIONS
CONGREGATIVE
CONGREGATOR
CONGREGATORS
CONGRESSED
CONGRESSES
CONGRESSING
CONGRESSIONAL
CONGRESSIONALLY
CONGRESSMAN
CONGRESSMEN
CONGRESSPEOPLE
CONGRESSPERSON
CONGRESSPERSONS
CONGRESSWOMAN
CONGRESSWOMEN
CONGRUENCE
CONGRUENCES
CONGRUENCIES
CONGRUENCY
CONGRUENTLY
CONGRUITIES
CONGRUOUSLY
CONGRUOUSNESS
CONGRUOUSNESSES
CONICITIES
CONIDIOPHORE
CONIDIOPHORES
CONIDIOPHOROUS
CONIDIOSPORE
CONIDIOSPORES
CONIFEROUS
CONIOLOGIES
CONIROSTRAL
CONJECTING
CONJECTURABLE
CONJECTURABLY
CONJECTURAL
CONJECTURALLY
CONJECTURE
CONJECTURED
CONJECTURER
CONJECTURERS
CONJECTURES
CONJECTURING
CONJOINERS
CONJOINING
CONJOINTLY
CONJUGABLE
CONJUGALITIES
CONJUGALITY
CONJUGALLY
CONJUGANTS
CONJUGATED
CONJUGATELY
CONJUGATENESS
CONJUGATENESSES
CONJUGATES
CONJUGATING
CONJUGATINGS
CONJUGATION
CONJUGATIONAL
CONJUGATIONALLY
CONJUGATIONS
CONJUGATIVE
CONJUGATOR
CONJUGATORS
CONJUNCTION
CONJUNCTIONAL
CONJUNCTIONALLY
CONJUNCTIONS
CONJUNCTIVA
CONJUNCTIVAE
CONJUNCTIVAL
CONJUNCTIVAS
CONJUNCTIVE
CONJUNCTIVELY
CONJUNCTIVENESS
CONJUNCTIVES
CONJUNCTIVITIS
CONJUNCTLY
CONJUNCTURAL
CONJUNCTURE
CONJUNCTURES
CONJURATION
CONJURATIONS
CONJURATOR
CONJURATORS
CONJUREMENT
CONJUREMENTS
CONJURINGS
CONLANGERS
CONNASCENCE
CONNASCENCES
CONNASCENCIES
CONNASCENCY
CONNASCENT
CONNATENESS
CONNATENESSES
CONNATIONS
CONNATURAL
CONNATURALISE
CONNATURALISED
CONNATURALISES
CONNATURALISING
CONNATURALITIES
CONNATURALITY
CONNATURALIZE
CONNATURALIZED
CONNATURALIZES
CONNATURALIZING
CONNATURALLY
CONNATURALNESS
CONNATURES
CONNECTABLE
CONNECTEDLY
CONNECTEDNESS
CONNECTEDNESSES
CONNECTERS
CONNECTIBLE
CONNECTING
CONNECTION

C

CONNECTIONAL
CONNECTIONISM
CONNECTIONISMS
CONNECTIONS
CONNECTIVE
CONNECTIVELY
CONNECTIVES
CONNECTIVITIES
CONNECTIVITY
CONNECTORS
CONNEXIONAL
CONNEXIONS
CONNIPTION
CONNIPTIONS
CONNIVANCE
CONNIVANCES
CONNIVANCIES
CONNIVANCY
CONNIVENCE
CONNIVENCES
CONNIVENCIES
CONNIVENCY
CONNIVENTLY
CONNIVERIES
CONNIVINGLY
CONNIVINGS
CONNOISSEUR
CONNOISSEURS
CONNOISSEURSHIP
CONNOTATED
CONNOTATES
CONNOTATING
CONNOTATION
CONNOTATIONAL
CONNOTATIONS
CONNOTATIVE
CONNOTATIVELY
CONNOTIVELY
CONNUBIALISM
CONNUBIALISMS
CONNUBIALITIES
CONNUBIALITY
CONNUBIALLY
CONNUMERATE
CONNUMERATED
CONNUMERATES
CONNUMERATING
CONNUMERATION
CONNUMERATIONS
CONOIDALLY
CONOIDICAL
CONOMINEES
CONOSCENTE
CONOSCENTI
CONQUERABILITY
CONQUERABLE
CONQUERABLENESS
CONQUERERS
CONQUERESS
CONQUERESSES
CONQUERING
CONQUERINGLY
CONQUERORS
CONQUISTADOR
CONQUISTADORES
CONQUISTADORS
CONSANGUINE
CONSANGUINEOUS
CONSANGUINITIES
CONSANGUINITY
CONSCIENCE
CONSCIENCELESS
CONSCIENCES
CONSCIENTIOUS
CONSCIENTIOUSLY
CONSCIENTISE
CONSCIENTISED
CONSCIENTISES
CONSCIENTISING
CONSCIENTIZE
CONSCIENTIZED
CONSCIENTIZES
CONSCIENTIZING
CONSCIONABILITY
CONSCIONABLE
CONSCIONABLY
CONSCIOUSES
CONSCIOUSLY
CONSCIOUSNESS
CONSCIOUSNESSES
CONSCRIBED
CONSCRIBES
CONSCRIBING
CONSCRIPTED
CONSCRIPTING
CONSCRIPTION
CONSCRIPTIONAL
CONSCRIPTIONIST
CONSCRIPTIONS
CONSCRIPTS
CONSECRATE
CONSECRATED
CONSECRATEDNESS
CONSECRATES
CONSECRATING
CONSECRATION
CONSECRATIONS
CONSECRATIVE
CONSECRATOR
CONSECRATORS
CONSECRATORY
CONSECTANEOUS
CONSECTARIES
CONSECTARY
CONSECUTION
CONSECUTIONS
CONSECUTIVE
CONSECUTIVELY
CONSECUTIVENESS
CONSENESCENCE
CONSENESCENCES
CONSENESCENCIES
CONSENESCENCY
CONSENSION
CONSENSIONS
CONSENSUAL
CONSENSUALLY
CONSENSUSES
CONSENTANEITIES
CONSENTANEITY
CONSENTANEOUS
CONSENTANEOUSLY
CONSENTERS
CONSENTIENCE
CONSENTIENCES
CONSENTIENT
CONSENTING
CONSENTINGLY
CONSEQUENCE
CONSEQUENCED
CONSEQUENCES
CONSEQUENCING
CONSEQUENT
CONSEQUENTIAL
CONSEQUENTIALLY
CONSEQUENTLY
CONSEQUENTS
CONSERVABLE
CONSERVANCIES
CONSERVANCY
CONSERVANT
CONSERVATION
CONSERVATIONAL
CONSERVATIONIST
CONSERVATIONS
CONSERVATISE
CONSERVATISED
CONSERVATISES
CONSERVATISING
CONSERVATISM
CONSERVATISMS
CONSERVATIVE
CONSERVATIVELY
CONSERVATIVES
CONSERVATIZE
CONSERVATIZED
CONSERVATIZES
CONSERVATIZING
CONSERVATOIRE
CONSERVATOIRES
CONSERVATOR
CONSERVATORIA
CONSERVATORIAL
CONSERVATORIES
CONSERVATORIUM
CONSERVATORIUMS
CONSERVATORS
CONSERVATORSHIP
CONSERVATORY
CONSERVATRICES
CONSERVATRIX
CONSERVATRIXES
CONSERVERS
CONSERVING
CONSIDERABLE
CONSIDERABLES
CONSIDERABLY
CONSIDERANCE
CONSIDERANCES
CONSIDERATE
CONSIDERATELY
CONSIDERATENESS
CONSIDERATION
CONSIDERATIONS
CONSIDERATIVE
CONSIDERATIVELY
CONSIDERED
CONSIDERER
CONSIDERERS
CONSIDERING
CONSIDERINGLY
CONSIGLIERE
CONSIGLIERES
CONSIGLIERI
CONSIGNABLE
CONSIGNATION
CONSIGNATIONS
CONSIGNATORIES
CONSIGNATORY
CONSIGNEES
CONSIGNERS
CONSIGNIFIED
CONSIGNIFIES
CONSIGNIFY
CONSIGNIFYING
CONSIGNING
CONSIGNMENT
CONSIGNMENTS
CONSIGNORS
CONSILIENCE
CONSILIENCES
CONSILIENT
CONSIMILAR
CONSIMILARITIES
CONSIMILARITY
CONSIMILITIES
CONSIMILITUDE
CONSIMILITUDES
CONSIMILITY
CONSISTENCE
CONSISTENCES
CONSISTENCIES
CONSISTENCY
CONSISTENT
CONSISTENTLY
CONSISTING
CONSISTORIAL
CONSISTORIAN
CONSISTORIES
CONSISTORY

CONSOCIATE
CONSOCIATED
CONSOCIATES
CONSOCIATING
CONSOCIATION
CONSOCIATIONAL
CONSOCIATIONS
CONSOLABLE
CONSOLATED
CONSOLATES
CONSOLATING
CONSOLATION
CONSOLATIONS
CONSOLATORIES
CONSOLATORY
CONSOLATRICES
CONSOLATRIX
CONSOLATRIXES
CONSOLEMENT
CONSOLEMENTS
CONSOLIDATE
CONSOLIDATED
CONSOLIDATES
CONSOLIDATING
CONSOLIDATION
CONSOLIDATIONS
CONSOLIDATIVE
CONSOLIDATOR
CONSOLIDATORS
CONSOLINGLY
CONSONANCE
CONSONANCES
CONSONANCIES
CONSONANCY
CONSONANTAL
CONSONANTALLY
CONSONANTLY
CONSONANTS
CONSORTABLE
CONSORTERS
CONSORTIAL
CONSORTING
CONSORTISM
CONSORTISMS
CONSORTIUM
CONSORTIUMS
CONSPECIFIC
CONSPECIFICS
CONSPECTUITIES
CONSPECTUITY
CONSPECTUS
CONSPECTUSES
CONSPICUITIES
CONSPICUITY
CONSPICUOUS
CONSPICUOUSLY
CONSPICUOUSNESS
CONSPIRACIES
CONSPIRACY
CONSPIRANT
CONSPIRANTS
CONSPIRATION
CONSPIRATIONAL
CONSPIRATIONS
CONSPIRATOR
CONSPIRATORIAL
CONSPIRATORS
CONSPIRATORY
CONSPIRATRESS
CONSPIRATRESSES
CONSPIRERS
CONSPIRING
CONSPIRINGLY
CONSPURCATION
CONSPURCATIONS
CONSTABLES
CONSTABLESHIP
CONSTABLESHIPS
CONSTABLEWICK
CONSTABLEWICKS
CONSTABULARIES
CONSTABULARY
CONSTANCIES
CONSTANTAN
CONSTANTANS
CONSTANTLY
CONSTATATION
CONSTATATIONS
CONSTATING
CONSTATIVE
CONSTATIVES
CONSTELLATE
CONSTELLATED
CONSTELLATES
CONSTELLATING
CONSTELLATION
CONSTELLATIONAL
CONSTELLATIONS
CONSTELLATORY
CONSTERING
CONSTERNATE
CONSTERNATED
CONSTERNATES
CONSTERNATING
CONSTERNATION
CONSTERNATIONS
CONSTIPATE
CONSTIPATED
CONSTIPATES
CONSTIPATING
CONSTIPATION
CONSTIPATIONS
CONSTITUENCIES
CONSTITUENCY
CONSTITUENT
CONSTITUENTLY
CONSTITUENTS
CONSTITUTE
CONSTITUTED
CONSTITUTER
CONSTITUTERS
CONSTITUTES
CONSTITUTING
CONSTITUTION
CONSTITUTIONAL
CONSTITUTIONALS
CONSTITUTIONIST
CONSTITUTIONS
CONSTITUTIVE
CONSTITUTIVELY
CONSTITUTOR
CONSTITUTORS
CONSTRAINABLE
CONSTRAINED
CONSTRAINEDLY
CONSTRAINER
CONSTRAINERS
CONSTRAINING
CONSTRAINS
CONSTRAINT
CONSTRAINTS
CONSTRICTED
CONSTRICTING
CONSTRICTION
CONSTRICTIONS
CONSTRICTIVE
CONSTRICTIVELY
CONSTRICTOR
CONSTRICTORS
CONSTRICTS
CONSTRINGE
CONSTRINGED
CONSTRINGENCE
CONSTRINGENCES
CONSTRINGENCIES
CONSTRINGENCY
CONSTRINGENT
CONSTRINGES
CONSTRINGING
CONSTRUABILITY
CONSTRUABLE
CONSTRUALS
CONSTRUCTABLE
CONSTRUCTED
CONSTRUCTER
CONSTRUCTERS
CONSTRUCTIBLE
CONSTRUCTING
CONSTRUCTION
CONSTRUCTIONAL
CONSTRUCTIONISM
CONSTRUCTIONIST
CONSTRUCTIONS
CONSTRUCTIVE
CONSTRUCTIVELY
CONSTRUCTIVISM
CONSTRUCTIVISMS
CONSTRUCTIVIST
CONSTRUCTIVISTS
CONSTRUCTOR
CONSTRUCTORS
CONSTRUCTS
CONSTRUCTURE
CONSTRUCTURES
CONSTRUERS
CONSTRUING
CONSTUPRATE
CONSTUPRATED
CONSTUPRATES
CONSTUPRATING
CONSTUPRATION
CONSTUPRATIONS
CONSUBSIST
CONSUBSISTED
CONSUBSISTING
CONSUBSISTS
CONSUBSTANTIAL
CONSUBSTANTIATE
CONSUETUDE
CONSUETUDES
CONSUETUDINARY
CONSULAGES
CONSULATES
CONSULSHIP
CONSULSHIPS
CONSULTABLE
CONSULTANCIES
CONSULTANCY
CONSULTANT
CONSULTANTS
CONSULTANTSHIP
CONSULTANTSHIPS
CONSULTATION
CONSULTATIONS
CONSULTATIVE
CONSULTATIVELY
CONSULTATORY
CONSULTEES
CONSULTERS
CONSULTING
CONSULTINGS
CONSULTIVE
CONSULTORS
CONSULTORY
CONSUMABLE
CONSUMABLES
CONSUMEDLY
CONSUMERISM
CONSUMERISMS
CONSUMERIST
CONSUMERISTIC
CONSUMERISTS
CONSUMERSHIP
CONSUMERSHIPS
CONSUMINGLY
CONSUMINGS
CONSUMMATE
CONSUMMATED
CONSUMMATELY
CONSUMMATES

CONSUMMATING
CONSUMMATION
CONSUMMATIONS
CONSUMMATIVE
CONSUMMATOR
CONSUMMATORS
CONSUMMATORY
CONSUMPTION
CONSUMPTIONS
CONSUMPTIVE
CONSUMPTIVELY
CONSUMPTIVENESS
CONSUMPTIVES
CONSUMPTIVITIES
CONSUMPTIVITY
CONTABESCENCE
CONTABESCENCES
CONTABESCENT
CONTACTABLE
CONTACTEES
CONTACTING
CONTACTLESS
CONTACTORS
CONTACTUAL
CONTACTUALLY
CONTADINAS
CONTADINOS
CONTAGIONIST
CONTAGIONISTS
CONTAGIONS
CONTAGIOUS
CONTAGIOUSLY
CONTAGIOUSNESS
CONTAINABLE
CONTAINERBOARD
CONTAINERBOARDS
CONTAINERISE
CONTAINERISED
CONTAINERISES
CONTAINERISING
CONTAINERIZE
CONTAINERIZED
CONTAINERIZES
CONTAINERIZING
CONTAINERLESS
CONTAINERPORT
CONTAINERPORTS
CONTAINERS
CONTAINERSHIP
CONTAINERSHIPS
CONTAINING
CONTAINMENT
CONTAINMENTS
CONTAMINABLE
CONTAMINANT
CONTAMINANTS
CONTAMINATE
CONTAMINATED
CONTAMINATES
CONTAMINATING
CONTAMINATION
CONTAMINATIONS
CONTAMINATIVE
CONTAMINATOR
CONTAMINATORS
CONTANGOED
CONTANGOES
CONTANGOING
CONTEMNERS
CONTEMNIBLE
CONTEMNIBLY
CONTEMNING
CONTEMNORS
CONTEMPERATION
CONTEMPERATIONS
CONTEMPERATURE
CONTEMPERATURES
CONTEMPERED
CONTEMPERING
CONTEMPERS
CONTEMPLABLE
CONTEMPLANT
CONTEMPLANTS
CONTEMPLATE
CONTEMPLATED
CONTEMPLATES
CONTEMPLATING
CONTEMPLATION
CONTEMPLATIONS
CONTEMPLATIST
CONTEMPLATISTS
CONTEMPLATIVE
CONTEMPLATIVELY
CONTEMPLATIVES
CONTEMPLATOR
CONTEMPLATORS
CONTEMPORANEAN
CONTEMPORANEANS
CONTEMPORANEITY
CONTEMPORANEOUS
CONTEMPORARIES
CONTEMPORARILY
CONTEMPORARY
CONTEMPORISE
CONTEMPORISED
CONTEMPORISES
CONTEMPORISING
CONTEMPORIZE
CONTEMPORIZED
CONTEMPORIZES
CONTEMPORIZING
CONTEMPTIBILITY
CONTEMPTIBLE
CONTEMPTIBLY
CONTEMPTUOUS
CONTEMPTUOUSLY
CONTENDENT
CONTENDENTS
CONTENDERS
CONTENDING
CONTENDINGLY
CONTENDINGS
CONTENEMENT
CONTENEMENTS
CONTENTATION
CONTENTATIONS
CONTENTEDLY
CONTENTEDNESS
CONTENTEDNESSES
CONTENTING
CONTENTION
CONTENTIONS
CONTENTIOUS
CONTENTIOUSLY
CONTENTIOUSNESS
CONTENTLESS
CONTENTMENT
CONTENTMENTS
CONTERMINAL
CONTERMINALLY
CONTERMINANT
CONTERMINATE
CONTERMINOUS
CONTERMINOUSLY
CONTESSERATION
CONTESSERATIONS
CONTESTABILITY
CONTESTABLE
CONTESTABLENESS
CONTESTABLY
CONTESTANT
CONTESTANTS
CONTESTATION
CONTESTATIONS
CONTESTERS
CONTESTING
CONTESTINGLY
CONTEXTLESS
CONTEXTUAL
CONTEXTUALISE
CONTEXTUALISED
CONTEXTUALISES
CONTEXTUALISING
CONTEXTUALIZE
CONTEXTUALIZED
CONTEXTUALIZES
CONTEXTUALIZING
CONTEXTUALLY
CONTEXTURAL
CONTEXTURE
CONTEXTURES
CONTIGNATION
CONTIGNATIONS
CONTIGUITIES
CONTIGUITY
CONTIGUOUS
CONTIGUOUSLY
CONTIGUOUSNESS
CONTINENCE
CONTINENCES
CONTINENCIES
CONTINENCY
CONTINENTAL
CONTINENTALISM
CONTINENTALISMS
CONTINENTALIST
CONTINENTALISTS
CONTINENTALLY
CONTINENTALS
CONTINENTLY
CONTINENTS
CONTINGENCE
CONTINGENCES
CONTINGENCIES
CONTINGENCY
CONTINGENT
CONTINGENTLY
CONTINGENTS
CONTINUABLE
CONTINUALITIES
CONTINUALITY
CONTINUALLY
CONTINUALNESS
CONTINUALNESSES
CONTINUANCE
CONTINUANCES
CONTINUANT
CONTINUANTS
CONTINUATE
CONTINUATION
CONTINUATIONS
CONTINUATIVE
CONTINUATIVELY
CONTINUATIVES
CONTINUATOR
CONTINUATORS
CONTINUEDLY
CONTINUEDNESS
CONTINUEDNESSES
CONTINUERS
CONTINUING
CONTINUINGLY
CONTINUITIES
CONTINUITY
CONTINUOUS
CONTINUOUSLY
CONTINUOUSNESS
CONTINUUMS
CONTORNIATE
CONTORNIATES
CONTORTEDLY
CONTORTEDNESS
CONTORTEDNESSES
CONTORTING
CONTORTION
CONTORTIONAL
CONTORTIONATE
CONTORTIONED
CONTORTIONISM
CONTORTIONISMS

CONTORTIONIST
CONTORTIONISTIC
CONTORTIONISTS
CONTORTIONS
CONTORTIVE
CONTOURING
CONTRABAND
CONTRABANDISM
CONTRABANDISMS
CONTRABANDIST
CONTRABANDISTS
CONTRABANDS
CONTRABASS
CONTRABASSES
CONTRABASSI
CONTRABASSIST
CONTRABASSISTS
CONTRABASSO
CONTRABASSOON
CONTRABASSOONS
CONTRABASSOS
CONTRABBASSI
CONTRABBASSO
CONTRABBASSOS
CONTRACEPTION
CONTRACEPTIONS
CONTRACEPTIVE
CONTRACEPTIVES
CONTRACLOCKWISE
CONTRACTABILITY
CONTRACTABLE
CONTRACTABLY
CONTRACTED
CONTRACTEDLY
CONTRACTEDNESS
CONTRACTIBILITY
CONTRACTIBLE
CONTRACTIBLY
CONTRACTILE
CONTRACTILITIES
CONTRACTILITY
CONTRACTING
CONTRACTION
CONTRACTIONAL
CONTRACTIONARY
CONTRACTIONS
CONTRACTIVE
CONTRACTIVELY
CONTRACTIVENESS
CONTRACTOR
CONTRACTORS
CONTRACTUAL
CONTRACTUALLY
CONTRACTURAL
CONTRACTURE
CONTRACTURES
CONTRACYCLICAL
CONTRADANCE
CONTRADANCES
CONTRADICT
CONTRADICTABLE
CONTRADICTED
CONTRADICTER
CONTRADICTERS
CONTRADICTING
CONTRADICTION
CONTRADICTIONS
CONTRADICTIOUS
CONTRADICTIVE
CONTRADICTIVELY
CONTRADICTOR
CONTRADICTORIES
CONTRADICTORILY
CONTRADICTORS
CONTRADICTORY
CONTRADICTS
CONTRAFAGOTTI
CONTRAFAGOTTO
CONTRAFAGOTTOS
CONTRAFLOW
CONTRAFLOWS
CONTRAGESTION
CONTRAGESTIONS
CONTRAGESTIVE
CONTRAGESTIVES
CONTRAHENT
CONTRAHENTS
CONTRAINDICANT
CONTRAINDICANTS
CONTRAINDICATE
CONTRAINDICATED
CONTRAINDICATES
CONTRALATERAL
CONTRALTOS
CONTRANATANT
CONTRAOCTAVE
CONTRAOCTAVES
CONTRAPLEX
CONTRAPOSITION
CONTRAPOSITIONS
CONTRAPOSITIVE
CONTRAPOSITIVES
CONTRAPPOSTO
CONTRAPPOSTOS
CONTRAPROP
CONTRAPROPELLER
CONTRAPROPS
CONTRAPTION
CONTRAPTIONS
CONTRAPUNTAL
CONTRAPUNTALIST
CONTRAPUNTALLY
CONTRAPUNTIST
CONTRAPUNTISTS
CONTRARIAN
CONTRARIANS
CONTRARIED
CONTRARIES
CONTRARIETIES
CONTRARIETY
CONTRARILY
CONTRARINESS
CONTRARINESSES
CONTRARIOUS
CONTRARIOUSLY
CONTRARIOUSNESS
CONTRARIWISE
CONTRARYING
CONTRASEXUAL
CONTRASEXUALS
CONTRASTABLE
CONTRASTABLY
CONTRASTED
CONTRASTIER
CONTRASTIEST
CONTRASTING
CONTRASTINGLY
CONTRASTIVE
CONTRASTIVELY
CONTRATERRENE
CONTRAVALLATION
CONTRAVENE
CONTRAVENED
CONTRAVENER
CONTRAVENERS
CONTRAVENES
CONTRAVENING
CONTRAVENTION
CONTRAVENTIONS
CONTRAYERVA
CONTRAYERVAS
CONTRECOUP
CONTRECOUPS
CONTREDANCE
CONTREDANCES
CONTREDANSE
CONTREDANSES
CONTRETEMPS
CONTRIBUTABLE
CONTRIBUTARIES
CONTRIBUTARY
CONTRIBUTE
CONTRIBUTED
CONTRIBUTES
CONTRIBUTING
CONTRIBUTION
CONTRIBUTIONS
CONTRIBUTIVE
CONTRIBUTIVELY
CONTRIBUTOR
CONTRIBUTORIES
CONTRIBUTORS
CONTRIBUTORY
CONTRISTATION
CONTRISTATIONS
CONTRISTED
CONTRISTING
CONTRITELY
CONTRITENESS
CONTRITENESSES
CONTRITION
CONTRITIONS
CONTRITURATE
CONTRITURATED
CONTRITURATES
CONTRITURATING
CONTRIVABLE
CONTRIVANCE
CONTRIVANCES
CONTRIVEMENT
CONTRIVEMENTS
CONTRIVERS
CONTRIVING
CONTROLLABILITY
CONTROLLABLE
CONTROLLABLY
CONTROLLED
CONTROLLER
CONTROLLERS
CONTROLLERSHIP
CONTROLLERSHIPS
CONTROLLING
CONTROLMENT
CONTROLMENTS
CONTROULED
CONTROULING
CONTROVERSE
CONTROVERSES
CONTROVERSIAL
CONTROVERSIALLY
CONTROVERSIES
CONTROVERSY
CONTROVERT
CONTROVERTED
CONTROVERTER
CONTROVERTERS
CONTROVERTIBLE
CONTROVERTIBLY
CONTROVERTING
CONTROVERTIST
CONTROVERTISTS
CONTROVERTS
CONTUBERNAL
CONTUBERNYAL
CONTUMACIES
CONTUMACIOUS
CONTUMACIOUSLY
CONTUMACITIES
CONTUMACITY
CONTUMELIES
CONTUMELIOUS
CONTUMELIOUSLY
CONTUNDING
CONTUSIONED
CONTUSIONS
CONUNDRUMS
CONURBATION
CONURBATIONS
CONVALESCE
CONVALESCED

CONVALESCENCE
CONVALESCENCES
CONVALESCENCIES
CONVALESCENCY
CONVALESCENT
CONVALESCENTLY
CONVALESCENTS
CONVALESCES
CONVALESCING
CONVECTING
CONVECTION
CONVECTIONAL
CONVECTIONS
CONVECTIVE
CONVECTORS
CONVENABLE
CONVENANCE
CONVENANCES
CONVENERSHIP
CONVENERSHIPS
CONVENIENCE
CONVENIENCES
CONVENIENCIES
CONVENIENCY
CONVENIENT
CONVENIENTLY
CONVENINGS
CONVENORSHIP
CONVENORSHIPS
CONVENTICLE
CONVENTICLED
CONVENTICLER
CONVENTICLERS
CONVENTICLES
CONVENTICLING
CONVENTING
CONVENTION
CONVENTIONAL
CONVENTIONALISE
CONVENTIONALISM
CONVENTIONALIST
CONVENTIONALITY
CONVENTIONALIZE
CONVENTIONALLY
CONVENTIONALS
CONVENTIONARY
CONVENTIONEER
CONVENTIONEERS
CONVENTIONER
CONVENTIONERS
CONVENTIONIST
CONVENTIONISTS
CONVENTIONS
CONVENTUAL
CONVENTUALLY
CONVENTUALS
CONVERGENCE
CONVERGENCES
CONVERGENCIES
CONVERGENCY
CONVERGENT
CONVERGING
CONVERSABLE
CONVERSABLENESS
CONVERSABLY
CONVERSANCE
CONVERSANCES
CONVERSANCIES
CONVERSANCY
CONVERSANT
CONVERSANTLY
CONVERSATION
CONVERSATIONAL
CONVERSATIONISM
CONVERSATIONIST
CONVERSATIONS
CONVERSATIVE
CONVERSAZIONE
CONVERSAZIONES
CONVERSAZIONI
CONVERSELY
CONVERSERS
CONVERSING
CONVERSION
CONVERSIONAL
CONVERSIONARY
CONVERSIONS
CONVERTAPLANE
CONVERTAPLANES
CONVERTEND
CONVERTENDS
CONVERTERS
CONVERTIBILITY
CONVERTIBLE
CONVERTIBLENESS
CONVERTIBLES
CONVERTIBLY
CONVERTING
CONVERTIPLANE
CONVERTIPLANES
CONVERTITE
CONVERTITES
CONVERTIVE
CONVERTOPLANE
CONVERTOPLANES
CONVERTORS
CONVEXEDLY
CONVEXITIES
CONVEXNESS
CONVEXNESSES
CONVEYABLE
CONVEYANCE
CONVEYANCER
CONVEYANCERS
CONVEYANCES
CONVEYANCING
CONVEYANCINGS
CONVEYORISATION
CONVEYORISE
CONVEYORISED
CONVEYORISES
CONVEYORISING
CONVEYORIZATION
CONVEYORIZE
CONVEYORIZED
CONVEYORIZES
CONVEYORIZING
CONVICINITIES
CONVICINITY
CONVICTABLE
CONVICTIBLE
CONVICTING
CONVICTION
CONVICTIONAL
CONVICTIONS
CONVICTISM
CONVICTISMS
CONVICTIVE
CONVICTIVELY
CONVINCEMENT
CONVINCEMENTS
CONVINCERS
CONVINCIBLE
CONVINCING
CONVINCINGLY
CONVINCINGNESS
CONVIVIALIST
CONVIVIALISTS
CONVIVIALITIES
CONVIVIALITY
CONVIVIALLY
CONVOCATED
CONVOCATES
CONVOCATING
CONVOCATION
CONVOCATIONAL
CONVOCATIONIST
CONVOCATIONISTS
CONVOCATIONS
CONVOCATIVE
CONVOCATOR
CONVOCATORS
CONVOLUTED
CONVOLUTEDLY
CONVOLUTEDNESS
CONVOLUTELY
CONVOLUTES
CONVOLUTING
CONVOLUTION
CONVOLUTIONAL
CONVOLUTIONARY
CONVOLUTIONS
CONVOLVING
CONVOLVULACEOUS
CONVOLVULI
CONVOLVULUS
CONVOLVULUSES
CONVULSANT
CONVULSANTS
CONVULSIBLE
CONVULSING
CONVULSION
CONVULSIONAL
CONVULSIONARIES
CONVULSIONARY
CONVULSIONIST
CONVULSIONISTS
CONVULSIONS
CONVULSIVE
CONVULSIVELY
CONVULSIVENESS
COOKHOUSES
COOKSHACKS
COOKSTOVES
COOLHEADED
COOLHOUSES
COOLINGNESS
COOLINGNESSES
COOLNESSES
COOMCEILED
COONHOUNDS
COOPERAGES
COOPERATED
COOPERATES
COOPERATING
COOPERATION
COOPERATIONIST
COOPERATIONISTS
COOPERATIONS
COOPERATIVE
COOPERATIVELY
COOPERATIVENESS
COOPERATIVES
COOPERATIVITIES
COOPERATIVITY
COOPERATOR
COOPERATORS
COOPERINGS
COOPTATION
COOPTATIONS
COOPTATIVE
COORDINANCE
COORDINANCES
COORDINATE
COORDINATED
COORDINATELY
COORDINATENESS
COORDINATES
COORDINATING
COORDINATION
COORDINATIONS
COORDINATIVE
COORDINATOR
COORDINATORS
COPARCENARIES
COPARCENARY
COPARCENER
COPARCENERIES
COPARCENERS
COPARCENERY

COPARCENIES
COPARENTED
COPARENTING
COPARTNERED
COPARTNERIES
COPARTNERING
COPARTNERS
COPARTNERSHIP
COPARTNERSHIPS
COPARTNERY
COPATRIOTS
COPAYMENTS
COPERNICIUM
COPERNICIUMS
COPESETTIC
COPESTONES
COPILOTING
COPINGSTONE
COPINGSTONES
COPIOUSNESS
COPIOUSNESSES
COPLAINTIFF
COPLAINTIFFS
COPLANARITIES
COPLANARITY
COPLOTTING
COPLOTTINGS
COPOLYMERIC
COPOLYMERISE
COPOLYMERISED
COPOLYMERISES
COPOLYMERISING
COPOLYMERIZE
COPOLYMERIZED
COPOLYMERIZES
COPOLYMERIZING
COPOLYMERS
COPPERASES
COPPERHEAD
COPPERHEADS
COPPERIEST
COPPERINGS
COPPERPLATE
COPPERPLATES
COPPERSMITH
COPPERSMITHS
COPPERWORK
COPPERWORKS
COPPERWORM
COPPERWORMS
COPPICINGS
COPRAEMIAS
COPRESENCE
COPRESENCES
COPRESENTED
COPRESENTING
COPRESENTS
COPRESIDENT
COPRESIDENTS
COPRINCIPAL
COPRINCIPALS
COPRISONER
COPRISONERS
COPROCESSING
COPROCESSINGS
COPROCESSOR
COPROCESSORS
COPRODUCED
COPRODUCER
COPRODUCERS
COPRODUCES
COPRODUCING
COPRODUCTION
COPRODUCTIONS
COPRODUCTS
COPROLALIA
COPROLALIAC
COPROLALIAS
COPROLITES
COPROLITHS
COPROLITIC
COPROLOGIES
COPROMOTER
COPROMOTERS
COPROPHAGAN
COPROPHAGANS
COPROPHAGIC
COPROPHAGIES
COPROPHAGIST
COPROPHAGISTS
COPROPHAGOUS
COPROPHAGY
COPROPHILIA
COPROPHILIAC
COPROPHILIACS
COPROPHILIAS
COPROPHILIC
COPROPHILOUS
COPROPRIETOR
COPROPRIETORS
COPROSPERITIES
COPROSPERITY
COPROSTEROL
COPROSTEROLS
COPSEWOODS
COPUBLISHED
COPUBLISHER
COPUBLISHERS
COPUBLISHES
COPUBLISHING
COPULATING
COPULATION
COPULATIONS
COPULATIVE
COPULATIVELY
COPULATIVES
COPULATORY
COPURIFIED
COPURIFIES
COPURIFYING
COPYCATTED
COPYCATTING
COPYEDITED
COPYEDITING
COPYFIGHTS
COPYGRAPHS
COPYHOLDER
COPYHOLDERS
COPYLEFTED
COPYLEFTING
COPYREADER
COPYREADERS
COPYREADING
COPYREADINGS
COPYRIGHTABLE
COPYRIGHTED
COPYRIGHTER
COPYRIGHTERS
COPYRIGHTING
COPYRIGHTS
COPYTAKERS
COPYWRITER
COPYWRITERS
COPYWRITING
COPYWRITINGS
COQUELICOT
COQUELICOTS
COQUETRIES
COQUETTING
COQUETTISH
COQUETTISHLY
COQUETTISHNESS
COQUIMBITE
COQUIMBITES
CORACIIFORM
CORADICATE
CORALBELLS
CORALBERRIES
CORALBERRY
CORALLACEOUS
CORALLIFEROUS
CORALLIFORM
CORALLIGENOUS
CORALLINES
CORALLITES
CORALLOIDAL
CORALLOIDS
CORALROOTS
CORALWORTS
CORBEILLES
CORBELINGS
CORBELLING
CORBELLINGS
CORBICULAE
CORBICULATE
CORDECTOMIES
CORDECTOMY
CORDELLING
CORDGRASSES
CORDIALISE
CORDIALISED
CORDIALISES
CORDIALISING
CORDIALITIES
CORDIALITY
CORDIALIZE
CORDIALIZED
CORDIALIZES
CORDIALIZING
CORDIALNESS
CORDIALNESSES
CORDIERITE
CORDIERITES
CORDILLERA
CORDILLERAN
CORDILLERAS
CORDLESSES
CORDOCENTESES
CORDOCENTESIS
CORDONNETS
CORDOTOMIES
CORDUROYED
CORDUROYING
CORDWAINER
CORDWAINERIES
CORDWAINERS
CORDWAINERY
CORDYLINES
CORECIPIENT
CORECIPIENTS
COREDEEMED
COREDEEMING
COREFERENTIAL
COREGONINE
CORELATING
CORELATION
CORELATIONS
CORELATIVE
CORELATIVES
CORELIGIONIST
CORELIGIONISTS
COREOPSISES
COREPRESSOR
COREPRESSORS
COREQUISITE
COREQUISITES
CORESEARCHER
CORESEARCHERS
CORESIDENT
CORESIDENTIAL
CORESIDENTS
CORESPONDENT
CORESPONDENTS
CORFHOUSES
CORIACEOUS
CORIANDERS
CORINTHIANISE
CORINTHIANISED
CORINTHIANISES
CORINTHIANISING

CORINTHIANIZE
CORINTHIANIZED
CORINTHIANIZES
CORINTHIANIZING
CORIVALLED
CORIVALLING
CORIVALRIES
CORIVALSHIP
CORIVALSHIPS
CORKBOARDS
CORKBORERS
CORKINESSES
CORKSCREWED
CORKSCREWING
CORKSCREWS
CORMOPHYTE
CORMOPHYTES
CORMOPHYTIC
CORMORANTS
CORNACEOUS
CORNBORERS
CORNBRAIDED
CORNBRAIDING
CORNBRAIDS
CORNBRANDIES
CORNBRANDY
CORNBRASHES
CORNBREADS
CORNCOCKLE
CORNCOCKLES
CORNCRAKES
CORNEITISES
CORNELIANS
CORNEMUSES
CORNERBACK
CORNERBACKS
CORNERINGS
CORNERSTONE
CORNERSTONES
CORNERWAYS
CORNERWISE
CORNETCIES
CORNETISTS
CORNETTINI
CORNETTINO
CORNETTINOS
CORNETTIST
CORNETTISTS
CORNFIELDS
CORNFLAKES
CORNFLOURS
CORNFLOWER
CORNFLOWERS
CORNHUSKER
CORNHUSKERS
CORNHUSKING
CORNHUSKINGS
CORNICHONS
CORNICINGS
CORNICULATE
CORNICULUM
CORNICULUMS
CORNIFEROUS
CORNIFICATION
CORNIFICATIONS
CORNIFYING
CORNIGEROUS
CORNINESSES
CORNOPEANS
CORNROWING
CORNSTALKS
CORNSTARCH
CORNSTARCHES
CORNSTONES
CORNUCOPIA
CORNUCOPIAN
CORNUCOPIAS
COROLLACEOUS
COROLLARIES
COROLLIFLORAL
COROLLIFLOROUS
COROLLIFORM
COROMANDEL
COROMANDELS
CORONAGRAPH
CORONAGRAPHS
CORONARIES
CORONATING
CORONATION
CORONATIONS
CORONAVIRUS
CORONAVIRUSES
CORONERSHIP
CORONERSHIPS
CORONOGRAPH
CORONOGRAPHS
COROTATING
COROTATION
COROTATIONS
CORPORALES
CORPORALITIES
CORPORALITY
CORPORALLY
CORPORALSHIP
CORPORALSHIPS
CORPORASES
CORPORATELY
CORPORATENESS
CORPORATENESSES
CORPORATES
CORPORATION
CORPORATIONS
CORPORATISE
CORPORATISED
CORPORATISES
CORPORATISING
CORPORATISM
CORPORATISMS
CORPORATIST
CORPORATISTS
CORPORATIVE
CORPORATIVISM
CORPORATIVISMS
CORPORATIZE
CORPORATIZED
CORPORATIZES
CORPORATIZING
CORPORATOR
CORPORATORS
CORPOREALISE
CORPOREALISED
CORPOREALISES
CORPOREALISING
CORPOREALISM
CORPOREALISMS
CORPOREALIST
CORPOREALISTS
CORPOREALITIES
CORPOREALITY
CORPOREALIZE
CORPOREALIZED
CORPOREALIZES
CORPOREALIZING
CORPOREALLY
CORPOREALNESS
CORPOREALNESSES
CORPOREITIES
CORPOREITY
CORPORIFICATION
CORPORIFIED
CORPORIFIES
CORPORIFYING
CORPOSANTS
CORPSELIKE
CORPULENCE
CORPULENCES
CORPULENCIES
CORPULENCY
CORPULENTLY
CORPUSCLES
CORPUSCULAR
CORPUSCULARIAN
CORPUSCULARIANS
CORPUSCULARITY
CORPUSCULE
CORPUSCULES
CORRALLING
CORRASIONS
CORRECTABLE
CORRECTEST
CORRECTIBLE
CORRECTING
CORRECTION
CORRECTIONAL
CORRECTIONER
CORRECTIONERS
CORRECTIONS
CORRECTITUDE
CORRECTITUDES
CORRECTIVE
CORRECTIVELY
CORRECTIVES
CORRECTNESS
CORRECTNESSES
CORRECTORS
CORRECTORY
CORREGIDOR
CORREGIDORS
CORRELATABLE
CORRELATED
CORRELATES
CORRELATING
CORRELATION
CORRELATIONAL
CORRELATIONS
CORRELATIVE
CORRELATIVELY
CORRELATIVENESS
CORRELATIVES
CORRELATIVITIES
CORRELATIVITY
CORRELATOR
CORRELATORS
CORRELIGIONIST
CORRELIGIONISTS
CORREPTION
CORREPTIONS
CORRESPOND
CORRESPONDED
CORRESPONDENCE
CORRESPONDENCES
CORRESPONDENCY
CORRESPONDENT
CORRESPONDENTLY
CORRESPONDENTS
CORRESPONDING
CORRESPONDINGLY
CORRESPONDS
CORRESPONSIVE
CORRIGENDA
CORRIGENDUM
CORRIGENTS
CORRIGIBILITIES
CORRIGIBILITY
CORRIGIBLE
CORRIGIBLY
CORRIVALLED
CORRIVALLING
CORRIVALRIES
CORRIVALRY
CORRIVALSHIP
CORRIVALSHIPS
CORROBORABLE
CORROBORANT
CORROBORATE
CORROBORATED
CORROBORATES
CORROBORATING
CORROBORATION
CORROBORATIONS

CORROBORATIVE
CORROBORATIVELY
CORROBORATIVES
CORROBORATOR
CORROBORATORS
CORROBORATORY
CORROBOREE
CORROBOREED
CORROBOREEING
CORROBOREES
CORRODANTS
CORRODENTS
CORRODIBILITIES
CORRODIBILITY
CORRODIBLE
CORROSIBILITIES
CORROSIBILITY
CORROSIBLE
CORROSIONS
CORROSIVELY
CORROSIVENESS
CORROSIVENESSES
CORROSIVES
CORRUGATED
CORRUGATES
CORRUGATING
CORRUGATION
CORRUGATIONS
CORRUGATOR
CORRUGATORS
CORRUPTERS
CORRUPTEST
CORRUPTIBILITY
CORRUPTIBLE
CORRUPTIBLENESS
CORRUPTIBLY
CORRUPTING
CORRUPTION
CORRUPTIONIST
CORRUPTIONISTS
CORRUPTIONS
CORRUPTIVE
CORRUPTIVELY
CORRUPTNESS
CORRUPTNESSES
CORRUPTORS
CORSELETTE
CORSELETTES
CORSETIERE
CORSETIERES
CORSETIERS
CORSETRIES
CORTICALLY
CORTICATED
CORTICATION
CORTICATIONS
CORTICOIDS
CORTICOLOUS
CORTICOSTEROID
CORTICOSTEROIDS
CORTICOSTERONE
CORTICOSTERONES
CORTICOTROPHIC
CORTICOTROPHIN
CORTICOTROPHINS
CORTICOTROPIC
CORTICOTROPIN
CORTICOTROPINS
CORTISONES
CORUSCATED
CORUSCATES
CORUSCATING
CORUSCATION
CORUSCATIONS
CORVETTING
CORYBANTES
CORYBANTIC
CORYBANTISM
CORYBANTISMS
CORYDALINE
CORYDALINES
CORYDALISES
CORYLOPSES
CORYLOPSIS
CORYMBOSELY
CORYNEBACTERIA
CORYNEBACTERIAL
CORYNEBACTERIUM
CORYNEFORM
CORYPHAEUS
CORYPHENES
COSCINOMANCIES
COSCINOMANCY
COSCRIPTED
COSCRIPTING
COSEISMALS
COSEISMICS
COSENTIENT
COSHERINGS
COSIGNATORIES
COSIGNATORY
COSIGNIFICATIVE
COSINESSES
COSMECEUTICAL
COSMECEUTICALS
COSMETICAL
COSMETICALLY
COSMETICIAN
COSMETICIANS
COSMETICISE
COSMETICISED
COSMETICISES
COSMETICISING
COSMETICISM
COSMETICISMS
COSMETICIZE
COSMETICIZED
COSMETICIZES
COSMETICIZING
COSMETICOLOGIES
COSMETICOLOGY
COSMETOLOGIES
COSMETOLOGIST
COSMETOLOGISTS
COSMETOLOGY
COSMICALLY
COSMOCHEMICAL
COSMOCHEMIST
COSMOCHEMISTRY
COSMOCHEMISTS
COSMOCRATIC
COSMOCRATS
COSMODROME
COSMODROMES
COSMOGENIC
COSMOGENIES
COSMOGONAL
COSMOGONIC
COSMOGONICAL
COSMOGONIES
COSMOGONIST
COSMOGONISTS
COSMOGRAPHER
COSMOGRAPHERS
COSMOGRAPHIC
COSMOGRAPHICAL
COSMOGRAPHIES
COSMOGRAPHIST
COSMOGRAPHISTS
COSMOGRAPHY
COSMOLATRIES
COSMOLATRY
COSMOLINED
COSMOLINES
COSMOLINING
COSMOLOGIC
COSMOLOGICAL
COSMOLOGICALLY
COSMOLOGIES
COSMOLOGIST
COSMOLOGISTS
COSMONAUTICS
COSMONAUTS
COSMOPLASTIC
COSMOPOLIS
COSMOPOLISES
COSMOPOLITAN
COSMOPOLITANISM
COSMOPOLITANS
COSMOPOLITE
COSMOPOLITES
COSMOPOLITIC
COSMOPOLITICAL
COSMOPOLITICS
COSMOPOLITISM
COSMOPOLITISMS
COSMORAMAS
COSMORAMIC
COSMOSPHERE
COSMOSPHERES
COSMOTHEISM
COSMOTHEISMS
COSMOTHETIC
COSMOTHETICAL
COSMOTRONS
COSPONSORED
COSPONSORING
COSPONSORS
COSPONSORSHIP
COSPONSORSHIPS
COSSETTING
COSTALGIAS
COSTARDMONGER
COSTARDMONGERS
COSTARRING
COSTEANING
COSTEANINGS
COSTERMONGER
COSTERMONGERS
COSTIVENESS
COSTIVENESSES
COSTLESSLY
COSTLINESS
COSTLINESSES
COSTMARIES
COSTOTOMIES
COSTUMERIES
COSTUMIERS
COSTUMINGS
COSURFACTANT
COSURFACTANTS
COTANGENTIAL
COTANGENTS
COTELETTES
COTEMPORANEOUS
COTEMPORARY
COTENANCIES
COTERMINOUS
COTERMINOUSLY
COTILLIONS
COTONEASTER
COTONEASTERS
COTRANSDUCE
COTRANSDUCED
COTRANSDUCES
COTRANSDUCING
COTRANSDUCTION
COTRANSDUCTIONS
COTRANSFER
COTRANSFERS
COTRANSPORT
COTRANSPORTED
COTRANSPORTING
COTRANSPORTS
COTRUSTEES
COTTABUSES
COTTAGIEST
COTTAGINGS
COTTERLESS
COTTIERISM

COTTIERISMS
COTTONADES
COTTONIEST
COTTONMOUTH
COTTONMOUTHS
COTTONOCRACIES
COTTONOCRACY
COTTONSEED
COTTONSEEDS
COTTONTAIL
COTTONTAILS
COTTONWEED
COTTONWEEDS
COTTONWOOD
COTTONWOODS
COTURNIXES
COTYLEDONAL
COTYLEDONARY
COTYLEDONOID
COTYLEDONOUS
COTYLEDONS
COTYLIFORM
COTYLOIDAL
COTYLOIDALS
COTYLOSAUR
COTYLOSAURS
COUCHETTES
COUCHSURFING
COUCHSURFINGS
COULIBIACA
COULIBIACAS
COULIBIACS
COULOMBMETER
COULOMBMETERS
COULOMETER
COULOMETERS
COULOMETRIC
COULOMETRICALLY
COULOMETRIES
COULOMETRY
COUMARILIC
COUMARONES
COUNCILLOR
COUNCILLORS
COUNCILLORSHIP
COUNCILLORSHIPS
COUNCILMAN
COUNCILMANIC
COUNCILMEN
COUNCILORS
COUNCILORSHIP
COUNCILORSHIPS
COUNCILWOMAN
COUNCILWOMEN
COUNSELABLE
COUNSELEES
COUNSELING
COUNSELINGS
COUNSELLABLE
COUNSELLED
COUNSELLEE
COUNSELLEES
COUNSELLING
COUNSELLINGS
COUNSELLOR
COUNSELLORS
COUNSELLORSHIP
COUNSELLORSHIPS
COUNSELORS
COUNSELORSHIP
COUNSELORSHIPS
COUNTABILITIES
COUNTABILITY
COUNTBACKS
COUNTDOWNS
COUNTENANCE
COUNTENANCED
COUNTENANCER
COUNTENANCERS
COUNTENANCES
COUNTENANCING
COUNTERACT
COUNTERACTED
COUNTERACTING
COUNTERACTION
COUNTERACTIONS
COUNTERACTIVE
COUNTERACTIVELY
COUNTERACTS
COUNTERAGENT
COUNTERAGENTS
COUNTERARGUE
COUNTERARGUED
COUNTERARGUES
COUNTERARGUING
COUNTERARGUMENT
COUNTERASSAULT
COUNTERASSAULTS
COUNTERATTACK
COUNTERATTACKED
COUNTERATTACKER
COUNTERATTACKS
COUNTERBALANCE
COUNTERBALANCED
COUNTERBALANCES
COUNTERBASE
COUNTERBASES
COUNTERBID
COUNTERBIDDER
COUNTERBIDDERS
COUNTERBIDS
COUNTERBLAST
COUNTERBLASTS
COUNTERBLOCKADE
COUNTERBLOW
COUNTERBLOWS
COUNTERBLUFF
COUNTERBLUFFS
COUNTERBOND
COUNTERBONDS
COUNTERBORE
COUNTERBORED
COUNTERBORES
COUNTERBORING
COUNTERBRACE
COUNTERBRACED
COUNTERBRACES
COUNTERBRACING
COUNTERBUFF
COUNTERBUFFED
COUNTERBUFFING
COUNTERBUFFS
COUNTERCAMPAIGN
COUNTERCHANGE
COUNTERCHANGED
COUNTERCHANGES
COUNTERCHANGING
COUNTERCHARGE
COUNTERCHARGED
COUNTERCHARGES
COUNTERCHARGING
COUNTERCHARM
COUNTERCHARMED
COUNTERCHARMING
COUNTERCHARMS
COUNTERCHECK
COUNTERCHECKED
COUNTERCHECKING
COUNTERCHECKS
COUNTERCLAIM
COUNTERCLAIMANT
COUNTERCLAIMED
COUNTERCLAIMING
COUNTERCLAIMS
COUNTERCOUP
COUNTERCOUPS
COUNTERCRIES
COUNTERCRY
COUNTERCULTURAL
COUNTERCULTURE
COUNTERCULTURES
COUNTERCURRENT
COUNTERCURRENTS
COUNTERCYCLICAL
COUNTERDEMAND
COUNTERDEMANDS
COUNTERDRAW
COUNTERDRAWING
COUNTERDRAWN
COUNTERDRAWS
COUNTERDREW
COUNTEREFFORT
COUNTEREFFORTS
COUNTEREVIDENCE
COUNTEREXAMPLE
COUNTEREXAMPLES
COUNTERFACTUAL
COUNTERFACTUALS
COUNTERFECT
COUNTERFEISANCE
COUNTERFEIT
COUNTERFEITED
COUNTERFEITER
COUNTERFEITERS
COUNTERFEITING
COUNTERFEITINGS
COUNTERFEITLY
COUNTERFEITS
COUNTERFESAUNCE
COUNTERFIRE
COUNTERFIRES
COUNTERFLOW
COUNTERFLOWS
COUNTERFOIL
COUNTERFOILS
COUNTERFORCE
COUNTERFORCES
COUNTERFORT
COUNTERFORTS
COUNTERGLOW
COUNTERGLOWS
COUNTERGUERILLA
COUNTERIMAGE
COUNTERIMAGES
COUNTERING
COUNTERINSTANCE
COUNTERION
COUNTERIONS
COUNTERIRRITANT
COUNTERLIGHT
COUNTERLIGHTS
COUNTERMAN
COUNTERMAND
COUNTERMANDABLE
COUNTERMANDED
COUNTERMANDING
COUNTERMANDS
COUNTERMARCH
COUNTERMARCHED
COUNTERMARCHES
COUNTERMARCHING
COUNTERMARK
COUNTERMARKS
COUNTERMEASURE
COUNTERMEASURES
COUNTERMELODIES
COUNTERMELODY
COUNTERMEMO
COUNTERMEMOS
COUNTERMEN
COUNTERMINE
COUNTERMINED
COUNTERMINES
COUNTERMINING
COUNTERMOTION
COUNTERMOTIONS
COUNTERMOVE
COUNTERMOVED
COUNTERMOVEMENT
COUNTERMOVES

COUNTERMOVING
COUNTERMURE
COUNTERMURED
COUNTERMURES
COUNTERMURING
COUNTERMYTH
COUNTERMYTHS
COUNTEROFFER
COUNTEROFFERS
COUNTERORDER
COUNTERORDERED
COUNTERORDERING
COUNTERORDERS
COUNTERPACE
COUNTERPACES
COUNTERPANE
COUNTERPANES
COUNTERPART
COUNTERPARTIES
COUNTERPARTS
COUNTERPARTY
COUNTERPEISE
COUNTERPEISED
COUNTERPEISES
COUNTERPEISING
COUNTERPETITION
COUNTERPICKET
COUNTERPICKETED
COUNTERPICKETS
COUNTERPLAN
COUNTERPLANNED
COUNTERPLANNING
COUNTERPLANS
COUNTERPLAY
COUNTERPLAYED
COUNTERPLAYER
COUNTERPLAYERS
COUNTERPLAYING
COUNTERPLAYS
COUNTERPLEA
COUNTERPLEAD
COUNTERPLEADED
COUNTERPLEADING
COUNTERPLEADS
COUNTERPLEAS
COUNTERPLED
COUNTERPLOT
COUNTERPLOTS
COUNTERPLOTTED
COUNTERPLOTTING
COUNTERPLOY
COUNTERPLOYS
COUNTERPOINT
COUNTERPOINTED
COUNTERPOINTING
COUNTERPOINTS
COUNTERPOISE
COUNTERPOISED
COUNTERPOISES
COUNTERPOISING
COUNTERPOSE
COUNTERPOSED
COUNTERPOSES
COUNTERPOSING
COUNTERPOWER
COUNTERPOWERS
COUNTERPRESSURE
COUNTERPROJECT
COUNTERPROJECTS
COUNTERPROOF
COUNTERPROOFS
COUNTERPROPOSAL
COUNTERPROTEST
COUNTERPROTESTS
COUNTERPUNCH
COUNTERPUNCHED
COUNTERPUNCHER
COUNTERPUNCHERS
COUNTERPUNCHES
COUNTERPUNCHING
COUNTERQUESTION
COUNTERRAID
COUNTERRAIDED
COUNTERRAIDING
COUNTERRAIDS
COUNTERRALLIED
COUNTERRALLIES
COUNTERRALLY
COUNTERRALLYING
COUNTERREACTION
COUNTERREFORM
COUNTERREFORMED
COUNTERREFORMER
COUNTERREFORMS
COUNTERRESPONSE
COUNTERSANK
COUNTERSCARP
COUNTERSCARPS
COUNTERSEAL
COUNTERSEALED
COUNTERSEALING
COUNTERSEALS
COUNTERSHADING
COUNTERSHADINGS
COUNTERSHAFT
COUNTERSHAFTS
COUNTERSHOT
COUNTERSHOTS
COUNTERSIGN
COUNTERSIGNED
COUNTERSIGNING
COUNTERSIGNS
COUNTERSINK
COUNTERSINKING
COUNTERSINKS
COUNTERSNIPER
COUNTERSNIPERS
COUNTERSPELL
COUNTERSPELLS
COUNTERSPIES
COUNTERSPY
COUNTERSPYING
COUNTERSPYINGS
COUNTERSTAIN
COUNTERSTAINED
COUNTERSTAINING
COUNTERSTAINS
COUNTERSTATE
COUNTERSTATED
COUNTERSTATES
COUNTERSTATING
COUNTERSTEP
COUNTERSTEPS
COUNTERSTRATEGY
COUNTERSTREAM
COUNTERSTREAMS
COUNTERSTRICKEN
COUNTERSTRIKE
COUNTERSTRIKES
COUNTERSTRIKING
COUNTERSTROKE
COUNTERSTROKES
COUNTERSTRUCK
COUNTERSTYLE
COUNTERSTYLES
COUNTERSUBJECT
COUNTERSUBJECTS
COUNTERSUE
COUNTERSUED
COUNTERSUES
COUNTERSUING
COUNTERSUIT
COUNTERSUITS
COUNTERSUNK
COUNTERTACTIC
COUNTERTACTICS
COUNTERTENDENCY
COUNTERTENOR
COUNTERTENORS
COUNTERTERROR
COUNTERTERRORS
COUNTERTHREAT
COUNTERTHREATS
COUNTERTHRUST
COUNTERTHRUSTS
COUNTERTOP
COUNTERTOPS
COUNTERTRADE
COUNTERTRADED
COUNTERTRADES
COUNTERTRADING
COUNTERTREND
COUNTERTRENDS
COUNTERTYPE
COUNTERTYPES
COUNTERVAIL
COUNTERVAILABLE
COUNTERVAILED
COUNTERVAILING
COUNTERVAILS
COUNTERVIEW
COUNTERVIEWS
COUNTERVIOLENCE
COUNTERWEIGH
COUNTERWEIGHED
COUNTERWEIGHING
COUNTERWEIGHS
COUNTERWEIGHT
COUNTERWEIGHTED
COUNTERWEIGHTS
COUNTERWORD
COUNTERWORDS
COUNTERWORK
COUNTERWORKED
COUNTERWORKER
COUNTERWORKERS
COUNTERWORKING
COUNTERWORKS
COUNTERWORLD
COUNTERWORLDS
COUNTESSES
COUNTINGHOUSE
COUNTINGHOUSES
COUNTLESSLY
COUNTLINES
COUNTRIFIED
COUNTROLLED
COUNTROLLING
COUNTRYFIED
COUNTRYISH
COUNTRYMAN
COUNTRYMEN
COUNTRYSEAT
COUNTRYSEATS
COUNTRYSIDE
COUNTRYSIDES
COUNTRYWIDE
COUNTRYWOMAN
COUNTRYWOMEN
COUNTSHIPS
COUPLEDOMS
COUPLEMENT
COUPLEMENTS
COUPONINGS
COURAGEFUL
COURAGEOUS
COURAGEOUSLY
COURAGEOUSNESS
COURANTOES
COURBARILS
COURBETTES
COURGETTES
COURIERING
COURSEBOOK
COURSEBOOKS
COURSEWARE
COURSEWARES
COURSEWORK
COURSEWORKS
COURTCRAFT

C

COURTCRAFTS
COURTEOUSLY
COURTEOUSNESS
COURTEOUSNESSES
COURTESANS
COURTESIED
COURTESIES
COURTESYING
COURTEZANS
COURTHOUSE
COURTHOUSES
COURTIERISM
COURTIERISMS
COURTIERLIKE
COURTIERLY
COURTLIEST
COURTLINESS
COURTLINESSES
COURTLINGS
COURTROOMS
COURTSHIPS
COURTSIDES
COURTYARDS
COUSCOUSES
COUSCOUSOU
COUSCOUSOUS
COUSINAGES
COUSINHOOD
COUSINHOODS
COUSINRIES
COUSINSHIP
COUSINSHIPS
COUTURIERE
COUTURIERES
COUTURIERS
COVALENCES
COVALENCIES
COVALENTLY
COVARIANCE
COVARIANCES
COVARIANTS
COVARIATES
COVARIATION
COVARIATIONS
COVELLINES
COVELLITES
COVENANTAL
COVENANTALLY
COVENANTED
COVENANTEE
COVENANTEES
COVENANTER
COVENANTERS
COVENANTING
COVENANTOR
COVENANTORS
COVERALLED
COVERMOUNT
COVERMOUNTED
COVERMOUNTING
COVERMOUNTS
COVERSINES
COVERSLIPS
COVERTNESS
COVERTNESSES
COVERTURES
COVETINGLY
COVETIVENESS
COVETIVENESSES
COVETOUSLY
COVETOUSNESS
COVETOUSNESSES
COWARDICES
COWARDLIER
COWARDLIEST
COWARDLINESS
COWARDLINESSES
COWARDRIES
COWARDSHIP
COWARDSHIPS
COWBERRIES
COWBOYINGS
COWCATCHER
COWCATCHERS
COWERINGLY
COWFEEDERS
COWFETERIA
COWFETERIAS
COWGRASSES
COWLSTAFFS
COWLSTAVES
COWPUNCHER
COWPUNCHERS
COXCOMBICAL
COXCOMBICALITY
COXCOMBICALLY
COXCOMBRIES
COXCOMICAL
COXINESSES
COXSWAINED
COXSWAINING
COYISHNESS
COYISHNESSES
COYOTILLOS
COZINESSES
CRABAPPLES
CRABBEDNESS
CRABBEDNESSES
CRABBINESS
CRABBINESSES
CRABEATERS
CRABGRASSES
CRABSTICKS
CRACKAJACK
CRACKAJACKS
CRACKBACKS
CRACKBERRIES
CRACKBERRY
CRACKBRAIN
CRACKBRAINED
CRACKBRAINS
CRACKDOWNS
CRACKERJACK
CRACKERJACKS
CRACKHEADS
CRACKLEWARE
CRACKLEWARES
CRACKLIEST
CRACKLINGS
CRACOVIENNE
CRACOVIENNES
CRADLESONG
CRADLESONGS
CRADLEWALK
CRADLEWALKS
CRAFTINESS
CRAFTINESSES
CRAFTMANSHIP
CRAFTMANSHIPS
CRAFTSMANLIKE
CRAFTSMANLY
CRAFTSMANSHIP
CRAFTSMANSHIPS
CRAFTSPEOPLE
CRAFTSPERSON
CRAFTSPERSONS
CRAFTSWOMAN
CRAFTSWOMEN
CRAFTWORKS
CRAGGEDNESS
CRAGGEDNESSES
CRAGGINESS
CRAGGINESSES
CRAIGFLUKE
CRAIGFLUKES
CRAKEBERRIES
CRAKEBERRY
CRAMBOCLINK
CRAMBOCLINKS
CRAMOISIES
CRAMPBARKS
CRAMPFISHES
CRAMPONING
CRAMPONNED
CRAMPONNING
CRAMPONNINGS
CRANACHANS
CRANBERRIES
CRANEFLIES
CRANESBILL
CRANESBILLS
CRANIECTOMIES
CRANIECTOMY
CRANIOCEREBRAL
CRANIOFACIAL
CRANIOGNOMIES
CRANIOGNOMY
CRANIOLOGICAL
CRANIOLOGICALLY
CRANIOLOGIES
CRANIOLOGIST
CRANIOLOGISTS
CRANIOLOGY
CRANIOMETER
CRANIOMETERS
CRANIOMETRIC
CRANIOMETRICAL
CRANIOMETRIES
CRANIOMETRIST
CRANIOMETRISTS
CRANIOMETRY
CRANIOPAGI
CRANIOPAGUS
CRANIOSACRAL
CRANIOSCOPIES
CRANIOSCOPIST
CRANIOSCOPISTS
CRANIOSCOPY
CRANIOTOMIES
CRANIOTOMY
CRANKBAITS
CRANKCASES
CRANKHANDLE
CRANKHANDLES
CRANKINESS
CRANKINESSES
CRANKNESSES
CRANKSHAFT
CRANKSHAFTS
CRANREUCHS
CRAPEHANGER
CRAPEHANGERS
CRAPEHANGING
CRAPEHANGINGS
CRAPSHOOTER
CRAPSHOOTERS
CRAPSHOOTS
CRAPULENCE
CRAPULENCES
CRAPULENTLY
CRAPULOSITIES
CRAPULOSITY
CRAPULOUSLY
CRAPULOUSNESS
CRAPULOUSNESSES
CRAQUELURE
CRAQUELURES
CRASHINGLY
CRASHWORTHIER
CRASHWORTHIEST
CRASHWORTHINESS
CRASHWORTHY
CRASSAMENTA
CRASSAMENTUM
CRASSITUDE
CRASSITUDES
CRASSNESSES
CRASSULACEAN
CRASSULACEOUS
CRATERIFORM

CRATERINGS
CRATERLESS
CRATERLETS
CRATERLIKE
CRAUNCHABLE
CRAUNCHIER
CRAUNCHIEST
CRAUNCHINESS
CRAUNCHINESSES
CRAUNCHING
CRAVATTING
CRAVENNESS
CRAVENNESSES
CRAWDADDIES
CRAWFISHED
CRAWFISHES
CRAWFISHING
CRAWLINGLY
CRAYFISHES
CRAYONISTS
CRAZINESSES
CRAZYWEEDS
CREAKINESS
CREAKINESSES
CREAKINGLY
CREAMERIES
CREAMINESS
CREAMINESSES
CREAMPUFFS
CREAMWARES
CREASELESS
CREASOTING
CREATIANISM
CREATIANISMS
CREATININE
CREATININES
CREATIONAL
CREATIONISM
CREATIONISMS
CREATIONIST
CREATIONISTIC
CREATIONISTS
CREATIVELY
CREATIVENESS
CREATIVENESSES
CREATIVITIES
CREATIVITY
CREATORSHIP
CREATORSHIPS
CREATRESSES
CREATRIXES
CREATUREHOOD
CREATUREHOODS
CREATURELINESS
CREATURELY
CREATURESHIP
CREATURESHIPS
CREDENTIAL
CREDENTIALED
CREDENTIALING
CREDENTIALINGS
CREDENTIALISM
CREDENTIALISMS
CREDENTIALLED
CREDENTIALLING
CREDENTIALLINGS
CREDENTIALS
CREDIBILITIES
CREDIBILITY
CREDIBLENESS
CREDIBLENESSES
CREDITABILITIES
CREDITABILITY
CREDITABLE
CREDITABLENESS
CREDITABLY
CREDITLESS
CREDITORSHIP
CREDITORSHIPS
CREDITWORTHIER
CREDITWORTHIEST
CREDITWORTHY
CREDULITIES
CREDULOUSLY
CREDULOUSNESS
CREDULOUSNESSES
CREEKSIDES
CREEPINESS
CREEPINESSES
CREEPINGLY
CREEPMOUSE
CREEPMOUSES
CREESHIEST
CREMAILLERE
CREMAILLERES
CREMASTERS
CREMATIONISM
CREMATIONISMS
CREMATIONIST
CREMATIONISTS
CREMATIONS
CREMATORIA
CREMATORIAL
CREMATORIES
CREMATORIUM
CREMATORIUMS
CREMOCARPS
CRENATIONS
CRENATURES
CRENELATED
CRENELATES
CRENELATING
CRENELATION
CRENELATIONS
CRENELLATE
CRENELLATED
CRENELLATES
CRENELLATING
CRENELLATION
CRENELLATIONS
CRENELLING
CRENULATED
CRENULATION
CRENULATIONS
CREOLISATION
CREOLISATIONS
CREOLISING
CREOLIZATION
CREOLIZATIONS
CREOLIZING
CREOPHAGIES
CREOPHAGOUS
CREOSOTING
CREPEHANGER
CREPEHANGERS
CREPEHANGING
CREPEHANGINGS
CREPINESSES
CREPITATED
CREPITATES
CREPITATING
CREPITATION
CREPITATIONS
CREPITATIVE
CREPITUSES
CREPOLINES
CREPUSCLES
CREPUSCULAR
CREPUSCULE
CREPUSCULES
CREPUSCULOUS
CRESCENDOED
CRESCENDOES
CRESCENDOING
CRESCENDOS
CRESCENTADE
CRESCENTADES
CRESCENTED
CRESCENTIC
CRESCIVELY
CRESCOGRAPH
CRESCOGRAPHS
CRESTFALLEN
CRESTFALLENLY
CRESTFALLENNESS
CRETACEOUS
CRETACEOUSES
CRETACEOUSLY
CRETINISED
CRETINISES
CRETINISING
CRETINISMS
CRETINIZED
CRETINIZES
CRETINIZING
CRETINOIDS
CREVASSING
CREWELISTS
CREWELLERIES
CREWELLERY
CREWELLING
CREWELLINGS
CREWELWORK
CREWELWORKS
CRIBRATION
CRIBRATIONS
CRIBRIFORM
CRICKETERS
CRICKETING
CRICKETINGS
CRIMEWAVES
CRIMINALESE
CRIMINALESES
CRIMINALISATION
CRIMINALISE
CRIMINALISED
CRIMINALISES
CRIMINALISING
CRIMINALIST
CRIMINALISTICS
CRIMINALISTS
CRIMINALITIES
CRIMINALITY
CRIMINALIZATION
CRIMINALIZE
CRIMINALIZED
CRIMINALIZES
CRIMINALIZING
CRIMINALLY
CRIMINATED
CRIMINATES
CRIMINATING
CRIMINATION
CRIMINATIONS
CRIMINATIVE
CRIMINATOR
CRIMINATORS
CRIMINATORY
CRIMINOGENIC
CRIMINOLOGIC
CRIMINOLOGICAL
CRIMINOLOGIES
CRIMINOLOGIST
CRIMINOLOGISTS
CRIMINOLOGY
CRIMINOUSNESS
CRIMINOUSNESSES
CRIMSONING
CRIMSONNESS
CRIMSONNESSES
CRINGELING
CRINGELINGS
CRINGEWORTHIER
CRINGEWORTHIEST
CRINGEWORTHY
CRINGINGLY
CRINICULTURAL
CRINIGEROUS
CRINKLEROOT
CRINKLEROOTS

C

CRINKLIEST
CRINOIDEAN
CRINOIDEANS
CRINOLETTE
CRINOLETTES
CRINOLINED
CRINOLINES
CRIPPLEWARE
CRIPPLEWARES
CRIPPLINGLY
CRIPPLINGS
CRISPATION
CRISPATIONS
CRISPATURE
CRISPATURES
CRISPBREAD
CRISPBREADS
CRISPENING
CRISPHEADS
CRISPINESS
CRISPINESSES
CRISPNESSES
CRISSCROSS
CRISSCROSSED
CRISSCROSSES
CRISSCROSSING
CRISTIFORM
CRISTOBALITE
CRISTOBALITES
CRITERIONS
CRITERIUMS
CRITHIDIAL
CRITHOMANCIES
CRITHOMANCY
CRITICALITIES
CRITICALITY
CRITICALLY
CRITICALNESS
CRITICALNESSES
CRITICASTER
CRITICASTERS
CRITICISABLE
CRITICISED
CRITICISER
CRITICISERS
CRITICISES
CRITICISING
CRITICISINGLY
CRITICISMS
CRITICIZABLE
CRITICIZED
CRITICIZER
CRITICIZERS
CRITICIZES
CRITICIZING
CRITICIZINGLY
CRITIQUING
CROAKINESS
CROAKINESSES
CROCHETERS
CROCHETING
CROCHETINGS
CROCIDOLITE
CROCIDOLITES
CROCKERIES
CROCODILES
CROCODILIAN
CROCODILIANS
CROCOISITE
CROCOISITES
CROCOSMIAS
CROISSANTS
CROKINOLES
CROOKBACKED
CROOKBACKS
CROOKEDEST
CROOKEDNESS
CROOKEDNESSES
CROOKERIES
CROOKNECKS
CROPDUSTER
CROPDUSTERS
CROPDUSTING
CROPDUSTINGS
CROQUANTES
CROQUETING
CROQUETTES
CROQUIGNOLE
CROQUIGNOLES
CROREPATIS
CROSSABILITIES
CROSSABILITY
CROSSANDRA
CROSSANDRAS
CROSSBANDED
CROSSBANDING
CROSSBANDINGS
CROSSBANDS
CROSSBARRED
CROSSBARRING
CROSSBARRINGS
CROSSBEAMS
CROSSBEARER
CROSSBEARERS
CROSSBENCH
CROSSBENCHER
CROSSBENCHERS
CROSSBENCHES
CROSSBILLS
CROSSBIRTH
CROSSBIRTHS
CROSSBITES
CROSSBITING
CROSSBITTEN
CROSSBONES
CROSSBOWER
CROSSBOWERS
CROSSBOWMAN
CROSSBOWMEN
CROSSBREDS
CROSSBREED
CROSSBREEDING
CROSSBREEDINGS
CROSSBREEDS
CROSSBUCKS
CROSSCHECK
CROSSCHECKED
CROSSCHECKING
CROSSCHECKS
CROSSCLAIM
CROSSCLAIMS
CROSSCOURT
CROSSCURRENT
CROSSCURRENTS
CROSSCUTTING
CROSSCUTTINGS
CROSSETTES
CROSSFALLS
CROSSFIELD
CROSSFIRES
CROSSFISHES
CROSSHAIRS
CROSSHATCH
CROSSHATCHED
CROSSHATCHES
CROSSHATCHING
CROSSHATCHINGS
CROSSHEADS
CROSSJACKS
CROSSLIGHT
CROSSLIGHTS
CROSSLINGUISTIC
CROSSNESSES
CROSSOPTERYGIAN
CROSSOVERS
CROSSPATCH
CROSSPATCHES
CROSSPIECE
CROSSPIECES
CROSSROADS
CROSSRUFFED
CROSSRUFFING
CROSSRUFFS
CROSSTALKS
CROSSTREES
CROSSWALKS
CROSSWINDS
CROSSWIRES
CROSSWORDS
CROSSWORTS
CROTALARIA
CROTALARIAS
CROTALISMS
CROTCHETED
CROTCHETEER
CROTCHETEERS
CROTCHETIER
CROTCHETIEST
CROTCHETINESS
CROTCHETINESSES
CROTONALDEHYDE
CROTONALDEHYDES
CROTONBUGS
CROUPINESS
CROUPINESSES
CROUSTADES
CROWBARRED
CROWBARRING
CROWBERRIES
CROWDEDNESS
CROWDEDNESSES
CROWDFUNDED
CROWDFUNDING
CROWDFUNDINGS
CROWDFUNDS
CROWDSOURCE
CROWDSOURCED
CROWDSOURCES
CROWDSOURCING
CROWDSOURCINGS
CROWKEEPER
CROWKEEPERS
CROWNLANDS
CROWNPIECE
CROWNPIECES
CROWNWORKS
CROWSTEPPED
CRUCIATELY
CRUCIFEROUS
CRUCIFIERS
CRUCIFIXES
CRUCIFIXION
CRUCIFIXIONS
CRUCIFORMLY
CRUCIFORMS
CRUCIFYING
CRUCIVERBAL
CRUCIVERBALISM
CRUCIVERBALISMS
CRUCIVERBALIST
CRUCIVERBALISTS
CRUDENESSES
CRUELNESSES
CRUISERWEIGHT
CRUISERWEIGHTS
CRUISEWAYS
CRUISEWEAR
CRUISEWEARS
CRUMBCLOTH
CRUMBCLOTHS
CRUMBLIEST
CRUMBLINESS
CRUMBLINESSES
CRUMBLINGS
CRUMMINESS
CRUMMINESSES
CRUMPLIEST
CRUMPLINGS
CRUNCHABLE
CRUNCHIEST

CRUNCHINESS
CRUNCHINESSES
CRUNCHINGS
CRUSHABILITIES
CRUSHABILITY
CRUSHINGLY
CRUSHPROOF
CRUSTACEAN
CRUSTACEANS
CRUSTACEOUS
CRUSTATION
CRUSTATIONS
CRUSTINESS
CRUSTINESSES
CRUTCHINGS
CRYMOTHERAPIES
CRYMOTHERAPY
CRYOBIOLOGICAL
CRYOBIOLOGIES
CRYOBIOLOGIST
CRYOBIOLOGISTS
CRYOBIOLOGY
CRYOCABLES
CRYOCONITE
CRYOCONITES
CRYOGENICALLY
CRYOGENICS
CRYOGENIES
CRYOGLOBULIN
CRYOGLOBULINS
CRYOHYDRATE
CRYOHYDRATES
CRYOMETERS
CRYOMETRIC
CRYOMETRIES
CRYONICALLY
CRYOPHILIC
CRYOPHORUS
CRYOPHORUSES
CRYOPHYSICS
CRYOPHYTES
CRYOPLANKTON
CRYOPLANKTONS
CRYOPRECIPITATE
CRYOPRESERVE
CRYOPRESERVED
CRYOPRESERVES
CRYOPRESERVING
CRYOPROBES
CRYOPROTECTANT
CRYOPROTECTANTS
CRYOPROTECTIVE
CRYOSCOPES
CRYOSCOPIC
CRYOSCOPIES
CRYOSTATIC
CRYOSURGEON
CRYOSURGEONS
CRYOSURGERIES
CRYOSURGERY
CRYOSURGICAL
CRYOTHERAPIES
CRYOTHERAPY
CRYPTAESTHESIA
CRYPTAESTHESIAS
CRYPTAESTHETIC
CRYPTANALYSES
CRYPTANALYSIS
CRYPTANALYST
CRYPTANALYSTS
CRYPTANALYTIC
CRYPTANALYTICAL
CRYPTARITHM
CRYPTARITHMS
CRYPTESTHESIA
CRYPTESTHESIAS
CRYPTESTHETIC
CRYPTICALLY
CRYPTOBIONT
CRYPTOBIONTS
CRYPTOBIOSES
CRYPTOBIOSIS
CRYPTOCLASTIC
CRYPTOCOCCAL
CRYPTOCOCCI
CRYPTOCOCCOSES
CRYPTOCOCCOSIS
CRYPTOCOCCUS
CRYPTOCURRENCY
CRYPTOGAMIAN
CRYPTOGAMIC
CRYPTOGAMIES
CRYPTOGAMIST
CRYPTOGAMISTS
CRYPTOGAMOUS
CRYPTOGAMS
CRYPTOGAMY
CRYPTOGENIC
CRYPTOGRAM
CRYPTOGRAMS
CRYPTOGRAPH
CRYPTOGRAPHER
CRYPTOGRAPHERS
CRYPTOGRAPHIC
CRYPTOGRAPHICAL
CRYPTOGRAPHIES
CRYPTOGRAPHIST
CRYPTOGRAPHISTS
CRYPTOGRAPHS
CRYPTOGRAPHY
CRYPTOLOGIC
CRYPTOLOGICAL
CRYPTOLOGIES
CRYPTOLOGIST
CRYPTOLOGISTS
CRYPTOLOGY
CRYPTOMERIA
CRYPTOMERIAS
CRYPTOMETER
CRYPTOMETERS
CRYPTOMNESIA
CRYPTOMNESIAS
CRYPTOMNESIC
CRYPTONYMOUS
CRYPTONYMS
CRYPTOPHYTE
CRYPTOPHYTES
CRYPTOPHYTIC
CRYPTORCHID
CRYPTORCHIDISM
CRYPTORCHIDISMS
CRYPTORCHIDS
CRYPTORCHISM
CRYPTORCHISMS
CRYPTOSPORIDIA
CRYPTOSPORIDIUM
CRYPTOZOIC
CRYPTOZOITE
CRYPTOZOITES
CRYPTOZOOLOGIES
CRYPTOZOOLOGIST
CRYPTOZOOLOGY
CRYSTALISABLE
CRYSTALISATION
CRYSTALISATIONS
CRYSTALISE
CRYSTALISED
CRYSTALISER
CRYSTALISERS
CRYSTALISES
CRYSTALISING
CRYSTALIZABLE
CRYSTALIZATION
CRYSTALIZATIONS
CRYSTALIZE
CRYSTALIZED
CRYSTALIZER
CRYSTALIZERS
CRYSTALIZES
CRYSTALIZING
CRYSTALLINE
CRYSTALLINES
CRYSTALLINITIES
CRYSTALLINITY
CRYSTALLISABLE
CRYSTALLISATION
CRYSTALLISE
CRYSTALLISED
CRYSTALLISER
CRYSTALLISERS
CRYSTALLISES
CRYSTALLISING
CRYSTALLITE
CRYSTALLITES
CRYSTALLITIC
CRYSTALLITIS
CRYSTALLITISES
CRYSTALLIZABLE
CRYSTALLIZATION
CRYSTALLIZE
CRYSTALLIZED
CRYSTALLIZER
CRYSTALLIZERS
CRYSTALLIZES
CRYSTALLIZING
CRYSTALLOGRAPHY
CRYSTALLOID
CRYSTALLOIDAL
CRYSTALLOIDS
CRYSTALLOMANCY
CTENOPHORAN
CTENOPHORANS
CTENOPHORE
CTENOPHORES
CUADRILLAS
CUBANELLES
CUBBYHOLES
CUBICALNESS
CUBICALNESSES
CUBICITIES
CUBISTICALLY
CUCKOLDING
CUCKOLDISE
CUCKOLDISED
CUCKOLDISES
CUCKOLDISING
CUCKOLDIZE
CUCKOLDIZED
CUCKOLDIZES
CUCKOLDIZING
CUCKOLDOMS
CUCKOLDRIES
CUCKOOFLOWER
CUCKOOFLOWERS
CUCKOOPINT
CUCKOOPINTS
CUCULIFORM
CUCULLATED
CUCULLATELY
CUCUMIFORM
CUCURBITACEOUS
CUCURBITAL
CUDDLESOME
CUDGELINGS
CUDGELLERS
CUDGELLING
CUDGELLINGS
CUFFUFFLES
CUIRASSIER
CUIRASSIERS
CUIRASSING
CUISINARTS
CUISINIERS
CULICIFORM
CULINARIAN
CULINARIANS
CULINARILY
CULLENDERS
CULMIFEROUS
CULMINATED

CULMINATES
CULMINATING
CULMINATION
CULMINATIONS
CULPABILITIES
CULPABILITY
CULPABLENESS
CULPABLENESSES
CULTISHNESS
CULTISHNESSES
CULTIVABILITIES
CULTIVABILITY
CULTIVABLE
CULTIVATABLE
CULTIVATED
CULTIVATES
CULTIVATING
CULTIVATION
CULTIVATIONS
CULTIVATOR
CULTIVATORS
CULTRIFORM
CULTURABLE
CULTURALLY
CULTURELESS
CULTURISTS
CULVERINEER
CULVERINEERS
CULVERTAGE
CULVERTAGES
CULVERTAILED
CULVERTING
CUMBERBUND
CUMBERBUNDS
CUMBERLESS
CUMBERMENT
CUMBERMENTS
CUMBERSOME
CUMBERSOMELY
CUMBERSOMENESS
CUMBRANCES
CUMBROUSLY
CUMBROUSNESS
CUMBROUSNESSES
CUMMERBUND
CUMMERBUNDS
CUMMINGTONITE
CUMMINGTONITES
CUMULATELY
CUMULATING
CUMULATION
CUMULATIONS
CUMULATIVE
CUMULATIVELY
CUMULATIVENESS
CUMULIFORM
CUMULOCIRRI
CUMULOCIRRUS
CUMULONIMBI
CUMULONIMBUS
CUMULONIMBUSES
CUMULOSTRATI
CUMULOSTRATUS
CUNCTATION
CUNCTATIONS
CUNCTATIOUS
CUNCTATIVE
CUNCTATORS
CUNCTATORY
CUNEIFORMS
CUNNILINCTUS
CUNNILINCTUSES
CUNNILINGUS
CUNNILINGUSES
CUNNINGEST
CUNNINGNESS
CUNNINGNESSES
CUPBEARERS
CUPBOARDED
CUPBOARDING
CUPELLATION
CUPELLATIONS
CUPFERRONS
CUPHOLDERS
CUPIDINOUS
CUPIDITIES
CUPRAMMONIUM
CUPRAMMONIUMS
CUPRESSUSES
CUPRIFEROUS
CUPRONICKEL
CUPRONICKELS
CUPULIFEROUS
CURABILITIES
CURABILITY
CURABLENESS
CURABLENESSES
CURANDERAS
CURANDEROS
CURARISATION
CURARISATIONS
CURARISING
CURARIZATION
CURARIZATIONS
CURARIZING
CURATESHIP
CURATESHIPS
CURATIVELY
CURATIVENESS
CURATIVENESSES
CURATORIAL
CURATORSHIP
CURATORSHIPS
CURATRIXES
CURBSTONES
CURCUMINES
CURDINESSES
CURETTAGES
CURETTEMENT
CURETTEMENTS
CURFUFFLED
CURFUFFLES
CURFUFFLING
CURIALISMS
CURIALISTIC
CURIALISTS
CURIETHERAPIES
CURIETHERAPY
CURIOSITIES
CURIOUSEST
CURIOUSNESS
CURIOUSNESSES
CURLICUING
CURLIEWURLIE
CURLIEWURLIES
CURLINESSES
CURLPAPERS
CURMUDGEON
CURMUDGEONLIER
CURMUDGEONLIEST
CURMUDGEONLY
CURMUDGEONS
CURMURRING
CURMURRINGS
CURNAPTIOUS
CURRAJONGS
CURRANTIER
CURRANTIEST
CURRAWONGS
CURREJONGS
CURRENCIES
CURRENTNESS
CURRENTNESSES
CURRICULAR
CURRICULUM
CURRICULUMS
CURRIERIES
CURRIJONGS
CURRISHNESS
CURRISHNESSES
CURRYCOMBED
CURRYCOMBING
CURRYCOMBS
CURSEDNESS
CURSEDNESSES
CURSELARIE
CURSIVENESS
CURSIVENESSES
CURSORINESS
CURSORINESSES
CURSTNESSES
CURTAILERS
CURTAILING
CURTAILMENT
CURTAILMENTS
CURTAINING
CURTAINLESS
CURTALAXES
CURTATIONS
CURTILAGES
CURTNESSES
CURTSEYING
CURVACEOUS
CURVACEOUSLY
CURVACEOUSNESS
CURVACIOUS
CURVACIOUSLY
CURVACIOUSNESS
CURVATIONS
CURVATURES
CURVEBALLED
CURVEBALLING
CURVEBALLS
CURVEDNESS
CURVEDNESSES
CURVETTING
CURVICAUDATE
CURVICOSTATE
CURVIFOLIATE
CURVILINEAL
CURVILINEALLY
CURVILINEAR
CURVILINEARITY
CURVILINEARLY
CURVINESSES
CURVIROSTRAL
CUSHINESSES
CUSHIONETS
CUSHIONIER
CUSHIONIEST
CUSHIONING
CUSHIONINGS
CUSHIONLESS
CUSPIDATED
CUSPIDATION
CUSPIDATIONS
CUSPIDORES
CUSSEDNESS
CUSSEDNESSES
CUSTARDIER
CUSTARDIEST
CUSTODIANS
CUSTODIANSHIP
CUSTODIANSHIPS
CUSTODIERS
CUSTOMABLE
CUSTOMARIES
CUSTOMARILY
CUSTOMARINESS
CUSTOMARINESSES
CUSTOMHOUSE
CUSTOMHOUSES
CUSTOMISATION
CUSTOMISATIONS
CUSTOMISED
CUSTOMISER
CUSTOMISERS
CUSTOMISES
CUSTOMISING
CUSTOMIZATION

CUSTOMIZATIONS
CUSTOMIZED
CUSTOMIZER
CUSTOMIZERS
CUSTOMIZES
CUSTOMIZING
CUSTOMSHOUSE
CUSTOMSHOUSES
CUSTUMARIES
CUTABILITIES
CUTABILITY
CUTANEOUSLY
CUTCHERIES
CUTCHERRIES
CUTENESSES
CUTGRASSES
CUTINISATION
CUTINISATIONS
CUTINISING
CUTINIZATION
CUTINIZATIONS
CUTINIZING
CUTTHROATS
CUTTLEBONE
CUTTLEBONES
CUTTLEFISH
CUTTLEFISHES
CYANAMIDES
CYANIDATION
CYANIDATIONS
CYANIDINGS
CYANOACETYLENE
CYANOACETYLENES
CYANOACRYLATE
CYANOACRYLATES
CYANOBACTERIA
CYANOBACTERIUM
CYANOCOBALAMIN
CYANOCOBALAMINE
CYANOCOBALAMINS
CYANOETHYLATE
CYANOETHYLATED
CYANOETHYLATES
CYANOETHYLATING
CYANOETHYLATION
CYANOGENAMIDE
CYANOGENAMIDES
CYANOGENESES
CYANOGENESIS
CYANOGENETIC
CYANOGENIC
CYANOHYDRIN
CYANOHYDRINS
CYANOMETER
CYANOMETERS
CYANOPHYTE
CYANOPHYTES
CYANOTYPES
CYANURATES
CYATHIFORM
CYBERATHLETE
CYBERATHLETES
CYBERATHLETICS
CYBERATTACK
CYBERATTACKS
CYBERBULLIES
CYBERBULLY
CYBERBULLYING
CYBERBULLYINGS
CYBERCAFES
CYBERCASTS
CYBERCHONDRIA
CYBERCHONDRIAC
CYBERCHONDRIACS
CYBERCHONDRIAS
CYBERCRIME
CYBERCRIMES
CYBERCRIMINAL
CYBERCRIMINALS
CYBERNATED
CYBERNATES
CYBERNATING
CYBERNATION
CYBERNATIONS
CYBERNAUTS
CYBERNETIC
CYBERNETICAL
CYBERNETICALLY
CYBERNETICIAN
CYBERNETICIANS
CYBERNETICIST
CYBERNETICISTS
CYBERNETICS
CYBERPHOBIA
CYBERPHOBIAS
CYBERPHOBIC
CYBERPORNS
CYBERPUNKS
CYBERSECURITIES
CYBERSECURITY
CYBERSEXES
CYBERSPACE
CYBERSPACES
CYBERSQUATTER
CYBERSQUATTERS
CYBERSQUATTING
CYBERSQUATTINGS
CYBERSTALKER
CYBERSTALKERS
CYBERSTALKING
CYBERSTALKINGS
CYBERTERRORISM
CYBERTERRORISMS
CYBERTERRORIST
CYBERTERRORISTS
CYBRARIANS
CYCADACEOUS
CYCADEOIDS
CYCADOPHYTE
CYCADOPHYTES
CYCLAMATES
CYCLANDELATE
CYCLANDELATES
CYCLANTHACEOUS
CYCLAZOCINE
CYCLAZOCINES
CYCLEPATHS
CYCLICALITIES
CYCLICALITY
CYCLICALLY
CYCLICISMS
CYCLICITIES
CYCLISATION
CYCLISATIONS
CYCLIZATION
CYCLIZATIONS
CYCLIZINES
CYCLOADDITION
CYCLOADDITIONS
CYCLOALIPHATIC
CYCLOALKANE
CYCLOALKANES
CYCLOBARBITONE
CYCLOBARBITONES
CYCLODEXTRIN
CYCLODEXTRINS
CYCLODIALYSES
CYCLODIALYSIS
CYCLODIENE
CYCLODIENES
CYCLOGENESES
CYCLOGENESIS
CYCLOGIROS
CYCLOGRAPH
CYCLOGRAPHIC
CYCLOGRAPHS
CYCLOHEXANE
CYCLOHEXANES
CYCLOHEXANONE
CYCLOHEXANONES
CYCLOHEXIMIDE
CYCLOHEXIMIDES
CYCLOHEXYLAMINE
CYCLOIDALLY
CYCLOIDIAN
CYCLOIDIANS
CYCLOLITHS
CYCLOMETER
CYCLOMETERS
CYCLOMETRIES
CYCLOMETRY
CYCLONICAL
CYCLONICALLY
CYCLONITES
CYCLOOLEFIN
CYCLOOLEFINIC
CYCLOOLEFINS
CYCLOPAEDIA
CYCLOPAEDIAS
CYCLOPAEDIC
CYCLOPAEDIST
CYCLOPAEDISTS
CYCLOPARAFFIN
CYCLOPARAFFINS
CYCLOPEDIA
CYCLOPEDIAS
CYCLOPEDIC
CYCLOPEDIST
CYCLOPEDISTS
CYCLOPENTADIENE
CYCLOPENTANE
CYCLOPENTANES
CYCLOPENTOLATE
CYCLOPENTOLATES
CYCLOPLEGIA
CYCLOPLEGIAS
CYCLOPLEGIC
CYCLOPROPANE
CYCLOPROPANES
CYCLORAMAS
CYCLORAMIC
CYCLOSERINE
CYCLOSERINES
CYCLOSPERMOUS
CYCLOSPORIN
CYCLOSPORINE
CYCLOSPORINES
CYCLOSPORINS
CYCLOSTOMATE
CYCLOSTOMATOUS
CYCLOSTOME
CYCLOSTOMES
CYCLOSTOMOUS
CYCLOSTYLE
CYCLOSTYLED
CYCLOSTYLES
CYCLOSTYLING
CYCLOTHYME
CYCLOTHYMES
CYCLOTHYMIA
CYCLOTHYMIAC
CYCLOTHYMIACS
CYCLOTHYMIAS
CYCLOTHYMIC
CYCLOTHYMICS
CYCLOTOMIC
CYCLOTRONS
CYLINDERED
CYLINDERING
CYLINDRACEOUS
CYLINDRICAL
CYLINDRICALITY
CYLINDRICALLY
CYLINDRICALNESS
CYLINDRICITIES
CYLINDRICITY
CYLINDRIFORM
CYLINDRITE
CYLINDRITES
CYLINDROID

C

CYLINDROIDS
CYMAGRAPHS
CYMBALEERS
CYMBALISTS
CYMBIDIUMS
CYMIFEROUS
CYMOGRAPHIC
CYMOGRAPHS
CYMOPHANES
CYMOPHANOUS
CYMOTRICHIES
CYMOTRICHOUS
CYMOTRICHY
CYNGHANEDD
CYNGHANEDDS
CYNICALNESS
CYNICALNESSES
CYNOMOLGUS
CYNOMOLGUSES
CYNOPHILIA
CYNOPHILIAS
CYNOPHILIST
CYNOPHILISTS
CYNOPHOBIA
CYNOPHOBIAS
CYNOPODOUS
CYPERACEOUS
CYPRINODONT
CYPRINODONTS
CYPRINOIDS
CYPRIPEDIA
CYPRIPEDIUM
CYPRIPEDIUMS
CYPROHEPTADINE
CYPROHEPTADINES
CYPROTERONE
CYPROTERONES
CYSTEAMINE
CYSTEAMINES
CYSTECTOMIES
CYSTECTOMY
CYSTICERCI
CYSTICERCOID
CYSTICERCOIDS
CYSTICERCOSES
CYSTICERCOSIS
CYSTICERCUS
CYSTIDEANS
CYSTINOSES
CYSTINOSIS
CYSTINURIA
CYSTINURIAS
CYSTITIDES
CYSTITISES
CYSTOCARPIC
CYSTOCARPS
CYSTOCELES
CYSTOGENOUS
CYSTOGRAPHIES
CYSTOGRAPHY
CYSTOLITHIASES
CYSTOLITHIASIS
CYSTOLITHS
CYSTOSCOPE
CYSTOSCOPES
CYSTOSCOPIC
CYSTOSCOPIES
CYSTOSCOPY
CYSTOSTOMIES
CYSTOSTOMY
CYSTOTOMIES
CYTOCHALASIN
CYTOCHALASINS
CYTOCHEMICAL
CYTOCHEMISTRIES
CYTOCHEMISTRY
CYTOCHROME
CYTOCHROMES
CYTODIAGNOSES
CYTODIAGNOSIS
CYTOGENESES
CYTOGENESIS
CYTOGENETIC
CYTOGENETICAL
CYTOGENETICALLY
CYTOGENETICIST
CYTOGENETICISTS
CYTOGENETICS
CYTOGENIES
CYTOKINESES
CYTOKINESIS
CYTOKINETIC
CYTOKININS
CYTOLOGICAL
CYTOLOGICALLY
CYTOLOGIES
CYTOLOGIST
CYTOLOGISTS
CYTOLYSINS
CYTOMEGALIC
CYTOMEGALOVIRUS
CYTOMEMBRANE
CYTOMEMBRANES
CYTOMETERS
CYTOMETRIC
CYTOMETRIES
CYTOPATHIC
CYTOPATHIES
CYTOPATHOGENIC
CYTOPATHOLOGIES
CYTOPATHOLOGY
CYTOPENIAS
CYTOPHILIC
CYTOPHOTOMETRIC
CYTOPHOTOMETRY
CYTOPLASMIC
CYTOPLASMICALLY
CYTOPLASMS
CYTOPLASTIC
CYTOPLASTS
CYTOSKELETAL
CYTOSKELETON
CYTOSKELETONS
CYTOSTATIC
CYTOSTATICALLY
CYTOSTATICS
CYTOTAXONOMIC
CYTOTAXONOMIES
CYTOTAXONOMIST
CYTOTAXONOMISTS
CYTOTAXONOMY
CYTOTECHNOLOGY
CYTOTOXICITIES
CYTOTOXICITY
CYTOTOXINS
CZAREVICHES
CZAREVITCH
CZAREVITCHES

D

DABBLINGLY
DACHSHUNDS
DACOITAGES
DACQUOISES
DACTYLICALLY
DACTYLIOGRAPHY
DACTYLIOLOGIES
DACTYLIOLOGY
DACTYLIOMANCIES
DACTYLIOMANCY
DACTYLISTS
DACTYLOGRAM
DACTYLOGRAMS
DACTYLOGRAPHER
DACTYLOGRAPHERS
DACTYLOGRAPHIC
DACTYLOGRAPHIES
DACTYLOGRAPHY
DACTYLOLOGIES
DACTYLOLOGY
DACTYLOSCOPIES
DACTYLOSCOPY
DAFFADOWNDILLY
DAFFINESSES
DAFFODILLIES
DAFFODILLY
DAFTNESSES
DAGGERBOARD
DAGGERBOARDS
DAGGERLIKE
DAGUERREAN
DAGUERREOTYPE
DAGUERREOTYPED
DAGUERREOTYPER
DAGUERREOTYPERS
DAGUERREOTYPES
DAGUERREOTYPIES
DAGUERREOTYPING
DAGUERREOTYPIST
DAGUERREOTYPY
DAHABEEAHS
DAHABEEYAH
DAHABEEYAHS
DAHABIYAHS
DAHABIYEHS
DAILINESSES
DAILYNESSES
DAINTINESS
DAINTINESSES
DAIRYMAIDS
DAISYWHEEL
DAISYWHEELS
DALLIANCES
DALMATIANS
DALTONIANS
DALTONISMS
DAMAGEABILITIES
DAMAGEABILITY
DAMAGEABLE
DAMAGINGLY
DAMASCEENE
DAMASCEENED
DAMASCEENES
DAMASCEENING
DAMASCENED
DAMASCENES
DAMASCENING
DAMASCENINGS
DAMASKEENED
DAMASKEENING
DAMASKEENS
DAMASKINED
DAMASKINING
DAMASQUINED
DAMASQUINING
DAMASQUINS
DAMINOZIDE
DAMINOZIDES
DAMNABILITIES
DAMNABILITY
DAMNABLENESS
DAMNABLENESSES
DAMNATIONS
DAMNEDESTS
DAMNIFICATION
DAMNIFICATIONS
DAMNIFYING
DAMOISELLE
DAMOISELLES
DAMPCOURSE
DAMPCOURSES
DAMPISHNESS
DAMPISHNESSES
DAMPNESSES
DAMSELFISH
DAMSELFISHES
DAMSELFLIES
DANCECORES
DANCEHALLS
DANCEWEARS
DANDELIONS
DANDIFICATION
DANDIFICATIONS
DANDIFYING
DANDIPRATS
DANDRUFFIER
DANDRUFFIEST
DANDYFUNKS
DANDYISHLY
DANDYPRATS
DANGERLESS
DANGEROUSLY
DANGEROUSNESS
DANGEROUSNESSES
DANGLINGLY
DANKNESSES
DANNEBROGS
DANTHONIAS
DAPPERLING
DAPPERLINGS
DAPPERNESS
DAPPERNESSES
DAREDEVILRIES
DAREDEVILRY
DAREDEVILS
DAREDEVILTRIES
DAREDEVILTRY
DARINGNESS
DARINGNESSES
DARKNESSES
DARLINGNESS
DARLINGNESSES
DARMSTADTIUM
DARMSTADTIUMS
DARNATIONS
DARNEDESTS
DARRAIGNED
DARRAIGNES
DARRAIGNING
DARRAIGNMENT
DARRAIGNMENTS
DARRAINING
DARRAYNING
DARTBOARDS
DARTITISES
DASHBOARDS
DASHLIGHTS
DASTARDIES
DASTARDLIER
DASTARDLIEST
DASTARDLINESS
DASTARDLINESSES
DASTARDNESS
DASTARDNESSES
DASYMETERS
DASYPAEDAL
DASYPHYLLOUS
DATABASING
DATABUSSES
DATAGLOVES
DATAMATION
DATAMATIONS
DATAVEILLANCE
DATAVEILLANCES
DATEDNESSES
DATELINING
DAUGHTERBOARD
DAUGHTERBOARDS
DAUGHTERHOOD
DAUGHTERHOODS
DAUGHTERLESS
DAUGHTERLIER
DAUGHTERLIEST
DAUGHTERLINESS
DAUGHTERLING
DAUGHTERLINGS
DAUGHTERLY
DAUNDERING
DAUNOMYCIN
DAUNOMYCINS
DAUNORUBICIN
DAUNORUBICINS
DAUNTINGLY
DAUNTLESSLY
DAUNTLESSNESS
DAUNTLESSNESSES
DAUNTONING
DAUPHINESS
DAUPHINESSES
DAVENPORTS
DAWDLINGLY
DAWSONITES
DAYCATIONS
DAYCENTRES
DAYDREAMED
DAYDREAMER
DAYDREAMERS
DAYDREAMIER
DAYDREAMIEST
DAYDREAMING
DAYDREAMINGS
DAYDREAMLIKE
DAYFLOWERS
DAYLIGHTED
DAYLIGHTING
DAYLIGHTINGS
DAYSAILERS
DAYSAILING
DAYSAILORS
DAYSPRINGS

D

DAYWORKERS
DAZEDNESSES
DAZZLEMENT
DAZZLEMENTS
DAZZLINGLY
DEACIDIFICATION
DEACIDIFIED
DEACIDIFIES
DEACIDIFYING
DEACONESSES
DEACONHOOD
DEACONHOODS
DEACONRIES
DEACONSHIP
DEACONSHIPS
DEACTIVATE
DEACTIVATED
DEACTIVATES
DEACTIVATING
DEACTIVATION
DEACTIVATIONS
DEACTIVATOR
DEACTIVATORS
DEADENINGLY
DEADENINGS
DEADHEADED
DEADHEADING
DEADHOUSES
DEADLIFTED
DEADLIFTING
DEADLIGHTS
DEADLINESS
DEADLINESSES
DEADLINING
DEADLOCKED
DEADLOCKING
DEADNESSES
DEADPANNED
DEADPANNER
DEADPANNERS
DEADPANNING
DEADSTOCKS
DEADSTROKE
DEADWATERS
DEADWEIGHT
DEADWEIGHTS
DEAERATING
DEAERATION
DEAERATIONS
DEAERATORS
DEAFENINGLY
DEAFENINGS
DEAFNESSES
DEALATIONS
DEALBATION
DEALBATIONS
DEALBREAKER
DEALBREAKERS
DEALERSHIP
DEALERSHIPS
DEALFISHES
DEALIGNING
DEALMAKERS
DEAMBULATORIES
DEAMBULATORY
DEAMINASES
DEAMINATED
DEAMINATES
DEAMINATING
DEAMINATION
DEAMINATIONS
DEAMINISATION
DEAMINISATIONS
DEAMINISED
DEAMINISES
DEAMINISING
DEAMINIZATION
DEAMINIZATIONS
DEAMINIZED
DEAMINIZES
DEAMINIZING
DEARBOUGHT
DEARNESSES
DEARTICULATE
DEARTICULATED
DEARTICULATES
DEARTICULATING
DEASPIRATE
DEASPIRATED
DEASPIRATES
DEASPIRATING
DEASPIRATION
DEASPIRATIONS
DEATHBLOWS
DEATHLESSLY
DEATHLESSNESS
DEATHLESSNESSES
DEATHLIEST
DEATHLINESS
DEATHLINESSES
DEATHTRAPS
DEATHWARDS
DEATHWATCH
DEATHWATCHES
DEATTRIBUTE
DEATTRIBUTED
DEATTRIBUTES
DEATTRIBUTING
DEBAGGINGS
DEBARCATION
DEBARCATIONS
DEBARKATION
DEBARKATIONS
DEBARMENTS
DEBARRASSED
DEBARRASSES
DEBARRASSING
DEBASEDNESS
DEBASEDNESSES
DEBASEMENT
DEBASEMENTS
DEBASINGLY
DEBATEABLE
DEBATEMENT
DEBATEMENTS
DEBATINGLY
DEBAUCHEDLY
DEBAUCHEDNESS
DEBAUCHEDNESSES
DEBAUCHEES
DEBAUCHERIES
DEBAUCHERS
DEBAUCHERY
DEBAUCHING
DEBAUCHMENT
DEBAUCHMENTS
DEBEARDING
DEBENTURED
DEBENTURES
DEBILITATE
DEBILITATED
DEBILITATES
DEBILITATING
DEBILITATION
DEBILITATIONS
DEBILITATIVE
DEBILITIES
DEBONAIRLY
DEBONAIRNESS
DEBONAIRNESSES
DEBONNAIRE
DEBOUCHING
DEBOUCHMENT
DEBOUCHMENTS
DEBOUCHURE
DEBOUCHURES
DEBRIDEMENT
DEBRIDEMENTS
DEBRIEFERS
DEBRIEFING
DEBRIEFINGS
DEBRUISING
DEBUGGINGS
DEBUTANTES
DECACHORDS
DECADENCES
DECADENCIES
DECADENTLY
DECAFFEINATE
DECAFFEINATED
DECAFFEINATES
DECAFFEINATING
DECAGONALLY
DECAGRAMME
DECAGRAMMES
DECAGYNIAN
DECAGYNOUS
DECAHEDRAL
DECAHEDRON
DECAHEDRONS
DECAHYDRATE
DECAHYDRATES
DECALCIFICATION
DECALCIFIED
DECALCIFIER
DECALCIFIERS
DECALCIFIES
DECALCIFYING
DECALCOMANIA
DECALCOMANIAS
DECALESCENCE
DECALESCENCES
DECALESCENT
DECALITERS
DECALITRES
DECALOGIST
DECALOGISTS
DECALOGUES
DECAMERONIC
DECAMEROUS
DECAMETERS
DECAMETHONIUM
DECAMETHONIUMS
DECAMETRES
DECAMETRIC
DECAMPMENT
DECAMPMENTS
DECANDRIAN
DECANDROUS
DECANEDIOIC
DECANICALLY
DECANTATED
DECANTATES
DECANTATING
DECANTATION
DECANTATIONS
DECAPITALISE
DECAPITALISED
DECAPITALISES
DECAPITALISING
DECAPITALIZE
DECAPITALIZED
DECAPITALIZES
DECAPITALIZING
DECAPITATE
DECAPITATED
DECAPITATES
DECAPITATING
DECAPITATION
DECAPITATIONS
DECAPITATOR
DECAPITATORS
DECAPODANS
DECAPODOUS
DECAPSULATE
DECAPSULATED
DECAPSULATES
DECAPSULATING
DECAPSULATION
DECAPSULATIONS

DECARBONATE
DECARBONATED
DECARBONATES
DECARBONATING
DECARBONATION
DECARBONATIONS
DECARBONATOR
DECARBONATORS
DECARBONISATION
DECARBONISE
DECARBONISED
DECARBONISER
DECARBONISERS
DECARBONISES
DECARBONISING
DECARBONIZATION
DECARBONIZE
DECARBONIZED
DECARBONIZER
DECARBONIZERS
DECARBONIZES
DECARBONIZING
DECARBOXYLASE
DECARBOXYLASES
DECARBOXYLATE
DECARBOXYLATED
DECARBOXYLATES
DECARBOXYLATING
DECARBOXYLATION
DECARBURATION
DECARBURATIONS
DECARBURISATION
DECARBURISE
DECARBURISED
DECARBURISES
DECARBURISING
DECARBURIZATION
DECARBURIZE
DECARBURIZED
DECARBURIZES
DECARBURIZING
DECARTELISE
DECARTELISED
DECARTELISES
DECARTELISING
DECARTELIZE
DECARTELIZED
DECARTELIZES
DECARTELIZING
DECASTERES
DECASTICHS
DECASTYLES
DECASUALISATION
DECASUALISE
DECASUALISED
DECASUALISES
DECASUALISING
DECASUALIZATION
DECASUALIZE
DECASUALIZED
DECASUALIZES
DECASUALIZING
DECASYLLABIC
DECASYLLABICS
DECASYLLABLE
DECASYLLABLES
DECATHLETE
DECATHLETES
DECATHLONS
DECAUDATED
DECAUDATES
DECAUDATING
DECEITFULLY
DECEITFULNESS
DECEITFULNESSES
DECEIVABILITIES
DECEIVABILITY
DECEIVABLE
DECEIVABLENESS
DECEIVABLY
DECEIVINGLY
DECEIVINGS
DECELERATE
DECELERATED
DECELERATES
DECELERATING
DECELERATION
DECELERATIONS
DECELERATOR
DECELERATORS
DECELEROMETER
DECELEROMETERS
DECELERONS
DECEMVIRAL
DECEMVIRATE
DECEMVIRATES
DECENARIES
DECENNARIES
DECENNIALLY
DECENNIALS
DECENNIUMS
DECENNOVAL
DECENTERED
DECENTERING
DECENTERINGS
DECENTNESS
DECENTNESSES
DECENTRALISE
DECENTRALISED
DECENTRALISES
DECENTRALISING
DECENTRALIST
DECENTRALISTS
DECENTRALIZE
DECENTRALIZED
DECENTRALIZES
DECENTRALIZING
DECENTRING
DECEPTIBILITIES
DECEPTIBILITY
DECEPTIBLE
DECEPTIONAL
DECEPTIONS
DECEPTIOUS
DECEPTIVELY
DECEPTIVENESS
DECEPTIVENESSES
DECEREBRATE
DECEREBRATED
DECEREBRATES
DECEREBRATING
DECEREBRATION
DECEREBRATIONS
DECEREBRISE
DECEREBRISED
DECEREBRISES
DECEREBRISING
DECEREBRIZE
DECEREBRIZED
DECEREBRIZES
DECEREBRIZING
DECERTIFICATION
DECERTIFIED
DECERTIFIES
DECERTIFYING
DECESSIONS
DECHEANCES
DECHLORINATE
DECHLORINATED
DECHLORINATES
DECHLORINATING
DECHLORINATION
DECHLORINATIONS
DECHRISTIANISE
DECHRISTIANISED
DECHRISTIANISES
DECHRISTIANIZE
DECHRISTIANIZED
DECHRISTIANIZES
DECIDABILITIES
DECIDABILITY
DECIDEDNESS
DECIDEDNESSES
DECIDUOUSLY
DECIDUOUSNESS
DECIDUOUSNESSES
DECIGRAMME
DECIGRAMMES
DECILITERS
DECILITRES
DECILLIONS
DECILLIONTH
DECILLIONTHS
DECIMALISATION
DECIMALISATIONS
DECIMALISE
DECIMALISED
DECIMALISES
DECIMALISING
DECIMALISM
DECIMALISMS
DECIMALIST
DECIMALISTS
DECIMALIZATION
DECIMALIZATIONS
DECIMALIZE
DECIMALIZED
DECIMALIZES
DECIMALIZING
DECIMATING
DECIMATION
DECIMATIONS
DECIMATORS
DECIMETERS
DECIMETRES
DECIMETRIC
DECINORMAL
DECIPHERABILITY
DECIPHERABLE
DECIPHERED
DECIPHERER
DECIPHERERS
DECIPHERING
DECIPHERMENT
DECIPHERMENTS
DECISIONAL
DECISIONED
DECISIONING
DECISIVELY
DECISIVENESS
DECISIVENESSES
DECISTERES
DECITIZENISE
DECITIZENISED
DECITIZENISES
DECITIZENISING
DECITIZENIZE
DECITIZENIZED
DECITIZENIZES
DECITIZENIZING
DECIVILISE
DECIVILISED
DECIVILISES
DECIVILISING
DECIVILIZE
DECIVILIZED
DECIVILIZES
DECIVILIZING
DECKCHAIRS
DECKHOUSES
DECLAIMANT
DECLAIMANTS
DECLAIMERS
DECLAIMING
DECLAIMINGS
DECLAMATION
DECLAMATIONS
DECLAMATORILY
DECLAMATORY
DECLARABLE

DECLARANTS
DECLARATION
DECLARATIONS
DECLARATIVE
DECLARATIVELY
DECLARATOR
DECLARATORILY
DECLARATORS
DECLARATORY
DECLAREDLY
DECLASSIFIABLE
DECLASSIFIED
DECLASSIFIES
DECLASSIFY
DECLASSIFYING
DECLASSING
DECLENSION
DECLENSIONAL
DECLENSIONALLY
DECLENSIONS
DECLINABLE
DECLINANTS
DECLINATION
DECLINATIONAL
DECLINATIONS
DECLINATOR
DECLINATORIES
DECLINATORS
DECLINATORY
DECLINATURE
DECLINATURES
DECLINISTS
DECLINOMETER
DECLINOMETERS
DECLIVITIES
DECLIVITOUS
DECLUTCHED
DECLUTCHES
DECLUTCHING
DECLUTTERED
DECLUTTERING
DECLUTTERS
DECOCTIBLE
DECOCTIONS
DECOCTURES
DECOHERENCE
DECOHERENCES
DECOHERERS
DECOLLATED
DECOLLATES
DECOLLATING
DECOLLATION
DECOLLATIONS
DECOLLATOR
DECOLLATORS
DECOLLETAGE
DECOLLETAGES
DECOLLETES
DECOLONISATION
DECOLONISATIONS
DECOLONISE
DECOLONISED
DECOLONISES
DECOLONISING
DECOLONIZATION
DECOLONIZATIONS
DECOLONIZE
DECOLONIZED
DECOLONIZES
DECOLONIZING
DECOLORANT
DECOLORANTS
DECOLORATE
DECOLORATED
DECOLORATES
DECOLORATING
DECOLORATION
DECOLORATIONS
DECOLORING
DECOLORISATION
DECOLORISATIONS
DECOLORISE
DECOLORISED
DECOLORISER
DECOLORISERS
DECOLORISES
DECOLORISING
DECOLORIZATION
DECOLORIZATIONS
DECOLORIZE
DECOLORIZED
DECOLORIZER
DECOLORIZERS
DECOLORIZES
DECOLORIZING
DECOLOURED
DECOLOURING
DECOLOURISATION
DECOLOURISE
DECOLOURISED
DECOLOURISES
DECOLOURISING
DECOLOURIZATION
DECOLOURIZE
DECOLOURIZED
DECOLOURIZES
DECOLOURIZING
DECOMMISSION
DECOMMISSIONED
DECOMMISSIONER
DECOMMISSIONERS
DECOMMISSIONING
DECOMMISSIONS
DECOMMITTED
DECOMMITTING
DECOMMUNISATION
DECOMMUNISE
DECOMMUNISED
DECOMMUNISES
DECOMMUNISING
DECOMMUNIZATION
DECOMMUNIZE
DECOMMUNIZED
DECOMMUNIZES
DECOMMUNIZING
DECOMPENSATE
DECOMPENSATED
DECOMPENSATES
DECOMPENSATING
DECOMPENSATION
DECOMPENSATIONS
DECOMPOSABILITY
DECOMPOSABLE
DECOMPOSED
DECOMPOSER
DECOMPOSERS
DECOMPOSES
DECOMPOSING
DECOMPOSITE
DECOMPOSITES
DECOMPOSITION
DECOMPOSITIONS
DECOMPOUND
DECOMPOUNDABLE
DECOMPOUNDED
DECOMPOUNDING
DECOMPOUNDS
DECOMPRESS
DECOMPRESSED
DECOMPRESSES
DECOMPRESSING
DECOMPRESSION
DECOMPRESSIONS
DECOMPRESSIVE
DECOMPRESSOR
DECOMPRESSORS
DECONCENTRATE
DECONCENTRATED
DECONCENTRATES
DECONCENTRATING
DECONCENTRATION
DECONDITION
DECONDITIONED
DECONDITIONING
DECONDITIONS
DECONGESTANT
DECONGESTANTS
DECONGESTED
DECONGESTING
DECONGESTION
DECONGESTIONS
DECONGESTIVE
DECONGESTS
DECONSECRATE
DECONSECRATED
DECONSECRATES
DECONSECRATING
DECONSECRATION
DECONSECRATIONS
DECONSTRUCT
DECONSTRUCTED
DECONSTRUCTING
DECONSTRUCTION
DECONSTRUCTIONS
DECONSTRUCTIVE
DECONSTRUCTOR
DECONSTRUCTORS
DECONSTRUCTS
DECONTAMINANT
DECONTAMINANTS
DECONTAMINATE
DECONTAMINATED
DECONTAMINATES
DECONTAMINATING
DECONTAMINATION
DECONTAMINATIVE
DECONTAMINATOR
DECONTAMINATORS
DECONTEXTUALISE
DECONTEXTUALIZE
DECONTROLLED
DECONTROLLING
DECONTROLS
DECORATING
DECORATINGS
DECORATION
DECORATIONS
DECORATIVE
DECORATIVELY
DECORATIVENESS
DECORATORS
DECOROUSLY
DECOROUSNESS
DECOROUSNESSES
DECORTICATE
DECORTICATED
DECORTICATES
DECORTICATING
DECORTICATION
DECORTICATIONS
DECORTICATOR
DECORTICATORS
DECOUPAGED
DECOUPAGES
DECOUPAGING
DECOUPLERS
DECOUPLING
DECOUPLINGS
DECRASSIFIED
DECRASSIFIES
DECRASSIFY
DECRASSIFYING
DECREASING
DECREASINGLY
DECREASINGS
DECREEABLE
DECREMENTAL
DECREMENTED
DECREMENTING
DECREMENTS

DECREPITATE
DECREPITATED
DECREPITATES
DECREPITATING
DECREPITATION
DECREPITATIONS
DECREPITLY
DECREPITNESS
DECREPITNESSES
DECREPITUDE
DECREPITUDES
DECRESCENCE
DECRESCENCES
DECRESCENDO
DECRESCENDOS
DECRESCENT
DECRETALIST
DECRETALISTS
DECRETISTS
DECRIMINALISE
DECRIMINALISED
DECRIMINALISES
DECRIMINALISING
DECRIMINALIZE
DECRIMINALIZED
DECRIMINALIZES
DECRIMINALIZING
DECROWNING
DECRUSTATION
DECRUSTATIONS
DECRYPTING
DECRYPTION
DECRYPTIONS
DECUMBENCE
DECUMBENCES
DECUMBENCIES
DECUMBENCY
DECUMBENTLY
DECUMBITURE
DECUMBITURES
DECUMULATION
DECUMULATIONS
DECURIONATE
DECURIONATES
DECURRENCIES
DECURRENCY
DECURRENTLY
DECURSIONS
DECURSIVELY
DECURVATION
DECURVATIONS
DECUSSATED
DECUSSATELY
DECUSSATES
DECUSSATING
DECUSSATION
DECUSSATIONS
DEDICATEDLY
DEDICATEES
DEDICATING
DEDICATION
DEDICATIONAL
DEDICATIONS
DEDICATIVE
DEDICATORIAL
DEDICATORS
DEDICATORY
DEDIFFERENTIATE
DEDRAMATISE
DEDRAMATISED
DEDRAMATISES
DEDRAMATISING
DEDRAMATIZE
DEDRAMATIZED
DEDRAMATIZES
DEDRAMATIZING
DEDUCEMENT
DEDUCEMENTS
DEDUCIBILITIES
DEDUCIBILITY
DEDUCIBLENESS
DEDUCIBLENESSES
DEDUCTIBILITIES
DEDUCTIBILITY
DEDUCTIBLE
DEDUCTIBLES
DEDUCTIONS
DEDUCTIVELY
DEDUPLICATE
DEDUPLICATED
DEDUPLICATES
DEDUPLICATING
DEDUPLICATION
DEDUPLICATIONS
DEEJAYINGS
DEEMSTERSHIP
DEEMSTERSHIPS
DEEPENINGS
DEEPFREEZE
DEEPFREEZES
DEEPFREEZING
DEEPFROZEN
DEEPNESSES
DEEPWATERMAN
DEEPWATERMEN
DEERBERRIES
DEERGRASSES
DEERHOUNDS
DEERSTALKER
DEERSTALKERS
DEERSTALKING
DEERSTALKINGS
DEFACEABLE
DEFACEMENT
DEFACEMENTS
DEFACINGLY
DEFAECATED
DEFAECATES
DEFAECATING
DEFAECATION
DEFAECATIONS
DEFAECATOR
DEFAECATORS
DEFALCATED
DEFALCATES
DEFALCATING
DEFALCATION
DEFALCATIONS
DEFALCATOR
DEFALCATORS
DEFAMATION
DEFAMATIONS
DEFAMATORILY
DEFAMATORY
DEFAULTERS
DEFAULTING
DEFEASANCE
DEFEASANCED
DEFEASANCES
DEFEASIBILITIES
DEFEASIBILITY
DEFEASIBLE
DEFEASIBLENESS
DEFEATISMS
DEFEATISTS
DEFEATURED
DEFEATURES
DEFEATURING
DEFECATING
DEFECATION
DEFECATIONS
DEFECATORS
DEFECTIBILITIES
DEFECTIBILITY
DEFECTIBLE
DEFECTIONIST
DEFECTIONISTS
DEFECTIONS
DEFECTIVELY
DEFECTIVENESS
DEFECTIVENESSES
DEFECTIVES
DEFEMINISATION
DEFEMINISATIONS
DEFEMINISE
DEFEMINISED
DEFEMINISES
DEFEMINISING
DEFEMINIZATION
DEFEMINIZATIONS
DEFEMINIZE
DEFEMINIZED
DEFEMINIZES
DEFEMINIZING
DEFENCELESS
DEFENCELESSLY
DEFENCELESSNESS
DEFENCEMAN
DEFENCEMEN
DEFENDABLE
DEFENDANTS
DEFENESTRATE
DEFENESTRATED
DEFENESTRATES
DEFENESTRATING
DEFENESTRATION
DEFENESTRATIONS
DEFENSATIVE
DEFENSATIVES
DEFENSELESS
DEFENSELESSLY
DEFENSELESSNESS
DEFENSEMAN
DEFENSEMEN
DEFENSIBILITIES
DEFENSIBILITY
DEFENSIBLE
DEFENSIBLENESS
DEFENSIBLY
DEFENSIVELY
DEFENSIVENESS
DEFENSIVENESSES
DEFENSIVES
DEFERENCES
DEFERENTIAL
DEFERENTIALLY
DEFERMENTS
DEFERRABLE
DEFERRABLES
DEFERVESCENCE
DEFERVESCENCES
DEFERVESCENCIES
DEFERVESCENCY
DEFEUDALISE
DEFEUDALISED
DEFEUDALISES
DEFEUDALISING
DEFEUDALIZE
DEFEUDALIZED
DEFEUDALIZES
DEFEUDALIZING
DEFIANTNESS
DEFIANTNESSES
DEFIBRILLATE
DEFIBRILLATED
DEFIBRILLATES
DEFIBRILLATING
DEFIBRILLATION
DEFIBRILLATIONS
DEFIBRILLATOR
DEFIBRILLATORS
DEFIBRINATE
DEFIBRINATED
DEFIBRINATES
DEFIBRINATING
DEFIBRINATION
DEFIBRINATIONS
DEFIBRINISE
DEFIBRINISED
DEFIBRINISES

D

DEFIBRINISING
DEFIBRINIZE
DEFIBRINIZED
DEFIBRINIZES
DEFIBRINIZING
DEFICIENCE
DEFICIENCES
DEFICIENCIES
DEFICIENCY
DEFICIENTLY
DEFICIENTNESS
DEFICIENTNESSES
DEFICIENTS
DEFILADING
DEFILEMENT
DEFILEMENTS
DEFILIATION
DEFILIATIONS
DEFINABILITIES
DEFINABILITY
DEFINEMENT
DEFINEMENTS
DEFINIENDA
DEFINIENDUM
DEFINIENTIA
DEFINITELY
DEFINITENESS
DEFINITENESSES
DEFINITION
DEFINITIONAL
DEFINITIONS
DEFINITISE
DEFINITISED
DEFINITISES
DEFINITISING
DEFINITIVE
DEFINITIVELY
DEFINITIVENESS
DEFINITIVES
DEFINITIZE
DEFINITIZED
DEFINITIZES
DEFINITIZING
DEFINITUDE
DEFINITUDES
DEFLAGRABILITY
DEFLAGRABLE
DEFLAGRATE
DEFLAGRATED
DEFLAGRATES
DEFLAGRATING
DEFLAGRATION
DEFLAGRATIONS
DEFLAGRATOR
DEFLAGRATORS
DEFLATIONARY
DEFLATIONIST
DEFLATIONISTS
DEFLATIONS
DEFLECTABLE
DEFLECTING
DEFLECTION
DEFLECTIONAL
DEFLECTIONS
DEFLECTIVE
DEFLECTORS
DEFLEXIONAL
DEFLEXIONS
DEFLEXURES
DEFLOCCULANT
DEFLOCCULANTS
DEFLOCCULATE
DEFLOCCULATED
DEFLOCCULATES
DEFLOCCULATING
DEFLOCCULATION
DEFLOCCULATIONS
DEFLORATED
DEFLORATES
DEFLORATING
DEFLORATION
DEFLORATIONS
DEFLOWERED
DEFLOWERER
DEFLOWERERS
DEFLOWERING
DEFLUXIONS
DEFOCUSING
DEFOCUSSED
DEFOCUSSES
DEFOCUSSING
DEFOLIANTS
DEFOLIATED
DEFOLIATES
DEFOLIATING
DEFOLIATION
DEFOLIATIONS
DEFOLIATOR
DEFOLIATORS
DEFORCEMENT
DEFORCEMENTS
DEFORCIANT
DEFORCIANTS
DEFORCIATION
DEFORCIATIONS
DEFORESTATION
DEFORESTATIONS
DEFORESTED
DEFORESTER
DEFORESTERS
DEFORESTING
DEFORMABILITIES
DEFORMABILITY
DEFORMABLE
DEFORMALISE
DEFORMALISED
DEFORMALISES
DEFORMALISING
DEFORMALIZE
DEFORMALIZED
DEFORMALIZES
DEFORMALIZING
DEFORMATION
DEFORMATIONAL
DEFORMATIONS
DEFORMATIVE
DEFORMEDLY
DEFORMEDNESS
DEFORMEDNESSES
DEFORMITIES
DEFRAGGERS
DEFRAGGING
DEFRAGGINGS
DEFRAGMENT
DEFRAGMENTED
DEFRAGMENTING
DEFRAGMENTS
DEFRAUDATION
DEFRAUDATIONS
DEFRAUDERS
DEFRAUDING
DEFRAUDMENT
DEFRAUDMENTS
DEFRAYABLE
DEFRAYMENT
DEFRAYMENTS
DEFREEZING
DEFRIENDED
DEFRIENDING
DEFROCKING
DEFROSTERS
DEFROSTING
DEFROSTINGS
DEFTNESSES
DEFUELLING
DEFUNCTION
DEFUNCTIONS
DEFUNCTIVE
DEFUNCTNESS
DEFUNCTNESSES
DEGARNISHED
DEGARNISHES
DEGARNISHING
DEGAUSSERS
DEGAUSSING
DEGAUSSINGS
DEGEARINGS
DEGENDERED
DEGENDERING
DEGENERACIES
DEGENERACY
DEGENERATE
DEGENERATED
DEGENERATELY
DEGENERATENESS
DEGENERATES
DEGENERATING
DEGENERATION
DEGENERATIONIST
DEGENERATIONS
DEGENERATIVE
DEGENEROUS
DEGLACIATED
DEGLACIATION
DEGLACIATIONS
DEGLAMORISATION
DEGLAMORISE
DEGLAMORISED
DEGLAMORISES
DEGLAMORISING
DEGLAMORIZATION
DEGLAMORIZE
DEGLAMORIZED
DEGLAMORIZES
DEGLAMORIZING
DEGLUTINATE
DEGLUTINATED
DEGLUTINATES
DEGLUTINATING
DEGLUTINATION
DEGLUTINATIONS
DEGLUTITION
DEGLUTITIONS
DEGLUTITIVE
DEGLUTITORY
DEGRADABILITIES
DEGRADABILITY
DEGRADABLE
DEGRADATION
DEGRADATIONS
DEGRADATIVE
DEGRADEDLY
DEGRADINGLY
DEGRADINGNESS
DEGRADINGNESSES
DEGRANULATION
DEGRANULATIONS
DEGREASANT
DEGREASANTS
DEGREASERS
DEGREASING
DEGREASINGS
DEGREELESS
DEGRESSION
DEGRESSIONS
DEGRESSIVE
DEGRESSIVELY
DEGRINGOLADE
DEGRINGOLADED
DEGRINGOLADES
DEGRINGOLADING
DEGRINGOLER
DEGRINGOLERED
DEGRINGOLERING
DEGRINGOLERS
DEGUSTATED
DEGUSTATES
DEGUSTATING
DEGUSTATION
DEGUSTATIONS

DEGUSTATORY
DEHISCENCE
DEHISCENCES
DEHORTATION
DEHORTATIONS
DEHORTATIVE
DEHORTATORY
DEHUMANISATION
DEHUMANISATIONS
DEHUMANISE
DEHUMANISED
DEHUMANISES
DEHUMANISING
DEHUMANIZATION
DEHUMANIZATIONS
DEHUMANIZE
DEHUMANIZED
DEHUMANIZES
DEHUMANIZING
DEHUMIDIFIED
DEHUMIDIFIER
DEHUMIDIFIERS
DEHUMIDIFIES
DEHUMIDIFY
DEHUMIDIFYING
DEHYDRATED
DEHYDRATER
DEHYDRATERS
DEHYDRATES
DEHYDRATING
DEHYDRATION
DEHYDRATIONS
DEHYDRATOR
DEHYDRATORS
DEHYDROGENASE
DEHYDROGENASES
DEHYDROGENATE
DEHYDROGENATED
DEHYDROGENATES
DEHYDROGENATING
DEHYDROGENATION
DEHYDROGENISE
DEHYDROGENISED
DEHYDROGENISES
DEHYDROGENISING
DEHYDROGENIZE
DEHYDROGENIZED
DEHYDROGENIZES
DEHYDROGENIZING
DEHYDRORETINOL
DEHYDRORETINOLS
DEHYPNOTISATION
DEHYPNOTISE
DEHYPNOTISED
DEHYPNOTISES
DEHYPNOTISING
DEHYPNOTIZATION
DEHYPNOTIZE
DEHYPNOTIZED
DEHYPNOTIZES
DEHYPNOTIZING
DEICTICALLY
DEIFICATION
DEIFICATIONS
DEINDEXATION
DEINDEXATIONS
DEINDEXING
DEINDIVIDUATION
DEINDUSTRIALISE
DEINDUSTRIALIZE
DEINONYCHUS
DEINONYCHUSES
DEINOSAURS
DEINOTHERE
DEINOTHERES
DEINOTHERIA
DEINOTHERIUM
DEINOTHERIUMS
DEIONISATION
DEIONISATIONS
DEIONISERS
DEIONISING
DEIONIZATION
DEIONIZATIONS
DEIONIZERS
DEIONIZING
DEIPNOSOPHIST
DEIPNOSOPHISTS
DEISTICALLY
DEJECTEDLY
DEJECTEDNESS
DEJECTEDNESSES
DEJECTIONS
DEKALITERS
DEKALITRES
DEKALOGIES
DEKAMETERS
DEKAMETRES
DEKAMETRIC
DELAMINATE
DELAMINATED
DELAMINATES
DELAMINATING
DELAMINATION
DELAMINATIONS
DELAPSIONS
DELASSEMENT
DELASSEMENTS
DELAYERING
DELAYERINGS
DELAYINGLY
DELECTABILITIES
DELECTABILITY
DELECTABLE
DELECTABLENESS
DELECTABLES
DELECTABLY
DELECTATED
DELECTATES
DELECTATING
DELECTATION
DELECTATIONS
DELEGACIES
DELEGATEES
DELEGATING
DELEGATION
DELEGATIONS
DELEGATORS
DELEGITIMATION
DELEGITIMATIONS
DELEGITIMISE
DELEGITIMISED
DELEGITIMISES
DELEGITIMISING
DELEGITIMIZE
DELEGITIMIZED
DELEGITIMIZES
DELEGITIMIZING
DELETERIOUS
DELETERIOUSLY
DELETERIOUSNESS
DELEVERAGE
DELEVERAGED
DELEVERAGES
DELEVERAGING
DELEVERAGINGS
DELFTWARES
DELIBATING
DELIBATION
DELIBATIONS
DELIBERATE
DELIBERATED
DELIBERATELY
DELIBERATENESS
DELIBERATES
DELIBERATING
DELIBERATION
DELIBERATIONS
DELIBERATIVE
DELIBERATIVELY
DELIBERATOR
DELIBERATORS
DELICACIES
DELICATELY
DELICATENESS
DELICATENESSES
DELICATESSEN
DELICATESSENS
DELICIOUSLY
DELICIOUSNESS
DELICIOUSNESSES
DELIGATION
DELIGATIONS
DELIGHTEDLY
DELIGHTEDNESS
DELIGHTEDNESSES
DELIGHTERS
DELIGHTFUL
DELIGHTFULLY
DELIGHTFULNESS
DELIGHTING
DELIGHTLESS
DELIGHTSOME
DELIMITATE
DELIMITATED
DELIMITATES
DELIMITATING
DELIMITATION
DELIMITATIONS
DELIMITATIVE
DELIMITERS
DELIMITING
DELINEABLE
DELINEATED
DELINEATES
DELINEATING
DELINEATION
DELINEATIONS
DELINEATIVE
DELINEATOR
DELINEATORS
DELINEAVIT
DELINQUENCIES
DELINQUENCY
DELINQUENT
DELINQUENTLY
DELINQUENTS
DELIQUESCE
DELIQUESCED
DELIQUESCENCE
DELIQUESCENCES
DELIQUESCENT
DELIQUESCES
DELIQUESCING
DELIQUIUMS
DELIRATION
DELIRATIONS
DELIRIFACIENT
DELIRIFACIENTS
DELIRIOUSLY
DELIRIOUSNESS
DELIRIOUSNESSES
DELITESCENCE
DELITESCENCES
DELITESCENT
DELIVERABILITY
DELIVERABLE
DELIVERABLES
DELIVERANCE
DELIVERANCES
DELIVERERS
DELIVERIES
DELIVERING
DELIVERYMAN
DELIVERYMEN
DELOCALISATION
DELOCALISATIONS
DELOCALISE
DELOCALISED
DELOCALISES

DELOCALISING
DELOCALIZATION
DELOCALIZATIONS
DELOCALIZE
DELOCALIZED
DELOCALIZES
DELOCALIZING
DELPHICALLY
DELPHINIUM
DELPHINIUMS
DELPHINOID
DELPHINOIDS
DELTIOLOGIES
DELTIOLOGIST
DELTIOLOGISTS
DELTIOLOGY
DELTOIDEUS
DELUDINGLY
DELUNDUNGS
DELUSIONAL
DELUSIONARY
DELUSIONIST
DELUSIONISTS
DELUSIVELY
DELUSIVENESS
DELUSIVENESSES
DELUSTERED
DELUSTERING
DELUSTRANT
DELUSTRANTS
DELUSTRING
DEMAGNETISATION
DEMAGNETISE
DEMAGNETISED
DEMAGNETISER
DEMAGNETISERS
DEMAGNETISES
DEMAGNETISING
DEMAGNETIZATION
DEMAGNETIZE
DEMAGNETIZED
DEMAGNETIZER
DEMAGNETIZERS
DEMAGNETIZES
DEMAGNETIZING
DEMAGOGICAL
DEMAGOGICALLY
DEMAGOGIES
DEMAGOGING
DEMAGOGISM
DEMAGOGISMS
DEMAGOGUED
DEMAGOGUERIES
DEMAGOGUERY
DEMAGOGUES
DEMAGOGUING
DEMAGOGUISM
DEMAGOGUISMS
DEMANDABLE
DEMANDANTS
DEMANDINGLY
DEMANDINGNESS
DEMANDINGNESSES
DEMANNINGS
DEMANTOIDS
DEMARCATED
DEMARCATES
DEMARCATING
DEMARCATION
DEMARCATIONS
DEMARCATOR
DEMARCATORS
DEMARKATION
DEMARKATIONS
DEMARKETED
DEMARKETING
DEMATERIALISE
DEMATERIALISED
DEMATERIALISES
DEMATERIALISING
DEMATERIALIZE
DEMATERIALIZED
DEMATERIALIZES
DEMATERIALIZING
DEMEANOURS
DEMEASNURE
DEMEASNURES
DEMENTATED
DEMENTATES
DEMENTATING
DEMENTEDLY
DEMENTEDNESS
DEMENTEDNESSES
DEMERGERED
DEMERGERING
DEMERITING
DEMERITORIOUS
DEMERITORIOUSLY
DEMERSIONS
DEMIBASTION
DEMIBASTIONS
DEMICANTON
DEMICANTONS
DEMIGODDESS
DEMIGODDESSES
DEMIGRATION
DEMIGRATIONS
DEMILITARISE
DEMILITARISED
DEMILITARISES
DEMILITARISING
DEMILITARIZE
DEMILITARIZED
DEMILITARIZES
DEMILITARIZING
DEMIMONDAINE
DEMIMONDAINES
DEMIMONDES
DEMINERALISE
DEMINERALISED
DEMINERALISER
DEMINERALISERS
DEMINERALISES
DEMINERALISING
DEMINERALIZE
DEMINERALIZED
DEMINERALIZER
DEMINERALIZERS
DEMINERALIZES
DEMINERALIZING
DEMIPIQUES
DEMIRELIEF
DEMIRELIEFS
DEMIREPDOM
DEMIREPDOMS
DEMISEMIQUAVER
DEMISEMIQUAVERS
DEMISSIONS
DEMISTINGS
DEMITASSES
DEMIURGEOUS
DEMIURGICAL
DEMIURGICALLY
DEMIURGUSES
DEMIVEGGES
DEMIVIERGE
DEMIVIERGES
DEMIVOLTES
DEMIWORLDS
DEMOBILISATION
DEMOBILISATIONS
DEMOBILISE
DEMOBILISED
DEMOBILISES
DEMOBILISING
DEMOBILIZATION
DEMOBILIZATIONS
DEMOBILIZE
DEMOBILIZED
DEMOBILIZES
DEMOBILIZING
DEMOCRACIES
DEMOCRATIC
DEMOCRATICAL
DEMOCRATICALLY
DEMOCRATIES
DEMOCRATIFIABLE
DEMOCRATISATION
DEMOCRATISE
DEMOCRATISED
DEMOCRATISER
DEMOCRATISERS
DEMOCRATISES
DEMOCRATISING
DEMOCRATIST
DEMOCRATISTS
DEMOCRATIZATION
DEMOCRATIZE
DEMOCRATIZED
DEMOCRATIZER
DEMOCRATIZERS
DEMOCRATIZES
DEMOCRATIZING
DEMODULATE
DEMODULATED
DEMODULATES
DEMODULATING
DEMODULATION
DEMODULATIONS
DEMODULATOR
DEMODULATORS
DEMOGRAPHER
DEMOGRAPHERS
DEMOGRAPHIC
DEMOGRAPHICAL
DEMOGRAPHICALLY
DEMOGRAPHICS
DEMOGRAPHIES
DEMOGRAPHIST
DEMOGRAPHISTS
DEMOGRAPHY
DEMOISELLE
DEMOISELLES
DEMOLISHED
DEMOLISHER
DEMOLISHERS
DEMOLISHES
DEMOLISHING
DEMOLISHMENT
DEMOLISHMENTS
DEMOLITION
DEMOLITIONIST
DEMOLITIONISTS
DEMOLITIONS
DEMOLOGIES
DEMONESSES
DEMONETARISE
DEMONETARISED
DEMONETARISES
DEMONETARISING
DEMONETARIZE
DEMONETARIZED
DEMONETARIZES
DEMONETARIZING
DEMONETISATION
DEMONETISATIONS
DEMONETISE
DEMONETISED
DEMONETISES
DEMONETISING
DEMONETIZATION
DEMONETIZATIONS
DEMONETIZE
DEMONETIZED
DEMONETIZES
DEMONETIZING
DEMONIACAL
DEMONIACALLY
DEMONIACISM
DEMONIACISMS

DEMONIANISM
DEMONIANISMS
DEMONICALLY
DEMONISATION
DEMONISATIONS
DEMONISING
DEMONIZATION
DEMONIZATIONS
DEMONIZING
DEMONOCRACIES
DEMONOCRACY
DEMONOLATER
DEMONOLATERS
DEMONOLATRIES
DEMONOLATRY
DEMONOLOGIC
DEMONOLOGICAL
DEMONOLOGIES
DEMONOLOGIST
DEMONOLOGISTS
DEMONOLOGY
DEMONOMANIA
DEMONOMANIAS
DEMONSTRABILITY
DEMONSTRABLE
DEMONSTRABLY
DEMONSTRATE
DEMONSTRATED
DEMONSTRATES
DEMONSTRATING
DEMONSTRATION
DEMONSTRATIONAL
DEMONSTRATIONS
DEMONSTRATIVE
DEMONSTRATIVELY
DEMONSTRATIVES
DEMONSTRATOR
DEMONSTRATORS
DEMONSTRATORY
DEMORALISATION
DEMORALISATIONS
DEMORALISE
DEMORALISED
DEMORALISER
DEMORALISERS
DEMORALISES
DEMORALISING
DEMORALISINGLY
DEMORALIZATION
DEMORALIZATIONS
DEMORALIZE
DEMORALIZED
DEMORALIZER
DEMORALIZERS
DEMORALIZES
DEMORALIZING
DEMORALIZINGLY
DEMOSCENES
DEMOTICIST
DEMOTICISTS
DEMOTIVATE
DEMOTIVATED
DEMOTIVATES
DEMOTIVATING
DEMOTIVATION
DEMOTIVATIONS
DEMOUNTABLE
DEMOUNTING
DEMULCENTS
DEMULSIFICATION
DEMULSIFIED
DEMULSIFIER
DEMULSIFIERS
DEMULSIFIES
DEMULSIFYING
DEMULTIPLEXER
DEMULTIPLEXERS
DEMURENESS
DEMURENESSES
DEMURRABLE
DEMURRAGES
DEMUTUALISATION
DEMUTUALISE
DEMUTUALISED
DEMUTUALISES
DEMUTUALISING
DEMUTUALIZATION
DEMUTUALIZE
DEMUTUALIZED
DEMUTUALIZES
DEMUTUALIZING
DEMYELINATE
DEMYELINATED
DEMYELINATES
DEMYELINATING
DEMYELINATION
DEMYELINATIONS
DEMYSTIFICATION
DEMYSTIFIED
DEMYSTIFIES
DEMYSTIFYING
DEMYTHIFICATION
DEMYTHIFIED
DEMYTHIFIES
DEMYTHIFYING
DEMYTHOLOGISE
DEMYTHOLOGISED
DEMYTHOLOGISER
DEMYTHOLOGISERS
DEMYTHOLOGISES
DEMYTHOLOGISING
DEMYTHOLOGIZE
DEMYTHOLOGIZED
DEMYTHOLOGIZER
DEMYTHOLOGIZERS
DEMYTHOLOGIZES
DEMYTHOLOGIZING
DENATIONALISE
DENATIONALISED
DENATIONALISES
DENATIONALISING
DENATIONALIZE
DENATIONALIZED
DENATIONALIZES
DENATIONALIZING
DENATURALISE
DENATURALISED
DENATURALISES
DENATURALISING
DENATURALIZE
DENATURALIZED
DENATURALIZES
DENATURALIZING
DENATURANT
DENATURANTS
DENATURATION
DENATURATIONS
DENATURING
DENATURISE
DENATURISED
DENATURISES
DENATURISING
DENATURIZE
DENATURIZED
DENATURIZES
DENATURIZING
DENAZIFICATION
DENAZIFICATIONS
DENAZIFIED
DENAZIFIES
DENAZIFYING
DENDRACHATE
DENDRACHATES
DENDRIFORM
DENDRIMERS
DENDRITICAL
DENDRITICALLY
DENDROBIUM
DENDROBIUMS
DENDROGLYPH
DENDROGLYPHS
DENDROGRAM
DENDROGRAMS
DENDROIDAL
DENDROLATRIES
DENDROLATRY
DENDROLOGIC
DENDROLOGICAL
DENDROLOGIES
DENDROLOGIST
DENDROLOGISTS
DENDROLOGOUS
DENDROLOGY
DENDROMETER
DENDROMETERS
DENDROPHIS
DENDROPHISES
DENEGATION
DENEGATIONS
DENERVATED
DENERVATES
DENERVATING
DENERVATION
DENERVATIONS
DENIABILITIES
DENIABILITY
DENIALISTS
DENIGRATED
DENIGRATES
DENIGRATING
DENIGRATION
DENIGRATIONS
DENIGRATIVE
DENIGRATOR
DENIGRATORS
DENIGRATORY
DENISATION
DENISATIONS
DENITRATED
DENITRATES
DENITRATING
DENITRATION
DENITRATIONS
DENITRIFICATION
DENITRIFICATOR
DENITRIFICATORS
DENITRIFIED
DENITRIFIER
DENITRIFIERS
DENITRIFIES
DENITRIFYING
DENIZATION
DENIZATIONS
DENIZENING
DENIZENSHIP
DENIZENSHIPS
DENOMINABLE
DENOMINATE
DENOMINATED
DENOMINATES
DENOMINATING
DENOMINATION
DENOMINATIONAL
DENOMINATIONS
DENOMINATIVE
DENOMINATIVELY
DENOMINATIVES
DENOMINATOR
DENOMINATORS
DENOTATING
DENOTATION
DENOTATIONS
DENOTATIVE
DENOTATIVELY
DENOTEMENT
DENOTEMENTS
DENOUEMENT
DENOUEMENTS
DENOUNCEMENT
DENOUNCEMENTS

DENOUNCERS
DENOUNCING
DENSENESSES
DENSIFICATION
DENSIFICATIONS
DENSIFIERS
DENSIFYING
DENSIMETER
DENSIMETERS
DENSIMETRIC
DENSIMETRIES
DENSIMETRY
DENSITOMETER
DENSITOMETERS
DENSITOMETRIC
DENSITOMETRIES
DENSITOMETRY
DENTALISED
DENTALISES
DENTALISING
DENTALITIES
DENTALIUMS
DENTALIZED
DENTALIZES
DENTALIZING
DENTATIONS
DENTICARES
DENTICULATE
DENTICULATED
DENTICULATELY
DENTICULATION
DENTICULATIONS
DENTIFRICE
DENTIFRICES
DENTIGEROUS
DENTILABIAL
DENTILINGUAL
DENTILINGUALS
DENTIROSTRAL
DENTISTRIES
DENTITIONS
DENTURISMS
DENTURISTS
DENUCLEARISE
DENUCLEARISED
DENUCLEARISES
DENUCLEARISING
DENUCLEARIZE
DENUCLEARIZED
DENUCLEARIZES
DENUCLEARIZING
DENUDATING
DENUDATION
DENUDATIONS
DENUDEMENT
DENUDEMENTS
DENUMERABILITY
DENUMERABLE
DENUMERABLY
DENUNCIATE
DENUNCIATED
DENUNCIATES
DENUNCIATING
DENUNCIATION
DENUNCIATIONS
DENUNCIATIVE
DENUNCIATOR
DENUNCIATORS
DENUNCIATORY
DEOBSTRUENT
DEOBSTRUENTS
DEODORANTS
DEODORISATION
DEODORISATIONS
DEODORISED
DEODORISER
DEODORISERS
DEODORISES
DEODORISING
DEODORIZATION
DEODORIZATIONS
DEODORIZED
DEODORIZER
DEODORIZERS
DEODORIZES
DEODORIZING
DEONTOLOGICAL
DEONTOLOGIES
DEONTOLOGIST
DEONTOLOGISTS
DEONTOLOGY
DEOPPILATE
DEOPPILATED
DEOPPILATES
DEOPPILATING
DEOPPILATION
DEOPPILATIONS
DEOPPILATIVE
DEOPPILATIVES
DEORBITING
DEOXIDATED
DEOXIDATES
DEOXIDATING
DEOXIDATION
DEOXIDATIONS
DEOXIDISATION
DEOXIDISATIONS
DEOXIDISED
DEOXIDISER
DEOXIDISERS
DEOXIDISES
DEOXIDISING
DEOXIDIZATION
DEOXIDIZATIONS
DEOXIDIZED
DEOXIDIZER
DEOXIDIZERS
DEOXIDIZES
DEOXIDIZING
DEOXYCORTONE
DEOXYCORTONES
DEOXYGENATE
DEOXYGENATED
DEOXYGENATES
DEOXYGENATING
DEOXYGENATION
DEOXYGENATIONS
DEOXYGENISE
DEOXYGENISED
DEOXYGENISES
DEOXYGENISING
DEOXYGENIZE
DEOXYGENIZED
DEOXYGENIZES
DEOXYGENIZING
DEOXYRIBOSE
DEOXYRIBOSES
DEPAINTING
DEPANNEURS
DEPARTEMENT
DEPARTEMENTS
DEPARTINGS
DEPARTMENT
DEPARTMENTAL
DEPARTMENTALISE
DEPARTMENTALISM
DEPARTMENTALIZE
DEPARTMENTALLY
DEPARTMENTS
DEPARTURES
DEPASTURED
DEPASTURES
DEPASTURING
DEPAUPERATE
DEPAUPERATED
DEPAUPERATES
DEPAUPERATING
DEPAUPERISE
DEPAUPERISED
DEPAUPERISES
DEPAUPERISING
DEPAUPERIZE
DEPAUPERIZED
DEPAUPERIZES
DEPAUPERIZING
DEPEINCTED
DEPEINCTING
DEPENDABILITIES
DEPENDABILITY
DEPENDABLE
DEPENDABLENESS
DEPENDABLY
DEPENDANCE
DEPENDANCES
DEPENDANCIES
DEPENDANCY
DEPENDANTS
DEPENDENCE
DEPENDENCES
DEPENDENCIES
DEPENDENCY
DEPENDENTLY
DEPENDENTS
DEPENDINGLY
DEPEOPLING
DEPERSONALISE
DEPERSONALISED
DEPERSONALISES
DEPERSONALISING
DEPERSONALIZE
DEPERSONALIZED
DEPERSONALIZES
DEPERSONALIZING
DEPHLEGMATE
DEPHLEGMATED
DEPHLEGMATES
DEPHLEGMATING
DEPHLEGMATION
DEPHLEGMATIONS
DEPHLEGMATOR
DEPHLEGMATORS
DEPHLOGISTICATE
DEPHOSPHORYLATE
DEPICTIONS
DEPICTURED
DEPICTURES
DEPICTURING
DEPIGMENTATION
DEPIGMENTATIONS
DEPIGMENTED
DEPIGMENTING
DEPIGMENTS
DEPILATING
DEPILATION
DEPILATIONS
DEPILATORIES
DEPILATORS
DEPILATORY
DEPLENISHED
DEPLENISHES
DEPLENISHING
DEPLETABLE
DEPLETIONS
DEPLORABILITIES
DEPLORABILITY
DEPLORABLE
DEPLORABLENESS
DEPLORABLY
DEPLORATION
DEPLORATIONS
DEPLORINGLY
DEPLOYABLE
DEPLOYMENT
DEPLOYMENTS
DEPLUMATION
DEPLUMATIONS
DEPOLARISATION
DEPOLARISATIONS
DEPOLARISE
DEPOLARISED

DEPOLARISER
DEPOLARISERS
DEPOLARISES
DEPOLARISING
DEPOLARIZATION
DEPOLARIZATIONS
DEPOLARIZE
DEPOLARIZED
DEPOLARIZER
DEPOLARIZERS
DEPOLARIZES
DEPOLARIZING
DEPOLISHED
DEPOLISHES
DEPOLISHING
DEPOLITICISE
DEPOLITICISED
DEPOLITICISES
DEPOLITICISING
DEPOLITICIZE
DEPOLITICIZED
DEPOLITICIZES
DEPOLITICIZING
DEPOLYMERISE
DEPOLYMERISED
DEPOLYMERISES
DEPOLYMERISING
DEPOLYMERIZE
DEPOLYMERIZED
DEPOLYMERIZES
DEPOLYMERIZING
DEPOPULATE
DEPOPULATED
DEPOPULATES
DEPOPULATING
DEPOPULATION
DEPOPULATIONS
DEPOPULATOR
DEPOPULATORS
DEPORTABLE
DEPORTATION
DEPORTATIONS
DEPORTMENT
DEPORTMENTS
DEPOSITARIES
DEPOSITARY
DEPOSITATION
DEPOSITATIONS
DEPOSITING
DEPOSITION
DEPOSITIONAL
DEPOSITIONS
DEPOSITIVE
DEPOSITORIES
DEPOSITORS
DEPOSITORY
DEPRAVATION
DEPRAVATIONS
DEPRAVEDLY
DEPRAVEDNESS
DEPRAVEDNESSES
DEPRAVEMENT
DEPRAVEMENTS
DEPRAVINGLY
DEPRAVITIES
DEPRECABLE
DEPRECATED
DEPRECATES
DEPRECATING
DEPRECATINGLY
DEPRECATION
DEPRECATIONS
DEPRECATIVE
DEPRECATIVELY
DEPRECATOR
DEPRECATORILY
DEPRECATORS
DEPRECATORY
DEPRECIABLE
DEPRECIATE
DEPRECIATED
DEPRECIATES
DEPRECIATING
DEPRECIATINGLY
DEPRECIATION
DEPRECIATIONS
DEPRECIATIVE
DEPRECIATOR
DEPRECIATORS
DEPRECIATORY
DEPREDATED
DEPREDATES
DEPREDATING
DEPREDATION
DEPREDATIONS
DEPREDATOR
DEPREDATORS
DEPREDATORY
DEPREHENDED
DEPREHENDING
DEPREHENDS
DEPRESSANT
DEPRESSANTS
DEPRESSIBLE
DEPRESSING
DEPRESSINGLY
DEPRESSION
DEPRESSIONS
DEPRESSIVE
DEPRESSIVELY
DEPRESSIVENESS
DEPRESSIVES
DEPRESSOMOTOR
DEPRESSOMOTORS
DEPRESSORS
DEPRESSURISE
DEPRESSURISED
DEPRESSURISES
DEPRESSURISING
DEPRESSURIZE
DEPRESSURIZED
DEPRESSURIZES
DEPRESSURIZING
DEPRIVABLE
DEPRIVATION
DEPRIVATIONS
DEPRIVATIVE
DEPRIVEMENT
DEPRIVEMENTS
DEPROGRAMED
DEPROGRAMING
DEPROGRAMME
DEPROGRAMMED
DEPROGRAMMER
DEPROGRAMMERS
DEPROGRAMMES
DEPROGRAMMING
DEPROGRAMS
DEPURATING
DEPURATION
DEPURATIONS
DEPURATIVE
DEPURATIVES
DEPURATORS
DEPURATORY
DEPUTATION
DEPUTATIONS
DEPUTISATION
DEPUTISATIONS
DEPUTISING
DEPUTIZATION
DEPUTIZATIONS
DEPUTIZING
DEQUEUEING
DERACIALISE
DERACIALISED
DERACIALISES
DERACIALISING
DERACIALIZE
DERACIALIZED
DERACIALIZES
DERACIALIZING
DERACINATE
DERACINATED
DERACINATES
DERACINATING
DERACINATION
DERACINATIONS
DERAIGNING
DERAIGNMENT
DERAIGNMENTS
DERAILLEUR
DERAILLEURS
DERAILMENT
DERAILMENTS
DERANGEMENT
DERANGEMENTS
DERATIONED
DERATIONING
DEREALISATION
DEREALISATIONS
DEREALIZATION
DEREALIZATIONS
DERECOGNISE
DERECOGNISED
DERECOGNISES
DERECOGNISING
DERECOGNITION
DERECOGNITIONS
DERECOGNIZE
DERECOGNIZED
DERECOGNIZES
DERECOGNIZING
DEREGISTER
DEREGISTERED
DEREGISTERING
DEREGISTERS
DEREGISTRATION
DEREGISTRATIONS
DEREGULATE
DEREGULATED
DEREGULATES
DEREGULATING
DEREGULATION
DEREGULATIONS
DEREGULATOR
DEREGULATORS
DEREGULATORY
DERELICTION
DERELICTIONS
DERELIGIONISE
DERELIGIONISED
DERELIGIONISES
DERELIGIONISING
DERELIGIONIZE
DERELIGIONIZED
DERELIGIONIZES
DERELIGIONIZING
DEREPRESSED
DEREPRESSES
DEREPRESSING
DEREPRESSION
DEREPRESSIONS
DEREQUISITION
DEREQUISITIONED
DEREQUISITIONS
DERESTRICT
DERESTRICTED
DERESTRICTING
DERESTRICTION
DERESTRICTIONS
DERESTRICTS
DERIDINGLY
DERISIVELY
DERISIVENESS
DERISIVENESSES
DERIVATING
DERIVATION
DERIVATIONAL
DERIVATIONIST

DERIVATIONISTS
DERIVATIONS
DERIVATISATION
DERIVATISATIONS
DERIVATISE
DERIVATISED
DERIVATISES
DERIVATISING
DERIVATIVE
DERIVATIVELY
DERIVATIVENESS
DERIVATIVES
DERIVATIZATION
DERIVATIZATIONS
DERIVATIZE
DERIVATIZED
DERIVATIZES
DERIVATIZING
DERMABRASION
DERMABRASIONS
DERMAPLANING
DERMAPLANINGS
DERMAPTERAN
DERMAPTERANS
DERMATITIDES
DERMATITIS
DERMATITISES
DERMATOGEN
DERMATOGENS
DERMATOGLYPHIC
DERMATOGLYPHICS
DERMATOGRAPHIA
DERMATOGRAPHIAS
DERMATOGRAPHIC
DERMATOGRAPHIES
DERMATOGRAPHY
DERMATOLOGIC
DERMATOLOGICAL
DERMATOLOGIES
DERMATOLOGIST
DERMATOLOGISTS
DERMATOLOGY
DERMATOMAL
DERMATOMES
DERMATOMIC
DERMATOMYOSITIS
DERMATOPHYTE
DERMATOPHYTES
DERMATOPHYTIC
DERMATOPHYTOSES
DERMATOPHYTOSIS
DERMATOPLASTIC
DERMATOPLASTIES
DERMATOPLASTY
DERMATOSES
DERMATOSIS
DERMESTIDS
DERMOGRAPHIES
DERMOGRAPHY
DEROGATELY
DEROGATING
DEROGATION
DEROGATIONS
DEROGATIVE
DEROGATIVELY
DEROGATORILY
DEROGATORINESS
DEROGATORY
DERRICKING
DERRINGERS
DESACRALISATION
DESACRALISE
DESACRALISED
DESACRALISES
DESACRALISING
DESACRALIZATION
DESACRALIZE
DESACRALIZED
DESACRALIZES
DESACRALIZING
DESAGREMENT
DESAGREMENTS
DESALINATE
DESALINATED
DESALINATES
DESALINATING
DESALINATION
DESALINATIONS
DESALINATOR
DESALINATORS
DESALINISATION
DESALINISATIONS
DESALINISE
DESALINISED
DESALINISES
DESALINISING
DESALINIZATION
DESALINIZATIONS
DESALINIZE
DESALINIZED
DESALINIZES
DESALINIZING
DESALTINGS
DESATURATE
DESATURATED
DESATURATES
DESATURATING
DESATURATION
DESATURATIONS
DESCANTERS
DESCANTING
DESCENDABLE
DESCENDANT
DESCENDANTS
DESCENDENT
DESCENDENTS
DESCENDERS
DESCENDEUR
DESCENDEURS
DESCENDIBLE
DESCENDING
DESCENDINGS
DESCENSION
DESCENSIONAL
DESCENSIONS
DESCHOOLED
DESCHOOLER
DESCHOOLERS
DESCHOOLING
DESCHOOLINGS
DESCRAMBLE
DESCRAMBLED
DESCRAMBLER
DESCRAMBLERS
DESCRAMBLES
DESCRAMBLING
DESCRIBABLE
DESCRIBERS
DESCRIBING
DESCRIPTION
DESCRIPTIONS
DESCRIPTIVE
DESCRIPTIVELY
DESCRIPTIVENESS
DESCRIPTIVISM
DESCRIPTIVISMS
DESCRIPTIVIST
DESCRIPTOR
DESCRIPTORS
DESCRIVING
DESECRATED
DESECRATER
DESECRATERS
DESECRATES
DESECRATING
DESECRATION
DESECRATIONS
DESECRATOR
DESECRATORS
DESEGREGATE
DESEGREGATED
DESEGREGATES
DESEGREGATING
DESEGREGATION
DESEGREGATIONS
DESELECTED
DESELECTING
DESELECTION
DESELECTIONS
DESENSITISATION
DESENSITISE
DESENSITISED
DESENSITISER
DESENSITISERS
DESENSITISES
DESENSITISING
DESENSITIZATION
DESENSITIZE
DESENSITIZED
DESENSITIZER
DESENSITIZERS
DESENSITIZES
DESENSITIZING
DESERPIDINE
DESERPIDINES
DESERTIFICATION
DESERTIFIED
DESERTIFIES
DESERTIFYING
DESERTIONS
DESERTISATION
DESERTISATIONS
DESERTIZATION
DESERTIZATIONS
DESERTLESS
DESERVEDLY
DESERVEDNESS
DESERVEDNESSES
DESERVINGLY
DESERVINGNESS
DESERVINGNESSES
DESERVINGS
DESEXUALISATION
DESEXUALISE
DESEXUALISED
DESEXUALISES
DESEXUALISING
DESEXUALIZATION
DESEXUALIZE
DESEXUALIZED
DESEXUALIZES
DESEXUALIZING
DESHABILLE
DESHABILLES
DESICCANTS
DESICCATED
DESICCATES
DESICCATING
DESICCATION
DESICCATIONS
DESICCATIVE
DESICCATIVES
DESICCATOR
DESICCATORS
DESIDERATA
DESIDERATE
DESIDERATED
DESIDERATES
DESIDERATING
DESIDERATION
DESIDERATIONS
DESIDERATIVE
DESIDERATIVES
DESIDERATUM
DESIDERIUM
DESIDERIUMS
DESIGNABLE
DESIGNATED
DESIGNATES
DESIGNATING

DESIGNATION
DESIGNATIONS
DESIGNATIVE
DESIGNATOR
DESIGNATORS
DESIGNATORY
DESIGNEDLY
DESIGNINGLY
DESIGNINGS
DESIGNLESS
DESIGNMENT
DESIGNMENTS
DESILVERED
DESILVERING
DESILVERISATION
DESILVERISE
DESILVERISED
DESILVERISES
DESILVERISING
DESILVERIZATION
DESILVERIZE
DESILVERIZED
DESILVERIZES
DESILVERIZING
DESINENCES
DESINENTIAL
DESIPIENCE
DESIPIENCES
DESIPRAMINE
DESIPRAMINES
DESIRABILITIES
DESIRABILITY
DESIRABLENESS
DESIRABLENESSES
DESIRABLES
DESIRELESS
DESIROUSLY
DESIROUSNESS
DESIROUSNESSES
DESISTANCE
DESISTANCES
DESISTENCE
DESISTENCES
DESKILLING
DESKILLINGS
DESMODIUMS
DESMODROMIC
DESMOSOMAL
DESMOSOMES
DESNOODING
DESOBLIGEANTE
DESOBLIGEANTES
DESOLATELY
DESOLATENESS
DESOLATENESSES
DESOLATERS
DESOLATING
DESOLATINGLY
DESOLATION
DESOLATIONS
DESOLATORS
DESOLATORY
DESORIENTE
DESORPTION
DESORPTIONS
DESOXYRIBOSE
DESOXYRIBOSES
DESPAIRERS
DESPAIRFUL
DESPAIRING
DESPAIRINGLY
DESPATCHED
DESPATCHER
DESPATCHERS
DESPATCHES
DESPATCHING
DESPERADOES
DESPERADOS
DESPERATELY
DESPERATENESS
DESPERATENESSES
DESPERATION
DESPERATIONS
DESPICABILITIES
DESPICABILITY
DESPICABLE
DESPICABLENESS
DESPICABLY
DESPIRITUALISE
DESPIRITUALISED
DESPIRITUALISES
DESPIRITUALIZE
DESPIRITUALIZED
DESPIRITUALIZES
DESPISABLE
DESPISEDNESS
DESPISEDNESSES
DESPISEMENT
DESPISEMENTS
DESPISINGLY
DESPITEFUL
DESPITEFULLY
DESPITEFULNESS
DESPITEOUS
DESPITEOUSLY
DESPITEOUSNESS
DESPOILERS
DESPOILING
DESPOILINGS
DESPOILMENT
DESPOILMENTS
DESPOLIATION
DESPOLIATIONS
DESPONDENCE
DESPONDENCES
DESPONDENCIES
DESPONDENCY
DESPONDENT
DESPONDENTLY
DESPONDING
DESPONDINGLY
DESPONDINGS
DESPOTATES
DESPOTICAL
DESPOTICALLY
DESPOTICALNESS
DESPOTISMS
DESPOTOCRACIES
DESPOTOCRACY
DESPUMATED
DESPUMATES
DESPUMATING
DESPUMATION
DESPUMATIONS
DESQUAMATE
DESQUAMATED
DESQUAMATES
DESQUAMATING
DESQUAMATION
DESQUAMATIONS
DESQUAMATIVE
DESQUAMATORIES
DESQUAMATORY
DESSERTSPOON
DESSERTSPOONFUL
DESSERTSPOONS
DESSIATINE
DESSIATINES
DESSIGNMENT
DESSIGNMENTS
DESSYATINE
DESSYATINES
DESSYATINS
DESTABILISATION
DESTABILISE
DESTABILISED
DESTABILISER
DESTABILISERS
DESTABILISES
DESTABILISING
DESTABILIZATION
DESTABILIZE
DESTABILIZED
DESTABILIZER
DESTABILIZERS
DESTABILIZES
DESTABILIZING
DESTAINING
DESTEMPERED
DESTEMPERING
DESTEMPERS
DESTINATED
DESTINATES
DESTINATING
DESTINATION
DESTINATIONS
DESTITUTED
DESTITUTENESS
DESTITUTENESSES
DESTITUTES
DESTITUTING
DESTITUTION
DESTITUTIONS
DESTOCKING
DESTREAMED
DESTREAMING
DESTRESSED
DESTRESSES
DESTRESSING
DESTROYABLE
DESTROYERS
DESTROYING
DESTRUCTED
DESTRUCTIBILITY
DESTRUCTIBLE
DESTRUCTING
DESTRUCTION
DESTRUCTIONAL
DESTRUCTIONIST
DESTRUCTIONISTS
DESTRUCTIONS
DESTRUCTIVE
DESTRUCTIVELY
DESTRUCTIVENESS
DESTRUCTIVES
DESTRUCTIVISM
DESTRUCTIVISMS
DESTRUCTIVIST
DESTRUCTIVISTS
DESTRUCTIVITIES
DESTRUCTIVITY
DESTRUCTOR
DESTRUCTORS
DESTRUCTOS
DESUETUDES
DESUGARING
DESULFURATE
DESULFURATED
DESULFURATES
DESULFURATING
DESULFURATION
DESULFURATIONS
DESULFURED
DESULFURING
DESULFURISATION
DESULFURISE
DESULFURISED
DESULFURISER
DESULFURISERS
DESULFURISES
DESULFURISING
DESULFURIZATION
DESULFURIZE
DESULFURIZED
DESULFURIZER
DESULFURIZERS
DESULFURIZES
DESULFURIZING
DESULPHURATE
DESULPHURATED

D

DESULPHURATES
DESULPHURATING
DESULPHURATION
DESULPHURATIONS
DESULPHURED
DESULPHURING
DESULPHURISE
DESULPHURISED
DESULPHURISER
DESULPHURISERS
DESULPHURISES
DESULPHURISING
DESULPHURIZE
DESULPHURIZED
DESULPHURIZER
DESULPHURIZERS
DESULPHURIZES
DESULPHURIZING
DESULPHURS
DESULTORILY
DESULTORINESS
DESULTORINESSES
DETACHABILITIES
DETACHABILITY
DETACHABLE
DETACHABLY
DETACHEDLY
DETACHEDNESS
DETACHEDNESSES
DETACHMENT
DETACHMENTS
DETAILEDLY
DETAILEDNESS
DETAILEDNESSES
DETAILINGS
DETAINABLE
DETAINMENT
DETAINMENTS
DETANGLERS
DETANGLING
DETASSELED
DETASSELING
DETASSELLED
DETASSELLING
DETECTABILITIES
DETECTABILITY
DETECTABLE
DETECTIBLE
DETECTIONS
DETECTIVELIKE
DETECTIVES
DETECTIVIST
DETECTIVISTS
DETECTOPHONE
DETECTOPHONES
DETECTORIST
DETECTORISTS
DETENTIONS
DETENTISTS
DETERGENCE
DETERGENCES
DETERGENCIES
DETERGENCY
DETERGENTS
DETERIORATE
DETERIORATED
DETERIORATES
DETERIORATING
DETERIORATION
DETERIORATIONS
DETERIORATIVE
DETERIORISM
DETERIORISMS
DETERIORITIES
DETERIORITY
DETERMENTS
DETERMINABILITY
DETERMINABLE
DETERMINABLY
DETERMINACIES
DETERMINACY
DETERMINANT
DETERMINANTAL
DETERMINANTS
DETERMINATE
DETERMINATED
DETERMINATELY
DETERMINATENESS
DETERMINATES
DETERMINATING
DETERMINATION
DETERMINATIONS
DETERMINATIVE
DETERMINATIVELY
DETERMINATIVES
DETERMINATOR
DETERMINATORS
DETERMINED
DETERMINEDLY
DETERMINEDNESS
DETERMINER
DETERMINERS
DETERMINES
DETERMINING
DETERMINISM
DETERMINISMS
DETERMINIST
DETERMINISTIC
DETERMINISTS
DETERRABILITIES
DETERRABILITY
DETERRABLE
DETERRENCE
DETERRENCES
DETERRENTLY
DETERRENTS
DETERSIONS
DETERSIVES
DETESTABILITIES
DETESTABILITY
DETESTABLE
DETESTABLENESS
DETESTABLY
DETESTATION
DETESTATIONS
DETHATCHED
DETHATCHES
DETHATCHING
DETHRONEMENT
DETHRONEMENTS
DETHRONERS
DETHRONING
DETHRONINGS
DETHRONISE
DETHRONISED
DETHRONISES
DETHRONISING
DETHRONIZE
DETHRONIZED
DETHRONIZES
DETHRONIZING
DETONABILITIES
DETONABILITY
DETONATABLE
DETONATING
DETONATION
DETONATIONS
DETONATIVE
DETONATORS
DETORSIONS
DETORTIONS
DETOXICANT
DETOXICANTS
DETOXICATE
DETOXICATED
DETOXICATES
DETOXICATING
DETOXICATION
DETOXICATIONS
DETOXIFICATION
DETOXIFICATIONS
DETOXIFIED
DETOXIFIES
DETOXIFYING
DETRACTING
DETRACTINGLY
DETRACTINGS
DETRACTION
DETRACTIONS
DETRACTIVE
DETRACTIVELY
DETRACTORS
DETRACTORY
DETRACTRESS
DETRACTRESSES
DETRAINING
DETRAINMENT
DETRAINMENTS
DETRAQUEES
DETRIBALISATION
DETRIBALISE
DETRIBALISED
DETRIBALISES
DETRIBALISING
DETRIBALIZATION
DETRIBALIZE
DETRIBALIZED
DETRIBALIZES
DETRIBALIZING
DETRIMENTAL
DETRIMENTALLY
DETRIMENTALS
DETRIMENTS
DETRITIONS
DETRITOVORE
DETRITOVORES
DETRUNCATE
DETRUNCATED
DETRUNCATES
DETRUNCATING
DETRUNCATION
DETRUNCATIONS
DETRUSIONS
DETUMESCENCE
DETUMESCENCES
DETUMESCENT
DEUTERAGONIST
DEUTERAGONISTS
DEUTERANOMALIES
DEUTERANOMALOUS
DEUTERANOMALY
DEUTERANOPE
DEUTERANOPES
DEUTERANOPIA
DEUTERANOPIAS
DEUTERANOPIC
DEUTERATED
DEUTERATES
DEUTERATING
DEUTERATION
DEUTERATIONS
DEUTERIDES
DEUTERIUMS
DEUTEROGAMIES
DEUTEROGAMIST
DEUTEROGAMISTS
DEUTEROGAMY
DEUTEROPLASM
DEUTEROPLASMS
DEUTEROSCOPIC
DEUTEROSCOPIES
DEUTEROSCOPY
DEUTEROSTOME
DEUTEROSTOMES
DEUTEROTOKIES
DEUTEROTOKY
DEUTOPLASM
DEUTOPLASMIC
DEUTOPLASMS
DEUTOPLASTIC

DEVALORISATION
DEVALORISATIONS
DEVALORISE
DEVALORISED
DEVALORISES
DEVALORISING
DEVALORIZATION
DEVALORIZATIONS
DEVALORIZE
DEVALORIZED
DEVALORIZES
DEVALORIZING
DEVALUATED
DEVALUATES
DEVALUATING
DEVALUATION
DEVALUATIONS
DEVANAGARI
DEVANAGARIS
DEVASTATED
DEVASTATES
DEVASTATING
DEVASTATINGLY
DEVASTATION
DEVASTATIONS
DEVASTATIVE
DEVASTATOR
DEVASTATORS
DEVASTAVIT
DEVASTAVITS
DEVELOPABLE
DEVELOPERS
DEVELOPING
DEVELOPMENT
DEVELOPMENTAL
DEVELOPMENTALLY
DEVELOPMENTS
DEVELOPPES
DEVERBATIVE
DEVERBATIVES
DEVIANCIES
DEVIATIONISM
DEVIATIONISMS
DEVIATIONIST
DEVIATIONISTS
DEVIATIONS
DEVILESSES
DEVILFISHES
DEVILISHLY
DEVILISHNESS
DEVILISHNESSES
DEVILMENTS
DEVILSHIPS
DEVILTRIES
DEVILWOODS
DEVIOUSNESS
DEVIOUSNESSES
DEVITALISATION
DEVITALISATIONS
DEVITALISE
DEVITALISED
DEVITALISES
DEVITALISING
DEVITALIZATION
DEVITALIZATIONS
DEVITALIZE
DEVITALIZED
DEVITALIZES
DEVITALIZING
DEVITRIFICATION
DEVITRIFIED
DEVITRIFIES
DEVITRIFYING
DEVOCALISE
DEVOCALISED
DEVOCALISES
DEVOCALISING
DEVOCALIZE
DEVOCALIZED
DEVOCALIZES
DEVOCALIZING
DEVOICINGS
DEVOLUTION
DEVOLUTIONARY
DEVOLUTIONIST
DEVOLUTIONISTS
DEVOLUTIONS
DEVOLVEMENT
DEVOLVEMENTS
DEVONPORTS
DEVOTEDNESS
DEVOTEDNESSES
DEVOTEMENT
DEVOTEMENTS
DEVOTIONAL
DEVOTIONALIST
DEVOTIONALISTS
DEVOTIONALITIES
DEVOTIONALITY
DEVOTIONALLY
DEVOTIONALNESS
DEVOTIONALS
DEVOTIONIST
DEVOTIONISTS
DEVOURINGLY
DEVOURMENT
DEVOURMENTS
DEVOUTNESS
DEVOUTNESSES
DEVVELLING
DEWATERERS
DEWATERING
DEWATERINGS
DEWBERRIES
DEWINESSES
DEXAMETHASONE
DEXAMETHASONES
DEXAMPHETAMINE
DEXAMPHETAMINES
DEXIOTROPIC
DEXTERITIES
DEXTEROUSLY
DEXTEROUSNESS
DEXTEROUSNESSES
DEXTERWISE
DEXTRALITIES
DEXTRALITY
DEXTRANASE
DEXTRANASES
DEXTROCARDIA
DEXTROCARDIAC
DEXTROCARDIACS
DEXTROCARDIAS
DEXTROGLUCOSE
DEXTROGLUCOSES
DEXTROGYRATE
DEXTROGYRE
DEXTROROTARY
DEXTROROTATION
DEXTROROTATIONS
DEXTROROTATORY
DEXTRORSAL
DEXTRORSELY
DEXTROUSLY
DEXTROUSNESS
DEXTROUSNESSES
DEZINCKING
DHARMSALAS
DHARMSHALA
DHARMSHALAS
DIABETICAL
DIABETOGENIC
DIABETOLOGIST
DIABETOLOGISTS
DIABLERIES
DIABOLICAL
DIABOLICALLY
DIABOLICALNESS
DIABOLISED
DIABOLISES
DIABOLISING
DIABOLISMS
DIABOLISTS
DIABOLIZED
DIABOLIZES
DIABOLIZING
DIABOLOGIES
DIABOLOLOGIES
DIABOLOLOGY
DIACATHOLICON
DIACATHOLICONS
DIACAUSTIC
DIACAUSTICS
DIACHRONIC
DIACHRONICALLY
DIACHRONIES
DIACHRONISM
DIACHRONISMS
DIACHRONISTIC
DIACHRONOUS
DIACHYLONS
DIACHYLUMS
DIACODIONS
DIACODIUMS
DIACONATES
DIACONICON
DIACONICONS
DIACOUSTIC
DIACOUSTICS
DIACRITICAL
DIACRITICALLY
DIACRITICS
DIACTINISM
DIACTINISMS
DIADELPHOUS
DIADOCHIES
DIADROMOUS
DIAGENESES
DIAGENESIS
DIAGENETIC
DIAGENETICALLY
DIAGEOTROPIC
DIAGEOTROPISM
DIAGEOTROPISMS
DIAGNOSABILITY
DIAGNOSABLE
DIAGNOSEABLE
DIAGNOSING
DIAGNOSTIC
DIAGNOSTICAL
DIAGNOSTICALLY
DIAGNOSTICIAN
DIAGNOSTICIANS
DIAGNOSTICS
DIAGOMETER
DIAGOMETERS
DIAGONALISABLE
DIAGONALISATION
DIAGONALISE
DIAGONALISED
DIAGONALISES
DIAGONALISING
DIAGONALIZABLE
DIAGONALIZATION
DIAGONALIZE
DIAGONALIZED
DIAGONALIZES
DIAGONALIZING
DIAGONALLY
DIAGRAMING
DIAGRAMMABLE
DIAGRAMMATIC
DIAGRAMMATICAL
DIAGRAMMED
DIAGRAMMING
DIAGRAPHIC
DIAHELIOTROPIC
DIAHELIOTROPISM
DIAKINESES
DIAKINESIS

D

DIALECTALLY
DIALECTICAL
DIALECTICALLY
DIALECTICIAN
DIALECTICIANS
DIALECTICISM
DIALECTICISMS
DIALECTICS
DIALECTOLOGICAL
DIALECTOLOGIES
DIALECTOLOGIST
DIALECTOLOGISTS
DIALECTOLOGY
DIALLAGOID
DIALOGICAL
DIALOGICALLY
DIALOGISED
DIALOGISES
DIALOGISING
DIALOGISMS
DIALOGISTIC
DIALOGISTICAL
DIALOGISTS
DIALOGITES
DIALOGIZED
DIALOGIZES
DIALOGIZING
DIALOGUERS
DIALOGUING
DIALYPETALOUS
DIALYSABILITIES
DIALYSABILITY
DIALYSABLE
DIALYSATES
DIALYSATION
DIALYSATIONS
DIALYTICALLY
DIALYZABILITIES
DIALYZABILITY
DIALYZABLE
DIALYZATES
DIALYZATION
DIALYZATIONS
DIAMAGNETIC
DIAMAGNETICALLY
DIAMAGNETISM
DIAMAGNETISMS
DIAMAGNETS
DIAMANTIFEROUS
DIAMANTINE
DIAMETRALLY
DIAMETRICAL
DIAMETRICALLY
DIAMONDBACK
DIAMONDBACKS
DIAMONDIFEROUS
DIAMONDING
DIAMORPHINE
DIAMORPHINES
DIANTHUSES
DIAPASONAL
DIAPASONIC
DIAPAUSING
DIAPEDESES
DIAPEDESIS
DIAPEDETIC
DIAPERINGS
DIAPHANEITIES
DIAPHANEITY
DIAPHANOMETER
DIAPHANOMETERS
DIAPHANOUS
DIAPHANOUSLY
DIAPHANOUSNESS
DIAPHONIES
DIAPHORASE
DIAPHORASES
DIAPHORESES
DIAPHORESIS
DIAPHORETIC
DIAPHORETICS
DIAPHOTOTROPIC
DIAPHOTOTROPIES
DIAPHOTOTROPISM
DIAPHOTOTROPY
DIAPHRAGMAL
DIAPHRAGMATIC
DIAPHRAGMATITIS
DIAPHRAGMED
DIAPHRAGMING
DIAPHRAGMITIS
DIAPHRAGMITISES
DIAPHRAGMS
DIAPHYSEAL
DIAPHYSIAL
DIAPIRISMS
DIAPOPHYSES
DIAPOPHYSIAL
DIAPOPHYSIS
DIAPOSITIVE
DIAPOSITIVES
DIAPYETICS
DIARCHICAL
DIARRHETIC
DIARRHOEAL
DIARRHOEAS
DIARRHOEIC
DIARTHRODIAL
DIARTHROSES
DIARTHROSIS
DIASCORDIUM
DIASCORDIUMS
DIASKEUAST
DIASKEUASTS
DIASTALSES
DIASTALSIS
DIASTALTIC
DIASTEMATA
DIASTEMATIC
DIASTEREOISOMER
DIASTEREOMER
DIASTEREOMERIC
DIASTEREOMERS
DIASTROPHIC
DIASTROPHICALLY
DIASTROPHISM
DIASTROPHISMS
DIATESSARON
DIATESSARONS
DIATHERMACIES
DIATHERMACY
DIATHERMAL
DIATHERMANCIES
DIATHERMANCY
DIATHERMANEITY
DIATHERMANOUS
DIATHERMIA
DIATHERMIAS
DIATHERMIC
DIATHERMIES
DIATHERMOUS
DIATOMACEOUS
DIATOMICITIES
DIATOMICITY
DIATOMISTS
DIATOMITES
DIATONICALLY
DIATONICISM
DIATONICISMS
DIATRETUMS
DIATRIBIST
DIATRIBISTS
DIATROPISM
DIATROPISMS
DIAZEUCTIC
DIAZOMETHANE
DIAZOMETHANES
DIAZONIUMS
DIAZOTISATION
DIAZOTISATIONS
DIAZOTISED
DIAZOTISES
DIAZOTISING
DIAZOTIZATION
DIAZOTIZATIONS
DIAZOTIZED
DIAZOTIZES
DIAZOTIZING
DIBASICITIES
DIBASICITY
DIBENZOFURAN
DIBENZOFURANS
DIBRANCHIATE
DIBRANCHIATES
DIBROMIDES
DICACITIES
DICACODYLS
DICARBOXYLIC
DICARPELLARY
DICASTERIES
DICENTRICS
DICEPHALISM
DICEPHALISMS
DICEPHALOUS
DICHASIALLY
DICHLAMYDEOUS
DICHLORACETIC
DICHLORIDE
DICHLORIDES
DICHLOROBENZENE
DICHLOROETHANE
DICHLOROETHANES
DICHLOROMETHANE
DICHLORVOS
DICHLORVOSES
DICHOGAMIC
DICHOGAMIES
DICHOGAMOUS
DICHONDRAS
DICHOTICALLY
DICHOTOMIC
DICHOTOMIES
DICHOTOMISATION
DICHOTOMISE
DICHOTOMISED
DICHOTOMISES
DICHOTOMISING
DICHOTOMIST
DICHOTOMISTS
DICHOTOMIZATION
DICHOTOMIZE
DICHOTOMIZED
DICHOTOMIZES
DICHOTOMIZING
DICHOTOMOUS
DICHOTOMOUSLY
DICHOTOMOUSNESS
DICHROISCOPE
DICHROISCOPES
DICHROISCOPIC
DICHROISMS
DICHROITES
DICHROITIC
DICHROMATE
DICHROMATES
DICHROMATIC
DICHROMATICISM
DICHROMATICISMS
DICHROMATICS
DICHROMATISM
DICHROMATISMS
DICHROMATS
DICHROMISM
DICHROMISMS
DICHROOSCOPE
DICHROOSCOPES
DICHROOSCOPIC
DICHROSCOPE
DICHROSCOPES
DICHROSCOPIC

DICKCISSEL
DICKCISSELS
DICKEYBIRD
DICKEYBIRDS
DICKYBIRDS
DICLINISMS
DICOTYLEDON
DICOTYLEDONOUS
DICOTYLEDONS
DICOUMARIN
DICOUMARINS
DICOUMAROL
DICOUMAROLS
DICROTISMS
DICTATIONAL
DICTATIONS
DICTATORIAL
DICTATORIALLY
DICTATORIALNESS
DICTATORSHIP
DICTATORSHIPS
DICTATRESS
DICTATRESSES
DICTATRICES
DICTATRIXES
DICTATURES
DICTIONALLY
DICTIONARIES
DICTIONARY
DICTYOGENS
DICTYOPTERAN
DICTYOPTERANS
DICTYOSOME
DICTYOSOMES
DICTYOSTELE
DICTYOSTELES
DICUMAROLS
DICYNODONT
DICYNODONTS
DIDACTICAL
DIDACTICALLY
DIDACTICISM
DIDACTICISMS
DIDACTYLISM
DIDACTYLISMS
DIDACTYLOUS
DIDASCALIC
DIDELPHIAN
DIDELPHIDS
DIDELPHINE
DIDELPHOUS
DIDGERIDOO
DIDGERIDOOS
DIDJERIDOO
DIDJERIDOOS
DIDJERIDUS
DIDRACHMAS
DIDYNAMIAN
DIDYNAMIES
DIDYNAMOUS
DIECIOUSLY
DIECIOUSNESS
DIECIOUSNESSES
DIEFFENBACHIA
DIEFFENBACHIAS
DIELECTRIC
DIELECTRICALLY
DIELECTRICS
DIENCEPHALA
DIENCEPHALIC
DIENCEPHALON
DIENCEPHALONS
DIESELINGS
DIESELISATION
DIESELISATIONS
DIESELISED
DIESELISES
DIESELISING
DIESELIZATION
DIESELIZATIONS
DIESELIZED
DIESELIZES
DIESELIZING
DIESELLING
DIESELLINGS
DIESINKERS
DIESTRUSES
DIETARIANS
DIETETICAL
DIETETICALLY
DIETHYLAMIDE
DIETHYLAMIDES
DIETHYLAMINE
DIETHYLAMINES
DIETHYLENE
DIETHYLENES
DIETICIANS
DIETITIANS
DIEZEUGMENON
DIEZEUGMENONS
DIFFARREATION
DIFFARREATIONS
DIFFERENCE
DIFFERENCED
DIFFERENCES
DIFFERENCIED
DIFFERENCIES
DIFFERENCING
DIFFERENCY
DIFFERENCYING
DIFFERENTIA
DIFFERENTIABLE
DIFFERENTIAE
DIFFERENTIAL
DIFFERENTIALLY
DIFFERENTIALS
DIFFERENTIATE
DIFFERENTIATED
DIFFERENTIATES
DIFFERENTIATING
DIFFERENTIATION
DIFFERENTIATOR
DIFFERENTIATORS
DIFFERENTLY
DIFFERENTNESS
DIFFERENTNESSES
DIFFICULTIES
DIFFICULTLY
DIFFICULTY
DIFFIDENCE
DIFFIDENCES
DIFFIDENTLY
DIFFORMITIES
DIFFORMITY
DIFFRACTED
DIFFRACTING
DIFFRACTION
DIFFRACTIONS
DIFFRACTIVE
DIFFRACTIVELY
DIFFRACTIVENESS
DIFFRACTOMETER
DIFFRACTOMETERS
DIFFRACTOMETRIC
DIFFRACTOMETRY
DIFFRANGIBILITY
DIFFRANGIBLE
DIFFUSEDLY
DIFFUSEDNESS
DIFFUSEDNESSES
DIFFUSENESS
DIFFUSENESSES
DIFFUSIBILITIES
DIFFUSIBILITY
DIFFUSIBLE
DIFFUSIBLENESS
DIFFUSIONAL
DIFFUSIONISM
DIFFUSIONISMS
DIFFUSIONIST
DIFFUSIONISTS
DIFFUSIONS
DIFFUSIVELY
DIFFUSIVENESS
DIFFUSIVENESSES
DIFFUSIVITIES
DIFFUSIVITY
DIFUNCTIONAL
DIFUNCTIONALS
DIGASTRICS
DIGESTANTS
DIGESTEDLY
DIGESTIBILITIES
DIGESTIBILITY
DIGESTIBLE
DIGESTIBLENESS
DIGESTIBLY
DIGESTIONAL
DIGESTIONS
DIGESTIVELY
DIGESTIVES
DIGITALINS
DIGITALISATION
DIGITALISATIONS
DIGITALISE
DIGITALISED
DIGITALISES
DIGITALISING
DIGITALISM
DIGITALISMS
DIGITALIZATION
DIGITALIZATIONS
DIGITALIZE
DIGITALIZED
DIGITALIZES
DIGITALIZING
DIGITATELY
DIGITATION
DIGITATIONS
DIGITIFORM
DIGITIGRADE
DIGITIGRADES
DIGITISATION
DIGITISATIONS
DIGITISERS
DIGITISING
DIGITIZATION
DIGITIZATIONS
DIGITIZERS
DIGITIZING
DIGITONINS
DIGITORIUM
DIGITORIUMS
DIGITOXIGENIN
DIGITOXIGENINS
DIGITOXINS
DIGLADIATE
DIGLADIATED
DIGLADIATES
DIGLADIATING
DIGLADIATION
DIGLADIATIONS
DIGLADIATOR
DIGLADIATORS
DIGLOSSIAS
DIGLYCERIDE
DIGLYCERIDES
DIGNIFICATION
DIGNIFICATIONS
DIGNIFIEDLY
DIGNIFIEDNESS
DIGNIFIEDNESSES
DIGNIFYING
DIGNITARIES
DIGONEUTIC
DIGONEUTISM
DIGONEUTISMS
DIGRAPHICALLY
DIGRESSERS
DIGRESSING

DIGRESSION
DIGRESSIONAL
DIGRESSIONARY
DIGRESSIONS
DIGRESSIVE
DIGRESSIVELY
DIGRESSIVENESS
DIHYBRIDISM
DIHYBRIDISMS
DIHYDROCODEINE
DIHYDROCODEINES
DIHYDROGEN
DIJUDICATE
DIJUDICATED
DIJUDICATES
DIJUDICATING
DIJUDICATION
DIJUDICATIONS
DILACERATE
DILACERATED
DILACERATES
DILACERATING
DILACERATION
DILACERATIONS
DILAPIDATE
DILAPIDATED
DILAPIDATES
DILAPIDATING
DILAPIDATION
DILAPIDATIONS
DILAPIDATOR
DILAPIDATORS
DILATABILITIES
DILATABILITY
DILATABLENESS
DILATABLENESSES
DILATANCIES
DILATATION
DILATATIONAL
DILATATIONS
DILATATORS
DILATOMETER
DILATOMETERS
DILATOMETRIC
DILATOMETRIES
DILATOMETRY
DILATORILY
DILATORINESS
DILATORINESSES
DILEMMATIC
DILETTANTE
DILETTANTEISH
DILETTANTEISM
DILETTANTEISMS
DILETTANTES
DILETTANTI
DILETTANTISH
DILETTANTISM
DILETTANTISMS
DILIGENCES
DILIGENTLY
DILLYDALLIED
DILLYDALLIES
DILLYDALLY
DILLYDALLYING
DILTIAZEMS
DILUCIDATE
DILUCIDATED
DILUCIDATES
DILUCIDATING
DILUCIDATION
DILUCIDATIONS
DILUTABLES
DILUTENESS
DILUTENESSES
DILUTIONARY
DILUVIALISM
DILUVIALISMS
DILUVIALIST
DILUVIALISTS
DIMENHYDRINATE
DIMENHYDRINATES
DIMENSIONAL
DIMENSIONALITY
DIMENSIONALLY
DIMENSIONED
DIMENSIONING
DIMENSIONLESS
DIMENSIONS
DIMERCAPROL
DIMERCAPROLS
DIMERISATION
DIMERISATIONS
DIMERISING
DIMERIZATION
DIMERIZATIONS
DIMERIZING
DIMETHOATE
DIMETHOATES
DIMETHYLAMINE
DIMETHYLAMINES
DIMETHYLANILINE
DIMIDIATED
DIMIDIATES
DIMIDIATING
DIMIDIATION
DIMIDIATIONS
DIMINISHABLE
DIMINISHED
DIMINISHES
DIMINISHING
DIMINISHINGLY
DIMINISHINGS
DIMINISHMENT
DIMINISHMENTS
DIMINUENDO
DIMINUENDOES
DIMINUENDOS
DIMINUTION
DIMINUTIONS
DIMINUTIVAL
DIMINUTIVE
DIMINUTIVELY
DIMINUTIVENESS
DIMINUTIVES
DIMORPHISM
DIMORPHISMS
DIMORPHOUS
DIMPLEMENT
DIMPLEMENTS
DINANDERIE
DINANDERIES
DINARCHIES
DINGDONGED
DINGDONGING
DINGINESSES
DINGLEBERRIES
DINGLEBERRY
DINITROBENZENE
DINITROBENZENES
DINITROGEN
DINITROPHENOL
DINITROPHENOLS
DINNERLESS
DINNERTIME
DINNERTIMES
DINNERWARE
DINNERWARES
DINOCERASES
DINOFLAGELLATE
DINOFLAGELLATES
DINOMANIAS
DINOSAURIAN
DINOSAURIC
DINOTHERES
DINOTHERIA
DINOTHERIUM
DINOTHERIUMS
DINOTURBATION
DINOTURBATIONS
DINUCLEOTIDE
DINUCLEOTIDES
DIOECIOUSLY
DIOECIOUSNESS
DIOECIOUSNESSES
DIOESTRUSES
DIOICOUSLY
DIOICOUSNESS
DIOICOUSNESSES
DIOPHYSITE
DIOPHYSITES
DIOPTOMETER
DIOPTOMETERS
DIOPTOMETRIES
DIOPTOMETRY
DIOPTRICAL
DIOPTRICALLY
DIORISTICAL
DIORISTICALLY
DIORTHOSES
DIORTHOSIS
DIORTHOTIC
DIOSCOREACEOUS
DIOSGENINS
DIOTHELETE
DIOTHELETES
DIOTHELETIC
DIOTHELETICAL
DIOTHELISM
DIOTHELISMS
DIOTHELITE
DIOTHELITES
DIOXONITRIC
DIPEPTIDASE
DIPEPTIDASES
DIPEPTIDES
DIPETALOUS
DIPHENHYDRAMINE
DIPHENYLAMINE
DIPHENYLAMINES
DIPHENYLENE
DIPHENYLENIMINE
DIPHENYLKETONE
DIPHENYLKETONES
DIPHOSGENE
DIPHOSGENES
DIPHOSPHATE
DIPHOSPHATES
DIPHTHERIA
DIPHTHERIAL
DIPHTHERIAS
DIPHTHERIC
DIPHTHERITIC
DIPHTHERITIS
DIPHTHERITISES
DIPHTHEROID
DIPHTHEROIDS
DIPHTHONGAL
DIPHTHONGALLY
DIPHTHONGED
DIPHTHONGIC
DIPHTHONGING
DIPHTHONGISE
DIPHTHONGISED
DIPHTHONGISES
DIPHTHONGISING
DIPHTHONGIZE
DIPHTHONGIZED
DIPHTHONGIZES
DIPHTHONGIZING
DIPHTHONGS
DIPHYCERCAL
DIPHYLETIC
DIPHYLLOUS
DIPHYODONT
DIPHYODONTS
DIPHYSITES
DIPHYSITISM
DIPHYSITISMS
DIPLEIDOSCOPE

DIPLEIDOSCOPES
DIPLOBIONT
DIPLOBIONTIC
DIPLOBIONTS
DIPLOBLASTIC
DIPLOCARDIAC
DIPLOCOCCAL
DIPLOCOCCI
DIPLOCOCCIC
DIPLOCOCCUS
DIPLODOCUS
DIPLODOCUSES
DIPLOGENESES
DIPLOGENESIS
DIPLOIDIES
DIPLOMACIES
DIPLOMAING
DIPLOMATED
DIPLOMATES
DIPLOMATESE
DIPLOMATESES
DIPLOMATIC
DIPLOMATICAL
DIPLOMATICALLY
DIPLOMATICS
DIPLOMATING
DIPLOMATISE
DIPLOMATISED
DIPLOMATISES
DIPLOMATISING
DIPLOMATIST
DIPLOMATISTS
DIPLOMATIZE
DIPLOMATIZED
DIPLOMATIZES
DIPLOMATIZING
DIPLOMATOLOGIES
DIPLOMATOLOGY
DIPLONEMAS
DIPLOPHASE
DIPLOPHASES
DIPLOSPEAK
DIPLOSPEAKS
DIPLOSTEMONOUS
DIPLOTENES
DIPNETTING
DIPPERFULS
DIPPINESSES

DIPRIONIDIAN
DIPROPELLANT
DIPROPELLANTS
DIPROTODON
DIPROTODONS
DIPROTODONT
DIPROTODONTID
DIPROTODONTIDS
DIPROTODONTS
DIPSOMANIA
DIPSOMANIAC
DIPSOMANIACAL
DIPSOMANIACS
DIPSOMANIAS
DIPSWITCHES
DIPTERISTS
DIPTEROCARP
DIPTEROCARPOUS
DIPTEROCARPS
DIPTEROSES
DIRECTEDNESS
DIRECTEDNESSES
DIRECTIONAL
DIRECTIONALITY
DIRECTIONLESS
DIRECTIONS
DIRECTIVES
DIRECTIVITIES
DIRECTIVITY
DIRECTNESS
DIRECTNESSES
DIRECTORATE
DIRECTORATES
DIRECTORIAL
DIRECTORIALLY
DIRECTORIES
DIRECTORSHIP
DIRECTORSHIPS
DIRECTRESS
DIRECTRESSES
DIRECTRICE
DIRECTRICES
DIRECTRIXES
DIREFULNESS
DIREFULNESSES
DIREMPTING
DIREMPTION
DIREMPTIONS

DIRENESSES
DIRIGIBILITIES
DIRIGIBILITY
DIRIGIBLES
DIRIGISMES
DIRTINESSES
DISABILITIES
DISABILITY
DISABLEMENT
DISABLEMENTS
DISABLISMS
DISABLISTS
DISABUSALS
DISABUSING
DISACCHARID
DISACCHARIDASE
DISACCHARIDASES
DISACCHARIDE
DISACCHARIDES
DISACCHARIDS
DISACCOMMODATE
DISACCOMMODATED
DISACCOMMODATES
DISACCORDANT
DISACCORDED
DISACCORDING
DISACCORDS
DISACCREDIT
DISACCREDITED
DISACCREDITING
DISACCREDITS
DISACCUSTOM
DISACCUSTOMED
DISACCUSTOMING
DISACCUSTOMS
DISACKNOWLEDGE
DISACKNOWLEDGED
DISACKNOWLEDGES
DISADORNED
DISADORNING
DISADVANCE
DISADVANCED
DISADVANCES
DISADVANCING
DISADVANTAGE
DISADVANTAGED
DISADVANTAGEOUS
DISADVANTAGES

DISADVANTAGING
DISADVENTURE
DISADVENTURES
DISADVENTUROUS
DISAFFECTED
DISAFFECTEDLY
DISAFFECTEDNESS
DISAFFECTING
DISAFFECTION
DISAFFECTIONATE
DISAFFECTIONS
DISAFFECTS
DISAFFILIATE
DISAFFILIATED
DISAFFILIATES
DISAFFILIATING
DISAFFILIATION
DISAFFILIATIONS
DISAFFIRMANCE
DISAFFIRMANCES
DISAFFIRMATION
DISAFFIRMATIONS
DISAFFIRMED
DISAFFIRMING
DISAFFIRMS
DISAFFOREST
DISAFFORESTED
DISAFFORESTING
DISAFFORESTMENT
DISAFFORESTS
DISAGGREGATE
DISAGGREGATED
DISAGGREGATES
DISAGGREGATING
DISAGGREGATION
DISAGGREGATIONS
DISAGGREGATIVE
DISAGREEABILITY
DISAGREEABLE
DISAGREEABLES
DISAGREEABLY
DISAGREEING
DISAGREEMENT
DISAGREEMENTS
DISALLOWABLE
DISALLOWANCE
DISALLOWANCES
DISALLOWED

DISALLOWING
DISALLYING
DISAMBIGUATE
DISAMBIGUATED
DISAMBIGUATES
DISAMBIGUATING
DISAMBIGUATION
DISAMBIGUATIONS
DISAMENITIES
DISAMENITY
DISANALOGIES
DISANALOGOUS
DISANALOGY
DISANCHORED
DISANCHORING
DISANCHORS
DISANIMATE
DISANIMATED
DISANIMATES
DISANIMATING
DISANNEXED
DISANNEXES
DISANNEXING
DISANNULLED
DISANNULLER
DISANNULLERS
DISANNULLING
DISANNULLINGS
DISANNULMENT
DISANNULMENTS
DISANOINTED
DISANOINTING
DISANOINTS
DISAPPAREL
DISAPPARELLED
DISAPPARELLING
DISAPPARELS
DISAPPEARANCE
DISAPPEARANCES
DISAPPEARED
DISAPPEARING
DISAPPEARS
DISAPPLICATION
DISAPPLICATIONS
DISAPPLIED
DISAPPLIES
DISAPPLYING
DISAPPOINT

DISAPPOINTED
DISAPPOINTEDLY
DISAPPOINTING
DISAPPOINTINGLY
DISAPPOINTMENT
DISAPPOINTMENTS
DISAPPOINTS
DISAPPROBATION
DISAPPROBATIONS
DISAPPROBATIVE
DISAPPROBATORY
DISAPPROPRIATE
DISAPPROPRIATED
DISAPPROPRIATES
DISAPPROVAL
DISAPPROVALS
DISAPPROVE
DISAPPROVED
DISAPPROVER
DISAPPROVERS
DISAPPROVES
DISAPPROVING
DISAPPROVINGLY
DISARMAMENT
DISARMAMENTS
DISARMINGLY
DISARRANGE
DISARRANGED
DISARRANGEMENT
DISARRANGEMENTS
DISARRANGES
DISARRANGING
DISARRAYED
DISARRAYING
DISARTICULATE
DISARTICULATED
DISARTICULATES
DISARTICULATING
DISARTICULATION
DISARTICULATOR
DISARTICULATORS
DISASSEMBLE
DISASSEMBLED
DISASSEMBLER
DISASSEMBLERS
DISASSEMBLES
DISASSEMBLIES
DISASSEMBLING
DISASSEMBLY
DISASSIMILATE
DISASSIMILATED
DISASSIMILATES
DISASSIMILATING
DISASSIMILATION
DISASSIMILATIVE
DISASSOCIATE
DISASSOCIATED
DISASSOCIATES
DISASSOCIATING
DISASSOCIATION
DISASSOCIATIONS
DISASTROUS
DISASTROUSLY
DISATTIRED
DISATTIRES
DISATTIRING
DISATTRIBUTION
DISATTRIBUTIONS
DISATTUNED
DISATTUNES
DISATTUNING
DISAUTHORISE
DISAUTHORISED
DISAUTHORISES
DISAUTHORISING
DISAUTHORIZE
DISAUTHORIZED
DISAUTHORIZES
DISAUTHORIZING
DISAVAUNCE
DISAVAUNCED
DISAVAUNCES
DISAVAUNCING
DISAVENTROUS
DISAVENTURE
DISAVENTURES
DISAVOUCHED
DISAVOUCHES
DISAVOUCHING
DISAVOWABLE
DISAVOWALS
DISAVOWEDLY
DISAVOWERS
DISAVOWING
DISBANDING
DISBANDMENT
DISBANDMENTS
DISBARKING
DISBARMENT
DISBARMENTS
DISBARRING
DISBELIEFS
DISBELIEVE
DISBELIEVED
DISBELIEVER
DISBELIEVERS
DISBELIEVES
DISBELIEVING
DISBELIEVINGLY
DISBENCHED
DISBENCHES
DISBENCHING
DISBENEFIT
DISBENEFITS
DISBOSOMED
DISBOSOMING
DISBOWELED
DISBOWELING
DISBOWELLED
DISBOWELLING
DISBRANCHED
DISBRANCHES
DISBRANCHING
DISBUDDING
DISBURDENED
DISBURDENING
DISBURDENMENT
DISBURDENMENTS
DISBURDENS
DISBURSABLE
DISBURSALS
DISBURSEMENT
DISBURSEMENTS
DISBURSERS
DISBURSING
DISBURTHEN
DISBURTHENED
DISBURTHENING
DISBURTHENS
DISCALCEATE
DISCALCEATES
DISCANDERING
DISCANDERINGS
DISCANDIED
DISCANDIES
DISCANDYING
DISCANDYINGS
DISCANTERS
DISCANTING
DISCAPACITATE
DISCAPACITATED
DISCAPACITATES
DISCAPACITATING
DISCARDABLE
DISCARDERS
DISCARDING
DISCARDMENT
DISCARDMENTS
DISCARNATE
DISCEPTATION
DISCEPTATIONS
DISCEPTATIOUS
DISCEPTATOR
DISCEPTATORIAL
DISCEPTATORS
DISCEPTING
DISCERNABLE
DISCERNABLY
DISCERNERS
DISCERNIBLE
DISCERNIBLY
DISCERNING
DISCERNINGLY
DISCERNMENT
DISCERNMENTS
DISCERPIBILITY
DISCERPIBLE
DISCERPING
DISCERPTIBLE
DISCERPTION
DISCERPTIONS
DISCERPTIVE
DISCHARGEABLE
DISCHARGED
DISCHARGEE
DISCHARGEES
DISCHARGER
DISCHARGERS
DISCHARGES
DISCHARGING
DISCHUFFED
DISCHURCHED
DISCHURCHES
DISCHURCHING
DISCIPLESHIP
DISCIPLESHIPS
DISCIPLINABLE
DISCIPLINAL
DISCIPLINANT
DISCIPLINANTS
DISCIPLINARIAN
DISCIPLINARIANS
DISCIPLINARILY
DISCIPLINARITY
DISCIPLINARIUM
DISCIPLINARIUMS
DISCIPLINARY
DISCIPLINE
DISCIPLINED
DISCIPLINER
DISCIPLINERS
DISCIPLINES
DISCIPLING
DISCIPLINING
DISCIPULAR
DISCISSION
DISCISSIONS
DISCLAIMED
DISCLAIMER
DISCLAIMERS
DISCLAIMING
DISCLAMATION
DISCLAMATIONS
DISCLIMAXES
DISCLOSERS
DISCLOSING
DISCLOSURE
DISCLOSURES
DISCOBOLOS
DISCOBOLUS
DISCOBOLUSES
DISCOGRAPHER
DISCOGRAPHERS
DISCOGRAPHIC
DISCOGRAPHICAL
DISCOGRAPHIES
DISCOGRAPHY
DISCOLOGIES
DISCOLOGIST
DISCOLOGISTS

DISCOLORATION
DISCOLORATIONS
DISCOLORED
DISCOLORING
DISCOLORMENT
DISCOLORMENTS
DISCOLOURATION
DISCOLOURATIONS
DISCOLOURED
DISCOLOURING
DISCOLOURMENT
DISCOLOURMENTS
DISCOLOURS
DISCOMBOBERATE
DISCOMBOBERATED
DISCOMBOBERATES
DISCOMBOBULATE
DISCOMBOBULATED
DISCOMBOBULATES
DISCOMEDUSAN
DISCOMEDUSANS
DISCOMFITED
DISCOMFITER
DISCOMFITERS
DISCOMFITING
DISCOMFITS
DISCOMFITURE
DISCOMFITURES
DISCOMFORT
DISCOMFORTABLE
DISCOMFORTED
DISCOMFORTING
DISCOMFORTS
DISCOMMEND
DISCOMMENDABLE
DISCOMMENDATION
DISCOMMENDED
DISCOMMENDING
DISCOMMENDS
DISCOMMISSION
DISCOMMISSIONED
DISCOMMISSIONS
DISCOMMODE
DISCOMMODED
DISCOMMODES
DISCOMMODING
DISCOMMODIOUS
DISCOMMODIOUSLY
DISCOMMODITIES
DISCOMMODITY
DISCOMMONED
DISCOMMONING
DISCOMMONS
DISCOMMUNITIES
DISCOMMUNITY
DISCOMPOSE
DISCOMPOSED
DISCOMPOSEDLY
DISCOMPOSES
DISCOMPOSING
DISCOMPOSINGLY
DISCOMPOSURE
DISCOMPOSURES
DISCOMYCETE
DISCOMYCETES
DISCOMYCETOUS
DISCONCERT
DISCONCERTED
DISCONCERTEDLY
DISCONCERTING
DISCONCERTINGLY
DISCONCERTION
DISCONCERTIONS
DISCONCERTMENT
DISCONCERTMENTS
DISCONCERTS
DISCONFIRM
DISCONFIRMATION
DISCONFIRMED
DISCONFIRMING
DISCONFIRMS
DISCONFORMABLE
DISCONFORMITIES
DISCONFORMITY
DISCONNECT
DISCONNECTED
DISCONNECTEDLY
DISCONNECTER
DISCONNECTERS
DISCONNECTING
DISCONNECTION
DISCONNECTIONS
DISCONNECTIVE
DISCONNECTS
DISCONNEXION
DISCONNEXIONS
DISCONSENT
DISCONSENTED
DISCONSENTING
DISCONSENTS
DISCONSOLATE
DISCONSOLATELY
DISCONSOLATION
DISCONSOLATIONS
DISCONTENT
DISCONTENTED
DISCONTENTEDLY
DISCONTENTFUL
DISCONTENTING
DISCONTENTMENT
DISCONTENTMENTS
DISCONTENTS
DISCONTIGUITIES
DISCONTIGUITY
DISCONTIGUOUS
DISCONTINUANCE
DISCONTINUANCES
DISCONTINUATION
DISCONTINUE
DISCONTINUED
DISCONTINUER
DISCONTINUERS
DISCONTINUES
DISCONTINUING
DISCONTINUITIES
DISCONTINUITY
DISCONTINUOUS
DISCONTINUOUSLY
DISCOPHILE
DISCOPHILES
DISCOPHORAN
DISCOPHORANS
DISCOPHOROUS
DISCORDANCE
DISCORDANCES
DISCORDANCIES
DISCORDANCY
DISCORDANT
DISCORDANTLY
DISCORDFUL
DISCORDING
DISCORPORATE
DISCORPORATED
DISCORPORATES
DISCORPORATING
DISCOTHEQUE
DISCOTHEQUES
DISCOUNSEL
DISCOUNSELLED
DISCOUNSELLING
DISCOUNSELS
DISCOUNTABLE
DISCOUNTED
DISCOUNTENANCE
DISCOUNTENANCED
DISCOUNTENANCES
DISCOUNTER
DISCOUNTERS
DISCOUNTING
DISCOURAGE
DISCOURAGEABLE
DISCOURAGED
DISCOURAGEMENT
DISCOURAGEMENTS
DISCOURAGER
DISCOURAGERS
DISCOURAGES
DISCOURAGING
DISCOURAGINGLY
DISCOURING
DISCOURSAL
DISCOURSED
DISCOURSER
DISCOURSERS
DISCOURSES
DISCOURSING
DISCOURSIVE
DISCOURTEISE
DISCOURTEOUS
DISCOURTEOUSLY
DISCOURTESIES
DISCOURTESY
DISCOVERABLE
DISCOVERED
DISCOVERER
DISCOVERERS
DISCOVERIES
DISCOVERING
DISCOVERTURE
DISCOVERTURES
DISCREDITABLE
DISCREDITABLY
DISCREDITED
DISCREDITING
DISCREDITS
DISCREETER
DISCREETEST
DISCREETLY
DISCREETNESS
DISCREETNESSES
DISCREPANCE
DISCREPANCES
DISCREPANCIES
DISCREPANCY
DISCREPANT
DISCREPANTLY
DISCRETELY
DISCRETENESS
DISCRETENESSES
DISCRETEST
DISCRETION
DISCRETIONAL
DISCRETIONALLY
DISCRETIONARILY
DISCRETIONARY
DISCRETIONS
DISCRETIVE
DISCRETIVELY
DISCRETIVES
DISCRIMINABLE
DISCRIMINABLY
DISCRIMINANT
DISCRIMINANTS
DISCRIMINATE
DISCRIMINATED
DISCRIMINATELY
DISCRIMINATES
DISCRIMINATING
DISCRIMINATION
DISCRIMINATIONS
DISCRIMINATIVE
DISCRIMINATOR
DISCRIMINATORS
DISCRIMINATORY
DISCROWNED
DISCROWNING
DISCULPATE
DISCULPATED
DISCULPATES
DISCULPATING

DISCUMBERED
DISCUMBERING
DISCUMBERS
DISCURSION
DISCURSIONS
DISCURSIST
DISCURSISTS
DISCURSIVE
DISCURSIVELY
DISCURSIVENESS
DISCURSORY
DISCURSUSES
DISCUSSABLE
DISCUSSANT
DISCUSSANTS
DISCUSSERS
DISCUSSIBLE
DISCUSSING
DISCUSSION
DISCUSSIONAL
DISCUSSIONS
DISCUSSIVE
DISCUSSIVES
DISCUTIENT
DISCUTIENTS
DISDAINFUL
DISDAINFULLY
DISDAINFULNESS
DISDAINING
DISEASEDNESS
DISEASEDNESSES
DISEASEFUL
DISECONOMIES
DISECONOMY
DISEMBARKATION
DISEMBARKATIONS
DISEMBARKED
DISEMBARKING
DISEMBARKMENT
DISEMBARKMENTS
DISEMBARKS
DISEMBARRASS
DISEMBARRASSED
DISEMBARRASSES
DISEMBARRASSING
DISEMBELLISH
DISEMBELLISHED
DISEMBELLISHES
DISEMBELLISHING
DISEMBITTER
DISEMBITTERED
DISEMBITTERING
DISEMBITTERS
DISEMBODIED
DISEMBODIES
DISEMBODIMENT
DISEMBODIMENTS
DISEMBODYING
DISEMBOGUE
DISEMBOGUED
DISEMBOGUEMENT
DISEMBOGUEMENTS
DISEMBOGUES
DISEMBOGUING
DISEMBOSOM
DISEMBOSOMED
DISEMBOSOMING
DISEMBOSOMS
DISEMBOWEL
DISEMBOWELED
DISEMBOWELING
DISEMBOWELLED
DISEMBOWELLING
DISEMBOWELMENT
DISEMBOWELMENTS
DISEMBOWELS
DISEMBRANGLE
DISEMBRANGLED
DISEMBRANGLES
DISEMBRANGLING
DISEMBROIL
DISEMBROILED
DISEMBROILING
DISEMBROILS
DISEMBURDEN
DISEMBURDENED
DISEMBURDENING
DISEMBURDENS
DISEMPLOYED
DISEMPLOYING
DISEMPLOYMENT
DISEMPLOYMENTS
DISEMPLOYS
DISEMPOWER
DISEMPOWERED
DISEMPOWERING
DISEMPOWERMENT
DISEMPOWERMENTS
DISEMPOWERS
DISEMVOWEL
DISEMVOWELLED
DISEMVOWELLING
DISEMVOWELS
DISENABLED
DISENABLEMENT
DISENABLEMENTS
DISENABLES
DISENABLING
DISENCHAIN
DISENCHAINED
DISENCHAINING
DISENCHAINS
DISENCHANT
DISENCHANTED
DISENCHANTER
DISENCHANTERS
DISENCHANTING
DISENCHANTINGLY
DISENCHANTMENT
DISENCHANTMENTS
DISENCHANTRESS
DISENCHANTS
DISENCLOSE
DISENCLOSED
DISENCLOSES
DISENCLOSING
DISENCUMBER
DISENCUMBERED
DISENCUMBERING
DISENCUMBERMENT
DISENCUMBERS
DISENCUMBRANCE
DISENCUMBRANCES
DISENDOWED
DISENDOWER
DISENDOWERS
DISENDOWING
DISENDOWMENT
DISENDOWMENTS
DISENFRANCHISE
DISENFRANCHISED
DISENFRANCHISES
DISENGAGED
DISENGAGEDNESS
DISENGAGEMENT
DISENGAGEMENTS
DISENGAGES
DISENGAGING
DISENNOBLE
DISENNOBLED
DISENNOBLES
DISENNOBLING
DISENROLLED
DISENROLLING
DISENROLLINGS
DISENSHROUD
DISENSHROUDED
DISENSHROUDING
DISENSHROUDS
DISENSLAVE
DISENSLAVED
DISENSLAVES
DISENSLAVING
DISENTAILED
DISENTAILING
DISENTAILMENT
DISENTAILMENTS
DISENTAILS
DISENTANGLE
DISENTANGLED
DISENTANGLEMENT
DISENTANGLES
DISENTANGLING
DISENTHRAL
DISENTHRALL
DISENTHRALLED
DISENTHRALLING
DISENTHRALLMENT
DISENTHRALLS
DISENTHRALMENT
DISENTHRALMENTS
DISENTHRALS
DISENTHRONE
DISENTHRONED
DISENTHRONES
DISENTHRONING
DISENTITLE
DISENTITLED
DISENTITLES
DISENTITLING
DISENTOMBED
DISENTOMBING
DISENTOMBS
DISENTRAIL
DISENTRAILED
DISENTRAILING
DISENTRAILS
DISENTRAIN
DISENTRAINED
DISENTRAINING
DISENTRAINMENT
DISENTRAINMENTS
DISENTRAINS
DISENTRANCE
DISENTRANCED
DISENTRANCEMENT
DISENTRANCES
DISENTRANCING
DISENTRAYLE
DISENTRAYLED
DISENTRAYLES
DISENTRAYLING
DISENTWINE
DISENTWINED
DISENTWINES
DISENTWINING
DISENVELOP
DISENVELOPED
DISENVELOPING
DISENVELOPS
DISENVIRON
DISENVIRONED
DISENVIRONING
DISENVIRONS
DISEPALOUS
DISEQUILIBRATE
DISEQUILIBRATED
DISEQUILIBRATES
DISEQUILIBRIA
DISEQUILIBRIUM
DISEQUILIBRIUMS
DISESPOUSE
DISESPOUSED
DISESPOUSES
DISESPOUSING
DISESTABLISH
DISESTABLISHED
DISESTABLISHES
DISESTABLISHING
DISESTEEMED

DISESTEEMING
DISESTEEMS
DISESTIMATION
DISESTIMATIONS
DISFAVORED
DISFAVORING
DISFAVOURED
DISFAVOURER
DISFAVOURERS
DISFAVOURING
DISFAVOURS
DISFEATURE
DISFEATURED
DISFEATUREMENT
DISFEATUREMENTS
DISFEATURES
DISFEATURING
DISFELLOWSHIP
DISFELLOWSHIPED
DISFELLOWSHIPS
DISFIGURATION
DISFIGURATIONS
DISFIGURED
DISFIGUREMENT
DISFIGUREMENTS
DISFIGURER
DISFIGURERS
DISFIGURES
DISFIGURING
DISFLESHED
DISFLESHES
DISFLESHING
DISFLUENCIES
DISFLUENCY
DISFORESTATION
DISFORESTATIONS
DISFORESTED
DISFORESTING
DISFORESTS
DISFORMING
DISFRANCHISE
DISFRANCHISED
DISFRANCHISES
DISFRANCHISING
DISFROCKED
DISFROCKING
DISFUNCTION
DISFUNCTIONAL
DISFUNCTIONS
DISFURNISH
DISFURNISHED
DISFURNISHES
DISFURNISHING
DISFURNISHMENT
DISFURNISHMENTS
DISGARNISH
DISGARNISHED
DISGARNISHES
DISGARNISHING
DISGARRISON
DISGARRISONED
DISGARRISONING
DISGARRISONS
DISGAVELLED
DISGAVELLING
DISGAVELLINGS
DISGESTING
DISGESTION
DISGESTIONS
DISGLORIFIED
DISGLORIFIES
DISGLORIFY
DISGLORIFYING
DISGORGEMENT
DISGORGEMENTS
DISGORGERS
DISGORGING
DISGOSPELLING
DISGOWNING
DISGRACEFUL
DISGRACEFULLY
DISGRACEFULNESS
DISGRACERS
DISGRACING
DISGRACIOUS
DISGRADATION
DISGRADATIONS
DISGRADING
DISGREGATION
DISGREGATIONS
DISGRUNTLE
DISGRUNTLED
DISGRUNTLEMENT
DISGRUNTLEMENTS
DISGRUNTLES
DISGRUNTLING
DISGUISABLE
DISGUISEDLY
DISGUISEDNESS
DISGUISEDNESSES
DISGUISELESS
DISGUISEMENT
DISGUISEMENTS
DISGUISERS
DISGUISING
DISGUISINGS
DISGUSTEDLY
DISGUSTEDNESS
DISGUSTEDNESSES
DISGUSTFUL
DISGUSTFULLY
DISGUSTFULNESS
DISGUSTING
DISGUSTINGLY
DISGUSTINGNESS
DISHABILITATE
DISHABILITATED
DISHABILITATES
DISHABILITATING
DISHABILITATION
DISHABILLE
DISHABILLES
DISHABITED
DISHABITING
DISHABLING
DISHALLOWED
DISHALLOWING
DISHALLOWS
DISHARMONIC
DISHARMONIES
DISHARMONIOUS
DISHARMONIOUSLY
DISHARMONISE
DISHARMONISED
DISHARMONISES
DISHARMONISING
DISHARMONIZE
DISHARMONIZED
DISHARMONIZES
DISHARMONIZING
DISHARMONY
DISHCLOTHS
DISHCLOUTS
DISHDASHAS
DISHDASHES
DISHEARTEN
DISHEARTENED
DISHEARTENING
DISHEARTENINGLY
DISHEARTENMENT
DISHEARTENMENTS
DISHEARTENS
DISHELMING
DISHERISON
DISHERISONS
DISHERITED
DISHERITING
DISHERITOR
DISHERITORS
DISHEVELED
DISHEVELING
DISHEVELLED
DISHEVELLING
DISHEVELMENT
DISHEVELMENTS
DISHOARDED
DISHOARDING
DISHONESTIES
DISHONESTLY
DISHONESTY
DISHONORABLE
DISHONORABLY
DISHONORARY
DISHONORED
DISHONORER
DISHONORERS
DISHONORING
DISHONOURABLE
DISHONOURABLY
DISHONOURED
DISHONOURER
DISHONOURERS
DISHONOURING
DISHONOURS
DISHORNING
DISHORSING
DISHOUSING
DISHTOWELS
DISHUMOURED
DISHUMOURING
DISHUMOURS
DISHWASHER
DISHWASHERS
DISHWATERS
DISILLUDED
DISILLUDES
DISILLUDING
DISILLUMINATE
DISILLUMINATED
DISILLUMINATES
DISILLUMINATING
DISILLUSION
DISILLUSIONARY
DISILLUSIONED
DISILLUSIONING
DISILLUSIONISE
DISILLUSIONISED
DISILLUSIONISES
DISILLUSIONIZE
DISILLUSIONIZED
DISILLUSIONIZES
DISILLUSIONMENT
DISILLUSIONS
DISILLUSIVE
DISIMAGINE
DISIMAGINED
DISIMAGINES
DISIMAGINING
DISIMMURED
DISIMMURES
DISIMMURING
DISIMPASSIONED
DISIMPRISON
DISIMPRISONED
DISIMPRISONING
DISIMPRISONMENT
DISIMPRISONS
DISIMPROVE
DISIMPROVED
DISIMPROVES
DISIMPROVING
DISINCARCERATE
DISINCARCERATED
DISINCARCERATES
DISINCENTIVE
DISINCENTIVES
DISINCLINATION
DISINCLINATIONS
DISINCLINE
DISINCLINED

DISINCLINES
DISINCLINING
DISINCLOSE
DISINCLOSED
DISINCLOSES
DISINCLOSING
DISINCORPORATE
DISINCORPORATED
DISINCORPORATES
DISINFECTANT
DISINFECTANTS
DISINFECTED
DISINFECTING
DISINFECTION
DISINFECTIONS
DISINFECTOR
DISINFECTORS
DISINFECTS
DISINFESTANT
DISINFESTANTS
DISINFESTATION
DISINFESTATIONS
DISINFESTED
DISINFESTING
DISINFESTS
DISINFLATION
DISINFLATIONARY
DISINFLATIONS
DISINFORMATION
DISINFORMATIONS
DISINFORMED
DISINFORMING
DISINFORMS
DISINGENUITIES
DISINGENUITY
DISINGENUOUS
DISINGENUOUSLY
DISINHERISON
DISINHERISONS
DISINHERIT
DISINHERITANCE
DISINHERITANCES
DISINHERITED
DISINHERITING
DISINHERITS
DISINHIBIT
DISINHIBITED
DISINHIBITING
DISINHIBITION
DISINHIBITIONS
DISINHIBITORY
DISINHIBITS
DISINHUMED
DISINHUMES
DISINHUMING
DISINTEGRABLE
DISINTEGRATE
DISINTEGRATED
DISINTEGRATES
DISINTEGRATING
DISINTEGRATION
DISINTEGRATIONS
DISINTEGRATIVE
DISINTEGRATOR
DISINTEGRATORS
DISINTEREST
DISINTERESTED
DISINTERESTEDLY
DISINTERESTING
DISINTERESTS
DISINTERMENT
DISINTERMENTS
DISINTERRED
DISINTERRING
DISINTHRAL
DISINTHRALLED
DISINTHRALLING
DISINTHRALLINGS
DISINTHRALS
DISINTOXICATE
DISINTOXICATED
DISINTOXICATES
DISINTOXICATING
DISINTOXICATION
DISINTRICATE
DISINTRICATED
DISINTRICATES
DISINTRICATING
DISINURING
DISINVENTED
DISINVENTING
DISINVENTS
DISINVESTED
DISINVESTING
DISINVESTITURE
DISINVESTITURES
DISINVESTMENT
DISINVESTMENTS
DISINVESTS
DISINVIGORATE
DISINVIGORATED
DISINVIGORATES
DISINVIGORATING
DISINVITED
DISINVITES
DISINVITING
DISINVOLVE
DISINVOLVED
DISINVOLVES
DISINVOLVING
DISJECTING
DISJECTION
DISJECTIONS
DISJOINABLE
DISJOINING
DISJOINTED
DISJOINTEDLY
DISJOINTEDNESS
DISJOINTING
DISJUNCTION
DISJUNCTIONS
DISJUNCTIVE
DISJUNCTIVELY
DISJUNCTIVES
DISJUNCTOR
DISJUNCTORS
DISJUNCTURE
DISJUNCTURES
DISLEAFING
DISLEAVING
DISLIKABLE
DISLIKEABLE
DISLIKEFUL
DISLIKENED
DISLIKENESS
DISLIKENESSES
DISLIKENING
DISLIMBING
DISLIMNING
DISLINKING
DISLOADING
DISLOCATED
DISLOCATEDLY
DISLOCATES
DISLOCATING
DISLOCATION
DISLOCATIONS
DISLODGEMENT
DISLODGEMENTS
DISLODGING
DISLODGMENT
DISLODGMENTS
DISLOIGNED
DISLOIGNING
DISLOYALLY
DISLOYALTIES
DISLOYALTY
DISLUSTRED
DISLUSTRES
DISLUSTRING
DISMALITIES
DISMALLEST
DISMALNESS
DISMALNESSES
DISMANNING
DISMANTLED
DISMANTLEMENT
DISMANTLEMENTS
DISMANTLER
DISMANTLERS
DISMANTLES
DISMANTLING
DISMANTLINGS
DISMASKING
DISMASTING
DISMASTMENT
DISMASTMENTS
DISMAYEDNESS
DISMAYEDNESSES
DISMAYFULLY
DISMAYINGLY
DISMAYLING
DISMEMBERED
DISMEMBERER
DISMEMBERERS
DISMEMBERING
DISMEMBERMENT
DISMEMBERMENTS
DISMEMBERS
DISMISSALS
DISMISSIBLE
DISMISSING
DISMISSION
DISMISSIONS
DISMISSIVE
DISMISSIVELY
DISMISSORY
DISMOUNTABLE
DISMOUNTED
DISMOUNTING
DISMUTATION
DISMUTATIONS
DISNATURALISE
DISNATURALISED
DISNATURALISES
DISNATURALISING
DISNATURALIZE
DISNATURALIZED
DISNATURALIZES
DISNATURALIZING
DISNATURED
DISNATURES
DISNATURING
DISNESTING
DISOBEDIENCE
DISOBEDIENCES
DISOBEDIENT
DISOBEDIENTLY
DISOBEYERS
DISOBEYING
DISOBLIGATION
DISOBLIGATIONS
DISOBLIGATORY
DISOBLIGED
DISOBLIGEMENT
DISOBLIGEMENTS
DISOBLIGES
DISOBLIGING
DISOBLIGINGLY
DISOBLIGINGNESS
DISOPERATION
DISOPERATIONS
DISORDERED
DISORDEREDLY
DISORDEREDNESS
DISORDERING
DISORDERLIES
DISORDERLINESS
DISORDERLY
DISORDINATE

DISORDINATELY
DISORGANIC
DISORGANISATION
DISORGANISE
DISORGANISED
DISORGANISER
DISORGANISERS
DISORGANISES
DISORGANISING
DISORGANIZATION
DISORGANIZE
DISORGANIZED
DISORGANIZER
DISORGANIZERS
DISORGANIZES
DISORGANIZING
DISORIENTATE
DISORIENTATED
DISORIENTATES
DISORIENTATING
DISORIENTATION
DISORIENTATIONS
DISORIENTED
DISORIENTING
DISORIENTS
DISOWNMENT
DISOWNMENTS
DISPARAGED
DISPARAGEMENT
DISPARAGEMENTS
DISPARAGER
DISPARAGERS
DISPARAGES
DISPARAGING
DISPARAGINGLY
DISPARATELY
DISPARATENESS
DISPARATENESSES
DISPARATES
DISPARITIES
DISPARKING
DISPARTING
DISPASSION
DISPASSIONATE
DISPASSIONATELY
DISPASSIONS
DISPATCHED
DISPATCHER
DISPATCHERS
DISPATCHES
DISPATCHFUL
DISPATCHING
DISPATHIES
DISPAUPERED
DISPAUPERING
DISPAUPERISE
DISPAUPERISED
DISPAUPERISES
DISPAUPERISING
DISPAUPERIZE
DISPAUPERIZED
DISPAUPERIZES
DISPAUPERIZING
DISPAUPERS
DISPELLERS
DISPELLING
DISPENCING
DISPENDING
DISPENSABILITY
DISPENSABLE
DISPENSABLENESS
DISPENSABLY
DISPENSARIES
DISPENSARY
DISPENSATION
DISPENSATIONAL
DISPENSATIONS
DISPENSATIVE
DISPENSATIVELY
DISPENSATOR
DISPENSATORIES
DISPENSATORILY
DISPENSATORS
DISPENSATORY
DISPENSERS
DISPENSING
DISPEOPLED
DISPEOPLES
DISPEOPLING
DISPERMOUS
DISPERSALS
DISPERSANT
DISPERSANTS
DISPERSEDLY
DISPERSEDNESS
DISPERSEDNESSES
DISPERSERS
DISPERSIBLE
DISPERSING
DISPERSION
DISPERSIONS
DISPERSIVE
DISPERSIVELY
DISPERSIVENESS
DISPERSOID
DISPERSOIDS
DISPIRITED
DISPIRITEDLY
DISPIRITEDNESS
DISPIRITING
DISPIRITINGLY
DISPIRITMENT
DISPIRITMENTS
DISPITEOUS
DISPITEOUSLY
DISPITEOUSNESS
DISPLACEABLE
DISPLACEMENT
DISPLACEMENTS
DISPLACERS
DISPLACING
DISPLANTATION
DISPLANTATIONS
DISPLANTED
DISPLANTING
DISPLAYABLE
DISPLAYERS
DISPLAYING
DISPLEASANCE
DISPLEASANCES
DISPLEASANT
DISPLEASANTED
DISPLEASANTING
DISPLEASANTS
DISPLEASED
DISPLEASEDLY
DISPLEASEDNESS
DISPLEASES
DISPLEASING
DISPLEASINGLY
DISPLEASINGNESS
DISPLEASURE
DISPLEASURED
DISPLEASURES
DISPLEASURING
DISPLENISH
DISPLENISHED
DISPLENISHES
DISPLENISHING
DISPLENISHMENT
DISPLENISHMENTS
DISPLODING
DISPLOSION
DISPLOSIONS
DISPLUMING
DISPONDAIC
DISPONDEES
DISPONGING
DISPORTING
DISPORTMENT
DISPORTMENTS
DISPOSABILITIES
DISPOSABILITY
DISPOSABLE
DISPOSABLENESS
DISPOSABLES
DISPOSEDLY
DISPOSINGLY
DISPOSINGS
DISPOSITION
DISPOSITIONAL
DISPOSITIONED
DISPOSITIONS
DISPOSITIVE
DISPOSITIVELY
DISPOSITIVES
DISPOSITOR
DISPOSITORS
DISPOSSESS
DISPOSSESSED
DISPOSSESSES
DISPOSSESSING
DISPOSSESSION
DISPOSSESSIONS
DISPOSSESSOR
DISPOSSESSORS
DISPOSSESSORY
DISPOSTING
DISPOSURES
DISPRAISED
DISPRAISER
DISPRAISERS
DISPRAISES
DISPRAISING
DISPRAISINGLY
DISPREADING
DISPREDDEN
DISPREDDING
DISPRINCED
DISPRISONED
DISPRISONING
DISPRISONS
DISPRIVACIED
DISPRIVILEGE
DISPRIVILEGED
DISPRIVILEGES
DISPRIVILEGING
DISPRIZING
DISPROFESS
DISPROFESSED
DISPROFESSES
DISPROFESSING
DISPROFITED
DISPROFITING
DISPROFITS
DISPROOVED
DISPROOVES
DISPROOVING
DISPROPERTIED
DISPROPERTIES
DISPROPERTY
DISPROPERTYING
DISPROPORTION
DISPROPORTIONAL
DISPROPORTIONED
DISPROPORTIONS
DISPROPRIATE
DISPROPRIATED
DISPROPRIATES
DISPROPRIATING
DISPROVABLE
DISPROVALS
DISPROVERS
DISPROVIDE
DISPROVIDED
DISPROVIDES
DISPROVIDING
DISPROVING
DISPUNGING
DISPURSING

DISPURVEYANCE
DISPURVEYANCES
DISPURVEYED
DISPURVEYING
DISPURVEYS
DISPUTABILITIES
DISPUTABILITY
DISPUTABLE
DISPUTABLENESS
DISPUTABLY
DISPUTANTS
DISPUTATION
DISPUTATIONS
DISPUTATIOUS
DISPUTATIOUSLY
DISPUTATIVE
DISPUTATIVELY
DISPUTATIVENESS
DISQUALIFIABLE
DISQUALIFIED
DISQUALIFIER
DISQUALIFIERS
DISQUALIFIES
DISQUALIFY
DISQUALIFYING
DISQUANTITIED
DISQUANTITIES
DISQUANTITY
DISQUANTITYING
DISQUIETED
DISQUIETEDLY
DISQUIETEDNESS
DISQUIETEN
DISQUIETENED
DISQUIETENING
DISQUIETENS
DISQUIETFUL
DISQUIETING
DISQUIETINGLY
DISQUIETIVE
DISQUIETLY
DISQUIETNESS
DISQUIETNESSES
DISQUIETOUS
DISQUIETUDE
DISQUIETUDES
DISQUISITION
DISQUISITIONAL
DISQUISITIONARY
DISQUISITIONS
DISQUISITIVE
DISQUISITORY
DISRANKING
DISREGARDED
DISREGARDER
DISREGARDERS
DISREGARDFUL
DISREGARDFULLY
DISREGARDING
DISREGARDS
DISRELATED
DISRELATION
DISRELATIONS
DISRELISHED
DISRELISHES
DISRELISHING
DISREMEMBER
DISREMEMBERED
DISREMEMBERING
DISREMEMBERS
DISREPAIRS
DISREPUTABILITY
DISREPUTABLE
DISREPUTABLY
DISREPUTATION
DISREPUTATIONS
DISREPUTES
DISRESPECT
DISRESPECTABLE
DISRESPECTED
DISRESPECTFUL
DISRESPECTFULLY
DISRESPECTING
DISRESPECTS
DISROBEMENT
DISROBEMENTS
DISROOTING
DISRUPTERS
DISRUPTING
DISRUPTION
DISRUPTIONS
DISRUPTIVE
DISRUPTIVELY
DISRUPTIVENESS
DISRUPTORS
DISSATISFACTION
DISSATISFACTORY
DISSATISFIED
DISSATISFIEDLY
DISSATISFIES
DISSATISFY
DISSATISFYING
DISSAVINGS
DISSEATING
DISSECTIBLE
DISSECTING
DISSECTINGS
DISSECTION
DISSECTIONS
DISSECTIVE
DISSECTORS
DISSEISEES
DISSEISING
DISSEISINS
DISSEISORS
DISSEIZEES
DISSEIZING
DISSEIZINS
DISSEIZORS
DISSELBOOM
DISSELBOOMS
DISSEMBLANCE
DISSEMBLANCES
DISSEMBLED
DISSEMBLER
DISSEMBLERS
DISSEMBLES
DISSEMBLIES
DISSEMBLING
DISSEMBLINGLY
DISSEMBLINGS
DISSEMINATE
DISSEMINATED
DISSEMINATES
DISSEMINATING
DISSEMINATION
DISSEMINATIONS
DISSEMINATIVE
DISSEMINATOR
DISSEMINATORS
DISSEMINULE
DISSEMINULES
DISSENSION
DISSENSIONS
DISSENSUSES
DISSENTERISH
DISSENTERISM
DISSENTERISMS
DISSENTERS
DISSENTIENCE
DISSENTIENCES
DISSENTIENCIES
DISSENTIENCY
DISSENTIENT
DISSENTIENTLY
DISSENTIENTS
DISSENTING
DISSENTINGLY
DISSENTION
DISSENTIONS
DISSENTIOUS
DISSEPIMENT
DISSEPIMENTAL
DISSEPIMENTS
DISSERTATE
DISSERTATED
DISSERTATES
DISSERTATING
DISSERTATION
DISSERTATIONAL
DISSERTATIONIST
DISSERTATIONS
DISSERTATIVE
DISSERTATOR
DISSERTATORS
DISSERTING
DISSERVICE
DISSERVICEABLE
DISSERVICES
DISSERVING
DISSEVERANCE
DISSEVERANCES
DISSEVERATION
DISSEVERATIONS
DISSEVERED
DISSEVERING
DISSEVERMENT
DISSEVERMENTS
DISSHEATHE
DISSHEATHED
DISSHEATHES
DISSHEATHING
DISSHIVERED
DISSHIVERING
DISSHIVERS
DISSIDENCE
DISSIDENCES
DISSIDENTLY
DISSIDENTS
DISSILIENCE
DISSILIENCES
DISSILIENT
DISSIMILAR
DISSIMILARITIES
DISSIMILARITY
DISSIMILARLY
DISSIMILARS
DISSIMILATE
DISSIMILATED
DISSIMILATES
DISSIMILATING
DISSIMILATION
DISSIMILATIONS
DISSIMILATIVE
DISSIMILATORY
DISSIMILES
DISSIMILITUDE
DISSIMILITUDES
DISSIMULATE
DISSIMULATED
DISSIMULATES
DISSIMULATING
DISSIMULATION
DISSIMULATIONS
DISSIMULATIVE
DISSIMULATOR
DISSIMULATORS
DISSIPABLE
DISSIPATED
DISSIPATEDLY
DISSIPATEDNESS
DISSIPATER
DISSIPATERS
DISSIPATES
DISSIPATING
DISSIPATION
DISSIPATIONS
DISSIPATIVE
DISSIPATOR
DISSIPATORS

DISSOCIABILITY
DISSOCIABLE
DISSOCIABLENESS
DISSOCIABLY
DISSOCIALISE
DISSOCIALISED
DISSOCIALISES
DISSOCIALISING
DISSOCIALITIES
DISSOCIALITY
DISSOCIALIZE
DISSOCIALIZED
DISSOCIALIZES
DISSOCIALIZING
DISSOCIATE
DISSOCIATED
DISSOCIATES
DISSOCIATING
DISSOCIATION
DISSOCIATIONS
DISSOCIATIVE
DISSOLUBILITIES
DISSOLUBILITY
DISSOLUBLE
DISSOLUBLENESS
DISSOLUTELY
DISSOLUTENESS
DISSOLUTENESSES
DISSOLUTES
DISSOLUTION
DISSOLUTIONISM
DISSOLUTIONISMS
DISSOLUTIONIST
DISSOLUTIONISTS
DISSOLUTIONS
DISSOLUTIVE
DISSOLVABILITY
DISSOLVABLE
DISSOLVABLENESS
DISSOLVENT
DISSOLVENTS
DISSOLVERS
DISSOLVING
DISSOLVINGS
DISSONANCE
DISSONANCES
DISSONANCIES
DISSONANCY
DISSONANTLY
DISSUADABLE
DISSUADERS
DISSUADING
DISSUASION
DISSUASIONS
DISSUASIVE
DISSUASIVELY
DISSUASIVENESS
DISSUASIVES
DISSUASORIES
DISSUASORY
DISSUNDERED
DISSUNDERING
DISSUNDERS
DISSYLLABIC
DISSYLLABIFIED
DISSYLLABIFIES
DISSYLLABIFY
DISSYLLABIFYING
DISSYLLABISM
DISSYLLABISMS
DISSYLLABLE
DISSYLLABLES
DISSYMMETRIC
DISSYMMETRICAL
DISSYMMETRIES
DISSYMMETRY
DISTAINING
DISTANCELESS
DISTANCING
DISTANTNESS
DISTANTNESSES
DISTASTEFUL
DISTASTEFULLY
DISTASTEFULNESS
DISTASTING
DISTELFINK
DISTELFINKS
DISTEMPERATE
DISTEMPERATURE
DISTEMPERATURES
DISTEMPERED
DISTEMPERING
DISTEMPERS
DISTENDERS
DISTENDING
DISTENSIBILITY
DISTENSIBLE
DISTENSILE
DISTENSION
DISTENSIONS
DISTENSIVE
DISTENTION
DISTENTIONS
DISTHRONED
DISTHRONES
DISTHRONING
DISTHRONISE
DISTHRONISED
DISTHRONISES
DISTHRONISING
DISTHRONIZE
DISTHRONIZED
DISTHRONIZES
DISTHRONIZING
DISTICHOUS
DISTICHOUSLY
DISTILLABLE
DISTILLAND
DISTILLANDS
DISTILLATE
DISTILLATES
DISTILLATION
DISTILLATIONS
DISTILLATORY
DISTILLERIES
DISTILLERS
DISTILLERY
DISTILLING
DISTILLINGS
DISTILMENT
DISTILMENTS
DISTINCTER
DISTINCTEST
DISTINCTION
DISTINCTIONS
DISTINCTIVE
DISTINCTIVELY
DISTINCTIVENESS
DISTINCTIVES
DISTINCTLY
DISTINCTNESS
DISTINCTNESSES
DISTINCTURE
DISTINCTURES
DISTINGUEE
DISTINGUISH
DISTINGUISHABLE
DISTINGUISHABLY
DISTINGUISHED
DISTINGUISHER
DISTINGUISHERS
DISTINGUISHES
DISTINGUISHING
DISTINGUISHMENT
DISTORTEDLY
DISTORTEDNESS
DISTORTEDNESSES
DISTORTERS
DISTORTING
DISTORTION
DISTORTIONAL
DISTORTIONS
DISTORTIVE
DISTRACTABLE
DISTRACTED
DISTRACTEDLY
DISTRACTEDNESS
DISTRACTER
DISTRACTERS
DISTRACTIBILITY
DISTRACTIBLE
DISTRACTING
DISTRACTINGLY
DISTRACTION
DISTRACTIONS
DISTRACTIVE
DISTRACTIVELY
DISTRACTOR
DISTRACTORS
DISTRAINABLE
DISTRAINED
DISTRAINEE
DISTRAINEES
DISTRAINER
DISTRAINERS
DISTRAINING
DISTRAINMENT
DISTRAINMENTS
DISTRAINOR
DISTRAINORS
DISTRAINTS
DISTRAUGHT
DISTRAUGHTLY
DISTRESSED
DISTRESSER
DISTRESSERS
DISTRESSES
DISTRESSFUL
DISTRESSFULLY
DISTRESSFULNESS
DISTRESSING
DISTRESSINGLY
DISTRESSINGS
DISTRIBUEND
DISTRIBUENDS
DISTRIBUTABLE
DISTRIBUTARIES
DISTRIBUTARY
DISTRIBUTE
DISTRIBUTED
DISTRIBUTEE
DISTRIBUTEES
DISTRIBUTER
DISTRIBUTERS
DISTRIBUTES
DISTRIBUTING
DISTRIBUTION
DISTRIBUTIONAL
DISTRIBUTIONS
DISTRIBUTIVE
DISTRIBUTIVELY
DISTRIBUTIVES
DISTRIBUTIVITY
DISTRIBUTOR
DISTRIBUTORS
DISTRIBUTORSHIP
DISTRICTED
DISTRICTING
DISTRINGAS
DISTRINGASES
DISTROUBLE
DISTROUBLED
DISTROUBLES
DISTROUBLING
DISTRUSTED
DISTRUSTER
DISTRUSTERS
DISTRUSTFUL
DISTRUSTFULLY
DISTRUSTFULNESS

D

DISTRUSTING
DISTRUSTLESS
DISTURBANCE
DISTURBANCES
DISTURBANT
DISTURBANTS
DISTURBATIVE
DISTURBERS
DISTURBING
DISTURBINGLY
DISUBSTITUTED
DISULFATES
DISULFIDES
DISULFIRAM
DISULFIRAMS
DISULFOTON
DISULFOTONS
DISULPHATE
DISULPHATES
DISULPHIDE
DISULPHIDES
DISULPHURET
DISULPHURETS
DISULPHURIC
DISUNIONIST
DISUNIONISTS
DISUNITERS
DISUNITIES
DISUNITING
DISUTILITIES
DISUTILITY
DISVALUING
DISVOUCHED
DISVOUCHES
DISVOUCHING
DISWORSHIP
DISWORSHIPED
DISWORSHIPING
DISWORSHIPPED
DISWORSHIPPING
DISWORSHIPS
DISYLLABIC
DISYLLABIFIED
DISYLLABIFIES
DISYLLABIFY
DISYLLABIFYING
DISYLLABISM
DISYLLABISMS
DISYLLABLE
DISYLLABLES
DITCHDIGGER
DITCHDIGGERS
DITCHWATER
DITCHWATERS
DITHEISTIC
DITHEISTICAL
DITHELETES
DITHELETIC
DITHELETICAL
DITHELETISM
DITHELETISMS
DITHELISMS
DITHELITISM
DITHELITISMS
DITHERIEST
DITHERINGS
DITHIOCARBAMATE
DITHIOCARBAMIC
DITHIONATE
DITHIONATES
DITHIONITE
DITHIONITES
DITHIONOUS
DITHYRAMBIC
DITHYRAMBICALLY
DITHYRAMBIST
DITHYRAMBISTS
DITHYRAMBS
DITRANSITIVE
DITRANSITIVES
DITRIGLYPH
DITRIGLYPHIC
DITRIGLYPHS
DITROCHEAN
DITROCHEES
DITSINESSES
DITTANDERS
DITTOGRAPHIC
DITTOGRAPHIES
DITTOGRAPHY
DITTOLOGIES
DITZINESSES
DIURETICALLY
DIURETICALNESS
DIURNALIST
DIURNALISTS
DIUTURNITIES
DIUTURNITY
DIVAGATING
DIVAGATION
DIVAGATIONS
DIVALENCES
DIVALENCIES
DIVARICATE
DIVARICATED
DIVARICATELY
DIVARICATES
DIVARICATING
DIVARICATINGLY
DIVARICATION
DIVARICATIONS
DIVARICATOR
DIVARICATORS
DIVEBOMBED
DIVEBOMBING
DIVELLICATE
DIVELLICATED
DIVELLICATES
DIVELLICATING
DIVERGEMENT
DIVERGEMENTS
DIVERGENCE
DIVERGENCES
DIVERGENCIES
DIVERGENCY
DIVERGENTLY
DIVERGINGLY
DIVERSENESS
DIVERSENESSES
DIVERSIFIABLE
DIVERSIFICATION
DIVERSIFIED
DIVERSIFIER
DIVERSIFIERS
DIVERSIFIES
DIVERSIFORM
DIVERSIFYING
DIVERSIONAL
DIVERSIONARY
DIVERSIONIST
DIVERSIONISTS
DIVERSIONS
DIVERSITIES
DIVERTIBILITIES
DIVERTIBILITY
DIVERTIBLE
DIVERTICULA
DIVERTICULAR
DIVERTICULATE
DIVERTICULATED
DIVERTICULITIS
DIVERTICULOSES
DIVERTICULOSIS
DIVERTICULUM
DIVERTIMENTI
DIVERTIMENTO
DIVERTIMENTOS
DIVERTINGLY
DIVERTISEMENT
DIVERTISEMENTS
DIVERTISSEMENT
DIVERTISSEMENTS
DIVESTIBLE
DIVESTITURE
DIVESTITURES
DIVESTMENT
DIVESTMENTS
DIVESTURES
DIVIDEDNESS
DIVIDEDNESSES
DIVIDENDLESS
DIVINATION
DIVINATIONS
DIVINATORIAL
DIVINATORS
DIVINATORY
DIVINENESS
DIVINENESSES
DIVINERESS
DIVINERESSES
DIVINIFIED
DIVINIFIES
DIVINIFYING
DIVINISATION
DIVINISATIONS
DIVINISING
DIVINITIES
DIVINIZATION
DIVINIZATIONS
DIVINIZING
DIVISIBILITIES
DIVISIBILITY
DIVISIBLENESS
DIVISIBLENESSES
DIVISIONAL
DIVISIONALLY
DIVISIONARY
DIVISIONISM
DIVISIONISMS
DIVISIONIST
DIVISIONISTS
DIVISIVELY
DIVISIVENESS
DIVISIVENESSES
DIVORCEABLE
DIVORCEMENT
DIVORCEMENTS
DIVULGATED
DIVULGATER
DIVULGATERS
DIVULGATES
DIVULGATING
DIVULGATION
DIVULGATIONS
DIVULGATOR
DIVULGATORS
DIVULGEMENT
DIVULGEMENTS
DIVULGENCE
DIVULGENCES
DIVULSIONS
DIZENMENTS
DIZZINESSES
DIZZYINGLY
DJELLABAHS
DOBSONFLIES
DOCENTSHIP
DOCENTSHIPS
DOCHMIACAL
DOCHMIUSES
DOCIBILITIES
DOCIBILITY
DOCIBLENESS
DOCIBLENESSES
DOCILITIES
DOCIMASIES
DOCIMASTIC
DOCIMOLOGIES
DOCIMOLOGY
DOCKISATION

DOCKISATIONS
DOCKIZATION
DOCKIZATIONS
DOCKMASTER
DOCKMASTERS
DOCKWALLOPER
DOCKWALLOPERS
DOCKWORKER
DOCKWORKERS
DOCQUETING
DOCTORANDS
DOCTORATED
DOCTORATES
DOCTORATING
DOCTORESSES
DOCTORINGS
DOCTORLESS
DOCTORSHIP
DOCTORSHIPS
DOCTRESSES
DOCTRINAIRE
DOCTRINAIRES
DOCTRINAIRISM
DOCTRINAIRISMS
DOCTRINALITIES
DOCTRINALITY
DOCTRINALLY
DOCTRINARIAN
DOCTRINARIANISM
DOCTRINARIANS
DOCTRINARISM
DOCTRINARISMS
DOCTRINISM
DOCTRINISMS
DOCTRINIST
DOCTRINISTS
DOCUDRAMAS
DOCUMENTABLE
DOCUMENTAL
DOCUMENTALIST
DOCUMENTALISTS
DOCUMENTARIAN
DOCUMENTARIANS
DOCUMENTARIES
DOCUMENTARILY
DOCUMENTARISE
DOCUMENTARISED
DOCUMENTARISES
DOCUMENTARISING
DOCUMENTARIST
DOCUMENTARISTS
DOCUMENTARIZE
DOCUMENTARIZED
DOCUMENTARIZES
DOCUMENTARIZING
DOCUMENTARY
DOCUMENTATION
DOCUMENTATIONAL
DOCUMENTATIONS
DOCUMENTED
DOCUMENTER
DOCUMENTERS
DOCUMENTING
DODDERIEST
DODDIPOLLS
DODDYPOLLS
DODECAGONAL
DODECAGONS
DODECAGYNIAN
DODECAGYNOUS
DODECAHEDRA
DODECAHEDRAL
DODECAHEDRON
DODECAHEDRONS
DODECANDROUS
DODECANOIC
DODECAPHONIC
DODECAPHONIES
DODECAPHONISM
DODECAPHONISMS
DODECAPHONIST
DODECAPHONISTS
DODECAPHONY
DODECASTYLE
DODECASTYLES
DODECASYLLABIC
DODECASYLLABLE
DODECASYLLABLES
DODGEBALLS
DODGINESSES
DOGARESSAS
DOGBERRIES
DOGBERRYISM
DOGBERRYISMS
DOGCATCHER
DOGCATCHERS
DOGFIGHTING
DOGFIGHTINGS
DOGGEDNESS
DOGGEDNESSES
DOGGINESSES
DOGGISHNESS
DOGGISHNESSES
DOGGONEDER
DOGGONEDEST
DOGLEGGING
DOGMATICAL
DOGMATICALLY
DOGMATICALNESS
DOGMATISATION
DOGMATISATIONS
DOGMATISED
DOGMATISER
DOGMATISERS
DOGMATISES
DOGMATISING
DOGMATISMS
DOGMATISTS
DOGMATIZATION
DOGMATIZATIONS
DOGMATIZED
DOGMATIZER
DOGMATIZERS
DOGMATIZES
DOGMATIZING
DOGMATOLOGIES
DOGMATOLOGY
DOGNAPINGS
DOGNAPPERS
DOGNAPPING
DOGNAPPINGS
DOGROBBERS
DOGSBODIED
DOGSBODIES
DOGSBODYING
DOGSBODYINGS
DOGSLEDDED
DOGSLEDDER
DOGSLEDDERS
DOGSLEDDING
DOGSLEDDINGS
DOGTROTTED
DOGTROTTING
DOGWATCHES
DOLABRIFORM
DOLCELATTE
DOLCELATTES
DOLCEMENTE
DOLEFULLER
DOLEFULLEST
DOLEFULNESS
DOLEFULNESSES
DOLESOMELY
DOLICHOCEPHAL
DOLICHOCEPHALIC
DOLICHOCEPHALS
DOLICHOCEPHALY
DOLICHOSAURUS
DOLICHOSAURUSES
DOLICHOSES
DOLICHURUS
DOLICHURUSES
DOLLARBIRD
DOLLARBIRDS
DOLLARFISH
DOLLARFISHES
DOLLARISATION
DOLLARISATIONS
DOLLARISED
DOLLARISES
DOLLARISING
DOLLARIZATION
DOLLARIZATIONS
DOLLARIZED
DOLLARIZES
DOLLARIZING
DOLLARLESS
DOLLAROCRACIES
DOLLAROCRACY
DOLLARSHIP
DOLLARSHIPS
DOLLHOUSES
DOLLINESSES
DOLLISHNESS
DOLLISHNESSES
DOLLYBIRDS
DOLOMITISATION
DOLOMITISATIONS
DOLOMITISE
DOLOMITISED
DOLOMITISES
DOLOMITISING
DOLOMITIZATION
DOLOMITIZATIONS
DOLOMITIZE
DOLOMITIZED
DOLOMITIZES
DOLOMITIZING
DOLORIFEROUS
DOLORIMETRIES
DOLORIMETRY
DOLOROUSLY
DOLOROUSNESS
DOLOROUSNESSES
DOLOSTONES
DOLPHINARIA
DOLPHINARIUM
DOLPHINARIUMS
DOLPHINETS
DOLPHINFISH
DOLPHINFISHES
DOLTISHNESS
DOLTISHNESSES
DOMESTICABLE
DOMESTICAL
DOMESTICALLY
DOMESTICATE
DOMESTICATED
DOMESTICATES
DOMESTICATING
DOMESTICATION
DOMESTICATIONS
DOMESTICATIVE
DOMESTICATOR
DOMESTICATORS
DOMESTICISE
DOMESTICISED
DOMESTICISES
DOMESTICISING
DOMESTICITIES
DOMESTICITY
DOMESTICIZE
DOMESTICIZED
DOMESTICIZES
DOMESTICIZING
DOMESTIQUE
DOMESTIQUES
DOMICILIARY
DOMICILIATE
DOMICILIATED

D

DOMICILIATES
DOMICILIATING
DOMICILIATION
DOMICILIATIONS
DOMICILING
DOMINANCES
DOMINANCIES
DOMINANTLY
DOMINATING
DOMINATINGLY
DOMINATION
DOMINATIONS
DOMINATIVE
DOMINATORS
DOMINATRICES
DOMINATRIX
DOMINATRIXES
DOMINEERED
DOMINEERING
DOMINEERINGLY
DOMINEERINGNESS
DOMINICKER
DOMINICKERS
DOMINIQUES
DONATARIES
DONATISTIC
DONATISTICAL
DONATORIES
DONENESSES
DONEPEZILS
DONKEYWORK
DONKEYWORKS
DONNICKERS
DONNISHNESS
DONNISHNESSES
DONNYBROOK
DONNYBROOKS
DONORSHIPS
DOODLEBUGS
DOOHICKEYS
DOOHICKIES
DOOMSAYERS
DOOMSAYING
DOOMSAYINGS
DOOMSDAYER
DOOMSDAYERS
DOOMWATCHED
DOOMWATCHER
DOOMWATCHERS
DOOMWATCHES
DOOMWATCHING
DOOMWATCHINGS
DOORFRAMES
DOORKEEPER
DOORKEEPERS
DOORKNOCKED
DOORKNOCKER
DOORKNOCKERS
DOORKNOCKING
DOORKNOCKS
DOORNBOOMS
DOORPLATES
DOORSTEPPED
DOORSTEPPER
DOORSTEPPERS
DOORSTEPPING
DOORSTEPPINGS
DOORSTONES
DOPAMINERGIC
DOPESHEETS
DOPEYNESSES
DOPINESSES
DOPPELGANGER
DOPPELGANGERS
DOPPLERITE
DOPPLERITES
DORBEETLES
DORKINESSES
DORMANCIES
DORMITIONS
DORMITIVES
DORMITORIES
DORONICUMS
DORSIBRANCHIATE
DORSIFEROUS
DORSIFIXED
DORSIFLEXED
DORSIFLEXES
DORSIFLEXING
DORSIFLEXION
DORSIFLEXIONS
DORSIGRADE
DORSIVENTRAL
DORSIVENTRALITY
DORSIVENTRALLY
DORSOLATERAL
DORSOLUMBAR
DORSOVENTRAL
DORSOVENTRALITY
DORSOVENTRALLY
DORTINESSES
DOSEMETERS
DOSIMETERS
DOSIMETRIC
DOSIMETRICIAN
DOSIMETRICIANS
DOSIMETRIES
DOSIMETRIST
DOSIMETRISTS
DOSIOLOGIES
DOSOLOGIES
DOSSHOUSES
DOTARDLIER
DOTARDLIEST
DOTCOMMERS
DOTTINESSES
DOUBLEHEADER
DOUBLEHEADERS
DOUBLENESS
DOUBLENESSES
DOUBLESPEAK
DOUBLESPEAKER
DOUBLESPEAKERS
DOUBLESPEAKS
DOUBLETHINK
DOUBLETHINKS
DOUBLETONS
DOUBLETREE
DOUBLETREES
DOUBTFULLY
DOUBTFULNESS
DOUBTFULNESSES
DOUBTINGLY
DOUBTLESSLY
DOUBTLESSNESS
DOUBTLESSNESSES
DOUCENESSES
DOUCEPERES
DOUCHEBAGS
DOUGHBALLS
DOUGHFACED
DOUGHFACES
DOUGHINESS
DOUGHINESSES
DOUGHNUTLIKE
DOUGHNUTTED
DOUGHNUTTING
DOUGHNUTTINGS
DOUGHTIEST
DOUGHTINESS
DOUGHTINESSES
DOULOCRACIES
DOULOCRACY
DOUPPIONIS
DOURNESSES
DOUROUCOULI
DOUROUCOULIS
DOVEISHNESS
DOVEISHNESSES
DOVETAILED
DOVETAILING
DOVETAILINGS
DOVISHNESS
DOVISHNESSES
DOWDINESSES
DOWELLINGS
DOWFNESSES
DOWITCHERS
DOWNBURSTS
DOWNCOMERS
DOWNCRYING
DOWNDRAFTS
DOWNDRAUGHT
DOWNDRAUGHTS
DOWNFALLEN
DOWNFORCES
DOWNGRADED
DOWNGRADES
DOWNGRADING
DOWNHEARTED
DOWNHEARTEDLY
DOWNHEARTEDNESS
DOWNHILLER
DOWNHILLERS
DOWNINESSES
DOWNLIGHTER
DOWNLIGHTERS
DOWNLIGHTS
DOWNLINKED
DOWNLINKING
DOWNLOADABLE
DOWNLOADED
DOWNLOADING
DOWNLOADINGS
DOWNLOOKED
DOWNPLAYED
DOWNPLAYING
DOWNRATING
DOWNREGULATION
DOWNREGULATIONS
DOWNRIGHTLY
DOWNRIGHTNESS
DOWNRIGHTNESSES
DOWNRUSHES
DOWNSCALED
DOWNSCALES
DOWNSCALING
DOWNSHIFTED
DOWNSHIFTER
DOWNSHIFTERS
DOWNSHIFTING
DOWNSHIFTINGS
DOWNSHIFTS
DOWNSIZERS
DOWNSIZING
DOWNSIZINGS
DOWNSLIDES
DOWNSLOPES
DOWNSPOUTS
DOWNSTAGES
DOWNSTAIRS
DOWNSTAIRSES
DOWNSTATER
DOWNSTATERS
DOWNSTATES
DOWNSTREAM
DOWNSTROKE
DOWNSTROKES
DOWNSWINGS
DOWNTHROWS
DOWNTOWNER
DOWNTOWNERS
DOWNTRENDED
DOWNTRENDING
DOWNTRENDS
DOWNTRODDEN
DOWNTURNED
DOWNVOTING
DOWNWARDLY
DOWNWARDNESS

DOWNWARDNESSES
DOWNWASHES
DOWNZONING
DOXOGRAPHER
DOXOGRAPHERS
DOXOGRAPHIC
DOXOGRAPHIES
DOXOGRAPHY
DOXOLOGICAL
DOXOLOGICALLY
DOXOLOGIES
DOXORUBICIN
DOXORUBICINS
DOXYCYCLINE
DOXYCYCLINES
DOZINESSES
DRABBINESS
DRABBINESSES
DRABBLINGS
DRABNESSES
DRACONIANISM
DRACONIANISMS
DRACONICALLY
DRACONISMS
DRACONITES
DRACONTIASES
DRACONTIASIS
DRACUNCULIASES
DRACUNCULIASIS
DRACUNCULUS
DRACUNCULUSES
DRAFTINESS
DRAFTINESSES
DRAFTSMANSHIP
DRAFTSMANSHIPS
DRAFTSPERSON
DRAFTSPERSONS
DRAFTSWOMAN
DRAFTSWOMEN
DRAGGINGLY
DRAGGLETAILED
DRAGHOUNDS
DRAGONESSES
DRAGONFLIES
DRAGONHEAD
DRAGONHEADS
DRAGONISED
DRAGONISES
DRAGONISING
DRAGONISMS
DRAGONIZED
DRAGONIZES
DRAGONIZING
DRAGONLIKE
DRAGONNADE
DRAGONNADED
DRAGONNADES
DRAGONNADING
DRAGONROOT
DRAGONROOTS
DRAGOONAGE
DRAGOONAGES
DRAGOONING
DRAGSTRIPS
DRAGSVILLE
DRAGSVILLES
DRAINBOARD
DRAINBOARDS
DRAINLAYER
DRAINLAYERS
DRAINPIPES
DRAKESTONE
DRAKESTONES
DRAMATICAL
DRAMATICALLY
DRAMATICISM
DRAMATICISMS
DRAMATISABLE
DRAMATISATION
DRAMATISATIONS
DRAMATISED
DRAMATISER
DRAMATISERS
DRAMATISES
DRAMATISING
DRAMATISTS
DRAMATIZABLE
DRAMATIZATION
DRAMATIZATIONS
DRAMATIZED
DRAMATIZER
DRAMATIZERS
DRAMATIZES
DRAMATIZING
DRAMATURGE
DRAMATURGES
DRAMATURGIC
DRAMATURGICAL
DRAMATURGICALLY
DRAMATURGIES
DRAMATURGIST
DRAMATURGISTS
DRAMATURGS
DRAMATURGY
DRAPABILITIES
DRAPABILITY
DRAPEABILITIES
DRAPEABILITY
DRAPERYING
DRASTICALLY
DRATCHELLS
DRAUGHTBOARD
DRAUGHTBOARDS
DRAUGHTERS
DRAUGHTIER
DRAUGHTIEST
DRAUGHTILY
DRAUGHTINESS
DRAUGHTINESSES
DRAUGHTING
DRAUGHTMAN
DRAUGHTMEN
DRAUGHTPROOF
DRAUGHTPROOFED
DRAUGHTPROOFING
DRAUGHTPROOFS
DRAUGHTSMAN
DRAUGHTSMANSHIP
DRAUGHTSMEN
DRAUGHTSPERSON
DRAUGHTSPERSONS
DRAUGHTSWOMAN
DRAUGHTSWOMEN
DRAWBRIDGE
DRAWBRIDGES
DRAWERFULS
DRAWKNIVES
DRAWLINGLY
DRAWLINGNESS
DRAWLINGNESSES
DRAWNWORKS
DRAWPLATES
DRAWSHAVES
DRAWSTRING
DRAWSTRINGS
DRAYHORSES
DREADFULLY
DREADFULNESS
DREADFULNESSES
DREADLESSLY
DREADLESSNESS
DREADLESSNESSES
DREADLOCKED
DREADLOCKS
DREADNAUGHT
DREADNAUGHTS
DREADNOUGHT
DREADNOUGHTS
DREAMBOATS
DREAMERIES
DREAMFULLY
DREAMFULNESS
DREAMFULNESSES
DREAMHOLES
DREAMINESS
DREAMINESSES
DREAMINGLY
DREAMLANDS
DREAMLESSLY
DREAMLESSNESS
DREAMLESSNESSES
DREAMTIMES
DREAMWHILE
DREAMWHILES
DREAMWORLD
DREAMWORLDS
DREARIHEAD
DREARIHEADS
DREARIHOOD
DREARIHOODS
DREARIMENT
DREARIMENTS
DREARINESS
DREARINESSES
DREARISOME
DRECKSILLS
DREGGINESS
DREGGINESSES
DREIKANTER
DREIKANTERS
DRENCHINGS
DREPANIUMS
DRERIHEADS
DRESSGUARD
DRESSGUARDS
DRESSINESS
DRESSINESSES
DRESSMAKER
DRESSMAKERS
DRESSMAKES
DRESSMAKING
DRESSMAKINGS
DRIBBLIEST
DRIBBLINGS
DRICKSIEST
DRIFTINGLY
DRIFTWOODS
DRILLABILITIES
DRILLABILITY
DRILLHOLES
DRILLMASTER
DRILLMASTERS
DRILLSHIPS
DRILLSTOCK
DRILLSTOCKS
DRINKABILITIES
DRINKABILITY
DRINKABLENESS
DRINKABLENESSES
DRINKABLES
DRIPSTONES
DRIVABILITIES
DRIVABILITY
DRIVEABILITIES
DRIVEABILITY
DRIVELINES
DRIVELLERS
DRIVELLING
DRIVENNESS
DRIVENNESSES
DRIVERLESS
DRIVESHAFT
DRIVESHAFTS
DRIVETHROUGH
DRIVETHROUGHS
DRIVETRAIN
DRIVETRAINS
DRIZZLIEST
DRIZZLINGLY
DROICHIEST

DROLLERIES
DROLLNESSES
DROMEDARES
DROMEDARIES
DROMOPHOBIA
DROMOPHOBIAS
DRONISHNESS
DRONISHNESSES
DRONKVERDRIET
DROOLWORTHIER
DROOLWORTHIEST
DROOLWORTHY
DROOPINESS
DROOPINESSES
DROOPINGLY
DROPCLOTHS
DROPFORGED
DROPFORGES
DROPFORGING
DROPKICKER
DROPKICKERS
DROPLIGHTS
DROPPERFUL
DROPPERFULS
DROPPERSFUL
DROPSICALLY
DROPSONDES
DROPSTONES
DROSERACEOUS
DROSOMETER
DROSOMETERS
DROSOPHILA
DROSOPHILAE
DROSOPHILAS
DROSSINESS
DROSSINESSES
DROUGHTIER
DROUGHTIEST
DROUGHTINESS
DROUGHTINESSES
DROUTHIEST
DROUTHINESS
DROUTHINESSES
DROWSIHEAD
DROWSIHEADS
DROWSIHEDS
DROWSINESS
DROWSINESSES
DRUCKENNESS
DRUCKENNESSES
DRUDGERIES
DRUDGINGLY
DRUGMAKERS
DRUGSTORES
DRUIDESSES
DRUMBEATER
DRUMBEATERS
DRUMBEATING
DRUMBEATINGS
DRUMBLEDOR
DRUMBLEDORS
DRUMBLEDRANE
DRUMBLEDRANES
DRUMFISHES
DRUMSTICKS
DRUNKALOGUE
DRUNKALOGUES
DRUNKATHON
DRUNKATHONS
DRUNKENNESS
DRUNKENNESSES
DRUNKOMETER
DRUNKOMETERS
DRUPACEOUS
DRYASDUSTS
DRYBEATING
DRYOPITHECINE
DRYOPITHECINES
DRYSALTERIES
DRYSALTERS
DRYSALTERY
DRYWALLERS
DRYWALLING
DRYWALLINGS
DUALISTICALLY
DUATHLETES
DUBIOSITIES
DUBIOUSNESS
DUBIOUSNESSES
DUBITANCIES
DUBITATING
DUBITATION
DUBITATIONS
DUBITATIVE
DUBITATIVELY
DUCHESSING
DUCKBOARDS
DUCKSHOVED
DUCKSHOVER
DUCKSHOVERS
DUCKSHOVES
DUCKSHOVING
DUCKSHOVINGS
DUCKWALKED
DUCKWALKING
DUCTILENESS
DUCTILENESSES
DUCTILITIES
DUDENESSES
DUENNASHIP
DUENNASHIPS
DUFFERDOMS
DUFFERISMS
DUIKERBOKS
DUKKERIPEN
DUKKERIPENS
DULCAMARAS
DULCETNESS
DULCETNESSES
DULCIFICATION
DULCIFICATIONS
DULCIFLUOUS
DULCIFYING
DULCILOQUIES
DULCILOQUY
DULCIMORES
DULCITUDES
DULLNESSES
DULLSVILLE
DULLSVILLES
DULOCRACIES
DUMBFOUNDED
DUMBFOUNDER
DUMBFOUNDERED
DUMBFOUNDERING
DUMBFOUNDERS
DUMBFOUNDING
DUMBFOUNDS
DUMBLEDORE
DUMBLEDORES
DUMBNESSES
DUMBSIZING
DUMBSTRICKEN
DUMBSTRUCK
DUMBWAITER
DUMBWAITERS
DUMFOUNDED
DUMFOUNDER
DUMFOUNDERED
DUMFOUNDERING
DUMFOUNDERS
DUMFOUNDING
DUMMELHEAD
DUMMELHEADS
DUMMINESSES
DUMORTIERITE
DUMORTIERITES
DUMOSITIES
DUMPINESSES
DUMPISHNESS
DUMPISHNESSES
DUMPTRUCKS
DUNDERFUNK
DUNDERFUNKS
DUNDERHEAD
DUNDERHEADED
DUNDERHEADISM
DUNDERHEADISMS
DUNDERHEADS
DUNDERPATE
DUNDERPATES
DUNDREARIES
DUNGEONERS
DUNGEONING
DUNIEWASSAL
DUNIEWASSALS
DUNIWASSAL
DUNIWASSALS
DUNNIEWASSAL
DUNNIEWASSALS
DUODECENNIAL
DUODECILLION
DUODECILLIONS
DUODECIMAL
DUODECIMALLY
DUODECIMALS
DUODECIMOS
DUODENECTOMIES
DUODENECTOMY
DUODENITIS
DUODENITISES
DUOPOLISTIC
DUOPOLISTS
DUOPSONIES
DUPABILITIES
DUPABILITY
DUPLEXINGS
DUPLEXITIES
DUPLICABILITIES
DUPLICABILITY
DUPLICABLE
DUPLICANDS
DUPLICATED
DUPLICATELY
DUPLICATES
DUPLICATING
DUPLICATION
DUPLICATIONS
DUPLICATIVE
DUPLICATOR
DUPLICATORS
DUPLICATURE
DUPLICATURES
DUPLICIDENT
DUPLICITIES
DUPLICITOUS
DUPLICITOUSLY
DURABILITIES
DURABILITY
DURABLENESS
DURABLENESSES
DURALUMINIUM
DURALUMINIUMS
DURALUMINS
DURATIONAL
DURCHKOMPONIERT
DURCHKOMPONIRT
DURICRUSTS
DUROMETERS
DUSKINESSES
DUSKISHNESS
DUSKISHNESSES
DUSKNESSES
DUSTCLOTHS
DUSTCOVERS
DUSTINESSES
DUSTSHEETS
DUSTSTORMS
DUTEOUSNESS
DUTEOUSNESSES

D

DUTIABILITIES
DUTIABILITY
DUTIFULNESS
DUTIFULNESSES
DUUMVIRATE
DUUMVIRATES
DWARFISHLY
DWARFISHNESS
DWARFISHNESSES
DWARFNESSES
DWINDLEMENT
DWINDLEMENTS
DYADICALLY
DYARCHICAL
DYEABILITIES
DYEABILITY
DYINGNESSES
DYNAMETERS
DYNAMICALLY
DYNAMICIST
DYNAMICISTS
DYNAMISING
DYNAMISTIC
DYNAMITARD
DYNAMITARDS
DYNAMITERS
DYNAMITING
DYNAMIZING
DYNAMOELECTRIC
DYNAMOGENESES
DYNAMOGENESIS
DYNAMOGENIES
DYNAMOGENY
DYNAMOGRAPH
DYNAMOGRAPHS
DYNAMOMETER
DYNAMOMETERS
DYNAMOMETRIC
DYNAMOMETRICAL
DYNAMOMETRIES
DYNAMOMETRY
DYNAMOTORS
DYNASTICAL
DYNASTICALLY
DYNASTICISM
DYNASTICISMS
DYNORPHINS
DYOPHYSITE
DYOPHYSITES
DYOTHELETE
DYOTHELETES
DYOTHELETIC
DYOTHELETICAL
DYOTHELETISM
DYOTHELETISMS
DYOTHELISM
DYOTHELISMS
DYOTHELITE
DYOTHELITES
DYOTHELITIC
DYOTHELITICAL
DYSAESTHESIA
DYSAESTHESIAS
DYSAESTHETIC
DYSARTHRIA
DYSARTHRIAS
DYSBINDINS
DYSCALCULIA
DYSCALCULIAS
DYSCHROIAS
DYSCRASIAS
DYSCRASITE
DYSCRASITES
DYSENTERIC
DYSENTERIES
DYSFUNCTION
DYSFUNCTIONAL
DYSFUNCTIONS
DYSGENESES
DYSGENESIS
DYSGRAPHIA
DYSGRAPHIAS
DYSGRAPHIC
DYSGRAPHICS
DYSHARMONIC
DYSKINESIA
DYSKINESIAS
DYSKINETIC
DYSLECTICS
DYSLOGISTIC
DYSLOGISTICALLY
DYSMENORRHEA
DYSMENORRHEAL
DYSMENORRHEAS
DYSMENORRHEIC
DYSMENORRHOEA
DYSMENORRHOEAL
DYSMENORRHOEAS
DYSMENORRHOEIC
DYSMORPHIC
DYSMORPHOPHOBIA
DYSMORPHOPHOBIC
DYSPAREUNIA
DYSPAREUNIAS
DYSPATHETIC
DYSPATHIES
DYSPEPSIAS
DYSPEPSIES
DYSPEPTICAL
DYSPEPTICALLY
DYSPEPTICS
DYSPHAGIAS
DYSPHAGIES
DYSPHASIAS
DYSPHASICS
DYSPHEMISM
DYSPHEMISMS
DYSPHEMISTIC
DYSPHONIAS
DYSPHORIAS
DYSPLASIAS
DYSPLASTIC
DYSPRACTIC
DYSPRAXIAS
DYSPROSIUM
DYSPROSIUMS
DYSRHYTHMIA
DYSRHYTHMIAS
DYSRHYTHMIC
DYSRHYTHMICS
DYSSYNERGIA
DYSSYNERGIAS
DYSSYNERGIC
DYSSYNERGIES
DYSSYNERGY
DYSTELEOLOGICAL
DYSTELEOLOGIES
DYSTELEOLOGIST
DYSTELEOLOGISTS
DYSTELEOLOGY
DYSTHESIAS
DYSTHYMIAC
DYSTHYMIACS
DYSTHYMIAS
DYSTHYMICS
DYSTOPIANS
DYSTROPHIA
DYSTROPHIAS
DYSTROPHIC
DYSTROPHIES
DYSTROPHIN
DYSTROPHINS
DZIGGETAIS

E

EAGERNESSES
EAGLEHAWKS
EAGLESTONE
EAGLESTONES
EAGLEWOODS
EARBASHERS
EARBASHING
EARBASHINGS
EARLIERISE
EARLIERISED
EARLIERISES
EARLIERISING
EARLIERIZE
EARLIERIZED
EARLIERIZES
EARLIERIZING
EARLINESSES
EARLYWOODS
EARMARKING
EARNESTNESS
EARNESTNESSES
EARSPLITTING
EARTHBOUND
EARTHENWARE
EARTHENWARES
EARTHFALLS
EARTHFLAXES
EARTHINESS
EARTHINESSES
EARTHLIEST
EARTHLIGHT
EARTHLIGHTS
EARTHLINESS
EARTHLINESSES
EARTHLINGS
EARTHMOVER
EARTHMOVERS
EARTHMOVING
EARTHMOVINGS
EARTHQUAKE
EARTHQUAKED
EARTHQUAKES
EARTHQUAKING
EARTHRISES
EARTHSHAKER
EARTHSHAKERS
EARTHSHAKING
EARTHSHAKINGLY
EARTHSHATTERING
EARTHSHINE
EARTHSHINES
EARTHSTARS
EARTHWARDS
EARTHWAXES
EARTHWOLVES
EARTHWOMAN
EARTHWOMEN
EARTHWORKS
EARTHWORMS
EARWIGGIER
EARWIGGIEST
EARWIGGING
EARWIGGINGS
EARWITNESS
EARWITNESSES
EASEFULNESS
EASEFULNESSES
EASINESSES
EASSELGATE
EASSELWARD
EASTERLIES
EASTERLING
EASTERLINGS
EASTERMOST
EASTERNERS
EASTERNMOST
EASTWARDLY
EASYGOINGNESS
EASYGOINGNESSES
EAVESDRIPS
EAVESDROPPED
EAVESDROPPER
EAVESDROPPERS
EAVESDROPPING
EAVESDROPPINGS
EAVESDROPS
EAVESTROUGH
EAVESTROUGHS
EBIONISING
EBIONITISM
EBIONITISMS
EBIONIZING
EBOULEMENT
EBOULEMENTS
EBRACTEATE
EBRACTEOLATE
EBRILLADES
EBRIOSITIES
EBULLIENCE
EBULLIENCES
EBULLIENCIES
EBULLIENCY
EBULLIENTLY
EBULLIOMETER
EBULLIOMETERS
EBULLIOMETRIES
EBULLIOMETRY
EBULLIOSCOPE
EBULLIOSCOPES
EBULLIOSCOPIC
EBULLIOSCOPICAL
EBULLIOSCOPIES
EBULLIOSCOPY
EBULLITION
EBULLITIONS
EBURNATION
EBURNATIONS
EBURNIFICATION
EBURNIFICATIONS
ECARDINATE
ECBLASTESES
ECBLASTESIS
ECCALEOBION
ECCALEOBIONS
ECCENTRICAL
ECCENTRICALLY
ECCENTRICITIES
ECCENTRICITY
ECCENTRICS
ECCHYMOSED
ECCHYMOSES
ECCHYMOSIS
ECCHYMOTIC
ECCLESIARCH
ECCLESIARCHS
ECCLESIAST
ECCLESIASTIC
ECCLESIASTICAL
ECCLESIASTICISM
ECCLESIASTICS
ECCLESIASTS
ECCLESIOLATER
ECCLESIOLATERS
ECCLESIOLATRIES
ECCLESIOLATRY
ECCLESIOLOGICAL
ECCLESIOLOGIES
ECCLESIOLOGIST
ECCLESIOLOGISTS
ECCLESIOLOGY
ECCOPROTIC
ECCOPROTICS
ECCREMOCARPUS
ECCREMOCARPUSES
ECCRINOLOGIES
ECCRINOLOGY
ECDYSIASTS
ECHELONING
ECHEVERIAS
ECHIDNINES
ECHINACEAS
ECHINOCOCCI
ECHINOCOCCOSES
ECHINOCOCCOSIS
ECHINOCOCCUS
ECHINODERM
ECHINODERMAL
ECHINODERMATOUS
ECHINODERMS
ECHIUROIDS
ECHOCARDIOGRAM
ECHOCARDIOGRAMS
ECHOGRAPHIES
ECHOGRAPHS
ECHOGRAPHY
ECHOICALLY
ECHOLALIAS
ECHOLOCATION
ECHOLOCATIONS
ECHOPRAXES
ECHOPRAXIA
ECHOPRAXIAS
ECHOPRAXIS
ECHOVIRUSES
ECLAIRCISSEMENT
ECLAMPSIAS
ECLAMPSIES
ECLECTICALLY
ECLECTICISM
ECLECTICISMS
ECLIPSISES
ECLIPTICALLY
ECOCATASTROPHE
ECOCATASTROPHES
ECOCENTRIC
ECOCLIMATE
ECOCLIMATES
ECOFEMINISM
ECOFEMINISMS
ECOFEMINIST
ECOFEMINISTS
ECOFRIENDLIER
ECOFRIENDLIEST
ECOFRIENDLY
ECOLOGICAL
ECOLOGICALLY
ECOLOGISTS
ECOMMERCES
ECOMOVEMENT
ECOMOVEMENTS

ECOMUSEUMS
ECONOBOXES
ECONOMETER
ECONOMETERS
ECONOMETRIC
ECONOMETRICAL
ECONOMETRICALLY
ECONOMETRICIAN
ECONOMETRICIANS
ECONOMETRICS
ECONOMETRIST
ECONOMETRISTS
ECONOMICAL
ECONOMICALLY
ECONOMISATION
ECONOMISATIONS
ECONOMISED
ECONOMISER
ECONOMISERS
ECONOMISES
ECONOMISING
ECONOMISMS
ECONOMISTIC
ECONOMISTS
ECONOMIZATION
ECONOMIZATIONS
ECONOMIZED
ECONOMIZER
ECONOMIZERS
ECONOMIZES
ECONOMIZING
ECOPHOBIAS
ECOPHYSIOLOGIES
ECOPHYSIOLOGY
ECOREGIONS
ECOSPECIES
ECOSPECIFIC
ECOSPHERES
ECOSSAISES
ECOSYSTEMS
ECOTARIANISM
ECOTARIANISMS
ECOTARIANS
ECOTECTURE
ECOTECTURES
ECOTERRORISM
ECOTERRORISMS
ECOTERRORIST
ECOTERRORISTS
ECOTOURING
ECOTOURISM
ECOTOURISMS
ECOTOURIST
ECOTOURISTS
ECOTOXICOLOGIES
ECOTOXICOLOGIST
ECOTOXICOLOGY
ECOTYPICALLY
ECPHONESES
ECPHONESIS
ECPHRACTIC
ECPHRACTICS
ECRITOIRES
ECSTASISED
ECSTASISES
ECSTASISING
ECSTASIZED
ECSTASIZES
ECSTASIZING
ECSTASYING
ECSTATICALLY
ECTHLIPSES
ECTHLIPSIS
ECTOBLASTIC
ECTOBLASTS
ECTOCRINES
ECTODERMAL
ECTODERMIC
ECTOENZYME
ECTOENZYMES
ECTOGENESES
ECTOGENESIS
ECTOGENETIC
ECTOGENICALLY
ECTOGENIES
ECTOGENOUS
ECTOMORPHIC
ECTOMORPHIES
ECTOMORPHS
ECTOMORPHY
ECTOMYCORRHIZA
ECTOMYCORRHIZAE
ECTOMYCORRHIZAS
ECTOPARASITE
ECTOPARASITES
ECTOPARASITIC
ECTOPHYTES
ECTOPHYTIC
ECTOPICALLY
ECTOPLASMIC
ECTOPLASMS
ECTOPLASTIC
ECTOPROCTS
ECTOSARCOUS
ECTOTHERMIC
ECTOTHERMS
ECTOTROPHIC
ECTROPIONS
ECTROPIUMS
ECTYPOGRAPHIES
ECTYPOGRAPHY
ECUMENICAL
ECUMENICALISM
ECUMENICALISMS
ECUMENICALLY
ECUMENICISM
ECUMENICISMS
ECUMENICIST
ECUMENICISTS
ECUMENICITIES
ECUMENICITY
ECUMENISMS
ECUMENISTS
ECZEMATOUS
EDACIOUSLY
EDACIOUSNESS
EDACIOUSNESSES
EDAPHICALLY
EDAPHOLOGIES
EDAPHOLOGY
EDELWEISSES
EDENTULATE
EDENTULOUS
EDGINESSES
EDIBILITIES
EDIBLENESS
EDIBLENESSES
EDIFICATION
EDIFICATIONS
EDIFICATORY
EDIFYINGLY
EDITIONING
EDITORIALISE
EDITORIALISED
EDITORIALISER
EDITORIALISERS
EDITORIALISES
EDITORIALISING
EDITORIALIST
EDITORIALISTS
EDITORIALIZE
EDITORIALIZED
EDITORIALIZER
EDITORIALIZERS
EDITORIALIZES
EDITORIALIZING
EDITORIALLY
EDITORIALS
EDITORSHIP
EDITORSHIPS
EDITRESSES
EDRIOPHTHALMIAN
EDRIOPHTHALMIC
EDRIOPHTHALMOUS
EDUCABILITIES
EDUCABILITY
EDUCATABILITIES
EDUCATABILITY
EDUCATABLE
EDUCATEDNESS
EDUCATEDNESSES
EDUCATIONAL
EDUCATIONALIST
EDUCATIONALISTS
EDUCATIONALLY
EDUCATIONESE
EDUCATIONESES
EDUCATIONIST
EDUCATIONISTS
EDUCATIONS
EDUCEMENTS
EDULCORANT
EDULCORATE
EDULCORATED
EDULCORATES
EDULCORATING
EDULCORATION
EDULCORATIONS
EDULCORATIVE
EDULCORATOR
EDULCORATORS
EDUTAINMENT
EDUTAINMENTS
EELGRASSES
EERINESSES
EFFACEABLE
EFFACEMENT
EFFACEMENTS
EFFECTIBLE
EFFECTIVELY
EFFECTIVENESS
EFFECTIVENESSES
EFFECTIVES
EFFECTIVITIES
EFFECTIVITY
EFFECTLESS
EFFECTUALITIES
EFFECTUALITY
EFFECTUALLY
EFFECTUALNESS
EFFECTUALNESSES
EFFECTUATE
EFFECTUATED
EFFECTUATES
EFFECTUATING
EFFECTUATION
EFFECTUATIONS
EFFEMINACIES
EFFEMINACY
EFFEMINATE
EFFEMINATED
EFFEMINATELY
EFFEMINATENESS
EFFEMINATES
EFFEMINATING
EFFEMINISE
EFFEMINISED
EFFEMINISES
EFFEMINISING
EFFEMINIZE
EFFEMINIZED
EFFEMINIZES
EFFEMINIZING
EFFERENCES
EFFERENTLY
EFFERVESCE
EFFERVESCED
EFFERVESCENCE
EFFERVESCENCES
EFFERVESCENCIES

EFFERVESCENCY
EFFERVESCENT
EFFERVESCENTLY
EFFERVESCES
EFFERVESCIBLE
EFFERVESCING
EFFERVESCINGLY
EFFETENESS
EFFETENESSES
EFFICACIES
EFFICACIOUS
EFFICACIOUSLY
EFFICACIOUSNESS
EFFICACITIES
EFFICACITY
EFFICIENCE
EFFICIENCES
EFFICIENCIES
EFFICIENCY
EFFICIENTLY
EFFICIENTS
EFFIERCING
EFFIGURATE
EFFIGURATION
EFFIGURATIONS
EFFLEURAGE
EFFLEURAGED
EFFLEURAGES
EFFLEURAGING
EFFLORESCE
EFFLORESCED
EFFLORESCENCE
EFFLORESCENCES
EFFLORESCENT
EFFLORESCES
EFFLORESCING
EFFLUENCES
EFFLUVIUMS
EFFLUXIONS
EFFORTFULLY
EFFORTFULNESS
EFFORTFULNESSES
EFFORTLESS
EFFORTLESSLY
EFFORTLESSNESS
EFFRONTERIES
EFFRONTERY
EFFULGENCE
EFFULGENCES
EFFULGENTLY
EFFUSIOMETER
EFFUSIOMETERS
EFFUSIVELY
EFFUSIVENESS
EFFUSIVENESSES
EGALITARIAN
EGALITARIANISM
EGALITARIANISMS
EGALITARIANS
EGAREMENTS
EGGBEATERS
EGGHEADEDNESS
EGGHEADEDNESSES
EGLANDULAR
EGLANDULOSE
EGLANTINES
EGOCENTRIC
EGOCENTRICAL
EGOCENTRICALLY
EGOCENTRICITIES
EGOCENTRICITY
EGOCENTRICS
EGOCENTRISM
EGOCENTRISMS
EGOISTICAL
EGOISTICALLY
EGOMANIACAL
EGOMANIACALLY
EGOMANIACS
EGOSURFING
EGOTHEISMS
EGOTISTICAL
EGOTISTICALLY
EGREGIOUSLY
EGREGIOUSNESS
EGREGIOUSNESSES
EGRESSIONS
EGRESSIVES
EGURGITATE
EGURGITATED
EGURGITATES
EGURGITATING
EICOSANOID
EICOSANOIDS
EIDERDOWNS
EIDETICALLY
EIDOGRAPHS
EIGENFREQUENCY
EIGENFUNCTION
EIGENFUNCTIONS
EIGENMODES
EIGENTONES
EIGENVALUE
EIGENVALUES
EIGENVECTOR
EIGENVECTORS
EIGHTBALLS
EIGHTEENMO
EIGHTEENMOS
EIGHTEENTH
EIGHTEENTHLY
EIGHTEENTHS
EIGHTFOILS
EIGHTIETHS
EIGHTPENCE
EIGHTPENCES
EIGHTPENNY
EIGHTSCORE
EIGHTSCORES
EIGHTSOMES
EINSTEINIUM
EINSTEINIUMS
EIRENICALLY
EIRENICONS
EISTEDDFOD
EISTEDDFODAU
EISTEDDFODIC
EISTEDDFODS
EJACULATED
EJACULATES
EJACULATING
EJACULATION
EJACULATIONS
EJACULATIVE
EJACULATOR
EJACULATORS
EJACULATORY
EJECTAMENTA
EJECTIVELY
EJECTMENTS
EKISTICIAN
EKISTICIANS
ELABORATED
ELABORATELY
ELABORATENESS
ELABORATENESSES
ELABORATES
ELABORATING
ELABORATION
ELABORATIONS
ELABORATIVE
ELABORATOR
ELABORATORIES
ELABORATORS
ELABORATORY
ELAEAGNUSES
ELAEOLITES
ELAEOPTENE
ELAEOPTENES
ELAIOSOMES
ELASMOBRANCH
ELASMOBRANCHS
ELASMOSAUR
ELASMOSAURS
ELASTANCES
ELASTICALLY
ELASTICATE
ELASTICATED
ELASTICATES
ELASTICATING
ELASTICATION
ELASTICATIONS
ELASTICISE
ELASTICISED
ELASTICISES
ELASTICISING
ELASTICITIES
ELASTICITY
ELASTICIZE
ELASTICIZED
ELASTICIZES
ELASTICIZING
ELASTICNESS
ELASTICNESSES
ELASTOMERIC
ELASTOMERS
ELATEDNESS
ELATEDNESSES
ELATERITES
ELATERIUMS
ELBOWROOMS
ELDERBERRIES
ELDERBERRY
ELDERCARES
ELDERFLOWER
ELDERFLOWERS
ELDERLINESS
ELDERLINESSES
ELDERSHIPS
ELECAMPANE
ELECAMPANES
ELECTABILITIES
ELECTABILITY
ELECTIONEER
ELECTIONEERED
ELECTIONEERER
ELECTIONEERERS
ELECTIONEERING
ELECTIONEERINGS
ELECTIONEERS
ELECTIVELY
ELECTIVENESS
ELECTIVENESSES
ELECTIVITIES
ELECTIVITY
ELECTORALLY
ELECTORATE
ELECTORATES
ELECTORESS
ELECTORESSES
ELECTORIAL
ELECTORIALLY
ELECTORSHIP
ELECTORSHIPS
ELECTRESSES
ELECTRICAL
ELECTRICALLY
ELECTRICALS
ELECTRICIAN
ELECTRICIANS
ELECTRICITIES
ELECTRICITY
ELECTRIFIABLE
ELECTRIFICATION
ELECTRIFIED
ELECTRIFIER
ELECTRIFIERS
ELECTRIFIES
ELECTRIFYING
ELECTRIFYINGLY

ELECTRISATION
ELECTRISATIONS
ELECTRISED
ELECTRISES
ELECTRISING
ELECTRIZATION
ELECTRIZATIONS
ELECTRIZED
ELECTRIZES
ELECTRIZING
ELECTROACOUSTIC
ELECTROACTIVE
ELECTROACTIVITY
ELECTROANALYSES
ELECTROANALYSIS
ELECTROANALYTIC
ELECTROBIOLOGY
ELECTROCAUTERY
ELECTROCEMENT
ELECTROCEMENTS
ELECTROCHEMIC
ELECTROCHEMICAL
ELECTROCHEMIST
ELECTROCHEMISTS
ELECTROCLASH
ELECTROCLASHES
ELECTROCULTURE
ELECTROCULTURES
ELECTROCUTE
ELECTROCUTED
ELECTROCUTES
ELECTROCUTING
ELECTROCUTION
ELECTROCUTIONS
ELECTROCYTE
ELECTROCYTES
ELECTRODEPOSIT
ELECTRODEPOSITS
ELECTRODERMAL
ELECTRODES
ELECTRODIALYSES
ELECTRODIALYSIS
ELECTRODIALYTIC
ELECTRODYNAMIC
ELECTRODYNAMICS
ELECTROFISHING
ELECTROFISHINGS
ELECTROFLUOR
ELECTROFLUORS
ELECTROFORM
ELECTROFORMED
ELECTROFORMING
ELECTROFORMINGS
ELECTROFORMS
ELECTROGEN
ELECTROGENESES
ELECTROGENESIS
ELECTROGENIC
ELECTROGENS
ELECTROGILDING
ELECTROGILDINGS
ELECTROGRAM
ELECTROGRAMS
ELECTROGRAPH
ELECTROGRAPHIC
ELECTROGRAPHIES
ELECTROGRAPHS
ELECTROGRAPHY
ELECTROING
ELECTROJET
ELECTROJETS
ELECTROKINETIC
ELECTROKINETICS
ELECTROLESS
ELECTROLIER
ELECTROLIERS
ELECTROLOGIES
ELECTROLOGIST
ELECTROLOGISTS
ELECTROLOGY
ELECTROLYSATION
ELECTROLYSE
ELECTROLYSED
ELECTROLYSER
ELECTROLYSERS
ELECTROLYSES
ELECTROLYSING
ELECTROLYSIS
ELECTROLYTE
ELECTROLYTES
ELECTROLYTIC
ELECTROLYTICS
ELECTROLYZATION
ELECTROLYZE
ELECTROLYZED
ELECTROLYZER
ELECTROLYZERS
ELECTROLYZES
ELECTROLYZING
ELECTROMAGNET
ELECTROMAGNETIC
ELECTROMAGNETS
ELECTROMER
ELECTROMERIC
ELECTROMERISM
ELECTROMERISMS
ELECTROMERS
ELECTROMETER
ELECTROMETERS
ELECTROMETRIC
ELECTROMETRICAL
ELECTROMETRIES
ELECTROMETRY
ELECTROMOTANCE
ELECTROMOTANCES
ELECTROMOTIVE
ELECTROMOTOR
ELECTROMOTORS
ELECTROMYOGRAM
ELECTROMYOGRAMS
ELECTROMYOGRAPH
ELECTRONEGATIVE
ELECTRONIC
ELECTRONICA
ELECTRONICALLY
ELECTRONICAS
ELECTRONICS
ELECTRONVOLT
ELECTRONVOLTS
ELECTROOSMOSES
ELECTROOSMOSIS
ELECTROOSMOTIC
ELECTROPHILE
ELECTROPHILES
ELECTROPHILIC
ELECTROPHONE
ELECTROPHONES
ELECTROPHONIC
ELECTROPHORESE
ELECTROPHORESED
ELECTROPHORESES
ELECTROPHORESIS
ELECTROPHORETIC
ELECTROPHORI
ELECTROPHORUS
ELECTROPHORUSES
ELECTROPLATE
ELECTROPLATED
ELECTROPLATER
ELECTROPLATERS
ELECTROPLATES
ELECTROPLATING
ELECTROPLATINGS
ELECTROPOLAR
ELECTROPOP
ELECTROPOPS
ELECTROPOSITIVE
ELECTROPUNCTURE
ELECTRORECEPTOR
ELECTRORHEOLOGY
ELECTROSCOPE
ELECTROSCOPES
ELECTROSCOPIC
ELECTROSHOCK
ELECTROSHOCKS
ELECTROSONDE
ELECTROSONDES
ELECTROSTATIC
ELECTROSTATICS
ELECTROSURGERY
ELECTROSURGICAL
ELECTROTECHNICS
ELECTROTHERAPY
ELECTROTHERMAL
ELECTROTHERMIC
ELECTROTHERMICS
ELECTROTHERMIES
ELECTROTHERMY
ELECTROTINT
ELECTROTINTS
ELECTROTONIC
ELECTROTONUS
ELECTROTONUSES
ELECTROTYPE
ELECTROTYPED
ELECTROTYPER
ELECTROTYPERS
ELECTROTYPES
ELECTROTYPIC
ELECTROTYPIES
ELECTROTYPING
ELECTROTYPIST
ELECTROTYPISTS
ELECTROTYPY
ELECTROVALENCE
ELECTROVALENCES
ELECTROVALENCY
ELECTROVALENT
ELECTROVALENTLY
ELECTROWEAK
ELECTROWINNING
ELECTROWINNINGS
ELECTUARIES
ELEDOISINS
ELEEMOSYNARY
ELEGANCIES
ELEGIACALLY
ELEMENTALISM
ELEMENTALISMS
ELEMENTALLY
ELEMENTALS
ELEMENTARILY
ELEMENTARINESS
ELEMENTARY
ELEOPTENES
ELEPHANTIASES
ELEPHANTIASIC
ELEPHANTIASIS
ELEPHANTINE
ELEPHANTOID
ELEPIDOTES
ELEUTHERARCH
ELEUTHERARCHS
ELEUTHERIAN
ELEUTHEROCOCCI
ELEUTHEROCOCCUS
ELEUTHERODACTYL
ELEUTHEROMANIA
ELEUTHEROMANIAS
ELEUTHEROPHOBIA
ELEUTHEROPHOBIC
ELEVATIONAL
ELEVATIONS
ELEVENTHLY
ELFISHNESS
ELFISHNESSES
ELICITABLE
ELICITATION
ELICITATIONS
ELIGIBILITIES

ELIGIBILITY
ELIMINABILITIES
ELIMINABILITY
ELIMINABLE
ELIMINANTS
ELIMINATED
ELIMINATES
ELIMINATING
ELIMINATION
ELIMINATIONS
ELIMINATIVE
ELIMINATIVISM
ELIMINATIVISMS
ELIMINATOR
ELIMINATORS
ELIMINATORY
ELLIPSOGRAPH
ELLIPSOGRAPHS
ELLIPSOIDAL
ELLIPSOIDS
ELLIPTICAL
ELLIPTICALLY
ELLIPTICALNESS
ELLIPTICALS
ELLIPTICITIES
ELLIPTICITY
ELOCUTIONARY
ELOCUTIONIST
ELOCUTIONISTS
ELOCUTIONS
ELOIGNMENT
ELOIGNMENTS
ELOINMENTS
ELONGATING
ELONGATION
ELONGATIONS
ELOPEMENTS
ELOQUENCES
ELOQUENTLY
ELSEWHITHER
ELUCIDATED
ELUCIDATES
ELUCIDATING
ELUCIDATION
ELUCIDATIONS
ELUCIDATIVE
ELUCIDATOR
ELUCIDATORS
ELUCIDATORY
ELUCUBRATE
ELUCUBRATED
ELUCUBRATES
ELUCUBRATING
ELUCUBRATION
ELUCUBRATIONS
ELUSIVENESS
ELUSIVENESSES
ELUSORINESS
ELUSORINESSES
ELUTRIATED
ELUTRIATES
ELUTRIATING
ELUTRIATION
ELUTRIATIONS
ELUTRIATOR
ELUTRIATORS
ELUVIATING
ELUVIATION
ELUVIATIONS
ELVISHNESS
ELVISHNESSES
ELYTRIFORM
ELYTRIGEROUS
EMACIATING
EMACIATION
EMACIATIONS
EMALANGENI
EMANATIONAL
EMANATIONS
EMANATISTS
EMANCIPATE
EMANCIPATED
EMANCIPATES
EMANCIPATING
EMANCIPATION
EMANCIPATIONIST
EMANCIPATIONS
EMANCIPATIVE
EMANCIPATOR
EMANCIPATORS
EMANCIPATORY
EMANCIPIST
EMANCIPISTS
EMARGINATE
EMARGINATED
EMARGINATELY
EMARGINATES
EMARGINATING
EMARGINATION
EMARGINATIONS
EMASCULATE
EMASCULATED
EMASCULATES
EMASCULATING
EMASCULATION
EMASCULATIONS
EMASCULATIVE
EMASCULATOR
EMASCULATORS
EMASCULATORY
EMBALLINGS
EMBALMINGS
EMBALMMENT
EMBALMMENTS
EMBANKMENT
EMBANKMENTS
EMBARCADERO
EMBARCADEROS
EMBARCATION
EMBARCATIONS
EMBARGOING
EMBARKATION
EMBARKATIONS
EMBARKMENT
EMBARKMENTS
EMBARQUEMENT
EMBARQUEMENTS
EMBARRASSABLE
EMBARRASSED
EMBARRASSEDLY
EMBARRASSES
EMBARRASSING
EMBARRASSINGLY
EMBARRASSMENT
EMBARRASSMENTS
EMBARRINGS
EMBASEMENT
EMBASEMENTS
EMBASSADES
EMBASSADOR
EMBASSADORS
EMBASSAGES
EMBATTLEMENT
EMBATTLEMENTS
EMBATTLING
EMBAYMENTS
EMBEDDINGS
EMBEDMENTS
EMBELLISHED
EMBELLISHER
EMBELLISHERS
EMBELLISHES
EMBELLISHING
EMBELLISHINGLY
EMBELLISHMENT
EMBELLISHMENTS
EMBEZZLEMENT
EMBEZZLEMENTS
EMBEZZLERS
EMBEZZLING
EMBIGGENED
EMBIGGENING
EMBITTERED
EMBITTERER
EMBITTERERS
EMBITTERING
EMBITTERINGS
EMBITTERMENT
EMBITTERMENTS
EMBLAZONED
EMBLAZONER
EMBLAZONERS
EMBLAZONING
EMBLAZONMENT
EMBLAZONMENTS
EMBLAZONRIES
EMBLAZONRY
EMBLEMATIC
EMBLEMATICAL
EMBLEMATICALLY
EMBLEMATISE
EMBLEMATISED
EMBLEMATISES
EMBLEMATISING
EMBLEMATIST
EMBLEMATISTS
EMBLEMATIZE
EMBLEMATIZED
EMBLEMATIZES
EMBLEMATIZING
EMBLEMENTS
EMBLEMISED
EMBLEMISES
EMBLEMISING
EMBLEMIZED
EMBLEMIZES
EMBLEMIZING
EMBLOOMING
EMBLOSSOMED
EMBLOSSOMING
EMBLOSSOMS
EMBODIMENT
EMBODIMENTS
EMBOITEMENT
EMBOITEMENTS
EMBOLDENED
EMBOLDENER
EMBOLDENERS
EMBOLDENING
EMBOLECTOMIES
EMBOLECTOMY
EMBOLISATION
EMBOLISATIONS
EMBOLISING
EMBOLISMAL
EMBOLISMIC
EMBOLIZATION
EMBOLIZATIONS
EMBOLIZING
EMBONPOINT
EMBONPOINTS
EMBORDERED
EMBORDERING
EMBOSCATAS
EMBOSOMING
EMBOSSABLE
EMBOSSINGS
EMBOSSMENT
EMBOSSMENTS
EMBOTHRIUM
EMBOTHRIUMS
EMBOUCHURE
EMBOUCHURES
EMBOUNDING
EMBOURGEOISE
EMBOURGEOISED
EMBOURGEOISES
EMBOURGEOISING
EMBOWELING
EMBOWELLED

EMBOWELLING
EMBOWELMENT
EMBOWELMENTS
EMBOWERING
EMBOWERMENT
EMBOWERMENTS
EMBOWMENTS
EMBRACEABLE
EMBRACEMENT
EMBRACEMENTS
EMBRACEORS
EMBRACERIES
EMBRACINGLY
EMBRACINGNESS
EMBRACINGNESSES
EMBRAIDING
EMBRANCHMENT
EMBRANCHMENTS
EMBRANGLED
EMBRANGLEMENT
EMBRANGLEMENTS
EMBRANGLES
EMBRANGLING
EMBRASURED
EMBRASURES
EMBRAZURES
EMBREADING
EMBREATHED
EMBREATHES
EMBREATHING
EMBRITTLED
EMBRITTLEMENT
EMBRITTLEMENTS
EMBRITTLES
EMBRITTLING
EMBROCATED
EMBROCATES
EMBROCATING
EMBROCATION
EMBROCATIONS
EMBROGLIOS
EMBROIDERED
EMBROIDERER
EMBROIDERERS
EMBROIDERIES
EMBROIDERING
EMBROIDERS
EMBROIDERY
EMBROILERS
EMBROILING
EMBROILMENT
EMBROILMENTS
EMBROWNING
EMBRUEMENT
EMBRUEMENTS
EMBRYECTOMIES
EMBRYECTOMY
EMBRYOGENESES
EMBRYOGENESIS
EMBRYOGENETIC
EMBRYOGENIC
EMBRYOGENIES
EMBRYOGENY
EMBRYOLOGIC
EMBRYOLOGICAL
EMBRYOLOGICALLY
EMBRYOLOGIES
EMBRYOLOGIST
EMBRYOLOGISTS
EMBRYOLOGY
EMBRYONATE
EMBRYONATED
EMBRYONICALLY
EMBRYOPHYTE
EMBRYOPHYTES
EMBRYOTICALLY
EMBRYOTOMIES
EMBRYOTOMY
EMBRYULCIA
EMBRYULCIAS
EMENDATING
EMENDATION
EMENDATIONS
EMENDATORS
EMENDATORY
EMERGENCES
EMERGENCIES
EMERGENTLY
EMETICALLY
EMETOPHOBIA
EMETOPHOBIAS
EMICATIONS
EMIGRATING
EMIGRATION
EMIGRATIONAL
EMIGRATIONIST
EMIGRATIONISTS
EMIGRATIONS
EMIGRATORY
EMINENCIES
EMINENTIAL
EMISSARIES
EMISSIVITIES
EMISSIVITY
EMITTANCES
EMMARBLING
EMMENAGOGIC
EMMENAGOGUE
EMMENAGOGUES
EMMENOLOGIES
EMMENOLOGY
EMMETROPES
EMMETROPIA
EMMETROPIAS
EMMETROPIC
EMOLLESCENCE
EMOLLESCENCES
EMOLLIATED
EMOLLIATES
EMOLLIATING
EMOLLIENCE
EMOLLIENCES
EMOLLIENTS
EMOLLITION
EMOLLITIONS
EMOLUMENTAL
EMOLUMENTARY
EMOLUMENTS
EMOTIONABLE
EMOTIONALISE
EMOTIONALISED
EMOTIONALISES
EMOTIONALISING
EMOTIONALISM
EMOTIONALISMS
EMOTIONALIST
EMOTIONALISTIC
EMOTIONALISTS
EMOTIONALITIES
EMOTIONALITY
EMOTIONALIZE
EMOTIONALIZED
EMOTIONALIZES
EMOTIONALIZING
EMOTIONALLY
EMOTIONLESS
EMOTIONLESSLY
EMOTIONLESSNESS
EMOTIVENESS
EMOTIVENESSES
EMOTIVISMS
EMOTIVITIES
EMPACKETED
EMPACKETING
EMPALEMENT
EMPALEMENTS
EMPANELING
EMPANELLED
EMPANELLING
EMPANELMENT
EMPANELMENTS
EMPANOPLIED
EMPANOPLIES
EMPANOPLYING
EMPARADISE
EMPARADISED
EMPARADISES
EMPARADISING
EMPARLAUNCE
EMPARLAUNCES
EMPASSIONATE
EMPASSIONED
EMPATHETIC
EMPATHETICALLY
EMPATHICALLY
EMPATHISED
EMPATHISES
EMPATHISING
EMPATHISTS
EMPATHIZED
EMPATHIZES
EMPATHIZING
EMPATRONED
EMPATRONING
EMPEACHING
EMPENNAGES
EMPEOPLING
EMPERISHED
EMPERISHES
EMPERISHING
EMPERISING
EMPERIZING
EMPERORSHIP
EMPERORSHIPS
EMPHASISED
EMPHASISES
EMPHASISING
EMPHASIZED
EMPHASIZES
EMPHASIZING
EMPHATICAL
EMPHATICALLY
EMPHATICALNESS
EMPHRACTIC
EMPHRACTICS
EMPHYSEMAS
EMPHYSEMATOUS
EMPHYSEMIC
EMPHYSEMICS
EMPHYTEUSES
EMPHYTEUSIS
EMPHYTEUTIC
EMPIECEMENT
EMPIECEMENTS
EMPIERCING
EMPIGHTING
EMPIRICALLY
EMPIRICALNESS
EMPIRICALNESSES
EMPIRICALS
EMPIRICISM
EMPIRICISMS
EMPIRICIST
EMPIRICISTS
EMPIRICUTIC
EMPLACEMENT
EMPLACEMENTS
EMPLASTERED
EMPLASTERING
EMPLASTERS
EMPLASTICS
EMPLASTRON
EMPLASTRONS
EMPLASTRUM
EMPLASTRUMS
EMPLEACHED
EMPLEACHES
EMPLEACHING
EMPLECTONS
EMPLECTUMS

EMPLONGING
EMPLOYABILITIES
EMPLOYABILITY
EMPLOYABLE
EMPLOYABLES
EMPLOYMENT
EMPLOYMENTS
EMPOISONED
EMPOISONING
EMPOISONMENT
EMPOISONMENTS
EMPOLDERED
EMPOLDERING
EMPOVERISH
EMPOVERISHED
EMPOVERISHER
EMPOVERISHERS
EMPOVERISHES
EMPOVERISHING
EMPOVERISHMENT
EMPOVERISHMENTS
EMPOWERING
EMPOWERMENT
EMPOWERMENTS
EMPRESSEMENT
EMPRESSEMENTS
EMPTINESSES
EMPURPLING
EMPYREUMATA
EMPYREUMATIC
EMPYREUMATICAL
EMPYREUMATISE
EMPYREUMATISED
EMPYREUMATISES
EMPYREUMATISING
EMPYREUMATIZE
EMPYREUMATIZED
EMPYREUMATIZES
EMPYREUMATIZING
EMULATIONS
EMULATIVELY
EMULATRESS
EMULATRESSES
EMULGENCES
EMULOUSNESS
EMULOUSNESSES
EMULSIFIABLE
EMULSIFICATION
EMULSIFICATIONS
EMULSIFIED
EMULSIFIER
EMULSIFIERS
EMULSIFIES
EMULSIFYING
EMULSIONISE
EMULSIONISED
EMULSIONISES
EMULSIONISING
EMULSIONIZE
EMULSIONIZED
EMULSIONIZES
EMULSIONIZING
EMULSOIDAL
EMUNCTIONS
EMUNCTORIES
ENABLEMENT
ENABLEMENTS
ENACTMENTS
ENALAPRILS
ENAMELINGS
ENAMELISTS
ENAMELLERS
ENAMELLING
ENAMELLINGS
ENAMELLIST
ENAMELLISTS
ENAMELWARE
ENAMELWARES
ENAMELWORK
ENAMELWORKS
ENAMORADOS
ENAMOURING
ENANTHEMAS
ENANTIODROMIA
ENANTIODROMIAS
ENANTIODROMIC
ENANTIOMER
ENANTIOMERIC
ENANTIOMERS
ENANTIOMORPH
ENANTIOMORPHIC
ENANTIOMORPHIES
ENANTIOMORPHISM
ENANTIOMORPHOUS
ENANTIOMORPHS
ENANTIOMORPHY
ENANTIOPATHIES
ENANTIOPATHY
ENANTIOSES
ENANTIOSIS
ENANTIOSTYLIES
ENANTIOSTYLOUS
ENANTIOSTYLY
ENANTIOTROPIC
ENANTIOTROPIES
ENANTIOTROPY
ENARRATION
ENARRATIONS
ENARTHRODIAL
ENARTHROSES
ENARTHROSIS
ENCAMPMENT
ENCAMPMENTS
ENCANTHISES
ENCAPSULATE
ENCAPSULATED
ENCAPSULATES
ENCAPSULATING
ENCAPSULATION
ENCAPSULATIONS
ENCAPSULED
ENCAPSULES
ENCAPSULING
ENCARNALISE
ENCARNALISED
ENCARNALISES
ENCARNALISING
ENCARNALIZE
ENCARNALIZED
ENCARNALIZES
ENCARNALIZING
ENCARPUSES
ENCASEMENT
ENCASEMENTS
ENCASHABLE
ENCASHMENT
ENCASHMENTS
ENCAUSTICALLY
ENCAUSTICS
ENCEPHALALGIA
ENCEPHALALGIAS
ENCEPHALIC
ENCEPHALIN
ENCEPHALINE
ENCEPHALINES
ENCEPHALINS
ENCEPHALITIC
ENCEPHALITIDES
ENCEPHALITIS
ENCEPHALITISES
ENCEPHALITOGEN
ENCEPHALITOGENS
ENCEPHALOCELE
ENCEPHALOCELES
ENCEPHALOGRAM
ENCEPHALOGRAMS
ENCEPHALOGRAPH
ENCEPHALOGRAPHS
ENCEPHALOGRAPHY
ENCEPHALOID
ENCEPHALOMA
ENCEPHALOMAS
ENCEPHALOMATA
ENCEPHALON
ENCEPHALONS
ENCEPHALOPATHIC
ENCEPHALOPATHY
ENCEPHALOTOMIES
ENCEPHALOTOMY
ENCEPHALOUS
ENCHAINING
ENCHAINMENT
ENCHAINMENTS
ENCHANTERS
ENCHANTING
ENCHANTINGLY
ENCHANTMENT
ENCHANTMENTS
ENCHANTRESS
ENCHANTRESSES
ENCHARGING
ENCHARMING
ENCHEASONS
ENCHEERING
ENCHEIRIDIA
ENCHEIRIDION
ENCHEIRIDIONS
ENCHILADAS
ENCHIRIDIA
ENCHIRIDION
ENCHIRIDIONS
ENCHONDROMA
ENCHONDROMAS
ENCHONDROMATA
ENCHONDROMATOUS
ENCINCTURE
ENCINCTURED
ENCINCTURES
ENCINCTURING
ENCIPHERED
ENCIPHERER
ENCIPHERERS
ENCIPHERING
ENCIPHERMENT
ENCIPHERMENTS
ENCIRCLEMENT
ENCIRCLEMENTS
ENCIRCLING
ENCLASPING
ENCLITICALLY
ENCLOISTER
ENCLOISTERED
ENCLOISTERING
ENCLOISTERS
ENCLOSABLE
ENCLOSURES
ENCLOTHING
ENCLOUDING
ENCODEMENT
ENCODEMENTS
ENCOIGNURE
ENCOIGNURES
ENCOLOURED
ENCOLOURING
ENCOLPIONS
ENCOLPIUMS
ENCOMENDERO
ENCOMENDEROS
ENCOMIASTIC
ENCOMIASTICAL
ENCOMIASTICALLY
ENCOMIASTS
ENCOMIENDA
ENCOMIENDAS
ENCOMPASSED
ENCOMPASSES
ENCOMPASSING
ENCOMPASSMENT
ENCOMPASSMENTS
ENCOPRESES

ENCOPRESIS
ENCOPRETIC
ENCOUNTERED
ENCOUNTERER
ENCOUNTERERS
ENCOUNTERING
ENCOUNTERS
ENCOURAGED
ENCOURAGEMENT
ENCOURAGEMENTS
ENCOURAGER
ENCOURAGERS
ENCOURAGES
ENCOURAGING
ENCOURAGINGLY
ENCOURAGINGS
ENCRADLING
ENCREASING
ENCRIMSONED
ENCRIMSONING
ENCRIMSONS
ENCRINITAL
ENCRINITES
ENCRINITIC
ENCROACHED
ENCROACHER
ENCROACHERS
ENCROACHES
ENCROACHING
ENCROACHINGLY
ENCROACHMENT
ENCROACHMENTS
ENCRUSTATION
ENCRUSTATIONS
ENCRUSTING
ENCRUSTMENT
ENCRUSTMENTS
ENCRYPTING
ENCRYPTION
ENCRYPTIONS
ENCULTURATE
ENCULTURATED
ENCULTURATES
ENCULTURATING
ENCULTURATION
ENCULTURATIONS
ENCULTURATIVE
ENCUMBERED
ENCUMBERING
ENCUMBERINGLY
ENCUMBERMENT
ENCUMBERMENTS
ENCUMBRANCE
ENCUMBRANCER
ENCUMBRANCERS
ENCUMBRANCES
ENCURTAINED
ENCURTAINING
ENCURTAINS
ENCYCLICAL
ENCYCLICALS
ENCYCLOPAEDIA
ENCYCLOPAEDIAS
ENCYCLOPAEDIC
ENCYCLOPAEDICAL
ENCYCLOPAEDISM
ENCYCLOPAEDISMS
ENCYCLOPAEDIST
ENCYCLOPAEDISTS
ENCYCLOPEDIA
ENCYCLOPEDIAN
ENCYCLOPEDIAS
ENCYCLOPEDIC
ENCYCLOPEDICAL
ENCYCLOPEDISM
ENCYCLOPEDISMS
ENCYCLOPEDIST
ENCYCLOPEDISTS
ENCYSTATION
ENCYSTATIONS
ENCYSTMENT
ENCYSTMENTS
ENDAMAGEMENT
ENDAMAGEMENTS
ENDAMAGING
ENDAMOEBAE
ENDAMOEBAS
ENDAMOEBIC
ENDANGERED
ENDANGERER
ENDANGERERS
ENDANGERING
ENDANGERMENT
ENDANGERMENTS
ENDARCHIES
ENDARTERECTOMY
ENDEARINGLY
ENDEARINGNESS
ENDEARINGNESSES
ENDEARMENT
ENDEARMENTS
ENDEAVORED
ENDEAVORER
ENDEAVORERS
ENDEAVORING
ENDEAVOURED
ENDEAVOURER
ENDEAVOURERS
ENDEAVOURING
ENDEAVOURMENT
ENDEAVOURMENTS
ENDEAVOURS
ENDECAGONS
ENDEIXISES
ENDEMICALLY
ENDEMICITIES
ENDEMICITY
ENDEMIOLOGIES
ENDEMIOLOGY
ENDENIZENED
ENDENIZENING
ENDENIZENS
ENDERGONIC
ENDERMATIC
ENDERMICAL
ENDLESSNESS
ENDLESSNESSES
ENDOBIOTIC
ENDOBLASTIC
ENDOBLASTS
ENDOCARDIA
ENDOCARDIAC
ENDOCARDIAL
ENDOCARDITIC
ENDOCARDITIDES
ENDOCARDITIS
ENDOCARDITISES
ENDOCARDIUM
ENDOCARPAL
ENDOCARPIC
ENDOCENTRIC
ENDOCHONDRAL
ENDOCHYLOUS
ENDOCRANIA
ENDOCRANIAL
ENDOCRANIUM
ENDOCRINAL
ENDOCRINES
ENDOCRINIC
ENDOCRINOLOGIC
ENDOCRINOLOGIES
ENDOCRINOLOGIST
ENDOCRINOLOGY
ENDOCRINOPATHIC
ENDOCRINOPATHY
ENDOCRINOUS
ENDOCRITIC
ENDOCUTICLE
ENDOCUTICLES
ENDOCYTOSES
ENDOCYTOSIS
ENDOCYTOTIC
ENDODERMAL
ENDODERMIC
ENDODERMIS
ENDODERMISES
ENDODONTAL
ENDODONTIC
ENDODONTICALLY
ENDODONTICS
ENDODONTIST
ENDODONTISTS
ENDOENZYME
ENDOENZYMES
ENDOGAMIES
ENDOGAMOUS
ENDOGENIES
ENDOGENOUS
ENDOGENOUSLY
ENDOLITHIC
ENDOLYMPHATIC
ENDOLYMPHS
ENDOMETRIA
ENDOMETRIAL
ENDOMETRIOSES
ENDOMETRIOSIS
ENDOMETRITIS
ENDOMETRITISES
ENDOMETRIUM
ENDOMITOSES
ENDOMITOSIS
ENDOMITOTIC
ENDOMIXISES
ENDOMORPHIC
ENDOMORPHIES
ENDOMORPHISM
ENDOMORPHISMS
ENDOMORPHS
ENDOMORPHY
ENDOMYCORRHIZA
ENDONEURIA
ENDONEURIUM
ENDONUCLEASE
ENDONUCLEASES
ENDONUCLEOLYTIC
ENDOPARASITE
ENDOPARASITES
ENDOPARASITIC
ENDOPARASITISM
ENDOPARASITISMS
ENDOPEPTIDASE
ENDOPEPTIDASES
ENDOPEROXIDE
ENDOPEROXIDES
ENDOPHAGIES
ENDOPHAGOUS
ENDOPHITIC
ENDOPHYLLOUS
ENDOPHYTES
ENDOPHYTIC
ENDOPHYTICALLY
ENDOPLASMIC
ENDOPLASMS
ENDOPLASTIC
ENDOPLEURA
ENDOPLEURAS
ENDOPODITE
ENDOPODITES
ENDOPOLYPLOID
ENDOPOLYPLOIDY
ENDOPROCTS
ENDORADIOSONDE
ENDORADIOSONDES
ENDORHIZAL
ENDORPHINS
ENDORSABLE
ENDORSATION
ENDORSATIONS
ENDORSEMENT
ENDORSEMENTS

ENDOSCOPES
ENDOSCOPIC
ENDOSCOPICALLY
ENDOSCOPIES
ENDOSCOPIST
ENDOSCOPISTS
ENDOSKELETAL
ENDOSKELETON
ENDOSKELETONS
ENDOSMOMETER
ENDOSMOMETERS
ENDOSMOMETRIC
ENDOSMOSES
ENDOSMOSIS
ENDOSMOTIC
ENDOSMOTICALLY
ENDOSPERMIC
ENDOSPERMS
ENDOSPORES
ENDOSPOROUS
ENDOSTEALLY
ENDOSTOSES
ENDOSTOSIS
ENDOSTYLES
ENDOSULFAN
ENDOSULFANS
ENDOSYMBIONT
ENDOSYMBIONTS
ENDOSYMBIOSES
ENDOSYMBIOSIS
ENDOSYMBIOTIC
ENDOTHECIA
ENDOTHECIAL
ENDOTHECIUM
ENDOTHELIA
ENDOTHELIAL
ENDOTHELIOID
ENDOTHELIOMA
ENDOTHELIOMAS
ENDOTHELIOMATA
ENDOTHELIUM
ENDOTHERMAL
ENDOTHERMIC
ENDOTHERMICALLY
ENDOTHERMIES
ENDOTHERMISM
ENDOTHERMISMS
ENDOTHERMS
ENDOTHERMY
ENDOTOXINS
ENDOTRACHEAL
ENDOTROPHIC
ENDOWMENTS
ENDPLAYING
ENDUNGEONED
ENDUNGEONING
ENDUNGEONS
ENDURABILITIES
ENDURABILITY
ENDURABLENESS
ENDURABLENESSES
ENDURANCES
ENDURINGLY
ENDURINGNESS
ENDURINGNESSES
ENERGETICAL
ENERGETICALLY
ENERGETICS
ENERGISATION
ENERGISATIONS
ENERGISERS
ENERGISING
ENERGIZATION
ENERGIZATIONS
ENERGIZERS
ENERGIZING
ENERGUMENS
ENERVATING
ENERVATION
ENERVATIONS
ENERVATIVE
ENERVATORS
ENFACEMENT
ENFACEMENTS
ENFEEBLEMENT
ENFEEBLEMENTS
ENFEEBLERS
ENFEEBLING
ENFELONING
ENFEOFFING
ENFEOFFMENT
ENFEOFFMENTS
ENFESTERED
ENFETTERED
ENFETTERING
ENFEVERING
ENFIERCING
ENFILADING
ENFLESHING
ENFLEURAGE
ENFLEURAGES
ENFLOWERED
ENFLOWERING
ENFOLDMENT
ENFOLDMENTS
ENFORCEABILITY
ENFORCEABLE
ENFORCEDLY
ENFORCEMENT
ENFORCEMENTS
ENFORESTED
ENFORESTING
ENFOULDERED
ENFRAMEMENT
ENFRAMEMENTS
ENFRANCHISE
ENFRANCHISED
ENFRANCHISEMENT
ENFRANCHISER
ENFRANCHISERS
ENFRANCHISES
ENFRANCHISING
ENFREEDOMED
ENFREEDOMING
ENFREEDOMS
ENFREEZING
ENGAGEMENT
ENGAGEMENTS
ENGAGINGLY
ENGAGINGNESS
ENGAGINGNESSES
ENGARLANDED
ENGARLANDING
ENGARLANDS
ENGARRISON
ENGARRISONED
ENGARRISONING
ENGARRISONS
ENGENDERED
ENGENDERER
ENGENDERERS
ENGENDERING
ENGENDERMENT
ENGENDERMENTS
ENGENDRURE
ENGENDRURES
ENGENDURES
ENGINEERED
ENGINEERING
ENGINEERINGS
ENGINERIES
ENGIRDLING
ENGLACIALLY
ENGLISHING
ENGLOOMING
ENGLUTTING
ENGORGEMENT
ENGORGEMENTS
ENGOUEMENT
ENGOUEMENTS
ENGOUMENTS
ENGRAFFING
ENGRAFTATION
ENGRAFTATIONS
ENGRAFTING
ENGRAFTMENT
ENGRAFTMENTS
ENGRAILING
ENGRAILMENT
ENGRAILMENTS
ENGRAINEDLY
ENGRAINEDNESS
ENGRAINEDNESSES
ENGRAINERS
ENGRAINING
ENGRAMMATIC
ENGRASPING
ENGRAVERIES
ENGRAVINGS
ENGRENAGES
ENGRIEVING
ENGROOVING
ENGROSSEDLY
ENGROSSERS
ENGROSSING
ENGROSSINGLY
ENGROSSMENT
ENGROSSMENTS
ENGUARDING
ENGULFMENT
ENGULFMENTS
ENGULPHING
ENGYSCOPES
ENHANCEMENT
ENHANCEMENTS
ENHARMONIC
ENHARMONICAL
ENHARMONICALLY
ENHEARSING
ENHEARTENED
ENHEARTENING
ENHEARTENS
ENHUNGERED
ENHUNGERING
ENHYDRITES
ENHYDRITIC
ENHYDROSES
ENHYPOSTASIA
ENHYPOSTASIAS
ENHYPOSTATIC
ENHYPOSTATISE
ENHYPOSTATISED
ENHYPOSTATISES
ENHYPOSTATISING
ENHYPOSTATIZE
ENHYPOSTATIZED
ENHYPOSTATIZES
ENHYPOSTATIZING
ENIGMATICAL
ENIGMATICALLY
ENIGMATISE
ENIGMATISED
ENIGMATISES
ENIGMATISING
ENIGMATIST
ENIGMATISTS
ENIGMATIZE
ENIGMATIZED
ENIGMATIZES
ENIGMATIZING
ENIGMATOGRAPHY
ENJAMBEMENT
ENJAMBEMENTS
ENJAMBMENT
ENJAMBMENTS
ENJOINDERS
ENJOINMENT
ENJOINMENTS
ENJOYABLENESS
ENJOYABLENESSES

ENJOYMENTS
ENKEPHALIN
ENKEPHALINE
ENKEPHALINES
ENKEPHALINS
ENKERNELLED
ENKERNELLING
ENKINDLERS
ENKINDLING
ENLACEMENT
ENLACEMENTS
ENLARGEABLE
ENLARGEDLY
ENLARGEDNESS
ENLARGEDNESSES
ENLARGEMENT
ENLARGEMENTS
ENLARGENED
ENLARGENING
ENLEVEMENT
ENLEVEMENTS
ENLIGHTENED
ENLIGHTENER
ENLIGHTENERS
ENLIGHTENING
ENLIGHTENMENT
ENLIGHTENMENTS
ENLIGHTENS
ENLIGHTING
ENLISTMENT
ENLISTMENTS
ENLIVENERS
ENLIVENING
ENLIVENMENT
ENLIVENMENTS
ENLUMINING
ENMESHMENT
ENMESHMENTS
ENNEAGONAL
ENNEAGRAMS
ENNEAHEDRA
ENNEAHEDRAL
ENNEAHEDRON
ENNEAHEDRONS
ENNEANDRIAN
ENNEANDROUS
ENNEASTYLE
ENNEATHLON
ENNEATHLONS
ENNOBLEMENT
ENNOBLEMENTS
ENOKIDAKES
ENOKITAKES
ENOLOGICAL
ENOLOGISTS
ENORMITIES
ENORMOUSLY
ENORMOUSNESS
ENORMOUSNESSES
ENOUNCEMENT
ENOUNCEMENTS
ENPHYTOTIC
ENQUEUEING
ENQUIRATION
ENQUIRATIONS
ENRAGEMENT
ENRAGEMENTS
ENRANCKLED
ENRANCKLES
ENRANCKLING
ENRAPTURED
ENRAPTURES
ENRAPTURING
ENRAUNGING
ENRAVISHED
ENRAVISHES
ENRAVISHING
ENREGIMENT
ENREGIMENTED
ENREGIMENTING
ENREGIMENTS
ENREGISTER
ENREGISTERED
ENREGISTERING
ENREGISTERS
ENRHEUMING
ENRICHMENT
ENRICHMENTS
ENROLLMENT
ENROLLMENTS
ENROLMENTS
ENROUGHING
ENROUNDING
ENSAMPLING
ENSANGUINATED
ENSANGUINE
ENSANGUINED
ENSANGUINES
ENSANGUINING
ENSCHEDULE
ENSCHEDULED
ENSCHEDULES
ENSCHEDULING
ENSCONCING
ENSCROLLED
ENSCROLLING
ENSEPULCHRE
ENSEPULCHRED
ENSEPULCHRES
ENSEPULCHRING
ENSERFMENT
ENSERFMENTS
ENSHEATHED
ENSHEATHES
ENSHEATHING
ENSHELLING
ENSHELTERED
ENSHELTERING
ENSHELTERS
ENSHIELDED
ENSHIELDING
ENSHRINEES
ENSHRINEMENT
ENSHRINEMENTS
ENSHRINING
ENSHROUDED
ENSHROUDING
ENSIGNCIES
ENSIGNSHIP
ENSIGNSHIPS
ENSILABILITIES
ENSILABILITY
ENSILAGEING
ENSILAGING
ENSLAVEMENT
ENSLAVEMENTS
ENSNAREMENT
ENSNAREMENTS
ENSNARLING
ENSORCELED
ENSORCELING
ENSORCELLED
ENSORCELLING
ENSORCELLMENT
ENSORCELLMENTS
ENSORCELLS
ENSOULMENT
ENSOULMENTS
ENSPHERING
ENSTAMPING
ENSTATITES
ENSTEEPING
ENSTRUCTURED
ENSWATHEMENT
ENSWATHEMENTS
ENSWATHING
ENSWEEPING
ENTABLATURE
ENTABLATURES
ENTABLEMENT
ENTABLEMENTS
ENTAILMENT
ENTAILMENTS
ENTAMOEBAE
ENTAMOEBAS
ENTANGLEMENT
ENTANGLEMENTS
ENTANGLERS
ENTANGLING
ENTELECHIES
ENTELLUSES
ENTENDERED
ENTENDERING
ENTERCHAUNGE
ENTERCHAUNGED
ENTERCHAUNGES
ENTERCHAUNGING
ENTERDEALE
ENTERDEALED
ENTERDEALES
ENTERDEALING
ENTERECTOMIES
ENTERECTOMY
ENTERITIDES
ENTERITISES
ENTEROBACTERIA
ENTEROBACTERIAL
ENTEROBACTERIUM
ENTEROBIASES
ENTEROBIASIS
ENTEROCELE
ENTEROCELES
ENTEROCENTESES
ENTEROCENTESIS
ENTEROCOCCAL
ENTEROCOCCI
ENTEROCOCCUS
ENTEROCOEL
ENTEROCOELE
ENTEROCOELES
ENTEROCOELIC
ENTEROCOELOUS
ENTEROCOELS
ENTEROCOLITIDES
ENTEROCOLITIS
ENTEROCOLITISES
ENTEROGASTRONE
ENTEROGASTRONES
ENTEROHEPATITIS
ENTEROKINASE
ENTEROKINASES
ENTEROLITH
ENTEROLITHS
ENTEROPATHIES
ENTEROPATHY
ENTEROPNEUST
ENTEROPNEUSTAL
ENTEROPNEUSTS
ENTEROPTOSES
ENTEROPTOSIS
ENTEROSTOMAL
ENTEROSTOMIES
ENTEROSTOMY
ENTEROTOMIES
ENTEROTOMY
ENTEROTOXIN
ENTEROTOXINS
ENTEROVIRAL
ENTEROVIRUS
ENTEROVIRUSES
ENTERPRISE
ENTERPRISED
ENTERPRISER
ENTERPRISERS
ENTERPRISES
ENTERPRISING
ENTERPRISINGLY
ENTERTAINED
ENTERTAINER
ENTERTAINERS

ENTERTAINING
ENTERTAININGLY
ENTERTAININGS
ENTERTAINMENT
ENTERTAINMENTS
ENTERTAINS
ENTERTAKEN
ENTERTAKES
ENTERTAKING
ENTERTISSUED
ENTHALPIES
ENTHRALDOM
ENTHRALDOMS
ENTHRALLED
ENTHRALLER
ENTHRALLERS
ENTHRALLING
ENTHRALLMENT
ENTHRALLMENTS
ENTHRALMENT
ENTHRALMENTS
ENTHRONEMENT
ENTHRONEMENTS
ENTHRONING
ENTHRONISATION
ENTHRONISATIONS
ENTHRONISE
ENTHRONISED
ENTHRONISES
ENTHRONISING
ENTHRONIZATION
ENTHRONIZATIONS
ENTHRONIZE
ENTHRONIZED
ENTHRONIZES
ENTHRONIZING
ENTHUSIASM
ENTHUSIASMS
ENTHUSIAST
ENTHUSIASTIC
ENTHUSIASTICAL
ENTHUSIASTS
ENTHYMEMATIC
ENTHYMEMATICAL
ENTHYMEMES
ENTICEABLE
ENTICEMENT
ENTICEMENTS
ENTICINGLY
ENTICINGNESS
ENTICINGNESSES
ENTIRENESS
ENTIRENESSES
ENTIRETIES
ENTITATIVE
ENTITLEMENT
ENTITLEMENTS
ENTOBLASTIC
ENTOBLASTS
ENTODERMAL
ENTODERMIC
ENTOILMENT
ENTOILMENTS
ENTOMBMENT
ENTOMBMENTS
ENTOMOFAUNA
ENTOMOFAUNAE
ENTOMOFAUNAS
ENTOMOLOGIC
ENTOMOLOGICAL
ENTOMOLOGICALLY
ENTOMOLOGIES
ENTOMOLOGISE
ENTOMOLOGISED
ENTOMOLOGISES
ENTOMOLOGISING
ENTOMOLOGIST
ENTOMOLOGISTS
ENTOMOLOGIZE
ENTOMOLOGIZED
ENTOMOLOGIZES
ENTOMOLOGIZING
ENTOMOLOGY
ENTOMOPHAGIES
ENTOMOPHAGOUS
ENTOMOPHAGY
ENTOMOPHILIES
ENTOMOPHILOUS
ENTOMOPHILY
ENTOMOSTRACAN
ENTOMOSTRACANS
ENTOMOSTRACOUS
ENTOPHYTAL
ENTOPHYTES
ENTOPHYTIC
ENTOPHYTOUS
ENTOPLASTRA
ENTOPLASTRAL
ENTOPLASTRON
ENTOPROCTS
ENTOURAGES
ENTRAILING
ENTRAINEMENT
ENTRAINEMENTS
ENTRAINERS
ENTRAINING
ENTRAINMENT
ENTRAINMENTS
ENTRAMMELED
ENTRAMMELING
ENTRAMMELLED
ENTRAMMELLING
ENTRAMMELS
ENTRANCEMENT
ENTRANCEMENTS
ENTRANCEWAY
ENTRANCEWAYS
ENTRANCING
ENTRANCINGLY
ENTRAPMENT
ENTRAPMENTS
ENTRAPPERS
ENTRAPPING
ENTREASURE
ENTREASURED
ENTREASURES
ENTREASURING
ENTREATABLE
ENTREATIES
ENTREATING
ENTREATINGLY
ENTREATINGS
ENTREATIVE
ENTREATMENT
ENTREATMENTS
ENTRECHATS
ENTRECOTES
ENTREMESSE
ENTREMESSES
ENTRENCHED
ENTRENCHER
ENTRENCHERS
ENTRENCHES
ENTRENCHING
ENTRENCHMENT
ENTRENCHMENTS
ENTREPRENEUR
ENTREPRENEURIAL
ENTREPRENEURS
ENTREPRENEUSE
ENTREPRENEUSES
ENTROPICALLY
ENTROPIONS
ENTROPIUMS
ENTRUSTING
ENTRUSTMENT
ENTRUSTMENTS
ENTWINEMENT
ENTWINEMENTS
ENTWISTING
ENUCLEATED
ENUCLEATES
ENUCLEATING
ENUCLEATION
ENUCLEATIONS
ENUMERABILITIES
ENUMERABILITY
ENUMERABLE
ENUMERATED
ENUMERATES
ENUMERATING
ENUMERATION
ENUMERATIONS
ENUMERATIVE
ENUMERATOR
ENUMERATORS
ENUNCIABLE
ENUNCIATED
ENUNCIATES
ENUNCIATING
ENUNCIATION
ENUNCIATIONS
ENUNCIATIVE
ENUNCIATIVELY
ENUNCIATOR
ENUNCIATORS
ENUNCIATORY
ENUREDNESS
ENUREDNESSES
ENUREMENTS
ENURESISES
ENVASSALLED
ENVASSALLING
ENVAULTING
ENVEIGLING
ENVELOPERS
ENVELOPING
ENVELOPMENT
ENVELOPMENTS
ENVENOMING
ENVENOMISATION
ENVENOMISATIONS
ENVENOMIZATION
ENVENOMIZATIONS
ENVERMEILED
ENVERMEILING
ENVERMEILS
ENVIABLENESS
ENVIABLENESSES
ENVIOUSNESS
ENVIOUSNESSES
ENVIRONICS
ENVIRONING
ENVIRONMENT
ENVIRONMENTAL
ENVIRONMENTALLY
ENVIRONMENTS
ENVISAGEMENT
ENVISAGEMENTS
ENVISAGING
ENVISIONED
ENVISIONING
ENVOYSHIPS
ENWALLOWED
ENWALLOWING
ENWHEELING
ENWRAPMENT
ENWRAPMENTS
ENWRAPPING
ENWRAPPINGS
ENWREATHED
ENWREATHES
ENWREATHING
ENZOOTICALLY
ENZYMATICALLY
ENZYMICALLY
ENZYMOLOGICAL
ENZYMOLOGIES
ENZYMOLOGIST
ENZYMOLOGISTS

ENZYMOLOGY
ENZYMOLYSES
ENZYMOLYSIS
ENZYMOLYTIC
EOHIPPUSES
EOSINOPHIL
EOSINOPHILE
EOSINOPHILES
EOSINOPHILIA
EOSINOPHILIAS
EOSINOPHILIC
EOSINOPHILOUS
EOSINOPHILS
EPAGOMENAL
EPANADIPLOSES
EPANADIPLOSIS
EPANALEPSES
EPANALEPSIS
EPANALEPTIC
EPANAPHORA
EPANAPHORAL
EPANAPHORAS
EPANODOSES
EPANORTHOSES
EPANORTHOSIS
EPANORTHOTIC
EPARCHATES
EPAULEMENT
EPAULEMENTS
EPAULETTED
EPAULETTES
EPEIROGENESES
EPEIROGENESIS
EPEIROGENETIC
EPEIROGENIC
EPEIROGENICALLY
EPEIROGENIES
EPEIROGENY
EPENCEPHALA
EPENCEPHALIC
EPENCEPHALON
EPENCEPHALONS
EPENTHESES
EPENTHESIS
EPENTHETIC
EPEOLATRIES
EPEXEGESES
EPEXEGESIS
EPEXEGETIC
EPEXEGETICAL
EPEXEGETICALLY
EPHEBOPHILE
EPHEBOPHILES
EPHEBOPHILIA
EPHEBOPHILIAS
EPHEDRINES
EPHEMERALITIES
EPHEMERALITY
EPHEMERALLY
EPHEMERALNESS
EPHEMERALNESSES
EPHEMERALS
EPHEMERIDES
EPHEMERIDIAN
EPHEMERIDS
EPHEMERIST
EPHEMERISTS
EPHEMERONS
EPHEMEROPTERAN
EPHEMEROPTERANS
EPHEMEROUS
EPHORALTIES
EPIBLASTIC
EPICALYCES
EPICALYXES
EPICANTHIC
EPICANTHUS
EPICARDIAC
EPICARDIAL
EPICARDIUM
EPICARDIUMS
EPICEDIANS
EPICENISMS
EPICENTERS
EPICENTRAL
EPICENTRES
EPICENTRUM
EPICHEIREMA
EPICHEIREMAS
EPICHEIREMATA
EPICHLOROHYDRIN
EPICONDYLE
EPICONDYLES
EPICONDYLITIS
EPICONDYLITISES
EPICONTINENTAL
EPICRANIUM
EPICRANIUMS
EPICUREANISM
EPICUREANISMS
EPICUREANS
EPICURISED
EPICURISES
EPICURISING
EPICURISMS
EPICURIZED
EPICURIZES
EPICURIZING
EPICUTICLE
EPICUTICLES
EPICUTICULAR
EPICYCLICAL
EPICYCLOID
EPICYCLOIDAL
EPICYCLOIDS
EPIDEICTIC
EPIDEICTICAL
EPIDEMICAL
EPIDEMICALLY
EPIDEMICITIES
EPIDEMICITY
EPIDEMIOLOGIC
EPIDEMIOLOGICAL
EPIDEMIOLOGIES
EPIDEMIOLOGIST
EPIDEMIOLOGISTS
EPIDEMIOLOGY
EPIDENDRONE
EPIDENDRONES
EPIDENDRUM
EPIDENDRUMS
EPIDERMISES
EPIDERMOID
EPIDERMOLYSES
EPIDERMOLYSIS
EPIDIASCOPE
EPIDIASCOPES
EPIDIDYMAL
EPIDIDYMIDES
EPIDIDYMIS
EPIDIDYMITIS
EPIDIDYMITISES
EPIDIORITE
EPIDIORITES
EPIDOSITES
EPIDOTISATION
EPIDOTISATIONS
EPIDOTISED
EPIDOTIZATION
EPIDOTIZATIONS
EPIDOTIZED
EPIGASTRIA
EPIGASTRIAL
EPIGASTRIC
EPIGASTRIUM
EPIGENESES
EPIGENESIS
EPIGENESIST
EPIGENESISTS
EPIGENETIC
EPIGENETICALLY
EPIGENETICIST
EPIGENETICISTS
EPIGENETICS
EPIGENISTS
EPIGENOMES
EPIGLOTTAL
EPIGLOTTIC
EPIGLOTTIDES
EPIGLOTTIS
EPIGLOTTISES
EPIGNATHOUS
EPIGONISMS
EPIGRAMMATIC
EPIGRAMMATICAL
EPIGRAMMATISE
EPIGRAMMATISED
EPIGRAMMATISER
EPIGRAMMATISERS
EPIGRAMMATISES
EPIGRAMMATISING
EPIGRAMMATISM
EPIGRAMMATISMS
EPIGRAMMATIST
EPIGRAMMATISTS
EPIGRAMMATIZE
EPIGRAMMATIZED
EPIGRAMMATIZER
EPIGRAMMATIZERS
EPIGRAMMATIZES
EPIGRAMMATIZING
EPIGRAPHED
EPIGRAPHER
EPIGRAPHERS
EPIGRAPHIC
EPIGRAPHICAL
EPIGRAPHICALLY
EPIGRAPHIES
EPIGRAPHING
EPIGRAPHIST
EPIGRAPHISTS
EPILATIONS
EPILEPSIES
EPILEPTICAL
EPILEPTICALLY
EPILEPTICS
EPILEPTIFORM
EPILEPTOGENIC
EPILEPTOID
EPILIMNION
EPILIMNIONS
EPILOBIUMS
EPILOGISED
EPILOGISES
EPILOGISING
EPILOGISTIC
EPILOGISTS
EPILOGIZED
EPILOGIZES
EPILOGIZING
EPILOGUING
EPILOGUISE
EPILOGUISED
EPILOGUISES
EPILOGUISING
EPILOGUIZE
EPILOGUIZED
EPILOGUIZES
EPILOGUIZING
EPIMELETIC
EPIMERASES
EPIMERISED
EPIMERISES
EPIMERISING
EPIMERISMS
EPIMERIZED
EPIMERIZES
EPIMERIZING
EPIMORPHIC
EPIMORPHOSES

EPIMORPHOSIS
EPINASTICALLY
EPINASTIES
EPINEPHRIN
EPINEPHRINE
EPINEPHRINES
EPINEPHRINS
EPINEURIAL
EPINEURIUM
EPINEURIUMS
EPINICIONS
EPINIKIANS
EPINIKIONS
EPIPELAGIC
EPIPETALOUS
EPIPHANIES
EPIPHANOUS
EPIPHENOMENA
EPIPHENOMENAL
EPIPHENOMENALLY
EPIPHENOMENON
EPIPHONEMA
EPIPHONEMAS
EPIPHRAGMS
EPIPHYLLOUS
EPIPHYSEAL
EPIPHYSIAL
EPIPHYTICAL
EPIPHYTICALLY
EPIPHYTISM
EPIPHYTISMS
EPIPHYTOLOGIES
EPIPHYTOLOGY
EPIPHYTOTIC
EPIPHYTOTICS
EPIPLASTRA
EPIPLASTRAL
EPIPLASTRON
EPIPOLISMS
EPIROGENETIC
EPIROGENIC
EPIROGENIES
EPIRRHEMAS
EPIRRHEMATA
EPIRRHEMATIC
EPISCOPACIES
EPISCOPACY
EPISCOPALIAN
EPISCOPALIANISM
EPISCOPALIANS
EPISCOPALISM
EPISCOPALISMS
EPISCOPALLY
EPISCOPANT
EPISCOPANTS
EPISCOPATE
EPISCOPATED
EPISCOPATES
EPISCOPATING
EPISCOPIES
EPISCOPISE
EPISCOPISED
EPISCOPISES
EPISCOPISING
EPISCOPIZE
EPISCOPIZED
EPISCOPIZES
EPISCOPIZING
EPISEMATIC
EPISEPALOUS
EPISIOTOMIES
EPISIOTOMY
EPISODICAL
EPISODICALLY
EPISOMALLY
EPISPASTIC
EPISPASTICS
EPISTASIES
EPISTAXISES
EPISTEMICALLY
EPISTEMICS
EPISTEMOLOGICAL
EPISTEMOLOGIES
EPISTEMOLOGIST
EPISTEMOLOGISTS
EPISTEMOLOGY
EPISTERNAL
EPISTERNUM
EPISTERNUMS
EPISTILBITE
EPISTILBITES
EPISTOLARIAN
EPISTOLARIANS
EPISTOLARIES
EPISTOLARY
EPISTOLATORY
EPISTOLERS
EPISTOLETS
EPISTOLICAL
EPISTOLISE
EPISTOLISED
EPISTOLISES
EPISTOLISING
EPISTOLIST
EPISTOLISTS
EPISTOLIZE
EPISTOLIZED
EPISTOLIZES
EPISTOLIZING
EPISTOLOGRAPHY
EPISTROPHE
EPISTROPHES
EPITAPHERS
EPITAPHIAL
EPITAPHIAN
EPITAPHING
EPITAPHIST
EPITAPHISTS
EPITAXIALLY
EPITHALAMIA
EPITHALAMIC
EPITHALAMION
EPITHALAMIUM
EPITHALAMIUMS
EPITHELIAL
EPITHELIALISE
EPITHELIALISED
EPITHELIALISES
EPITHELIALISING
EPITHELIALIZE
EPITHELIALIZED
EPITHELIALIZES
EPITHELIALIZING
EPITHELIOID
EPITHELIOMA
EPITHELIOMAS
EPITHELIOMATA
EPITHELIOMATOUS
EPITHELISATION
EPITHELISATIONS
EPITHELISE
EPITHELISED
EPITHELISES
EPITHELISING
EPITHELIUM
EPITHELIUMS
EPITHELIZATION
EPITHELIZATIONS
EPITHELIZE
EPITHELIZED
EPITHELIZES
EPITHELIZING
EPITHEMATA
EPITHERMAL
EPITHETICAL
EPITHETICALLY
EPITHETING
EPITHETONS
EPITHYMETIC
EPITOMICAL
EPITOMISATION
EPITOMISATIONS
EPITOMISED
EPITOMISER
EPITOMISERS
EPITOMISES
EPITOMISING
EPITOMISTS
EPITOMIZATION
EPITOMIZATIONS
EPITOMIZED
EPITOMIZER
EPITOMIZERS
EPITOMIZES
EPITOMIZING
EPITRACHELION
EPITRACHELIONS
EPITROCHOID
EPITROCHOIDS
EPIZEUXISES
EPIZOOTICALLY
EPIZOOTICS
EPIZOOTIES
EPIZOOTIOLOGIC
EPIZOOTIOLOGIES
EPIZOOTIOLOGY
EPONYCHIUM
EPONYCHIUMS
EPONYMOUSLY
EPOXIDATION
EPOXIDATIONS
EPOXIDISED
EPOXIDISES
EPOXIDISING
EPOXIDIZED
EPOXIDIZES
EPOXIDIZING
EPROUVETTE
EPROUVETTES
EPULATIONS
EPURATIONS
EQUABILITIES
EQUABILITY
EQUABLENESS
EQUABLENESSES
EQUALISATION
EQUALISATIONS
EQUALISERS
EQUALISING
EQUALITARIAN
EQUALITARIANISM
EQUALITARIANS
EQUALITIES
EQUALIZATION
EQUALIZATIONS
EQUALIZERS
EQUALIZING
EQUALNESSES
EQUANIMITIES
EQUANIMITY
EQUANIMOUS
EQUANIMOUSLY
EQUATABILITIES
EQUATABILITY
EQUATIONAL
EQUATIONALLY
EQUATORIAL
EQUATORIALLY
EQUATORIALS
EQUATORWARD
EQUESTRIAN
EQUESTRIANISM
EQUESTRIANISMS
EQUESTRIANS
EQUESTRIENNE
EQUESTRIENNES
EQUIANGULAR
EQUIANGULARITY
EQUIBALANCE
EQUIBALANCED

EQUIBALANCES
EQUIBALANCING
EQUICALORIC
EQUIDIFFERENT
EQUIDISTANCE
EQUIDISTANCES
EQUIDISTANT
EQUIDISTANTLY
EQUIFINALLY
EQUILATERAL
EQUILATERALLY
EQUILATERALS
EQUILIBRANT
EQUILIBRANTS
EQUILIBRATE
EQUILIBRATED
EQUILIBRATES
EQUILIBRATING
EQUILIBRATION
EQUILIBRATIONS
EQUILIBRATOR
EQUILIBRATORS
EQUILIBRATORY
EQUILIBRIA
EQUILIBRIST
EQUILIBRISTIC
EQUILIBRISTS
EQUILIBRITIES
EQUILIBRITY
EQUILIBRIUM
EQUILIBRIUMS
EQUIMOLECULAR
EQUIMULTIPLE
EQUIMULTIPLES
EQUINITIES
EQUINOCTIAL
EQUINOCTIALLY
EQUINOCTIALS
EQUINUMEROUS
EQUIPAGING
EQUIPARATE
EQUIPARATED
EQUIPARATES
EQUIPARATING
EQUIPARATION
EQUIPARATIONS
EQUIPARTITION
EQUIPARTITIONS
EQUIPMENTS
EQUIPOISED
EQUIPOISES
EQUIPOISING
EQUIPOLLENCE
EQUIPOLLENCES
EQUIPOLLENCIES
EQUIPOLLENCY
EQUIPOLLENT
EQUIPOLLENTLY
EQUIPOLLENTS
EQUIPONDERANCE
EQUIPONDERANCES
EQUIPONDERANCY
EQUIPONDERANT
EQUIPONDERATE
EQUIPONDERATED
EQUIPONDERATES
EQUIPONDERATING
EQUIPOTENT
EQUIPOTENTIAL
EQUIPOTENTIALS
EQUIPROBABILITY
EQUIPROBABLE
EQUISETACEOUS
EQUISETIFORM
EQUISETUMS
EQUITABILITIES
EQUITABILITY
EQUITABLENESS
EQUITABLENESSES
EQUITATION
EQUITATIONS
EQUIVALENCE
EQUIVALENCES
EQUIVALENCIES
EQUIVALENCY
EQUIVALENT
EQUIVALENTLY
EQUIVALENTS
EQUIVOCACIES
EQUIVOCACY
EQUIVOCALITIES
EQUIVOCALITY
EQUIVOCALLY
EQUIVOCALNESS
EQUIVOCALNESSES
EQUIVOCATE
EQUIVOCATED
EQUIVOCATES
EQUIVOCATING
EQUIVOCATINGLY
EQUIVOCATION
EQUIVOCATIONS
EQUIVOCATOR
EQUIVOCATORS
EQUIVOCATORY
EQUIVOQUES
ERADIATING
ERADIATION
ERADIATIONS
ERADICABLE
ERADICABLY
ERADICANTS
ERADICATED
ERADICATES
ERADICATING
ERADICATION
ERADICATIONS
ERADICATIVE
ERADICATOR
ERADICATORS
ERASABILITIES
ERASABILITY
ERASEMENTS
ERECTILITIES
ERECTILITY
ERECTNESSES
EREMACAUSES
EREMACAUSIS
EREMITICAL
EREMITISMS
EREMURUSES
ERETHISMIC
ERETHISTIC
ERGASTOPLASM
ERGASTOPLASMIC
ERGASTOPLASMS
ERGATANDROMORPH
ERGATANERS
ERGATIVITIES
ERGATIVITY
ERGATOCRACIES
ERGATOCRACY
ERGATOGYNE
ERGATOGYNES
ERGATOMORPH
ERGATOMORPHIC
ERGATOMORPHS
ERGODICITIES
ERGODICITY
ERGOGRAPHS
ERGOMANIAC
ERGOMANIACS
ERGOMANIAS
ERGOMETERS
ERGOMETRIC
ERGOMETRIES
ERGONOMICALLY
ERGONOMICS
ERGONOMIST
ERGONOMISTS
ERGONOVINE
ERGONOVINES
ERGOPHOBIA
ERGOPHOBIAS
ERGOSTEROL
ERGOSTEROLS
ERGOTAMINE
ERGOTAMINES
ERGOTISING
ERGOTIZING
ERICACEOUS
ERINACEOUS
ERIOMETERS
ERIOPHOROUS
ERIOPHORUM
ERIOPHORUMS
ERIOPHYIDS
ERIOSTEMON
ERIOSTEMONS
ERISTICALLY
ERODIBILITIES
ERODIBILITY
EROGENEITIES
EROGENEITY
EROSIONALLY
EROSIVENESS
EROSIVENESSES
EROSIVITIES
EROTICALLY
EROTICISATION
EROTICISATIONS
EROTICISED
EROTICISES
EROTICISING
EROTICISMS
EROTICISTS
EROTICIZATION
EROTICIZATIONS
EROTICIZED
EROTICIZES
EROTICIZING
EROTISATION
EROTISATIONS
EROTIZATION
EROTIZATIONS
EROTOGENIC
EROTOGENOUS
EROTOLOGICAL
EROTOLOGIES
EROTOLOGIST
EROTOLOGISTS
EROTOMANIA
EROTOMANIAC
EROTOMANIACS
EROTOMANIAS
EROTOPHOBIA
EROTOPHOBIAS
ERRANTRIES
ERRATICALLY
ERRATICISM
ERRATICISMS
ERRONEOUSLY
ERRONEOUSNESS
ERRONEOUSNESSES
ERUBESCENCE
ERUBESCENCES
ERUBESCENCIES
ERUBESCENCY
ERUBESCENT
ERUBESCITE
ERUBESCITES
ERUCTATING
ERUCTATION
ERUCTATIONS
ERUCTATIVE
ERUDITENESS
ERUDITENESSES
ERUDITIONS
ERUPTIONAL
ERUPTIVELY

E

ERUPTIVENESS
ERUPTIVENESSES
ERUPTIVITIES
ERUPTIVITY
ERVALENTAS
ERYSIPELAS
ERYSIPELASES
ERYSIPELATOUS
ERYSIPELOID
ERYSIPELOIDS
ERYTHEMATIC
ERYTHEMATOUS
ERYTHORBATE
ERYTHORBATES
ERYTHORBIC
ERYTHRAEMIA
ERYTHRAEMIAS
ERYTHREMIA
ERYTHREMIAS
ERYTHRINAS
ERYTHRISMAL
ERYTHRISMS
ERYTHRISTIC
ERYTHRITES
ERYTHRITIC
ERYTHRITOL
ERYTHRITOLS
ERYTHROBLAST
ERYTHROBLASTIC
ERYTHROBLASTS
ERYTHROCYTE
ERYTHROCYTES
ERYTHROCYTIC
ERYTHROMELALGIA
ERYTHROMYCIN
ERYTHROMYCINS
ERYTHRONIUM
ERYTHRONIUMS
ERYTHROPENIA
ERYTHROPENIAS
ERYTHROPHOBIA
ERYTHROPHOBIAS
ERYTHROPOIESES
ERYTHROPOIESIS
ERYTHROPOIETIC
ERYTHROPOIETIN
ERYTHROPOIETINS
ERYTHROPSIA
ERYTHROPSIAS
ERYTHROSIN
ERYTHROSINE
ERYTHROSINES
ERYTHROSINS
ESCABECHES
ESCADRILLE
ESCADRILLES
ESCALADERS
ESCALADING
ESCALADOES
ESCALATING
ESCALATION
ESCALATIONS
ESCALATORS
ESCALATORY
ESCALLONIA
ESCALLONIAS
ESCALLOPED
ESCALLOPING
ESCALOPING
ESCAMOTAGE
ESCAMOTAGES
ESCAPADOES
ESCAPELESS
ESCAPEMENT
ESCAPEMENTS
ESCAPOLOGIES
ESCAPOLOGIST
ESCAPOLOGISTS
ESCAPOLOGY
ESCARMOUCHE
ESCARMOUCHES
ESCARPMENT
ESCARPMENTS
ESCHAROTIC
ESCHAROTICS
ESCHATOLOGIC
ESCHATOLOGICAL
ESCHATOLOGIES
ESCHATOLOGIST
ESCHATOLOGISTS
ESCHATOLOGY
ESCHEATABLE
ESCHEATAGE
ESCHEATAGES
ESCHEATING
ESCHEATMENT
ESCHEATMENTS
ESCHEATORS
ESCHSCHOLTZIA
ESCHSCHOLTZIAS
ESCHSCHOLZIA
ESCHSCHOLZIAS
ESCLANDRES
ESCOPETTES
ESCORTAGES
ESCRIBANOS
ESCRITOIRE
ESCRITOIRES
ESCRITORIAL
ESCUTCHEON
ESCUTCHEONED
ESCUTCHEONS
ESEMPLASIES
ESEMPLASTIC
ESEMPLASTICALLY
ESOPHAGEAL
ESOPHAGITIDES
ESOPHAGITIS
ESOPHAGITISES
ESOPHAGOSCOPE
ESOPHAGOSCOPES
ESOPHAGOSCOPIES
ESOPHAGOSCOPY
ESOPHAGUSES
ESOTERICALLY
ESOTERICAS
ESOTERICISM
ESOTERICISMS
ESOTERICIST
ESOTERICISTS
ESOTERISMS
ESOTROPIAS
ESPADRILLE
ESPADRILLES
ESPAGNOLES
ESPAGNOLETTE
ESPAGNOLETTES
ESPALIERED
ESPALIERING
ESPECIALLY
ESPERANCES
ESPIEGLERIE
ESPIEGLERIES
ESPIONAGES
ESPLANADES
ESPRESSIVO
ESQUIRESSES
ESSAYETTES
ESSAYISTIC
ESSENTIALISE
ESSENTIALISED
ESSENTIALISES
ESSENTIALISING
ESSENTIALISM
ESSENTIALISMS
ESSENTIALIST
ESSENTIALISTS
ESSENTIALITIES
ESSENTIALITY
ESSENTIALIZE
ESSENTIALIZED
ESSENTIALIZES
ESSENTIALIZING
ESSENTIALLY
ESSENTIALNESS
ESSENTIALNESSES
ESSENTIALS
ESTABLISHABLE
ESTABLISHED
ESTABLISHER
ESTABLISHERS
ESTABLISHES
ESTABLISHING
ESTABLISHMENT
ESTABLISHMENTS
ESTAFETTES
ESTAMINETS
ESTANCIERO
ESTANCIEROS
ESTATESMAN
ESTATESMEN
ESTERIFICATION
ESTERIFICATIONS
ESTERIFIED
ESTERIFIES
ESTERIFYING
ESTERISATION
ESTERISATIONS
ESTERIZATION
ESTERIZATIONS
ESTHESIOGEN
ESTHESIOGENS
ESTHESISES
ESTHETICAL
ESTHETICALLY
ESTHETICIAN
ESTHETICIANS
ESTHETICISM
ESTHETICISMS
ESTIMABLENESS
ESTIMABLENESSES
ESTIMATING
ESTIMATION
ESTIMATIONS
ESTIMATIVE
ESTIMATORS
ESTIPULATE
ESTIVATING
ESTIVATION
ESTIVATIONS
ESTIVATORS
ESTOPPAGES
ESTRADIOLS
ESTRAMAZONE
ESTRAMAZONES
ESTRANGEDNESS
ESTRANGEDNESSES
ESTRANGELO
ESTRANGELOS
ESTRANGEMENT
ESTRANGEMENTS
ESTRANGERS
ESTRANGHELO
ESTRANGHELOS
ESTRANGING
ESTRAPADES
ESTREATING
ESTREPEMENT
ESTREPEMENTS
ESTRIBUTOR
ESTRIBUTORS
ESTRILDIDS
ESTROGENIC
ESTROGENICALLY
ESURIENCES
ESURIENCIES
ESURIENTLY
ETEPIMELETIC
ETERNALISATION
ETERNALISATIONS

ETERNALISE
ETERNALISED
ETERNALISES
ETERNALISING
ETERNALIST
ETERNALISTS
ETERNALITIES
ETERNALITY
ETERNALIZATION
ETERNALIZATIONS
ETERNALIZE
ETERNALIZED
ETERNALIZES
ETERNALIZING
ETERNALNESS
ETERNALNESSES
ETERNISATION
ETERNISATIONS
ETERNISING
ETERNITIES
ETERNIZATION
ETERNIZATIONS
ETERNIZING
ETHAMBUTOL
ETHAMBUTOLS
ETHANEDIOIC
ETHANEDIOL
ETHANEDIOLS
ETHANOATES
ETHANOLAMINE
ETHANOLAMINES
ETHEOSTOMINE
ETHEREALISATION
ETHEREALISE
ETHEREALISED
ETHEREALISES
ETHEREALISING
ETHEREALITIES
ETHEREALITY
ETHEREALIZATION
ETHEREALIZE
ETHEREALIZED
ETHEREALIZES
ETHEREALIZING
ETHEREALLY
ETHEREALNESS
ETHEREALNESSES
ETHERIFICATION
ETHERIFICATIONS
ETHERIFIED
ETHERIFIES
ETHERIFYING
ETHERISATION
ETHERISATIONS
ETHERISERS
ETHERISING
ETHERIZATION
ETHERIZATIONS
ETHERIZERS
ETHERIZING
ETHEROMANIA
ETHEROMANIAC
ETHEROMANIACS
ETHEROMANIAS
ETHICALITIES
ETHICALITY
ETHICALNESS
ETHICALNESSES
ETHICISING
ETHICIZING
ETHIONAMIDE
ETHIONAMIDES
ETHIONINES
ETHNARCHIES
ETHNICALLY
ETHNICISMS
ETHNICITIES
ETHNOBIOLOGIES
ETHNOBIOLOGY
ETHNOBOTANICAL
ETHNOBOTANIES
ETHNOBOTANIST
ETHNOBOTANISTS
ETHNOBOTANY
ETHNOCENTRIC
ETHNOCENTRICITY
ETHNOCENTRISM
ETHNOCENTRISMS
ETHNOCIDES
ETHNOGENIC
ETHNOGENIES
ETHNOGENIST
ETHNOGENISTS
ETHNOGRAPHER
ETHNOGRAPHERS
ETHNOGRAPHIC
ETHNOGRAPHICA
ETHNOGRAPHICAL
ETHNOGRAPHIES
ETHNOGRAPHY
ETHNOHISTORIAN
ETHNOHISTORIANS
ETHNOHISTORIC
ETHNOHISTORICAL
ETHNOHISTORIES
ETHNOHISTORY
ETHNOLINGUIST
ETHNOLINGUISTIC
ETHNOLINGUISTS
ETHNOLOGIC
ETHNOLOGICAL
ETHNOLOGICALLY
ETHNOLOGIES
ETHNOLOGIST
ETHNOLOGISTS
ETHNOMEDICINE
ETHNOMEDICINES
ETHNOMUSICOLOGY
ETHNOSCIENCE
ETHNOSCIENCES
ETHOLOGICAL
ETHOLOGICALLY
ETHOLOGIES
ETHOLOGIST
ETHOLOGISTS
ETHOXYETHANE
ETHOXYETHANES
ETHYLAMINE
ETHYLAMINES
ETHYLATING
ETHYLATION
ETHYLATIONS
ETHYLBENZENE
ETHYLBENZENES
ETIOLATING
ETIOLATION
ETIOLATIONS
ETIOLOGICAL
ETIOLOGICALLY
ETIOLOGIES
ETIOLOGIST
ETIOLOGISTS
ETIQUETTES
ETONOGESTREL
ETONOGESTRELS
ETOURDERIE
ETOURDERIES
ETRANGERES
ETYMOLOGICA
ETYMOLOGICAL
ETYMOLOGICALLY
ETYMOLOGICON
ETYMOLOGICUM
ETYMOLOGIES
ETYMOLOGISE
ETYMOLOGISED
ETYMOLOGISES
ETYMOLOGISING
ETYMOLOGIST
ETYMOLOGISTS
ETYMOLOGIZE
ETYMOLOGIZED
ETYMOLOGIZES
ETYMOLOGIZING
EUBACTERIA
EUBACTERIUM
EUCALYPTOL
EUCALYPTOLE
EUCALYPTOLES
EUCALYPTOLS
EUCALYPTUS
EUCALYPTUSES
EUCARYOTES
EUCARYOTIC
EUCHARISES
EUCHARISTIC
EUCHLORINE
EUCHLORINES
EUCHLORINS
EUCHOLOGIA
EUCHOLOGIES
EUCHOLOGION
EUCHROMATIC
EUCHROMATIN
EUCHROMATINS
EUCRYPHIAS
EUDAEMONIA
EUDAEMONIAS
EUDAEMONIC
EUDAEMONICS
EUDAEMONIES
EUDAEMONISM
EUDAEMONISMS
EUDAEMONIST
EUDAEMONISTIC
EUDAEMONISTICAL
EUDAEMONISTS
EUDAIMONISM
EUDAIMONISMS
EUDEMONIAS
EUDEMONICS
EUDEMONISM
EUDEMONISMS
EUDEMONIST
EUDEMONISTIC
EUDEMONISTICAL
EUDEMONISTS
EUDIALYTES
EUDICOTYLEDON
EUDICOTYLEDONS
EUDIOMETER
EUDIOMETERS
EUDIOMETRIC
EUDIOMETRICAL
EUDIOMETRICALLY
EUDIOMETRIES
EUDIOMETRY
EUGENECIST
EUGENECISTS
EUGENICALLY
EUGENICIST
EUGENICISTS
EUGEOSYNCLINAL
EUGEOSYNCLINE
EUGEOSYNCLINES
EUGLENOIDS
EUGLOBULIN
EUGLOBULINS
EUHARMONIC
EUHEMERISE
EUHEMERISED
EUHEMERISES
EUHEMERISING
EUHEMERISM
EUHEMERISMS
EUHEMERIST
EUHEMERISTIC
EUHEMERISTS
EUHEMERIZE
EUHEMERIZED

EUHEMERIZES
EUHEMERIZING
EUKARYOTES
EUKARYOTIC
EULOGISERS
EULOGISING
EULOGISTIC
EULOGISTICAL
EULOGISTICALLY
EULOGIZERS
EULOGIZING
EUMELANINS
EUNUCHISED
EUNUCHISES
EUNUCHISING
EUNUCHISMS
EUNUCHIZED
EUNUCHIZES
EUNUCHIZING
EUNUCHOIDISM
EUNUCHOIDISMS
EUNUCHOIDS
EUONYMUSES
EUPATORIUM
EUPATORIUMS
EUPATRIDAE
EUPEPTICITIES
EUPEPTICITY
EUPHAUSIACEAN
EUPHAUSIACEANS
EUPHAUSIDS
EUPHAUSIID
EUPHAUSIIDS
EUPHEMISED
EUPHEMISER
EUPHEMISERS
EUPHEMISES
EUPHEMISING
EUPHEMISMS
EUPHEMISTIC
EUPHEMISTICALLY
EUPHEMISTS
EUPHEMIZED
EUPHEMIZER
EUPHEMIZERS
EUPHEMIZES
EUPHEMIZING
EUPHONICAL
EUPHONICALLY
EUPHONIOUS
EUPHONIOUSLY
EUPHONIOUSNESS
EUPHONISED
EUPHONISES
EUPHONISING
EUPHONISMS
EUPHONIUMS
EUPHONIZED
EUPHONIZES
EUPHONIZING
EUPHORBIACEOUS
EUPHORBIAS
EUPHORBIUM
EUPHORBIUMS
EUPHORIANT
EUPHORIANTS
EUPHORICALLY
EUPHRASIAS
EUPHRASIES
EUPHUISING
EUPHUISTIC
EUPHUISTICAL
EUPHUISTICALLY
EUPHUIZING
EUPLASTICS
EUPLOIDIES
EURHYTHMIC
EURHYTHMICAL
EURHYTHMICS
EURHYTHMIES
EURHYTHMIST
EURHYTHMISTS
EUROCHEQUE
EUROCHEQUES
EUROCREDIT
EUROCREDITS
EUROCREEPS
EUROCURRENCIES
EUROCURRENCY
EURODEPOSIT
EURODEPOSITS
EURODOLLAR
EURODOLLARS
EUROMARKET
EUROMARKETS
EUROPHILES
EUROPHILIA
EUROPHILIAS
EUROPHOBIA
EUROPHOBIAS
EUROPHOBIC
EUROTERMINAL
EUROTERMINALS
EURYBATHIC
EURYHALINE
EURYOECIOUS
EURYPTERID
EURYPTERIDS
EURYPTEROID
EURYPTEROIDS
EURYTHERMAL
EURYTHERMIC
EURYTHERMOUS
EURYTHERMS
EURYTHMICAL
EURYTHMICS
EURYTHMIES
EURYTHMIST
EURYTHMISTS
EUSPORANGIATE
EUSTATICALLY
EUSTRESSES
EUTECTOIDS
EUTHANASED
EUTHANASES
EUTHANASIA
EUTHANASIAS
EUTHANASIAST
EUTHANASIASTS
EUTHANASIC
EUTHANASIES
EUTHANASING
EUTHANATISE
EUTHANATISED
EUTHANATISES
EUTHANATISING
EUTHANATIZE
EUTHANATIZED
EUTHANATIZES
EUTHANATIZING
EUTHANAZED
EUTHANAZES
EUTHANAZING
EUTHANISED
EUTHANISES
EUTHANISING
EUTHANIZED
EUTHANIZES
EUTHANIZING
EUTHENISTS
EUTHERIANS
EUTHYROIDS
EUTRAPELIA
EUTRAPELIAS
EUTRAPELIES
EUTROPHICATION
EUTROPHICATIONS
EUTROPHIES
EVACUATING
EVACUATION
EVACUATIONS
EVACUATIVE
EVACUATIVES
EVACUATORS
EVAGATIONS
EVAGINATED
EVAGINATES
EVAGINATING
EVAGINATION
EVAGINATIONS
EVALUATING
EVALUATION
EVALUATIONS
EVALUATIVE
EVALUATORS
EVANESCENCE
EVANESCENCES
EVANESCENT
EVANESCENTLY
EVANESCING
EVANGELARIUM
EVANGELARIUMS
EVANGELIAR
EVANGELIARIES
EVANGELIARION
EVANGELIARIONS
EVANGELIARIUM
EVANGELIARIUMS
EVANGELIARS
EVANGELIARY
EVANGELICAL
EVANGELICALISM
EVANGELICALISMS
EVANGELICALLY
EVANGELICALNESS
EVANGELICALS
EVANGELICISM
EVANGELICISMS
EVANGELIES
EVANGELISATION
EVANGELISATIONS
EVANGELISE
EVANGELISED
EVANGELISER
EVANGELISERS
EVANGELISES
EVANGELISING
EVANGELISM
EVANGELISMS
EVANGELIST
EVANGELISTARIES
EVANGELISTARION
EVANGELISTARY
EVANGELISTIC
EVANGELISTS
EVANGELIZATION
EVANGELIZATIONS
EVANGELIZE
EVANGELIZED
EVANGELIZER
EVANGELIZERS
EVANGELIZES
EVANGELIZING
EVANISHING
EVANISHMENT
EVANISHMENTS
EVANITIONS
EVAPORABILITIES
EVAPORABILITY
EVAPORABLE
EVAPORATED
EVAPORATES
EVAPORATING
EVAPORATION
EVAPORATIONS
EVAPORATIVE
EVAPORATOR
EVAPORATORS
EVAPORIMETER
EVAPORIMETERS

EVAPORITES
EVAPORITIC
EVAPOROGRAPH
EVAPOROGRAPHS
EVAPOROMETER
EVAPOROMETERS
EVASIVENESS
EVASIVENESSES
EVECTIONAL
EVENEMENTS
EVENHANDED
EVENHANDEDLY
EVENHANDEDNESS
EVENNESSES
EVENTFULLY
EVENTFULNESS
EVENTFULNESSES
EVENTRATED
EVENTRATES
EVENTRATING
EVENTRATION
EVENTRATIONS
EVENTUALISE
EVENTUALISED
EVENTUALISES
EVENTUALISING
EVENTUALITIES
EVENTUALITY
EVENTUALIZE
EVENTUALIZED
EVENTUALIZES
EVENTUALIZING
EVENTUALLY
EVENTUATED
EVENTUATES
EVENTUATING
EVENTUATION
EVENTUATIONS
EVERBLOOMING
EVERDURING
EVERGLADES
EVERGREENS
EVERLASTING
EVERLASTINGLY
EVERLASTINGNESS
EVERLASTINGS
EVERYDAYNESS
EVERYDAYNESSES
EVERYPLACE
EVERYTHING
EVERYWHENCE
EVERYWHERE
EVERYWHITHER
EVERYWOMAN
EVERYWOMEN
EVIDENCING
EVIDENTIAL
EVIDENTIALLY
EVIDENTIARY
EVILDOINGS
EVILNESSES
EVINCEMENT
EVINCEMENTS
EVISCERATE
EVISCERATED
EVISCERATES
EVISCERATING
EVISCERATION
EVISCERATIONS
EVISCERATOR
EVISCERATORS
EVITATIONS
EVITERNALLY
EVITERNITIES
EVITERNITY
EVOCATIONS
EVOCATIVELY
EVOCATIVENESS
EVOCATIVENESSES
EVOLUTIONAL
EVOLUTIONARILY
EVOLUTIONARY
EVOLUTIONISM
EVOLUTIONISMS
EVOLUTIONIST
EVOLUTIONISTIC
EVOLUTIONISTS
EVOLUTIONS
EVOLVEMENT
EVOLVEMENTS
EVONYMUSES
EVULGATING
EXACERBATE
EXACERBATED
EXACERBATES
EXACERBATING
EXACERBATION
EXACERBATIONS
EXACERBESCENCE
EXACERBESCENCES
EXACTINGLY
EXACTINGNESS
EXACTINGNESSES
EXACTITUDE
EXACTITUDES
EXACTMENTS
EXACTNESSES
EXACTRESSES
EXAGGERATE
EXAGGERATED
EXAGGERATEDLY
EXAGGERATEDNESS
EXAGGERATES
EXAGGERATING
EXAGGERATINGLY
EXAGGERATION
EXAGGERATIONS
EXAGGERATIVE
EXAGGERATOR
EXAGGERATORS
EXAGGERATORY
EXAHERTZES
EXALBUMINOUS
EXALTATION
EXALTATIONS
EXALTEDNESS
EXALTEDNESSES
EXAMINABILITIES
EXAMINABILITY
EXAMINABLE
EXAMINANTS
EXAMINATES
EXAMINATION
EXAMINATIONAL
EXAMINATIONS
EXAMINATOR
EXAMINATORS
EXAMINERSHIP
EXAMINERSHIPS
EXANIMATION
EXANIMATIONS
EXANTHEMAS
EXANTHEMATA
EXANTHEMATIC
EXANTHEMATOUS
EXARATIONS
EXARCHATES
EXARCHISTS
EXASPERATE
EXASPERATED
EXASPERATEDLY
EXASPERATER
EXASPERATERS
EXASPERATES
EXASPERATING
EXASPERATINGLY
EXASPERATION
EXASPERATIONS
EXASPERATIVE
EXASPERATOR
EXASPERATORS
EXCAMBIONS
EXCAMBIUMS
EXCARNATED
EXCARNATES
EXCARNATING
EXCARNATION
EXCARNATIONS
EXCAVATING
EXCAVATION
EXCAVATIONAL
EXCAVATIONS
EXCAVATORS
EXCEEDABLE
EXCEEDINGLY
EXCELLENCE
EXCELLENCES
EXCELLENCIES
EXCELLENCY
EXCELLENTLY
EXCELSIORS
EXCENTRICS
EXCEPTANTS
EXCEPTIONABLE
EXCEPTIONABLY
EXCEPTIONAL
EXCEPTIONALISM
EXCEPTIONALISMS
EXCEPTIONALITY
EXCEPTIONALLY
EXCEPTIONALNESS
EXCEPTIONALS
EXCEPTIONS
EXCEPTIOUS
EXCEPTLESS
EXCERPTERS
EXCERPTIBLE
EXCERPTING
EXCERPTINGS
EXCERPTION
EXCERPTIONS
EXCERPTORS
EXCESSIVELY
EXCESSIVENESS
EXCESSIVENESSES
EXCHANGEABILITY
EXCHANGEABLE
EXCHANGEABLY
EXCHANGERS
EXCHANGING
EXCHEQUERED
EXCHEQUERING
EXCHEQUERS
EXCIPIENTS
EXCISIONAL
EXCITABILITIES
EXCITABILITY
EXCITABLENESS
EXCITABLENESSES
EXCITANCIES
EXCITATION
EXCITATIONS
EXCITATIVE
EXCITATORY
EXCITEDNESS
EXCITEDNESSES
EXCITEMENT
EXCITEMENTS
EXCITINGLY
EXCLAIMERS
EXCLAIMING
EXCLAMATION
EXCLAMATIONAL
EXCLAMATIONS
EXCLAMATIVE
EXCLAMATIVES
EXCLAMATORILY
EXCLAMATORY
EXCLAUSTRATION
EXCLAUSTRATIONS

EXCLOSURES
EXCLUDABILITIES
EXCLUDABILITY
EXCLUDABLE
EXCLUDIBLE
EXCLUSIONARY
EXCLUSIONISM
EXCLUSIONISMS
EXCLUSIONIST
EXCLUSIONISTS
EXCLUSIONS
EXCLUSIVELY
EXCLUSIVENESS
EXCLUSIVENESSES
EXCLUSIVES
EXCLUSIVISM
EXCLUSIVISMS
EXCLUSIVIST
EXCLUSIVISTS
EXCLUSIVITIES
EXCLUSIVITY
EXCOGITABLE
EXCOGITATE
EXCOGITATED
EXCOGITATES
EXCOGITATING
EXCOGITATION
EXCOGITATIONS
EXCOGITATIVE
EXCOGITATOR
EXCOGITATORS
EXCOMMUNICABLE
EXCOMMUNICATE
EXCOMMUNICATED
EXCOMMUNICATES
EXCOMMUNICATING
EXCOMMUNICATION
EXCOMMUNICATIVE
EXCOMMUNICATOR
EXCOMMUNICATORS
EXCOMMUNICATORY
EXCOMMUNION
EXCOMMUNIONS
EXCORIATED
EXCORIATES
EXCORIATING
EXCORIATION
EXCORIATIONS
EXCORTICATE
EXCORTICATED
EXCORTICATES
EXCORTICATING
EXCORTICATION
EXCORTICATIONS
EXCREMENTA
EXCREMENTAL
EXCREMENTITIAL
EXCREMENTITIOUS
EXCREMENTS
EXCREMENTUM
EXCRESCENCE
EXCRESCENCES
EXCRESCENCIES
EXCRESCENCY
EXCRESCENT
EXCRESCENTIAL
EXCRESCENTLY
EXCRETIONS
EXCRETORIES
EXCRUCIATE
EXCRUCIATED
EXCRUCIATES
EXCRUCIATING
EXCRUCIATINGLY
EXCRUCIATION
EXCRUCIATIONS
EXCULPABLE
EXCULPATED
EXCULPATES
EXCULPATING
EXCULPATION
EXCULPATIONS
EXCULPATORY
EXCURSIONED
EXCURSIONING
EXCURSIONISE
EXCURSIONISED
EXCURSIONISES
EXCURSIONISING
EXCURSIONIST
EXCURSIONISTS
EXCURSIONIZE
EXCURSIONIZED
EXCURSIONIZES
EXCURSIONIZING
EXCURSIONS
EXCURSIVELY
EXCURSIVENESS
EXCURSIVENESSES
EXCURSUSES
EXCUSABLENESS
EXCUSABLENESSES
EXCUSATORY
EXECRABLENESS
EXECRABLENESSES
EXECRATING
EXECRATION
EXECRATIONS
EXECRATIVE
EXECRATIVELY
EXECRATORS
EXECRATORY
EXECUTABLE
EXECUTABLES
EXECUTANCIES
EXECUTANCY
EXECUTANTS
EXECUTARIES
EXECUTIONER
EXECUTIONERS
EXECUTIONS
EXECUTIVELY
EXECUTIVES
EXECUTORIAL
EXECUTORSHIP
EXECUTORSHIPS
EXECUTRESS
EXECUTRESSES
EXECUTRICES
EXECUTRIES
EXECUTRIXES
EXEGETICAL
EXEGETICALLY
EXEGETISTS
EXEMPLARILY
EXEMPLARINESS
EXEMPLARINESSES
EXEMPLARITIES
EXEMPLARITY
EXEMPLIFIABLE
EXEMPLIFICATION
EXEMPLIFICATIVE
EXEMPLIFIED
EXEMPLIFIER
EXEMPLIFIERS
EXEMPLIFIES
EXEMPLIFYING
EXEMPTIONS
EXENTERATE
EXENTERATED
EXENTERATES
EXENTERATING
EXENTERATION
EXENTERATIONS
EXEQUATURS
EXERCISABLE
EXERCISERS
EXERCISING
EXERCITATION
EXERCITATIONS
EXERCYCLES
EXERGAMING
EXERGAMINGS
EXERTAINMENT
EXERTAINMENTS
EXFILTRATE
EXFILTRATED
EXFILTRATES
EXFILTRATING
EXFOLIANTS
EXFOLIATED
EXFOLIATES
EXFOLIATING
EXFOLIATION
EXFOLIATIONS
EXFOLIATIVE
EXFOLIATOR
EXFOLIATORS
EXHALATION
EXHALATIONS
EXHAUSTEDLY
EXHAUSTERS
EXHAUSTIBILITY
EXHAUSTIBLE
EXHAUSTING
EXHAUSTINGLY
EXHAUSTION
EXHAUSTIONS
EXHAUSTIVE
EXHAUSTIVELY
EXHAUSTIVENESS
EXHAUSTIVITIES
EXHAUSTIVITY
EXHAUSTLESS
EXHAUSTLESSLY
EXHAUSTLESSNESS
EXHEREDATE
EXHEREDATED
EXHEREDATES
EXHEREDATING
EXHEREDATION
EXHEREDATIONS
EXHIBITERS
EXHIBITING
EXHIBITION
EXHIBITIONER
EXHIBITIONERS
EXHIBITIONISM
EXHIBITIONISMS
EXHIBITIONIST
EXHIBITIONISTIC
EXHIBITIONISTS
EXHIBITIONS
EXHIBITIVE
EXHIBITIVELY
EXHIBITORS
EXHIBITORY
EXHILARANT
EXHILARANTS
EXHILARATE
EXHILARATED
EXHILARATES
EXHILARATING
EXHILARATINGLY
EXHILARATION
EXHILARATIONS
EXHILARATIVE
EXHILARATOR
EXHILARATORS
EXHILARATORY
EXHORTATION
EXHORTATIONS
EXHORTATIVE
EXHORTATORY
EXHUMATING
EXHUMATION
EXHUMATIONS
EXIGENCIES
EXIGUITIES
EXIGUOUSLY

EXIGUOUSNESS
EXIGUOUSNESSES
EXILEMENTS
EXIMIOUSLY
EXISTENCES
EXISTENTIAL
EXISTENTIALISM
EXISTENTIALISMS
EXISTENTIALIST
EXISTENTIALISTS
EXISTENTIALLY
EXISTENTIALS
EXOBIOLOGICAL
EXOBIOLOGIES
EXOBIOLOGIST
EXOBIOLOGISTS
EXOBIOLOGY
EXOCENTRIC
EXOCUTICLE
EXOCUTICLES
EXOCYTOSED
EXOCYTOSES
EXOCYTOSING
EXOCYTOSIS
EXOCYTOTIC
EXODERMISES
EXODONTIAS
EXODONTICS
EXODONTIST
EXODONTISTS
EXOENZYMES
EXOERYTHROCYTIC
EXOGENETIC
EXOGENISMS
EXOGENOUSLY
EXONERATED
EXONERATES
EXONERATING
EXONERATION
EXONERATIONS
EXONERATIVE
EXONERATOR
EXONERATORS
EXONUCLEASE
EXONUCLEASES
EXONUMISTS
EXOPARASITE
EXOPARASITES
EXOPARASITIC
EXOPEPTIDASE
EXOPEPTIDASES
EXOPHAGIES
EXOPHAGOUS
EXOPHTHALMIA
EXOPHTHALMIAS
EXOPHTHALMIC
EXOPHTHALMOS
EXOPHTHALMOSES
EXOPHTHALMUS
EXOPHTHALMUSES
EXOPLANETS
EXOPODITES
EXOPODITIC
EXORABILITIES
EXORABILITY
EXORATIONS
EXORBITANCE
EXORBITANCES
EXORBITANCIES
EXORBITANCY
EXORBITANT
EXORBITANTLY
EXORBITATE
EXORBITATED
EXORBITATES
EXORBITATING
EXORCISERS
EXORCISING
EXORCISTIC
EXORCISTICAL
EXORCIZERS
EXORCIZING
EXOSKELETAL
EXOSKELETON
EXOSKELETONS
EXOSPHERES
EXOSPHERIC
EXOSPHERICAL
EXOSPORIUM
EXOSPOROUS
EXOTERICAL
EXOTERICALLY
EXOTERICISM
EXOTERICISMS
EXOTHERMAL
EXOTHERMALLY
EXOTHERMIC
EXOTHERMICALLY
EXOTHERMICITIES
EXOTHERMICITY
EXOTICALLY
EXOTICISED
EXOTICISES
EXOTICISING
EXOTICISMS
EXOTICISTS
EXOTICIZED
EXOTICIZES
EXOTICIZING
EXOTICNESS
EXOTICNESSES
EXOTROPIAS
EXPANDABILITIES
EXPANDABILITY
EXPANDABLE
EXPANSIBILITIES
EXPANSIBILITY
EXPANSIBLE
EXPANSIBLY
EXPANSIONAL
EXPANSIONARY
EXPANSIONISM
EXPANSIONISMS
EXPANSIONIST
EXPANSIONISTIC
EXPANSIONISTS
EXPANSIONS
EXPANSIVELY
EXPANSIVENESS
EXPANSIVENESSES
EXPANSIVITIES
EXPANSIVITY
EXPATIATED
EXPATIATES
EXPATIATING
EXPATIATION
EXPATIATIONS
EXPATIATIVE
EXPATIATOR
EXPATIATORS
EXPATIATORY
EXPATRIATE
EXPATRIATED
EXPATRIATES
EXPATRIATING
EXPATRIATION
EXPATRIATIONS
EXPATRIATISM
EXPATRIATISMS
EXPECTABLE
EXPECTABLY
EXPECTANCE
EXPECTANCES
EXPECTANCIES
EXPECTANCY
EXPECTANTLY
EXPECTANTS
EXPECTATION
EXPECTATIONAL
EXPECTATIONS
EXPECTATIVE
EXPECTATIVES
EXPECTEDLY
EXPECTEDNESS
EXPECTEDNESSES
EXPECTINGLY
EXPECTINGS
EXPECTORANT
EXPECTORANTS
EXPECTORATE
EXPECTORATED
EXPECTORATES
EXPECTORATING
EXPECTORATION
EXPECTORATIONS
EXPECTORATIVE
EXPECTORATIVES
EXPECTORATOR
EXPECTORATORS
EXPEDIENCE
EXPEDIENCES
EXPEDIENCIES
EXPEDIENCY
EXPEDIENTIAL
EXPEDIENTIALLY
EXPEDIENTLY
EXPEDIENTS
EXPEDITATE
EXPEDITATED
EXPEDITATES
EXPEDITATING
EXPEDITATION
EXPEDITATIONS
EXPEDITELY
EXPEDITERS
EXPEDITING
EXPEDITION
EXPEDITIONARY
EXPEDITIONS
EXPEDITIOUS
EXPEDITIOUSLY
EXPEDITIOUSNESS
EXPEDITIVE
EXPEDITORS
EXPELLABLE
EXPELLANTS
EXPELLENTS
EXPENDABILITIES
EXPENDABILITY
EXPENDABLE
EXPENDABLES
EXPENDABLY
EXPENDITURE
EXPENDITURES
EXPENSIVELY
EXPENSIVENESS
EXPENSIVENESSES
EXPERIENCE
EXPERIENCEABLE
EXPERIENCED
EXPERIENCELESS
EXPERIENCER
EXPERIENCERS
EXPERIENCES
EXPERIENCING
EXPERIENTIAL
EXPERIENTIALISM
EXPERIENTIALIST
EXPERIENTIALLY
EXPERIMENT
EXPERIMENTAL
EXPERIMENTALISE
EXPERIMENTALISM
EXPERIMENTALIST
EXPERIMENTALIZE
EXPERIMENTALLY
EXPERIMENTATION
EXPERIMENTATIVE
EXPERIMENTED
EXPERIMENTER

E

EXPERIMENTERS
EXPERIMENTING
EXPERIMENTIST
EXPERIMENTISTS
EXPERIMENTS
EXPERTISED
EXPERTISES
EXPERTISING
EXPERTISMS
EXPERTIZED
EXPERTIZES
EXPERTIZING
EXPERTNESS
EXPERTNESSES
EXPIATIONS
EXPIRATION
EXPIRATIONS
EXPIRATORY
EXPISCATED
EXPISCATES
EXPISCATING
EXPISCATION
EXPISCATIONS
EXPISCATORY
EXPLAINABLE
EXPLAINERS
EXPLAINING
EXPLANATION
EXPLANATIONS
EXPLANATIVE
EXPLANATIVELY
EXPLANATORILY
EXPLANATORY
EXPLANTATION
EXPLANTATIONS
EXPLANTING
EXPLETIVELY
EXPLETIVES
EXPLICABLE
EXPLICABLY
EXPLICATED
EXPLICATES
EXPLICATING
EXPLICATION
EXPLICATIONS
EXPLICATIVE
EXPLICATIVELY
EXPLICATOR
EXPLICATORS
EXPLICATORY
EXPLICITLY
EXPLICITNESS
EXPLICITNESSES
EXPLOITABLE
EXPLOITAGE
EXPLOITAGES
EXPLOITATION
EXPLOITATIONS
EXPLOITATIVE
EXPLOITATIVELY
EXPLOITERS
EXPLOITING
EXPLOITIVE
EXPLORATION
EXPLORATIONAL
EXPLORATIONIST
EXPLORATIONISTS
EXPLORATIONS
EXPLORATIVE
EXPLORATIVELY
EXPLORATORY
EXPLOSIBLE
EXPLOSIONS
EXPLOSIVELY
EXPLOSIVENESS
EXPLOSIVENESSES
EXPLOSIVES
EXPONENTIAL
EXPONENTIALLY
EXPONENTIALS
EXPONENTIATION
EXPONENTIATIONS
EXPORTABILITIES
EXPORTABILITY
EXPORTABLE
EXPORTATION
EXPORTATIONS
EXPOSEDNESS
EXPOSEDNESSES
EXPOSITING
EXPOSITION
EXPOSITIONAL
EXPOSITIONS
EXPOSITIVE
EXPOSITIVELY
EXPOSITORILY
EXPOSITORS
EXPOSITORY
EXPOSITRESS
EXPOSITRESSES
EXPOSTULATE
EXPOSTULATED
EXPOSTULATES
EXPOSTULATING
EXPOSTULATINGLY
EXPOSTULATION
EXPOSTULATIONS
EXPOSTULATIVE
EXPOSTULATOR
EXPOSTULATORS
EXPOSTULATORY
EXPOSTURES
EXPOUNDERS
EXPOUNDING
EXPRESSAGE
EXPRESSAGES
EXPRESSERS
EXPRESSIBLE
EXPRESSING
EXPRESSION
EXPRESSIONAL
EXPRESSIONISM
EXPRESSIONISMS
EXPRESSIONIST
EXPRESSIONISTIC
EXPRESSIONISTS
EXPRESSIONLESS
EXPRESSIONS
EXPRESSIVE
EXPRESSIVELY
EXPRESSIVENESS
EXPRESSIVITIES
EXPRESSIVITY
EXPRESSMAN
EXPRESSMEN
EXPRESSNESS
EXPRESSNESSES
EXPRESSURE
EXPRESSURES
EXPRESSWAY
EXPRESSWAYS
EXPROBRATE
EXPROBRATED
EXPROBRATES
EXPROBRATING
EXPROBRATION
EXPROBRATIONS
EXPROBRATIVE
EXPROBRATORY
EXPROMISSION
EXPROMISSIONS
EXPROMISSOR
EXPROMISSORS
EXPROPRIABLE
EXPROPRIATE
EXPROPRIATED
EXPROPRIATES
EXPROPRIATING
EXPROPRIATION
EXPROPRIATIONS
EXPROPRIATOR
EXPROPRIATORS
EXPUGNABLE
EXPUGNATION
EXPUGNATIONS
EXPULSIONS
EXPUNCTING
EXPUNCTION
EXPUNCTIONS
EXPURGATED
EXPURGATES
EXPURGATING
EXPURGATION
EXPURGATIONS
EXPURGATOR
EXPURGATORIAL
EXPURGATORS
EXPURGATORY
EXQUISITELY
EXQUISITENESS
EXQUISITENESSES
EXQUISITES
EXSANGUINATE
EXSANGUINATED
EXSANGUINATES
EXSANGUINATING
EXSANGUINATION
EXSANGUINATIONS
EXSANGUINE
EXSANGUINED
EXSANGUINEOUS
EXSANGUINITIES
EXSANGUINITY
EXSANGUINOUS
EXSCINDING
EXSECTIONS
EXSERTIONS
EXSICCANTS
EXSICCATED
EXSICCATES
EXSICCATING
EXSICCATION
EXSICCATIONS
EXSICCATIVE
EXSICCATOR
EXSICCATORS
EXSOLUTION
EXSOLUTIONS
EXSTIPULATE
EXSTROPHIES
EXSUFFLATE
EXSUFFLATED
EXSUFFLATES
EXSUFFLATING
EXSUFFLATION
EXSUFFLATIONS
EXSUFFLICATE
EXTEMPORAL
EXTEMPORALLY
EXTEMPORANEITY
EXTEMPORANEOUS
EXTEMPORARILY
EXTEMPORARINESS
EXTEMPORARY
EXTEMPORES
EXTEMPORISATION
EXTEMPORISE
EXTEMPORISED
EXTEMPORISER
EXTEMPORISERS
EXTEMPORISES
EXTEMPORISING
EXTEMPORIZATION
EXTEMPORIZE
EXTEMPORIZED
EXTEMPORIZER
EXTEMPORIZERS
EXTEMPORIZES
EXTEMPORIZING
EXTENDABILITIES

EXTENDABILITY
EXTENDABLE
EXTENDEDLY
EXTENDEDNESS
EXTENDEDNESSES
EXTENDIBILITIES
EXTENDIBILITY
EXTENDIBLE
EXTENSIBILITIES
EXTENSIBILITY
EXTENSIBLE
EXTENSIBLENESS
EXTENSIFICATION
EXTENSIMETER
EXTENSIMETERS
EXTENSIONAL
EXTENSIONALISM
EXTENSIONALISMS
EXTENSIONALITY
EXTENSIONALLY
EXTENSIONIST
EXTENSIONISTS
EXTENSIONS
EXTENSITIES
EXTENSIVELY
EXTENSIVENESS
EXTENSIVENESSES
EXTENSIVISATION
EXTENSIVIZATION
EXTENSOMETER
EXTENSOMETERS
EXTENUATED
EXTENUATES
EXTENUATING
EXTENUATINGLY
EXTENUATINGS
EXTENUATION
EXTENUATIONS
EXTENUATIVE
EXTENUATIVES
EXTENUATOR
EXTENUATORS
EXTENUATORY
EXTERIORISATION
EXTERIORISE
EXTERIORISED
EXTERIORISES
EXTERIORISING
EXTERIORITIES
EXTERIORITY
EXTERIORIZATION
EXTERIORIZE
EXTERIORIZED
EXTERIORIZES
EXTERIORIZING
EXTERIORLY
EXTERMINABLE
EXTERMINATE
EXTERMINATED
EXTERMINATES
EXTERMINATING
EXTERMINATION
EXTERMINATIONS
EXTERMINATIVE
EXTERMINATOR
EXTERMINATORS
EXTERMINATORY
EXTERMINED
EXTERMINES
EXTERMINING
EXTERNALISATION
EXTERNALISE
EXTERNALISED
EXTERNALISES
EXTERNALISING
EXTERNALISM
EXTERNALISMS
EXTERNALIST
EXTERNALISTS
EXTERNALITIES
EXTERNALITY
EXTERNALIZATION
EXTERNALIZE
EXTERNALIZED
EXTERNALIZES
EXTERNALIZING
EXTERNALLY
EXTERNSHIP
EXTERNSHIPS
EXTEROCEPTIVE
EXTEROCEPTOR
EXTEROCEPTORS
EXTERRITORIAL
EXTERRITORIALLY
EXTINCTING
EXTINCTION
EXTINCTIONS
EXTINCTIVE
EXTINCTURE
EXTINCTURES
EXTINGUISH
EXTINGUISHABLE
EXTINGUISHANT
EXTINGUISHANTS
EXTINGUISHED
EXTINGUISHER
EXTINGUISHERS
EXTINGUISHES
EXTINGUISHING
EXTINGUISHMENT
EXTINGUISHMENTS
EXTIRPABLE
EXTIRPATED
EXTIRPATES
EXTIRPATING
EXTIRPATION
EXTIRPATIONS
EXTIRPATIVE
EXTIRPATOR
EXTIRPATORS
EXTIRPATORY
EXTOLLINGLY
EXTOLMENTS
EXTORSIVELY
EXTORTIONARY
EXTORTIONATE
EXTORTIONATELY
EXTORTIONER
EXTORTIONERS
EXTORTIONIST
EXTORTIONISTS
EXTORTIONS
EXTRABOLDS
EXTRACANONICAL
EXTRACELLULAR
EXTRACELLULARLY
EXTRACORPOREAL
EXTRACRANIAL
EXTRACTABILITY
EXTRACTABLE
EXTRACTANT
EXTRACTANTS
EXTRACTIBLE
EXTRACTING
EXTRACTION
EXTRACTIONS
EXTRACTIVE
EXTRACTIVELY
EXTRACTIVES
EXTRACTORS
EXTRACURRICULAR
EXTRADITABLE
EXTRADITED
EXTRADITES
EXTRADITING
EXTRADITION
EXTRADITIONS
EXTRADOSES
EXTRADOTAL
EXTRADURAL
EXTRADURALS
EXTRAEMBRYONIC
EXTRAFLORAL
EXTRAFORANEOUS
EXTRAGALACTIC
EXTRAHEPATIC
EXTRAJUDICIAL
EXTRAJUDICIALLY
EXTRALEGAL
EXTRALEGALLY
EXTRALIMITAL
EXTRALIMITARY
EXTRALINGUISTIC
EXTRALITERARY
EXTRALITIES
EXTRALOGICAL
EXTRAMARITAL
EXTRAMARITALLY
EXTRAMETRICAL
EXTRAMUNDANE
EXTRAMURAL
EXTRAMURALLY
EXTRAMUSICAL
EXTRANEITIES
EXTRANEITY
EXTRANEOUS
EXTRANEOUSLY
EXTRANEOUSNESS
EXTRANUCLEAR
EXTRAORDINAIRE
EXTRAORDINARIES
EXTRAORDINARILY
EXTRAORDINARY
EXTRAPOLATE
EXTRAPOLATED
EXTRAPOLATES
EXTRAPOLATING
EXTRAPOLATION
EXTRAPOLATIONS
EXTRAPOLATIVE
EXTRAPOLATOR
EXTRAPOLATORS
EXTRAPOLATORY
EXTRAPOSED
EXTRAPOSES
EXTRAPOSING
EXTRAPOSITION
EXTRAPOSITIONS
EXTRAPYRAMIDAL
EXTRASENSORY
EXTRASOLAR
EXTRASYSTOLE
EXTRASYSTOLES
EXTRATEXTUAL
EXTRATROPICAL
EXTRAUTERINE
EXTRAVAGANCE
EXTRAVAGANCES
EXTRAVAGANCIES
EXTRAVAGANCY
EXTRAVAGANT
EXTRAVAGANTLY
EXTRAVAGANZA
EXTRAVAGANZAS
EXTRAVAGATE
EXTRAVAGATED
EXTRAVAGATES
EXTRAVAGATING
EXTRAVAGATION
EXTRAVAGATIONS
EXTRAVASATE
EXTRAVASATED
EXTRAVASATES
EXTRAVASATING
EXTRAVASATION
EXTRAVASATIONS
EXTRAVASCULAR
EXTRAVEHICULAR
EXTRAVERSION
EXTRAVERSIONS

EXTRAVERSIVE
EXTRAVERSIVELY
EXTRAVERTED
EXTRAVERTING
EXTRAVERTLY
EXTRAVERTS
EXTREATING
EXTREMENESS
EXTREMENESSES
EXTREMISMS
EXTREMISTS
EXTREMITIES
EXTREMOPHILE
EXTREMOPHILES
EXTRICABLE
EXTRICATED
EXTRICATES
EXTRICATING
EXTRICATION
EXTRICATIONS
EXTRINSICAL
EXTRINSICALITY
EXTRINSICALLY
EXTRINSICALS
EXTROPIANS
EXTROVERSION
EXTROVERSIONS
EXTROVERSIVE
EXTROVERSIVELY
EXTROVERTED
EXTROVERTING
EXTROVERTLY
EXTROVERTS
EXTRUDABILITIES
EXTRUDABILITY
EXTRUDABLE
EXTRUSIBLE
EXTRUSIONS
EXTUBATING
EXUBERANCE
EXUBERANCES
EXUBERANCIES
EXUBERANCY
EXUBERANTLY
EXUBERATED
EXUBERATES
EXUBERATING
EXUDATIONS
EXULCERATE
EXULCERATED
EXULCERATES
EXULCERATING
EXULCERATION
EXULCERATIONS
EXULTANCES
EXULTANCIES
EXULTANTLY
EXULTATION
EXULTATIONS
EXULTINGLY
EXURBANITE
EXURBANITES
EXUVIATING
EXUVIATION
EXUVIATIONS
EYEBALLING
EYEBRIGHTS
EYEBROWING
EYEBROWLESS
EYEDNESSES
EYEDROPPER
EYEDROPPERS
EYEGLASSES
EYELETEERS
EYELETTING
EYEOPENERS
EYEPATCHES
EYEPOPPERS
EYESHADOWS
EYESTRAINS
EYESTRINGS
EYEWITNESS
EYEWITNESSED
EYEWITNESSES
EYEWITNESSING

F

FABRICANTS
FABRICATED
FABRICATES
FABRICATING
FABRICATION
FABRICATIONS
FABRICATIVE
FABRICATOR
FABRICATORS
FABRICKING
FABRICKINGS
FABULATING
FABULATORS
FABULISING
FABULISTIC
FABULIZING
FABULOSITIES
FABULOSITY
FABULOUSLY
FABULOUSNESS
FABULOUSNESSES
FACEBOOKED
FACEBOOKING
FACECLOTHS
FACELESSNESS
FACELESSNESSES
FACELIFTED
FACELIFTING
FACEPALMED
FACEPALMING
FACEPLANTED
FACEPLANTING
FACEPLANTS
FACEPLATES
FACEPRINTS
FACETIMING
FACETIOUSLY
FACETIOUSNESS
FACETIOUSNESSES
FACEWORKER
FACEWORKERS
FACIALISTS
FACILENESS
FACILENESSES
FACILITATE
FACILITATED
FACILITATES
FACILITATING
FACILITATION
FACILITATIONS
FACILITATIVE
FACILITATOR
FACILITATORS
FACILITATORY
FACILITIES
FACINERIOUS
FACINOROUS
FACINOROUSNESS
FACSIMILED
FACSIMILEING
FACSIMILES
FACSIMILIST
FACSIMILISTS
FACTICITIES
FACTIONALISE
FACTIONALISED
FACTIONALISES
FACTIONALISING
FACTIONALISM
FACTIONALISMS
FACTIONALIST
FACTIONALISTS
FACTIONALIZE
FACTIONALIZED
FACTIONALIZES
FACTIONALIZING
FACTIONALLY
FACTIONARIES
FACTIONARY
FACTIONIST
FACTIONISTS
FACTIOUSLY
FACTIOUSNESS
FACTIOUSNESSES
FACTITIOUS
FACTITIOUSLY
FACTITIOUSNESS
FACTITIVELY
FACTORABILITIES
FACTORABILITY
FACTORABLE
FACTORAGES
FACTORIALLY
FACTORIALS
FACTORINGS
FACTORISATION
FACTORISATIONS
FACTORISED
FACTORISES
FACTORISING
FACTORIZATION
FACTORIZATIONS
FACTORIZED
FACTORIZES
FACTORIZING
FACTORSHIP
FACTORSHIPS
FACTORYLIKE
FACTSHEETS
FACTUALISM
FACTUALISMS
FACTUALIST
FACTUALISTIC
FACTUALISTS
FACTUALITIES
FACTUALITY
FACTUALNESS
FACTUALNESSES
FACULTATIVE
FACULTATIVELY
FACUNDITIES
FADDINESSES
FADDISHNESS
FADDISHNESSES
FADEDNESSES
FADELESSLY
FADOMETERS
FAGGOTINGS
FAGOTTISTS
FAINEANCES
FAINEANCIES
FAINEANTISE
FAINEANTISES
FAINNESSES
FAINTHEARTED
FAINTHEARTEDLY
FAINTINGLY
FAINTISHNESS
FAINTISHNESSES
FAINTNESSES
FAIRGROUND
FAIRGROUNDS
FAIRLEADER
FAIRLEADERS
FAIRNESSES
FAIRNITICKLE
FAIRNITICKLES
FAIRNITICLE
FAIRNITICLES
FAIRNYTICKLE
FAIRNYTICKLES
FAIRNYTICLE
FAIRNYTICLES
FAIRYFLOSS
FAIRYFLOSSES
FAIRYHOODS
FAIRYLANDS
FAITHCURES
FAITHFULLY
FAITHFULNESS
FAITHFULNESSES
FAITHLESSLY
FAITHLESSNESS
FAITHLESSNESSES
FAITHWORTHIER
FAITHWORTHIEST
FAITHWORTHINESS
FAITHWORTHY
FALANGISMS
FALANGISTS
FALCATIONS
FALCONIFORM
FALCONOIDS
FALCONRIES
FALDERALED
FALDERALING
FALDISTORIES
FALDISTORY
FALDSTOOLS
FALLACIOUS
FALLACIOUSLY
FALLACIOUSNESS
FALLALERIES
FALLALISHLY
FALLBOARDS
FALLFISHES
FALLIBILISM
FALLIBILISMS
FALLIBILIST
FALLIBILISTS
FALLIBILITIES
FALLIBILITY
FALLIBLENESS
FALLIBLENESSES
FALLOWNESS
FALLOWNESSES
FALSEFACES
FALSEHOODS
FALSENESSES
FALSEWORKS
FALSIDICAL
FALSIFIABILITY
FALSIFIABLE
FALSIFICATION
FALSIFICATIONS
FALSIFIERS
FALSIFYING
FALTERINGLY
FALTERINGS
FAMILIARISATION

FAMILIARISE
FAMILIARISED
FAMILIARISER
FAMILIARISERS
FAMILIARISES
FAMILIARISING
FAMILIARITIES
FAMILIARITY
FAMILIARIZATION
FAMILIARIZE
FAMILIARIZED
FAMILIARIZER
FAMILIARIZERS
FAMILIARIZES
FAMILIARIZING
FAMILIARLY
FAMILIARNESS
FAMILIARNESSES
FAMILISTIC
FAMISHMENT
FAMISHMENTS
FAMOUSNESS
FAMOUSNESSES
FANATICALLY
FANATICALNESS
FANATICALNESSES
FANATICISATION
FANATICISATIONS
FANATICISE
FANATICISED
FANATICISES
FANATICISING
FANATICISM
FANATICISMS
FANATICIZATION
FANATICIZATIONS
FANATICIZE
FANATICIZED
FANATICIZES
FANATICIZING
FANCIFULLY
FANCIFULNESS
FANCIFULNESSES
FANCIFYING
FANCINESSES
FANCYWORKS
FANDABIDOZI
FANDANGLES
FANDANGOES
FANFARADES
FANFARONADE
FANFARONADED
FANFARONADES
FANFARONADING
FANFARONAS
FANFOLDING
FANTABULOUS
FANTASISED
FANTASISER
FANTASISERS
FANTASISES
FANTASISING
FANTASISTS
FANTASIZED
FANTASIZER
FANTASIZERS
FANTASIZES
FANTASIZING
FANTASMALLY
FANTASMICALLY
FANTASQUES
FANTASTICAL
FANTASTICALITY
FANTASTICALLY
FANTASTICALNESS
FANTASTICATE
FANTASTICATED
FANTASTICATES
FANTASTICATING
FANTASTICATION
FANTASTICATIONS
FANTASTICISM
FANTASTICISMS
FANTASTICO
FANTASTICOES
FANTASTICS
FANTASTRIES
FANTASYING
FANTASYLAND
FANTASYLANDS
FANTOCCINI
FARADISATION
FARADISATIONS
FARADISERS
FARADISING
FARADIZATION
FARADIZATIONS
FARADIZERS
FARADIZING
FARANDINES
FARANDOLES
FARAWAYNESS
FARAWAYNESSES
FARBOROUGH
FARBOROUGHS
FARCEMEATS
FARCICALITIES
FARCICALITY
FARCICALLY
FARCICALNESS
FARCICALNESSES
FARCIFYING
FAREWELLED
FAREWELLING
FARFETCHEDNESS
FARINACEOUS
FARINOSELY
FARKLEBERRIES
FARKLEBERRY
FARMERESSES
FARMERETTE
FARMERETTES
FARMHOUSES
FARMSTEADS
FARMWORKER
FARMWORKERS
FARNARKELED
FARNARKELING
FARNARKELINGS
FARNARKELS
FARRAGINOUS
FARRANDINE
FARRANDINES
FARRIERIES
FARROWINGS
FARSIGHTED
FARSIGHTEDLY
FARSIGHTEDNESS
FARTHERMORE
FARTHERMOST
FARTHINGALE
FARTHINGALES
FARTHINGLAND
FARTHINGLANDS
FARTHINGLESS
FARTHINGSWORTH
FARTHINGSWORTHS
FASCIATELY
FASCIATION
FASCIATIONS
FASCICULAR
FASCICULARLY
FASCICULATE
FASCICULATED
FASCICULATELY
FASCICULATION
FASCICULATIONS
FASCICULES
FASCICULUS
FASCIITISES
FASCINATED
FASCINATEDLY
FASCINATES
FASCINATING
FASCINATINGLY
FASCINATION
FASCINATIONS
FASCINATIVE
FASCINATOR
FASCINATORS
FASCIOLIASES
FASCIOLIASIS
FASCISTICALLY
FASCITISES
FASHIONABILITY
FASHIONABLE
FASHIONABLENESS
FASHIONABLES
FASHIONABLY
FASHIONERS
FASHIONIER
FASHIONIEST
FASHIONING
FASHIONIST
FASHIONISTA
FASHIONISTAS
FASHIONISTS
FASHIONMONGER
FASHIONMONGERS
FASHIONMONGING
FASHIOUSNESS
FASHIOUSNESSES
FASTBALLER
FASTBALLERS
FASTENINGS
FASTIDIOUS
FASTIDIOUSLY
FASTIDIOUSNESS
FASTIGIATE
FASTIGIATED
FASTIGIUMS
FASTNESSES
FATALISTIC
FATALISTICALLY
FATALITIES
FATALNESSES
FATBRAINED
FATEFULNESS
FATEFULNESSES
FATHEADEDLY
FATHEADEDNESS
FATHEADEDNESSES
FATHERHOOD
FATHERHOODS
FATHERINGS
FATHERLAND
FATHERLANDS
FATHERLESS
FATHERLESSNESS
FATHERLIER
FATHERLIEST
FATHERLIKE
FATHERLINESS
FATHERLINESSES
FATHERSHIP
FATHERSHIPS
FATHOMABLE
FATHOMETER
FATHOMETERS
FATHOMLESS
FATHOMLESSLY
FATHOMLESSNESS
FATIDICALLY
FATIGABILITIES
FATIGABILITY
FATIGABLENESS
FATIGABLENESSES
FATIGATING
FATIGUABLE
FATIGUABLENESS

FATIGUELESS
FATIGUINGLY
FATISCENCE
FATISCENCES
FATSHEDERA
FATSHEDERAS
FATTENABLE
FATTENINGS
FATTINESSES
FATUOUSNESS
FATUOUSNESSES
FAUCETRIES
FAULCHIONS
FAULTFINDER
FAULTFINDERS
FAULTFINDING
FAULTFINDINGS
FAULTINESS
FAULTINESSES
FAULTLESSLY
FAULTLESSNESS
FAULTLESSNESSES
FAULTLINES
FAUNISTICALLY
FAUXBOURDON
FAUXBOURDONS
FAUXMANCES
FAVORABLENESS
FAVORABLENESSES
FAVOREDNESS
FAVOREDNESSES
FAVORINGLY
FAVORITISM
FAVORITISMS
FAVOURABLE
FAVOURABLENESS
FAVOURABLY
FAVOUREDNESS
FAVOUREDNESSES
FAVOURINGLY
FAVOURITES
FAVOURITISM
FAVOURITISMS
FAVOURLESS
FAWNINGNESS
FAWNINGNESSES
FAZENDEIRO
FAZENDEIROS
FEARFULLER
FEARFULLEST
FEARFULNESS
FEARFULNESSES
FEARLESSLY
FEARLESSNESS
FEARLESSNESSES
FEARMONGER
FEARMONGERING
FEARMONGERINGS
FEARMONGERS
FEARNAUGHT
FEARNAUGHTS
FEARNOUGHT
FEARNOUGHTS
FEARSOMELY
FEARSOMENESS
FEARSOMENESSES
FEASIBILITIES
FEASIBILITY
FEASIBLENESS
FEASIBLENESSES
FEATEOUSLY
FEATHERBED
FEATHERBEDDED
FEATHERBEDDING
FEATHERBEDDINGS
FEATHERBEDS
FEATHERBRAIN
FEATHERBRAINED
FEATHERBRAINS
FEATHEREDGE
FEATHEREDGED
FEATHEREDGES
FEATHEREDGING
FEATHERHEAD
FEATHERHEADED
FEATHERHEADS
FEATHERIER
FEATHERIEST
FEATHERINESS
FEATHERINESSES
FEATHERING
FEATHERINGS
FEATHERLESS
FEATHERLIGHT
FEATHERSTITCH
FEATHERSTITCHED
FEATHERSTITCHES
FEATHERWEIGHT
FEATHERWEIGHTS
FEATLINESS
FEATLINESSES
FEATURELESS
FEATURELESSNESS
FEATURETTE
FEATURETTES
FEBRICITIES
FEBRICULAS
FEBRICULES
FEBRIFACIENT
FEBRIFACIENTS
FEBRIFEROUS
FEBRIFUGAL
FEBRIFUGES
FEBRILITIES
FECKLESSLY
FECKLESSNESS
FECKLESSNESSES
FECULENCES
FECULENCIES
FECUNDATED
FECUNDATES
FECUNDATING
FECUNDATION
FECUNDATIONS
FECUNDATOR
FECUNDATORS
FECUNDATORY
FECUNDITIES
FEDERACIES
FEDERALESE
FEDERALESES
FEDERALISATION
FEDERALISATIONS
FEDERALISE
FEDERALISED
FEDERALISES
FEDERALISING
FEDERALISM
FEDERALISMS
FEDERALIST
FEDERALISTIC
FEDERALISTS
FEDERALIZATION
FEDERALIZATIONS
FEDERALIZE
FEDERALIZED
FEDERALIZES
FEDERALIZING
FEDERARIES
FEDERATING
FEDERATION
FEDERATIONS
FEDERATIVE
FEDERATIVELY
FEDERATORS
FEEBLEMINDED
FEEBLEMINDEDLY
FEEBLENESS
FEEBLENESSES
FEEDGRAINS
FEEDINGSTUFF
FEEDINGSTUFFS
FEEDSTOCKS
FEEDSTUFFS
FEEDTHROUGH
FEEDTHROUGHS
FEEDWATERS
FEELINGLESS
FEELINGNESS
FEELINGNESSES
FEIGNEDNESS
FEIGNEDNESSES
FEIGNINGLY
FEISTINESS
FEISTINESSES
FELDSCHARS
FELDSCHERS
FELDSPATHIC
FELDSPATHOID
FELDSPATHOIDS
FELDSPATHOSE
FELDSPATHS
FELICITATE
FELICITATED
FELICITATES
FELICITATING
FELICITATION
FELICITATIONS
FELICITATOR
FELICITATORS
FELICITIES
FELICITOUS
FELICITOUSLY
FELICITOUSNESS
FELINENESS
FELINENESSES
FELINITIES
FELLATIONS
FELLATRICES
FELLATRIXES
FELLFIELDS
FELLMONGER
FELLMONGERED
FELLMONGERIES
FELLMONGERING
FELLMONGERINGS
FELLMONGERS
FELLMONGERY
FELLNESSES
FELLOWSHIP
FELLOWSHIPED
FELLOWSHIPING
FELLOWSHIPPED
FELLOWSHIPPING
FELLOWSHIPS
FELLWALKER
FELLWALKERS
FELONIOUSLY
FELONIOUSNESS
FELONIOUSNESSES
FELQUISTES
FELSPATHIC
FELSPATHOID
FELSPATHOIDS
FELSPATHOSE
FEMALENESS
FEMALENESSES
FEMALITIES
FEMETARIES
FEMINACIES
FEMINALITIES
FEMINALITY
FEMINEITIES
FEMINILITIES
FEMINILITY
FEMININELY
FEMININENESS
FEMININENESSES
FEMININISM
FEMININISMS

FEMININITIES
FEMININITY
FEMINISATION
FEMINISATIONS
FEMINISING
FEMINISTIC
FEMINITIES
FEMINIZATION
FEMINIZATIONS
FEMINIZING
FEMTOSECOND
FEMTOSECONDS
FENCELESSNESS
FENCELESSNESSES
FENCELINES
FENCEWIRES
FENDERLESS
FENESTELLA
FENESTELLAE
FENESTELLAS
FENESTRALS
FENESTRATE
FENESTRATED
FENESTRATES
FENESTRATING
FENESTRATION
FENESTRATIONS
FENNELFLOWER
FENNELFLOWERS
FENUGREEKS
FEOFFMENTS
FERACITIES
FERETORIES
FERMENTABILITY
FERMENTABLE
FERMENTATION
FERMENTATIONS
FERMENTATIVE
FERMENTATIVELY
FERMENTERS
FERMENTESCIBLE
FERMENTING
FERMENTITIOUS
FERMENTIVE
FERMENTORS
FERNALLIES
FERNITICKLE
FERNITICKLES
FERNITICLE
FERNITICLES
FERNTICKLE
FERNTICKLED
FERNTICKLES
FERNTICLED
FERNTICLES
FERNYTICKLE
FERNYTICKLES
FERNYTICLE
FERNYTICLES
FEROCIOUSLY
FEROCIOUSNESS
FEROCIOUSNESSES
FEROCITIES
FERRANDINE
FERRANDINES
FERREDOXIN
FERREDOXINS
FERRELLING
FERRETIEST
FERRETINGS
FERRICYANIC
FERRICYANIDE
FERRICYANIDES
FERRICYANOGEN
FERRICYANOGENS
FERRIFEROUS
FERRIMAGNET
FERRIMAGNETIC
FERRIMAGNETISM
FERRIMAGNETISMS
FERRIMAGNETS
FERROCENES
FERROCHROME
FERROCHROMES
FERROCHROMIUM
FERROCHROMIUMS
FERROCONCRETE
FERROCONCRETES
FERROCYANIC
FERROCYANIDE
FERROCYANIDES
FERROCYANOGEN
FERROCYANOGENS
FERROELECTRIC
FERROELECTRICS
FERROGRAMS
FERROGRAPHIES
FERROGRAPHY
FERROMAGNESIAN
FERROMAGNET
FERROMAGNETIC
FERROMAGNETISM
FERROMAGNETISMS
FERROMAGNETS
FERROMANGANESE
FERROMANGANESES
FERROMOLYBDENUM
FERRONICKEL
FERRONICKELS
FERRONIERE
FERRONIERES
FERRONNIERE
FERRONNIERES
FERROPRUSSIATE
FERROPRUSSIATES
FERROSILICON
FERROSILICONS
FERROSOFERRIC
FERROTYPED
FERROTYPES
FERROTYPING
FERRUGINEOUS
FERRUGINOUS
FERRYBOATS
FERTIGATED
FERTIGATES
FERTIGATING
FERTIGATION
FERTIGATIONS
FERTILENESS
FERTILENESSES
FERTILISABLE
FERTILISATION
FERTILISATIONS
FERTILISED
FERTILISER
FERTILISERS
FERTILISES
FERTILISING
FERTILITIES
FERTILIZABLE
FERTILIZATION
FERTILIZATIONS
FERTILIZED
FERTILIZER
FERTILIZERS
FERTILIZES
FERTILIZING
FERULACEOUS
FERVENCIES
FERVENTEST
FERVENTNESS
FERVENTNESSES
FERVESCENT
FERVIDITIES
FERVIDNESS
FERVIDNESSES
FESCENNINE
FESTILOGIES
FESTINATED
FESTINATELY
FESTINATES
FESTINATING
FESTINATION
FESTINATIONS
FESTIVALGOER
FESTIVALGOERS
FESTIVENESS
FESTIVENESSES
FESTIVITIES
FESTOLOGIES
FESTOONERIES
FESTOONERY
FESTOONING
FESTSCHRIFT
FESTSCHRIFTEN
FESTSCHRIFTS
FETCHINGLY
FETICHISED
FETICHISES
FETICHISING
FETICHISMS
FETICHISTIC
FETICHISTS
FETICHIZED
FETICHIZES
FETICHIZING
FETIDITIES
FETIDNESSES
FETIPAROUS
FETISHISATION
FETISHISATIONS
FETISHISED
FETISHISES
FETISHISING
FETISHISMS
FETISHISTIC
FETISHISTICALLY
FETISHISTS
FETISHIZATION
FETISHIZATIONS
FETISHIZED
FETISHIZES
FETISHIZING
FETOLOGIES
FETOLOGIST
FETOLOGISTS
FETOPROTEIN
FETOPROTEINS
FETOSCOPES
FETOSCOPIES
FETTERLESS
FETTERLOCK
FETTERLOCKS
FETTUCCINE
FETTUCCINES
FETTUCCINI
FETTUCCINIS
FETTUCINES
FETTUCINIS
FEUDALISATION
FEUDALISATIONS
FEUDALISED
FEUDALISES
FEUDALISING
FEUDALISMS
FEUDALISTIC
FEUDALISTS
FEUDALITIES
FEUDALIZATION
FEUDALIZATIONS
FEUDALIZED
FEUDALIZES
FEUDALIZING
FEUDATORIES
FEUILLETES
FEUILLETON
FEUILLETONISM
FEUILLETONISMS
FEUILLETONIST

FEUILLETONISTIC
FEUILLETONISTS
FEUILLETONS
FEVERISHLY
FEVERISHNESS
FEVERISHNESSES
FEVEROUSLY
FEVERROOTS
FEVERWEEDS
FEVERWORTS
FIANCAILLES
FIANCHETTI
FIANCHETTO
FIANCHETTOED
FIANCHETTOES
FIANCHETTOING
FIANCHETTOS
FIBERBOARD
FIBERBOARDS
FIBERFILLS
FIBERGLASS
FIBERGLASSED
FIBERGLASSES
FIBERGLASSING
FIBERISATION
FIBERISATIONS
FIBERISING
FIBERIZATION
FIBERIZATIONS
FIBERIZING
FIBERSCOPE
FIBERSCOPES
FIBREBOARD
FIBREBOARDS
FIBREFILLS
FIBREGLASS
FIBREGLASSED
FIBREGLASSES
FIBREGLASSING
FIBREOPTIC
FIBRESCOPE
FIBRESCOPES
FIBRILLARY
FIBRILLATE
FIBRILLATED
FIBRILLATES
FIBRILLATING
FIBRILLATION
FIBRILLATIONS
FIBRILLIFORM
FIBRILLINS
FIBRILLOSE
FIBRILLOUS
FIBRINOGEN
FIBRINOGENIC
FIBRINOGENOUS
FIBRINOGENS
FIBRINOIDS
FIBRINOLYSES
FIBRINOLYSIN
FIBRINOLYSINS
FIBRINOLYSIS
FIBRINOLYTIC
FIBRINOPEPTIDE
FIBRINOPEPTIDES
FIBROBLAST
FIBROBLASTIC
FIBROBLASTS
FIBROCARTILAGE
FIBROCARTILAGES
FIBROCEMENT
FIBROCEMENTS
FIBROCYSTIC
FIBROCYTES
FIBROLINES
FIBROLITES
FIBROMATOUS
FIBROMYALGIA
FIBROMYALGIAS
FIBRONECTIN
FIBRONECTINS
FIBROSARCOMA
FIBROSARCOMAS
FIBROSARCOMATA
FIBROSITIS
FIBROSITISES
FIBROUSNESS
FIBROUSNESSES
FIBROVASCULAR
FICKLENESS
FICKLENESSES
FICTIONALISE
FICTIONALISED
FICTIONALISES
FICTIONALISING
FICTIONALITIES
FICTIONALITY
FICTIONALIZE
FICTIONALIZED
FICTIONALIZES
FICTIONALIZING
FICTIONALLY
FICTIONEER
FICTIONEERING
FICTIONEERINGS
FICTIONEERS
FICTIONISATION
FICTIONISATIONS
FICTIONISE
FICTIONISED
FICTIONISES
FICTIONISING
FICTIONIST
FICTIONISTS
FICTIONIZATION
FICTIONIZATIONS
FICTIONIZE
FICTIONIZED
FICTIONIZES
FICTIONIZING
FICTITIOUS
FICTITIOUSLY
FICTITIOUSNESS
FICTIVENESS
FICTIVENESSES
FIDDIOUSED
FIDDIOUSES
FIDDIOUSING
FIDDLEBACK
FIDDLEBACKS
FIDDLEDEDEE
FIDDLEDEEDEE
FIDDLEHEAD
FIDDLEHEADS
FIDDLENECK
FIDDLENECKS
FIDDLESTICK
FIDDLESTICKS
FIDDLEWOOD
FIDDLEWOODS
FIDEICOMMISSA
FIDEICOMMISSARY
FIDEICOMMISSUM
FIDELISMOS
FIDELISTAS
FIDELITIES
FIDGETIEST
FIDGETINESS
FIDGETINESSES
FIDGETINGLY
FIDUCIALLY
FIDUCIARIES
FIDUCIARILY
FIELDBOOTS
FIELDCRAFT
FIELDCRAFTS
FIELDFARES
FIELDMOUSE
FIELDPIECE
FIELDPIECES
FIELDSTONE
FIELDSTONES
FIELDSTRIP
FIELDSTRIPPED
FIELDSTRIPPING
FIELDSTRIPS
FIELDVOLES
FIELDWARDS
FIELDWORKER
FIELDWORKERS
FIELDWORKS
FIENDISHLY
FIENDISHNESS
FIENDISHNESSES
FIERCENESS
FIERCENESSES
FIERINESSES
FIFTEENERS
FIFTEENTHLY
FIFTEENTHS
FIGHTBACKS
FIGURABILITIES
FIGURABILITY
FIGURANTES
FIGURATELY
FIGURATION
FIGURATIONS
FIGURATIVE
FIGURATIVELY
FIGURATIVENESS
FIGUREHEAD
FIGUREHEADS
FIGURELESS
FIGUREWORK
FIGUREWORKS
FILAGGRINS
FILAGREEING
FILAMENTARY
FILAMENTOUS
FILARIASES
FILARIASIS
FILATORIES
FILCHINGLY
FILEFISHES
FILIALNESS
FILIALNESSES
FILIATIONS
FILIBUSTER
FILIBUSTERED
FILIBUSTERER
FILIBUSTERERS
FILIBUSTERING
FILIBUSTERINGS
FILIBUSTERISM
FILIBUSTERISMS
FILIBUSTEROUS
FILIBUSTERS
FILICINEAN
FILIGRAINS
FILIGRANES
FILIGREEING
FILIOPIETISTIC
FILIPENDULOUS
FILLAGREED
FILLAGREEING
FILLAGREES
FILLESTERS
FILLIPEENS
FILLISTERS
FILMGOINGS
FILMICALLY
FILMINESSES
FILMMAKERS
FILMMAKING
FILMMAKINGS
FILMOGRAPHIES
FILMOGRAPHY
FILMSETTER
FILMSETTERS
FILMSETTING

FILMSETTINGS
FILMSTRIPS
FILOPLUMES
FILOPODIUM
FILOSELLES
FILOVIRUSES
FILTERABILITIES
FILTERABILITY
FILTERABLE
FILTERABLENESS
FILTHINESS
FILTHINESSES
FILTRABILITIES
FILTRABILITY
FILTRABLENESS
FILTRABLENESSES
FILTRATABLE
FILTRATING
FILTRATION
FILTRATIONS
FIMBRIATED
FIMBRIATES
FIMBRIATING
FIMBRIATION
FIMBRIATIONS
FIMBRILLATE
FIMICOLOUS
FINABLENESS
FINABLENESSES
FINAGLINGS
FINALISATION
FINALISATIONS
FINALISERS
FINALISING
FINALISTIC
FINALITIES
FINALIZATION
FINALIZATIONS
FINALIZERS
FINALIZING
FINANCIALIST
FINANCIALISTS
FINANCIALLY
FINANCIALS
FINANCIERED
FINANCIERING
FINANCIERS
FINANCINGS
FINEABLENESS
FINEABLENESSES
FINENESSES
FINESSINGS
FINGERBOARD
FINGERBOARDS
FINGERBOWL
FINGERBOWLS
FINGERBREADTH
FINGERBREADTHS
FINGERGLASS
FINGERGLASSES
FINGERGUARD
FINGERGUARDS
FINGERHOLD
FINGERHOLDS
FINGERHOLE
FINGERHOLES
FINGERINGS
FINGERLESS
FINGERLIKE
FINGERLING
FINGERLINGS
FINGERMARK
FINGERMARKS
FINGERNAIL
FINGERNAILS
FINGERPICK
FINGERPICKED
FINGERPICKING
FINGERPICKINGS
FINGERPICKS
FINGERPLATE
FINGERPLATES
FINGERPOST
FINGERPOSTS
FINGERPRINT
FINGERPRINTED
FINGERPRINTING
FINGERPRINTINGS
FINGERPRINTS
FINGERSTALL
FINGERSTALLS
FINGERTIPS
FINICALITIES
FINICALITY
FINICALNESS
FINICALNESSES
FINICKETIER
FINICKETIEST
FINICKIEST
FINICKINESS
FINICKINESSES
FINICKINGS
FINISHINGS
FINITENESS
FINITENESSES
FINNICKIER
FINNICKIEST
FINNOCHIOS
FINOCCHIOS
FIORATURAE
FIREBALLER
FIREBALLERS
FIREBALLING
FIREBOARDS
FIREBOMBED
FIREBOMBER
FIREBOMBERS
FIREBOMBING
FIREBOMBINGS
FIREBRANDS
FIREBREAKS
FIREBRICKS
FIREBUSHES
FIRECRACKER
FIRECRACKERS
FIRECRESTS
FIREDRAGON
FIREDRAGONS
FIREDRAKES
FIREFANGED
FIREFANGING
FIREFIGHTER
FIREFIGHTERS
FIREFIGHTING
FIREFIGHTINGS
FIREFIGHTS
FIREFLOATS
FIREFLOODS
FIREGUARDS
FIREHOUSES
FIRELIGHTER
FIRELIGHTERS
FIRELIGHTS
FIREPLACED
FIREPLACES
FIREPOWERS
FIREPROOFED
FIREPROOFING
FIREPROOFINGS
FIREPROOFS
FIRESCAPED
FIRESCAPES
FIRESCAPING
FIRESCAPINGS
FIRESCREEN
FIRESCREENS
FIRESTONES
FIRESTORMS
FIRETHORNS
FIRETRUCKS
FIREWALLED
FIREWALLING
FIREWARDEN
FIREWARDENS
FIREWATERS
FIRMAMENTAL
FIRMAMENTS
FIRMNESSES
FIRSTBORNS
FIRSTFRUITS
FIRSTLINGS
FIRSTNESSES
FISCALISTS
FISHABILITIES
FISHABILITY
FISHBURGER
FISHBURGERS
FISHERFOLK
FISHERWOMAN
FISHERWOMEN
FISHFINGER
FISHFINGERS
FISHIFYING
FISHINESSES
FISHMONGER
FISHMONGERS
FISHPLATES
FISHTAILED
FISHTAILING
FISHWIFELIER
FISHWIFELIEST
FISHWIFELY
FISHYBACKS
FISSICOSTATE
FISSILINGUAL
FISSILITIES
FISSIONABILITY
FISSIONABLE
FISSIONABLES
FISSIONING
FISSIPALMATE
FISSIPARISM
FISSIPARISMS
FISSIPARITIES
FISSIPARITY
FISSIPAROUS
FISSIPAROUSLY
FISSIPAROUSNESS
FISSIPEDAL
FISSIPEDES
FISSIROSTRAL
FISTFIGHTS
FISTICUFFED
FISTICUFFING
FISTICUFFS
FITFULNESS
FITFULNESSES
FITTINGNESS
FITTINGNESSES
FIVEFINGER
FIVEFINGERS
FIVEPENCES
FIXEDNESSES
FIXTURELESS
FIZGIGGING
FIZZENLESS
FIZZINESSES
FLABBERGAST
FLABBERGASTED
FLABBERGASTING
FLABBERGASTS
FLABBINESS
FLABBINESSES
FLABELLATE
FLABELLATION
FLABELLATIONS
FLABELLIFORM
FLACCIDEST
FLACCIDITIES
FLACCIDITY

FLACCIDNESS
FLACCIDNESSES
FLACKERIES
FLACKERING
FLACKETING
FLAFFERING
FLAGELLANT
FLAGELLANTISM
FLAGELLANTISMS
FLAGELLANTS
FLAGELLATE
FLAGELLATED
FLAGELLATES
FLAGELLATING
FLAGELLATION
FLAGELLATIONS
FLAGELLATOR
FLAGELLATORS
FLAGELLATORY
FLAGELLIFEROUS
FLAGELLIFORM
FLAGELLINS
FLAGELLOMANIA
FLAGELLOMANIAC
FLAGELLOMANIACS
FLAGELLOMANIAS
FLAGELLUMS
FLAGEOLETS
FLAGGINESS
FLAGGINESSES
FLAGGINGLY
FLAGITATED
FLAGITATES
FLAGITATING
FLAGITATION
FLAGITATIONS
FLAGITIOUS
FLAGITIOUSLY
FLAGITIOUSNESS
FLAGRANCES
FLAGRANCIES
FLAGRANTLY
FLAGRANTNESS
FLAGRANTNESSES
FLAGSTAFFS
FLAGSTAVES
FLAGSTICKS
FLAGSTONES
FLAKINESSES
FLAMBEEING
FLAMBOYANCE
FLAMBOYANCES
FLAMBOYANCIES
FLAMBOYANCY
FLAMBOYANT
FLAMBOYANTE
FLAMBOYANTES
FLAMBOYANTLY
FLAMBOYANTS
FLAMEPROOF
FLAMEPROOFED
FLAMEPROOFER
FLAMEPROOFERS
FLAMEPROOFING
FLAMEPROOFS
FLAMETHROWER
FLAMETHROWERS
FLAMINGOES
FLAMINICAL
FLAMMABILITIES
FLAMMABILITY
FLAMMABLES
FLAMMIFEROUS
FLAMMULATED
FLAMMULATION
FLAMMULATIONS
FLANCHINGS
FLANCONADE
FLANCONADES
FLANGELESS
FLANKERING
FLANNELBOARD
FLANNELBOARDS
FLANNELETS
FLANNELETTE
FLANNELETTES
FLANNELGRAPH
FLANNELGRAPHS
FLANNELING
FLANNELLED
FLANNELLIER
FLANNELLIEST
FLANNELLING
FLANNELMOUTHED
FLAPDOODLE
FLAPDOODLES
FLAPPERHOOD
FLAPPERHOODS
FLAPPERISH
FLAPTRACKS
FLAREBACKS
FLASHBACKED
FLASHBACKING
FLASHBACKS
FLASHBANGS
FLASHBOARD
FLASHBOARDS
FLASHBULBS
FLASHCARDS
FLASHCUBES
FLASHFORWARD
FLASHFORWARDS
FLASHINESS
FLASHINESSES
FLASHLAMPS
FLASHLIGHT
FLASHLIGHTS
FLASHMOBBING
FLASHMOBBINGS
FLASHOVERS
FLASHPACKER
FLASHPACKERS
FLASHPOINT
FLASHPOINTS
FLASHTUBES
FLATBREADS
FLATFISHES
FLATFOOTED
FLATFOOTING
FLATLANDER
FLATLANDERS
FLATLINERS
FLATLINING
FLATNESSES
FLATPICKED
FLATPICKING
FLATSCREEN
FLATSCREENS
FLATSHARES
FLATTENERS
FLATTENING
FLATTERABLE
FLATTERERS
FLATTERIES
FLATTERING
FLATTERINGLY
FLATTEROUS
FLATTEROUSLY
FLATULENCE
FLATULENCES
FLATULENCIES
FLATULENCY
FLATULENTLY
FLATWASHES
FLATWATERS
FLAUGHTERED
FLAUGHTERING
FLAUGHTERS
FLAUGHTING
FLAUNCHING
FLAUNCHINGS
FLAUNTIEST
FLAUNTINESS
FLAUNTINESSES
FLAUNTINGLY
FLAVANONES
FLAVESCENT
FLAVIVIRUS
FLAVIVIRUSES
FLAVONOIDS
FLAVOPROTEIN
FLAVOPROTEINS
FLAVOPURPURIN
FLAVOPURPURINS
FLAVORFULLY
FLAVORIEST
FLAVORINGS
FLAVORISTS
FLAVORLESS
FLAVORSOME
FLAVOURDYNAMICS
FLAVOURERS
FLAVOURFUL
FLAVOURFULLY
FLAVOURIER
FLAVOURIEST
FLAVOURING
FLAVOURINGS
FLAVOURIST
FLAVOURISTS
FLAVOURLESS
FLAVOURSOME
FLAWLESSLY
FLAWLESSNESS
FLAWLESSNESSES
FLEAHOPPER
FLEAHOPPERS
FLECHETTES
FLECKERING
FLECTIONAL
FLECTIONLESS
FLEDGELING
FLEDGELINGS
FLEDGLINGS
FLEECELESS
FLEECHINGS
FLEECHMENT
FLEECHMENTS
FLEECINESS
FLEECINESSES
FLEERINGLY
FLEETINGLY
FLEETINGNESS
FLEETINGNESSES
FLEETNESSES
FLEHMENING
FLEMISHING
FLEROVIUMS
FLESHHOODS
FLESHINESS
FLESHINESSES
FLESHLIEST
FLESHLINESS
FLESHLINESSES
FLESHLINGS
FLESHMENTS
FLESHMONGER
FLESHMONGERS
FLESHWORMS
FLETCHINGS
FLEURETTES
FLEXECUTIVE
FLEXECUTIVES
FLEXIBILITIES
FLEXIBILITY
FLEXIBLENESS
FLEXIBLENESSES
FLEXICURITIES
FLEXICURITY
FLEXIHOURS

F

FLEXIONLESS
FLEXITARIAN
FLEXITARIANISM
FLEXITARIANISMS
FLEXITARIANS
FLEXITIMES
FLEXOGRAPHIC
FLEXOGRAPHIES
FLEXOGRAPHY
FLEXTIMERS
FLEXUOUSLY
FLIBBERTIGIBBET
FLICHTERED
FLICHTERING
FLICKERIER
FLICKERIEST
FLICKERING
FLICKERINGLY
FLICKERTAIL
FLICKERTAILS
FLIGHTIEST
FLIGHTINESS
FLIGHTINESSES
FLIGHTLESS
FLIMFLAMMED
FLIMFLAMMER
FLIMFLAMMERIES
FLIMFLAMMERS
FLIMFLAMMERY
FLIMFLAMMING
FLIMSINESS
FLIMSINESSES
FLINCHINGLY
FLINCHINGS
FLINDERING
FLINDERSIA
FLINDERSIAS
FLINTHEADS
FLINTIFIED
FLINTIFIES
FLINTIFYING
FLINTINESS
FLINTINESSES
FLINTLOCKS
FLIPBOARDS
FLIPCHARTS
FLIPFLOPPED
FLIPFLOPPING
FLIPPANCIES
FLIPPANTLY
FLIPPANTNESS
FLIPPANTNESSES
FLIRTATION
FLIRTATIONS
FLIRTATIOUS
FLIRTATIOUSLY
FLIRTATIOUSNESS
FLIRTINGLY
FLITTERING
FLITTERMICE
FLITTERMOUSE
FLOATABILITIES
FLOATABILITY
FLOATATION
FLOATATIONS
FLOATBASES
FLOATINGLY
FLOATPLANE
FLOATPLANES
FLOCCILLATION
FLOCCILLATIONS
FLOCCULANT
FLOCCULANTS
FLOCCULATE
FLOCCULATED
FLOCCULATES
FLOCCULATING
FLOCCULATION
FLOCCULATIONS
FLOCCULATOR
FLOCCULATORS
FLOCCULENCE
FLOCCULENCES
FLOCCULENCIES
FLOCCULENCY
FLOCCULENT
FLOCCULENTLY
FLOODGATES
FLOODLIGHT
FLOODLIGHTED
FLOODLIGHTING
FLOODLIGHTINGS
FLOODLIGHTS
FLOODMARKS
FLOODPLAIN
FLOODPLAINS
FLOODTIDES
FLOODWALLS
FLOODWATER
FLOODWATERS
FLOORBOARD
FLOORBOARDS
FLOORCLOTH
FLOORCLOTHS
FLOORDROBE
FLOORDROBES
FLOORHEADS
FLOORSHOWS
FLOORWALKER
FLOORWALKERS
FLOPHOUSES
FLOPPINESS
FLOPPINESSES
FLOPTICALS
FLORENTINE
FLORENTINES
FLORESCENCE
FLORESCENCES
FLORESCENT
FLORIATION
FLORIATIONS
FLORIBUNDA
FLORIBUNDAS
FLORICANES
FLORICULTURAL
FLORICULTURE
FLORICULTURES
FLORICULTURIST
FLORICULTURISTS
FLORIDEANS
FLORIDEOUS
FLORIDITIES
FLORIDNESS
FLORIDNESSES
FLORIFEROUS
FLORIFEROUSNESS
FLORIGENIC
FLORILEGIA
FLORILEGIUM
FLORISTICALLY
FLORISTICS
FLORISTRIES
FLOSCULOUS
FLOTATIONS
FLOUNCIEST
FLOUNCINGS
FLOUNDERED
FLOUNDERING
FLOURISHED
FLOURISHER
FLOURISHERS
FLOURISHES
FLOURISHIER
FLOURISHIEST
FLOURISHING
FLOURISHINGLY
FLOUTINGLY
FLOUTINGSTOCK
FLOUTINGSTOCKS
FLOWCHARTING
FLOWCHARTINGS
FLOWCHARTS
FLOWERAGES
FLOWERBEDS
FLOWERETTE
FLOWERETTES
FLOWERHORN
FLOWERIEST
FLOWERINESS
FLOWERINESSES
FLOWERINGS
FLOWERLESS
FLOWERLIKE
FLOWERPOTS
FLOWINGNESS
FLOWINGNESSES
FLOWMETERS
FLOWSTONES
FLUCTUATED
FLUCTUATES
FLUCTUATING
FLUCTUATION
FLUCTUATIONAL
FLUCTUATIONS
FLUEGELHORN
FLUEGELHORNS
FLUENTNESS
FLUENTNESSES
FLUFFBALLS
FLUFFINESS
FLUFFINESSES
FLUGELHORN
FLUGELHORNIST
FLUGELHORNISTS
FLUGELHORNS
FLUIDEXTRACT
FLUIDEXTRACTS
FLUIDIFIED
FLUIDIFIES
FLUIDIFYING
FLUIDISATION
FLUIDISATIONS
FLUIDISERS
FLUIDISING
FLUIDITIES
FLUIDIZATION
FLUIDIZATIONS
FLUIDIZERS
FLUIDIZING
FLUIDNESSES
FLUKINESSES
FLUMMERIES
FLUMMOXING
FLUNITRAZEPAM
FLUNITRAZEPAMS
FLUNKEYDOM
FLUNKEYDOMS
FLUNKEYISH
FLUNKEYISM
FLUNKEYISMS
FLUNKYISMS
FLUORAPATITE
FLUORAPATITES
FLUORESCED
FLUORESCEIN
FLUORESCEINE
FLUORESCEINES
FLUORESCEINS
FLUORESCENCE
FLUORESCENCES
FLUORESCENT
FLUORESCENTS
FLUORESCER
FLUORESCERS
FLUORESCES
FLUORESCING
FLUORIDATE
FLUORIDATED
FLUORIDATES
FLUORIDATING

FLUORIDATION
FLUORIDATIONS
FLUORIDISE
FLUORIDISED
FLUORIDISES
FLUORIDISING
FLUORIDIZE
FLUORIDIZED
FLUORIDIZES
FLUORIDIZING
FLUORIMETER
FLUORIMETERS
FLUORIMETRIC
FLUORIMETRIES
FLUORIMETRY
FLUORINATE
FLUORINATED
FLUORINATES
FLUORINATING
FLUORINATION
FLUORINATIONS
FLUOROACETATE
FLUOROACETATES
FLUOROCARBON
FLUOROCARBONS
FLUOROCHROME
FLUOROCHROMES
FLUOROGRAPHIC
FLUOROGRAPHIES
FLUOROGRAPHY
FLUOROMETER
FLUOROMETERS
FLUOROMETRIC
FLUOROMETRIES
FLUOROMETRY
FLUOROPHORE
FLUOROPHORES
FLUOROPHOSPHATE
FLUOROSCOPE
FLUOROSCOPED
FLUOROSCOPES
FLUOROSCOPIC
FLUOROSCOPIES
FLUOROSCOPING
FLUOROSCOPIST
FLUOROSCOPISTS
FLUOROSCOPY
FLUOROTYPE
FLUOROTYPES
FLUOROURACIL
FLUOROURACILS
FLUORSPARS
FLUOXETINE
FLUOXETINES
FLUPHENAZINE
FLUPHENAZINES
FLUSHNESSES
FLUSHWORKS
FLUSTEREDLY
FLUSTERIER
FLUSTERIEST
FLUSTERING
FLUSTERMENT
FLUSTERMENTS
FLUSTRATED
FLUSTRATES
FLUSTRATING
FLUSTRATION
FLUSTRATIONS
FLUTEMOUTH
FLUTEMOUTHS
FLUTTERBOARD
FLUTTERBOARDS
FLUTTERERS
FLUTTERIER
FLUTTERIEST
FLUTTERING
FLUTTERINGLY
FLUTTERINGS
FLUVIALIST
FLUVIALISTS
FLUVIATILE
FLUVIOMARINE
FLUVOXAMINE
FLUVOXAMINES
FLUXIONALLY
FLUXIONARY
FLUXIONIST
FLUXIONISTS
FLUXMETERS
FLYBLOWING
FLYBRIDGES
FLYCATCHER
FLYCATCHERS
FLYFISHERS
FLYPITCHER
FLYPITCHERS
FLYPITCHES
FLYPOSTERS
FLYPOSTING
FLYPOSTINGS
FLYRODDERS
FLYSCREENS
FLYSPECKED
FLYSPECKING
FLYSTRIKES
FLYSWATTER
FLYSWATTERS
FLYWEIGHTS
FOAMFLOWER
FOAMFLOWERS
FOAMINESSES
FOCALISATION
FOCALISATIONS
FOCALISING
FOCALIZATION
FOCALIZATIONS
FOCALIZING
FOCIMETERS
FOCOMETERS
FODDERINGS
FOEDERATUS
FOETATIONS
FOETICIDAL
FOETICIDES
FOETIDNESS
FOETIDNESSES
FOETIPAROUS
FOETOSCOPIES
FOETOSCOPY
FOGGINESSES
FOGRAMITES
FOGRAMITIES
FOILSWOMAN
FOILSWOMEN
FOISONLESS
FOLIACEOUS
FOLIATIONS
FOLIATURES
FOLKINESSES
FOLKISHNESS
FOLKISHNESSES
FOLKLORISH
FOLKLORIST
FOLKLORISTIC
FOLKLORISTS
FOLKSINESS
FOLKSINESSES
FOLKSINGER
FOLKSINGERS
FOLKSINGING
FOLKSINGINGS
FOLKSONOMIES
FOLKSONOMY
FOLKTRONICA
FOLKTRONICAS
FOLLICULAR
FOLLICULATE
FOLLICULATED
FOLLICULIN
FOLLICULINS
FOLLICULITIS
FOLLICULITISES
FOLLICULOSE
FOLLICULOUS
FOLLOWABLE
FOLLOWERSHIP
FOLLOWERSHIPS
FOLLOWINGS
FOLLOWSHIP
FOLLOWSHIPS
FOMENTATION
FOMENTATIONS
FONCTIONNAIRE
FONCTIONNAIRES
FONDLINGLY
FONDNESSES
FONTANELLE
FONTANELLES
FONTICULUS
FONTINALIS
FONTINALISES
FOODLESSNESS
FOODLESSNESSES
FOODSTUFFS
FOOLBEGGED
FOOLFISHES
FOOLHARDIER
FOOLHARDIEST
FOOLHARDILY
FOOLHARDINESS
FOOLHARDINESSES
FOOLHARDISE
FOOLHARDISES
FOOLHARDIZE
FOOLHARDIZES
FOOLISHEST
FOOLISHNESS
FOOLISHNESSES
FOOTBALLENE
FOOTBALLENES
FOOTBALLER
FOOTBALLERS
FOOTBALLING
FOOTBALLIST
FOOTBALLISTS
FOOTBOARDS
FOOTBRAKES
FOOTBREADTH
FOOTBREADTHS
FOOTBRIDGE
FOOTBRIDGES
FOOTCLOTHS
FOOTDRAGGER
FOOTDRAGGERS
FOOTDRAGGING
FOOTDRAGGINGS
FOOTFAULTED
FOOTFAULTING
FOOTFAULTS
FOOTGUARDS
FOOTLAMBERT
FOOTLAMBERTS
FOOTLESSLY
FOOTLESSNESS
FOOTLESSNESSES
FOOTLIGHTS
FOOTLOCKER
FOOTLOCKERS
FOOTNOTING
FOOTPLATEMAN
FOOTPLATEMEN
FOOTPLATES
FOOTPLATEWOMAN
FOOTPLATEWOMEN
FOOTPRINTS
FOOTSLOGGED
FOOTSLOGGER
FOOTSLOGGERS
FOOTSLOGGING

FOOTSLOGGINGS
FOOTSORENESS
FOOTSORENESSES
FOOTSTALKS
FOOTSTALLS
FOOTSTOCKS
FOOTSTONES
FOOTSTOOLED
FOOTSTOOLS
FOOTWEARIER
FOOTWEARIEST
FOPPISHNESS
FOPPISHNESSES
FORAMINATED
FORAMINIFER
FORAMINIFERA
FORAMINIFERAL
FORAMINIFERAN
FORAMINIFERANS
FORAMINIFEROUS
FORAMINIFERS
FORAMINOUS
FORBEARANCE
FORBEARANCES
FORBEARANT
FORBEARERS
FORBEARING
FORBEARINGLY
FORBIDDALS
FORBIDDANCE
FORBIDDANCES
FORBIDDENLY
FORBIDDERS
FORBIDDING
FORBIDDINGLY
FORBIDDINGNESS
FORBIDDINGS
FORCEDNESS
FORCEDNESSES
FORCEFULLY
FORCEFULNESS
FORCEFULNESSES
FORCEMEATS
FORCEPSLIKE
FORCIBILITIES
FORCIBILITY
FORCIBLENESS
FORCIBLENESSES
FORCIPATED
FORCIPATION
FORCIPATIONS
FOREARMING
FOREBITTER
FOREBITTERS
FOREBODEMENT
FOREBODEMENTS
FOREBODERS
FOREBODIES
FOREBODING
FOREBODINGLY
FOREBODINGNESS
FOREBODINGS
FOREBRAINS
FORECABINS
FORECADDIE
FORECADDIES
FORECARRIAGE
FORECARRIAGES
FORECASTABLE
FORECASTED
FORECASTER
FORECASTERS
FORECASTING
FORECASTINGS
FORECASTLE
FORECASTLES
FORECHECKED
FORECHECKER
FORECHECKERS
FORECHECKING
FORECHECKS
FORECHOSEN
FORECLOSABLE
FORECLOSED
FORECLOSES
FORECLOSING
FORECLOSURE
FORECLOSURES
FORECLOTHS
FORECOURSE
FORECOURSES
FORECOURTS
FOREDAMNED
FOREDATING
FOREDOOMED
FOREDOOMING
FOREFATHER
FOREFATHERLY
FOREFATHERS
FOREFEELING
FOREFEELINGLY
FOREFENDED
FOREFENDING
FOREFINGER
FOREFINGERS
FOREFRONTS
FOREGATHER
FOREGATHERED
FOREGATHERING
FOREGATHERS
FOREGLEAMS
FOREGOINGS
FOREGONENESS
FOREGONENESSES
FOREGROUND
FOREGROUNDED
FOREGROUNDING
FOREGROUNDS
FOREHANDED
FOREHANDEDLY
FOREHANDEDNESS
FOREHANDING
FOREHENTING
FOREHOOVES
FOREIGNERS
FOREIGNISM
FOREIGNISMS
FOREIGNNESS
FOREIGNNESSES
FOREJUDGED
FOREJUDGEMENT
FOREJUDGEMENTS
FOREJUDGES
FOREJUDGING
FOREJUDGMENT
FOREJUDGMENTS
FOREKNOWABLE
FOREKNOWING
FOREKNOWINGLY
FOREKNOWLEDGE
FOREKNOWLEDGES
FORELADIES
FORELAYING
FORELENDING
FORELIFTED
FORELIFTING
FORELOCKED
FORELOCKING
FOREMANSHIP
FOREMANSHIPS
FOREMASTMAN
FOREMASTMEN
FOREMEANING
FOREMENTIONED
FOREMOTHER
FOREMOTHERS
FORENIGHTS
FORENSICALITIES
FORENSICALITY
FORENSICALLY
FOREORDAIN
FOREORDAINED
FOREORDAINING
FOREORDAINMENT
FOREORDAINMENTS
FOREORDAINS
FOREORDINATION
FOREORDINATIONS
FOREPASSED
FOREPAYMENT
FOREPAYMENTS
FOREPLANNED
FOREPLANNING
FOREPOINTED
FOREPOINTING
FOREPOINTS
FOREQUARTER
FOREQUARTERS
FOREREACHED
FOREREACHES
FOREREACHING
FOREREADING
FOREREADINGS
FORERUNNER
FORERUNNERS
FORERUNNING
FORESAYING
FORESEEABILITY
FORESEEABLE
FORESEEING
FORESEEINGLY
FORESHADOW
FORESHADOWED
FORESHADOWER
FORESHADOWERS
FORESHADOWING
FORESHADOWINGS
FORESHADOWS
FORESHANKS
FORESHEETS
FORESHEWED
FORESHEWING
FORESHOCKS
FORESHORES
FORESHORTEN
FORESHORTENED
FORESHORTENING
FORESHORTENINGS
FORESHORTENS
FORESHOWED
FORESHOWING
FORESIGHTED
FORESIGHTEDLY
FORESIGHTEDNESS
FORESIGHTFUL
FORESIGHTLESS
FORESIGHTS
FORESIGNIFIED
FORESIGNIFIES
FORESIGNIFY
FORESIGNIFYING
FORESKIRTS
FORESLACKED
FORESLACKING
FORESLACKS
FORESLOWED
FORESLOWING
FORESPEAKING
FORESPEAKS
FORESPENDING
FORESPENDS
FORESPOKEN
FORESTAGES
FORESTAIRS
FORESTALLED
FORESTALLER
FORESTALLERS
FORESTALLING
FORESTALLINGS
FORESTALLMENT

FORESTALLMENTS
FORESTALLS
FORESTALMENT
FORESTALMENTS
FORESTATION
FORESTATIONS
FORESTAYSAIL
FORESTAYSAILS
FORESTLAND
FORESTLANDS
FORESTLESS
FORESTRIES
FORESWEARING
FORESWEARS
FORETASTED
FORETASTES
FORETASTING
FORETAUGHT
FORETEACHES
FORETEACHING
FORETELLER
FORETELLERS
FORETELLING
FORETHINKER
FORETHINKERS
FORETHINKING
FORETHINKS
FORETHOUGHT
FORETHOUGHTFUL
FORETHOUGHTS
FORETOKENED
FORETOKENING
FORETOKENINGS
FORETOKENS
FORETOPMAN
FORETOPMAST
FORETOPMASTS
FORETOPMEN
FORETRIANGLE
FORETRIANGLES
FOREVERMORE
FOREVERNESS
FOREVERNESSES
FOREVOUCHED
FOREWARDED
FOREWARDING
FOREWARNED
FOREWARNER
FOREWARNERS
FOREWARNING
FOREWARNINGLY
FOREWARNINGS
FOREWEIGHED
FOREWEIGHING
FOREWEIGHS
FORFAIRING
FORFAITERS
FORFAITING
FORFAITINGS
FORFEITABLE
FORFEITERS
FORFEITING
FORFEITURE
FORFEITURES
FORFENDING
FORFEUCHEN
FORFICULATE
FORFOUGHEN
FORFOUGHTEN
FORGATHERED
FORGATHERING
FORGATHERS
FORGEABILITIES
FORGEABILITY
FORGETFULLY
FORGETFULNESS
FORGETFULNESSES
FORGETTABLE
FORGETTERIES
FORGETTERS
FORGETTERY
FORGETTING
FORGETTINGLY
FORGETTINGS
FORGIVABLE
FORGIVABLY
FORGIVENESS
FORGIVENESSES
FORGIVINGLY
FORGIVINGNESS
FORGIVINGNESSES
FORGOTTENNESS
FORGOTTENNESSES
FORHAILING
FORHENTING
FORHOOIEING
FORINSECAL
FORISFAMILIATE
FORISFAMILIATED
FORISFAMILIATES
FORJUDGING
FORJUDGMENT
FORJUDGMENTS
FORKEDNESS
FORKEDNESSES
FORKINESSES
FORKLIFTED
FORKLIFTING
FORLENDING
FORLORNEST
FORLORNNESS
FORLORNNESSES
FORMABILITIES
FORMABILITY
FORMALDEHYDE
FORMALDEHYDES
FORMALINES
FORMALISABLE
FORMALISATION
FORMALISATIONS
FORMALISED
FORMALISER
FORMALISERS
FORMALISES
FORMALISING
FORMALISMS
FORMALISTIC
FORMALISTICALLY
FORMALISTS
FORMALITER
FORMALITIES
FORMALIZABLE
FORMALIZATION
FORMALIZATIONS
FORMALIZED
FORMALIZER
FORMALIZERS
FORMALIZES
FORMALIZING
FORMALNESS
FORMALNESSES
FORMAMIDES
FORMATIONAL
FORMATIONS
FORMATIVELY
FORMATIVENESS
FORMATIVENESSES
FORMATIVES
FORMATTERS
FORMATTING
FORMATTINGS
FORMFITTING
FORMICARIA
FORMICARIES
FORMICARIUM
FORMICATED
FORMICATES
FORMICATING
FORMICATION
FORMICATIONS
FORMIDABILITIES
FORMIDABILITY
FORMIDABLE
FORMIDABLENESS
FORMIDABLY
FORMLESSLY
FORMLESSNESS
FORMLESSNESSES
FORMULAICALLY
FORMULARIES
FORMULARISATION
FORMULARISE
FORMULARISED
FORMULARISER
FORMULARISERS
FORMULARISES
FORMULARISING
FORMULARISTIC
FORMULARIZATION
FORMULARIZE
FORMULARIZED
FORMULARIZER
FORMULARIZERS
FORMULARIZES
FORMULARIZING
FORMULATED
FORMULATES
FORMULATING
FORMULATION
FORMULATIONS
FORMULATOR
FORMULATORS
FORMULISED
FORMULISES
FORMULISING
FORMULISMS
FORMULISTIC
FORMULISTS
FORMULIZED
FORMULIZES
FORMULIZING
FORNICATED
FORNICATES
FORNICATING
FORNICATION
FORNICATIONS
FORNICATOR
FORNICATORS
FORNICATRESS
FORNICATRESSES
FORSAKENLY
FORSAKENNESS
FORSAKENNESSES
FORSAKINGS
FORSLACKED
FORSLACKING
FORSLOEING
FORSLOWING
FORSPEAKING
FORSPENDING
FORSTERITE
FORSTERITES
FORSWEARER
FORSWEARERS
FORSWEARING
FORSWINKED
FORSWINKING
FORSWORNNESS
FORSWORNNESSES
FORSYTHIAS
FORTALICES
FORTEPIANIST
FORTEPIANISTS
FORTEPIANO
FORTEPIANOS
FORTHCOMES
FORTHCOMING
FORTHCOMINGNESS
FORTHGOING
FORTHGOINGS

F

FORTHINKING
FORTHOUGHT
FORTHRIGHT
FORTHRIGHTLY
FORTHRIGHTNESS
FORTHRIGHTS
FORTIFIABLE
FORTIFICATION
FORTIFICATIONS
FORTIFIERS
FORTIFYING
FORTIFYINGLY
FORTILAGES
FORTISSIMI
FORTISSIMO
FORTISSIMOS
FORTISSISSIMO
FORTITUDES
FORTITUDINOUS
FORTNIGHTLIES
FORTNIGHTLY
FORTNIGHTS
FORTRESSED
FORTRESSES
FORTRESSING
FORTRESSLIKE
FORTUITIES
FORTUITISM
FORTUITISMS
FORTUITIST
FORTUITISTS
FORTUITOUS
FORTUITOUSLY
FORTUITOUSNESS
FORTUNATELY
FORTUNATENESS
FORTUNATENESSES
FORTUNATES
FORTUNELESS
FORTUNISED
FORTUNISES
FORTUNISING
FORTUNIZED
FORTUNIZES
FORTUNIZING
FORWANDERED
FORWANDERING
FORWANDERS
FORWARDERS
FORWARDEST
FORWARDING
FORWARDINGS
FORWARDNESS
FORWARDNESSES
FORWARNING
FORWASTING
FORWEARIED
FORWEARIES
FORWEARYING
FOSCARNETS
FOSSICKERS
FOSSICKING
FOSSICKINGS
FOSSILIFEROUS
FOSSILISABLE
FOSSILISATION
FOSSILISATIONS
FOSSILISED
FOSSILISES
FOSSILISING
FOSSILIZABLE
FOSSILIZATION
FOSSILIZATIONS
FOSSILIZED
FOSSILIZES
FOSSILIZING
FOSTERAGES
FOSTERINGS
FOSTERLING
FOSTERLINGS
FOSTRESSES
FOTHERGILLA
FOTHERGILLAS
FOUDROYANT
FOUGHTIEST
FOULBROODS
FOULDERING
FOULMOUTHED
FOULNESSES
FOUNDATION
FOUNDATIONAL
FOUNDATIONALLY
FOUNDATIONARY
FOUNDATIONER
FOUNDATIONERS
FOUNDATIONLESS
FOUNDATIONS
FOUNDERING
FOUNDEROUS
FOUNDLINGS
FOUNDRESSES
FOUNTAINED
FOUNTAINHEAD
FOUNTAINHEADS
FOUNTAINING
FOUNTAINLESS
FOURCHETTE
FOURCHETTES
FOURDRINIER
FOURDRINIERS
FOURFOLDNESS
FOURFOLDNESSES
FOURPENCES
FOURPENNIES
FOURPLEXES
FOURRAGERE
FOURRAGERES
FOURSCORTH
FOURSQUARE
FOURSQUARELY
FOURSQUARENESS
FOURTEENER
FOURTEENERS
FOURTEENTH
FOURTEENTHLY
FOURTEENTHS
FOVEOLATED
FOXBERRIES
FOXHUNTERS
FOXHUNTING
FOXHUNTINGS
FOXINESSES
FOXTROTTED
FOXTROTTING
FOZINESSES
FRABJOUSLY
FRACTALITIES
FRACTALITY
FRACTIONAL
FRACTIONALISE
FRACTIONALISED
FRACTIONALISES
FRACTIONALISING
FRACTIONALISM
FRACTIONALISMS
FRACTIONALIST
FRACTIONALISTS
FRACTIONALIZE
FRACTIONALIZED
FRACTIONALIZES
FRACTIONALIZING
FRACTIONALLY
FRACTIONARY
FRACTIONATE
FRACTIONATED
FRACTIONATES
FRACTIONATING
FRACTIONATION
FRACTIONATIONS
FRACTIONATOR
FRACTIONATORS
FRACTIONED
FRACTIONING
FRACTIONISATION
FRACTIONISE
FRACTIONISED
FRACTIONISES
FRACTIONISING
FRACTIONIZATION
FRACTIONIZE
FRACTIONIZED
FRACTIONIZES
FRACTIONIZING
FRACTIONLET
FRACTIONLETS
FRACTIOUSLY
FRACTIOUSNESS
FRACTIOUSNESSES
FRACTOCUMULI
FRACTOCUMULUS
FRACTOGRAPHIES
FRACTOGRAPHY
FRACTOSTRATI
FRACTOSTRATUS
FRACTURABLE
FRACTURERS
FRACTURING
FRAGILENESS
FRAGILENESSES
FRAGILITIES
FRAGMENTAL
FRAGMENTALLY
FRAGMENTARILY
FRAGMENTARINESS
FRAGMENTARY
FRAGMENTATE
FRAGMENTATED
FRAGMENTATES
FRAGMENTATING
FRAGMENTATION
FRAGMENTATIONS
FRAGMENTED
FRAGMENTING
FRAGMENTISE
FRAGMENTISED
FRAGMENTISES
FRAGMENTISING
FRAGMENTIZE
FRAGMENTIZED
FRAGMENTIZES
FRAGMENTIZING
FRAGRANCED
FRAGRANCES
FRAGRANCIES
FRAGRANCING
FRAGRANTLY
FRAGRANTNESS
FRAGRANTNESSES
FRAICHEURS
FRAILNESSES
FRAMBESIAS
FRAMBOESIA
FRAMBOESIAS
FRAMBOISES
FRAMESHIFT
FRAMESHIFTS
FRAMEWORKS
FRANCHISED
FRANCHISEE
FRANCHISEES
FRANCHISEMENT
FRANCHISEMENTS
FRANCHISER
FRANCHISERS
FRANCHISES
FRANCHISING
FRANCHISOR
FRANCHISORS
FRANCISATION
FRANCISATIONS

FRANCISING
FRANCIZATION
FRANCIZATIONS
FRANCIZING
FRANCOLINS
FRANCOMANIA
FRANCOMANIAS
FRANCOPHIL
FRANCOPHILE
FRANCOPHILES
FRANCOPHILS
FRANCOPHOBE
FRANCOPHOBES
FRANCOPHOBIA
FRANCOPHOBIAS
FRANCOPHONE
FRANCOPHONES
FRANGIBILITIES
FRANGIBILITY
FRANGIBLENESS
FRANGIBLENESSES
FRANGIPANE
FRANGIPANES
FRANGIPANI
FRANGIPANIS
FRANGIPANNI
FRANKALMOIGN
FRANKALMOIGNS
FRANKFORTS
FRANKFURTER
FRANKFURTERS
FRANKFURTS
FRANKINCENSE
FRANKINCENSES
FRANKLINITE
FRANKLINITES
FRANKNESSES
FRANKPLEDGE
FRANKPLEDGES
FRANSERIAS
FRANTICALLY
FRANTICNESS
FRANTICNESSES
FRATCHETIER
FRATCHETIEST
FRATCHIEST
FRATERNALISM
FRATERNALISMS
FRATERNALLY
FRATERNISATION
FRATERNISATIONS
FRATERNISE
FRATERNISED
FRATERNISER
FRATERNISERS
FRATERNISES
FRATERNISING
FRATERNITIES
FRATERNITY
FRATERNIZATION
FRATERNIZATIONS
FRATERNIZE
FRATERNIZED
FRATERNIZER
FRATERNIZERS
FRATERNIZES
FRATERNIZING
FRATRICIDAL
FRATRICIDE
FRATRICIDES
FRAUDFULLY
FRAUDSTERS
FRAUDULENCE
FRAUDULENCES
FRAUDULENCIES
FRAUDULENCY
FRAUDULENT
FRAUDULENTLY
FRAUDULENTNESS
FRAUGHTAGE
FRAUGHTAGES
FRAUGHTEST
FRAUGHTING
FRAXINELLA
FRAXINELLAS
FREAKERIES
FREAKINESS
FREAKINESSES
FREAKISHLY
FREAKISHNESS
FREAKISHNESSES
FRECKLIEST
FRECKLINGS
FREEBASERS
FREEBASING
FREEBOARDS
FREEBOOTED
FREEBOOTER
FREEBOOTERIES
FREEBOOTERS
FREEBOOTERY
FREEBOOTIES
FREEBOOTING
FREEBOOTINGS
FREECOOLING
FREECOOLINGS
FREECYCLED
FREECYCLES
FREECYCLING
FREEDIVERS
FREEDIVING
FREEDIVINGS
FREEDWOMAN
FREEDWOMEN
FREEGANISM
FREEGANISMS
FREEHANDED
FREEHANDEDLY
FREEHANDEDNESS
FREEHEARTED
FREEHEARTEDLY
FREEHOLDER
FREEHOLDERS
FREELANCED
FREELANCER
FREELANCERS
FREELANCES
FREELANCING
FREELOADED
FREELOADER
FREELOADERS
FREELOADING
FREELOADINGS
FREEMARTIN
FREEMARTINS
FREEMASONIC
FREEMASONRIES
FREEMASONRY
FREEMASONS
FREENESSES
FREEPHONES
FREESHEETS
FREESTANDING
FREESTONES
FREESTYLED
FREESTYLER
FREESTYLERS
FREESTYLES
FREESTYLING
FREESTYLINGS
FREETHINKER
FREETHINKERS
FREETHINKING
FREETHINKINGS
FREEWHEELED
FREEWHEELER
FREEWHEELERS
FREEWHEELING
FREEWHEELINGLY
FREEWHEELINGS
FREEWHEELS
FREEWRITES
FREEWRITING
FREEWRITINGS
FREEWRITTEN
FREEZINGLY
FREIGHTAGE
FREIGHTAGES
FREIGHTERS
FREIGHTING
FREIGHTLESS
FREMESCENCE
FREMESCENCES
FREMESCENT
FREMITUSES
FRENCHIFICATION
FRENCHIFIED
FRENCHIFIES
FRENCHIFYING
FRENETICAL
FRENETICALLY
FRENETICISM
FRENETICISMS
FRENETICNESS
FRENETICNESSES
FRENZIEDLY
FREQUENCES
FREQUENCIES
FREQUENTABLE
FREQUENTATION
FREQUENTATIONS
FREQUENTATIVE
FREQUENTATIVES
FREQUENTED
FREQUENTER
FREQUENTERS
FREQUENTEST
FREQUENTING
FREQUENTLY
FREQUENTNESS
FREQUENTNESSES
FRESCOINGS
FRESCOISTS
FRESHENERS
FRESHENING
FRESHERDOM
FRESHERDOMS
FRESHMANSHIP
FRESHMANSHIPS
FRESHNESSES
FRESHWATER
FRESHWATERS
FRETBOARDS
FRETFULNESS
FRETFULNESSES
FRIABILITIES
FRIABILITY
FRIABLENESS
FRIABLENESSES
FRIARBIRDS
FRICANDEAU
FRICANDEAUS
FRICANDEAUX
FRICANDOES
FRICASSEED
FRICASSEEING
FRICASSEES
FRICATIVES
FRICTIONAL
FRICTIONALLY
FRICTIONLESS
FRICTIONLESSLY
FRIEDCAKES
FRIENDINGS
FRIENDLESS
FRIENDLESSNESS
FRIENDLIER
FRIENDLIES
FRIENDLIEST
FRIENDLILY

FRIENDLINESS
FRIENDLINESSES
FRIENDSHIP
FRIENDSHIPS
FRIEZELIKE
FRIGATOONS
FRIGHTENED
FRIGHTENER
FRIGHTENERS
FRIGHTENING
FRIGHTENINGLY
FRIGHTFULLY
FRIGHTFULNESS
FRIGHTFULNESSES
FRIGHTSOME
FRIGIDARIA
FRIGIDARIUM
FRIGIDITIES
FRIGIDNESS
FRIGIDNESSES
FRIGORIFIC
FRIGORIFICO
FRIGORIFICOS
FRIKKADELS
FRILLERIES
FRILLINESS
FRILLINESSES
FRINGELESS
FRINGELIKE
FRINGILLACEOUS
FRINGILLID
FRINGILLIFORM
FRINGILLINE
FRIPONNERIE
FRIPONNERIES
FRIPPERERS
FRIPPERIES
FRISKINESS
FRISKINESSES
FRISKINGLY
FRITHBORHS
FRITHSOKEN
FRITHSOKENS
FRITHSTOOL
FRITHSTOOLS
FRITILLARIA
FRITILLARIAS
FRITILLARIES
FRITILLARY
FRITTERERS
FRITTERING
FRIVOLITIES
FRIVOLLERS
FRIVOLLING
FRIVOLOUSLY
FRIVOLOUSNESS
FRIVOLOUSNESSES
FRIZZINESS
FRIZZINESSES
FRIZZLIEST
FRIZZLINESS
FRIZZLINESSES
FROGFISHES
FROGGERIES
FROGHOPPER
FROGHOPPERS
FROGMARCHED
FROGMARCHES
FROGMARCHING
FROGMOUTHS
FROGSPAWNS
FROLICKERS
FROLICKIER
FROLICKIEST
FROLICKING
FROLICSOME
FROLICSOMELY
FROLICSOMENESS
FROMENTIES
FRONDESCENCE
FRONDESCENCES
FRONDESCENT
FRONDIFEROUS
FRONTAGERS
FRONTALITIES
FRONTALITY
FRONTBENCHER
FRONTBENCHERS
FRONTCOURT
FRONTCOURTS
FRONTENISES
FRONTIERED
FRONTIERING
FRONTIERSMAN
FRONTIERSMEN
FRONTIERSWOMAN
FRONTIERSWOMEN
FRONTISPIECE
FRONTISPIECED
FRONTISPIECES
FRONTISPIECING
FRONTLESSLY
FRONTLINES
FRONTLISTS
FRONTOGENESES
FRONTOGENESIS
FRONTOGENETIC
FRONTOLYSES
FRONTOLYSIS
FRONTPAGED
FRONTPAGES
FRONTPAGING
FRONTRUNNER
FRONTRUNNERS
FRONTRUNNING
FRONTRUNNINGS
FRONTWARDS
FROSTBITES
FROSTBITING
FROSTBITINGS
FROSTBITTEN
FROSTBOUND
FROSTFISHES
FROSTINESS
FROSTINESSES
FROSTLINES
FROSTWORKS
FROTHERIES
FROTHINESS
FROTHINESSES
FROUGHIEST
FROUZINESS
FROUZINESSES
FROWARDNESS
FROWARDNESSES
FROWNINGLY
FROWSINESS
FROWSINESSES
FROWSTIEST
FROWSTINESS
FROWSTINESSES
FROWZINESS
FROWZINESSES
FROZENNESS
FROZENNESSES
FRUCTIFEROUS
FRUCTIFEROUSLY
FRUCTIFICATION
FRUCTIFICATIONS
FRUCTIFIED
FRUCTIFIER
FRUCTIFIERS
FRUCTIFIES
FRUCTIFYING
FRUCTIVOROUS
FRUCTUARIES
FRUCTUATED
FRUCTUATES
FRUCTUATING
FRUCTUATION
FRUCTUATIONS
FRUCTUOUSLY
FRUCTUOUSNESS
FRUCTUOUSNESSES
FRUGALISTA
FRUGALISTAS
FRUGALISTS
FRUGALITIES
FRUGALNESS
FRUGALNESSES
FRUGIFEROUS
FRUGIVORES
FRUGIVOROUS
FRUITARIAN
FRUITARIANISM
FRUITARIANISMS
FRUITARIANS
FRUITCAKES
FRUITERERS
FRUITERESS
FRUITERESSES
FRUITERIES
FRUITFULLER
FRUITFULLEST
FRUITFULLY
FRUITFULNESS
FRUITFULNESSES
FRUITINESS
FRUITINESSES
FRUITLESSLY
FRUITLESSNESS
FRUITLESSNESSES
FRUITWOODS
FRUITWORMS
FRUMENTACEOUS
FRUMENTARIOUS
FRUMENTATION
FRUMENTATIONS
FRUMENTIES
FRUMPINESS
FRUMPINESSES
FRUMPISHLY
FRUMPISHNESS
FRUMPISHNESSES
FRUSEMIDES
FRUSTRATED
FRUSTRATER
FRUSTRATERS
FRUSTRATES
FRUSTRATING
FRUSTRATINGLY
FRUSTRATION
FRUSTRATIONS
FRUTESCENCE
FRUTESCENCES
FRUTESCENT
FRUTIFYING
FUCIVOROUS
FUCOXANTHIN
FUCOXANTHINS
FUGACIOUSLY
FUGACIOUSNESS
FUGACIOUSNESSES
FUGACITIES
FUGGINESSES
FUGITATION
FUGITATIONS
FUGITIVELY
FUGITIVENESS
FUGITIVENESSES
FUGITOMETER
FUGITOMETERS
FULFILLERS
FULFILLING
FULFILLINGS
FULFILLMENT
FULFILLMENTS
FULFILMENT
FULFILMENTS
FULGENCIES

FULGURATED
FULGURATES
FULGURATING
FULGURATION
FULGURATIONS
FULGURITES
FULIGINOSITIES
FULIGINOSITY
FULIGINOUS
FULIGINOUSLY
FULIGINOUSNESS
FULLBLOODS
FULLERENES
FULLERIDES
FULLERITES
FULLMOUTHED
FULLNESSES
FULMINANTS
FULMINATED
FULMINATES
FULMINATING
FULMINATION
FULMINATIONS
FULMINATOR
FULMINATORS
FULMINATORY
FULMINEOUS
FULSOMENESS
FULSOMENESSES
FUMATORIES
FUMATORIUM
FUMATORIUMS
FUMBLINGLY
FUMBLINGNESS
FUMBLINGNESSES
FUMIGATING
FUMIGATION
FUMIGATIONS
FUMIGATORS
FUMIGATORY
FUMITORIES
FUMOSITIES
FUNAMBULATE
FUNAMBULATED
FUNAMBULATES
FUNAMBULATING
FUNAMBULATION
FUNAMBULATIONS
FUNAMBULATOR
FUNAMBULATORS
FUNAMBULATORY
FUNAMBULISM
FUNAMBULISMS
FUNAMBULIST
FUNAMBULISTS
FUNCTIONAL
FUNCTIONALISM
FUNCTIONALISMS
FUNCTIONALIST
FUNCTIONALISTIC
FUNCTIONALISTS
FUNCTIONALITIES
FUNCTIONALITY
FUNCTIONALLY
FUNCTIONALS
FUNCTIONARIES
FUNCTIONARY
FUNCTIONATE
FUNCTIONATED
FUNCTIONATES
FUNCTIONATING
FUNCTIONED
FUNCTIONING
FUNCTIONLESS
FUNDAMENTAL
FUNDAMENTALISM
FUNDAMENTALISMS
FUNDAMENTALIST
FUNDAMENTALISTS
FUNDAMENTALITY
FUNDAMENTALLY
FUNDAMENTALNESS
FUNDAMENTALS
FUNDAMENTS
FUNDHOLDER
FUNDHOLDERS
FUNDHOLDING
FUNDHOLDINGS
FUNDRAISED
FUNDRAISER
FUNDRAISERS
FUNDRAISES
FUNDRAISING
FUNDRAISINGS
FUNEREALLY
FUNGIBILITIES
FUNGIBILITY
FUNGICIDAL
FUNGICIDALLY
FUNGICIDES
FUNGISTATIC
FUNGISTATICALLY
FUNGISTATS
FUNGOSITIES
FUNICULARS
FUNICULATE
FUNKINESSES
FUNNELFORM
FUNNELLING
FUNNINESSES
FURACIOUSNESS
FURACIOUSNESSES
FURACITIES
FURALDEHYDE
FURALDEHYDES
FURANOSIDE
FURANOSIDES
FURAZOLIDONE
FURAZOLIDONES
FURBEARERS
FURBELOWED
FURBELOWING
FURBISHERS
FURBISHING
FURCATIONS
FURCIFEROUS
FURFURACEOUS
FURFURACEOUSLY
FURFURALDEHYDE
FURFURALDEHYDES
FURFUROLES
FURIOSITIES
FURIOUSNESS
FURIOUSNESSES
FURLOUGHED
FURLOUGHING
FURMENTIES
FURNIMENTS
FURNISHERS
FURNISHING
FURNISHINGS
FURNISHMENT
FURNISHMENTS
FURNITURES
FUROSEMIDE
FUROSEMIDES
FURRIERIES
FURRINESSES
FURROWIEST
FURROWLESS
FURSHLUGGINER
FURTHCOMING
FURTHCOMINGS
FURTHERANCE
FURTHERANCES
FURTHERERS
FURTHERING
FURTHERMORE
FURTHERMOST
FURTHERSOME
FURTIVENESS
FURTIVENESSES
FURUNCULAR
FURUNCULOSES
FURUNCULOSIS
FURUNCULOUS
FUSHIONLESS
FUSIBILITIES
FUSIBILITY
FUSIBLENESS
FUSIBLENESSES
FUSILLADED
FUSILLADES
FUSILLADING
FUSILLATION
FUSILLATIONS
FUSIONISMS
FUSIONISTS
FUSIONLESS
FUSSBUDGET
FUSSBUDGETIER
FUSSBUDGETIEST
FUSSBUDGETS
FUSSBUDGETY
FUSSINESSES
FUSTANELLA
FUSTANELLAS
FUSTANELLE
FUSTANELLES
FUSTIANISE
FUSTIANISED
FUSTIANISES
FUSTIANISING
FUSTIANIST
FUSTIANISTS
FUSTIANIZE
FUSTIANIZED
FUSTIANIZES
FUSTIANIZING
FUSTIGATED
FUSTIGATES
FUSTIGATING
FUSTIGATION
FUSTIGATIONS
FUSTIGATOR
FUSTIGATORS
FUSTIGATORY
FUSTILARIAN
FUSTILARIANS
FUSTILIRIAN
FUSTILIRIANS
FUSTILLIRIAN
FUSTILLIRIANS
FUSTINESSES
FUSULINIDS
FUTILENESS
FUTILENESSES
FUTILITARIAN
FUTILITARIANISM
FUTILITARIANS
FUTILITIES
FUTURELESS
FUTURELESSNESS
FUTURISTIC
FUTURISTICALLY
FUTURISTICS
FUTURITIES
FUTURITION
FUTURITIONS
FUTUROLOGICAL
FUTUROLOGIES
FUTUROLOGIST
FUTUROLOGISTS
FUTUROLOGY
FUZZINESSES

F

G

GABAPENTIN
GABAPENTINS
GABARDINES
GABBINESSES
GABBLEMENT
GABBLEMENTS
GABBROITIC
GABERDINES
GABERLUNZIE
GABERLUNZIES
GABIONADES
GABIONAGES
GABIONNADE
GABIONNADES
GADGETEERS
GADGETIEST
GADGETRIES
GADOLINITE
GADOLINITES
GADOLINIUM
GADOLINIUMS
GADROONING
GADROONINGS
GADZOOKERIES
GADZOOKERY
GAELICISED
GAELICISES
GAELICISING
GAELICISMS
GAELICIZED
GAELICIZES
GAELICIZING
GAILLARDIA
GAILLARDIAS
GAINFULNESS
GAINFULNESSES
GAINGIVING
GAINGIVINGS
GAINLESSNESS
GAINLESSNESSES
GAINLINESS
GAINLINESSES
GAINSAYERS
GAINSAYING
GAINSAYINGS
GAINSHARING
GAINSHARINGS
GAINSTRIVE
GAINSTRIVED
GAINSTRIVEN
GAINSTRIVES
GAINSTRIVING
GAINSTROVE
GAITERLESS
GALABIYAHS
GALACTAGOGUE
GALACTAGOGUES
GALACTICOS
GALACTOMETER
GALACTOMETERS
GALACTOMETRIES
GALACTOMETRY
GALACTOPHOROUS
GALACTOPOIESES
GALACTOPOIESIS
GALACTOPOIETIC
GALACTOPOIETICS
GALACTORRHEA
GALACTORRHEAS
GALACTORRHOEA
GALACTORRHOEAS
GALACTOSAEMIA
GALACTOSAEMIAS
GALACTOSAEMIC
GALACTOSAMINE
GALACTOSAMINES
GALACTOSEMIA
GALACTOSEMIAS
GALACTOSEMIC
GALACTOSES
GALACTOSIDASE
GALACTOSIDASES
GALACTOSIDE
GALACTOSIDES
GALACTOSYL
GALACTOSYLS
GALANTAMINE
GALANTAMINES
GALANTINES
GALAVANTED
GALAVANTING
GALDRAGONS
GALENGALES
GALENICALS
GALEOPITHECINE
GALEOPITHECOID
GALIMATIAS
GALIMATIASES
GALINGALES
GALIONGEES
GALIVANTED
GALIVANTING
GALLABEAHS
GALLABIAHS
GALLABIEHS
GALLABIYAH
GALLABIYAHS
GALLABIYAS
GALLABIYEH
GALLABIYEHS
GALLAMINES
GALLANTEST
GALLANTING
GALLANTNESS
GALLANTNESSES
GALLANTRIES
GALLBLADDER
GALLBLADDERS
GALLEASSES
GALLERISTS
GALLERYGOER
GALLERYGOERS
GALLERYING
GALLERYITE
GALLERYITES
GALLIAMBIC
GALLIAMBICS
GALLIARDISE
GALLIARDISES
GALLIASSES
GALLICISATION
GALLICISATIONS
GALLICISED
GALLICISES
GALLICISING
GALLICISMS
GALLICIZATION
GALLICIZATIONS
GALLICIZED
GALLICIZES
GALLICIZING
GALLIGASKINS
GALLIMAUFRIES
GALLIMAUFRY
GALLINACEAN
GALLINACEANS
GALLINACEOUS
GALLINAZOS
GALLINIPPER
GALLINIPPERS
GALLINULES
GALLISISED
GALLISISES
GALLISISING
GALLISIZED
GALLISIZES
GALLISIZING
GALLIVANTED
GALLIVANTING
GALLIVANTS
GALLIWASPS
GALLOGLASS
GALLOGLASSES
GALLONAGES
GALLOPADED
GALLOPADES
GALLOPADING
GALLOWGLASS
GALLOWGLASSES
GALLOWSNESS
GALLOWSNESSES
GALLSICKNESS
GALLSICKNESSES
GALLSTONES
GALLUMPHED
GALLUMPHING
GALLYGASKINS
GALRAVAGED
GALRAVAGES
GALRAVAGING
GALRAVITCH
GALRAVITCHED
GALRAVITCHES
GALRAVITCHING
GALUMPHERS
GALUMPHING
GALVANICAL
GALVANICALLY
GALVANISATION
GALVANISATIONS
GALVANISED
GALVANISER
GALVANISERS
GALVANISES
GALVANISING
GALVANISMS
GALVANISTS
GALVANIZATION
GALVANIZATIONS
GALVANIZED
GALVANIZER
GALVANIZERS
GALVANIZES
GALVANIZING
GALVANOMETER
GALVANOMETERS
GALVANOMETRIC
GALVANOMETRICAL
GALVANOMETRIES
GALVANOMETRY

GALVANOPLASTIC
GALVANOPLASTIES
GALVANOPLASTY
GALVANOSCOPE
GALVANOSCOPES
GALVANOSCOPIC
GALVANOSCOPIES
GALVANOSCOPY
GALVANOTROPIC
GALVANOTROPISM
GALVANOTROPISMS
GAMAHUCHED
GAMAHUCHES
GAMAHUCHING
GAMARUCHED
GAMARUCHES
GAMARUCHING
GAMBADOING
GAMBOLLING
GAMEBREAKER
GAMEBREAKERS
GAMEFISHES
GAMEKEEPER
GAMEKEEPERS
GAMEKEEPING
GAMEKEEPINGS
GAMENESSES
GAMESMANSHIP
GAMESMANSHIPS
GAMESOMELY
GAMESOMENESS
GAMESOMENESSES
GAMETANGIA
GAMETANGIAL
GAMETANGIUM
GAMETICALLY
GAMETOCYTE
GAMETOCYTES
GAMETOGENESES
GAMETOGENESIS
GAMETOGENIC
GAMETOGENIES
GAMETOGENOUS
GAMETOGENY
GAMETOPHORE
GAMETOPHORES
GAMETOPHORIC
GAMETOPHYTE
GAMETOPHYTES
GAMETOPHYTIC
GAMEYNESSES
GAMIFICATION
GAMIFICATIONS
GAMINERIES
GAMINESQUE
GAMINESSES
GAMMERSTANG
GAMMERSTANGS
GAMMOCKING
GAMMONINGS
GAMOGENESES
GAMOGENESIS
GAMOGENETIC
GAMOGENETICAL
GAMOGENETICALLY
GAMOPETALOUS
GAMOPHYLLOUS
GAMOSEPALOUS
GAMOTROPIC
GAMOTROPISM
GAMOTROPISMS
GAMYNESSES
GANDERISMS
GANGBANGED
GANGBANGER
GANGBANGERS
GANGBANGING
GANGBOARDS
GANGBUSTER
GANGBUSTERS
GANGBUSTING
GANGBUSTINGS
GANGLIATED
GANGLIFORM
GANGLIONATED
GANGLIONIC
GANGLIOSIDE
GANGLIOSIDES
GANGMASTER
GANGMASTERS
GANGPLANKS
GANGRENING
GANGRENOUS
GANGSHAGGED
GANGSHAGGING
GANGSTERDOM
GANGSTERDOMS
GANGSTERISH
GANGSTERISM
GANGSTERISMS
GANGSTERLAND
GANGSTERLANDS
GANNETRIES
GANNISTERS
GANTELOPES
GANTLETING
GAOLBREAKING
GAOLBREAKS
GAOLBROKEN
GAOLERESSES
GARAGISTES
GARBAGEMAN
GARBAGEMEN
GARBAGIEST
GARBOLOGIES
GARBOLOGIST
GARBOLOGISTS
GARBURATOR
GARBURATORS
GARDENFULS
GARDENINGS
GARDENLESS
GARDEROBES
GARGANTUAN
GARGANTUAS
GARGARISED
GARGARISES
GARGARISING
GARGARISMS
GARGARIZED
GARGARIZES
GARGARIZING
GARGOYLISM
GARGOYLISMS
GARIBALDIS
GARISHNESS
GARISHNESSES
GARLANDAGE
GARLANDAGES
GARLANDING
GARLANDLESS
GARLANDRIES
GARLICKIER
GARLICKIEST
GARLICKING
GARMENTING
GARMENTLESS
GARMENTURE
GARMENTURES
GARNETIFEROUS
GARNIERITE
GARNIERITES
GARNISHEED
GARNISHEEING
GARNISHEEMENT
GARNISHEEMENTS
GARNISHEES
GARNISHERS
GARNISHING
GARNISHINGS
GARNISHMENT
GARNISHMENTS
GARNISHORS
GARNISHRIES
GARNITURES
GAROTTINGS
GARRETEERS
GARRISONED
GARRISONING
GARROTTERS
GARROTTING
GARROTTINGS
GARRULITIES
GARRULOUSLY
GARRULOUSNESS
GARRULOUSNESSES
GARRYOWENS
GASBAGGING
GASCONADED
GASCONADER
GASCONADERS
GASCONADES
GASCONADING
GASCONISMS
GASEOUSNESS
GASEOUSNESSES
GASHLINESS
GASHLINESSES
GASHOLDERS
GASIFIABLE
GASIFICATION
GASIFICATIONS
GASLIGHTED
GASLIGHTING
GASOMETERS
GASOMETRIC
GASOMETRICAL
GASOMETRIES
GASPEREAUS
GASPEREAUX
GASPINESSES
GASSINESSES
GASTEROPOD
GASTEROPODOUS
GASTEROPODS
GASTHAUSER
GASTHAUSES
GASTIGHTNESS
GASTIGHTNESSES
GASTNESSES
GASTRAEUMS
GASTRALGIA
GASTRALGIAS
GASTRALGIC
GASTRECTOMIES
GASTRECTOMY
GASTRITIDES
GASTRITISES
GASTROCNEMII
GASTROCNEMIUS
GASTROCOLIC
GASTRODUODENAL
GASTROENTERIC
GASTROENTERITIC
GASTROENTERITIS
GASTROLITH
GASTROLITHS
GASTROLOGER
GASTROLOGERS
GASTROLOGICAL
GASTROLOGIES
GASTROLOGIST
GASTROLOGISTS
GASTROLOGY
GASTROMANCIES
GASTROMANCY
GASTRONOME
GASTRONOMER
GASTRONOMERS
GASTRONOMES

GASTRONOMIC
GASTRONOMICAL
GASTRONOMICALLY
GASTRONOMICS
GASTRONOMIES
GASTRONOMIST
GASTRONOMISTS
GASTRONOMY
GASTROPODAN
GASTROPODANS
GASTROPODOUS
GASTROPODS
GASTROPORN
GASTROPORNS
GASTROPUBS
GASTROSCOPE
GASTROSCOPES
GASTROSCOPIC
GASTROSCOPIES
GASTROSCOPIST
GASTROSCOPISTS
GASTROSCOPY
GASTROSOPH
GASTROSOPHER
GASTROSOPHERS
GASTROSOPHIES
GASTROSOPHS
GASTROSOPHY
GASTROSTOMIES
GASTROSTOMY
GASTROTOMIES
GASTROTOMY
GASTROTRICH
GASTROTRICHS
GASTROVASCULAR
GASTRULATE
GASTRULATED
GASTRULATES
GASTRULATING
GASTRULATION
GASTRULATIONS
GATECRASHED
GATECRASHER
GATECRASHERS
GATECRASHES
GATECRASHING
GATEHOUSES
GATEKEEPER
GATEKEEPERS
GATEKEEPING
GATEKEEPINGS
GATHERABLE
GATHERINGS
GAUCHENESS
GAUCHENESSES
GAUCHERIES
GAUDEAMUSES
GAUDINESSES
GAUFFERING
GAUFFERINGS
GAULEITERS
GAULTHERIA
GAULTHERIAS
GAUNTLETED
GAUNTLETING
GAUNTNESSES
GAUSSMETER
GAUSSMETERS
GAUZINESSES
GAVELKINDS
GAWKIHOODS
GAWKINESSES
GAWKISHNESS
GAWKISHNESSES
GAYCATIONS
GAZEHOUNDS
GAZETTEERED
GAZETTEERING
GAZETTEERISH
GAZETTEERS
GAZILLIONAIRE
GAZILLIONAIRES
GAZILLIONS
GAZUMPINGS
GAZUNDERED
GAZUNDERER
GAZUNDERERS
GAZUNDERING
GEALOUSIES
GEANTICLINAL
GEANTICLINE
GEANTICLINES
GEARCHANGE
GEARCHANGES
GEARSHIFTS
GEARSTICKS
GEARWHEELS
GEEKINESSES
GEEKSPEAKS
GEFUFFLING
GEGENSCHEIN
GEGENSCHEINS
GEHLENITES
GEITONOGAMIES
GEITONOGAMOUS
GEITONOGAMY
GELANDESPRUNG
GELANDESPRUNGS
GELATINATE
GELATINATED
GELATINATES
GELATINATING
GELATINATION
GELATINATIONS
GELATINISATION
GELATINISATIONS
GELATINISE
GELATINISED
GELATINISER
GELATINISERS
GELATINISES
GELATINISING
GELATINIZATION
GELATINIZATIONS
GELATINIZE
GELATINIZED
GELATINIZER
GELATINIZERS
GELATINIZES
GELATINIZING
GELATINOID
GELATINOIDS
GELATINOUS
GELATINOUSLY
GELATINOUSNESS
GELIDITIES
GELIDNESSES
GELIGNITES
GELLIFLOWRE
GELLIFLOWRES
GELSEMINES
GELSEMININE
GELSEMININES
GELSEMIUMS
GEMEINSCHAFT
GEMEINSCHAFTEN
GEMEINSCHAFTS
GEMFIBROZIL
GEMFIBROZILS
GEMINATELY
GEMINATING
GEMINATION
GEMINATIONS
GEMMACEOUS
GEMMATIONS
GEMMIFEROUS
GEMMINESSES
GEMMIPAROUS
GEMMIPAROUSLY
GEMMOLOGICAL
GEMMOLOGIES
GEMMOLOGIST
GEMMOLOGISTS
GEMMULATION
GEMMULATIONS
GEMOLOGICAL
GEMOLOGIES
GEMOLOGIST
GEMOLOGISTS
GEMUTLICHKEIT
GEMUTLICHKEITS
GENDARMERIE
GENDARMERIES
GENDARMERY
GENDERISED
GENDERISES
GENDERISING
GENDERIZED
GENDERIZES
GENDERIZING
GENDERLESS
GENDERQUEER
GENDERQUEERS
GENEALOGIC
GENEALOGICAL
GENEALOGICALLY
GENEALOGIES
GENEALOGISE
GENEALOGISED
GENEALOGISES
GENEALOGISING
GENEALOGIST
GENEALOGISTS
GENEALOGIZE
GENEALOGIZED
GENEALOGIZES
GENEALOGIZING
GENECOLOGIES
GENECOLOGY
GENERALATE
GENERALATES
GENERALCIES
GENERALISABLE
GENERALISATION
GENERALISATIONS
GENERALISE
GENERALISED
GENERALISER
GENERALISERS
GENERALISES
GENERALISING
GENERALISM
GENERALISMS
GENERALISSIMO
GENERALISSIMOS
GENERALIST
GENERALISTS
GENERALITIES
GENERALITY
GENERALIZABLE
GENERALIZATION
GENERALIZATIONS
GENERALIZE
GENERALIZED
GENERALIZER
GENERALIZERS
GENERALIZES
GENERALIZING
GENERALLED
GENERALLING
GENERALNESS
GENERALNESSES
GENERALSHIP
GENERALSHIPS
GENERATING
GENERATION
GENERATIONAL
GENERATIONALLY
GENERATIONISM
GENERATIONISMS

GENERATIONS
GENERATIVE
GENERATORS
GENERATRICES
GENERATRIX
GENERICALLY
GENERICNESS
GENERICNESSES
GENEROSITIES
GENEROSITY
GENEROUSLY
GENEROUSNESS
GENEROUSNESSES
GENETHLIAC
GENETHLIACAL
GENETHLIACALLY
GENETHLIACON
GENETHLIACONS
GENETHLIACS
GENETHLIALOGIC
GENETHLIALOGIES
GENETHLIALOGY
GENETICALLY
GENETICIST
GENETICISTS
GENETOTROPHIC
GENETRICES
GENETRIXES
GENEVRETTE
GENEVRETTES
GENIALISED
GENIALISES
GENIALISING
GENIALITIES
GENIALIZED
GENIALIZES
GENIALIZING
GENIALNESS
GENIALNESSES
GENICULATE
GENICULATED
GENICULATELY
GENICULATES
GENICULATING
GENICULATION
GENICULATIONS
GENISTEINS
GENITALIAL
GENITIVALLY
GENITIVELY
GENITOURINARY
GENITRICES
GENITRIXES
GENLOCKING
GENLOCKINGS
GENOCIDAIRE
GENOCIDAIRES
GENOPHOBIA
GENOPHOBIAS
GENOTYPICAL
GENOTYPICALLY
GENOTYPICITIES
GENOTYPICITY
GENOTYPING
GENOUILLERE
GENOUILLERES
GENSDARMES
GENTAMICIN
GENTAMICINS
GENTEELEST
GENTEELISE
GENTEELISED
GENTEELISES
GENTEELISH
GENTEELISING
GENTEELISM
GENTEELISMS
GENTEELIZE
GENTEELIZED
GENTEELIZES
GENTEELIZING
GENTEELNESS
GENTEELNESSES
GENTIANACEOUS
GENTIANELLA
GENTIANELLAS
GENTILESSE
GENTILESSES
GENTILHOMME
GENTILISED
GENTILISES
GENTILISING
GENTILISMS
GENTILITIAL
GENTILITIAN
GENTILITIES
GENTILITIOUS
GENTILIZED
GENTILIZES
GENTILIZING
GENTILSHOMMES
GENTLEFOLK
GENTLEFOLKS
GENTLEHOOD
GENTLEHOODS
GENTLEMANHOOD
GENTLEMANHOODS
GENTLEMANLIER
GENTLEMANLIEST
GENTLEMANLIKE
GENTLEMANLINESS
GENTLEMANLY
GENTLEMANSHIP
GENTLEMANSHIPS
GENTLENESS
GENTLENESSE
GENTLENESSES
GENTLEPERSON
GENTLEPERSONS
GENTLEWOMAN
GENTLEWOMANLIER
GENTLEWOMANLY
GENTLEWOMEN
GENTRIFICATION
GENTRIFICATIONS
GENTRIFIED
GENTRIFIER
GENTRIFIERS
GENTRIFIES
GENTRIFYING
GENUFLECTED
GENUFLECTING
GENUFLECTION
GENUFLECTIONS
GENUFLECTOR
GENUFLECTORS
GENUFLECTS
GENUFLEXION
GENUFLEXIONS
GENUINENESS
GENUINENESSES
GEOBOTANIC
GEOBOTANICAL
GEOBOTANIES
GEOBOTANIST
GEOBOTANISTS
GEOCACHERS
GEOCACHING
GEOCACHINGS
GEOCARPIES
GEOCENTRIC
GEOCENTRICAL
GEOCENTRICALLY
GEOCENTRICISM
GEOCENTRICISMS
GEOCHEMICAL
GEOCHEMICALLY
GEOCHEMIST
GEOCHEMISTRIES
GEOCHEMISTRY
GEOCHEMISTS
GEOCHRONOLOGIC
GEOCHRONOLOGIES
GEOCHRONOLOGIST
GEOCHRONOLOGY
GEOCORONAE
GEOCORONAS
GEODEMOGRAPHICS
GEODESICAL
GEODESISTS
GEODETICAL
GEODETICALLY
GEODYNAMIC
GEODYNAMICAL
GEODYNAMICIST
GEODYNAMICISTS
GEODYNAMICS
GEOENGINEERING
GEOENGINEERINGS
GEOGNOSIES
GEOGNOSTIC
GEOGNOSTICAL
GEOGNOSTICALLY
GEOGRAPHER
GEOGRAPHERS
GEOGRAPHIC
GEOGRAPHICAL
GEOGRAPHICALLY
GEOGRAPHIES
GEOHYDROLOGIC
GEOHYDROLOGIES
GEOHYDROLOGIST
GEOHYDROLOGISTS
GEOHYDROLOGY
GEOLATRIES
GEOLINGUISTICS
GEOLOCATION
GEOLOCATIONS
GEOLOGIANS
GEOLOGICAL
GEOLOGICALLY
GEOLOGISED
GEOLOGISES
GEOLOGISING
GEOLOGISTS
GEOLOGIZED
GEOLOGIZES
GEOLOGIZING
GEOMAGNETIC
GEOMAGNETICALLY
GEOMAGNETISM
GEOMAGNETISMS
GEOMAGNETIST
GEOMAGNETISTS
GEOMANCERS
GEOMANCIES
GEOMECHANICS
GEOMEDICAL
GEOMEDICINE
GEOMEDICINES
GEOMETRICAL
GEOMETRICALLY
GEOMETRICIAN
GEOMETRICIANS
GEOMETRICS
GEOMETRIDS
GEOMETRIES
GEOMETRISATION
GEOMETRISATIONS
GEOMETRISE
GEOMETRISED
GEOMETRISES
GEOMETRISING
GEOMETRIST
GEOMETRISTS
GEOMETRIZATION
GEOMETRIZATIONS
GEOMETRIZE
GEOMETRIZED
GEOMETRIZES

GEOMETRIZING
GEOMORPHIC
GEOMORPHOGENIC
GEOMORPHOGENIES
GEOMORPHOGENIST
GEOMORPHOGENY
GEOMORPHOLOGIC
GEOMORPHOLOGIES
GEOMORPHOLOGIST
GEOMORPHOLOGY
GEOPHAGIAS
GEOPHAGIES
GEOPHAGISM
GEOPHAGISMS
GEOPHAGIST
GEOPHAGISTS
GEOPHAGOUS
GEOPHILOUS
GEOPHYSICAL
GEOPHYSICALLY
GEOPHYSICIST
GEOPHYSICISTS
GEOPHYSICS
GEOPOLITICAL
GEOPOLITICALLY
GEOPOLITICIAN
GEOPOLITICIANS
GEOPOLITICS
GEOPONICAL
GEOPRESSURED
GEORGETTES
GEOSCIENCE
GEOSCIENCES
GEOSCIENTIFIC
GEOSCIENTIST
GEOSCIENTISTS
GEOSPATIAL
GEOSPHERES
GEOSTATICS
GEOSTATIONARY
GEOSTRATEGIC
GEOSTRATEGICAL
GEOSTRATEGIES
GEOSTRATEGIST
GEOSTRATEGISTS
GEOSTRATEGY
GEOSTROPHIC
GEOSTROPHICALLY
GEOSYNCHRONOUS
GEOSYNCLINAL
GEOSYNCLINE
GEOSYNCLINES
GEOTACTICAL
GEOTACTICALLY
GEOTAGGING
GEOTECHNIC
GEOTECHNICAL
GEOTECHNICS
GEOTECHNOLOGIES
GEOTECHNOLOGY
GEOTECTONIC
GEOTECTONICALLY
GEOTECTONICS
GEOTEXTILE
GEOTEXTILES
GEOTHERMAL
GEOTHERMALLY
GEOTHERMIC
GEOTHERMOMETER
GEOTHERMOMETERS
GEOTROPICALLY
GEOTROPISM
GEOTROPISMS
GERANIACEOUS
GERATOLOGICAL
GERATOLOGIES
GERATOLOGIST
GERATOLOGISTS
GERATOLOGY
GERFALCONS
GERIATRICIAN
GERIATRICIANS
GERIATRICS
GERIATRIST
GERIATRISTS
GERMANDERS
GERMANENESS
GERMANENESSES
GERMANISATION
GERMANISATIONS
GERMANISED
GERMANISES
GERMANISING
GERMANITES
GERMANIUMS
GERMANIZATION
GERMANIZATIONS
GERMANIZED
GERMANIZES
GERMANIZING
GERMICIDAL
GERMICIDES
GERMINABILITIES
GERMINABILITY
GERMINABLE
GERMINALLY
GERMINATED
GERMINATES
GERMINATING
GERMINATION
GERMINATIONS
GERMINATIVE
GERMINATOR
GERMINATORS
GERMINESSES
GERMPLASMS
GERONTOCRACIES
GERONTOCRACY
GERONTOCRAT
GERONTOCRATIC
GERONTOCRATS
GERONTOLOGIC
GERONTOLOGICAL
GERONTOLOGIES
GERONTOLOGIST
GERONTOLOGISTS
GERONTOLOGY
GERONTOMORPHIC
GERONTOPHIL
GERONTOPHILE
GERONTOPHILES
GERONTOPHILIA
GERONTOPHILIAS
GERONTOPHILS
GERONTOPHOBE
GERONTOPHOBES
GERONTOPHOBIA
GERONTOPHOBIAS
GERRYMANDER
GERRYMANDERED
GERRYMANDERER
GERRYMANDERERS
GERRYMANDERING
GERRYMANDERINGS
GERRYMANDERS
GERUNDIVAL
GERUNDIVELY
GERUNDIVES
GESELLSCHAFT
GESELLSCHAFTEN
GESELLSCHAFTS
GESNERIADS
GESSAMINES
GESTALTISM
GESTALTISMS
GESTALTIST
GESTALTISTS
GESTATIONAL
GESTATIONS
GESTATORIAL
GESTICULANT
GESTICULATE
GESTICULATED
GESTICULATES
GESTICULATING
GESTICULATION
GESTICULATIONS
GESTICULATIVE
GESTICULATOR
GESTICULATORS
GESTICULATORY
GESTURALLY
GESUNDHEIT
GETTERINGS
GEWURZTRAMINER
GEWURZTRAMINERS
GEYSERITES
GHASTFULLY
GHASTLIEST
GHASTLINESS
GHASTLINESSES
GHASTNESSES
GHETTOISATION
GHETTOISATIONS
GHETTOISED
GHETTOISES
GHETTOISING
GHETTOIZATION
GHETTOIZATIONS
GHETTOIZED
GHETTOIZES
GHETTOIZING
GHOSTLIEST
GHOSTLINESS
GHOSTLINESSES
GHOSTWRITE
GHOSTWRITER
GHOSTWRITERS
GHOSTWRITES
GHOSTWRITING
GHOSTWRITTEN
GHOSTWROTE
GHOULISHLY
GHOULISHNESS
GHOULISHNESSES
GIANTESSES
GIANTHOODS
GIANTLIEST
GIANTSHIPS
GIARDIASES
GIARDIASIS
GIBBERELLIC
GIBBERELLIN
GIBBERELLINS
GIBBERINGS
GIBBERISHES
GIBBETTING
GIBBOSITIES
GIBBOUSNESS
GIBBOUSNESSES
GIDDINESSES
GIFTEDNESS
GIFTEDNESSES
GIFTWRAPPED
GIFTWRAPPING
GIFTWRAPPINGS
GIGACYCLES
GIGAHERTZES
GIGANTESQUE
GIGANTICALLY
GIGANTICIDE
GIGANTICIDES
GIGANTICNESS
GIGANTICNESSES
GIGANTISMS
GIGANTOLOGIES
GIGANTOLOGY
GIGANTOMACHIA
GIGANTOMACHIAS
GIGANTOMACHIES

GIGANTOMACHY
GIGGLESOME
GIGGLINGLY
GIGMANITIES
GILDSWOMAN
GILDSWOMEN
GILLFLIRTS
GILLIFLOWER
GILLIFLOWERS
GILLNETTED
GILLNETTER
GILLNETTERS
GILLNETTING
GILLRAVAGE
GILLRAVAGED
GILLRAVAGES
GILLRAVAGING
GILLRAVITCH
GILLRAVITCHED
GILLRAVITCHES
GILLRAVITCHING
GILLYFLOWER
GILLYFLOWERS
GILRAVAGED
GILRAVAGER
GILRAVAGERS
GILRAVAGES
GILRAVAGING
GILRAVITCH
GILRAVITCHED
GILRAVITCHES
GILRAVITCHING
GILSONITES
GIMBALLING
GIMCRACKERIES
GIMCRACKERY
GIMMICKIER
GIMMICKIEST
GIMMICKING
GIMMICKRIES
GINGELLIES
GINGERADES
GINGERBREAD
GINGERBREADED
GINGERBREADIER
GINGERBREADIEST
GINGERBREADS
GINGERBREADY
GINGERIEST
GINGERLIER
GINGERLIEST
GINGERLINESS
GINGERLINESSES
GINGERROOT
GINGERROOTS
GINGERSNAP
GINGERSNAPS
GINGIVECTOMIES
GINGIVECTOMY
GINGIVITIS
GINGIVITISES
GINGLIMOID
GIPSYHOODS
GIPSYWORTS
GIRANDOLAS
GIRANDOLES
GIRDLECAKE
GIRDLECAKES
GIRDLESCONE
GIRDLESCONES
GIRDLESTEAD
GIRDLESTEADS
GIRLFRIEND
GIRLFRIENDS
GIRLISHNESS
GIRLISHNESSES
GIRTHLINES
GISMOLOGIES
GITTARONES
GITTERNING
GIVENNESSES
GIZMOLOGIES
GLABRESCENT
GLABROUSNESS
GLABROUSNESSES
GLACIALIST
GLACIALISTS
GLACIATING
GLACIATION
GLACIATIONS
GLACIOLOGIC
GLACIOLOGICAL
GLACIOLOGIES
GLACIOLOGIST
GLACIOLOGISTS
GLACIOLOGY
GLADDENERS
GLADDENING
GLADFULNESS
GLADFULNESSES
GLADIATORIAL
GLADIATORIAN
GLADIATORS
GLADIATORSHIP
GLADIATORSHIPS
GLADIATORY
GLADIOLUSES
GLADNESSES
GLADSOMELY
GLADSOMENESS
GLADSOMENESSES
GLADSOMEST
GLADSTONES
GLADWRAPPED
GLADWRAPPING
GLAIKETNESS
GLAIKETNESSES
GLAIKITNESS
GLAIKITNESSES
GLAIRINESS
GLAIRINESSES
GLAMORISATION
GLAMORISATIONS
GLAMORISED
GLAMORISER
GLAMORISERS
GLAMORISES
GLAMORISING
GLAMORIZATION
GLAMORIZATIONS
GLAMORIZED
GLAMORIZER
GLAMORIZERS
GLAMORIZES
GLAMORIZING
GLAMOROUSLY
GLAMOROUSNESS
GLAMOROUSNESSES
GLAMOURING
GLAMOURISE
GLAMOURISED
GLAMOURISES
GLAMOURISING
GLAMOURIZE
GLAMOURIZED
GLAMOURIZES
GLAMOURIZING
GLAMOURLESS
GLAMOUROUS
GLAMOUROUSLY
GLAMOUROUSNESS
GLAMOURPUSS
GLAMOURPUSSES
GLANCINGLY
GLANDEROUS
GLANDIFEROUS
GLANDIFORM
GLANDULARLY
GLANDULIFEROUS
GLANDULOUS
GLANDULOUSLY
GLARINESSES
GLARINGNESS
GLARINGNESSES
GLASNOSTIAN
GLASNOSTIC
GLASSBLOWER
GLASSBLOWERS
GLASSBLOWING
GLASSBLOWINGS
GLASSCLOTH
GLASSCLOTHS
GLASSCUTTER
GLASSCUTTERS
GLASSHOUSE
GLASSHOUSES
GLASSIFIED
GLASSIFIES
GLASSIFYING
GLASSINESS
GLASSINESSES
GLASSMAKER
GLASSMAKERS
GLASSMAKING
GLASSMAKINGS
GLASSPAPER
GLASSPAPERED
GLASSPAPERING
GLASSPAPERS
GLASSWARES
GLASSWORKER
GLASSWORKERS
GLASSWORKS
GLASSWORMS
GLASSWORTS
GLASSYHEADED
GLAUBERITE
GLAUBERITES
GLAUCESCENCE
GLAUCESCENCES
GLAUCESCENT
GLAUCOMATOUS
GLAUCONITE
GLAUCONITES
GLAUCONITIC
GLAUCOUSLY
GLAUCOUSNESS
GLAUCOUSNESSES
GLAZIERIES
GLAZINESSES
GLEAMINGLY
GLEEFULNESS
GLEEFULNESSES
GLEEMAIDEN
GLEEMAIDENS
GLEGNESSES
GLEISATION
GLEISATIONS
GLEIZATION
GLEIZATIONS
GLENDOVEER
GLENDOVEERS
GLENGARRIES
GLIBNESSES
GLIDEPATHS
GLIMMERIER
GLIMMERIEST
GLIMMERING
GLIMMERINGLY
GLIMMERINGS
GLIOBLASTOMA
GLIOBLASTOMAS
GLIOBLASTOMATA
GLIOMATOSES
GLIOMATOSIS
GLIOMATOUS
GLISSADERS
GLISSADING
GLISSANDOS
GLISTENING

G

GLISTENINGLY
GLISTERING
GLISTERINGLY
GLITCHIEST
GLITTERAND
GLITTERATI
GLITTERIER
GLITTERIEST
GLITTERING
GLITTERINGLY
GLITTERINGS
GLITZINESS
GLITZINESSES
GLOATINGLY
GLOBALISATION
GLOBALISATIONS
GLOBALISED
GLOBALISES
GLOBALISING
GLOBALISMS
GLOBALISTS
GLOBALIZATION
GLOBALIZATIONS
GLOBALIZED
GLOBALIZES
GLOBALIZING
GLOBEFISHES
GLOBEFLOWER
GLOBEFLOWERS
GLOBESITIES
GLOBETROTS
GLOBETROTTED
GLOBETROTTER
GLOBETROTTERS
GLOBETROTTING
GLOBETROTTINGS
GLOBIGERINA
GLOBIGERINAE
GLOBIGERINAS
GLOBOSENESS
GLOBOSENESSES
GLOBOSITIES
GLOBULARITIES
GLOBULARITY
GLOBULARLY
GLOBULARNESS
GLOBULARNESSES
GLOBULIFEROUS
GLOBULITES
GLOCHIDIATE
GLOCHIDIUM
GLOCKENSPIEL
GLOCKENSPIELS
GLOMERATED
GLOMERATES
GLOMERATING
GLOMERATION
GLOMERATIONS
GLOMERULAR
GLOMERULATE
GLOMERULES
GLOMERULUS
GLOOMFULLY
GLOOMINESS
GLOOMINESSES
GLOOMSTERS
GLORIFIABLE
GLORIFICATION
GLORIFICATIONS
GLORIFIERS
GLORIFYING
GLORIOUSLY
GLORIOUSNESS
GLORIOUSNESSES
GLOSSARIAL
GLOSSARIALLY
GLOSSARIES
GLOSSARIST
GLOSSARISTS
GLOSSATORS
GLOSSECTOMIES
GLOSSECTOMY
GLOSSEMATICS
GLOSSINESS
GLOSSINESSES
GLOSSINGLY
GLOSSITISES
GLOSSODYNIA
GLOSSODYNIAS
GLOSSOGRAPHER
GLOSSOGRAPHERS
GLOSSOGRAPHICAL
GLOSSOGRAPHIES
GLOSSOGRAPHY
GLOSSOLALIA
GLOSSOLALIAS
GLOSSOLALIST
GLOSSOLALISTS
GLOSSOLARYNGEAL
GLOSSOLOGICAL
GLOSSOLOGIES
GLOSSOLOGIST
GLOSSOLOGISTS
GLOSSOLOGY
GLOTTIDEAN
GLOTTOGONIC
GLOTTOLOGIES
GLOTTOLOGY
GLOVEBOXES
GLOWERINGLY
GLOWSTICKS
GLUCINIUMS
GLUCOCORTICOID
GLUCOCORTICOIDS
GLUCOKINASE
GLUCOKINASES
GLUCONATES
GLUCONEOGENESES
GLUCONEOGENESIS
GLUCONEOGENIC
GLUCOPHORE
GLUCOPHORES
GLUCOPROTEIN
GLUCOPROTEINS
GLUCOSAMINE
GLUCOSAMINES
GLUCOSIDAL
GLUCOSIDASE
GLUCOSIDASES
GLUCOSIDES
GLUCOSIDIC
GLUCOSURIA
GLUCOSURIAS
GLUCOSURIC
GLUCURONIC
GLUCURONIDASE
GLUCURONIDASES
GLUCURONIDE
GLUCURONIDES
GLUEYNESSES
GLUINESSES
GLUMACEOUS
GLUMIFEROUS
GLUMNESSES
GLUTAMATES
GLUTAMINASE
GLUTAMINASES
GLUTAMINES
GLUTAMINIC
GLUTARALDEHYDE
GLUTARALDEHYDES
GLUTATHIONE
GLUTATHIONES
GLUTETHIMIDE
GLUTETHIMIDES
GLUTINOSITIES
GLUTINOSITY
GLUTINOUSLY
GLUTINOUSNESS
GLUTINOUSNESSES
GLUTTINGLY
GLUTTONIES
GLUTTONISE
GLUTTONISED
GLUTTONISES
GLUTTONISH
GLUTTONISING
GLUTTONIZE
GLUTTONIZED
GLUTTONIZES
GLUTTONIZING
GLUTTONOUS
GLUTTONOUSLY
GLUTTONOUSNESS
GLYCAEMIAS
GLYCATIONS
GLYCERALDEHYDE
GLYCERALDEHYDES
GLYCERIDES
GLYCERIDIC
GLYCERINATE
GLYCERINATED
GLYCERINATES
GLYCERINATING
GLYCERINES
GLYCOCOLLS
GLYCOGENESES
GLYCOGENESIS
GLYCOGENETIC
GLYCOGENIC
GLYCOGENOLYSES
GLYCOGENOLYSIS
GLYCOGENOLYTIC
GLYCOLIPID
GLYCOLIPIDS
GLYCOLYSES
GLYCOLYSIS
GLYCOLYTIC
GLYCONEOGENESES
GLYCONEOGENESIS
GLYCOPEPTIDE
GLYCOPEPTIDES
GLYCOPHYTE
GLYCOPHYTES
GLYCOPHYTIC
GLYCOPROTEIN
GLYCOPROTEINS
GLYCOSIDASE
GLYCOSIDASES
GLYCOSIDES
GLYCOSIDIC
GLYCOSIDICALLY
GLYCOSURIA
GLYCOSURIAS
GLYCOSURIC
GLYCOSYLATE
GLYCOSYLATED
GLYCOSYLATES
GLYCOSYLATING
GLYCOSYLATION
GLYCOSYLATIONS
GLYOXALINE
GLYOXALINES
GLYPHOGRAPH
GLYPHOGRAPHER
GLYPHOGRAPHERS
GLYPHOGRAPHIC
GLYPHOGRAPHICAL
GLYPHOGRAPHIES
GLYPHOGRAPHS
GLYPHOGRAPHY
GLYPHOSATE
GLYPHOSATES
GLYPTODONT
GLYPTODONTS
GLYPTOGRAPHER
GLYPTOGRAPHERS
GLYPTOGRAPHIC
GLYPTOGRAPHICAL
GLYPTOGRAPHIES

GLYPTOGRAPHY
GLYPTOTHECA
GLYPTOTHECAE
GMELINITES
GNAPHALIUM
GNAPHALIUMS
GNASHINGLY
GNATCATCHER
GNATCATCHERS
GNATHONICAL
GNATHONICALLY
GNATHOSTOMATOUS
GNATHOSTOME
GNATHOSTOMES
GNEISSITIC
GNETOPHYTE
GNETOPHYTES
GNOMICALLY
GNOMONICAL
GNOMONICALLY
GNOMONOLOGIES
GNOMONOLOGY
GNOSEOLOGIES
GNOSEOLOGY
GNOSIOLOGIES
GNOSIOLOGY
GNOSTICALLY
GNOSTICISM
GNOSTICISMS
GNOTOBIOLOGICAL
GNOTOBIOLOGIES
GNOTOBIOLOGY
GNOTOBIOSES
GNOTOBIOSIS
GNOTOBIOTE
GNOTOBIOTES
GNOTOBIOTIC
GNOTOBIOTICALLY
GNOTOBIOTICS
GOALKEEPER
GOALKEEPERS
GOALKEEPING
GOALKEEPINGS
GOALKICKER
GOALKICKERS
GOALKICKING
GOALKICKINGS
GOALMOUTHS
GOALSCORER
GOALSCORERS
GOALTENDER
GOALTENDERS
GOALTENDING
GOALTENDINGS
GOATFISHES
GOATISHNESS
GOATISHNESSES
GOATSBEARD
GOATSBEARDS
GOATSUCKER
GOATSUCKERS
GOBBELINES
GOBBLEDEGOOK
GOBBLEDEGOOKS
GOBBLEDYGOOK
GOBBLEDYGOOKS
GOBSMACKED
GOBSTOPPER
GOBSTOPPERS
GOCHUJANGS
GODAMMNDEST
GODCHILDREN
GODDAMMING
GODDAMNDEST
GODDAMNEDEST
GODDAMNING
GODDAUGHTER
GODDAUGHTERS
GODDESSHOOD
GODDESSHOODS
GODFATHERED
GODFATHERING
GODFATHERS
GODFORSAKEN
GODLESSNESS
GODLESSNESSES
GODLIKENESS
GODLIKENESSES
GODLINESSES
GODMOTHERED
GODMOTHERING
GODMOTHERS
GODPARENTS
GODROONING
GODROONINGS
GOFFERINGS
GOGGLEBOXES
GOITROGENIC
GOITROGENICITY
GOITROGENS
GOLDARNING
GOLDBEATER
GOLDBEATERS
GOLDBRICKED
GOLDBRICKING
GOLDBRICKS
GOLDCRESTS
GOLDENBERRIES
GOLDENBERRY
GOLDENEYES
GOLDENNESS
GOLDENNESSES
GOLDENRODS
GOLDENSEAL
GOLDENSEALS
GOLDFIELDS
GOLDFINCHES
GOLDFINNIES
GOLDFISHES
GOLDILOCKS
GOLDILOCKSES
GOLDMINERS
GOLDSINNIES
GOLDSMITHERIES
GOLDSMITHERY
GOLDSMITHRIES
GOLDSMITHRY
GOLDSMITHS
GOLDSPINKS
GOLDSTICKS
GOLDSTONES
GOLDTHREAD
GOLDTHREADS
GOLIARDERIES
GOLIARDERY
GOLIARDIES
GOLIATHISE
GOLIATHISED
GOLIATHISES
GOLIATHISING
GOLIATHIZE
GOLIATHIZED
GOLIATHIZES
GOLIATHIZING
GOLOMYNKAS
GOLOPTIOUS
GOLUPTIOUS
GOMBEENISM
GOMBEENISMS
GONADECTOMIES
GONADECTOMISED
GONADECTOMIZED
GONADECTOMY
GONADOTROPHIC
GONADOTROPHIN
GONADOTROPHINS
GONADOTROPIC
GONADOTROPIN
GONADOTROPINS
GONDOLIERS
GONENESSES
GONFALONIER
GONFALONIERS
GONGORISTIC
GONIATITES
GONIATITOID
GONIATITOIDS
GONIMOBLAST
GONIMOBLASTS
GONIOMETER
GONIOMETERS
GONIOMETRIC
GONIOMETRICAL
GONIOMETRICALLY
GONIOMETRIES
GONIOMETRY
GONIOSCOPE
GONIOSCOPES
GONOCOCCAL
GONOCOCCIC
GONOCOCCOID
GONOCOCCUS
GONOPHORES
GONOPHORIC
GONOPHOROUS
GONORRHEAL
GONORRHEAS
GONORRHEIC
GONORRHOEA
GONORRHOEAL
GONORRHOEAS
GONORRHOEIC
GOODFELLAS
GOODFELLOW
GOODFELLOWS
GOODFELLOWSHIP
GOODFELLOWSHIPS
GOODINESSES
GOODLIHEAD
GOODLIHEADS
GOODLINESS
GOODLINESSES
GOODLYHEAD
GOODLYHEADS
GOODNESSES
GOODNIGHTS
GOODWILLED
GOOEYNESSES
GOOFINESSES
GOOGLEWHACK
GOOGLEWHACKS
GOOGOLPLEX
GOOGOLPLEXES
GOOINESSES
GOONEYBIRD
GOONEYBIRDS
GOOPINESSES
GOOSANDERS
GOOSEBERRIES
GOOSEBERRY
GOOSEFISHES
GOOSEFLESH
GOOSEFLESHES
GOOSEFOOTS
GOOSEGRASS
GOOSEGRASSES
GOOSEHERDS
GOOSENECKED
GOOSENECKS
GOOSINESSES
GOPHERWOOD
GOPHERWOODS
GORBELLIES
GORBLIMEYS
GORBLIMIES
GOREHOUNDS
GORGEOUSLY
GORGEOUSNESS
GORGEOUSNESSES
GORGONEION

G

GORGONIANS
GORGONISED
GORGONISES
GORGONISING
GORGONIZED
GORGONIZES
GORGONIZING
GORILLAGRAM
GORILLAGRAMS
GORINESSES
GORMANDISE
GORMANDISED
GORMANDISER
GORMANDISERS
GORMANDISES
GORMANDISING
GORMANDISINGS
GORMANDISM
GORMANDISMS
GORMANDIZE
GORMANDIZED
GORMANDIZER
GORMANDIZERS
GORMANDIZES
GORMANDIZING
GORMANDIZINGS
GOSLARITES
GOSPELISED
GOSPELISES
GOSPELISING
GOSPELIZED
GOSPELIZES
GOSPELIZING
GOSPELLERS
GOSPELLIER
GOSPELLIEST
GOSPELLING
GOSPELLINGS
GOSPELLISE
GOSPELLISED
GOSPELLISES
GOSPELLISING
GOSPELLIZE
GOSPELLIZED
GOSPELLIZES
GOSPELLIZING
GOSSAMERIER
GOSSAMERIEST
GOSSIPIEST
GOSSIPINGLY
GOSSIPINGS
GOSSIPMONGER
GOSSIPMONGERS
GOSSIPPERS
GOSSIPPING
GOSSIPRIES
GOTHICALLY
GOTHICISED
GOTHICISES
GOTHICISING
GOTHICISMS
GOTHICIZED
GOTHICIZES
GOTHICIZING
GOURDINESS
GOURDINESSES
GOURMANDISE
GOURMANDISED
GOURMANDISES
GOURMANDISING
GOURMANDISM
GOURMANDISMS
GOURMANDIZE
GOURMANDIZED
GOURMANDIZES
GOURMANDIZING
GOUTINESSES
GOUVERNANTE
GOUVERNANTES
GOVERNABILITIES
GOVERNABILITY
GOVERNABLE
GOVERNABLENESS
GOVERNALLS
GOVERNANCE
GOVERNANCES
GOVERNANTE
GOVERNANTES
GOVERNESSED
GOVERNESSES
GOVERNESSIER
GOVERNESSIEST
GOVERNESSING
GOVERNESSY
GOVERNMENT
GOVERNMENTAL
GOVERNMENTALISE
GOVERNMENTALISM
GOVERNMENTALIST
GOVERNMENTALIZE
GOVERNMENTALLY
GOVERNMENTESE
GOVERNMENTESES
GOVERNMENTS
GOVERNORATE
GOVERNORATES
GOVERNORSHIP
GOVERNORSHIPS
GOWDSPINKS
GOWPENFULS
GRACEFULLER
GRACEFULLEST
GRACEFULLY
GRACEFULNESS
GRACEFULNESSES
GRACELESSLY
GRACELESSNESS
GRACELESSNESSES
GRACILENESS
GRACILENESSES
GRACILITIES
GRACIOSITIES
GRACIOSITY
GRACIOUSLY
GRACIOUSNESS
GRACIOUSNESSES
GRADABILITIES
GRADABILITY
GRADABLENESS
GRADABLENESSES
GRADATIONAL
GRADATIONALLY
GRADATIONED
GRADATIONS
GRADATORIES
GRADDANING
GRADELIEST
GRADIENTER
GRADIENTERS
GRADIOMETER
GRADIOMETERS
GRADUALISM
GRADUALISMS
GRADUALIST
GRADUALISTIC
GRADUALISTS
GRADUALITIES
GRADUALITY
GRADUALNESS
GRADUALNESSES
GRADUATESHIP
GRADUATESHIPS
GRADUATING
GRADUATION
GRADUATIONS
GRADUATORS
GRAECISING
GRAECIZING
GRAFFITIED
GRAFFITIING
GRAFFITING
GRAFFITIST
GRAFFITISTS
GRAINFIELD
GRAINFIELDS
GRAININESS
GRAININESSES
GRALLATORIAL
GRALLOCHED
GRALLOCHING
GRAMERCIES
GRAMICIDIN
GRAMICIDINS
GRAMINACEOUS
GRAMINEOUS
GRAMINICOLOUS
GRAMINIVOROUS
GRAMINOLOGIES
GRAMINOLOGY
GRAMMALOGUE
GRAMMALOGUES
GRAMMARIAN
GRAMMARIANS
GRAMMARLESS
GRAMMATICAL
GRAMMATICALITY
GRAMMATICALLY
GRAMMATICALNESS
GRAMMATICASTER
GRAMMATICASTERS
GRAMMATICISE
GRAMMATICISED
GRAMMATICISES
GRAMMATICISING
GRAMMATICISM
GRAMMATICISMS
GRAMMATICIZE
GRAMMATICIZED
GRAMMATICIZES
GRAMMATICIZING
GRAMMATIST
GRAMMATISTS
GRAMMATOLOGIES
GRAMMATOLOGIST
GRAMMATOLOGISTS
GRAMMATOLOGY
GRAMOPHONE
GRAMOPHONES
GRAMOPHONIC
GRAMOPHONICALLY
GRAMOPHONIES
GRAMOPHONIST
GRAMOPHONISTS
GRAMOPHONY
GRANADILLA
GRANADILLAS
GRANDADDIES
GRANDAUNTS
GRANDBABIES
GRANDCHILD
GRANDCHILDREN
GRANDDADDIES
GRANDDADDY
GRANDDAUGHTER
GRANDDAUGHTERS
GRANDEESHIP
GRANDEESHIPS
GRANDFATHER
GRANDFATHERED
GRANDFATHERING
GRANDFATHERLIER
GRANDFATHERLY
GRANDFATHERS
GRANDIFLORA
GRANDIFLORAS
GRANDILOQUENCE
GRANDILOQUENCES
GRANDILOQUENT
GRANDILOQUENTLY
GRANDILOQUOUS

G

GRANDIOSELY
GRANDIOSENESS
GRANDIOSENESSES
GRANDIOSITIES
GRANDIOSITY
GRANDMAMAS
GRANDMAMMA
GRANDMAMMAS
GRANDMASTER
GRANDMASTERS
GRANDMOTHER
GRANDMOTHERLIER
GRANDMOTHERLY
GRANDMOTHERS
GRANDNEPHEW
GRANDNEPHEWS
GRANDNESSES
GRANDNIECE
GRANDNIECES
GRANDPAPAS
GRANDPARENT
GRANDPARENTAL
GRANDPARENTHOOD
GRANDPARENTS
GRANDSIRES
GRANDSTAND
GRANDSTANDED
GRANDSTANDER
GRANDSTANDERS
GRANDSTANDING
GRANDSTANDINGS
GRANDSTANDS
GRANDSTOOD
GRANDUNCLE
GRANDUNCLES
GRANGERISATION
GRANGERISATIONS
GRANGERISE
GRANGERISED
GRANGERISER
GRANGERISERS
GRANGERISES
GRANGERISING
GRANGERISM
GRANGERISMS
GRANGERIZATION
GRANGERIZATIONS
GRANGERIZE
GRANGERIZED
GRANGERIZER
GRANGERIZERS
GRANGERIZES
GRANGERIZING
GRANITELIKE
GRANITEWARE
GRANITEWARES
GRANITIFICATION
GRANITIFORM
GRANITISATION
GRANITISATIONS
GRANITISED
GRANITISES
GRANITISING
GRANITITES
GRANITIZATION
GRANITIZATIONS
GRANITIZED
GRANITIZES
GRANITIZING
GRANITOIDS
GRANIVORES
GRANIVOROUS
GRANNIEING
GRANODIORITE
GRANODIORITES
GRANODIORITIC
GRANOLITHIC
GRANOLITHICS
GRANOLITHS
GRANOPHYRE
GRANOPHYRES
GRANOPHYRIC
GRANTSMANSHIP
GRANTSMANSHIPS
GRANULARITIES
GRANULARITY
GRANULARLY
GRANULATED
GRANULATER
GRANULATERS
GRANULATES
GRANULATING
GRANULATION
GRANULATIONS
GRANULATIVE
GRANULATOR
GRANULATORS
GRANULIFEROUS
GRANULIFORM
GRANULITES
GRANULITIC
GRANULITISATION
GRANULITIZATION
GRANULOCYTE
GRANULOCYTES
GRANULOCYTIC
GRANULOMAS
GRANULOMATA
GRANULOMATOUS
GRANULOSES
GRANULOSIS
GRAPEFRUIT
GRAPEFRUITS
GRAPELOUSE
GRAPESEEDS
GRAPESHOTS
GRAPESTONE
GRAPESTONES
GRAPETREES
GRAPEVINES
GRAPHEMICALLY
GRAPHEMICS
GRAPHICACIES
GRAPHICACY
GRAPHICALLY
GRAPHICALNESS
GRAPHICALNESSES
GRAPHICNESS
GRAPHICNESSES
GRAPHITISABLE
GRAPHITISATION
GRAPHITISATIONS
GRAPHITISE
GRAPHITISED
GRAPHITISES
GRAPHITISING
GRAPHITIZABLE
GRAPHITIZATION
GRAPHITIZATIONS
GRAPHITIZE
GRAPHITIZED
GRAPHITIZES
GRAPHITIZING
GRAPHITOID
GRAPHOLECT
GRAPHOLECTS
GRAPHOLOGIC
GRAPHOLOGICAL
GRAPHOLOGIES
GRAPHOLOGIST
GRAPHOLOGISTS
GRAPHOLOGY
GRAPHOMANIA
GRAPHOMANIAS
GRAPHOMOTOR
GRAPHOPHOBIA
GRAPHOPHOBIAS
GRAPINESSES
GRAPLEMENT
GRAPLEMENTS
GRAPPLINGS
GRAPTOLITE
GRAPTOLITES
GRAPTOLITIC
GRASPINGLY
GRASPINGNESS
GRASPINGNESSES
GRASSBIRDS
GRASSFINCH
GRASSFINCHES
GRASSHOOKS
GRASSHOPPER
GRASSHOPPERS
GRASSINESS
GRASSINESSES
GRASSLANDS
GRASSPLOTS
GRASSQUITS
GRASSROOTS
GRASSWRACK
GRASSWRACKS
GRATEFULLER
GRATEFULLEST
GRATEFULLY
GRATEFULNESS
GRATEFULNESSES
GRATICULATION
GRATICULATIONS
GRATICULES
GRATIFICATION
GRATIFICATIONS
GRATIFIERS
GRATIFYING
GRATIFYINGLY
GRATILLITIES
GRATILLITY
GRATINATED
GRATINATES
GRATINATING
GRATINEEING
GRATITUDES
GRATUITIES
GRATUITOUS
GRATUITOUSLY
GRATUITOUSNESS
GRATULATED
GRATULATES
GRATULATING
GRATULATION
GRATULATIONS
GRATULATORY
GRAUNCHERS
GRAUNCHING
GRAVADLAXES
GRAVEDIGGER
GRAVEDIGGERS
GRAVELLIER
GRAVELLIEST
GRAVELLING
GRAVENESSES
GRAVEOLENT
GRAVEROBBER
GRAVEROBBERS
GRAVESIDES
GRAVESITES
GRAVESTONE
GRAVESTONES
GRAVEYARDS
GRAVIDITIES
GRAVIDNESS
GRAVIDNESSES
GRAVIMETER
GRAVIMETERS
GRAVIMETRIC
GRAVIMETRICAL
GRAVIMETRICALLY
GRAVIMETRIES
GRAVIMETRY
GRAVIPERCEPTION
GRAVITASES

GRAVITATED
GRAVITATER
GRAVITATERS
GRAVITATES
GRAVITATING
GRAVITATION
GRAVITATIONAL
GRAVITATIONALLY
GRAVITATIONS
GRAVITATIVE
GRAVITINOS
GRAVITOMETER
GRAVITOMETERS
GRAYBEARDED
GRAYBEARDS
GRAYFISHES
GRAYHEADED
GRAYHOUNDS
GRAYLISTED
GRAYLISTING
GRAYNESSES
GRAYSTONES
GRAYWACKES
GRAYWATERS
GRAYWETHER
GRAYWETHERS
GREASEBALL
GREASEBALLS
GREASEBAND
GREASEBANDS
GREASEBUSH
GREASEBUSHES
GREASELESS
GREASEPAINT
GREASEPAINTS
GREASEPROOF
GREASEPROOFS
GREASEWOOD
GREASEWOODS
GREASINESS
GREASINESSES
GREATCOATED
GREATCOATS
GREATENING
GREATHEARTED
GREATHEARTEDLY
GREATNESSES
GRECIANISE
GRECIANISED
GRECIANISES
GRECIANISING
GRECIANIZE
GRECIANIZED
GRECIANIZES
GRECIANIZING
GREEDHEADS
GREEDINESS
GREEDINESSES
GREENBACKER
GREENBACKERS
GREENBACKISM
GREENBACKISMS
GREENBACKS
GREENBELTS
GREENBONES
GREENBOTTLE
GREENBOTTLES
GREENBRIER
GREENBRIERS
GREENCLOTH
GREENCLOTHS
GREENERIES
GREENFIELD
GREENFIELDS
GREENFINCH
GREENFINCHES
GREENFLIES
GREENGAGES
GREENGROCER
GREENGROCERIES
GREENGROCERS
GREENGROCERY
GREENHANDS
GREENHEADS
GREENHEART
GREENHEARTS
GREENHORNS
GREENHOUSE
GREENHOUSES
GREENISHNESS
GREENISHNESSES
GREENKEEPER
GREENKEEPERS
GREENLIGHT
GREENLIGHTED
GREENLIGHTING
GREENLIGHTS
GREENLINGS
GREENMAILED
GREENMAILER
GREENMAILERS
GREENMAILING
GREENMAILS
GREENNESSES
GREENOCKITE
GREENOCKITES
GREENROOMS
GREENSANDS
GREENSHANK
GREENSHANKS
GREENSICKNESS
GREENSICKNESSES
GREENSKEEPER
GREENSKEEPERS
GREENSOMES
GREENSPEAK
GREENSPEAKS
GREENSTICK
GREENSTONE
GREENSTONES
GREENSTUFF
GREENSTUFFS
GREENSWARD
GREENSWARDS
GREENWASHED
GREENWASHES
GREENWASHING
GREENWASHINGS
GREENWEEDS
GREENWINGS
GREENWOODS
GREGARIANISM
GREGARIANISMS
GREGARINES
GREGARINIAN
GREGARIOUS
GREGARIOUSLY
GREGARIOUSNESS
GREISENISATION
GREISENISATIONS
GREISENISE
GREISENISED
GREISENISES
GREISENISING
GREISENIZATION
GREISENIZATIONS
GREISENIZE
GREISENIZED
GREISENIZES
GREISENIZING
GREMOLATAS
GRENADIERS
GRENADILLA
GRENADILLAS
GRENADINES
GRESSORIAL
GRESSORIOUS
GREVILLEAS
GREWHOUNDS
GREWSOMEST
GREYBEARDED
GREYBEARDS
GREYHEADED
GREYHOUNDS
GREYLISTED
GREYLISTING
GREYNESSES
GREYSCALES
GREYSTONES
GREYWACKES
GREYWETHER
GREYWETHERS
GRIDDLEBREAD
GRIDDLEBREADS
GRIDDLECAKE
GRIDDLECAKES
GRIDIRONED
GRIDIRONING
GRIDLOCKED
GRIDLOCKING
GRIEVANCES
GRIEVINGLY
GRIEVOUSLY
GRIEVOUSNESS
GRIEVOUSNESSES
GRIFFINISH
GRIFFINISM
GRIFFINISMS
GRILLERIES
GRILLROOMS
GRILLSTEAK
GRILLSTEAKS
GRILLWORKS
GRIMACINGLY
GRIMALKINS
GRIMINESSES
GRIMLOOKED
GRIMNESSES
GRINDELIAS
GRINDERIES
GRINDHOUSE
GRINDHOUSES
GRINDINGLY
GRINDSTONE
GRINDSTONES
GRINNINGLY
GRIPPINGLY
GRISAILLES
GRISEOFULVIN
GRISEOFULVINS
GRISLINESS
GRISLINESSES
GRISTLIEST
GRISTLINESS
GRISTLINESSES
GRISTMILLS
GRITSTONES
GRITTINESS
GRITTINESSES
GRIVATIONS
GRIZZLIEST
GROANINGLY
GROATSWORTH
GROATSWORTHS
GROCETERIA
GROCETERIAS
GROGGERIES
GROGGINESS
GROGGINESSES
GROMMETING
GROOVELESS
GROOVELIKE
GROOVINESS
GROOVINESSES
GROSGRAINS
GROSSIERETE
GROSSIERETES
GROSSNESSES
GROSSULARITE
GROSSULARITES

GROSSULARS
GROTESQUELY
GROTESQUENESS
GROTESQUENESSES
GROTESQUER
GROTESQUERIE
GROTESQUERIES
GROTESQUERY
GROTESQUES
GROTESQUEST
GROTTINESS
GROTTINESSES
GROUCHIEST
GROUCHINESS
GROUCHINESSES
GROUNDAGES
GROUNDBAIT
GROUNDBAITED
GROUNDBAITING
GROUNDBAITS
GROUNDBREAKER
GROUNDBREAKERS
GROUNDBREAKING
GROUNDBREAKINGS
GROUNDBURST
GROUNDBURSTS
GROUNDEDLY
GROUNDFISH
GROUNDFISHES
GROUNDHOGS
GROUNDINGS
GROUNDLESS
GROUNDLESSLY
GROUNDLESSNESS
GROUNDLING
GROUNDLINGS
GROUNDMASS
GROUNDMASSES
GROUNDNUTS
GROUNDOUTS
GROUNDPLOT
GROUNDPLOTS
GROUNDPROX
GROUNDPROXES
GROUNDSELL
GROUNDSELLS
GROUNDSELS
GROUNDSHARE
GROUNDSHARED
GROUNDSHARES
GROUNDSHARING
GROUNDSHEET
GROUNDSHEETS
GROUNDSILL
GROUNDSILLS
GROUNDSKEEPER
GROUNDSKEEPERS
GROUNDSMAN
GROUNDSMEN
GROUNDSPEED
GROUNDSPEEDS
GROUNDSWELL
GROUNDSWELLS
GROUNDWATER
GROUNDWATERS
GROUNDWOOD
GROUNDWOODS
GROUNDWORK
GROUNDWORKS
GROUPTHINK
GROUPTHINKS
GROUPUSCULE
GROUPUSCULES
GROUPWARES
GROUPWORKS
GROUSELIKE
GROVELINGLY
GROVELINGS
GROVELLERS
GROVELLING
GROVELLINGLY
GROVELLINGS
GROWLERIES
GROWLINESS
GROWLINESSES
GROWLINGLY
GROWTHIEST
GROWTHINESS
GROWTHINESSES
GROWTHISTS
GRUBBINESS
GRUBBINESSES
GRUBSTAKED
GRUBSTAKER
GRUBSTAKERS
GRUBSTAKES
GRUBSTAKING
GRUBSTREET
GRUDGELESS
GRUDGINGLY
GRUELINGLY
GRUELLINGLY
GRUELLINGS
GRUESOMELY
GRUESOMENESS
GRUESOMENESSES
GRUESOMEST
GRUFFNESSES
GRUMBLIEST
GRUMBLINGLY
GRUMBLINGS
GRUMMETING
GRUMNESSES
GRUMPINESS
GRUMPINESSES
GRUMPISHLY
GRUMPISHNESS
GRUMPISHNESSES
GRUNTINGLY
GUACAMOLES
GUACHAMOLE
GUACHAMOLES
GUACHAROES
GUANABANAS
GUANAZOLOS
GUANETHIDINE
GUANETHIDINES
GUANIDINES
GUANIFEROUS
GUANOSINES
GUARANTEED
GUARANTEEING
GUARANTEES
GUARANTIED
GUARANTIES
GUARANTORS
GUARANTYING
GUARDEDNESS
GUARDEDNESSES
GUARDHOUSE
GUARDHOUSES
GUARDIANSHIP
GUARDIANSHIPS
GUARDRAILS
GUARDROOMS
GUARDSHIPS
GUARISHING
GUAYABERAS
GUBERNACULA
GUBERNACULAR
GUBERNACULUM
GUBERNATION
GUBERNATIONS
GUBERNATOR
GUBERNATORIAL
GUBERNATORS
GUBERNIYAS
GUDGEONING
GUERDONERS
GUERDONING
GUERILLAISM
GUERILLAISMS
GUERRILLAISM
GUERRILLAISMS
GUERRILLAS
GUERRILLERO
GUERRILLEROS
GUESSINGLY
GUESSTIMATE
GUESSTIMATED
GUESSTIMATES
GUESSTIMATING
GUESSWORKS
GUESTBOOKS
GUESTENING
GUESTHOUSE
GUESTHOUSES
GUESTIMATE
GUESTIMATED
GUESTIMATES
GUESTIMATING
GUIDEBOOKS
GUIDELINES
GUIDEPOSTS
GUIDESHIPS
GUIDEWORDS
GUIDWILLIE
GUILDHALLS
GUILDSHIPS
GUILDSWOMAN
GUILDSWOMEN
GUILEFULLY
GUILEFULNESS
GUILEFULNESSES
GUILELESSLY
GUILELESSNESS
GUILELESSNESSES
GUILLEMETS
GUILLEMOTS
GUILLOCHED
GUILLOCHES
GUILLOCHING
GUILLOTINE
GUILLOTINED
GUILLOTINER
GUILLOTINERS
GUILLOTINES
GUILLOTINING
GUILTINESS
GUILTINESSES
GUILTLESSLY
GUILTLESSNESS
GUILTLESSNESSES
GUITARFISH
GUITARFISHES
GUITARISTS
GULLIBILITIES
GULLIBILITY
GULOSITIES
GUMMIFEROUS
GUMMINESSES
GUMMOSITIES
GUMSHIELDS
GUMSHOEING
GUMSUCKERS
GUNCOTTONS
GUNFIGHTER
GUNFIGHTERS
GUNFIGHTING
GUNFIGHTINGS
GUNKHOLING
GUNMANSHIP
GUNMANSHIPS
GUNNERSHIP
GUNNERSHIPS
GUNNYSACKS
GUNPOWDERIER
GUNPOWDERIEST
GUNPOWDERS
GUNPOWDERY

G

GUNRUNNERS
GUNRUNNING
GUNRUNNINGS
GUNSLINGER
GUNSLINGERS
GUNSLINGING
GUNSLINGINGS
GUNSMITHING
GUNSMITHINGS
GURGITATION
GURGITATIONS
GUSHINESSES
GUSSETINGS
GUSTATIONS
GUSTATORILY
GUSTINESSES
GUTBUCKETS
GUTLESSNESS
GUTLESSNESSES
GUTSINESSES
GUTTATIONS
GUTTERBLOOD
GUTTERBLOODS
GUTTERIEST
GUTTERINGS
GUTTERSNIPE
GUTTERSNIPES
GUTTERSNIPISH
GUTTIFEROUS
GUTTURALISATION
GUTTURALISE
GUTTURALISED
GUTTURALISES
GUTTURALISING
GUTTURALISM
GUTTURALISMS
GUTTURALITIES
GUTTURALITY
GUTTURALIZATION
GUTTURALIZE
GUTTURALIZED
GUTTURALIZES
GUTTURALIZING
GUTTURALLY
GUTTURALNESS
GUTTURALNESSES
GYMNASIARCH
GYMNASIARCHS
GYMNASIAST
GYMNASIASTS
GYMNASIUMS
GYMNASTICAL
GYMNASTICALLY
GYMNASTICS
GYMNORHINAL
GYMNOSOPHIES
GYMNOSOPHIST
GYMNOSOPHISTS
GYMNOSOPHS
GYMNOSOPHY
GYMNOSPERM
GYMNOSPERMIES
GYMNOSPERMOUS
GYMNOSPERMS
GYMNOSPERMY
GYNAECEUMS
GYNAECOCRACIES
GYNAECOCRACY
GYNAECOCRATIC
GYNAECOLOGIC
GYNAECOLOGICAL
GYNAECOLOGIES
GYNAECOLOGIST
GYNAECOLOGISTS
GYNAECOLOGY
GYNAECOMAST
GYNAECOMASTIA
GYNAECOMASTIAS
GYNAECOMASTIES
GYNAECOMASTS
GYNAECOMASTY
GYNANDRIES
GYNANDRISM
GYNANDRISMS
GYNANDROMORPH
GYNANDROMORPHIC
GYNANDROMORPHS
GYNANDROMORPHY
GYNANDROUS
GYNARCHIES
GYNECOCRACIES
GYNECOCRACY
GYNECOCRATIC
GYNECOLOGIC
GYNECOLOGICAL
GYNECOLOGIES
GYNECOLOGIST
GYNECOLOGISTS
GYNECOLOGY
GYNECOMASTIA
GYNECOMASTIAS
GYNIATRICS
GYNIATRIES
GYNIOLATRIES
GYNIOLATRY
GYNOCRACIES
GYNOCRATIC
GYNODIOECIOUS
GYNODIOECISM
GYNODIOECISMS
GYNOGENESES
GYNOGENESIS
GYNOGENETIC
GYNOMONOECIOUS
GYNOMONOECISM
GYNOMONOECISMS
GYNOPHOBES
GYNOPHOBIA
GYNOPHOBIAS
GYNOPHOBIC
GYNOPHOBICS
GYNOPHORES
GYNOPHORIC
GYNOSTEMIA
GYNOSTEMIUM
GYPSIFEROUS
GYPSOPHILA
GYPSOPHILAS
GYPSYHOODS
GYPSYWORTS
GYRATIONAL
GYRFALCONS
GYROCOMPASS
GYROCOMPASSES
GYROCOPTER
GYROCOPTERS
GYROFREQUENCIES
GYROFREQUENCY
GYROMAGNETIC
GYROMAGNETISM
GYROMAGNETISMS
GYROMANCIES
GYROPILOTS
GYROPLANES
GYROSCOPES
GYROSCOPIC
GYROSCOPICALLY
GYROSCOPICS
GYROSTABILISER
GYROSTABILISERS
GYROSTABILIZER
GYROSTABILIZERS
GYROSTATIC
GYROSTATICALLY
GYROSTATICS
GYROVAGUES

HAANEPOOTS
HABERDASHER
HABERDASHERIES
HABERDASHERS
HABERDASHERY
HABERDINES
HABERGEONS
HABILATORY
HABILIMENT
HABILIMENTS
HABILITATE
HABILITATED
HABILITATES
HABILITATING
HABILITATION
HABILITATIONS
HABILITATOR
HABILITATORS
HABITABILITIES
HABITABILITY
HABITABLENESS
HABITABLENESSES
HABITATION
HABITATIONAL
HABITATIONS
HABITAUNCE
HABITAUNCES
HABITUALLY
HABITUALNESS
HABITUALNESSES
HABITUATED
HABITUATES
HABITUATING
HABITUATION
HABITUATIONS
HABITUDINAL
HACENDADOS
HACIENDADO
HACIENDADOS
HACKAMORES
HACKBERRIES
HACKBUTEER
HACKBUTEERS
HACKBUTTER
HACKBUTTERS
HACKERAZZI
HACKERAZZIS
HACKERAZZO
HACKMATACK
HACKMATACKS
HACKNEYING
HACKNEYISM
HACKNEYISMS
HACKNEYMAN
HACKNEYMEN
HACKSAWING
HACKTIVISM
HACKTIVISMS
HACKTIVIST
HACKTIVISTS
HACQUETONS
HADROSAURS
HADROSAURUS
HADROSAURUSES
HAECCEITIES
HAEMACHROME
HAEMACHROMES
HAEMACYTOMETER
HAEMACYTOMETERS
HAEMAGGLUTINATE
HAEMAGGLUTININ
HAEMAGGLUTININS
HAEMAGOGUE
HAEMAGOGUES
HAEMANGIOMA
HAEMANGIOMAS
HAEMANGIOMATA
HAEMATEINS
HAEMATEMESES
HAEMATEMESIS
HAEMATINIC
HAEMATINICS
HAEMATITES
HAEMATITIC
HAEMATOBLAST
HAEMATOBLASTIC
HAEMATOBLASTS
HAEMATOCELE
HAEMATOCELES
HAEMATOCRIT
HAEMATOCRITS
HAEMATOCRYAL
HAEMATOGENESES
HAEMATOGENESIS
HAEMATOGENETIC
HAEMATOGENIC
HAEMATOGENOUS
HAEMATOLOGIC
HAEMATOLOGICAL
HAEMATOLOGIES
HAEMATOLOGIST
HAEMATOLOGISTS
HAEMATOLOGY
HAEMATOLYSES
HAEMATOLYSIS
HAEMATOMAS
HAEMATOMATA
HAEMATOPHAGOUS
HAEMATOPOIESES
HAEMATOPOIESIS
HAEMATOPOIETIC
HAEMATOSES
HAEMATOSIS
HAEMATOTHERMAL
HAEMATOXYLIC
HAEMATOXYLIN
HAEMATOXYLINS
HAEMATOXYLON
HAEMATOXYLONS
HAEMATOZOA
HAEMATOZOON
HAEMATURIA
HAEMATURIAS
HAEMATURIC
HAEMOCHROME
HAEMOCHROMES
HAEMOCOELS
HAEMOCONIA
HAEMOCONIAS
HAEMOCYANIN
HAEMOCYANINS
HAEMOCYTES
HAEMOCYTOMETER
HAEMOCYTOMETERS
HAEMODIALYSER
HAEMODIALYSERS
HAEMODIALYSES
HAEMODIALYSIS
HAEMODIALYZER
HAEMODIALYZERS
HAEMODILUTION
HAEMODILUTIONS
HAEMODYNAMIC
HAEMODYNAMICS
HAEMOFLAGELLATE
HAEMOGLOBIN
HAEMOGLOBINS
HAEMOGLOBINURIA
HAEMOGLOBINURIC
HAEMOLYMPH
HAEMOLYMPHS
HAEMOLYSED
HAEMOLYSES
HAEMOLYSIN
HAEMOLYSING
HAEMOLYSINS
HAEMOLYSIS
HAEMOLYTIC
HAEMOLYZED
HAEMOLYZES
HAEMOLYZING
HAEMOPHILE
HAEMOPHILES
HAEMOPHILIA
HAEMOPHILIAC
HAEMOPHILIACS
HAEMOPHILIAS
HAEMOPHILIC
HAEMOPHILIOID
HAEMOPHOBIA
HAEMOPHOBIAS
HAEMOPOIESES
HAEMOPOIESIS
HAEMOPOIETIC
HAEMOPROTEIN
HAEMOPROTEINS
HAEMOPTYSES
HAEMOPTYSIS
HAEMORRHAGE
HAEMORRHAGED
HAEMORRHAGES
HAEMORRHAGIC
HAEMORRHAGING
HAEMORRHAGINGS
HAEMORRHOID
HAEMORRHOIDAL
HAEMORRHOIDS
HAEMOSIDERIN
HAEMOSIDERINS
HAEMOSTASES
HAEMOSTASIA
HAEMOSTASIAS
HAEMOSTASIS
HAEMOSTATIC
HAEMOSTATICS
HAEMOSTATS
HAEMOTOXIC
HAEMOTOXIN
HAEMOTOXINS
HAGBERRIES
HAGBUTEERS
HAGBUTTERS
HAGGADICAL
HAGGADISTIC
HAGGADISTS
HAGGARDNESS
HAGGARDNESSES
HAGGISHNESS
HAGGISHNESSES
HAGIARCHIES

HAGIOCRACIES
HAGIOCRACY
HAGIOGRAPHER
HAGIOGRAPHERS
HAGIOGRAPHIC
HAGIOGRAPHICAL
HAGIOGRAPHIES
HAGIOGRAPHIST
HAGIOGRAPHISTS
HAGIOGRAPHY
HAGIOLATER
HAGIOLATERS
HAGIOLATRIES
HAGIOLATROUS
HAGIOLATRY
HAGIOLOGIC
HAGIOLOGICAL
HAGIOLOGIES
HAGIOLOGIST
HAGIOLOGISTS
HAGIOSCOPE
HAGIOSCOPES
HAGIOSCOPIC
HAILSTONES
HAILSTORMS
HAIRBRAINED
HAIRBREADTH
HAIRBREADTHS
HAIRBRUSHES
HAIRCLOTHS
HAIRCUTTER
HAIRCUTTERS
HAIRCUTTING
HAIRCUTTINGS
HAIRDRESSER
HAIRDRESSERS
HAIRDRESSING
HAIRDRESSINGS
HAIRDRIERS
HAIRDRYERS
HAIRINESSES
HAIRLESSES
HAIRLESSNESS
HAIRLESSNESSES
HAIRPIECES
HAIRSBREADTH
HAIRSBREADTHS
HAIRSPLITTER
HAIRSPLITTERS
HAIRSPLITTING
HAIRSPLITTINGS
HAIRSPRAYS
HAIRSPRING
HAIRSPRINGS
HAIRSTREAK
HAIRSTREAKS
HAIRSTYLES
HAIRSTYLING
HAIRSTYLINGS
HAIRSTYLIST
HAIRSTYLISTS
HAIRWEAVING
HAIRWEAVINGS
HAIRYBACKS
HALACHISTS
HALAKHISTS
HALBERDIER
HALBERDIERS
HALCYONIAN
HALENESSES
HALFENDEALE
HALFENDEALES
HALFHEARTED
HALFHEARTEDLY
HALFHEARTEDNESS
HALFNESSES
HALFPENNIES
HALFPENNYWORTH
HALFPENNYWORTHS
HALFSERIOUSLY
HALFTRACKS
HALFWITTED
HALFWITTEDLY
HALFWITTEDNESS
HALIEUTICS
HALIPLANKTON
HALIPLANKTONS
HALLALLING
HALLEFLINTA
HALLEFLINTAS
HALLELUIAH
HALLELUIAHS
HALLELUJAH
HALLELUJAHS
HALLMARKED
HALLMARKING
HALLOWEDNESS
HALLOWEDNESSES
HALLOYSITE
HALLOYSITES
HALLSTANDS
HALLUCINANT
HALLUCINANTS
HALLUCINATE
HALLUCINATED
HALLUCINATES
HALLUCINATING
HALLUCINATION
HALLUCINATIONAL
HALLUCINATIONS
HALLUCINATIVE
HALLUCINATOR
HALLUCINATORS
HALLUCINATORY
HALLUCINOGEN
HALLUCINOGENIC
HALLUCINOGENICS
HALLUCINOGENS
HALLUCINOSES
HALLUCINOSIS
HALOBIONTIC
HALOBIONTS
HALOBIOTIC
HALOCARBON
HALOCARBONS
HALOCLINES
HALOGENATE
HALOGENATED
HALOGENATES
HALOGENATING
HALOGENATION
HALOGENATIONS
HALOGENOID
HALOGENOUS
HALOGETONS
HALOMORPHIC
HALOPERIDOL
HALOPERIDOLS
HALOPHILES
HALOPHILIC
HALOPHILIES
HALOPHILOUS
HALOPHOBES
HALOPHYTES
HALOPHYTIC
HALOPHYTISM
HALOPHYTISMS
HALOTHANES
HALTERBREAK
HALTERBREAKING
HALTERBREAKS
HALTERBROKE
HALTERBROKEN
HALTERNECK
HALTERNECKS
HALTINGNESS
HALTINGNESSES
HAMADRYADES
HAMADRYADS
HAMADRYASES
HAMAMELIDACEOUS
HAMAMELISES
HAMANTASCH
HAMANTASCHEN
HAMARTHRITIS
HAMARTHRITISES
HAMARTIOLOGIES
HAMARTIOLOGY
HAMBURGERS
HAMESUCKEN
HAMESUCKENS
HAMFATTERED
HAMFATTERING
HAMFATTERS
HAMMERCLOTH
HAMMERCLOTHS
HAMMERHEAD
HAMMERHEADED
HAMMERHEADS
HAMMERINGS
HAMMERKOPS
HAMMERLESS
HAMMERLOCK
HAMMERLOCKS
HAMMERSTONE
HAMMERSTONES
HAMMERTOES
HAMMINESSES
HAMPEREDNESS
HAMPEREDNESSES
HAMSHACKLE
HAMSHACKLED
HAMSHACKLES
HAMSHACKLING
HAMSTRINGED
HAMSTRINGING
HAMSTRINGS
HANDBAGGED
HANDBAGGING
HANDBAGGINGS
HANDBALLED
HANDBALLER
HANDBALLERS
HANDBALLING
HANDBARROW
HANDBARROWS
HANDBASKET
HANDBASKETS
HANDBRAKES
HANDBREADTH
HANDBREADTHS
HANDCLASPS
HANDCRAFTED
HANDCRAFTING
HANDCRAFTS
HANDCRAFTSMAN
HANDCRAFTSMEN
HANDCUFFED
HANDCUFFING
HANDEDNESS
HANDEDNESSES
HANDFASTED
HANDFASTING
HANDFASTINGS
HANDFEEDING
HANDGLASSES
HANDICAPPED
HANDICAPPER
HANDICAPPERS
HANDICAPPING
HANDICRAFT
HANDICRAFTER
HANDICRAFTERS
HANDICRAFTS
HANDICRAFTSMAN
HANDICRAFTSMEN
HANDICUFFS
HANDINESSES
HANDIWORKS
HANDKERCHER

HANDKERCHERS
HANDKERCHIEF
HANDKERCHIEFS
HANDKERCHIEVES
HANDLANGER
HANDLANGERS
HANDLEABLE
HANDLEBARS
HANDLELESS
HANDLINERS
HANDMAIDEN
HANDMAIDENS
HANDPASSED
HANDPASSES
HANDPASSING
HANDPHONES
HANDPICKED
HANDPICKING
HANDPRESSES
HANDPRINTS
HANDSBREADTH
HANDSBREADTHS
HANDSELING
HANDSELLED
HANDSELLING
HANDSHAKES
HANDSHAKING
HANDSHAKINGS
HANDSOMELY
HANDSOMENESS
HANDSOMENESSES
HANDSOMEST
HANDSPIKES
HANDSPRING
HANDSPRINGS
HANDSTAFFS
HANDSTAMPED
HANDSTAMPING
HANDSTAMPS
HANDSTANDS
HANDSTAVES
HANDSTROKE
HANDSTROKES
HANDSTURNS
HANDTOWELS
HANDWHEELS
HANDWORKED
HANDWORKER
HANDWORKERS
HANDWRINGER
HANDWRINGERS
HANDWRITES
HANDWRITING
HANDWRITINGS
HANDWRITTEN
HANDWROUGHT
HANDYPERSON
HANDYPERSONS
HANDYWORKS
HANGABILITIES
HANGABILITY
HANGARAGES
HANKERINGS
HANSARDISE
HANSARDISED
HANSARDISES
HANSARDISING
HANSARDIZE
HANSARDIZED
HANSARDIZES
HANSARDIZING
HANSELLING
HANTAVIRUS
HANTAVIRUSES
HAPAXANTHIC
HAPAXANTHOUS
HAPHAZARDLY
HAPHAZARDNESS
HAPHAZARDNESSES
HAPHAZARDRIES
HAPHAZARDRY
HAPHAZARDS
HAPHTARAHS
HAPHTAROTH
HAPLESSNESS
HAPLESSNESSES
HAPLOBIONT
HAPLOBIONTIC
HAPLOBIONTS
HAPLOGRAPHIES
HAPLOGRAPHY
HAPLOIDIES
HAPLOLOGIC
HAPLOLOGIES
HAPLOSTEMONOUS
HAPLOTYPES
HAPPENCHANCE
HAPPENCHANCES
HAPPENINGS
HAPPENSTANCE
HAPPENSTANCES
HAPPINESSES
HAPTOGLOBIN
HAPTOGLOBINS
HAPTOTROPIC
HAPTOTROPISM
HAPTOTROPISMS
HARAMZADAS
HARAMZADIS
HARANGUERS
HARANGUING
HARASSEDLY
HARASSINGLY
HARASSINGS
HARASSMENT
HARASSMENTS
HARBINGERED
HARBINGERING
HARBINGERS
HARBORAGES
HARBORFULS
HARBORLESS
HARBORMASTER
HARBORMASTERS
HARBORSIDE
HARBOURAGE
HARBOURAGES
HARBOURERS
HARBOURFUL
HARBOURFULS
HARBOURING
HARBOURLESS
HARBOURSIDE
HARBOURSIDES
HARDBACKED
HARDBOARDS
HARDBODIES
HARDBOUNDS
HARDCOVERS
HARDENINGS
HARDFISTED
HARDGRASSES
HARDHANDED
HARDHANDEDNESS
HARDHEADED
HARDHEADEDLY
HARDHEADEDNESS
HARDHEARTED
HARDHEARTEDLY
HARDHEARTEDNESS
HARDIHEADS
HARDIHOODS
HARDIMENTS
HARDINESSES
HARDINGGRASS
HARDINGGRASSES
HARDLINERS
HARDMOUTHED
HARDNESSES
HARDSCAPES
HARDSCRABBLE
HARDSCRABBLES
HARDSTANDING
HARDSTANDINGS
HARDSTANDS
HARDWAREMAN
HARDWAREMEN
HARDWIRING
HARDWORKING
HAREBRAINED
HARESTAILS
HARIOLATED
HARIOLATES
HARIOLATING
HARIOLATION
HARIOLATIONS
HARLEQUINADE
HARLEQUINADES
HARLEQUINED
HARLEQUINING
HARLEQUINS
HARLOTRIES
HARMALINES
HARMATTANS
HARMDOINGS
HARMFULNESS
HARMFULNESSES
HARMLESSLY
HARMLESSNESS
HARMLESSNESSES
HARMOLODIC
HARMOLODICS
HARMONICAL
HARMONICALLY
HARMONICAS
HARMONICHORD
HARMONICHORDS
HARMONICIST
HARMONICISTS
HARMONICON
HARMONICONS
HARMONIOUS
HARMONIOUSLY
HARMONIOUSNESS
HARMONIPHON
HARMONIPHONE
HARMONIPHONES
HARMONIPHONS
HARMONISABLE
HARMONISATION
HARMONISATIONS
HARMONISED
HARMONISER
HARMONISERS
HARMONISES
HARMONISING
HARMONISTIC
HARMONISTICALLY
HARMONISTS
HARMONIUMIST
HARMONIUMISTS
HARMONIUMS
HARMONIZABLE
HARMONIZATION
HARMONIZATIONS
HARMONIZED
HARMONIZER
HARMONIZERS
HARMONIZES
HARMONIZING
HARMONOGRAM
HARMONOGRAMS
HARMONOGRAPH
HARMONOGRAPHS
HARMONOMETER
HARMONOMETERS
HARMOSTIES
HARMOTOMES
HARNESSERS
HARNESSING

H

HARNESSLESS
HARPOONEER
HARPOONEERS
HARPOONERS
HARPOONING
HARPSICHORD
HARPSICHORDIST
HARPSICHORDISTS
HARPSICHORDS
HARQUEBUSE
HARQUEBUSES
HARQUEBUSIER
HARQUEBUSIERS
HARQUEBUSS
HARQUEBUSSES
HARROWINGLY
HARROWINGS
HARROWMENT
HARROWMENTS
HARRUMPHED
HARRUMPHING
HARSHENING
HARSHNESSES
HARTBEESES
HARTBEESTS
HARTEBEEST
HARTEBEESTS
HARTSHORNS
HARUMPHING
HARUSPICAL
HARUSPICATE
HARUSPICATED
HARUSPICATES
HARUSPICATING
HARUSPICATION
HARUSPICATIONS
HARUSPICES
HARUSPICIES
HARVESTABLE
HARVESTERS
HARVESTING
HARVESTINGS
HARVESTLESS
HARVESTMAN
HARVESTMEN
HARVESTTIME
HARVESTTIMES
HASENPFEFFER
HASENPFEFFERS
HASHEESHES
HASSOCKIER
HASSOCKIEST
HASTEFULLY
HASTINESSES
HATBRUSHES
HATCHABILITIES
HATCHABILITY
HATCHBACKS
HATCHELING
HATCHELLED
HATCHELLER
HATCHELLERS
HATCHELLING
HATCHERIES
HATCHETIER
HATCHETIEST
HATCHETTITE
HATCHETTITES
HATCHLINGS
HATCHMENTS
HATEFULNESS
HATEFULNESSES
HATELESSNESS
HATELESSNESSES
HATEWORTHIER
HATEWORTHIEST
HATEWORTHY
HATINATORS
HATLESSNESS
HATLESSNESSES
HAUBERGEON
HAUBERGEONS
HAUGHTIEST
HAUGHTINESS
HAUGHTINESSES
HAUNTINGLY
HAUSFRAUEN
HAUSSMANNISE
HAUSSMANNISED
HAUSSMANNISES
HAUSSMANNISING
HAUSSMANNIZE
HAUSSMANNIZED
HAUSSMANNIZES
HAUSSMANNIZING
HAUSTELLATE
HAUSTELLUM
HAUSTORIAL
HAUSTORIUM
HAVERSACKS
HAVERSINES
HAWFINCHES
HAWKISHNESS
HAWKISHNESSES
HAWKSBEARD
HAWKSBEARDS
HAWKSBILLS
HAWSEHOLES
HAWSEPIPES
HAWTHORNIER
HAWTHORNIEST
HAYCATIONS
HAYMAKINGS
HAZARDABLE
HAZARDIZES
HAZARDOUSLY
HAZARDOUSNESS
HAZARDOUSNESSES
HAZARDRIES
HAZELWOODS
HAZINESSES
HEADACHIER
HEADACHIEST
HEADBANGED
HEADBANGING
HEADBANGINGS
HEADBOARDS
HEADBOROUGH
HEADBOROUGHS
HEADCHAIRS
HEADCHEESE
HEADCHEESES
HEADCLOTHS
HEADCOUNTS
HEADDRESSES
HEADFISHES
HEADFOREMOST
HEADFRAMES
HEADGUARDS
HEADHUNTED
HEADHUNTER
HEADHUNTERS
HEADHUNTING
HEADHUNTINGS
HEADINESSES
HEADLEASES
HEADLESSNESS
HEADLESSNESSES
HEADLIGHTS
HEADLINERS
HEADLINING
HEADMASTER
HEADMASTERLIER
HEADMASTERLIEST
HEADMASTERLY
HEADMASTERS
HEADMASTERSHIP
HEADMASTERSHIPS
HEADMISTRESS
HEADMISTRESSES
HEADMISTRESSIER
HEADMISTRESSY
HEADPEACES
HEADPHONES
HEADPIECES
HEADQUARTER
HEADQUARTERED
HEADQUARTERING
HEADQUARTERS
HEADREACHED
HEADREACHES
HEADREACHING
HEADSCARVES
HEADSHAKES
HEADSHEETS
HEADSHRINKER
HEADSHRINKERS
HEADSPACES
HEADSPRING
HEADSPRINGS
HEADSQUARE
HEADSQUARES
HEADSTALLS
HEADSTANDS
HEADSTICKS
HEADSTOCKS
HEADSTONES
HEADSTREAM
HEADSTREAMS
HEADSTRONG
HEADSTRONGLY
HEADSTRONGNESS
HEADTEACHER
HEADTEACHERS
HEADWAITER
HEADWAITERS
HEADWATERS
HEADWORKER
HEADWORKERS
HEALTHCARE
HEALTHCARES
HEALTHFULLY
HEALTHFULNESS
HEALTHFULNESSES
HEALTHIEST
HEALTHINESS
HEALTHINESSES
HEALTHISMS
HEALTHLESS
HEALTHLESSNESS
HEALTHSOME
HEAPSTEADS
HEARKENERS
HEARKENING
HEARTACHES
HEARTBEATS
HEARTBREAK
HEARTBREAKER
HEARTBREAKERS
HEARTBREAKING
HEARTBREAKINGLY
HEARTBREAKS
HEARTBROKE
HEARTBROKEN
HEARTBROKENLY
HEARTBROKENNESS
HEARTBURNING
HEARTBURNINGS
HEARTBURNS
HEARTENERS
HEARTENING
HEARTENINGLY
HEARTHRUGS
HEARTHSTONE
HEARTHSTONES
HEARTIKINS
HEARTINESS
HEARTINESSES
HEARTLANDS
HEARTLESSLY

HEARTLESSNESS
HEARTLESSNESSES
HEARTLINGS
HEARTRENDING
HEARTRENDINGLY
HEARTSEASE
HEARTSEASES
HEARTSEEDS
HEARTSICKNESS
HEARTSICKNESSES
HEARTSINKS
HEARTSOMELY
HEARTSOMENESS
HEARTSOMENESSES
HEARTSORES
HEARTSTRING
HEARTSTRINGS
HEARTTHROB
HEARTTHROBS
HEARTWARMING
HEARTWATER
HEARTWATERS
HEARTWOODS
HEARTWORMS
HEATEDNESS
HEATEDNESSES
HEATHBERRIES
HEATHBERRY
HEATHBIRDS
HEATHCOCKS
HEATHENDOM
HEATHENDOMS
HEATHENESSE
HEATHENESSES
HEATHENISE
HEATHENISED
HEATHENISES
HEATHENISH
HEATHENISHLY
HEATHENISHNESS
HEATHENISING
HEATHENISM
HEATHENISMS
HEATHENIZE
HEATHENIZED
HEATHENIZES
HEATHENIZING
HEATHENNESS
HEATHENNESSES
HEATHENRIES
HEATHERIER
HEATHERIEST
HEATHFOWLS
HEATHLANDS
HEATSTROKE
HEATSTROKES
HEAVENLIER
HEAVENLIEST
HEAVENLINESS
HEAVENLINESSES
HEAVENWARD
HEAVENWARDS
HEAVINESSES
HEAVYHEARTED
HEAVYHEARTEDLY
HEAVYWEIGHT
HEAVYWEIGHTS
HEBDOMADAL
HEBDOMADALLY
HEBDOMADAR
HEBDOMADARIES
HEBDOMADARS
HEBDOMADARY
HEBDOMADER
HEBDOMADERS
HEBEPHRENIA
HEBEPHRENIAC
HEBEPHRENIACS
HEBEPHRENIAS
HEBEPHRENIC
HEBEPHRENICS
HEBETATING
HEBETATION
HEBETATIONS
HEBETATIVE
HEBETUDINOSITY
HEBETUDINOUS
HEBRAISATION
HEBRAISATIONS
HEBRAISING
HEBRAIZATION
HEBRAIZATIONS
HEBRAIZING
HECKELPHONE
HECKELPHONES
HECOGENINS
HECTICALLY
HECTOCOTYLI
HECTOCOTYLUS
HECTOGRAMME
HECTOGRAMMES
HECTOGRAMS
HECTOGRAPH
HECTOGRAPHED
HECTOGRAPHIC
HECTOGRAPHIES
HECTOGRAPHING
HECTOGRAPHS
HECTOGRAPHY
HECTOLITER
HECTOLITERS
HECTOLITRE
HECTOLITRES
HECTOMETER
HECTOMETERS
HECTOMETRE
HECTOMETRES
HECTORINGLY
HECTORINGS
HECTORISMS
HECTORSHIP
HECTORSHIPS
HECTOSTERE
HECTOSTERES
HEDGEBILLS
HEDGEHOPPED
HEDGEHOPPER
HEDGEHOPPERS
HEDGEHOPPING
HEDGEHOPPINGS
HEDONICALLY
HEDONISTIC
HEDONISTICALLY
HEDYPHANES
HEDYSARUMS
HEEDFULNESS
HEEDFULNESSES
HEEDINESSES
HEEDLESSLY
HEEDLESSNESS
HEEDLESSNESSES
HEELPIECES
HEELPLATES
HEFTINESSES
HEGEMONIAL
HEGEMONICAL
HEGEMONIES
HEGEMONISM
HEGEMONISMS
HEGEMONIST
HEGEMONISTS
HEGUMENIES
HEGUMENOSES
HEIGHTENED
HEIGHTENER
HEIGHTENERS
HEIGHTENING
HEIGHTISMS
HEINOUSNESS
HEINOUSNESSES
HEKTOGRAMS
HELDENTENOR
HELDENTENORS
HELIACALLY
HELIANTHEMUM
HELIANTHEMUMS
HELIANTHUS
HELIANTHUSES
HELIBUSSES
HELICHRYSUM
HELICHRYSUMS
HELICITIES
HELICLINES
HELICOGRAPH
HELICOGRAPHS
HELICOIDAL
HELICOIDALLY
HELICONIAS
HELICOPTED
HELICOPTER
HELICOPTERED
HELICOPTERING
HELICOPTERS
HELICOPTING
HELICTITES
HELIDROMES
HELILIFTED
HELILIFTING
HELIOCENTRIC
HELIOCENTRICISM
HELIOCENTRICITY
HELIOCHROME
HELIOCHROMES
HELIOCHROMIC
HELIOCHROMIES
HELIOCHROMY
HELIOGRAMS
HELIOGRAPH
HELIOGRAPHED
HELIOGRAPHER
HELIOGRAPHERS
HELIOGRAPHIC
HELIOGRAPHICAL
HELIOGRAPHIES
HELIOGRAPHING
HELIOGRAPHS
HELIOGRAPHY
HELIOGRAVURE
HELIOGRAVURES
HELIOLATER
HELIOLATERS
HELIOLATRIES
HELIOLATROUS
HELIOLATRY
HELIOLITHIC
HELIOLOGIES
HELIOMETER
HELIOMETERS
HELIOMETRIC
HELIOMETRICAL
HELIOMETRICALLY
HELIOMETRIES
HELIOMETRY
HELIOPAUSE
HELIOPAUSES
HELIOPHILOUS
HELIOPHOBIC
HELIOPHYTE
HELIOPHYTES
HELIOSCIOPHYTE
HELIOSCIOPHYTES
HELIOSCOPE
HELIOSCOPES
HELIOSCOPIC
HELIOSPHERE
HELIOSPHERES
HELIOSTATIC
HELIOSTATS
HELIOTACTIC
HELIOTAXES

HELIOTAXIS
HELIOTHERAPIES
HELIOTHERAPY
HELIOTROPE
HELIOTROPES
HELIOTROPIC
HELIOTROPICAL
HELIOTROPICALLY
HELIOTROPIES
HELIOTROPIN
HELIOTROPINS
HELIOTROPISM
HELIOTROPISMS
HELIOTROPY
HELIOTYPED
HELIOTYPES
HELIOTYPIC
HELIOTYPIES
HELIOTYPING
HELIOZOANS
HELIPILOTS
HELISKIING
HELISKIINGS
HELISPHERIC
HELISPHERICAL
HELLACIOUS
HELLACIOUSLY
HELLBENDER
HELLBENDERS
HELLBROTHS
HELLDIVERS
HELLEBORES
HELLEBORINE
HELLEBORINES
HELLENISATION
HELLENISATIONS
HELLENISED
HELLENISES
HELLENISING
HELLENIZATION
HELLENIZATIONS
HELLENIZED
HELLENIZES
HELLENIZING
HELLGRAMITE
HELLGRAMITES
HELLGRAMMITE
HELLGRAMMITES
HELLHOUNDS
HELLISHNESS
HELLISHNESSES
HELLSCAPES
HELMETINGS
HELMETLIKE
HELMINTHIASES
HELMINTHIASIS
HELMINTHIC
HELMINTHICS
HELMINTHOID
HELMINTHOLOGIC
HELMINTHOLOGIES
HELMINTHOLOGIST
HELMINTHOLOGY
HELMINTHOUS
HELMSMANSHIP
HELMSMANSHIPS
HELOPHYTES
HELPFULNESS
HELPFULNESSES
HELPLESSLY
HELPLESSNESS
HELPLESSNESSES
HELVETIUMS
HEMACHROME
HEMACHROMES
HEMACYTOMETER
HEMACYTOMETERS
HEMAGGLUTINATE
HEMAGGLUTINATED
HEMAGGLUTINATES
HEMAGGLUTININ
HEMAGGLUTININS
HEMAGOGUES
HEMANGIOMA
HEMANGIOMAS
HEMANGIOMATA
HEMATEMESES
HEMATEMESIS
HEMATINICS
HEMATOBLAST
HEMATOBLASTIC
HEMATOBLASTS
HEMATOCELE
HEMATOCELES
HEMATOCRIT
HEMATOCRITS
HEMATOCRYAL
HEMATOGENESES
HEMATOGENESIS
HEMATOGENETIC
HEMATOGENIC
HEMATOGENOUS
HEMATOLOGIC
HEMATOLOGICAL
HEMATOLOGIES
HEMATOLOGIST
HEMATOLOGISTS
HEMATOLOGY
HEMATOLYSES
HEMATOLYSIS
HEMATOMATA
HEMATOPHAGOUS
HEMATOPOIESES
HEMATOPOIESIS
HEMATOPOIETIC
HEMATOPORPHYRIN
HEMATOTHERMAL
HEMATOXYLIN
HEMATOXYLINS
HEMATOZOON
HEMATURIAS
HEMELYTRAL
HEMELYTRON
HEMELYTRUM
HEMERALOPIA
HEMERALOPIAS
HEMERALOPIC
HEMEROCALLIS
HEMEROCALLISES
HEMERYTHRIN
HEMERYTHRINS
HEMIACETAL
HEMIACETALS
HEMIALGIAS
HEMIANOPIA
HEMIANOPIAS
HEMIANOPIC
HEMIANOPSIA
HEMIANOPSIAS
HEMIANOPTIC
HEMICELLULOSE
HEMICELLULOSES
HEMICHORDATE
HEMICHORDATES
HEMICRANIA
HEMICRANIAS
HEMICRYPTOPHYTE
HEMICRYSTALLINE
HEMICYCLES
HEMICYCLIC
HEMIELYTRA
HEMIELYTRAL
HEMIELYTRON
HEMIHEDRAL
HEMIHEDRIES
HEMIHEDRISM
HEMIHEDRISMS
HEMIHEDRON
HEMIHEDRONS
HEMIHYDRATE
HEMIHYDRATED
HEMIHYDRATES
HEMIMETABOLOUS
HEMIMORPHIC
HEMIMORPHIES
HEMIMORPHISM
HEMIMORPHISMS
HEMIMORPHITE
HEMIMORPHITES
HEMIMORPHY
HEMIONUSES
HEMIOPSIAS
HEMIPARASITE
HEMIPARASITES
HEMIPARASITIC
HEMIPLEGIA
HEMIPLEGIAS
HEMIPLEGIC
HEMIPLEGICS
HEMIPTERAL
HEMIPTERAN
HEMIPTERANS
HEMIPTERON
HEMIPTERONS
HEMIPTEROUS
HEMISPACES
HEMISPHERE
HEMISPHERES
HEMISPHERIC
HEMISPHERICAL
HEMISPHEROID
HEMISPHEROIDAL
HEMISPHEROIDS
HEMISTICHAL
HEMISTICHS
HEMITERPENE
HEMITERPENES
HEMITROPAL
HEMITROPES
HEMITROPIC
HEMITROPIES
HEMITROPISM
HEMITROPISMS
HEMITROPOUS
HEMIZYGOUS
HEMOCHROMATOSES
HEMOCHROMATOSIS
HEMOCHROME
HEMOCHROMES
HEMOCONIAS
HEMOCYANIN
HEMOCYANINS
HEMOCYTOMETER
HEMOCYTOMETERS
HEMODIALYSES
HEMODIALYSIS
HEMODIALYZER
HEMODIALYZERS
HEMODILUTION
HEMODILUTIONS
HEMODYNAMIC
HEMODYNAMICALLY
HEMODYNAMICS
HEMOFLAGELLATE
HEMOFLAGELLATES
HEMOGLOBIN
HEMOGLOBINS
HEMOGLOBINURIA
HEMOGLOBINURIAS
HEMOGLOBINURIC
HEMOLYMPHS
HEMOLYSING
HEMOLYSINS
HEMOLYZING
HEMOPHILES
HEMOPHILIA
HEMOPHILIAC
HEMOPHILIACS
HEMOPHILIAS
HEMOPHILIC

HEMOPHILICS
HEMOPHILIOID
HEMOPOIESES
HEMOPOIESIS
HEMOPOIETIC
HEMOPROTEIN
HEMOPROTEINS
HEMOPTYSES
HEMOPTYSIS
HEMORRHAGE
HEMORRHAGED
HEMORRHAGES
HEMORRHAGIC
HEMORRHAGING
HEMORRHAGINGS
HEMORRHOID
HEMORRHOIDAL
HEMORRHOIDALS
HEMORRHOIDS
HEMOSIDERIN
HEMOSIDERINS
HEMOSTASES
HEMOSTASIA
HEMOSTASIAS
HEMOSTASIS
HEMOSTATIC
HEMOSTATICS
HEMOTOXINS
HEMSTITCHED
HEMSTITCHER
HEMSTITCHERS
HEMSTITCHES
HEMSTITCHING
HENCEFORTH
HENCEFORWARD
HENCEFORWARDS
HENCHPERSON
HENCHPERSONS
HENCHWOMAN
HENCHWOMEN
HENDECAGON
HENDECAGONAL
HENDECAGONS
HENDECAHEDRA
HENDECAHEDRON
HENDECAHEDRONS
HENDECASYLLABIC
HENDECASYLLABLE
HENDIADYSES
HENOTHEISM
HENOTHEISMS
HENOTHEIST
HENOTHEISTIC
HENOTHEISTS
HENPECKERIES
HENPECKERY
HENPECKING
HEORTOLOGICAL
HEORTOLOGIES
HEORTOLOGIST
HEORTOLOGISTS
HEORTOLOGY
HEPARINISED
HEPARINIZED
HEPARINOID
HEPATECTOMIES
HEPATECTOMISED
HEPATECTOMIZED
HEPATECTOMY
HEPATICOLOGICAL
HEPATICOLOGIES
HEPATICOLOGIST
HEPATICOLOGISTS
HEPATICOLOGY
HEPATISATION
HEPATISATIONS
HEPATISING
HEPATITIDES
HEPATITISES
HEPATIZATION
HEPATIZATIONS
HEPATIZING
HEPATOCELLULAR
HEPATOCYTE
HEPATOCYTES
HEPATOGENOUS
HEPATOLOGIES
HEPATOLOGIST
HEPATOLOGISTS
HEPATOLOGY
HEPATOMATA
HEPATOMEGALIES
HEPATOMEGALY
HEPATOPANCREAS
HEPATOSCOPIES
HEPATOSCOPY
HEPATOTOXIC
HEPATOTOXICITY
HEPHTHEMIMER
HEPHTHEMIMERAL
HEPHTHEMIMERS
HEPTACHLOR
HEPTACHLORS
HEPTACHORD
HEPTACHORDS
HEPTADECANOIC
HEPTAGLOTS
HEPTAGONAL
HEPTAGYNOUS
HEPTAHEDRA
HEPTAHEDRAL
HEPTAHEDRON
HEPTAHEDRONS
HEPTAMEROUS
HEPTAMETER
HEPTAMETERS
HEPTAMETRICAL
HEPTANDROUS
HEPTANGULAR
HEPTAPODIC
HEPTAPODIES
HEPTARCHAL
HEPTARCHIC
HEPTARCHIES
HEPTARCHIST
HEPTARCHISTS
HEPTASTICH
HEPTASTICHS
HEPTASYLLABIC
HEPTATHLETE
HEPTATHLETES
HEPTATHLON
HEPTATHLONS
HEPTATONIC
HEPTAVALENT
HERALDICALLY
HERALDISTS
HERALDRIES
HERALDSHIP
HERALDSHIPS
HERBACEOUS
HERBACEOUSLY
HERBALISMS
HERBALISTS
HERBARIANS
HERBARIUMS
HERBICIDAL
HERBICIDALLY
HERBICIDES
HERBIVORES
HERBIVORIES
HERBIVOROUS
HERBIVOROUSLY
HERBIVOROUSNESS
HERBOLOGIES
HERBORISATION
HERBORISATIONS
HERBORISED
HERBORISES
HERBORISING
HERBORISTS
HERBORIZATION
HERBORIZATIONS
HERBORIZED
HERBORIZES
HERBORIZING
HERCOGAMIES
HERCOGAMOUS
HERCULESES
HERCYNITES
HEREABOUTS
HEREAFTERS
HEREDITABILITY
HEREDITABLE
HEREDITABLY
HEREDITAMENT
HEREDITAMENTS
HEREDITARIAN
HEREDITARIANISM
HEREDITARIANIST
HEREDITARIANS
HEREDITARILY
HEREDITARINESS
HEREDITARY
HEREDITIES
HEREDITIST
HEREDITISTS
HEREINABOVE
HEREINAFTER
HEREINBEFORE
HEREINBELOW
HERENESSES
HERESIARCH
HERESIARCHS
HERESIOGRAPHER
HERESIOGRAPHERS
HERESIOGRAPHIES
HERESIOGRAPHY
HERESIOLOGIES
HERESIOLOGIST
HERESIOLOGISTS
HERESIOLOGY
HERESTHETIC
HERESTHETICAL
HERESTHETICIAN
HERESTHETICIANS
HERESTHETICS
HERETICALLY
HERETICATE
HERETICATED
HERETICATES
HERETICATING
HERETOFORE
HERETOFORES
HERETRICES
HERETRIXES
HERIOTABLE
HERITABILITIES
HERITABILITY
HERITRESSES
HERITRICES
HERITRIXES
HERKOGAMIES
HERMANDADS
HERMAPHRODITE
HERMAPHRODITES
HERMAPHRODITIC
HERMAPHRODITISM
HERMATYPIC
HERMENEUTIC
HERMENEUTICAL
HERMENEUTICALLY
HERMENEUTICS
HERMENEUTIST
HERMENEUTISTS
HERMETICAL
HERMETICALLY
HERMETICISM
HERMETICISMS
HERMETICITIES

HERMETICITY
HERMETISMS
HERMETISTS
HERMITAGES
HERMITESSES
HERMITICAL
HERMITICALLY
HERMITISMS
HERMITRIES
HERNIATING
HERNIATION
HERNIATIONS
HERNIORRHAPHIES
HERNIORRHAPHY
HERNIOTOMIES
HERNIOTOMY
HEROICALLY
HEROICALNESS
HEROICALNESSES
HEROICISED
HEROICISES
HEROICISING
HEROICIZED
HEROICIZES
HEROICIZING
HEROICNESS
HEROICNESSES
HEROICOMIC
HEROICOMICAL
HEROINISMS
HERONSHAWS
HERPESVIRUS
HERPESVIRUSES
HERPETOFAUNA
HERPETOFAUNAE
HERPETOFAUNAS
HERPETOLOGIC
HERPETOLOGICAL
HERPETOLOGIES
HERPETOLOGIST
HERPETOLOGISTS
HERPETOLOGY
HERRENVOLK
HERRENVOLKS
HERRIMENTS
HERRINGBONE
HERRINGBONED
HERRINGBONES
HERRINGBONING
HERRINGERS
HERRYMENTS
HERSTORIES
HESITANCES
HESITANCIES
HESITANTLY
HESITATERS
HESITATING
HESITATINGLY
HESITATION
HESITATIONS
HESITATIVE
HESITATORS
HESITATORY
HESPERIDIA
HESPERIDIN
HESPERIDINS
HESPERIDIUM
HESSONITES
HETAERISMIC
HETAERISMS
HETAERISTIC
HETAERISTS
HETAIRISMIC
HETAIRISMS
HETAIRISTIC
HETAIRISTS
HETERARCHIES
HETERARCHY
HETERAUXESES
HETERAUXESIS
HETEROAROMATIC
HETEROATOM
HETEROATOMS
HETEROAUXIN
HETEROAUXINS
HETEROBLASTIC
HETEROBLASTIES
HETEROBLASTY
HETEROCARPOUS
HETEROCERCAL
HETEROCERCALITY
HETEROCERCIES
HETEROCERCY
HETEROCHROMATIC
HETEROCHROMATIN
HETEROCHROMOUS
HETEROCHRONIC
HETEROCHRONIES
HETEROCHRONISM
HETEROCHRONISMS
HETEROCHRONOUS
HETEROCHRONY
HETEROCLITE
HETEROCLITES
HETEROCLITIC
HETEROCLITOUS
HETEROCONT
HETEROCONTS
HETEROCYCLE
HETEROCYCLES
HETEROCYCLIC
HETEROCYCLICS
HETEROCYST
HETEROCYSTOUS
HETEROCYSTS
HETERODACTYL
HETERODACTYLOUS
HETERODACTYLS
HETERODONT
HETERODOXIES
HETERODOXY
HETERODUPLEX
HETERODUPLEXES
HETERODYNE
HETERODYNED
HETERODYNES
HETERODYNING
HETEROECIOUS
HETEROECISM
HETEROECISMS
HETEROFLEXIBLE
HETEROFLEXIBLES
HETEROGAMETE
HETEROGAMETES
HETEROGAMETIC
HETEROGAMETIES
HETEROGAMETY
HETEROGAMIES
HETEROGAMOUS
HETEROGAMY
HETEROGENEITIES
HETEROGENEITY
HETEROGENEOUS
HETEROGENEOUSLY
HETEROGENESES
HETEROGENESIS
HETEROGENETIC
HETEROGENIC
HETEROGENIES
HETEROGENOUS
HETEROGENY
HETEROGONIC
HETEROGONIES
HETEROGONOUS
HETEROGONOUSLY
HETEROGONY
HETEROGRAFT
HETEROGRAFTS
HETEROGRAPHIC
HETEROGRAPHICAL
HETEROGRAPHIES
HETEROGRAPHY
HETEROGYNOUS
HETEROKARYON
HETEROKARYONS
HETEROKARYOSES
HETEROKARYOSIS
HETEROKARYOTIC
HETEROKONT
HETEROKONTAN
HETEROKONTS
HETEROLECITHAL
HETEROLOGIES
HETEROLOGOUS
HETEROLOGOUSLY
HETEROLOGY
HETEROLYSES
HETEROLYSIS
HETEROLYTIC
HETEROMEROUS
HETEROMORPHIC
HETEROMORPHIES
HETEROMORPHISM
HETEROMORPHISMS
HETEROMORPHOUS
HETEROMORPHY
HETERONOMIES
HETERONOMOUS
HETERONOMOUSLY
HETERONOMY
HETERONORMATIVE
HETERONYMOUS
HETERONYMOUSLY
HETERONYMS
HETEROOUSIAN
HETEROOUSIANS
HETEROPHIL
HETEROPHILE
HETEROPHILES
HETEROPHILS
HETEROPHONIES
HETEROPHONY
HETEROPHYLLIES
HETEROPHYLLOUS
HETEROPHYLLY
HETEROPLASIA
HETEROPLASIAS
HETEROPLASTIC
HETEROPLASTIES
HETEROPLASTY
HETEROPLOID
HETEROPLOIDIES
HETEROPLOIDS
HETEROPLOIDY
HETEROPODS
HETEROPOLAR
HETEROPOLARITY
HETEROPTERAN
HETEROPTERANS
HETEROPTEROUS
HETEROSCEDASTIC
HETEROSCIAN
HETEROSCIANS
HETEROSEXISM
HETEROSEXISMS
HETEROSEXIST
HETEROSEXISTS
HETEROSEXUAL
HETEROSEXUALITY
HETEROSEXUALLY
HETEROSEXUALS
HETEROSOCIAL
HETEROSOCIALITY
HETEROSOMATOUS
HETEROSPECIFIC
HETEROSPECIFICS
HETEROSPORIES
HETEROSPOROUS
HETEROSPORY
HETEROSTROPHIC

HETEROSTROPHIES
HETEROSTROPHY
HETEROSTYLED
HETEROSTYLIES
HETEROSTYLISM
HETEROSTYLISMS
HETEROSTYLOUS
HETEROSTYLY
HETEROTACTIC
HETEROTACTOUS
HETEROTAXES
HETEROTAXIA
HETEROTAXIAS
HETEROTAXIC
HETEROTAXIES
HETEROTAXIS
HETEROTAXY
HETEROTHALLIC
HETEROTHALLIES
HETEROTHALLISM
HETEROTHALLISMS
HETEROTHALLY
HETEROTHERMAL
HETEROTOPIA
HETEROTOPIAS
HETEROTOPIC
HETEROTOPIES
HETEROTOPOUS
HETEROTOPY
HETEROTROPH
HETEROTROPHIC
HETEROTROPHIES
HETEROTROPHS
HETEROTROPHY
HETEROTYPIC
HETEROTYPICAL
HETEROUSIAN
HETEROUSIANS
HETEROZYGOSES
HETEROZYGOSIS
HETEROZYGOSITY
HETEROZYGOTE
HETEROZYGOTES
HETEROZYGOUS
HETHERWARD
HETMANATES
HETMANSHIP
HETMANSHIPS
HEULANDITE
HEULANDITES
HEURISTICALLY
HEURISTICS
HEXACHLORETHANE
HEXACHLORIDE
HEXACHLORIDES
HEXACHLOROPHANE
HEXACHLOROPHENE
HEXACHORDS
HEXACOSANOIC
HEXACTINAL
HEXACTINELLID
HEXACTINELLIDS
HEXADACTYLIC
HEXADACTYLOUS
HEXADECANE
HEXADECANES
HEXADECANOIC
HEXADECIMAL
HEXADECIMALS
HEXADECYLS
HEXAEMERIC
HEXAEMERON
HEXAEMERONS
HEXAFLUORIDE
HEXAFLUORIDES
HEXAGONALLY
HEXAGRAMMOID
HEXAGRAMMOIDS
HEXAGYNIAN
HEXAGYNOUS
HEXAHEDRAL
HEXAHEDRON
HEXAHEDRONS
HEXAHEMERIC
HEXAHEMERON
HEXAHEMERONS
HEXAHYDRATE
HEXAHYDRATED
HEXAHYDRATES
HEXAMERISM
HEXAMERISMS
HEXAMEROUS
HEXAMETERS
HEXAMETHONIUM
HEXAMETHONIUMS
HEXAMETRAL
HEXAMETRIC
HEXAMETRICAL
HEXAMETRISE
HEXAMETRISED
HEXAMETRISES
HEXAMETRISING
HEXAMETRIST
HEXAMETRISTS
HEXAMETRIZE
HEXAMETRIZED
HEXAMETRIZES
HEXAMETRIZING
HEXANDRIAN
HEXANDROUS
HEXANGULAR
HEXAPLARIAN
HEXAPLARIC
HEXAPLOIDIES
HEXAPLOIDS
HEXAPLOIDY
HEXAPODIES
HEXARCHIES
HEXASTICHAL
HEXASTICHIC
HEXASTICHON
HEXASTICHONS
HEXASTICHS
HEXASTYLES
HEXATEUCHAL
HEXATHLONS
HEXAVALENT
HEXOBARBITAL
HEXOBARBITALS
HEXOKINASE
HEXOKINASES
HEXOSAMINIDASE
HEXOSAMINIDASES
HEXYLRESORCINOL
HIBAKUSHAS
HIBERNACLE
HIBERNACLES
HIBERNACULA
HIBERNACULUM
HIBERNATED
HIBERNATES
HIBERNATING
HIBERNATION
HIBERNATIONS
HIBERNATOR
HIBERNATORS
HIBERNICISATION
HIBERNICISE
HIBERNICISED
HIBERNICISES
HIBERNICISING
HIBERNICIZATION
HIBERNICIZE
HIBERNICIZED
HIBERNICIZES
HIBERNICIZING
HIBERNISATION
HIBERNISATIONS
HIBERNISED
HIBERNISES
HIBERNISING
HIBERNIZATION
HIBERNIZATIONS
HIBERNIZED
HIBERNIZES
HIBERNIZING
HIBISCUSES
HICCOUGHED
HICCOUGHING
HICCUPIEST
HICCUPPING
HIDALGOISH
HIDALGOISM
HIDALGOISMS
HIDDENITES
HIDDENMOST
HIDDENNESS
HIDDENNESSES
HIDEOSITIES
HIDEOUSNESS
HIDEOUSNESSES
HIERACIUMS
HIERACOSPHINGES
HIERACOSPHINX
HIERACOSPHINXES
HIERARCHAL
HIERARCHIC
HIERARCHICAL
HIERARCHICALLY
HIERARCHIES
HIERARCHISE
HIERARCHISED
HIERARCHISES
HIERARCHISING
HIERARCHISM
HIERARCHISMS
HIERARCHIZE
HIERARCHIZED
HIERARCHIZES
HIERARCHIZING
HIERATICAL
HIERATICALLY
HIERATICAS
HIEROCRACIES
HIEROCRACY
HIEROCRATIC
HIEROCRATICAL
HIEROCRATS
HIERODULES
HIERODULIC
HIEROGLYPH
HIEROGLYPHED
HIEROGLYPHIC
HIEROGLYPHICAL
HIEROGLYPHICS
HIEROGLYPHING
HIEROGLYPHIST
HIEROGLYPHISTS
HIEROGLYPHS
HIEROGRAMMAT
HIEROGRAMMATE
HIEROGRAMMATES
HIEROGRAMMATIC
HIEROGRAMMATIST
HIEROGRAMMATS
HIEROGRAMS
HIEROGRAPH
HIEROGRAPHER
HIEROGRAPHERS
HIEROGRAPHIC
HIEROGRAPHICAL
HIEROGRAPHIES
HIEROGRAPHS
HIEROGRAPHY
HIEROLATRIES
HIEROLATRY
HIEROLOGIC
HIEROLOGICAL
HIEROLOGIES
HIEROLOGIST

H

HIEROLOGISTS
HIEROMANCIES
HIEROMANCY
HIEROPHANT
HIEROPHANTIC
HIEROPHANTS
HIEROPHOBIA
HIEROPHOBIAS
HIEROPHOBIC
HIEROPHOBICS
HIEROSCOPIES
HIEROSCOPY
HIERURGICAL
HIERURGIES
HIGHBALLED
HIGHBALLING
HIGHBINDER
HIGHBINDERS
HIGHBLOODED
HIGHBROWED
HIGHBROWISM
HIGHBROWISMS
HIGHBUSHES
HIGHCHAIRS
HIGHERMOST
HIGHFALUTIN
HIGHFALUTING
HIGHFALUTINGS
HIGHFALUTINS
HIGHFLIERS
HIGHFLYERS
HIGHJACKED
HIGHJACKER
HIGHJACKERS
HIGHJACKING
HIGHJACKINGS
HIGHLANDER
HIGHLANDERS
HIGHLIGHTED
HIGHLIGHTER
HIGHLIGHTERS
HIGHLIGHTING
HIGHLIGHTS
HIGHNESSES
HIGHTAILED
HIGHTAILING
HIGHWAYMAN
HIGHWAYMEN
HIGHWROUGHT
HIJACKINGS
HILARIOUSLY
HILARIOUSNESS
HILARIOUSNESSES
HILARITIES
HILLBILLIES
HILLCRESTS
HILLINESSES
HILLOCKIER
HILLOCKIEST
HILLSLOPES
HILLWALKER
HILLWALKERS
HILLWALKING
HILLWALKINGS
HINDBERRIES
HINDBRAINS
HINDCASTED
HINDCASTING
HINDERANCE
HINDERANCES
HINDERINGLY
HINDERINGS
HINDERLAND
HINDERLANDS
HINDERLANS
HINDERLINGS
HINDERLINS
HINDERMOST
HINDFOREMOST
HINDQUARTER
HINDQUARTERS
HINDRANCES
HINDSHANKS
HINDSIGHTS
HINTERLAND
HINTERLANDS
HIPPEASTRUM
HIPPEASTRUMS
HIPPIATRIC
HIPPIATRICS
HIPPIATRIES
HIPPIATRIST
HIPPIATRISTS
HIPPIEDOMS
HIPPIENESS
HIPPIENESSES
HIPPINESSES
HIPPOCAMPAL
HIPPOCAMPI
HIPPOCAMPUS
HIPPOCENTAUR
HIPPOCENTAURS
HIPPOCRASES
HIPPOCREPIAN
HIPPOCREPIANS
HIPPODAMES
HIPPODAMIST
HIPPODAMISTS
HIPPODAMOUS
HIPPODROME
HIPPODROMES
HIPPODROMIC
HIPPOGRIFF
HIPPOGRIFFS
HIPPOGRYPH
HIPPOGRYPHS
HIPPOLOGIES
HIPPOLOGIST
HIPPOLOGISTS
HIPPOMANES
HIPPOPHAGIES
HIPPOPHAGIST
HIPPOPHAGISTS
HIPPOPHAGOUS
HIPPOPHAGY
HIPPOPHILE
HIPPOPHILES
HIPPOPHOBE
HIPPOPHOBES
HIPPOPOTAMI
HIPPOPOTAMIAN
HIPPOPOTAMIC
HIPPOPOTAMUS
HIPPOPOTAMUSES
HIPPURITES
HIPPURITIC
HIPSTERISM
HIPSTERISMS
HIRCOCERVUS
HIRCOCERVUSES
HIRCOSITIES
HIRSELLING
HIRSELLINGS
HIRSUTENESS
HIRSUTENESSES
HIRSUTISMS
HIRUDINEAN
HIRUDINEANS
HIRUDINOID
HIRUDINOUS
HISPANICISE
HISPANICISED
HISPANICISES
HISPANICISING
HISPANICISM
HISPANICISMS
HISPANICIZE
HISPANICIZED
HISPANICIZES
HISPANICIZING
HISPANIDAD
HISPANIDADS
HISPANIOLISE
HISPANIOLISED
HISPANIOLISES
HISPANIOLISING
HISPANIOLIZE
HISPANIOLIZED
HISPANIOLIZES
HISPANIOLIZING
HISPANISMS
HISPIDITIES
HISTAMINASE
HISTAMINASES
HISTAMINERGIC
HISTAMINES
HISTAMINIC
HISTIDINES
HISTIOCYTE
HISTIOCYTES
HISTIOCYTIC
HISTIOLOGIES
HISTIOLOGY
HISTIOPHOROID
HISTOBLAST
HISTOBLASTS
HISTOCHEMICAL
HISTOCHEMICALLY
HISTOCHEMIST
HISTOCHEMISTRY
HISTOCHEMISTS
HISTOCOMPATIBLE
HISTOGENESES
HISTOGENESIS
HISTOGENETIC
HISTOGENIC
HISTOGENICALLY
HISTOGENIES
HISTOGRAMS
HISTOLOGIC
HISTOLOGICAL
HISTOLOGICALLY
HISTOLOGIES
HISTOLOGIST
HISTOLOGISTS
HISTOLYSES
HISTOLYSIS
HISTOLYTIC
HISTOLYTICALLY
HISTOPATHOLOGIC
HISTOPATHOLOGY
HISTOPHYSIOLOGY
HISTOPLASMOSES
HISTOPLASMOSIS
HISTORIANS
HISTORIATED
HISTORICAL
HISTORICALLY
HISTORICALNESS
HISTORICISE
HISTORICISED
HISTORICISES
HISTORICISING
HISTORICISM
HISTORICISMS
HISTORICIST
HISTORICISTS
HISTORICITIES
HISTORICITY
HISTORICIZE
HISTORICIZED
HISTORICIZES
HISTORICIZING
HISTORIETTE
HISTORIETTES
HISTORIFIED
HISTORIFIES
HISTORIFYING
HISTORIOGRAPHER
HISTORIOGRAPHIC

HISTORIOGRAPHY
HISTORIOLOGIES
HISTORIOLOGY
HISTORISMS
HISTORYING
HISTRIONIC
HISTRIONICAL
HISTRIONICALLY
HISTRIONICISM
HISTRIONICISMS
HISTRIONICS
HISTRIONISM
HISTRIONISMS
HITCHHIKED
HITCHHIKER
HITCHHIKERS
HITCHHIKES
HITCHHIKING
HITCHHIKINGS
HITHERMOST
HITHERSIDE
HITHERSIDES
HITHERWARD
HITHERWARDS
HOACTZINES
HOARFROSTS
HOARHOUNDS
HOARINESSES
HOARSENESS
HOARSENESSES
HOARSENING
HOBBITRIES
HOBBLEBUSH
HOBBLEBUSHES
HOBBLEDEHOY
HOBBLEDEHOYDOM
HOBBLEDEHOYDOMS
HOBBLEDEHOYHOOD
HOBBLEDEHOYISH
HOBBLEDEHOYISM
HOBBLEDEHOYISMS
HOBBLEDEHOYS
HOBBLINGLY
HOBBYHORSE
HOBBYHORSED
HOBBYHORSES
HOBBYHORSING
HOBGOBLINISM
HOBGOBLINISMS
HOBGOBLINRIES
HOBGOBLINRY
HOBGOBLINS
HOBJOBBERS
HOBJOBBING
HOBJOBBINGS
HOBNAILING
HOBNOBBERS
HOBNOBBIER
HOBNOBBIEST
HOBNOBBING
HOCHMAGANDIES
HOCHMAGANDY
HODGEPODGE
HODGEPODGES
HODMANDODS
HODOGRAPHIC
HODOGRAPHS
HODOMETERS
HODOMETRIES
HODOSCOPES
HOGGISHNESS
HOGGISHNESSES
HOIDENISHNESS
HOIDENISHNESSES
HOJATOLESLAM
HOJATOLESLAMS
HOJATOLISLAM
HOJATOLISLAMS
HOKEYNESSES
HOKEYPOKEY
HOKEYPOKEYS
HOKINESSES
HOKYPOKIES
HOLARCHIES
HOLDERBATS
HOLDERSHIP
HOLDERSHIPS
HOLIDAYERS
HOLIDAYING
HOLIDAYMAKER
HOLIDAYMAKERS
HOLINESSES
HOLISTICALLY
HOLLANDAISE
HOLLANDAISES
HOLLOWARES
HOLLOWNESS
HOLLOWNESSES
HOLLOWWARE
HOLLOWWARES
HOLLYHOCKS
HOLOBENTHIC
HOLOBLASTIC
HOLOBLASTICALLY
HOLOCAINES
HOLOCAUSTAL
HOLOCAUSTIC
HOLOCAUSTS
HOLOCRYSTALLINE
HOLODISCUS
HOLODISCUSES
HOLOENZYME
HOLOENZYMES
HOLOGAMIES
HOLOGRAPHED
HOLOGRAPHER
HOLOGRAPHERS
HOLOGRAPHIC
HOLOGRAPHICALLY
HOLOGRAPHIES
HOLOGRAPHING
HOLOGRAPHS
HOLOGRAPHY
HOLOGYNIES
HOLOHEDRAL
HOLOHEDRISM
HOLOHEDRISMS
HOLOHEDRON
HOLOHEDRONS
HOLOMETABOLIC
HOLOMETABOLISM
HOLOMETABOLISMS
HOLOMETABOLOUS
HOLOMORPHIC
HOLOPHOTAL
HOLOPHOTES
HOLOPHRASE
HOLOPHRASES
HOLOPHRASTIC
HOLOPHYTES
HOLOPHYTIC
HOLOPHYTISM
HOLOPHYTISMS
HOLOPLANKTON
HOLOPLANKTONS
HOLOSTERIC
HOLOTHURIAN
HOLOTHURIANS
HOLSTERING
HOLYSTONED
HOLYSTONES
HOLYSTONING
HOMALOGRAPHIC
HOMALOIDAL
HOMEBIRTHS
HOMEBODIES
HOMEBUYERS
HOMECOMERS
HOMECOMING
HOMECOMINGS
HOMECRAFTS
HOMELESSNESS
HOMELESSNESSES
HOMELINESS
HOMELINESSES
HOMEMAKERS
HOMEMAKING
HOMEMAKINGS
HOMEOBOXES
HOMEOMERIC
HOMEOMERIES
HOMEOMEROUS
HOMEOMORPH
HOMEOMORPHIC
HOMEOMORPHIES
HOMEOMORPHISM
HOMEOMORPHISMS
HOMEOMORPHOUS
HOMEOMORPHS
HOMEOMORPHY
HOMEOPATHIC
HOMEOPATHICALLY
HOMEOPATHIES
HOMEOPATHIST
HOMEOPATHISTS
HOMEOPATHS
HOMEOPATHY
HOMEOSTASES
HOMEOSTASIS
HOMEOSTATIC
HOMEOTELEUTON
HOMEOTELEUTONS
HOMEOTHERM
HOMEOTHERMAL
HOMEOTHERMIC
HOMEOTHERMIES
HOMEOTHERMISM
HOMEOTHERMISMS
HOMEOTHERMOUS
HOMEOTHERMS
HOMEOTHERMY
HOMEOTYPIC
HOMEOTYPICAL
HOMEOWNERS
HOMEOWNERSHIP
HOMEOWNERSHIPS
HOMEPLACES
HOMEPORTED
HOMEPORTING
HOMESCHOOL
HOMESCHOOLED
HOMESCHOOLER
HOMESCHOOLERS
HOMESCHOOLING
HOMESCHOOLS
HOMESCREETCH
HOMESCREETCHES
HOMESHORING
HOMESHORINGS
HOMESICKNESS
HOMESICKNESSES
HOMESOURCING
HOMESOURCINGS
HOMESTALLS
HOMESTANDS
HOMESTEADED
HOMESTEADER
HOMESTEADERS
HOMESTEADING
HOMESTEADINGS
HOMESTEADS
HOMESTRETCH
HOMESTRETCHES
HOMEWORKER
HOMEWORKERS
HOMEWORKING
HOMEWORKINGS
HOMEYNESSES
HOMICIDALLY
HOMILETICAL

H

HOMILETICALLY
HOMILETICS
HOMINESSES
HOMINISATION
HOMINISATIONS
HOMINISING
HOMINIZATION
HOMINIZATIONS
HOMINIZING
HOMOBLASTIC
HOMOBLASTIES
HOMOBLASTY
HOMOCENTRIC
HOMOCENTRICALLY
HOMOCERCAL
HOMOCERCIES
HOMOCHLAMYDEOUS
HOMOCHROMATIC
HOMOCHROMATISM
HOMOCHROMATISMS
HOMOCHROMIES
HOMOCHROMOUS
HOMOCHROMY
HOMOCYCLIC
HOMOCYSTEINE
HOMOCYSTEINES
HOMOEOMERIC
HOMOEOMERIES
HOMOEOMEROUS
HOMOEOMERY
HOMOEOMORPH
HOMOEOMORPHIC
HOMOEOMORPHIES
HOMOEOMORPHISM
HOMOEOMORPHISMS
HOMOEOMORPHOUS
HOMOEOMORPHS
HOMOEOMORPHY
HOMOEOPATH
HOMOEOPATHIC
HOMOEOPATHIES
HOMOEOPATHIST
HOMOEOPATHISTS
HOMOEOPATHS
HOMOEOPATHY
HOMOEOSTASES
HOMOEOSTASIS
HOMOEOSTATIC
HOMOEOTELEUTON
HOMOEOTELEUTONS
HOMOEOTHERM
HOMOEOTHERMAL
HOMOEOTHERMIC
HOMOEOTHERMOUS
HOMOEOTHERMS
HOMOEOTYPIC
HOMOEOTYPICAL
HOMOEROTIC
HOMOEROTICISM
HOMOEROTICISMS
HOMOEROTISM
HOMOEROTISMS
HOMOGAMETIC
HOMOGAMIES
HOMOGAMOUS
HOMOGENATE
HOMOGENATES
HOMOGENEITIES
HOMOGENEITY
HOMOGENEOUS
HOMOGENEOUSLY
HOMOGENEOUSNESS
HOMOGENESES
HOMOGENESIS
HOMOGENETIC
HOMOGENETICAL
HOMOGENIES
HOMOGENISATION
HOMOGENISATIONS
HOMOGENISE
HOMOGENISED
HOMOGENISER
HOMOGENISERS
HOMOGENISES
HOMOGENISING
HOMOGENIZATION
HOMOGENIZATIONS
HOMOGENIZE
HOMOGENIZED
HOMOGENIZER
HOMOGENIZERS
HOMOGENIZES
HOMOGENIZING
HOMOGENOUS
HOMOGONIES
HOMOGONOUS
HOMOGONOUSLY
HOMOGRAFTS
HOMOGRAPHIC
HOMOGRAPHIES
HOMOGRAPHS
HOMOGRAPHY
HOMOIOMEROUS
HOMOIOTHERM
HOMOIOTHERMAL
HOMOIOTHERMIC
HOMOIOTHERMIES
HOMOIOTHERMS
HOMOIOTHERMY
HOMOIOUSIAN
HOMOIOUSIANS
HOMOLOGATE
HOMOLOGATED
HOMOLOGATES
HOMOLOGATING
HOMOLOGATION
HOMOLOGATIONS
HOMOLOGICAL
HOMOLOGICALLY
HOMOLOGIES
HOMOLOGISE
HOMOLOGISED
HOMOLOGISER
HOMOLOGISERS
HOMOLOGISES
HOMOLOGISING
HOMOLOGIZE
HOMOLOGIZED
HOMOLOGIZER
HOMOLOGIZERS
HOMOLOGIZES
HOMOLOGIZING
HOMOLOGOUMENA
HOMOLOGOUS
HOMOLOGRAPHIC
HOMOLOGUES
HOMOLOGUMENA
HOMOLOSINE
HOMOMORPHIC
HOMOMORPHIES
HOMOMORPHISM
HOMOMORPHISMS
HOMOMORPHOSES
HOMOMORPHOSIS
HOMOMORPHOUS
HOMOMORPHS
HOMOMORPHY
HOMONUCLEAR
HOMONYMIES
HOMONYMITIES
HOMONYMITY
HOMONYMOUS
HOMONYMOUSLY
HOMOOUSIAN
HOMOOUSIANS
HOMOPHILES
HOMOPHOBES
HOMOPHOBIA
HOMOPHOBIAS
HOMOPHOBIC
HOMOPHONES
HOMOPHONIC
HOMOPHONICALLY
HOMOPHONIES
HOMOPHONOUS
HOMOPHYLIES
HOMOPHYLLIC
HOMOPLASIES
HOMOPLASMIES
HOMOPLASMY
HOMOPLASTIC
HOMOPLASTICALLY
HOMOPLASTIES
HOMOPLASTY
HOMOPOLARITIES
HOMOPOLARITY
HOMOPOLYMER
HOMOPOLYMERIC
HOMOPOLYMERS
HOMOPTERAN
HOMOPTERANS
HOMOPTEROUS
HOMORGANIC
HOMOSCEDASTIC
HOMOSEXUAL
HOMOSEXUALISM
HOMOSEXUALISMS
HOMOSEXUALIST
HOMOSEXUALISTS
HOMOSEXUALITIES
HOMOSEXUALITY
HOMOSEXUALLY
HOMOSEXUALS
HOMOSOCIAL
HOMOSOCIALITIES
HOMOSOCIALITY
HOMOSPORIES
HOMOSPOROUS
HOMOSTYLIES
HOMOTAXIAL
HOMOTAXIALLY
HOMOTHALLIC
HOMOTHALLIES
HOMOTHALLISM
HOMOTHALLISMS
HOMOTHALLY
HOMOTHERMAL
HOMOTHERMIC
HOMOTHERMIES
HOMOTHERMOUS
HOMOTHERMY
HOMOTONIES
HOMOTONOUS
HOMOTRANSPLANT
HOMOTRANSPLANTS
HOMOTYPIES
HOMOUSIANS
HOMOZYGOSES
HOMOZYGOSIS
HOMOZYGOSITIES
HOMOZYGOSITY
HOMOZYGOTE
HOMOZYGOTES
HOMOZYGOTIC
HOMOZYGOUS
HOMOZYGOUSLY
HOMUNCULAR
HOMUNCULES
HOMUNCULUS
HONESTNESS
HONESTNESSES
HONEYBELLS
HONEYBUNCH
HONEYBUNCHES
HONEYCOMBED
HONEYCOMBING
HONEYCOMBINGS
HONEYCOMBS
HONEYCREEPER
HONEYCREEPERS

HONEYDEWED
HONEYEATER
HONEYEATERS
HONEYGUIDE
HONEYGUIDES
HONEYMONTH
HONEYMONTHED
HONEYMONTHING
HONEYMONTHS
HONEYMOONED
HONEYMOONER
HONEYMOONERS
HONEYMOONING
HONEYMOONS
HONEYSUCKER
HONEYSUCKERS
HONEYSUCKLE
HONEYSUCKLED
HONEYSUCKLES
HONEYTRAPS
HONORABILITIES
HONORABILITY
HONORABLENESS
HONORABLENESSES
HONORARIES
HONORARILY
HONORARIUM
HONORARIUMS
HONORIFICAL
HONORIFICALLY
HONORIFICS
HONOURABILITIES
HONOURABILITY
HONOURABLE
HONOURABLENESS
HONOURABLY
HONOURLESS
HOODEDNESS
HOODEDNESSES
HOODLUMISH
HOODLUMISM
HOODLUMISMS
HOODOOISMS
HOODWINKED
HOODWINKER
HOODWINKERS
HOODWINKING
HOOFPRINTS
HOOKCHECKS
HOOKEDNESS
HOOKEDNESSES
HOOLACHANS
HOOLIGANISM
HOOLIGANISMS
HOOPSKIRTS
HOOTANANNIE
HOOTANANNIES
HOOTANANNY
HOOTENANNIE
HOOTENANNIES
HOOTENANNY
HOOTNANNIE
HOOTNANNIES
HOOVERINGS
HOPEFULNESS
HOPEFULNESSES
HOPELESSLY
HOPELESSNESS
HOPELESSNESSES
HOPLOLOGIES
HOPLOLOGIST
HOPLOLOGISTS
HOPPERCARS
HOPPINESSES
HOPSACKING
HOPSACKINGS
HOPSCOTCHED
HOPSCOTCHES
HOPSCOTCHING
HOREHOUNDS
HORIATIKIS
HORIZONLESS
HORIZONTAL
HORIZONTALITIES
HORIZONTALITY
HORIZONTALLY
HORIZONTALNESS
HORIZONTALS
HORMOGONIA
HORMOGONIUM
HORMONALLY
HORMONELIKE
HORNBLENDE
HORNBLENDES
HORNBLENDIC
HORNEDNESS
HORNEDNESSES
HORNFELSES
HORNFISHES
HORNINESSES
HORNLESSNESS
HORNLESSNESSES
HORNSTONES
HORNSWOGGLE
HORNSWOGGLED
HORNSWOGGLES
HORNSWOGGLING
HORNWRACKS
HORNYHEADS
HORNYWINKS
HOROGRAPHER
HOROGRAPHERS
HOROGRAPHIES
HOROGRAPHY
HOROLOGERS
HOROLOGICAL
HOROLOGIES
HOROLOGION
HOROLOGIONS
HOROLOGIST
HOROLOGISTS
HOROLOGIUM
HOROMETRICAL
HOROMETRIES
HOROSCOPES
HOROSCOPIC
HOROSCOPIES
HOROSCOPIST
HOROSCOPISTS
HORRENDOUS
HORRENDOUSLY
HORRENDOUSNESS
HORRIBLENESS
HORRIBLENESSES
HORRIDNESS
HORRIDNESSES
HORRIFICALLY
HORRIFICATION
HORRIFICATIONS
HORRIFYING
HORRIFYINGLY
HORRIPILANT
HORRIPILATE
HORRIPILATED
HORRIPILATES
HORRIPILATING
HORRIPILATION
HORRIPILATIONS
HORRISONANT
HORRISONOUS
HORSEBACKS
HORSEBEANS
HORSEBOXES
HORSEFEATHERS
HORSEFLESH
HORSEFLESHES
HORSEFLIES
HORSEHAIRS
HORSEHEADS
HORSEHIDES
HORSELAUGH
HORSELAUGHS
HORSELEECH
HORSELEECHES
HORSEMANSHIP
HORSEMANSHIPS
HORSEMEATS
HORSEMINTS
HORSEPLAYER
HORSEPLAYERS
HORSEPLAYS
HORSEPONDS
HORSEPOWER
HORSEPOWERS
HORSEPOXES
HORSERACES
HORSERADISH
HORSERADISHES
HORSESHITS
HORSESHOED
HORSESHOEING
HORSESHOEINGS
HORSESHOER
HORSESHOERS
HORSESHOES
HORSETAILS
HORSEWEEDS
HORSEWHIPPED
HORSEWHIPPER
HORSEWHIPPERS
HORSEWHIPPING
HORSEWHIPS
HORSEWOMAN
HORSEWOMEN
HORSINESSES
HORTATIONS
HORTATIVELY
HORTATORILY
HORTENSIAS
HORTICULTURAL
HORTICULTURALLY
HORTICULTURE
HORTICULTURES
HORTICULTURIST
HORTICULTURISTS
HOSANNAING
HOSPITABLE
HOSPITABLENESS
HOSPITABLY
HOSPITAGES
HOSPITALER
HOSPITALERS
HOSPITALES
HOSPITALISATION
HOSPITALISE
HOSPITALISED
HOSPITALISES
HOSPITALISING
HOSPITALIST
HOSPITALISTS
HOSPITALITIES
HOSPITALITY
HOSPITALIZATION
HOSPITALIZE
HOSPITALIZED
HOSPITALIZES
HOSPITALIZING
HOSPITALLER
HOSPITALLERS
HOSTELINGS
HOSTELLERS
HOSTELLING
HOSTELLINGS
HOSTELRIES
HOSTESSING
HOSTILITIES
HOTCHPOTCH
HOTCHPOTCHES
HOTDOGGERS
HOTDOGGING

HOTELLINGS
HOTFOOTING
HOTHEADEDLY
HOTHEADEDNESS
HOTHEADEDNESSES
HOTHOUSING
HOTHOUSINGS
HOTPRESSED
HOTPRESSES
HOTPRESSING
HOTTENTOTS
HOUGHMAGANDIE
HOUGHMAGANDIES
HOUNDFISHES
HOURGLASSES
HOURPLATES
HOUSEBOATER
HOUSEBOATERS
HOUSEBOATS
HOUSEBOUND
HOUSEBREAK
HOUSEBREAKER
HOUSEBREAKERS
HOUSEBREAKING
HOUSEBREAKINGS
HOUSEBREAKS
HOUSEBROKE
HOUSEBROKEN
HOUSECARLS
HOUSECLEAN
HOUSECLEANED
HOUSECLEANING
HOUSECLEANINGS
HOUSECLEANS
HOUSECOATS
HOUSECRAFT
HOUSECRAFTS
HOUSEDRESS
HOUSEDRESSES
HOUSEFATHER
HOUSEFATHERS
HOUSEFLIES
HOUSEFRONT
HOUSEFRONTS
HOUSEGUEST
HOUSEGUESTS
HOUSEHOLDER
HOUSEHOLDERS
HOUSEHOLDERSHIP
HOUSEHOLDS
HOUSEHUSBAND
HOUSEHUSBANDS
HOUSEKEEPER
HOUSEKEEPERS
HOUSEKEEPING
HOUSEKEEPINGS
HOUSEKEEPS
HOUSELEEKS
HOUSELESSNESS
HOUSELESSNESSES
HOUSELIGHTS
HOUSELINES
HOUSELINGS
HOUSELLING
HOUSELLINGS
HOUSEMAIDS
HOUSEMASTER
HOUSEMASTERS
HOUSEMATES
HOUSEMISTRESS
HOUSEMISTRESSES
HOUSEMOTHER
HOUSEMOTHERS
HOUSEPAINTER
HOUSEPAINTERS
HOUSEPARENT
HOUSEPARENTS
HOUSEPERSON
HOUSEPERSONS
HOUSEPLANT
HOUSEPLANTS
HOUSEROOMS
HOUSESITTING
HOUSEWARES
HOUSEWARMING
HOUSEWARMINGS
HOUSEWIFELIER
HOUSEWIFELIEST
HOUSEWIFELINESS
HOUSEWIFELY
HOUSEWIFERIES
HOUSEWIFERY
HOUSEWIFESHIP
HOUSEWIFESHIPS
HOUSEWIFESKEP
HOUSEWIFESKEPS
HOUSEWIFEY
HOUSEWIFIER
HOUSEWIFIEST
HOUSEWIVES
HOUSEWORKER
HOUSEWORKERS
HOUSEWORKS
HOUSEWRAPS
HOUSTONIAS
HOVERBOARD
HOVERBOARDS
HOVERCRAFT
HOVERCRAFTS
HOVERFLIES
HOVERINGLY
HOVERPORTS
HOVERTRAIN
HOVERTRAINS
HOWLROUNDS
HOWSOMDEVER
HOWSOMEVER
HOWTOWDIES
HOYDENHOOD
HOYDENHOODS
HOYDENISHNESS
HOYDENISHNESSES
HOYDENISMS
HUBRISTICALLY
HUCKABACKS
HUCKLEBERRIES
HUCKLEBERRY
HUCKLEBERRYING
HUCKLEBERRYINGS
HUCKLEBONE
HUCKLEBONES
HUCKSTERAGE
HUCKSTERAGES
HUCKSTERED
HUCKSTERESS
HUCKSTERESSES
HUCKSTERIES
HUCKSTERING
HUCKSTERISM
HUCKSTERISMS
HUCKSTRESS
HUCKSTRESSES
HUDIBRASTIC
HUFFINESSES
HUFFISHNESS
HUFFISHNESSES
HUGENESSES
HUGEOUSNESS
HUGEOUSNESSES
HULLABALLOO
HULLABALLOOS
HULLABALOO
HULLABALOOS
HUMANENESS
HUMANENESSES
HUMANHOODS
HUMANISATION
HUMANISATIONS
HUMANISERS
HUMANISING
HUMANISTIC
HUMANISTICALLY
HUMANITARIAN
HUMANITARIANISM
HUMANITARIANIST
HUMANITARIANS
HUMANITIES
HUMANIZATION
HUMANIZATIONS
HUMANIZERS
HUMANIZING
HUMANKINDS
HUMANNESSES
HUMBLEBEES
HUMBLEBRAG
HUMBLEBRAGGED
HUMBLEBRAGGING
HUMBLEBRAGS
HUMBLENESS
HUMBLENESSES
HUMBLESSES
HUMBLINGLY
HUMBUCKERS
HUMBUGGABLE
HUMBUGGERIES
HUMBUGGERS
HUMBUGGERY
HUMBUGGING
HUMDINGERS
HUMDRUMNESS
HUMDRUMNESSES
HUMDUDGEON
HUMDUDGEONS
HUMDURGEON
HUMDURGEONS
HUMECTANTS
HUMECTATED
HUMECTATES
HUMECTATING
HUMECTATION
HUMECTATIONS
HUMECTIVES
HUMGRUFFIAN
HUMGRUFFIANS
HUMGRUFFIN
HUMGRUFFINS
HUMICOLOUS
HUMIDIFICATION
HUMIDIFICATIONS
HUMIDIFIED
HUMIDIFIER
HUMIDIFIERS
HUMIDIFIES
HUMIDIFYING
HUMIDISTAT
HUMIDISTATS
HUMIDITIES
HUMIDNESSES
HUMIFICATION
HUMIFICATIONS
HUMILIATED
HUMILIATES
HUMILIATING
HUMILIATINGLY
HUMILIATION
HUMILIATIONS
HUMILIATIVE
HUMILIATOR
HUMILIATORS
HUMILIATORY
HUMILITIES
HUMMELLERS
HUMMELLING
HUMMELLINGS
HUMMINGBIRD
HUMMINGBIRDS
HUMMOCKIER
HUMMOCKIEST
HUMMOCKING
HUMORALISM

HUMORALISMS
HUMORALIST
HUMORALISTS
HUMORESQUE
HUMORESQUES
HUMORISTIC
HUMORLESSLY
HUMORLESSNESS
HUMORLESSNESSES
HUMOROUSLY
HUMOROUSNESS
HUMOROUSNESSES
HUMORSOMENESS
HUMORSOMENESSES
HUMOURLESS
HUMOURLESSLY
HUMOURLESSNESS
HUMOURSOME
HUMOURSOMENESS
HUMPBACKED
HUMPINESSES
HUNCHBACKED
HUNCHBACKS
HUNDREDERS
HUNDREDFOLD
HUNDREDFOLDS
HUNDREDORS
HUNDREDTHS
HUNDREDWEIGHT
HUNDREDWEIGHTS
HUNGERINGLY
HUNGRINESS
HUNGRINESSES
HUNTIEGOWK
HUNTIEGOWKED
HUNTIEGOWKING
HUNTIEGOWKS
HUNTRESSES
HUNTSMANSHIP
HUNTSMANSHIPS
HUPAITHRIC
HURLBARROW
HURLBARROWS
HURRICANES
HURRICANOES
HURRIEDNESS
HURRIEDNESSES
HURRYINGLY
HURTFULNESS
HURTFULNESSES
HURTLEBERRIES
HURTLEBERRY
HURTLESSLY
HURTLESSNESS
HURTLESSNESSES
HUSBANDAGE
HUSBANDAGES
HUSBANDERS
HUSBANDING
HUSBANDLAND
HUSBANDLANDS
HUSBANDLESS
HUSBANDLIER
HUSBANDLIEST
HUSBANDLIKE
HUSBANDMAN
HUSBANDMEN
HUSBANDRIES
HUSHABYING
HUSHPUPPIES
HUSKINESSES
HYACINTHINE
HYALINISATION
HYALINISATIONS
HYALINISED
HYALINISES
HYALINISING
HYALINIZATION
HYALINIZATIONS
HYALINIZED
HYALINIZES
HYALINIZING
HYALOMELAN
HYALOMELANE
HYALOMELANES
HYALOMELANS
HYALONEMAS
HYALOPHANE
HYALOPHANES
HYALOPLASM
HYALOPLASMIC
HYALOPLASMS
HYALURONIC
HYALURONIDASE
HYALURONIDASES
HYBRIDISABLE
HYBRIDISATION
HYBRIDISATIONS
HYBRIDISED
HYBRIDISER
HYBRIDISERS
HYBRIDISES
HYBRIDISING
HYBRIDISMS
HYBRIDISTS
HYBRIDITIES
HYBRIDIZABLE
HYBRIDIZATION
HYBRIDIZATIONS
HYBRIDIZED
HYBRIDIZER
HYBRIDIZERS
HYBRIDIZES
HYBRIDIZING
HYBRIDOMAS
HYBRIDOMATA
HYDANTOINS
HYDATHODES
HYDATIDIFORM
HYDNOCARPATE
HYDNOCARPATES
HYDNOCARPIC
HYDRAEMIAS
HYDRAGOGUE
HYDRAGOGUES
HYDRALAZINE
HYDRALAZINES
HYDRANGEAS
HYDRARGYRAL
HYDRARGYRIA
HYDRARGYRIAS
HYDRARGYRIC
HYDRARGYRISM
HYDRARGYRISMS
HYDRARGYRUM
HYDRARGYRUMS
HYDRARTHROSES
HYDRARTHROSIS
HYDRASTINE
HYDRASTINES
HYDRASTININE
HYDRASTININES
HYDRASTISES
HYDRATIONS
HYDRAULICALLY
HYDRAULICKED
HYDRAULICKING
HYDRAULICKINGS
HYDRAULICS
HYDRAZIDES
HYDRAZINES
HYDRICALLY
HYDROACOUSTICS
HYDROBIOLOGICAL
HYDROBIOLOGIES
HYDROBIOLOGIST
HYDROBIOLOGISTS
HYDROBIOLOGY
HYDROBROMIC
HYDROCARBON
HYDROCARBONS
HYDROCASTS
HYDROCELES
HYDROCELLULOSE
HYDROCELLULOSES
HYDROCEPHALI
HYDROCEPHALIC
HYDROCEPHALICS
HYDROCEPHALIES
HYDROCEPHALOID
HYDROCEPHALOUS
HYDROCEPHALUS
HYDROCEPHALUSES
HYDROCEPHALY
HYDROCHLORIC
HYDROCHLORIDE
HYDROCHLORIDES
HYDROCHORE
HYDROCHORES
HYDROCHORIC
HYDROCODONE
HYDROCODONES
HYDROCOLLOID
HYDROCOLLOIDAL
HYDROCOLLOIDS
HYDROCORAL
HYDROCORALLINE
HYDROCORALLINES
HYDROCORALS
HYDROCORTISONE
HYDROCORTISONES
HYDROCRACK
HYDROCRACKED
HYDROCRACKER
HYDROCRACKERS
HYDROCRACKING
HYDROCRACKINGS
HYDROCRACKS
HYDROCYANIC
HYDRODYNAMIC
HYDRODYNAMICAL
HYDRODYNAMICIST
HYDRODYNAMICS
HYDROELASTIC
HYDROELECTRIC
HYDROEXTRACTOR
HYDROEXTRACTORS
HYDROFLUORIC
HYDROFOILS
HYDROFORMING
HYDROFORMINGS
HYDROGENASE
HYDROGENASES
HYDROGENATE
HYDROGENATED
HYDROGENATES
HYDROGENATING
HYDROGENATION
HYDROGENATIONS
HYDROGENATOR
HYDROGENATORS
HYDROGENISATION
HYDROGENISE
HYDROGENISED
HYDROGENISES
HYDROGENISING
HYDROGENIZATION
HYDROGENIZE
HYDROGENIZED
HYDROGENIZES
HYDROGENIZING
HYDROGENOLYSES
HYDROGENOLYSIS
HYDROGENOUS
HYDROGEOLOGICAL
HYDROGEOLOGIES
HYDROGEOLOGIST
HYDROGEOLOGISTS
HYDROGEOLOGY
HYDROGRAPH

H

HYDROGRAPHER
HYDROGRAPHERS
HYDROGRAPHIC
HYDROGRAPHICAL
HYDROGRAPHIES
HYDROGRAPHS
HYDROGRAPHY
HYDROKINETIC
HYDROKINETICAL
HYDROKINETICS
HYDROLASES
HYDROLOGIC
HYDROLOGICAL
HYDROLOGICALLY
HYDROLOGIES
HYDROLOGIST
HYDROLOGISTS
HYDROLYSABLE
HYDROLYSATE
HYDROLYSATES
HYDROLYSATION
HYDROLYSATIONS
HYDROLYSED
HYDROLYSER
HYDROLYSERS
HYDROLYSES
HYDROLYSING
HYDROLYSIS
HYDROLYTES
HYDROLYTIC
HYDROLYTICALLY
HYDROLYZABLE
HYDROLYZATE
HYDROLYZATES
HYDROLYZATION
HYDROLYZATIONS
HYDROLYZED
HYDROLYZER
HYDROLYZERS
HYDROLYZES
HYDROLYZING
HYDROMAGNETIC
HYDROMAGNETICS
HYDROMANCER
HYDROMANCERS
HYDROMANCIES
HYDROMANCY
HYDROMANIA
HYDROMANIAS
HYDROMANTIC
HYDROMECHANICAL
HYDROMECHANICS
HYDROMEDUSA
HYDROMEDUSAE
HYDROMEDUSAN
HYDROMEDUSANS
HYDROMEDUSAS
HYDROMEDUSOID
HYDROMEDUSOIDS
HYDROMETALLURGY
HYDROMETEOR
HYDROMETEORS
HYDROMETER
HYDROMETERS
HYDROMETRIC
HYDROMETRICAL
HYDROMETRICALLY
HYDROMETRIES
HYDROMETRY
HYDROMORPHIC
HYDRONAUTS
HYDRONEPHROSES
HYDRONEPHROSIS
HYDRONEPHROTIC
HYDRONICALLY
HYDRONIUMS
HYDROPATHIC
HYDROPATHICAL
HYDROPATHICALLY
HYDROPATHICS
HYDROPATHIES
HYDROPATHIST
HYDROPATHISTS
HYDROPATHS
HYDROPATHY
HYDROPEROXIDE
HYDROPEROXIDES
HYDROPHANE
HYDROPHANES
HYDROPHANOUS
HYDROPHILE
HYDROPHILES
HYDROPHILIC
HYDROPHILICITY
HYDROPHILIES
HYDROPHILITE
HYDROPHILITES
HYDROPHILOUS
HYDROPHILY
HYDROPHOBIA
HYDROPHOBIAS
HYDROPHOBIC
HYDROPHOBICITY
HYDROPHOBOUS
HYDROPHONE
HYDROPHONES
HYDROPHYTE
HYDROPHYTES
HYDROPHYTIC
HYDROPHYTON
HYDROPHYTONS
HYDROPHYTOUS
HYDROPLANE
HYDROPLANED
HYDROPLANES
HYDROPLANING
HYDROPNEUMATIC
HYDROPOLYP
HYDROPOLYPS
HYDROPONIC
HYDROPONICALLY
HYDROPONICS
HYDROPOWER
HYDROPOWERS
HYDROPSIES
HYDROPULTS
HYDROQUINOL
HYDROQUINOLS
HYDROQUINONE
HYDROQUINONES
HYDROSCOPE
HYDROSCOPES
HYDROSCOPIC
HYDROSCOPICAL
HYDROSERES
HYDROSOLIC
HYDROSOMAL
HYDROSOMATA
HYDROSOMATOUS
HYDROSOMES
HYDROSPACE
HYDROSPACES
HYDROSPHERE
HYDROSPHERES
HYDROSPHERIC
HYDROSTATIC
HYDROSTATICAL
HYDROSTATICALLY
HYDROSTATICS
HYDROSTATS
HYDROSULPHATE
HYDROSULPHATES
HYDROSULPHIDE
HYDROSULPHIDES
HYDROSULPHITE
HYDROSULPHITES
HYDROSULPHURIC
HYDROSULPHUROUS
HYDROTACTIC
HYDROTAXES
HYDROTAXIS
HYDROTHECA
HYDROTHECAE
HYDROTHERAPIC
HYDROTHERAPIES
HYDROTHERAPIST
HYDROTHERAPISTS
HYDROTHERAPY
HYDROTHERMAL
HYDROTHERMALLY
HYDROTHORACES
HYDROTHORACIC
HYDROTHORAX
HYDROTHORAXES
HYDROTROPIC
HYDROTROPICALLY
HYDROTROPISM
HYDROTROPISMS
HYDROVANES
HYDROXIDES
HYDROXIUMS
HYDROXONIUM
HYDROXONIUMS
HYDROXYACETIC
HYDROXYAPATITE
HYDROXYAPATITES
HYDROXYBUTYRATE
HYDROXYCITRIC
HYDROXYLAMINE
HYDROXYLAMINES
HYDROXYLAPATITE
HYDROXYLASE
HYDROXYLASES
HYDROXYLATE
HYDROXYLATED
HYDROXYLATES
HYDROXYLATING
HYDROXYLATION
HYDROXYLATIONS
HYDROXYLIC
HYDROXYPROLINE
HYDROXYPROLINES
HYDROXYUREA
HYDROXYUREAS
HYDROXYZINE
HYDROXYZINES
HYDROZINCITE
HYDROZINCITES
HYDROZOANS
HYETOGRAPH
HYETOGRAPHIC
HYETOGRAPHICAL
HYETOGRAPHIES
HYETOGRAPHS
HYETOGRAPHY
HYETOLOGIES
HYETOMETER
HYETOMETERS
HYETOMETROGRAPH
HYGIENICALLY
HYGIENISTS
HYGRISTORS
HYGROCHASIES
HYGROCHASTIC
HYGROCHASY
HYGRODEIKS
HYGROGRAPH
HYGROGRAPHIC
HYGROGRAPHICAL
HYGROGRAPHS
HYGROLOGIES
HYGROMETER
HYGROMETERS
HYGROMETRIC
HYGROMETRICAL
HYGROMETRICALLY
HYGROMETRIES
HYGROMETRY
HYGROPHILE
HYGROPHILES

H

HYGROPHILOUS
HYGROPHOBE
HYGROPHOBES
HYGROPHYTE
HYGROPHYTES
HYGROPHYTIC
HYGROSCOPE
HYGROSCOPES
HYGROSCOPIC
HYGROSCOPICAL
HYGROSCOPICALLY
HYGROSCOPICITY
HYGROSTATS
HYLOGENESES
HYLOGENESIS
HYLOMORPHIC
HYLOMORPHISM
HYLOMORPHISMS
HYLOPATHISM
HYLOPATHISMS
HYLOPATHIST
HYLOPATHISTS
HYLOPHAGOUS
HYLOPHYTES
HYLOTHEISM
HYLOTHEISMS
HYLOTHEIST
HYLOTHEISTS
HYLOTOMOUS
HYLOZOICAL
HYLOZOISMS
HYLOZOISTIC
HYLOZOISTICALLY
HYLOZOISTS
HYMENAEANS
HYMENEALLY
HYMENOPHORE
HYMENOPHORES
HYMENOPLASTIES
HYMENOPLASTY
HYMENOPTERA
HYMENOPTERAN
HYMENOPTERANS
HYMENOPTERON
HYMENOPTERONS
HYMENOPTEROUS
HYMNODICAL
HYMNODISTS
HYMNOGRAPHER
HYMNOGRAPHERS
HYMNOGRAPHIES
HYMNOGRAPHY
HYMNOLOGIC
HYMNOLOGICAL
HYMNOLOGIES
HYMNOLOGIST
HYMNOLOGISTS
HYOPLASTRA
HYOPLASTRAL
HYOPLASTRON
HYOSCYAMINE
HYOSCYAMINES
HYOSCYAMUS
HYOSCYAMUSES
HYPABYSSAL
HYPABYSSALLY
HYPAESTHESIA
HYPAESTHESIAS
HYPAESTHESIC
HYPAETHRAL
HYPAETHRON
HYPAETHRONS
HYPALGESIA
HYPALGESIAS
HYPALGESIC
HYPALLACTIC
HYPALLAGES
HYPANTHIAL
HYPANTHIUM
HYPERACIDITIES
HYPERACIDITY
HYPERACTION
HYPERACTIONS
HYPERACTIVE
HYPERACTIVES
HYPERACTIVITIES
HYPERACTIVITY
HYPERACUITIES
HYPERACUITY
HYPERACUSES
HYPERACUSIS
HYPERACUTE
HYPERACUTENESS
HYPERADRENALISM
HYPERAEMIA
HYPERAEMIAS
HYPERAEMIC
HYPERAESTHESIA
HYPERAESTHESIAS
HYPERAESTHESIC
HYPERAESTHETIC
HYPERAGGRESSIVE
HYPERALERT
HYPERALGESIA
HYPERALGESIAS
HYPERALGESIC
HYPERAROUSAL
HYPERAROUSALS
HYPERAWARE
HYPERAWARENESS
HYPERBARIC
HYPERBARICALLY
HYPERBATIC
HYPERBATICALLY
HYPERBATON
HYPERBATONS
HYPERBOLAE
HYPERBOLAEON
HYPERBOLAEONS
HYPERBOLAS
HYPERBOLES
HYPERBOLIC
HYPERBOLICAL
HYPERBOLICALLY
HYPERBOLISE
HYPERBOLISED
HYPERBOLISES
HYPERBOLISING
HYPERBOLISM
HYPERBOLISMS
HYPERBOLIST
HYPERBOLISTS
HYPERBOLIZE
HYPERBOLIZED
HYPERBOLIZES
HYPERBOLIZING
HYPERBOLOID
HYPERBOLOIDAL
HYPERBOLOIDS
HYPERBOREAN
HYPERBOREANS
HYPERCALCAEMIA
HYPERCALCAEMIAS
HYPERCALCAEMIC
HYPERCALCEMIA
HYPERCALCEMIAS
HYPERCALCEMIC
HYPERCAPNIA
HYPERCAPNIAS
HYPERCAPNIC
HYPERCARBIA
HYPERCARBIAS
HYPERCATABOLISM
HYPERCATALECTIC
HYPERCATALEXES
HYPERCATALEXIS
HYPERCAUTIOUS
HYPERCHARGE
HYPERCHARGED
HYPERCHARGES
HYPERCHARGING
HYPERCIVILISED
HYPERCIVILIZED
HYPERCOAGULABLE
HYPERCOLOUR
HYPERCOLOURS
HYPERCOMPLEX
HYPERCONSCIOUS
HYPERCORRECT
HYPERCORRECTION
HYPERCORRECTLY
HYPERCRITIC
HYPERCRITICAL
HYPERCRITICALLY
HYPERCRITICISE
HYPERCRITICISED
HYPERCRITICISES
HYPERCRITICISM
HYPERCRITICISMS
HYPERCRITICIZE
HYPERCRITICIZED
HYPERCRITICIZES
HYPERCRITICS
HYPERCUBES
HYPERDACTYL
HYPERDACTYLIES
HYPERDACTYLY
HYPERDORIAN
HYPERDULIA
HYPERDULIAS
HYPERDULIC
HYPERDULICAL
HYPEREFFICIENT
HYPEREMESES
HYPEREMESIS
HYPEREMETIC
HYPEREMIAS
HYPEREMOTIONAL
HYPERENDEMIC
HYPERENERGETIC
HYPERESTHESIA
HYPERESTHESIAS
HYPERESTHETIC
HYPEREUTECTIC
HYPEREUTECTOID
HYPEREXCITABLE
HYPEREXCITED
HYPEREXCITEMENT
HYPEREXCRETION
HYPEREXCRETIONS
HYPEREXTEND
HYPEREXTENDED
HYPEREXTENDING
HYPEREXTENDS
HYPEREXTENSION
HYPEREXTENSIONS
HYPERFASTIDIOUS
HYPERFOCAL
HYPERFUNCTION
HYPERFUNCTIONAL
HYPERFUNCTIONS
HYPERGAMIES
HYPERGAMOUS
HYPERGEOMETRIC
HYPERGLYCAEMIA
HYPERGLYCAEMIAS
HYPERGLYCAEMIC
HYPERGLYCEMIA
HYPERGLYCEMIAS
HYPERGLYCEMIC
HYPERGOLIC
HYPERGOLICALLY
HYPERHIDROSES
HYPERHIDROSIS
HYPERICINS
HYPERICUMS
HYPERIDROSES
HYPERIDROSIS
HYPERIMMUNE
HYPERIMMUNISE

HYPERIMMUNISED
HYPERIMMUNISES
HYPERIMMUNISING
HYPERIMMUNIZE
HYPERIMMUNIZED
HYPERIMMUNIZES
HYPERIMMUNIZING
HYPERINFLATED
HYPERINFLATION
HYPERINFLATIONS
HYPERINOSES
HYPERINOSIS
HYPERINOTIC
HYPERINSULINISM
HYPERINTENSE
HYPERINVOLUTION
HYPERIRRITABLE
HYPERKERATOSES
HYPERKERATOSIS
HYPERKERATOTIC
HYPERKINESES
HYPERKINESIA
HYPERKINESIAS
HYPERKINESIS
HYPERKINETIC
HYPERLINKED
HYPERLINKING
HYPERLINKS
HYPERLIPEMIA
HYPERLIPEMIAS
HYPERLIPEMIC
HYPERLIPIDAEMIA
HYPERLIPIDEMIA
HYPERLIPIDEMIAS
HYPERLYDIAN
HYPERMANIA
HYPERMANIAS
HYPERMANIC
HYPERMARKET
HYPERMARKETS
HYPERMARTS
HYPERMASCULINE
HYPERMEDIA
HYPERMEDIAS
HYPERMETABOLIC
HYPERMETABOLISM
HYPERMETER
HYPERMETERS
HYPERMETRIC
HYPERMETRICAL
HYPERMETROPIA
HYPERMETROPIAS
HYPERMETROPIC
HYPERMETROPICAL
HYPERMETROPIES
HYPERMETROPY
HYPERMILING
HYPERMILINGS
HYPERMNESIA
HYPERMNESIAS
HYPERMNESIC
HYPERMOBILITIES
HYPERMOBILITY
HYPERMODERN
HYPERMODERNISM
HYPERMODERNISMS
HYPERMODERNIST
HYPERMODERNISTS
HYPERMUTABILITY
HYPERMUTABLE
HYPERNATRAEMIA
HYPERNATRAEMIAS
HYPERNOVAE
HYPERNOVAS
HYPERNYMIES
HYPEROPIAS
HYPEROREXIA
HYPEROREXIAS
HYPEROSMIA
HYPEROSMIAS
HYPEROSTOSES
HYPEROSTOSIS
HYPEROSTOSISES
HYPEROSTOTIC
HYPEROXIDE
HYPEROXIDES
HYPERPARASITE
HYPERPARASITES
HYPERPARASITIC
HYPERPARASITISM
HYPERPHAGIA
HYPERPHAGIAS
HYPERPHAGIC
HYPERPHRYGIAN
HYPERPHYSICAL
HYPERPHYSICALLY
HYPERPIGMENTED
HYPERPITUITARY
HYPERPLANE
HYPERPLANES
HYPERPLASIA
HYPERPLASIAS
HYPERPLASTIC
HYPERPLOID
HYPERPLOIDIES
HYPERPLOIDS
HYPERPLOIDY
HYPERPNEAS
HYPERPNEIC
HYPERPNOEA
HYPERPNOEAS
HYPERPOLARISE
HYPERPOLARISED
HYPERPOLARISES
HYPERPOLARISING
HYPERPOLARIZE
HYPERPOLARIZED
HYPERPOLARIZES
HYPERPOLARIZING
HYPERPOWER
HYPERPOWERS
HYPERPRODUCER
HYPERPRODUCERS
HYPERPRODUCTION
HYPERPROSEXIA
HYPERPROSEXIAS
HYPERPYRETIC
HYPERPYREXIA
HYPERPYREXIAL
HYPERPYREXIAS
HYPERRATIONAL
HYPERREACTIVE
HYPERREACTIVITY
HYPERREACTOR
HYPERREACTORS
HYPERREALISM
HYPERREALISMS
HYPERREALIST
HYPERREALISTIC
HYPERREALISTS
HYPERREALITIES
HYPERREALITY
HYPERREALS
HYPERRESPONSIVE
HYPERROMANTIC
HYPERROMANTICS
HYPERSALINE
HYPERSALINITIES
HYPERSALINITY
HYPERSALIVATION
HYPERSARCOMA
HYPERSARCOMAS
HYPERSARCOMATA
HYPERSARCOSES
HYPERSARCOSIS
HYPERSECRETION
HYPERSECRETIONS
HYPERSENSITISE
HYPERSENSITISED
HYPERSENSITISES
HYPERSENSITIVE
HYPERSENSITIZE
HYPERSENSITIZED
HYPERSENSITIZES
HYPERSENSUAL
HYPERSEXUAL
HYPERSEXUALITY
HYPERSOMNIA
HYPERSOMNIAS
HYPERSOMNOLENCE
HYPERSONIC
HYPERSONICALLY
HYPERSONICS
HYPERSPACE
HYPERSPACES
HYPERSPATIAL
HYPERSTATIC
HYPERSTHENE
HYPERSTHENES
HYPERSTHENIA
HYPERSTHENIAS
HYPERSTHENIC
HYPERSTHENITE
HYPERSTHENITES
HYPERSTIMULATE
HYPERSTIMULATED
HYPERSTIMULATES
HYPERSTRESS
HYPERSTRESSES
HYPERSURFACE
HYPERSURFACES
HYPERTENSE
HYPERTENSION
HYPERTENSIONS
HYPERTENSIVE
HYPERTENSIVES
HYPERTEXTS
HYPERTHERMAL
HYPERTHERMIA
HYPERTHERMIAS
HYPERTHERMIC
HYPERTHERMIES
HYPERTHERMY
HYPERTHYMIA
HYPERTHYMIAS
HYPERTHYROID
HYPERTHYROIDISM
HYPERTHYROIDS
HYPERTONIA
HYPERTONIAS
HYPERTONIC
HYPERTONICITIES
HYPERTONICITY
HYPERTROPHIC
HYPERTROPHICAL
HYPERTROPHIED
HYPERTROPHIES
HYPERTROPHOUS
HYPERTROPHY
HYPERTROPHYING
HYPERTYPICAL
HYPERURBANISM
HYPERURBANISMS
HYPERURICAEMIA
HYPERURICAEMIAS
HYPERURICEMIA
HYPERURICEMIAS
HYPERVELOCITIES
HYPERVELOCITY
HYPERVENTILATE
HYPERVENTILATED
HYPERVENTILATES
HYPERVIGILANCE
HYPERVIGILANCES
HYPERVIGILANT
HYPERVIRULENT
HYPERVISCOSITY
HYPESTHESIA
HYPESTHESIAS
HYPESTHESIC

HYPHENATED
HYPHENATES
HYPHENATING
HYPHENATION
HYPHENATIONS
HYPHENISATION
HYPHENISATIONS
HYPHENISED
HYPHENISES
HYPHENISING
HYPHENISMS
HYPHENIZATION
HYPHENIZATIONS
HYPHENIZED
HYPHENIZES
HYPHENIZING
HYPHENLESS
HYPNAGOGIC
HYPNOANALYSES
HYPNOANALYSIS
HYPNOANALYTIC
HYPNOBIRTHING
HYPNOBIRTHINGS
HYPNOGENESES
HYPNOGENESIS
HYPNOGENETIC
HYPNOGENIC
HYPNOGENIES
HYPNOGENOUS
HYPNOGOGIC
HYPNOIDISE
HYPNOIDISED
HYPNOIDISES
HYPNOIDISING
HYPNOIDIZE
HYPNOIDIZED
HYPNOIDIZES
HYPNOIDIZING
HYPNOLOGIC
HYPNOLOGICAL
HYPNOLOGIES
HYPNOLOGIST
HYPNOLOGISTS
HYPNOPAEDIA
HYPNOPAEDIAS
HYPNOPHOBIA
HYPNOPHOBIAS
HYPNOPOMPIC
HYPNOTHERAPIES
HYPNOTHERAPIST
HYPNOTHERAPISTS
HYPNOTHERAPY
HYPNOTICALLY
HYPNOTISABILITY
HYPNOTISABLE
HYPNOTISATION
HYPNOTISATIONS
HYPNOTISED
HYPNOTISER
HYPNOTISERS
HYPNOTISES
HYPNOTISING
HYPNOTISMS
HYPNOTISTIC
HYPNOTISTS
HYPNOTIZABILITY
HYPNOTIZABLE
HYPNOTIZATION
HYPNOTIZATIONS
HYPNOTIZED
HYPNOTIZER
HYPNOTIZERS
HYPNOTIZES
HYPNOTIZING
HYPOACIDITIES
HYPOACIDITY
HYPOAEOLIAN
HYPOALLERGENIC
HYPOBLASTIC
HYPOBLASTS
HYPOCALCAEMIA
HYPOCALCAEMIAS
HYPOCALCAEMIC
HYPOCALCEMIA
HYPOCALCEMIAS
HYPOCALCEMIC
HYPOCAUSTS
HYPOCENTER
HYPOCENTERS
HYPOCENTRAL
HYPOCENTRE
HYPOCENTRES
HYPOCHLORITE
HYPOCHLORITES
HYPOCHLOROUS
HYPOCHONDRIA
HYPOCHONDRIAC
HYPOCHONDRIACAL
HYPOCHONDRIACS
HYPOCHONDRIAS
HYPOCHONDRIASES
HYPOCHONDRIASIS
HYPOCHONDRIASM
HYPOCHONDRIASMS
HYPOCHONDRIAST
HYPOCHONDRIASTS
HYPOCHONDRIUM
HYPOCORISM
HYPOCORISMA
HYPOCORISMAS
HYPOCORISMS
HYPOCORISTIC
HYPOCORISTICAL
HYPOCOTYLOUS
HYPOCOTYLS
HYPOCRISIES
HYPOCRITES
HYPOCRITIC
HYPOCRITICAL
HYPOCRITICALLY
HYPOCRYSTALLINE
HYPOCYCLOID
HYPOCYCLOIDAL
HYPOCYCLOIDS
HYPODERMAL
HYPODERMAS
HYPODERMIC
HYPODERMICALLY
HYPODERMICS
HYPODERMIS
HYPODERMISES
HYPODIPLOID
HYPODIPLOIDIES
HYPODIPLOIDY
HYPODORIAN
HYPOEUTECTIC
HYPOEUTECTOID
HYPOGAEOUS
HYPOGASTRIA
HYPOGASTRIC
HYPOGASTRIUM
HYPOGENOUS
HYPOGLOSSAL
HYPOGLOSSALS
HYPOGLYCAEMIA
HYPOGLYCAEMIAS
HYPOGLYCAEMIC
HYPOGLYCEMIA
HYPOGLYCEMIAS
HYPOGLYCEMIC
HYPOGLYCEMICS
HYPOGNATHISM
HYPOGNATHISMS
HYPOGNATHOUS
HYPOGYNIES
HYPOGYNOUS
HYPOKALEMIA
HYPOKALEMIAS
HYPOKALEMIC
HYPOLIMNIA
HYPOLIMNION
HYPOLIMNIONS
HYPOLYDIAN
HYPOMAGNESAEMIA
HYPOMAGNESEMIA
HYPOMAGNESEMIAS
HYPOMANIAS
HYPOMANICS
HYPOMENORRHEA
HYPOMENORRHEAS
HYPOMENORRHOEA
HYPOMENORRHOEAS
HYPOMIXOLYDIAN
HYPOMORPHIC
HYPOMORPHS
HYPONASTIC
HYPONASTICALLY
HYPONASTIES
HYPONATRAEMIA
HYPONATRAEMIAS
HYPONITRITE
HYPONITRITES
HYPONITROUS
HYPONYMIES
HYPOPHARYNGES
HYPOPHARYNX
HYPOPHARYNXES
HYPOPHOSPHATE
HYPOPHOSPHATES
HYPOPHOSPHITE
HYPOPHOSPHITES
HYPOPHOSPHORIC
HYPOPHOSPHOROUS
HYPOPHRYGIAN
HYPOPHYGES
HYPOPHYSEAL
HYPOPHYSECTOMY
HYPOPHYSES
HYPOPHYSIAL
HYPOPHYSIS
HYPOPITUITARISM
HYPOPITUITARY
HYPOPLASIA
HYPOPLASIAS
HYPOPLASTIC
HYPOPLASTIES
HYPOPLASTRA
HYPOPLASTRON
HYPOPLASTY
HYPOPLOIDIES
HYPOPLOIDS
HYPOPLOIDY
HYPOPNOEAS
HYPOSENSITISE
HYPOSENSITISED
HYPOSENSITISES
HYPOSENSITISING
HYPOSENSITIZE
HYPOSENSITIZED
HYPOSENSITIZES
HYPOSENSITIZING
HYPOSPADIAS
HYPOSPADIASES
HYPOSTASES
HYPOSTASIS
HYPOSTASISATION
HYPOSTASISE
HYPOSTASISED
HYPOSTASISES
HYPOSTASISING
HYPOSTASIZATION
HYPOSTASIZE
HYPOSTASIZED
HYPOSTASIZES
HYPOSTASIZING
HYPOSTATIC
HYPOSTATICAL
HYPOSTATICALLY
HYPOSTATISATION
HYPOSTATISE

HYPOSTATISED
HYPOSTATISES
HYPOSTATISING
HYPOSTATIZATION
HYPOSTATIZE
HYPOSTATIZED
HYPOSTATIZES
HYPOSTATIZING
HYPOSTHENIA
HYPOSTHENIAS
HYPOSTHENIC
HYPOSTOMES
HYPOSTRESS
HYPOSTRESSES
HYPOSTROPHE
HYPOSTROPHES
HYPOSTYLES
HYPOSULPHATE
HYPOSULPHATES
HYPOSULPHITE
HYPOSULPHITES
HYPOSULPHURIC
HYPOSULPHUROUS
HYPOTACTIC
HYPOTENSION
HYPOTENSIONS
HYPOTENSIVE
HYPOTENSIVES
HYPOTENUSE
HYPOTENUSES
HYPOTHALAMI
HYPOTHALAMIC
HYPOTHALAMUS
HYPOTHECAE
HYPOTHECARY
HYPOTHECATE
HYPOTHECATED
HYPOTHECATES
HYPOTHECATING
HYPOTHECATION
HYPOTHECATIONS
HYPOTHECATOR
HYPOTHECATORS
HYPOTHENUSE
HYPOTHENUSES
HYPOTHERMAL
HYPOTHERMIA
HYPOTHERMIAS
HYPOTHERMIC
HYPOTHESES
HYPOTHESIS
HYPOTHESISE
HYPOTHESISED
HYPOTHESISER
HYPOTHESISERS
HYPOTHESISES
HYPOTHESISING
HYPOTHESIST
HYPOTHESISTS
HYPOTHESIZE
HYPOTHESIZED
HYPOTHESIZER
HYPOTHESIZERS
HYPOTHESIZES
HYPOTHESIZING
HYPOTHETIC
HYPOTHETICAL
HYPOTHETICALLY
HYPOTHETISE
HYPOTHETISED
HYPOTHETISES
HYPOTHETISING
HYPOTHETIZE
HYPOTHETIZED
HYPOTHETIZES
HYPOTHETIZING
HYPOTHYMIA
HYPOTHYMIAS
HYPOTHYROID
HYPOTHYROIDISM
HYPOTHYROIDISMS
HYPOTHYROIDS
HYPOTONIAS
HYPOTONICITIES
HYPOTONICITY
HYPOTROCHOID
HYPOTROCHOIDS
HYPOTYPOSES
HYPOTYPOSIS
HYPOVENTILATION
HYPOXAEMIA
HYPOXAEMIAS
HYPOXAEMIC
HYPOXANTHINE
HYPOXANTHINES
HYPOXEMIAS
HYPSOCHROME
HYPSOCHROMES
HYPSOCHROMIC
HYPSOGRAPHIC
HYPSOGRAPHICAL
HYPSOGRAPHIES
HYPSOGRAPHY
HYPSOMETER
HYPSOMETERS
HYPSOMETRIC
HYPSOMETRICAL
HYPSOMETRICALLY
HYPSOMETRIES
HYPSOMETRIST
HYPSOMETRISTS
HYPSOMETRY
HYPSOPHOBE
HYPSOPHOBES
HYPSOPHOBIA
HYPSOPHOBIAS
HYPSOPHYLL
HYPSOPHYLLARY
HYPSOPHYLLS
HYRACOIDEAN
HYRACOIDEANS
HYSTERANTHOUS
HYSTERECTOMIES
HYSTERECTOMISE
HYSTERECTOMISED
HYSTERECTOMISES
HYSTERECTOMIZE
HYSTERECTOMIZED
HYSTERECTOMIZES
HYSTERECTOMY
HYSTERESES
HYSTERESIAL
HYSTERESIS
HYSTERETIC
HYSTERETICALLY
HYSTERICAL
HYSTERICALLY
HYSTERICKY
HYSTERITIS
HYSTERITISES
HYSTEROGENIC
HYSTEROGENIES
HYSTEROGENY
HYSTEROIDAL
HYSTEROMANIA
HYSTEROMANIAS
HYSTEROTOMIES
HYSTEROTOMY
HYSTRICOMORPH
HYSTRICOMORPHIC
HYSTRICOMORPHS

I

IAMBICALLY
IAMBOGRAPHER
IAMBOGRAPHERS
IATROCHEMICAL
IATROCHEMIST
IATROCHEMISTRY
IATROCHEMISTS
IATROGENIC
IATROGENICALLY
IATROGENICITIES
IATROGENICITY
IATROGENIES
IBUPROFENS
ICEBOATERS
ICEBOATING
ICEBOATINGS
ICEBREAKER
ICEBREAKERS
ICEBREAKING
ICEFISHING
ICHNEUMONS
ICHNOFOSSIL
ICHNOFOSSILS
ICHNOGRAPHIC
ICHNOGRAPHICAL
ICHNOGRAPHIES
ICHNOGRAPHY
ICHNOLITES
ICHNOLOGICAL
ICHNOLOGIES
ICHTHYOCOLLA
ICHTHYOCOLLAS
ICHTHYODORULITE
ICHTHYODORYLITE
ICHTHYOFAUNA
ICHTHYOFAUNAE
ICHTHYOFAUNAL
ICHTHYOFAUNAS
ICHTHYOIDAL
ICHTHYOIDS
ICHTHYOLATRIES
ICHTHYOLATROUS
ICHTHYOLATRY
ICHTHYOLITE
ICHTHYOLITES
ICHTHYOLITIC
ICHTHYOLOGIC
ICHTHYOLOGICAL
ICHTHYOLOGIES
ICHTHYOLOGIST
ICHTHYOLOGISTS
ICHTHYOLOGY
ICHTHYOPHAGIES
ICHTHYOPHAGIST
ICHTHYOPHAGISTS
ICHTHYOPHAGOUS
ICHTHYOPHAGY
ICHTHYOPSID
ICHTHYOPSIDAN
ICHTHYOPSIDANS
ICHTHYOPSIDS
ICHTHYORNIS
ICHTHYORNISES
ICHTHYOSAUR
ICHTHYOSAURI
ICHTHYOSAURIAN
ICHTHYOSAURIANS
ICHTHYOSAURS
ICHTHYOSAURUS
ICHTHYOSAURUSES
ICHTHYOSES
ICHTHYOSIS
ICHTHYOTIC
ICKINESSES
ICONICALLY
ICONICITIES
ICONIFYING
ICONOCLASM
ICONOCLASMS
ICONOCLAST
ICONOCLASTIC
ICONOCLASTS
ICONOGRAPHER
ICONOGRAPHERS
ICONOGRAPHIC
ICONOGRAPHICAL
ICONOGRAPHIES
ICONOGRAPHY
ICONOLATER
ICONOLATERS
ICONOLATRIES
ICONOLATROUS
ICONOLATRY
ICONOLOGICAL
ICONOLOGIES
ICONOLOGIST
ICONOLOGISTS
ICONOMACHIES
ICONOMACHIST
ICONOMACHISTS
ICONOMACHY
ICONOMATIC
ICONOMATICISM
ICONOMATICISMS
ICONOMETER
ICONOMETERS
ICONOMETRIES
ICONOMETRY
ICONOPHILISM
ICONOPHILISMS
ICONOPHILIST
ICONOPHILISTS
ICONOSCOPE
ICONOSCOPES
ICONOSTASES
ICONOSTASIS
ICOSAHEDRA
ICOSAHEDRAL
ICOSAHEDRON
ICOSAHEDRONS
ICOSANDRIAN
ICOSANDROUS
ICOSITETRAHEDRA
ICTERICALS
ICTERITIOUS
IDEALISATION
IDEALISATIONS
IDEALISERS
IDEALISING
IDEALISTIC
IDEALISTICALLY
IDEALITIES
IDEALIZATION
IDEALIZATIONS
IDEALIZERS
IDEALIZING
IDEALNESSES
IDEALOGIES
IDEALOGUES
IDEATIONAL
IDEATIONALLY
IDEMPOTENCIES
IDEMPOTENCY
IDEMPOTENT
IDEMPOTENTS
IDENTICALLY
IDENTICALNESS
IDENTICALNESSES
IDENTIFIABLE
IDENTIFIABLY
IDENTIFICATION
IDENTIFICATIONS
IDENTIFIED
IDENTIFIER
IDENTIFIERS
IDENTIFIES
IDENTIFYING
IDENTIKITS
IDENTITIES
IDEOGRAMIC
IDEOGRAMMATIC
IDEOGRAMMIC
IDEOGRAPHIC
IDEOGRAPHICAL
IDEOGRAPHICALLY
IDEOGRAPHIES
IDEOGRAPHS
IDEOGRAPHY
IDEOLOGICAL
IDEOLOGICALLY
IDEOLOGIES
IDEOLOGISE
IDEOLOGISED
IDEOLOGISES
IDEOLOGISING
IDEOLOGIST
IDEOLOGISTS
IDEOLOGIZE
IDEOLOGIZED
IDEOLOGIZES
IDEOLOGIZING
IDEOLOGUES
IDEOPHONES
IDEOPOLISES
IDEOPRAXIST
IDEOPRAXISTS
IDIOBLASTIC
IDIOBLASTS
IDIOGLOSSIA
IDIOGLOSSIAS
IDIOGRAPHIC
IDIOGRAPHS
IDIOLECTAL
IDIOLECTIC
IDIOMATICAL
IDIOMATICALLY
IDIOMATICALNESS
IDIOMATICNESS
IDIOMATICNESSES
IDIOMORPHIC
IDIOMORPHICALLY
IDIOMORPHISM
IDIOMORPHISMS
IDIOPATHIC
IDIOPATHICALLY
IDIOPATHIES
IDIOPHONES
IDIOPHONIC
IDIOPLASMATIC
IDIOPLASMIC

IDIOPLASMS
IDIORHYTHMIC
IDIORRHYTHMIC
IDIOSYNCRASIES
IDIOSYNCRASY
IDIOSYNCRATIC
IDIOSYNCRATICAL
IDIOTHERMOUS
IDIOTICALLY
IDIOTICALNESS
IDIOTICALNESSES
IDIOTICONS
IDLENESSES
IDOLATRESS
IDOLATRESSES
IDOLATRIES
IDOLATRISE
IDOLATRISED
IDOLATRISER
IDOLATRISERS
IDOLATRISES
IDOLATRISING
IDOLATRIZE
IDOLATRIZED
IDOLATRIZER
IDOLATRIZERS
IDOLATRIZES
IDOLATRIZING
IDOLATROUS
IDOLATROUSLY
IDOLATROUSNESS
IDOLISATION
IDOLISATIONS
IDOLIZATION
IDOLIZATIONS
IDOLOCLAST
IDOLOCLASTS
IDONEITIES
IDOXURIDINE
IDOXURIDINES
IDYLLICALLY
IFFINESSES
IGNESCENTS
IGNIMBRITE
IGNIMBRITES
IGNIPOTENT
IGNITABILITIES
IGNITABILITY
IGNITIBILITIES
IGNITIBILITY
IGNOBILITIES
IGNOBILITY
IGNOBLENESS
IGNOBLENESSES
IGNOMINIES
IGNOMINIOUS
IGNOMINIOUSLY
IGNOMINIOUSNESS
IGNORAMUSES
IGNORANCES
IGNORANTLY
IGNORANTNESS
IGNORANTNESSES
IGNORATION
IGNORATIONS
IGUANODONS
ILEOSTOMIES
ILLAQUEABLE
ILLAQUEATE
ILLAQUEATED
ILLAQUEATES
ILLAQUEATING
ILLAQUEATION
ILLAQUEATIONS
ILLATIVELY
ILLAUDABLE
ILLAUDABLY
ILLAWARRAS
ILLEGALISATION
ILLEGALISATIONS
ILLEGALISE
ILLEGALISED
ILLEGALISES
ILLEGALISING
ILLEGALITIES
ILLEGALITY
ILLEGALIZATION
ILLEGALIZATIONS
ILLEGALIZE
ILLEGALIZED
ILLEGALIZES
ILLEGALIZING
ILLEGIBILITIES
ILLEGIBILITY
ILLEGIBLENESS
ILLEGIBLENESSES
ILLEGITIMACIES
ILLEGITIMACY
ILLEGITIMATE
ILLEGITIMATED
ILLEGITIMATELY
ILLEGITIMATES
ILLEGITIMATING
ILLEGITIMATION
ILLEGITIMATIONS
ILLIBERALISE
ILLIBERALISED
ILLIBERALISES
ILLIBERALISING
ILLIBERALISM
ILLIBERALISMS
ILLIBERALITIES
ILLIBERALITY
ILLIBERALIZE
ILLIBERALIZED
ILLIBERALIZES
ILLIBERALIZING
ILLIBERALLY
ILLIBERALNESS
ILLIBERALNESSES
ILLICITNESS
ILLICITNESSES
ILLIMITABILITY
ILLIMITABLE
ILLIMITABLENESS
ILLIMITABLY
ILLIMITATION
ILLIMITATIONS
ILLIQUATION
ILLIQUATIONS
ILLIQUIDITIES
ILLIQUIDITY
ILLITERACIES
ILLITERACY
ILLITERATE
ILLITERATELY
ILLITERATENESS
ILLITERATES
ILLOCUTION
ILLOCUTIONARY
ILLOCUTIONS
ILLOGICALITIES
ILLOGICALITY
ILLOGICALLY
ILLOGICALNESS
ILLOGICALNESSES
ILLUMINABLE
ILLUMINANCE
ILLUMINANCES
ILLUMINANT
ILLUMINANTS
ILLUMINATE
ILLUMINATED
ILLUMINATES
ILLUMINATI
ILLUMINATING
ILLUMINATINGLY
ILLUMINATION
ILLUMINATIONAL
ILLUMINATIONS
ILLUMINATIVE
ILLUMINATO
ILLUMINATOR
ILLUMINATORS
ILLUMINERS
ILLUMINING
ILLUMINISM
ILLUMINISMS
ILLUMINIST
ILLUMINISTS
ILLUSIONAL
ILLUSIONARY
ILLUSIONED
ILLUSIONISM
ILLUSIONISMS
ILLUSIONIST
ILLUSIONISTIC
ILLUSIONISTS
ILLUSIVELY
ILLUSIVENESS
ILLUSIVENESSES
ILLUSORILY
ILLUSORINESS
ILLUSORINESSES
ILLUSTRATABLE
ILLUSTRATE
ILLUSTRATED
ILLUSTRATEDS
ILLUSTRATES
ILLUSTRATING
ILLUSTRATION
ILLUSTRATIONAL
ILLUSTRATIONS
ILLUSTRATIVE
ILLUSTRATIVELY
ILLUSTRATOR
ILLUSTRATORS
ILLUSTRATORY
ILLUSTRIOUS
ILLUSTRIOUSLY
ILLUSTRIOUSNESS
ILLUSTRISSIMO
ILLUVIATED
ILLUVIATES
ILLUVIATING
ILLUVIATION
ILLUVIATIONS
IMAGINABLE
IMAGINABLENESS
IMAGINABLY
IMAGINARIES
IMAGINARILY
IMAGINARINESS
IMAGINARINESSES
IMAGINATION
IMAGINATIONAL
IMAGINATIONS
IMAGINATIVE
IMAGINATIVELY
IMAGINATIVENESS
IMAGINEERED
IMAGINEERING
IMAGINEERS
IMAGININGS
IMAGINISTS
IMAGISTICALLY
IMBALANCED
IMBALANCES
IMBECILELY
IMBECILICALLY
IMBECILITIES
IMBECILITY
IMBIBITION
IMBIBITIONAL
IMBIBITIONS
IMBITTERED
IMBITTERING
IMBOLDENED
IMBOLDENING
IMBORDERED

IMBORDERING
IMBOSOMING
IMBOWERING
IMBRANGLED
IMBRANGLES
IMBRANGLING
IMBRICATED
IMBRICATELY
IMBRICATES
IMBRICATING
IMBRICATION
IMBRICATIONS
IMBROCCATA
IMBROCCATAS
IMBROGLIOS
IMBROWNING
IMBRUEMENT
IMBRUEMENTS
IMBUEMENTS
IMIDAZOLES
IMINAZOLES
IMINOUREAS
IMIPRAMINE
IMIPRAMINES
IMITABILITIES
IMITABILITY
IMITABLENESS
IMITABLENESSES
IMITANCIES
IMITATIONAL
IMITATIONS
IMITATIVELY
IMITATIVENESS
IMITATIVENESSES
IMMACULACIES
IMMACULACY
IMMACULATE
IMMACULATELY
IMMACULATENESS
IMMANACLED
IMMANACLES
IMMANACLING
IMMANATION
IMMANATIONS
IMMANENCES
IMMANENCIES
IMMANENTAL
IMMANENTISM
IMMANENTISMS
IMMANENTIST
IMMANENTISTIC
IMMANENTISTS
IMMANENTLY
IMMANITIES
IMMANTLING
IMMARCESCIBLE
IMMARGINATE
IMMATERIAL
IMMATERIALISE
IMMATERIALISED
IMMATERIALISES
IMMATERIALISING
IMMATERIALISM
IMMATERIALISMS
IMMATERIALIST
IMMATERIALISTS
IMMATERIALITIES
IMMATERIALITY
IMMATERIALIZE
IMMATERIALIZED
IMMATERIALIZES
IMMATERIALIZING
IMMATERIALLY
IMMATERIALNESS
IMMATURELY
IMMATURENESS
IMMATURENESSES
IMMATUREST
IMMATURITIES
IMMATURITY
IMMEASURABILITY
IMMEASURABLE
IMMEASURABLY
IMMEASURED
IMMEDIACIES
IMMEDIATELY
IMMEDIATENESS
IMMEDIATENESSES
IMMEDIATISM
IMMEDIATISMS
IMMEDICABLE
IMMEDICABLENESS
IMMEDICABLY
IMMEMORIAL
IMMEMORIALLY
IMMENSENESS
IMMENSENESSES
IMMENSITIES
IMMENSURABILITY
IMMENSURABLE
IMMERGENCE
IMMERGENCES
IMMERITOUS
IMMERSIBLE
IMMERSIONISM
IMMERSIONISMS
IMMERSIONIST
IMMERSIONISTS
IMMERSIONS
IMMETHODICAL
IMMETHODICALLY
IMMIGRANCIES
IMMIGRANCY
IMMIGRANTS
IMMIGRATED
IMMIGRATES
IMMIGRATING
IMMIGRATION
IMMIGRATIONAL
IMMIGRATIONS
IMMIGRATOR
IMMIGRATORS
IMMIGRATORY
IMMINENCES
IMMINENCIES
IMMINENTLY
IMMINENTNESS
IMMINENTNESSES
IMMINGLING
IMMINUTION
IMMINUTIONS
IMMISCIBILITIES
IMMISCIBILITY
IMMISCIBLE
IMMISCIBLY
IMMISERATION
IMMISERATIONS
IMMISERISATION
IMMISERISATIONS
IMMISERISE
IMMISERISED
IMMISERISES
IMMISERISING
IMMISERIZATION
IMMISERIZATIONS
IMMISERIZE
IMMISERIZED
IMMISERIZES
IMMISERIZING
IMMISSIONS
IMMITIGABILITY
IMMITIGABLE
IMMITIGABLY
IMMITTANCE
IMMITTANCES
IMMIXTURES
IMMOBILISATION
IMMOBILISATIONS
IMMOBILISE
IMMOBILISED
IMMOBILISER
IMMOBILISERS
IMMOBILISES
IMMOBILISING
IMMOBILISM
IMMOBILISMS
IMMOBILITIES
IMMOBILITY
IMMOBILIZATION
IMMOBILIZATIONS
IMMOBILIZE
IMMOBILIZED
IMMOBILIZER
IMMOBILIZERS
IMMOBILIZES
IMMOBILIZING
IMMODERACIES
IMMODERACY
IMMODERATE
IMMODERATELY
IMMODERATENESS
IMMODERATION
IMMODERATIONS
IMMODESTER
IMMODESTEST
IMMODESTIES
IMMODESTLY
IMMOLATING
IMMOLATION
IMMOLATIONS
IMMOLATORS
IMMOMENTOUS
IMMORALISM
IMMORALISMS
IMMORALIST
IMMORALISTS
IMMORALITIES
IMMORALITY
IMMORTALISATION
IMMORTALISE
IMMORTALISED
IMMORTALISER
IMMORTALISERS
IMMORTALISES
IMMORTALISING
IMMORTALITIES
IMMORTALITY
IMMORTALIZATION
IMMORTALIZE
IMMORTALIZED
IMMORTALIZER
IMMORTALIZERS
IMMORTALIZES
IMMORTALIZING
IMMORTALLY
IMMORTELLE
IMMORTELLES
IMMOTILITIES
IMMOTILITY
IMMOVABILITIES
IMMOVABILITY
IMMOVABLENESS
IMMOVABLENESSES
IMMOVABLES
IMMOVEABILITIES
IMMOVEABILITY
IMMOVEABLE
IMMOVEABLENESS
IMMOVEABLES
IMMOVEABLY
IMMUNIFACIENT
IMMUNISATION
IMMUNISATIONS
IMMUNISERS
IMMUNISING
IMMUNITIES
IMMUNIZATION
IMMUNIZATIONS
IMMUNIZERS
IMMUNIZING

IMMUNOASSAY
IMMUNOASSAYABLE
IMMUNOASSAYIST
IMMUNOASSAYISTS
IMMUNOASSAYS
IMMUNOBLOT
IMMUNOBLOTS
IMMUNOBLOTTING
IMMUNOBLOTTINGS
IMMUNOCHEMICAL
IMMUNOCHEMIST
IMMUNOCHEMISTRY
IMMUNOCHEMISTS
IMMUNOCOMPETENT
IMMUNOCOMPLEX
IMMUNOCOMPLEXES
IMMUNODEFICIENT
IMMUNODIAGNOSES
IMMUNODIAGNOSIS
IMMUNODIFFUSION
IMMUNOGENESES
IMMUNOGENESIS
IMMUNOGENETIC
IMMUNOGENETICAL
IMMUNOGENETICS
IMMUNOGENIC
IMMUNOGENICALLY
IMMUNOGENICITY
IMMUNOGENS
IMMUNOGLOBULIN
IMMUNOGLOBULINS
IMMUNOLOGIC
IMMUNOLOGICAL
IMMUNOLOGICALLY
IMMUNOLOGIES
IMMUNOLOGIST
IMMUNOLOGISTS
IMMUNOLOGY
IMMUNOMODULATOR
IMMUNOPATHOLOGY
IMMUNOPHORESES
IMMUNOPHORESIS
IMMUNOREACTION
IMMUNOREACTIONS
IMMUNOREACTIVE
IMMUNOSORBENT
IMMUNOSORBENTS
IMMUNOSTIMULANT
IMMUNOSUPPRESS
IMMUNOTHERAPIES
IMMUNOTHERAPY
IMMUNOTOXIC
IMMUNOTOXIN
IMMUNOTOXINS
IMMUREMENT
IMMUREMENTS
IMMUTABILITIES
IMMUTABILITY
IMMUTABLENESS
IMMUTABLENESSES
IMPACTIONS
IMPACTITES
IMPAINTING
IMPAIRABLE
IMPAIRINGS
IMPAIRMENT
IMPAIRMENTS
IMPALEMENT
IMPALEMENTS
IMPALPABILITIES
IMPALPABILITY
IMPALPABLE
IMPALPABLY
IMPALUDISM
IMPALUDISMS
IMPANATION
IMPANATIONS
IMPANELING
IMPANELLED
IMPANELLING
IMPANELMENT
IMPANELMENTS
IMPANNELLED
IMPANNELLING
IMPARADISE
IMPARADISED
IMPARADISES
IMPARADISING
IMPARIDIGITATE
IMPARIPINNATE
IMPARISYLLABIC
IMPARITIES
IMPARKATION
IMPARKATIONS
IMPARLANCE
IMPARLANCES
IMPARTABLE
IMPARTATION
IMPARTATIONS
IMPARTIALITIES
IMPARTIALITY
IMPARTIALLY
IMPARTIALNESS
IMPARTIALNESSES
IMPARTIBILITIES
IMPARTIBILITY
IMPARTIBLE
IMPARTIBLY
IMPARTMENT
IMPARTMENTS
IMPASSABILITIES
IMPASSABILITY
IMPASSABLE
IMPASSABLENESS
IMPASSABLY
IMPASSIBILITIES
IMPASSIBILITY
IMPASSIBLE
IMPASSIBLENESS
IMPASSIBLY
IMPASSIONATE
IMPASSIONED
IMPASSIONEDLY
IMPASSIONEDNESS
IMPASSIONING
IMPASSIONS
IMPASSIVELY
IMPASSIVENESS
IMPASSIVENESSES
IMPASSIVITIES
IMPASSIVITY
IMPASTATION
IMPASTATIONS
IMPATIENCE
IMPATIENCES
IMPATIENTLY
IMPEACHABILITY
IMPEACHABLE
IMPEACHERS
IMPEACHING
IMPEACHMENT
IMPEACHMENTS
IMPEARLING
IMPECCABILITIES
IMPECCABILITY
IMPECCABLE
IMPECCABLY
IMPECCANCIES
IMPECCANCY
IMPECUNIOSITIES
IMPECUNIOSITY
IMPECUNIOUS
IMPECUNIOUSLY
IMPECUNIOUSNESS
IMPEDANCES
IMPEDIMENT
IMPEDIMENTA
IMPEDIMENTAL
IMPEDIMENTARY
IMPEDIMENTS
IMPEDINGLY
IMPEDITIVE
IMPELLENTS
IMPENDENCE
IMPENDENCES
IMPENDENCIES
IMPENDENCY
IMPENETRABILITY
IMPENETRABLE
IMPENETRABLY
IMPENETRATE
IMPENETRATED
IMPENETRATES
IMPENETRATING
IMPENETRATION
IMPENETRATIONS
IMPENITENCE
IMPENITENCES
IMPENITENCIES
IMPENITENCY
IMPENITENT
IMPENITENTLY
IMPENITENTNESS
IMPENITENTS
IMPERATIVAL
IMPERATIVE
IMPERATIVELY
IMPERATIVENESS
IMPERATIVES
IMPERATORIAL
IMPERATORIALLY
IMPERATORS
IMPERATORSHIP
IMPERATORSHIPS
IMPERCEABLE
IMPERCEIVABLE
IMPERCEPTIBLE
IMPERCEPTIBLY
IMPERCEPTION
IMPERCEPTIONS
IMPERCEPTIVE
IMPERCEPTIVELY
IMPERCEPTIVITY
IMPERCIPIENCE
IMPERCIPIENCES
IMPERCIPIENT
IMPERCIPIENTLY
IMPERFECTER
IMPERFECTEST
IMPERFECTIBLE
IMPERFECTION
IMPERFECTIONS
IMPERFECTIVE
IMPERFECTIVELY
IMPERFECTIVES
IMPERFECTLY
IMPERFECTNESS
IMPERFECTNESSES
IMPERFECTS
IMPERFORABLE
IMPERFORATE
IMPERFORATED
IMPERFORATION
IMPERFORATIONS
IMPERIALISE
IMPERIALISED
IMPERIALISES
IMPERIALISING
IMPERIALISM
IMPERIALISMS
IMPERIALIST
IMPERIALISTIC
IMPERIALISTS
IMPERIALITIES
IMPERIALITY
IMPERIALIZE
IMPERIALIZED
IMPERIALIZES
IMPERIALIZING
IMPERIALLY

IMPERIALNESS
IMPERIALNESSES
IMPERILING
IMPERILLED
IMPERILLING
IMPERILMENT
IMPERILMENTS
IMPERIOUSLY
IMPERIOUSNESS
IMPERIOUSNESSES
IMPERISHABILITY
IMPERISHABLE
IMPERISHABLES
IMPERISHABLY
IMPERMANENCE
IMPERMANENCES
IMPERMANENCIES
IMPERMANENCY
IMPERMANENT
IMPERMANENTLY
IMPERMEABILITY
IMPERMEABLE
IMPERMEABLENESS
IMPERMEABLY
IMPERMISSIBLE
IMPERMISSIBLY
IMPERSCRIPTIBLE
IMPERSEVERANT
IMPERSISTENT
IMPERSONAL
IMPERSONALISE
IMPERSONALISED
IMPERSONALISES
IMPERSONALISING
IMPERSONALITIES
IMPERSONALITY
IMPERSONALIZE
IMPERSONALIZED
IMPERSONALIZES
IMPERSONALIZING
IMPERSONALLY
IMPERSONATE
IMPERSONATED
IMPERSONATES
IMPERSONATING
IMPERSONATION
IMPERSONATIONS
IMPERSONATOR
IMPERSONATORS
IMPERTINENCE
IMPERTINENCES
IMPERTINENCIES
IMPERTINENCY
IMPERTINENT
IMPERTINENTLY
IMPERTURBABLE
IMPERTURBABLY
IMPERTURBATION
IMPERTURBATIONS
IMPERVIABILITY
IMPERVIABLE
IMPERVIABLENESS
IMPERVIOUS
IMPERVIOUSLY
IMPERVIOUSNESS
IMPETICOSSED
IMPETICOSSES
IMPETICOSSING
IMPETIGINES
IMPETIGINOUS
IMPETRATED
IMPETRATES
IMPETRATING
IMPETRATION
IMPETRATIONS
IMPETRATIVE
IMPETRATOR
IMPETRATORS
IMPETRATORY
IMPETUOSITIES
IMPETUOSITY
IMPETUOUSLY
IMPETUOUSNESS
IMPETUOUSNESSES
IMPICTURED
IMPIERCEABLE
IMPIGNORATE
IMPIGNORATED
IMPIGNORATES
IMPIGNORATING
IMPIGNORATION
IMPIGNORATIONS
IMPINGEMENT
IMPINGEMENTS
IMPIOUSNESS
IMPIOUSNESSES
IMPISHNESS
IMPISHNESSES
IMPLACABILITIES
IMPLACABILITY
IMPLACABLE
IMPLACABLENESS
IMPLACABLY
IMPLACENTAL
IMPLANTABLE
IMPLANTATION
IMPLANTATIONS
IMPLANTERS
IMPLANTING
IMPLAUSIBILITY
IMPLAUSIBLE
IMPLAUSIBLENESS
IMPLAUSIBLY
IMPLEACHED
IMPLEACHES
IMPLEACHING
IMPLEADABLE
IMPLEADERS
IMPLEADING
IMPLEDGING
IMPLEMENTAL
IMPLEMENTATION
IMPLEMENTATIONS
IMPLEMENTED
IMPLEMENTER
IMPLEMENTERS
IMPLEMENTING
IMPLEMENTOR
IMPLEMENTORS
IMPLEMENTS
IMPLETIONS
IMPLEXIONS
IMPLEXUOUS
IMPLICATED
IMPLICATES
IMPLICATING
IMPLICATION
IMPLICATIONAL
IMPLICATIONS
IMPLICATIVE
IMPLICATIVELY
IMPLICATIVENESS
IMPLICATURE
IMPLICATURES
IMPLICITIES
IMPLICITLY
IMPLICITNESS
IMPLICITNESSES
IMPLODENTS
IMPLORATION
IMPLORATIONS
IMPLORATOR
IMPLORATORS
IMPLORATORY
IMPLORINGLY
IMPLOSIONS
IMPLOSIVELY
IMPLOSIVES
IMPLUNGING
IMPOCKETED
IMPOCKETING
IMPOLDERED
IMPOLDERING
IMPOLICIES
IMPOLITELY
IMPOLITENESS
IMPOLITENESSES
IMPOLITEST
IMPOLITICAL
IMPOLITICALLY
IMPOLITICLY
IMPOLITICNESS
IMPOLITICNESSES
IMPONDERABILIA
IMPONDERABILITY
IMPONDERABLE
IMPONDERABLES
IMPONDERABLY
IMPONDEROUS
IMPORTABILITIES
IMPORTABILITY
IMPORTABLE
IMPORTANCE
IMPORTANCES
IMPORTANCIES
IMPORTANCY
IMPORTANTLY
IMPORTATION
IMPORTATIONS
IMPORTINGS
IMPORTUNACIES
IMPORTUNACY
IMPORTUNATE
IMPORTUNATELY
IMPORTUNATENESS
IMPORTUNED
IMPORTUNELY
IMPORTUNER
IMPORTUNERS
IMPORTUNES
IMPORTUNING
IMPORTUNINGS
IMPORTUNITIES
IMPORTUNITY
IMPOSINGLY
IMPOSINGNESS
IMPOSINGNESSES
IMPOSITION
IMPOSITIONS
IMPOSSIBILISM
IMPOSSIBILISMS
IMPOSSIBILIST
IMPOSSIBILISTS
IMPOSSIBILITIES
IMPOSSIBILITY
IMPOSSIBLE
IMPOSSIBLENESS
IMPOSSIBLES
IMPOSSIBLY
IMPOSTHUMATE
IMPOSTHUMATED
IMPOSTHUMATES
IMPOSTHUMATING
IMPOSTHUMATION
IMPOSTHUMATIONS
IMPOSTHUME
IMPOSTHUMED
IMPOSTHUMES
IMPOSTOROUS
IMPOSTROUS
IMPOSTUMATE
IMPOSTUMATED
IMPOSTUMATES
IMPOSTUMATING
IMPOSTUMATION
IMPOSTUMATIONS
IMPOSTUMED
IMPOSTUMES
IMPOSTURES
IMPOSTUROUS

IMPOTENCES
IMPOTENCIES
IMPOTENTLY
IMPOTENTNESS
IMPOTENTNESSES
IMPOUNDABLE
IMPOUNDAGE
IMPOUNDAGES
IMPOUNDERS
IMPOUNDING
IMPOUNDMENT
IMPOUNDMENTS
IMPOVERISH
IMPOVERISHED
IMPOVERISHER
IMPOVERISHERS
IMPOVERISHES
IMPOVERISHING
IMPOVERISHMENT
IMPOVERISHMENTS
IMPOWERING
IMPRACTICABLE
IMPRACTICABLY
IMPRACTICAL
IMPRACTICALITY
IMPRACTICALLY
IMPRACTICALNESS
IMPRECATED
IMPRECATES
IMPRECATING
IMPRECATION
IMPRECATIONS
IMPRECATORY
IMPRECISELY
IMPRECISENESS
IMPRECISENESSES
IMPRECISION
IMPRECISIONS
IMPREDICATIVE
IMPREGNABILITY
IMPREGNABLE
IMPREGNABLENESS
IMPREGNABLY
IMPREGNANT
IMPREGNANTS
IMPREGNATABLE
IMPREGNATE
IMPREGNATED
IMPREGNATES
IMPREGNATING
IMPREGNATION
IMPREGNATIONS
IMPREGNATOR
IMPREGNATORS
IMPREGNING
IMPRESARIO
IMPRESARIOS
IMPRESCRIPTIBLE
IMPRESCRIPTIBLY
IMPRESSERS
IMPRESSIBILITY
IMPRESSIBLE
IMPRESSING
IMPRESSION
IMPRESSIONABLE
IMPRESSIONAL
IMPRESSIONALLY
IMPRESSIONISM
IMPRESSIONISMS
IMPRESSIONIST
IMPRESSIONISTIC
IMPRESSIONISTS
IMPRESSIONS
IMPRESSIVE
IMPRESSIVELY
IMPRESSIVENESS
IMPRESSMENT
IMPRESSMENTS
IMPRESSURE
IMPRESSURES
IMPRIMATUR
IMPRIMATURS
IMPRINTERS
IMPRINTING
IMPRINTINGS
IMPRISONABLE
IMPRISONED
IMPRISONER
IMPRISONERS
IMPRISONING
IMPRISONMENT
IMPRISONMENTS
IMPROBABILITIES
IMPROBABILITY
IMPROBABLE
IMPROBABLENESS
IMPROBABLY
IMPROBATION
IMPROBATIONS
IMPROBITIES
IMPROMPTUS
IMPROPERER
IMPROPEREST
IMPROPERLY
IMPROPERNESS
IMPROPERNESSES
IMPROPRIATE
IMPROPRIATED
IMPROPRIATES
IMPROPRIATING
IMPROPRIATION
IMPROPRIATIONS
IMPROPRIATOR
IMPROPRIATORS
IMPROPRIETIES
IMPROPRIETY
IMPROVABILITIES
IMPROVABILITY
IMPROVABLE
IMPROVABLENESS
IMPROVABLY
IMPROVEMENT
IMPROVEMENTS
IMPROVIDENCE
IMPROVIDENCES
IMPROVIDENT
IMPROVIDENTLY
IMPROVINGLY
IMPROVISATE
IMPROVISATED
IMPROVISATES
IMPROVISATING
IMPROVISATION
IMPROVISATIONAL
IMPROVISATIONS
IMPROVISATOR
IMPROVISATORE
IMPROVISATORES
IMPROVISATORI
IMPROVISATORIAL
IMPROVISATORS
IMPROVISATORY
IMPROVISATRICE
IMPROVISATRICES
IMPROVISATRIX
IMPROVISATRIXES
IMPROVISED
IMPROVISER
IMPROVISERS
IMPROVISES
IMPROVISING
IMPROVISOR
IMPROVISORS
IMPROVVISATORE
IMPROVVISATORES
IMPROVVISATRICE
IMPRUDENCE
IMPRUDENCES
IMPRUDENTLY
IMPSONITES
IMPUDENCES
IMPUDENCIES
IMPUDENTLY
IMPUDENTNESS
IMPUDENTNESSES
IMPUDICITIES
IMPUDICITY
IMPUGNABLE
IMPUGNATION
IMPUGNATIONS
IMPUGNMENT
IMPUGNMENTS
IMPUISSANCE
IMPUISSANCES
IMPUISSANT
IMPULSIONS
IMPULSIVELY
IMPULSIVENESS
IMPULSIVENESSES
IMPULSIVITIES
IMPULSIVITY
IMPUNDULUS
IMPUNITIES
IMPURENESS
IMPURENESSES
IMPURITIES
IMPURPLING
IMPUTABILITIES
IMPUTABILITY
IMPUTABLENESS
IMPUTABLENESSES
IMPUTATION
IMPUTATIONS
IMPUTATIVE
IMPUTATIVELY
INABILITIES
INABSTINENCE
INABSTINENCES
INACCESSIBILITY
INACCESSIBLE
INACCESSIBLY
INACCURACIES
INACCURACY
INACCURATE
INACCURATELY
INACCURATENESS
INACTIVATE
INACTIVATED
INACTIVATES
INACTIVATING
INACTIVATION
INACTIVATIONS
INACTIVELY
INACTIVENESS
INACTIVENESSES
INACTIVITIES
INACTIVITY
INADAPTABLE
INADAPTATION
INADAPTATIONS
INADAPTIVE
INADEQUACIES
INADEQUACY
INADEQUATE
INADEQUATELY
INADEQUATENESS
INADEQUATES
INADMISSIBILITY
INADMISSIBLE
INADMISSIBLY
INADVERTENCE
INADVERTENCES
INADVERTENCIES
INADVERTENCY
INADVERTENT
INADVERTENTLY
INADVISABILITY
INADVISABLE
INADVISABLENESS
INADVISABLY

INALIENABILITY
INALIENABLE
INALIENABLENESS
INALIENABLY
INALTERABILITY
INALTERABLE
INALTERABLENESS
INALTERABLY
INAMORATAS
INAMORATOS
INANENESSES
INANIMATELY
INANIMATENESS
INANIMATENESSES
INANIMATION
INANIMATIONS
INANITIONS
INAPPARENT
INAPPARENTLY
INAPPEASABLE
INAPPELLABLE
INAPPETENCE
INAPPETENCES
INAPPETENCIES
INAPPETENCY
INAPPETENT
INAPPLICABILITY
INAPPLICABLE
INAPPLICABLY
INAPPOSITE
INAPPOSITELY
INAPPOSITENESS
INAPPRECIABLE
INAPPRECIABLY
INAPPRECIATION
INAPPRECIATIONS
INAPPRECIATIVE
INAPPREHENSIBLE
INAPPREHENSION
INAPPREHENSIONS
INAPPREHENSIVE
INAPPROACHABLE
INAPPROACHABLY
INAPPROPRIATE
INAPPROPRIATELY
INAPTITUDE
INAPTITUDES
INAPTNESSES
INARGUABLE
INARGUABLY
INARTICULACIES
INARTICULACY
INARTICULATE
INARTICULATELY
INARTICULATES
INARTICULATION
INARTICULATIONS
INARTIFICIAL
INARTIFICIALLY
INARTISTIC
INARTISTICALLY
INATTENTION
INATTENTIONS
INATTENTIVE
INATTENTIVELY
INATTENTIVENESS
INAUDIBILITIES
INAUDIBILITY
INAUDIBLENESS
INAUDIBLENESSES
INAUGURALS
INAUGURATE
INAUGURATED
INAUGURATES
INAUGURATING
INAUGURATION
INAUGURATIONS
INAUGURATOR
INAUGURATORS
INAUGURATORY
INAURATING
INAUSPICIOUS
INAUSPICIOUSLY
INAUTHENTIC
INAUTHENTICITY
INBOUNDING
INBREATHED
INBREATHES
INBREATHING
INBREEDERS
INBREEDING
INBREEDINGS
INBRINGING
INBRINGINGS
INBURSTING
INCALCULABILITY
INCALCULABLE
INCALCULABLY
INCALESCENCE
INCALESCENCES
INCALESCENT
INCANDESCE
INCANDESCED
INCANDESCENCE
INCANDESCENCES
INCANDESCENCIES
INCANDESCENCY
INCANDESCENT
INCANDESCENTLY
INCANDESCENTS
INCANDESCES
INCANDESCING
INCANTATION
INCANTATIONAL
INCANTATIONS
INCANTATOR
INCANTATORS
INCANTATORY
INCAPABILITIES
INCAPABILITY
INCAPABLENESS
INCAPABLENESSES
INCAPABLES
INCAPACIOUS
INCAPACIOUSNESS
INCAPACITANT
INCAPACITANTS
INCAPACITATE
INCAPACITATED
INCAPACITATES
INCAPACITATING
INCAPACITATION
INCAPACITATIONS
INCAPACITIES
INCAPACITY
INCAPSULATE
INCAPSULATED
INCAPSULATES
INCAPSULATING
INCAPSULATION
INCAPSULATIONS
INCARCERATE
INCARCERATED
INCARCERATES
INCARCERATING
INCARCERATION
INCARCERATIONS
INCARCERATOR
INCARCERATORS
INCARDINATE
INCARDINATED
INCARDINATES
INCARDINATING
INCARDINATION
INCARDINATIONS
INCARNADINE
INCARNADINED
INCARNADINES
INCARNADINING
INCARNATED
INCARNATES
INCARNATING
INCARNATION
INCARNATIONS
INCARVILLEA
INCARVILLEAS
INCASEMENT
INCASEMENTS
INCATENATE
INCATENATED
INCATENATES
INCATENATING
INCATENATION
INCATENATIONS
INCAUTIONS
INCAUTIOUS
INCAUTIOUSLY
INCAUTIOUSNESS
INCEDINGLY
INCENDIARIES
INCENDIARISM
INCENDIARISMS
INCENDIARY
INCENDIVITIES
INCENDIVITY
INCENSATION
INCENSATIONS
INCENSEMENT
INCENSEMENTS
INCENSORIES
INCENTIVELY
INCENTIVES
INCENTIVISATION
INCENTIVISE
INCENTIVISED
INCENTIVISES
INCENTIVISING
INCENTIVIZATION
INCENTIVIZE
INCENTIVIZED
INCENTIVIZES
INCENTIVIZING
INCEPTIONS
INCEPTIVELY
INCEPTIVES
INCERTAINTIES
INCERTAINTY
INCERTITUDE
INCERTITUDES
INCESSANCIES
INCESSANCY
INCESSANTLY
INCESSANTNESS
INCESSANTNESSES
INCESTUOUS
INCESTUOUSLY
INCESTUOUSNESS
INCHARITABLE
INCHOATELY
INCHOATENESS
INCHOATENESSES
INCHOATING
INCHOATION
INCHOATIONS
INCHOATIVE
INCHOATIVELY
INCHOATIVES
INCIDENCES
INCIDENTAL
INCIDENTALLY
INCIDENTALNESS
INCIDENTALS
INCINERATE
INCINERATED
INCINERATES
INCINERATING
INCINERATION
INCINERATIONS
INCINERATOR
INCINERATORS

INCIPIENCE
INCIPIENCES
INCIPIENCIES
INCIPIENCY
INCIPIENTLY
INCISIFORM
INCISIVELY
INCISIVENESS
INCISIVENESSES
INCISORIAL
INCITATION
INCITATIONS
INCITATIVE
INCITATIVES
INCITEMENT
INCITEMENTS
INCITINGLY
INCIVILITIES
INCIVILITY
INCLASPING
INCLEMENCIES
INCLEMENCY
INCLEMENTLY
INCLEMENTNESS
INCLEMENTNESSES
INCLINABLE
INCLINABLENESS
INCLINATION
INCLINATIONAL
INCLINATIONS
INCLINATORIA
INCLINATORIUM
INCLINATORY
INCLININGS
INCLINOMETER
INCLINOMETERS
INCLIPPING
INCLOSABLE
INCLOSURES
INCLUDABLE
INCLUDEDNESS
INCLUDEDNESSES
INCLUDIBLE
INCLUSIONS
INCLUSIVELY
INCLUSIVENESS
INCLUSIVENESSES
INCLUSIVITIES
INCLUSIVITY
INCOAGULABLE
INCOERCIBLE
INCOGITABILITY
INCOGITABLE
INCOGITANCIES
INCOGITANCY
INCOGITANT
INCOGITATIVE
INCOGNISABLE
INCOGNISANCE
INCOGNISANCES
INCOGNISANT
INCOGNITAS
INCOGNITOS
INCOGNIZABLE
INCOGNIZANCE
INCOGNIZANCES
INCOGNIZANT
INCOHERENCE
INCOHERENCES
INCOHERENCIES
INCOHERENCY
INCOHERENT
INCOHERENTLY
INCOHERENTNESS
INCOHESIVE
INCOMBUSTIBLE
INCOMBUSTIBLES
INCOMBUSTIBLY
INCOMMENSURABLE
INCOMMENSURABLY
INCOMMENSURATE
INCOMMISCIBLE
INCOMMODED
INCOMMODES
INCOMMODING
INCOMMODIOUS
INCOMMODIOUSLY
INCOMMODITIES
INCOMMODITY
INCOMMUNICABLE
INCOMMUNICABLY
INCOMMUNICADO
INCOMMUNICATIVE
INCOMMUTABILITY
INCOMMUTABLE
INCOMMUTABLY
INCOMPARABILITY
INCOMPARABLE
INCOMPARABLY
INCOMPARED
INCOMPATIBILITY
INCOMPATIBLE
INCOMPATIBLES
INCOMPATIBLY
INCOMPETENCE
INCOMPETENCES
INCOMPETENCIES
INCOMPETENCY
INCOMPETENT
INCOMPETENTLY
INCOMPETENTS
INCOMPLETE
INCOMPLETELY
INCOMPLETENESS
INCOMPLETION
INCOMPLETIONS
INCOMPLIANCE
INCOMPLIANCES
INCOMPLIANCIES
INCOMPLIANCY
INCOMPLIANT
INCOMPLIANTLY
INCOMPOSED
INCOMPOSITE
INCOMPOSSIBLE
INCOMPREHENSION
INCOMPREHENSIVE
INCOMPRESSIBLE
INCOMPRESSIBLY
INCOMPUTABILITY
INCOMPUTABLE
INCOMPUTABLY
INCOMUNICADO
INCONCEIVABLE
INCONCEIVABLES
INCONCEIVABLY
INCONCINNITIES
INCONCINNITY
INCONCINNOUS
INCONCLUSION
INCONCLUSIONS
INCONCLUSIVE
INCONCLUSIVELY
INCONDENSABLE
INCONDENSIBLE
INCONDITELY
INCONFORMITIES
INCONFORMITY
INCONGRUENCE
INCONGRUENCES
INCONGRUENT
INCONGRUENTLY
INCONGRUITIES
INCONGRUITY
INCONGRUOUS
INCONGRUOUSLY
INCONGRUOUSNESS
INCONSCIENT
INCONSCIENTLY
INCONSCIONABLE
INCONSCIOUS
INCONSECUTIVE
INCONSECUTIVELY
INCONSEQUENCE
INCONSEQUENCES
INCONSEQUENT
INCONSEQUENTIAL
INCONSEQUENTLY
INCONSIDERABLE
INCONSIDERABLY
INCONSIDERATE
INCONSIDERATELY
INCONSIDERATION
INCONSISTENCE
INCONSISTENCES
INCONSISTENCIES
INCONSISTENCY
INCONSISTENT
INCONSISTENTLY
INCONSOLABILITY
INCONSOLABLE
INCONSOLABLY
INCONSONANCE
INCONSONANCES
INCONSONANT
INCONSONANTLY
INCONSPICUOUS
INCONSPICUOUSLY
INCONSTANCIES
INCONSTANCY
INCONSTANT
INCONSTANTLY
INCONSTRUABLE
INCONSUMABLE
INCONSUMABLY
INCONTESTABLE
INCONTESTABLY
INCONTIGUOUS
INCONTIGUOUSLY
INCONTINENCE
INCONTINENCES
INCONTINENCIES
INCONTINENCY
INCONTINENT
INCONTINENTLY
INCONTROLLABLE
INCONTROLLABLY
INCONVENIENCE
INCONVENIENCED
INCONVENIENCES
INCONVENIENCIES
INCONVENIENCING
INCONVENIENCY
INCONVENIENT
INCONVENIENTLY
INCONVERSABLE
INCONVERSANT
INCONVERTIBLE
INCONVERTIBLY
INCONVINCIBLE
INCONVINCIBLY
INCOORDINATE
INCOORDINATION
INCOORDINATIONS
INCORONATE
INCORONATED
INCORONATION
INCORONATIONS
INCORPORABLE
INCORPORAL
INCORPORALL
INCORPORATE
INCORPORATED
INCORPORATES
INCORPORATING
INCORPORATION
INCORPORATIONS
INCORPORATIVE
INCORPORATOR
INCORPORATORS

INCORPOREAL
INCORPOREALITY
INCORPOREALLY
INCORPOREITIES
INCORPOREITY
INCORPSING
INCORRECTLY
INCORRECTNESS
INCORRECTNESSES
INCORRIGIBILITY
INCORRIGIBLE
INCORRIGIBLES
INCORRIGIBLY
INCORRODIBLE
INCORROSIBLE
INCORRUPTED
INCORRUPTIBLE
INCORRUPTIBLES
INCORRUPTIBLY
INCORRUPTION
INCORRUPTIONS
INCORRUPTIVE
INCORRUPTLY
INCORRUPTNESS
INCORRUPTNESSES
INCRASSATE
INCRASSATED
INCRASSATES
INCRASSATING
INCRASSATION
INCRASSATIONS
INCRASSATIVE
INCRASSATIVES
INCREASABLE
INCREASEDLY
INCREASEFUL
INCREASERS
INCREASING
INCREASINGLY
INCREASINGS
INCREATELY
INCREDIBILITIES
INCREDIBILITY
INCREDIBLE
INCREDIBLENESS
INCREDIBLY
INCREDULITIES
INCREDULITY
INCREDULOUS
INCREDULOUSLY
INCREDULOUSNESS
INCREMATED
INCREMATES
INCREMATING
INCREMATION
INCREMATIONS
INCREMENTAL
INCREMENTALISM
INCREMENTALISMS
INCREMENTALIST
INCREMENTALISTS
INCREMENTALLY
INCREMENTALS
INCREMENTED
INCREMENTING
INCREMENTS
INCRESCENT
INCRETIONARY
INCRETIONS
INCRIMINATE
INCRIMINATED
INCRIMINATES
INCRIMINATING
INCRIMINATION
INCRIMINATIONS
INCRIMINATOR
INCRIMINATORS
INCRIMINATORY
INCROSSBRED
INCROSSBREDS
INCROSSBREED
INCROSSBREEDING
INCROSSBREEDS
INCROSSING
INCRUSTANT
INCRUSTANTS
INCRUSTATION
INCRUSTATIONS
INCRUSTING
INCRUSTMENT
INCRUSTMENTS
INCUBATING
INCUBATION
INCUBATIONAL
INCUBATIONS
INCUBATIVE
INCUBATORS
INCUBATORY
INCULCATED
INCULCATES
INCULCATING
INCULCATION
INCULCATIONS
INCULCATIVE
INCULCATOR
INCULCATORS
INCULCATORY
INCULPABILITIES
INCULPABILITY
INCULPABLE
INCULPABLENESS
INCULPABLY
INCULPATED
INCULPATES
INCULPATING
INCULPATION
INCULPATIONS
INCULPATIVE
INCULPATORY
INCUMBENCIES
INCUMBENCY
INCUMBENTLY
INCUMBENTS
INCUMBERED
INCUMBERING
INCUMBERINGLY
INCUMBRANCE
INCUMBRANCER
INCUMBRANCERS
INCUMBRANCES
INCUNABLES
INCUNABULA
INCUNABULAR
INCUNABULIST
INCUNABULISTS
INCUNABULUM
INCURABILITIES
INCURABILITY
INCURABLENESS
INCURABLENESSES
INCURABLES
INCURIOSITIES
INCURIOSITY
INCURIOUSLY
INCURIOUSNESS
INCURIOUSNESSES
INCURRABLE
INCURRENCE
INCURRENCES
INCURSIONS
INCURVATED
INCURVATES
INCURVATING
INCURVATION
INCURVATIONS
INCURVATURE
INCURVATURES
INCURVITIES
INDAGATING
INDAGATION
INDAGATIONS
INDAGATIVE
INDAGATORS
INDAGATORY
INDAPAMIDE
INDAPAMIDES
INDEBTEDNESS
INDEBTEDNESSES
INDECENCIES
INDECENTER
INDECENTEST
INDECENTLY
INDECIDUATE
INDECIDUOUS
INDECIPHERABLE
INDECIPHERABLY
INDECISION
INDECISIONS
INDECISIVE
INDECISIVELY
INDECISIVENESS
INDECLINABLE
INDECLINABLY
INDECOMPOSABLE
INDECOROUS
INDECOROUSLY
INDECOROUSNESS
INDECORUMS
INDEFATIGABLE
INDEFATIGABLY
INDEFEASIBILITY
INDEFEASIBLE
INDEFEASIBLY
INDEFECTIBILITY
INDEFECTIBLE
INDEFECTIBLY
INDEFENSIBILITY
INDEFENSIBLE
INDEFENSIBLY
INDEFINABILITY
INDEFINABLE
INDEFINABLENESS
INDEFINABLES
INDEFINABLY
INDEFINITE
INDEFINITELY
INDEFINITENESS
INDEFINITES
INDEHISCENCE
INDEHISCENCES
INDEHISCENT
INDELIBILITIES
INDELIBILITY
INDELIBLENESS
INDELIBLENESSES
INDELICACIES
INDELICACY
INDELICATE
INDELICATELY
INDELICATENESS
INDEMNIFICATION
INDEMNIFIED
INDEMNIFIER
INDEMNIFIERS
INDEMNIFIES
INDEMNIFYING
INDEMNITIES
INDEMONSTRABLE
INDEMONSTRABLY
INDENTATION
INDENTATIONS
INDENTIONS
INDENTURED
INDENTURES
INDENTURESHIP
INDENTURESHIPS
INDENTURING
INDEPENDENCE
INDEPENDENCES
INDEPENDENCIES

INDEPENDENCY
INDEPENDENT
INDEPENDENTLY
INDEPENDENTS
INDESCRIBABLE
INDESCRIBABLES
INDESCRIBABLY
INDESIGNATE
INDESTRUCTIBLE
INDESTRUCTIBLY
INDETECTABLE
INDETECTIBLE
INDETERMINABLE
INDETERMINABLY
INDETERMINACIES
INDETERMINACY
INDETERMINATE
INDETERMINATELY
INDETERMINATION
INDETERMINED
INDETERMINISM
INDETERMINISMS
INDETERMINIST
INDETERMINISTIC
INDETERMINISTS
INDEXATION
INDEXATIONS
INDEXICALS
INDEXTERITIES
INDEXTERITY
INDEXTROUS
INDICATABLE
INDICATING
INDICATION
INDICATIONAL
INDICATIONS
INDICATIVE
INDICATIVELY
INDICATIVES
INDICATORS
INDICATORY
INDICOLITE
INDICOLITES
INDICTABLE
INDICTABLY
INDICTIONAL
INDICTIONS
INDICTMENT
INDICTMENTS
INDIFFERENCE
INDIFFERENCES
INDIFFERENCIES
INDIFFERENCY
INDIFFERENT
INDIFFERENTISM
INDIFFERENTISMS
INDIFFERENTIST
INDIFFERENTISTS
INDIFFERENTLY
INDIFFERENTS
INDIGENCES
INDIGENCIES
INDIGENISATION
INDIGENISATIONS
INDIGENISE
INDIGENISED
INDIGENISES
INDIGENISING
INDIGENITIES
INDIGENITY
INDIGENIZATION
INDIGENIZATIONS
INDIGENIZE
INDIGENIZED
INDIGENIZES
INDIGENIZING
INDIGENOUS
INDIGENOUSLY
INDIGENOUSNESS
INDIGENTLY
INDIGESTED
INDIGESTIBILITY
INDIGESTIBLE
INDIGESTIBLES
INDIGESTIBLY
INDIGESTING
INDIGESTION
INDIGESTIONS
INDIGESTIVE
INDIGNANCE
INDIGNANCES
INDIGNANTLY
INDIGNATION
INDIGNATIONS
INDIGNIFIED
INDIGNIFIES
INDIGNIFYING
INDIGNITIES
INDIGOLITE
INDIGOLITES
INDIGOTINS
INDINAVIRS
INDIRECTION
INDIRECTIONS
INDIRECTLY
INDIRECTNESS
INDIRECTNESSES
INDIRUBINS
INDISCERNIBLE
INDISCERNIBLY
INDISCERPTIBLE
INDISCIPLINABLE
INDISCIPLINE
INDISCIPLINED
INDISCIPLINES
INDISCOVERABLE
INDISCREET
INDISCREETER
INDISCREETEST
INDISCREETLY
INDISCREETNESS
INDISCRETE
INDISCRETELY
INDISCRETENESS
INDISCRETION
INDISCRETIONARY
INDISCRETIONS
INDISCRIMINATE
INDISPENSABLE
INDISPENSABLES
INDISPENSABLY
INDISPOSED
INDISPOSEDNESS
INDISPOSES
INDISPOSING
INDISPOSITION
INDISPOSITIONS
INDISPUTABILITY
INDISPUTABLE
INDISPUTABLY
INDISSOCIABLE
INDISSOCIABLY
INDISSOLUBILITY
INDISSOLUBLE
INDISSOLUBLY
INDISSOLVABLE
INDISSUADABLE
INDISSUADABLY
INDISTINCT
INDISTINCTION
INDISTINCTIONS
INDISTINCTIVE
INDISTINCTIVELY
INDISTINCTLY
INDISTINCTNESS
INDISTRIBUTABLE
INDITEMENT
INDITEMENTS
INDIVERTIBLE
INDIVERTIBLY
INDIVIDABLE
INDIVIDUAL
INDIVIDUALISE
INDIVIDUALISED
INDIVIDUALISER
INDIVIDUALISERS
INDIVIDUALISES
INDIVIDUALISING
INDIVIDUALISM
INDIVIDUALISMS
INDIVIDUALIST
INDIVIDUALISTIC
INDIVIDUALISTS
INDIVIDUALITIES
INDIVIDUALITY
INDIVIDUALIZE
INDIVIDUALIZED
INDIVIDUALIZER
INDIVIDUALIZERS
INDIVIDUALIZES
INDIVIDUALIZING
INDIVIDUALLY
INDIVIDUALS
INDIVIDUATE
INDIVIDUATED
INDIVIDUATES
INDIVIDUATING
INDIVIDUATION
INDIVIDUATIONS
INDIVIDUATOR
INDIVIDUATORS
INDIVIDUUM
INDIVISIBILITY
INDIVISIBLE
INDIVISIBLENESS
INDIVISIBLES
INDIVISIBLY
INDOCILITIES
INDOCILITY
INDOCTRINATE
INDOCTRINATED
INDOCTRINATES
INDOCTRINATING
INDOCTRINATION
INDOCTRINATIONS
INDOCTRINATOR
INDOCTRINATORS
INDOLEACETIC
INDOLEBUTYRIC
INDOLENCES
INDOLENCIES
INDOLENTLY
INDOMETACIN
INDOMETACINS
INDOMETHACIN
INDOMETHACINS
INDOMITABILITY
INDOMITABLE
INDOMITABLENESS
INDOMITABLY
INDOPHENOL
INDOPHENOLS
INDORSABLE
INDORSATION
INDORSATIONS
INDORSEMENT
INDORSEMENTS
INDRAUGHTS
INDRENCHED
INDRENCHES
INDRENCHING
INDUBITABILITY
INDUBITABLE
INDUBITABLENESS
INDUBITABLY
INDUCEMENT
INDUCEMENTS
INDUCIBILITIES
INDUCIBILITY
INDUCTANCE

I

INDUCTANCES
INDUCTILITIES
INDUCTILITY
INDUCTIONAL
INDUCTIONS
INDUCTIVELY
INDUCTIVENESS
INDUCTIVENESSES
INDUCTIVITIES
INDUCTIVITY
INDULGENCE
INDULGENCED
INDULGENCES
INDULGENCIES
INDULGENCING
INDULGENCY
INDULGENTLY
INDULGINGLY
INDUMENTUM
INDUMENTUMS
INDUPLICATE
INDUPLICATED
INDUPLICATION
INDUPLICATIONS
INDURATING
INDURATION
INDURATIONS
INDURATIVE
INDUSTRIAL
INDUSTRIALISE
INDUSTRIALISED
INDUSTRIALISES
INDUSTRIALISING
INDUSTRIALISM
INDUSTRIALISMS
INDUSTRIALIST
INDUSTRIALISTS
INDUSTRIALIZE
INDUSTRIALIZED
INDUSTRIALIZES
INDUSTRIALIZING
INDUSTRIALLY
INDUSTRIALS
INDUSTRIES
INDUSTRIOUS
INDUSTRIOUSLY
INDUSTRIOUSNESS
INDUSTRYWIDE
INDWELLERS
INDWELLING
INDWELLINGS
INEARTHING
INEBRIANTS
INEBRIATED
INEBRIATES
INEBRIATING
INEBRIATION
INEBRIATIONS
INEBRIETIES
INEDIBILITIES
INEDIBILITY
INEDUCABILITIES
INEDUCABILITY
INEDUCABLE
INEFFABILITIES
INEFFABILITY
INEFFABLENESS
INEFFABLENESSES
INEFFACEABILITY
INEFFACEABLE
INEFFACEABLY
INEFFECTIVE
INEFFECTIVELY
INEFFECTIVENESS
INEFFECTUAL
INEFFECTUALITY
INEFFECTUALLY
INEFFECTUALNESS
INEFFICACIES
INEFFICACIOUS
INEFFICACIOUSLY
INEFFICACITIES
INEFFICACITY
INEFFICACY
INEFFICIENCIES
INEFFICIENCY
INEFFICIENT
INEFFICIENTLY
INEFFICIENTS
INEGALITARIAN
INEGALITARIANS
INELABORATE
INELABORATED
INELABORATELY
INELABORATES
INELABORATING
INELASTICALLY
INELASTICITIES
INELASTICITY
INELEGANCE
INELEGANCES
INELEGANCIES
INELEGANCY
INELEGANTLY
INELIGIBILITIES
INELIGIBILITY
INELIGIBLE
INELIGIBLENESS
INELIGIBLES
INELIGIBLY
INELOQUENCE
INELOQUENCES
INELOQUENT
INELOQUENTLY
INELUCTABILITY
INELUCTABLE
INELUCTABLY
INELUDIBILITIES
INELUDIBILITY
INELUDIBLE
INELUDIBLY
INENARRABLE
INEPTITUDE
INEPTITUDES
INEPTNESSES
INEQUALITIES
INEQUALITY
INEQUATION
INEQUATIONS
INEQUIPOTENT
INEQUITABLE
INEQUITABLENESS
INEQUITABLY
INEQUITIES
INEQUIVALVE
INEQUIVALVED
INERADICABILITY
INERADICABLE
INERADICABLY
INERASABLE
INERASABLY
INERASIBLE
INERASIBLY
INERRABILITIES
INERRABILITY
INERRABLENESS
INERRABLENESSES
INERRANCIES
INERTIALLY
INERTNESSES
INESCAPABLE
INESCAPABLY
INESCULENT
INESCUTCHEON
INESCUTCHEONS
INESSENTIAL
INESSENTIALITY
INESSENTIALS
INESTIMABILITY
INESTIMABLE
INESTIMABLENESS
INESTIMABLY
INEVITABILITIES
INEVITABILITY
INEVITABLE
INEVITABLENESS
INEVITABLES
INEVITABLY
INEXACTITUDE
INEXACTITUDES
INEXACTNESS
INEXACTNESSES
INEXCITABLE
INEXCUSABILITY
INEXCUSABLE
INEXCUSABLENESS
INEXCUSABLY
INEXECRABLE
INEXECUTABLE
INEXECUTION
INEXECUTIONS
INEXHAUSTED
INEXHAUSTIBLE
INEXHAUSTIBLY
INEXHAUSTIVE
INEXISTANT
INEXISTENCE
INEXISTENCES
INEXISTENCIES
INEXISTENCY
INEXISTENT
INEXORABILITIES
INEXORABILITY
INEXORABLE
INEXORABLENESS
INEXORABLY
INEXPANSIBLE
INEXPECTANCIES
INEXPECTANCY
INEXPECTANT
INEXPECTATION
INEXPECTATIONS
INEXPEDIENCE
INEXPEDIENCES
INEXPEDIENCIES
INEXPEDIENCY
INEXPEDIENT
INEXPEDIENTLY
INEXPENSIVE
INEXPENSIVELY
INEXPENSIVENESS
INEXPERIENCE
INEXPERIENCED
INEXPERIENCES
INEXPERTLY
INEXPERTNESS
INEXPERTNESSES
INEXPIABLE
INEXPIABLENESS
INEXPIABLY
INEXPLAINABLE
INEXPLAINABLY
INEXPLICABILITY
INEXPLICABLE
INEXPLICABLY
INEXPLICIT
INEXPLICITLY
INEXPLICITNESS
INEXPRESSIBLE
INEXPRESSIBLES
INEXPRESSIBLY
INEXPRESSIVE
INEXPRESSIVELY
INEXPUGNABILITY
INEXPUGNABLE
INEXPUGNABLY
INEXPUNGIBLE
INEXTENDED
INEXTENSIBILITY
INEXTENSIBLE

I

INEXTENSION
INEXTENSIONS
INEXTIRPABLE
INEXTRICABILITY
INEXTRICABLE
INEXTRICABLY
INFALLIBILISM
INFALLIBILISMS
INFALLIBILIST
INFALLIBILISTS
INFALLIBILITIES
INFALLIBILITY
INFALLIBLE
INFALLIBLENESS
INFALLIBLES
INFALLIBLY
INFAMISING
INFAMIZING
INFAMONISE
INFAMONISED
INFAMONISES
INFAMONISING
INFAMONIZE
INFAMONIZED
INFAMONIZES
INFAMONIZING
INFAMOUSLY
INFAMOUSNESS
INFAMOUSNESSES
INFANGTHIEF
INFANGTHIEFS
INFANTEERS
INFANTHOOD
INFANTHOODS
INFANTICIDAL
INFANTICIDE
INFANTICIDES
INFANTILISATION
INFANTILISE
INFANTILISED
INFANTILISES
INFANTILISING
INFANTILISM
INFANTILISMS
INFANTILITIES
INFANTILITY
INFANTILIZATION
INFANTILIZE
INFANTILIZED
INFANTILIZES
INFANTILIZING
INFANTRIES
INFANTRYMAN
INFANTRYMEN
INFARCTION
INFARCTIONS
INFATUATED
INFATUATEDLY
INFATUATES
INFATUATING
INFATUATION
INFATUATIONS
INFEASIBILITIES
INFEASIBILITY
INFEASIBLE
INFEASIBLENESS
INFECTANTS
INFECTIONS
INFECTIOUS
INFECTIOUSLY
INFECTIOUSNESS
INFECTIVELY
INFECTIVENESS
INFECTIVENESSES
INFECTIVITIES
INFECTIVITY
INFECUNDITIES
INFECUNDITY
INFEFTMENT
INFEFTMENTS
INFELICITIES
INFELICITOUS
INFELICITOUSLY
INFELICITY
INFEOFFING
INFERENCES
INFERENCING
INFERENCINGS
INFERENTIAL
INFERENTIALLY
INFERIORITIES
INFERIORITY
INFERIORLY
INFERNALITIES
INFERNALITY
INFERNALLY
INFERRABLE
INFERRIBLE
INFERTILELY
INFERTILITIES
INFERTILITY
INFESTANTS
INFESTATION
INFESTATIONS
INFEUDATION
INFEUDATIONS
INFIBULATE
INFIBULATED
INFIBULATES
INFIBULATING
INFIBULATION
INFIBULATIONS
INFIDELITIES
INFIDELITY
INFIELDERS
INFIELDSMAN
INFIELDSMEN
INFIGHTERS
INFIGHTING
INFIGHTINGS
INFILLINGS
INFILTRATE
INFILTRATED
INFILTRATES
INFILTRATING
INFILTRATION
INFILTRATIONS
INFILTRATIVE
INFILTRATOR
INFILTRATORS
INFINITANT
INFINITARY
INFINITATE
INFINITATED
INFINITATES
INFINITATING
INFINITELY
INFINITENESS
INFINITENESSES
INFINITESIMAL
INFINITESIMALLY
INFINITESIMALS
INFINITIES
INFINITIVAL
INFINITIVALLY
INFINITIVE
INFINITIVELY
INFINITIVES
INFINITUDE
INFINITUDES
INFIRMARER
INFIRMARERS
INFIRMARIAN
INFIRMARIANS
INFIRMARIES
INFIRMITIES
INFIRMNESS
INFIRMNESSES
INFIXATION
INFIXATIONS
INFLAMABLE
INFLAMINGLY
INFLAMMABILITY
INFLAMMABLE
INFLAMMABLENESS
INFLAMMABLES
INFLAMMABLY
INFLAMMATION
INFLAMMATIONS
INFLAMMATORILY
INFLAMMATORY
INFLATABLE
INFLATABLES
INFLATEDLY
INFLATEDNESS
INFLATEDNESSES
INFLATINGLY
INFLATIONARY
INFLATIONISM
INFLATIONISMS
INFLATIONIST
INFLATIONISTS
INFLATIONS
INFLATUSES
INFLECTABLE
INFLECTEDNESS
INFLECTEDNESSES
INFLECTING
INFLECTION
INFLECTIONAL
INFLECTIONALLY
INFLECTIONLESS
INFLECTIONS
INFLECTIVE
INFLECTORS
INFLEXIBILITIES
INFLEXIBILITY
INFLEXIBLE
INFLEXIBLENESS
INFLEXIBLY
INFLEXIONAL
INFLEXIONALLY
INFLEXIONLESS
INFLEXIONS
INFLEXURES
INFLICTABLE
INFLICTERS
INFLICTING
INFLICTION
INFLICTIONS
INFLICTIVE
INFLICTORS
INFLORESCENCE
INFLORESCENCES
INFLORESCENT
INFLOWINGS
INFLUENCEABLE
INFLUENCED
INFLUENCER
INFLUENCERS
INFLUENCES
INFLUENCING
INFLUENTIAL
INFLUENTIALLY
INFLUENTIALS
INFLUENZAL
INFLUENZAS
INFLUXIONS
INFOGRAPHIC
INFOGRAPHICS
INFOLDINGS
INFOLDMENT
INFOLDMENTS
INFOMANIAS
INFOMERCIAL
INFOMERCIALS
INFOPRENEURIAL
INFORMABLE
INFORMALITIES
INFORMALITY

INFORMALLY
INFORMANTS
INFORMATICIAN
INFORMATICIANS
INFORMATICS
INFORMATION
INFORMATIONAL
INFORMATIONALLY
INFORMATIONS
INFORMATISATION
INFORMATISE
INFORMATISED
INFORMATISES
INFORMATISING
INFORMATIVE
INFORMATIVELY
INFORMATIVENESS
INFORMATIZATION
INFORMATIZE
INFORMATIZED
INFORMATIZES
INFORMATIZING
INFORMATORILY
INFORMATORY
INFORMEDLY
INFORMIDABLE
INFORMINGLY
INFORTUNES
INFOSPHERE
INFOSPHERES
INFOTAINMENT
INFOTAINMENTS
INFRACOSTAL
INFRACTING
INFRACTION
INFRACTIONS
INFRACTORS
INFRAGRANT
INFRAHUMAN
INFRAHUMANS
INFRALAPSARIAN
INFRALAPSARIANS
INFRAMAXILLARY
INFRANGIBILITY
INFRANGIBLE
INFRANGIBLENESS
INFRANGIBLY
INFRAORBITAL
INFRAPOSED
INFRAPOSITION
INFRAPOSITIONS
INFRASONIC
INFRASOUND
INFRASOUNDS
INFRASPECIFIC
INFRASTRUCTURAL
INFRASTRUCTURE
INFRASTRUCTURES
INFREQUENCE
INFREQUENCES
INFREQUENCIES
INFREQUENCY
INFREQUENT
INFREQUENTLY
INFRINGEMENT
INFRINGEMENTS
INFRINGERS
INFRINGING
INFRUCTUOUS
INFRUCTUOUSLY
INFUNDIBULA
INFUNDIBULAR
INFUNDIBULATE
INFUNDIBULIFORM
INFUNDIBULUM
INFURIATED
INFURIATELY
INFURIATES
INFURIATING
INFURIATINGLY
INFURIATION
INFURIATIONS
INFUSCATED
INFUSIBILITIES
INFUSIBILITY
INFUSIBLENESS
INFUSIBLENESSES
INFUSIONISM
INFUSIONISMS
INFUSIONIST
INFUSIONISTS
INFUSORIAL
INFUSORIAN
INFUSORIANS
INFUSORIES
INGATHERED
INGATHERER
INGATHERERS
INGATHERING
INGATHERINGS
INGEMINATE
INGEMINATED
INGEMINATES
INGEMINATING
INGEMINATION
INGEMINATIONS
INGENERATE
INGENERATED
INGENERATES
INGENERATING
INGENERATION
INGENERATIONS
INGENIOUSLY
INGENIOUSNESS
INGENIOUSNESSES
INGENUITIES
INGENUOUSLY
INGENUOUSNESS
INGENUOUSNESSES
INGESTIBLE
INGESTIONS
INGLENEUKS
INGLENOOKS
INGLORIOUS
INGLORIOUSLY
INGLORIOUSNESS
INGRAFTATION
INGRAFTATIONS
INGRAFTING
INGRAFTMENT
INGRAFTMENTS
INGRAINEDLY
INGRAINEDNESS
INGRAINEDNESSES
INGRAINERS
INGRAINING
INGRATEFUL
INGRATIATE
INGRATIATED
INGRATIATES
INGRATIATING
INGRATIATINGLY
INGRATIATION
INGRATIATIONS
INGRATIATORY
INGRATITUDE
INGRATITUDES
INGRAVESCENCE
INGRAVESCENCES
INGRAVESCENT
INGREDIENT
INGREDIENTS
INGRESSION
INGRESSIONS
INGRESSIVE
INGRESSIVENESS
INGRESSIVES
INGROOVING
INGROSSING
INGROUNDED
INGROUNDING
INGROWNNESS
INGROWNNESSES
INGULFMENT
INGULFMENTS
INGULPHING
INGURGITATE
INGURGITATED
INGURGITATES
INGURGITATING
INGURGITATION
INGURGITATIONS
INHABITABILITY
INHABITABLE
INHABITANCE
INHABITANCES
INHABITANCIES
INHABITANCY
INHABITANT
INHABITANTS
INHABITATION
INHABITATIONS
INHABITERS
INHABITING
INHABITIVENESS
INHABITORS
INHABITRESS
INHABITRESSES
INHALATION
INHALATIONAL
INHALATIONS
INHALATORIUM
INHALATORIUMS
INHALATORS
INHARMONIC
INHARMONICAL
INHARMONICITIES
INHARMONICITY
INHARMONIES
INHARMONIOUS
INHARMONIOUSLY
INHAUSTING
INHEARSING
INHERENCES
INHERENCIES
INHERENTLY
INHERITABILITY
INHERITABLE
INHERITABLENESS
INHERITABLY
INHERITANCE
INHERITANCES
INHERITING
INHERITORS
INHERITRESS
INHERITRESSES
INHERITRICES
INHERITRIX
INHERITRIXES
INHIBITABLE
INHIBITEDLY
INHIBITERS
INHIBITING
INHIBITION
INHIBITIONS
INHIBITIVE
INHIBITORS
INHIBITORY
INHOLDINGS
INHOMOGENEITIES
INHOMOGENEITY
INHOMOGENEOUS
INHOSPITABLE
INHOSPITABLY
INHOSPITALITIES
INHOSPITALITY
INHUMANELY
INHUMANEST
INHUMANITIES
INHUMANITY

INHUMANNESS
INHUMANNESSES
INHUMATING
INHUMATION
INHUMATIONS
INIMICALITIES
INIMICALITY
INIMICALLY
INIMICALNESS
INIMICALNESSES
INIMICITIOUS
INIMITABILITIES
INIMITABILITY
INIMITABLE
INIMITABLENESS
INIMITABLY
INIQUITIES
INIQUITOUS
INIQUITOUSLY
INIQUITOUSNESS
INITIALERS
INITIALING
INITIALISATION
INITIALISATIONS
INITIALISE
INITIALISED
INITIALISES
INITIALISING
INITIALISM
INITIALISMS
INITIALIZATION
INITIALIZATIONS
INITIALIZE
INITIALIZED
INITIALIZES
INITIALIZING
INITIALLED
INITIALLER
INITIALLERS
INITIALLING
INITIALNESS
INITIALNESSES
INITIATING
INITIATION
INITIATIONS
INITIATIVE
INITIATIVELY
INITIATIVES
INITIATORIES
INITIATORS
INITIATORY
INITIATRESS
INITIATRESSES
INITIATRICES
INITIATRIX
INITIATRIXES
INJECTABLE
INJECTABLES
INJECTANTS
INJECTIONS
INJELLYING
INJOINTING
INJUDICIAL
INJUDICIALLY
INJUDICIOUS
INJUDICIOUSLY
INJUDICIOUSNESS
INJUNCTING
INJUNCTION
INJUNCTIONS
INJUNCTIVE
INJUNCTIVELY
INJURIOUSLY
INJURIOUSNESS
INJURIOUSNESSES
INJUSTICES
INKBERRIES
INKHOLDERS
INKINESSES
INMARRIAGE
INMARRIAGES
INMIGRANTS
INNATENESS
INNATENESSES
INNAVIGABLE
INNAVIGABLY
INNERMOSTS
INNERNESSES
INNERSOLES
INNERSPRING
INNERVATED
INNERVATES
INNERVATING
INNERVATION
INNERVATIONS
INNERWEARS
INNKEEPERS
INNOCENCES
INNOCENCIES
INNOCENTER
INNOCENTEST
INNOCENTLY
INNOCUITIES
INNOCUOUSLY
INNOCUOUSNESS
INNOCUOUSNESSES
INNOMINABLE
INNOMINABLES
INNOMINATE
INNOVATING
INNOVATION
INNOVATIONAL
INNOVATIONIST
INNOVATIONISTS
INNOVATIONS
INNOVATIVE
INNOVATIVELY
INNOVATIVENESS
INNOVATORS
INNOVATORY
INNOXIOUSLY
INNOXIOUSNESS
INNOXIOUSNESSES
INNUENDOED
INNUENDOES
INNUENDOING
INNUMERABILITY
INNUMERABLE
INNUMERABLENESS
INNUMERABLY
INNUMERACIES
INNUMERACY
INNUMERATE
INNUMERATES
INNUMEROUS
INNUTRIENT
INNUTRITION
INNUTRITIONS
INNUTRITIOUS
INOBEDIENCE
INOBEDIENCES
INOBEDIENT
INOBEDIENTLY
INOBSERVABLE
INOBSERVANCE
INOBSERVANCES
INOBSERVANT
INOBSERVANTLY
INOBSERVATION
INOBSERVATIONS
INOBTRUSIVE
INOBTRUSIVELY
INOBTRUSIVENESS
INOCCUPATION
INOCCUPATIONS
INOCULABILITIES
INOCULABILITY
INOCULABLE
INOCULANTS
INOCULATED
INOCULATES
INOCULATING
INOCULATION
INOCULATIONS
INOCULATIVE
INOCULATOR
INOCULATORS
INOCULATORY
INODOROUSLY
INODOROUSNESS
INODOROUSNESSES
INOFFENSIVE
INOFFENSIVELY
INOFFENSIVENESS
INOFFICIOUS
INOFFICIOUSLY
INOFFICIOUSNESS
INOPERABILITIES
INOPERABILITY
INOPERABLE
INOPERABLENESS
INOPERABLY
INOPERATIVE
INOPERATIVENESS
INOPERCULATE
INOPERCULATES
INOPPORTUNE
INOPPORTUNELY
INOPPORTUNENESS
INOPPORTUNITIES
INOPPORTUNITY
INORDINACIES
INORDINACY
INORDINATE
INORDINATELY
INORDINATENESS
INORDINATION
INORDINATIONS
INORGANICALLY
INORGANICS
INORGANISATION
INORGANISATIONS
INORGANISED
INORGANIZATION
INORGANIZATIONS
INORGANIZED
INOSCULATE
INOSCULATED
INOSCULATES
INOSCULATING
INOSCULATION
INOSCULATIONS
INOSILICATE
INOSILICATES
INPATIENTS
INPAYMENTS
INPOURINGS
INQUIETING
INQUIETUDE
INQUIETUDES
INQUILINES
INQUILINIC
INQUILINICS
INQUILINISM
INQUILINISMS
INQUILINITIES
INQUILINITY
INQUILINOUS
INQUINATED
INQUINATES
INQUINATING
INQUINATION
INQUINATIONS
INQUIRATION
INQUIRATIONS
INQUIRENDO
INQUIRENDOS
INQUIRINGLY
INQUISITION
INQUISITIONAL

INQUISITIONIST
INQUISITIONISTS
INQUISITIONS
INQUISITIVE
INQUISITIVELY
INQUISITIVENESS
INQUISITOR
INQUISITORIAL
INQUISITORIALLY
INQUISITORS
INQUISITRESS
INQUISITRESSES
INQUISITURIENT
INRUSHINGS
INSALIVATE
INSALIVATED
INSALIVATES
INSALIVATING
INSALIVATION
INSALIVATIONS
INSALUBRIOUS
INSALUBRIOUSLY
INSALUBRITIES
INSALUBRITY
INSALUTARY
INSANENESS
INSANENESSES
INSANITARINESS
INSANITARY
INSANITATION
INSANITATIONS
INSANITIES
INSATIABILITIES
INSATIABILITY
INSATIABLE
INSATIABLENESS
INSATIABLY
INSATIATELY
INSATIATENESS
INSATIATENESSES
INSATIETIES
INSCIENCES
INSCONCING
INSCRIBABLE
INSCRIBABLENESS
INSCRIBERS
INSCRIBING
INSCRIPTION
INSCRIPTIONAL
INSCRIPTIONS
INSCRIPTIVE
INSCRIPTIVELY
INSCROLLED
INSCROLLING
INSCRUTABILITY
INSCRUTABLE
INSCRUTABLENESS
INSCRUTABLY
INSCULPING
INSCULPTURE
INSCULPTURED
INSCULPTURES
INSCULPTURING
INSECTARIA
INSECTARIES
INSECTARIUM
INSECTARIUMS
INSECTICIDAL
INSECTICIDALLY
INSECTICIDE
INSECTICIDES
INSECTIFORM
INSECTIFUGE
INSECTIFUGES
INSECTIONS
INSECTIVORE
INSECTIVORES
INSECTIVOROUS
INSECTOLOGIES
INSECTOLOGIST
INSECTOLOGISTS
INSECTOLOGY
INSECURELY
INSECURENESS
INSECURENESSES
INSECUREST
INSECURITIES
INSECURITY
INSELBERGE
INSELBERGS
INSEMINATE
INSEMINATED
INSEMINATES
INSEMINATING
INSEMINATION
INSEMINATIONS
INSEMINATOR
INSEMINATORS
INSENSATELY
INSENSATENESS
INSENSATENESSES
INSENSIBILITIES
INSENSIBILITY
INSENSIBLE
INSENSIBLENESS
INSENSIBLY
INSENSITIVE
INSENSITIVELY
INSENSITIVENESS
INSENSITIVITIES
INSENSITIVITY
INSENSUOUS
INSENTIENCE
INSENTIENCES
INSENTIENCIES
INSENTIENCY
INSENTIENT
INSEPARABILITY
INSEPARABLE
INSEPARABLENESS
INSEPARABLES
INSEPARABLY
INSEPARATE
INSERTABLE
INSERTIONAL
INSERTIONS
INSESSORIAL
INSEVERABLE
INSHEATHED
INSHEATHES
INSHEATHING
INSHELLING
INSHELTERED
INSHELTERING
INSHELTERS
INSHIPPING
INSHRINEMENT
INSHRINEMENTS
INSHRINING
INSIDIOUSLY
INSIDIOUSNESS
INSIDIOUSNESSES
INSIGHTFUL
INSIGHTFULLY
INSIGNIFICANCE
INSIGNIFICANCES
INSIGNIFICANCY
INSIGNIFICANT
INSIGNIFICANTLY
INSIGNIFICATIVE
INSINCERELY
INSINCERER
INSINCEREST
INSINCERITIES
INSINCERITY
INSINEWING
INSINUATED
INSINUATES
INSINUATING
INSINUATINGLY
INSINUATION
INSINUATIONS
INSINUATIVE
INSINUATOR
INSINUATORS
INSINUATORY
INSIPIDEST
INSIPIDITIES
INSIPIDITY
INSIPIDNESS
INSIPIDNESSES
INSIPIENCE
INSIPIENCES
INSIPIENTLY
INSISTENCE
INSISTENCES
INSISTENCIES
INSISTENCY
INSISTENTLY
INSISTINGLY
INSNAREMENT
INSNAREMENTS
INSOBRIETIES
INSOBRIETY
INSOCIABILITIES
INSOCIABILITY
INSOCIABLE
INSOCIABLY
INSOLATING
INSOLATION
INSOLATIONS
INSOLENCES
INSOLENTLY
INSOLIDITIES
INSOLIDITY
INSOLUBILISE
INSOLUBILISED
INSOLUBILISES
INSOLUBILISING
INSOLUBILITIES
INSOLUBILITY
INSOLUBILIZE
INSOLUBILIZED
INSOLUBILIZES
INSOLUBILIZING
INSOLUBLENESS
INSOLUBLENESSES
INSOLUBLES
INSOLVABILITIES
INSOLVABILITY
INSOLVABLE
INSOLVABLY
INSOLVENCIES
INSOLVENCY
INSOLVENTS
INSOMNIACS
INSOMNIOUS
INSOMNOLENCE
INSOMNOLENCES
INSOUCIANCE
INSOUCIANCES
INSOUCIANT
INSOUCIANTLY
INSOULMENT
INSOULMENTS
INSOURCING
INSOURCINGS
INSPANNING
INSPECTABLE
INSPECTING
INSPECTINGLY
INSPECTION
INSPECTIONAL
INSPECTIONS
INSPECTIVE
INSPECTORAL
INSPECTORATE
INSPECTORATES
INSPECTORIAL
INSPECTORS

INSPECTORSHIP
INSPECTORSHIPS
INSPHERING
INSPIRABLE
INSPIRATION
INSPIRATIONAL
INSPIRATIONALLY
INSPIRATIONISM
INSPIRATIONISMS
INSPIRATIONIST
INSPIRATIONISTS
INSPIRATIONS
INSPIRATIVE
INSPIRATOR
INSPIRATORS
INSPIRATORY
INSPIRINGLY
INSPIRITED
INSPIRITER
INSPIRITERS
INSPIRITING
INSPIRITINGLY
INSPIRITMENT
INSPIRITMENTS
INSPISSATE
INSPISSATED
INSPISSATES
INSPISSATING
INSPISSATION
INSPISSATIONS
INSPISSATOR
INSPISSATORS
INSTABILITIES
INSTABILITY
INSTAGRAMMED
INSTAGRAMMING
INSTAGRAMS
INSTALLANT
INSTALLANTS
INSTALLATION
INSTALLATIONS
INSTALLERS
INSTALLING
INSTALLMENT
INSTALLMENTS
INSTALMENT
INSTALMENTS
INSTANCIES
INSTANCING
INSTANTANEITIES
INSTANTANEITY
INSTANTANEOUS
INSTANTANEOUSLY
INSTANTIAL
INSTANTIATE
INSTANTIATED
INSTANTIATES
INSTANTIATING
INSTANTIATION
INSTANTIATIONS
INSTANTNESS
INSTANTNESSES
INSTARRING
INSTATEMENT
INSTATEMENTS
INSTAURATION
INSTAURATIONS
INSTAURATOR
INSTAURATORS
INSTIGATED
INSTIGATES
INSTIGATING
INSTIGATINGLY
INSTIGATION
INSTIGATIONS
INSTIGATIVE
INSTIGATOR
INSTIGATORS
INSTILLATION
INSTILLATIONS
INSTILLERS
INSTILLING
INSTILLMENT
INSTILLMENTS
INSTILMENT
INSTILMENTS
INSTINCTIVE
INSTINCTIVELY
INSTINCTIVITIES
INSTINCTIVITY
INSTINCTUAL
INSTINCTUALLY
INSTITORIAL
INSTITUTED
INSTITUTER
INSTITUTERS
INSTITUTES
INSTITUTING
INSTITUTION
INSTITUTIONAL
INSTITUTIONALLY
INSTITUTIONARY
INSTITUTIONS
INSTITUTIST
INSTITUTISTS
INSTITUTIVE
INSTITUTIVELY
INSTITUTOR
INSTITUTORS
INSTREAMING
INSTREAMINGS
INSTRESSED
INSTRESSES
INSTRESSING
INSTRUCTED
INSTRUCTIBLE
INSTRUCTING
INSTRUCTION
INSTRUCTIONAL
INSTRUCTIONS
INSTRUCTIVE
INSTRUCTIVELY
INSTRUCTIVENESS
INSTRUCTOR
INSTRUCTORS
INSTRUCTORSHIP
INSTRUCTORSHIPS
INSTRUCTRESS
INSTRUCTRESSES
INSTRUMENT
INSTRUMENTAL
INSTRUMENTALISM
INSTRUMENTALIST
INSTRUMENTALITY
INSTRUMENTALLY
INSTRUMENTALS
INSTRUMENTATION
INSTRUMENTED
INSTRUMENTING
INSTRUMENTS
INSUBJECTION
INSUBJECTIONS
INSUBORDINATE
INSUBORDINATELY
INSUBORDINATES
INSUBORDINATION
INSUBSTANTIAL
INSUBSTANTIALLY
INSUFFERABLE
INSUFFERABLY
INSUFFICIENCE
INSUFFICIENCES
INSUFFICIENCIES
INSUFFICIENCY
INSUFFICIENT
INSUFFICIENTLY
INSUFFLATE
INSUFFLATED
INSUFFLATES
INSUFFLATING
INSUFFLATION
INSUFFLATIONS
INSUFFLATOR
INSUFFLATORS
INSULARISM
INSULARISMS
INSULARITIES
INSULARITY
INSULATING
INSULATION
INSULATIONS
INSULATORS
INSULINASE
INSULINASES
INSULSITIES
INSULTABLE
INSULTINGLY
INSULTMENT
INSULTMENTS
INSUPERABILITY
INSUPERABLE
INSUPERABLENESS
INSUPERABLY
INSUPPORTABLE
INSUPPORTABLY
INSUPPRESSIBLE
INSUPPRESSIBLY
INSURABILITIES
INSURABILITY
INSURANCER
INSURANCERS
INSURANCES
INSURGENCE
INSURGENCES
INSURGENCIES
INSURGENCY
INSURGENTLY
INSURGENTS
INSURMOUNTABLE
INSURMOUNTABLY
INSURRECTION
INSURRECTIONAL
INSURRECTIONARY
INSURRECTIONISM
INSURRECTIONIST
INSURRECTIONS
INSUSCEPTIBLE
INSUSCEPTIBLY
INSUSCEPTIVE
INSUSCEPTIVELY
INSWATHING
INSWINGERS
INTACTNESS
INTACTNESSES
INTAGLIATED
INTAGLIOED
INTAGLIOES
INTAGLIOING
INTANGIBILITIES
INTANGIBILITY
INTANGIBLE
INTANGIBLENESS
INTANGIBLES
INTANGIBLY
INTEGRABILITIES
INTEGRABILITY
INTEGRABLE
INTEGRALITIES
INTEGRALITY
INTEGRALLY
INTEGRANDS
INTEGRANTS
INTEGRATED
INTEGRATES
INTEGRATING
INTEGRATION
INTEGRATIONIST
INTEGRATIONISTS
INTEGRATIONS
INTEGRATIVE

INTEGRATOR
INTEGRATORS
INTEGRITIES
INTEGUMENT
INTEGUMENTAL
INTEGUMENTARY
INTEGUMENTS
INTELLECTED
INTELLECTION
INTELLECTIONS
INTELLECTIVE
INTELLECTIVELY
INTELLECTS
INTELLECTUAL
INTELLECTUALISE
INTELLECTUALISM
INTELLECTUALIST
INTELLECTUALITY
INTELLECTUALIZE
INTELLECTUALLY
INTELLECTUALS
INTELLIGENCE
INTELLIGENCER
INTELLIGENCERS
INTELLIGENCES
INTELLIGENT
INTELLIGENTIAL
INTELLIGENTLY
INTELLIGENTSIA
INTELLIGENTSIAS
INTELLIGENTZIA
INTELLIGENTZIAS
INTELLIGIBILITY
INTELLIGIBLE
INTELLIGIBLY
INTEMERATE
INTEMERATELY
INTEMERATENESS
INTEMPERANCE
INTEMPERANCES
INTEMPERANT
INTEMPERANTS
INTEMPERATE
INTEMPERATELY
INTEMPERATENESS
INTEMPESTIVE
INTEMPESTIVELY
INTEMPESTIVITY
INTENDANCE
INTENDANCES
INTENDANCIES
INTENDANCY
INTENDANTS
INTENDEDLY
INTENDERED
INTENDERING
INTENDMENT
INTENDMENTS
INTENERATE
INTENERATED
INTENERATES
INTENERATING
INTENERATION
INTENERATIONS
INTENSATED
INTENSATES
INTENSATING
INTENSATIVE
INTENSATIVES
INTENSENESS
INTENSENESSES
INTENSIFICATION
INTENSIFIED
INTENSIFIER
INTENSIFIERS
INTENSIFIES
INTENSIFYING
INTENSIONAL
INTENSIONALITY
INTENSIONALLY
INTENSIONS
INTENSITIES
INTENSITIVE
INTENSITIVES
INTENSIVELY
INTENSIVENESS
INTENSIVENESSES
INTENSIVES
INTENTIONAL
INTENTIONALITY
INTENTIONALLY
INTENTIONED
INTENTIONS
INTENTNESS
INTENTNESSES
INTERABANG
INTERABANGS
INTERACTANT
INTERACTANTS
INTERACTED
INTERACTING
INTERACTION
INTERACTIONAL
INTERACTIONISM
INTERACTIONISMS
INTERACTIONIST
INTERACTIONISTS
INTERACTIONS
INTERACTIVE
INTERACTIVELY
INTERACTIVITIES
INTERACTIVITY
INTERAGENCY
INTERALLELIC
INTERALLIED
INTERAMBULACRA
INTERAMBULACRAL
INTERAMBULACRUM
INTERANIMATION
INTERANIMATIONS
INTERANNUAL
INTERARCHED
INTERARCHES
INTERARCHING
INTERATOMIC
INTERBASIN
INTERBEDDED
INTERBEDDING
INTERBEDDINGS
INTERBEHAVIOR
INTERBEHAVIORAL
INTERBEHAVIORS
INTERBEHAVIOUR
INTERBEHAVIOURS
INTERBLEND
INTERBLENDED
INTERBLENDING
INTERBLENDS
INTERBOROUGH
INTERBRAIN
INTERBRAINS
INTERBRANCH
INTERBREED
INTERBREEDING
INTERBREEDINGS
INTERBREEDS
INTERBROKER
INTERCALAR
INTERCALARILY
INTERCALARY
INTERCALATE
INTERCALATED
INTERCALATES
INTERCALATING
INTERCALATION
INTERCALATIONS
INTERCALATIVE
INTERCAMPUS
INTERCASTE
INTERCEDED
INTERCEDENT
INTERCEDER
INTERCEDERS
INTERCEDES
INTERCEDING
INTERCELLULAR
INTERCENSAL
INTERCEPTED
INTERCEPTER
INTERCEPTERS
INTERCEPTING
INTERCEPTION
INTERCEPTIONS
INTERCEPTIVE
INTERCEPTOR
INTERCEPTORS
INTERCEPTS
INTERCESSION
INTERCESSIONAL
INTERCESSIONS
INTERCESSOR
INTERCESSORIAL
INTERCESSORS
INTERCESSORY
INTERCHAIN
INTERCHAINED
INTERCHAINING
INTERCHAINS
INTERCHANGE
INTERCHANGEABLE
INTERCHANGEABLY
INTERCHANGED
INTERCHANGEMENT
INTERCHANGER
INTERCHANGERS
INTERCHANGES
INTERCHANGING
INTERCHANNEL
INTERCHAPTER
INTERCHAPTERS
INTERCHURCH
INTERCIPIENT
INTERCIPIENTS
INTERCLASS
INTERCLAVICLE
INTERCLAVICLES
INTERCLAVICULAR
INTERCLUDE
INTERCLUDED
INTERCLUDES
INTERCLUDING
INTERCLUSION
INTERCLUSIONS
INTERCLUSTER
INTERCOASTAL
INTERCOLLEGIATE
INTERCOLLINE
INTERCOLONIAL
INTERCOLONIALLY
INTERCOLUMNAR
INTERCOMMUNAL
INTERCOMMUNE
INTERCOMMUNED
INTERCOMMUNES
INTERCOMMUNING
INTERCOMMUNION
INTERCOMMUNIONS
INTERCOMMUNITY
INTERCOMPANY
INTERCOMPARE
INTERCOMPARED
INTERCOMPARES
INTERCOMPARING
INTERCOMPARISON
INTERCONNECT
INTERCONNECTED
INTERCONNECTING
INTERCONNECTION
INTERCONNECTOR
INTERCONNECTORS

INTERCONNECTS
INTERCONNEXION
INTERCONNEXIONS
INTERCONVERSION
INTERCONVERT
INTERCONVERTED
INTERCONVERTING
INTERCONVERTS
INTERCOOLED
INTERCOOLER
INTERCOOLERS
INTERCOOLING
INTERCOOLS
INTERCORPORATE
INTERCORRELATE
INTERCORRELATED
INTERCORRELATES
INTERCORTICAL
INTERCOSTAL
INTERCOSTALLY
INTERCOSTALS
INTERCOUNTRY
INTERCOUNTY
INTERCOUPLE
INTERCOURSE
INTERCOURSES
INTERCRATER
INTERCROPPED
INTERCROPPING
INTERCROPS
INTERCROSS
INTERCROSSED
INTERCROSSES
INTERCROSSING
INTERCRURAL
INTERCULTURAL
INTERCULTURALLY
INTERCULTURE
INTERCULTURES
INTERCURRENCE
INTERCURRENCES
INTERCURRENT
INTERCURRENTLY
INTERCURRENTS
INTERCUTTING
INTERDASHED
INTERDASHES
INTERDASHING
INTERDEALER
INTERDEALERS
INTERDEALING
INTERDEALS
INTERDEALT
INTERDENTAL
INTERDENTALLY
INTERDEPEND
INTERDEPENDED
INTERDEPENDENCE
INTERDEPENDENCY
INTERDEPENDENT
INTERDEPENDING
INTERDEPENDS
INTERDIALECTAL
INTERDICTED
INTERDICTING
INTERDICTION
INTERDICTIONS
INTERDICTIVE
INTERDICTIVELY
INTERDICTOR
INTERDICTORS
INTERDICTORY
INTERDICTS
INTERDIFFUSE
INTERDIFFUSED
INTERDIFFUSES
INTERDIFFUSING
INTERDIFFUSION
INTERDIFFUSIONS
INTERDIGITAL
INTERDIGITATE
INTERDIGITATED
INTERDIGITATES
INTERDIGITATING
INTERDIGITATION
INTERDINED
INTERDINES
INTERDINING
INTERDISTRICT
INTERDIVISIONAL
INTERDOMINION
INTERELECTRODE
INTERELECTRON
INTERELECTRONIC
INTEREPIDEMIC
INTERESSED
INTERESSES
INTERESSING
INTERESTED
INTERESTEDLY
INTERESTEDNESS
INTERESTING
INTERESTINGLY
INTERESTINGNESS
INTERETHNIC
INTERFACED
INTERFACES
INTERFACIAL
INTERFACIALLY
INTERFACING
INTERFACINGS
INTERFACULTY
INTERFAITH
INTERFAMILIAL
INTERFAMILY
INTERFASCICULAR
INTERFEMORAL
INTERFERED
INTERFERENCE
INTERFERENCES
INTERFERENTIAL
INTERFERER
INTERFERERS
INTERFERES
INTERFERING
INTERFERINGLY
INTERFEROGRAM
INTERFEROGRAMS
INTERFEROMETER
INTERFEROMETERS
INTERFEROMETRIC
INTERFEROMETRY
INTERFERON
INTERFERONS
INTERFERTILE
INTERFERTILITY
INTERFIBER
INTERFIBRE
INTERFILED
INTERFILES
INTERFILING
INTERFLOWED
INTERFLOWING
INTERFLOWS
INTERFLUENCE
INTERFLUENCES
INTERFLUENT
INTERFLUOUS
INTERFLUVE
INTERFLUVES
INTERFLUVIAL
INTERFOLDED
INTERFOLDING
INTERFOLDS
INTERFOLIATE
INTERFOLIATED
INTERFOLIATES
INTERFOLIATING
INTERFRATERNITY
INTERFRETTED
INTERFRONTAL
INTERFUSED
INTERFUSES
INTERFUSING
INTERFUSION
INTERFUSIONS
INTERGALACTIC
INTERGENERATION
INTERGENERIC
INTERGLACIAL
INTERGLACIALS
INTERGRADATION
INTERGRADATIONS
INTERGRADE
INTERGRADED
INTERGRADES
INTERGRADIENT
INTERGRADING
INTERGRAFT
INTERGRAFTED
INTERGRAFTING
INTERGRAFTS
INTERGRANULAR
INTERGROUP
INTERGROUPS
INTERGROWING
INTERGROWN
INTERGROWS
INTERGROWTH
INTERGROWTHS
INTERINDIVIDUAL
INTERINDUSTRY
INTERINFLUENCE
INTERINFLUENCED
INTERINFLUENCES
INTERINVOLVE
INTERINVOLVED
INTERINVOLVES
INTERINVOLVING
INTERIONIC
INTERIORISATION
INTERIORISE
INTERIORISED
INTERIORISES
INTERIORISING
INTERIORITIES
INTERIORITY
INTERIORIZATION
INTERIORIZE
INTERIORIZED
INTERIORIZES
INTERIORIZING
INTERIORLY
INTERISLAND
INTERJACENCIES
INTERJACENCY
INTERJACENT
INTERJACULATE
INTERJACULATED
INTERJACULATES
INTERJACULATING
INTERJACULATORY
INTERJECTED
INTERJECTING
INTERJECTION
INTERJECTIONAL
INTERJECTIONARY
INTERJECTIONS
INTERJECTOR
INTERJECTORS
INTERJECTORY
INTERJECTS
INTERJECTURAL
INTERJOINED
INTERJOINING
INTERJOINS
INTERKINESES
INTERKINESIS
INTERKNITS
INTERKNITTED

INTERKNITTING
INTERKNOTS
INTERKNOTTED
INTERKNOTTING
INTERLACED
INTERLACEDLY
INTERLACEMENT
INTERLACEMENTS
INTERLACES
INTERLACING
INTERLACUSTRINE
INTERLAMINAR
INTERLAMINATE
INTERLAMINATED
INTERLAMINATES
INTERLAMINATING
INTERLAMINATION
INTERLAPPED
INTERLAPPING
INTERLARDED
INTERLARDING
INTERLARDS
INTERLAYER
INTERLAYERED
INTERLAYERING
INTERLAYERINGS
INTERLAYERS
INTERLAYING
INTERLEAVE
INTERLEAVED
INTERLEAVES
INTERLEAVING
INTERLENDING
INTERLENDS
INTERLEUKIN
INTERLEUKINS
INTERLIBRARY
INTERLINEAL
INTERLINEALLY
INTERLINEAR
INTERLINEARLY
INTERLINEARS
INTERLINEATE
INTERLINEATED
INTERLINEATES
INTERLINEATING
INTERLINEATION
INTERLINEATIONS
INTERLINED
INTERLINER
INTERLINERS
INTERLINES
INTERLINGUA
INTERLINGUAL
INTERLINGUALLY
INTERLINGUAS
INTERLINING
INTERLININGS
INTERLINKED
INTERLINKING
INTERLINKS
INTERLOANS
INTERLOBULAR
INTERLOCAL
INTERLOCATION
INTERLOCATIONS
INTERLOCKED
INTERLOCKER
INTERLOCKERS
INTERLOCKING
INTERLOCKS
INTERLOCUTION
INTERLOCUTIONS
INTERLOCUTOR
INTERLOCUTORILY
INTERLOCUTORS
INTERLOCUTORY
INTERLOCUTRESS
INTERLOCUTRICE
INTERLOCUTRICES
INTERLOCUTRIX
INTERLOCUTRIXES
INTERLOOPED
INTERLOOPING
INTERLOOPS
INTERLOPED
INTERLOPER
INTERLOPERS
INTERLOPES
INTERLOPING
INTERLUDED
INTERLUDES
INTERLUDIAL
INTERLUDING
INTERLUNAR
INTERLUNARY
INTERLUNATION
INTERLUNATIONS
INTERMARGINAL
INTERMARRIAGE
INTERMARRIAGES
INTERMARRIED
INTERMARRIES
INTERMARRY
INTERMARRYING
INTERMATTED
INTERMATTING
INTERMAXILLA
INTERMAXILLAE
INTERMAXILLARY
INTERMEDDLE
INTERMEDDLED
INTERMEDDLER
INTERMEDDLERS
INTERMEDDLES
INTERMEDDLING
INTERMEDIA
INTERMEDIACIES
INTERMEDIACY
INTERMEDIAL
INTERMEDIARIES
INTERMEDIARY
INTERMEDIATE
INTERMEDIATED
INTERMEDIATELY
INTERMEDIATES
INTERMEDIATING
INTERMEDIATION
INTERMEDIATIONS
INTERMEDIATOR
INTERMEDIATORS
INTERMEDIATORY
INTERMEDIN
INTERMEDINS
INTERMEDIUM
INTERMEDIUMS
INTERMEMBRANE
INTERMENSTRUAL
INTERMENTS
INTERMESHED
INTERMESHES
INTERMESHING
INTERMETALLIC
INTERMETALLICS
INTERMEZZI
INTERMEZZO
INTERMEZZOS
INTERMIGRATION
INTERMIGRATIONS
INTERMINABILITY
INTERMINABLE
INTERMINABLY
INTERMINGLE
INTERMINGLED
INTERMINGLES
INTERMINGLING
INTERMISSION
INTERMISSIONS
INTERMISSIVE
INTERMITOTIC
INTERMITTED
INTERMITTENCE
INTERMITTENCES
INTERMITTENCIES
INTERMITTENCY
INTERMITTENT
INTERMITTENTLY
INTERMITTER
INTERMITTERS
INTERMITTING
INTERMITTINGLY
INTERMITTOR
INTERMITTORS
INTERMIXED
INTERMIXES
INTERMIXING
INTERMIXTURE
INTERMIXTURES
INTERMODAL
INTERMODULATION
INTERMOLECULAR
INTERMONTANE
INTERMOUNTAIN
INTERMUNDANE
INTERMURED
INTERMURES
INTERMURING
INTERMUSCULAR
INTERNALISATION
INTERNALISE
INTERNALISED
INTERNALISES
INTERNALISING
INTERNALITIES
INTERNALITY
INTERNALIZATION
INTERNALIZE
INTERNALIZED
INTERNALIZES
INTERNALIZING
INTERNALLY
INTERNALNESS
INTERNALNESSES
INTERNATIONAL
INTERNATIONALLY
INTERNATIONALS
INTERNECINE
INTERNECIVE
INTERNEURAL
INTERNEURON
INTERNEURONAL
INTERNEURONS
INTERNISTS
INTERNMENT
INTERNMENTS
INTERNODAL
INTERNODES
INTERNODIAL
INTERNSHIP
INTERNSHIPS
INTERNUCLEAR
INTERNUCLEON
INTERNUCLEONIC
INTERNUCLEOTIDE
INTERNUNCIAL
INTERNUNCIO
INTERNUNCIOS
INTEROBSERVER
INTEROCEAN
INTEROCEANIC
INTEROCEPTION
INTEROCEPTIONS
INTEROCEPTIVE
INTEROCEPTOR
INTEROCEPTORS
INTEROCULAR
INTEROFFICE
INTEROPERABLE
INTEROPERATIVE
INTERORBITAL

INTERORGAN
INTEROSCULANT
INTEROSCULATE
INTEROSCULATED
INTEROSCULATES
INTEROSCULATING
INTEROSCULATION
INTEROSSEAL
INTEROSSEOUS
INTERPAGED
INTERPAGES
INTERPAGING
INTERPANDEMIC
INTERPARIETAL
INTERPARISH
INTERPAROCHIAL
INTERPAROXYSMAL
INTERPARTICLE
INTERPARTY
INTERPELLANT
INTERPELLANTS
INTERPELLATE
INTERPELLATED
INTERPELLATES
INTERPELLATING
INTERPELLATION
INTERPELLATIONS
INTERPELLATOR
INTERPELLATORS
INTERPENETRABLE
INTERPENETRANT
INTERPENETRATE
INTERPENETRATED
INTERPENETRATES
INTERPERCEPTUAL
INTERPERMEATE
INTERPERMEATED
INTERPERMEATES
INTERPERMEATING
INTERPERSONAL
INTERPERSONALLY
INTERPETIOLAR
INTERPHALANGEAL
INTERPHASE
INTERPHASES
INTERPHONE
INTERPHONES
INTERPILASTER
INTERPILASTERS
INTERPLANETARY
INTERPLANT
INTERPLANTED
INTERPLANTING
INTERPLANTS
INTERPLAYED
INTERPLAYING
INTERPLAYS
INTERPLEAD
INTERPLEADED
INTERPLEADER
INTERPLEADERS
INTERPLEADING
INTERPLEADS
INTERPLEURAL
INTERPLUVIAL
INTERPLUVIALS
INTERPOINT
INTERPOINTS
INTERPOLABLE
INTERPOLAR
INTERPOLATE
INTERPOLATED
INTERPOLATER
INTERPOLATERS
INTERPOLATES
INTERPOLATING
INTERPOLATION
INTERPOLATIONS
INTERPOLATIVE
INTERPOLATOR
INTERPOLATORS
INTERPONED
INTERPONES
INTERPONING
INTERPOPULATION
INTERPOSABLE
INTERPOSAL
INTERPOSALS
INTERPOSED
INTERPOSER
INTERPOSERS
INTERPOSES
INTERPOSING
INTERPOSITION
INTERPOSITIONS
INTERPRETABLE
INTERPRETABLY
INTERPRETATE
INTERPRETATED
INTERPRETATES
INTERPRETATING
INTERPRETATION
INTERPRETATIONS
INTERPRETATIVE
INTERPRETED
INTERPRETER
INTERPRETERS
INTERPRETERSHIP
INTERPRETESS
INTERPRETESSES
INTERPRETING
INTERPRETIVE
INTERPRETIVELY
INTERPRETRESS
INTERPRETRESSES
INTERPRETS
INTERPROVINCIAL
INTERPROXIMAL
INTERPSYCHIC
INTERPUNCTION
INTERPUNCTIONS
INTERPUNCTUATE
INTERPUNCTUATED
INTERPUNCTUATES
INTERPUPILLARY
INTERQUARTILE
INTERRACIAL
INTERRACIALLY
INTERRADIAL
INTERRADIALLY
INTERRADII
INTERRADIUS
INTERRADIUSES
INTERRAILED
INTERRAILER
INTERRAILERS
INTERRAILING
INTERRAILS
INTERRAMAL
INTERREGAL
INTERREGES
INTERREGIONAL
INTERREGNA
INTERREGNAL
INTERREGNUM
INTERREGNUMS
INTERRELATE
INTERRELATED
INTERRELATEDLY
INTERRELATES
INTERRELATING
INTERRELATION
INTERRELATIONS
INTERRELIGIOUS
INTERRENAL
INTERROBANG
INTERROBANGS
INTERROGABLE
INTERROGANT
INTERROGANTS
INTERROGATE
INTERROGATED
INTERROGATEE
INTERROGATEES
INTERROGATES
INTERROGATING
INTERROGATINGLY
INTERROGATION
INTERROGATIONAL
INTERROGATIONS
INTERROGATIVE
INTERROGATIVELY
INTERROGATIVES
INTERROGATOR
INTERROGATORIES
INTERROGATORILY
INTERROGATORS
INTERROGATORY
INTERROGEE
INTERROGEES
INTERRUPTED
INTERRUPTEDLY
INTERRUPTER
INTERRUPTERS
INTERRUPTIBLE
INTERRUPTING
INTERRUPTION
INTERRUPTIONS
INTERRUPTIVE
INTERRUPTIVELY
INTERRUPTOR
INTERRUPTORS
INTERRUPTS
INTERSCAPULAR
INTERSCHOLASTIC
INTERSCHOOL
INTERSCRIBE
INTERSCRIBED
INTERSCRIBES
INTERSCRIBING
INTERSECTED
INTERSECTING
INTERSECTION
INTERSECTIONAL
INTERSECTIONS
INTERSECTS
INTERSEGMENT
INTERSEGMENTAL
INTERSEGMENTS
INTERSENSORY
INTERSEPTAL
INTERSERTAL
INTERSERTED
INTERSERTING
INTERSERTS
INTERSERVICE
INTERSESSION
INTERSESSIONS
INTERSEXES
INTERSEXUAL
INTERSEXUALISM
INTERSEXUALISMS
INTERSEXUALITY
INTERSEXUALLY
INTERSEXUALS
INTERSIDEREAL
INTERSOCIETAL
INTERSOCIETY
INTERSPACE
INTERSPACED
INTERSPACES
INTERSPACING
INTERSPATIAL
INTERSPATIALLY
INTERSPECIES
INTERSPECIFIC
INTERSPERSAL
INTERSPERSALS
INTERSPERSE
INTERSPERSED

INTERSPERSEDLY
INTERSPERSES
INTERSPERSING
INTERSPERSION
INTERSPERSIONS
INTERSPINAL
INTERSPINOUS
INTERSTADIAL
INTERSTADIALS
INTERSTAGE
INTERSTATE
INTERSTATES
INTERSTATION
INTERSTELLAR
INTERSTELLARY
INTERSTERILE
INTERSTERILITY
INTERSTICE
INTERSTICES
INTERSTIMULUS
INTERSTITIAL
INTERSTITIALLY
INTERSTITIALS
INTERSTRAIN
INTERSTRAND
INTERSTRATIFIED
INTERSTRATIFIES
INTERSTRATIFY
INTERSUBJECTIVE
INTERSYSTEM
INTERTANGLE
INTERTANGLED
INTERTANGLEMENT
INTERTANGLES
INTERTANGLING
INTERTARSAL
INTERTENTACULAR
INTERTERMINAL
INTERTERMS
INTERTEXTS
INTERTEXTUAL
INTERTEXTUALITY
INTERTEXTUALLY
INTERTEXTURE
INTERTEXTURES
INTERTIDAL
INTERTIDALLY
INTERTILLAGE
INTERTILLAGES
INTERTILLED
INTERTILLING
INTERTILLS
INTERTISSUED
INTERTRAFFIC
INTERTRAFFICS
INTERTRIAL
INTERTRIBAL
INTERTRIGO
INTERTRIGOS
INTERTROOP
INTERTROPICAL
INTERTWINE
INTERTWINED
INTERTWINEMENT
INTERTWINEMENTS
INTERTWINES
INTERTWINING
INTERTWININGLY
INTERTWININGS
INTERTWIST
INTERTWISTED
INTERTWISTING
INTERTWISTINGLY
INTERTWISTS
INTERUNION
INTERUNIONS
INTERUNIVERSITY
INTERURBAN
INTERVALES
INTERVALLEY
INTERVALLIC
INTERVALLUM
INTERVALLUMS
INTERVALOMETER
INTERVALOMETERS
INTERVARSITY
INTERVEINED
INTERVEINING
INTERVEINS
INTERVENED
INTERVENER
INTERVENERS
INTERVENES
INTERVENIENT
INTERVENING
INTERVENOR
INTERVENORS
INTERVENTION
INTERVENTIONAL
INTERVENTIONISM
INTERVENTIONIST
INTERVENTIONS
INTERVENTOR
INTERVENTORS
INTERVERTEBRAL
INTERVIEWED
INTERVIEWEE
INTERVIEWEES
INTERVIEWER
INTERVIEWERS
INTERVIEWING
INTERVIEWS
INTERVILLAGE
INTERVISIBILITY
INTERVISIBLE
INTERVISITATION
INTERVITAL
INTERVOCALIC
INTERVOLVE
INTERVOLVED
INTERVOLVES
INTERVOLVING
INTERWEAVE
INTERWEAVED
INTERWEAVEMENT
INTERWEAVEMENTS
INTERWEAVER
INTERWEAVERS
INTERWEAVES
INTERWEAVING
INTERWINDING
INTERWINDS
INTERWORKED
INTERWORKING
INTERWORKINGS
INTERWORKS
INTERWOUND
INTERWOVEN
INTERWREATHE
INTERWREATHED
INTERWREATHES
INTERWREATHING
INTERWROUGHT
INTERZONAL
INTERZONES
INTESTACIES
INTESTATES
INTESTINAL
INTESTINALLY
INTESTINES
INTHRALLED
INTHRALLING
INTHRONING
INTIFADAHS
INTIFADEHS
INTIMACIES
INTIMATELY
INTIMATENESS
INTIMATENESSES
INTIMATERS
INTIMATING
INTIMATION
INTIMATIONS
INTIMIDATE
INTIMIDATED
INTIMIDATES
INTIMIDATING
INTIMIDATINGLY
INTIMIDATION
INTIMIDATIONS
INTIMIDATOR
INTIMIDATORS
INTIMIDATORY
INTIMISTES
INTIMITIES
INTINCTION
INTINCTIONS
INTITULING
INTOLERABILITY
INTOLERABLE
INTOLERABLENESS
INTOLERABLY
INTOLERANCE
INTOLERANCES
INTOLERANT
INTOLERANTLY
INTOLERANTNESS
INTOLERANTS
INTOLERATION
INTOLERATIONS
INTONATING
INTONATION
INTONATIONAL
INTONATIONS
INTONATORS
INTONINGLY
INTORSIONS
INTORTIONS
INTOXICABLE
INTOXICANT
INTOXICANTS
INTOXICATE
INTOXICATED
INTOXICATEDLY
INTOXICATES
INTOXICATING
INTOXICATINGLY
INTOXICATION
INTOXICATIONS
INTOXICATIVE
INTOXICATOR
INTOXICATORS
INTOXIMETER
INTOXIMETERS
INTRACAPSULAR
INTRACARDIAC
INTRACARDIAL
INTRACARDIALLY
INTRACAVITARY
INTRACELLULAR
INTRACELLULARLY
INTRACEREBRAL
INTRACEREBRALLY
INTRACOMPANY
INTRACRANIAL
INTRACRANIALLY
INTRACTABILITY
INTRACTABLE
INTRACTABLENESS
INTRACTABLY
INTRACUTANEOUS
INTRADERMAL
INTRADERMALLY
INTRADERMIC
INTRADERMICALLY
INTRADOSES
INTRAFALLOPIAN
INTRAFASCICULAR
INTRAGALACTIC
INTRAGENIC

INTRAMEDULLARY
INTRAMERCURIAL
INTRAMOLECULAR
INTRAMUNDANE
INTRAMURAL
INTRAMURALLY
INTRAMURALS
INTRAMUSCULAR
INTRAMUSCULARLY
INTRANASAL
INTRANASALLY
INTRANATIONAL
INTRANSIGEANCE
INTRANSIGEANCES
INTRANSIGEANT
INTRANSIGEANTLY
INTRANSIGEANTS
INTRANSIGENCE
INTRANSIGENCES
INTRANSIGENCIES
INTRANSIGENCY
INTRANSIGENT
INTRANSIGENTISM
INTRANSIGENTIST
INTRANSIGENTLY
INTRANSIGENTS
INTRANSITIVE
INTRANSITIVELY
INTRANSITIVES
INTRANSITIVITY
INTRANSMISSIBLE
INTRANSMUTABLE
INTRANUCLEAR
INTRAOCULAR
INTRAOCULARLY
INTRAPARIETAL
INTRAPARTUM
INTRAPERITONEAL
INTRAPERSONAL
INTRAPETIOLAR
INTRAPLATE
INTRAPOPULATION
INTRAPRENEUR
INTRAPRENEURIAL
INTRAPRENEURS
INTRAPSYCHIC
INTRASEXUAL
INTRASPECIES
INTRASPECIFIC
INTRASTATE
INTRATELLURIC
INTRATHECAL
INTRATHECALLY
INTRATHORACIC
INTRAUTERINE
INTRAVASATION
INTRAVASATIONS
INTRAVASCULAR
INTRAVASCULARLY
INTRAVENOUS
INTRAVENOUSLY
INTRAVERSABLE
INTRAVITAL
INTRAVITALLY
INTRAVITAM
INTRAZONAL
INTREATFULL
INTREATING
INTREATINGLY
INTREATMENT
INTREATMENTS
INTRENCHANT
INTRENCHED
INTRENCHER
INTRENCHERS
INTRENCHES
INTRENCHING
INTRENCHMENT
INTRENCHMENTS
INTREPIDITIES
INTREPIDITY
INTREPIDLY
INTREPIDNESS
INTREPIDNESSES
INTRICACIES
INTRICATELY
INTRICATENESS
INTRICATENESSES
INTRIGANTE
INTRIGANTES
INTRIGANTS
INTRIGUANT
INTRIGUANTE
INTRIGUANTES
INTRIGUANTS
INTRIGUERS
INTRIGUING
INTRIGUINGLY
INTRINSICAL
INTRINSICALITY
INTRINSICALLY
INTRINSICALNESS
INTRINSICATE
INTRODUCED
INTRODUCER
INTRODUCERS
INTRODUCES
INTRODUCIBLE
INTRODUCING
INTRODUCTION
INTRODUCTIONS
INTRODUCTIVE
INTRODUCTORILY
INTRODUCTORY
INTROFYING
INTROGRESSANT
INTROGRESSANTS
INTROGRESSION
INTROGRESSIONS
INTROGRESSIVE
INTROITUSES
INTROJECTED
INTROJECTING
INTROJECTION
INTROJECTIONS
INTROJECTIVE
INTROJECTS
INTROMISSIBLE
INTROMISSION
INTROMISSIONS
INTROMISSIVE
INTROMITTED
INTROMITTENT
INTROMITTER
INTROMITTERS
INTROMITTING
INTRORSELY
INTROSPECT
INTROSPECTED
INTROSPECTING
INTROSPECTION
INTROSPECTIONAL
INTROSPECTIONS
INTROSPECTIVE
INTROSPECTIVELY
INTROSPECTS
INTROSUSCEPTION
INTROVERSIBLE
INTROVERSION
INTROVERSIONS
INTROVERSIVE
INTROVERSIVELY
INTROVERTED
INTROVERTING
INTROVERTIVE
INTROVERTS
INTRUDINGLY
INTRUSIONAL
INTRUSIONIST
INTRUSIONISTS
INTRUSIONS
INTRUSIVELY
INTRUSIVENESS
INTRUSIVENESSES
INTRUSIVES
INTRUSTING
INTRUSTMENT
INTRUSTMENTS
INTUBATING
INTUBATION
INTUBATIONS
INTUITABLE
INTUITIONAL
INTUITIONALISM
INTUITIONALISMS
INTUITIONALIST
INTUITIONALISTS
INTUITIONALLY
INTUITIONISM
INTUITIONISMS
INTUITIONIST
INTUITIONISTS
INTUITIONS
INTUITIVELY
INTUITIVENESS
INTUITIVENESSES
INTUITIVISM
INTUITIVISMS
INTUMESCED
INTUMESCENCE
INTUMESCENCES
INTUMESCENCIES
INTUMESCENCY
INTUMESCENT
INTUMESCES
INTUMESCING
INTURBIDATE
INTURBIDATED
INTURBIDATES
INTURBIDATING
INTUSSUSCEPT
INTUSSUSCEPTED
INTUSSUSCEPTING
INTUSSUSCEPTION
INTUSSUSCEPTIVE
INTUSSUSCEPTS
INTWINEMENT
INTWINEMENTS
INTWISTING
INUMBRATED
INUMBRATES
INUMBRATING
INUNCTIONS
INUNDATING
INUNDATION
INUNDATIONS
INUNDATORS
INUNDATORY
INURBANELY
INURBANITIES
INURBANITY
INUREDNESS
INUREDNESSES
INUREMENTS
INURNMENTS
INUSITATION
INUSITATIONS
INUTILITIES
INUTTERABLE
INVAGINABLE
INVAGINATE
INVAGINATED
INVAGINATES
INVAGINATING
INVAGINATION
INVAGINATIONS
INVALIDATE
INVALIDATED
INVALIDATES
INVALIDATING

INVALIDATION
INVALIDATIONS
INVALIDATOR
INVALIDATORS
INVALIDEST
INVALIDHOOD
INVALIDHOODS
INVALIDING
INVALIDINGS
INVALIDISM
INVALIDISMS
INVALIDITIES
INVALIDITY
INVALIDNESS
INVALIDNESSES
INVALUABLE
INVALUABLENESS
INVALUABLY
INVARIABILITIES
INVARIABILITY
INVARIABLE
INVARIABLENESS
INVARIABLES
INVARIABLY
INVARIANCE
INVARIANCES
INVARIANCIES
INVARIANCY
INVARIANTS
INVASIVELY
INVASIVENESS
INVASIVENESSES
INVEAGLING
INVECTIVELY
INVECTIVENESS
INVECTIVENESSES
INVECTIVES
INVEIGHERS
INVEIGHING
INVEIGLEMENT
INVEIGLEMENTS
INVEIGLERS
INVEIGLING
INVENDIBILITIES
INVENDIBILITY
INVENDIBLE
INVENTABLE
INVENTIBLE
INVENTIONAL
INVENTIONLESS
INVENTIONS
INVENTIVELY
INVENTIVENESS
INVENTIVENESSES
INVENTORIABLE
INVENTORIAL
INVENTORIALLY
INVENTORIED
INVENTORIES
INVENTORYING
INVENTRESS
INVENTRESSES
INVERACITIES
INVERACITY
INVERITIES
INVERNESSES
INVERSIONS
INVERTASES
INVERTEBRAL
INVERTEBRATE
INVERTEBRATES
INVERTEDLY
INVERTIBILITIES
INVERTIBILITY
INVERTIBLE
INVESTABLE
INVESTIBLE
INVESTIGABLE
INVESTIGATE
INVESTIGATED
INVESTIGATES
INVESTIGATING
INVESTIGATION
INVESTIGATIONAL
INVESTIGATIONS
INVESTIGATIVE
INVESTIGATOR
INVESTIGATORS
INVESTIGATORY
INVESTITIVE
INVESTITURE
INVESTITURES
INVESTMENT
INVESTMENTS
INVETERACIES
INVETERACY
INVETERATE
INVETERATELY
INVETERATENESS
INVIABILITIES
INVIABILITY
INVIABLENESS
INVIABLENESSES
INVIDIOUSLY
INVIDIOUSNESS
INVIDIOUSNESSES
INVIGILATE
INVIGILATED
INVIGILATES
INVIGILATING
INVIGILATION
INVIGILATIONS
INVIGILATOR
INVIGILATORS
INVIGORANT
INVIGORANTS
INVIGORATE
INVIGORATED
INVIGORATES
INVIGORATING
INVIGORATINGLY
INVIGORATION
INVIGORATIONS
INVIGORATIVE
INVIGORATIVELY
INVIGORATOR
INVIGORATORS
INVINCIBILITIES
INVINCIBILITY
INVINCIBLE
INVINCIBLENESS
INVINCIBLY
INVIOLABILITIES
INVIOLABILITY
INVIOLABLE
INVIOLABLENESS
INVIOLABLY
INVIOLACIES
INVIOLATED
INVIOLATELY
INVIOLATENESS
INVIOLATENESSES
INVISIBILITIES
INVISIBILITY
INVISIBLENESS
INVISIBLENESSES
INVISIBLES
INVITATION
INVITATIONAL
INVITATIONALS
INVITATIONS
INVITATORIES
INVITATORY
INVITEMENT
INVITEMENTS
INVITINGLY
INVITINGNESS
INVITINGNESSES
INVOCATING
INVOCATION
INVOCATIONAL
INVOCATIONS
INVOCATIVE
INVOCATORS
INVOCATORY
INVOICINGS
INVOLUCELLA
INVOLUCELLATE
INVOLUCELLATED
INVOLUCELLUM
INVOLUCELS
INVOLUCRAL
INVOLUCRATE
INVOLUCRES
INVOLUCRUM
INVOLUNTARILY
INVOLUNTARINESS
INVOLUNTARY
INVOLUTEDLY
INVOLUTELY
INVOLUTING
INVOLUTION
INVOLUTIONAL
INVOLUTIONS
INVOLVEDLY
INVOLVEMENT
INVOLVEMENTS
INVULNERABILITY
INVULNERABLE
INVULNERABLY
INVULTUATION
INVULTUATIONS
INWARDNESS
INWARDNESSES
INWORKINGS
INWRAPMENT
INWRAPMENTS
INWRAPPING
INWRAPPINGS
INWREATHED
INWREATHES
INWREATHING
IODINATING
IODINATION
IODINATIONS
IODISATION
IODISATIONS
IODIZATION
IODIZATIONS
IODOMETRIC
IODOMETRICAL
IODOMETRICALLY
IODOMETRIES
IONICITIES
IONISATION
IONISATIONS
IONIZATION
IONIZATIONS
IONOPAUSES
IONOPHORES
IONOPHORESES
IONOPHORESIS
IONOSONDES
IONOSPHERE
IONOSPHERES
IONOSPHERIC
IONOSPHERICALLY
IONOTROPIC
IONOTROPIES
IONTOPHORESES
IONTOPHORESIS
IONTOPHORETIC
IPECACUANHA
IPECACUANHAS
IPRATROPIUM
IPRATROPIUMS
IPRINDOLES
IPRONIAZID
IPRONIAZIDS
IPSELATERAL

IPSILATERAL
IPSILATERALLY
IRACUNDITIES
IRACUNDITY
IRACUNDULOUS
IRASCIBILITIES
IRASCIBILITY
IRASCIBLENESS
IRASCIBLENESSES
IRATENESSES
IREFULNESS
IREFULNESSES
IRENICALLY
IRENICISMS
IRENOLOGIES
IRIDACEOUS
IRIDECTOMIES
IRIDECTOMY
IRIDESCENCE
IRIDESCENCES
IRIDESCENT
IRIDESCENTLY
IRIDISATION
IRIDISATIONS
IRIDIZATION
IRIDIZATIONS
IRIDOCYTES
IRIDOLOGIES
IRIDOLOGIST
IRIDOLOGISTS
IRIDOSMINE
IRIDOSMINES
IRIDOSMIUM
IRIDOSMIUMS
IRIDOTOMIES
IRISATIONS
IRKSOMENESS
IRKSOMENESSES
IRONFISTED
IRONHANDED
IRONHEARTED
IRONICALLY
IRONICALNESS
IRONICALNESSES
IRONMASTER
IRONMASTERS
IRONMONGER
IRONMONGERIES
IRONMONGERS
IRONMONGERY
IRONNESSES
IRONSMITHS
IRONSTONES
IRONWORKER
IRONWORKERS
IRRADIANCE
IRRADIANCES
IRRADIANCIES
IRRADIANCY
IRRADIATED
IRRADIATES
IRRADIATING
IRRADIATION
IRRADIATIONS
IRRADIATIVE
IRRADIATOR
IRRADIATORS
IRRADICABLE
IRRADICABLY
IRRADICATE
IRRADICATED
IRRADICATES
IRRADICATING
IRRATIONAL
IRRATIONALISE
IRRATIONALISED
IRRATIONALISES
IRRATIONALISING
IRRATIONALISM
IRRATIONALISMS
IRRATIONALIST
IRRATIONALISTIC
IRRATIONALISTS
IRRATIONALITIES
IRRATIONALITY
IRRATIONALIZE
IRRATIONALIZED
IRRATIONALIZES
IRRATIONALIZING
IRRATIONALLY
IRRATIONALNESS
IRRATIONALS
IRREALISABLE
IRREALITIES
IRREALIZABLE
IRREBUTTABLE
IRRECEPTIVE
IRRECIPROCAL
IRRECIPROCITIES
IRRECIPROCITY
IRRECLAIMABLE
IRRECLAIMABLY
IRRECOGNISABLE
IRRECOGNITION
IRRECOGNITIONS
IRRECOGNIZABLE
IRRECONCILABLE
IRRECONCILABLES
IRRECONCILABLY
IRRECONCILED
IRRECONCILEMENT
IRRECOVERABLE
IRRECOVERABLY
IRRECUSABLE
IRRECUSABLY
IRREDEEMABILITY
IRREDEEMABLE
IRREDEEMABLES
IRREDEEMABLY
IRREDENTAS
IRREDENTISM
IRREDENTISMS
IRREDENTIST
IRREDENTISTS
IRREDUCIBILITY
IRREDUCIBLE
IRREDUCIBLENESS
IRREDUCIBLY
IRREDUCTIBILITY
IRREDUCTION
IRREDUCTIONS
IRREFLECTION
IRREFLECTIONS
IRREFLECTIVE
IRREFLEXION
IRREFLEXIONS
IRREFLEXIVE
IRREFORMABILITY
IRREFORMABLE
IRREFORMABLY
IRREFRAGABILITY
IRREFRAGABLE
IRREFRAGABLY
IRREFRANGIBLE
IRREFRANGIBLY
IRREFUTABILITY
IRREFUTABLE
IRREFUTABLENESS
IRREFUTABLY
IRREGARDLESS
IRREGULARITIES
IRREGULARITY
IRREGULARLY
IRREGULARS
IRRELATION
IRRELATIONS
IRRELATIVE
IRRELATIVELY
IRRELATIVENESS
IRRELEVANCE
IRRELEVANCES
IRRELEVANCIES
IRRELEVANCY
IRRELEVANT
IRRELEVANTLY
IRRELIEVABLE
IRRELIGION
IRRELIGIONIST
IRRELIGIONISTS
IRRELIGIONS
IRRELIGIOUS
IRRELIGIOUSLY
IRRELIGIOUSNESS
IRREMEABLE
IRREMEABLY
IRREMEDIABLE
IRREMEDIABLY
IRREMISSIBILITY
IRREMISSIBLE
IRREMISSIBLY
IRREMISSION
IRREMISSIONS
IRREMISSIVE
IRREMOVABILITY
IRREMOVABLE
IRREMOVABLENESS
IRREMOVABLY
IRRENOWNED
IRREPAIRABLE
IRREPARABILITY
IRREPARABLE
IRREPARABLENESS
IRREPARABLY
IRREPEALABILITY
IRREPEALABLE
IRREPEALABLY
IRREPLACEABLE
IRREPLACEABLY
IRREPLEVIABLE
IRREPLEVISABLE
IRREPREHENSIBLE
IRREPREHENSIBLY
IRREPRESSIBLE
IRREPRESSIBLY
IRREPROACHABLE
IRREPROACHABLY
IRREPRODUCIBLE
IRREPROVABLE
IRREPROVABLY
IRRESISTANCE
IRRESISTANCES
IRRESISTIBILITY
IRRESISTIBLE
IRRESISTIBLY
IRRESOLUBILITY
IRRESOLUBLE
IRRESOLUBLY
IRRESOLUTE
IRRESOLUTELY
IRRESOLUTENESS
IRRESOLUTION
IRRESOLUTIONS
IRRESOLVABILITY
IRRESOLVABLE
IRRESOLVABLY
IRRESPECTIVE
IRRESPECTIVELY
IRRESPIRABLE
IRRESPONSIBLE
IRRESPONSIBLES
IRRESPONSIBLY
IRRESPONSIVE
IRRESPONSIVELY
IRRESTRAINABLE
IRRESUSCITABLE
IRRESUSCITABLY
IRRETENTION
IRRETENTIONS
IRRETENTIVE
IRRETENTIVENESS

IRRETRIEVABLE
IRRETRIEVABLY
IRREVERENCE
IRREVERENCES
IRREVERENT
IRREVERENTIAL
IRREVERENTLY
IRREVERSIBILITY
IRREVERSIBLE
IRREVERSIBLY
IRREVOCABILITY
IRREVOCABLE
IRREVOCABLENESS
IRREVOCABLY
IRRIDENTAS
IRRIGATING
IRRIGATION
IRRIGATIONAL
IRRIGATIONS
IRRIGATIVE
IRRIGATORS
IRRITABILITIES
IRRITABILITY
IRRITABLENESS
IRRITABLENESSES
IRRITANCIES
IRRITATEDLY
IRRITATING
IRRITATINGLY
IRRITATION
IRRITATIONS
IRRITATIVE
IRRITATORS
IRROTATIONAL
IRRUPTIONS
IRRUPTIVELY
IRUKANDJIS
ISABELLINE
ISABELLINES
ISALLOBARIC
ISALLOBARS
ISAPOSTOLIC
ISCHAEMIAS
ISCHURETIC
ISCHURETICS
ISEIKONIAS
ISENTROPIC
ISENTROPICALLY
ISINGLASSES
ISLOMANIAS
ISMATICALNESS
ISMATICALNESSES
ISOAGGLUTININ
ISOAGGLUTININS
ISOALLOXAZINE
ISOALLOXAZINES
ISOAMINILE
ISOAMINILES
ISOANTIBODIES
ISOANTIBODY
ISOANTIGEN
ISOANTIGENIC
ISOANTIGENS
ISOBARISMS
ISOBAROMETRIC
ISOBILATERAL
ISOBUTANES
ISOBUTENES
ISOBUTYLENE
ISOBUTYLENES
ISOCALORIC
ISOCARBOXAZID
ISOCARBOXAZIDS
ISOCHASMIC
ISOCHEIMAL
ISOCHEIMALS
ISOCHEIMENAL
ISOCHEIMENALS
ISOCHEIMIC
ISOCHIMALS
ISOCHROMATIC
ISOCHROMOSOME
ISOCHROMOSOMES
ISOCHRONAL
ISOCHRONALLY
ISOCHRONES
ISOCHRONISE
ISOCHRONISED
ISOCHRONISES
ISOCHRONISING
ISOCHRONISM
ISOCHRONISMS
ISOCHRONIZE
ISOCHRONIZED
ISOCHRONIZES
ISOCHRONIZING
ISOCHRONOUS
ISOCHRONOUSLY
ISOCHROOUS
ISOCLINALS
ISOCLINICS
ISOCRACIES
ISOCRYMALS
ISOCYANATE
ISOCYANATES
ISOCYANIDE
ISOCYANIDES
ISODIAMETRIC
ISODIAMETRICAL
ISODIAPHERE
ISODIAPHERES
ISODIMORPHIC
ISODIMORPHISM
ISODIMORPHISMS
ISODIMORPHOUS
ISODONTALS
ISODYNAMIC
ISODYNAMICS
ISOELECTRIC
ISOELECTRONIC
ISOENZYMATIC
ISOENZYMES
ISOENZYMIC
ISOFLAVONE
ISOFLAVONES
ISOGAMETES
ISOGAMETIC
ISOGENETIC
ISOGEOTHERM
ISOGEOTHERMAL
ISOGEOTHERMALS
ISOGEOTHERMIC
ISOGEOTHERMICS
ISOGEOTHERMS
ISOGLOSSAL
ISOGLOSSES
ISOGLOSSIC
ISOGLOTTAL
ISOGLOTTIC
ISOGRAFTED
ISOGRAFTING
ISOHYETALS
ISOIMMUNISATION
ISOIMMUNIZATION
ISOKINETIC
ISOKONTANS
ISOLABILITIES
ISOLABILITY
ISOLATABLE
ISOLATIONISM
ISOLATIONISMS
ISOLATIONIST
ISOLATIONISTS
ISOLATIONS
ISOLECITHAL
ISOLEUCINE
ISOLEUCINES
ISOMAGNETIC
ISOMAGNETICS
ISOMERASES
ISOMERISATION
ISOMERISATIONS
ISOMERISED
ISOMERISES
ISOMERISING
ISOMERISMS
ISOMERIZATION
ISOMERIZATIONS
ISOMERIZED
ISOMERIZES
ISOMERIZING
ISOMETRICAL
ISOMETRICALLY
ISOMETRICS
ISOMETRIES
ISOMETROPIA
ISOMETROPIAS
ISOMORPHIC
ISOMORPHICALLY
ISOMORPHISM
ISOMORPHISMS
ISOMORPHOUS
ISONIAZIDE
ISONIAZIDES
ISONIAZIDS
ISONITRILE
ISONITRILES
ISOOCTANES
ISOPACHYTE
ISOPACHYTES
ISOPERIMETER
ISOPERIMETERS
ISOPERIMETRICAL
ISOPERIMETRIES
ISOPERIMETRY
ISOPIESTIC
ISOPIESTICALLY
ISOPLETHIC
ISOPLUVIAL
ISOPLUVIALS
ISOPOLITIES
ISOPRENALINE
ISOPRENALINES
ISOPRENOID
ISOPRENOIDS
ISOPROPYLS
ISOPROTERENOL
ISOPROTERENOLS
ISOPTERANS
ISOPTEROUS
ISOPYCNALS
ISOPYCNICS
ISORHYTHMIC
ISOSEISMAL
ISOSEISMALS
ISOSEISMIC
ISOSEISMICS
ISOSMOTICALLY
ISOSPONDYLOUS
ISOSPORIES
ISOSPOROUS
ISOSTACIES
ISOSTASIES
ISOSTATICALLY
ISOSTEMONOUS
ISOSTHENURIA
ISOSTHENURIAS
ISOTENISCOPE
ISOTENISCOPES
ISOTHERALS
ISOTHERMAL
ISOTHERMALLY
ISOTHERMALS
ISOTONICALLY
ISOTONICITIES
ISOTONICITY
ISOTOPICALLY
ISOTRETINOIN
ISOTRETINOINS
ISOTROPICALLY

ISOTROPIES
ISOTROPISM
ISOTROPISMS
ISOTROPOUS
ISOXSUPRINE
ISOXSUPRINES
ISPAGHULAS
ITACOLUMITE
ITACOLUMITES
ITALIANATE
ITALIANATED
ITALIANATES
ITALIANATING
ITALIANISE
ITALIANISED
ITALIANISES
ITALIANISING
ITALIANIZE
ITALIANIZED
ITALIANIZES
ITALIANIZING
ITALICISATION
ITALICISATIONS
ITALICISED
ITALICISES
ITALICISING
ITALICIZATION
ITALICIZATIONS
ITALICIZED
ITALICIZES
ITALICIZING
ITCHINESSES
ITEMISATION
ITEMISATIONS
ITEMIZATION
ITEMIZATIONS
ITERATIONS
ITERATIVELY
ITERATIVENESS
ITERATIVENESSES
ITEROPARITIES
ITEROPARITY
ITEROPAROUS
ITHYPHALLI
ITHYPHALLIC
ITHYPHALLICS
ITHYPHALLUS
ITHYPHALLUSES
ITINERACIES
ITINERANCIES
ITINERANCY
ITINERANTLY
ITINERANTS
ITINERARIES
ITINERATED
ITINERATES
ITINERATING
ITINERATION
ITINERATIONS
IVERMECTIN
IVERMECTINS
IVORYBILLS
IVORYWOODS
IZVESTIYAS

J

JABBERINGLY
JABBERINGS
JABBERWOCK
JABBERWOCKIES
JABBERWOCKS
JABBERWOCKY
JABORANDIS
JABOTICABA
JABOTICABAS
JACARANDAS
JACKALLING
JACKALOPES
JACKANAPES
JACKANAPESES
JACKAROOED
JACKAROOING
JACKASSERIES
JACKASSERY
JACKBOOTED
JACKBOOTING
JACKEROOED
JACKEROOING
JACKETLESS
JACKFISHES
JACKFRUITS
JACKHAMMER
JACKHAMMERED
JACKHAMMERING
JACKHAMMERS
JACKKNIFED
JACKKNIFES
JACKKNIFING
JACKKNIVES
JACKLIGHTED
JACKLIGHTING
JACKLIGHTS
JACKPLANES
JACKPOTTED
JACKPOTTING
JACKRABBIT
JACKRABBITS
JACKROLLED
JACKROLLING
JACKSCREWS
JACKSHAFTS
JACKSMELTS
JACKSMITHS
JACKSNIPES
JACKSTAFFS
JACKSTAVES
JACKSTONES
JACKSTRAWS
JACQUERIES
JACTATIONS
JACTITATION
JACTITATIONS
JACULATING
JACULATION
JACULATIONS
JACULATORS
JACULATORY
JADEDNESSES
JADISHNESS
JADISHNESSES
JAGDWURSTS
JAGGEDNESS
JAGGEDNESSES
JAGGHERIES
JAGHIRDARS
JAGUARONDI
JAGUARONDIS
JAGUARUNDI
JAGUARUNDIS
JAILBREAKER
JAILBREAKERS
JAILBREAKING
JAILBREAKS
JAILBROKEN
JAILERESSES
JAILHOUSES
JAILORESSES
JALOALLOFANE
JALOALLOFANES
JAMAHIRIYA
JAMAHIRIYAS
JAMBALAYAS
JAMBOKKING
JAMBOLANAS
JAMBUSTERS
JANISARIES
JANISSARIES
JANITORIAL
JANITORSHIP
JANITORSHIPS
JANITRESSES
JANITRIXES
JANIZARIAN
JANIZARIES
JANNEYINGS
JAPANISING
JAPANIZING
JAPONAISERIE
JAPONAISERIES
JARDINIERE
JARDINIERES
JARGONEERS
JARGONELLE
JARGONELLES
JARGONIEST
JARGONISATION
JARGONISATIONS
JARGONISED
JARGONISES
JARGONISING
JARGONISTIC
JARGONISTS
JARGONIZATION
JARGONIZATIONS
JARGONIZED
JARGONIZES
JARGONIZING
JARLSBERGS
JAROVISING
JAROVIZING
JASMONATES
JASPERIEST
JASPERISED
JASPERISES
JASPERISING
JASPERIZED
JASPERIZES
JASPERIZING
JASPERWARE
JASPERWARES
JASPIDEOUS
JASPILITES
JAUNDICING
JAUNTINESS
JAUNTINESSES
JAUNTINGLY
JAVELINING
JAWBATIONS
JAWBONINGS
JAWBREAKER
JAWBREAKERS
JAWBREAKING
JAWBREAKINGLY
JAWCRUSHER
JAWCRUSHERS
JAYHAWKERS
JAYWALKERS
JAYWALKING
JAYWALKINGS
JAZZINESSES
JEALOUSEST
JEALOUSHOOD
JEALOUSHOODS
JEALOUSIES
JEALOUSING
JEALOUSNESS
JEALOUSNESSES
JEANSWEARS
JEISTIECOR
JEISTIECORS
JEJUNENESS
JEJUNENESSES
JEJUNITIES
JEJUNOSTOMIES
JEJUNOSTOMY
JELLIFICATION
JELLIFICATIONS
JELLIFYING
JELLYBEANS
JELLYFISHES
JELLYGRAPH
JELLYGRAPHED
JELLYGRAPHING
JELLYGRAPHS
JELLYROLLS
JEMMINESSES
JENNETINGS
JEOPARDERS
JEOPARDIED
JEOPARDIES
JEOPARDING
JEOPARDISE
JEOPARDISED
JEOPARDISES
JEOPARDISING
JEOPARDIZE
JEOPARDIZED
JEOPARDIZES
JEOPARDIZING
JEOPARDOUS
JEOPARDOUSLY
JEOPARDYING
JEQUERITIES
JEQUIRITIES
JERFALCONS
JERKINESSES
JERKINHEAD
JERKINHEADS
JERKWATERS
JERRYMANDER
JERRYMANDERED
JERRYMANDERING
JERRYMANDERS
JESSAMINES
JESSERANTS
JETSTREAMS

JETTATURAS
JETTINESSES
JETTISONABLE
JETTISONED
JETTISONING
JEWELFISHES
JEWELLERIES
JEWELWEEDS
JICKAJOGGED
JICKAJOGGING
JICKAJOGGINGS
JIGAJIGGED
JIGAJIGGING
JIGAJOGGED
JIGAJOGGING
JIGAMAREES
JIGGERMAST
JIGGERMASTS
JIGGUMBOBS
JILLFLIRTS
JIMPNESSES
JIMSONWEED
JIMSONWEEDS
JINGOISTIC
JINGOISTICALLY
JINRICKSHA
JINRICKSHAS
JINRICKSHAW
JINRICKSHAWS
JINRIKISHA
JINRIKISHAS
JINRIKSHAS
JITTERBUGGED
JITTERBUGGING
JITTERBUGS
JITTERIEST
JITTERINESS
JITTERINESSES
JOBCENTRES
JOBERNOWLS
JOBHOLDERS
JOBLESSNESS
JOBLESSNESSES
JOBSEEKERS
JOBSWORTHS
JOCKEYISMS
JOCKEYSHIP
JOCKEYSHIPS
JOCKSTRAPS
JOCKTELEGS
JOCOSENESS
JOCOSENESSES
JOCOSERIOUS
JOCOSITIES
JOCULARITIES
JOCULARITY
JOCULATORS
JOCUNDITIES
JOCUNDNESS
JOCUNDNESSES
JOGTROTTED
JOGTROTTING
JOHANNESES
JOHNNYCAKE
JOHNNYCAKES
JOHNSONGRASS
JOHNSONGRASSES
JOINTEDNESS
JOINTEDNESSES
JOINTNESSES
JOINTRESSES
JOINTURESS
JOINTURESSES
JOINTURING
JOINTWEEDS
JOINTWORMS
JOKESMITHS
JOKINESSES
JOLIOTIUMS
JOLLEYINGS
JOLLIFICATION
JOLLIFICATIONS
JOLLIFYING
JOLLIMENTS
JOLLINESSES
JOLLYBOATS
JOLLYHEADS
JOLTERHEAD
JOLTERHEADS
JONNYCAKES
JOSEPHINITE
JOSEPHINITES
JOSTLEMENT
JOSTLEMENTS
JOUISANCES
JOURNALESE
JOURNALESES
JOURNALING
JOURNALINGS
JOURNALISATION
JOURNALISATIONS
JOURNALISE
JOURNALISED
JOURNALISER
JOURNALISERS
JOURNALISES
JOURNALISING
JOURNALISM
JOURNALISMS
JOURNALIST
JOURNALISTIC
JOURNALISTS
JOURNALIZATION
JOURNALIZATIONS
JOURNALIZE
JOURNALIZED
JOURNALIZER
JOURNALIZERS
JOURNALIZES
JOURNALIZING
JOURNALLED
JOURNALLING
JOURNALLINGS
JOURNEYERS
JOURNEYING
JOURNEYMAN
JOURNEYMEN
JOURNEYWORK
JOURNEYWORKS
JOUYSAUNCE
JOUYSAUNCES
JOVIALITIES
JOVIALNESS
JOVIALNESSES
JOVIALTIES
JOVYSAUNCE
JOVYSAUNCES
JOWLINESSES
JOYFULLEST
JOYFULNESS
JOYFULNESSES
JOYLESSNESS
JOYLESSNESSES
JOYOUSNESS
JOYOUSNESSES
JOYPOPPERS
JOYPOPPING
JOYRIDINGS
JUBILANCES
JUBILANCIES
JUBILANTLY
JUBILARIAN
JUBILARIANS
JUBILATING
JUBILATION
JUBILATIONS
JUDDERIEST
JUDGEMENTAL
JUDGEMENTALLY
JUDGEMENTS
JUDGESHIPS
JUDGMATICAL
JUDGMATICALLY
JUDGMENTAL
JUDGMENTALLY
JUDICATION
JUDICATIONS
JUDICATIVE
JUDICATORIAL
JUDICATORIES
JUDICATORS
JUDICATORY
JUDICATURE
JUDICATURES
JUDICIALLY
JUDICIARIES
JUDICIARILY
JUDICIOUSLY
JUDICIOUSNESS
JUDICIOUSNESSES
JUGGERNAUT
JUGGERNAUTS
JUGGLERIES
JUGGLINGLY
JUGLANDACEOUS
JUGULATING
JUGULATION
JUGULATIONS
JUICEHEADS
JUICINESSES
JULIENNING
JUMBLINGLY
JUMBOISING
JUMBOIZING
JUMHOURIYA
JUMHOURIYAS
JUMPINESSES
JUNCACEOUS
JUNCTIONAL
JUNEATINGS
JUNGLEGYMS
JUNGLELIKE
JUNIORATES
JUNIORITIES
JUNKERDOMS
JUNKETEERED
JUNKETEERING
JUNKETEERS
JUNKETINGS
JUNKETTERS
JUNKETTING
JUNKINESSES
JURIDICALLY
JURISCONSULT
JURISCONSULTS
JURISDICTION
JURISDICTIONAL
JURISDICTIONS
JURISDICTIVE
JURISPRUDENCE
JURISPRUDENCES
JURISPRUDENT
JURISPRUDENTIAL
JURISPRUDENTS
JURISTICAL
JURISTICALLY
JUSTICESHIP
JUSTICESHIPS
JUSTICIABILITY
JUSTICIABLE
JUSTICIALISM
JUSTICIALISMS
JUSTICIARIES
JUSTICIARS
JUSTICIARSHIP
JUSTICIARSHIPS
JUSTICIARY
JUSTIFIABILITY
JUSTIFIABLE
JUSTIFIABLENESS

JUSTIFIABLY
JUSTIFICATION
JUSTIFICATIONS
JUSTIFICATIVE
JUSTIFICATOR
JUSTIFICATORS
JUSTIFICATORY
JUSTIFIERS
JUSTIFYING
JUSTNESSES
JUVENESCENCE
JUVENESCENCES
JUVENESCENT
JUVENILELY
JUVENILENESS
JUVENILENESSES
JUVENILITIES
JUVENILITY
JUXTAPOSED
JUXTAPOSES
JUXTAPOSING
JUXTAPOSITION
JUXTAPOSITIONAL
JUXTAPOSITIONS

J

K

KABALISTIC
KABARAGOYA
KABARAGOYAS
KABBALISMS
KABBALISTIC
KABBALISTS
KABELJOUWS
KACHUMBERS
KADAITCHAS
KAFFEEKLATSCH
KAFFEEKLATSCHES
KAHIKATEAS
KAHIKATOAS
KAIKAWAKAS
KAIKOMAKOS
KAILYAIRDS
KAINOGENESES
KAINOGENESIS
KAINOGENETIC
KAIROMONES
KAISERDOMS
KAISERISMS
KAISERSHIP
KAISERSHIPS
KAKISTOCRACIES
KAKISTOCRACY
KALAMKARIS
KALANCHOES
KALASHNIKOV
KALASHNIKOVS
KALEIDOPHONE
KALEIDOPHONES
KALEIDOSCOPE
KALEIDOSCOPES
KALEIDOSCOPIC
KALENDARED
KALENDARING
KALIPHATES
KALLIKREIN
KALLIKREINS
KALLITYPES
KALSOMINED
KALSOMINES
KALSOMINING
KAMELAUKION
KAMELAUKIONS
KAMERADING
KANAMYCINS
KANGAROOED
KANGAROOING
KANTIKOYED
KANTIKOYING
KAOLINISED
KAOLINISES
KAOLINISING
KAOLINITES
KAOLINITIC
KAOLINIZED
KAOLINIZES
KAOLINIZING
KAOLINOSES
KAOLINOSIS
KAPELLMEISTER
KAPELLMEISTERS
KARABINERS
KARANGAING
KARATEISTS
KARMICALLY
KARSTIFICATION
KARSTIFICATIONS
KARSTIFIED
KARSTIFIES
KARSTIFYING
KARUHIRUHI
KARUHIRUHIS
KARYOGAMIC
KARYOGAMIES
KARYOGRAMS
KARYOKINESES
KARYOKINESIS
KARYOKINETIC
KARYOLOGIC
KARYOLOGICAL
KARYOLOGIES
KARYOLOGIST
KARYOLOGISTS
KARYOLYMPH
KARYOLYMPHS
KARYOLYSES
KARYOLYSIS
KARYOLYTIC
KARYOMAPPING
KARYOMAPPINGS
KARYOPLASM
KARYOPLASMIC
KARYOPLASMS
KARYOSOMES
KARYOTYPED
KARYOTYPES
KARYOTYPIC
KARYOTYPICAL
KARYOTYPICALLY
KARYOTYPING
KATABOLICALLY
KATABOLISM
KATABOLISMS
KATABOTHRON
KATABOTHRONS
KATADROMOUS
KATATHERMOMETER
KATAVOTHRON
KATAVOTHRONS
KATHAKALIS
KATHAREVOUSA
KATHAREVOUSAS
KATHAROMETER
KATHAROMETERS
KATZENJAMMER
KATZENJAMMERS
KAWANATANGA
KAWANATANGAS
KAZATSKIES
KAZILLIONS
KEELHALING
KEELHAULED
KEELHAULING
KEELHAULINGS
KEELIVINES
KEELYVINES
KEENNESSES
KEEPERLESS
KEEPERSHIP
KEEPERSHIPS
KEEPSAKIER
KEEPSAKIEST
KEESHONDEN
KEFUFFLING
KEKERENGUS
KELPFISHES
KELYPHITIC
KENNELLING
KENNETTING
KENOGENESES
KENOGENESIS
KENOGENETIC
KENOGENETICALLY
KENOPHOBIA
KENOPHOBIAS
KENOTICIST
KENOTICISTS
KENSPECKLE
KENTLEDGES
KERATECTOMIES
KERATECTOMY
KERATINISATION
KERATINISATIONS
KERATINISE
KERATINISED
KERATINISES
KERATINISING
KERATINIZATION
KERATINIZATIONS
KERATINIZE
KERATINIZED
KERATINIZES
KERATINIZING
KERATINOPHILIC
KERATINOUS
KERATITIDES
KERATITISES
KERATOGENOUS
KERATOMATA
KERATOMETER
KERATOMETERS
KERATOPHYRE
KERATOPHYRES
KERATOPLASTIC
KERATOPLASTIES
KERATOPLASTY
KERATOTOMIES
KERATOTOMY
KERAUNOGRAPH
KERAUNOGRAPHS
KERBLOOEYS
KERBSTONES
KERCHIEFED
KERCHIEFING
KERCHIEVES
KERFUFFLED
KERFUFFLES
KERFUFFLING
KERMESITES
KERNELLIER
KERNELLIEST
KERNELLING
KERNICTERUS
KERNICTERUSES
KERNMANTEL
KERPLUNKED
KERPLUNKING
KERSANTITE
KERSANTITES
KERSEYMERE
KERSEYMERES
KERYGMATIC
KETCHUPIER
KETCHUPIEST
KETOACIDOSES
KETOACIDOSIS
KETOGENESES

KETOGENESIS
KETONAEMIA
KETONAEMIAS
KETONEMIAS
KETONURIAS
KETOSTEROID
KETOSTEROIDS
KETTLEBELL
KETTLEBELLS
KETTLEDRUM
KETTLEDRUMMER
KETTLEDRUMMERS
KETTLEDRUMS
KETTLEFULS
KETTLESTITCH
KETTLESTITCHES
KEYBOARDED
KEYBOARDER
KEYBOARDERS
KEYBOARDING
KEYBOARDINGS
KEYBOARDIST
KEYBOARDISTS
KEYBUTTONS
KEYLOGGERS
KEYLOGGING
KEYLOGGINGS
KEYPRESSES
KEYPUNCHED
KEYPUNCHER
KEYPUNCHERS
KEYPUNCHES
KEYPUNCHING
KEYSTONING
KEYSTROKED
KEYSTROKES
KEYSTROKING
KEYSTROKINGS
KEYWORKERS
KHALIFATES
KHANSAMAHS
KHEDIVATES
KHEDIVIATE
KHEDIVIATES
KHIDMUTGAR
KHIDMUTGARS
KHITMUTGAR
KHITMUTGARS
KHUSKHUSES
KIBBITZERS
KIBBITZING
KIBBUTZNIK
KIBBUTZNIKS
KICKABOUTS
KICKAROUND
KICKAROUNDS
KICKBOARDS
KICKBOXERS
KICKBOXING
KICKBOXINGS
KICKFLIPPED
KICKFLIPPING
KICKPLATES
KICKSHAWSES
KICKSORTER
KICKSORTERS
KICKSTANDS
KICKSTARTED
KICKSTARTING
KICKSTARTS
KIDDIEWINK
KIDDIEWINKIE
KIDDIEWINKIES
KIDDIEWINKS
KIDDISHNESS
KIDDISHNESSES
KIDDYWINKS
KIDNAPINGS
KIDNAPPEES
KIDNAPPERS
KIDNAPPING
KIDNAPPINGS
KIDNEYLIKE
KIDOLOGIES
KIDOLOGIST
KIDOLOGISTS
KIESELGUHR
KIESELGUHRS
KIESELGURS
KIESERITES
KILDERKINS
KILLIFISHES
KILLIKINICK
KILLIKINICKS
KILOCALORIE
KILOCALORIES
KILOCURIES
KILOCYCLES
KILOGAUSSES
KILOGRAMME
KILOGRAMMES
KILOHERTZES
KILOJOULES
KILOLITERS
KILOLITRES
KILOMETERS
KILOMETRES
KILOMETRIC
KILOMETRICAL
KILOPARSEC
KILOPARSECS
KILOPASCAL
KILOPASCALS
KILOTONNES
KIMBERLITE
KIMBERLITES
KINAESTHESES
KINAESTHESIA
KINAESTHESIAS
KINAESTHESIS
KINAESTHETIC
KINDERGARTEN
KINDERGARTENER
KINDERGARTENERS
KINDERGARTENS
KINDERGARTNER
KINDERGARTNERS
KINDERSPIEL
KINDERSPIELS
KINDHEARTED
KINDHEARTEDLY
KINDHEARTEDNESS
KINDLESSLY
KINDLINESS
KINDLINESSES
KINDNESSES
KINDREDNESS
KINDREDNESSES
KINDREDSHIP
KINDREDSHIPS
KINEMATICAL
KINEMATICALLY
KINEMATICS
KINEMATOGRAPH
KINEMATOGRAPHER
KINEMATOGRAPHIC
KINEMATOGRAPHS
KINEMATOGRAPHY
KINESCOPED
KINESCOPES
KINESCOPING
KINESIATRIC
KINESIATRICS
KINESIOLOGIES
KINESIOLOGIST
KINESIOLOGISTS
KINESIOLOGY
KINESIPATH
KINESIPATHIC
KINESIPATHIES
KINESIPATHIST
KINESIPATHISTS
KINESIPATHS
KINESIPATHY
KINESITHERAPIES
KINESITHERAPY
KINESTHESES
KINESTHESIA
KINESTHESIAS
KINESTHESIS
KINESTHETIC
KINESTHETICALLY
KINETHEODOLITE
KINETHEODOLITES
KINETICALLY
KINETICIST
KINETICISTS
KINETOCHORE
KINETOCHORES
KINETOGRAPH
KINETOGRAPHS
KINETONUCLEI
KINETONUCLEUS
KINETONUCLEUSES
KINETOPLAST
KINETOPLASTS
KINETOSCOPE
KINETOSCOPES
KINETOSOME
KINETOSOMES
KINGCRAFTS
KINGDOMLESS
KINGFISHER
KINGFISHERS
KINGFISHES
KINGLIHOOD
KINGLIHOODS
KINGLINESS
KINGLINESSES
KINGMAKERS
KINGSNAKES
KINKINESSES
KINNIKINIC
KINNIKINICK
KINNIKINICKS
KINNIKINICS
KINNIKINNICK
KINNIKINNICKS
KINTLEDGES
KIRBIGRIPS
KIRKYAIRDS
KIRSCHWASSER
KIRSCHWASSERS
KISSAGRAMS
KISSOGRAMS
KISSPEPTIN
KISSPEPTINS
KITCHENALIA
KITCHENALIAS
KITCHENDOM
KITCHENDOMS
KITCHENERS
KITCHENETS
KITCHENETTE
KITCHENETTES
KITCHENING
KITCHENMAID
KITCHENMAIDS
KITCHENWARE
KITCHENWARES
KITEBOARDS
KITESURFER
KITESURFERS
KITESURFING
KITESURFINGS
KITSCHIEST
KITSCHIFIED
KITSCHIFIES
KITSCHIFYING
KITSCHNESS

KITSCHNESSES
KITTENIEST
KITTENISHLY
KITTENISHNESS
KITTENISHNESSES
KITTIWAKES
KIWIFRUITS
KIWISPORTS
KLANGFARBE
KLANGFARBES
KLEBSIELLA
KLEBSIELLAS
KLEINHUISIE
KLEINHUISIES
KLENDUSITIES
KLENDUSITY
KLEPHTISMS
KLEPTOCRACIES
KLEPTOCRACY
KLEPTOCRATIC
KLEPTOMANIA
KLEPTOMANIAC
KLEPTOMANIACS
KLEPTOMANIAS
KLETTERSCHUH
KLETTERSCHUHE
KLINOSTATS
KLIPSPRINGER
KLIPSPRINGERS
KLONDIKERS
KLONDIKING
KLONDYKERS
KLONDYKING
KLOOCHMANS
KLOOTCHMAN
KLOOTCHMANS
KLOOTCHMEN
KLUTZINESS
KLUTZINESSES
KNACKERIES
KNACKERING
KNACKINESS
KNACKINESSES
KNACKWURST
KNACKWURSTS
KNAGGINESS
KNAGGINESSES
KNAPSACKED
KNAVESHIPS
KNAVISHNESS
KNAVISHNESSES
KNEEBOARDED
KNEEBOARDING
KNEEBOARDS
KNEECAPPED
KNEECAPPING
KNEECAPPINGS
KNEEPIECES
KNEVELLING
KNICKERBOCKER
KNICKERBOCKERS
KNICKKNACK
KNICKKNACKS
KNICKPOINT
KNICKPOINTS
KNIFEPOINT
KNIFEPOINTS
KNIFERESTS
KNIGHTAGES
KNIGHTHEAD
KNIGHTHEADS
KNIGHTHOOD
KNIGHTHOODS
KNIGHTLESS
KNIGHTLIER
KNIGHTLIEST
KNIGHTLINESS
KNIGHTLINESSES
KNIPHOFIAS
KNOBBINESS
KNOBBINESSES
KNOBBLIEST
KNOBKERRIE
KNOBKERRIES
KNOBSTICKS
KNOCKABOUT
KNOCKABOUTS
KNOCKBACKS
KNOCKDOWNS
KNOCKWURST
KNOCKWURSTS
KNOTGRASSES
KNOTTINESS
KNOTTINESSES
KNOWABLENESS
KNOWABLENESSES
KNOWINGEST
KNOWINGNESS
KNOWINGNESSES
KNOWLEDGABILITY
KNOWLEDGABLE
KNOWLEDGABLY
KNOWLEDGEABLE
KNOWLEDGEABLY
KNOWLEDGED
KNOWLEDGES
KNOWLEDGING
KNUBBLIEST
KNUCKLEBALL
KNUCKLEBALLER
KNUCKLEBALLERS
KNUCKLEBALLS
KNUCKLEBONE
KNUCKLEBONES
KNUCKLEDUSTER
KNUCKLEDUSTERS
KNUCKLEHEAD
KNUCKLEHEADED
KNUCKLEHEADS
KNUCKLIEST
KOEKSISTER
KOEKSISTERS
KOHLRABIES
KOHUTUHUTU
KOHUTUHUTUS
KOLINSKIES
KOLKHOZNIK
KOLKHOZNIKI
KOLKHOZNIKS
KOMONDOROCK
KOMONDOROK
KOMPROMATS
KONIMETERS
KONIOLOGIES
KONISCOPES
KOOKABURRA
KOOKABURRAS
KOOKINESSES
KOTAHITANGA
KOTAHITANGAS
KOTTABOSES
KOTUKUTUKU
KOTUKUTUKUS
KOULIBIACA
KOULIBIACAS
KOURBASHED
KOURBASHES
KOURBASHING
KOUSKOUSES
KOWHAIWHAI
KOWHAIWHAIS
KRAKOWIAKS
KRAUTROCKS
KREASOTING
KREMLINOLOGIES
KREMLINOLOGIST
KREMLINOLOGISTS
KREMLINOLOGY
KREOSOTING
KRIEGSPIEL
KRIEGSPIELS
KRIEGSSPIEL
KRIEGSSPIELS
KROMESKIES
KRUGERRAND
KRUGERRANDS
KRUMMHORNS
KRYOMETERS
KRYPTONITE
KRYPTONITES
KUMARAHOUS
KUMMERBUND
KUMMERBUNDS
KUNDALINIS
KURBASHING
KURCHATOVIUM
KURCHATOVIUMS
KURDAITCHA
KURDAITCHAS
KURFUFFLED
KURFUFFLES
KURFUFFLING
KURRAJONGS
KURTOSISES
KVETCHIEST
KVETCHINESS
KVETCHINESSES
KVETCHINGS
KWASHIORKOR
KWASHIORKORS
KYANISATION
KYANISATIONS
KYANIZATION
KYANIZATIONS
KYMOGRAPHIC
KYMOGRAPHIES
KYMOGRAPHS
KYMOGRAPHY

L

LABANOTATION
LABANOTATIONS
LABDACISMS
LABEFACTATION
LABEFACTATIONS
LABEFACTION
LABEFACTIONS
LABELLABLE
LABELLINGS
LABELLISTS
LABELMATES
LABIALISATION
LABIALISATIONS
LABIALISED
LABIALISES
LABIALISING
LABIALISMS
LABIALITIES
LABIALIZATION
LABIALIZATIONS
LABIALIZED
LABIALIZES
LABIALIZING
LABILITIES
LABIODENTAL
LABIODENTALS
LABIONASAL
LABIONASALS
LABIOVELAR
LABIOVELARS
LABORATORIES
LABORATORY
LABOREDNESS
LABOREDNESSES
LABORINGLY
LABORIOUSLY
LABORIOUSNESS
LABORIOUSNESSES
LABORSAVING
LABOUREDLY
LABOUREDNESS
LABOUREDNESSES
LABOURINGLY
LABOURISMS
LABOURISTS
LABOURITES
LABOURSAVING
LABOURSOME
LABRADOODLE
LABRADOODLES
LABRADORESCENT
LABRADORITE
LABRADORITES
LABYRINTHAL
LABYRINTHIAN
LABYRINTHIC
LABYRINTHICAL
LABYRINTHICALLY
LABYRINTHINE
LABYRINTHITIS
LABYRINTHITISES
LABYRINTHODONT
LABYRINTHODONTS
LABYRINTHS
LACCOLITES
LACCOLITHIC
LACCOLITHS
LACCOLITIC
LACEMAKERS
LACEMAKING
LACEMAKINGS
LACERABILITIES
LACERABILITY
LACERATING
LACERATION
LACERATIONS
LACERATIVE
LACERTIANS
LACERTILIAN
LACERTILIANS
LACERTINES
LACHRYMALS
LACHRYMARIES
LACHRYMARY
LACHRYMATION
LACHRYMATIONS
LACHRYMATOR
LACHRYMATORIES
LACHRYMATORS
LACHRYMATORY
LACHRYMOSE
LACHRYMOSELY
LACHRYMOSITIES
LACHRYMOSITY
LACINESSES
LACINIATED
LACINIATION
LACINIATIONS
LACKADAISICAL
LACKADAISICALLY
LACKADAISY
LACKLUSTER
LACKLUSTERS
LACKLUSTRE
LACKLUSTRES
LACONICALLY
LACONICISM
LACONICISMS
LACQUERERS
LACQUERING
LACQUERINGS
LACQUERWARE
LACQUERWARES
LACQUERWORK
LACQUERWORKS
LACQUEYING
LACRIMARIES
LACRIMATION
LACRIMATIONS
LACRIMATOR
LACRIMATORS
LACRIMATORY
LACRYMATOR
LACRYMATORS
LACRYMATORY
LACTALBUMIN
LACTALBUMINS
LACTARIANS
LACTATIONAL
LACTATIONALLY
LACTATIONS
LACTESCENCE
LACTESCENCES
LACTESCENT
LACTIFEROUS
LACTIFEROUSNESS
LACTIFLUOUS
LACTIVISMS
LACTIVISTS
LACTOBACILLI
LACTOBACILLUS
LACTOFLAVIN
LACTOFLAVINS
LACTOGENIC
LACTOGLOBULIN
LACTOGLOBULINS
LACTOMETER
LACTOMETERS
LACTOPROTEIN
LACTOPROTEINS
LACTOSCOPE
LACTOSCOPES
LACTOSURIA
LACTOSURIAS
LACTOVEGETARIAN
LACTULOSES
LACUNOSITIES
LACUNOSITY
LACUSTRINE
LADDERIEST
LADDERLIKE
LADDERPROOF
LADDISHNESS
LADDISHNESSES
LADIESWEAR
LADIESWEARS
LADYFINGER
LADYFINGERS
LADYFISHES
LADYLIKENESS
LADYLIKENESSES
LADYNESSES
LAEOTROPIC
LAEVIGATED
LAEVIGATES
LAEVIGATING
LAEVOGYRATE
LAEVOROTARY
LAEVOROTATION
LAEVOROTATIONS
LAEVOROTATORY
LAEVULOSES
LAGENIFORM
LAGERPHONE
LAGERPHONES
LAGGARDLIER
LAGGARDLIEST
LAGGARDNESS
LAGGARDNESSES
LAGNIAPPES
LAGOMORPHIC
LAGOMORPHOUS
LAGOMORPHS
LAICISATION
LAICISATIONS
LAICIZATION
LAICIZATIONS
LAIRDLIEST
LAIRDSHIPS
LAKEFRONTS
LAKESHORES
LALAPALOOZA
LALAPALOOZAS
LALLAPALOOZA
LALLAPALOOZAS
LALLATIONS
LALLYGAGGED
LALLYGAGGING
LAMASERAIS
LAMASERIES

L

LAMBASTING
LAMBDACISM
LAMBDACISMS
LAMBDOIDAL
LAMBENCIES
LAMBITIVES
LAMBREQUIN
LAMBREQUINS
LAMBRUSCOS
LAMBSWOOLS
LAMEBRAINED
LAMEBRAINS
LAMELLARLY
LAMELLATED
LAMELLATELY
LAMELLATION
LAMELLATIONS
LAMELLIBRANCH
LAMELLIBRANCHS
LAMELLICORN
LAMELLICORNS
LAMELLIFORM
LAMELLIROSTRAL
LAMELLIROSTRATE
LAMELLOSITIES
LAMELLOSITY
LAMENESSES
LAMENTABLE
LAMENTABLENESS
LAMENTABLY
LAMENTATION
LAMENTATIONS
LAMENTEDLY
LAMENTINGLY
LAMENTINGS
LAMESTREAM
LAMESTREAMS
LAMINARIAN
LAMINARIANS
LAMINARIAS
LAMINARINS
LAMINARISE
LAMINARISED
LAMINARISES
LAMINARISING
LAMINARIZE
LAMINARIZED
LAMINARIZES
LAMINARIZING
LAMINATING
LAMINATION
LAMINATIONS
LAMINATORS
LAMINECTOMIES
LAMINECTOMY
LAMINGTONS
LAMINITISES
LAMMERGEIER
LAMMERGEIERS
LAMMERGEYER
LAMMERGEYERS
LAMPADARIES
LAMPADEDROMIES
LAMPADEDROMY
LAMPADEPHORIA
LAMPADEPHORIAS
LAMPADISTS
LAMPADOMANCIES
LAMPADOMANCY
LAMPBLACKED
LAMPBLACKING
LAMPBLACKS
LAMPHOLDER
LAMPHOLDERS
LAMPLIGHTER
LAMPLIGHTERS
LAMPLIGHTS
LAMPOONERIES
LAMPOONERS
LAMPOONERY
LAMPOONING
LAMPOONIST
LAMPOONISTS
LAMPROPHYRE
LAMPROPHYRES
LAMPROPHYRIC
LAMPSHADES
LAMPSHELLS
LAMPSTANDS
LANCEJACKS
LANCEOLATE
LANCEOLATED
LANCEOLATELY
LANCEWOODS
LANCINATED
LANCINATES
LANCINATING
LANCINATION
LANCINATIONS
LANDAMMANN
LANDAMMANNS
LANDAMMANS
LANDAULETS
LANDAULETTE
LANDAULETTES
LANDBOARDING
LANDBOARDINGS
LANDBOARDS
LANDDAMNED
LANDDAMNES
LANDDAMNING
LANDDROSES
LANDDROSTS
LANDFILLED
LANDFILLING
LANDFILLINGS
LANDFORCES
LANDGRAVATE
LANDGRAVATES
LANDGRAVES
LANDGRAVIATE
LANDGRAVIATES
LANDGRAVINE
LANDGRAVINES
LANDHOLDER
LANDHOLDERS
LANDHOLDING
LANDHOLDINGS
LANDLADIES
LANDLESSNESS
LANDLESSNESSES
LANDLOCKED
LANDLOPERS
LANDLORDISM
LANDLORDISMS
LANDLUBBER
LANDLUBBERLY
LANDLUBBERS
LANDLUBBING
LANDMARKED
LANDMARKING
LANDMASSES
LANDMINING
LANDMININGS
LANDOWNERS
LANDOWNERSHIP
LANDOWNERSHIPS
LANDOWNING
LANDOWNINGS
LANDSCAPED
LANDSCAPER
LANDSCAPERS
LANDSCAPES
LANDSCAPING
LANDSCAPINGS
LANDSCAPIST
LANDSCAPISTS
LANDSHARKS
LANDSKIPPED
LANDSKIPPING
LANDSKNECHT
LANDSKNECHTS
LANDSLIDDEN
LANDSLIDES
LANDSLIDING
LANDWAITER
LANDWAITERS
LANDWASHES
LANGBEINITE
LANGBEINITES
LANGLAUFER
LANGLAUFERS
LANGOSTINO
LANGOSTINOS
LANGOUSTES
LANGOUSTINE
LANGOUSTINES
LANGRIDGES
LANGSPIELS
LANGUAGELESS
LANGUAGING
LANGUESCENT
LANGUETTES
LANGUIDNESS
LANGUIDNESSES
LANGUISHED
LANGUISHER
LANGUISHERS
LANGUISHES
LANGUISHING
LANGUISHINGLY
LANGUISHINGS
LANGUISHMENT
LANGUISHMENTS
LANGUOROUS
LANGUOROUSLY
LANGUOROUSNESS
LANIFEROUS
LANIGEROUS
LANKINESSES
LANKNESSES
LANOSITIES
LANSQUENET
LANSQUENETS
LANTERLOOS
LANTERNING
LANTERNIST
LANTERNISTS
LANTHANIDE
LANTHANIDES
LANTHANONS
LANTHANUMS
LANUGINOSE
LANUGINOUS
LANUGINOUSNESS
LANZKNECHT
LANZKNECHTS
LAODICEANS
LAPAROSCOPE
LAPAROSCOPES
LAPAROSCOPIC
LAPAROSCOPIES
LAPAROSCOPIST
LAPAROSCOPISTS
LAPAROSCOPY
LAPAROTOMIES
LAPAROTOMY
LAPIDARIAN
LAPIDARIES
LAPIDARIST
LAPIDARISTS
LAPIDATING
LAPIDATION
LAPIDATIONS
LAPIDESCENCE
LAPIDESCENCES
LAPIDESCENT
LAPIDICOLOUS
LAPIDIFICATION
LAPIDIFICATIONS

LAPIDIFIED
LAPIDIFIES
LAPIDIFYING
LAPILLIFORM
LAPSTRAKES
LAPSTREAKS
LARCENISTS
LARCENOUSLY
LARCHWOODS
LARDACEOUS
LARDALITES
LARGEHEARTED
LARGEMOUTH
LARGEMOUTHS
LARGENESSES
LARGHETTOS
LARGITIONS
LARKINESSES
LARKISHNESS
LARKISHNESSES
LARRIKINISM
LARRIKINISMS
LARVACEOUS
LARVICIDAL
LARVICIDED
LARVICIDES
LARVICIDING
LARVIKITES
LARVIPAROUS
LARYNGEALLY
LARYNGEALS
LARYNGECTOMEE
LARYNGECTOMEES
LARYNGECTOMIES
LARYNGECTOMISED
LARYNGECTOMIZED
LARYNGECTOMY
LARYNGISMUS
LARYNGISMUSES
LARYNGITIC
LARYNGITIDES
LARYNGITIS
LARYNGITISES
LARYNGOLOGIC
LARYNGOLOGICAL
LARYNGOLOGIES
LARYNGOLOGIST
LARYNGOLOGISTS
LARYNGOLOGY
LARYNGOPHONIES
LARYNGOPHONY
LARYNGOSCOPE
LARYNGOSCOPES
LARYNGOSCOPIC
LARYNGOSCOPIES
LARYNGOSCOPIST
LARYNGOSCOPISTS
LARYNGOSCOPY
LARYNGOSPASM
LARYNGOSPASMS
LARYNGOTOMIES
LARYNGOTOMY
LASCIVIOUS
LASCIVIOUSLY
LASCIVIOUSNESS
LASERDISCS
LASERDISKS
LASERWORTS
LASSITUDES
LASTINGNESS
LASTINGNESSES
LATCHSTRING
LATCHSTRINGS
LATECOMERS
LATEENRIGGED
LATENESSES
LATENSIFICATION
LATERALING
LATERALISATION
LATERALISATIONS
LATERALISE
LATERALISED
LATERALISES
LATERALISING
LATERALITIES
LATERALITY
LATERALIZATION
LATERALIZATIONS
LATERALIZE
LATERALIZED
LATERALIZES
LATERALIZING
LATERALLED
LATERALLING
LATERBORNS
LATERIGRADE
LATERISATION
LATERISATIONS
LATERISING
LATERITIOUS
LATERIZATION
LATERIZATIONS
LATERIZING
LATEROVERSION
LATEROVERSIONS
LATESCENCE
LATESCENCES
LATHERIEST
LATHYRISMS
LATHYRITIC
LATHYRUSES
LATICIFEROUS
LATICIFERS
LATICLAVES
LATIFUNDIA
LATIFUNDIO
LATIFUNDIOS
LATIFUNDIUM
LATIMERIAS
LATINISATION
LATINISATIONS
LATINISING
LATINITIES
LATINIZATION
LATINIZATIONS
LATINIZING
LATIROSTRAL
LATIROSTRATE
LATISEPTATE
LATITANCIES
LATITATION
LATITATIONS
LATITUDINAL
LATITUDINALLY
LATITUDINARIAN
LATITUDINARIANS
LATITUDINOUS
LATRATIONS
LATROCINIA
LATROCINIES
LATROCINIUM
LATTERMATH
LATTERMATHS
LATTERMOST
LATTICEWORK
LATTICEWORKS
LATTICINGS
LATTICINIO
LAUDABILITIES
LAUDABILITY
LAUDABLENESS
LAUDABLENESSES
LAUDATIONS
LAUDATIVES
LAUDATORIES
LAUGHABLENESS
LAUGHABLENESSES
LAUGHINGLY
LAUGHINGSTOCK
LAUGHINGSTOCKS
LAUGHLINES
LAUGHWORTHIER
LAUGHWORTHIEST
LAUGHWORTHY
LAUNCEGAYE
LAUNCEGAYES
LAUNCHINGS
LAUNCHPADS
LAUNDERERS
LAUNDERETTE
LAUNDERETTES
LAUNDERING
LAUNDERINGS
LAUNDRESSES
LAUNDRETTE
LAUNDRETTES
LAUNDRYMAN
LAUNDRYMEN
LAUNDRYWOMAN
LAUNDRYWOMEN
LAURACEOUS
LAURDALITE
LAURDALITES
LAUREATESHIP
LAUREATESHIPS
LAUREATING
LAUREATION
LAUREATIONS
LAURELLING
LAURUSTINE
LAURUSTINES
LAURUSTINUS
LAURUSTINUSES
LAURVIKITE
LAURVIKITES
LAVALIERES
LAVALLIERE
LAVALLIERES
LAVATIONAL
LAVATORIAL
LAVATORIES
LAVENDERED
LAVENDERING
LAVERBREAD
LAVERBREADS
LAVEROCKED
LAVEROCKING
LAVISHMENT
LAVISHMENTS
LAVISHNESS
LAVISHNESSES
LAVOLTAING
LAWBREAKER
LAWBREAKERS
LAWBREAKING
LAWBREAKINGS
LAWFULNESS
LAWFULNESSES
LAWGIVINGS
LAWLESSNESS
LAWLESSNESSES
LAWMAKINGS
LAWMONGERS
LAWNMOWERS
LAWRENCIUM
LAWRENCIUMS
LAWYERINGS
LAWYERLIER
LAWYERLIEST
LAWYERLIKE
LAXATIVENESS
LAXATIVENESSES
LAYBACKING
LAYMANISED
LAYMANISES
LAYMANISING
LAYMANIZED
LAYMANIZES
LAYMANIZING
LAYPERSONS

L

LAZARETTES
LAZARETTOS
LAZINESSES
LEACHABILITIES
LEACHABILITY
LEADENNESS
LEADENNESSES
LEADERBOARD
LEADERBOARDS
LEADERENES
LEADERETTE
LEADERETTES
LEADERLESS
LEADERSHIP
LEADERSHIPS
LEADPLANTS
LEADSCREWS
LEAFCUTTER
LEAFCUTTERS
LEAFHOPPER
LEAFHOPPERS
LEAFINESSES
LEAFLESSNESS
LEAFLESSNESSES
LEAFLETEER
LEAFLETEERS
LEAFLETERS
LEAFLETING
LEAFLETTED
LEAFLETTING
LEAFSTALKS
LEAGUERING
LEAKINESSES
LEANNESSES
LEAPFROGGED
LEAPFROGGING
LEARINESSES
LEARNABILITIES
LEARNABILITY
LEARNEDNESS
LEARNEDNESSES
LEASEBACKS
LEASEHOLDER
LEASEHOLDERS
LEASEHOLDS
LEASTAWAYS
LEATHERBACK
LEATHERBACKS
LEATHERBOUND
LEATHERETTE
LEATHERETTES
LEATHERGOODS
LEATHERHEAD
LEATHERHEADS
LEATHERIER
LEATHERIEST
LEATHERINESS
LEATHERINESSES
LEATHERING
LEATHERINGS
LEATHERJACKET
LEATHERJACKETS
LEATHERLEAF
LEATHERLEAFS
LEATHERLEAVES
LEATHERLIKE
LEATHERNECK
LEATHERNECKS
LEATHERWOOD
LEATHERWOODS
LEATHERWORK
LEATHERWORKS
LEAVENINGS
LEBENSRAUM
LEBENSRAUMS
LECHEROUSLY
LECHEROUSNESS
LECHEROUSNESSES
LECITHINASE
LECITHINASES
LECTIONARIES
LECTIONARY
LECTISTERNIA
LECTISTERNIUM
LECTISTERNIUMS
LECTORATES
LECTORSHIP
LECTORSHIPS
LECTOTYPES
LECTRESSES
LECTURESHIP
LECTURESHIPS
LECYTHIDACEOUS
LECYTHISES
LEDERHOSEN
LEECHCRAFT
LEECHCRAFTS
LEERINESSES
LEETSPEAKS
LEFTWARDLY
LEGALISATION
LEGALISATIONS
LEGALISERS
LEGALISING
LEGALISTIC
LEGALISTICALLY
LEGALITIES
LEGALIZATION
LEGALIZATIONS
LEGALIZERS
LEGALIZING
LEGATARIES
LEGATESHIP
LEGATESHIPS
LEGATIONARY
LEGATISSIMO
LEGATORIAL
LEGENDARIES
LEGENDARILY
LEGENDISED
LEGENDISES
LEGENDISING
LEGENDISTS
LEGENDIZED
LEGENDIZES
LEGENDIZING
LEGENDRIES
LEGERDEMAIN
LEGERDEMAINIST
LEGERDEMAINISTS
LEGERDEMAINS
LEGERITIES
LEGGINESSES
LEGIBILITIES
LEGIBILITY
LEGIBLENESS
LEGIBLENESSES
LEGIONARIES
LEGIONELLA
LEGIONELLAE
LEGIONELLAS
LEGIONNAIRE
LEGIONNAIRES
LEGISLATED
LEGISLATES
LEGISLATING
LEGISLATION
LEGISLATIONS
LEGISLATIVE
LEGISLATIVELY
LEGISLATIVES
LEGISLATOR
LEGISLATORIAL
LEGISLATORS
LEGISLATORSHIP
LEGISLATORSHIPS
LEGISLATRESS
LEGISLATRESSES
LEGISLATURE
LEGISLATURES
LEGITIMACIES
LEGITIMACY
LEGITIMATE
LEGITIMATED
LEGITIMATELY
LEGITIMATENESS
LEGITIMATES
LEGITIMATING
LEGITIMATION
LEGITIMATIONS
LEGITIMATISE
LEGITIMATISED
LEGITIMATISES
LEGITIMATISING
LEGITIMATIZE
LEGITIMATIZED
LEGITIMATIZES
LEGITIMATIZING
LEGITIMATOR
LEGITIMATORS
LEGITIMISATION
LEGITIMISATIONS
LEGITIMISE
LEGITIMISED
LEGITIMISER
LEGITIMISERS
LEGITIMISES
LEGITIMISING
LEGITIMISM
LEGITIMISMS
LEGITIMIST
LEGITIMISTIC
LEGITIMISTS
LEGITIMIZATION
LEGITIMIZATIONS
LEGITIMIZE
LEGITIMIZED
LEGITIMIZER
LEGITIMIZERS
LEGITIMIZES
LEGITIMIZING
LEGLESSNESS
LEGLESSNESSES
LEGUMINOUS
LEGWARMERS
LEIOMYOMAS
LEIOMYOMATA
LEIOTRICHIES
LEIOTRICHOUS
LEIOTRICHY
LEISHMANIA
LEISHMANIAE
LEISHMANIAL
LEISHMANIAS
LEISHMANIASES
LEISHMANIASIS
LEISHMANIOSES
LEISHMANIOSIS
LEISTERING
LEISURABLE
LEISURABLY
LEISURELIER
LEISURELIEST
LEISURELINESS
LEISURELINESSES
LEISUREWEAR
LEISUREWEARS
LEITMOTIFS
LEITMOTIVS
LEMMATISATION
LEMMATISATIONS
LEMMATISED
LEMMATISES
LEMMATISING
LEMMATIZATION
LEMMATIZATIONS
LEMMATIZED
LEMMATIZES
LEMMATIZING
LEMMINGLIKE

LEMNISCATE
LEMNISCATES
LEMONFISHES
LEMONGRASS
LEMONGRASSES
LEMONWOODS
LENGTHENED
LENGTHENER
LENGTHENERS
LENGTHENING
LENGTHIEST
LENGTHINESS
LENGTHINESSES
LENGTHSMAN
LENGTHSMEN
LENGTHWAYS
LENGTHWISE
LENIENCIES
LENITIVELY
LENOCINIUM
LENOCINIUMS
LENTAMENTE
LENTICELLATE
LENTICULAR
LENTICULARLY
LENTICULARS
LENTICULES
LENTIGINES
LENTIGINOSE
LENTIGINOUS
LENTISSIMO
LENTIVIRUS
LENTIVIRUSES
LEONTIASES
LEONTIASIS
LEONTOPODIUM
LEONTOPODIUMS
LEOPARDESS
LEOPARDESSES
LEOPARDSKIN
LEOPARDSKINS
LEPIDODENDROID
LEPIDODENDROIDS
LEPIDOLITE
LEPIDOLITES
LEPIDOMELANE
LEPIDOMELANES
LEPIDOPTERA
LEPIDOPTERAN
LEPIDOPTERANS
LEPIDOPTERIST
LEPIDOPTERISTS
LEPIDOPTEROLOGY
LEPIDOPTERON
LEPIDOPTERONS
LEPIDOPTEROUS
LEPIDOSIREN
LEPIDOSIRENS
LEPRECHAUN
LEPRECHAUNISH
LEPRECHAUNS
LEPRECHAWN
LEPRECHAWNS
LEPROMATOUS
LEPROSARIA
LEPROSARIUM
LEPROSARIUMS
LEPROSERIE
LEPROSERIES
LEPROSITIES
LEPROUSNESS
LEPROUSNESSES
LEPTOCEPHALI
LEPTOCEPHALIC
LEPTOCEPHALOUS
LEPTOCEPHALUS
LEPTOCERCAL
LEPTODACTYL
LEPTODACTYLOUS
LEPTODACTYLS
LEPTOKURTIC
LEPTOPHOSES
LEPTOPHYLLOUS
LEPTORRHINE
LEPTOSOMATIC
LEPTOSOMES
LEPTOSOMIC
LEPTOSPIRAL
LEPTOSPIRE
LEPTOSPIRES
LEPTOSPIROSES
LEPTOSPIROSIS
LEPTOTENES
LESBIANISM
LESBIANISMS
LESPEDEZAS
LESSEESHIP
LESSEESHIPS
LESSENINGS
LESSONINGS
LETHALITIES
LETHARGICAL
LETHARGICALLY
LETHARGIED
LETHARGIES
LETHARGISE
LETHARGISED
LETHARGISES
LETHARGISING
LETHARGIZE
LETHARGIZED
LETHARGIZES
LETHARGIZING
LETHIFEROUS
LETROZOLES
LETTERBOXED
LETTERBOXES
LETTERBOXING
LETTERBOXINGS
LETTERFORM
LETTERFORMS
LETTERHEAD
LETTERHEADS
LETTERINGS
LETTERLESS
LETTERPRESS
LETTERPRESSES
LETTERSETS
LETTERSPACING
LETTERSPACINGS
LEUCAEMIAS
LEUCAEMOGEN
LEUCAEMOGENESES
LEUCAEMOGENESIS
LEUCAEMOGENIC
LEUCAEMOGENS
LEUCHAEMIA
LEUCHAEMIAS
LEUCITOHEDRA
LEUCITOHEDRON
LEUCITOHEDRONS
LEUCOBLAST
LEUCOBLASTS
LEUCOCIDIN
LEUCOCIDINS
LEUCOCRATIC
LEUCOCYTES
LEUCOCYTHAEMIA
LEUCOCYTHAEMIAS
LEUCOCYTIC
LEUCOCYTOLYSES
LEUCOCYTOLYSIS
LEUCOCYTOPENIA
LEUCOCYTOPENIAS
LEUCOCYTOSES
LEUCOCYTOSIS
LEUCOCYTOTIC
LEUCODEPLETED
LEUCODERMA
LEUCODERMAL
LEUCODERMAS
LEUCODERMIA
LEUCODERMIAS
LEUCODERMIC
LEUCOMAINE
LEUCOMAINES
LEUCOPENIA
LEUCOPENIAS
LEUCOPENIC
LEUCOPLAKIA
LEUCOPLAKIAS
LEUCOPLAKIC
LEUCOPLAST
LEUCOPLASTID
LEUCOPLASTIDS
LEUCOPLASTS
LEUCOPOIESES
LEUCOPOIESIS
LEUCOPOIETIC
LEUCORRHOEA
LEUCORRHOEAL
LEUCORRHOEAS
LEUCOTOMES
LEUCOTOMIES
LEUKAEMIAS
LEUKAEMOGEN
LEUKAEMOGENESES
LEUKAEMOGENESIS
LEUKAEMOGENIC
LEUKAEMOGENS
LEUKEMOGEN
LEUKEMOGENESES
LEUKEMOGENESIS
LEUKEMOGENIC
LEUKEMOGENS
LEUKOBLAST
LEUKOBLASTS
LEUKOCIDIN
LEUKOCIDINS
LEUKOCYTES
LEUKOCYTIC
LEUKOCYTOLYSES
LEUKOCYTOLYSIS
LEUKOCYTOPENIA
LEUKOCYTOPENIAS
LEUKOCYTOSES
LEUKOCYTOSIS
LEUKOCYTOTIC
LEUKODEPLETED
LEUKODERMA
LEUKODERMAL
LEUKODERMAS
LEUKODERMIC
LEUKODYSTROPHY
LEUKOPENIA
LEUKOPENIAS
LEUKOPENIC
LEUKOPLAKIA
LEUKOPLAKIAS
LEUKOPLAKIC
LEUKOPOIESES
LEUKOPOIESIS
LEUKOPOIETIC
LEUKORRHEA
LEUKORRHEAL
LEUKORRHEAS
LEUKOTOMES
LEUKOTOMIES
LEUKOTRIENE
LEUKOTRIENES
LEVANTINES
LEVELHEADED
LEVELHEADEDNESS
LEVELLINGS
LEVELNESSES
LEVERAGING
LEVIATHANS
LEVIGATING
LEVIGATION
LEVIGATIONS

LEVIGATORS
LEVIRATICAL
LEVIRATION
LEVIRATIONS
LEVITATING
LEVITATION
LEVITATIONAL
LEVITATIONS
LEVITATORS
LEVITICALLY
LEVOROTARY
LEVOROTATORY
LEWDNESSES
LEXICALISATION
LEXICALISATIONS
LEXICALISE
LEXICALISED
LEXICALISES
LEXICALISING
LEXICALITIES
LEXICALITY
LEXICALIZATION
LEXICALIZATIONS
LEXICALIZE
LEXICALIZED
LEXICALIZES
LEXICALIZING
LEXICOGRAPHER
LEXICOGRAPHERS
LEXICOGRAPHIC
LEXICOGRAPHICAL
LEXICOGRAPHIES
LEXICOGRAPHIST
LEXICOGRAPHISTS
LEXICOGRAPHY
LEXICOLOGICAL
LEXICOLOGICALLY
LEXICOLOGIES
LEXICOLOGIST
LEXICOLOGISTS
LEXICOLOGY
LEXIGRAPHIC
LEXIGRAPHICAL
LEXIGRAPHIES
LEXIGRAPHY
LEYLANDIIS
LHERZOLITE
LHERZOLITES
LIABILITIES
LIABLENESS
LIABLENESSES
LIBATIONAL
LIBATIONARY
LIBECCHIOS
LIBELLANTS
LIBELLINGS
LIBELLOUSLY
LIBELOUSLY
LIBERALISATION
LIBERALISATIONS
LIBERALISE
LIBERALISED
LIBERALISER
LIBERALISERS
LIBERALISES
LIBERALISING
LIBERALISM
LIBERALISMS
LIBERALIST
LIBERALISTIC
LIBERALISTS
LIBERALITIES
LIBERALITY
LIBERALIZATION
LIBERALIZATIONS
LIBERALIZE
LIBERALIZED
LIBERALIZER
LIBERALIZERS
LIBERALIZES
LIBERALIZING
LIBERALNESS
LIBERALNESSES
LIBERATING
LIBERATION
LIBERATIONISM
LIBERATIONISMS
LIBERATIONIST
LIBERATIONISTS
LIBERATIONS
LIBERATORS
LIBERATORY
LIBERTARIAN
LIBERTARIANISM
LIBERTARIANISMS
LIBERTARIANS
LIBERTICIDAL
LIBERTICIDE
LIBERTICIDES
LIBERTINAGE
LIBERTINAGES
LIBERTINES
LIBERTINISM
LIBERTINISMS
LIBIDINALLY
LIBIDINIST
LIBIDINISTS
LIBIDINOSITIES
LIBIDINOSITY
LIBIDINOUS
LIBIDINOUSLY
LIBIDINOUSNESS
LIBRAIRIES
LIBRARIANS
LIBRARIANSHIP
LIBRARIANSHIPS
LIBRATIONAL
LIBRATIONS
LIBRETTIST
LIBRETTISTS
LICENSABLE
LICENSURES
LICENTIATE
LICENTIATES
LICENTIATESHIP
LICENTIATESHIPS
LICENTIATION
LICENTIATIONS
LICENTIOUS
LICENTIOUSLY
LICENTIOUSNESS
LICHANOSES
LICHENISMS
LICHENISTS
LICHENOLOGICAL
LICHENOLOGIES
LICHENOLOGIST
LICHENOLOGISTS
LICHENOLOGY
LICHTLYING
LICITNESSES
LICKERISHLY
LICKERISHNESS
LICKERISHNESSES
LICKPENNIES
LICKSPITTLE
LICKSPITTLES
LIDOCAINES
LIEBFRAUMILCH
LIEBFRAUMILCHS
LIENHOLDER
LIENHOLDERS
LIENTERIES
LIEUTENANCIES
LIEUTENANCY
LIEUTENANT
LIEUTENANTRIES
LIEUTENANTRY
LIEUTENANTS
LIEUTENANTSHIP
LIEUTENANTSHIPS
LIFEBLOODS
LIFEBOATMAN
LIFEBOATMEN
LIFEGUARDED
LIFEGUARDING
LIFEGUARDS
LIFEHACKED
LIFEHACKER
LIFEHACKERS
LIFEHACKING
LIFELESSLY
LIFELESSNESS
LIFELESSNESSES
LIFELIKENESS
LIFELIKENESSES
LIFEMANSHIP
LIFEMANSHIPS
LIFESAVERS
LIFESAVING
LIFESAVINGS
LIFESTYLER
LIFESTYLERS
LIFESTYLES
LIFEWORLDS
LIGAMENTAL
LIGAMENTARY
LIGAMENTOUS
LIGATURING
LIGHTBULBS
LIGHTENERS
LIGHTENING
LIGHTENINGS
LIGHTERAGE
LIGHTERAGES
LIGHTERING
LIGHTERMAN
LIGHTERMEN
LIGHTFACED
LIGHTFACES
LIGHTFASTNESS
LIGHTFASTNESSES
LIGHTHEARTED
LIGHTHEARTEDLY
LIGHTHOUSE
LIGHTHOUSEMAN
LIGHTHOUSEMEN
LIGHTHOUSES
LIGHTLYING
LIGHTNESSES
LIGHTNINGED
LIGHTNINGS
LIGHTPLANE
LIGHTPLANES
LIGHTPROOF
LIGHTSHIPS
LIGHTSOMELY
LIGHTSOMENESS
LIGHTSOMENESSES
LIGHTTIGHT
LIGHTWEIGHT
LIGHTWEIGHTS
LIGHTWOODS
LIGNICOLOUS
LIGNIFICATION
LIGNIFICATIONS
LIGNIFYING
LIGNIPERDOUS
LIGNIVOROUS
LIGNOCAINE
LIGNOCAINES
LIGNOCELLULOSE
LIGNOCELLULOSES
LIGNOCELLULOSIC
LIGNOSULFONATE
LIGNOSULFONATES
LIGULIFLORAL
LIGUSTRUMS
LIKABILITIES
LIKABILITY

LIKABLENESS
LIKABLENESSES
LIKEABILITIES
LIKEABILITY
LIKEABLENESS
LIKEABLENESSES
LIKELIHOOD
LIKELIHOODS
LIKELINESS
LIKELINESSES
LIKENESSES
LILANGENIS
LILIACEOUS
LILLIPUTIAN
LILLIPUTIANS
LILTINGNESS
LILTINGNESSES
LIMACIFORM
LIMACOLOGIES
LIMACOLOGIST
LIMACOLOGISTS
LIMACOLOGY
LIMBERNESS
LIMBERNESSES
LIMBURGITE
LIMBURGITES
LIMELIGHTED
LIMELIGHTER
LIMELIGHTERS
LIMELIGHTING
LIMELIGHTS
LIMERENCES
LIMESCALES
LIMESTONES
LIMEWASHES
LIMEWATERS
LIMICOLINE
LIMICOLOUS
LIMINESSES
LIMITABLENESS
LIMITABLENESSES
LIMITARIAN
LIMITARIANS
LIMITATION
LIMITATIONAL
LIMITATIONS
LIMITATIVE
LIMITEDNESS
LIMITEDNESSES
LIMITINGLY
LIMITLESSLY
LIMITLESSNESS
LIMITLESSNESSES
LIMITROPHE
LIMIVOROUS
LIMNOLOGIC
LIMNOLOGICAL
LIMNOLOGICALLY
LIMNOLOGIES
LIMNOLOGIST
LIMNOLOGISTS
LIMNOPHILOUS
LIMOUSINES
LIMPIDITIES
LIMPIDNESS
LIMPIDNESSES
LIMPNESSES
LINCOMYCIN
LINCOMYCINS
LINCRUSTAS
LINEALITIES
LINEAMENTAL
LINEAMENTS
LINEARISATION
LINEARISATIONS
LINEARISED
LINEARISES
LINEARISING
LINEARITIES
LINEARIZATION
LINEARIZATIONS
LINEARIZED
LINEARIZES
LINEARIZING
LINEATIONS
LINEBACKER
LINEBACKERS
LINEBACKING
LINEBACKINGS
LINEBREEDING
LINEBREEDINGS
LINECASTER
LINECASTERS
LINECASTING
LINECASTINGS
LINENFOLDS
LINEOLATED
LINERBOARD
LINERBOARDS
LINESCORES
LINGBERRIES
LINGERINGLY
LINGERINGS
LINGONBERRIES
LINGONBERRY
LINGUIFORM
LINGUISTER
LINGUISTERS
LINGUISTIC
LINGUISTICAL
LINGUISTICALLY
LINGUISTICIAN
LINGUISTICIANS
LINGUISTICS
LINGUISTRIES
LINGUISTRY
LINGULATED
LINISHINGS
LINKSLANDS
LINOLEATES
LINOTYPERS
LINOTYPING
LINTSTOCKS
LINTWHITES
LIONCELLES
LIONFISHES
LIONHEARTED
LIONHEARTEDNESS
LIONISATION
LIONISATIONS
LIONIZATION
LIONIZATIONS
LIPECTOMIES
LIPGLOSSES
LIPIDOPLAST
LIPIDOPLASTS
LIPOCHROME
LIPOCHROMES
LIPODYSTROPHIES
LIPODYSTROPHY
LIPOGENESES
LIPOGENESIS
LIPOGRAMMATIC
LIPOGRAMMATISM
LIPOGRAMMATISMS
LIPOGRAMMATIST
LIPOGRAMMATISTS
LIPOGRAPHIES
LIPOGRAPHY
LIPOMATOSES
LIPOMATOSIS
LIPOMATOUS
LIPOPHILIC
LIPOPLASTS
LIPOPROTEIN
LIPOPROTEINS
LIPOSCULPTURE
LIPOSCULPTURES
LIPOSUCKED
LIPOSUCKING
LIPOSUCTION
LIPOSUCTIONS
LIPOTROPIC
LIPOTROPIES
LIPOTROPIN
LIPOTROPINS
LIPPINESSES
LIPPITUDES
LIPREADERS
LIPREADING
LIPREADINGS
LIPSTICKED
LIPSTICKING
LIQUATIONS
LIQUEFACIENT
LIQUEFACIENTS
LIQUEFACTION
LIQUEFACTIONS
LIQUEFACTIVE
LIQUEFIABLE
LIQUEFIERS
LIQUEFYING
LIQUESCENCE
LIQUESCENCES
LIQUESCENCIES
LIQUESCENCY
LIQUESCENT
LIQUESCING
LIQUEURING
LIQUIDAMBAR
LIQUIDAMBARS
LIQUIDATED
LIQUIDATES
LIQUIDATING
LIQUIDATION
LIQUIDATIONISM
LIQUIDATIONISMS
LIQUIDATIONIST
LIQUIDATIONISTS
LIQUIDATIONS
LIQUIDATOR
LIQUIDATORS
LIQUIDIEST
LIQUIDISED
LIQUIDISER
LIQUIDISERS
LIQUIDISES
LIQUIDISING
LIQUIDITIES
LIQUIDIZED
LIQUIDIZER
LIQUIDIZERS
LIQUIDIZES
LIQUIDIZING
LIQUIDNESS
LIQUIDNESSES
LIQUIDUSES
LIQUIFACTION
LIQUIFACTIONS
LIQUIFACTIVE
LIQUIFIABLE
LIQUIFIERS
LIQUIFYING
LIQUORICES
LIQUORISHLY
LIQUORISHNESS
LIQUORISHNESSES
LIRIODENDRA
LIRIODENDRON
LIRIODENDRONS
LISSENCEPHALOUS
LISSOMENESS
LISSOMENESSES
LISSOMNESS
LISSOMNESSES
LISSOTRICHOUS
LISTENABILITIES
LISTENABILITY
LISTENABLE
LISTENERSHIP

LISTENERSHIPS
LISTENINGS
LISTERIOSES
LISTERIOSIS
LISTLESSLY
LISTLESSNESS
LISTLESSNESSES
LITENESSES
LITERACIES
LITERALISATION
LITERALISATIONS
LITERALISE
LITERALISED
LITERALISER
LITERALISERS
LITERALISES
LITERALISING
LITERALISM
LITERALISMS
LITERALIST
LITERALISTIC
LITERALISTS
LITERALITIES
LITERALITY
LITERALIZATION
LITERALIZATIONS
LITERALIZE
LITERALIZED
LITERALIZER
LITERALIZERS
LITERALIZES
LITERALIZING
LITERALNESS
LITERALNESSES
LITERARILY
LITERARINESS
LITERARINESSES
LITERARYISM
LITERARYISMS
LITERATELY
LITERATENESS
LITERATENESSES
LITERATION
LITERATIONS
LITERATORS
LITERATURE
LITERATURED
LITERATURES
LITEROSITIES
LITEROSITY
LITHENESSES
LITHESOMENESS
LITHESOMENESSES
LITHIFICATION
LITHIFICATIONS
LITHIFYING
LITHISTIDS
LITHOCHROMATIC
LITHOCHROMATICS
LITHOCHROMIES
LITHOCHROMY
LITHOCLAST
LITHOCLASTS
LITHOCYSTS
LITHODOMOUS
LITHOGENOUS
LITHOGLYPH
LITHOGLYPHS
LITHOGRAPH
LITHOGRAPHED
LITHOGRAPHER
LITHOGRAPHERS
LITHOGRAPHIC
LITHOGRAPHICAL
LITHOGRAPHIES
LITHOGRAPHING
LITHOGRAPHS
LITHOGRAPHY
LITHOLAPAXIES
LITHOLAPAXY
LITHOLATRIES
LITHOLATROUS
LITHOLATRY
LITHOLOGIC
LITHOLOGICAL
LITHOLOGICALLY
LITHOLOGIES
LITHOLOGIST
LITHOLOGISTS
LITHOMANCIES
LITHOMANCY
LITHOMARGE
LITHOMARGES
LITHOMETEOR
LITHOMETEORS
LITHONTHRYPTIC
LITHONTHRYPTICS
LITHONTRIPTIC
LITHONTRIPTICS
LITHONTRIPTIST
LITHONTRIPTISTS
LITHONTRIPTOR
LITHONTRIPTORS
LITHOPHAGOUS
LITHOPHANE
LITHOPHANES
LITHOPHILOUS
LITHOPHYSA
LITHOPHYSAE
LITHOPHYSE
LITHOPHYSES
LITHOPHYTE
LITHOPHYTES
LITHOPHYTIC
LITHOPONES
LITHOPRINT
LITHOPRINTS
LITHOSPERMUM
LITHOSPERMUMS
LITHOSPHERE
LITHOSPHERES
LITHOSPHERIC
LITHOSTATIC
LITHOTOMES
LITHOTOMIC
LITHOTOMICAL
LITHOTOMIES
LITHOTOMIST
LITHOTOMISTS
LITHOTOMOUS
LITHOTRIPSIES
LITHOTRIPSY
LITHOTRIPTER
LITHOTRIPTERS
LITHOTRIPTIC
LITHOTRIPTICS
LITHOTRIPTIST
LITHOTRIPTISTS
LITHOTRIPTOR
LITHOTRIPTORS
LITHOTRITE
LITHOTRITES
LITHOTRITIC
LITHOTRITICS
LITHOTRITIES
LITHOTRITISE
LITHOTRITISED
LITHOTRITISES
LITHOTRITISING
LITHOTRITIST
LITHOTRITISTS
LITHOTRITIZE
LITHOTRITIZED
LITHOTRITIZES
LITHOTRITIZING
LITHOTRITOR
LITHOTRITORS
LITHOTRITY
LITHOTYPES
LITIGATING
LITIGATION
LITIGATIONS
LITIGATORS
LITIGIOUSLY
LITIGIOUSNESS
LITIGIOUSNESSES
LITTERATEUR
LITTERATEURS
LITTERBAGS
LITTERBUGS
LITTERIEST
LITTERMATE
LITTERMATES
LITTLENECK
LITTLENECKS
LITTLENESS
LITTLENESSES
LITTLEWORTH
LITURGICAL
LITURGICALLY
LITURGIOLOGIES
LITURGIOLOGIST
LITURGIOLOGISTS
LITURGIOLOGY
LITURGISMS
LITURGISTIC
LITURGISTS
LIVABILITIES
LIVABILITY
LIVABLENESS
LIVABLENESSES
LIVEABILITIES
LIVEABILITY
LIVEABLENESS
LIVEABLENESSES
LIVEBLOGGED
LIVEBLOGGER
LIVEBLOGGERS
LIVEBLOGGING
LIVEBLOGGINGS
LIVELIHEAD
LIVELIHEADS
LIVELIHOOD
LIVELIHOODS
LIVELINESS
LIVELINESSES
LIVENESSES
LIVERISHLY
LIVERISHNESS
LIVERISHNESSES
LIVERLEAVES
LIVERMORIUM
LIVERMORIUMS
LIVERWORTS
LIVERWURST
LIVERWURSTS
LIVESTOCKS
LIVESTREAM
LIVESTREAMED
LIVESTREAMING
LIVESTREAMS
LIVETRAPPED
LIVETRAPPING
LIVIDITIES
LIVIDNESSES
LIVINGNESS
LIVINGNESSES
LIVRAISONS
LIXIVIATED
LIXIVIATES
LIXIVIATING
LIXIVIATION
LIXIVIATIONS
LOADMASTER
LOADMASTERS
LOADSAMONEY
LOADSAMONEYS
LOADSAMONIES
LOADSPACES
LOADSTONES

LOAMINESSES
LOANSHIFTS
LOATHEDNESS
LOATHEDNESSES
LOATHFULNESS
LOATHFULNESSES
LOATHINGLY
LOATHLIEST
LOATHLINESS
LOATHLINESSES
LOATHNESSES
LOATHSOMELY
LOATHSOMENESS
LOATHSOMENESSES
LOBECTOMIES
LOBLOLLIES
LOBOTOMIES
LOBOTOMISE
LOBOTOMISED
LOBOTOMISES
LOBOTOMISING
LOBOTOMIZE
LOBOTOMIZED
LOBOTOMIZES
LOBOTOMIZING
LOBSCOUSES
LOBSTERERS
LOBSTERING
LOBSTERINGS
LOBSTERLIKE
LOBSTERMAN
LOBSTERMEN
LOBTAILING
LOBTAILINGS
LOBULATION
LOBULATIONS
LOCALISABILITY
LOCALISABLE
LOCALISATION
LOCALISATIONS
LOCALISERS
LOCALISING
LOCALISTIC
LOCALITIES
LOCALIZABILITY
LOCALIZABLE
LOCALIZATION
LOCALIZATIONS
LOCALIZERS
LOCALIZING
LOCALNESSES
LOCATEABLE
LOCATIONAL
LOCATIONALLY
LOCKHOUSES
LOCKKEEPER
LOCKKEEPERS
LOCKMAKERS
LOCKSMITHERIES
LOCKSMITHERY
LOCKSMITHING
LOCKSMITHINGS
LOCKSMITHS
LOCKSTITCH
LOCKSTITCHED
LOCKSTITCHES
LOCKSTITCHING
LOCOMOBILE
LOCOMOBILES
LOCOMOBILITIES
LOCOMOBILITY
LOCOMOTING
LOCOMOTION
LOCOMOTIONS
LOCOMOTIVE
LOCOMOTIVELY
LOCOMOTIVENESS
LOCOMOTIVES
LOCOMOTIVITIES
LOCOMOTIVITY
LOCOMOTORS
LOCOMOTORY
LOCOPLANTS
LOCORESTIVE
LOCULAMENT
LOCULAMENTS
LOCULATION
LOCULATIONS
LOCULICIDAL
LOCUTIONARY
LOCUTORIES
LODESTONES
LODGEMENTS
LODGEPOLES
LOFTINESSES
LOGAGRAPHIA
LOGAGRAPHIAS
LOGANBERRIES
LOGANBERRY
LOGANIACEOUS
LOGAOEDICS
LOGARITHMIC
LOGARITHMICAL
LOGARITHMICALLY
LOGARITHMS
LOGGERHEAD
LOGGERHEADED
LOGGERHEADS
LOGICALITIES
LOGICALITY
LOGICALNESS
LOGICALNESSES
LOGICISING
LOGICIZING
LOGINESSES
LOGISTICAL
LOGISTICALLY
LOGISTICIAN
LOGISTICIANS
LOGJAMMING
LOGJAMMINGS
LOGNORMALITIES
LOGNORMALITY
LOGNORMALLY
LOGOCENTRISM
LOGOCENTRISMS
LOGODAEDALIC
LOGODAEDALIES
LOGODAEDALUS
LOGODAEDALUSES
LOGODAEDALY
LOGOGRAMMATIC
LOGOGRAPHER
LOGOGRAPHERS
LOGOGRAPHIC
LOGOGRAPHICAL
LOGOGRAPHICALLY
LOGOGRAPHIES
LOGOGRAPHS
LOGOGRAPHY
LOGOGRIPHIC
LOGOGRIPHS
LOGOMACHIES
LOGOMACHIST
LOGOMACHISTS
LOGOPAEDIC
LOGOPAEDICS
LOGOPEDICS
LOGOPHILES
LOGORRHEAS
LOGORRHEIC
LOGORRHOEA
LOGORRHOEAS
LOGOTHETES
LOGOTYPIES
LOGROLLERS
LOGROLLING
LOGROLLINGS
LOINCLOTHS
LOITERINGLY
LOITERINGS
LOLLAPALOOSA
LOLLAPALOOSAS
LOLLAPALOOZA
LOLLAPALOOZAS
LOLLOPIEST
LOLLYGAGGED
LOLLYGAGGING
LOMENTACEOUS
LONELINESS
LONELINESSES
LONENESSES
LONESOMELY
LONESOMENESS
LONESOMENESSES
LONGAEVOUS
LONGANIMITIES
LONGANIMITY
LONGANIMOUS
LONGBOARDS
LONGBOWMAN
LONGBOWMEN
LONGCLOTHS
LONGEVITIES
LONGHAIRED
LONGHEADED
LONGHEADEDNESS
LONGHOUSES
LONGICAUDATE
LONGICORNS
LONGINQUITIES
LONGINQUITY
LONGIPENNATE
LONGIROSTRAL
LONGITUDES
LONGITUDINAL
LONGITUDINALLY
LONGJUMPED
LONGJUMPING
LONGLEAVES
LONGLINERS
LONGLISTED
LONGLISTING
LONGNESSES
LONGPRIMER
LONGPRIMERS
LONGSHOREMAN
LONGSHOREMEN
LONGSHORING
LONGSHORINGS
LONGSIGHTED
LONGSIGHTEDNESS
LONGSOMELY
LONGSOMENESS
LONGSOMENESSES
LONGWEARING
LOOKALIKES
LOONINESSES
LOOPHOLING
LOOPINESSES
LOOSEBOXES
LOOSENESSES
LOOSENINGS
LOOSESTRIFE
LOOSESTRIFES
LOOYENWORK
LOOYENWORKS
LOPGRASSES
LOPHOBRANCH
LOPHOBRANCHIATE
LOPHOBRANCHS
LOPHOPHORATE
LOPHOPHORE
LOPHOPHORES
LOPSIDEDLY
LOPSIDEDNESS
LOPSIDEDNESSES
LOQUACIOUS
LOQUACIOUSLY
LOQUACIOUSNESS

L

LOQUACITIES
LORAZEPAMS
LORDLINESS
LORDLINESSES
LORDOLATRIES
LORDOLATRY
LORGNETTES
LORICATING
LORICATION
LORICATIONS
LORNNESSES
LOSABLENESS
LOSABLENESSES
LOSSMAKERS
LOSSMAKING
LOSTNESSES
LOTHNESSES
LOTUSLANDS
LOUDHAILER
LOUDHAILERS
LOUDMOUTHED
LOUDMOUTHS
LOUDNESSES
LOUDSPEAKER
LOUDSPEAKERS
LOUNDERING
LOUNDERINGS
LOUNGEWEAR
LOUNGEWEARS
LOUNGINGLY
LOUSEWORTS
LOUSINESSES
LOUTISHNESS
LOUTISHNESSES
LOVABILITIES
LOVABILITY
LOVABLENESS
LOVABLENESSES
LOVASTATIN
LOVASTATINS
LOVEABILITIES
LOVEABILITY
LOVEABLENESS
LOVEABLENESSES
LOVELESSLY
LOVELESSNESS
LOVELESSNESSES
LOVELIGHTS
LOVELIHEAD
LOVELIHEADS
LOVELINESS
LOVELINESSES
LOVELORNNESS
LOVELORNNESSES
LOVEMAKERS
LOVEMAKING
LOVEMAKINGS
LOVESICKNESS
LOVESICKNESSES
LOVESTRUCK
LOVEWORTHIER
LOVEWORTHIES
LOVEWORTHIEST
LOVEWORTHY
LOVINGNESS
LOVINGNESSES
LOWBALLING
LOWBALLINGS
LOWBROWISM
LOWBROWISMS
LOWERCASED
LOWERCASES
LOWERCASING
LOWERCLASSMAN
LOWERCLASSMEN
LOWERINGLY
LOWLANDERS
LOWLIGHTED
LOWLIGHTING
LOWLIHEADS
LOWLINESSES
LOWSENINGS
LOXODROMES
LOXODROMIC
LOXODROMICAL
LOXODROMICALLY
LOXODROMICS
LOXODROMIES
LOYALNESSES
LOZENGIEST
LUBBERLIER
LUBBERLIEST
LUBBERLINESS
LUBBERLINESSES
LUBRICANTS
LUBRICATED
LUBRICATES
LUBRICATING
LUBRICATION
LUBRICATIONAL
LUBRICATIONS
LUBRICATIVE
LUBRICATOR
LUBRICATORS
LUBRICIOUS
LUBRICIOUSLY
LUBRICITIES
LUBRICOUSLY
LUBRITORIA
LUBRITORIUM
LUBRITORIUMS
LUCIDITIES
LUCIDNESSES
LUCIFERASE
LUCIFERASES
LUCIFERINS
LUCIFEROUS
LUCIFUGOUS
LUCKENBOOTH
LUCKENBOOTHS
LUCKENGOWAN
LUCKENGOWANS
LUCKINESSES
LUCKLESSLY
LUCKLESSNESS
LUCKLESSNESSES
LUCKPENNIES
LUCRATIVELY
LUCRATIVENESS
LUCRATIVENESSES
LUCTATIONS
LUCUBRATED
LUCUBRATES
LUCUBRATING
LUCUBRATION
LUCUBRATIONS
LUCUBRATOR
LUCUBRATORS
LUCULENTLY
LUDICROUSLY
LUDICROUSNESS
LUDICROUSNESSES
LUETICALLY
LUFTMENSCH
LUFTMENSCHEN
LUGUBRIOUS
LUGUBRIOUSLY
LUGUBRIOUSNESS
LUKEWARMISH
LUKEWARMLY
LUKEWARMNESS
LUKEWARMNESSES
LUKEWARMTH
LUKEWARMTHS
LULLABYING
LUMBAGINOUS
LUMBERINGLY
LUMBERINGNESS
LUMBERINGNESSES
LUMBERINGS
LUMBERJACK
LUMBERJACKET
LUMBERJACKETS
LUMBERJACKS
LUMBERSOME
LUMBERSOMENESS
LUMBERYARD
LUMBERYARDS
LUMBOSACRAL
LUMBRICALES
LUMBRICALIS
LUMBRICALISES
LUMBRICALS
LUMBRICIFORM
LUMBRICOID
LUMBRICUSES
LUMINAIRES
LUMINANCES
LUMINARIAS
LUMINARIES
LUMINARISM
LUMINARISMS
LUMINARIST
LUMINARISTS
LUMINATION
LUMINATIONS
LUMINESCED
LUMINESCENCE
LUMINESCENCES
LUMINESCENT
LUMINESCES
LUMINESCING
LUMINIFEROUS
LUMINOSITIES
LUMINOSITY
LUMINOUSLY
LUMINOUSNESS
LUMINOUSNESSES
LUMISTEROL
LUMISTEROLS
LUMPECTOMIES
LUMPECTOMY
LUMPFISHES
LUMPINESSES
LUMPISHNESS
LUMPISHNESSES
LUMPSUCKER
LUMPSUCKERS
LUNARNAUTS
LUNATICALLY
LUNCHBOXES
LUNCHBREAK
LUNCHBREAKS
LUNCHEONED
LUNCHEONETTE
LUNCHEONETTES
LUNCHEONING
LUNCHMEATS
LUNCHPAILS
LUNCHROOMS
LUNCHTIMES
LUNGFISHES
LUNINESSES
LUNKHEADED
LURIDNESSES
LUSCIOUSLY
LUSCIOUSNESS
LUSCIOUSNESSES
LUSHNESSES
LUSKISHNESS
LUSKISHNESSES
LUSTERLESS
LUSTERWARE
LUSTERWARES
LUSTFULNESS
LUSTFULNESSES
LUSTIHEADS
LUSTIHOODS
LUSTINESSES
LUSTRATING

LUSTRATION
LUSTRATIONS
LUSTRATIVE
LUSTRELESS
LUSTREWARE
LUSTREWARES
LUSTROUSLY
LUSTROUSNESS
LUSTROUSNESSES
LUTEINISATION
LUTEINISATIONS
LUTEINISED
LUTEINISES
LUTEINISING
LUTEINIZATION
LUTEINIZATIONS
LUTEINIZED
LUTEINIZES
LUTEINIZING
LUTEOTROPHIC
LUTEOTROPHIN
LUTEOTROPHINS
LUTEOTROPIC
LUTEOTROPIN
LUTEOTROPINS
LUTESTRING
LUTESTRINGS
LUVVIEDOMS
LUXULIANITE
LUXULIANITES
LUXULLIANITE
LUXULLIANITES
LUXULYANITE
LUXULYANITES
LUXURIANCE
LUXURIANCES
LUXURIANCIES
LUXURIANCY
LUXURIANTLY
LUXURIATED
LUXURIATES
LUXURIATING
LUXURIATION
LUXURIATIONS
LUXURIOUSLY
LUXURIOUSNESS
LUXURIOUSNESSES
LYCANTHROPE
LYCANTHROPES
LYCANTHROPIC
LYCANTHROPIES
LYCANTHROPIST
LYCANTHROPISTS
LYCANTHROPY
LYCHNOSCOPE
LYCHNOSCOPES
LYCOPODIUM
LYCOPODIUMS
LYMPHADENITIS
LYMPHADENITISES
LYMPHADENOPATHY
LYMPHANGIAL
LYMPHANGIOGRAM
LYMPHANGIOGRAMS
LYMPHANGIOMA
LYMPHANGIOMAS
LYMPHANGIOMATA
LYMPHANGITIC
LYMPHANGITIDES
LYMPHANGITIS
LYMPHANGITISES
LYMPHATICALLY
LYMPHATICS
LYMPHOADENOMA
LYMPHOADENOMAS
LYMPHOADENOMATA
LYMPHOBLAST
LYMPHOBLASTIC
LYMPHOBLASTS
LYMPHOCYTE
LYMPHOCYTES
LYMPHOCYTIC
LYMPHOCYTOPENIA
LYMPHOCYTOSES
LYMPHOCYTOSIS
LYMPHOCYTOTIC
LYMPHOGRAM
LYMPHOGRAMS
LYMPHOGRANULOMA
LYMPHOGRAPHIC
LYMPHOGRAPHIES
LYMPHOGRAPHY
LYMPHOKINE
LYMPHOKINES
LYMPHOMATA
LYMPHOMATOID
LYMPHOMATOSES
LYMPHOMATOSIS
LYMPHOMATOUS
LYMPHOPENIA
LYMPHOPENIAS
LYMPHOPOIESES
LYMPHOPOIESIS
LYMPHOPOIETIC
LYMPHOSARCOMA
LYMPHOSARCOMAS
LYMPHOSARCOMATA
LYMPHOTROPHIC
LYOPHILISATION
LYOPHILISATIONS
LYOPHILISE
LYOPHILISED
LYOPHILISER
LYOPHILISERS
LYOPHILISES
LYOPHILISING
LYOPHILIZATION
LYOPHILIZATIONS
LYOPHILIZE
LYOPHILIZED
LYOPHILIZER
LYOPHILIZERS
LYOPHILIZES
LYOPHILIZING
LYOSORPTION
LYOSORPTIONS
LYRICALNESS
LYRICALNESSES
LYRICISING
LYRICIZING
LYSERGIDES
LYSIGENETIC
LYSIGENOUS
LYSIMETERS
LYSIMETRIC
LYSOGENICITIES
LYSOGENICITY
LYSOGENIES
LYSOGENISATION
LYSOGENISATIONS
LYSOGENISE
LYSOGENISED
LYSOGENISES
LYSOGENISING
LYSOGENIZATION
LYSOGENIZATIONS
LYSOGENIZE
LYSOGENIZED
LYSOGENIZES
LYSOGENIZING
LYSOLECITHIN
LYSOLECITHINS
LYTHRACEOUS

M

MACABERESQUE
MACADAMIAS
MACADAMISATION
MACADAMISATIONS
MACADAMISE
MACADAMISED
MACADAMISER
MACADAMISERS
MACADAMISES
MACADAMISING
MACADAMIZATION
MACADAMIZATIONS
MACADAMIZE
MACADAMIZED
MACADAMIZER
MACADAMIZERS
MACADAMIZES
MACADAMIZING
MACARISING
MACARIZING
MACARONICALLY
MACARONICS
MACARONIES
MACCARONIES
MACCARONIS
MACCHERONCINI
MACCHERONCINIS
MACCHIATOS
MACEBEARER
MACEBEARERS
MACEDOINES
MACERANDUBA
MACERANDUBAS
MACERATERS
MACERATING
MACERATION
MACERATIONS
MACERATIVE
MACERATORS
MACHAIRODONT
MACHAIRODONTS
MACHIAVELIAN
MACHIAVELIANS
MACHIAVELLIAN
MACHIAVELLIANS
MACHICOLATE
MACHICOLATED
MACHICOLATES
MACHICOLATING
MACHICOLATION
MACHICOLATIONS
MACHINABILITIES
MACHINABILITY
MACHINABLE
MACHINATED
MACHINATES
MACHINATING
MACHINATION
MACHINATIONS
MACHINATOR
MACHINATORS
MACHINEABILITY
MACHINEABLE
MACHINEGUN
MACHINEGUNNED
MACHINEGUNNING
MACHINEGUNS
MACHINELESS
MACHINELIKE
MACHINEMAN
MACHINEMEN
MACHINERIES
MACHINIMAS
MACHININGS
MACHINISTS
MACHMETERS
MACHTPOLITIK
MACHTPOLITIKS
MACINTOSHES
MACKINTOSH
MACKINTOSHES
MACONOCHIE
MACONOCHIES
MACRENCEPHALIA
MACRENCEPHALIAS
MACRENCEPHALIES
MACRENCEPHALY
MACROAGGREGATE
MACROAGGREGATED
MACROAGGREGATES
MACROBIOTA
MACROBIOTAS
MACROBIOTE
MACROBIOTES
MACROBIOTIC
MACROBIOTICS
MACROCARPA
MACROCARPAS
MACROCEPHALIA
MACROCEPHALIAS
MACROCEPHALIC
MACROCEPHALIES
MACROCEPHALOUS
MACROCEPHALY
MACROCLIMATE
MACROCLIMATES
MACROCLIMATIC
MACROCODES
MACROCOPIES
MACROCOSMIC
MACROCOSMICALLY
MACROCOSMS
MACROCYCLE
MACROCYCLES
MACROCYCLIC
MACROCYSTS
MACROCYTES
MACROCYTIC
MACROCYTOSES
MACROCYTOSIS
MACRODACTYL
MACRODACTYLIC
MACRODACTYLIES
MACRODACTYLOUS
MACRODACTYLS
MACRODACTYLY
MACRODIAGONAL
MACRODIAGONALS
MACRODOMES
MACROECONOMIC
MACROECONOMICS
MACROEVOLUTION
MACROEVOLUTIONS
MACROFAUNA
MACROFAUNAE
MACROFAUNAS
MACROFLORA
MACROFLORAE
MACROFLORAS
MACROFOSSIL
MACROFOSSILS
MACROGAMETE
MACROGAMETES
MACROGLIAS
MACROGLOBULIN
MACROGLOBULINS
MACROGRAPH
MACROGRAPHIC
MACROGRAPHS
MACROLIDES
MACROLOGIES
MACROMARKETING
MACROMARKETINGS
MACROMERES
MACROMOLECULAR
MACROMOLECULE
MACROMOLECULES
MACROMOLES
MACROMUTATION
MACROMUTATIONS
MACRONUCLEAR
MACRONUCLEI
MACRONUCLEUS
MACRONUCLEUSES
MACRONUTRIENT
MACRONUTRIENTS
MACROPHAGE
MACROPHAGES
MACROPHAGIC
MACROPHAGOUS
MACROPHOTOGRAPH
MACROPHYLA
MACROPHYLUM
MACROPHYSICS
MACROPHYTE
MACROPHYTES
MACROPHYTIC
MACROPINACOID
MACROPINACOIDS
MACROPINAKOID
MACROPINAKOIDS
MACROPRISM
MACROPRISMS
MACROPRUDENTIAL
MACROPSIAS
MACROPTEROUS
MACROSCALE
MACROSCALES
MACROSCOPIC
MACROSCOPICALLY
MACROSOCIOLOGY
MACROSPORANGIA
MACROSPORANGIUM
MACROSPORE
MACROSPORES
MACROSTRUCTURAL
MACROSTRUCTURE
MACROSTRUCTURES
MACROZAMIA
MACROZAMIAS
MACTATIONS
MACULATING
MACULATION
MACULATIONS
MACULATURE
MACULATURES
MADBRAINED
MADDENINGLY
MADDENINGNESS
MADDENINGNESSES

MADEFACTION
MADEFACTIONS
MADELEINES
MADEMOISELLE
MADEMOISELLES
MADERISATION
MADERISATIONS
MADERISING
MADERIZATION
MADERIZATIONS
MADERIZING
MADONNAISH
MADONNAWISE
MADRASSAHS
MADREPORAL
MADREPORES
MADREPORIAN
MADREPORIANS
MADREPORIC
MADREPORITE
MADREPORITES
MADREPORITIC
MADRIGALESQUE
MADRIGALIAN
MADRIGALIST
MADRIGALISTS
MADRILENES
MAELSTROMS
MAENADICALLY
MAENADISMS
MAFFICKERS
MAFFICKING
MAFFICKINGS
MAGALOGUES
MAGAZINIST
MAGAZINISTS
MAGDALENES
MAGGOTIEST
MAGGOTORIA
MAGGOTORIUM
MAGIANISMS
MAGISTERIAL
MAGISTERIALLY
MAGISTERIALNESS
MAGISTERIES
MAGISTERIUM
MAGISTERIUMS
MAGISTRACIES
MAGISTRACY
MAGISTRALITIES
MAGISTRALITY
MAGISTRALLY
MAGISTRALS
MAGISTRAND
MAGISTRANDS
MAGISTRATE
MAGISTRATES
MAGISTRATESHIP
MAGISTRATESHIPS
MAGISTRATIC
MAGISTRATICAL
MAGISTRATICALLY
MAGISTRATURE
MAGISTRATURES
MAGMATISMS
MAGNALIUMS
MAGNANIMITIES
MAGNANIMITY
MAGNANIMOUS
MAGNANIMOUSLY
MAGNANIMOUSNESS
MAGNATESHIP
MAGNATESHIPS
MAGNESITES
MAGNESIUMS
MAGNESSTONE
MAGNESSTONES
MAGNETICAL
MAGNETICALLY
MAGNETICIAN
MAGNETICIANS
MAGNETISABLE
MAGNETISATION
MAGNETISATIONS
MAGNETISED
MAGNETISER
MAGNETISERS
MAGNETISES
MAGNETISING
MAGNETISMS
MAGNETISTS
MAGNETITES
MAGNETITIC
MAGNETIZABLE
MAGNETIZATION
MAGNETIZATIONS
MAGNETIZED
MAGNETIZER
MAGNETIZERS
MAGNETIZES
MAGNETIZING
MAGNETOCHEMICAL
MAGNETOELECTRIC
MAGNETOGRAPH
MAGNETOGRAPHS
MAGNETOMETER
MAGNETOMETERS
MAGNETOMETRIC
MAGNETOMETRIES
MAGNETOMETRY
MAGNETOMOTIVE
MAGNETOPAUSE
MAGNETOPAUSES
MAGNETOSPHERE
MAGNETOSPHERES
MAGNETOSPHERIC
MAGNETOSTATIC
MAGNETOSTATICS
MAGNETRONS
MAGNIFIABLE
MAGNIFICAL
MAGNIFICALLY
MAGNIFICAT
MAGNIFICATION
MAGNIFICATIONS
MAGNIFICATS
MAGNIFICENCE
MAGNIFICENCES
MAGNIFICENT
MAGNIFICENTLY
MAGNIFICENTNESS
MAGNIFICOES
MAGNIFICOS
MAGNIFIERS
MAGNIFYING
MAGNILOQUENCE
MAGNILOQUENCES
MAGNILOQUENT
MAGNILOQUENTLY
MAGNITUDES
MAGNITUDINOUS
MAGNOLIACEOUS
MAHARAJAHS
MAHARANEES
MAHARISHIS
MAHATMAISM
MAHATMAISMS
MAHLSTICKS
MAHOGANIES
MAIASAURAS
MAIDENHAIR
MAIDENHAIRS
MAIDENHEAD
MAIDENHEADS
MAIDENHOOD
MAIDENHOODS
MAIDENLIER
MAIDENLIEST
MAIDENLIKE
MAIDENLINESS
MAIDENLINESSES
MAIDENWEED
MAIDENWEEDS
MAIDISHNESS
MAIDISHNESSES
MAIDSERVANT
MAIDSERVANTS
MAIEUTICAL
MAILABILITIES
MAILABILITY
MAILCOACHES
MAILGRAMMED
MAILGRAMMING
MAILMERGED
MAILMERGES
MAILMERGING
MAILPOUCHES
MAILSHOTTED
MAILSHOTTING
MAIMEDNESS
MAIMEDNESSES
MAINBRACES
MAINFRAMES
MAINLANDER
MAINLANDERS
MAINLINERS
MAINLINING
MAINLININGS
MAINPERNOR
MAINPERNORS
MAINPRISED
MAINPRISES
MAINPRISING
MAINSHEETS
MAINSPRING
MAINSPRINGS
MAINSTAGES
MAINSTREAM
MAINSTREAMED
MAINSTREAMING
MAINSTREAMINGS
MAINSTREAMS
MAINSTREETING
MAINSTREETINGS
MAINTAINABILITY
MAINTAINABLE
MAINTAINED
MAINTAINER
MAINTAINERS
MAINTAINING
MAINTENANCE
MAINTENANCED
MAINTENANCES
MAINTENANCING
MAINTOPMAST
MAINTOPMASTS
MAINTOPSAIL
MAINTOPSAILS
MAISONETTE
MAISONETTES
MAISONNETTE
MAISONNETTES
MAISTERDOME
MAISTERDOMES
MAISTERING
MAISTRINGS
MAJESTICAL
MAJESTICALLY
MAJESTICALNESS
MAJESTICNESS
MAJESTICNESSES
MAJOLICAWARE
MAJOLICAWARES
MAJORDOMOS
MAJORETTES
MAJORETTING
MAJORETTINGS
MAJORITAIRE
MAJORITAIRES
MAJORITARIAN

MAJORITARIANISM
MAJORITARIANS
MAJORITIES
MAJORSHIPS
MAJUSCULAR
MAJUSCULES
MAKEREADIES
MAKESHIFTS
MAKEWEIGHT
MAKEWEIGHTS
MAKUNOUCHI
MAKUNOUCHIS
MALABSORPTION
MALABSORPTIONS
MALACHITES
MALACOLOGICAL
MALACOLOGIES
MALACOLOGIST
MALACOLOGISTS
MALACOLOGY
MALACOPHILIES
MALACOPHILOUS
MALACOPHILY
MALACOPHYLLOUS
MALACOPTERYGIAN
MALACOSTRACAN
MALACOSTRACANS
MALACOSTRACOUS
MALADAPTATION
MALADAPTATIONS
MALADAPTED
MALADAPTIVE
MALADAPTIVELY
MALADDRESS
MALADDRESSES
MALADJUSTED
MALADJUSTIVE
MALADJUSTMENT
MALADJUSTMENTS
MALADMINISTER
MALADMINISTERED
MALADMINISTERS
MALADROITLY
MALADROITNESS
MALADROITNESSES
MALADROITS
MALAGUENAS
MALAGUETTA
MALAGUETTAS
MALAKATOONE
MALAKATOONES
MALAPERTLY
MALAPERTNESS
MALAPERTNESSES
MALAPPORTIONED
MALAPPROPRIATE
MALAPPROPRIATED
MALAPPROPRIATES
MALAPROPIAN
MALAPROPISM
MALAPROPISMS
MALAPROPIST
MALAPROPISTS
MALAPROPOS
MALARIOLOGIES
MALARIOLOGIST
MALARIOLOGISTS
MALARIOLOGY
MALASSIMILATION
MALATHIONS
MALAXATING
MALAXATION
MALAXATIONS
MALAXATORS
MALCONFORMATION
MALCONTENT
MALCONTENTED
MALCONTENTEDLY
MALCONTENTS
MALDEPLOYMENT
MALDEPLOYMENTS
MALDISTRIBUTION
MALEDICENT
MALEDICTED
MALEDICTING
MALEDICTION
MALEDICTIONS
MALEDICTIVE
MALEDICTORY
MALEFACTION
MALEFACTIONS
MALEFACTOR
MALEFACTORS
MALEFACTORY
MALEFACTRESS
MALEFACTRESSES
MALEFFECTS
MALEFICALLY
MALEFICENCE
MALEFICENCES
MALEFICENT
MALEFICIAL
MALENESSES
MALENGINES
MALENTENDU
MALENTENDUS
MALEVOLENCE
MALEVOLENCES
MALEVOLENT
MALEVOLENTLY
MALFEASANCE
MALFEASANCES
MALFEASANT
MALFEASANTS
MALFORMATION
MALFORMATIONS
MALFUNCTION
MALFUNCTIONED
MALFUNCTIONING
MALFUNCTIONINGS
MALFUNCTIONS
MALICIOUSLY
MALICIOUSNESS
MALICIOUSNESSES
MALIGNANCE
MALIGNANCES
MALIGNANCIES
MALIGNANCY
MALIGNANTLY
MALIGNANTS
MALIGNITIES
MALIGNMENT
MALIGNMENTS
MALIMPRINTED
MALIMPRINTING
MALIMPRINTINGS
MALINGERED
MALINGERER
MALINGERERS
MALINGERIES
MALINGERING
MALLANDERS
MALLEABILITIES
MALLEABILITY
MALLEABLENESS
MALLEABLENESSES
MALLEATING
MALLEATION
MALLEATIONS
MALLEIFORM
MALLEMAROKING
MALLEMAROKINGS
MALLEMUCKS
MALLENDERS
MALLEOLUSES
MALLOPHAGOUS
MALLOWPUFF
MALLOWPUFFS
MALMSTONES
MALNOURISHED
MALNUTRITION
MALNUTRITIONS
MALOCCLUDED
MALOCCLUSION
MALOCCLUSIONS
MALODOROUS
MALODOROUSLY
MALODOROUSNESS
MALOLACTIC
MALONYLUREA
MALONYLUREAS
MALPIGHIACEOUS
MALPIGHIAS
MALPOSITION
MALPOSITIONS
MALPRACTICE
MALPRACTICES
MALPRACTITIONER
MALPRESENTATION
MALTALENTS
MALTINESSES
MALTODEXTRIN
MALTODEXTRINS
MALTREATED
MALTREATER
MALTREATERS
MALTREATING
MALTREATMENT
MALTREATMENTS
MALVACEOUS
MALVERSATION
MALVERSATIONS
MALVOISIES
MAMAGUYING
MAMILLATED
MAMILLATION
MAMILLATIONS
MAMILLIFORM
MAMMALIANS
MAMMALIFEROUS
MAMMALITIES
MAMMALOGICAL
MAMMALOGIES
MAMMALOGIST
MAMMALOGISTS
MAMMAPLASTIES
MAMMAPLASTY
MAMMECTOMIES
MAMMECTOMY
MAMMETRIES
MAMMIFEROUS
MAMMILLARIA
MAMMILLARIAS
MAMMILLARY
MAMMILLATE
MAMMILLATED
MAMMILLATION
MAMMILLATIONS
MAMMILLIFORM
MAMMITIDES
MAMMOCKING
MAMMOGENIC
MAMMOGRAMS
MAMMOGRAPH
MAMMOGRAPHIC
MAMMOGRAPHIES
MAMMOGRAPHS
MAMMOGRAPHY
MAMMONISMS
MAMMONISTIC
MAMMONISTS
MAMMONITES
MAMMOPLASTIES
MAMMOPLASTY
MANAGEABILITIES
MANAGEABILITY
MANAGEABLE
MANAGEABLENESS
MANAGEABLY
MANAGEMENT

MANAGEMENTAL
MANAGEMENTS
MANAGERESS
MANAGERESSES
MANAGERIAL
MANAGERIALISM
MANAGERIALISMS
MANAGERIALIST
MANAGERIALISTS
MANAGERIALLY
MANAGERSHIP
MANAGERSHIPS
MANCHESTER
MANCHESTERS
MANCHINEEL
MANCHINEELS
MANCIPATED
MANCIPATES
MANCIPATING
MANCIPATION
MANCIPATIONS
MANCIPATORY
MANDAMUSED
MANDAMUSES
MANDAMUSING
MANDARINATE
MANDARINATES
MANDARINES
MANDARINIC
MANDARINISM
MANDARINISMS
MANDATARIES
MANDATORIES
MANDATORILY
MANDIBULAR
MANDIBULATE
MANDIBULATED
MANDIBULATES
MANDILIONS
MANDIOCCAS
MANDOLINES
MANDOLINIST
MANDOLINISTS
MANDRAGORA
MANDRAGORAS
MANDUCABLE
MANDUCATED
MANDUCATES
MANDUCATING
MANDUCATION
MANDUCATIONS
MANDUCATORY
MANDYLIONS
MANEUVERABILITY
MANEUVERABLE
MANEUVERED
MANEUVERER
MANEUVERERS
MANEUVERING
MANEUVERINGS
MANFULLEST
MANFULNESS
MANFULNESSES
MANGABEIRA
MANGABEIRAS
MANGALSUTRA
MANGALSUTRAS
MANGANATES
MANGANESES
MANGANESIAN
MANGANIFEROUS
MANGANITES
MANGELWURZEL
MANGELWURZELS
MANGEMANGE
MANGEMANGES
MANGETOUTS
MANGINESSES
MANGOLDWURZEL
MANGOLDWURZELS
MANGOSTANS
MANGOSTEEN
MANGOSTEENS
MANGOUSTES
MANGULATED
MANGULATES
MANGULATING
MANHANDLED
MANHANDLES
MANHANDLING
MANHATTANS
MANHUNTERS
MANIACALLY
MANICOTTIS
MANICURING
MANICURIST
MANICURISTS
MANIFESTABLE
MANIFESTANT
MANIFESTANTS
MANIFESTATION
MANIFESTATIONAL
MANIFESTATIONS
MANIFESTATIVE
MANIFESTED
MANIFESTER
MANIFESTERS
MANIFESTIBLE
MANIFESTING
MANIFESTLY
MANIFESTNESS
MANIFESTNESSES
MANIFESTOED
MANIFESTOES
MANIFESTOING
MANIFESTOS
MANIFOLDED
MANIFOLDER
MANIFOLDERS
MANIFOLDING
MANIFOLDLY
MANIFOLDNESS
MANIFOLDNESSES
MANIPULABILITY
MANIPULABLE
MANIPULARS
MANIPULATABLE
MANIPULATE
MANIPULATED
MANIPULATES
MANIPULATING
MANIPULATION
MANIPULATIONS
MANIPULATIVE
MANIPULATIVELY
MANIPULATIVES
MANIPULATOR
MANIPULATORS
MANIPULATORY
MANLINESSES
MANNEQUINS
MANNERISMS
MANNERISTIC
MANNERISTICAL
MANNERISTICALLY
MANNERISTS
MANNERLESS
MANNERLESSNESS
MANNERLIER
MANNERLIEST
MANNERLINESS
MANNERLINESSES
MANNIFEROUS
MANNISHNESS
MANNISHNESSES
MANOEUVERED
MANOEUVERING
MANOEUVERS
MANOEUVRABILITY
MANOEUVRABLE
MANOEUVRED
MANOEUVRER
MANOEUVRERS
MANOEUVRES
MANOEUVRING
MANOEUVRINGS
MANOMETERS
MANOMETRIC
MANOMETRICAL
MANOMETRICALLY
MANOMETRIES
MANORIALISM
MANORIALISMS
MANOSCOPIES
MANRIKIGUSARI
MANRIKIGUSARIS
MANSCAPING
MANSCAPINGS
MANSERVANT
MANSIONARIES
MANSIONARY
MANSLAUGHTER
MANSLAUGHTERS
MANSLAYERS
MANSONRIES
MANSPLAINED
MANSPLAINING
MANSPLAININGS
MANSPLAINS
MANSPREADING
MANSPREADINGS
MANSPREADS
MANSUETUDE
MANSUETUDES
MANTELLETTA
MANTELLETTAS
MANTELPIECE
MANTELPIECES
MANTELSHELF
MANTELSHELVES
MANTELTREE
MANTELTREES
MANTICALLY
MANTICORAS
MANTICORES
MANTLETREE
MANTLETREES
MANTYHOSES
MANUBRIUMS
MANUFACTORIES
MANUFACTORY
MANUFACTURABLE
MANUFACTURAL
MANUFACTURE
MANUFACTURED
MANUFACTURER
MANUFACTURERS
MANUFACTURES
MANUFACTURING
MANUFACTURINGS
MANUMISSION
MANUMISSIONS
MANUMITTED
MANUMITTER
MANUMITTERS
MANUMITTING
MANURANCES
MANUSCRIPT
MANUSCRIPTS
MANZANILLA
MANZANILLAS
MANZANITAS
MAPMAKINGS
MAPPEMONDS
MAQUILADORA
MAQUILADORAS
MAQUILLAGE
MAQUILLAGES
MAQUISARDS
MARABUNTAS

MARANATHAS
MARASCHINO
MARASCHINOS
MARASMUSES
MARATHONER
MARATHONERS
MARATHONING
MARATHONINGS
MARAUDINGS
MARBELISED
MARBELISES
MARBELISING
MARBELIZED
MARBELIZES
MARBELIZING
MARBLEISED
MARBLEISES
MARBLEISING
MARBLEIZED
MARBLEIZES
MARBLEIZING
MARBLEWOOD
MARBLEWOODS
MARCANTANT
MARCANTANTS
MARCASITES
MARCASITICAL
MARCATISSIMO
MARCELLERS
MARCELLING
MARCESCENCE
MARCESCENCES
MARCESCENT
MARCESCIBLE
MARCHANTIA
MARCHANTIAS
MARCHIONESS
MARCHIONESSES
MARCHLANDS
MARCHPANES
MARCONIGRAM
MARCONIGRAMS
MARCONIGRAPH
MARCONIGRAPHED
MARCONIGRAPHING
MARCONIGRAPHS
MARCONIING
MARESCHALS
MARGARINES
MARGARITAS
MARGARITES
MARGARITIC
MARGARITIFEROUS
MARGENTING
MARGHERITA
MARGHERITAS
MARGINALIA
MARGINALISATION
MARGINALISE
MARGINALISED
MARGINALISES
MARGINALISING
MARGINALISM
MARGINALISMS
MARGINALIST
MARGINALISTS
MARGINALITIES
MARGINALITY
MARGINALIZATION
MARGINALIZE
MARGINALIZED
MARGINALIZES
MARGINALIZING
MARGINALLY
MARGINATED
MARGINATES
MARGINATING
MARGINATION
MARGINATIONS
MARGRAVATE
MARGRAVATES
MARGRAVIAL
MARGRAVIATE
MARGRAVIATES
MARGRAVINE
MARGRAVINES
MARGUERITA
MARGUERITAS
MARGUERITE
MARGUERITES
MARIALITES
MARICULTURE
MARICULTURES
MARICULTURIST
MARICULTURISTS
MARIGRAPHS
MARIHUANAS
MARIJUANAS
MARIMBAPHONE
MARIMBAPHONES
MARIMBISTS
MARINADING
MARINATING
MARINATION
MARINATIONS
MARIONBERRIES
MARIONBERRY
MARIONETTE
MARIONETTES
MARISCHALLED
MARISCHALLING
MARISCHALS
MARIVAUDAGE
MARIVAUDAGES
MARKEDNESS
MARKEDNESSES
MARKETABILITIES
MARKETABILITY
MARKETABLE
MARKETABLENESS
MARKETABLY
MARKETEERS
MARKETINGS
MARKETISATION
MARKETISATIONS
MARKETISED
MARKETISES
MARKETISING
MARKETIZATION
MARKETIZATIONS
MARKETIZED
MARKETIZES
MARKETIZING
MARKETPLACE
MARKETPLACES
MARKSMANSHIP
MARKSMANSHIPS
MARKSWOMAN
MARKSWOMEN
MARLACIOUS
MARLINESPIKE
MARLINESPIKES
MARLINGSPIKE
MARLINGSPIKES
MARLINSPIKE
MARLINSPIKES
MARLSTONES
MARMALADES
MARMALISED
MARMALISES
MARMALISING
MARMALIZED
MARMALIZES
MARMALIZING
MARMARISED
MARMARISES
MARMARISING
MARMARIZED
MARMARIZES
MARMARIZING
MARMAROSES
MARMAROSIS
MARMELISED
MARMELISES
MARMELISING
MARMELIZED
MARMELIZES
MARMELIZING
MARMOREALLY
MAROONINGS
MARPRELATE
MARPRELATED
MARPRELATES
MARPRELATING
MARQUESSATE
MARQUESSATES
MARQUESSES
MARQUETERIE
MARQUETERIES
MARQUETRIES
MARQUISATE
MARQUISATES
MARQUISETTE
MARQUISETTES
MARRIAGEABILITY
MARRIAGEABLE
MARROWBONE
MARROWBONES
MARROWFATS
MARROWIEST
MARROWLESS
MARROWSKIED
MARROWSKIES
MARROWSKYING
MARSEILLES
MARSHALCIES
MARSHALERS
MARSHALING
MARSHALLED
MARSHALLER
MARSHALLERS
MARSHALLING
MARSHALLINGS
MARSHALSHIP
MARSHALSHIPS
MARSHBUCKS
MARSHELDER
MARSHELDERS
MARSHINESS
MARSHINESSES
MARSHLANDER
MARSHLANDERS
MARSHLANDS
MARSHLOCKS
MARSHLOCKSES
MARSHMALLOW
MARSHMALLOWIER
MARSHMALLOWIEST
MARSHMALLOWS
MARSHMALLOWY
MARSHWORTS
MARSIPOBRANCH
MARSIPOBRANCHS
MARSQUAKES
MARSUPIALIAN
MARSUPIALIANS
MARSUPIALS
MARSUPIANS
MARTELLANDO
MARTELLANDOS
MARTELLATO
MARTELLATOS
MARTELLING
MARTENSITE
MARTENSITES
MARTENSITIC
MARTENSITICALLY
MARTIALISM
MARTIALISMS
MARTIALIST

M

MARTIALISTS
MARTIALNESS
MARTIALNESSES
MARTINETISH
MARTINETISM
MARTINETISMS
MARTINGALE
MARTINGALES
MARTINGALS
MARTYRDOMS
MARTYRISATION
MARTYRISATIONS
MARTYRISED
MARTYRISES
MARTYRISING
MARTYRIZATION
MARTYRIZATIONS
MARTYRIZED
MARTYRIZES
MARTYRIZING
MARTYROLOGIC
MARTYROLOGICAL
MARTYROLOGIES
MARTYROLOGIST
MARTYROLOGISTS
MARTYROLOGY
MARVELLERS
MARVELLING
MARVELLOUS
MARVELLOUSLY
MARVELLOUSNESS
MARVELOUSLY
MARVELOUSNESS
MARVELOUSNESSES
MARZIPANNED
MARZIPANNING
MASCARAING
MASCARPONE
MASCARPONES
MASCULINELY
MASCULINENESS
MASCULINENESSES
MASCULINES
MASCULINISATION
MASCULINISE
MASCULINISED
MASCULINISES
MASCULINISING
MASCULINIST
MASCULINISTS
MASCULINITIES
MASCULINITY
MASCULINIZATION
MASCULINIZE
MASCULINIZED
MASCULINIZES
MASCULINIZING
MASCULISTS
MASHGICHIM
MASKALLONGE
MASKALLONGES
MASKALONGE
MASKALONGES
MASKANONGE
MASKANONGES
MASKINONGE
MASKINONGES
MASKIROVKA
MASKIROVKAS
MASOCHISMS
MASOCHISTIC
MASOCHISTICALLY
MASOCHISTS
MASONICALLY
MASQUERADE
MASQUERADED
MASQUERADER
MASQUERADERS
MASQUERADES
MASQUERADING
MASSACRERS
MASSACRING
MASSAGISTS
MASSARANDUBA
MASSARANDUBAS
MASSASAUGA
MASSASAUGAS
MASSERANDUBA
MASSERANDUBAS
MASSETERIC
MASSIFICATION
MASSIFICATIONS
MASSINESSES
MASSIVENESS
MASSIVENESSES
MASSOTHERAPIES
MASSOTHERAPIST
MASSOTHERAPISTS
MASSOTHERAPY
MASSPRIEST
MASSPRIESTS
MASSYMORES
MASTECTOMIES
MASTECTOMY
MASTERATES
MASTERCLASS
MASTERCLASSES
MASTERDOMS
MASTERFULLY
MASTERFULNESS
MASTERFULNESSES
MASTERHOOD
MASTERHOODS
MASTERINGS
MASTERLESS
MASTERLIER
MASTERLIEST
MASTERLINESS
MASTERLINESSES
MASTERMIND
MASTERMINDED
MASTERMINDING
MASTERMINDS
MASTERPIECE
MASTERPIECES
MASTERSHIP
MASTERSHIPS
MASTERSINGER
MASTERSINGERS
MASTERSTROKE
MASTERSTROKES
MASTERWORK
MASTERWORKS
MASTERWORT
MASTERWORTS
MASTHEADED
MASTHEADING
MASTHOUSES
MASTICABLE
MASTICATED
MASTICATES
MASTICATING
MASTICATION
MASTICATIONS
MASTICATOR
MASTICATORIES
MASTICATORS
MASTICATORY
MASTIGOPHORAN
MASTIGOPHORANS
MASTIGOPHORE
MASTIGOPHORES
MASTIGOPHORIC
MASTIGOPHOROUS
MASTITIDES
MASTITISES
MASTODONIC
MASTODONTIC
MASTODONTS
MASTODYNIA
MASTODYNIAS
MASTOIDECTOMIES
MASTOIDECTOMY
MASTOIDITIDES
MASTOIDITIS
MASTOIDITISES
MASTOPEXIES
MASTURBATE
MASTURBATED
MASTURBATES
MASTURBATING
MASTURBATION
MASTURBATIONS
MASTURBATOR
MASTURBATORS
MASTURBATORY
MATACHINAS
MATAGOURIS
MATCHBOARD
MATCHBOARDING
MATCHBOARDINGS
MATCHBOARDS
MATCHBOOKS
MATCHBOXES
MATCHLESSLY
MATCHLESSNESS
MATCHLESSNESSES
MATCHLOCKS
MATCHMAKER
MATCHMAKERS
MATCHMAKES
MATCHMAKING
MATCHMAKINGS
MATCHMARKED
MATCHMARKING
MATCHMARKS
MATCHPLAYS
MATCHSTICK
MATCHSTICKS
MATCHWOODS
MATELASSES
MATELLASSE
MATELLASSES
MATELOTTES
MATERFAMILIAS
MATERFAMILIASES
MATERIALISATION
MATERIALISE
MATERIALISED
MATERIALISER
MATERIALISERS
MATERIALISES
MATERIALISING
MATERIALISM
MATERIALISMS
MATERIALIST
MATERIALISTIC
MATERIALISTICAL
MATERIALISTS
MATERIALITIES
MATERIALITY
MATERIALIZATION
MATERIALIZE
MATERIALIZED
MATERIALIZER
MATERIALIZERS
MATERIALIZES
MATERIALIZING
MATERIALLY
MATERIALNESS
MATERIALNESSES
MATERNALISM
MATERNALISMS
MATERNALISTIC
MATERNALLY
MATERNITIES
MATEYNESSES
MATFELLONS
MATGRASSES
MATHEMATIC

MATHEMATICAL
MATHEMATICALLY
MATHEMATICIAN
MATHEMATICIANS
MATHEMATICISE
MATHEMATICISED
MATHEMATICISES
MATHEMATICISING
MATHEMATICISM
MATHEMATICISMS
MATHEMATICIZE
MATHEMATICIZED
MATHEMATICIZES
MATHEMATICIZING
MATHEMATICS
MATHEMATISATION
MATHEMATISE
MATHEMATISED
MATHEMATISES
MATHEMATISING
MATHEMATIZATION
MATHEMATIZE
MATHEMATIZED
MATHEMATIZES
MATHEMATIZING
MATINESSES
MATRESFAMILIAS
MATRIARCHAL
MATRIARCHALISM
MATRIARCHALISMS
MATRIARCHATE
MATRIARCHATES
MATRIARCHIC
MATRIARCHIES
MATRIARCHS
MATRIARCHY
MATRICIDAL
MATRICIDES
MATRICLINIC
MATRICLINOUS
MATRICULANT
MATRICULANTS
MATRICULAR
MATRICULAS
MATRICULATE
MATRICULATED
MATRICULATES
MATRICULATING
MATRICULATION
MATRICULATIONS
MATRICULATOR
MATRICULATORS
MATRICULATORY
MATRIFOCAL
MATRIFOCALITIES
MATRIFOCALITY
MATRILINEAL
MATRILINEALLY
MATRILINEAR
MATRILINIES
MATRILOCAL
MATRILOCALITIES
MATRILOCALITY
MATRILOCALLY
MATRIMONIAL
MATRIMONIALLY
MATRIMONIES
MATRIOSHKA
MATRIOSHKAS
MATRIOSHKI
MATROCLINAL
MATROCLINIC
MATROCLINIES
MATROCLINOUS
MATROCLINY
MATRONAGES
MATRONHOOD
MATRONHOODS
MATRONISED
MATRONISES
MATRONISING
MATRONIZED
MATRONIZES
MATRONIZING
MATRONLIER
MATRONLIEST
MATRONLINESS
MATRONLINESSES
MATRONSHIP
MATRONSHIPS
MATRONYMIC
MATRONYMICS
MATROYSHKA
MATROYSHKAS
MATRYOSHKA
MATRYOSHKAS
MATRYOSHKI
MATSUTAKES
MATTAMORES
MATTERIEST
MATTERLESS
MATTIFYING
MATTRASSES
MATTRESSES
MATURATING
MATURATION
MATURATIONAL
MATURATIONS
MATURATIVE
MATURENESS
MATURENESSES
MATURITIES
MATUTINALLY
MAUDLINISM
MAUDLINISMS
MAUDLINNESS
MAUDLINNESSES
MAULSTICKS
MAUMETRIES
MAUNDERERS
MAUNDERING
MAUNDERINGS
MAUSOLEUMS
MAVERICKED
MAVERICKING
MAVOURNEEN
MAVOURNEENS
MAVOURNINS
MAWKISHNESS
MAWKISHNESSES
MAWMETRIES
MAXIDRESSES
MAXILLARIES
MAXILLIPED
MAXILLIPEDARY
MAXILLIPEDE
MAXILLIPEDES
MAXILLIPEDS
MAXILLOFACIAL
MAXILLULAE
MAXIMALIST
MAXIMALISTS
MAXIMAPHILIES
MAXIMAPHILY
MAXIMATION
MAXIMATIONS
MAXIMISATION
MAXIMISATIONS
MAXIMISERS
MAXIMISING
MAXIMIZATION
MAXIMIZATIONS
MAXIMIZERS
MAXIMIZING
MAYFLOWERS
MAYONNAISE
MAYONNAISES
MAYORALTIES
MAYORESSES
MAYORSHIPS
MAYSTERDOME
MAYSTERDOMES
MAZARINADE
MAZARINADES
MAZEDNESSES
MAZINESSES
MEADOWIEST
MEADOWLAND
MEADOWLANDS
MEADOWLARK
MEADOWLARKS
MEADOWSWEET
MEADOWSWEETS
MEAGERNESS
MEAGERNESSES
MEAGRENESS
MEAGRENESSES
MEALINESSES
MEALYMOUTHED
MEANDERERS
MEANDERING
MEANDERINGLY
MEANDERINGS
MEANINGFUL
MEANINGFULLY
MEANINGFULNESS
MEANINGLESS
MEANINGLESSLY
MEANINGLESSNESS
MEANNESSES
MEANWHILES
MEASLINESS
MEASLINESSES
MEASURABILITIES
MEASURABILITY
MEASURABLE
MEASURABLENESS
MEASURABLY
MEASUREDLY
MEASUREDNESS
MEASUREDNESSES
MEASURELESS
MEASURELESSLY
MEASURELESSNESS
MEASUREMENT
MEASUREMENTS
MEASURINGS
MEATINESSES
MEATLOAVES
MEATPACKER
MEATPACKERS
MEATPACKING
MEATPACKINGS
MEATSCREEN
MEATSCREENS
MEATSPACES
MECAMYLAMINE
MECAMYLAMINES
MECHANICAL
MECHANICALISM
MECHANICALISMS
MECHANICALLY
MECHANICALNESS
MECHANICALS
MECHANICIAN
MECHANICIANS
MECHANISABLE
MECHANISATION
MECHANISATIONS
MECHANISED
MECHANISER
MECHANISERS
MECHANISES
MECHANISING
MECHANISMS
MECHANISTIC
MECHANISTICALLY
MECHANISTS
MECHANIZABLE
MECHANIZATION

MECHANIZATIONS
MECHANIZED
MECHANIZER
MECHANIZERS
MECHANIZES
MECHANIZING
MECHANOCHEMICAL
MECHANOMORPHISM
MECHANORECEPTOR
MECHANOTHERAPY
MECHATRONIC
MECHATRONICS
MECLIZINES
MECONOPSES
MECONOPSIS
MEDAILLONS
MEDALLIONED
MEDALLIONING
MEDALLIONS
MEDALLISTS
MEDALPLAYS
MEDDLESOME
MEDDLESOMELY
MEDDLESOMENESS
MEDDLINGLY
MEDEVACING
MEDEVACKED
MEDEVACKING
MEDIAEVALISM
MEDIAEVALISMS
MEDIAEVALIST
MEDIAEVALISTIC
MEDIAEVALISTS
MEDIAEVALLY
MEDIAEVALS
MEDIAGENIC
MEDIASTINA
MEDIASTINAL
MEDIASTINUM
MEDIATENESS
MEDIATENESSES
MEDIATIONAL
MEDIATIONS
MEDIATISATION
MEDIATISATIONS
MEDIATISED
MEDIATISES
MEDIATISING
MEDIATIZATION
MEDIATIZATIONS
MEDIATIZED
MEDIATIZES
MEDIATIZING
MEDIATORIAL
MEDIATORIALLY
MEDIATORSHIP
MEDIATORSHIPS
MEDIATRESS
MEDIATRESSES
MEDIATRICES
MEDIATRIXES
MEDICALISATION
MEDICALISATIONS
MEDICALISE
MEDICALISED
MEDICALISES
MEDICALISING
MEDICALIZATION
MEDICALIZATIONS
MEDICALIZE
MEDICALIZED
MEDICALIZES
MEDICALIZING
MEDICAMENT
MEDICAMENTAL
MEDICAMENTALLY
MEDICAMENTARY
MEDICAMENTED
MEDICAMENTING
MEDICAMENTOUS
MEDICAMENTS
MEDICASTER
MEDICASTERS
MEDICATING
MEDICATION
MEDICATIONS
MEDICATIVE
MEDICINABLE
MEDICINALLY
MEDICINALS
MEDICINERS
MEDICINING
MEDICOLEGAL
MEDIEVALISM
MEDIEVALISMS
MEDIEVALIST
MEDIEVALISTIC
MEDIEVALISTS
MEDIEVALLY
MEDIOCRACIES
MEDIOCRACY
MEDIOCRITIES
MEDIOCRITY
MEDITATING
MEDITATION
MEDITATIONS
MEDITATIVE
MEDITATIVELY
MEDITATIVENESS
MEDITATORS
MEDITERRANEAN
MEDIUMISTIC
MEDIUMSHIP
MEDIUMSHIPS
MEDIVACING
MEDIVACKED
MEDIVACKING
MEDRESSEHS
MEDULLATED
MEDULLOBLASTOMA
MEDUSIFORM
MEEKNESSES
MEERSCHAUM
MEERSCHAUMS
MEETINGHOUSE
MEETINGHOUSES
MEETNESSES
MEFLOQUINE
MEFLOQUINES
MEGACEPHALIC
MEGACEPHALIES
MEGACEPHALOUS
MEGACEPHALY
MEGACHURCH
MEGACHURCHES
MEGACITIES
MEGACORPORATION
MEGACURIES
MEGACYCLES
MEGADEATHS
MEGAFARADS
MEGAFAUNAE
MEGAFAUNAL
MEGAFAUNAS
MEGAFLORAE
MEGAFLORAS
MEGAGAMETE
MEGAGAMETES
MEGAGAMETOPHYTE
MEGAGAUSSES
MEGAHERBIVORE
MEGAHERBIVORES
MEGAHERTZES
MEGAJOULES
MEGAKARYOCYTE
MEGAKARYOCYTES
MEGAKARYOCYTIC
MEGALITHIC
MEGALITRES
MEGALOBLAST
MEGALOBLASTIC
MEGALOBLASTS
MEGALOCARDIA
MEGALOCARDIAS
MEGALOCEPHALIC
MEGALOCEPHALIES
MEGALOCEPHALOUS
MEGALOCEPHALY
MEGALODONS
MEGALOMANIA
MEGALOMANIAC
MEGALOMANIACAL
MEGALOMANIACS
MEGALOMANIAS
MEGALOMANIC
MEGALOPOLIS
MEGALOPOLISES
MEGALOPOLITAN
MEGALOPOLITANS
MEGALOPSES
MEGALOSAUR
MEGALOSAURI
MEGALOSAURIAN
MEGALOSAURIANS
MEGALOSAURS
MEGALOSAURUS
MEGANEWTON
MEGANEWTONS
MEGAPARSEC
MEGAPARSECS
MEGAPHONED
MEGAPHONES
MEGAPHONIC
MEGAPHONICALLY
MEGAPHONING
MEGAPHYLLS
MEGAPIXELS
MEGAPLEXES
MEGAPROJECT
MEGAPROJECTS
MEGAQUAKES
MEGASCOPES
MEGASCOPIC
MEGASCOPICALLY
MEGASPORANGIA
MEGASPORANGIUM
MEGASPORES
MEGASPORIC
MEGASPOROPHYLL
MEGASPOROPHYLLS
MEGASTORES
MEGASTORMS
MEGASTRUCTURE
MEGASTRUCTURES
MEGATECHNOLOGY
MEGATHERES
MEGATHERIAN
MEGATHRUST
MEGATONNAGE
MEGATONNAGES
MEGAVERTEBRATE
MEGAVERTEBRATES
MEGAVITAMIN
MEGAVITAMINS
MEIOFAUNAE
MEIOFAUNAL
MEIOFAUNAS
MEIOSPORES
MEIOTICALLY
MEITNERIUM
MEITNERIUMS
MEKOMETERS
MELACONITE
MELACONITES
MELALEUCAS
MELAMPODES
MELANAEMIA
MELANAEMIAS
MELANCHOLIA
MELANCHOLIAC

MELANCHOLIACS
MELANCHOLIAE
MELANCHOLIAS
MELANCHOLIC
MELANCHOLICALLY
MELANCHOLICS
MELANCHOLIES
MELANCHOLILY
MELANCHOLINESS
MELANCHOLIOUS
MELANCHOLY
MELANISATION
MELANISATIONS
MELANISING
MELANISTIC
MELANIZATION
MELANIZATIONS
MELANIZING
MELANOBLAST
MELANOBLASTS
MELANOCHROI
MELANOCHROIC
MELANOCHROOUS
MELANOCYTE
MELANOCYTES
MELANOGENESES
MELANOGENESIS
MELANOMATA
MELANOPHORE
MELANOPHORES
MELANOSITIES
MELANOSITY
MELANOSOME
MELANOSOMES
MELANOTROPIN
MELANOTROPINS
MELANTERITE
MELANTERITES
MELANURIAS
MELAPHYRES
MELASTOMACEOUS
MELASTOMES
MELATONINS
MELIACEOUS
MELICOTTON
MELICOTTONS
MELIORABLE
MELIORATED
MELIORATES
MELIORATING
MELIORATION
MELIORATIONS
MELIORATIVE
MELIORATIVES
MELIORATOR
MELIORATORS
MELIORISMS
MELIORISTIC
MELIORISTS
MELIORITIES
MELIPHAGOUS
MELISMATIC
MELLIFEROUS
MELLIFICATION
MELLIFICATIONS
MELLIFLUENCE
MELLIFLUENCES
MELLIFLUENT
MELLIFLUENTLY
MELLIFLUOUS
MELLIFLUOUSLY
MELLIFLUOUSNESS
MELLIPHAGOUS
MELLIVOROUS
MELLOPHONE
MELLOPHONES
MELLOTRONS
MELLOWIEST
MELLOWNESS
MELLOWNESSES
MELLOWSPEAK
MELLOWSPEAKS
MELOCOTONS
MELOCOTOON
MELOCOTOONS
MELODICALLY
MELODIOUSLY
MELODIOUSNESS
MELODIOUSNESSES
MELODISERS
MELODISING
MELODIZERS
MELODIZING
MELODRAMAS
MELODRAMATIC
MELODRAMATICS
MELODRAMATISE
MELODRAMATISED
MELODRAMATISES
MELODRAMATISING
MELODRAMATIST
MELODRAMATISTS
MELODRAMATIZE
MELODRAMATIZED
MELODRAMATIZES
MELODRAMATIZING
MELODRAMES
MELOMANIAC
MELOMANIACS
MELOMANIAS
MELONGENES
MELOXICAMS
MELPHALANS
MELTABILITIES
MELTABILITY
MELTINGNESS
MELTINGNESSES
MELTWATERS
MELUNGEONS
MEMBERLESS
MEMBERSHIP
MEMBERSHIPS
MEMBRANACEOUS
MEMBRANEOUS
MEMBRANOUS
MEMBRANOUSLY
MEMOIRISMS
MEMOIRISTS
MEMORABILE
MEMORABILIA
MEMORABILITIES
MEMORABILITY
MEMORABLENESS
MEMORABLENESSES
MEMORANDUM
MEMORANDUMS
MEMORATIVE
MEMORIALISATION
MEMORIALISE
MEMORIALISED
MEMORIALISER
MEMORIALISERS
MEMORIALISES
MEMORIALISING
MEMORIALIST
MEMORIALISTS
MEMORIALIZATION
MEMORIALIZE
MEMORIALIZED
MEMORIALIZER
MEMORIALIZERS
MEMORIALIZES
MEMORIALIZING
MEMORIALLY
MEMORISABLE
MEMORISATION
MEMORISATIONS
MEMORISERS
MEMORISING
MEMORIZABLE
MEMORIZATION
MEMORIZATIONS
MEMORIZERS
MEMORIZING
MEMORIZINGS
MENACINGLY
MENADIONES
MENAGERIES
MENAQUINONE
MENAQUINONES
MENARCHEAL
MENARCHIAL
MENDACIOUS
MENDACIOUSLY
MENDACIOUSNESS
MENDACITIES
MENDELEVIUM
MENDELEVIUMS
MENDICANCIES
MENDICANCY
MENDICANTS
MENDICITIES
MENINGIOMA
MENINGIOMAS
MENINGIOMATA
MENINGITIC
MENINGITIDES
MENINGITIS
MENINGITISES
MENINGOCELE
MENINGOCELES
MENINGOCOCCAL
MENINGOCOCCI
MENINGOCOCCIC
MENINGOCOCCUS
MENISCECTOMIES
MENISCECTOMY
MENISCUSES
MENISPERMACEOUS
MENISPERMUM
MENISPERMUMS
MENOLOGIES
MENOMINEES
MENOPAUSAL
MENOPAUSES
MENOPAUSIC
MENOPOLISES
MENORRHAGIA
MENORRHAGIAS
MENORRHAGIC
MENORRHEAS
MENORRHOEA
MENORRHOEAS
MENSCHIEST
MENSERVANTS
MENSTRUALLY
MENSTRUATE
MENSTRUATED
MENSTRUATES
MENSTRUATING
MENSTRUATION
MENSTRUATIONS
MENSTRUOUS
MENSTRUUMS
MENSURABILITIES
MENSURABILITY
MENSURABLE
MENSURATION
MENSURATIONAL
MENSURATIONS
MENSURATIVE
MENTALESES
MENTALISMS
MENTALISTIC
MENTALISTICALLY
MENTALISTS
MENTALITIES
MENTATIONS
MENTHACEOUS
MENTHOLATED

MENTICIDES
MENTIONABLE
MENTIONERS
MENTIONING
MENTONNIERE
MENTONNIERES
MENTORINGS
MENTORSHIP
MENTORSHIPS
MENUISIERS
MEPACRINES
MEPERIDINE
MEPERIDINES
MEPHITICAL
MEPHITICALLY
MEPHITISES
MEPHITISMS
MEPROBAMATE
MEPROBAMATES
MERBROMINS
MERCANTILE
MERCANTILISM
MERCANTILISMS
MERCANTILIST
MERCANTILISTIC
MERCANTILISTS
MERCAPTANS
MERCAPTIDE
MERCAPTIDES
MERCAPTOPURINE
MERCAPTOPURINES
MERCENARIES
MERCENARILY
MERCENARINESS
MERCENARINESSES
MERCENARISM
MERCENARISMS
MERCERISATION
MERCERISATIONS
MERCERISED
MERCERISER
MERCERISERS
MERCERISES
MERCERISING
MERCERIZATION
MERCERIZATIONS
MERCERIZED
MERCERIZER
MERCERIZERS
MERCERIZES
MERCERIZING
MERCHANDISE
MERCHANDISED
MERCHANDISER
MERCHANDISERS
MERCHANDISES
MERCHANDISING
MERCHANDISINGS
MERCHANDIZE
MERCHANDIZED
MERCHANDIZER
MERCHANDIZERS
MERCHANDIZES
MERCHANDIZING
MERCHANDIZINGS
MERCHANTABILITY
MERCHANTABLE
MERCHANTED
MERCHANTING
MERCHANTINGS
MERCHANTLIKE
MERCHANTMAN
MERCHANTMEN
MERCHANTRIES
MERCHANTRY
MERCHILDREN
MERCIFULLY
MERCIFULNESS
MERCIFULNESSES
MERCIFYING
MERCILESSLY
MERCILESSNESS
MERCILESSNESSES
MERCURATED
MERCURATES
MERCURATING
MERCURATION
MERCURATIONS
MERCURIALISE
MERCURIALISED
MERCURIALISES
MERCURIALISING
MERCURIALISM
MERCURIALISMS
MERCURIALIST
MERCURIALISTS
MERCURIALITIES
MERCURIALITY
MERCURIALIZE
MERCURIALIZED
MERCURIALIZES
MERCURIALIZING
MERCURIALLY
MERCURIALNESS
MERCURIALNESSES
MERCURIALS
MERCURISED
MERCURISES
MERCURISING
MERCURIZED
MERCURIZES
MERCURIZING
MERDIVOROUS
MEREOLOGICAL
MEREOLOGIES
MERESTONES
MERETRICIOUS
MERETRICIOUSLY
MERGANSERS
MERIDIONAL
MERIDIONALITIES
MERIDIONALITY
MERIDIONALLY
MERIDIONALS
MERISTEMATIC
MERISTICALLY
MERITOCRACIES
MERITOCRACY
MERITOCRAT
MERITOCRATIC
MERITOCRATS
MERITORIOUS
MERITORIOUSLY
MERITORIOUSNESS
MERMAIDENS
MEROBLASTIC
MEROBLASTICALLY
MEROGENESES
MEROGENESIS
MEROGENETIC
MEROGONIES
MEROMORPHIC
MEROMYOSIN
MEROMYOSINS
MERONYMIES
MEROPIDANS
MEROPLANKTON
MEROPLANKTONS
MEROZOITES
MERPEOPLES
MERRIMENTS
MERRINESSES
MERRYMAKER
MERRYMAKERS
MERRYMAKING
MERRYMAKINGS
MERRYTHOUGHT
MERRYTHOUGHTS
MERVEILLEUSE
MERVEILLEUSES
MERVEILLEUX
MERVEILLEUXES
MESALLIANCE
MESALLIANCES
MESATICEPHALIC
MESATICEPHALIES
MESATICEPHALOUS
MESATICEPHALY
MESCALINES
MESCALISMS
MESDEMOISELLES
MESENCEPHALA
MESENCEPHALIC
MESENCEPHALON
MESENCEPHALONS
MESENCHYMAL
MESENCHYMATOUS
MESENCHYME
MESENCHYMES
MESENTERIAL
MESENTERIC
MESENTERIES
MESENTERITIS
MESENTERITISES
MESENTERON
MESENTERONIC
MESHUGAASEN
MESHUGASEN
MESHUGGENAH
MESHUGGENAHS
MESHUGGENEH
MESHUGGENEHS
MESHUGGENER
MESHUGGENERS
MESITYLENE
MESITYLENES
MESMERICAL
MESMERICALLY
MESMERISATION
MESMERISATIONS
MESMERISED
MESMERISER
MESMERISERS
MESMERISES
MESMERISING
MESMERISMS
MESMERISTS
MESMERIZATION
MESMERIZATIONS
MESMERIZED
MESMERIZER
MESMERIZERS
MESMERIZES
MESMERIZING
MESNALTIES
MESOAMERICAN
MESOBENTHOS
MESOBENTHOSES
MESOBLASTIC
MESOBLASTS
MESOCEPHALIC
MESOCEPHALICS
MESOCEPHALIES
MESOCEPHALISM
MESOCEPHALISMS
MESOCEPHALOUS
MESOCEPHALY
MESOCRANIES
MESOCRATIC
MESOCYCLONE
MESOCYCLONES
MESODERMAL
MESODERMIC
MESOGASTRIA
MESOGASTRIC
MESOGASTRIUM
MESOGLOEAS
MESOGNATHIES
MESOGNATHISM
MESOGNATHISMS

MESOGNATHOUS
MESOGNATHY
MESOHIPPUS
MESOHIPPUSES
MESOKURTIC
MESOMERISM
MESOMERISMS
MESOMORPHIC
MESOMORPHIES
MESOMORPHISM
MESOMORPHISMS
MESOMORPHOUS
MESOMORPHS
MESOMORPHY
MESONEPHRIC
MESONEPHROI
MESONEPHROS
MESONEPHROSES
MESOPAUSES
MESOPELAGIC
MESOPHILES
MESOPHILIC
MESOPHYLLIC
MESOPHYLLOUS
MESOPHYLLS
MESOPHYTES
MESOPHYTIC
MESOSCAPHE
MESOSCAPHES
MESOSPHERE
MESOSPHERES
MESOSPHERIC
MESOTHELIA
MESOTHELIAL
MESOTHELIOMA
MESOTHELIOMAS
MESOTHELIOMATA
MESOTHELIUM
MESOTHELIUMS
MESOTHERAPIES
MESOTHERAPY
MESOTHORACES
MESOTHORACIC
MESOTHORAX
MESOTHORAXES
MESOTHORIUM
MESOTHORIUMS
MESOTROPHIC
MESQUINERIE
MESQUINERIES
MESSAGINGS
MESSALINES
MESSEIGNEURS
MESSENGERED
MESSENGERING
MESSENGERS
MESSIAHSHIP
MESSIAHSHIPS
MESSIANICALLY
MESSIANISM
MESSIANISMS
MESSINESSES
MESTRANOLS
METABISULPHITE
METABISULPHITES
METABOLICALLY
METABOLIES
METABOLISABLE
METABOLISE
METABOLISED
METABOLISES
METABOLISING
METABOLISM
METABOLISMS
METABOLITE
METABOLITES
METABOLIZABLE
METABOLIZE
METABOLIZED
METABOLIZES
METABOLIZING
METABOLOME
METABOLOMES
METABOLOMICS
METABOTROPIC
METACARPAL
METACARPALS
METACARPUS
METACENTER
METACENTERS
METACENTRE
METACENTRES
METACENTRIC
METACENTRICS
METACERCARIA
METACERCARIAE
METACERCARIAL
METACERCARIAS
METACHROMATIC
METACHROMATISM
METACHROMATISMS
METACHRONISM
METACHRONISMS
METACHROSES
METACHROSIS
METACINNABARITE
METACOGNITION
METACOGNITIONS
METACOMPUTER
METACOMPUTERS
METACOMPUTING
METACOMPUTINGS
METAETHICAL
METAETHICS
METAFEMALE
METAFEMALES
METAFICTION
METAFICTIONAL
METAFICTIONIST
METAFICTIONISTS
METAFICTIONS
METAGALACTIC
METAGALAXIES
METAGALAXY
METAGENESES
METAGENESIS
METAGENETIC
METAGENETICALLY
METAGNATHISM
METAGNATHISMS
METAGNATHOUS
METAGRABOLISE
METAGRABOLISED
METAGRABOLISES
METAGRABOLISING
METAGRABOLIZE
METAGRABOLIZED
METAGRABOLIZES
METAGRABOLIZING
METAGROBOLISE
METAGROBOLISED
METAGROBOLISES
METAGROBOLISING
METAGROBOLIZE
METAGROBOLIZED
METAGROBOLIZES
METAGROBOLIZING
METALANGUAGE
METALANGUAGES
METALDEHYDE
METALDEHYDES
METALEPSES
METALEPSIS
METALEPTIC
METALEPTICAL
METALHEADS
METALINGUISTIC
METALINGUISTICS
METALISATION
METALISATIONS
METALISING
METALIZATION
METALIZATIONS
METALIZING
METALLICALLY
METALLIDING
METALLIDINGS
METALLIFEROUS
METALLINGS
METALLISATION
METALLISATIONS
METALLISED
METALLISES
METALLISING
METALLISTS
METALLIZATION
METALLIZATIONS
METALLIZED
METALLIZES
METALLIZING
METALLOCENE
METALLOCENES
METALLOGENETIC
METALLOGENIC
METALLOGENIES
METALLOGENY
METALLOGRAPHER
METALLOGRAPHERS
METALLOGRAPHIC
METALLOGRAPHIES
METALLOGRAPHIST
METALLOGRAPHY
METALLOIDAL
METALLOIDS
METALLOPHONE
METALLOPHONES
METALLURGIC
METALLURGICAL
METALLURGICALLY
METALLURGIES
METALLURGIST
METALLURGISTS
METALLURGY
METALMARKS
METALSMITH
METALSMITHS
METALWARES
METALWORKER
METALWORKERS
METALWORKING
METALWORKINGS
METALWORKS
METAMATERIAL
METAMATERIALS
METAMATHEMATICS
METAMERICALLY
METAMERISM
METAMERISMS
METAMICTISATION
METAMICTIZATION
METAMORPHIC
METAMORPHICALLY
METAMORPHISM
METAMORPHISMS
METAMORPHIST
METAMORPHISTS
METAMORPHOSE
METAMORPHOSED
METAMORPHOSES
METAMORPHOSING
METAMORPHOSIS
METAMORPHOUS
METANALYSES
METANALYSIS
METANARRATIVE
METANARRATIVES
METANEPHRIC
METANEPHROI
METANEPHROS
METAPERIODIC

METAPHASES
METAPHORIC
METAPHORICAL
METAPHORICALLY
METAPHORIST
METAPHORISTS
METAPHOSPHATE
METAPHOSPHATES
METAPHOSPHORIC
METAPHRASE
METAPHRASED
METAPHRASES
METAPHRASING
METAPHRASIS
METAPHRAST
METAPHRASTIC
METAPHRASTICAL
METAPHRASTS
METAPHYSIC
METAPHYSICAL
METAPHYSICALLY
METAPHYSICIAN
METAPHYSICIANS
METAPHYSICISE
METAPHYSICISED
METAPHYSICISES
METAPHYSICISING
METAPHYSICIST
METAPHYSICISTS
METAPHYSICIZE
METAPHYSICIZED
METAPHYSICIZES
METAPHYSICIZING
METAPHYSICS
METAPLASES
METAPLASIA
METAPLASIAS
METAPLASIS
METAPLASMIC
METAPLASMS
METAPLASTIC
METAPOLITICAL
METAPOLITICS
METAPROTEIN
METAPROTEINS
METAPSYCHIC
METAPSYCHICAL
METAPSYCHICS
METAPSYCHOLOGY
METARCHONS
METASEQUOIA
METASEQUOIAS
METASILICATE
METASILICATES
METASILICIC
METASOMATA
METASOMATIC
METASOMATISM
METASOMATISMS
METASOMATOSES
METASOMATOSIS
METASTABILITIES
METASTABILITY
METASTABLE
METASTABLES
METASTABLY
METASTASES
METASTASIS
METASTASISE
METASTASISED
METASTASISES
METASTASISING
METASTASIZE
METASTASIZED
METASTASIZES
METASTASIZING
METASTATIC
METASTATICALLY
METATARSAL
METATARSALS
METATARSUS
METATHEORETICAL
METATHEORIES
METATHEORY
METATHERIAN
METATHERIANS
METATHESES
METATHESIS
METATHESISE
METATHESISED
METATHESISES
METATHESISING
METATHESIZE
METATHESIZED
METATHESIZES
METATHESIZING
METATHETIC
METATHETICAL
METATHETICALLY
METATHORACES
METATHORACIC
METATHORAX
METATHORAXES
METATUNGSTIC
METAVANADIC
METAVERSES
METAXYLEMS
METECDYSES
METECDYSIS
METEMPIRIC
METEMPIRICAL
METEMPIRICALLY
METEMPIRICISM
METEMPIRICISMS
METEMPIRICIST
METEMPIRICISTS
METEMPIRICS
METEMPSYCHOSES
METEMPSYCHOSIS
METEMPSYCHOSIST
METENCEPHALA
METENCEPHALIC
METENCEPHALON
METENCEPHALONS
METEORICALLY
METEORISMS
METEORISTS
METEORITAL
METEORITES
METEORITIC
METEORITICAL
METEORITICIST
METEORITICISTS
METEORITICS
METEOROGRAM
METEOROGRAMS
METEOROGRAPH
METEOROGRAPHIC
METEOROGRAPHS
METEOROIDAL
METEOROIDS
METEOROLITE
METEOROLITES
METEOROLOGIC
METEOROLOGICAL
METEOROLOGIES
METEOROLOGIST
METEOROLOGISTS
METEOROLOGY
METERSTICK
METERSTICKS
METESTICKS
METESTROUS
METESTRUSES
METFORMINS
METHACRYLATE
METHACRYLATES
METHACRYLIC
METHADONES
METHAEMOGLOBIN
METHAEMOGLOBINS
METHAMPHETAMINE
METHANAMIDE
METHANAMIDES
METHANATION
METHANATIONS
METHANOMETER
METHANOMETERS
METHANOYLS
METHAQUALONE
METHAQUALONES
METHEDRINE
METHEDRINES
METHEGLINS
METHEMOGLOBIN
METHEMOGLOBINS
METHENAMINE
METHENAMINES
METHICILLIN
METHICILLINS
METHINKETH
METHIONINE
METHIONINES
METHODICAL
METHODICALLY
METHODICALNESS
METHODISATION
METHODISATIONS
METHODISED
METHODISER
METHODISERS
METHODISES
METHODISING
METHODISMS
METHODISTIC
METHODISTS
METHODIZATION
METHODIZATIONS
METHODIZED
METHODIZER
METHODIZERS
METHODIZES
METHODIZING
METHODOLOGICAL
METHODOLOGIES
METHODOLOGIST
METHODOLOGISTS
METHODOLOGY
METHOMANIA
METHOMANIAS
METHOTREXATE
METHOTREXATES
METHOXIDES
METHOXYBENZENE
METHOXYBENZENES
METHOXYCHLOR
METHOXYCHLORS
METHOXYFLURANE
METHOXYFLURANES
METHYLAMINE
METHYLAMINES
METHYLASES
METHYLATED
METHYLATES
METHYLATING
METHYLATION
METHYLATIONS
METHYLATOR
METHYLATORS
METHYLCELLULOSE
METHYLDOPA
METHYLDOPAS
METHYLENES
METHYLMERCURIES
METHYLMERCURY
METHYLPHENIDATE
METHYLPHENOL
METHYLPHENOLS
METHYLTHIONINE
METHYLTHIONINES

METHYLXANTHINE
METHYLXANTHINES
METHYSERGIDE
METHYSERGIDES
METICULOSITIES
METICULOSITY
METICULOUS
METICULOUSLY
METICULOUSNESS
METOCLOPRAMIDE
METOCLOPRAMIDES
METOESTROUS
METOESTRUS
METOESTRUSES
METONYMICAL
METONYMICALLY
METONYMIES
METOPOSCOPIC
METOPOSCOPICAL
METOPOSCOPIES
METOPOSCOPIST
METOPOSCOPISTS
METOPOSCOPY
METRALGIAS
METRESTICK
METRESTICKS
METRICALLY
METRICATED
METRICATES
METRICATING
METRICATION
METRICATIONS
METRICIANS
METRICISED
METRICISES
METRICISING
METRICISMS
METRICISTS
METRICIZED
METRICIZES
METRICIZING
METRIFICATION
METRIFICATIONS
METRIFIERS
METRIFONATE
METRIFONATES
METRIFYING
METRITISES
METROLOGIC
METROLOGICAL
METROLOGICALLY
METROLOGIES
METROLOGIST
METROLOGISTS
METROMANIA
METROMANIAS
METRONIDAZOLE
METRONIDAZOLES
METRONOMES
METRONOMIC
METRONOMICAL
METRONOMICALLY
METRONYMIC
METRONYMICS
METROPLEXES
METROPOLIS
METROPOLISES
METROPOLITAN
METROPOLITANATE
METROPOLITANISE
METROPOLITANISM
METROPOLITANIZE
METROPOLITANS
METROPOLITICAL
METRORRHAGIA
METRORRHAGIAS
METROSEXUAL
METROSEXUALS
METROSTYLE
METROSTYLES
METTLESOME
METTLESOMENESS
MEZCALINES
MEZZALUNAS
MEZZANINES
MEZZOTINTED
MEZZOTINTER
MEZZOTINTERS
MEZZOTINTING
MEZZOTINTO
MEZZOTINTOS
MEZZOTINTS
MIAROLITIC
MIASMATICAL
MIASMATOUS
MIASMICALLY
MICRIFYING
MICROAEROPHILE
MICROAEROPHILES
MICROAEROPHILIC
MICROAGGRESSION
MICROAMPERE
MICROAMPERES
MICROANALYSES
MICROANALYSIS
MICROANALYST
MICROANALYSTS
MICROANALYTIC
MICROANALYTICAL
MICROANATOMICAL
MICROANATOMIES
MICROANATOMY
MICROARRAY
MICROARRAYS
MICROBALANCE
MICROBALANCES
MICROBAROGRAPH
MICROBAROGRAPHS
MICROBEADS
MICROBEAMS
MICROBIOLOGIC
MICROBIOLOGICAL
MICROBIOLOGIES
MICROBIOLOGIST
MICROBIOLOGISTS
MICROBIOLOGY
MICROBIOME
MICROBIOMES
MICROBIOTA
MICROBIOTAS
MICROBLOGGER
MICROBLOGGERS
MICROBLOGGING
MICROBLOGGINGS
MICROBLOGS
MICROBREWER
MICROBREWERIES
MICROBREWERS
MICROBREWERY
MICROBREWING
MICROBREWINGS
MICROBREWS
MICROBUBBLES
MICROBURST
MICROBURSTS
MICROBUSES
MICROBUSSES
MICROCAPSULE
MICROCAPSULES
MICROCARDS
MICROCASSETTE
MICROCASSETTES
MICROCELEBRITY
MICROCEPHAL
MICROCEPHALIC
MICROCEPHALICS
MICROCEPHALIES
MICROCEPHALOUS
MICROCEPHALS
MICROCEPHALY
MICROCHEMICAL
MICROCHEMISTRY
MICROCHIPPED
MICROCHIPPING
MICROCHIPS
MICROCIRCUIT
MICROCIRCUITRY
MICROCIRCUITS
MICROCLIMATE
MICROCLIMATES
MICROCLIMATIC
MICROCLINE
MICROCLINES
MICROCOCCAL
MICROCOCCI
MICROCOCCUS
MICROCODES
MICROCOMPONENT
MICROCOMPONENTS
MICROCOMPUTER
MICROCOMPUTERS
MICROCOMPUTING
MICROCOMPUTINGS
MICROCOPIED
MICROCOPIES
MICROCOPYING
MICROCOPYINGS
MICROCOSMIC
MICROCOSMICAL
MICROCOSMICALLY
MICROCOSMOS
MICROCOSMOSES
MICROCOSMS
MICROCRACK
MICROCRACKED
MICROCRACKING
MICROCRACKINGS
MICROCRACKS
MICROCRYSTAL
MICROCRYSTALS
MICROCULTURAL
MICROCULTURE
MICROCULTURES
MICROCURIE
MICROCURIES
MICROCYTES
MICROCYTIC
MICRODETECTION
MICRODETECTIONS
MICRODETECTOR
MICRODETECTORS
MICRODISSECTION
MICRODONTOUS
MICRODRIVE
MICRODRIVES
MICRODRONE
MICRODRONES
MICROEARTHQUAKE
MICROECONOMIC
MICROECONOMICS
MICROELECTRODE
MICROELECTRODES
MICROELECTRONIC
MICROELEMENT
MICROELEMENTS
MICROEVOLUTION
MICROEVOLUTIONS
MICROFARAD
MICROFARADS
MICROFAUNA
MICROFAUNAE
MICROFAUNAL
MICROFAUNAS
MICROFELSITIC
MICROFIBER
MICROFIBERS
MICROFIBRE
MICROFIBRES
MICROFIBRIL
MICROFIBRILLAR

M

MICROFIBRILS
MICROFICHE
MICROFICHES
MICROFILAMENT
MICROFILAMENTS
MICROFILARIA
MICROFILARIAE
MICROFILARIAL
MICROFILING
MICROFILINGS
MICROFILMABLE
MICROFILMED
MICROFILMER
MICROFILMERS
MICROFILMING
MICROFILMS
MICROFILTER
MICROFILTERS
MICROFLOPPIES
MICROFLOPPY
MICROFLORA
MICROFLORAE
MICROFLORAL
MICROFLORAS
MICROFORMS
MICROFOSSIL
MICROFOSSILS
MICROFUNGI
MICROFUNGUS
MICROFUNGUSES
MICROGAMETE
MICROGAMETES
MICROGAMETOCYTE
MICROGENERATION
MICROGLIAS
MICROGRAMS
MICROGRANITE
MICROGRANITES
MICROGRANITIC
MICROGRAPH
MICROGRAPHED
MICROGRAPHER
MICROGRAPHERS
MICROGRAPHIC
MICROGRAPHICS
MICROGRAPHIES
MICROGRAPHING
MICROGRAPHS
MICROGRAPHY
MICROGRAVITIES
MICROGRAVITY
MICROGREENS
MICROGROOVE
MICROGROOVES
MICROHABITAT
MICROHABITATS
MICROIMAGE
MICROIMAGES
MICROINCHES
MICROINJECT
MICROINJECTED
MICROINJECTING
MICROINJECTION
MICROINJECTIONS
MICROINJECTS
MICROLIGHT
MICROLIGHTING
MICROLIGHTINGS
MICROLIGHTS
MICROLITER
MICROLITERS
MICROLITES
MICROLITHIC
MICROLITHS
MICROLITIC
MICROLITRE
MICROLITRES
MICROLOANS
MICROLOGIC
MICROLOGICAL
MICROLOGICALLY
MICROLOGIES
MICROLOGIST
MICROLOGISTS
MICROLUCES
MICROLUXES
MICROMANAGE
MICROMANAGED
MICROMANAGEMENT
MICROMANAGER
MICROMANAGERS
MICROMANAGES
MICROMANAGING
MICROMARKETING
MICROMARKETINGS
MICROMERES
MICROMESHES
MICROMETEORITE
MICROMETEORITES
MICROMETEORITIC
MICROMETEOROID
MICROMETEOROIDS
MICROMETER
MICROMETERS
MICROMETHOD
MICROMETHODS
MICROMETRE
MICROMETRES
MICROMETRIC
MICROMETRICAL
MICROMETRIES
MICROMETRY
MICROMICROCURIE
MICROMICROFARAD
MICROMILLIMETRE
MICROMINIATURE
MICROMINIS
MICROMOLAR
MICROMOLES
MICROMORPHOLOGY
MICROMORTS
MICRONATION
MICRONATIONS
MICRONEEDLE
MICRONEEDLES
MICRONISATION
MICRONISATIONS
MICRONISED
MICRONISES
MICRONISING
MICRONIZATION
MICRONIZATIONS
MICRONIZED
MICRONIZES
MICRONIZING
MICRONUCLEI
MICRONUCLEUS
MICRONUCLEUSES
MICRONUTRIENT
MICRONUTRIENTS
MICROORGANISM
MICROORGANISMS
MICROPARASITE
MICROPARASITES
MICROPARASITIC
MICROPARTICLE
MICROPARTICLES
MICROPARTIES
MICROPARTY
MICROPAYMENT
MICROPAYMENTS
MICROPEGMATITE
MICROPEGMATITES
MICROPEGMATITIC
MICROPHAGE
MICROPHAGES
MICROPHAGOUS
MICROPHONE
MICROPHONES
MICROPHONIC
MICROPHONICS
MICROPHOTOGRAPH
MICROPHOTOMETER
MICROPHOTOMETRY
MICROPHYLL
MICROPHYLLOUS
MICROPHYLLS
MICROPHYSICAL
MICROPHYSICALLY
MICROPHYSICIST
MICROPHYSICISTS
MICROPHYSICS
MICROPHYTE
MICROPHYTES
MICROPHYTIC
MICROPIPET
MICROPIPETS
MICROPIPETTE
MICROPIPETTES
MICROPLANKTON
MICROPLANKTONS
MICROPLASTIC
MICROPLASTICS
MICROPOLIS
MICROPOLISES
MICROPORES
MICROPOROSITIES
MICROPOROSITY
MICROPOROUS
MICROPOWER
MICROPOWERS
MICROPRINT
MICROPRINTED
MICROPRINTING
MICROPRINTINGS
MICROPRINTS
MICROPRISM
MICROPRISMS
MICROPROBE
MICROPROBES
MICROPROCESSING
MICROPROCESSOR
MICROPROCESSORS
MICROPROGRAM
MICROPROGRAMS
MICROPROJECTION
MICROPROJECTOR
MICROPROJECTORS
MICROPSIAS
MICROPTEROUS
MICROPUBLISHER
MICROPUBLISHERS
MICROPUBLISHING
MICROPULSATION
MICROPULSATIONS
MICROPUMPS
MICROPUNCTURE
MICROPUNCTURES
MICROPYLAR
MICROPYLES
MICROPYROMETER
MICROPYROMETERS
MICROQUAKE
MICROQUAKES
MICRORADIOGRAPH
MICROREADER
MICROREADERS
MICROSATELLITE
MICROSATELLITES
MICROSCALE
MICROSCALES
MICROSCOPE
MICROSCOPES
MICROSCOPIC
MICROSCOPICAL
MICROSCOPICALLY
MICROSCOPIES
MICROSCOPIST
MICROSCOPISTS
MICROSCOPY

MICROSECOND
MICROSECONDS
MICROSEISM
MICROSEISMIC
MICROSEISMICAL
MICROSEISMICITY
MICROSEISMS
MICROSITES
MICROSKIRT
MICROSKIRTS
MICROSLEEP
MICROSLEEPS
MICROSMATIC
MICROSOMAL
MICROSOMES
MICROSPECIES
MICROSPHERE
MICROSPHERES
MICROSPHERICAL
MICROSPORANGIA
MICROSPORANGIUM
MICROSPORE
MICROSPORES
MICROSPORIC
MICROSPORIDIAN
MICROSPOROCYTE
MICROSPOROCYTES
MICROSPOROPHYLL
MICROSPOROUS
MICROSTATE
MICROSTATES
MICROSTOMATOUS
MICROSTOMOUS
MICROSTRUCTURAL
MICROSTRUCTURE
MICROSTRUCTURES
MICROSURGEON
MICROSURGEONS
MICROSURGERIES
MICROSURGERY
MICROSURGICAL
MICROSWITCH
MICROSWITCHES
MICROTECHNIC
MICROTECHNICS
MICROTECHNIQUE
MICROTECHNIQUES
MICROTECHNOLOGY
MICROTOMES
MICROTOMIC
MICROTOMICAL
MICROTOMIES
MICROTOMIST
MICROTOMISTS
MICROTONAL
MICROTONALITIES
MICROTONALITY
MICROTONALLY
MICROTONES
MICROTUBES
MICROTUBULAR
MICROTUBULE
MICROTUBULES
MICROTUNNELLING
MICROVASCULAR
MICROVILLAR
MICROVILLI
MICROVILLOUS
MICROVILLUS
MICROVOLTS
MICROWATTS
MICROWAVABLE
MICROWAVEABLE
MICROWAVED
MICROWAVES
MICROWAVING
MICROWIRES
MICROWORLD
MICROWORLDS
MICROWRITER
MICROWRITERS
MICRURGIES
MICTURATED
MICTURATES
MICTURATING
MICTURITION
MICTURITIONS
MIDDELMANNETJIE
MIDDELSKOT
MIDDELSKOTS
MIDDENSTEAD
MIDDENSTEADS
MIDDLEBREAKER
MIDDLEBREAKERS
MIDDLEBROW
MIDDLEBROWED
MIDDLEBROWISM
MIDDLEBROWISMS
MIDDLEBROWS
MIDDLEBUSTER
MIDDLEBUSTERS
MIDDLEMOST
MIDDLEWARE
MIDDLEWARES
MIDDLEWEIGHT
MIDDLEWEIGHTS
MIDDLINGLY
MIDFIELDER
MIDFIELDERS
MIDIBUSSES
MIDINETTES
MIDISKIRTS
MIDLANDERS
MIDLATITUDE
MIDLATITUDES
MIDLITTORAL
MIDLITTORALS
MIDNIGHTLY
MIDRASHOTH
MIDSAGITTAL
MIDSECTION
MIDSECTIONS
MIDSHIPMAN
MIDSHIPMATE
MIDSHIPMATES
MIDSHIPMEN
MIDSTORIES
MIDSTREAMS
MIDSUMMERS
MIDWATCHES
MIDWESTERN
MIDWIFERIES
MIDWINTERS
MIFEPRISTONE
MIFEPRISTONES
MIFFINESSES
MIGHTINESS
MIGHTINESSES
MIGMATITES
MIGNONETTE
MIGNONETTES
MIGRAINEUR
MIGRAINEURS
MIGRAINOUS
MIGRATIONAL
MIGRATIONIST
MIGRATIONISTS
MIGRATIONS
MILDEWIEST
MILDNESSES
MILEOMETER
MILEOMETERS
MILESTONES
MILITANCES
MILITANCIES
MILITANTLY
MILITANTNESS
MILITANTNESSES
MILITARIES
MILITARILY
MILITARISATION
MILITARISATIONS
MILITARISE
MILITARISED
MILITARISES
MILITARISING
MILITARISM
MILITARISMS
MILITARIST
MILITARISTIC
MILITARISTS
MILITARIZATION
MILITARIZATIONS
MILITARIZE
MILITARIZED
MILITARIZES
MILITARIZING
MILITATING
MILITATION
MILITATIONS
MILITIAMAN
MILITIAMEN
MILKFISHES
MILKINESSES
MILKSHAKES
MILKSOPISM
MILKSOPISMS
MILKSOPPIER
MILKSOPPIEST
MILKSOPPING
MILKTOASTS
MILLBOARDS
MILLEFEUILLE
MILLEFEUILLES
MILLEFIORI
MILLEFIORIS
MILLEFLEUR
MILLEFLEURS
MILLENARIAN
MILLENARIANISM
MILLENARIANISMS
MILLENARIANS
MILLENARIES
MILLENARISM
MILLENARISMS
MILLENNIAL
MILLENNIALISM
MILLENNIALISMS
MILLENNIALIST
MILLENNIALISTS
MILLENNIALLY
MILLENNIALS
MILLENNIANISM
MILLENNIANISMS
MILLENNIARISM
MILLENNIARISMS
MILLENNIUM
MILLENNIUMS
MILLEPEDES
MILLEPORES
MILLERITES
MILLESIMAL
MILLESIMALLY
MILLESIMALS
MILLHOUSES
MILLIAMPERE
MILLIAMPERES
MILLIARIES
MILLICURIE
MILLICURIES
MILLIDEGREE
MILLIDEGREES
MILLIGRAMME
MILLIGRAMMES
MILLIGRAMS
MILLIHENRIES
MILLIHENRY
MILLIHENRYS
MILLILAMBERT
MILLILAMBERTS

MILLILITER
MILLILITERS
MILLILITRE
MILLILITRES
MILLILUCES
MILLILUXES
MILLIMETER
MILLIMETERS
MILLIMETRE
MILLIMETRES
MILLIMICRON
MILLIMICRONS
MILLIMOLAR
MILLIMOLES
MILLINERIES
MILLIONAIRE
MILLIONAIRES
MILLIONAIRESS
MILLIONAIRESSES
MILLIONARY
MILLIONFOLD
MILLIONNAIRE
MILLIONNAIRES
MILLIONNAIRESS
MILLIONTHS
MILLIOSMOL
MILLIOSMOLS
MILLIPEDES
MILLIPROBE
MILLIPROBES
MILLIRADIAN
MILLIRADIANS
MILLIROENTGEN
MILLIROENTGENS
MILLISECOND
MILLISECONDS
MILLISIEVERT
MILLISIEVERTS
MILLIVOLTS
MILLIWATTS
MILLOCRACIES
MILLOCRACY
MILLOCRATS
MILLSCALES
MILLSTONES
MILLSTREAM
MILLSTREAMS
MILLWHEELS
MILLWRIGHT
MILLWRIGHTS
MILOMETERS
MILQUETOAST
MILQUETOASTS
MIMEOGRAPH
MIMEOGRAPHED
MIMEOGRAPHING
MIMEOGRAPHS
MIMETICALLY
MIMIVIRUSES
MIMMICKING
MIMOGRAPHER
MIMOGRAPHERS
MIMOGRAPHIES
MIMOGRAPHY
MIMOSACEOUS
MINACIOUSLY
MINACITIES
MINATORIAL
MINATORIALLY
MINATORILY
MINAUDERIE
MINAUDERIES
MINAUDIERE
MINAUDIERES
MINCEMEATS
MINDBLOWER
MINDBLOWERS
MINDEDNESS
MINDEDNESSES
MINDFULNESS
MINDFULNESSES
MINDLESSLY
MINDLESSNESS
MINDLESSNESSES
MINDSCAPES
MINDSHARES
MINEFIELDS
MINEHUNTER
MINEHUNTERS
MINELAYERS
MINELAYING
MINELAYINGS
MINERALISABLE
MINERALISATION
MINERALISATIONS
MINERALISE
MINERALISED
MINERALISER
MINERALISERS
MINERALISES
MINERALISING
MINERALIST
MINERALISTS
MINERALIZABLE
MINERALIZATION
MINERALIZATIONS
MINERALIZE
MINERALIZED
MINERALIZER
MINERALIZERS
MINERALIZES
MINERALIZING
MINERALOGIC
MINERALOGICAL
MINERALOGICALLY
MINERALOGIES
MINERALOGISE
MINERALOGISED
MINERALOGISES
MINERALOGISING
MINERALOGIST
MINERALOGISTS
MINERALOGIZE
MINERALOGIZED
MINERALOGIZES
MINERALOGIZING
MINERALOGY
MINESHAFTS
MINESTONES
MINESTRONE
MINESTRONES
MINESWEEPER
MINESWEEPERS
MINESWEEPING
MINESWEEPINGS
MINEWORKER
MINEWORKERS
MINGIMINGI
MINGIMINGIS
MINGINESSES
MINGLEMENT
MINGLEMENTS
MINGLINGLY
MINIATIONS
MINIATURED
MINIATURES
MINIATURING
MINIATURISATION
MINIATURISE
MINIATURISED
MINIATURISES
MINIATURISING
MINIATURIST
MINIATURISTIC
MINIATURISTS
MINIATURIZATION
MINIATURIZE
MINIATURIZED
MINIATURIZES
MINIATURIZING
MINIBIKERS
MINIBREAKS
MINIBUDGET
MINIBUDGETS
MINIBUSSES
MINICABBING
MINICABBINGS
MINICALCULATOR
MINICALCULATORS
MINICASSETTE
MINICASSETTES
MINICOMPUTER
MINICOMPUTERS
MINICOURSE
MINICOURSES
MINIDISHES
MINIDRESSES
MINIFICATION
MINIFICATIONS
MINIFLOPPIES
MINIFLOPPY
MINIMALISM
MINIMALISMS
MINIMALIST
MINIMALISTIC
MINIMALISTS
MINIMARKET
MINIMARKETS
MINIMAXING
MINIMISATION
MINIMISATIONS
MINIMISERS
MINIMISING
MINIMIZATION
MINIMIZATIONS
MINIMIZERS
MINIMIZING
MINIRUGBIES
MINISCHOOL
MINISCHOOLS
MINISCULES
MINISERIES
MINISKIRTED
MINISKIRTS
MINISTATES
MINISTERED
MINISTERIA
MINISTERIAL
MINISTERIALIST
MINISTERIALISTS
MINISTERIALLY
MINISTERING
MINISTERIUM
MINISTERSHIP
MINISTERSHIPS
MINISTRANT
MINISTRANTS
MINISTRATION
MINISTRATIONS
MINISTRATIVE
MINISTRESS
MINISTRESSES
MINISTRIES
MINISTROKE
MINISTROKES
MINISYSTEM
MINISYSTEMS
MINITOWERS
MINITRACKS
MINIVOLLEY
MINIVOLLEYS
MINNESINGER
MINNESINGERS
MINNICKING
MINNOCKING
MINORITAIRE
MINORITAIRES
MINORITIES
MINORSHIPS
MINOXIDILS

MINSTRELSIES
MINSTRELSY
MINUSCULAR
MINUSCULES
MINUTENESS
MINUTENESSES
MIRABELLES
MIRABILISES
MIRACIDIAL
MIRACIDIUM
MIRACULOUS
MIRACULOUSLY
MIRACULOUSNESS
MIRANDISED
MIRANDISES
MIRANDISING
MIRANDIZED
MIRANDIZES
MIRANDIZING
MIRIFICALLY
MIRINESSES
MIRKINESSES
MIRRORINGS
MIRRORLIKE
MIRRORWISE
MIRTHFULLY
MIRTHFULNESS
MIRTHFULNESSES
MIRTHLESSLY
MIRTHLESSNESS
MIRTHLESSNESSES
MISACCEPTATION
MISACCEPTATIONS
MISADAPTED
MISADAPTING
MISADDRESS
MISADDRESSED
MISADDRESSES
MISADDRESSING
MISADJUSTED
MISADJUSTING
MISADJUSTS
MISADVENTURE
MISADVENTURED
MISADVENTURER
MISADVENTURERS
MISADVENTURES
MISADVENTUROUS
MISADVERTENCE
MISADVERTENCES
MISADVICES
MISADVISED
MISADVISEDLY
MISADVISEDNESS
MISADVISES
MISADVISING
MISALIGNED
MISALIGNING
MISALIGNMENT
MISALIGNMENTS
MISALLEGED
MISALLEGES
MISALLEGING
MISALLIANCE
MISALLIANCES
MISALLOCATE
MISALLOCATED
MISALLOCATES
MISALLOCATING
MISALLOCATION
MISALLOCATIONS
MISALLOTMENT
MISALLOTMENTS
MISALLOTTED
MISALLOTTING
MISALLYING
MISALTERED
MISALTERING
MISANALYSES
MISANALYSIS
MISANDRIES
MISANDRIST
MISANDRISTS
MISANDROUS
MISANTHROPE
MISANTHROPES
MISANTHROPIC
MISANTHROPICAL
MISANTHROPIES
MISANTHROPIST
MISANTHROPISTS
MISANTHROPOS
MISANTHROPOSES
MISANTHROPY
MISAPPLICATION
MISAPPLICATIONS
MISAPPLIED
MISAPPLIES
MISAPPLYING
MISAPPRAISAL
MISAPPRAISALS
MISAPPRECIATE
MISAPPRECIATED
MISAPPRECIATES
MISAPPRECIATING
MISAPPRECIATION
MISAPPRECIATIVE
MISAPPREHEND
MISAPPREHENDED
MISAPPREHENDING
MISAPPREHENDS
MISAPPREHENSION
MISAPPREHENSIVE
MISAPPROPRIATE
MISAPPROPRIATED
MISAPPROPRIATES
MISARRANGE
MISARRANGED
MISARRANGEMENT
MISARRANGEMENTS
MISARRANGES
MISARRANGING
MISARTICULATE
MISARTICULATED
MISARTICULATES
MISARTICULATING
MISASSAYED
MISASSAYING
MISASSEMBLE
MISASSEMBLED
MISASSEMBLES
MISASSEMBLING
MISASSIGNED
MISASSIGNING
MISASSIGNS
MISASSUMED
MISASSUMES
MISASSUMING
MISASSUMPTION
MISASSUMPTIONS
MISATONING
MISATTRIBUTE
MISATTRIBUTED
MISATTRIBUTES
MISATTRIBUTING
MISATTRIBUTION
MISATTRIBUTIONS
MISAUNTERS
MISAVERRED
MISAVERRING
MISAWARDED
MISAWARDING
MISBALANCE
MISBALANCED
MISBALANCES
MISBALANCING
MISBECOMES
MISBECOMING
MISBECOMINGNESS
MISBEGINNING
MISBEGOTTEN
MISBEHAVED
MISBEHAVER
MISBEHAVERS
MISBEHAVES
MISBEHAVING
MISBEHAVIOR
MISBEHAVIORS
MISBEHAVIOUR
MISBEHAVIOURS
MISBELIEFS
MISBELIEVE
MISBELIEVED
MISBELIEVER
MISBELIEVERS
MISBELIEVES
MISBELIEVING
MISBESEEMED
MISBESEEMING
MISBESEEMS
MISBESTOWAL
MISBESTOWALS
MISBESTOWED
MISBESTOWING
MISBESTOWS
MISBIASING
MISBIASSED
MISBIASSES
MISBIASSING
MISBILLING
MISBINDING
MISBRANDED
MISBRANDING
MISBUILDING
MISBUTTONED
MISBUTTONING
MISBUTTONS
MISCALCULATE
MISCALCULATED
MISCALCULATES
MISCALCULATING
MISCALCULATION
MISCALCULATIONS
MISCALCULATOR
MISCALCULATORS
MISCALLERS
MISCALLING
MISCANTHUS
MISCANTHUSES
MISCAPTION
MISCAPTIONED
MISCAPTIONING
MISCAPTIONS
MISCARRIAGE
MISCARRIAGES
MISCARRIED
MISCARRIES
MISCARRYING
MISCASTING
MISCATALOG
MISCATALOGED
MISCATALOGING
MISCATALOGS
MISCEGENATE
MISCEGENATED
MISCEGENATES
MISCEGENATING
MISCEGENATION
MISCEGENATIONAL
MISCEGENATIONS
MISCEGENATOR
MISCEGENATORS
MISCEGENES
MISCEGENETIC
MISCEGENIST
MISCEGENISTS
MISCEGINES
MISCELLANARIAN
MISCELLANARIANS
MISCELLANEA

MISCELLANEOUS
MISCELLANEOUSLY
MISCELLANIES
MISCELLANIST
MISCELLANISTS
MISCELLANY
MISCHALLENGE
MISCHALLENGES
MISCHANCED
MISCHANCEFUL
MISCHANCES
MISCHANCIER
MISCHANCIEST
MISCHANCING
MISCHANNEL
MISCHANNELED
MISCHANNELING
MISCHANNELLED
MISCHANNELLING
MISCHANNELS
MISCHANTER
MISCHANTERS
MISCHARACTERISE
MISCHARACTERIZE
MISCHARGED
MISCHARGES
MISCHARGING
MISCHIEFED
MISCHIEFING
MISCHIEVOUS
MISCHIEVOUSLY
MISCHIEVOUSNESS
MISCHMETAL
MISCHMETALS
MISCHOICES
MISCHOOSES
MISCHOOSING
MISCIBILITIES
MISCIBILITY
MISCITATION
MISCITATIONS
MISCLAIMED
MISCLAIMING
MISCLASSED
MISCLASSES
MISCLASSIFIED
MISCLASSIFIES
MISCLASSIFY
MISCLASSIFYING
MISCLASSING
MISCOINING
MISCOLORED
MISCOLORING
MISCOLOURED
MISCOLOURING
MISCOLOURS
MISCOMPREHEND
MISCOMPREHENDED
MISCOMPREHENDS
MISCOMPUTATION
MISCOMPUTATIONS
MISCOMPUTE
MISCOMPUTED
MISCOMPUTES
MISCOMPUTING
MISCONCEIT
MISCONCEITED
MISCONCEITING
MISCONCEITS
MISCONCEIVE
MISCONCEIVED
MISCONCEIVER
MISCONCEIVERS
MISCONCEIVES
MISCONCEIVING
MISCONCEPTION
MISCONCEPTIONS
MISCONDUCT
MISCONDUCTED
MISCONDUCTING
MISCONDUCTS
MISCONJECTURE
MISCONJECTURED
MISCONJECTURES
MISCONJECTURING
MISCONNECT
MISCONNECTED
MISCONNECTING
MISCONNECTION
MISCONNECTIONS
MISCONNECTS
MISCONSTER
MISCONSTERED
MISCONSTERING
MISCONSTERS
MISCONSTRUCT
MISCONSTRUCTED
MISCONSTRUCTING
MISCONSTRUCTION
MISCONSTRUCTS
MISCONSTRUE
MISCONSTRUED
MISCONSTRUES
MISCONSTRUING
MISCONTENT
MISCONTENTED
MISCONTENTING
MISCONTENTMENT
MISCONTENTMENTS
MISCONTENTS
MISCOOKING
MISCOPYING
MISCORRECT
MISCORRECTED
MISCORRECTING
MISCORRECTION
MISCORRECTIONS
MISCORRECTS
MISCORRELATION
MISCORRELATIONS
MISCOUNSEL
MISCOUNSELLED
MISCOUNSELLING
MISCOUNSELLINGS
MISCOUNSELS
MISCOUNTED
MISCOUNTING
MISCREANCE
MISCREANCES
MISCREANCIES
MISCREANCY
MISCREANTS
MISCREATED
MISCREATES
MISCREATING
MISCREATION
MISCREATIONS
MISCREATIVE
MISCREATOR
MISCREATORS
MISCREAUNCE
MISCREAUNCES
MISCREDITED
MISCREDITING
MISCREDITS
MISCUTTING
MISDEALERS
MISDEALING
MISDEEMFUL
MISDEEMING
MISDEEMINGS
MISDEFINED
MISDEFINES
MISDEFINING
MISDEMEANANT
MISDEMEANANTS
MISDEMEANED
MISDEMEANING
MISDEMEANOR
MISDEMEANORS
MISDEMEANOUR
MISDEMEANOURS
MISDEMEANS
MISDESCRIBE
MISDESCRIBED
MISDESCRIBES
MISDESCRIBING
MISDESCRIPTION
MISDESCRIPTIONS
MISDESERTS
MISDEVELOP
MISDEVELOPED
MISDEVELOPING
MISDEVELOPS
MISDEVOTION
MISDEVOTIONS
MISDIAGNOSE
MISDIAGNOSED
MISDIAGNOSES
MISDIAGNOSING
MISDIAGNOSIS
MISDIALING
MISDIALLED
MISDIALLING
MISDIETING
MISDIGHTED
MISDIGHTING
MISDIRECTED
MISDIRECTING
MISDIRECTION
MISDIRECTIONS
MISDIRECTS
MISDISTRIBUTION
MISDIVIDED
MISDIVIDES
MISDIVIDING
MISDIVISION
MISDIVISIONS
MISDOUBTED
MISDOUBTFUL
MISDOUBTING
MISDRAWING
MISDRAWINGS
MISDREADED
MISDREADING
MISDRIVING
MISEDITING
MISEDUCATE
MISEDUCATED
MISEDUCATES
MISEDUCATING
MISEDUCATION
MISEDUCATIONS
MISEMPHASES
MISEMPHASIS
MISEMPHASISE
MISEMPHASISED
MISEMPHASISES
MISEMPHASISING
MISEMPHASIZE
MISEMPHASIZED
MISEMPHASIZES
MISEMPHASIZING
MISEMPLOYED
MISEMPLOYING
MISEMPLOYMENT
MISEMPLOYMENTS
MISEMPLOYS
MISENROLLED
MISENROLLING
MISENROLLS
MISENTERED
MISENTERING
MISENTREAT
MISENTREATED
MISENTREATING
MISENTREATS
MISENTRIES
MISERABILISM
MISERABILISMS

MISERABILIST
MISERABILISTS
MISERABLENESS
MISERABLENESSES
MISERABLES
MISERABLISM
MISERABLISMS
MISERABLIST
MISERABLISTS
MISERICORD
MISERICORDE
MISERICORDES
MISERICORDS
MISERLIEST
MISERLINESS
MISERLINESSES
MISESTEEMED
MISESTEEMING
MISESTEEMS
MISESTIMATE
MISESTIMATED
MISESTIMATES
MISESTIMATING
MISESTIMATION
MISESTIMATIONS
MISEVALUATE
MISEVALUATED
MISEVALUATES
MISEVALUATING
MISEVALUATION
MISEVALUATIONS
MISFALLING
MISFARINGS
MISFEASANCE
MISFEASANCES
MISFEASORS
MISFEATURE
MISFEATURED
MISFEATURES
MISFEATURING
MISFEEDING
MISFEIGNED
MISFEIGNING
MISFIELDED
MISFIELDING
MISFITTING
MISFOCUSED
MISFOCUSES
MISFOCUSING
MISFOCUSSED
MISFOCUSSES
MISFOCUSSING
MISFOLDING
MISFORMATION
MISFORMATIONS
MISFORMING
MISFORTUNE
MISFORTUNED
MISFORTUNES
MISFRAMING
MISFUNCTION
MISFUNCTIONED
MISFUNCTIONING
MISFUNCTIONS
MISGAUGING
MISGENDERED
MISGENDERING
MISGENDERS
MISGIVINGS
MISGOVERNANCE
MISGOVERNANCES
MISGOVERNAUNCE
MISGOVERNAUNCES
MISGOVERNED
MISGOVERNING
MISGOVERNMENT
MISGOVERNMENTS
MISGOVERNOR
MISGOVERNORS
MISGOVERNS
MISGRADING
MISGRAFTED
MISGRAFTING
MISGROWING
MISGROWTHS
MISGUESSED
MISGUESSES
MISGUESSING
MISGUGGLED
MISGUGGLES
MISGUGGLING
MISGUIDANCE
MISGUIDANCES
MISGUIDEDLY
MISGUIDEDNESS
MISGUIDEDNESSES
MISGUIDERS
MISGUIDING
MISHALLOWED
MISHANDLED
MISHANDLES
MISHANDLING
MISHANDLINGS
MISHANTERS
MISHAPPENED
MISHAPPENING
MISHAPPENS
MISHAPPING
MISHEARING
MISHEGAASEN
MISHGUGGLE
MISHGUGGLED
MISHGUGGLES
MISHGUGGLING
MISHITTING
MISHMASHES
MISHMOSHES
MISHUGASES
MISIDENTIFIED
MISIDENTIFIES
MISIDENTIFY
MISIDENTIFYING
MISIMPRESSION
MISIMPRESSIONS
MISIMPROVE
MISIMPROVED
MISIMPROVEMENT
MISIMPROVEMENTS
MISIMPROVES
MISIMPROVING
MISINFERRED
MISINFERRING
MISINFORMANT
MISINFORMANTS
MISINFORMATION
MISINFORMATIONS
MISINFORMED
MISINFORMER
MISINFORMERS
MISINFORMING
MISINFORMS
MISINSTRUCT
MISINSTRUCTED
MISINSTRUCTING
MISINSTRUCTION
MISINSTRUCTIONS
MISINSTRUCTS
MISINTELLIGENCE
MISINTENDED
MISINTENDING
MISINTENDS
MISINTERPRET
MISINTERPRETED
MISINTERPRETER
MISINTERPRETERS
MISINTERPRETING
MISINTERPRETS
MISINTERRED
MISINTERRING
MISJOINDER
MISJOINDERS
MISJOINING
MISJUDGEMENT
MISJUDGEMENTS
MISJUDGERS
MISJUDGING
MISJUDGMENT
MISJUDGMENTS
MISKEEPING
MISKENNING
MISKICKING
MISKNOWING
MISKNOWLEDGE
MISKNOWLEDGES
MISLABELED
MISLABELING
MISLABELLED
MISLABELLING
MISLABORED
MISLABORING
MISLABOURED
MISLABOURING
MISLABOURS
MISLEADERS
MISLEADING
MISLEADINGLY
MISLEARNED
MISLEARNING
MISLEEKING
MISLIGHTED
MISLIGHTING
MISLIKINGS
MISLIPPENED
MISLIPPENING
MISLIPPENS
MISLOCATED
MISLOCATES
MISLOCATING
MISLOCATION
MISLOCATIONS
MISLODGING
MISLUCKING
MISMANAGED
MISMANAGEMENT
MISMANAGEMENTS
MISMANAGER
MISMANAGERS
MISMANAGES
MISMANAGING
MISMANNERS
MISMARKING
MISMARRIAGE
MISMARRIAGES
MISMARRIED
MISMARRIES
MISMARRYING
MISMATCHED
MISMATCHES
MISMATCHING
MISMATCHMENT
MISMATCHMENTS
MISMATINGS
MISMEASURE
MISMEASURED
MISMEASUREMENT
MISMEASUREMENTS
MISMEASURES
MISMEASURING
MISMEETING
MISMETRING
MISNOMERED
MISNOMERING
MISNUMBERED
MISNUMBERING
MISNUMBERS
MISOBSERVANCE
MISOBSERVANCES
MISOBSERVE
MISOBSERVED
MISOBSERVES

MISOBSERVING
MISOCAPNIC
MISOGAMIES
MISOGAMIST
MISOGAMISTS
MISOGYNIES
MISOGYNIST
MISOGYNISTIC
MISOGYNISTICAL
MISOGYNISTS
MISOGYNOUS
MISOLOGIES
MISOLOGIST
MISOLOGISTS
MISONEISMS
MISONEISTIC
MISONEISTS
MISORDERED
MISORDERING
MISORIENTATION
MISORIENTATIONS
MISORIENTED
MISORIENTING
MISORIENTS
MISPACKAGE
MISPACKAGED
MISPACKAGES
MISPACKAGING
MISPAINTED
MISPAINTING
MISPARSING
MISPARTING
MISPATCHED
MISPATCHES
MISPATCHING
MISPENNING
MISPERCEIVE
MISPERCEIVED
MISPERCEIVES
MISPERCEIVING
MISPERCEPTION
MISPERCEPTIONS
MISPERSUADE
MISPERSUADED
MISPERSUADES
MISPERSUADING
MISPERSUASION
MISPERSUASIONS
MISPHRASED
MISPHRASES
MISPHRASING
MISPICKELS
MISPLACEMENT
MISPLACEMENTS
MISPLACING
MISPLANNED
MISPLANNING
MISPLANTED
MISPLANTING
MISPLAYING
MISPLEADED
MISPLEADING
MISPLEADINGS
MISPLEASED
MISPLEASES
MISPLEASING
MISPOINTED
MISPOINTING
MISPOISING
MISPOSITION
MISPOSITIONED
MISPOSITIONING
MISPOSITIONS
MISPRAISED
MISPRAISES
MISPRAISING
MISPRICING
MISPRINTED
MISPRINTING
MISPRISING
MISPRISION
MISPRISIONS
MISPRIZERS
MISPRIZING
MISPROGRAM
MISPROGRAMED
MISPROGRAMING
MISPROGRAMMED
MISPROGRAMMING
MISPROGRAMS
MISPRONOUNCE
MISPRONOUNCED
MISPRONOUNCES
MISPRONOUNCING
MISPROPORTION
MISPROPORTIONED
MISPROPORTIONS
MISPUNCTUATE
MISPUNCTUATED
MISPUNCTUATES
MISPUNCTUATING
MISPUNCTUATION
MISPUNCTUATIONS
MISQUOTATION
MISQUOTATIONS
MISQUOTERS
MISQUOTING
MISRAISING
MISREADING
MISREADINGS
MISRECKONED
MISRECKONING
MISRECKONINGS
MISRECKONS
MISRECOLLECTION
MISRECORDED
MISRECORDING
MISRECORDS
MISREFERENCE
MISREFERENCED
MISREFERENCES
MISREFERENCING
MISREFERRED
MISREFERRING
MISREGARDED
MISREGARDING
MISREGARDS
MISREGISTER
MISREGISTERED
MISREGISTERING
MISREGISTERS
MISREGISTRATION
MISRELATED
MISRELATES
MISRELATING
MISRELATION
MISRELATIONS
MISRELYING
MISREMEMBER
MISREMEMBERED
MISREMEMBERING
MISREMEMBERS
MISRENDERED
MISRENDERING
MISRENDERS
MISREPORTED
MISREPORTER
MISREPORTERS
MISREPORTING
MISREPORTS
MISREPRESENT
MISREPRESENTED
MISREPRESENTER
MISREPRESENTERS
MISREPRESENTING
MISREPRESENTS
MISROUTEING
MISROUTING
MISSAYINGS
MISSEATING
MISSEEMING
MISSEEMINGS
MISSELLING
MISSELLINGS
MISSENDING
MISSENSING
MISSETTING
MISSHAPENLY
MISSHAPENNESS
MISSHAPENNESSES
MISSHAPERS
MISSHAPING
MISSHEATHED
MISSILEERS
MISSILEMAN
MISSILEMEN
MISSILERIES
MISSILRIES
MISSIOLOGIES
MISSIOLOGY
MISSIONARIES
MISSIONARISE
MISSIONARISED
MISSIONARISES
MISSIONARISING
MISSIONARIZE
MISSIONARIZED
MISSIONARIZES
MISSIONARIZING
MISSIONARY
MISSIONERS
MISSIONING
MISSIONISATION
MISSIONISATIONS
MISSIONISE
MISSIONISED
MISSIONISER
MISSIONISERS
MISSIONISES
MISSIONISING
MISSIONIZATION
MISSIONIZATIONS
MISSIONIZE
MISSIONIZED
MISSIONIZER
MISSIONIZERS
MISSIONIZES
MISSIONIZING
MISSISHNESS
MISSISHNESSES
MISSORTING
MISSOUNDED
MISSOUNDING
MISSPACING
MISSPEAKING
MISSPELLED
MISSPELLING
MISSPELLINGS
MISSPENDER
MISSPENDERS
MISSPENDING
MISSTAMPED
MISSTAMPING
MISSTARTED
MISSTARTING
MISSTATEMENT
MISSTATEMENTS
MISSTATING
MISSTEERED
MISSTEERING
MISSTEPPED
MISSTEPPING
MISSTOPPED
MISSTOPPING
MISSTRICKEN
MISSTRIKES
MISSTRIKING
MISSTYLING
MISSUITING
MISSUMMATION

M

MISSUMMATIONS
MISTAKABLE
MISTAKABLY
MISTAKEABLE
MISTAKEABLY
MISTAKENLY
MISTAKENNESS
MISTAKENNESSES
MISTAKINGS
MISTEACHES
MISTEACHING
MISTELLING
MISTEMPERED
MISTEMPERING
MISTEMPERS
MISTENDING
MISTERMING
MISTHINKING
MISTHOUGHT
MISTHOUGHTS
MISTHROWING
MISTIGRISES
MISTIMINGS
MISTINESSES
MISTITLING
MISTLETOES
MISTOUCHED
MISTOUCHES
MISTOUCHING
MISTRACING
MISTRAINED
MISTRAINING
MISTRANSCRIBE
MISTRANSCRIBED
MISTRANSCRIBES
MISTRANSCRIBING
MISTRANSLATE
MISTRANSLATED
MISTRANSLATES
MISTRANSLATING
MISTRANSLATION
MISTRANSLATIONS
MISTRAYNED
MISTREADING
MISTREADINGS
MISTREATED
MISTREATING
MISTREATMENT
MISTREATMENTS
MISTRESSED
MISTRESSES
MISTRESSING
MISTRESSLESS
MISTRESSLIER
MISTRESSLIEST
MISTRESSLY
MISTRUSTED
MISTRUSTER
MISTRUSTERS
MISTRUSTFUL
MISTRUSTFULLY
MISTRUSTFULNESS
MISTRUSTING
MISTRUSTINGLY
MISTRUSTLESS
MISTRYSTED
MISTRYSTING
MISTUTORED
MISTUTORING
MISUNDERSTAND
MISUNDERSTANDS
MISUNDERSTOOD
MISUTILISATION
MISUTILISATIONS
MISUTILIZATION
MISUTILIZATIONS
MISVALUING
MISVENTURE
MISVENTURES
MISVENTUROUS
MISVOCALISATION
MISVOCALIZATION
MISWANDRED
MISWEENING
MISWENDING
MISWORDING
MISWORDINGS
MISWORSHIP
MISWORSHIPPED
MISWORSHIPPING
MISWORSHIPPINGS
MISWORSHIPS
MISWRITING
MISWRITTEN
MITERWORTS
MITHRADATIC
MITHRIDATE
MITHRIDATES
MITHRIDATIC
MITHRIDATISE
MITHRIDATISED
MITHRIDATISES
MITHRIDATISING
MITHRIDATISM
MITHRIDATISMS
MITHRIDATIZE
MITHRIDATIZED
MITHRIDATIZES
MITHRIDATIZING
MITIGATING
MITIGATION
MITIGATIONS
MITIGATIVE
MITIGATIVES
MITIGATORS
MITIGATORY
MITOCHONDRIA
MITOCHONDRIAL
MITOCHONDRION
MITOGENETIC
MITOGENICITIES
MITOGENICITY
MITOMYCINS
MITOTICALLY
MITRAILLES
MITRAILLEUR
MITRAILLEURS
MITRAILLEUSE
MITRAILLEUSES
MITREWORTS
MITTIMUSES
MIXABILITIES
MIXABILITY
MIXEDNESSES
MIXMASTERS
MIXOBARBARIC
MIXOLOGIES
MIXOLOGIST
MIXOLOGISTS
MIXOLYDIAN
MIXOTROPHIC
MIZENMASTS
MIZZENMAST
MIZZENMASTS
MIZZONITES
MNEMONICAL
MNEMONICALLY
MNEMONISTS
MNEMOTECHNIC
MNEMOTECHNICS
MNEMOTECHNIST
MNEMOTECHNISTS
MOBCASTING
MOBCASTINGS
MOBILISABLE
MOBILISATION
MOBILISATIONS
MOBILISERS
MOBILISING
MOBILITIES
MOBILIZABLE
MOBILIZATION
MOBILIZATIONS
MOBILIZERS
MOBILIZING
MOBLOGGERS
MOBOCRACIES
MOBOCRATIC
MOBOCRATICAL
MOCHINESSES
MOCKERNUTS
MOCKINGBIRD
MOCKINGBIRDS
MOCKUMENTARIES
MOCKUMENTARY
MODAFINILS
MODALISTIC
MODALITIES
MODELLINGS
MODELLISTS
MODERATELY
MODERATENESS
MODERATENESSES
MODERATING
MODERATION
MODERATIONS
MODERATISM
MODERATISMS
MODERATORS
MODERATORSHIP
MODERATORSHIPS
MODERATRICES
MODERATRIX
MODERATRIXES
MODERNISATION
MODERNISATIONS
MODERNISED
MODERNISER
MODERNISERS
MODERNISES
MODERNISING
MODERNISMS
MODERNISTIC
MODERNISTICALLY
MODERNISTS
MODERNITIES
MODERNIZATION
MODERNIZATIONS
MODERNIZED
MODERNIZER
MODERNIZERS
MODERNIZES
MODERNIZING
MODERNNESS
MODERNNESSES
MODIFIABILITIES
MODIFIABILITY
MODIFIABLE
MODIFIABLENESS
MODIFICATION
MODIFICATIONS
MODIFICATIVE
MODIFICATORY
MODILLIONS
MODISHNESS
MODISHNESSES
MODULABILITIES
MODULABILITY
MODULARISED
MODULARITIES
MODULARITY
MODULARIZED
MODULATING
MODULATION
MODULATIONS
MODULATIVE
MODULATORS
MODULATORY
MOISTENERS
MOISTENING

MOISTIFIED
MOISTIFIES
MOISTIFYING
MOISTNESSES
MOISTURELESS
MOISTURISE
MOISTURISED
MOISTURISER
MOISTURISERS
MOISTURISES
MOISTURISING
MOISTURIZE
MOISTURIZED
MOISTURIZER
MOISTURIZERS
MOISTURIZES
MOISTURIZING
MOITHERING
MOLALITIES
MOLARITIES
MOLASSESES
MOLDABILITIES
MOLDABILITY
MOLDAVITES
MOLDBOARDS
MOLDINESSES
MOLECATCHER
MOLECATCHERS
MOLECULARITIES
MOLECULARITY
MOLECULARLY
MOLENDINAR
MOLENDINARIES
MOLENDINARS
MOLENDINARY
MOLESTATION
MOLESTATIONS
MOLIMINOUS
MOLLIFIABLE
MOLLIFICATION
MOLLIFICATIONS
MOLLIFIERS
MOLLIFYING
MOLLITIOUS
MOLLUSCANS
MOLLUSCICIDAL
MOLLUSCICIDE
MOLLUSCICIDES
MOLLUSCOID
MOLLUSCOIDAL
MOLLUSCOIDS
MOLLUSCOUS
MOLLUSKANS
MOLLYCODDLE
MOLLYCODDLED
MOLLYCODDLER
MOLLYCODDLERS
MOLLYCODDLES
MOLLYCODDLING
MOLLYCODDLINGS
MOLLYHAWKS
MOLLYMAWKS
MOLOCHISED
MOLOCHISES
MOLOCHISING
MOLOCHIZED
MOLOCHIZES
MOLOCHIZING
MOLYBDATES
MOLYBDENITE
MOLYBDENITES
MOLYBDENOSES
MOLYBDENOSIS
MOLYBDENOUS
MOLYBDENUM
MOLYBDENUMS
MOLYBDOSES
MOLYBDOSIS
MOMENTANEOUS
MOMENTARILY
MOMENTARINESS
MOMENTARINESSES
MOMENTOUSLY
MOMENTOUSNESS
MOMENTOUSNESSES
MOMPRENEUR
MOMPRENEURS
MONACHISMS
MONACHISTS
MONACTINAL
MONACTINES
MONADELPHOUS
MONADICALLY
MONADIFORM
MONADISTIC
MONADNOCKS
MONADOLOGIES
MONADOLOGY
MONANDRIES
MONANDROUS
MONANTHOUS
MONARCHALLY
MONARCHIAL
MONARCHICAL
MONARCHICALLY
MONARCHIES
MONARCHISE
MONARCHISED
MONARCHISES
MONARCHISING
MONARCHISM
MONARCHISMS
MONARCHIST
MONARCHISTIC
MONARCHISTS
MONARCHIZE
MONARCHIZED
MONARCHIZES
MONARCHIZING
MONASTERIAL
MONASTERIES
MONASTICAL
MONASTICALLY
MONASTICISM
MONASTICISMS
MONAURALLY
MONCHIQUITE
MONCHIQUITES
MONDEGREEN
MONDEGREENS
MONECIOUSLY
MONERGISMS
MONESTROUS
MONETARILY
MONETARISM
MONETARISMS
MONETARIST
MONETARISTS
MONETISATION
MONETISATIONS
MONETISING
MONETIZATION
MONETIZATIONS
MONETIZING
MONEYBELTS
MONEYBOXES
MONEYCHANGER
MONEYCHANGERS
MONEYGRUBBING
MONEYGRUBBINGS
MONEYLENDER
MONEYLENDERS
MONEYLENDING
MONEYLENDINGS
MONEYMAKER
MONEYMAKERS
MONEYMAKING
MONEYMAKINGS
MONEYSPINNING
MONEYWORTS
MONGERINGS
MONGRELISATION
MONGRELISATIONS
MONGRELISE
MONGRELISED
MONGRELISER
MONGRELISERS
MONGRELISES
MONGRELISING
MONGRELISM
MONGRELISMS
MONGRELIZATION
MONGRELIZATIONS
MONGRELIZE
MONGRELIZED
MONGRELIZER
MONGRELIZERS
MONGRELIZES
MONGRELIZING
MONGRELLIER
MONGRELLIEST
MONILIASES
MONILIASIS
MONILIFORM
MONISTICAL
MONISTICALLY
MONITORIAL
MONITORIALLY
MONITORIES
MONITORING
MONITORINGS
MONITORSHIP
MONITORSHIPS
MONITRESSES
MONKEYGLAND
MONKEYISMS
MONKEYPODS
MONKEYPOTS
MONKEYPOXES
MONKEYSHINE
MONKEYSHINES
MONKFISHES
MONKISHNESS
MONKISHNESSES
MONKSHOODS
MONOACIDIC
MONOAMINERGIC
MONOAMINES
MONOATOMIC
MONOBLEPSES
MONOBLEPSIS
MONOCARBOXYLIC
MONOCARDIAN
MONOCARDIANS
MONOCARPELLARY
MONOCARPIC
MONOCARPOUS
MONOCEROSES
MONOCEROUS
MONOCHASIA
MONOCHASIAL
MONOCHASIUM
MONOCHLAMYDEOUS
MONOCHLORIDE
MONOCHLORIDES
MONOCHORDS
MONOCHROIC
MONOCHROICS
MONOCHROMASIES
MONOCHROMASY
MONOCHROMAT
MONOCHROMATE
MONOCHROMATES
MONOCHROMATIC
MONOCHROMATICS
MONOCHROMATISM
MONOCHROMATISMS
MONOCHROMATOR
MONOCHROMATORS
MONOCHROMATS

MONOCHROME
MONOCHROMES
MONOCHROMIC
MONOCHROMICAL
MONOCHROMIES
MONOCHROMIST
MONOCHROMISTS
MONOCHROMY
MONOCLINAL
MONOCLINALLY
MONOCLINALS
MONOCLINES
MONOCLINIC
MONOCLINISM
MONOCLINISMS
MONOCLINOUS
MONOCLONAL
MONOCLONALS
MONOCOQUES
MONOCOTYLEDON
MONOCOTYLEDONS
MONOCOTYLS
MONOCRACIES
MONOCRATIC
MONOCROPPED
MONOCROPPING
MONOCRYSTAL
MONOCRYSTALLINE
MONOCRYSTALS
MONOCULARLY
MONOCULARS
MONOCULOUS
MONOCULTURAL
MONOCULTURE
MONOCULTURES
MONOCYCLES
MONOCYCLIC
MONOCYTOID
MONODACTYLOUS
MONODELPHIAN
MONODELPHIANS
MONODELPHIC
MONODELPHOUS
MONODICALLY
MONODISPERSE
MONODRAMAS
MONODRAMATIC
MONOECIOUS
MONOECIOUSLY
MONOECISMS
MONOESTERS
MONOFILAMENT
MONOFILAMENTS
MONOGAMIES
MONOGAMIST
MONOGAMISTIC
MONOGAMISTS
MONOGAMOUS
MONOGAMOUSLY
MONOGAMOUSNESS
MONOGASTRIC
MONOGENEAN
MONOGENEANS
MONOGENESES
MONOGENESIS
MONOGENETIC
MONOGENICALLY
MONOGENIES
MONOGENISM
MONOGENISMS
MONOGENIST
MONOGENISTIC
MONOGENISTS
MONOGENOUS
MONOGLYCERIDE
MONOGLYCERIDES
MONOGONIES
MONOGRAMED
MONOGRAMING
MONOGRAMMATIC
MONOGRAMMED
MONOGRAMMER
MONOGRAMMERS
MONOGRAMMING
MONOGRAPHED
MONOGRAPHER
MONOGRAPHERS
MONOGRAPHIC
MONOGRAPHICAL
MONOGRAPHICALLY
MONOGRAPHIES
MONOGRAPHING
MONOGRAPHIST
MONOGRAPHISTS
MONOGRAPHS
MONOGRAPHY
MONOGYNIAN
MONOGYNIES
MONOGYNIST
MONOGYNISTS
MONOGYNOUS
MONOHYBRID
MONOHYBRIDS
MONOHYDRATE
MONOHYDRATED
MONOHYDRATES
MONOHYDRIC
MONOHYDROGEN
MONOHYDROXY
MONOICOUSLY
MONOLATERS
MONOLATRIES
MONOLATRIST
MONOLATRISTS
MONOLATROUS
MONOLAYERS
MONOLINGUAL
MONOLINGUALISM
MONOLINGUALISMS
MONOLINGUALS
MONOLINGUIST
MONOLINGUISTS
MONOLITHIC
MONOLITHICALLY
MONOLOGGED
MONOLOGGING
MONOLOGICAL
MONOLOGIES
MONOLOGISE
MONOLOGISED
MONOLOGISES
MONOLOGISING
MONOLOGIST
MONOLOGISTS
MONOLOGIZE
MONOLOGIZED
MONOLOGIZES
MONOLOGIZING
MONOLOGUED
MONOLOGUES
MONOLOGUING
MONOLOGUISE
MONOLOGUISED
MONOLOGUISES
MONOLOGUISING
MONOLOGUIST
MONOLOGUISTS
MONOLOGUIZE
MONOLOGUIZED
MONOLOGUIZES
MONOLOGUIZING
MONOMACHIA
MONOMACHIAS
MONOMACHIES
MONOMANIAC
MONOMANIACAL
MONOMANIACALLY
MONOMANIACS
MONOMANIAS
MONOMEROUS
MONOMETALLIC
MONOMETALLISM
MONOMETALLISMS
MONOMETALLIST
MONOMETALLISTS
MONOMETERS
MONOMETRIC
MONOMETRICAL
MONOMOLECULAR
MONOMOLECULARLY
MONOMORPHEMIC
MONOMORPHIC
MONOMORPHISM
MONOMORPHISMS
MONOMORPHOUS
MONOMYARIAN
MONOMYARIANS
MONONUCLEAR
MONONUCLEARS
MONONUCLEATE
MONONUCLEATED
MONONUCLEOSES
MONONUCLEOSIS
MONONUCLEOTIDE
MONONUCLEOTIDES
MONOPETALOUS
MONOPHAGIES
MONOPHAGOUS
MONOPHASES
MONOPHASIC
MONOPHOBIA
MONOPHOBIAS
MONOPHOBIC
MONOPHOBICS
MONOPHONIC
MONOPHONICALLY
MONOPHONIES
MONOPHOSPHATE
MONOPHOSPHATES
MONOPHTHONG
MONOPHTHONGAL
MONOPHTHONGISE
MONOPHTHONGISED
MONOPHTHONGISES
MONOPHTHONGIZE
MONOPHTHONGIZED
MONOPHTHONGIZES
MONOPHTHONGS
MONOPHYLETIC
MONOPHYLIES
MONOPHYLLOUS
MONOPHYODONT
MONOPHYODONTS
MONOPHYSITE
MONOPHYSITES
MONOPHYSITIC
MONOPHYSITISM
MONOPHYSITISMS
MONOPITCHES
MONOPLANES
MONOPLEGIA
MONOPLEGIAS
MONOPLEGIC
MONOPLEGICS
MONOPLOIDS
MONOPODIAL
MONOPODIALLY
MONOPODIAS
MONOPODIES
MONOPODIUM
MONOPOLIES
MONOPOLISATION
MONOPOLISATIONS
MONOPOLISE
MONOPOLISED
MONOPOLISER
MONOPOLISERS
MONOPOLISES
MONOPOLISING
MONOPOLISM

MONOPOLISMS
MONOPOLIST
MONOPOLISTIC
MONOPOLISTS
MONOPOLIZATION
MONOPOLIZATIONS
MONOPOLIZE
MONOPOLIZED
MONOPOLIZER
MONOPOLIZERS
MONOPOLIZES
MONOPOLIZING
MONOPRINTS
MONOPRIONIDIAN
MONOPROPELLANT
MONOPROPELLANTS
MONOPSONIES
MONOPSONIST
MONOPSONISTIC
MONOPSONISTS
MONOPTERAL
MONOPTEROI
MONOPTERON
MONOPTEROS
MONOPTEROSES
MONOPTOTES
MONOPULSES
MONORCHIDISM
MONORCHIDISMS
MONORCHIDS
MONORCHISM
MONORCHISMS
MONORHINAL
MONORHINES
MONORHYMED
MONORHYMES
MONOSACCHARIDE
MONOSACCHARIDES
MONOSATURATED
MONOSEMIES
MONOSEPALOUS
MONOSKIERS
MONOSKIING
MONOSKIINGS
MONOSODIUM
MONOSOMICS
MONOSOMIES
MONOSPACED
MONOSPECIFIC
MONOSPECIFICITY
MONOSPERMAL
MONOSPERMOUS
MONOSTABLE
MONOSTELES
MONOSTELIC
MONOSTELIES
MONOSTICHIC
MONOSTICHOUS
MONOSTICHS
MONOSTOMOUS
MONOSTROPHE
MONOSTROPHES
MONOSTROPHIC
MONOSTROPHICS
MONOSTYLAR
MONOSTYLOUS
MONOSYLLABIC
MONOSYLLABICITY
MONOSYLLABISM
MONOSYLLABISMS
MONOSYLLABLE
MONOSYLLABLES
MONOSYMMETRIC
MONOSYMMETRICAL
MONOSYMMETRIES
MONOSYMMETRY
MONOSYNAPTIC
MONOTASKED
MONOTASKING
MONOTASKINGS
MONOTELEPHONE
MONOTELEPHONES
MONOTERPENE
MONOTERPENES
MONOTHALAMIC
MONOTHALAMOUS
MONOTHECAL
MONOTHECOUS
MONOTHEISM
MONOTHEISMS
MONOTHEIST
MONOTHEISTIC
MONOTHEISTICAL
MONOTHEISTS
MONOTHELETE
MONOTHELETES
MONOTHELETIC
MONOTHELETICAL
MONOTHELETISM
MONOTHELETISMS
MONOTHELISM
MONOTHELISMS
MONOTHELITE
MONOTHELITES
MONOTHELITISM
MONOTHELITISMS
MONOTHERAPIES
MONOTHERAPY
MONOTOCOUS
MONOTONICALLY
MONOTONICITIES
MONOTONICITY
MONOTONIES
MONOTONING
MONOTONISE
MONOTONISED
MONOTONISES
MONOTONISING
MONOTONIZE
MONOTONIZED
MONOTONIZES
MONOTONIZING
MONOTONOUS
MONOTONOUSLY
MONOTONOUSNESS
MONOTREMATOUS
MONOTREMES
MONOTRICHIC
MONOTRICHOUS
MONOTROCHS
MONOUNSATURATE
MONOUNSATURATED
MONOUNSATURATES
MONOVALENCE
MONOVALENCES
MONOVALENCIES
MONOVALENCY
MONOVALENT
MONOXYLONS
MONOXYLOUS
MONOZYGOTIC
MONOZYGOUS
MONSEIGNEUR
MONSEIGNEURS
MONSIGNORI
MONSIGNORIAL
MONSIGNORS
MONSTERING
MONSTERINGS
MONSTRANCE
MONSTRANCES
MONSTROSITIES
MONSTROSITY
MONSTROUSLY
MONSTROUSNESS
MONSTROUSNESSES
MONSTRUOSITIES
MONSTRUOSITY
MONSTRUOUS
MONTADALES
MONTAGNARD
MONTAGNARDS
MONTBRETIA
MONTBRETIAS
MONTELIMAR
MONTELIMARS
MONTGOLFIER
MONTGOLFIERS
MONTHLINGS
MONTICELLITE
MONTICELLITES
MONTICOLOUS
MONTICULATE
MONTICULES
MONTICULOUS
MONTICULUS
MONTICULUSES
MONTMORILLONITE
MONUMENTAL
MONUMENTALISE
MONUMENTALISED
MONUMENTALISES
MONUMENTALISING
MONUMENTALITIES
MONUMENTALITY
MONUMENTALIZE
MONUMENTALIZED
MONUMENTALIZES
MONUMENTALIZING
MONUMENTALLY
MONUMENTED
MONUMENTING
MONZONITES
MONZONITIC
MOODINESSES
MOONCALVES
MOONCHILDREN
MOONCRAFTS
MOONFISHES
MOONFLOWER
MOONFLOWERS
MOONINESSES
MOONLIGHTED
MOONLIGHTER
MOONLIGHTERS
MOONLIGHTING
MOONLIGHTINGS
MOONLIGHTS
MOONPHASES
MOONQUAKES
MOONRAKERS
MOONRAKING
MOONRAKINGS
MOONSCAPES
MOONSHINED
MOONSHINER
MOONSHINERS
MOONSHINES
MOONSHINIER
MOONSHINIEST
MOONSHINING
MOONSHININGS
MOONSTONES
MOONSTRICKEN
MOONSTRIKE
MOONSTRIKES
MOONSTRUCK
MOONWALKED
MOONWALKER
MOONWALKERS
MOONWALKING
MOORBUZZARD
MOORBUZZARDS
MOOSEBIRDS
MOOSEHAIRS
MOOSEHIDES
MOOSEWOODS
MOOSEYARDS
MOOTNESSES
MOPINESSES

MOPISHNESS
MOPISHNESSES
MORALISATION
MORALISATIONS
MORALISERS
MORALISING
MORALISINGS
MORALISTIC
MORALISTICALLY
MORALITIES
MORALIZATION
MORALIZATIONS
MORALIZERS
MORALIZING
MORALIZINGS
MORASSIEST
MORATORIUM
MORATORIUMS
MORBIDEZZA
MORBIDEZZAS
MORBIDITIES
MORBIDNESS
MORBIDNESSES
MORBIFEROUS
MORBIFICALLY
MORBILLIFORM
MORBILLIVIRUS
MORBILLIVIRUSES
MORBILLOUS
MORDACIOUS
MORDACIOUSLY
MORDACIOUSNESS
MORDACITIES
MORDANCIES
MORDANTING
MORENESSES
MORGANATIC
MORGANATICALLY
MORGANITES
MORGELLONS
MORGENSTERN
MORGENSTERNS
MORIBUNDITIES
MORIBUNDITY
MORIBUNDLY
MORIGERATE
MORIGERATED
MORIGERATES
MORIGERATING
MORIGERATION
MORIGERATIONS
MORIGEROUS
MORONICALLY
MORONITIES
MOROSENESS
MOROSENESSES
MOROSITIES
MORPHACTIN
MORPHACTINS
MORPHALLAXES
MORPHALLAXIS
MORPHEMICALLY
MORPHEMICS
MORPHINISM
MORPHINISMS
MORPHINOMANIA
MORPHINOMANIAC
MORPHINOMANIACS
MORPHINOMANIAS
MORPHOGENESES
MORPHOGENESIS
MORPHOGENETIC
MORPHOGENIC
MORPHOGENIES
MORPHOGENS
MORPHOGENY
MORPHOGRAPHER
MORPHOGRAPHERS
MORPHOGRAPHIES
MORPHOGRAPHY
MORPHOLINE
MORPHOLINES
MORPHOLINO
MORPHOLINOS
MORPHOLOGIC
MORPHOLOGICAL
MORPHOLOGICALLY
MORPHOLOGIES
MORPHOLOGIST
MORPHOLOGISTS
MORPHOLOGY
MORPHOMETRIC
MORPHOMETRICS
MORPHOMETRIES
MORPHOMETRY
MORPHOPHONEME
MORPHOPHONEMES
MORPHOPHONEMIC
MORPHOPHONEMICS
MORPHOPHONOLOGY
MORPHOSYNTAX
MORPHOSYNTAXES
MORPHOTROPIC
MORPHOTROPIES
MORPHOTROPY
MORSELLING
MORSELLINGS
MORTADELLA
MORTADELLAS
MORTADELLE
MORTALISED
MORTALISES
MORTALISING
MORTALITIES
MORTALIZED
MORTALIZES
MORTALIZING
MORTARBOARD
MORTARBOARDS
MORTARIEST
MORTARLESS
MORTCLOTHS
MORTGAGEABLE
MORTGAGEES
MORTGAGERS
MORTGAGING
MORTGAGORS
MORTICIANS
MORTIFEROUS
MORTIFEROUSNESS
MORTIFICATION
MORTIFICATIONS
MORTIFIERS
MORTIFYING
MORTIFYINGLY
MORTIFYINGS
MORTUARIES
MORULATION
MORULATIONS
MOSAICALLY
MOSAICISMS
MOSAICISTS
MOSAICKING
MOSAICKINGS
MOSAICLIKE
MOSASAURUS
MOSBOLLETJIE
MOSBOLLETJIES
MOSCHATELS
MOSCHIFEROUS
MOSCOVIUMS
MOSKONFYTS
MOSQUITOES
MOSQUITOEY
MOSQUITOFISH
MOSQUITOFISHES
MOSQUITOIER
MOSQUITOIEST
MOSSBACKED
MOSSBLUITER
MOSSBLUITERS
MOSSBUNKER
MOSSBUNKERS
MOSSINESSES
MOSSPLANTS
MOSSTROOPER
MOSSTROOPERS
MOTETTISTS
MOTHBALLED
MOTHBALLING
MOTHERBOARD
MOTHERBOARDS
MOTHERCRAFT
MOTHERCRAFTS
MOTHERESES
MOTHERFUCKER
MOTHERFUCKERS
MOTHERFUCKING
MOTHERHOOD
MOTHERHOODS
MOTHERHOUSE
MOTHERHOUSES
MOTHERIEST
MOTHERINGS
MOTHERLAND
MOTHERLANDS
MOTHERLESS
MOTHERLESSNESS
MOTHERLIER
MOTHERLIEST
MOTHERLINESS
MOTHERLINESSES
MOTHERWORT
MOTHERWORTS
MOTHPROOFED
MOTHPROOFER
MOTHPROOFERS
MOTHPROOFING
MOTHPROOFS
MOTILITIES
MOTIONISTS
MOTIONLESS
MOTIONLESSLY
MOTIONLESSNESS
MOTIVATING
MOTIVATION
MOTIVATIONAL
MOTIVATIONALLY
MOTIVATIONS
MOTIVATIVE
MOTIVATORS
MOTIVELESS
MOTIVELESSLY
MOTIVELESSNESS
MOTIVITIES
MOTOCROSSES
MOTONEURON
MOTONEURONAL
MOTONEURONS
MOTORBICYCLE
MOTORBICYCLES
MOTORBIKED
MOTORBIKES
MOTORBIKING
MOTORBOATED
MOTORBOATER
MOTORBOATERS
MOTORBOATING
MOTORBOATINGS
MOTORBOATS
MOTORBUSES
MOTORBUSSES
MOTORCADED
MOTORCADES
MOTORCADING
MOTORCOACH
MOTORCOACHES
MOTORCYCLE
MOTORCYCLED
MOTORCYCLES

MOTORCYCLING
MOTORCYCLINGS
MOTORCYCLIST
MOTORCYCLISTS
MOTORHOMES
MOTORICALLY
MOTORISATION
MOTORISATIONS
MOTORISING
MOTORIZATION
MOTORIZATIONS
MOTORIZING
MOTORMOUTH
MOTORMOUTHS
MOTORSHIPS
MOTORTRUCK
MOTORTRUCKS
MOTOSCAFOS
MOUCHARABIES
MOUCHARABY
MOUDIEWART
MOUDIEWARTS
MOUDIEWORT
MOUDIEWORTS
MOUDIWARTS
MOUDIWORTS
MOULDABILITIES
MOULDABILITY
MOULDBOARD
MOULDBOARDS
MOULDERING
MOULDINESS
MOULDINESSES
MOULDWARPS
MOULDYWARP
MOULDYWARPS
MOUNDBIRDS
MOUNTAINBOARD
MOUNTAINBOARDER
MOUNTAINBOARDS
MOUNTAINED
MOUNTAINEER
MOUNTAINEERED
MOUNTAINEERING
MOUNTAINEERINGS
MOUNTAINEERS
MOUNTAINIER
MOUNTAINIEST
MOUNTAINOUS
MOUNTAINOUSLY
MOUNTAINOUSNESS
MOUNTAINSIDE
MOUNTAINSIDES
MOUNTAINTOP
MOUNTAINTOPS
MOUNTEBANK
MOUNTEBANKED
MOUNTEBANKERIES
MOUNTEBANKERY
MOUNTEBANKING
MOUNTEBANKINGS
MOUNTEBANKISM
MOUNTEBANKISMS
MOUNTEBANKS
MOUNTENANCE
MOUNTENANCES
MOUNTENAUNCE
MOUNTENAUNCES
MOURNFULLER
MOURNFULLEST
MOURNFULLY
MOURNFULNESS
MOURNFULNESSES
MOURNINGLY
MOURNIVALS
MOURVEDRES
MOUSEBIRDS
MOUSEOVERS
MOUSEPIECE
MOUSEPIECES
MOUSETAILS
MOUSETRAPPED
MOUSETRAPPING
MOUSETRAPPINGS
MOUSETRAPS
MOUSINESSES
MOUSQUETAIRE
MOUSQUETAIRES
MOUSSELIKE
MOUSSELINE
MOUSSELINES
MOUSTACHED
MOUSTACHES
MOUSTACHIAL
MOUSTACHIO
MOUSTACHIOED
MOUSTACHIOS
MOUTHBREATHER
MOUTHBREATHERS
MOUTHBREEDER
MOUTHBREEDERS
MOUTHBROODER
MOUTHBROODERS
MOUTHFEELS
MOUTHPARTS
MOUTHPIECE
MOUTHPIECES
MOUTHWASHES
MOUTHWATERING
MOUTHWATERINGLY
MOUVEMENTE
MOVABILITIES
MOVABILITY
MOVABLENESS
MOVABLENESSES
MOVEABILITIES
MOVEABILITY
MOVEABLENESS
MOVEABLENESSES
MOVELESSLY
MOVELESSNESS
MOVELESSNESSES
MOVIEGOERS
MOVIEGOING
MOVIEGOINGS
MOVIELANDS
MOVIEMAKER
MOVIEMAKERS
MOVIEMAKING
MOVIEMAKINGS
MOWBURNING
MOWBURNINGS
MOWDIEWART
MOWDIEWARTS
MOWDIEWORT
MOWDIEWORTS
MOXIBUSTION
MOXIBUSTIONS
MOYGASHELS
MOZZARELLA
MOZZARELLAS
MRIDAMGAMS
MRIDANGAMS
MUCEDINOUS
MUCHNESSES
MUCIDITIES
MUCIDNESSES
MUCIFEROUS
MUCILAGINOUS
MUCILAGINOUSLY
MUCINOGENS
MUCKAMUCKED
MUCKAMUCKING
MUCKAMUCKS
MUCKENDERS
MUCKINESSES
MUCKRAKERS
MUCKRAKING
MUCKRAKINGS
MUCKSPREAD
MUCKSPREADER
MUCKSPREADERS
MUCKSPREADING
MUCKSPREADS
MUCKSWEATS
MUCKYMUCKS
MUCOCUTANEOUS
MUCOLYTICS
MUCOMEMBRANOUS
MUCOPEPTIDE
MUCOPEPTIDES
MUCOPROTEIN
MUCOPROTEINS
MUCOPURULENT
MUCOSANGUINEOUS
MUCOSITIES
MUCOVISCIDOSES
MUCOVISCIDOSIS
MUCRONATED
MUCRONATION
MUCRONATIONS
MUDCAPPING
MUDCAPPINGS
MUDDINESSES
MUDDLEDNESS
MUDDLEDNESSES
MUDDLEHEAD
MUDDLEHEADED
MUDDLEHEADEDLY
MUDDLEHEADS
MUDDLEMENT
MUDDLEMENTS
MUDDLINGLY
MUDHOPPERS
MUDLARKING
MUDLOGGERS
MUDLOGGING
MUDLOGGINGS
MUDPUPPIES
MUDSKIPPER
MUDSKIPPERS
MUDSLINGER
MUDSLINGERS
MUDSLINGING
MUDSLINGINGS
MUFFETTEES
MUFFINEERS
MUGEARITES
MUGGINESSES
MUGWUMPERIES
MUGWUMPERY
MUGWUMPISH
MUGWUMPISM
MUGWUMPISMS
MUJAHEDDIN
MUJAHEDEEN
MUJAHIDEEN
MUKHABARAT
MUKHABARATS
MULBERRIES
MULIEBRITIES
MULIEBRITY
MULISHNESS
MULISHNESSES
MULLAHISMS
MULLARKIES
MULLIGATAWNIES
MULLIGATAWNY
MULLIGRUBS
MULLIONING
MULLOCKIER
MULLOCKIEST
MULTANGULAR
MULTANIMOUS
MULTARTICULATE
MULTEITIES
MULTIACCESS
MULTIACCESSES
MULTIAGENCY
MULTIANGULAR

MULTIARMED
MULTIARTICULATE
MULTIAUTHOR
MULTIAXIAL
MULTIBARREL
MULTIBARRELED
MULTIBARRELLED
MULTIBARRELS
MULTIBILLION
MULTIBLADED
MULTIBRANCHED
MULTIBUILDING
MULTICAMERATE
MULTICAMPUS
MULTICAPITATE
MULTICARBON
MULTICASTS
MULTICAULINE
MULTICAUSAL
MULTICELLED
MULTICELLULAR
MULTICENTER
MULTICENTRAL
MULTICENTRE
MULTICENTRIC
MULTICHAIN
MULTICHAMBERED
MULTICHANNEL
MULTICHARACTER
MULTICIDES
MULTICIPITAL
MULTICLIENT
MULTICOATED
MULTICOLOR
MULTICOLORED
MULTICOLORS
MULTICOLOUR
MULTICOLOURED
MULTICOLOURS
MULTICOLUMN
MULTICOMPONENT
MULTICONDUCTOR
MULTICOPIES
MULTICOSTATE
MULTICOUNTY
MULTICOURSE
MULTICULTI
MULTICULTIS
MULTICULTURAL
MULTICULTURALLY
MULTICURIE
MULTICURRENCIES
MULTICURRENCY
MULTICUSPID
MULTICUSPIDATE
MULTICUSPIDS
MULTICYCLE
MULTICYCLES
MULTICYLINDER
MULTIDENTATE
MULTIDIALECTAL
MULTIDIGITATE
MULTIDISCIPLINE
MULTIDIVISIONAL
MULTIDOMAIN
MULTIELECTRODE
MULTIELEMENT
MULTIEMPLOYER
MULTIEMPLOYERS
MULTIENGINE
MULTIENGINED
MULTIENZYME
MULTIETHNIC
MULTIETHNICS
MULTIFACED
MULTIFACETED
MULTIFACTOR
MULTIFACTORIAL
MULTIFAMILIES
MULTIFAMILY
MULTIFARIOUS
MULTIFARIOUSLY
MULTIFIDLY
MULTIFIDOUS
MULTIFILAMENT
MULTIFILAMENTS
MULTIFLASH
MULTIFLORA
MULTIFLORAS
MULTIFLOROUS
MULTIFOCAL
MULTIFOCALS
MULTIFOILS
MULTIFOLIATE
MULTIFOLIOLATE
MULTIFORMITIES
MULTIFORMITY
MULTIFORMS
MULTIFREQUENCY
MULTIFUNCTION
MULTIFUNCTIONAL
MULTIGENES
MULTIGENIC
MULTIGRADE
MULTIGRADES
MULTIGRAIN
MULTIGRAVIDA
MULTIGRAVIDAE
MULTIGRAVIDAS
MULTIGROUP
MULTIHEADED
MULTIHOSPITAL
MULTIHULLS
MULTIJUGATE
MULTIJUGOUS
MULTILANES
MULTILATERAL
MULTILATERALISM
MULTILATERALIST
MULTILATERALLY
MULTILAYER
MULTILAYERED
MULTILAYERS
MULTILEVEL
MULTILEVELED
MULTILEVELLED
MULTILINEAL
MULTILINEAR
MULTILINES
MULTILINGUAL
MULTILINGUALISM
MULTILINGUALLY
MULTILINGUIST
MULTILINGUISTS
MULTILOBATE
MULTILOBED
MULTILOBES
MULTILOBULAR
MULTILOBULATE
MULTILOCATIONAL
MULTILOCULAR
MULTILOCULATE
MULTILOQUENCE
MULTILOQUENCES
MULTILOQUENT
MULTILOQUIES
MULTILOQUOUS
MULTILOQUY
MULTIMANNED
MULTIMEDIA
MULTIMEDIAS
MULTIMEGATON
MULTIMEGAWATT
MULTIMEGAWATTS
MULTIMEMBER
MULTIMETALLIC
MULTIMETER
MULTIMETERS
MULTIMILLENNIAL
MULTIMILLION
MULTIMODAL
MULTIMODES
MULTIMOLECULAR
MULTINATION
MULTINATIONAL
MULTINATIONALS
MULTINOMIAL
MULTINOMIALS
MULTINOMINAL
MULTINUCLEAR
MULTINUCLEATE
MULTINUCLEATED
MULTINUCLEOLAR
MULTINUCLEOLATE
MULTIORGASMIC
MULTIPACKS
MULTIPANED
MULTIPARAE
MULTIPARAMETER
MULTIPARAS
MULTIPARITIES
MULTIPARITY
MULTIPAROUS
MULTIPARTICLE
MULTIPARTITE
MULTIPARTY
MULTIPARTYISM
MULTIPARTYISMS
MULTIPEDES
MULTIPHASE
MULTIPHASIC
MULTIPHOTON
MULTIPICTURE
MULTIPIECE
MULTIPISTON
MULTIPLANE
MULTIPLANES
MULTIPLANT
MULTIPLAYER
MULTIPLAYERS
MULTIPLETS
MULTIPLEXED
MULTIPLEXER
MULTIPLEXERS
MULTIPLEXES
MULTIPLEXING
MULTIPLEXINGS
MULTIPLEXOR
MULTIPLEXORS
MULTIPLIABLE
MULTIPLICABLE
MULTIPLICAND
MULTIPLICANDS
MULTIPLICATE
MULTIPLICATES
MULTIPLICATION
MULTIPLICATIONS
MULTIPLICATIVE
MULTIPLICATOR
MULTIPLICATORS
MULTIPLICITIES
MULTIPLICITY
MULTIPLIED
MULTIPLIER
MULTIPLIERS
MULTIPLIES
MULTIPLYING
MULTIPOINT
MULTIPOLAR
MULTIPOLARITIES
MULTIPOLARITY
MULTIPOLES
MULTIPOTENT
MULTIPOTENTIAL
MULTIPOWER
MULTIPRESENCE
MULTIPRESENCES
MULTIPRESENT
MULTIPROBLEM
MULTIPROCESSING

MULTIPROCESSOR
MULTIPROCESSORS
MULTIPRODUCT
MULTIPRONGED
MULTIPURPOSE
MULTIRACIAL
MULTIRACIALISM
MULTIRACIALISMS
MULTIRACIALLY
MULTIRAMIFIED
MULTIRANGE
MULTIREGIONAL
MULTIRELIGIOUS
MULTIROOMED
MULTISCIENCE
MULTISCIENCES
MULTISCREEN
MULTISCREENS
MULTISENSE
MULTISENSORY
MULTISEPTATE
MULTISERIAL
MULTISERIATE
MULTISERVICE
MULTISIDED
MULTISKILL
MULTISKILLED
MULTISKILLING
MULTISKILLINGS
MULTISKILLS
MULTISONANT
MULTISOURCE
MULTISPECIES
MULTISPECTRAL
MULTISPEED
MULTISPIRAL
MULTISPORT
MULTISTAGE
MULTISTANDARD
MULTISTATE
MULTISTEMMED
MULTISTOREY
MULTISTOREYS
MULTISTORIED
MULTISTORIES
MULTISTORY
MULTISTRANDED
MULTISTRIKE
MULTISTRIKES
MULTISULCATE
MULTISYLLABIC
MULTISYSTEM
MULTITALENTED
MULTITASKED
MULTITASKING
MULTITASKINGS
MULTITASKS
MULTITERMINAL
MULTITHREADING
MULTITHREADINGS
MULTITIERED
MULTITONED
MULTITONES
MULTITOOLS
MULTITOWERED
MULTITRACK
MULTITRACKED
MULTITRACKING
MULTITRACKS
MULTITRILLION
MULTITRILLIONS
MULTITUDES
MULTITUDINARY
MULTITUDINOUS
MULTITUDINOUSLY
MULTIUNION
MULTIUTILITIES
MULTIUTILITY
MULTIVALENCE
MULTIVALENCES
MULTIVALENCIES
MULTIVALENCY
MULTIVALENT
MULTIVALENTS
MULTIVARIABLE
MULTIVARIATE
MULTIVARIOUS
MULTIVERSE
MULTIVERSES
MULTIVERSITIES
MULTIVERSITY
MULTIVIBRATOR
MULTIVIBRATORS
MULTIVIOUS
MULTIVITAMIN
MULTIVITAMINS
MULTIVOCAL
MULTIVOCALS
MULTIVOLTINE
MULTIVOLUME
MULTIWARHEAD
MULTIWAVELENGTH
MULTIWINDOW
MULTIWINDOWS
MULTOCULAR
MULTUNGULATE
MULTUNGULATES
MUMBLEMENT
MUMBLEMENTS
MUMBLETYPEG
MUMBLETYPEGS
MUMBLINGLY
MUMCHANCES
MUMMERINGS
MUMMICHOGS
MUMMIFICATION
MUMMIFICATIONS
MUMMIFORMS
MUMMIFYING
MUMPISHNESS
MUMPISHNESSES
MUMPRENEUR
MUMPRENEURS
MUMPSIMUSES
MUMSINESSES
MUNCHABLES
MUNDANENESS
MUNDANENESSES
MUNDANITIES
MUNDIFICATION
MUNDIFICATIONS
MUNDIFICATIVE
MUNDIFICATIVES
MUNDIFYING
MUNDUNGUSES
MUNICIPALISE
MUNICIPALISED
MUNICIPALISES
MUNICIPALISING
MUNICIPALISM
MUNICIPALISMS
MUNICIPALIST
MUNICIPALISTS
MUNICIPALITIES
MUNICIPALITY
MUNICIPALIZE
MUNICIPALIZED
MUNICIPALIZES
MUNICIPALIZING
MUNICIPALLY
MUNICIPALS
MUNIFICENCE
MUNIFICENCES
MUNIFICENT
MUNIFICENTLY
MUNIFICENTNESS
MUNIFIENCE
MUNIFIENCES
MUNITIONED
MUNITIONEER
MUNITIONEERS
MUNITIONER
MUNITIONERS
MUNITIONETTE
MUNITIONETTES
MUNITIONING
MURDERABILIA
MURDERBALL
MURDERBALLS
MURDERESSES
MURDEROUSLY
MURDEROUSNESS
MURDEROUSNESSES
MURGEONING
MURKINESSES
MURMURATION
MURMURATIONS
MURMURINGLY
MURMURINGS
MURMUROUSLY
MURTHERERS
MURTHERING
MUSCADELLE
MUSCADELLES
MUSCADINES
MUSCARDINE
MUSCARDINES
MUSCARINES
MUSCARINIC
MUSCATORIA
MUSCATORIUM
MUSCAVADOS
MUSCOLOGIES
MUSCOVADOS
MUSCOVITES
MUSCULARITIES
MUSCULARITY
MUSCULARLY
MUSCULATION
MUSCULATIONS
MUSCULATURE
MUSCULATURES
MUSCULOSKELETAL
MUSEOLOGICAL
MUSEOLOGIES
MUSEOLOGIST
MUSEOLOGISTS
MUSHINESSES
MUSHMOUTHS
MUSHROOMED
MUSHROOMER
MUSHROOMERS
MUSHROOMIER
MUSHROOMIEST
MUSHROOMING
MUSHROOMINGS
MUSICALISATION
MUSICALISATIONS
MUSICALISE
MUSICALISED
MUSICALISES
MUSICALISING
MUSICALITIES
MUSICALITY
MUSICALIZATION
MUSICALIZATIONS
MUSICALIZE
MUSICALIZED
MUSICALIZES
MUSICALIZING
MUSICALNESS
MUSICALNESSES
MUSICIANER
MUSICIANERS
MUSICIANLIER
MUSICIANLIEST
MUSICIANLY
MUSICIANSHIP
MUSICIANSHIPS
MUSICOLOGICAL

MUSICOLOGICALLY
MUSICOLOGIES
MUSICOLOGIST
MUSICOLOGISTS
MUSICOLOGY
MUSICOTHERAPIES
MUSICOTHERAPY
MUSKELLUNGE
MUSKELLUNGES
MUSKETEERS
MUSKETOONS
MUSKETRIES
MUSKINESSES
MUSKMELONS
MUSQUASHES
MUSQUETOON
MUSQUETOONS
MUSSELCRACKER
MUSSELCRACKERS
MUSSINESSES
MUSSITATED
MUSSITATES
MUSSITATING
MUSSITATION
MUSSITATIONS
MUSTACHIOED
MUSTACHIOS
MUSTARDIER
MUSTARDIEST
MUSTELINES
MUSTINESSES
MUTABILITIES
MUTABILITY
MUTABLENESS
MUTABLENESSES
MUTAGENESES
MUTAGENESIS
MUTAGENICALLY
MUTAGENICITIES
MUTAGENICITY
MUTAGENISE
MUTAGENISED
MUTAGENISES
MUTAGENISING
MUTAGENIZE
MUTAGENIZED
MUTAGENIZES
MUTAGENIZING
MUTATIONAL
MUTATIONALLY
MUTATIONIST
MUTATIONISTS
MUTENESSES
MUTESSARIF
MUTESSARIFAT
MUTESSARIFATS
MUTESSARIFS
MUTILATING
MUTILATION
MUTILATIONS
MUTILATIVE
MUTILATORS
MUTINEERED
MUTINEERING
MUTINOUSLY
MUTINOUSNESS
MUTINOUSNESSES
MUTOSCOPES
MUTTERATION
MUTTERATIONS
MUTTERINGLY
MUTTERINGS
MUTTONBIRD
MUTTONBIRDER
MUTTONBIRDERS
MUTTONBIRDS
MUTTONCHOPS
MUTTONFISH
MUTTONFISHES
MUTTONHEAD
MUTTONHEADED
MUTTONHEADS
MUTTONIEST
MUTUALISATION
MUTUALISATIONS
MUTUALISED
MUTUALISES
MUTUALISING
MUTUALISMS
MUTUALISTIC
MUTUALISTS
MUTUALITIES
MUTUALIZATION
MUTUALIZATIONS
MUTUALIZED
MUTUALIZES
MUTUALIZING
MUTUALNESS
MUTUALNESSES
MUZZINESSES
MYASTHENIA
MYASTHENIAS
MYASTHENIC
MYASTHENICS
MYCETOLOGIES
MYCETOLOGY
MYCETOMATA
MYCETOMATOUS
MYCETOPHAGOUS
MYCETOZOAN
MYCETOZOANS
MYCOBACTERIA
MYCOBACTERIAL
MYCOBACTERIUM
MYCOBIONTS
MYCODOMATIA
MYCODOMATIUM
MYCOFLORAE
MYCOFLORAS
MYCOLOGICAL
MYCOLOGICALLY
MYCOLOGIES
MYCOLOGIST
MYCOLOGISTS
MYCOPHAGIES
MYCOPHAGIST
MYCOPHAGISTS
MYCOPHAGOUS
MYCOPHILES
MYCOPLASMA
MYCOPLASMAL
MYCOPLASMAS
MYCOPLASMATA
MYCOPLASMOSES
MYCOPLASMOSIS
MYCORHIZAE
MYCORHIZAL
MYCORHIZAS
MYCORRHIZA
MYCORRHIZAE
MYCORRHIZAL
MYCORRHIZAS
MYCOTOXICOLOGY
MYCOTOXICOSES
MYCOTOXICOSIS
MYCOTOXINS
MYCOTOXOLOGIES
MYCOTOXOLOGY
MYCOTROPHIC
MYCOVIRUSES
MYDRIATICS
MYELENCEPHALA
MYELENCEPHALIC
MYELENCEPHALON
MYELENCEPHALONS
MYELINATED
MYELITIDES
MYELITISES
MYELOBLAST
MYELOBLASTIC
MYELOBLASTS
MYELOCYTES
MYELOCYTIC
MYELOFIBROSES
MYELOFIBROSIS
MYELOFIBROTIC
MYELOGENOUS
MYELOGRAMS
MYELOGRAPHIES
MYELOGRAPHY
MYELOMATOID
MYELOMATOUS
MYELOPATHIC
MYELOPATHIES
MYELOPATHY
MYIOPHILIES
MYIOPHILOUS
MYLOHYOIDS
MYLONITISATION
MYLONITISATIONS
MYLONITISE
MYLONITISED
MYLONITISES
MYLONITISING
MYLONITIZATION
MYLONITIZATIONS
MYLONITIZE
MYLONITIZED
MYLONITIZES
MYLONITIZING
MYOBLASTIC
MYOCARDIAL
MYOCARDIOGRAPH
MYOCARDIOGRAPHS
MYOCARDIOPATHY
MYOCARDITIS
MYOCARDITISES
MYOCARDIUM
MYOCLONUSES
MYOELECTRIC
MYOELECTRICAL
MYOFIBRILLAR
MYOFIBRILS
MYOFILAMENT
MYOFILAMENTS
MYOGLOBINS
MYOGRAPHIC
MYOGRAPHICAL
MYOGRAPHICALLY
MYOGRAPHIES
MYOGRAPHIST
MYOGRAPHISTS
MYOINOSITOL
MYOINOSITOLS
MYOLOGICAL
MYOLOGISTS
MYOMANCIES
MYOMECTOMIES
MYOMECTOMY
MYOPATHIES
MYOPHILIES
MYOPHILOUS
MYOPICALLY
MYOSITISES
MYOSOTISES
MYOSTATINS
MYRIADFOLD
MYRIADFOLDS
MYRIAPODAN
MYRIAPODOUS
MYRINGITIS
MYRINGITISES
MYRINGOSCOPE
MYRINGOSCOPES
MYRINGOTOMIES
MYRINGOTOMY
MYRIORAMAS
MYRIOSCOPE
MYRIOSCOPES
MYRISTICIVOROUS

MYRMECOCHORIES
MYRMECOCHORY
MYRMECOLOGIC
MYRMECOLOGICAL
MYRMECOLOGIES
MYRMECOLOGIST
MYRMECOLOGISTS
MYRMECOLOGY
MYRMECOPHAGOUS
MYRMECOPHILE
MYRMECOPHILES
MYRMECOPHILIES
MYRMECOPHILOUS
MYRMECOPHILY
MYRMIDONES
MYRMIDONIAN
MYROBALANS
MYRTACEOUS
MYSOPHOBIA
MYSOPHOBIAS
MYSTAGOGIC
MYSTAGOGICAL
MYSTAGOGICALLY
MYSTAGOGIES
MYSTAGOGUE
MYSTAGOGUES
MYSTAGOGUS
MYSTAGOGUSES
MYSTERIOUS
MYSTERIOUSLY
MYSTERIOUSNESS
MYSTICALLY
MYSTICALNESS
MYSTICALNESSES
MYSTICETES
MYSTICISMS
MYSTIFICATION
MYSTIFICATIONS
MYSTIFIERS
MYSTIFYING
MYSTIFYINGLY
MYTHICALLY
MYTHICISATION
MYTHICISATIONS
MYTHICISED
MYTHICISER
MYTHICISERS
MYTHICISES
MYTHICISING
MYTHICISMS
MYTHICISTS
MYTHICIZATION
MYTHICIZATIONS
MYTHICIZED
MYTHICIZER
MYTHICIZERS
MYTHICIZES
MYTHICIZING
MYTHMAKERS
MYTHMAKING
MYTHMAKINGS
MYTHOGENESES
MYTHOGENESIS
MYTHOGRAPHER
MYTHOGRAPHERS
MYTHOGRAPHIES
MYTHOGRAPHY
MYTHOLOGER
MYTHOLOGERS
MYTHOLOGIAN
MYTHOLOGIANS
MYTHOLOGIC
MYTHOLOGICAL
MYTHOLOGICALLY
MYTHOLOGIES
MYTHOLOGISATION
MYTHOLOGISE
MYTHOLOGISED
MYTHOLOGISER
MYTHOLOGISERS
MYTHOLOGISES
MYTHOLOGISING
MYTHOLOGIST
MYTHOLOGISTS
MYTHOLOGIZATION
MYTHOLOGIZE
MYTHOLOGIZED
MYTHOLOGIZER
MYTHOLOGIZERS
MYTHOLOGIZES
MYTHOLOGIZING
MYTHOMANES
MYTHOMANIA
MYTHOMANIAC
MYTHOMANIACS
MYTHOMANIAS
MYTHOPOEIA
MYTHOPOEIAS
MYTHOPOEIC
MYTHOPOEISM
MYTHOPOEISMS
MYTHOPOEIST
MYTHOPOEISTS
MYTHOPOESES
MYTHOPOESIS
MYTHOPOETIC
MYTHOPOETICAL
MYTHOPOETS
MYTILIFORM
MYXAMOEBAE
MYXAMOEBAS
MYXEDEMATOUS
MYXOEDEMAS
MYXOEDEMATOUS
MYXOEDEMIC
MYXOMATOSES
MYXOMATOSIS
MYXOMATOUS
MYXOMYCETE
MYXOMYCETES
MYXOMYCETOUS
MYXOVIRUSES

N

NABOBERIES
NABOBESSES
NACHTMAALS
NAFFNESSES
NAIFNESSES
NAILBITERS
NAILBRUSHES
NAISSANCES
NAIVENESSES
NAKEDNESSES
NALBUPHINE
NALBUPHINES
NALORPHINE
NALORPHINES
NALTREXONE
NALTREXONES
NAMAYCUSHES
NAMECHECKED
NAMECHECKING
NAMECHECKS
NAMELESSLY
NAMELESSNESS
NAMELESSNESSES
NAMEPLATES
NAMEWORTHIER
NAMEWORTHIEST
NAMEWORTHY
NANDROLONE
NANDROLONES
NANISATION
NANISATIONS
NANIZATION
NANIZATIONS
NANNOPLANKTON
NANNOPLANKTONS
NANOGRAMME
NANOGRAMMES
NANOGRASSES
NANOMATERIAL
NANOMATERIALS
NANOMETERS
NANOMETRES
NANOPARTICLE
NANOPARTICLES
NANOPHYSICS
NANOPLANKTON
NANOPLANKTONS
NANOPUBLISHING
NANOPUBLISHINGS
NANOSECOND
NANOSECONDS
NANOTECHNOLOGY
NANOTESLAS
NANOWORLDS
NAPHTHALENE
NAPHTHALENES
NAPHTHALIC
NAPHTHALIN
NAPHTHALINE
NAPHTHALINES
NAPHTHALINS
NAPHTHALISE
NAPHTHALISED
NAPHTHALISES
NAPHTHALISING
NAPHTHALIZE
NAPHTHALIZED
NAPHTHALIZES
NAPHTHALIZING
NAPHTHENES
NAPHTHENIC
NAPHTHYLAMINE
NAPHTHYLAMINES
NAPOLEONITE
NAPOLEONITES
NAPPINESSES
NAPRAPATHIES
NAPRAPATHY
NARCISSISM
NARCISSISMS
NARCISSIST
NARCISSISTIC
NARCISSISTS
NARCISSUSES
NARCOANALYSES
NARCOANALYSIS
NARCOCATHARSES
NARCOCATHARSIS
NARCOHYPNOSES
NARCOHYPNOSIS
NARCOLEPSIES
NARCOLEPSY
NARCOLEPTIC
NARCOLEPTICS
NARCOSYNTHESES
NARCOSYNTHESIS
NARCOTERRORISM
NARCOTERRORISMS
NARCOTERRORIST
NARCOTERRORISTS
NARCOTICALLY
NARCOTINES
NARCOTISATION
NARCOTISATIONS
NARCOTISED
NARCOTISES
NARCOTISING
NARCOTISMS
NARCOTISTS
NARCOTIZATION
NARCOTIZATIONS
NARCOTIZED
NARCOTIZES
NARCOTIZING
NARGHILIES
NARGHILLIES
NARGUILEHS
NARRATABLE
NARRATIONAL
NARRATIONS
NARRATIVELY
NARRATIVES
NARRATOLOGICAL
NARRATOLOGIES
NARRATOLOGIST
NARRATOLOGISTS
NARRATOLOGY
NARROWBAND
NARROWBANDS
NARROWCAST
NARROWCASTED
NARROWCASTING
NARROWCASTINGS
NARROWCASTS
NARROWINGS
NARROWNESS
NARROWNESSES
NASALISATION
NASALISATIONS
NASALISING
NASALITIES
NASALIZATION
NASALIZATIONS
NASALIZING
NASCENCIES
NASEBERRIES
NASOFRONTAL
NASOGASTRIC
NASOLACRYMAL
NASOPHARYNGEAL
NASOPHARYNGES
NASOPHARYNX
NASOPHARYNXES
NASTINESSES
NASTURTIUM
NASTURTIUMS
NATALITIAL
NATALITIES
NATATIONAL
NATATORIAL
NATATORIUM
NATATORIUMS
NATHELESSE
NATIONALISATION
NATIONALISE
NATIONALISED
NATIONALISER
NATIONALISERS
NATIONALISES
NATIONALISING
NATIONALISM
NATIONALISMS
NATIONALIST
NATIONALISTIC
NATIONALISTS
NATIONALITIES
NATIONALITY
NATIONALIZATION
NATIONALIZE
NATIONALIZED
NATIONALIZER
NATIONALIZERS
NATIONALIZES
NATIONALIZING
NATIONALLY
NATIONHOOD
NATIONHOODS
NATIONLESS
NATIONWIDE
NATIVENESS
NATIVENESSES
NATIVISTIC
NATIVITIES
NATRIURESES
NATRIURESIS
NATRIURESISES
NATRIURETIC
NATRIURETICS
NATROLITES
NATTERIEST
NATTERJACK
NATTERJACKS
NATTINESSES
NATURALISATION
NATURALISATIONS
NATURALISE
NATURALISED
NATURALISES
NATURALISING
NATURALISM

NATURALISMS
NATURALIST
NATURALISTIC
NATURALISTS
NATURALIZATION
NATURALIZATIONS
NATURALIZE
NATURALIZED
NATURALIZES
NATURALIZING
NATURALNESS
NATURALNESSES
NATURISTIC
NATUROPATH
NATUROPATHIC
NATUROPATHIES
NATUROPATHS
NATUROPATHY
NAUGAHYDES
NAUGHTIEST
NAUGHTINESS
NAUGHTINESSES
NAUMACHIAE
NAUMACHIAS
NAUMACHIES
NAUPLIIFORM
NAUSEATING
NAUSEATINGLY
NAUSEATION
NAUSEATIONS
NAUSEATIVE
NAUSEOUSLY
NAUSEOUSNESS
NAUSEOUSNESSES
NAUTICALLY
NAUTILOIDS
NAUTILUSES
NAVARCHIES
NAVELWORTS
NAVICULARE
NAVICULARES
NAVICULARS
NAVIGABILITIES
NAVIGABILITY
NAVIGABLENESS
NAVIGABLENESSES
NAVIGATING
NAVIGATION
NAVIGATIONAL
NAVIGATIONALLY
NAVIGATIONS
NAVIGATORS
NAYSAYINGS
NAZIFICATION
NAZIFICATIONS
NEANDERTAL
NEANDERTALER
NEANDERTALERS
NEANDERTALS
NEANDERTHAL
NEANDERTHALER
NEANDERTHALERS
NEANDERTHALOID
NEANDERTHALS
NEAPOLITAN
NEAPOLITANS
NEARNESSES
NEARSHORED
NEARSHORES
NEARSHORING
NEARSIGHTED
NEARSIGHTEDLY
NEARSIGHTEDNESS
NEARTHROSES
NEARTHROSIS
NEATNESSES
NEBBISHERS
NEBBISHIER
NEBBISHIEST
NEBENKERNS
NEBUCHADNEZZAR
NEBUCHADNEZZARS
NEBULISATION
NEBULISATIONS
NEBULISERS
NEBULISING
NEBULIZATION
NEBULIZATIONS
NEBULIZERS
NEBULIZING
NEBULOSITIES
NEBULOSITY
NEBULOUSLY
NEBULOUSNESS
NEBULOUSNESSES
NECESSAIRE
NECESSAIRES
NECESSARIAN
NECESSARIANISM
NECESSARIANISMS
NECESSARIANS
NECESSARIES
NECESSARILY
NECESSARINESS
NECESSARINESSES
NECESSITARIAN
NECESSITARIANS
NECESSITATE
NECESSITATED
NECESSITATES
NECESSITATING
NECESSITATION
NECESSITATIONS
NECESSITATIVE
NECESSITIED
NECESSITIES
NECESSITOUS
NECESSITOUSLY
NECESSITOUSNESS
NECKCLOTHS
NECKERCHIEF
NECKERCHIEFS
NECKERCHIEVES
NECKLACING
NECKLACINGS
NECKPIECES
NECKVERSES
NECROBIOSES
NECROBIOSIS
NECROBIOTIC
NECROGRAPHER
NECROGRAPHERS
NECROLATER
NECROLATERS
NECROLATRIES
NECROLATRY
NECROLOGIC
NECROLOGICAL
NECROLOGIES
NECROLOGIST
NECROLOGISTS
NECROMANCER
NECROMANCERS
NECROMANCIES
NECROMANCY
NECROMANIA
NECROMANIAC
NECROMANIACS
NECROMANIAS
NECROMANTIC
NECROMANTICAL
NECROMANTICALLY
NECROPHAGOUS
NECROPHILE
NECROPHILES
NECROPHILIA
NECROPHILIAC
NECROPHILIACS
NECROPHILIAS
NECROPHILIC
NECROPHILIES
NECROPHILISM
NECROPHILISMS
NECROPHILOUS
NECROPHILS
NECROPHILY
NECROPHOBE
NECROPHOBES
NECROPHOBIA
NECROPHOBIAS
NECROPHOBIC
NECROPHOROUS
NECROPOLEIS
NECROPOLES
NECROPOLIS
NECROPOLISES
NECROPSIED
NECROPSIES
NECROPSYING
NECROSCOPIC
NECROSCOPICAL
NECROSCOPIES
NECROSCOPY
NECROTISED
NECROTISES
NECROTISING
NECROTIZED
NECROTIZES
NECROTIZING
NECROTOMIES
NECROTROPH
NECROTROPHIC
NECROTROPHS
NECTAREOUS
NECTAREOUSNESS
NECTARIFEROUS
NECTARINES
NECTARIVOROUS
NECTOCALYCES
NECTOCALYX
NEEDCESSITIES
NEEDCESSITY
NEEDFULNESS
NEEDFULNESSES
NEEDINESSES
NEEDLECORD
NEEDLECORDS
NEEDLECRAFT
NEEDLECRAFTS
NEEDLEFISH
NEEDLEFISHES
NEEDLEFULS
NEEDLELESS
NEEDLELIKE
NEEDLEPOINT
NEEDLEPOINTED
NEEDLEPOINTING
NEEDLEPOINTS
NEEDLESSLY
NEEDLESSNESS
NEEDLESSNESSES
NEEDLESTICK
NEEDLESTICKS
NEEDLEWOMAN
NEEDLEWOMEN
NEEDLEWORK
NEEDLEWORKER
NEEDLEWORKERS
NEEDLEWORKS
NEESBERRIES
NEFARIOUSLY
NEFARIOUSNESS
NEFARIOUSNESSES
NEGATIONAL
NEGATIONIST
NEGATIONISTS
NEGATIVELY
NEGATIVENESS
NEGATIVENESSES
NEGATIVING

NEGATIVISM
NEGATIVISMS
NEGATIVIST
NEGATIVISTIC
NEGATIVISTS
NEGATIVITIES
NEGATIVITY
NEGLECTABLE
NEGLECTEDNESS
NEGLECTEDNESSES
NEGLECTERS
NEGLECTFUL
NEGLECTFULLY
NEGLECTFULNESS
NEGLECTING
NEGLECTINGLY
NEGLECTION
NEGLECTIONS
NEGLECTIVE
NEGLECTORS
NEGLIGEABLE
NEGLIGENCE
NEGLIGENCES
NEGLIGENTLY
NEGLIGIBILITIES
NEGLIGIBILITY
NEGLIGIBLE
NEGLIGIBLENESS
NEGLIGIBLY
NEGOCIANTS
NEGOTIABILITIES
NEGOTIABILITY
NEGOTIABLE
NEGOTIANTS
NEGOTIATED
NEGOTIATES
NEGOTIATING
NEGOTIATION
NEGOTIATIONS
NEGOTIATOR
NEGOTIATORS
NEGOTIATORY
NEGOTIATRESS
NEGOTIATRESSES
NEGOTIATRICES
NEGOTIATRIX
NEGOTIATRIXES
NEGRITUDES
NEIGHBORED
NEIGHBORHOOD
NEIGHBORHOODS
NEIGHBORING
NEIGHBORLESS
NEIGHBORLIER
NEIGHBORLIEST
NEIGHBORLINESS
NEIGHBORLY
NEIGHBOURED
NEIGHBOURHOOD
NEIGHBOURHOODS
NEIGHBOURING
NEIGHBOURLESS
NEIGHBOURLIER
NEIGHBOURLIEST
NEIGHBOURLINESS
NEIGHBOURLY
NEIGHBOURS
NELUMBIUMS
NEMATHELMINTH
NEMATHELMINTHIC
NEMATHELMINTHS
NEMATICIDAL
NEMATICIDE
NEMATICIDES
NEMATOBLAST
NEMATOBLASTS
NEMATOCIDAL
NEMATOCIDE
NEMATOCIDES
NEMATOCYST
NEMATOCYSTIC
NEMATOCYSTS
NEMATODIRIASES
NEMATODIRIASIS
NEMATODIRUS
NEMATODIRUSES
NEMATOLOGICAL
NEMATOLOGIES
NEMATOLOGIST
NEMATOLOGISTS
NEMATOLOGY
NEMATOPHORE
NEMATOPHORES
NEMERTEANS
NEMERTIANS
NEMERTINES
NEMOPHILAS
NEOANTHROPIC
NEOARSPHENAMINE
NEOCAPITALISM
NEOCAPITALISMS
NEOCAPITALIST
NEOCAPITALISTS
NEOCLASSIC
NEOCLASSICAL
NEOCLASSICISM
NEOCLASSICISMS
NEOCLASSICIST
NEOCLASSICISTS
NEOCOLONIAL
NEOCOLONIALISM
NEOCOLONIALISMS
NEOCOLONIALIST
NEOCOLONIALISTS
NEOCONSERVATISM
NEOCONSERVATIVE
NEOCORTEXES
NEOCORTICAL
NEOCORTICES
NEODYMIUMS
NEOGENESES
NEOGENESIS
NEOGENETIC
NEOGOTHICS
NEOGRAMMARIAN
NEOGRAMMARIANS
NEOLIBERAL
NEOLIBERALISM
NEOLIBERALISMS
NEOLIBERALS
NEOLITHICS
NEOLOGIANS
NEOLOGICAL
NEOLOGICALLY
NEOLOGISED
NEOLOGISES
NEOLOGISING
NEOLOGISMS
NEOLOGISTIC
NEOLOGISTICAL
NEOLOGISTICALLY
NEOLOGISTS
NEOLOGIZED
NEOLOGIZES
NEOLOGIZING
NEONATALLY
NEONATICIDE
NEONATICIDES
NEONATOLOGIES
NEONATOLOGIST
NEONATOLOGISTS
NEONATOLOGY
NEONOMIANISM
NEONOMIANISMS
NEONOMIANS
NEOORTHODOX
NEOORTHODOXIES
NEOORTHODOXY
NEOPAGANISE
NEOPAGANISED
NEOPAGANISES
NEOPAGANISING
NEOPAGANISM
NEOPAGANISMS
NEOPAGANIZE
NEOPAGANIZED
NEOPAGANIZES
NEOPAGANIZING
NEOPHILIAC
NEOPHILIACS
NEOPHILIAS
NEOPHOBIAS
NEOPILINAS
NEOPLASIAS
NEOPLASTIC
NEOPLASTICISM
NEOPLASTICISMS
NEOPLASTICIST
NEOPLASTICISTS
NEOPLASTIES
NEOREALISM
NEOREALISMS
NEOREALIST
NEOREALISTIC
NEOREALISTS
NEOSTIGMINE
NEOSTIGMINES
NEOTEINIAS
NEOTERICAL
NEOTERICALLY
NEOTERICALS
NEOTERISED
NEOTERISES
NEOTERISING
NEOTERISMS
NEOTERISTS
NEOTERIZED
NEOTERIZES
NEOTERIZING
NEOTROPICS
NEOVITALISM
NEOVITALISMS
NEOVITALIST
NEOVITALISTS
NEPENTHEAN
NEPHALISMS
NEPHALISTS
NEPHELINES
NEPHELINIC
NEPHELINITE
NEPHELINITES
NEPHELINITIC
NEPHELITES
NEPHELOMETER
NEPHELOMETERS
NEPHELOMETRIC
NEPHELOMETRIES
NEPHELOMETRY
NEPHOGRAMS
NEPHOGRAPH
NEPHOGRAPHS
NEPHOLOGIC
NEPHOLOGICAL
NEPHOLOGIES
NEPHOLOGIST
NEPHOLOGISTS
NEPHOSCOPE
NEPHOSCOPES
NEPHRALGIA
NEPHRALGIAS
NEPHRALGIC
NEPHRALGIES
NEPHRECTOMIES
NEPHRECTOMISE
NEPHRECTOMISED
NEPHRECTOMISES
NEPHRECTOMISING
NEPHRECTOMIZE
NEPHRECTOMIZED
NEPHRECTOMIZES

NEPHRECTOMIZING
NEPHRECTOMY
NEPHRIDIAL
NEPHRIDIUM
NEPHRITICAL
NEPHRITICS
NEPHRITIDES
NEPHRITISES
NEPHROBLASTOMA
NEPHROBLASTOMAS
NEPHROLEPIS
NEPHROLEPISES
NEPHROLOGICAL
NEPHROLOGIES
NEPHROLOGIST
NEPHROLOGISTS
NEPHROLOGY
NEPHROPATHIC
NEPHROPATHIES
NEPHROPATHY
NEPHROPEXIES
NEPHROPEXY
NEPHROPTOSES
NEPHROPTOSIS
NEPHROSCOPE
NEPHROSCOPES
NEPHROSCOPIES
NEPHROSCOPY
NEPHROSTOME
NEPHROSTOMES
NEPHROTICS
NEPHROTOMIES
NEPHROTOMY
NEPHROTOXIC
NEPHROTOXICITY
NEPOTISTIC
NEPTUNIUMS
NERDINESSES
NERVATIONS
NERVATURES
NERVELESSLY
NERVELESSNESS
NERVELESSNESSES
NERVINESSES
NERVOSITIES
NERVOUSNESS
NERVOUSNESSES
NERVURATION
NERVURATIONS
NESCIENCES
NESHNESSES
NESSELRODE
NESSELRODES
NETBALLERS
NETHERLINGS
NETHERMORE
NETHERMORES
NETHERMOST
NETHERSTOCK
NETHERSTOCKS
NETHERWARD
NETHERWARDS
NETHERWORLD
NETHERWORLDS
NETIQUETTE
NETIQUETTES
NETMINDERS
NETSURFERS
NETSURFING
NETSURFINGS
NETTLELIKE
NETTLESOME
NETWORKERS
NETWORKING
NETWORKINGS
NEURALGIAS
NEURAMINIC
NEURAMINIDASE
NEURAMINIDASES
NEURASTHENIA
NEURASTHENIAC
NEURASTHENIACS
NEURASTHENIAS
NEURASTHENIC
NEURASTHENICS
NEURATIONS
NEURECTOMIES
NEURECTOMY
NEURILEMMA
NEURILEMMAL
NEURILEMMAS
NEURILITIES
NEURITIDES
NEURITISES
NEUROACTIVE
NEUROANATOMIC
NEUROANATOMICAL
NEUROANATOMIES
NEUROANATOMIST
NEUROANATOMISTS
NEUROANATOMY
NEUROBIOLOGICAL
NEUROBIOLOGIES
NEUROBIOLOGIST
NEUROBIOLOGISTS
NEUROBIOLOGY
NEUROBLAST
NEUROBLASTOMA
NEUROBLASTOMAS
NEUROBLASTOMATA
NEUROBLASTS
NEUROCHEMICAL
NEUROCHEMICALS
NEUROCHEMIST
NEUROCHEMISTRY
NEUROCHEMISTS
NEUROCHIPS
NEUROCOELE
NEUROCOELES
NEUROCOELS
NEUROCOGNITIVE
NEUROCOMPUTER
NEUROCOMPUTERS
NEUROCOMPUTING
NEUROCOMPUTINGS
NEURODIVERSITY
NEUROECTODERMAL
NEUROENDOCRINE
NEUROETHOLOGIES
NEUROETHOLOGY
NEUROFEEDBACK
NEUROFEEDBACKS
NEUROFIBRIL
NEUROFIBRILAR
NEUROFIBRILLAR
NEUROFIBRILLARY
NEUROFIBRILS
NEUROFIBROMA
NEUROFIBROMAS
NEUROFIBROMATA
NEUROGENESES
NEUROGENESIS
NEUROGENIC
NEUROGENICALLY
NEUROGLIAL
NEUROGLIAS
NEUROGRAMS
NEUROHORMONAL
NEUROHORMONE
NEUROHORMONES
NEUROHUMOR
NEUROHUMORAL
NEUROHUMORS
NEUROHUMOUR
NEUROHUMOURS
NEUROHYPNOLOGY
NEUROHYPOPHYSES
NEUROHYPOPHYSIS
NEUROLEMMA
NEUROLEMMAS
NEUROLEPTIC
NEUROLEPTICS
NEUROLINGUIST
NEUROLINGUISTIC
NEUROLINGUISTS
NEUROLOGIC
NEUROLOGICAL
NEUROLOGICALLY
NEUROLOGIES
NEUROLOGIST
NEUROLOGISTS
NEUROLYSES
NEUROLYSIS
NEUROMARKETING
NEUROMARKETINGS
NEUROMASTS
NEUROMATOUS
NEUROMOTOR
NEUROMUSCULAR
NEUROPATHIC
NEUROPATHICAL
NEUROPATHICALLY
NEUROPATHIES
NEUROPATHIST
NEUROPATHISTS
NEUROPATHOLOGIC
NEUROPATHOLOGY
NEUROPATHS
NEUROPATHY
NEUROPEPTIDE
NEUROPEPTIDES
NEUROPHYSIOLOGY
NEUROPLASM
NEUROPLASMS
NEUROPSYCHIATRY
NEUROPSYCHOLOGY
NEUROPTERA
NEUROPTERAN
NEUROPTERANS
NEUROPTERIST
NEUROPTERISTS
NEUROPTERON
NEUROPTERONS
NEUROPTEROUS
NEURORADIOLOGY
NEUROSCIENCE
NEUROSCIENCES
NEUROSCIENTIFIC
NEUROSCIENTIST
NEUROSCIENTISTS
NEUROSECRETION
NEUROSECRETIONS
NEUROSECRETORY
NEUROSENSORY
NEUROSPORA
NEUROSPORAS
NEUROSURGEON
NEUROSURGEONS
NEUROSURGERIES
NEUROSURGERY
NEUROSURGICAL
NEUROSURGICALLY
NEUROSYPHILIS
NEUROSYPHILISES
NEUROTICALLY
NEUROTICISM
NEUROTICISMS
NEUROTOMIES
NEUROTOMIST
NEUROTOMISTS
NEUROTOXIC
NEUROTOXICITIES
NEUROTOXICITY
NEUROTOXIN
NEUROTOXINS
NEUROTROPHIC
NEUROTROPHIES
NEUROTROPHY
NEUROTROPIC
NEUROTYPICAL

NEUROVASCULAR
NEURULATION
NEURULATIONS
NEURYPNOLOGIES
NEURYPNOLOGY
NEUTERINGS
NEUTRALISATION
NEUTRALISATIONS
NEUTRALISE
NEUTRALISED
NEUTRALISER
NEUTRALISERS
NEUTRALISES
NEUTRALISING
NEUTRALISM
NEUTRALISMS
NEUTRALIST
NEUTRALISTIC
NEUTRALISTS
NEUTRALITIES
NEUTRALITY
NEUTRALIZATION
NEUTRALIZATIONS
NEUTRALIZE
NEUTRALIZED
NEUTRALIZER
NEUTRALIZERS
NEUTRALIZES
NEUTRALIZING
NEUTRALNESS
NEUTRALNESSES
NEUTRETTOS
NEUTRINOLESS
NEUTROPENIA
NEUTROPENIAS
NEUTROPHIL
NEUTROPHILE
NEUTROPHILES
NEUTROPHILIC
NEUTROPHILS
NEVERMINDS
NEVERTHELESS
NEVERTHEMORE
NEWFANGLED
NEWFANGLEDLY
NEWFANGLEDNESS
NEWFANGLENESS
NEWFANGLENESSES
NEWFANGLES
NEWISHNESS
NEWISHNESSES
NEWMARKETS
NEWSAGENCIES
NEWSAGENCY
NEWSAGENTS
NEWSBREAKS
NEWSCASTER
NEWSCASTERS
NEWSCASTING
NEWSCASTINGS
NEWSDEALER
NEWSDEALERS
NEWSFLASHES
NEWSGROUPS
NEWSHOUNDS
NEWSINESSES
NEWSLETTER
NEWSLETTERS
NEWSMAGAZINE
NEWSMAGAZINES
NEWSMAKERS
NEWSMONGER
NEWSMONGERS
NEWSPAPERDOM
NEWSPAPERDOMS
NEWSPAPERED
NEWSPAPERING
NEWSPAPERISM
NEWSPAPERISMS
NEWSPAPERMAN
NEWSPAPERMEN
NEWSPAPERS
NEWSPAPERWOMAN
NEWSPAPERWOMEN
NEWSPEOPLE
NEWSPERSON
NEWSPERSONS
NEWSPRINTS
NEWSREADER
NEWSREADERS
NEWSSHEETS
NEWSSTANDS
NEWSTRADES
NEWSWEEKLIES
NEWSWEEKLY
NEWSWORTHIER
NEWSWORTHIEST
NEWSWORTHINESS
NEWSWORTHY
NEWSWRITING
NEWSWRITINGS
NEXTNESSES
NIACINAMIDE
NIACINAMIDES
NIAISERIES
NIALAMIDES
NIBBLINGLY
NICCOLITES
NICENESSES
NICKELIFEROUS
NICKELINES
NICKELISED
NICKELISES
NICKELISING
NICKELIZED
NICKELIZES
NICKELIZING
NICKELLING
NICKELODEON
NICKELODEONS
NICKERNUTS
NICKNAMERS
NICKNAMING
NICKPOINTS
NICKSTICKS
NICKUMPOOP
NICKUMPOOPS
NICOMPOOPS
NICOTIANAS
NICOTINAMIDE
NICOTINAMIDES
NICOTINISM
NICOTINISMS
NICROSILAL
NICROSILALS
NICTATIONS
NICTITATED
NICTITATES
NICTITATING
NICTITATION
NICTITATIONS
NIDAMENTAL
NIDAMENTUM
NIDDERINGS
NIDDERLING
NIDDERLINGS
NIDERLINGS
NIDICOLOUS
NIDIFICATE
NIDIFICATED
NIDIFICATES
NIDIFICATING
NIDIFICATION
NIDIFICATIONS
NIDIFUGOUS
NIDULATION
NIDULATIONS
NIFEDIPINE
NIFEDIPINES
NIFFNAFFED
NIFFNAFFING
NIFTINESSES
NIGGARDING
NIGGARDISE
NIGGARDISES
NIGGARDIZE
NIGGARDIZES
NIGGARDLIER
NIGGARDLIEST
NIGGARDLINESS
NIGGARDLINESSES
NIGGLINGLY
NIGHNESSES
NIGHTBIRDS
NIGHTBLIND
NIGHTCLASS
NIGHTCLASSES
NIGHTCLOTHES
NIGHTCLUBBED
NIGHTCLUBBER
NIGHTCLUBBERS
NIGHTCLUBBING
NIGHTCLUBBINGS
NIGHTCLUBS
NIGHTDRESS
NIGHTDRESSES
NIGHTFALLS
NIGHTFARING
NIGHTFIRES
NIGHTGEARS
NIGHTGLOWS
NIGHTGOWNS
NIGHTHAWKS
NIGHTINGALE
NIGHTINGALES
NIGHTLIFES
NIGHTLIVES
NIGHTMARES
NIGHTMARIER
NIGHTMARIEST
NIGHTMARISH
NIGHTMARISHLY
NIGHTMARISHNESS
NIGHTPIECE
NIGHTPIECES
NIGHTRIDER
NIGHTRIDERS
NIGHTRIDING
NIGHTRIDINGS
NIGHTSCOPE
NIGHTSCOPES
NIGHTSHADE
NIGHTSHADES
NIGHTSHIRT
NIGHTSHIRTS
NIGHTSIDES
NIGHTSPOTS
NIGHTSTAND
NIGHTSTANDS
NIGHTSTICK
NIGHTSTICKS
NIGHTTIDES
NIGHTTIMES
NIGHTWALKER
NIGHTWALKERS
NIGHTWATCHMAN
NIGHTWATCHMEN
NIGHTWEARS
NIGRESCENCE
NIGRESCENCES
NIGRESCENT
NIGRIFYING
NIGRITUDES
NIGROMANCIES
NIGROMANCY
NIGROSINES
NIHILISTIC
NIHILITIES
NIKETHAMIDE
NIKETHAMIDES

NILPOTENTS
NIMBLENESS
NIMBLENESSES
NIMBLESSES
NIMBLEWITS
NIMBLEWITTED
NIMBOSTRATI
NIMBOSTRATUS
NIMBYNESSES
NINCOMPOOP
NINCOMPOOPERIES
NINCOMPOOPERY
NINCOMPOOPS
NINEPENCES
NINEPENNIES
NINESCORES
NINETEENTH
NINETEENTHLIES
NINETEENTHLY
NINETEENTHS
NINETIETHS
NINHYDRINS
NINNYHAMMER
NINNYHAMMERS
NIPCHEESES
NIPPERKINS
NIPPINESSES
NIPPLEWORT
NIPPLEWORTS
NISBERRIES
NITPICKERS
NITPICKIER
NITPICKIEST
NITPICKING
NITPICKINGS
NITRAMINES
NITRANILINE
NITRANILINES
NITRATINES
NITRATIONS
NITRAZEPAM
NITRAZEPAMS
NITRIDINGS
NITRIFIABLE
NITRIFICATION
NITRIFICATIONS
NITRIFIERS
NITRIFYING
NITROBACTERIA
NITROBACTERIUM
NITROBENZENE
NITROBENZENES
NITROCELLULOSE
NITROCELLULOSES
NITROCHLOROFORM
NITROCOTTON
NITROCOTTONS
NITROFURAN
NITROFURANS
NITROGELATIN
NITROGELATINE
NITROGELATINES
NITROGELATINS
NITROGENASE
NITROGENASES
NITROGENISATION
NITROGENISE
NITROGENISED
NITROGENISES
NITROGENISING
NITROGENIZATION
NITROGENIZE
NITROGENIZED
NITROGENIZES
NITROGENIZING
NITROGENOUS
NITROGLYCERIN
NITROGLYCERINE
NITROGLYCERINES
NITROGLYCERINS
NITROMETER
NITROMETERS
NITROMETHANE
NITROMETHANES
NITROMETRIC
NITROPARAFFIN
NITROPARAFFINS
NITROPHILOUS
NITROSAMINE
NITROSAMINES
NITROSATION
NITROSATIONS
NITROTOLUENE
NITROTOLUENES
NITWITTEDNESS
NITWITTEDNESSES
NITWITTERIES
NITWITTERY
NOBBINESSES
NOBILESSES
NOBILITATE
NOBILITATED
NOBILITATES
NOBILITATING
NOBILITATION
NOBILITATIONS
NOBILITIES
NOBLENESSES
NOBLEWOMAN
NOBLEWOMEN
NOCHELLING
NOCICEPTIVE
NOCICEPTOR
NOCICEPTORS
NOCIRECEPTOR
NOCIRECEPTORS
NOCTAMBULATION
NOCTAMBULATIONS
NOCTAMBULISM
NOCTAMBULISMS
NOCTAMBULIST
NOCTAMBULISTS
NOCTILUCAE
NOCTILUCAS
NOCTILUCENCE
NOCTILUCENCES
NOCTILUCENT
NOCTILUCOUS
NOCTIVAGANT
NOCTIVAGANTS
NOCTIVAGATION
NOCTIVAGATIONS
NOCTIVAGOUS
NOCTUARIES
NOCTURNALITIES
NOCTURNALITY
NOCTURNALLY
NOCTURNALS
NOCUOUSNESS
NOCUOUSNESSES
NODALISING
NODALITIES
NODALIZING
NODOSITIES
NODULATION
NODULATIONS
NOEMATICAL
NOEMATICALLY
NOGOODNIKS
NOISELESSLY
NOISELESSNESS
NOISELESSNESSES
NOISEMAKER
NOISEMAKERS
NOISEMAKING
NOISEMAKINGS
NOISINESSES
NOISOMENESS
NOISOMENESSES
NOMADICALLY
NOMADISATION
NOMADISATIONS
NOMADISING
NOMADIZATION
NOMADIZATIONS
NOMADIZING
NOMARCHIES
NOMENCLATIVE
NOMENCLATOR
NOMENCLATORIAL
NOMENCLATORS
NOMENCLATURAL
NOMENCLATURE
NOMENCLATURES
NOMENKLATURA
NOMENKLATURAS
NOMINALISATION
NOMINALISATIONS
NOMINALISE
NOMINALISED
NOMINALISES
NOMINALISING
NOMINALISM
NOMINALISMS
NOMINALIST
NOMINALISTIC
NOMINALISTS
NOMINALIZATION
NOMINALIZATIONS
NOMINALIZE
NOMINALIZED
NOMINALIZES
NOMINALIZING
NOMINATELY
NOMINATING
NOMINATION
NOMINATIONS
NOMINATIVAL
NOMINATIVALLY
NOMINATIVE
NOMINATIVELY
NOMINATIVES
NOMINATORS
NOMOCRACIES
NOMOGENIES
NOMOGRAPHER
NOMOGRAPHERS
NOMOGRAPHIC
NOMOGRAPHICAL
NOMOGRAPHICALLY
NOMOGRAPHIES
NOMOGRAPHS
NOMOGRAPHY
NOMOLOGICAL
NOMOLOGICALLY
NOMOLOGIES
NOMOLOGIST
NOMOLOGISTS
NOMOTHETES
NOMOTHETIC
NOMOTHETICAL
NONABRASIVE
NONABSORBABLE
NONABSORBENT
NONABSORPTIVE
NONABSTRACT
NONACADEMIC
NONACADEMICS
NONACCEPTANCE
NONACCEPTANCES
NONACCIDENTAL
NONACCOUNTABLE
NONACCREDITED
NONACCRUAL
NONACHIEVEMENT
NONACHIEVEMENTS
NONACQUISITIVE
NONACTINGS
NONACTIONS
NONACTIVATED

NONADAPTIVE
NONADDICTIVE
NONADDICTS
NONADDITIVE
NONADDITIVITIES
NONADDITIVITY
NONADHESIVE
NONADIABATIC
NONADJACENT
NONADMIRER
NONADMIRERS
NONADMISSION
NONADMISSIONS
NONAESTHETIC
NONAFFILIATED
NONAFFLUENT
NONAGENARIAN
NONAGENARIANS
NONAGESIMAL
NONAGESIMALS
NONAGGRESSION
NONAGGRESSIONS
NONAGGRESSIVE
NONAGRICULTURAL
NONALCOHOLIC
NONALGEBRAIC
NONALIGNED
NONALIGNMENT
NONALIGNMENTS
NONALLELIC
NONALLERGENIC
NONALLERGIC
NONALPHABETIC
NONALUMINIUM
NONALUMINUM
NONAMBIGUOUS
NONANALYTIC
NONANATOMIC
NONANSWERED
NONANSWERING
NONANSWERS
NONANTAGONISTIC
NONANTIBIOTIC
NONANTIBIOTICS
NONANTIGENIC
NONAPPEARANCE
NONAPPEARANCES
NONAQUATIC
NONAQUEOUS
NONARBITRARY
NONARCHITECT
NONARCHITECTS
NONARCHITECTURE
NONARGUMENT
NONARGUMENTS
NONARISTOCRATIC
NONAROMATIC
NONAROMATICS
NONARRIVAL
NONARRIVALS
NONARTISTIC
NONARTISTS
NONASCETIC
NONASCETICS
NONASPIRIN
NONASSERTIVE
NONASSOCIATED
NONASTRONOMICAL
NONATHLETE
NONATHLETES
NONATHLETIC
NONATTACHED
NONATTACHMENT
NONATTACHMENTS
NONATTENDANCE
NONATTENDANCES
NONATTENDER
NONATTENDERS
NONATTRIBUTABLE
NONAUDITORY
NONAUTHORS
NONAUTOMATED
NONAUTOMATIC
NONAUTOMOTIVE
NONAUTONOMOUS
NONAVAILABILITY
NONBACTERIAL
NONBANKING
NONBARBITURATE
NONBARBITURATES
NONBEARING
NONBEHAVIORAL
NONBEHAVIOURAL
NONBELIEFS
NONBELIEVER
NONBELIEVERS
NONBELLIGERENCY
NONBELLIGERENT
NONBELLIGERENTS
NONBETTING
NONBINDING
NONBIOGRAPHICAL
NONBIOLOGICAL
NONBIOLOGICALLY
NONBIOLOGIST
NONBIOLOGISTS
NONBONDING
NONBOTANIST
NONBOTANISTS
NONBREAKABLE
NONBREATHING
NONBREEDER
NONBREEDERS
NONBREEDING
NONBROADCAST
NONBUILDING
NONBURNABLE
NONBUSINESS
NONCABINET
NONCALLABLE
NONCALORIC
NONCANCELABLE
NONCANCELLABLE
NONCANCEROUS
NONCANDIDACIES
NONCANDIDACY
NONCANDIDATE
NONCANDIDATES
NONCAPITAL
NONCAPITALIST
NONCAPITALISTS
NONCARBOHYDRATE
NONCARCINOGEN
NONCARCINOGENIC
NONCARCINOGENS
NONCARDIAC
NONCARRIER
NONCARRIERS
NONCELEBRATION
NONCELEBRATIONS
NONCELEBRITIES
NONCELEBRITY
NONCELLULAR
NONCELLULOSIC
NONCELLULOSICS
NONCENTRAL
NONCERTIFICATED
NONCERTIFIED
NONCHALANCE
NONCHALANCES
NONCHALANT
NONCHALANTLY
NONCHARACTER
NONCHARACTERS
NONCHARISMATIC
NONCHARISMATICS
NONCHAUVINIST
NONCHAUVINISTS
NONCHEMICAL
NONCHEMICALS
NONCHROMOSOMAL
NONCHURCHED
NONCHURCHES
NONCHURCHGOER
NONCHURCHGOERS
NONCHURCHING
NONCIRCULAR
NONCIRCULATING
NONCITIZEN
NONCITIZENS
NONCLANDESTINE
NONCLASSES
NONCLASSICAL
NONCLASSIFIED
NONCLASSROOM
NONCLERICAL
NONCLINICAL
NONCLOGGING
NONCOERCIVE
NONCOGNITIVE
NONCOGNITIVISM
NONCOGNITIVISMS
NONCOHERENT
NONCOINCIDENCE
NONCOINCIDENCES
NONCOLLECTOR
NONCOLLECTORS
NONCOLLEGE
NONCOLLEGIATE
NONCOLLINEAR
NONCOLORED
NONCOLORFAST
NONCOLOURED
NONCOLOURFAST
NONCOLOURS
NONCOMBATANT
NONCOMBATANTS
NONCOMBATIVE
NONCOMBUSTIBLE
NONCOMBUSTIBLES
NONCOMMERCIAL
NONCOMMISSIONED
NONCOMMITMENT
NONCOMMITMENTS
NONCOMMITTAL
NONCOMMITTALLY
NONCOMMITTALS
NONCOMMITTED
NONCOMMUNICANT
NONCOMMUNICANTS
NONCOMMUNIST
NONCOMMUNISTS
NONCOMMUNITY
NONCOMMUTATIVE
NONCOMPARABLE
NONCOMPATIBLE
NONCOMPETITION
NONCOMPETITIONS
NONCOMPETITIVE
NONCOMPETITOR
NONCOMPETITORS
NONCOMPLETION
NONCOMPLETIONS
NONCOMPLEX
NONCOMPLIANCE
NONCOMPLIANCES
NONCOMPLICATED
NONCOMPLYING
NONCOMPLYINGS
NONCOMPOSER
NONCOMPOSERS
NONCOMPOUND
NONCOMPRESSIBLE
NONCOMPUTER
NONCOMPUTERISED
NONCOMPUTERIZED
NONCONCEPTUAL
NONCONCERN
NONCONCERNS
NONCONCLUSION

NONCONCLUSIONS
NONCONCURRED
NONCONCURRENCE
NONCONCURRENCES
NONCONCURRENT
NONCONCURRING
NONCONCURS
NONCONDENSABLE
NONCONDITIONED
NONCONDUCTING
NONCONDUCTION
NONCONDUCTIONS
NONCONDUCTIVE
NONCONDUCTOR
NONCONDUCTORS
NONCONFERENCE
NONCONFIDENCE
NONCONFIDENCES
NONCONFIDENTIAL
NONCONFLICTING
NONCONFORM
NONCONFORMANCE
NONCONFORMANCES
NONCONFORMED
NONCONFORMER
NONCONFORMERS
NONCONFORMING
NONCONFORMINGS
NONCONFORMISM
NONCONFORMISMS
NONCONFORMIST
NONCONFORMISTS
NONCONFORMITIES
NONCONFORMITY
NONCONFORMS
NONCONGRUENT
NONCONJUGATED
NONCONNECTION
NONCONNECTIONS
NONCONSCIOUS
NONCONSECUTIVE
NONCONSENSUAL
NONCONSERVATION
NONCONSERVATIVE
NONCONSOLIDATED
NONCONSTANT
NONCONSTRUCTION
NONCONSTRUCTIVE
NONCONSUMER
NONCONSUMERS
NONCONSUMING
NONCONSUMPTION
NONCONSUMPTIONS
NONCONSUMPTIVE
NONCONTACT
NONCONTACTS
NONCONTAGIOUS
NONCONTEMPORARY
NONCONTIGUOUS
NONCONTINGENT
NONCONTINUOUS
NONCONTRACT
NONCONTRACTUAL
NONCONTRIBUTING
NONCONTRIBUTORY
NONCONTROLLABLE
NONCONTROLLED
NONCONTROLLING
NONCONVENTIONAL
NONCONVERTIBLE
NONCOOPERATION
NONCOOPERATIONS
NONCOOPERATIVE
NONCOOPERATOR
NONCOOPERATORS
NONCOPLANAR
NONCORPORATE
NONCORRELATION
NONCORRELATIONS
NONCORRODIBLE
NONCORRODING
NONCORROSIVE
NONCOUNTRIES
NONCOUNTRY
NONCOVERAGE
NONCOVERAGES
NONCREATIVE
NONCREATIVITIES
NONCREATIVITY
NONCREDENTIALED
NONCRIMINAL
NONCRIMINALS
NONCRITICAL
NONCROSSOVER
NONCROSSOVERS
NONCRUSHABLE
NONCRYSTALLINE
NONCULINARY
NONCULTIVATED
NONCULTIVATION
NONCULTIVATIONS
NONCULTURAL
NONCUMULATIVE
NONCURRENT
NONCUSTODIAL
NONCUSTOMER
NONCUSTOMERS
NONCYCLICAL
NONDANCERS
NONDEALERS
NONDECEPTIVE
NONDECISION
NONDECISIONS
NONDECREASING
NONDEDUCTIBLE
NONDEDUCTIVE
NONDEFENCE
NONDEFENSE
NONDEFERRABLE
NONDEFORMING
NONDEGENERATE
NONDEGRADABLE
NONDELEGATE
NONDELEGATES
NONDELIBERATE
NONDELINQUENT
NONDELINQUENTS
NONDELIVERIES
NONDELIVERY
NONDEMANDING
NONDEMANDS
NONDEMOCRATIC
NONDEPARTMENTAL
NONDEPENDENT
NONDEPENDENTS
NONDEPLETABLE
NONDEPLETING
NONDEPOSITION
NONDEPOSITIONS
NONDEPRESSED
NONDERIVATIVE
NONDESCRIPT
NONDESCRIPTIVE
NONDESCRIPTLY
NONDESCRIPTNESS
NONDESCRIPTS
NONDESTRUCTIVE
NONDETACHABLE
NONDEVELOPMENT
NONDEVELOPMENTS
NONDEVIANT
NONDIABETIC
NONDIABETICS
NONDIALYSABLE
NONDIALYZABLE
NONDIAPAUSING
NONDIDACTIC
NONDIFFUSIBLE
NONDIMENSIONAL
NONDIPLOMATIC
NONDIRECTED
NONDIRECTIONAL
NONDIRECTIVE
NONDISABLED
NONDISCLOSURE
NONDISCLOSURES
NONDISCOUNT
NONDISCURSIVE
NONDISJUNCTION
NONDISJUNCTIONS
NONDISPERSIVE
NONDISRUPTIVE
NONDISTINCTIVE
NONDIVERGENT
NONDIVERSIFIED
NONDIVIDING
NONDOCTORS
NONDOCTRINAIRE
NONDOCUMENTARY
NONDOGMATIC
NONDOMESTIC
NONDOMICILED
NONDOMINANT
NONDORMANT
NONDRAMATIC
NONDRINKER
NONDRINKERS
NONDRINKING
NONDRIVERS
NONDURABLE
NONDURABLES
NONEARNING
NONECONOMIC
NONECONOMIST
NONECONOMISTS
NONEDIBLES
NONEDITORIAL
NONEDUCATION
NONEDUCATIONAL
NONEFFECTIVE
NONEFFECTIVES
NONELASTIC
NONELECTED
NONELECTION
NONELECTIONS
NONELECTIVE
NONELECTRIC
NONELECTRICAL
NONELECTRICALS
NONELECTRICS
NONELECTROLYTE
NONELECTROLYTES
NONELECTRONIC
NONELEMENTARY
NONEMERGENCIES
NONEMERGENCY
NONEMOTIONAL
NONEMPHATIC
NONEMPIRICAL
NONEMPLOYEE
NONEMPLOYEES
NONEMPLOYMENT
NONEMPLOYMENTS
NONENCAPSULATED
NONENFORCEMENT
NONENFORCEMENTS
NONENGAGEMENT
NONENGAGEMENTS
NONENGINEERING
NONENTITIES
NONENTRIES
NONENZYMATIC
NONENZYMIC
NONEQUILIBRIA
NONEQUILIBRIUM
NONEQUILIBRIUMS
NONEQUIVALENCE
NONEQUIVALENCES
NONEQUIVALENT
NONESSENTIAL

NONESSENTIALS
NONESTABLISHED
NONESTERIFIED
NONESUCHES
NONETHELESS
NONETHICAL
NONETHNICS
NONEVALUATIVE
NONEVIDENCE
NONEVIDENCES
NONEXCLUSIVE
NONEXECUTIVE
NONEXECUTIVES
NONEXEMPTS
NONEXISTENCE
NONEXISTENCES
NONEXISTENT
NONEXISTENTIAL
NONEXISTENTS
NONEXPENDABLE
NONEXPERIMENTAL
NONEXPERTS
NONEXPLANATORY
NONEXPLOITATION
NONEXPLOITATIVE
NONEXPLOITIVE
NONEXPLOSIVE
NONEXPOSED
NONFACTORS
NONFACTUAL
NONFACULTIES
NONFACULTY
NONFAMILIAL
NONFAMILIES
NONFARMERS
NONFATTENING
NONFEASANCE
NONFEASANCES
NONFEDERAL
NONFEDERATED
NONFEEDING
NONFEMINIST
NONFEMINISTS
NONFERROUS
NONFICTION
NONFICTIONAL
NONFICTIONALLY
NONFICTIONS
NONFIGURATIVE
NONFILAMENTOUS
NONFILTERABLE
NONFINANCIAL
NONFISSIONABLE
NONFLAMMABILITY
NONFLAMMABLE
NONFLOWERING
NONFLUENCIES
NONFLUENCY
NONFLUORESCENT
NONFORFEITABLE
NONFORFEITURE
NONFORFEITURES
NONFREEZING
NONFRIVOLOUS
NONFULFILLMENT
NONFULFILLMENTS
NONFULFILMENT
NONFULFILMENTS
NONFUNCTIONAL
NONFUNCTIONING
NONGASEOUS
NONGENETIC
NONGENITAL
NONGEOMETRICAL
NONGLAMOROUS
NONGOLFERS
NONGONOCOCCAL
NONGOVERNMENT
NONGOVERNMENTAL
NONGRADUATE
NONGRADUATES
NONGRAMMATICAL
NONGRANULAR
NONGREGARIOUS
NONGROWING
NONGROWTHS
NONHAEMOLYTIC
NONHALOGENATED
NONHAPPENING
NONHAPPENINGS
NONHARMONIC
NONHAZARDOUS
NONHEMOLYTIC
NONHEREDITARY
NONHIERARCHICAL
NONHISTONE
NONHISTORICAL
NONHOMOGENEITY
NONHOMOGENEOUS
NONHOMOLOGOUS
NONHOMOSEXUAL
NONHOMOSEXUALS
NONHORMONAL
NONHOSPITAL
NONHOSPITALISED
NONHOSPITALIZED
NONHOSTILE
NONHOUSING
NONHUNTERS
NONHUNTING
NONHYGROSCOPIC
NONHYSTERICAL
NONIDENTICAL
NONIDENTITIES
NONIDENTITY
NONIDEOLOGICAL
NONILLIONS
NONILLIONTH
NONILLIONTHS
NONIMITATIVE
NONIMMIGRANT
NONIMMIGRANTS
NONIMPACTS
NONIMPLICATION
NONIMPLICATIONS
NONIMPORTATION
NONIMPORTATIONS
NONINCLUSION
NONINCLUSIONS
NONINCREASING
NONINCUMBENT
NONINCUMBENTS
NONINDEPENDENCE
NONINDICTABLE
NONINDIGENOUS
NONINDIVIDUAL
NONINDIVIDUALS
NONINDUCTIVE
NONINDUSTRIAL
NONINDUSTRY
NONINFECTED
NONINFECTIOUS
NONINFECTIVE
NONINFESTED
NONINFLAMMABLE
NONINFLAMMATORY
NONINFLATIONARY
NONINFLECTIONAL
NONINFLUENCE
NONINFLUENCES
NONINFORMATION
NONINFORMATIONS
NONINFRINGEMENT
NONINITIAL
NONINITIATE
NONINITIATES
NONINSECTICIDAL
NONINSECTS
NONINSTALLMENT
NONINSTALLMENTS
NONINSTALMENT
NONINSTRUMENTAL
NONINSURANCE
NONINSURANCES
NONINSURED
NONINTEGRAL
NONINTEGRATED
NONINTELLECTUAL
NONINTERACTING
NONINTERACTIVE
NONINTERCOURSE
NONINTERCOURSES
NONINTEREST
NONINTERFERENCE
NONINTERSECTING
NONINTERVENTION
NONINTIMIDATING
NONINTOXICANT
NONINTOXICANTS
NONINTOXICATING
NONINTRUSIVE
NONINTUITIVE
NONINVASIVE
NONINVOLVED
NONINVOLVEMENT
NONINVOLVEMENTS
NONIONISING
NONIONIZING
NONIRRADIATED
NONIRRIGATED
NONIRRITANT
NONIRRITANTS
NONIRRITATING
NONJOINDER
NONJOINDERS
NONJOINERS
NONJUDGEMENTAL
NONJUDGMENTAL
NONJUDICIAL
NONJUSTICIABLE
NONKOSHERS
NONLADDERING
NONLANDOWNER
NONLANDOWNERS
NONLANGUAGE
NONLANGUAGES
NONLAWYERS
NONLEGUMES
NONLEGUMINOUS
NONLEXICAL
NONLIBRARIAN
NONLIBRARIANS
NONLIBRARY
NONLINEARITIES
NONLINEARITY
NONLINGUISTIC
NONLIQUIDS
NONLITERAL
NONLITERARY
NONLITERATE
NONLITERATES
NONLIVINGS
NONLOGICAL
NONLOGICALLY
NONLUMINOUS
NONMAGNETIC
NONMAINSTREAM
NONMALICIOUS
NONMALIGNANT
NONMALLEABLE
NONMANAGEMENT
NONMANAGERIAL
NONMANDATORY
NONMARITAL
NONMARKETS
NONMATERIAL
NONMATHEMATICAL
NONMATRICULATED
NONMEANINGFUL
NONMEASURABLE

NONMECHANICAL
NONMECHANISTIC
NONMEDICAL
NONMEETING
NONMEETINGS
NONMEMBERS
NONMEMBERSHIP
NONMEMBERSHIPS
NONMERCURIAL
NONMETALLIC
NONMETAMERIC
NONMETAPHORICAL
NONMETRICAL
NONMETROPOLITAN
NONMICROBIAL
NONMIGRANT
NONMIGRANTS
NONMIGRATORY
NONMILITANT
NONMILITANTS
NONMILITARY
NONMIMETIC
NONMINORITIES
NONMINORITY
NONMODERNS
NONMOLECULAR
NONMONETARIST
NONMONETARISTS
NONMONETARY
NONMONOGAMOUS
NONMORTALS
NONMOTILITIES
NONMOTILITY
NONMOTORISED
NONMOTORIZED
NONMUNICIPAL
NONMUSICAL
NONMUSICALS
NONMUSICIAN
NONMUSICIANS
NONMUTANTS
NONMYELINATED
NONMYSTICAL
NONNARRATIVE
NONNATIONAL
NONNATIONALS
NONNATIVES
NONNATURAL
NONNECESSITIES
NONNECESSITY
NONNEGATIVE
NONNEGLIGENT
NONNEGOTIABLE
NONNEGOTIABLES
NONNETWORK
NONNITROGENOUS
NONNORMATIVE
NONNUCLEAR
NONNUCLEATED
NONNUMERICAL
NONNUTRITIOUS
NONNUTRITIVE
NONOBJECTIVE
NONOBJECTIVISM
NONOBJECTIVISMS
NONOBJECTIVIST
NONOBJECTIVISTS
NONOBJECTIVITY
NONOBSCENE
NONOBSERVANCE
NONOBSERVANCES
NONOBSERVANT
NONOBVIOUS
NONOBVIOUSES
NONOCCUPATIONAL
NONOCCURRENCE
NONOCCURRENCES
NONOFFICIAL
NONOFFICIALS
NONOPERATIC
NONOPERATING
NONOPERATIONAL
NONOPERATIVE
NONOPTIMAL
NONORGANIC
NONORGASMIC
NONORTHODOX
NONOVERLAPPING
NONOXIDISING
NONOXIDIZING
NONPARALLEL
NONPARAMETRIC
NONPARASITIC
NONPAREILS
NONPARENTS
NONPARITIES
NONPARTICIPANT
NONPARTICIPANTS
NONPARTIES
NONPARTISAN
NONPARTISANSHIP
NONPARTIZAN
NONPARTIZANSHIP
NONPASSERINE
NONPASSIVE
NONPATHOGENIC
NONPAYMENT
NONPAYMENTS
NONPECUNIARY
NONPERFORMANCE
NONPERFORMANCES
NONPERFORMER
NONPERFORMERS
NONPERFORMING
NONPERISHABLE
NONPERISHABLES
NONPERMANENT
NONPERMISSIVE
NONPERSISTENT
NONPERSONAL
NONPERSONS
NONPETROLEUM
NONPHILOSOPHER
NONPHILOSOPHERS
NONPHONEMIC
NONPHONETIC
NONPHOSPHATE
NONPHOTOGRAPHIC
NONPHYSICAL
NONPHYSICIAN
NONPHYSICIANS
NONPLASTIC
NONPLASTICS
NONPLAYERS
NONPLAYING
NONPLUSING
NONPLUSSED
NONPLUSSES
NONPLUSSING
NONPOISONOUS
NONPOLARISABLE
NONPOLARIZABLE
NONPOLITICAL
NONPOLITICALLY
NONPOLITICIAN
NONPOLITICIANS
NONPOLLUTING
NONPOPULAR
NONPORTABLE
NONPOSSESSION
NONPOSSESSIONS
NONPRACTICAL
NONPRACTICING
NONPRACTISING
NONPREGNANT
NONPREHENSILE
NONPRESCRIPTION
NONPRINTING
NONPROBLEM
NONPROBLEMS
NONPRODUCING
NONPRODUCTIVE
NONPRODUCTIVITY
NONPROFESSIONAL
NONPROFESSORIAL
NONPROFITS
NONPROGRAM
NONPROGRAMMER
NONPROGRAMMERS
NONPROGRESSIVE
NONPROPRIETARY
NONPROSSED
NONPROSSES
NONPROSSING
NONPROTEIN
NONPSYCHIATRIC
NONPSYCHIATRIST
NONPSYCHOTIC
NONPUNITIVE
NONPURPOSIVE
NONQUANTIFIABLE
NONQUANTITATIVE
NONRACIALLY
NONRACISMS
NONRADIOACTIVE
NONRAILROAD
NONRANDOMNESS
NONRANDOMNESSES
NONRATIONAL
NONREACTIVE
NONREACTOR
NONREACTORS
NONREADERS
NONREADING
NONREADINGS
NONREALISTIC
NONRECEIPT
NONRECEIPTS
NONRECIPROCAL
NONRECOGNITION
NONRECOGNITIONS
NONRECOMBINANT
NONRECOMBINANTS
NONRECOURSE
NONRECOVERABLE
NONRECURRENT
NONRECURRING
NONRECYCLABLE
NONRECYCLABLES
NONREDUCING
NONREDUNDANT
NONREFILLABLE
NONREFLECTING
NONREFLECTIVE
NONREFLEXIVE
NONREFUNDABLE
NONREGIMENTAL
NONREGULATED
NONREGULATION
NONREIGNING
NONRELATIVE
NONRELATIVES
NONRELATIVISTIC
NONRELEVANT
NONRELIGIOUS
NONRENEWABLE
NONRENEWAL
NONRENEWALS
NONREPAYABLE
NONREPRODUCTIVE
NONRESIDENCE
NONRESIDENCES
NONRESIDENCIES
NONRESIDENCY
NONRESIDENT
NONRESIDENTIAL
NONRESIDENTS
NONRESISTANCE
NONRESISTANCES
NONRESISTANT

NONRESISTANTS
NONRESONANT
NONRESPONDENT
NONRESPONDENTS
NONRESPONDER
NONRESPONDERS
NONRESPONSE
NONRESPONSES
NONRESPONSIVE
NONRESTRICTED
NONRESTRICTIVE
NONRETRACTILE
NONRETROACTIVE
NONRETURNABLE
NONRETURNABLES
NONREUSABLE
NONREVERSIBLE
NONRHOTICITIES
NONRHOTICITY
NONRIOTERS
NONRIOTING
NONROTATING
NONROUTINE
NONRUMINANT
NONRUMINANTS
NONRUNNERS
NONSALABLE
NONSALEABLE
NONSAPONIFIABLE
NONSCHEDULED
NONSCIENCE
NONSCIENCES
NONSCIENTIFIC
NONSCIENTIST
NONSCIENTISTS
NONSEASONAL
NONSECRETOR
NONSECRETORS
NONSECRETORY
NONSECRETS
NONSECTARIAN
NONSEDIMENTABLE
NONSEGREGATED
NONSEGREGATION
NONSEGREGATIONS
NONSELECTED
NONSELECTIVE
NONSENSATIONAL
NONSENSICAL
NONSENSICALITY
NONSENSICALLY
NONSENSICALNESS
NONSENSITIVE
NONSENSUOUS
NONSENTENCE
NONSENTENCES
NONSEPTATE
NONSEQUENTIAL
NONSERIALS
NONSERIOUS
NONSHRINKABLE
NONSIGNERS
NONSIGNIFICANT
NONSIGNIFICANTS
NONSIMULTANEOUS
NONSINKABLE
NONSINUSOIDAL
NONSKATERS
NONSKELETAL
NONSKILLED
NONSMOKERS
NONSMOKING
NONSOCIALIST
NONSOCIALISTS
NONSOLUTION
NONSOLUTIONS
NONSOLVENT
NONSPATIAL
NONSPEAKER
NONSPEAKERS
NONSPEAKING
NONSPECIALIST
NONSPECIALISTS
NONSPECIFIC
NONSPECIFICALLY
NONSPECIFICITY
NONSPECTACULAR
NONSPECTRAL
NONSPECULAR
NONSPECULATIVE
NONSPEECHES
NONSPHERICAL
NONSPORTING
NONSTAINING
NONSTANDARD
NONSTAPLES
NONSTARTER
NONSTARTERS
NONSTATIONARY
NONSTATISTICAL
NONSTATIVE
NONSTATIVES
NONSTATUTORY
NONSTELLAR
NONSTEROID
NONSTEROIDAL
NONSTEROIDS
NONSTORIES
NONSTRATEGIC
NONSTRIATED
NONSTRIKING
NONSTRUCTURAL
NONSTRUCTURED
NONSTUDENT
NONSTUDENTS
NONSUBJECT
NONSUBJECTIVE
NONSUBJECTS
NONSUBSIDISED
NONSUBSIDIZED
NONSUCCESS
NONSUCCESSES
NONSUITING
NONSUPERVISORY
NONSUPPORT
NONSUPPORTS
NONSURGICAL
NONSWIMMER
NONSWIMMERS
NONSYLLABIC
NONSYLLABICS
NONSYMBOLIC
NONSYMMETRIC
NONSYMMETRICAL
NONSYNCHRONOUS
NONSYSTEMATIC
NONSYSTEMIC
NONSYSTEMS
NONTACTICAL
NONTALKERS
NONTAXABLE
NONTEACHING
NONTECHNICAL
NONTEMPORAL
NONTENURED
NONTERMINAL
NONTERMINALS
NONTERMINATING
NONTEXTUAL
NONTHEATRICAL
NONTHEISMS
NONTHEISTIC
NONTHEISTS
NONTHEOLOGICAL
NONTHEORETICAL
NONTHERAPEUTIC
NONTHERMAL
NONTHINKING
NONTHINKINGS
NONTHREATENING
NONTOBACCO
NONTOTALITARIAN
NONTRADING
NONTRADITIONAL
NONTRANSFERABLE
NONTRANSITIVE
NONTREATMENT
NONTREATMENTS
NONTRIVIAL
NONTROPICAL
NONTURBULENT
NONTYPICAL
NONUNANIMOUS
NONUNIFORM
NONUNIFORMITIES
NONUNIFORMITY
NONUNIONISED
NONUNIONISM
NONUNIONISMS
NONUNIONIST
NONUNIONISTS
NONUNIONIZED
NONUNIQUENESS
NONUNIQUENESSES
NONUNIVERSAL
NONUNIVERSITY
NONUTILITARIAN
NONUTILITIES
NONUTILITY
NONUTOPIAN
NONVALIDITIES
NONVALIDITY
NONVANISHING
NONVASCULAR
NONVECTORS
NONVEGETARIAN
NONVEGETARIANS
NONVENEREAL
NONVENOMOUS
NONVERBALLY
NONVETERAN
NONVETERANS
NONVIEWERS
NONVINTAGE
NONVINTAGES
NONVIOLENCE
NONVIOLENCES
NONVIOLENT
NONVIOLENTLY
NONVIRGINS
NONVISCOUS
NONVOCATIONAL
NONVOLATILE
NONVOLCANIC
NONVOLUNTARY
NONWINNING
NONWORKERS
NONWORKING
NONWRITERS
NONYELLOWING
NOODLEDOMS
NOOGENESES
NOOGENESIS
NOOMETRIES
NOOSPHERES
NOOTROPICS
NORADRENALIN
NORADRENALINE
NORADRENALINES
NORADRENALINS
NORADRENERGIC
NORDICITIES
NOREPINEPHRINE
NOREPINEPHRINES
NORETHINDRONE
NORETHINDRONES
NORETHISTERONE
NORETHISTERONES
NORMALCIES
NORMALISABLE

N

NORMALISATION
NORMALISATIONS
NORMALISED
NORMALISER
NORMALISERS
NORMALISES
NORMALISING
NORMALITIES
NORMALIZABLE
NORMALIZATION
NORMALIZATIONS
NORMALIZED
NORMALIZER
NORMALIZERS
NORMALIZES
NORMALIZING
NORMATIVELY
NORMATIVENESS
NORMATIVENESSES
NORMOGLYCAEMIA
NORMOGLYCAEMIAS
NORMOGLYCAEMIC
NORMOGLYCEMIA
NORMOGLYCEMIAS
NORMOGLYCEMIC
NORMOTENSION
NORMOTENSIONS
NORMOTENSIVE
NORMOTENSIVES
NORMOTHERMIA
NORMOTHERMIAS
NORMOTHERMIC
NOROVIRUSES
NORSELLERS
NORSELLING
NORTHBOUND
NORTHCOUNTRYMAN
NORTHCOUNTRYMEN
NORTHEASTER
NORTHEASTERLIES
NORTHEASTERLY
NORTHEASTERN
NORTHEASTERS
NORTHEASTS
NORTHEASTWARD
NORTHEASTWARDLY
NORTHEASTWARDS
NORTHERING
NORTHERLIES
NORTHERLINESS
NORTHERLINESSES
NORTHERMOST
NORTHERNER
NORTHERNERS
NORTHERNISE
NORTHERNISED
NORTHERNISES
NORTHERNISING
NORTHERNISM
NORTHERNISMS
NORTHERNIZE
NORTHERNIZED
NORTHERNIZES
NORTHERNIZING
NORTHERNMOST
NORTHLANDS
NORTHWARDLY
NORTHWARDS
NORTHWESTER
NORTHWESTERLIES
NORTHWESTERLY
NORTHWESTERN
NORTHWESTERS
NORTHWESTS
NORTHWESTWARD
NORTHWESTWARDLY
NORTHWESTWARDS
NORTRIPTYLINE
NORTRIPTYLINES
NOSEBANDED
NOSEBLEEDING
NOSEBLEEDINGS
NOSEBLEEDS
NOSEDIVING
NOSEGUARDS
NOSEPIECES
NOSEWHEELS
NOSINESSES
NOSOCOMIAL
NOSOGRAPHER
NOSOGRAPHERS
NOSOGRAPHIC
NOSOGRAPHIES
NOSOGRAPHY
NOSOLOGICAL
NOSOLOGICALLY
NOSOLOGIES
NOSOLOGIST
NOSOLOGISTS
NOSOPHOBIA
NOSOPHOBIAS
NOSTALGIAS
NOSTALGICALLY
NOSTALGICS
NOSTALGIST
NOSTALGISTS
NOSTOLOGIC
NOSTOLOGICAL
NOSTOLOGIES
NOSTOMANIA
NOSTOMANIAS
NOSTOPATHIES
NOSTOPATHY
NOSTRADAMIC
NOTABILITIES
NOTABILITY
NOTABLENESS
NOTABLENESSES
NOTAPHILIC
NOTAPHILIES
NOTAPHILISM
NOTAPHILISMS
NOTAPHILIST
NOTAPHILISTS
NOTARIALLY
NOTARISATION
NOTARISATIONS
NOTARISING
NOTARIZATION
NOTARIZATIONS
NOTARIZING
NOTARYSHIP
NOTARYSHIPS
NOTATIONAL
NOTCHBACKS
NOTCHELING
NOTCHELLED
NOTCHELLING
NOTEBANDIS
NOTEDNESSES
NOTEPAPERS
NOTEWORTHIER
NOTEWORTHIEST
NOTEWORTHILY
NOTEWORTHINESS
NOTEWORTHY
NOTHINGARIAN
NOTHINGARIANISM
NOTHINGARIANS
NOTHINGISM
NOTHINGISMS
NOTHINGNESS
NOTHINGNESSES
NOTICEABILITIES
NOTICEABILITY
NOTICEABLE
NOTICEABLY
NOTICEBOARD
NOTICEBOARDS
NOTIFIABLE
NOTIFICATION
NOTIFICATIONS
NOTIONALIST
NOTIONALISTS
NOTIONALITIES
NOTIONALITY
NOTIONALLY
NOTIONISTS
NOTOCHORDAL
NOTOCHORDS
NOTODONTID
NOTODONTIDS
NOTONECTAL
NOTORIETIES
NOTORIOUSLY
NOTORIOUSNESS
NOTORIOUSNESSES
NOTORNISES
NOTOTHERIUM
NOTOTHERIUMS
NOTOUNGULATE
NOTOUNGULATES
NOTUNGULATE
NOTUNGULATES
NOTWITHSTANDING
NOTWORKING
NOTWORKINGS
NOUGATINES
NOUMENALISM
NOUMENALISMS
NOUMENALIST
NOUMENALISTS
NOUMENALITIES
NOUMENALITY
NOUMENALLY
NOURISHABLE
NOURISHERS
NOURISHING
NOURISHINGLY
NOURISHMENT
NOURISHMENTS
NOURITURES
NOURRITURE
NOURRITURES
NOUSELLING
NOVACULITE
NOVACULITES
NOVELETTES
NOVELETTISH
NOVELETTIST
NOVELETTISTS
NOVELISATION
NOVELISATIONS
NOVELISERS
NOVELISING
NOVELISTIC
NOVELISTICALLY
NOVELIZATION
NOVELIZATIONS
NOVELIZERS
NOVELIZING
NOVEMDECILLION
NOVEMDECILLIONS
NOVENARIES
NOVICEHOOD
NOVICEHOODS
NOVICESHIP
NOVICESHIPS
NOVICIATES
NOVITIATES
NOVOBIOCIN
NOVOBIOCINS
NOVOCAINES
NOVOCENTENARIES
NOVOCENTENARY
NOVODAMUSES
NOWCASTING
NOWCASTINGS
NOXIOUSNESS
NOXIOUSNESSES

NUBBINESSES
NUBIFEROUS
NUBIGENOUS
NUBILITIES
NUCIFEROUS
NUCIVOROUS
NUCLEARISATION
NUCLEARISATIONS
NUCLEARISE
NUCLEARISED
NUCLEARISES
NUCLEARISING
NUCLEARIZATION
NUCLEARIZATIONS
NUCLEARIZE
NUCLEARIZED
NUCLEARIZES
NUCLEARIZING
NUCLEATING
NUCLEATION
NUCLEATIONS
NUCLEATORS
NUCLEOCAPSID
NUCLEOCAPSIDS
NUCLEOLATE
NUCLEOLATED
NUCLEONICALLY
NUCLEONICS
NUCLEOPHILE
NUCLEOPHILES
NUCLEOPHILIC
NUCLEOPHILICITY
NUCLEOPLASM
NUCLEOPLASMATIC
NUCLEOPLASMIC
NUCLEOPLASMS
NUCLEOPROTEIN
NUCLEOPROTEINS
NUCLEOSIDE
NUCLEOSIDES
NUCLEOSOMAL
NUCLEOSOME
NUCLEOSOMES
NUCLEOSYNTHESES
NUCLEOSYNTHESIS
NUCLEOSYNTHETIC
NUCLEOTIDASE
NUCLEOTIDASES
NUCLEOTIDE
NUCLEOTIDES
NUDENESSES
NUDIBRANCH
NUDIBRANCHIATE
NUDIBRANCHIATES
NUDIBRANCHS
NUDICAUDATE
NUDICAULOUS
NUGATORINESS
NUGATORINESSES
NUGGETIEST
NUGGETTING
NUISANCERS
NULLIFICATION
NULLIFICATIONS
NULLIFIDIAN
NULLIFIDIANS
NULLIFIERS
NULLIFYING
NULLIPARAE
NULLIPARAS
NULLIPARITIES
NULLIPARITY
NULLIPAROUS
NULLIPORES
NULLNESSES
NUMBERABLE
NUMBERINGS
NUMBERLESS
NUMBERLESSLY
NUMBERLESSNESS
NUMBERPLATE
NUMBERPLATES
NUMBFISHES
NUMBNESSES
NUMBNUTSES
NUMBSKULLED
NUMBSKULLS
NUMERABILITIES
NUMERABILITY
NUMERACIES
NUMERAIRES
NUMERATING
NUMERATION
NUMERATIONS
NUMERATIVE
NUMERATORS
NUMERICALLY
NUMEROLOGICAL
NUMEROLOGIES
NUMEROLOGIST
NUMEROLOGISTS
NUMEROLOGY
NUMEROSITIES
NUMEROSITY
NUMEROUSLY
NUMEROUSNESS
NUMEROUSNESSES
NUMINOUSES
NUMINOUSNESS
NUMINOUSNESSES
NUMISMATIC
NUMISMATICALLY
NUMISMATICS
NUMISMATIST
NUMISMATISTS
NUMISMATOLOGIES
NUMISMATOLOGIST
NUMISMATOLOGY
NUMMULATED
NUMMULATION
NUMMULATIONS
NUMMULINES
NUMMULITES
NUMMULITIC
NUMSKULLED
NUNCIATURE
NUNCIATURES
NUNCUPATED
NUNCUPATES
NUNCUPATING
NUNCUPATION
NUNCUPATIONS
NUNCUPATIVE
NUNCUPATORY
NUNNATIONS
NUNNISHNESS
NUNNISHNESSES
NUPTIALITIES
NUPTIALITY
NURSEHOUND
NURSEHOUNDS
NURSELINGS
NURSEMAIDED
NURSEMAIDING
NURSEMAIDS
NURSERYMAID
NURSERYMAIDS
NURSERYMAN
NURSERYMEN
NURTURABLE
NURTURANCE
NURTURANCES
NUTATIONAL
NUTBUTTERS
NUTCRACKER
NUTCRACKERS
NUTGRASSES
NUTHATCHES
NUTJOBBERS
NUTMEGGIER
NUTMEGGIEST
NUTMEGGING
NUTPECKERS
NUTRACEUTICAL
NUTRACEUTICALS
NUTRIGENETICS
NUTRIGENOMICS
NUTRIMENTAL
NUTRIMENTS
NUTRITIONAL
NUTRITIONALLY
NUTRITIONARY
NUTRITIONIST
NUTRITIONISTS
NUTRITIONS
NUTRITIOUS
NUTRITIOUSLY
NUTRITIOUSNESS
NUTRITIVELY
NUTRITIVES
NUTTINESSES
NYCHTHEMERAL
NYCHTHEMERON
NYCHTHEMERONS
NYCTAGINACEOUS
NYCTALOPES
NYCTALOPIA
NYCTALOPIAS
NYCTALOPIC
NYCTANTHOUS
NYCTINASTIC
NYCTINASTIES
NYCTINASTY
NYCTITROPIC
NYCTITROPISM
NYCTITROPISMS
NYCTOPHOBIA
NYCTOPHOBIAS
NYCTOPHOBIC
NYMPHAEACEOUS
NYMPHAEUMS
NYMPHALIDS
NYMPHETTES
NYMPHLIEST
NYMPHOLEPSIES
NYMPHOLEPSY
NYMPHOLEPT
NYMPHOLEPTIC
NYMPHOLEPTS
NYMPHOMANIA
NYMPHOMANIAC
NYMPHOMANIACAL
NYMPHOMANIACS
NYMPHOMANIAS
NYSTAGMOID
NYSTAGMUSES

O

OAFISHNESS
OAFISHNESSES
OAKENSHAWS
OAKINESSES
OARSMANSHIP
OARSMANSHIPS
OASTHOUSES
OBBLIGATOS
OBCOMPRESSED
OBDURACIES
OBDURATELY
OBDURATENESS
OBDURATENESSES
OBDURATING
OBDURATION
OBDURATIONS
OBEDIENCES
OBEDIENTIAL
OBEDIENTIARIES
OBEDIENTIARY
OBEDIENTLY
OBEISANCES
OBEISANTLY
OBELISCOID
OBELISKOID
OBESENESSES
OBESOGENIC
OBFUSCATED
OBFUSCATES
OBFUSCATING
OBFUSCATION
OBFUSCATIONS
OBFUSCATORY
OBITUARIES
OBITUARIST
OBITUARISTS
OBJECTIFICATION
OBJECTIFIED
OBJECTIFIES
OBJECTIFYING
OBJECTIONABLE
OBJECTIONABLY
OBJECTIONS
OBJECTIVAL
OBJECTIVATE
OBJECTIVATED
OBJECTIVATES
OBJECTIVATING
OBJECTIVATION
OBJECTIVATIONS
OBJECTIVELY
OBJECTIVENESS
OBJECTIVENESSES
OBJECTIVES
OBJECTIVISE
OBJECTIVISED
OBJECTIVISES
OBJECTIVISING
OBJECTIVISM
OBJECTIVISMS
OBJECTIVIST
OBJECTIVISTIC
OBJECTIVISTS
OBJECTIVITIES
OBJECTIVITY
OBJECTIVIZE
OBJECTIVIZED
OBJECTIVIZES
OBJECTIVIZING
OBJECTLESS
OBJECTLESSNESS
OBJURATION
OBJURATIONS
OBJURGATED
OBJURGATES
OBJURGATING
OBJURGATION
OBJURGATIONS
OBJURGATIVE
OBJURGATOR
OBJURGATORS
OBJURGATORY
OBLANCEOLATE
OBLATENESS
OBLATENESSES
OBLATIONAL
OBLIGATELY
OBLIGATING
OBLIGATION
OBLIGATIONAL
OBLIGATIONS
OBLIGATIVE
OBLIGATORILY
OBLIGATORINESS
OBLIGATORS
OBLIGATORY
OBLIGEMENT
OBLIGEMENTS
OBLIGINGLY
OBLIGINGNESS
OBLIGINGNESSES
OBLIQUATION
OBLIQUATIONS
OBLIQUENESS
OBLIQUENESSES
OBLIQUITIES
OBLIQUITOUS
OBLITERATE
OBLITERATED
OBLITERATES
OBLITERATING
OBLITERATION
OBLITERATIONS
OBLITERATIVE
OBLITERATOR
OBLITERATORS
OBLIVIOUSLY
OBLIVIOUSNESS
OBLIVIOUSNESSES
OBLIVISCENCE
OBLIVISCENCES
OBMUTESCENCE
OBMUTESCENCES
OBMUTESCENT
OBNOXIOUSLY
OBNOXIOUSNESS
OBNOXIOUSNESSES
OBNUBILATE
OBNUBILATED
OBNUBILATES
OBNUBILATING
OBNUBILATION
OBNUBILATIONS
OBREPTIONS
OBREPTITIOUS
OBSCENENESS
OBSCENENESSES
OBSCENITIES
OBSCURANTIC
OBSCURANTISM
OBSCURANTISMS
OBSCURANTIST
OBSCURANTISTS
OBSCURANTS
OBSCURATION
OBSCURATIONS
OBSCUREMENT
OBSCUREMENTS
OBSCURENESS
OBSCURENESSES
OBSCURITIES
OBSECRATED
OBSECRATES
OBSECRATING
OBSECRATION
OBSECRATIONS
OBSEQUIOUS
OBSEQUIOUSLY
OBSEQUIOUSNESS
OBSERVABILITIES
OBSERVABILITY
OBSERVABLE
OBSERVABLENESS
OBSERVABLES
OBSERVABLY
OBSERVANCE
OBSERVANCES
OBSERVANCIES
OBSERVANCY
OBSERVANTLY
OBSERVANTS
OBSERVATION
OBSERVATIONAL
OBSERVATIONALLY
OBSERVATIONS
OBSERVATIVE
OBSERVATOR
OBSERVATORIES
OBSERVATORS
OBSERVATORY
OBSERVINGLY
OBSESSIONAL
OBSESSIONALLY
OBSESSIONIST
OBSESSIONISTS
OBSESSIONS
OBSESSIVELY
OBSESSIVENESS
OBSESSIVENESSES
OBSESSIVES
OBSIDIONAL
OBSIDIONARY
OBSIGNATED
OBSIGNATES
OBSIGNATING
OBSIGNATION
OBSIGNATIONS
OBSIGNATORY
OBSOLESCED
OBSOLESCENCE
OBSOLESCENCES
OBSOLESCENT
OBSOLESCENTLY
OBSOLESCES
OBSOLESCING
OBSOLETELY
OBSOLETENESS
OBSOLETENESSES
OBSOLETING
OBSOLETION

O

OBSOLETIONS
OBSOLETISM
OBSOLETISMS
OBSTETRICAL
OBSTETRICALLY
OBSTETRICIAN
OBSTETRICIANS
OBSTETRICS
OBSTINACIES
OBSTINATELY
OBSTINATENESS
OBSTINATENESSES
OBSTIPATION
OBSTIPATIONS
OBSTREPERATE
OBSTREPERATED
OBSTREPERATES
OBSTREPERATING
OBSTREPEROUS
OBSTREPEROUSLY
OBSTRICTION
OBSTRICTIONS
OBSTROPALOUS
OBSTROPULOUS
OBSTRUCTED
OBSTRUCTER
OBSTRUCTERS
OBSTRUCTING
OBSTRUCTINGLY
OBSTRUCTION
OBSTRUCTIONAL
OBSTRUCTIONALLY
OBSTRUCTIONISM
OBSTRUCTIONISMS
OBSTRUCTIONIST
OBSTRUCTIONISTS
OBSTRUCTIONS
OBSTRUCTIVE
OBSTRUCTIVELY
OBSTRUCTIVENESS
OBSTRUCTIVES
OBSTRUCTOR
OBSTRUCTORS
OBSTRUENTS
OBTAINABILITIES
OBTAINABILITY
OBTAINABLE
OBTAINMENT
OBTAINMENTS
OBTEMPERATE
OBTEMPERATED
OBTEMPERATES
OBTEMPERATING
OBTEMPERED
OBTEMPERING
OBTENTIONS
OBTESTATION
OBTESTATIONS
OBTRUDINGS
OBTRUNCATE
OBTRUNCATED
OBTRUNCATES
OBTRUNCATING
OBTRUSIONS
OBTRUSIVELY
OBTRUSIVENESS
OBTRUSIVENESSES
OBTUNDENTS
OBTUNDITIES
OBTURATING
OBTURATION
OBTURATIONS
OBTURATORS
OBTUSENESS
OBTUSENESSES
OBTUSITIES
OBUMBRATED
OBUMBRATES
OBUMBRATING
OBUMBRATION
OBUMBRATIONS
OBVENTIONS
OBVERSIONS
OBVIATIONS
OBVIOUSNESS
OBVIOUSNESSES
OBVOLUTION
OBVOLUTIONS
OBVOLUTIVE
OCCASIONAL
OCCASIONALISM
OCCASIONALISMS
OCCASIONALIST
OCCASIONALISTS
OCCASIONALITIES
OCCASIONALITY
OCCASIONALLY
OCCASIONED
OCCASIONER
OCCASIONERS
OCCASIONING
OCCIDENTAL
OCCIDENTALISE
OCCIDENTALISED
OCCIDENTALISES
OCCIDENTALISING
OCCIDENTALISM
OCCIDENTALISMS
OCCIDENTALIST
OCCIDENTALISTS
OCCIDENTALIZE
OCCIDENTALIZED
OCCIDENTALIZES
OCCIDENTALIZING
OCCIDENTALLY
OCCIDENTALS
OCCIPITALLY
OCCIPITALS
OCCLUDENTS
OCCLUSIONS
OCCLUSIVENESS
OCCLUSIVENESSES
OCCLUSIVES
OCCULTATION
OCCULTATIONS
OCCULTISMS
OCCULTISTS
OCCULTNESS
OCCULTNESSES
OCCUPANCES
OCCUPANCIES
OCCUPATING
OCCUPATION
OCCUPATIONAL
OCCUPATIONALLY
OCCUPATIONS
OCCUPATIVE
OCCURRENCE
OCCURRENCES
OCCURRENTS
OCEANARIUM
OCEANARIUMS
OCEANFRONT
OCEANFRONTS
OCEANGOING
OCEANOGRAPHER
OCEANOGRAPHERS
OCEANOGRAPHIC
OCEANOGRAPHICAL
OCEANOGRAPHIES
OCEANOGRAPHY
OCEANOLOGICAL
OCEANOLOGIES
OCEANOLOGIST
OCEANOLOGISTS
OCEANOLOGY
OCELLATION
OCELLATIONS
OCHLOCRACIES
OCHLOCRACY
OCHLOCRATIC
OCHLOCRATICAL
OCHLOCRATICALLY
OCHLOCRATS
OCHLOPHOBIA
OCHLOPHOBIAC
OCHLOPHOBIACS
OCHLOPHOBIAS
OCHLOPHOBIC
OCHLOPHOBICS
OCHRACEOUS
OCHROLEUCOUS
OCTACHORDAL
OCTACHORDS
OCTAGONALLY
OCTAHEDRAL
OCTAHEDRALLY
OCTAHEDRITE
OCTAHEDRITES
OCTAHEDRON
OCTAHEDRONS
OCTAMEROUS
OCTAMETERS
OCTANDRIAN
OCTANDROUS
OCTANEDIOIC
OCTANGULAR
OCTAPEPTIDE
OCTAPEPTIDES
OCTAPLOIDIES
OCTAPLOIDS
OCTAPLOIDY
OCTAPODIES
OCTARCHIES
OCTASTICHON
OCTASTICHONS
OCTASTICHOUS
OCTASTICHS
OCTASTROPHIC
OCTASTYLES
OCTAVALENT
OCTENNIALLY
OCTILLIONS
OCTILLIONTH
OCTILLIONTHS
OCTINGENARIES
OCTINGENARY
OCTINGENTENARY
OCTOCENTENARIES
OCTOCENTENARY
OCTODECILLION
OCTODECILLIONS
OCTODECIMO
OCTODECIMOS
OCTOGENARIAN
OCTOGENARIANS
OCTOGENARIES
OCTOGENARY
OCTOGYNOUS
OCTOHEDRON
OCTOHEDRONS
OCTONARIAN
OCTONARIANS
OCTONARIES
OCTONARIUS
OCTONOCULAR
OCTOPETALOUS
OCTOPLOIDS
OCTOPODANS
OCTOPODOUS
OCTOPUSHER
OCTOPUSHERS
OCTOPUSHES
OCTOSEPALOUS
OCTOSTICHOUS
OCTOSTYLES
OCTOSYLLABIC
OCTOSYLLABICS
OCTOSYLLABLE
OCTOSYLLABLES

OCTOTHORPS
OCTUPLICATE
OCTUPLICATES
OCULARISTS
OCULOMOTOR
ODALISQUES
ODDSMAKERS
ODIOUSNESS
ODIOUSNESSES
ODOMETRIES
ODONATISTS
ODONATOLOGIES
ODONATOLOGIST
ODONATOLOGISTS
ODONATOLOGY
ODONTALGIA
ODONTALGIAS
ODONTALGIC
ODONTALGIES
ODONTOBLAST
ODONTOBLASTIC
ODONTOBLASTS
ODONTOCETE
ODONTOCETES
ODONTOGENIC
ODONTOGENIES
ODONTOGENY
ODONTOGLOSSUM
ODONTOGLOSSUMS
ODONTOGRAPH
ODONTOGRAPHIES
ODONTOGRAPHS
ODONTOGRAPHY
ODONTOLITE
ODONTOLITES
ODONTOLOGIC
ODONTOLOGICAL
ODONTOLOGIES
ODONTOLOGIST
ODONTOLOGISTS
ODONTOLOGY
ODONTOMATA
ODONTOMATOUS
ODONTOPHOBIA
ODONTOPHOBIAS
ODONTOPHORAL
ODONTOPHORAN
ODONTOPHORANS
ODONTOPHORE
ODONTOPHORES
ODONTOPHOROUS
ODONTORHYNCHOUS
ODONTORNITHES
ODONTOSTOMATOUS
ODORIFEROUS
ODORIFEROUSLY
ODORIFEROUSNESS
ODORIMETRIES
ODORIMETRY
ODORIPHORE
ODORIPHORES
ODOROUSNESS
ODOROUSNESSES
OECOLOGICAL
OECOLOGICALLY
OECOLOGIES
OECOLOGIST
OECOLOGISTS
OECUMENICAL
OECUMENICALLY
OEDEMATOSE
OEDEMATOUS
OEDOMETERS
OENOLOGICAL
OENOLOGIES
OENOLOGIST
OENOLOGISTS
OENOMANCIES
OENOMANIAS
OENOMETERS
OENOPHILES
OENOPHILIES
OENOPHILIST
OENOPHILISTS
OENOTHERAS
OESOPHAGEAL
OESOPHAGITIS
OESOPHAGITISES
OESOPHAGOSCOPE
OESOPHAGOSCOPES
OESOPHAGOSCOPY
OESOPHAGUS
OESOPHAGUSES
OESTRADIOL
OESTRADIOLS
OESTROGENIC
OESTROGENICALLY
OESTROGENS
OFFENCEFUL
OFFENCELESS
OFFENDEDLY
OFFENDRESS
OFFENDRESSES
OFFENSELESS
OFFENSIVELY
OFFENSIVENESS
OFFENSIVENESSES
OFFENSIVES
OFFERTORIES
OFFHANDEDLY
OFFHANDEDNESS
OFFHANDEDNESSES
OFFICEHOLDER
OFFICEHOLDERS
OFFICERING
OFFICIALDOM
OFFICIALDOMS
OFFICIALESE
OFFICIALESES
OFFICIALISM
OFFICIALISMS
OFFICIALITIES
OFFICIALITY
OFFICIALLY
OFFICIALTIES
OFFICIALTY
OFFICIANTS
OFFICIARIES
OFFICIATED
OFFICIATES
OFFICIATING
OFFICIATION
OFFICIATIONS
OFFICIATOR
OFFICIATORS
OFFICINALLY
OFFICINALS
OFFICIOUSLY
OFFICIOUSNESS
OFFICIOUSNESSES
OFFISHNESS
OFFISHNESSES
OFFLOADING
OFFPRINTED
OFFPRINTING
OFFSADDLED
OFFSADDLES
OFFSADDLING
OFFSCOURING
OFFSCOURINGS
OFFSEASONS
OFFSETABLE
OFFSETTING
OFFSETTINGS
OFFSHORING
OFFSHORINGS
OFFSPRINGS
OFTENNESSES
OFTENTIMES
OGANESSONS
OILINESSES
OINOLOGIES
OLDFANGLED
OLEAGINOUS
OLEAGINOUSLY
OLEAGINOUSNESS
OLEANDOMYCIN
OLEANDOMYCINS
OLECRANONS
OLEIFEROUS
OLEOGRAPHIC
OLEOGRAPHIES
OLEOGRAPHS
OLEOGRAPHY
OLEOMARGARIN
OLEOMARGARINE
OLEOMARGARINES
OLEOMARGARINS
OLEOPHILIC
OLEORESINOUS
OLEORESINS
OLERACEOUS
OLFACTIBLE
OLFACTIONS
OLFACTOLOGIES
OLFACTOLOGIST
OLFACTOLOGISTS
OLFACTOLOGY
OLFACTOMETER
OLFACTOMETERS
OLFACTOMETRIES
OLFACTOMETRY
OLFACTORIES
OLFACTRONICS
OLIGAEMIAS
OLIGARCHAL
OLIGARCHIC
OLIGARCHICAL
OLIGARCHICALLY
OLIGARCHIES
OLIGOCHAETE
OLIGOCHAETES
OLIGOCHROME
OLIGOCHROMES
OLIGOCLASE
OLIGOCLASES
OLIGOCYTHAEMIA
OLIGOCYTHAEMIAS
OLIGODENDROCYTE
OLIGODENDROGLIA
OLIGOGENES
OLIGOMERIC
OLIGOMERISATION
OLIGOMERIZATION
OLIGOMEROUS
OLIGONUCLEOTIDE
OLIGOPEPTIDE
OLIGOPEPTIDES
OLIGOPHAGIES
OLIGOPHAGOUS
OLIGOPHAGY
OLIGOPOLIES
OLIGOPOLISTIC
OLIGOPSONIES
OLIGOPSONISTIC
OLIGOPSONY
OLIGOSACCHARIDE
OLIGOSPERMIA
OLIGOSPERMIAS
OLIGOTROPHIC
OLIGOTROPHIES
OLIGOTROPHY
OLIGURESES
OLIGURESIS
OLIGURETIC
OLINGUITOS
OLIVACEOUS
OLIVENITES
OLIVEWOODS
OLIVINITIC

O

OLOGOANING
OLOLIUQUIS
OMBROGENOUS
OMBROMETER
OMBROMETERS
OMBROPHILE
OMBROPHILES
OMBROPHILOUS
OMBROPHILS
OMBROPHOBE
OMBROPHOBES
OMBROPHOBOUS
OMBUDSMANSHIP
OMBUDSMANSHIPS
OMINOUSNESS
OMINOUSNESSES
OMISSIVENESS
OMISSIVENESSES
OMITTANCES
OMMATIDIAL
OMMATIDIUM
OMMATOPHORE
OMMATOPHORES
OMMATOPHOROUS
OMNIBENEVOLENCE
OMNIBENEVOLENT
OMNIBUSSES
OMNICOMPETENCE
OMNICOMPETENCES
OMNICOMPETENT
OMNIDIRECTIONAL
OMNIFARIOUS
OMNIFARIOUSLY
OMNIFARIOUSNESS
OMNIFEROUS
OMNIFICENCE
OMNIFICENCES
OMNIFICENT
OMNIFORMITIES
OMNIFORMITY
OMNIGENOUS
OMNIPARITIES
OMNIPARITY
OMNIPAROUS
OMNIPATIENT
OMNIPOTENCE
OMNIPOTENCES
OMNIPOTENCIES
OMNIPOTENCY
OMNIPOTENT
OMNIPOTENTLY
OMNIPOTENTS
OMNIPRESENCE
OMNIPRESENCES
OMNIPRESENT
OMNIRANGES
OMNISCIENCE
OMNISCIENCES
OMNISCIENT
OMNISCIENTLY
OMNISHAMBLES
OMNIVORIES
OMNIVOROUS
OMNIVOROUSLY
OMNIVOROUSNESS
OMOPHAGIAS
OMOPHAGIES
OMOPHAGOUS
OMOPHORION
OMOPLATOSCOPIES
OMOPLATOSCOPY
OMPHACITES
OMPHALOMANCIES
OMPHALOMANCY
OMPHALOSKEPSES
OMPHALOSKEPSIS
ONAGRACEOUS
ONBOARDING
ONBOARDINGS
ONCHOCERCIASES
ONCHOCERCIASIS
ONCOGENESES
ONCOGENESIS
ONCOGENETICIST
ONCOGENETICISTS
ONCOGENICITIES
ONCOGENICITY
ONCOGENOUS
ONCOLOGICAL
ONCOLOGIES
ONCOLOGIST
ONCOLOGISTS
ONCOLYTICS
ONCOMETERS
ONCORNAVIRUS
ONCORNAVIRUSES
ONCOTOMIES
ONCOVIRUSES
ONDOGRAPHS
ONEIRICALLY
ONEIROCRITIC
ONEIROCRITICAL
ONEIROCRITICISM
ONEIROCRITICS
ONEIRODYNIA
ONEIRODYNIAS
ONEIROLOGIES
ONEIROLOGY
ONEIROMANCER
ONEIROMANCERS
ONEIROMANCIES
ONEIROMANCY
ONEIROSCOPIES
ONEIROSCOPIST
ONEIROSCOPISTS
ONEIROSCOPY
ONEROUSNESS
ONEROUSNESSES
ONGOINGNESS
ONGOINGNESSES
ONIONSKINS
ONOCENTAUR
ONOCENTAURS
ONOMASIOLOGIES
ONOMASIOLOGY
ONOMASTICALLY
ONOMASTICIAN
ONOMASTICIANS
ONOMASTICON
ONOMASTICONS
ONOMASTICS
ONOMATOLOGIES
ONOMATOLOGIST
ONOMATOLOGISTS
ONOMATOLOGY
ONOMATOPOEIA
ONOMATOPOEIAS
ONOMATOPOEIC
ONOMATOPOESES
ONOMATOPOESIS
ONOMATOPOETIC
ONOMATOPOIESES
ONOMATOPOIESIS
ONSETTINGS
ONSHORINGS
ONSLAUGHTS
ONTOGENESES
ONTOGENESIS
ONTOGENETIC
ONTOGENETICALLY
ONTOGENICALLY
ONTOGENIES
ONTOLOGICAL
ONTOLOGICALLY
ONTOLOGIES
ONTOLOGIST
ONTOLOGISTS
ONYCHITISES
ONYCHOCRYPTOSES
ONYCHOCRYPTOSIS
ONYCHOMANCIES
ONYCHOMANCY
ONYCHOPHAGIES
ONYCHOPHAGIST
ONYCHOPHAGISTS
ONYCHOPHAGY
ONYCHOPHORAN
ONYCHOPHORANS
OOGAMOUSLY
OOJAMAFLIP
OOJAMAFLIPS
OOMPAHPAHS
OOPHORECTOMIES
OOPHORECTOMISE
OOPHORECTOMISED
OOPHORECTOMISES
OOPHORECTOMIZE
OOPHORECTOMIZED
OOPHORECTOMIZES
OOPHORECTOMY
OOPHORITIC
OOPHORITIS
OOPHORITISES
OOZINESSES
OPACIFIERS
OPACIFYING
OPALESCENCE
OPALESCENCES
OPALESCENT
OPALESCENTLY
OPALESCING
OPAQUENESS
OPAQUENESSES
OPEIDOSCOPE
OPEIDOSCOPES
OPENABILITIES
OPENABILITY
OPENHANDED
OPENHANDEDLY
OPENHANDEDNESS
OPENHEARTED
OPENHEARTEDLY
OPENHEARTEDNESS
OPENMOUTHED
OPENMOUTHEDLY
OPENMOUTHEDNESS
OPENNESSES
OPERABILITIES
OPERABILITY
OPERAGOERS
OPERAGOING
OPERAGOINGS
OPERATICALLY
OPERATIONAL
OPERATIONALISM
OPERATIONALISMS
OPERATIONALIST
OPERATIONALISTS
OPERATIONALLY
OPERATIONISM
OPERATIONISMS
OPERATIONIST
OPERATIONISTS
OPERATIONS
OPERATISED
OPERATISES
OPERATISING
OPERATIVELY
OPERATIVENESS
OPERATIVENESSES
OPERATIVES
OPERATIVITIES
OPERATIVITY
OPERATIZED
OPERATIZES
OPERATIZING
OPERATORLESS
OPERCULARS
OPERCULATE
OPERCULATED

O

OPERCULUMS
OPERETTIST
OPERETTISTS
OPEROSENESS
OPEROSENESSES
OPEROSITIES
OPHICALCITE
OPHICALCITES
OPHICLEIDE
OPHICLEIDES
OPHIDIARIA
OPHIDIARIUM
OPHIDIARIUMS
OPHIOLATER
OPHIOLATERS
OPHIOLATRIES
OPHIOLATROUS
OPHIOLATRY
OPHIOLITES
OPHIOLITIC
OPHIOLOGIC
OPHIOLOGICAL
OPHIOLOGIES
OPHIOLOGIST
OPHIOLOGISTS
OPHIOMORPH
OPHIOMORPHIC
OPHIOMORPHOUS
OPHIOMORPHS
OPHIOPHAGOUS
OPHIOPHILIST
OPHIOPHILISTS
OPHIUROIDS
OPHTHALMIA
OPHTHALMIAS
OPHTHALMIC
OPHTHALMIST
OPHTHALMISTS
OPHTHALMITIS
OPHTHALMITISES
OPHTHALMOLOGIC
OPHTHALMOLOGIES
OPHTHALMOLOGIST
OPHTHALMOLOGY
OPHTHALMOMETER
OPHTHALMOMETERS
OPHTHALMOMETRY
OPHTHALMOPHOBIA
OPHTHALMOPLEGIA
OPHTHALMOSCOPE
OPHTHALMOSCOPES
OPHTHALMOSCOPIC
OPHTHALMOSCOPY
OPINICUSES
OPINIONATE
OPINIONATED
OPINIONATEDLY
OPINIONATEDNESS
OPINIONATELY
OPINIONATES
OPINIONATING
OPINIONATIVE
OPINIONATIVELY
OPINIONATOR
OPINIONATORS
OPINIONIST
OPINIONISTS
OPISOMETER
OPISOMETERS
OPISTHOBRANCH
OPISTHOBRANCHS
OPISTHOCOELIAN
OPISTHOCOELOUS
OPISTHODOMOI
OPISTHODOMOS
OPISTHOGLOSSAL
OPISTHOGNATHISM
OPISTHOGNATHOUS
OPISTHOGRAPH
OPISTHOGRAPHIC
OPISTHOGRAPHIES
OPISTHOGRAPHS
OPISTHOGRAPHY
OPISTHOSOMA
OPISTHOSOMATA
OPISTHOTONIC
OPISTHOTONOS
OPISTHOTONOSES
OPOBALSAMS
OPODELDOCS
OPOPANAXES
OPOTHERAPIES
OPOTHERAPY
OPPIGNERATE
OPPIGNERATED
OPPIGNERATES
OPPIGNERATING
OPPIGNERATION
OPPIGNERATIONS
OPPIGNORATE
OPPIGNORATED
OPPIGNORATES
OPPIGNORATING
OPPIGNORATION
OPPIGNORATIONS
OPPILATING
OPPILATION
OPPILATIONS
OPPILATIVE
OPPONENCIES
OPPORTUNELY
OPPORTUNENESS
OPPORTUNENESSES
OPPORTUNISM
OPPORTUNISMS
OPPORTUNIST
OPPORTUNISTIC
OPPORTUNISTS
OPPORTUNITIES
OPPORTUNITY
OPPOSABILITIES
OPPOSABILITY
OPPOSELESS
OPPOSINGLY
OPPOSITELY
OPPOSITENESS
OPPOSITENESSES
OPPOSITION
OPPOSITIONAL
OPPOSITIONIST
OPPOSITIONISTS
OPPOSITIONLESS
OPPOSITIONS
OPPOSITIVE
OPPRESSING
OPPRESSINGLY
OPPRESSION
OPPRESSIONS
OPPRESSIVE
OPPRESSIVELY
OPPRESSIVENESS
OPPRESSORS
OPPROBRIOUS
OPPROBRIOUSLY
OPPROBRIOUSNESS
OPPROBRIUM
OPPROBRIUMS
OPPUGNANCIES
OPPUGNANCY
OPPUGNANTLY
OPPUGNANTS
OPSIMATHIES
OPSIOMETER
OPSIOMETERS
OPSOMANIAC
OPSOMANIACS
OPSOMANIAS
OPSONIFICATION
OPSONIFICATIONS
OPSONIFIED
OPSONIFIES
OPSONIFYING
OPSONISATION
OPSONISATIONS
OPSONISING
OPSONIZATION
OPSONIZATIONS
OPSONIZING
OPTATIVELY
OPTIMALISATION
OPTIMALISATIONS
OPTIMALISE
OPTIMALISED
OPTIMALISES
OPTIMALISING
OPTIMALITIES
OPTIMALITY
OPTIMALIZATION
OPTIMALIZATIONS
OPTIMALIZE
OPTIMALIZED
OPTIMALIZES
OPTIMALIZING
OPTIMISATION
OPTIMISATIONS
OPTIMISERS
OPTIMISING
OPTIMISTIC
OPTIMISTICAL
OPTIMISTICALLY
OPTIMIZATION
OPTIMIZATIONS
OPTIMIZERS
OPTIMIZING
OPTIONALITIES
OPTIONALITY
OPTIONALLY
OPTOACOUSTIC
OPTOELECTRONIC
OPTOELECTRONICS
OPTOKINETIC
OPTOLOGIES
OPTOLOGIST
OPTOLOGISTS
OPTOMETERS
OPTOMETRIC
OPTOMETRICAL
OPTOMETRIES
OPTOMETRIST
OPTOMETRISTS
OPTOPHONES
OPULENCIES
ORACULARITIES
ORACULARITY
ORACULARLY
ORACULARNESS
ORACULARNESSES
ORACULOUSLY
ORACULOUSNESS
ORACULOUSNESSES
ORANGEADES
ORANGERIES
ORANGEWOOD
ORANGEWOODS
ORANGUTANS
ORATORIANS
ORATORICAL
ORATORICALLY
ORATRESSES
ORBICULARES
ORBICULARIS
ORBICULARITIES
ORBICULARITY
ORBICULARLY
ORBICULATE
ORBICULATED
ORCHARDING
ORCHARDINGS
ORCHARDIST
ORCHARDISTS

ORCHARDMAN
ORCHARDMEN
ORCHESOGRAPHIES
ORCHESOGRAPHY
ORCHESTICS
ORCHESTRAL
ORCHESTRALIST
ORCHESTRALISTS
ORCHESTRALLY
ORCHESTRAS
ORCHESTRATE
ORCHESTRATED
ORCHESTRATER
ORCHESTRATERS
ORCHESTRATES
ORCHESTRATING
ORCHESTRATION
ORCHESTRATIONAL
ORCHESTRATIONS
ORCHESTRATOR
ORCHESTRATORS
ORCHESTRIC
ORCHESTRINA
ORCHESTRINAS
ORCHESTRION
ORCHESTRIONS
ORCHIDACEOUS
ORCHIDECTOMIES
ORCHIDECTOMY
ORCHIDEOUS
ORCHIDISTS
ORCHIDLIKE
ORCHIDOLOGIES
ORCHIDOLOGIST
ORCHIDOLOGISTS
ORCHIDOLOGY
ORCHIDOMANIA
ORCHIDOMANIAC
ORCHIDOMANIACS
ORCHIDOMANIAS
ORCHIECTOMIES
ORCHIECTOMY
ORCHITISES
ORDAINABLE
ORDAINMENT
ORDAINMENTS
ORDERLINESS
ORDERLINESSES
ORDINAIRES
ORDINANCES
ORDINARIER
ORDINARIES
ORDINARIEST
ORDINARILY
ORDINARINESS
ORDINARINESSES
ORDINATELY
ORDINATING
ORDINATION
ORDINATIONS
ORDONNANCE
ORDONNANCES
ORECCHIETTE
ORECCHIETTES
ORECCHIETTI
OREOGRAPHIC
OREOGRAPHICAL
OREOGRAPHICALLY
OREOGRAPHIES
OREOGRAPHY
OREOLOGICAL
OREOLOGIES
OREOLOGIST
OREOLOGISTS
OREPEARCHED
OREPEARCHES
OREPEARCHING
ORGANELLES
ORGANICALLY
ORGANICISM
ORGANICISMS
ORGANICIST
ORGANICISTIC
ORGANICISTS
ORGANICITIES
ORGANICITY
ORGANISABILITY
ORGANISABLE
ORGANISATION
ORGANISATIONAL
ORGANISATIONS
ORGANISERS
ORGANISING
ORGANISINGS
ORGANISMAL
ORGANISMALLY
ORGANISMIC
ORGANISMICALLY
ORGANISTRUM
ORGANISTRUMS
ORGANITIES
ORGANIZABILITY
ORGANIZABLE
ORGANIZATION
ORGANIZATIONAL
ORGANIZATIONS
ORGANIZERS
ORGANIZING
ORGANIZINGS
ORGANOCHLORINE
ORGANOCHLORINES
ORGANOGENESES
ORGANOGENESIS
ORGANOGENETIC
ORGANOGENIES
ORGANOGENY
ORGANOGRAM
ORGANOGRAMS
ORGANOGRAPHIC
ORGANOGRAPHICAL
ORGANOGRAPHIES
ORGANOGRAPHIST
ORGANOGRAPHISTS
ORGANOGRAPHY
ORGANOLEPTIC
ORGANOLOGICAL
ORGANOLOGIES
ORGANOLOGIST
ORGANOLOGISTS
ORGANOLOGY
ORGANOMERCURIAL
ORGANOMETALLIC
ORGANOMETALLICS
ORGANOPHOSPHATE
ORGANOSOLS
ORGANOTHERAPIES
ORGANOTHERAPY
ORGANZINES
ORGASMICALLY
ORGASTICALLY
ORGIASTICALLY
ORICALCHES
ORICHALCEOUS
ORIENTALISE
ORIENTALISED
ORIENTALISES
ORIENTALISING
ORIENTALISM
ORIENTALISMS
ORIENTALIST
ORIENTALISTS
ORIENTALITIES
ORIENTALITY
ORIENTALIZE
ORIENTALIZED
ORIENTALIZES
ORIENTALIZING
ORIENTALLY
ORIENTATED
ORIENTATES
ORIENTATING
ORIENTATION
ORIENTATIONAL
ORIENTATIONALLY
ORIENTATIONS
ORIENTATOR
ORIENTATORS
ORIENTEERED
ORIENTEERING
ORIENTEERINGS
ORIENTEERS
ORIFLAMMES
ORIGINALITIES
ORIGINALITY
ORIGINALLY
ORIGINATED
ORIGINATES
ORIGINATING
ORIGINATION
ORIGINATIONS
ORIGINATIVE
ORIGINATIVELY
ORIGINATOR
ORIGINATORS
ORINASALLY
ORISMOLOGICAL
ORISMOLOGIES
ORISMOLOGY
ORNAMENTAL
ORNAMENTALLY
ORNAMENTALS
ORNAMENTATION
ORNAMENTATIONS
ORNAMENTED
ORNAMENTER
ORNAMENTERS
ORNAMENTING
ORNAMENTIST
ORNAMENTISTS
ORNATENESS
ORNATENESSES
ORNERINESS
ORNERINESSES
ORNITHICHNITE
ORNITHICHNITES
ORNITHINES
ORNITHISCHIAN
ORNITHISCHIANS
ORNITHODELPHIAN
ORNITHODELPHIC
ORNITHODELPHOUS
ORNITHOGALUM
ORNITHOGALUMS
ORNITHOLOGIC
ORNITHOLOGICAL
ORNITHOLOGIES
ORNITHOLOGIST
ORNITHOLOGISTS
ORNITHOLOGY
ORNITHOMANCIES
ORNITHOMANCY
ORNITHOMANTIC
ORNITHOMORPH
ORNITHOMORPHIC
ORNITHOMORPHS
ORNITHOPHILIES
ORNITHOPHILOUS
ORNITHOPHILY
ORNITHOPHOBIA
ORNITHOPHOBIAS
ORNITHOPOD
ORNITHOPODS
ORNITHOPTER
ORNITHOPTERS
ORNITHORHYNCHUS
ORNITHOSAUR
ORNITHOSAURS
ORNITHOSCOPIES
ORNITHOSCOPY
ORNITHOSES

ORNITHOSIS
OROBANCHACEOUS
OROGENESES
OROGENESIS
OROGENETIC
OROGENETICALLY
OROGENICALLY
OROGRAPHER
OROGRAPHERS
OROGRAPHIC
OROGRAPHICAL
OROGRAPHICALLY
OROGRAPHIES
OROLOGICAL
OROLOGICALLY
OROLOGISTS
OROMAXILLARY
OROPHARYNGEAL
OROPHARYNGES
OROPHARYNX
OROPHARYNXES
OROROTUNDITIES
OROROTUNDITY
OROTUNDITIES
OROTUNDITY
ORPHANAGES
ORPHANHOOD
ORPHANHOODS
ORPHANISMS
ORPHARIONS
ORPHEOREON
ORPHEOREONS
ORPHICALLY
ORRISROOTS
ORTANIQUES
ORTHOBORATE
ORTHOBORATES
ORTHOBORIC
ORTHOCAINE
ORTHOCAINES
ORTHOCENTER
ORTHOCENTERS
ORTHOCENTRE
ORTHOCENTRES
ORTHOCEPHALIC
ORTHOCEPHALIES
ORTHOCEPHALOUS
ORTHOCEPHALY
ORTHOCHROMATIC
ORTHOCHROMATISM
ORTHOCLASE
ORTHOCLASES
ORTHOCLASTIC
ORTHOCOUSINS
ORTHODIAGONAL
ORTHODIAGONALS
ORTHODONTIA
ORTHODONTIAS
ORTHODONTIC
ORTHODONTICALLY
ORTHODONTICS
ORTHODONTIST
ORTHODONTISTS
ORTHODOXES
ORTHODOXIES
ORTHODOXLY
ORTHODROMIC
ORTHODROMICS
ORTHODROMIES
ORTHODROMY
ORTHOEPICAL
ORTHOEPICALLY
ORTHOEPIES
ORTHOEPIST
ORTHOEPISTS
ORTHOGENESES
ORTHOGENESIS
ORTHOGENETIC
ORTHOGENIC
ORTHOGENICALLY
ORTHOGENICS
ORTHOGNATHIC
ORTHOGNATHIES
ORTHOGNATHISM
ORTHOGNATHISMS
ORTHOGNATHOUS
ORTHOGNATHY
ORTHOGONAL
ORTHOGONALISE
ORTHOGONALISED
ORTHOGONALISES
ORTHOGONALISING
ORTHOGONALITIES
ORTHOGONALITY
ORTHOGONALIZE
ORTHOGONALIZED
ORTHOGONALIZES
ORTHOGONALIZING
ORTHOGONALLY
ORTHOGRADE
ORTHOGRAPH
ORTHOGRAPHER
ORTHOGRAPHERS
ORTHOGRAPHIC
ORTHOGRAPHICAL
ORTHOGRAPHIES
ORTHOGRAPHIST
ORTHOGRAPHISTS
ORTHOGRAPHS
ORTHOGRAPHY
ORTHOHYDROGEN
ORTHOHYDROGENS
ORTHOMOLECULAR
ORTHOMORPHIC
ORTHONORMAL
ORTHOPAEDIC
ORTHOPAEDICAL
ORTHOPAEDICALLY
ORTHOPAEDICS
ORTHOPAEDIES
ORTHOPAEDIST
ORTHOPAEDISTS
ORTHOPAEDY
ORTHOPEDIA
ORTHOPEDIAS
ORTHOPEDIC
ORTHOPEDICAL
ORTHOPEDICALLY
ORTHOPEDICS
ORTHOPEDIES
ORTHOPEDIST
ORTHOPEDISTS
ORTHOPHOSPHATE
ORTHOPHOSPHATES
ORTHOPHOSPHORIC
ORTHOPHYRE
ORTHOPHYRES
ORTHOPHYRIC
ORTHOPINAKOID
ORTHOPINAKOIDS
ORTHOPNOEA
ORTHOPNOEAS
ORTHOPRAXES
ORTHOPRAXIES
ORTHOPRAXIS
ORTHOPRAXY
ORTHOPRISM
ORTHOPRISMS
ORTHOPSYCHIATRY
ORTHOPTERA
ORTHOPTERAN
ORTHOPTERANS
ORTHOPTERIST
ORTHOPTERISTS
ORTHOPTEROID
ORTHOPTEROIDS
ORTHOPTEROLOGY
ORTHOPTERON
ORTHOPTEROUS
ORTHOPTERS
ORTHOPTICS
ORTHOPTIST
ORTHOPTISTS
ORTHOPYROXENE
ORTHOPYROXENES
ORTHOREXIA
ORTHOREXIAS
ORTHORHOMBIC
ORTHOSCOPE
ORTHOSCOPES
ORTHOSCOPIC
ORTHOSILICATE
ORTHOSILICATES
ORTHOSILICIC
ORTHOSTATIC
ORTHOSTICHIES
ORTHOSTICHOUS
ORTHOSTICHY
ORTHOTISTS
ORTHOTONES
ORTHOTONESES
ORTHOTONESIS
ORTHOTONIC
ORTHOTOPIC
ORTHOTROPIC
ORTHOTROPIES
ORTHOTROPISM
ORTHOTROPISMS
ORTHOTROPOUS
ORTHOTROPY
ORTHOTUNGSTIC
ORTHOVANADIC
ORYCTOLOGIES
ORYCTOLOGY
OSCILLATED
OSCILLATES
OSCILLATING
OSCILLATION
OSCILLATIONAL
OSCILLATIONS
OSCILLATIVE
OSCILLATOR
OSCILLATORS
OSCILLATORY
OSCILLOGRAM
OSCILLOGRAMS
OSCILLOGRAPH
OSCILLOGRAPHIC
OSCILLOGRAPHIES
OSCILLOGRAPHS
OSCILLOGRAPHY
OSCILLOSCOPE
OSCILLOSCOPES
OSCILLOSCOPIC
OSCITANCES
OSCITANCIES
OSCITANTLY
OSCITATING
OSCITATION
OSCITATIONS
OSCULATING
OSCULATION
OSCULATIONS
OSCULATORIES
OSCULATORY
OSMETERIUM
OSMIDROSES
OSMIDROSIS
OSMIRIDIUM
OSMIRIDIUMS
OSMOLALITIES
OSMOLALITY
OSMOLARITIES
OSMOLARITY
OSMOMETERS
OSMOMETRIC
OSMOMETRICALLY
OSMOMETRIES
OSMOREGULATION
OSMOREGULATIONS

O

OSMOREGULATORY
OSMOTICALLY
OSMUNDINES
OSSIFEROUS
OSSIFICATION
OSSIFICATIONS
OSSIFRAGAS
OSSIFRAGES
OSSIVOROUS
OSTEICHTHYAN
OSTEICHTHYANS
OSTEITIDES
OSTEITISES
OSTENSIBILITIES
OSTENSIBILITY
OSTENSIBLE
OSTENSIBLY
OSTENSIVELY
OSTENSORIA
OSTENSORIES
OSTENSORIUM
OSTENTATION
OSTENTATIONS
OSTENTATIOUS
OSTENTATIOUSLY
OSTEOARTHRITIC
OSTEOARTHRITICS
OSTEOARTHRITIS
OSTEOARTHROSES
OSTEOARTHROSIS
OSTEOBLAST
OSTEOBLASTIC
OSTEOBLASTS
OSTEOCLASES
OSTEOCLASIS
OSTEOCLAST
OSTEOCLASTIC
OSTEOCLASTS
OSTEOCOLLA
OSTEOCOLLAS
OSTEOCYTES
OSTEODERMAL
OSTEODERMATOUS
OSTEODERMIC
OSTEODERMOUS
OSTEODERMS
OSTEOFIBROSES
OSTEOFIBROSIS
OSTEOGENESES
OSTEOGENESIS
OSTEOGENETIC
OSTEOGENIC
OSTEOGENIES
OSTEOGENOUS
OSTEOGRAPHIES
OSTEOGRAPHY
OSTEOLOGICAL
OSTEOLOGICALLY
OSTEOLOGIES
OSTEOLOGIST
OSTEOLOGISTS
OSTEOMALACIA
OSTEOMALACIAL
OSTEOMALACIAS
OSTEOMALACIC
OSTEOMYELITIS
OSTEOMYELITISES
OSTEOPATHIC
OSTEOPATHICALLY
OSTEOPATHIES
OSTEOPATHIST
OSTEOPATHISTS
OSTEOPATHS
OSTEOPATHY
OSTEOPETROSES
OSTEOPETROSIS
OSTEOPHYTE
OSTEOPHYTES
OSTEOPHYTIC
OSTEOPLASTIC
OSTEOPLASTIES
OSTEOPLASTY
OSTEOPOROSES
OSTEOPOROSIS
OSTEOPOROTIC
OSTEOSARCOMA
OSTEOSARCOMAS
OSTEOSARCOMATA
OSTEOSISES
OSTEOTOMES
OSTEOTOMIES
OSTLERESSES
OSTRACEANS
OSTRACEOUS
OSTRACISABLE
OSTRACISED
OSTRACISER
OSTRACISERS
OSTRACISES
OSTRACISING
OSTRACISMS
OSTRACIZABLE
OSTRACIZED
OSTRACIZER
OSTRACIZERS
OSTRACIZES
OSTRACIZING
OSTRACODAN
OSTRACODERM
OSTRACODERMS
OSTRACODES
OSTRACODOUS
OSTREACEOUS
OSTREICULTURE
OSTREICULTURES
OSTREICULTURIST
OSTREOPHAGE
OSTREOPHAGES
OSTREOPHAGIES
OSTREOPHAGOUS
OSTREOPHAGY
OSTRICHISM
OSTRICHISMS
OSTRICHLIKE
OTHERGATES
OTHERGUESS
OTHERNESSES
OTHERWHERE
OTHERWHILE
OTHERWHILES
OTHERWORLD
OTHERWORLDISH
OTHERWORLDLIER
OTHERWORLDLIEST
OTHERWORLDLY
OTHERWORLDS
OTIOSENESS
OTIOSENESSES
OTIOSITIES
OTOLARYNGOLOGY
OTOLOGICAL
OTOLOGISTS
OTOPLASTIES
OTORRHOEAS
OTOSCLEROSES
OTOSCLEROSIS
OTOSCOPIES
OTOTOXICITIES
OTOTOXICITY
OTTERHOUND
OTTERHOUNDS
OTTRELITES
OUANANICHE
OUANANICHES
OUBLIETTES
OUGHTLINGS
OUGHTNESSES
OUROBOROSES
OUROLOGIES
OUROSCOPIES
OUTACHIEVE
OUTACHIEVED
OUTACHIEVES
OUTACHIEVING
OUTARGUING
OUTBACKERS
OUTBALANCE
OUTBALANCED
OUTBALANCES
OUTBALANCING
OUTBARGAIN
OUTBARGAINED
OUTBARGAINING
OUTBARGAINS
OUTBARKING
OUTBARRING
OUTBAWLING
OUTBEAMING
OUTBEGGING
OUTBIDDERS
OUTBIDDING
OUTBITCHED
OUTBITCHES
OUTBITCHING
OUTBLAZING
OUTBLEATED
OUTBLEATING
OUTBLESSED
OUTBLESSES
OUTBLESSING
OUTBLOOMED
OUTBLOOMING
OUTBLUFFED
OUTBLUFFING
OUTBLUSHED
OUTBLUSHES
OUTBLUSHING
OUTBLUSTER
OUTBLUSTERED
OUTBLUSTERING
OUTBLUSTERS
OUTBOASTED
OUTBOASTING
OUTBRAGGED
OUTBRAGGING
OUTBRAVING
OUTBRAWLED
OUTBRAWLING
OUTBRAZENED
OUTBRAZENING
OUTBRAZENS
OUTBREAKING
OUTBREATHE
OUTBREATHED
OUTBREATHES
OUTBREATHING
OUTBREEDING
OUTBREEDINGS
OUTBRIBING
OUTBUILDING
OUTBUILDINGS
OUTBULGING
OUTBULKING
OUTBULLIED
OUTBULLIES
OUTBULLYING
OUTBURNING
OUTBURSTING
OUTCALLING
OUTCAPERED
OUTCAPERING
OUTCASTEING
OUTCASTING
OUTCATCHES
OUTCATCHING
OUTCAVILED
OUTCAVILING
OUTCAVILLED
OUTCAVILLING
OUTCHARGED

OUTCHARGES
OUTCHARGING
OUTCHARMED
OUTCHARMING
OUTCHEATED
OUTCHEATING
OUTCHIDDEN
OUTCHIDING
OUTCLASSED
OUTCLASSES
OUTCLASSING
OUTCLIMBED
OUTCLIMBING
OUTCOACHED
OUTCOACHES
OUTCOACHING
OUTCOMPETE
OUTCOMPETED
OUTCOMPETES
OUTCOMPETING
OUTCOOKING
OUTCOUNTED
OUTCOUNTING
OUTCRAFTIED
OUTCRAFTIES
OUTCRAFTYING
OUTCRAWLED
OUTCRAWLING
OUTCROPPED
OUTCROPPING
OUTCROPPINGS
OUTCROSSED
OUTCROSSES
OUTCROSSING
OUTCROSSINGS
OUTCROWDED
OUTCROWDING
OUTCROWING
OUTCURSING
OUTDACIOUS
OUTDANCING
OUTDATEDLY
OUTDATEDNESS
OUTDATEDNESSES
OUTDAZZLED
OUTDAZZLES
OUTDAZZLING
OUTDEBATED
OUTDEBATES
OUTDEBATING
OUTDELIVER
OUTDELIVERED
OUTDELIVERING
OUTDELIVERS
OUTDESIGNED
OUTDESIGNING
OUTDESIGNS
OUTDISTANCE
OUTDISTANCED
OUTDISTANCES
OUTDISTANCING
OUTDODGING
OUTDOORSIER
OUTDOORSIEST
OUTDOORSMAN
OUTDOORSMANSHIP
OUTDOORSMEN
OUTDRAGGED
OUTDRAGGING
OUTDRAWING
OUTDREAMED
OUTDREAMING
OUTDRESSED
OUTDRESSES
OUTDRESSING
OUTDRINKING
OUTDRIVING
OUTDROPPED
OUTDROPPING
OUTDUELING
OUTDUELLED
OUTDUELLING
OUTDWELLED
OUTDWELLING
OUTEARNING
OUTECHOING
OUTERCOATS
OUTERCOURSE
OUTERCOURSES
OUTERWEARS
OUTFABLING
OUTFANGTHIEF
OUTFANGTHIEVES
OUTFASTING
OUTFAWNING
OUTFEASTED
OUTFEASTING
OUTFEELING
OUTFENCING
OUTFIELDER
OUTFIELDERS
OUTFIGHTING
OUTFIGHTINGS
OUTFIGURED
OUTFIGURES
OUTFIGURING
OUTFINDING
OUTFISHING
OUTFITTERS
OUTFITTING
OUTFITTINGS
OUTFLANKED
OUTFLANKING
OUTFLASHED
OUTFLASHES
OUTFLASHING
OUTFLINGING
OUTFLOATED
OUTFLOATING
OUTFLOWING
OUTFLOWINGS
OUTFLUSHED
OUTFLUSHES
OUTFLUSHING
OUTFOOLING
OUTFOOTING
OUTFROWNED
OUTFROWNING
OUTFUMBLED
OUTFUMBLES
OUTFUMBLING
OUTGAINING
OUTGALLOPED
OUTGALLOPING
OUTGALLOPS
OUTGAMBLED
OUTGAMBLES
OUTGAMBLING
OUTGASSING
OUTGASSINGS
OUTGENERAL
OUTGENERALED
OUTGENERALING
OUTGENERALLED
OUTGENERALLING
OUTGENERALS
OUTGIVINGS
OUTGLARING
OUTGLEAMED
OUTGLEAMING
OUTGLITTER
OUTGLITTERED
OUTGLITTERING
OUTGLITTERS
OUTGLOWING
OUTGNAWING
OUTGOINGNESS
OUTGOINGNESSES
OUTGRINNED
OUTGRINNING
OUTGROSSED
OUTGROSSES
OUTGROSSING
OUTGROWING
OUTGROWTHS
OUTGUESSED
OUTGUESSES
OUTGUESSING
OUTGUIDING
OUTGUNNING
OUTGUSHING
OUTHANDLED
OUTHANDLES
OUTHANDLING
OUTHARBORS
OUTHAULERS
OUTHEARING
OUTHITTING
OUTHOMERED
OUTHOMERING
OUTHOWLING
OUTHUMORED
OUTHUMORING
OUTHUMOURED
OUTHUMOURING
OUTHUMOURS
OUTHUNTING
OUTHUSTLED
OUTHUSTLES
OUTHUSTLING
OUTINTRIGUE
OUTINTRIGUED
OUTINTRIGUES
OUTINTRIGUING
OUTJESTING
OUTJETTING
OUTJETTINGS
OUTJINXING
OUTJOCKEYED
OUTJOCKEYING
OUTJOCKEYS
OUTJUGGLED
OUTJUGGLES
OUTJUGGLING
OUTJUMPING
OUTJUTTING
OUTJUTTINGS
OUTKEEPING
OUTKICKING
OUTKILLING
OUTKISSING
OUTLANDERS
OUTLANDISH
OUTLANDISHLY
OUTLANDISHNESS
OUTLASHING
OUTLASTING
OUTLAUGHED
OUTLAUGHING
OUTLAUNCED
OUTLAUNCES
OUTLAUNCHED
OUTLAUNCHES
OUTLAUNCHING
OUTLAUNCING
OUTLAWRIES
OUTLEADING
OUTLEAPING
OUTLEARNED
OUTLEARNING
OUTLODGING
OUTLODGINGS
OUTLOOKING
OUTLUSTERED
OUTLUSTERING
OUTLUSTERS
OUTLUSTRED
OUTLUSTRES
OUTLUSTRING
OUTMANEUVER

O

OUTMANEUVERED
OUTMANEUVERING
OUTMANEUVERS
OUTMANIPULATE
OUTMANIPULATED
OUTMANIPULATES
OUTMANIPULATING
OUTMANNING
OUTMANOEUVRE
OUTMANOEUVRED
OUTMANOEUVRES
OUTMANOEUVRING
OUTMANTLED
OUTMANTLES
OUTMANTLING
OUTMARCHED
OUTMARCHES
OUTMARCHING
OUTMARRIAGE
OUTMARRIAGES
OUTMASTERED
OUTMASTERING
OUTMASTERS
OUTMATCHED
OUTMATCHES
OUTMATCHING
OUTMEASURE
OUTMEASURED
OUTMEASURES
OUTMEASURING
OUTMODEDLY
OUTMODEDNESS
OUTMODEDNESSES
OUTMUSCLED
OUTMUSCLES
OUTMUSCLING
OUTNIGHTED
OUTNIGHTING
OUTNUMBERED
OUTNUMBERING
OUTNUMBERS
OUTOFFICES
OUTORGANISE
OUTORGANISED
OUTORGANISES
OUTORGANISING
OUTORGANIZE
OUTORGANIZED
OUTORGANIZES
OUTORGANIZING
OUTPAINTED
OUTPAINTING
OUTPASSING
OUTPASSION
OUTPASSIONED
OUTPASSIONING
OUTPASSIONS
OUTPATIENT
OUTPATIENTS
OUTPEEPING
OUTPEERING
OUTPEOPLED
OUTPEOPLES
OUTPEOPLING
OUTPERFORM
OUTPERFORMED
OUTPERFORMING
OUTPERFORMS
OUTPITCHED
OUTPITCHES
OUTPITCHING
OUTPITYING
OUTPLACEMENT
OUTPLACEMENTS
OUTPLACERS
OUTPLACING
OUTPLANNED
OUTPLANNING
OUTPLAYING
OUTPLODDED
OUTPLODDING
OUTPLOTTED
OUTPLOTTING
OUTPOINTED
OUTPOINTING
OUTPOLITICK
OUTPOLITICKED
OUTPOLITICKING
OUTPOLITICKS
OUTPOLLING
OUTPOPULATE
OUTPOPULATED
OUTPOPULATES
OUTPOPULATING
OUTPORTERS
OUTPOURERS
OUTPOURING
OUTPOURINGS
OUTPOWERED
OUTPOWERING
OUTPRAYING
OUTPREACHED
OUTPREACHES
OUTPREACHING
OUTPREENED
OUTPREENING
OUTPRESSED
OUTPRESSES
OUTPRESSING
OUTPRICING
OUTPRIZING
OUTPRODUCE
OUTPRODUCED
OUTPRODUCES
OUTPRODUCING
OUTPROMISE
OUTPROMISED
OUTPROMISES
OUTPROMISING
OUTPSYCHED
OUTPSYCHING
OUTPULLING
OUTPUNCHED
OUTPUNCHES
OUTPUNCHING
OUTPURSUED
OUTPURSUES
OUTPURSUING
OUTPUSHING
OUTPUTTING
OUTQUARTERS
OUTQUOTING
OUTRAGEOUS
OUTRAGEOUSLY
OUTRAGEOUSNESS
OUTRAISING
OUTRANGING
OUTRANKING
OUTREACHED
OUTREACHES
OUTREACHING
OUTREADING
OUTREASONED
OUTREASONING
OUTREASONS
OUTREBOUND
OUTREBOUNDED
OUTREBOUNDING
OUTREBOUNDS
OUTRECKONED
OUTRECKONING
OUTRECKONS
OUTRECUIDANCE
OUTRECUIDANCES
OUTREDDENED
OUTREDDENING
OUTREDDENS
OUTREDDING
OUTREDDINGS
OUTREIGNED
OUTREIGNING
OUTRELIEFS
OUTREPRODUCE
OUTREPRODUCED
OUTREPRODUCES
OUTREPRODUCING
OUTRIDINGS
OUTRIGGERS
OUTRIGGING
OUTRIGGINGS
OUTRIGHTLY
OUTRINGING
OUTRIVALED
OUTRIVALING
OUTRIVALLED
OUTRIVALLING
OUTROARING
OUTROCKING
OUTROLLING
OUTROOPERS
OUTROOTING
OUTRUNNERS
OUTRUNNING
OUTRUSHING
OUTSAILING
OUTSAVORED
OUTSAVORING
OUTSAVOURED
OUTSAVOURING
OUTSAVOURS
OUTSCHEMED
OUTSCHEMES
OUTSCHEMING
OUTSCOLDED
OUTSCOLDING
OUTSCOOPED
OUTSCOOPING
OUTSCORING
OUTSCORNED
OUTSCORNING
OUTSCREAMED
OUTSCREAMING
OUTSCREAMS
OUTSELLING
OUTSERVING
OUTSETTING
OUTSETTINGS
OUTSETTLEMENT
OUTSETTLEMENTS
OUTSHAMING
OUTSHINING
OUTSHOOTING
OUTSHOUTED
OUTSHOUTING
OUTSIDERNESS
OUTSIDERNESSES
OUTSINGING
OUTSINNING
OUTSITTING
OUTSKATING
OUTSLEEPING
OUTSLICKED
OUTSLICKING
OUTSMARTED
OUTSMARTING
OUTSMELLED
OUTSMELLING
OUTSMILING
OUTSMOKING
OUTSNORING
OUTSOARING
OUTSOURCED
OUTSOURCES
OUTSOURCING
OUTSOURCINGS
OUTSPANNED
OUTSPANNING
OUTSPARKLE
OUTSPARKLED
OUTSPARKLES

OUTSPARKLING
OUTSPEAKING
OUTSPECKLE
OUTSPECKLES
OUTSPEEDED
OUTSPEEDING
OUTSPELLED
OUTSPELLING
OUTSPENDING
OUTSPOKENLY
OUTSPOKENNESS
OUTSPOKENNESSES
OUTSPORTED
OUTSPORTING
OUTSPREADING
OUTSPREADS
OUTSPRINGING
OUTSPRINGS
OUTSPRINTED
OUTSPRINTING
OUTSPRINTS
OUTSTANDING
OUTSTANDINGLY
OUTSTARING
OUTSTARTED
OUTSTARTING
OUTSTATING
OUTSTATION
OUTSTATIONS
OUTSTAYING
OUTSTEERED
OUTSTEERING
OUTSTEPPED
OUTSTEPPING
OUTSTRAINED
OUTSTRAINING
OUTSTRAINS
OUTSTRETCH
OUTSTRETCHED
OUTSTRETCHES
OUTSTRETCHING
OUTSTRIDDEN
OUTSTRIDED
OUTSTRIDES
OUTSTRIDING
OUTSTRIKES
OUTSTRIKING
OUTSTRIPPED
OUTSTRIPPING
OUTSTRIVEN
OUTSTRIVES
OUTSTRIVING
OUTSTROKES
OUTSTUDIED
OUTSTUDIES
OUTSTUDYING
OUTSTUNTED
OUTSTUNTING
OUTSULKING
OUTSUMMING
OUTSWEARING
OUTSWEEPING
OUTSWEETEN
OUTSWEETENED
OUTSWEETENING
OUTSWEETENS
OUTSWELLED
OUTSWELLING
OUTSWIMMING
OUTSWINGER
OUTSWINGERS
OUTSWINGING
OUTSWOLLEN
OUTTALKING
OUTTASKING
OUTTELLING
OUTTHANKED
OUTTHANKING
OUTTHIEVED
OUTTHIEVES
OUTTHIEVING
OUTTHINKING
OUTTHOUGHT
OUTTHROBBED
OUTTHROBBING
OUTTHROWING
OUTTHRUSTED
OUTTHRUSTING
OUTTHRUSTS
OUTTONGUED
OUTTONGUES
OUTTONGUING
OUTTOPPING
OUTTOWERED
OUTTOWERING
OUTTRADING
OUTTRAVELED
OUTTRAVELING
OUTTRAVELLED
OUTTRAVELLING
OUTTRAVELS
OUTTRICKED
OUTTRICKING
OUTTROTTED
OUTTROTTING
OUTTRUMPED
OUTTRUMPING
OUTVALUING
OUTVAUNTED
OUTVAUNTING
OUTVENOMED
OUTVENOMING
OUTVILLAIN
OUTVILLAINED
OUTVILLAINING
OUTVILLAINS
OUTVOICING
OUTWAITING
OUTWALKING
OUTWARDNESS
OUTWARDNESSES
OUTWARRING
OUTWASTING
OUTWATCHED
OUTWATCHES
OUTWATCHING
OUTWEARIED
OUTWEARIES
OUTWEARING
OUTWEARYING
OUTWEEDING
OUTWEEPING
OUTWEIGHED
OUTWEIGHING
OUTWELLING
OUTWHIRLED
OUTWHIRLING
OUTWICKING
OUTWILLING
OUTWINDING
OUTWINGING
OUTWINNING
OUTWISHING
OUTWITTING
OUTWORKERS
OUTWORKING
OUTWORTHED
OUTWORTHING
OUTWRESTED
OUTWRESTING
OUTWRESTLE
OUTWRESTLED
OUTWRESTLES
OUTWRESTLING
OUTWRITING
OUTWRITTEN
OUTWROUGHT
OUTYELLING
OUTYELPING
OUTYIELDED
OUTYIELDING
OUVIRANDRA
OUVIRANDRAS
OVALBUMINS
OVALNESSES
OVARIECTOMIES
OVARIECTOMISED
OVARIECTOMIZED
OVARIECTOMY
OVARIOTOMIES
OVARIOTOMIST
OVARIOTOMISTS
OVARIOTOMY
OVARITIDES
OVARITISES
OVERABOUND
OVERABOUNDED
OVERABOUNDING
OVERABOUNDS
OVERABSTRACT
OVERABUNDANCE
OVERABUNDANCES
OVERABUNDANT
OVERACCENTUATE
OVERACCENTUATED
OVERACCENTUATES
OVERACHIEVE
OVERACHIEVED
OVERACHIEVEMENT
OVERACHIEVER
OVERACHIEVERS
OVERACHIEVES
OVERACHIEVING
OVERACTING
OVERACTION
OVERACTIONS
OVERACTIVE
OVERACTIVITIES
OVERACTIVITY
OVERADJUSTMENT
OVERADJUSTMENTS
OVERADVERTISE
OVERADVERTISED
OVERADVERTISES
OVERADVERTISING
OVERADVERTIZE
OVERADVERTIZED
OVERADVERTIZES
OVERADVERTIZING
OVERAGGRESSIVE
OVERAMBITIOUS
OVERAMPLIFIED
OVERANALYSE
OVERANALYSED
OVERANALYSES
OVERANALYSING
OVERANALYSIS
OVERANALYTICAL
OVERANALYZE
OVERANALYZED
OVERANALYZES
OVERANALYZING
OVERANXIETIES
OVERANXIETY
OVERANXIOUS
OVERAPPLICATION
OVERARCHED
OVERARCHES
OVERARCHING
OVERARMING
OVERAROUSAL
OVERAROUSALS
OVERARRANGE
OVERARRANGED
OVERARRANGES
OVERARRANGING
OVERARTICULATE
OVERARTICULATED
OVERARTICULATES
OVERASSERT

O

OVERASSERTED
OVERASSERTING
OVERASSERTION
OVERASSERTIONS
OVERASSERTIVE
OVERASSERTS
OVERASSESSMENT
OVERASSESSMENTS
OVERATTENTION
OVERATTENTIONS
OVERATTENTIVE
OVERBAKING
OVERBALANCE
OVERBALANCED
OVERBALANCES
OVERBALANCING
OVERBEARING
OVERBEARINGLY
OVERBEARINGNESS
OVERBEATEN
OVERBEATING
OVERBEJEWELED
OVERBEJEWELLED
OVERBETTED
OVERBETTING
OVERBETTINGS
OVERBIDDEN
OVERBIDDER
OVERBIDDERS
OVERBIDDING
OVERBIDDINGS
OVERBILLED
OVERBILLING
OVERBLANKET
OVERBLANKETS
OVERBLEACH
OVERBLEACHED
OVERBLEACHES
OVERBLEACHING
OVERBLOUSE
OVERBLOUSES
OVERBLOWING
OVERBOILED
OVERBOILING
OVERBOLDLY
OVERBOOKED
OVERBOOKING
OVERBOOKINGS
OVERBORROW
OVERBORROWED
OVERBORROWING
OVERBORROWS
OVERBOUGHT
OVERBOUNDED
OVERBOUNDING
OVERBOUNDS
OVERBRAKED
OVERBRAKES
OVERBRAKING
OVERBREATHING
OVERBREATHINGS
OVERBREEDING
OVERBREEDS
OVERBRIDGE
OVERBRIDGED
OVERBRIDGES
OVERBRIDGING
OVERBRIEFED
OVERBRIEFING
OVERBRIEFS
OVERBRIGHT
OVERBRIMMED
OVERBRIMMING
OVERBROWED
OVERBROWING
OVERBROWSE
OVERBROWSED
OVERBROWSES
OVERBROWSING
OVERBRUTAL
OVERBUILDING
OVERBUILDS
OVERBULKED
OVERBULKING
OVERBURDEN
OVERBURDENED
OVERBURDENING
OVERBURDENS
OVERBURDENSOME
OVERBURNED
OVERBURNING
OVERBURTHEN
OVERBURTHENED
OVERBURTHENING
OVERBURTHENS
OVERBUSIED
OVERBUSIES
OVERBUSYING
OVERBUYING
OVERCALLED
OVERCALLING
OVERCANOPIED
OVERCANOPIES
OVERCANOPY
OVERCANOPYING
OVERCAPACITIES
OVERCAPACITY
OVERCAPITALISE
OVERCAPITALISED
OVERCAPITALISES
OVERCAPITALIZE
OVERCAPITALIZED
OVERCAPITALIZES
OVERCAREFUL
OVERCARRIED
OVERCARRIES
OVERCARRYING
OVERCASTED
OVERCASTING
OVERCASTINGS
OVERCATCHES
OVERCATCHING
OVERCAUGHT
OVERCAUTION
OVERCAUTIONS
OVERCAUTIOUS
OVERCAUTIOUSLY
OVERCENTRALISE
OVERCENTRALISED
OVERCENTRALISES
OVERCENTRALIZE
OVERCENTRALIZED
OVERCENTRALIZES
OVERCHARGE
OVERCHARGED
OVERCHARGES
OVERCHARGING
OVERCHARGINGS
OVERCHECKS
OVERCHILLED
OVERCHILLING
OVERCHILLS
OVERCIVILISED
OVERCIVILIZED
OVERCLAIMED
OVERCLAIMING
OVERCLAIMS
OVERCLASSES
OVERCLASSIFIED
OVERCLASSIFIES
OVERCLASSIFY
OVERCLASSIFYING
OVERCLEANED
OVERCLEANING
OVERCLEANS
OVERCLEARED
OVERCLEARING
OVERCLEARS
OVERCLEVER
OVERCLOCKED
OVERCLOCKER
OVERCLOCKERS
OVERCLOCKING
OVERCLOCKINGS
OVERCLOCKS
OVERCLOUDED
OVERCLOUDING
OVERCLOUDS
OVERCLOYED
OVERCLOYING
OVERCLUBBED
OVERCLUBBING
OVERCOACHED
OVERCOACHES
OVERCOACHING
OVERCOATING
OVERCOATINGS
OVERCOLORED
OVERCOLORING
OVERCOLORS
OVERCOLOUR
OVERCOLOURED
OVERCOLOURING
OVERCOLOURS
OVERCOMERS
OVERCOMING
OVERCOMMIT
OVERCOMMITMENT
OVERCOMMITMENTS
OVERCOMMITS
OVERCOMMITTED
OVERCOMMITTING
OVERCOMMUNICATE
OVERCOMPENSATE
OVERCOMPENSATED
OVERCOMPENSATES
OVERCOMPLEX
OVERCOMPLIANCE
OVERCOMPLIANCES
OVERCOMPLICATE
OVERCOMPLICATED
OVERCOMPLICATES
OVERCOMPRESS
OVERCOMPRESSED
OVERCOMPRESSES
OVERCOMPRESSING
OVERCONCERN
OVERCONCERNED
OVERCONCERNING
OVERCONCERNS
OVERCONFIDENCE
OVERCONFIDENCES
OVERCONFIDENT
OVERCONFIDENTLY
OVERCONSCIOUS
OVERCONSTRUCT
OVERCONSTRUCTED
OVERCONSTRUCTS
OVERCONSUME
OVERCONSUMED
OVERCONSUMES
OVERCONSUMING
OVERCONSUMPTION
OVERCONTROL
OVERCONTROLLED
OVERCONTROLLING
OVERCONTROLS
OVERCOOKED
OVERCOOKING
OVERCOOLED
OVERCOOLING
OVERCORRECT
OVERCORRECTED
OVERCORRECTING
OVERCORRECTION
OVERCORRECTIONS
OVERCORRECTS
OVERCOUNTED
OVERCOUNTING
OVERCOUNTS

OVERCOVERED
OVERCOVERING
OVERCOVERS
OVERCRAMMED
OVERCRAMMING
OVERCRAMMINGS
OVERCRAWED
OVERCRAWING
OVERCREDULITIES
OVERCREDULITY
OVERCREDULOUS
OVERCRITICAL
OVERCROPPED
OVERCROPPING
OVERCROWDED
OVERCROWDING
OVERCROWDINGS
OVERCROWDS
OVERCROWED
OVERCROWING
OVERCULTIVATION
OVERCURING
OVERCUTTING
OVERCUTTINGS
OVERDARING
OVERDECKED
OVERDECKING
OVERDECORATE
OVERDECORATED
OVERDECORATES
OVERDECORATING
OVERDECORATION
OVERDECORATIONS
OVERDEEPENING
OVERDELICATE
OVERDEMANDING
OVERDEPENDENCE
OVERDEPENDENCES
OVERDEPENDENT
OVERDESIGN
OVERDESIGNED
OVERDESIGNING
OVERDESIGNS
OVERDETERMINED
OVERDEVELOP
OVERDEVELOPED
OVERDEVELOPING
OVERDEVELOPMENT
OVERDEVELOPS
OVERDEVIATE
OVERDEVIATED
OVERDEVIATES
OVERDEVIATING
OVERDIAGNOSES
OVERDIAGNOSIS
OVERDILUTED
OVERDIRECT
OVERDIRECTED
OVERDIRECTING
OVERDIRECTS
OVERDISCOUNT
OVERDISCOUNTED
OVERDISCOUNTING
OVERDISCOUNTS
OVERDIVERSITIES
OVERDIVERSITY
OVERDOCUMENT
OVERDOCUMENTED
OVERDOCUMENTING
OVERDOCUMENTS
OVERDOMINANCE
OVERDOMINANCES
OVERDOMINANT
OVERDOSAGE
OVERDOSAGES
OVERDOSING
OVERDRAFTS
OVERDRAMATIC
OVERDRAMATISE
OVERDRAMATISED
OVERDRAMATISES
OVERDRAMATISING
OVERDRAMATIZE
OVERDRAMATIZED
OVERDRAMATIZES
OVERDRAMATIZING
OVERDRAUGHT
OVERDRAUGHTS
OVERDRAWING
OVERDRESSED
OVERDRESSES
OVERDRESSING
OVERDRINKING
OVERDRINKS
OVERDRIVEN
OVERDRIVES
OVERDRIVING
OVERDRYING
OVERDUBBED
OVERDUBBING
OVERDUSTED
OVERDUSTING
OVERDYEING
OVEREAGERNESS
OVEREAGERNESSES
OVEREARNEST
OVEREASIER
OVEREASIEST
OVEREATERS
OVEREATING
OVEREATINGS
OVEREDITED
OVEREDITING
OVEREDUCATE
OVEREDUCATED
OVEREDUCATES
OVEREDUCATING
OVEREDUCATION
OVEREDUCATIONS
OVEREFFUSIVE
OVEREGGING
OVERELABORATE
OVERELABORATED
OVERELABORATES
OVERELABORATING
OVERELABORATION
OVEREMBELLISH
OVEREMBELLISHED
OVEREMBELLISHES
OVEREMOTED
OVEREMOTES
OVEREMOTING
OVEREMOTIONAL
OVEREMPHASES
OVEREMPHASIS
OVEREMPHASISE
OVEREMPHASISED
OVEREMPHASISES
OVEREMPHASISING
OVEREMPHASIZE
OVEREMPHASIZED
OVEREMPHASIZES
OVEREMPHASIZING
OVEREMPHATIC
OVEREMPLOYMENT
OVEREMPLOYMENTS
OVERENAMORED
OVERENAMOURED
OVERENCOURAGE
OVERENCOURAGED
OVERENCOURAGES
OVERENCOURAGING
OVERENERGETIC
OVERENGINEER
OVERENGINEERED
OVERENGINEERING
OVERENGINEERS
OVERENROLLED
OVERENTERTAINED
OVERENTHUSIASM
OVERENTHUSIASMS
OVEREQUIPPED
OVEREQUIPPING
OVEREQUIPS
OVERESTIMATE
OVERESTIMATED
OVERESTIMATES
OVERESTIMATING
OVERESTIMATION
OVERESTIMATIONS
OVEREVALUATION
OVEREVALUATIONS
OVEREXAGGERATE
OVEREXAGGERATED
OVEREXAGGERATES
OVEREXCITABLE
OVEREXCITE
OVEREXCITED
OVEREXCITEMENT
OVEREXCITEMENTS
OVEREXCITES
OVEREXCITING
OVEREXERCISE
OVEREXERCISED
OVEREXERCISES
OVEREXERCISING
OVEREXERTED
OVEREXERTING
OVEREXERTION
OVEREXERTIONS
OVEREXERTS
OVEREXPAND
OVEREXPANDED
OVEREXPANDING
OVEREXPANDS
OVEREXPANSION
OVEREXPANSIONS
OVEREXPECTATION
OVEREXPLAIN
OVEREXPLAINED
OVEREXPLAINING
OVEREXPLAINS
OVEREXPLICIT
OVEREXPLOIT
OVEREXPLOITED
OVEREXPLOITING
OVEREXPLOITS
OVEREXPOSE
OVEREXPOSED
OVEREXPOSES
OVEREXPOSING
OVEREXPOSURE
OVEREXPOSURES
OVEREXTEND
OVEREXTENDED
OVEREXTENDING
OVEREXTENDS
OVEREXTENSION
OVEREXTENSIONS
OVEREXTRACTION
OVEREXTRACTIONS
OVEREXTRAVAGANT
OVEREXUBERANT
OVEREYEING
OVERFACILE
OVERFALLEN
OVERFALLING
OVERFAMILIAR
OVERFAMILIARITY
OVERFASTIDIOUS
OVERFATIGUE
OVERFATIGUED
OVERFATIGUES
OVERFATIGUING
OVERFAVORED
OVERFAVORING
OVERFAVORS
OVERFAVOUR
OVERFAVOURED
OVERFAVOURING

O

OVERFAVOURS
OVERFEARED
OVERFEARING
OVERFEEDING
OVERFEEDINGS
OVERFERTILISE
OVERFERTILISED
OVERFERTILISES
OVERFERTILISING
OVERFERTILIZE
OVERFERTILIZED
OVERFERTILIZES
OVERFERTILIZING
OVERFILLED
OVERFILLING
OVERFINENESS
OVERFINENESSES
OVERFINISHED
OVERFISHED
OVERFISHES
OVERFISHING
OVERFISHINGS
OVERFLIGHT
OVERFLIGHTS
OVERFLOODED
OVERFLOODING
OVERFLOODS
OVERFLOURISH
OVERFLOURISHED
OVERFLOURISHES
OVERFLOURISHING
OVERFLOWED
OVERFLOWING
OVERFLOWINGLY
OVERFLOWINGS
OVERFLUSHES
OVERFLYING
OVERFOCUSED
OVERFOCUSES
OVERFOCUSING
OVERFOCUSSED
OVERFOCUSSES
OVERFOCUSSING
OVERFOLDED
OVERFOLDING
OVERFONDLY
OVERFONDNESS
OVERFONDNESSES
OVERFORWARD
OVERFORWARDNESS
OVERFRAUGHT
OVERFREEDOM
OVERFREEDOMS
OVERFREELY
OVERFREIGHT
OVERFREIGHTING
OVERFREIGHTS
OVERFULFIL
OVERFULFILL
OVERFULFILLED
OVERFULFILLING
OVERFULFILLS
OVERFULFILS
OVERFULLNESS
OVERFULLNESSES
OVERFULNESS
OVERFULNESSES
OVERFUNDED
OVERFUNDING
OVERFUNDINGS
OVERFUSSIER
OVERFUSSIEST
OVERGALLED
OVERGALLING
OVERGANGING
OVERGARMENT
OVERGARMENTS
OVERGEARED
OVERGEARING
OVERGENERALISE
OVERGENERALISED
OVERGENERALISES
OVERGENERALIZE
OVERGENERALIZED
OVERGENERALIZES
OVERGENEROSITY
OVERGENEROUS
OVERGENEROUSLY
OVERGETTING
OVERGILDED
OVERGILDING
OVERGIRDED
OVERGIRDING
OVERGIVING
OVERGLAMORISE
OVERGLAMORISED
OVERGLAMORISES
OVERGLAMORISING
OVERGLAMORIZE
OVERGLAMORIZED
OVERGLAMORIZES
OVERGLAMORIZING
OVERGLANCE
OVERGLANCED
OVERGLANCES
OVERGLANCING
OVERGLAZED
OVERGLAZES
OVERGLAZING
OVERGLOOMED
OVERGLOOMING
OVERGLOOMS
OVERGOADED
OVERGOADING
OVERGOINGS
OVERGORGED
OVERGORGES
OVERGORGING
OVERGOVERN
OVERGOVERNED
OVERGOVERNING
OVERGOVERNS
OVERGRADED
OVERGRADES
OVERGRADING
OVERGRAINED
OVERGRAINER
OVERGRAINERS
OVERGRAINING
OVERGRAINS
OVERGRASSED
OVERGRASSES
OVERGRASSING
OVERGRAZED
OVERGRAZES
OVERGRAZING
OVERGRAZINGS
OVERGREEDIER
OVERGREEDIEST
OVERGREEDY
OVERGREENED
OVERGREENING
OVERGREENS
OVERGROUND
OVERGROWING
OVERGROWTH
OVERGROWTHS
OVERHAILED
OVERHAILES
OVERHAILING
OVERHALING
OVERHANDED
OVERHANDING
OVERHANDLE
OVERHANDLED
OVERHANDLES
OVERHANDLING
OVERHANGING
OVERHAPPIER
OVERHAPPIEST
OVERHARVEST
OVERHARVESTED
OVERHARVESTING
OVERHARVESTS
OVERHASTES
OVERHASTILY
OVERHASTINESS
OVERHASTINESSES
OVERHATING
OVERHAULED
OVERHAULING
OVERHEAPED
OVERHEAPING
OVERHEARING
OVERHEATED
OVERHEATING
OVERHEATINGS
OVERHENTING
OVERHITTING
OVERHOLDING
OVERHOLIER
OVERHOLIEST
OVERHOMOGENISE
OVERHOMOGENISED
OVERHOMOGENISES
OVERHOMOGENIZE
OVERHOMOGENIZED
OVERHOMOGENIZES
OVERHONORED
OVERHONORING
OVERHONORS
OVERHONOUR
OVERHONOURED
OVERHONOURING
OVERHONOURS
OVERHOPING
OVERHUNTED
OVERHUNTING
OVERHUNTINGS
OVERHYPING
OVERIDEALISE
OVERIDEALISED
OVERIDEALISES
OVERIDEALISING
OVERIDEALIZE
OVERIDEALIZED
OVERIDEALIZES
OVERIDEALIZING
OVERIDENTIFIED
OVERIDENTIFIES
OVERIDENTIFY
OVERIDENTIFYING
OVERIMAGINATIVE
OVERIMPRESS
OVERIMPRESSED
OVERIMPRESSES
OVERIMPRESSING
OVERINCLINED
OVERINDULGE
OVERINDULGED
OVERINDULGENCE
OVERINDULGENCES
OVERINDULGENT
OVERINDULGES
OVERINDULGING
OVERINFLATE
OVERINFLATED
OVERINFLATES
OVERINFLATING
OVERINFLATION
OVERINFLATIONS
OVERINFORM
OVERINFORMED
OVERINFORMING
OVERINFORMS
OVERINGENIOUS
OVERINGENUITIES
OVERINGENUITY
OVERINSISTENT
OVERINSURANCE

OVERINSURANCES
OVERINSURE
OVERINSURED
OVERINSURES
OVERINSURING
OVERINTENSE
OVERINTENSITIES
OVERINTENSITY
OVERINVESTMENT
OVERINVESTMENTS
OVERISSUANCE
OVERISSUANCES
OVERISSUED
OVERISSUES
OVERISSUING
OVERJOYING
OVERJUMPED
OVERJUMPING
OVERKEEPING
OVERKILLED
OVERKILLING
OVERKINDNESS
OVERKINDNESSES
OVERLABORED
OVERLABORING
OVERLABORS
OVERLABOUR
OVERLABOURED
OVERLABOURING
OVERLABOURS
OVERLADING
OVERLANDED
OVERLANDER
OVERLANDERS
OVERLANDING
OVERLAPPED
OVERLAPPING
OVERLARDED
OVERLARDING
OVERLAUNCH
OVERLAUNCHED
OVERLAUNCHES
OVERLAUNCHING
OVERLAVISH
OVERLAYING
OVERLAYINGS
OVERLEAPED
OVERLEAPING
OVERLEARNED
OVERLEARNING
OVERLEARNS
OVERLEARNT
OVERLEATHER
OVERLEATHERS
OVERLEAVEN
OVERLEAVENED
OVERLEAVENING
OVERLEAVENS
OVERLENDING
OVERLENGTH
OVERLENGTHEN
OVERLENGTHENED
OVERLENGTHENING
OVERLENGTHENS
OVERLENGTHS
OVERLETTING
OVERLEVERAGED
OVERLIGHTED
OVERLIGHTING
OVERLIGHTS
OVERLITERAL
OVERLITERARY
OVERLIVING
OVERLOADED
OVERLOADING
OVERLOCKED
OVERLOCKER
OVERLOCKERS
OVERLOCKING
OVERLOCKINGS
OVERLOOKED
OVERLOOKER
OVERLOOKERS
OVERLOOKING
OVERLORDED
OVERLORDING
OVERLORDSHIP
OVERLORDSHIPS
OVERLOVING
OVERMANAGE
OVERMANAGED
OVERMANAGES
OVERMANAGING
OVERMANIES
OVERMANNED
OVERMANNERED
OVERMANNING
OVERMANNINGS
OVERMANTEL
OVERMANTELS
OVERMASTED
OVERMASTER
OVERMASTERED
OVERMASTERING
OVERMASTERS
OVERMASTING
OVERMATCHED
OVERMATCHES
OVERMATCHING
OVERMATTER
OVERMATTERS
OVERMATURE
OVERMATURITIES
OVERMATURITY
OVERMEASURE
OVERMEASURED
OVERMEASURES
OVERMEASURING
OVERMEDICATE
OVERMEDICATED
OVERMEDICATES
OVERMEDICATING
OVERMEDICATION
OVERMEDICATIONS
OVERMELTED
OVERMELTING
OVERMERRIER
OVERMERRIEST
OVERMIGHTIER
OVERMIGHTIEST
OVERMIGHTY
OVERMILKED
OVERMILKING
OVERMINING
OVERMIXING
OVERMODEST
OVERMODESTLY
OVERMOUNTED
OVERMOUNTING
OVERMOUNTS
OVERMUCHES
OVERMULTIPLIED
OVERMULTIPLIES
OVERMULTIPLY
OVERMULTIPLYING
OVERMULTITUDE
OVERMULTITUDED
OVERMULTITUDES
OVERMULTITUDING
OVERMUSCLED
OVERNAMING
OVERNETTED
OVERNETTING
OVERNETTINGS
OVERNICELY
OVERNICENESS
OVERNICENESSES
OVERNIGHTED
OVERNIGHTER
OVERNIGHTERS
OVERNIGHTING
OVERNIGHTS
OVERNOURISH
OVERNOURISHED
OVERNOURISHES
OVERNOURISHING
OVERNUTRITION
OVERNUTRITIONS
OVEROBVIOUS
OVEROFFICE
OVEROFFICED
OVEROFFICES
OVEROFFICING
OVEROPERATE
OVEROPERATED
OVEROPERATES
OVEROPERATING
OVEROPINIONATED
OVEROPTIMISM
OVEROPTIMISMS
OVEROPTIMIST
OVEROPTIMISTIC
OVEROPTIMISTS
OVERORCHESTRATE
OVERORGANISE
OVERORGANISED
OVERORGANISES
OVERORGANISING
OVERORGANIZE
OVERORGANIZED
OVERORGANIZES
OVERORGANIZING
OVERORNAMENT
OVERORNAMENTED
OVERORNAMENTING
OVERORNAMENTS
OVERPACKAGE
OVERPACKAGED
OVERPACKAGES
OVERPACKAGING
OVERPACKED
OVERPACKING
OVERPAINTED
OVERPAINTING
OVERPAINTS
OVERPARTED
OVERPARTICULAR
OVERPARTING
OVERPASSED
OVERPASSES
OVERPASSING
OVERPAYING
OVERPAYMENT
OVERPAYMENTS
OVERPEDALED
OVERPEDALING
OVERPEDALLED
OVERPEDALLING
OVERPEDALLINGS
OVERPEDALS
OVERPEERED
OVERPEERING
OVERPEOPLE
OVERPEOPLED
OVERPEOPLES
OVERPEOPLING
OVERPERCHED
OVERPERCHES
OVERPERCHING
OVERPERSUADE
OVERPERSUADED
OVERPERSUADES
OVERPERSUADING
OVERPERSUASION
OVERPERSUASIONS
OVERPESSIMISTIC
OVERPICTURE
OVERPICTURED
OVERPICTURES
OVERPICTURING

O

OVERPITCHED
OVERPITCHES
OVERPITCHING
OVERPLACED
OVERPLAIDED
OVERPLAIDS
OVERPLANNED
OVERPLANNING
OVERPLANNINGS
OVERPLANTED
OVERPLANTING
OVERPLANTS
OVERPLAYED
OVERPLAYING
OVERPLOTTED
OVERPLOTTING
OVERPLOTTINGS
OVERPLUSES
OVERPLUSSES
OVERPLYING
OVERPOISED
OVERPOISES
OVERPOISING
OVERPOPULATE
OVERPOPULATED
OVERPOPULATES
OVERPOPULATING
OVERPOPULATION
OVERPOPULATIONS
OVERPOSTED
OVERPOSTING
OVERPOTENT
OVERPOWERED
OVERPOWERING
OVERPOWERINGLY
OVERPOWERS
OVERPRAISE
OVERPRAISED
OVERPRAISES
OVERPRAISING
OVERPRECISE
OVERPREPARATION
OVERPREPARE
OVERPREPARED
OVERPREPARES
OVERPREPARING
OVERPRESCRIBE
OVERPRESCRIBED
OVERPRESCRIBES
OVERPRESCRIBING
OVERPRESSED
OVERPRESSES
OVERPRESSING
OVERPRESSURE
OVERPRESSURES
OVERPRICED
OVERPRICES
OVERPRICING
OVERPRINTED
OVERPRINTING
OVERPRINTS
OVERPRIVILEGED
OVERPRIZED
OVERPRIZES
OVERPRIZING
OVERPROCESS
OVERPROCESSED
OVERPROCESSES
OVERPROCESSING
OVERPRODUCE
OVERPRODUCED
OVERPRODUCES
OVERPRODUCING
OVERPRODUCTION
OVERPRODUCTIONS
OVERPROGRAM
OVERPROGRAMED
OVERPROGRAMING
OVERPROGRAMMED
OVERPROGRAMMING
OVERPROGRAMS
OVERPROMISE
OVERPROMISED
OVERPROMISES
OVERPROMISING
OVERPROMOTE
OVERPROMOTED
OVERPROMOTES
OVERPROMOTING
OVERPROOFS
OVERPROPORTION
OVERPROPORTIONS
OVERPROTECT
OVERPROTECTED
OVERPROTECTING
OVERPROTECTION
OVERPROTECTIONS
OVERPROTECTIVE
OVERPROTECTS
OVERPUMPED
OVERPUMPING
OVERQUALIFIED
OVERRACKED
OVERRACKING
OVERRAKING
OVERRANKED
OVERRANKING
OVERRASHLY
OVERRASHNESS
OVERRASHNESSES
OVERRATING
OVERRAUGHT
OVERREACHED
OVERREACHER
OVERREACHERS
OVERREACHES
OVERREACHING
OVERREACTED
OVERREACTING
OVERREACTION
OVERREACTIONS
OVERREACTS
OVERREADING
OVERRECKON
OVERRECKONED
OVERRECKONING
OVERRECKONS
OVERREDDED
OVERREDDING
OVERREFINE
OVERREFINED
OVERREFINEMENT
OVERREFINEMENTS
OVERREFINES
OVERREFINING
OVERREGULATE
OVERREGULATED
OVERREGULATES
OVERREGULATING
OVERREGULATION
OVERREGULATIONS
OVERRELIANCE
OVERRELIANCES
OVERRENNING
OVERREPORT
OVERREPORTED
OVERREPORTING
OVERREPORTS
OVERREPRESENTED
OVERRESPOND
OVERRESPONDED
OVERRESPONDING
OVERRESPONDS
OVERRIDDEN
OVERRIDERS
OVERRIDING
OVERRIPENED
OVERRIPENESS
OVERRIPENESSES
OVERRIPENING
OVERRIPENS
OVERROASTED
OVERROASTING
OVERROASTS
OVERRUFFED
OVERRUFFING
OVERRULERS
OVERRULING
OVERRULINGS
OVERRUNNER
OVERRUNNERS
OVERRUNNING
OVERSAILED
OVERSAILING
OVERSALTED
OVERSALTING
OVERSANGUINE
OVERSATURATE
OVERSATURATED
OVERSATURATES
OVERSATURATING
OVERSATURATION
OVERSATURATIONS
OVERSAUCED
OVERSAUCES
OVERSAUCING
OVERSAVING
OVERSCALED
OVERSCHUTCHT
OVERSCORED
OVERSCORES
OVERSCORING
OVERSCRUPULOUS
OVERSCUTCHED
OVERSECRETION
OVERSECRETIONS
OVERSEEDED
OVERSEEDING
OVERSEEING
OVERSELLING
OVERSENSITIVE
OVERSENSITIVITY
OVERSERIOUS
OVERSERIOUSLY
OVERSERVICE
OVERSERVICED
OVERSERVICES
OVERSERVICING
OVERSETTING
OVERSEWING
OVERSHADED
OVERSHADES
OVERSHADING
OVERSHADOW
OVERSHADOWED
OVERSHADOWING
OVERSHADOWS
OVERSHARED
OVERSHARES
OVERSHARING
OVERSHINES
OVERSHINING
OVERSHIRTS
OVERSHOOTING
OVERSHOOTS
OVERSHOWER
OVERSHOWERED
OVERSHOWERING
OVERSHOWERS
OVERSIGHTS
OVERSIMPLE
OVERSIMPLIFIED
OVERSIMPLIFIES
OVERSIMPLIFY
OVERSIMPLIFYING
OVERSIMPLISTIC
OVERSIMPLY
OVERSIZING
OVERSKATED
OVERSKATES

OVERSKATING
OVERSKIPPED
OVERSKIPPING
OVERSKIRTS
OVERSLAUGH
OVERSLAUGHED
OVERSLAUGHING
OVERSLAUGHS
OVERSLEEPING
OVERSLEEPS
OVERSLEEVE
OVERSLEEVES
OVERSLIPPED
OVERSLIPPING
OVERSMOKED
OVERSMOKES
OVERSMOKING
OVERSOAKED
OVERSOAKING
OVERSOLICITOUS
OVERSOWING
OVERSPECIALISE
OVERSPECIALISED
OVERSPECIALISES
OVERSPECIALIZE
OVERSPECIALIZED
OVERSPECIALIZES
OVERSPECULATE
OVERSPECULATED
OVERSPECULATES
OVERSPECULATING
OVERSPECULATION
OVERSPENDER
OVERSPENDERS
OVERSPENDING
OVERSPENDINGS
OVERSPENDS
OVERSPICED
OVERSPICES
OVERSPICING
OVERSPILLED
OVERSPILLING
OVERSPILLS
OVERSPREAD
OVERSPREADING
OVERSPREADS
OVERSTABILITIES
OVERSTABILITY
OVERSTAFFED
OVERSTAFFING
OVERSTAFFINGS
OVERSTAFFS
OVERSTAINED
OVERSTAINING
OVERSTAINS
OVERSTANDING
OVERSTANDS
OVERSTARED
OVERSTARES
OVERSTARING
OVERSTATED
OVERSTATEMENT
OVERSTATEMENTS
OVERSTATES
OVERSTATING
OVERSTAYED
OVERSTAYER
OVERSTAYERS
OVERSTAYING
OVERSTEERED
OVERSTEERING
OVERSTEERS
OVERSTEPPED
OVERSTEPPING
OVERSTIMULATE
OVERSTIMULATED
OVERSTIMULATES
OVERSTIMULATING
OVERSTIMULATION
OVERSTINKING
OVERSTINKS
OVERSTIRRED
OVERSTIRRING
OVERSTOCKED
OVERSTOCKING
OVERSTOCKS
OVERSTOREY
OVERSTOREYS
OVERSTORIES
OVERSTRAIN
OVERSTRAINED
OVERSTRAINING
OVERSTRAINS
OVERSTRESS
OVERSTRESSED
OVERSTRESSES
OVERSTRESSING
OVERSTRETCH
OVERSTRETCHED
OVERSTRETCHES
OVERSTRETCHING
OVERSTREWED
OVERSTREWING
OVERSTREWN
OVERSTREWS
OVERSTRIDDEN
OVERSTRIDE
OVERSTRIDES
OVERSTRIDING
OVERSTRIKE
OVERSTRIKES
OVERSTRIKING
OVERSTRODE
OVERSTRONG
OVERSTROOKE
OVERSTRUCK
OVERSTRUCTURED
OVERSTRUNG
OVERSTUDIED
OVERSTUDIES
OVERSTUDYING
OVERSTUFFED
OVERSTUFFING
OVERSTUFFS
OVERSUBSCRIBE
OVERSUBSCRIBED
OVERSUBSCRIBES
OVERSUBSCRIBING
OVERSUBTLE
OVERSUBTLETIES
OVERSUBTLETY
OVERSUDSED
OVERSUDSES
OVERSUDSING
OVERSUPPED
OVERSUPPING
OVERSUPPLIED
OVERSUPPLIES
OVERSUPPLY
OVERSUPPLYING
OVERSUSPICIOUS
OVERSWAYED
OVERSWAYING
OVERSWEARING
OVERSWEARS
OVERSWEETEN
OVERSWEETENED
OVERSWEETENING
OVERSWEETENS
OVERSWEETNESS
OVERSWEETNESSES
OVERSWELLED
OVERSWELLING
OVERSWELLS
OVERSWIMMING
OVERSWINGING
OVERSWINGS
OVERSWOLLEN
OVERTAKING
OVERTAKINGS
OVERTALKATIVE
OVERTALKED
OVERTALKING
OVERTASKED
OVERTASKING
OVERTAUGHT
OVERTAXATION
OVERTAXATIONS
OVERTAXING
OVERTEACHES
OVERTEACHING
OVERTEDIOUS
OVERTEEMED
OVERTEEMING
OVERTHINKING
OVERTHINKS
OVERTHINNED
OVERTHINNING
OVERTHOUGHT
OVERTHROWER
OVERTHROWERS
OVERTHROWING
OVERTHROWN
OVERTHROWS
OVERTHRUST
OVERTHRUSTS
OVERTHWART
OVERTHWARTED
OVERTHWARTING
OVERTHWARTS
OVERTIGHTEN
OVERTIGHTENED
OVERTIGHTENING
OVERTIGHTENS
OVERTIMELY
OVERTIMERS
OVERTIMING
OVERTIPPED
OVERTIPPING
OVERTIRING
OVERTNESSES
OVERTOILED
OVERTOILING
OVERTOPPED
OVERTOPPING
OVERTOPPINGS
OVERTOWERED
OVERTOWERING
OVERTOWERS
OVERTRADED
OVERTRADES
OVERTRADING
OVERTRADINGS
OVERTRAINED
OVERTRAINING
OVERTRAINS
OVERTREATED
OVERTREATING
OVERTREATMENT
OVERTREATMENTS
OVERTREATS
OVERTRICKS
OVERTRIMMED
OVERTRIMMING
OVERTRIPPED
OVERTRIPPING
OVERTRUMPED
OVERTRUMPING
OVERTRUMPS
OVERTRUSTED
OVERTRUSTING
OVERTRUSTS
OVERTURING
OVERTURNED
OVERTURNER
OVERTURNERS
OVERTURNING
OVERTYPING
OVERURGING
OVERUTILISATION

O

OVERUTILISE
OVERUTILISED
OVERUTILISES
OVERUTILISING
OVERUTILIZATION
OVERUTILIZE
OVERUTILIZED
OVERUTILIZES
OVERUTILIZING
OVERVALUATION
OVERVALUATIONS
OVERVALUED
OVERVALUES
OVERVALUING
OVERVEILED
OVERVEILING
OVERVIOLENT
OVERVOLTAGE
OVERVOLTAGES
OVERVOTING
OVERWARIER
OVERWARIEST
OVERWARMED
OVERWARMING
OVERWASHES
OVERWATCHED
OVERWATCHES
OVERWATCHING
OVERWATERED
OVERWATERING
OVERWATERS
OVERWEARIED
OVERWEARIES
OVERWEARING
OVERWEARYING
OVERWEATHER
OVERWEATHERED
OVERWEATHERING
OVERWEATHERS
OVERWEENED
OVERWEENING
OVERWEENINGLY
OVERWEENINGNESS
OVERWEENINGS
OVERWEIGHED
OVERWEIGHING
OVERWEIGHS
OVERWEIGHT
OVERWEIGHTED
OVERWEIGHTING
OVERWEIGHTS
OVERWETTED
OVERWETTING
OVERWHELMED
OVERWHELMING
OVERWHELMINGLY
OVERWHELMINGS
OVERWHELMS
OVERWILIER
OVERWILIEST
OVERWINDED
OVERWINDING
OVERWINGED
OVERWINGING
OVERWINTER
OVERWINTERED
OVERWINTERING
OVERWINTERS
OVERWISELY
OVERWITHHELD
OVERWITHHOLD
OVERWITHHOLDING
OVERWITHHOLDS
OVERWORKED
OVERWORKING
OVERWRAPPED
OVERWRAPPING
OVERWRESTED
OVERWRESTING
OVERWRESTLE
OVERWRESTLED
OVERWRESTLES
OVERWRESTLING
OVERWRESTS
OVERWRITES
OVERWRITING
OVERWRITTEN
OVERWROUGHT
OVERYEARED
OVERYEARING
OVERZEALOUS
OVERZEALOUSLY
OVERZEALOUSNESS
OVIPARITIES
OVIPAROUSLY
OVIPOSITED
OVIPOSITING
OVIPOSITION
OVIPOSITIONAL
OVIPOSITIONS
OVIPOSITOR
OVIPOSITORS
OVIRAPTORS
OVOVIVIPARITIES
OVOVIVIPARITY
OVOVIVIPAROUS
OVOVIVIPAROUSLY
OVULATIONS
OVULIFEROUS
OWERLOUPEN
OWERLOUPING
OWERLOUPIT
OWLISHNESS
OWLISHNESSES
OWNERSHIPS
OWRECOMING
OXACILLINS
OXALACETATE
OXALACETATES
OXALOACETATE
OXALOACETATES
OXALOACETIC
OXIDATIONAL
OXIDATIONS
OXIDATIVELY
OXIDIMETRIC
OXIDIMETRIES
OXIDIMETRY
OXIDISABLE
OXIDISATION
OXIDISATIONS
OXIDIZABLE
OXIDIZATION
OXIDIZATIONS
OXIDOREDUCTASE
OXIDOREDUCTASES
OXIMETRIES
OXYACETYLENE
OXYACETYLENES
OXYCEPHALIC
OXYCEPHALIES
OXYCEPHALOUS
OXYCEPHALY
OXYCODONES
OXYGENASES
OXYGENATED
OXYGENATES
OXYGENATING
OXYGENATION
OXYGENATIONS
OXYGENATOR
OXYGENATORS
OXYGENISED
OXYGENISER
OXYGENISERS
OXYGENISES
OXYGENISING
OXYGENIZED
OXYGENIZER
OXYGENIZERS
OXYGENIZES
OXYGENIZING
OXYGENLESS
OXYHAEMOGLOBIN
OXYHAEMOGLOBINS
OXYHEMOGLOBIN
OXYHEMOGLOBINS
OXYHYDROGEN
OXYHYDROGENS
OXYMORONIC
OXYMORONICALLY
OXYPHENBUTAZONE
OXYRHYNCHUS
OXYRHYNCHUSES
OXYSULPHIDE
OXYSULPHIDES
OXYTETRACYCLINE
OXYURIASES
OXYURIASIS
OYSTERCATCHER
OYSTERCATCHERS
OYSTERINGS
OZOCERITES
OZOKERITES
OZONATIONS
OZONIFEROUS
OZONISATION
OZONISATIONS
OZONIZATION
OZONIZATIONS
OZONOLYSES
OZONOLYSIS
OZONOSPHERE
OZONOSPHERES

P

PACEMAKERS
PACEMAKING
PACEMAKINGS
PACESETTER
PACESETTERS
PACESETTING
PACESETTINGS
PACHYCARPOUS
PACHYDACTYL
PACHYDACTYLOUS
PACHYDERMAL
PACHYDERMATOUS
PACHYDERMIA
PACHYDERMIAS
PACHYDERMIC
PACHYDERMOUS
PACHYDERMS
PACHYMENINGITIS
PACHYMETER
PACHYMETERS
PACHYSANDRA
PACHYSANDRAS
PACHYTENES
PACIFIABLE
PACIFICALLY
PACIFICATE
PACIFICATED
PACIFICATES
PACIFICATING
PACIFICATION
PACIFICATIONS
PACIFICATOR
PACIFICATORS
PACIFICATORY
PACIFICISM
PACIFICISMS
PACIFICIST
PACIFICISTS
PACIFISTIC
PACIFISTICALLY
PACKABILITIES
PACKABILITY
PACKAGINGS
PACKBOARDS
PACKCLOTHS
PACKETISED
PACKETISES
PACKETISING
PACKETIZED
PACKETIZES
PACKETIZING
PACKFRAMES
PACKHORSES
PACKINGHOUSE
PACKINGHOUSES
PACKNESSES
PACKSADDLE
PACKSADDLES
PACKSHEETS
PACKSTAFFS
PACKTHREAD
PACKTHREADS
PACLITAXEL
PACLITAXELS
PACTIONING
PADDLEBALL
PADDLEBALLS
PADDLEBOARD
PADDLEBOARDS
PADDLEBOAT
PADDLEBOATS
PADDLEFISH
PADDLEFISHES
PADDOCKING
PADDYMELON
PADDYMELONS
PADDYWACKED
PADDYWACKING
PADDYWACKS
PADDYWHACK
PADDYWHACKS
PADEMELONS
PADEREROES
PADLOCKING
PADRONISMS
PADYMELONS
PAEDAGOGIC
PAEDAGOGUE
PAEDAGOGUES
PAEDERASTIC
PAEDERASTIES
PAEDERASTS
PAEDERASTY
PAEDEUTICS
PAEDIATRIC
PAEDIATRICIAN
PAEDIATRICIANS
PAEDIATRICS
PAEDIATRIES
PAEDIATRIST
PAEDIATRISTS
PAEDOBAPTISM
PAEDOBAPTISMS
PAEDOBAPTIST
PAEDOBAPTISTS
PAEDODONTIC
PAEDODONTICS
PAEDOGENESES
PAEDOGENESIS
PAEDOGENETIC
PAEDOGENIC
PAEDOLOGICAL
PAEDOLOGIES
PAEDOLOGIST
PAEDOLOGISTS
PAEDOMORPHIC
PAEDOMORPHISM
PAEDOMORPHISMS
PAEDOMORPHOSES
PAEDOMORPHOSIS
PAEDOPHILE
PAEDOPHILES
PAEDOPHILIA
PAEDOPHILIAC
PAEDOPHILIACS
PAEDOPHILIAS
PAEDOPHILIC
PAEDOPHILICS
PAEDOTRIBE
PAEDOTRIBES
PAEDOTROPHIES
PAEDOTROPHY
PAGANISATION
PAGANISATIONS
PAGANISERS
PAGANISING
PAGANISTIC
PAGANISTICALLY
PAGANIZATION
PAGANIZATIONS
PAGANIZERS
PAGANIZING
PAGEANTRIES
PAGINATING
PAGINATION
PAGINATIONS
PAIDEUTICS
PAILLASSES
PAILLETTES
PAINFULLER
PAINFULLEST
PAINFULNESS
PAINFULNESSES
PAINKILLER
PAINKILLERS
PAINKILLING
PAINLESSLY
PAINLESSNESS
PAINLESSNESSES
PAINSTAKER
PAINSTAKERS
PAINSTAKING
PAINSTAKINGLY
PAINSTAKINGNESS
PAINSTAKINGS
PAINTBALLING
PAINTBALLINGS
PAINTBALLS
PAINTBOXES
PAINTBRUSH
PAINTBRUSHES
PAINTERLINESS
PAINTERLINESSES
PAINTINESS
PAINTINESSES
PAINTRESSES
PAINTWORKS
PAKIRIKIRI
PAKIRIKIRIS
PALACINKES
PALAEANTHROPIC
PALAEBIOLOGIES
PALAEBIOLOGIST
PALAEBIOLOGISTS
PALAEBIOLOGY
PALAEETHNOLOGY
PALAEOANTHROPIC
PALAEOBIOLOGIC
PALAEOBIOLOGIES
PALAEOBIOLOGIST
PALAEOBIOLOGY
PALAEOBOTANIC
PALAEOBOTANICAL
PALAEOBOTANIES
PALAEOBOTANIST
PALAEOBOTANISTS
PALAEOBOTANY
PALAEOCLIMATE
PALAEOCLIMATES
PALAEOCLIMATIC
PALAEOCRYSTIC
PALAEOCURRENT
PALAEOCURRENTS
PALAEOECOLOGIC
PALAEOECOLOGIES
PALAEOECOLOGIST
PALAEOECOLOGY
PALAEOETHNOLOGY
PALAEOGAEA
PALAEOGAEAS

PALAEOGEOGRAPHY
PALAEOGRAPHER
PALAEOGRAPHERS
PALAEOGRAPHIC
PALAEOGRAPHICAL
PALAEOGRAPHIES
PALAEOGRAPHIST
PALAEOGRAPHISTS
PALAEOGRAPHY
PALAEOLIMNOLOGY
PALAEOLITH
PALAEOLITHIC
PALAEOLITHS
PALAEOLOGIES
PALAEOLOGY
PALAEOMAGNETIC
PALAEOMAGNETISM
PALAEOMAGNETIST
PALAEONTOGRAPHY
PALAEONTOLOGIES
PALAEONTOLOGIST
PALAEONTOLOGY
PALAEOPATHOLOGY
PALAEOPEDOLOGY
PALAEOPHYTOLOGY
PALAEOSOLS
PALAEOTYPE
PALAEOTYPES
PALAEOTYPIC
PALAEOZOOLOGIES
PALAEOZOOLOGIST
PALAEOZOOLOGY
PALAESTRAE
PALAESTRAL
PALAESTRAS
PALAESTRIC
PALAESTRICAL
PALAFITTES
PALAGONITE
PALAGONITES
PALAMPORES
PALANKEENS
PALANQUINS
PALATABILITIES
PALATABILITY
PALATABLENESS
PALATABLENESSES
PALATALISATION
PALATALISATIONS
PALATALISE
PALATALISED
PALATALISES
PALATALISING
PALATALIZATION
PALATALIZATIONS
PALATALIZE
PALATALIZED
PALATALIZES
PALATALIZING
PALATIALLY
PALATIALNESS
PALATIALNESSES
PALATINATE
PALATINATES
PALAVERERS
PALAVERING
PALEACEOUS
PALEMPORES
PALENESSES
PALEOBIOLOGIC
PALEOBIOLOGICAL
PALEOBIOLOGIES
PALEOBIOLOGIST
PALEOBIOLOGISTS
PALEOBIOLOGY
PALEOBOTANIC
PALEOBOTANICAL
PALEOBOTANIES
PALEOBOTANIST
PALEOBOTANISTS
PALEOBOTANY
PALEOECOLOGIC
PALEOECOLOGICAL
PALEOECOLOGIES
PALEOECOLOGIST
PALEOECOLOGISTS
PALEOECOLOGY
PALEOGEOGRAPHIC
PALEOGEOGRAPHY
PALEOGRAPHER
PALEOGRAPHERS
PALEOGRAPHIC
PALEOGRAPHICAL
PALEOGRAPHIES
PALEOGRAPHY
PALEOLITHIC
PALEOLITHS
PALEOLOGIES
PALEOMAGNETIC
PALEOMAGNETISM
PALEOMAGNETISMS
PALEOMAGNETIST
PALEOMAGNETISTS
PALEONTOLOGIC
PALEONTOLOGICAL
PALEONTOLOGIES
PALEONTOLOGIST
PALEONTOLOGISTS
PALEONTOLOGY
PALEOPATHOLOGY
PALEOZOOLOGICAL
PALEOZOOLOGIES
PALEOZOOLOGIST
PALEOZOOLOGISTS
PALEOZOOLOGY
PALFRENIER
PALFRENIERS
PALIFICATION
PALIFICATIONS
PALILALIAS
PALILLOGIES
PALIMONIES
PALIMPSEST
PALIMPSESTS
PALINDROME
PALINDROMES
PALINDROMIC
PALINDROMICAL
PALINDROMIST
PALINDROMISTS
PALINGENESES
PALINGENESIA
PALINGENESIAS
PALINGENESIES
PALINGENESIS
PALINGENESIST
PALINGENESISTS
PALINGENESY
PALINGENETIC
PALINGENETICAL
PALINODIES
PALINOPIAS
PALINOPSIA
PALINOPSIAS
PALISADING
PALISADOED
PALISADOES
PALISADOING
PALISANDER
PALISANDERS
PALLADIOUS
PALLADIUMS
PALLASITES
PALLBEARER
PALLBEARERS
PALLESCENCE
PALLESCENCES
PALLESCENT
PALLETISATION
PALLETISATIONS
PALLETISED
PALLETISER
PALLETISERS
PALLETISES
PALLETISING
PALLETIZATION
PALLETIZATIONS
PALLETIZED
PALLETIZER
PALLETIZERS
PALLETIZES
PALLETIZING
PALLIAMENT
PALLIAMENTS
PALLIASSES
PALLIATING
PALLIATION
PALLIATIONS
PALLIATIVE
PALLIATIVELY
PALLIATIVES
PALLIATORS
PALLIATORY
PALLIDITIES
PALLIDNESS
PALLIDNESSES
PALMACEOUS
PALMATIFID
PALMATIONS
PALMATIPARTITE
PALMATISECT
PALMCORDER
PALMCORDERS
PALMERWORM
PALMERWORMS
PALMETTOES
PALMHOUSES
PALMIFICATION
PALMIFICATIONS
PALMIPEDES
PALMISTERS
PALMISTRIES
PALMITATES
PALMPRINTS
PALOVERDES
PALPABILITIES
PALPABILITY
PALPABLENESS
PALPABLENESSES
PALPATIONS
PALPEBRATE
PALPEBRATED
PALPEBRATES
PALPEBRATING
PALPITATED
PALPITATES
PALPITATING
PALPITATION
PALPITATIONS
PALSGRAVES
PALSGRAVINE
PALSGRAVINES
PALTRINESS
PALTRINESSES
PALUDAMENT
PALUDAMENTA
PALUDAMENTS
PALUDAMENTUM
PALUDAMENTUMS
PALUDICOLOUS
PALUDINOUS
PALUSTRIAN
PALUSTRINE
PALYNOLOGIC
PALYNOLOGICAL
PALYNOLOGICALLY
PALYNOLOGIES
PALYNOLOGIST
PALYNOLOGISTS
PALYNOLOGY

PAMPELMOOSE
PAMPELMOOSES
PAMPELMOUSE
PAMPELMOUSES
PAMPEREDNESS
PAMPEREDNESSES
PAMPERINGS
PAMPHLETED
PAMPHLETEER
PAMPHLETEERED
PAMPHLETEERING
PAMPHLETEERINGS
PAMPHLETEERS
PAMPHLETING
PAMPOOTIES
PANACHAEAS
PANAESTHESIA
PANAESTHESIAS
PANAESTHETISM
PANAESTHETISMS
PANARITIUM
PANARITIUMS
PANARTHRITIS
PANARTHRITISES
PANATELLAS
PANBROILED
PANBROILING
PANCHAYATS
PANCHROMATIC
PANCHROMATISM
PANCHROMATISMS
PANCOSMISM
PANCOSMISMS
PANCRATIAN
PANCRATIAST
PANCRATIASTS
PANCRATIST
PANCRATISTS
PANCRATIUM
PANCRATIUMS
PANCREASES
PANCREATECTOMY
PANCREATIC
PANCREATIN
PANCREATINS
PANCREATITIDES
PANCREATITIS
PANCREATITISES
PANCREOZYMIN
PANCREOZYMINS
PANCYTOPENIA
PANCYTOPENIAS
PANDAEMONIUM
PANDAEMONIUMS
PANDANACEOUS
PANDANUSES
PANDATIONS
PANDECTIST
PANDECTISTS
PANDEMONIAC
PANDEMONIACAL
PANDEMONIAN
PANDEMONIANS
PANDEMONIC
PANDEMONIUM
PANDEMONIUMS
PANDERESSES
PANDERINGS
PANDERISMS
PANDERMITE
PANDERMITES
PANDICULATION
PANDICULATIONS
PANDOWDIES
PANDURATED
PANDURIFORM
PANEGOISMS
PANEGYRICA
PANEGYRICAL
PANEGYRICALLY
PANEGYRICON
PANEGYRICS
PANEGYRIES
PANEGYRISE
PANEGYRISED
PANEGYRISES
PANEGYRISING
PANEGYRIST
PANEGYRISTS
PANEGYRIZE
PANEGYRIZED
PANEGYRIZES
PANEGYRIZING
PANELLINGS
PANELLISED
PANELLISTS
PANELLIZED
PANENTHEISM
PANENTHEISMS
PANENTHEIST
PANENTHEISTS
PANESTHESIA
PANESTHESIAS
PANETELLAS
PANETTONES
PANFISHING
PANFISHINGS
PANGENESES
PANGENESIS
PANGENETIC
PANGENETICALLY
PANGRAMMATIST
PANGRAMMATISTS
PANHANDLED
PANHANDLER
PANHANDLERS
PANHANDLES
PANHANDLING
PANHARMONICON
PANHARMONICONS
PANHELLENIC
PANHELLENION
PANHELLENIONS
PANHELLENIUM
PANHELLENIUMS
PANICKIEST
PANICMONGER
PANICMONGERS
PANICULATE
PANICULATED
PANICULATELY
PANIDIOMORPHIC
PANIFICATION
PANIFICATIONS
PANISLAMIST
PANJANDARUM
PANJANDARUMS
PANJANDRUM
PANJANDRUMS
PANLEUCOPENIA
PANLEUCOPENIAS
PANLEUKOPENIA
PANLEUKOPENIAS
PANLOGISMS
PANMIXISES
PANNICULUS
PANNICULUSES
PANNIKELLS
PANOMPHAEAN
PANOPHOBIA
PANOPHOBIAS
PANOPHTHALMIA
PANOPHTHALMIAS
PANOPHTHALMITIS
PANOPTICAL
PANOPTICALLY
PANOPTICON
PANOPTICONS
PANORAMICALLY
PANPHARMACON
PANPHARMACONS
PANPSYCHISM
PANPSYCHISMS
PANPSYCHIST
PANPSYCHISTIC
PANPSYCHISTS
PANRADIOMETER
PANRADIOMETERS
PANSEXUALISM
PANSEXUALISMS
PANSEXUALIST
PANSEXUALISTS
PANSEXUALITIES
PANSEXUALITY
PANSEXUALS
PANSOPHICAL
PANSOPHICALLY
PANSOPHIES
PANSOPHISM
PANSOPHISMS
PANSOPHIST
PANSOPHISTS
PANSPERMATIC
PANSPERMATISM
PANSPERMATISMS
PANSPERMATIST
PANSPERMATISTS
PANSPERMIA
PANSPERMIAS
PANSPERMIC
PANSPERMIES
PANSPERMISM
PANSPERMISMS
PANSPERMIST
PANSPERMISTS
PANTAGAMIES
PANTAGRAPH
PANTAGRAPHS
PANTALEONS
PANTALETTED
PANTALETTES
PANTALONES
PANTALOONED
PANTALOONERIES
PANTALOONERY
PANTALOONS
PANTDRESSES
PANTECHNICON
PANTECHNICONS
PANTHEISMS
PANTHEISTIC
PANTHEISTICAL
PANTHEISTICALLY
PANTHEISTS
PANTHENOLS
PANTHEOLOGIES
PANTHEOLOGIST
PANTHEOLOGISTS
PANTHEOLOGY
PANTHERESS
PANTHERESSES
PANTHERINE
PANTHERISH
PANTIHOSES
PANTILINGS
PANTISOCRACIES
PANTISOCRACY
PANTISOCRAT
PANTISOCRATIC
PANTISOCRATICAL
PANTISOCRATIST
PANTISOCRATISTS
PANTISOCRATS
PANTOFFLES
PANTOGRAPH
PANTOGRAPHER
PANTOGRAPHERS
PANTOGRAPHIC
PANTOGRAPHICAL
PANTOGRAPHIES

PANTOGRAPHS
PANTOGRAPHY
PANTOMIMED
PANTOMIMES
PANTOMIMIC
PANTOMIMICAL
PANTOMIMICALLY
PANTOMIMING
PANTOMIMIST
PANTOMIMISTS
PANTOPHAGIES
PANTOPHAGIST
PANTOPHAGISTS
PANTOPHAGOUS
PANTOPHAGY
PANTOPHOBIA
PANTOPHOBIAS
PANTOPRAGMATIC
PANTOPRAGMATICS
PANTOSCOPE
PANTOSCOPES
PANTOSCOPIC
PANTOTHENATE
PANTOTHENATES
PANTOTHENIC
PANTOUFLES
PANTROPICAL
PANTRYMAID
PANTRYMAIDS
PANTSUITED
PANTYHOSES
PANTYWAIST
PANTYWAISTS
PANZEROTTI
PANZEROTTO
PANZEROTTOS
PANZOOTICS
PAPALISING
PAPALIZING
PAPAPRELATIST
PAPAPRELATISTS
PAPAVERACEOUS
PAPAVERINE
PAPAVERINES
PAPAVEROUS
PAPERBACKED
PAPERBACKER
PAPERBACKERS
PAPERBACKING
PAPERBACKS
PAPERBARKS
PAPERBOARD
PAPERBOARDS
PAPERBOUND
PAPERBOUNDS
PAPERCLIPS
PAPERGIRLS
PAPERHANGER
PAPERHANGERS
PAPERHANGING
PAPERHANGINGS
PAPERINESS
PAPERINESSES
PAPERKNIFE
PAPERKNIVES
PAPERMAKER
PAPERMAKERS
PAPERMAKING
PAPERMAKINGS
PAPERWARES
PAPERWEIGHT
PAPERWEIGHTS
PAPERWORKS
PAPETERIES
PAPILIONACEOUS
PAPILLATED
PAPILLIFEROUS
PAPILLIFORM
PAPILLITIS
PAPILLITISES
PAPILLOMAS
PAPILLOMATA
PAPILLOMATOSES
PAPILLOMATOSIS
PAPILLOMATOUS
PAPILLOMAVIRUS
PAPILLOTES
PAPILLULATE
PAPILLULES
PAPOVAVIRUS
PAPOVAVIRUSES
PAPPARDELLE
PAPPARDELLES
PAPRIKASES
PAPRIKASHES
PAPULATION
PAPULATIONS
PAPULIFEROUS
PAPYRACEOUS
PAPYROLOGICAL
PAPYROLOGIES
PAPYROLOGIST
PAPYROLOGISTS
PAPYROLOGY
PARABAPTISM
PARABAPTISMS
PARABEMATA
PARABEMATIC
PARABIOSES
PARABIOSIS
PARABIOTIC
PARABIOTICALLY
PARABLASTIC
PARABLASTS
PARABLEPSES
PARABLEPSIES
PARABLEPSIS
PARABLEPSY
PARABLEPTIC
PARABOLANUS
PARABOLANUSES
PARABOLICAL
PARABOLICALLY
PARABOLISATION
PARABOLISATIONS
PARABOLISE
PARABOLISED
PARABOLISES
PARABOLISING
PARABOLIST
PARABOLISTS
PARABOLIZATION
PARABOLIZATIONS
PARABOLIZE
PARABOLIZED
PARABOLIZES
PARABOLIZING
PARABOLOID
PARABOLOIDAL
PARABOLOIDS
PARABRAKES
PARACASEIN
PARACASEINS
PARACENTESES
PARACENTESIS
PARACETAMOL
PARACETAMOLS
PARACHRONISM
PARACHRONISMS
PARACHUTED
PARACHUTES
PARACHUTIC
PARACHUTING
PARACHUTINGS
PARACHUTIST
PARACHUTISTS
PARACLETES
PARACROSTIC
PARACROSTICS
PARACYANOGEN
PARACYANOGENS
PARADIDDLE
PARADIDDLED
PARADIDDLES
PARADIDDLING
PARADIGMATIC
PARADIGMATICAL
PARADISAIC
PARADISAICAL
PARADISAICALLY
PARADISEAN
PARADISIAC
PARADISIACAL
PARADISIACALLY
PARADISIAL
PARADISIAN
PARADISICAL
PARADOCTOR
PARADOCTORS
PARADOXERS
PARADOXICAL
PARADOXICALITY
PARADOXICALLY
PARADOXICALNESS
PARADOXIDIAN
PARADOXIES
PARADOXIST
PARADOXISTS
PARADOXOLOGIES
PARADOXOLOGY
PARADOXURE
PARADOXURES
PARADOXURINE
PARADOXURINES
PARADROPPED
PARADROPPING
PARAENESES
PARAENESIS
PARAENETIC
PARAENETICAL
PARAESTHESIA
PARAESTHESIAS
PARAESTHETIC
PARAFFINED
PARAFFINES
PARAFFINIC
PARAFFINIER
PARAFFINIEST
PARAFFINING
PARAFFINOID
PARAGENESES
PARAGENESIA
PARAGENESIAS
PARAGENESIS
PARAGENETIC
PARAGENETICALLY
PARAGLIDED
PARAGLIDER
PARAGLIDERS
PARAGLIDES
PARAGLIDING
PARAGLIDINGS
PARAGLOSSA
PARAGLOSSAE
PARAGLOSSAL
PARAGLOSSATE
PARAGNATHISM
PARAGNATHISMS
PARAGNATHOUS
PARAGNOSES
PARAGNOSIS
PARAGOGICAL
PARAGOGICALLY
PARAGOGUES
PARAGONING
PARAGONITE
PARAGONITES
PARAGRAMMATIST
PARAGRAMMATISTS
PARAGRAPHED

PARAGRAPHER
PARAGRAPHERS
PARAGRAPHIA
PARAGRAPHIAS
PARAGRAPHIC
PARAGRAPHICAL
PARAGRAPHICALLY
PARAGRAPHING
PARAGRAPHIST
PARAGRAPHISTS
PARAGRAPHS
PARAHELIOTROPIC
PARAHYDROGEN
PARAHYDROGENS
PARAINFLUENZA
PARAINFLUENZAS
PARAJOURNALISM
PARAJOURNALISMS
PARAKEELYA
PARAKEELYAS
PARAKELIAS
PARAKITING
PARAKITINGS
PARALALIAS
PARALANGUAGE
PARALANGUAGES
PARALDEHYDE
PARALDEHYDES
PARALEGALS
PARALEIPOMENA
PARALEIPOMENON
PARALEIPSES
PARALEIPSIS
PARALEXIAS
PARALIMNION
PARALIMNIONS
PARALINGUISTIC
PARALINGUISTICS
PARALIPOMENA
PARALIPOMENON
PARALIPSES
PARALIPSIS
PARALLACTIC
PARALLACTICAL
PARALLACTICALLY
PARALLAXES
PARALLELED
PARALLELEPIPED
PARALLELEPIPEDA
PARALLELEPIPEDS
PARALLELING
PARALLELINGS
PARALLELISE
PARALLELISED
PARALLELISES
PARALLELISING
PARALLELISM
PARALLELISMS
PARALLELIST
PARALLELISTIC
PARALLELISTS
PARALLELIZE
PARALLELIZED
PARALLELIZES
PARALLELIZING
PARALLELLED
PARALLELLING
PARALLELLY
PARALLELOGRAM
PARALLELOGRAMS
PARALLELOPIPED
PARALLELOPIPEDA
PARALLELOPIPEDS
PARALLELWISE
PARALOGIAS
PARALOGIES
PARALOGISE
PARALOGISED
PARALOGISES
PARALOGISING
PARALOGISM
PARALOGISMS
PARALOGIST
PARALOGISTIC
PARALOGISTS
PARALOGIZE
PARALOGIZED
PARALOGIZES
PARALOGIZING
PARALOGUES
PARALYMPIC
PARALYMPICS
PARALYSATION
PARALYSATIONS
PARALYSERS
PARALYSING
PARALYSINGLY
PARALYTICALLY
PARALYTICS
PARALYZATION
PARALYZATIONS
PARALYZERS
PARALYZING
PARALYZINGLY
PARAMAECIA
PARAMAECIUM
PARAMAGNET
PARAMAGNETIC
PARAMAGNETISM
PARAMAGNETISMS
PARAMAGNETS
PARAMASTOID
PARAMASTOIDS
PARAMATTAS
PARAMECIUM
PARAMECIUMS
PARAMEDICAL
PARAMEDICALS
PARAMEDICO
PARAMEDICOS
PARAMEDICS
PARAMENSTRUA
PARAMENSTRUUM
PARAMENSTRUUMS
PARAMETERISE
PARAMETERISED
PARAMETERISES
PARAMETERISING
PARAMETERIZE
PARAMETERIZED
PARAMETERIZES
PARAMETERIZING
PARAMETERS
PARAMETRAL
PARAMETRIC
PARAMETRICAL
PARAMETRICALLY
PARAMETRISATION
PARAMETRISE
PARAMETRISED
PARAMETRISES
PARAMETRISING
PARAMETRIZATION
PARAMETRIZE
PARAMETRIZED
PARAMETRIZES
PARAMETRIZING
PARAMILITARIES
PARAMILITARY
PARAMNESIA
PARAMNESIAS
PARAMOECIA
PARAMOECIUM
PARAMORPHIC
PARAMORPHINE
PARAMORPHINES
PARAMORPHISM
PARAMORPHISMS
PARAMORPHOUS
PARAMORPHS
PARAMOUNCIES
PARAMOUNCY
PARAMOUNTCIES
PARAMOUNTCY
PARAMOUNTLY
PARAMOUNTS
PARAMYLUMS
PARAMYXOVIRUS
PARAMYXOVIRUSES
PARANEPHRIC
PARANEPHROS
PARANEPHROSES
PARANOEICS
PARANOIACS
PARANOICALLY
PARANOIDAL
PARANORMAL
PARANORMALITIES
PARANORMALITY
PARANORMALLY
PARANORMALS
PARANTHELIA
PARANTHELION
PARANTHROPUS
PARANTHROPUSES
PARANYMPHS
PARAPARESES
PARAPARESIS
PARAPARETIC
PARAPENTES
PARAPENTING
PARAPENTINGS
PARAPERIODIC
PARAPHASIA
PARAPHASIAS
PARAPHASIC
PARAPHERNALIA
PARAPHILIA
PARAPHILIAC
PARAPHILIACS
PARAPHILIAS
PARAPHIMOSES
PARAPHIMOSIS
PARAPHONIA
PARAPHONIAS
PARAPHONIC
PARAPHRASABLE
PARAPHRASE
PARAPHRASED
PARAPHRASER
PARAPHRASERS
PARAPHRASES
PARAPHRASING
PARAPHRAST
PARAPHRASTIC
PARAPHRASTICAL
PARAPHRASTS
PARAPHRAXES
PARAPHRAXIA
PARAPHRAXIAS
PARAPHRAXIS
PARAPHRENIA
PARAPHRENIAS
PARAPHYSATE
PARAPHYSES
PARAPHYSIS
PARAPINEAL
PARAPLANNER
PARAPLANNERS
PARAPLEGIA
PARAPLEGIAS
PARAPLEGIC
PARAPLEGICS
PARAPODIAL
PARAPODIUM
PARAPOPHYSES
PARAPOPHYSIAL
PARAPOPHYSIS
PARAPRAXES
PARAPRAXIS

PARAPRAXISES
PARAPSYCHIC
PARAPSYCHICAL
PARAPSYCHISM
PARAPSYCHISMS
PARAPSYCHOLOGY
PARAPSYCHOSES
PARAPSYCHOSIS
PARAQUADRATE
PARAQUADRATES
PARAQUITOS
PARARHYMES
PARAROSANILINE
PARAROSANILINES
PARARTHRIA
PARARTHRIAS
PARASAILED
PARASAILING
PARASAILINGS
PARASCENDER
PARASCENDERS
PARASCENDING
PARASCENDINGS
PARASCENIA
PARASCENIUM
PARASCEVES
PARASCIENCE
PARASCIENCES
PARASELENAE
PARASELENE
PARASELENIC
PARASEXUAL
PARASEXUALITIES
PARASEXUALITY
PARASHIOTH
PARASITAEMIA
PARASITAEMIAS
PARASITICAL
PARASITICALLY
PARASITICALNESS
PARASITICIDAL
PARASITICIDE
PARASITICIDES
PARASITISATION
PARASITISATIONS
PARASITISE
PARASITISED
PARASITISES
PARASITISING
PARASITISM
PARASITISMS
PARASITIZATION
PARASITIZATIONS
PARASITIZE
PARASITIZED
PARASITIZES
PARASITIZING
PARASITOID
PARASITOIDS
PARASITOLOGIC
PARASITOLOGICAL
PARASITOLOGIES
PARASITOLOGIST
PARASITOLOGISTS
PARASITOLOGY
PARASITOSES
PARASITOSIS
PARASKIING
PARASKIINGS
PARASOMNIA
PARASOMNIAS
PARASPHENOID
PARASPHENOIDS
PARASTATAL
PARASTATALS
PARASTICHIES
PARASTICHOUS
PARASTICHY
PARASUICIDE
PARASUICIDES
PARASYMBIONT
PARASYMBIONTS
PARASYMBIOSES
PARASYMBIOSIS
PARASYMBIOTIC
PARASYMPATHETIC
PARASYNAPSES
PARASYNAPSIS
PARASYNAPTIC
PARASYNTHESES
PARASYNTHESIS
PARASYNTHETA
PARASYNTHETIC
PARASYNTHETON
PARATACTIC
PARATACTICAL
PARATACTICALLY
PARATANIWHA
PARATANIWHAS
PARATHESES
PARATHESIS
PARATHIONS
PARATHORMONE
PARATHORMONES
PARATHYROID
PARATHYROIDS
PARATROOPER
PARATROOPERS
PARATROOPS
PARATUNGSTIC
PARATYPHOID
PARATYPHOIDS
PARAWALKER
PARAWALKERS
PARBOILING
PARBREAKED
PARBREAKING
PARBUCKLED
PARBUCKLES
PARBUCKLING
PARCELLING
PARCELWISE
PARCENARIES
PARCHEDNESS
PARCHEDNESSES
PARCHEESIS
PARCHMENTIER
PARCHMENTIEST
PARCHMENTISE
PARCHMENTISED
PARCHMENTISES
PARCHMENTISING
PARCHMENTIZE
PARCHMENTIZED
PARCHMENTIZES
PARCHMENTIZING
PARCHMENTS
PARCHMENTY
PARCIMONIES
PARDALISES
PARDALOTES
PARDONABLE
PARDONABLENESS
PARDONABLY
PARDONINGS
PARDONLESS
PAREGORICS
PAREIDOLIA
PAREIDOLIAS
PARENCEPHALA
PARENCEPHALON
PARENCHYMA
PARENCHYMAL
PARENCHYMAS
PARENCHYMATA
PARENCHYMATOUS
PARENTAGES
PARENTALLY
PARENTERAL
PARENTERALLY
PARENTHESES
PARENTHESIS
PARENTHESISE
PARENTHESISED
PARENTHESISES
PARENTHESISING
PARENTHESIZE
PARENTHESIZED
PARENTHESIZES
PARENTHESIZING
PARENTHETIC
PARENTHETICAL
PARENTHETICALLY
PARENTHOOD
PARENTHOODS
PARENTINGS
PARENTLESS
PARESTHESIA
PARESTHESIAS
PARESTHETIC
PARFLECHES
PARFLESHES
PARFOCALISE
PARFOCALISED
PARFOCALISES
PARFOCALISING
PARFOCALITIES
PARFOCALITY
PARFOCALIZE
PARFOCALIZED
PARFOCALIZES
PARFOCALIZING
PARGASITES
PARGETINGS
PARGETTERS
PARGETTING
PARGETTINGS
PARGYLINES
PARHELIACAL
PARHELIONS
PARHYPATES
PARIPINNATE
PARISCHANE
PARISCHANES
PARISCHANS
PARISHIONER
PARISHIONERS
PARISYLLABIC
PARKINSONIAN
PARKINSONIANS
PARKINSONISM
PARKINSONISMS
PARKLEAVES
PARLEMENTS
PARLEYVOOED
PARLEYVOOING
PARLEYVOOS
PARLIAMENT
PARLIAMENTARIAN
PARLIAMENTARILY
PARLIAMENTARISM
PARLIAMENTARY
PARLIAMENTING
PARLIAMENTINGS
PARLIAMENTS
PARLOURMAID
PARLOURMAIDS
PARLOUSNESS
PARLOUSNESSES
PARMACITIE
PARMACITIES
PARMIGIANA
PARMIGIANO
PARMIGIANOS
PAROCCIPITAL
PAROCCIPITALS
PAROCHIALISE
PAROCHIALISED
PAROCHIALISES
PAROCHIALISING

PAROCHIALISM
PAROCHIALISMS
PAROCHIALITIES
PAROCHIALITY
PAROCHIALIZE
PAROCHIALIZED
PAROCHIALIZES
PAROCHIALIZING
PAROCHIALLY
PAROCHINES
PARODISTIC
PAROECIOUS
PAROECISMS
PAROEMIACS
PAROEMIOGRAPHER
PAROEMIOGRAPHY
PAROEMIOLOGIES
PAROEMIOLOGY
PARONOMASIA
PARONOMASIAS
PARONOMASIES
PARONOMASTIC
PARONOMASTICAL
PARONOMASY
PARONYCHIA
PARONYCHIAL
PARONYCHIAS
PARONYMIES
PARONYMOUS
PARONYMOUSLY
PAROTIDITIC
PAROTIDITIS
PAROTIDITISES
PAROTITIDES
PAROTITISES
PAROXETINE
PAROXETINES
PAROXYSMAL
PAROXYSMALLY
PAROXYSMIC
PAROXYTONE
PAROXYTONES
PAROXYTONIC
PARQUETING
PARQUETRIES
PARQUETTED
PARQUETTING
PARRAKEETS
PARRAMATTA
PARRAMATTAS
PARRHESIAS
PARRICIDAL
PARRICIDES
PARRITCHES
PARROCKING
PARROQUETS
PARROTFISH
PARROTFISHES
PARROTIEST
PARROTRIES
PARSIMONIES
PARSIMONIOUS
PARSIMONIOUSLY
PARSONAGES
PARSONICAL
PARTAKINGS
PARTHENOCARPIC
PARTHENOCARPIES
PARTHENOCARPOUS
PARTHENOCARPY
PARTHENOGENESES
PARTHENOGENESIS
PARTHENOGENETIC
PARTHENOSPORE
PARTHENOSPORES
PARTIALISE
PARTIALISED
PARTIALISES
PARTIALISING
PARTIALISM
PARTIALISMS
PARTIALIST
PARTIALISTS
PARTIALITIES
PARTIALITY
PARTIALIZE
PARTIALIZED
PARTIALIZES
PARTIALIZING
PARTIALLED
PARTIALLING
PARTIALNESS
PARTIALNESSES
PARTIBILITIES
PARTIBILITY
PARTICIPABLE
PARTICIPANT
PARTICIPANTLY
PARTICIPANTS
PARTICIPATE
PARTICIPATED
PARTICIPATES
PARTICIPATING
PARTICIPATION
PARTICIPATIONAL
PARTICIPATIONS
PARTICIPATIVE
PARTICIPATOR
PARTICIPATORS
PARTICIPATORY
PARTICIPIAL
PARTICIPIALLY
PARTICIPIALS
PARTICIPLE
PARTICIPLES
PARTICLEBOARD
PARTICLEBOARDS
PARTICOLORED
PARTICOLOURED
PARTICULAR
PARTICULARISE
PARTICULARISED
PARTICULARISER
PARTICULARISERS
PARTICULARISES
PARTICULARISING
PARTICULARISM
PARTICULARISMS
PARTICULARIST
PARTICULARISTIC
PARTICULARISTS
PARTICULARITIES
PARTICULARITY
PARTICULARIZE
PARTICULARIZED
PARTICULARIZER
PARTICULARIZERS
PARTICULARIZES
PARTICULARIZING
PARTICULARLY
PARTICULARNESS
PARTICULARS
PARTICULATE
PARTICULATES
PARTISANLY
PARTISANSHIP
PARTISANSHIPS
PARTITIONED
PARTITIONER
PARTITIONERS
PARTITIONING
PARTITIONIST
PARTITIONISTS
PARTITIONMENT
PARTITIONMENTS
PARTITIONS
PARTITIVELY
PARTITIVES
PARTITURAS
PARTIZANLY
PARTIZANSHIP
PARTIZANSHIPS
PARTNERING
PARTNERINGS
PARTNERLESS
PARTNERSHIP
PARTNERSHIPS
PARTRIDGEBERRY
PARTRIDGES
PARTURIENCIES
PARTURIENCY
PARTURIENT
PARTURIENTS
PARTURIFACIENT
PARTURIFACIENTS
PARTURITION
PARTURITIONS
PARTYGOERS
PARURETICS
PARVANIMITIES
PARVANIMITY
PARVIFOLIATE
PARVOLINES
PARVOVIRUS
PARVOVIRUSES
PASIGRAPHIC
PASIGRAPHICAL
PASIGRAPHIES
PASIGRAPHY
PASODOBLES
PASQUEFLOWER
PASQUEFLOWERS
PASQUILANT
PASQUILANTS
PASQUILERS
PASQUILLED
PASQUILLING
PASQUINADE
PASQUINADED
PASQUINADER
PASQUINADERS
PASQUINADES
PASQUINADING
PASSABLENESS
PASSABLENESSES
PASSACAGLIA
PASSACAGLIAS
PASSAGEWAY
PASSAGEWAYS
PASSAGEWORK
PASSAGEWORKS
PASSALONGS
PASSAMENTED
PASSAMENTING
PASSAMENTS
PASSAMEZZO
PASSAMEZZOS
PASSEMEASURE
PASSEMEASURES
PASSEMENTED
PASSEMENTERIE
PASSEMENTERIES
PASSEMENTING
PASSEMENTS
PASSENGERS
PASSEPIEDS
PASSERIFORM
PASSERINES
PASSIBILITIES
PASSIBILITY
PASSIBLENESS
PASSIBLENESSES
PASSIFLORA
PASSIFLORACEOUS
PASSIFLORAS
PASSIMETER
PASSIMETERS
PASSIONALS
PASSIONARIES
PASSIONARY

PASSIONATE
PASSIONATED
PASSIONATELY
PASSIONATENESS
PASSIONATES
PASSIONATING
PASSIONFLOWER
PASSIONFLOWERS
PASSIONING
PASSIONLESS
PASSIONLESSLY
PASSIONLESSNESS
PASSIVATED
PASSIVATES
PASSIVATING
PASSIVATION
PASSIVATIONS
PASSIVENESS
PASSIVENESSES
PASSIVISMS
PASSIVISTS
PASSIVITIES
PASSMENTED
PASSMENTING
PASSPORTED
PASSPORTING
PASTEBOARD
PASTEBOARDS
PASTEDOWNS
PASTELISTS
PASTELLIST
PASTELLISTS
PASTEURELLA
PASTEURELLAE
PASTEURELLAS
PASTEURISATION
PASTEURISATIONS
PASTEURISE
PASTEURISED
PASTEURISER
PASTEURISERS
PASTEURISES
PASTEURISING
PASTEURISM
PASTEURISMS
PASTEURIZATION
PASTEURIZATIONS
PASTEURIZE
PASTEURIZED
PASTEURIZER
PASTEURIZERS
PASTEURIZES
PASTEURIZING
PASTICCIOS
PASTICHEUR
PASTICHEURS
PASTINESSES
PASTITSIOS
PASTNESSES
PASTORALES
PASTORALISM
PASTORALISMS
PASTORALIST
PASTORALISTS
PASTORALLY
PASTORALNESS
PASTORALNESSES
PASTORATES
PASTORIUMS
PASTORLIER
PASTORLIEST
PASTORSHIP
PASTORSHIPS
PASTOURELLE
PASTOURELLES
PASTRYCOOK
PASTRYCOOKS
PASTURABLE
PASTURAGES
PASTURELAND
PASTURELANDS
PASTURELESS
PATAPHYSICS
PATCHBOARD
PATCHBOARDS
PATCHCOCKE
PATCHCOCKES
PATCHERIES
PATCHINESS
PATCHINESSES
PATCHOCKES
PATCHOULIES
PATCHOULIS
PATCHWORKED
PATCHWORKING
PATCHWORKS
PATELLECTOMIES
PATELLECTOMY
PATELLIFORM
PATENTABILITIES
PATENTABILITY
PATENTABLE
PATERCOVES
PATEREROES
PATERFAMILIAS
PATERFAMILIASES
PATERNALISM
PATERNALISMS
PATERNALIST
PATERNALISTIC
PATERNALISTS
PATERNALLY
PATERNITIES
PATERNOSTER
PATERNOSTERS
PATHBREAKING
PATHETICAL
PATHETICALLY
PATHFINDER
PATHFINDERS
PATHFINDING
PATHFINDINGS
PATHLESSNESS
PATHLESSNESSES
PATHOBIOLOGIES
PATHOBIOLOGY
PATHOGENES
PATHOGENESES
PATHOGENESIS
PATHOGENETIC
PATHOGENIC
PATHOGENICITIES
PATHOGENICITY
PATHOGENIES
PATHOGENOUS
PATHOGNOMIES
PATHOGNOMONIC
PATHOGNOMY
PATHOGRAPHIES
PATHOGRAPHY
PATHOLOGIC
PATHOLOGICAL
PATHOLOGICALLY
PATHOLOGIES
PATHOLOGISE
PATHOLOGISED
PATHOLOGISES
PATHOLOGISING
PATHOLOGIST
PATHOLOGISTS
PATHOLOGIZE
PATHOLOGIZED
PATHOLOGIZES
PATHOLOGIZING
PATHOPHOBIA
PATHOPHOBIAS
PATHOPHYSIOLOGY
PATIBULARY
PATIENTEST
PATIENTING
PATINATING
PATINATION
PATINATIONS
PATINISING
PATINIZING
PATISSERIE
PATISSERIES
PATISSIERS
PATRESFAMILIAS
PATRIALISATION
PATRIALISATIONS
PATRIALISE
PATRIALISED
PATRIALISES
PATRIALISING
PATRIALISM
PATRIALISMS
PATRIALITIES
PATRIALITY
PATRIALIZATION
PATRIALIZATIONS
PATRIALIZE
PATRIALIZED
PATRIALIZES
PATRIALIZING
PATRIARCHAL
PATRIARCHALISM
PATRIARCHALISMS
PATRIARCHALLY
PATRIARCHATE
PATRIARCHATES
PATRIARCHIES
PATRIARCHISM
PATRIARCHISMS
PATRIARCHS
PATRIARCHY
PATRIATING
PATRIATION
PATRIATIONS
PATRICIANLY
PATRICIANS
PATRICIATE
PATRICIATES
PATRICIDAL
PATRICIDES
PATRICLINIC
PATRICLINOUS
PATRIFOCAL
PATRIFOCALITIES
PATRIFOCALITY
PATRILINEAGE
PATRILINEAGES
PATRILINEAL
PATRILINEALLY
PATRILINEAR
PATRILINEARLY
PATRILINIES
PATRILOCAL
PATRILOCALLY
PATRIMONIAL
PATRIMONIALLY
PATRIMONIES
PATRIOTICALLY
PATRIOTISM
PATRIOTISMS
PATRISTICAL
PATRISTICALLY
PATRISTICISM
PATRISTICISMS
PATRISTICS
PATROCLINAL
PATROCLINIC
PATROCLINIES
PATROCLINOUS
PATROCLINY
PATROLLERS
PATROLLING
PATROLOGICAL
PATROLOGIES
PATROLOGIST

PATROLOGISTS
PATROLWOMAN
PATROLWOMEN
PATRONAGED
PATRONAGES
PATRONAGING
PATRONESSES
PATRONISATION
PATRONISATIONS
PATRONISED
PATRONISER
PATRONISERS
PATRONISES
PATRONISING
PATRONISINGLY
PATRONIZATION
PATRONIZATIONS
PATRONIZED
PATRONIZER
PATRONIZERS
PATRONIZES
PATRONIZING
PATRONIZINGLY
PATRONLESS
PATRONLIER
PATRONLIEST
PATRONYMIC
PATRONYMICS
PATROONSHIP
PATROONSHIPS
PATTERNING
PATTERNINGS
PATTERNLESS
PATTRESSES
PATULOUSLY
PATULOUSNESS
PATULOUSNESSES
PAUCILOQUENT
PAUGHTIEST
PAULOWNIAS
PAUNCHIEST
PAUNCHINESS
PAUNCHINESSES
PAUPERDOMS
PAUPERESSES
PAUPERISATION
PAUPERISATIONS
PAUPERISED
PAUPERISES
PAUPERISING
PAUPERISMS
PAUPERIZATION
PAUPERIZATIONS
PAUPERIZED
PAUPERIZES
PAUPERIZING
PAUPIETTES
PAUSEFULLY
PAUSELESSLY
PAVEMENTED
PAVEMENTING
PAVILIONED
PAVILIONING
PAVONAZZOS
PAWKINESSES
PAWNBROKER
PAWNBROKERS
PAWNBROKING
PAWNBROKINGS
PAWNTICKET
PAWNTICKETS
PAYCHEQUES
PAYMASTERS
PAYNIMRIES
PAYSAGISTS
PEABERRIES
PEACEABLENESS
PEACEABLENESSES
PEACEFULLER
PEACEFULLEST
PEACEFULLY
PEACEFULNESS
PEACEFULNESSES
PEACEKEEPER
PEACEKEEPERS
PEACEKEEPING
PEACEKEEPINGS
PEACELESSNESS
PEACELESSNESSES
PEACEMAKER
PEACEMAKERS
PEACEMAKING
PEACEMAKINGS
PEACETIMES
PEACHBLOWS
PEACHERINO
PEACHERINOS
PEACHINESS
PEACHINESSES
PEACOCKERIES
PEACOCKERY
PEACOCKIER
PEACOCKIEST
PEACOCKING
PEACOCKISH
PEAKEDNESS
PEAKEDNESSES
PEAKINESSES
PEANUTTIER
PEANUTTIEST
PEARLASHES
PEARLESCENCE
PEARLESCENCES
PEARLESCENT
PEARLINESS
PEARLINESSES
PEARLWARES
PEARLWORTS
PEARMONGER
PEARMONGERS
PEARTNESSES
PEASANTIER
PEASANTIEST
PEASANTRIES
PEASHOOTER
PEASHOOTERS
PEASOUPERS
PEBBLEDASH
PEBBLEDASHED
PEBBLEDASHES
PEBBLEDASHING
PEBBLEWEAVE
PEBBLEWEAVES
PECCABILITIES
PECCABILITY
PECCADILLO
PECCADILLOES
PECCADILLOS
PECCANCIES
PECKISHNESS
PECKISHNESSES
PECTINACEOUS
PECTINATED
PECTINATELY
PECTINATION
PECTINATIONS
PECTINESTERASE
PECTINESTERASES
PECTINEUSES
PECTISABLE
PECTISATION
PECTISATIONS
PECTIZABLE
PECTIZATION
PECTIZATIONS
PECTOLITES
PECTORALLY
PECTORILOQUIES
PECTORILOQUY
PECULATING
PECULATION
PECULATIONS
PECULATORS
PECULIARISE
PECULIARISED
PECULIARISES
PECULIARISING
PECULIARITIES
PECULIARITY
PECULIARIZE
PECULIARIZED
PECULIARIZES
PECULIARIZING
PECULIARLY
PECUNIARILY
PEDAGOGICAL
PEDAGOGICALLY
PEDAGOGICS
PEDAGOGIES
PEDAGOGISM
PEDAGOGISMS
PEDAGOGUED
PEDAGOGUERIES
PEDAGOGUERY
PEDAGOGUES
PEDAGOGUING
PEDAGOGUISH
PEDAGOGUISHNESS
PEDAGOGUISM
PEDAGOGUISMS
PEDALBOATS
PEDALLINGS
PEDANTICAL
PEDANTICALLY
PEDANTICISE
PEDANTICISED
PEDANTICISES
PEDANTICISING
PEDANTICISM
PEDANTICISMS
PEDANTICIZE
PEDANTICIZED
PEDANTICIZES
PEDANTICIZING
PEDANTISED
PEDANTISES
PEDANTISING
PEDANTISMS
PEDANTIZED
PEDANTIZES
PEDANTIZING
PEDANTOCRACIES
PEDANTOCRACY
PEDANTOCRAT
PEDANTOCRATIC
PEDANTOCRATS
PEDANTRIES
PEDDLERIES
PEDERASTIC
PEDERASTIES
PEDEREROES
PEDESTALED
PEDESTALING
PEDESTALLED
PEDESTALLING
PEDESTRIAN
PEDESTRIANISE
PEDESTRIANISED
PEDESTRIANISES
PEDESTRIANISING
PEDESTRIANISM
PEDESTRIANISMS
PEDESTRIANIZE
PEDESTRIANIZED
PEDESTRIANIZES
PEDESTRIANIZING
PEDESTRIANS
PEDETENTOUS
PEDIATRICIAN
PEDIATRICIANS

PEDIATRICS
PEDIATRIST
PEDIATRISTS
PEDICELLARIA
PEDICELLARIAE
PEDICELLATE
PEDICULATE
PEDICULATED
PEDICULATES
PEDICULATION
PEDICULATIONS
PEDICULOSES
PEDICULOSIS
PEDICULOUS
PEDICURING
PEDICURIST
PEDICURISTS
PEDIMENTAL
PEDIMENTED
PEDIPALPUS
PEDOGENESES
PEDOGENESIS
PEDOGENETIC
PEDOLOGICAL
PEDOLOGIES
PEDOLOGIST
PEDOLOGISTS
PEDOMETERS
PEDOPHILES
PEDOPHILIA
PEDOPHILIAC
PEDOPHILIACS
PEDOPHILIAS
PEDOPHILIC
PEDOPHILICS
PEDUNCULAR
PEDUNCULATE
PEDUNCULATED
PEDUNCULATION
PEDUNCULATIONS
PEELGARLIC
PEELGARLICS
PEERLESSLY
PEERLESSNESS
PEERLESSNESSES
PEEVISHNESS
PEEVISHNESSES
PEGMATITES
PEGMATITIC
PEIRASTICALLY
PEJORATING
PEJORATION
PEJORATIONS
PEJORATIVE
PEJORATIVELY
PEJORATIVES
PELARGONIC
PELARGONIUM
PELARGONIUMS
PELECYPODS
PELLAGRINS
PELLAGROUS
PELLETIFIED
PELLETIFIES
PELLETIFYING
PELLETISATION
PELLETISATIONS
PELLETISED
PELLETISER
PELLETISERS
PELLETISES
PELLETISING
PELLETIZATION
PELLETIZATIONS
PELLETIZED
PELLETIZER
PELLETIZERS
PELLETIZES
PELLETIZING
PELLICULAR
PELLITORIES
PELLUCIDITIES
PELLUCIDITY
PELLUCIDLY
PELLUCIDNESS
PELLUCIDNESSES
PELMANISMS
PELOLOGIES
PELOTHERAPIES
PELOTHERAPY
PELTATIONS
PELTMONGER
PELTMONGERS
PELVIMETER
PELVIMETERS
PELVIMETRIES
PELVIMETRY
PELYCOSAUR
PELYCOSAURS
PEMPHIGOID
PEMPHIGOIDS
PEMPHIGOUS
PEMPHIGUSES
PENALISATION
PENALISATIONS
PENALISING
PENALITIES
PENALIZATION
PENALIZATIONS
PENALIZING
PENANNULAR
PENCILINGS
PENCILLERS
PENCILLING
PENCILLINGS
PENDENCIES
PENDENTIVE
PENDENTIVES
PENDICLERS
PENDRAGONS
PENDRAGONSHIP
PENDRAGONSHIPS
PENDULATED
PENDULATES
PENDULATING
PENDULOSITIES
PENDULOSITY
PENDULOUSLY
PENDULOUSNESS
PENDULOUSNESSES
PENELOPISE
PENELOPISED
PENELOPISES
PENELOPISING
PENELOPIZE
PENELOPIZED
PENELOPIZES
PENELOPIZING
PENEPLAINS
PENEPLANATION
PENEPLANATIONS
PENEPLANES
PENETRABILITIES
PENETRABILITY
PENETRABLE
PENETRABLENESS
PENETRABLY
PENETRALIA
PENETRALIAN
PENETRANCE
PENETRANCES
PENETRANCIES
PENETRANCY
PENETRANTS
PENETRATED
PENETRATES
PENETRATING
PENETRATINGLY
PENETRATION
PENETRATIONS
PENETRATIVE
PENETRATIVELY
PENETRATIVENESS
PENETRATOR
PENETRATORS
PENETROMETER
PENETROMETERS
PENFRIENDS
PENGUINERIES
PENGUINERY
PENGUINRIES
PENHOLDERS
PENICILLAMINE
PENICILLAMINES
PENICILLATE
PENICILLATELY
PENICILLATION
PENICILLATIONS
PENICILLIA
PENICILLIFORM
PENICILLIN
PENICILLINASE
PENICILLINASES
PENICILLINS
PENICILLIUM
PENICILLIUMS
PENICILLUS
PENINSULAR
PENINSULARITIES
PENINSULARITY
PENINSULAS
PENINSULATE
PENINSULATED
PENINSULATES
PENINSULATING
PENISTONES
PENITENCES
PENITENCIES
PENITENTIAL
PENITENTIALLY
PENITENTIALS
PENITENTIARIES
PENITENTIARY
PENITENTLY
PENMANSHIP
PENMANSHIPS
PENNACEOUS
PENNALISMS
PENNATULACEOUS
PENNATULAE
PENNATULAS
PENNILESSLY
PENNILESSNESS
PENNILESSNESSES
PENNILLION
PENNINITES
PENNONCELLE
PENNONCELLES
PENNONCELS
PENNYCRESS
PENNYCRESSES
PENNYLANDS
PENNYROYAL
PENNYROYALS
PENNYWEIGHT
PENNYWEIGHTS
PENNYWHISTLE
PENNYWHISTLES
PENNYWINKLE
PENNYWINKLES
PENNYWORTH
PENNYWORTHS
PENNYWORTS
PENOLOGICAL
PENOLOGICALLY
PENOLOGIES
PENOLOGIST
PENOLOGISTS
PENONCELLE
PENONCELLES

PENPUSHERS
PENPUSHING
PENPUSHINGS
PENSEROSOS
PENSIEROSO
PENSILENESS
PENSILENESSES
PENSILITIES
PENSIONABLE
PENSIONARIES
PENSIONARY
PENSIONEER
PENSIONERS
PENSIONING
PENSIONLESS
PENSIONNAT
PENSIONNATS
PENSIVENESS
PENSIVENESSES
PENSTEMONS
PENTABARBITAL
PENTABARBITALS
PENTACHORD
PENTACHORDS
PENTACRINOID
PENTACRINOIDS
PENTACTINAL
PENTACYCLIC
PENTADACTYL
PENTADACTYLE
PENTADACTYLES
PENTADACTYLIC
PENTADACTYLIES
PENTADACTYLISM
PENTADACTYLISMS
PENTADACTYLOUS
PENTADACTYLS
PENTADACTYLY
PENTADELPHOUS
PENTAGONAL
PENTAGONALLY
PENTAGONALS
PENTAGRAMS
PENTAGRAPH
PENTAGRAPHS
PENTAGYNIAN
PENTAGYNOUS
PENTAHEDRA
PENTAHEDRAL
PENTAHEDRON
PENTAHEDRONS
PENTAHYDRATE
PENTAHYDRATES
PENTALOGIES
PENTALPHAS
PENTAMERIES
PENTAMERISM
PENTAMERISMS
PENTAMEROUS
PENTAMETER
PENTAMETERS
PENTAMIDINE
PENTAMIDINES
PENTANDRIAN
PENTANDROUS
PENTANGLES
PENTANGULAR
PENTAPEPTIDE
PENTAPEPTIDES
PENTAPLOID
PENTAPLOIDIES
PENTAPLOIDS
PENTAPLOIDY
PENTAPODIC
PENTAPODIES
PENTAPOLIS
PENTAPOLISES
PENTAPOLITAN
PENTAPRISM
PENTAPRISMS
PENTAQUARK
PENTAQUARKS
PENTARCHICAL
PENTARCHIES
PENTASTICH
PENTASTICHOUS
PENTASTICHS
PENTASTYLE
PENTASTYLES
PENTASYLLABIC
PENTATEUCHAL
PENTATHLETE
PENTATHLETES
PENTATHLON
PENTATHLONS
PENTATHLUM
PENTATHLUMS
PENTATOMIC
PENTATONIC
PENTAVALENCE
PENTAVALENCES
PENTAVALENCIES
PENTAVALENCY
PENTAVALENT
PENTAZOCINE
PENTAZOCINES
PENTECONTER
PENTECONTERS
PENTETERIC
PENTHEMIMER
PENTHEMIMERAL
PENTHEMIMERS
PENTHOUSED
PENTHOUSES
PENTHOUSING
PENTIMENTI
PENTIMENTO
PENTLANDITE
PENTLANDITES
PENTOBARBITAL
PENTOBARBITALS
PENTOBARBITONE
PENTOBARBITONES
PENTOSANES
PENTOSIDES
PENTOXIDES
PENTSTEMON
PENTSTEMONS
PENTYLENES
PENULTIMAS
PENULTIMATE
PENULTIMATELY
PENULTIMATES
PENUMBROUS
PENURIOUSLY
PENURIOUSNESS
PENURIOUSNESSES
PEOPLEHOOD
PEOPLEHOODS
PEOPLELESS
PEPEROMIAS
PEPPERBOXES
PEPPERCORN
PEPPERCORNIER
PEPPERCORNIEST
PEPPERCORNS
PEPPERCORNY
PEPPERGRASS
PEPPERGRASSES
PEPPERIDGE
PEPPERIDGES
PEPPERIEST
PEPPERINESS
PEPPERINESSES
PEPPERINGS
PEPPERMILL
PEPPERMILLS
PEPPERMINT
PEPPERMINTIER
PEPPERMINTIEST
PEPPERMINTS
PEPPERMINTY
PEPPERONIS
PEPPERTREE
PEPPERTREES
PEPPERWORT
PEPPERWORTS
PEPPINESSES
PEPSINATED
PEPSINATES
PEPSINATING
PEPSINOGEN
PEPSINOGENS
PEPTALKING
PEPTICITIES
PEPTIDASES
PEPTIDOGLYCAN
PEPTIDOGLYCANS
PEPTISABLE
PEPTISATION
PEPTISATIONS
PEPTIZABLE
PEPTIZATION
PEPTIZATIONS
PEPTONISATION
PEPTONISATIONS
PEPTONISED
PEPTONISER
PEPTONISERS
PEPTONISES
PEPTONISING
PEPTONIZATION
PEPTONIZATIONS
PEPTONIZED
PEPTONIZER
PEPTONIZERS
PEPTONIZES
PEPTONIZING
PERACIDITIES
PERACIDITY
PERADVENTURE
PERADVENTURES
PERAEOPODS
PERAMBULATE
PERAMBULATED
PERAMBULATES
PERAMBULATING
PERAMBULATION
PERAMBULATIONS
PERAMBULATOR
PERAMBULATORS
PERAMBULATORY
PERBORATES
PERCALINES
PERCEIVABILITY
PERCEIVABLE
PERCEIVABLY
PERCEIVERS
PERCEIVING
PERCEIVINGS
PERCENTAGE
PERCENTAGES
PERCENTILE
PERCENTILES
PERCEPTIBILITY
PERCEPTIBLE
PERCEPTIBLY
PERCEPTION
PERCEPTIONAL
PERCEPTIONS
PERCEPTIVE
PERCEPTIVELY
PERCEPTIVENESS
PERCEPTIVITIES
PERCEPTIVITY
PERCEPTUAL
PERCEPTUALLY
PERCHERIES
PERCHERONS
PERCHLORATE

P

PERCHLORATES
PERCHLORIC
PERCHLORIDE
PERCHLORIDES
PERCHLOROETHENE
PERCIFORMS
PERCIPIENCE
PERCIPIENCES
PERCIPIENCIES
PERCIPIENCY
PERCIPIENT
PERCIPIENTLY
PERCIPIENTS
PERCOCTING
PERCOIDEAN
PERCOIDEANS
PERCOLABLE
PERCOLATED
PERCOLATES
PERCOLATING
PERCOLATION
PERCOLATIONS
PERCOLATIVE
PERCOLATOR
PERCOLATORS
PERCURRENT
PERCURSORY
PERCUSSANT
PERCUSSING
PERCUSSION
PERCUSSIONAL
PERCUSSIONIST
PERCUSSIONISTS
PERCUSSIONS
PERCUSSIVE
PERCUSSIVELY
PERCUSSIVENESS
PERCUSSORS
PERCUTANEOUS
PERCUTANEOUSLY
PERCUTIENT
PERCUTIENTS
PERDENDOSI
PERDITIONABLE
PERDITIONS
PERDUELLION
PERDUELLIONS
PERDURABILITIES
PERDURABILITY
PERDURABLE
PERDURABLY
PERDURANCE
PERDURANCES
PERDURATION
PERDURATIONS
PEREGRINATE
PEREGRINATED
PEREGRINATES
PEREGRINATING
PEREGRINATION
PEREGRINATIONS
PEREGRINATOR
PEREGRINATORS
PEREGRINATORY
PEREGRINES
PEREGRINITIES
PEREGRINITY
PEREIOPODS
PEREMPTORILY
PEREMPTORINESS
PEREMPTORY
PERENNATED
PERENNATES
PERENNATING
PERENNATION
PERENNATIONS
PERENNIALITIES
PERENNIALITY
PERENNIALLY
PERENNIALS
PERENNIBRANCH
PERENNIBRANCHS
PERENNITIES
PERESTROIKA
PERESTROIKAS
PERFECTATION
PERFECTATIONS
PERFECTERS
PERFECTEST
PERFECTIBILIAN
PERFECTIBILIANS
PERFECTIBILISM
PERFECTIBILISMS
PERFECTIBILIST
PERFECTIBILISTS
PERFECTIBILITY
PERFECTIBLE
PERFECTING
PERFECTION
PERFECTIONATE
PERFECTIONATED
PERFECTIONATES
PERFECTIONATING
PERFECTIONISM
PERFECTIONISMS
PERFECTIONIST
PERFECTIONISTIC
PERFECTIONISTS
PERFECTIONS
PERFECTIVE
PERFECTIVELY
PERFECTIVENESS
PERFECTIVES
PERFECTIVITIES
PERFECTIVITY
PERFECTNESS
PERFECTNESSES
PERFECTORS
PERFERVIDITIES
PERFERVIDITY
PERFERVIDLY
PERFERVIDNESS
PERFERVIDNESSES
PERFERVORS
PERFERVOUR
PERFERVOURS
PERFICIENT
PERFICIENTS
PERFIDIOUS
PERFIDIOUSLY
PERFIDIOUSNESS
PERFLUOROCARBON
PERFOLIATE
PERFOLIATION
PERFOLIATIONS
PERFORABLE
PERFORANSES
PERFORATED
PERFORATES
PERFORATING
PERFORATION
PERFORATIONS
PERFORATIVE
PERFORATOR
PERFORATORS
PERFORATORY
PERFORATUS
PERFORATUSES
PERFORMABILITY
PERFORMABLE
PERFORMANCE
PERFORMANCES
PERFORMATIVE
PERFORMATIVELY
PERFORMATIVES
PERFORMATORY
PERFORMERS
PERFORMING
PERFORMINGS
PERFUMELESS
PERFUMERIES
PERFUMIERS
PERFUMIEST
PERFUNCTORILY
PERFUNCTORINESS
PERFUNCTORY
PERFUSATES
PERFUSIONIST
PERFUSIONISTS
PERFUSIONS
PERGAMENEOUS
PERGAMENTACEOUS
PERGUNNAHS
PERIASTRON
PERIASTRONS
PERIBLASTS
PERICARDIA
PERICARDIAC
PERICARDIAL
PERICARDIAN
PERICARDITIC
PERICARDITIDES
PERICARDITIS
PERICARDITISES
PERICARDIUM
PERICARDIUMS
PERICARPIAL
PERICARPIC
PERICENTER
PERICENTERS
PERICENTRAL
PERICENTRE
PERICENTRES
PERICENTRIC
PERICHAETIA
PERICHAETIAL
PERICHAETIUM
PERICHONDRAL
PERICHONDRIA
PERICHONDRIAL
PERICHONDRIUM
PERICHORESES
PERICHORESIS
PERICHYLOUS
PERICLASES
PERICLASTIC
PERICLINAL
PERICLINES
PERICLITATE
PERICLITATED
PERICLITATES
PERICLITATING
PERICRANIA
PERICRANIAL
PERICRANIUM
PERICRANIUMS
PERICULOUS
PERICYCLES
PERICYCLIC
PERICYNTHIA
PERICYNTHION
PERICYNTHIONS
PERIDERMAL
PERIDERMIC
PERIDESMIA
PERIDESMIUM
PERIDINIAN
PERIDINIANS
PERIDINIUM
PERIDINIUMS
PERIDOTITE
PERIDOTITES
PERIDOTITIC
PERIDROMES
PERIEGESES
PERIEGESIS
PERIGASTRIC
PERIGASTRITIS
PERIGASTRITISES
PERIGENESES

PERIGENESIS
PERIGLACIAL
PERIGONIAL
PERIGONIUM
PERIGYNIES
PERIGYNOUS
PERIHELIAL
PERIHELION
PERIHEPATIC
PERIHEPATITIS
PERIHEPATITISES
PERIKARYAL
PERIKARYON
PERILOUSLY
PERILOUSNESS
PERILOUSNESSES
PERILYMPHS
PERIMENOPAUSAL
PERIMENOPAUSE
PERIMENOPAUSES
PERIMETERS
PERIMETRAL
PERIMETRIC
PERIMETRICAL
PERIMETRICALLY
PERIMETRIES
PERIMORPHIC
PERIMORPHISM
PERIMORPHISMS
PERIMORPHOUS
PERIMORPHS
PERIMYSIUM
PERINAEUMS
PERINATALLY
PERINEPHRIA
PERINEPHRIC
PERINEPHRITIS
PERINEPHRITISES
PERINEPHRIUM
PERINEURAL
PERINEURIA
PERINEURIAL
PERINEURITIC
PERINEURITIS
PERINEURITISES
PERINEURIUM
PERIODATES
PERIODICAL
PERIODICALIST
PERIODICALISTS
PERIODICALLY
PERIODICALS
PERIODICITIES
PERIODICITY
PERIODIDES
PERIODISATION
PERIODISATIONS
PERIODISED
PERIODISES
PERIODISING
PERIODIZATION
PERIODIZATIONS
PERIODIZED
PERIODIZES
PERIODIZING
PERIODONTAL
PERIODONTALLY
PERIODONTIA
PERIODONTIAS
PERIODONTIC
PERIODONTICALLY
PERIODONTICS
PERIODONTIST
PERIODONTISTS
PERIODONTITIS
PERIODONTITISES
PERIODONTOLOGY
PERIONYCHIA
PERIONYCHIUM
PERIOSTEAL
PERIOSTEUM
PERIOSTITIC
PERIOSTITIDES
PERIOSTITIS
PERIOSTITISES
PERIOSTRACUM
PERIOSTRACUMS
PERIPATETIC
PERIPATETICAL
PERIPATETICALLY
PERIPATETICISM
PERIPATETICISMS
PERIPATETICS
PERIPATUSES
PERIPETEIA
PERIPETEIAN
PERIPETEIAS
PERIPETIAN
PERIPETIAS
PERIPETIES
PERIPHERAL
PERIPHERALITIES
PERIPHERALITY
PERIPHERALLY
PERIPHERALS
PERIPHERIC
PERIPHERICAL
PERIPHERIES
PERIPHONIC
PERIPHRASE
PERIPHRASED
PERIPHRASES
PERIPHRASING
PERIPHRASIS
PERIPHRASTIC
PERIPHRASTICAL
PERIPHYTIC
PERIPHYTON
PERIPHYTONS
PERIPLASMS
PERIPLASTS
PERIPLUSES
PERIPROCTS
PERIPTERAL
PERIPTERIES
PERISARCAL
PERISARCOUS
PERISCIANS
PERISCOPES
PERISCOPIC
PERISCOPICALLY
PERISELENIA
PERISELENIUM
PERISHABILITIES
PERISHABILITY
PERISHABLE
PERISHABLENESS
PERISHABLES
PERISHABLY
PERISHINGLY
PERISPERMAL
PERISPERMIC
PERISPERMS
PERISPOMENA
PERISPOMENON
PERISPOMENONS
PERISSODACTYL
PERISSODACTYLE
PERISSODACTYLES
PERISSODACTYLIC
PERISSODACTYLS
PERISSOLOGIES
PERISSOLOGY
PERISSOSYLLABIC
PERISTALITH
PERISTALITHS
PERISTALSES
PERISTALSIS
PERISTALTIC
PERISTALTICALLY
PERISTERITE
PERISTERITES
PERISTERONIC
PERISTOMAL
PERISTOMATIC
PERISTOMES
PERISTOMIAL
PERISTREPHIC
PERISTYLAR
PERISTYLES
PERITECTIC
PERITECTICS
PERITHECIA
PERITHECIAL
PERITHECIUM
PERITONAEA
PERITONAEAL
PERITONAEUM
PERITONAEUMS
PERITONEAL
PERITONEALLY
PERITONEOSCOPY
PERITONEUM
PERITONEUMS
PERITONITIC
PERITONITIS
PERITONITISES
PERITRACKS
PERITRICHA
PERITRICHOUS
PERITRICHOUSLY
PERITRICHS
PERITYPHLITIS
PERITYPHLITISES
PERIVITELLINE
PERIWIGGED
PERIWIGGING
PERIWINKLE
PERIWINKLES
PERJINKETY
PERJINKITIES
PERJINKITY
PERJURIOUS
PERJURIOUSLY
PERKINESSES
PERLEMOENS
PERLOCUTION
PERLOCUTIONARY
PERLOCUTIONS
PERLUSTRATE
PERLUSTRATED
PERLUSTRATES
PERLUSTRATING
PERLUSTRATION
PERLUSTRATIONS
PERMABEARS
PERMABULLS
PERMACULTURE
PERMACULTURES
PERMAFROST
PERMAFROSTS
PERMALINKS
PERMALLOYS
PERMANENCE
PERMANENCES
PERMANENCIES
PERMANENCY
PERMANENTLY
PERMANENTNESS
PERMANENTNESSES
PERMANENTS
PERMANGANATE
PERMANGANATES
PERMANGANIC
PERMEABILITIES
PERMEABILITY
PERMEABLENESS
PERMEABLENESSES
PERMEAMETER
PERMEAMETERS

PERMEANCES
PERMEATING
PERMEATION
PERMEATIONS
PERMEATIVE
PERMEATORS
PERMETHRIN
PERMETHRINS
PERMILLAGE
PERMILLAGES
PERMISSIBILITY
PERMISSIBLE
PERMISSIBLENESS
PERMISSIBLY
PERMISSION
PERMISSIONS
PERMISSIVE
PERMISSIVELY
PERMISSIVENESS
PERMITTANCE
PERMITTANCES
PERMITTEES
PERMITTERS
PERMITTING
PERMITTIVITIES
PERMITTIVITY
PERMUTABILITIES
PERMUTABILITY
PERMUTABLE
PERMUTABLENESS
PERMUTABLY
PERMUTATED
PERMUTATES
PERMUTATING
PERMUTATION
PERMUTATIONAL
PERMUTATIONS
PERNANCIES
PERNICIOUS
PERNICIOUSLY
PERNICIOUSNESS
PERNICKETIER
PERNICKETIEST
PERNICKETINESS
PERNICKETY
PERNOCTATE
PERNOCTATED
PERNOCTATES
PERNOCTATING
PERNOCTATION
PERNOCTATIONS
PERONEUSES
PERORATING
PERORATION
PERORATIONAL
PERORATIONS
PERORATORS
PEROVSKIAS
PEROVSKITE
PEROVSKITES
PEROXIDASE
PEROXIDASES
PEROXIDATION
PEROXIDATIONS
PEROXIDING
PEROXIDISE
PEROXIDISED
PEROXIDISES
PEROXIDISING
PEROXIDIZE
PEROXIDIZED
PEROXIDIZES
PEROXIDIZING
PEROXISOMAL
PEROXISOME
PEROXISOMES
PEROXYSULPHURIC
PERPENDICULAR
PERPENDICULARLY
PERPENDICULARS
PERPENDING
PERPETRABLE
PERPETRATE
PERPETRATED
PERPETRATES
PERPETRATING
PERPETRATION
PERPETRATIONS
PERPETRATOR
PERPETRATORS
PERPETUABLE
PERPETUALISM
PERPETUALISMS
PERPETUALIST
PERPETUALISTS
PERPETUALITIES
PERPETUALITY
PERPETUALLY
PERPETUALS
PERPETUANCE
PERPETUANCES
PERPETUATE
PERPETUATED
PERPETUATES
PERPETUATING
PERPETUATION
PERPETUATIONS
PERPETUATOR
PERPETUATORS
PERPETUITIES
PERPETUITY
PERPHENAZINE
PERPHENAZINES
PERPLEXEDLY
PERPLEXEDNESS
PERPLEXEDNESSES
PERPLEXERS
PERPLEXING
PERPLEXINGLY
PERPLEXITIES
PERPLEXITY
PERQUISITE
PERQUISITES
PERQUISITION
PERQUISITIONS
PERQUISITOR
PERQUISITORS
PERRUQUIER
PERRUQUIERS
PERSCRUTATION
PERSCRUTATIONS
PERSECUTED
PERSECUTEE
PERSECUTEES
PERSECUTES
PERSECUTING
PERSECUTION
PERSECUTIONS
PERSECUTIVE
PERSECUTOR
PERSECUTORS
PERSECUTORY
PERSEITIES
PERSELINES
PERSEVERANCE
PERSEVERANCES
PERSEVERANT
PERSEVERATE
PERSEVERATED
PERSEVERATES
PERSEVERATING
PERSEVERATION
PERSEVERATIONS
PERSEVERATIVE
PERSEVERATOR
PERSEVERATORS
PERSEVERED
PERSEVERES
PERSEVERING
PERSEVERINGLY
PERSICARIA
PERSICARIAS
PERSIENNES
PERSIFLAGE
PERSIFLAGES
PERSIFLEUR
PERSIFLEURS
PERSIMMONS
PERSISTENCE
PERSISTENCES
PERSISTENCIES
PERSISTENCY
PERSISTENT
PERSISTENTLY
PERSISTENTS
PERSISTERS
PERSISTING
PERSISTINGLY
PERSISTIVE
PERSNICKETIER
PERSNICKETIEST
PERSNICKETINESS
PERSNICKETY
PERSONABLE
PERSONABLENESS
PERSONABLY
PERSONAGES
PERSONALIA
PERSONALISATION
PERSONALISE
PERSONALISED
PERSONALISES
PERSONALISING
PERSONALISM
PERSONALISMS
PERSONALIST
PERSONALISTIC
PERSONALISTS
PERSONALITIES
PERSONALITY
PERSONALIZATION
PERSONALIZE
PERSONALIZED
PERSONALIZES
PERSONALIZING
PERSONALLY
PERSONALTIES
PERSONALTY
PERSONATED
PERSONATES
PERSONATING
PERSONATINGS
PERSONATION
PERSONATIONS
PERSONATIVE
PERSONATOR
PERSONATORS
PERSONHOOD
PERSONHOODS
PERSONIFIABLE
PERSONIFICATION
PERSONIFIED
PERSONIFIER
PERSONIFIERS
PERSONIFIES
PERSONIFYING
PERSONISED
PERSONISES
PERSONISING
PERSONIZED
PERSONIZES
PERSONIZING
PERSONNELS
PERSONPOWER
PERSONPOWERS
PERSPECTIVAL
PERSPECTIVE
PERSPECTIVELY
PERSPECTIVES
PERSPECTIVISM

PERSPECTIVISMS
PERSPECTIVIST
PERSPECTIVISTS
PERSPICACIOUS
PERSPICACIOUSLY
PERSPICACITIES
PERSPICACITY
PERSPICUITIES
PERSPICUITY
PERSPICUOUS
PERSPICUOUSLY
PERSPICUOUSNESS
PERSPIRABLE
PERSPIRATE
PERSPIRATED
PERSPIRATES
PERSPIRATING
PERSPIRATION
PERSPIRATIONS
PERSPIRATORY
PERSPIRIER
PERSPIRIEST
PERSPIRING
PERSPIRINGLY
PERSTRINGE
PERSTRINGED
PERSTRINGES
PERSTRINGING
PERSUADABILITY
PERSUADABLE
PERSUADERS
PERSUADING
PERSUASIBILITY
PERSUASIBLE
PERSUASION
PERSUASIONS
PERSUASIVE
PERSUASIVELY
PERSUASIVENESS
PERSUASIVES
PERSUASORY
PERSULFATE
PERSULFATES
PERSULFURIC
PERSULPHATE
PERSULPHATES
PERSULPHURIC
PERSWADING

PERTAINING
PERTINACIOUS
PERTINACIOUSLY
PERTINACITIES
PERTINACITY
PERTINENCE
PERTINENCES
PERTINENCIES
PERTINENCY
PERTINENTLY
PERTINENTS
PERTNESSES
PERTURBABLE
PERTURBABLY
PERTURBANCE
PERTURBANCES
PERTURBANT
PERTURBANTS
PERTURBATE
PERTURBATED
PERTURBATES
PERTURBATING
PERTURBATION
PERTURBATIONAL
PERTURBATIONS
PERTURBATIVE
PERTURBATOR
PERTURBATORIES
PERTURBATORS
PERTURBATORY
PERTURBEDLY
PERTURBERS
PERTURBING
PERTURBINGLY
PERTUSIONS
PERTUSSISES
PERVASIONS
PERVASIVELY
PERVASIVENESS
PERVASIVENESSES
PERVERSELY
PERVERSENESS
PERVERSENESSES
PERVERSEST
PERVERSION
PERVERSIONS
PERVERSITIES
PERVERSITY

PERVERSIVE
PERVERTEDLY
PERVERTEDNESS
PERVERTEDNESSES
PERVERTERS
PERVERTIBLE
PERVERTING
PERVIATING
PERVICACIES
PERVICACIOUS
PERVICACITIES
PERVICACITY
PERVIOUSLY
PERVIOUSNESS
PERVIOUSNESSES
PESCATARIAN
PESCATARIANS
PESCETARIAN
PESCETARIANS
PESHMERGAS
PESKINESSES
PESSIMISMS
PESSIMISTIC
PESSIMISTICAL
PESSIMISTICALLY
PESSIMISTS
PESTERINGLY
PESTERMENT
PESTERMENTS
PESTHOUSES
PESTICIDAL
PESTICIDES
PESTIFEROUS
PESTIFEROUSLY
PESTIFEROUSNESS
PESTILENCE
PESTILENCES
PESTILENTIAL
PESTILENTIALLY
PESTILENTLY
PESTOLOGICAL
PESTOLOGIES
PESTOLOGIST
PESTOLOGISTS
PETAHERTZES
PETALIFEROUS
PETALODIES
PETALOMANIA

PETALOMANIAS
PETAMETERS
PETAMETRES
PETAURINES
PETAURISTS
PETCHARIES
PETERSHAMS
PETHIDINES
PETIOLATED
PETIOLULES
PETITENESS
PETITENESSES
PETITIONARY
PETITIONED
PETITIONER
PETITIONERS
PETITIONING
PETITIONINGS
PETITIONIST
PETITIONISTS
PETNAPINGS
PETNAPPERS
PETNAPPING
PETNAPPINGS
PETRICHORS
PETRIFACTION
PETRIFACTIONS
PETRIFACTIVE
PETRIFICATION
PETRIFICATIONS
PETRIFIERS
PETRIFYING
PETRISSAGE
PETRISSAGES
PETROCHEMICAL
PETROCHEMICALLY
PETROCHEMICALS
PETROCHEMIST
PETROCHEMISTRY
PETROCHEMISTS
PETROCURRENCIES
PETROCURRENCY
PETRODOLLAR
PETRODOLLARS
PETRODROME
PETRODROMES
PETROGENESES
PETROGENESIS

PETROGENETIC
PETROGENIES
PETROGLYPH
PETROGLYPHIC
PETROGLYPHIES
PETROGLYPHS
PETROGLYPHY
PETROGRAMS
PETROGRAPHER
PETROGRAPHERS
PETROGRAPHIC
PETROGRAPHICAL
PETROGRAPHIES
PETROGRAPHY
PETROLAGES
PETROLATUM
PETROLATUMS
PETROLEOUS
PETROLEUMS
PETROLEURS
PETROLEUSE
PETROLEUSES
PETROLHEAD
PETROLHEADS
PETROLIFEROUS
PETROLLING
PETROLOGIC
PETROLOGICAL
PETROLOGICALLY
PETROLOGIES
PETROLOGIST
PETROLOGISTS
PETROMONEY
PETROMONEYS
PETROMONIES
PETRONELLA
PETRONELLAS
PETROPHYSICAL
PETROPHYSICIST
PETROPHYSICISTS
PETROPHYSICS
PETROPOUNDS
PETROSTATE
PETROSTATES
PETTEDNESS
PETTEDNESSES
PETTICHAPS
PETTICHAPSES

P

PETTICOATED
PETTICOATS
PETTIFOGGED
PETTIFOGGER
PETTIFOGGERIES
PETTIFOGGERS
PETTIFOGGERY
PETTIFOGGING
PETTIFOGGINGS
PETTINESSES
PETTISHNESS
PETTISHNESSES
PETULANCES
PETULANCIES
PETULANTLY
PEWHOLDERS
PEWTERIEST
PHACOLITES
PHACOLITHS
PHAELONION
PHAELONIONS
PHAENOGAMIC
PHAENOGAMOUS
PHAENOGAMS
PHAENOLOGIES
PHAENOLOGY
PHAENOMENA
PHAENOMENON
PHAENOTYPE
PHAENOTYPED
PHAENOTYPES
PHAENOTYPING
PHAEOMELANIN
PHAEOMELANINS
PHAGEDAENA
PHAGEDAENAS
PHAGEDAENIC
PHAGEDENAS
PHAGEDENIC
PHAGOCYTES
PHAGOCYTIC
PHAGOCYTICAL
PHAGOCYTISE
PHAGOCYTISED
PHAGOCYTISES
PHAGOCYTISING
PHAGOCYTISM
PHAGOCYTISMS
PHAGOCYTIZE
PHAGOCYTIZED
PHAGOCYTIZES
PHAGOCYTIZING
PHAGOCYTOSE
PHAGOCYTOSED
PHAGOCYTOSES
PHAGOCYTOSING
PHAGOCYTOSIS
PHAGOCYTOTIC
PHAGOMANIA
PHAGOMANIAC
PHAGOMANIACS
PHAGOMANIAS
PHAGOPHOBIA
PHAGOPHOBIAS
PHAGOSOMES
PHALANGEAL
PHALANGERS
PHALANGIDS
PHALANGIST
PHALANGISTS
PHALANSTERIAN
PHALANSTERIANS
PHALANSTERIES
PHALANSTERISM
PHALANSTERISMS
PHALANSTERIST
PHALANSTERISTS
PHALANSTERY
PHALAROPES
PHALLICALLY
PHALLICISM
PHALLICISMS
PHALLICIST
PHALLICISTS
PHALLOCENTRIC
PHALLOCENTRISM
PHALLOCENTRISMS
PHALLOCRAT
PHALLOCRATIC
PHALLOCRATS
PHALLOIDIN
PHALLOIDINS
PHANEROGAM
PHANEROGAMIC
PHANEROGAMOUS
PHANEROGAMS
PHANEROPHYTE
PHANEROPHYTES
PHANSIGARS
PHANTASIAST
PHANTASIASTS
PHANTASIED
PHANTASIES
PHANTASIME
PHANTASIMES
PHANTASIMS
PHANTASMAGORIA
PHANTASMAGORIAL
PHANTASMAGORIAS
PHANTASMAGORIC
PHANTASMAGORIES
PHANTASMAGORY
PHANTASMAL
PHANTASMALIAN
PHANTASMALITIES
PHANTASMALITY
PHANTASMALLY
PHANTASMATA
PHANTASMIC
PHANTASMICAL
PHANTASMICALLY
PHANTASTIC
PHANTASTICS
PHANTASTRIES
PHANTASTRY
PHANTASYING
PHANTOMATIC
PHANTOMISH
PHANTOMLIKE
PHANTOSMES
PHARISAICAL
PHARISAICALLY
PHARISAICALNESS
PHARISAISM
PHARISAISMS
PHARISEEISM
PHARISEEISMS
PHARMACEUTIC
PHARMACEUTICAL
PHARMACEUTICALS
PHARMACEUTICS
PHARMACEUTIST
PHARMACEUTISTS
PHARMACIES
PHARMACIST
PHARMACISTS
PHARMACODYNAMIC
PHARMACOGENOMIC
PHARMACOGNOSIES
PHARMACOGNOSIST
PHARMACOGNOSTIC
PHARMACOGNOSY
PHARMACOKINETIC
PHARMACOLOGIC
PHARMACOLOGICAL
PHARMACOLOGIES
PHARMACOLOGIST
PHARMACOLOGISTS
PHARMACOLOGY
PHARMACOPEIA
PHARMACOPEIAL
PHARMACOPEIAS
PHARMACOPOEIA
PHARMACOPOEIAL
PHARMACOPOEIAN
PHARMACOPOEIANS
PHARMACOPOEIAS
PHARMACOPOEIC
PHARMACOPOEIST
PHARMACOPOEISTS
PHARMACOPOLIST
PHARMACOPOLISTS
PHARMACOTHERAPY
PHARYNGALS
PHARYNGEAL
PHARYNGEALS
PHARYNGITIC
PHARYNGITIDES
PHARYNGITIS
PHARYNGITISES
PHARYNGOLOGICAL
PHARYNGOLOGIES
PHARYNGOLOGIST
PHARYNGOLOGISTS
PHARYNGOLOGY
PHARYNGOSCOPE
PHARYNGOSCOPES
PHARYNGOSCOPIC
PHARYNGOSCOPIES
PHARYNGOSCOPY
PHARYNGOTOMIES
PHARYNGOTOMY
PHASCOGALE
PHASCOGALES
PHASEDOWNS
PHASEOLINS
PHATICALLY
PHEASANTRIES
PHEASANTRY
PHELLODERM
PHELLODERMAL
PHELLODERMS
PHELLOGENETIC
PHELLOGENIC
PHELLOGENS
PHELLOPLASTIC
PHELLOPLASTICS
PHELONIONS
PHENACAINE
PHENACAINES
PHENACETIN
PHENACETINS
PHENACITES
PHENAKISMS
PHENAKISTOSCOPE
PHENAKITES
PHENANTHRENE
PHENANTHRENES
PHENARSAZINE
PHENARSAZINES
PHENAZINES
PHENCYCLIDINE
PHENCYCLIDINES
PHENETICIST
PHENETICISTS
PHENETIDINE
PHENETIDINES
PHENETOLES
PHENFORMIN
PHENFORMINS
PHENGOPHOBIA
PHENGOPHOBIAS
PHENMETRAZINE
PHENMETRAZINES
PHENOBARBITAL
PHENOBARBITALS
PHENOBARBITONE
PHENOBARBITONES
PHENOBARBS
PHENOCOPIES

PHENOCRYST
PHENOCRYSTIC
PHENOCRYSTS
PHENOLATED
PHENOLATES
PHENOLATING
PHENOLOGICAL
PHENOLOGICALLY
PHENOLOGIES
PHENOLOGIST
PHENOLOGISTS
PHENOLPHTHALEIN
PHENOMENAL
PHENOMENALISE
PHENOMENALISED
PHENOMENALISES
PHENOMENALISING
PHENOMENALISM
PHENOMENALISMS
PHENOMENALIST
PHENOMENALISTIC
PHENOMENALISTS
PHENOMENALITIES
PHENOMENALITY
PHENOMENALIZE
PHENOMENALIZED
PHENOMENALIZES
PHENOMENALIZING
PHENOMENALLY
PHENOMENAS
PHENOMENISE
PHENOMENISED
PHENOMENISES
PHENOMENISING
PHENOMENISM
PHENOMENISMS
PHENOMENIST
PHENOMENISTS
PHENOMENIZE
PHENOMENIZED
PHENOMENIZES
PHENOMENIZING
PHENOMENOLOGIES
PHENOMENOLOGIST
PHENOMENOLOGY
PHENOMENON
PHENOMENONS
PHENOTHIAZINE
PHENOTHIAZINES
PHENOTYPED
PHENOTYPES
PHENOTYPIC
PHENOTYPICAL
PHENOTYPICALLY
PHENOTYPING
PHENOXIDES
PHENTOLAMINE
PHENTOLAMINES
PHENYLALANIN
PHENYLALANINE
PHENYLALANINES
PHENYLALANINS
PHENYLAMINE
PHENYLAMINES
PHENYLBUTAZONE
PHENYLBUTAZONES
PHENYLENES
PHENYLEPHRINE
PHENYLEPHRINES
PHENYLKETONURIA
PHENYLKETONURIC
PHENYLMETHYL
PHENYLMETHYLS
PHENYLTHIOUREA
PHENYLTHIOUREAS
PHENYTOINS
PHEROMONAL
PHEROMONES
PHIALIFORM
PHILADELPHUS
PHILADELPHUSES
PHILANDERED
PHILANDERER
PHILANDERERS
PHILANDERING
PHILANDERINGS
PHILANDERS
PHILANTHROPE
PHILANTHROPES
PHILANTHROPIC
PHILANTHROPICAL
PHILANTHROPIES
PHILANTHROPIST
PHILANTHROPISTS
PHILANTHROPOID
PHILANTHROPOIDS
PHILANTHROPY
PHILATELIC
PHILATELICALLY
PHILATELIES
PHILATELIST
PHILATELISTS
PHILAVERIES
PHILHARMONIC
PHILHARMONICS
PHILHELLENE
PHILHELLENES
PHILHELLENIC
PHILHELLENISM
PHILHELLENISMS
PHILHELLENIST
PHILHELLENISTS
PHILHORSES
PHILIPPICS
PHILIPPINA
PHILIPPINAS
PHILIPPINE
PHILIPPINES
PHILISTIAS
PHILISTINE
PHILISTINES
PHILISTINISM
PHILISTINISMS
PHILLABEGS
PHILLIBEGS
PHILLIPSITE
PHILLIPSITES
PHILLUMENIES
PHILLUMENIST
PHILLUMENISTS
PHILLUMENY
PHILODENDRA
PHILODENDRON
PHILODENDRONS
PHILOGYNIES
PHILOGYNIST
PHILOGYNISTS
PHILOGYNOUS
PHILOLOGER
PHILOLOGERS
PHILOLOGIAN
PHILOLOGIANS
PHILOLOGIC
PHILOLOGICAL
PHILOLOGICALLY
PHILOLOGIES
PHILOLOGIST
PHILOLOGISTS
PHILOLOGUE
PHILOLOGUES
PHILOMATHIC
PHILOMATHICAL
PHILOMATHIES
PHILOMATHS
PHILOMATHY
PHILOMELAS
PHILOPENAS
PHILOPOENA
PHILOPOENAS
PHILOSOPHASTER
PHILOSOPHASTERS
PHILOSOPHE
PHILOSOPHER
PHILOSOPHERESS
PHILOSOPHERS
PHILOSOPHES
PHILOSOPHESS
PHILOSOPHESSES
PHILOSOPHIC
PHILOSOPHICAL
PHILOSOPHICALLY
PHILOSOPHIES
PHILOSOPHISE
PHILOSOPHISED
PHILOSOPHISER
PHILOSOPHISERS
PHILOSOPHISES
PHILOSOPHISING
PHILOSOPHISINGS
PHILOSOPHISM
PHILOSOPHISMS
PHILOSOPHIST
PHILOSOPHISTIC
PHILOSOPHISTS
PHILOSOPHIZE
PHILOSOPHIZED
PHILOSOPHIZER
PHILOSOPHIZERS
PHILOSOPHIZES
PHILOSOPHIZING
PHILOSOPHIZINGS
PHILOSOPHY
PHILOXENIA
PHILOXENIAS
PHILTERING
PHISNOMIES
PHLEBECTOMIES
PHLEBECTOMY
PHLEBITIDES
PHLEBITISES
PHLEBOGRAM
PHLEBOGRAMS
PHLEBOGRAPHIC
PHLEBOGRAPHIES
PHLEBOGRAPHY
PHLEBOLITE
PHLEBOLITES
PHLEBOLOGIES
PHLEBOLOGY
PHLEBOSCLEROSES
PHLEBOSCLEROSIS
PHLEBOTOMIC
PHLEBOTOMICAL
PHLEBOTOMIES
PHLEBOTOMISE
PHLEBOTOMISED
PHLEBOTOMISES
PHLEBOTOMISING
PHLEBOTOMIST
PHLEBOTOMISTS
PHLEBOTOMIZE
PHLEBOTOMIZED
PHLEBOTOMIZES
PHLEBOTOMIZING
PHLEBOTOMY
PHLEGMAGOGIC
PHLEGMAGOGICS
PHLEGMAGOGUE
PHLEGMAGOGUES
PHLEGMASIA
PHLEGMASIAS
PHLEGMATIC
PHLEGMATICAL
PHLEGMATICALLY
PHLEGMATICNESS
PHLEGMIEST
PHLEGMONIC
PHLEGMONOID
PHLEGMONOUS
PHLOGISTIC

PHLOGISTICATE
PHLOGISTICATED
PHLOGISTICATES
PHLOGISTICATING
PHLOGISTON
PHLOGISTONS
PHLOGOPITE
PHLOGOPITES
PHLORIZINS
PHLYCTAENA
PHLYCTAENAE
PHLYCTENAE
PHOCOMELIA
PHOCOMELIAS
PHOCOMELIC
PHOCOMELIES
PHOENIXISM
PHOENIXISMS
PHOENIXLIKE
PHOLIDOSES
PHOLIDOSIS
PHONASTHENIA
PHONASTHENIAS
PHONATHONS
PHONATIONS
PHONAUTOGRAPH
PHONAUTOGRAPHIC
PHONAUTOGRAPHS
PHONECARDS
PHONEMATIC
PHONEMATICALLY
PHONEMICALLY
PHONEMICISATION
PHONEMICISE
PHONEMICISED
PHONEMICISES
PHONEMICISING
PHONEMICIST
PHONEMICISTS
PHONEMICIZATION
PHONEMICIZE
PHONEMICIZED
PHONEMICIZES
PHONEMICIZING
PHONENDOSCOPE
PHONENDOSCOPES
PHONETICAL
PHONETICALLY
PHONETICIAN
PHONETICIANS
PHONETICISATION
PHONETICISE
PHONETICISED
PHONETICISES
PHONETICISING
PHONETICISM
PHONETICISMS
PHONETICIST
PHONETICISTS
PHONETICIZATION
PHONETICIZE
PHONETICIZED
PHONETICIZES
PHONETICIZING
PHONETISATION
PHONETISATIONS
PHONETISED
PHONETISES
PHONETISING
PHONETISMS
PHONETISTS
PHONETIZATION
PHONETIZATIONS
PHONETIZED
PHONETIZES
PHONETIZING
PHONEYNESS
PHONEYNESSES
PHONICALLY
PHONINESSES
PHONMETERS
PHONOCAMPTIC
PHONOCAMPTICS
PHONOCARDIOGRAM
PHONOCHEMISTRY
PHONOFIDDLE
PHONOFIDDLES
PHONOGRAMIC
PHONOGRAMICALLY
PHONOGRAMMIC
PHONOGRAMS
PHONOGRAPH
PHONOGRAPHER
PHONOGRAPHERS
PHONOGRAPHIC
PHONOGRAPHIES
PHONOGRAPHIST
PHONOGRAPHISTS
PHONOGRAPHS
PHONOGRAPHY
PHONOLITES
PHONOLITIC
PHONOLOGIC
PHONOLOGICAL
PHONOLOGICALLY
PHONOLOGIES
PHONOLOGIST
PHONOLOGISTS
PHONOMETER
PHONOMETERS
PHONOMETRIC
PHONOMETRICAL
PHONOPHOBIA
PHONOPHOBIAS
PHONOPHORE
PHONOPHORES
PHONOPORES
PHONOSCOPE
PHONOSCOPES
PHONOTACTIC
PHONOTACTICS
PHONOTYPED
PHONOTYPER
PHONOTYPERS
PHONOTYPES
PHONOTYPIC
PHONOTYPICAL
PHONOTYPIES
PHONOTYPING
PHONOTYPIST
PHONOTYPISTS
PHORMINGES
PHOSGENITE
PHOSGENITES
PHOSPHATASE
PHOSPHATASES
PHOSPHATED
PHOSPHATES
PHOSPHATIC
PHOSPHATIDE
PHOSPHATIDES
PHOSPHATIDIC
PHOSPHATIDYL
PHOSPHATIDYLS
PHOSPHATING
PHOSPHATISATION
PHOSPHATISE
PHOSPHATISED
PHOSPHATISES
PHOSPHATISING
PHOSPHATIZATION
PHOSPHATIZE
PHOSPHATIZED
PHOSPHATIZES
PHOSPHATIZING
PHOSPHATURIA
PHOSPHATURIAS
PHOSPHATURIC
PHOSPHENES
PHOSPHIDES
PHOSPHINES
PHOSPHITES
PHOSPHOCREATIN
PHOSPHOCREATINE
PHOSPHOCREATINS
PHOSPHOKINASE
PHOSPHOKINASES
PHOSPHOLIPASE
PHOSPHOLIPASES
PHOSPHOLIPID
PHOSPHOLIPIDS
PHOSPHONIC
PHOSPHONIUM
PHOSPHONIUMS
PHOSPHOPROTEIN
PHOSPHOPROTEINS
PHOSPHORATE
PHOSPHORATED
PHOSPHORATES
PHOSPHORATING
PHOSPHORES
PHOSPHORESCE
PHOSPHORESCED
PHOSPHORESCENCE
PHOSPHORESCENT
PHOSPHORESCES
PHOSPHORESCING
PHOSPHORET
PHOSPHORETS
PHOSPHORETTED
PHOSPHORIC
PHOSPHORISE
PHOSPHORISED
PHOSPHORISES
PHOSPHORISING
PHOSPHORISM
PHOSPHORISMS
PHOSPHORITE
PHOSPHORITES
PHOSPHORITIC
PHOSPHORIZE
PHOSPHORIZED
PHOSPHORIZES
PHOSPHORIZING
PHOSPHOROLYSES
PHOSPHOROLYSIS
PHOSPHOROLYTIC
PHOSPHOROSCOPE
PHOSPHOROSCOPES
PHOSPHOROUS
PHOSPHORUS
PHOSPHORUSES
PHOSPHORYL
PHOSPHORYLASE
PHOSPHORYLASES
PHOSPHORYLATE
PHOSPHORYLATED
PHOSPHORYLATES
PHOSPHORYLATING
PHOSPHORYLATION
PHOSPHORYLATIVE
PHOSPHORYLS
PHOSPHURET
PHOSPHURETS
PHOSPHURETTED
PHOTICALLY
PHOTOACTINIC
PHOTOACTIVE
PHOTOAUTOTROPH
PHOTOAUTOTROPHS
PHOTOBATHIC
PHOTOBIOLOGIC
PHOTOBIOLOGICAL
PHOTOBIOLOGIES
PHOTOBIOLOGIST
PHOTOBIOLOGISTS
PHOTOBIOLOGY
PHOTOBLOGGED
PHOTOBLOGGING
PHOTOBLOGS

P

PHOTOBOMBED
PHOTOBOMBING
PHOTOBOMBS
PHOTOCALLS
PHOTOCARDS
PHOTOCATALYSES
PHOTOCATALYSIS
PHOTOCATALYTIC
PHOTOCATHODE
PHOTOCATHODES
PHOTOCELLS
PHOTOCHEMICAL
PHOTOCHEMICALLY
PHOTOCHEMIST
PHOTOCHEMISTRY
PHOTOCHEMISTS
PHOTOCHROMIC
PHOTOCHROMICS
PHOTOCHROMIES
PHOTOCHROMISM
PHOTOCHROMISMS
PHOTOCHROMY
PHOTOCOMPOSE
PHOTOCOMPOSED
PHOTOCOMPOSER
PHOTOCOMPOSERS
PHOTOCOMPOSES
PHOTOCOMPOSING
PHOTOCONDUCTING
PHOTOCONDUCTION
PHOTOCONDUCTIVE
PHOTOCONDUCTOR
PHOTOCONDUCTORS
PHOTOCOPIABLE
PHOTOCOPIED
PHOTOCOPIER
PHOTOCOPIERS
PHOTOCOPIES
PHOTOCOPYING
PHOTOCOPYINGS
PHOTOCURRENT
PHOTOCURRENTS
PHOTODEGRADABLE
PHOTODETECTOR
PHOTODETECTORS
PHOTODIODE
PHOTODIODES
PHOTODISKS
PHOTODISSOCIATE
PHOTODUPLICATE
PHOTODUPLICATED
PHOTODUPLICATES
PHOTODYNAMIC
PHOTODYNAMICS
PHOTOELASTIC
PHOTOELASTICITY
PHOTOELECTRIC
PHOTOELECTRICAL
PHOTOELECTRODE
PHOTOELECTRODES
PHOTOELECTRON
PHOTOELECTRONIC
PHOTOELECTRONS
PHOTOEMISSION
PHOTOEMISSIONS
PHOTOEMISSIVE
PHOTOENGRAVE
PHOTOENGRAVED
PHOTOENGRAVER
PHOTOENGRAVERS
PHOTOENGRAVES
PHOTOENGRAVING
PHOTOENGRAVINGS
PHOTOEXCITATION
PHOTOEXCITED
PHOTOFINISHER
PHOTOFINISHERS
PHOTOFINISHING
PHOTOFINISHINGS
PHOTOFISSION
PHOTOFISSIONS
PHOTOFLASH
PHOTOFLASHES
PHOTOFLOOD
PHOTOFLOODS
PHOTOFLUOROGRAM
PHOTOGELATIN
PHOTOGELATINE
PHOTOGENES
PHOTOGENIC
PHOTOGENICALLY
PHOTOGENIES
PHOTOGEOLOGIC
PHOTOGEOLOGICAL
PHOTOGEOLOGIES
PHOTOGEOLOGIST
PHOTOGEOLOGISTS
PHOTOGEOLOGY
PHOTOGLYPH
PHOTOGLYPHIC
PHOTOGLYPHIES
PHOTOGLYPHS
PHOTOGLYPHY
PHOTOGRAMMETRIC
PHOTOGRAMMETRY
PHOTOGRAMS
PHOTOGRAPH
PHOTOGRAPHED
PHOTOGRAPHER
PHOTOGRAPHERS
PHOTOGRAPHIC
PHOTOGRAPHICAL
PHOTOGRAPHIES
PHOTOGRAPHING
PHOTOGRAPHIST
PHOTOGRAPHISTS
PHOTOGRAPHS
PHOTOGRAPHY
PHOTOGRAVURE
PHOTOGRAVURES
PHOTOINDUCED
PHOTOINDUCTION
PHOTOINDUCTIONS
PHOTOINDUCTIVE
PHOTOIONISATION
PHOTOIONISE
PHOTOIONISED
PHOTOIONISES
PHOTOIONISING
PHOTOIONIZATION
PHOTOIONIZE
PHOTOIONIZED
PHOTOIONIZES
PHOTOIONIZING
PHOTOJOURNALISM
PHOTOJOURNALIST
PHOTOKINESES
PHOTOKINESIS
PHOTOKINETIC
PHOTOLITHO
PHOTOLITHOGRAPH
PHOTOLITHOS
PHOTOLUMINESCE
PHOTOLUMINESCED
PHOTOLUMINESCES
PHOTOLYSABLE
PHOTOLYSED
PHOTOLYSES
PHOTOLYSING
PHOTOLYSIS
PHOTOLYTIC
PHOTOLYTICALLY
PHOTOLYZABLE
PHOTOLYZED
PHOTOLYZES
PHOTOLYZING
PHOTOMACHINE
PHOTOMACHINES
PHOTOMACROGRAPH
PHOTOMAPPED
PHOTOMAPPING
PHOTOMASKS
PHOTOMECHANICAL
PHOTOMETER
PHOTOMETERS
PHOTOMETRIC
PHOTOMETRICALLY
PHOTOMETRIES
PHOTOMETRIST
PHOTOMETRISTS
PHOTOMETRY
PHOTOMICROGRAPH
PHOTOMONTAGE
PHOTOMONTAGES
PHOTOMOSAIC
PHOTOMOSAICS
PHOTOMULTIPLIER
PHOTOMURAL
PHOTOMURALS
PHOTONASTIC
PHOTONASTIES
PHOTONASTY
PHOTONEGATIVE
PHOTONEUTRON
PHOTONEUTRONS
PHOTONOVEL
PHOTONOVELS
PHOTONUCLEAR
PHOTOOXIDATION
PHOTOOXIDATIONS
PHOTOOXIDATIVE
PHOTOOXIDISE
PHOTOOXIDISED
PHOTOOXIDISES
PHOTOOXIDISING
PHOTOOXIDIZE
PHOTOOXIDIZED
PHOTOOXIDIZES
PHOTOOXIDIZING
PHOTOPERIOD
PHOTOPERIODIC
PHOTOPERIODISM
PHOTOPERIODISMS
PHOTOPERIODS
PHOTOPHASE
PHOTOPHASES
PHOTOPHILIC
PHOTOPHILIES
PHOTOPHILOUS
PHOTOPHILS
PHOTOPHILY
PHOTOPHOBE
PHOTOPHOBES
PHOTOPHOBIA
PHOTOPHOBIAS
PHOTOPHOBIC
PHOTOPHONE
PHOTOPHONES
PHOTOPHONIC
PHOTOPHONIES
PHOTOPHONY
PHOTOPHORE
PHOTOPHORES
PHOTOPHORESES
PHOTOPHORESIS
PHOTOPLAYS
PHOTOPOLYMER
PHOTOPOLYMERS
PHOTOPOSITIVE
PHOTOPRODUCT
PHOTOPRODUCTION
PHOTOPRODUCTS
PHOTOPSIAS
PHOTOPSIES
PHOTOREACTION
PHOTOREACTIONS
PHOTOREACTIVE
PHOTOREALISM
PHOTOREALISMS
PHOTOREALIST

PHOTOREALISTIC
PHOTOREALISTS
PHOTORECEPTION
PHOTORECEPTIONS
PHOTORECEPTIVE
PHOTORECEPTOR
PHOTORECEPTORS
PHOTOREDUCE
PHOTOREDUCED
PHOTOREDUCES
PHOTOREDUCING
PHOTOREDUCTION
PHOTOREDUCTIONS
PHOTOREFRACTIVE
PHOTORESIST
PHOTORESISTS
PHOTOSCANNED
PHOTOSCANNING
PHOTOSCANS
PHOTOSENSITISE
PHOTOSENSITISED
PHOTOSENSITISER
PHOTOSENSITISES
PHOTOSENSITIVE
PHOTOSENSITIZE
PHOTOSENSITIZED
PHOTOSENSITIZER
PHOTOSENSITIZES
PHOTOSENSOR
PHOTOSENSORS
PHOTOSETTER
PHOTOSETTERS
PHOTOSETTING
PHOTOSETTINGS
PHOTOSHOOT
PHOTOSHOOTS
PHOTOSHOPPED
PHOTOSHOPPING
PHOTOSHOPS
PHOTOSPHERE
PHOTOSPHERES
PHOTOSPHERIC
PHOTOSTATED
PHOTOSTATIC
PHOTOSTATING
PHOTOSTATS
PHOTOSTATTED
PHOTOSTATTING
PHOTOSYNTHATE
PHOTOSYNTHATES
PHOTOSYNTHESES
PHOTOSYNTHESIS
PHOTOSYNTHESISE
PHOTOSYNTHESIZE
PHOTOSYNTHETIC
PHOTOSYSTEM
PHOTOSYSTEMS
PHOTOTACTIC
PHOTOTACTICALLY
PHOTOTAXES
PHOTOTAXIES
PHOTOTAXIS
PHOTOTELEGRAM
PHOTOTELEGRAMS
PHOTOTELEGRAPH
PHOTOTELEGRAPHS
PHOTOTELEGRAPHY
PHOTOTHERAPIES
PHOTOTHERAPY
PHOTOTHERMAL
PHOTOTHERMALLY
PHOTOTHERMIC
PHOTOTONIC
PHOTOTONUS
PHOTOTONUSES
PHOTOTOPOGRAPHY
PHOTOTOXIC
PHOTOTOXICITIES
PHOTOTOXICITY
PHOTOTRANSISTOR
PHOTOTROPE
PHOTOTROPES
PHOTOTROPH
PHOTOTROPHIC
PHOTOTROPHS
PHOTOTROPIC
PHOTOTROPICALLY
PHOTOTROPIES
PHOTOTROPISM
PHOTOTROPISMS
PHOTOTROPY
PHOTOTUBES
PHOTOTYPED
PHOTOTYPES
PHOTOTYPESET
PHOTOTYPESETS
PHOTOTYPESETTER
PHOTOTYPIC
PHOTOTYPICALLY
PHOTOTYPIES
PHOTOTYPING
PHOTOTYPOGRAPHY
PHOTOVOLTAIC
PHOTOVOLTAICS
PHOTOXYLOGRAPHY
PHOTOZINCOGRAPH
PHRAGMOPLAST
PHRAGMOPLASTS
PHRASELESS
PHRASEMAKER
PHRASEMAKERS
PHRASEMAKING
PHRASEMAKINGS
PHRASEMONGER
PHRASEMONGERING
PHRASEMONGERS
PHRASEOGRAM
PHRASEOGRAMS
PHRASEOGRAPH
PHRASEOGRAPHIC
PHRASEOGRAPHIES
PHRASEOGRAPHS
PHRASEOGRAPHY
PHRASEOLOGIC
PHRASEOLOGICAL
PHRASEOLOGIES
PHRASEOLOGIST
PHRASEOLOGISTS
PHRASEOLOGY
PHREAKINGS
PHREATOPHYTE
PHREATOPHYTES
PHREATOPHYTIC
PHRENESIAC
PHRENETICAL
PHRENETICALLY
PHRENETICNESS
PHRENETICNESSES
PHRENETICS
PHRENITIDES
PHRENITISES
PHRENOLOGIC
PHRENOLOGICAL
PHRENOLOGICALLY
PHRENOLOGIES
PHRENOLOGISE
PHRENOLOGISED
PHRENOLOGISES
PHRENOLOGISING
PHRENOLOGIST
PHRENOLOGISTS
PHRENOLOGIZE
PHRENOLOGIZED
PHRENOLOGIZES
PHRENOLOGIZING
PHRENOLOGY
PHRENSICAL
PHRENSYING
PHRONTISTERIES
PHRONTISTERY
PHTHALATES
PHTHALEINS
PHTHALOCYANIN
PHTHALOCYANINE
PHTHALOCYANINES
PHTHALOCYANINS
PHTHIRIASES
PHTHIRIASIS
PHTHISICAL
PHTHISICKY
PHYCOBILIN
PHYCOBILINS
PHYCOBIONT
PHYCOBIONTS
PHYCOCYANIN
PHYCOCYANINS
PHYCOCYANS
PHYCOERYTHRIN
PHYCOERYTHRINS
PHYCOLOGICAL
PHYCOLOGIES
PHYCOLOGIST
PHYCOLOGISTS
PHYCOMYCETE
PHYCOMYCETES
PHYCOMYCETOUS
PHYCOPHAEIN
PHYCOPHAEINS
PHYCOXANTHIN
PHYCOXANTHINS
PHYLACTERIC
PHYLACTERICAL
PHYLACTERIES
PHYLACTERY
PHYLARCHIES
PHYLAXISES
PHYLESISES
PHYLETICALLY
PHYLLARIES
PHYLLOCLAD
PHYLLOCLADE
PHYLLOCLADES
PHYLLOCLADS
PHYLLODIAL
PHYLLODIES
PHYLLODIUM
PHYLLOMANIA
PHYLLOMANIAS
PHYLLOPHAGOUS
PHYLLOPLANE
PHYLLOPLANES
PHYLLOPODS
PHYLLOQUINONE
PHYLLOQUINONES
PHYLLOSILICATE
PHYLLOSILICATES
PHYLLOSPHERE
PHYLLOSPHERES
PHYLLOTACTIC
PHYLLOTACTICAL
PHYLLOTAXES
PHYLLOTAXIES
PHYLLOTAXIS
PHYLLOTAXY
PHYLLOXERA
PHYLLOXERAE
PHYLLOXERAS
PHYLOGENESES
PHYLOGENESIS
PHYLOGENETIC
PHYLOGENIC
PHYLOGENIES
PHYSALISES
PHYSHARMONICA
PHYSHARMONICAS
PHYSIATRIC
PHYSIATRICAL
PHYSIATRICS
PHYSIATRIES
PHYSIATRIST

P

PHYSIATRISTS
PHYSICALISM
PHYSICALISMS
PHYSICALIST
PHYSICALISTIC
PHYSICALISTS
PHYSICALITIES
PHYSICALITY
PHYSICALLY
PHYSICALNESS
PHYSICALNESSES
PHYSICIANCIES
PHYSICIANCY
PHYSICIANER
PHYSICIANERS
PHYSICIANS
PHYSICIANSHIP
PHYSICIANSHIPS
PHYSICISMS
PHYSICISTS
PHYSICKING
PHYSICOCHEMICAL
PHYSIOCRACIES
PHYSIOCRACY
PHYSIOCRAT
PHYSIOCRATIC
PHYSIOCRATS
PHYSIOGNOMIC
PHYSIOGNOMICAL
PHYSIOGNOMIES
PHYSIOGNOMIST
PHYSIOGNOMISTS
PHYSIOGNOMY
PHYSIOGRAPHER
PHYSIOGRAPHERS
PHYSIOGRAPHIC
PHYSIOGRAPHICAL
PHYSIOGRAPHIES
PHYSIOGRAPHY
PHYSIOLATER
PHYSIOLATERS
PHYSIOLATRIES
PHYSIOLATRY
PHYSIOLOGIC
PHYSIOLOGICAL
PHYSIOLOGICALLY
PHYSIOLOGIES
PHYSIOLOGIST
PHYSIOLOGISTS
PHYSIOLOGUS
PHYSIOLOGUSES
PHYSIOLOGY
PHYSIOPATHOLOGY
PHYSIOTHERAPIES
PHYSIOTHERAPIST
PHYSIOTHERAPY
PHYSITHEISM
PHYSITHEISMS
PHYSITHEISTIC
PHYSOCLISTOUS
PHYSOSTIGMIN
PHYSOSTIGMINE
PHYSOSTIGMINES
PHYSOSTIGMINS
PHYSOSTOMOUS
PHYTOALEXIN
PHYTOALEXINS
PHYTOBENTHOS
PHYTOBENTHOSES
PHYTOCHEMICAL
PHYTOCHEMICALLY
PHYTOCHEMICALS
PHYTOCHEMIST
PHYTOCHEMISTRY
PHYTOCHEMISTS
PHYTOCHROME
PHYTOCHROMES
PHYTOESTROGEN
PHYTOESTROGENS
PHYTOFLAGELLATE
PHYTOGENESES
PHYTOGENESIS
PHYTOGENETIC
PHYTOGENETICAL
PHYTOGENIC
PHYTOGENIES
PHYTOGEOGRAPHER
PHYTOGEOGRAPHIC
PHYTOGEOGRAPHY
PHYTOGRAPHER
PHYTOGRAPHERS
PHYTOGRAPHIC
PHYTOGRAPHIES
PHYTOGRAPHY
PHYTOHORMONE
PHYTOHORMONES
PHYTOLITHS
PHYTOLOGICAL
PHYTOLOGICALLY
PHYTOLOGIES
PHYTOLOGIST
PHYTOLOGISTS
PHYTONADIONE
PHYTONADIONES
PHYTOPATHOGEN
PHYTOPATHOGENIC
PHYTOPATHOGENS
PHYTOPATHOLOGY
PHYTOPHAGIC
PHYTOPHAGIES
PHYTOPHAGOUS
PHYTOPHAGY
PHYTOPLANKTER
PHYTOPLANKTERS
PHYTOPLANKTON
PHYTOPLANKTONIC
PHYTOPLANKTONS
PHYTOSANITARY
PHYTOSOCIOLOGY
PHYTOSTEROL
PHYTOSTEROLS
PHYTOTHERAPIES
PHYTOTHERAPY
PHYTOTOMIES
PHYTOTOMIST
PHYTOTOMISTS
PHYTOTOXIC
PHYTOTOXICITIES
PHYTOTOXICITY
PHYTOTOXIN
PHYTOTOXINS
PHYTOTRONS
PIACULARITIES
PIACULARITY
PIANISSIMI
PIANISSIMO
PIANISSIMOS
PIANISSISSIMO
PIANISTICALLY
PIANOFORTE
PIANOFORTES
PIANOLISTS
PICADILLOS
PICARESQUE
PICARESQUES
PICAROONED
PICAROONING
PICAYUNISH
PICAYUNISHLY
PICAYUNISHNESS
PICCADILLIES
PICCADILLO
PICCADILLOES
PICCADILLOS
PICCADILLS
PICCADILLY
PICCALILLI
PICCALILLIS
PICCOLOIST
PICCOLOISTS
PICHICIAGO
PICHICIAGOS
PICHICIEGO
PICHICIEGOS
PICHOLINES
PICKABACKED
PICKABACKING
PICKABACKS
PICKADILLIES
PICKADILLO
PICKADILLOES
PICKADILLOS
PICKADILLS
PICKADILLY
PICKAPACKED
PICKAPACKING
PICKAPACKS
PICKAROONS
PICKBACKED
PICKBACKING
PICKEDNESS
PICKEDNESSES
PICKEERERS
PICKEERING
PICKELHAUBE
PICKELHAUBES
PICKERELWEED
PICKERELWEEDS
PICKETBOAT
PICKETBOATS
PICKETINGS
PICKINESSES
PICKPOCKET
PICKPOCKETED
PICKPOCKETING
PICKPOCKETS
PICKTHANKS
PICNICKERS
PICNICKIER
PICNICKIEST
PICNICKING
PICOCURIES
PICOFARADS
PICOMETERS
PICOMETRES
PICORNAVIRUS
PICORNAVIRUSES
PICOSECOND
PICOSECONDS
PICOWAVING
PICQUETING
PICROCARMINE
PICROCARMINES
PICROTOXIN
PICROTOXINS
PICTARNIES
PICTOGRAMS
PICTOGRAPH
PICTOGRAPHIC
PICTOGRAPHIES
PICTOGRAPHS
PICTOGRAPHY
PICTORIALISE
PICTORIALISED
PICTORIALISES
PICTORIALISING
PICTORIALISM
PICTORIALISMS
PICTORIALIST
PICTORIALISTS
PICTORIALIZE
PICTORIALIZED
PICTORIALIZES
PICTORIALIZING
PICTORIALLY
PICTORIALNESS
PICTORIALNESSES
PICTORIALS
PICTORICAL
PICTORICALLY

P

PICTUREGOER
PICTUREGOERS
PICTUREPHONE
PICTUREPHONES
PICTURESQUE
PICTURESQUELY
PICTURESQUENESS
PICTURISATION
PICTURISATIONS
PICTURISED
PICTURISES
PICTURISING
PICTURIZATION
PICTURIZATIONS
PICTURIZED
PICTURIZES
PICTURIZING
PIDDLINGLY
PIDGINISATION
PIDGINISATIONS
PIDGINISED
PIDGINISES
PIDGINISING
PIDGINIZATION
PIDGINIZATIONS
PIDGINIZED
PIDGINIZES
PIDGINIZING
PIECEMEALED
PIECEMEALING
PIECEMEALS
PIECEWORKER
PIECEWORKERS
PIECEWORKS
PIEDMONTITE
PIEDMONTITES
PIEDNESSES
PIEMONTITE
PIEMONTITES
PIEPOWDERS
PIERCEABLE
PIERCINGLY
PIERCINGNESS
PIERCINGNESSES
PIERRETTES
PIETISTICAL
PIETISTICALLY
PIEZOCHEMISTRY
PIEZOELECTRIC
PIEZOMAGNETIC
PIEZOMAGNETISM
PIEZOMAGNETISMS
PIEZOMETER
PIEZOMETERS
PIEZOMETRIC
PIEZOMETRICALLY
PIEZOMETRIES
PIEZOMETRY
PIFFERAROS
PIGEONHOLE
PIGEONHOLED
PIGEONHOLER
PIGEONHOLERS
PIGEONHOLES
PIGEONHOLING
PIGEONITES
PIGEONRIES
PIGEONWING
PIGEONWINGS
PIGGINESSES
PIGGISHNESS
PIGGISHNESSES
PIGGYBACKED
PIGGYBACKING
PIGGYBACKS
PIGHEADEDLY
PIGHEADEDNESS
PIGHEADEDNESSES
PIGMENTARY
PIGMENTATION
PIGMENTATIONS
PIGMENTING
PIGMENTOSA
PIGMENTOSAS
PIGNERATED
PIGNERATES
PIGNERATING
PIGNERATION
PIGNERATIONS
PIGNORATED
PIGNORATES
PIGNORATING
PIGNORATION
PIGNORATIONS
PIGSCONCES
PIGSTICKED
PIGSTICKER
PIGSTICKERS
PIGSTICKING
PIGSTICKINGS
PIKEPERCHES
PIKESTAFFS
PIKESTAVES
PILASTERED
PILEORHIZA
PILEORHIZAS
PILFERABLE
PILFERAGES
PILFERINGLY
PILFERINGS
PILFERPROOF
PILGARLICK
PILGARLICKS
PILGARLICKY
PILGARLICS
PILGRIMAGE
PILGRIMAGED
PILGRIMAGER
PILGRIMAGERS
PILGRIMAGES
PILGRIMAGING
PILGRIMERS
PILGRIMING
PILGRIMISE
PILGRIMISED
PILGRIMISES
PILGRIMISING
PILGRIMIZE
PILGRIMIZED
PILGRIMIZES
PILGRIMIZING
PILIFEROUS
PILLAGINGS
PILLARISTS
PILLARLESS
PILLICOCKS
PILLIONING
PILLIONIST
PILLIONISTS
PILLIWINKS
PILLORISED
PILLORISES
PILLORISING
PILLORIZED
PILLORIZES
PILLORIZING
PILLORYING
PILLOWCASE
PILLOWCASES
PILLOWIEST
PILLOWSLIP
PILLOWSLIPS
PILNIEWINKS
PILOCARPIN
PILOCARPINE
PILOCARPINES
PILOCARPINS
PILOSITIES
PILOTFISHES
PILOTHOUSE
PILOTHOUSES
PIMPERNELS
PIMPLINESS
PIMPLINESSES
PIMPMOBILE
PIMPMOBILES
PINACOIDAL
PINACOTHECA
PINACOTHECAE
PINAKOIDAL
PINAKOTHEK
PINAKOTHEKS
PINBALLING
PINCERLIKE
PINCHBECKS
PINCHCOCKS
PINCHCOMMONS
PINCHCOMMONSES
PINCHFISTS
PINCHINGLY
PINCHPENNIES
PINCHPENNY
PINCHPOINT
PINCHPOINTS
PINCUSHION
PINCUSHIONS
PINEALECTOMIES
PINEALECTOMISE
PINEALECTOMISED
PINEALECTOMISES
PINEALECTOMIZE
PINEALECTOMIZED
PINEALECTOMIZES
PINEALECTOMY
PINEAPPLES
PINFEATHER
PINFEATHERS
PINFOLDING
PINGRASSES
PINGUEFIED
PINGUEFIES
PINGUEFYING
PINGUIDITIES
PINGUIDITY
PINGUITUDE
PINGUITUDES
PINHEADEDNESS
PINHEADEDNESSES
PINHOOKERS
PINKERTONS
PINKINESSES
PINKISHNESS
PINKISHNESSES
PINKNESSES
PINNACLING
PINNATIFID
PINNATIFIDLY
PINNATIONS
PINNATIPARTITE
PINNATIPED
PINNATISECT
PINNIEWINKLE
PINNIEWINKLES
PINNIPEDES
PINNIPEDIAN
PINNIPEDIANS
PINNULATED
PINNYWINKLE
PINNYWINKLES
PINOCYTOSES
PINOCYTOSIS
PINOCYTOTIC
PINOCYTOTICALLY
PINPOINTED
PINPOINTING
PINPRICKED
PINPRICKING
PINSETTERS
PINSPOTTED
PINSPOTTER

PINSPOTTERS
PINSPOTTING
PINSTRIPED
PINSTRIPES
PINTADERAS
PINTUCKING
PINTUCKINGS
PINWHEELED
PINWHEELING
PINWRENCHES
PIONEERING
PIOUSNESSES
PIPECLAYED
PIPECLAYING
PIPEFISHES
PIPEFITTER
PIPEFITTERS
PIPEFITTING
PIPEFITTINGS
PIPELINING
PIPELININGS
PIPERACEOUS
PIPERAZINE
PIPERAZINES
PIPERIDINE
PIPERIDINES
PIPERONALS
PIPESTONES
PIPINESSES
PIPISTRELLE
PIPISTRELLES
PIPISTRELS
PIPIWHARAUROA
PIPIWHARAUROAS
PIPSISSEWA
PIPSISSEWAS
PIPSQUEAKS
PIQUANCIES
PIQUANTNESS
PIQUANTNESSES
PIRACETAMS
PIRATICALLY
PIRLICUING
PIROPLASMA
PIROPLASMATA
PIROPLASMS
PIROUETTED
PIROUETTER
PIROUETTERS
PIROUETTES
PIROUETTING
PISCATORIAL
PISCATORIALLY
PISCATRIXES
PISCICOLOUS
PISCICULTURAL
PISCICULTURALLY
PISCICULTURE
PISCICULTURES
PISCICULTURIST
PISCICULTURISTS
PISCIFAUNA
PISCIFAUNAE
PISCIFAUNAS
PISCIVORES
PISCIVOROUS
PISSASPHALT
PISSASPHALTS
PISTACHIOS
PISTAREENS
PISTILLARY
PISTILLATE
PISTILLODE
PISTILLODES
PISTOLEERS
PISTOLEROS
PISTOLIERS
PISTOLLING
PITAPATTED
PITAPATTING
PITCHBENDS
PITCHBLENDE
PITCHBLENDES
PITCHERFUL
PITCHERFULS
PITCHERSFUL
PITCHFORKED
PITCHFORKING
PITCHFORKS
PITCHINESS
PITCHINESSES
PITCHOMETER
PITCHOMETERS
PITCHPERSON
PITCHPERSONS
PITCHPINES
PITCHPIPES
PITCHPOLED
PITCHPOLES
PITCHPOLING
PITCHSTONE
PITCHSTONES
PITCHWOMAN
PITCHWOMEN
PITEOUSNESS
PITEOUSNESSES
PITHECANTHROPI
PITHECANTHROPUS
PITHECOIDS
PITHINESSES
PITIABLENESS
PITIABLENESSES
PITIFULLER
PITIFULLEST
PITIFULNESS
PITIFULNESSES
PITILESSLY
PITILESSNESS
PITILESSNESSES
PITTOSPORUM
PITTOSPORUMS
PITUITARIES
PITUITRINS
PITYRIASES
PITYRIASIS
PITYROSPORUM
PITYROSPORUMS
PIWAKAWAKA
PIWAKAWAKAS
PIXELATING
PIXELATION
PIXELATIONS
PIXELLATED
PIXELLATES
PIXELLATING
PIXELLATION
PIXELLATIONS
PIXILATING
PIXILATION
PIXILATIONS
PIXILLATED
PIXILLATES
PIXILLATING
PIXILLATION
PIXILLATIONS
PIXINESSES
PIZAZZIEST
PIZZAZZIER
PIZZAZZIEST
PIZZICATOS
PLACABILITIES
PLACABILITY
PLACABLENESS
PLACABLENESSES
PLACARDING
PLACATINGLY
PLACATIONS
PLACEHOLDER
PLACEHOLDERS
PLACEKICKED
PLACEKICKER
PLACEKICKERS
PLACEKICKING
PLACEKICKS
PLACELESSLY
PLACEMENTS
PLACENTALS
PLACENTATE
PLACENTATION
PLACENTATIONS
PLACENTIFORM
PLACENTOLOGIES
PLACENTOLOGY
PLACIDITIES
PLACIDNESS
PLACIDNESSES
PLACODERMS
PLAGIARIES
PLAGIARISE
PLAGIARISED
PLAGIARISER
PLAGIARISERS
PLAGIARISES
PLAGIARISING
PLAGIARISM
PLAGIARISMS
PLAGIARIST
PLAGIARISTIC
PLAGIARISTS
PLAGIARIZE
PLAGIARIZED
PLAGIARIZER
PLAGIARIZERS
PLAGIARIZES
PLAGIARIZING
PLAGIOCEPHALIES
PLAGIOCEPHALY
PLAGIOCLASE
PLAGIOCLASES
PLAGIOCLASTIC
PLAGIOCLIMAX
PLAGIOCLIMAXES
PLAGIOSTOMATOUS
PLAGIOSTOME
PLAGIOSTOMES
PLAGIOSTOMOUS
PLAGIOTROPIC
PLAGIOTROPISM
PLAGIOTROPISMS
PLAGIOTROPOUS
PLAGUELIKE
PLAGUESOME
PLAINCHANT
PLAINCHANTS
PLAINCLOTHES
PLAINCLOTHESMAN
PLAINCLOTHESMEN
PLAINNESSES
PLAINSONGS
PLAINSPOKEN
PLAINSPOKENNESS
PLAINSTANES
PLAINSTONES
PLAINTEXTS
PLAINTIFFS
PLAINTIVELY
PLAINTIVENESS
PLAINTIVENESSES
PLAINTLESS
PLAINWORKS
PLAISTERED
PLAISTERING
PLANARIANS
PLANARITIES
PLANATIONS
PLANCHETTE
PLANCHETTES
PLANELOADS
PLANENESSES
PLANESIDES

PLANETARIA
PLANETARIES
PLANETARIUM
PLANETARIUMS
PLANETESIMAL
PLANETESIMALS
PLANETICAL
PLANETLIKE
PLANETOIDAL
PLANETOIDS
PLANETOLOGICAL
PLANETOLOGIES
PLANETOLOGIST
PLANETOLOGISTS
PLANETOLOGY
PLANETWIDE
PLANGENCIES
PLANGENTLY
PLANIGRAMS
PLANIGRAPH
PLANIGRAPHIES
PLANIGRAPHS
PLANIGRAPHY
PLANIMETER
PLANIMETERS
PLANIMETRIC
PLANIMETRICAL
PLANIMETRICALLY
PLANIMETRIES
PLANIMETRY
PLANISHERS
PLANISHING
PLANISPHERE
PLANISPHERES
PLANISPHERIC
PLANKTONIC
PLANLESSLY
PLANLESSNESS
PLANLESSNESSES
PLANOBLAST
PLANOBLASTS
PLANOCONVEX
PLANOGAMETE
PLANOGAMETES
PLANOGRAMS
PLANOGRAPHIC
PLANOGRAPHIES
PLANOGRAPHY
PLANOMETER
PLANOMETERS
PLANOMETRIC
PLANOMETRICALLY
PLANOMETRIES
PLANOMETRY
PLANTAGINACEOUS
PLANTATION
PLANTATIONS
PLANTIGRADE
PLANTIGRADES
PLANTLINGS
PLANTOCRACIES
PLANTOCRACY
PLANTSWOMAN
PLANTSWOMEN
PLANULIFORM
PLAQUETTES
PLASMAGELS
PLASMAGENE
PLASMAGENES
PLASMAGENIC
PLASMALEMMA
PLASMALEMMAS
PLASMAPHERESES
PLASMAPHERESIS
PLASMASOLS
PLASMATICAL
PLASMINOGEN
PLASMINOGENS
PLASMODESM
PLASMODESMA
PLASMODESMAS
PLASMODESMATA
PLASMODESMS
PLASMODIAL
PLASMODIUM
PLASMOGAMIES
PLASMOGAMY
PLASMOLYSE
PLASMOLYSED
PLASMOLYSES
PLASMOLYSING
PLASMOLYSIS
PLASMOLYTIC
PLASMOLYTICALLY
PLASMOLYZE
PLASMOLYZED
PLASMOLYZES
PLASMOLYZING
PLASMOSOMA
PLASMOSOMATA
PLASMOSOME
PLASMOSOMES
PLASTERBOARD
PLASTERBOARDS
PLASTERERS
PLASTERIER
PLASTERIEST
PLASTERINESS
PLASTERINESSES
PLASTERING
PLASTERINGS
PLASTERSTONE
PLASTERSTONES
PLASTERWORK
PLASTERWORKS
PLASTICALLY
PLASTICATED
PLASTICENE
PLASTICENES
PLASTICINE
PLASTICINES
PLASTICISATION
PLASTICISATIONS
PLASTICISE
PLASTICISED
PLASTICISER
PLASTICISERS
PLASTICISES
PLASTICISING
PLASTICITIES
PLASTICITY
PLASTICIZATION
PLASTICIZATIONS
PLASTICIZE
PLASTICIZED
PLASTICIZER
PLASTICIZERS
PLASTICIZES
PLASTICIZING
PLASTICKIER
PLASTICKIEST
PLASTIDIAL
PLASTIDULE
PLASTIDULES
PLASTILINA
PLASTILINAS
PLASTINATION
PLASTINATIONS
PLASTIQUES
PLASTISOLS
PLASTOCYANIN
PLASTOCYANINS
PLASTOGAMIES
PLASTOGAMY
PLASTOMETER
PLASTOMETERS
PLASTOMETRIC
PLASTOMETRIES
PLASTOMETRY
PLASTOQUINONE
PLASTOQUINONES
PLATANACEOUS
PLATEAUING
PLATEGLASS
PLATEGLASSES
PLATELAYER
PLATELAYERS
PLATELAYING
PLATELAYINGS
PLATEMAKER
PLATEMAKERS
PLATEMAKING
PLATEMAKINGS
PLATEMARKED
PLATEMARKING
PLATEMARKS
PLATERESQUE
PLATFORMED
PLATFORMER
PLATFORMERS
PLATFORMING
PLATFORMINGS
PLATINIFEROUS
PLATINIRIDIUM
PLATINIRIDIUMS
PLATINISATION
PLATINISATIONS
PLATINISED
PLATINISES
PLATINISING
PLATINIZATION
PLATINIZATIONS
PLATINIZED
PLATINIZES
PLATINIZING
PLATINOCYANIC
PLATINOCYANIDE
PLATINOCYANIDES
PLATINOIDS
PLATINOTYPE
PLATINOTYPES
PLATITUDES
PLATITUDINAL
PLATITUDINARIAN
PLATITUDINISE
PLATITUDINISED
PLATITUDINISER
PLATITUDINISERS
PLATITUDINISES
PLATITUDINISING
PLATITUDINIZE
PLATITUDINIZED
PLATITUDINIZER
PLATITUDINIZERS
PLATITUDINIZES
PLATITUDINIZING
PLATITUDINOUS
PLATITUDINOUSLY
PLATONICALLY
PLATONISMS
PLATOONING
PLATTELAND
PLATTELANDS
PLATTERFUL
PLATTERFULS
PLATTERSFUL
PLATYCEPHALIC
PLATYCEPHALOUS
PLATYFISHES
PLATYHELMINTH
PLATYHELMINTHIC
PLATYHELMINTHS
PLATYKURTIC
PLATYPUSES
PLATYRRHINE
PLATYRRHINES
PLATYRRHINIAN
PLATYRRHINIANS
PLAUDITORY
PLAUSIBILITIES

PLAUSIBILITY
PLAUSIBLENESS
PLAUSIBLENESSES
PLAYABILITIES
PLAYABILITY
PLAYACTING
PLAYACTINGS
PLAYACTORS
PLAYBUSSES
PLAYDOUGHS
PLAYFELLOW
PLAYFELLOWS
PLAYFIELDS
PLAYFULNESS
PLAYFULNESSES
PLAYGOINGS
PLAYGROUND
PLAYGROUNDS
PLAYGROUPS
PLAYHOUSES
PLAYLEADER
PLAYLEADERS
PLAYLISTED
PLAYLISTING
PLAYMAKERS
PLAYMAKING
PLAYMAKINGS
PLAYREADER
PLAYREADERS
PLAYSCHOOL
PLAYSCHOOLS
PLAYTHINGS
PLAYWRIGHT
PLAYWRIGHTING
PLAYWRIGHTINGS
PLAYWRIGHTS
PLAYWRITING
PLAYWRITINGS
PLEADINGLY
PLEASANCES
PLEASANTER
PLEASANTEST
PLEASANTLY
PLEASANTNESS
PLEASANTNESSES
PLEASANTRIES
PLEASANTRY
PLEASINGLY
PLEASINGNESS
PLEASINGNESSES
PLEASURABILITY
PLEASURABLE
PLEASURABLENESS
PLEASURABLY
PLEASUREFUL
PLEASURELESS
PLEASURERS
PLEASURING
PLEBEIANISE
PLEBEIANISED
PLEBEIANISES
PLEBEIANISING
PLEBEIANISM
PLEBEIANISMS
PLEBEIANIZE
PLEBEIANIZED
PLEBEIANIZES
PLEBEIANIZING
PLEBEIANLY
PLEBIFICATION
PLEBIFICATIONS
PLEBIFYING
PLEBISCITARY
PLEBISCITE
PLEBISCITES
PLECOPTERAN
PLECOPTERANS
PLECOPTEROUS
PLECTOGNATH
PLECTOGNATHIC
PLECTOGNATHOUS
PLECTOGNATHS
PLECTOPTEROUS
PLEDGEABLE
PLEINAIRISM
PLEINAIRISMS
PLEINAIRIST
PLEINAIRISTS
PLEIOCHASIA
PLEIOCHASIUM
PLEIOMERIES
PLEIOMEROUS
PLEIOTAXIES
PLEIOTROPIC
PLEIOTROPIES
PLEIOTROPISM
PLEIOTROPISMS
PLEIOTROPY
PLENARTIES
PLENILUNAR
PLENILUNES
PLENIPOTENCE
PLENIPOTENCES
PLENIPOTENCIES
PLENIPOTENCY
PLENIPOTENT
PLENIPOTENTIAL
PLENIPOTENTIARY
PLENISHERS
PLENISHING
PLENISHINGS
PLENISHMENT
PLENISHMENTS
PLENITUDES
PLENITUDINOUS
PLENTEOUSLY
PLENTEOUSNESS
PLENTEOUSNESSES
PLENTIFULLY
PLENTIFULNESS
PLENTIFULNESSES
PLENTITUDE
PLENTITUDES
PLEOCHROIC
PLEOCHROISM
PLEOCHROISMS
PLEOMORPHIC
PLEOMORPHIES
PLEOMORPHISM
PLEOMORPHISMS
PLEOMORPHOUS
PLEOMORPHY
PLEONASTES
PLEONASTIC
PLEONASTICAL
PLEONASTICALLY
PLEONECTIC
PLEONEXIAS
PLEROCERCOID
PLEROCERCOIDS
PLEROMATIC
PLEROPHORIA
PLEROPHORIAS
PLEROPHORIES
PLEROPHORY
PLESIOSAUR
PLESIOSAURIAN
PLESIOSAURIANS
PLESIOSAURS
PLESSIMETER
PLESSIMETERS
PLESSIMETRIC
PLESSIMETRIES
PLESSIMETRY
PLETHORICAL
PLETHORICALLY
PLETHYSMOGRAM
PLETHYSMOGRAMS
PLETHYSMOGRAPH
PLETHYSMOGRAPHS
PLETHYSMOGRAPHY
PLEURAPOPHYSES
PLEURAPOPHYSIS
PLEURISIES
PLEURITICAL
PLEURITICS
PLEURITISES
PLEUROCARPOUS
PLEUROCENTESES
PLEUROCENTESIS
PLEURODONT
PLEURODONTS
PLEURODYNIA
PLEURODYNIAS
PLEURONIAS
PLEUROPNEUMONIA
PLEUROTOMIES
PLEUROTOMY
PLEUSTONIC
PLEXIGLASS
PLEXIGLASSES
PLEXIMETER
PLEXIMETERS
PLEXIMETRIC
PLEXIMETRIES
PLEXIMETRY
PLIABILITIES
PLIABILITY
PLIABLENESS
PLIABLENESSES
PLIANTNESS
PLIANTNESSES
PLICATENESS
PLICATENESSES
PLICATIONS
PLICATURES
PLODDINGLY
PLODDINGNESS
PLODDINGNESSES
PLOTLESSNESS
PLOTLESSNESSES
PLOTTERING
PLOTTINGLY
PLOUGHABLE
PLOUGHBACK
PLOUGHBACKS
PLOUGHBOYS
PLOUGHGATE
PLOUGHGATES
PLOUGHHEAD
PLOUGHHEADS
PLOUGHINGS
PLOUGHLAND
PLOUGHLANDS
PLOUGHMANSHIP
PLOUGHMANSHIPS
PLOUGHSHARE
PLOUGHSHARES
PLOUGHSTAFF
PLOUGHSTAFFS
PLOUGHTAIL
PLOUGHTAILS
PLOUGHWISE
PLOUGHWRIGHT
PLOUGHWRIGHTS
PLOUTERING
PLOVERIEST
PLOWMANSHIP
PLOWMANSHIPS
PLOWSHARES
PLOWSTAFFS
PLOWTERING
PLOWWRIGHT
PLOWWRIGHTS
PLUCKINESS
PLUCKINESSES
PLUGBOARDS
PLUGUGLIES
PLUMASSIER
PLUMASSIERS

PLUMBAGINACEOUS
PLUMBAGINOUS
PLUMBERIES
PLUMBIFEROUS
PLUMBISOLVENCY
PLUMBISOLVENT
PLUMBNESSES
PLUMBOSOLVENCY
PLUMBOSOLVENT
PLUMDAMASES
PLUMIGEROUS
PLUMMETING
PLUMOSITIES
PLUMPENING
PLUMPNESSES
PLUMULACEOUS
PLUMULARIAN
PLUMULARIANS
PLUNDERABLE
PLUNDERAGE
PLUNDERAGES
PLUNDERERS
PLUNDERING
PLUNDEROUS
PLUPERFECT
PLUPERFECTS
PLURALISATION
PLURALISATIONS
PLURALISED
PLURALISER
PLURALISERS
PLURALISES
PLURALISING
PLURALISMS
PLURALISTIC
PLURALISTICALLY
PLURALISTS
PLURALITIES
PLURALIZATION
PLURALIZATIONS
PLURALIZED
PLURALIZER
PLURALIZERS
PLURALIZES
PLURALIZING
PLURILITERAL
PLURILOCULAR
PLURIPARAE
PLURIPARAS
PLURIPOTENT
PLURIPRESENCE
PLURIPRESENCES
PLURISERIAL
PLURISERIATE
PLUSHINESS
PLUSHINESSES
PLUSHNESSES
PLUTOCRACIES
PLUTOCRACY
PLUTOCRATIC
PLUTOCRATICAL
PLUTOCRATICALLY
PLUTOCRATS
PLUTOLATRIES
PLUTOLATRY
PLUTOLOGIES
PLUTOLOGIST
PLUTOLOGISTS
PLUTONISMS
PLUTONIUMS
PLUTONOMIES
PLUTONOMIST
PLUTONOMISTS
PLUVIOMETER
PLUVIOMETERS
PLUVIOMETRIC
PLUVIOMETRICAL
PLUVIOMETRIES
PLUVIOMETRY
PLYOMETRIC
PLYOMETRICS
PNEUMATHODE
PNEUMATHODES
PNEUMATICAL
PNEUMATICALLY
PNEUMATICITIES
PNEUMATICITY
PNEUMATICS
PNEUMATOLOGICAL
PNEUMATOLOGIES
PNEUMATOLOGIST
PNEUMATOLOGISTS
PNEUMATOLOGY
PNEUMATOLYSES
PNEUMATOLYSIS
PNEUMATOLYTIC
PNEUMATOMETER
PNEUMATOMETERS
PNEUMATOMETRIES
PNEUMATOMETRY
PNEUMATOPHORE
PNEUMATOPHORES
PNEUMECTOMIES
PNEUMECTOMY
PNEUMOBACILLI
PNEUMOBACILLUS
PNEUMOCOCCAL
PNEUMOCOCCI
PNEUMOCOCCUS
PNEUMOCONIOSES
PNEUMOCONIOSIS
PNEUMOCONIOTIC
PNEUMOCONIOTICS
PNEUMOCYSTIS
PNEUMOCYSTISES
PNEUMODYNAMICS
PNEUMOGASTRIC
PNEUMOGASTRICS
PNEUMOGRAM
PNEUMOGRAMS
PNEUMOGRAPH
PNEUMOGRAPHS
PNEUMOKONIOSES
PNEUMOKONIOSIS
PNEUMONECTOMIES
PNEUMONECTOMY
PNEUMONIAS
PNEUMONICS
PNEUMONITIDES
PNEUMONITIS
PNEUMONITISES
PNEUMONOLOGIES
PNEUMONOLOGIST
PNEUMONOLOGISTS
PNEUMONOLOGY
PNEUMOTHORACES
PNEUMOTHORAX
PNEUMOTHORAXES
POACHINESS
POACHINESSES
POCKETABLE
POCKETBIKE
POCKETBIKES
POCKETBOOK
POCKETBOOKS
POCKETFULS
POCKETKNIFE
POCKETKNIVES
POCKETLESS
POCKETPHONE
POCKETPHONES
POCKETSFUL
POCKMANKIES
POCKMANTIE
POCKMANTIES
POCKMARKED
POCKMARKING
POCKPITTED
POCOCURANTE
POCOCURANTEISM
POCOCURANTEISMS
POCOCURANTES
POCOCURANTISM
POCOCURANTISMS
POCOCURANTIST
POCOCURANTISTS
POCULIFORM
PODAGRICAL
PODARGUSES
PODCASTERS
PODCASTING
PODCASTINGS
PODGINESSES
PODIATRIES
PODIATRIST
PODIATRISTS
PODOCONIOSES
PODOCONIOSIS
PODOLOGIES
PODOLOGIST
PODOLOGISTS
PODOPHTHALMOUS
PODOPHYLIN
PODOPHYLINS
PODOPHYLLI
PODOPHYLLIN
PODOPHYLLINS
PODOPHYLLUM
PODOPHYLLUMS
PODOSPHERE
PODOSPHERES
PODSOLISATION
PODSOLISATIONS
PODSOLISED
PODSOLISES
PODSOLISING
PODSOLIZATION
PODSOLIZATIONS
PODSOLIZED
PODSOLIZES
PODSOLIZING
PODZOLISATION
PODZOLISATIONS
PODZOLISED
PODZOLISES
PODZOLISING
PODZOLIZATION
PODZOLIZATIONS
PODZOLIZED
PODZOLIZES
PODZOLIZING
POENOLOGIES
POETASTERIES
POETASTERING
POETASTERINGS
POETASTERS
POETASTERY
POETASTRIES
POETICALLY
POETICALNESS
POETICALNESSES
POETICISED
POETICISES
POETICISING
POETICISMS
POETICIZED
POETICIZES
POETICIZING
POETICULES
POETRESSES
POGONOPHORAN
POGONOPHORANS
POGONOTOMIES
POGONOTOMY
POGROMISTS
POHUTUKAWA
POHUTUKAWAS
POIGNADOES
POIGNANCES
POIGNANCIES

POIGNANTLY
POIKILITIC
POIKILOCYTE
POIKILOCYTES
POIKILOTHERM
POIKILOTHERMAL
POIKILOTHERMIC
POIKILOTHERMIES
POIKILOTHERMISM
POIKILOTHERMS
POIKILOTHERMY
POINCIANAS
POINSETTIA
POINSETTIAS
POINTEDNESS
POINTEDNESSES
POINTELLES
POINTILLES
POINTILLISM
POINTILLISME
POINTILLISMES
POINTILLISMS
POINTILLIST
POINTILLISTE
POINTILLISTES
POINTILLISTIC
POINTILLISTS
POINTLESSLY
POINTLESSNESS
POINTLESSNESSES
POISONABLE
POISONINGS
POISONOUSLY
POISONOUSNESS
POISONOUSNESSES
POISONWOOD
POISONWOODS
POKEBERRIES
POKELOGANS
POKERISHLY
POKERWORKS
POKINESSES
POLARIMETER
POLARIMETERS
POLARIMETRIC
POLARIMETRIES
POLARIMETRY
POLARISABILITY
POLARISABLE
POLARISATION
POLARISATIONS
POLARISCOPE
POLARISCOPES
POLARISCOPIC
POLARISERS
POLARISING
POLARITIES
POLARIZABILITY
POLARIZABLE
POLARIZATION
POLARIZATIONS
POLARIZERS
POLARIZING
POLAROGRAM
POLAROGRAMS
POLAROGRAPH
POLAROGRAPHIC
POLAROGRAPHIES
POLAROGRAPHS
POLAROGRAPHY
POLEMARCHS
POLEMICALLY
POLEMICISE
POLEMICISED
POLEMICISES
POLEMICISING
POLEMICIST
POLEMICISTS
POLEMICIZE
POLEMICIZED
POLEMICIZES
POLEMICIZING
POLEMISING
POLEMIZING
POLEMONIACEOUS
POLEMONIUM
POLEMONIUMS
POLIANITES
POLICEWOMAN
POLICEWOMEN
POLICYHOLDER
POLICYHOLDERS
POLICYMAKER
POLICYMAKERS
POLIOMYELITIDES
POLIOMYELITIS
POLIOMYELITISES
POLIORCETIC
POLIORCETICS
POLIOVIRUS
POLIOVIRUSES
POLISHABLE
POLISHINGS
POLISHMENT
POLISHMENTS
POLITBUROS
POLITENESS
POLITENESSES
POLITESSES
POLITICALISE
POLITICALISED
POLITICALISES
POLITICALISING
POLITICALIZE
POLITICALIZED
POLITICALIZES
POLITICALIZING
POLITICALLY
POLITICASTER
POLITICASTERS
POLITICIAN
POLITICIANS
POLITICISATION
POLITICISATIONS
POLITICISE
POLITICISED
POLITICISES
POLITICISING
POLITICIZATION
POLITICIZATIONS
POLITICIZE
POLITICIZED
POLITICIZES
POLITICIZING
POLITICKED
POLITICKER
POLITICKERS
POLITICKING
POLITICKINGS
POLITICOES
POLITIQUES
POLLARDING
POLLENATED
POLLENATES
POLLENATING
POLLENIFEROUS
POLLENISER
POLLENISERS
POLLENIZER
POLLENIZERS
POLLENOSES
POLLENOSIS
POLLICITATION
POLLICITATIONS
POLLINATED
POLLINATES
POLLINATING
POLLINATION
POLLINATIONS
POLLINATOR
POLLINATORS
POLLINIFEROUS
POLLINISED
POLLINISER
POLLINISERS
POLLINISES
POLLINISING
POLLINIZED
POLLINIZER
POLLINIZERS
POLLINIZES
POLLINIZING
POLLINOSES
POLLINOSIS
POLLTAKERS
POLLUCITES
POLLUSIONS
POLLUTANTS
POLLUTEDLY
POLLUTEDNESS
POLLUTEDNESSES
POLLUTIONS
POLLYANNAISH
POLLYANNAISM
POLLYANNAISMS
POLLYANNAS
POLLYANNISH
POLONAISES
POLONISING
POLONIZING
POLTERGEIST
POLTERGEISTS
POLTROONERIES
POLTROONERY
POLVERINES
POLYACRYLAMIDE
POLYACRYLAMIDES
POLYACTINAL
POLYACTINE
POLYACTINES
POLYADELPHOUS
POLYALCOHOL
POLYALCOHOLS
POLYAMIDES
POLYAMINES
POLYAMORIES
POLYAMOROUS
POLYANDRIES
POLYANDROUS
POLYANTHAS
POLYANTHUS
POLYANTHUSES
POLYARCHIES
POLYARTHRITIDES
POLYARTHRITIS
POLYARTHRITISES
POLYATOMIC
POLYAXIALS
POLYAXONIC
POLYBAGGED
POLYBAGGING
POLYBASITE
POLYBASITES
POLYBUTADIENE
POLYBUTADIENES
POLYCARBONATE
POLYCARBONATES
POLYCARBOXYLATE
POLYCARBOXYLIC
POLYCARPELLARY
POLYCARPIC
POLYCARPIES
POLYCARPOUS
POLYCENTRIC
POLYCENTRICS
POLYCENTRISM
POLYCENTRISMS
POLYCHAETE
POLYCHAETES
POLYCHAETOUS

P

POLYCHASIA
POLYCHASIUM
POLYCHETES
POLYCHETOUS
POLYCHLORINATED
POLYCHLOROPRENE
POLYCHOTOMIES
POLYCHOTOMOUS
POLYCHOTOMY
POLYCHREST
POLYCHRESTS
POLYCHROIC
POLYCHROISM
POLYCHROISMS
POLYCHROMATIC
POLYCHROMATISM
POLYCHROMATISMS
POLYCHROME
POLYCHROMED
POLYCHROMES
POLYCHROMIC
POLYCHROMIES
POLYCHROMING
POLYCHROMOUS
POLYCHROMY
POLYCISTRONIC
POLYCLINIC
POLYCLINICS
POLYCLONAL
POLYCLONALS
POLYCOTTON
POLYCOTTONS
POLYCOTYLEDON
POLYCOTYLEDONS
POLYCROTIC
POLYCROTISM
POLYCROTISMS
POLYCRYSTAL
POLYCRYSTALLINE
POLYCRYSTALS
POLYCULTURE
POLYCULTURES
POLYCYCLIC
POLYCYCLICS
POLYCYSTIC
POLYCYTHAEMIA
POLYCYTHAEMIAS
POLYCYTHEMIA
POLYCYTHEMIAS
POLYCYTHEMIC
POLYDACTYL
POLYDACTYLIES
POLYDACTYLISM
POLYDACTYLISMS
POLYDACTYLOUS
POLYDACTYLS
POLYDACTYLY
POLYDAEMONISM
POLYDAEMONISMS
POLYDEMONISM
POLYDEMONISMS
POLYDIPSIA
POLYDIPSIAS
POLYDIPSIC
POLYDISPERSE
POLYDISPERSITY
POLYELECTROLYTE
POLYEMBRYONATE
POLYEMBRYONIC
POLYEMBRYONIES
POLYEMBRYONY
POLYESTERS
POLYESTROUS
POLYETHENE
POLYETHENES
POLYETHYLENE
POLYETHYLENES
POLYGALACEOUS
POLYGAMIES
POLYGAMISE
POLYGAMISED
POLYGAMISES
POLYGAMISING
POLYGAMIST
POLYGAMISTS
POLYGAMIZE
POLYGAMIZED
POLYGAMIZES
POLYGAMIZING
POLYGAMOUS
POLYGAMOUSLY
POLYGENESES
POLYGENESIS
POLYGENETIC
POLYGENETICALLY
POLYGENIES
POLYGENISM
POLYGENISMS
POLYGENIST
POLYGENISTS
POLYGENOUS
POLYGLOTISM
POLYGLOTISMS
POLYGLOTTAL
POLYGLOTTIC
POLYGLOTTISM
POLYGLOTTISMS
POLYGLOTTOUS
POLYGLOTTS
POLYGONACEOUS
POLYGONALLY
POLYGONATUM
POLYGONATUMS
POLYGONIES
POLYGONUMS
POLYGRAPHED
POLYGRAPHER
POLYGRAPHERS
POLYGRAPHIC
POLYGRAPHICALLY
POLYGRAPHIES
POLYGRAPHING
POLYGRAPHIST
POLYGRAPHISTS
POLYGRAPHS
POLYGRAPHY
POLYGYNIAN
POLYGYNIES
POLYGYNIST
POLYGYNISTS
POLYGYNOUS
POLYHALITE
POLYHALITES
POLYHEDRAL
POLYHEDRIC
POLYHEDRON
POLYHEDRONS
POLYHEDROSES
POLYHEDROSIS
POLYHISTOR
POLYHISTORIAN
POLYHISTORIANS
POLYHISTORIC
POLYHISTORIES
POLYHISTORS
POLYHISTORY
POLYHYBRID
POLYHYBRIDS
POLYHYDRIC
POLYHYDROXY
POLYIMIDES
POLYISOPRENE
POLYISOPRENES
POLYLEMMAS
POLYLINGUAL
POLYLYSINE
POLYLYSINES
POLYMASTIA
POLYMASTIAS
POLYMASTIC
POLYMASTICS
POLYMASTIES
POLYMASTISM
POLYMASTISMS
POLYMATHIC
POLYMATHIES
POLYMERASE
POLYMERASES
POLYMERIDE
POLYMERIDES
POLYMERIES
POLYMERISATION
POLYMERISATIONS
POLYMERISE
POLYMERISED
POLYMERISES
POLYMERISING
POLYMERISM
POLYMERISMS
POLYMERIZATION
POLYMERIZATIONS
POLYMERIZE
POLYMERIZED
POLYMERIZES
POLYMERIZING
POLYMEROUS
POLYMORPHIC
POLYMORPHICALLY
POLYMORPHISM
POLYMORPHISMS
POLYMORPHOUS
POLYMORPHOUSLY
POLYMORPHS
POLYMYOSITIS
POLYMYOSITISES
POLYMYXINS
POLYNEURITIDES
POLYNEURITIS
POLYNEURITISES
POLYNOMIAL
POLYNOMIALISM
POLYNOMIALISMS
POLYNOMIALS
POLYNUCLEAR
POLYNUCLEATE
POLYNUCLEOTIDE
POLYNUCLEOTIDES
POLYOLEFIN
POLYOLEFINS
POLYOMINOES
POLYOMINOS
POLYONYMIC
POLYONYMIES
POLYONYMOUS
POLYPARIES
POLYPARIUM
POLYPEPTIDE
POLYPEPTIDES
POLYPEPTIDIC
POLYPETALOUS
POLYPHAGIA
POLYPHAGIAS
POLYPHAGIES
POLYPHAGOUS
POLYPHARMACIES
POLYPHARMACY
POLYPHASIC
POLYPHENOL
POLYPHENOLIC
POLYPHENOLS
POLYPHLOESBOEAN
POLYPHLOISBIC
POLYPHONES
POLYPHONIC
POLYPHONICALLY
POLYPHONIES
POLYPHONIST
POLYPHONISTS
POLYPHONOUS
POLYPHONOUSLY

POLYPHOSPHORIC
POLYPHYLETIC
POLYPHYLLOUS
POLYPHYODONT
POLYPIDOMS
POLYPLOIDAL
POLYPLOIDIC
POLYPLOIDIES
POLYPLOIDS
POLYPLOIDY
POLYPODIES
POLYPODOUS
POLYPROPENE
POLYPROPENES
POLYPROPYLENE
POLYPROPYLENES
POLYPROTODONT
POLYPROTODONTS
POLYPTYCHS
POLYRHYTHM
POLYRHYTHMIC
POLYRHYTHMS
POLYRIBOSOMAL
POLYRIBOSOME
POLYRIBOSOMES
POLYSACCHARIDE
POLYSACCHARIDES
POLYSACCHAROSE
POLYSACCHAROSES
POLYSEMANT
POLYSEMANTS
POLYSEMIES
POLYSEMOUS
POLYSEPALOUS
POLYSILOXANE
POLYSILOXANES
POLYSOMICS
POLYSOMIES
POLYSORBATE
POLYSORBATES
POLYSTICHOUS
POLYSTYLAR
POLYSTYLES
POLYSTYRENE
POLYSTYRENES
POLYSULFIDE
POLYSULFIDES
POLYSULPHIDE
POLYSULPHIDES
POLYSYLLABIC
POLYSYLLABICAL
POLYSYLLABICISM
POLYSYLLABISM
POLYSYLLABISMS
POLYSYLLABLE
POLYSYLLABLES
POLYSYLLOGISM
POLYSYLLOGISMS
POLYSYNAPTIC
POLYSYNDETON
POLYSYNDETONS
POLYSYNTHESES
POLYSYNTHESIS
POLYSYNTHESISM
POLYSYNTHESISMS
POLYSYNTHETIC
POLYSYNTHETICAL
POLYSYNTHETISM
POLYSYNTHETISMS
POLYTECHNIC
POLYTECHNICAL
POLYTECHNICS
POLYTENIES
POLYTHALAMOUS
POLYTHEISM
POLYTHEISMS
POLYTHEIST
POLYTHEISTIC
POLYTHEISTICAL
POLYTHEISTS
POLYTHENES
POLYTOCOUS
POLYTONALISM
POLYTONALISMS
POLYTONALIST
POLYTONALISTS
POLYTONALITIES
POLYTONALITY
POLYTONALLY
POLYTROPHIC
POLYTUNNEL
POLYTUNNELS
POLYTYPICAL
POLYTYPING
POLYUNSATURATE
POLYUNSATURATED
POLYUNSATURATES
POLYURETHAN
POLYURETHANE
POLYURETHANES
POLYURETHANS
POLYVALENCE
POLYVALENCES
POLYVALENCIES
POLYVALENCY
POLYVALENT
POLYVINYLIDENE
POLYVINYLIDENES
POLYVINYLS
POLYWATERS
POLYZOARIA
POLYZOARIAL
POLYZOARIES
POLYZOARIUM
POMATUMING
POMEGRANATE
POMEGRANATES
POMICULTURE
POMICULTURES
POMIFEROUS
POMMELLING
POMOERIUMS
POMOLOGICAL
POMOLOGICALLY
POMOLOGIES
POMOLOGIST
POMOLOGISTS
POMOSEXUAL
POMOSEXUALS
POMPADOURED
POMPADOURS
POMPELMOOSE
POMPELMOOSES
POMPELMOUS
POMPELMOUSE
POMPELMOUSES
POMPHOLYGOUS
POMPHOLYXES
POMPOSITIES
POMPOUSNESS
POMPOUSNESSES
PONDERABILITIES
PONDERABILITY
PONDERABLE
PONDERABLES
PONDERABLY
PONDERANCE
PONDERANCES
PONDERANCIES
PONDERANCY
PONDERATED
PONDERATES
PONDERATING
PONDERATION
PONDERATIONS
PONDERINGLY
PONDERMENT
PONDERMENTS
PONDEROSAS
PONDEROSITIES
PONDEROSITY
PONDEROUSLY
PONDEROUSNESS
PONDEROUSNESSES
PONDOKKIES
PONEROLOGIES
PONEROLOGY
PONIARDING
PONTIANACS
PONTIANAKS
PONTICELLO
PONTICELLOS
PONTIFICAL
PONTIFICALITIES
PONTIFICALITY
PONTIFICALLY
PONTIFICALS
PONTIFICATE
PONTIFICATED
PONTIFICATES
PONTIFICATING
PONTIFICATION
PONTIFICATIONS
PONTIFICATOR
PONTIFICATORS
PONTIFICES
PONTIFYING
PONTLEVISES
PONTONEERS
PONTONIERS
PONTONNIER
PONTONNIERS
PONTOONERS
PONTOONING
PONYTAILED
POORHOUSES
POORMOUTHED
POORMOUTHING
POORMOUTHS
POORNESSES
POPLINETTE
POPLINETTES
POPMOBILITIES
POPMOBILITY
POPPERINGS
POPPYCOCKS
POPPYHEADS
POPULARISATION
POPULARISATIONS
POPULARISE
POPULARISED
POPULARISER
POPULARISERS
POPULARISES
POPULARISING
POPULARIST
POPULARITIES
POPULARITY
POPULARIZATION
POPULARIZATIONS
POPULARIZE
POPULARIZED
POPULARIZER
POPULARIZERS
POPULARIZES
POPULARIZING
POPULATING
POPULATION
POPULATIONAL
POPULATIONS
POPULISTIC
POPULOUSLY
POPULOUSNESS
POPULOUSNESSES
PORBEAGLES
PORCELAINEOUS
PORCELAINISE
PORCELAINISED
PORCELAINISES
PORCELAINISING

PORCELAINIZE
PORCELAINIZED
PORCELAINIZES
PORCELAINIZING
PORCELAINLIKE
PORCELAINOUS
PORCELAINS
PORCELANEOUS
PORCELLANEOUS
PORCELLANISE
PORCELLANISED
PORCELLANISES
PORCELLANISING
PORCELLANITE
PORCELLANITES
PORCELLANIZE
PORCELLANIZED
PORCELLANIZES
PORCELLANIZING
PORCELLANOUS
PORCHETTAS
PORCUPINES
PORCUPINIER
PORCUPINIEST
PORCUPINISH
PORIFERANS
PORIFEROUS
PORINESSES
PORISMATIC
PORISMATICAL
PORISTICAL
PORKINESSES
PORLOCKING
PORNIFICATION
PORNIFICATIONS
PORNOCRACIES
PORNOCRACY
PORNOGRAPHER
PORNOGRAPHERS
PORNOGRAPHIC
PORNOGRAPHIES
PORNOGRAPHY
PORNOTOPIA
PORNOTOPIAN
PORNOTOPIAS
POROGAMIES
POROMERICS
POROSCOPES
POROSCOPIC
POROSCOPIES
POROSITIES
POROUSNESS
POROUSNESSES
PORPENTINE
PORPENTINES
PORPHYRIAS
PORPHYRIES
PORPHYRINS
PORPHYRIOS
PORPHYRITE
PORPHYRITES
PORPHYRITIC
PORPHYROGENITE
PORPHYROGENITES
PORPHYROID
PORPHYROIDS
PORPHYROPSIN
PORPHYROPSINS
PORPHYROUS
PORPOISING
PORRACEOUS
PORRECTING
PORRECTION
PORRECTIONS
PORRENGERS
PORRIDGIER
PORRIDGIEST
PORRIGINOUS
PORRINGERS
PORTABELLA
PORTABELLAS
PORTABELLO
PORTABELLOS
PORTABILITIES
PORTABILITY
PORTAMENTI
PORTAMENTO
PORTAPACKS
PORTATIVES
PORTCULLIS
PORTCULLISED
PORTCULLISES
PORTCULLISING
PORTENDING
PORTENTOUS
PORTENTOUSLY
PORTENTOUSNESS
PORTEOUSES
PORTERAGES
PORTERESSES
PORTERHOUSE
PORTERHOUSES
PORTFOLIOS
PORTHORSES
PORTHOUSES
PORTIONERS
PORTIONING
PORTIONIST
PORTIONISTS
PORTIONLESS
PORTLINESS
PORTLINESSES
PORTMANTEAU
PORTMANTEAUS
PORTMANTEAUX
PORTMANTLE
PORTMANTLES
PORTMANTUA
PORTMANTUAS
PORTOBELLO
PORTOBELLOS
PORTOLANOS
PORTRAITED
PORTRAITING
PORTRAITIST
PORTRAITISTS
PORTRAITURE
PORTRAITURES
PORTRAYABLE
PORTRAYALS
PORTRAYERS
PORTRAYING
PORTREEVES
PORTRESSES
PORTULACACEOUS
PORTULACAS
PORWIGGLES
POSHNESSES
POSITIONAL
POSITIONALLY
POSITIONED
POSITIONING
POSITIONINGS
POSITIVELY
POSITIVENESS
POSITIVENESSES
POSITIVEST
POSITIVISM
POSITIVISMS
POSITIVIST
POSITIVISTIC
POSITIVISTS
POSITIVITIES
POSITIVITY
POSITRONIUM
POSITRONIUMS
POSOLOGICAL
POSOLOGIES
POSSESSABLE
POSSESSEDLY
POSSESSEDNESS
POSSESSEDNESSES
POSSESSING
POSSESSION
POSSESSIONAL
POSSESSIONARY
POSSESSIONATE
POSSESSIONATES
POSSESSIONED
POSSESSIONLESS
POSSESSIONS
POSSESSIVE
POSSESSIVELY
POSSESSIVENESS
POSSESSIVES
POSSESSORS
POSSESSORSHIP
POSSESSORSHIPS
POSSESSORY
POSSIBILISM
POSSIBILISMS
POSSIBILIST
POSSIBILISTS
POSSIBILITIES
POSSIBILITY
POSSIBLEST
POSTABORTION
POSTACCIDENT
POSTADOLESCENT
POSTADOLESCENTS
POSTAMPUTATION
POSTAPOCALYPTIC
POSTARREST
POSTATOMIC
POSTATTACK
POSTBELLUM
POSTBIBLICAL
POSTBOURGEOIS
POSTBUSSES
POSTCAPITALIST
POSTCARDED
POSTCARDING
POSTCARDLIKE
POSTCLASSIC
POSTCLASSICAL
POSTCODING
POSTCOITAL
POSTCOLLEGE
POSTCOLLEGIATE
POSTCOLONIAL
POSTCONCEPTION
POSTCONCERT
POSTCONQUEST
POSTCONSONANTAL
POSTCONVENTION
POSTCOPULATORY
POSTCORONARY
POSTCRANIAL
POSTCRANIALLY
POSTCRISIS
POSTDATING
POSTDEADLINE
POSTDEBATE
POSTDEBUTANTE
POSTDELIVERY
POSTDEPRESSION
POSTDEVALUATION
POSTDILUVIAL
POSTDILUVIAN
POSTDILUVIANS
POSTDIVESTITURE
POSTDIVORCE
POSTDOCTORAL
POSTDOCTORALS
POSTDOCTORATE
POSTDOCTORATES
POSTEDITING
POSTEDITINGS
POSTELECTION
POSTEMBRYONAL

POSTEMBRYONIC
POSTEMERGENCE
POSTEMERGENCY
POSTEPILEPTIC
POSTERIORITIES
POSTERIORITY
POSTERIORLY
POSTERIORS
POSTERISATION
POSTERISATIONS
POSTERISED
POSTERISES
POSTERISING
POSTERITIES
POSTERIZATION
POSTERIZATIONS
POSTERIZED
POSTERIZES
POSTERIZING
POSTEROLATERAL
POSTERUPTIVE
POSTEXERCISE
POSTEXILIAN
POSTEXILIC
POSTEXPERIENCE
POSTEXPOSURE
POSTFEMINISM
POSTFEMINISMS
POSTFEMINIST
POSTFEMINISTS
POSTFIXING
POSTFLIGHT
POSTFORMED
POSTFORMING
POSTFRACTURE
POSTFREEZE
POSTGANGLIONIC
POSTGLACIAL
POSTGRADUATE
POSTGRADUATES
POSTGRADUATION
POSTGRADUATIONS
POSTHARVEST
POSTHASTES
POSTHEATED
POSTHEATING
POSTHEMORRHAGIC
POSTHOLDER
POSTHOLDERS
POSTHOLIDAY
POSTHOLOCAUST
POSTHORSES
POSTHOSPITAL
POSTHOUSES
POSTHUMOUS
POSTHUMOUSLY
POSTHUMOUSNESS
POSTHYPNOTIC
POSTILIONS
POSTILLATE
POSTILLATED
POSTILLATES
POSTILLATING
POSTILLATION
POSTILLATIONS
POSTILLATOR
POSTILLATORS
POSTILLERS
POSTILLING
POSTILLION
POSTILLIONS
POSTIMPACT
POSTIMPERIAL
POSTINAUGURAL
POSTINDUSTRIAL
POSTINFECTION
POSTINJECTION
POSTINOCULATION
POSTIRRADIATION
POSTISCHEMIC
POSTISOLATION
POSTLANDING
POSTLAPSARIAN
POSTLAUNCH
POSTLIBERATION
POSTLIMINARY
POSTLIMINIA
POSTLIMINIARY
POSTLIMINIES
POSTLIMINIOUS
POSTLIMINIUM
POSTLIMINOUS
POSTLIMINY
POSTLITERATE
POSTMARITAL
POSTMARKED
POSTMARKING
POSTMASTECTOMY
POSTMASTER
POSTMASTERS
POSTMASTERSHIP
POSTMASTERSHIPS
POSTMATING
POSTMEDIEVAL
POSTMENOPAUSAL
POSTMENSTRUAL
POSTMERIDIAN
POSTMIDNIGHT
POSTMILLENARIAN
POSTMILLENNIAL
POSTMISTRESS
POSTMISTRESSES
POSTMODERN
POSTMODERNISM
POSTMODERNISMS
POSTMODERNIST
POSTMODERNISTS
POSTMODERNS
POSTMODIFIED
POSTMODIFIES
POSTMODIFY
POSTMODIFYING
POSTMORTEM
POSTMORTEMS
POSTNATALLY
POSTNEONATAL
POSTNUPTIAL
POSTOCULAR
POSTOCULARS
POSTOPERATIVE
POSTOPERATIVELY
POSTORBITAL
POSTORGASMIC
POSTPARTUM
POSTPERSON
POSTPERSONS
POSTPOLLINATION
POSTPONABLE
POSTPONEMENT
POSTPONEMENTS
POSTPONENCE
POSTPONENCES
POSTPONERS
POSTPONING
POSTPOSING
POSTPOSITION
POSTPOSITIONAL
POSTPOSITIONS
POSTPOSITIVE
POSTPOSITIVELY
POSTPOSITIVES
POSTPRANDIAL
POSTPRIMARY
POSTPRISON
POSTPRODUCTION
POSTPRODUCTIONS
POSTPUBERTIES
POSTPUBERTY
POSTPUBESCENT
POSTPUBESCENTS
POSTRECESSION
POSTRETIREMENT
POSTRIDERS
POSTROMANTIC
POSTROMANTICS
POSTSCENIUM
POSTSCENIUMS
POSTSCRIPT
POSTSCRIPTS
POSTSEASON
POSTSEASONS
POSTSECONDARY
POSTSTIMULATION
POSTSTIMULATORY
POSTSTIMULUS
POSTSTRIKE
POSTSURGICAL
POSTSYNAPTIC
POSTSYNCED
POSTSYNCHRONISE
POSTSYNCHRONIZE
POSTSYNCING
POSTTENSION
POSTTENSIONED
POSTTENSIONING
POSTTENSIONS
POSTTRANSFUSION
POSTTRAUMATIC
POSTTREATMENT
POSTTREATMENTS
POSTULANCIES
POSTULANCY
POSTULANTS
POSTULANTSHIP
POSTULANTSHIPS
POSTULATED
POSTULATES
POSTULATING
POSTULATION
POSTULATIONAL
POSTULATIONALLY
POSTULATIONS
POSTULATOR
POSTULATORS
POSTULATORY
POSTULATUM
POSTURINGS
POSTURISED
POSTURISES
POSTURISING
POSTURISTS
POSTURIZED
POSTURIZES
POSTURIZING
POSTVACCINAL
POSTVACCINATION
POSTVAGOTOMY
POSTVASECTOMY
POSTVOCALIC
POSTWEANING
POSTWORKSHOP
POTABILITIES
POTABILITY
POTABLENESS
POTABLENESSES
POTAMOGETON
POTAMOGETONS
POTAMOLOGICAL
POTAMOLOGIES
POTAMOLOGIST
POTAMOLOGISTS
POTAMOLOGY
POTASSIUMS
POTATOBUGS
POTBELLIED
POTBELLIES
POTBOILERS
POTBOILING
POTBOILINGS
POTENTATES

POTENTIALITIES
POTENTIALITY
POTENTIALLY
POTENTIALS
POTENTIARIES
POTENTIARY
POTENTIATE
POTENTIATED
POTENTIATES
POTENTIATING
POTENTIATION
POTENTIATIONS
POTENTIATOR
POTENTIATORS
POTENTILLA
POTENTILLAS
POTENTIOMETER
POTENTIOMETERS
POTENTIOMETRIC
POTENTIOMETRIES
POTENTIOMETRY
POTENTISED
POTENTISES
POTENTISING
POTENTIZED
POTENTIZES
POTENTIZING
POTENTNESS
POTENTNESSES
POTHECARIES
POTHERIEST
POTHOLDERS
POTHOLINGS
POTHUNTERS
POTHUNTING
POTHUNTINGS
POTICARIES
POTICHOMANIA
POTICHOMANIAS
POTLATCHED
POTLATCHES
POTLATCHING
POTOMETERS
POTPOURRIS
POTSHOTTING
POTSHOTTINGS
POTTERINGLY
POTTERINGS
POTTINESSES
POTTINGARS
POTTINGERS
POTTYMOUTH
POTTYMOUTHS
POTWALLERS
POULTERERS
POULTICING
POULTROONE
POULTROONES
POULTRYMAN
POULTRYMEN
POUNDCAKES
POURBOIRES
POURPARLER
POURPARLERS
POURPOINTS
POURSEWING
POURTRAHED
POURTRAICT
POURTRAICTS
POURTRAYED
POURTRAYING
POUSOWDIES
POUSSETTED
POUSSETTES
POUSSETTING
POUTASSOUS
POUTHERING
POWDERIEST
POWDERINGS
POWDERLESS
POWDERLIKE
POWELLISED
POWELLISES
POWELLISING
POWELLITES
POWELLIZED
POWELLIZES
POWELLIZING
POWERBANDS
POWERBOATING
POWERBOATINGS
POWERBOATS
POWERFULLY
POWERFULNESS
POWERFULNESSES
POWERHOUSE
POWERHOUSES
POWERLESSLY
POWERLESSNESS
POWERLESSNESSES
POWERLIFTER
POWERLIFTERS
POWERLIFTING
POWERLIFTINGS
POWERPLAYS
POWERTRAIN
POWERTRAINS
POWSOWDIES
POXVIRUSES
POZZOLANAS
POZZOLANIC
POZZUOLANA
POZZUOLANAS
PRACHARAKS
PRACTICABILITY
PRACTICABLE
PRACTICABLENESS
PRACTICABLY
PRACTICALISM
PRACTICALISMS
PRACTICALIST
PRACTICALISTS
PRACTICALITIES
PRACTICALITY
PRACTICALLY
PRACTICALNESS
PRACTICALNESSES
PRACTICALS
PRACTICERS
PRACTICIAN
PRACTICIANS
PRACTICING
PRACTICKED
PRACTICKING
PRACTICUMS
PRACTIQUES
PRACTISANT
PRACTISANTS
PRACTISERS
PRACTISING
PRACTITIONER
PRACTITIONERS
PRACTOLOLS
PRAEAMBLES
PRAECOCIAL
PRAECORDIAL
PRAEDIALITIES
PRAEDIALITY
PRAEFECTORIAL
PRAELECTED
PRAELECTING
PRAELUDIUM
PRAEMUNIRE
PRAEMUNIRES
PRAENOMENS
PRAENOMINA
PRAENOMINAL
PRAENOMINALLY
PRAEPOSTOR
PRAEPOSTORS
PRAESIDIUM
PRAESIDIUMS
PRAETORIAL
PRAETORIAN
PRAETORIANS
PRAETORIUM
PRAETORIUMS
PRAETORSHIP
PRAETORSHIPS
PRAGMATICAL
PRAGMATICALITY
PRAGMATICALLY
PRAGMATICALNESS
PRAGMATICISM
PRAGMATICISMS
PRAGMATICIST
PRAGMATICISTS
PRAGMATICS
PRAGMATISATION
PRAGMATISATIONS
PRAGMATISE
PRAGMATISED
PRAGMATISER
PRAGMATISERS
PRAGMATISES
PRAGMATISING
PRAGMATISM
PRAGMATISMS
PRAGMATIST
PRAGMATISTIC
PRAGMATISTS
PRAGMATIZATION
PRAGMATIZATIONS
PRAGMATIZE
PRAGMATIZED
PRAGMATIZER
PRAGMATIZERS
PRAGMATIZES
PRAGMATIZING
PRAISEACHS
PRAISELESS
PRAISEWORTHIER
PRAISEWORTHIEST
PRAISEWORTHILY
PRAISEWORTHY
PRAISINGLY
PRALLTRILLER
PRALLTRILLERS
PRANAYAMAS
PRANCINGLY
PRANDIALLY
PRANKINGLY
PRANKISHLY
PRANKISHNESS
PRANKISHNESSES
PRANKSTERS
PRASEODYMIUM
PRASEODYMIUMS
PRATFALLEN
PRATFALLING
PRATINCOLE
PRATINCOLES
PRATTLEBOX
PRATTLEBOXES
PRATTLEMENT
PRATTLEMENTS
PRATTLINGLY
PRAXEOLOGICAL
PRAXEOLOGIES
PRAXEOLOGY
PRAXINOSCOPE
PRAXINOSCOPES
PRAYERFULLY
PRAYERFULNESS
PRAYERFULNESSES
PRAYERLESS
PRAYERLESSLY
PRAYERLESSNESS
PREABSORBED
PREABSORBING

PREABSORBS
PREACCUSED
PREACCUSES
PREACCUSING
PREACHABLE
PREACHERSHIP
PREACHERSHIPS
PREACHIEST
PREACHIFIED
PREACHIFIES
PREACHIFYING
PREACHIFYINGS
PREACHINESS
PREACHINESSES
PREACHINGLY
PREACHINGS
PREACHMENT
PREACHMENTS
PREACQUAINT
PREACQUAINTANCE
PREACQUAINTED
PREACQUAINTING
PREACQUAINTS
PREACQUISITION
PREADAMITE
PREADAMITES
PREADAPTATION
PREADAPTATIONS
PREADAPTED
PREADAPTING
PREADAPTIVE
PREADJUSTED
PREADJUSTING
PREADJUSTS
PREADMISSION
PREADMISSIONS
PREADMITTED
PREADMITTING
PREADMONISH
PREADMONISHED
PREADMONISHES
PREADMONISHING
PREADMONITION
PREADMONITIONS
PREADOLESCENCE
PREADOLESCENCES
PREADOLESCENT
PREADOLESCENTS
PREADOPTED
PREADOPTING
PREAGRICULTURAL
PREALLOTTED
PREALLOTTING
PREALTERED
PREALTERING
PREAMBLING
PREAMBULARY
PREAMBULATE
PREAMBULATED
PREAMBULATES
PREAMBULATING
PREAMBULATORY
PREAMPLIFIER
PREAMPLIFIERS
PREANAESTHETIC
PREANAESTHETICS
PREANESTHETIC
PREANNOUNCE
PREANNOUNCED
PREANNOUNCES
PREANNOUNCING
PREAPPLIED
PREAPPLIES
PREAPPLYING
PREAPPOINT
PREAPPOINTED
PREAPPOINTING
PREAPPOINTS
PREAPPROVE
PREAPPROVED
PREAPPROVES
PREAPPROVING
PREARRANGE
PREARRANGED
PREARRANGEMENT
PREARRANGEMENTS
PREARRANGES
PREARRANGING
PREASSEMBLED
PREASSIGNED
PREASSIGNING
PREASSIGNS
PREASSURANCE
PREASSURANCES
PREASSURED
PREASSURES
PREASSURING
PREATTUNED
PREATTUNES
PREATTUNING
PREAUDIENCE
PREAUDIENCES
PREAVERRED
PREAVERRING
PREAXIALLY
PREBENDARIES
PREBENDARY
PREBIBLICAL
PREBIDDING
PREBIDDINGS
PREBILLING
PREBINDING
PREBIOLOGIC
PREBIOLOGICAL
PREBIOTICS
PREBLESSED
PREBLESSES
PREBLESSING
PREBOARDED
PREBOARDING
PREBOILING
PREBOOKING
PREBREAKFAST
PREBUDGETS
PREBUILDING
PREBUTTALS
PRECALCULI
PRECALCULUS
PRECALCULUSES
PRECANCELED
PRECANCELING
PRECANCELLATION
PRECANCELLED
PRECANCELLING
PRECANCELS
PRECANCEROUS
PRECANCERS
PRECAPITALIST
PRECARIATS
PRECARIOUS
PRECARIOUSLY
PRECARIOUSNESS
PRECASTING
PRECAUTION
PRECAUTIONAL
PRECAUTIONARY
PRECAUTIONED
PRECAUTIONING
PRECAUTIONS
PRECAUTIOUS
PRECEDENCE
PRECEDENCES
PRECEDENCIES
PRECEDENCY
PRECEDENTED
PRECEDENTIAL
PRECEDENTIALLY
PRECEDENTLY
PRECEDENTS
PRECENSORED
PRECENSORING
PRECENSORS
PRECENTING
PRECENTORIAL
PRECENTORS
PRECENTORSHIP
PRECENTORSHIPS
PRECENTRESS
PRECENTRESSES
PRECENTRICES
PRECENTRIX
PRECENTRIXES
PRECEPTIAL
PRECEPTIVE
PRECEPTIVELY
PRECEPTORAL
PRECEPTORATE
PRECEPTORATES
PRECEPTORIAL
PRECEPTORIALS
PRECEPTORIES
PRECEPTORS
PRECEPTORSHIP
PRECEPTORSHIPS
PRECEPTORY
PRECEPTRESS
PRECEPTRESSES
PRECESSING
PRECESSION
PRECESSIONAL
PRECESSIONALLY
PRECESSIONS
PRECHARGED
PRECHARGES
PRECHARGING
PRECHECKED
PRECHECKING
PRECHILLED
PRECHILLING
PRECHOOSES
PRECHOOSING
PRECHRISTIAN
PRECIEUSES
PRECIOSITIES
PRECIOSITY
PRECIOUSES
PRECIOUSLY
PRECIOUSNESS
PRECIOUSNESSES
PRECIPICED
PRECIPICES
PRECIPITABILITY
PRECIPITABLE
PRECIPITANCE
PRECIPITANCES
PRECIPITANCIES
PRECIPITANCY
PRECIPITANT
PRECIPITANTLY
PRECIPITANTNESS
PRECIPITANTS
PRECIPITATE
PRECIPITATED
PRECIPITATELY
PRECIPITATENESS
PRECIPITATES
PRECIPITATING
PRECIPITATION
PRECIPITATIONS
PRECIPITATIVE
PRECIPITATOR
PRECIPITATORS
PRECIPITIN
PRECIPITINOGEN
PRECIPITINOGENS
PRECIPITINS
PRECIPITOUS
PRECIPITOUSLY
PRECIPITOUSNESS
PRECISENESS

P

PRECISENESSES
PRECISIANISM
PRECISIANISMS
PRECISIANIST
PRECISIANISTS
PRECISIANS
PRECISIONISM
PRECISIONISMS
PRECISIONIST
PRECISIONISTS
PRECISIONS
PRECLASSICAL
PRECLEANED
PRECLEANING
PRECLEARANCE
PRECLEARANCES
PRECLEARED
PRECLEARING
PRECLINICAL
PRECLINICALLY
PRECLUDABLE
PRECLUDING
PRECLUSION
PRECLUSIONS
PRECLUSIVE
PRECLUSIVELY
PRECOCIALS
PRECOCIOUS
PRECOCIOUSLY
PRECOCIOUSNESS
PRECOCITIES
PRECOGNISANT
PRECOGNISE
PRECOGNISED
PRECOGNISES
PRECOGNISING
PRECOGNITION
PRECOGNITIONS
PRECOGNITIVE
PRECOGNIZANT
PRECOGNIZE
PRECOGNIZED
PRECOGNIZES
PRECOGNIZING
PRECOGNOSCE
PRECOGNOSCED
PRECOGNOSCES
PRECOGNOSCING
PRECOLLEGE
PRECOLLEGIATE
PRECOLONIAL
PRECOMBUSTION
PRECOMBUSTIONS
PRECOMMITMENT
PRECOMMITMENTS
PRECOMPETITIVE
PRECOMPOSE
PRECOMPOSED
PRECOMPOSES
PRECOMPOSING
PRECOMPUTE
PRECOMPUTED
PRECOMPUTER
PRECOMPUTES
PRECOMPUTING
PRECONCEIT
PRECONCEITED
PRECONCEITING
PRECONCEITS
PRECONCEIVE
PRECONCEIVED
PRECONCEIVES
PRECONCEIVING
PRECONCEPTION
PRECONCEPTIONS
PRECONCERT
PRECONCERTED
PRECONCERTEDLY
PRECONCERTING
PRECONCERTS
PRECONCILIAR
PRECONDEMN
PRECONDEMNED
PRECONDEMNING
PRECONDEMNS
PRECONDITION
PRECONDITIONED
PRECONDITIONING
PRECONDITIONS
PRECONISATION
PRECONISATIONS
PRECONISED
PRECONISES
PRECONISING
PRECONIZATION
PRECONIZATIONS
PRECONIZED
PRECONIZES
PRECONIZING
PRECONQUEST
PRECONSCIOUS
PRECONSCIOUSES
PRECONSCIOUSLY
PRECONSONANTAL
PRECONSTRUCT
PRECONSTRUCTED
PRECONSTRUCTING
PRECONSTRUCTION
PRECONSTRUCTS
PRECONSUME
PRECONSUMED
PRECONSUMES
PRECONSUMING
PRECONTACT
PRECONTACTS
PRECONTRACT
PRECONTRACTED
PRECONTRACTING
PRECONTRACTS
PRECONVENTION
PRECONVICTION
PRECONVICTIONS
PRECOOKERS
PRECOOKING
PRECOOLING
PRECOPULATORY
PRECORDIAL
PRECREASED
PRECREASES
PRECREASING
PRECRITICAL
PRECURRERS
PRECURSING
PRECURSIVE
PRECURSORS
PRECURSORY
PRECUTTING
PRECYCLING
PREDACEOUS
PREDACEOUSNESS
PREDACIOUS
PREDACIOUSNESS
PREDACITIES
PREDATIONS
PREDATISMS
PREDATORILY
PREDATORINESS
PREDATORINESSES
PREDECEASE
PREDECEASED
PREDECEASES
PREDECEASING
PREDECESSOR
PREDECESSORS
PREDEDUCTED
PREDEDUCTING
PREDEDUCTS
PREDEFINED
PREDEFINES
PREDEFINING
PREDEFINITION
PREDEFINITIONS
PREDELIVERIES
PREDELIVERY
PREDENTARY
PREDENTATE
PREDEPARTURE
PREDEPOSIT
PREDEPOSITED
PREDEPOSITING
PREDEPOSITS
PREDESIGNATE
PREDESIGNATED
PREDESIGNATES
PREDESIGNATING
PREDESIGNATION
PREDESIGNATIONS
PREDESIGNATORY
PREDESIGNED
PREDESIGNING
PREDESIGNS
PREDESTINABLE
PREDESTINARIAN
PREDESTINARIANS
PREDESTINATE
PREDESTINATED
PREDESTINATES
PREDESTINATING
PREDESTINATION
PREDESTINATIONS
PREDESTINATIVE
PREDESTINATOR
PREDESTINATORS
PREDESTINE
PREDESTINED
PREDESTINES
PREDESTINIES
PREDESTINING
PREDESTINY
PREDETERMINABLE
PREDETERMINATE
PREDETERMINE
PREDETERMINED
PREDETERMINER
PREDETERMINERS
PREDETERMINES
PREDETERMINING
PREDETERMINISM
PREDETERMINISMS
PREDEVALUATION
PREDEVELOP
PREDEVELOPED
PREDEVELOPING
PREDEVELOPMENT
PREDEVELOPMENTS
PREDEVELOPS
PREDEVOTED
PREDEVOTES
PREDEVOTING
PREDIABETES
PREDIABETESES
PREDIABETIC
PREDIABETICS
PREDIALITIES
PREDIALITY
PREDICABILITIES
PREDICABILITY
PREDICABLE
PREDICABLENESS
PREDICABLES
PREDICAMENT
PREDICAMENTAL
PREDICAMENTS
PREDICANTS
PREDICATED
PREDICATES
PREDICATING
PREDICATION
PREDICATIONS
PREDICATIVE

PREDICATIVELY
PREDICATOR
PREDICATORS
PREDICATORY
PREDICTABILITY
PREDICTABLE
PREDICTABLENESS
PREDICTABLY
PREDICTERS
PREDICTING
PREDICTION
PREDICTIONS
PREDICTIVE
PREDICTIVELY
PREDICTORS
PREDIGESTED
PREDIGESTING
PREDIGESTION
PREDIGESTIONS
PREDIGESTS
PREDIKANTS
PREDILECTED
PREDILECTION
PREDILECTIONS
PREDINNERS
PREDISCHARGE
PREDISCOVERIES
PREDISCOVERY
PREDISPOSAL
PREDISPOSALS
PREDISPOSE
PREDISPOSED
PREDISPOSES
PREDISPOSING
PREDISPOSITION
PREDISPOSITIONS
PREDNISOLONE
PREDNISOLONES
PREDNISONE
PREDNISONES
PREDOCTORAL
PREDOMINANCE
PREDOMINANCES
PREDOMINANCIES
PREDOMINANCY
PREDOMINANT
PREDOMINANTLY
PREDOMINATE
PREDOMINATED
PREDOMINATELY
PREDOMINATES
PREDOMINATING
PREDOMINATION
PREDOMINATIONS
PREDOMINATOR
PREDOMINATORS
PREDOOMING
PREDRILLED
PREDRILLING
PREDYNASTIC
PREECLAMPSIA
PREECLAMPSIAS
PREECLAMPTIC
PREEDITING
PREELECTED
PREELECTING
PREELECTION
PREELECTRIC
PREEMBARGO
PREEMERGENCE
PREEMERGENT
PREEMINENCE
PREEMINENCES
PREEMINENT
PREEMINENTLY
PREEMPLOYMENT
PREEMPTING
PREEMPTION
PREEMPTIONS
PREEMPTIVE
PREEMPTIVELY
PREEMPTORS
PREENACTED
PREENACTING
PREENROLLMENT
PREERECTED
PREERECTING
PREESTABLISH
PREESTABLISHED
PREESTABLISHES
PREESTABLISHING
PREETHICAL
PREEXCITED
PREEXCITES
PREEXCITING
PREEXEMPTED
PREEXEMPTING
PREEXEMPTS
PREEXISTED
PREEXISTENCE
PREEXISTENCES
PREEXISTENT
PREEXISTING
PREEXPERIMENT
PREEXPOSED
PREEXPOSES
PREEXPOSING
PREFABBING
PREFABRICATE
PREFABRICATED
PREFABRICATES
PREFABRICATING
PREFABRICATION
PREFABRICATIONS
PREFABRICATOR
PREFABRICATORS
PREFASCIST
PREFATORIAL
PREFATORIALLY
PREFATORILY
PREFECTORIAL
PREFECTSHIP
PREFECTSHIPS
PREFECTURAL
PREFECTURE
PREFECTURES
PREFERABILITIES
PREFERABILITY
PREFERABLE
PREFERABLENESS
PREFERABLY
PREFERENCE
PREFERENCES
PREFERENTIAL
PREFERENTIALISM
PREFERENTIALIST
PREFERENTIALITY
PREFERENTIALLY
PREFERMENT
PREFERMENTS
PREFERRABLE
PREFERRERS
PREFERRING
PREFIGURATE
PREFIGURATED
PREFIGURATES
PREFIGURATING
PREFIGURATION
PREFIGURATIONS
PREFIGURATIVE
PREFIGURATIVELY
PREFIGURED
PREFIGUREMENT
PREFIGUREMENTS
PREFIGURES
PREFIGURING
PREFINANCE
PREFINANCED
PREFINANCES
PREFINANCING
PREFINANCINGS
PREFIXALLY
PREFIXIONS
PREFIXTURE
PREFIXTURES
PREFLIGHTED
PREFLIGHTING
PREFLIGHTS
PREFLORATION
PREFLORATIONS
PREFOCUSED
PREFOCUSES
PREFOCUSING
PREFOCUSSED
PREFOCUSSES
PREFOCUSSING
PREFOLIATION
PREFOLIATIONS
PREFORMATION
PREFORMATIONISM
PREFORMATIONIST
PREFORMATIONS
PREFORMATIVE
PREFORMATIVES
PREFORMATS
PREFORMATTED
PREFORMATTING
PREFORMING
PREFORMULATE
PREFORMULATED
PREFORMULATES
PREFORMULATING
PREFRANKED
PREFRANKING
PREFREEZES
PREFREEZING
PREFRESHMAN
PREFRESHMEN
PREFRONTAL
PREFRONTALS
PREFULGENT
PREFUNDING
PREGANGLIONIC
PREGENITAL
PREGLACIAL
PREGNABILITIES
PREGNABILITY
PREGNANCES
PREGNANCIES
PREGNANTLY
PREGNENOLONE
PREGNENOLONES
PREGROWTHS
PREGUIDING
PREGUSTATION
PREGUSTATIONS
PREHALLUCES
PREHANDLED
PREHANDLES
PREHANDLING
PREHARDENED
PREHARDENING
PREHARDENS
PREHARVEST
PREHARVESTS
PREHEADACHE
PREHEATERS
PREHEATING
PREHEMINENCE
PREHEMINENCES
PREHENDING
PREHENSIBLE
PREHENSILE
PREHENSILITIES
PREHENSILITY
PREHENSION
PREHENSIONS
PREHENSIVE
PREHENSORIAL
PREHENSORS

P

PREHENSORY
PREHISTORIAN
PREHISTORIANS
PREHISTORIC
PREHISTORICAL
PREHISTORICALLY
PREHISTORIES
PREHISTORY
PREHOLIDAY
PREHOMINID
PREHOMINIDS
PREIGNITION
PREIGNITIONS
PREIMPLANTATION
PREIMPOSED
PREIMPOSES
PREIMPOSING
PREINAUGURAL
PREINDUCTION
PREINDUSTRIAL
PREINFORMED
PREINFORMING
PREINFORMS
PREINSERTED
PREINSERTING
PREINSERTS
PREINTERVIEW
PREINTERVIEWED
PREINTERVIEWING
PREINTERVIEWS
PREINVASION
PREINVITED
PREINVITES
PREINVITING
PREJUDGEMENT
PREJUDGEMENTS
PREJUDGERS
PREJUDGING
PREJUDGMENT
PREJUDGMENTS
PREJUDICANT
PREJUDICATE
PREJUDICATED
PREJUDICATES
PREJUDICATING
PREJUDICATION
PREJUDICATIONS
PREJUDICATIVE
PREJUDICED
PREJUDICES
PREJUDICIAL
PREJUDICIALLY
PREJUDICIALNESS
PREJUDICING
PREJUDIZES
PREKINDERGARTEN
PRELAPSARIAN
PRELATESHIP
PRELATESHIPS
PRELATESSES
PRELATICAL
PRELATICALLY
PRELATIONS
PRELATISED
PRELATISES
PRELATISING
PRELATISMS
PRELATISTS
PRELATIZED
PRELATIZES
PRELATIZING
PRELATURES
PRELAUNCHED
PRELAUNCHES
PRELAUNCHING
PRELECTING
PRELECTION
PRELECTIONS
PRELECTORS
PRELEXICAL
PRELIBATION
PRELIBATIONS
PRELIMINARIES
PRELIMINARILY
PRELIMINARY
PRELIMITED
PRELIMITING
PRELINGUAL
PRELINGUALLY
PRELITERACIES
PRELITERACY
PRELITERARY
PRELITERATE
PRELITERATES
PRELOADING
PRELOCATED
PRELOCATES
PRELOCATING
PRELOGICAL
PRELUDIOUS
PRELUNCHEON
PRELUNCHEONS
PRELUSIONS
PRELUSIVELY
PRELUSORILY
PREMALIGNANT
PREMANDIBULAR
PREMANDIBULARS
PREMANUFACTURE
PREMANUFACTURED
PREMANUFACTURES
PREMARITAL
PREMARITALLY
PREMARKETED
PREMARKETING
PREMARKETS
PREMARRIAGE
PREMATURELY
PREMATURENESS
PREMATURENESSES
PREMATURES
PREMATURITIES
PREMATURITY
PREMAXILLA
PREMAXILLAE
PREMAXILLARIES
PREMAXILLARY
PREMAXILLAS
PREMEASURE
PREMEASURED
PREMEASURES
PREMEASURING
PREMEDICAL
PREMEDICALLY
PREMEDICATE
PREMEDICATED
PREMEDICATES
PREMEDICATING
PREMEDICATION
PREMEDICATIONS
PREMEDIEVAL
PREMEDITATE
PREMEDITATED
PREMEDITATEDLY
PREMEDITATES
PREMEDITATING
PREMEDITATION
PREMEDITATIONS
PREMEDITATIVE
PREMEDITATOR
PREMEDITATORS
PREMEIOTIC
PREMENOPAUSAL
PREMENSTRUAL
PREMENSTRUALLY
PREMIERING
PREMIERSHIP
PREMIERSHIPS
PREMIGRATION
PREMILLENARIAN
PREMILLENARIANS
PREMILLENNIAL
PREMILLENNIALLY
PREMILLENNIALS
PREMISSING
PREMODIFICATION
PREMODIFIED
PREMODIFIES
PREMODIFYING
PREMOISTEN
PREMOISTENED
PREMOISTENING
PREMOISTENS
PREMOLDING
PREMONISHED
PREMONISHES
PREMONISHING
PREMONISHMENT
PREMONISHMENTS
PREMONITION
PREMONITIONS
PREMONITIVE
PREMONITOR
PREMONITORILY
PREMONITORS
PREMONITORY
PREMOTIONS
PREMOULDED
PREMOULDING
PREMOVEMENT
PREMOVEMENTS
PREMUNITION
PREMUNITIONS
PREMYCOTIC
PRENATALLY
PRENEGOTIATE
PRENEGOTIATED
PRENEGOTIATES
PRENEGOTIATING
PRENEGOTIATION
PRENEGOTIATIONS
PRENOMINAL
PRENOMINALLY
PRENOMINATE
PRENOMINATED
PRENOMINATES
PRENOMINATING
PRENOMINATION
PRENOMINATIONS
PRENOTIFICATION
PRENOTIFIED
PRENOTIFIES
PRENOTIFYING
PRENOTIONS
PRENTICESHIP
PRENTICESHIPS
PRENTICING
PRENUMBERED
PRENUMBERING
PRENUMBERS
PRENUPTIAL
PRENUPTIALS
PREOBTAINED
PREOBTAINING
PREOBTAINS
PREOCCUPANCIES
PREOCCUPANCY
PREOCCUPANT
PREOCCUPANTS
PREOCCUPATE
PREOCCUPATED
PREOCCUPATES
PREOCCUPATING
PREOCCUPATION
PREOCCUPATIONS
PREOCCUPIED
PREOCCUPIES
PREOCCUPYING
PREOCULARS
PREOPENING

PREOPERATIONAL
PREOPERATIVE
PREOPERATIVELY
PREOPTIONS
PREORDAINED
PREORDAINING
PREORDAINMENT
PREORDAINMENTS
PREORDAINS
PREORDERED
PREORDERING
PREORDINANCE
PREORDINANCES
PREORDINATION
PREORDINATIONS
PREOVULATORY
PREPACKAGE
PREPACKAGED
PREPACKAGES
PREPACKAGING
PREPACKING
PREPARATION
PREPARATIONS
PREPARATIVE
PREPARATIVELY
PREPARATIVES
PREPARATOR
PREPARATORILY
PREPARATORS
PREPARATORY
PREPAREDLY
PREPAREDNESS
PREPAREDNESSES
PREPASTING
PREPATELLAR
PREPAYABLE
PREPAYMENT
PREPAYMENTS
PREPENSELY
PREPENSING
PREPENSIVE
PREPERFORMANCE
PREPLACING
PREPLANNED
PREPLANNING
PREPLANTING
PREPOLLENCE
PREPOLLENCES
PREPOLLENCIES
PREPOLLENCY
PREPOLLENT
PREPOLLICES
PREPONDERANCE
PREPONDERANCES
PREPONDERANCIES
PREPONDERANCY
PREPONDERANT
PREPONDERANTLY
PREPONDERATE
PREPONDERATED
PREPONDERATELY
PREPONDERATES
PREPONDERATING
PREPONDERATION
PREPONDERATIONS
PREPORTION
PREPORTIONED
PREPORTIONING
PREPORTIONS
PREPOSITION
PREPOSITIONAL
PREPOSITIONALLY
PREPOSITIONS
PREPOSITIVE
PREPOSITIVELY
PREPOSITIVES
PREPOSITOR
PREPOSITORS
PREPOSSESS
PREPOSSESSED
PREPOSSESSES
PREPOSSESSING
PREPOSSESSINGLY
PREPOSSESSION
PREPOSSESSIONS
PREPOSTEROUS
PREPOSTEROUSLY
PREPOSTORS
PREPOTENCE
PREPOTENCES
PREPOTENCIES
PREPOTENCY
PREPOTENTLY
PREPPINESS
PREPPINESSES
PREPRANDIAL
PREPREPARED
PREPRESIDENTIAL
PREPRESSES
PREPRICING
PREPRIMARIES
PREPRIMARY
PREPRINTED
PREPRINTING
PREPROCESS
PREPROCESSED
PREPROCESSES
PREPROCESSING
PREPROCESSOR
PREPROCESSORS
PREPRODUCTION
PREPRODUCTIONS
PREPROFESSIONAL
PREPROGRAM
PREPROGRAMED
PREPROGRAMING
PREPROGRAMMED
PREPROGRAMMING
PREPROGRAMMINGS
PREPROGRAMS
PREPSYCHEDELIC
PREPUBERAL
PREPUBERTAL
PREPUBERTIES
PREPUBERTY
PREPUBESCENCE
PREPUBESCENCES
PREPUBESCENT
PREPUBESCENTS
PREPUBLICATION
PREPUBLICATIONS
PREPUNCHED
PREPUNCHES
PREPUNCHING
PREPUNCTUAL
PREPURCHASE
PREPURCHASED
PREPURCHASES
PREPURCHASING
PREQUALIFIED
PREQUALIFIES
PREQUALIFY
PREQUALIFYING
PREREADING
PRERECESSION
PRERECORDED
PRERECORDING
PRERECORDS
PREREGISTER
PREREGISTERED
PREREGISTERING
PREREGISTERS
PREREGISTRATION
PREREHEARSAL
PREREHEARSALS
PRERELEASE
PRERELEASED
PRERELEASES
PRERELEASING
PREREQUIRE
PREREQUIRED
PREREQUIRES
PREREQUIRING
PREREQUISITE
PREREQUISITES
PRERETIREMENT
PREREVIEWED
PREREVIEWING
PREREVIEWS
PREREVISIONIST
PREREVOLUTION
PRERINSING
PREROGATIVE
PREROGATIVED
PREROGATIVELY
PREROGATIVES
PREROMANTIC
PREROMANTICS
PRESAGEFUL
PRESAGEFULLY
PRESAGEMENT
PRESAGEMENTS
PRESANCTIFIED
PRESANCTIFIES
PRESANCTIFY
PRESANCTIFYING
PRESBYACOUSES
PRESBYACOUSIS
PRESBYACUSES
PRESBYACUSIS
PRESBYCOUSES
PRESBYCOUSIS
PRESBYCUSES
PRESBYCUSIS
PRESBYOPES
PRESBYOPIA
PRESBYOPIAS
PRESBYOPIC
PRESBYOPICS
PRESBYOPIES
PRESBYTERAL
PRESBYTERATE
PRESBYTERATES
PRESBYTERIAL
PRESBYTERIALLY
PRESBYTERIALS
PRESBYTERIAN
PRESBYTERIANISE
PRESBYTERIANISM
PRESBYTERIANIZE
PRESBYTERIANS
PRESBYTERIES
PRESBYTERS
PRESBYTERSHIP
PRESBYTERSHIPS
PRESBYTERY
PRESBYTISM
PRESBYTISMS
PRESCHEDULE
PRESCHEDULED
PRESCHEDULES
PRESCHEDULING
PRESCHOOLER
PRESCHOOLERS
PRESCHOOLS
PRESCIENCE
PRESCIENCES
PRESCIENTIFIC
PRESCIENTLY
PRESCINDED
PRESCINDENT
PRESCINDING
PRESCISSION
PRESCISSIONS
PRESCORING
PRESCREENED
PRESCREENING
PRESCREENS
PRESCRIBED
PRESCRIBER

P

PRESCRIBERS
PRESCRIBES
PRESCRIBING
PRESCRIBINGS
PRESCRIPTIBLE
PRESCRIPTION
PRESCRIPTIONS
PRESCRIPTIVE
PRESCRIPTIVELY
PRESCRIPTIVISM
PRESCRIPTIVISMS
PRESCRIPTIVIST
PRESCRIPTIVISTS
PRESCRIPTS
PRESEASONS
PRESELECTED
PRESELECTING
PRESELECTION
PRESELECTIONS
PRESELECTOR
PRESELECTORS
PRESELECTS
PRESELLING
PRESENSION
PRESENSIONS
PRESENTABILITY
PRESENTABLE
PRESENTABLENESS
PRESENTABLY
PRESENTATION
PRESENTATIONAL
PRESENTATIONISM
PRESENTATIONIST
PRESENTATIONS
PRESENTATIVE
PRESENTEEISM
PRESENTEEISMS
PRESENTEES
PRESENTENCE
PRESENTENCED
PRESENTENCES
PRESENTENCING
PRESENTERS
PRESENTIAL
PRESENTIALITIES
PRESENTIALITY
PRESENTIALLY
PRESENTIENT
PRESENTIMENT
PRESENTIMENTAL
PRESENTIMENTS
PRESENTING
PRESENTISM
PRESENTISMS
PRESENTIST
PRESENTISTS
PRESENTIVE
PRESENTIVENESS
PRESENTIVES
PRESENTMENT
PRESENTMENTS
PRESENTNESS
PRESENTNESSES
PRESERVABILITY
PRESERVABLE
PRESERVABLY
PRESERVATION
PRESERVATIONIST
PRESERVATIONS
PRESERVATIVE
PRESERVATIVES
PRESERVATORIES
PRESERVATORY
PRESERVERS
PRESERVICE
PRESERVING
PRESETTING
PRESETTLED
PRESETTLEMENT
PRESETTLES
PRESETTLING
PRESHAPING
PRESHIPPED
PRESHIPPING
PRESHOWING
PRESHRINKING
PRESHRINKS
PRESHRUNKEN
PRESIDENCIES
PRESIDENCY
PRESIDENTESS
PRESIDENTESSES
PRESIDENTIAL
PRESIDENTIALLY
PRESIDENTS
PRESIDENTSHIP
PRESIDENTSHIPS
PRESIDIARY
PRESIDIUMS
PRESIFTING
PRESIGNALED
PRESIGNALING
PRESIGNALLED
PRESIGNALLING
PRESIGNALS
PRESIGNIFIED
PRESIGNIFIES
PRESIGNIFY
PRESIGNIFYING
PRESLAUGHTER
PRESLICING
PRESOAKING
PRESOLVING
PRESORTING
PRESPECIFIED
PRESPECIFIES
PRESPECIFY
PRESPECIFYING
PRESSBOARD
PRESSBOARDS
PRESSGANGS
PRESSINGLY
PRESSINGNESS
PRESSINGNESSES
PRESSMARKS
PRESSROOMS
PRESSURELESS
PRESSURING
PRESSURISATION
PRESSURISATIONS
PRESSURISE
PRESSURISED
PRESSURISER
PRESSURISERS
PRESSURISES
PRESSURISING
PRESSURIZATION
PRESSURIZATIONS
PRESSURIZE
PRESSURIZED
PRESSURIZER
PRESSURIZERS
PRESSURIZES
PRESSURIZING
PRESSWOMAN
PRESSWOMEN
PRESSWORKS
PRESTAMPED
PRESTAMPING
PRESTATION
PRESTATIONS
PRESTERILISE
PRESTERILISED
PRESTERILISES
PRESTERILISING
PRESTERILIZE
PRESTERILIZED
PRESTERILIZES
PRESTERILIZING
PRESTERNUM
PRESTERNUMS
PRESTIDIGITATOR
PRESTIGEFUL
PRESTIGIATOR
PRESTIGIATORS
PRESTIGIOUS
PRESTIGIOUSLY
PRESTIGIOUSNESS
PRESTISSIMO
PRESTISSIMOS
PRESTORAGE
PRESTORING
PRESTRESSED
PRESTRESSES
PRESTRESSING
PRESTRICTION
PRESTRICTIONS
PRESTRUCTURE
PRESTRUCTURED
PRESTRUCTURES
PRESTRUCTURING
PRESUMABLE
PRESUMABLY
PRESUMEDLY
PRESUMINGLY
PRESUMMITS
PRESUMPTION
PRESUMPTIONS
PRESUMPTIVE
PRESUMPTIVELY
PRESUMPTIVENESS
PRESUMPTUOUS
PRESUMPTUOUSLY
PRESUPPOSE
PRESUPPOSED
PRESUPPOSES
PRESUPPOSING
PRESUPPOSITION
PRESUPPOSITIONS
PRESURGERY
PRESURMISE
PRESURMISES
PRESURVEYED
PRESURVEYING
PRESURVEYS
PRESWEETEN
PRESWEETENED
PRESWEETENING
PRESWEETENS
PRESYMPTOMATIC
PRESYNAPTIC
PRESYNAPTICALLY
PRETASTING
PRETELEVISION
PRETELLING
PRETENCELESS
PRETENDANT
PRETENDANTS
PRETENDEDLY
PRETENDENT
PRETENDENTS
PRETENDERS
PRETENDERSHIP
PRETENDERSHIPS
PRETENDING
PRETENDINGLY
PRETENSELESS
PRETENSION
PRETENSIONED
PRETENSIONING
PRETENSIONLESS
PRETENSIONS
PRETENSIVE
PRETENTIOUS
PRETENTIOUSLY
PRETENTIOUSNESS
PRETERHUMAN
PRETERISTS
PRETERITENESS
PRETERITENESSES

PRETERITES
PRETERITION
PRETERITIONS
PRETERITIVE
PRETERMINAL
PRETERMINATION
PRETERMINATIONS
PRETERMISSION
PRETERMISSIONS
PRETERMITS
PRETERMITTED
PRETERMITTER
PRETERMITTERS
PRETERMITTING
PRETERNATURAL
PRETERNATURALLY
PRETERPERFECT
PRETERPERFECTS
PRETESTING
PRETEXTING
PRETEXTINGS
PRETHEATER
PRETHEATRE
PRETORIANS
PRETORSHIP
PRETORSHIPS
PRETOURNAMENT
PRETRAINED
PRETRAINING
PRETREATED
PRETREATING
PRETREATMENT
PRETREATMENTS
PRETRIMMED
PRETRIMMING
PRETTIFICATION
PRETTIFICATIONS
PRETTIFIED
PRETTIFIER
PRETTIFIERS
PRETTIFIES
PRETTIFYING
PRETTINESS
PRETTINESSES
PRETTYISMS
PRETZELLED
PRETZELLING
PREUNIFICATION
PREUNITING
PREUNIVERSITY
PREVAILERS
PREVAILING
PREVAILINGLY
PREVAILMENT
PREVAILMENTS
PREVALENCE
PREVALENCES
PREVALENCIES
PREVALENCY
PREVALENTLY
PREVALENTNESS
PREVALENTNESSES
PREVALENTS
PREVALUING
PREVARICATE
PREVARICATED
PREVARICATES
PREVARICATING
PREVARICATION
PREVARICATIONS
PREVARICATOR
PREVARICATORS
PREVENANCIES
PREVENANCY
PREVENIENCE
PREVENIENCES
PREVENIENT
PREVENIENTLY
PREVENTABILITY
PREVENTABLE
PREVENTABLY
PREVENTATIVE
PREVENTATIVES
PREVENTERS
PREVENTIBILITY
PREVENTIBLE
PREVENTIBLY
PREVENTING
PREVENTION
PREVENTIONS
PREVENTIVE
PREVENTIVELY
PREVENTIVENESS
PREVENTIVES
PREVIEWERS
PREVIEWING
PREVIOUSLY
PREVIOUSNESS
PREVIOUSNESSES
PREVISIONAL
PREVISIONARY
PREVISIONED
PREVISIONING
PREVISIONS
PREVISITED
PREVISITING
PREVOCALIC
PREVOCALICALLY
PREVOCATIONAL
PREWARMING
PREWARNING
PREWASHING
PREWEANING
PREWEIGHED
PREWEIGHING
PREWORKING
PREWRAPPED
PREWRAPPING
PREWRITING
PREWRITINGS
PREWRITTEN
PRICELESSLY
PRICELESSNESS
PRICELESSNESSES
PRICINESSES
PRICKLIEST
PRICKLINESS
PRICKLINESSES
PRICKLINGS
PRICKWOODS
PRIDEFULLY
PRIDEFULNESS
PRIDEFULNESSES
PRIESTCRAFT
PRIESTCRAFTS
PRIESTESSES
PRIESTHOOD
PRIESTHOODS
PRIESTLIER
PRIESTLIEST
PRIESTLIKE
PRIESTLINESS
PRIESTLINESSES
PRIESTLING
PRIESTLINGS
PRIESTSHIP
PRIESTSHIPS
PRIGGERIES
PRIGGISHLY
PRIGGISHNESS
PRIGGISHNESSES
PRIMAEVALLY
PRIMALITIES
PRIMAQUINE
PRIMAQUINES
PRIMARINESS
PRIMARINESSES
PRIMATESHIP
PRIMATESHIPS
PRIMATIALS
PRIMATICAL
PRIMATOLOGICAL
PRIMATOLOGIES
PRIMATOLOGIST
PRIMATOLOGISTS
PRIMATOLOGY
PRIMAVERAS
PRIMENESSES
PRIMEVALLY
PRIMIGENIAL
PRIMIGRAVIDA
PRIMIGRAVIDAE
PRIMIGRAVIDAS
PRIMIPARAE
PRIMIPARAS
PRIMIPARITIES
PRIMIPARITY
PRIMIPAROUS
PRIMITIVELY
PRIMITIVENESS
PRIMITIVENESSES
PRIMITIVES
PRIMITIVISM
PRIMITIVISMS
PRIMITIVIST
PRIMITIVISTIC
PRIMITIVISTS
PRIMITIVITIES
PRIMITIVITY
PRIMNESSES
PRIMOGENIAL
PRIMOGENIT
PRIMOGENITAL
PRIMOGENITARY
PRIMOGENITIVE
PRIMOGENITIVES
PRIMOGENITOR
PRIMOGENITORS
PRIMOGENITRICES
PRIMOGENITRIX
PRIMOGENITRIXES
PRIMOGENITS
PRIMOGENITURE
PRIMOGENITURES
PRIMORDIAL
PRIMORDIALISM
PRIMORDIALISMS
PRIMORDIALITIES
PRIMORDIALITY
PRIMORDIALLY
PRIMORDIALS
PRIMORDIUM
PRIMROSIER
PRIMROSIEST
PRIMROSING
PRIMULACEOUS
PRIMULINES
PRINCEDOMS
PRINCEHOOD
PRINCEHOODS
PRINCEKINS
PRINCELETS
PRINCELIER
PRINCELIEST
PRINCELIKE
PRINCELINESS
PRINCELINESSES
PRINCELING
PRINCELINGS
PRINCESHIP
PRINCESHIPS
PRINCESSES
PRINCESSLIER
PRINCESSLIEST
PRINCESSLY
PRINCIFIED
PRINCIPALITIES
PRINCIPALITY
PRINCIPALLY
PRINCIPALNESS

PRINCIPALNESSES
PRINCIPALS
PRINCIPALSHIP
PRINCIPALSHIPS
PRINCIPATE
PRINCIPATES
PRINCIPIAL
PRINCIPIUM
PRINCIPLED
PRINCIPLES
PRINCIPLING
PRINTABILITIES
PRINTABILITY
PRINTABLENESS
PRINTABLENESSES
PRINTERIES
PRINTHEADS
PRINTMAKER
PRINTMAKERS
PRINTMAKING
PRINTMAKINGS
PRINTWHEEL
PRINTWHEELS
PRINTWORKS
PRIORESSES
PRIORITIES
PRIORITISATION
PRIORITISATIONS
PRIORITISE
PRIORITISED
PRIORITISES
PRIORITISING
PRIORITIZATION
PRIORITIZATIONS
PRIORITIZE
PRIORITIZED
PRIORITIZES
PRIORITIZING
PRIORSHIPS
PRISMATICAL
PRISMATICALLY
PRISMATOID
PRISMATOIDAL
PRISMATOIDS
PRISMOIDAL
PRISONMENT
PRISONMENTS
PRISSINESS
PRISSINESSES
PRISTINELY
PRIVATDOCENT
PRIVATDOCENTS
PRIVATDOZENT
PRIVATDOZENTS
PRIVATEERED
PRIVATEERING
PRIVATEERINGS
PRIVATEERS
PRIVATEERSMAN
PRIVATEERSMEN
PRIVATENESS
PRIVATENESSES
PRIVATIONS
PRIVATISATION
PRIVATISATIONS
PRIVATISED
PRIVATISER
PRIVATISERS
PRIVATISES
PRIVATISING
PRIVATISMS
PRIVATISTS
PRIVATIVELY
PRIVATIVES
PRIVATIZATION
PRIVATIZATIONS
PRIVATIZED
PRIVATIZER
PRIVATIZERS
PRIVATIZES
PRIVATIZING
PRIVILEGED
PRIVILEGES
PRIVILEGING
PRIZEFIGHT
PRIZEFIGHTER
PRIZEFIGHTERS
PRIZEFIGHTING
PRIZEFIGHTINGS
PRIZEFIGHTS
PRIZEWINNER
PRIZEWINNERS
PRIZEWINNING
PRIZEWOMAN
PRIZEWOMEN
PROABORTION
PROACTIONS
PROAIRESES
PROAIRESIS
PROBABILIORISM
PROBABILIORISMS
PROBABILIORIST
PROBABILIORISTS
PROBABILISM
PROBABILISMS
PROBABILIST
PROBABILISTIC
PROBABILISTS
PROBABILITIES
PROBABILITY
PROBATIONAL
PROBATIONALLY
PROBATIONARIES
PROBATIONARY
PROBATIONER
PROBATIONERS
PROBATIONERSHIP
PROBATIONS
PROBATIVELY
PROBENECID
PROBENECIDS
PROBIOTICS
PROBLEMATIC
PROBLEMATICAL
PROBLEMATICALLY
PROBLEMATICS
PROBLEMIST
PROBLEMISTS
PROBOSCIDEAN
PROBOSCIDEANS
PROBOSCIDES
PROBOSCIDIAN
PROBOSCIDIANS
PROBOSCISES
PROBOULEUTIC
PROBUSINESS
PROCACIOUS
PROCACITIES
PROCAMBIAL
PROCAMBIUM
PROCAMBIUMS
PROCAPITALIST
PROCARBAZINE
PROCARBAZINES
PROCARYONS
PROCARYOTE
PROCARYOTES
PROCARYOTIC
PROCATHEDRAL
PROCATHEDRALS
PROCEDURAL
PROCEDURALLY
PROCEDURALS
PROCEDURES
PROCEEDERS
PROCEEDING
PROCEEDINGS
PROCELEUSMATIC
PROCELEUSMATICS
PROCELLARIAN
PROCELLARIANS
PROCEPHALIC
PROCERCOID
PROCERCOIDS
PROCEREBRA
PROCEREBRAL
PROCEREBRUM
PROCEREBRUMS
PROCERITIES
PROCESSABILITY
PROCESSABLE
PROCESSERS
PROCESSIBILITY
PROCESSIBLE
PROCESSING
PROCESSINGS
PROCESSION
PROCESSIONAL
PROCESSIONALIST
PROCESSIONALLY
PROCESSIONALS
PROCESSIONARIES
PROCESSIONARY
PROCESSIONED
PROCESSIONER
PROCESSIONERS
PROCESSIONING
PROCESSIONINGS
PROCESSIONS
PROCESSORS
PROCESSUAL
PROCHRONISM
PROCHRONISMS
PROCIDENCE
PROCIDENCES
PROCLAIMANT
PROCLAIMANTS
PROCLAIMED
PROCLAIMER
PROCLAIMERS
PROCLAIMING
PROCLAMATION
PROCLAMATIONS
PROCLAMATORY
PROCLITICS
PROCLIVITIES
PROCLIVITY
PROCOELOUS
PROCONSULAR
PROCONSULATE
PROCONSULATES
PROCONSULS
PROCONSULSHIP
PROCONSULSHIPS
PROCRASTINATE
PROCRASTINATED
PROCRASTINATES
PROCRASTINATING
PROCRASTINATION
PROCRASTINATIVE
PROCRASTINATOR
PROCRASTINATORS
PROCRASTINATORY
PROCREANTS
PROCREATED
PROCREATES
PROCREATING
PROCREATION
PROCREATIONAL
PROCREATIONS
PROCREATIVE
PROCREATIVENESS
PROCREATOR
PROCREATORS
PROCRUSTEAN
PROCRYPSES
PROCRYPSIS
PROCRYPTIC
PROCRYPTICALLY
PROCTALGIA

PROCTALGIAS
PROCTITIDES
PROCTITISES
PROCTODAEA
PROCTODAEAL
PROCTODAEUM
PROCTODAEUMS
PROCTODEAL
PROCTODEUM
PROCTODEUMS
PROCTOLOGIC
PROCTOLOGICAL
PROCTOLOGIES
PROCTOLOGIST
PROCTOLOGISTS
PROCTOLOGY
PROCTORAGE
PROCTORAGES
PROCTORIAL
PROCTORIALLY
PROCTORING
PROCTORISE
PROCTORISED
PROCTORISES
PROCTORISING
PROCTORIZE
PROCTORIZED
PROCTORIZES
PROCTORIZING
PROCTORSHIP
PROCTORSHIPS
PROCTOSCOPE
PROCTOSCOPES
PROCTOSCOPIC
PROCTOSCOPIES
PROCTOSCOPY
PROCUMBENT
PROCURABLE
PROCURACIES
PROCURANCE
PROCURANCES
PROCURATION
PROCURATIONS
PROCURATOR
PROCURATORIAL
PROCURATORIES
PROCURATORS
PROCURATORSHIP
PROCURATORSHIPS
PROCURATORY
PROCUREMENT
PROCUREMENTS
PROCURESSES
PROCUREURS
PROCURINGS
PROCYONIDS
PRODIGALISE
PRODIGALISED
PRODIGALISES
PRODIGALISING
PRODIGALITIES
PRODIGALITY
PRODIGALIZE
PRODIGALIZED
PRODIGALIZES
PRODIGALIZING
PRODIGALLY
PRODIGIOSITIES
PRODIGIOSITY
PRODIGIOUS
PRODIGIOUSLY
PRODIGIOUSNESS
PRODITORIOUS
PRODNOSING
PRODROMATA
PRODUCEMENT
PRODUCEMENTS
PRODUCIBILITIES
PRODUCIBILITY
PRODUCIBLE
PRODUCTIBILITY
PRODUCTILE
PRODUCTION
PRODUCTIONAL
PRODUCTIONS
PRODUCTIVE
PRODUCTIVELY
PRODUCTIVENESS
PRODUCTIVITIES
PRODUCTIVITY
PROEMBRYOS
PROENZYMES
PROESTRUSES
PROFANATION
PROFANATIONS
PROFANATORY
PROFANENESS
PROFANENESSES
PROFANITIES
PROFASCIST
PROFECTITIOUS
PROFEMINIST
PROFESSEDLY
PROFESSING
PROFESSION
PROFESSIONAL
PROFESSIONALISE
PROFESSIONALISM
PROFESSIONALIST
PROFESSIONALIZE
PROFESSIONALLY
PROFESSIONALS
PROFESSIONS
PROFESSORATE
PROFESSORATES
PROFESSORESS
PROFESSORESSES
PROFESSORIAL
PROFESSORIALLY
PROFESSORIAT
PROFESSORIATE
PROFESSORIATES
PROFESSORIATS
PROFESSORS
PROFESSORSHIP
PROFESSORSHIPS
PROFFERERS
PROFFERING
PROFICIENCE
PROFICIENCES
PROFICIENCIES
PROFICIENCY
PROFICIENT
PROFICIENTLY
PROFICIENTS
PROFILINGS
PROFILISTS
PROFITABILITIES
PROFITABILITY
PROFITABLE
PROFITABLENESS
PROFITABLY
PROFITEERED
PROFITEERING
PROFITEERINGS
PROFITEERS
PROFITEROLE
PROFITEROLES
PROFITINGS
PROFITLESS
PROFITLESSLY
PROFITWISE
PROFLIGACIES
PROFLIGACY
PROFLIGATE
PROFLIGATELY
PROFLIGATES
PROFLUENCE
PROFLUENCES
PROFOUNDER
PROFOUNDEST
PROFOUNDLY
PROFOUNDNESS
PROFOUNDNESSES
PROFULGENT
PROFUNDITIES
PROFUNDITY
PROFUSENESS
PROFUSENESSES
PROFUSIONS
PROGENITIVE
PROGENITIVENESS
PROGENITOR
PROGENITORIAL
PROGENITORS
PROGENITORSHIP
PROGENITORSHIPS
PROGENITRESS
PROGENITRESSES
PROGENITRICES
PROGENITRIX
PROGENITRIXES
PROGENITURE
PROGENITURES
PROGESTATIONAL
PROGESTERONE
PROGESTERONES
PROGESTINS
PROGESTOGEN
PROGESTOGENIC
PROGESTOGENS
PROGGINSES
PROGLOTTIC
PROGLOTTID
PROGLOTTIDEAN
PROGLOTTIDES
PROGLOTTIDS
PROGLOTTIS
PROGNATHIC
PROGNATHISM
PROGNATHISMS
PROGNATHOUS
PROGNOSING
PROGNOSTIC
PROGNOSTICATE
PROGNOSTICATED
PROGNOSTICATES
PROGNOSTICATING
PROGNOSTICATION
PROGNOSTICATIVE
PROGNOSTICATOR
PROGNOSTICATORS
PROGNOSTICS
PROGRADATION
PROGRADATIONS
PROGRADING
PROGRAMABLE
PROGRAMERS
PROGRAMING
PROGRAMINGS
PROGRAMMABILITY
PROGRAMMABLE
PROGRAMMABLES
PROGRAMMATIC
PROGRAMMED
PROGRAMMER
PROGRAMMERS
PROGRAMMES
PROGRAMMING
PROGRAMMINGS
PROGRESSED
PROGRESSES
PROGRESSING
PROGRESSION
PROGRESSIONAL
PROGRESSIONALLY
PROGRESSIONARY
PROGRESSIONISM
PROGRESSIONISMS
PROGRESSIONIST

PROGRESSIONISTS
PROGRESSIONS
PROGRESSISM
PROGRESSISMS
PROGRESSIST
PROGRESSISTS
PROGRESSIVE
PROGRESSIVELY
PROGRESSIVENESS
PROGRESSIVES
PROGRESSIVISM
PROGRESSIVISMS
PROGRESSIVIST
PROGRESSIVISTIC
PROGRESSIVISTS
PROGRESSIVITIES
PROGRESSIVITY
PROGYMNASIA
PROGYMNASIUM
PROGYMNASIUMS
PROHIBITED
PROHIBITER
PROHIBITERS
PROHIBITING
PROHIBITION
PROHIBITIONARY
PROHIBITIONISM
PROHIBITIONISMS
PROHIBITIONIST
PROHIBITIONISTS
PROHIBITIONS
PROHIBITIVE
PROHIBITIVELY
PROHIBITIVENESS
PROHIBITOR
PROHIBITORS
PROHIBITORY
PROINSULIN
PROINSULINS
PROJECTABLE
PROJECTILE
PROJECTILES
PROJECTING
PROJECTINGS
PROJECTION
PROJECTIONAL
PROJECTIONIST
PROJECTIONISTS
PROJECTIONS
PROJECTISATION
PROJECTISATIONS
PROJECTIVE
PROJECTIVELY
PROJECTIVITIES
PROJECTIVITY
PROJECTIZATION
PROJECTIZATIONS
PROJECTMENT
PROJECTMENTS
PROJECTORS
PROJECTURE
PROJECTURES
PROKARYONS
PROKARYOTE
PROKARYOTES
PROKARYOTIC
PROKARYOTS
PROLACTINS
PROLAMINES
PROLAPSING
PROLAPSUSES
PROLATENESS
PROLATENESSES
PROLATIONS
PROLEGOMENA
PROLEGOMENAL
PROLEGOMENARY
PROLEGOMENON
PROLEGOMENOUS
PROLEPTICAL
PROLEPTICALLY
PROLETARIAN
PROLETARIANISE
PROLETARIANISED
PROLETARIANISES
PROLETARIANISM
PROLETARIANISMS
PROLETARIANIZE
PROLETARIANIZED
PROLETARIANIZES
PROLETARIANNESS
PROLETARIANS
PROLETARIAT
PROLETARIATE
PROLETARIATES
PROLETARIATS
PROLETARIES
PROLICIDAL
PROLICIDES
PROLIFERATE
PROLIFERATED
PROLIFERATES
PROLIFERATING
PROLIFERATION
PROLIFERATIONS
PROLIFERATIVE
PROLIFEROUS
PROLIFEROUSLY
PROLIFICACIES
PROLIFICACY
PROLIFICAL
PROLIFICALLY
PROLIFICATION
PROLIFICATIONS
PROLIFICITIES
PROLIFICITY
PROLIFICNESS
PROLIFICNESSES
PROLIXIOUS
PROLIXITIES
PROLIXNESS
PROLIXNESSES
PROLOCUTION
PROLOCUTIONS
PROLOCUTOR
PROLOCUTORS
PROLOCUTORSHIP
PROLOCUTORSHIPS
PROLOCUTRICES
PROLOCUTRIX
PROLOCUTRIXES
PROLOGISED
PROLOGISES
PROLOGISING
PROLOGISTS
PROLOGIZED
PROLOGIZES
PROLOGIZING
PROLOGUING
PROLOGUISE
PROLOGUISED
PROLOGUISES
PROLOGUISING
PROLOGUIZE
PROLOGUIZED
PROLOGUIZES
PROLOGUIZING
PROLONGABLE
PROLONGATE
PROLONGATED
PROLONGATES
PROLONGATING
PROLONGATION
PROLONGATIONS
PROLONGERS
PROLONGING
PROLONGMENT
PROLONGMENTS
PROLUSIONS
PROMACHOSES
PROMENADED
PROMENADER
PROMENADERS
PROMENADES
PROMENADING
PROMETHAZINE
PROMETHAZINES
PROMETHEUM
PROMETHEUMS
PROMETHIUM
PROMETHIUMS
PROMILITARY
PROMINENCE
PROMINENCES
PROMINENCIES
PROMINENCY
PROMINENTLY
PROMINENTNESS
PROMINENTNESSES
PROMINENTS
PROMISCUITIES
PROMISCUITY
PROMISCUOUS
PROMISCUOUSLY
PROMISCUOUSNESS
PROMISEFUL
PROMISELESS
PROMISINGLY
PROMISSIVE
PROMISSORILY
PROMISSORS
PROMISSORY
PROMONARCHIST
PROMONTORIES
PROMONTORY
PROMOTABILITIES
PROMOTABILITY
PROMOTABLE
PROMOTIONAL
PROMOTIONS
PROMOTIVENESS
PROMOTIVENESSES
PROMPTBOOK
PROMPTBOOKS
PROMPTINGS
PROMPTITUDE
PROMPTITUDES
PROMPTNESS
PROMPTNESSES
PROMPTUARIES
PROMPTUARY
PROMPTURES
PROMULGATE
PROMULGATED
PROMULGATES
PROMULGATING
PROMULGATION
PROMULGATIONS
PROMULGATOR
PROMULGATORS
PROMULGING
PROMUSCIDATE
PROMUSCIDES
PROMYCELIA
PROMYCELIAL
PROMYCELIUM
PRONATIONS
PRONATORES
PRONENESSES
PRONEPHRIC
PRONEPHROI
PRONEPHROS
PRONEPHROSES
PRONGBUCKS
PRONGHORNS
PRONOMINAL
PRONOMINALISE
PRONOMINALISED
PRONOMINALISES
PRONOMINALISING

PRONOMINALIZE
PRONOMINALIZED
PRONOMINALIZES
PRONOMINALIZING
PRONOMINALLY
PRONOUNCEABLE
PRONOUNCED
PRONOUNCEDLY
PRONOUNCEMENT
PRONOUNCEMENTS
PRONOUNCER
PRONOUNCERS
PRONOUNCES
PRONOUNCING
PRONOUNCINGS
PRONUCLEAR
PRONUCLEARIST
PRONUCLEARISTS
PRONUCLEUS
PRONUCLEUSES
PRONUNCIAMENTO
PRONUNCIAMENTOS
PRONUNCIATION
PRONUNCIATIONAL
PRONUNCIATIONS
PRONUNCIOS
PROOEMIONS
PROOEMIUMS
PROOFREADER
PROOFREADERS
PROOFREADING
PROOFREADINGS
PROOFREADS
PROOFROOMS
PROPAEDEUTIC
PROPAEDEUTICAL
PROPAEDEUTICS
PROPAGABILITIES
PROPAGABILITY
PROPAGABLE
PROPAGABLENESS
PROPAGANDA
PROPAGANDAS
PROPAGANDISE
PROPAGANDISED
PROPAGANDISER
PROPAGANDISERS
PROPAGANDISES
PROPAGANDISING
PROPAGANDISM
PROPAGANDISMS
PROPAGANDIST
PROPAGANDISTIC
PROPAGANDISTS
PROPAGANDIZE
PROPAGANDIZED
PROPAGANDIZER
PROPAGANDIZERS
PROPAGANDIZES
PROPAGANDIZING
PROPAGATED
PROPAGATES
PROPAGATING
PROPAGATION
PROPAGATIONAL
PROPAGATIONS
PROPAGATIVE
PROPAGATOR
PROPAGATORS
PROPAGULES
PROPAGULUM
PROPANEDIOIC
PROPANONES
PROPAROXYTONE
PROPAROXYTONES
PROPELLANT
PROPELLANTS
PROPELLENT
PROPELLENTS
PROPELLERS
PROPELLING
PROPELLINGS
PROPELLORS
PROPELMENT
PROPELMENTS
PROPENDENT
PROPENDING
PROPENSELY
PROPENSENESS
PROPENSENESSES
PROPENSION
PROPENSIONS
PROPENSITIES
PROPENSITY
PROPENSIVE
PROPERDINS
PROPERISPOMENA
PROPERISPOMENON
PROPERNESS
PROPERNESSES
PROPERTIED
PROPERTIES
PROPERTYING
PROPERTYLESS
PROPHECIES
PROPHESIABLE
PROPHESIED
PROPHESIER
PROPHESIERS
PROPHESIES
PROPHESYING
PROPHESYINGS
PROPHETESS
PROPHETESSES
PROPHETHOOD
PROPHETHOODS
PROPHETICAL
PROPHETICALLY
PROPHETICISM
PROPHETICISMS
PROPHETISM
PROPHETISMS
PROPHETSHIP
PROPHETSHIPS
PROPHYLACTIC
PROPHYLACTICS
PROPHYLAXES
PROPHYLAXIS
PROPINQUITIES
PROPINQUITY
PROPIONATE
PROPIONATES
PROPITIABLE
PROPITIATE
PROPITIATED
PROPITIATES
PROPITIATING
PROPITIATION
PROPITIATIONS
PROPITIATIOUS
PROPITIATIVE
PROPITIATOR
PROPITIATORIES
PROPITIATORILY
PROPITIATORS
PROPITIATORY
PROPITIOUS
PROPITIOUSLY
PROPITIOUSNESS
PROPLASTID
PROPLASTIDS
PROPODEONS
PROPODEUMS
PROPOLISES
PROPONENTS
PROPORTION
PROPORTIONABLE
PROPORTIONABLY
PROPORTIONAL
PROPORTIONALITY
PROPORTIONALLY
PROPORTIONALS
PROPORTIONATE
PROPORTIONATED
PROPORTIONATELY
PROPORTIONATES
PROPORTIONATING
PROPORTIONED
PROPORTIONING
PROPORTIONINGS
PROPORTIONLESS
PROPORTIONMENT
PROPORTIONMENTS
PROPORTIONS
PROPOSABLE
PROPOSITAE
PROPOSITION
PROPOSITIONAL
PROPOSITIONALLY
PROPOSITIONED
PROPOSITIONING
PROPOSITIONS
PROPOSITUS
PROPOUNDED
PROPOUNDER
PROPOUNDERS
PROPOUNDING
PROPOXYPHENE
PROPOXYPHENES
PROPRAETOR
PROPRAETORIAL
PROPRAETORIAN
PROPRAETORS
PROPRANOLOL
PROPRANOLOLS
PROPRETORS
PROPRIETARIES
PROPRIETARILY
PROPRIETARY
PROPRIETIES
PROPRIETOR
PROPRIETORIAL
PROPRIETORIALLY
PROPRIETORS
PROPRIETORSHIP
PROPRIETORSHIPS
PROPRIETRESS
PROPRIETRESSES
PROPRIETRICES
PROPRIETRIX
PROPRIETRIXES
PROPRIOCEPTION
PROPRIOCEPTIONS
PROPRIOCEPTIVE
PROPRIOCEPTOR
PROPRIOCEPTORS
PROPROCTOR
PROPROCTORS
PROPUGNATION
PROPUGNATIONS
PROPULSION
PROPULSIONS
PROPULSIVE
PROPULSORS
PROPULSORY
PROPYLAEUM
PROPYLAMINE
PROPYLAMINES
PROPYLENES
PROPYLITES
PROPYLITISATION
PROPYLITISE
PROPYLITISED
PROPYLITISES
PROPYLITISING
PROPYLITIZATION
PROPYLITIZE
PROPYLITIZED
PROPYLITIZES
PROPYLITIZING

PRORATABLE
PRORATIONS
PRORECTORS
PROROGATED
PROROGATES
PROROGATING
PROROGATION
PROROGATIONS
PROROGUING
PROSAICALLY
PROSAICALNESS
PROSAICALNESSES
PROSAICISM
PROSAICISMS
PROSAICNESS
PROSAICNESSES
PROSATEURS
PROSAUROPOD
PROSAUROPODS
PROSCENIUM
PROSCENIUMS
PROSCIUTTI
PROSCIUTTO
PROSCIUTTOS
PROSCRIBED
PROSCRIBER
PROSCRIBERS
PROSCRIBES
PROSCRIBING
PROSCRIPTION
PROSCRIPTIONS
PROSCRIPTIVE
PROSCRIPTIVELY
PROSCRIPTS
PROSECTING
PROSECTORIAL
PROSECTORS
PROSECTORSHIP
PROSECTORSHIPS
PROSECUTABLE
PROSECUTED
PROSECUTES
PROSECUTING
PROSECUTION
PROSECUTIONS
PROSECUTOR
PROSECUTORIAL
PROSECUTORS
PROSECUTRICES
PROSECUTRIX
PROSECUTRIXES
PROSELYTED
PROSELYTES
PROSELYTIC
PROSELYTING
PROSELYTISATION
PROSELYTISE
PROSELYTISED
PROSELYTISER
PROSELYTISERS
PROSELYTISES
PROSELYTISING
PROSELYTISM
PROSELYTISMS
PROSELYTIZATION
PROSELYTIZE
PROSELYTIZED
PROSELYTIZER
PROSELYTIZERS
PROSELYTIZES
PROSELYTIZING
PROSEMINAR
PROSEMINARS
PROSENCEPHALA
PROSENCEPHALIC
PROSENCEPHALON
PROSENCHYMA
PROSENCHYMAS
PROSENCHYMATA
PROSENCHYMATOUS
PROSEUCHAE
PROSIFYING
PROSILIENCIES
PROSILIENCY
PROSILIENT
PROSIMIANS
PROSINESSES
PROSLAMBANOMENE
PROSLAVERY
PROSOBRANCH
PROSOBRANCHS
PROSODIANS
PROSODICAL
PROSODICALLY
PROSODISTS
PROSOPAGNOSIA
PROSOPAGNOSIAS
PROSOPOGRAPHER
PROSOPOGRAPHERS
PROSOPOGRAPHIES
PROSOPOGRAPHY
PROSOPOPEIA
PROSOPOPEIAL
PROSOPOPEIAS
PROSOPOPOEIA
PROSOPOPOEIAL
PROSOPOPOEIAS
PROSPECTED
PROSPECTING
PROSPECTINGS
PROSPECTION
PROSPECTIONS
PROSPECTIVE
PROSPECTIVELY
PROSPECTIVENESS
PROSPECTIVES
PROSPECTLESS
PROSPECTOR
PROSPECTORS
PROSPECTUS
PROSPECTUSES
PROSPERING
PROSPERITIES
PROSPERITY
PROSPEROUS
PROSPEROUSLY
PROSPEROUSNESS
PROSTACYCLIN
PROSTACYCLINS
PROSTAGLANDIN
PROSTAGLANDINS
PROSTANTHERA
PROSTANTHERAS
PROSTATECTOMIES
PROSTATECTOMY
PROSTATISM
PROSTATISMS
PROSTATITIS
PROSTATITISES
PROSTERNUM
PROSTERNUMS
PROSTHESES
PROSTHESIS
PROSTHETIC
PROSTHETICALLY
PROSTHETICS
PROSTHETIST
PROSTHETISTS
PROSTHODONTIA
PROSTHODONTIAS
PROSTHODONTICS
PROSTHODONTIST
PROSTHODONTISTS
PROSTITUTE
PROSTITUTED
PROSTITUTES
PROSTITUTING
PROSTITUTION
PROSTITUTIONS
PROSTITUTOR
PROSTITUTORS
PROSTOMIAL
PROSTOMIUM
PROSTRATED
PROSTRATES
PROSTRATING
PROSTRATION
PROSTRATIONS
PROSYLLOGISM
PROSYLLOGISMS
PROTACTINIUM
PROTACTINIUMS
PROTAGONISM
PROTAGONISMS
PROTAGONIST
PROTAGONISTS
PROTAMINES
PROTANDRIES
PROTANDROUS
PROTANOMALIES
PROTANOMALOUS
PROTANOMALY
PROTANOPES
PROTANOPIA
PROTANOPIAS
PROTANOPIC
PROTEACEOUS
PROTECTANT
PROTECTANTS
PROTECTERS
PROTECTING
PROTECTINGLY
PROTECTION
PROTECTIONISM
PROTECTIONISMS
PROTECTIONIST
PROTECTIONISTS
PROTECTIONS
PROTECTIVE
PROTECTIVELY
PROTECTIVENESS
PROTECTIVES
PROTECTORAL
PROTECTORATE
PROTECTORATES
PROTECTORIAL
PROTECTORIES
PROTECTORLESS
PROTECTORS
PROTECTORSHIP
PROTECTORSHIPS
PROTECTORY
PROTECTRESS
PROTECTRESSES
PROTECTRICES
PROTECTRIX
PROTECTRIXES
PROTEIFORM
PROTEINACEOUS
PROTEINASE
PROTEINASES
PROTEINOUS
PROTEINURIA
PROTEINURIAS
PROTENDING
PROTENSION
PROTENSIONS
PROTENSITIES
PROTENSITY
PROTENSIVE
PROTENSIVELY
PROTEOCLASTIC
PROTEOGLYCAN
PROTEOGLYCANS
PROTEOLYSE
PROTEOLYSED
PROTEOLYSES
PROTEOLYSING
PROTEOLYSIS
PROTEOLYTIC

P

PROTEOLYTICALLY
PROTEOMICS
PROTERANDRIES
PROTERANDROUS
PROTERANDRY
PROTEROGYNIES
PROTEROGYNOUS
PROTEROGYNY
PROTERVITIES
PROTERVITY
PROTESTANT
PROTESTANTS
PROTESTATION
PROTESTATIONS
PROTESTERS
PROTESTING
PROTESTINGLY
PROTESTORS
PROTHALAMIA
PROTHALAMION
PROTHALAMIUM
PROTHALLIA
PROTHALLIAL
PROTHALLIC
PROTHALLIUM
PROTHALLOID
PROTHALLUS
PROTHALLUSES
PROTHETICALLY
PROTHONOTARIAL
PROTHONOTARIAT
PROTHONOTARIATS
PROTHONOTARIES
PROTHONOTARY
PROTHORACES
PROTHORACIC
PROTHORAXES
PROTHROMBIN
PROTHROMBINS
PROTISTANS
PROTISTOLOGIES
PROTISTOLOGIST
PROTISTOLOGISTS
PROTISTOLOGY
PROTOACTINIUM
PROTOACTINIUMS
PROTOAVISES
PROTOCHORDATE
PROTOCHORDATES
PROTOCOCCAL
PROTOCOLED
PROTOCOLIC
PROTOCOLING
PROTOCOLISE
PROTOCOLISED
PROTOCOLISES
PROTOCOLISING
PROTOCOLIST
PROTOCOLISTS
PROTOCOLIZE
PROTOCOLIZED
PROTOCOLIZES
PROTOCOLIZING
PROTOCOLLED
PROTOCOLLING
PROTOCTIST
PROTOCTISTS
PROTODERMS
PROTOGALAXIES
PROTOGALAXY
PROTOGENIC
PROTOGINES
PROTOGYNIES
PROTOGYNOUS
PROTOHISTORIAN
PROTOHISTORIANS
PROTOHISTORIC
PROTOHISTORIES
PROTOHISTORY
PROTOHUMAN
PROTOHUMANS
PROTOLANGUAGE
PROTOLANGUAGES
PROTOLITHIC
PROTOMARTYR
PROTOMARTYRS
PROTOMORPHIC
PROTONATED
PROTONATES
PROTONATING
PROTONATION
PROTONATIONS
PROTONEMAL
PROTONEMATA
PROTONEMATAL
PROTONOTARIAL
PROTONOTARIAT
PROTONOTARIATS
PROTONOTARIES
PROTONOTARY
PROTOPATHIC
PROTOPATHIES
PROTOPATHY
PROTOPHILIC
PROTOPHLOEM
PROTOPHLOEMS
PROTOPHYTE
PROTOPHYTES
PROTOPHYTIC
PROTOPLANET
PROTOPLANETARY
PROTOPLANETS
PROTOPLASM
PROTOPLASMAL
PROTOPLASMATIC
PROTOPLASMIC
PROTOPLASMS
PROTOPLAST
PROTOPLASTIC
PROTOPLASTS
PROTOPORPHYRIN
PROTOPORPHYRINS
PROTOSPATAIRE
PROTOSPATAIRES
PROTOSPATHAIRE
PROTOSPATHAIRES
PROTOSPATHARIUS
PROTOSTARS
PROTOSTELE
PROTOSTELES
PROTOSTELIC
PROTOSTOME
PROTOSTOMES
PROTOTHERIAN
PROTOTHERIANS
PROTOTROPH
PROTOTROPHIC
PROTOTROPHIES
PROTOTROPHS
PROTOTROPHY
PROTOTYPAL
PROTOTYPED
PROTOTYPES
PROTOTYPIC
PROTOTYPICAL
PROTOTYPICALLY
PROTOTYPING
PROTOXIDES
PROTOXYLEM
PROTOXYLEMS
PROTOZOANS
PROTOZOOLOGICAL
PROTOZOOLOGIES
PROTOZOOLOGIST
PROTOZOOLOGISTS
PROTOZOOLOGY
PROTOZOONS
PROTRACTED
PROTRACTEDLY
PROTRACTEDNESS
PROTRACTIBLE
PROTRACTILE
PROTRACTING
PROTRACTION
PROTRACTIONS
PROTRACTIVE
PROTRACTOR
PROTRACTORS
PROTREPTIC
PROTREPTICAL
PROTREPTICS
PROTRUDABLE
PROTRUDENT
PROTRUDING
PROTRUSIBLE
PROTRUSILE
PROTRUSION
PROTRUSIONS
PROTRUSIVE
PROTRUSIVELY
PROTRUSIVENESS
PROTUBERANCE
PROTUBERANCES
PROTUBERANCIES
PROTUBERANCY
PROTUBERANT
PROTUBERANTLY
PROTUBERATE
PROTUBERATED
PROTUBERATES
PROTUBERATING
PROTUBERATION
PROTUBERATIONS
PROUDHEARTED
PROUDNESSES
PROUSTITES
PROVABILITIES
PROVABILITY
PROVABLENESS
PROVABLENESSES
PROVANTING
PROVASCULAR
PROVEABILITIES
PROVEABILITY
PROVECTION
PROVECTIONS
PROVEDITOR
PROVEDITORE
PROVEDITORES
PROVEDITORS
PROVEDORES
PROVENANCE
PROVENANCES
PROVENDERED
PROVENDERING
PROVENDERS
PROVENIENCE
PROVENIENCES
PROVENTRICULAR
PROVENTRICULI
PROVENTRICULUS
PROVERBIAL
PROVERBIALISE
PROVERBIALISED
PROVERBIALISES
PROVERBIALISING
PROVERBIALISM
PROVERBIALISMS
PROVERBIALIST
PROVERBIALISTS
PROVERBIALIZE
PROVERBIALIZED
PROVERBIALIZES
PROVERBIALIZING
PROVERBIALLY
PROVERBING
PROVIDABLE
PROVIDENCE
PROVIDENCES
PROVIDENTIAL

P

PROVIDENTIALLY
PROVIDENTLY
PROVINCEWIDE
PROVINCIAL
PROVINCIALISE
PROVINCIALISED
PROVINCIALISES
PROVINCIALISING
PROVINCIALISM
PROVINCIALISMS
PROVINCIALIST
PROVINCIALISTS
PROVINCIALITIES
PROVINCIALITY
PROVINCIALIZE
PROVINCIALIZED
PROVINCIALIZES
PROVINCIALIZING
PROVINCIALLY
PROVINCIALS
PROVIRUSES
PROVISIONAL
PROVISIONALLY
PROVISIONALS
PROVISIONARIES
PROVISIONARY
PROVISIONED
PROVISIONER
PROVISIONERS
PROVISIONING
PROVISIONS
PROVISORILY
PROVITAMIN
PROVITAMINS
PROVOCABLE
PROVOCANTS
PROVOCATEUR
PROVOCATEURS
PROVOCATION
PROVOCATIONS
PROVOCATIVE
PROVOCATIVELY
PROVOCATIVENESS
PROVOCATIVES
PROVOCATOR
PROVOCATORS
PROVOCATORY
PROVOKABLE
PROVOKEMENT
PROVOKEMENTS
PROVOKINGLY
PROVOLONES
PROVOSTRIES
PROVOSTSHIP
PROVOSTSHIPS
PROWLINGLY
PROXIMALLY
PROXIMATELY
PROXIMATENESS
PROXIMATENESSES
PROXIMATION
PROXIMATIONS
PROXIMITIES
PROZYMITES
PRUDENTIAL
PRUDENTIALISM
PRUDENTIALISMS
PRUDENTIALIST
PRUDENTIALISTS
PRUDENTIALITIES
PRUDENTIALITY
PRUDENTIALLY
PRUDENTIALS
PRUDISHNESS
PRUDISHNESSES
PRURIENCES
PRURIENCIES
PRURIENTLY
PRURIGINOUS
PRURITUSES
PRUSSIANISATION
PRUSSIANISE
PRUSSIANISED
PRUSSIANISES
PRUSSIANISING
PRUSSIANIZATION
PRUSSIANIZE
PRUSSIANIZED
PRUSSIANIZES
PRUSSIANIZING
PRUSSIATES
PSALIGRAPHIES
PSALIGRAPHY
PSALMBOOKS
PSALMODICAL
PSALMODIES
PSALMODISE
PSALMODISED
PSALMODISES
PSALMODISING
PSALMODIST
PSALMODISTS
PSALMODIZE
PSALMODIZED
PSALMODIZES
PSALMODIZING
PSALTERIAN
PSALTERIES
PSALTERIUM
PSALTRESSES
PSAMMOPHIL
PSAMMOPHILE
PSAMMOPHILES
PSAMMOPHILOUS
PSAMMOPHILS
PSAMMOPHYTE
PSAMMOPHYTES
PSAMMOPHYTIC
PSELLISMUS
PSELLISMUSES
PSEPHOANALYSES
PSEPHOANALYSIS
PSEPHOLOGICAL
PSEPHOLOGICALLY
PSEPHOLOGIES
PSEPHOLOGIST
PSEPHOLOGISTS
PSEPHOLOGY
PSEUDAESTHESIA
PSEUDAESTHESIAS
PSEUDARTHROSES
PSEUDARTHROSIS
PSEUDEPIGRAPH
PSEUDEPIGRAPHA
PSEUDEPIGRAPHIC
PSEUDEPIGRAPHON
PSEUDEPIGRAPHS
PSEUDEPIGRAPHY
PSEUDERIES
PSEUDIMAGINES
PSEUDIMAGO
PSEUDIMAGOES
PSEUDIMAGOS
PSEUDOACID
PSEUDOACIDS
PSEUDOALLELE
PSEUDOALLELES
PSEUDOARTHROSES
PSEUDOARTHROSIS
PSEUDOBULB
PSEUDOBULBS
PSEUDOCARP
PSEUDOCARPOUS
PSEUDOCARPS
PSEUDOCIDE
PSEUDOCIDES
PSEUDOCLASSIC
PSEUDOCLASSICS
PSEUDOCODE
PSEUDOCODES
PSEUDOCOEL
PSEUDOCOELOMATE
PSEUDOCOELS
PSEUDOCYESES
PSEUDOCYESIS
PSEUDOEPHEDRINE
PSEUDOGRAPH
PSEUDOGRAPHIES
PSEUDOGRAPHS
PSEUDOGRAPHY
PSEUDOLOGIA
PSEUDOLOGIAS
PSEUDOLOGIES
PSEUDOLOGUE
PSEUDOLOGUES
PSEUDOLOGY
PSEUDOMARTYR
PSEUDOMARTYRS
PSEUDOMEMBRANE
PSEUDOMEMBRANES
PSEUDOMONAD
PSEUDOMONADES
PSEUDOMONADS
PSEUDOMONAS
PSEUDOMORPH
PSEUDOMORPHIC
PSEUDOMORPHISM
PSEUDOMORPHISMS
PSEUDOMORPHOUS
PSEUDOMORPHS
PSEUDOMUTUALITY
PSEUDONYMITIES
PSEUDONYMITY
PSEUDONYMOUS
PSEUDONYMOUSLY
PSEUDONYMS
PSEUDOPODAL
PSEUDOPODIA
PSEUDOPODIAL
PSEUDOPODIUM
PSEUDOPODS
PSEUDOPREGNANCY
PSEUDOPREGNANT
PSEUDORANDOM
PSEUDOSCALAR
PSEUDOSCALARS
PSEUDOSCIENCE
PSEUDOSCIENCES
PSEUDOSCIENTIST
PSEUDOSCOPE
PSEUDOSCOPES
PSEUDOSCORPION
PSEUDOSCORPIONS
PSEUDOSOLUTION
PSEUDOSOLUTIONS
PSEUDOSYMMETRY
PSEUDOVECTOR
PSEUDOVECTORS
PSILANTHROPIC
PSILANTHROPIES
PSILANTHROPISM
PSILANTHROPISMS
PSILANTHROPIST
PSILANTHROPISTS
PSILANTHROPY
PSILOCYBIN
PSILOCYBINS
PSILOMELANE
PSILOMELANES
PSILOPHYTE
PSILOPHYTES
PSILOPHYTIC
PSITTACINE
PSITTACINES
PSITTACOSES
PSITTACOSIS
PSITTACOTIC
PSORIATICS
PSYCHAGOGUE
PSYCHAGOGUES

PSYCHASTHENIA
PSYCHASTHENIAS
PSYCHASTHENIC
PSYCHASTHENICS
PSYCHEDELIA
PSYCHEDELIAS
PSYCHEDELIC
PSYCHEDELICALLY
PSYCHEDELICS
PSYCHIATER
PSYCHIATERS
PSYCHIATRIC
PSYCHIATRICAL
PSYCHIATRICALLY
PSYCHIATRIES
PSYCHIATRIST
PSYCHIATRISTS
PSYCHIATRY
PSYCHICALLY
PSYCHICISM
PSYCHICISMS
PSYCHICIST
PSYCHICISTS
PSYCHOACOUSTIC
PSYCHOACOUSTICS
PSYCHOACTIVE
PSYCHOANALYSE
PSYCHOANALYSED
PSYCHOANALYSER
PSYCHOANALYSERS
PSYCHOANALYSES
PSYCHOANALYSING
PSYCHOANALYSIS
PSYCHOANALYST
PSYCHOANALYSTS
PSYCHOANALYTIC
PSYCHOANALYZE
PSYCHOANALYZED
PSYCHOANALYZER
PSYCHOANALYZERS
PSYCHOANALYZES
PSYCHOANALYZING
PSYCHOBABBLE
PSYCHOBABBLED
PSYCHOBABBLER
PSYCHOBABBLERS
PSYCHOBABBLES
PSYCHOBABBLING
PSYCHOBILLIES
PSYCHOBILLY
PSYCHOBIOGRAPHY
PSYCHOBIOLOGIC
PSYCHOBIOLOGIES
PSYCHOBIOLOGIST
PSYCHOBIOLOGY
PSYCHOCHEMICAL
PSYCHOCHEMICALS
PSYCHOCHEMISTRY
PSYCHODELIA
PSYCHODELIAS
PSYCHODELIC
PSYCHODELICALLY
PSYCHODRAMA
PSYCHODRAMAS
PSYCHODRAMATIC
PSYCHODYNAMIC
PSYCHODYNAMICS
PSYCHOGALVANIC
PSYCHOGASES
PSYCHOGENESES
PSYCHOGENESIS
PSYCHOGENETIC
PSYCHOGENETICAL
PSYCHOGENETICS
PSYCHOGENIC
PSYCHOGENICALLY
PSYCHOGERIATRIC
PSYCHOGNOSES
PSYCHOGNOSIS
PSYCHOGNOSTIC
PSYCHOGONIES
PSYCHOGONY
PSYCHOGRAM
PSYCHOGRAMS
PSYCHOGRAPH
PSYCHOGRAPHIC
PSYCHOGRAPHICAL
PSYCHOGRAPHICS
PSYCHOGRAPHIES
PSYCHOGRAPHS
PSYCHOGRAPHY
PSYCHOHISTORIAN
PSYCHOHISTORIES
PSYCHOHISTORY
PSYCHOKINESES
PSYCHOKINESIS
PSYCHOKINETIC
PSYCHOLINGUIST
PSYCHOLINGUISTS
PSYCHOLOGIC
PSYCHOLOGICAL
PSYCHOLOGICALLY
PSYCHOLOGIES
PSYCHOLOGISE
PSYCHOLOGISED
PSYCHOLOGISES
PSYCHOLOGISING
PSYCHOLOGISM
PSYCHOLOGISMS
PSYCHOLOGIST
PSYCHOLOGISTIC
PSYCHOLOGISTS
PSYCHOLOGIZE
PSYCHOLOGIZED
PSYCHOLOGIZES
PSYCHOLOGIZING
PSYCHOLOGY
PSYCHOMACHIA
PSYCHOMACHIAS
PSYCHOMACHIES
PSYCHOMACHY
PSYCHOMETER
PSYCHOMETERS
PSYCHOMETRIC
PSYCHOMETRICAL
PSYCHOMETRICIAN
PSYCHOMETRICS
PSYCHOMETRIES
PSYCHOMETRIST
PSYCHOMETRISTS
PSYCHOMETRY
PSYCHOMOTOR
PSYCHONEUROSES
PSYCHONEUROSIS
PSYCHONEUROTIC
PSYCHONEUROTICS
PSYCHONOMIC
PSYCHONOMICS
PSYCHOPATH
PSYCHOPATHIC
PSYCHOPATHICS
PSYCHOPATHIES
PSYCHOPATHIST
PSYCHOPATHISTS
PSYCHOPATHOLOGY
PSYCHOPATHS
PSYCHOPATHY
PSYCHOPHILIES
PSYCHOPHILY
PSYCHOPHYSICAL
PSYCHOPHYSICIST
PSYCHOPHYSICS
PSYCHOPOMP
PSYCHOPOMPS
PSYCHOSEXUAL
PSYCHOSEXUALITY
PSYCHOSEXUALLY
PSYCHOSOCIAL
PSYCHOSOCIALLY
PSYCHOSOCIOLOGY
PSYCHOSOMATIC
PSYCHOSOMATICS
PSYCHOSOMIMETIC
PSYCHOSURGEON
PSYCHOSURGEONS
PSYCHOSURGERIES
PSYCHOSURGERY
PSYCHOSURGICAL
PSYCHOSYNTHESES
PSYCHOSYNTHESIS
PSYCHOTECHNICS
PSYCHOTHERAPIES
PSYCHOTHERAPIST
PSYCHOTHERAPY
PSYCHOTICALLY
PSYCHOTICISM
PSYCHOTICISMS
PSYCHOTICS
PSYCHOTOMIMETIC
PSYCHOTOXIC
PSYCHOTROPIC
PSYCHOTROPICS
PSYCHROMETER
PSYCHROMETERS
PSYCHROMETRIC
PSYCHROMETRICAL
PSYCHROMETRIES
PSYCHROMETRY
PSYCHROPHILIC
PTARMIGANS
PTERANODON
PTERANODONS
PTERIDINES
PTERIDOLOGICAL
PTERIDOLOGIES
PTERIDOLOGIST
PTERIDOLOGISTS
PTERIDOLOGY
PTERIDOMANIA
PTERIDOMANIAS
PTERIDOPHILIST
PTERIDOPHILISTS
PTERIDOPHYTE
PTERIDOPHYTES
PTERIDOPHYTIC
PTERIDOPHYTOUS
PTERIDOSPERM
PTERIDOSPERMS
PTERODACTYL
PTERODACTYLE
PTERODACTYLES
PTERODACTYLS
PTEROSAURIAN
PTEROSAURIANS
PTEROSAURS
PTERYGIALS
PTERYGIUMS
PTERYGOIDS
PTERYLOGRAPHIC
PTERYLOGRAPHIES
PTERYLOGRAPHY
PTERYLOSES
PTERYLOSIS
PTOCHOCRACIES
PTOCHOCRACY
PTYALAGOGIC
PTYALAGOGUE
PTYALAGOGUES
PTYALISING
PTYALIZING
PUBCRAWLER
PUBCRAWLERS
PUBERULENT
PUBERULOUS
PUBESCENCE
PUBESCENCES
PUBLICALLY
PUBLICATION
PUBLICATIONS
PUBLICISED

P

PUBLICISES
PUBLICISING
PUBLICISTS
PUBLICITIES
PUBLICIZED
PUBLICIZES
PUBLICIZING
PUBLICNESS
PUBLICNESSES
PUBLISHABLE
PUBLISHERS
PUBLISHING
PUBLISHINGS
PUBLISHMENT
PUBLISHMENTS
PUCCINIACEOUS
PUCKERIEST
PUCKEROOED
PUCKISHNESS
PUCKISHNESSES
PUDDENINGS
PUDDINGIER
PUDDINGIEST
PUDGINESSES
PUDIBUNDITIES
PUDIBUNDITY
PUDICITIES
PUERILISMS
PUERILITIES
PUERPERALLY
PUERPERIUM
PUFFERFISH
PUFFERFISHES
PUFFINESSES
PUFFTALOONAS
PUFTALOONAS
PUFTALOONIES
PUFTALOONS
PUGGINESSES
PUGILISTIC
PUGILISTICAL
PUGILISTICALLY
PUGNACIOUS
PUGNACIOUSLY
PUGNACIOUSNESS
PUGNACITIES
PUISSANCES
PUISSANTLY
PUISSAUNCE
PUISSAUNCES
PULCHRITUDE
PULCHRITUDES
PULCHRITUDINOUS
PULLULATED
PULLULATES
PULLULATING
PULLULATION
PULLULATIONS
PULMOBRANCH
PULMOBRANCHIATE
PULMOBRANCHS
PULMONATES
PULMONOLOGIES
PULMONOLOGIST
PULMONOLOGISTS
PULMONOLOGY
PULPBOARDS
PULPIFYING
PULPINESSES
PULPITEERED
PULPITEERING
PULPITEERS
PULPITRIES
PULPSTONES
PULSATANCE
PULSATANCES
PULSATILITIES
PULSATILITY
PULSATILLA
PULSATILLAS
PULSATIONS
PULSATIVELY
PULSEBEATS
PULSELESSNESS
PULSELESSNESSES
PULSIMETER
PULSIMETERS
PULSOMETER
PULSOMETERS
PULTACEOUS
PULTRUDING
PULTRUSION
PULTRUSIONS
PULVERABLE
PULVERATION
PULVERATIONS
PULVERINES
PULVERISABLE
PULVERISATION
PULVERISATIONS
PULVERISED
PULVERISER
PULVERISERS
PULVERISES
PULVERISING
PULVERIZABLE
PULVERIZATION
PULVERIZATIONS
PULVERIZED
PULVERIZER
PULVERIZERS
PULVERIZES
PULVERIZING
PULVERULENCE
PULVERULENCES
PULVERULENT
PULVILISED
PULVILIZED
PULVILLIFORM
PULVILLING
PULVILLIOS
PULVINATED
PULVINULES
PUMICATING
PUMMELLING
PUMMELLINGS
PUMPERNICKEL
PUMPERNICKELS
PUMPHOUSES
PUMPKINSEED
PUMPKINSEEDS
PUNCHBALLS
PUNCHBOARD
PUNCHBOARDS
PUNCHBOWLS
PUNCHINELLO
PUNCHINELLOES
PUNCHINELLOS
PUNCHINESS
PUNCHINESSES
PUNCHLINES
PUNCTATION
PUNCTATIONS
PUNCTATORS
PUNCTILIOS
PUNCTILIOUS
PUNCTILIOUSLY
PUNCTILIOUSNESS
PUNCTUALIST
PUNCTUALISTS
PUNCTUALITIES
PUNCTUALITY
PUNCTUALLY
PUNCTUATED
PUNCTUATES
PUNCTUATING
PUNCTUATION
PUNCTUATIONIST
PUNCTUATIONISTS
PUNCTUATIONS
PUNCTUATIVE
PUNCTUATOR
PUNCTUATORS
PUNCTULATE
PUNCTULATED
PUNCTULATES
PUNCTULATING
PUNCTULATION
PUNCTULATIONS
PUNCTURABLE
PUNCTURATION
PUNCTURATIONS
PUNCTURERS
PUNCTURING
PUNDIGRION
PUNDIGRIONS
PUNDITRIES
PUNDONORES
PUNGENCIES
PUNICACEOUS
PUNINESSES
PUNISHABILITIES
PUNISHABILITY
PUNISHABLE
PUNISHINGLY
PUNISHMENT
PUNISHMENTS
PUNITIVELY
PUNITIVENESS
PUNITIVENESSES
PUNKINESSES
PUPIGEROUS
PUPILABILITIES
PUPILABILITY
PUPILARITIES
PUPILARITY
PUPILLAGES
PUPILLARITIES
PUPILLARITY
PUPILLATED
PUPILLATES
PUPILLATING
PUPILSHIPS
PUPIPAROUS
PUPPETEERED
PUPPETEERING
PUPPETEERS
PUPPETLIKE
PUPPETRIES
PUPPYHOODS
PURBLINDLY
PURBLINDNESS
PURBLINDNESSES
PURCHASABILITY
PURCHASABLE
PURCHASERS
PURCHASING
PURCHASINGS
PURDONIUMS
PUREBLOODS
PURENESSES
PURGATIONS
PURGATIVELY
PURGATIVES
PURGATORIAL
PURGATORIALLY
PURGATORIAN
PURGATORIANS
PURGATORIES
PURIFICATION
PURIFICATIONS
PURIFICATIVE
PURIFICATOR
PURIFICATORS
PURIFICATORY
PURISTICAL
PURISTICALLY
PURITANICAL
PURITANICALLY
PURITANICALNESS

PURITANISE
PURITANISED
PURITANISES
PURITANISING
PURITANISM
PURITANISMS
PURITANIZE
PURITANIZED
PURITANIZES
PURITANIZING
PURLICUING
PURLOINERS
PURLOINING
PUROMYCINS
PURPLEHEART
PURPLEHEARTS
PURPLENESS
PURPLENESSES
PURPORTEDLY
PURPORTING
PURPORTLESS
PURPOSEFUL
PURPOSEFULLY
PURPOSEFULNESS
PURPOSELESS
PURPOSELESSLY
PURPOSELESSNESS
PURPOSIVELY
PURPOSIVENESS
PURPOSIVENESSES
PURPRESTURE
PURPRESTURES
PURSERSHIP
PURSERSHIPS
PURSINESSES
PURSUANCES
PURSUANTLY
PURSUINGLY
PURSUIVANT
PURSUIVANTS
PURTENANCE
PURTENANCES
PURULENCES
PURULENCIES
PURULENTLY
PURVEYANCE
PURVEYANCES
PUSCHKINIA
PUSCHKINIAS
PUSHCHAIRS
PUSHFULNESS
PUSHFULNESSES
PUSHINESSES
PUSHINGNESS
PUSHINGNESSES
PUSILLANIMITIES
PUSILLANIMITY
PUSILLANIMOUS
PUSILLANIMOUSLY
PUSSYFOOTED
PUSSYFOOTER
PUSSYFOOTERS
PUSSYFOOTING
PUSSYFOOTINGS
PUSSYFOOTS
PUSTULANTS
PUSTULATED
PUSTULATES
PUSTULATING
PUSTULATION
PUSTULATIONS
PUTANGITANGI
PUTANGITANGIS
PUTATIVELY
PUTONGHUAS
PUTREFACIENT
PUTREFACTION
PUTREFACTIONS
PUTREFACTIVE
PUTREFIABLE
PUTREFIERS
PUTREFYING
PUTRESCENCE
PUTRESCENCES
PUTRESCENT
PUTRESCIBILITY
PUTRESCIBLE
PUTRESCIBLES
PUTRESCINE
PUTRESCINES
PUTRIDITIES
PUTRIDNESS
PUTRIDNESSES
PUTRIFICATION
PUTRIFICATIONS
PUTSCHISTS
PUTTYROOTS
PUZZLEDOMS
PUZZLEHEADED
PUZZLEMENT
PUZZLEMENTS
PUZZLINGLY
PUZZOLANAS
PYCNIDIOSPORE
PYCNIDIOSPORES
PYCNOCONIDIA
PYCNOCONIDIUM
PYCNODYSOSTOSES
PYCNODYSOSTOSIS
PYCNOGONID
PYCNOGONIDS
PYCNOGONOID
PYCNOGONOIDS
PYCNOMETER
PYCNOMETERS
PYCNOMETRIC
PYCNOSOMES
PYCNOSPORE
PYCNOSPORES
PYCNOSTYLE
PYCNOSTYLES
PYELITISES
PYELOGRAMS
PYELOGRAPHIC
PYELOGRAPHIES
PYELOGRAPHY
PYELONEPHRITIC
PYELONEPHRITIS
PYGARGUSES
PYGOSTYLES
PYKNODYSOSTOSES
PYKNODYSOSTOSIS
PYKNOMETER
PYKNOMETERS
PYKNOSOMES
PYLORECTOMIES
PYLORECTOMY
PYOGENESES
PYOGENESIS
PYORRHOEAL
PYORRHOEAS
PYORRHOEIC
PYRACANTHA
PYRACANTHAS
PYRACANTHS
PYRALIDIDS
PYRAMIDALLY
PYRAMIDICAL
PYRAMIDICALLY
PYRAMIDING
PYRAMIDION
PYRAMIDIONS
PYRAMIDIST
PYRAMIDISTS
PYRAMIDOLOGIES
PYRAMIDOLOGIST
PYRAMIDOLOGISTS
PYRAMIDOLOGY
PYRAMIDONS
PYRANOMETER
PYRANOMETERS
PYRANOSIDE
PYRANOSIDES
PYRARGYRITE
PYRARGYRITES
PYRENEITES
PYRENOCARP
PYRENOCARPS
PYRENOMYCETOUS
PYRETHRINS
PYRETHROID
PYRETHROIDS
PYRETHRUMS
PYRETOLOGIES
PYRETOLOGY
PYRETOTHERAPIES
PYRETOTHERAPY
PYRGEOMETER
PYRGEOMETERS
PYRHELIOMETER
PYRHELIOMETERS
PYRHELIOMETRIC
PYRIDOXALS
PYRIDOXAMINE
PYRIDOXAMINES
PYRIDOXINE
PYRIDOXINES
PYRIDOXINS
PYRIMETHAMINE
PYRIMETHAMINES
PYRIMIDINE
PYRIMIDINES
PYRITHIAMINE
PYRITHIAMINES
PYRITIFEROUS
PYRITISING
PYRITIZING
PYRITOHEDRA
PYRITOHEDRAL
PYRITOHEDRON
PYRITOHEDRONS
PYROBALLOGIES
PYROBALLOGY
PYROCATECHIN
PYROCATECHINS
PYROCATECHOL
PYROCATECHOLS
PYROCERAMS
PYROCHEMICAL
PYROCHEMICALLY
PYROCLASTIC
PYROCLASTICS
PYROCLASTS
PYROELECTRIC
PYROELECTRICITY
PYROELECTRICS
PYROGALLATE
PYROGALLATES
PYROGALLIC
PYROGALLOL
PYROGALLOLS
PYROGENETIC
PYROGENICITIES
PYROGENICITY
PYROGENOUS
PYROGNOSTIC
PYROGNOSTICS
PYROGRAPHER
PYROGRAPHERS
PYROGRAPHIC
PYROGRAPHIES
PYROGRAPHY
PYROGRAVURE
PYROGRAVURES
PYROKINESES
PYROKINESIS
PYROLATERS
PYROLATRIES
PYROLIGNEOUS
PYROLIGNIC

P

PYROLISING
PYROLIZING
PYROLOGIES
PYROLUSITE
PYROLUSITES
PYROLYSABLE
PYROLYSATE
PYROLYSATES
PYROLYSERS
PYROLYSING
PYROLYTICALLY
PYROLYZABLE
PYROLYZATE
PYROLYZATES
PYROLYZERS
PYROLYZING
PYROMAGNETIC
PYROMANCER
PYROMANCERS
PYROMANCIES
PYROMANIAC
PYROMANIACAL
PYROMANIACS
PYROMANIAS
PYROMANTIC
PYROMERIDE
PYROMERIDES
PYROMETALLURGY
PYROMETERS
PYROMETRIC
PYROMETRICAL
PYROMETRICALLY
PYROMETRIES
PYROMORPHITE
PYROMORPHITES
PYRONINOPHILIC
PYROPHOBIA
PYROPHOBIAS
PYROPHOBIC
PYROPHOBICS
PYROPHONES
PYROPHORIC
PYROPHOROUS
PYROPHORUS
PYROPHORUSES
PYROPHOSPHATE
PYROPHOSPHATES
PYROPHOSPHORIC
PYROPHOTOGRAPH
PYROPHOTOGRAPHS
PYROPHOTOGRAPHY
PYROPHOTOMETER
PYROPHOTOMETERS
PYROPHOTOMETRY
PYROPHYLLITE
PYROPHYLLITES
PYROSCOPES
PYROSTATIC
PYROSULFITE
PYROSULFITES
PYROSULPHATE
PYROSULPHATES
PYROSULPHURIC
PYROTARTARIC
PYROTARTRATE
PYROTARTRATES
PYROTECHNIC
PYROTECHNICAL
PYROTECHNICALLY
PYROTECHNICIAN
PYROTECHNICIANS
PYROTECHNICS
PYROTECHNIES
PYROTECHNIST
PYROTECHNISTS
PYROTECHNY
PYROVANADIC
PYROXENITE
PYROXENITES
PYROXENITIC
PYROXENOID
PYROXENOIDS
PYROXYLINE
PYROXYLINES
PYROXYLINS
PYRRHICIST
PYRRHICISTS
PYRRHOTINE
PYRRHOTINES
PYRRHOTITE
PYRRHOTITES
PYRRHULOXIA
PYRRHULOXIAS
PYRROLIDINE
PYRROLIDINES
PYTHOGENIC
PYTHONESSES
PYTHONOMORPH
PYTHONOMORPHS

Q

QABALISTIC
QINGHAOSUS
QUACKERIES
QUACKSALVER
QUACKSALVERS
QUACKSALVING
QUADCOPTER
QUADCOPTERS
QUADPLEXES
QUADRAGENARIAN
QUADRAGENARIANS
QUADRAGESIMAL
QUADRANGLE
QUADRANGLES
QUADRANGULAR
QUADRANGULARLY
QUADRANTAL
QUADRANTES
QUADRAPHONIC
QUADRAPHONICS
QUADRAPHONIES
QUADRAPHONY
QUADRAPLEGIA
QUADRAPLEGIAS
QUADRAPLEGIC
QUADRAPLEGICS
QUADRASONIC
QUADRASONICS
QUADRATICAL
QUADRATICALLY
QUADRATICS
QUADRATING
QUADRATRICES
QUADRATRIX
QUADRATRIXES
QUADRATURA
QUADRATURE
QUADRATURES
QUADRATUSES
QUADRELLAS
QUADRENNIA
QUADRENNIAL
QUADRENNIALLY
QUADRENNIALS
QUADRENNIUM
QUADRENNIUMS
QUADRICEPS
QUADRICEPSES
QUADRICIPITAL
QUADRICONE
QUADRICONES
QUADRIENNIA
QUADRIENNIAL
QUADRIENNIUM
QUADRIENNIUMS
QUADRIFARIOUS
QUADRIFOLIATE
QUADRIFORM
QUADRIGEMINAL
QUADRIGEMINATE
QUADRIGEMINOUS
QUADRILATERAL
QUADRILATERALS
QUADRILINGUAL
QUADRILITERAL
QUADRILITERALS
QUADRILLED
QUADRILLER
QUADRILLERS
QUADRILLES
QUADRILLING
QUADRILLION
QUADRILLIONS
QUADRILLIONTH
QUADRILLIONTHS
QUADRILOCULAR
QUADRINGENARIES
QUADRINGENARY
QUADRINOMIAL
QUADRINOMIALS
QUADRIPARTITE
QUADRIPARTITION
QUADRIPHONIC
QUADRIPHONICS
QUADRIPLEGIA
QUADRIPLEGIAS
QUADRIPLEGIC
QUADRIPLEGICS
QUADRIPOLE
QUADRIPOLES
QUADRIREME
QUADRIREMES
QUADRISECT
QUADRISECTED
QUADRISECTING
QUADRISECTION
QUADRISECTIONS
QUADRISECTS
QUADRISYLLABIC
QUADRISYLLABICS
QUADRISYLLABLE
QUADRISYLLABLES
QUADRIVALENCE
QUADRIVALENCES
QUADRIVALENCIES
QUADRIVALENCY
QUADRIVALENT
QUADRIVALENTS
QUADRIVIAL
QUADRIVIUM
QUADRIVIUMS
QUADROPHONIC
QUADROPHONICS
QUADROPHONIES
QUADROPHONY
QUADRUMANE
QUADRUMANES
QUADRUMANOUS
QUADRUMANS
QUADRUMVIR
QUADRUMVIRATE
QUADRUMVIRATES
QUADRUMVIRS
QUADRUPEDAL
QUADRUPEDS
QUADRUPLED
QUADRUPLES
QUADRUPLET
QUADRUPLETS
QUADRUPLEX
QUADRUPLEXED
QUADRUPLEXES
QUADRUPLEXING
QUADRUPLICATE
QUADRUPLICATED
QUADRUPLICATES
QUADRUPLICATING
QUADRUPLICATION
QUADRUPLICITIES
QUADRUPLICITY
QUADRUPLIES
QUADRUPLING
QUADRUPOLE
QUADRUPOLES
QUAESITUMS
QUAESTIONARIES
QUAESTIONARY
QUAESTORIAL
QUAESTORSHIP
QUAESTORSHIPS
QUAESTUARIES
QUAESTUARY
QUAGGINESS
QUAGGINESSES
QUAGMIRIER
QUAGMIRIEST
QUAGMIRING
QUAINTNESS
QUAINTNESSES
QUAKINESSES
QUALIFIABLE
QUALIFICATION
QUALIFICATIONS
QUALIFICATIVE
QUALIFICATIVES
QUALIFICATOR
QUALIFICATORS
QUALIFICATORY
QUALIFIEDLY
QUALIFIERS
QUALIFYING
QUALIFYINGS
QUALITATIVE
QUALITATIVELY
QUALMISHLY
QUALMISHNESS
QUALMISHNESSES
QUANDARIES
QUANGOCRACIES
QUANGOCRACY
QUANTIFIABLE
QUANTIFICATION
QUANTIFICATIONS
QUANTIFIED
QUANTIFIER
QUANTIFIERS
QUANTIFIES
QUANTIFYING
QUANTISATION
QUANTISATIONS
QUANTISERS
QUANTISING
QUANTITATE
QUANTITATED
QUANTITATES
QUANTITATING
QUANTITATION
QUANTITATIONS
QUANTITATIVE
QUANTITATIVELY
QUANTITIES
QUANTITIVE
QUANTITIVELY
QUANTIVALENCE
QUANTIVALENCES
QUANTIVALENT
QUANTIZATION
QUANTIZATIONS
QUANTIZERS
QUANTIZING

QUANTOMETER
QUANTOMETERS
QUAQUAVERSAL
QUAQUAVERSALLY
QUARANTINE
QUARANTINED
QUARANTINES
QUARANTINING
QUARENDENS
QUARENDERS
QUARRELERS
QUARRELING
QUARRELINGS
QUARRELLED
QUARRELLER
QUARRELLERS
QUARRELLING
QUARRELLINGS
QUARRELLOUS
QUARRELSOME
QUARRELSOMELY
QUARRELSOMENESS
QUARRENDER
QUARRENDERS
QUARRIABLE
QUARRINGTON
QUARRINGTONS
QUARRYINGS
QUARRYMASTER
QUARRYMASTERS
QUARTATION
QUARTATIONS
QUARTERAGE
QUARTERAGES
QUARTERBACK
QUARTERBACKED
QUARTERBACKING
QUARTERBACKINGS
QUARTERBACKS
QUARTERDECK
QUARTERDECKER
QUARTERDECKERS
QUARTERDECKS
QUARTERERS
QUARTERFINAL
QUARTERFINALIST
QUARTERFINALS
QUARTERING
QUARTERINGS
QUARTERLIES
QUARTERLIFE
QUARTERLIGHT
QUARTERLIGHTS
QUARTERMASTER
QUARTERMASTERS
QUARTERMISTRESS
QUARTERSAW
QUARTERSAWED
QUARTERSAWING
QUARTERSAWN
QUARTERSAWS
QUARTERSTAFF
QUARTERSTAFFS
QUARTERSTAVES
QUARTETTES
QUARTODECIMAN
QUARTODECIMANS
QUARTZIEST
QUARTZIFEROUS
QUARTZITES
QUARTZITIC
QUASICRYSTAL
QUASICRYSTALS
QUASIPARTICLE
QUASIPARTICLES
QUASIPERIODIC
QUATERCENTENARY
QUATERNARIES
QUATERNARY
QUATERNATE
QUATERNION
QUATERNIONIST
QUATERNIONISTS
QUATERNIONS
QUATERNITIES
QUATERNITY
QUATORZAIN
QUATORZAINS
QUATREFEUILLE
QUATREFEUILLES
QUATREFOIL
QUATREFOILS
QUATTROCENTISM
QUATTROCENTISMS
QUATTROCENTIST
QUATTROCENTISTS
QUATTROCENTO
QUATTROCENTOS
QUAVERIEST
QUAVERINGLY
QUAVERINGS
QUEACHIEST
QUEASINESS
QUEASINESSES
QUEBRACHOS
QUEECHIEST
QUEENCAKES
QUEENCRAFT
QUEENCRAFTS
QUEENFISHES
QUEENHOODS
QUEENLIEST
QUEENLINESS
QUEENLINESSES
QUEENSHIPS
QUEENSIDES
QUEERCORES
QUEERITIES
QUEERNESSES
QUELQUECHOSE
QUELQUECHOSES
QUENCHABLE
QUENCHINGS
QUENCHLESS
QUENCHLESSLY
QUERCETINS
QUERCETUMS
QUERCITINS
QUERCITRON
QUERCITRONS
QUERIMONIES
QUERIMONIOUS
QUERIMONIOUSLY
QUERNSTONE
QUERNSTONES
QUERSPRUNG
QUERSPRUNGS
QUERULOUSLY
QUERULOUSNESS
QUERULOUSNESSES
QUERYINGLY
QUESADILLA
QUESADILLAS
QUESTINGLY
QUESTIONABILITY
QUESTIONABLE
QUESTIONABLY
QUESTIONARIES
QUESTIONARY
QUESTIONED
QUESTIONEE
QUESTIONEES
QUESTIONER
QUESTIONERS
QUESTIONING
QUESTIONINGLY
QUESTIONINGS
QUESTIONIST
QUESTIONISTS
QUESTIONLESS
QUESTIONLESSLY
QUESTIONNAIRE
QUESTIONNAIRES
QUESTORIAL
QUESTORSHIP
QUESTORSHIPS
QUESTRISTS
QUIBBLINGLY
QUIBBLINGS
QUICKBEAMS
QUICKENERS
QUICKENING
QUICKENINGS
QUICKLIMES
QUICKNESSES
QUICKSANDS
QUICKSILVER
QUICKSILVERED
QUICKSILVERIER
QUICKSILVERIEST
QUICKSILVERING
QUICKSILVERINGS
QUICKSILVERISH
QUICKSILVERS
QUICKSILVERY
QUICKSTEPPED
QUICKSTEPPING
QUICKSTEPS
QUICKTHORN
QUICKTHORNS
QUIDDANIED
QUIDDANIES
QUIDDANYING
QUIDDITATIVE
QUIDDITCHES
QUIDDITIES
QUIESCENCE
QUIESCENCES
QUIESCENCIES
QUIESCENCY
QUIESCENTLY
QUIETENERS
QUIETENING
QUIETENINGS
QUIETISTIC
QUIETNESSES
QUILLBACKS
QUILLWORKS
QUILLWORTS
QUINACRINE
QUINACRINES
QUINALBARBITONE
QUINAQUINA
QUINAQUINAS
QUINCENTENARIES
QUINCENTENARY
QUINCENTENNIAL
QUINCENTENNIALS
QUINCUNCIAL
QUINCUNCIALLY
QUINCUNXES
QUINCUNXIAL
QUINDECAGON
QUINDECAGONS
QUINDECAPLET
QUINDECAPLETS
QUINDECENNIAL
QUINDECENNIALS
QUINDECILLION
QUINDECILLIONS
QUINGENTENARIES
QUINGENTENARY
QUINIDINES
QUINOLINES
QUINOLONES
QUINQUAGENARIAN
QUINQUAGESIMAL
QUINQUECOSTATE
QUINQUEFARIOUS
QUINQUEFOLIATE

Q

QUINQUENNIA
QUINQUENNIAD
QUINQUENNIADS
QUINQUENNIAL
QUINQUENNIALLY
QUINQUENNIALS
QUINQUENNIUM
QUINQUENNIUMS
QUINQUEPARTITE
QUINQUEREME
QUINQUEREMES
QUINQUEVALENCE
QUINQUEVALENCES
QUINQUEVALENCY
QUINQUEVALENT
QUINQUINAS
QUINQUIVALENCE
QUINQUIVALENCES
QUINQUIVALENCY
QUINQUIVALENT
QUINTESSENCE
QUINTESSENCES
QUINTESSENTIAL
QUINTESSENTIALS
QUINTETTES
QUINTILLION
QUINTILLIONS
QUINTILLIONTH
QUINTILLIONTHS
QUINTUPLED
QUINTUPLES
QUINTUPLET
QUINTUPLETS
QUINTUPLICATE
QUINTUPLICATED
QUINTUPLICATES
QUINTUPLICATING
QUINTUPLICATION
QUINTUPLIES
QUINTUPLING
QUIRISTERS
QUIRKINESS
QUIRKINESSES
QUISLINGISM
QUISLINGISMS
QUITCLAIMED
QUITCLAIMING
QUITCLAIMS
QUITTANCED
QUITTANCES
QUITTANCING
QUIVERFULS
QUIVERIEST
QUIVERINGLY
QUIVERINGS
QUIVERSFUL
QUIXOTICAL
QUIXOTICALLY
QUIXOTISMS
QUIXOTRIES
QUIZMASTER
QUIZMASTERS
QUIZZERIES
QUIZZICALITIES
QUIZZICALITY
QUIZZICALLY
QUIZZIFICATION
QUIZZIFICATIONS
QUIZZIFIED
QUIZZIFIES
QUIZZIFYING
QUIZZINESS
QUIZZINESSES
QUODLIBETARIAN
QUODLIBETARIANS
QUODLIBETIC
QUODLIBETICAL
QUODLIBETICALLY
QUODLIBETS
QUOTABILITIES
QUOTABILITY
QUOTABLENESS
QUOTABLENESSES
QUOTATIONS
QUOTATIOUS
QUOTATIVES
QUOTEWORTHIER
QUOTEWORTHIEST
QUOTEWORTHY
QUOTIDIANS
QUOTITIONS

Q

R

RABATMENTS
RABATTEMENT
RABATTEMENTS
RABATTINGS
RABBINATES
RABBINICAL
RABBINICALLY
RABBINISMS
RABBINISTIC
RABBINISTS
RABBINITES
RABBITBRUSH
RABBITBRUSHES
RABBITFISH
RABBITFISHES
RABBITIEST
RABBITINGS
RABBITRIES
RABBLEMENT
RABBLEMENTS
RABIDITIES
RABIDNESSES
RACCAHOUTS
RACECOURSE
RACECOURSES
RACEGOINGS
RACEHORSES
RACEMATION
RACEMATIONS
RACEMISATION
RACEMISATIONS
RACEMISING
RACEMIZATION
RACEMIZATIONS
RACEMIZING
RACEMOSELY
RACEMOUSLY
RACETRACKER
RACETRACKERS
RACETRACKS
RACEWALKED
RACEWALKER
RACEWALKERS
RACEWALKING
RACEWALKINGS
RACHIOTOMIES
RACHIOTOMY
RACHISCHISES
RACHISCHISIS
RACHITIDES
RACHITISES
RACIALISED
RACIALISES
RACIALISING
RACIALISMS
RACIALISTIC
RACIALISTS
RACIALIZED
RACIALIZES
RACIALIZING
RACIATIONS
RACINESSES
RACKABONES
RACKETEERED
RACKETEERING
RACKETEERINGS
RACKETEERS
RACKETIEST
RACKETRIES
RACONTEURING
RACONTEURINGS
RACONTEURS
RACONTEUSE
RACONTEUSES
RACQUETBALL
RACQUETBALLS
RACQUETING
RACTOPAMINE
RACTOPAMINES
RADARSCOPE
RADARSCOPES
RADIALISATION
RADIALISATIONS
RADIALISED
RADIALISES
RADIALISING
RADIALITIES
RADIALIZATION
RADIALIZATIONS
RADIALIZED
RADIALIZES
RADIALIZING
RADIANCIES
RADIATIONAL
RADIATIONLESS
RADIATIONS
RADICALISATION
RADICALISATIONS
RADICALISE
RADICALISED
RADICALISES
RADICALISING
RADICALISM
RADICALISMS
RADICALISTIC
RADICALITIES
RADICALITY
RADICALIZATION
RADICALIZATIONS
RADICALIZE
RADICALIZED
RADICALIZES
RADICALIZING
RADICALNESS
RADICALNESSES
RADICATING
RADICATION
RADICATIONS
RADICCHIOS
RADICELLOSE
RADICICOLOUS
RADICIFORM
RADICIVOROUS
RADICULOSE
RADIESTHESIA
RADIESTHESIAS
RADIESTHESIST
RADIESTHESISTS
RADIESTHETIC
RADIOACTIVATE
RADIOACTIVATED
RADIOACTIVATES
RADIOACTIVATING
RADIOACTIVATION
RADIOACTIVE
RADIOACTIVELY
RADIOACTIVITIES
RADIOACTIVITY
RADIOAUTOGRAPH
RADIOAUTOGRAPHS
RADIOAUTOGRAPHY
RADIOBIOLOGIC
RADIOBIOLOGICAL
RADIOBIOLOGIES
RADIOBIOLOGIST
RADIOBIOLOGISTS
RADIOBIOLOGY
RADIOCARBON
RADIOCARBONS
RADIOCHEMICAL
RADIOCHEMICALLY
RADIOCHEMIST
RADIOCHEMISTRY
RADIOCHEMISTS
RADIOECOLOGIES
RADIOECOLOGY
RADIOELEMENT
RADIOELEMENTS
RADIOGENIC
RADIOGOLDS
RADIOGONIOMETER
RADIOGONIOMETRY
RADIOGRAMS
RADIOGRAPH
RADIOGRAPHED
RADIOGRAPHER
RADIOGRAPHERS
RADIOGRAPHIC
RADIOGRAPHIES
RADIOGRAPHING
RADIOGRAPHS
RADIOGRAPHY
RADIOIODINE
RADIOIODINES
RADIOISOTOPE
RADIOISOTOPES
RADIOISOTOPIC
RADIOLABEL
RADIOLABELED
RADIOLABELING
RADIOLABELLED
RADIOLABELLING
RADIOLABELS
RADIOLARIAN
RADIOLARIANS
RADIOLOCATION
RADIOLOCATIONAL
RADIOLOCATIONS
RADIOLOGIC
RADIOLOGICAL
RADIOLOGICALLY
RADIOLOGIES
RADIOLOGIST
RADIOLOGISTS
RADIOLUCENCIES
RADIOLUCENCY
RADIOLUCENT
RADIOLYSES
RADIOLYSIS
RADIOLYTIC
RADIOMETER
RADIOMETERS
RADIOMETRIC
RADIOMETRICALLY
RADIOMETRIES
RADIOMETRY
RADIOMICROMETER
RADIOMIMETIC
RADIONUCLIDE
RADIONUCLIDES

RADIOPACITIES
RADIOPACITY
RADIOPAGER
RADIOPAGERS
RADIOPAGING
RADIOPAGINGS
RADIOPAQUE
RADIOPHONE
RADIOPHONES
RADIOPHONIC
RADIOPHONICALLY
RADIOPHONICS
RADIOPHONIES
RADIOPHONIST
RADIOPHONISTS
RADIOPHONY
RADIOPHOSPHORUS
RADIOPHOTO
RADIOPHOTOS
RADIOPROTECTION
RADIOPROTECTIVE
RADIORESISTANT
RADIOSCOPE
RADIOSCOPES
RADIOSCOPIC
RADIOSCOPICALLY
RADIOSCOPIES
RADIOSCOPY
RADIOSENSITISE
RADIOSENSITISED
RADIOSENSITISES
RADIOSENSITIVE
RADIOSENSITIZE
RADIOSENSITIZED
RADIOSENSITIZES
RADIOSONDE
RADIOSONDES
RADIOSTRONTIUM
RADIOSTRONTIUMS
RADIOTELEGRAM
RADIOTELEGRAMS
RADIOTELEGRAPH
RADIOTELEGRAPHS
RADIOTELEGRAPHY
RADIOTELEMETER
RADIOTELEMETERS
RADIOTELEMETRIC
RADIOTELEMETRY
RADIOTELEPHONE
RADIOTELEPHONED
RADIOTELEPHONES
RADIOTELEPHONIC
RADIOTELEPHONY
RADIOTELETYPE
RADIOTELETYPES
RADIOTHERAPIES
RADIOTHERAPIST
RADIOTHERAPISTS
RADIOTHERAPY
RADIOTHERMIES
RADIOTHERMY
RADIOTHONS
RADIOTHORIUM
RADIOTHORIUMS
RADIOTOXIC
RADIOTRACER
RADIOTRACERS
RADULIFORM
RAFFINATES
RAFFINOSES
RAFFISHNESS
RAFFISHNESSES
RAFFLESIAS
RAFTERINGS
RAGAMUFFIN
RAGAMUFFINS
RAGGAMUFFIN
RAGGAMUFFINS
RAGGEDIEST
RAGGEDNESS
RAGGEDNESSES
RAGMATICAL
RAGPICKERS
RAILBUSSES
RAILLERIES
RAILROADED
RAILROADER
RAILROADERS
RAILROADING
RAILROADINGS
RAILWAYMAN
RAILWAYMEN
RAILWORKER
RAILWORKERS
RAINBOWIER
RAINBOWIEST
RAINBOWLIKE
RAINCHECKS
RAINFOREST
RAINFORESTS
RAININESSES
RAINMAKERS
RAINMAKING
RAINMAKINGS
RAINPROOFED
RAINPROOFING
RAINPROOFS
RAINSPOUTS
RAINSQUALL
RAINSQUALLS
RAINSTICKS
RAINSTORMS
RAINWASHED
RAINWASHES
RAINWASHING
RAINWATERS
RAISINIEST
RAISONNEUR
RAISONNEURS
RAIYATWARI
RAIYATWARIS
RAJAHSHIPS
RAJPRAMUKH
RAJPRAMUKHS
RAKEHELLIER
RAKEHELLIEST
RAKESHAMES
RAKISHNESS
RAKISHNESSES
RALLENTANDI
RALLENTANDO
RALLENTANDOS
RALLYCROSS
RALLYCROSSES
RALLYINGLY
RAMAPITHECINE
RAMAPITHECINES
RAMBLINGLY
RAMBOUILLET
RAMBOUILLETS
RAMBUNCTIOUS
RAMBUNCTIOUSLY
RAMENTACEOUS
RAMGUNSHOCH
RAMIFICATION
RAMIFICATIONS
RAMMISHNESS
RAMMISHNESSES
RAMOSITIES
RAMPACIOUS
RAMPAGEOUS
RAMPAGEOUSLY
RAMPAGEOUSNESS
RAMPAGINGS
RAMPALLIAN
RAMPALLIANS
RAMPANCIES
RAMPARTING
RAMPAUGING
RAMRODDING
RAMSHACKLE
RANCELLING
RANCHERIAS
RANCHERIES
RANCHETTES
RANCHLANDS
RANCIDITIES
RANCIDNESS
RANCIDNESSES
RANCOROUSLY
RANCOROUSNESS
RANCOROUSNESSES
RANDINESSES
RANDOMISATION
RANDOMISATIONS
RANDOMISED
RANDOMISER
RANDOMISERS
RANDOMISES
RANDOMISING
RANDOMIZATION
RANDOMIZATIONS
RANDOMIZED
RANDOMIZER
RANDOMIZERS
RANDOMIZES
RANDOMIZING
RANDOMNESS
RANDOMNESSES
RANDOMWISE
RANGATIRAS
RANGATIRATANGA
RANGATIRATANGAS
RANGEFINDER
RANGEFINDERS
RANGEFINDING
RANGEFINDINGS
RANGELANDS
RANGERSHIP
RANGERSHIPS
RANGINESSES
RANIVOROUS
RANKNESSES
RANKSHIFTED
RANKSHIFTING
RANKSHIFTS
RANSACKERS
RANSACKING
RANSACKINGS
RANSHACKLE
RANSHACKLED
RANSHACKLES
RANSHACKLING
RANSHAKLED
RANSHAKLES
RANSHAKLING
RANSOMABLE
RANSOMLESS
RANSOMWARE
RANSOMWARES
RANTERISMS
RANTIPOLED
RANTIPOLES
RANTIPOLING
RANUNCULACEOUS
RANUNCULUS
RANUNCULUSES
RAPACIOUSLY
RAPACIOUSNESS
RAPACIOUSNESSES
RAPACITIES
RAPIDITIES
RAPIDNESSES
RAPIERLIKE
RAPPELLING
RAPPELLINGS
RAPPORTAGE
RAPPORTAGES
RAPPORTEUR
RAPPORTEURS

R

RAPPROCHEMENT
RAPPROCHEMENTS
RAPSCALLION
RAPSCALLIONS
RAPTATORIAL
RAPTNESSES
RAPTURELESS
RAPTURISED
RAPTURISES
RAPTURISING
RAPTURISTS
RAPTURIZED
RAPTURIZES
RAPTURIZING
RAPTUROUSLY
RAPTUROUSNESS
RAPTUROUSNESSES
RAREFACTION
RAREFACTIONAL
RAREFACTIONS
RAREFACTIVE
RAREFIABLE
RAREFICATION
RAREFICATIONAL
RAREFICATIONS
RARENESSES
RASCAILLES
RASCALDOMS
RASCALISMS
RASCALITIES
RASCALLIER
RASCALLIEST
RASCALLION
RASCALLIONS
RASHNESSES
RASPATORIES
RASPBERRIES
RASPINESSES
RASTAFARIAN
RASTAFARIANS
RASTAFARIS
RASTERISED
RASTERISES
RASTERISING
RASTERIZED
RASTERIZES
RASTERIZING
RATABILITIES
RATABILITY
RATABLENESS
RATABLENESSES
RATAPLANNED
RATAPLANNING
RATATOUILLE
RATATOUILLES
RATBAGGERIES
RATBAGGERY
RATCHETING
RATEABILITIES
RATEABILITY
RATEABLENESS
RATEABLENESSES
RATEMETERS
RATEPAYERS
RATHERIPES
RATHSKELLER
RATHSKELLERS
RATIFIABLE
RATIFICATION
RATIFICATIONS
RATIOCINATE
RATIOCINATED
RATIOCINATES
RATIOCINATING
RATIOCINATION
RATIOCINATIONS
RATIOCINATIVE
RATIOCINATOR
RATIOCINATORS
RATIOCINATORY
RATIONALES
RATIONALISABLE
RATIONALISATION
RATIONALISE
RATIONALISED
RATIONALISER
RATIONALISERS
RATIONALISES
RATIONALISING
RATIONALISM
RATIONALISMS
RATIONALIST
RATIONALISTIC
RATIONALISTS
RATIONALITIES
RATIONALITY
RATIONALIZABLE
RATIONALIZATION
RATIONALIZE
RATIONALIZED
RATIONALIZER
RATIONALIZERS
RATIONALIZES
RATIONALIZING
RATIONALLY
RATIONALNESS
RATIONALNESSES
RATIONINGS
RATTENINGS
RATTINESSES
RATTLEBAGS
RATTLEBOXES
RATTLEBRAIN
RATTLEBRAINED
RATTLEBRAINS
RATTLEPODS
RATTLESNAKE
RATTLESNAKES
RATTLETRAP
RATTLETRAPS
RATTLINGLY
RATTOONING
RAUCOUSNESS
RAUCOUSNESSES
RAUNCHIEST
RAUNCHINESS
RAUNCHINESSES
RAUWOLFIAS
RAVAGEMENT
RAVAGEMENTS
RAVELLIEST
RAVELLINGS
RAVELMENTS
RAVENINGLY
RAVENOUSLY
RAVENOUSNESS
RAVENOUSNESSES
RAVIGOTTES
RAVISHINGLY
RAVISHMENT
RAVISHMENTS
RAWINSONDE
RAWINSONDES
RAWMAISHES
RAYGRASSES
RAYLESSNESS
RAYLESSNESSES
RAZMATAZES
RAZORBACKS
RAZORBILLS
RAZORCLAMS
RAZORFISHES
RAZZAMATAZZ
RAZZAMATAZZES
RAZZBERRIES
RAZZMATAZZ
RAZZMATAZZES
REABSORBED
REABSORBING
REABSORPTION
REABSORPTIONS
REACCEDING
REACCELERATE
REACCELERATED
REACCELERATES
REACCELERATING
REACCENTED
REACCENTING
REACCEPTED
REACCEPTING
REACCESSION
REACCESSIONS
REACCLAIMED
REACCLAIMING
REACCLAIMS
REACCLIMATISE
REACCLIMATISED
REACCLIMATISES
REACCLIMATISING
REACCLIMATIZE
REACCLIMATIZED
REACCLIMATIZES
REACCLIMATIZING
REACCREDIT
REACCREDITATION
REACCREDITED
REACCREDITING
REACCREDITS
REACCUSING
REACCUSTOM
REACCUSTOMED
REACCUSTOMING
REACCUSTOMS
REACQUAINT
REACQUAINTANCE
REACQUAINTANCES
REACQUAINTED
REACQUAINTING
REACQUAINTS
REACQUIRED
REACQUIRES
REACQUIRING
REACQUISITION
REACQUISITIONS
REACTANCES
REACTIONAL
REACTIONARIES
REACTIONARISM
REACTIONARISMS
REACTIONARIST
REACTIONARISTS
REACTIONARY
REACTIONARYISM
REACTIONARYISMS
REACTIONISM
REACTIONISMS
REACTIONIST
REACTIONISTS
REACTIVATE
REACTIVATED
REACTIVATES
REACTIVATING
REACTIVATION
REACTIVATIONS
REACTIVELY
REACTIVENESS
REACTIVENESSES
REACTIVITIES
REACTIVITY
REACTUATED
REACTUATES
REACTUATING
READABILITIES
READABILITY
READABLENESS
READABLENESSES
READAPTATION
READAPTATIONS
READAPTING
READDICTED

READDICTING
READDRESSED
READDRESSES
READDRESSING
READERLIER
READERLIEST
READERSHIP
READERSHIPS
READINESSES
READJUSTABLE
READJUSTED
READJUSTER
READJUSTERS
READJUSTING
READJUSTMENT
READJUSTMENTS
READMISSION
READMISSIONS
READMITTANCE
READMITTANCES
READMITTED
READMITTING
READOPTING
READOPTION
READOPTIONS
READORNING
READVANCED
READVANCES
READVANCING
READVERTISE
READVERTISED
READVERTISEMENT
READVERTISES
READVERTISING
READVERTIZE
READVERTIZED
READVERTIZEMENT
READVERTIZES
READVERTIZING
READVISING
READYMADES
REAEDIFIED
REAEDIFIES
REAEDIFYED
REAEDIFYES
REAEDIFYING
REAFFIRMATION
REAFFIRMATIONS
REAFFIRMED
REAFFIRMING
REAFFIXING
REAFFOREST
REAFFORESTATION
REAFFORESTED
REAFFORESTING
REAFFORESTS
REAGENCIES
REAGGREGATE
REAGGREGATED
REAGGREGATES
REAGGREGATING
REAGGREGATION
REAGGREGATIONS
REALIGNING
REALIGNMENT
REALIGNMENTS
REALISABILITIES
REALISABILITY
REALISABLE
REALISABLY
REALISATION
REALISATIONS
REALISTICALLY
REALIZABILITIES
REALIZABILITY
REALIZABLE
REALIZABLY
REALIZATION
REALIZATIONS
REALLOCATE
REALLOCATED
REALLOCATES
REALLOCATING
REALLOCATION
REALLOCATIONS
REALLOTMENT
REALLOTMENTS
REALLOTTED
REALLOTTING
REALNESSES
REALPOLITIK
REALPOLITIKER
REALPOLITIKERS
REALPOLITIKS
REALTERING
REAMENDING
REAMENDMENT
REAMENDMENTS
REANALYSED
REANALYSES
REANALYSING
REANALYSIS
REANALYZED
REANALYZES
REANALYZING
REANIMATED
REANIMATES
REANIMATING
REANIMATION
REANIMATIONS
REANNEXATION
REANNEXATIONS
REANNEXING
REANOINTED
REANOINTING
REANSWERED
REANSWERING
REAPPARELED
REAPPARELING
REAPPARELLED
REAPPARELLING
REAPPARELS
REAPPEARANCE
REAPPEARANCES
REAPPEARED
REAPPEARING
REAPPLICATION
REAPPLICATIONS
REAPPLYING
REAPPOINTED
REAPPOINTING
REAPPOINTMENT
REAPPOINTMENTS
REAPPOINTS
REAPPORTION
REAPPORTIONED
REAPPORTIONING
REAPPORTIONMENT
REAPPORTIONS
REAPPRAISAL
REAPPRAISALS
REAPPRAISE
REAPPRAISED
REAPPRAISEMENT
REAPPRAISEMENTS
REAPPRAISER
REAPPRAISERS
REAPPRAISES
REAPPRAISING
REAPPROPRIATE
REAPPROPRIATED
REAPPROPRIATES
REAPPROPRIATING
REAPPROVED
REAPPROVES
REAPPROVING
REARGUARDS
REARGUMENT
REARGUMENTS
REARHORSES
REARMAMENT
REARMAMENTS
REAROUSALS
REAROUSING
REARRANGED
REARRANGEMENT
REARRANGEMENTS
REARRANGER
REARRANGERS
REARRANGES
REARRANGING
REARRESTED
REARRESTING
REARTICULATE
REARTICULATED
REARTICULATES
REARTICULATING
REASCENDED
REASCENDING
REASCENSION
REASCENSIONS
REASONABILITIES
REASONABILITY
REASONABLE
REASONABLENESS
REASONABLY
REASONEDLY
REASONINGS
REASONLESS
REASONLESSLY
REASSAILED
REASSAILING
REASSEMBLAGE
REASSEMBLAGES
REASSEMBLE
REASSEMBLED
REASSEMBLES
REASSEMBLIES
REASSEMBLING
REASSEMBLY
REASSERTED
REASSERTING
REASSERTION
REASSERTIONS
REASSESSED
REASSESSES
REASSESSING
REASSESSMENT
REASSESSMENTS
REASSIGNED
REASSIGNING
REASSIGNMENT
REASSIGNMENTS
REASSORTED
REASSORTING
REASSORTMENT
REASSORTMENTS
REASSUMING
REASSUMPTION
REASSUMPTIONS
REASSURANCE
REASSURANCES
REASSURERS
REASSURING
REASSURINGLY
REASTINESS
REASTINESSES
REATTACHED
REATTACHES
REATTACHING
REATTACHMENT
REATTACHMENTS
REATTACKED
REATTACKING
REATTAINED
REATTAINING
REATTEMPTED
REATTEMPTING
REATTEMPTS
REATTRIBUTE

R

REATTRIBUTED
REATTRIBUTES
REATTRIBUTING
REATTRIBUTION
REATTRIBUTIONS
REAUTHORISATION
REAUTHORISE
REAUTHORISED
REAUTHORISES
REAUTHORISING
REAUTHORIZATION
REAUTHORIZE
REAUTHORIZED
REAUTHORIZES
REAUTHORIZING
REAVAILING
REAWAKENED
REAWAKENING
REAWAKENINGS
REBALANCED
REBALANCES
REBALANCING
REBAPTISED
REBAPTISES
REBAPTISING
REBAPTISMS
REBAPTIZED
REBAPTIZES
REBAPTIZING
REBARBATIVE
REBARBATIVELY
REBATEABLE
REBATEMENT
REBATEMENTS
REBBETZINS
REBEGINNING
REBELLIONS
REBELLIOUS
REBELLIOUSLY
REBELLIOUSNESS
REBELLOWED
REBELLOWING
REBIRTHERS
REBIRTHING
REBIRTHINGS
REBLENDING
REBLOCHONS
REBLOOMERS
REBLOOMING
REBLOSSOMED
REBLOSSOMING
REBLOSSOMS
REBOARDING
REBOATIONS
REBORROWED
REBORROWING
REBOTTLING
REBOUNDERS
REBOUNDING
REBOUNDINGS
REBRANCHED
REBRANCHES
REBRANCHING
REBRANDING
REBRANDINGS
REBREEDING
REBROADCAST
REBROADCASTED
REBROADCASTING
REBROADCASTS
REBUILDING
REBUILDINGS
REBUKEFULLY
REBUKINGLY
REBUTMENTS
REBUTTABLE
REBUTTONED
REBUTTONING
RECALCITRANCE
RECALCITRANCES
RECALCITRANCIES
RECALCITRANCY
RECALCITRANT
RECALCITRANTS
RECALCITRATE
RECALCITRATED
RECALCITRATES
RECALCITRATING
RECALCITRATION
RECALCITRATIONS
RECALCULATE
RECALCULATED
RECALCULATES
RECALCULATING
RECALCULATION
RECALCULATIONS
RECALESCED
RECALESCENCE
RECALESCENCES
RECALESCENT
RECALESCES
RECALESCING
RECALIBRATE
RECALIBRATED
RECALIBRATES
RECALIBRATING
RECALIBRATION
RECALIBRATIONS
RECALLABILITIES
RECALLABILITY
RECALLABLE
RECALLMENT
RECALLMENTS
RECALMENTS
RECANALISATION
RECANALISATIONS
RECANALISE
RECANALISED
RECANALISES
RECANALISING
RECANALIZATION
RECANALIZATIONS
RECANALIZE
RECANALIZED
RECANALIZES
RECANALIZING
RECANTATION
RECANTATIONS
RECAPITALISE
RECAPITALISED
RECAPITALISES
RECAPITALISING
RECAPITALIZE
RECAPITALIZED
RECAPITALIZES
RECAPITALIZING
RECAPITULATE
RECAPITULATED
RECAPITULATES
RECAPITULATING
RECAPITULATION
RECAPITULATIONS
RECAPITULATIVE
RECAPITULATORY
RECAPPABLE
RECAPTIONS
RECAPTURED
RECAPTURER
RECAPTURERS
RECAPTURES
RECAPTURING
RECARPETED
RECARPETING
RECARRYING
RECATALOGED
RECATALOGING
RECATALOGS
RECATALOGUE
RECATALOGUED
RECATALOGUES
RECATALOGUING
RECATCHING
RECAUTIONED
RECAUTIONING
RECAUTIONS
RECEIPTING
RECEIPTORS
RECEIVABILITIES
RECEIVABILITY
RECEIVABLE
RECEIVABLENESS
RECEIVABLES
RECEIVERSHIP
RECEIVERSHIPS
RECEIVINGS
RECEMENTED
RECEMENTING
RECENSIONS
RECENSORED
RECENSORING
RECENTNESS
RECENTNESSES
RECENTRIFUGE
RECENTRIFUGED
RECENTRIFUGES
RECENTRIFUGING
RECENTRING
RECEPTACLE
RECEPTACLES
RECEPTACULA
RECEPTACULAR
RECEPTACULUM
RECEPTIBILITIES
RECEPTIBILITY
RECEPTIBLE
RECEPTIONIST
RECEPTIONISTS
RECEPTIONS
RECEPTIVELY
RECEPTIVENESS
RECEPTIVENESSES
RECEPTIVITIES
RECEPTIVITY
RECERTIFICATION
RECERTIFIED
RECERTIFIES
RECERTIFYING
RECESSIONAL
RECESSIONALS
RECESSIONARY
RECESSIONISTA
RECESSIONISTAS
RECESSIONS
RECESSIVELY
RECESSIVENESS
RECESSIVENESSES
RECESSIVES
RECHALLENGE
RECHALLENGED
RECHALLENGES
RECHALLENGING
RECHANGING
RECHANNELED
RECHANNELING
RECHANNELLED
RECHANNELLING
RECHANNELS
RECHARGEABLE
RECHARGERS
RECHARGING
RECHARTERED
RECHARTERING
RECHARTERS
RECHARTING
RECHAUFFES
RECHEATING
RECHECKING
RECHIPPING
RECHIPPINGS
RECHOOSING

R

RECHOREOGRAPH
RECHOREOGRAPHED
RECHOREOGRAPHS
RECHRISTEN
RECHRISTENED
RECHRISTENING
RECHRISTENS
RECHROMATOGRAPH
RECIDIVISM
RECIDIVISMS
RECIDIVIST
RECIDIVISTIC
RECIDIVISTS
RECIDIVOUS
RECIPIENCE
RECIPIENCES
RECIPIENCIES
RECIPIENCY
RECIPIENTS
RECIPROCAL
RECIPROCALITIES
RECIPROCALITY
RECIPROCALLY
RECIPROCALS
RECIPROCANT
RECIPROCANTS
RECIPROCATE
RECIPROCATED
RECIPROCATES
RECIPROCATING
RECIPROCATION
RECIPROCATIONS
RECIPROCATIVE
RECIPROCATOR
RECIPROCATORS
RECIPROCATORY
RECIPROCITIES
RECIPROCITY
RECIRCLING
RECIRCULATE
RECIRCULATED
RECIRCULATES
RECIRCULATING
RECIRCULATION
RECIRCULATIONS
RECITALIST
RECITALISTS
RECITATION
RECITATIONIST
RECITATIONISTS
RECITATIONS
RECITATIVE
RECITATIVES
RECITATIVI
RECITATIVO
RECITATIVOS
RECKLESSLY
RECKLESSNESS
RECKLESSNESSES
RECKONINGS
RECLADDING
RECLAIMABLE
RECLAIMABLY
RECLAIMANT
RECLAIMANTS
RECLAIMERS
RECLAIMING
RECLAMATION
RECLAMATIONS
RECLASPING
RECLASSIFIED
RECLASSIFIES
RECLASSIFY
RECLASSIFYING
RECLEANING
RECLIMBING
RECLINABLE
RECLINATION
RECLINATIONS
RECLOSABLE
RECLOTHING
RECLUSENESS
RECLUSENESSES
RECLUSIONS
RECLUSIVELY
RECLUSIVENESS
RECLUSIVENESSES
RECLUSORIES
RECODIFICATION
RECODIFICATIONS
RECODIFIED
RECODIFIES
RECODIFYING
RECOGNISABILITY
RECOGNISABLE
RECOGNISABLY
RECOGNISANCE
RECOGNISANCES
RECOGNISANT
RECOGNISED
RECOGNISEE
RECOGNISEES
RECOGNISER
RECOGNISERS
RECOGNISES
RECOGNISING
RECOGNISOR
RECOGNISORS
RECOGNITION
RECOGNITIONS
RECOGNITIVE
RECOGNITORY
RECOGNIZABILITY
RECOGNIZABLE
RECOGNIZABLY
RECOGNIZANCE
RECOGNIZANCES
RECOGNIZANT
RECOGNIZED
RECOGNIZEE
RECOGNIZEES
RECOGNIZER
RECOGNIZERS
RECOGNIZES
RECOGNIZING
RECOGNIZOR
RECOGNIZORS
RECOILLESS
RECOINAGES
RECOLLECTED
RECOLLECTEDLY
RECOLLECTEDNESS
RECOLLECTING
RECOLLECTION
RECOLLECTIONS
RECOLLECTIVE
RECOLLECTIVELY
RECOLLECTS
RECOLONISATION
RECOLONISATIONS
RECOLONISE
RECOLONISED
RECOLONISES
RECOLONISING
RECOLONIZATION
RECOLONIZATIONS
RECOLONIZE
RECOLONIZED
RECOLONIZES
RECOLONIZING
RECOLORING
RECOLOURED
RECOLOURING
RECOMBINANT
RECOMBINANTS
RECOMBINATION
RECOMBINATIONAL
RECOMBINATIONS
RECOMBINED
RECOMBINES
RECOMBINING
RECOMFORTED
RECOMFORTING
RECOMFORTLESS
RECOMFORTS
RECOMFORTURE
RECOMFORTURES
RECOMMENCE
RECOMMENCED
RECOMMENCEMENT
RECOMMENCEMENTS
RECOMMENCES
RECOMMENCING
RECOMMENDABLE
RECOMMENDABLY
RECOMMENDATION
RECOMMENDATIONS
RECOMMENDATORY
RECOMMENDED
RECOMMENDER
RECOMMENDERS
RECOMMENDING
RECOMMENDS
RECOMMISSION
RECOMMISSIONED
RECOMMISSIONING
RECOMMISSIONS
RECOMMITMENT
RECOMMITMENTS
RECOMMITTAL
RECOMMITTALS
RECOMMITTED
RECOMMITTING
RECOMPACTED
RECOMPACTING
RECOMPACTS
RECOMPENCE
RECOMPENCES
RECOMPENSABLE
RECOMPENSE
RECOMPENSED
RECOMPENSER
RECOMPENSERS
RECOMPENSES
RECOMPENSING
RECOMPILATION
RECOMPILATIONS
RECOMPILED
RECOMPILES
RECOMPILING
RECOMPOSED
RECOMPOSES
RECOMPOSING
RECOMPOSITION
RECOMPOSITIONS
RECOMPRESS
RECOMPRESSED
RECOMPRESSES
RECOMPRESSING
RECOMPRESSION
RECOMPRESSIONS
RECOMPUTATION
RECOMPUTATIONS
RECOMPUTED
RECOMPUTES
RECOMPUTING
RECONCEIVE
RECONCEIVED
RECONCEIVES
RECONCEIVING
RECONCENTRATE
RECONCENTRATED
RECONCENTRATES
RECONCENTRATING
RECONCENTRATION
RECONCEPTION
RECONCEPTIONS
RECONCEPTUALISE
RECONCEPTUALIZE
RECONCILABILITY

R

RECONCILABLE
RECONCILABLY
RECONCILED
RECONCILEMENT
RECONCILEMENTS
RECONCILER
RECONCILERS
RECONCILES
RECONCILIATION
RECONCILIATIONS
RECONCILIATORY
RECONCILING
RECONDENSATION
RECONDENSATIONS
RECONDENSE
RECONDENSED
RECONDENSES
RECONDENSING
RECONDITELY
RECONDITENESS
RECONDITENESSES
RECONDITION
RECONDITIONED
RECONDITIONING
RECONDITIONS
RECONDUCTED
RECONDUCTING
RECONDUCTS
RECONFERRED
RECONFERRING
RECONFIGURATION
RECONFIGURE
RECONFIGURED
RECONFIGURES
RECONFIGURING
RECONFINED
RECONFINES
RECONFINING
RECONFIRMATION
RECONFIRMATIONS
RECONFIRMED
RECONFIRMING
RECONFIRMS
RECONNAISSANCE
RECONNAISSANCES
RECONNECTED
RECONNECTING
RECONNECTION
RECONNECTIONS
RECONNECTS
RECONNOISSANCE
RECONNOISSANCES
RECONNOITER
RECONNOITERED
RECONNOITERER
RECONNOITERERS
RECONNOITERING
RECONNOITERS
RECONNOITRE
RECONNOITRED
RECONNOITRER
RECONNOITRERS
RECONNOITRES
RECONNOITRING
RECONNOITRINGS
RECONQUERED
RECONQUERING
RECONQUERS
RECONQUEST
RECONQUESTS
RECONSECRATE
RECONSECRATED
RECONSECRATES
RECONSECRATING
RECONSECRATION
RECONSECRATIONS
RECONSIDER
RECONSIDERATION
RECONSIDERED
RECONSIDERING
RECONSIDERS
RECONSIGNED
RECONSIGNING
RECONSIGNS
RECONSOLED
RECONSOLES
RECONSOLIDATE
RECONSOLIDATED
RECONSOLIDATES
RECONSOLIDATING
RECONSOLIDATION
RECONSOLING
RECONSTITUENT
RECONSTITUENTS
RECONSTITUTABLE
RECONSTITUTE
RECONSTITUTED
RECONSTITUTES
RECONSTITUTING
RECONSTITUTION
RECONSTITUTIONS
RECONSTRUCT
RECONSTRUCTED
RECONSTRUCTIBLE
RECONSTRUCTING
RECONSTRUCTION
RECONSTRUCTIONS
RECONSTRUCTIVE
RECONSTRUCTOR
RECONSTRUCTORS
RECONSTRUCTS
RECONSULTED
RECONSULTING
RECONSULTS
RECONTACTED
RECONTACTING
RECONTACTS
RECONTAMINATE
RECONTAMINATED
RECONTAMINATES
RECONTAMINATING
RECONTAMINATION
RECONTEXTUALISE
RECONTEXTUALIZE
RECONTINUE
RECONTINUED
RECONTINUES
RECONTINUING
RECONTOURED
RECONTOURING
RECONTOURS
RECONVALESCE
RECONVALESCED
RECONVALESCENCE
RECONVALESCENT
RECONVALESCES
RECONVALESCING
RECONVENED
RECONVENES
RECONVENING
RECONVERSION
RECONVERSIONS
RECONVERTED
RECONVERTING
RECONVERTS
RECONVEYANCE
RECONVEYANCES
RECONVEYED
RECONVEYING
RECONVICTED
RECONVICTING
RECONVICTION
RECONVICTIONS
RECONVICTS
RECONVINCE
RECONVINCED
RECONVINCES
RECONVINCING
RECORDABLE
RECORDATION
RECORDATIONS
RECORDERSHIP
RECORDERSHIPS
RECORDINGS
RECORDISTS
RECOUNTALS
RECOUNTERS
RECOUNTING
RECOUNTMENT
RECOUNTMENTS
RECOUPABLE
RECOUPLING
RECOUPMENT
RECOUPMENTS
RECOURSING
RECOVERABILITY
RECOVERABLE
RECOVERABLENESS
RECOVEREES
RECOVERERS
RECOVERIES
RECOVERING
RECOVERORS
RECOWERING
RECREANCES
RECREANCIES
RECREANTLY
RECREATING
RECREATION
RECREATIONAL
RECREATIONALLY
RECREATIONIST
RECREATIONISTS
RECREATIONS
RECREATIVE
RECREATIVELY
RECREATORS
RECREMENTAL
RECREMENTITIAL
RECREMENTITIOUS
RECREMENTS
RECRIMINATE
RECRIMINATED
RECRIMINATES
RECRIMINATING
RECRIMINATION
RECRIMINATIONS
RECRIMINATIVE
RECRIMINATOR
RECRIMINATORS
RECRIMINATORY
RECROSSING
RECROWNING
RECRUDESCE
RECRUDESCED
RECRUDESCENCE
RECRUDESCENCES
RECRUDESCENCIES
RECRUDESCENCY
RECRUDESCENT
RECRUDESCES
RECRUDESCING
RECRUITABLE
RECRUITALS
RECRUITERS
RECRUITING
RECRUITINGS
RECRUITMENT
RECRUITMENTS
RECRYSTALLISE
RECRYSTALLISED
RECRYSTALLISES
RECRYSTALLISING
RECRYSTALLIZE
RECRYSTALLIZED
RECRYSTALLIZES
RECRYSTALLIZING
RECTANGLED
RECTANGLES
RECTANGULAR

R

RECTANGULARITY
RECTANGULARLY
RECTIFIABILITY
RECTIFIABLE
RECTIFICATION
RECTIFICATIONS
RECTIFIERS
RECTIFYING
RECTILINEAL
RECTILINEALLY
RECTILINEAR
RECTILINEARITY
RECTILINEARLY
RECTIPETALIES
RECTIPETALITIES
RECTIPETALITY
RECTIPETALY
RECTIROSTRAL
RECTISERIAL
RECTITISES
RECTITUDES
RECTITUDINOUS
RECTOCELES
RECTORATES
RECTORESSES
RECTORIALS
RECTORSHIP
RECTORSHIPS
RECTRESSES
RECTRICIAL
RECULTIVATE
RECULTIVATED
RECULTIVATES
RECULTIVATING
RECUMBENCE
RECUMBENCES
RECUMBENCIES
RECUMBENCY
RECUMBENTLY
RECUPERABLE
RECUPERATE
RECUPERATED
RECUPERATES
RECUPERATING
RECUPERATION
RECUPERATIONS
RECUPERATIVE
RECUPERATOR
RECUPERATORS
RECUPERATORY
RECURELESS
RECURRENCE
RECURRENCES
RECURRENCIES
RECURRENCY
RECURRENTLY
RECURRINGLY
RECURSIONS
RECURSIVELY
RECURSIVENESS
RECURSIVENESSES
RECURVIROSTRAL
RECUSANCES
RECUSANCIES
RECUSATION
RECUSATIONS
RECYCLABLE
RECYCLABLES
RECYCLATES
RECYCLEABLE
RECYCLEABLES
RECYCLINGS
RECYCLISTS
REDACTIONAL
REDACTIONS
REDACTORIAL
REDAMAGING
REDARGUING
REDBAITERS
REDBAITING
REDBELLIES
REDBREASTS
REDCURRANT
REDCURRANTS
REDDISHNESS
REDDISHNESSES
REDECIDING
REDECORATE
REDECORATED
REDECORATES
REDECORATING
REDECORATION
REDECORATIONS
REDECORATOR
REDECORATORS
REDECRAFTS
REDEDICATE
REDEDICATED
REDEDICATES
REDEDICATING
REDEDICATION
REDEDICATIONS
REDEEMABILITIES
REDEEMABILITY
REDEEMABLE
REDEEMABLENESS
REDEEMABLY
REDEEMLESS
REDEFEATED
REDEFEATING
REDEFECTED
REDEFECTING
REDEFINING
REDEFINITION
REDEFINITIONS
REDELIVERANCE
REDELIVERANCES
REDELIVERED
REDELIVERER
REDELIVERERS
REDELIVERIES
REDELIVERING
REDELIVERS
REDELIVERY
REDEMANDED
REDEMANDING
REDEMPTIBLE
REDEMPTION
REDEMPTIONAL
REDEMPTIONER
REDEMPTIONERS
REDEMPTIONS
REDEMPTIVE
REDEMPTIVELY
REDEMPTORY
REDEPLOYED
REDEPLOYING
REDEPLOYMENT
REDEPLOYMENTS
REDEPOSITED
REDEPOSITING
REDEPOSITS
REDESCENDED
REDESCENDING
REDESCENDS
REDESCRIBE
REDESCRIBED
REDESCRIBES
REDESCRIBING
REDESCRIPTION
REDESCRIPTIONS
REDESIGNED
REDESIGNING
REDETERMINATION
REDETERMINE
REDETERMINED
REDETERMINES
REDETERMINING
REDEVELOPED
REDEVELOPER
REDEVELOPERS
REDEVELOPING
REDEVELOPMENT
REDEVELOPMENTS
REDEVELOPS
REDIALLING
REDICTATED
REDICTATES
REDICTATING
REDIGESTED
REDIGESTING
REDIGESTION
REDIGESTIONS
REDIGRESSED
REDIGRESSES
REDIGRESSING
REDINGOTES
REDINTEGRATE
REDINTEGRATED
REDINTEGRATES
REDINTEGRATING
REDINTEGRATION
REDINTEGRATIONS
REDINTEGRATIVE
REDIRECTED
REDIRECTING
REDIRECTION
REDIRECTIONS
REDISBURSE
REDISBURSED
REDISBURSES
REDISBURSING
REDISCOUNT
REDISCOUNTABLE
REDISCOUNTED
REDISCOUNTING
REDISCOUNTS
REDISCOVER
REDISCOVERED
REDISCOVERER
REDISCOVERERS
REDISCOVERIES
REDISCOVERING
REDISCOVERS
REDISCOVERY
REDISCUSSED
REDISCUSSES
REDISCUSSING
REDISPLAYED
REDISPLAYING
REDISPLAYS
REDISPOSED
REDISPOSES
REDISPOSING
REDISPOSITION
REDISPOSITIONS
REDISSOLUTION
REDISSOLUTIONS
REDISSOLVE
REDISSOLVED
REDISSOLVES
REDISSOLVING
REDISTILLATION
REDISTILLATIONS
REDISTILLED
REDISTILLING
REDISTILLS
REDISTRIBUTE
REDISTRIBUTED
REDISTRIBUTES
REDISTRIBUTING
REDISTRIBUTION
REDISTRIBUTIONS
REDISTRIBUTIVE
REDISTRICT
REDISTRICTED
REDISTRICTING
REDISTRICTINGS
REDISTRICTS
REDIVIDING

R

REDIVISION
REDIVISIONS
REDIVORCED
REDIVORCES
REDIVORCING
REDLININGS
REDOLENCES
REDOLENCIES
REDOLENTLY
REDOUBLEMENT
REDOUBLEMENTS
REDOUBLERS
REDOUBLING
REDOUBTABLE
REDOUBTABLENESS
REDOUBTABLY
REDOUBTING
REDOUNDING
REDOUNDINGS
REDRAFTING
REDREAMING
REDRESSABLE
REDRESSALS
REDRESSERS
REDRESSIBLE
REDRESSING
REDRESSIVE
REDRESSORS
REDRILLING
REDRUTHITE
REDRUTHITES
REDSHIFTED
REDSHIRTED
REDSHIRTING
REDSTREAKS
REDUCIBILITIES
REDUCIBILITY
REDUCIBLENESS
REDUCIBLENESSES
REDUCTANTS
REDUCTASES
REDUCTIONAL
REDUCTIONISM
REDUCTIONISMS
REDUCTIONIST
REDUCTIONISTIC
REDUCTIONISTS
REDUCTIONS
REDUCTIVELY
REDUCTIVENESS
REDUCTIVENESSES
REDUCTIVES
REDUNDANCE
REDUNDANCES
REDUNDANCIES
REDUNDANCY
REDUNDANTLY
REDUPLICATE
REDUPLICATED
REDUPLICATES
REDUPLICATING
REDUPLICATION
REDUPLICATIONS
REDUPLICATIVE
REDUPLICATIVELY
REEDIFYING
REEDINESSES
REEDITIONS
REEDUCATED
REEDUCATES
REEDUCATING
REEDUCATION
REEDUCATIONS
REEDUCATIVE
REEFPOINTS
REEJECTING
REELECTING
REELECTION
REELECTIONS
REELEVATED
REELEVATES
REELEVATING
REELIGIBILITIES
REELIGIBILITY
REELIGIBLE
REEMBARKED
REEMBARKING
REEMBODIED
REEMBODIES
REEMBODYING
REEMBRACED
REEMBRACES
REEMBRACING
REEMBROIDER
REEMBROIDERED
REEMBROIDERING
REEMBROIDERS
REEMERGENCE
REEMERGENCES
REEMERGING
REEMISSION
REEMISSIONS
REEMITTING
REEMPHASES
REEMPHASIS
REEMPHASISE
REEMPHASISED
REEMPHASISES
REEMPHASISING
REEMPHASIZE
REEMPHASIZED
REEMPHASIZES
REEMPHASIZING
REEMPLOYED
REEMPLOYING
REEMPLOYMENT
REEMPLOYMENTS
REENACTING
REENACTMENT
REENACTMENTS
REENACTORS
REENCOUNTER
REENCOUNTERED
REENCOUNTERING
REENCOUNTERS
REENDOWING
REENERGISE
REENERGISED
REENERGISES
REENERGISING
REENERGIZE
REENERGIZED
REENERGIZES
REENERGIZING
REENFORCED
REENFORCES
REENFORCING
REENGAGEMENT
REENGAGEMENTS
REENGAGING
REENGINEER
REENGINEERED
REENGINEERING
REENGINEERS
REENGRAVED
REENGRAVES
REENGRAVING
REENJOYING
REENLARGED
REENLARGES
REENLARGING
REENLISTED
REENLISTING
REENLISTMENT
REENLISTMENTS
REENROLLED
REENROLLING
REENSLAVED
REENSLAVES
REENSLAVING
REENTERING
REENTHRONE
REENTHRONED
REENTHRONES
REENTHRONING
REENTRANCE
REENTRANCES
REENTRANTS
REEQUIPMENT
REEQUIPMENTS
REEQUIPPED
REEQUIPPING
REERECTING
REESCALATE
REESCALATED
REESCALATES
REESCALATING
REESCALATION
REESCALATIONS
REESTABLISH
REESTABLISHED
REESTABLISHES
REESTABLISHING
REESTABLISHMENT
REESTIMATE
REESTIMATED
REESTIMATES
REESTIMATING
REEVALUATE
REEVALUATED
REEVALUATES
REEVALUATING
REEVALUATION
REEVALUATIONS
REEVESHIPS
REEXAMINATION
REEXAMINATIONS
REEXAMINED
REEXAMINES
REEXAMINING
REEXECUTED
REEXECUTES
REEXECUTING
REEXHIBITED
REEXHIBITING
REEXHIBITS
REEXPELLED
REEXPELLING
REEXPERIENCE
REEXPERIENCED
REEXPERIENCES
REEXPERIENCING
REEXPLAINED
REEXPLAINING
REEXPLAINS
REEXPLORED
REEXPLORES
REEXPLORING
REEXPORTATION
REEXPORTATIONS
REEXPORTED
REEXPORTING
REEXPOSING
REEXPOSURE
REEXPOSURES
REEXPRESSED
REEXPRESSES
REEXPRESSING
REFASHIONED
REFASHIONING
REFASHIONMENT
REFASHIONMENTS
REFASHIONS
REFASTENED
REFASTENING
REFECTIONER
REFECTIONERS
REFECTIONS
REFECTORIAN
REFECTORIANS

REFECTORIES
REFEEDINGS
REFEREEING
REFEREEINGS
REFERENCED
REFERENCER
REFERENCERS
REFERENCES
REFERENCING
REFERENCINGS
REFERENDARIES
REFERENDARY
REFERENDUM
REFERENDUMS
REFERENTIAL
REFERENTIALITY
REFERENTIALLY
REFERRABLE
REFERRIBLE
REFIGHTING
REFIGURING
REFILLABLE
REFILTERED
REFILTERING
REFINANCED
REFINANCES
REFINANCING
REFINANCINGS
REFINEDNESS
REFINEDNESSES
REFINEMENT
REFINEMENTS
REFINERIES
REFINISHED
REFINISHER
REFINISHERS
REFINISHES
REFINISHING
REFITMENTS
REFITTINGS
REFLAGGING
REFLATIONARY
REFLATIONS
REFLECTANCE
REFLECTANCES
REFLECTERS
REFLECTING
REFLECTINGLY
REFLECTION
REFLECTIONAL
REFLECTIONLESS
REFLECTIONS
REFLECTIVE
REFLECTIVELY
REFLECTIVENESS
REFLECTIVITIES
REFLECTIVITY
REFLECTOGRAM
REFLECTOGRAMS
REFLECTOGRAPH
REFLECTOGRAPHS
REFLECTOGRAPHY
REFLECTOMETER
REFLECTOMETERS
REFLECTOMETRIES
REFLECTOMETRY
REFLECTORISE
REFLECTORISED
REFLECTORISES
REFLECTORISING
REFLECTORIZE
REFLECTORIZED
REFLECTORIZES
REFLECTORIZING
REFLECTORS
REFLEXIBILITIES
REFLEXIBILITY
REFLEXIBLE
REFLEXIONAL
REFLEXIONS
REFLEXIVELY
REFLEXIVENESS
REFLEXIVENESSES
REFLEXIVES
REFLEXIVITIES
REFLEXIVITY
REFLEXOLOGICAL
REFLEXOLOGIES
REFLEXOLOGIST
REFLEXOLOGISTS
REFLEXOLOGY
REFLOATING
REFLOODING
REFLOWERED
REFLOWERING
REFLOWERINGS
REFLOWINGS
REFLUENCES
REFOCILLATE
REFOCILLATED
REFOCILLATES
REFOCILLATING
REFOCILLATION
REFOCILLATIONS
REFOCUSING
REFOCUSSED
REFOCUSSES
REFOCUSSING
REFORESTATION
REFORESTATIONS
REFORESTED
REFORESTING
REFORMABILITIES
REFORMABILITY
REFORMABLE
REFORMADES
REFORMADOES
REFORMADOS
REFORMATES
REFORMATION
REFORMATIONAL
REFORMATIONIST
REFORMATIONISTS
REFORMATIONS
REFORMATIVE
REFORMATORIES
REFORMATORY
REFORMATTED
REFORMATTING
REFORMINGS
REFORMISMS
REFORMISTS
REFORMULATE
REFORMULATED
REFORMULATES
REFORMULATING
REFORMULATION
REFORMULATIONS
REFORTIFICATION
REFORTIFIED
REFORTIFIES
REFORTIFYING
REFOULEMENT
REFOULEMENTS
REFOUNDATION
REFOUNDATIONS
REFOUNDERS
REFOUNDING
REFRACTABLE
REFRACTARIES
REFRACTARY
REFRACTILE
REFRACTING
REFRACTION
REFRACTIONS
REFRACTIVE
REFRACTIVELY
REFRACTIVENESS
REFRACTIVITIES
REFRACTIVITY
REFRACTOMETER
REFRACTOMETERS
REFRACTOMETRIC
REFRACTOMETRIES
REFRACTOMETRY
REFRACTORIES
REFRACTORILY
REFRACTORINESS
REFRACTORS
REFRACTORY
REFRACTURE
REFRACTURED
REFRACTURES
REFRACTURING
REFRAINERS
REFRAINING
REFRAINMENT
REFRAINMENTS
REFRANGIBILITY
REFRANGIBLE
REFRANGIBLENESS
REFREEZING
REFRESHENED
REFRESHENER
REFRESHENERS
REFRESHENING
REFRESHENS
REFRESHERS
REFRESHFUL
REFRESHFULLY
REFRESHING
REFRESHINGLY
REFRESHMENT
REFRESHMENTS
REFRIGERANT
REFRIGERANTS
REFRIGERATE
REFRIGERATED
REFRIGERATES
REFRIGERATING
REFRIGERATION
REFRIGERATIONS
REFRIGERATIVE
REFRIGERATOR
REFRIGERATORIES
REFRIGERATORS
REFRIGERATORY
REFRINGENCE
REFRINGENCES
REFRINGENCIES
REFRINGENCY
REFRINGENT
REFRINGING
REFRONTING
REFUELABLE
REFUELINGS
REFUELLABLE
REFUELLING
REFUELLINGS
REFUGEEISM
REFUGEEISMS
REFULGENCE
REFULGENCES
REFULGENCIES
REFULGENCY
REFULGENTLY
REFUNDABILITIES
REFUNDABILITY
REFUNDABLE
REFUNDINGS
REFUNDMENT
REFUNDMENTS
REFURBISHED
REFURBISHER
REFURBISHERS
REFURBISHES
REFURBISHING
REFURBISHINGS
REFURBISHMENT
REFURBISHMENTS

REFURNISHED
REFURNISHES
REFURNISHING
REFUSENIKS
REFUTABILITIES
REFUTABILITY
REFUTATION
REFUTATIONS
REGAINABLE
REGAINMENT
REGAINMENTS
REGALEMENT
REGALEMENTS
REGALITIES
REGALNESSES
REGARDABLE
REGARDFULLY
REGARDFULNESS
REGARDFULNESSES
REGARDLESS
REGARDLESSLY
REGARDLESSNESS
REGATHERED
REGATHERING
REGELATING
REGELATION
REGELATIONS
REGENERABLE
REGENERACIES
REGENERACY
REGENERATE
REGENERATED
REGENERATELY
REGENERATENESS
REGENERATES
REGENERATING
REGENERATION
REGENERATIONS
REGENERATIVE
REGENERATIVELY
REGENERATOR
REGENERATORS
REGENERATORY
REGENTSHIP
REGENTSHIPS
REGGAETONS
REGIMENTAL
REGIMENTALLY
REGIMENTALS
REGIMENTATION
REGIMENTATIONS
REGIMENTED
REGIMENTING
REGIONALISATION
REGIONALISE
REGIONALISED
REGIONALISES
REGIONALISING
REGIONALISM
REGIONALISMS
REGIONALIST
REGIONALISTIC
REGIONALISTS
REGIONALIZATION
REGIONALIZE
REGIONALIZED
REGIONALIZES
REGIONALIZING
REGIONALLY
REGISSEURS
REGISTERABLE
REGISTERED
REGISTERER
REGISTERERS
REGISTERING
REGISTRABLE
REGISTRANT
REGISTRANTS
REGISTRARIES
REGISTRARS
REGISTRARSHIP
REGISTRARSHIPS
REGISTRARY
REGISTRATION
REGISTRATIONAL
REGISTRATIONS
REGISTRIES
REGLORIFIED
REGLORIFIES
REGLORIFYING
REGLOSSING
REGNANCIES
REGRAFTING
REGRANTING
REGRATINGS
REGREDIENCE
REGREDIENCES
REGREENING
REGREETING
REGRESSING
REGRESSION
REGRESSIONS
REGRESSIVE
REGRESSIVELY
REGRESSIVENESS
REGRESSIVITIES
REGRESSIVITY
REGRESSORS
REGRETFULLY
REGRETFULNESS
REGRETFULNESSES
REGRETTABLE
REGRETTABLY
REGRETTERS
REGRETTING
REGRINDING
REGROOMING
REGROOVING
REGROUPING
REGROUPINGS
REGUERDONED
REGUERDONING
REGUERDONS
REGULARISATION
REGULARISATIONS
REGULARISE
REGULARISED
REGULARISES
REGULARISING
REGULARITIES
REGULARITY
REGULARIZATION
REGULARIZATIONS
REGULARIZE
REGULARIZED
REGULARIZES
REGULARIZING
REGULATING
REGULATION
REGULATIONS
REGULATIVE
REGULATIVELY
REGULATORS
REGULATORY
REGULISING
REGULIZING
REGURGITANT
REGURGITANTS
REGURGITATE
REGURGITATED
REGURGITATES
REGURGITATING
REGURGITATION
REGURGITATIONS
REHABILITANT
REHABILITANTS
REHABILITATE
REHABILITATED
REHABILITATES
REHABILITATING
REHABILITATION
REHABILITATIONS
REHABILITATIVE
REHABILITATOR
REHABILITATORS
REHAMMERED
REHAMMERING
REHANDLING
REHANDLINGS
REHARDENED
REHARDENING
REHEARINGS
REHEARSALS
REHEARSERS
REHEARSING
REHEARSINGS
REHEATINGS
REHOSPITALISE
REHOSPITALISED
REHOSPITALISES
REHOSPITALISING
REHOSPITALIZE
REHOSPITALIZED
REHOSPITALIZES
REHOSPITALIZING
REHOUSINGS
REHUMANISE
REHUMANISED
REHUMANISES
REHUMANISING
REHUMANIZE
REHUMANIZED
REHUMANIZES
REHUMANIZING
REHYDRATABLE
REHYDRATED
REHYDRATES
REHYDRATING
REHYDRATION
REHYDRATIONS
REHYPNOTISE
REHYPNOTISED
REHYPNOTISES
REHYPNOTISING
REHYPNOTIZE
REHYPNOTIZED
REHYPNOTIZES
REHYPNOTIZING
REICHSMARK
REICHSMARKS
REIDENTIFIED
REIDENTIFIES
REIDENTIFY
REIDENTIFYING
REIFICATION
REIFICATIONS
REIFICATORY
REIGNITING
REIGNITION
REIGNITIONS
REILLUMINE
REILLUMINED
REILLUMINES
REILLUMING
REILLUMINING
REIMAGINED
REIMAGINES
REIMAGINING
REIMBURSABLE
REIMBURSED
REIMBURSEMENT
REIMBURSEMENTS
REIMBURSER
REIMBURSERS
REIMBURSES
REIMBURSING
REIMMERSED
REIMMERSES
REIMMERSING
REIMPLANTATION

REIMPLANTATIONS
REIMPLANTED
REIMPLANTING
REIMPLANTS
REIMPORTATION
REIMPORTATIONS
REIMPORTED
REIMPORTER
REIMPORTERS
REIMPORTING
REIMPOSING
REIMPOSITION
REIMPOSITIONS
REIMPRESSION
REIMPRESSIONS
REINCARNATE
REINCARNATED
REINCARNATES
REINCARNATING
REINCARNATION
REINCARNATIONS
REINCITING
REINCORPORATE
REINCORPORATED
REINCORPORATES
REINCORPORATING
REINCORPORATION
REINCREASE
REINCREASED
REINCREASES
REINCREASING
REINCURRED
REINCURRING
REINDEXING
REINDICTED
REINDICTING
REINDICTMENT
REINDICTMENTS
REINDUCING
REINDUCTED
REINDUCTING
REINDUSTRIALISE
REINDUSTRIALIZE
REINFECTED
REINFECTING
REINFECTION
REINFECTIONS
REINFESTATION
REINFESTATIONS
REINFLAMED
REINFLAMES
REINFLAMING
REINFLATED
REINFLATES
REINFLATING
REINFLATION
REINFLATIONS
REINFORCEABLE
REINFORCED
REINFORCEMENT
REINFORCEMENTS
REINFORCER
REINFORCERS
REINFORCES
REINFORCING
REINFORMED
REINFORMING
REINFUNDED
REINFUNDING
REINFUSING
REINHABITED
REINHABITING
REINHABITS
REINITIATE
REINITIATED
REINITIATES
REINITIATING
REINJECTED
REINJECTING
REINJECTION
REINJECTIONS
REINJURIES
REINJURING
REINNERVATE
REINNERVATED
REINNERVATES
REINNERVATING
REINNERVATION
REINNERVATIONS
REINOCULATE
REINOCULATED
REINOCULATES
REINOCULATING
REINOCULATION
REINOCULATIONS
REINSERTED
REINSERTING
REINSERTION
REINSERTIONS
REINSPECTED
REINSPECTING
REINSPECTION
REINSPECTIONS
REINSPECTS
REINSPIRED
REINSPIRES
REINSPIRING
REINSPIRIT
REINSPIRITED
REINSPIRITING
REINSPIRITS
REINSTALLATION
REINSTALLATIONS
REINSTALLED
REINSTALLING
REINSTALLS
REINSTALMENT
REINSTALMENTS
REINSTATED
REINSTATEMENT
REINSTATEMENTS
REINSTATES
REINSTATING
REINSTATION
REINSTATIONS
REINSTATOR
REINSTATORS
REINSTITUTE
REINSTITUTED
REINSTITUTES
REINSTITUTING
REINSTITUTION
REINSTITUTIONS
REINSURANCE
REINSURANCES
REINSURERS
REINSURING
REINTEGRATE
REINTEGRATED
REINTEGRATES
REINTEGRATING
REINTEGRATION
REINTEGRATIONS
REINTEGRATIVE
REINTERMENT
REINTERMENTS
REINTERPRET
REINTERPRETED
REINTERPRETING
REINTERPRETS
REINTERRED
REINTERRING
REINTERROGATE
REINTERROGATED
REINTERROGATES
REINTERROGATING
REINTERROGATION
REINTERVIEW
REINTERVIEWED
REINTERVIEWING
REINTERVIEWS
REINTRODUCE
REINTRODUCED
REINTRODUCES
REINTRODUCING
REINTRODUCTION
REINTRODUCTIONS
REINVADING
REINVASION
REINVASIONS
REINVENTED
REINVENTING
REINVENTION
REINVENTIONS
REINVESTED
REINVESTIGATE
REINVESTIGATED
REINVESTIGATES
REINVESTIGATING
REINVESTIGATION
REINVESTING
REINVESTMENT
REINVESTMENTS
REINVIGORATE
REINVIGORATED
REINVIGORATES
REINVIGORATING
REINVIGORATION
REINVIGORATIONS
REINVIGORATOR
REINVIGORATORS
REINVITING
REINVOKING
REINVOLVED
REINVOLVES
REINVOLVING
REIOYNDURE
REIOYNDURES
REISSUABLE
REISTAFELS
REITERANCE
REITERANCES
REITERATED
REITERATEDLY
REITERATES
REITERATING
REITERATION
REITERATIONS
REITERATIVE
REITERATIVELY
REITERATIVES
REJACKETED
REJACKETING
REJECTABLE
REJECTAMENTA
REJECTIBLE
REJECTINGLY
REJECTIONIST
REJECTIONISTS
REJECTIONS
REJIGGERED
REJIGGERING
REJOICEFUL
REJOICEMENT
REJOICEMENTS
REJOICINGLY
REJOICINGS
REJOINDERS
REJOINDURE
REJOINDURES
REJONEADOR
REJONEADORA
REJONEADORAS
REJONEADORES
REJOURNING
REJUGGLING
REJUSTIFIED
REJUSTIFIES
REJUSTIFYING
REJUVENATE

REJUVENATED
REJUVENATES
REJUVENATING
REJUVENATION
REJUVENATIONS
REJUVENATOR
REJUVENATORS
REJUVENESCE
REJUVENESCED
REJUVENESCENCE
REJUVENESCENCES
REJUVENESCENT
REJUVENESCES
REJUVENESCING
REJUVENISE
REJUVENISED
REJUVENISES
REJUVENISING
REJUVENIZE
REJUVENIZED
REJUVENIZES
REJUVENIZING
REKEYBOARD
REKEYBOARDED
REKEYBOARDING
REKEYBOARDS
REKINDLING
REKINDLINGS
REKNITTING
REKNITTINGS
REKNOTTING
REKNOTTINGS
RELABELING
RELABELLED
RELABELLING
RELACQUERED
RELACQUERING
RELACQUERS
RELANDSCAPE
RELANDSCAPED
RELANDSCAPES
RELANDSCAPING
RELATEDNESS
RELATEDNESSES
RELATIONAL
RELATIONALLY
RELATIONISM
RELATIONISMS
RELATIONIST
RELATIONISTS
RELATIONLESS
RELATIONSHIP
RELATIONSHIPS
RELATIVELY
RELATIVENESS
RELATIVENESSES
RELATIVISATION
RELATIVISATIONS
RELATIVISE
RELATIVISED
RELATIVISES
RELATIVISING
RELATIVISM
RELATIVISMS
RELATIVIST
RELATIVISTIC
RELATIVISTS
RELATIVITIES
RELATIVITIST
RELATIVITISTS
RELATIVITY
RELATIVIZATION
RELATIVIZATIONS
RELATIVIZE
RELATIVIZED
RELATIVIZES
RELATIVIZING
RELAUNCHED
RELAUNCHES
RELAUNCHING
RELAUNDERED
RELAUNDERING
RELAUNDERS
RELAXATION
RELAXATIONS
RELAXATIVE
RELAXATIVES
RELAXEDNESS
RELAXEDNESSES
RELEARNING
RELEASABLE
RELEASEMENT
RELEASEMENTS
RELEGATABLE
RELEGATING
RELEGATION
RELEGATIONS
RELENTINGS
RELENTLESS
RELENTLESSLY
RELENTLESSNESS
RELENTMENT
RELENTMENTS
RELETTERED
RELETTERING
RELEVANCES
RELEVANCIES
RELEVANTLY
RELIABILITIES
RELIABILITY
RELIABLENESS
RELIABLENESSES
RELICENSED
RELICENSES
RELICENSING
RELICENSURE
RELICENSURES
RELICTIONS
RELIEFLESS
RELIEVABLE
RELIEVEDLY
RELIGHTING
RELIGIEUSE
RELIGIEUSES
RELIGIONARIES
RELIGIONARY
RELIGIONER
RELIGIONERS
RELIGIONISE
RELIGIONISED
RELIGIONISES
RELIGIONISING
RELIGIONISM
RELIGIONISMS
RELIGIONIST
RELIGIONISTS
RELIGIONIZE
RELIGIONIZED
RELIGIONIZES
RELIGIONIZING
RELIGIONLESS
RELIGIOSELY
RELIGIOSITIES
RELIGIOSITY
RELIGIOSOS
RELIGIOUSES
RELIGIOUSLY
RELIGIOUSNESS
RELIGIOUSNESSES
RELINQUISH
RELINQUISHED
RELINQUISHER
RELINQUISHERS
RELINQUISHES
RELINQUISHING
RELINQUISHMENT
RELINQUISHMENTS
RELIQUAIRE
RELIQUAIRES
RELIQUARIES
RELIQUEFIED
RELIQUEFIES
RELIQUEFYING
RELIQUIFIED
RELIQUIFIES
RELIQUIFYING
RELISHABLE
RELISTENED
RELISTENING
RELIVERING
RELLISHING
RELOCATABLE
RELOCATEES
RELOCATING
RELOCATION
RELOCATIONS
RELOCATORS
RELUBRICATE
RELUBRICATED
RELUBRICATES
RELUBRICATING
RELUBRICATION
RELUBRICATIONS
RELUCTANCE
RELUCTANCES
RELUCTANCIES
RELUCTANCY
RELUCTANTLY
RELUCTATED
RELUCTATES
RELUCTATING
RELUCTATION
RELUCTATIONS
RELUCTIVITIES
RELUCTIVITY
RELUMINING
REMAILINGS
REMAINDERED
REMAINDERING
REMAINDERMAN
REMAINDERMEN
REMAINDERS
REMANDMENT
REMANDMENTS
REMANENCES
REMANENCIES
REMANUFACTURE
REMANUFACTURED
REMANUFACTURER
REMANUFACTURERS
REMANUFACTURES
REMANUFACTURING
REMARKABILITIES
REMARKABILITY
REMARKABLE
REMARKABLENESS
REMARKABLES
REMARKABLY
REMARKETED
REMARKETING
REMARRIAGE
REMARRIAGES
REMARRYING
REMASTERED
REMASTERING
REMATCHING
REMATERIALISE
REMATERIALISED
REMATERIALISES
REMATERIALISING
REMATERIALIZE
REMATERIALIZED
REMATERIALIZES
REMATERIALIZING
REMEASURED
REMEASUREMENT
REMEASUREMENTS
REMEASURES
REMEASURING
REMEDIABILITIES

REMEDIABILITY
REMEDIABLE
REMEDIABLY
REMEDIALLY
REMEDIATED
REMEDIATES
REMEDIATING
REMEDIATION
REMEDIATIONS
REMEDILESS
REMEDILESSLY
REMEDILESSNESS
REMEMBERABILITY
REMEMBERABLE
REMEMBERABLY
REMEMBERED
REMEMBERER
REMEMBERERS
REMEMBERING
REMEMBRANCE
REMEMBRANCER
REMEMBRANCERS
REMEMBRANCES
REMERCYING
REMIGATING
REMIGATION
REMIGATIONS
REMIGRATED
REMIGRATES
REMIGRATING
REMIGRATION
REMIGRATIONS
REMILITARISE
REMILITARISED
REMILITARISES
REMILITARISING
REMILITARIZE
REMILITARIZED
REMILITARIZES
REMILITARIZING
REMINERALISE
REMINERALISED
REMINERALISES
REMINERALISING
REMINERALIZE
REMINERALIZED
REMINERALIZES
REMINERALIZING
REMINISCED
REMINISCENCE
REMINISCENCES
REMINISCENT
REMINISCENTIAL
REMINISCENTLY
REMINISCENTS
REMINISCER
REMINISCERS
REMINISCES
REMINISCING
REMISSIBILITIES
REMISSIBILITY
REMISSIBLE
REMISSIBLENESS
REMISSIBLY
REMISSIONS
REMISSIVELY
REMISSNESS
REMISSNESSES
REMITMENTS
REMITTABLE
REMITTANCE
REMITTANCES
REMITTENCE
REMITTENCES
REMITTENCIES
REMITTENCY
REMITTENTLY
REMIXTURES
REMOBILISATION
REMOBILISATIONS
REMOBILISE
REMOBILISED
REMOBILISES
REMOBILISING
REMOBILIZATION
REMOBILIZATIONS
REMOBILIZE
REMOBILIZED
REMOBILIZES
REMOBILIZING
REMODELERS
REMODELING
REMODELINGS
REMODELLED
REMODELLER
REMODELLERS
REMODELLING
REMODELLINGS
REMODIFIED
REMODIFIES
REMODIFYING
REMOISTENED
REMOISTENING
REMOISTENS
REMONETISATION
REMONETISATIONS
REMONETISE
REMONETISED
REMONETISES
REMONETISING
REMONETIZATION
REMONETIZATIONS
REMONETIZE
REMONETIZED
REMONETIZES
REMONETIZING
REMONSTRANCE
REMONSTRANCES
REMONSTRANT
REMONSTRANTLY
REMONSTRANTS
REMONSTRATE
REMONSTRATED
REMONSTRATES
REMONSTRATING
REMONSTRATINGLY
REMONSTRATION
REMONSTRATIONS
REMONSTRATIVE
REMONSTRATIVELY
REMONSTRATOR
REMONSTRATORS
REMONSTRATORY
REMONTANTS
REMONTOIRE
REMONTOIRES
REMONTOIRS
REMORALISATION
REMORALISATIONS
REMORALISE
REMORALISED
REMORALISES
REMORALISING
REMORALIZATION
REMORALIZATIONS
REMORALIZE
REMORALIZED
REMORALIZES
REMORALIZING
REMORSEFUL
REMORSEFULLY
REMORSEFULNESS
REMORSELESS
REMORSELESSLY
REMORSELESSNESS
REMORTGAGE
REMORTGAGED
REMORTGAGES
REMORTGAGING
REMOTENESS
REMOTENESSES
REMOTIVATE
REMOTIVATED
REMOTIVATES
REMOTIVATING
REMOTIVATION
REMOTIVATIONS
REMOULADES
REMOULDING
REMOUNTING
REMOUNTINGS
REMOVABILITIES
REMOVABILITY
REMOVABLENESS
REMOVABLENESSES
REMOVALIST
REMOVALISTS
REMOVEABLE
REMOVEDNESS
REMOVEDNESSES
REMUNERABILITY
REMUNERABLE
REMUNERATE
REMUNERATED
REMUNERATES
REMUNERATING
REMUNERATION
REMUNERATIONS
REMUNERATIVE
REMUNERATIVELY
REMUNERATOR
REMUNERATORS
REMUNERATORY
REMURMURED
REMURMURING
REMYTHOLOGISE
REMYTHOLOGISED
REMYTHOLOGISES
REMYTHOLOGISING
REMYTHOLOGIZE
REMYTHOLOGIZED
REMYTHOLOGIZES
REMYTHOLOGIZING
RENAISSANCE
RENAISSANCES
RENASCENCE
RENASCENCES
RENATIONALISE
RENATIONALISED
RENATIONALISES
RENATIONALISING
RENATIONALIZE
RENATIONALIZED
RENATIONALIZES
RENATIONALIZING
RENATURATION
RENATURATIONS
RENATURING
RENCONTRED
RENCONTRES
RENCONTRING
RENCOUNTER
RENCOUNTERED
RENCOUNTERING
RENCOUNTERS
RENDERABLE
RENDERINGS
RENDEZVOUS
RENDEZVOUSED
RENDEZVOUSES
RENDEZVOUSING
RENDITIONED
RENDITIONING
RENDITIONS
RENEAGUING
RENEGADING
RENEGADOES
RENEGATION
RENEGATIONS
RENEGOTIABLE

RENEGOTIATE
RENEGOTIATED
RENEGOTIATES
RENEGOTIATING
RENEGOTIATION
RENEGOTIATIONS
RENEWABILITIES
RENEWABILITY
RENEWABLES
RENEWEDNESS
RENEWEDNESSES
RENFORCING
RENITENCES
RENITENCIES
RENOGRAPHIC
RENOGRAPHIES
RENOGRAPHY
RENOMINATE
RENOMINATED
RENOMINATES
RENOMINATING
RENOMINATION
RENOMINATIONS
RENORMALISATION
RENORMALISE
RENORMALISED
RENORMALISES
RENORMALISING
RENORMALIZATION
RENORMALIZE
RENORMALIZED
RENORMALIZES
RENORMALIZING
RENOSTERVELD
RENOSTERVELDS
RENOTIFIED
RENOTIFIES
RENOTIFYING
RENOUNCEABLE
RENOUNCEMENT
RENOUNCEMENTS
RENOUNCERS
RENOUNCING
RENOVASCULAR
RENOVATING
RENOVATION
RENOVATIONS
RENOVATIVE
RENOVATORS
RENSSELAERITE
RENSSELAERITES
RENTABILITIES
RENTABILITY
RENTALLERS
RENUMBERED
RENUMBERING
RENUNCIATE
RENUNCIATES
RENUNCIATION
RENUNCIATIONS
RENUNCIATIVE
RENUNCIATORY
RENVERSEMENT
RENVERSEMENTS
RENVERSING
REOBJECTED
REOBJECTING
REOBSERVED
REOBSERVES
REOBSERVING
REOBTAINED
REOBTAINING
REOCCUPATION
REOCCUPATIONS
REOCCUPIED
REOCCUPIES
REOCCUPYING
REOCCURRED
REOCCURRENCE
REOCCURRENCES
REOCCURRING
REOFFENDED
REOFFENDER
REOFFENDERS
REOFFENDING
REOFFERING
REOPENINGS
REOPERATED
REOPERATES
REOPERATING
REOPERATION
REOPERATIONS
REOPPOSING
REORCHESTRATE
REORCHESTRATED
REORCHESTRATES
REORCHESTRATING
REORCHESTRATION
REORDAINED
REORDAINING
REORDERING
REORDINATION
REORDINATIONS
REORGANISATION
REORGANISATIONS
REORGANISE
REORGANISED
REORGANISER
REORGANISERS
REORGANISES
REORGANISING
REORGANIZATION
REORGANIZATIONS
REORGANIZE
REORGANIZED
REORGANIZER
REORGANIZERS
REORGANIZES
REORGANIZING
REORIENTATE
REORIENTATED
REORIENTATES
REORIENTATING
REORIENTATION
REORIENTATIONS
REORIENTED
REORIENTING
REOUTFITTED
REOUTFITTING
REOVIRUSES
REOXIDATION
REOXIDATIONS
REOXIDISED
REOXIDISES
REOXIDISING
REOXIDIZED
REOXIDIZES
REOXIDIZING
REOXYGENATE
REOXYGENATED
REOXYGENATES
REOXYGENATING
REPACIFIED
REPACIFIES
REPACIFYING
REPACKAGED
REPACKAGER
REPACKAGERS
REPACKAGES
REPACKAGING
REPAGINATE
REPAGINATED
REPAGINATES
REPAGINATING
REPAGINATION
REPAGINATIONS
REPAINTING
REPAINTINGS
REPAIRABILITIES
REPAIRABILITY
REPAIRABLE
REPANELING
REPANELLED
REPANELLING
REPAPERING
REPARABILITIES
REPARABILITY
REPARATION
REPARATIONS
REPARATIVE
REPARATORY
REPARTEEING
REPARTITION
REPARTITIONED
REPARTITIONING
REPARTITIONS
REPASSAGES
REPASTURES
REPATCHING
REPATRIATE
REPATRIATED
REPATRIATES
REPATRIATING
REPATRIATION
REPATRIATIONS
REPATRIATOR
REPATRIATORS
REPATTERNED
REPATTERNING
REPATTERNS
REPAYMENTS
REPEALABLE
REPEATABILITIES
REPEATABILITY
REPEATABLE
REPEATEDLY
REPEATINGS
REPECHAGES
REPELLANCE
REPELLANCES
REPELLANCIES
REPELLANCY
REPELLANTLY
REPELLANTS
REPELLENCE
REPELLENCES
REPELLENCIES
REPELLENCY
REPELLENTLY
REPELLENTS
REPELLINGLY
REPENTANCE
REPENTANCES
REPENTANTLY
REPENTANTS
REPENTINGLY
REPEOPLING
REPERCUSSED
REPERCUSSES
REPERCUSSING
REPERCUSSION
REPERCUSSIONS
REPERCUSSIVE
REPERTOIRE
REPERTOIRES
REPERTORIAL
REPERTORIES
REPERUSALS
REPERUSING
REPETITEUR
REPETITEURS
REPETITEUSE
REPETITEUSES
REPETITION
REPETITIONAL
REPETITIONARY
REPETITIONS
REPETITIOUS
REPETITIOUSLY
REPETITIOUSNESS

R

REPETITIVE
REPETITIVELY
REPETITIVENESS
REPHOTOGRAPH
REPHOTOGRAPHED
REPHOTOGRAPHING
REPHOTOGRAPHS
REPHRASING
REPHRASINGS
REPIGMENTED
REPIGMENTING
REPIGMENTS
REPINEMENT
REPINEMENTS
REPININGLY
REPLACEABILITY
REPLACEABLE
REPLACEMENT
REPLACEMENTS
REPLANNING
REPLANTATION
REPLANTATIONS
REPLANTING
REPLASTERED
REPLASTERING
REPLASTERS
REPLEADERS
REPLEADING
REPLEDGING
REPLENISHABLE
REPLENISHED
REPLENISHER
REPLENISHERS
REPLENISHES
REPLENISHING
REPLENISHMENT
REPLENISHMENTS
REPLETENESS
REPLETENESSES
REPLETIONS
REPLEVIABLE
REPLEVINED
REPLEVINING
REPLEVISABLE
REPLEVYING
REPLICABILITIES
REPLICABILITY
REPLICABLE
REPLICANTS
REPLICASES
REPLICATED
REPLICATES
REPLICATING
REPLICATION
REPLICATIONS
REPLICATIVE
REPLICATOR
REPLICATORS
REPLOTTING
REPLOUGHED
REPLOUGHING
REPLUMBING
REPLUNGING
REPOINTING
REPOINTINGS
REPOLARISATION
REPOLARISATIONS
REPOLARISE
REPOLARISED
REPOLARISES
REPOLARISING
REPOLARIZATION
REPOLARIZATIONS
REPOLARIZE
REPOLARIZED
REPOLARIZES
REPOLARIZING
REPOLISHED
REPOLISHES
REPOLISHING
REPOPULARISE
REPOPULARISED
REPOPULARISES
REPOPULARISING
REPOPULARIZE
REPOPULARIZED
REPOPULARIZES
REPOPULARIZING
REPOPULATE
REPOPULATED
REPOPULATES
REPOPULATING
REPOPULATION
REPOPULATIONS
REPORTABLE
REPORTAGES
REPORTEDLY
REPORTINGLY
REPORTINGS
REPORTORIAL
REPORTORIALLY
REPOSEDNESS
REPOSEDNESSES
REPOSEFULLY
REPOSEFULNESS
REPOSEFULNESSES
REPOSITING
REPOSITION
REPOSITIONED
REPOSITIONING
REPOSITIONS
REPOSITORIES
REPOSITORS
REPOSITORY
REPOSSESSED
REPOSSESSES
REPOSSESSING
REPOSSESSION
REPOSSESSIONS
REPOSSESSOR
REPOSSESSORS
REPOTTINGS
REPOUSSAGE
REPOUSSAGES
REPOUSSOIR
REPOUSSOIRS
REPOWERING
REPREEVING
REPREHENDABLE
REPREHENDED
REPREHENDER
REPREHENDERS
REPREHENDING
REPREHENDS
REPREHENSIBLE
REPREHENSIBLY
REPREHENSION
REPREHENSIONS
REPREHENSIVE
REPREHENSIVELY
REPREHENSORY
REPRESENTABLE
REPRESENTAMEN
REPRESENTAMENS
REPRESENTANT
REPRESENTANTS
REPRESENTATION
REPRESENTATIONS
REPRESENTATIVE
REPRESENTATIVES
REPRESENTED
REPRESENTEE
REPRESENTEES
REPRESENTER
REPRESENTERS
REPRESENTING
REPRESENTMENT
REPRESENTMENTS
REPRESENTOR
REPRESENTORS
REPRESENTS
REPRESSERS
REPRESSIBILITY
REPRESSIBLE
REPRESSIBLY
REPRESSING
REPRESSION
REPRESSIONIST
REPRESSIONISTS
REPRESSIONS
REPRESSIVE
REPRESSIVELY
REPRESSIVENESS
REPRESSORS
REPRESSURISE
REPRESSURISED
REPRESSURISES
REPRESSURISING
REPRESSURIZE
REPRESSURIZED
REPRESSURIZES
REPRESSURIZING
REPRIEVABLE
REPRIEVALS
REPRIEVERS
REPRIEVING
REPRIMANDED
REPRIMANDING
REPRIMANDS
REPRINTERS
REPRINTING
REPRISTINATE
REPRISTINATED
REPRISTINATES
REPRISTINATING
REPRISTINATION
REPRISTINATIONS
REPRIVATISATION
REPRIVATISE
REPRIVATISED
REPRIVATISES
REPRIVATISING
REPRIVATIZATION
REPRIVATIZE
REPRIVATIZED
REPRIVATIZES
REPRIVATIZING
REPROACHABLE
REPROACHABLY
REPROACHED
REPROACHER
REPROACHERS
REPROACHES
REPROACHFUL
REPROACHFULLY
REPROACHFULNESS
REPROACHING
REPROACHINGLY
REPROACHLESS
REPROBACIES
REPROBANCE
REPROBANCES
REPROBATED
REPROBATER
REPROBATERS
REPROBATES
REPROBATING
REPROBATION
REPROBATIONARY
REPROBATIONS
REPROBATIVE
REPROBATIVELY
REPROBATOR
REPROBATORS
REPROBATORY
REPROCESSED
REPROCESSES
REPROCESSING
REPROCESSINGS
REPRODUCED

REPRODUCER
REPRODUCERS
REPRODUCES
REPRODUCIBILITY
REPRODUCIBLE
REPRODUCIBLES
REPRODUCIBLY
REPRODUCING
REPRODUCTION
REPRODUCTIONS
REPRODUCTIVE
REPRODUCTIVELY
REPRODUCTIVES
REPRODUCTIVITY
REPROGRAMED
REPROGRAMING
REPROGRAMMABLE
REPROGRAMME
REPROGRAMMED
REPROGRAMMES
REPROGRAMMING
REPROGRAMS
REPROGRAPHER
REPROGRAPHERS
REPROGRAPHIC
REPROGRAPHICS
REPROGRAPHIES
REPROGRAPHY
REPROOFING
REPROVABLE
REPROVINGLY
REPROVISION
REPROVISIONED
REPROVISIONING
REPROVISIONS
REPTATIONS
REPTILIANLY
REPTILIANS
REPTILIFEROUS
REPTILIFORM
REPTILIOUS
REPTILOIDS
REPUBLICAN
REPUBLICANISE
REPUBLICANISED
REPUBLICANISES
REPUBLICANISING
REPUBLICANISM
REPUBLICANISMS
REPUBLICANIZE
REPUBLICANIZED
REPUBLICANIZES
REPUBLICANIZING
REPUBLICANS
REPUBLICATION
REPUBLICATIONS
REPUBLISHED
REPUBLISHER
REPUBLISHERS
REPUBLISHES
REPUBLISHING
REPUDIABLE
REPUDIATED
REPUDIATES
REPUDIATING
REPUDIATION
REPUDIATIONIST
REPUDIATIONISTS
REPUDIATIONS
REPUDIATIVE
REPUDIATOR
REPUDIATORS
REPUGNANCE
REPUGNANCES
REPUGNANCIES
REPUGNANCY
REPUGNANTLY
REPULSIONS
REPULSIVELY
REPULSIVENESS
REPULSIVENESSES
REPUNCTUATION
REPUNCTUATIONS
REPURCHASE
REPURCHASED
REPURCHASES
REPURCHASING
REPURIFIED
REPURIFIES
REPURIFYING
REPURPOSED
REPURPOSES
REPURPOSING
REPURSUING
REPUTABILITIES
REPUTABILITY
REPUTATION
REPUTATIONAL
REPUTATIONLESS
REPUTATIONS
REPUTATIVE
REPUTATIVELY
REPUTELESS
REQUALIFIED
REQUALIFIES
REQUALIFYING
REQUESTERS
REQUESTING
REQUESTORS
REQUICKENED
REQUICKENING
REQUICKENS
REQUIESCAT
REQUIESCATS
REQUIGHTED
REQUIGHTING
REQUIRABLE
REQUIREMENT
REQUIREMENTS
REQUIRINGS
REQUISITELY
REQUISITENESS
REQUISITENESSES
REQUISITES
REQUISITION
REQUISITIONARY
REQUISITIONED
REQUISITIONING
REQUISITIONIST
REQUISITIONISTS
REQUISITIONS
REQUISITOR
REQUISITORIES
REQUISITORS
REQUISITORY
REQUITABLE
REQUITEFUL
REQUITELESS
REQUITEMENT
REQUITEMENTS
REQUITTING
REQUOYLING
RERADIATED
RERADIATES
RERADIATING
RERADIATION
RERADIATIONS
RERAILINGS
REREADINGS
REREBRACES
RERECORDED
RERECORDING
REREDORTER
REREDORTERS
REREDOSSES
REREGISTER
REREGISTERED
REREGISTERING
REREGISTERS
REREGISTRATION
REREGISTRATIONS
REREGULATE
REREGULATED
REREGULATES
REREGULATING
REREGULATION
REREGULATIONS
RERELEASED
RERELEASES
RERELEASING
REREMINDED
REREMINDING
REREPEATED
REREPEATING
REREVIEWED
REREVIEWING
REREVISING
REROUTEING
RESADDLING
RESALEABLE
RESALUTING
RESAMPLING
RESCHEDULE
RESCHEDULED
RESCHEDULES
RESCHEDULING
RESCHEDULINGS
RESCHOOLED
RESCHOOLING
RESCINDABLE
RESCINDERS
RESCINDING
RESCINDMENT
RESCINDMENTS
RESCISSIBLE
RESCISSION
RESCISSIONS
RESCISSORY
RESCREENED
RESCREENING
RESCRIPTED
RESCRIPTING
RESCRIPTION
RESCRIPTIONS
RESCULPTED
RESCULPTING
RESEALABLE
RESEARCHABLE
RESEARCHED
RESEARCHER
RESEARCHERS
RESEARCHES
RESEARCHFUL
RESEARCHING
RESEARCHIST
RESEARCHISTS
RESEASONED
RESEASONING
RESECTABILITIES
RESECTABILITY
RESECTABLE
RESECTIONAL
RESECTIONS
RESECURING
RESEGREGATE
RESEGREGATED
RESEGREGATES
RESEGREGATING
RESEGREGATION
RESEGREGATIONS
RESEIZURES
RESELECTED
RESELECTING
RESELECTION
RESELECTIONS
RESEMBLANCE
RESEMBLANCES
RESEMBLANT
RESEMBLERS
RESEMBLING

RESENSITISE
RESENSITISED
RESENSITISES
RESENSITISING
RESENSITIZE
RESENSITIZED
RESENSITIZES
RESENSITIZING
RESENTENCE
RESENTENCED
RESENTENCES
RESENTENCING
RESENTFULLY
RESENTFULNESS
RESENTFULNESSES
RESENTINGLY
RESENTMENT
RESENTMENTS
RESERPINES
RESERVABLE
RESERVATION
RESERVATIONIST
RESERVATIONISTS
RESERVATIONS
RESERVATORIES
RESERVATORY
RESERVEDLY
RESERVEDNESS
RESERVEDNESSES
RESERVICED
RESERVICES
RESERVICING
RESERVISTS
RESERVOIRED
RESERVOIRING
RESERVOIRS
RESETTABLE
RESETTLEMENT
RESETTLEMENTS
RESETTLING
RESHAPINGS
RESHARPENED
RESHARPENING
RESHARPENS
RESHINGLED
RESHINGLES
RESHINGLING
RESHIPMENT
RESHIPMENTS
RESHIPPERS
RESHIPPING
RESHOOTING
RESHOWERED
RESHOWERING
RESHOWINGS
RESHUFFLED
RESHUFFLES
RESHUFFLING
RESIDENCES
RESIDENCIES
RESIDENTER
RESIDENTERS
RESIDENTIAL
RESIDENTIALLY
RESIDENTIARIES
RESIDENTIARY
RESIDENTSHIP
RESIDENTSHIPS
RESIDUALLY
RESIGHTING
RESIGNATION
RESIGNATIONS
RESIGNEDLY
RESIGNEDNESS
RESIGNEDNESSES
RESIGNMENT
RESIGNMENTS
RESILEMENT
RESILEMENTS
RESILIENCE
RESILIENCES
RESILIENCIES
RESILIENCY
RESILIENTLY
RESILVERED
RESILVERING
RESINATING
RESINIFEROUS
RESINIFICATION
RESINIFICATIONS
RESINIFIED
RESINIFIES
RESINIFYING
RESINISING
RESINIZING
RESINOUSLY
RESINOUSNESS
RESINOUSNESSES
RESIPISCENCE
RESIPISCENCES
RESIPISCENCIES
RESIPISCENCY
RESIPISCENT
RESISTANCE
RESISTANCES
RESISTANTS
RESISTENTS
RESISTIBILITIES
RESISTIBILITY
RESISTIBLE
RESISTIBLY
RESISTINGLY
RESISTIVELY
RESISTIVENESS
RESISTIVENESSES
RESISTIVITIES
RESISTIVITY
RESISTLESS
RESISTLESSLY
RESISTLESSNESS
RESITTINGS
RESITUATED
RESITUATES
RESITUATING
RESKETCHED
RESKETCHES
RESKETCHING
RESKILLING
RESKILLINGS
RESKINNING
RESMELTING
RESMOOTHED
RESMOOTHING
RESNATRONS
RESOCIALISATION
RESOCIALISE
RESOCIALISED
RESOCIALISES
RESOCIALISING
RESOCIALIZATION
RESOCIALIZE
RESOCIALIZED
RESOCIALIZES
RESOCIALIZING
RESOFTENED
RESOFTENING
RESOLDERED
RESOLDERING
RESOLIDIFIED
RESOLIDIFIES
RESOLIDIFY
RESOLIDIFYING
RESOLUBILITIES
RESOLUBILITY
RESOLUBLENESS
RESOLUBLENESSES
RESOLUTELY
RESOLUTENESS
RESOLUTENESSES
RESOLUTEST
RESOLUTION
RESOLUTIONER
RESOLUTIONERS
RESOLUTIONIST
RESOLUTIONISTS
RESOLUTIONS
RESOLUTIVE
RESOLVABILITIES
RESOLVABILITY
RESOLVABLE
RESOLVABLENESS
RESOLVEDLY
RESOLVEDNESS
RESOLVEDNESSES
RESOLVENTS
RESONANCES
RESONANTLY
RESONATING
RESONATION
RESONATIONS
RESONATORS
RESORBENCE
RESORBENCES
RESORCINAL
RESORCINOL
RESORCINOLS
RESORPTION
RESORPTIONS
RESORPTIVE
RESOUNDING
RESOUNDINGLY
RESOURCEFUL
RESOURCEFULLY
RESOURCEFULNESS
RESOURCELESS
RESOURCING
RESOURCINGS
RESPEAKING
RESPECIFIED
RESPECIFIES
RESPECIFYING
RESPECTABILISE
RESPECTABILISED
RESPECTABILISES
RESPECTABILITY
RESPECTABILIZE
RESPECTABILIZED
RESPECTABILIZES
RESPECTABLE
RESPECTABLENESS
RESPECTABLES
RESPECTABLY
RESPECTANT
RESPECTERS
RESPECTFUL
RESPECTFULLY
RESPECTFULNESS
RESPECTING
RESPECTIVE
RESPECTIVELY
RESPECTIVENESS
RESPECTLESS
RESPELLING
RESPELLINGS
RESPIRABILITIES
RESPIRABILITY
RESPIRABLE
RESPIRATION
RESPIRATIONAL
RESPIRATIONS
RESPIRATOR
RESPIRATORS
RESPIRATORY
RESPIRITUALISE
RESPIRITUALISED
RESPIRITUALISES
RESPIRITUALIZE
RESPIRITUALIZED
RESPIRITUALIZES
RESPIROLOGIES

R

RESPIROLOGIST
RESPIROLOGISTS
RESPIROLOGY
RESPIROMETER
RESPIROMETERS
RESPIROMETRIC
RESPIROMETRIES
RESPIROMETRY
RESPITELESS
RESPLENDED
RESPLENDENCE
RESPLENDENCES
RESPLENDENCIES
RESPLENDENCY
RESPLENDENT
RESPLENDENTLY
RESPLENDING
RESPLICING
RESPLITTING
RESPONDENCE
RESPONDENCES
RESPONDENCIES
RESPONDENCY
RESPONDENT
RESPONDENTIA
RESPONDENTIAS
RESPONDENTS
RESPONDERS
RESPONDING
RESPONSELESS
RESPONSERS
RESPONSIBILITY
RESPONSIBLE
RESPONSIBLENESS
RESPONSIBLY
RESPONSIONS
RESPONSIVE
RESPONSIVELY
RESPONSIVENESS
RESPONSORIAL
RESPONSORIALS
RESPONSORIES
RESPONSORS
RESPONSORY
RESPONSUMS
RESPOOLING
RESPOTTING
RESPRAYING
RESPREADING
RESPRINGING
RESPROUTED
RESPROUTING
RESSALDARS
RESSENTIMENT
RESSENTIMENTS
RESTABILISE
RESTABILISED
RESTABILISES
RESTABILISING
RESTABILIZE
RESTABILIZED
RESTABILIZES
RESTABILIZING
RESTABLING
RESTACKING
RESTAFFING
RESTAMPING
RESTARTABLE
RESTARTERS
RESTARTING
RESTATEMENT
RESTATEMENTS
RESTATIONED
RESTATIONING
RESTATIONS
RESTAURANT
RESTAURANTEUR
RESTAURANTEURS
RESTAURANTS
RESTAURATEUR
RESTAURATEURS
RESTAURATION
RESTAURATIONS
RESTEMMING
RESTFULLER
RESTFULLEST
RESTFULNESS
RESTFULNESSES
RESTHARROW
RESTHARROWS
RESTIMULATE
RESTIMULATED
RESTIMULATES
RESTIMULATING
RESTIMULATION
RESTIMULATIONS
RESTITCHED
RESTITCHES
RESTITCHING
RESTITUTED
RESTITUTES
RESTITUTING
RESTITUTION
RESTITUTIONISM
RESTITUTIONISMS
RESTITUTIONIST
RESTITUTIONISTS
RESTITUTIONS
RESTITUTIVE
RESTITUTOR
RESTITUTORS
RESTITUTORY
RESTIVENESS
RESTIVENESSES
RESTLESSLY
RESTLESSNESS
RESTLESSNESSES
RESTOCKING
RESTORABLE
RESTORABLENESS
RESTORATION
RESTORATIONISM
RESTORATIONISMS
RESTORATIONIST
RESTORATIONISTS
RESTORATIONS
RESTORATIVE
RESTORATIVELY
RESTORATIVES
RESTRAINABLE
RESTRAINED
RESTRAINEDLY
RESTRAINEDNESS
RESTRAINER
RESTRAINERS
RESTRAINING
RESTRAININGS
RESTRAINTS
RESTRENGTHEN
RESTRENGTHENED
RESTRENGTHENING
RESTRENGTHENS
RESTRESSED
RESTRESSES
RESTRESSING
RESTRETCHED
RESTRETCHES
RESTRETCHING
RESTRICKEN
RESTRICTED
RESTRICTEDLY
RESTRICTEDNESS
RESTRICTING
RESTRICTION
RESTRICTIONISM
RESTRICTIONISMS
RESTRICTIONIST
RESTRICTIONISTS
RESTRICTIONS
RESTRICTIVE
RESTRICTIVELY
RESTRICTIVENESS
RESTRICTIVES
RESTRIKING
RESTRINGED
RESTRINGEING
RESTRINGENT
RESTRINGENTS
RESTRINGES
RESTRINGING
RESTRIVING
RESTRUCTURE
RESTRUCTURED
RESTRUCTURES
RESTRUCTURING
RESTRUCTURINGS
RESTUDYING
RESTUFFING
RESTUMPING
RESUBJECTED
RESUBJECTING
RESUBJECTS
RESUBMISSION
RESUBMISSIONS
RESUBMITTED
RESUBMITTING
RESULTANTLY
RESULTANTS
RESULTATIVE
RESULTATIVES
RESULTLESS
RESULTLESSNESS
RESUMMONED
RESUMMONING
RESUMPTION
RESUMPTIONS
RESUMPTIVE
RESUMPTIVELY
RESUPINATE
RESUPINATION
RESUPINATIONS
RESUPPLIED
RESUPPLIES
RESUPPLYING
RESURFACED
RESURFACER
RESURFACERS
RESURFACES
RESURFACING
RESURGENCE
RESURGENCES
RESURRECTED
RESURRECTING
RESURRECTION
RESURRECTIONAL
RESURRECTIONARY
RESURRECTIONISE
RESURRECTIONISM
RESURRECTIONIST
RESURRECTIONIZE
RESURRECTIONS
RESURRECTIVE
RESURRECTOR
RESURRECTORS
RESURRECTS
RESURVEYED
RESURVEYING
RESUSCITABLE
RESUSCITANT
RESUSCITANTS
RESUSCITATE
RESUSCITATED
RESUSCITATES
RESUSCITATING
RESUSCITATION
RESUSCITATIONS
RESUSCITATIVE
RESUSCITATOR
RESUSCITATORS
RESUSPENDED

RESUSPENDING
RESUSPENDS
RESVERATROL
RESVERATROLS
RESWALLOWED
RESWALLOWING
RESWALLOWS
RESYNCHRONISE
RESYNCHRONISED
RESYNCHRONISES
RESYNCHRONISING
RESYNCHRONIZE
RESYNCHRONIZED
RESYNCHRONIZES
RESYNCHRONIZING
RESYNTHESES
RESYNTHESIS
RESYNTHESISE
RESYNTHESISED
RESYNTHESISES
RESYNTHESISING
RESYNTHESIZE
RESYNTHESIZED
RESYNTHESIZES
RESYNTHESIZING
RESYSTEMATISE
RESYSTEMATISED
RESYSTEMATISES
RESYSTEMATISING
RESYSTEMATIZE
RESYSTEMATIZED
RESYSTEMATIZES
RESYSTEMATIZING
RETACKLING
RETAILINGS
RETAILMENT
RETAILMENTS
RETAILORED
RETAILORING
RETAINABLE
RETAINERSHIP
RETAINERSHIPS
RETAINMENT
RETAINMENTS
RETALIATED
RETALIATES
RETALIATING
RETALIATION
RETALIATIONIST
RETALIATIONISTS
RETALIATIONS
RETALIATIVE
RETALIATOR
RETALIATORS
RETALIATORY
RETALLYING
RETARDANTS
RETARDATION
RETARDATIONS
RETARDATIVE
RETARDATORY
RETARDMENT
RETARDMENTS
RETARGETED
RETARGETING
RETEACHING
RETELLINGS
RETEMPERED
RETEMPERING
RETENTIONIST
RETENTIONISTS
RETENTIONS
RETENTIVELY
RETENTIVENESS
RETENTIVENESSES
RETENTIVES
RETENTIVITIES
RETENTIVITY
RETESTIFIED
RETESTIFIES
RETESTIFYING
RETEXTURED
RETEXTURES
RETEXTURING
RETHINKERS
RETHINKING
RETHINKINGS
RETHREADED
RETHREADING
RETICELLAS
RETICENCES
RETICENCIES
RETICENTLY
RETICULARLY
RETICULARY
RETICULATE
RETICULATED
RETICULATELY
RETICULATES
RETICULATING
RETICULATION
RETICULATIONS
RETICULOCYTE
RETICULOCYTES
RETICULUMS
RETIGHTENED
RETIGHTENING
RETIGHTENS
RETINACULA
RETINACULAR
RETINACULUM
RETINALITE
RETINALITES
RETINISPORA
RETINISPORAS
RETINITIDES
RETINITISES
RETINOBLASTOMA
RETINOBLASTOMAS
RETINOPATHIES
RETINOPATHY
RETINOSCOPE
RETINOSCOPES
RETINOSCOPIC
RETINOSCOPIES
RETINOSCOPIST
RETINOSCOPISTS
RETINOSCOPY
RETINOSPORA
RETINOSPORAS
RETINOTECTAL
RETIRACIES
RETIREDNESS
RETIREDNESSES
RETIREMENT
RETIREMENTS
RETIRINGLY
RETIRINGNESS
RETIRINGNESSES
RETORSIONS
RETORTIONS
RETOTALING
RETOTALLED
RETOTALLING
RETOUCHABLE
RETOUCHERS
RETOUCHING
RETOUCHINGS
RETRACEABLE
RETRACEMENT
RETRACEMENTS
RETRACKING
RETRACTABILITY
RETRACTABLE
RETRACTATION
RETRACTATIONS
RETRACTIBILITY
RETRACTIBLE
RETRACTILE
RETRACTILITIES
RETRACTILITY
RETRACTING
RETRACTION
RETRACTIONS
RETRACTIVE
RETRACTIVELY
RETRACTORS
RETRAINABLE
RETRAINEES
RETRAINING
RETRAININGS
RETRANSFER
RETRANSFERRED
RETRANSFERRING
RETRANSFERS
RETRANSFORM
RETRANSFORMED
RETRANSFORMING
RETRANSFORMS
RETRANSFUSE
RETRANSFUSED
RETRANSFUSES
RETRANSFUSING
RETRANSLATE
RETRANSLATED
RETRANSLATES
RETRANSLATING
RETRANSLATION
RETRANSLATIONS
RETRANSMISSION
RETRANSMISSIONS
RETRANSMIT
RETRANSMITS
RETRANSMITTED
RETRANSMITTING
RETREADING
RETREATANT
RETREATANTS
RETREATERS
RETREATING
RETRENCHABLE
RETRENCHED
RETRENCHES
RETRENCHING
RETRENCHMENT
RETRENCHMENTS
RETRIBUTED
RETRIBUTES
RETRIBUTING
RETRIBUTION
RETRIBUTIONS
RETRIBUTIVE
RETRIBUTIVELY
RETRIBUTOR
RETRIBUTORS
RETRIBUTORY
RETRIEVABILITY
RETRIEVABLE
RETRIEVABLENESS
RETRIEVABLY
RETRIEVALS
RETRIEVEMENT
RETRIEVEMENTS
RETRIEVERS
RETRIEVING
RETRIEVINGS
RETRIMMING
RETROACTED
RETROACTING
RETROACTION
RETROACTIONS
RETROACTIVE
RETROACTIVELY
RETROACTIVENESS
RETROACTIVITIES
RETROACTIVITY
RETROBULBAR
RETROCEDED
RETROCEDENCE
RETROCEDENCES

R

RETROCEDENT
RETROCEDES
RETROCEDING
RETROCESSION
RETROCESSIONS
RETROCESSIVE
RETROCHOIR
RETROCHOIRS
RETROCOGNITION
RETROCOGNITIONS
RETRODICTED
RETRODICTING
RETRODICTION
RETRODICTIONS
RETRODICTIVE
RETRODICTS
RETROENGINE
RETROENGINES
RETROFIRED
RETROFIRES
RETROFIRING
RETROFITTED
RETROFITTING
RETROFITTINGS
RETROFLECTED
RETROFLECTION
RETROFLECTIONS
RETROFLEXED
RETROFLEXES
RETROFLEXING
RETROFLEXION
RETROFLEXIONS
RETROGRADATION
RETROGRADATIONS
RETROGRADE
RETROGRADED
RETROGRADELY
RETROGRADES
RETROGRADING
RETROGRESS
RETROGRESSED
RETROGRESSES
RETROGRESSING
RETROGRESSION
RETROGRESSIONAL
RETROGRESSIONS
RETROGRESSIVE
RETROGRESSIVELY
RETROJECTED
RETROJECTING
RETROJECTION
RETROJECTIONS
RETROJECTS
RETROLENTAL
RETROMINGENCIES
RETROMINGENCY
RETROMINGENT
RETROMINGENTS
RETROPACKS
RETROPERITONEAL
RETROPHILIA
RETROPHILIAC
RETROPHILIACS
RETROPHILIAS
RETROPULSION
RETROPULSIONS
RETROPULSIVE
RETROREFLECTION
RETROREFLECTIVE
RETROREFLECTOR
RETROREFLECTORS
RETROROCKET
RETROROCKETS
RETRORSELY
RETROSEXUAL
RETROSEXUALS
RETROSPECT
RETROSPECTED
RETROSPECTING
RETROSPECTION
RETROSPECTIONS
RETROSPECTIVE
RETROSPECTIVELY
RETROSPECTIVES
RETROSPECTS
RETROUSSAGE
RETROUSSAGES
RETROVERSE
RETROVERSION
RETROVERSIONS
RETROVERTED
RETROVERTING
RETROVERTS
RETROVIRAL
RETROVIRUS
RETROVIRUSES
RETURNABILITIES
RETURNABILITY
RETURNABLE
RETURNABLES
RETURNLESS
RETWEETING
RETWISTING
REUNIFICATION
REUNIFICATIONS
REUNIFYING
REUNIONISM
REUNIONISMS
REUNIONIST
REUNIONISTIC
REUNIONISTS
REUNITABLE
REUPHOLSTER
REUPHOLSTERED
REUPHOLSTERING
REUPHOLSTERS
REUPTAKING
REUSABILITIES
REUSABILITY
REUTILISATION
REUTILISATIONS
REUTILISED
REUTILISES
REUTILISING
REUTILIZATION
REUTILIZATIONS
REUTILIZED
REUTILIZES
REUTILIZING
REUTTERING
REVACCINATE
REVACCINATED
REVACCINATES
REVACCINATING
REVACCINATION
REVACCINATIONS
REVALENTAS
REVALIDATE
REVALIDATED
REVALIDATES
REVALIDATING
REVALIDATION
REVALIDATIONS
REVALORISATION
REVALORISATIONS
REVALORISE
REVALORISED
REVALORISES
REVALORISING
REVALORIZATION
REVALORIZATIONS
REVALORIZE
REVALORIZED
REVALORIZES
REVALORIZING
REVALUATED
REVALUATES
REVALUATING
REVALUATION
REVALUATIONS
REVAMPINGS
REVANCHISM
REVANCHISMS
REVANCHIST
REVANCHISTS
REVARNISHED
REVARNISHES
REVARNISHING
REVEALABILITIES
REVEALABILITY
REVEALABLE
REVEALINGLY
REVEALINGNESS
REVEALINGNESSES
REVEALINGS
REVEALMENT
REVEALMENTS
REVEGETATE
REVEGETATED
REVEGETATES
REVEGETATING
REVEGETATION
REVEGETATIONS
REVELATION
REVELATIONAL
REVELATIONIST
REVELATIONISTS
REVELATIONS
REVELATIVE
REVELATORS
REVELATORY
REVELLINGS
REVELMENTS
REVENDICATE
REVENDICATED
REVENDICATES
REVENDICATING
REVENDICATION
REVENDICATIONS
REVENGEFUL
REVENGEFULLY
REVENGEFULNESS
REVENGELESS
REVENGEMENT
REVENGEMENTS
REVENGINGLY
REVENGINGS
REVERBATORIES
REVERBATORY
REVERBERANT
REVERBERANTLY
REVERBERATE
REVERBERATED
REVERBERATES
REVERBERATING
REVERBERATION
REVERBERATIONS
REVERBERATIVE
REVERBERATOR
REVERBERATORIES
REVERBERATORS
REVERBERATORY
REVERENCED
REVERENCER
REVERENCERS
REVERENCES
REVERENCING
REVERENTIAL
REVERENTIALLY
REVERENTLY
REVERENTNESS
REVERENTNESSES
REVERIFIED
REVERIFIES
REVERIFYING
REVERSEDLY
REVERSELESS
REVERSIBILITIES
REVERSIBILITY
REVERSIBLE

REVERSIBLES
REVERSIBLY
REVERSINGS
REVERSIONAL
REVERSIONALLY
REVERSIONARIES
REVERSIONARY
REVERSIONER
REVERSIONERS
REVERSIONS
REVERSISES
REVERTANTS
REVERTIBLE
REVESTIARIES
REVESTIARY
REVESTRIES
REVETMENTS
REVIBRATED
REVIBRATES
REVIBRATING
REVICTUALED
REVICTUALING
REVICTUALLED
REVICTUALLING
REVICTUALS
REVIEWABLE
REVILEMENT
REVILEMENTS
REVILINGLY
REVINDICATE
REVINDICATED
REVINDICATES
REVINDICATING
REVINDICATION
REVINDICATIONS
REVIOLATED
REVIOLATES
REVIOLATING
REVISIONAL
REVISIONARY
REVISIONISM
REVISIONISMS
REVISIONIST
REVISIONISTS
REVISITANT
REVISITANTS
REVISITATION
REVISITATIONS
REVISITING
REVISUALISATION
REVISUALIZATION
REVITALISATION
REVITALISATIONS
REVITALISE
REVITALISED
REVITALISES
REVITALISING
REVITALIZATION
REVITALIZATIONS
REVITALIZE
REVITALIZED
REVITALIZES
REVITALIZING
REVIVABILITIES
REVIVABILITY
REVIVALISM
REVIVALISMS
REVIVALIST
REVIVALISTIC
REVIVALISTS
REVIVEMENT
REVIVEMENTS
REVIVESCENCE
REVIVESCENCES
REVIVESCENCIES
REVIVESCENCY
REVIVESCENT
REVIVIFICATION
REVIVIFICATIONS
REVIVIFIED
REVIVIFIES
REVIVIFYING
REVIVINGLY
REVIVISCENCE
REVIVISCENCES
REVIVISCENCIES
REVIVISCENCY
REVIVISCENT
REVOCABILITIES
REVOCABILITY
REVOCABLENESS
REVOCABLENESSES
REVOCATION
REVOCATIONS
REVOCATORY
REVOKABILITIES
REVOKABILITY
REVOKEMENT
REVOKEMENTS
REVOLTINGLY
REVOLUTION
REVOLUTIONAL
REVOLUTIONARIES
REVOLUTIONARILY
REVOLUTIONARY
REVOLUTIONER
REVOLUTIONERS
REVOLUTIONISE
REVOLUTIONISED
REVOLUTIONISER
REVOLUTIONISERS
REVOLUTIONISES
REVOLUTIONISING
REVOLUTIONISM
REVOLUTIONISMS
REVOLUTIONIST
REVOLUTIONISTS
REVOLUTIONIZE
REVOLUTIONIZED
REVOLUTIONIZER
REVOLUTIONIZERS
REVOLUTIONIZES
REVOLUTIONIZING
REVOLUTIONS
REVOLVABLE
REVOLVABLY
REVOLVENCIES
REVOLVENCY
REVOLVINGLY
REVOLVINGS
REVULSIONARY
REVULSIONS
REVULSIVELY
REVULSIVES
REWAKENING
REWARDABLE
REWARDABLENESS
REWARDINGLY
REWARDLESS
REWATERING
REWEIGHING
REWIDENING
REWILDINGS
REWINDINGS
REWORDINGS
REWORKINGS
REWRAPPING
REWRITABLE
REWRITEABLE
RHABDOCOELE
RHABDOCOELES
RHABDOLITH
RHABDOLITHS
RHABDOMANCER
RHABDOMANCERS
RHABDOMANCIES
RHABDOMANCY
RHABDOMANTIST
RHABDOMANTISTS
RHABDOMERE
RHABDOMERES
RHABDOMYOMA
RHABDOMYOMAS
RHABDOMYOMATA
RHABDOSPHERE
RHABDOSPHERES
RHABDOVIRUS
RHABDOVIRUSES
RHACHIDIAL
RHACHILLAS
RHACHITISES
RHADAMANTHINE
RHAGADIFORM
RHAMNACEOUS
RHAMPHOTHECA
RHAMPHOTHECAE
RHAPONTICS
RHAPSODICAL
RHAPSODICALLY
RHAPSODIES
RHAPSODISE
RHAPSODISED
RHAPSODISES
RHAPSODISING
RHAPSODIST
RHAPSODISTIC
RHAPSODISTS
RHAPSODIZE
RHAPSODIZED
RHAPSODIZES
RHAPSODIZING
RHEOCHORDS
RHEOLOGICAL
RHEOLOGICALLY
RHEOLOGIES
RHEOLOGIST
RHEOLOGISTS
RHEOMETERS
RHEOMETRIC
RHEOMETRICAL
RHEOMETRIES
RHEOMORPHIC
RHEOMORPHISM
RHEOMORPHISMS
RHEOPHILES
RHEORECEPTOR
RHEORECEPTORS
RHEOSCOPES
RHEOSTATIC
RHEOTACTIC
RHEOTROPES
RHEOTROPIC
RHEOTROPISM
RHEOTROPISMS
RHETORICAL
RHETORICALLY
RHETORICIAN
RHETORICIANS
RHETORISED
RHETORISES
RHETORISING
RHETORIZED
RHETORIZES
RHETORIZING
RHEUMATEESE
RHEUMATEESES
RHEUMATICAL
RHEUMATICALLY
RHEUMATICKY
RHEUMATICS
RHEUMATISE
RHEUMATISES
RHEUMATISM
RHEUMATISMAL
RHEUMATISMS
RHEUMATIZE
RHEUMATIZES
RHEUMATOID
RHEUMATOIDALLY
RHEUMATOLOGICAL

RHEUMATOLOGIES
RHEUMATOLOGIST
RHEUMATOLOGISTS
RHEUMATOLOGY
RHIGOLENES
RHINENCEPHALA
RHINENCEPHALIC
RHINENCEPHALON
RHINENCEPHALONS
RHINESTONE
RHINESTONED
RHINESTONES
RHINITIDES
RHINITISES
RHINOCERICAL
RHINOCEROI
RHINOCEROS
RHINOCEROSES
RHINOCEROT
RHINOCEROTE
RHINOCEROTES
RHINOCEROTIC
RHINOLALIA
RHINOLALIAS
RHINOLITHS
RHINOLOGICAL
RHINOLOGIES
RHINOLOGIST
RHINOLOGISTS
RHINOPHONIA
RHINOPHONIAS
RHINOPHYMA
RHINOPHYMAS
RHINOPLASTIC
RHINOPLASTIES
RHINOPLASTY
RHINORRHAGIA
RHINORRHAGIAS
RHINORRHOEA
RHINORRHOEAL
RHINORRHOEAS
RHINOSCLEROMA
RHINOSCLEROMAS
RHINOSCLEROMATA
RHINOSCOPE
RHINOSCOPES
RHINOSCOPIC
RHINOSCOPIES
RHINOSCOPY
RHINOTHECA
RHINOTHECAE
RHINOVIRUS
RHINOVIRUSES
RHIPIDIONS
RHIPIDIUMS
RHIZANTHOUS
RHIZOCARPIC
RHIZOCARPOUS
RHIZOCARPS
RHIZOCAULS
RHIZOCEPHALAN
RHIZOCEPHALANS
RHIZOCEPHALOUS
RHIZOCTONIA
RHIZOCTONIAS
RHIZOGENETIC
RHIZOGENIC
RHIZOGENOUS
RHIZOMATOUS
RHIZOMORPH
RHIZOMORPHOUS
RHIZOMORPHS
RHIZOPHAGOUS
RHIZOPHILOUS
RHIZOPHORE
RHIZOPHORES
RHIZOPLANE
RHIZOPLANES
RHIZOPODAN
RHIZOPODANS
RHIZOPODOUS
RHIZOPUSES
RHIZOSPHERE
RHIZOSPHERES
RHIZOTOMIES
RHODAMINES
RHODANATES
RHODANISED
RHODANISES
RHODANISING
RHODANIZED
RHODANIZES
RHODANIZING
RHODOCHROSITE
RHODOCHROSITES
RHODODAPHNE
RHODODAPHNES
RHODODENDRA
RHODODENDRON
RHODODENDRONS
RHODOLITES
RHODOMONTADE
RHODOMONTADED
RHODOMONTADES
RHODOMONTADING
RHODONITES
RHODOPHANE
RHODOPHANES
RHODOPSINS
RHOEADINES
RHOICISSUS
RHOICISSUSES
RHOMBENCEPHALA
RHOMBENCEPHALON
RHOMBENPORPHYR
RHOMBENPORPHYRS
RHOMBENPORPHYRY
RHOMBOHEDRA
RHOMBOHEDRAL
RHOMBOHEDRON
RHOMBOHEDRONS
RHOMBOIDAL
RHOMBOIDEI
RHOMBOIDES
RHOMBOIDEUS
RHOMBPORPHYRIES
RHOMBPORPHYRY
RHOPALISMS
RHOPALOCERAL
RHOPALOCEROUS
RHOTACISED
RHOTACISES
RHOTACISING
RHOTACISMS
RHOTACISTIC
RHOTACISTS
RHOTACIZED
RHOTACIZES
RHOTACIZING
RHOTICITIES
RHUBARBIER
RHUBARBIEST
RHUBARBING
RHUBARBINGS
RHUMBATRON
RHUMBATRONS
RHYMESTERS
RHYNCHOCOEL
RHYNCHOCOELS
RHYNCHODONT
RHYNCHOPHORE
RHYNCHOPHORES
RHYNCHOPHOROUS
RHYPAROGRAPHER
RHYPAROGRAPHERS
RHYPAROGRAPHIC
RHYPAROGRAPHIES
RHYPAROGRAPHY
RHYTHMICAL
RHYTHMICALLY
RHYTHMICITIES
RHYTHMICITY
RHYTHMISATION
RHYTHMISATIONS
RHYTHMISED
RHYTHMISES
RHYTHMISING
RHYTHMISTS
RHYTHMIZATION
RHYTHMIZATIONS
RHYTHMIZED
RHYTHMIZES
RHYTHMIZING
RHYTHMLESS
RHYTHMOMETER
RHYTHMOMETERS
RHYTHMOPOEIA
RHYTHMOPOEIAS
RHYTHMUSES
RHYTIDECTOMIES
RHYTIDECTOMY
RHYTIDOMES
RIBALDRIES
RIBATTUTAS
RIBAUDRIES
RIBAVIRINS
RIBBONFISH
RIBBONFISHES
RIBBONIEST
RIBBONLIKE
RIBBONRIES
RIBBONWOOD
RIBBONWOODS
RIBGRASSES
RIBOFLAVIN
RIBOFLAVINE
RIBOFLAVINES
RIBOFLAVINS
RIBONUCLEASE
RIBONUCLEASES
RIBONUCLEIC
RIBONUCLEOSIDE
RIBONUCLEOSIDES
RIBONUCLEOTIDE
RIBONUCLEOTIDES
RICEFIELDS
RICEGRASSES
RICERCARES
RICERCATAS
RICHNESSES
RICINOLEIC
RICKBURNER
RICKBURNERS
RICKETIEST
RICKETINESS
RICKETINESSES
RICKETTIER
RICKETTIEST
RICKETTSIA
RICKETTSIAE
RICKETTSIAL
RICKETTSIAS
RICKSTANDS
RICKSTICKS
RICOCHETED
RICOCHETING
RICOCHETTED
RICOCHETTING
RIDABILITIES
RIDABILITY
RIDDLINGLY
RIDERSHIPS
RIDESHARING
RIDESHARINGS
RIDGEBACKS
RIDGELINES
RIDGELINGS
RIDGEPOLES
RIDGETREES
RIDICULERS

RIDICULING
RIDICULOUS
RIDICULOUSLY
RIDICULOUSNESS
RIEBECKITE
RIEBECKITES
RIFACIMENTI
RIFACIMENTO
RIFACIMENTOS
RIFAMPICIN
RIFAMPICINS
RIFAMYCINS
RIFENESSES
RIFLEBIRDS
RIGAMAROLE
RIGAMAROLES
RIGHTABLENESS
RIGHTABLENESSES
RIGHTENING
RIGHTEOUSLY
RIGHTEOUSNESS
RIGHTEOUSNESSES
RIGHTFULLY
RIGHTFULNESS
RIGHTFULNESSES
RIGHTNESSES
RIGHTSIZED
RIGHTSIZES
RIGHTSIZING
RIGHTSIZINGS
RIGHTWARDLY
RIGHTWARDS
RIGIDIFICATION
RIGIDIFICATIONS
RIGIDIFIED
RIGIDIFIES
RIGIDIFYING
RIGIDISING
RIGIDITIES
RIGIDIZING
RIGIDNESSES
RIGMAROLES
RIGORISTIC
RIGOROUSLY
RIGOROUSNESS
RIGOROUSNESSES
RIGSDALERS
RIGWIDDIES
RIGWOODIES
RIJKSDAALER
RIJKSDAALERS
RIJSTAFELS
RIJSTTAFEL
RIJSTTAFELS
RIMINESSES
RIMOSITIES
RINDERPEST
RINDERPESTS
RINFORZANDO
RINGBARKED
RINGBARKING
RINGHALSES
RINGLEADER
RINGLEADERS
RINGLETIER
RINGLETIEST
RINGMASTER
RINGMASTERS
RINGSIDERS
RINGSTANDS
RINGSTRAKED
RINGTOSSES
RINKHALSES
RINSABILITIES
RINSABILITY
RINSIBILITIES
RINSIBILITY
RINTHEREOUT
RINTHEREOUTS
RIOTOUSNESS
RIOTOUSNESSES
RIPENESSES
RIPIDOLITE
RIPIDOLITES
RIPIENISTS
RIPPLINGLY
RIPRAPPING
RIPSNORTER
RIPSNORTERS
RIPSNORTING
RIPSNORTINGLY
RISIBILITIES
RISIBILITY
RISKINESSES
RISORGIMENTO
RISORGIMENTOS
RISTRETTOS
RITARDANDI
RITARDANDO
RITARDANDOS
RITONAVIRS
RITORNELLE
RITORNELLES
RITORNELLI
RITORNELLO
RITORNELLOS
RITORNELLS
RITOURNELLE
RITOURNELLES
RITUALISATION
RITUALISATIONS
RITUALISED
RITUALISES
RITUALISING
RITUALISMS
RITUALISTIC
RITUALISTICALLY
RITUALISTS
RITUALIZATION
RITUALIZATIONS
RITUALIZED
RITUALIZES
RITUALIZING
RITUXIMABS
RITZINESSES
RIVALESSES
RIVALISING
RIVALITIES
RIVALIZING
RIVALSHIPS
RIVERBANKS
RIVERBOATS
RIVERCRAFT
RIVERCRAFTS
RIVERFRONT
RIVERFRONTS
RIVERHEADS
RIVERSCAPE
RIVERSCAPES
RIVERSIDES
RIVERWALKS
RIVERWARDS
RIVERWEEDS
RIVERWORTHIER
RIVERWORTHIEST
RIVERWORTHINESS
RIVERWORTHY
RIVETINGLY
ROADABILITIES
ROADABILITY
ROADBLOCKED
ROADBLOCKING
ROADBLOCKS
ROADCRAFTS
ROADHEADER
ROADHEADERS
ROADHOLDING
ROADHOLDINGS
ROADHOUSES
ROADMAKING
ROADMAKINGS
ROADMENDER
ROADMENDERS
ROADROLLER
ROADROLLERS
ROADRUNNER
ROADRUNNERS
ROADSTEADS
ROADWORTHIER
ROADWORTHIES
ROADWORTHIEST
ROADWORTHINESS
ROADWORTHY
ROBERDSMAN
ROBERDSMEN
ROBERTSMAN
ROBERTSMEN
ROBORATING
ROBOTICALLY
ROBOTISATION
ROBOTISATIONS
ROBOTISING
ROBOTIZATION
ROBOTIZATIONS
ROBOTIZING
ROBUSTIOUS
ROBUSTIOUSLY
ROBUSTIOUSNESS
ROBUSTNESS
ROBUSTNESSES
ROCAMBOLES
ROCKABILLIES
ROCKABILLY
ROCKBURSTS
ROCKCRESSES
ROCKETEERS
ROCKETRIES
ROCKETSONDE
ROCKETSONDES
ROCKFISHES
ROCKHOPPER
ROCKHOPPERS
ROCKHOUNDING
ROCKHOUNDINGS
ROCKHOUNDS
ROCKINESSES
ROCKSHAFTS
ROCKSLIDES
ROCKSTEADIES
ROCKSTEADY
ROCKWATERS
RODENTICIDE
RODENTICIDES
RODFISHERS
RODFISHING
RODFISHINGS
RODGERSIAS
RODOMONTADE
RODOMONTADED
RODOMONTADER
RODOMONTADERS
RODOMONTADES
RODOMONTADING
ROENTGENISATION
ROENTGENISE
ROENTGENISED
ROENTGENISES
ROENTGENISING
ROENTGENIUM
ROENTGENIUMS
ROENTGENIZATION
ROENTGENIZE
ROENTGENIZED
ROENTGENIZES
ROENTGENIZING
ROENTGENOGRAM
ROENTGENOGRAMS
ROENTGENOGRAPH
ROENTGENOGRAPHS
ROENTGENOGRAPHY

ROENTGENOLOGIC
ROENTGENOLOGIES
ROENTGENOLOGIST
ROENTGENOLOGY
ROENTGENOPAQUE
ROENTGENOSCOPE
ROENTGENOSCOPES
ROENTGENOSCOPIC
ROENTGENOSCOPY
ROGUESHIPS
ROGUISHNESS
ROGUISHNESSES
ROISTERERS
ROISTERING
ROISTERINGS
ROISTEROUS
ROISTEROUSLY
ROLLCOLLAR
ROLLCOLLARS
ROLLERBALL
ROLLERBALLS
ROLLERBLADE
ROLLERBLADED
ROLLERBLADER
ROLLERBLADERS
ROLLERBLADES
ROLLERBLADING
ROLLERBLADINGS
ROLLERCOASTER
ROLLERCOASTERED
ROLLERCOASTERS
ROLLERDROME
ROLLERDROMES
ROLLICKIER
ROLLICKIEST
ROLLICKING
ROLLICKINGS
ROLLOCKING
ROLLOCKINGS
ROMANCICAL
ROMANCINGS
ROMANESCOS
ROMANICITE
ROMANICITES
ROMANISATION
ROMANISATIONS
ROMANISING
ROMANIZATION
ROMANIZATIONS
ROMANIZING
ROMANTICAL
ROMANTICALITIES
ROMANTICALITY
ROMANTICALLY
ROMANTICISATION
ROMANTICISE
ROMANTICISED
ROMANTICISES
ROMANTICISING
ROMANTICISM
ROMANTICISMS
ROMANTICIST
ROMANTICISTS
ROMANTICIZATION
ROMANTICIZE
ROMANTICIZED
ROMANTICIZES
ROMANTICIZING
ROMELDALES
ROMPISHNESS
ROMPISHNESSES
RONDOLETTO
RONDOLETTOS
RONTGENISATION
RONTGENISATIONS
RONTGENISE
RONTGENISED
RONTGENISES
RONTGENISING
RONTGENIZATION
RONTGENIZATIONS
RONTGENIZE
RONTGENIZED
RONTGENIZES
RONTGENIZING
RONTGENOGRAM
RONTGENOGRAMS
RONTGENOGRAPH
RONTGENOGRAPHS
RONTGENOGRAPHY
RONTGENOLOGICAL
RONTGENOLOGIES
RONTGENOLOGIST
RONTGENOLOGISTS
RONTGENOLOGY
RONTGENOPAQUE
RONTGENOSCOPE
RONTGENOSCOPES
RONTGENOSCOPIC
RONTGENOSCOPIES
RONTGENOSCOPY
RONTGENOTHERAPY
ROOFLESSNESS
ROOFLESSNESSES
ROOFSCAPES
ROOMINESSES
ROOTEDNESS
ROOTEDNESSES
ROOTINESSES
ROOTLESSNESS
ROOTLESSNESSES
ROOTSERVER
ROOTSERVERS
ROOTSINESS
ROOTSINESSES
ROOTSTALKS
ROOTSTOCKS
ROPEDANCER
ROPEDANCERS
ROPEDANCING
ROPEDANCINGS
ROPEWALKER
ROPEWALKERS
ROPINESSES
ROQUEFORTS
ROQUELAURE
ROQUELAURES
ROSANILINE
ROSANILINES
ROSANILINS
ROSEBUSHES
ROSEFINCHES
ROSEFISHES
ROSEMALING
ROSEMALINGS
ROSEMARIES
ROSETTINGS
ROSEWATERS
ROSINESSES
ROSINWEEDS
ROSMARINES
ROSTELLATE
ROSTELLUMS
ROSTERINGS
ROSTROCARINATE
ROSTROCARINATES
ROTACHUTES
ROTAMETERS
ROTAPLANES
ROTATIONAL
ROTATIVELY
ROTAVATING
ROTAVATORS
ROTAVIRUSES
ROTGRASSES
ROTIFERANS
ROTIFEROUS
ROTISSERIE
ROTISSERIED
ROTISSERIEING
ROTISSERIES
ROTOGRAPHED
ROTOGRAPHING
ROTOGRAPHS
ROTOGRAVURE
ROTOGRAVURES
ROTORCRAFT
ROTORCRAFTS
ROTOSCOPED
ROTOSCOPES
ROTOSCOPING
ROTOTILLED
ROTOTILLER
ROTOTILLERS
ROTOTILLING
ROTOVATING
ROTOVATORS
ROTTENNESS
ROTTENNESSES
ROTTENSTONE
ROTTENSTONED
ROTTENSTONES
ROTTENSTONING
ROTTWEILER
ROTTWEILERS
ROTUNDITIES
ROTUNDNESS
ROTUNDNESSES
ROUGHBACKS
ROUGHCASTED
ROUGHCASTER
ROUGHCASTERS
ROUGHCASTING
ROUGHCASTS
ROUGHDRIED
ROUGHDRIES
ROUGHDRYING
ROUGHENING
ROUGHHEWED
ROUGHHEWING
ROUGHHOUSE
ROUGHHOUSED
ROUGHHOUSES
ROUGHHOUSING
ROUGHHOUSINGS
ROUGHNECKED
ROUGHNECKING
ROUGHNECKS
ROUGHNESSES
ROUGHRIDER
ROUGHRIDERS
ROULETTING
ROUNCEVALS
ROUNDABOUT
ROUNDABOUTATION
ROUNDABOUTED
ROUNDABOUTEDLY
ROUNDABOUTILITY
ROUNDABOUTING
ROUNDABOUTLY
ROUNDABOUTNESS
ROUNDABOUTS
ROUNDARCHED
ROUNDBALLS
ROUNDEDNESS
ROUNDEDNESSES
ROUNDELAYS
ROUNDHANDS
ROUNDHEADED
ROUNDHEADEDNESS
ROUNDHEELS
ROUNDHOUSE
ROUNDHOUSES
ROUNDNESSES
ROUNDTABLE
ROUNDTABLES
ROUNDTRIPPING
ROUNDTRIPPINGS
ROUNDTRIPS
ROUNDWOODS

ROUNDWORMS
ROUSEABOUT
ROUSEABOUTS
ROUSEDNESS
ROUSEDNESSES
ROUSEMENTS
ROUSSETTES
ROUSTABOUT
ROUSTABOUTS
ROUTEMARCH
ROUTEMARCHED
ROUTEMARCHES
ROUTEMARCHING
ROUTINEERS
ROUTINISATION
ROUTINISATIONS
ROUTINISED
ROUTINISES
ROUTINISING
ROUTINISMS
ROUTINISTS
ROUTINIZATION
ROUTINIZATIONS
ROUTINIZED
ROUTINIZES
ROUTINIZING
ROWANBERRIES
ROWANBERRY
ROWDINESSES
ROWDYDOWED
ROWDYDOWING
ROYALISING
ROYALISTIC
ROYALIZING
ROYALMASTS
ROYSTERERS
ROYSTERING
ROYSTEROUS
RUBBERIEST
RUBBERISED
RUBBERISES
RUBBERISING
RUBBERIZED
RUBBERIZES
RUBBERIZING
RUBBERLIKE
RUBBERNECK
RUBBERNECKED
RUBBERNECKER
RUBBERNECKERS
RUBBERNECKING
RUBBERNECKS
RUBBERWEAR
RUBBERWEARS
RUBBISHIER
RUBBISHIEST
RUBBISHING
RUBBISHLIER
RUBBISHLIEST
RUBBLEWORK
RUBBLEWORKS
RUBEFACIENT
RUBEFACIENTS
RUBEFACTION
RUBEFACTIONS
RUBELLITES
RUBESCENCE
RUBESCENCES
RUBIACEOUS
RUBICELLES
RUBICONING
RUBICUNDITIES
RUBICUNDITY
RUBIGINOSE
RUBIGINOUS
RUBRICALLY
RUBRICATED
RUBRICATES
RUBRICATING
RUBRICATION
RUBRICATIONS
RUBRICATOR
RUBRICATORS
RUBRICIANS
RUBYTHROAT
RUBYTHROATS
RUCTATIONS
RUDBECKIAS
RUDDERHEAD
RUDDERHEADS
RUDDERLESS
RUDDERPOST
RUDDERPOSTS
RUDDERSTOCK
RUDDERSTOCKS
RUDDINESSES
RUDENESSES
RUDIMENTAL
RUDIMENTALLY
RUDIMENTARILY
RUDIMENTARINESS
RUDIMENTARY
RUEFULNESS
RUEFULNESSES
RUFESCENCE
RUFESCENCES
RUFFIANING
RUFFIANISH
RUFFIANISM
RUFFIANISMS
RUGGEDISATION
RUGGEDISATIONS
RUGGEDISED
RUGGEDISES
RUGGEDISING
RUGGEDIZATION
RUGGEDIZATIONS
RUGGEDIZED
RUGGEDIZES
RUGGEDIZING
RUGGEDNESS
RUGGEDNESSES
RUGOSITIES
RUINATIONS
RUINOUSNESS
RUINOUSNESSES
RULERSHIPS
RUMBLEDETHUMP
RUMBLEDETHUMPS
RUMBLEGUMPTION
RUMBLEGUMPTIONS
RUMBLINGLY
RUMBULLION
RUMBULLIONS
RUMBUNCTIOUS
RUMBUSTICAL
RUMBUSTIOUS
RUMBUSTIOUSLY
RUMBUSTIOUSNESS
RUMELGUMPTION
RUMELGUMPTIONS
RUMFUSTIAN
RUMFUSTIANS
RUMGUMPTION
RUMGUMPTIONS
RUMINANTLY
RUMINATING
RUMINATINGLY
RUMINATION
RUMINATIONS
RUMINATIVE
RUMINATIVELY
RUMINATORS
RUMLEGUMPTION
RUMLEGUMPTIONS
RUMMELGUMPTION
RUMMELGUMPTIONS
RUMMINESSES
RUMMISHING
RUMMLEGUMPTION
RUMMLEGUMPTIONS
RUMORMONGER
RUMORMONGERING
RUMORMONGERINGS
RUMORMONGERS
RUMRUNNERS
RUNAROUNDS
RUNECRAFTS
RUNNINESSES
RUNTINESSES
RUPESTRIAN
RUPICOLINE
RUPICOLOUS
RUPTURABLE
RUPTUREWORT
RUPTUREWORTS
RURALISATION
RURALISATIONS
RURALISING
RURALITIES
RURALIZATION
RURALIZATIONS
RURALIZING
RURALNESSES
RURIDECANAL
RUSHINESSES
RUSHLIGHTS
RUSSETIEST
RUSSETINGS
RUSSETTING
RUSSETTINGS
RUSSIFYING
RUSTBUCKET
RUSTBUCKETS
RUSTICALLY
RUSTICATED
RUSTICATES
RUSTICATING
RUSTICATINGS
RUSTICATION
RUSTICATIONS
RUSTICATOR
RUSTICATORS
RUSTICISED
RUSTICISES
RUSTICISING
RUSTICISMS
RUSTICITIES
RUSTICIZED
RUSTICIZES
RUSTICIZING
RUSTICWORK
RUSTICWORKS
RUSTINESSES
RUSTLINGLY
RUSTPROOFED
RUSTPROOFING
RUSTPROOFINGS
RUSTPROOFS
RUTHENIOUS
RUTHENIUMS
RUTHERFORD
RUTHERFORDIUM
RUTHERFORDIUMS
RUTHERFORDS
RUTHFULNESS
RUTHFULNESSES
RUTHLESSLY
RUTHLESSNESS
RUTHLESSNESSES
RUTTINESSES
RUTTISHNESS
RUTTISHNESSES
RYBAUDRYES
RYEGRASSES

S

SABADILLAS
SABBATARIAN
SABBATICAL
SABBATICALS
SABBATISED
SABBATISES
SABBATISING
SABBATISMS
SABBATIZED
SABBATIZES
SABBATIZING
SABERMETRICIAN
SABERMETRICIANS
SABERMETRICS
SABLEFISHES
SABOTAGING
SABRETACHE
SABRETACHES
SABREWINGS
SABULOSITIES
SABULOSITY
SABURRATION
SABURRATIONS
SACAHUISTA
SACAHUISTAS
SACAHUISTE
SACAHUISTES
SACCADICALLY
SACCHARASE
SACCHARASES
SACCHARATE
SACCHARATED
SACCHARATES
SACCHARIDE
SACCHARIDES
SACCHARIFEROUS
SACCHARIFIED
SACCHARIFIES
SACCHARIFY
SACCHARIFYING
SACCHARIMETER
SACCHARIMETERS
SACCHARIMETRIES
SACCHARIMETRY
SACCHARINE
SACCHARINELY
SACCHARINES
SACCHARINITIES
SACCHARINITY
SACCHARINS
SACCHARISATION
SACCHARISATIONS
SACCHARISE
SACCHARISED
SACCHARISES
SACCHARISING
SACCHARIZATION
SACCHARIZATIONS
SACCHARIZE
SACCHARIZED
SACCHARIZES
SACCHARIZING
SACCHAROID
SACCHAROIDAL
SACCHAROIDS
SACCHAROMETER
SACCHAROMETERS
SACCHAROMETRIES
SACCHAROMETRY
SACCHAROMYCES
SACCHAROMYCETES
SACCHAROSE
SACCHAROSES
SACCHARUMS
SACCULATED
SACCULATION
SACCULATIONS
SACCULIFORM
SACERDOTAL
SACERDOTALISE
SACERDOTALISED
SACERDOTALISES
SACERDOTALISING
SACERDOTALISM
SACERDOTALISMS
SACERDOTALIST
SACERDOTALISTS
SACERDOTALIZE
SACERDOTALIZED
SACERDOTALIZES
SACERDOTALIZING
SACERDOTALLY
SACHEMDOMS
SACHEMSHIP
SACHEMSHIPS
SACKCLOTHS
SACRALGIAS
SACRALISATION
SACRALISATIONS
SACRALISED
SACRALISES
SACRALISING
SACRALITIES
SACRALIZATION
SACRALIZATIONS
SACRALIZED
SACRALIZES
SACRALIZING
SACRAMENTAL
SACRAMENTALISM
SACRAMENTALISMS
SACRAMENTALIST
SACRAMENTALISTS
SACRAMENTALITY
SACRAMENTALLY
SACRAMENTALNESS
SACRAMENTALS
SACRAMENTARIAN
SACRAMENTARIANS
SACRAMENTARIES
SACRAMENTARY
SACRAMENTED
SACRAMENTING
SACRAMENTS
SACRARIUMS
SACREDNESS
SACREDNESSES
SACRIFICEABLE
SACRIFICED
SACRIFICER
SACRIFICERS
SACRIFICES
SACRIFICIAL
SACRIFICIALLY
SACRIFICING
SACRIFYING
SACRILEGES
SACRILEGIOUS
SACRILEGIOUSLY
SACRILEGIST
SACRILEGISTS
SACRISTANS
SACRISTIES
SACROCOCCYGEAL
SACROCOSTAL
SACROCOSTALS
SACROILIAC
SACROILIACS
SACROILIITIS
SACROILIITISES
SACROSANCT
SACROSANCTITIES
SACROSANCTITY
SACROSANCTNESS
SADDLEBACK
SADDLEBACKED
SADDLEBACKS
SADDLEBAGS
SADDLEBILL
SADDLEBILLS
SADDLEBOWS
SADDLEBRED
SADDLEBREDS
SADDLECLOTH
SADDLECLOTHS
SADDLELESS
SADDLERIES
SADDLEROOM
SADDLEROOMS
SADDLETREE
SADDLETREES
SADISTICALLY
SADOMASOCHISM
SADOMASOCHISMS
SADOMASOCHIST
SADOMASOCHISTIC
SADOMASOCHISTS
SAFECRACKER
SAFECRACKERS
SAFECRACKING
SAFECRACKINGS
SAFEGUARDED
SAFEGUARDING
SAFEGUARDS
SAFEKEEPING
SAFEKEEPINGS
SAFELIGHTS
SAFENESSES
SAFFLOWERS
SAFFRONIER
SAFFRONIEST
SAFRANINES
SAGACIOUSLY
SAGACIOUSNESS
SAGACIOUSNESSES
SAGACITIES
SAGANASHES
SAGAPENUMS
SAGEBRUSHES
SAGENESSES
SAGINATING
SAGINATION
SAGINATIONS
SAGITTALLY
SAGITTARIES
SAGITTIFORM
SAILBOARDED
SAILBOARDER
SAILBOARDERS
SAILBOARDING

SAILBOARDINGS
SAILBOARDS
SAILBOATER
SAILBOATERS
SAILBOATING
SAILBOATINGS
SAILCLOTHS
SAILFISHES
SAILMAKERS
SAILMAKING
SAILMAKINGS
SAILORINGS
SAILORLESS
SAILORLIER
SAILORLIEST
SAILORLIKE
SAILPLANED
SAILPLANER
SAILPLANERS
SAILPLANES
SAILPLANING
SAILPLANINGS
SAINTESSES
SAINTFOINS
SAINTHOODS
SAINTLIEST
SAINTLINESS
SAINTLINESSES
SAINTLINGS
SAINTPAULIA
SAINTPAULIAS
SAINTSHIPS
SALABILITIES
SALABILITY
SALABLENESS
SALABLENESSES
SALACIOUSLY
SALACIOUSNESS
SALACIOUSNESSES
SALACITIES
SALAMANDER
SALAMANDERS
SALAMANDRIAN
SALAMANDRIANS
SALAMANDRINE
SALAMANDROID
SALAMANDROIDS
SALANGANES
SALBUTAMOL
SALBUTAMOLS
SALEABILITIES
SALEABILITY
SALEABLENESS
SALEABLENESSES
SALERATUSES
SALESCLERK
SALESCLERKS
SALESGIRLS
SALESLADIES
SALESMANSHIP
SALESMANSHIPS
SALESPEOPLE
SALESPERSON
SALESPERSONS
SALESROOMS
SALESWOMAN
SALESWOMEN
SALIAUNCES
SALICACEOUS
SALICETUMS
SALICIONAL
SALICIONALS
SALICORNIA
SALICORNIAS
SALICYLAMIDE
SALICYLAMIDES
SALICYLATE
SALICYLATED
SALICYLATES
SALICYLATING
SALICYLISM
SALICYLISMS
SALIENCIES
SALIENTIAN
SALIENTIANS
SALIFEROUS
SALIFIABLE
SALIFICATION
SALIFICATIONS
SALIMETERS
SALIMETRIC
SALIMETRIES
SALINISATION
SALINISATIONS
SALINISING
SALINITIES
SALINIZATION
SALINIZATIONS
SALINIZING
SALINOMETER
SALINOMETERS
SALINOMETRIC
SALINOMETRIES
SALINOMETRY
SALIVATING
SALIVATION
SALIVATIONS
SALIVATORS
SALLENDERS
SALLOWIEST
SALLOWNESS
SALLOWNESSES
SALLYPORTS
SALMAGUNDI
SALMAGUNDIES
SALMAGUNDIS
SALMAGUNDY
SALMANASER
SALMANASERS
SALMANAZAR
SALMANAZARS
SALMONBERRIES
SALMONBERRY
SALMONELLA
SALMONELLAE
SALMONELLAS
SALMONELLOSES
SALMONELLOSIS
SALMONIEST
SALMONOIDS
SALOMETERS
SALOPETTES
SALPIGLOSSES
SALPIGLOSSIS
SALPIGLOSSISES
SALPINGECTOMIES
SALPINGECTOMY
SALPINGIAN
SALPINGITIC
SALPINGITIS
SALPINGITISES
SALSOLACEOUS
SALSUGINOUS
SALTARELLI
SALTARELLO
SALTARELLOS
SALTATIONISM
SALTATIONISMS
SALTATIONIST
SALTATIONISTS
SALTATIONS
SALTATORIAL
SALTATORIOUS
SALTBUSHES
SALTCELLAR
SALTCELLARS
SALTCHUCKER
SALTCHUCKERS
SALTCHUCKS
SALTFISHES
SALTIGRADE
SALTIGRADES
SALTIMBANCO
SALTIMBANCOS
SALTIMBOCCA
SALTIMBOCCAS
SALTINESSES
SALTIREWISE
SALTISHNESS
SALTISHNESSES
SALTNESSES
SALTPETERS
SALTPETREMAN
SALTPETREMEN
SALTPETRES
SALTSHAKER
SALTSHAKERS
SALTWATERS
SALUBRIOUS
SALUBRIOUSLY
SALUBRIOUSNESS
SALUBRITIES
SALURETICS
SALUTARILY
SALUTARINESS
SALUTARINESSES
SALUTATION
SALUTATIONAL
SALUTATIONS
SALUTATORIAN
SALUTATORIANS
SALUTATORIES
SALUTATORILY
SALUTATORY
SALUTIFEROUS
SALVABILITIES
SALVABILITY
SALVABLENESS
SALVABLENESSES
SALVAGEABILITY
SALVAGEABLE
SALVARSANS
SALVATIONAL
SALVATIONISM
SALVATIONISMS
SALVATIONIST
SALVATIONISTS
SALVATIONS
SALVATORIES
SALVERFORM
SALVIFICAL
SALVIFICALLY
SALVINIACEOUS
SAMARIFORM
SAMARITANS
SAMARSKITE
SAMARSKITES
SAMENESSES
SAMEYNESSES
SAMNITISES
SAMPLERIES
SANATORIUM
SANATORIUMS
SANBENITOS
SANCTIFIABLE
SANCTIFICATION
SANCTIFICATIONS
SANCTIFIED
SANCTIFIEDLY
SANCTIFIER
SANCTIFIERS
SANCTIFIES
SANCTIFYING
SANCTIFYINGLY
SANCTIFYINGS
SANCTIMONIES
SANCTIMONIOUS
SANCTIMONIOUSLY
SANCTIMONY
SANCTIONABLE

SANCTIONED
SANCTIONEER
SANCTIONEERS
SANCTIONER
SANCTIONERS
SANCTIONING
SANCTIONLESS
SANCTITIES
SANCTITUDE
SANCTITUDES
SANCTUARIES
SANCTUARISE
SANCTUARISED
SANCTUARISES
SANCTUARISING
SANCTUARIZE
SANCTUARIZED
SANCTUARIZES
SANCTUARIZING
SANDALLING
SANDALWOOD
SANDALWOODS
SANDARACHS
SANDBAGGED
SANDBAGGER
SANDBAGGERS
SANDBAGGING
SANDBLASTED
SANDBLASTER
SANDBLASTERS
SANDBLASTING
SANDBLASTINGS
SANDBLASTS
SANDCASTLE
SANDCASTLES
SANDCRACKS
SANDERLING
SANDERLINGS
SANDERSWOOD
SANDERSWOODS
SANDFISHES
SANDGLASSES
SANDGROPER
SANDGROPERS
SANDGROUSE
SANDGROUSES
SANDINESSES
SANDLOTTER
SANDLOTTERS
SANDPAINTING
SANDPAINTINGS
SANDPAPERED
SANDPAPERIER
SANDPAPERIEST
SANDPAPERING
SANDPAPERINGS
SANDPAPERS
SANDPAPERY
SANDPIPERS
SANDSPOUTS
SANDSTONES
SANDSTORMS
SANDSUCKER
SANDSUCKERS
SANDWICHED
SANDWICHES
SANDWICHING
SANENESSES
SANGFROIDS
SANGUIFEROUS
SANGUIFICATION
SANGUIFICATIONS
SANGUIFIED
SANGUIFIES
SANGUIFYING
SANGUINARIA
SANGUINARIAS
SANGUINARILY
SANGUINARINESS
SANGUINARY
SANGUINELY
SANGUINENESS
SANGUINENESSES
SANGUINEOUS
SANGUINEOUSNESS
SANGUINING
SANGUINITIES
SANGUINITY
SANGUINIVOROUS
SANGUINOLENCIES
SANGUINOLENCY
SANGUINOLENT
SANGUIVOROUS
SANITARIAN
SANITARIANISM
SANITARIANISMS
SANITARIANS
SANITARIES
SANITARILY
SANITARINESS
SANITARINESSES
SANITARIST
SANITARISTS
SANITARIUM
SANITARIUMS
SANITATING
SANITATION
SANITATIONIST
SANITATIONISTS
SANITATIONS
SANITISATION
SANITISATIONS
SANITISERS
SANITISING
SANITIZATION
SANITIZATIONS
SANITIZERS
SANITIZING
SANITORIUM
SANITORIUMS
SANNYASINS
SANSCULOTTE
SANSCULOTTERIE
SANSCULOTTERIES
SANSCULOTTES
SANSCULOTTIC
SANSCULOTTIDES
SANSCULOTTISH
SANSCULOTTISM
SANSCULOTTISMS
SANSCULOTTIST
SANSCULOTTISTS
SANSEVIERIA
SANSEVIERIAS
SANTALACEOUS
SANTOLINAS
SANTONICAS
SAPANWOODS
SAPIDITIES
SAPIDNESSES
SAPIENCIES
SAPIENTIAL
SAPIENTIALLY
SAPINDACEOUS
SAPLESSNESS
SAPLESSNESSES
SAPODILLAS
SAPOGENINS
SAPONACEOUS
SAPONACEOUSNESS
SAPONARIAS
SAPONIFIABLE
SAPONIFICATION
SAPONIFICATIONS
SAPONIFIED
SAPONIFIER
SAPONIFIERS
SAPONIFIES
SAPONIFYING
SAPOTACEOUS
SAPPANWOOD
SAPPANWOODS
SAPPERMENT
SAPPHIRINE
SAPPHIRINES
SAPPINESSES
SAPRAEMIAS
SAPROBIONT
SAPROBIONTS
SAPROBIOTIC
SAPROBITIES
SAPROGENIC
SAPROGENICITIES
SAPROGENICITY
SAPROGENOUS
SAPROLEGNIA
SAPROLEGNIAS
SAPROLITES
SAPROLITIC
SAPROPELIC
SAPROPELITE
SAPROPELITES
SAPROPHAGOUS
SAPROPHYTE
SAPROPHYTES
SAPROPHYTIC
SAPROPHYTICALLY
SAPROPHYTISM
SAPROPHYTISMS
SAPROTROPH
SAPROTROPHIC
SAPROTROPHS
SAPSUCKERS
SARABANDES
SARBACANES
SARCASTICALLY
SARCENCHYMATOUS
SARCENCHYME
SARCENCHYMES
SARCOCARPS
SARCOCOLLA
SARCOCOLLAS
SARCOCYSTIS
SARCOCYSTISES
SARCOIDOSES
SARCOIDOSIS
SARCOLEMMA
SARCOLEMMAL
SARCOLEMMAS
SARCOLEMMATA
SARCOLOGIES
SARCOMATOID
SARCOMATOSES
SARCOMATOSIS
SARCOMATOUS
SARCOMERES
SARCOPENIA
SARCOPENIAS
SARCOPHAGAL
SARCOPHAGI
SARCOPHAGOUS
SARCOPHAGUS
SARCOPHAGUSES
SARCOPLASM
SARCOPLASMIC
SARCOPLASMS
SARCOSOMAL
SARCOSOMES
SARDONIANS
SARDONICAL
SARDONICALLY
SARDONICISM
SARDONICISMS
SARDONYXES
SARGASSOES
SARGASSUMS
SARKINESSES
SARMENTACEOUS
SARMENTOSE
SARMENTOUS

S

SARPANCHES
SARRACENIA
SARRACENIACEOUS
SARRACENIAS
SARRUSOPHONE
SARRUSOPHONES
SARSAPARILLA
SARSAPARILLAS
SARTORIALLY
SARTORIUSES
SASKATOONS
SASQUATCHES
SASSAFRASES
SASSARARAS
SASSINESSES
SASSOLITES
SASSYWOODS
SATANICALLY
SATANICALNESS
SATANICALNESSES
SATANITIES
SATANOLOGIES
SATANOLOGY
SATANOPHANIES
SATANOPHANY
SATANOPHOBIA
SATANOPHOBIAS
SATCHELFUL
SATCHELFULS
SATCHELLED
SATCHELSFUL
SATEDNESSES
SATELLITED
SATELLITES
SATELLITIC
SATELLITING
SATELLITISE
SATELLITISED
SATELLITISES
SATELLITISING
SATELLITIUM
SATELLITIUMS
SATELLITIZE
SATELLITIZED
SATELLITIZES
SATELLITIZING
SATIABILITIES
SATIABILITY
SATIATIONS
SATINETTAS
SATINETTES
SATINFLOWER
SATINFLOWERS
SATINWOODS
SATIRICALLY
SATIRICALNESS
SATIRICALNESSES
SATIRISABLE
SATIRISATION
SATIRISATIONS
SATIRISERS
SATIRISING
SATIRIZABLE
SATIRIZATION
SATIRIZATIONS
SATIRIZERS
SATIRIZING
SATISFACTION
SATISFACTIONS
SATISFACTORILY
SATISFACTORY
SATISFIABLE
SATISFICED
SATISFICER
SATISFICERS
SATISFICES
SATISFICING
SATISFICINGS
SATISFIERS
SATISFYING
SATISFYINGLY
SATURABILITIES
SATURABILITY
SATURATERS
SATURATING
SATURATION
SATURATIONS
SATURATORS
SATURNALIA
SATURNALIAN
SATURNALIANLY
SATURNALIAS
SATURNIIDS
SATURNINELY
SATURNINITIES
SATURNINITY
SATURNISMS
SATURNISTS
SATYAGRAHA
SATYAGRAHAS
SATYAGRAHI
SATYAGRAHIS
SATYRESQUE
SATYRESSES
SATYRIASES
SATYRIASIS
SAUCEBOATS
SAUCEBOXES
SAUCERFULS
SAUCERLESS
SAUCERLIKE
SAUCINESSES
SAUCISSONS
SAUERBRATEN
SAUERBRATENS
SAUERKRAUT
SAUERKRAUTS
SAUNTERERS
SAUNTERING
SAUNTERINGLY
SAUNTERINGS
SAURISCHIAN
SAURISCHIANS
SAUROGNATHOUS
SAUROPODOUS
SAUROPSIDAN
SAUROPSIDANS
SAUROPTERYGIAN
SAUROPTERYGIANS
SAUSSURITE
SAUSSURITES
SAUSSURITIC
SAVABLENESS
SAVABLENESSES
SAVAGEDOMS
SAVAGENESS
SAVAGENESSES
SAVAGERIES
SAVEABLENESS
SAVEABLENESSES
SAVEGARDED
SAVEGARDING
SAVINGNESS
SAVINGNESSES
SAVORINESS
SAVORINESSES
SAVOURIEST
SAVOURINESS
SAVOURINESSES
SAVOURLESS
SAVVINESSES
SAWBONESES
SAWDUSTIER
SAWDUSTIEST
SAWDUSTING
SAWGRASSES
SAWMILLERS
SAWTIMBERS
SAXICAVOUS
SAXICOLINE
SAXICOLOUS
SAXIFRAGACEOUS
SAXIFRAGES
SAXITOXINS
SAXOPHONES
SAXOPHONIC
SAXOPHONIST
SAXOPHONISTS
SCABBARDED
SCABBARDING
SCABBARDLESS
SCABBEDNESS
SCABBEDNESSES
SCABBINESS
SCABBINESSES
SCABERULOUS
SCABIOUSES
SCABRIDITIES
SCABRIDITY
SCABROUSLY
SCABROUSNESS
SCABROUSNESSES
SCAFFOLAGE
SCAFFOLAGES
SCAFFOLDAGE
SCAFFOLDAGES
SCAFFOLDED
SCAFFOLDER
SCAFFOLDERS
SCAFFOLDING
SCAFFOLDINGS
SCAGLIOLAS
SCAITHLESS
SCALABILITIES
SCALABILITY
SCALABLENESS
SCALABLENESSES
SCALARIFORM
SCALARIFORMLY
SCALATIONS
SCALDBERRIES
SCALDBERRY
SCALDFISHES
SCALDHEADS
SCALDSHIPS
SCALEBOARD
SCALEBOARDS
SCALENOHEDRA
SCALENOHEDRON
SCALENOHEDRONS
SCALETAILS
SCALEWORKS
SCALINESSES
SCALLAWAGS
SCALLOPERS
SCALLOPING
SCALLOPINGS
SCALLOPINI
SCALLOPINIS
SCALLYWAGS
SCALOGRAMS
SCALOPPINE
SCALOPPINES
SCALOPPINI
SCALPELLIC
SCALPELLIFORM
SCALPRIFORM
SCAMBAITING
SCAMBAITINGS
SCAMBLINGLY
SCAMBLINGS
SCAMMONIATE
SCAMMONIES
SCAMPERERS
SCAMPERING
SCAMPERINGS
SCAMPISHLY
SCAMPISHNESS
SCAMPISHNESSES
SCANDALING

S

SCANDALISATION
SCANDALISATIONS
SCANDALISE
SCANDALISED
SCANDALISER
SCANDALISERS
SCANDALISES
SCANDALISING
SCANDALIZATION
SCANDALIZATIONS
SCANDALIZE
SCANDALIZED
SCANDALIZER
SCANDALIZERS
SCANDALIZES
SCANDALIZING
SCANDALLED
SCANDALLING
SCANDALMONGER
SCANDALMONGERS
SCANDALOUS
SCANDALOUSLY
SCANDALOUSNESS
SCANSORIAL
SCANTINESS
SCANTINESSES
SCANTITIES
SCANTLINGS
SCANTNESSES
SCAPEGALLOWS
SCAPEGALLOWSES
SCAPEGOATED
SCAPEGOATING
SCAPEGOATINGS
SCAPEGOATISM
SCAPEGOATISMS
SCAPEGOATS
SCAPEGRACE
SCAPEGRACES
SCAPEMENTS
SCAPEWHEEL
SCAPEWHEELS
SCAPHOCEPHALI
SCAPHOCEPHALIC
SCAPHOCEPHALICS
SCAPHOCEPHALIES
SCAPHOCEPHALISM
SCAPHOCEPHALOUS
SCAPHOCEPHALUS
SCAPHOCEPHALY
SCAPHOPODS
SCAPIGEROUS
SCAPOLITES
SCAPULARIES
SCAPULATED
SCAPULIMANCIES
SCAPULIMANCY
SCAPULIMANTIC
SCAPULOMANCIES
SCAPULOMANCY
SCAPULOMANTIC
SCARABAEAN
SCARABAEANS
SCARABAEID
SCARABAEIDS
SCARABAEIST
SCARABAEISTS
SCARABAEOID
SCARABAEOIDS
SCARABAEUS
SCARABAEUSES
SCARABOIDS
SCARAMOUCH
SCARAMOUCHE
SCARAMOUCHED
SCARAMOUCHES
SCARAMOUCHING
SCARCEMENT
SCARCEMENTS
SCARCENESS
SCARCENESSES
SCARCITIES
SCARECROWS
SCAREHEADS
SCAREMONGER
SCAREMONGERING
SCAREMONGERINGS
SCAREMONGERS
SCAREWARES
SCARFISHES
SCARFSKINS
SCARIFICATION
SCARIFICATIONS
SCARIFICATOR
SCARIFICATORS
SCARIFIERS
SCARIFYING
SCARIFYINGLY
SCARINESSES
SCARLATINA
SCARLATINAL
SCARLATINAS
SCARLETING
SCARPERING
SCATHEFULNESS
SCATHEFULNESSES
SCATHELESS
SCATHINGLY
SCATOLOGIC
SCATOLOGICAL
SCATOLOGIES
SCATOLOGIST
SCATOLOGISTS
SCATOPHAGIES
SCATOPHAGOUS
SCATOPHAGY
SCATTERABLE
SCATTERATION
SCATTERATIONS
SCATTERBRAIN
SCATTERBRAINED
SCATTERBRAINS
SCATTEREDLY
SCATTERERS
SCATTERGOOD
SCATTERGOODS
SCATTERGRAM
SCATTERGRAMS
SCATTERGUN
SCATTERGUNS
SCATTERIER
SCATTERIEST
SCATTERING
SCATTERINGLY
SCATTERINGS
SCATTERLING
SCATTERLINGS
SCATTERMOUCH
SCATTERMOUCHES
SCATTEROMETER
SCATTEROMETERS
SCATTERSHOT
SCATTINESS
SCATTINESSES
SCATURIENT
SCAVENGERED
SCAVENGERIES
SCAVENGERING
SCAVENGERINGS
SCAVENGERS
SCAVENGERY
SCAVENGING
SCAVENGINGS
SCAZONTICS
SCELERATES
SCENARISATION
SCENARISATIONS
SCENARISED
SCENARISES
SCENARISING
SCENARISTS
SCENARIZATION
SCENARIZATIONS
SCENARIZED
SCENARIZES
SCENARIZING
SCENESHIFTER
SCENESHIFTERS
SCENESTERS
SCENICALLY
SCENOGRAPHER
SCENOGRAPHERS
SCENOGRAPHIC
SCENOGRAPHICAL
SCENOGRAPHIES
SCENOGRAPHY
SCENTLESSNESS
SCENTLESSNESSES
SCEPTERING
SCEPTERLESS
SCEPTICALLY
SCEPTICISM
SCEPTICISMS
SCEPTRELESS
SCEUOPHYLACIA
SCEUOPHYLACIUM
SCEUOPHYLACIUMS
SCEUOPHYLAX
SCEUOPHYLAXES
SCHADENFREUDE
SCHADENFREUDES
SCHALSTEIN
SCHALSTEINS
SCHAPPEING
SCHATCHENS
SCHECHITAH
SCHECHITAHS
SCHECHITAS
SCHECKLATON
SCHECKLATONS
SCHEDULERS
SCHEDULING
SCHEDULINGS
SCHEELITES
SCHEFFLERA
SCHEFFLERAS
SCHEMATICAL
SCHEMATICALLY
SCHEMATICS
SCHEMATISATION
SCHEMATISATIONS
SCHEMATISE
SCHEMATISED
SCHEMATISES
SCHEMATISING
SCHEMATISM
SCHEMATISMS
SCHEMATIST
SCHEMATISTS
SCHEMATIZATION
SCHEMATIZATIONS
SCHEMATIZE
SCHEMATIZED
SCHEMATIZES
SCHEMATIZING
SCHEMINGLY
SCHEMOZZLE
SCHEMOZZLED
SCHEMOZZLES
SCHEMOZZLING
SCHERZANDI
SCHERZANDO
SCHERZANDOS
SCHIAVONES
SCHILLERISATION
SCHILLERISE
SCHILLERISED
SCHILLERISES
SCHILLERISING
SCHILLERIZATION

S

SCHILLERIZE
SCHILLERIZED
SCHILLERIZES
SCHILLERIZING
SCHILLINGS
SCHINDYLESES
SCHINDYLESIS
SCHINDYLETIC
SCHIPPERKE
SCHIPPERKES
SCHISMATIC
SCHISMATICAL
SCHISMATICALLY
SCHISMATICALS
SCHISMATICS
SCHISMATISE
SCHISMATISED
SCHISMATISES
SCHISMATISING
SCHISMATIZE
SCHISMATIZED
SCHISMATIZES
SCHISMATIZING
SCHISTOSITIES
SCHISTOSITY
SCHISTOSOMAL
SCHISTOSOME
SCHISTOSOMES
SCHISTOSOMIASES
SCHISTOSOMIASIS
SCHIZAEACEOUS
SCHIZANTHUS
SCHIZANTHUSES
SCHIZOCARP
SCHIZOCARPIC
SCHIZOCARPOUS
SCHIZOCARPS
SCHIZOGENESES
SCHIZOGENESIS
SCHIZOGENETIC
SCHIZOGENIC
SCHIZOGNATHOUS
SCHIZOGONIC
SCHIZOGONIES
SCHIZOGONOUS
SCHIZOGONY
SCHIZOIDAL
SCHIZOMYCETE
SCHIZOMYCETES
SCHIZOMYCETIC
SCHIZOMYCETOUS
SCHIZOPHRENE
SCHIZOPHRENES
SCHIZOPHRENETIC
SCHIZOPHRENIA
SCHIZOPHRENIAS
SCHIZOPHRENIC
SCHIZOPHRENICS
SCHIZOPHYCEOUS
SCHIZOPHYTE
SCHIZOPHYTES
SCHIZOPHYTIC
SCHIZOPODAL
SCHIZOPODOUS
SCHIZOPODS
SCHIZOTHYMIA
SCHIZOTHYMIAS
SCHIZOTHYMIC
SCHLEMIELS
SCHLEMIHLS
SCHLEPPERS
SCHLEPPIER
SCHLEPPIEST
SCHLEPPING
SCHLIERENS
SCHLIMAZEL
SCHLIMAZELS
SCHLOCKERS
SCHLOCKEYS
SCHLOCKIER
SCHLOCKIEST
SCHLUMBERGERA
SCHLUMBERGERAS
SCHLUMPIER
SCHLUMPIEST
SCHLUMPING
SCHMALTZES
SCHMALTZIER
SCHMALTZIEST
SCHMALZIER
SCHMALZIEST
SCHMEARING
SCHMECKERS
SCHMECKING
SCHMEERING
SCHMICKEST
SCHMOOSING
SCHMOOZERS
SCHMOOZIER
SCHMOOZIEST
SCHMOOZING
SCHMUCKIER
SCHMUCKIEST
SCHMUCKING
SCHMUTTERS
SCHNAPPERS
SCHNAPPSES
SCHNAUZERS
SCHNITZELS
SCHNOODLES
SCHNORKELED
SCHNORKELING
SCHNORKELLED
SCHNORKELLING
SCHNORKELS
SCHNORRERS
SCHNORRING
SCHNOZZLES
SCHOLARCHS
SCHOLARLIER
SCHOLARLIEST
SCHOLARLINESS
SCHOLARLINESSES
SCHOLARSHIP
SCHOLARSHIPS
SCHOLASTIC
SCHOLASTICAL
SCHOLASTICALLY
SCHOLASTICATE
SCHOLASTICATES
SCHOLASTICISM
SCHOLASTICISMS
SCHOLASTICS
SCHOLIASTIC
SCHOLIASTS
SCHOOLBAGS
SCHOOLBOOK
SCHOOLBOOKS
SCHOOLBOYISH
SCHOOLBOYS
SCHOOLCHILD
SCHOOLCHILDREN
SCHOOLCRAFT
SCHOOLCRAFTS
SCHOOLDAYS
SCHOOLERIES
SCHOOLFELLOW
SCHOOLFELLOWS
SCHOOLGIRL
SCHOOLGIRLISH
SCHOOLGIRLS
SCHOOLGOING
SCHOOLGOINGS
SCHOOLHOUSE
SCHOOLHOUSES
SCHOOLINGS
SCHOOLKIDS
SCHOOLMAID
SCHOOLMAIDS
SCHOOLMARM
SCHOOLMARMISH
SCHOOLMARMS
SCHOOLMASTER
SCHOOLMASTERED
SCHOOLMASTERING
SCHOOLMASTERISH
SCHOOLMASTERLY
SCHOOLMASTERS
SCHOOLMATE
SCHOOLMATES
SCHOOLMISTRESS
SCHOOLMISTRESSY
SCHOOLROOM
SCHOOLROOMS
SCHOOLTEACHER
SCHOOLTEACHERS
SCHOOLTEACHING
SCHOOLTEACHINGS
SCHOOLTIDE
SCHOOLTIDES
SCHOOLTIME
SCHOOLTIMES
SCHOOLWARD
SCHOOLWARDS
SCHOOLWORK
SCHOOLWORKS
SCHOOLYARD
SCHOOLYARDS
SCHORLACEOUS
SCHORLOMITE
SCHORLOMITES
SCHOTTISCHE
SCHOTTISCHES
SCHRECKLICH
SCHTUPPING
SCHUSSBOOMER
SCHUSSBOOMERS
SCHVITZING
SCHWARMEREI
SCHWARMEREIS
SCHWARMERISCH
SCHWARZLOT
SCHWARZLOTS
SCIAENOIDS
SCIAMACHIES
SCIENTIFIC
SCIENTIFICAL
SCIENTIFICALLY
SCIENTIFICITIES
SCIENTIFICITY
SCIENTISED
SCIENTISES
SCIENTISING
SCIENTISMS
SCIENTISTIC
SCIENTISTS
SCIENTIZED
SCIENTIZES
SCIENTIZING
SCINCOIDIAN
SCINCOIDIANS
SCINDAPSUS
SCINDAPSUSES
SCINTIGRAM
SCINTIGRAMS
SCINTIGRAPHIC
SCINTIGRAPHIES
SCINTIGRAPHY
SCINTILLAE
SCINTILLANT
SCINTILLANTLY
SCINTILLAS
SCINTILLASCOPE
SCINTILLASCOPES
SCINTILLATE
SCINTILLATED
SCINTILLATES
SCINTILLATING
SCINTILLATINGLY
SCINTILLATION

SCINTILLATIONS
SCINTILLATOR
SCINTILLATORS
SCINTILLISCAN
SCINTILLISCANS
SCINTILLOMETER
SCINTILLOMETERS
SCINTILLON
SCINTILLONS
SCINTILLOSCOPE
SCINTILLOSCOPES
SCINTISCAN
SCINTISCANNER
SCINTISCANNERS
SCINTISCANS
SCIOLISTIC
SCIOMACHIES
SCIOMANCER
SCIOMANCERS
SCIOMANCIES
SCIOMANTIC
SCIOPHYTES
SCIOPHYTIC
SCIOSOPHIES
SCIRRHOSITIES
SCIRRHOSITY
SCIRRHUSES
SCISSIPARITIES
SCISSIPARITY
SCISSORERS
SCISSORING
SCISSORTAIL
SCISSORTAILS
SCISSORWISE
SCITAMINEOUS
SCLAUNDERS
SCLEREIDES
SCLERENCHYMA
SCLERENCHYMAS
SCLERENCHYMATA
SCLERIASES
SCLERIASIS
SCLERITISES
SCLEROCAULIES
SCLEROCAULOUS
SCLEROCAULY
SCLERODERM
SCLERODERMA
SCLERODERMAS
SCLERODERMATA
SCLERODERMATOUS
SCLERODERMIA
SCLERODERMIAS
SCLERODERMIC
SCLERODERMITE
SCLERODERMITES
SCLERODERMOUS
SCLERODERMS
SCLEROMALACIA
SCLEROMALACIAS
SCLEROMATA
SCLEROMETER
SCLEROMETERS
SCLEROMETRIC
SCLEROPHYLL
SCLEROPHYLLIES
SCLEROPHYLLOUS
SCLEROPHYLLS
SCLEROPHYLLY
SCLEROPROTEIN
SCLEROPROTEINS
SCLEROSING
SCLEROTALS
SCLEROTIAL
SCLEROTICS
SCLEROTINS
SCLEROTIOID
SCLEROTISATION
SCLEROTISATIONS
SCLEROTISE
SCLEROTISED
SCLEROTISES
SCLEROTISING
SCLEROTITIS
SCLEROTITISES
SCLEROTIUM
SCLEROTIZATION
SCLEROTIZATIONS
SCLEROTIZE
SCLEROTIZED
SCLEROTIZES
SCLEROTIZING
SCLEROTOMIES
SCLEROTOMY
SCOFFINGLY
SCOLDINGLY
SCOLECIFORM
SCOLECITES
SCOLLOPING
SCOLOPACEOUS
SCOLOPENDRA
SCOLOPENDRAS
SCOLOPENDRID
SCOLOPENDRIDS
SCOLOPENDRIFORM
SCOLOPENDRINE
SCOLOPENDRIUM
SCOLOPENDRIUMS
SCOLYTOIDS
SCOMBROIDS
SCOMFISHED
SCOMFISHES
SCOMFISHING
SCONCHEONS
SCOOTCHING
SCOOTERING
SCOOTERIST
SCOOTERISTS
SCOPELOIDS
SCOPOLAMINE
SCOPOLAMINES
SCOPOLINES
SCOPOPHILIA
SCOPOPHILIAC
SCOPOPHILIACS
SCOPOPHILIAS
SCOPOPHILIC
SCOPOPHOBIA
SCOPOPHOBIAS
SCOPTOPHILIA
SCOPTOPHILIAS
SCOPTOPHOBIA
SCOPTOPHOBIAS
SCORBUTICALLY
SCORCHINGLY
SCORCHINGNESS
SCORCHINGNESSES
SCORCHINGS
SCORDATURA
SCORDATURAS
SCOREBOARD
SCOREBOARDS
SCORECARDS
SCOREKEEPER
SCOREKEEPERS
SCORELINES
SCORESHEET
SCORESHEETS
SCORIACEOUS
SCORIFICATION
SCORIFICATIONS
SCORIFIERS
SCORIFYING
SCORNFULLY
SCORNFULNESS
SCORNFULNESSES
SCORODITES
SCORPAENID
SCORPAENIDS
SCORPAENOID
SCORPAENOIDS
SCORPIOIDS
SCORPIONIC
SCORZONERA
SCORZONERAS
SCOTODINIA
SCOTODINIAS
SCOTOMATOUS
SCOTOMETER
SCOTOMETERS
SCOUNDRELLIER
SCOUNDRELLIEST
SCOUNDRELLY
SCOUNDRELS
SCOURGINGS
SCOUTCRAFT
SCOUTCRAFTS
SCOUTHERED
SCOUTHERING
SCOUTHERINGS
SCOUTMASTER
SCOUTMASTERS
SCOWDERING
SCOWDERINGS
SCOWLINGLY
SCOWTHERED
SCOWTHERING
SCRABBLERS
SCRABBLIER
SCRABBLIEST
SCRABBLING
SCRABBLINGS
SCRAGGEDNESS
SCRAGGEDNESSES
SCRAGGIEST
SCRAGGINESS
SCRAGGINESSES
SCRAGGLIER
SCRAGGLIEST
SCRAGGLING
SCRAICHING
SCRAIGHING
SCRAMBLERS
SCRAMBLING
SCRAMBLINGLY
SCRAMBLINGS
SCRANCHING
SCRANNIEST
SCRAPBOOKED
SCRAPBOOKING
SCRAPBOOKINGS
SCRAPBOOKS
SCRAPEGOOD
SCRAPEGOODS
SCRAPEGUTS
SCRAPEPENNIES
SCRAPEPENNY
SCRAPERBOARD
SCRAPERBOARDS
SCRAPHEAPS
SCRAPPAGES
SCRAPPIEST
SCRAPPINESS
SCRAPPINESSES
SCRAPPINGS
SCRAPYARDS
SCRATCHBACK
SCRATCHBACKS
SCRATCHBOARD
SCRATCHBOARDS
SCRATCHBUILD
SCRATCHBUILDER
SCRATCHBUILDERS
SCRATCHBUILDING
SCRATCHBUILDS
SCRATCHBUILT
SCRATCHCARD
SCRATCHCARDS
SCRATCHERS
SCRATCHIER

SCRATCHIES
SCRATCHIEST
SCRATCHILY
SCRATCHINESS
SCRATCHINESSES
SCRATCHING
SCRATCHINGLY
SCRATCHINGS
SCRATCHLESS
SCRATCHPLATE
SCRATCHPLATES
SCRATTLING
SCRAUCHING
SCRAUGHING
SCRAVELING
SCRAVELLED
SCRAVELLING
SCRAWLIEST
SCRAWLINGLY
SCRAWLINGS
SCRAWNIEST
SCRAWNINESS
SCRAWNINESSES
SCREAKIEST
SCREAKINGS
SCREAMINGLY
SCREAMINGS
SCREECHERS
SCREECHIER
SCREECHIEST
SCREECHING
SCREEDINGS
SCREENABLE
SCREENAGER
SCREENAGERS
SCREENCAST
SCREENCASTS
SCREENCRAFT
SCREENCRAFTS
SCREENFULS
SCREENINGS
SCREENLAND
SCREENLANDS
SCREENLIKE
SCREENPLAY
SCREENPLAYS
SCREENSAVER
SCREENSAVERS
SCREENSHOT
SCREENSHOTS
SCREENSHOTTED
SCREENSHOTTING
SCREENWRITER
SCREENWRITERS
SCREENWRITING
SCREENWRITINGS
SCREEVINGS
SCREICHING
SCREIGHING
SCREWBALLS
SCREWBEANS
SCREWDRIVER
SCREWDRIVERS
SCREWHEADS
SCREWINESS
SCREWINESSES
SCREWWORMS
SCRIBACIOUS
SCRIBACIOUSNESS
SCRIBBLEMENT
SCRIBBLEMENTS
SCRIBBLERS
SCRIBBLIER
SCRIBBLIEST
SCRIBBLING
SCRIBBLINGLY
SCRIBBLINGS
SCRIECHING
SCRIEVEBOARD
SCRIEVEBOARDS
SCRIGGLIER
SCRIGGLIEST
SCRIGGLING
SCRIMMAGED
SCRIMMAGER
SCRIMMAGERS
SCRIMMAGES
SCRIMMAGING
SCRIMPIEST
SCRIMPINESS
SCRIMPINESSES
SCRIMPINGS
SCRIMPNESS
SCRIMPNESSES
SCRIMSHANDER
SCRIMSHANDERED
SCRIMSHANDERING
SCRIMSHANDERS
SCRIMSHANDIED
SCRIMSHANDIES
SCRIMSHANDY
SCRIMSHANDYING
SCRIMSHANK
SCRIMSHANKED
SCRIMSHANKER
SCRIMSHANKERS
SCRIMSHANKING
SCRIMSHANKS
SCRIMSHAWED
SCRIMSHAWING
SCRIMSHAWS
SCRIMSHONER
SCRIMSHONERS
SCRIPHOLDER
SCRIPHOLDERS
SCRIPOPHILE
SCRIPOPHILES
SCRIPOPHILIES
SCRIPOPHILIST
SCRIPOPHILISTS
SCRIPOPHILY
SCRIPPAGES
SCRIPTORIA
SCRIPTORIAL
SCRIPTORIUM
SCRIPTORIUMS
SCRIPTURAL
SCRIPTURALISM
SCRIPTURALISMS
SCRIPTURALIST
SCRIPTURALISTS
SCRIPTURALLY
SCRIPTURES
SCRIPTURISM
SCRIPTURISMS
SCRIPTURIST
SCRIPTURISTS
SCRIPTWRITER
SCRIPTWRITERS
SCRIPTWRITING
SCRIPTWRITINGS
SCRITCHING
SCRITCHINGS
SCRIVEBOARD
SCRIVEBOARDS
SCRIVENERS
SCRIVENERSHIP
SCRIVENERSHIPS
SCRIVENING
SCRIVENINGS
SCROBBLING
SCROBICULAR
SCROBICULATE
SCROBICULATED
SCROBICULE
SCROBICULES
SCROFULOUS
SCROFULOUSLY
SCROFULOUSNESS
SCROGGIEST
SCROLLABLE
SCROLLINGS
SCROLLWISE
SCROLLWORK
SCROLLWORKS
SCROOCHING
SCROOTCHED
SCROOTCHES
SCROOTCHING
SCROPHULARIA
SCROPHULARIAS
SCROUNGERS
SCROUNGIER
SCROUNGIEST
SCROUNGING
SCROUNGINGS
SCROWDGING
SCRUBBABLE
SCRUBBIEST
SCRUBBINESS
SCRUBBINESSES
SCRUBBINGS
SCRUBLANDS
SCRUBWOMAN
SCRUBWOMEN
SCRUFFIEST
SCRUFFINESS
SCRUFFINESSES
SCRUMDOWNS
SCRUMMAGED
SCRUMMAGER
SCRUMMAGERS
SCRUMMAGES
SCRUMMAGING
SCRUMMIEST
SCRUMPLING
SCRUMPOXES
SCRUMPTIOUS
SCRUMPTIOUSLY
SCRUMPTIOUSNESS
SCRUNCHEON
SCRUNCHEONS
SCRUNCHIER
SCRUNCHIES
SCRUNCHIEST
SCRUNCHING
SCRUNCHINGS
SCRUNCHINS
SCRUNCHION
SCRUNCHIONS
SCRUNTIEST
SCRUPLELESS
SCRUPULOSITIES
SCRUPULOSITY
SCRUPULOUS
SCRUPULOUSLY
SCRUPULOUSNESS
SCRUTABILITIES
SCRUTABILITY
SCRUTATORS
SCRUTINEER
SCRUTINEERS
SCRUTINIES
SCRUTINISE
SCRUTINISED
SCRUTINISER
SCRUTINISERS
SCRUTINISES
SCRUTINISING
SCRUTINISINGLY
SCRUTINIZE
SCRUTINIZED
SCRUTINIZER
SCRUTINIZERS
SCRUTINIZES
SCRUTINIZING
SCRUTINIZINGLY
SCRUTINOUS
SCRUTINOUSLY
SCRUTOIRES

S

SCUDDALERS
SCUFFLINGS
SCULDUDDERIES
SCULDUDDERY
SCULDUDDRIES
SCULDUDDRY
SCULDUGGERIES
SCULDUGGERY
SCULLERIES
SCULPTINGS
SCULPTRESS
SCULPTRESSES
SCULPTURAL
SCULPTURALLY
SCULPTURED
SCULPTURES
SCULPTURESQUE
SCULPTURESQUELY
SCULPTURING
SCULPTURINGS
SCUMBERING
SCUMBLINGS
SCUMFISHED
SCUMFISHES
SCUMFISHING
SCUNCHEONS
SCUNGILLIS
SCUNNERING
SCUPPERING
SCUPPERNONG
SCUPPERNONGS
SCURFINESS
SCURFINESSES
SCURRILITIES
SCURRILITY
SCURRILOUS
SCURRILOUSLY
SCURRILOUSNESS
SCURRIOURS
SCURVINESS
SCURVINESSES
SCUTATIONS
SCUTCHEONLESS
SCUTCHEONS
SCUTCHINGS
SCUTELLATE
SCUTELLATED
SCUTELLATION
SCUTELLATIONS
SCUTTERING
SCUTTLEBUTT
SCUTTLEBUTTS
SCUTTLEFUL
SCUTTLEFULS
SCUTTLINGS
SCUZZBALLS
SCYPHIFORM
SCYPHISTOMA
SCYPHISTOMAE
SCYPHISTOMAS
SCYPHOZOAN
SCYPHOZOANS
SCYTHELIKE
SDEIGNFULL
SDEIGNFULLY
SDRUCCIOLA
SEABEACHES
SEABORGIUM
SEABORGIUMS
SEABOTTLES
SEACHANGER
SEACHANGERS
SEACUNNIES
SEAFARINGS
SEAGRASSES
SEALIFTING
SEALPOINTS
SEAMANLIER
SEAMANLIEST
SEAMANLIKE
SEAMANSHIP
SEAMANSHIPS
SEAMINESSES
SEAMLESSLY
SEAMLESSNESS
SEAMLESSNESSES
SEAMSTRESS
SEAMSTRESSES
SEAMSTRESSIES
SEAMSTRESSY
SEANNACHIE
SEANNACHIES
SEAQUARIUM
SEAQUARIUMS
SEARCHABLE
SEARCHINGLY
SEARCHINGNESS
SEARCHINGNESSES
SEARCHINGS
SEARCHLESS
SEARCHLIGHT
SEARCHLIGHTS
SEAREDNESS
SEAREDNESSES
SEARNESSES
SEASICKEST
SEASICKNESS
SEASICKNESSES
SEASONABILITIES
SEASONABILITY
SEASONABLE
SEASONABLENESS
SEASONABLY
SEASONALITIES
SEASONALITY
SEASONALLY
SEASONALNESS
SEASONALNESSES
SEASONINGS
SEASONLESS
SEASTRANDS
SEAWEEDIER
SEAWEEDIEST
SEAWORTHIER
SEAWORTHIEST
SEAWORTHINESS
SEAWORTHINESSES
SEBIFEROUS
SEBORRHEAL
SEBORRHEAS
SEBORRHEIC
SEBORRHOEA
SEBORRHOEAL
SEBORRHOEAS
SEBORRHOEIC
SECERNENTS
SECERNMENT
SECERNMENTS
SECESSIONAL
SECESSIONISM
SECESSIONISMS
SECESSIONIST
SECESSIONISTS
SECESSIONS
SECLUDEDLY
SECLUDEDNESS
SECLUDEDNESSES
SECLUSIONIST
SECLUSIONISTS
SECLUSIONS
SECLUSIVELY
SECLUSIVENESS
SECLUSIVENESSES
SECOBARBITAL
SECOBARBITALS
SECONDARIES
SECONDARILY
SECONDARINESS
SECONDARINESSES
SECONDHAND
SECONDINGS
SECONDMENT
SECONDMENTS
SECRETAGES
SECRETAGOGIC
SECRETAGOGUE
SECRETAGOGUES
SECRETAIRE
SECRETAIRES
SECRETARIAL
SECRETARIAT
SECRETARIATE
SECRETARIATES
SECRETARIATS
SECRETARIES
SECRETARYSHIP
SECRETARYSHIPS
SECRETIONAL
SECRETIONARY
SECRETIONS
SECRETIVELY
SECRETIVENESS
SECRETIVENESSES
SECRETNESS
SECRETNESSES
SECRETORIES
SECTARIANISE
SECTARIANISED
SECTARIANISES
SECTARIANISING
SECTARIANISM
SECTARIANISMS
SECTARIANIZE
SECTARIANIZED
SECTARIANIZES
SECTARIANIZING
SECTARIANS
SECTILITIES
SECTIONALISE
SECTIONALISED
SECTIONALISES
SECTIONALISING
SECTIONALISM
SECTIONALISMS
SECTIONALIST
SECTIONALISTS
SECTIONALIZE
SECTIONALIZED
SECTIONALIZES
SECTIONALIZING
SECTIONALLY
SECTIONALS
SECTIONING
SECTIONISATION
SECTIONISATIONS
SECTIONISE
SECTIONISED
SECTIONISES
SECTIONISING
SECTIONIZATION
SECTIONIZATIONS
SECTIONIZE
SECTIONIZED
SECTIONIZES
SECTIONIZING
SECTORIALS
SECTORISATION
SECTORISATIONS
SECTORISED
SECTORISES
SECTORISING
SECTORIZATION
SECTORIZATIONS
SECTORIZED
SECTORIZES
SECTORIZING
SECULARISATION
SECULARISATIONS
SECULARISE
SECULARISED

SECULARISER
SECULARISERS
SECULARISES
SECULARISING
SECULARISM
SECULARISMS
SECULARIST
SECULARISTIC
SECULARISTS
SECULARITIES
SECULARITY
SECULARIZATION
SECULARIZATIONS
SECULARIZE
SECULARIZED
SECULARIZER
SECULARIZERS
SECULARIZES
SECULARIZING
SECUNDINES
SECUNDOGENITURE
SECURANCES
SECUREMENT
SECUREMENTS
SECURENESS
SECURENESSES
SECURIFORM
SECURITANS
SECURITIES
SECURITISATION
SECURITISATIONS
SECURITISE
SECURITISED
SECURITISES
SECURITISING
SECURITIZATION
SECURITIZATIONS
SECURITIZE
SECURITIZED
SECURITIZES
SECURITIZING
SECUROCRAT
SECUROCRATS
SEDATENESS
SEDATENESSES
SEDENTARILY
SEDENTARINESS
SEDENTARINESSES
SEDGELANDS
SEDIGITATED
SEDIMENTABLE
SEDIMENTARILY
SEDIMENTARY
SEDIMENTATION
SEDIMENTATIONS
SEDIMENTED
SEDIMENTING
SEDIMENTOLOGIC
SEDIMENTOLOGIES
SEDIMENTOLOGIST
SEDIMENTOLOGY
SEDIMENTOUS
SEDITIONARIES
SEDITIONARY
SEDITIOUSLY
SEDITIOUSNESS
SEDITIOUSNESSES
SEDUCEABLE
SEDUCEMENT
SEDUCEMENTS
SEDUCINGLY
SEDUCTIONS
SEDUCTIVELY
SEDUCTIVENESS
SEDUCTIVENESSES
SEDUCTRESS
SEDUCTRESSES
SEDULITIES
SEDULOUSLY
SEDULOUSNESS
SEDULOUSNESSES
SEECATCHES
SEECATCHIE
SEEDEATERS
SEEDINESSES
SEEDNESSES
SEEDSTOCKS
SEEMELESSE
SEEMINGNESS
SEEMINGNESSES
SEEMLIHEAD
SEEMLIHEADS
SEEMLIHEDS
SEEMLINESS
SEEMLINESSES
SEEMLYHEDS
SEERSUCKER
SEERSUCKERS
SEETHINGLY
SEGHOLATES
SEGMENTALLY
SEGMENTARY
SEGMENTATE
SEGMENTATION
SEGMENTATIONS
SEGMENTING
SEGREGABLE
SEGREGANTS
SEGREGATED
SEGREGATES
SEGREGATING
SEGREGATION
SEGREGATIONAL
SEGREGATIONIST
SEGREGATIONISTS
SEGREGATIONS
SEGREGATIVE
SEGREGATOR
SEGREGATORS
SEGUIDILLA
SEGUIDILLAS
SEIGNEURIAL
SEIGNEURIE
SEIGNEURIES
SEIGNIORAGE
SEIGNIORAGES
SEIGNIORALTIES
SEIGNIORALTY
SEIGNIORIAL
SEIGNIORIES
SEIGNIORSHIP
SEIGNIORSHIPS
SEIGNORAGE
SEIGNORAGES
SEIGNORIAL
SEIGNORIES
SEISMICALLY
SEISMICITIES
SEISMICITY
SEISMOGRAM
SEISMOGRAMS
SEISMOGRAPH
SEISMOGRAPHER
SEISMOGRAPHERS
SEISMOGRAPHIC
SEISMOGRAPHICAL
SEISMOGRAPHIES
SEISMOGRAPHS
SEISMOGRAPHY
SEISMOLOGIC
SEISMOLOGICAL
SEISMOLOGICALLY
SEISMOLOGIES
SEISMOLOGIST
SEISMOLOGISTS
SEISMOLOGY
SEISMOMETER
SEISMOMETERS
SEISMOMETRIC
SEISMOMETRICAL
SEISMOMETRIES
SEISMOMETRY
SEISMONASTIC
SEISMONASTIES
SEISMONASTY
SEISMOSCOPE
SEISMOSCOPES
SEISMOSCOPIC
SELACHIANS
SELAGINELLA
SELAGINELLAS
SELDOMNESS
SELDOMNESSES
SELECTABLE
SELECTIONIST
SELECTIONISTS
SELECTIONS
SELECTIVELY
SELECTIVENESS
SELECTIVENESSES
SELECTIVITIES
SELECTIVITY
SELECTNESS
SELECTNESSES
SELECTORATE
SELECTORATES
SELECTORIAL
SELEGILINE
SELEGILINES
SELENIFEROUS
SELENOCENTRIC
SELENODONT
SELENODONTS
SELENOGRAPH
SELENOGRAPHER
SELENOGRAPHERS
SELENOGRAPHIC
SELENOGRAPHICAL
SELENOGRAPHIES
SELENOGRAPHIST
SELENOGRAPHISTS
SELENOGRAPHS
SELENOGRAPHY
SELENOLOGICAL
SELENOLOGIES
SELENOLOGIST
SELENOLOGISTS
SELENOLOGY
SELFISHNESS
SELFISHNESSES
SELFLESSLY
SELFLESSNESS
SELFLESSNESSES
SELFNESSES
SELFSAMENESS
SELFSAMENESSES
SELLOTAPED
SELLOTAPES
SELLOTAPING
SELTZOGENE
SELTZOGENES
SELVEDGING
SEMAINIERS
SEMANTEMES
SEMANTICAL
SEMANTICALLY
SEMANTICIST
SEMANTICISTS
SEMANTIDES
SEMANTRONS
SEMAPHORED
SEMAPHORES
SEMAPHORIC
SEMAPHORICAL
SEMAPHORICALLY
SEMAPHORING
SEMASIOLOGICAL
SEMASIOLOGIES
SEMASIOLOGIST
SEMASIOLOGISTS

S

SEMASIOLOGY
SEMATOLOGIES
SEMATOLOGY
SEMBLABLES
SEMBLANCES
SEMBLATIVE
SEMEIOLOGIC
SEMEIOLOGICAL
SEMEIOLOGIES
SEMEIOLOGIST
SEMEIOLOGISTS
SEMEIOLOGY
SEMEIOTICALLY
SEMEIOTICIAN
SEMEIOTICIANS
SEMEIOTICS
SEMELPARITIES
SEMELPARITY
SEMELPAROUS
SEMESTERED
SEMESTERING
SEMESTERINGS
SEMESTRIAL
SEMIABSTRACT
SEMIABSTRACTION
SEMIANGLES
SEMIANNUAL
SEMIANNUALLY
SEMIAQUATIC
SEMIARBOREAL
SEMIARIDITIES
SEMIARIDITY
SEMIAUTOMATED
SEMIAUTOMATIC
SEMIAUTOMATICS
SEMIAUTONOMOUS
SEMIBASEMENT
SEMIBASEMENTS
SEMIBREVES
SEMICARBAZIDE
SEMICARBAZIDES
SEMICARBAZONE
SEMICARBAZONES
SEMICENTENNIAL
SEMICENTENNIALS
SEMICHORUS
SEMICHORUSES
SEMICIRCLE
SEMICIRCLED
SEMICIRCLES
SEMICIRCULAR
SEMICIRCULARLY
SEMICIRQUE
SEMICIRQUES
SEMICIVILISED
SEMICIVILIZED
SEMICLASSIC
SEMICLASSICAL
SEMICLASSICS
SEMICOLONIAL
SEMICOLONIALISM
SEMICOLONIES
SEMICOLONS
SEMICOLONY
SEMICOMATOSE
SEMICOMMERCIAL
SEMICONDUCTING
SEMICONDUCTION
SEMICONDUCTIONS
SEMICONDUCTOR
SEMICONDUCTORS
SEMICONSCIOUS
SEMICONSCIOUSLY
SEMICONSONANT
SEMICONSONANTS
SEMICRYSTALLIC
SEMICRYSTALLINE
SEMICYLINDER
SEMICYLINDERS
SEMICYLINDRICAL
SEMIDARKNESS
SEMIDARKNESSES
SEMIDEIFIED
SEMIDEIFIES
SEMIDEIFYING
SEMIDEPONENT
SEMIDEPONENTS
SEMIDESERT
SEMIDESERTS
SEMIDETACHED
SEMIDETACHEDS
SEMIDIAMETER
SEMIDIAMETERS
SEMIDIURNAL
SEMIDIVINE
SEMIDOCUMENTARY
SEMIDOMINANT
SEMIDRIEST
SEMIDRYING
SEMIDWARFS
SEMIDWARVES
SEMIELLIPTICAL
SEMIEMPIRICAL
SEMIEVERGREEN
SEMIFEUDAL
SEMIFINALIST
SEMIFINALISTS
SEMIFINALS
SEMIFINISHED
SEMIFITTED
SEMIFLEXIBLE
SEMIFLUIDIC
SEMIFLUIDITIES
SEMIFLUIDITY
SEMIFLUIDS
SEMIFORMAL
SEMIFREDDI
SEMIFREDDO
SEMIFREDDOS
SEMIGLOBES
SEMIGLOBULAR
SEMIGLOSSES
SEMIGROUPS
SEMIHOBOES
SEMILEGENDARY
SEMILETHAL
SEMILETHALS
SEMILIQUID
SEMILIQUIDS
SEMILITERATE
SEMILITERATES
SEMILOGARITHMIC
SEMILUCENT
SEMILUNATE
SEMILUSTROUS
SEMIMANUFACTURE
SEMIMENSTRUAL
SEMIMETALLIC
SEMIMETALS
SEMIMONASTIC
SEMIMONTHLIES
SEMIMONTHLY
SEMIMYSTICAL
SEMINALITIES
SEMINALITY
SEMINARIAL
SEMINARIAN
SEMINARIANS
SEMINARIES
SEMINARIST
SEMINARISTS
SEMINATING
SEMINATION
SEMINATIONS
SEMINATURAL
SEMINIFEROUS
SEMINOMADIC
SEMINOMADS
SEMINOMATA
SEMINUDITIES
SEMINUDITY
SEMIOCHEMICAL
SEMIOCHEMICALS
SEMIOFFICIAL
SEMIOFFICIALLY
SEMIOLOGIC
SEMIOLOGICAL
SEMIOLOGICALLY
SEMIOLOGIES
SEMIOLOGIST
SEMIOLOGISTS
SEMIOPAQUE
SEMIOTICALLY
SEMIOTICIAN
SEMIOTICIANS
SEMIOTICIST
SEMIOTICISTS
SEMIOVIPAROUS
SEMIPALMATE
SEMIPALMATED
SEMIPALMATION
SEMIPALMATIONS
SEMIPARASITE
SEMIPARASITES
SEMIPARASITIC
SEMIPARASITISM
SEMIPARASITISMS
SEMIPELLUCID
SEMIPERIMETER
SEMIPERIMETERS
SEMIPERMANENT
SEMIPERMEABLE
SEMIPLUMES
SEMIPOLITICAL
SEMIPOPULAR
SEMIPORCELAIN
SEMIPORCELAINS
SEMIPORNOGRAPHY
SEMIPOSTAL
SEMIPOSTALS
SEMIPRECIOUS
SEMIPRIVATE
SEMIPUBLIC
SEMIQUAVER
SEMIQUAVERS
SEMIREFINED
SEMIRELIGIOUS
SEMIRETIRED
SEMIRETIREMENT
SEMIRETIREMENTS
SEMIROUNDS
SEMISACRED
SEMISECRET
SEMISEDENTARY
SEMISHRUBBY
SEMISKILLED
SEMISOLIDS
SEMISOLUSES
SEMISUBMERSIBLE
SEMISYNTHETIC
SEMITERETE
SEMITERRESTRIAL
SEMITONALLY
SEMITONICALLY
SEMITRAILER
SEMITRAILERS
SEMITRANSLUCENT
SEMITRANSPARENT
SEMITROPIC
SEMITROPICAL
SEMITROPICS
SEMITRUCKS
SEMIVITREOUS
SEMIVOCALIC
SEMIVOWELS
SEMIWEEKLIES
SEMIWEEKLY
SEMIYEARLY
SEMPERVIVUM
SEMPERVIVUMS

SEMPITERNAL
SEMPITERNALLY
SEMPITERNITIES
SEMPITERNITY
SEMPITERNUM
SEMPITERNUMS
SEMPSTERING
SEMPSTERINGS
SEMPSTRESS
SEMPSTRESSES
SEMPSTRESSING
SEMPSTRESSINGS
SENARMONTITE
SENARMONTITES
SENATORIAL
SENATORIALLY
SENATORIAN
SENATORSHIP
SENATORSHIPS
SENECTITUDE
SENECTITUDES
SENESCENCE
SENESCENCES
SENESCHALS
SENESCHALSHIP
SENESCHALSHIPS
SENHORITAS
SENILITIES
SENIORITIES
SENNACHIES
SENSATIONAL
SENSATIONALISE
SENSATIONALISED
SENSATIONALISES
SENSATIONALISM
SENSATIONALISMS
SENSATIONALIST
SENSATIONALISTS
SENSATIONALIZE
SENSATIONALIZED
SENSATIONALIZES
SENSATIONALLY
SENSATIONISM
SENSATIONISMS
SENSATIONIST
SENSATIONISTS
SENSATIONLESS
SENSATIONS
SENSELESSLY
SENSELESSNESS
SENSELESSNESSES
SENSIBILIA
SENSIBILITIES
SENSIBILITY
SENSIBLENESS
SENSIBLENESSES
SENSIBLEST
SENSITISATION
SENSITISATIONS
SENSITISED
SENSITISER
SENSITISERS
SENSITISES
SENSITISING
SENSITIVELY
SENSITIVENESS
SENSITIVENESSES
SENSITIVES
SENSITIVITIES
SENSITIVITY
SENSITIZATION
SENSITIZATIONS
SENSITIZED
SENSITIZER
SENSITIZERS
SENSITIZES
SENSITIZING
SENSITOMETER
SENSITOMETERS
SENSITOMETRIC
SENSITOMETRIES
SENSITOMETRY
SENSOMOTOR
SENSORIALLY
SENSORIMOTOR
SENSORINEURAL
SENSORIUMS
SENSUALISATION
SENSUALISATIONS
SENSUALISE
SENSUALISED
SENSUALISES
SENSUALISING
SENSUALISM
SENSUALISMS
SENSUALIST
SENSUALISTIC
SENSUALISTS
SENSUALITIES
SENSUALITY
SENSUALIZATION
SENSUALIZATIONS
SENSUALIZE
SENSUALIZED
SENSUALIZES
SENSUALIZING
SENSUALNESS
SENSUALNESSES
SENSUOSITIES
SENSUOSITY
SENSUOUSLY
SENSUOUSNESS
SENSUOUSNESSES
SENTENCERS
SENTENCING
SENTENCINGS
SENTENTIAE
SENTENTIAL
SENTENTIALLY
SENTENTIOUS
SENTENTIOUSLY
SENTENTIOUSNESS
SENTIENCES
SENTIENCIES
SENTIENTLY
SENTIMENTAL
SENTIMENTALISE
SENTIMENTALISED
SENTIMENTALISES
SENTIMENTALISM
SENTIMENTALISMS
SENTIMENTALIST
SENTIMENTALISTS
SENTIMENTALITY
SENTIMENTALIZE
SENTIMENTALIZED
SENTIMENTALIZES
SENTIMENTALLY
SENTIMENTS
SENTINELED
SENTINELING
SENTINELLED
SENTINELLING
SEPALODIES
SEPARABILITIES
SEPARABILITY
SEPARABLENESS
SEPARABLENESSES
SEPARATELY
SEPARATENESS
SEPARATENESSES
SEPARATING
SEPARATION
SEPARATIONISM
SEPARATIONISMS
SEPARATIONIST
SEPARATIONISTS
SEPARATIONS
SEPARATISM
SEPARATISMS
SEPARATIST
SEPARATISTIC
SEPARATISTS
SEPARATIVE
SEPARATIVELY
SEPARATIVENESS
SEPARATORIES
SEPARATORS
SEPARATORY
SEPARATRICES
SEPARATRIX
SEPARATUMS
SEPIOLITES
SEPIOSTAIRE
SEPIOSTAIRES
SEPTATIONS
SEPTAVALENT
SEPTEMVIRATE
SEPTEMVIRATES
SEPTEMVIRI
SEPTEMVIRS
SEPTENARIES
SEPTENARII
SEPTENARIUS
SEPTENDECILLION
SEPTENNATE
SEPTENNATES
SEPTENNIAL
SEPTENNIALLY
SEPTENNIUM
SEPTENNIUMS
SEPTENTRIAL
SEPTENTRION
SEPTENTRIONAL
SEPTENTRIONALLY
SEPTENTRIONES
SEPTENTRIONS
SEPTICAEMIA
SEPTICAEMIAS
SEPTICAEMIC
SEPTICALLY
SEPTICEMIA
SEPTICEMIAS
SEPTICEMIC
SEPTICIDAL
SEPTICIDALLY
SEPTICITIES
SEPTIFEROUS
SEPTIFRAGAL
SEPTILATERAL
SEPTILLION
SEPTILLIONS
SEPTILLIONTH
SEPTILLIONTHS
SEPTIMOLES
SEPTIVALENT
SEPTUAGENARIAN
SEPTUAGENARIANS
SEPTUAGENARIES
SEPTUAGENARY
SEPTUPLETS
SEPTUPLICATE
SEPTUPLICATES
SEPTUPLING
SEPULCHERED
SEPULCHERING
SEPULCHERS
SEPULCHRAL
SEPULCHRALLY
SEPULCHRED
SEPULCHRES
SEPULCHRING
SEPULCHROUS
SEPULTURAL
SEPULTURED
SEPULTURES
SEPULTURING
SEQUACIOUS
SEQUACIOUSLY
SEQUACIOUSNESS

SEQUACITIES
SEQUELISED
SEQUELISES
SEQUELISING
SEQUELIZED
SEQUELIZES
SEQUELIZING
SEQUENCERS
SEQUENCIES
SEQUENCING
SEQUENCINGS
SEQUENTIAL
SEQUENTIALITIES
SEQUENTIALITY
SEQUENTIALLY
SEQUESTERED
SEQUESTERING
SEQUESTERS
SEQUESTRABLE
SEQUESTRAL
SEQUESTRANT
SEQUESTRANTS
SEQUESTRATE
SEQUESTRATED
SEQUESTRATES
SEQUESTRATING
SEQUESTRATION
SEQUESTRATIONS
SEQUESTRATOR
SEQUESTRATORS
SEQUESTRUM
SEQUESTRUMS
SERAPHICAL
SERAPHICALLY
SERAPHINES
SERASKIERATE
SERASKIERATES
SERASKIERS
SERENADERS
SERENADING
SERENATING
SERENDIPITIES
SERENDIPITIST
SERENDIPITISTS
SERENDIPITOUS
SERENDIPITOUSLY
SERENDIPITY
SERENENESS
SERENENESSES
SERENITIES
SERGEANCIES
SERGEANTIES
SERGEANTSHIP
SERGEANTSHIPS
SERIALISATION
SERIALISATIONS
SERIALISED
SERIALISES
SERIALISING
SERIALISMS
SERIALISTS
SERIALITIES
SERIALIZATION
SERIALIZATIONS
SERIALIZED
SERIALIZES
SERIALIZING
SERIATIONS
SERICICULTURE
SERICICULTURES
SERICICULTURIST
SERICITISATION
SERICITISATIONS
SERICITIZATION
SERICITIZATIONS
SERICTERIA
SERICTERIUM
SERICULTURAL
SERICULTURE
SERICULTURES
SERICULTURIST
SERICULTURISTS
SERIGRAPHER
SERIGRAPHERS
SERIGRAPHIC
SERIGRAPHIES
SERIGRAPHS
SERIGRAPHY
SERINETTES
SERIOCOMIC
SERIOCOMICAL
SERIOCOMICALLY
SERIOUSNESS
SERIOUSNESSES
SERJEANCIES
SERJEANTIES
SERJEANTRIES
SERJEANTRY
SERJEANTSHIP
SERJEANTSHIPS
SERMONEERS
SERMONETTE
SERMONETTES
SERMONICAL
SERMONINGS
SERMONISED
SERMONISER
SERMONISERS
SERMONISES
SERMONISING
SERMONISINGS
SERMONIZED
SERMONIZER
SERMONIZERS
SERMONIZES
SERMONIZING
SERMONIZINGS
SEROCONVERSION
SEROCONVERSIONS
SEROCONVERT
SEROCONVERTED
SEROCONVERTING
SEROCONVERTS
SERODIAGNOSES
SERODIAGNOSIS
SERODIAGNOSTIC
SEROGROUPS
SEROLOGICAL
SEROLOGICALLY
SEROLOGIES
SEROLOGIST
SEROLOGISTS
SERONEGATIVE
SERONEGATIVITY
SEROPOSITIVE
SEROPOSITIVITY
SEROPURULENT
SEROSITIES
SEROTAXONOMIES
SEROTAXONOMY
SEROTHERAPIES
SEROTHERAPY
SEROTINIES
SEROTINOUS
SEROTONERGIC
SEROTONINERGIC
SEROTONINS
SEROTYPING
SEROTYPINGS
SEROUSNESS
SEROUSNESSES
SERPENTIFORM
SERPENTINE
SERPENTINED
SERPENTINELY
SERPENTINES
SERPENTINIC
SERPENTINING
SERPENTININGLY
SERPENTININGS
SERPENTINISE
SERPENTINISED
SERPENTINISES
SERPENTINISING
SERPENTINITE
SERPENTINITES
SERPENTINIZE
SERPENTINIZED
SERPENTINIZES
SERPENTINIZING
SERPENTINOUS
SERPENTISE
SERPENTISED
SERPENTISES
SERPENTISING
SERPENTIZE
SERPENTIZED
SERPENTIZES
SERPENTIZING
SERPENTLIKE
SERPENTRIES
SERPIGINES
SERPIGINOUS
SERPIGINOUSLY
SERPULITES
SERRADELLA
SERRADELLAS
SERRADILLA
SERRADILLAS
SERRANOIDS
SERRASALMO
SERRASALMOS
SERRATIONS
SERRATIROSTRAL
SERRATULATE
SERRATURES
SERRATUSES
SERREFILES
SERRICORNS
SERRIEDNESS
SERRIEDNESSES
SERRULATED
SERRULATION
SERRULATIONS
SERTULARIAN
SERTULARIANS
SERVANTHOOD
SERVANTHOODS
SERVANTING
SERVANTLESS
SERVANTRIES
SERVANTSHIP
SERVANTSHIPS
SERVEWARES
SERVICEABILITY
SERVICEABLE
SERVICEABLENESS
SERVICEABLY
SERVICEBERRIES
SERVICEBERRY
SERVICELESS
SERVICEMAN
SERVICEMEN
SERVICEWOMAN
SERVICEWOMEN
SERVICINGS
SERVIETTES
SERVILENESS
SERVILENESSES
SERVILISMS
SERVILITIES
SERVITORIAL
SERVITORSHIP
SERVITORSHIPS
SERVITRESS
SERVITRESSES
SERVITUDES
SERVOCONTROL
SERVOCONTROLS
SERVOMECHANICAL

S

SERVOMECHANISM
SERVOMECHANISMS
SERVOMOTOR
SERVOMOTORS
SESQUIALTER
SESQUIALTERA
SESQUIALTERAS
SESQUIALTERS
SESQUICARBONATE
SESQUICENTENARY
SESQUIOXIDE
SESQUIOXIDES
SESQUIPEDAL
SESQUIPEDALIAN
SESQUIPEDALIANS
SESQUIPEDALITY
SESQUIPEDALS
SESQUIPLICATE
SESQUISULPHIDE
SESQUISULPHIDES
SESQUITERPENE
SESQUITERPENES
SESQUITERTIA
SESQUITERTIAS
SESSILITIES
SESSIONALLY
SESTERTIUM
SESTERTIUS
SETACEOUSLY
SETIFEROUS
SETIGEROUS
SETTERWORT
SETTERWORTS
SETTLEABLE
SETTLEDNESS
SETTLEDNESSES
SETTLEMENT
SETTLEMENTS
SEVENPENCE
SEVENPENCES
SEVENPENNIES
SEVENPENNY
SEVENTEENS
SEVENTEENTH
SEVENTEENTHLY
SEVENTEENTHS
SEVENTIETH
SEVENTIETHS
SEVERABILITIES
SEVERABILITY
SEVERALFOLD
SEVERALTIES
SEVERANCES
SEVERENESS
SEVERENESSES
SEVERITIES
SEWABILITIES
SEWABILITY
SEXAGENARIAN
SEXAGENARIANS
SEXAGENARIES
SEXAGENARY
SEXAGESIMAL
SEXAGESIMALLY
SEXAGESIMALS
SEXAHOLICS
SEXANGULAR
SEXANGULARLY
SEXAVALENT
SEXCAPADES
SEXCENTENARIES
SEXCENTENARY
SEXDECILLION
SEXDECILLIONS
SEXENNIALLY
SEXENNIALS
SEXERCISES
SEXINESSES
SEXIVALENT
SEXLESSNESS
SEXLESSNESSES
SEXLOCULAR
SEXOLOGICAL
SEXOLOGIES
SEXOLOGIST
SEXOLOGISTS
SEXPARTITE
SEXPLOITATION
SEXPLOITATIONS
SEXTARIUSES
SEXTILLION
SEXTILLIONS
SEXTILLIONTH
SEXTILLIONTHS
SEXTODECIMO
SEXTODECIMOS
SEXTONESSES
SEXTONSHIP
SEXTONSHIPS
SEXTUPLETS
SEXTUPLICATE
SEXTUPLICATED
SEXTUPLICATES
SEXTUPLICATING
SEXTUPLIED
SEXTUPLIES
SEXTUPLING
SEXTUPLYING
SEXUALISATION
SEXUALISATIONS
SEXUALISED
SEXUALISES
SEXUALISING
SEXUALISMS
SEXUALISTS
SEXUALITIES
SEXUALIZATION
SEXUALIZATIONS
SEXUALIZED
SEXUALIZES
SEXUALIZING
SFORZANDOS
SHABBINESS
SHABBINESSES
SHABRACQUE
SHABRACQUES
SHACKLEBONE
SHACKLEBONES
SHACKTOWNS
SHADBERRIES
SHADBUSHES
SHADCHANIM
SHADINESSES
SHADKHANIM
SHADOWBOXED
SHADOWBOXES
SHADOWBOXING
SHADOWCAST
SHADOWCASTED
SHADOWCASTING
SHADOWCASTINGS
SHADOWCASTS
SHADOWGRAPH
SHADOWGRAPHIES
SHADOWGRAPHS
SHADOWGRAPHY
SHADOWIEST
SHADOWINESS
SHADOWINESSES
SHADOWINGS
SHADOWLESS
SHADOWLIKE
SHAGGEDNESS
SHAGGEDNESSES
SHAGGINESS
SHAGGINESSES
SHAGGYMANE
SHAGGYMANES
SHAGREENED
SHAGTASTIC
SHAHTOOSHES
SHAKEDOWNS
SHAKINESSES
SHAKUHACHI
SHAKUHACHIS
SHALLOWEST
SHALLOWING
SHALLOWINGS
SHALLOWNESS
SHALLOWNESSES
SHAMANISMS
SHAMANISTIC
SHAMANISTS
SHAMATEURISM
SHAMATEURISMS
SHAMATEURS
SHAMBLIEST
SHAMBLINGS
SHAMBOLICALLY
SHAMEFACED
SHAMEFACEDLY
SHAMEFACEDNESS
SHAMEFASTNESS
SHAMEFASTNESSES
SHAMEFULLY
SHAMEFULNESS
SHAMEFULNESSES
SHAMELESSLY
SHAMELESSNESS
SHAMELESSNESSES
SHAMEWORTHIER
SHAMEWORTHIEST
SHAMEWORTHY
SHAMIANAHS
SHAMIYANAH
SHAMIYANAHS
SHAMMASHIM
SHAMOISING
SHAMPOOERS
SHAMPOOING
SHANACHIES
SHANDRYDAN
SHANDRYDANS
SHANDYGAFF
SHANDYGAFFS
SHANGHAIED
SHANGHAIER
SHANGHAIERS
SHANGHAIING
SHANKBONES
SHANKPIECE
SHANKPIECES
SHANTYTOWN
SHANTYTOWNS
SHAPELESSLY
SHAPELESSNESS
SHAPELESSNESSES
SHAPELIEST
SHAPELINESS
SHAPELINESSES
SHAPESHIFTER
SHAPESHIFTERS
SHAPESHIFTING
SHAPESHIFTINGS
SHAPEWEARS
SHARAWADGI
SHARAWADGIS
SHARAWAGGI
SHARAWAGGIS
SHAREABILITIES
SHAREABILITY
SHARECROPPED
SHARECROPPER
SHARECROPPERS
SHARECROPPING
SHARECROPPINGS
SHARECROPS
SHAREFARMER
SHAREFARMERS
SHAREHOLDER

SHAREHOLDERS
SHAREHOLDING
SHAREHOLDINGS
SHAREMILKER
SHAREMILKERS
SHARENTING
SHARENTINGS
SHAREWARES
SHARKSKINS
SHARKSUCKER
SHARKSUCKERS
SHARPBENDER
SHARPBENDERS
SHARPENERS
SHARPENING
SHARPENINGS
SHARPNESSES
SHARPSHOOTER
SHARPSHOOTERS
SHARPSHOOTING
SHARPSHOOTINGS
SHARPTAILS
SHASHLICKS
SHATOOSHES
SHATTERERS
SHATTERIER
SHATTERIEST
SHATTERING
SHATTERINGLY
SHATTERPROOF
SHAUCHLIER
SHAUCHLIEST
SHAUCHLING
SHAVASANAS
SHAVELINGS
SHAVETAILS
SHEARLINGS
SHEARWATER
SHEARWATERS
SHEATFISHES
SHEATHBILL
SHEATHBILLS
SHEATHFISH
SHEATHFISHES
SHEATHIEST
SHEATHINGS
SHEATHLESS
SHEATHLIKE
SHEBAGGING
SHEBAGGINGS
SHEBEENERS
SHEBEENING
SHEBEENINGS
SHECHITAHS
SHECKLATON
SHECKLATONS
SHEEPBERRIES
SHEEPBERRY
SHEEPCOTES
SHEEPFOLDS
SHEEPHEADS
SHEEPHERDER
SHEEPHERDERS
SHEEPHERDING
SHEEPHERDINGS
SHEEPISHLY
SHEEPISHNESS
SHEEPISHNESSES
SHEEPSHANK
SHEEPSHANKS
SHEEPSHEAD
SHEEPSHEADS
SHEEPSHEARER
SHEEPSHEARERS
SHEEPSHEARING
SHEEPSHEARINGS
SHEEPSKINS
SHEEPTRACK
SHEEPTRACKS
SHEEPWALKS
SHEERNESSES
SHEETROCKED
SHEETROCKING
SHEETROCKS
SHEIKHDOMS
SHELDDUCKS
SHELDRAKES
SHELFROOMS
SHELFTALKER
SHELFTALKERS
SHELLACKED
SHELLACKER
SHELLACKERS
SHELLACKING
SHELLACKINGS
SHELLBACKS
SHELLBARKS
SHELLBOUND
SHELLCRACKER
SHELLCRACKERS
SHELLDRAKE
SHELLDRAKES
SHELLDUCKS
SHELLFIRES
SHELLFISHERIES
SHELLFISHERY
SHELLFISHES
SHELLINESS
SHELLINESSES
SHELLPROOF
SHELLSHOCK
SHELLSHOCKED
SHELLSHOCKS
SHELLWORKS
SHELLYCOAT
SHELLYCOATS
SHELTERBELT
SHELTERBELTS
SHELTERERS
SHELTERIER
SHELTERIEST
SHELTERING
SHELTERINGS
SHELTERLESS
SHEMOZZLED
SHEMOZZLES
SHEMOZZLING
SHENANIGAN
SHENANIGANS
SHEPHERDED
SHEPHERDESS
SHEPHERDESSES
SHEPHERDING
SHEPHERDINGS
SHEPHERDLESS
SHEPHERDLING
SHEPHERDLINGS
SHERARDISATION
SHERARDISATIONS
SHERARDISE
SHERARDISED
SHERARDISES
SHERARDISING
SHERARDIZATION
SHERARDIZATIONS
SHERARDIZE
SHERARDIZED
SHERARDIZES
SHERARDIZING
SHEREEFIAN
SHERGOTTITE
SHERGOTTITES
SHERIFFALTIES
SHERIFFALTY
SHERIFFDOM
SHERIFFDOMS
SHERIFFSHIP
SHERIFFSHIPS
SHERLOCKED
SHERLOCKING
SHEWBREADS
SHIBBOLETH
SHIBBOLETHS
SHIBUICHIS
SHIDDUCHIM
SHIELDINGS
SHIELDLESS
SHIELDLIKE
SHIELDLING
SHIELDLINGS
SHIELDRAKE
SHIELDRAKES
SHIELDWALL
SHIELDWALLS
SHIFTINESS
SHIFTINESSES
SHIFTLESSLY
SHIFTLESSNESS
SHIFTLESSNESSES
SHIFTSTICK
SHIFTSTICKS
SHIFTWORKS
SHIGELLOSES
SHIGELLOSIS
SHIKARRING
SHILLABERS
SHILLALAHS
SHILLELAGH
SHILLELAGHS
SHILLELAHS
SHILLINGLESS
SHILLINGSWORTH
SHILLINGSWORTHS
SHILLYSHALLIED
SHILLYSHALLIER
SHILLYSHALLIERS
SHILLYSHALLIES
SHILLYSHALLY
SHILLYSHALLYING
SHIMMERIER
SHIMMERIEST
SHIMMERING
SHIMMERINGLY
SHIMMERINGS
SHIMOZZLES
SHINGLIEST
SHINGLINGS
SHINGUARDS
SHININESSES
SHININGNESS
SHININGNESSES
SHINLEAVES
SHINNERIES
SHINNEYING
SHINPLASTER
SHINPLASTERS
SHINSPLINTS
SHIPBOARDS
SHIPBROKER
SHIPBROKERS
SHIPBUILDER
SHIPBUILDERS
SHIPBUILDING
SHIPBUILDINGS
SHIPFITTER
SHIPFITTERS
SHIPLAPPED
SHIPLAPPING
SHIPLAPPINGS
SHIPMASTER
SHIPMASTERS
SHIPOWNERS
SHIPPOUNDS
SHIPWRECKED
SHIPWRECKING
SHIPWRECKS
SHIPWRIGHT
SHIPWRIGHTS
SHIRETOWNS
SHIRRALEES

SHIRTBANDS
SHIRTDRESS
SHIRTDRESSES
SHIRTFRONT
SHIRTFRONTED
SHIRTFRONTING
SHIRTFRONTS
SHIRTINESS
SHIRTINESSES
SHIRTMAKER
SHIRTMAKERS
SHIRTSLEEVE
SHIRTSLEEVED
SHIRTSLEEVES
SHIRTTAILED
SHIRTTAILING
SHIRTTAILS
SHIRTWAIST
SHIRTWAISTED
SHIRTWAISTER
SHIRTWAISTERS
SHIRTWAISTS
SHITCANNED
SHITCANNING
SHITHOUSES
SHITSTORMS
SHITTIMWOOD
SHITTIMWOODS
SHITTINESS
SHITTINESSES
SHIVAREEING
SHIVERIEST
SHIVERINGLY
SHIVERINGS
SHLEMIEHLS
SHLEMOZZLE
SHLEMOZZLED
SHLEMOZZLES
SHLEMOZZLING
SHLEPPIEST
SHLIMAZELS
SHLOCKIEST
SHLUMPIEST
SHMALTZIER
SHMALTZIEST
SHMOOZIEST
SHMUCKIEST
SHOALINESS
SHOALINESSES
SHOALNESSES
SHOCKABILITIES
SHOCKABILITY
SHOCKHEADED
SHOCKINGLY
SHOCKINGNESS
SHOCKINGNESSES
SHOCKPROOF
SHOCKSTALL
SHOCKSTALLS
SHOCKUMENTARIES
SHOCKUMENTARY
SHODDINESS
SHODDINESSES
SHOEBLACKS
SHOEBRUSHES
SHOEHORNED
SHOEHORNING
SHOEMAKERS
SHOEMAKING
SHOEMAKINGS
SHOESHINES
SHOESTRING
SHOESTRINGS
SHOGGLIEST
SHOGUNATES
SHONGOLOLO
SHONGOLOLOS
SHOOGIEING
SHOOGLIEST
SHOOTAROUND
SHOOTAROUNDS
SHOOTDOWNS
SHOPAHOLIC
SHOPAHOLICS
SHOPAHOLISM
SHOPAHOLISMS
SHOPBOARDS
SHOPBREAKER
SHOPBREAKERS
SHOPBREAKING
SHOPBREAKINGS
SHOPFITTER
SHOPFITTERS
SHOPFRONTS
SHOPHOUSES
SHOPKEEPER
SHOPKEEPERS
SHOPKEEPING
SHOPKEEPINGS
SHOPLIFTED
SHOPLIFTER
SHOPLIFTERS
SHOPLIFTING
SHOPLIFTINGS
SHOPSOILED
SHOPWALKER
SHOPWALKERS
SHOPWINDOW
SHOPWINDOWS
SHOREBIRDS
SHOREFRONT
SHOREFRONTS
SHORELINES
SHORESIDES
SHOREWARDS
SHOREWEEDS
SHORTARSES
SHORTBOARD
SHORTBOARDS
SHORTBREAD
SHORTBREADS
SHORTCAKES
SHORTCHANGE
SHORTCHANGED
SHORTCHANGER
SHORTCHANGERS
SHORTCHANGES
SHORTCHANGING
SHORTCOMING
SHORTCOMINGS
SHORTCRUST
SHORTCUTTING
SHORTENERS
SHORTENING
SHORTENINGS
SHORTFALLS
SHORTGOWNS
SHORTHAIRED
SHORTHAIRS
SHORTHANDED
SHORTHANDS
SHORTHEADS
SHORTHORNS
SHORTLISTED
SHORTLISTING
SHORTLISTS
SHORTNESSES
SHORTSHEET
SHORTSHEETED
SHORTSHEETING
SHORTSHEETS
SHORTSIGHTED
SHORTSIGHTEDLY
SHORTSTOPS
SHORTSWORD
SHORTSWORDS
SHORTWAVED
SHORTWAVES
SHORTWAVING
SHOTCRETES
SHOTFIRERS
SHOTGUNNED
SHOTGUNNER
SHOTGUNNERS
SHOTGUNNING
SHOTMAKERS
SHOTMAKING
SHOTMAKINGS
SHOULDERED
SHOULDERING
SHOULDERINGS
SHOUTHERED
SHOUTHERING
SHOUTINGLY
SHOUTLINES
SHOVELBOARD
SHOVELBOARDS
SHOVELFULS
SHOVELHEAD
SHOVELHEADS
SHOVELLERS
SHOVELLING
SHOVELNOSE
SHOVELNOSES
SHOVELSFUL
SHOWBIZZES
SHOWBIZZIER
SHOWBIZZIEST
SHOWBOATED
SHOWBOATER
SHOWBOATERS
SHOWBOATING
SHOWBREADS
SHOWCASING
SHOWERHEAD
SHOWERHEADS
SHOWERIEST
SHOWERINESS
SHOWERINESSES
SHOWERINGS
SHOWERLESS
SHOWERPROOF
SHOWERPROOFED
SHOWERPROOFING
SHOWERPROOFINGS
SHOWERPROOFS
SHOWGROUND
SHOWGROUNDS
SHOWINESSES
SHOWJUMPED
SHOWJUMPER
SHOWJUMPERS
SHOWJUMPING
SHOWJUMPINGS
SHOWMANCES
SHOWMANLIER
SHOWMANLIEST
SHOWMANSHIP
SHOWMANSHIPS
SHOWPIECES
SHOWPLACES
SHOWROOMING
SHOWROOMINGS
SHOWSTOPPER
SHOWSTOPPERS
SHOWSTOPPING
SHREDDIEST
SHREDDINGS
SHREWDNESS
SHREWDNESSES
SHREWISHLY
SHREWISHNESS
SHREWISHNESSES
SHREWMOUSE
SHRIECHING
SHRIEKIEST
SHRIEKINGLY
SHRIEKINGS
SHRIEVALTIES
SHRIEVALTY

S

SHRILLIEST
SHRILLINGS
SHRILLNESS
SHRILLNESSES
SHRIMPIEST
SHRIMPINGS
SHRIMPLIKE
SHRINELIKE
SHRINKABLE
SHRINKAGES
SHRINKFLATION
SHRINKFLATIONS
SHRINKINGLY
SHRINKPACK
SHRINKPACKS
SHRITCHING
SHRIVELING
SHRIVELLED
SHRIVELLING
SHROFFAGES
SHROUDIEST
SHROUDINGS
SHROUDLESS
SHRUBBERIED
SHRUBBERIES
SHRUBBIEST
SHRUBBINESS
SHRUBBINESSES
SHRUBLANDS
SHTETELACH
SHTICKIEST
SHTREIMELS
SHUBUNKINS
SHUDDERIER
SHUDDERIEST
SHUDDERING
SHUDDERINGLY
SHUDDERINGS
SHUDDERSOME
SHUFFLEBOARD
SHUFFLEBOARDS
SHUFFLINGLY
SHUFFLINGS
SHUNAMITISM
SHUNAMITISMS
SHUNPIKERS
SHUNPIKING
SHUNPIKINGS
SHUTTERBUG
SHUTTERBUGS
SHUTTERING
SHUTTERINGS
SHUTTERLESS
SHUTTLECOCK
SHUTTLECOCKED
SHUTTLECOCKING
SHUTTLECOCKS
SHUTTLELESS
SHUTTLEWISE
SHYLOCKING
SIALAGOGIC
SIALAGOGUE
SIALAGOGUES
SIALOGOGIC
SIALOGOGUE
SIALOGOGUES
SIALOGRAMS
SIALOGRAPHIES
SIALOGRAPHY
SIALOLITHS
SIALORRHOEA
SIALORRHOEAS
SIBILANCES
SIBILANCIES
SIBILANTLY
SIBILATING
SIBILATION
SIBILATIONS
SIBILATORS
SIBILATORY
SICCATIVES
SICILIANAS
SICILIANOS
SICILIENNE
SICILIENNES
SICKENINGLY
SICKENINGS
SICKERNESS
SICKERNESSES
SICKISHNESS
SICKISHNESSES
SICKLEBILL
SICKLEBILLS
SICKLEMIAS
SICKLINESS
SICKLINESSES
SICKNESSES
SICKNURSED
SICKNURSES
SICKNURSING
SICKNURSINGS
SIDDHUISMS
SIDEARMERS
SIDEARMING
SIDEBOARDS
SIDEBURNED
SIDECHAIRS
SIDECHECKS
SIDEDNESSES
SIDEDRESSES
SIDELEVERS
SIDELIGHTS
SIDELINERS
SIDELINING
SIDEPIECES
SIDERATING
SIDERATION
SIDERATIONS
SIDEREALLY
SIDEROLITE
SIDEROLITES
SIDEROPENIA
SIDEROPENIAS
SIDEROPHILE
SIDEROPHILES
SIDEROPHILIC
SIDEROPHILIN
SIDEROPHILINS
SIDEROSTAT
SIDEROSTATIC
SIDEROSTATS
SIDESADDLE
SIDESADDLES
SIDESHOOTS
SIDESLIPPED
SIDESLIPPING
SIDESPLITS
SIDESPLITTING
SIDESPLITTINGLY
SIDESTEPPED
SIDESTEPPER
SIDESTEPPERS
SIDESTEPPING
SIDESTEPPINGS
SIDESTREAM
SIDESTROKE
SIDESTROKES
SIDESWIPED
SIDESWIPER
SIDESWIPERS
SIDESWIPES
SIDESWIPING
SIDETABLES
SIDETRACKED
SIDETRACKING
SIDETRACKS
SIDEWHEELER
SIDEWHEELERS
SIDEWHEELS
SIDEWINDER
SIDEWINDERS
SIEGECRAFT
SIEGECRAFTS
SIEGEWORKS
SIFFLEUSES
SIGHTLESSLY
SIGHTLESSNESS
SIGHTLESSNESSES
SIGHTLIEST
SIGHTLINES
SIGHTLINESS
SIGHTLINESSES
SIGHTSCREEN
SIGHTSCREENS
SIGHTSEEING
SIGHTSEEINGS
SIGHTSEERS
SIGHTWORTHIER
SIGHTWORTHIEST
SIGHTWORTHY
SIGILLARIAN
SIGILLARIANS
SIGILLARID
SIGILLARIDS
SIGILLATION
SIGILLATIONS
SIGMATIONS
SIGMATISMS
SIGMATRONS
SIGMOIDALLY
SIGMOIDECTOMIES
SIGMOIDECTOMY
SIGMOIDOSCOPE
SIGMOIDOSCOPES
SIGMOIDOSCOPIC
SIGMOIDOSCOPIES
SIGMOIDOSCOPY
SIGNALINGS
SIGNALISATION
SIGNALISATIONS
SIGNALISED
SIGNALISES
SIGNALISING
SIGNALIZATION
SIGNALIZATIONS
SIGNALIZED
SIGNALIZES
SIGNALIZING
SIGNALLERS
SIGNALLING
SIGNALLINGS
SIGNALMENT
SIGNALMENTS
SIGNATORIES
SIGNATURES
SIGNBOARDS
SIGNEURIES
SIGNIFIABLE
SIGNIFICANCE
SIGNIFICANCES
SIGNIFICANCIES
SIGNIFICANCY
SIGNIFICANT
SIGNIFICANTLY
SIGNIFICANTS
SIGNIFICATE
SIGNIFICATES
SIGNIFICATION
SIGNIFICATIONS
SIGNIFICATIVE
SIGNIFICATIVELY
SIGNIFICATOR
SIGNIFICATORS
SIGNIFICATORY
SIGNIFIEDS
SIGNIFIERS
SIGNIFYING
SIGNIFYINGS
SIGNIORIES
SIGNORINAS

SIGNPOSTED
SIGNPOSTING
SIGNPOSTINGS
SIKORSKIES
SILDENAFIL
SILDENAFILS
SILENTIARIES
SILENTIARY
SILENTNESS
SILENTNESSES
SILHOUETTE
SILHOUETTED
SILHOUETTES
SILHOUETTING
SILHOUETTIST
SILHOUETTISTS
SILICATING
SILICICOLOUS
SILICIFEROUS
SILICIFICATION
SILICIFICATIONS
SILICIFIED
SILICIFIES
SILICIFYING
SILICONISED
SILICONIZED
SILICOTICS
SILICULOSE
SILIQUACEOUS
SILKALENES
SILKALINES
SILKGROWER
SILKGROWERS
SILKINESSES
SILKOLINES
SILKSCREEN
SILKSCREENED
SILKSCREENING
SILKSCREENS
SILLIMANITE
SILLIMANITES
SILLINESSES
SILTATIONS
SILTSTONES
SILVERBACK
SILVERBACKS
SILVERBERRIES
SILVERBERRY
SILVERBILL
SILVERBILLS
SILVEREYES
SILVERFISH
SILVERFISHES
SILVERHORN
SILVERHORNS
SILVERIEST
SILVERINESS
SILVERINESSES
SILVERINGS
SILVERISED
SILVERISES
SILVERISING
SILVERIZED
SILVERIZES
SILVERIZING
SILVERLING
SILVERLINGS
SILVERPOINT
SILVERPOINTS
SILVERSIDE
SILVERSIDES
SILVERSKIN
SILVERSKINS
SILVERSMITH
SILVERSMITHING
SILVERSMITHINGS
SILVERSMITHS
SILVERTAIL
SILVERTAILS
SILVERTIPS
SILVERWARE
SILVERWARES
SILVERWEED
SILVERWEEDS
SILVESTRIAN
SILVICULTURAL
SILVICULTURALLY
SILVICULTURE
SILVICULTURES
SILVICULTURIST
SILVICULTURISTS
SILYMARINS
SIMAROUBACEOUS
SIMAROUBAS
SIMARUBACEOUS
SIMILARITIES
SIMILARITY
SIMILATIVE
SIMILISING
SIMILITUDE
SIMILITUDES
SIMILIZING
SIMILLIMUM
SIMILLIMUMS
SIMONIACAL
SIMONIACALLY
SIMONISING
SIMONIZING
SIMPERINGLY
SIMPERINGS
SIMPLEMINDED
SIMPLEMINDEDLY
SIMPLENESS
SIMPLENESSES
SIMPLESSES
SIMPLETONS
SIMPLICIAL
SIMPLICIALLY
SIMPLICIDENTATE
SIMPLICITER
SIMPLICITIES
SIMPLICITY
SIMPLIFIABLE
SIMPLIFICATION
SIMPLIFICATIONS
SIMPLIFICATIVE
SIMPLIFICATOR
SIMPLIFICATORS
SIMPLIFIED
SIMPLIFIER
SIMPLIFIERS
SIMPLIFIES
SIMPLIFYING
SIMPLISTES
SIMPLISTIC
SIMPLISTICALLY
SIMULACRES
SIMULACRUM
SIMULACRUMS
SIMULATING
SIMULATION
SIMULATIONS
SIMULATIVE
SIMULATIVELY
SIMULATORS
SIMULATORY
SIMULCASTED
SIMULCASTING
SIMULCASTS
SIMULTANEITIES
SIMULTANEITY
SIMULTANEOUS
SIMULTANEOUSES
SIMULTANEOUSLY
SIMVASTATIN
SIMVASTATINS
SINANTHROPUS
SINANTHROPUSES
SINARCHISM
SINARCHISMS
SINARCHIST
SINARCHISTS
SINARQUISM
SINARQUISMS
SINARQUIST
SINARQUISTS
SINCERENESS
SINCERENESSES
SINCERITIES
SINCIPITAL
SINDONOLOGIES
SINDONOLOGIST
SINDONOLOGISTS
SINDONOLOGY
SINDONOPHANIES
SINDONOPHANY
SINECURISM
SINECURISMS
SINECURIST
SINECURISTS
SINEWINESS
SINEWINESSES
SINFONIETTA
SINFONIETTAS
SINFULNESS
SINFULNESSES
SINGABLENESS
SINGABLENESSES
SINGALONGS
SINGLEDOMS
SINGLEHOOD
SINGLEHOODS
SINGLENESS
SINGLENESSES
SINGLESTICK
SINGLESTICKS
SINGLETONS
SINGLETRACK
SINGLETRACKS
SINGLETREE
SINGLETREES
SINGSONGED
SINGSONGIER
SINGSONGIEST
SINGSONGING
SINGSPIELS
SINGULARISATION
SINGULARISE
SINGULARISED
SINGULARISES
SINGULARISING
SINGULARISM
SINGULARISMS
SINGULARIST
SINGULARISTS
SINGULARITIES
SINGULARITY
SINGULARIZATION
SINGULARIZE
SINGULARIZED
SINGULARIZES
SINGULARIZING
SINGULARLY
SINGULARNESS
SINGULARNESSES
SINGULTUSES
SINICISING
SINICIZING
SINISTERITIES
SINISTERITY
SINISTERLY
SINISTERNESS
SINISTERNESSES
SINISTERWISE
SINISTRALITIES
SINISTRALITY
SINISTRALLY
SINISTRALS
SINISTRODEXTRAL
SINISTRORSAL

S

SINISTRORSALLY
SINISTRORSE
SINISTRORSELY
SINISTROUS
SINISTROUSLY
SINLESSNESS
SINLESSNESSES
SINNINGIAS
SINOATRIAL
SINOLOGICAL
SINOLOGIES
SINOLOGIST
SINOLOGISTS
SINOLOGUES
SINSEMILLA
SINSEMILLAS
SINTERABILITIES
SINTERABILITY
SINTERIEST
SINUATIONS
SINUITISES
SINUOSITIES
SINUOUSNESS
SINUOUSNESSES
SINUPALLIAL
SINUPALLIATE
SINUSITISES
SINUSOIDAL
SINUSOIDALLY
SIPHONAGES
SIPHONOGAM
SIPHONOGAMIES
SIPHONOGAMS
SIPHONOGAMY
SIPHONOPHORE
SIPHONOPHORES
SIPHONOPHOROUS
SIPHONOSTELE
SIPHONOSTELES
SIPHONOSTELIC
SIPHUNCLES
SIPUNCULID
SIPUNCULIDS
SIPUNCULOID
SIPUNCULOIDS
SIRENISING
SIRENIZING
SIRONISING
SIRONIZING
SISERARIES
SISSINESSES
SISSYNESSES
SISTERHOOD
SISTERHOODS
SISTERLESS
SISTERLIER
SISTERLIEST
SISTERLIKE
SISTERLINESS
SISTERLINESSES
SITATUNGAS
SITIOLOGIES
SITIOPHOBIA
SITIOPHOBIAS
SITOLOGIES
SITOPHOBIA
SITOPHOBIAS
SITOSTEROL
SITOSTEROLS
SITUATIONAL
SITUATIONALLY
SITUATIONISM
SITUATIONISMS
SITUATIONS
SITUTUNGAS
SITZKRIEGS
SIXPENNIES
SIXTEENERS
SIXTEENMOS
SIXTEENTHLY
SIXTEENTHS
SIZABLENESS
SIZABLENESSES
SIZARSHIPS
SIZEABLENESS
SIZEABLENESSES
SIZINESSES
SIZZLINGLY
SJAMBOKING
SJAMBOKKED
SJAMBOKKING
SKAITHLESS
SKALDSHIPS
SKANKINESS
SKANKINESSES
SKATEBOARD
SKATEBOARDED
SKATEBOARDER
SKATEBOARDERS
SKATEBOARDING
SKATEBOARDINGS
SKATEBOARDS
SKATEPARKS
SKATEPUNKS
SKEDADDLED
SKEDADDLER
SKEDADDLERS
SKEDADDLES
SKEDADDLING
SKELDERING
SKELETALLY
SKELETOGENOUS
SKELETONIC
SKELETONISE
SKELETONISED
SKELETONISER
SKELETONISERS
SKELETONISES
SKELETONISING
SKELETONIZE
SKELETONIZED
SKELETONIZER
SKELETONIZERS
SKELETONIZES
SKELETONIZING
SKELLOCHED
SKELLOCHING
SKELTERING
SKEPTICALLY
SKEPTICALNESS
SKEPTICALNESSES
SKEPTICISM
SKEPTICISMS
SKETCHABILITIES
SKETCHABILITY
SKETCHABLE
SKETCHBOOK
SKETCHBOOKS
SKETCHIEST
SKETCHINESS
SKETCHINESSES
SKETCHPADS
SKEUOMORPH
SKEUOMORPHIC
SKEUOMORPHISM
SKEUOMORPHISMS
SKEUOMORPHS
SKEWBACKED
SKEWNESSES
SKIAGRAPHS
SKIAMACHIES
SKIASCOPES
SKIASCOPIES
SKIBOBBERS
SKIBOBBING
SKIBOBBINGS
SKIDDOOING
SKIDOOINGS
SKIJORINGS
SKIJUMPERS
SKIKJORERS
SKIKJORING
SKIKJORINGS
SKILFULNESS
SKILFULNESSES
SKILLCENTRE
SKILLCENTRES
SKILLESSNESS
SKILLESSNESSES
SKILLFULLY
SKILLFULNESS
SKILLFULNESSES
SKILLIGALEE
SKILLIGALEES
SKILLIGOLEE
SKILLIGOLEES
SKIMBOARDED
SKIMBOARDER
SKIMBOARDERS
SKIMBOARDING
SKIMBOARDS
SKIMMINGLY
SKIMMINGTON
SKIMMINGTONS
SKIMOBILED
SKIMOBILES
SKIMOBILING
SKIMPINESS
SKIMPINESSES
SKIMPINGLY
SKINFLICKS
SKINFLINTIER
SKINFLINTIEST
SKINFLINTS
SKINFLINTY
SKINNINESS
SKINNINESSES
SKINTIGHTER
SKINTIGHTEST
SKINTIGHTS
SKIPPERING
SKIPPERINGS
SKIPPINGLY
SKIRMISHED
SKIRMISHER
SKIRMISHERS
SKIRMISHES
SKIRMISHING
SKIRMISHINGS
SKITTERIER
SKITTERIEST
SKITTERING
SKITTISHLY
SKITTISHNESS
SKITTISHNESSES
SKORDALIAS
SKREEGHING
SKREIGHING
SKRIECHING
SKRIEGHING
SKRIMMAGED
SKRIMMAGES
SKRIMMAGING
SKRIMSHANK
SKRIMSHANKED
SKRIMSHANKER
SKRIMSHANKERS
SKRIMSHANKING
SKRIMSHANKS
SKULDUDDERIES
SKULDUDDERY
SKULDUGGERIES
SKULDUGGERY
SKULKINGLY
SKULLDUGGERIES
SKULLDUGGERY
SKUMMERING
SKUNKBIRDS
SKUNKWEEDS
SKUTTERUDITE

S

SKUTTERUDITES
SKYBRIDGES
SKYDIVINGS
SKYJACKERS
SKYJACKING
SKYJACKINGS
SKYLARKERS
SKYLARKING
SKYLARKINGS
SKYLIGHTED
SKYROCKETED
SKYROCKETING
SKYROCKETS
SKYSCRAPER
SKYSCRAPERS
SKYSURFERS
SKYSURFING
SKYSURFINGS
SKYWATCHED
SKYWATCHES
SKYWATCHING
SKYWRITERS
SKYWRITING
SKYWRITINGS
SKYWRITTEN
SLABBERERS
SLABBERIER
SLABBERIEST
SLABBERING
SLABBINESS
SLABBINESSES
SLABSTONES
SLACKENERS
SLACKENING
SLACKENINGS
SLACKLINING
SLACKLININGS
SLACKNESSES
SLACKTIVISM
SLACKTIVISMS
SLACKTIVIST
SLACKTIVISTS
SLACTIVISM
SLACTIVISMS
SLACTIVIST
SLACTIVISTS
SLAISTERED
SLAISTERIES
SLAISTERING
SLALOMISTS
SLAMDANCED
SLAMDANCES
SLAMDANCING
SLAMMAKINS
SLAMMERKIN
SLAMMERKINS
SLANDERERS
SLANDERING
SLANDEROUS
SLANDEROUSLY
SLANDEROUSNESS
SLANGINESS
SLANGINESSES
SLANGINGLY
SLANGUAGES
SLANTENDICULAR
SLANTINDICULAR
SLANTINGLY
SLANTINGWAYS
SLAPDASHED
SLAPDASHES
SLAPDASHING
SLAPHAPPIER
SLAPHAPPIEST
SLAPSTICKS
SLASHFESTS
SLASHINGLY
SLATHERING
SLATINESSES
SLATTERING
SLATTERNLIER
SLATTERNLIEST
SLATTERNLINESS
SLATTERNLY
SLAUGHTERABLE
SLAUGHTERED
SLAUGHTERER
SLAUGHTERERS
SLAUGHTERHOUSE
SLAUGHTERHOUSES
SLAUGHTERIES
SLAUGHTERING
SLAUGHTERMAN
SLAUGHTERMEN
SLAUGHTEROUS
SLAUGHTEROUSLY
SLAUGHTERS
SLAUGHTERY
SLAVEHOLDER
SLAVEHOLDERS
SLAVEHOLDING
SLAVEHOLDINGS
SLAVERINGLY
SLAVERINGS
SLAVISHNESS
SLAVISHNESSES
SLAVOCRACIES
SLAVOCRACY
SLAVOCRATS
SLAVOPHILE
SLAVOPHILES
SLAVOPHILS
SLEAZEBAGS
SLEAZEBALL
SLEAZEBALLS
SLEAZINESS
SLEAZINESSES
SLEDGEHAMMER
SLEDGEHAMMERED
SLEDGEHAMMERING
SLEDGEHAMMERS
SLEECHIEST
SLEEKENING
SLEEKNESSES
SLEEKSTONE
SLEEKSTONES
SLEEPINESS
SLEEPINESSES
SLEEPLESSLY
SLEEPLESSNESS
SLEEPLESSNESSES
SLEEPOVERS
SLEEPSUITS
SLEEPWALKED
SLEEPWALKER
SLEEPWALKERS
SLEEPWALKING
SLEEPWALKINGS
SLEEPWALKS
SLEEPWEARS
SLEEPYHEAD
SLEEPYHEADED
SLEEPYHEADS
SLEETINESS
SLEETINESSES
SLEEVEHAND
SLEEVEHANDS
SLEEVELESS
SLEEVELETS
SLEEVELIKE
SLEIGHINGS
SLENDEREST
SLENDERISE
SLENDERISED
SLENDERISES
SLENDERISING
SLENDERIZE
SLENDERIZED
SLENDERIZES
SLENDERIZING
SLENDERNESS
SLENDERNESSES
SLEUTHHOUND
SLEUTHHOUNDS
SLEUTHINGS
SLICKENERS
SLICKENING
SLICKENSIDE
SLICKENSIDED
SLICKENSIDES
SLICKNESSES
SLICKROCKS
SLICKSTERS
SLICKSTONE
SLICKSTONES
SLIDDERIER
SLIDDERIEST
SLIDDERING
SLIDESHOWS
SLIGHTINGLY
SLIGHTNESS
SLIGHTNESSES
SLIMEBALLS
SLIMINESSES
SLIMNASTICS
SLIMNESSES
SLIMPSIEST
SLINGBACKS
SLINGSHOTS
SLINGSTONE
SLINGSTONES
SLINKINESS
SLINKINESSES
SLINKSKINS
SLINKWEEDS
SLIPCOVERED
SLIPCOVERING
SLIPCOVERS
SLIPDRESSES
SLIPFORMED
SLIPFORMING
SLIPNOOSES
SLIPPERIER
SLIPPERIEST
SLIPPERILY
SLIPPERINESS
SLIPPERINESSES
SLIPPERING
SLIPPERWORT
SLIPPERWORTS
SLIPPINESS
SLIPPINESSES
SLIPSHEETED
SLIPSHEETING
SLIPSHEETS
SLIPSHODDINESS
SLIPSHODNESS
SLIPSHODNESSES
SLIPSLOPPIER
SLIPSLOPPIEST
SLIPSLOPPY
SLIPSTREAM
SLIPSTREAMED
SLIPSTREAMING
SLIPSTREAMS
SLITHERIER
SLITHERIEST
SLITHERING
SLIVOVICAS
SLIVOVICES
SLIVOVITZES
SLIVOWITZES
SLOBBERERS
SLOBBERIER
SLOBBERIEST
SLOBBERING
SLOBBISHNESS
SLOBBISHNESSES
SLOCKDOLAGER
SLOCKDOLAGERS

SLOCKDOLIGER
SLOCKDOLIGERS
SLOCKDOLOGER
SLOCKDOLOGERS
SLOCKENING
SLOEBUSHES
SLOETHORNS
SLOGANEERED
SLOGANEERING
SLOGANEERINGS
SLOGANEERS
SLOGANISED
SLOGANISES
SLOGANISING
SLOGANISINGS
SLOGANIZED
SLOGANIZES
SLOGANIZING
SLOGANIZINGS
SLOMMOCKED
SLOMMOCKING
SLOPESIDES
SLOPINGNESS
SLOPINGNESSES
SLOPPINESS
SLOPPINESSES
SLOPWORKER
SLOPWORKERS
SLOTHFULLY
SLOTHFULNESS
SLOTHFULNESSES
SLOUCHIEST
SLOUCHINESS
SLOUCHINESSES
SLOUCHINGLY
SLOUGHIEST
SLOVENLIER
SLOVENLIEST
SLOVENLIKE
SLOVENLINESS
SLOVENLINESSES
SLOVENRIES
SLOWCOACHES
SLOWNESSES
SLUBBERING
SLUBBERINGLY
SLUBBERINGS
SLUGGABEDS
SLUGGARDISE
SLUGGARDISED
SLUGGARDISES
SLUGGARDISING
SLUGGARDIZE
SLUGGARDIZED
SLUGGARDIZES
SLUGGARDIZING
SLUGGARDLIER
SLUGGARDLIEST
SLUGGARDLINESS
SLUGGARDLY
SLUGGARDNESS
SLUGGARDNESSES
SLUGGISHLY
SLUGGISHNESS
SLUGGISHNESSES
SLUGHORNES
SLUICEGATE
SLUICEGATES
SLUICELIKE
SLUICEWAYS
SLUMBERERS
SLUMBERFUL
SLUMBERIER
SLUMBERIEST
SLUMBERING
SLUMBERINGLY
SLUMBERINGS
SLUMBERLAND
SLUMBERLANDS
SLUMBERLESS
SLUMBEROUS
SLUMBEROUSLY
SLUMBEROUSNESS
SLUMBERSOME
SLUMBROUSLY
SLUMBROUSNESS
SLUMBROUSNESSES
SLUMGULLION
SLUMGULLIONS
SLUMMOCKED
SLUMMOCKING
SLUMPFLATION
SLUMPFLATIONARY
SLUMPFLATIONS
SLUNGSHOTS
SLUSHINESS
SLUSHINESSES
SLUTCHIEST
SLUTTERIES
SLUTTINESS
SLUTTINESSES
SLUTTISHLY
SLUTTISHNESS
SLUTTISHNESSES
SMACKDOWNS
SMACKEROOS
SMACKHEADS
SMALLCLOTHES
SMALLHOLDER
SMALLHOLDERS
SMALLHOLDING
SMALLHOLDINGS
SMALLMOUTH
SMALLMOUTHS
SMALLNESSES
SMALLPOXES
SMALLSWORD
SMALLSWORDS
SMALMINESS
SMALMINESSES
SMARAGDINE
SMARAGDITE
SMARAGDITES
SMARMINESS
SMARMINESSES
SMARTARSED
SMARTARSES
SMARTASSES
SMARTENING
SMARTINGLY
SMARTMOUTH
SMARTMOUTHS
SMARTNESSES
SMARTPHONE
SMARTPHONES
SMARTWATCH
SMARTWATCHES
SMARTWEEDS
SMARTYPANTS
SMASHEROOS
SMASHINGLY
SMASHMOUTH
SMATTERERS
SMATTERING
SMATTERINGLY
SMATTERINGS
SMEARCASES
SMEARINESS
SMEARINESSES
SMELLINESS
SMELLINESSES
SMELTERIES
SMICKERING
SMICKERINGS
SMIERCASES
SMIFLIGATE
SMIFLIGATED
SMIFLIGATES
SMIFLIGATING
SMILACACEOUS
SMILINGNESS
SMILINGNESSES
SMIRKINGLY
SMITHCRAFT
SMITHCRAFTS
SMITHEREEN
SMITHEREENED
SMITHEREENING
SMITHEREENS
SMITHERIES
SMITHSONITE
SMITHSONITES
SMOKEBOARD
SMOKEBOARDS
SMOKEBOXES
SMOKEBUSHES
SMOKEHOODS
SMOKEHOUSE
SMOKEHOUSES
SMOKEJACKS
SMOKELESSLY
SMOKELESSNESS
SMOKELESSNESSES
SMOKEPROOF
SMOKESCREEN
SMOKESCREENS
SMOKESTACK
SMOKESTACKS
SMOKETIGHT
SMOKINESSES
SMOLDERING
SMOOCHIEST
SMOOTHABLE
SMOOTHBORE
SMOOTHBORED
SMOOTHBORES
SMOOTHENED
SMOOTHENING
SMOOTHINGS
SMOOTHNESS
SMOOTHNESSES
SMOOTHPATE
SMOOTHPATES
SMORGASBORD
SMORGASBORDS
SMORREBROD
SMORREBRODS
SMOTHERERS
SMOTHERIER
SMOTHERIEST
SMOTHERINESS
SMOTHERINESSES
SMOTHERING
SMOTHERINGLY
SMOTHERINGS
SMOULDERED
SMOULDERING
SMOULDERINGLY
SMOULDERINGS
SMOULDRIER
SMOULDRIEST
SMUDGELESS
SMUDGINESS
SMUDGINESSES
SMUGGERIES
SMUGGLINGS
SMUGNESSES
SMUTCHIEST
SMUTTINESS
SMUTTINESSES
SNACKETTES
SNAGGLETEETH
SNAGGLETOOTH
SNAGGLETOOTHED
SNAILERIES
SNAILFISHES
SNAKEBIRDS
SNAKEBITES
SNAKEBITTEN
SNAKEFISHES

SNAKEHEADS
SNAKEMOUTH
SNAKEMOUTHS
SNAKEROOTS
SNAKESKINS
SNAKESTONE
SNAKESTONES
SNAKEWEEDS
SNAKEWOODS
SNAKINESSES
SNAKISHNESS
SNAKISHNESSES
SNAPDRAGON
SNAPDRAGONS
SNAPHANCES
SNAPHAUNCE
SNAPHAUNCES
SNAPHAUNCH
SNAPHAUNCHES
SNAPPERING
SNAPPINESS
SNAPPINESSES
SNAPPINGLY
SNAPPISHLY
SNAPPISHNESS
SNAPPISHNESSES
SNAPSHOOTER
SNAPSHOOTERS
SNAPSHOOTING
SNAPSHOOTINGS
SNAPSHOTTED
SNAPSHOTTING
SNARLINGLY
SNATCHIEST
SNATCHINGLY
SNATCHINGS
SNAZZINESS
SNAZZINESSES
SNEAKBOXES
SNEAKINESS
SNEAKINESSES
SNEAKINGLY
SNEAKINGNESS
SNEAKINGNESSES
SNEAKISHLY
SNEAKISHNESS
SNEAKISHNESSES
SNEAKSBIES
SNEERINGLY
SNEESHINGS
SNEEZELESS
SNEEZEWEED
SNEEZEWEEDS
SNEEZEWOOD
SNEEZEWOODS
SNEEZEWORT
SNEEZEWORTS
SNICKERERS
SNICKERIER
SNICKERIEST
SNICKERING
SNICKERSNEE
SNICKERSNEED
SNICKERSNEEING
SNICKERSNEES
SNIDENESSES
SNIFFINESS
SNIFFINESSES
SNIFFINGLY
SNIFFISHLY
SNIFFISHNESS
SNIFFISHNESSES
SNIFFLIEST
SNIFTERING
SNIGGERERS
SNIGGERING
SNIGGERINGLY
SNIGGERINGS
SNIGGLINGS
SNIPEFISHES
SNIPERSCOPE
SNIPERSCOPES
SNIPPERSNAPPER
SNIPPERSNAPPERS
SNIPPETIER
SNIPPETIEST
SNIPPETINESS
SNIPPETINESSES
SNIPPINESS
SNIPPINESSES
SNITCHIEST
SNIVELIEST
SNIVELINGS
SNIVELLERS
SNIVELLIER
SNIVELLIEST
SNIVELLING
SNIVELLINGS
SNOBBERIES
SNOBBISHLY
SNOBBISHNESS
SNOBBISHNESSES
SNOBBOCRACIES
SNOBBOCRACY
SNOBOCRACIES
SNOBOCRACY
SNOBOGRAPHER
SNOBOGRAPHERS
SNOBOGRAPHIES
SNOBOGRAPHY
SNOCOACHES
SNOLLYGOSTER
SNOLLYGOSTERS
SNOOKERING
SNOOPERSCOPE
SNOOPERSCOPES
SNOOTINESS
SNOOTINESSES
SNORKELERS
SNORKELING
SNORKELINGS
SNORKELLED
SNORKELLER
SNORKELLERS
SNORKELLING
SNORKELLINGS
SNORTINGLY
SNOTTERIES
SNOTTERING
SNOTTINESS
SNOTTINESSES
SNOWBALLED
SNOWBALLING
SNOWBERRIES
SNOWBLADER
SNOWBLADERS
SNOWBLADES
SNOWBLADING
SNOWBLADINGS
SNOWBLINKS
SNOWBLOWER
SNOWBLOWERS
SNOWBOARDED
SNOWBOARDER
SNOWBOARDERS
SNOWBOARDING
SNOWBOARDINGS
SNOWBOARDS
SNOWBRUSHES
SNOWBUSHES
SNOWCAPPED
SNOWCLONES
SNOWCOACHES
SNOWDRIFTS
SNOWFIELDS
SNOWFLAKES
SNOWFLECKS
SNOWFLICKS
SNOWGLOBES
SNOWINESSES
SNOWMAKERS
SNOWMAKING
SNOWMOBILE
SNOWMOBILED
SNOWMOBILER
SNOWMOBILERS
SNOWMOBILES
SNOWMOBILING
SNOWMOBILINGS
SNOWMOBILIST
SNOWMOBILISTS
SNOWMOULDS
SNOWPLOUGH
SNOWPLOUGHED
SNOWPLOUGHING
SNOWPLOUGHS
SNOWPLOWED
SNOWPLOWING
SNOWSCAPES
SNOWSHOEING
SNOWSHOEINGS
SNOWSHOERS
SNOWSLIDES
SNOWSNAKES
SNOWSTORMS
SNOWSURFING
SNOWSURFINGS
SNOWTUBING
SNOWTUBINGS
SNUBBINESS
SNUBBINESSES
SNUBBINGLY
SNUBNESSES
SNUFFBOXES
SNUFFINESS
SNUFFINESSES
SNUFFLIEST
SNUFFLINGS
SNUGGERIES
SNUGGLIEST
SNUGNESSES
SOAPBERRIES
SOAPBOXING
SOAPDISHES
SOAPFISHES
SOAPFLAKES
SOAPINESSES
SOAPOLALLIE
SOAPOLALLIES
SOAPSTONES
SOAPSUDSIER
SOAPSUDSIEST
SOBERINGLY
SOBERISING
SOBERIZING
SOBERNESSES
SOBERSIDED
SOBERSIDEDNESS
SOBERSIDES
SOBOLIFEROUS
SOBRIETIES
SOBRIQUETS
SOCDOLAGER
SOCDOLAGERS
SOCDOLIGER
SOCDOLIGERS
SOCDOLOGER
SOCDOLOGERS
SOCIABILITIES
SOCIABILITY
SOCIABLENESS
SOCIABLENESSES
SOCIALISABLE
SOCIALISATION
SOCIALISATIONS
SOCIALISED
SOCIALISER
SOCIALISERS
SOCIALISES
SOCIALISING

SOCIALISINGS
SOCIALISMS
SOCIALISTIC
SOCIALISTICALLY
SOCIALISTS
SOCIALITES
SOCIALITIES
SOCIALIZABLE
SOCIALIZATION
SOCIALIZATIONS
SOCIALIZED
SOCIALIZER
SOCIALIZERS
SOCIALIZES
SOCIALIZING
SOCIALIZINGS
SOCIALNESS
SOCIALNESSES
SOCIATIONS
SOCIETALLY
SOCIOBIOLOGICAL
SOCIOBIOLOGIES
SOCIOBIOLOGIST
SOCIOBIOLOGISTS
SOCIOBIOLOGY
SOCIOCULTURAL
SOCIOCULTURALLY
SOCIOECONOMIC
SOCIOGRAMS
SOCIOHISTORICAL
SOCIOLECTS
SOCIOLINGUIST
SOCIOLINGUISTIC
SOCIOLINGUISTS
SOCIOLOGESE
SOCIOLOGESES
SOCIOLOGIC
SOCIOLOGICAL
SOCIOLOGICALLY
SOCIOLOGIES
SOCIOLOGISM
SOCIOLOGISMS
SOCIOLOGIST
SOCIOLOGISTIC
SOCIOLOGISTS
SOCIOMETRIC
SOCIOMETRIES
SOCIOMETRIST
SOCIOMETRISTS
SOCIOMETRY
SOCIOPATHIC
SOCIOPATHIES
SOCIOPATHS
SOCIOPATHY
SOCIOPOLITICAL
SOCIORELIGIOUS
SOCIOSEXUAL
SOCKDOLAGER
SOCKDOLAGERS
SOCKDOLIGER
SOCKDOLIGERS
SOCKDOLOGER
SOCKDOLOGERS
SODALITIES
SODBUSTERS
SODDENNESS
SODDENNESSES
SODICITIES
SODOMISING
SODOMITICAL
SODOMITICALLY
SODOMIZING
SOFTBALLER
SOFTBALLERS
SOFTBOUNDS
SOFTCOVERS
SOFTENINGS
SOFTHEADED
SOFTHEADEDLY
SOFTHEADEDNESS
SOFTHEARTED
SOFTHEARTEDLY
SOFTHEARTEDNESS
SOFTNESSES
SOFTSCAPES
SOFTSHELLS
SOGDOLAGER
SOGDOLAGERS
SOGDOLIGER
SOGDOLIGERS
SOGDOLOGER
SOGDOLOGERS
SOGGINESSES
SOILINESSES
SOJOURNERS
SOJOURNING
SOJOURNINGS
SOJOURNMENT
SOJOURNMENTS
SOKEMANRIES
SOLACEMENT
SOLACEMENTS
SOLANACEOUS
SOLARIMETER
SOLARIMETERS
SOLARISATION
SOLARISATIONS
SOLARISING
SOLARIZATION
SOLARIZATIONS
SOLARIZING
SOLDATESQUE
SOLDERABILITIES
SOLDERABILITY
SOLDERABLE
SOLDERINGS
SOLDIERIES
SOLDIERING
SOLDIERINGS
SOLDIERLIER
SOLDIERLIEST
SOLDIERLIKE
SOLDIERLINESS
SOLDIERLINESSES
SOLDIERSHIP
SOLDIERSHIPS
SOLECISING
SOLECISTIC
SOLECISTICAL
SOLECISTICALLY
SOLECIZING
SOLEMNESSES
SOLEMNIFICATION
SOLEMNIFIED
SOLEMNIFIES
SOLEMNIFYING
SOLEMNISATION
SOLEMNISATIONS
SOLEMNISED
SOLEMNISER
SOLEMNISERS
SOLEMNISES
SOLEMNISING
SOLEMNITIES
SOLEMNIZATION
SOLEMNIZATIONS
SOLEMNIZED
SOLEMNIZER
SOLEMNIZERS
SOLEMNIZES
SOLEMNIZING
SOLEMNNESS
SOLEMNNESSES
SOLENESSES
SOLENETTES
SOLENODONS
SOLENOIDAL
SOLENOIDALLY
SOLEPLATES
SOLEPRINTS
SOLFATARAS
SOLFATARIC
SOLFEGGIOS
SOLFERINOS
SOLICITANT
SOLICITANTS
SOLICITATION
SOLICITATIONS
SOLICITIES
SOLICITING
SOLICITINGS
SOLICITORS
SOLICITORSHIP
SOLICITORSHIPS
SOLICITOUS
SOLICITOUSLY
SOLICITOUSNESS
SOLICITUDE
SOLICITUDES
SOLIDARISM
SOLIDARISMS
SOLIDARIST
SOLIDARISTIC
SOLIDARISTS
SOLIDARITIES
SOLIDARITY
SOLIDATING
SOLIDIFIABLE
SOLIDIFICATION
SOLIDIFICATIONS
SOLIDIFIED
SOLIDIFIER
SOLIDIFIERS
SOLIDIFIES
SOLIDIFYING
SOLIDITIES
SOLIDNESSES
SOLIDUNGULATE
SOLIDUNGULATES
SOLIDUNGULOUS
SOLIFIDIAN
SOLIFIDIANISM
SOLIFIDIANISMS
SOLIFIDIANS
SOLIFLUCTION
SOLIFLUCTIONS
SOLIFLUXION
SOLIFLUXIONS
SOLILOQUIES
SOLILOQUISE
SOLILOQUISED
SOLILOQUISER
SOLILOQUISERS
SOLILOQUISES
SOLILOQUISING
SOLILOQUIST
SOLILOQUISTS
SOLILOQUIZE
SOLILOQUIZED
SOLILOQUIZER
SOLILOQUIZERS
SOLILOQUIZES
SOLILOQUIZING
SOLIPEDOUS
SOLIPSISMS
SOLIPSISTIC
SOLIPSISTICALLY
SOLIPSISTS
SOLITAIRES
SOLITARIAN
SOLITARIANS
SOLITARIES
SOLITARILY
SOLITARINESS
SOLITARINESSES
SOLITUDINARIAN
SOLITUDINARIANS
SOLITUDINOUS
SOLIVAGANT
SOLIVAGANTS

S

SOLLICKERS
SOLMISATION
SOLMISATIONS
SOLMIZATION
SOLMIZATIONS
SOLONCHAKS
SOLONETSES
SOLONETZES
SOLONETZIC
SOLONISATION
SOLONISATIONS
SOLONIZATION
SOLONIZATIONS
SOLSTITIAL
SOLSTITIALLY
SOLUBILISATION
SOLUBILISATIONS
SOLUBILISE
SOLUBILISED
SOLUBILISES
SOLUBILISING
SOLUBILITIES
SOLUBILITY
SOLUBILIZATION
SOLUBILIZATIONS
SOLUBILIZE
SOLUBILIZED
SOLUBILIZES
SOLUBILIZING
SOLUBLENESS
SOLUBLENESSES
SOLUTIONAL
SOLUTIONED
SOLUTIONING
SOLUTIONIST
SOLUTIONISTS
SOLVABILITIES
SOLVABILITY
SOLVABLENESS
SOLVABLENESSES
SOLVATIONS
SOLVENCIES
SOLVENTLESS
SOLVOLYSES
SOLVOLYSIS
SOLVOLYTIC
SOMAESTHESIA
SOMAESTHESIAS
SOMAESTHESIS
SOMAESTHESISES
SOMAESTHETIC
SOMASCOPES
SOMATICALLY
SOMATOGENIC
SOMATOLOGIC
SOMATOLOGICAL
SOMATOLOGICALLY
SOMATOLOGIES
SOMATOLOGIST
SOMATOLOGISTS
SOMATOLOGY
SOMATOMEDIN
SOMATOMEDINS
SOMATOPLASM
SOMATOPLASMS
SOMATOPLASTIC
SOMATOPLEURAL
SOMATOPLEURE
SOMATOPLEURES
SOMATOPLEURIC
SOMATOSENSORY
SOMATOSTATIN
SOMATOSTATINS
SOMATOTENSIC
SOMATOTONIA
SOMATOTONIAS
SOMATOTONIC
SOMATOTONICS
SOMATOTROPHIC
SOMATOTROPHIN
SOMATOTROPHINS
SOMATOTROPIC
SOMATOTROPIN
SOMATOTROPINE
SOMATOTROPINES
SOMATOTROPINS
SOMATOTYPE
SOMATOTYPED
SOMATOTYPES
SOMATOTYPING
SOMBERNESS
SOMBERNESSES
SOMBRENESS
SOMBRENESSES
SOMBRERITE
SOMBRERITES
SOMEBODIES
SOMEPLACES
SOMERSAULT
SOMERSAULTED
SOMERSAULTING
SOMERSAULTS
SOMERSETED
SOMERSETING
SOMERSETTED
SOMERSETTING
SOMESTHESIA
SOMESTHESIAS
SOMESTHESIS
SOMESTHESISES
SOMESTHETIC
SOMETHINGS
SOMEWHENCE
SOMEWHERES
SOMEWHILES
SOMEWHITHER
SOMMELIERS
SOMNAMBULANCE
SOMNAMBULANCES
SOMNAMBULANT
SOMNAMBULANTS
SOMNAMBULAR
SOMNAMBULARY
SOMNAMBULATE
SOMNAMBULATED
SOMNAMBULATES
SOMNAMBULATING
SOMNAMBULATION
SOMNAMBULATIONS
SOMNAMBULATOR
SOMNAMBULATORS
SOMNAMBULE
SOMNAMBULES
SOMNAMBULIC
SOMNAMBULISM
SOMNAMBULISMS
SOMNAMBULIST
SOMNAMBULISTIC
SOMNAMBULISTS
SOMNIATING
SOMNIATIVE
SOMNIATORY
SOMNIFACIENT
SOMNIFACIENTS
SOMNIFEROUS
SOMNIFEROUSLY
SOMNILOQUENCE
SOMNILOQUENCES
SOMNILOQUIES
SOMNILOQUISE
SOMNILOQUISED
SOMNILOQUISES
SOMNILOQUISING
SOMNILOQUISM
SOMNILOQUISMS
SOMNILOQUIST
SOMNILOQUISTS
SOMNILOQUIZE
SOMNILOQUIZED
SOMNILOQUIZES
SOMNILOQUIZING
SOMNILOQUOUS
SOMNILOQUY
SOMNOLENCE
SOMNOLENCES
SOMNOLENCIES
SOMNOLENCY
SOMNOLENTLY
SOMNOLESCENT
SONGCRAFTS
SONGFULNESS
SONGFULNESSES
SONGLESSLY
SONGOLOLOS
SONGSHEETS
SONGSMITHS
SONGSTRESS
SONGSTRESSES
SONGWRITER
SONGWRITERS
SONGWRITING
SONGWRITINGS
SONICATING
SONICATION
SONICATIONS
SONICATORS
SONIFEROUS
SONNETEERING
SONNETEERINGS
SONNETEERS
SONNETISED
SONNETISES
SONNETISING
SONNETIZED
SONNETIZES
SONNETIZING
SONNETTING
SONOFABITCH
SONOGRAPHER
SONOGRAPHERS
SONOGRAPHIES
SONOGRAPHS
SONOGRAPHY
SONOMETERS
SONORITIES
SONOROUSLY
SONOROUSNESS
SONOROUSNESSES
SOOTERKINS
SOOTFLAKES
SOOTHERING
SOOTHFASTLY
SOOTHFASTNESS
SOOTHFASTNESSES
SOOTHINGLY
SOOTHINGNESS
SOOTHINGNESSES
SOOTHSAYER
SOOTHSAYERS
SOOTHSAYING
SOOTHSAYINGS
SOOTINESSES
SOPAIPILLA
SOPAIPILLAS
SOPAPILLAS
SOPHISTERS
SOPHISTICAL
SOPHISTICALLY
SOPHISTICATE
SOPHISTICATED
SOPHISTICATEDLY
SOPHISTICATES
SOPHISTICATING
SOPHISTICATION
SOPHISTICATIONS
SOPHISTICATOR
SOPHISTICATORS
SOPHISTRIES
SOPHOMORES
SOPHOMORIC

SOPHOMORICAL
SOPORIFEROUS
SOPORIFEROUSLY
SOPORIFICALLY
SOPORIFICS
SOPPINESSES
SOPRANINOS
SOPRANISTS
SORBABILITIES
SORBABILITY
SORBEFACIENT
SORBEFACIENTS
SORBITISATION
SORBITISATIONS
SORBITISED
SORBITISES
SORBITISING
SORBITIZATION
SORBITIZATIONS
SORBITIZED
SORBITIZES
SORBITIZING
SORCERESSES
SORDAMENTE
SORDIDNESS
SORDIDNESSES
SOREHEADED
SOREHEADEDLY
SOREHEADEDNESS
SORENESSES
SORICIDENT
SORORIALLY
SORORICIDAL
SORORICIDE
SORORICIDES
SORORISING
SORORITIES
SORORIZING
SORRINESSES
SORROWFULLY
SORROWFULNESS
SORROWFULNESSES
SORROWINGS
SORROWLESS
SORTATIONS
SORTILEGER
SORTILEGERS
SORTILEGES
SORTILEGIES
SORTITIONS
SOSTENUTOS
SOTERIOLOGIC
SOTERIOLOGICAL
SOTERIOLOGIES
SOTERIOLOGY
SOTTISHNESS
SOTTISHNESSES
SOTTISIERS
SOUBRETTES
SOUBRETTISH
SOUBRIQUET
SOUBRIQUETS
SOULDIERED
SOULDIERING
SOULFULNESS
SOULFULNESSES
SOULLESSLY
SOULLESSNESS
SOULLESSNESSES
SOUNDALIKE
SOUNDALIKES
SOUNDBITES
SOUNDBOARD
SOUNDBOARDS
SOUNDBOXES
SOUNDCARDS
SOUNDINGLY
SOUNDLESSLY
SOUNDLESSNESS
SOUNDLESSNESSES
SOUNDNESSES
SOUNDPOSTS
SOUNDPROOF
SOUNDPROOFED
SOUNDPROOFING
SOUNDPROOFINGS
SOUNDPROOFS
SOUNDSCAPE
SOUNDSCAPES
SOUNDSTAGE
SOUNDSTAGES
SOUNDTRACK
SOUNDTRACKED
SOUNDTRACKING
SOUNDTRACKS
SOUPINESSES
SOUPSPOONS
SOURCEBOOK
SOURCEBOOKS
SOURCELESS
SOURDELINE
SOURDELINES
SOURDOUGHS
SOURNESSES
SOURPUSSES
SOUSAPHONE
SOUSAPHONES
SOUSAPHONIST
SOUSAPHONISTS
SOUTENEURS
SOUTERRAIN
SOUTERRAINS
SOUTHBOUND
SOUTHEASTER
SOUTHEASTERLIES
SOUTHEASTERLY
SOUTHEASTERN
SOUTHEASTERS
SOUTHEASTS
SOUTHEASTWARD
SOUTHEASTWARDS
SOUTHERING
SOUTHERLIES
SOUTHERLINESS
SOUTHERLINESSES
SOUTHERMOST
SOUTHERNER
SOUTHERNERS
SOUTHERNISE
SOUTHERNISED
SOUTHERNISES
SOUTHERNISING
SOUTHERNISM
SOUTHERNISMS
SOUTHERNIZE
SOUTHERNIZED
SOUTHERNIZES
SOUTHERNIZING
SOUTHERNLY
SOUTHERNMOST
SOUTHERNNESS
SOUTHERNNESSES
SOUTHERNWOOD
SOUTHERNWOODS
SOUTHLANDER
SOUTHLANDERS
SOUTHLANDS
SOUTHSAYING
SOUTHWARDLY
SOUTHWARDS
SOUTHWESTER
SOUTHWESTERLIES
SOUTHWESTERLY
SOUTHWESTERN
SOUTHWESTERS
SOUTHWESTS
SOUTHWESTWARD
SOUTHWESTWARDLY
SOUTHWESTWARDS
SOUVENIRED
SOUVENIRING
SOUVLAKIAS
SOVENANCES
SOVEREIGNLY
SOVEREIGNS
SOVEREIGNTIES
SOVEREIGNTIST
SOVEREIGNTISTS
SOVEREIGNTY
SOVIETISATION
SOVIETISATIONS
SOVIETISED
SOVIETISES
SOVIETISING
SOVIETISMS
SOVIETISTIC
SOVIETISTS
SOVIETIZATION
SOVIETIZATIONS
SOVIETIZED
SOVIETIZES
SOVIETIZING
SOVIETOLOGICAL
SOVIETOLOGIST
SOVIETOLOGISTS
SOVRANTIES
SOWBELLIES
SOYBURGERS
SPACEBANDS
SPACEBORNE
SPACECRAFT
SPACECRAFTS
SPACEFARING
SPACEFARINGS
SPACEFLIGHT
SPACEFLIGHTS
SPACEPLANE
SPACEPLANES
SPACEPORTS
SPACESHIPS
SPACESUITS
SPACETIMES
SPACEWALKED
SPACEWALKER
SPACEWALKERS
SPACEWALKING
SPACEWALKS
SPACEWOMAN
SPACEWOMEN
SPACINESSES
SPACIOUSLY
SPACIOUSNESS
SPACIOUSNESSES
SPADASSINS
SPADEFISHES
SPADEFOOTS
SPADEWORKS
SPADICEOUS
SPADICIFLORAL
SPADILLIOS
SPAGHETTIFIED
SPAGHETTIFIES
SPAGHETTIFY
SPAGHETTIFYING
SPAGHETTILIKE
SPAGHETTINI
SPAGHETTINIS
SPAGHETTIS
SPAGIRISTS
SPAGYRICAL
SPAGYRICALLY
SPAGYRISTS
SPALLATION
SPALLATIONS
SPANAEMIAS
SPANAKOPITA
SPANAKOPITAS
SPANCELING
SPANCELLED
SPANCELLING

S

SPANGHEWED
SPANGHEWING
SPANGLIEST
SPANGLINGS
SPANIELLED
SPANIELLING
SPANIOLATE
SPANIOLATED
SPANIOLATES
SPANIOLATING
SPANIOLISE
SPANIOLISED
SPANIOLISES
SPANIOLISING
SPANIOLIZE
SPANIOLIZED
SPANIOLIZES
SPANIOLIZING
SPANKINGLY
SPANOKOPITA
SPANOKOPITAS
SPARAGMATIC
SPARAGRASS
SPARAGRASSES
SPARAXISES
SPARENESSES
SPARGANIUM
SPARGANIUMS
SPARINGNESS
SPARINGNESSES
SPARKISHLY
SPARKLEBERRIES
SPARKLEBERRY
SPARKLESSLY
SPARKLIEST
SPARKLINGLY
SPARKLINGS
SPARKPLUGGED
SPARKPLUGGING
SPARKPLUGS
SPARROWFART
SPARROWFARTS
SPARROWGRASS
SPARROWGRASSES
SPARROWHAWK
SPARROWHAWKS
SPARROWLIKE
SPARSENESS
SPARSENESSES
SPARSITIES
SPARTEINES
SPARTERIES
SPARTICLES
SPASMATICAL
SPASMODICAL
SPASMODICALLY
SPASMODIST
SPASMODISTS
SPASMOLYTIC
SPASMOLYTICS
SPASTICALLY
SPASTICITIES
SPASTICITY
SPATANGOID
SPATANGOIDS
SPATCHCOCK
SPATCHCOCKED
SPATCHCOCKING
SPATCHCOCKS
SPATHACEOUS
SPATHIPHYLLUM
SPATHIPHYLLUMS
SPATHULATE
SPATIALISATION
SPATIALISATIONS
SPATIALITIES
SPATIALITY
SPATIALIZATION
SPATIALIZATIONS
SPATIOTEMPORAL
SPATTERDASH
SPATTERDASHES
SPATTERDOCK
SPATTERDOCKS
SPATTERING
SPATTERWORK
SPATTERWORKS
SPEAKEASIES
SPEAKERINE
SPEAKERINES
SPEAKERPHONE
SPEAKERPHONES
SPEAKERSHIP
SPEAKERSHIPS
SPEAKINGLY
SPEARCARRIER
SPEARCARRIERS
SPEARFISHED
SPEARFISHES
SPEARFISHING
SPEARHEADED
SPEARHEADING
SPEARHEADS
SPEARMINTS
SPEARWORTS
SPECIALEST
SPECIALISATION
SPECIALISATIONS
SPECIALISE
SPECIALISED
SPECIALISER
SPECIALISERS
SPECIALISES
SPECIALISING
SPECIALISM
SPECIALISMS
SPECIALIST
SPECIALISTIC
SPECIALISTS
SPECIALITIES
SPECIALITY
SPECIALIZATION
SPECIALIZATIONS
SPECIALIZE
SPECIALIZED
SPECIALIZER
SPECIALIZERS
SPECIALIZES
SPECIALIZING
SPECIALLED
SPECIALLING
SPECIALNESS
SPECIALNESSES
SPECIALOGUE
SPECIALOGUES
SPECIALTIES
SPECIATING
SPECIATION
SPECIATIONAL
SPECIATIONS
SPECIESISM
SPECIESISMS
SPECIESIST
SPECIESISTS
SPECIFIABLE
SPECIFICAL
SPECIFICALLY
SPECIFICATE
SPECIFICATED
SPECIFICATES
SPECIFICATING
SPECIFICATION
SPECIFICATIONS
SPECIFICATIVE
SPECIFICATORY
SPECIFICITIES
SPECIFICITY
SPECIFIERS
SPECIFYING
SPECIOCIDE
SPECIOCIDES
SPECIOSITIES
SPECIOSITY
SPECIOUSLY
SPECIOUSNESS
SPECIOUSNESSES
SPECKLEDNESS
SPECKLEDNESSES
SPECKSIONEER
SPECKSIONEERS
SPECKTIONEER
SPECKTIONEERS
SPECTACLED
SPECTACLES
SPECTACULAR
SPECTACULARITY
SPECTACULARLY
SPECTACULARS
SPECTATING
SPECTATORIAL
SPECTATORS
SPECTATORSHIP
SPECTATORSHIPS
SPECTATRESS
SPECTATRESSES
SPECTATRICES
SPECTATRIX
SPECTATRIXES
SPECTINOMYCIN
SPECTINOMYCINS
SPECTRALITIES
SPECTRALITY
SPECTRALLY
SPECTRALNESS
SPECTRALNESSES
SPECTROGRAM
SPECTROGRAMS
SPECTROGRAPH
SPECTROGRAPHIC
SPECTROGRAPHIES
SPECTROGRAPHS
SPECTROGRAPHY
SPECTROLOGICAL
SPECTROLOGIES
SPECTROLOGY
SPECTROMETER
SPECTROMETERS
SPECTROMETRIC
SPECTROMETRIES
SPECTROMETRY
SPECTROSCOPE
SPECTROSCOPES
SPECTROSCOPIC
SPECTROSCOPICAL
SPECTROSCOPIES
SPECTROSCOPIST
SPECTROSCOPISTS
SPECTROSCOPY
SPECULARITIES
SPECULARITY
SPECULARLY
SPECULATED
SPECULATES
SPECULATING
SPECULATION
SPECULATIONS
SPECULATIST
SPECULATISTS
SPECULATIVE
SPECULATIVELY
SPECULATIVENESS
SPECULATOR
SPECULATORS
SPECULATORY
SPECULATRICE
SPECULATRICES
SPECULATRIX
SPECULATRIXES
SPEECHCRAFT
SPEECHCRAFTS

SPEECHFULNESS
SPEECHFULNESSES
SPEECHIFICATION
SPEECHIFIED
SPEECHIFIER
SPEECHIFIERS
SPEECHIFIES
SPEECHIFYING
SPEECHIFYINGS
SPEECHLESS
SPEECHLESSLY
SPEECHLESSNESS
SPEECHMAKER
SPEECHMAKERS
SPEECHMAKING
SPEECHMAKINGS
SPEECHWRITER
SPEECHWRITERS
SPEEDBALLED
SPEEDBALLING
SPEEDBALLINGS
SPEEDBALLS
SPEEDBOATING
SPEEDBOATINGS
SPEEDBOATS
SPEEDFREAK
SPEEDFREAKS
SPEEDFULLY
SPEEDINESS
SPEEDINESSES
SPEEDOMETER
SPEEDOMETERS
SPEEDREADING
SPEEDREADS
SPEEDSKATING
SPEEDSKATINGS
SPEEDSTERS
SPEEDWALKS
SPEEDWELLS
SPELAEOLOGICAL
SPELAEOLOGIES
SPELAEOLOGIST
SPELAEOLOGISTS
SPELAEOLOGY
SPELAEOTHEM
SPELAEOTHEMS
SPELDERING
SPELDRINGS
SPELEOLOGICAL
SPELEOLOGIES
SPELEOLOGIST
SPELEOLOGISTS
SPELEOLOGY
SPELEOTHEM
SPELEOTHEMS
SPELEOTHERAPIES
SPELEOTHERAPY
SPELLBINDER
SPELLBINDERS
SPELLBINDING
SPELLBINDINGLY
SPELLBINDS
SPELLBOUND
SPELLCHECK
SPELLCHECKED
SPELLCHECKER
SPELLCHECKERS
SPELLCHECKING
SPELLCHECKS
SPELLDOWNS
SPELLICANS
SPELLINGLY
SPELLSTOPT
SPELUNKERS
SPELUNKING
SPELUNKINGS
SPENDTHRIFT
SPENDTHRIFTS
SPERMACETI
SPERMACETIS
SPERMADUCT
SPERMADUCTS
SPERMAGONIA
SPERMAGONIUM
SPERMAPHYTE
SPERMAPHYTES
SPERMAPHYTIC
SPERMARIES
SPERMARIUM
SPERMATHECA
SPERMATHECAE
SPERMATHECAL
SPERMATHECAS
SPERMATIAL
SPERMATICAL
SPERMATICALLY
SPERMATICS
SPERMATIDS
SPERMATIUM
SPERMATOBLAST
SPERMATOBLASTIC
SPERMATOBLASTS
SPERMATOCELE
SPERMATOCELES
SPERMATOCIDAL
SPERMATOCIDE
SPERMATOCIDES
SPERMATOCYTE
SPERMATOCYTES
SPERMATOGENESES
SPERMATOGENESIS
SPERMATOGENETIC
SPERMATOGENIC
SPERMATOGENIES
SPERMATOGENOUS
SPERMATOGENY
SPERMATOGONIA
SPERMATOGONIAL
SPERMATOGONIUM
SPERMATOPHORAL
SPERMATOPHORE
SPERMATOPHORES
SPERMATOPHYTE
SPERMATOPHYTES
SPERMATOPHYTIC
SPERMATORRHEA
SPERMATORRHEAS
SPERMATORRHOEA
SPERMATORRHOEAS
SPERMATOTHECA
SPERMATOTHECAE
SPERMATOTHECAS
SPERMATOZOA
SPERMATOZOAL
SPERMATOZOAN
SPERMATOZOANS
SPERMATOZOIC
SPERMATOZOID
SPERMATOZOIDS
SPERMATOZOON
SPERMICIDAL
SPERMICIDE
SPERMICIDES
SPERMIDUCT
SPERMIDUCTS
SPERMIOGENESES
SPERMIOGENESIS
SPERMIOGENETIC
SPERMOGONE
SPERMOGONES
SPERMOGONIA
SPERMOGONIUM
SPERMOPHILE
SPERMOPHILES
SPERMOPHYTE
SPERMOPHYTES
SPERMOPHYTIC
SPERRYLITE
SPERRYLITES
SPESSARTINE
SPESSARTINES
SPESSARTITE
SPESSARTITES
SPETSNAZES
SPETZNAZES
SPEWINESSES
SPHACELATE
SPHACELATED
SPHACELATES
SPHACELATING
SPHACELATION
SPHACELATIONS
SPHACELUSES
SPHAERIDIA
SPHAERIDIUM
SPHAERITES
SPHAEROCRYSTAL
SPHAEROCRYSTALS
SPHAEROSIDERITE
SPHAGNICOLOUS
SPHAGNOLOGIES
SPHAGNOLOGIST
SPHAGNOLOGISTS
SPHAGNOLOGY
SPHAIRISTIKE
SPHAIRISTIKES
SPHALERITE
SPHALERITES
SPHENDONES
SPHENODONS
SPHENODONT
SPHENODONTS
SPHENOGRAM
SPHENOGRAMS
SPHENOIDAL
SPHENOPSID
SPHENOPSIDS
SPHERELESS
SPHERELIKE
SPHERICALITIES
SPHERICALITY
SPHERICALLY
SPHERICALNESS
SPHERICALNESSES
SPHERICITIES
SPHERICITY
SPHERISTERION
SPHERISTERIONS
SPHEROCYTE
SPHEROCYTES
SPHEROCYTOSES
SPHEROCYTOSIS
SPHEROIDAL
SPHEROIDALLY
SPHEROIDICALLY
SPHEROIDICITIES
SPHEROIDICITY
SPHEROIDISATION
SPHEROIDISE
SPHEROIDISED
SPHEROIDISES
SPHEROIDISING
SPHEROIDIZATION
SPHEROIDIZE
SPHEROIDIZED
SPHEROIDIZES
SPHEROIDIZING
SPHEROMETER
SPHEROMETERS
SPHEROPLAST
SPHEROPLASTS
SPHERULITE
SPHERULITES
SPHERULITIC
SPHINCTERAL
SPHINCTERIAL
SPHINCTERIC
SPHINCTERS
SPHINGOMYELIN
SPHINGOMYELINS

SPHINGOSINE
SPHINGOSINES
SPHINXLIKE
SPHRAGISTIC
SPHRAGISTICS
SPHYGMOGRAM
SPHYGMOGRAMS
SPHYGMOGRAPH
SPHYGMOGRAPHIC
SPHYGMOGRAPHIES
SPHYGMOGRAPHS
SPHYGMOGRAPHY
SPHYGMOLOGIES
SPHYGMOLOGY
SPHYGMOMETER
SPHYGMOMETERS
SPHYGMOPHONE
SPHYGMOPHONES
SPHYGMOSCOPE
SPHYGMOSCOPES
SPHYGMUSES
SPICEBERRIES
SPICEBERRY
SPICEBUSHES
SPICILEGES
SPICINESSES
SPICULATED
SPICULATION
SPICULATIONS
SPIDERIEST
SPIDERLIKE
SPIDERWEBS
SPIDERWOOD
SPIDERWOODS
SPIDERWORK
SPIDERWORKS
SPIDERWORT
SPIDERWORTS
SPIEGELEISEN
SPIEGELEISENS
SPIFFINESS
SPIFFINESSES
SPIFFLICATE
SPIFFLICATED
SPIFFLICATES
SPIFFLICATING
SPIFFLICATION
SPIFFLICATIONS
SPIFLICATE
SPIFLICATED
SPIFLICATES
SPIFLICATING
SPIFLICATION
SPIFLICATIONS
SPIKEFISHES
SPIKENARDS
SPIKINESSES
SPILLIKINS
SPILLOVERS
SPILOSITES
SPINACENES
SPINACEOUS
SPINACHIER
SPINACHIEST
SPINACHLIKE
SPINARAMAS
SPINDLELEGS
SPINDLESHANKS
SPINDLIEST
SPINDLINGS
SPINDRIFTS
SPINELESSLY
SPINELESSNESS
SPINELESSNESSES
SPINESCENCE
SPINESCENCES
SPINESCENT
SPINIFEROUS
SPINIFEXES
SPINIGEROUS
SPINIGRADE
SPINIGRADES
SPININESSES
SPINMEISTER
SPINMEISTERS
SPINNAKERS
SPINNERETS
SPINNERETTE
SPINNERETTES
SPINNERIES
SPINNERULE
SPINNERULES
SPINOSITIES
SPINSTERDOM
SPINSTERDOMS
SPINSTERHOOD
SPINSTERHOODS
SPINSTERIAL
SPINSTERIAN
SPINSTERISH
SPINSTERLIER
SPINSTERLIEST
SPINSTERLY
SPINSTERSHIP
SPINSTERSHIPS
SPINSTRESS
SPINSTRESSES
SPINTHARISCOPE
SPINTHARISCOPES
SPINULESCENT
SPINULIFEROUS
SPIRACULAR
SPIRACULATE
SPIRACULUM
SPIRALIFORM
SPIRALISER
SPIRALISERS
SPIRALISMS
SPIRALISTS
SPIRALITIES
SPIRALIZER
SPIRALIZERS
SPIRALLING
SPIRASTERS
SPIRATIONS
SPIRIFEROUS
SPIRILLOSES
SPIRILLOSIS
SPIRITEDLY
SPIRITEDNESS
SPIRITEDNESSES
SPIRITINGS
SPIRITISMS
SPIRITISTIC
SPIRITISTS
SPIRITLESS
SPIRITLESSLY
SPIRITLESSNESS
SPIRITOUSNESS
SPIRITOUSNESSES
SPIRITUALISE
SPIRITUALISED
SPIRITUALISER
SPIRITUALISERS
SPIRITUALISES
SPIRITUALISING
SPIRITUALISM
SPIRITUALISMS
SPIRITUALIST
SPIRITUALISTIC
SPIRITUALISTS
SPIRITUALITIES
SPIRITUALITY
SPIRITUALIZE
SPIRITUALIZED
SPIRITUALIZER
SPIRITUALIZERS
SPIRITUALIZES
SPIRITUALIZING
SPIRITUALLY
SPIRITUALNESS
SPIRITUALNESSES
SPIRITUALS
SPIRITUALTIES
SPIRITUALTY
SPIRITUELLE
SPIRITUOSITIES
SPIRITUOSITY
SPIRITUOUS
SPIRITUOUSNESS
SPIRITUSES
SPIRKETTING
SPIRKETTINGS
SPIROCHAETAEMIA
SPIROCHAETAL
SPIROCHAETE
SPIROCHAETES
SPIROCHAETOSES
SPIROCHAETOSIS
SPIROCHETAL
SPIROCHETE
SPIROCHETES
SPIROCHETOSES
SPIROCHETOSIS
SPIROGRAMS
SPIROGRAPH
SPIROGRAPHIC
SPIROGRAPHIES
SPIROGRAPHS
SPIROGRAPHY
SPIROGYRAS
SPIROMETER
SPIROMETERS
SPIROMETRIC
SPIROMETRIES
SPIROMETRY
SPIRONOLACTONE
SPIRONOLACTONES
SPIROPHORE
SPIROPHORES
SPIRULINAE
SPIRULINAS
SPISSITUDE
SPISSITUDES
SPITBALLED
SPITBALLING
SPITCHCOCK
SPITCHCOCKED
SPITCHCOCKING
SPITCHCOCKS
SPITCHERED
SPITCHERING
SPITEFULLER
SPITEFULLEST
SPITEFULLY
SPITEFULNESS
SPITEFULNESSES
SPITSTICKER
SPITSTICKERS
SPITTLEBUG
SPITTLEBUGS
SPITTLIEST
SPIVVERIES
SPLANCHNIC
SPLANCHNOCELE
SPLANCHNOCELES
SPLANCHNOLOGIES
SPLANCHNOLOGY
SPLASHBACK
SPLASHBACKS
SPLASHBOARD
SPLASHBOARDS
SPLASHDOWN
SPLASHDOWNS
SPLASHIEST
SPLASHINESS
SPLASHINESSES
SPLASHINGS
SPLASHPROOF
SPLATCHING

SPLATTERED
SPLATTERING
SPLATTERPUNK
SPLATTERPUNKS
SPLATTINGS
SPLAYFOOTED
SPLAYFOOTEDLY
SPLEENFULLY
SPLEENIEST
SPLEENLESS
SPLEENLIKE
SPLEENSTONE
SPLEENSTONES
SPLEENWORT
SPLEENWORTS
SPLENATIVE
SPLENDIDER
SPLENDIDEST
SPLENDIDIOUS
SPLENDIDLY
SPLENDIDNESS
SPLENDIDNESSES
SPLENDIDOUS
SPLENDIFEROUS
SPLENDIFEROUSLY
SPLENDOROUS
SPLENDOURS
SPLENDROUS
SPLENECTOMIES
SPLENECTOMISE
SPLENECTOMISED
SPLENECTOMISES
SPLENECTOMISING
SPLENECTOMIZE
SPLENECTOMIZED
SPLENECTOMIZES
SPLENECTOMIZING
SPLENECTOMY
SPLENETICAL
SPLENETICALLY
SPLENETICS
SPLENISATION
SPLENISATIONS
SPLENITISES
SPLENIUSES
SPLENIZATION
SPLENIZATIONS
SPLENOMEGALIES
SPLENOMEGALY
SPLEUCHANS
SPLINTERED
SPLINTERIER
SPLINTERIEST
SPLINTERING
SPLINTLIKE
SPLINTWOOD
SPLINTWOODS
SPLITTINGS
SPLITTISMS
SPLITTISTS
SPLODGIEST
SPLODGINESS
SPLODGINESSES
SPLOOSHING
SPLOTCHIER
SPLOTCHIEST
SPLOTCHILY
SPLOTCHINESS
SPLOTCHINESSES
SPLOTCHING
SPLURGIEST
SPLUTTERED
SPLUTTERER
SPLUTTERERS
SPLUTTERIER
SPLUTTERIEST
SPLUTTERING
SPLUTTERINGLY
SPLUTTERINGS
SPODOGRAMS
SPODOMANCIES
SPODOMANCY
SPODOMANTIC
SPODUMENES
SPOILFIVES
SPOILSPORT
SPOILSPORTS
SPOKESHAVE
SPOKESHAVES
SPOKESMANSHIP
SPOKESMANSHIPS
SPOKESPEOPLE
SPOKESPERSON
SPOKESPERSONS
SPOKESWOMAN
SPOKESWOMEN
SPOLIATING
SPOLIATION
SPOLIATIONS
SPOLIATIVE
SPOLIATORS
SPOLIATORY
SPONDAICAL
SPONDOOLICKS
SPONDULICKS
SPONDYLITIC
SPONDYLITICS
SPONDYLITIDES
SPONDYLITIS
SPONDYLITISES
SPONDYLOLYSES
SPONDYLOLYSIS
SPONDYLOSES
SPONDYLOSIS
SPONDYLOSISES
SPONDYLOUS
SPONGEABLE
SPONGEBAGS
SPONGELIKE
SPONGEWARE
SPONGEWARES
SPONGEWOOD
SPONGEWOODS
SPONGICOLOUS
SPONGIFORM
SPONGINESS
SPONGINESSES
SPONGIOBLAST
SPONGIOBLASTIC
SPONGIOBLASTS
SPONGOLOGIES
SPONGOLOGIST
SPONGOLOGISTS
SPONGOLOGY
SPONSIONAL
SPONSORIAL
SPONSORING
SPONSORSHIP
SPONSORSHIPS
SPONTANEITIES
SPONTANEITY
SPONTANEOUS
SPONTANEOUSLY
SPONTANEOUSNESS
SPOOFERIES
SPOOKERIES
SPOOKINESS
SPOOKINESSES
SPOONBAITS
SPOONBILLS
SPOONDRIFT
SPOONDRIFTS
SPOONERISM
SPOONERISMS
SPOONHOOKS
SPOONWORMS
SPORADICAL
SPORADICALLY
SPORADICALNESS
SPORANGIAL
SPORANGIOLA
SPORANGIOLE
SPORANGIOLES
SPORANGIOLUM
SPORANGIOPHORE
SPORANGIOPHORES
SPORANGIOSPORE
SPORANGIOSPORES
SPORANGIUM
SPORICIDAL
SPORICIDES
SPORIDESMS
SPOROCARPS
SPOROCYSTIC
SPOROCYSTS
SPOROCYTES
SPOROGENESES
SPOROGENESIS
SPOROGENIC
SPOROGENIES
SPOROGENOUS
SPOROGONIA
SPOROGONIAL
SPOROGONIC
SPOROGONIES
SPOROGONIUM
SPOROPHORE
SPOROPHORES
SPOROPHORIC
SPOROPHOROUS
SPOROPHYLL
SPOROPHYLLS
SPOROPHYLS
SPOROPHYTE
SPOROPHYTES
SPOROPHYTIC
SPOROPOLLENIN
SPOROPOLLENINS
SPOROTRICHOSES
SPOROTRICHOSIS
SPOROZOANS
SPOROZOITE
SPOROZOITES
SPORTABILITIES
SPORTABILITY
SPORTANCES
SPORTBIKES
SPORTCASTER
SPORTCASTERS
SPORTCOATS
SPORTFISHERMAN
SPORTFISHERMEN
SPORTFISHING
SPORTFISHINGS
SPORTFULLY
SPORTFULNESS
SPORTFULNESSES
SPORTINESS
SPORTINESSES
SPORTINGLY
SPORTIVELY
SPORTIVENESS
SPORTIVENESSES
SPORTSCAST
SPORTSCASTER
SPORTSCASTERS
SPORTSCASTS
SPORTSMANLIER
SPORTSMANLIEST
SPORTSMANLIKE
SPORTSMANLY
SPORTSMANSHIP
SPORTSMANSHIPS
SPORTSPEOPLE
SPORTSPERSON
SPORTSPERSONS
SPORTSWEAR
SPORTSWEARS
SPORTSWOMAN
SPORTSWOMEN

S

SPORTSWRITER
SPORTSWRITERS
SPORTSWRITING
SPORTSWRITINGS
SPORULATED
SPORULATES
SPORULATING
SPORULATION
SPORULATIONS
SPORULATIVE
SPOTLESSLY
SPOTLESSNESS
SPOTLESSNESSES
SPOTLIGHTED
SPOTLIGHTING
SPOTLIGHTS
SPOTTEDNESS
SPOTTEDNESSES
SPOTTINESS
SPOTTINESSES
SPOUSELESS
SPOYLEFULL
SPRACHGEFUHL
SPRACHGEFUHLS
SPRACKLING
SPRADDLING
SPRANGLING
SPRATTLING
SPRAUCHLED
SPRAUCHLES
SPRAUCHLING
SPRAUNCIER
SPRAUNCIEST
SPRAWLIEST
SPREADABILITIES
SPREADABILITY
SPREADABLE
SPREADEAGLED
SPREADINGLY
SPREADINGS
SPREADSHEET
SPREADSHEETS
SPREAGHERIES
SPREAGHERY
SPREATHING
SPRECHERIES
SPRECHGESANG
SPRECHGESANGS
SPRECHSTIMME
SPRECHSTIMMES
SPREETHING
SPREKELIAS
SPRIGGIEST
SPRIGHTFUL
SPRIGHTFULLY
SPRIGHTFULNESS
SPRIGHTING
SPRIGHTLESS
SPRIGHTLIER
SPRIGHTLIEST
SPRIGHTLINESS
SPRIGHTLINESSES
SPRIGTAILS
SPRINGALDS
SPRINGBOARD
SPRINGBOARDS
SPRINGBOKS
SPRINGBUCK
SPRINGBUCKS
SPRINGEING
SPRINGHAAS
SPRINGHALT
SPRINGHALTS
SPRINGHASE
SPRINGHEAD
SPRINGHEADS
SPRINGHOUSE
SPRINGHOUSES
SPRINGIEST
SPRINGINESS
SPRINGINESSES
SPRINGINGS
SPRINGKEEPER
SPRINGKEEPERS
SPRINGLESS
SPRINGLETS
SPRINGLIKE
SPRINGTAIL
SPRINGTAILS
SPRINGTIDE
SPRINGTIDES
SPRINGTIME
SPRINGTIMES
SPRINGWATER
SPRINGWATERS
SPRINGWOOD
SPRINGWOODS
SPRINGWORT
SPRINGWORTS
SPRINKLERED
SPRINKLERING
SPRINKLERS
SPRINKLING
SPRINKLINGS
SPRINTINGS
SPRITEFULLY
SPRITEFULNESS
SPRITEFULNESSES
SPRITELIER
SPRITELIEST
SPRITSAILS
SPRITZIEST
SPROUTINGS
SPRUCENESS
SPRUCENESSES
SPRYNESSES
SPUILZIEING
SPULEBLADE
SPULEBLADES
SPULYIEING
SPULZIEING
SPUMESCENCE
SPUMESCENCES
SPUMESCENT
SPUNBONDED
SPUNKINESS
SPUNKINESSES
SPURGALLED
SPURGALLING
SPURIOSITIES
SPURIOSITY
SPURIOUSLY
SPURIOUSNESS
SPURIOUSNESSES
SPUTTERERS
SPUTTERIER
SPUTTERIEST
SPUTTERING
SPUTTERINGLY
SPUTTERINGS
SPYCATCHER
SPYCATCHERS
SPYGLASSES
SPYMASTERS
SQUABASHED
SQUABASHER
SQUABASHERS
SQUABASHES
SQUABASHING
SQUABBIEST
SQUABBLERS
SQUABBLING
SQUABBLINGS
SQUADOOSHES
SQUADRONAL
SQUADRONED
SQUADRONES
SQUADRONING
SQUAILINGS
SQUALIDEST
SQUALIDITIES
SQUALIDITY
SQUALIDNESS
SQUALIDNESSES
SQUALLIEST
SQUALLINGS
SQUAMATION
SQUAMATIONS
SQUAMELLAS
SQUAMIFORM
SQUAMOSALS
SQUAMOSELY
SQUAMOSENESS
SQUAMOSENESSES
SQUAMOSITIES
SQUAMOSITY
SQUAMOUSLY
SQUAMOUSNESS
SQUAMOUSNESSES
SQUAMULOSE
SQUANDERED
SQUANDERER
SQUANDERERS
SQUANDERING
SQUANDERINGLY
SQUANDERINGS
SQUANDERMANIA
SQUANDERMANIAS
SQUAREHEAD
SQUAREHEADS
SQUARENESS
SQUARENESSES
SQUAREWISE
SQUARISHLY
SQUARISHNESS
SQUARISHNESSES
SQUARSONAGE
SQUARSONAGES
SQUASHABLE
SQUASHIEST
SQUASHINESS
SQUASHINESSES
SQUATNESSES
SQUATTERED
SQUATTERING
SQUATTIEST
SQUATTINESS
SQUATTINESSES
SQUATTINGS
SQUATTLING
SQUATTOCRACIES
SQUATTOCRACY
SQUAWBUSHES
SQUAWFISHES
SQUAWKIEST
SQUAWKINGS
SQUAWROOTS
SQUEAKERIES
SQUEAKIEST
SQUEAKINESS
SQUEAKINESSES
SQUEAKINGLY
SQUEAKINGS
SQUEALINGS
SQUEAMISHLY
SQUEAMISHNESS
SQUEAMISHNESSES
SQUEEGEEING
SQUEEZABILITIES
SQUEEZABILITY
SQUEEZABLE
SQUEEZIEST
SQUEEZINGS
SQUEGGINGS
SQUELCHERS
SQUELCHIER
SQUELCHIEST
SQUELCHING
SQUELCHINGS
SQUETEAGUE

SQUETEAGUES
SQUIBBINGS
SQUIDGIEST
SQUIFFIEST
SQUIGGLERS
SQUIGGLIER
SQUIGGLIEST
SQUIGGLING
SQUILGEEING
SQUILLIONS
SQUINANCIES
SQUINCHING
SQUINNIEST
SQUINNYING
SQUINTIEST
SQUINTINGLY
SQUINTINGS
SQUIRALITIES
SQUIRALITY
SQUIRALTIES
SQUIRARCHAL
SQUIRARCHICAL
SQUIRARCHIES
SQUIRARCHS
SQUIRARCHY
SQUIREAGES
SQUIREARCH
SQUIREARCHAL
SQUIREARCHICAL
SQUIREARCHIES
SQUIREARCHS
SQUIREARCHY
SQUIREDOMS
SQUIREHOOD
SQUIREHOODS
SQUIRELIKE
SQUIRELING
SQUIRELINGS
SQUIRESHIP
SQUIRESHIPS
SQUIRESSES
SQUIRMIEST
SQUIRMINGLY
SQUIRRELED
SQUIRRELFISH
SQUIRRELFISHES
SQUIRRELIER
SQUIRRELIEST
SQUIRRELING
SQUIRRELLED
SQUIRRELLIER
SQUIRRELLIEST
SQUIRRELLING
SQUIRRELLY
SQUIRTINGS
SQUISHIEST
SQUISHINESS
SQUISHINESSES
SQUOOSHIER
SQUOOSHIEST
SQUOOSHING
STABBINGLY
STABILATES
STABILISATION
STABILISATIONS
STABILISATOR
STABILISATORS
STABILISED
STABILISER
STABILISERS
STABILISES
STABILISING
STABILITIES
STABILIZATION
STABILIZATIONS
STABILIZATOR
STABILIZATORS
STABILIZED
STABILIZER
STABILIZERS
STABILIZES
STABILIZING
STABLEBOYS
STABLEMATE
STABLEMATES
STABLENESS
STABLENESSES
STABLISHED
STABLISHES
STABLISHING
STABLISHMENT
STABLISHMENTS
STACATIONS
STACCATISSIMO
STACKROOMS
STACKYARDS
STACTOMETER
STACTOMETERS
STADDLESTONE
STADDLESTONES
STADHOLDER
STADHOLDERATE
STADHOLDERATES
STADHOLDERS
STADHOLDERSHIP
STADHOLDERSHIPS
STADIOMETER
STADIOMETERS
STADTHOLDER
STADTHOLDERATE
STADTHOLDERATES
STADTHOLDERS
STADTHOLDERSHIP
STAFFRIDER
STAFFRIDERS
STAFFROOMS
STAGECOACH
STAGECOACHES
STAGECOACHING
STAGECOACHINGS
STAGECOACHMAN
STAGECOACHMEN
STAGECRAFT
STAGECRAFTS
STAGEHANDS
STAGEHEADS
STAGESTRUCK
STAGFLATION
STAGFLATIONARY
STAGFLATIONS
STAGGERBUSH
STAGGERBUSHES
STAGGERERS
STAGGERIER
STAGGERIEST
STAGGERING
STAGGERINGLY
STAGGERINGS
STAGHOUNDS
STAGINESSES
STAGNANCES
STAGNANCIES
STAGNANTLY
STAGNATING
STAGNATION
STAGNATIONS
STAIDNESSES
STAINABILITIES
STAINABILITY
STAINLESSES
STAINLESSLY
STAINLESSNESS
STAINLESSNESSES
STAINPROOF
STAIRCASED
STAIRCASES
STAIRCASING
STAIRCASINGS
STAIRFOOTS
STAIRHEADS
STAIRLIFTS
STAIRSTEPPED
STAIRSTEPPING
STAIRSTEPS
STAIRWELLS
STAIRWORKS
STAKEHOLDER
STAKEHOLDERS
STAKHANOVISM
STAKHANOVISMS
STAKHANOVITE
STAKHANOVITES
STAKTOMETER
STAKTOMETERS
STALACTICAL
STALACTIFORM
STALACTITAL
STALACTITE
STALACTITED
STALACTITES
STALACTITIC
STALACTITICAL
STALACTITICALLY
STALACTITIFORM
STALACTITIOUS
STALAGMITE
STALAGMITES
STALAGMITIC
STALAGMITICAL
STALAGMITICALLY
STALAGMOMETER
STALAGMOMETERS
STALAGMOMETRIES
STALAGMOMETRY
STALEMATED
STALEMATES
STALEMATING
STALENESSES
STALKINESS
STALKINESSES
STALLENGER
STALLENGERS
STALLHOLDER
STALLHOLDERS
STALLINGER
STALLINGERS
STALLMASTER
STALLMASTERS
STALWARTLY
STALWARTNESS
STALWARTNESSES
STALWORTHS
STAMINEOUS
STAMINIFEROUS
STAMINODES
STAMINODIA
STAMINODIES
STAMINODIUM
STAMMERERS
STAMMERING
STAMMERINGLY
STAMMERINGS
STAMPEDERS
STAMPEDING
STAMPEDOED
STAMPEDOING
STANCHABLE
STANCHELLED
STANCHELLING
STANCHERED
STANCHERING
STANCHINGS
STANCHIONED
STANCHIONING
STANCHIONS
STANCHLESS
STANCHNESS
STANCHNESSES
STANDARDBRED
STANDARDBREDS

STANDARDISATION
STANDARDISE
STANDARDISED
STANDARDISER
STANDARDISERS
STANDARDISES
STANDARDISING
STANDARDIZATION
STANDARDIZE
STANDARDIZED
STANDARDIZER
STANDARDIZERS
STANDARDIZES
STANDARDIZING
STANDARDLESS
STANDARDLY
STANDDOWNS
STANDFASTS
STANDFIRST
STANDFIRSTS
STANDGALES
STANDISHES
STANDOFFISH
STANDOFFISHLY
STANDOFFISHNESS
STANDOVERS
STANDPATTER
STANDPATTERS
STANDPATTISM
STANDPATTISMS
STANDPIPES
STANDPOINT
STANDPOINTS
STANDSTILL
STANDSTILLS
STANNARIES
STANNATORS
STANNIFEROUS
STANNOTYPE
STANNOTYPES
STAPEDECTOMIES
STAPEDECTOMY
STAPEDIUSES
STAPHYLINE
STAPHYLINID
STAPHYLINIDS
STAPHYLITIS
STAPHYLITISES
STAPHYLOCOCCAL
STAPHYLOCOCCI
STAPHYLOCOCCIC
STAPHYLOCOCCUS
STAPHYLOMA
STAPHYLOMAS
STAPHYLOMATA
STAPHYLOPLASTIC
STAPHYLOPLASTY
STAPHYLORRHAPHY
STARBOARDED
STARBOARDING
STARBOARDS
STARBURSTS
STARCHEDLY
STARCHEDNESS
STARCHEDNESSES
STARCHIEST
STARCHINESS
STARCHINESSES
STARCHLIKE
STARDRIFTS
STARFISHED
STARFISHES
STARFLOWER
STARFLOWERS
STARFRUITS
STARFUCKER
STARFUCKERS
STARFUCKING
STARFUCKINGS
STARGAZERS
STARGAZING
STARGAZINGS
STARKENING
STARKNESSES
STARLIGHTED
STARLIGHTS
STARMONGER
STARMONGERS
STAROSTIES
STARRINESS
STARRINESSES
STARSHINES
STARSTONES
STARSTRUCK
STARTINGLY
STARTLEMENT
STARTLEMENTS
STARTLIEST
STARTLINGLY
STARTLINGS
STARVATION
STARVATIONS
STARVELING
STARVELINGS
STASIDIONS
STASIMORPHIES
STASIMORPHY
STATECRAFT
STATECRAFTS
STATEHOODS
STATEHOUSE
STATEHOUSES
STATELESSNESS
STATELESSNESSES
STATELIEST
STATELINESS
STATELINESSES
STATEMENTED
STATEMENTING
STATEMENTINGS
STATEMENTS
STATEROOMS
STATESMANLIER
STATESMANLIEST
STATESMANLIKE
STATESMANLY
STATESMANSHIP
STATESMANSHIPS
STATESPERSON
STATESPERSONS
STATESWOMAN
STATESWOMEN
STATICALLY
STATICKIER
STATICKIEST
STATIONARIES
STATIONARILY
STATIONARINESS
STATIONARY
STATIONERIES
STATIONERS
STATIONERY
STATIONING
STATIONMASTER
STATIONMASTERS
STATISTICAL
STATISTICALLY
STATISTICIAN
STATISTICIANS
STATISTICS
STATOBLAST
STATOBLASTS
STATOCYSTS
STATOLATRIES
STATOLATRY
STATOLITHIC
STATOLITHS
STATOSCOPE
STATOSCOPES
STATUARIES
STATUESQUE
STATUESQUELY
STATUESQUENESS
STATUETTES
STATUSIEST
STATUTABLE
STATUTABLY
STATUTORILY
STAUNCHABLE
STAUNCHERS
STAUNCHEST
STAUNCHING
STAUNCHINGS
STAUNCHLESS
STAUNCHNESS
STAUNCHNESSES
STAUROLITE
STAUROLITES
STAUROLITIC
STAUROSCOPE
STAUROSCOPES
STAUROSCOPIC
STAVESACRE
STAVESACRES
STAVUDINES
STAYCATION
STAYCATIONS
STAYMAKERS
STEADFASTLY
STEADFASTNESS
STEADFASTNESSES
STEADINESS
STEADINESSES
STEAKETTES
STEAKHOUSE
STEAKHOUSES
STEALINGLY
STEALTHFUL
STEALTHIER
STEALTHIEST
STEALTHILY
STEALTHINESS
STEALTHINESSES
STEALTHING
STEALTHINGS
STEAMBOATS
STEAMERING
STEAMFITTER
STEAMFITTERS
STEAMINESS
STEAMINESSES
STEAMPUNKS
STEAMROLLED
STEAMROLLER
STEAMROLLERED
STEAMROLLERING
STEAMROLLERS
STEAMROLLING
STEAMROLLS
STEAMSHIPS
STEAMTIGHT
STEAMTIGHTNESS
STEAROPTENE
STEAROPTENES
STEARSMATE
STEARSMATES
STEATOCELE
STEATOCELES
STEATOLYSES
STEATOLYSIS
STEATOMATOUS
STEATOPYGA
STEATOPYGAS
STEATOPYGIA
STEATOPYGIAS
STEATOPYGIC
STEATOPYGOUS
STEATORRHEA
STEATORRHEAS
STEATORRHOEA

STEATORRHOEAS
STEDFASTLY
STEDFASTNESS
STEDFASTNESSES
STEELHEADS
STEELINESS
STEELINESSES
STEELMAKER
STEELMAKERS
STEELMAKING
STEELMAKINGS
STEELWARES
STEELWORKER
STEELWORKERS
STEELWORKING
STEELWORKINGS
STEELWORKS
STEELYARDS
STEENBRASES
STEENBUCKS
STEENKIRKS
STEEPDOWNE
STEEPEDOWNE
STEEPENING
STEEPINESS
STEEPINESSES
STEEPLEBUSH
STEEPLEBUSHES
STEEPLECHASE
STEEPLECHASED
STEEPLECHASER
STEEPLECHASERS
STEEPLECHASES
STEEPLECHASING
STEEPLECHASINGS
STEEPLEJACK
STEEPLEJACKS
STEEPNESSES
STEERAGEWAY
STEERAGEWAYS
STEERLINGS
STEERSMATE
STEERSMATES
STEGANOGRAM
STEGANOGRAMS
STEGANOGRAPH
STEGANOGRAPHER
STEGANOGRAPHERS
STEGANOGRAPHIC
STEGANOGRAPHIES
STEGANOGRAPHIST
STEGANOGRAPHS
STEGANOGRAPHY
STEGANOPOD
STEGANOPODOUS
STEGANOPODS
STEGNOTICS
STEGOCARPOUS
STEGOCEPHALIAN
STEGOCEPHALIANS
STEGOCEPHALOUS
STEGODONTS
STEGOMYIAS
STEGOPHILIST
STEGOPHILISTS
STEGOSAURIAN
STEGOSAURIANS
STEGOSAURS
STEGOSAURUS
STEGOSAURUSES
STEINBOCKS
STEINKIRKS
STELLARATOR
STELLARATORS
STELLATELY
STELLERIDAN
STELLERIDANS
STELLERIDS
STELLIFEROUS
STELLIFIED
STELLIFIES
STELLIFORM
STELLIFYING
STELLIFYINGS
STELLIONATE
STELLIONATES
STELLULARLY
STELLULATE
STEMMATOUS
STEMMERIES
STEMWINDER
STEMWINDERS
STENCHIEST
STENCILERS
STENCILING
STENCILINGS
STENCILLED
STENCILLER
STENCILLERS
STENCILLING
STENCILLINGS
STENOBATHIC
STENOBATHS
STENOCARDIA
STENOCARDIAS
STENOCHROME
STENOCHROMES
STENOCHROMIES
STENOCHROMY
STENOGRAPH
STENOGRAPHED
STENOGRAPHER
STENOGRAPHERS
STENOGRAPHIC
STENOGRAPHICAL
STENOGRAPHIES
STENOGRAPHING
STENOGRAPHIST
STENOGRAPHISTS
STENOGRAPHS
STENOGRAPHY
STENOHALINE
STENOPAEIC
STENOPETALOUS
STENOPHAGOUS
STENOPHYLLOUS
STENOTHERM
STENOTHERMAL
STENOTHERMS
STENOTOPIC
STENOTROPIC
STENOTYPED
STENOTYPER
STENOTYPERS
STENOTYPES
STENOTYPIC
STENOTYPIES
STENOTYPING
STENOTYPIST
STENOTYPISTS
STENTMASTER
STENTMASTERS
STENTORIAN
STEPBAIRNS
STEPBROTHER
STEPBROTHERS
STEPCHILDREN
STEPDANCER
STEPDANCERS
STEPDANCING
STEPDANCINGS
STEPDAUGHTER
STEPDAUGHTERS
STEPFAMILIES
STEPFAMILY
STEPFATHER
STEPFATHERS
STEPHANITE
STEPHANITES
STEPHANOTIS
STEPHANOTISES
STEPLADDER
STEPLADDERS
STEPMOTHER
STEPMOTHERLIER
STEPMOTHERLIEST
STEPMOTHERLY
STEPMOTHERS
STEPPARENT
STEPPARENTING
STEPPARENTINGS
STEPPARENTS
STEPSISTER
STEPSISTERS
STEPSTOOLS
STERADIANS
STERCORACEOUS
STERCORANISM
STERCORANISMS
STERCORANIST
STERCORANISTS
STERCORARIES
STERCORARIOUS
STERCORARY
STERCORATE
STERCORATED
STERCORATES
STERCORATING
STERCORICOLOUS
STERCULIACEOUS
STERCULIAS
STEREOACUITIES
STEREOACUITY
STEREOBATE
STEREOBATES
STEREOBATIC
STEREOBLIND
STEREOCARD
STEREOCARDS
STEREOCHEMICAL
STEREOCHEMISTRY
STEREOCHROME
STEREOCHROMED
STEREOCHROMES
STEREOCHROMIES
STEREOCHROMING
STEREOCHROMY
STEREOGNOSES
STEREOGNOSIS
STEREOGRAM
STEREOGRAMS
STEREOGRAPH
STEREOGRAPHED
STEREOGRAPHIC
STEREOGRAPHICAL
STEREOGRAPHIES
STEREOGRAPHING
STEREOGRAPHS
STEREOGRAPHY
STEREOISOMER
STEREOISOMERIC
STEREOISOMERISM
STEREOISOMERS
STEREOISOMETRIC
STEREOLOGICAL
STEREOLOGICALLY
STEREOLOGIES
STEREOLOGY
STEREOMETER
STEREOMETERS
STEREOMETRIC
STEREOMETRICAL
STEREOMETRIES
STEREOMETRY
STEREOPHONIC
STEREOPHONIES
STEREOPHONY
STEREOPSES
STEREOPSIS
STEREOPTICON

S

STEREOPTICONS
STEREOPTICS
STEREOREGULAR
STEREOSCOPE
STEREOSCOPES
STEREOSCOPIC
STEREOSCOPICAL
STEREOSCOPIES
STEREOSCOPIST
STEREOSCOPISTS
STEREOSCOPY
STEREOSONIC
STEREOSPECIFIC
STEREOTACTIC
STEREOTACTICAL
STEREOTAXES
STEREOTAXIA
STEREOTAXIAS
STEREOTAXIC
STEREOTAXICALLY
STEREOTAXIS
STEREOTOMIES
STEREOTOMY
STEREOTROPIC
STEREOTROPISM
STEREOTROPISMS
STEREOTYPE
STEREOTYPED
STEREOTYPER
STEREOTYPERS
STEREOTYPES
STEREOTYPIC
STEREOTYPICAL
STEREOTYPICALLY
STEREOTYPIES
STEREOTYPING
STEREOTYPINGS
STEREOTYPIST
STEREOTYPISTS
STEREOTYPY
STEREOVISION
STEREOVISIONS
STERICALLY
STERIGMATA
STERILANTS
STERILISABLE
STERILISATION
STERILISATIONS
STERILISED
STERILISER
STERILISERS
STERILISES
STERILISING
STERILITIES
STERILIZABLE
STERILIZATION
STERILIZATIONS
STERILIZED
STERILIZER
STERILIZERS
STERILIZES
STERILIZING
STERLINGLY
STERLINGNESS
STERLINGNESSES
STERNALGIA
STERNALGIAS
STERNALGIC
STERNBOARD
STERNBOARDS
STERNEBRAE
STERNFASTS
STERNFOREMOST
STERNNESSES
STERNOCOSTAL
STERNOTRIBE
STERNPORTS
STERNPOSTS
STERNSHEET
STERNSHEETS
STERNUTATION
STERNUTATIONS
STERNUTATIVE
STERNUTATIVES
STERNUTATOR
STERNUTATORIES
STERNUTATORS
STERNUTATORY
STERNWARDS
STERNWORKS
STEROIDOGENESES
STEROIDOGENESIS
STEROIDOGENIC
STERTOROUS
STERTOROUSLY
STERTOROUSNESS
STETHOSCOPE
STETHOSCOPES
STETHOSCOPIC
STETHOSCOPIES
STETHOSCOPIST
STETHOSCOPISTS
STETHOSCOPY
STEVEDORED
STEVEDORES
STEVEDORING
STEVEDORINGS
STEVENGRAPH
STEVENGRAPHS
STEWARDESS
STEWARDESSES
STEWARDING
STEWARDRIES
STEWARDSHIP
STEWARDSHIPS
STEWARTRIES
STIACCIATO
STIACCIATOS
STIBIALISM
STIBIALISMS
STICCADOES
STICCATOES
STICHARION
STICHARIONS
STICHICALLY
STICHIDIUM
STICHOLOGIES
STICHOLOGY
STICHOMETRIC
STICHOMETRICAL
STICHOMETRIES
STICHOMETRY
STICHOMYTHIA
STICHOMYTHIAS
STICHOMYTHIC
STICHOMYTHIES
STICHOMYTHY
STICKABILITIES
STICKABILITY
STICKBALLS
STICKERING
STICKHANDLE
STICKHANDLED
STICKHANDLER
STICKHANDLERS
STICKHANDLES
STICKHANDLING
STICKHANDLINGS
STICKINESS
STICKINESSES
STICKLEADER
STICKLEADERS
STICKLEBACK
STICKLEBACKS
STICKLINGS
STICKSEEDS
STICKTIGHT
STICKTIGHTS
STICKWEEDS
STICKWORKS
STICKYBEAK
STICKYBEAKED
STICKYBEAKING
STICKYBEAKS
STIDDIEING
STIFFENERS
STIFFENING
STIFFENINGS
STIFFNESSES
STIFFWARES
STIFLINGLY
STIGMARIAN
STIGMARIANS
STIGMASTEROL
STIGMASTEROLS
STIGMATICAL
STIGMATICALLY
STIGMATICS
STIGMATIFEROUS
STIGMATISATION
STIGMATISATIONS
STIGMATISE
STIGMATISED
STIGMATISER
STIGMATISERS
STIGMATISES
STIGMATISING
STIGMATISM
STIGMATISMS
STIGMATIST
STIGMATISTS
STIGMATIZATION
STIGMATIZATIONS
STIGMATIZE
STIGMATIZED
STIGMATIZER
STIGMATIZERS
STIGMATIZES
STIGMATIZING
STIGMATOPHILIA
STIGMATOPHILIAS
STIGMATOPHILIST
STIGMATOSE
STILBESTROL
STILBESTROLS
STILBOESTROL
STILBOESTROLS
STILETTOED
STILETTOES
STILETTOING
STILLATORIES
STILLATORY
STILLBIRTH
STILLBIRTHS
STILLBORNS
STILLHOUSE
STILLHOUSES
STILLICIDE
STILLICIDES
STILLIFORM
STILLNESSES
STILLROOMS
STILPNOSIDERITE
STILTBIRDS
STILTEDNESS
STILTEDNESSES
STILTINESS
STILTINESSES
STIMPMETER
STIMPMETERS
STIMULABLE
STIMULANCIES
STIMULANCY
STIMULANTS
STIMULATED
STIMULATER
STIMULATERS
STIMULATES
STIMULATING
STIMULATINGLY

STIMULATION
STIMULATIONS
STIMULATIVE
STIMULATIVES
STIMULATOR
STIMULATORS
STIMULATORY
STINGAREES
STINGBULLS
STINGFISHES
STINGINESS
STINGINESSES
STINGINGLY
STINGINGNESS
STINGINGNESSES
STINKBIRDS
STINKEROOS
STINKHORNS
STINKINGLY
STINKINGNESS
STINKINGNESSES
STINKSTONE
STINKSTONES
STINKWEEDS
STINKWOODS
STINTEDNESS
STINTEDNESSES
STINTINGLY
STIPELLATE
STIPENDIARIES
STIPENDIARY
STIPENDIATE
STIPENDIATED
STIPENDIATES
STIPENDIATING
STIPITIFORM
STIPPLINGS
STIPULABLE
STIPULACEOUS
STIPULATED
STIPULATES
STIPULATING
STIPULATION
STIPULATIONS
STIPULATOR
STIPULATORS
STIPULATORY
STIRABOUTS
STIRPICULTURE
STIRPICULTURES
STIRRINGLY
STITCHCRAFT
STITCHCRAFTS
STITCHERIES
STITCHINGS
STITCHWORK
STITCHWORKS
STITCHWORT
STITCHWORTS
STOCCADOES
STOCHASTIC
STOCHASTICALLY
STOCKADING
STOCKBREEDER
STOCKBREEDERS
STOCKBREEDING
STOCKBREEDINGS
STOCKBROKER
STOCKBROKERAGE
STOCKBROKERAGES
STOCKBROKERS
STOCKBROKING
STOCKBROKINGS
STOCKFISHES
STOCKHOLDER
STOCKHOLDERS
STOCKHOLDING
STOCKHOLDINGS
STOCKHORNS
STOCKHORSE
STOCKHORSES
STOCKINESS
STOCKINESSES
STOCKINETS
STOCKINETTE
STOCKINETTES
STOCKINGED
STOCKINGER
STOCKINGERS
STOCKINGLESS
STOCKISHLY
STOCKISHNESS
STOCKISHNESSES
STOCKJOBBER
STOCKJOBBERIES
STOCKJOBBERS
STOCKJOBBERY
STOCKJOBBING
STOCKJOBBINGS
STOCKKEEPER
STOCKKEEPERS
STOCKLISTS
STOCKLOCKS
STOCKPILED
STOCKPILER
STOCKPILERS
STOCKPILES
STOCKPILING
STOCKPILINGS
STOCKPUNISHT
STOCKROOMS
STOCKROUTE
STOCKROUTES
STOCKTAKEN
STOCKTAKES
STOCKTAKING
STOCKTAKINGS
STOCKWORKS
STOCKYARDS
STODGINESS
STODGINESSES
STOECHIOLOGICAL
STOECHIOLOGIES
STOECHIOLOGY
STOECHIOMETRIC
STOECHIOMETRIES
STOECHIOMETRY
STOICALNESS
STOICALNESSES
STOICHEIOLOGIES
STOICHEIOLOGY
STOICHEIOMETRIC
STOICHEIOMETRY
STOICHIOLOGICAL
STOICHIOLOGIES
STOICHIOLOGY
STOICHIOMETRIC
STOICHIOMETRIES
STOICHIOMETRY
STOITERING
STOKEHOLDS
STOKEHOLES
STOLENWISE
STOLIDITIES
STOLIDNESS
STOLIDNESSES
STOLONIFEROUS
STOMACHACHE
STOMACHACHES
STOMACHALS
STOMACHERS
STOMACHFUL
STOMACHFULNESS
STOMACHFULS
STOMACHICAL
STOMACHICS
STOMACHIER
STOMACHIEST
STOMACHING
STOMACHLESS
STOMACHOUS
STOMATITIC
STOMATITIDES
STOMATITIS
STOMATITISES
STOMATODAEA
STOMATODAEUM
STOMATOGASTRIC
STOMATOLOGICAL
STOMATOLOGIES
STOMATOLOGIST
STOMATOLOGISTS
STOMATOLOGY
STOMATOPLASTIES
STOMATOPLASTY
STOMATOPOD
STOMATOPODS
STOMODAEAL
STOMODAEUM
STOMODAEUMS
STOMODEUMS
STONEBOATS
STONEBORER
STONEBORERS
STONEBRASH
STONEBRASHES
STONEBREAK
STONEBREAKER
STONEBREAKERS
STONEBREAKS
STONECASTS
STONECHATS
STONECROPS
STONECUTTER
STONECUTTERS
STONECUTTING
STONECUTTINGS
STONEFISHES
STONEFLIES
STONEGROUND
STONEHANDS
STONEHORSE
STONEHORSES
STONELESSNESS
STONELESSNESSES
STONEMASON
STONEMASONRIES
STONEMASONRY
STONEMASONS
STONESHOTS
STONEWALLED
STONEWALLER
STONEWALLERS
STONEWALLING
STONEWALLINGS
STONEWALLS
STONEWARES
STONEWASHED
STONEWASHES
STONEWASHING
STONEWORKER
STONEWORKERS
STONEWORKS
STONEWORTS
STONINESSES
STONISHING
STONKERING
STONYHEARTED
STOOLBALLS
STOOPBALLS
STOOPINGLY
STOPLIGHTS
STOPPERING
STOPWATCHES
STORECARDS
STOREFRONT
STOREFRONTS
STOREHOUSE
STOREHOUSES
STOREKEEPER

STOREKEEPERS
STOREKEEPING
STOREKEEPINGS
STOREROOMS
STORESHIPS
STORIETTES
STORIOLOGIES
STORIOLOGIST
STORIOLOGISTS
STORIOLOGY
STORKSBILL
STORKSBILLS
STORMBIRDS
STORMBOUND
STORMCOCKS
STORMFULLY
STORMFULNESS
STORMFULNESSES
STORMINESS
STORMINESSES
STORMPROOF
STORMSTAYED
STORYBOARD
STORYBOARDED
STORYBOARDING
STORYBOARDS
STORYBOOKS
STORYETTES
STORYLINES
STORYTELLER
STORYTELLERS
STORYTELLING
STORYTELLINGS
STORYTIMES
STOTTERING
STOUTENING
STOUTHEARTED
STOUTHEARTEDLY
STOUTHERIE
STOUTHERIES
STOUTHRIEF
STOUTHRIEFS
STOUTNESSES
STOVEPIPES
STOVEWOODS
STRABISMAL
STRABISMIC
STRABISMICAL
STRABISMOMETER
STRABISMOMETERS
STRABISMUS
STRABISMUSES
STRABOMETER
STRABOMETERS
STRABOTOMIES
STRABOTOMY
STRACCHINI
STRACCHINO
STRADDLEBACK
STRADDLERS
STRADDLING
STRAGGLERS
STRAGGLIER
STRAGGLIEST
STRAGGLING
STRAGGLINGLY
STRAGGLINGS
STRAICHTER
STRAICHTEST
STRAIGHTAWAY
STRAIGHTAWAYS
STRAIGHTBRED
STRAIGHTBREDS
STRAIGHTED
STRAIGHTEDGE
STRAIGHTEDGED
STRAIGHTEDGES
STRAIGHTEN
STRAIGHTENED
STRAIGHTENER
STRAIGHTENERS
STRAIGHTENING
STRAIGHTENS
STRAIGHTER
STRAIGHTEST
STRAIGHTFORTH
STRAIGHTFORWARD
STRAIGHTING
STRAIGHTISH
STRAIGHTJACKET
STRAIGHTJACKETS
STRAIGHTLACED
STRAIGHTLY
STRAIGHTNESS
STRAIGHTNESSES
STRAIGHTWAY
STRAIGHTWAYS
STRAINEDLY
STRAININGS
STRAITENED
STRAITENING
STRAITJACKET
STRAITJACKETED
STRAITJACKETING
STRAITJACKETS
STRAITLACED
STRAITLACEDLY
STRAITLACEDNESS
STRAITNESS
STRAITNESSES
STRAITWAISTCOAT
STRAMACONS
STRAMASHED
STRAMASHES
STRAMASHING
STRAMAZONS
STRAMINEOUS
STRAMONIES
STRAMONIUM
STRAMONIUMS
STRANDEDNESS
STRANDEDNESSES
STRANDFLAT
STRANDFLATS
STRANDLINE
STRANDLINES
STRANDWOLF
STRANDWOLVES
STRANGENESS
STRANGENESSES
STRANGERED
STRANGERING
STRANGLEHOLD
STRANGLEHOLDS
STRANGLEMENT
STRANGLEMENTS
STRANGLERS
STRANGLING
STRANGULATE
STRANGULATED
STRANGULATES
STRANGULATING
STRANGULATION
STRANGULATIONS
STRANGURIES
STRAPHANGED
STRAPHANGER
STRAPHANGERS
STRAPHANGING
STRAPHANGINGS
STRAPHANGS
STRAPLESSES
STRAPLINES
STRAPONTIN
STRAPONTINS
STRAPPADOED
STRAPPADOES
STRAPPADOING
STRAPPADOS
STRAPPIEST
STRAPPINGS
STRAPWORTS
STRATAGEMS
STRATEGETIC
STRATEGETICAL
STRATEGICAL
STRATEGICALLY
STRATEGICS
STRATEGIES
STRATEGISE
STRATEGISED
STRATEGISES
STRATEGISING
STRATEGIST
STRATEGISTS
STRATEGIZE
STRATEGIZED
STRATEGIZES
STRATEGIZING
STRATHSPEY
STRATHSPEYS
STRATICULATE
STRATICULATION
STRATICULATIONS
STRATIFICATION
STRATIFICATIONS
STRATIFIED
STRATIFIES
STRATIFORM
STRATIFYING
STRATIGRAPHER
STRATIGRAPHERS
STRATIGRAPHIC
STRATIGRAPHICAL
STRATIGRAPHIES
STRATIGRAPHIST
STRATIGRAPHISTS
STRATIGRAPHY
STRATOCRACIES
STRATOCRACY
STRATOCRAT
STRATOCRATIC
STRATOCRATS
STRATOCUMULI
STRATOCUMULUS
STRATOPAUSE
STRATOPAUSES
STRATOSPHERE
STRATOSPHERES
STRATOSPHERIC
STRATOSPHERICAL
STRATOTANKER
STRATOTANKERS
STRATOVOLCANO
STRATOVOLCANOES
STRATOVOLCANOS
STRAUCHTED
STRAUCHTER
STRAUCHTEST
STRAUCHTING
STRAUGHTED
STRAUGHTER
STRAUGHTEST
STRAUGHTING
STRAVAGING
STRAVAIGED
STRAVAIGER
STRAVAIGERS
STRAVAIGING
STRAWBERRIES
STRAWBERRY
STRAWBOARD
STRAWBOARDS
STRAWFLOWER
STRAWFLOWERS
STRAWWEIGHT
STRAWWEIGHTS
STRAWWORMS
STRAYLINGS
STREAKIEST

S

STREAKINESS
STREAKINESSES
STREAKINGS
STREAKLIKE
STREAMBEDS
STREAMERED
STREAMIEST
STREAMINESS
STREAMINESSES
STREAMINGLY
STREAMINGS
STREAMLESS
STREAMLETS
STREAMLIKE
STREAMLINE
STREAMLINED
STREAMLINER
STREAMLINERS
STREAMLINES
STREAMLING
STREAMLINGS
STREAMLINING
STREAMLININGS
STREAMSIDE
STREAMSIDES
STREETAGES
STREETBOYS
STREETCARS
STREETFULS
STREETIEST
STREETKEEPER
STREETKEEPERS
STREETLAMP
STREETLAMPS
STREETLIGHT
STREETLIGHTS
STREETROOM
STREETROOMS
STREETSCAPE
STREETSCAPES
STREETSMART
STREETWALKER
STREETWALKERS
STREETWALKING
STREETWALKINGS
STREETWARD
STREETWARDS
STREETWEAR
STREETWEARS
STREETWISE
STREIGNING
STRELITZES
STRELITZIA
STRELITZIAS
STRENGTHEN
STRENGTHENED
STRENGTHENER
STRENGTHENERS
STRENGTHENING
STRENGTHENINGS
STRENGTHENS
STRENGTHFUL
STRENGTHLESS
STRENUITIES
STRENUOSITIES
STRENUOSITY
STRENUOUSLY
STRENUOUSNESS
STRENUOUSNESSES
STREPEROUS
STREPHOSYMBOLIA
STREPITANT
STREPITATION
STREPITATIONS
STREPITOSO
STREPITOUS
STREPSIPTEROUS
STREPTOBACILLI
STREPTOBACILLUS
STREPTOCARPUS
STREPTOCARPUSES
STREPTOCOCCAL
STREPTOCOCCI
STREPTOCOCCIC
STREPTOCOCCUS
STREPTOKINASE
STREPTOKINASES
STREPTOLYSIN
STREPTOLYSINS
STREPTOMYCES
STREPTOMYCETE
STREPTOMYCETES
STREPTOMYCIN
STREPTOMYCINS
STREPTOSOLEN
STREPTOSOLENS
STREPTOTHRICIN
STREPTOTHRICINS
STRESSBUSTER
STRESSBUSTERS
STRESSBUSTING
STRESSFULLY
STRESSFULNESS
STRESSFULNESSES
STRESSIEST
STRESSLESS
STRESSLESSNESS
STRETCHABILITY
STRETCHABLE
STRETCHERED
STRETCHERING
STRETCHERS
STRETCHIER
STRETCHIEST
STRETCHINESS
STRETCHINESSES
STRETCHING
STRETCHINGS
STRETCHLESS
STRETCHMARKS
STREWMENTS
STRIATIONS
STRIATURES
STRICKENLY
STRICKLING
STRICTIONS
STRICTNESS
STRICTNESSES
STRICTURED
STRICTURES
STRIDDLING
STRIDELEGGED
STRIDELEGS
STRIDENCES
STRIDENCIES
STRIDENTLY
STRIDEWAYS
STRIDULANCE
STRIDULANCES
STRIDULANT
STRIDULANTLY
STRIDULATE
STRIDULATED
STRIDULATES
STRIDULATING
STRIDULATION
STRIDULATIONS
STRIDULATOR
STRIDULATORS
STRIDULATORY
STRIDULOUS
STRIDULOUSLY
STRIDULOUSNESS
STRIFELESS
STRIGIFORM
STRIKEBOUND
STRIKEBREAKER
STRIKEBREAKERS
STRIKEBREAKING
STRIKEBREAKINGS
STRIKELESS
STRIKEOUTS
STRIKEOVER
STRIKEOVERS
STRIKINGLY
STRIKINGNESS
STRIKINGNESSES
STRINGBOARD
STRINGBOARDS
STRINGCOURSE
STRINGCOURSES
STRINGENCIES
STRINGENCY
STRINGENDO
STRINGENTLY
STRINGENTNESS
STRINGENTNESSES
STRINGHALT
STRINGHALTED
STRINGHALTS
STRINGIEST
STRINGINESS
STRINGINESSES
STRINGINGS
STRINGLESS
STRINGLIKE
STRINGPIECE
STRINGPIECES
STRINGYBARK
STRINGYBARKS
STRINKLING
STRINKLINGS
STRIPAGRAM
STRIPAGRAMS
STRIPELESS
STRIPINESS
STRIPINESSES
STRIPLINGS
STRIPOGRAM
STRIPOGRAMS
STRIPPABLE
STRIPPAGRAM
STRIPPAGRAMS
STRIPPERGRAM
STRIPPERGRAMS
STRIPPINGS
STRIPTEASE
STRIPTEASER
STRIPTEASERS
STRIPTEASES
STRIVINGLY
STROBILACEOUS
STROBILATE
STROBILATED
STROBILATES
STROBILATING
STROBILATION
STROBILATIONS
STROBILIFORM
STROBILINE
STROBILISATION
STROBILISATIONS
STROBILIZATION
STROBILIZATIONS
STROBILOID
STROBILUSES
STROBOSCOPE
STROBOSCOPES
STROBOSCOPIC
STROBOSCOPICAL
STROBOTRON
STROBOTRONS
STRODDLING
STROGANOFF
STROGANOFFS
STROKEPLAY
STROLLINGS
STROMATOLITE
STROMATOLITES
STROMATOLITIC

STROMATOUS
STROMBULIFEROUS
STROMBULIFORM
STROMBUSES
STRONGARMED
STRONGARMING
STRONGARMS
STRONGBOXES
STRONGHOLD
STRONGHOLDS
STRONGNESS
STRONGNESSES
STRONGPOINT
STRONGPOINTS
STRONGROOM
STRONGROOMS
STRONGYLES
STRONGYLOID
STRONGYLOIDOSES
STRONGYLOIDOSIS
STRONGYLOIDS
STRONGYLOSES
STRONGYLOSIS
STRONTIANITE
STRONTIANITES
STRONTIANS
STRONTIUMS
STROPHANTHIN
STROPHANTHINS
STROPHANTHUS
STROPHANTHUSES
STROPHICAL
STROPHIOLATE
STROPHIOLATED
STROPHIOLE
STROPHIOLES
STROPHOIDS
STROPHULUS
STROPPIEST
STROPPINESS
STROPPINESSES
STROUDINGS
STROUPACHS
STRUCTURAL
STRUCTURALISE
STRUCTURALISED
STRUCTURALISES
STRUCTURALISING
STRUCTURALISM
STRUCTURALISMS
STRUCTURALIST
STRUCTURALISTS
STRUCTURALIZE
STRUCTURALIZED
STRUCTURALIZES
STRUCTURALIZING
STRUCTURALLY
STRUCTURATION
STRUCTURATIONS
STRUCTURED
STRUCTURELESS
STRUCTURES
STRUCTURING
STRUGGLERS
STRUGGLING
STRUGGLINGLY
STRUGGLINGS
STRUMITISES
STRUMPETED
STRUMPETING
STRUTHIOID
STRUTHIOIDS
STRUTHIOUS
STRUTTINGLY
STRUTTINGS
STRYCHNIAS
STRYCHNINE
STRYCHNINED
STRYCHNINES
STRYCHNINING
STRYCHNINISM
STRYCHNINISMS
STRYCHNISM
STRYCHNISMS
STUBBINESS
STUBBINESSES
STUBBLIEST
STUBBORNED
STUBBORNER
STUBBORNEST
STUBBORNING
STUBBORNLY
STUBBORNNESS
STUBBORNNESSES
STUCCOWORK
STUCCOWORKS
STUDDINGSAIL
STUDDINGSAILS
STUDENTIER
STUDENTIEST
STUDENTRIES
STUDENTSHIP
STUDENTSHIPS
STUDFISHES
STUDHORSES
STUDIEDNESS
STUDIEDNESSES
STUDIOUSLY
STUDIOUSNESS
STUDIOUSNESSES
STUFFINESS
STUFFINESSES
STULTIFICATION
STULTIFICATIONS
STULTIFIED
STULTIFIER
STULTIFIERS
STULTIFIES
STULTIFYING
STUMBLEBUM
STUMBLEBUMS
STUMBLIEST
STUMBLINGLY
STUMPINESS
STUMPINESSES
STUMPWORKS
STUNNINGLY
STUNTEDNESS
STUNTEDNESSES
STUNTWOMAN
STUNTWOMEN
STUPEFACIENT
STUPEFACIENTS
STUPEFACTION
STUPEFACTIONS
STUPEFACTIVE
STUPEFIERS
STUPEFYING
STUPEFYINGLY
STUPENDIOUS
STUPENDOUS
STUPENDOUSLY
STUPENDOUSNESS
STUPIDITIES
STUPIDNESS
STUPIDNESSES
STUPRATING
STUPRATION
STUPRATIONS
STURDINESS
STURDINESSES
STUTTERERS
STUTTERING
STUTTERINGLY
STUTTERINGS
STYLEBOOKS
STYLELESSNESS
STYLELESSNESSES
STYLIFEROUS
STYLISATION
STYLISATIONS
STYLISHNESS
STYLISHNESSES
STYLISTICALLY
STYLISTICS
STYLITISMS
STYLIZATION
STYLIZATIONS
STYLOBATES
STYLOGRAPH
STYLOGRAPHIC
STYLOGRAPHICAL
STYLOGRAPHIES
STYLOGRAPHS
STYLOGRAPHY
STYLOLITES
STYLOLITIC
STYLOMETRIES
STYLOMETRY
STYLOPHONE
STYLOPHONES
STYLOPISED
STYLOPISES
STYLOPISING
STYLOPIZED
STYLOPIZES
STYLOPIZING
STYLOPODIA
STYLOPODIUM
STYLOSTIXES
STYLOSTIXIS
STYPTICITIES
STYPTICITY
STYRACACEOUS
STYROFOAMS
SUABILITIES
SUASIVENESS
SUASIVENESSES
SUAVENESSES
SUAVEOLENT
SUBABDOMINAL
SUBACETATE
SUBACETATES
SUBACIDITIES
SUBACIDITY
SUBACIDNESS
SUBACIDNESSES
SUBACTIONS
SUBACUTELY
SUBADOLESCENT
SUBADOLESCENTS
SUBAERIALLY
SUBAFFLUENT
SUBAGENCIES
SUBAGGREGATE
SUBAGGREGATES
SUBAGGREGATION
SUBAGGREGATIONS
SUBAHDARIES
SUBAHSHIPS
SUBALLIANCE
SUBALLIANCES
SUBALLOCATION
SUBALLOCATIONS
SUBALTERNANT
SUBALTERNANTS
SUBALTERNATE
SUBALTERNATES
SUBALTERNATION
SUBALTERNATIONS
SUBALTERNITIES
SUBALTERNITY
SUBALTERNS
SUBANGULAR
SUBANTARCTIC
SUBAPOSTOLIC
SUBAPPEARANCE
SUBAPPEARANCES
SUBAQUATIC
SUBAQUEOUS

S

SUBARACHNOID
SUBARACHNOIDAL
SUBARACHNOIDS
SUBARBOREAL
SUBARBORESCENT
SUBARCTICS
SUBARCUATE
SUBARCUATION
SUBARCUATIONS
SUBARRATION
SUBARRATIONS
SUBARRHATION
SUBARRHATIONS
SUBARTICLE
SUBARTICLES
SUBASSEMBLE
SUBASSEMBLED
SUBASSEMBLES
SUBASSEMBLIES
SUBASSEMBLING
SUBASSEMBLY
SUBASSOCIATION
SUBASSOCIATIONS
SUBATMOSPHERIC
SUBATOMICS
SUBAUDIBLE
SUBAUDITION
SUBAUDITIONS
SUBAURICULAR
SUBAVERAGE
SUBAXILLARY
SUBBASEMENT
SUBBASEMENTS
SUBBITUMINOUS
SUBBRANCHES
SUBBUREAUS
SUBBUREAUX
SUBCABINET
SUBCABINETS
SUBCALIBER
SUBCALIBRE
SUBCANTORS
SUBCAPSULAR
SUBCARDINAL
SUBCARDINALS
SUBCARRIER
SUBCARRIERS
SUBCATEGORIES
SUBCATEGORISE
SUBCATEGORISED
SUBCATEGORISES
SUBCATEGORISING
SUBCATEGORIZE
SUBCATEGORIZED
SUBCATEGORIZES
SUBCATEGORIZING
SUBCATEGORY
SUBCAVITIES
SUBCEILING
SUBCEILINGS
SUBCELESTIAL
SUBCELESTIALS
SUBCELLARS
SUBCELLULAR
SUBCENTERS
SUBCENTRAL
SUBCENTRALLY
SUBCENTRES
SUBCEPTION
SUBCEPTIONS
SUBCHANTER
SUBCHANTERS
SUBCHAPTER
SUBCHAPTERS
SUBCHARTER
SUBCHARTERED
SUBCHARTERING
SUBCHARTERS
SUBCHASERS
SUBCHELATE
SUBCHLORIDE
SUBCHLORIDES
SUBCIRCUIT
SUBCIRCUITS
SUBCIVILISATION
SUBCIVILISED
SUBCIVILIZATION
SUBCIVILIZED
SUBCLASSED
SUBCLASSES
SUBCLASSIFIED
SUBCLASSIFIES
SUBCLASSIFY
SUBCLASSIFYING
SUBCLASSING
SUBCLAUSES
SUBCLAVIAN
SUBCLAVIANS
SUBCLAVICULAR
SUBCLIMACTIC
SUBCLIMAXES
SUBCLINICAL
SUBCLINICALLY
SUBCLUSTER
SUBCLUSTERED
SUBCLUSTERING
SUBCLUSTERS
SUBCOLLECTION
SUBCOLLECTIONS
SUBCOLLEGE
SUBCOLLEGES
SUBCOLLEGIATE
SUBCOLONIES
SUBCOMMISSION
SUBCOMMISSIONED
SUBCOMMISSIONER
SUBCOMMISSIONS
SUBCOMMITTEE
SUBCOMMITTEES
SUBCOMMUNITIES
SUBCOMMUNITY
SUBCOMPACT
SUBCOMPACTS
SUBCOMPONENT
SUBCOMPONENTS
SUBCONSCIOUS
SUBCONSCIOUSES
SUBCONSCIOUSLY
SUBCONSULS
SUBCONTIGUOUS
SUBCONTINENT
SUBCONTINENTAL
SUBCONTINENTS
SUBCONTINUOUS
SUBCONTRACT
SUBCONTRACTED
SUBCONTRACTING
SUBCONTRACTINGS
SUBCONTRACTOR
SUBCONTRACTORS
SUBCONTRACTS
SUBCONTRAOCTAVE
SUBCONTRARIES
SUBCONTRARIETY
SUBCONTRARY
SUBCOOLING
SUBCORDATE
SUBCORIACEOUS
SUBCORTEXES
SUBCORTICAL
SUBCORTICES
SUBCOSTALS
SUBCOUNTIES
SUBCRANIAL
SUBCRITICAL
SUBCRUSTAL
SUBCULTURAL
SUBCULTURALLY
SUBCULTURE
SUBCULTURED
SUBCULTURES
SUBCULTURING
SUBCURATIVE
SUBCUTANEOUS
SUBCUTANEOUSLY
SUBCUTISES
SUBDEACONATE
SUBDEACONATES
SUBDEACONRIES
SUBDEACONRY
SUBDEACONS
SUBDEACONSHIP
SUBDEACONSHIPS
SUBDEALERS
SUBDEANERIES
SUBDEANERY
SUBDEBUTANTE
SUBDEBUTANTES
SUBDECANAL
SUBDECISION
SUBDECISIONS
SUBDELIRIA
SUBDELIRIOUS
SUBDELIRIUM
SUBDELIRIUMS
SUBDEPARTMENT
SUBDEPARTMENTS
SUBDEPUTIES
SUBDERMALLY
SUBDEVELOPMENT
SUBDEVELOPMENTS
SUBDIACONAL
SUBDIACONATE
SUBDIACONATES
SUBDIALECT
SUBDIALECTS
SUBDIRECTOR
SUBDIRECTORS
SUBDISCIPLINE
SUBDISCIPLINES
SUBDISTRICT
SUBDISTRICTS
SUBDIVIDABLE
SUBDIVIDED
SUBDIVIDER
SUBDIVIDERS
SUBDIVIDES
SUBDIVIDING
SUBDIVISIBLE
SUBDIVISION
SUBDIVISIONAL
SUBDIVISIONS
SUBDIVISIVE
SUBDOMINANT
SUBDOMINANTS
SUBDUCTING
SUBDUCTION
SUBDUCTIONS
SUBDUEDNESS
SUBDUEDNESSES
SUBDUEMENT
SUBDUEMENTS
SUBDUPLICATE
SUBECONOMIC
SUBECONOMIES
SUBECONOMY
SUBEDITING
SUBEDITORIAL
SUBEDITORS
SUBEDITORSHIP
SUBEDITORSHIPS
SUBEMPLOYED
SUBEMPLOYMENT
SUBEMPLOYMENTS
SUBENTRIES
SUBEPIDERMAL
SUBEQUATORIAL
SUBERISATION
SUBERISATIONS
SUBERISING

S

SUBERIZATION
SUBERIZATIONS
SUBERIZING
SUBFACTORIAL
SUBFACTORIALS
SUBFAMILIES
SUBFERTILE
SUBFERTILITIES
SUBFERTILITY
SUBFEUDATION
SUBFEUDATIONS
SUBFEUDATORY
SUBFOLDERS
SUBFOSSILS
SUBFREEZING
SUBFUSCOUS
SUBGENERATION
SUBGENERATIONS
SUBGENERIC
SUBGENERICALLY
SUBGENUSES
SUBGLACIAL
SUBGLACIALLY
SUBGLOBOSE
SUBGLOBULAR
SUBGOVERNMENT
SUBGOVERNMENTS
SUBGROUPED
SUBGROUPING
SUBHARMONIC
SUBHARMONICS
SUBHASTATION
SUBHASTATIONS
SUBHEADING
SUBHEADINGS
SUBIMAGINAL
SUBIMAGINES
SUBIMAGOES
SUBINCISED
SUBINCISES
SUBINCISING
SUBINCISION
SUBINCISIONS
SUBINDEXES
SUBINDICATE
SUBINDICATED
SUBINDICATES
SUBINDICATING
SUBINDICATION
SUBINDICATIONS
SUBINDICATIVE
SUBINDICES
SUBINDUSTRIES
SUBINDUSTRY
SUBINFEUDATE
SUBINFEUDATED
SUBINFEUDATES
SUBINFEUDATING
SUBINFEUDATION
SUBINFEUDATIONS
SUBINFEUDATORY
SUBINFEUDED
SUBINFEUDING
SUBINFEUDS
SUBINHIBITORY
SUBINSINUATION
SUBINSINUATIONS
SUBINSPECTOR
SUBINSPECTORS
SUBINTELLECTION
SUBINTELLIGENCE
SUBINTELLIGITUR
SUBINTERVAL
SUBINTERVALS
SUBINTRANT
SUBINTRODUCE
SUBINTRODUCED
SUBINTRODUCES
SUBINTRODUCING
SUBINVOLUTION
SUBINVOLUTIONS
SUBIRRIGATE
SUBIRRIGATED
SUBIRRIGATES
SUBIRRIGATING
SUBIRRIGATION
SUBIRRIGATIONS
SUBITANEOUS
SUBITISING
SUBITIZING
SUBJACENCIES
SUBJACENCY
SUBJACENTLY
SUBJECTABILITY
SUBJECTABLE
SUBJECTIFIED
SUBJECTIFIES
SUBJECTIFY
SUBJECTIFYING
SUBJECTING
SUBJECTION
SUBJECTIONS
SUBJECTIVE
SUBJECTIVELY
SUBJECTIVENESS
SUBJECTIVES
SUBJECTIVISE
SUBJECTIVISED
SUBJECTIVISES
SUBJECTIVISING
SUBJECTIVISM
SUBJECTIVISMS
SUBJECTIVIST
SUBJECTIVISTIC
SUBJECTIVISTS
SUBJECTIVITIES
SUBJECTIVITY
SUBJECTIVIZE
SUBJECTIVIZED
SUBJECTIVIZES
SUBJECTIVIZING
SUBJECTLESS
SUBJECTSHIP
SUBJECTSHIPS
SUBJOINDER
SUBJOINDERS
SUBJOINING
SUBJUGABLE
SUBJUGATED
SUBJUGATES
SUBJUGATING
SUBJUGATION
SUBJUGATIONS
SUBJUGATOR
SUBJUGATORS
SUBJUNCTION
SUBJUNCTIONS
SUBJUNCTIVE
SUBJUNCTIVELY
SUBJUNCTIVES
SUBKINGDOM
SUBKINGDOMS
SUBLANCEOLATE
SUBLANGUAGE
SUBLANGUAGES
SUBLAPSARIAN
SUBLAPSARIANISM
SUBLAPSARIANS
SUBLATIONS
SUBLEASING
SUBLESSEES
SUBLESSORS
SUBLETHALLY
SUBLETTERS
SUBLETTING
SUBLETTINGS
SUBLIBRARIAN
SUBLIBRARIANS
SUBLICENSE
SUBLICENSED
SUBLICENSES
SUBLICENSING
SUBLIEUTENANCY
SUBLIEUTENANT
SUBLIEUTENANTS
SUBLIMABLE
SUBLIMATED
SUBLIMATES
SUBLIMATING
SUBLIMATION
SUBLIMATIONS
SUBLIMENESS
SUBLIMENESSES
SUBLIMINAL
SUBLIMINALLY
SUBLIMINALS
SUBLIMINGS
SUBLIMISED
SUBLIMISES
SUBLIMISING
SUBLIMITIES
SUBLIMIZED
SUBLIMIZES
SUBLIMIZING
SUBLINEATION
SUBLINEATIONS
SUBLINGUAL
SUBLITERACIES
SUBLITERACY
SUBLITERARY
SUBLITERATE
SUBLITERATES
SUBLITERATURE
SUBLITERATURES
SUBLITTORAL
SUBLITTORALS
SUBLUXATED
SUBLUXATES
SUBLUXATING
SUBLUXATION
SUBLUXATIONS
SUBMANAGER
SUBMANAGERS
SUBMANDIBULAR
SUBMANDIBULARS
SUBMANIFOLD
SUBMANIFOLDS
SUBMARGINAL
SUBMARGINALLY
SUBMARINED
SUBMARINER
SUBMARINERS
SUBMARINES
SUBMARINING
SUBMARKETS
SUBMATRICES
SUBMATRIXES
SUBMAXILLARIES
SUBMAXILLARY
SUBMAXIMAL
SUBMEDIANT
SUBMEDIANTS
SUBMENTUMS
SUBMERGEMENT
SUBMERGEMENTS
SUBMERGENCE
SUBMERGENCES
SUBMERGIBILITY
SUBMERGIBLE
SUBMERGIBLES
SUBMERGING
SUBMERSIBILITY
SUBMERSIBLE
SUBMERSIBLES
SUBMERSING
SUBMERSION
SUBMERSIONS
SUBMETACENTRIC
SUBMETACENTRICS
SUBMICROGRAM

S

SUBMICRONS
SUBMICROSCOPIC
SUBMILLIMETER
SUBMILLIMETERS
SUBMILLIMETRE
SUBMILLIMETRES
SUBMINIATURE
SUBMINIATURES
SUBMINIATURISE
SUBMINIATURISED
SUBMINIATURISES
SUBMINIATURIZE
SUBMINIATURIZED
SUBMINIATURIZES
SUBMINIMAL
SUBMINISTER
SUBMINISTERED
SUBMINISTERING
SUBMINISTERS
SUBMISSIBLE
SUBMISSION
SUBMISSIONS
SUBMISSIVE
SUBMISSIVELY
SUBMISSIVENESS
SUBMISSNESS
SUBMISSNESSES
SUBMITTABLE
SUBMITTALS
SUBMITTERS
SUBMITTING
SUBMITTINGS
SUBMOLECULE
SUBMOLECULES
SUBMONTANE
SUBMONTANELY
SUBMUCOSAE
SUBMUCOSAL
SUBMUCOSAS
SUBMULTIPLE
SUBMULTIPLES
SUBMUNITION
SUBMUNITIONS
SUBNASCENT
SUBNATIONAL
SUBNATURAL
SUBNETWORK
SUBNETWORKED
SUBNETWORKING
SUBNETWORKS
SUBNORMALITIES
SUBNORMALITY
SUBNORMALLY
SUBNORMALS
SUBNUCLEAR
SUBNUCLEUS
SUBNUCLEUSES
SUBOCCIPITAL
SUBOCEANIC
SUBOCTAVES
SUBOCTUPLE
SUBOFFICER
SUBOFFICERS
SUBOFFICES
SUBOPERCULA
SUBOPERCULAR
SUBOPERCULUM
SUBOPERCULUMS
SUBOPTIMAL
SUBOPTIMISATION
SUBOPTIMISE
SUBOPTIMISED
SUBOPTIMISES
SUBOPTIMISING
SUBOPTIMIZATION
SUBOPTIMIZE
SUBOPTIMIZED
SUBOPTIMIZES
SUBOPTIMIZING
SUBOPTIMUM
SUBOPTIMUMS
SUBORBICULAR
SUBORBITAL
SUBORDINAL
SUBORDINANCIES
SUBORDINANCY
SUBORDINARIES
SUBORDINARY
SUBORDINATE
SUBORDINATED
SUBORDINATELY
SUBORDINATENESS
SUBORDINATES
SUBORDINATING
SUBORDINATION
SUBORDINATIONS
SUBORDINATIVE
SUBORDINATOR
SUBORDINATORS
SUBORGANISATION
SUBORGANIZATION
SUBORNATION
SUBORNATIONS
SUBORNATIVE
SUBOSCINES
SUBPANATION
SUBPANATIONS
SUBPARAGRAPH
SUBPARAGRAPHS
SUBPARALLEL
SUBPENAING
SUBPERIODS
SUBPHRENIC
SUBPHYLUMS
SUBPOENAED
SUBPOENAING
SUBPOPULATION
SUBPOPULATIONS
SUBPOTENCIES
SUBPOTENCY
SUBPREFECT
SUBPREFECTS
SUBPREFECTURE
SUBPREFECTURES
SUBPRIMATE
SUBPRIMATES
SUBPRINCIPAL
SUBPRINCIPALS
SUBPRIORESS
SUBPRIORESSES
SUBPROBLEM
SUBPROBLEMS
SUBPROCESS
SUBPROCESSES
SUBPRODUCT
SUBPRODUCTS
SUBPROFESSIONAL
SUBPROGRAM
SUBPROGRAMS
SUBPROJECT
SUBPROJECTS
SUBPROLETARIAT
SUBPROLETARIATS
SUBRATIONAL
SUBREFERENCE
SUBREFERENCES
SUBREGIONAL
SUBREGIONS
SUBRENTING
SUBREPTION
SUBREPTIONS
SUBREPTITIOUS
SUBREPTITIOUSLY
SUBREPTIVE
SUBROGATED
SUBROGATES
SUBROGATING
SUBROGATION
SUBROGATIONS
SUBROUTINE
SUBROUTINES
SUBSAMPLED
SUBSAMPLES
SUBSAMPLING
SUBSATELLITE
SUBSATELLITES
SUBSATURATED
SUBSATURATION
SUBSATURATIONS
SUBSCAPULAR
SUBSCAPULARS
SUBSCHEMATA
SUBSCIENCE
SUBSCIENCES
SUBSCRIBABLE
SUBSCRIBED
SUBSCRIBER
SUBSCRIBERS
SUBSCRIBES
SUBSCRIBING
SUBSCRIBINGS
SUBSCRIPTION
SUBSCRIPTIONS
SUBSCRIPTIVE
SUBSCRIPTS
SUBSECRETARIES
SUBSECRETARY
SUBSECTION
SUBSECTIONS
SUBSECTORS
SUBSEGMENT
SUBSEGMENTS
SUBSEIZURE
SUBSEIZURES
SUBSELLIUM
SUBSENSIBLE
SUBSENTENCE
SUBSENTENCES
SUBSEQUENCE
SUBSEQUENCES
SUBSEQUENT
SUBSEQUENTIAL
SUBSEQUENTLY
SUBSEQUENTNESS
SUBSEQUENTS
SUBSERVIENCE
SUBSERVIENCES
SUBSERVIENCIES
SUBSERVIENCY
SUBSERVIENT
SUBSERVIENTLY
SUBSERVIENTS
SUBSERVING
SUBSESSILE
SUBSHRUBBY
SUBSIDENCE
SUBSIDENCES
SUBSIDENCIES
SUBSIDENCY
SUBSIDIARIAT
SUBSIDIARIATS
SUBSIDIARIES
SUBSIDIARILY
SUBSIDIARINESS
SUBSIDIARITIES
SUBSIDIARITY
SUBSIDIARY
SUBSIDISABLE
SUBSIDISATION
SUBSIDISATIONS
SUBSIDISED
SUBSIDISER
SUBSIDISERS
SUBSIDISES
SUBSIDISING
SUBSIDIZABLE
SUBSIDIZATION
SUBSIDIZATIONS
SUBSIDIZED
SUBSIDIZER

SUBSIDIZERS
SUBSIDIZES
SUBSIDIZING
SUBSISTENCE
SUBSISTENCES
SUBSISTENT
SUBSISTENTIAL
SUBSISTERS
SUBSISTING
SUBSOCIALLY
SUBSOCIETIES
SUBSOCIETY
SUBSOILERS
SUBSOILING
SUBSOILINGS
SUBSONICALLY
SUBSPECIALISE
SUBSPECIALISED
SUBSPECIALISES
SUBSPECIALISING
SUBSPECIALIST
SUBSPECIALISTS
SUBSPECIALITIES
SUBSPECIALITY
SUBSPECIALIZE
SUBSPECIALIZED
SUBSPECIALIZES
SUBSPECIALIZING
SUBSPECIALTIES
SUBSPECIALTY
SUBSPECIES
SUBSPECIFIC
SUBSPECIFICALLY
SUBSPINOUS
SUBSPONTANEOUS
SUBSTANCELESS
SUBSTANCES
SUBSTANDARD
SUBSTANTIAL
SUBSTANTIALISE
SUBSTANTIALISED
SUBSTANTIALISES
SUBSTANTIALISM
SUBSTANTIALISMS
SUBSTANTIALIST
SUBSTANTIALISTS
SUBSTANTIALITY
SUBSTANTIALIZE
SUBSTANTIALIZED
SUBSTANTIALIZES
SUBSTANTIALLY
SUBSTANTIALNESS
SUBSTANTIALS
SUBSTANTIATE
SUBSTANTIATED
SUBSTANTIATES
SUBSTANTIATING
SUBSTANTIATION
SUBSTANTIATIONS
SUBSTANTIATIVE
SUBSTANTIATOR
SUBSTANTIATORS
SUBSTANTIVAL
SUBSTANTIVALLY
SUBSTANTIVE
SUBSTANTIVELY
SUBSTANTIVENESS
SUBSTANTIVES
SUBSTANTIVISE
SUBSTANTIVISED
SUBSTANTIVISES
SUBSTANTIVISING
SUBSTANTIVITIES
SUBSTANTIVITY
SUBSTANTIVIZE
SUBSTANTIVIZED
SUBSTANTIVIZES
SUBSTANTIVIZING
SUBSTATION
SUBSTATIONS
SUBSTELLAR
SUBSTERNAL
SUBSTITUENT
SUBSTITUENTS
SUBSTITUTABLE
SUBSTITUTE
SUBSTITUTED
SUBSTITUTES
SUBSTITUTING
SUBSTITUTION
SUBSTITUTIONAL
SUBSTITUTIONARY
SUBSTITUTIONS
SUBSTITUTIVE
SUBSTITUTIVELY
SUBSTITUTIVITY
SUBSTRACTED
SUBSTRACTING
SUBSTRACTION
SUBSTRACTIONS
SUBSTRACTOR
SUBSTRACTORS
SUBSTRACTS
SUBSTRATAL
SUBSTRATES
SUBSTRATIVE
SUBSTRATOSPHERE
SUBSTRATUM
SUBSTRATUMS
SUBSTRUCTED
SUBSTRUCTING
SUBSTRUCTION
SUBSTRUCTIONS
SUBSTRUCTS
SUBSTRUCTURAL
SUBSTRUCTURE
SUBSTRUCTURES
SUBSULTIVE
SUBSULTORILY
SUBSULTORY
SUBSULTUSES
SUBSUMABLE
SUBSUMPTION
SUBSUMPTIONS
SUBSUMPTIVE
SUBSURFACE
SUBSURFACES
SUBSYSTEMS
SUBTACKSMAN
SUBTACKSMEN
SUBTANGENT
SUBTANGENTS
SUBTEMPERATE
SUBTENANCIES
SUBTENANCY
SUBTENANTS
SUBTENDING
SUBTENURES
SUBTERFUGE
SUBTERFUGES
SUBTERMINAL
SUBTERNATURAL
SUBTERRAIN
SUBTERRAINS
SUBTERRANE
SUBTERRANEAN
SUBTERRANEANLY
SUBTERRANEANS
SUBTERRANEOUS
SUBTERRANEOUSLY
SUBTERRANES
SUBTERRENE
SUBTERRENES
SUBTERRESTRIAL
SUBTERRESTRIALS
SUBTEXTUAL
SUBTHERAPEUTIC
SUBTHRESHOLD
SUBTILENESS
SUBTILENESSES
SUBTILISATION
SUBTILISATIONS
SUBTILISED
SUBTILISER
SUBTILISERS
SUBTILISES
SUBTILISIN
SUBTILISING
SUBTILISINS
SUBTILITIES
SUBTILIZATION
SUBTILIZATIONS
SUBTILIZED
SUBTILIZER
SUBTILIZERS
SUBTILIZES
SUBTILIZING
SUBTILTIES
SUBTITLING
SUBTITLINGS
SUBTITULAR
SUBTLENESS
SUBTLENESSES
SUBTLETIES
SUBTOTALED
SUBTOTALING
SUBTOTALLED
SUBTOTALLING
SUBTOTALLY
SUBTRACTED
SUBTRACTER
SUBTRACTERS
SUBTRACTING
SUBTRACTION
SUBTRACTIONS
SUBTRACTIVE
SUBTRACTOR
SUBTRACTORS
SUBTRAHEND
SUBTRAHENDS
SUBTREASURER
SUBTREASURERS
SUBTREASURIES
SUBTREASURY
SUBTRIANGULAR
SUBTRIPLICATE
SUBTROPICAL
SUBTROPICALLY
SUBTROPICS
SUBTRUDING
SUBTWEETED
SUBTWEETING
SUBTYPICAL
SUBUMBRELLA
SUBUMBRELLAR
SUBUMBRELLAS
SUBUNGULATE
SUBUNGULATES
SUBURBANISATION
SUBURBANISE
SUBURBANISED
SUBURBANISES
SUBURBANISING
SUBURBANISM
SUBURBANISMS
SUBURBANITE
SUBURBANITES
SUBURBANITIES
SUBURBANITY
SUBURBANIZATION
SUBURBANIZE
SUBURBANIZED
SUBURBANIZES
SUBURBANIZING
SUBURBICARIAN
SUBVARIETIES
SUBVARIETY
SUBVASSALS
SUBVENTION
SUBVENTIONARY

SUBVENTIONS
SUBVERSALS
SUBVERSING
SUBVERSION
SUBVERSIONARIES
SUBVERSIONARY
SUBVERSIONS
SUBVERSIVE
SUBVERSIVELY
SUBVERSIVENESS
SUBVERSIVES
SUBVERTEBRAL
SUBVERTERS
SUBVERTICAL
SUBVERTING
SUBVIRUSES
SUBVISIBLE
SUBVITREOUS
SUBVOCALISATION
SUBVOCALISE
SUBVOCALISED
SUBVOCALISES
SUBVOCALISING
SUBVOCALIZATION
SUBVOCALIZE
SUBVOCALIZED
SUBVOCALIZES
SUBVOCALIZING
SUBVOCALLY
SUBWARDENS
SUBWOOFERS
SUBWRITERS
SUCCEDANEA
SUCCEDANEOUS
SUCCEDANEUM
SUCCEDANEUMS
SUCCEDENTS
SUCCEEDABLE
SUCCEEDERS
SUCCEEDING
SUCCEEDINGLY
SUCCENTORS
SUCCENTORSHIP
SUCCENTORSHIPS
SUCCESSANTLY
SUCCESSFUL
SUCCESSFULLY
SUCCESSFULNESS
SUCCESSION
SUCCESSIONAL
SUCCESSIONALLY
SUCCESSIONIST
SUCCESSIONISTS
SUCCESSIONLESS
SUCCESSIONS
SUCCESSIVE
SUCCESSIVELY
SUCCESSIVENESS
SUCCESSLESS
SUCCESSLESSLY
SUCCESSLESSNESS
SUCCESSORAL
SUCCESSORS
SUCCESSORSHIP
SUCCESSORSHIPS
SUCCINATES
SUCCINCTER
SUCCINCTEST
SUCCINCTLY
SUCCINCTNESS
SUCCINCTNESSES
SUCCINCTORIA
SUCCINCTORIES
SUCCINCTORIUM
SUCCINCTORIUMS
SUCCINCTORY
SUCCINITES
SUCCINYLCHOLINE
SUCCORABLE
SUCCORLESS
SUCCOTASHES
SUCCOURABLE
SUCCOURERS
SUCCOURING
SUCCOURLESS
SUCCUBUSES
SUCCULENCE
SUCCULENCES
SUCCULENCIES
SUCCULENCY
SUCCULENTLY
SUCCULENTS
SUCCUMBERS
SUCCUMBING
SUCCURSALE
SUCCURSALES
SUCCURSALS
SUCCUSSATION
SUCCUSSATIONS
SUCCUSSING
SUCCUSSION
SUCCUSSIONS
SUCCUSSIVE
SUCHNESSES
SUCKERFISH
SUCKERFISHES
SUCKFISHES
SUCKHOLING
SUCKINESSES
SUCRALFATE
SUCRALFATES
SUCRALOSES
SUCTIONING
SUCTORIANS
SUDATORIES
SUDATORIUM
SUDATORIUMS
SUDDENNESS
SUDDENNESSES
SUDDENTIES
SUDORIFEROUS
SUDORIFICS
SUDORIPAROUS
SUEABILITIES
SUEABILITY
SUFFERABLE
SUFFERABLENESS
SUFFERABLY
SUFFERANCE
SUFFERANCES
SUFFERINGLY
SUFFERINGS
SUFFICIENCE
SUFFICIENCES
SUFFICIENCIES
SUFFICIENCY
SUFFICIENT
SUFFICIENTLY
SUFFICIENTS
SUFFICINGNESS
SUFFICINGNESSES
SUFFIGANCE
SUFFIGANCES
SUFFISANCE
SUFFISANCES
SUFFIXATION
SUFFIXATIONS
SUFFIXIONS
SUFFLATING
SUFFLATION
SUFFLATIONS
SUFFOCATED
SUFFOCATES
SUFFOCATING
SUFFOCATINGLY
SUFFOCATINGS
SUFFOCATION
SUFFOCATIONS
SUFFOCATIVE
SUFFRAGANS
SUFFRAGANSHIP
SUFFRAGANSHIPS
SUFFRAGETTE
SUFFRAGETTES
SUFFRAGETTISM
SUFFRAGETTISMS
SUFFRAGISM
SUFFRAGISMS
SUFFRAGIST
SUFFRAGISTS
SUFFRUTESCENT
SUFFRUTICOSE
SUFFUMIGATE
SUFFUMIGATED
SUFFUMIGATES
SUFFUMIGATING
SUFFUMIGATION
SUFFUMIGATIONS
SUFFUSIONS
SUGARALLIE
SUGARALLIES
SUGARBERRIES
SUGARBERRY
SUGARBUSHES
SUGARCANES
SUGARCOATED
SUGARCOATING
SUGARCOATS
SUGARHOUSE
SUGARHOUSES
SUGARINESS
SUGARINESSES
SUGARLOAVES
SUGARPLUMS
SUGGESTERS
SUGGESTIBILITY
SUGGESTIBLE
SUGGESTIBLENESS
SUGGESTIBLY
SUGGESTING
SUGGESTION
SUGGESTIONISE
SUGGESTIONISED
SUGGESTIONISES
SUGGESTIONISING
SUGGESTIONISM
SUGGESTIONISMS
SUGGESTIONIST
SUGGESTIONISTS
SUGGESTIONIZE
SUGGESTIONIZED
SUGGESTIONIZES
SUGGESTIONIZING
SUGGESTIONS
SUGGESTIVE
SUGGESTIVELY
SUGGESTIVENESS
SUICIDALLY
SUICIDOLOGIES
SUICIDOLOGIST
SUICIDOLOGISTS
SUICIDOLOGY
SUITABILITIES
SUITABILITY
SUITABLENESS
SUITABLENESSES
SUITRESSES
SULCALISED
SULCALISES
SULCALISING
SULCALIZED
SULCALIZES
SULCALIZING
SULCATIONS
SULFACETAMIDE
SULFACETAMIDES
SULFADIAZINE
SULFADIAZINES
SULFADIMIDINE
SULFADIMIDINES

SULFADOXINE
SULFADOXINES
SULFAMETHAZINE
SULFAMETHAZINES
SULFANILAMIDE
SULFANILAMIDES
SULFATASES
SULFATHIAZOLE
SULFATHIAZOLES
SULFATIONS
SULFHYDRYL
SULFHYDRYLS
SULFINPYRAZONE
SULFINPYRAZONES
SULFONAMIDE
SULFONAMIDES
SULFONATED
SULFONATES
SULFONATING
SULFONATION
SULFONATIONS
SULFONIUMS
SULFONMETHANE
SULFONMETHANES
SULFONYLUREA
SULFONYLUREAS
SULFOXIDES
SULFURATED
SULFURATES
SULFURATING
SULFURATION
SULFURATIONS
SULFUREOUS
SULFURETED
SULFURETING
SULFURETTED
SULFURETTING
SULFURIEST
SULFURISATION
SULFURISATIONS
SULFURISED
SULFURISES
SULFURISING
SULFURIZATION
SULFURIZATIONS
SULFURIZED
SULFURIZES
SULFURIZING
SULFUROUSLY
SULFUROUSNESS
SULFUROUSNESSES
SULKINESSES
SULLENNESS
SULLENNESSES
SULPHACETAMIDE
SULPHACETAMIDES
SULPHADIAZINE
SULPHADIAZINES
SULPHADOXINE
SULPHADOXINES
SULPHANILAMIDE
SULPHANILAMIDES
SULPHATASE
SULPHATASES
SULPHATHIAZOLE
SULPHATHIAZOLES
SULPHATING
SULPHATION
SULPHATIONS
SULPHHYDRYL
SULPHHYDRYLS
SULPHINPYRAZONE
SULPHINYLS
SULPHONAMIDE
SULPHONAMIDES
SULPHONATE
SULPHONATED
SULPHONATES
SULPHONATING
SULPHONATION
SULPHONATIONS
SULPHONIUM
SULPHONIUMS
SULPHONMETHANE
SULPHONMETHANES
SULPHONYLS
SULPHONYLUREA
SULPHONYLUREAS
SULPHOXIDE
SULPHOXIDES
SULPHURATE
SULPHURATED
SULPHURATES
SULPHURATING
SULPHURATION
SULPHURATIONS
SULPHURATOR
SULPHURATORS
SULPHUREOUS
SULPHUREOUSLY
SULPHUREOUSNESS
SULPHURETED
SULPHURETING
SULPHURETS
SULPHURETTED
SULPHURETTING
SULPHURIER
SULPHURIEST
SULPHURING
SULPHURISATION
SULPHURISATIONS
SULPHURISE
SULPHURISED
SULPHURISES
SULPHURISING
SULPHURIZATION
SULPHURIZATIONS
SULPHURIZE
SULPHURIZED
SULPHURIZES
SULPHURIZING
SULPHUROUS
SULPHUROUSLY
SULPHUROUSNESS
SULPHURWORT
SULPHURWORTS
SULPHURYLS
SULTANATES
SULTANESSES
SULTANSHIP
SULTANSHIPS
SULTRINESS
SULTRINESSES
SUMBITCHES
SUMMABILITIES
SUMMABILITY
SUMMARINESS
SUMMARINESSES
SUMMARISABLE
SUMMARISATION
SUMMARISATIONS
SUMMARISED
SUMMARISER
SUMMARISERS
SUMMARISES
SUMMARISING
SUMMARISTS
SUMMARIZABLE
SUMMARIZATION
SUMMARIZATIONS
SUMMARIZED
SUMMARIZER
SUMMARIZERS
SUMMARIZES
SUMMARIZING
SUMMATIONAL
SUMMATIONS
SUMMERHOUSE
SUMMERHOUSES
SUMMERIEST
SUMMERINESS
SUMMERINESSES
SUMMERINGS
SUMMERLESS
SUMMERLIER
SUMMERLIEST
SUMMERLIKE
SUMMERLONG
SUMMERSAULT
SUMMERSAULTED
SUMMERSAULTING
SUMMERSAULTS
SUMMERSETS
SUMMERSETTED
SUMMERSETTING
SUMMERTIDE
SUMMERTIDES
SUMMERTIME
SUMMERTIMES
SUMMERWEIGHT
SUMMERWOOD
SUMMERWOODS
SUMMITEERS
SUMMITLESS
SUMMITRIES
SUMMONABLE
SUMMONSING
SUMPHISHNESS
SUMPHISHNESSES
SUMPSIMUSES
SUMPTUOSITIES
SUMPTUOSITY
SUMPTUOUSLY
SUMPTUOUSNESS
SUMPTUOUSNESSES
SUNBATHERS
SUNBATHING
SUNBATHINGS
SUNBEAMIER
SUNBEAMIEST
SUNBERRIES
SUNBONNETED
SUNBONNETS
SUNBURNING
SUNDERABLE
SUNDERANCE
SUNDERANCES
SUNDERINGS
SUNDERMENT
SUNDERMENTS
SUNDOWNERS
SUNDOWNING
SUNDRENCHED
SUNDRESSES
SUNFLOWERS
SUNGAZINGS
SUNGLASSES
SUNLESSNESS
SUNLESSNESSES
SUNLOUNGER
SUNLOUNGERS
SUNNINESSES
SUNPORCHES
SUNRISINGS
SUNSCREENING
SUNSCREENINGS
SUNSCREENS
SUNSEEKERS
SUNSETTING
SUNSETTINGS
SUNSHINIER
SUNSHINIEST
SUNSPOTTED
SUNSTROKES
SUNTANNING
SUNTANNINGS
SUNWORSHIPPER
SUNWORSHIPPERS
SUOVETAURILIA
SUOVETAURILIAS

SUPERABILITIES
SUPERABILITY
SUPERABLENESS
SUPERABLENESSES
SUPERABOUND
SUPERABOUNDED
SUPERABOUNDING
SUPERABOUNDS
SUPERABSORBENT
SUPERABSORBENTS
SUPERABUNDANCE
SUPERABUNDANCES
SUPERABUNDANT
SUPERABUNDANTLY
SUPERACHIEVER
SUPERACHIEVERS
SUPERACTIVE
SUPERACTIVITIES
SUPERACTIVITY
SUPERACUTE
SUPERADDED
SUPERADDING
SUPERADDITION
SUPERADDITIONAL
SUPERADDITIONS
SUPERAGENCIES
SUPERAGENCY
SUPERAGENT
SUPERAGENTS
SUPERALLOY
SUPERALLOYS
SUPERALTAR
SUPERALTARS
SUPERALTERN
SUPERALTERNS
SUPERAMBITIOUS
SUPERANNUABLE
SUPERANNUATE
SUPERANNUATED
SUPERANNUATES
SUPERANNUATING
SUPERANNUATION
SUPERANNUATIONS
SUPERATHLETE
SUPERATHLETES
SUPERATING
SUPERATION
SUPERATIONS
SUPERATOMS
SUPERBANKS
SUPERBAZAAR
SUPERBAZAARS
SUPERBAZAR
SUPERBAZARS
SUPERBIKES
SUPERBITCH
SUPERBITCHES
SUPERBITIES
SUPERBLOCK
SUPERBLOCKS
SUPERBNESS
SUPERBNESSES
SUPERBOARD
SUPERBOARDS
SUPERBOMBER
SUPERBOMBERS
SUPERBOMBS
SUPERBRAIN
SUPERBRAINS
SUPERBRATS
SUPERBRIGHT
SUPERBUREAUCRAT
SUPERCABINET
SUPERCABINETS
SUPERCALENDER
SUPERCALENDERED
SUPERCALENDERS
SUPERCARGO
SUPERCARGOES
SUPERCARGOS
SUPERCARGOSHIP
SUPERCARGOSHIPS
SUPERCARRIER
SUPERCARRIERS
SUPERCAUTIOUS
SUPERCEDED
SUPERCEDES
SUPERCEDING
SUPERCELESTIAL
SUPERCELLS
SUPERCENTER
SUPERCENTERS
SUPERCHARGE
SUPERCHARGED
SUPERCHARGER
SUPERCHARGERS
SUPERCHARGES
SUPERCHARGING
SUPERCHERIE
SUPERCHERIES
SUPERCHURCH
SUPERCHURCHES
SUPERCILIARIES
SUPERCILIARY
SUPERCILIOUS
SUPERCILIOUSLY
SUPERCITIES
SUPERCIVILISED
SUPERCIVILIZED
SUPERCLASS
SUPERCLASSES
SUPERCLEAN
SUPERCLUBS
SUPERCLUSTER
SUPERCLUSTERS
SUPERCOILED
SUPERCOILING
SUPERCOILS
SUPERCOLLIDER
SUPERCOLLIDERS
SUPERCOLOSSAL
SUPERCOLUMNAR
SUPERCOMPUTER
SUPERCOMPUTERS
SUPERCOMPUTING
SUPERCOMPUTINGS
SUPERCONDUCT
SUPERCONDUCTED
SUPERCONDUCTING
SUPERCONDUCTION
SUPERCONDUCTIVE
SUPERCONDUCTOR
SUPERCONDUCTORS
SUPERCONDUCTS
SUPERCONFIDENCE
SUPERCONFIDENT
SUPERCONTINENT
SUPERCONTINENTS
SUPERCONVENIENT
SUPERCOOLED
SUPERCOOLING
SUPERCOOLS
SUPERCOVER
SUPERCOVERS
SUPERCRIMINAL
SUPERCRIMINALS
SUPERCRITICAL
SUPERCURRENT
SUPERCURRENTS
SUPERDAINTIER
SUPERDAINTIEST
SUPERDAINTY
SUPERDELEGATE
SUPERDELEGATES
SUPERDELUXE
SUPERDENSE
SUPERDIPLOMAT
SUPERDIPLOMATS
SUPERDOMINANT
SUPERDOMINANTS
SUPEREFFECTIVE
SUPEREFFICIENCY
SUPEREFFICIENT
SUPEREGOIST
SUPEREGOISTS
SUPERELASTIC
SUPERELEVATE
SUPERELEVATED
SUPERELEVATES
SUPERELEVATING
SUPERELEVATION
SUPERELEVATIONS
SUPERELITE
SUPERELITES
SUPEREMINENCE
SUPEREMINENCES
SUPEREMINENT
SUPEREMINENTLY
SUPEREROGANT
SUPEREROGATE
SUPEREROGATED
SUPEREROGATES
SUPEREROGATING
SUPEREROGATION
SUPEREROGATIONS
SUPEREROGATIVE
SUPEREROGATOR
SUPEREROGATORS
SUPEREROGATORY
SUPERESSENTIAL
SUPERETTES
SUPEREVIDENT
SUPEREXALT
SUPEREXALTATION
SUPEREXALTED
SUPEREXALTING
SUPEREXALTS
SUPEREXCELLENCE
SUPEREXCELLENT
SUPEREXPENSIVE
SUPEREXPRESS
SUPEREXPRESSES
SUPERFAMILIES
SUPERFAMILY
SUPERFARMS
SUPERFATTED
SUPERFECTA
SUPERFECTAS
SUPERFEMALE
SUPERFEMALES
SUPERFETATE
SUPERFETATED
SUPERFETATES
SUPERFETATING
SUPERFETATION
SUPERFETATIONS
SUPERFICIAL
SUPERFICIALISE
SUPERFICIALISED
SUPERFICIALISES
SUPERFICIALITY
SUPERFICIALIZE
SUPERFICIALIZED
SUPERFICIALIZES
SUPERFICIALLY
SUPERFICIALNESS
SUPERFICIALS
SUPERFICIES
SUPERFINENESS
SUPERFINENESSES
SUPERFIRMS
SUPERFIXES
SUPERFLACK
SUPERFLACKS
SUPERFLUID
SUPERFLUIDITIES
SUPERFLUIDITY
SUPERFLUIDS
SUPERFLUITIES
SUPERFLUITY

S

SUPERFLUOUS
SUPERFLUOUSLY
SUPERFLUOUSNESS
SUPERFLUXES
SUPERFOETATION
SUPERFOETATIONS
SUPERFOODS
SUPERFRONTAL
SUPERFRONTALS
SUPERFUNDS
SUPERFUSED
SUPERFUSES
SUPERFUSING
SUPERFUSION
SUPERFUSIONS
SUPERGENES
SUPERGIANT
SUPERGIANTS
SUPERGLACIAL
SUPERGLUED
SUPERGLUEING
SUPERGLUES
SUPERGLUING
SUPERGOVERNMENT
SUPERGRAPHICS
SUPERGRASS
SUPERGRASSES
SUPERGRAVITIES
SUPERGRAVITY
SUPERGROUP
SUPERGROUPS
SUPERGROWTH
SUPERGROWTHS
SUPERHARDEN
SUPERHARDENED
SUPERHARDENING
SUPERHARDENS
SUPERHEATED
SUPERHEATER
SUPERHEATERS
SUPERHEATING
SUPERHEATS
SUPERHEAVIES
SUPERHEAVY
SUPERHELICAL
SUPERHELICES
SUPERHELIX
SUPERHELIXES
SUPERHEROES
SUPERHEROINE
SUPERHEROINES
SUPERHETERODYNE
SUPERHIGHWAY
SUPERHIGHWAYS
SUPERHIVES
SUPERHUMAN
SUPERHUMANISE
SUPERHUMANISED
SUPERHUMANISES
SUPERHUMANISING
SUPERHUMANITIES
SUPERHUMANITY
SUPERHUMANIZE
SUPERHUMANIZED
SUPERHUMANIZES
SUPERHUMANIZING
SUPERHUMANLY
SUPERHUMANNESS
SUPERHUMANS
SUPERHUMERAL
SUPERHUMERALS
SUPERHYPED
SUPERHYPES
SUPERHYPING
SUPERIMPORTANT
SUPERIMPOSABLE
SUPERIMPOSE
SUPERIMPOSED
SUPERIMPOSES
SUPERIMPOSING
SUPERIMPOSITION
SUPERINCUMBENCE
SUPERINCUMBENCY
SUPERINCUMBENT
SUPERINDIVIDUAL
SUPERINDUCE
SUPERINDUCED
SUPERINDUCEMENT
SUPERINDUCES
SUPERINDUCING
SUPERINDUCTION
SUPERINDUCTIONS
SUPERINFECT
SUPERINFECTED
SUPERINFECTING
SUPERINFECTION
SUPERINFECTIONS
SUPERINFECTS
SUPERINSULATED
SUPERINTEND
SUPERINTENDED
SUPERINTENDENCE
SUPERINTENDENCY
SUPERINTENDENT
SUPERINTENDENTS
SUPERINTENDING
SUPERINTENDS
SUPERINTENSITY
SUPERIORESS
SUPERIORESSES
SUPERIORITIES
SUPERIORITY
SUPERIORLY
SUPERIORSHIP
SUPERIORSHIPS
SUPERJACENT
SUPERJOCKS
SUPERJUMBO
SUPERJUMBOS
SUPERKINGDOM
SUPERKINGDOMS
SUPERLARGE
SUPERLATIVE
SUPERLATIVELY
SUPERLATIVENESS
SUPERLATIVES
SUPERLAWYER
SUPERLAWYERS
SUPERLIGHT
SUPERLINER
SUPERLINERS
SUPERLOADS
SUPERLOBBYIST
SUPERLOBBYISTS
SUPERLOYALIST
SUPERLOYALISTS
SUPERLUMINAL
SUPERLUNAR
SUPERLUNARY
SUPERLUXURIES
SUPERLUXURIOUS
SUPERLUXURY
SUPERLYING
SUPERMACHO
SUPERMAJORITIES
SUPERMAJORITY
SUPERMALES
SUPERMARKET
SUPERMARKETS
SUPERMARTS
SUPERMASCULINE
SUPERMASSIVE
SUPERMAXES
SUPERMEMBRANE
SUPERMEMBRANES
SUPERMICRO
SUPERMICROS
SUPERMILITANT
SUPERMILITANTS
SUPERMINDS
SUPERMINIS
SUPERMINISTER
SUPERMINISTERS
SUPERMODEL
SUPERMODELS
SUPERMODERN
SUPERMOONS
SUPERMOTOS
SUPERMUNDANE
SUPERNACULA
SUPERNACULAR
SUPERNACULUM
SUPERNALLY
SUPERNANNIES
SUPERNANNY
SUPERNATANT
SUPERNATANTS
SUPERNATATION
SUPERNATATIONS
SUPERNATED
SUPERNATES
SUPERNATING
SUPERNATION
SUPERNATIONAL
SUPERNATIONALLY
SUPERNATIONS
SUPERNATURAL
SUPERNATURALISE
SUPERNATURALISM
SUPERNATURALIST
SUPERNATURALIZE
SUPERNATURALLY
SUPERNATURALS
SUPERNATURE
SUPERNATURES
SUPERNORMAL
SUPERNORMALITY
SUPERNORMALLY
SUPERNOVAE
SUPERNOVAS
SUPERNUMERARIES
SUPERNUMERARY
SUPERNURSE
SUPERNURSES
SUPERNUTRIENT
SUPERNUTRIENTS
SUPERNUTRITION
SUPERNUTRITIONS
SUPEROCTAVE
SUPEROCTAVES
SUPERORDER
SUPERORDERS
SUPERORDINAL
SUPERORDINARY
SUPERORDINATE
SUPERORDINATED
SUPERORDINATES
SUPERORDINATING
SUPERORDINATION
SUPERORGANIC
SUPERORGANICISM
SUPERORGANICIST
SUPERORGANISM
SUPERORGANISMS
SUPERORGASM
SUPERORGASMS
SUPEROVULATE
SUPEROVULATED
SUPEROVULATES
SUPEROVULATING
SUPEROVULATION
SUPEROVULATIONS
SUPEROXIDE
SUPEROXIDES
SUPERPARASITISM
SUPERPARTICLE
SUPERPARTICLES
SUPERPATRIOT
SUPERPATRIOTIC
SUPERPATRIOTISM

S

SUPERPATRIOTS
SUPERPEOPLE
SUPERPERSON
SUPERPERSONAL
SUPERPERSONS
SUPERPHENOMENA
SUPERPHENOMENON
SUPERPHONE
SUPERPHONES
SUPERPHOSPHATE
SUPERPHOSPHATES
SUPERPHYLA
SUPERPHYLUM
SUPERPHYSICAL
SUPERPIMPS
SUPERPLANE
SUPERPLANES
SUPERPLASTIC
SUPERPLASTICITY
SUPERPLASTICS
SUPERPLAYER
SUPERPLAYERS
SUPERPLUSES
SUPERPOLITE
SUPERPOLYMER
SUPERPOLYMERS
SUPERPORTS
SUPERPOSABLE
SUPERPOSED
SUPERPOSES
SUPERPOSING
SUPERPOSITION
SUPERPOSITIONS
SUPERPOWER
SUPERPOWERED
SUPERPOWERFUL
SUPERPOWERS
SUPERPRAISE
SUPERPRAISED
SUPERPRAISES
SUPERPRAISING
SUPERPREMIUM
SUPERPREMIUMS
SUPERPROFIT
SUPERPROFITS
SUPERQUALITIES
SUPERQUALITY
SUPERRACES
SUPERREALISM
SUPERREALISMS
SUPERREALIST
SUPERREALISTS
SUPERREFINE
SUPERREFINED
SUPERREFINES
SUPERREFINING
SUPERREGIONAL
SUPERREGIONALS
SUPERROADS
SUPERROMANTIC
SUPERSAFETIES
SUPERSAFETY
SUPERSALES
SUPERSALESMAN
SUPERSALESMEN
SUPERSALTS
SUPERSATURATE
SUPERSATURATED
SUPERSATURATES
SUPERSATURATING
SUPERSATURATION
SUPERSAURS
SUPERSAVER
SUPERSAVERS
SUPERSCALAR
SUPERSCALE
SUPERSCHOOL
SUPERSCHOOLS
SUPERSCOUT
SUPERSCOUTS
SUPERSCREEN
SUPERSCREENS
SUPERSCRIBE
SUPERSCRIBED
SUPERSCRIBES
SUPERSCRIBING
SUPERSCRIPT
SUPERSCRIPTION
SUPERSCRIPTIONS
SUPERSCRIPTS
SUPERSECRECIES
SUPERSECRECY
SUPERSECRET
SUPERSECRETS
SUPERSEDABLE
SUPERSEDEAS
SUPERSEDEASES
SUPERSEDED
SUPERSEDENCE
SUPERSEDENCES
SUPERSEDER
SUPERSEDERE
SUPERSEDERES
SUPERSEDERS
SUPERSEDES
SUPERSEDING
SUPERSEDURE
SUPERSEDURES
SUPERSELLER
SUPERSELLERS
SUPERSELLING
SUPERSELLS
SUPERSENSIBLE
SUPERSENSIBLY
SUPERSENSITIVE
SUPERSENSORY
SUPERSENSUAL
SUPERSESSION
SUPERSESSIONS
SUPERSEXES
SUPERSEXUALITY
SUPERSHARP
SUPERSHOWS
SUPERSINGER
SUPERSINGERS
SUPERSIZED
SUPERSIZES
SUPERSIZING
SUPERSLEUTH
SUPERSLEUTHS
SUPERSLICK
SUPERSMART
SUPERSMOOTH
SUPERSONIC
SUPERSONICALLY
SUPERSONICS
SUPERSOUND
SUPERSOUNDS
SUPERSPECIAL
SUPERSPECIALIST
SUPERSPECIALS
SUPERSPECIES
SUPERSPECTACLE
SUPERSPECTACLES
SUPERSPEED
SUPERSPEEDS
SUPERSPIES
SUPERSTARDOM
SUPERSTARDOMS
SUPERSTARS
SUPERSTATE
SUPERSTATES
SUPERSTATION
SUPERSTATIONS
SUPERSTIMULATE
SUPERSTIMULATED
SUPERSTIMULATES
SUPERSTITION
SUPERSTITIONS
SUPERSTITIOUS
SUPERSTITIOUSLY
SUPERSTOCK
SUPERSTOCKS
SUPERSTORE
SUPERSTORES
SUPERSTORM
SUPERSTORMS
SUPERSTRATA
SUPERSTRATUM
SUPERSTRATUMS
SUPERSTRENGTH
SUPERSTRENGTHS
SUPERSTRIKE
SUPERSTRIKES
SUPERSTRING
SUPERSTRINGS
SUPERSTRONG
SUPERSTRUCT
SUPERSTRUCTED
SUPERSTRUCTING
SUPERSTRUCTION
SUPERSTRUCTIONS
SUPERSTRUCTIVE
SUPERSTRUCTS
SUPERSTRUCTURAL
SUPERSTRUCTURE
SUPERSTRUCTURES
SUPERSTUDS
SUPERSUBTILE
SUPERSUBTLE
SUPERSUBTLETIES
SUPERSUBTLETY
SUPERSURGEON
SUPERSURGEONS
SUPERSWEET
SUPERSYMMETRIC
SUPERSYMMETRIES
SUPERSYMMETRY
SUPERSYSTEM
SUPERSYSTEMS
SUPERTANKER
SUPERTANKERS
SUPERTAXES
SUPERTEACHER
SUPERTEACHERS
SUPERTERRANEAN
SUPERTERRIFIC
SUPERTHICK
SUPERTHRILLER
SUPERTHRILLERS
SUPERTIGHT
SUPERTITLE
SUPERTITLES
SUPERTONIC
SUPERTONICS
SUPERTRAMS
SUPERTRUCK
SUPERTRUCKS
SUPERTWIST
SUPERTWISTS
SUPERUSERS
SUPERVENED
SUPERVENES
SUPERVENIENCE
SUPERVENIENCES
SUPERVENIENT
SUPERVENING
SUPERVENTION
SUPERVENTIONS
SUPERVIRILE
SUPERVIRTUOSI
SUPERVIRTUOSO
SUPERVIRTUOSOS
SUPERVIRULENT
SUPERVISAL
SUPERVISALS
SUPERVISED
SUPERVISEE
SUPERVISEES
SUPERVISES

S

SUPERVISING
SUPERVISION
SUPERVISIONS
SUPERVISOR
SUPERVISORS
SUPERVISORSHIP
SUPERVISORSHIPS
SUPERVISORY
SUPERVOLUTE
SUPERWAIFS
SUPERWAVES
SUPERWEAPON
SUPERWEAPONS
SUPERWEEDS
SUPERWIDES
SUPERWIVES
SUPERWOMAN
SUPERWOMEN
SUPINATING
SUPINATION
SUPINATIONS
SUPINATORS
SUPINENESS
SUPINENESSES
SUPPEAGOES
SUPPEDANEA
SUPPEDANEUM
SUPPERLESS
SUPPERTIME
SUPPERTIMES
SUPPLANTATION
SUPPLANTATIONS
SUPPLANTED
SUPPLANTER
SUPPLANTERS
SUPPLANTING
SUPPLEJACK
SUPPLEJACKS
SUPPLEMENT
SUPPLEMENTAL
SUPPLEMENTALLY
SUPPLEMENTALS
SUPPLEMENTARIES
SUPPLEMENTARILY
SUPPLEMENTARY
SUPPLEMENTATION
SUPPLEMENTED
SUPPLEMENTER
SUPPLEMENTERS
SUPPLEMENTING
SUPPLEMENTS
SUPPLENESS
SUPPLENESSES
SUPPLETION
SUPPLETIONS
SUPPLETIVE
SUPPLETIVES
SUPPLETORILY
SUPPLETORY
SUPPLIABLE
SUPPLIANCE
SUPPLIANCES
SUPPLIANTLY
SUPPLIANTS
SUPPLICANT
SUPPLICANTS
SUPPLICATE
SUPPLICATED
SUPPLICATES
SUPPLICATING
SUPPLICATINGLY
SUPPLICATION
SUPPLICATIONS
SUPPLICATORY
SUPPLICATS
SUPPLICAVIT
SUPPLICAVITS
SUPPLYMENT
SUPPLYMENTS
SUPPORTABILITY
SUPPORTABLE
SUPPORTABLENESS
SUPPORTABLY
SUPPORTANCE
SUPPORTANCES
SUPPORTERS
SUPPORTING
SUPPORTINGS
SUPPORTIVE
SUPPORTIVELY
SUPPORTIVENESS
SUPPORTLESS
SUPPORTMENT
SUPPORTMENTS
SUPPORTRESS
SUPPORTRESSES
SUPPORTURE
SUPPORTURES
SUPPOSABLE
SUPPOSABLY
SUPPOSEDLY
SUPPOSINGS
SUPPOSITION
SUPPOSITIONAL
SUPPOSITIONALLY
SUPPOSITIONARY
SUPPOSITIONLESS
SUPPOSITIONS
SUPPOSITIOUS
SUPPOSITIOUSLY
SUPPOSITITIOUS
SUPPOSITIVE
SUPPOSITIVELY
SUPPOSITIVES
SUPPOSITORIES
SUPPOSITORY
SUPPRESSANT
SUPPRESSANTS
SUPPRESSED
SUPPRESSEDLY
SUPPRESSER
SUPPRESSERS
SUPPRESSES
SUPPRESSIBILITY
SUPPRESSIBLE
SUPPRESSING
SUPPRESSION
SUPPRESSIONS
SUPPRESSIVE
SUPPRESSIVENESS
SUPPRESSOR
SUPPRESSORS
SUPPURATED
SUPPURATES
SUPPURATING
SUPPURATION
SUPPURATIONS
SUPPURATIVE
SUPPURATIVES
SUPRACHIASMIC
SUPRACHOROIDAL
SUPRACILIARY
SUPRACOSTAL
SUPRACRUSTAL
SUPRAGLOTTAL
SUPRALAPSARIAN
SUPRALAPSARIANS
SUPRALIMINAL
SUPRALIMINALLY
SUPRALUNAR
SUPRAMAXILLARY
SUPRAMOLECULAR
SUPRAMOLECULE
SUPRAMOLECULES
SUPRAMUNDANE
SUPRANATIONAL
SUPRANATIONALLY
SUPRAOPTIC
SUPRAORBITAL
SUPRAPUBIC
SUPRARATIONAL
SUPRARENAL
SUPRARENALS
SUPRASEGMENTAL
SUPRASENSIBLE
SUPRATEMPORAL
SUPRAVITAL
SUPRAVITALLY
SUPREMACIES
SUPREMACISM
SUPREMACISMS
SUPREMACIST
SUPREMACISTS
SUPREMATISM
SUPREMATISMS
SUPREMATIST
SUPREMATISTS
SUPREMENESS
SUPREMENESSES
SUPREMITIES
SURADDITION
SURADDITIONS
SURBASEMENT
SURBASEMENTS
SURBEDDING
SURCEASING
SURCHARGED
SURCHARGEMENT
SURCHARGEMENTS
SURCHARGER
SURCHARGERS
SURCHARGES
SURCHARGING
SURCINGLED
SURCINGLES
SURCINGLING
SURCULUSES
SUREFOOTED
SUREFOOTEDLY
SUREFOOTEDNESS
SURENESSES
SURETYSHIP
SURETYSHIPS
SURFACELESS
SURFACEMAN
SURFACEMEN
SURFACINGS
SURFACTANT
SURFACTANTS
SURFBOARDED
SURFBOARDER
SURFBOARDERS
SURFBOARDING
SURFBOARDINGS
SURFBOARDS
SURFCASTER
SURFCASTERS
SURFCASTING
SURFCASTINGS
SURFEITERS
SURFEITING
SURFEITINGS
SURFFISHES
SURFPERCHES
SURFRIDDEN
SURFRIDERS
SURFRIDING
SURFRIDINGS
SURGEONCIES
SURGEONFISH
SURGEONFISHES
SURGEONSHIP
SURGEONSHIPS
SURGICALLY
SURJECTION
SURJECTIONS
SURJECTIVE
SURLINESSES
SURMASTERS
SURMISABLE

SURMISINGS
SURMISTRESS
SURMISTRESSES
SURMOUNTABLE
SURMOUNTED
SURMOUNTER
SURMOUNTERS
SURMOUNTING
SURMOUNTINGS
SURMULLETS
SURNOMINAL
SURPASSABLE
SURPASSERS
SURPASSING
SURPASSINGLY
SURPASSINGNESS
SURPLUSAGE
SURPLUSAGES
SURPLUSING
SURPLUSSED
SURPLUSSES
SURPLUSSING
SURPRINTED
SURPRINTING
SURPRISALS
SURPRISEDLY
SURPRISERS
SURPRISING
SURPRISINGLY
SURPRISINGNESS
SURPRISINGS
SURPRIZING
SURQUEDIES
SURQUEDRIES
SURREALISM
SURREALISMS
SURREALIST
SURREALISTIC
SURREALISTS
SURREBUTTAL
SURREBUTTALS
SURREBUTTED
SURREBUTTER
SURREBUTTERS
SURREBUTTING
SURREJOINDER
SURREJOINDERS
SURREJOINED
SURREJOINING
SURREJOINS
SURRENDERED
SURRENDEREE
SURRENDEREES
SURRENDERER
SURRENDERERS
SURRENDERING
SURRENDEROR
SURRENDERORS
SURRENDERS
SURRENDRIES
SURREPTITIOUS
SURREPTITIOUSLY
SURROGACIES
SURROGATED
SURROGATES
SURROGATESHIP
SURROGATESHIPS
SURROGATING
SURROGATION
SURROGATIONS
SURROGATUM
SURROGATUMS
SURROUNDED
SURROUNDING
SURROUNDINGS
SURTARBRAND
SURTARBRANDS
SURTURBRAND
SURTURBRANDS
SURVEILING
SURVEILLANCE
SURVEILLANCES
SURVEILLANT
SURVEILLANTS
SURVEILLED
SURVEILLES
SURVEILLING
SURVEYABLE
SURVEYANCE
SURVEYANCES
SURVEYINGS
SURVEYORSHIP
SURVEYORSHIPS
SURVIEWING
SURVIVABILITIES
SURVIVABILITY
SURVIVABLE
SURVIVALISM
SURVIVALISMS
SURVIVALIST
SURVIVALISTS
SURVIVANCE
SURVIVANCES
SURVIVORSHIP
SURVIVORSHIPS
SUSCEPTANCE
SUSCEPTANCES
SUSCEPTIBILITY
SUSCEPTIBLE
SUSCEPTIBLENESS
SUSCEPTIBLY
SUSCEPTIVE
SUSCEPTIVENESS
SUSCEPTIVITIES
SUSCEPTIVITY
SUSCEPTORS
SUSCIPIENT
SUSCIPIENTS
SUSCITATED
SUSCITATES
SUSCITATING
SUSCITATION
SUSCITATIONS
SUSPECTABLE
SUSPECTEDLY
SUSPECTEDNESS
SUSPECTEDNESSES
SUSPECTERS
SUSPECTFUL
SUSPECTING
SUSPECTLESS
SUSPENDERED
SUSPENDERS
SUSPENDIBILITY
SUSPENDIBLE
SUSPENDING
SUSPENSEFUL
SUSPENSEFULLY
SUSPENSEFULNESS
SUSPENSELESS
SUSPENSERS
SUSPENSIBILITY
SUSPENSIBLE
SUSPENSION
SUSPENSIONS
SUSPENSIVE
SUSPENSIVELY
SUSPENSIVENESS
SUSPENSOID
SUSPENSOIDS
SUSPENSORIA
SUSPENSORIAL
SUSPENSORIES
SUSPENSORIUM
SUSPENSORS
SUSPENSORY
SUSPERCOLLATE
SUSPERCOLLATED
SUSPERCOLLATES
SUSPERCOLLATING
SUSPICIONAL
SUSPICIONED
SUSPICIONING
SUSPICIONLESS
SUSPICIONS
SUSPICIOUS
SUSPICIOUSLY
SUSPICIOUSNESS
SUSPIRATION
SUSPIRATIONS
SUSPIRIOUS
SUSTAINABILITY
SUSTAINABLE
SUSTAINABLY
SUSTAINEDLY
SUSTAINERS
SUSTAINING
SUSTAININGLY
SUSTAININGS
SUSTAINMENT
SUSTAINMENTS
SUSTENANCE
SUSTENANCES
SUSTENTACULA
SUSTENTACULAR
SUSTENTACULUM
SUSTENTATE
SUSTENTATED
SUSTENTATES
SUSTENTATING
SUSTENTATION
SUSTENTATIONS
SUSTENTATIVE
SUSTENTATOR
SUSTENTATORS
SUSTENTION
SUSTENTIONS
SUSTENTIVE
SUSURRATED
SUSURRATES
SUSURRATING
SUSURRATION
SUSURRATIONS
SUSURRUSES
SUTLERSHIP
SUTLERSHIPS
SUTTEEISMS
SUTTLETIES
SUTURATION
SUTURATIONS
SUZERAINTIES
SUZERAINTY
SVARABHAKTI
SVARABHAKTIS
SVELTENESS
SVELTENESSES
SWAGGERERS
SWAGGERING
SWAGGERINGLY
SWAGGERINGS
SWAINISHNESS
SWAINISHNESSES
SWALLOWABLE
SWALLOWERS
SWALLOWING
SWALLOWTAIL
SWALLOWTAILS
SWALLOWWORT
SWALLOWWORTS
SWAMPINESS
SWAMPINESSES
SWAMPLANDS
SWANKINESS
SWANKINESSES
SWANNERIES
SWANSDOWNS
SWARAJISMS
SWARAJISTS
SWARTHIEST
SWARTHINESS

S

SWARTHINESSES
SWARTHNESS
SWARTHNESSES
SWARTNESSES
SWASHBUCKLE
SWASHBUCKLED
SWASHBUCKLER
SWASHBUCKLERS
SWASHBUCKLES
SWASHBUCKLING
SWASHWORKS
SWATCHBOOK
SWATCHBOOKS
SWATHEABLE
SWATTERING
SWAYBACKED
SWEARWORDS
SWEATBANDS
SWEATBOXES
SWEATERDRESS
SWEATERDRESSES
SWEATINESS
SWEATINESSES
SWEATPANTS
SWEATSHIRT
SWEATSHIRTS
SWEATSHOPS
SWEATSUITS
SWEEPBACKS
SWEEPINGLY
SWEEPINGNESS
SWEEPINGNESSES
SWEEPSTAKE
SWEEPSTAKES
SWEETBREAD
SWEETBREADS
SWEETBRIAR
SWEETBRIARS
SWEETBRIER
SWEETBRIERS
SWEETCORNS
SWEETENERS
SWEETENING
SWEETENINGS
SWEETFISHES
SWEETHEART
SWEETHEARTED
SWEETHEARTING
SWEETHEARTINGS
SWEETHEARTS
SWEETIEWIFE
SWEETIEWIVES
SWEETISHLY
SWEETISHNESS
SWEETISHNESSES
SWEETMEATS
SWEETNESSES
SWEETSHOPS
SWEETVELDS
SWEETWATER
SWEETWATERS
SWEETWOODS
SWEIRNESSES
SWELLFISHES
SWELLHEADED
SWELLHEADEDNESS
SWELLHEADS
SWELLINGLY
SWELTERING
SWELTERINGLY
SWELTERINGS
SWELTRIEST
SWEPTWINGS
SWERVELESS
SWIFTNESSES
SWIMFEEDER
SWIMFEEDERS
SWIMMERETS
SWIMMINGLY
SWIMMINGNESS
SWIMMINGNESSES
SWINDLINGS
SWINEHERDS
SWINEHOODS
SWINEPOXES
SWINESTONE
SWINESTONES
SWINGBEATS
SWINGBOATS
SWINGEINGLY
SWINGINGER
SWINGINGEST
SWINGINGLY
SWINGLETREE
SWINGLETREES
SWINGLINGS
SWINGOMETER
SWINGOMETERS
SWINGTREES
SWINISHNESS
SWINISHNESSES
SWIRLINGLY
SWISHINGLY
SWITCHABLE
SWITCHBACK
SWITCHBACKED
SWITCHBACKING
SWITCHBACKS
SWITCHBLADE
SWITCHBLADES
SWITCHBOARD
SWITCHBOARDS
SWITCHEROO
SWITCHEROOS
SWITCHGEAR
SWITCHGEARS
SWITCHGIRL
SWITCHGIRLS
SWITCHGRASS
SWITCHGRASSES
SWITCHIEST
SWITCHINGS
SWITCHLIKE
SWITCHOVER
SWITCHOVERS
SWITCHYARD
SWITCHYARDS
SWITHERING
SWIVELBLOCK
SWIVELBLOCKS
SWIVELLING
SWOLLENNESS
SWOLLENNESSES
SWOONINGLY
SWOOPSTAKE
SWORDBEARER
SWORDBEARERS
SWORDBILLS
SWORDCRAFT
SWORDCRAFTS
SWORDFERNS
SWORDFISHES
SWORDPLAYER
SWORDPLAYERS
SWORDPLAYS
SWORDPROOF
SWORDSMANSHIP
SWORDSMANSHIPS
SWORDSTICK
SWORDSTICKS
SWORDSWOMAN
SWORDSWOMEN
SWORDTAILS
SYBARITICAL
SYBARITICALLY
SYBARITISH
SYBARITISM
SYBARITISMS
SYCOPHANCIES
SYCOPHANCY
SYCOPHANTIC
SYCOPHANTICAL
SYCOPHANTICALLY
SYCOPHANTISE
SYCOPHANTISED
SYCOPHANTISES
SYCOPHANTISH
SYCOPHANTISHLY
SYCOPHANTISING
SYCOPHANTISM
SYCOPHANTISMS
SYCOPHANTIZE
SYCOPHANTIZED
SYCOPHANTIZES
SYCOPHANTIZING
SYCOPHANTLIER
SYCOPHANTLIEST
SYCOPHANTLY
SYCOPHANTRIES
SYCOPHANTRY
SYCOPHANTS
SYLLABARIA
SYLLABARIES
SYLLABARIUM
SYLLABICAL
SYLLABICALLY
SYLLABICATE
SYLLABICATED
SYLLABICATES
SYLLABICATING
SYLLABICATION
SYLLABICATIONS
SYLLABICITIES
SYLLABICITY
SYLLABIFICATION
SYLLABIFIED
SYLLABIFIES
SYLLABIFYING
SYLLABISED
SYLLABISES
SYLLABISING
SYLLABISMS
SYLLABIZED
SYLLABIZES
SYLLABIZING
SYLLABLING
SYLLABOGRAM
SYLLABOGRAMS
SYLLABOGRAPHIES
SYLLABOGRAPHY
SYLLABUSES
SYLLEPTICAL
SYLLEPTICALLY
SYLLOGISATION
SYLLOGISATIONS
SYLLOGISED
SYLLOGISER
SYLLOGISERS
SYLLOGISES
SYLLOGISING
SYLLOGISMS
SYLLOGISTIC
SYLLOGISTICAL
SYLLOGISTICALLY
SYLLOGISTICS
SYLLOGISTS
SYLLOGIZATION
SYLLOGIZATIONS
SYLLOGIZED
SYLLOGIZER
SYLLOGIZERS
SYLLOGIZES
SYLLOGIZING
SYLPHIDINE
SYLVANITES
SYLVESTRAL
SYLVESTRIAN
SYLVICULTURAL
SYLVICULTURE
SYLVICULTURES

SYLVINITES
SYMBIONTIC
SYMBIONTICALLY
SYMBIOTICAL
SYMBIOTICALLY
SYMBOLICAL
SYMBOLICALLY
SYMBOLICALNESS
SYMBOLISATION
SYMBOLISATIONS
SYMBOLISED
SYMBOLISER
SYMBOLISERS
SYMBOLISES
SYMBOLISING
SYMBOLISMS
SYMBOLISTIC
SYMBOLISTICAL
SYMBOLISTICALLY
SYMBOLISTS
SYMBOLIZATION
SYMBOLIZATIONS
SYMBOLIZED
SYMBOLIZER
SYMBOLIZERS
SYMBOLIZES
SYMBOLIZING
SYMBOLLING
SYMBOLOGICAL
SYMBOLOGIES
SYMBOLOGIST
SYMBOLOGISTS
SYMBOLOGRAPHIES
SYMBOLOGRAPHY
SYMBOLOLATRIES
SYMBOLOLATRY
SYMBOLOLOGIES
SYMBOLOLOGY
SYMMETALISM
SYMMETALISMS
SYMMETALLIC
SYMMETALLISM
SYMMETALLISMS
SYMMETRIAN
SYMMETRIANS
SYMMETRICAL
SYMMETRICALLY
SYMMETRICALNESS
SYMMETRIES
SYMMETRISATION
SYMMETRISATIONS
SYMMETRISE
SYMMETRISED
SYMMETRISES
SYMMETRISING
SYMMETRIZATION
SYMMETRIZATIONS
SYMMETRIZE
SYMMETRIZED
SYMMETRIZES
SYMMETRIZING
SYMMETROPHOBIA
SYMMETROPHOBIAS
SYMPATHECTOMIES
SYMPATHECTOMY
SYMPATHETIC
SYMPATHETICAL
SYMPATHETICALLY
SYMPATHETICS
SYMPATHIES
SYMPATHINS
SYMPATHIQUE
SYMPATHISE
SYMPATHISED
SYMPATHISER
SYMPATHISERS
SYMPATHISES
SYMPATHISING
SYMPATHIZE
SYMPATHIZED
SYMPATHIZER
SYMPATHIZERS
SYMPATHIZES
SYMPATHIZING
SYMPATHOLYTIC
SYMPATHOLYTICS
SYMPATHOMIMETIC
SYMPATRICALLY
SYMPATRIES
SYMPETALIES
SYMPETALOUS
SYMPHILIES
SYMPHILISM
SYMPHILISMS
SYMPHILOUS
SYMPHONICALLY
SYMPHONIES
SYMPHONION
SYMPHONIONS
SYMPHONIOUS
SYMPHONIOUSLY
SYMPHONIST
SYMPHONISTS
SYMPHYLOUS
SYMPHYSEAL
SYMPHYSEOTOMIES
SYMPHYSEOTOMY
SYMPHYSIAL
SYMPHYSIOTOMIES
SYMPHYSIOTOMY
SYMPHYSTIC
SYMPIESOMETER
SYMPIESOMETERS
SYMPLASTIC
SYMPODIALLY
SYMPOSIACS
SYMPOSIARCH
SYMPOSIARCHS
SYMPOSIAST
SYMPOSIASTS
SYMPOSIUMS
SYMPTOMATIC
SYMPTOMATICAL
SYMPTOMATICALLY
SYMPTOMATISE
SYMPTOMATISED
SYMPTOMATISES
SYMPTOMATISING
SYMPTOMATIZE
SYMPTOMATIZED
SYMPTOMATIZES
SYMPTOMATIZING
SYMPTOMATOLOGIC
SYMPTOMATOLOGY
SYMPTOMLESS
SYMPTOMOLOGICAL
SYMPTOMOLOGIES
SYMPTOMOLOGY
SYNADELPHITE
SYNADELPHITES
SYNAERESES
SYNAERESIS
SYNAESTHESES
SYNAESTHESIA
SYNAESTHESIAS
SYNAESTHESIS
SYNAESTHETIC
SYNAGOGICAL
SYNAGOGUES
SYNALEPHAS
SYNALLAGMATIC
SYNALOEPHA
SYNALOEPHAS
SYNANDRIUM
SYNANDROUS
SYNANTHEROUS
SYNANTHESES
SYNANTHESIS
SYNANTHETIC
SYNANTHIES
SYNANTHOUS
SYNAPHEIAS
SYNAPOSEMATIC
SYNAPOSEMATISM
SYNAPOSEMATISMS
SYNAPTASES
SYNAPTICAL
SYNAPTICALLY
SYNAPTOSOMAL
SYNAPTOSOME
SYNAPTOSOMES
SYNARCHIES
SYNARTHRODIAL
SYNARTHRODIALLY
SYNARTHROSES
SYNARTHROSIS
SYNASTRIES
SYNAXARION
SYNBIOTICS
SYNCARPIES
SYNCARPOUS
SYNCHONDROSES
SYNCHONDROSIS
SYNCHORESES
SYNCHORESIS
SYNCHROFLASH
SYNCHROFLASHES
SYNCHROMESH
SYNCHROMESHES
SYNCHRONAL
SYNCHRONEITIES
SYNCHRONEITY
SYNCHRONIC
SYNCHRONICAL
SYNCHRONICALLY
SYNCHRONICITIES
SYNCHRONICITY
SYNCHRONIES
SYNCHRONISATION
SYNCHRONISE
SYNCHRONISED
SYNCHRONISER
SYNCHRONISERS
SYNCHRONISES
SYNCHRONISING
SYNCHRONISM
SYNCHRONISMS
SYNCHRONISTIC
SYNCHRONISTICAL
SYNCHRONIZATION
SYNCHRONIZE
SYNCHRONIZED
SYNCHRONIZER
SYNCHRONIZERS
SYNCHRONIZES
SYNCHRONIZING
SYNCHRONOLOGIES
SYNCHRONOLOGY
SYNCHRONOSCOPE
SYNCHRONOSCOPES
SYNCHRONOUS
SYNCHRONOUSLY
SYNCHRONOUSNESS
SYNCHROSCOPE
SYNCHROSCOPES
SYNCHROTRON
SYNCHROTRONS
SYNCLASTIC
SYNCLINALS
SYNCLINORIA
SYNCLINORIUM
SYNCOPATED
SYNCOPATES
SYNCOPATING
SYNCOPATION
SYNCOPATIONS
SYNCOPATIVE
SYNCOPATOR
SYNCOPATORS
SYNCRETISATION

SYNCRETISATIONS
SYNCRETISE
SYNCRETISED
SYNCRETISES
SYNCRETISING
SYNCRETISM
SYNCRETISMS
SYNCRETIST
SYNCRETISTIC
SYNCRETISTS
SYNCRETIZATION
SYNCRETIZATIONS
SYNCRETIZE
SYNCRETIZED
SYNCRETIZES
SYNCRETIZING
SYNDACTYLIES
SYNDACTYLISM
SYNDACTYLISMS
SYNDACTYLOUS
SYNDACTYLS
SYNDACTYLY
SYNDERESES
SYNDERESIS
SYNDESISES
SYNDESMOSES
SYNDESMOSIS
SYNDESMOTIC
SYNDETICAL
SYNDETICALLY
SYNDICALISM
SYNDICALISMS
SYNDICALIST
SYNDICALISTIC
SYNDICALISTS
SYNDICATED
SYNDICATES
SYNDICATING
SYNDICATION
SYNDICATIONS
SYNDICATOR
SYNDICATORS
SYNDICSHIP
SYNDICSHIPS
SYNDIOTACTIC
SYNDYASMIAN
SYNECDOCHE
SYNECDOCHES
SYNECDOCHIC
SYNECDOCHICAL
SYNECDOCHICALLY
SYNECDOCHISM
SYNECDOCHISMS
SYNECOLOGIC
SYNECOLOGICAL
SYNECOLOGICALLY
SYNECOLOGIES
SYNECOLOGIST
SYNECOLOGISTS
SYNECOLOGY
SYNECPHONESES
SYNECPHONESIS
SYNECTICALLY
SYNEIDESES
SYNEIDESIS
SYNERGETIC
SYNERGETICALLY
SYNERGICALLY
SYNERGISED
SYNERGISES
SYNERGISING
SYNERGISMS
SYNERGISTIC
SYNERGISTICALLY
SYNERGISTS
SYNERGIZED
SYNERGIZES
SYNERGIZING
SYNESTHESIA
SYNESTHESIAS
SYNESTHETIC
SYNGENESES
SYNGENESIOUS
SYNGENESIS
SYNGENETIC
SYNGNATHOUS
SYNKARYONIC
SYNKARYONS
SYNODICALLY
SYNOECETES
SYNOECIOSES
SYNOECIOSIS
SYNOECIOUS
SYNOECISED
SYNOECISES
SYNOECISING
SYNOECISMS
SYNOECIZED
SYNOECIZES
SYNOECIZING
SYNOECOLOGIES
SYNOECOLOGY
SYNOEKETES
SYNONYMATIC
SYNONYMICAL
SYNONYMICON
SYNONYMICONS
SYNONYMIES
SYNONYMISE
SYNONYMISED
SYNONYMISES
SYNONYMISING
SYNONYMIST
SYNONYMISTS
SYNONYMITIES
SYNONYMITY
SYNONYMIZE
SYNONYMIZED
SYNONYMIZES
SYNONYMIZING
SYNONYMOUS
SYNONYMOUSLY
SYNONYMOUSNESS
SYNOPSISED
SYNOPSISES
SYNOPSISING
SYNOPSIZED
SYNOPSIZES
SYNOPSIZING
SYNOPTICAL
SYNOPTICALLY
SYNOPTISTIC
SYNOPTISTS
SYNOSTOSES
SYNOSTOSIS
SYNOVIALLY
SYNOVITISES
SYNSEPALOUS
SYNTACTICAL
SYNTACTICALLY
SYNTACTICS
SYNTAGMATA
SYNTAGMATIC
SYNTAGMATITE
SYNTAGMATITES
SYNTECTICAL
SYNTENOSES
SYNTENOSIS
SYNTERESES
SYNTERESIS
SYNTEXISES
SYNTHESISATION
SYNTHESISATIONS
SYNTHESISE
SYNTHESISED
SYNTHESISER
SYNTHESISERS
SYNTHESISES
SYNTHESISING
SYNTHESIST
SYNTHESISTS
SYNTHESIZATION
SYNTHESIZATIONS
SYNTHESIZE
SYNTHESIZED
SYNTHESIZER
SYNTHESIZERS
SYNTHESIZES
SYNTHESIZING
SYNTHESPIAN
SYNTHESPIANS
SYNTHETASE
SYNTHETASES
SYNTHETICAL
SYNTHETICALLY
SYNTHETICISM
SYNTHETICISMS
SYNTHETICS
SYNTHETISATION
SYNTHETISATIONS
SYNTHETISE
SYNTHETISED
SYNTHETISER
SYNTHETISERS
SYNTHETISES
SYNTHETISING
SYNTHETISM
SYNTHETISMS
SYNTHETIST
SYNTHETISTS
SYNTHETIZATION
SYNTHETIZATIONS
SYNTHETIZE
SYNTHETIZED
SYNTHETIZER
SYNTHETIZERS
SYNTHETIZES
SYNTHETIZING
SYNTHRONUS
SYNTONICALLY
SYNTONISED
SYNTONISES
SYNTONISING
SYNTONIZED
SYNTONIZES
SYNTONIZING
SYPHERINGS
SYPHILISATION
SYPHILISATIONS
SYPHILISED
SYPHILISES
SYPHILISING
SYPHILITIC
SYPHILITICALLY
SYPHILITICS
SYPHILIZATION
SYPHILIZATIONS
SYPHILIZED
SYPHILIZES
SYPHILIZING
SYPHILOLOGIES
SYPHILOLOGIST
SYPHILOLOGISTS
SYPHILOLOGY
SYPHILOMAS
SYPHILOMATA
SYPHILOPHOBIA
SYPHILOPHOBIAS
SYPHONAGES
SYRINGITIS
SYRINGITISES
SYRINGOMYELIA
SYRINGOMYELIAS
SYRINGOMYELIC
SYRINGOTOMIES
SYRINGOTOMY
SYSSARCOSES
SYSSARCOSIS
SYSSARCOTIC
SYSTEMATIC

SYSTEMATICAL
SYSTEMATICALLY
SYSTEMATICIAN
SYSTEMATICIANS
SYSTEMATICNESS
SYSTEMATICS
SYSTEMATISATION
SYSTEMATISE
SYSTEMATISED
SYSTEMATISER
SYSTEMATISERS
SYSTEMATISES
SYSTEMATISING
SYSTEMATISM
SYSTEMATISMS
SYSTEMATIST
SYSTEMATISTS
SYSTEMATIZATION
SYSTEMATIZE
SYSTEMATIZED
SYSTEMATIZER
SYSTEMATIZERS
SYSTEMATIZES
SYSTEMATIZING
SYSTEMATOLOGIES
SYSTEMATOLOGY
SYSTEMICALLY
SYSTEMISATION
SYSTEMISATIONS
SYSTEMISED
SYSTEMISER
SYSTEMISERS
SYSTEMISES
SYSTEMISING
SYSTEMIZATION
SYSTEMIZATIONS
SYSTEMIZED
SYSTEMIZER
SYSTEMIZERS
SYSTEMIZES
SYSTEMIZING
SYSTEMLESS
SYZYGETICALLY

S

T

TABASHEERS
TABBOULEHS
TABBYHOODS
TABEFACTION
TABEFACTIONS
TABELLIONS
TABERNACLE
TABERNACLED
TABERNACLES
TABERNACLING
TABERNACULAR
TABESCENCE
TABESCENCES
TABLANETTE
TABLANETTES
TABLATURES
TABLECLOTH
TABLECLOTHS
TABLELANDS
TABLEMATES
TABLESPOON
TABLESPOONFUL
TABLESPOONFULS
TABLESPOONS
TABLESPOONSFUL
TABLETOPPED
TABLETTING
TABLEWARES
TABLOIDIER
TABLOIDIEST
TABOGGANED
TABOGGANING
TABOPARESES
TABOPARESIS
TABULARISATION
TABULARISATIONS
TABULARISE
TABULARISED
TABULARISES
TABULARISING
TABULARIZATION
TABULARIZATIONS
TABULARIZE
TABULARIZED
TABULARIZES
TABULARIZING
TABULATING
TABULATION
TABULATIONS
TABULATORS
TABULATORY
TACAMAHACS
TACHEOMETER
TACHEOMETERS
TACHEOMETRIC
TACHEOMETRICAL
TACHEOMETRIES
TACHEOMETRY
TACHISTOSCOPE
TACHISTOSCOPES
TACHISTOSCOPIC
TACHOGRAMS
TACHOGRAPH
TACHOGRAPHS
TACHOMETER
TACHOMETERS
TACHOMETRIC
TACHOMETRICAL
TACHOMETRICALLY
TACHOMETRIES
TACHOMETRY
TACHYARRHYTHMIA
TACHYCARDIA
TACHYCARDIAC
TACHYCARDIAS
TACHYGRAPH
TACHYGRAPHER
TACHYGRAPHERS
TACHYGRAPHIC
TACHYGRAPHICAL
TACHYGRAPHIES
TACHYGRAPHIST
TACHYGRAPHISTS
TACHYGRAPHS
TACHYGRAPHY
TACHYLITES
TACHYLITIC
TACHYLYTES
TACHYLYTIC
TACHYMETER
TACHYMETERS
TACHYMETRIC
TACHYMETRICAL
TACHYMETRICALLY
TACHYMETRIES
TACHYMETRY
TACHYPHASIA
TACHYPHASIAS
TACHYPHRASIA
TACHYPHRASIAS
TACHYPHYLAXES
TACHYPHYLAXIS
TACHYPNEAS
TACHYPNOEA
TACHYPNOEAS
TACITNESSES
TACITURNITIES
TACITURNITY
TACITURNLY
TACKBOARDS
TACKETIEST
TACKIFIERS
TACKIFYING
TACKINESSES
TACMAHACKS
TACTFULNESS
TACTFULNESSES
TACTICALLY
TACTICIANS
TACTICITIES
TACTILISTS
TACTILITIES
TACTLESSLY
TACTLESSNESS
TACTLESSNESSES
TACTUALITIES
TACTUALITY
TADALAFILS
TAEKWONDOS
TAENIACIDE
TAENIACIDES
TAENIAFUGE
TAENIAFUGES
TAFFETASES
TAFFETIEST
TAFFETISED
TAFFETIZED
TAGLIARINI
TAGLIARINIS
TAGLIATELLE
TAGLIATELLES
TAHSILDARS
TAIKONAUTS
TAILBOARDS
TAILCOATED
TAILENDERS
TAILGATERS
TAILGATING
TAILGATINGS
TAILHOPPING
TAILHOPPINGS
TAILLESSLY
TAILLESSNESS
TAILLESSNESSES
TAILLIGHTS
TAILORBIRD
TAILORBIRDS
TAILORESSES
TAILORINGS
TAILORMADE
TAILORMAKE
TAILORMAKES
TAILORMAKING
TAILPIECES
TAILPIPING
TAILPLANES
TAILSLIDES
TAILSPINNED
TAILSPINNING
TAILSTOCKS
TAILWATERS
TAILWHEELS
TAINTLESSLY
TAKINGNESS
TAKINGNESSES
TALBOTYPES
TALEBEARER
TALEBEARERS
TALEBEARING
TALEBEARINGS
TALEGALLAS
TALENTLESS
TALETELLER
TALETELLERS
TALETELLING
TALETELLINGS
TALISMANIC
TALISMANICAL
TALISMANICALLY
TALKABILITIES
TALKABILITY
TALKATHONS
TALKATIVELY
TALKATIVENESS
TALKATIVENESSES
TALKINESSES
TALLGRASSES
TALLIATING
TALLNESSES
TALLOWIEST
TALLYHOING
TALLYSHOPS
TALLYWOMAN
TALLYWOMEN
TALMUDISMS
TAMABILITIES
TAMABILITY
TAMABLENESS
TAMABLENESSES
TAMARILLOS

TAMBOURERS
TAMBOURINE
TAMBOURINES
TAMBOURING
TAMBOURINIST
TAMBOURINISTS
TAMBOURINS
TAMEABILITIES
TAMEABILITY
TAMEABLENESS
TAMEABLENESSES
TAMELESSNESS
TAMELESSNESSES
TAMENESSES
TAMOXIFENS
TAMPERINGS
TAMPERPROOF
TAMPONADES
TAMPONAGES
TANDEMWISE
TANGENCIES
TANGENTALLY
TANGENTIAL
TANGENTIALITIES
TANGENTIALITY
TANGENTIALLY
TANGERINES
TANGHININS
TANGIBILITIES
TANGIBILITY
TANGIBLENESS
TANGIBLENESSES
TANGINESSES
TANGLEFOOT
TANGLEFOOTS
TANGLEMENT
TANGLEMENTS
TANGLESOME
TANGLEWEED
TANGLEWEEDS
TANGLINGLY
TANISTRIES
TANKBUSTER
TANKBUSTERS
TANKBUSTING
TANKBUSTINGS
TANOREXICS
TANTALATES
TANTALISATION
TANTALISATIONS
TANTALISED
TANTALISER
TANTALISERS
TANTALISES
TANTALISING
TANTALISINGLY
TANTALISINGS
TANTALISMS
TANTALITES
TANTALIZATION
TANTALIZATIONS
TANTALIZED
TANTALIZER
TANTALIZERS
TANTALIZES
TANTALIZING
TANTALIZINGLY
TANTALIZINGS
TANTALUSES
TANTAMOUNT
TANTARARAS
TANZANITES
TAPERINGLY
TAPERNESSES
TAPERSTICK
TAPERSTICKS
TAPESCRIPT
TAPESCRIPTS
TAPESTRIED
TAPESTRIES
TAPESTRYING
TAPHEPHOBIA
TAPHEPHOBIAS
TAPHEPHOBIC
TAPHONOMIC
TAPHONOMICAL
TAPHONOMIES
TAPHONOMIST
TAPHONOMISTS
TAPHOPHOBIA
TAPHOPHOBIAS
TAPHROGENESES
TAPHROGENESIS
TAPOTEMENT
TAPOTEMENTS
TAPSALTEERIE
TAPSALTEERIES
TAPSIETEERIE
TAPSIETEERIES
TAPSTRESSES
TARABISHES
TARADIDDLE
TARADIDDLES
TARAMASALATA
TARAMASALATAS
TARANTARAED
TARANTARAING
TARANTARAS
TARANTASES
TARANTASSES
TARANTELLA
TARANTELLAS
TARANTISMS
TARANTISTS
TARANTULAE
TARANTULAS
TARATANTARA
TARATANTARAED
TARATANTARAING
TARATANTARAS
TARAXACUMS
TARBOGGINED
TARBOGGINING
TARBOGGINS
TARBOOSHES
TARBOUCHES
TARBOUSHES
TARDIGRADE
TARDIGRADES
TARDINESSES
TARGETABLE
TARGETEERS
TARGETINGS
TARGETITIS
TARGETITISES
TARGETLESS
TARIFFICATION
TARIFFICATIONS
TARIFFLESS
TARMACADAM
TARMACADAMS
TARMACKING
TARNATIONS
TARNISHABLE
TARNISHERS
TARNISHING
TARPAULING
TARPAULINGS
TARPAULINS
TARRADIDDLE
TARRADIDDLES
TARRIANCES
TARRINESSES
TARSALGIAS
TARSOMETATARSAL
TARSOMETATARSI
TARSOMETATARSUS
TARTANALIA
TARTANALIAS
TARTANRIES
TARTAREOUS
TARTARISATION
TARTARISATIONS
TARTARISED
TARTARISES
TARTARISING
TARTARIZATION
TARTARIZATIONS
TARTARIZED
TARTARIZES
TARTARIZING
TARTINESSES
TARTNESSES
TARTRAZINE
TARTRAZINES
TASEOMETER
TASEOMETERS
TASIMETERS
TASIMETRIC
TASIMETRIES
TASKMASTER
TASKMASTERS
TASKMISTRESS
TASKMISTRESSES
TASSELIEST
TASSELLIER
TASSELLIEST
TASSELLING
TASSELLINGS
TASTEFULLY
TASTEFULNESS
TASTEFULNESSES
TASTELESSLY
TASTELESSNESS
TASTELESSNESSES
TASTEMAKER
TASTEMAKERS
TASTINESSES
TATAHASHES
TATPURUSHA
TATPURUSHAS
TATTERDEMALION
TATTERDEMALIONS
TATTERDEMALLION
TATTERIEST
TATTERSALL
TATTERSALLS
TATTINESSES
TATTLETALE
TATTLETALED
TATTLETALES
TATTLETALING
TATTLINGLY
TATTOOISTS
TAUNTINGLY
TAUROBOLIA
TAUROBOLIUM
TAUROMACHIAN
TAUROMACHIES
TAUROMACHY
TAUROMORPHOUS
TAUTNESSES
TAUTOCHRONE
TAUTOCHRONES
TAUTOCHRONISM
TAUTOCHRONISMS
TAUTOCHRONOUS
TAUTOLOGIC
TAUTOLOGICAL
TAUTOLOGICALLY
TAUTOLOGIES
TAUTOLOGISE
TAUTOLOGISED
TAUTOLOGISES
TAUTOLOGISING
TAUTOLOGISM
TAUTOLOGISMS
TAUTOLOGIST
TAUTOLOGISTS
TAUTOLOGIZE

TAUTOLOGIZED
TAUTOLOGIZES
TAUTOLOGIZING
TAUTOLOGOUS
TAUTOLOGOUSLY
TAUTOMERIC
TAUTOMERISM
TAUTOMERISMS
TAUTOMETRIC
TAUTOMETRICAL
TAUTONYMIC
TAUTONYMIES
TAUTONYMOUS
TAUTOPHONIC
TAUTOPHONICAL
TAUTOPHONIES
TAUTOPHONY
TAWDRINESS
TAWDRINESSES
TAWHEOWHEO
TAWHEOWHEOS
TAWNINESSES
TAXABILITIES
TAXABILITY
TAXABLENESS
TAXABLENESSES
TAXAMETERS
TAXATIONAL
TAXIDERMAL
TAXIDERMIC
TAXIDERMIES
TAXIDERMISE
TAXIDERMISED
TAXIDERMISES
TAXIDERMISING
TAXIDERMIST
TAXIDERMISTS
TAXIDERMIZE
TAXIDERMIZED
TAXIDERMIZES
TAXIDERMIZING
TAXIMETERS
TAXIPLANES
TAXONOMERS
TAXONOMICAL
TAXONOMICALLY
TAXONOMIES
TAXONOMIST
TAXONOMISTS
TAXPAYINGS
TAYASSUIDS
TAYBERRIES
TCHOTCHKES
TCHOUKBALL
TCHOUKBALLS
TEABERRIES
TEACHABILITIES
TEACHABILITY
TEACHABLENESS
TEACHABLENESSES
TEACHERLESS
TEACHERLIER
TEACHERLIEST
TEACHERSHIP
TEACHERSHIPS
TEACUPFULS
TEACUPSFUL
TEAKETTLES
TEARFULNESS
TEARFULNESSES
TEARGASSED
TEARGASSES
TEARGASSING
TEARINESSES
TEARJERKER
TEARJERKERS
TEARLESSLY
TEARSHEETS
TEARSTAINED
TEARSTAINS
TEARSTRIPS
TEASELINGS
TEASELLERS
TEASELLING
TEASELLINGS
TEASPOONFUL
TEASPOONFULS
TEASPOONSFUL
TEATASTERS
TEAZELLING
TECHINESSES
TECHNETIUM
TECHNETIUMS
TECHNETRONIC
TECHNICALISE
TECHNICALISED
TECHNICALISES
TECHNICALISING
TECHNICALITIES
TECHNICALITY
TECHNICALIZE
TECHNICALIZED
TECHNICALIZES
TECHNICALIZING
TECHNICALLY
TECHNICALNESS
TECHNICALNESSES
TECHNICALS
TECHNICIAN
TECHNICIANS
TECHNICISE
TECHNICISED
TECHNICISES
TECHNICISING
TECHNICISM
TECHNICISMS
TECHNICIST
TECHNICISTS
TECHNICIZE
TECHNICIZED
TECHNICIZES
TECHNICIZING
TECHNICOLOUR
TECHNICOLOURED
TECHNIKONS
TECHNIQUES
TECHNOBABBLE
TECHNOBABBLES
TECHNOCRACIES
TECHNOCRACY
TECHNOCRAT
TECHNOCRATIC
TECHNOCRATS
TECHNOFEAR
TECHNOFEARS
TECHNOGRAPHIES
TECHNOGRAPHY
TECHNOJUNKIE
TECHNOJUNKIES
TECHNOLOGIC
TECHNOLOGICAL
TECHNOLOGICALLY
TECHNOLOGIES
TECHNOLOGISE
TECHNOLOGISED
TECHNOLOGISES
TECHNOLOGISING
TECHNOLOGIST
TECHNOLOGISTS
TECHNOLOGIZE
TECHNOLOGIZED
TECHNOLOGIZES
TECHNOLOGIZING
TECHNOLOGY
TECHNOMANIA
TECHNOMANIAC
TECHNOMANIACS
TECHNOMANIAS
TECHNOMUSIC
TECHNOMUSICS
TECHNOPHILE
TECHNOPHILES
TECHNOPHILIA
TECHNOPHILIAS
TECHNOPHOBE
TECHNOPHOBES
TECHNOPHOBIA
TECHNOPHOBIAS
TECHNOPHOBIC
TECHNOPHOBICS
TECHNOPOLE
TECHNOPOLES
TECHNOPOLIS
TECHNOPOLISES
TECHNOPOLITAN
TECHNOPOLITANS
TECHNOPOPS
TECHNOSPEAK
TECHNOSPEAKS
TECHNOSTRESS
TECHNOSTRESSES
TECHNOSTRUCTURE
TECTIBRANCH
TECTIBRANCHIATE
TECTIBRANCHS
TECTONICALLY
TECTONISMS
TECTRICIAL
TEDIOSITIES
TEDIOUSNESS
TEDIOUSNESSES
TEDIOUSOME
TEEMINGNESS
TEEMINGNESSES
TEENTSIEST
TEENYBOPPER
TEENYBOPPERS
TEETERBOARD
TEETERBOARDS
TEETHRIDGE
TEETHRIDGES
TEETOTALED
TEETOTALER
TEETOTALERS
TEETOTALING
TEETOTALISM
TEETOTALISMS
TEETOTALIST
TEETOTALISTS
TEETOTALLED
TEETOTALLER
TEETOTALLERS
TEETOTALLING
TEETOTALLY
TEGUMENTAL
TEGUMENTARY
TEHSILDARS
TEICHOPSIA
TEICHOPSIAS
TEINOSCOPE
TEINOSCOPES
TEKNONYMIES
TEKNONYMOUS
TELAESTHESIA
TELAESTHESIAS
TELAESTHETIC
TELANGIECTASES
TELANGIECTASIA
TELANGIECTASIAS
TELANGIECTASIS
TELANGIECTATIC
TELAUTOGRAPHIC
TELAUTOGRAPHIES
TELAUTOGRAPHY
TELEARCHICS
TELEBANKING
TELEBANKINGS
TELEBRIDGE
TELEBRIDGES
TELECAMERA

TELECAMERAS
TELECASTED
TELECASTER
TELECASTERS
TELECASTING
TELECHIRIC
TELECOMMAND
TELECOMMANDS
TELECOMMUTE
TELECOMMUTED
TELECOMMUTER
TELECOMMUTERS
TELECOMMUTES
TELECOMMUTING
TELECOMMUTINGS
TELECONFERENCE
TELECONFERENCES
TELECONNECTION
TELECONNECTIONS
TELECONTROL
TELECONTROLS
TELECONVERTER
TELECONVERTERS
TELECOPIES
TELECOTTAGE
TELECOTTAGES
TELECOTTAGING
TELECOTTAGINGS
TELECOURSE
TELECOURSES
TELEDILDONICS
TELEFACSIMILE
TELEFACSIMILES
TELEFAXING
TELEFERIQUE
TELEFERIQUES
TELEGENICALLY
TELEGNOSES
TELEGNOSIS
TELEGNOSTIC
TELEGONIES
TELEGONOUS
TELEGRAMMATIC
TELEGRAMMED
TELEGRAMMIC
TELEGRAMMING
TELEGRAPHED
TELEGRAPHER
TELEGRAPHERS
TELEGRAPHESE
TELEGRAPHESES
TELEGRAPHIC
TELEGRAPHICALLY
TELEGRAPHIES
TELEGRAPHING
TELEGRAPHIST
TELEGRAPHISTS
TELEGRAPHS
TELEGRAPHY
TELEHEALTH
TELEHEALTHS
TELEJOURNALISM
TELEJOURNALISMS
TELEJOURNALIST
TELEJOURNALISTS
TELEKINESES
TELEKINESIS
TELEKINETIC
TELEKINETICALLY
TELEMARKED
TELEMARKETER
TELEMARKETERS
TELEMARKETING
TELEMARKETINGS
TELEMARKING
TELEMATICS
TELEMEDICINE
TELEMEDICINES
TELEMEETING
TELEMEETINGS
TELEMESSAGE
TELEMESSAGES
TELEMETERED
TELEMETERING
TELEMETERS
TELEMETRIC
TELEMETRICAL
TELEMETRICALLY
TELEMETRIES
TELENCEPHALA
TELENCEPHALIC
TELENCEPHALON
TELENCEPHALONS
TELEOLOGIC
TELEOLOGICAL
TELEOLOGICALLY
TELEOLOGIES
TELEOLOGISM
TELEOLOGISMS
TELEOLOGIST
TELEOLOGISTS
TELEONOMIC
TELEONOMIES
TELEOSAURIAN
TELEOSAURIANS
TELEOSAURS
TELEOSTEAN
TELEOSTEANS
TELEOSTOME
TELEOSTOMES
TELEOSTOMOUS
TELEPATHED
TELEPATHIC
TELEPATHICALLY
TELEPATHIES
TELEPATHING
TELEPATHISE
TELEPATHISED
TELEPATHISES
TELEPATHISING
TELEPATHIST
TELEPATHISTS
TELEPATHIZE
TELEPATHIZED
TELEPATHIZES
TELEPATHIZING
TELEPHEMES
TELEPHERIQUE
TELEPHERIQUES
TELEPHONED
TELEPHONER
TELEPHONERS
TELEPHONES
TELEPHONIC
TELEPHONICALLY
TELEPHONIES
TELEPHONING
TELEPHONIST
TELEPHONISTS
TELEPHONITIS
TELEPHONITISES
TELEPHOTOGRAPH
TELEPHOTOGRAPHS
TELEPHOTOGRAPHY
TELEPHOTOS
TELEPOINTS
TELEPORTATION
TELEPORTATIONS
TELEPORTED
TELEPORTING
TELEPRESENCE
TELEPRESENCES
TELEPRINTED
TELEPRINTER
TELEPRINTERS
TELEPRINTING
TELEPRINTS
TELEPROCESSING
TELEPROCESSINGS
TELERECORD
TELERECORDED
TELERECORDING
TELERECORDINGS
TELERECORDS
TELERGICALLY
TELEROBOTS
TELESCIENCE
TELESCIENCES
TELESCOPED
TELESCOPES
TELESCOPIC
TELESCOPICAL
TELESCOPICALLY
TELESCOPIES
TELESCOPIFORM
TELESCOPING
TELESCOPIST
TELESCOPISTS
TELESCREEN
TELESCREENS
TELESELLING
TELESELLINGS
TELESERVICES
TELESHOPPED
TELESHOPPING
TELESHOPPINGS
TELESMATIC
TELESMATICAL
TELESMATICALLY
TELESOFTWARE
TELESOFTWARES
TELESTEREOSCOPE
TELESTHESIA
TELESTHESIAS
TELESTHETIC
TELESTICHS
TELESURGERIES
TELESURGERY
TELETYPESETTING
TELETYPEWRITER
TELETYPEWRITERS
TELETYPING
TELEUTOSPORE
TELEUTOSPORES
TELEUTOSPORIC
TELEVANGELICAL
TELEVANGELISM
TELEVANGELISMS
TELEVANGELIST
TELEVANGELISTS
TELEVERITE
TELEVERITES
TELEVIEWED
TELEVIEWER
TELEVIEWERS
TELEVIEWING
TELEVIEWINGS
TELEVISERS
TELEVISING
TELEVISION
TELEVISIONAL
TELEVISIONALLY
TELEVISIONARY
TELEVISIONS
TELEVISORS
TELEVISUAL
TELEVISUALLY
TELEWORKED
TELEWORKER
TELEWORKERS
TELEWORKING
TELEWORKINGS
TELEWRITER
TELEWRITERS
TELFERAGES
TELICITIES
TELIOSPORE
TELIOSPORES
TELLERSHIP
TELLERSHIPS

TELLURATES
TELLURETTED
TELLURIANS
TELLURIDES
TELLURIONS
TELLURISED
TELLURISES
TELLURISING
TELLURITES
TELLURIUMS
TELLURIZED
TELLURIZES
TELLURIZING
TELLUROMETER
TELLUROMETERS
TELNETTING
TELOCENTRIC
TELOCENTRICS
TELOMERASE
TELOMERASES
TELOMERISATION
TELOMERISATIONS
TELOMERIZATION
TELOMERIZATIONS
TELOPHASES
TELOPHASIC
TELPHERAGE
TELPHERAGES
TELPHERING
TELPHERLINE
TELPHERLINES
TELPHERMAN
TELPHERMEN
TELPHERWAY
TELPHERWAYS
TEMAZEPAMS
TEMERARIOUS
TEMERARIOUSLY
TEMERARIOUSNESS
TEMERITIES
TEMEROUSLY
TEMPERABILITIES
TEMPERABILITY
TEMPERABLE
TEMPERALITIE
TEMPERALITIES
TEMPERAMENT
TEMPERAMENTAL
TEMPERAMENTALLY
TEMPERAMENTFUL
TEMPERAMENTS
TEMPERANCE
TEMPERANCES
TEMPERATED
TEMPERATELY
TEMPERATENESS
TEMPERATENESSES
TEMPERATES
TEMPERATING
TEMPERATIVE
TEMPERATURE
TEMPERATURES
TEMPERINGS
TEMPESTING
TEMPESTIVE
TEMPESTUOUS
TEMPESTUOUSLY
TEMPESTUOUSNESS
TEMPOLABILE
TEMPORALISE
TEMPORALISED
TEMPORALISES
TEMPORALISING
TEMPORALITIES
TEMPORALITY
TEMPORALIZE
TEMPORALIZED
TEMPORALIZES
TEMPORALIZING
TEMPORALLY
TEMPORALNESS
TEMPORALNESSES
TEMPORALTIES
TEMPORALTY
TEMPORANEOUS
TEMPORARIES
TEMPORARILY
TEMPORARINESS
TEMPORARINESSES
TEMPORISATION
TEMPORISATIONS
TEMPORISED
TEMPORISER
TEMPORISERS
TEMPORISES
TEMPORISING
TEMPORISINGLY
TEMPORISINGS
TEMPORIZATION
TEMPORIZATIONS
TEMPORIZED
TEMPORIZER
TEMPORIZERS
TEMPORIZES
TEMPORIZING
TEMPORIZINGLY
TEMPORIZINGS
TEMPTABILITIES
TEMPTABILITY
TEMPTABLENESS
TEMPTABLENESSES
TEMPTATION
TEMPTATIONS
TEMPTATIOUS
TEMPTINGLY
TEMPTINGNESS
TEMPTINGNESSES
TEMPTRESSES
TEMULENCES
TEMULENCIES
TEMULENTLY
TENABILITIES
TENABILITY
TENABLENESS
TENABLENESSES
TENACIOUSLY
TENACIOUSNESS
TENACIOUSNESSES
TENACITIES
TENACULUMS
TENAILLONS
TENANTABLE
TENANTLESS
TENANTRIES
TENANTSHIP
TENANTSHIPS
TENDENCIAL
TENDENCIALLY
TENDENCIES
TENDENCIOUS
TENDENCIOUSLY
TENDENCIOUSNESS
TENDENTIAL
TENDENTIALLY
TENDENTIOUS
TENDENTIOUSLY
TENDENTIOUSNESS
TENDERABLE
TENDERFEET
TENDERFOOT
TENDERFOOTS
TENDERHEARTED
TENDERHEARTEDLY
TENDERINGS
TENDERISATION
TENDERISATIONS
TENDERISED
TENDERISER
TENDERISERS
TENDERISES
TENDERISING
TENDERIZATION
TENDERIZATIONS
TENDERIZED
TENDERIZER
TENDERIZERS
TENDERIZES
TENDERIZING
TENDERLING
TENDERLINGS
TENDERLOIN
TENDERLOINS
TENDERNESS
TENDERNESSES
TENDEROMETER
TENDEROMETERS
TENDINITIDES
TENDINITIS
TENDINITISES
TENDONITIDES
TENDONITIS
TENDONITISES
TENDOVAGINITIS
TENDRESSES
TENDRILLAR
TENDRILLED
TENDRILLIER
TENDRILLIEST
TENDRILLOUS
TENDRILOUS
TENEBRIFIC
TENEBRIONID
TENEBRIONIDS
TENEBRIOUS
TENEBRIOUSNESS
TENEBRISMS
TENEBRISTS
TENEBRITIES
TENEBROSITIES
TENEBROSITY
TENEBROUSNESS
TENEBROUSNESSES
TENEMENTAL
TENEMENTARY
TENEMENTED
TENESMUSES
TENIACIDES
TENIAFUGES
TENNANTITE
TENNANTITES
TENNESSINE
TENNESSINES
TENORRHAPHIES
TENORRHAPHY
TENOSYNOVITIS
TENOSYNOVITISES
TENOTOMIES
TENOTOMIST
TENOTOMISTS
TENOVAGINITIS
TENOVAGINITISES
TENPINNERS
TENPOUNDER
TENPOUNDERS
TENSENESSES
TENSIBILITIES
TENSIBILITY
TENSIBLENESS
TENSIBLENESSES
TENSILENESS
TENSILENESSES
TENSILITIES
TENSIMETER
TENSIMETERS
TENSIOMETER
TENSIOMETERS
TENSIOMETRIC
TENSIOMETRIES
TENSIOMETRY
TENSIONALLY

T

TENSIONERS
TENSIONING
TENSIONLESS
TENTACULAR
TENTACULATE
TENTACULIFEROUS
TENTACULITE
TENTACULITES
TENTACULOID
TENTACULUM
TENTATIONS
TENTATIVELY
TENTATIVENESS
TENTATIVENESSES
TENTATIVES
TENTERHOOK
TENTERHOOKS
TENTIGINOUS
TENTMAKERS
TENUIROSTRAL
TENUOUSNESS
TENUOUSNESSES
TENURIALLY
TEPEFACTION
TEPEFACTIONS
TEPHIGRAMS
TEPHROITES
TEPHROMANCIES
TEPHROMANCY
TEPIDARIUM
TEPIDITIES
TEPIDNESSES
TERAHERTZES
TERAMETERS
TERATOCARCINOMA
TERATOGENESES
TERATOGENESIS
TERATOGENIC
TERATOGENICIST
TERATOGENICISTS
TERATOGENICITY
TERATOGENIES
TERATOGENS
TERATOGENY
TERATOLOGIC
TERATOLOGICAL
TERATOLOGIES
TERATOLOGIST
TERATOLOGISTS
TERATOLOGY
TERATOMATA
TERATOMATOUS
TERATOPHOBIA
TERATOPHOBIAS
TERCENTENARIES
TERCENTENARY
TERCENTENNIAL
TERCENTENNIALS
TEREBINTHINE
TEREBINTHS
TEREBRANTS
TEREBRATED
TEREBRATES
TEREBRATING
TEREBRATION
TEREBRATIONS
TEREBRATULA
TEREBRATULAE
TEREBRATULAS
TEREPHTHALATE
TEREPHTHALATES
TEREPHTHALIC
TERGIVERSANT
TERGIVERSANTS
TERGIVERSATE
TERGIVERSATED
TERGIVERSATES
TERGIVERSATING
TERGIVERSATION
TERGIVERSATIONS
TERGIVERSATOR
TERGIVERSATORS
TERGIVERSATORY
TERMAGANCIES
TERMAGANCY
TERMAGANTLY
TERMAGANTS
TERMINABILITIES
TERMINABILITY
TERMINABLE
TERMINABLENESS
TERMINABLY
TERMINALLY
TERMINATED
TERMINATES
TERMINATING
TERMINATION
TERMINATIONAL
TERMINATIONS
TERMINATIVE
TERMINATIVELY
TERMINATOR
TERMINATORS
TERMINATORY
TERMINISMS
TERMINISTS
TERMINOLOGICAL
TERMINOLOGIES
TERMINOLOGIST
TERMINOLOGISTS
TERMINOLOGY
TERMINUSES
TERMITARIA
TERMITARIES
TERMITARIUM
TERMITARIUMS
TERNEPLATE
TERNEPLATES
TEROTECHNOLOGY
TERPENELESS
TERPENOIDS
TERPINEOLS
TERPOLYMER
TERPOLYMERS
TERPSICHOREAL
TERPSICHOREAN
TERRACELESS
TERRACETTE
TERRACETTES
TERRACINGS
TERRACOTTA
TERRACOTTAS
TERRAFORMED
TERRAFORMING
TERRAFORMINGS
TERRAFORMS
TERRAMARAS
TERRAMARES
TERRAQUEOUS
TERRARIUMS
TERREMOTIVE
TERREPLEIN
TERREPLEINS
TERRESTRIAL
TERRESTRIALLY
TERRESTRIALNESS
TERRESTRIALS
TERRIBILITIES
TERRIBILITY
TERRIBLENESS
TERRIBLENESSES
TERRICOLES
TERRICOLOUS
TERRIFICALLY
TERRIFIERS
TERRIFYING
TERRIFYINGLY
TERRIGENOUS
TERRITORIAL
TERRITORIALISE
TERRITORIALISED
TERRITORIALISES
TERRITORIALISM
TERRITORIALISMS
TERRITORIALIST
TERRITORIALISTS
TERRITORIALITY
TERRITORIALIZE
TERRITORIALIZED
TERRITORIALIZES
TERRITORIALLY
TERRITORIALS
TERRITORIED
TERRITORIES
TERRORISATION
TERRORISATIONS
TERRORISED
TERRORISER
TERRORISERS
TERRORISES
TERRORISING
TERRORISMS
TERRORISTIC
TERRORISTS
TERRORIZATION
TERRORIZATIONS
TERRORIZED
TERRORIZER
TERRORIZERS
TERRORIZES
TERRORIZING
TERRORLESS
TERSANCTUS
TERSANCTUSES
TERSENESSES
TERTIARIES
TERVALENCIES
TERVALENCY
TESCHENITE
TESCHENITES
TESSARAGLOT
TESSELATED
TESSELATES
TESSELATING
TESSELLATE
TESSELLATED
TESSELLATES
TESSELLATING
TESSELLATION
TESSELLATIONS
TESSERACTS
TESSITURAS
TESTABILITIES
TESTABILITY
TESTACEANS
TESTACEOUS
TESTAMENTAL
TESTAMENTAR
TESTAMENTARILY
TESTAMENTARY
TESTAMENTS
TESTATIONS
TESTATRICES
TESTATRIXES
TESTCROSSED
TESTCROSSES
TESTCROSSING
TESTERNING
TESTICULAR
TESTICULATE
TESTICULATED
TESTIFICATE
TESTIFICATES
TESTIFICATION
TESTIFICATIONS
TESTIFICATOR
TESTIFICATORS
TESTIFICATORY
TESTIFIERS
TESTIFYING

TESTIMONIAL
TESTIMONIALISE
TESTIMONIALISED
TESTIMONIALISES
TESTIMONIALIZE
TESTIMONIALIZED
TESTIMONIALIZES
TESTIMONIALS
TESTIMONIED
TESTIMONIES
TESTIMONYING
TESTINESSES
TESTOSTERONE
TESTOSTERONES
TESTUDINAL
TESTUDINARY
TESTUDINEOUS
TESTUDINES
TETANICALLY
TETANISATION
TETANISATIONS
TETANISING
TETANIZATION
TETANIZATIONS
TETANIZING
TETARTOHEDRAL
TETARTOHEDRALLY
TETARTOHEDRISM
TETARTOHEDRISMS
TETCHINESS
TETCHINESSES
TETHERBALL
TETHERBALLS
TETRABASIC
TETRABASICITIES
TETRABASICITY
TETRABORATE
TETRABORATES
TETRABRACH
TETRABRACHS
TETRABRANCHIATE
TETRACAINE
TETRACAINES
TETRACHLORIDE
TETRACHLORIDES
TETRACHORD
TETRACHORDAL
TETRACHORDS
TETRACHOTOMIES
TETRACHOTOMOUS
TETRACHOTOMY
TETRACTINAL
TETRACTINALS
TETRACTINE
TETRACTINES
TETRACYCLIC
TETRACYCLINE
TETRACYCLINES
TETRADACTYL
TETRADACTYLIES
TETRADACTYLOUS
TETRADACTYLS
TETRADACTYLY
TETRADITES
TETRADRACHM
TETRADRACHMS
TETRADYMITE
TETRADYMITES
TETRADYNAMOUS
TETRAETHYL
TETRAETHYLLEAD
TETRAETHYLLEADS
TETRAETHYLS
TETRAFLUORIDE
TETRAFLUORIDES
TETRAGONAL
TETRAGONALLY
TETRAGONALNESS
TETRAGONOUS
TETRAGRAMMATON
TETRAGRAMMATONS
TETRAGRAMS
TETRAGYNIAN
TETRAGYNOUS
TETRAHEDRA
TETRAHEDRAL
TETRAHEDRALLY
TETRAHEDRITE
TETRAHEDRITES
TETRAHEDRON
TETRAHEDRONS
TETRAHYDROFURAN
TETRAHYMENA
TETRAHYMENAS
TETRALOGIES
TETRAMERAL
TETRAMERIC
TETRAMERISM
TETRAMERISMS
TETRAMEROUS
TETRAMETER
TETRAMETERS
TETRAMETHYL
TETRAMETHYLLEAD
TETRAMORPHIC
TETRANDRIAN
TETRANDROUS
TETRAPLEGIA
TETRAPLEGIAS
TETRAPLEGIC
TETRAPLOID
TETRAPLOIDIES
TETRAPLOIDS
TETRAPLOIDY
TETRAPODIC
TETRAPODIES
TETRAPODOUS
TETRAPOLIS
TETRAPOLISES
TETRAPOLITAN
TETRAPTERAN
TETRAPTEROUS
TETRAPTOTE
TETRAPTOTES
TETRAPYRROLE
TETRAPYRROLES
TETRARCHATE
TETRARCHATES
TETRARCHIC
TETRARCHICAL
TETRARCHIES
TETRASEMIC
TETRASPORANGIA
TETRASPORANGIUM
TETRASPORE
TETRASPORES
TETRASPORIC
TETRASPOROUS
TETRASTICH
TETRASTICHAL
TETRASTICHIC
TETRASTICHOUS
TETRASTICHS
TETRASTYLE
TETRASTYLES
TETRASYLLABIC
TETRASYLLABICAL
TETRASYLLABLE
TETRASYLLABLES
TETRATHEISM
TETRATHEISMS
TETRATHLON
TETRATHLONS
TETRATOMIC
TETRAVALENCE
TETRAVALENCES
TETRAVALENCIES
TETRAVALENCY
TETRAVALENT
TETRAVALENTS
TETRAZOLIUM
TETRAZOLIUMS
TETRAZZINI
TETRODOTOXIN
TETRODOTOXINS
TETROTOXIN
TETROTOXINS
TETROXIDES
TEUTONISED
TEUTONISES
TEUTONISING
TEUTONIZED
TEUTONIZES
TEUTONIZING
TEXTBOOKISH
TEXTPHONES
TEXTSPEAKS
TEXTUALISM
TEXTUALISMS
TEXTUALIST
TEXTUALISTS
TEXTUARIES
TEXTURALLY
TEXTURELESS
TEXTURINGS
TEXTURISED
TEXTURISES
TEXTURISING
TEXTURIZED
TEXTURIZES
TEXTURIZING
THALAMENCEPHALA
THALAMICALLY
THALAMIFLORAL
THALASSAEMIA
THALASSAEMIAS
THALASSAEMIC
THALASSAEMICS
THALASSEMIA
THALASSEMIAS
THALASSEMIC
THALASSEMICS
THALASSIAN
THALASSIANS
THALASSOCRACIES
THALASSOCRACY
THALASSOCRAT
THALASSOCRATS
THALASSOGRAPHER
THALASSOGRAPHIC
THALASSOGRAPHY
THALASSOTHERAPY
THALATTOCRACIES
THALATTOCRACY
THALICTRUM
THALICTRUMS
THALIDOMIDE
THALIDOMIDES
THALLIFORM
THALLOPHYTE
THALLOPHYTES
THALLOPHYTIC
THANATISMS
THANATISTS
THANATOGNOMONIC
THANATOGRAPHIES
THANATOGRAPHY
THANATOLOGICAL
THANATOLOGIES
THANATOLOGIST
THANATOLOGISTS
THANATOLOGY
THANATOPHOBIA
THANATOPHOBIAS
THANATOPSES
THANATOPSIS
THANATOSES
THANATOSIS
THANEHOODS
THANESHIPS

T

THANKFULLER
THANKFULLEST
THANKFULLY
THANKFULNESS
THANKFULNESSES
THANKLESSLY
THANKLESSNESS
THANKLESSNESSES
THANKSGIVER
THANKSGIVERS
THANKSGIVING
THANKSGIVINGS
THANKWORTHIER
THANKWORTHIEST
THANKWORTHILY
THANKWORTHINESS
THANKWORTHY
THARBOROUGH
THARBOROUGHS
THATCHIEST
THATCHINGS
THATCHLESS
THATNESSES
THAUMASITE
THAUMASITES
THAUMATINS
THAUMATOGENIES
THAUMATOGENY
THAUMATOGRAPHY
THAUMATOLATRIES
THAUMATOLATRY
THAUMATOLOGIES
THAUMATOLOGY
THAUMATROPE
THAUMATROPES
THAUMATROPICAL
THAUMATURGE
THAUMATURGES
THAUMATURGIC
THAUMATURGICAL
THAUMATURGICS
THAUMATURGIES
THAUMATURGISM
THAUMATURGISMS
THAUMATURGIST
THAUMATURGISTS
THAUMATURGUS
THAUMATURGUSES
THAUMATURGY
THEANTHROPIC
THEANTHROPIES
THEANTHROPISM
THEANTHROPISMS
THEANTHROPIST
THEANTHROPISTS
THEANTHROPY
THEARCHIES
THEATERGOER
THEATERGOERS
THEATERGOING
THEATERGOINGS
THEATERLAND
THEATERLANDS
THEATREGOER
THEATREGOERS
THEATREGOING
THEATREGOINGS
THEATRELAND
THEATRELANDS
THEATRICAL
THEATRICALISE
THEATRICALISED
THEATRICALISES
THEATRICALISING
THEATRICALISM
THEATRICALISMS
THEATRICALITIES
THEATRICALITY
THEATRICALIZE
THEATRICALIZED
THEATRICALIZES
THEATRICALIZING
THEATRICALLY
THEATRICALNESS
THEATRICALS
THEATRICISE
THEATRICISED
THEATRICISES
THEATRICISING
THEATRICISM
THEATRICISMS
THEATRICIZE
THEATRICIZED
THEATRICIZES
THEATRICIZING
THEATROMANIA
THEATROMANIAS
THEATROPHONE
THEATROPHONES
THECODONTS
THEFTUOUSLY
THEGNLIEST
THEIRSELVES
THEISTICAL
THEISTICALLY
THELEMENTS
THELITISES
THELYTOKIES
THELYTOKOUS
THEMATICALLY
THEMATISATION
THEMATISATIONS
THEMATISED
THEMATISES
THEMATISING
THEMATIZATION
THEMATIZATIONS
THEMATIZED
THEMATIZES
THEMATIZING
THEMSELVES
THENABOUTS
THENARDITE
THENARDITES
THENCEFORTH
THENCEFORWARD
THENCEFORWARDS
THEOBROMINE
THEOBROMINES
THEOCENTRIC
THEOCENTRICISM
THEOCENTRICISMS
THEOCENTRICITY
THEOCENTRISM
THEOCENTRISMS
THEOCRACIES
THEOCRASIES
THEOCRATIC
THEOCRATICAL
THEOCRATICALLY
THEODICEAN
THEODICEANS
THEODICIES
THEODOLITE
THEODOLITES
THEODOLITIC
THEOGONICAL
THEOGONIES
THEOGONIST
THEOGONISTS
THEOLOGASTER
THEOLOGASTERS
THEOLOGATE
THEOLOGATES
THEOLOGERS
THEOLOGIAN
THEOLOGIANS
THEOLOGICAL
THEOLOGICALLY
THEOLOGIES
THEOLOGISATION
THEOLOGISATIONS
THEOLOGISE
THEOLOGISED
THEOLOGISER
THEOLOGISERS
THEOLOGISES
THEOLOGISING
THEOLOGIST
THEOLOGISTS
THEOLOGIZATION
THEOLOGIZATIONS
THEOLOGIZE
THEOLOGIZED
THEOLOGIZER
THEOLOGIZERS
THEOLOGIZES
THEOLOGIZING
THEOLOGOUMENA
THEOLOGOUMENON
THEOLOGUES
THEOMACHIES
THEOMACHIST
THEOMACHISTS
THEOMANCIES
THEOMANIAC
THEOMANIACS
THEOMANIAS
THEOMANTIC
THEOMORPHIC
THEOMORPHISM
THEOMORPHISMS
THEONOMIES
THEONOMOUS
THEOPATHETIC
THEOPATHIC
THEOPATHIES
THEOPHAGIES
THEOPHAGOUS
THEOPHANIC
THEOPHANIES
THEOPHANOUS
THEOPHOBIA
THEOPHOBIAC
THEOPHOBIACS
THEOPHOBIAS
THEOPHOBIST
THEOPHOBISTS
THEOPHORIC
THEOPHYLLINE
THEOPHYLLINES
THEOPNEUST
THEOPNEUSTIC
THEOPNEUSTIES
THEOPNEUSTY
THEORBISTS
THEOREMATIC
THEOREMATICAL
THEOREMATICALLY
THEOREMATIST
THEOREMATISTS
THEORETICAL
THEORETICALLY
THEORETICIAN
THEORETICIANS
THEORETICS
THEORIQUES
THEORISATION
THEORISATIONS
THEORISERS
THEORISING
THEORIZATION
THEORIZATIONS
THEORIZERS
THEORIZING
THEOSOPHER
THEOSOPHERS
THEOSOPHIC
THEOSOPHICAL
THEOSOPHICALLY

THEOSOPHIES
THEOSOPHISE
THEOSOPHISED
THEOSOPHISES
THEOSOPHISING
THEOSOPHISM
THEOSOPHISMS
THEOSOPHIST
THEOSOPHISTICAL
THEOSOPHISTS
THEOSOPHIZE
THEOSOPHIZED
THEOSOPHIZES
THEOSOPHIZING
THEOTECHNIC
THEOTECHNIES
THEOTECHNY
THERALITES
THERAPEUSES
THERAPEUSIS
THERAPEUTIC
THERAPEUTICAL
THERAPEUTICALLY
THERAPEUTICS
THERAPEUTIST
THERAPEUTISTS
THERAPISED
THERAPISES
THERAPISING
THERAPISTS
THERAPIZED
THERAPIZES
THERAPIZING
THERAPSIDS
THEREABOUT
THEREABOUTS
THEREAFTER
THEREAGAINST
THEREAMONG
THEREANENT
THEREBESIDE
THEREINAFTER
THEREINBEFORE
THERENESSES
THERETHROUGH
THERETOFORE
THEREUNDER
THEREWITHAL
THEREWITHIN
THERIANTHROPIC
THERIANTHROPISM
THERIOLATRIES
THERIOLATRY
THERIOMORPH
THERIOMORPHIC
THERIOMORPHISM
THERIOMORPHISMS
THERIOMORPHOSES
THERIOMORPHOSIS
THERIOMORPHOUS
THERIOMORPHS
THERMAESTHESIA
THERMAESTHESIAS
THERMALISATION
THERMALISATIONS
THERMALISE
THERMALISED
THERMALISES
THERMALISING
THERMALIZATION
THERMALIZATIONS
THERMALIZE
THERMALIZED
THERMALIZES
THERMALIZING
THERMESTHESIA
THERMESTHESIAS
THERMETTES
THERMICALLY
THERMIDORS
THERMIONIC
THERMIONICS
THERMISTOR
THERMISTORS
THERMOBALANCE
THERMOBALANCES
THERMOBARIC
THERMOBAROGRAPH
THERMOBAROMETER
THERMOCHEMICAL
THERMOCHEMIST
THERMOCHEMISTRY
THERMOCHEMISTS
THERMOCHROMIC
THERMOCHROMIES
THERMOCHROMISM
THERMOCHROMISMS
THERMOCHROMY
THERMOCLINE
THERMOCLINES
THERMOCOUPLE
THERMOCOUPLES
THERMODURIC
THERMODYNAMIC
THERMODYNAMICAL
THERMODYNAMICS
THERMOELECTRIC
THERMOELECTRON
THERMOELECTRONS
THERMOELEMENT
THERMOELEMENTS
THERMOFORM
THERMOFORMABLE
THERMOFORMED
THERMOFORMING
THERMOFORMS
THERMOGENESES
THERMOGENESIS
THERMOGENETIC
THERMOGENIC
THERMOGENOUS
THERMOGRAM
THERMOGRAMS
THERMOGRAPH
THERMOGRAPHER
THERMOGRAPHERS
THERMOGRAPHIC
THERMOGRAPHIES
THERMOGRAPHS
THERMOGRAPHY
THERMOHALINE
THERMOJUNCTION
THERMOJUNCTIONS
THERMOLABILE
THERMOLABILITY
THERMOLOGIES
THERMOLOGY
THERMOLYSES
THERMOLYSIS
THERMOLYTIC
THERMOMAGNETIC
THERMOMETER
THERMOMETERS
THERMOMETRIC
THERMOMETRICAL
THERMOMETRIES
THERMOMETRY
THERMOMOTOR
THERMOMOTORS
THERMONASTIES
THERMONASTY
THERMONUCLEAR
THERMOPERIODIC
THERMOPERIODISM
THERMOPHIL
THERMOPHILE
THERMOPHILES
THERMOPHILIC
THERMOPHILOUS
THERMOPHILS
THERMOPHYLLOUS
THERMOPILE
THERMOPILES
THERMOPLASTIC
THERMOPLASTICS
THERMORECEPTOR
THERMORECEPTORS
THERMOREGULATE
THERMOREGULATED
THERMOREGULATES
THERMOREGULATOR
THERMOREMANENCE
THERMOREMANENT
THERMOSCOPE
THERMOSCOPES
THERMOSCOPIC
THERMOSCOPICAL
THERMOSETS
THERMOSETTING
THERMOSIPHON
THERMOSIPHONS
THERMOSPHERE
THERMOSPHERES
THERMOSPHERIC
THERMOSTABILITY
THERMOSTABLE
THERMOSTAT
THERMOSTATED
THERMOSTATIC
THERMOSTATICS
THERMOSTATING
THERMOSTATS
THERMOSTATTED
THERMOSTATTING
THERMOTACTIC
THERMOTAXES
THERMOTAXIC
THERMOTAXIS
THERMOTENSILE
THERMOTHERAPIES
THERMOTHERAPY
THERMOTICAL
THERMOTICS
THERMOTOLERANT
THERMOTROPIC
THERMOTROPICS
THERMOTROPISM
THERMOTROPISMS
THEROLOGIES
THEROPHYTE
THEROPHYTES
THEROPODAN
THEROPODANS
THERSITICAL
THESAURUSES
THESMOTHETE
THESMOTHETES
THETICALLY
THEURGICAL
THEURGICALLY
THEURGISTS
THIABENDAZOLE
THIABENDAZOLES
THIAMINASE
THIAMINASES
THICKENERS
THICKENING
THICKENINGS
THICKETIER
THICKETIEST
THICKHEADED
THICKHEADEDNESS
THICKHEADS
THICKLEAVES
THICKNESSES
THICKSKINS
THIEVERIES
THIEVISHLY
THIEVISHNESS
THIEVISHNESSES

THIGHBONES
THIGMOTACTIC
THIGMOTAXES
THIGMOTAXIS
THIGMOTROPIC
THIGMOTROPISM
THIGMOTROPISMS
THIMBLEBERRIES
THIMBLEBERRY
THIMBLEFUL
THIMBLEFULS
THIMBLERIG
THIMBLERIGGED
THIMBLERIGGER
THIMBLERIGGERS
THIMBLERIGGING
THIMBLERIGGINGS
THIMBLERIGS
THIMBLESFUL
THIMBLEWEED
THIMBLEWEEDS
THIMBLEWIT
THIMBLEWITS
THIMBLEWITTED
THIMEROSAL
THIMEROSALS
THINGAMABOB
THINGAMABOBS
THINGAMAJIG
THINGAMAJIGS
THINGAMIES
THINGAMYBOB
THINGAMYBOBS
THINGAMYJIG
THINGAMYJIGS
THINGHOODS
THINGINESS
THINGINESSES
THINGLINESS
THINGLINESSES
THINGNESSES
THINGUMABOB
THINGUMABOBS
THINGUMAJIG
THINGUMAJIGS
THINGUMBOB
THINGUMBOBS
THINGUMMIES
THINGUMMYBOB
THINGUMMYBOBS
THINGUMMYJIG
THINGUMMYJIGS
THINKABLENESS
THINKABLENESSES
THINKINGLY
THINKINGNESS
THINKINGNESSES
THINKPIECE
THINKPIECES
THINNESSES
THIOALCOHOL
THIOALCOHOLS
THIOBACILLI
THIOBACILLUS
THIOBARBITURATE
THIOCARBAMIDE
THIOCARBAMIDES
THIOCYANATE
THIOCYANATES
THIOCYANIC
THIODIGLYCOL
THIODIGLYCOLS
THIOFURANS
THIOPENTAL
THIOPENTALS
THIOPENTONE
THIOPENTONES
THIOPHENES
THIORIDAZINE
THIORIDAZINES
THIOSINAMINE
THIOSINAMINES
THIOSULFATE
THIOSULFATES
THIOSULFURIC
THIOSULPHATE
THIOSULPHATES
THIOSULPHURIC
THIOURACIL
THIOURACILS
THIRDBOROUGH
THIRDBOROUGHS
THIRDSTREAM
THIRDSTREAMS
THIRSTIEST
THIRSTINESS
THIRSTINESSES
THIRSTLESS
THIRTEENTH
THIRTEENTHLY
THIRTEENTHS
THIRTIETHS
THIRTYFOLD
THIRTYSOMETHING
THISNESSES
THISTLEDOWN
THISTLEDOWNS
THISTLIEST
THITHERWARD
THITHERWARDS
THIXOTROPE
THIXOTROPES
THIXOTROPIC
THIXOTROPIES
THIXOTROPY
THOLEIITES
THOLEIITIC
THOLOBATES
THORACENTESES
THORACENTESIS
THORACICALLY
THORACOCENTESES
THORACOCENTESIS
THORACOPLASTIES
THORACOPLASTY
THORACOSCOPE
THORACOSCOPES
THORACOSTOMIES
THORACOSTOMY
THORACOTOMIES
THORACOTOMY
THORIANITE
THORIANITES
THORNBACKS
THORNBILLS
THORNBIRDS
THORNBUSHES
THORNHEDGE
THORNHEDGES
THORNINESS
THORNINESSES
THORNPROOF
THORNPROOFS
THORNTAILS
THORNTREES
THOROUGHBASS
THOROUGHBASSES
THOROUGHBRACE
THOROUGHBRACED
THOROUGHBRACES
THOROUGHBRED
THOROUGHBREDS
THOROUGHER
THOROUGHEST
THOROUGHFARE
THOROUGHFARES
THOROUGHGOING
THOROUGHGOINGLY
THOROUGHLY
THOROUGHNESS
THOROUGHNESSES
THOROUGHPACED
THOROUGHPIN
THOROUGHPINS
THOROUGHWAX
THOROUGHWAXES
THOROUGHWORT
THOROUGHWORTS
THOUGHTCAST
THOUGHTCASTS
THOUGHTFUL
THOUGHTFULLY
THOUGHTFULNESS
THOUGHTLESS
THOUGHTLESSLY
THOUGHTLESSNESS
THOUGHTWAY
THOUGHTWAYS
THOUSANDFOLD
THOUSANDFOLDS
THOUSANDTH
THOUSANDTHS
THRAIPINGS
THRALLDOMS
THRAPPLING
THRASHIEST
THRASHINGS
THRASONICAL
THRASONICALLY
THREADBARE
THREADBARENESS
THREADBARER
THREADBAREST
THREADFINS
THREADIEST
THREADINESS
THREADINESSES
THREADLESS
THREADLIKE
THREADMAKER
THREADMAKERS
THREADWORM
THREADWORMS
THREATENED
THREATENER
THREATENERS
THREATENING
THREATENINGLY
THREATENINGS
THREEFOLDNESS
THREEFOLDNESSES
THREENESSES
THREEPEATED
THREEPEATING
THREEPEATS
THREEPENCE
THREEPENCES
THREEPENCEWORTH
THREEPENNIES
THREEPENNY
THREEPENNYWORTH
THREEQUELS
THREESCORE
THREESCORES
THREESOMES
THREMMATOLOGIES
THREMMATOLOGY
THRENETICAL
THRENODIAL
THRENODIES
THRENODIST
THRENODISTS
THREONINES
THRESHINGS
THRESHOLDS
THRIFTIEST
THRIFTINESS
THRIFTINESSES
THRIFTLESS
THRIFTLESSLY

THRIFTLESSNESS
THRILLIEST
THRILLINGLY
THRILLINGNESS
THRILLINGNESSES
THRIVELESS
THRIVINGLY
THRIVINGNESS
THRIVINGNESSES
THROATIEST
THROATINESS
THROATINESSES
THROATLASH
THROATLASHES
THROATLATCH
THROATLATCHES
THROATWORT
THROATWORTS
THROBBINGLY
THROBBINGS
THROMBOCYTE
THROMBOCYTES
THROMBOCYTIC
THROMBOEMBOLIC
THROMBOEMBOLISM
THROMBOGEN
THROMBOGENS
THROMBOKINASE
THROMBOKINASES
THROMBOLYSES
THROMBOLYSIS
THROMBOLYTIC
THROMBOLYTICS
THROMBOPHILIA
THROMBOPHILIAS
THROMBOPLASTIC
THROMBOPLASTIN
THROMBOPLASTINS
THROMBOSED
THROMBOSES
THROMBOSING
THROMBOSIS
THROMBOTIC
THROMBOXANE
THROMBOXANES
THRONELESS
THRONGINGS
THROPPLING
THROTTLEABLE
THROTTLEHOLD
THROTTLEHOLDS
THROTTLERS
THROTTLING
THROTTLINGS
THROUGHFARE
THROUGHFARES
THROUGHGAUN
THROUGHGAUNS
THROUGHITHER
THROUGHOTHER
THROUGHOUT
THROUGHPUT
THROUGHPUTS
THROUGHWAY
THROUGHWAYS
THROWAWAYS
THROWBACKS
THROWDOWNS
THROWOVERS
THROWSTERS
THRUMMIEST
THRUMMINGLY
THRUMMINGS
THRUPENNIES
THRUPPENCE
THRUPPENCES
THRUPPENNIES
THRUPPENNY
THRUSHLIKE
THRUSTINGS
THRUTCHING
THUDDINGLY
THUGGERIES
THUMBHOLES
THUMBIKINS
THUMBLINGS
THUMBNAILS
THUMBPIECE
THUMBPIECES
THUMBPRINT
THUMBPRINTS
THUMBSCREW
THUMBSCREWS
THUMBSTALL
THUMBSTALLS
THUMBTACKED
THUMBTACKING
THUMBTACKS
THUMBWHEEL
THUMBWHEELS
THUMPINGLY
THUNBERGIA
THUNBERGIAS
THUNDERBIRD
THUNDERBIRDS
THUNDERBOLT
THUNDERBOLTS
THUNDERBOX
THUNDERBOXES
THUNDERCLAP
THUNDERCLAPS
THUNDERCLOUD
THUNDERCLOUDS
THUNDERERS
THUNDERFLASH
THUNDERFLASHES
THUNDERHEAD
THUNDERHEADS
THUNDERIER
THUNDERIEST
THUNDERING
THUNDERINGLY
THUNDERINGS
THUNDERLESS
THUNDEROUS
THUNDEROUSLY
THUNDEROUSNESS
THUNDERSHOWER
THUNDERSHOWERS
THUNDERSTONE
THUNDERSTONES
THUNDERSTORM
THUNDERSTORMS
THUNDERSTRICKEN
THUNDERSTRIKE
THUNDERSTRIKES
THUNDERSTRIKING
THUNDERSTROKE
THUNDERSTROKES
THUNDERSTRUCK
THURIFEROUS
THURIFICATION
THURIFICATIONS
THURIFYING
THUSNESSES
THWACKINGS
THWARTEDLY
THWARTINGLY
THWARTINGS
THWARTSHIP
THWARTSHIPS
THWARTWAYS
THWARTWISE
THYLACINES
THYLAKOIDS
THYMECTOMIES
THYMECTOMISE
THYMECTOMISED
THYMECTOMISES
THYMECTOMISING
THYMECTOMIZE
THYMECTOMIZED
THYMECTOMIZES
THYMECTOMIZING
THYMECTOMY
THYMELAEACEOUS
THYMIDINES
THYMIDYLIC
THYMOCYTES
THYRATRONS
THYRISTORS
THYROCALCITONIN
THYROGLOBULIN
THYROGLOBULINS
THYROIDECTOMIES
THYROIDECTOMY
THYROIDITIDES
THYROIDITIS
THYROIDITISES
THYROTOXICOSES
THYROTOXICOSIS
THYROTROPHIC
THYROTROPHIN
THYROTROPHINS
THYROTROPIC
THYROTROPIN
THYROTROPINS
THYROXINES
THYRSOIDAL
THYSANOPTEROUS
THYSANURAN
THYSANURANS
THYSANUROUS
TIBIOFIBULA
TIBIOFIBULAE
TIBIOFIBULAS
TIBIOTARSI
TIBIOTARSUS
TIBOUCHINA
TIBOUCHINAS
TICHORRHINE
TICHORRHINES
TICKETINGS
TICKETLESS
TICKETTYBOO
TICKLEASSES
TICKLISHLY
TICKLISHNESS
TICKLISHNESSES
TICKTACKED
TICKTACKING
TICKTACKTOE
TICKTACKTOES
TICKTOCKED
TICKTOCKING
TICTACKING
TICTOCKING
TIDDLEDYWINK
TIDDLEDYWINKS
TIDDLEYWINK
TIDDLEYWINKS
TIDDLYWINK
TIDDLYWINKS
TIDEWAITER
TIDEWAITERS
TIDEWATERS
TIDINESSES
TIDIVATING
TIDIVATION
TIDIVATIONS
TIEBREAKER
TIEBREAKERS
TIEMANNITE
TIEMANNITES
TIERCELETS
TIERCERONS
TIGERISHLY
TIGERISHNESS
TIGERISHNESSES
TIGERLIEST

TIGERWOODS
TIGGYWINKLE
TIGGYWINKLES
TIGHTASSED
TIGHTASSES
TIGHTENERS
TIGHTENING
TIGHTENINGS
TIGHTFISTED
TIGHTFISTEDNESS
TIGHTISHLY
TIGHTNESSES
TIGHTROPES
TIGHTWIRES
TIGRISHNESS
TIGRISHNESSES
TIKINAGANS
TIKOLOSHES
TIKTAALIKS
TILEFISHES
TILIACEOUS
TILLANDSIA
TILLANDSIAS
TILLERINGS
TILLERLESS
TILTMETERS
TILTROTORS
TIMBERDOODLE
TIMBERDOODLES
TIMBERHEAD
TIMBERHEADS
TIMBERIEST
TIMBERINGS
TIMBERLAND
TIMBERLANDS
TIMBERLINE
TIMBERLINES
TIMBERWORK
TIMBERWORKS
TIMBERYARD
TIMBERYARDS
TIMBRELLED
TIMBROLOGIES
TIMBROLOGIST
TIMBROLOGISTS
TIMBROLOGY
TIMBROMANIA
TIMBROMANIAC
TIMBROMANIACS
TIMBROMANIAS
TIMBROPHILIES
TIMBROPHILIST
TIMBROPHILISTS
TIMBROPHILY
TIMEFRAMES
TIMEKEEPER
TIMEKEEPERS
TIMEKEEPING
TIMEKEEPINGS
TIMELESSLY
TIMELESSNESS
TIMELESSNESSES
TIMELINESS
TIMELINESSES
TIMENOGUYS
TIMEPASSED
TIMEPASSES
TIMEPASSING
TIMEPIECES
TIMEPLEASER
TIMEPLEASERS
TIMESAVERS
TIMESAVING
TIMESCALES
TIMESERVER
TIMESERVERS
TIMESERVING
TIMESERVINGS
TIMESHARES
TIMESHIFTED
TIMESHIFTING
TIMESHIFTS
TIMESTAMPED
TIMESTAMPING
TIMESTAMPS
TIMETABLED
TIMETABLES
TIMETABLING
TIMETABLINGS
TIMEWORKER
TIMEWORKERS
TIMIDITIES
TIMIDNESSES
TIMOCRACIES
TIMOCRATIC
TIMOCRATICAL
TIMOROUSLY
TIMOROUSNESS
TIMOROUSNESSES
TIMPANISTS
TINCTORIAL
TINCTORIALLY
TINCTURING
TINDERBOXES
TINDERIEST
TINGLINGLY
TINGUAITES
TININESSES
TINKERINGS
TINKERTOYS
TINKLINGLY
TINNINESSES
TINNITUSES
TINPLATING
TINSELIEST
TINSELLIER
TINSELLIEST
TINSELLING
TINSELRIES
TINSMITHING
TINSMITHINGS
TINTINESSES
TINTINNABULA
TINTINNABULANT
TINTINNABULAR
TINTINNABULARY
TINTINNABULATE
TINTINNABULATED
TINTINNABULATES
TINTINNABULOUS
TINTINNABULUM
TINTOMETER
TINTOMETERS
TINTOOKIES
TIPPYTOEING
TIPSIFYING
TIPSINESSES
TIPTRONICS
TIRAILLEUR
TIRAILLEURS
TIREDNESSES
TIRELESSLY
TIRELESSNESS
TIRELESSNESSES
TIREMAKERS
TIRESOMELY
TIRESOMENESS
TIRESOMENESSES
TIROCINIUM
TIROCINIUMS
TITANESSES
TITANICALLY
TITANIFEROUS
TITANOSAUR
TITANOSAURS
TITANOTHERE
TITANOTHERES
TITARAKURA
TITARAKURAS
TITHINGMAN
TITHINGMEN
TITILLATED
TITILLATES
TITILLATING
TITILLATINGLY
TITILLATION
TITILLATIONS
TITILLATIVE
TITILLATOR
TITILLATORS
TITIPOUNAMU
TITIPOUNAMUS
TITIVATING
TITIVATION
TITIVATIONS
TITIVATORS
TITLEHOLDER
TITLEHOLDERS
TITLEHOLDING
TITRATABLE
TITRATIONS
TITRIMETRIC
TITTERINGLY
TITTERINGS
TITTIVATED
TITTIVATES
TITTIVATING
TITTIVATION
TITTIVATIONS
TITTIVATOR
TITTIVATORS
TITTLEBATS
TITTUPIEST
TITTUPPIER
TITTUPPIEST
TITTUPPING
TITUBANCIES
TITUBATING
TITUBATION
TITUBATIONS
TITULARIES
TITULARITIES
TITULARITY
TOADEATERS
TOADFISHES
TOADFLAXES
TOADGRASSES
TOADRUSHES
TOADSTONES
TOADSTOOLS
TOASTMASTER
TOASTMASTERS
TOASTMISTRESS
TOASTMISTRESSES
TOBACCANALIAN
TOBACCANALIANS
TOBACCOLESS
TOBACCONIST
TOBACCONISTS
TOBOGGANED
TOBOGGANER
TOBOGGANERS
TOBOGGANING
TOBOGGANINGS
TOBOGGANIST
TOBOGGANISTS
TOBOGGINED
TOBOGGINING
TOCCATELLA
TOCCATELLAS
TOCCATINAS
TOCHERLESS
TOCOLOGIES
TOCOPHEROL
TOCOPHEROLS
TOCOPHOBIA
TOCOPHOBIAS
TODDLERHOOD
TODDLERHOODS
TOENAILING

TOERAGGERS
TOFFISHNESS
TOFFISHNESSES
TOGAVIRUSES
TOGETHERNESS
TOGETHERNESSES
TOILETINGS
TOILETRIES
TOILFULNESS
TOILFULNESSES
TOILINETTE
TOILINETTES
TOILSOMELY
TOILSOMENESS
TOILSOMENESSES
TOKENISTIC
TOKOLOGIES
TOKOLOSHES
TOKOLOSHIS
TOKOPHOBIA
TOKOPHOBIAS
TOKTOKKIES
TOLBUTAMIDE
TOLBUTAMIDES
TOLERABILITIES
TOLERABILITY
TOLERABLENESS
TOLERABLENESSES
TOLERANCES
TOLERANTLY
TOLERATING
TOLERATION
TOLERATIONISM
TOLERATIONISMS
TOLERATIONIST
TOLERATIONISTS
TOLERATIONS
TOLERATIVE
TOLERATORS
TOLLBOOTHS
TOLLBRIDGE
TOLLBRIDGES
TOLLDISHES
TOLLGATING
TOLLHOUSES
TOLLKEEPER
TOLLKEEPERS
TOLUIDIDES
TOLUIDINES
TOMAHAWKED
TOMAHAWKING
TOMATILLOES
TOMATILLOS
TOMATOIEST
TOMBOYISHLY
TOMBOYISHNESS
TOMBOYISHNESSES
TOMBSTONES
TOMBSTONING
TOMBSTONINGS
TOMCATTING
TOMCATTINGS
TOMFOOLERIES
TOMFOOLERY
TOMFOOLING
TOMFOOLISH
TOMFOOLISHNESS
TOMOGRAPHIC
TOMOGRAPHIES
TOMOGRAPHS
TOMOGRAPHY
TONALITIES
TONALITIVE
TONELESSLY
TONELESSNESS
TONELESSNESSES
TONETICALLY
TONGUELESS
TONGUELETS
TONGUELIKE
TONGUESTER
TONGUESTERS
TONICITIES
TONISHNESS
TONISHNESSES
TONNISHNESS
TONNISHNESSES
TONOMETERS
TONOMETRIC
TONOMETRIES
TONOPLASTS
TONSILITIS
TONSILITISES
TONSILLARY
TONSILLECTOMIES
TONSILLECTOMY
TONSILLITIC
TONSILLITIDES
TONSILLITIS
TONSILLITISES
TONSILLOTOMIES
TONSILLOTOMY
TOOLCHESTS
TOOLHOLDER
TOOLHOLDERS
TOOLHOUSES
TOOLMAKERS
TOOLMAKING
TOOLMAKINGS
TOOLPUSHER
TOOLPUSHERS
TOOLPUSHES
TOOTHACHES
TOOTHBRUSH
TOOTHBRUSHES
TOOTHBRUSHING
TOOTHBRUSHINGS
TOOTHCOMBS
TOOTHFISHES
TOOTHINESS
TOOTHINESSES
TOOTHPASTE
TOOTHPASTES
TOOTHPICKS
TOOTHSHELL
TOOTHSHELLS
TOOTHSOMELY
TOOTHSOMENESS
TOOTHSOMENESSES
TOOTHWASHES
TOOTHWORTS
TOPAGNOSES
TOPAGNOSIA
TOPAGNOSIAS
TOPAGNOSIS
TOPARCHIES
TOPAZOLITE
TOPAZOLITES
TOPCROSSES
TOPDRESSING
TOPDRESSINGS
TOPECTOMIES
TOPGALLANT
TOPGALLANTS
TOPHACEOUS
TOPIARISTS
TOPICALITIES
TOPICALITY
TOPKNOTTED
TOPLESSNESS
TOPLESSNESSES
TOPLOFTICAL
TOPLOFTIER
TOPLOFTIEST
TOPLOFTILY
TOPLOFTINESS
TOPLOFTINESSES
TOPMAKINGS
TOPMINNOWS
TOPNOTCHER
TOPNOTCHERS
TOPOCENTRIC
TOPOCHEMISTRIES
TOPOCHEMISTRY
TOPOGRAPHER
TOPOGRAPHERS
TOPOGRAPHIC
TOPOGRAPHICAL
TOPOGRAPHICALLY
TOPOGRAPHIES
TOPOGRAPHS
TOPOGRAPHY
TOPOISOMERASE
TOPOISOMERASES
TOPOLOGICAL
TOPOLOGICALLY
TOPOLOGIES
TOPOLOGIST
TOPOLOGISTS
TOPOMETRIES
TOPONYMICAL
TOPONYMICS
TOPONYMIES
TOPONYMIST
TOPONYMISTS
TOPOPHILIA
TOPOPHILIAS
TOPSCORING
TOPSOILING
TOPSOILINGS
TOPSTITCHED
TOPSTITCHES
TOPSTITCHING
TOPWORKING
TORBANITES
TORBERNITE
TORBERNITES
TORCHBEARER
TORCHBEARERS
TORCHIERES
TORCHLIGHT
TORCHLIGHTS
TORCHWOODS
TORMENTEDLY
TORMENTERS
TORMENTILS
TORMENTING
TORMENTINGLY
TORMENTINGS
TORMENTORS
TORMENTUMS
TOROIDALLY
TOROSITIES
TORPEDINOUS
TORPEDOERS
TORPEDOING
TORPEDOIST
TORPEDOISTS
TORPEFYING
TORPESCENCE
TORPESCENCES
TORPESCENT
TORPIDITIES
TORPIDNESS
TORPIDNESSES
TORPITUDES
TORPORIFIC
TORREFACTION
TORREFACTIONS
TORREFYING
TORRENTIAL
TORRENTIALITIES
TORRENTIALITY
TORRENTIALLY
TORRENTUOUS
TORRIDITIES
TORRIDNESS
TORRIDNESSES
TORRIFYING
TORSIBILITIES

T

TORSIBILITY
TORSIOGRAPH
TORSIOGRAPHS
TORSIONALLY
TORTELLINI
TORTELLINIS
TORTFEASOR
TORTFEASORS
TORTICOLLAR
TORTICOLLIS
TORTICOLLISES
TORTILITIES
TORTILLONS
TORTIOUSLY
TORTOISESHELL
TORTOISESHELLS
TORTRICIDS
TORTUOSITIES
TORTUOSITY
TORTUOUSLY
TORTUOUSNESS
TORTUOUSNESSES
TORTUREDLY
TORTURESOME
TORTURINGLY
TORTURINGS
TORTUROUSLY
TOSSICATED
TOSTICATED
TOSTICATION
TOSTICATIONS
TOTALISATION
TOTALISATIONS
TOTALISATOR
TOTALISATORS
TOTALISERS
TOTALISING
TOTALISTIC
TOTALITARIAN
TOTALITARIANISE
TOTALITARIANISM
TOTALITARIANIZE
TOTALITARIANS
TOTALITIES
TOTALIZATION
TOTALIZATIONS
TOTALIZATOR
TOTALIZATORS
TOTALIZERS
TOTALIZING
TOTAQUINES
TOTEMICALLY
TOTEMISTIC
TOTIPALMATE
TOTIPALMATION
TOTIPALMATIONS
TOTIPOTENCIES
TOTIPOTENCY
TOTIPOTENT
TOTTERIEST
TOTTERINGLY
TOTTERINGS
TOUCHABLENESS
TOUCHABLENESSES
TOUCHBACKS
TOUCHDOWNS
TOUCHHOLES
TOUCHINESS
TOUCHINESSES
TOUCHINGLY
TOUCHINGNESS
TOUCHINGNESSES
TOUCHLINES
TOUCHMARKS
TOUCHPAPER
TOUCHPAPERS
TOUCHSCREEN
TOUCHSCREENS
TOUCHSTONE
TOUCHSTONES
TOUCHTONES
TOUCHWOODS
TOUGHENERS
TOUGHENING
TOUGHENINGS
TOUGHNESSES
TOURBILLION
TOURBILLIONS
TOURBILLON
TOURBILLONS
TOURISTICALLY
TOURISTIER
TOURISTIEST
TOURMALINE
TOURMALINES
TOURMALINIC
TOURNAMENT
TOURNAMENTS
TOURNEYERS
TOURNEYING
TOURNIQUET
TOURNIQUETS
TOURTIERES
TOVARICHES
TOVARISCHES
TOVARISHES
TOWARDLINESS
TOWARDLINESSES
TOWARDNESS
TOWARDNESSES
TOWELETTES
TOWELLINGS
TOWERINGLY
TOWNHOUSES
TOWNSCAPED
TOWNSCAPES
TOWNSCAPING
TOWNSCAPINGS
TOWNSFOLKS
TOWNSPEOPLE
TOWNSPEOPLES
TOWNSWOMAN
TOWNSWOMEN
TOXALBUMIN
TOXALBUMINS
TOXAPHENES
TOXICATION
TOXICATIONS
TOXICITIES
TOXICOGENIC
TOXICOLOGIC
TOXICOLOGICAL
TOXICOLOGICALLY
TOXICOLOGIES
TOXICOLOGIST
TOXICOLOGISTS
TOXICOLOGY
TOXICOMANIA
TOXICOMANIAS
TOXICOPHAGOUS
TOXICOPHOBIA
TOXICOPHOBIAS
TOXIGENICITIES
TOXIGENICITY
TOXIPHAGOUS
TOXIPHOBIA
TOXIPHOBIAC
TOXIPHOBIACS
TOXIPHOBIAS
TOXOCARIASES
TOXOCARIASIS
TOXOPHILIES
TOXOPHILITE
TOXOPHILITES
TOXOPHILITIC
TOXOPLASMA
TOXOPLASMAS
TOXOPLASMIC
TOXOPLASMOSES
TOXOPLASMOSIS
TOYISHNESS
TOYISHNESSES
TRABEATION
TRABEATIONS
TRABECULAE
TRABECULAR
TRABECULAS
TRABECULATE
TRABECULATED
TRACASSERIE
TRACASSERIES
TRACEABILITIES
TRACEABILITY
TRACEABLENESS
TRACEABLENESSES
TRACELESSLY
TRACHEARIAN
TRACHEARIANS
TRACHEARIES
TRACHEATED
TRACHEATES
TRACHEIDAL
TRACHEIDES
TRACHEITIDES
TRACHEITIS
TRACHEITISES
TRACHELATE
TRACHEOLAR
TRACHEOLES
TRACHEOPHYTE
TRACHEOPHYTES
TRACHEOSCOPIES
TRACHEOSCOPY
TRACHEOSTOMIES
TRACHEOSTOMY
TRACHEOTOMIES
TRACHEOTOMY
TRACHINUSES
TRACHITISES
TRACHOMATOUS
TRACHYPTERUS
TRACHYPTERUSES
TRACHYTOID
TRACKBALLS
TRACKERBALL
TRACKERBALLS
TRACKLAYER
TRACKLAYERS
TRACKLAYING
TRACKLAYINGS
TRACKLEMENT
TRACKLEMENTS
TRACKLESSLY
TRACKLESSNESS
TRACKLESSNESSES
TRACKROADS
TRACKSIDES
TRACKSUITS
TRACKWALKER
TRACKWALKERS
TRACTABILITIES
TRACTABILITY
TRACTABLENESS
TRACTABLENESSES
TRACTARIAN
TRACTARIANS
TRACTATORS
TRACTILITIES
TRACTILITY
TRACTIONAL
TRACTORATION
TRACTORATIONS
TRACTORFEED
TRACTORFEEDS
TRACTRICES
TRADECRAFT
TRADECRAFTS
TRADEMARKED
TRADEMARKING
TRADEMARKS

TRADENAMES
TRADERSHIP
TRADERSHIPS
TRADESCANTIA
TRADESCANTIAS
TRADESFOLK
TRADESFOLKS
TRADESMANLIKE
TRADESPEOPLE
TRADESPEOPLES
TRADESPERSON
TRADESPERSONS
TRADESWOMAN
TRADESWOMEN
TRADITIONAL
TRADITIONALISE
TRADITIONALISED
TRADITIONALISES
TRADITIONALISM
TRADITIONALISMS
TRADITIONALIST
TRADITIONALISTS
TRADITIONALITY
TRADITIONALIZE
TRADITIONALIZED
TRADITIONALIZES
TRADITIONALLY
TRADITIONARILY
TRADITIONARY
TRADITIONER
TRADITIONERS
TRADITIONIST
TRADITIONISTS
TRADITIONLESS
TRADITIONS
TRADITORES
TRADUCEMENT
TRADUCEMENTS
TRADUCIANISM
TRADUCIANISMS
TRADUCIANIST
TRADUCIANISTIC
TRADUCIANISTS
TRADUCIANS
TRADUCIBLE
TRADUCINGLY
TRADUCINGS
TRADUCTION
TRADUCTIONS
TRADUCTIVE
TRAFFICABILITY
TRAFFICABLE
TRAFFICATOR
TRAFFICATORS
TRAFFICKED
TRAFFICKER
TRAFFICKERS
TRAFFICKIER
TRAFFICKIEST
TRAFFICKING
TRAFFICKINGS
TRAFFICLESS
TRAGACANTH
TRAGACANTHS
TRAGEDIANS
TRAGEDIENNE
TRAGEDIENNES
TRAGELAPHINE
TRAGELAPHS
TRAGICALLY
TRAGICALNESS
TRAGICALNESSES
TRAGICOMEDIES
TRAGICOMEDY
TRAGICOMIC
TRAGICOMICAL
TRAGICOMICALLY
TRAILBASTON
TRAILBASTONS
TRAILBLAZER
TRAILBLAZERS
TRAILBLAZING
TRAILBLAZINGS
TRAILBREAKER
TRAILBREAKERS
TRAILERABLE
TRAILERING
TRAILERINGS
TRAILERIST
TRAILERISTS
TRAILERITE
TRAILERITES
TRAILHEADS
TRAILINGLY
TRAINABILITIES
TRAINABILITY
TRAINBANDS
TRAINBEARER
TRAINBEARERS
TRAINEESHIP
TRAINEESHIPS
TRAINLOADS
TRAINSPOTTER
TRAINSPOTTERISH
TRAINSPOTTERS
TRAIPSINGS
TRAITORESS
TRAITORESSES
TRAITORHOOD
TRAITORHOODS
TRAITORISM
TRAITORISMS
TRAITOROUS
TRAITOROUSLY
TRAITOROUSNESS
TRAITORSHIP
TRAITORSHIPS
TRAITRESSES
TRAJECTILE
TRAJECTING
TRAJECTION
TRAJECTIONS
TRAJECTORIES
TRAJECTORY
TRALATICIOUS
TRALATITIOUS
TRAMELLING
TRAMMELERS
TRAMMELING
TRAMMELLED
TRAMMELLER
TRAMMELLERS
TRAMMELLING
TRAMONTANA
TRAMONTANAS
TRAMONTANE
TRAMONTANES
TRAMPETTES
TRAMPLINGS
TRAMPOLINE
TRAMPOLINED
TRAMPOLINER
TRAMPOLINERS
TRAMPOLINES
TRAMPOLINING
TRAMPOLININGS
TRAMPOLINIST
TRAMPOLINISTS
TRAMPOLINS
TRANCELIKE
TRANQUILER
TRANQUILEST
TRANQUILISATION
TRANQUILISE
TRANQUILISED
TRANQUILISER
TRANQUILISERS
TRANQUILISES
TRANQUILISING
TRANQUILISINGLY
TRANQUILITIES
TRANQUILITY
TRANQUILIZATION
TRANQUILIZE
TRANQUILIZED
TRANQUILIZER
TRANQUILIZERS
TRANQUILIZES
TRANQUILIZING
TRANQUILIZINGLY
TRANQUILLER
TRANQUILLEST
TRANQUILLISE
TRANQUILLISED
TRANQUILLISER
TRANQUILLISERS
TRANQUILLISES
TRANQUILLISING
TRANQUILLITIES
TRANQUILLITY
TRANQUILLIZE
TRANQUILLIZED
TRANQUILLIZER
TRANQUILLIZERS
TRANQUILLIZES
TRANQUILLIZING
TRANQUILLY
TRANQUILNESS
TRANQUILNESSES
TRANSACTED
TRANSACTING
TRANSACTINIDE
TRANSACTINIDES
TRANSACTION
TRANSACTIONAL
TRANSACTIONALLY
TRANSACTIONS
TRANSACTOR
TRANSACTORS
TRANSALPINE
TRANSALPINES
TRANSAMINASE
TRANSAMINASES
TRANSAMINATION
TRANSAMINATIONS
TRANSANDEAN
TRANSANDINE
TRANSATLANTIC
TRANSAXLES
TRANSCALENCIES
TRANSCALENCY
TRANSCALENT
TRANSCAUCASIAN
TRANSCEIVER
TRANSCEIVERS
TRANSCENDED
TRANSCENDENCE
TRANSCENDENCES
TRANSCENDENCIES
TRANSCENDENCY
TRANSCENDENT
TRANSCENDENTAL
TRANSCENDENTALS
TRANSCENDENTLY
TRANSCENDENTS
TRANSCENDING
TRANSCENDINGLY
TRANSCENDS
TRANSCODED
TRANSCODER
TRANSCODERS
TRANSCODES
TRANSCODING
TRANSCRANIAL
TRANSCRIBABLE
TRANSCRIBE
TRANSCRIBED
TRANSCRIBER
TRANSCRIBERS
TRANSCRIBES

TRANSCRIBING
TRANSCRIPT
TRANSCRIPTASE
TRANSCRIPTASES
TRANSCRIPTION
TRANSCRIPTIONAL
TRANSCRIPTIONS
TRANSCRIPTIVE
TRANSCRIPTIVELY
TRANSCRIPTOME
TRANSCRIPTOMES
TRANSCRIPTS
TRANSCULTURAL
TRANSCURRENT
TRANSCUTANEOUS
TRANSDERMAL
TRANSDUCED
TRANSDUCER
TRANSDUCERS
TRANSDUCES
TRANSDUCING
TRANSDUCTANT
TRANSDUCTANTS
TRANSDUCTION
TRANSDUCTIONAL
TRANSDUCTIONS
TRANSDUCTOR
TRANSDUCTORS
TRANSECTED
TRANSECTING
TRANSECTION
TRANSECTIONS
TRANSENNAS
TRANSEPTAL
TRANSEPTATE
TRANSEPTED
TRANSEXUAL
TRANSEXUALISM
TRANSEXUALISMS
TRANSEXUALITIES
TRANSEXUALITY
TRANSEXUALS
TRANSFECTED
TRANSFECTING
TRANSFECTION
TRANSFECTIONS
TRANSFECTS
TRANSFERABILITY
TRANSFERABLE
TRANSFERAL
TRANSFERALS
TRANSFERASE
TRANSFERASES
TRANSFEREE
TRANSFEREES
TRANSFERENCE
TRANSFERENCES
TRANSFERENTIAL
TRANSFEROR
TRANSFERORS
TRANSFERRABLE
TRANSFERRAL
TRANSFERRALS
TRANSFERRED
TRANSFERRER
TRANSFERRERS
TRANSFERRIBLE
TRANSFERRIN
TRANSFERRING
TRANSFERRINS
TRANSFIGURATION
TRANSFIGURE
TRANSFIGURED
TRANSFIGUREMENT
TRANSFIGURES
TRANSFIGURING
TRANSFINITE
TRANSFIXED
TRANSFIXES
TRANSFIXING
TRANSFIXION
TRANSFIXIONS
TRANSFORMABLE
TRANSFORMATION
TRANSFORMATIONS
TRANSFORMATIVE
TRANSFORMED
TRANSFORMER
TRANSFORMERS
TRANSFORMING
TRANSFORMINGS
TRANSFORMISM
TRANSFORMISMS
TRANSFORMIST
TRANSFORMISTIC
TRANSFORMISTS
TRANSFORMS
TRANSFUSABLE
TRANSFUSED
TRANSFUSER
TRANSFUSERS
TRANSFUSES
TRANSFUSIBLE
TRANSFUSING
TRANSFUSION
TRANSFUSIONAL
TRANSFUSIONIST
TRANSFUSIONISTS
TRANSFUSIONS
TRANSFUSIVE
TRANSFUSIVELY
TRANSGENDER
TRANSGENDERED
TRANSGENDERS
TRANSGENES
TRANSGENESES
TRANSGENESIS
TRANSGENIC
TRANSGENICS
TRANSGRESS
TRANSGRESSED
TRANSGRESSES
TRANSGRESSING
TRANSGRESSION
TRANSGRESSIONAL
TRANSGRESSIONS
TRANSGRESSIVE
TRANSGRESSIVELY
TRANSGRESSOR
TRANSGRESSORS
TRANSHIPMENT
TRANSHIPMENTS
TRANSHIPPED
TRANSHIPPER
TRANSHIPPERS
TRANSHIPPING
TRANSHIPPINGS
TRANSHISTORICAL
TRANSHUMANCE
TRANSHUMANCES
TRANSHUMANT
TRANSHUMANTS
TRANSHUMED
TRANSHUMES
TRANSHUMING
TRANSIENCE
TRANSIENCES
TRANSIENCIES
TRANSIENCY
TRANSIENTLY
TRANSIENTNESS
TRANSIENTNESSES
TRANSIENTS
TRANSILIENCE
TRANSILIENCES
TRANSILIENCIES
TRANSILIENCY
TRANSILIENT
TRANSILLUMINATE
TRANSISTHMIAN
TRANSISTOR
TRANSISTORISE
TRANSISTORISED
TRANSISTORISES
TRANSISTORISING
TRANSISTORIZE
TRANSISTORIZED
TRANSISTORIZES
TRANSISTORIZING
TRANSISTORS
TRANSITABLE
TRANSITING
TRANSITION
TRANSITIONAL
TRANSITIONALLY
TRANSITIONALS
TRANSITIONARY
TRANSITIONED
TRANSITIONING
TRANSITIONS
TRANSITIVE
TRANSITIVELY
TRANSITIVENESS
TRANSITIVES
TRANSITIVITIES
TRANSITIVITY
TRANSITORILY
TRANSITORINESS
TRANSITORY
TRANSLATABILITY
TRANSLATABLE
TRANSLATED
TRANSLATES
TRANSLATING
TRANSLATION
TRANSLATIONAL
TRANSLATIONALLY
TRANSLATIONS
TRANSLATIVE
TRANSLATIVES
TRANSLATOR
TRANSLATORIAL
TRANSLATORS
TRANSLATORY
TRANSLEITHAN
TRANSLITERATE
TRANSLITERATED
TRANSLITERATES
TRANSLITERATING
TRANSLITERATION
TRANSLITERATOR
TRANSLITERATORS
TRANSLOCATE
TRANSLOCATED
TRANSLOCATES
TRANSLOCATING
TRANSLOCATION
TRANSLOCATIONS
TRANSLUCENCE
TRANSLUCENCES
TRANSLUCENCIES
TRANSLUCENCY
TRANSLUCENT
TRANSLUCENTLY
TRANSLUCID
TRANSLUCIDITIES
TRANSLUCIDITY
TRANSLUMENAL
TRANSLUMINAL
TRANSLUNAR
TRANSLUNARY
TRANSMANCHE
TRANSMARINE
TRANSMEMBRANE
TRANSMEWED
TRANSMEWING
TRANSMIGRANT
TRANSMIGRANTS
TRANSMIGRATE
TRANSMIGRATED

TRANSMIGRATES
TRANSMIGRATING
TRANSMIGRATION
TRANSMIGRATIONS
TRANSMIGRATIVE
TRANSMIGRATOR
TRANSMIGRATORS
TRANSMIGRATORY
TRANSMISSIBLE
TRANSMISSION
TRANSMISSIONAL
TRANSMISSIONS
TRANSMISSIVE
TRANSMISSIVELY
TRANSMISSIVITY
TRANSMISSOMETER
TRANSMITTABLE
TRANSMITTAL
TRANSMITTALS
TRANSMITTANCE
TRANSMITTANCES
TRANSMITTANCIES
TRANSMITTANCY
TRANSMITTED
TRANSMITTER
TRANSMITTERS
TRANSMITTIBLE
TRANSMITTING
TRANSMITTIVITY
TRANSMOGRIFIED
TRANSMOGRIFIES
TRANSMOGRIFY
TRANSMOGRIFYING
TRANSMONTANE
TRANSMONTANES
TRANSMOUNTAIN
TRANSMOVED
TRANSMOVES
TRANSMOVING
TRANSMUNDANE
TRANSMUTABILITY
TRANSMUTABLE
TRANSMUTABLY
TRANSMUTATION
TRANSMUTATIONAL
TRANSMUTATIONS
TRANSMUTATIVE
TRANSMUTED
TRANSMUTER
TRANSMUTERS
TRANSMUTES
TRANSMUTING
TRANSNATIONAL
TRANSNATURAL
TRANSOCEANIC
TRANSONICS
TRANSPACIFIC
TRANSPADANE
TRANSPARENCE
TRANSPARENCES
TRANSPARENCIES
TRANSPARENCY
TRANSPARENT
TRANSPARENTISE
TRANSPARENTISED
TRANSPARENTISES
TRANSPARENTIZE
TRANSPARENTIZED
TRANSPARENTIZES
TRANSPARENTLY
TRANSPARENTNESS
TRANSPERSON
TRANSPERSONAL
TRANSPERSONS
TRANSPHOBIA
TRANSPHOBIAS
TRANSPHOBIC
TRANSPICUOUS
TRANSPICUOUSLY
TRANSPIERCE
TRANSPIERCED
TRANSPIERCES
TRANSPIERCING
TRANSPIRABLE
TRANSPIRATION
TRANSPIRATIONAL
TRANSPIRATIONS
TRANSPIRATORY
TRANSPIRED
TRANSPIRES
TRANSPIRING
TRANSPLACENTAL
TRANSPLANT
TRANSPLANTABLE
TRANSPLANTATION
TRANSPLANTED
TRANSPLANTER
TRANSPLANTERS
TRANSPLANTING
TRANSPLANTINGS
TRANSPLANTS
TRANSPOLAR
TRANSPONDER
TRANSPONDERS
TRANSPONDOR
TRANSPONDORS
TRANSPONTINE
TRANSPORTABLE
TRANSPORTAL
TRANSPORTALS
TRANSPORTANCE
TRANSPORTANCES
TRANSPORTATION
TRANSPORTATIONS
TRANSPORTED
TRANSPORTEDLY
TRANSPORTEDNESS
TRANSPORTER
TRANSPORTERS
TRANSPORTING
TRANSPORTINGLY
TRANSPORTINGS
TRANSPORTIVE
TRANSPORTS
TRANSPOSABILITY
TRANSPOSABLE
TRANSPOSAL
TRANSPOSALS
TRANSPOSED
TRANSPOSER
TRANSPOSERS
TRANSPOSES
TRANSPOSING
TRANSPOSINGS
TRANSPOSITION
TRANSPOSITIONAL
TRANSPOSITIONS
TRANSPOSITIVE
TRANSPOSON
TRANSPOSONS
TRANSPUTER
TRANSPUTERS
TRANSSEXUAL
TRANSSEXUALISM
TRANSSEXUALISMS
TRANSSEXUALITY
TRANSSEXUALS
TRANSSHAPE
TRANSSHAPED
TRANSSHAPES
TRANSSHAPING
TRANSSHIPMENT
TRANSSHIPMENTS
TRANSSHIPPED
TRANSSHIPPER
TRANSSHIPPERS
TRANSSHIPPING
TRANSSHIPPINGS
TRANSSHIPS
TRANSSONIC
TRANSTHORACIC
TRANSUBSTANTIAL
TRANSUDATE
TRANSUDATES
TRANSUDATION
TRANSUDATIONS
TRANSUDATORY
TRANSUDING
TRANSUMING
TRANSUMPTION
TRANSUMPTIONS
TRANSUMPTIVE
TRANSUMPTS
TRANSURANIAN
TRANSURANIC
TRANSURANICS
TRANSURANIUM
TRANSURETHRAL
TRANSVAGINAL
TRANSVALUATE
TRANSVALUATED
TRANSVALUATES
TRANSVALUATING
TRANSVALUATION
TRANSVALUATIONS
TRANSVALUE
TRANSVALUED
TRANSVALUER
TRANSVALUERS
TRANSVALUES
TRANSVALUING
TRANSVERSAL
TRANSVERSALITY
TRANSVERSALLY
TRANSVERSALS
TRANSVERSE
TRANSVERSED
TRANSVERSELY
TRANSVERSENESS
TRANSVERSES
TRANSVERSING
TRANSVERSION
TRANSVERSIONS
TRANSVERTER
TRANSVERTERS
TRANSVESTED
TRANSVESTIC
TRANSVESTING
TRANSVESTISM
TRANSVESTISMS
TRANSVESTIST
TRANSVESTISTS
TRANSVESTITE
TRANSVESTITES
TRANSVESTITISM
TRANSVESTITISMS
TRANSVESTS
TRANSWOMAN
TRANSWOMEN
TRAPANNERS
TRAPANNING
TRAPESINGS
TRAPEZIFORM
TRAPEZISTS
TRAPEZIUMS
TRAPEZIUSES
TRAPEZOHEDRA
TRAPEZOHEDRAL
TRAPEZOHEDRON
TRAPEZOHEDRONS
TRAPEZOIDAL
TRAPEZOIDS
TRAPNESTED
TRAPNESTING
TRAPPINESS
TRAPPINESSES
TRAPSHOOTER
TRAPSHOOTERS
TRAPSHOOTING
TRAPSHOOTINGS

TRASHERIES
TRASHINESS
TRASHINESSES
TRASHTRIES
TRATTORIAS
TRAUCHLING
TRAUMATICALLY
TRAUMATISATION
TRAUMATISATIONS
TRAUMATISE
TRAUMATISED
TRAUMATISES
TRAUMATISING
TRAUMATISM
TRAUMATISMS
TRAUMATIZATION
TRAUMATIZATIONS
TRAUMATIZE
TRAUMATIZED
TRAUMATIZES
TRAUMATIZING
TRAUMATOLOGICAL
TRAUMATOLOGIES
TRAUMATOLOGY
TRAUMATONASTIES
TRAUMATONASTY
TRAVAILING
TRAVELATOR
TRAVELATORS
TRAVELINGS
TRAVELLERS
TRAVELLING
TRAVELLINGS
TRAVELOGUE
TRAVELOGUES
TRAVERSABLE
TRAVERSALS
TRAVERSERS
TRAVERSING
TRAVERSINGS
TRAVERTINE
TRAVERTINES
TRAVERTINS
TRAVESTIED
TRAVESTIES
TRAVESTYING
TRAVOLATOR
TRAVOLATORS
TRAWLERMAN
TRAWLERMEN
TRAYCLOTHS
TRAYMOBILE
TRAYMOBILES
TRAZODONES
TREACHERER
TREACHERERS
TREACHERIES
TREACHEROUS
TREACHEROUSLY
TREACHEROUSNESS
TREACHETOUR
TREACHETOURS
TREACHOURS
TREACLIEST
TREACLINESS
TREACLINESSES
TREADLINGS
TREADMILLS
TREADWHEEL
TREADWHEELS
TREASONABLE
TREASONABLENESS
TREASONABLY
TREASONOUS
TREASURABLE
TREASURELESS
TREASURERS
TREASURERSHIP
TREASURERSHIPS
TREASURIES
TREASURING
TREATABILITIES
TREATABILITY
TREATMENTS
TREATYLESS
TREBBIANOS
TREBLENESS
TREBLENESSES
TREBUCHETS
TREBUCKETS
TRECENTIST
TRECENTISTS
TREDECILLION
TREDECILLIONS
TREDRILLES
TREEHOPPER
TREEHOPPERS
TREEHOUSES
TREELESSNESS
TREELESSNESSES
TREENWARES
TREGETOURS
TREHALOSES
TREILLAGED
TREILLAGES
TREKSCHUIT
TREKSCHUITS
TRELLISING
TRELLISWORK
TRELLISWORKS
TREMATODES
TREMATOIDS
TREMBLEMENT
TREMBLEMENTS
TREMBLIEST
TREMBLINGLY
TREMBLINGS
TREMENDOUS
TREMENDOUSLY
TREMENDOUSNESS
TREMOLANDI
TREMOLANDO
TREMOLANDOS
TREMOLANTS
TREMOLITES
TREMOLITIC
TREMORLESS
TREMULANTS
TREMULATED
TREMULATES
TREMULATING
TREMULOUSLY
TREMULOUSNESS
TREMULOUSNESSES
TRENCHANCIES
TRENCHANCY
TRENCHANTLY
TRENCHARDS
TRENCHERMAN
TRENCHERMEN
TRENDIFIED
TRENDIFIES
TRENDIFYING
TRENDINESS
TRENDINESSES
TRENDSETTER
TRENDSETTERS
TRENDSETTING
TRENDSETTINGS
TRENDYISMS
TREPANATION
TREPANATIONS
TREPANNERS
TREPANNING
TREPANNINGS
TREPHINATION
TREPHINATIONS
TREPHINERS
TREPHINING
TREPHININGS
TREPIDATION
TREPIDATIONS
TREPIDATORY
TREPONEMAL
TREPONEMAS
TREPONEMATA
TREPONEMATOSES
TREPONEMATOSIS
TREPONEMATOUS
TREPONEMES
TRESPASSED
TRESPASSER
TRESPASSERS
TRESPASSES
TRESPASSING
TRESTLETREE
TRESTLETREES
TRESTLEWORK
TRESTLEWORKS
TRETINOINS
TREVALLIES
TRIABLENESS
TRIABLENESSES
TRIACETATE
TRIACETATES
TRIACONTER
TRIACONTERS
TRIACTINAL
TRIADELPHOUS
TRIADICALLY
TRIALITIES
TRIALLINGS
TRIALLISTS
TRIALOGUES
TRIALWARES
TRIAMCINOLONE
TRIAMCINOLONES
TRIANDRIAN
TRIANDROUS
TRIANGULAR
TRIANGULARITIES
TRIANGULARITY
TRIANGULARLY
TRIANGULATE
TRIANGULATED
TRIANGULATELY
TRIANGULATES
TRIANGULATING
TRIANGULATION
TRIANGULATIONS
TRIAPSIDAL
TRIARCHIES
TRIATHLETE
TRIATHLETES
TRIATHLONS
TRIATOMICALLY
TRIAXIALITIES
TRIAXIALITY
TRIBADISMS
TRIBALISMS
TRIBALISTIC
TRIBALISTS
TRIBESPEOPLE
TRIBESWOMAN
TRIBESWOMEN
TRIBOELECTRIC
TRIBOLOGICAL
TRIBOLOGIES
TRIBOLOGIST
TRIBOLOGISTS
TRIBOMETER
TRIBOMETERS
TRIBRACHIAL
TRIBRACHIC
TRIBROMOETHANOL
TRIBROMOMETHANE
TRIBULATED
TRIBULATES
TRIBULATING
TRIBULATION

TRIBULATIONS
TRIBUNATES
TRIBUNESHIP
TRIBUNESHIPS
TRIBUNICIAL
TRIBUNICIAN
TRIBUNITIAL
TRIBUNITIAN
TRIBUTARIES
TRIBUTARILY
TRIBUTARINESS
TRIBUTARINESSES
TRICAMERAL
TRICARBOXYLIC
TRICARPELLARY
TRICENTENARIES
TRICENTENARY
TRICENTENNIAL
TRICENTENNIALS
TRICEPHALOUS
TRICERATOPS
TRICERATOPSES
TRICERIONS
TRICHIASES
TRICHIASIS
TRICHINELLA
TRICHINELLAE
TRICHINELLAS
TRICHINIASES
TRICHINIASIS
TRICHINISATION
TRICHINISATIONS
TRICHINISE
TRICHINISED
TRICHINISES
TRICHINISING
TRICHINIZATION
TRICHINIZATIONS
TRICHINIZE
TRICHINIZED
TRICHINIZES
TRICHINIZING
TRICHINOSE
TRICHINOSED
TRICHINOSES
TRICHINOSING
TRICHINOSIS
TRICHINOTIC
TRICHINOUS
TRICHLORACETIC
TRICHLORFON
TRICHLORFONS
TRICHLORIDE
TRICHLORIDES
TRICHLOROACETIC
TRICHLOROETHANE
TRICHLORPHON
TRICHLORPHONS
TRICHOBACTERIA
TRICHOCYST
TRICHOCYSTIC
TRICHOCYSTS
TRICHOGYNE
TRICHOGYNES
TRICHOGYNIAL
TRICHOGYNIC
TRICHOLOGICAL
TRICHOLOGIES
TRICHOLOGIST
TRICHOLOGISTS
TRICHOLOGY
TRICHOMONACIDAL
TRICHOMONACIDE
TRICHOMONACIDES
TRICHOMONAD
TRICHOMONADAL
TRICHOMONADS
TRICHOMONAL
TRICHOMONIASES
TRICHOMONIASIS
TRICHOPHYTON
TRICHOPHYTONS
TRICHOPHYTOSES
TRICHOPHYTOSIS
TRICHOPTERAN
TRICHOPTERANS
TRICHOPTERIST
TRICHOPTERISTS
TRICHOPTEROUS
TRICHOTHECENE
TRICHOTHECENES
TRICHOTOMIC
TRICHOTOMIES
TRICHOTOMISE
TRICHOTOMISED
TRICHOTOMISES
TRICHOTOMISING
TRICHOTOMIZE
TRICHOTOMIZED
TRICHOTOMIZES
TRICHOTOMIZING
TRICHOTOMOUS
TRICHOTOMOUSLY
TRICHOTOMY
TRICHROISM
TRICHROISMS
TRICHROMAT
TRICHROMATIC
TRICHROMATISM
TRICHROMATISMS
TRICHROMATS
TRICHROMIC
TRICHROMICS
TRICHRONOUS
TRICHURIASES
TRICHURIASIS
TRICKERIES
TRICKINESS
TRICKINESSES
TRICKISHLY
TRICKISHNESS
TRICKISHNESSES
TRICKLIEST
TRICKLINGLY
TRICKLINGS
TRICKSIEST
TRICKSINESS
TRICKSINESSES
TRICKSTERING
TRICKSTERINGS
TRICKSTERS
TRICKTRACK
TRICKTRACKS
TRICLINIUM
TRICLOSANS
TRICOLETTE
TRICOLETTES
TRICOLORED
TRICOLOURED
TRICOLOURS
TRICONSONANTAL
TRICONSONANTIC
TRICORNERED
TRICORPORATE
TRICORPORATED
TRICOSTATE
TRICOTEUSE
TRICOTEUSES
TRICOTINES
TRICROTISM
TRICROTISMS
TRICROTOUS
TRICUSPIDAL
TRICUSPIDATE
TRICUSPIDS
TRICYCLERS
TRICYCLICS
TRICYCLING
TRICYCLINGS
TRICYCLIST
TRICYCLISTS
TRIDACTYLOUS
TRIDENTATE
TRIDIMENSIONAL
TRIDOMINIA
TRIDOMINIUM
TRIDOMINIUMS
TRIDYMITES
TRIENNIALLY
TRIENNIALS
TRIENNIUMS
TRIERARCHAL
TRIERARCHIES
TRIERARCHS
TRIERARCHY
TRIETHIODIDE
TRIETHIODIDES
TRIETHYLAMINE
TRIETHYLAMINES
TRIFACIALS
TRIFARIOUS
TRIFFIDIAN
TRIFFIDIER
TRIFFIDIEST
TRIFLINGLY
TRIFLINGNESS
TRIFLINGNESSES
TRIFLUOPERAZINE
TRIFLURALIN
TRIFLURALINS
TRIFOLIATE
TRIFOLIATED
TRIFOLIOLATE
TRIFOLIUMS
TRIFURCATE
TRIFURCATED
TRIFURCATES
TRIFURCATING
TRIFURCATION
TRIFURCATIONS
TRIGAMISTS
TRIGEMINAL
TRIGEMINALS
TRIGEMINUS
TRIGGERFISH
TRIGGERFISHES
TRIGGERING
TRIGGERLESS
TRIGGERMAN
TRIGGERMEN
TRIGLYCERIDE
TRIGLYCERIDES
TRIGLYPHIC
TRIGLYPHICAL
TRIGNESSES
TRIGONALLY
TRIGONOMETER
TRIGONOMETERS
TRIGONOMETRIC
TRIGONOMETRICAL
TRIGONOMETRIES
TRIGONOMETRY
TRIGRAMMATIC
TRIGRAMMIC
TRIGRAPHIC
TRIHALOMETHANE
TRIHALOMETHANES
TRIHEDRALS
TRIHEDRONS
TRIHYBRIDS
TRIHYDRATE
TRIHYDRATED
TRIHYDRATES
TRIHYDROXY
TRIIODOMETHANE
TRIIODOMETHANES
TRILATERAL
TRILATERALISM
TRILATERALISMS
TRILATERALIST

T

TRILATERALISTS
TRILATERALLY
TRILATERALS
TRILATERATION
TRILATERATIONS
TRILINEATE
TRILINGUAL
TRILINGUALISM
TRILINGUALISMS
TRILINGUALLY
TRILITERAL
TRILITERALISM
TRILITERALISMS
TRILITERALS
TRILITHONS
TRILLIONAIRE
TRILLIONAIRES
TRILLIONTH
TRILLIONTHS
TRILOBATED
TRILOBITES
TRILOBITIC
TRILOCULAR
TRIMERISMS
TRIMESTERS
TRIMESTRAL
TRIMESTRIAL
TRIMETHADIONE
TRIMETHADIONES
TRIMETHOPRIM
TRIMETHOPRIMS
TRIMETHYLAMINE
TRIMETHYLAMINES
TRIMETHYLENE
TRIMETHYLENES
TRIMETRICAL
TRIMETROGON
TRIMETROGONS
TRIMMINGLY
TRIMNESSES
TRIMOLECULAR
TRIMONTHLY
TRIMORPHIC
TRIMORPHISM
TRIMORPHISMS
TRIMORPHOUS
TRIMPHONES
TRINACRIAN
TRINACRIFORM
TRINISCOPE
TRINISCOPES
TRINITARIAN
TRINITARIANS
TRINITRATE
TRINITRATES
TRINITRINS
TRINITROBENZENE
TRINITROCRESOL
TRINITROCRESOLS
TRINITROPHENOL
TRINITROPHENOLS
TRINITROTOLUENE
TRINITROTOLUOL
TRINITROTOLUOLS
TRINKETERS
TRINKETING
TRINKETINGS
TRINKETRIES
TRINOCULAR
TRINOMIALISM
TRINOMIALISMS
TRINOMIALIST
TRINOMIALISTS
TRINOMIALLY
TRINOMIALS
TRINUCLEOTIDE
TRINUCLEOTIDES
TRIOECIOUS
TRIOXOBORIC
TRIOXYGENS
TRIPALMITIN
TRIPALMITINS
TRIPARTISM
TRIPARTISMS
TRIPARTITE
TRIPARTITELY
TRIPARTITION
TRIPARTITIONS
TRIPEHOUND
TRIPEHOUNDS
TRIPERSONAL
TRIPERSONALISM
TRIPERSONALISMS
TRIPERSONALIST
TRIPERSONALISTS
TRIPERSONALITY
TRIPETALOUS
TRIPHAMMER
TRIPHAMMERS
TRIPHENYLAMINE
TRIPHENYLAMINES
TRIPHIBIOUS
TRIPHOSPHATE
TRIPHOSPHATES
TRIPHTHONG
TRIPHTHONGAL
TRIPHTHONGS
TRIPHYLITE
TRIPHYLITES
TRIPHYLLOUS
TRIPINNATE
TRIPINNATELY
TRIPITAKAS
TRIPLENESS
TRIPLENESSES
TRIPLETAIL
TRIPLETAILS
TRIPLEXING
TRIPLICATE
TRIPLICATED
TRIPLICATES
TRIPLICATING
TRIPLICATION
TRIPLICATIONS
TRIPLICITIES
TRIPLICITY
TRIPLOBLASTIC
TRIPLOIDIES
TRIPMETERS
TRIPPERIER
TRIPPERIEST
TRIPPERISH
TRIPPINGLY
TRIPTEROUS
TRIPTYQUES
TRIPUDIARY
TRIPUDIATE
TRIPUDIATED
TRIPUDIATES
TRIPUDIATING
TRIPUDIATION
TRIPUDIATIONS
TRIQUETRAE
TRIQUETRAL
TRIQUETRAS
TRIQUETROUS
TRIQUETROUSLY
TRIQUETRUM
TRIRADIATE
TRIRADIATELY
TRISACCHARIDE
TRISACCHARIDES
TRISAGIONS
TRISECTING
TRISECTION
TRISECTIONS
TRISECTORS
TRISECTRICES
TRISECTRIX
TRISKELION
TRISKELIONS
TRISOCTAHEDRA
TRISOCTAHEDRAL
TRISOCTAHEDRON
TRISOCTAHEDRONS
TRISTEARIN
TRISTEARINS
TRISTESSES
TRISTFULLY
TRISTFULNESS
TRISTFULNESSES
TRISTICHIC
TRISTICHOUS
TRISTIMULUS
TRISUBSTITUTED
TRISULCATE
TRISULFIDE
TRISULFIDES
TRISULPHIDE
TRISULPHIDES
TRISYLLABIC
TRISYLLABICAL
TRISYLLABICALLY
TRISYLLABLE
TRISYLLABLES
TRITAGONIST
TRITAGONISTS
TRITANOPES
TRITANOPIA
TRITANOPIAS
TRITANOPIC
TRITENESSES
TRITERNATE
TRITHEISMS
TRITHEISTIC
TRITHEISTICAL
TRITHEISTS
TRITHIONATE
TRITHIONATES
TRITHIONIC
TRITIATING
TRITIATION
TRITIATIONS
TRITICALES
TRITICALLY
TRITICALNESS
TRITICALNESSES
TRITICEOUS
TRITICISMS
TRITUBERCULAR
TRITUBERCULATE
TRITUBERCULIES
TRITUBERCULISM
TRITUBERCULISMS
TRITUBERCULY
TRITURABLE
TRITURATED
TRITURATES
TRITURATING
TRITURATION
TRITURATIONS
TRITURATOR
TRITURATORS
TRIUMPHALISM
TRIUMPHALISMS
TRIUMPHALIST
TRIUMPHALISTS
TRIUMPHALS
TRIUMPHANT
TRIUMPHANTLY
TRIUMPHERIES
TRIUMPHERS
TRIUMPHERY
TRIUMPHING
TRIUMPHINGS
TRIUMVIRAL
TRIUMVIRATE
TRIUMVIRATES
TRIUMVIRIES
TRIUNITIES

T

TRIVALENCE
TRIVALENCES
TRIVALENCIES
TRIVALENCY
TRIVALVULAR
TRIVIALISATION
TRIVIALISATIONS
TRIVIALISE
TRIVIALISED
TRIVIALISES
TRIVIALISING
TRIVIALISM
TRIVIALISMS
TRIVIALIST
TRIVIALISTS
TRIVIALITIES
TRIVIALITY
TRIVIALIZATION
TRIVIALIZATIONS
TRIVIALIZE
TRIVIALIZED
TRIVIALIZES
TRIVIALIZING
TRIVIALNESS
TRIVIALNESSES
TRIWEEKLIES
TROCHAICALLY
TROCHANTER
TROCHANTERAL
TROCHANTERIC
TROCHANTERS
TROCHEAMETER
TROCHEAMETERS
TROCHELMINTH
TROCHELMINTHS
TROCHILUSES
TROCHISCUS
TROCHISCUSES
TROCHLEARS
TROCHOIDAL
TROCHOIDALLY
TROCHOMETER
TROCHOMETERS
TROCHOPHORE
TROCHOPHORES
TROCHOSPHERE
TROCHOSPHERES
TROCHOTRON
TROCHOTRONS
TROCTOLITE
TROCTOLITES
TROGLODYTE
TROGLODYTES
TROGLODYTIC
TROGLODYTICAL
TROGLODYTISM
TROGLODYTISMS
TROLLEYBUS
TROLLEYBUSES
TROLLEYBUSSES
TROLLEYING
TROLLIUSES
TROLLOPEES
TROLLOPIER
TROLLOPIEST
TROLLOPING
TROLLOPISH
TROMBICULID
TROMBICULIDS
TROMBIDIASES
TROMBIDIASIS
TROMBONIST
TROMBONISTS
TROMOMETER
TROMOMETERS
TROMOMETRIC
TROOPSHIPS
TROOSTITES
TROPAEOLIN
TROPAEOLINS
TROPAEOLUM
TROPAEOLUMS
TROPARIONS
TROPEOLINS
TROPHALLACTIC
TROPHALLAXES
TROPHALLAXIS
TROPHESIAL
TROPHESIES
TROPHICALLY
TROPHOBIOSES
TROPHOBIOSIS
TROPHOBIOTIC
TROPHOBLAST
TROPHOBLASTIC
TROPHOBLASTS
TROPHOLOGIES
TROPHOLOGY
TROPHONEUROSES
TROPHONEUROSIS
TROPHOPLASM
TROPHOPLASMS
TROPHOTACTIC
TROPHOTAXES
TROPHOTAXIS
TROPHOTROPIC
TROPHOTROPISM
TROPHOTROPISMS
TROPHOZOITE
TROPHOZOITES
TROPICALISATION
TROPICALISE
TROPICALISED
TROPICALISES
TROPICALISING
TROPICALITIES
TROPICALITY
TROPICALIZATION
TROPICALIZE
TROPICALIZED
TROPICALIZES
TROPICALIZING
TROPICALLY
TROPICBIRD
TROPICBIRDS
TROPISMATIC
TROPOCOLLAGEN
TROPOCOLLAGENS
TROPOLOGIC
TROPOLOGICAL
TROPOLOGICALLY
TROPOLOGIES
TROPOMYOSIN
TROPOMYOSINS
TROPOPAUSE
TROPOPAUSES
TROPOPHILOUS
TROPOPHYTE
TROPOPHYTES
TROPOPHYTIC
TROPOSCATTER
TROPOSCATTERS
TROPOSPHERE
TROPOSPHERES
TROPOSPHERIC
TROPOTAXES
TROPOTAXIS
TROTHPLIGHT
TROTHPLIGHTED
TROTHPLIGHTING
TROTHPLIGHTS
TROUBADOUR
TROUBADOURS
TROUBLEDLY
TROUBLEFREE
TROUBLEMAKER
TROUBLEMAKERS
TROUBLEMAKING
TROUBLEMAKINGS
TROUBLESHOOT
TROUBLESHOOTER
TROUBLESHOOTERS
TROUBLESHOOTING
TROUBLESHOOTS
TROUBLESHOT
TROUBLESOME
TROUBLESOMELY
TROUBLESOMENESS
TROUBLINGS
TROUBLOUSLY
TROUBLOUSNESS
TROUBLOUSNESSES
TROUGHINGS
TROUGHLIKE
TROUNCINGS
TROUSERING
TROUSERINGS
TROUSERLESS
TROUSSEAUS
TROUSSEAUX
TROUTLINGS
TROUTSTONE
TROUTSTONES
TROUVAILLE
TROUVAILLES
TROWELLERS
TROWELLING
TRUANTINGS
TRUANTRIES
TRUANTSHIP
TRUANTSHIPS
TRUCKLINES
TRUCKLINGS
TRUCKLOADS
TRUCKMASTER
TRUCKMASTERS
TRUCKSTOPS
TRUCULENCE
TRUCULENCES
TRUCULENCIES
TRUCULENCY
TRUCULENTLY
TRUEHEARTED
TRUEHEARTEDNESS
TRUENESSES
TRUEPENNIES
TRUFFLINGS
TRUMPERIES
TRUMPETERS
TRUMPETING
TRUMPETINGS
TRUMPETLIKE
TRUMPETWEED
TRUMPETWEEDS
TRUNCATELY
TRUNCATING
TRUNCATINGS
TRUNCATION
TRUNCATIONS
TRUNCHEONED
TRUNCHEONER
TRUNCHEONERS
TRUNCHEONING
TRUNCHEONS
TRUNKFISHES
TRUNKSLEEVE
TRUNKSLEEVES
TRUNKWORKS
TRUNNIONED
TRUSTABILITIES
TRUSTABILITY
TRUSTAFARIAN
TRUSTAFARIANS
TRUSTBUSTER
TRUSTBUSTERS
TRUSTBUSTING
TRUSTBUSTINGS
TRUSTEEING
TRUSTEESHIP
TRUSTEESHIPS

TRUSTFULLY
TRUSTFULNESS
TRUSTFULNESSES
TRUSTINESS
TRUSTINESSES
TRUSTINGLY
TRUSTINGNESS
TRUSTINGNESSES
TRUSTLESSLY
TRUSTLESSNESS
TRUSTLESSNESSES
TRUSTWORTHIER
TRUSTWORTHIEST
TRUSTWORTHILY
TRUSTWORTHINESS
TRUSTWORTHY
TRUTHFULLY
TRUTHFULNESS
TRUTHFULNESSES
TRUTHINESS
TRUTHINESSES
TRUTHLESSNESS
TRUTHLESSNESSES
TRYINGNESS
TRYINGNESSES
TRYPAFLAVINE
TRYPAFLAVINES
TRYPANOCIDAL
TRYPANOCIDE
TRYPANOCIDES
TRYPANOSOMAL
TRYPANOSOME
TRYPANOSOMES
TRYPANOSOMIASES
TRYPANOSOMIASIS
TRYPANOSOMIC
TRYPARSAMIDE
TRYPARSAMIDES
TRYPSINOGEN
TRYPSINOGENS
TRYPTAMINE
TRYPTAMINES
TRYPTOPHAN
TRYPTOPHANE
TRYPTOPHANES
TRYPTOPHANS
TSAREVICHES
TSAREVITCH
TSAREVITCHES
TSCHERNOSEM
TSCHERNOSEMS
TSESAREVICH
TSESAREVICHES
TSESAREVITCH
TSESAREVITCHES
TSESAREVNA
TSESAREVNAS
TSESAREWICH
TSESAREWICHES
TSESAREWITCH
TSESAREWITCHES
TSOTSITAAL
TSOTSITAALS
TSUNAMIGENIC
TSUTSUGAMUSHI
TSUTSUGAMUSHIS
TUBBINESSES
TUBECTOMIES
TUBERACEOUS
TUBERCULAR
TUBERCULARLY
TUBERCULARS
TUBERCULATE
TUBERCULATED
TUBERCULATELY
TUBERCULATION
TUBERCULATIONS
TUBERCULES
TUBERCULIN
TUBERCULINS
TUBERCULISATION
TUBERCULISE
TUBERCULISED
TUBERCULISES
TUBERCULISING
TUBERCULIZATION
TUBERCULIZE
TUBERCULIZED
TUBERCULIZES
TUBERCULIZING
TUBERCULOID
TUBERCULOMA
TUBERCULOMAS
TUBERCULOMATA
TUBERCULOSE
TUBERCULOSED
TUBERCULOSES
TUBERCULOSIS
TUBERCULOUS
TUBERCULOUSLY
TUBERCULUM
TUBERIFEROUS
TUBERIFORM
TUBEROSITIES
TUBEROSITY
TUBICOLOUS
TUBIFICIDS
TUBIFLOROUS
TUBOCURARINE
TUBOCURARINES
TUBOPLASTIES
TUBOPLASTY
TUBULARIAN
TUBULARIANS
TUBULARITIES
TUBULARITY
TUBULATING
TUBULATION
TUBULATIONS
TUBULATORS
TUBULATURE
TUBULATURES
TUBULIFLORAL
TUBULIFLOROUS
TUBULOUSLY
TUCKAMORES
TUCKERBAGS
TUCKERBOXES
TUFFACEOUS
TUFFTAFFETA
TUFFTAFFETAS
TUFFTAFFETIES
TUFFTAFFETY
TUFTAFFETA
TUFTAFFETAS
TUFTAFFETIES
TUFTAFFETY
TUILLETTES
TUILYIEING
TUILZIEING
TUITIONARY
TULARAEMIA
TULARAEMIAS
TULARAEMIC
TULAREMIAS
TULIPOMANIA
TULIPOMANIAS
TULIPWOODS
TUMATAKURU
TUMATAKURUS
TUMBLEBUGS
TUMBLEDOWN
TUMBLEHOME
TUMBLEHOMES
TUMBLERFUL
TUMBLERFULS
TUMBLERSFUL
TUMBLESETS
TUMBLEWEED
TUMBLEWEEDS
TUMEFACIENT
TUMEFACTION
TUMEFACTIONS
TUMESCENCE
TUMESCENCES
TUMESCENTLY
TUMIDITIES
TUMIDNESSES
TUMORGENIC
TUMORGENICITIES
TUMORGENICITY
TUMORIGENESES
TUMORIGENESIS
TUMORIGENIC
TUMORIGENICITY
TUMULOSITIES
TUMULOSITY
TUMULTUARY
TUMULTUATE
TUMULTUATED
TUMULTUATES
TUMULTUATING
TUMULTUATION
TUMULTUATIONS
TUMULTUOUS
TUMULTUOUSLY
TUMULTUOUSNESS
TUNABILITIES
TUNABILITY
TUNABLENESS
TUNABLENESSES
TUNBELLIED
TUNBELLIES
TUNEFULNESS
TUNEFULNESSES
TUNELESSLY
TUNELESSNESS
TUNELESSNESSES
TUNESMITHS
TUNGSTATES
TUNGSTITES
TUNNELINGS
TUNNELLERS
TUNNELLIKE
TUNNELLING
TUNNELLINGS
TUPPENNIES
TUPTOWINGS
TURACOVERDIN
TURACOVERDINS
TURANGAWAEWAE
TURANGAWAEWAES
TURBELLARIAN
TURBELLARIANS
TURBIDIMETER
TURBIDIMETERS
TURBIDIMETRIC
TURBIDIMETRIES
TURBIDIMETRY
TURBIDITES
TURBIDITIES
TURBIDNESS
TURBIDNESSES
TURBINACIOUS
TURBINATED
TURBINATES
TURBINATION
TURBINATIONS
TURBOCHARGED
TURBOCHARGER
TURBOCHARGERS
TURBOCHARGING
TURBOCHARGINGS
TURBOELECTRIC
TURBOGENERATOR
TURBOGENERATORS
TURBOMACHINERY
TURBOPROPS
TURBOSHAFT
TURBOSHAFTS

TURBULATOR
TURBULATORS
TURBULENCE
TURBULENCES
TURBULENCIES
TURBULENCY
TURBULENTLY
TURCOPOLES
TURCOPOLIER
TURCOPOLIERS
TURDUCKENS
TURFGRASSES
TURFINESSES
TURFSKIING
TURFSKIINGS
TURGENCIES
TURGESCENCE
TURGESCENCES
TURGESCENCIES
TURGESCENCY
TURGESCENT
TURGIDITIES
TURGIDNESS
TURGIDNESSES
TURMOILING
TURNABOUTS
TURNAGAINS
TURNAROUND
TURNAROUNDS
TURNBROACH
TURNBROACHES
TURNBUCKLE
TURNBUCKLES
TURNIPIEST
TURNROUNDS
TURNSTILES
TURNSTONES
TURNTABLES
TURNTABLIST
TURNTABLISTS
TURNVEREIN
TURNVEREINS
TUROPHILES
TURPENTINE
TURPENTINED
TURPENTINES
TURPENTINIER
TURPENTINIEST
TURPENTINING
TURPENTINY
TURPITUDES
TURQUOISES
TURRIBANTS
TURRICULATE
TURRICULATED
TURTLEBACK
TURTLEBACKS
TURTLEDOVE
TURTLEDOVES
TURTLEHEAD
TURTLEHEADS
TURTLENECK
TURTLENECKED
TURTLENECKS
TUSSOCKIER
TUSSOCKIEST
TUTELARIES
TUTIORISMS
TUTIORISTS
TUTORESSES
TUTORIALLY
TUTORISING
TUTORIZING
TUTORSHIPS
TUTOYERING
TUTWORKERS
TUTWORKMAN
TUTWORKMEN
TWADDLIEST
TWADDLINGS
TWALPENNIES
TWANGINGLY
TWANGLINGLY
TWANGLINGS
TWATTLINGS
TWAYBLADES
TWEEDINESS
TWEEDINESSES
TWEEDLEDEE
TWEEDLEDEED
TWEEDLEDEEING
TWEEDLEDEES
TWEENAGERS
TWEENESSES
TWELVEFOLD
TWELVEMONTH
TWELVEMONTHS
TWENTIETHS
TWENTYFOLD
TWENTYFOLDS
TWICHILDREN
TWIDDLIEST
TWIDDLINGS
TWILIGHTED
TWILIGHTING
TWINBERRIES
TWINFLOWER
TWINFLOWERS
TWINKLIEST
TWINKLINGS
TWISTABILITIES
TWISTABILITY
TWITCHIEST
TWITCHINGS
TWITTERATI
TWITTERERS
TWITTERIER
TWITTERIEST
TWITTERING
TWITTERINGLY
TWITTERINGS
TWITTINGLY
TWOFOLDNESS
TWOFOLDNESSES
TWOPENCEWORTH
TWOPENCEWORTHS
TWOPENNIES
TWOSEATERS
TYCOONATES
TYCOONERIES
TYLECTOMIES
TYMPANIFORM
TYMPANISTS
TYMPANITES
TYMPANITESES
TYMPANITIC
TYMPANITIS
TYMPANITISES
TYNDALLIMETRIES
TYNDALLIMETRY
TYPECASTER
TYPECASTERS
TYPECASTING
TYPECASTINGS
TYPEFOUNDER
TYPEFOUNDERS
TYPEFOUNDING
TYPEFOUNDINGS
TYPEFOUNDRIES
TYPEFOUNDRY
TYPESCRIPT
TYPESCRIPTS
TYPESETTER
TYPESETTERS
TYPESETTING
TYPESETTINGS
TYPESTYLES
TYPEWRITER
TYPEWRITERS
TYPEWRITES
TYPEWRITING
TYPEWRITINGS
TYPEWRITTEN
TYPHACEOUS
TYPHLITISES
TYPHLOLOGIES
TYPHLOLOGY
TYPHLOSOLE
TYPHLOSOLES
TYPHOGENIC
TYPHOIDINS
TYPICALITIES
TYPICALITY
TYPICALNESS
TYPICALNESSES
TYPIFICATION
TYPIFICATIONS
TYPOGRAPHED
TYPOGRAPHER
TYPOGRAPHERS
TYPOGRAPHIA
TYPOGRAPHIC
TYPOGRAPHICAL
TYPOGRAPHICALLY
TYPOGRAPHIES
TYPOGRAPHING
TYPOGRAPHIST
TYPOGRAPHISTS
TYPOGRAPHS
TYPOGRAPHY
TYPOLOGICAL
TYPOLOGICALLY
TYPOLOGIES
TYPOLOGIST
TYPOLOGISTS
TYPOMANIAS
TYPOTHETAE
TYRANNESSES
TYRANNICAL
TYRANNICALLY
TYRANNICALNESS
TYRANNICIDAL
TYRANNICIDE
TYRANNICIDES
TYRANNISED
TYRANNISER
TYRANNISERS
TYRANNISES
TYRANNISING
TYRANNIZED
TYRANNIZER
TYRANNIZERS
TYRANNIZES
TYRANNIZING
TYRANNOSAUR
TYRANNOSAURS
TYRANNOSAURUS
TYRANNOSAURUSES
TYRANNOUSLY
TYRANNOUSNESS
TYRANNOUSNESSES
TYREMAKERS
TYROCIDINE
TYROCIDINES
TYROCIDINS
TYROGLYPHID
TYROGLYPHIDS
TYROPITTAS
TYROSINASE
TYROSINASES
TYROTHRICIN
TYROTHRICINS

U

UBERSEXUAL
UBERSEXUALS
UBIQUARIAN
UBIQUINONE
UBIQUINONES
UBIQUITARIAN
UBIQUITARIANISM
UBIQUITARIANS
UBIQUITARY
UBIQUITIES
UBIQUITINATION
UBIQUITINATIONS
UBIQUITINS
UBIQUITOUS
UBIQUITOUSLY
UBIQUITOUSNESS
UDOMETRIES
UFOLOGICAL
UFOLOGISTS
UGLIFICATION
UGLIFICATIONS
UGLINESSES
UGSOMENESS
UGSOMENESSES
UINTAHITES
UINTATHERE
UINTATHERES
UITLANDERS
ULCERATING
ULCERATION
ULCERATIONS
ULCERATIVE
ULCEROGENIC
ULCEROUSLY
ULCEROUSNESS
ULCEROUSNESSES
ULOTRICHIES
ULOTRICHOUS
ULSTERETTE
ULSTERETTES
ULTERIORLY
ULTIMACIES
ULTIMATELY
ULTIMATENESS
ULTIMATENESSES
ULTIMATING
ULTIMATUMS
ULTIMOGENITURE
ULTIMOGENITURES
ULTRABASIC
ULTRABASICS
ULTRACAREFUL
ULTRACASUAL
ULTRACAUTIOUS
ULTRACENTRIFUGE
ULTRACIVILISED
ULTRACIVILIZED
ULTRACLEAN
ULTRACOMMERCIAL
ULTRACOMPACT
ULTRACOMPETENT
ULTRACONVENIENT
ULTRACREPIDATE
ULTRACREPIDATED
ULTRACREPIDATES
ULTRACRITICAL
ULTRADEMOCRATIC
ULTRADENSE
ULTRADISTANCE
ULTRADISTANT
ULTRADRIER
ULTRADRIEST
ULTRADRYER
ULTRADRYEST
ULTRAEFFICIENT
ULTRAENERGETIC
ULTRAEXCLUSIVE
ULTRAFAMILIAR
ULTRAFASTIDIOUS
ULTRAFEMININE
ULTRAFICHE
ULTRAFICHES
ULTRAFILTER
ULTRAFILTERED
ULTRAFILTERING
ULTRAFILTERS
ULTRAFILTRATE
ULTRAFILTRATES
ULTRAFILTRATION
ULTRAGLAMOROUS
ULTRAHAZARDOUS
ULTRAHEATED
ULTRAHEATING
ULTRAHEATS
ULTRAHEAVIER
ULTRAHEAVIEST
ULTRAHEAVY
ULTRAHUMAN
ULTRAISTIC
ULTRALARGE
ULTRALEFTISM
ULTRALEFTISMS
ULTRALEFTIST
ULTRALEFTISTS
ULTRALEFTS
ULTRALIBERAL
ULTRALIBERALISM
ULTRALIBERALS
ULTRALIGHT
ULTRALIGHTS
ULTRAMAFIC
ULTRAMARATHON
ULTRAMARATHONER
ULTRAMARATHONS
ULTRAMARINE
ULTRAMARINES
ULTRAMASCULINE
ULTRAMICRO
ULTRAMICROMETER
ULTRAMICROSCOPE
ULTRAMICROSCOPY
ULTRAMICROTOME
ULTRAMICROTOMES
ULTRAMICROTOMY
ULTRAMILITANT
ULTRAMILITANTS
ULTRAMINIATURE
ULTRAMODERN
ULTRAMODERNISM
ULTRAMODERNISMS
ULTRAMODERNIST
ULTRAMODERNISTS
ULTRAMONTANE
ULTRAMONTANES
ULTRAMONTANISM
ULTRAMONTANISMS
ULTRAMONTANIST
ULTRAMONTANISTS
ULTRAMUNDANE
ULTRANATIONAL
ULTRAORTHODOX
ULTRAPATRIOTIC
ULTRAPHYSICAL
ULTRAPOWERFUL
ULTRAPRACTICAL
ULTRAPRECISE
ULTRAPRECISION
ULTRAPRECISIONS
ULTRAQUIET
ULTRARADICAL
ULTRARADICALS
ULTRARAPID
ULTRARAREFIED
ULTRARATIONAL
ULTRAREALISM
ULTRAREALISMS
ULTRAREALIST
ULTRAREALISTIC
ULTRAREALISTS
ULTRAREFINED
ULTRARELIABLE
ULTRARIGHT
ULTRARIGHTISM
ULTRARIGHTISMS
ULTRARIGHTIST
ULTRARIGHTISTS
ULTRARIGHTS
ULTRAROMANTIC
ULTRAROYALIST
ULTRAROYALISTS
ULTRASECRET
ULTRASENSITIVE
ULTRASENSUAL
ULTRASERIOUS
ULTRASHARP
ULTRASHORT
ULTRASIMPLE
ULTRASLICK
ULTRASMALL
ULTRASMART
ULTRASMOOTH
ULTRASONIC
ULTRASONICALLY
ULTRASONICS
ULTRASONOGRAPHY
ULTRASOUND
ULTRASOUNDS
ULTRASTRUCTURAL
ULTRASTRUCTURE
ULTRASTRUCTURES
ULTRATINIER
ULTRATINIEST
ULTRAVACUA
ULTRAVACUUM
ULTRAVACUUMS
ULTRAVIOLENCE
ULTRAVIOLENCES
ULTRAVIOLENT
ULTRAVIOLET
ULTRAVIOLETS
ULTRAVIRILE
ULTRAVIRILITIES
ULTRAVIRILITY
ULTRAVIRUS
ULTRAVIRUSES
ULTRAWIDEBAND
ULTRAWIDEBANDS
ULTRONEOUS
ULTRONEOUSLY
ULTRONEOUSNESS

U

ULULATIONS
UMBELLATED
UMBELLATELY
UMBELLIFER
UMBELLIFEROUS
UMBELLIFERS
UMBELLULATE
UMBELLULES
UMBILICALLY
UMBILICALS
UMBILICATE
UMBILICATED
UMBILICATION
UMBILICATIONS
UMBILICUSES
UMBILIFORM
UMBONATION
UMBONATIONS
UMBRACULATE
UMBRACULIFORM
UMBRACULUM
UMBRAGEOUS
UMBRAGEOUSLY
UMBRAGEOUSNESS
UMBRATICAL
UMBRATILES
UMBRATILOUS
UMBRELLAED
UMBRELLAING
UMBRELLOES
UMBRIFEROUS
UMPIRESHIP
UMPIRESHIPS
UMPTEENTHS
UNABASHEDLY
UNABATEDLY
UNABBREVIATED
UNABOLISHED
UNABRIDGED
UNABROGATED
UNABSOLVED
UNABSORBED
UNABSORBENT
UNACADEMIC
UNACADEMICALLY
UNACCENTED
UNACCENTUATED
UNACCEPTABILITY
UNACCEPTABLE
UNACCEPTABLY
UNACCEPTANCE
UNACCEPTANCES
UNACCEPTED
UNACCLIMATED
UNACCLIMATISED
UNACCLIMATIZED
UNACCOMMODATED
UNACCOMMODATING
UNACCOMPANIED
UNACCOMPLISHED
UNACCOUNTABLE
UNACCOUNTABLY
UNACCOUNTED
UNACCREDITED
UNACCULTURATED
UNACCUSABLE
UNACCUSABLY
UNACCUSTOMED
UNACCUSTOMEDLY
UNACHIEVABLE
UNACHIEVED
UNACKNOWLEDGED
UNACQUAINT
UNACQUAINTANCE
UNACQUAINTANCES
UNACQUAINTED
UNACQUAINTING
UNACQUAINTS
UNACTIVING
UNACTORISH
UNACTUATED
UNADAPTABLE
UNADDRESSED
UNADJUDICATED
UNADJUSTED
UNADMIRING
UNADMITTED
UNADMONISHED
UNADOPTABLE
UNADULTERATE
UNADULTERATED
UNADULTERATEDLY
UNADVENTROUS
UNADVENTUROUS
UNADVENTUROUSLY
UNADVERTISED
UNADVERTIZED
UNADVISABLE
UNADVISABLENESS
UNADVISABLY
UNADVISEDLY
UNADVISEDNESS
UNADVISEDNESSES
UNAESTHETIC
UNAFFECTED
UNAFFECTEDLY
UNAFFECTEDNESS
UNAFFECTING
UNAFFECTIONATE
UNAFFILIATED
UNAFFLUENT
UNAFFORDABLE
UNAGGRESSIVE
UNAGREEABLE
UNALIENABLE
UNALIENABLY
UNALIENATED
UNALLEVIATED
UNALLOCATED
UNALLOTTED
UNALLOWABLE
UNALLURING
UNALTERABILITY
UNALTERABLE
UNALTERABLENESS
UNALTERABLY
UNALTERING
UNAMBIGUOUS
UNAMBIGUOUSLY
UNAMBITIOUS
UNAMBITIOUSLY
UNAMBIVALENT
UNAMBIVALENTLY
UNAMENABLE
UNAMENDABLE
UNAMIABILITIES
UNAMIABILITY
UNAMIABLENESS
UNAMIABLENESSES
UNAMORTISED
UNAMORTIZED
UNAMPLIFIED
UNAMUSABLE
UNAMUSINGLY
UNANAESTHETISED
UNANAESTHETIZED
UNANALYSABLE
UNANALYSED
UNANALYTIC
UNANALYTICAL
UNANALYZABLE
UNANALYZED
UNANCHORED
UNANCHORING
UNANESTHETISED
UNANESTHETIZED
UNANIMATED
UNANIMITIES
UNANIMOUSLY
UNANIMOUSNESS
UNANIMOUSNESSES
UNANNEALED
UNANNOTATED
UNANNOUNCED
UNANSWERABILITY
UNANSWERABLE
UNANSWERABLY
UNANSWERED
UNANTICIPATED
UNANTICIPATEDLY
UNAPOLOGETIC
UNAPOLOGISING
UNAPOLOGIZING
UNAPOSTOLIC
UNAPOSTOLICAL
UNAPOSTOLICALLY
UNAPPALLED
UNAPPARELLED
UNAPPARELLING
UNAPPARELS
UNAPPARENT
UNAPPEALABLE
UNAPPEALABLY
UNAPPEALING
UNAPPEALINGLY
UNAPPEASABLE
UNAPPEASABLY
UNAPPEASED
UNAPPETISING
UNAPPETISINGLY
UNAPPETIZING
UNAPPETIZINGLY
UNAPPLAUSIVE
UNAPPLICABLE
UNAPPOINTED
UNAPPRECIATED
UNAPPRECIATION
UNAPPRECIATIONS
UNAPPRECIATIVE
UNAPPREHENDED
UNAPPREHENSIBLE
UNAPPREHENSIVE
UNAPPRISED
UNAPPROACHABLE
UNAPPROACHABLY
UNAPPROACHED
UNAPPROPRIATE
UNAPPROPRIATED
UNAPPROPRIATES
UNAPPROPRIATING
UNAPPROVED
UNAPPROVING
UNAPPROVINGLY
UNAPTNESSES
UNARGUABLE
UNARGUABLY
UNARMOURED
UNARRANGED
UNARROGANT
UNARTFULLY
UNARTICULATE
UNARTICULATED
UNARTIFICIAL
UNARTIFICIALLY
UNARTISTIC
UNARTISTLIKE
UNASCENDABLE
UNASCENDED
UNASCENDIBLE
UNASCERTAINABLE
UNASCERTAINED
UNASHAMEDLY
UNASHAMEDNESS
UNASHAMEDNESSES
UNASPIRATED
UNASPIRING
UNASPIRINGLY
UNASPIRINGNESS
UNASSAILABILITY
UNASSAILABLE

UNASSAILABLY
UNASSAILED
UNASSEMBLED
UNASSERTIVE
UNASSERTIVELY
UNASSIGNABLE
UNASSIGNED
UNASSIMILABLE
UNASSIMILATED
UNASSISTED
UNASSISTEDLY
UNASSISTING
UNASSOCIATED
UNASSUAGEABLE
UNASSUAGED
UNASSUMING
UNASSUMINGLY
UNASSUMINGNESS
UNATHLETIC
UNATONABLE
UNATTACHED
UNATTAINABLE
UNATTAINABLY
UNATTAINTED
UNATTEMPTED
UNATTENDED
UNATTENDING
UNATTENTIVE
UNATTENUATED
UNATTESTED
UNATTRACTIVE
UNATTRACTIVELY
UNATTRIBUTABLE
UNATTRIBUTED
UNAUGMENTED
UNAUSPICIOUS
UNAUTHENTIC
UNAUTHENTICATED
UNAUTHENTICITY
UNAUTHORISED
UNAUTHORITATIVE
UNAUTHORIZED
UNAUTOMATED
UNAVAILABILITY
UNAVAILABLE
UNAVAILABLENESS
UNAVAILABLY
UNAVAILING
UNAVAILINGLY
UNAVAILINGNESS
UNAVERTABLE
UNAVERTIBLE
UNAVOIDABILITY
UNAVOIDABLE
UNAVOIDABLENESS
UNAVOIDABLY
UNAVOWEDLY
UNAWAKENED
UNAWAKENING
UNAWARENESS
UNAWARENESSES
UNBAILABLE
UNBALANCED
UNBALANCES
UNBALANCING
UNBALLASTED
UNBANDAGED
UNBANDAGES
UNBANDAGING
UNBANNINGS
UNBAPTISED
UNBAPTISES
UNBAPTISING
UNBAPTIZED
UNBAPTIZES
UNBAPTIZING
UNBARBERED
UNBARRICADE
UNBARRICADED
UNBARRICADES
UNBARRICADING
UNBATTERED
UNBEARABLE
UNBEARABLENESS
UNBEARABLY
UNBEATABLE
UNBEATABLY
UNBEAUTIFUL
UNBEAUTIFULLY
UNBEAVERED
UNBECOMING
UNBECOMINGLY
UNBECOMINGNESS
UNBECOMINGS
UNBEDIMMED
UNBEDINNED
UNBEFITTING
UNBEFRIENDED
UNBEGETTING
UNBEGINNING
UNBEGOTTEN
UNBEGUILED
UNBEGUILES
UNBEGUILING
UNBEHOLDEN
UNBEKNOWNST
UNBELIEVABILITY
UNBELIEVABLE
UNBELIEVABLY
UNBELIEVED
UNBELIEVER
UNBELIEVERS
UNBELIEVES
UNBELIEVING
UNBELIEVINGLY
UNBELIEVINGNESS
UNBELLIGERENT
UNBENDABLE
UNBENDINGLY
UNBENDINGNESS
UNBENDINGNESSES
UNBENDINGS
UNBENEFICED
UNBENEFICIAL
UNBENEFITED
UNBENEFITTED
UNBENIGHTED
UNBENIGNANT
UNBENIGNLY
UNBESEEMED
UNBESEEMING
UNBESEEMINGLY
UNBESOUGHT
UNBESPEAKING
UNBESPEAKS
UNBESPOKEN
UNBESTOWED
UNBETRAYED
UNBETTERABLE
UNBETTERED
UNBEWAILED
UNBIASEDLY
UNBIASEDNESS
UNBIASEDNESSES
UNBIASINGS
UNBIASSEDLY
UNBIASSEDNESS
UNBIASSEDNESSES
UNBIASSING
UNBIASSINGS
UNBIBLICAL
UNBINDINGS
UNBIRTHDAY
UNBIRTHDAYS
UNBISHOPED
UNBISHOPING
UNBLAMABLE
UNBLAMABLY
UNBLAMEABLE
UNBLAMEABLY
UNBLEACHED
UNBLEMISHED
UNBLENCHED
UNBLENCHING
UNBLESSEDNESS
UNBLESSEDNESSES
UNBLESSING
UNBLINDFOLD
UNBLINDFOLDED
UNBLINDFOLDING
UNBLINDFOLDS
UNBLINDING
UNBLINKING
UNBLINKINGLY
UNBLISSFUL
UNBLOCKING
UNBLOODIED
UNBLOODIER
UNBLOODIEST
UNBLUSHING
UNBLUSHINGLY
UNBLUSHINGNESS
UNBOASTFUL
UNBONNETED
UNBONNETING
UNBORROWED
UNBOSOMERS
UNBOSOMING
UNBOTTLING
UNBOTTOMED
UNBOUNCIER
UNBOUNCIEST
UNBOUNDEDLY
UNBOUNDEDNESS
UNBOUNDEDNESSES
UNBOWDLERISED
UNBOWDLERIZED
UNBRACKETED
UNBRAIDING
UNBRANCHED
UNBREACHABLE
UNBREACHED
UNBREAKABLE
UNBREATHABLE
UNBREATHED
UNBREATHING
UNBREECHED
UNBREECHES
UNBREECHING
UNBRIBABLE
UNBRIDGEABLE
UNBRIDLEDLY
UNBRIDLEDNESS
UNBRIDLEDNESSES
UNBRIDLING
UNBRILLIANT
UNBROKENLY
UNBROKENNESS
UNBROKENNESSES
UNBROTHERLIKE
UNBROTHERLY
UNBUCKLING
UNBUDGEABLE
UNBUDGEABLY
UNBUDGETED
UNBUDGINGLY
UNBUFFERED
UNBUILDABLE
UNBUILDING
UNBULKIEST
UNBUNDLERS
UNBUNDLING
UNBUNDLINGS
UNBURDENED
UNBURDENING
UNBUREAUCRATIC
UNBURNABLE
UNBURNISHED
UNBURROWED
UNBURROWING

UNBURTHENED
UNBURTHENING
UNBURTHENS
UNBUSINESSLIKE
UNBUTTERED
UNBUTTONED
UNBUTTONING
UNCALCIFIED
UNCALCINED
UNCALCULATED
UNCALCULATING
UNCALIBRATED
UNCALLOUSED
UNCANCELED
UNCANCELLED
UNCANDIDLY
UNCANDIDNESS
UNCANDIDNESSES
UNCANDOURS
UNCANNIEST
UNCANNINESS
UNCANNINESSES
UNCANONICAL
UNCANONICALNESS
UNCANONISE
UNCANONISED
UNCANONISES
UNCANONISING
UNCANONIZE
UNCANONIZED
UNCANONIZES
UNCANONIZING
UNCAPITALISED
UNCAPITALIZED
UNCAPSIZABLE
UNCAPTIONED
UNCAPTIVATED
UNCAPTURABLE
UNCARPETED
UNCASTRATED
UNCATALOGED
UNCATALOGUED
UNCATCHABLE
UNCATCHIER
UNCATCHIEST
UNCATEGORISABLE
UNCATEGORIZABLE
UNCEASINGLY
UNCEASINGNESS
UNCEASINGNESSES
UNCELEBRATED
UNCENSORED
UNCENSORIOUS
UNCENSURED
UNCEREBRAL
UNCEREMONIOUS
UNCEREMONIOUSLY
UNCERTAINLY
UNCERTAINNESS
UNCERTAINNESSES
UNCERTAINTIES
UNCERTAINTY
UNCERTIFICATED
UNCERTIFIED
UNCHAINING
UNCHAIRING
UNCHALLENGEABLE
UNCHALLENGEABLY
UNCHALLENGED
UNCHALLENGING
UNCHANCIER
UNCHANCIEST
UNCHANGEABILITY
UNCHANGEABLE
UNCHANGEABLY
UNCHANGING
UNCHANGINGLY
UNCHANGINGNESS
UNCHANNELED
UNCHANNELLED
UNCHAPERONED
UNCHARGING
UNCHARIEST
UNCHARISMATIC
UNCHARITABLE
UNCHARITABLY
UNCHARITIES
UNCHARMING
UNCHARNELLED
UNCHARNELLING
UNCHARNELS
UNCHARTERED
UNCHASTELY
UNCHASTENED
UNCHASTENESS
UNCHASTENESSES
UNCHASTEST
UNCHASTISABLE
UNCHASTISED
UNCHASTITIES
UNCHASTITY
UNCHASTIZABLE
UNCHASTIZED
UNCHAUVINISTIC
UNCHECKABLE
UNCHECKING
UNCHEERFUL
UNCHEERFULLY
UNCHEERFULNESS
UNCHEWABLE
UNCHILDING
UNCHILDLIKE
UNCHIVALROUS
UNCHIVALROUSLY
UNCHLORINATED
UNCHOREOGRAPHED
UNCHRISTEN
UNCHRISTENED
UNCHRISTENING
UNCHRISTENS
UNCHRISTIAN
UNCHRISTIANED
UNCHRISTIANING
UNCHRISTIANISE
UNCHRISTIANISED
UNCHRISTIANISES
UNCHRISTIANIZE
UNCHRISTIANIZED
UNCHRISTIANIZES
UNCHRISTIANLIKE
UNCHRISTIANLY
UNCHRISTIANS
UNCHRONICLED
UNCHRONOLOGICAL
UNCHURCHED
UNCHURCHES
UNCHURCHING
UNCHURCHLY
UNCILIATED
UNCINARIAS
UNCINARIASES
UNCINARIASIS
UNCINEMATIC
UNCIPHERED
UNCIPHERING
UNCIRCULATED
UNCIRCUMCISED
UNCIRCUMCISION
UNCIRCUMCISIONS
UNCIRCUMSCRIBED
UNCIVILISED
UNCIVILISEDLY
UNCIVILISEDNESS
UNCIVILITIES
UNCIVILITY
UNCIVILIZED
UNCIVILIZEDLY
UNCIVILIZEDNESS
UNCIVILNESS
UNCIVILNESSES
UNCLAMPING
UNCLARIFIED
UNCLARITIES
UNCLASPING
UNCLASSICAL
UNCLASSIER
UNCLASSIEST
UNCLASSIFIABLE
UNCLASSIFIED
UNCLEANEST
UNCLEANLIER
UNCLEANLIEST
UNCLEANLINESS
UNCLEANLINESSES
UNCLEANNESS
UNCLEANNESSES
UNCLEANSED
UNCLEAREST
UNCLEARNESS
UNCLEARNESSES
UNCLENCHED
UNCLENCHES
UNCLENCHING
UNCLERICAL
UNCLESHIPS
UNCLIMBABLE
UNCLIMBABLENESS
UNCLINCHED
UNCLINCHES
UNCLINCHING
UNCLIPPING
UNCLOAKING
UNCLOGGING
UNCLOISTER
UNCLOISTERED
UNCLOISTERING
UNCLOISTERS
UNCLOTHING
UNCLOUDEDLY
UNCLOUDEDNESS
UNCLOUDEDNESSES
UNCLOUDIER
UNCLOUDIEST
UNCLOUDING
UNCLUBABLE
UNCLUBBABLE
UNCLUTCHED
UNCLUTCHES
UNCLUTCHING
UNCLUTTERED
UNCLUTTERING
UNCLUTTERS
UNCOALESCE
UNCOALESCED
UNCOALESCES
UNCOALESCING
UNCOATINGS
UNCODIFIED
UNCOERCIVE
UNCOERCIVELY
UNCOFFINED
UNCOFFINING
UNCOLLECTABLE
UNCOLLECTABLES
UNCOLLECTED
UNCOLLECTIBLE
UNCOLLECTIBLES
UNCOLOURED
UNCOMATABLE
UNCOMBATIVE
UNCOMBINED
UNCOMBINES
UNCOMBINING
UNCOMEATABLE
UNCOMELIER
UNCOMELIEST
UNCOMELINESS
UNCOMELINESSES
UNCOMFIEST
UNCOMFORTABLE

UNCOMFORTABLY
UNCOMFORTED
UNCOMMENDABLE
UNCOMMENDABLY
UNCOMMENDED
UNCOMMERCIAL
UNCOMMITTED
UNCOMMONER
UNCOMMONEST
UNCOMMONLY
UNCOMMONNESS
UNCOMMONNESSES
UNCOMMUNICABLE
UNCOMMUNICATED
UNCOMMUNICATIVE
UNCOMMUTED
UNCOMPACTED
UNCOMPANIED
UNCOMPANIONABLE
UNCOMPANIONED
UNCOMPASSIONATE
UNCOMPELLED
UNCOMPELLING
UNCOMPENSATED
UNCOMPETITIVE
UNCOMPLACENT
UNCOMPLAINING
UNCOMPLAININGLY
UNCOMPLAISANT
UNCOMPLAISANTLY
UNCOMPLETED
UNCOMPLIANT
UNCOMPLICATED
UNCOMPLIMENTARY
UNCOMPLYING
UNCOMPOSABLE
UNCOMPOUNDED
UNCOMPREHENDED
UNCOMPREHENDING
UNCOMPREHENSIVE
UNCOMPROMISABLE
UNCOMPROMISING
UNCOMPUTERISED
UNCOMPUTERIZED
UNCONCEALABLE
UNCONCEALED
UNCONCEALING
UNCONCEIVABLE
UNCONCEIVABLY
UNCONCEIVED
UNCONCERNED
UNCONCERNEDLY
UNCONCERNEDNESS
UNCONCERNING
UNCONCERNMENT
UNCONCERNMENTS
UNCONCERNS
UNCONCERTED
UNCONCILIATORY
UNCONCLUSIVE
UNCONCOCTED
UNCONDITIONAL
UNCONDITIONALLY
UNCONDITIONED
UNCONDUCIVE
UNCONFEDERATED
UNCONFESSED
UNCONFINABLE
UNCONFINED
UNCONFINEDLY
UNCONFINES
UNCONFINING
UNCONFIRMED
UNCONFORMABLE
UNCONFORMABLY
UNCONFORMING
UNCONFORMITIES
UNCONFORMITY
UNCONFOUNDED
UNCONFUSED
UNCONFUSEDLY
UNCONFUSES
UNCONFUSING
UNCONGEALED
UNCONGEALING
UNCONGEALS
UNCONGENIAL
UNCONGENIALITY
UNCONJECTURED
UNCONJUGAL
UNCONJUGATED
UNCONJUNCTIVE
UNCONNECTED
UNCONNECTEDLY
UNCONNECTEDNESS
UNCONNIVING
UNCONQUERABLE
UNCONQUERABLY
UNCONQUERED
UNCONSCIENTIOUS
UNCONSCIONABLE
UNCONSCIONABLY
UNCONSCIOUS
UNCONSCIOUSES
UNCONSCIOUSLY
UNCONSCIOUSNESS
UNCONSECRATE
UNCONSECRATED
UNCONSECRATES
UNCONSECRATING
UNCONSENTANEOUS
UNCONSENTING
UNCONSIDERED
UNCONSIDERING
UNCONSOLED
UNCONSOLIDATED
UNCONSTANT
UNCONSTRAINABLE
UNCONSTRAINED
UNCONSTRAINEDLY
UNCONSTRAINT
UNCONSTRAINTS
UNCONSTRICTED
UNCONSTRUCTED
UNCONSTRUCTIVE
UNCONSUMED
UNCONSUMMATED
UNCONTAINABLE
UNCONTAMINATED
UNCONTEMNED
UNCONTEMPLATED
UNCONTEMPORARY
UNCONTENTIOUS
UNCONTESTABLE
UNCONTESTED
UNCONTRACTED
UNCONTRADICTED
UNCONTRIVED
UNCONTROLLABLE
UNCONTROLLABLY
UNCONTROLLED
UNCONTROLLEDLY
UNCONTROVERSIAL
UNCONTROVERTED
UNCONVENTIONAL
UNCONVERSABLE
UNCONVERSANT
UNCONVERTED
UNCONVERTIBLE
UNCONVICTED
UNCONVINCED
UNCONVINCING
UNCONVINCINGLY
UNCONVOYED
UNCOOPERATIVE
UNCOOPERATIVELY
UNCOORDINATED
UNCOPYRIGHTABLE
UNCOQUETTISH
UNCORRECTABLE
UNCORRECTED
UNCORRELATED
UNCORROBORATED
UNCORRUPTED
UNCORSETED
UNCOSTLIER
UNCOSTLIEST
UNCOUNSELLED
UNCOUNTABLE
UNCOUPLERS
UNCOUPLING
UNCOURAGEOUS
UNCOURTEOUS
UNCOURTLIER
UNCOURTLIEST
UNCOURTLINESS
UNCOURTLINESSES
UNCOUTHEST
UNCOUTHNESS
UNCOUTHNESSES
UNCOVENANTED
UNCOVERING
UNCRAZIEST
UNCREATEDNESS
UNCREATEDNESSES
UNCREATING
UNCREATIVE
UNCREDENTIALED
UNCREDIBLE
UNCREDITABLE
UNCREDITED
UNCRIPPLED
UNCRITICAL
UNCRITICALLY
UNCROSSABLE
UNCROSSING
UNCROWNING
UNCRUMPLED
UNCRUMPLES
UNCRUMPLING
UNCRUSHABLE
UNCRYSTALLISED
UNCRYSTALLIZED
UNCTIONLESS
UNCTUOSITIES
UNCTUOSITY
UNCTUOUSLY
UNCTUOUSNESS
UNCTUOUSNESSES
UNCUCKOLDED
UNCULTIVABLE
UNCULTIVATABLE
UNCULTIVATED
UNCULTURED
UNCUMBERED
UNCURBABLE
UNCURTAILED
UNCURTAINED
UNCURTAINING
UNCURTAINS
UNCUSTOMARILY
UNCUSTOMARY
UNCUSTOMED
UNCYNICALLY
UNDANCEABLE
UNDAUNTABLE
UNDAUNTEDLY
UNDAUNTEDNESS
UNDAUNTEDNESSES
UNDAUNTING
UNDAZZLING
UNDEBARRED
UNDEBATABLE
UNDEBATABLY
UNDEBAUCHED
UNDECADENT
UNDECAGONS
UNDECEIVABLE
UNDECEIVED
UNDECEIVER

UNDECEIVERS
UNDECEIVES
UNDECEIVING
UNDECIDABILITY
UNDECIDABLE
UNDECIDEDLY
UNDECIDEDNESS
UNDECIDEDNESSES
UNDECIDEDS
UNDECILLION
UNDECILLIONS
UNDECIMOLE
UNDECIMOLES
UNDECIPHERABLE
UNDECIPHERED
UNDECISIVE
UNDECLARED
UNDECLINING
UNDECOMPOSABLE
UNDECOMPOSED
UNDECORATED
UNDEDICATED
UNDEFEATABLE
UNDEFEATED
UNDEFENDED
UNDEFINABLE
UNDEFOLIATED
UNDEFORMED
UNDEIFYING
UNDELAYING
UNDELECTABLE
UNDELEGATED
UNDELETING
UNDELIBERATE
UNDELIGHTED
UNDELIGHTFUL
UNDELIGHTS
UNDELIVERABLE
UNDELIVERED
UNDEMANDING
UNDEMARCATED
UNDEMOCRATIC
UNDEMONSTRABLE
UNDEMONSTRATED
UNDEMONSTRATIVE
UNDENIABLE
UNDENIABLENESS
UNDENIABLY
UNDEPENDABLE
UNDEPENDING
UNDEPLORED
UNDEPRAVED
UNDEPRECIATED
UNDEPRESSED
UNDEPRIVED
UNDERACHIEVE
UNDERACHIEVED
UNDERACHIEVER
UNDERACHIEVERS
UNDERACHIEVES
UNDERACHIEVING
UNDERACTED
UNDERACTING
UNDERACTION
UNDERACTIONS
UNDERACTIVE
UNDERACTIVITIES
UNDERACTIVITY
UNDERACTOR
UNDERACTORS
UNDERAGENT
UNDERAGENTS
UNDERBAKED
UNDERBAKES
UNDERBAKING
UNDERBEARER
UNDERBEARERS
UNDERBEARING
UNDERBEARINGS
UNDERBEARS
UNDERBELLIES
UNDERBELLY
UNDERBIDDER
UNDERBIDDERS
UNDERBIDDING
UNDERBITES
UNDERBITING
UNDERBITTEN
UNDERBLANKET
UNDERBLANKETS
UNDERBODIES
UNDERBORNE
UNDERBOSSES
UNDERBOUGH
UNDERBOUGHS
UNDERBOUGHT
UNDERBREATH
UNDERBREATHS
UNDERBREEDING
UNDERBREEDINGS
UNDERBRIDGE
UNDERBRIDGES
UNDERBRIMS
UNDERBRUSH
UNDERBRUSHED
UNDERBRUSHES
UNDERBRUSHING
UNDERBUDDED
UNDERBUDDING
UNDERBUDGET
UNDERBUDGETED
UNDERBUDGETING
UNDERBUDGETS
UNDERBUILD
UNDERBUILDER
UNDERBUILDERS
UNDERBUILDING
UNDERBUILDS
UNDERBUILT
UNDERBURNT
UNDERBUSHED
UNDERBUSHES
UNDERBUSHING
UNDERBUYING
UNDERCAPITALISE
UNDERCAPITALIZE
UNDERCARDS
UNDERCARRIAGE
UNDERCARRIAGES
UNDERCARTS
UNDERCASTS
UNDERCHARGE
UNDERCHARGED
UNDERCHARGES
UNDERCHARGING
UNDERCLASS
UNDERCLASSES
UNDERCLASSMAN
UNDERCLASSMEN
UNDERCLAYS
UNDERCLIFF
UNDERCLIFFS
UNDERCLOTHE
UNDERCLOTHED
UNDERCLOTHES
UNDERCLOTHING
UNDERCLOTHINGS
UNDERCLUBBED
UNDERCLUBBING
UNDERCLUBS
UNDERCOATED
UNDERCOATING
UNDERCOATINGS
UNDERCOATS
UNDERCOOKED
UNDERCOOKING
UNDERCOOKS
UNDERCOOLED
UNDERCOOLING
UNDERCOOLS
UNDERCOUNT
UNDERCOUNTED
UNDERCOUNTING
UNDERCOUNTS
UNDERCOVER
UNDERCOVERT
UNDERCOVERTS
UNDERCRACKERS
UNDERCREST
UNDERCRESTED
UNDERCRESTING
UNDERCRESTS
UNDERCROFT
UNDERCROFTS
UNDERCURRENT
UNDERCURRENTS
UNDERCUTTING
UNDERDAMPER
UNDERDAMPERS
UNDERDECKS
UNDERDELIVER
UNDERDELIVERED
UNDERDELIVERING
UNDERDELIVERS
UNDERDEVELOP
UNDERDEVELOPED
UNDERDEVELOPING
UNDERDEVELOPS
UNDERDOERS
UNDERDOING
UNDERDOSED
UNDERDOSES
UNDERDOSING
UNDERDRAIN
UNDERDRAINAGE
UNDERDRAINAGES
UNDERDRAINED
UNDERDRAINING
UNDERDRAINS
UNDERDRAWERS
UNDERDRAWING
UNDERDRAWINGS
UNDERDRAWN
UNDERDRAWS
UNDERDRESS
UNDERDRESSED
UNDERDRESSES
UNDERDRESSING
UNDERDRIVE
UNDERDRIVES
UNDEREARTH
UNDEREARTHS
UNDEREATEN
UNDEREATING
UNDEREDUCATED
UNDEREMPHASES
UNDEREMPHASIS
UNDEREMPHASISE
UNDEREMPHASISED
UNDEREMPHASISES
UNDEREMPHASIZE
UNDEREMPHASIZED
UNDEREMPHASIZES
UNDEREMPLOYED
UNDEREMPLOYMENT
UNDERESTIMATE
UNDERESTIMATED
UNDERESTIMATES
UNDERESTIMATING
UNDERESTIMATION
UNDEREXPLOIT
UNDEREXPLOITED
UNDEREXPLOITING
UNDEREXPLOITS
UNDEREXPOSE
UNDEREXPOSED
UNDEREXPOSES
UNDEREXPOSING
UNDEREXPOSURE
UNDEREXPOSURES

UNDERFEEDING
UNDERFEEDINGS
UNDERFEEDS
UNDERFELTS
UNDERFINANCED
UNDERFINISHED
UNDERFIRED
UNDERFIRES
UNDERFIRING
UNDERFISHED
UNDERFISHES
UNDERFISHING
UNDERFLOOR
UNDERFLOWS
UNDERFONGED
UNDERFONGING
UNDERFONGS
UNDERFOOTED
UNDERFOOTING
UNDERFOOTS
UNDERFULFIL
UNDERFULFILL
UNDERFULFILLED
UNDERFULFILLING
UNDERFULFILLS
UNDERFULFILS
UNDERFUNDED
UNDERFUNDING
UNDERFUNDINGS
UNDERFUNDS
UNDERGARMENT
UNDERGARMENTS
UNDERGIRDED
UNDERGIRDING
UNDERGIRDS
UNDERGLAZE
UNDERGLAZES
UNDERGOERS
UNDERGOING
UNDERGOWNS
UNDERGRADS
UNDERGRADUATE
UNDERGRADUATES
UNDERGRADUETTE
UNDERGRADUETTES
UNDERGROUND
UNDERGROUNDER
UNDERGROUNDERS
UNDERGROUNDS
UNDERGROVE
UNDERGROVES
UNDERGROWN
UNDERGROWTH
UNDERGROWTHS
UNDERHAIRS
UNDERHANDED
UNDERHANDEDLY
UNDERHANDEDNESS
UNDERHANDING
UNDERHANDS
UNDERHEATED
UNDERHEATING
UNDERHEATS
UNDERHONEST
UNDERINFLATED
UNDERINFLATION
UNDERINFLATIONS
UNDERINSURE
UNDERINSURED
UNDERINSURES
UNDERINSURING
UNDERINVEST
UNDERINVESTED
UNDERINVESTING
UNDERINVESTMENT
UNDERINVESTS
UNDERJAWED
UNDERKEEPER
UNDERKEEPERS
UNDERKEEPING
UNDERKEEPS
UNDERKILLS
UNDERKINGDOM
UNDERKINGDOMS
UNDERKINGS
UNDERLAPPED
UNDERLAPPING
UNDERLAYER
UNDERLAYERS
UNDERLAYING
UNDERLAYMENT
UNDERLAYMENTS
UNDERLEASE
UNDERLEASED
UNDERLEASES
UNDERLEASING
UNDERLEAVES
UNDERLETTER
UNDERLETTERS
UNDERLETTING
UNDERLETTINGS
UNDERLEVERAGED
UNDERLIERS
UNDERLINED
UNDERLINEN
UNDERLINENS
UNDERLINES
UNDERLINGS
UNDERLINING
UNDERLININGS
UNDERLOADED
UNDERLOADING
UNDERLOADS
UNDERLOOKER
UNDERLOOKERS
UNDERLYING
UNDERLYINGLY
UNDERMANNED
UNDERMANNING
UNDERMANNINGS
UNDERMASTED
UNDERMEANING
UNDERMEANINGS
UNDERMENTIONED
UNDERMINDE
UNDERMINDED
UNDERMINDES
UNDERMINDING
UNDERMINED
UNDERMINER
UNDERMINERS
UNDERMINES
UNDERMINING
UNDERMININGS
UNDERNAMED
UNDERNEATH
UNDERNEATHS
UNDERNICENESS
UNDERNICENESSES
UNDERNOTED
UNDERNOTES
UNDERNOTING
UNDERNOURISH
UNDERNOURISHED
UNDERNOURISHES
UNDERNOURISHING
UNDERNTIME
UNDERNTIMES
UNDERNUTRITION
UNDERNUTRITIONS
UNDEROCCUPIED
UNDERPAINTING
UNDERPAINTINGS
UNDERPANTS
UNDERPARTS
UNDERPASSES
UNDERPASSION
UNDERPASSIONS
UNDERPAYING
UNDERPAYMENT
UNDERPAYMENTS
UNDERPEEPED
UNDERPEEPING
UNDERPEEPS
UNDERPEOPLED
UNDERPERFORM
UNDERPERFORMED
UNDERPERFORMING
UNDERPERFORMS
UNDERPINNED
UNDERPINNING
UNDERPINNINGS
UNDERPITCH
UNDERPLANT
UNDERPLANTED
UNDERPLANTING
UNDERPLANTS
UNDERPLAYED
UNDERPLAYING
UNDERPLAYS
UNDERPLOTS
UNDERPOPULATED
UNDERPOWERED
UNDERPRAISE
UNDERPRAISED
UNDERPRAISES
UNDERPRAISING
UNDERPREPARED
UNDERPRICE
UNDERPRICED
UNDERPRICES
UNDERPRICING
UNDERPRICINGS
UNDERPRISE
UNDERPRISED
UNDERPRISES
UNDERPRISING
UNDERPRIVILEGED
UNDERPRIZE
UNDERPRIZED
UNDERPRIZES
UNDERPRIZING
UNDERPRODUCE
UNDERPRODUCED
UNDERPRODUCES
UNDERPRODUCING
UNDERPRODUCTION
UNDERPROOF
UNDERPROPPED
UNDERPROPPER
UNDERPROPPERS
UNDERPROPPING
UNDERPROPS
UNDERPUBLICISED
UNDERPUBLICIZED
UNDERQUALIFIED
UNDERQUOTE
UNDERQUOTED
UNDERQUOTES
UNDERQUOTING
UNDERRATED
UNDERRATES
UNDERRATING
UNDERREACT
UNDERREACTED
UNDERREACTING
UNDERREACTION
UNDERREACTIONS
UNDERREACTS
UNDERREPORT
UNDERREPORTED
UNDERREPORTING
UNDERREPORTS
UNDERRUNNING
UNDERRUNNINGS
UNDERSATURATED
UNDERSAYING
UNDERSCORE
UNDERSCORED
UNDERSCORES

U

UNDERSCORING
UNDERSCORINGS
UNDERSCRUB
UNDERSCRUBS
UNDERSEALED
UNDERSEALING
UNDERSEALINGS
UNDERSEALS
UNDERSECRETARY
UNDERSELLER
UNDERSELLERS
UNDERSELLING
UNDERSELLS
UNDERSELVES
UNDERSENSE
UNDERSENSES
UNDERSERVED
UNDERSETTING
UNDERSEXED
UNDERSHAPEN
UNDERSHERIFF
UNDERSHERIFFS
UNDERSHIRT
UNDERSHIRTED
UNDERSHIRTS
UNDERSHOOT
UNDERSHOOTING
UNDERSHOOTS
UNDERSHORTS
UNDERSHRUB
UNDERSHRUBS
UNDERSIDES
UNDERSIGNED
UNDERSIGNING
UNDERSIGNS
UNDERSIZED
UNDERSKIES
UNDERSKINKER
UNDERSKINKERS
UNDERSKIRT
UNDERSKIRTS
UNDERSLEEVE
UNDERSLEEVES
UNDERSLUNG
UNDERSOILS
UNDERSONGS
UNDERSOWED
UNDERSOWING
UNDERSPEND
UNDERSPENDING
UNDERSPENDINGS
UNDERSPENDS
UNDERSPENT
UNDERSPINS
UNDERSTAFFED
UNDERSTAFFING
UNDERSTAFFINGS
UNDERSTAND
UNDERSTANDABLE
UNDERSTANDABLY
UNDERSTANDED
UNDERSTANDER
UNDERSTANDERS
UNDERSTANDING
UNDERSTANDINGLY
UNDERSTANDINGS
UNDERSTANDS
UNDERSTATE
UNDERSTATED
UNDERSTATEDLY
UNDERSTATEMENT
UNDERSTATEMENTS
UNDERSTATES
UNDERSTATING
UNDERSTEER
UNDERSTEERED
UNDERSTEERING
UNDERSTEERS
UNDERSTOCK
UNDERSTOCKED
UNDERSTOCKING
UNDERSTOCKS
UNDERSTOOD
UNDERSTOREY
UNDERSTOREYS
UNDERSTORIES
UNDERSTORY
UNDERSTRAPPER
UNDERSTRAPPERS
UNDERSTRAPPING
UNDERSTRATA
UNDERSTRATUM
UNDERSTRATUMS
UNDERSTRENGTH
UNDERSTUDIED
UNDERSTUDIES
UNDERSTUDY
UNDERSTUDYING
UNDERSUBSCRIBED
UNDERSUPPLIED
UNDERSUPPLIES
UNDERSUPPLY
UNDERSUPPLYING
UNDERSURFACE
UNDERSURFACES
UNDERTAKABLE
UNDERTAKEN
UNDERTAKER
UNDERTAKERS
UNDERTAKES
UNDERTAKING
UNDERTAKINGS
UNDERTAXED
UNDERTAXES
UNDERTAXING
UNDERTENANCIES
UNDERTENANCY
UNDERTENANT
UNDERTENANTS
UNDERTHINGS
UNDERTHIRST
UNDERTHIRSTS
UNDERTHRUST
UNDERTHRUSTING
UNDERTHRUSTS
UNDERTIMED
UNDERTIMES
UNDERTINTS
UNDERTONED
UNDERTONES
UNDERTRICK
UNDERTRICKS
UNDERTRUMP
UNDERTRUMPED
UNDERTRUMPING
UNDERTRUMPS
UNDERUSING
UNDERUTILISE
UNDERUTILISED
UNDERUTILISES
UNDERUTILISING
UNDERUTILIZE
UNDERUTILIZED
UNDERUTILIZES
UNDERUTILIZING
UNDERVALUATION
UNDERVALUATIONS
UNDERVALUE
UNDERVALUED
UNDERVALUER
UNDERVALUERS
UNDERVALUES
UNDERVALUING
UNDERVESTS
UNDERVIEWER
UNDERVIEWERS
UNDERVOICE
UNDERVOICES
UNDERVOTES
UNDERWATER
UNDERWATERS
UNDERWEARS
UNDERWEIGHT
UNDERWEIGHTS
UNDERWHELM
UNDERWHELMED
UNDERWHELMING
UNDERWHELMS
UNDERWINGS
UNDERWIRED
UNDERWIRES
UNDERWIRING
UNDERWIRINGS
UNDERWOODS
UNDERWOOLS
UNDERWORKED
UNDERWORKER
UNDERWORKERS
UNDERWORKING
UNDERWORKS
UNDERWORLD
UNDERWORLDS
UNDERWRITE
UNDERWRITER
UNDERWRITERS
UNDERWRITES
UNDERWRITING
UNDERWRITINGS
UNDERWRITTEN
UNDERWROTE
UNDERWROUGHT
UNDESCENDABLE
UNDESCENDED
UNDESCENDIBLE
UNDESCRIBABLE
UNDESCRIBED
UNDESCRIED
UNDESERVED
UNDESERVEDLY
UNDESERVEDNESS
UNDESERVER
UNDESERVERS
UNDESERVES
UNDESERVING
UNDESERVINGLY
UNDESIGNATED
UNDESIGNED
UNDESIGNEDLY
UNDESIGNEDNESS
UNDESIGNING
UNDESIRABILITY
UNDESIRABLE
UNDESIRABLENESS
UNDESIRABLES
UNDESIRABLY
UNDESIRING
UNDESIROUS
UNDESPAIRING
UNDESPAIRINGLY
UNDESPATCHED
UNDESPOILED
UNDESTROYED
UNDETECTABLE
UNDETECTED
UNDETERMINABLE
UNDETERMINATE
UNDETERMINATION
UNDETERMINED
UNDETERRED
UNDEVELOPED
UNDEVIATING
UNDEVIATINGLY
UNDIAGNOSABLE
UNDIAGNOSED
UNDIALECTICAL
UNDIDACTIC
UNDIFFERENCED
UNDIGESTED
UNDIGESTIBLE
UNDIGHTING

UNDIGNIFIED
UNDIGNIFIES
UNDIGNIFYING
UNDIMINISHABLE
UNDIMINISHED
UNDIPLOMATIC
UNDIRECTED
UNDISAPPOINTING
UNDISCERNED
UNDISCERNEDLY
UNDISCERNIBLE
UNDISCERNIBLY
UNDISCERNING
UNDISCERNINGS
UNDISCHARGED
UNDISCIPLINABLE
UNDISCIPLINE
UNDISCIPLINED
UNDISCIPLINES
UNDISCLOSED
UNDISCOMFITED
UNDISCORDANT
UNDISCORDING
UNDISCOURAGED
UNDISCOVERABLE
UNDISCOVERABLY
UNDISCOVERED
UNDISCUSSABLE
UNDISCUSSED
UNDISCUSSIBLE
UNDISGUISABLE
UNDISGUISED
UNDISGUISEDLY
UNDISHONOURED
UNDISMANTLED
UNDISMAYED
UNDISORDERED
UNDISPATCHED
UNDISPENSED
UNDISPOSED
UNDISPUTABLE
UNDISPUTED
UNDISPUTEDLY
UNDISSEMBLED
UNDISSOCIATED
UNDISSOLVED
UNDISSOLVING
UNDISTEMPERED
UNDISTILLED
UNDISTINCTIVE
UNDISTINGUISHED
UNDISTORTED
UNDISTRACTED
UNDISTRACTEDLY
UNDISTRACTING
UNDISTRIBUTED
UNDISTURBED
UNDISTURBEDLY
UNDISTURBING
UNDIVERSIFIED
UNDIVERTED
UNDIVERTING
UNDIVESTED
UNDIVESTEDLY
UNDIVIDABLE
UNDIVIDEDLY
UNDIVIDEDNESS
UNDIVIDEDNESSES
UNDIVORCED
UNDIVULGED
UNDOCTORED
UNDOCTRINAIRE
UNDOCTRINAIRES
UNDOCUMENTED
UNDOGMATIC
UNDOGMATICALLY
UNDOMESTIC
UNDOMESTICATE
UNDOMESTICATED
UNDOMESTICATES
UNDOMESTICATING
UNDOUBLING
UNDOUBTABLE
UNDOUBTEDLY
UNDOUBTFUL
UNDOUBTING
UNDOUBTINGLY
UNDRAINABLE
UNDRAMATIC
UNDRAMATICALLY
UNDRAMATISED
UNDRAMATIZED
UNDREADING
UNDREAMING
UNDRESSING
UNDRESSINGS
UNDRINKABLE
UNDRIVEABLE
UNDROOPING
UNDROSSIER
UNDROSSIEST
UNDULANCES
UNDULANCIES
UNDULATELY
UNDULATING
UNDULATINGLY
UNDULATION
UNDULATIONIST
UNDULATIONISTS
UNDULATIONS
UNDULATORS
UNDULATORY
UNDUPLICATED
UNDUTIFULLY
UNDUTIFULNESS
UNDUTIFULNESSES
UNDYINGNESS
UNDYINGNESSES
UNEARMARKED
UNEARTHING
UNEARTHLIER
UNEARTHLIEST
UNEARTHLINESS
UNEARTHLINESSES
UNEASINESS
UNEASINESSES
UNEATABLENESS
UNEATABLENESSES
UNECCENTRIC
UNECLIPSED
UNECOLOGICAL
UNECONOMIC
UNECONOMICAL
UNEDIFYING
UNEDUCABLE
UNEDUCATED
UNEFFECTED
UNELABORATE
UNELABORATED
UNELECTABLE
UNELECTRIFIED
UNEMBARRASSED
UNEMBELLISHED
UNEMBITTERED
UNEMBODIED
UNEMOTIONAL
UNEMOTIONALLY
UNEMOTIONED
UNEMPHASISED
UNEMPHASIZED
UNEMPHATIC
UNEMPHATICALLY
UNEMPIRICAL
UNEMPLOYABILITY
UNEMPLOYABLE
UNEMPLOYABLES
UNEMPLOYED
UNEMPLOYEDS
UNEMPLOYMENT
UNEMPLOYMENTS
UNENCHANTED
UNENCLOSED
UNENCOURAGING
UNENCUMBERED
UNENDANGERED
UNENDEARED
UNENDEARING
UNENDINGLY
UNENDINGNESS
UNENDINGNESSES
UNENDURABLE
UNENDURABLENESS
UNENDURABLY
UNENFORCEABLE
UNENFORCED
UNENJOYABLE
UNENLARGED
UNENLIGHTENED
UNENLIGHTENING
UNENQUIRING
UNENRICHED
UNENSLAVED
UNENTAILED
UNENTERPRISING
UNENTERTAINED
UNENTERTAINING
UNENTHRALLED
UNENTHUSIASTIC
UNENTITLED
UNENVIABLE
UNENVIABLY
UNEQUALLED
UNEQUIPPED
UNEQUITABLE
UNEQUIVOCABLE
UNEQUIVOCABLY
UNEQUIVOCAL
UNEQUIVOCALLY
UNEQUIVOCALNESS
UNERASABLE
UNERRINGLY
UNERRINGNESS
UNERRINGNESSES
UNESCAPABLE
UNESCORTED
UNESSENCED
UNESSENCES
UNESSENCING
UNESSENTIAL
UNESSENTIALLY
UNESSENTIALS
UNESTABLISHED
UNESTHETIC
UNETHICALLY
UNEVALUATED
UNEVANGELICAL
UNEVENNESS
UNEVENNESSES
UNEVENTFUL
UNEVENTFULLY
UNEVENTFULNESS
UNEVIDENCED
UNEXACTING
UNEXAGGERATED
UNEXAMINED
UNEXAMPLED
UNEXCAVATED
UNEXCELLED
UNEXCEPTIONABLE
UNEXCEPTIONABLY
UNEXCEPTIONAL
UNEXCEPTIONALLY
UNEXCITABLE
UNEXCITING
UNEXCLUDED
UNEXCLUSIVE
UNEXCLUSIVELY
UNEXECUTED
UNEXEMPLIFIED
UNEXERCISED

U

UNEXHAUSTED
UNEXPANDED
UNEXPECTANT
UNEXPECTED
UNEXPECTEDLY
UNEXPECTEDNESS
UNEXPENDED
UNEXPENSIVE
UNEXPENSIVELY
UNEXPERIENCED
UNEXPERIENT
UNEXPIATED
UNEXPLAINABLE
UNEXPLAINED
UNEXPLODED
UNEXPLOITED
UNEXPLORED
UNEXPRESSED
UNEXPRESSIBLE
UNEXPRESSIVE
UNEXPUGNABLE
UNEXPURGATED
UNEXTENDED
UNEXTENUATED
UNEXTINGUISHED
UNEXTRAORDINARY
UNFADINGLY
UNFADINGNESS
UNFADINGNESSES
UNFAILINGLY
UNFAILINGNESS
UNFAILINGNESSES
UNFAIRNESS
UNFAIRNESSES
UNFAITHFUL
UNFAITHFULLY
UNFAITHFULNESS
UNFALLIBLE
UNFALSIFIABLE
UNFALTERING
UNFALTERINGLY
UNFAMILIAR
UNFAMILIARITIES
UNFAMILIARITY
UNFAMILIARLY
UNFANCIEST
UNFASHIONABLE
UNFASHIONABLY
UNFASHIONED
UNFASTENED
UNFASTENING
UNFASTIDIOUS
UNFATHERED
UNFATHERLIER
UNFATHERLIEST
UNFATHERLY
UNFATHOMABLE
UNFATHOMABLY
UNFATHOMED
UNFAULTIER
UNFAULTIEST
UNFAVORABLE
UNFAVORABLENESS
UNFAVORABLY
UNFAVORITE
UNFAVOURABLE
UNFAVOURABLY
UNFAVOURED
UNFAVOURITE
UNFEARFULLY
UNFEASIBLE
UNFEATHERED
UNFEATURED
UNFEELINGLY
UNFEELINGNESS
UNFEELINGNESSES
UNFEIGNEDLY
UNFEIGNEDNESS
UNFEIGNEDNESSES
UNFEIGNING
UNFELLOWED
UNFEMININE
UNFERMENTED
UNFERTILISED
UNFERTILIZED
UNFETTERED
UNFETTERING
UNFEUDALISE
UNFEUDALISED
UNFEUDALISES
UNFEUDALISING
UNFEUDALIZE
UNFEUDALIZED
UNFEUDALIZES
UNFEUDALIZING
UNFILIALLY
UNFILLABLE
UNFILLETED
UNFILTERABLE
UNFILTERED
UNFILTRABLE
UNFINDABLE
UNFINISHED
UNFINISHING
UNFINISHINGS
UNFITNESSES
UNFITTEDNESS
UNFITTEDNESSES
UNFITTINGLY
UNFIXEDNESS
UNFIXEDNESSES
UNFIXITIES
UNFLAGGING
UNFLAGGINGLY
UNFLAMBOYANT
UNFLAPPABILITY
UNFLAPPABLE
UNFLAPPABLENESS
UNFLAPPABLY
UNFLASHIER
UNFLASHIEST
UNFLATTERING
UNFLATTERINGLY
UNFLAVORED
UNFLAVOURED
UNFLESHING
UNFLESHLIER
UNFLESHLIEST
UNFLINCHING
UNFLINCHINGLY
UNFLUSHING
UNFLUSTERED
UNFOCUSSED
UNFOLDINGS
UNFOLDMENT
UNFOLDMENTS
UNFOLLOWED
UNFOLLOWING
UNFORBIDDEN
UNFORCEDLY
UNFORCIBLE
UNFORDABLE
UNFOREBODING
UNFOREKNOWABLE
UNFOREKNOWN
UNFORESEEABLE
UNFORESEEING
UNFORESEEN
UNFORESKINNED
UNFORESTED
UNFORETOLD
UNFOREWARNED
UNFORFEITED
UNFORGETTABLE
UNFORGETTABLY
UNFORGIVABLE
UNFORGIVABLY
UNFORGIVEN
UNFORGIVENESS
UNFORGIVENESSES
UNFORGIVING
UNFORGIVINGNESS
UNFORGOTTEN
UNFORMALISED
UNFORMALIZED
UNFORMATTED
UNFORMIDABLE
UNFORMULATED
UNFORSAKEN
UNFORTHCOMING
UNFORTIFIED
UNFORTUNATE
UNFORTUNATELY
UNFORTUNATENESS
UNFORTUNATES
UNFORTUNED
UNFORTUNES
UNFOSSILIFEROUS
UNFOSSILISED
UNFOSSILIZED
UNFOSTERED
UNFOUGHTEN
UNFOUNDEDLY
UNFOUNDEDNESS
UNFOUNDEDNESSES
UNFRANCHISED
UNFRAUGHTED
UNFRAUGHTING
UNFRAUGHTS
UNFREEDOMS
UNFREEZING
UNFREEZINGS
UNFREQUENT
UNFREQUENTED
UNFREQUENTING
UNFREQUENTLY
UNFREQUENTS
UNFRIENDED
UNFRIENDEDNESS
UNFRIENDING
UNFRIENDLIER
UNFRIENDLIEST
UNFRIENDLILY
UNFRIENDLINESS
UNFRIENDLY
UNFRIENDSHIP
UNFRIENDSHIPS
UNFRIGHTED
UNFRIGHTENED
UNFRIVOLOUS
UNFROCKING
UNFRUCTUOUS
UNFRUITFUL
UNFRUITFULLY
UNFRUITFULNESS
UNFULFILLABLE
UNFULFILLED
UNFULFILLING
UNFUNNIEST
UNFURNISHED
UNFURNISHES
UNFURNISHING
UNFURROWED
UNFUSSIEST
UNGAINLIER
UNGAINLIEST
UNGAINLINESS
UNGAINLINESSES
UNGAINSAID
UNGAINSAYABLE
UNGALLANTLY
UNGARMENTED
UNGARNERED
UNGARNISHED
UNGARTERED
UNGATHERED
UNGENEROSITIES
UNGENEROSITY
UNGENEROUS
UNGENEROUSLY

U

UNGENITURED
UNGENTEELLY
UNGENTILITIES
UNGENTILITY
UNGENTLEMANLIER
UNGENTLEMANLIKE
UNGENTLEMANLY
UNGENTLENESS
UNGENTLENESSES
UNGENTLEST
UNGENTRIFIED
UNGENUINENESS
UNGENUINENESSES
UNGERMINATED
UNGETATABLE
UNGHOSTLIER
UNGHOSTLIEST
UNGIMMICKY
UNGIRTHING
UNGLACIATED
UNGLAMORISED
UNGLAMORIZED
UNGLAMOROUS
UNGLITZIER
UNGLITZIEST
UNGODLIEST
UNGODLINESS
UNGODLINESSES
UNGOVERNABLE
UNGOVERNABLY
UNGOVERNED
UNGRACEFUL
UNGRACEFULLY
UNGRACEFULNESS
UNGRACIOUS
UNGRACIOUSLY
UNGRACIOUSNESS
UNGRAMMATIC
UNGRAMMATICAL
UNGRAMMATICALLY
UNGRASPABLE
UNGRATEFUL
UNGRATEFULLY
UNGRATEFULNESS
UNGRATIFIED
UNGREEDIER
UNGREEDIEST
UNGREENEST
UNGROUNDED
UNGROUNDEDLY
UNGROUNDEDNESS
UNGROUPING
UNGRUDGING
UNGRUDGINGLY
UNGUARDEDLY
UNGUARDEDNESS
UNGUARDEDNESSES
UNGUARDING
UNGUENTARIA
UNGUENTARIES
UNGUENTARIUM
UNGUENTARY
UNGUERDONED
UNGUESSABLE
UNGUICULATE
UNGUICULATED
UNGUICULATES
UNGUILTIER
UNGUILTIEST
UNGULIGRADE
UNHABITABLE
UNHABITUATED
UNHACKNEYED
UNHALLOWED
UNHALLOWING
UNHAMPERED
UNHANDIEST
UNHANDINESS
UNHANDINESSES
UNHANDSELLED
UNHANDSOME
UNHANDSOMELY
UNHANDSOMENESS
UNHAPPENED
UNHAPPENING
UNHAPPENINGS
UNHAPPIEST
UNHAPPINESS
UNHAPPINESSES
UNHAPPYING
UNHARBOURED
UNHARBOURING
UNHARBOURS
UNHARDENED
UNHARDIEST
UNHARMFULLY
UNHARMONIOUS
UNHARNESSED
UNHARNESSES
UNHARNESSING
UNHARVESTED
UNHASTIEST
UNHATTINGS
UNHAZARDED
UNHAZARDOUS
UNHEALABLE
UNHEALTHFUL
UNHEALTHFULLY
UNHEALTHFULNESS
UNHEALTHIER
UNHEALTHIEST
UNHEALTHILY
UNHEALTHINESS
UNHEALTHINESSES
UNHEARSING
UNHEARTING
UNHEEDEDLY
UNHEEDFULLY
UNHEEDIEST
UNHEEDINGLY
UNHELMETED
UNHELPABLE
UNHELPFULLY
UNHELPFULNESS
UNHELPFULNESSES
UNHERALDED
UNHEROICAL
UNHEROICALLY
UNHESITATING
UNHESITATINGLY
UNHIDEBOUND
UNHINDERED
UNHINGEMENT
UNHINGEMENTS
UNHISTORIC
UNHISTORICAL
UNHITCHING
UNHOARDING
UNHOLINESS
UNHOLINESSES
UNHOLSTERED
UNHOLSTERING
UNHOLSTERS
UNHOMELIER
UNHOMELIEST
UNHOMELIKE
UNHOMOGENISED
UNHOMOGENIZED
UNHONOURED
UNHOPEFULLY
UNHOSPITABLE
UNHOUSELED
UNHOUZZLED
UNHUMANISE
UNHUMANISED
UNHUMANISES
UNHUMANISING
UNHUMANIZE
UNHUMANIZED
UNHUMANIZES
UNHUMANIZING
UNHUMOROUS
UNHURRIEDLY
UNHURRYING
UNHURTFULLY
UNHURTFULNESS
UNHURTFULNESSES
UNHUSBANDED
UNHYDROLYSED
UNHYDROLYZED
UNHYGIENIC
UNHYPHENATED
UNHYSTERICAL
UNHYSTERICALLY
UNIAXIALLY
UNICAMERAL
UNICAMERALISM
UNICAMERALISMS
UNICAMERALIST
UNICAMERALISTS
UNICAMERALLY
UNICELLULAR
UNICELLULARITY
UNICENTRAL
UNICOLORATE
UNICOLORED
UNICOLOROUS
UNICOLOURED
UNICOSTATE
UNICYCLING
UNICYCLIST
UNICYCLISTS
UNIDEALISM
UNIDEALISMS
UNIDEALISTIC
UNIDENTIFIABLE
UNIDENTIFIED
UNIDEOLOGICAL
UNIDIMENSIONAL
UNIDIOMATIC
UNIDIOMATICALLY
UNIDIRECTIONAL
UNIFICATION
UNIFICATIONS
UNIFLOROUS
UNIFOLIATE
UNIFOLIOLATE
UNIFORMEST
UNIFORMING
UNIFORMITARIAN
UNIFORMITARIANS
UNIFORMITIES
UNIFORMITY
UNIFORMNESS
UNIFORMNESSES
UNIGENITURE
UNIGENITURES
UNIGNORABLE
UNILABIATE
UNILATERAL
UNILATERALISM
UNILATERALISMS
UNILATERALIST
UNILATERALISTS
UNILATERALITIES
UNILATERALITY
UNILATERALLY
UNILINGUAL
UNILINGUALISM
UNILINGUALISMS
UNILINGUALIST
UNILINGUALISTS
UNILINGUALS
UNILITERAL
UNILLUMINATED
UNILLUMINATING
UNILLUMINED
UNILLUSIONED
UNILLUSTRATED
UNILOBULAR

UNILOCULAR
UNIMAGINABLE
UNIMAGINABLY
UNIMAGINATIVE
UNIMAGINATIVELY
UNIMAGINED
UNIMMORTAL
UNIMMUNISED
UNIMMUNIZED
UNIMOLECULAR
UNIMPAIRED
UNIMPARTED
UNIMPASSIONED
UNIMPEACHABLE
UNIMPEACHABLY
UNIMPEACHED
UNIMPEDEDLY
UNIMPLORED
UNIMPORTANCE
UNIMPORTANCES
UNIMPORTANT
UNIMPORTUNED
UNIMPOSING
UNIMPREGNATED
UNIMPRESSED
UNIMPRESSIBLE
UNIMPRESSIVE
UNIMPRISONED
UNIMPROVED
UNIMPUGNABLE
UNINAUGURATED
UNINCHANTED
UNINCLOSED
UNINCORPORATED
UNINCUMBERED
UNINDEARED
UNINDENTED
UNINDICTED
UNINFECTED
UNINFLAMED
UNINFLAMMABLE
UNINFLATED
UNINFLECTED
UNINFLUENCED
UNINFLUENTIAL
UNINFORCEABLE
UNINFORCED
UNINFORMATIVE
UNINFORMATIVELY
UNINFORMED
UNINFORMING
UNINGRATIATING
UNINHABITABLE
UNINHABITED
UNINHIBITED
UNINHIBITEDLY
UNINHIBITEDNESS
UNINITIATE
UNINITIATED
UNINITIATES
UNINOCULATED
UNINQUIRING
UNINQUISITIVE
UNINSCRIBED
UNINSPECTED
UNINSPIRED
UNINSPIRING
UNINSTALLED
UNINSTALLING
UNINSTALLS
UNINSTRUCTED
UNINSTRUCTIVE
UNINSULATED
UNINSURABLE
UNINSUREDS
UNINTEGRATED
UNINTELLECTUAL
UNINTELLIGENCE
UNINTELLIGENCES
UNINTELLIGENT
UNINTELLIGENTLY
UNINTELLIGIBLE
UNINTELLIGIBLY
UNINTENDED
UNINTENTIONAL
UNINTENTIONALLY
UNINTEREST
UNINTERESTED
UNINTERESTEDLY
UNINTERESTING
UNINTERESTINGLY
UNINTERESTS
UNINTERMITTED
UNINTERMITTEDLY
UNINTERMITTING
UNINTERPRETABLE
UNINTERPRETED
UNINTERRUPTED
UNINTERRUPTEDLY
UNINTIMIDATED
UNINTOXICATING
UNINTRODUCED
UNINUCLEAR
UNINUCLEATE
UNINVENTIVE
UNINVESTED
UNINVIDIOUS
UNINVITING
UNINVOLVED
UNIONISATION
UNIONISATIONS
UNIONISERS
UNIONISING
UNIONISTIC
UNIONIZATION
UNIONIZATIONS
UNIONIZERS
UNIONIZING
UNIPARENTAL
UNIPARENTALLY
UNIPARTITE
UNIPERSONAL
UNIPERSONALITY
UNIPOLARITIES
UNIPOLARITY
UNIQUENESS
UNIQUENESSES
UNIRONICALLY
UNIRRADIATED
UNIRRIGATED
UNISEPTATE
UNISERIALLY
UNISERIATE
UNISERIATELY
UNISEXUALITIES
UNISEXUALITY
UNISEXUALLY
UNISONALLY
UNISONANCE
UNISONANCES
UNITARIANISM
UNITARIANISMS
UNITARIANS
UNITARITIES
UNITEDNESS
UNITEDNESSES
UNITHOLDER
UNITHOLDERS
UNITISATION
UNITISATIONS
UNITIZATION
UNITIZATIONS
UNIVALENCE
UNIVALENCES
UNIVALENCIES
UNIVALENCY
UNIVALENTS
UNIVALVULAR
UNIVARIANT
UNIVARIATE
UNIVERSALISABLE
UNIVERSALISE
UNIVERSALISED
UNIVERSALISES
UNIVERSALISING
UNIVERSALISM
UNIVERSALISMS
UNIVERSALIST
UNIVERSALISTIC
UNIVERSALISTS
UNIVERSALITIES
UNIVERSALITY
UNIVERSALIZABLE
UNIVERSALIZE
UNIVERSALIZED
UNIVERSALIZES
UNIVERSALIZING
UNIVERSALLY
UNIVERSALNESS
UNIVERSALNESSES
UNIVERSALS
UNIVERSITARIAN
UNIVERSITIES
UNIVERSITY
UNIVOCALLY
UNIVOLTINE
UNJAUNDICED
UNJOINTING
UNJUSTIFIABLE
UNJUSTIFIABLY
UNJUSTIFIED
UNJUSTNESS
UNJUSTNESSES
UNKEMPTNESS
UNKEMPTNESSES
UNKENNELED
UNKENNELING
UNKENNELLED
UNKENNELLING
UNKINDLIER
UNKINDLIEST
UNKINDLINESS
UNKINDLINESSES
UNKINDNESS
UNKINDNESSES
UNKINGLIER
UNKINGLIEST
UNKINGLIKE
UNKNIGHTED
UNKNIGHTING
UNKNIGHTLIER
UNKNIGHTLIEST
UNKNIGHTLINESS
UNKNIGHTLY
UNKNITTING
UNKNOTTING
UNKNOWABILITIES
UNKNOWABILITY
UNKNOWABLE
UNKNOWABLENESS
UNKNOWABLES
UNKNOWABLY
UNKNOWINGLY
UNKNOWINGNESS
UNKNOWINGNESSES
UNKNOWINGS
UNKNOWLEDGEABLE
UNKNOWNNESS
UNKNOWNNESSES
UNLABELLED
UNLABORING
UNLABORIOUS
UNLABOURED
UNLABOURING
UNLADYLIKE
UNLAMENTED
UNLATCHING
UNLAUNDERED
UNLAWFULLY
UNLAWFULNESS

UNLAWFULNESSES
UNLEARNABLE
UNLEARNEDLY
UNLEARNEDNESS
UNLEARNEDNESSES
UNLEARNING
UNLEASHING
UNLEAVENED
UNLEISURED
UNLEISURELY
UNLESSONED
UNLETTABLE
UNLETTERED
UNLEVELING
UNLEVELLED
UNLEVELLING
UNLIBERATED
UNLIBIDINOUS
UNLICENSED
UNLIFELIKE
UNLIGHTENED
UNLIGHTSOME
UNLIKEABLE
UNLIKELIER
UNLIKELIEST
UNLIKELIHOOD
UNLIKELIHOODS
UNLIKELINESS
UNLIKELINESSES
UNLIKENESS
UNLIKENESSES
UNLIMBERED
UNLIMBERING
UNLIMITEDLY
UNLIMITEDNESS
UNLIMITEDNESSES
UNLIQUEFIED
UNLIQUIDATED
UNLIQUORED
UNLISTENABLE
UNLISTENED
UNLISTENING
UNLITERARY
UNLIVEABLE
UNLIVELIER
UNLIVELIEST
UNLIVELINESS
UNLIVELINESSES
UNLOADINGS
UNLOCALISED
UNLOCALIZED
UNLOCKABLE
UNLOOSENED
UNLOOSENING
UNLORDLIER
UNLORDLIEST
UNLOVEABLE
UNLOVELIER
UNLOVELIEST
UNLOVELINESS
UNLOVELINESSES
UNLOVERLIKE
UNLOVINGLY
UNLOVINGNESS
UNLOVINGNESSES
UNLUCKIEST
UNLUCKINESS
UNLUCKINESSES
UNLUXURIANT
UNLUXURIOUS
UNMACADAMISED
UNMACADAMIZED
UNMAGNIFIED
UNMAIDENLY
UNMAILABLE
UNMAINTAINABLE
UNMAINTAINED
UNMALICIOUS
UNMALICIOUSLY
UNMALLEABILITY
UNMALLEABLE
UNMANACLED
UNMANACLES
UNMANACLING
UNMANAGEABLE
UNMANAGEABLY
UNMANFULLY
UNMANIPULATED
UNMANLIEST
UNMANLINESS
UNMANLINESSES
UNMANNERED
UNMANNEREDLY
UNMANNERLIER
UNMANNERLIEST
UNMANNERLINESS
UNMANNERLY
UNMANTLING
UNMANUFACTURED
UNMARKETABLE
UNMARRIABLE
UNMARRIAGEABLE
UNMARRIEDS
UNMARRYING
UNMASCULINE
UNMASKINGS
UNMASTERED
UNMATCHABLE
UNMATCHING
UNMATERIAL
UNMATERIALISED
UNMATERIALIZED
UNMATERNAL
UNMATHEMATICAL
UNMATRICULATED
UNMEANINGLY
UNMEANINGNESS
UNMEANINGNESSES
UNMEASURABLE
UNMEASURABLY
UNMEASURED
UNMEASUREDLY
UNMECHANIC
UNMECHANICAL
UNMECHANISE
UNMECHANISED
UNMECHANISES
UNMECHANISING
UNMECHANIZE
UNMECHANIZED
UNMECHANIZES
UNMECHANIZING
UNMEDIATED
UNMEDICATED
UNMEDICINABLE
UNMEDITATED
UNMEETNESS
UNMEETNESSES
UNMELLOWED
UNMELODIOUS
UNMELODIOUSNESS
UNMEMORABLE
UNMEMORABLY
UNMENTIONABLE
UNMENTIONABLES
UNMENTIONABLY
UNMENTIONED
UNMERCENARY
UNMERCHANTABLE
UNMERCIFUL
UNMERCIFULLY
UNMERCIFULNESS
UNMERITABLE
UNMERITEDLY
UNMERITING
UNMERRIEST
UNMETABOLISED
UNMETABOLIZED
UNMETALLED
UNMETAPHORICAL
UNMETAPHYSICAL
UNMETHODICAL
UNMETHODISED
UNMETHODIZED
UNMETRICAL
UNMILITARY
UNMINDFULLY
UNMINDFULNESS
UNMINDFULNESSES
UNMINGLING
UNMINISTERIAL
UNMIRACULOUS
UNMISSABLE
UNMISTAKABLE
UNMISTAKABLY
UNMISTAKEABLE
UNMISTAKEABLY
UNMISTRUSTFUL
UNMITERING
UNMITIGABLE
UNMITIGABLY
UNMITIGATED
UNMITIGATEDLY
UNMITIGATEDNESS
UNMODERATED
UNMODERNISED
UNMODERNIZED
UNMODIFIABLE
UNMODIFIED
UNMODULATED
UNMOISTENED
UNMOLESTED
UNMONITORED
UNMORALISED
UNMORALISING
UNMORALITIES
UNMORALITY
UNMORALIZED
UNMORALIZING
UNMORTGAGED
UNMORTIFIED
UNMORTISED
UNMORTISES
UNMORTISING
UNMOTHERLIER
UNMOTHERLIEST
UNMOTHERLY
UNMOTIVATED
UNMOULDING
UNMOUNTING
UNMOVEABLE
UNMOVEABLY
UNMUFFLING
UNMUNITIONED
UNMURMURING
UNMURMURINGLY
UNMUSICALLY
UNMUSICALNESS
UNMUSICALNESSES
UNMUTILATED
UNMUZZLING
UNMUZZLINGS
UNMYELINATED
UNNAMEABLE
UNNATIVING
UNNATURALISE
UNNATURALISED
UNNATURALISES
UNNATURALISING
UNNATURALIZE
UNNATURALIZED
UNNATURALIZES
UNNATURALIZING
UNNATURALLY
UNNATURALNESS
UNNATURALNESSES
UNNAVIGABLE
UNNAVIGATED
UNNECESSARILY
UNNECESSARINESS

UNNECESSARY
UNNEEDFULLY
UNNEGOTIABLE
UNNEIGHBORED
UNNEIGHBORLY
UNNEIGHBOURED
UNNEIGHBOURLY
UNNERVINGLY
UNNEUROTIC
UNNEWSWORTHIER
UNNEWSWORTHIEST
UNNEWSWORTHY
UNNILHEXIUM
UNNILHEXIUMS
UNNILPENTIUM
UNNILPENTIUMS
UNNILQUADIUM
UNNILQUADIUMS
UNNILSEPTIUM
UNNILSEPTIUMS
UNNOISIEST
UNNOTICEABLE
UNNOTICEABLY
UNNOTICING
UNNOURISHED
UNNOURISHING
UNNUMBERED
UNNURTURED
UNOBEDIENT
UNOBJECTIONABLE
UNOBJECTIONABLY
UNOBLIGING
UNOBNOXIOUS
UNOBSCURED
UNOBSERVABLE
UNOBSERVABLES
UNOBSERVANCE
UNOBSERVANCES
UNOBSERVANT
UNOBSERVED
UNOBSERVEDLY
UNOBSERVING
UNOBSTRUCTED
UNOBSTRUCTIVE
UNOBTAINABLE
UNOBTAINED
UNOBTRUSIVE
UNOBTRUSIVELY
UNOBTRUSIVENESS
UNOCCUPIED
UNOFFENDED
UNOFFENDING
UNOFFENSIVE
UNOFFICERED
UNOFFICIAL
UNOFFICIALLY
UNOFFICIOUS
UNOPENABLE
UNOPERATIVE
UNOPPOSING
UNOPPRESSIVE
UNORDAINED
UNORDERING
UNORDINARY
UNORGANISED
UNORGANIZED
UNORIGINAL
UNORIGINALITIES
UNORIGINALITY
UNORIGINALS
UNORIGINATE
UNORIGINATED
UNORNAMENTAL
UNORNAMENTED
UNORTHODOX
UNORTHODOXIES
UNORTHODOXLY
UNORTHODOXY
UNOSSIFIED
UNOSTENTATIOUS
UNOVERCOME
UNOVERTHROWN
UNOXIDISED
UNOXIDIZED
UNOXYGENATED
UNPACIFIED
UNPACKINGS
UNPAINTABLE
UNPAINTING
UNPALATABILITY
UNPALATABLE
UNPALATABLY
UNPAMPERED
UNPANELLED
UNPANELLING
UNPANNELLED
UNPANNELLING
UNPAPERING
UNPARADISE
UNPARADISED
UNPARADISES
UNPARADISING
UNPARAGONED
UNPARALLEL
UNPARALLELED
UNPARASITISED
UNPARASITIZED
UNPARDONABLE
UNPARDONABLY
UNPARDONED
UNPARDONING
UNPARENTAL
UNPARENTED
UNPARLIAMENTARY
UNPASSABLE
UNPASSABLENESS
UNPASSIONATE
UNPASSIONED
UNPASTEURISED
UNPASTEURIZED
UNPASTORAL
UNPASTURED
UNPATENTABLE
UNPATENTED
UNPATHETIC
UNPATHWAYED
UNPATRIOTIC
UNPATRIOTICALLY
UNPATRONISED
UNPATRONIZED
UNPATTERNED
UNPAVILIONED
UNPEACEABLE
UNPEACEABLENESS
UNPEACEFUL
UNPEACEFULLY
UNPEDANTIC
UNPEDIGREED
UNPEERABLE
UNPENSIONED
UNPEOPLING
UNPEPPERED
UNPERCEIVABLE
UNPERCEIVABLY
UNPERCEIVED
UNPERCEIVEDLY
UNPERCEPTIVE
UNPERCHING
UNPERFECTED
UNPERFECTION
UNPERFECTIONS
UNPERFECTLY
UNPERFECTNESS
UNPERFECTNESSES
UNPERFORATED
UNPERFORMABLE
UNPERFORMED
UNPERFORMING
UNPERFUMED
UNPERILOUS
UNPERISHABLE
UNPERISHED
UNPERISHING
UNPERJURED
UNPERPETRATED
UNPERPLEXED
UNPERPLEXES
UNPERPLEXING
UNPERSECUTED
UNPERSONED
UNPERSONING
UNPERSUADABLE
UNPERSUADED
UNPERSUASIVE
UNPERTURBED
UNPERVERTED
UNPERVERTING
UNPERVERTS
UNPHILOSOPHIC
UNPHILOSOPHICAL
UNPHONETIC
UNPICKABLE
UNPICTURESQUE
UNPIGMENTED
UNPILLARED
UNPILLOWED
UNPITIFULLY
UNPITIFULNESS
UNPITIFULNESSES
UNPITYINGLY
UNPLAITING
UNPLASTERED
UNPLASTICISED
UNPLASTICIZED
UNPLAUSIBLE
UNPLAUSIBLY
UNPLAUSIVE
UNPLAYABLE
UNPLEASANT
UNPLEASANTLY
UNPLEASANTNESS
UNPLEASANTRIES
UNPLEASANTRY
UNPLEASING
UNPLEASINGLY
UNPLEASURABLE
UNPLEASURABLY
UNPLOUGHED
UNPLUGGING
UNPLUMBING
UNPOETICAL
UNPOETICALLY
UNPOETICALNESS
UNPOISONED
UNPOISONING
UNPOLARISABLE
UNPOLARISED
UNPOLARIZABLE
UNPOLARIZED
UNPOLICIED
UNPOLISHABLE
UNPOLISHED
UNPOLISHES
UNPOLISHING
UNPOLITELY
UNPOLITENESS
UNPOLITENESSES
UNPOLITICAL
UNPOLLUTED
UNPOPULARITIES
UNPOPULARITY
UNPOPULARLY
UNPOPULATED
UNPOPULOUS
UNPORTIONED
UNPOSSESSED
UNPOSSESSING
UNPOSSIBLE
UNPOWDERED
UNPRACTICABLE

UNPRACTICAL
UNPRACTICALITY
UNPRACTICALLY
UNPRACTICALNESS
UNPRACTICED
UNPRACTISED
UNPRACTISEDNESS
UNPRAISEWORTHY
UNPRAISING
UNPREACHED
UNPREACHES
UNPREACHING
UNPRECEDENTED
UNPRECEDENTEDLY
UNPREDESTINED
UNPREDICTABLE
UNPREDICTABLES
UNPREDICTABLY
UNPREDICTED
UNPREDICTING
UNPREDICTS
UNPREFERRED
UNPREGNANT
UNPREJUDICED
UNPREJUDICEDLY
UNPRELATICAL
UNPREMEDITABLE
UNPREMEDITATED
UNPREMEDITATION
UNPREOCCUPIED
UNPREPARED
UNPREPAREDLY
UNPREPAREDNESS
UNPREPARES
UNPREPARING
UNPREPOSSESSED
UNPREPOSSESSING
UNPRESCRIBED
UNPRESENTABLE
UNPRESSURED
UNPRESSURISED
UNPRESSURIZED
UNPRESUMING
UNPRESUMPTUOUS
UNPRETENDING
UNPRETENDINGLY
UNPRETENTIOUS
UNPRETENTIOUSLY
UNPRETTIER
UNPRETTIEST
UNPRETTINESS
UNPRETTINESSES
UNPREVAILING
UNPREVENTABLE
UNPREVENTED
UNPRIESTED
UNPRIESTING
UNPRIESTLIER
UNPRIESTLIEST
UNPRIESTLY
UNPRINCELIER
UNPRINCELIEST
UNPRINCELY
UNPRINCIPLED
UNPRINTABLE
UNPRINTABLENESS
UNPRINTABLY
UNPRISABLE
UNPRISONED
UNPRISONING
UNPRIVILEGED
UNPRIZABLE
UNPROBLEMATIC
UNPROCEDURAL
UNPROCESSED
UNPROCLAIMED
UNPROCURABLE
UNPRODUCED
UNPRODUCTIVE
UNPRODUCTIVELY
UNPRODUCTIVITY
UNPROFANED
UNPROFESSED
UNPROFESSIONAL
UNPROFESSIONALS
UNPROFITABILITY
UNPROFITABLE
UNPROFITABLY
UNPROFITED
UNPROFITING
UNPROFITINGS
UNPROGRAMMABLE
UNPROGRAMMED
UNPROGRESSIVE
UNPROGRESSIVELY
UNPROHIBITED
UNPROJECTED
UNPROLIFIC
UNPROMISED
UNPROMISING
UNPROMISINGLY
UNPROMPTED
UNPRONOUNCEABLE
UNPRONOUNCED
UNPROPERLY
UNPROPERTIED
UNPROPHETIC
UNPROPHETICAL
UNPROPITIOUS
UNPROPITIOUSLY
UNPROPORTIONATE
UNPROPORTIONED
UNPROPOSED
UNPROPPING
UNPROSPEROUS
UNPROSPEROUSLY
UNPROTECTED
UNPROTECTEDNESS
UNPROTESTANTISE
UNPROTESTANTIZE
UNPROTESTED
UNPROTESTING
UNPROVABLE
UNPROVIDED
UNPROVIDEDLY
UNPROVIDENT
UNPROVIDES
UNPROVIDING
UNPROVISIONED
UNPROVOCATIVE
UNPROVOKED
UNPROVOKEDLY
UNPROVOKES
UNPROVOKING
UNPUBLICISED
UNPUBLICIZED
UNPUBLISHABLE
UNPUBLISHED
UNPUCKERED
UNPUCKERING
UNPUNCTUAL
UNPUNCTUALITIES
UNPUNCTUALITY
UNPUNCTUATED
UNPUNISHABLE
UNPUNISHABLY
UNPUNISHED
UNPURCHASABLE
UNPURCHASEABLE
UNPURCHASED
UNPURIFIED
UNPURPOSED
UNPURVAIDE
UNPURVEYED
UNPUTDOWNABLE
UNPUZZLING
UNQUALIFIABLE
UNQUALIFIED
UNQUALIFIEDLY
UNQUALIFIEDNESS
UNQUALIFIES
UNQUALIFYING
UNQUALITED
UNQUALITIED
UNQUANTIFIABLE
UNQUANTIFIED
UNQUANTISED
UNQUANTIZED
UNQUARRIED
UNQUEENING
UNQUEENLIER
UNQUEENLIEST
UNQUEENLIKE
UNQUENCHABLE
UNQUENCHABLY
UNQUENCHED
UNQUESTIONABLE
UNQUESTIONABLY
UNQUESTIONED
UNQUESTIONING
UNQUESTIONINGLY
UNQUICKENED
UNQUIETEST
UNQUIETING
UNQUIETNESS
UNQUIETNESSES
UNQUOTABLE
UNRANSOMED
UNRATIFIED
UNRAVELING
UNRAVELLED
UNRAVELLER
UNRAVELLERS
UNRAVELLING
UNRAVELLINGS
UNRAVELMENT
UNRAVELMENTS
UNRAVISHED
UNREACHABLE
UNREACTIVE
UNREADABILITIES
UNREADABILITY
UNREADABLE
UNREADABLENESS
UNREADABLY
UNREADIEST
UNREADINESS
UNREADINESSES
UNREALISABLE
UNREALISED
UNREALISES
UNREALISING
UNREALISMS
UNREALISTIC
UNREALISTICALLY
UNREALITIES
UNREALIZABLE
UNREALIZED
UNREALIZES
UNREALIZING
UNREASONABLE
UNREASONABLY
UNREASONED
UNREASONING
UNREASONINGLY
UNRECALLABLE
UNRECALLED
UNRECALLING
UNRECAPTURABLE
UNRECEIPTED
UNRECEIVED
UNRECEPTIVE
UNRECIPROCATED
UNRECKONABLE
UNRECKONED
UNRECLAIMABLE
UNRECLAIMABLY
UNRECLAIMED
UNRECOGNISABLE
UNRECOGNISABLY

U

UNRECOGNISED
UNRECOGNISING
UNRECOGNIZABLE
UNRECOGNIZABLY
UNRECOGNIZED
UNRECOGNIZING
UNRECOLLECTED
UNRECOMMENDABLE
UNRECOMMENDED
UNRECOMPENSED
UNRECONCILABLE
UNRECONCILABLY
UNRECONCILED
UNRECONCILIABLE
UNRECONSTRUCTED
UNRECORDED
UNRECOUNTED
UNRECOVERABLE
UNRECOVERABLY
UNRECOVERED
UNRECTIFIED
UNRECURING
UNRECYCLABLE
UNRECYCLABLES
UNREDEEMABLE
UNREDEEMED
UNREDRESSED
UNREDUCIBLE
UNREFLECTED
UNREFLECTING
UNREFLECTINGLY
UNREFLECTIVE
UNREFLECTIVELY
UNREFORMABLE
UNREFORMED
UNREFRACTED
UNREFRESHED
UNREFRESHING
UNREFRIGERATED
UNREGARDED
UNREGARDING
UNREGENERACIES
UNREGENERACY
UNREGENERATE
UNREGENERATED
UNREGENERATELY
UNREGENERATES
UNREGIMENTED
UNREGISTERED
UNREGRETTED
UNREGULATED
UNREHEARSED
UNREINFORCED
UNREJOICED
UNREJOICING
UNRELATIVE
UNRELEASED
UNRELENTING
UNRELENTINGLY
UNRELENTINGNESS
UNRELENTOR
UNRELENTORS
UNRELIABILITIES
UNRELIABILITY
UNRELIABLE
UNRELIABLENESS
UNRELIABLY
UNRELIEVABLE
UNRELIEVED
UNRELIEVEDLY
UNRELIGIOUS
UNRELIGIOUSLY
UNRELISHED
UNRELUCTANT
UNREMAINING
UNREMARKABLE
UNREMARKABLY
UNREMARKED
UNREMEDIED
UNREMEMBERED
UNREMEMBERING
UNREMINISCENT
UNREMITTED
UNREMITTEDLY
UNREMITTENT
UNREMITTENTLY
UNREMITTING
UNREMITTINGLY
UNREMITTINGNESS
UNREMORSEFUL
UNREMORSEFULLY
UNREMORSELESS
UNREMOVABLE
UNREMUNERATIVE
UNRENDERED
UNRENOWNED
UNREPAIRABLE
UNREPAIRED
UNREPEALABLE
UNREPEALED
UNREPEATABLE
UNREPEATED
UNREPELLED
UNREPENTANCE
UNREPENTANCES
UNREPENTANT
UNREPENTANTLY
UNREPENTED
UNREPENTING
UNREPENTINGLY
UNREPINING
UNREPININGLY
UNREPLACEABLE
UNREPLENISHED
UNREPORTABLE
UNREPORTED
UNREPOSEFUL
UNREPOSING
UNREPRESENTED
UNREPRESSED
UNREPRIEVABLE
UNREPRIEVED
UNREPRIMANDED
UNREPROACHED
UNREPROACHFUL
UNREPROACHING
UNREPRODUCIBLE
UNREPROVABLE
UNREPROVED
UNREPROVING
UNREPUGNANT
UNREPULSABLE
UNREQUESTED
UNREQUIRED
UNREQUISITE
UNREQUITED
UNREQUITEDLY
UNRESCINDED
UNRESENTED
UNRESENTFUL
UNRESENTING
UNRESERVED
UNRESERVEDLY
UNRESERVEDNESS
UNRESERVES
UNRESISTANT
UNRESISTED
UNRESISTIBLE
UNRESISTING
UNRESISTINGLY
UNRESOLVABLE
UNRESOLVED
UNRESOLVEDNESS
UNRESPECTABLE
UNRESPECTABLES
UNRESPECTED
UNRESPECTIVE
UNRESPITED
UNRESPONSIVE
UNRESPONSIVELY
UNRESTFULNESS
UNRESTFULNESSES
UNRESTINGLY
UNRESTINGNESS
UNRESTINGNESSES
UNRESTORED
UNRESTRAINABLE
UNRESTRAINED
UNRESTRAINEDLY
UNRESTRAINT
UNRESTRAINTS
UNRESTRICTED
UNRESTRICTEDLY
UNRETARDED
UNRETENTIVE
UNRETIRING
UNRETOUCHED
UNRETURNABLE
UNRETURNED
UNRETURNING
UNRETURNINGLY
UNREVEALABLE
UNREVEALED
UNREVEALING
UNREVENGED
UNREVENGEFUL
UNREVEREND
UNREVERENT
UNREVERSED
UNREVERTED
UNREVIEWABLE
UNREVIEWED
UNREVOLUTIONARY
UNREWARDED
UNREWARDEDLY
UNREWARDING
UNRHETORICAL
UNRHYTHMIC
UNRHYTHMICAL
UNRHYTHMICALLY
UNRIDDLEABLE
UNRIDDLERS
UNRIDDLING
UNRIDEABLE
UNRIGHTEOUS
UNRIGHTEOUSLY
UNRIGHTEOUSNESS
UNRIGHTFUL
UNRIGHTFULLY
UNRIGHTFULNESS
UNRIGHTING
UNRIPENESS
UNRIPENESSES
UNRIPPINGS
UNRIVALLED
UNRIVETING
UNRIVETTED
UNRIVETTING
UNROADWORTHY
UNROMANISED
UNROMANIZED
UNROMANTIC
UNROMANTICAL
UNROMANTICALLY
UNROMANTICISED
UNROMANTICIZED
UNROOSTING
UNROUNDING
UNRUFFABLE
UNRUFFLEDNESS
UNRUFFLEDNESSES
UNRUFFLING
UNRULIMENT
UNRULIMENTS
UNRULINESS
UNRULINESSES
UNRUPTURED
UNSADDLING
UNSAFENESS
UNSAFENESSES

U

UNSAFETIES
UNSAILORLIKE
UNSAINTING
UNSAINTLIER
UNSAINTLIEST
UNSAINTLINESS
UNSAINTLINESSES
UNSALABILITIES
UNSALABILITY
UNSALARIED
UNSALEABILITIES
UNSALEABILITY
UNSALEABLE
UNSALEABLY
UNSALVAGEABLE
UNSANCTIFIED
UNSANCTIFIES
UNSANCTIFY
UNSANCTIFYING
UNSANCTIONED
UNSANDALLED
UNSANITARY
UNSATIABLE
UNSATIATED
UNSATIATING
UNSATIRICAL
UNSATISFACTION
UNSATISFACTIONS
UNSATISFACTORY
UNSATISFIABLE
UNSATISFIED
UNSATISFIEDNESS
UNSATISFYING
UNSATURATE
UNSATURATED
UNSATURATES
UNSATURATION
UNSATURATIONS
UNSAVORIER
UNSAVORIEST
UNSAVORILY
UNSAVORINESS
UNSAVORINESSES
UNSAVOURIER
UNSAVOURIEST
UNSAVOURILY
UNSAVOURINESS
UNSAVOURINESSES
UNSAYABLES
UNSCABBARD
UNSCABBARDED
UNSCABBARDING
UNSCABBARDS
UNSCALABLE
UNSCARIEST
UNSCAVENGERED
UNSCEPTRED
UNSCHEDULED
UNSCHOLARLIKE
UNSCHOLARLY
UNSCHOOLED
UNSCIENTIFIC
UNSCISSORED
UNSCORCHED
UNSCOTTIFIED
UNSCRAMBLE
UNSCRAMBLED
UNSCRAMBLER
UNSCRAMBLERS
UNSCRAMBLES
UNSCRAMBLING
UNSCRATCHED
UNSCREENED
UNSCREWING
UNSCRIPTED
UNSCRIPTURAL
UNSCRIPTURALLY
UNSCRUPLED
UNSCRUPULOSITY
UNSCRUPULOUS
UNSCRUPULOUSLY
UNSCRUTINISED
UNSCRUTINIZED
UNSCULPTURED
UNSEALABLE
UNSEARCHABLE
UNSEARCHABLES
UNSEARCHABLY
UNSEARCHED
UNSEASONABLE
UNSEASONABLY
UNSEASONED
UNSEASONEDNESS
UNSEASONING
UNSEAWORTHINESS
UNSEAWORTHY
UNSECONDED
UNSECRETED
UNSECRETING
UNSECTARIAN
UNSECTARIANISM
UNSECTARIANISMS
UNSECTARIANS
UNSEEMINGS
UNSEEMLIER
UNSEEMLIEST
UNSEEMLINESS
UNSEEMLINESSES
UNSEGMENTED
UNSEGREGATED
UNSEISABLE
UNSEIZABLE
UNSELECTED
UNSELECTIVE
UNSELECTIVELY
UNSELFCONSCIOUS
UNSELFISHLY
UNSELFISHNESS
UNSELFISHNESSES
UNSELLABLE
UNSEMINARIED
UNSENSATIONAL
UNSENSIBLE
UNSENSIBLY
UNSENSITISED
UNSENSITIVE
UNSENSITIZED
UNSENSUALISE
UNSENSUALISED
UNSENSUALISES
UNSENSUALISING
UNSENSUALIZE
UNSENSUALIZED
UNSENSUALIZES
UNSENSUALIZING
UNSENTENCED
UNSENTIMENTAL
UNSEPARABLE
UNSEPARATED
UNSEPULCHRED
UNSERIOUSNESS
UNSERIOUSNESSES
UNSERVICEABLE
UNSETTLEDLY
UNSETTLEDNESS
UNSETTLEDNESSES
UNSETTLEMENT
UNSETTLEMENTS
UNSETTLING
UNSETTLINGLY
UNSETTLINGS
UNSHACKLED
UNSHACKLES
UNSHACKLING
UNSHADOWABLE
UNSHADOWED
UNSHADOWING
UNSHAKABLE
UNSHAKABLENESS
UNSHAKABLY
UNSHAKEABLE
UNSHAKEABLENESS
UNSHAKEABLY
UNSHAKENLY
UNSHAPELIER
UNSHAPELIEST
UNSHARPENED
UNSHEATHED
UNSHEATHES
UNSHEATHING
UNSHELLING
UNSHELTERED
UNSHIELDED
UNSHIFTING
UNSHINGLED
UNSHIPPING
UNSHOCKABLE
UNSHOOTING
UNSHOTTING
UNSHOUTING
UNSHOWERED
UNSHOWIEST
UNSHRINKABLE
UNSHRINKING
UNSHRINKINGLY
UNSHROUDED
UNSHROUDING
UNSHRUBBED
UNSHUNNABLE
UNSHUTTERED
UNSHUTTERING
UNSHUTTERS
UNSHUTTING
UNSIGHTEDLY
UNSIGHTING
UNSIGHTLIER
UNSIGHTLIEST
UNSIGHTLINESS
UNSIGHTLINESSES
UNSINEWING
UNSINKABLE
UNSINNOWED
UNSISTERED
UNSISTERLINESS
UNSISTERLY
UNSIZEABLE
UNSKILFULLY
UNSKILFULNESS
UNSKILFULNESSES
UNSKILLFUL
UNSKILLFULLY
UNSKILLFULNESS
UNSLAKABLE
UNSLEEPING
UNSLEEPINGS
UNSLINGING
UNSLIPPING
UNSLUICING
UNSLUMBERING
UNSLUMBROUS
UNSMILINGLY
UNSMIRCHED
UNSMOKABLE
UNSMOOTHED
UNSMOOTHING
UNSMOTHERABLE
UNSNAGGING
UNSNAPPING
UNSNARLING
UNSNECKING
UNSOBERING
UNSOCIABILITIES
UNSOCIABILITY
UNSOCIABLE
UNSOCIABLENESS
UNSOCIABLY
UNSOCIALISED
UNSOCIALISM
UNSOCIALISMS
UNSOCIALITIES

U

UNSOCIALITY
UNSOCIALIZED
UNSOCIALLY
UNSOCKETED
UNSOCKETING
UNSOFTENED
UNSOFTENING
UNSOLDERED
UNSOLDERING
UNSOLDIERLIKE
UNSOLDIERLY
UNSOLICITED
UNSOLICITOUS
UNSOLIDITIES
UNSOLIDITY
UNSOLVABLE
UNSONSIEST
UNSOPHISTICATE
UNSOPHISTICATED
UNSOUNDABLE
UNSOUNDEST
UNSOUNDNESS
UNSOUNDNESSES
UNSPARINGLY
UNSPARINGNESS
UNSPARINGNESSES
UNSPARRING
UNSPEAKABLE
UNSPEAKABLENESS
UNSPEAKABLY
UNSPEAKING
UNSPECIALISED
UNSPECIALIZED
UNSPECIFIABLE
UNSPECIFIC
UNSPECIFICALLY
UNSPECIFIED
UNSPECTACLED
UNSPECTACULAR
UNSPECULATIVE
UNSPELLING
UNSPHERING
UNSPIRITED
UNSPIRITUAL
UNSPIRITUALISE
UNSPIRITUALISED
UNSPIRITUALISES
UNSPIRITUALIZE
UNSPIRITUALIZED
UNSPIRITUALIZES
UNSPIRITUALLY
UNSPLINTERABLE
UNSPOOLING
UNSPORTING
UNSPORTSMANLIKE
UNSPOTTEDNESS
UNSPOTTEDNESSES
UNSPRINKLED
UNSTABLENESS
UNSTABLENESSES
UNSTABLEST
UNSTACKING
UNSTAIDNESS
UNSTAIDNESSES
UNSTAINABLE
UNSTANCHABLE
UNSTANCHED
UNSTANDARDISED
UNSTANDARDIZED
UNSTARCHED
UNSTARCHES
UNSTARCHING
UNSTARRIER
UNSTARRIEST
UNSTARTLING
UNSTATESMANLIKE
UNSTATUTABLE
UNSTATUTABLY
UNSTAUNCHABLE
UNSTAUNCHED
UNSTEADFAST
UNSTEADFASTLY
UNSTEADFASTNESS
UNSTEADIED
UNSTEADIER
UNSTEADIES
UNSTEADIEST
UNSTEADILY
UNSTEADINESS
UNSTEADINESSES
UNSTEADYING
UNSTEELING
UNSTEPPING
UNSTERCORATED
UNSTEREOTYPED
UNSTERILISED
UNSTERILIZED
UNSTICKING
UNSTIFFENED
UNSTIFFENING
UNSTIFFENS
UNSTIGMATISED
UNSTIGMATIZED
UNSTIMULATED
UNSTINTING
UNSTINTINGLY
UNSTITCHED
UNSTITCHES
UNSTITCHING
UNSTOCKING
UNSTOCKINGED
UNSTOOPING
UNSTOPPABLE
UNSTOPPABLY
UNSTOPPERED
UNSTOPPERING
UNSTOPPERS
UNSTOPPING
UNSTRAINED
UNSTRAPPED
UNSTRAPPING
UNSTRATIFIED
UNSTREAMED
UNSTRENGTHENED
UNSTRESSED
UNSTRESSES
UNSTRESSING
UNSTRIATED
UNSTRINGED
UNSTRINGING
UNSTRIPPED
UNSTRIPPING
UNSTRUCTURED
UNSTUFFIER
UNSTUFFIEST
UNSUBDUABLE
UNSUBJECTED
UNSUBJECTING
UNSUBJECTS
UNSUBLIMATED
UNSUBLIMED
UNSUBMERGED
UNSUBMISSIVE
UNSUBMITTING
UNSUBSCRIBE
UNSUBSCRIBED
UNSUBSCRIBER
UNSUBSCRIBERS
UNSUBSCRIBES
UNSUBSCRIBING
UNSUBSIDISED
UNSUBSIDIZED
UNSUBSTANTIAL
UNSUBSTANTIALLY
UNSUBSTANTIATED
UNSUBTLEST
UNSUCCEEDED
UNSUCCESSES
UNSUCCESSFUL
UNSUCCESSFULLY
UNSUCCESSIVE
UNSUCCOURED
UNSUFFERABLE
UNSUFFICIENT
UNSUITABILITIES
UNSUITABILITY
UNSUITABLE
UNSUITABLENESS
UNSUITABLY
UNSUMMERED
UNSUMMONED
UNSUNNIEST
UNSUPERFLUOUS
UNSUPERVISED
UNSUPPLENESS
UNSUPPLENESSES
UNSUPPLIED
UNSUPPORTABLE
UNSUPPORTED
UNSUPPORTEDLY
UNSUPPOSABLE
UNSUPPRESSED
UNSURFACED
UNSURMISED
UNSURMOUNTABLE
UNSURPASSABLE
UNSURPASSABLY
UNSURPASSED
UNSURPRISED
UNSURPRISING
UNSURPRISINGLY
UNSURVEYED
UNSUSCEPTIBLE
UNSUSPECTED
UNSUSPECTEDLY
UNSUSPECTEDNESS
UNSUSPECTING
UNSUSPECTINGLY
UNSUSPENDED
UNSUSPICION
UNSUSPICIONS
UNSUSPICIOUS
UNSUSPICIOUSLY
UNSUSTAINABLE
UNSUSTAINABLY
UNSUSTAINED
UNSUSTAINING
UNSWADDLED
UNSWADDLES
UNSWADDLING
UNSWALLOWED
UNSWATHING
UNSWAYABLE
UNSWEARING
UNSWEARINGS
UNSWEETENED
UNSWERVING
UNSWERVINGLY
UNSYLLABLED
UNSYMMETRICAL
UNSYMMETRICALLY
UNSYMMETRIES
UNSYMMETRISED
UNSYMMETRIZED
UNSYMMETRY
UNSYMPATHETIC
UNSYMPATHIES
UNSYMPATHISING
UNSYMPATHIZING
UNSYMPATHY
UNSYNCHRONISED
UNSYNCHRONIZED
UNSYSTEMATIC
UNSYSTEMATICAL
UNSYSTEMATISED
UNSYSTEMATIZED
UNSYSTEMIC
UNTACKLING
UNTAILORED
UNTAINTEDLY

UNTAINTEDNESS
UNTAINTEDNESSES
UNTAINTING
UNTALENTED
UNTAMABLENESS
UNTAMABLENESSES
UNTAMEABLE
UNTAMEABLENESS
UNTAMEABLY
UNTAMEDNESS
UNTAMEDNESSES
UNTANGIBLE
UNTANGLING
UNTARNISHED
UNTASTEFUL
UNTEACHABLE
UNTEACHABLENESS
UNTEACHING
UNTEARABLE
UNTECHNICAL
UNTELLABLE
UNTEMPERED
UNTEMPERING
UNTENABILITIES
UNTENABILITY
UNTENABLENESS
UNTENABLENESSES
UNTENANTABLE
UNTENANTED
UNTENANTING
UNTENDERED
UNTENDERLY
UNTENTIEST
UNTERMINATED
UNTERRESTRIAL
UNTERRIFIED
UNTERRIFYING
UNTESTABLE
UNTETHERED
UNTETHERING
UNTHANKFUL
UNTHANKFULLY
UNTHANKFULNESS
UNTHATCHED
UNTHATCHES
UNTHATCHING
UNTHEOLOGICAL
UNTHEORETICAL
UNTHICKENED
UNTHINKABILITY
UNTHINKABLE
UNTHINKABLENESS
UNTHINKABLY
UNTHINKING
UNTHINKINGLY
UNTHINKINGNESS
UNTHOROUGH
UNTHOUGHTFUL
UNTHOUGHTFULLY
UNTHREADED
UNTHREADING
UNTHREATENED
UNTHREATENING
UNTHRESHED
UNTHRIFTIER
UNTHRIFTIEST
UNTHRIFTIHEAD
UNTHRIFTIHEADS
UNTHRIFTILY
UNTHRIFTINESS
UNTHRIFTINESSES
UNTHRIFTYHEAD
UNTHRIFTYHEADS
UNTHRIFTYHED
UNTHRIFTYHEDS
UNTHRONING
UNTIDINESS
UNTIDINESSES
UNTILLABLE
UNTIMBERED
UNTIMELIER
UNTIMELIEST
UNTIMELINESS
UNTIMELINESSES
UNTIMEOUSLY
UNTINCTURED
UNTIRINGLY
UNTOCHERED
UNTOGETHER
UNTORMENTED
UNTORTURED
UNTOUCHABILITY
UNTOUCHABLE
UNTOUCHABLES
UNTOWARDLINESS
UNTOWARDLY
UNTOWARDNESS
UNTOWARDNESSES
UNTRACEABLE
UNTRACKING
UNTRACTABLE
UNTRACTABLENESS
UNTRADITIONAL
UNTRADITIONALLY
UNTRAMMELED
UNTRAMMELLED
UNTRAMPLED
UNTRANQUIL
UNTRANSFERABLE
UNTRANSFERRABLE
UNTRANSFORMED
UNTRANSLATABLE
UNTRANSLATABLY
UNTRANSLATED
UNTRANSMIGRATED
UNTRANSMISSIBLE
UNTRANSMITTED
UNTRANSMUTABLE
UNTRANSMUTED
UNTRANSPARENT
UNTRAVELED
UNTRAVELLED
UNTRAVERSABLE
UNTRAVERSED
UNTREADING
UNTREASURE
UNTREASURED
UNTREASURES
UNTREASURING
UNTREATABLE
UNTREMBLING
UNTREMBLINGLY
UNTREMENDOUS
UNTREMULOUS
UNTRENCHED
UNTRENDIER
UNTRENDIEST
UNTRESPASSING
UNTRIMMING
UNTROUBLED
UNTROUBLEDLY
UNTRUENESS
UNTRUENESSES
UNTRUSSERS
UNTRUSSING
UNTRUSSINGS
UNTRUSTFUL
UNTRUSTIER
UNTRUSTIEST
UNTRUSTINESS
UNTRUSTINESSES
UNTRUSTING
UNTRUSTWORTHILY
UNTRUSTWORTHY
UNTRUTHFUL
UNTRUTHFULLY
UNTRUTHFULNESS
UNTUCKERED
UNTUMULTUOUS
UNTUNABLENESS
UNTUNABLENESSES
UNTUNEABLE
UNTUNEFULLY
UNTUNEFULNESS
UNTUNEFULNESSES
UNTURNABLE
UNTWISTING
UNTWISTINGS
UNTYPICALLY
UNTYREABLE
UNUNUNIUMS
UNUPLIFTED
UNUSEFULLY
UNUSEFULNESS
UNUSEFULNESSES
UNUSUALNESS
UNUSUALNESSES
UNUTILISED
UNUTILIZED
UNUTTERABLE
UNUTTERABLENESS
UNUTTERABLES
UNUTTERABLY
UNVACCINATED
UNVALUABLE
UNVANQUISHABLE
UNVANQUISHED
UNVARIABLE
UNVARIEGATED
UNVARNISHED
UNVARYINGLY
UNVEILINGS
UNVENDIBLE
UNVENERABLE
UNVENTILATED
UNVERACIOUS
UNVERACITIES
UNVERACITY
UNVERBALISED
UNVERBALIZED
UNVERIFIABILITY
UNVERIFIABLE
UNVERIFIED
UNVIOLATED
UNVIRTUOUS
UNVIRTUOUSLY
UNVISITABLE
UNVISORING
UNVITIATED
UNVITRIFIABLE
UNVITRIFIED
UNVIZARDED
UNVIZARDING
UNVOCALISED
UNVOCALIZED
UNVOICINGS
UNVOYAGEABLE
UNVULGARISE
UNVULGARISED
UNVULGARISES
UNVULGARISING
UNVULGARIZE
UNVULGARIZED
UNVULGARIZES
UNVULGARIZING
UNVULNERABLE
UNWANDERING
UNWARENESS
UNWARENESSES
UNWARINESS
UNWARINESSES
UNWARRANTABLE
UNWARRANTABLY
UNWARRANTED
UNWARRANTEDLY
UNWASHEDNESS
UNWASHEDNESSES
UNWATCHABLE
UNWATCHFUL
UNWATCHFULLY

UNWATCHFULNESS
UNWATERING
UNWAVERING
UNWAVERINGLY
UNWEAKENED
UNWEAPONED
UNWEAPONING
UNWEARABLE
UNWEARABLES
UNWEARIABLE
UNWEARIABLY
UNWEARIEDLY
UNWEARIEDNESS
UNWEARIEDNESSES
UNWEARIEST
UNWEARYING
UNWEARYINGLY
UNWEATHERED
UNWEDGABLE
UNWEDGEABLE
UNWEETINGLY
UNWEIGHING
UNWEIGHTED
UNWEIGHTING
UNWEIGHTINGS
UNWELCOMED
UNWELCOMELY
UNWELCOMENESS
UNWELCOMENESSES
UNWELCOMING
UNWELLNESS
UNWELLNESSES
UNWESTERNISED
UNWESTERNIZED
UNWHISTLEABLE
UNWHOLESOME
UNWHOLESOMELY
UNWHOLESOMENESS
UNWIELDIER
UNWIELDIEST
UNWIELDILY
UNWIELDINESS
UNWIELDINESSES
UNWIELDLILY
UNWIELDLINESS
UNWIELDLINESSES
UNWIFELIER
UNWIFELIEST
UNWIFELIKE
UNWILLINGLY
UNWILLINGNESS
UNWILLINGNESSES
UNWINDABLE
UNWINDINGS
UNWINKINGLY
UNWINNABLE
UNWINNOWED
UNWISENESS
UNWISENESSES
UNWITCHING
UNWITHDRAWING
UNWITHERED
UNWITHERING
UNWITHHELD
UNWITHHOLDEN
UNWITHHOLDING
UNWITHSTOOD
UNWITNESSED
UNWITTIEST
UNWITTINGLY
UNWITTINGNESS
UNWITTINGNESSES
UNWOMANING
UNWOMANLIER
UNWOMANLIEST
UNWOMANLINESS
UNWOMANLINESSES
UNWONTEDLY
UNWONTEDNESS
UNWONTEDNESSES
UNWORKABILITIES
UNWORKABILITY
UNWORKABLE
UNWORKMANLIKE
UNWORLDLIER
UNWORLDLIEST
UNWORLDLINESS
UNWORLDLINESSES
UNWORSHIPFUL
UNWORSHIPPED
UNWORTHIER
UNWORTHIES
UNWORTHIEST
UNWORTHILY
UNWORTHINESS
UNWORTHINESSES
UNWOUNDABLE
UNWRAPPING
UNWREATHED
UNWREATHES
UNWREATHING
UNWRINKLED
UNWRINKLES
UNWRINKLING
UNYIELDING
UNYIELDINGLY
UNYIELDINGNESS
UPBRAIDERS
UPBRAIDING
UPBRAIDINGLY
UPBRAIDINGS
UPBREAKING
UPBRINGING
UPBRINGINGS
UPBUILDERS
UPBUILDING
UPBUILDINGS
UPBUOYANCE
UPBUOYANCES
UPBURSTING
UPCATCHING
UPCHEERING
UPCHUCKING
UPCLIMBING
UPCOUNTRIES
UPDATEABLE
UPDRAGGING
UPDRAGGINGS
UPDRAUGHTS
UPFILLINGS
UPFLASHING
UPFLINGING
UPFOLLOWED
UPFOLLOWING
UPGATHERED
UPGATHERING
UPGRADABILITIES
UPGRADABILITY
UPGRADABLE
UPGRADATION
UPGRADATIONS
UPGRADEABILITY
UPGRADEABLE
UPGROWINGS
UPHEAPINGS
UPHILLWARD
UPHOARDING
UPHOISTING
UPHOLDINGS
UPHOLSTERED
UPHOLSTERER
UPHOLSTERERS
UPHOLSTERIES
UPHOLSTERING
UPHOLSTERS
UPHOLSTERY
UPHOLSTRESS
UPHOLSTRESSES
UPHOORDING
UPKNITTING
UPLIFTINGLY
UPLIFTINGS
UPLIGHTERS
UPLIGHTING
UPLIGHTINGS
UPLINKINGS
UPMANSHIPS
UPMARKETED
UPMARKETING
UPPERCASED
UPPERCASES
UPPERCASING
UPPERCLASSMAN
UPPERCLASSMEN
UPPERCUTTING
UPPERPARTS
UPPERWORKS
UPPISHNESS
UPPISHNESSES
UPPITINESS
UPPITINESSES
UPPITYNESS
UPPITYNESSES
UPPROPPING
UPREACHING
UPRIGHTEOUSLY
UPRIGHTING
UPRIGHTNESS
UPRIGHTNESSES
UPROARIOUS
UPROARIOUSLY
UPROARIOUSNESS
UPROOTEDNESS
UPROOTEDNESSES
UPROOTINGS
UPSETTABLE
UPSETTINGLY
UPSETTINGS
UPSHIFTING
UPSHOOTING
UPSIDEOWNE
UPSITTINGS
UPSKILLING
UPSKIRTING
UPSKIRTINGS
UPSPEAKING
UPSPEARING
UPSPRINGING
UPSTANDING
UPSTANDINGNESS
UPSTARTING
UPSTEPPING
UPSTEPPINGS
UPSTIRRING
UPSTREAMED
UPSTREAMING
UPSTRETCHED
UPSURGENCE
UPSURGENCES
UPSWARMING
UPSWEEPING
UPSWELLING
UPSWINGING
UPTALKINGS
UPTHROWING
UPTHRUSTED
UPTHRUSTING
UPTHUNDERED
UPTHUNDERING
UPTHUNDERS
UPTIGHTEST
UPTIGHTNESS
UPTIGHTNESSES
UPTITLINGS
UPTRAINING
UPTURNINGS
UPVALUATION
UPVALUATIONS
UPWARDNESS
UPWARDNESSES

UPWELLINGS
UPWHIRLING
URALITISATION
URALITISATIONS
URALITISED
URALITISES
URALITISING
URALITIZATION
URALITIZATIONS
URALITIZED
URALITIZES
URALITIZING
URANALYSES
URANALYSIS
URANINITES
URANOGRAPHER
URANOGRAPHERS
URANOGRAPHIC
URANOGRAPHICAL
URANOGRAPHIES
URANOGRAPHIST
URANOGRAPHISTS
URANOGRAPHY
URANOLOGIES
URANOMETRIES
URANOMETRY
URANOPLASTIES
URANOPLASTY
URBANENESS
URBANENESSES
URBANISATION
URBANISATIONS
URBANISING
URBANISTIC
URBANISTICALLY
URBANITIES
URBANIZATION
URBANIZATIONS
URBANIZING
URBANOLOGIES
URBANOLOGIST
URBANOLOGISTS
URBANOLOGY
URCEOLUSES
UREDINIOSPORE
UREDINIOSPORES
UREDINIUMS
UREDIOSPORE
UREDIOSPORES
UREDOSORUS
UREDOSPORE
UREDOSPORES
UREOTELISM
UREOTELISMS
URETERITIS
URETERITISES
URETHANING
URETHRITIC
URETHRITIDES
URETHRITIS
URETHRITISES
URETHROSCOPE
URETHROSCOPES
URETHROSCOPIC
URETHROSCOPIES
URETHROSCOPY
URICOSURIC
URICOTELIC
URICOTELISM
URICOTELISMS
URINALYSES
URINALYSIS
URINATIONS
URINIFEROUS
URINIPAROUS
URINOGENITAL
URINOLOGIES
URINOMETER
URINOMETERS
URINOSCOPIES
URINOSCOPY
UROBILINOGEN
UROBILINOGENS
UROBOROSES
UROCHORDAL
UROCHORDATE
UROCHORDATES
UROCHROMES
URODYNAMICS
UROGENITAL
UROGENITALS
UROGRAPHIC
UROGRAPHIES
UROKINASES
UROLAGNIAS
UROLITHIASES
UROLITHIASIS
UROLOGICAL
UROLOGISTS
UROPOIESES
UROPOIESIS
UROPYGIUMS
UROSCOPIES
UROSCOPIST
UROSCOPISTS
UROSTEGITE
UROSTEGITES
UROSTHENIC
UROSTOMIES
URTICACEOUS
URTICARIAL
URTICARIAS
URTICARIOUS
URTICATING
URTICATION
URTICATIONS
USABILITIES
USABLENESS
USABLENESSES
USEABILITIES
USEABILITY
USEABLENESS
USEABLENESSES
USEFULNESS
USEFULNESSES
USELESSNESS
USELESSNESSES
USHERESSES
USHERETTES
USHERSHIPS
USQUEBAUGH
USQUEBAUGHS
USTILAGINEOUS
USTILAGINOUS
USTULATING
USTULATION
USTULATIONS
USUALNESSES
USUCAPIENT
USUCAPIENTS
USUCAPIONS
USUCAPTIBLE
USUCAPTING
USUCAPTION
USUCAPTIONS
USUFRUCTED
USUFRUCTING
USUFRUCTUARIES
USUFRUCTUARY
USURIOUSLY
USURIOUSNESS
USURIOUSNESSES
USURPATION
USURPATIONS
USURPATIVE
USURPATORY
USURPATURE
USURPATURES
USURPINGLY
UTERECTOMIES
UTERECTOMY
UTERITISES
UTEROGESTATION
UTEROGESTATIONS
UTEROTOMIES
UTILISABLE
UTILISATION
UTILISATIONS
UTILITARIAN
UTILITARIANISE
UTILITARIANISED
UTILITARIANISES
UTILITARIANISM
UTILITARIANISMS
UTILITARIANIZE
UTILITARIANIZED
UTILITARIANIZES
UTILITARIANS
UTILIZABLE
UTILIZATION
UTILIZATIONS
UTOPIANISE
UTOPIANISED
UTOPIANISER
UTOPIANISERS
UTOPIANISES
UTOPIANISING
UTOPIANISM
UTOPIANISMS
UTOPIANIZE
UTOPIANIZED
UTOPIANIZER
UTOPIANIZERS
UTOPIANIZES
UTOPIANIZING
UTRICULARIA
UTRICULARIAS
UTRICULATE
UTRICULITIS
UTRICULITISES
UTTERABLENESS
UTTERABLENESSES
UTTERANCES
UTTERMOSTS
UTTERNESSES
UVAROVITES
UVULITISES
UXORICIDAL
UXORICIDES
UXORILOCAL
UXORIOUSLY
UXORIOUSNESS
UXORIOUSNESSES

V

VACANTNESS
VACANTNESSES
VACATIONED
VACATIONER
VACATIONERS
VACATIONING
VACATIONIST
VACATIONISTS
VACATIONLAND
VACATIONLANDS
VACATIONLESS
VACCINATED
VACCINATES
VACCINATING
VACCINATION
VACCINATIONS
VACCINATOR
VACCINATORS
VACCINATORY
VACCINIUMS
VACILLATED
VACILLATES
VACILLATING
VACILLATINGLY
VACILLATION
VACILLATIONS
VACILLATOR
VACILLATORS
VACILLATORY
VACUATIONS
VACUOLATED
VACUOLATION
VACUOLATIONS
VACUOLISATION
VACUOLISATIONS
VACUOLIZATION
VACUOLIZATIONS
VACUOUSNESS
VACUOUSNESSES
VAGABONDAGE
VAGABONDAGES
VAGABONDED
VAGABONDING
VAGABONDISE
VAGABONDISED
VAGABONDISES
VAGABONDISH
VAGABONDISING
VAGABONDISM
VAGABONDISMS
VAGABONDIZE
VAGABONDIZED
VAGABONDIZES
VAGABONDIZING
VAGARIOUSLY
VAGILITIES
VAGINECTOMIES
VAGINECTOMY
VAGINICOLINE
VAGINICOLOUS
VAGINISMUS
VAGINISMUSES
VAGINITIDES
VAGINITISES
VAGOTOMIES
VAGOTONIAS
VAGOTROPIC
VAGRANCIES
VAGRANTNESS
VAGRANTNESSES
VAGUENESSES
VAINGLORIED
VAINGLORIES
VAINGLORIOUS
VAINGLORIOUSLY
VAINGLORYING
VAINNESSES
VAIVODESHIP
VAIVODESHIPS
VAJAZZLING
VAJAZZLINGS
VALEDICTION
VALEDICTIONS
VALEDICTORIAN
VALEDICTORIANS
VALEDICTORIES
VALEDICTORY
VALENTINES
VALERIANACEOUS
VALETUDINARIAN
VALETUDINARIANS
VALETUDINARIES
VALETUDINARY
VALIANCIES
VALIANTNESS
VALIANTNESSES
VALIDATING
VALIDATION
VALIDATIONS
VALIDATORS
VALIDATORY
VALIDITIES
VALIDNESSES
VALLATIONS
VALLECULAE
VALLECULAR
VALLECULAS
VALLECULATE
VALORISATION
VALORISATIONS
VALORISING
VALORIZATION
VALORIZATIONS
VALORIZING
VALOROUSLY
VALPOLICELLA
VALPOLICELLAS
VALPROATES
VALUABLENESS
VALUABLENESSES
VALUATIONAL
VALUATIONALLY
VALUATIONS
VALUELESSNESS
VALUELESSNESSES
VALVASSORS
VALVULITIS
VALVULITISES
VAMPIRISED
VAMPIRISES
VAMPIRISING
VAMPIRISMS
VAMPIRIZED
VAMPIRIZES
VAMPIRIZING
VANADIATES
VANADINITE
VANADINITES
VANASPATIS
VANCOMYCIN
VANCOMYCINS
VANDALISATION
VANDALISATIONS
VANDALISED
VANDALISES
VANDALISING
VANDALISMS
VANDALISTIC
VANDALIZATION
VANDALIZATIONS
VANDALIZED
VANDALIZES
VANDALIZING
VANGUARDISM
VANGUARDISMS
VANGUARDIST
VANGUARDISTS
VANISHINGLY
VANISHINGS
VANISHMENT
VANISHMENTS
VANITORIES
VANPOOLING
VANPOOLINGS
VANQUISHABLE
VANQUISHED
VANQUISHER
VANQUISHERS
VANQUISHES
VANQUISHING
VANQUISHMENT
VANQUISHMENTS
VANTAGELESS
VANTBRACES
VANTBRASSES
VAPIDITIES
VAPIDNESSES
VAPORABILITIES
VAPORABILITY
VAPORESCENCE
VAPORESCENCES
VAPORESCENT
VAPORETTOS
VAPORIFORM
VAPORIMETER
VAPORIMETERS
VAPORISABLE
VAPORISATION
VAPORISATIONS
VAPORISERS
VAPORISHNESS
VAPORISHNESSES
VAPORISING
VAPORIZABLE
VAPORIZATION
VAPORIZATIONS
VAPORIZERS
VAPORIZING
VAPOROSITIES
VAPOROSITY
VAPOROUSLY
VAPOROUSNESS
VAPOROUSNESSES
VAPORWARES
VAPOURABILITIES
VAPOURABILITY
VAPOURABLE
VAPOURIEST
VAPOURINGLY
VAPOURINGS

V

VAPOURISHNESS
VAPOURISHNESSES
VAPOURLESS
VAPOURWARE
VAPOURWARES
VAPULATING
VAPULATION
VAPULATIONS
VARIABILITIES
VARIABILITY
VARIABLENESS
VARIABLENESSES
VARIATIONAL
VARIATIONALLY
VARIATIONIST
VARIATIONISTS
VARIATIONS
VARICELLAR
VARICELLAS
VARICELLATE
VARICELLOID
VARICELLOUS
VARICOCELE
VARICOCELES
VARICOLORED
VARICOLOURED
VARICOSITIES
VARICOSITY
VARICOTOMIES
VARICOTOMY
VARIEDNESS
VARIEDNESSES
VARIEGATED
VARIEGATES
VARIEGATING
VARIEGATION
VARIEGATIONS
VARIEGATOR
VARIEGATORS
VARIETALLY
VARIFOCALS
VARIFORMLY
VARIOLATED
VARIOLATES
VARIOLATING
VARIOLATION
VARIOLATIONS
VARIOLATOR
VARIOLATORS
VARIOLISATION
VARIOLISATIONS
VARIOLITES
VARIOLITIC
VARIOLIZATION
VARIOLIZATIONS
VARIOLOIDS
VARIOMETER
VARIOMETERS
VARIOUSNESS
VARIOUSNESSES
VARISCITES
VARITYPING
VARITYPIST
VARITYPISTS
VARLETESSES
VARLETRIES
VARNISHERS
VARNISHIER
VARNISHIEST
VARNISHING
VARNISHINGS
VARSOVIENNE
VARSOVIENNES
VASCULARISATION
VASCULARISE
VASCULARISED
VASCULARISES
VASCULARISING
VASCULARITIES
VASCULARITY
VASCULARIZATION
VASCULARIZE
VASCULARIZED
VASCULARIZES
VASCULARIZING
VASCULARLY
VASCULATURE
VASCULATURES
VASCULIFORM
VASCULITIDES
VASCULITIS
VASCULITISES
VASECTOMIES
VASECTOMISE
VASECTOMISED
VASECTOMISES
VASECTOMISING
VASECTOMIZE
VASECTOMIZED
VASECTOMIZES
VASECTOMIZING
VASELINING
VASOACTIVE
VASOACTIVITIES
VASOACTIVITY
VASOCONSTRICTOR
VASODILATATION
VASODILATATIONS
VASODILATATORY
VASODILATION
VASODILATIONS
VASODILATOR
VASODILATORS
VASODILATORY
VASOINHIBITOR
VASOINHIBITORS
VASOINHIBITORY
VASOPRESSIN
VASOPRESSINS
VASOPRESSOR
VASOPRESSORS
VASOSPASMS
VASOSPASTIC
VASOTOCINS
VASOTOMIES
VASSALAGES
VASSALESSES
VASSALISED
VASSALISES
VASSALISING
VASSALIZED
VASSALIZES
VASSALIZING
VASSALLING
VASSALRIES
VASTIDITIES
VASTITUDES
VASTNESSES
VATICINATE
VATICINATED
VATICINATES
VATICINATING
VATICINATION
VATICINATIONS
VATICINATOR
VATICINATORS
VATICINATORY
VAUDEVILLE
VAUDEVILLEAN
VAUDEVILLEANS
VAUDEVILLES
VAUDEVILLIAN
VAUDEVILLIANS
VAUDEVILLIST
VAUDEVILLISTS
VAULTINGLY
VAUNTERIES
VAUNTINGLY
VAVASORIES
VECTOGRAPH
VECTOGRAPHS
VECTORIALLY
VECTORINGS
VECTORISATION
VECTORISATIONS
VECTORISED
VECTORISES
VECTORISING
VECTORIZATION
VECTORIZATIONS
VECTORIZED
VECTORIZES
VECTORIZING
VECTORSCOPE
VECTORSCOPES
VEDUTISTAS
VEGEBURGER
VEGEBURGERS
VEGETABLES
VEGETABLIER
VEGETABLIEST
VEGETARIAN
VEGETARIANISM
VEGETARIANISMS
VEGETARIANS
VEGETATING
VEGETATINGS
VEGETATION
VEGETATIONAL
VEGETATIONS
VEGETATIOUS
VEGETATIVE
VEGETATIVELY
VEGETATIVENESS
VEGGIEBURGER
VEGGIEBURGERS
VEHEMENCES
VEHEMENCIES
VEHEMENTLY
VEILLEUSES
VEINSTONES
VEINSTUFFS
VELARISATION
VELARISATIONS
VELARISING
VELARIZATION
VELARIZATIONS
VELARIZING
VELDSCHOEN
VELDSCHOENS
VELDSKOENS
VELITATION
VELITATIONS
VELLEITIES
VELLENAGES
VELLICATED
VELLICATES
VELLICATING
VELLICATION
VELLICATIONS
VELLICATIVE
VELOCIMETER
VELOCIMETERS
VELOCIMETRIES
VELOCIMETRY
VELOCIPEDE
VELOCIPEDEAN
VELOCIPEDEANS
VELOCIPEDED
VELOCIPEDER
VELOCIPEDERS
VELOCIPEDES
VELOCIPEDIAN
VELOCIPEDIANS
VELOCIPEDING
VELOCIPEDIST
VELOCIPEDISTS
VELOCIRAPTOR
VELOCIRAPTORS
VELOCITIES

VELODROMES
VELOUTINES
VELUTINOUS
VELVETEENED
VELVETEENS
VELVETIEST
VELVETINESS
VELVETINESSES
VELVETINGS
VELVETLIKE
VENALITIES
VENATICALLY
VENATIONAL
VENATORIAL
VENDETTIST
VENDETTISTS
VENDIBILITIES
VENDIBILITY
VENDIBLENESS
VENDIBLENESSES
VENDITATION
VENDITATIONS
VENDITIONS
VENEERINGS
VENEFICALLY
VENEFICIOUS
VENEFICIOUSLY
VENEFICOUS
VENEFICOUSLY
VENENATING
VENEPUNCTURE
VENEPUNCTURES
VENERABILITIES
VENERABILITY
VENERABLENESS
VENERABLENESSES
VENERABLES
VENERATING
VENERATION
VENERATIONAL
VENERATIONS
VENERATIVE
VENERATIVENESS
VENERATORS
VENEREALLY
VENEREOLOGICAL
VENEREOLOGIES
VENEREOLOGIST
VENEREOLOGISTS
VENEREOLOGY
VENESECTION
VENESECTIONS
VENGEANCES
VENGEFULLY
VENGEFULNESS
VENGEFULNESSES
VENGEMENTS
VENIALITIES
VENIALNESS
VENIALNESSES
VENIPUNCTURE
VENIPUNCTURES
VENISECTION
VENISECTIONS
VENOGRAPHIC
VENOGRAPHICAL
VENOGRAPHIES
VENOGRAPHY
VENOLOGIES
VENOMOUSLY
VENOMOUSNESS
VENOMOUSNESSES
VENOSCLEROSES
VENOSCLEROSIS
VENOSITIES
VENOUSNESS
VENOUSNESSES
VENTIDUCTS
VENTIFACTS
VENTILABLE
VENTILATED
VENTILATES
VENTILATING
VENTILATION
VENTILATIONS
VENTILATIVE
VENTILATOR
VENTILATORS
VENTILATORY
VENTOSITIES
VENTRICLES
VENTRICOSE
VENTRICOSITIES
VENTRICOSITY
VENTRICOUS
VENTRICULAR
VENTRICULE
VENTRICULES
VENTRICULI
VENTRICULUS
VENTRILOQUAL
VENTRILOQUIAL
VENTRILOQUIALLY
VENTRILOQUIES
VENTRILOQUISE
VENTRILOQUISED
VENTRILOQUISES
VENTRILOQUISING
VENTRILOQUISM
VENTRILOQUISMS
VENTRILOQUIST
VENTRILOQUISTIC
VENTRILOQUISTS
VENTRILOQUIZE
VENTRILOQUIZED
VENTRILOQUIZES
VENTRILOQUIZING
VENTRILOQUOUS
VENTRILOQUY
VENTRIPOTENT
VENTROLATERAL
VENTROMEDIAL
VENTURESOME
VENTURESOMELY
VENTURESOMENESS
VENTURINGLY
VENTURINGS
VENTUROUSLY
VENTUROUSNESS
VENTUROUSNESSES
VERACIOUSLY
VERACIOUSNESS
VERACIOUSNESSES
VERACITIES
VERANDAHED
VERAPAMILS
VERATRIDINE
VERATRIDINES
VERATRINES
VERBALISATION
VERBALISATIONS
VERBALISED
VERBALISER
VERBALISERS
VERBALISES
VERBALISING
VERBALISMS
VERBALISTIC
VERBALISTS
VERBALITIES
VERBALIZATION
VERBALIZATIONS
VERBALIZED
VERBALIZER
VERBALIZERS
VERBALIZES
VERBALIZING
VERBALLING
VERBARIANS
VERBASCUMS
VERBENACEOUS
VERBERATED
VERBERATES
VERBERATING
VERBERATION
VERBERATIONS
VERBICIDES
VERBIFICATION
VERBIFICATIONS
VERBIFYING
VERBIGERATE
VERBIGERATED
VERBIGERATES
VERBIGERATING
VERBIGERATION
VERBIGERATIONS
VERBOSENESS
VERBOSENESSES
VERBOSITIES
VERDANCIES
VERDIGRISED
VERDIGRISES
VERDIGRISING
VERDURELESS
VERGEBOARD
VERGEBOARDS
VERGENCIES
VERGERSHIP
VERGERSHIPS
VERIDICALITIES
VERIDICALITY
VERIDICALLY
VERIDICOUS
VERIFIABILITIES
VERIFIABILITY
VERIFIABLE
VERIFIABLENESS
VERIFIABLY
VERIFICATION
VERIFICATIONS
VERIFICATIVE
VERIFICATORY
VERISIMILAR
VERISIMILARLY
VERISIMILITIES
VERISIMILITUDE
VERISIMILITUDES
VERISIMILITY
VERISIMILOUS
VERITABLENESS
VERITABLENESSES
VERJUICING
VERKRAMPTE
VERKRAMPTES
VERMEILING
VERMEILLED
VERMEILLES
VERMEILLING
VERMICELLI
VERMICELLIS
VERMICIDAL
VERMICIDES
VERMICULAR
VERMICULARLY
VERMICULATE
VERMICULATED
VERMICULATES
VERMICULATING
VERMICULATION
VERMICULATIONS
VERMICULES
VERMICULITE
VERMICULITES
VERMICULOUS
VERMICULTURE
VERMICULTURES
VERMIFUGAL
VERMIFUGES
VERMILIONED
VERMILIONING

VERMILIONS
VERMILLING
VERMILLION
VERMILLIONS
VERMINATED
VERMINATES
VERMINATING
VERMINATION
VERMINATIONS
VERMINIEST
VERMINOUSLY
VERMINOUSNESS
VERMINOUSNESSES
VERMIVOROUS
VERNACULAR
VERNACULARISE
VERNACULARISED
VERNACULARISES
VERNACULARISING
VERNACULARISM
VERNACULARISMS
VERNACULARIST
VERNACULARISTS
VERNACULARITIES
VERNACULARITY
VERNACULARIZE
VERNACULARIZED
VERNACULARIZES
VERNACULARIZING
VERNACULARLY
VERNACULARS
VERNALISATION
VERNALISATIONS
VERNALISED
VERNALISES
VERNALISING
VERNALITIES
VERNALIZATION
VERNALIZATIONS
VERNALIZED
VERNALIZES
VERNALIZING
VERNATIONS
VERNISSAGE
VERNISSAGES
VERRUCIFORM
VERRUCOSITIES
VERRUCOSITY
VERSABILITIES
VERSABILITY
VERSATILELY
VERSATILENESS
VERSATILENESSES
VERSATILITIES
VERSATILITY
VERSICOLOR
VERSICOLORED
VERSICOLOUR
VERSICOLOURED
VERSICULAR
VERSIFICATION
VERSIFICATIONS
VERSIFICATOR
VERSIFICATORS
VERSIFIERS
VERSIFYING
VERSIONERS
VERSIONING
VERSIONINGS
VERSIONIST
VERSIONISTS
VERSLIBRIST
VERSLIBRISTE
VERSLIBRISTES
VERSLIBRISTS
VERTEBRALLY
VERTEBRATE
VERTEBRATED
VERTEBRATES
VERTEBRATION
VERTEBRATIONS
VERTICALITIES
VERTICALITY
VERTICALLY
VERTICALNESS
VERTICALNESSES
VERTICILLASTER
VERTICILLASTERS
VERTICILLATE
VERTICILLATED
VERTICILLATELY
VERTICILLATION
VERTICILLATIONS
VERTICILLIUM
VERTICILLIUMS
VERTICITIES
VERTIGINES
VERTIGINOUS
VERTIGINOUSLY
VERTIGINOUSNESS
VERTIPORTS
VERUMONTANA
VERUMONTANUM
VERUMONTANUMS
VESICATING
VESICATION
VESICATIONS
VESICATORIES
VESICATORY
VESICULARITIES
VESICULARITY
VESICULARLY
VESICULATE
VESICULATED
VESICULATES
VESICULATING
VESICULATION
VESICULATIONS
VESICULOSE
VESPERTILIAN
VESPERTILIONID
VESPERTILIONIDS
VESPERTILIONINE
VESPERTINAL
VESPERTINE
VESPIARIES
VESTIARIES
VESTIBULAR
VESTIBULED
VESTIBULES
VESTIBULING
VESTIBULITIS
VESTIBULITISES
VESTIBULUM
VESTIGIALLY
VESTIMENTAL
VESTIMENTARY
VESTIMENTS
VESTITURES
VESTMENTAL
VESTMENTED
VESUVIANITE
VESUVIANITES
VETCHLINGS
VETERINARIAN
VETERINARIANS
VETERINARIES
VETERINARY
VETTURINOS
VEXATIOUSLY
VEXATIOUSNESS
VEXATIOUSNESSES
VEXEDNESSES
VEXILLARIES
VEXILLATION
VEXILLATIONS
VEXILLOLOGIC
VEXILLOLOGICAL
VEXILLOLOGIES
VEXILLOLOGIST
VEXILLOLOGISTS
VEXILLOLOGY
VEXINGNESS
VEXINGNESSES
VIABILITIES
VIBRACULAR
VIBRACULARIA
VIBRACULARIUM
VIBRACULOID
VIBRACULUM
VIBRAHARPIST
VIBRAHARPISTS
VIBRAHARPS
VIBRANCIES
VIBRAPHONE
VIBRAPHONES
VIBRAPHONIST
VIBRAPHONISTS
VIBRATILITIES
VIBRATILITY
VIBRATINGLY
VIBRATIONAL
VIBRATIONLESS
VIBRATIONS
VIBRATIUNCLE
VIBRATIUNCLES
VIBRATOLESS
VIBROFLOTATION
VIBROFLOTATIONS
VIBROGRAPH
VIBROGRAPHS
VIBROMETER
VIBROMETERS
VICARESSES
VICARIANCE
VICARIANCES
VICARIANTS
VICARIATES
VICARIOUSLY
VICARIOUSNESS
VICARIOUSNESSES
VICARLIEST
VICARSHIPS
VICEGERENCIES
VICEGERENCY
VICEGERENT
VICEGERENTS
VICEREGALLY
VICEREGENT
VICEREGENTS
VICEREINES
VICEROYALTIES
VICEROYALTY
VICEROYSHIP
VICEROYSHIPS
VICHYSSOIS
VICHYSSOISE
VICHYSSOISES
VICINITIES
VICIOSITIES
VICIOUSNESS
VICIOUSNESSES
VICISSITUDE
VICISSITUDES
VICISSITUDINARY
VICISSITUDINOUS
VICOMTESSE
VICOMTESSES
VICTIMHOOD
VICTIMHOODS
VICTIMISATION
VICTIMISATIONS
VICTIMISED
VICTIMISER
VICTIMISERS
VICTIMISES
VICTIMISING
VICTIMIZATION
VICTIMIZATIONS
VICTIMIZED

V

VICTIMIZER
VICTIMIZERS
VICTIMIZES
VICTIMIZING
VICTIMLESS
VICTIMOLOGIES
VICTIMOLOGIST
VICTIMOLOGISTS
VICTIMOLOGY
VICTORESSES
VICTORIANA
VICTORIANAS
VICTORINES
VICTORIOUS
VICTORIOUSLY
VICTORIOUSNESS
VICTORYLESS
VICTRESSES
VICTUALAGE
VICTUALAGES
VICTUALERS
VICTUALING
VICTUALLAGE
VICTUALLAGES
VICTUALLED
VICTUALLER
VICTUALLERS
VICTUALLESS
VICTUALLING
VIDEOCASSETTE
VIDEOCASSETTES
VIDEOCONFERENCE
VIDEODISCS
VIDEODISKS
VIDEOGRAMS
VIDEOGRAPHER
VIDEOGRAPHERS
VIDEOGRAPHIES
VIDEOGRAPHY
VIDEOLANDS
VIDEOPHILE
VIDEOPHILES
VIDEOPHONE
VIDEOPHONES
VIDEOPHONIC
VIDEOTAPED
VIDEOTAPES
VIDEOTAPING
VIDEOTELEPHONE
VIDEOTELEPHONES
VIDEOTEXES
VIDEOTEXTS
VIDEOTHEQUE
VIDEOTHEQUES
VIDSCREENS
VIEWERSHIP
VIEWERSHIPS
VIEWFINDER
VIEWFINDERS
VIEWINESSES
VIEWLESSLY
VIEWPHONES
VIEWPOINTS
VIGILANCES
VIGILANTES
VIGILANTISM
VIGILANTISMS
VIGILANTLY
VIGILANTNESS
VIGILANTNESSES
VIGINTILLION
VIGINTILLIONS
VIGNETTERS
VIGNETTING
VIGNETTINGS
VIGNETTIST
VIGNETTISTS
VIGORISHES
VIGOROUSLY
VIGOROUSNESS
VIGOROUSNESSES
VIKINGISMS
VILDNESSES
VILENESSES
VILIFICATION
VILIFICATIONS
VILIPENDED
VILIPENDER
VILIPENDERS
VILIPENDING
VILLAGERIES
VILLAGIEST
VILLAGIOES
VILLAGISATION
VILLAGISATIONS
VILLAGIZATION
VILLAGIZATIONS
VILLAGREES
VILLAINAGE
VILLAINAGES
VILLAINESS
VILLAINESSES
VILLAINIES
VILLAINOUS
VILLAINOUSLY
VILLAINOUSNESS
VILLANAGES
VILLANELLA
VILLANELLAS
VILLANELLE
VILLANELLES
VILLANOUSLY
VILLEGGIATURA
VILLEGGIATURAS
VILLEINAGE
VILLEINAGES
VILLENAGES
VILLIACOES
VILLIAGOES
VILLICATION
VILLICATIONS
VILLOSITIES
VINAIGRETTE
VINAIGRETTES
VINBLASTINE
VINBLASTINES
VINCIBILITIES
VINCIBILITY
VINCIBLENESS
VINCIBLENESSES
VINCRISTINE
VINCRISTINES
VINDEMIATE
VINDEMIATED
VINDEMIATES
VINDEMIATING
VINDICABILITIES
VINDICABILITY
VINDICABLE
VINDICATED
VINDICATES
VINDICATING
VINDICATION
VINDICATIONS
VINDICATIVE
VINDICATIVENESS
VINDICATOR
VINDICATORILY
VINDICATORS
VINDICATORY
VINDICATRESS
VINDICATRESSES
VINDICTIVE
VINDICTIVELY
VINDICTIVENESS
VINEDRESSER
VINEDRESSERS
VINEGARETTE
VINEGARETTES
VINEGARIER
VINEGARIEST
VINEGARING
VINEGARISH
VINEGARRETTE
VINEGARRETTES
VINEGARROON
VINEGARROONS
VINEYARDIST
VINEYARDISTS
VINICULTURAL
VINICULTURE
VINICULTURES
VINICULTURIST
VINICULTURISTS
VINIFEROUS
VINIFICATION
VINIFICATIONS
VINIFICATOR
VINIFICATORS
VINOLOGIES
VINOLOGIST
VINOLOGISTS
VINOSITIES
VINTAGINGS
VINYLCYANIDE
VINYLCYANIDES
VINYLIDENE
VINYLIDENES
VIOLABILITIES
VIOLABILITY
VIOLABLENESS
VIOLABLENESSES
VIOLACEOUS
VIOLATIONS
VIOLENTING
VIOLINISTIC
VIOLINISTICALLY
VIOLINISTS
VIOLONCELLI
VIOLONCELLIST
VIOLONCELLISTS
VIOLONCELLO
VIOLONCELLOS
VIOSTEROLS
VIPASSANAS
VIPERFISHES
VIPERIFORM
VIPERISHLY
VIPEROUSLY
VIRAGINIAN
VIRAGINOUS
VIRALITIES
VIREONINES
VIRESCENCE
VIRESCENCES
VIRGINALIST
VIRGINALISTS
VIRGINALLED
VIRGINALLING
VIRGINALLY
VIRGINHOOD
VIRGINHOODS
VIRGINITIES
VIRGINIUMS
VIRIDESCENCE
VIRIDESCENCES
VIRIDESCENT
VIRIDITIES
VIRILESCENCE
VIRILESCENCES
VIRILESCENT
VIRILISATION
VIRILISATIONS
VIRILISING
VIRILITIES
VIRILIZATION
VIRILIZATIONS
VIRILIZING
VIROLOGICAL
VIROLOGICALLY

VIROLOGIES
VIROLOGIST
VIROLOGISTS
VIRTUALISATION
VIRTUALISATIONS
VIRTUALISE
VIRTUALISED
VIRTUALISES
VIRTUALISING
VIRTUALISM
VIRTUALISMS
VIRTUALIST
VIRTUALISTS
VIRTUALITIES
VIRTUALITY
VIRTUALIZATION
VIRTUALIZATIONS
VIRTUALIZE
VIRTUALIZED
VIRTUALIZES
VIRTUALIZING
VIRTUELESS
VIRTUOSITIES
VIRTUOSITY
VIRTUOSOSHIP
VIRTUOSOSHIPS
VIRTUOUSLY
VIRTUOUSNESS
VIRTUOUSNESSES
VIRULENCES
VIRULENCIES
VIRULENTLY
VIRULIFEROUS
VISAGISTES
VISCACHERA
VISCACHERAS
VISCERALLY
VISCERATED
VISCERATES
VISCERATING
VISCEROMOTOR
VISCEROPTOSES
VISCEROPTOSIS
VISCEROTONIA
VISCEROTONIAS
VISCEROTONIC
VISCIDITIES
VISCIDNESS
VISCIDNESSES
VISCOELASTIC
VISCOELASTICITY
VISCOMETER
VISCOMETERS
VISCOMETRIC
VISCOMETRICAL
VISCOMETRIES
VISCOMETRY
VISCOSIMETER
VISCOSIMETERS
VISCOSIMETRIC
VISCOSIMETRICAL
VISCOSIMETRIES
VISCOSIMETRY
VISCOSITIES
VISCOUNTCIES
VISCOUNTCY
VISCOUNTESS
VISCOUNTESSES
VISCOUNTIES
VISCOUNTSHIP
VISCOUNTSHIPS
VISCOUSNESS
VISCOUSNESSES
VISIBILITIES
VISIBILITY
VISIBLENESS
VISIBLENESSES
VISIOGENIC
VISIONALLY
VISIONARIES
VISIONARINESS
VISIONARINESSES
VISIONINGS
VISIONISTS
VISIONLESS
VISIOPHONE
VISIOPHONES
VISITATION
VISITATIONAL
VISITATIONS
VISITATIVE
VISITATORIAL
VISITATORS
VISITORIAL
VISITRESSES
VISUALISATION
VISUALISATIONS
VISUALISED
VISUALISER
VISUALISERS
VISUALISES
VISUALISING
VISUALISTS
VISUALITIES
VISUALIZATION
VISUALIZATIONS
VISUALIZED
VISUALIZER
VISUALIZERS
VISUALIZES
VISUALIZING
VITALISATION
VITALISATIONS
VITALISERS
VITALISING
VITALISTIC
VITALISTICALLY
VITALITIES
VITALIZATION
VITALIZATIONS
VITALIZERS
VITALIZING
VITALNESSES
VITAMINISE
VITAMINISED
VITAMINISES
VITAMINISING
VITAMINIZE
VITAMINIZED
VITAMINIZES
VITAMINIZING
VITASCOPES
VITATIVENESS
VITATIVENESSES
VITELLARIES
VITELLICLE
VITELLICLES
VITELLIGENOUS
VITELLINES
VITELLOGENESES
VITELLOGENESIS
VITELLOGENIC
VITELLUSES
VITIATIONS
VITICETUMS
VITICOLOUS
VITICULTURAL
VITICULTURALLY
VITICULTURE
VITICULTURER
VITICULTURERS
VITICULTURES
VITICULTURIST
VITICULTURISTS
VITIFEROUS
VITILITIGATE
VITILITIGATED
VITILITIGATES
VITILITIGATING
VITILITIGATION
VITILITIGATIONS
VITIOSITIES
VITRAILLED
VITRAILLIST
VITRAILLISTS
VITRECTOMIES
VITRECTOMY
VITREORETINAL
VITREOSITIES
VITREOSITY
VITREOUSES
VITREOUSLY
VITREOUSNESS
VITREOUSNESSES
VITRESCENCE
VITRESCENCES
VITRESCENT
VITRESCIBILITY
VITRESCIBLE
VITRIFACTION
VITRIFACTIONS
VITRIFACTURE
VITRIFACTURES
VITRIFIABILITY
VITRIFIABLE
VITRIFICATION
VITRIFICATIONS
VITRIFYING
VITRIOLATE
VITRIOLATED
VITRIOLATES
VITRIOLATING
VITRIOLATION
VITRIOLATIONS
VITRIOLING
VITRIOLISATION
VITRIOLISATIONS
VITRIOLISE
VITRIOLISED
VITRIOLISES
VITRIOLISING
VITRIOLIZATION
VITRIOLIZATIONS
VITRIOLIZE
VITRIOLIZED
VITRIOLIZES
VITRIOLIZING
VITRIOLLED
VITRIOLLING
VITUPERABLE
VITUPERATE
VITUPERATED
VITUPERATES
VITUPERATING
VITUPERATION
VITUPERATIONS
VITUPERATIVE
VITUPERATIVELY
VITUPERATOR
VITUPERATORS
VITUPERATORY
VIVACIOUSLY
VIVACIOUSNESS
VIVACIOUSNESSES
VIVACISSIMO
VIVACITIES
VIVANDIERE
VIVANDIERES
VIVANDIERS
VIVERRINES
VIVIANITES
VIVIDITIES
VIVIDNESSES
VIVIFICATION
VIVIFICATIONS
VIVIPARIES
VIVIPARISM
VIVIPARISMS
VIVIPARITIES
VIVIPARITY

VIVIPAROUS
VIVIPAROUSLY
VIVIPAROUSNESS
VIVISECTED
VIVISECTING
VIVISECTION
VIVISECTIONAL
VIVISECTIONALLY
VIVISECTIONIST
VIVISECTIONISTS
VIVISECTIONS
VIVISECTIVE
VIVISECTOR
VIVISECTORIA
VIVISECTORIUM
VIVISECTORIUMS
VIVISECTORS
VIVISEPULTURE
VIVISEPULTURES
VIXENISHLY
VIXENISHNESS
VIXENISHNESSES
VIZIERATES
VIZIERSHIP
VIZIERSHIPS
VIZIRSHIPS
VOCABULARIAN
VOCABULARIANS
VOCABULARIED
VOCABULARIES
VOCABULARY
VOCABULIST
VOCABULISTS
VOCALICALLY
VOCALISATION
VOCALISATIONS
VOCALISERS
VOCALISING
VOCALITIES
VOCALIZATION
VOCALIZATIONS
VOCALIZERS
VOCALIZING
VOCALNESSES
VOCATIONAL
VOCATIONALISM
VOCATIONALISMS
VOCATIONALIST
VOCATIONALISTS
VOCATIONALLY
VOCATIVELY
VOCICULTURAL
VOCIFERANCE
VOCIFERANCES
VOCIFERANT
VOCIFERANTS
VOCIFERATE
VOCIFERATED
VOCIFERATES
VOCIFERATING
VOCIFERATION
VOCIFERATIONS
VOCIFERATOR
VOCIFERATORS
VOCIFEROSITIES
VOCIFEROSITY
VOCIFEROUS
VOCIFEROUSLY
VOCIFEROUSNESS
VODCASTERS
VODCASTING
VODCASTINGS
VOETGANGER
VOETGANGERS
VOETSTOETS
VOETSTOOTS
VOGUISHNESS
VOGUISHNESSES
VOICEFULNESS
VOICEFULNESSES
VOICELESSLY
VOICELESSNESS
VOICELESSNESSES
VOICEMAILS
VOICEOVERS
VOICEPRINT
VOICEPRINTS
VOIDABLENESS
VOIDABLENESSES
VOIDNESSES
VOISINAGES
VOITURIERS
VOIVODESHIP
VOIVODESHIPS
VOLATILENESS
VOLATILENESSES
VOLATILISABLE
VOLATILISATION
VOLATILISATIONS
VOLATILISE
VOLATILISED
VOLATILISES
VOLATILISING
VOLATILITIES
VOLATILITY
VOLATILIZABLE
VOLATILIZATION
VOLATILIZATIONS
VOLATILIZE
VOLATILIZED
VOLATILIZES
VOLATILIZING
VOLCANICALLY
VOLCANICITIES
VOLCANICITY
VOLCANISATION
VOLCANISATIONS
VOLCANISED
VOLCANISES
VOLCANISING
VOLCANISMS
VOLCANISTS
VOLCANIZATION
VOLCANIZATIONS
VOLCANIZED
VOLCANIZES
VOLCANIZING
VOLCANOLOGIC
VOLCANOLOGICAL
VOLCANOLOGIES
VOLCANOLOGIST
VOLCANOLOGISTS
VOLCANOLOGY
VOLITATING
VOLITATION
VOLITATIONAL
VOLITATIONS
VOLITIONAL
VOLITIONALLY
VOLITIONARY
VOLITIONLESS
VOLITORIAL
VOLKSLIEDER
VOLKSRAADS
VOLLEYBALL
VOLLEYBALLS
VOLPLANING
VOLTAMETER
VOLTAMETERS
VOLTAMETRIC
VOLTAMMETER
VOLTAMMETERS
VOLTIGEURS
VOLTINISMS
VOLTMETERS
VOLUBILITIES
VOLUBILITY
VOLUBLENESS
VOLUBLENESSES
VOLUMENOMETER
VOLUMENOMETERS
VOLUMETERS
VOLUMETRIC
VOLUMETRICAL
VOLUMETRICALLY
VOLUMETRIES
VOLUMINOSITIES
VOLUMINOSITY
VOLUMINOUS
VOLUMINOUSLY
VOLUMINOUSNESS
VOLUMISERS
VOLUMISING
VOLUMIZERS
VOLUMIZING
VOLUMOMETER
VOLUMOMETERS
VOLUNTARIES
VOLUNTARILY
VOLUNTARINESS
VOLUNTARINESSES
VOLUNTARISM
VOLUNTARISMS
VOLUNTARIST
VOLUNTARISTIC
VOLUNTARISTS
VOLUNTARYISM
VOLUNTARYISMS
VOLUNTARYIST
VOLUNTARYISTS
VOLUNTATIVE
VOLUNTATIVES
VOLUNTEERED
VOLUNTEERING
VOLUNTEERISM
VOLUNTEERISMS
VOLUNTEERS
VOLUNTOURISM
VOLUNTOURISMS
VOLUPTUARIES
VOLUPTUARY
VOLUPTUOSITIES
VOLUPTUOSITY
VOLUPTUOUS
VOLUPTUOUSLY
VOLUPTUOUSNESS
VOLUTATION
VOLUTATIONS
VOLVULUSES
VOMERONASAL
VOMITORIES
VOMITORIUM
VOMITURITION
VOMITURITIONS
VOODOOISMS
VOODOOISTIC
VOODOOISTS
VOORKAMERS
VOORTREKKER
VOORTREKKERS
VORACIOUSLY
VORACIOUSNESS
VORACIOUSNESSES
VORACITIES
VORAGINOUS
VORTICALLY
VORTICELLA
VORTICELLAE
VORTICELLAS
VORTICISMS
VORTICISTS
VORTICITIES
VORTICULAR
VORTIGINOUS
VOTARESSES
VOTIVENESS
VOTIVENESSES
VOUCHERING
VOUCHSAFED
VOUCHSAFEMENT

VOUCHSAFEMENTS
VOUCHSAFES
VOUCHSAFING
VOUCHSAFINGS
VOUSSOIRED
VOUSSOIRING
VOUTSAFING
VOWELISATION
VOWELISATIONS
VOWELISING
VOWELIZATION
VOWELIZATIONS
VOWELIZING
VOWELLIEST
VOYAGEABLE
VOYEURISMS
VOYEURISTIC
VOYEURISTICALLY
VRAICKINGS
VRAISEMBLANCE
VRAISEMBLANCES
VRYSTATERS
VULCANICITIES
VULCANICITY
VULCANISABLE
VULCANISATE
VULCANISATES
VULCANISATION
VULCANISATIONS
VULCANISED
VULCANISER
VULCANISERS
VULCANISES
VULCANISING
VULCANISMS
VULCANISTS
VULCANITES
VULCANIZABLE
VULCANIZATE
VULCANIZATES
VULCANIZATION
VULCANIZATIONS
VULCANIZED
VULCANIZER
VULCANIZERS
VULCANIZES
VULCANIZING
VULCANOLOGIC
VULCANOLOGICAL
VULCANOLOGIES
VULCANOLOGIST
VULCANOLOGISTS
VULCANOLOGY
VULGARIANS
VULGARISATION
VULGARISATIONS
VULGARISED
VULGARISER
VULGARISERS
VULGARISES
VULGARISING
VULGARISMS
VULGARITIES
VULGARIZATION
VULGARIZATIONS
VULGARIZED
VULGARIZER
VULGARIZERS
VULGARIZES
VULGARIZING
VULNERABILITIES
VULNERABILITY
VULNERABLE
VULNERABLENESS
VULNERABLY
VULNERARIES
VULNERATED
VULNERATES
VULNERATING
VULNERATION
VULNERATIONS
VULPECULAR
VULPICIDES
VULPINISMS
VULPINITES
VULTURISMS
VULVITISES
VULVOVAGINAL
VULVOVAGINITIS

V

W

WACKINESSES
WADSETTERS
WADSETTING
WAFFLESTOMPER
WAFFLESTOMPERS
WAGELESSNESS
WAGELESSNESSES
WAGENBOOMS
WAGEWORKER
WAGEWORKERS
WAGGISHNESS
WAGGISHNESSES
WAGGLINGLY
WAGGONETTE
WAGGONETTES
WAGGONLESS
WAGGONLOAD
WAGGONLOADS
WAGHALTERS
WAGONETTES
WAGONLOADS
WAGONWRIGHT
WAGONWRIGHTS
WAINSCOTED
WAINSCOTING
WAINSCOTINGS
WAINSCOTTED
WAINSCOTTING
WAINSCOTTINGS
WAINWRIGHT
WAINWRIGHTS
WAISTBANDS
WAISTBELTS
WAISTCLOTH
WAISTCLOTHS
WAISTCOATED
WAISTCOATEER
WAISTCOATEERS
WAISTCOATING
WAISTCOATINGS
WAISTCOATS
WAISTLINES
WAITERAGES
WAITERHOOD
WAITERHOODS
WAITERINGS
WAITLISTED
WAITLISTING
WAITPEOPLE
WAITPERSON
WAITPERSONS
WAITRESSED
WAITRESSES
WAITRESSING
WAITRESSINGS
WAITSTAFFS
WAKEBOARDED
WAKEBOARDER
WAKEBOARDERS
WAKEBOARDING
WAKEBOARDINGS
WAKEBOARDS
WAKEFULNESS
WAKEFULNESSES
WALDFLUTES
WALDGRAVES
WALDGRAVINE
WALDGRAVINES
WALDSTERBEN
WALDSTERBENS
WALKABOUTS
WALKATHONS
WALKINGSTICK
WALKINGSTICKS
WALKSHORTS
WALLBOARDS
WALLCHARTS
WALLCLIMBER
WALLCLIMBERS
WALLCOVERING
WALLCOVERINGS
WALLFISHES
WALLFLOWER
WALLFLOWERS
WALLOPINGS
WALLOWINGS
WALLPAPERED
WALLPAPERING
WALLPAPERS
WALLPEPPER
WALLPEPPERS
WALLPOSTER
WALLPOSTERS
WALLYBALLS
WALLYDRAGS
WALLYDRAIGLE
WALLYDRAIGLES
WALNUTWOOD
WALNUTWOODS
WAMBENGERS
WAMBLINESS
WAMBLINESSES
WAMBLINGLY
WAMPISHING
WAMPUMPEAG
WAMPUMPEAGS
WANCHANCIE
WANDERINGLY
WANDERINGS
WANDERLUST
WANDERLUSTS
WANRESTFUL
WANTHRIVEN
WANTONISED
WANTONISES
WANTONISING
WANTONIZED
WANTONIZES
WANTONIZING
WANTONNESS
WANTONNESSES
WANWORDIER
WANWORDIEST
WAPENSCHAW
WAPENSCHAWS
WAPENSHAWS
WAPENTAKES
WAPINSCHAW
WAPINSCHAWS
WAPINSHAWS
WAPPENSCHAW
WAPPENSCHAWING
WAPPENSCHAWINGS
WAPPENSCHAWS
WAPPENSHAW
WAPPENSHAWING
WAPPENSHAWINGS
WAPPENSHAWS
WARBLINGLY
WARBONNETS
WARCHALKER
WARCHALKERS
WARCHALKING
WARCHALKINGS
WARDENRIES
WARDENSHIP
WARDENSHIPS
WARDERSHIP
WARDERSHIPS
WARDRESSES
WARDROBERS
WARDROBING
WAREHOUSED
WAREHOUSEMAN
WAREHOUSEMEN
WAREHOUSER
WAREHOUSERS
WAREHOUSES
WAREHOUSING
WAREHOUSINGS
WARFARINGS
WARGAMINGS
WARIBASHIS
WARINESSES
WARLIKENESS
WARLIKENESSES
WARLOCKRIES
WARLORDISM
WARLORDISMS
WARMBLOODS
WARMHEARTED
WARMHEARTEDNESS
WARMNESSES
WARMONGERING
WARMONGERINGS
WARMONGERS
WARRANDICE
WARRANDICES
WARRANDING
WARRANTABILITY
WARRANTABLE
WARRANTABLENESS
WARRANTABLY
WARRANTEES
WARRANTERS
WARRANTIED
WARRANTIES
WARRANTING
WARRANTINGS
WARRANTISE
WARRANTISED
WARRANTISES
WARRANTISING
WARRANTIZE
WARRANTIZED
WARRANTIZES
WARRANTIZING
WARRANTLESS
WARRANTORS
WARRANTYING
WARRIORESS
WARRIORESSES
WASHABILITIES
WASHABILITY
WASHATERIA
WASHATERIAS
WASHBASINS
WASHBOARDS
WASHCLOTHS
WASHERWOMAN

W

WASHERWOMEN
WASHETERIA
WASHETERIAS
WASHHOUSES
WASHINESSES
WASHINGTONIA
WASHINGTONIAS
WASHSTANDS
WASPINESSES
WASPISHNESS
WASPISHNESSES
WASSAILERS
WASSAILING
WASSAILINGS
WASSAILRIES
WASTEBASKET
WASTEBASKETS
WASTEFULLY
WASTEFULNESS
WASTEFULNESSES
WASTELANDS
WASTENESSES
WASTEPAPER
WASTEPAPERS
WASTERFULLY
WASTERFULNESS
WASTERFULNESSES
WASTEWATER
WASTEWATERS
WASTEWEIRS
WASTNESSES
WATCHABLES
WATCHBANDS
WATCHBOXES
WATCHCASES
WATCHCRIES
WATCHDOGGED
WATCHDOGGING
WATCHDOGGINGS
WATCHFULLY
WATCHFULNESS
WATCHFULNESSES
WATCHGLASS
WATCHGLASSES
WATCHGUARD
WATCHGUARDS
WATCHLISTS
WATCHMAKER
WATCHMAKERS
WATCHMAKING
WATCHMAKINGS
WATCHSPRING
WATCHSPRINGS
WATCHSTRAP
WATCHSTRAPS
WATCHTOWER
WATCHTOWERS
WATCHWORDS
WATERBIRDS
WATERBOARDING
WATERBOARDINGS
WATERBORNE
WATERBRAIN
WATERBRAINS
WATERBUCKS
WATERBUSES
WATERBUSSES
WATERCOLOR
WATERCOLORIST
WATERCOLORISTS
WATERCOLORS
WATERCOLOUR
WATERCOLOURIST
WATERCOLOURISTS
WATERCOLOURS
WATERCOOLER
WATERCOOLERS
WATERCOURSE
WATERCOURSES
WATERCRAFT
WATERCRAFTS
WATERCRESS
WATERCRESSES
WATERDRIVE
WATERDRIVES
WATERFALLS
WATERFINDER
WATERFINDERS
WATERFLOOD
WATERFLOODED
WATERFLOODING
WATERFLOODINGS
WATERFLOODS
WATERFOWLER
WATERFOWLERS
WATERFOWLING
WATERFOWLINGS
WATERFOWLS
WATERFRONT
WATERFRONTS
WATERGATES
WATERGLASS
WATERGLASSES
WATERHEADS
WATERHOLES
WATERINESS
WATERINESSES
WATERISHNESS
WATERISHNESSES
WATERLEAFS
WATERLEAVES
WATERLESSNESS
WATERLESSNESSES
WATERLILIES
WATERLINES
WATERLOGGED
WATERLOGGING
WATERLOGGINGS
WATERMANSHIP
WATERMANSHIPS
WATERMARKED
WATERMARKING
WATERMARKS
WATERMELON
WATERMELONS
WATERMILLS
WATERPOWER
WATERPOWERS
WATERPOXES
WATERPROOF
WATERPROOFED
WATERPROOFER
WATERPROOFERS
WATERPROOFING
WATERPROOFINGS
WATERPROOFNESS
WATERPROOFS
WATERQUAKE
WATERQUAKES
WATERSCAPE
WATERSCAPES
WATERSHEDS
WATERSIDER
WATERSIDERS
WATERSIDES
WATERSKIING
WATERSKIINGS
WATERSMEET
WATERSMEETS
WATERSPOUT
WATERSPOUTS
WATERTHRUSH
WATERTHRUSHES
WATERTIGHT
WATERTIGHTNESS
WATERWEEDS
WATERWHEEL
WATERWHEELS
WATERWORKS
WATERZOOIS
WATTLEBARK
WATTLEBARKS
WATTLEBIRD
WATTLEBIRDS
WATTLEWORK
WATTLEWORKS
WATTMETERS
WAULKMILLS
WAVEFRONTS
WAVEGUIDES
WAVELENGTH
WAVELENGTHS
WAVELESSLY
WAVELLITES
WAVEMETERS
WAVERINGLY
WAVERINGNESS
WAVERINGNESSES
WAVESHAPES
WAVETABLES
WAVINESSES
WAXBERRIES
WAXFLOWERS
WAXINESSES
WAXWORKERS
WAYFARINGS
WAYMARKING
WAYMENTING
WAYWARDNESS
WAYWARDNESSES
WAYZGOOSES
WEAKENINGS
WEAKFISHES
WEAKHEARTED
WEAKISHNESS
WEAKISHNESSES
WEAKLINESS
WEAKLINESSES
WEAKNESSES
WEALTHIEST
WEALTHINESS
WEALTHINESSES
WEALTHLESS
WEAPONEERED
WEAPONEERING
WEAPONEERINGS
WEAPONEERS
WEAPONISED
WEAPONISES
WEAPONISING
WEAPONIZED
WEAPONIZES
WEAPONIZING
WEAPONLESS
WEAPONRIES
WEARABILITIES
WEARABILITY
WEARIFULLY
WEARIFULNESS
WEARIFULNESSES
WEARILESSLY
WEARINESSES
WEARISOMELY
WEARISOMENESS
WEARISOMENESSES
WEARYINGLY
WEASELIEST
WEASELLERS
WEASELLIER
WEASELLIEST
WEASELLING
WEATHERABILITY
WEATHERABLE
WEATHERBOARD
WEATHERBOARDED
WEATHERBOARDING
WEATHERBOARDS
WEATHERCAST
WEATHERCASTER
WEATHERCASTERS

WEATHERCASTS
WEATHERCLOTH
WEATHERCLOTHS
WEATHERCOCK
WEATHERCOCKED
WEATHERCOCKING
WEATHERCOCKS
WEATHERERS
WEATHERGIRL
WEATHERGIRLS
WEATHERGLASS
WEATHERGLASSES
WEATHERING
WEATHERINGS
WEATHERISATION
WEATHERISATIONS
WEATHERISE
WEATHERISED
WEATHERISES
WEATHERISING
WEATHERIZATION
WEATHERIZATIONS
WEATHERIZE
WEATHERIZED
WEATHERIZES
WEATHERIZING
WEATHERLIER
WEATHERLIEST
WEATHERLINESS
WEATHERLINESSES
WEATHERMAN
WEATHERMEN
WEATHERMOST
WEATHEROMETER
WEATHEROMETERS
WEATHERPERSON
WEATHERPERSONS
WEATHERPROOF
WEATHERPROOFED
WEATHERPROOFING
WEATHERPROOFS
WEATHERWOMAN
WEATHERWOMEN
WEATHERWORN
WEAVERBIRD
WEAVERBIRDS
WEBCASTERS
WEBCASTING
WEBCASTINGS
WEBCHATTED
WEBCHATTING
WEBLIOGRAPHIES
WEBLIOGRAPHY
WEBLOGGERS
WEBLOGGING
WEBLOGGINGS
WEBMASTERS
WEEDICIDES
WEEDINESSES
WEEDKILLER
WEEDKILLERS
WEEKENDERS
WEEKENDING
WEEKENDINGS
WEEKNIGHTS
WEELDLESSE
WEEPINESSES
WEEVILIEST
WEEVILLIER
WEEVILLIEST
WEIGHBOARD
WEIGHBOARDS
WEIGHBRIDGE
WEIGHBRIDGES
WEIGHTAGES
WEIGHTIEST
WEIGHTINESS
WEIGHTINESSES
WEIGHTINGS
WEIGHTLESS
WEIGHTLESSLY
WEIGHTLESSNESS
WEIGHTLIFTER
WEIGHTLIFTERS
WEIGHTLIFTING
WEIGHTLIFTINGS
WEIMARANER
WEIMARANERS
WEIRDNESSES
WEISENHEIMER
WEISENHEIMERS
WELCOMENESS
WELCOMENESSES
WELCOMINGLY
WELDABILITIES
WELDABILITY
WELDMESHES
WELFARISMS
WELFARISTIC
WELFARISTS
WELFARITES
WELLBEINGS
WELLHOUSES
WELLINGTON
WELLINGTONIA
WELLINGTONIAS
WELLINGTONS
WELLNESSES
WELLSPRING
WELLSPRINGS
WELTANSCHAUUNG
WELTANSCHAUUNGS
WELTERWEIGHT
WELTERWEIGHTS
WELTSCHMERZ
WELTSCHMERZES
WELWITSCHIA
WELWITSCHIAS
WENSLEYDALE
WENSLEYDALES
WENTLETRAP
WENTLETRAPS
WEREWOLFERIES
WEREWOLFERY
WEREWOLFISH
WEREWOLFISM
WEREWOLFISMS
WEREWOLVES
WERNERITES
WERWOLFISH
WESTERINGS
WESTERLIES
WESTERLINESS
WESTERLINESSES
WESTERNERS
WESTERNISATION
WESTERNISATIONS
WESTERNISE
WESTERNISED
WESTERNISES
WESTERNISING
WESTERNISM
WESTERNISMS
WESTERNIZATION
WESTERNIZATIONS
WESTERNIZE
WESTERNIZED
WESTERNIZES
WESTERNIZING
WESTERNMOST
WESTWARDLY
WETTABILITIES
WETTABILITY
WHAIKORERO
WHAIKOREROS
WHAKAPAPAS
WHALEBACKS
WHALEBOATS
WHALEBONES
WHAREPUNIS
WHARFINGER
WHARFINGERS
WHARFMASTER
WHARFMASTERS
WHATABOUTERIES
WHATABOUTERY
WHATABOUTISM
WHATABOUTISMS
WHATABOUTS
WHATCHAMACALLIT
WHATNESSES
WHATSERNAME
WHATSERNAMES
WHATSHERNAME
WHATSHERNAMES
WHATSHISNAME
WHATSHISNAMES
WHATSISNAME
WHATSISNAMES
WHATSITSNAME
WHATSITSNAMES
WHATSOEVER
WHATSOMEVER
WHEATFIELD
WHEATFIELDS
WHEATGERMS
WHEATGRASS
WHEATGRASSES
WHEATLANDS
WHEATMEALS
WHEATWORMS
WHEEDLESOME
WHEEDLINGLY
WHEEDLINGS
WHEELBARROW
WHEELBARROWED
WHEELBARROWING
WHEELBARROWS
WHEELBASES
WHEELCHAIR
WHEELCHAIRS
WHEELHORSE
WHEELHORSES
WHEELHOUSE
WHEELHOUSES
WHEELSPINS
WHEELWORKS
WHEELWRIGHT
WHEELWRIGHTS
WHEESHTING
WHEEZINESS
WHEEZINESSES
WHEEZINGLY
WHENCEFORTH
WHENCESOEVER
WHENSOEVER
WHEREABOUT
WHEREABOUTS
WHEREAFTER
WHEREAGAINST
WHEREFORES
WHEREINSOEVER
WHERENESSES
WHERESOEVER
WHERETHROUGH
WHEREUNDER
WHEREUNTIL
WHEREWITHAL
WHEREWITHALS
WHEREWITHS
WHERRETING
WHERRITING
WHETSTONES
WHEWELLITE
WHEWELLITES
WHEYISHNESS
WHEYISHNESSES
WHICHSOEVER
WHICKERING
WHIDDERING

W

WHIFFLERIES
WHIFFLETREE
WHIFFLETREES
WHIFFLINGS
WHIGGAMORE
WHIGGAMORES
WHIGMALEERIE
WHIGMALEERIES
WHIGMALEERY
WHILLYWHAED
WHILLYWHAING
WHILLYWHAS
WHILLYWHAW
WHILLYWHAWED
WHILLYWHAWING
WHILLYWHAWS
WHIMBERRIES
WHIMPERERS
WHIMPERING
WHIMPERINGLY
WHIMPERINGS
WHIMSICALITIES
WHIMSICALITY
WHIMSICALLY
WHIMSICALNESS
WHIMSICALNESSES
WHIMSINESS
WHIMSINESSES
WHINBERRIES
WHINGDINGS
WHINGEINGLY
WHINGEINGS
WHININESSES
WHINSTONES
WHIPCORDIER
WHIPCORDIEST
WHIPCRACKS
WHIPLASHED
WHIPLASHES
WHIPLASHING
WHIPPERSNAPPER
WHIPPERSNAPPERS
WHIPPETING
WHIPPETINGS
WHIPPINESS
WHIPPINESSES
WHIPPLETREE
WHIPPLETREES
WHIPPOORWILL
WHIPPOORWILLS
WHIPSAWING
WHIPSNAKES
WHIPSTAFFS
WHIPSTALLED
WHIPSTALLING
WHIPSTALLS
WHIPSTITCH
WHIPSTITCHED
WHIPSTITCHES
WHIPSTITCHING
WHIPSTOCKS
WHIPTAILED
WHIRLABOUT
WHIRLABOUTS
WHIRLBLAST
WHIRLBLASTS
WHIRLIGIGS
WHIRLINGLY
WHIRLPOOLS
WHIRLWINDS
WHIRLYBIRD
WHIRLYBIRDS
WHIRRETING
WHISKERANDO
WHISKERANDOED
WHISKERANDOS
WHISKERIER
WHISKERIEST
WHISKEYFIED
WHISKIFIED
WHISPERERS
WHISPERIER
WHISPERIEST
WHISPERING
WHISPERINGLY
WHISPERINGS
WHISPEROUSLY
WHISTLEABLE
WHISTLEBLOWING
WHISTLEBLOWINGS
WHISTLINGLY
WHISTLINGS
WHITEBAITS
WHITEBASSES
WHITEBEAMS
WHITEBEARD
WHITEBEARDS
WHITEBOARD
WHITEBOARDS
WHITEBOYISM
WHITEBOYISMS
WHITECOATS
WHITECOMBS
WHITEDAMPS
WHITEFACES
WHITEFISHES
WHITEFLIES
WHITEHEADS
WHITELISTED
WHITELISTING
WHITELISTS
WHITENESSES
WHITENINGS
WHITESMITH
WHITESMITHS
WHITETAILS
WHITETHORN
WHITETHORNS
WHITETHROAT
WHITETHROATS
WHITEWALLS
WHITEWARES
WHITEWASHED
WHITEWASHER
WHITEWASHERS
WHITEWASHES
WHITEWASHING
WHITEWASHINGS
WHITEWATER
WHITEWINGS
WHITEWOODS
WHITEYWOOD
WHITEYWOODS
WHITHERING
WHITHERSOEVER
WHITHERWARD
WHITHERWARDS
WHITISHNESS
WHITISHNESSES
WHITLEATHER
WHITLEATHERS
WHITTAWERS
WHITTERICK
WHITTERICKS
WHITTERING
WHITTLINGS
WHIZZBANGS
WHIZZINGLY
WHODUNITRIES
WHODUNITRY
WHODUNNITRIES
WHODUNNITRY
WHODUNNITS
WHOLEFOODS
WHOLEGRAIN
WHOLEGRAINS
WHOLEHEARTED
WHOLEHEARTEDLY
WHOLEMEALS
WHOLENESSES
WHOLESALED
WHOLESALER
WHOLESALERS
WHOLESALES
WHOLESALING
WHOLESALINGS
WHOLESOMELY
WHOLESOMENESS
WHOLESOMENESSES
WHOLESOMER
WHOLESOMEST
WHOLESTITCH
WHOLESTITCHES
WHOLEWHEAT
WHOMSOEVER
WHOREHOUSE
WHOREHOUSES
WHOREMASTER
WHOREMASTERIES
WHOREMASTERLY
WHOREMASTERS
WHOREMASTERY
WHOREMISTRESS
WHOREMISTRESSES
WHOREMONGER
WHOREMONGERIES
WHOREMONGERS
WHOREMONGERY
WHORISHNESS
WHORISHNESSES
WHORTLEBERRIES
WHORTLEBERRY
WHOSESOEVER
WHUNSTANES
WHYDUNNITS
WICKEDNESS
WICKEDNESSES
WICKERWORK
WICKERWORKS
WICKETKEEPER
WICKETKEEPERS
WICKTHINGS
WIDDERSHINS
WIDEAWAKES
WIDEBODIES
WIDECHAPPED
WIDEMOUTHED
WIDENESSES
WIDERSHINS
WIDESCREEN
WIDESPREAD
WIDOWBIRDS
WIDOWERHOOD
WIDOWERHOODS
WIDOWHOODS
WIELDINESS
WIELDINESSES
WIENERWURST
WIENERWURSTS
WIFELINESS
WIFELINESSES
WIGWAGGERS
WIGWAGGING
WIKIALITIES
WIKITORIAL
WIKITORIALS
WILDCATTED
WILDCATTER
WILDCATTERS
WILDCATTING
WILDCATTINGS
WILDEBEEST
WILDEBEESTS
WILDERMENT
WILDERMENTS
WILDERNESS
WILDERNESSES
WILDFLOWER
WILDFLOWERS
WILDFOWLER

W

WILDFOWLERS
WILDFOWLING
WILDFOWLINGS
WILDGRAVES
WILDNESSES
WILFULNESS
WILFULNESSES
WILINESSES
WILLEMITES
WILLFULNESS
WILLFULNESSES
WILLIEWAUGHT
WILLIEWAUGHTS
WILLINGEST
WILLINGNESS
WILLINGNESSES
WILLOWHERB
WILLOWHERBS
WILLOWIEST
WILLOWLIKE
WILLOWWARE
WILLOWWARES
WILLPOWERS
WIMPINESSES
WIMPISHNESS
WIMPISHNESSES
WINCEYETTE
WINCEYETTES
WINCHESTER
WINCHESTERS
WINCOPIPES
WINDBAGGERIES
WINDBAGGERY
WINDBLASTS
WINDBREAKER
WINDBREAKERS
WINDBREAKS
WINDBURNED
WINDBURNING
WINDCHEATER
WINDCHEATERS
WINDCHILLS
WINDFALLEN
WINDFLOWER
WINDFLOWERS
WINDGALLED
WINDHOVERS
WINDINESSES
WINDJAMMER
WINDJAMMERS
WINDJAMMING
WINDJAMMINGS
WINDLASSED
WINDLASSES
WINDLASSING
WINDLESSLY
WINDLESSNESS
WINDLESSNESSES
WINDLESTRAE
WINDLESTRAES
WINDLESTRAW
WINDLESTRAWS
WINDMILLED
WINDMILLING
WINDOWIEST
WINDOWINGS
WINDOWLESS
WINDOWPANE
WINDOWPANES
WINDOWSILL
WINDOWSILLS
WINDPROOFED
WINDPROOFING
WINDPROOFS
WINDROWERS
WINDROWING
WINDSCREEN
WINDSCREENS
WINDSHAKES
WINDSHIELD
WINDSHIELDS
WINDSTORMS
WINDSUCKER
WINDSUCKERS
WINDSURFED
WINDSURFER
WINDSURFERS
WINDSURFING
WINDSURFINGS
WINDTHROWS
WINEBERRIES
WINEBIBBER
WINEBIBBERS
WINEBIBBING
WINEBIBBINGS
WINEGLASSES
WINEGLASSFUL
WINEGLASSFULS
WINEGROWER
WINEGROWERS
WINEGROWING
WINEGROWINGS
WINEMAKERS
WINEMAKING
WINEMAKINGS
WINEPRESSES
WINGCHAIRS
WINGLESSNESS
WINGLESSNESSES
WINGSPREAD
WINGSPREADS
WINNABILITIES
WINNABILITY
WINNINGEST
WINNINGNESS
WINNINGNESSES
WINNOWINGS
WINSOMENESS
WINSOMENESSES
WINTERBERRIES
WINTERBERRY
WINTERBOURNE
WINTERBOURNES
WINTERCRESS
WINTERCRESSES
WINTERFEED
WINTERFEEDING
WINTERFEEDS
WINTERGREEN
WINTERGREENS
WINTERIEST
WINTERINESS
WINTERINESSES
WINTERISATION
WINTERISATIONS
WINTERISED
WINTERISES
WINTERISING
WINTERIZATION
WINTERIZATIONS
WINTERIZED
WINTERIZES
WINTERIZING
WINTERKILL
WINTERKILLED
WINTERKILLING
WINTERKILLINGS
WINTERKILLS
WINTERLESS
WINTERLIER
WINTERLIEST
WINTERLINESS
WINTERLINESSES
WINTERTIDE
WINTERTIDES
WINTERTIME
WINTERTIMES
WINTERWEIGHT
WINTRINESS
WINTRINESSES
WIREDRAWER
WIREDRAWERS
WIREDRAWING
WIREDRAWINGS
WIREFRAMES
WIREGRASSES
WIREHAIRED
WIRELESSED
WIRELESSES
WIRELESSING
WIRELESSLY
WIREPHOTOS
WIREPULLER
WIREPULLERS
WIREPULLING
WIREPULLINGS
WIRETAPPED
WIRETAPPER
WIRETAPPERS
WIRETAPPING
WIRETAPPINGS
WIREWALKER
WIREWALKERS
WIREWORKER
WIREWORKERS
WIREWORKING
WIREWORKINGS
WIRINESSES
WISECRACKED
WISECRACKER
WISECRACKERS
WISECRACKING
WISECRACKS
WISENESSES
WISENHEIMER
WISENHEIMERS
WISHFULNESS
WISHFULNESSES
WISHTONWISH
WISHTONWISHES
WISPINESSES
WISTFULNESS
WISTFULNESSES
WITBLITSES
WITCHBROOM
WITCHBROOMS
WITCHCRAFT
WITCHCRAFTS
WITCHERIES
WITCHETTIES
WITCHGRASS
WITCHGRASSES
WITCHHOODS
WITCHINGLY
WITCHKNOTS
WITCHWEEDS
WITENAGEMOT
WITENAGEMOTE
WITENAGEMOTES
WITENAGEMOTS
WITGATBOOM
WITGATBOOMS
WITHDRAWABLE
WITHDRAWAL
WITHDRAWALS
WITHDRAWER
WITHDRAWERS
WITHDRAWING
WITHDRAWMENT
WITHDRAWMENTS
WITHDRAWNNESS
WITHDRAWNNESSES
WITHEREDNESS
WITHEREDNESSES
WITHERINGLY
WITHERINGS
WITHERITES
WITHERSHINS
WITHHOLDEN
WITHHOLDER

W

WITHHOLDERS
WITHHOLDING
WITHHOLDMENT
WITHHOLDMENTS
WITHINDOORS
WITHOUTDOORS
WITHSTANDER
WITHSTANDERS
WITHSTANDING
WITHSTANDS
WITHYWINDS
WITLESSNESS
WITLESSNESSES
WITNESSABLE
WITNESSERS
WITNESSING
WITTICISMS
WITTINESSES
WITWANTONED
WITWANTONING
WITWANTONS
WIZARDLIER
WIZARDLIEST
WIZARDRIES
WOADWAXENS
WOBBEGONGS
WOBBLINESS
WOBBLINESSES
WOEBEGONENESS
WOEBEGONENESSES
WOEFULLEST
WOEFULNESS
WOEFULNESSES
WOFULNESSES
WOLFBERRIES
WOLFFISHES
WOLFHOUNDS
WOLFISHNESS
WOLFISHNESSES
WOLFRAMITE
WOLFRAMITES
WOLFSBANES
WOLLASTONITE
WOLLASTONITES
WOLVERENES
WOLVERINES
WOMANFULLY
WOMANHOODS
WOMANISERS
WOMANISHLY
WOMANISHNESS
WOMANISHNESSES
WOMANISING
WOMANISINGS
WOMANIZERS
WOMANIZING
WOMANIZINGS
WOMANKINDS
WOMANLIEST
WOMANLINESS
WOMANLINESSES
WOMANNESSES
WOMANPOWER
WOMANPOWERS
WOMENFOLKS
WOMENKINDS
WOMENSWEAR
WOMENSWEARS
WONDERFULLY
WONDERFULNESS
WONDERFULNESSES
WONDERINGLY
WONDERINGS
WONDERKIDS
WONDERLAND
WONDERLANDS
WONDERLESS
WONDERMENT
WONDERMENTS
WONDERMONGER
WONDERMONGERING
WONDERMONGERS
WONDERSTRUCK
WONDERWORK
WONDERWORKS
WONDROUSLY
WONDROUSNESS
WONDROUSNESSES
WONKINESSES
WONTEDNESS
WONTEDNESSES
WOODBLOCKS
WOODBORERS
WOODBURYTYPE
WOODBURYTYPES
WOODCARVER
WOODCARVERS
WOODCARVING
WOODCARVINGS
WOODCHOPPER
WOODCHOPPERS
WOODCHUCKS
WOODCRAFTS
WOODCRAFTSMAN
WOODCRAFTSMEN
WOODCUTTER
WOODCUTTERS
WOODCUTTING
WOODCUTTINGS
WOODENHEAD
WOODENHEADED
WOODENHEADS
WOODENNESS
WOODENNESSES
WOODENTOPS
WOODENWARE
WOODENWARES
WOODGRAINS
WOODGROUSE
WOODGROUSES
WOODHORSES
WOODHOUSES
WOODINESSES
WOODLANDER
WOODLANDERS
WOODLESSNESS
WOODLESSNESSES
WOODNESSES
WOODPECKER
WOODPECKERS
WOODPRINTS
WOODREEVES
WOODRUSHES
WOODSCREWS
WOODSHEDDED
WOODSHEDDING
WOODSHEDDINGS
WOODSHOCKS
WOODSHRIKE
WOODSHRIKES
WOODSMOKES
WOODSPITES
WOODSTONES
WOODSTOVES
WOODSWALLOW
WOODSWALLOWS
WOODTHRUSH
WOODTHRUSHES
WOODWAXENS
WOODWORKER
WOODWORKERS
WOODWORKING
WOODWORKINGS
WOOLGATHERER
WOOLGATHERERS
WOOLGATHERING
WOOLGATHERINGS
WOOLGROWER
WOOLGROWERS
WOOLGROWING
WOOLGROWINGS
WOOLINESSES
WOOLLINESS
WOOLLINESSES
WOOLLYBACK
WOOLLYBACKS
WOOLLYBUTT
WOOLLYBUTTS
WOOLLYFOOT
WOOLLYFOOTS
WOOLSORTER
WOOLSORTERS
WOOMERANGS
WOOZINESSES
WORCESTERBERRY
WORCESTERS
WORDBREAKS
WORDCOUNTS
WORDINESSES
WORDISHNESS
WORDISHNESSES
WORDLESSLY
WORDLESSNESS
WORDLESSNESSES
WORDMONGER
WORDMONGERS
WORDSEARCH
WORDSEARCHES
WORDSMITHERIES
WORDSMITHERY
WORDSMITHS
WORKABILITIES
WORKABILITY
WORKABLENESS
WORKABLENESSES
WORKAHOLIC
WORKAHOLICS
WORKAHOLISM
WORKAHOLISMS
WORKAROUND
WORKAROUNDS
WORKBASKET
WORKBASKETS
WORKBENCHES
WORKERISTS
WORKERLESS
WORKFELLOW
WORKFELLOWS
WORKFORCES
WORKGROUPS
WORKHORSES
WORKHOUSES
WORKINGMAN
WORKINGMEN
WORKINGWOMAN
WORKINGWOMEN
WORKLESSNESS
WORKLESSNESSES
WORKMANLIER
WORKMANLIEST
WORKMANLIKE
WORKMANSHIP
WORKMANSHIPS
WORKMASTER
WORKMASTERS
WORKMISTRESS
WORKMISTRESSES
WORKPEOPLE
WORKPIECES
WORKPLACES
WORKPRINTS
WORKSHEETS
WORKSHOPPED
WORKSHOPPING
WORKSPACES
WORKSTATION
WORKSTATIONS
WORKSTREAM
WORKSTREAMS
WORKTABLES

W

WORKWATCHER
WORKWATCHERS
WORLDBEATS
WORLDLIEST
WORLDLINESS
WORLDLINESSES
WORLDLINGS
WORLDSCALE
WORLDSCALES
WORLDVIEWS
WORMINESSES
WORMWHEELS
WORNNESSES
WORRIMENTS
WORRISOMELY
WORRISOMENESS
WORRISOMENESSES
WORRYINGLY
WORRYWARTS
WORSENESSES
WORSENINGS
WORSHIPABLE
WORSHIPERS
WORSHIPFUL
WORSHIPFULLY
WORSHIPFULNESS
WORSHIPING
WORSHIPLESS
WORSHIPPED
WORSHIPPER
WORSHIPPERS
WORSHIPPING
WORTHINESS
WORTHINESSES
WORTHLESSLY
WORTHLESSNESS
WORTHLESSNESSES
WORTHWHILE
WORTHWHILENESS
WOUNDINGLY
WOUNDWORTS
WRAITHLIKE
WRANGLERSHIP
WRANGLERSHIPS
WRANGLESOME
WRANGLINGS
WRAPAROUND
WRAPAROUNDS
WRAPPERING
WRAPROUNDS
WRATHFULLY
WRATHFULNESS
WRATHFULNESSES
WRATHINESS
WRATHINESSES
WREATHIEST
WREATHLESS
WREATHLIKE
WRECKFISHES
WRECKMASTER
WRECKMASTERS
WRENCHINGLY
WRENCHINGS
WRESTLINGS
WRETCHEDER
WRETCHEDEST
WRETCHEDLY
WRETCHEDNESS
WRETCHEDNESSES
WRIGGLIEST
WRIGGLINGS
WRINKLELESS
WRINKLIEST
WRISTBANDS
WRISTLOCKS
WRISTWATCH
WRISTWATCHES
WRITEDOWNS
WRITERESSES
WRITERLIER
WRITERLIEST
WRITERSHIP
WRITERSHIPS
WRITHINGLY
WRONGDOERS
WRONGDOING
WRONGDOINGS
WRONGFULLY
WRONGFULNESS
WRONGFULNESSES
WRONGHEADED
WRONGHEADEDLY
WRONGHEADEDNESS
WRONGNESSES
WRONGOUSLY
WULFENITES
WUNDERKIND
WUNDERKINDER
WUNDERKINDS
WYANDOTTES
WYLIECOATS

W

X

XANTHATION
XANTHATIONS
XANTHOCHROIA
XANTHOCHROIAS
XANTHOCHROIC
XANTHOCHROID
XANTHOCHROIDS
XANTHOCHROISM
XANTHOCHROISMS
XANTHOCHROMIA
XANTHOCHROMIAS
XANTHOCHROOUS
XANTHOMATA
XANTHOMATOUS
XANTHOMELANOUS
XANTHOPHYL
XANTHOPHYLL
XANTHOPHYLLOUS
XANTHOPHYLLS
XANTHOPHYLS
XANTHOPSIA
XANTHOPSIAS
XANTHOPTERIN
XANTHOPTERINE
XANTHOPTERINES
XANTHOPTERINS
XANTHOXYLS
XENARTHRAL
XENOBIOTIC
XENOBIOTICS
XENOBLASTS
XENOCRYSTS
XENODIAGNOSES
XENODIAGNOSIS
XENODIAGNOSTIC
XENODOCHIUM
XENODOCHIUMS
XENOGAMIES
XENOGAMOUS
XENOGENEIC
XENOGENESES
XENOGENESIS
XENOGENETIC
XENOGENIES
XENOGENOUS
XENOGLOSSIA
XENOGLOSSIAS
XENOGLOSSIES
XENOGLOSSY
XENOGRAFTS
XENOLITHIC
XENOMANIAS
XENOMENIAS
XENOMORPHIC
XENOMORPHICALLY
XENOPHILES
XENOPHOBES
XENOPHOBIA
XENOPHOBIAS
XENOPHOBIC
XENOPHOBICALLY
XENOPHOBIES
XENOPLASTIC
XENOTRANSPLANT
XENOTRANSPLANTS
XENOTROPIC
XERANTHEMUM
XERANTHEMUMS
XERISCAPED
XERISCAPES
XERISCAPING
XEROCHASIES
XERODERMAE
XERODERMAS
XERODERMATIC
XERODERMATOUS
XERODERMIA
XERODERMIAS
XERODERMIC
XEROGRAPHER
XEROGRAPHERS
XEROGRAPHIC
XEROGRAPHICALLY
XEROGRAPHIES
XEROGRAPHY
XEROMORPHIC
XEROMORPHOUS
XEROMORPHS
XEROPHAGIES
XEROPHILES
XEROPHILIES
XEROPHILOUS
XEROPHTHALMIA
XEROPHTHALMIAS
XEROPHTHALMIC
XEROPHYTES
XEROPHYTIC
XEROPHYTICALLY
XEROPHYTISM
XEROPHYTISMS
XERORADIOGRAPHY
XEROSTOMAS
XEROSTOMATA
XEROSTOMIA
XEROSTOMIAS
XEROTHERMIC
XEROTRIPSES
XEROTRIPSIS
XIPHIHUMERALIS
XIPHIPLASTRA
XIPHIPLASTRAL
XIPHIPLASTRALS
XIPHIPLASTRON
XIPHISTERNA
XIPHISTERNUM
XIPHISTERNUMS
XIPHOPAGIC
XIPHOPAGOUS
XIPHOPAGUS
XIPHOPAGUSES
XIPHOPHYLLOUS
XIPHOSURAN
XIPHOSURANS
XYLOBALSAMUM
XYLOBALSAMUMS
XYLOCARPOUS
XYLOCHROME
XYLOCHROMES
XYLOGENOUS
XYLOGRAPHED
XYLOGRAPHER
XYLOGRAPHERS
XYLOGRAPHIC
XYLOGRAPHICAL
XYLOGRAPHIES
XYLOGRAPHING
XYLOGRAPHS
XYLOGRAPHY
XYLOIDINES
XYLOLOGIES
XYLOMETERS
XYLOPHAGAN
XYLOPHAGANS
XYLOPHAGES
XYLOPHAGOUS
XYLOPHILOUS
XYLOPHONES
XYLOPHONIC
XYLOPHONIST
XYLOPHONISTS
XYLOPYROGRAPHY
XYLORIMBAS
XYLOTOMIES
XYLOTOMIST
XYLOTOMISTS
XYLOTOMOUS
XYLOTYPOGRAPHIC
XYLOTYPOGRAPHY
XYRIDACEOUS

Y

YACHTSMANSHIP
YACHTSMANSHIPS
YACHTSWOMAN
YACHTSWOMEN
YAFFINGALE
YAFFINGALES
YAMMERINGS
YARBOROUGH
YARBOROUGHS
YARDLIGHTS
YARDMASTER
YARDMASTERS
YARDSTICKS
YATTERINGLY
YATTERINGS
YEARNINGLY
YEASTINESS
YEASTINESSES
YELLOCHING
YELLOWBACK
YELLOWBACKS
YELLOWBARK
YELLOWBARKS
YELLOWBIRD
YELLOWBIRDS
YELLOWCAKE
YELLOWCAKES
YELLOWFINS
YELLOWHAMMER
YELLOWHAMMERS
YELLOWHEAD
YELLOWHEADS
YELLOWIEST
YELLOWISHNESS
YELLOWISHNESSES
YELLOWLEGS
YELLOWNESS
YELLOWNESSES
YELLOWTAIL
YELLOWTAILS
YELLOWTHROAT
YELLOWTHROATS
YELLOWWARE
YELLOWWARES
YELLOWWEED
YELLOWWEEDS
YELLOWWOOD
YELLOWWOODS
YELLOWWORT
YELLOWWORTS
YEOMANRIES
YERSINIOSES
YERSINIOSIS
YESTERDAYS
YESTEREVEN
YESTEREVENING
YESTEREVENINGS
YESTEREVENS
YESTEREVES
YESTERMORN
YESTERMORNING
YESTERMORNINGS
YESTERMORNS
YESTERNIGHT
YESTERNIGHTS
YESTERYEAR
YESTERYEARS
YIELDABLENESS
YIELDABLENESSES
YIELDINGLY
YIELDINGNESS
YIELDINGNESSES
YOCTOSECOND
YOCTOSECONDS
YODELLINGS
YOHIMBINES
YOKEFELLOW
YOKEFELLOWS
YOTTABYTES
YOUNGBERRIES
YOUNGBERRY
YOUNGLINGS
YOUNGNESSES
YOUNGSTERS
YOURSELVES
YOUTHENING
YOUTHFULLY
YOUTHFULNESS
YOUTHFULNESSES
YOUTHHEADS
YOUTHHOODS
YOUTHQUAKE
YOUTHQUAKES
YPSILIFORM
YTHUNDERED
YTTERBITES
YTTERBIUMS
YTTRIFEROUS
YUCKINESSES
YUMBERRIES
YUMMINESSES
YUPPIEDOMS
YUPPIFICATION
YUPPIFICATIONS
YUPPIFYING

Z

ZABAGLIONE
ZABAGLIONES
ZALAMBDODONT
ZALAMBDODONTS
ZAMBOORAKS
ZAMINDARIES
ZAMINDARIS
ZANAMIVIRS
ZANINESSES
ZANTEDESCHIA
ZANTEDESCHIAS
ZANTEWOODS
ZANTHOXYLS
ZANTHOXYLUM
ZANTHOXYLUMS
ZAPATEADOS
ZAPOTILLAS
ZEALOTISMS
ZEALOTRIES
ZEALOUSNESS
ZEALOUSNESSES
ZEBRAFISHES
ZEBRAWOODS
ZEBRINNIES
ZEITGEBERS
ZEITGEISTIER
ZEITGEISTIEST
ZEITGEISTS
ZEITGEISTY
ZELATRICES
ZELATRIXES
ZELOPHOBIA
ZELOPHOBIAS
ZELOPHOBIC
ZELOPHOBICS
ZELOTYPIAS
ZEMINDARIES
ZEMINDARIS
ZEOLITIFORM
ZEPTOSECOND
ZEPTOSECONDS
ZESTFULNESS
ZESTFULNESSES
ZESTINESSES
ZETTABYTES
ZEUGLODONT
ZEUGLODONTS
ZEUGMATICALLY
ZIBELLINES
ZIDOVUDINE
ZIDOVUDINES
ZIGZAGGEDNESS
ZIGZAGGEDNESSES
ZIGZAGGERIES
ZIGZAGGERS
ZIGZAGGERY
ZIGZAGGIER
ZIGZAGGIEST
ZIGZAGGING
ZILLIONAIRE
ZILLIONAIRES
ZILLIONTHS
ZINCIFEROUS
ZINCIFICATION
ZINCIFICATIONS
ZINCIFYING
ZINCKENITE
ZINCKENITES
ZINCKIFICATION
ZINCKIFICATIONS
ZINCKIFIED
ZINCKIFIES
ZINCKIFYING
ZINCOGRAPH
ZINCOGRAPHER
ZINCOGRAPHERS
ZINCOGRAPHIC
ZINCOGRAPHICAL
ZINCOGRAPHIES
ZINCOGRAPHS
ZINCOGRAPHY
ZINCOLYSES
ZINCOLYSIS
ZINFANDELS
ZINGIBERACEOUS
ZINJANTHROPI
ZINJANTHROPUS
ZINJANTHROPUSES
ZINKENITES
ZINKIFEROUS
ZINKIFICATION
ZINKIFICATIONS
ZINKIFYING
ZINZIBERACEOUS
ZIPLOCKING
ZIPPINESSES
ZIRCALLOYS
ZIRCONIUMS
ZITHERISTS
ZIZYPHUSES
ZOANTHARIAN
ZOANTHARIANS
ZOANTHROPIC
ZOANTHROPIES
ZOANTHROPY
ZOECHROMES
ZOMBIELIKE
ZOMBIFICATION
ZOMBIFICATIONS
ZOMBIFYING
ZOOCEPHALIC
ZOOCHEMICAL
ZOOCHEMISTRIES
ZOOCHEMISTRY
ZOOCHORIES
ZOOCHOROUS
ZOOCULTURE
ZOOCULTURES
ZOODENDRIA
ZOODENDRIUM
ZOOGAMETES
ZOOGEOGRAPHER
ZOOGEOGRAPHERS
ZOOGEOGRAPHIC
ZOOGEOGRAPHICAL
ZOOGEOGRAPHIES
ZOOGEOGRAPHY
ZOOGLOEOID
ZOOGONIDIA
ZOOGONIDIUM
ZOOGRAFTING
ZOOGRAFTINGS
ZOOGRAPHER
ZOOGRAPHERS
ZOOGRAPHIC
ZOOGRAPHICAL
ZOOGRAPHIES
ZOOGRAPHIST
ZOOGRAPHISTS
ZOOKEEPERS
ZOOLATRIAS
ZOOLATRIES
ZOOLATROUS
ZOOLOGICAL
ZOOLOGICALLY
ZOOLOGISTS
ZOOMAGNETIC
ZOOMAGNETISM
ZOOMAGNETISMS
ZOOMANCIES
ZOOMETRICAL
ZOOMETRIES
ZOOMORPHIC
ZOOMORPHIES
ZOOMORPHISM
ZOOMORPHISMS
ZOONOMISTS
ZOOPATHIES
ZOOPATHOLOGIES
ZOOPATHOLOGY
ZOOPERISTS
ZOOPHAGANS
ZOOPHAGIES
ZOOPHAGOUS
ZOOPHILIAS
ZOOPHILIES
ZOOPHILISM
ZOOPHILISMS
ZOOPHILIST
ZOOPHILISTS
ZOOPHILOUS
ZOOPHOBIAS
ZOOPHOBOUS
ZOOPHYSIOLOGIES
ZOOPHYSIOLOGIST
ZOOPHYSIOLOGY
ZOOPHYTICAL
ZOOPHYTOID
ZOOPHYTOLOGICAL
ZOOPHYTOLOGIES
ZOOPHYTOLOGIST
ZOOPHYTOLOGISTS
ZOOPHYTOLOGY
ZOOPLANKTER
ZOOPLANKTERS
ZOOPLANKTON
ZOOPLANKTONIC
ZOOPLANKTONS
ZOOPLASTIC
ZOOPLASTIES
ZOOPSYCHOLOGIES
ZOOPSYCHOLOGY
ZOOSCOPIES
ZOOSPERMATIC
ZOOSPERMIA
ZOOSPERMIUM
ZOOSPORANGIA
ZOOSPORANGIAL
ZOOSPORANGIUM
ZOOSPOROUS
ZOOSTEROLS
ZOOTECHNICAL
ZOOTECHNICS
ZOOTECHNIES
ZOOTHAPSES
ZOOTHAPSIS
ZOOTHECIAL
ZOOTHECIUM
ZOOTHEISMS
ZOOTHEISTIC

Z

ZOOTHERAPIES
ZOOTHERAPY
ZOOTOMICAL
ZOOTOMICALLY
ZOOTOMISTS
ZOOTROPHIC
ZOOTROPHIES
ZOOTSUITER
ZOOTSUITERS
ZOOXANTHELLA
ZOOXANTHELLAE
ZORBONAUTS
ZUCCHETTOS
ZUGZWANGED
ZUGZWANGING
ZUMBOORUKS
ZWANZIGERS
ZWISCHENZUG
ZWISCHENZUGS
ZWITTERION
ZWITTERIONIC
ZWITTERIONS
ZYGANTRUMS
ZYGAPOPHYSEAL
ZYGAPOPHYSES
ZYGAPOPHYSIAL
ZYGAPOPHYSIS
ZYGOBRANCH
ZYGOBRANCHIATE
ZYGOBRANCHIATES
ZYGOBRANCHS
ZYGOCACTUS
ZYGOCACTUSES
ZYGOCARDIAC
ZYGODACTYL
ZYGODACTYLIC
ZYGODACTYLISM
ZYGODACTYLISMS
ZYGODACTYLOUS
ZYGODACTYLS
ZYGOMATICS
ZYGOMORPHIC
ZYGOMORPHIES
ZYGOMORPHISM
ZYGOMORPHISMS
ZYGOMORPHOUS
ZYGOMORPHY
ZYGOMYCETE
ZYGOMYCETES
ZYGOMYCETOUS
ZYGOPHYLLACEOUS
ZYGOPHYTES
ZYGOPLEURAL
ZYGOSITIES
ZYGOSPERMS
ZYGOSPHENE
ZYGOSPHENES
ZYGOSPORES
ZYGOSPORIC
ZYGOTICALLY
ZYMOGENESES
ZYMOGENESIS
ZYMOLOGICAL
ZYMOLOGIES
ZYMOLOGIST
ZYMOLOGISTS
ZYMOMETERS
ZYMOSIMETER
ZYMOSIMETERS
ZYMOTECHNIC
ZYMOTECHNICAL
ZYMOTECHNICS
ZYMOTICALLY